American Places
DICTIONARY

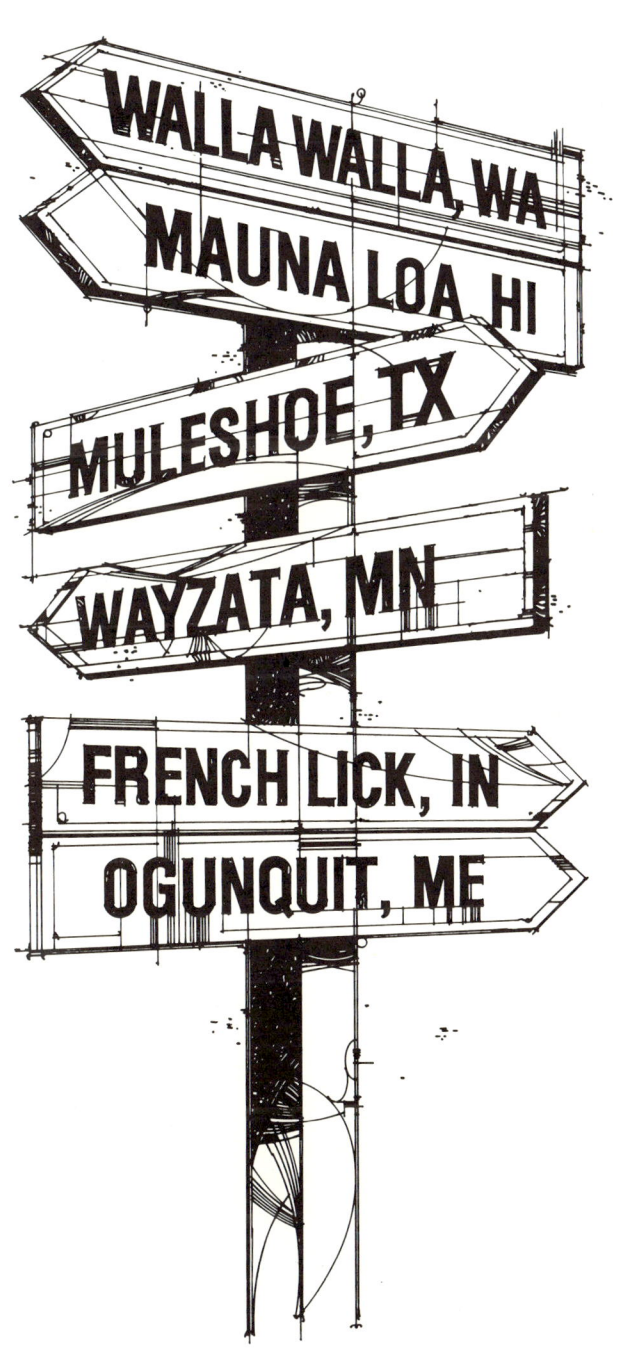

American Places Dictionary

A Guide to 45,000 Populated Places, Natural Features, and Other Places in the United States

Covering States, Counties, Cities, Towns, Townships, Villages, and Boroughs, as well as Indian Reservations, Military Bases, and Major Geographical Features, the Entries Providing Description, Precise Location, and Name Origin Information, and Supplemented by Maps & Indexes

in Four Volumes

Volume Three: Midwest

Illinois	Minnesota
Indiana	Missouri
Iowa	Ohio
Michigan	Wisconsin

Edited by

Frank R. Abate

SAN DIEGO PUBLIC LIBRARY
LA JOLLA BRANCH

Omnigraphics, Inc.
Penobscot Building • Detroit, Michigan 48226

Editorial Staff

Frank R. Abate, *Editor*

Jacquelyn S. Goodwin, Katherine M. Isaacs, and Elizabeth J. Jewell, *Associate Editors*

Margaret Mary Missar, *Research*

Terri Finkeldey and Christine Kelley, *Editorial Assistants*

Additional Editorial Services provided by Sachem Publishing Associates, Inc., Guilford, CT
Data Processing and Typesetting: Weimer Graphics, Indianapolis, IN

Omnigraphics, Inc.

Eric Berger, *Vice President, Production*
Laurie Lanzen Harris, *Editorial Director*
Peter E. Ruffner, *Vice President, Administration*
James A. Sellgren, *Vice President, Operations & Finance*

Frederick G. Ruffner, Jr., *Publisher*

Copyright © 1994 Omnigraphics, Inc.

Library of Congress Cataloging-in-Publication Data

> American places dictionary : a guide to 45,000 populated places, natural features, and other places in the United States . . . in four volumes / Frank R. Abate, editor.
> p. cm.
> Includes indexes.
> Contents: v. 1. Northeast — v. 2. South — v. 3. Midwest — v. 4. West. Appendices & index.
> ISBN 1-55888-747-4 (lib. bdg. : alk. paper : set). — ISBN 1-55888-146-8 (lib. bdg. : alk. paper : v. 1). — ISBN 1-55888-147-6 (lib. bdg. : alk. paper : v. 2). — ISBN 1-55888-148-4 (lib. bdg. : alk. paper : v. 3). — ISBN 1-55888-149-2 (lib. bdg. : alk. paper : v. 4)
> 1. United States—Gazetteers. I. Abate, Frank R.
> E154.A48 1994
> 917.3'003—dc20
> 93-12306
> CIP

Grateful acknowledgment is made to Dr. Kelsie Harder for permission to use the name origin information from his book, *Illustrated Dictionary of Place Names: United States and Canada* (copyright © 1974 by Kelsie Harder).

The information in this publication was compiled from sources considered reliable. While every possible effort has been made to ensure reliability, the publisher will not assume liability for damages caused by inaccuracies in the data, and makes no warranty, express or implied, on the accuracy of the information contained herein.

This book is printed on acid-free paper meeting the ANSI Z38.48 Standard. The infinity symbol that appears above indicates that the paper in this book meets that standard.

Printed in the United States of America

Contents

Volume Three: Midwest

Foreword vii

Introduction & How to Use This Book xv
   Organization of Entries by County xv
   Coverage xvi
   Contents of the Four Volumes xviii
   Entry Presentation and Information in *APD* xix
   Name Origin Information xxii
   Hierarchy of Government in the United States xxv

Editor's Miscellany:
   American Places and American Names—Curiosities and Peculiarities xxxiii

Bibliography xli

American Places Dictionary-Midwest:
   Illinois 3
   Indiana 171
   Iowa 275
   Michigan 363
   Minnesota 479
   Missouri 635
   Ohio 785
   Wisconsin 925

(Statewide Index at the end of each state section)

Foreword:

Patterns and Practices in the Naming of American Places

Place names in the United States reflect the attitudes, ambitions, and desires of the namers, who themselves were uprooted from their homes in other countries or from their former homes in eastern states as they moved westward across the North American continent. That they found the land occupied already is also reflected in the Amerindian-derived names (names used by Native Americans) that dot the landscape. The southwestern areas—Texas, New Mexico, Arizona, and California—were settled by Spaniards, who also assigned names as did their English-speaking counterparts who were moving west. Primarily, however, the names now existing came from European languages, the namers being of European descent who sought new living conditions, more freedom, and more space to live out their dreams. From their point of view, they had a new land to settle and, hence, names to give. George R. Stewart, in his *Names on the Land,* wrote that "the names lay thickly over the land, and the Americans spoke them, great and little, easily and carelessly—Virginia, Susquehanna, Rio Grande, Deadman Creek, Sugarloaf Hill, Detroit, Wall Street—not thinking how they came to be."

And they did come to be. A good instance of the way naming occurred comes from the story of how **Hope**, county seat of Hempstead County, Arkansas, received its name. The name also is indicative of how names somehow interact historically, alluding to other names and other places. Hope appears to be an abstract name, symbolizing the thoughts of desire and expectation, placing faith in the future, all in all a good name. Established in 1874, the Arkansas city of Hope was named not necessarily in allegorical anticipation but for Hope Loughborough, daughter of James Loughborough, a director of the Cairo and Fulton Railroad. This is simple enough and a standard naming method, that of giving to a place the name of a loved one, such as a wife, daughter, sometimes a son, and many such names exist in the United States. But the former county seat of Hempstead County, **Washington**, named for George Washington, was called the "birthplace of Texas," because Stephen F. Austin resided there and held court before he went to Texas. James Bowie also lived in Washington, Arkansas, before he, too, went to Texas. Before leaving Bowie engaged a certain James Black to craft a special knife for him.

The citizens of Washington, however, would not cooperate with the railway officials, who took their revenge by building Hope and bypassing Washington. Hope became the county seat and the boyhood home of U.S. President Bill Clinton, while Washington became another hamlet. Intertwined here, with many meaningful connotations, are names that have become important for places. Hope is second only to **Union** as the abstract name most often used in the United States. **Austin** became the name for the capital of Texas and a county. Bowie went to his destiny at the Alamo, as well as being remembered for his Bowie knife and also by a county name in Texas.

Sometimes the bizarre occurs. **California**, the county seat of Moniteau County, Missouri, was to be established in 1834 as **Boonesborough**, for Daniel Boone, the frontiersman. But another **Boonesborough** existed in Missouri, so the name was not approved by postal officials, who often forced the alteration or wholesale change of place names before they could be made official. A man happened along who offered a jug of whiskey if the people would name the town for him. The offer was accepted. His name was California Wilson. An extreme case, no doubt, but indeed many honorific names were bestowed by town officials in recognition of the owner or purveyor of the land on which the town was first platted. **Lovewell**, Kansas, for instance, was named for Thomas Lovewell, who gave land for the railroad, a church, and a school. **Chardon**, Ohio, was named for Peter Chardon Brooks, who donated the site. Thomas Bell granted the land that became **Bellville**, Texas. **Phil Campbell**, Alabama, was named for the man who built a depot and railroad spur to the town in exchange for its being given his name.

Occasionally, town leaders will name the place for a wealthy person in hope of obtaining favors (money included). For instance, **Vanderbilt**, Tennessee, was named for Cornelius Vanderbilt, in the hope that this would persuade him and his family to live there during summer months. Vanderbilt chose Asheville, North Carolina, for that purpose, whereupon **Vanderbilt**, Tennessee, changed its name to **Ervin**, honoring Dr. J. N. Ervin, who had donated land for the courthouse. All along, the post office had been called **Erwin**, for Jesse B. Erwin, the first county-court clerk. When the town was incorporated, **Erwin** was made official, the excuse being that it was close enough to **Ervin**.

A close examination of the names in *American Places Dictionary* will reveal many patterns. It will also reveal psychological aspects of the minds of the namers and give insight into the character of the historical period in which the patterns occur. In the colonial years, from the time settlers began to arrive from Europe in the 17th century to the end of the Revolutionary War in 1783, place names indicated three distinct patterns: descriptive, those based on English royalty, and English transfer names. Also, a few religious names appeared (**Bethel**, **Canaan**, **Providence**), but the three larger patterns dominated.

The descriptive names always reflect the point of view of the namer, for what is now **Trout Brook** could just as easily have been **Birch Brook**. Descriptive names were attached especially to features, seldom to habitation places, unless a community developed around a feature, usually a spring or other watercourse, such as **Big Spring** and **Deep River**. The descriptive names were merely identifiers, serving the purpose of immediacy; some were actually translated from an Amerindian name.

English royalty names contributed many of the major names in the original colonies: **New York** (state and city) and **Albany** for James, Duke of York and Albany, later King James II of England; **Brunswick**, for one of the titles of the British royal house of Hanover; **Buckingham**, in reference to the title of George Villiers and later of his son; **Elizabeth** (New Jersey) for the wife of Sir George Carteret; **Cape Ann** (Massachusetts) for the wife of James I; **Annapolis** (Maryland) and **Anne Arundel County** (Virginia) for Anne Arundell, daughter of Lord Thomas Arundell of Wardour and wife of Cecilius Calvert, Lord Baltimore; **North Carolina**, **South Carolina**, **Cape Charles** (Virginia), **Charles River** (Massachusetts), **Charles City** (Virginia), and **Charles City County** (Virginia), for Charles I; **Charleston** and **Charleston County** (South Carolina) are named for Charles II. Such a list could go on for pages.

English county and town names used during these years show both nostalgia for the former homes of colonists and also the desire to perpetuate the names. Among the more well known transfers are **New England**, **Chester** (Connecticut, Massachusetts, Pennsylvania, and throughout the United States; at least forty other municipalities are named **Chester**), **Durham** (Connecticut, New Hampshire, New York, North Carolina, and nine other states), **Winchester** (Connecticut, Massachusetts, New Hampshire, Virginia, and twelve other states), **Kent** (Connecticut, Delaware, Florida, Maryland, New York, Rhode Island, and nine other states), **Norfolk** (Connecticut, Massachusetts, New York, Virginia, and three other states), **Dover** (Delaware, New Hampshire, New Jersey, North Carolina, Pennsylvania, and twenty other states), **New London** (Connecticut, New Hampshire, North Carolina, Pennsylvania, and six other states), **Plymouth** (Connecticut, Massachusetts, New Hampshire, Pennsylvania, Virginia, and seventeen other states), **Cumberland** (Maryland, Pennsylvania, Rhode Island, and seven other states), **Portland** (Connecticut, New York, Pennsylvania, and thirteen other states), **Essex** (Connecticut, Massachusetts, New York, and five other states), and **Bristol** (Connecticut, New York, New Hampshire, Rhode Island, and sixteen other states).

Other English place name transfers are not so well known, but still were quite popular. Examples include **Farmington** (Connecticut, Delaware, New Hampshire, New York, North Carolina, Pennsylvania, and sixteen other states), **Enfield** (Connecticut, New Hampshire, New York, North Carolina, and Illinois), **Glastonbury** (Connecticut), **Newington** (Connecticut, Georgia, and New Hampshire), **Torrington** (Connecticut), **Litchfield** (Connecticut, New York, New Hampshire, and seven other states), **Haddam** (Connecticut), **Killingworth** (from **Kenilworth;** Connecticut), **Guilford** (Connecticut, New York, and nine other states), **Derby** (Connecticut and three other states), and many more. **Brentford** (South Dakota) shows that the practice continued beyond colonial times. In some cases, particularly as Americans moved westward, the names were actually given in honor of the American town the pioneers had left behind, rather than for the original English name.

After the Revolutionary War, places began to be named for war heroes and leaders. This occurred especially in the new states being formed west of the Appalachian Mountains and were influenced strongly by the fervor of patriotism that swept through the former colonies. County names especially reflect this commemorative movement, with the major leaders all being so honored: (George) **Washington** (31 counties), (Benjamin) **Franklin** (23 counties), (Thomas) **Jefferson** (25 counties), (General Nathanael) **Greene** (17 counties), (Alexander) **Hamilton** (eight counties), (German-born French soldier Johann, Baron de Kalb, who fought with the Americans during the war) **DeKalb** (ten counties), (Patrick) **Henry** (ten counties), (James) **Madison** (20 counties), (General Richard) **Montgomery** (16 counties), (General Francis "The Swamp Fox") **Marion** (17 counties), (General Daniel) **Morgan** (9 counties), (Polish soldier Count Casimir, who also fought with the Americans) **Pulaski** (7 counties), (General Israel) **Putnam** (9 counties), and (General "Mad Anthony") **Wayne** (16 counties). The Marquis de **LaFayette**, French statesman and aide to Washington, is commemorated in 17 U.S. counties, and a host of cities and towns, some using only the **Fayette** portion of his name.

Names of other heroes from the American Revolution, now obscure, dot the maps of states: (soldier Anthony) **Bledsoe** (Tennessee), (Kentucky soldier and statesman John) **Adair** (Louisiana, Kentucky, Missouri), (Major General Ethan) **Allen** (Ohio), (soldier and U.S. Senator John) **Armstrong** (Pennsylvania), (soldier Nicholas) **Herkimer** (New York), (Sergeant William) **Jasper** (8 counties), (soldier and U.S. Representative Joseph) **McDowell** (North Carolina), (General Hugh)

Mercer (six counties), (soldier John) **Newton** (Georgia, Indiana), (one of the captors of British spy John Andre, soldier John) **Paulding** (Georgia, Oklahoma), (General Thomas) **Person** (North Carolina), and (soldier and U.S. Representative Andrew) **Pickins** (Alabama, Georgia, South Carolina) are examples.

Signers of the Declaration of Independence were among the most commemorated: (John) **Adams** (eight counties), (Carter) **Braxton** (Virginia), (Charles) **Carroll** (11 counties), (Benjamin) **Franklin** (23 counties), (Button) **Gwinnett** and (Lyman) **Hall** (Georgia), (John) **Hancock** (10 counties), (Benjamin) **Harrison** (West Virginia), (Samuel) **Huntington** (Indiana), (Thomas) **Jefferson** (25 counties), (Richard Henry) **Lee** (Georgia, Illinois), (Thomas) **McKean** (Pennsylvania), (Robert Hunter) **Morris** (New Jersey), (Thomas) **Nelson** (Virginia, Kentucky), (Benjamin) **Rush** (Indiana), (George) **Walton** (Georgia), and (George) **Wythe** (Virginia).

The same was true after the War of 1812, with counties being named for leaders and heroes, including (Andrew) **Jackson** (21 counties); (John) **Coffee** (Alabama, Tennessee); (Stephen F.) **Decatur** (five counties); (Oliver Hazard) **Perry** (10 counties); (Thomas) **McDonough** and (William, who also fought in the Black Hawk War of 1832) **McHenry** (Illinois); (James) **Lawrence** (11 counties); (Alexander) **Macomb** (Michigan); (Virgil) **McCracken,** (James) **Meade,** and (Alney) **McLean** (Kentucky); (William) **Moore** (Tennessee); and (Zebulon) **Pike** (10 counties).

In the so-called Military Tract of upstate New York, as noted by George R. Stewart in *Names on the Land,* many names from Greco-Roman history and culture were given by the state land commissioners. Though they themselves probably were not steeped in the classics, perhaps the influence of a name already assigned, **Seneca Lake** (itself of Amerindian origin, not classical, but converted into a classical name from Mohegan—with a Dutch spelling—**Sinneken**, or **Sinnegar**, or **Sennicky**), started the trend. Along with nearby **Troy, Seneca** seems to have been the catalyst to the naming of 23 townships on classical or literary models: **Lysander, Hannibal, Cato, Camillus, Cicero, Manlius, Marcellus, Aurelius, Romulus, Scipio, Sempronius, Tully, Fabius, Ovid, Homer, Solon, Hector, Ulysses, Virgil,** and **Cincinnatus.** After exhausting their store of classical names, they added the English literary greats, improvising with **Milton, Locke,** and **Dryden.** Once the precedent was set in New York, the custom of using classical or literary names became common and a pattern throughout the United States.

The use of suffixes in places has continued from the time of **Jamestown** to the present: **Elizabethtown, Youngstown,** and **Austintown,** plus the many **-towns** that were shortened to **-ton** (**Charles Town** to **Charleston**). The suffixes -boro, -burg(h), -ville, -field, and -polis yielded, among hundreds of others, **Hatboro** (Pennsylvania), **Pittsburgh** (Pennsylvania and elsewhere), **Bloomfield** (Illinois and elsewhere), and **Annapolis** (Maryland).

As befits a new country with a strong religious base, biblical names became common between the Revolutionary War and the Civil War, including **Bethel** (possibly the most popular biblical name), **Shiloh, Bethlehem, Corinth, Dothan, Ephrata, Jerusalem, Joseph, Mary, Salem, Zion,** and **Zoar,** along with many names assigned by the Church of Latter-Day Saints in Utah. In parts of the country already settled by Spanish speakers, the names of saints prevailed, many such names having been given by Spanish explorers for the saint's day, or day of naming: **San Luis Obispo, Santa Rosa, San Francisco, San Diego, San Gabriel, San Bernardino, San Juan, San Rafael,** and **Santa Barbara,** as well as many others in the western states. In Florida, **Saint Augustine** survives from the Spanish colonial era there, the oldest continuously inhabited settlement in the United States.

In the middle states and in Louisiana and in areas bordering Quebec in Canada, French names of saints survive, among them **St. Bernard Parish** (Louisiana), **Lake St. Catherine** (Vermont), **St. Croix County** (Wisconsin), **Ste. Genevieve County** (Missouri), and, probably the most famous French-derived name, **St. Lawrence River** (anglicized from **St. Laurent**), given originally to a harbor by explorer Jacques Cartier on the saint's day, August 10, 1535, and then spread to the gulf, the river, and places along the river. But not much direct use of honorific saints' names occurred after the Revolutionary War, except humorously or facetiously. Some that are apparently saint's names actually have a more mundane explanation, such as **St. John** (Kansas) for John Pierce St. John, a prohibitionist; **St. James** (Missouri), probably for Thomas James, founder; and **St. George** (South Carolina), for James George, first settler.

The coming of the railroads in the mid-nineteenth century and the resulting explosion of new settlements dictated the need for many, many names, spread hastily and almost indiscriminately across the United States. The name origins of many of these towns are opaque, forgotten or buried in stored files of long discontinued railway offices. Railway officials, clerks, engineers, even some company presidents were entrusted with the practical necessity of naming stations along a line. Perhaps rough guidelines existed, but generally the namer was left to his or her devices, and these included names of superiors, female friends, male friends, family members, names from back East, foreign names, spelling deviations, back formations, blends, and personal whim. A few examples include **Mitchell** (Indiana), for a chief surveyor; **Conroe** (Texas), for a sawmill owner; **Crete** (Illinois) and **Corfu** (Washington), for the Mediterranean islands; **Creston** (Louisiana), for the highest point along the line; **Cressona** (Pennsylvania), for John Champman Cresson, president of a railroad; and **Depot** (Oregon), when inspiration ends.

After the Civil War **Lincoln** became the most popular name in the United States, commemorating the martyred president, although the giving of this honorific for Abraham Lincoln was far less common in the South. But **Lincoln**, for Benjamin Lincoln, commander of the American forces in the South during the Revolutionary War, does occur in southern states and several southern counties have his name. The continuing popularity of **Lincoln** is such that it still surpasses **Washington** as the name most often given to places needing a name, especially housing developments.

Names commemorating state and local politicians (legislators, state officials, and governors) represent a naming pattern of sizeable proportions. These names perpetuate the memory of the authors of bills, of friends in state legislatures, of those courted for political favors, and of self-aggrandizing legislators. A representative selection includes **Alexander County** (North Carolina), **Allen County** and **Anderson County** (Kansas), **Ashville** (Alabama), **Casey** and **Menard** (Illinois), **Morgan** (Utah), **Rabun** (Georgia), **Miller County** (Missouri), and **Pitkin** (Colorado).

Place names in the twentieth century generally were given by land developers and realtors, who are not apt to follow traditional patterns. Rather, they name to impress potential customers, the name somehow appealing to nostalgia, to Amerindian themes, to prestige, to love of nature, to snobbery, or to what is aesthetically pleasing. The names are self-consciously selected, sometimes invented. Examples of these types of names (typically with British connotations) would include **Cambridge Estates, Berkeley Grove, Essex Homes, Strathmore Village,** and **Brentwood-in-the-**

Pines. Nature names include **Tanglewood, Woodland Acres, Oak Manor, Seaside Shores, Sunset Hills, Cedar Farms**, and **Beechwood Lawns**. Amerindian names have strong appeal, but not necessarily to the Amerindians. Still, **Connetquot Park, Haccabauk Park, St. Regis Homes**, and **Winnesunk Gardens** indicate that such names have prestige value. Land development names strove to avoid the coarse, vulgar, or deviant; as a result, they have an innocence or blandness about them. This new wave of promotional naming has largely supplanted such older, unprepossessing examples as **Hog Hollow, Skunk Creek, Duck Pond.** Similarly, ethnic names that could possibly intimidate have given way to carefully sanitized ones.

Some influence in assigning place names was wielded by the U.S. Post Office Department, and also by the U.S. Board on Geographic Names, an interdepartmental agency composed of federal government officials. In the latter part of the nineteenth century, postal officials decided that names of places should be short, yielding the likes of **Ink** (Missouri), **Fry** (Texas), **Ono** and **Igo** (California), **Roy** (New Mexico), and **Ely** (Nevada). Some "original" names were changed by postal officials, either because the same name was already in use in the same state or out of bureaucratic propriety. One postal regulation stipulated that for "names consisting of more than one word, it is desirable to combine them into one word," resulting in **Mountpleasant, Boilingsprings, Bigprairie, Bigflat, Beaverdam, Bearcreek, Bonaire, Musselshell, Warmsprings, Plentywood, Forestgrove, Coscob, Glenlyon**, and **Polebridge**. Many have been changed back to two words, but many still exist unchanged. Apostrophes, with few exceptions—**Martha's Vineyard, D'hanis, O'brien**, and **O'Fallon**—have been eliminated through official guidelines. On the whole, however, the U.S. Board on Geographic Names has, at least in recent years, approved local preferences on names.

Names deriving from Amerindian languages have been popular since the earliest days of European settlement. The Amerindians had their own names (sometimes many, designating different locales along a single river) for geographical features, and many of these were used by the invaders, especially river names, such as **Potomac, Rappahanock, Susquehanna, Connecticut, Mohawk, Pomperaug, Naugatuck, Mystic**, and **Willimantic**. The names changed as they were filtered through the pronunciation and spellings of the English, French, or Dutch settlers, and were used without any consciousness of original meaning. Only later did an interest in the etymology of the place names develop, but by then the original meaning and pronunciation had been lost in so many instances that origins were either guessed at or romanticized. Still, the influence of Amerindian names led to several states having Amerindian-derived names, including two in the colonies—**Connecticut** and **Massachusetts**. The reasons why settlers retained and accepted Amerindian names are complicated. A practical reason was that the names were already there. Also, during the late eighteenth and early nineteenth centuries, Enlightenment and Romantic thinkers tended to idealize the Amerindians as "noble savages," symbolizing the goodness of natural life.

On the other hand, some Europeans looked upon the Amerindians as enemies and savages whose names should not be used for places. This attitude is shown in such states as Kentucky, which has few Amerindian-derived names. Whatever the reasons, the Europeans retained or gave Amerindian names to thousands of places, including the state name, **Indiana**. Such names as **Rockaway, Cherokee, Chickasaw, Apache, Ute, Creek, Iroquois, Minnewashka, Cathlamet, Catoctin, Edisto, Erie, Guyandot, Hassayampa, Manitou**, and **Winnebago** may only resemble the original names, but stand at least as commemoratives of the many Amerindian groups in the United States, all now woven into the country's fabric of names.

The geographical names in the United States have an unsurpassed variety. The ethnic mix of peoples has produced names not only from the four main linguistic sources (Amerindian, English, Spanish, and French) but also from the languages of immigrants who have settled throughout the fifty states. Germans, Swedes, Italians, Hungarians, Dutch, Russians, Polynesians, Japanese, Chinese, Czechs, Slovaks, Greeks, Norwegians, Danes, Hindus, and Middle Easterners have contributed to the named places, and their legacy appears on the pages of *American Places Dictionary.* Above all, the wonder is the assimilation of these names into acceptance in an expanse of land so varied and with peoples of such different national backgrounds. In this rich mix of names is the culture of a nation, its history, psychology, folklore, and perhaps its destiny.

Kelsie B. Harder
*State University of
New York at Potsdam*

October 1993

Introduction & How to Use This Book

American Places Dictionary (APD) provides comprehensive coverage of places throughout the United States that are the subject of frequent inquiry. Included among the 45,000 entries are:

Political Entities

- States

- Counties and County Equivalents

- Legally Incorporated Places: e.g., cities; towns in New England; etc.

- Unincorporated Places: e.g., townships and villages in some states; Census Designated Places (CDPs) in certain states; etc.

American Indian Reservations

Major U.S. Military Installations

Major U.S. Geographic Features: mountains and ranges, rivers, natural landmarks, etc.

This Introduction will first discuss the overall organization and contents of *APD*; then explain the entry presentation and information given at the state, county, and place levels; and finally touch on two major areas covered in *APD*: name origin information and the variety of government structures in the United States.

Organization of Entries by County

Each volume of *APD* covers the states of one region of the country, with each state presented alphabetically in its own section. In each state section entries appear *alphabetically by county*. This organization brings together entries that are closely related.

Unique Arrangement by County

There are few, if any, major reference books that present material by county. The county-by-county organization of APD was deliberately chosen to meet the needs of the many users who are interested in the local context. Within a county the places tend to be closely linked historically, culturally, and economically. The county-by-county organization of APD provides 3,141 county profiles covering the entire United States. This allows quick comparison and cross-study at the county level, and brings out clearly the interrelationship of entries. Thus population, land and water area, population density, historical background, and name origins can be easily compared. In metropolitan areas, suburbs and other communities are listed with their near neighbors.

State Indexes and National Index

For those needing alphabetical access to the populated places in a state, or all the populated places (and other entries) in the United States, both state indexes and a national index are provided. *State indexes*, including all places and counties listed alphabetically, are at the end of each state section. Volume Four contains a *national index*, covering all places and counties in the entire United States.

Coverage

Populated Places

Volumes One through Four of *APD* offer comprehensive coverage of populated places in the United States that have a functioning government, as well as many other inhabited places. No population limit or other arbitrary cutoff was applied to limit the coverage of *APD*. Every city, town or township, borough, or village was included—no matter its size—if it had legal, incorporated status. In addition, thousands of unincorporated townships and other places also have entries. Such places are common in many states and, despite their lack of formal legal status, residents of them often say they are "from. . . ." Our editorial goal in *APD* was to cover U.S. populated places as comprehensively as possible while still giving a substantial amount of reliable data in each entry.

In some states selecting entries for comprehensive coverage presented difficulties, particularly for areas in the western U.S., where many vast tracts of inhabited land have no incorporated places. The editors of *APD* relied on baseline data from the U.S. Bureau of the Census, one of whose many tasks it is to keep track of all the inhabited places in the U.S. that have a functioning government and many less formally defined places that do not. As it is the purpose of the decennial censuses conducted by the Bureau to count all the inhabitants of the U.S., no inhabited area can be overlooked. Unincorporated places and districts must be given some status and name for purposes of the Census.

Another problem confronted the editors when it was discovered that some widely known places, such as La Jolla and Hollywood, California, were not incorporated cities and therefore had no census data from which to create an entry. For the fifty or so best-known of these unincorporated places, the editors placed a cross-reference in the county listing for the place, directing the reader to the incorporated place where data covering it was included. These unincorporated places also appear in the state and national indexes, with cross-references to the relevant entries.

Other Places and Features

In addition, other U.S. places that merit particular attention—American Indian reservations, major military installations, and major geographic features (see list of types below)—are each covered in separate Appendices in Volume Four. As many of these places are so vast that they cover all or parts of several counties, entering them in the state entries of Volumes One through

Four would have been impracticable. Stilltext, many of these places have important historical and cultural links to the populated places covered in Volumes One through Four, and are often referred to in the name origin or other information for populated places in *APD*. In addition, the American Indian reservations and military installations are themselves populated places.

Appendix A: American Indian Reservations

Appendix A of Volume Four has entries for each of the more than 300 American Indian reservations throughout the United States.

Appendix B: Military Installations

Appendix B of Volume Four has entries for more than 100 major U.S. military installations in the United States. In addition to the basic information given for each, the entries also note which facilities are scheduled to be affected by the 1993 recommendations of the Base Closure Commission.

Appendix C: Major Geographic Features

Appendix C of Volume Four has entries for more than 600 major geographic features across the United States. These include natural features on both land and water. In addition, some sizable features of human construction, such as dams and reservoirs, are also included. Many of these features are frequently referred to in written works, have historical significance, or are popular tourist spots. We have not included national parks as such, although some natural features found within national parks (e.g., Old Faithful, the geyser) do have entries.

The following types of major features are covered:

bays	deserts	oceans	seas
beaches	gaps	passes	sounds
canals	glaciers	peninsulas	trails
capes	gorges	plains	valleys
canyons	gulfs	plateaus	volcanoes
caves	islands	regions	waterfalls
currents	lakes	reservoirs	
dams	mountain ranges and peaks	rivers	

Contents of the Four Volumes

The complete *APD* is a four-volume set, organized as follows:

Volume One-Northeast:
    Connecticut
    Delaware
    District of Columbia (also in Vol. Two)
    Maine
    Maryland
    Massachusetts
    New Hampshire
    New Jersey
    New York
    Pennsylvania
    Rhode Island
    Vermont

Volume Two-South:
    Alabama
    Arkansas
    District of Columbia (also in Vol. One)
    Florida
    Georgia
    Kentucky
    Louisiana
    Mississippi
    North Carolina
    Oklahoma
    South Carolina
    Tennessee
    Texas
    Virginia
    West Virginia

Volume Three-Midwest:
    Illinois
    Indiana
    Iowa
    Michigan
    Minnesota
    Missouri
    Ohio
    Wisconsin

Volume Four-West:
    Alaska
    Arizona
    California
    Colorado
    Hawaii
    Idaho
    Kansas
    Montana
    Nebraska
    Nevada
    New Mexico
    North Dakota
    Oregon
    South Dakota
    Utah
    Washington
    Wyoming

Appendices & Index
Appendix A: American Indian Reservations
Appendix B: Major U.S. Military Installations
Appendix C: Major U.S. Geographic Features

Index: Including entries for Volumes One through Four and the Appendices

Entry Presentation and Information in *APD*

Entries for States

In each regional volume the states appear in alphabetic order, each in its own section. There is a section for each of the 50 states, plus a section for Washington, D.C., which appears in both Volume One (Northeast) and Volume Two (South).

Each state section opens with the state seal, followed by a one-page map showing the state and county boundaries and the names of neighboring states or provinces. Each map includes latitude and longitude references in the margins and a scale of miles and kilometers.

Opposite the map page is the state entry information and introductory information. Entries at the state level include the following basic information:

Population: in 1990 and 1980; 1990 rank among the 50 states; percent change from 1980 to 1990; projections for 1995 and 2000 (data from the U.S. Bureau of the Census).

Area: for land and water, in square miles; rank among the 50 states (data from the U.S. Bureau of the Census).

Coastline: number of miles of coastline, as applicable, as reported by the state and other sources.

Elevation: highest and lowest points (data from U.S. Geological Survey and other sources).
State capital: with county
Largest city: with population
Second largest city: with population
Largest county: with population

Housing: number of units, number occupied, percentage vacant (data from the U.S. Bureau of the Census).

Distribution of population by race and Hispanic origin: percentages for White, Black, Hispanic (may be of any race), Native American, Asian and Pacific islander, Other (data from the U.S. Bureau of the Census).

Admission date: with order of admission.

Location: descriptive, noting bordering states, provinces, and bodies of water.

Name Origin: concise account of state name origin.

State Symbols or Emblems: as given by state authorities.

State motto and nickname(s): as given by state authorities.

Telephone Area code(s): with indication of where used if multiple.

Time Zone(s): with indication of where used if multiple.

Abbreviations: both official postal and traditional.

Part of (region): the region or regions that the state is generally considered to be part of.

Following this standard presentation of basic data is a brief introductory essay. Generally, these essays follow a standard outline and include information on local government (counties and municipalities), settlement history and early development, and later history through the twentieth century. They close with a discussion of the state's boundaries, including any peculiarities or disputes with other states.

The state introduction closes with a list of all the counties and, for those states that have them, a list of all multi-county places. The multi-county places are municipalities or census designated places (CDPs) whose area lies within more than one county. Typically, multi-county places have a large portion in one county, with a smaller portion in a second county, often without any population residing there. For each multi-county place the population of the entire place and of each county portion is given. For further discussion of the multi-county places in the United States, see under "Counties" in the discussion below on **Hierarchy of Government in the United States**.

Entries for Counties or County Equivalents

Following the state introduction, each county appears alphabetically, followed by the populated places that are in that county. Each county has an entry that gives the following basic information:

Name
County Seat: with ZIP code
Population (1990 Census; 1980 Census)
Population density (per square mile)
Land area and water area (square miles)
Area code
Descriptive location
Background and establishment
Name origin

Entries for Places below the County Level

In compiling material for the populated places below the county level, which comprise the bulk of the entries in *APD*, the editorial policy was to include as much information as could be reliably reported for each data element in the entry. At minimum, entries in *APD* provide the following for each incorporated populated place below the county level:

Name
Status: city, town, township, etc.

Population (1990 Census)
Land area and water area (square miles)
Latitude and longitude
Population density (per square mile)
Area code (given with county entry)

For some unincorporated places, only name and some 1990 census data are given.

For larger places, particularly for those with a population above 10,000, the amount of data provided is greater, and normally also includes:

ZIP code
Population (1980 Census)

Aside from the statistical data, many entries also include:

Other Information: location, founder, dates of incorporation, etc.
Name Origin: as available; date of naming and previous names given whenever possible.

A typical "full" entry for a municipality in *APD* looks like this:

> **Worcester** City
> **ZIP:** 01601   **Lat:** 42-16-10 N **Long:** 71-48-32 W
> **Pop:** 169,759 (1990); 161,799 (1980)   **Pop Density:** 4514.9
> **Land:** 37.6 sq. mi.; **Water:** 1.0 sq. mi.   **Elev:** 480 ft.
> In central MA, 15 mi. west of Boston. Second largest city in MA: settled 1673; incorporated as town 1722; as city 1848. Diverse industrial city: machinery and machine tools, fabricated metals, printed materials, and chemicals, plastics, and abrasives.
> **Name origin:** Either for the town of Worcester or for Worcestershire, the county in England in which it is located.

The various elements of an entry may be explained as follows:

Name: the full legal name for the place, or the common name for unincorporated places. In some cases the popular form of the name is given.

Status: (to the right of the name) the legal status of the incorporated place—e.g., City, Town, Township, Village, Borough—according to local use. The types of incorporated places in the state are discussed in each state introduction under the heading *Municipalities*. In the case of unincorporated places, status may be given as "populated place" if official or legal status could not be verified. Certain unincorporated places for which the U.S. Bureau of the Census reports population figures and other data, known as Census Designated Places, are identified as "CDP". *U.S. military installations with resident population* are identified as "Military Facility".

Population (1990 Census): the population reported by the U.S. Bureau of the Census for the decennial census of April 1, 1990. (1980 Census): the population reported by the U.S. Bureau of the Census for the decennial census of April 1, 1980, as corrected, for comparison with 1990. If the populated place is new since 1980 (or its boundaries changed between the 1980 and the 1990 censuses), 1980 data is not given.

Land area and water area (square miles): as provided by the U.S. Bureau of the Census.

Latitude and longitude: in degrees, minutes, and seconds; as provided by the U.S. Bureau of the Census.

Population density (per square mile): calculated by dividing the 1990 population by the land area in square miles.

Telephone Area code (given with county entry).

ZIP code: as reported by the U.S. Postal Service.

Other information: for state capitals, larger cities, county seats, commercial and industrial centers, and municipalities of historic or cultural significance, descriptive location and other background information are also provided. As often as possible, when reliable information could be obtained, incorporation dates of municipalities are also provided.

Name origin: given when reliable information could be obtained and verified.

Data given in *APD* for population (1990, 1980; 1995 and 2000 projections for states), for housing and population distribution (for states), and for latitude and longitude is from published reports or data files provided by the U.S. Bureau of the Census.

Land and water area measurement are from data files provided by the U.S. Bureau of the Census. The Bureau calculates area measurements by computer based on information from the TIGER geographic data base.

Water area measurements include all water, unlike previous Census measurements, which included only inland water. As a result, total water area reported, especially for coastal states, has increased from previous Census figures. Water area measurements from the 1990 Census include inland, coastal, Great Lakes (including Lake St. Clair), and territorial water (from the 3-mile limit to the shoreline or base lines that delimit inland and coastal waters).

Name Origin Information

This element of entry information was the greatest challenge to compile and remains an unfinished (perhaps never to be finished) task. Sources for the data are variable in quality and reliability, and are often very difficult to obtain. Many tend to deal with names within a state, county, or region, and it is typically difficult to acquire books or locally published material regarding name origins. Aside from the initial problem of acquiring or accessing any good source material, the information provided in the sources was often found to be incomplete, conflicting, or lacking in credibility.

"Onomastic Fact"

We have attempted to present *the reason a particular name was given to a place*, what Prof. Kelsie Harder (see "Foreword") has termed the "onomastic fact." Whenever possible, we have also indicated who gave the name and the date it was bestowed. Former names for a place, if known, are also indicated.

Occasionally the onomastic fact is easy to determine, well documented, and well known. More often the determination requires a study of history and biography, a sense for the settlement pattern within a state or region, and an understanding of the tenor of the times in which the naming was done. Some sensitivity for language and knowledge of naming practices also proves useful. For most of the name origins, we have relied upon Kelsie Harder's *Illustrated Dictionary of Place Names: United States and Canada* (1976).

What we have *not* done is to trace the etymology in terms of the linguistic roots of the names themselves. Such work is certainly legitimate and important, often fascinating, but is beyond the requirements of determining onomastic fact. We have been content with determining and presenting, as often as possible, when and why a place was named.

Borrowed Names

If the name was borrowed from another U.S. place, the entry indicates this. The onomastic fact for the eponymous place, if known, is given under its entry. If the place is not an entry in *APD* (e.g., a small river whose name is used for a populated place), we have attempted to give the onomastic fact, if known, within the name origin information for the populated place.

The editorial policy for name origins in *APD* was to present as much material as we could reliably offer, but to say nothing if reliable information could not be obtained. We were able to give such information for all states, counties, and a majority of the larger cities, as well as many smaller places, perhaps 10,000 entries overall. Thus many entries in *APD* lack name origin data. We hope that this feature can be augmented in subsequent editions of the book. We encourage users who have such information on a place, county, region, or state to notify the publisher. Please mail correspondence to:

>Editor, *American Places Dictionary*
>Omnigraphics, Inc.
>Penobscot Bldg.
>Detroit, MI 48226

Variability by Region

For some states name origin material is abundant and well researched. This generally reflects the interests of a local expert, or a set of experts over the years, who had access to good historical sources and who devoted prodigious amounts of research time and scholarly effort to producing publications of quality, knowing that their audience would likely be a small, albeit devoted one. For the names of counties and municipalities, the New England states have perhaps the best coverage of any single region, perhaps reflecting the relative simplicity or lack of complications for the names (many are of English origin), the existence of good historical records, and the geographic compactness of the region and its states. Other states have been blessed by the scholarship of particular researchers, so that the name origins and other information for places in Kentucky, Oregon, and California are generally better documented and widely available, thanks to the efforts of Robert Rennick, Lewis McArthur (father and son), and Erwin Gudde, to name but a notable few.

"American Indian" Names

This is an area fraught with controversy, even regarding the question of how to refer to these names. While recent developments have led some to favor such terms as *Amerindian* or *Native American* to refer to these names and the languages from which they originate, *APD* uses the more traditional forms *Indian* or *American Indian* when speaking in general of such names, or, whenever possible, notes a specific language or people.

Putting aside the issue of style, more critical to understanding the origin of names is the fact that American Indian languages have been less well documented and studied. Several reasons may be cited for this, including the fact that these languages were rarely recorded in writing by native speakers, so that records for them, if they exist, are generally sparse and very often second-hand, in the form of observations by Europeans or Americans. As a result, place names of American Indian origin generally have come down to us as if through a filter.

Another factor results from cultural differences regarding the use of names. As a rule, American Indian naming practices differed greatly from the tradition of the European cultures. Whereas the European explorers and settlers made a great issue of naming features and places and dutifully recording everything—as evidence of a claim, for convenience of future reference, and out of pride—it seems that American Indian cultures did not follow and in fact may have been opposed to the practice of systematically assigning names to particular places. Additionally, Indian naming seems to have been more localized, so that a river, for example, may have been referred to in several if not many ways along its entire course, each "name" reflecting local experience.

As Lewis L. McArthur notes in his Introduction to *Oregon Geographic Names,* Sixth Edition:

A good deal of nonsense has been written about the meaning of Indian names. The late Lewis A. McArthur knew many Indians. They eked out a living amidst hard circumstances and it seems improbable that Oregon Indians ever made up geographic names because of "moonlight filtering through trees," "sunshine dancing on the water," "rose petals floating on water" and "water rippling over pebbles." Competent researchers have found that most Indian names were based on much more practical and everyday matters.

What often can be said about an American place name is that it originates from an earlier Indian name or term. Beyond that the situation becomes much murkier. It has been the practice of *APD* to avoid speculation about names of American Indian origin. We have on occasion reported what is believed about certain names, but maintain that it is perilous to assert the original meaning of many American Indian names.

Hierarchy of Government in the United States

The organization of *APD* into state sections, county groupings, and entries for the individual places themselves repeats the pattern of government administration of the entire country below the federal level. This hierarchy of government starts at the state level, and at each level the entire territory of the United States is included in some administrative entity. Thus the "mosaic of governments" is complete at the state, county, and place levels. The primary reason for this bit of bureaucratic thoroughness is to ensure that all the U.S. population is included in each decennial census at every level, allowing for statistical integrity and (technically) equitable distribution of federal benefits at each level.

States

Most people are quite familiar with the state government level—50 states, plus the District of Columbia. This is the top level covered by *APD*, which has entries for each of these 51 entities.

Four of the states refer to themselves as commonwealths: Kentucky, Massachusetts, Pennsylvania, and Virginia.

There are no entries in *APD* for Puerto Rico or any territories or possessions of the United States.

Counties and County Equivalents

Below the state level are the counties or county equivalents, of which there are 3,141 in the entire United States. This total includes the District of Columbia government as a state and a county equivalent. If one considers Washington, D.C., also as a city, then the nation's capital is the only place that functions technically at all three government levels.

States without Counties or with County Equivalents

In certain states the county level of government is somewhat different from the "normal" pattern, as outlined for each state listed below.

In Louisiana, the parishes provide the equivalent of county government in other states.

In Connecticut and Rhode Island, county government has actually been abolished, but county boundaries still are used administratively, and counties are still recognized popularly.

In Maryland, the city of Baltimore is independent and serves as a county equivalent.

In Virginia, 41 independent cities serve as county equivalents; there are also 95 counties.

In Missouri, the city of St. Louis is an independent city and serves as a county equivalent.

In Nevada, Carson City is an independent city and serves as a county equivalent.

In Alaska there are no counties as such. Areas with some concentration of population are called boroughs and do provide government administration. Most of the territory of the state is included in large tracts called census areas, which have been designated by the U.S. Bureau of the Census.

In Hawaii alone among the states, all local government is at the county level. There are no incorporated municipalities. The four main islands—Oahu, Hawaii, Kauai, and Maui—are essentially each treated as counties. The island of Oahu and most of the smaller Hawaiian Islands are all governed by the consolidated government called the City and County of Honolulu. Also, a small part of Molokai Island is administered by the state Department of Health as Kalawao County, and is occupied by patients with Hansen's disease, or leprosy. This is the site of the noted leper colony ministered to by Father Joseph Damien (1840–89).

Two other variations on the standard county pattern, city-county consolidations and multi-county places, lead to the discussion of municipalities and other sub-county entities.

City-County Consolidations

A number of cities have consolidated their government with the county, and the two are largely functionally equivalent. These city-county consolidations are:

Anchorage, AK (city consolidated with Anchorage Borough)

Juneau, AK (city consolidated with Juneau Borough)

Sitka, AK (city consolidated with Sitka Borough)

San Francisco, CA (city consolidated with San Francisco County)

Denver, CO (city consolidated with Denver County)

Jacksonville, FL (city consolidated with Duval County, but the municipalities of Atlantic Beach, Baldwin, Jacksonville Beach, and Neptune Beach remain as separate entities in the county)

Columbus, GA (city consolidated with Muscogee County; Bibb City also consolidated with the county, but is a separate entity)

Honolulu, HI (city and county consolidated as the City and County of Honolulu)

Indianapolis, IN (city government consolidated with Marion County; the four suburbs of Beech Grove, Lawrence, Southport, and Speedway maintain independent status, and 13 other suburbs have quasi-independent status)

Lexington, KY (city consolidated with Fayette County as Lexington Fayette Urban County)

Baton Rouge, LA (city consolidated with East Baton Rouge Parish, but not coextensive)

Houma, LA (city consolidated with Terrebonne Parish, but not coextensive)

New Orleans, LA (city consolidated with Orleans Parish)

Nantucket, MA (town coextensive with Nantucket County; the whole of Nantucket Island)

Suffolk County, MA (government consolidated with city of Boston, but not coextensive)

Anaconda, MT (consolidated with Deer Lodge County as Anaconda-Deer Lodge County)

Butte, MT (consolidated with Silver Bow County as Butte-Silver Bow; Walkerville remains a separate municipality)

Yellowstone National Park, MT (administered by the National Park Service, but considered as a county equivalent)

Philadelphia, PA (city consolidated with Philadelphia County)

Lynchburg, TN (consolidated with Moore County as Lynchburg, Moore County)

Nashville, TN (city consolidated with Davidson County; six suburban cities continue as separate municipalities for certain purposes)

Multi-County Places

As noted above, a number of municipalities in the United States cover an area that is in more than one county. Typically, multi-county places have a large portion in one county, with a smaller portion in a second county, often without any population residing in the second county. The total number of multi-county places in the United States is 923, broken down as follows:

2-county places: 855
3-county places: 60
4-county places: 5*
5-county places: 3**

 * Broomfield, CO; Allentown, GA; Barrington Hills, IL; Kansas City, MO; High Point, NC
** New York, NY (its five boroughs are county equivalents); Oklahoma City, OK; Dallas, TX

Municipalities and Other Sub-county Entities

Owing to the diverse and varied settlement of the United States (and to the diverse and varied nature of its settlers), no two states treat their sub-county populated places in exactly the same way administratively. In different regions of the nation, government below the county level is represented by cities, towns, villages, townships, boroughs, and other administrative entities.

In the western and southern states particularly many populated areas are not administered by any government below the county level. These places are not cities or towns, but often have established popular names, even if they lack legal boundaries.

Taken as a whole, the variety of local governments and other populated districts reflects the long and varied history of settlement in the United States. But the situation also means a complicated burden for the federal agencies, such as the U.S. Bureau of the Census, that have to deal with this patchwork of local administration or, in some cases, lack thereof. Two common problems encountered at the sub-county level are discussed here to illustrate the kinds of unexpected peculiarities that arise in compiling entries for these places.

"Same Name, Same County" (Entries with Asterisks)

Frequently in *APD* there will be two entries for places in a single county, that will have the same name. This may seem puzzling, but reflects the fact that, in many states, local government or administrative units may overlap or divide certain functions. In states where land was surveyed into townships prior to much of the subsequent settlement, the township pattern was established before incorporated places were in existence or even necessary. As townships became settled, centers of population desired corporate status and legal standing as a government. Depending on the state, the incorporated place might be called a town, village, borough, or city. Frequently, places that were incorporated as towns would develop and grow to the point where they would want to become cities, often gaining thereby a greater amount of autonomy under state law. But as the incorporated places—cities, towns, villages, or whatever—became established, the original township pattern usually remained. Very often, the incorporated area might be only part (the most densely settled part) of a township. Also very often, the township name was adopted by the new incorporated place. The result usually is two places with the same name in the same county. Examples include Chevy Chase, MD; Farmington, NH; Grosse Pointe, MI; Green Bay, WI.

Our policy for this situation has been to retain both places if they are recognized by the state as incorporated. Naturally, they will come together alphabetically as entries within their county. One of the two entries, normally the one of lesser administrative function (and often smaller population), will appear second and be marked with an asterisk.

The Differing Use of *Borough* in Five States

One example of variation among the states can be seen in the use of the term *borough* in conjunction with other terms for municipalities in five states. Each has populated places called boroughs, but they differ greatly in function and relationship to other administrative units.

Alaska: the 16 boroughs are actually county equivalents; three are governmentally consolidated with cities (Anchorage, Juneau, Sitka).

Connecticut: the 11 boroughs are incorporated places; but are actually part of a town and not entirely independent. The borough of Naugatuck is coextensive with the town of the same name.

New Jersey: the 252 boroughs function as municipalities. New Jersey's cities, towns, townships, and villages are other types of municipalities.

New York: the five boroughs that make up New York City—Manhattan, Brooklyn, the Bronx, Queens, and Staten Island—function as parts of the city and county equivalents. Manhattan is coextensive with New York County, Brooklyn is coextensive with Kings County, and Staten Island is coextensive with Richmond County. Borough and county names are the same for the Bronx and Queens.

Pennsylvania: the 966 boroughs function as municipalities, along with 55 cities and one town. Pennsylvania also has 1,549 townships, which are similar in character to townships in New England (see below).

In *APD* we have attempted to present as much sub-county administrative detail as possible for populated places. As a result, many places that might normally be thought of as a single city or town may have two (or more) entries in *APD*. In the introductions for the individual states some of the nature of each state's municipalities is noted.

In the following paragraphs we shall attempt to suggest something of the complexity of the local administrative hierarchy that must be taken into account in any comprehensive treatment of U.S. populated places nationwide.

Minor Civil Divisions (MCDs) in 28 States

In 28 states the sub-county entities are functioning local governments or other sub-county administrative entities, broadly referred to as minor civil divisions (MCDs). In these states the U.S. Bureau of the Census tracks population totals within these established local boundaries. The names and relationships of the sub-county populated places in these 28 states varies regionally and from state to state.

In the Northeast (the six New England states, New York, New Jersey, and Pennsylvania), counties are generally divided into towns or townships. Typically, these are much more important administratively than the counties (hence, the vestigial counties of Connecticut and Rhode Island, noted above). Towns in the Northeast are typically incorporated, legal entities, and in most of these states there are very few areas that lie outside the boundaries of some town or township (except for some incorporated cities). In northern New England some sparsely inhabited or uninhabited districts provide sub-county boundaries. These areas are called plantations, gores, grants, unorganized territory (in northern Maine), or locations and purchases (in New Hampshire).

In the six Great Lakes states (Ohio, Michigan, Indiana, Illinois, Wisconsin, and Minnesota) and six other central states (Iowa, Kansas, Missouri, Nebraska, North Dakota, and South Dakota) the division into townships (called *towns* in Wisconsin) is the typical pattern. Compared to the Northeast, however, the townships in most of these states are generally of considerably less administrative importance than the counties. The towns or townships of the central states may or may not be incorporated, and less often have the authority to levy taxes or otherwise carry on the governmental functions of their counterparts in the Northeast. The exception is Wisconsin, where the towns function in a manner very similar to New England towns.

In North Carolina and Arkansas townships and unorganized territories provide sub-county boundaries where there are no incorporated places such as cities.

In some so-called "MCD states," the Census Bureau tracks population within the boundaries of other existing administrative districts, which vary in designation by state; these are listed as "Populated Places" in *APD*.

Census County Divisions (CCDs) in 21 States

In 21 states the U.S. Bureau of the Census, in cooperation with state and local officials, has established statistical entities below the county level for states that do not have MCDs or where MCDs are not adequate for reporting sub-county statistics. These statistical entities are called Census County Divisions (CCDs). The 21 "CCD states" are primarily in the South and the West, where, except for the incorporated places, much of the area below the county level is unincorporated. CCDs were created solely for statistical purposes, and are not normally used or referred to by the resident population. They have no legal functions and are not units of government. CCDs do have names, however, based on a place, county, or well-known local name. The Census County Divisions exist to maintain statistical integrity—and a complete "mosaic" at the sub-county level.

The 21 CCD states are as follows:

Alabama	Georgia	New Mexico	Utah
Arizona	Hawaii	Oklahoma	Washington
California	Idaho	Oregon	Wyoming
Colorado	Kentucky	South Carolina	
Delaware	Montana	Tennessee	
Florida	Nevada	Texas	

Census Subareas in Alaska

In Alaska the Census Bureau and the state delineated census subareas as statistical subdivisions of the county equivalent boroughs and census areas.

Census Designated Places (CDPs)

Another statistical entity used by the Census Bureau is called the Census Designated Place (CDP). CDPs, delineated in 49 states, are densely settled concentrations of population that are identifiable by name, but are not legally incorporated places. Like CCDs, their names are generally reflective of local usage, but they have no legal status.

In *APD* we have included entries for CDPs where they provide additional detail and do not cause potential confusion because of close similarity of the CDP name with an actual municipality within the same county. One state in which they are particularly noticeable is Hawaii, where there are no legally incorporated places besides the City and County of Honolulu. All other populated places in Hawaii that are entries are based on CDPs.

Conclusion

The melting pot that has become the United States of America reveals itself in many facets of our culture, not the least of which are historical settlement patterns, the place names given to settlements, and the diverse systems of organization and administration. As we delve deeper into why the United States, or the individual states, were set up as they were, we see more and more diversity. Establishing order in the midst of the state-by-state variation, as the Bureau of the Census has done with minor civil divisions and census county divisions (and census areas in Alaska), is a necessary task of government.

* * * * *

Acknowledgments

The compilation of *American Places Dictionary* would not have been possible without the vision, inspiration, and diligence of many individuals and organizations. Foremost among all those who had a role in the work is Fred Ruffner, publisher and president of Omnigraphics, Inc., who conceived of the project originally and whose support for it was unwavering despite unforeseen delays and setbacks. Other key personnel at Omnigraphics included Laurie Harris, editorial director; Jim Sellgren, operations; Jane Steele, promotion; and Eric Berger, production manager. The concern for quality that they exhibited, as well as their patience with the editor, are much appreciated.

Assisting the editorial process in all its details was Chuck Lacy of Weimer Graphics, Indianapolis, Indiana, who met the formidable challenge of the data processing and typesetting with exceptional skill and efficiency. Mr. Lacy helped conceive and implement the procedures to process, consolidate, sort, and typeset a massive body of data. The quality and efficiency of his work were never compromised by the demands imposed by editorial and publishing specifications.

We also wish to recognize the assistance provided by a number of specialists in federal agencies, including especially, at the Bureau of the Census, Marie Pees, of the Population Division; Don Hirschfeld (retired) and Joel Miller, of the Geography Division; and, at the National Institute of Standards and Technology, Henry Tom. These highly skilled, dedicated, and profoundly knowledgeable professionals promptly and ably responded to our many inquiries into the vagaries of U.S. populated places. Their work, and that of others like them in various federal agencies, is indispensable to the creation of place name reference tools.

Officials in state and local government nationwide, far too numerous to mention, assisted throughout the editorial process, sometimes answering single, focused inquiries, often sending enormously important publications and other data from their files. This state-specific information was vital to our work, especially given the complexity and variation across the United States in the way government and administration function below the federal level.

While the invaluable contributions of each of the individuals mentioned cannot be overemphasized, we must add that the responsibility for any errors or omissions in *American Places Dictionary* rests solely with the editor.

We encourage users of this dictionary to send suggestions on how the work might be improved, expanded, or made more accessible in subsequent editions.

                Editor, *American Places Dictionary*
                Omnigraphics, Inc.
                Penobscot Bldg.
                Detroit, MI, 48226

                                    Frank R. Abate
                                          Editor

Old Saybrook, Connecticut
April 1994

Editor's Miscellany:

American Places and American Names—
Curiosities and Peculiarities

In the course of compiling and editing *American Places Dictionary* the editorial staff came upon many fascinating tidbits and facts about the United States. Collectively, this grab-bag of trivia, history, odd names, and other surprises lacks a coherent theme, and while the material seemed inappropriate for the Introduction, we could not resist the opportunity to present what we found. Hence, this brief miscellany, a collection of unrelated details that we felt should not go unrecorded.

This brief list reveals the variety of items included here and serves as a handy summary:

I. Early U.S. Capitals
II. Geopolitical Peculiarities
III. Unusual Official State Symbols
IV. Historical Development and Changes in Counties
V. Some Out-of-the-Ordinary Place Names
VI. First Name/Last Name Places

I. Early U.S. Capitals

In the earliest years of U.S. history there was no permanent federal capital. This situation lasted from the signing of the Declaration of Independence in 1776 until 1800, when the federal government settled into the newly established Washington, D.C. The different meeting places of the Continental Congress, the Congress of the Confederation (authorized under the Articles of Confederation), and later the U.S. Congress (under the U.S. Constitution, from March 4, 1789) in these years, a total of eight different cities in four states, are listed below, with the span of first and last meeting dates in each place:

Philadelphia:	September 5, 1774 to December 12, 1776
Baltimore:	December 20, 1776 to March 4, 1777
Philadelphia:	March 5, 1777 to September 18, 1777
Lancaster, PA:	September 27, 1777 (one day only)
York, PA:	September 30, 1777 to June 27, 1778
Philadelphia:	July 2, 1778 to June 21, 1783
Princeton, NJ:	June 30, 1783 to November 4, 1783
Annapolis, MD:	November 26, 1783 to June 3, 1784
Trenton, NJ:	November 1, 1784 to December 24, 1784

New York City: January 11, 1785 to August 12, 1790
Philadelphia: December 6, 1790 to May 14, 1800

II. Geopolitical Peculiarities

The following section describes a number of instances of geopolitical peculiarities across the U.S. Some of these unusual or unique border patterns are rather obvious on a map of the United States, while others are quite hard to find except on very detailed maps. Several different kinds of situations are described, some affecting several states and others peculiar to a single state.

Panhandles and Other Border Extensions

The following states have panhandles or border extensions of some sort. A panhandle is generally defined as a projecting, relatively narrow strip of land that is surrounded by the territory of other states or a water boundary, but is not a peninsula.

Alabama	Missouri
Alaska	New Mexico
Florida	Oklahoma
Idaho	Pennsylvania
Maryland	Texas
Mississippi	West Virginia

Two "classic" panhandles are those of Oklahoma and Florida, projecting as long narrow strips to the west in each case, and truly resembling panhandles when viewed on a map. The panhandle of **Oklahoma** was ceded to the U.S. by Texas before Texas was admitted to the Union. It was part of Oklahoma Territory by 1890, called the Public Land Strip, sometimes referred to as "No Man's Land." **Florida's** panhandle, the area west of the Apalachicola River, was part of the original Spanish province that extended west to the Mississippi River. When Spain ceded Florida to Great Britain in 1763, the territory was divided into West Florida and East Florida along the river. West Florida was later reduced in extent as western portions to the Mississippi River became part of Louisiana, Mississippi, and Alabama.

The other commonly referred to panhandle, that of **Texas**, was created when the state sold a portion of its original northwest territory to the federal government in 1850. The new boundary lines of northwest Texas were set by survey, and left a distinctive broad panhandle that projects northward.

The panhandle of **Alaska**, extending southeast from the 141st meridian, is a remnant of the boundaries established by Great Britain and Russia in a convention of 1825. The territory, including this panhandle, was purchased by the United States from Russia in 1867, and the United States consistently maintained claim to the region despite objection over the years from Canada. The dispute was settled by an international tribunal in 1903.

West Virginia is the only state to have two panhandles, one extending north between Ohio and Pennsylvania near Wheeling, the other east, bordering Virginia to the south and Maryland to the north.

Western **Maryland**, from Hagerstown west, extends like a panhandle between West Virginia and Pennsylvania. In addition, Maryland is also cut by Chesapeake Bay, so that to the east there is a portion on the Delmarva Peninsula (see below) that is separated from the rest of the state. This region of the state is called the Eastern Shore.

Missouri has a distinctive portion at its southeast corner that is called the "bootheel" because of its shape. It lies below the line of 36 degrees, 30 minutes north latitude that marks the rest of Missouri's southern border. The eastern border of the bootheel is the Mississippi River, and the western the St. Francis River. This portion became a part of Missouri on its admission to statehood. Prominent landowner J. Hardeman Walker, founder of Caruthersville, an important town in the region, was influential in having this addition become part of the state.

The panhandle of **Idaho** is the result of a reduction to the original Idaho territory prior to statehood in 1890. This narrow area, lying between Idaho's western border with Washington and the Bitterroot Range of the Rockies, was left when land to the east of the Bitterroot Range was made part of the Territory of Montana in 1864.

The extreme southwestern corner of **New Mexico**, extending below its long southern boundary with Texas at 32 degrees north latitude, was an addition made to the original territory of 1850. The land was acquired from Mexico in the Gadsden Purchase of 1853, negotiated for the United States by James Gadsden, who wanted to ensure a good route for a southern railroad to the Pacific. The bulk of the Gadsden Purchase became part of the Territory of Arizona (1863) along its southern border with Mexico.

While they are not truly panhandles, Pennsylvania, Alabama, and Mississippi each have narrow projections that give the states access to water. The "Erie Triangle" of **Pennsylvania**, once a part of New York but ceded to the federal government in 1781, was purchased from the U.S. by Pennsylvania on March 3, 1792, to give the state a broader land access to Lake Erie. The purchase price was $151,640.25, and the deed was signed by George Washington. **Alabama** and **Mississippi** each have projections to the Gulf of Mexico that are a part of what was once called West Florida, originally part of the Spanish province of Florida. The land, to the west of the Perdido River, was occupied by the United States in 1812, and eventually was added to the territories of Alabama and Mississippi.

The Four Corners: Utah, Colorado, New Mexico, Arizona

One corner of each of these four states, each of which has very regular, straight borders, meets at a point referred to as the Four Corners. The point is the intersection of 37 degrees north latitude and 109 degrees, 2 minutes west longitude. The longitude is exactly 32 degrees west of Washington, D.C. The spot is marked by a prominent boundary monument, and is the only point in the U.S. common to four states.

Portions of Land Separated from the Rest of the State along Rivers

In a number of places, particularly along major rivers such as the Mississippi and Missouri, small portions of certain states are separated from the rest of the state owing to changes over the years in the course of the rivers. Natural events such as floods and earthquakes bring about these changes in river channels. The situation arises when two states have fixed their border along the channel of a river. Whenever the river changes course, an area of land that was once on one side of the river is left on the other. There are many such places along the southern course of the Mississippi River to the Gulf of Mexico, affecting, on the eastern banks, Kentucky, Tennessee, and Mississippi, and on the western banks Missouri, Arkansas, and Louisiana.

Kentucky–Missouri–Tennessee at New Madrid

A small portion of extreme southwestern Kentucky lies isolated from the rest of the state along the course of the Mississippi River near New Madrid, Missouri. This is the result of a change in the course of the river caused by the noted earthquake of 1811, whose epicenter was at New Madrid. From this part of Kentucky one can cross by land into Tennessee or by river to Missouri, but must pass through one of these two states to get to the rest of Kentucky.

Iowa–Nebraska at Omaha

A small portion of Iowa is separated from the rest of the state near Omaha, Nebraska. The border between the states is the Missouri River. When the river changed course in 1877, moving to its present channel, it isolated a portion of what had been on the eastern bank, also leaving a small lake, Carter Lake, as a remnant of the former channel. This small portion on the western bank of the Missouri is still part of Iowa.

Delmarva Peninsula

This peninsula extends between Chesapeake Bay to the west and Delaware Bay and the Atlantic Ocean to the east. It is divided among three states, Delaware, Maryland, and Virginia, hence the name, a combination of the first syllables of the first two states with the standard abbreviation letters for Virginia. The extreme southern portion of the peninsula has been a part of Virginia since colonial days, although it is totally separated from the rest of the state. The exact border with Maryland was a source of controversy from colonial times until 1972, when both states finally agreed on a well-defined boundary.

Going *South* from the United States into Canada—Detroit to Windsor

Owing to the natural course of the Detroit River, which forms the international boundary between southeastern Michigan and the Canadian province of Ontario, travelers crossing the border from Detroit into Canada, using either the Ambassador Bridge or the Detroit-Windsor tunnel under the river, are actually going nearly due south. Excepting in Alaska, this is the only instance of a major border crossing between the two countries where one travels south to reach Canada.

The Notch in the Connecticut–Massachusetts Border

The generally straight west-east border line between Connecticut and Massachusetts is broken by a notch north of Hartford, Connecticut. The Massachusetts town of Southwick extends into this notch; hence it is sometimes referred to as the "Southwick jog." In Connecticut it is sometimes referred to as the "Suffield gap," as it lies between the towns of Suffield and Granby. The area within the notch became part of Massachusetts in 1803 by ruling of a survey commission formed by both states. The commission determined that Massachusetts had lost territory owing to errors in the previous surveys that had set the straight-line border between the states. The notch was intended to compensate Massachusetts with an area equivalent to that lost.

Arc-of-a-Circle Border between Delaware and Pennsylvania

Most of Delaware's short northern border with Pennsylvania is the arc of a circle, the center of which is some 12 miles to the south at New Castle, Delaware. This unusual boundary line was fixed by a survey authorized in 1701 by William Penn. It is the only instance of such a border shape in the United States.

Michigan's Upper Peninsula

A portion of the state of Michigan shares a border with Wisconsin but is not connected to the rest of the state. Michigan's Upper Peninsula separates Lake Michigan from Lake Superior and extends to the Canadian province of Ontario at Sault Ste. Marie and to the Lower Peninsula of the state at the Straits of Mackinac and the entrance to Lake Huron. It was not a part of the original Michigan Territory organized in 1805, but was added as part of an extension of Michigan Territory in 1818. Wisconsin Territory was created in 1836 from the western portion of this extension, but the Upper Peninsula was retained by Michigan upon its admission to statehood in 1837. Subsequent disputes over the exact border line with Wisconsin raged for many years, finally being settled in 1948 after U.S. Supreme Court intervention and approval of the U.S. Congress.

Portion of Minnesota North of the 49th Parallel—The "Northwest Angle"

Minnesota's Lake of the Woods County includes an area of about 124 square miles, called the Northwest Angle, that is non-contiguous with the rest of the state. This area can only be reached from the rest of Minnesota by boat or by traveling through or over part of Canada (Manitoba or Ontario). Excepting Alaska, it is the northernmost tract of the United States, wholly above the forty-ninth parallel. This area became part of the United States because inaccurate maps were used during treaty negotiations with the British in 1783 and 1818. In 1917 the International Joint Commission between the United States and Canada described the situation as a "politico-geographical curiosity of a boundary."

Portion of New Hampshire North of the Forty-Fifth Parallel—Pittsburg, N.H.

This small portion of northern New Hampshire extends north of 45 degrees north latitude, which is the general line for the international boundary between the Canadian province of Quebec and the U.S. states of New York and Vermont. The area above the forty-fifth parallel was disputed for many years by New Hampshire and Canada. In 1829 the settlers in the region organized an independent republic known as the Indian Stream Territory. This government was in effect until New Hampshire took control in 1835. The area is now the town of Pittsburg, N.H., the largest town (in area) in the state, population 901 (in 1990).

III. Unusual Official State Symbols (by state)

Each state introduction provides a complete list of official state symbols. Some of the more unusual ones are listed here.

Alaska
  sport: dog mushing (sled-dog racing)
Arizona
  neckwear: bola tie
Connecticut
  hero: Nathan Hale
  ship: Nautilus (first nuclear submarine)
Idaho
  horse: Appaloosa
Maryland
  sport: jousting
Massachusetts
  bean: baked navy bean (Boston baked beans)
  cat: tabby
  heroine: Deborah Samson
  horse: Morgan
  muffin: corn
Michigan
  soil: Kalkaska soil series
Minnesota
  muffin: blueberry
Missouri
  musical instrument: fiddle
New Mexico
  cookie: biscochito
  vegetables: frijol (pinto bean) and chile (pepper)
Ohio
  rock song: "Hang On Sloopy"
Pennsylvania
  flagship: Niagara (U.S. Brig)
Vermont
  horse: Morgan
Wisconsin
  dog: American water spaniel
  soil: Antigo silt loam

IV. Historical Development and Changes in Counties

The counties of the U.S. today appear fairly stable and unchanging. In fact, from the 1950 Census through 1993 the total number of counties in the U.S. increased only from 3,112 to 3,143, a net gain of 31, or about one percent. But this apparent stability does not reflect the historical development and increase in counties over the decades from the founding of the nation, especially in the states east of the Rockies. The story is an exceedingly complicated one geographically, as large areas were broken up to form new, more compact entities. The number of counties in a state proliferated as the state was settled by pioneers or by residents seeking open land or new horizons. Very often, as previously unsettled territory was reached, it became inconvenient for the residents to make the journey to the county seat to register births, deaths, and marriages, or to file a suit or make a claim in court. In agricultural, pre-industrial America, any day away from the livestock on the farm was a serious inconvenience, and more than a day nearly impossible to arrange or too costly to bear. The farmers' need to be within a day's ride of the county seat was frequently the reason for the formation of new counties, with county seats nearer the newer settlers.

V. Some Out-of-the-Ordinary Place Names

The following list is highly selective, and reflects only a sampling of what struck us as most noteworthy.

Aubbeenaubbee, IN
Bee Branch, MO
Beisizl, ND
Coffee Springs, AL
Correctionville, IA
Dismal, NC
Dog Ear, SD
Dry Prong, LA
East and West Chillisquaque, PA
East Loony, MO
Fair Play, MO
Farr West, UT
Flippin, AR
Funks Grove, IL

Gun Barrel City, TX
Haymow, NE
Humansville, MO
Kaaawa, HI
Magnetic Springs, OH
Mule Barn, OK
Nanty-Glo, PA
New Diggins, WI
Nodaway, IA
Oil Trough, AR
Omphghent, IL
One Road, SD
Oolagah, OK
Pecan Gap, TX
Pe Ell, WA
Quewhiffle, NC
Roasting Ear, AR
Skedee, OK
Sleepy Eye, MN
Snee Oosh, WA
Sni-A-Bar, MO
Snow Shoe, PA
Sopchoppy, FL
Sublimity, OR
Teec Nos Pos, AZ
Tightwad, MO
Turnback, MO
Tywappity, MO
Uncertain, TX
Weeki Wachee, FL
What Cheer, IA
White Eyes, OH

VI. First Name/Last Name Municipalities (by state)

The pattern of the following place names suggests a person's name, and in some cases that is clearly behind the origin of the name. In any case, these are distinctive.

Alabama:
   Phil Campbell
Arkansas:
   Ben Lomond
   Lou Norris
   Reed Keathly
   Joe Burleson
California:
   Ben Lomond
Florida:
   Mary Esther
   Anna Maria
   Jan Phyl Village
Georgia:
   Warner Robins
Indiana:
   Dick Johnson
Louisiana:
   Jean Lafitte
Missouri:
   Jim Henry
Oklahoma:
   John Day
   Gene Autry
Pennsylvania:
   Jim Thorpe
   Henry Clay
   Glen Campbell
Texas:
   Robert Lee
   Tom Bean
   Seth Ward
   George West
Virginia:
   Jack Jonett
   Samuel Miller
   Patrick Henry
West Virginia:
   Jane Lew

Selected Bibliography

In addition to the sources listed below, the editors consulted various printed sources issued by state and local governments, government assoications, etc., including "blue books" or state government manuals, state and municipal directories, and informational brochures.

The *Flying the Colors* series, published by Clements Research II of Dallas, TX (published from 1987 to 1991) was also consulted for the following states: AL, AZ, CA, CT, FL, GA, IL, IN, IA, KS, KY, MA, MI, MO, NH, NJ, NY, NC, PA, SC, TX, VA, WA, WI.

Abate, Frank R., ed. *Omni Gazetteer of the United States of America*, 11 vols. Detroit: Omnigraphics, 1991.

Adams, James N., compiler, and Keller, William E. *Illinois Place Names*. Springfield: Illinois State Historical Society, 1989.

Andriot, Jay, compiler. *Township Atlas of the United States*. McLean, VA: Documents Index, 1991.

Baker, Ronald L., and Carmony, Marvin. *Indiana Place Names*. Bloomington: Indiana University Press, 1975.

Barnes, Will C. *Arizona Place Names*. Tucson: University of Arizona Press, 1988.

Beck, Warren A., and Haase, Ynez D. *Historical Atlas of California*. Norman: University of Oklahoma Press, 1974.

—. *Historical Atlas of New Mexico*. Norman: University of Oklahoma Press, 1969.

Bentley, Elizabeth Petty. *County Courthouse Book*. Baltimore: Genealogical Publishing Co., 1990.

Bloid, John T. *Gazetteer of the State of Michigan*. New York: Arno Press, 1975 (reprint).

Bloodworth, Bertha E. and Morris, Alton C. *Places in the Sun*. Gainesville: University Presses of Florida, 1978.

Boone, Lalia. *Idaho Place Names: A Geographical Dictionary*. Moscow, ID: University of Idaho Press, 1988.

Browning, Peter. *Place Names of the Sierra Nevada, from Abbot to Zumwalt*.

—. *Yosemite Place Names: The Historic Background of Geographic Names in Yosemite National Park*. Lafayette, CA: Great West Books, 1988.

Carlson, Helen S. *Nevada Place Names: A Geographical Dictionary*. Reno: University of Nevada Press, 1974.

Cheney, Roberta Carkeek. *Names on the Face of Montana: The Story of Montana's Place Names*. Missoula, MT: Mountain Press, 1983.

Chernow, Barbara A., and Vallasi, George A., eds. *Columbia Encyclopedia*, 5th ed. New York: Columbia University Press, 1993.

Confederation of American Indians, compilers. *Indian Reservations: A State and Federal Handbook*. Jefferson, NC: McFarland, 1986.

Coulet du Gard, Rene, and Western, Dominique C. *Handbook of American Counties, Parishes and Independent Cities.* Newark, DE: Editions des Deux Mondes, 1981.

Dean, Ernie. *Arkansas Place Names.* Branson, MO: Ozarks Mountaineer, 1986.

Espenshade, A. Howry. *Pennsylvania Place Names.* Harrisburg: Evangelical Press, 1925.

Evinger, William R. *Directory of Military Bases in the U.S.* Phoenix, AZ: Oryx Press, 1991.

Fitzpatrick, Lilian L. *Nebraska Place Names.* Lincoln: University of Nebraska Press, 1960.

Foscue, Virginia O. *Place Names in Alabama.* Tuscaloosa: University of Alabama Press, 1989.

Fullerton, Ralph O. *Place Names of Tennessee.* Nashville: Tennessee Division of Geology, 1974.

Gannett, Henry. *Geographic Dictionary of Connecticut and Rhode Island.* Baltimore: Genealogical Publishing, 1978 (reprint).

—. *Origin of Certain Place Names in the United States,* 2nd ed. Williamstown, MA: Corner House, 1978 (reprint).

Gard, Robert, and Sorden, L.G. *Romance of Wisconsin Placenames.* Minocqua, WI: Heartland Press, 1988.

Gudde, Erwin G. *California Place Names: The Origin and Etymology of Current Geographical Names.* Berkeley: University of California Press, 1949.

Hagemann, James. *Heritage of Virginia: The Story of Place Names in the Old Dominion.* West Chester, PA: Whitford Press, 1986.

Halverson, F. Douglas, compiler. *County Histories of the United States Giving Present Name, Date Formed, Parent County, and County Seat.* (unpublished manuscript, n.d.)

Hanson, Gerald T., and Moneyhon, Carl H. *Historical Atlas of Arkansas.* Norman: University of Oklahoma Press, 1989.

Harder, Kelsie B., ed. *Illustrated Dictionary of Place Names, United States and Canada.* New York: Facts On File, 1985.

Harris, William H., and Levey, Judith S., eds. *New Columbia Encyclopedia.* New York: Columbia University Press, 1975.

Hart, James D. *Companion to California.* New York: Oxford University Press, 1978.

Heck, L.W.; Wraight, A.J.; Orth, D.J.; Carter, J.R.; Van Winkle, L.G.; and Hazen, Janet. *Delaware Place Names.* Geological Survey and Coast & Geodetic Survey, 1966.

Hitchman, Robert. *Place Names of Washington.* Washington State Historical Society, 1985.

Hunt, Elmer Munson. *New Hampshire Town Names and Whence They Came.* Peterborough, NH: Noone House, 1970.

Indian Service Population and Labor Force Estimates. U.S. Dept. of the Interior, Bureau of Indian Affairs (report), 1991.

Kaminkow, Marion J. *Maryland A to Z: A Topographical Dictionary.* Baltimore: Magna Carta Book Co., 1985.

Kane, Joseph Nathan. *American Counties,* 4th ed. Metuchen, NJ: Scarecrow Press, 1983.

Kenny, Hamill. *Placenames of Maryland: Their Origin and Meaning.* Baltimore: Museum and Library of Maryland History, Maryland Historical Society, 1984.

Krakow, Kenneth K. *Georgia Place-Names.* Macon, GA: Winship Press, 1975.

Lekisch, Barbara. *Tahoe Place Names: The Origin and History of Names in the Lake Tahoe Basin.* Lafayette, CA: Great West Books, 1988.

McArthur, Lewis A. *Oregon Geographic Names,* 6th ed. Oregon Historical Society Press, 1992.

McCoy, Sondra Van Meter, and Hults, Jan. *1001 Kansas Place Names*. University Press of Kansas, 1989.

Morris, Allen. *Florida Place Names*. Coral Gables: University of Miami, 1974.

Morris, John W.; Goins, Charles R.; and McReynolds, Edwin C. *Historical Atlas of Oklahoma*. Norman: University of Oklahoma Press, 1969.

National Gazetteer of the United States of America, United States Concise. U.S. Geological Survey in cooperation with U.S. Board on Geographic Names, 1990.

Neuffer, Claude Henry. *Names in South Carolina: Vols. I-XII, 1954-1965*. University of South Carolina, 1967.

Neuffer, Claude and Irene. *Correct Mispronunciations of Some South Carolina Names*. Columbia: University of South Carolina, 1983.

Origin of New Jersey Place Names. Reprinted by NJ Public Library Commission, Trenton, 1945.

Orth, Donald J. *Dictionary of Alaska Place Names*. U.S. Geological Survey, Dept. of the Interior, 1967.

Paisano, Edna; Greendeer-Lee, Joan; Cowles, June; and Carroll, Debbie. *American Indian and Alaska Native Areas*. Population Division, Bureau of Census, 1990.

Palmer, T.S., ed. *Place Names of the Death Valley Region in California and Nevada*. Morongo Valley, CA: Sagebrush Press, 1980.

Palmetto Place Names. South Carolina Education Association, n.d.

Payne, Roger L. *Place Names of the Outer Banks*. Washington, NC: Thomas A. Williams, 1985.

Pearce, T.M., ed. *New Mexico Place Names: A Geographical Dictionary*. University of New Mexico Press, 1965.

Perkey, Elton A. *Perkey's Nebraska Place Names*. Lincoln: Nebraska State Historical Society, 1982.

Phillips, James W. *Washington State Place Names*. Seattle: University of Washington Press, 1971.

Powell William S. *North Carolina Gazetteer: A Dictionary of Tar Heel Places*. Chapel Hill: University of North Carolina Press, 1968.

Pukui, Mary Kawena, and Elbert, Samuel H. *Hawaiian Dictionary: Hawaiian-English, English-Hawaiian*, rev. ed. Honolulu: University of Hawaii Press, 1986.

Pukui, Mary Kawena; Elbert, Samuel H.; and Mookini, Esther T. *Place Names of Hawaii*. Honolulu: University of Hawaii Press, 1974.

Quimby, Myron J. *Scratch Ankle, U.S.A.: American Place Names and their Derivation*. New York: A.S. Barnes, 1969.

Rafferty, Milton D. *Historical Atlas of Missouri*. Norman: University of Oklahoma Press, 1982.

Ramsey, Robert L. *Our Storehouse of Missouri Place Names*. Columbia: University of Missouri Press, 1973.

Read, William A. *Florida Place-names of Indian Origin and Seminole Personal Names*. Baton Rouge: Louisiana State University, 1934.

Rennick, Robert M. *Kentucky Place Names*. University Press of Kentucky, 1984.

Rippley, La Verne J., and Schmeissner, Rainer H. *German Place Names in Minnesota (Deutsche Ortsnamen in Minnesota)*. Northfield, MN: St. Olaf College, 1989.

Romig, Walter. *Michigan Place Names: The History of the Founding and the Naming of More than Five Thousand Past and Present Michigan Communities.* Detroit: Wayne State University Press, 1986.

Rydjord, John. *Indian Place-Names: Their Origin, Evolution, and Meanings, Collected in Kansas from the Siouan, Algonquian, Shoshonean, Caddoan, Iroquoian, and Other Tongues.* Norman: University of Oklahoma Press, 1968.

—. *Kansas Place-Names.* Norman: University of Oklahoma Press, 1972.

Savela, Judith A., ed. *Michigan Municipalities.* Sterling Heights Public Library, MI, 1989.

Scott, James W., and De Lorme, Roland L. *Historical Atlas of Washington.* Norman: University of Oklahoma Press, 1988.

Seltzer, Leon E., ed. *Columbia Lippincott Gazetteer of the World.* New York: Columbia University Press, 1952.

Shirk, George H. *Oklahoma Place Names*, 2nd ed. Norman: University of Oklahoma Press, 1965.

Sixth Report of the United States Geographic Board, 1890 to 1932. U.S. Government Printing Office; reprinted by Gale Research, 1967.

Sneve, Virginia Driving Hawk, ed. *South Dakota Geographic Names.* Sioux Falls, SD: Brevet Press, 1973.

Snyder, John P. *The Story of New Jersey's Civil Boundaries, 1606-1968.* Trenton: Bureau of Geology and Topography, 1969.

Socolofsky, Homer E., and Self, Huber. *Historical Atlas of Kansas*, 2nd ed. Norman: University of Oklahoma Press, 1972.

Stephens, A. Ray, and Holmes, William M. *Historical Atlas of Texas.* Norman: University of Oklahoma Press, 1989.

Stewart, George R. *American Place-Names: A Concise and Selective Dictionary for the Continental United States of America.* New York: Oxford University Press, 1970.

—. *Names on the Land: A Historical Account of Place-Naming in the United States.* Boston: Houghton Mifflin, 1967.

Swift, Esther Munroe. *Vermont Place-Names.* Brattleboro: Stephen Greene Press, 1977.

Tarpley, Fred. *1001 Texas Place Names.* Austin: University of Texas Press, 1980.

—. *Place Names of Northeast Texas.* Commerce, TX: East Texas State University, 1969.

Tilden, Freeman; revised and expanded by Paul Schullery. *National Parks: The Classic Book on the National Parks, National Monuments, & Historic Sites.* New York: Alfred A. Knopf, 1986.

Upham, Warren. *Minnesota Geographic Names: Their Origin and Historic Significance.* St. Paul: Minnesota Historical Society, 1969.

Urbanek, Mae. *Wyoming Place Names.* Missoula, MT: Mountain Press, 1988.

Van Cott, John W. *Utah Place Names: A Comprehensive Guide to the Origins of Geographic Names.* Salt Lake City: University of Utah Press, 1990.

Van Zandt, Franklin K. *Boundaries of the United States and the Several States.* Geological Survey, U.S. Dept. of the Interior, 1976.

Vermont Year Book. Chester, VT: The National Survey, 1992.

Vogel, Virgil J. *Indian Names in Michigan.* Ann Arbor: University of Michigan Press, 1986.

—. *Iowa Place Names of Indian Origin.* Iowa City: University of Iowa Press, 1983.

Walker, Henry P., and Bufkin, Don. *Historical Atlas of Arizona*. Norman: University of Oklahoma Press, 1979.

Warmsley, Arthur J. *Connecticut Post Offices and Postmarks*. Portland, CT (private publication), 1977.

Webster's New Geographical Dictionary. Springfield, MA: Merriam-Webster, 1988.

Worldmark Encyclopedia of the States, 2nd ed. New York: John Wiley & Sons, 1986.

Who Was Who in America: Historical Volume 1607-1896, rev. ed. Chicago: Marquis Who's Who, 1967

Wick, Doulgas A. *North Dakota Place Names*. Hedemarken Collectibles, 1988.

Illinois

ILLINOIS

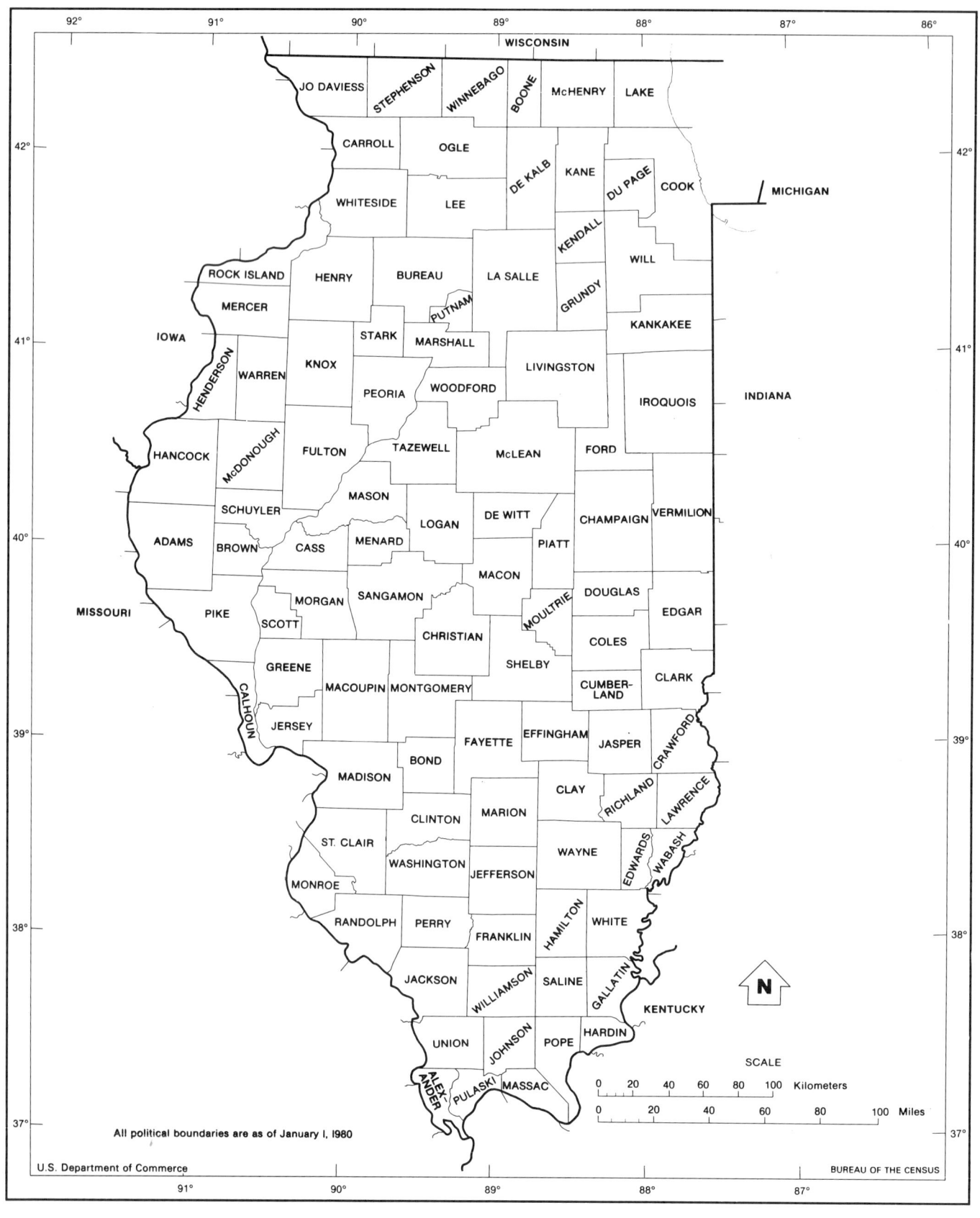

Illinois

Population: 11,430,602 (1990); 11,426,518 (1980)
Population rank (1990): 6
Percent population change (1980-1990): 0.0
Population projection: 11,814,000 (1995); 11,887,000 (2000)

Area: total: 57,918 sq. mi.; 55,593 sq. mi. land, 2,325 sq. mi. water
Area rank: 25
Highest elevation: 1,235 ft., Charles Mound (Jo Daviess County)
Lowest point: 279 ft., along the Mississippi River (Alexander County)

State capital: Springfield (Sangamon County)
Largest city: Chicago (2,783,726)
Second largest city: Rockford (139,426)
Largest county: Cook (5,105,067)

Total housing units: 4,506,275
No. of occupied housing units: 4,202,240
Vacant housing units (%): 6.7
Distribution of population by race and Hispanic origin (%):
  White: 78.3
  Black: 14.8
  Hispanic (any race): 7.9
  Native American: 0.2
  Asian/Pacific: 2.5
  Other: 4.2

Admission date: December 3, 1818 (21st state).

Location: In the east-central United States, bordering Kentucky, Missouri, Iowa, Wisconsin, Lake Michigan, and Indiana.

Name Origin: For an Indian tribe who called themselves the *Iliniwek* 'men; warriors.' The French called them *Illini* and added the suffix *-ois* to denote the tribe.

State animal: white-tailed deer *(Odocoileus virginianus)*
State bird: cardinal *(Cardinalis cardinalis)*
State dance: square dance
State fish: bluegill *(Lepomis macrochirus)*
State flower: violet
State fossil: Tully Monster *(Tullimonstrum gregarium)*
State insect: monarch butterfly *(Danaus plexippus)*
State mineral: fluorite
State song: "Illinois"
State tree: white oak *(Quercus alba)*

State motto: State Sovereignty, National Union

State nickname: Prairie State; Land of Lincoln

Area codes: 217 (Springfield), 309 (Peoria), 312 (Chicago), 618 (southern IL), 708 (Waukegan), 815 (Rockford)
Time zone: Central
Abbreviations: IL (postal); Ill. (traditional)
Part of (region): Great Lakes, Midwest

Local Government

Counties

Illinois has 102 counties. The New England township system was made optional by the 1848 constitution and eventually 85 counties, including Cook County, adopted the idea.

Municipalities

Illinois has more units of local government and administration than any other state, including 1,279 cities, towns, and villages; 1,433 townships; 1,049 school districts; and 2,602 special districts. Most of the cities are administered by city managers; some are governed by elected commissioners or aldermen, or by a mayor and council.

Settlement History and Early Development

The area of present-day Illinois was occupied by Indians 10,000 years ago. The Hopewellian culture (between 500 B.C. and A.D. 500) and the Middle Mississippian culture (about A.D. 900) built huge burial and temple mounds; the largest known prehistoric earthwork in the U.S. is Monk's Mound, located near Cahokia in the southwestern part of the state. These early civilizations died out and were replaced by seminomadic Algonquian-speaking tribes. When the first European explorers arrived in the late seventeenth century, they found the Cahokia, Kaskaskia, Michigamea, Moingwena, Peoria, and Tamaroa tribes, which had formed the Illinois Confederacy, and also Chippewa, Ottawa, Potawatomi, Sauk (Sac), Fox, Winnebago, Kickapoo, Maxcouten, Piankashaw, and Shawnee.

In 1673 two Frenchmen from Quebec, Fr. Jacques Marquette, a Jesuit missionary, and Louis Jolliet, an explorer, were probably the first white men to enter the Illinois area in their journey to find and trace the Mississippi River. While French missions and trading posts were established subsequently, the first permanent settlement was a mission built by French priests at Cahokia (near present-day St. Louis) in 1699, followed in 1703 by one at Kaskaskia. In 1717 Illinois became part of the French colony of Louisiana. At the end of the French and Indian Wars, the Treaty of Paris (1763) ceded the Illinois country to the British, but they established no settlements.

The American Revolution and War of 1812

The French settlers of Illinois were Loyalist, but did not resist the band of Virginia frontiersmen called the "Big Knives," led by George Rogers Clark, who captured the British forts at Cakohia and Kaskaskia in 1778. Present-day Illinois thus became a county of Virginia. Most of the French settlers fled to Missouri, but many of the "Big Knives" returned to settle after the war, as did colonists from Kentucky, Maryland, Tennessee, and Virginia.

In 1784 Virginia ceded the Illinois region to the federal government, and three years later it became part of the Northwest Territory. In 1800 Illinois was included in the Indiana Territory. Nine years later the Illinois Territory, including present-day Wisconsin, was formed, and a territorial legislature was established in 1812.

During this period the Indians became more and more enraged at the whites for their seizure of so much Indian land. When the U.S. Congress declared war on Great Britain in 1812 the Indians sided with the British. In August 1812, the Potawatomi Indians killed many American settlers and soldiers withdrawing from Fort Dearborn.

Statehood

On December 3, 1818, Illinois became the 21st state of the Union. The capital was moved from Kaskaskia to Vandalia in 1820 and to Springfield in 1839. At the time of admittance, only the southern third of the state was settled. The final defeat of the Indian tribes in the Black Hawk War of 1832 led to most of the Indians being settled west of the Mississippi and opened the fertile prairies to settlers from other states, especially Kentucky. The federal government owned most of the land and sold it on easy terms to prospective farmers. Other settlers were attracted to the lead deposits around Galena and the rich northern (now dairy) section of the state. The Erie Canal, completed in 1835, and the Illinois and Michigan Canal, completed in 1848, facilitated travel and shipping to the east and brought Yankee entrepreneurs west. During the 1850s rail lines were extended to carry produce to market and to link the major cities.

The Civil War

The debates between Abraham Lincoln and Stephen A. Douglas, campaigning for the U.S. Senate, brought national attention to the state, which was sharply divided over slavery and was dangerous territory for abolitionists and escaped slaves. Despite the number of Confederate sympathizers in the southern part of the state, Illinois remained with the Union. It sent about 260,000 men to serve in its armies and contributed huge quantities of food, feed, and horses. The stronghanded wartime administration of Republican Governor Richard Yates guaranteed full support for the president, but his forcible suppression of Democratic dissenters left a legacy of bitter feuds that troubled the southern third of the state for decades.

Business and Commerce

Economic and population growth expanded greatly after 1865. Railroad construction increased, attracting more entrepreneurs whose new businesses, forges, mills, and factories attracted Irish, Polish, and Czech immigrants to cities such as Chicago, Joliet, and Rockford. By 1870 Chicago, a tiny hamlet before the railroads, had become the largest grain and meat-packing center in the U.S. Small towns prospered, building banks, grain elevators, retail shops, courthouses, and schools.

During the second half of the nineteenth century Illinois was a center of the American labor movement, with workers fighting for child-labor laws and the eight-hour workday. Union organizing led to the Haymarket riot in 1886 and the Pullman strike in 1894; the latter was suppressed by federal troops. After the turn of the century Illinois became a center of the Progressive movement, which advocated laws to redress such problems as unsafe working conditions, monopolies in business, political corruption, and the problems of the poor.

Chicago's downtown section was destroyed by the great fire of 1871, but the city was rebuilt, and both business and cultural institutions flourished, as Chicago demonstrated during the World's Columbian Exposition in 1893. The state enjoyed prosperity in the early twentieth century, except for the slums in the cities (where many immigrants lived when they first arrived) and the southern part of the state, where both farming and the coal industry declined. During Prohibition the state—especially the Chicago and Joliet areas—was a center of illegal activity. Many famous gangsters, such as Al Capone, not only provided illegal alcohol but also became involved in a variety of other criminal activities.

Illinois, like the rest of the country, experienced renewed prosperity during and after World War II. In 1942 Enrico Fermi and other scientists at the University of Chicago engineered the first controlled nuclear chain reaction, and since then Illinois has been a center of nuclear energy and physics research.

The opening of the Saint Lawrence Seaway in 1959 made Chicago a major port for overseas shipping. Recent decades have seen the rapid growth of several metropolitan areas in Illinois, including the cities of Moline, Springfield, Peoria, Decatur, and Rockford. The state manufactures a wide variety of goods, including household appliances, tractors and other farm machinery, and diesel engines. It is also a transportation hub for both air and rail traffic.

State Boundaries

The Northwest Ordinance of 1787 fixed the northern boundary of the future state of Illinois at a line west from the southern tip of Lake Michigan. Nathaniel Pope, territorial delegate to Congress (1816–19), succeeded in having this extended to the present northern boundary.

Illinois Counties

Adams	DuPage	Jo Daviess	McHenry	Saline
Alexander	Edgar	Johnson	McLean	Sangamon
Bond	Edwards	Kane	Menard	Schuyler
Boone	Effingham	Kankakee	Mercer	Scott
Brown	Fayette	Kendall	Monroe	Shelby
Bureau	Ford	Knox	Montgomery	Stark
Calhoun	Franklin	Lake	Morgan	Stephenson
Carroll	Fulton	La Salle	Moultrie	Tazewell
Cass	Gallatin	Lawrence	Ogle	Union
Champaign	Greene	Lee	Peoria	Vermilion
Christian	Grundy	Livingston	Perry	Wabash
Clark	Hamilton	Logan	Piatt	Warren
Clay	Hancock	Macon	Pike	Washington
Clinton	Hardin	Macoupin	Pope	Wayne
Coles	Henderson	Madison	Pulaski	White
Cook	Henry	Marion	Putnam	Whiteside
Crawford	Iroquois	Marshall	Randolph	Will
Cumberland	Jackson	Mason	Richland	Williamson
DeKalb	Jasper	Massac	Rock Island	Winnebago
De Witt	Jefferson	McDonough	St. Clair	Woodford
Douglas	Jersey			

ILLINOIS   *American Places Dictionary*

Multi-County Places

The following Illinois places are in more than one county. Given here is the total population for each multi-county place, and the names of the counties it is in.

Alexis, pop. 908; Warren (526), Mercer (382)
Algonquin, pop. 11,663; McHenry (10,194), Kane (1,469)
Allerton, pop. 274; Vermilion (274), Champaign (0)
Arlington Heights, pop. 75,460; Cook (75,460), Lake (0)
Arthur, pop. 2,112; Douglas (1,365), Moultrie (747)
Atwood, pop. 1,253; Piatt (651), Douglas (602)
Aurora, pop. 99,581; Kane (84,770), DuPage (14,811)
Barrington, pop. 9,504; Cook (5,159), Lake (4,345)
Barrington Hills, pop. 4,202; Cook (2,130), McHenry (1,223), Lake (698), Kane (151)
Bartlett, pop. 19,373; DuPage (12,086), Cook (7,276), Kane (11)
Batavia, pop. 17,076; Kane (17,076), DuPage (0)
Bensenville, pop. 17,767; DuPage (17,767), Cook (0)
Bolingbrook, pop. 40,843; Will (39,371), DuPage (1,472)
Brighton, pop. 2,270; Macoupin (1,967), Jersey (303)
Buffalo Grove, pop. 36,427; Lake (21,930), Cook (14,497)
Burr Ridge, pop. 7,669; DuPage (4,596), Cook (3,073)
Cabery, pop. 268; Ford (183), Kankakee (85)
Casey, pop. 2,914; Clark (2,908), Cumberland (6)
Centralia, pop. 14,274; Marion (11,487), Clinton (2,787)
Channahon, pop. 4,266; Will (4,266), Grundy (0)
Chebanse, pop. 1,082; Iroquois (657), Kankakee (425)
Chicago, pop. 2,783,726; Cook (2,783,726), DuPage (0)
Coal Valley, pop. 2,683; Rock Island (2,632), Henry (51)
Collinsville, pop. 22,446; Madison (20,100), St. Clair (2,346)
Dallas City, pop. 1,037; Hancock (840), Henderson (197)
Dalzell, pop. 587; Bureau (587), La Salle (0)
Deer Creek, pop. 630; Tazewell (630), Woodford (0)
Deerfield, pop. 17,327; Lake (17,327), Cook (0)
Diamond, pop. 1,077; Grundy (1,077), Will (0)
Donnellson, pop. 167; Montgomery (167), Bond (0)
Dwight, pop. 4,230; Livingston (4,230), Grundy (0)
East Dundee, pop. 2,721; Kane (2,718), Cook (3)
Elgin, pop. 77,010; Kane (61,610), Cook (15,400)
Elk Grove Village, pop. 33,429; Cook (33,429), DuPage (0)
Fairmont City, pop. 2,140; St. Clair (2,101), Madison (39)
Farina, pop. 575; Fayette (575), Marion (0)
Fox Lake, pop. 7,478; Lake (7,430), McHenry (48)
Fox River Valley Gardens, pop. 665; McHenry (566), Lake (99)
Freeman Spur, pop. 290; Franklin (153), Williamson (137)
Godley, pop. 322; Will (272), Grundy (50)
Goodfield, pop. 454; Woodford (453), Tazewell (1)
Grayville, pop. 2,043; White (1,133), Edwards (910)
Hanover Park, pop. 32,895; Cook (18,662), DuPage (14,233)
Harvel, pop. 213; Montgomery (148), Christian (65)
Hinsdale, pop. 16,029; DuPage (13,956), Cook (2,073)
Hoffman Estates, pop. 46,561; Cook (46,561), Kane (0)
Island Lake, pop. 4,449; McHenry (2,466), Lake (1,983)
Ivesdale, pop. 339; Champaign (339), Piatt (0)
Keyesport, pop. 440; Clinton (246), Bond (194)
Lakemoor, pop. 1,322; McHenry (1,061), Lake (261)
Lake Summerset, pop. 1,296; Winnebago (687), Stephenson (609)

Lee, pop. 319; Lee (176), DeKalb (143)
London Mills, pop. 485; Fulton (473), Knox (12)
Macedonia, pop. 58; Hamilton (33), Franklin (25)
Madison, pop. 4,629; Madison (4,623), St. Clair (6)
Maple Park, pop. 641; Kane (637), DeKalb (4)
Millington, pop. 470; Kendall (258), La Salle (212)
Mill Shoals, pop. 247; White (247), Wayne (0)
Minooka, pop. 2,561; Grundy (1,757), Will (804)
Montgomery, pop. 4,267; Kane (3,675), Kendall (592)
Montrose, pop. 306; Effingham (306), Cumberland (0)
Moweaqua, pop. 1,785; Shelby (1,785), Christian (0)
Naperville, pop. 85,351; DuPage (72,931), Will (12,420)
New Baden, pop. 2,602; Clinton (2,529), St. Clair (73)
Oak Brook, pop. 9,178; DuPage (9,178), Cook (0)
Panama, pop. 294; Montgomery (157), Bond (137)
Park Forest, pop. 24,656; Cook (21,347), Will (3,309)
Pekin, pop. 32,254; Tazewell (32,254), Peoria (0)
Peoria Heights, pop. 6,930; Peoria (6,887), Woodford (43), Tazewell (0)
Pierron, pop. 554; Bond (533), Madison (21)
Plymouth, pop. 521; Hancock (518), McDonough (3)
Reddick, pop. 208; Kankakee (182), Livingston (26)
Reynolds, pop. 583; Rock Island (506), Mercer (77)
Roselle, pop. 20,819; DuPage (17,499), Cook (3,320)
St. Charles, pop. 22,501; Kane (22,491), DuPage (10)
Sandwich, pop. 5,567; DeKalb (5,566), Kendall (1)
San Jose, pop. 519; Mason (360), Logan (159)
Sauk Village, pop. 9,926; Cook (9,926), Will (0)
Schaumburg, pop. 68,586; Cook (68,586), DuPage (0)
Seneca, pop. 1,878; La Salle (1,878), Grundy (0)
Somonauk, pop. 1,263; DeKalb (1,031), La Salle (232)
Steger, pop. 8,584; Will (5,576), Cook (3,008)
Stonefort, pop. 311; Williamson (178), Saline (133)
Streator, pop. 14,121; La Salle (14,028), Livingston (93)
Tinley Park, pop. 37,121; Cook (37,040), Will (81)
University Park, pop. 6,204; Will (6,204), Cook (0)
Virden, pop. 3,635; Macoupin (3,614), Sangamon (21)
Wamac, pop. 1,501; Marion (730), Clinton (641), Washington (130)
Washburn, pop. 1,075; Woodford (1,040), Marshall (35)
Wayne, pop. 1,541; Kane (823), DuPage (718)
Wenona, pop. 950; Marshall (939), La Salle (11)
Wheeling, pop. 29,911; Cook (29,911), Lake (0)
Willow Springs, pop. 4,509; Cook (4,509), DuPage (0)
Woodridge, pop. 26,256; DuPage (26,232), Will (24)

ILLINOIS, Adams County   *American Places Dictionary*

Adams County
County Seat: Quincy (ZIP: 62301)

Pop: 66,090 (1990); 71,622 (1980)   **Pop Density:** 77.1
Land: 856.7 sq. mi.; **Water:** 14.6 sq. mi.   **Area Code:** 217

On west-central border of IL west of Springfield; organized Jan 13, 1825 from Pike County. Highland County organized from Adams and Marquette counties in 1847 and eliminated in 1848. Marquette County organized in 1843 from Adams County and eliminated in 1847.

Name origin: For John Quincy Adams (1767–1848), sixth U.S. president.

Beverly   Township
Lat: 39-48-35 N **Long:** 90-58-36 W
Pop: 363 (1990); 390 (1980)   **Pop Density:** 9.9
Land: 36.6 sq. mi.; **Water:** 0.0 sq. mi.

Burton   Township
Lat: 39-53-19 N **Long:** 91-12-17 W
Pop: 815 (1990); 959 (1980)   **Pop Density:** 21.4
Land: 38.1 sq. mi.; **Water:** 0.0 sq. mi.

Camp Point   Town
ZIP: 62320   **Lat:** 40-02-16 N **Long:** 91-03-59 W
Pop: 1,230 (1990); 1,285 (1980)   **Pop Density:** 1366.7
Land: 0.9 sq. mi.; **Water:** 0.0 sq. mi.   **Elev:** 743 ft.
In west-central IL, 29 mi. northeast of Quincy. Settled 1870 by German immigrants. Not coextensive with the town of the same name.

*Camp Point   Township
Lat: 40-04-13 N **Long:** 91-05-16 W
Pop: 1,622 (1990); 1,832 (1980)   **Pop Density:** 43.1
Land: 37.6 sq. mi.; **Water:** 0.1 sq. mi.

Clayton   Village
ZIP: 62324   **Lat:** 40-01-49 N **Long:** 90-57-28 W
Pop: 726 (1990); 889 (1980)   **Pop Density:** 806.7
Land: 0.9 sq. mi.; **Water:** 0.0 sq. mi.   **Elev:** 736 ft.
Not coextensive with the town of the same name.

*Clayton   Township
Lat: 40-03-37 N **Long:** 90-58-22 W
Pop: 990 (1990); 1,218 (1980)   **Pop Density:** 26.8
Land: 36.9 sq. mi.; **Water:** 0.0 sq. mi.

Coatsburg   Village
ZIP: 62325   **Lat:** 40-01-56 N **Long:** 91-09-33 W
Pop: 201 (1990); 258 (1980)   **Pop Density:** 2010.0
Land: 0.1 sq. mi.; **Water:** 0.0 sq. mi.   **Elev:** 761 ft.

Columbus   Village
ZIP: 62328   **Lat:** 39-59-17 N **Long:** 91-08-47 W
Pop: 88 (1990); 92 (1980)   **Pop Density:** 293.3
Land: 0.3 sq. mi.; **Water:** 0.0 sq. mi.
Not coextensive with the town of the same name.

*Columbus   Township
Lat: 39-58-25 N **Long:** 91-05-40 W
Pop: 500 (1990); 531 (1980)   **Pop Density:** 13.4
Land: 37.3 sq. mi.; **Water:** 0.1 sq. mi.

Concord   Township
Lat: 39-58-12 N **Long:** 90-58-29 W
Pop: 231 (1990); 294 (1980)   **Pop Density:** 6.2
Land: 37.1 sq. mi.; **Water:** 0.0 sq. mi.

Ellington   Township
Lat: 39-58-45 N **Long:** 91-18-46 W
Pop: 2,796 (1990); 3,296 (1980)   **Pop Density:** 79.9
Land: 35.0 sq. mi.; **Water:** 0.0 sq. mi.

Fall Creek   Township
Lat: 39-48-33 N **Long:** 91-20-11 W
Pop: 568 (1990); 701 (1980)   **Pop Density:** 15.5
Land: 36.6 sq. mi.; **Water:** 2.3 sq. mi.

Gilmer   Township
Lat: 39-58-29 N **Long:** 91-12-20 W
Pop: 1,107 (1990); 1,005 (1980)   **Pop Density:** 29.9
Land: 37.0 sq. mi.; **Water:** 0.1 sq. mi.

Golden   Village
ZIP: 62339   **Lat:** 40-06-35 N **Long:** 91-01-06 W
Pop: 565 (1990); 558 (1980)   **Pop Density:** 941.7
Land: 0.6 sq. mi.; **Water:** 0.0 sq. mi.

Honey Creek   Township
Lat: 40-03-44 N **Long:** 91-12-09 W
Pop: 700 (1990); 808 (1980)   **Pop Density:** 19.1
Land: 36.7 sq. mi.; **Water:** 0.0 sq. mi.

Houston   Township
Lat: 40-08-35 N **Long:** 91-05-24 W
Pop: 287 (1990); 288 (1980)   **Pop Density:** 7.6
Land: 38.0 sq. mi.; **Water:** 0.0 sq. mi.

Keene   Township
Lat: 40-09-37 N **Long:** 91-12-12 W
Pop: 634 (1990); 772 (1980)   **Pop Density:** 17.5
Land: 36.3 sq. mi.; **Water:** 0.1 sq. mi.

La Prairie   Village
ZIP: 62346   **Lat:** 40-08-49 N **Long:** 91-00-09 W
Pop: 68 (1990); 90 (1980)   **Pop Density:** 340.0
Land: 0.2 sq. mi.; **Water:** 0.0 sq. mi.

Liberty   Village
ZIP: 62347   **Lat:** 39-52-50 N **Long:** 91-06-28 W
Pop: 541 (1990); 587 (1980)   **Pop Density:** 1803.3
Land: 0.3 sq. mi.; **Water:** 0.0 sq. mi.   **Elev:** 757 ft.
Not coextensive with the town of the same name.

*Liberty   Township
Lat: 39-53-12 N **Long:** 91-05-33 W
Pop: 1,156 (1990); 1,261 (1980)   **Pop Density:** 31.4
Land: 36.8 sq. mi.; **Water:** 0.0 sq. mi.

Lima   Village
ZIP: 62348   **Lat:** 40-10-36 N **Long:** 91-22-30 W
Pop: 120 (1990); 166 (1980)   **Pop Density:** 600.0
Land: 0.2 sq. mi.; **Water:** 0.0 sq. mi.   **Elev:** 659 ft.
Not coextensive with the town of the same name.

American Places Dictionary   ILLINOIS, Alexander County

*Lima
Township
Lat: 40-10-12 N **Long:** 91-23-31 W
Pop: 569 (1990); 677 (1980)   **Pop Density:** 10.3
Land: 55.2 sq. mi.; **Water:** 2.4 sq. mi.

Loraine
Village
ZIP: 62349   **Lat:** 40-09-11 N **Long:** 91-13-20 W
Pop: 331 (1990); 382 (1980)   **Pop Density:** 413.8
Land: 0.8 sq. mi.; **Water:** 0.0 sq. mi.

McKee
Township
Lat: 39-53-14 N **Long:** 90-58-54 W
Pop: 205 (1990); 239 (1980)   **Pop Density:** 5.7
Land: 36.0 sq. mi.; **Water:** 0.1 sq. mi.

Melrose
Township
ZIP: 62301   **Lat:** 39-53-06 N **Long:** 91-20-39 W
Pop: 6,098 (1990); 6,616 (1980)   **Pop Density:** 130.9
Land: 46.6 sq. mi.; **Water:** 1.5 sq. mi.

Mendon
Village
ZIP: 62351   **Lat:** 40-05-20 N **Long:** 91-17-03 W
Pop: 854 (1990); 979 (1980)   **Pop Density:** 1220.0
Land: 0.7 sq. mi.; **Water:** 0.0 sq. mi.
Not coextensive with the town of the same name.

*Mendon
Township
Lat: 40-05-19 N **Long:** 91-17-40 W
Pop: 1,475 (1990); 1,597 (1980)   **Pop Density:** 40.2
Land: 36.7 sq. mi.; **Water:** 0.0 sq. mi.

Northeast
Township
Lat: 40-08-38 N **Long:** 90-58-23 W
Pop: 869 (1990); 950 (1980)   **Pop Density:** 23.5
Land: 37.0 sq. mi.; **Water:** 0.0 sq. mi.

Payson
Town
ZIP: 62360   **Lat:** 39-49-00 N **Long:** 91-14-38 W
Pop: 1,114 (1990); 1,065 (1980)   **Pop Density:** 1012.7
Land: 1.1 sq. mi.; **Water:** 0.0 sq. mi.
In west-central IL, 12 mi. southeast of Quincy. Not coextensive with the town of the same name.

*Payson
Township
Lat: 39-47-59 N **Long:** 91-12-26 W
Pop: 1,926 (1990); 1,911 (1980)   **Pop Density:** 50.3
Land: 38.3 sq. mi.; **Water:** 0.0 sq. mi.

Plainville
Village
ZIP: 62365   **Lat:** 39-47-02 N **Long:** 91-10-53 W
Pop: 261 (1990); 289 (1980)   **Pop Density:** 1305.0
Land: 0.2 sq. mi.; **Water:** 0.0 sq. mi.   **Elev:** 693 ft.

Quincy
City
ZIP: 62301   **Lat:** 39-56-00 N **Long:** 91-23-18 W
Pop: 39,681 (1990); 42,554 (1980)   **Pop Density:** 3124.5
Land: 12.7 sq. mi.; **Water:** 0.8 sq. mi.
In west-central IL on the Mississippi River bluffs at the MO border, 90 mi. west of Springfield. County seat. Founded 1825; incorporated Feb 21, 1839. Coextensive with the township of the same name.
Name origin: For John Quincy Adams (1767–1848), sixth U.S. president.

*Quincy
Township
ZIP: 62301   **Lat:** 39-56-00 N **Long:** 91-23-18 W
Pop: 39,681 (1990); 42,554 (1980)   **Pop Density:** 3124.5
Land: 12.7 sq. mi.; **Water:** 0.8 sq. mi.

Richfield
Township
Lat: 39-47-35 N **Long:** 91-04-56 W
Pop: 431 (1990); 471 (1980)   **Pop Density:** 11.3
Land: 38.1 sq. mi.; **Water:** 0.0 sq. mi.

Riverside
Township
Lat: 39-59-50 N **Long:** 91-25-38 W
Pop: 2,016 (1990); 2,252 (1980)   **Pop Density:** 110.2
Land: 18.3 sq. mi.; **Water:** 3.5 sq. mi.

Ursa
Village
ZIP: 62376   **Lat:** 40-04-28 N **Long:** 91-22-14 W
Pop: 506 (1990); 454 (1980)   **Pop Density:** 843.3
Land: 0.6 sq. mi.; **Water:** 0.0 sq. mi.
Not coextensive with the town of the same name.

*Ursa
Township
Lat: 40-04-55 N **Long:** 91-24-22 W
Pop: 1,051 (1990); 1,000 (1980)   **Pop Density:** 18.1
Land: 58.0 sq. mi.; **Water:** 3.4 sq. mi.

Alexander County
County Seat: Cairo (**ZIP:** 62914)

Pop: 10,626 (1990); 12,264 (1980)   **Pop Density:** 44.9
Land: 236.4 sq. mi.; **Water:** 16.2 sq. mi.   **Area Code:** 618
On the southwest border southwest of Carbondale; organized Mar 4, 1819 from Johnson County.
Name origin: For William M. Alexander, an early settler and IL legislator (1820–24).

Cairo
City
ZIP: 62914   **Lat:** 36-59-51 N **Long:** 89-10-39 W
Pop: 4,846 (1990); 5,931 (1980)   **Pop Density:** 821.4
Land: 5.9 sq. mi.; **Water:** 2.1 sq. mi.
In southwestern IL at the confluence of the Ohio and Mississippi rivers. French colony established 1702, with fort and tannery; eventually wiped out by disease; next settled 1818.
Name origin: Named in 1818 by a St. Louis merchant who thought it resembled Cairo, Egypt.

East Cape Girardeau
Village
ZIP: 62957   **Lat:** 37-17-24 N **Long:** 89-28-58 W
Pop: 451 (1990); 539 (1980)   **Pop Density:** 225.5
Land: 2.0 sq. mi.; **Water:** 0.0 sq. mi.

Tamms
Village
ZIP: 62988   **Lat:** 37-14-20 N **Long:** 89-16-03 W
Pop: 748 (1990); 826 (1980)   **Pop Density:** 356.2
Land: 2.1 sq. mi.; **Water:** 0.0 sq. mi.

ILLINOIS, Alexander County

Thebes
Village
ZIP: 62990 Lat: 37-12-38 N Long: 89-27-11 W
Pop: 461 (1990); 455 (1980) Pop Density: 256.1
Land: 1.8 sq. mi.; Water: 0.5 sq. mi.

Bond County
County Seat: Greenville (ZIP: 62246)

Pop: 14,991 (1990); 16,224 (1980) Pop Density: 39.4
Land: 380.2 sq. mi.; Water: 2.5 sq. mi. Area Code: 618

In south-central IL northeast of Belleville; organized Jan 4, 1817 (prior to statehood) from Madison County.

Name origin: For Shadrach Bond (1773–1832), IL legislator and first governor (1818–22).

Burgess
Township
Lat: 38-46-42 N Long: 89-32-36 W
Pop: 2,163 (1990); 2,052 (1980) Pop Density: 58.1
Land: 37.2 sq. mi.; Water: 0.1 sq. mi.

Central
Township
ZIP: 62246 Lat: 38-52-14 N Long: 89-25-51 W
Pop: 6,023 (1990); 6,396 (1980) Pop Density: 162.3
Land: 37.1 sq. mi.; Water: 0.0 sq. mi.

Donnellson
Village
Lat: 39-01-35 N Long: 89-28-28 W
Pop: 0 (1990); 25 (1980)
Land: 0.03 sq. mi.; Water: 0.0 sq. mi. Elev: 611 ft.
Part of the town is also in Montgomery County.

Greenville
City
ZIP: 62246 Lat: 38-53-21 N Long: 89-24-05 W
Pop: 4,806 (1990); 5,271 (1980) Pop Density: 1848.5
Land: 2.6 sq. mi.; Water: 0.0 sq. mi.
In south-central IL on Shoal Creek, 47 mi. east-northeast of East St. Louis.

Keyesport
Village
Lat: 38-44-41 N Long: 89-16-28 W
Pop: 194 (1990); 188 (1980) Pop Density: 970.0
Land: 0.2 sq. mi.; Water: 0.0 sq. mi. Elev: 453 ft.
Part of the town is also in Clinton County.

Lagrange
Township
Lat: 38-58-30 N Long: 89-25-50 W
Pop: 803 (1990); 768 (1980) Pop Density: 17.6
Land: 45.6 sq. mi.; Water: 0.9 sq. mi.

Mills
Township
Lat: 38-47-18 N Long: 89-25-15 W
Pop: 487 (1990); 574 (1980) Pop Density: 13.4
Land: 36.4 sq. mi.; Water: 0.0 sq. mi.

Mulberry Grove
Town
ZIP: 62262 Lat: 38-55-27 N Long: 89-16-02 W
Pop: 660 (1990); 707 (1980) Pop Density: 660.0
Land: 1.0 sq. mi.; Water: 0.0 sq. mi.
Not coextensive with the town of the same name.
Name origin: For its descriptive connotations.

*Mulberry Grove
Township
Lat: 38-58-05 N Long: 89-18-46 W
Pop: 1,247 (1990); 1,406 (1980) Pop Density: 26.5
Land: 47.0 sq. mi.; Water: 0.4 sq. mi.

Old Ripley
Village
ZIP: 62275 Lat: 38-53-32 N Long: 89-34-22 W
Pop: 95 (1990); 149 (1980) Pop Density: 950.0
Land: 0.1 sq. mi.; Water: 0.0 sq. mi.
Not coextensive with the town of the same name.

*Old Ripley
Township
Lat: 38-52-34 N Long: 89-33-29 W
Pop: 784 (1990); 887 (1980) Pop Density: 18.0
Land: 43.6 sq. mi.; Water: 0.0 sq. mi.

Panama
Village
Lat: 39-01-27 N Long: 89-31-31 W
Pop: 137 (1990); 394 (1980) Pop Density: 685.0
Land: 0.2 sq. mi.; Water: 0.0 sq. mi. Elev: 596 ft.
Part of the town is also in Montgomery County.

Pierron
Village
Lat: 38-46-43 N Long: 89-33-24 W
Pop: 533 (1990); 524 (1980) Pop Density: 761.4
Land: 0.7 sq. mi.; Water: 0.0 sq. mi.
Part of the town is also in Madison County.

Pleasant Mound
Township
Lat: 38-52-53 N Long: 89-18-50 W
Pop: 1,106 (1990); 1,316 (1980) Pop Density: 29.3
Land: 37.8 sq. mi.; Water: 0.1 sq. mi.

Pocahontas
Town
ZIP: 62275 Lat: 38-49-28 N Long: 89-32-20 W
Pop: 837 (1990); 866 (1980) Pop Density: 1046.3
Land: 0.8 sq. mi.; Water: 0.0 sq. mi. Elev: 570 ft.
In southwestern IL, 30 mi. west of Vandalia.
Name origin: For the famous daughter (c. 1595–1617) of Chief Powhatan of VA, who prevented the execution of Capt. John Smith in 1608.

Shoal Creek
Township
Lat: 38-58-29 N Long: 89-33-35 W
Pop: 1,803 (1990); 2,204 (1980) Pop Density: 31.0
Land: 58.2 sq. mi.; Water: 0.0 sq. mi.

Smithboro
Village
ZIP: 62284 Lat: 38-53-41 N Long: 89-20-28 W
Pop: 201 (1990); 236 (1980) Pop Density: 201.0
Land: 1.0 sq. mi.; Water: 0.0 sq. mi.

American Places Dictionary — ILLINOIS, Boone County

Sorento — Town
ZIP: 62086   Lat: 38-59-59 N   Long: 89-34-21 W
Pop: 596 (1990); 677 (1980)   Pop Density: 1192.0
Land: 0.5 sq. mi.; Water: 0.0 sq. mi.
Name origin: For Sorrento, Italy, with a spelling variation.

Tamalco — Township
Lat: 38-46-49 N   Long: 89-18-47 W
Pop: 575 (1990); 621 (1980)   Pop Density: 15.5
Land: 37.2 sq. mi.; Water: 0.9 sq. mi.

Boone County
County Seat: Belvidere (ZIP: 61008)

Pop: 30,806 (1990); 28,630 (1980)   Pop Density: 109.5
Land: 281.4 sq. mi.; Water: 0.6 sq. mi.   Area Code: 815
On the north-central border of IL east of Rockford; organized Mar 4, 1837 from Winnebago County.
Name origin: For Daniel Boone (1734?–1820), U.S. frontiersman and KY pioneer.

Belvidere — City
ZIP: 61008   Lat: 42-15-09 N   Long: 88-50-53 W
Pop: 15,958 (1990); 15,176 (1980)   Pop Density: 2901.5
Land: 5.5 sq. mi.; Water: 0.1 sq. mi.
In northern IL, 75 mi. northwest of Chicago; county seat. Incorporated Jun 23, 1852. Not coextensive with the town of the same name.

***Belvidere** — Township
ZIP: 61008   Lat: 42-17-00 N   Long: 88-53-25 W
Pop: 19,782 (1990); 18,729 (1980)   Pop Density: 543.5
Land: 36.4 sq. mi.; Water: 0.2 sq. mi.

Bonus — Township
Lat: 42-17-02 N   Long: 88-46-25 W
Pop: 1,951 (1990); 1,848 (1980)   Pop Density: 54.6
Land: 35.7 sq. mi.; Water: 0.1 sq. mi.

Boone — Township
Lat: 42-22-14 N   Long: 88-44-59 W
Pop: 1,410 (1990); 1,430 (1980)   Pop Density: 58.5
Land: 24.1 sq. mi.; Water: 0.0 sq. mi.

Caledonia — Township
Lat: 42-22-15 N   Long: 88-54-05 W
Pop: 1,491 (1990); 1,129 (1980)   Pop Density: 62.1
Land: 24.0 sq. mi.; Water: 0.3 sq. mi.

Capron — Village
ZIP: 61012   Lat: 42-23-55 N   Long: 88-44-33 W
Pop: 682 (1990); 678 (1980)   Pop Density: 1136.7
Land: 0.6 sq. mi.; Water: 0.0 sq. mi.

Flora — Township
Lat: 42-11-33 N   Long: 88-53-25 W
Pop: 1,698 (1990); 1,451 (1980)   Pop Density: 46.5
Land: 36.5 sq. mi.; Water: 0.0 sq. mi.

LeRoy — Township
Lat: 42-27-29 N   Long: 88-45-52 W
Pop: 519 (1990); 509 (1980)   Pop Density: 16.6
Land: 31.3 sq. mi.; Water: 0.0 sq. mi.

Manchester — Township
Lat: 42-27-35 N   Long: 88-52-58 W
Pop: 939 (1990); 901 (1980)   Pop Density: 28.0
Land: 33.5 sq. mi.; Water: 0.0 sq. mi.

Poplar Grove — Town
ZIP: 61065   Lat: 42-22-02 N   Long: 88-49-22 W
Pop: 743 (1990); 818 (1980)   Pop Density: 571.5
Land: 1.3 sq. mi.; Water: 0.0 sq. mi.
Not coextensive with the town of the same name.
Name origin: For its descriptive connotations.

***Poplar Grove** — Township
Lat: 42-22-11 N   Long: 88-49-22 W
Pop: 1,984 (1990); 1,683 (1980)   Pop Density: 83.7
Land: 23.7 sq. mi.; Water: 0.0 sq. mi.

Spring — Township
Lat: 42-11-49 N   Long: 88-45-25 W
Pop: 1,032 (1990); 950 (1980)   Pop Density: 28.6
Land: 36.1 sq. mi.; Water: 0.0 sq. mi.

ILLINOIS, Brown County   *American Places Dictionary*

Brown County
County Seat: Mt. Sterling (ZIP: 62353)

Pop: 5,836 (1990); 5,411 (1980) **Pop Density:** 19.1
Land: 305.7 sq. mi.; **Water:** 1.6 sq. mi. **Area Code:** 217
In west-central IL east of Quincy; organized Feb 1, 1839 from Schuyler County.
Name origin: For Gen. Jacob Jennings Brown (1775–1828), an officer in the War of 1812 and commander of the U.S. Army (1821–28).

Buckhorn — Township
Lat: 39-53-06 N Long: 90-51-28 W
Pop: 103 (1990); 120 (1980) **Pop Density:** 2.7
Land: 37.9 sq. mi.; **Water:** 0.1 sq. mi.

Cooperstown — Township
Lat: 39-57-48 N Long: 90-36-54 W
Pop: 360 (1990); 376 (1980) **Pop Density:** 8.9
Land: 40.6 sq. mi.; **Water:** 0.8 sq. mi.

Elkhorn — Township
Lat: 39-52-58 N Long: 90-43-51 W
Pop: 282 (1990); 371 (1980) **Pop Density:** 7.5
Land: 37.4 sq. mi.; **Water:** 0.0 sq. mi.

Lee — Township
Lat: 39-58-29 N Long: 90-51-01 W
Pop: 372 (1990); 461 (1980) **Pop Density:** 9.9
Land: 37.6 sq. mi.; **Water:** 0.0 sq. mi.

Missouri — Township
Lat: 40-03-39 N Long: 90-44-40 W
Pop: 157 (1990); 204 (1980) **Pop Density:** 4.4
Land: 35.4 sq. mi.; **Water:** 0.0 sq. mi.

Mound Station — Village
Lat: 40-00-24 N Long: 90-52-23 W
Pop: 147 (1990); 175 (1980) **Pop Density:** 294.0
Land: 0.5 sq. mi.; **Water:** 0.0 sq. mi.

Mount Sterling — Town
ZIP: 62353 Lat: 39-59-04 N Long: 90-45-49 W
Pop: 1,922 (1990); 2,186 (1980) **Pop Density:** 1922.0
Land: 1.0 sq. mi.; **Water:** 0.0 sq. mi.
Settled 1830. Not coextensive with the town of the same name.
Name origin: Named by first settler Robert Curry, for the "sterling" quality of the soil.

*Mount Sterling — Township
Lat: 39-58-22 N Long: 90-44-53 W
Pop: 3,408 (1990); 2,678 (1980) **Pop Density:** 91.6
Land: 37.2 sq. mi.; **Water:** 0.1 sq. mi.

Pea Ridge — Township
Lat: 40-03-37 N Long: 90-50-52 W
Pop: 167 (1990); 184 (1980) **Pop Density:** 4.5
Land: 37.4 sq. mi.; **Water:** 0.0 sq. mi.

Ripley — Village
Lat: 40-01-29 N Long: 90-38-15 W
Pop: 103 (1990); 149 (1980) **Pop Density:** 257.5
Land: 0.4 sq. mi.; **Water:** 0.0 sq. mi. **Elev:** 557 ft.
Not coextensive with the town of the same name.

*Ripley — Township
Lat: 40-01-33 N Long: 90-39-31 W
Pop: 133 (1990); 181 (1980) **Pop Density:** 21.8
Land: 6.1 sq. mi.; **Water:** 0.0 sq. mi.

Versailles — Village
ZIP: 62378 Lat: 39-53-01 N Long: 90-39-31 W
Pop: 480 (1990); 513 (1980) **Pop Density:** 533.3
Land: 0.9 sq. mi.; **Water:** 0.0 sq. mi.
Not coextensive with the town of the same name.

*Versailles — Township
Lat: 39-53-04 N Long: 90-37-43 W
Pop: 854 (1990); 836 (1980) **Pop Density:** 23.7
Land: 36.1 sq. mi.; **Water:** 0.6 sq. mi.

Bureau County
County Seat: Princeton (ZIP: 61356)

Pop: 35,688 (1990); 39,114 (1980) **Pop Density:** 41.1
Land: 868.6 sq. mi.; **Water:** 4.7 sq. mi. **Area Code:** 815
In north-central IL east of Moline; organized Feb 28, 1837 from Putnam County.
Name origin: Anglicized version of Pierre de Bureo (Buero), a French trader with the Indians.

Arispie — Township
Lat: 41-16-32 N Long: 89-27-04 W
Pop: 806 (1990); 989 (1980) **Pop Density:** 22.2
Land: 36.3 sq. mi.; **Water:** 0.2 sq. mi.

Arlington — Village
ZIP: 61312 Lat: 41-28-16 N Long: 89-14-53 W
Pop: 200 (1990); 236 (1980) **Pop Density:** 500.0
Land: 0.4 sq. mi.; **Water:** 0.0 sq. mi.

Berlin
Township
Lat: 41-26-46 N **Long:** 89-20-08 W
Pop: 821 (1990); 843 (1980) **Pop Density:** 22.4
Land: 36.6 sq. mi.; **Water:** 0.0 sq. mi.

Buda
Village
ZIP: 61314 **Lat:** 41-19-39 N **Long:** 89-40-42 W
Pop: 563 (1990); 668 (1980) **Pop Density:** 563.0
Land: 1.0 sq. mi.; **Water:** 0.0 sq. mi. **Elev:** 752 ft.

Bureau
Township
Lat: 41-26-50 N **Long:** 89-33-59 W
Pop: 316 (1990); 382 (1980) **Pop Density:** 8.8
Land: 36.1 sq. mi.; **Water:** 0.0 sq. mi.

Bureau Junction
Village
Lat: 41-17-16 N **Long:** 89-21-51 W
Pop: 350 (1990); 455 (1980) **Pop Density:** 250.0
Land: 1.4 sq. mi.; **Water:** 0.1 sq. mi.

Cherry
Village
ZIP: 61317 **Lat:** 41-25-46 N **Long:** 89-12-48 W
Pop: 487 (1990); 541 (1980) **Pop Density:** 811.7
Land: 0.6 sq. mi.; **Water:** 0.0 sq. mi.

Clarion
Township
Lat: 41-32-16 N **Long:** 89-13-30 W
Pop: 446 (1990); 448 (1980) **Pop Density:** 12.6
Land: 35.3 sq. mi.; **Water:** 0.0 sq. mi.

Concord
Township
Lat: 41-21-59 N **Long:** 89-41-12 W
Pop: 1,722 (1990); 2,023 (1980) **Pop Density:** 47.8
Land: 36.0 sq. mi.; **Water:** 0.2 sq. mi.

Dalzell
Village
ZIP: 61320 **Lat:** 41-21-26 N **Long:** 89-10-45 W
Pop: 587 (1990); 679 (1980) **Pop Density:** 838.6
Land: 0.7 sq. mi.; **Water:** 0.0 sq. mi.
Part of the town is also in La Salle County.

De Pue
Town
ZIP: 61322 **Lat:** 41-19-46 N **Long:** 89-17-44 W
Pop: 1,729 (1990); 1,873 (1980) **Pop Density:** 640.4
Land: 2.7 sq. mi.; **Water:** 0.3 sq. mi. **Elev:** 472 ft.
Founded early 1800s on a glacial moraine by the Illinois River.
Name origin: Also spelled De Pue. Previously called Sherman and Trenton.

Dover
Village
ZIP: 61323 **Lat:** 41-26-03 N **Long:** 89-23-44 W
Pop: 163 (1990); 213 (1980) **Pop Density:** 543.3
Land: 0.3 sq. mi.; **Water:** 0.0 sq. mi.
Not coextensive with the town of the same name.

*Dover
Township
Lat: 41-26-59 N **Long:** 89-27-17 W
Pop: 632 (1990); 649 (1980) **Pop Density:** 17.1
Land: 36.9 sq. mi.; **Water:** 0.0 sq. mi.

Fairfield
Township
Lat: 41-32-25 N **Long:** 89-48-45 W
Pop: 427 (1990); 457 (1980) **Pop Density:** 11.8
Land: 36.3 sq. mi.; **Water:** 0.0 sq. mi.

Gold
Township
Lat: 41-27-49 N **Long:** 89-47-49 W
Pop: 216 (1990); 278 (1980) **Pop Density:** 6.0
Land: 36.1 sq. mi.; **Water:** 0.0 sq. mi.

Greenville
Township
Lat: 41-32-27 N **Long:** 89-41-29 W
Pop: 370 (1990); 493 (1980) **Pop Density:** 10.1
Land: 36.5 sq. mi.; **Water:** 0.0 sq. mi.

Hall
Township
ZIP: 61362 **Lat:** 41-22-01 N **Long:** 89-13-02 W
Pop: 8,094 (1990); 8,788 (1980) **Pop Density:** 217.6
Land: 37.2 sq. mi.; **Water:** 0.7 sq. mi.

Hollowayville
Village
ZIP: 61356 **Lat:** 41-21-53 N **Long:** 89-17-40 W
Pop: 37 (1990); 92 (1980) **Pop Density:** 740.0
Land: 0.05 sq. mi.; **Water:** 0.0 sq. mi.

Indiantown
Township
Lat: 41-16-41 N **Long:** 89-34-07 W
Pop: 781 (1990); 905 (1980) **Pop Density:** 21.5
Land: 36.3 sq. mi.; **Water:** 0.1 sq. mi.

Ladd
Town
ZIP: 61329 **Lat:** 41-22-57 N **Long:** 89-12-51 W
Pop: 1,283 (1990); 1,337 (1980) **Pop Density:** 986.9
Land: 1.3 sq. mi.; **Water:** 0.0 sq. mi.
Founded 1890.
Name origin: For railroad builder George Ladd.

La Moille
Village
Lat: 41-31-48 N **Long:** 89-16-51 W
Pop: 654 (1990); 734 (1980) **Pop Density:** 654.0
Land: 1.0 sq. mi.; **Water:** 0.0 sq. mi. **Elev:** 750 ft.
Not coextensive with the town of the same name.

*La Moille
Township
Lat: 41-32-15 N **Long:** 89-20-06 W
Pop: 1,103 (1990); 1,254 (1980) **Pop Density:** 29.3
Land: 37.6 sq. mi.; **Water:** 0.0 sq. mi.

Leepertown
Township
Lat: 41-17-01 N **Long:** 89-21-36 W
Pop: 398 (1990); 525 (1980) **Pop Density:** 25.8
Land: 15.4 sq. mi.; **Water:** 3.1 sq. mi.

Macon
Township
Lat: 41-16-19 N **Long:** 89-41-18 W
Pop: 271 (1990); 371 (1980) **Pop Density:** 7.4
Land: 36.6 sq. mi.; **Water:** 0.0 sq. mi.

Malden
Village
ZIP: 61337 **Lat:** 41-25-29 N **Long:** 89-22-12 W
Pop: 370 (1990); 359 (1980) **Pop Density:** 1233.3
Land: 0.3 sq. mi.; **Water:** 0.0 sq. mi.

Manlius
Village
ZIP: 61338 **Lat:** 41-27-20 N **Long:** 89-40-04 W
Pop: 365 (1990); 439 (1980) **Pop Density:** 1216.7
Land: 0.3 sq. mi.; **Water:** 0.0 sq. mi.
Not coextensive with the town of the same name.

*Manlius
Township
Lat: 41-27-11 N **Long:** 89-40-44 W
Pop: 731 (1990); 830 (1980) **Pop Density:** 20.2
Land: 36.2 sq. mi.; **Water:** 0.0 sq. mi.

Milo
Township
Lat: 41-10-58 N **Long:** 89-35-04 W
Pop: 232 (1990); 336 (1980) **Pop Density:** 6.6
Land: 35.0 sq. mi.; **Water:** 0.0 sq. mi.

Mineral
Village
ZIP: 61344   **Lat:** 41-22-54 N   **Long:** 89-50-11 W
Pop: 250 (1990); 325 (1980)   **Pop Density:** 833.3
Land: 0.3 sq. mi.; **Water:** 0.0 sq. mi.

Not coextensive with the town of the same name.

*Mineral
Township
               Lat: 41-21-44 N   **Long:** 89-48-06 W
Pop: 603 (1990); 673 (1980)   **Pop Density:** 16.8
Land: 36.0 sq. mi.; **Water:** 0.1 sq. mi.

Neponset
Village
ZIP: 61345   **Lat:** 41-17-49 N   **Long:** 89-47-24 W
Pop: 529 (1990); 575 (1980)   **Pop Density:** 529.0
Land: 1.0 sq. mi.; **Water:** 0.0 sq. mi.

Not coextensive with the town of the same name.

*Neponset
Township
               Lat: 41-16-48 N   **Long:** 89-47-39 W
Pop: 819 (1990); 1,031 (1980)   **Pop Density:** 22.7
Land: 36.1 sq. mi.; **Water:** 0.0 sq. mi.

New Bedford
Village
ZIP: 61346   **Lat:** 41-30-42 N   **Long:** 89-43-02 W
Pop: 65 (1990); 152 (1980)   **Pop Density:** 325.0
Land: 0.2 sq. mi.; **Water:** 0.0 sq. mi.

Ohio
Village
ZIP: 61349   **Lat:** 41-33-24 N   **Long:** 89-27-34 W
Pop: 426 (1990); 544 (1980)   **Pop Density:** 608.6
Land: 0.7 sq. mi.; **Water:** 0.0 sq. mi.

Not coextensive with the town of the same name.

*Ohio
Township
               Lat: 41-32-24 N   **Long:** 89-27-24 W
Pop: 897 (1990); 1,012 (1980)   **Pop Density:** 23.6
Land: 38.0 sq. mi.; **Water:** 0.0 sq. mi.

Princeton
Town
ZIP: 61356   **Lat:** 41-22-42 N   **Long:** 89-28-00 W
Pop: 7,197 (1990); 7,342 (1980)   **Pop Density:** 1893.9
Land: 3.8 sq. mi.; **Water:** 0.0 sq. mi.

In north-central IL, southwest of Chicago. Settled 1833; incorporated Feb 8, 1849. Strong abolitionist community before Civil War. Not coextensive with the town of the same name.

Name origin: For Princeton, NJ.

*Princeton
Township
ZIP: 61356   **Lat:** 41-21-51 N   **Long:** 89-26-59 W
Pop: 8,966 (1990); 9,302 (1980)   **Pop Density:** 245.0
Land: 36.6 sq. mi.; **Water:** 0.0 sq. mi.

Seatonville
Village
ZIP: 61359   **Lat:** 41-21-49 N   **Long:** 89-16-22 W
Pop: 259 (1990); 369 (1980)   **Pop Density:** 647.5
Land: 0.4 sq. mi.; **Water:** 0.0 sq. mi.

Selby
Township
               Lat: 41-21-44 N   **Long:** 89-19-53 W
Pop: 2,461 (1990); 2,683 (1980)   **Pop Density:** 68.4
Land: 36.0 sq. mi.; **Water:** 0.2 sq. mi.

Sheffield
Village
ZIP: 61361   **Lat:** 41-21-25 N   **Long:** 89-44-22 W
Pop: 951 (1990); 1,130 (1980)   **Pop Density:** 951.0
Land: 1.0 sq. mi.; **Water:** 0.0 sq. mi.

Spring Valley
Town
ZIP: 61362   **Lat:** 41-19-34 N   **Long:** 89-11-56 W
Pop: 5,246 (1990); 5,822 (1980)   **Pop Density:** 1380.5
Land: 3.8 sq. mi.; **Water:** 0.0 sq. mi.

In north-central IL on the Illinois River, northeast of Peoria.

Tiskilwa
Village
ZIP: 61368   **Lat:** 41-17-33 N   **Long:** 89-30-28 W
Pop: 830 (1990); 990 (1980)   **Pop Density:** 1660.0
Land: 0.5 sq. mi.; **Water:** 0.0 sq. mi.   **Elev:** 512 ft.

Walnut
Village
ZIP: 61376   **Lat:** 41-33-24 N   **Long:** 89-35-27 W
Pop: 1,463 (1990); 1,513 (1980)   **Pop Density:** 2090.0
Land: 0.7 sq. mi.; **Water:** 0.0 sq. mi.

Not coextensive with the town of the same name.

*Walnut
Township
               Lat: 41-32-23 N   **Long:** 89-33-55 W
Pop: 1,894 (1990); 2,000 (1980)   **Pop Density:** 51.5
Land: 36.8 sq. mi.; **Water:** 0.0 sq. mi.

Westfield
Township
               Lat: 41-27-33 N   **Long:** 89-13-19 W
Pop: 1,044 (1990); 1,131 (1980)   **Pop Density:** 30.1
Land: 34.7 sq. mi.; **Water:** 0.0 sq. mi.

Wheatland
Township
               Lat: 41-11-58 N   **Long:** 89-30-00 W
Pop: 155 (1990); 185 (1980)   **Pop Density:** 8.7
Land: 17.8 sq. mi.; **Water:** 0.0 sq. mi.

Wyanet
Town
ZIP: 61379   **Lat:** 41-21-36 N   **Long:** 89-35-01 W
Pop: 1,017 (1990); 1,069 (1980)   **Pop Density:** 924.5
Land: 1.1 sq. mi.; **Water:** 0.0 sq. mi.

In north-central IL on the Illinois and Mississippi Canal, southwest of Chicago. Not coextensive with the town of the same name.

*Wyanet
Township
               Lat: 41-22-00 N   **Long:** 89-34-13 W
Pop: 1,483 (1990); 1,526 (1980)   **Pop Density:** 41.1
Land: 36.1 sq. mi.; **Water:** 0.0 sq. mi.

Calhoun County
County Seat: Hardin (ZIP: 62047)

Pop: 5,322 (1990); 5,867 (1980)   **Pop Density:** 21.0
Land: 253.8 sq. mi.; **Water:** 29.9 sq. mi.   **Area Code:** 618
On west-central border of IL southwest of Springfield; organized Jan 10, 1825 from Pike County.
Name origin: For John Caldwell Calhoun (1782–1850), U.S. statesman and champion of Southern causes.

Batchtown — Village
ZIP: 62006   **Lat:** 39-01-58 N   **Long:** 90-39-14 W
Pop: 225 (1990); 254 (1980)   **Pop Density:** 118.4
Land: 1.9 sq. mi.; **Water:** 0.0 sq. mi.

Brussels — Village
ZIP: 62013   **Lat:** 38-57-03 N   **Long:** 90-35-19 W
Pop: 125 (1990); 168 (1980)   **Pop Density:** 250.0
Land: 0.5 sq. mi.; **Water:** 0.0 sq. mi.

Hamburg — Town
ZIP: 62045   **Lat:** 39-13-58 N   **Long:** 90-42-56 W
Pop: 150 (1990); 166 (1980)   **Pop Density:** 300.0
Land: 0.5 sq. mi.; **Water:** 0.1 sq. mi.   **Elev:** 445 ft.
Founded 1852 by Artois Hamilton.
Name origin: For Hamburg, Germany.

Hardin — Town
ZIP: 62047   **Lat:** 39-09-26 N   **Long:** 90-37-23 W
Pop: 1,071 (1990); 1,107 (1980)   **Pop Density:** 535.5
Land: 2.0 sq. mi.; **Water:** 0.2 sq. mi.
Name origin: For Col. John J. Hardin, killed leading a charge of 1st IL Volunteers to Buena Vista during the Mexican War.

Kampsville — Village
ZIP: 62053   **Lat:** 39-18-34 N   **Long:** 90-37-30 W
Pop: 399 (1990); 423 (1980)   **Pop Density:** 199.5
Land: 2.0 sq. mi.; **Water:** 0.2 sq. mi.   **Elev:** 438 ft.

Carroll County
County Seat: Mount Carroll (ZIP: 61053)

Pop: 16,805 (1990); 18,779 (1980)   **Pop Density:** 37.8
Land: 444.2 sq. mi.; **Water:** 21.6 sq. mi.   **Area Code:** 815
On the northwest border of IL southwest of Rockford; organized Feb 22, 1839 from Jo Daviess County.
Name origin: For Charles Carroll (1737–1832), a signer of the Declaration of Independence, U.S. senator from MD (1789–92), and founder of the Baltimore and Ohio Railroad.

Chadwick — Village
ZIP: 61014   **Lat:** 42-00-50 N   **Long:** 89-53-20 W
Pop: 557 (1990); 631 (1980)   **Pop Density:** 1856.7
Land: 0.3 sq. mi.; **Water:** 0.0 sq. mi.

Cherry Grove-Shannon — Township
Lat: 42-09-29 N   **Long:** 89-46-29 W
Pop: 1,535 (1990); 1,607 (1980)   **Pop Density:** 28.7
Land: 53.5 sq. mi.; **Water:** 0.0 sq. mi.

Elkhorn Grove — Township
Lat: 41-58-46 N   **Long:** 89-42-48 W
Pop: 243 (1990); 260 (1980)   **Pop Density:** 12.5
Land: 19.4 sq. mi.; **Water:** 0.0 sq. mi.

Fairhaven — Township
Lat: 41-58-53 N   **Long:** 89-55-38 W
Pop: 994 (1990); 1,113 (1980)   **Pop Density:** 26.2
Land: 38.0 sq. mi.; **Water:** 0.0 sq. mi.

Freedom — Township
Lat: 42-09-14 N   **Long:** 89-55-10 W
Pop: 433 (1990); 395 (1980)   **Pop Density:** 12.1
Land: 35.7 sq. mi.; **Water:** 0.6 sq. mi.

Lanark — Town
ZIP: 61046   **Lat:** 42-06-10 N   **Long:** 89-49-55 W
Pop: 1,382 (1990); 1,483 (1980)   **Pop Density:** 1382.0
Land: 1.0 sq. mi.; **Water:** 0.0 sq. mi.

Milledgeville — Town
ZIP: 61051   **Lat:** 41-57-49 N   **Long:** 89-46-32 W
Pop: 1,076 (1990); 1,209 (1980)   **Pop Density:** 1793.3
Land: 0.6 sq. mi.; **Water:** 0.0 sq. mi.
Incorporated May 24, 1887.
Name origin: For the sawmill built in 1834 by early settler Jesse Kester at the end of the village.

Mount Carroll — City
ZIP: 61053   **Lat:** 42-05-43 N   **Long:** 89-58-36 W
Pop: 1,726 (1990); 1,936 (1980)   **Pop Density:** 958.9
Land: 1.8 sq. mi.; **Water:** 0.0 sq. mi.
Not coextensive with the town of the same name.

*Mount Carroll — Township
Lat: 42-04-10 N   **Long:** 90-01-51 W
Pop: 2,467 (1990); 2,693 (1980)   **Pop Density:** 66.0
Land: 37.4 sq. mi.; **Water:** 0.1 sq. mi.

ILLINOIS, Carroll County

Rock Creek-Lima
Township
Lat: 42-04-13 N Long: 89-46-13 W
Pop: 2,016 (1990); 2,199 (1980) Pop Density: 37.3
Land: 54.0 sq. mi.; Water: 0.0 sq. mi.

Salem
Township
Lat: 42-03-37 N Long: 89-55-24 W
Pop: 396 (1990); 459 (1980) Pop Density: 11.1
Land: 35.6 sq. mi.; Water: 0.0 sq. mi.

Savanna
Town
ZIP: 61074 Lat: 42-05-24 N Long: 90-08-23 W
Pop: 3,819 (1990); 4,529 (1980) Pop Density: 1591.2
Land: 2.4 sq. mi.; Water: 0.1 sq. mi. Elev: 606 ft.
In northwestern IL on the Mississippi River. Founded 1828. Not coextensive with the town of the same name.
Name origin: Descriptively named for the grassy plains.

*Savanna
Township
Lat: 42-04-08 N Long: 90-07-38 W
Pop: 4,483 (1990); 5,247 (1980) Pop Density: 334.6
Land: 13.4 sq. mi.; Water: 7.6 sq. mi.

Shannon
Village
ZIP: 61078 Lat: 42-09-07 N Long: 89-44-24 W
Pop: 887 (1990); 938 (1980) Pop Density: 1774.0
Land: 0.5 sq. mi.; Water: 0.0 sq. mi.

Thomson
Village
ZIP: 61285 Lat: 41-57-26 N Long: 90-06-11 W
Pop: 538 (1990); 911 (1980) Pop Density: 672.5
Land: 0.8 sq. mi.; Water: 0.0 sq. mi.

Washington
Township
Lat: 42-09-50 N Long: 90-10-11 W
Pop: 445 (1990); 473 (1980) Pop Density: 12.6
Land: 35.4 sq. mi.; Water: 4.3 sq. mi.

Woodland
Township
Lat: 42-09-09 N Long: 90-02-50 W
Pop: 376 (1990); 382 (1980) Pop Density: 10.3
Land: 36.6 sq. mi.; Water: 0.0 sq. mi.

Wysox
Township
Lat: 41-58-27 N Long: 89-48-13 W
Pop: 1,549 (1990); 1,679 (1980) Pop Density: 41.0
Land: 37.8 sq. mi.; Water: 0.0 sq. mi.

York
Township
Lat: 41-57-53 N Long: 90-03-45 W
Pop: 1,868 (1990); 2,272 (1980) Pop Density: 39.3
Land: 47.5 sq. mi.; Water: 8.9 sq. mi.

Cass County
County Seat: Virginia (ZIP: 62691)

Pop: 13,437 (1990); 15,084 (1980) Pop Density: 35.7
Land: 376.0 sq. mi.; Water: 7.8 sq. mi. Area Code: 217
In west-central IL northwest of Springfield; organized Mar 3, 1837 from Morgan County.
Name origin: For Gen. Lewis Cass (1782–1866), OH legislator, military and civil governor of MI Territory (1913–31), U.S. secretary of war (1831–36), and U.S. secretary of state (1857–60).

Arenzville
Village
ZIP: 62611 Lat: 39-52-44 N Long: 90-22-19 W
Pop: 432 (1990); 495 (1980) Pop Density: 540.0
Land: 0.8 sq. mi.; Water: 0.0 sq. mi.
Founded 1840; incorporated 1893. Not coextensive with the town of the same name.
Name origin: For Francis Arenz.

*Arenzville
Township
Lat: 39-55-13 N Long: 90-20-06 W
Pop: 857 (1990); 1,020 (1980) Pop Density: 23.5
Land: 36.5 sq. mi.; Water: 0.0 sq. mi.

Ashland
Village
ZIP: 62612 Lat: 39-53-19 N Long: 90-00-31 W
Pop: 1,257 (1990); 1,351 (1980) Pop Density: 1795.7
Land: 0.7 sq. mi.; Water: 0.0 sq. mi.
Platted 1857; incorporated 1869. Not coextensive with the town of the same name.
Name origin: For Ashland, KY.

*Ashland
Township
Lat: 39-55-06 N Long: 90-01-55 W
Pop: 1,356 (1990); 1,479 (1980) Pop Density: 75.8
Land: 17.9 sq. mi.; Water: 0.0 sq. mi.

Beardstown
City
ZIP: 62618 Lat: 40-00-15 N Long: 90-25-04 W
Pop: 5,270 (1990); 6,338 (1980) Pop Density: 1817.2
Land: 2.9 sq. mi.; Water: 0.0 sq. mi.
In central IL on the Illinois River, northwest of Springfield. Settled 1819 as a ferry crossing; incorporated Jul 21, 1837. Not coextensive with the town of the same name.
Name origin: Named for Thomas Beard, founder. Originally known as Beard's Ferry.

*Beardstown
Township
ZIP: 62618 Lat: 40-00-08 N Long: 90-26-05 W
Pop: 6,280 (1990); 7,232 (1980) Pop Density: 244.4
Land: 25.7 sq. mi.; Water: 3.6 sq. mi.

Bluff Springs
Township
Lat: 40-02-07 N Long: 90-20-48 W
Pop: 751 (1990); 720 (1980) Pop Density: 13.0
Land: 57.8 sq. mi.; Water: 2.0 sq. mi.

Chandlerville
Village
ZIP: 62627 Lat: 40-02-53 N Long: 90-09-02 W
Pop: 689 (1990); 842 (1980) Pop Density: 689.0
Land: 1.0 sq. mi.; Water: 0.0 sq. mi. Elev: 464 ft.
Not coextensive with the town of the same name.
Name origin: For first settler Dr. Charles Chandler, who

hired young Abraham Lincoln (1809–65), sixteenth U.S. president, to survey his land.

*Chandlerville
Township
Lat: 40-03-57 N Long: 90-03-31 W
Pop: 715 (1990); 758 (1980) **Pop Density:** 28.4
Land: 25.2 sq. mi.; **Water:** 0.3 sq. mi.

Hagener
Township
Lat: 39-55-15 N Long: 90-27-41 W
Pop: 432 (1990); 456 (1980) **Pop Density:** 9.0
Land: 47.9 sq. mi.; **Water:** 1.8 sq. mi.

Newmansville
Township
Lat: 40-00-24 N Long: 90-01-16 W
Pop: 64 (1990); 123 (1980) **Pop Density:** 3.6
Land: 17.7 sq. mi.; **Water:** 0.0 sq. mi.

Panther Creek
Township
Lat: 40-00-10 N Long: 90-06-22 W
Pop: 289 (1990); 457 (1980) **Pop Density:** 8.2
Land: 35.4 sq. mi.; **Water:** 0.1 sq. mi.

Philadelphia
Township
Lat: 39-55-07 N Long: 90-06-54 W
Pop: 270 (1990); 296 (1980) **Pop Density:** 7.5
Land: 36.2 sq. mi.; **Water:** 0.0 sq. mi.

Sangamon Valley
Township
Lat: 40-00-33 N Long: 90-12-52 W
Pop: 380 (1990); 380 (1980) **Pop Density:** 9.5
Land: 39.8 sq. mi.; **Water:** 0.1 sq. mi.

Virginia
City
ZIP: 62691 Lat: 39-57-02 N Long: 90-12-40 W
Pop: 1,767 (1990); 1,825 (1980) **Pop Density:** 1767.0
Land: 1.0 sq. mi.; **Water:** 0.0 sq. mi. **Elev:** 622 ft.
Not coextensive with the town of the same name.
Name origin: For the state.

*Virginia
Township
Lat: 39-55-15 N Long: 90-13-20 W
Pop: 2,043 (1990); 2,163 (1980) **Pop Density:** 57.1
Land: 35.8 sq. mi.; **Water:** 0.0 sq. mi.

Champaign County
County Seat: Urbana (ZIP: 61801)

Pop: 173,025 (1990); 168,392 (1980) **Pop Density:** 173.5
Land: 997.2 sq. mi.; **Water:** 0.4 sq. mi. **Area Code:** 217
In east-central IL west of Danville; organized Feb 20, 1833 from Vermilion County.
Name origin: For the county in OH, from French *campagne* 'field, plain.'

Allerton
Village
Lat: 39-55-04 N Long: 87-56-34 W
Pop: 0 (1990); 8 (1980)
Land: 0.1 sq. mi.; **Water:** 0.0 sq. mi.
Part of the town is also in Vermilion County.

Ayers
Township
Lat: 39-54-57 N Long: 87-57-58 W
Pop: 481 (1990); 503 (1980) **Pop Density:** 21.1
Land: 22.8 sq. mi.; **Water:** 0.0 sq. mi.

Bondville
Village
ZIP: 61815 Lat: 40-06-41 N Long: 88-22-07 W
Pop: 354 (1990); 442 (1980) **Pop Density:** 1180.0
Land: 0.3 sq. mi.; **Water:** 0.0 sq. mi. **Elev:** 719 ft.

Broadlands
Village
ZIP: 61816 Lat: 39-54-30 N Long: 87-59-43 W
Pop: 340 (1990); 346 (1980) **Pop Density:** 1133.3
Land: 0.3 sq. mi.; **Water:** 0.0 sq. mi.
Name origin: For its descriptive connotations.

Brown
Township
Lat: 40-21-31 N Long: 88-24-42 W
Pop: 1,488 (1990); 1,616 (1980) **Pop Density:** 40.9
Land: 36.4 sq. mi.; **Water:** 0.0 sq. mi.

Champaign
City
ZIP: 61820 Lat: 40-06-46 N Long: 88-15-53 W
Pop: 63,502 (1990); 58,267 (1980) **Pop Density:** 4884.8
Land: 13.0 sq. mi.; **Water:** 0.0 sq. mi.
In east-central IL, west of sister city, Urbana. Settled 1854; incorporated Feb 21, 1861. Site of University of Illinois at Urbana–Champaign.
Name origin: For Champaign County, OH.

*Champaign
Township
ZIP: 61820 Lat: 40-05-36 N Long: 88-18-27 W
Pop: 8,864 (1990); 8,212 (1980) **Pop Density:** 360.3
Land: 24.6 sq. mi.; **Water:** 0.1 sq. mi.

Colfax
Township
Lat: 40-01-07 N Long: 88-23-57 W
Pop: 271 (1990); 355 (1980) **Pop Density:** 7.5
Land: 36.3 sq. mi.; **Water:** 0.0 sq. mi.

Compromise
Township
Lat: 40-15-56 N Long: 88-00-46 W
Pop: 1,525 (1990); 1,588 (1980) **Pop Density:** 31.7
Land: 48.1 sq. mi.; **Water:** 0.0 sq. mi.

Condit
Township
Lat: 40-16-27 N Long: 88-17-56 W
Pop: 467 (1990); 477 (1980) **Pop Density:** 12.9
Land: 36.2 sq. mi.; **Water:** 0.0 sq. mi.

Crittenden
Township
Lat: 39-55-32 N Long: 88-11-14 W
Pop: 315 (1990); 312 (1980) **Pop Density:** 8.6
Land: 36.6 sq. mi.; **Water:** 0.0 sq. mi.

Cunningham
Township
ZIP: 61801 Lat: 40-06-30 N Long: 88-12-18 W
Pop: 36,344 (1990); 35,978 (1980) **Pop Density:** 4659.5
Land: 7.8 sq. mi.; **Water:** 0.0 sq. mi.
In east-central IL, coextensive with Urbana.

East Bend
Township
Lat: 40-21-24 N Long: 88-17-37 W
Pop: 814 (1990); 817 (1980) **Pop Density:** 22.4
Land: 36.4 sq. mi.; **Water:** 0.0 sq. mi.

ILLINOIS, Champaign County

Fisher — Village
ZIP: 61843   **Lat:** 40-18-56 N   **Long:** 88-20-54 W
Pop: 1,526 (1990); 1,572 (1980)   **Pop Density:** 1526.0
Land: 1.0 sq. mi.; **Water:** 0.0 sq. mi.
Name origin: For its founder, Robert Fisher.

Foosland — Village
ZIP: 61845   **Lat:** 40-21-37 N   **Long:** 88-25-43 W
Pop: 132 (1990); 153 (1980)   **Pop Density:** 1320.0
Land: 0.1 sq. mi.; **Water:** 0.0 sq. mi.   **Elev:** 740 ft.

Gifford — Village
ZIP: 61847   **Lat:** 40-18-23 N   **Long:** 88-01-17 W
Pop: 845 (1990); 848 (1980)   **Pop Density:** 1690.0
Land: 0.5 sq. mi.; **Water:** 0.0 sq. mi.

Harwood — Township
Lat: 40-21-47 N   **Long:** 88-03-06 W
Pop: 589 (1990); 625 (1980)   **Pop Density:** 16.0
Land: 36.7 sq. mi.; **Water:** 0.0 sq. mi.

Hensley — Township
Lat: 40-10-41 N   **Long:** 88-17-12 W
Pop: 1,073 (1990); 1,254 (1980)   **Pop Density:** 32.9
Land: 32.6 sq. mi.; **Water:** 0.0 sq. mi.

Homer — Village
ZIP: 61849   **Lat:** 40-01-54 N   **Long:** 87-57-32 W
Pop: 1,264 (1990); 1,279 (1980)   **Pop Density:** 1264.0
Land: 1.0 sq. mi.; **Water:** 0.0 sq. mi.

Ivesdale — Village
ZIP: 61851   **Lat:** 39-56-43 N   **Long:** 88-27-19 W
Pop: 339 (1990); 337 (1980)   **Pop Density:** 565.0
Land: 0.6 sq. mi.; **Water:** 0.0 sq. mi.
Part of the town is also in Piatt County.

Kerr — Township
Lat: 40-21-35 N   **Long:** 87-57-47 W
Pop: 200 (1990); 177 (1980)   **Pop Density:** 8.8
Land: 22.7 sq. mi.; **Water:** 0.0 sq. mi.

Lake of the Woods — CDP
Lat: 40-12-23 N   **Long:** 88-22-06 W
Pop: 2,748 (1990); 2,443 (1980)   **Pop Density:** 1374.0
Land: 2.0 sq. mi.; **Water:** 0.0 sq. mi.

Longview — Village
Lat: 39-53-07 N   **Long:** 88-03-59 W
Pop: 180 (1990); 207 (1980)   **Pop Density:** 900.0
Land: 0.2 sq. mi.; **Water:** 0.0 sq. mi.

Ludlow — Village
ZIP: 60949   **Lat:** 40-23-10 N   **Long:** 88-07-34 W
Pop: 323 (1990); 397 (1980)   **Pop Density:** 1076.7
Land: 0.3 sq. mi.; **Water:** 0.0 sq. mi.
Not coextensive with the town of the same name.

*Ludlow — Township
Lat: 40-21-10 N   **Long:** 88-10-00 W
Pop: 4,744 (1990); 5,114 (1980)   **Pop Density:** 129.3
Land: 36.7 sq. mi.; **Water:** 0.0 sq. mi.

Mahomet — Village
ZIP: 61853   **Lat:** 40-11-37 N   **Long:** 88-24-06 W
Pop: 3,103 (1990); 1,986 (1980)   **Pop Density:** 1349.1
Land: 2.3 sq. mi.; **Water:** 0.0 sq. mi.   **Elev:** 714 ft.
Not coextensive with the town of the same name.

*Mahomet — Township
ZIP: 61853   **Lat:** 40-11-07 N   **Long:** 88-24-23 W
Pop: 8,440 (1990); 6,909 (1980)   **Pop Density:** 256.5
Land: 32.9 sq. mi.; **Water:** 0.1 sq. mi.

Newcomb — Township
Lat: 40-16-14 N   **Long:** 88-24-26 W
Pop: 921 (1990); 805 (1980)   **Pop Density:** 25.5
Land: 36.1 sq. mi.; **Water:** 0.0 sq. mi.

Ogden — Village
ZIP: 61859   **Lat:** 40-06-55 N   **Long:** 87-57-20 W
Pop: 671 (1990); 818 (1980)   **Pop Density:** 1118.3
Land: 0.6 sq. mi.; **Water:** 0.0 sq. mi.
Not coextensive with the town of the same name.

*Ogden — Township
Lat: 40-08-48 N   **Long:** 87-58-17 W
Pop: 1,397 (1990); 1,574 (1980)   **Pop Density:** 37.1
Land: 37.7 sq. mi.; **Water:** 0.0 sq. mi.

Pesotum — Town
ZIP: 61863   **Lat:** 39-54-46 N   **Long:** 88-16-26 W
Pop: 558 (1990); 651 (1980)   **Pop Density:** 930.0
Land: 0.6 sq. mi.; **Water:** 0.0 sq. mi.
Not coextensive with the town of the same name.

*Pesotum — Township
Lat: 39-55-13 N   **Long:** 88-17-45 W
Pop: 931 (1990); 994 (1980)   **Pop Density:** 26.5
Land: 35.1 sq. mi.; **Water:** 0.0 sq. mi.

Philo — Town
ZIP: 61864   **Lat:** 40-00-11 N   **Long:** 88-09-28 W
Pop: 1,028 (1990); 973 (1980)   **Pop Density:** 1468.6
Land: 0.7 sq. mi.; **Water:** 0.0 sq. mi.   **Elev:** 737 ft.
In east-central IL between the Embarras and Vermilion rivers; a suburb of Champaign-Urbana. Not coextensive with the town of the same name.

*Philo — Township
Lat: 40-00-37 N   **Long:** 88-10-55 W
Pop: 1,480 (1990); 1,483 (1980)   **Pop Density:** 40.4
Land: 36.6 sq. mi.; **Water:** 0.0 sq. mi.

Rantoul — City
ZIP: 61866   **Lat:** 40-18-12 N   **Long:** 88-09-19 W
Pop: 17,212 (1990); 20,161 (1980)   **Pop Density:** 2607.9
Land: 6.6 sq. mi.; **Water:** 0.0 sq. mi.
In east-central IL, 13 mi. north of Champaign-Urbana. Incorporated 1869. Not coextensive with the town of the same name.
Name origin: For Robert Rantoul, early railroad executive of the Illinois Central Railroad.

*Rantoul — Township
ZIP: 61866   **Lat:** 40-16-21 N   **Long:** 88-09-56 W
Pop: 15,691 (1990); 18,139 (1980)   **Pop Density:** 320.2
Land: 49.0 sq. mi.; **Water:** 0.0 sq. mi.

Raymond — Township
Lat: 39-55-30 N   **Long:** 88-04-04 W
Pop: 459 (1990); 529 (1980)   **Pop Density:** 12.6
Land: 36.3 sq. mi.; **Water:** 0.0 sq. mi.

Royal — Village
ZIP: 61871   **Lat:** 40-11-31 N   **Long:** 87-58-16 W
Pop: 217 (1990); 274 (1980)   **Pop Density:** 1085.0
Land: 0.2 sq. mi.; **Water:** 0.0 sq. mi.

American Places Dictionary — ILLINOIS, Christian County

Sadorus — Village
ZIP: 61872 Lat: 39-58-01 N Long: 88-20-43 W
Pop: 469 (1990); 435 (1980) Pop Density: 586.3
Land: 0.8 sq. mi.; Water: 0.0 sq. mi. Elev: 690 ft.
Not coextensive with the town of the same name.

*Sadorus — Township
Lat: 39-55-50 N Long: 88-23-48 W
Pop: 1,126 (1990); 1,189 (1980) Pop Density: 29.6
Land: 38.0 sq. mi.; Water: 0.0 sq. mi.

St. Joseph — Village
ZIP: 61873 Lat: 40-06-45 N Long: 88-02-26 W
Pop: 2,052 (1990); 1,900 (1980) Pop Density: 2565.0
Land: 0.8 sq. mi.; Water: 0.0 sq. mi.
Not coextensive with the town of the same name.

*St. Joseph — Township
Lat: 40-06-09 N Long: 88-03-45 W
Pop: 3,694 (1990); 3,612 (1980) Pop Density: 101.2
Land: 36.5 sq. mi.; Water: 0.0 sq. mi.

Savoy — Town
ZIP: 61874 Lat: 40-03-54 N Long: 88-15-09 W
Pop: 2,674 (1990); 2,126 (1980) Pop Density: 2228.3
Land: 1.2 sq. mi.; Water: 0.0 sq. mi. Elev: 738 ft.

Scott — Township
Lat: 40-06-15 N Long: 88-23-51 W
Pop: 1,059 (1990); 1,094 (1980) Pop Density: 29.6
Land: 35.8 sq. mi.; Water: 0.0 sq. mi.

Sidney — Town
ZIP: 61877 Lat: 40-01-27 N Long: 88-04-18 W
Pop: 1,027 (1990); 886 (1980) Pop Density: 2054.0
Land: 0.5 sq. mi.; Water: 0.0 sq. mi. Elev: 672 ft.
Not coextensive with the town of the same name.

*Sidney — Township
Lat: 40-00-38 N Long: 88-03-59 W
Pop: 1,521 (1990); 1,358 (1980) Pop Density: 41.7
Land: 36.5 sq. mi.; Water: 0.0 sq. mi.

Somer — Township
Lat: 40-10-48 N Long: 88-11-12 W
Pop: 1,282 (1990); 1,238 (1980) Pop Density: 37.5
Land: 34.2 sq. mi.; Water: 0.0 sq. mi.

South Homer — Township
Lat: 40-01-23 N Long: 87-58-19 W
Pop: 1,624 (1990); 1,617 (1980) Pop Density: 57.4
Land: 28.3 sq. mi.; Water: 0.0 sq. mi.

Stanton — Township
Lat: 40-11-13 N Long: 88-03-53 W
Pop: 474 (1990); 513 (1980) Pop Density: 13.7
Land: 34.7 sq. mi.; Water: 0.0 sq. mi.

Thomasboro — Town
ZIP: 61878 Lat: 40-14-38 N Long: 88-11-12 W
Pop: 1,250 (1990); 1,242 (1980) Pop Density: 1250.0
Land: 1.0 sq. mi.; Water: 0.0 sq. mi.

Tolono — Town
ZIP: 61880 Lat: 39-59-10 N Long: 88-15-46 W
Pop: 2,605 (1990); 2,434 (1980) Pop Density: 1736.7
Land: 1.5 sq. mi.; Water: 0.0 sq. mi. Elev: 31 ft.
Not coextensive with the town of the same name.
Name origin: Name coined by J. B. Calhoun of the Illinois Central Railroad.

*Tolono — Township
Lat: 40-01-04 N Long: 88-17-55 W
Pop: 3,574 (1990); 3,410 (1980) Pop Density: 100.7
Land: 35.5 sq. mi.; Water: 0.0 sq. mi.

Urbana — City
ZIP: 61801 Lat: 40-06-30 N Long: 88-12-18 W
Pop: 36,344 (1990); 35,978 (1980) Pop Density: 4659.5
Land: 7.8 sq. mi.; Water: 0.0 sq. mi.
In east-central IL, 80 mi. northeast of Springfield. County seat. Coextensive with Cunningham, but not coextensive with the town of the same name. Incorporated Feb 20, 1833.
Name origin: Probably from the Latin for 'urban' or 'citified.'

*Urbana — Township
ZIP: 61801 Lat: 40-05-54 N Long: 88-10-24 W
Pop: 8,675 (1990); 8,633 (1980) Pop Density: 316.6
Land: 27.4 sq. mi.; Water: 0.0 sq. mi.

Christian County
County Seat: Taylorville (ZIP: 62568)

Pop: 34,418 (1990); 36,446 (1980) Pop Density: 48.5
Land: 709.1 sq. mi.; Water: 6.7 sq. mi. Area Code: 217
In central IL southwest of Decatur; organized as Dane County Feb 15, 1839 from Sangamon County; name changed Feb 1, 1840.
Name origin: For the county in KY, named for Col. William Christian (1743–86), army officer, Indian fighter, and legislator; brother-in-law of Patrick Henry (1736–99).

Assumption — City
ZIP: 62510 Lat: 39-31-04 N Long: 89-02-54 W
Pop: 1,244 (1990); 1,283 (1980) Pop Density: 1382.2
Land: 0.9 sq. mi.; Water: 0.0 sq. mi. Elev: 647 ft.
Not coextensive with the town of the same name.

*Assumption — Township
Lat: 39-30-57 N Long: 89-04-42 W
Pop: 1,595 (1990); 1,645 (1980) Pop Density: 37.4
Land: 42.7 sq. mi.; Water: 0.0 sq. mi.

ILLINOIS, Christian County

Bear Creek Township
Lat: 39-28-42 N Long: 89-24-57 W
Pop: 607 (1990); 675 (1980) Pop Density: 17.0
Land: 35.8 sq. mi.; Water: 0.0 sq. mi.

Buckhart Township
Lat: 39-39-43 N Long: 89-20-09 W
Pop: 1,730 (1990); 2,114 (1980) Pop Density: 29.5
Land: 58.7 sq. mi.; Water: 0.0 sq. mi.

Bulpitt Village
ZIP: 62517 Lat: 39-35-29 N Long: 89-25-30 W
Pop: 206 (1990); 301 (1980) Pop Density: 2060.0
Land: 0.1 sq. mi.; Water: 0.0 sq. mi.

Edinburg Village
ZIP: 62531 Lat: 39-39-28 N Long: 89-23-22 W
Pop: 982 (1990); 1,231 (1980) Pop Density: 1964.0
Land: 0.5 sq. mi.; Water: 0.0 sq. mi.
Incorporated 1872.
Name origin: For the city in Scotland.

Greenwood Township
Lat: 39-23-58 N Long: 89-18-16 W
Pop: 242 (1990); 279 (1980) Pop Density: 6.6
Land: 36.7 sq. mi.; Water: 0.0 sq. mi.

Harvel Village
ZIP: 62538 Lat: 39-21-34 N Long: 89-31-35 W
Pop: 65 (1990); 75 (1980) Pop Density: 216.7
Land: 0.3 sq. mi.; Water: 0.0 sq. mi.
Part of the town is also in Montgomery County.

Jeiseyville Village
Lat: 39-34-38 N Long: 89-24-26 W
Pop: 126 (1990); 178 (1980) Pop Density: 1260.0
Land: 0.1 sq. mi.; Water: 0.0 sq. mi.

Johnson Township
Lat: 39-29-02 N Long: 89-18-49 W
Pop: 565 (1990); 607 (1980) Pop Density: 15.9
Land: 35.6 sq. mi.; Water: 1.7 sq. mi.

Kincaid Town
ZIP: 62540 Lat: 39-35-19 N Long: 89-24-51 W
Pop: 1,353 (1990); 1,591 (1980) Pop Density: 2255.0
Land: 0.6 sq. mi.; Water: 0.0 sq. mi.
Name origin: For James R. Kincaid of Springfield, a planner of the town.

King Township
Lat: 39-26-37 N Long: 89-30-14 W
Pop: 271 (1990); 322 (1980) Pop Density: 7.4
Land: 36.7 sq. mi.; Water: 0.0 sq. mi.

Locust Township
Lat: 39-28-50 N Long: 89-11-39 W
Pop: 656 (1990); 745 (1980) Pop Density: 18.3
Land: 35.8 sq. mi.; Water: 0.3 sq. mi.

May Township
Lat: 39-33-53 N Long: 89-11-35 W
Pop: 1,307 (1990); 1,468 (1980) Pop Density: 35.9
Land: 36.4 sq. mi.; Water: 0.1 sq. mi.

Morrisonville Town
ZIP: 62546 Lat: 39-25-16 N Long: 89-27-28 W
Pop: 1,113 (1990); 1,208 (1980) Pop Density: 1113.0
Land: 1.0 sq. mi.; Water: 0.0 sq. mi.
Name origin: Named by and for its founder, Civil War veteran Col. J.L.D. Morrison, son-in-law of Thomas Carlin, sixth governor of IL (1838–42).

Mosquito Township
Lat: 39-45-20 N Long: 89-11-45 W
Pop: 420 (1990); 434 (1980) Pop Density: 9.0
Land: 46.6 sq. mi.; Water: 0.0 sq. mi.

Mount Auburn Village
ZIP: 62547 Lat: 39-45-57 N Long: 89-15-39 W
Pop: 544 (1990); 598 (1980) Pop Density: 544.0
Land: 1.0 sq. mi.; Water: 0.0 sq. mi. Elev: 628 ft.
Not coextensive with the town of the same name.

***Mount Auburn** Township
Lat: 39-43-50 N Long: 89-19-42 W
Pop: 1,112 (1990); 1,215 (1980) Pop Density: 24.3
Land: 45.7 sq. mi.; Water: 0.0 sq. mi.

Moweaqua Village
ZIP: 62550 Lat: 39-37-15 N Long: 89-01-37 W
Pop: 0 (1990); 1,922 (1980)
Land: 0.04 sq. mi.; Water: 0.0 sq. mi.
Part of the town is also in Shelby County.
Name origin: From the Potawatomi term probably meaning 'weeping woman' or 'wolf woman.'

Owaneco Village
ZIP: 62555 Lat: 39-28-52 N Long: 89-11-39 W
Pop: 260 (1990); 285 (1980) Pop Density: 520.0
Land: 0.5 sq. mi.; Water: 0.0 sq. mi. Elev: 624 ft.

Palmer Village
ZIP: 62556 Lat: 39-27-30 N Long: 89-24-28 W
Pop: 275 (1990); 278 (1980) Pop Density: 275.0
Land: 1.0 sq. mi.; Water: 0.0 sq. mi.

Pana City
ZIP: 62557 Lat: 39-23-11 N Long: 89-04-42 W
Pop: 5,796 (1990); 6,040 (1980) Pop Density: 2415.0
Land: 2.4 sq. mi.; Water: 0.0 sq. mi. Elev: 700 ft.
Incorporated Feb 16, 1857. Not coextensive with the town of the same name.

***Pana** Township
ZIP: 62557 Lat: 39-24-18 N Long: 89-04-48 W
Pop: 7,081 (1990); 7,019 (1980) Pop Density: 144.2
Land: 49.1 sq. mi.; Water: 0.2 sq. mi.

Prairieton Township
Lat: 39-36-41 N Long: 89-05-00 W
Pop: 537 (1990); 459 (1980) Pop Density: 14.7
Land: 36.5 sq. mi.; Water: 0.0 sq. mi.

Ricks Township
Lat: 39-23-18 N Long: 89-25-30 W
Pop: 1,348 (1990); 1,449 (1980) Pop Density: 37.4
Land: 36.0 sq. mi.; Water: 0.0 sq. mi.

Rosamond Township
Lat: 39-23-22 N Long: 89-11-09 W
Pop: 443 (1990); 469 (1980) Pop Density: 12.3
Land: 36.1 sq. mi.; Water: 0.0 sq. mi.

South Fork Township
Lat: 39-35-11 N Long: 89-27-20 W
Pop: 2,629 (1990); 3,151 (1980) Pop Density: 42.5
Land: 61.9 sq. mi.; Water: 3.9 sq. mi.

Stonington — Village
ZIP: 62567   Lat: 39-38-20 N   Long: 89-11-31 W
Pop: 1,006 (1990); 1,184 (1980)   Pop Density: 2515.0
Land: 0.4 sq. mi.; Water: 0.0 sq. mi.
Not coextensive with the town of the same name.

*Stonington — Township
Lat: 39-39-25 N   Long: 89-12-07 W
Pop: 1,280 (1990); 1,462 (1980)   Pop Density: 35.4
Land: 36.2 sq. mi.; Water: 0.0 sq. mi.

Taylorville — City
ZIP: 62568   Lat: 39-31-17 N   Long: 89-15-43 W
Pop: 11,133 (1990); 11,386 (1980)   Pop Density: 1568.0
Land: 7.1 sq. mi.; Water: 2.0 sq. mi.   Elev: 634 ft.
In central IL, 25 mi. southwest of Springfield. County seat. Incorporated Jan. 25, 1881. Not coextensive with the town of the same name.
Name origin: For Zachary Taylor (1784–1850), twelfth U.S. president.

*Taylorville — Township
ZIP: 62568   Lat: 39-34-04 N   Long: 89-19-03 W
Pop: 12,595 (1990); 12,933 (1980)   Pop Density: 295.7
Land: 42.6 sq. mi.; Water: 0.3 sq. mi.

Tovey — Village
ZIP: 62570   Lat: 39-35-15 N   Long: 89-26-57 W
Pop: 533 (1990); 598 (1980)   Pop Density: 2665.0
Land: 0.2 sq. mi.; Water: 0.0 sq. mi.

Clark County
County Seat: Marshall (ZIP: 62441)

Pop: 15,921 (1990); 16,913 (1980)   Pop Density: 31.7
Land: 501.5 sq. mi.; Water: 3.4 sq. mi.   Area Code: 217
On the east-central border of IL south of Danville; organized Mar 22, 1819 from Crawford County.
Name origin: For Gen. George Rogers Clark (1752–1818), officer in the Revolutionary War and frontiersman in the Northwest Territory.

Anderson — Township
Lat: 39-18-19 N   Long: 87-43-48 W
Pop: 335 (1990); 396 (1980)   Pop Density: 10.4
Land: 32.3 sq. mi.; Water: 0.4 sq. mi.

Auburn — Township
Lat: 39-21-50 N   Long: 87-48-37 W
Pop: 278 (1990); 310 (1980)   Pop Density: 17.6
Land: 15.8 sq. mi.; Water: 0.0 sq. mi.

Casey — City
ZIP: 62420   Lat: 39-18-09 N   Long: 87-59-21 W
Pop: 2,908 (1990); 3,007 (1980)   Pop Density: 1384.8
Land: 2.1 sq. mi.; Water: 0.0 sq. mi.
Incorporated 1871. Part of the town is also in Cumberland County. Not coextensive with the township of the same name.
Name origin: For Zadoc Casey, 19th-century IL lieutenant governor, U.S. representative, and state legislator.

*Casey — Township
Lat: 39-18-18 N   Long: 87-57-33 W
Pop: 4,021 (1990); 4,219 (1980)   Pop Density: 111.1
Land: 36.2 sq. mi.; Water: 0.1 sq. mi.

Darwin — Township
Lat: 39-18-00 N   Long: 87-38-31 W
Pop: 372 (1990); 435 (1980)   Pop Density: 13.7
Land: 27.2 sq. mi.; Water: 0.4 sq. mi.

Dolson — Township
Lat: 39-26-48 N   Long: 87-50-32 W
Pop: 310 (1990); 336 (1980)   Pop Density: 9.0
Land: 34.5 sq. mi.; Water: 1.2 sq. mi.

Douglas — Township
Lat: 39-28-10 N   Long: 87-44-46 W
Pop: 166 (1990); 170 (1980)   Pop Density: 9.4
Land: 17.7 sq. mi.; Water: 0.0 sq. mi.

Johnson — Township
Lat: 39-12-49 N   Long: 87-57-12 W
Pop: 363 (1990); 394 (1980)   Pop Density: 9.9
Land: 36.5 sq. mi.; Water: 0.1 sq. mi.

Marshall — Town
ZIP: 62441   Lat: 39-23-46 N   Long: 87-41-24 W
Pop: 3,555 (1990); 3,379 (1980)   Pop Density: 1316.7
Land: 2.7 sq. mi.; Water: 0.0 sq. mi.   Elev: 641 ft.
Incorporated Feb 10, 1853. Not coextensive with the town of the same name.
Name origin: For U.S. Chief Justice John Marshall (1755–1835).

*Marshall — Township
Lat: 39-24-08 N   Long: 87-44-14 W
Pop: 4,491 (1990); 4,373 (1980)   Pop Density: 141.7
Land: 31.7 sq. mi.; Water: 0.1 sq. mi.

Martinsville — Town
ZIP: 62442   Lat: 39-20-10 N   Long: 87-52-48 W
Pop: 1,161 (1990); 1,298 (1980)   Pop Density: 774.0
Land: 1.5 sq. mi.; Water: 0.0 sq. mi.
In eastern IL on the north fork of the Embarras River, 28 mi. southwest of Terre Haute, IN. Not coextensive with the town of the same name.
Name origin: For Joseph Martin, who platted it in 1833.

*Martinsville — Township
Lat: 39-19-21 N   Long: 87-51-21 W
Pop: 1,624 (1990); 1,815 (1980)   Pop Density: 38.9
Land: 41.7 sq. mi.; Water: 0.1 sq. mi.

Melrose — Township
Lat: 39-12-59 N   Long: 87-44-02 W
Pop: 371 (1990); 396 (1980)   Pop Density: 11.3
Land: 32.9 sq. mi.; Water: 0.1 sq. mi.

ILLINOIS, Clark County *American Places Dictionary*

Orange
Township
Lat: 39-13-22 N **Long:** 87-50-53 W
Pop: 257 (1990); 326 (1980) **Pop Density:** 6.9
Land: 37.1 sq. mi.; **Water:** 0.0 sq. mi.

Parker
Township
Lat: 39-23-12 N **Long:** 87-56-53 W
Pop: 218 (1990); 248 (1980) **Pop Density:** 6.1
Land: 35.9 sq. mi.; **Water:** 0.0 sq. mi.

Wabash
Township
Lat: 39-24-38 N **Long:** 87-36-15 W
Pop: 1,670 (1990); 1,903 (1980) **Pop Density:** 22.9
Land: 73.0 sq. mi.; **Water:** 0.1 sq. mi.

Westfield
Village
ZIP: 62474 **Lat:** 39-27-19 N **Long:** 87-59-48 W
Pop: 676 (1990); 733 (1980) **Pop Density:** 676.0
Land: 1.0 sq. mi.; **Water:** 0.0 sq. mi.
Not coextensive with the town of the same name.

*Westfield
Township
Lat: 39-27-31 N **Long:** 87-57-37 W
Pop: 824 (1990); 882 (1980) **Pop Density:** 46.3
Land: 17.8 sq. mi.; **Water:** 0.0 sq. mi.

York
Township
Lat: 39-13-15 N **Long:** 87-38-13 W
Pop: 621 (1990); 710 (1980) **Pop Density:** 19.8
Land: 31.3 sq. mi.; **Water:** 0.6 sq. mi.

Clay County
County Seat: Louisville (ZIP: 62858)

Pop: 14,460 (1990); 15,283 (1980) **Pop Density:** 30.8
Land: 469.3 sq. mi.; **Water:** 0.6 sq. mi. **Area Code:** 618
In east-central IL west of Olney; organized Dec 23, 1824 from Lawrence, Wayne, and Fayette counties.
Name origin: For Henry Clay (1777–1852), U.S. senator from KY, known as the "Great Pacificator" for his advocacy of compromise to avert national crises.

Bible Grove
Township
Lat: 38-52-11 N **Long:** 88-24-57 W
Pop: 417 (1990); 444 (1980) **Pop Density:** 11.7
Land: 35.6 sq. mi.; **Water:** 0.0 sq. mi.

Blair
Township
Lat: 38-51-50 N **Long:** 88-31-34 W
Pop: 589 (1990); 620 (1980) **Pop Density:** 16.3
Land: 36.2 sq. mi.; **Water:** 0.0 sq. mi.

Clay City
Village
ZIP: 62824 **Lat:** 38-41-07 N **Long:** 88-21-04 W
Pop: 929 (1990); 1,038 (1980) **Pop Density:** 546.5
Land: 1.7 sq. mi.; **Water:** 0.0 sq. mi. **Elev:** 433 ft.
Settled early 1830s. Not coextensive with the town of the same name.
Name origin: For the county.

*Clay City
Township
Lat: 38-39-35 N **Long:** 88-19-14 W
Pop: 1,356 (1990); 1,494 (1980) **Pop Density:** 33.3
Land: 40.7 sq. mi.; **Water:** 0.1 sq. mi.

Flora
City
ZIP: 62839 **Lat:** 38-40-13 N **Long:** 88-28-43 W
Pop: 5,054 (1990); 5,379 (1980) **Pop Density:** 1263.5
Land: 4.0 sq. mi.; **Water:** 0.0 sq. mi.
Incorporated Feb 27, 1867.

Harter
Township
ZIP: 62839 **Lat:** 38-39-52 N **Long:** 88-31-50 W
Pop: 6,591 (1990); 6,879 (1980) **Pop Density:** 117.9
Land: 55.9 sq. mi.; **Water:** 0.1 sq. mi.

Hoosier
Township
Lat: 38-46-48 N **Long:** 88-24-59 W
Pop: 409 (1990); 426 (1980) **Pop Density:** 11.5
Land: 35.6 sq. mi.; **Water:** 0.0 sq. mi.

Iola
Village
ZIP: 62847 **Lat:** 38-50-04 N **Long:** 88-37-39 W
Pop: 163 (1990); 178 (1980) **Pop Density:** 163.0
Land: 1.0 sq. mi.; **Water:** 0.0 sq. mi. **Elev:** 524 ft.

Larkinsburg
Township
Lat: 38-52-32 N **Long:** 88-38-12 W
Pop: 634 (1990); 650 (1980) **Pop Density:** 17.1
Land: 37.1 sq. mi.; **Water:** 0.1 sq. mi.

Louisville
Town
ZIP: 62858 **Lat:** 38-46-10 N **Long:** 88-30-26 W
Pop: 1,098 (1990); 1,166 (1980) **Pop Density:** 1568.6
Land: 0.7 sq. mi.; **Water:** 0.0 sq. mi.
In southeast-central IL on the Little Wabash River. Incorporated March 1, 1867. Not coextensive with the town of the same name.
Name origin: For a man named Lewis, who owned a gristmill on the river; with a spelling variation.

*Louisville
Township
Lat: 38-47-07 N **Long:** 88-31-55 W
Pop: 1,676 (1990); 1,835 (1980) **Pop Density:** 45.8
Land: 36.6 sq. mi.; **Water:** 0.0 sq. mi.

Oskaloosa
Township
Lat: 38-47-06 N **Long:** 88-37-45 W
Pop: 335 (1990); 353 (1980) **Pop Density:** 8.9
Land: 37.5 sq. mi.; **Water:** 0.0 sq. mi.

Pixley
Township
Lat: 38-47-28 N **Long:** 88-18-37 W
Pop: 712 (1990); 842 (1980) **Pop Density:** 15.8
Land: 45.1 sq. mi.; **Water:** 0.0 sq. mi.

Sailor Springs
Village
Lat: 38-45-53 N **Long:** 88-21-31 W
Pop: 136 (1990); 159 (1980) **Pop Density:** 453.3
Land: 0.3 sq. mi.; **Water:** 0.0 sq. mi.

Songer — Township
Lat: 38-41-18 N Long: 88-38-09 W
Pop: 375 (1990); 342 (1980) **Pop Density:** 10.1
Land: 37.3 sq. mi.; **Water:** 0.1 sq. mi.

Stanford — Township
Lat: 38-39-51 N Long: 88-25-05 W
Pop: 680 (1990); 690 (1980) **Pop Density:** 12.8
Land: 53.1 sq. mi.; **Water:** 0.0 sq. mi.

Xenia — Village
ZIP: 62899 Lat: 38-38-12 N Long: 88-38-13 W
Pop: 424 (1990); 475 (1980) **Pop Density:** 848.0
Land: 0.5 sq. mi.; **Water:** 0.0 sq. mi.
Not coextensive with the town of the same name.

*Xenia — Township
Lat: 38-37-52 N Long: 88-38-27 W
Pop: 686 (1990); 708 (1980) **Pop Density:** 37.1
Land: 18.5 sq. mi.; **Water:** 0.0 sq. mi.

Clinton County
County Seat: Carlyle (ZIP: 62231)

Pop: 33,944 (1990); 32,617 (1980) **Pop Density:** 71.6
Land: 474.3 sq. mi.; **Water:** 29.2 sq. mi. **Area Code:** 618
In south-central IL, east of St. Louis, MO; organized Dec 27, 1824 from Washington, Bond, and Fayette counties.
Name origin: For DeWitt Clinton (1769–1828), governor of NY (1817–21; 1825–28) and supporter of the Erie Canal.

Albers — Village
ZIP: 62215 Lat: 38-32-41 N Long: 89-36-54 W
Pop: 700 (1990); 663 (1980) **Pop Density:** 1166.7
Land: 0.6 sq. mi.; **Water:** 0.0 sq. mi. **Elev:** 434 ft.
In southwestern IL, 21 mi. east of East St. Louis.

Aviston — Village
ZIP: 62216 Lat: 38-36-28 N Long: 89-36-22 W
Pop: 924 (1990); 846 (1980) **Pop Density:** 3080.0
Land: 0.3 sq. mi.; **Water:** 0.0 sq. mi. **Elev:** 473 ft.

Bartelso — Village
ZIP: 62218 Lat: 38-32-11 N Long: 89-28-06 W
Pop: 412 (1990); 389 (1980) **Pop Density:** 1373.3
Land: 0.3 sq. mi.; **Water:** 0.0 sq. mi.

Beckemeyer — Village
ZIP: 62219 Lat: 38-36-18 N Long: 89-26-02 W
Pop: 1,070 (1990); 1,119 (1980) **Pop Density:** 2140.0
Land: 0.5 sq. mi.; **Water:** 0.0 sq. mi.
Established 1905.
Name origin: For the Beckemeyer family, who owned a large portion of coal-producing land.

Breese — City
ZIP: 62230 Lat: 38-36-39 N Long: 89-31-20 W
Pop: 3,567 (1990); 3,516 (1980) **Pop Density:** 1981.7
Land: 1.8 sq. mi.; **Water:** 0.0 sq. mi. **Elev:** 452 ft.
Settled c. 1860; incorporated 1905. Not coextensive with the town of the same name.
Name origin: For Judge Sidney Breese, an IL jurist who once lived here.

*Breese — Township
Lat: 38-36-37 N Long: 89-32-09 W
Pop: 4,612 (1990); 4,677 (1980) **Pop Density:** 123.0
Land: 37.5 sq. mi.; **Water:** 0.0 sq. mi.

Brookside — Township
ZIP: 62801 Lat: 38-32-13 N Long: 89-11-46 W
Pop: 5,458 (1990); 4,557 (1980) **Pop Density:** 224.6
Land: 24.3 sq. mi.; **Water:** 0.0 sq. mi.

Carlyle — Town
ZIP: 62231 Lat: 38-37-08 N Long: 89-22-20 W
Pop: 3,474 (1990); 3,388 (1980) **Pop Density:** 1654.3
Land: 2.1 sq. mi.; **Water:** 0.0 sq. mi.
In south-central IL, 35 mi. east of St. Louis. Incorporated 1836. Not coextensive with the town of the same name.
Name origin: Named by English settlers for Thomas Carlyle (1795–1881), Scottish historian.

*Carlyle — Township
Lat: 38-36-35 N Long: 89-21-32 W
Pop: 3,951 (1990); 3,805 (1980) **Pop Density:** 222.0
Land: 17.8 sq. mi.; **Water:** 2.8 sq. mi.

Centralia — City
ZIP: 62801 Lat: 38-31-36 N Long: 89-09-20 W
Pop: 2,787 (1990); 2,773 (1980) **Pop Density:** 2322.5
Land: 1.2 sq. mi.; **Water:** 0.0 sq. mi.
In south-central IL, 20 mi. northwest of Mount Vernon, 60 mi. east of St. Louis, MO. Founded 1853 by members of the Illinois Central Railroad System; incorporated Feb 18, 1859. Part of the town is also in Marion County.
Name origin: For either the railroad or its central location; (Latinized suffixes were common in the 1800s).

Clement — Township
Lat: 38-36-37 N Long: 89-17-34 W
Pop: 502 (1990); 500 (1980) **Pop Density:** 27.6
Land: 18.2 sq. mi.; **Water:** 6.3 sq. mi.

Damiansville — Village
ZIP: 62215 Lat: 38-30-34 N Long: 89-37-27 W
Pop: 379 (1990); 396 (1980) **Pop Density:** 1895.0
Land: 0.2 sq. mi.; **Water:** 0.0 sq. mi.

East Fork — Township
Lat: 38-41-57 N Long: 89-11-49 W
Pop: 435 (1990); 442 (1980) **Pop Density:** 13.8
Land: 31.6 sq. mi.; **Water:** 6.0 sq. mi.

ILLINOIS, Clinton County

Germantown — Village
ZIP: 62245   Lat: 38-33-08 N   Long: 89-32-15 W
Pop: 1,167 (1990); 1,191 (1980)   Pop Density: 2334.0
Land: 0.5 sq. mi.; Water: 0.0 sq. mi.   Elev: 432 ft.
Not coextensive with the town of the same name.

*Germantown — Township
Lat: 38-31-03 N   Long: 89-32-22 W
Pop: 1,931 (1990); 1,904 (1980)   Pop Density: 50.4
Land: 38.3 sq. mi.; Water: 0.3 sq. mi.

Hoffman — Village
ZIP: 62250   Lat: 38-32-18 N   Long: 89-15-46 W
Pop: 492 (1990); 467 (1980)   Pop Density: 1640.0
Land: 0.3 sq. mi.; Water: 0.0 sq. mi.

Huey — Village
ZIP: 62252   Lat: 38-36-19 N   Long: 89-17-29 W
Pop: 210 (1990); 215 (1980)   Pop Density: 1050.0
Land: 0.2 sq. mi.; Water: 0.0 sq. mi.

Irishtown — Township
Lat: 38-41-24 N   Long: 89-18-36 W
Pop: 889 (1990); 838 (1980)   Pop Density: 34.6
Land: 25.7 sq. mi.; Water: 13.0 sq. mi.

Keyesport — Village
Lat: 38-44-13 N   Long: 89-16-45 W
Pop: 246 (1990); 311 (1980)   Pop Density: 1230.0
Land: 0.2 sq. mi.; Water: 0.0 sq. mi.   Elev: 453 ft.
Part of the town is also in Bond County.

Lake — Township
Lat: 38-32-12 N   Long: 89-19-25 W
Pop: 943 (1990); 974 (1980)   Pop Density: 31.6
Land: 29.8 sq. mi.; Water: 0.1 sq. mi.

Looking Glass — Township
ZIP: 62265   Lat: 38-30-41 N   Long: 89-39-20 W
Pop: 5,096 (1990); 4,882 (1980)   Pop Density: 101.3
Land: 50.3 sq. mi.; Water: 0.4 sq. mi.

Meridian — Township
Lat: 38-36-29 N   Long: 89-11-48 W
Pop: 684 (1990); 699 (1980)   Pop Density: 18.6
Land: 36.8 sq. mi.; Water: 0.1 sq. mi.

New Baden — Town
ZIP: 62265   Lat: 38-32-12 N   Long: 89-41-45 W
Pop: 2,529 (1990); 2,437 (1980)   Pop Density: 3161.3
Land: 0.8 sq. mi.; Water: 0.0 sq. mi.   Elev: 462 ft.
Part of the town is also in St. Clair County.
Name origin: Named in 1855 by German immigrants for the German spa.

St. Rose — Township
Lat: 38-41-50 N   Long: 89-31-54 W
Pop: 1,230 (1990); 1,256 (1980)   Pop Density: 32.8
Land: 37.5 sq. mi.; Water: 0.0 sq. mi.

Santa Fe — Township
Lat: 38-31-41 N   Long: 89-26-05 W
Pop: 1,112 (1990); 1,101 (1980)   Pop Density: 43.8
Land: 25.4 sq. mi.; Water: 0.2 sq. mi.

Sugar Creek — Township
Lat: 38-36-55 N   Long: 89-39-08 W
Pop: 4,775 (1990); 4,628 (1980)   Pop Density: 130.8
Land: 36.5 sq. mi.; Water: 0.0 sq. mi.

Trenton — Town
ZIP: 62293   Lat: 38-36-24 N   Long: 89-40-53 W
Pop: 2,481 (1990); 2,504 (1980)   Pop Density: 2756.7
Land: 0.9 sq. mi.; Water: 0.0 sq. mi.   Elev: 497 ft.
Incorporated 1865.
Name origin: For Trenton, NJ.

Wade — Township
Lat: 38-36-30 N   Long: 89-26-04 W
Pop: 1,792 (1990); 1,771 (1980)   Pop Density: 62.0
Land: 28.9 sq. mi.; Water: 0.0 sq. mi.

Wamac — Town
ZIP: 62801   Lat: 38-30-38 N   Long: 89-08-48 W
Pop: 641 (1990); 753 (1980)   Pop Density: 3205.0
Land: 0.2 sq. mi.; Water: 0.0 sq. mi.
In southern IL, east of St. Louis, MO. Part of the town is also in Washington and Marion counties.
Name origin: An acronym for Washington, Marion, and Clinton counties, which converge here.

Wheatfield — Township
Lat: 38-41-37 N   Long: 89-25-39 W
Pop: 534 (1990); 583 (1980)   Pop Density: 15.0
Land: 35.5 sq. mi.; Water: 0.0 sq. mi.

Coles County
County Seat: Charleston (ZIP: 61920)

Pop: 51,644 (1990); 52,260 (1980)   Pop Density: 101.6
Land: 508.3 sq. mi.; Water: 1.8 sq. mi.   Area Code: 217
In east-central IL south of Urbana; organized Dec 25, 1830 from Clark and Edgar counties.
Name origin: For Edward Coles (1768–1868), humanitarian and IL governor (1822–26).

Ashmore — Village
ZIP: 61912   Lat: 39-31-51 N   Long: 88-01-13 W
Pop: 800 (1990); 883 (1980)   Pop Density: 1000.0
Land: 0.8 sq. mi.; Water: 0.0 sq. mi.   Elev: 696 ft.
Not coextensive with the town of the same name.

*Ashmore — Township
Lat: 39-31-46 N   Long: 88-02-00 W
Pop: 1,467 (1990); 1,552 (1980)   Pop Density: 27.4
Land: 53.6 sq. mi.; Water: 0.1 sq. mi.

Charleston
City
ZIP: 61920 Lat: 39-29-05 N Long: 88-10-33 W
Pop: 20,398 (1990); 19,355 (1980) Pop Density: 2794.2
Land: 7.3 sq. mi.; Water: 0.7 sq. mi. Elev: 686 ft.

In east-central IL on the Little Wabash River, 45 mi. southeast of Decatur. County seat. Settled 1826 by Benjamin Parker; incorporated Mar 2, 1839. Not coextensive with the town of the same name.

Name origin: For Charles Morton, its first postmaster and founder.

*Charleston
Township
ZIP: 61920 Lat: 39-28-51 N Long: 88-11-15 W
Pop: 22,031 (1990); 21,121 (1980) Pop Density: 595.4
Land: 37.0 sq. mi.; Water: 0.4 sq. mi.

East Oakland
Township
Lat: 39-38-03 N Long: 88-01-16 W
Pop: 1,447 (1990); 1,564 (1980) Pop Density: 36.9
Land: 39.2 sq. mi.; Water: 0.1 sq. mi.

Humboldt
Village
ZIP: 61931 Lat: 39-36-18 N Long: 88-19-10 W
Pop: 470 (1990); 499 (1980) Pop Density: 783.3
Land: 0.6 sq. mi.; Water: 0.0 sq. mi.

Not coextensive with the town of the same name.

*Humboldt
Township
Lat: 39-35-12 N Long: 88-18-17 W
Pop: 1,346 (1990); 1,482 (1980) Pop Density: 25.1
Land: 53.6 sq. mi.; Water: 0.0 sq. mi.

Hutton
Township
Lat: 39-25-20 N Long: 88-05-31 W
Pop: 778 (1990); 853 (1980) Pop Density: 14.2
Land: 54.6 sq. mi.; Water: 0.5 sq. mi.

Lafayette
Township
Lat: 39-28-55 N Long: 88-18-13 W
Pop: 3,991 (1990); 3,865 (1980) Pop Density: 110.6
Land: 36.1 sq. mi.; Water: 0.1 sq. mi.

Lerna
Village
ZIP: 62440 Lat: 39-25-04 N Long: 88-17-20 W
Pop: 301 (1990); 386 (1980) Pop Density: 3010.0
Land: 0.1 sq. mi.; Water: 0.0 sq. mi. Elev: 754 ft.

Mattoon
City
ZIP: 61938 Lat: 39-28-37 N Long: 88-22-07 W
Pop: 18,441 (1990); 19,293 (1980) Pop Density: 2752.4
Land: 6.7 sq. mi.; Water: 0.0 sq. mi. Elev: 726 ft.

In east-central IL, 40 mi. south of Champaign. Incorporated Feb 22, 1859. Not coextensive with the town of the same name.

Name origin: For railroad engineer and landowner William Mattoon.

*Mattoon
Township
ZIP: 61938 Lat: 39-28-39 N Long: 88-24-41 W
Pop: 16,560 (1990); 17,383 (1980) Pop Density: 458.7
Land: 36.1 sq. mi.; Water: 0.0 sq. mi.

Morgan
Township
Lat: 39-35-44 N Long: 88-06-36 W
Pop: 403 (1990); 425 (1980) Pop Density: 15.3
Land: 26.4 sq. mi.; Water: 0.0 sq. mi.

North Okaw
Township
Lat: 39-35-10 N Long: 88-25-02 W
Pop: 849 (1990); 1,072 (1980) Pop Density: 15.6
Land: 54.4 sq. mi.; Water: 0.0 sq. mi.

Oakland
Town
ZIP: 61943 Lat: 39-39-27 N Long: 88-01-35 W
Pop: 996 (1990); 1,035 (1980) Pop Density: 1245.0
Land: 0.8 sq. mi.; Water: 0.0 sq. mi. Elev: 656 ft.

Paradise
Township
Lat: 39-24-22 N Long: 88-25-02 W
Pop: 1,156 (1990); 1,171 (1980) Pop Density: 49.4
Land: 23.4 sq. mi.; Water: 0.5 sq. mi.

Pleasant Grove
Township
Lat: 39-24-13 N Long: 88-16-13 W
Pop: 1,283 (1990); 1,342 (1980) Pop Density: 30.8
Land: 41.7 sq. mi.; Water: 0.0 sq. mi.

Seven Hickory
Township
Lat: 39-35-10 N Long: 88-11-11 W
Pop: 333 (1990); 430 (1980) Pop Density: 6.4
Land: 52.1 sq. mi.; Water: 0.0 sq. mi.

Cook County
County Seat: Chicago (ZIP: 60602)

Pop: 5,105,070 (1990); 5,253,630 (1980) Pop Density: 5398.4
Land: 945.7 sq. mi.; Water: 689.2 sq. mi. Area Code: 312

On the northeast border of IL bounded on east by the western shore of Lake Michigan; organized Jan 15, 1831 from Putnam County.

Name origin: For Daniel Pope Cook (1794–1827), first attorney general of IL and U.S. representative (1819–27).

Alsip
Suburban village
ZIP: 60658 Lat: 41-40-13 N Long: 87-44-08 W
Pop: 18,227 (1990); 17,134 (1980) Pop Density: 2893.2
Land: 6.3 sq. mi.; Water: 0.2 sq. mi.

In northeastern IL, 15 mi. southwest of Chicago. Incorporated 1927.

Name origin: For Frank Alsip, 18th-century founder of Alsip Brick Company (the Alsips did not live here.)

Arlington Heights
Residential village
ZIP: 60005 Lat: 42-05-41 N Long: 87-58-55 W
Pop: 75,460 (1990); 66,116 (1980) Pop Density: 4658.0
Land: 16.2 sq. mi.; Water: 0.0 sq. mi.

In northeastern IL, 20 mi. northwest of Chicago. Settled 1830s; incorporated 1887. Site of Arlington Park Race Track. Part of the town is also in Lake County.

Name origin: For Arlington, VA.

ILLINOIS, Cook County

Barrington
Township
ZIP: 60010 Lat: 42-06-41 N Long: 88-10-45 W
Pop: 13,034 (1990); 9,600 (1980) Pop Density: 372.4
Land: 35.0 sq. mi.; Water: 1.0 sq. mi.
Incorporated 1959.
Name origin: From nearby Barrington.

*Barrington
Village
ZIP: 60010 Lat: 42-08-43 N Long: 88-07-41 W
Pop: 5,159 (1990); 4,955 (1980) Pop Density: 2149.6
Land: 2.4 sq. mi.; Water: 0.1 sq. mi.
Incorporated 1959. In northeastern IL, a residential suburb 30 mi. northwest of Chicago. Founded 1845. Not coextensive with the township of the same name in Cook County. Part of the town is also in Lake County.
Name origin: For Great Barrington, MA.

Barrington Hills
Village
ZIP: 60010 Lat: 42-07-17 N Long: 88-12-02 W
Pop: 2,130 (1990); 1,980 (1980) Pop Density: 122.4
Land: 17.4 sq. mi.; Water: 0.5 sq. mi. Elev: 877 ft.
Part of the town is also in Kane, Lake, and McHenry counties.
Name origin: For nearby Barrington.

Bartlett
Village
ZIP: 60103 Lat: 41-59-50 N Long: 88-12-42 W
Pop: 7,276 (1990); 4,705 (1980) Pop Density: 1692.1
Land: 4.3 sq. mi.; Water: 0.1 sq. mi.
In northeastern IL, 30 mi. northwest of Chicago; a manufacturing and residential suburb. Founded 1873; incorporated 1891. Part of the town is also in DuPage and Kane counties.
Name origin: For founder Luther Bartlett, its first postmaster, who bought the site in 1844.

Bedford Park
Village
ZIP: 60501 Lat: 41-46-11 N Long: 87-47-52 W
Pop: 566 (1990); 988 (1980) Pop Density: 94.3
Land: 6.0 sq. mi.; Water: 0.1 sq. mi.
Incorporated 1940.

Bellwood
Industrial village
ZIP: 60104 Lat: 41-52-58 N Long: 87-52-34 W
Pop: 20,241 (1990); 19,811 (1980) Pop Density: 8433.8
Land: 2.4 sq. mi.; Water: 0.0 sq. mi.
In northeastern IL, a residential suburb 12 mi. west of Chicago. Incorporated 1900.

Bensenville
Village
ZIP: 60106 Lat: 41-56-58 N Long: 87-55-04 W
Pop: 0 (1990); 3 (1980)
Land: 0.2 sq. mi.; Water: 0.0 sq. mi.
In northeastern IL on Salt Creek, 18 mi. northwest of Chicago. Incorporated 1894. Part of the town is also in DuPage County.

Berkeley
Village
ZIP: 60163 Lat: 41-53-18 N Long: 87-54-44 W
Pop: 5,137 (1990); 5,467 (1980) Pop Density: 3669.3
Land: 1.4 sq. mi.; Water: 0.0 sq. mi.
Incorporated 1924.
Name origin: For Berkeley, CA.

Berwyn
Residential city
ZIP: 60402 Lat: 41-50-32 N Long: 87-47-27 W
Pop: 45,426 (1990); 46,849 (1980) Pop Density: 11647.7
Land: 3.9 sq. mi.; Water: 0.0 sq. mi.
In northeastern IL, 8 mi. west of Chicago. Pre-planned by two realtors. Incorporated Nov 15, 1901. Coextensive with the town of the same name.
Name origin: For Berwyn, PA.

*Berwyn
Township
ZIP: 60402 Lat: 41-50-32 N Long: 87-47-27 W
Pop: 45,426 (1990); 46,849 (1980) Pop Density: 11647.7
Land: 3.9 sq. mi.; Water: 0.0 sq. mi.

Bloom
Township
ZIP: 60411 Lat: 41-31-02 N Long: 87-36-02 W
Pop: 95,029 (1990); 101,424 (1980) Pop Density: 2039.2
Land: 46.6 sq. mi.; Water: 0.2 sq. mi.

Blue Island
City
ZIP: 60406 Lat: 41-39-30 N Long: 87-40-53 W
Pop: 21,203 (1990); 21,855 (1980) Pop Density: 5300.8
Land: 4.0 sq. mi.; Water: 0.1 sq. mi.
In northeastern IL, 12 mi. south of Chicago. First settled 1835 by German and Italian pioneers. Incorporated Feb 24, 1843.
Name origin: Descriptive of a blue-iris-covered hill that, from a distance, resembled an island. Previously called Portland.

Bremen
Township
ZIP: 60426 Lat: 41-36-14 N Long: 87-44-01 W
Pop: 107,803 (1990); 109,023 (1980) Pop Density: 2859.5
Land: 37.7 sq. mi.; Water: 0.1 sq. mi.
Name origin: Probably for Bremen, Germany.

Bridgeview
Village
ZIP: 60455 Lat: 41-44-19 N Long: 87-48-21 W
Pop: 14,402 (1990); 14,155 (1980) Pop Density: 3512.7
Land: 4.1 sq. mi.; Water: 0.0 sq. mi.
In northeastern IL, 55 mi. southwest of Chicago. Incorporated 1947.

Broadview
Residential suburb
ZIP: 60153 Lat: 41-51-28 N Long: 87-51-21 W
Pop: 8,713 (1990); 8,618 (1980) Pop Density: 4840.6
Land: 1.8 sq. mi.; Water: 0.0 sq. mi.
In northeastern IL, west of Chicago. Incorporated as village 1910.
Name origin: For a station of the Illinois Central Railway.

Brookfield
Residential village
ZIP: 60513 Lat: 41-49-27 N Long: 87-50-51 W
Pop: 18,876 (1990); 19,395 (1980) Pop Density: 6089.0
Land: 3.1 sq. mi.; Water: 0.0 sq. mi.
In northeastern IL on Salt Creek, 10 mi. southwest of Chicago. Founded 1893, following extensive land purchases by the Ogden, Armour, McCormick, and Rockefeller families. Site of Chicago Zoological Park. Incorporated 1893.
Name origin: For its descriptive connotations. Previously called Grossdale.

Buffalo Grove
Residential suburb
ZIP: 60089 Lat: 42-08-35 N Long: 87-58-19 W
Pop: 14,497 (1990); 13,144 (1980) Pop Density: 6589.5
Land: 2.2 sq. mi.; Water: 0.0 sq. mi.
In northeastern IL, 25 mi. northwest of Chicago. Incorporated 1958. Part of the town is also in Lake County.
Name origin: For the once-present American bison.

Burbank — City
ZIP: 60459 **Lat:** 41-44-38 N **Long:** 87-46-08 W
Pop: 27,600 (1990); 28,462 (1980) **Pop Density:** 6731.7
Land: 4.1 sq. mi.; **Water:** 0.0 sq. mi. **Elev:** 622 ft.

In northeastern IL, 10 mi. southwest of Chicago. Incorporated Apr 10, 1970.

Name origin: For Luther Burbank (1849–1926), experimental horticulturalist.

Burnham — Village
ZIP: 60633 **Lat:** 41-38-17 N **Long:** 87-32-28 W
Pop: 3,916 (1990); 4,030 (1980) **Pop Density:** 2061.1
Land: 1.9 sq. mi.; **Water:** 0.1 sq. mi.

Burr Ridge — Village
ZIP: 60521 **Lat:** 41-45-32 N **Long:** 87-54-34 W
Pop: 3,073 (1990); 1,548 (1980) **Pop Density:** 1396.8
Land: 2.2 sq. mi.; **Water:** 0.0 sq. mi.

Part of the town is also in DuPage County.

Calumet — Township
ZIP: 60406 **Lat:** 41-39-27 N **Long:** 87-39-13 W
Pop: 21,000 (1990); 21,637 (1980) **Pop Density:** 4666.7
Land: 4.5 sq. mi.; **Water:** 0.3 sq. mi.

Name origin: For the long-stemmed Indian peace pipe; from the French term *chalemel* 'straw' or 'little reed'; later in Amerindian French extended to 'pipe.'

Calumet City — City
ZIP: 60409 **Lat:** 41-36-42 N **Long:** 87-32-58 W
Pop: 37,840 (1990); 39,697 (1980) **Pop Density:** 5183.6
Land: 7.3 sq. mi.; **Water:** 0.1 sq. mi. **Elev:** 589 ft.

In northeastern IL on the IN border, 20 mi. southeast of Chicago. Incorporated Jul 22, 1911.

Name origin: Previously named West Hammond.

Calumet Park — Village
ZIP: 60643 **Lat:** 41-39-50 N **Long:** 87-39-23 W
Pop: 8,418 (1990); 8,788 (1980) **Pop Density:** 7652.7
Land: 1.1 sq. mi.; **Water:** 0.0 sq. mi.

Name origin: Named in 1925. Originally known as Burr Oak.

Chicago — City
ZIP: 60607 **Lat:** 41-50-04 N **Long:** 87-40-55 W
Pop: 2,783,726 (1990); 3,005,061 (1980)
Pop Density: 12377.6
Land: 224.9 sq. mi.; **Water:** 6.8 sq. mi. **Elev:** 596 ft.

In northeastern IL on Lake Michigan; featuring Chicago Sanitary and Ship Canal. County seat; incorporated Feb 11, 1835. Part of the city is also in DuPage County. Third largest U.S. city, biggest transportation center, and one of busiest ports in the U.S. Financial capital of the Midwest and world's capital in futures trading; home to the Chicago Board of Trade, the oldest U.S. financial exchange. Site of the great fire of 1871 and the Haymarket riot in 1886. Produces food products, fabricated metals, chemicals, and iron and steel. Home of DePaul and Loyola universities, Illinois Institute of Technology, University of Chicago, Chicago Zoological Park, Lincoln Park Zoo, Natural History Museum, Comiskey Park (Chicago White Sox), Wrigley Field (Chicago Cubs), world's tallest building: 110-story Sears Tower. Downtown area called *the Loop*.

Name origin: From an Algonquian term meaning 'garlic field.'

Chicago Heights — City
ZIP: 60411 **Lat:** 41-30-35 N **Long:** 87-38-15 W
Pop: 33,072 (1990); 37,026 (1980) **Pop Density:** 3674.7
Land: 9.0 sq. mi.; **Water:** 0.0 sq. mi.

In northeastern IL near Indiana border, 25 mi. south of Chicago. Incorporated Sep 29, 1892.

Chicago Ridge — Village
ZIP: 60415 **Lat:** 41-42-08 N **Long:** 87-46-43 W
Pop: 13,643 (1990); 13,473 (1980) **Pop Density:** 6201.4
Land: 2.2 sq. mi.; **Water:** 0.0 sq. mi.

In northeastern IL, 15 mi. southwest of Chicago. Incorporated 1914.

Cicero — Town
ZIP: 60650 **Lat:** 41-50-39 N **Long:** 87-45-35 W
Pop: 67,436 (1990); 61,232 (1980) **Pop Density:** 11626.9
Land: 5.8 sq. mi.; **Water:** 0.0 sq. mi. **Elev:** 606 ft.

In northeastern IL, 8 mi. southwest of Chicago. Founded 1857; incorporated Feb 28, 1867. Coextensive with the township.

Name origin: For Marcus Tullius Cicero (106–43 B.C.), the great Roman orator.

*Cicero — Township
ZIP: 60650 **Lat:** 41-50-39 N **Long:** 87-45-35 W
Pop: 67,436 (1990); 61,232 (1980) **Pop Density:** 11626.9
Land: 5.8 sq. mi.; **Water:** 0.0 sq. mi.

Country Club Hills — Village
ZIP: 60478 **Lat:** 41-33-47 N **Long:** 87-43-30 W
Pop: 15,431 (1990); 14,676 (1980) **Pop Density:** 3354.6
Land: 4.6 sq. mi.; **Water:** 0.0 sq. mi.

In northeastern IL, 25 mi. south of Chicago. Incorporated Jul 15, 1958.

Name origin: Named in 1958 by its developers.

Countryside — Village
ZIP: 60525 **Lat:** 41-46-35 N **Long:** 87-52-35 W
Pop: 5,716 (1990); 6,242 (1980) **Pop Density:** 2286.4
Land: 2.5 sq. mi.; **Water:** 0.0 sq. mi.

Incorporated Apr 26, 1960.

Name origin: Descriptive of its early rural history.

Crestwood — Village
ZIP: 60445 **Lat:** 41-38-42 N **Long:** 87-44-25 W
Pop: 10,823 (1990); 10,852 (1980) **Pop Density:** 3607.7
Land: 3.0 sq. mi.; **Water:** 0.1 sq. mi.

In northeastern IL, 15 mi. southwest of Chicago. Incorporated 1928.

Name origin: Named in the 1950s by its developers.

Deerfield — Village
ZIP: 60015 **Lat:** 42-09-02 N **Long:** 87-51-02 W
Pop: 0 (1990); 2 (1980)
Land: 0.5 sq. mi.; **Water:** 0.0 sq. mi.

In northeastern IL, 25 mi. northwest of Chicago. Founded 1836 on the site of a Potawatomi Indian village; incorporated 1903. Part of the town is also in Lake County.

Name origin: For its descriptive connotations.

Des Plaines — City
ZIP: 60016 **Lat:** 42-02-04 N **Long:** 87-54-03 W
Pop: 53,223 (1990); 53,568 (1980) **Pop Density:** 3748.1
Land: 14.2 sq. mi.; **Water:** 0.1 sq. mi.

In northeastern IL on the Des Plaines River, 15 mi. north-

ILLINOIS, Cook County

west of Chicago. Founded in the 1830s; incorporated Apr 15, 1869.

Name origin: Named in 1869 for its river. Previously called Rand, for Socrates Rand, its first settler.

Dixmoor
ZIP: 60426   **Lat:** 41-37-54 N   **Long:** 87-40-04 W   Village
Pop: 3,647 (1990); 4,175 (1980)   **Pop Density:** 3039.2
Land: 1.2 sq. mi.; **Water:** 0.0 sq. mi.

In northeastern IL, south of Chicago. Incorporated 1922.

Name origin: Also spelled Dixmore.

Dolton
ZIP: 60419   **Lat:** 41-37-45 N   **Long:** 87-35-55 W   Village
Pop: 23,930 (1990); 24,766 (1980)   **Pop Density:** 5317.8
Land: 4.5 sq. mi.; **Water:** 0.1 sq. mi.

In northeastern IL, 15 mi. south of Chicago. Incorporated 1892.

Name origin: For its founder, Andrew H. Dolton.

East Dundee
Lat: 42-05-25 N   **Long:** 88-14-06 W   Village
Pop: 3 (1990); 2,618 (1980)   **Pop Density:** 30.0
Land: 0.1 sq. mi.; **Water:** 0.0 sq. mi.

Part of the town is also in Kane County.

East Hazel Crest
ZIP: 60429   **Lat:** 41-34-34 N   **Long:** 87-38-58 W   Village
Pop: 1,570 (1990); 1,362 (1980)   **Pop Density:** 1962.5
Land: 0.8 sq. mi.; **Water:** 0.0 sq. mi.

Elgin
ZIP: 60120   **Lat:** 42-01-53 N   **Long:** 88-14-46 W   City
Pop: 15,400 (1990); 11,020 (1980)   **Pop Density:** 2610.2
Land: 5.9 sq. mi.; **Water:** 0.1 sq. mi.

Founded in 1835 by James and Hezekiah Gifford, two settlers from New York. Incorporated 1854. Part of the town is also in Kane County.

Elk Grove
ZIP: 60007   **Lat:** 42-01-47 N   **Long:** 87-58-37 W   Township
Pop: 87,857 (1990); 88,283 (1980)   **Pop Density:** 3149.0
Land: 27.9 sq. mi.; **Water:** 0.3 sq. mi.

Elk Grove Village
ZIP: 60007   **Lat:** 42-00-32 N   **Long:** 87-59-35 W   Village
Pop: 33,429 (1990); 28,679 (1980)   **Pop Density:** 3342.9
Land: 10.0 sq. mi.; **Water:** 0.1 sq. mi.

In northeastern IL, a northwestern suburb of Chicago. Part of the town is also in DuPage County.

Name origin: Until 1960 Elk Grove Village was little more than a cornfield with scattered houses. That year Centrex Construction Company, a community planning enterprise, laid out a new town.

Elmwood Park
ZIP: 60635   **Lat:** 41-55-20 N   **Long:** 87-48-59 W   Village
Pop: 23,206 (1990); 24,016 (1980)   **Pop Density:** 12213.7
Land: 1.9 sq. mi.; **Water:** 0.0 sq. mi.

In northeastern IL, a western suburb of Chicago. Incorporated 1914.

Evanston
ZIP: 60201   **Lat:** 42-02-46 N   **Long:** 87-41-40 W   City
Pop: 73,233 (1990); 73,706 (1980)   **Pop Density:** 9388.8
Land: 7.8 sq. mi.; **Water:** 0.0 sq. mi.

In northeastern IL, 15 mi. north of Chicago. Incorporated Feb 17, 1857. Coextensive with the town of the same name. Site of Northwestern University.

Name origin: For John Evans, a founder of Northwestern University. Previously called Ridgeville.

*Evanston
ZIP: 60201   **Lat:** 42-02-46 N   **Long:** 87-41-40 W   Township
Pop: 73,233 (1990); 73,706 (1980)   **Pop Density:** 9388.8
Land: 7.8 sq. mi.; **Water:** 0.0 sq. mi.

Evergreen Park
ZIP: 60642   **Lat:** 41-43-15 N   **Long:** 87-42-03 W   Village
Pop: 20,874 (1990); 22,260 (1980)   **Pop Density:** 6523.1
Land: 3.2 sq. mi.; **Water:** 0.0 sq. mi.

In northeastern IL, 10 mi. southwest of Chicago. Incorporated 1893.

Name origin: Descriptively named.

Flossmoor
ZIP: 60422   **Lat:** 41-32-21 N   **Long:** 87-41-03 W   Village
Pop: 8,651 (1990); 8,423 (1980)   **Pop Density:** 2544.4
Land: 3.4 sq. mi.; **Water:** 0.0 sq. mi.   **Elev:** 674 ft.

Name origin: From a Scottish term meaning 'gently rolling countryside.' Also spelled Flossmore.

Ford Heights
ZIP: 60411   **Lat:** 41-30-34 N   **Long:** 87-35-20 W   Village
Pop: 4,259 (1990); 5,347 (1980)   **Pop Density:** 4259.0
Land: 1.0 sq. mi.; **Water:** 0.0 sq. mi.

Forest Park
ZIP: 60130   **Lat:** 41-52-08 N   **Long:** 87-48-53 W   Village
Pop: 14,918 (1990); 15,177 (1980)   **Pop Density:** 6215.8
Land: 2.4 sq. mi.; **Water:** 0.0 sq. mi.

In northeastern IL on the Des Plaines River, a western suburb of Chicago. Incorporated 1907.

Name origin: Descriptively named to promote settlement. Previously called Harlem.

Forest View
Lat: 41-48-23 N   **Long:** 87-46-51 W   Village
Pop: 743 (1990); 764 (1980)   **Pop Density:** 743.0
Land: 1.0 sq. mi.; **Water:** 0.1 sq. mi.

Franklin Park
ZIP: 60131   **Lat:** 41-56-07 N   **Long:** 87-52-41 W   Village
Pop: 18,485 (1990); 17,507 (1980)   **Pop Density:** 4018.5
Land: 4.6 sq. mi.; **Water:** 0.0 sq. mi.

In northeastern IL on the Des Plaines River, a residential suburb 15 mi. northwest of Chicago. Incorporated 1892.

Name origin: For a 19th-century Chicago real estate developer.

Glencoe
ZIP: 60022   **Lat:** 42-08-04 N   **Long:** 87-45-48 W   Village
Pop: 8,499 (1990); 9,200 (1980)   **Pop Density:** 2236.6
Land: 3.8 sq. mi.; **Water:** 0.1 sq. mi.

In northeastern IL, a northern suburb of Chicago, on the western shore of Lake Michigan. Founded 1836; incorporated as village 1869.

Name origin: A composite of *glen* suggestive of the site, and *coe* the maiden name of the wife of one of its founders, Walter S. Gurnee.

Glenview — Village
ZIP: 60025 **Lat:** 42-04-46 N **Long:** 87-48-54 W
Pop: 37,093 (1990); 32,060 (1980) **Pop Density:** 3091.1
Land: 12.0 sq. mi.; **Water:** 0.0 sq. mi.

In northeastern IL, 15 mi. northwest of Chicago. Incorporated 1899. Site of Glenview Naval Air Station.

Glenwood — Village
ZIP: 60425 **Lat:** 41-32-45 N **Long:** 87-37-01 W
Pop: 9,289 (1990); 10,538 (1980) **Pop Density:** 4222.3
Land: 2.2 sq. mi.; **Water:** 0.0 sq. mi.

In northeastern IL near the IN border, 20 mi. southeast of Chicago. Settled 1846.

Name origin: For its once-wooded glens.

Golf — Village
ZIP: 60029 **Lat:** 42-03-31 N **Long:** 87-47-11 W
Pop: 454 (1990); 482 (1980) **Pop Density:** 1135.0
Land: 0.4 sq. mi.; **Water:** 0.0 sq. mi.

Hanover — Township
ZIP: 60103 **Lat:** 42-01-40 N **Long:** 88-12-14 W
Pop: 62,308 (1990); 47,717 (1980) **Pop Density:** 1859.9
Land: 33.5 sq. mi.; **Water:** 0.2 sq. mi.

Hanover Park — City
ZIP: 60103 **Lat:** 42-00-04 N **Long:** 88-08-41 W
Pop: 18,662 (1990); 18,158 (1980) **Pop Density:** 6020.0
Land: 3.1 sq. mi.; **Water:** 0.0 sq. mi.

In northeastern IL, 25 mi. northwest of Chicago. Incorporated 1958. Part of the town is also in DuPage County.

Name origin: For the British royal house whose line began with George I (1660–1727), Duke of Hanover.

Harvey — City
ZIP: 60426 **Lat:** 41-36-26 N **Long:** 87-39-06 W
Pop: 29,771 (1990); 35,810 (1980) **Pop Density:** 4801.8
Land: 6.2 sq. mi.; **Water:** 0.0 sq. mi.

In northeastern IL, 20 mi. south of Chicago. Founded 1890; incorporated Jun 18, 1891. Industrial and manufacturing city.

Name origin: For Chicago land developer Turlington W. Harvey, its founder.

Harwood Heights — City
ZIP: 60656 **Lat:** 41-57-58 N **Long:** 87-48-19 W
Pop: 7,680 (1990); 8,228 (1980) **Pop Density:** 9600.0
Land: 0.8 sq. mi.; **Water:** 0.0 sq. mi.

Incorporated 1947.

Name origin: From the first syllable of Harlem and the *wood* of Norwood Park Township.

Hazel Crest — City
ZIP: 60429 **Lat:** 41-34-20 N **Long:** 87-41-21 W
Pop: 13,334 (1990); 13,973 (1980) **Pop Density:** 3921.8
Land: 3.4 sq. mi.; **Water:** 0.0 sq. mi. **Elev:** 648 ft.

In northeastern IL, 20 mi. southwest of Chicago. Incorporated 1911.

Name origin: For the area's hazel (*Corylus*) bushes.

Hickory Hills — City
ZIP: 60457 **Lat:** 41-43-25 N **Long:** 87-49-41 W
Pop: 13,021 (1990); 13,778 (1980) **Pop Density:** 4650.4
Land: 2.8 sq. mi.; **Water:** 0.0 sq. mi.

In northeastern IL, a residential suburb 15 mi. southwest of Chicago. Incorporated Sep 8, 1951.

Name origin: Descriptively named in 1951 by its incorporators.

Hillside — City
ZIP: 60162 **Lat:** 41-52-15 N **Long:** 87-53-54 W
Pop: 7,672 (1990); 8,279 (1980) **Pop Density:** 3653.3
Land: 2.1 sq. mi.; **Water:** 0.0 sq. mi. **Elev:** 659 ft.

Name origin: Named in 1905 by the railroad.

Hinsdale — City
ZIP: 60521 **Lat:** 41-47-44 N **Long:** 87-54-49 W
Pop: 2,073 (1990); 2,414 (1980) **Pop Density:** 2303.3
Land: 0.9 sq. mi.; **Water:** 0.0 sq. mi.

In northeastern IL, 15 mi. west of Chicago. Incorporated 1873. Part of the town is also in DuPage County.

Name origin: For H. W. Hinsdale, a director of the Burlington Railroad.

Hodgkins — Town
ZIP: 60525 **Lat:** 41-46-14 N **Long:** 87-51-22 W
Pop: 1,963 (1990); 2,005 (1980) **Pop Density:** 934.8
Land: 2.1 sq. mi.; **Water:** 0.1 sq. mi.

Hoffman Estates — Village
ZIP: 60196 **Lat:** 42-03-52 N **Long:** 88-08-17 W
Pop: 46,561 (1990); 37,272 (1980) **Pop Density:** 2503.3
Land: 18.6 sq. mi.; **Water:** 0.2 sq. mi.

Incorporated 1959. Part of the town is also in Kane County.

Hometown — City
ZIP: 60456 **Lat:** 41-43-56 N **Long:** 87-43-52 W
Pop: 4,769 (1990); 5,324 (1980) **Pop Density:** 9538.0
Land: 0.5 sq. mi.; **Water:** 0.0 sq. mi.

In northeastern IL, a residential suburb southwest of Chicago.

Name origin: Named in 1950 by its developers.

Homewood — City
ZIP: 60430 **Lat:** 41-33-30 N **Long:** 87-39-40 W
Pop: 19,278 (1990); 19,724 (1980) **Pop Density:** 3707.3
Land: 5.2 sq. mi.; **Water:** 0.0 sq. mi.

In northeastern IL, 22 mi. southeast of Chicago. Incorporated 1893.

Name origin: For Homewood, PA.

Indian Head Park — Village
ZIP: 60525 **Lat:** 41-46-03 N **Long:** 87-53-50 W
Pop: 3,503 (1990); 2,915 (1980) **Pop Density:** 4378.8
Land: 0.8 sq. mi.; **Water:** 0.0 sq. mi.

Inverness — Town
ZIP: 60067 **Lat:** 42-06-54 N **Long:** 88-06-02 W
Pop: 6,503 (1990); 4,046 (1980) **Pop Density:** 1066.1
Land: 6.1 sq. mi.; **Water:** 0.1 sq. mi. **Elev:** 853 ft.

Name origin: For Inverness, Scotland.

Justice — Village
ZIP: 60458 **Lat:** 41-44-47 N **Long:** 87-50-07 W
Pop: 11,137 (1990); 10,552 (1980) **Pop Density:** 3840.3
Land: 2.9 sq. mi.; **Water:** 0.0 sq. mi.

In northeastern IL, 14 mi. southwest of Chicago. Incorporated 1911.

Name origin: For the belief in the "righteous treatment" of its citizens.

Kenilworth — Town
ZIP: 60043 **Lat:** 42-05-20 N **Long:** 87-42-53 W
Pop: 2,402 (1990); 2,708 (1980) **Pop Density:** 4003.3
Land: 0.6 sq. mi.; **Water:** 0.0 sq. mi.

In northeastern IL, 17 mi. northwest of Chicago.

ILLINOIS, Cook County

La Grange — City
ZIP: 60525   **Lat:** 41-48-28 N **Long:** 87-52-24 W
Pop: 15,362 (1990); 15,693 (1980)   **Pop Density:** 6144.8
Land: 2.5 sq. mi.; **Water:** 0.0 sq. mi.

In northeastern IL, 13 mi. west of Chicago. Incorporated 1879.
Name origin: For LaGrange, TN, former home of the city's first president, Franklin D. Cossitt.

La Grange Park — City
ZIP: 60525   **Lat:** 41-49-53 N **Long:** 87-52-17 W
Pop: 12,861 (1990); 13,359 (1980)   **Pop Density:** 5591.7
Land: 2.3 sq. mi.; **Water:** 0.0 sq. mi.

In northeastern IL on Salt Creek, 12 mi. west of Chicago. Incorporated 1892.
Name origin: For nearby La Grange.

Lansing — City
ZIP: 60438   **Lat:** 41-34-03 N **Long:** 87-32-44 W
Pop: 28,086 (1990); 29,039 (1980)   **Pop Density:** 4255.5
Land: 6.6 sq. mi.; **Water:** 0.1 sq. mi.   **Elev:** 630 ft.

In northeastern IL on the IN border, 20 mi. southeast of Chicago. Founded 1864; incorporated 1893.
Name origin: For either the founding brothers, John and Henry Lansing, or possibly for American Revolution hero and NY legislator John Lansing.

Lemont — City
ZIP: 60439   **Lat:** 41-40-12 N **Long:** 87-59-29 W
Pop: 7,348 (1990); 5,640 (1980)   **Pop Density:** 1884.1
Land: 3.9 sq. mi.; **Water:** 0.1 sq. mi.

In northeastern IL along the Illinois and Michigan Canal, 25 mi. southwest of Chicago. Not coextensive with the town of the same name.
Name origin: From French 'the mountain'; reason for the name is unknown.

*Lemont — Township
ZIP: 60439   **Lat:** 41-39-52 N **Long:** 87-57-48 W
Pop: 11,537 (1990); 8,850 (1980)   **Pop Density:** 574.0
Land: 20.1 sq. mi.; **Water:** 0.7 sq. mi.

Leyden — Township
ZIP: 60131   **Lat:** 41-56-16 N **Long:** 87-52-06 W
Pop: 89,142 (1990); 91,572 (1980)   **Pop Density:** 4502.1
Land: 19.8 sq. mi.; **Water:** 0.0 sq. mi.

Lincolnwood — City
ZIP: 60646   **Lat:** 42-00-21 N **Long:** 87-43-58 W
Pop: 11,365 (1990); 11,921 (1980)   **Pop Density:** 4209.3
Land: 2.7 sq. mi.; **Water:** 0.0 sq. mi.

In northeastern IL, 12 mi. northwest of Chicago. Incorporated Sept 29, 1911.
Name origin: For Abraham Lincoln (1809–65), sixteenth U.S. president.

Lynwood — Town
ZIP: 60411   **Lat:** 41-31-35 N **Long:** 87-32-31 W
Pop: 6,535 (1990); 4,195 (1980)   **Pop Density:** 1519.8
Land: 4.3 sq. mi.; **Water:** 0.1 sq. mi.

Incorporated December 23, 1959.
Name origin: Named by its developers.

Lyons — City
ZIP: 60534   **Lat:** 41-48-42 N **Long:** 87-49-07 W
Pop: 9,828 (1990); 9,925 (1980)   **Pop Density:** 4467.3
Land: 2.2 sq. mi.; **Water:** 0.0 sq. mi.

In northeastern IL on the Des Plaines River, 8 mi. west of Chicago. Post office established February 29, 1848. Not coextensive with the town of the same name.
Name origin: For either Lyons, France, or a local community member.

*Lyons — Township
ZIP: 60525   **Lat:** 41-46-29 N **Long:** 87-51-34 W
Pop: 105,004 (1990); 105,317 (1980)   **Pop Density:** 2884.7
Land: 36.4 sq. mi.; **Water:** 0.6 sq. mi.

Maine — Township
ZIP: 60016   **Lat:** 42-01-59 N **Long:** 87-51-52 W
Pop: 128,837 (1990); 130,676 (1980)   **Pop Density:** 4955.3
Land: 26.0 sq. mi.; **Water:** 0.2 sq. mi.

Markham — City
ZIP: 60426   **Lat:** 41-35-57 N **Long:** 87-41-28 W
Pop: 13,136 (1990); 15,172 (1980)   **Pop Density:** 2526.2
Land: 5.2 sq. mi.; **Water:** 0.0 sq. mi.

In northeastern IL, 20 mi. south of Chicago. Incorporated Oct 23, 1925.
Name origin: For Charles H. Markham, president of the Illinois Central Railroad.

Matteson — City
ZIP: 60443   **Lat:** 41-30-39 N **Long:** 87-44-15 W
Pop: 11,378 (1990); 10,223 (1980)   **Pop Density:** 1750.5
Land: 6.5 sq. mi.; **Water:** 0.1 sq. mi.   **Elev:** 693 ft.

In northeastern IL, 25 mi. south of Chicago. Founded in the 1850s by German settlers. Incorporated Mar 20, 1889.
Name origin: For Joel A. Matteson, IL governor (1853–57).

Maywood — City
ZIP: 60153   **Lat:** 41-52-48 N **Long:** 87-50-40 W
Pop: 27,139 (1990); 27,998 (1980)   **Pop Density:** 10051.5
Land: 2.7 sq. mi.; **Water:** 0.0 sq. mi.

In northeastern IL on the Des Plaines River, 10 mi. west of Chicago. Founded in the 1860s by a group of New Englanders; incorporated 1881.
Name origin: For May Nichols, daughter of the leading founder Col. W. T. Nichols, plus *wood* for the plentiful forests.

McCook — Village
     Lat: 41-47-34 N **Long:** 87-50-08 W
Pop: 235 (1990); 303 (1980)   **Pop Density:** 90.4
Land: 2.6 sq. mi.; **Water:** 0.0 sq. mi.

Melrose Park — City
ZIP: 60160   **Lat:** 41-54-10 N **Long:** 87-51-48 W
Pop: 20,859 (1990); 20,735 (1980)   **Pop Density:** 4966.4
Land: 4.2 sq. mi.; **Water:** 0.0 sq. mi.

In northeastern IL, 15 mi. west of Chicago. Incorporated 1893.
Name origin: Named by incorporators, probably for Melrose Roxburghshire, Scotland, or for Melrose Abbey in Scotland.

Merrionette Park — Town
ZIP: 60655   **Lat:** 41-40-49 N **Long:** 87-41-59 W
Pop: 2,065 (1990); 2,054 (1980)   **Pop Density:** 5162.5
Land: 0.4 sq. mi.; **Water:** 0.0 sq. mi.

Name origin: For its subdivider, J. E. Merrion.

Midlothian — City
ZIP: 60445   **Lat:** 41-37-34 N   **Long:** 87-43-27 W
Pop: 14,372 (1990); 14,274 (1980)   **Pop Density:** 5132.9
Land: 2.8 sq. mi.; **Water:** 0.0 sq. mi.

In northeastern IL, 18 mi. south of Chicago. Incorporated 1927.
Name origin: For a golf course built here in 1898 by George R. Thorne, then head of Montgomery Ward, which was named for either the Scottish shire or Sir Walter Scott's (1771–1832) *The Heart of Midlothian*.

Morton Grove — City
ZIP: 60053   **Lat:** 42-02-32 N   **Long:** 87-47-20 W
Pop: 22,408 (1990); 23,747 (1980)   **Pop Density:** 4393.7
Land: 5.1 sq. mi.; **Water:** 0.0 sq. mi.

In northeastern IL on the Chicago River, 15 mi. northwest of Chicago. Incorporated 1895.
Name origin: For either Levi P. Morton (1824–1920), official of the Chicago, Milwaukee, & St. Paul Railroad and vice president under Benjamin Harrison (1889–93), or possibly for Marcus Morton, MA governor (1840–44).

Mount Prospect — City
ZIP: 60056   **Lat:** 42-03-55 N   **Long:** 87-56-15 W
Pop: 53,170 (1990); 52,634 (1980)   **Pop Density:** 5162.1
Land: 10.3 sq. mi.; **Water:** 0.0 sq. mi.

In northeastern IL, 20 mi. northwest of Chicago. Incorporated 1917.
Name origin: Descriptive of a local geographic feature.

New Trier — Township
ZIP: 60093   **Lat:** 42-06-06 N   **Long:** 87-44-41 W
Pop: 54,705 (1990); 58,216 (1980)   **Pop Density:** 3419.1
Land: 16.0 sq. mi.; **Water:** 0.3 sq. mi.

Niles — City
ZIP: 60648   **Lat:** 42-01-37 N   **Long:** 87-48-34 W
Pop: 28,284 (1990); 30,363 (1980)   **Pop Density:** 4876.6
Land: 5.8 sq. mi.; **Water:** 0.0 sq. mi.

In northeastern IL on the Chicago River, 15 mi. north of Chicago. Incorporated 1899. Not coextensive with the town of the same name.
Name origin: For Niles, NY. Previously named Dutchman's Point and Lyttleton's Point.

*Niles — Township
ZIP: 60076   **Lat:** 42-01-56 N   **Long:** 87-45-29 W
Pop: 96,412 (1990); 99,447 (1980)   **Pop Density:** 4547.7
Land: 21.2 sq. mi.; **Water:** 0.0 sq. mi.

Norridge — Village
ZIP: 60634   **Lat:** 41-57-53 N   **Long:** 87-49-21 W
Pop: 14,459 (1990); 16,483 (1980)   **Pop Density:** 8032.8
Land: 1.8 sq. mi.; **Water:** 0.0 sq. mi.

In northeastern IL, a residential suburb 10 mi. northwest of Chicago. Incorporated 1948.
Name origin: A combination of the names of two nearby residential areas: Norwood and Park Ridge.

Northbrook — City
ZIP: 60062   **Lat:** 42-07-46 N   **Long:** 87-49-58 W
Pop: 32,308 (1990); 30,778 (1980)   **Pop Density:** 2564.1
Land: 12.6 sq. mi.; **Water:** 0.0 sq. mi.

In northeastern IL, a residential suburb northwest of Chicago. Incorporated 1923.

Northfield — Village
ZIP: 60093   **Lat:** 42-06-02 N   **Long:** 87-46-43 W
Pop: 4,635 (1990); 4,887 (1980)   **Pop Density:** 1655.4
Land: 2.8 sq. mi.; **Water:** 0.0 sq. mi.

In northeastern IL, 15 mi. north of Chicago. Not coextensive with the town of the same name.
Name origin: For its descriptive connotations.

*Northfield — Township
ZIP: 60025   **Lat:** 42-06-25 N   **Long:** 87-49-56 W
Pop: 78,186 (1990); 74,243 (1980)   **Pop Density:** 2279.5
Land: 34.3 sq. mi.; **Water:** 0.3 sq. mi.

Northlake — City
ZIP: 60164   **Lat:** 41-54-49 N   **Long:** 87-54-13 W
Pop: 12,505 (1990); 12,166 (1980)   **Pop Density:** 4168.3
Land: 3.0 sq. mi.; **Water:** 0.0 sq. mi.

In northeastern IL, 15 mi. west of Chicago. Incorporated Apr 23, 1949. Not coextensive with the town of the same name.
Name origin: For its descriptive connotations.

North Riverside — Village
ZIP: 60546   **Lat:** 41-50-51 N   **Long:** 87-49-29 W
Pop: 6,005 (1990); 6,764 (1980)   **Pop Density:** 4003.3
Land: 1.5 sq. mi.; **Water:** 0.0 sq. mi.

Norwood Park — Township
ZIP: 60656   **Lat:** 41-58-06 N   **Long:** 87-49-03 W
Pop: 25,600 (1990); 28,070 (1980)   **Pop Density:** 6918.9
Land: 3.7 sq. mi.; **Water:** 0.0 sq. mi.

Oak Brook — Town
ZIP: 60521   **Lat:** 41-51-38 N   **Long:** 87-55-10 W
Pop: 0 (1990); 6,676 (1980)
Land: 0.01 sq. mi.; **Water:** 0.0 sq. mi.

Part of the town is in DuPage County.
Name origin: For the Oakbrook polo club.

Oak Forest — City
ZIP: 60452   **Lat:** 41-36-23 N   **Long:** 87-45-09 W
Pop: 26,203 (1990); 25,040 (1980)   **Pop Density:** 4852.4
Land: 5.4 sq. mi.; **Water:** 0.1 sq. mi.

In northeastern IL, a residential suburb 20 mi. southwest of Chicago. Incorporated May 10, 1947.
Name origin: Descriptively named for the early forest cover.

Oak Lawn — City
ZIP: 60453   **Lat:** 41-42-54 N   **Long:** 87-45-07 W
Pop: 56,182 (1990); 60,590 (1980)   **Pop Density:** 6688.3
Land: 8.4 sq. mi.; **Water:** 0.0 sq. mi.

In northeastern IL, 12 mi. southwest of Chicago. Incorporated 1909.
Name origin: For its descriptive connotations.

Oak Park — City
ZIP: 60302   **Lat:** 41-53-15 N   **Long:** 87-47-22 W
Pop: 53,648 (1990); 54,887 (1980)   **Pop Density:** 11414.5
Land: 4.7 sq. mi.; **Water:** 0.0 sq. mi.

In northeastern IL, 10 mi. west of Chicago. Founded 1833; incorporated 1901. Coextensive with the town of the same name.
Name origin: Initially called Oak Ridge, for the slight, tree-covered rise that has since disappeared due to grading and building.

*Oak Park — Township
ZIP: 60302   **Lat:** 41-53-15 N   **Long:** 87-47-22 W
Pop: 53,648 (1990); 54,887 (1980)   **Pop Density:** 11414.5
Land: 4.7 sq. mi.; **Water:** 0.0 sq. mi.

ILLINOIS, Cook County

Olympia Fields — Town
ZIP: 60461 Lat: 41-31-02 N Long: 87-41-34 W
Pop: 4,248 (1990); 4,146 (1980) Pop Density: 1464.8
Land: 2.9 sq. mi.; Water: 0.0 sq. mi.
Developed 1926.

Orland — Township
ZIP: 60462 Lat: 41-36-06 N Long: 87-51-12 W
Pop: 69,542 (1990); 42,588 (1980) Pop Density: 1942.5
Land: 35.8 sq. mi.; Water: 0.7 sq. mi.
Name origin: Probably for Orland, ME.

Orland Hills — Village
ZIP: 60477 Lat: 41-35-33 N Long: 87-50-34 W
Pop: 5,510 (1990); 2,784 (1980) Pop Density: 5009.1
Land: 1.1 sq. mi.; Water: 0.0 sq. mi.

Orland Park — Village
ZIP: 60462 Lat: 41-36-37 N Long: 87-51-02 W
Pop: 35,720 (1990); 23,045 (1980) Pop Density: 2665.7
Land: 13.4 sq. mi.; Water: 0.2 sq. mi.
In northeastern IL, 25 mi. southwest of Chicago. Incorporated 1892.
Name origin: Probably for Orland, ME.

Palatine — Town
ZIP: 60067 Lat: 42-06-44 N Long: 88-02-34 W
Pop: 39,253 (1990); 32,171 (1980) Pop Density: 3964.9
Land: 9.9 sq. mi.; Water: 0.1 sq. mi. Elev: 741 ft.
In northeastern IL, a residential suburb 30 mi. northwest of Chicago. Incorporated 1869. Not coextensive with the town of the same name.
Name origin: For the Rhine Palatinate, Germany.

*Palatine — Township
ZIP: 60067 Lat: 42-06-38 N Long: 88-03-47 W
Pop: 103,273 (1990); 83,201 (1980) Pop Density: 2892.8
Land: 35.7 sq. mi.; Water: 0.3 sq. mi.

Palos — Township
ZIP: 60464 Lat: 41-41-05 N Long: 87-51-10 W
Pop: 50,916 (1990); 46,412 (1980) Pop Density: 1501.9
Land: 33.9 sq. mi.; Water: 1.4 sq. mi.

Palos Heights — Town
ZIP: 60463 Lat: 41-39-55 N Long: 87-47-49 W
Pop: 11,478 (1990); 11,096 (1980) Pop Density: 3279.4
Land: 3.5 sq. mi.; Water: 0.1 sq. mi.
In northeastern IL, 15 mi. southwest of Chicago. Incorporated Apr 16, 1959.
Name origin: Probably named by Melanchon A. Powell for Palos, Spain, home of one of his ancestors and where Christopher Columbus (1451–1506) begun his historic voyage. Previously called Trenton.

Palos Hills — City
ZIP: 60465 Lat: 41-41-51 N Long: 87-49-34 W
Pop: 17,803 (1990); 16,654 (1980) Pop Density: 4238.8
Land: 4.2 sq. mi.; Water: 0.1 sq. mi.
In northeastern IL, 15 mi. southwest of Chicago. Incorporated Jan 26, 1959.

Palos Park — Village
ZIP: 60464 Lat: 41-39-52 N Long: 87-50-39 W
Pop: 4,199 (1990); 3,150 (1980) Pop Density: 1199.7
Land: 3.5 sq. mi.; Water: 0.0 sq. mi.

Park Forest — Village
ZIP: 60466 Lat: 41-29-04 N Long: 87-41-05 W
Pop: 21,347 (1990); 22,911 (1980) Pop Density: 5473.6
Land: 3.9 sq. mi.; Water: 0.0 sq. mi.
In northeastern IL, 28 mi. south of Chicago. Incorporated 1949. Part of the town is also in Will County.

Park Ridge — City
ZIP: 60068 Lat: 42-00-42 N Long: 87-50-38 W
Pop: 36,175 (1990); 38,704 (1980) Pop Density: 5242.8
Land: 6.9 sq. mi.; Water: 0.0 sq. mi.
In northeastern IL, 10 mi. northwest of Chicago. Incorporated Feb 22, 1873.
Name origin: Descriptive and promotional.

Phoenix — Village
ZIP: 60426 Lat: 41-36-44 N Long: 87-37-49 W
Pop: 2,217 (1990); 2,850 (1980) Pop Density: 4434.0
Land: 0.5 sq. mi.; Water: 0.0 sq. mi.

Posen — Town
ZIP: 60469 Lat: 41-37-41 N Long: 87-41-08 W
Pop: 4,226 (1990); 4,642 (1980) Pop Density: 3841.8
Land: 1.1 sq. mi.; Water: 0.0 sq. mi.
In northeastern IL, a Chicago suburb.
Name origin: For Posen, Poland.

Prospect Heights — City
ZIP: 60070 Lat: 42-06-08 N Long: 87-55-29 W
Pop: 15,239 (1990); 11,823 (1980) Pop Density: 3544.0
Land: 4.3 sq. mi.; Water: 0.0 sq. mi. Elev: 668 ft.
In northeastern IL near Chicago. Incorporated Feb 2, 1976.
Name origin: Promotional and descriptive.

Proviso — Township
ZIP: 60160 Lat: 41-51-52 N Long: 87-52-13 W
Pop: 152,443 (1990); 156,519 (1980) Pop Density: 5132.8
Land: 29.7 sq. mi.; Water: 0.0 sq. mi.

Rich — Township
ZIP: 60471 Lat: 41-30-44 N Long: 87-43-56 W
Pop: 61,458 (1990); 58,730 (1980) Pop Density: 1688.4
Land: 36.4 sq. mi.; Water: 0.2 sq. mi.

Richton Park — Village
ZIP: 60471 Lat: 41-28-55 N Long: 87-43-41 W
Pop: 10,523 (1990); 9,403 (1980) Pop Density: 3758.2
Land: 2.8 sq. mi.; Water: 0.0 sq. mi.
In northeastern IL, 28 mi. south of Chicago. Incorporated 1926.

Riverdale — Village
ZIP: 60627 Lat: 41-38-40 N Long: 87-38-04 W
Pop: 13,671 (1990); 13,233 (1980) Pop Density: 3797.5
Land: 3.6 sq. mi.; Water: 0.1 sq. mi.
In northeastern IL on the Little Calumet River, 14 mi. south of Chicago. Incorporated 1892.
Name origin: Descriptively named in 1848 by Frederick C. Schmidt.

River Forest — Village
ZIP: 60305 Lat: 41-53-41 N Long: 87-49-08 W
Pop: 11,669 (1990); 12,392 (1980) Pop Density: 4667.6
Land: 2.5 sq. mi.; Water: 0.0 sq. mi.
In northeastern IL on the Des Plaines River, 10 mi. west of Chicago. Incorporated 1880. Coextensive with the town of the same name.
Name origin: Descriptive of the forest along the river.

*River Forest — Township
ZIP: 60305　**Lat:** 41-53-41 N　**Long:** 87-49-08 W
Pop: 11,669 (1990); 12,392 (1980)　**Pop Density:** 4667.6
Land: 2.5 sq. mi.; **Water:** 0.0 sq. mi.

River Grove — City
ZIP: 60171　**Lat:** 41-55-26 N　**Long:** 87-50-15 W
Pop: 9,961 (1990); 10,368 (1980)　**Pop Density:** 4150.4
Land: 2.4 sq. mi.; **Water:** 0.0 sq. mi.
In northeastern IL on the Des Plaines River, a suburb of Chicago.
Name origin: For its descriptive connotations.

Riverside — City
ZIP: 60546　**Lat:** 41-49-51 N　**Long:** 87-48-57 W
Pop: 8,774 (1990); 9,236 (1980)　**Pop Density:** 4387.0
Land: 2.0 sq. mi.; **Water:** 0.0 sq. mi.
In northeastern IL on the Des Plaines River, 8 mi. west of Chicago. Not coextensive with the town of the same name.
Name origin: Descriptive of its location.

*Riverside — Township
ZIP: 60546　**Lat:** 41-50-09 N　**Long:** 87-49-23 W
Pop: 15,240 (1990); 15,930 (1980)　**Pop Density:** 3810.0
Land: 4.0 sq. mi.; **Water:** 0.0 sq. mi.

Robbins — City
ZIP: 60472　**Lat:** 41-38-34 N　**Long:** 87-42-29 W
Pop: 7,498 (1990); 8,853 (1980)　**Pop Density:** 4998.7
Land: 1.5 sq. mi.; **Water:** 0.0 sq. mi.
In northeastern IL, near Blue Island, a Chicago suburb.

Rolling Meadows — City
ZIP: 60008　**Lat:** 42-04-30 N　**Long:** 88-01-30 W
Pop: 22,591 (1990); 20,167 (1980)　**Pop Density:** 4262.5
Land: 5.3 sq. mi.; **Water:** 0.0 sq. mi.
In northeastern IL, 25 mi. northwest of Chicago. Incorporated Mar 2, 1955.
Name origin: Promotional and descriptive.

Roselle — Village
ZIP: 60172　**Lat:** 41-59-35 N　**Long:** 88-04-03 W
Pop: 3,320 (1990); 2,416 (1980)　**Pop Density:** 5533.3
Land: 0.6 sq. mi.; **Water:** 0.0 sq. mi.
In northeastern IL, 25 mi. northwest of Chicago. Incorporated 1922. Part of the town is also in DuPage County.
Name origin: For Roselle Hough (1827–98), a prominent Chicago citizen.

Rosemont — Village
ZIP: 60018　**Lat:** 41-59-20 N　**Long:** 87-52-17 W
Pop: 3,995 (1990); 4,137 (1980)　**Pop Density:** 2350.0
Land: 1.7 sq. mi.; **Water:** 0.0 sq. mi.

Sauk Village — Village
ZIP: 60411　**Lat:** 41-29-18 N　**Long:** 87-33-56 W
Pop: 9,926 (1990); 10,906 (1980)　**Pop Density:** 3817.7
Land: 2.6 sq. mi.; **Water:** 0.0 sq. mi.
In northeastern IL near the IN border, 28 mi. south of Chicago. Part of the town is also in Will County.
Name origin: For the Sauk Indians.

Schaumburg — Village
ZIP: 60193　**Lat:** 42-01-58 N　**Long:** 88-05-00 W
Pop: 68,586 (1990); 53,338 (1980)　**Pop Density:** 3667.7
Land: 18.7 sq. mi.; **Water:** 0.2 sq. mi.　**Elev:** 799 ft.
In northeastern IL, 28 mi. northwest of Chicago. Incorporated 1956. Part of the town is also in DuPage County. Not coextensive with the township of the same name.
Name origin: For a local citizen named Schaum.

*Schaumburg — Township
ZIP: 60194　**Lat:** 42-01-40 N　**Long:** 88-05-18 W
Pop: 127,625 (1990); 103,920 (1980)　**Pop Density:** 4170.8
Land: 30.6 sq. mi.; **Water:** 0.3 sq. mi.

Schiller Park — Village
ZIP: 60176　**Lat:** 41-57-35 N　**Long:** 87-52-12 W
Pop: 11,189 (1990); 11,458 (1980)　**Pop Density:** 3996.1
Land: 2.8 sq. mi.; **Water:** 0.0 sq. mi.
In northeastern IL on the Des Plaines River, 10 mi. northwest of Chicago. Incorporated 1914.
Name origin: Named by early citizens for the German poet and composer Johann von Schiller (1759–1805).

Skokie — City
ZIP: 60077　**Lat:** 42-02-13 N　**Long:** 87-44-23 W
Pop: 59,432 (1990); 60,278 (1980)　**Pop Density:** 5943.2
Land: 10.0 sq. mi.; **Water:** 0.0 sq. mi.
In northeastern IL, 15 mi. northwest of Chicago. Incorporated 1888.
Name origin: From a Potawatomi (Algonquian) word meaning 'marsh.' Previously called Niles Carter.

South Barrington — Village
ZIP: 60010　**Lat:** 42-05-14 N　**Long:** 88-09-10 W
Pop: 2,937 (1990); 1,168 (1980)　**Pop Density:** 466.2
Land: 6.3 sq. mi.; **Water:** 0.3 sq. mi.　**Elev:** 858 ft.

South Chicago Heights — Village
ZIP: 60411　**Lat:** 41-28-59 N　**Long:** 87-38-14 W
Pop: 3,597 (1990); 3,932 (1980)　**Pop Density:** 2398.0
Land: 1.5 sq. mi.; **Water:** 0.0 sq. mi.　**Elev:** 717 ft.

South Holland — City
ZIP: 60473　**Lat:** 41-35-51 N　**Long:** 87-36-04 W
Pop: 22,105 (1990); 24,977 (1980)　**Pop Density:** 3028.1
Land: 7.3 sq. mi.; **Water:** 0.0 sq. mi.
In northeastern IL on the Little Calumet River, 20 mi. south of Chicago. Settled 1840 by Dutch farmers; incorporated 1894.
Name origin: For the settlers' native country.

Steger — Village
ZIP: 60475　**Lat:** 41-28-22 N　**Long:** 87-38-01 W
Pop: 3,008 (1990); 3,414 (1980)　**Pop Density:** 5013.3
Land: 0.6 sq. mi.; **Water:** 0.0 sq. mi.　**Elev:** 715 ft.
Part of the town is also in Will County.
Name origin: For piano maker John Steger.

Stickney — Village
ZIP: 60402　**Lat:** 41-49-04 N　**Long:** 87-46-22 W
Pop: 5,678 (1990); 5,893 (1980)　**Pop Density:** 2988.4
Land: 1.9 sq. mi.; **Water:** 0.0 sq. mi.　**Elev:** 604 ft.
In northeastern IL, 10 mi. southwest of Chicago. Not coextensive with the town of the same name.

*Stickney — Township
ZIP: 60402　**Lat:** 41-46-24 N　**Long:** 87-46-07 W
Pop: 37,297 (1990); 38,757 (1980)　**Pop Density:** 2983.8
Land: 12.5 sq. mi.; **Water:** 0.2 sq. mi.

Stone Park — Village
ZIP: 60165　**Lat:** 41-54-15 N　**Long:** 87-52-49 W
Pop: 4,383 (1990); 4,273 (1980)　**Pop Density:** 14610.0
Land: 0.3 sq. mi.; **Water:** 0.0 sq. mi.

ILLINOIS, Cook County

Streamwood — Village
ZIP: 60107   **Lat:** 42-01-14 N   **Long:** 88-10-24 W
Pop: 30,987 (1990); 23,456 (1980)   **Pop Density:** 4556.9
Land: 6.8 sq. mi.; **Water:** 0.0 sq. mi.

In northeastern IL, 30 mi. northwest of Chicago. Incorporated Feb 11, 1957.
Name origin: For the Stream family.

Summit — Village
ZIP: 60501   **Lat:** 41-47-05 N   **Long:** 87-48-58 W
Pop: 9,971 (1990); 10,110 (1980)   **Pop Density:** 4748.1
Land: 2.1 sq. mi.; **Water:** 0.2 sq. mi.

In northeastern IL on the Illinois and Michigan Canal, 12 mi. southwest of Chicago.

Thornton — Town
ZIP: 60476   **Lat:** 41-34-26 N   **Long:** 87-37-07 W
Pop: 2,778 (1990); 3,024 (1980)   **Pop Density:** 1157.5
Land: 2.4 sq. mi.; **Water:** 0.0 sq. mi.   **Elev:** 603 ft.

In northeastern IL on the Little Calumet River, 22 mi. south of Chicago. Not coextensive with the town of the same name.

*Thornton — Township
ZIP: 60476   **Lat:** 41-36-05 N   **Long:** 87-36-00 W
Pop: 175,896 (1990); 191,359 (1980)   **Pop Density:** 3742.5
Land: 47.0 sq. mi.; **Water:** 0.5 sq. mi.

Tinley Park — Village
ZIP: 60477   **Lat:** 41-34-35 N   **Long:** 87-47-57 W
Pop: 37,040 (1990); 26,158 (1980)   **Pop Density:** 3898.9
Land: 9.5 sq. mi.; **Water:** 0.0 sq. mi.   **Elev:** 698 ft.

In northeastern IL, a residential suburb 20 mi. southwest of Chicago. Incorporated 1892. Part of the town is also in Will County.
Name origin: For the Tinley brothers, Rock Island Railroad executives.

University Park — Village
ZIP: 60466   **Lat:** 41-28-16 N   **Long:** 87-43-38 W
Pop: 0 (1990); 2 (1980)
Land: 0.1 sq. mi.; **Water:** 0.0 sq. mi.

Part of the town is also in Will County.

Westchester — Village
ZIP: 60154   **Lat:** 41-51-03 N   **Long:** 87-53-13 W
Pop: 17,301 (1990); 17,730 (1980)   **Pop Density:** 5581.0
Land: 3.1 sq. mi.; **Water:** 0.0 sq. mi.

In northeastern IL, a residential suburb 12 mi. west of Chicago. Incorporated 1925.
Name origin: For Chester, England.

Western Springs — City
ZIP: 60558   **Lat:** 41-48-12 N   **Long:** 87-54-02 W
Pop: 11,984 (1990); 12,876 (1980)   **Pop Density:** 4609.2
Land: 2.6 sq. mi.; **Water:** 0.0 sq. mi.   **Elev:** 673 ft.

In northeastern IL near Salt Creek, 15 mi. southwest of Chicago. Incorporated 1886.
Name origin: For once-present mineral springs, believed to have been medicinal.

Wheeling — City
ZIP: 60090   **Lat:** 42-07-49 N   **Long:** 87-55-25 W
Pop: 29,911 (1990); 23,242 (1980)   **Pop Density:** 3692.7
Land: 8.1 sq. mi.; **Water:** 0.0 sq. mi.

In northeastern IL, 20 mi. northwest of Chicago. Settled 1830 as a country store. Incorporated 1894. Part of the town is also in Lake County.
Name origin: For Wheeling, WV.

*Wheeling — Township
ZIP: 60090   **Lat:** 42-06-37 N   **Long:** 87-56-50 W
Pop: 148,641 (1990); 129,853 (1980)   **Pop Density:** 4140.4
Land: 35.9 sq. mi.; **Water:** 0.1 sq. mi.

Willow Springs — Town
ZIP: 60480   **Lat:** 41-43-59 N   **Long:** 87-52-41 W
Pop: 4,509 (1990); 4,147 (1980)   **Pop Density:** 1366.4
Land: 3.3 sq. mi.; **Water:** 0.1 sq. mi.

Part of the town is also in DuPage County.
Name origin: For its descriptive connotations.

Wilmette — Residential village
ZIP: 60091   **Lat:** 42-04-37 N   **Long:** 87-43-42 W
Pop: 26,690 (1990); 28,221 (1980)   **Pop Density:** 4942.6
Land: 5.4 sq. mi.; **Water:** 0.0 sq. mi.

In northeastern IL on Lake Michigan, 15 mi. northwest of Chicago. Settled 1829; incorporated 1872.
Name origin: For Archange Ouilmette, the Indian wife of French Canadian Antoine Ouilmette, Chicago's first non-Indian settler, who gained the land under a government treaty.

Winnetka — Village
ZIP: 60093   **Lat:** 42-06-23 N   **Long:** 87-44-33 W
Pop: 12,174 (1990); 12,772 (1980)   **Pop Density:** 3203.7
Land: 3.8 sq. mi.; **Water:** 0.1 sq. mi.

In northeastern IL on Lake Michigan, 20 mi. north of Chicago. Incorporated 1869.

Worth — Residential Village
ZIP: 60482   **Lat:** 41-41-14 N   **Long:** 87-47-33 W
Pop: 11,208 (1990); 11,592 (1980)   **Pop Density:** 4670.0
Land: 2.4 sq. mi.; **Water:** 0.0 sq. mi.

In northeastern IL, 16 mi. southwest of Chicago. Incorporated 1914. Not coextensive with the town of the same name.
Name origin: For Gen. William Jenkins Worth (1794–1849) of Mexican War fame.

*Worth — Township
ZIP: 60482   **Lat:** 41-41-20 N   **Long:** 87-44-42 W
Pop: 151,144 (1990); 158,157 (1980)   **Pop Density:** 4738.1
Land: 31.9 sq. mi.; **Water:** 0.4 sq. mi.

> ## Crawford County
> **County Seat: Robinson (ZIP: 62454)**
>
> **Pop:** 19,464 (1990); 20,818 (1980)   **Pop Density:** 43.9
> **Land:** 443.6 sq. mi.; **Water:** 2.2 sq. mi.   **Area Code:** 618
>
> On the east-central border of IL northeast of Olney; organized Dec 31, 1816 (prior to statehood) from Edwards County.
>
> **Name origin:** For William Harris Crawford (1772–1834), U.S. senator from GA (1807-13), U.S. secretary of war (1815–16), and U.S. secretary of the treasury (1816–25).

Flat Rock — Village
ZIP: 62427   Lat: 38-54-15 N   Long: 87-40-21 W
Pop: 421 (1990); 493 (1980)   Pop Density: 526.3
Land: 0.8 sq. mi.; Water: 0.0 sq. mi.

Honey Creek — Township
Lat: 38-54-10 N   Long: 87-43-42 W
Pop: 1,497 (1990); 1,476 (1980)   Pop Density: 30.9
Land: 48.4 sq. mi.; Water: 0.0 sq. mi.

Hutsonville — Village
ZIP: 62433   Lat: 39-06-31 N   Long: 87-39-38 W
Pop: 622 (1990); 705 (1980)   Pop Density: 888.6
Land: 0.7 sq. mi.; Water: 0.0 sq. mi.
Not coextensive with the town of the same name.

***Hutsonville** — Township
Lat: 39-07-03 N   Long: 87-41-03 W
Pop: 1,333 (1990); 1,438 (1980)   Pop Density: 36.1
Land: 36.9 sq. mi.; Water: 0.7 sq. mi.

Lamotte — Township
Lat: 39-00-53 N   Long: 87-37-11 W
Pop: 2,413 (1990); 2,579 (1980)   Pop Density: 47.6
Land: 50.7 sq. mi.; Water: 0.6 sq. mi.

Licking — Township
Lat: 39-07-28 N   Long: 87-53-42 W
Pop: 324 (1990); 401 (1980)   Pop Density: 8.8
Land: 36.8 sq. mi.; Water: 0.0 sq. mi.

Martin — Township
Lat: 38-54-38 N   Long: 87-51-54 W
Pop: 606 (1990); 669 (1980)   Pop Density: 14.2
Land: 42.6 sq. mi.; Water: 0.0 sq. mi.

Montgomery — Township
Lat: 38-54-34 N   Long: 87-35-54 W
Pop: 676 (1990); 791 (1980)   Pop Density: 12.5
Land: 54.1 sq. mi.; Water: 0.5 sq. mi.

Oblong — Town
ZIP: 62449   Lat: 39-00-07 N   Long: 87-54-30 W
Pop: 1,616 (1990); 1,840 (1980)   Pop Density: 1795.6
Land: 0.9 sq. mi.; Water: 0.0 sq. mi.   Elev: 524 ft.
In southeastern IL in the Wabash River valley, southeast of Champaign. Not coextensive with the town of the same name.

Name origin: For its shape in relation to the nearby Embarras River.

***Oblong** — Township
Lat: 39-00-28 N   Long: 87-52-51 W
Pop: 2,977 (1990); 3,222 (1980)   Pop Density: 51.9
Land: 57.4 sq. mi.; Water: 0.0 sq. mi.

Palestine — Town
ZIP: 62451   Lat: 39-00-07 N   Long: 87-36-43 W
Pop: 1,619 (1990); 1,718 (1980)   Pop Density: 2312.9
Land: 0.7 sq. mi.; Water: 0.0 sq. mi.   Elev: 450 ft.

Name origin: For the ancient country in southwest Asia, the biblical Holy Land.

Prairie — Township
Lat: 39-07-14 N   Long: 87-47-30 W
Pop: 694 (1990); 782 (1980)   Pop Density: 15.6
Land: 44.5 sq. mi.; Water: 0.1 sq. mi.

Robinson — Town
ZIP: 62454   Lat: 39-00-28 N   Long: 87-44-25 W
Pop: 6,740 (1990); 7,285 (1980)   Pop Density: 1925.7
Land: 3.5 sq. mi.; Water: 0.1 sq. mi.
Not coextensive with the town of the same name.

Name origin: For U.S. Sen. John McCracken Robinson.

***Robinson** — Township
ZIP: 62454   Lat: 39-00-49 N   Long: 87-44-59 W
Pop: 8,842 (1990); 9,349 (1980)   Pop Density: 154.3
Land: 57.3 sq. mi.; Water: 0.2 sq. mi.
Incorporated Jan 16, 1875.

Southwest — Township
Lat: 38-51-52 N   Long: 87-52-14 W
Pop: 102 (1990); 111 (1980)   Pop Density: 6.8
Land: 15.0 sq. mi.; Water: 0.0 sq. mi.

Stoy — Village
ZIP: 62464   Lat: 38-59-48 N   Long: 87-50-00 W
Pop: 135 (1990); 167 (1980)   Pop Density: 150.0
Land: 0.9 sq. mi.; Water: 0.0 sq. mi.   Elev: 467 ft.

ILLINOIS, Cumberland County

Cumberland County
County Seat: Toledo (ZIP: 62468)

Pop: 10,670 (1990); 11,062 (1980) **Pop Density:** 30.8
Land: 346.0 sq. mi.; **Water:** 1.0 sq. mi. **Area Code:** 217
In east-central IL south of Urbana; organized Mar 2, 1843 from Coles County.
Name origin: For the Cumberland Road.

Casey — City
ZIP: 62420 **Lat:** 39-17-36 N **Long:** 88-00-51 W
Pop: 6 (1990); 19 (1980) **Pop Density:** 60.0
Land: 0.1 sq. mi.; **Water:** 0.0 sq. mi.
Incorporated 1871. Part of the town is also in Clark County.
Name origin: For Zadoc Casey, 19th-century IL lieutenant governor, U.S. representative, and state legislator.

Cottonwood — Township
Lat: 39-20-48 N **Long:** 88-15-07 W
Pop: 529 (1990); 556 (1980) **Pop Density:** 16.2
Land: 32.6 sq. mi.; **Water:** 0.0 sq. mi.

Crooked Creek — Township
Lat: 39-13-14 N **Long:** 88-03-07 W
Pop: 414 (1990); 545 (1980) **Pop Density:** 12.1
Land: 34.2 sq. mi.; **Water:** 0.0 sq. mi.

Greenup — City
ZIP: 62428 **Lat:** 39-14-52 N **Long:** 88-09-35 W
Pop: 1,616 (1990); 1,655 (1980) **Pop Density:** 1010.0
Land: 1.6 sq. mi.; **Water:** 0.0 sq. mi. **Elev:** 543 ft.
Incorporated 1836. Not coextensive with the town of the same name.
Name origin: For William C. Greenup, first clerk of the IL Territorial Legislature.

*Greenup — Township
Lat: 39-13-22 N **Long:** 88-09-14 W
Pop: 2,500 (1990); 2,587 (1980) **Pop Density:** 52.6
Land: 47.5 sq. mi.; **Water:** 0.0 sq. mi.

Jewett — Village
ZIP: 62436 **Lat:** 39-12-27 N **Long:** 88-14-34 W
Pop: 194 (1990); 230 (1980) **Pop Density:** 194.0
Land: 1.0 sq. mi.; **Water:** 0.0 sq. mi.

Montrose — Village
ZIP: 62445 **Lat:** 39-10-25 N **Long:** 88-22-30 W
Pop: 0 (1990); 321 (1980)
Land: 0.1 sq. mi.; **Water:** 0.0 sq. mi.
Part of the town is also in Effingham County.

Neoga — City
ZIP: 62447 **Lat:** 39-19-17 N **Long:** 88-27-05 W
Pop: 1,678 (1990); 1,736 (1980) **Pop Density:** 1290.8
Land: 1.3 sq. mi.; **Water:** 0.0 sq. mi.
Not coextensive with the town of the same name.

*Neoga — Township
Lat: 39-19-23 N **Long:** 88-24-05 W
Pop: 2,952 (1990); 2,958 (1980) **Pop Density:** 54.0
Land: 54.7 sq. mi.; **Water:** 0.8 sq. mi.

Spring Point — Township
Lat: 39-13-38 N **Long:** 88-24-04 W
Pop: 1,131 (1990); 1,092 (1980) **Pop Density:** 20.2
Land: 55.9 sq. mi.; **Water:** 0.0 sq. mi.

Sumpter — Township
Lat: 39-16-27 N **Long:** 88-15-04 W
Pop: 1,872 (1990); 1,970 (1980) **Pop Density:** 41.0
Land: 45.7 sq. mi.; **Water:** 0.0 sq. mi.

Toledo — Town
ZIP: 62468 **Lat:** 39-16-27 N **Long:** 88-14-33 W
Pop: 1,199 (1990); 1,284 (1980) **Pop Density:** 1498.8
Land: 0.8 sq. mi.; **Water:** 0.0 sq. mi.
Name origin: For Toledo, OH.

Union — Township
Lat: 39-20-01 N **Long:** 88-05-07 W
Pop: 698 (1990); 771 (1980) **Pop Density:** 13.2
Land: 52.7 sq. mi.; **Water:** 0.1 sq. mi.

Woodbury — Township
Lat: 39-12-09 N **Long:** 88-15-55 W
Pop: 574 (1990); 583 (1980) **Pop Density:** 25.3
Land: 22.7 sq. mi.; **Water:** 0.0 sq. mi.

DeKalb County
County Seat: Sycamore (ZIP: 60178)

Pop: 77,932 (1990); 74,628 (1980)   **Pop Density:** 122.9
Land: 634.2 sq. mi.; **Water:** 0.8 sq. mi.   **Area Code:** 815
In north-central IL, west of Chicago; organized Mar 4, 1837 from Kane County.
Name origin: For Johann (1721–80), Baron de Kalb, German-born French soldier who fought with the Americans during the Revolutionary War.

Afton
Township
Lat: 41-51-05 N   **Long:** 88-46-40 W
Pop: 665 (1990); 605 (1980)   **Pop Density:** 18.9
Land: 35.2 sq. mi.; **Water:** 0.0 sq. mi.

Clinton
Township
Lat: 41-45-49 N   **Long:** 88-46-34 W
Pop: 1,521 (1990); 1,451 (1980)   **Pop Density:** 43.2
Land: 35.2 sq. mi.; **Water:** 0.0 sq. mi.

Cortland
Town
ZIP: 60112   **Lat:** 41-55-38 N   **Long:** 88-41-40 W
Pop: 963 (1990); 1,019 (1980)   **Pop Density:** 875.5
Land: 1.1 sq. mi.; **Water:** 0.0 sq. mi.
Not coextensive with the town of the same name.

*Cortland
Township
Lat: 41-56-29 N   **Long:** 88-39-44 W
Pop: 4,637 (1990); 4,297 (1980)   **Pop Density:** 131.4
Land: 35.3 sq. mi.; **Water:** 0.0 sq. mi.

De Kalb
City
ZIP: 60115   **Lat:** 41-55-50 N   **Long:** 88-45-06 W
Pop: 34,925 (1990); 33,157 (1980)   **Pop Density:** 4365.6
Land: 8.0 sq. mi.; **Water:** 0.0 sq. mi.
In north-central IL, 55 mi. west of Chicago. Incorporated Feb 2, 1861. Not coextensive with the town of the same name.
Name origin: For Johann (1721–80), Baron de Kalb, German-born French officer who served with the Americans in the American Revolution. Previously called Barb City.

*De Kalb
Township
ZIP: 60115   **Lat:** 41-56-13 N   **Long:** 88-46-20 W
Pop: 38,710 (1990); 36,375 (1980)   **Pop Density:** 1096.6
Land: 35.3 sq. mi.; **Water:** 0.1 sq. mi.

Franklin
Township
Lat: 42-06-31 N   **Long:** 88-52-55 W
Pop: 1,879 (1990); 1,891 (1980)   **Pop Density:** 51.9
Land: 36.2 sq. mi.; **Water:** 0.0 sq. mi.

Genoa
City
ZIP: 60135   **Lat:** 42-05-51 N   **Long:** 88-41-23 W
Pop: 3,083 (1990); 3,276 (1980)   **Pop Density:** 2569.2
Land: 1.2 sq. mi.; **Water:** 0.0 sq. mi.
Not coextensive with the town of the same name.

*Genoa
Township
Lat: 42-06-18 N   **Long:** 88-38-35 W
Pop: 4,210 (1990); 4,195 (1980)   **Pop Density:** 116.3
Land: 36.2 sq. mi.; **Water:** 0.0 sq. mi.

Hinckley
Town
ZIP: 60520   **Lat:** 41-46-10 N   **Long:** 88-38-30 W
Pop: 1,682 (1990); 1,447 (1980)   **Pop Density:** 2402.9
Land: 0.7 sq. mi.; **Water:** 0.0 sq. mi.
Name origin: For a 19th-century railroad official, F. G. Hinckley.

Kingston
Village
ZIP: 60145   **Lat:** 42-05-57 N   **Long:** 88-45-24 W
Pop: 562 (1990); 618 (1980)   **Pop Density:** 936.7
Land: 0.6 sq. mi.; **Water:** 0.0 sq. mi.   **Elev:** 791 ft.
Not coextensive with the town of the same name.

*Kingston
Township
Lat: 42-06-40 N   **Long:** 88-45-54 W
Pop: 1,955 (1990); 1,809 (1980)   **Pop Density:** 54.3
Land: 36.0 sq. mi.; **Water:** 0.0 sq. mi.

Kirkland
Town
ZIP: 60146   **Lat:** 42-05-32 N   **Long:** 88-51-16 W
Pop: 1,011 (1990); 1,155 (1980)   **Pop Density:** 1011.0
Land: 1.0 sq. mi.; **Water:** 0.0 sq. mi.   **Elev:** 764 ft.
In northern IL on the south branch of the Kishwaukee River, 18 mi. southeast of Rockford.

Lee
Village
ZIP: 60530   **Lat:** 41-47-35 N   **Long:** 88-56-21 W
Pop: 143 (1990); 145 (1980)   **Pop Density:** 1430.0
Land: 0.1 sq. mi.; **Water:** 0.0 sq. mi.
Part of the town is also in Lee County.

Malta
Village
ZIP: 60150   **Lat:** 41-55-48 N   **Long:** 88-51-47 W
Pop: 865 (1990); 995 (1980)   **Pop Density:** 2162.5
Land: 0.4 sq. mi.; **Water:** 0.0 sq. mi.
Not coextensive with the town of the same name.

*Malta
Township
Lat: 41-55-58 N   **Long:** 88-52-58 W
Pop: 1,335 (1990); 1,484 (1980)   **Pop Density:** 38.1
Land: 35.0 sq. mi.; **Water:** 0.0 sq. mi.

Maple Park
Village
ZIP: 60151   **Lat:** 41-54-02 N   **Long:** 88-36-07 W
Pop: 4 (1990); 637 (1980)   **Pop Density:** 133.3
Land: 0.03 sq. mi.; **Water:** 0.0 sq. mi.
Part of the town is also in Kane County.

Mayfield
Township
Lat: 42-01-11 N   **Long:** 88-46-23 W
Pop: 741 (1990); 769 (1980)   **Pop Density:** 21.1
Land: 35.2 sq. mi.; **Water:** 0.0 sq. mi.

Milan
Township
Lat: 41-50-42 N   **Long:** 88-52-36 W
Pop: 373 (1990); 413 (1980)   **Pop Density:** 10.6
Land: 35.3 sq. mi.; **Water:** 0.0 sq. mi.

Paw Paw
Township
Lat: 41-40-32 N   **Long:** 88-52-55 W
Pop: 384 (1990); 398 (1980)   **Pop Density:** 10.1
Land: 37.9 sq. mi.; **Water:** 0.0 sq. mi.

ILLINOIS, DeKalb County   *American Places Dictionary*

Pierce
Township
Lat: 41-50-53 N **Long:** 88-39-29 W
Pop: 506 (1990); 512 (1980)   **Pop Density:** 14.4
Land: 35.1 sq. mi.; **Water:** 0.0 sq. mi.

Sandwich
Town
ZIP: 60548   **Lat:** 41-38-52 N **Long:** 88-37-25 W
Pop: 5,566 (1990); 5,353 (1980)   **Pop Density:** 2420.0
Land: 2.3 sq. mi.; **Water:** 0.0 sq. mi.
Incorporated Feb 21, 1859. In northeastern IL, 55 mi. west of Chicago. Part of the town is also in Kendall County. Not coextensive with the township of the same name.
Name origin: Named by early settlers, for Sandwich, MA.

*Sandwich
Township
ZIP: 60548   **Lat:** 41-40-20 N **Long:** 88-37-47 W
Pop: 5,990 (1990); 5,743 (1980)   **Pop Density:** 389.0
Land: 15.4 sq. mi.; **Water:** 0.0 sq. mi.

Shabbona
Town
ZIP: 60550   **Lat:** 41-45-53 N **Long:** 88-52-35 W
Pop: 897 (1990); 851 (1980)   **Pop Density:** 747.5
Land: 1.2 sq. mi.; **Water:** 0.0 sq. mi.
Not coextensive with the town of the same name.
Name origin: For the Potawatomi Indian chief who befriended early settlers. Meaning of the name is unknown.

*Shabbona
Township
Lat: 41-45-36 N **Long:** 88-53-04 W
Pop: 1,379 (1990); 1,372 (1980)   **Pop Density:** 39.7
Land: 34.7 sq. mi.; **Water:** 0.5 sq. mi.

Somonauk
Town
ZIP: 60552   **Lat:** 41-38-04 N **Long:** 88-40-58 W
Pop: 1,031 (1990); 1,107 (1980)   **Pop Density:** 2577.5
Land: 0.4 sq. mi.; **Water:** 0.0 sq. mi.
Part of the town is also in La Salle County. Not coextensive with the township of the same name.
Name origin: From a Potawatomi term probably meaning 'pawpaw,' a fruit-bearing tree *Asimina triloba*.

*Somonauk
Township
Lat: 41-40-19 N **Long:** 88-41-07 W
Pop: 1,543 (1990); 1,610 (1980)   **Pop Density:** 79.5
Land: 19.4 sq. mi.; **Water:** 0.0 sq. mi.

South Grove
Township
Lat: 42-01-24 N **Long:** 88-53-19 W
Pop: 461 (1990); 532 (1980)   **Pop Density:** 13.4
Land: 34.5 sq. mi.; **Water:** 0.0 sq. mi.

Squaw Grove
Township
Lat: 41-45-28 N **Long:** 88-39-21 W
Pop: 2,387 (1990); 2,175 (1980)   **Pop Density:** 68.0
Land: 35.1 sq. mi.; **Water:** 0.0 sq. mi.

Sycamore
City
ZIP: 60178   **Lat:** 41-58-54 N **Long:** 88-41-44 W
Pop: 9,708 (1990); 9,219 (1980)   **Pop Density:** 2623.8
Land: 3.7 sq. mi.; **Water:** 0.0 sq. mi.
Incorporated Feb 21, 1859. Not coextensive with the town of the same name.

*Sycamore
Township
ZIP: 60178   **Lat:** 42-01-20 N **Long:** 88-39-03 W
Pop: 8,843 (1990); 8,549 (1980)   **Pop Density:** 257.1
Land: 34.4 sq. mi.; **Water:** 0.1 sq. mi.

Victor
Township
Lat: 41-40-02 N **Long:** 88-45-57 W
Pop: 413 (1990); 448 (1980)   **Pop Density:** 12.6
Land: 32.9 sq. mi.; **Water:** 0.0 sq. mi.

Waterman
Village
ZIP: 60556   **Lat:** 41-46-09 N **Long:** 88-46-23 W
Pop: 1,074 (1990); 943 (1980)   **Pop Density:** 895.0
Land: 1.2 sq. mi.; **Water:** 0.0 sq. mi.

De Witt County
County Seat: Clinton (ZIP: 61727)

Pop: 16,516 (1990); 18,108 (1980)   **Pop Density:** 41.5
Land: 397.6 sq. mi.; **Water:** 7.6 sq. mi.   **Area Code:** 217
In central IL north of Decatur; organized Mar 1, 1839 from McLean and Macon counties.
Name origin: For DeWitt Clinton (1769–1828), governor of NY (1817–21; 1825–28) and supporter of the Erie Canal.

Barnett
Township
Lat: 40-10-25 N **Long:** 89-05-43 W
Pop: 493 (1990); 571 (1980)   **Pop Density:** 13.2
Land: 37.4 sq. mi.; **Water:** 0.0 sq. mi.

Clinton
City
ZIP: 61727   **Lat:** 40-09-01 N **Long:** 88-57-41 W
Pop: 7,437 (1990); 8,014 (1980)   **Pop Density:** 2860.4
Land: 2.6 sq. mi.; **Water:** 0.0 sq. mi.
In central IL, 19 mi. north of Decatur. Settled 1836; incorporated Feb 15, 1855.
Name origin: For NY Gov. DeWitt Clinton (1769–1828), supporter of the Erie Canal.

Clintonia
Township
ZIP: 61727   **Lat:** 40-10-44 N **Long:** 88-58-14 W
Pop: 7,860 (1990); 8,524 (1980)   **Pop Density:** 262.0
Land: 30.0 sq. mi.; **Water:** 0.0 sq. mi.

Creek
Township
Lat: 40-05-26 N **Long:** 88-51-20 W
Pop: 412 (1990); 489 (1980)   **Pop Density:** 11.6
Land: 35.5 sq. mi.; **Water:** 1.4 sq. mi.

De Witt
Township
Lat: 40-11-01 N **Long:** 88-44-52 W
Pop: 417 (1990); 469 (1980)   **Pop Density:** 12.7
Land: 32.8 sq. mi.; **Water:** 2.3 sq. mi.

ILLINOIS, Douglas County

*De Witt — Village
Lat: 40-11-03 N Long: 88-47-09 W
Pop: 122 (1990); 232 (1980) Pop Density: 406.7
Land: 0.3 sq. mi.; Water: 0.0 sq. mi. Elev: 735 ft.

Farmer City — City
ZIP: 61842 Lat: 40-14-39 N Long: 88-38-28 W
Pop: 2,114 (1990); 2,252 (1980) Pop Density: 1510.0
Land: 1.4 sq. mi.; Water: 0.0 sq. mi. Elev: 724 ft.
Name origin: Named in 1869 (just before the railroad laid tracks through it) because all the residents were farmers. Originally known as Mount Pleasant, Hurley's Grove, and Santa Ana.

Harp — Township
Lat: 40-11-06 N Long: 88-51-30 W
Pop: 250 (1990); 270 (1980) Pop Density: 8.0
Land: 31.2 sq. mi.; Water: 3.6 sq. mi.

Kenney — Village
ZIP: 61749 Lat: 40-05-53 N Long: 89-05-09 W
Pop: 390 (1990); 443 (1980) Pop Density: 1300.0
Land: 0.3 sq. mi.; Water: 0.0 sq. mi. Elev: 650 ft.

Nixon — Township
Lat: 40-06-21 N Long: 88-45-18 W
Pop: 579 (1990); 720 (1980) Pop Density: 21.0
Land: 27.6 sq. mi.; Water: 0.0 sq. mi.

Rutledge — Township
Lat: 40-15-31 N Long: 88-45-33 W
Pop: 189 (1990); 229 (1980) Pop Density: 7.7
Land: 24.4 sq. mi.; Water: 0.0 sq. mi.

Santa Anna — Township
Lat: 40-14-22 N Long: 88-38-54 W
Pop: 2,550 (1990); 2,706 (1980) Pop Density: 91.1
Land: 28.0 sq. mi.; Water: 0.1 sq. mi.

Texas — Township
Lat: 40-05-41 N Long: 88-58-35 W
Pop: 1,028 (1990); 1,012 (1980) Pop Density: 28.9
Land: 35.6 sq. mi.; Water: 0.1 sq. mi.

Tunbridge — Township
Lat: 40-05-34 N Long: 89-05-16 W
Pop: 789 (1990); 872 (1980) Pop Density: 21.1
Land: 37.4 sq. mi.; Water: 0.0 sq. mi.

Wapella — Village
ZIP: 61777 Lat: 40-13-16 N Long: 88-57-42 W
Pop: 608 (1990); 768 (1980) Pop Density: 1216.0
Land: 0.5 sq. mi.; Water: 0.0 sq. mi. Elev: 748 ft.
Not coextensive with the town of the same name.

*Wapella — Township
Lat: 40-15-01 N Long: 88-58-36 W
Pop: 1,031 (1990); 1,165 (1980) Pop Density: 35.7
Land: 28.9 sq. mi.; Water: 0.0 sq. mi.

Waynesville — Village
ZIP: 61778 Lat: 40-14-27 N Long: 89-07-29 W
Pop: 440 (1990); 569 (1980) Pop Density: 1466.7
Land: 0.3 sq. mi.; Water: 0.0 sq. mi.
Not coextensive with the town of the same name.

*Waynesville — Township
Lat: 40-15-20 N Long: 89-05-18 W
Pop: 768 (1990); 884 (1980) Pop Density: 31.5
Land: 24.4 sq. mi.; Water: 0.0 sq. mi.

Weldon — Village
ZIP: 61882 Lat: 40-07-17 N Long: 88-45-01 W
Pop: 361 (1990); 531 (1980) Pop Density: 1203.3
Land: 0.3 sq. mi.; Water: 0.0 sq. mi.

Wilson — Township
Lat: 40-15-38 N Long: 88-52-17 W
Pop: 150 (1990); 197 (1980) Pop Density: 6.1
Land: 24.5 sq. mi.; Water: 0.0 sq. mi.

Douglas County
County Seat: Tuscola (ZIP: 61953)

Pop: 19,464 (1990); 19,774 (1980) Pop Density: 46.7
Land: 416.9 sq. mi.; Water: 0.6 sq. mi. Area Code: 217
In east-central IL, east of Decator; organized Feb 8, 1859 from Coles County.
Name origin: For Stephen Arnold Douglas (1813–61), U.S. orator and statesman.

Arcola — City
ZIP: 61910 Lat: 39-41-04 N Long: 88-18-13 W
Pop: 2,678 (1990); 2,714 (1980) Pop Density: 1912.9
Land: 1.4 sq. mi.; Water: 0.0 sq. mi. Elev: 678 ft.
In east-central IL. Platted 1855; incorporated 1865. Not coextensive with the town of the same name.
Name origin: For Arcole, Italy, with a spelling variation.

*Arcola — Township
Lat: 39-42-21 N Long: 88-17-17 W
Pop: 3,132 (1990); 3,219 (1980) Pop Density: 58.3
Land: 53.7 sq. mi.; Water: 0.1 sq. mi.

Arthur — Village
ZIP: 61911 Lat: 39-42-50 N Long: 88-27-54 W
Pop: 1,365 (1990); 1,332 (1980) Pop Density: 1950.0
Land: 0.7 sq. mi.; Water: 0.0 sq. mi. Elev: 662 ft.
In east-central IL, 32 mi. southwest of Urbana. Village platted 1873; incorporated 1877. Originally an Amish colony. Part of the town is also in Moultrie County.
Name origin: For either a prominent early settler or Chester A. Arthur (1829–86), twenty-first U.S. president.

ILLINOIS, Douglas County

Atwood
Village
ZIP: 61913   Lat: 39-47-50 N   Long: 88-27-34 W
Pop: 602 (1990); 632 (1980)   Pop Density: 2006.7
Land: 0.3 sq. mi.; Water: 0.0 sq. mi.
Established 1874; incorporated 1884. Part of the town is also in Piatt County.
Name origin: The name recalls a dense woods once found on the site: "at-wood."

Bourbon
Township
Lat: 39-42-11 N   Long: 88-24-51 W
Pop: 3,318 (1990); 3,043 (1980)   Pop Density: 77.0
Land: 43.1 sq. mi.; Water: 0.0 sq. mi.

Bowdre
Township
Lat: 39-42-46 N   Long: 88-08-55 W
Pop: 811 (1990); 872 (1980)   Pop Density: 16.9
Land: 48.1 sq. mi.; Water: 0.0 sq. mi.

Camargo
Village
ZIP: 61919   Lat: 39-47-58 N   Long: 88-10-00 W
Pop: 372 (1990); 428 (1980)   Pop Density: 286.2
Land: 1.3 sq. mi.; Water: 0.0 sq. mi.
Not coextensive with the town of the same name.

*Camargo
Township
Lat: 39-49-31 N   Long: 88-10-01 W
Pop: 3,716 (1990); 3,591 (1980)   Pop Density: 96.3
Land: 38.6 sq. mi.; Water: 0.1 sq. mi.

Garrett
Village
ZIP: 61913   Lat: 39-47-48 N   Long: 88-25-31 W
Pop: 169 (1990); 205 (1980)   Pop Density: 1690.0
Land: 0.1 sq. mi.; Water: 0.0 sq. mi.
Not coextensive with the town of the same name.

*Garrett
Township
Lat: 39-49-14 N   Long: 88-23-56 W
Pop: 1,466 (1990); 1,519 (1980)   Pop Density: 28.0
Land: 52.3 sq. mi.; Water: 0.1 sq. mi.

Hindsboro
Village
ZIP: 61930   Lat: 39-41-03 N   Long: 88-08-03 W
Pop: 346 (1990); 407 (1980)   Pop Density: 1153.3
Land: 0.3 sq. mi.; Water: 0.0 sq. mi.   Elev: 649 ft.

Murdock
Township
Lat: 39-49-11 N   Long: 88-04-52 W
Pop: 374 (1990); 383 (1980)   Pop Density: 12.1
Land: 30.8 sq. mi.; Water: 0.0 sq. mi.

Newman
Town
ZIP: 61942   Lat: 39-47-50 N   Long: 87-59-15 W
Pop: 960 (1990); 1,079 (1980)   Pop Density: 1600.0
Land: 0.6 sq. mi.; Water: 0.0 sq. mi.   Elev: 646 ft.
Founded 1857. Not coextensive with the town of the same name.
Name origin: For B. Newman, son-in-law of Methodist circuit rider Peter Cartwright (1785–1872).

*Newman
Township
Lat: 39-49-43 N   Long: 87-59-19 W
Pop: 1,248 (1990); 1,391 (1980)   Pop Density: 30.7
Land: 40.6 sq. mi.; Water: 0.0 sq. mi.

Sargent
Township
Lat: 39-43-34 N   Long: 88-02-15 W
Pop: 343 (1990); 399 (1980)   Pop Density: 7.3
Land: 47.0 sq. mi.; Water: 0.1 sq. mi.

Tuscola
City
ZIP: 61953   Lat: 39-47-51 N   Long: 88-16-53 W
Pop: 4,155 (1990); 3,839 (1980)   Pop Density: 3196.2
Land: 1.3 sq. mi.; Water: 0.0 sq. mi.
Not coextensive with the town of the same name.
Name origin: From a Choctaw Indian term probably meaning 'warriors.'

*Tuscola
Township
ZIP: 61953   Lat: 39-49-00 N   Long: 88-17-11 W
Pop: 5,056 (1990); 5,357 (1980)   Pop Density: 80.8
Land: 62.6 sq. mi.; Water: 0.1 sq. mi.

Villa Grove
Town
ZIP: 61956   Lat: 39-51-49 N   Long: 88-09-34 W
Pop: 2,734 (1990); 2,707 (1980)   Pop Density: 3037.8
Land: 0.9 sq. mi.; Water: 0.0 sq. mi.

DuPage County
County Seat: Wheaton (ZIP: 60187)

Pop: 781,666 (1990); 658,858 (1980)   Pop Density: 2337.2
Land: 334.4 sq. mi.; Water: 2.4 sq. mi.   Area Code: 708
In northeast IL, west of Chicago; organized Feb 9, 1839 from Cook County.
Name origin: For the DuPage River, from the French name of a local Indian chief.

Addison
Village
ZIP: 60101   Lat: 41-55-50 N   Long: 88-00-31 W
Pop: 32,058 (1990); 29,826 (1980)   Pop Density: 3727.7
Land: 8.6 sq. mi.; Water: 0.0 sq. mi.   Elev: 691 ft.
In northeastern IL, 18 mi. west of Chicago. Not coextensive with the town of the same name.
Name origin: For 18th-century British essayist Joseph Addison. Incorporated 1884.

*Addison
Township
ZIP: 60101   Lat: 41-56-51 N   Long: 87-58-48 W
Pop: 82,727 (1990); 82,862 (1980)   Pop Density: 2561.2
Land: 32.3 sq. mi.; Water: 0.1 sq. mi.

Aurora
Industrial city
ZIP: 60507   Lat: 41-45-56 N   Long: 88-14-22 W
Pop: 14,811 (1990); 1,683 (1980)   Pop Density: 1276.8
Land: 11.6 sq. mi.; Water: 0.2 sq. mi.   Elev: 676 ft.
In northeastern IL on the Fox River, an industrial suburb 35

mi. west of Chicago. Town incorporated Feb 8, 1853. Part of the town is also in Kane County.
Name origin: For the Roman goddess of dawn.

Bartlett
Village
ZIP: 60103 **Lat:** 41-58-08 N **Long:** 88-12-01 W
Pop: 12,086 (1990); 8,549 (1980) **Pop Density:** 1299.6
Land: 9.3 sq. mi.; **Water:** 0.0 sq. mi.

In northeastern IL, 30 mi. northwest of Chicago; a manufacturing and residential suburb. Founded 1873; incorporated 1891. Part of the town is also in Cook and Kane counties.
Name origin: For founder Luther Bartlett, its first postmaster, who bought the site in 1844.

Batavia
Industrial city
ZIP: 60510 **Lat:** 41-51-43 N **Long:** 88-15-37 W
Pop: 0 (1990); 12,574 (1980)
Land: 0.03 sq. mi.; **Water:** 0.0 sq. mi. **Elev:** 716 ft.

In northeastern IL on the Fox River, 35 mi. west of Chicago. Founded 1834. Incorporated Jul 27, 1872. Part of the town is also in Kane County.
Name origin: Possibly for Batavia, NY.

Bensenville
Village
ZIP: 60106 **Lat:** 41-57-26 N **Long:** 87-56-40 W
Pop: 17,767 (1990); 16,103 (1980) **Pop Density:** 3172.7
Land: 5.6 sq. mi.; **Water:** 0.0 sq. mi.

In northeastern IL on Salt Creek, 18 mi. northwest of Chicago. Incorporated 1894. Part of the town is also in Cook County.

Bloomingdale
Village
ZIP: 60108 **Lat:** 41-56-56 N **Long:** 88-05-11 W
Pop: 16,614 (1990); 12,656 (1980) **Pop Density:** 2595.9
Land: 6.4 sq. mi.; **Water:** 0.0 sq. mi.

In northeastern IL, a suburb 25 mi. west of Chicago. Incorporated 1923. Not coextensive with the town of the same name.
Name origin: For its descriptive connotations.

*Bloomingdale
Township
ZIP: 60108 **Lat:** 41-56-40 N **Long:** 88-05-19 W
Pop: 96,050 (1990); 79,623 (1980) **Pop Density:** 2721.0
Land: 35.3 sq. mi.; **Water:** 0.2 sq. mi.

Bolingbrook
Village
ZIP: 60440 **Lat:** 41-43-55 N **Long:** 88-02-53 W
Pop: 1,472 (1990); 1,154 (1980) **Pop Density:** 3680.0
Land: 0.4 sq. mi.; **Water:** 0.0 sq. mi. **Elev:** 703 ft.

In northeastern IL, 25 mi. southwest of Chicago. Incorporated 1965. Part of the town is also in Will County.
Name origin: For Bolingbroke, Lincolnshire, England, and for the Bolingbroke family; spelling change reflects pronunciation.

Burr Ridge
Village
ZIP: 60521 **Lat:** 41-44-56 N **Long:** 87-55-32 W
Pop: 4,596 (1990); 2,290 (1980) **Pop Density:** 1242.2
Land: 3.7 sq. mi.; **Water:** 0.0 sq. mi.

Part of the town is also in Cook County.

Carol Stream
Residential suburb
ZIP: 60188 **Lat:** 41-55-00 N **Long:** 88-07-51 W
Pop: 31,716 (1990); 15,472 (1980) **Pop Density:** 4066.2
Land: 7.8 sq. mi.; **Water:** 0.0 sq. mi.

In northeastern IL, 25 mi. west of Chicago. Incorporated 1959.
Name origin: For the daughter of developer Jay Stream.

Chicago
City
ZIP: 60620 **Lat:** 41-58-44 N **Long:** 87-55-46 W
Pop: 0 (1990); 11 (1980)
Land: 2.3 sq. mi.; **Water:** 0.0 sq. mi. **Elev:** 596 ft.

In northeastern IL on Lake Michigan; featuring Chicago Sanitary and Ship Canal. County seat; incorporated Feb 11, 1835. Part of the city is also in Cook County. Third largest U.S. city, biggest transportation center, and one of busiest ports in the U.S. Financial capital of the Midwest and world's capital in futures trading; home to the Chicago Board of Trade, the oldest U.S. financial exchange. Site of the great fire of 1871 and the Haymarket riot in 1886. Produces food products, fabricated metals, chemicals, and iron and steel. Home of DePaul and Loyola universities, Illinois Institute of Technology, University of Chicago, Chicago Zoological Park, Lincoln Park Zoo, Natural History Museum, Comiskey Park (Chicago White Sox), Wrigley Field (Chicago Cubs), world's tallest building: 110-story Sears Tower. Downtown area called *the Loop*. Part of the city is also in Cook County.
Name origin: From an Algonquian term meaning 'garlic field.'

Clarendon Hills
Village
ZIP: 60514 **Lat:** 41-47-54 N **Long:** 87-57-27 W
Pop: 6,994 (1990); 6,870 (1980) **Pop Density:** 4114.1
Land: 1.7 sq. mi.; **Water:** 0.0 sq. mi.

In northeastern IL, west of Chicago. Incorporated 1924.
Name origin: For Clarendon Hills, England.

Darien
City
ZIP: 60559 **Lat:** 41-44-57 N **Long:** 87-58-34 W
Pop: 18,341 (1990); 14,956 (1980) **Pop Density:** 3987.2
Land: 4.6 sq. mi.; **Water:** 0.0 sq. mi. **Elev:** 756 ft.

In northeastern IL, 15 mi. southwest of Chicago. Incorporated Dec 16, 1969.

Downers Grove
Village
ZIP: 60515 **Lat:** 41-47-49 N **Long:** 88-01-02 W
Pop: 46,858 (1990); 42,259 (1980) **Pop Density:** 3445.4
Land: 13.6 sq. mi.; **Water:** 0.0 sq. mi.

In northeastern IL, 20 mi. west of Chicago. Incorporated 1873. Not coextensive with the town of the same name.
Name origin: For town founder Pierce Downer.

*Downers Grove
Township
ZIP: 60559 **Lat:** 41-45-14 N **Long:** 87-58-32 W
Pop: 137,862 (1990); 122,865 (1980) **Pop Density:** 2724.5
Land: 50.6 sq. mi.; **Water:** 0.6 sq. mi.

Elk Grove Village
Village
ZIP: 60007 **Lat:** 41-59-21 N **Long:** 87-57-31 W
Pop: 0 (1990)
Land: 0.7 sq. mi.; **Water:** 0.0 sq. mi.

In northeastern IL, a northwestern suburb of Chicago. Part of the town is also in Cook County.
Name origin: Until 1960 Elk Grove Village was little more than a cornfield with scattered houses. That year Centrex Construction Company, a community planning enterprise, laid out a new town.

Elmhurst — City
ZIP: 60126   **Lat:** 41-53-52 N   **Long:** 87-56-37 W
Pop: 42,029 (1990); 44,276 (1980)   **Pop Density:** 4161.3
Land: 10.1 sq. mi.; **Water:** 0.0 sq. mi.

In northeastern IL, 8 miles east of Wheaton. Founded in 1843; incorporated Jun 5, 1882.
Name origin: For the stately elms that lined the city's boulevards.

Glenbard South — CDP
Lat: 41-49-46 N   **Long:** 88-03-58 W
Pop: 3,957 (1990)   **Pop Density:** 3043.8
Land: 1.3 sq. mi.; **Water:** 0.0 sq. mi.

Glendale Heights — City
ZIP: 60139   **Lat:** 41-55-12 N   **Long:** 88-04-43 W
Pop: 27,973 (1990); 23,251 (1980)   **Pop Density:** 5484.9
Land: 5.1 sq. mi.; **Water:** 0.0 sq. mi.   **Elev:** 762 ft.

In northeastern IL, a residential suburb 20 mi. west of Chicago. Incorporated 1959.
Name origin: Descriptively named by incorporators.

Glen Ellyn — Village
ZIP: 60137   **Lat:** 41-51-59 N   **Long:** 88-03-45 W
Pop: 24,944 (1990); 23,691 (1980)   **Pop Density:** 4023.2
Land: 6.2 sq. mi.; **Water:** 0.0 sq. mi.

In northeastern IL, 25 mi. west of Chicago. Platted 1851. Originally a stagecoach stop. Incorporated 1892.
Name origin: For the glen at the base of Cooper Hill and Ellyn, the wife of a founder.

Hanover Park — City
ZIP: 60103   **Lat:** 41-58-06 N   **Long:** 88-08-48 W
Pop: 14,233 (1990); 10,561 (1980)   **Pop Density:** 4744.3
Land: 3.0 sq. mi.; **Water:** 0.0 sq. mi.

In northeastern IL, 25 mi. northwest of Chicago. Incorporated 1958. Part of the town is also in Cook County.
Name origin: For the British royal house whose line began with George I (1660–1727), Duke of Hanover.

Hinsdale — City
ZIP: 60521   **Lat:** 41-48-05 N   **Long:** 87-55-53 W
Pop: 13,956 (1990); 14,312 (1980)   **Pop Density:** 3771.9
Land: 3.7 sq. mi.; **Water:** 0.0 sq. mi.

In northeastern IL, 15 mi. west of Chicago. Incorporated 1873. Part of the town is also in Cook County.
Name origin: For H. W. Hinsdale, a director of the Burlington Railroad.

Itasca — City
ZIP: 60143   **Lat:** 41-58-36 N   **Long:** 88-01-06 W
Pop: 6,947 (1990); 7,129 (1980)   **Pop Density:** 1543.8
Land: 4.5 sq. mi.; **Water:** 0.1 sq. mi.

Part of the town is also in Cook County.

Lisle — City
ZIP: 60532   **Lat:** 41-47-30 N   **Long:** 88-05-15 W
Pop: 19,512 (1990); 13,638 (1980)   **Pop Density:** 3307.1
Land: 5.9 sq. mi.; **Water:** 0.0 sq. mi.

In northeastern IL on the Du Page River, 25 mi. west of Chicago. Incorporated 1956. Not coextensive with the town of the same name.

*Lisle — Township
ZIP: 60532   **Lat:** 41-46-17 N   **Long:** 88-05-19 W
Pop: 108,452 (1990); 82,575 (1980)   **Pop Density:** 3029.4
Land: 35.8 sq. mi.; **Water:** 0.1 sq. mi.

Lombard — City
ZIP: 60148   **Lat:** 41-52-29 N   **Long:** 88-00-53 W
Pop: 39,408 (1990); 36,879 (1980)   **Pop Density:** 4237.4
Land: 9.3 sq. mi.; **Water:** 0.0 sq. mi.

In northeastern IL, 20 mi. west of Chicago. Settled 1834 by Winslow Churchill; incorporated March 29, 1869.
Name origin: City named for Josiah L. Lombard, who platted the town in the early 1860s.

Medinah — CDP
Lat: 41-58-31 N   **Long:** 88-03-20 W
Pop: 2,512 (1990)   **Pop Density:** 1570.0
Land: 1.6 sq. mi.; **Water:** 0.0 sq. mi.

Milton — Township
ZIP: 60187   **Lat:** 41-51-30 N   **Long:** 88-05-22 W
Pop: 108,148 (1990); 97,302 (1980)   **Pop Density:** 3081.1
Land: 35.1 sq. mi.; **Water:** 0.1 sq. mi.

Naperville — City
ZIP: 60566   **Lat:** 41-46-21 N   **Long:** 88-09-20 W
Pop: 72,931 (1990); 41,700 (1980)   **Pop Density:** 3198.7
Land: 22.8 sq. mi.; **Water:** 0.1 sq. mi.

In northeastern IL, 30 mi. west of Chicago. Incorporated Feb 7, 1857. Part of the town is also in Will County. Not coextensive with the township of the same name.
Name origin: For its founder, Capt. Joseph Naper, who built a sawmill and platted the townsite in 1832.

*Naperville — Township
ZIP: 60540   **Lat:** 41-46-18 N   **Long:** 88-12-20 W
Pop: 49,533 (1990); 21,053 (1980)   **Pop Density:** 1395.3
Land: 35.5 sq. mi.; **Water:** 0.4 sq. mi.

Oak Brook — Town
ZIP: 60521   **Lat:** 41-50-12 N   **Long:** 87-57-09 W
Pop: 9,178 (1990); 6,676 (1980)   **Pop Density:** 1119.3
Land: 8.2 sq. mi.; **Water:** 0.1 sq. mi.

Part of the town is in Cook County.
Name origin: For the Oakbrook polo club.

Oakbrook Terrace — City
ZIP: 60181   **Lat:** 41-51-11 N   **Long:** 87-58-07 W
Pop: 1,907 (1990); 2,285 (1980)   **Pop Density:** 1589.2
Land: 1.2 sq. mi.; **Water:** 0.0 sq. mi.

Roselle — Village
ZIP: 60172   **Lat:** 41-58-47 N   **Long:** 88-05-02 W
Pop: 17,499 (1990); 14,618 (1980)   **Pop Density:** 4374.8
Land: 4.0 sq. mi.; **Water:** 0.0 sq. mi.

In northeastern IL, 25 mi. northwest of Chicago. Incorporated 1922. Part of the town is also in Cook County.
Name origin: For Roselle Hough (1827–98), a prominent Chicago citizen.

St. Charles — Town
Lat: 41-55-07 N   **Long:** 88-15-22 W
Pop: 10 (1990); 21 (1980)   **Pop Density:** 33.3
Land: 0.3 sq. mi.; **Water:** 0.0 sq. mi.

In northeastern IL on the Fox River, 33 mi. northwest of Chicago. Incorporated Feb 9, 1839. Part of the town is also in Kane County.
Name origin: For Charlestown, NH. Name was changed to avoid confusion with Charleston, IL.

Schaumburg
Village
ZIP: 60194 **Lat:** 41-59-21 N **Long:** 88-05-50 W
Pop: 0 (1990); 17 (1980)
Land: 0.1 sq. mi.; **Water:** 0.0 sq. mi. **Elev:** 799 ft.
In northeastern IL, 28 mi. northwest of Chicago. Incorporated 1956. Part of the town is also in Cook County.
Name origin: For a local citizen named Schaum.

Villa Park
City
ZIP: 60181 **Lat:** 41-53-07 N **Long:** 87-58-41 W
Pop: 22,253 (1990); 23,155 (1980) **Pop Density:** 4837.6
Land: 4.6 sq. mi.; **Water:** 0.0 sq. mi.
In northeastern IL, 18 mi. west of Chicago. Incorporated 1914.

Warrenville
Town
ZIP: 60555 **Lat:** 41-49-12 N **Long:** 88-11-10 W
Pop: 11,333 (1990); 7,519 (1980) **Pop Density:** 2138.3
Land: 5.3 sq. mi.; **Water:** 0.1 sq. mi.
In northeastern IL on the Du Page River, 30 mi. south of Chicago. Incorporated Sep 20, 1967.
Name origin: For Daniel Warren (1780–1866), named by his son, who was a founder and leading citizen.

Wayne
Town
ZIP: 60184 **Lat:** 41-56-50 N **Long:** 88-14-29 W
Pop: 718 (1990); 460 (1980) **Pop Density:** 287.2
Land: 2.5 sq. mi.; **Water:** 0.0 sq. mi.
Part of the town is in Kane County.
Name origin: For Gen. "Mad Anthony" Wayne (1745–96) of Revolutionary War fame.

*Wayne
Township
ZIP: 60185 **Lat:** 41-56-46 N **Long:** 88-12-00 W
Pop: 40,379 (1990); 23,246 (1980) **Pop Density:** 1109.3
Land: 36.4 sq. mi.; **Water:** 0.1 sq. mi.

West Chicago
City
ZIP: 60185 **Lat:** 41-53-23 N **Long:** 88-13-22 W
Pop: 14,796 (1990); 12,550 (1980) **Pop Density:** 1557.5
Land: 9.5 sq. mi.; **Water:** 0.0 sq. mi. **Elev:** 784 ft.
In northeastern IL, 25 mi. west of Chicago. Incorporated May 31, 1873.

Westmont
City
ZIP: 60559 **Lat:** 41-47-49 N **Long:** 87-58-30 W
Pop: 21,228 (1990); 17,353 (1980) **Pop Density:** 4824.5
Land: 4.4 sq. mi.; **Water:** 0.0 sq. mi.
In northeastern IL, 20 mi. southwest of Chicago. Incorporated 1921.

Wheaton
City
ZIP: 60187 **Lat:** 41-51-21 N **Long:** 88-06-27 W
Pop: 51,464 (1990); 43,043 (1980) **Pop Density:** 4636.4
Land: 11.1 sq. mi.; **Water:** 0.0 sq. mi.
In northeastern IL, 25 mi. west of Chicago. County seat. Settled 1838; incorporated Feb 24, 1859.
Name origin: For first settlers, Warren and Jesse Wheaton.

Willowbrook
Village
ZIP: 60521 **Lat:** 41-45-42 N **Long:** 87-56-46 W
Pop: 8,598 (1990); 4,953 (1980) **Pop Density:** 3439.2
Land: 2.5 sq. mi.; **Water:** 0.0 sq. mi. **Elev:** 710 ft.

Willow Springs
Village
Lat: 41-42-42 N **Long:** 87-55-26 W
Pop: 0 (1990)
Land: 0.3 sq. mi.; **Water:** 0.0 sq. mi.
Part of the town is also in Cook County.
Name origin: For its descriptive connotations.

Winfield
Town
ZIP: 60190 **Lat:** 41-52-16 N **Long:** 88-09-13 W
Pop: 7,096 (1990); 4,422 (1980) **Pop Density:** 3225.5
Land: 2.2 sq. mi.; **Water:** 0.0 sq. mi.
In northeastern IL near the West Branch of the Du Page River, 28 mi. west of Chicago. Not coextensive with the town of the same name.
Name origin: For Gen. Winfield Scott (1786–1866) of Mexican War fame.

*Winfield
Township
ZIP: 60185 **Lat:** 41-51-23 N **Long:** 88-12-15 W
Pop: 37,969 (1990); 28,940 (1980) **Pop Density:** 1066.5
Land: 35.6 sq. mi.; **Water:** 0.7 sq. mi.

Wood Dale
Town
ZIP: 60191 **Lat:** 41-57-57 N **Long:** 87-58-51 W
Pop: 12,425 (1990); 11,251 (1980) **Pop Density:** 2889.5
Land: 4.3 sq. mi.; **Water:** 0.0 sq. mi. **Elev:** 696 ft.
In northeastern IL on Salt Creek, 20 mi. northwest of Chicago. Incorporated Oct 20, 1928.
Name origin: Descriptive and promotional.

Woodridge
Village
ZIP: 60517 **Lat:** 41-44-38 N **Long:** 88-02-30 W
Pop: 26,232 (1990); 21,763 (1980) **Pop Density:** 3801.7
Land: 6.9 sq. mi.; **Water:** 0.0 sq. mi.
In northeastern IL, 24 mi. southwest of Chicago. Incorporated 1959. Part of the town is also in Will County.
Name origin: Descriptive and promotional.

York
Township
ZIP: 60181 **Lat:** 41-51-38 N **Long:** 87-58-31 W
Pop: 120,546 (1990); 120,381 (1980) **Pop Density:** 3395.7
Land: 35.5 sq. mi.; **Water:** 0.1 sq. mi.

ILLINOIS, Edgar County *American Places Dictionary*

> ## Edgar County
> **County Seat: Paris (ZIP: 61944)**
>
> **Pop:** 19,595 (1990); 21,725 (1980)　　　　**Pop Density:** 31.4
> **Land:** 623.6 sq. mi.; **Water:** 0.6 sq. mi.　　**Area Code:** 217
> On the east-central border of IL south of Danville; organized Jan 3, 1823 from Clark County.
> **Name origin:** For John Edgar, pioneer merchant and politician.

Brocton　　　　　　　　　　　　　　Village
ZIP: 61917　　　　Lat: 39-42-58 N **Long:** 87-55-59 W
Pop: 322 (1990); 393 (1980)　　**Pop Density:** 536.7
Land: 0.6 sq. mi.; **Water:** 0.0 sq. mi.

Brouilletts Creek　　　　　　　　Township
　　　　　　　　Lat: 39-44-47 N **Long:** 87-34-52 W
Pop: 253 (1990); 307 (1980)　　**Pop Density:** 7.9
Land: 32.0 sq. mi.; **Water:** 0.0 sq. mi.

Buck　　　　　　　　　　　　　　Township
　　　　　　　　Lat: 39-38-29 N **Long:** 87-49-36 W
Pop: 366 (1990); 293 (1980)　　**Pop Density:** 10.7
Land: 34.3 sq. mi.; **Water:** 0.0 sq. mi.

Chrisman　　　　　　　　　　　　　　City
ZIP: 61924　　　　Lat: 39-48-14 N **Long:** 87-40-27 W
Pop: 1,136 (1990); 1,413 (1980)　　**Pop Density:** 1622.9
Land: 0.7 sq. mi.; **Water:** 0.0 sq. mi.
Name origin: For Matthias Chrisman, who platted it in 1872.

Edgar　　　　　　　　　　　　　　Township
　　　　　　　　Lat: 39-44-20 N **Long:** 87-42-04 W
Pop: 547 (1990); 630 (1980)　　**Pop Density:** 9.9
Land: 55.4 sq. mi.; **Water:** 0.0 sq. mi.

Elbridge　　　　　　　　　　　　Township
　　　　　　　　Lat: 39-31-50 N **Long:** 87-35-15 W
Pop: 672 (1990); 733 (1980)　　**Pop Density:** 15.4
Land: 43.5 sq. mi.; **Water:** 0.1 sq. mi.

Embarrass　　　　　　　　　　　Township
　　　　　　　　Lat: 39-40-22 N **Long:** 87-55-04 W
Pop: 696 (1990); 943 (1980)　　**Pop Density:** 15.7
Land: 44.2 sq. mi.; **Water:** 0.0 sq. mi.

Grandview　　　　　　　　　　　Township
　　　　　　　　Lat: 39-32-17 N **Long:** 87-49-24 W
Pop: 601 (1990); 650 (1980)　　**Pop Density:** 13.3
Land: 45.1 sq. mi.; **Water:** 0.1 sq. mi.

Hume　　　　　　　　　　　　　　Village
ZIP: 61932　　　　Lat: 39-47-51 N **Long:** 87-52-07 W
Pop: 406 (1990); 483 (1980)　　**Pop Density:** 812.0
Land: 0.5 sq. mi.; **Water:** 0.0 sq. mi.

Hunter　　　　　　　　　　　　Township
　　　　　　　　Lat: 39-40-16 N **Long:** 87-35-05 W
Pop: 269 (1990); 330 (1980)　　**Pop Density:** 8.9
Land: 30.2 sq. mi.; **Water:** 0.0 sq. mi.

Kansas　　　　　　　　　　　　　　Town
ZIP: 61933　　　　Lat: 39-33-13 N **Long:** 87-56-23 W
Pop: 887 (1990); 791 (1980)　　**Pop Density:** 887.0
Land: 1.0 sq. mi.; **Water:** 0.0 sq. mi.
Not coextensive with the town of the same name.
Name origin: For the Kansa Indians, a Sioux tribe.

*Kansas　　　　　　　　　　　　Township
　　　　　　　　Lat: 39-32-46 N **Long:** 87-55-38 W
Pop: 1,114 (1990); 1,097 (1980)　　**Pop Density:** 27.4
Land: 40.6 sq. mi.; **Water:** 0.0 sq. mi.

Metcalf　　　　　　　　　　　　　Village
ZIP: 61940　　　　Lat: 39-48-00 N **Long:** 87-48-28 W
Pop: 227 (1990); 278 (1980)　　**Pop Density:** 378.3
Land: 0.6 sq. mi.; **Water:** 0.0 sq. mi.

Paris　　　　　　　　　　　　　　City
ZIP: 61944　　　　Lat: 39-36-55 N **Long:** 87-41-29 W
Pop: 8,987 (1990); 9,885 (1980)　　**Pop Density:** 2139.8
Land: 4.2 sq. mi.; **Water:** 0.4 sq. mi.　　**Elev:** 726 ft.
In east-central IL, 40 mi. southeast of Champaign. County seat. Incorporated Feb 12, 1853. Not coextensive with the town of the same name.
Name origin: For Paris, KY

*Paris　　　　　　　　　　　　Township
ZIP: 61944　　　　Lat: 39-37-50 N **Long:** 87-42-33 W
Pop: 10,380 (1990); 11,354 (1980)　　**Pop Density:** 230.7
Land: 45.0 sq. mi.; **Water:** 0.4 sq. mi.

Prairie　　　　　　　　　　　　Township
　　　　　　　　Lat: 39-50-26 N **Long:** 87-35-26 W
Pop: 315 (1990); 392 (1980)　　**Pop Density:** 8.8
Land: 36.0 sq. mi.; **Water:** 0.0 sq. mi.

Redmon　　　　　　　　　　　　　Village
　　　　　　　　Lat: 39-38-41 N **Long:** 87-51-42 W
Pop: 201 (1990); 224 (1980)　　**Pop Density:** 2010.0
Land: 0.1 sq. mi.; **Water:** 0.0 sq. mi.　　**Elev:** 690 ft.

Ross　　　　　　　　　　　　　　Township
　　　　　　　　Lat: 39-50-24 N **Long:** 87-43-00 W
Pop: 1,556 (1990); 1,747 (1980)　　**Pop Density:** 42.4
Land: 36.7 sq. mi.; **Water:** 0.0 sq. mi.

Shiloh　　　　　　　　　　　　Township
　　　　　　　　Lat: 39-44-41 N **Long:** 87-51-13 W
Pop: 247 (1990); 356 (1980)　　**Pop Density:** 4.2
Land: 58.3 sq. mi.; **Water:** 0.0 sq. mi.

Stratton　　　　　　　　　　　Township
　　　　　　　　Lat: 39-36-25 N **Long:** 87-35-27 W
Pop: 594 (1990); 671 (1980)　　**Pop Density:** 24.0
Land: 24.8 sq. mi.; **Water:** 0.0 sq. mi.

Symmes　　　　　　　　　　　　Township
　　　　　　　　Lat: 39-31-44 N **Long:** 87-42-17 W
Pop: 1,136 (1990); 1,206 (1980)　　**Pop Density:** 26.8
Land: 42.4 sq. mi.; **Water:** 0.0 sq. mi.

Vermilion　　　　　　　　　　　Village
ZIP: 61955　　　　Lat: 39-34-47 N **Long:** 87-35-14 W
Pop: 283 (1990); 299 (1980)　　**Pop Density:** 353.8
Land: 0.8 sq. mi.; **Water:** 0.0 sq. mi.

Young America   Township
Lat: 39-50-20 N   **Long:** 87-50-43 W
Pop: 849 (1990); 1,016 (1980)   **Pop Density:** 15.4
Land: 55.2 sq. mi.; **Water:** 0.0 sq. mi.

Edwards County
County Seat: Albion (ZIP: 62806)

Pop: 7,440 (1990); 7,961 (1980)   **Pop Density:** 33.5
Land: 222.4 sq. mi.; **Water:** 0.3 sq. mi.   **Area Code:** 618
In southeastern IL, south of Olney; organized Nov 28, 1814 (prior to statehood) from Madison and Gallatin counties.
Name origin: For Ninian Edwards (1775–1833), KY legislator and jurist, and territorial (1809–18) and civil (1826–30) governor of IL.

Albion   City
ZIP: 62806   **Lat:** 38-22-34 N   **Long:** 88-03-25 W
Pop: 2,116 (1990); 2,285 (1980)   **Pop Density:** 1007.6
Land: 2.1 sq. mi.; **Water:** 0.0 sq. mi.
In southeastern IL, south of Olney. Founded 1818 by English colonizers Morris Birkbeck and George Flower; incorporated 1869.
Name origin: From the ancient and poetic name for England.

Bone Gap   Village
ZIP: 62815   **Lat:** 38-26-41 N   **Long:** 87-59-52 W
Pop: 271 (1990); 350 (1980)   **Pop Density:** 387.1
Land: 0.7 sq. mi.; **Water:** 0.0 sq. mi.   **Elev:** 462 ft.

Browns   Village
ZIP: 62818   **Lat:** 38-22-39 N   **Long:** 87-59-00 W
Pop: 207 (1990); 213 (1980)   **Pop Density:** 690.0
Land: 0.3 sq. mi.; **Water:** 0.0 sq. mi.

Grayville   City
ZIP: 62844   **Lat:** 38-16-05 N   **Long:** 87-59-45 W
Pop: 910 (1990); 1,064 (1980)   **Pop Density:** 1137.5
Land: 0.8 sq. mi.; **Water:** 0.0 sq. mi.
Part of the town is also in White County.

West Salem   Village
ZIP: 62476   **Lat:** 38-31-12 N   **Long:** 88-00-31 W
Pop: 1,042 (1990); 1,145 (1980)   **Pop Density:** 651.3
Land: 1.6 sq. mi.; **Water:** 0.0 sq. mi.

Effingham County
County Seat: Effingham (ZIP: 62401)

Pop: 31,704 (1990); 30,944 (1980)   **Pop Density:** 66.2
Land: 478.7 sq. mi.; **Water:** 1.2 sq. mi.   **Area Code:** 217
In central IL southeast of Decatur; organized Feb 15, 1831 from Fayette and Crawford counties.
Name origin: For either Thomas Howard (1746–91), 3rd Earl of Effingham, who supported the Americans during the Revolutionary War, or Gen. Edward Effingham, who resigned from the British Army rather than fight the colonists.

Altamont   City
ZIP: 62411   **Lat:** 39-03-28 N   **Long:** 88-44-54 W
Pop: 2,296 (1990); 2,389 (1980)   **Pop Density:** 2087.3
Land: 1.1 sq. mi.; **Water:** 0.0 sq. mi.   **Elev:** 619 ft.
Incorporated as village 1872, as city 1901.
Name origin: From the Latin for 'high mountain,' for a highland area one mile to the west.

Banner   Township
Lat: 39-11-55 N   **Long:** 88-38-06 W
Pop: 539 (1990); 543 (1980)   **Pop Density:** 29.9
Land: 18.0 sq. mi.; **Water:** 0.0 sq. mi.

Beecher City   Village
ZIP: 62414   **Lat:** 39-11-11 N   **Long:** 88-47-15 W
Pop: 437 (1990); 492 (1980)   **Pop Density:** 485.6
Land: 0.9 sq. mi.; **Water:** 0.0 sq. mi.

Bishop   Township
Lat: 39-02-54 N   **Long:** 88-25-14 W
Pop: 1,200 (1990); 1,190 (1980)   **Pop Density:** 34.3
Land: 35.0 sq. mi.; **Water:** 0.0 sq. mi.

Dieterich   Village
ZIP: 62424   **Lat:** 39-03-34 N   **Long:** 88-22-55 W
Pop: 568 (1990); 633 (1980)   **Pop Density:** 473.3
Land: 1.2 sq. mi.; **Water:** 0.0 sq. mi.   **Elev:** 591 ft.

ILLINOIS, Effingham County

Douglas
Township
ZIP: 62401 Lat: 39-10-03 N Long: 88-31-57 W
Pop: 12,566 (1990); 12,156 (1980) Pop Density: 374.0
Land: 33.6 sq. mi.; Water: 0.1 sq. mi.

Edgewood
Village
ZIP: 62426 Lat: 38-55-18 N Long: 88-39-50 W
Pop: 502 (1990); 574 (1980) Pop Density: 502.0
Land: 1.0 sq. mi.; Water: 0.0 sq. mi.

Effingham
City
ZIP: 62401 Lat: 39-07-10 N Long: 88-33-03 W
Pop: 11,851 (1990); 11,270 (1980) Pop Density: 1742.8
Land: 6.8 sq. mi.; Water: 0.1 sq. mi. Elev: 592 ft.
Incorporated 1861.

Name origin: Named in honor of Thomas Howard (1746–91), 3rd Earl of Effingham, who supported the Americans during the Revolutionary War.

Jackson
Township
Lat: 39-02-58 N Long: 88-38-04 W
Pop: 1,023 (1990); 951 (1980) Pop Density: 27.3
Land: 37.5 sq. mi.; Water: 0.0 sq. mi.

Liberty
Township
Lat: 39-11-35 N Long: 88-44-56 W
Pop: 734 (1990); 874 (1980) Pop Density: 40.8
Land: 18.0 sq. mi.; Water: 0.0 sq. mi.

Lucas
Township
Lat: 38-57-42 N Long: 88-24-32 W
Pop: 439 (1990); 517 (1980) Pop Density: 12.4
Land: 35.4 sq. mi.; Water: 0.0 sq. mi.

Mason
Town
ZIP: 62443 Lat: 38-57-11 N Long: 88-37-31 W
Pop: 387 (1990); 480 (1980) Pop Density: 351.8
Land: 1.1 sq. mi.; Water: 0.0 sq. mi.

In south-central IL near the Little Wabash River, southeast of Decatur. Incorporated Feb 15, 1865. Not coextensive with the town of the same name.

*Mason
Township
Lat: 38-57-32 N Long: 88-38-06 W
Pop: 1,411 (1990); 1,524 (1980) Pop Density: 37.9
Land: 37.2 sq. mi.; Water: 0.0 sq. mi.

Moccasin
Township
Lat: 39-07-44 N Long: 88-45-08 W
Pop: 454 (1990); 496 (1980) Pop Density: 12.8
Land: 35.6 sq. mi.; Water: 0.0 sq. mi.

Montrose
Village
ZIP: 62445 Lat: 39-09-56 N Long: 88-22-42 W
Pop: 306 (1990); 321 (1980) Pop Density: 510.0
Land: 0.6 sq. mi.; Water: 0.0 sq. mi.
Part of the town is also in Cumberland County.

Mound
Township
Lat: 39-02-39 N Long: 88-44-58 W
Pop: 3,413 (1990); 3,504 (1980) Pop Density: 92.2
Land: 37.0 sq. mi.; Water: 0.1 sq. mi.

St. Francis
Township
Lat: 39-07-52 N Long: 88-24-26 W
Pop: 1,263 (1990); 1,200 (1980) Pop Density: 39.0
Land: 32.4 sq. mi.; Water: 0.0 sq. mi.

Shumway
Village
ZIP: 62461 Lat: 39-10-59 N Long: 88-39-10 W
Pop: 243 (1990); 278 (1980) Pop Density: 810.0
Land: 0.3 sq. mi.; Water: 0.0 sq. mi. Elev: 655 ft.

Summit
Township
Lat: 39-07-42 N Long: 88-38-07 W
Pop: 2,665 (1990); 2,289 (1980) Pop Density: 79.3
Land: 33.6 sq. mi.; Water: 0.9 sq. mi.

Teutopolis
Town
ZIP: 62467 Lat: 39-07-55 N Long: 88-28-42 W
Pop: 1,417 (1990); 1,414 (1980) Pop Density: 1180.8
Land: 1.2 sq. mi.; Water: 0.0 sq. mi. Elev: 604 ft.

Established in 1839 by a group of Germans from Cincinnati, OH. Not coextensive with the town of the same name.

Name origin: A combination of the prefix *Teuto* 'German' and the suffix *polis* Greek for 'city.'

*Teutopolis
Township
Lat: 39-07-47 N Long: 88-29-51 W
Pop: 2,332 (1990); 2,276 (1980) Pop Density: 137.2
Land: 17.0 sq. mi.; Water: 0.0 sq. mi.

Union
Township
Lat: 38-57-33 N Long: 88-31-19 W
Pop: 534 (1990); 588 (1980) Pop Density: 14.9
Land: 35.8 sq. mi.; Water: 0.0 sq. mi.

Watson
Village
ZIP: 62473 Lat: 39-01-32 N Long: 88-34-10 W
Pop: 646 (1990); 551 (1980) Pop Density: 717.8
Land: 0.9 sq. mi.; Water: 0.0 sq. mi. Elev: 561 ft.
Not coextensive with the town of the same name.

*Watson
Township
Lat: 39-02-39 N Long: 88-31-15 W
Pop: 2,711 (1990); 2,360 (1980) Pop Density: 75.7
Land: 35.8 sq. mi.; Water: 0.0 sq. mi.

West
Township
Lat: 38-57-41 N Long: 88-45-04 W
Pop: 420 (1990); 476 (1980) Pop Density: 11.4
Land: 36.9 sq. mi.; Water: 0.0 sq. mi.

Fayette County
County Seat: Vandalia (ZIP: 62471)

Pop: 20,893 (1990); 22,167 (1980) **Pop Density:** 29.2
Land: 716.5 sq. mi.; **Water:** 8.9 sq. mi. **Area Code:** 618
In south-central IL northeast of St. Louis, MO; organized Feb 14, 1821 from Bond, Jefferson, Wayne, and Clark counties.
Name origin: For the Marquis de Lafayette (1757–1834), French statesman and soldier who fought with the Americans during the Revolutionary War.

Avena
Township
Lat: 39-02-34 N **Long:** 88-51-44 W
Pop: 2,091 (1990); 2,335 (1980) **Pop Density:** 57.6
Land: 36.3 sq. mi.; **Water:** 0.2 sq. mi.

Bear Grove
Township
Lat: 38-57-37 N **Long:** 89-11-29 W
Pop: 623 (1990); 653 (1980) **Pop Density:** 16.7
Land: 37.4 sq. mi.; **Water:** 0.1 sq. mi.

Bingham
Village
ZIP: 62011 **Lat:** 39-06-46 N **Long:** 89-12-42 W
Pop: 98 (1990); 128 (1980) **Pop Density:** 326.7
Land: 0.3 sq. mi.; **Water:** 0.0 sq. mi. **Elev:** 600 ft.

Bowling Green
Township
Lat: 39-11-39 N **Long:** 88-56-39 W
Pop: 425 (1990); 467 (1980) **Pop Density:** 16.7
Land: 25.5 sq. mi.; **Water:** 0.0 sq. mi.

Brownstown
Village
ZIP: 62418 **Lat:** 38-59-46 N **Long:** 88-57-12 W
Pop: 668 (1990); 708 (1980) **Pop Density:** 1113.3
Land: 0.6 sq. mi.; **Water:** 0.0 sq. mi. **Elev:** 586 ft.

Carson
Township
Lat: 39-08-07 N **Long:** 89-00-05 W
Pop: 170 (1990); 208 (1980) **Pop Density:** 9.6
Land: 17.8 sq. mi.; **Water:** 0.0 sq. mi.

Farina
Village
ZIP: 62838 **Lat:** 38-49-59 N **Long:** 88-46-33 W
Pop: 575 (1990); 594 (1980) **Pop Density:** 479.2
Land: 1.2 sq. mi.; **Water:** 0.0 sq. mi.
Part of the town is also in Marion County.

Hurricane
Township
Lat: 39-11-04 N **Long:** 89-11-59 W
Pop: 235 (1990); 229 (1980) **Pop Density:** 8.7
Land: 27.0 sq. mi.; **Water:** 0.0 sq. mi.

Kaskaskia
Township
Lat: 38-51-56 N **Long:** 89-05-12 W
Pop: 593 (1990); 676 (1980) **Pop Density:** 17.3
Land: 34.3 sq. mi.; **Water:** 0.0 sq. mi.

La Clede
Township
Lat: 38-52-18 N **Long:** 88-45-00 W
Pop: 925 (1990); 1,055 (1980) **Pop Density:** 25.1
Land: 36.9 sq. mi.; **Water:** 0.0 sq. mi.

Lone Grove
Township
Lat: 38-52-03 N **Long:** 88-51-51 W
Pop: 725 (1990); 752 (1980) **Pop Density:** 19.6
Land: 36.9 sq. mi.; **Water:** 0.0 sq. mi.

Loudon
Township
Lat: 39-08-25 N **Long:** 88-52-18 W
Pop: 826 (1990); 871 (1980) **Pop Density:** 13.8
Land: 59.8 sq. mi.; **Water:** 0.0 sq. mi.

Otego
Township
Lat: 38-57-08 N **Long:** 88-58-45 W
Pop: 1,347 (1990); 1,435 (1980) **Pop Density:** 38.2
Land: 35.3 sq. mi.; **Water:** 0.1 sq. mi.

Pope
Township
Lat: 38-47-22 N **Long:** 89-11-04 W
Pop: 250 (1990); 233 (1980) **Pop Density:** 9.8
Land: 25.4 sq. mi.; **Water:** 4.9 sq. mi.

Ramsey
Town
ZIP: 62080 **Lat:** 39-08-37 N **Long:** 89-06-35 W
Pop: 963 (1990); 1,058 (1980) **Pop Density:** 963.0
Land: 1.0 sq. mi.; **Water:** 0.0 sq. mi.
In south-central IL, 12 mi. north of Vandalia. Not coextensive with the town of the same name.

*Ramsey
Township
Lat: 39-09-10 N **Long:** 89-04-40 W
Pop: 1,743 (1990); 1,918 (1980) **Pop Density:** 32.0
Land: 54.4 sq. mi.; **Water:** 0.1 sq. mi.

St. Elmo
City
ZIP: 62458 **Lat:** 39-01-28 N **Long:** 88-51-11 W
Pop: 1,473 (1990); 1,611 (1980) **Pop Density:** 1841.3
Land: 0.8 sq. mi.; **Water:** 0.0 sq. mi.

St. Peter
Village
Lat: 38-52-02 N **Long:** 88-51-06 W
Pop: 353 (1990); 372 (1980) **Pop Density:** 706.0
Land: 0.5 sq. mi.; **Water:** 0.0 sq. mi. **Elev:** 591 ft.

Sefton
Township
Lat: 39-02-52 N **Long:** 88-59-32 W
Pop: 577 (1990); 645 (1980) **Pop Density:** 11.6
Land: 49.8 sq. mi.; **Water:** 0.0 sq. mi.

Seminary
Township
Lat: 38-51-22 N **Long:** 89-12-12 W
Pop: 529 (1990); 616 (1980) **Pop Density:** 11.8
Land: 44.9 sq. mi.; **Water:** 2.0 sq. mi.

Shafter
Township
Lat: 39-02-37 N **Long:** 89-11-08 W
Pop: 416 (1990); 549 (1980) **Pop Density:** 11.7
Land: 35.6 sq. mi.; **Water:** 0.7 sq. mi.

Sharon
Township
Lat: 39-02-42 N **Long:** 89-05-51 W
Pop: 1,837 (1990); 1,527 (1980) **Pop Density:** 74.4
Land: 24.7 sq. mi.; **Water:** 0.4 sq. mi.

ILLINOIS, Fayette County

South Hurricane
Township
Lat: 39-06-56 N **Long:** 89-11-48 W
Pop: 330 (1990); 409 (1980) **Pop Density:** 12.2
Land: 27.1 sq. mi.; **Water:** 0.0 sq. mi.

Vandalia
City
ZIP: 62471 **Lat:** 38-58-51 N **Long:** 89-06-04 W
Pop: 6,114 (1990); 5,338 (1980) **Pop Density:** 1175.8
Land: 5.2 sq. mi.; **Water:** 0.0 sq. mi.
In south-central IL on the Kaskaskia River, 30 mi. north of Centralia. The second state capital (1819–39). Incorporated Feb 15, 1821. Not coextensive with the town of the same name.

*Vandalia
Township
ZIP: 62471 **Lat:** 38-57-20 N **Long:** 89-05-15 W
Pop: 6,339 (1990); 6,636 (1980) **Pop Density:** 180.6
Land: 35.1 sq. mi.; **Water:** 0.3 sq. mi.

Wheatland
Township
Lat: 38-57-21 N **Long:** 88-51-33 W
Pop: 510 (1990); 513 (1980) **Pop Density:** 13.9
Land: 36.6 sq. mi.; **Water:** 0.0 sq. mi.

Wilberton
Township
Lat: 38-52-00 N **Long:** 88-58-36 W
Pop: 402 (1990); 440 (1980) **Pop Density:** 11.3
Land: 35.6 sq. mi.; **Water:** 0.0 sq. mi.

Ford County
County Seat: Paxton (ZIP: 60957)

Pop: 14,275 (1990); 15,265 (1980) **Pop Density:** 29.4
Land: 485.9 sq. mi.; **Water:** 0.5 sq. mi. **Area Code:** 217
In east-central IL east of Bloomington; organized Feb 17, 1859 from Vermilion County.
Name origin: For Thomas Ford (1800–1850), jurist on the IL Supreme Court (1840) and governor (1842–46).

Brenton
Township
Lat: 40-42-56 N **Long:** 88-10-45 W
Pop: 994 (1990); 1,073 (1980) **Pop Density:** 27.5
Land: 36.1 sq. mi.; **Water:** 0.0 sq. mi.

Button
Township
Lat: 40-26-54 N **Long:** 87-59-35 W
Pop: 299 (1990); 335 (1980) **Pop Density:** 8.8
Land: 34.0 sq. mi.; **Water:** 0.1 sq. mi.

Cabery
Village
ZIP: 60919 **Lat:** 40-59-38 N **Long:** 88-12-12 W
Pop: 183 (1990); 219 (1980) **Pop Density:** 915.0
Land: 0.2 sq. mi.; **Water:** 0.0 sq. mi. **Elev:** 698 ft.
Part of the town is also in Kankakee County.

Dix
Township
Lat: 40-27-57 N **Long:** 88-17-29 W
Pop: 711 (1990); 792 (1980) **Pop Density:** 13.2
Land: 54.0 sq. mi.; **Water:** 0.0 sq. mi.

Drummer
Township
Lat: 40-27-51 N **Long:** 88-24-15 W
Pop: 3,897 (1990); 4,071 (1980) **Pop Density:** 72.7
Land: 53.6 sq. mi.; **Water:** 0.1 sq. mi.

Elliott
Village
ZIP: 60933 **Lat:** 40-27-50 N **Long:** 88-16-29 W
Pop: 309 (1990); 370 (1980) **Pop Density:** 618.0
Land: 0.5 sq. mi.; **Water:** 0.0 sq. mi. **Elev:** 781 ft.

Gibson City
City
ZIP: 60936 **Lat:** 40-27-56 N **Long:** 88-22-42 W
Pop: 3,396 (1990); 3,498 (1980) **Pop Density:** 1617.1
Land: 2.1 sq. mi.; **Water:** 0.0 sq. mi.

Kempton
Village
ZIP: 60946 **Lat:** 40-56-08 N **Long:** 88-14-08 W
Pop: 219 (1990); 265 (1980) **Pop Density:** 1095.0
Land: 0.2 sq. mi.; **Water:** 0.0 sq. mi.

Lyman
Township
Lat: 40-37-19 N **Long:** 88-10-28 W
Pop: 617 (1990); 688 (1980) **Pop Density:** 14.6
Land: 42.2 sq. mi.; **Water:** 0.1 sq. mi.

Melvin
Village
ZIP: 60952 **Lat:** 40-34-16 N **Long:** 88-14-50 W
Pop: 466 (1990); 519 (1980) **Pop Density:** 1553.3
Land: 0.3 sq. mi.; **Water:** 0.0 sq. mi.

Mona
Township
Lat: 40-53-21 N **Long:** 88-10-55 W
Pop: 383 (1990); 479 (1980) **Pop Density:** 10.6
Land: 36.2 sq. mi.; **Water:** 0.0 sq. mi.

Patton
Township
ZIP: 60957 **Lat:** 40-26-47 N **Long:** 88-08-22 W
Pop: 5,226 (1990); 5,327 (1980) **Pop Density:** 85.3
Land: 61.3 sq. mi.; **Water:** 0.1 sq. mi.

Paxton
Town
ZIP: 60957 **Lat:** 40-27-30 N **Long:** 88-05-58 W
Pop: 4,289 (1990); 4,258 (1980) **Pop Density:** 1864.8
Land: 2.3 sq. mi.; **Water:** 0.0 sq. mi.
In east-central IL on the Vermilion River, 25 mi. northeast of Urbana. Settled 1853 by Swedish immigrants.

Peach Orchard
Township
Lat: 40-34-33 N **Long:** 88-16-36 W
Pop: 654 (1990); 700 (1980) **Pop Density:** 26.9
Land: 24.3 sq. mi.; **Water:** 0.0 sq. mi.

Pella
Township
Lat: 40-48-26 N **Long:** 88-10-35 W
Pop: 206 (1990); 285 (1980) **Pop Density:** 5.7
Land: 36.2 sq. mi.; **Water:** 0.0 sq. mi.

Piper City
Village
ZIP: 60959 **Lat:** 40-45-20 N **Long:** 88-11-15 W
Pop: 760 (1990); 905 (1980) **Pop Density:** 1266.7
Land: 0.6 sq. mi.; **Water:** 0.0 sq. mi. **Elev:** 668 ft.

Roberts   Village
ZIP: 60962   **Lat:** 40-36-50 N   **Long:** 88-11-00 W
Pop: 397 (1990); 422 (1980)   **Pop Density:** 794.0
Land: 0.5 sq. mi.; **Water:** 0.0 sq. mi.

Rogers   Township
     Lat: 40-58-18 N   **Long:** 88-10-45 W
Pop: 460 (1990); 569 (1980)   **Pop Density:** 19.0
Land: 24.2 sq. mi.; **Water:** 0.0 sq. mi.

Sibley   Village
ZIP: 61773   **Lat:** 40-35-15 N   **Long:** 88-22-41 W
Pop: 359 (1990); 370 (1980)   **Pop Density:** 718.0
Land: 0.5 sq. mi.; **Water:** 0.0 sq. mi.   **Elev:** 813 ft.

Sullivant   Township
     Lat: 40-34-30 N   **Long:** 88-23-01 W
Pop: 608 (1990); 692 (1980)   **Pop Density:** 12.9
Land: 47.2 sq. mi.; **Water:** 0.1 sq. mi.

Wall   Township
     Lat: 40-31-24 N   **Long:** 88-10-56 W
Pop: 220 (1990); 254 (1980)   **Pop Density:** 6.0
Land: 36.5 sq. mi.; **Water:** 0.0 sq. mi.

Franklin County
County Seat: Benton (ZIP: 62812)

Pop: 40,319 (1990); 43,201 (1980)   **Pop Density:** 97.8
Land: 412.1 sq. mi.; **Water:** 19.3 sq. mi.   **Area Code:** 618
In south-central IL northeast of Carbondale; organized Jan 2, 1818 (prior to statehood) from White and Gallatin counties.
Name origin: For Benjamin Franklin (1706–90), U.S. patriot, diplomat, and statesman.

Barren   Township
     Lat: 38-05-13 N   **Long:** 88-59-33 W
Pop: 467 (1990); 503 (1980)   **Pop Density:** 21.9
Land: 21.3 sq. mi.; **Water:** 14.8 sq. mi.

Benton   City
ZIP: 62812   **Lat:** 38-00-25 N   **Long:** 88-55-06 W
Pop: 7,216 (1990); 7,778 (1980)   **Pop Density:** 1472.7
Land: 4.9 sq. mi.; **Water:** 0.1 sq. mi.
Founded 1840. Not coextensive with the town of the same name.
Name origin: For Thomas Hart Benton (1782–1858), U.S. senator from MO.

*****Benton**   Township
ZIP: 62812   **Lat:** 37-59-44 N   **Long:** 88-52-09 W
Pop: 9,190 (1990); 9,754 (1980)   **Pop Density:** 253.2
Land: 36.3 sq. mi.; **Water:** 0.4 sq. mi.

Browning   Township
     Lat: 37-59-25 N   **Long:** 88-58-57 W
Pop: 2,318 (1990); 2,446 (1980)   **Pop Density:** 64.0
Land: 36.2 sq. mi.; **Water:** 0.2 sq. mi.

Buckner   Village
ZIP: 62819   **Lat:** 37-58-51 N   **Long:** 89-00-56 W
Pop: 478 (1990); 520 (1980)   **Pop Density:** 531.1
Land: 0.9 sq. mi.; **Water:** 0.0 sq. mi.   **Elev:** 410 ft.

Cave   Township
     Lat: 37-54-24 N   **Long:** 88-45-27 W
Pop: 1,580 (1990); 1,587 (1980)   **Pop Density:** 44.1
Land: 35.8 sq. mi.; **Water:** 0.7 sq. mi.

Christopher   City
ZIP: 62822   **Lat:** 37-58-21 N   **Long:** 89-03-06 W
Pop: 2,774 (1990); 3,086 (1980)   **Pop Density:** 2311.7
Land: 1.2 sq. mi.; **Water:** 0.0 sq. mi.
Incorporated 1910.

Denning   Township
ZIP: 62896   **Lat:** 37-54-28 N   **Long:** 88-59-02 W
Pop: 5,261 (1990); 5,728 (1980)   **Pop Density:** 144.5
Land: 36.4 sq. mi.; **Water:** 0.5 sq. mi.

Eastern   Township
     Lat: 37-59-47 N   **Long:** 88-45-40 W
Pop: 602 (1990); 602 (1980)   **Pop Density:** 16.6
Land: 36.2 sq. mi.; **Water:** 0.0 sq. mi.

Ewing   Village
ZIP: 62836   **Lat:** 38-05-21 N   **Long:** 88-51-07 W
Pop: 264 (1990); 321 (1980)   **Pop Density:** 264.0
Land: 1.0 sq. mi.; **Water:** 0.0 sq. mi.   **Elev:** 471 ft.
Not coextensive with the town of the same name.

*****Ewing**   Township
     Lat: 38-04-44 N   **Long:** 88-52-42 W
Pop: 1,263 (1990); 1,350 (1980)   **Pop Density:** 34.8
Land: 36.3 sq. mi.; **Water:** 1.7 sq. mi.

Frankfort   Township
ZIP: 62896   **Lat:** 37-54-06 N   **Long:** 88-52-08 W
Pop: 7,317 (1990); 8,018 (1980)   **Pop Density:** 199.4
Land: 36.7 sq. mi.; **Water:** 0.3 sq. mi.

Freeman Spur   Village
     Lat: 37-51-50 N   **Long:** 88-59-59 W
Pop: 153 (1990); 178 (1980)   **Pop Density:** 765.0
Land: 0.2 sq. mi.; **Water:** 0.0 sq. mi.
Part of the town is also in Williamson County.

Goode   Township
     Lat: 38-04-49 N   **Long:** 89-05-04 W
Pop: 2,844 (1990); 3,063 (1980)   **Pop Density:** 101.2
Land: 28.1 sq. mi.; **Water:** 0.1 sq. mi.

Hanaford   Village
     Lat: 37-57-30 N   **Long:** 88-50-07 W
Pop: 380 (1990); 328 (1980)   **Pop Density:** 380.0
Land: 1.0 sq. mi.; **Water:** 0.0 sq. mi.

ILLINOIS, Franklin County

Macedonia
Village
Lat: 38-03-08 N Long: 88-42-28 W
Pop: 25 (1990); 23 (1980) **Pop Density:** 250.0
Land: 0.1 sq. mi.; **Water:** 0.0 sq. mi.
Part of the town is also in Hamilton County.

North City
Village
Lat: 37-59-28 N Long: 89-03-41 W
Pop: 538 (1990); 404 (1980) **Pop Density:** 336.3
Land: 1.6 sq. mi.; **Water:** 0.0 sq. mi.

Northern
Township
Lat: 38-05-07 N Long: 88-45-30 W
Pop: 393 (1990); 433 (1980) **Pop Density:** 10.7
Land: 36.6 sq. mi.; **Water:** 0.0 sq. mi.

Orient
City
Lat: 37-54-59 N Long: 88-58-31 W
Pop: 428 (1990); 480 (1980) **Pop Density:** 713.3
Land: 0.6 sq. mi.; **Water:** 0.0 sq. mi.

Royalton
Town
ZIP: 62983 Lat: 37-52-39 N Long: 89-06-48 W
Pop: 1,191 (1990); 1,320 (1980) **Pop Density:** 1082.7
Land: 1.1 sq. mi.; **Water:** 0.0 sq. mi. **Elev:** 391 ft.

Sesser
Town
ZIP: 62884 Lat: 38-05-24 N Long: 89-03-01 W
Pop: 2,087 (1990); 2,238 (1980) **Pop Density:** 2087.0
Land: 1.0 sq. mi.; **Water:** 0.0 sq. mi.
Name origin: For railroad surveyor John Sesser.

Six Mile
Township
Lat: 37-54-37 N Long: 89-05-26 W
Pop: 3,846 (1990); 4,088 (1980) **Pop Density:** 105.1
Land: 36.6 sq. mi.; **Water:** 0.3 sq. mi.

Thompsonville
Village
ZIP: 62890 Lat: 37-54-50 N Long: 88-45-42 W
Pop: 602 (1990); 610 (1980) **Pop Density:** 301.0
Land: 2.0 sq. mi.; **Water:** 0.0 sq. mi.

Tyrone
Township
ZIP: 62822 Lat: 37-59-33 N Long: 89-05-34 W
Pop: 5,238 (1990); 5,629 (1980) **Pop Density:** 147.1
Land: 35.6 sq. mi.; **Water:** 0.2 sq. mi.

Valier
Town
ZIP: 62891 Lat: 38-01-03 N Long: 89-02-36 W
Pop: 708 (1990); 729 (1980) **Pop Density:** 643.6
Land: 1.1 sq. mi.; **Water:** 0.0 sq. mi.

West City
Village
ZIP: 62812 Lat: 37-59-45 N Long: 88-56-55 W
Pop: 747 (1990); 886 (1980) **Pop Density:** 466.9
Land: 1.6 sq. mi.; **Water:** 0.0 sq. mi.

West Frankfort
City
ZIP: 62896 Lat: 37-54-02 N Long: 88-55-45 W
Pop: 8,526 (1990); 9,437 (1980) **Pop Density:** 2030.0
Land: 4.2 sq. mi.; **Water:** 0.0 sq. mi. **Elev:** 401 ft.
Incorporated Mar 16, 1901.

Zeigler
Town
ZIP: 62999 Lat: 37-53-59 N Long: 89-03-09 W
Pop: 1,746 (1990); 1,858 (1980) **Pop Density:** 1940.0
Land: 0.9 sq. mi.; **Water:** 0.0 sq. mi.
Name origin: For the Zeigler Coal Company.

Fulton County
County Seat: Lewistown (ZIP: 61542)

Pop: 38,080 (1990); 43,687 (1980) **Pop Density:** 44.0
Land: 865.7 sq. mi.; **Water:** 17.0 sq. mi. **Area Code:** 309
In north-central IL, southwest of Peoria; organized Jan 18, 1823 from Pike County.
Name origin: For Robert Fulton (1765–1815), builder of the *Clermont*, the first commercially successful steamboat.

Astoria
Town
ZIP: 61501 Lat: 40-13-41 N Long: 90-21-21 W
Pop: 1,205 (1990); 1,370 (1980) **Pop Density:** 2008.3
Land: 0.6 sq. mi.; **Water:** 0.0 sq. mi.
Not coextensive with the town of the same name.
Name origin: For John Jacob Astor.

*Astoria
Township
ZIP: 61501 Lat: 40-13-53 N Long: 90-23-57 W
Pop: 1,608 (1990); 1,844 (1980) **Pop Density:** 44.4
Land: 36.2 sq. mi.; **Water:** 0.4 sq. mi.

Avon
Village
ZIP: 61415 Lat: 40-39-43 N Long: 90-26-07 W
Pop: 957 (1990); 1,019 (1980) **Pop Density:** 2392.5
Land: 0.4 sq. mi.; **Water:** 0.0 sq. mi.
Founded 1852.
Name origin: For the English river.

Banner
Village
ZIP: 61520 Lat: 40-30-52 N Long: 89-54-37 W
Pop: 160 (1990); 224 (1980) **Pop Density:** 533.3
Land: 0.3 sq. mi.; **Water:** 0.0 sq. mi. **Elev:** 475 ft.
Not coextensive with the town of the same name.

*Banner
Township
Lat: 40-29-49 N Long: 89-56-03 W
Pop: 424 (1990); 580 (1980) **Pop Density:** 14.9
Land: 28.5 sq. mi.; **Water:** 5.6 sq. mi.

Bernadotte
Township
Lat: 40-24-24 N Long: 90-16-14 W
Pop: 313 (1990); 409 (1980) **Pop Density:** 8.3
Land: 37.7 sq. mi.; **Water:** 0.0 sq. mi.

Bryant
Village
ZIP: 61519 Lat: 40-27-55 N Long: 90-05-40 W
Pop: 273 (1990); 333 (1980) **Pop Density:** 910.0
Land: 0.3 sq. mi.; **Water:** 0.0 sq. mi.

ILLINOIS, Fulton County

Buckheart — Township
Lat: 40-29-44 N Long: 90-02-53 W
Pop: 1,577 (1990); 1,885 (1980)   Pop Density: 45.4
Land: 34.7 sq. mi.; Water: 1.0 sq. mi.

Canton — City
ZIP: 61520   Lat: 40-33-45 N Long: 90-02-24 W
Pop: 13,922 (1990); 14,626 (1980)   Pop Density: 1907.1
Land: 7.3 sq. mi.; Water: 0.2 sq. mi.

In west-central IL, 25 mi. southwest of Peoria. Settled 1825 by Isaac Swan, a native New Yorker who surveyed out a number of lots here. Incorporated Feb 8, 1849. Not coextensive with the town of the same name.
Name origin: Named by Swan, who believed it to be exactly opposite, globally, from Canton, China.

***Canton** — Township
ZIP: 61520   Lat: 40-34-53 N Long: 90-02-47 W
Pop: 14,880 (1990); 16,065 (1980)   Pop Density: 428.8
Land: 34.7 sq. mi.; Water: 0.9 sq. mi.

Cass — Township
Lat: 40-29-40 N Long: 90-16-54 W
Pop: 647 (1990); 863 (1980)   Pop Density: 16.4
Land: 39.4 sq. mi.; Water: 0.1 sq. mi.

Cuba — City
ZIP: 61427   Lat: 40-29-36 N Long: 90-11-35 W
Pop: 1,440 (1990); 1,648 (1980)   Pop Density: 2880.0
Land: 0.5 sq. mi.; Water: 0.0 sq. mi.
Name origin: For the country in the Caribbean.

Deerfield — Township
Lat: 40-34-38 N Long: 90-15-31 W
Pop: 343 (1990); 448 (1980)   Pop Density: 10.0
Land: 34.2 sq. mi.; Water: 0.2 sq. mi.

Dunfermline — Village
ZIP: 61524   Lat: 40-29-27 N Long: 90-01-57 W
Pop: 259 (1990); 313 (1980)   Pop Density: 2590.0
Land: 0.1 sq. mi.; Water: 0.0 sq. mi.

Ellisville — Village
Lat: 40-37-37 N Long: 90-18-20 W
Pop: 116 (1990); 168 (1980)   Pop Density: 386.7
Land: 0.3 sq. mi.; Water: 0.0 sq. mi.
Not coextensive with the town of the same name.

***Ellisville** — Township
Lat: 40-39-49 N Long: 90-18-02 W
Pop: 222 (1990); 309 (1980)   Pop Density: 16.0
Land: 13.9 sq. mi.; Water: 0.0 sq. mi.

Fairview — Village
ZIP: 61432   Lat: 40-39-01 N Long: 90-11-27 W
Pop: 510 (1990); 594 (1980)   Pop Density: 121.4
Land: 4.2 sq. mi.; Water: 0.1 sq. mi.
Not coextensive with the town of the same name.

***Fairview** — Township
Lat: 40-40-08 N Long: 90-09-01 W
Pop: 702 (1990); 864 (1980)   Pop Density: 19.7
Land: 35.6 sq. mi.; Water: 0.4 sq. mi.

Farmers — Township
Lat: 40-24-47 N Long: 90-23-51 W
Pop: 429 (1990); 520 (1980)   Pop Density: 11.9
Land: 36.1 sq. mi.; Water: 0.1 sq. mi.

Farmington — City
ZIP: 61531   Lat: 40-41-51 N Long: 90-00-24 W
Pop: 2,535 (1990); 3,118 (1980)   Pop Density: 2112.5
Land: 1.2 sq. mi.; Water: 0.0 sq. mi.   Elev: 752 ft.
Not coextensive with the town of the same name.

***Farmington** — Township
Lat: 40-39-50 N Long: 90-03-17 W
Pop: 3,469 (1990); 4,184 (1980)   Pop Density: 97.4
Land: 35.6 sq. mi.; Water: 0.2 sq. mi.

Harris — Township
Lat: 40-29-59 N Long: 90-23-32 W
Pop: 421 (1990); 545 (1980)   Pop Density: 12.3
Land: 34.2 sq. mi.; Water: 0.2 sq. mi.

Ipava — Village
ZIP: 61441   Lat: 40-21-07 N Long: 90-19-23 W
Pop: 483 (1990); 661 (1980)   Pop Density: 1610.0
Land: 0.3 sq. mi.; Water: 0.0 sq. mi.

Isabel — Township
Lat: 40-18-26 N Long: 90-09-46 W
Pop: 247 (1990); 299 (1980)   Pop Density: 8.5
Land: 29.2 sq. mi.; Water: 0.1 sq. mi.

Joshua — Township
Lat: 40-34-49 N Long: 90-09-28 W
Pop: 495 (1990); 601 (1980)   Pop Density: 14.2
Land: 34.8 sq. mi.; Water: 0.7 sq. mi.

Kerton — Township
Lat: 40-14-29 N Long: 90-10-54 W
Pop: 123 (1990); 176 (1980)   Pop Density: 5.1
Land: 24.3 sq. mi.; Water: 2.6 sq. mi.

Lee — Township
Lat: 40-35-14 N Long: 90-23-31 W
Pop: 310 (1990); 393 (1980)   Pop Density: 8.3
Land: 37.2 sq. mi.; Water: 0.0 sq. mi.

Lewistown — City
ZIP: 61542   Lat: 40-23-48 N Long: 90-09-19 W
Pop: 2,572 (1990); 2,758 (1980)   Pop Density: 1428.9
Land: 1.8 sq. mi.; Water: 0.0 sq. mi.
Not coextensive with the town of the same name.

***Lewistown** — Township
Lat: 40-24-37 N Long: 90-09-33 W
Pop: 3,243 (1990); 3,547 (1980)   Pop Density: 91.4
Land: 35.5 sq. mi.; Water: 0.0 sq. mi.

Liverpool — Village
ZIP: 61543   Lat: 40-23-25 N Long: 90-00-05 W
Pop: 129 (1990); 243 (1980)   Pop Density: 1290.0
Land: 0.1 sq. mi.; Water: 0.0 sq. mi.
Not coextensive with the town of the same name.

***Liverpool** — Township
Lat: 40-24-44 N Long: 90-02-07 W
Pop: 730 (1990); 924 (1980)   Pop Density: 18.1
Land: 40.3 sq. mi.; Water: 1.8 sq. mi.

London Mills — Town
ZIP: 61544   Lat: 40-42-33 N Long: 90-16-06 W
Pop: 473 (1990); 569 (1980)   Pop Density: 788.3
Land: 0.6 sq. mi.; Water: 0.0 sq. mi.   Elev: 533 ft.
Incorporated November 27, 1883. Part of the town is also in Knox County.

ILLINOIS, Fulton County

Marietta
Village
ZIP: 61459   **Lat:** 40-29-59 N   **Long:** 90-23-32 W
Pop: 142 (1990); 192 (1980)   **Pop Density:** 473.3
Land: 0.3 sq. mi.; **Water:** 0.0 sq. mi.

Norris
Village
ZIP: 61553   **Lat:** 40-37-31 N   **Long:** 90-01-53 W
Pop: 212 (1990); 276 (1980)   **Pop Density:** 706.7
Land: 0.3 sq. mi.; **Water:** 0.0 sq. mi.

Orion
Township
Lat: 40-35-02 N   **Long:** 89-55-52 W
Pop: 1,105 (1990); 1,313 (1980)   **Pop Density:** 30.3
Land: 36.5 sq. mi.; **Water:** 0.4 sq. mi.

Pleasant
Township
Lat: 40-19-07 N   **Long:** 90-16-29 W
Pop: 839 (1990); 1,038 (1980)   **Pop Density:** 22.6
Land: 37.2 sq. mi.; **Water:** 0.0 sq. mi.

Putman
Township
Lat: 40-29-35 N   **Long:** 90-09-36 W
Pop: 2,169 (1990); 2,479 (1980)   **Pop Density:** 64.6
Land: 33.6 sq. mi.; **Water:** 1.6 sq. mi.

St. David
Village
Lat: 40-29-31 N   **Long:** 90-03-04 W
Pop: 603 (1990); 786 (1980)   **Pop Density:** 2010.0
Land: 0.3 sq. mi.; **Water:** 0.0 sq. mi.   **Elev:** 630 ft.

Smithfield
Village
ZIP: 61477   **Lat:** 40-28-27 N   **Long:** 90-17-42 W
Pop: 277 (1990); 340 (1980)   **Pop Density:** 554.0
Land: 0.5 sq. mi.; **Water:** 0.0 sq. mi.

Table Grove
Village
ZIP: 61482   **Lat:** 40-21-56 N   **Long:** 90-25-29 W
Pop: 408 (1990); 489 (1980)   **Pop Density:** 1360.0
Land: 0.3 sq. mi.; **Water:** 0.0 sq. mi.   **Elev:** 734 ft.

Union
Township
Lat: 40-39-50 N   **Long:** 90-23-45 W
Pop: 1,205 (1990); 1,332 (1980)   **Pop Density:** 32.9
Land: 36.6 sq. mi.; **Water:** 0.0 sq. mi.

Vermont
Town
ZIP: 61484   **Lat:** 40-17-45 N   **Long:** 90-25-41 W
Pop: 806 (1990); 885 (1980)   **Pop Density:** 620.0
Land: 1.3 sq. mi.; **Water:** 0.0 sq. mi.   **Elev:** 697 ft.
Not coextensive with the town of the same name.
Name origin: For the state.

*Vermont
Township
Lat: 40-19-10 N   **Long:** 90-23-30 W
Pop: 1,112 (1990); 1,276 (1980)   **Pop Density:** 30.3
Land: 36.7 sq. mi.; **Water:** 0.1 sq. mi.

Waterford
Township
Lat: 40-20-49 N   **Long:** 90-06-36 W
Pop: 236 (1990); 316 (1980)   **Pop Density:** 11.2
Land: 21.0 sq. mi.; **Water:** 0.2 sq. mi.

Woodland
Township
Lat: 40-13-38 N   **Long:** 90-16-35 W
Pop: 485 (1990); 603 (1980)   **Pop Density:** 12.8
Land: 38.0 sq. mi.; **Water:** 0.2 sq. mi.

Young Hickory
Township
Lat: 40-40-26 N   **Long:** 90-14-57 W
Pop: 746 (1990); 874 (1980)   **Pop Density:** 30.8
Land: 24.2 sq. mi.; **Water:** 0.0 sq. mi.

Gallatin County
County Seat: Shawneetown (ZIP: 62984)

Pop: 6,909 (1990); 7,590 (1980)   **Pop Density:** 21.3
Land: 323.7 sq. mi.; **Water:** 4.7 sq. mi.   **Area Code:** 618

On the southeast border of IL; organized Sep 14, 1812 (prior to statehood) from Randolph County.

Name origin: For Abraham Alfonse Albert Gallatin (1761–1849), Swiss-born U.S. representative from PA (1795–1801), U.S. secretary of treasury (1801–14), and U.S. minister to France (1815–23) and to Great Britain (1826–27).

Asbury
Township
Lat: 37-53-16 N   **Long:** 88-12-45 W
Pop: 158 (1990); 174 (1980)   **Pop Density:** 8.8
Land: 17.9 sq. mi.; **Water:** 0.0 sq. mi.

Bowlesville
Township
Lat: 37-38-42 N   **Long:** 88-12-49 W
Pop: 216 (1990); 211 (1980)   **Pop Density:** 5.6
Land: 38.8 sq. mi.; **Water:** 1.1 sq. mi.

Eagle Creek
Township
Lat: 37-38-30 N   **Long:** 88-19-33 W
Pop: 207 (1990); 191 (1980)   **Pop Density:** 5.6
Land: 37.1 sq. mi.; **Water:** 0.2 sq. mi.

Equality
Village
ZIP: 62934   **Lat:** 37-44-09 N   **Long:** 88-20-35 W
Pop: 748 (1990); 831 (1980)   **Pop Density:** 831.1
Land: 0.9 sq. mi.; **Water:** 0.0 sq. mi.
Not coextensive with the town of the same name.

*Equality
Township
Lat: 37-44-02 N   **Long:** 88-18-49 W
Pop: 1,023 (1990); 1,137 (1980)   **Pop Density:** 27.6
Land: 37.0 sq. mi.; **Water:** 0.3 sq. mi.

Gold Hill
Township
Lat: 37-44-11 N   **Long:** 88-12-42 W
Pop: 2,123 (1990); 2,301 (1980)   **Pop Density:** 60.5
Land: 35.1 sq. mi.; **Water:** 0.1 sq. mi.

American Places Dictionary   ILLINOIS, Greene County

Junction — Village
ZIP: 62954   Lat: 37-43-22 N   Long: 88-14-16 W
Pop: 201 (1990); 192 (1980)   Pop Density: 223.3
Land: 0.9 sq. mi.; Water: 0.0 sq. mi.   Elev: 363 ft.

New Haven — Village
ZIP: 62867   Lat: 37-54-00 N   Long: 88-07-40 W
Pop: 459 (1990); 559 (1980)   Pop Density: 382.5
Land: 1.2 sq. mi.; Water: 0.0 sq. mi.
Not coextensive with the town of the same name.

*New Haven — Township
Lat: 37-50-35 N   Long: 88-05-56 W
Pop: 545 (1990); 654 (1980)   Pop Density: 12.5
Land: 43.7 sq. mi.; Water: 1.8 sq. mi.

North Fork — Township
Lat: 37-49-10 N   Long: 88-19-11 W
Pop: 592 (1990); 633 (1980)   Pop Density: 16.2
Land: 36.5 sq. mi.; Water: 0.3 sq. mi.

Old Shawneetown — Village
Lat: 37-41-48 N   Long: 88-08-16 W
Pop: 356 (1990); 396 (1980)   Pop Density: 712.0
Land: 0.5 sq. mi.; Water: 0.0 sq. mi.   Elev: 370 ft.

Omaha — Village
ZIP: 62871   Lat: 37-53-23 N   Long: 88-18-15 W
Pop: 273 (1990); 295 (1980)   Pop Density: 341.3
Land: 0.8 sq. mi.; Water: 0.0 sq. mi.
Not coextensive with the town of the same name.

*Omaha — Township
Lat: 37-52-52 N   Long: 88-18-44 W
Pop: 484 (1990); 504 (1980)   Pop Density: 26.0
Land: 18.6 sq. mi.; Water: 0.1 sq. mi.

Ridgway — Town
ZIP: 62979   Lat: 37-47-52 N   Long: 88-15-37 W
Pop: 1,103 (1990); 1,245 (1980)   Pop Density: 1225.6
Land: 0.9 sq. mi.; Water: 0.0 sq. mi.
Not coextensive with the town of the same name.
Name origin: For naturalist Dr. Robert Ridgway (1850–1929).

*Ridgway — Township
Lat: 37-49-13 N   Long: 88-12-48 W
Pop: 1,094 (1990); 1,239 (1980)   Pop Density: 30.7
Land: 35.6 sq. mi.; Water: 0.0 sq. mi.

Shawnee — Township
Lat: 37-44-59 N   Long: 88-06-17 W
Pop: 467 (1990); 546 (1980)   Pop Density: 19.9
Land: 23.5 sq. mi.; Water: 0.8 sq. mi.

Shawneetown — City
ZIP: 62984   Lat: 37-42-46 N   Long: 88-09-55 W
Pop: 1,575 (1990); 1,841 (1980)   Pop Density: 1312.5
Land: 1.2 sq. mi.; Water: 0.0 sq. mi.
Name origin: For the Shawnee Indians.

Greene County
County Seat: Carrollton (ZIP: 62016)

Pop: 15,317 (1990); 16,661 (1980)   Pop Density: 28.2
Land: 543.1 sq. mi.; Water: 3.2 sq. mi.   Area Code: 217
In west-central IL northwest of Alton; organized Jan 20, 1821 from Madison County.
Name origin: For Gen. Nathanael Greene (1742–86), hero of the Revolutionary War, quartermaster general (1778–80), and commander of the Army of the South (1780).

Athensville — Township
Lat: 39-28-54 N   Long: 90-12-19 W
Pop: 391 (1990); 445 (1980)   Pop Density: 11.0
Land: 35.7 sq. mi.; Water: 0.0 sq. mi.

Bluffdale — Township
Lat: 39-18-48 N   Long: 90-33-04 W
Pop: 694 (1990); 742 (1980)   Pop Density: 15.5
Land: 44.7 sq. mi.; Water: 0.8 sq. mi.

Carrollton — City
ZIP: 62016   Lat: 39-17-52 N   Long: 90-24-24 W
Pop: 2,507 (1990); 2,816 (1980)   Pop Density: 1671.3
Land: 1.5 sq. mi.; Water: 0.0 sq. mi.
In western IL, 30 mi. north-northwest of Alton. Settled 1818. Not coextensive with the town of the same name.
Name origin: For Charles Carroll (1737–1832), signer of the Declaration of Independence.

*Carrollton — Township
Lat: 39-18-45 N   Long: 90-25-52 W
Pop: 3,075 (1990); 3,375 (1980)   Pop Density: 69.1
Land: 44.5 sq. mi.; Water: 0.0 sq. mi.

Eldred — Village
ZIP: 62027   Lat: 39-17-10 N   Long: 90-33-11 W
Pop: 254 (1990); 286 (1980)   Pop Density: 2540.0
Land: 0.1 sq. mi.; Water: 0.0 sq. mi.   Elev: 454 ft.

Greenfield — City
ZIP: 62044   Lat: 39-20-39 N   Long: 90-12-27 W
Pop: 1,162 (1990); 1,090 (1980)   Pop Density: 726.3
Land: 1.6 sq. mi.; Water: 0.1 sq. mi.

Hillview — Village
ZIP: 62050   Lat: 39-26-58 N   Long: 90-32-16 W
Pop: 271 (1990); 328 (1980)   Pop Density: 338.8
Land: 0.8 sq. mi.; Water: 0.0 sq. mi.

Kane — Village
ZIP: 62054   Lat: 39-11-25 N   Long: 90-21-04 W
Pop: 456 (1990); 445 (1980)   Pop Density: 912.0
Land: 0.5 sq. mi.; Water: 0.0 sq. mi.
Not coextensive with the town of the same name.

ILLINOIS, Greene County

*Kane
Township
Lat: 39-12-43 N **Long:** 90-23-11 W
Pop: 1,044 (1990); 1,124 (1980) **Pop Density:** 21.3
Land: 49.0 sq. mi.; **Water:** 0.0 sq. mi.

Linder
Township
Lat: 39-17-56 N **Long:** 90-18-44 W
Pop: 300 (1990); 339 (1980) **Pop Density:** 8.7
Land: 34.6 sq. mi.; **Water:** 0.0 sq. mi.

Patterson
Township
Lat: 39-28-57 N **Long:** 90-31-39 W
Pop: 795 (1990); 919 (1980) **Pop Density:** 16.9
Land: 47.1 sq. mi.; **Water:** 0.5 sq. mi.

Rockbridge
Village
ZIP: 62081 **Lat:** 39-16-22 N **Long:** 90-12-32 W
Pop: 212 (1990); 258 (1980) **Pop Density:** 117.8
Land: 1.8 sq. mi.; **Water:** 0.0 sq. mi. **Elev:** 542 ft.
Not coextensive with the town of the same name.

*Rockbridge
Township
Lat: 39-17-18 N **Long:** 90-12-50 W
Pop: 1,797 (1990); 1,833 (1980) **Pop Density:** 37.8
Land: 47.6 sq. mi.; **Water:** 0.1 sq. mi.

Roodhouse
Town
ZIP: 62082 **Lat:** 39-29-04 N **Long:** 90-22-24 W
Pop: 2,139 (1990); 2,364 (1980) **Pop Density:** 1944.5
Land: 1.1 sq. mi.; **Water:** 0.0 sq. mi.
In southwestern IL, 20 mi. south of Jacksonville. Not coextensive with the town of the same name.
Name origin: For its founder, John Roodhouse.

*Roodhouse
Township
Lat: 39-29-41 N **Long:** 90-21-11 W
Pop: 2,542 (1990); 2,827 (1980) **Pop Density:** 64.2
Land: 39.6 sq. mi.; **Water:** 0.0 sq. mi.

Rubicon
Township
Lat: 39-23-48 N **Long:** 90-12-26 W
Pop: 339 (1990); 414 (1980) **Pop Density:** 9.5
Land: 35.8 sq. mi.; **Water:** 0.1 sq. mi.

Walkerville
Township
Lat: 39-23-29 N **Long:** 90-33-01 W
Pop: 244 (1990); 285 (1980) **Pop Density:** 6.3
Land: 39.0 sq. mi.; **Water:** 0.6 sq. mi.

White Hall
Town
ZIP: 62092 **Lat:** 39-26-14 N **Long:** 90-24-14 W
Pop: 2,814 (1990); 2,935 (1980) **Pop Density:** 1172.5
Land: 2.4 sq. mi.; **Water:** 0.0 sq. mi.
Founded 1820. Not coextensive with the town of the same name.
Name origin: For the home of an early postmaster.

*White Hall
Township
Lat: 39-25-20 N **Long:** 90-23-44 W
Pop: 3,296 (1990); 3,425 (1980) **Pop Density:** 78.3
Land: 42.1 sq. mi.; **Water:** 0.1 sq. mi.

Wilmington
Village
Lat: 39-28-56 N **Long:** 90-29-22 W
Pop: 129 (1990); 185 (1980) **Pop Density:** 161.3
Land: 0.8 sq. mi.; **Water:** 0.0 sq. mi.

Woodville
Township
Lat: 39-12-25 N **Long:** 90-31-41 W
Pop: 454 (1990); 522 (1980) **Pop Density:** 9.6
Land: 47.5 sq. mi.; **Water:** 0.8 sq. mi.

Wrights
Township
Lat: 39-23-20 N **Long:** 90-19-13 W
Pop: 346 (1990); 411 (1980) **Pop Density:** 9.6
Land: 35.9 sq. mi.; **Water:** 0.0 sq. mi.

Grundy County
County Seat: Morris (ZIP: 60450)

Pop: 32,337 (1990); 30,582 (1980) **Pop Density:** 77.0
Land: 420.1 sq. mi.; **Water:** 10.3 sq. mi. **Area Code:** 815
In northeast IL, southwest of Chicago; established Feb 17, 1841 from La Salle County.
Name origin: For Felix Grundy (1777–1840), chief justice of KY Supreme Court, U.S. senator from TN (1829–38; 1839–40), and U.S. Attorney General (1838–39).

Aux Sable
Township
Lat: 41-25-20 N **Long:** 88-18-39 W
Pop: 3,284 (1990); 2,767 (1980) **Pop Density:** 113.2
Land: 29.0 sq. mi.; **Water:** 1.3 sq. mi.

Braceville
Village
ZIP: 60407 **Lat:** 41-13-27 N **Long:** 88-15-58 W
Pop: 587 (1990); 721 (1980) **Pop Density:** 451.5
Land: 1.3 sq. mi.; **Water:** 0.0 sq. mi.
Not coextensive with the town of the same name.

*Braceville
Township
Lat: 41-14-43 N **Long:** 88-16-35 W
Pop: 3,637 (1990); 3,637 (1980) **Pop Density:** 202.1
Land: 18.0 sq. mi.; **Water:** 0.1 sq. mi.

Carbon Hill
Village
ZIP: 60416 **Lat:** 41-17-46 N **Long:** 88-17-58 W
Pop: 362 (1990); 406 (1980) **Pop Density:** 1810.0
Land: 0.2 sq. mi.; **Water:** 0.0 sq. mi.

Channahon
Village
ZIP: 60410 **Lat:** 41-24-00 N **Long:** 88-16-35 W
Pop: 0 (1990); 3,788 (1980)
Land: 0.1 sq. mi.; **Water:** 0.2 sq. mi.
Part of the town is also in Will County.
Name origin: From an Indian term probably meaning 'meeting of the waters,' referring to the confluence of the Illinois and Kankakee rivers.

Coal City
City
ZIP: 60416 Lat: 41-17-17 N Long: 88-16-41 W
Pop: 3,907 (1990); 3,028 (1980) Pop Density: 1860.5
Land: 2.1 sq. mi.; Water: 0.0 sq. mi.

In northeastern IL, 21 mi. south-southwest of Joliet. Founded 1875 as a site for bituminous coal mining.

Diamond
Village
ZIP: 60416 Lat: 41-17-19 N Long: 88-15-25 W
Pop: 1,077 (1990); 1,170 (1980) Pop Density: 2154.0
Land: 0.5 sq. mi.; Water: 0.0 sq. mi.

Part of the town is also in Will County.

Dwight
Village
ZIP: 60420 Lat: 41-06-47 N Long: 88-25-05 W
Pop: 0 (1990); 29 (1980)
Land: 0.3 sq. mi.; Water: 0.0 sq. mi. Elev: 640 ft.

Founded in 1854. Part of the town is also in Livingston County.
Name origin: Named for a civil engineer who worked on the nearby railroad.

East Brooklyn
Village
ZIP: 60474 Lat: 41-10-20 N Long: 88-15-56 W
Pop: 80 (1990); 84 (1980) Pop Density: 1600.0
Land: 0.05 sq. mi.; Water: 0.0 sq. mi.

Erienna
Township
Lat: 41-20-58 N Long: 88-31-37 W
Pop: 924 (1990); 609 (1980) Pop Density: 44.2
Land: 20.9 sq. mi.; Water: 0.5 sq. mi.

Felix
Township
Lat: 41-18-39 N Long: 88-16-42 W
Pop: 3,869 (1990); 3,721 (1980) Pop Density: 339.4
Land: 11.4 sq. mi.; Water: 0.7 sq. mi.

Gardner
Town
ZIP: 60424 Lat: 41-11-15 N Long: 88-18-43 W
Pop: 1,237 (1990); 1,322 (1980) Pop Density: 1237.0
Land: 1.0 sq. mi.; Water: 0.0 sq. mi.

Garfield
Township
Lat: 41-09-46 N Long: 88-19-45 W
Pop: 1,404 (1990); 1,520 (1980) Pop Density: 77.1
Land: 18.2 sq. mi.; Water: 0.0 sq. mi.

Godley
Village
Lat: 41-14-16 N Long: 88-15-01 W
Pop: 50 (1990); 51 (1980) Pop Density: 100.0
Land: 0.5 sq. mi.; Water: 0.0 sq. mi.

Part of the town is also in Will County.

Goodfarm
Township
Lat: 41-09-11 N Long: 88-24-49 W
Pop: 324 (1990); 408 (1980) Pop Density: 9.1
Land: 35.8 sq. mi.; Water: 0.0 sq. mi.

Goose Lake
Township
Lat: 41-21-18 N Long: 88-18-39 W
Pop: 1,483 (1990); 1,236 (1980) Pop Density: 60.0
Land: 24.7 sq. mi.; Water: 5.3 sq. mi.

Greenfield
Township
Lat: 41-09-32 N Long: 88-16-25 W
Pop: 969 (1990); 1,030 (1980) Pop Density: 54.7
Land: 17.7 sq. mi.; Water: 0.4 sq. mi.

Highland
Township
Lat: 41-09-13 N Long: 88-32-07 W
Pop: 363 (1990); 431 (1980) Pop Density: 10.1
Land: 36.0 sq. mi.; Water: 0.0 sq. mi.

Kinsman
Village
ZIP: 60437 Lat: 41-11-26 N Long: 88-34-11 W
Pop: 112 (1990); 153 (1980) Pop Density: 1120.0
Land: 0.1 sq. mi.; Water: 0.0 sq. mi.

Maine
Township
Lat: 41-14-39 N Long: 88-19-54 W
Pop: 222 (1990); 216 (1980) Pop Density: 12.3
Land: 18.0 sq. mi.; Water: 0.0 sq. mi.

Mazon
Town
ZIP: 60444 Lat: 41-14-22 N Long: 88-25-29 W
Pop: 764 (1990); 828 (1980) Pop Density: 1910.0
Land: 0.4 sq. mi.; Water: 0.0 sq. mi. Elev: 586 ft.

Incorporated April 30, 1895. Not coextensive with the town of the same name.

*Mazon
Township
Lat: 41-14-28 N Long: 88-25-03 W
Pop: 1,287 (1990); 1,406 (1980) Pop Density: 36.3
Land: 35.5 sq. mi.; Water: 0.0 sq. mi.

Minooka
Town
ZIP: 60447 Lat: 41-27-21 N Long: 88-15-49 W
Pop: 1,757 (1990); 1,427 (1980) Pop Density: 1464.2
Land: 1.2 sq. mi.; Water: 0.0 sq. mi.

Incorporated Mar 27, 1869. Part of the town is also in Will County.
Name origin: From the Delaware term *mino* meaning 'good' and *oki* meaning 'land.'

Morris
City
ZIP: 60450 Lat: 41-22-07 N Long: 88-25-39 W
Pop: 10,270 (1990); 8,833 (1980) Pop Density: 1867.3
Land: 5.5 sq. mi.; Water: 0.3 sq. mi. Elev: 519 ft.

In northeastern IL on the Illinois River, 20 mi. southwest of Joliet. Incorporated Feb 12, 1853. Not coextensive with the town of the same name.
Name origin: For Isaac N. Morris, a commissioner for the Illinois and Michigan Canal (1848).

*Morris
Township
ZIP: 60450 Lat: 41-21-51 N Long: 88-24-26 W
Pop: 7,876 (1990); 7,337 (1980) Pop Density: 2187.8
Land: 3.6 sq. mi.; Water: 0.3 sq. mi.

Nettle Creek
Township
Lat: 41-24-40 N Long: 88-32-52 W
Pop: 345 (1990); 366 (1980) Pop Density: 9.6
Land: 35.8 sq. mi.; Water: 0.0 sq. mi.

Norman
Township
Lat: 41-18-03 N Long: 88-31-30 W
Pop: 213 (1990); 200 (1980) Pop Density: 12.5
Land: 17.0 sq. mi.; Water: 0.5 sq. mi.

Saratoga
Township
Lat: 41-24-36 N Long: 88-25-14 W
Pop: 3,181 (1990); 2,695 (1980) Pop Density: 88.1
Land: 36.1 sq. mi.; Water: 0.1 sq. mi.

ILLINOIS, Grundy County

Seneca
Town
Lat: 41-18-23 N **Long:** 88-35-18 W
Pop: 0 (1990); 2,098 (1980)
Land: 0.03 sq. mi.; **Water:** 0.0 sq. mi.
Part of the town is also in La Salle County.
Name origin: For the Seneca Indians.

South Wilmington
Village
ZIP: 60474 **Lat:** 41-10-27 N **Long:** 88-16-34 W
Pop: 698 (1990); 747 (1980) **Pop Density:** 2326.7
Land: 0.3 sq. mi.; **Water:** 0.0 sq. mi.

Verona
Village
ZIP: 60479 **Lat:** 41-12-56 N **Long:** 88-30-18 W
Pop: 242 (1990); 251 (1980) **Pop Density:** 2420.0
Land: 0.1 sq. mi.; **Water:** 0.0 sq. mi.

Vienna
Township
Lat: 41-14-41 N **Long:** 88-31-54 W
Pop: 556 (1990); 613 (1980) **Pop Density:** 15.6
Land: 35.6 sq. mi.; **Water:** 0.0 sq. mi.

Wauponsee
Township
Lat: 41-19-16 N **Long:** 88-25-07 W
Pop: 2,400 (1990); 2,390 (1980) **Pop Density:** 88.9
Land: 27.0 sq. mi.; **Water:** 0.9 sq. mi.

Hamilton County
County Seat: McLeansboro (ZIP: 62859)

Pop: 8,499 (1990); 9,172 (1980) **Pop Density:** 19.5
Land: 435.2 sq. mi.; **Water:** 0.7 sq. mi. **Area Code:** 618
In southeastern IL northeast of Carbondale; organized Feb 8, 1821 from White County.

Name origin: For Alexander Hamilton (1757–1804), first U.S. secretary of the treasury (1789–95).

Beaver Creek
Township
Lat: 38-10-21 N **Long:** 88-25-37 W
Pop: 286 (1990); 346 (1980) **Pop Density:** 7.9
Land: 36.4 sq. mi.; **Water:** 0.0 sq. mi.

Belle Prairie City
Town
Lat: 38-13-23 N **Long:** 88-33-05 W
Pop: 64 (1990); 58 (1980) **Pop Density:** 160.0
Land: 0.4 sq. mi.; **Water:** 0.0 sq. mi.

Broughton
Village
ZIP: 62817 **Lat:** 37-56-02 N **Long:** 88-27-40 W
Pop: 218 (1990); 263 (1980) **Pop Density:** 114.7
Land: 1.9 sq. mi.; **Water:** 0.0 sq. mi. **Elev:** 378 ft.

Crook
Township
Lat: 38-04-42 N **Long:** 88-25-59 W
Pop: 366 (1990); 429 (1980) **Pop Density:** 10.2
Land: 35.8 sq. mi.; **Water:** 0.1 sq. mi.

Crouch
Township
Lat: 38-13-32 N **Long:** 88-30-02 W
Pop: 395 (1990); 482 (1980) **Pop Density:** 8.3
Land: 47.5 sq. mi.; **Water:** 0.0 sq. mi.

Dahlgren
Village
ZIP: 62828 **Lat:** 38-11-54 N **Long:** 88-41-02 W
Pop: 512 (1990); 508 (1980) **Pop Density:** 512.0
Land: 1.0 sq. mi.; **Water:** 0.0 sq. mi.
Not coextensive with the town of the same name.

*Dahlgren
Township
Lat: 38-11-08 N **Long:** 88-38-28 W
Pop: 1,232 (1990); 1,178 (1980) **Pop Density:** 22.7
Land: 54.3 sq. mi.; **Water:** 0.1 sq. mi.

Flannigan
Township
Lat: 37-59-44 N **Long:** 88-38-56 W
Pop: 258 (1990); 254 (1980) **Pop Density:** 7.1
Land: 36.2 sq. mi.; **Water:** 0.1 sq. mi.

Knight Prairie
Township
Lat: 38-04-37 N **Long:** 88-39-30 W
Pop: 490 (1990); 498 (1980) **Pop Density:** 13.4
Land: 36.5 sq. mi.; **Water:** 0.0 sq. mi.

Macedonia
Village
Lat: 38-03-07 N **Long:** 88-42-07 W
Pop: 33 (1990); 47 (1980) **Pop Density:** 330.0
Land: 0.1 sq. mi.; **Water:** 0.0 sq. mi.
Part of the town is also in Franklin County.

Mayberry
Township
Lat: 37-58-42 N **Long:** 88-25-46 W
Pop: 548 (1990); 585 (1980) **Pop Density:** 10.0
Land: 54.7 sq. mi.; **Water:** 0.0 sq. mi.

McLeansboro
City
ZIP: 62859 **Lat:** 38-05-32 N **Long:** 88-31-58 W
Pop: 2,677 (1990); 2,960 (1980) **Pop Density:** 1274.8
Land: 2.1 sq. mi.; **Water:** 0.0 sq. mi.
Not coextensive with the town of the same name.

*McLeansboro
Township
Lat: 38-04-51 N **Long:** 88-32-27 W
Pop: 3,728 (1990); 4,022 (1980) **Pop Density:** 104.4
Land: 35.7 sq. mi.; **Water:** 0.3 sq. mi.

South Crouch
Township
Lat: 38-09-23 N **Long:** 88-31-33 W
Pop: 263 (1990); 328 (1980) **Pop Density:** 10.5
Land: 25.1 sq. mi.; **Water:** 0.0 sq. mi.

South Flannigan
Township
Lat: 37-55-49 N **Long:** 88-39-19 W
Pop: 155 (1990); 158 (1980) **Pop Density:** 8.4
Land: 18.4 sq. mi.; **Water:** 0.0 sq. mi.

South Twigg Township
Lat: 37-55-50 N Long: 88-31-59 W
Pop: 184 (1990); 200 (1980) Pop Density: 10.0
Land: 18.4 sq. mi.; Water: 0.0 sq. mi.

Twigg Township
Lat: 37-59-42 N Long: 88-32-26 W
Pop: 594 (1990); 692 (1980) Pop Density: 16.4
Land: 36.3 sq. mi.; Water: 0.0 sq. mi.

Hancock County
County Seat: Carthage (ZIP: 62321)

Pop: 21,373 (1990); 23,877 (1980) Pop Density: 26.9
Land: 794.7 sq. mi.; Water: 19.9 sq. mi. Area Code: 217

On the west-central border of IL north of Quincy; organized Jan 13, 1825 from Pike County and unorganized territory.

Name origin: For John Hancock (1737–93), noted signer of the Declaration of Independence, governor of MA (1780–85; 1787–93), and statesman.

Appanoose Township
Lat: 40-35-24 N Long: 91-17-54 W
Pop: 672 (1990); 730 (1980) Pop Density: 26.4
Land: 25.5 sq. mi.; Water: 4.8 sq. mi.

Augusta Village
ZIP: 62311 Lat: 40-13-51 N Long: 90-56-56 W
Pop: 614 (1990); 764 (1980) Pop Density: 877.1
Land: 0.7 sq. mi.; Water: 0.0 sq. mi. Elev: 668 ft.
Founded 1834; incorporated 1859. Not coextensive with the town of the same name.

*Augusta Township
Lat: 40-13-58 N Long: 90-58-18 W
Pop: 867 (1990); 997 (1980) Pop Density: 22.9
Land: 37.9 sq. mi.; Water: 0.1 sq. mi.

Basco Village
ZIP: 62313 Lat: 40-19-36 N Long: 91-11-56 W
Pop: 99 (1990); 155 (1980) Pop Density: 495.0
Land: 0.2 sq. mi.; Water: 0.0 sq. mi.

Bear Creek Township
Lat: 40-19-42 N Long: 91-11-54 W
Pop: 399 (1990); 454 (1980) Pop Density: 11.0
Land: 36.4 sq. mi.; Water: 0.0 sq. mi.

Bentley Town
Lat: 40-20-40 N Long: 91-06-39 W
Pop: 36 (1990); 49 (1980) Pop Density: 360.0
Land: 0.1 sq. mi.; Water: 0.0 sq. mi.

Bowen Village
ZIP: 62316 Lat: 40-13-55 N Long: 91-03-48 W
Pop: 462 (1990); 525 (1980) Pop Density: 1155.0
Land: 0.4 sq. mi.; Water: 0.0 sq. mi.

Carthage City
ZIP: 62321 Lat: 40-24-51 N Long: 91-08-06 W
Pop: 2,657 (1990); 2,978 (1980) Pop Density: 1660.6
Land: 1.6 sq. mi.; Water: 0.0 sq. mi.
Laid out 1833. Not coextensive with the town of the same name.
Name origin: For the ancient Phoenician city in northern Africa.

*Carthage Township
Lat: 40-24-53 N Long: 91-05-21 W
Pop: 3,122 (1990); 3,495 (1980) Pop Density: 77.5
Land: 40.3 sq. mi.; Water: 0.1 sq. mi.

Chili Township
Lat: 40-14-40 N Long: 91-05-18 W
Pop: 693 (1990); 773 (1980) Pop Density: 18.3
Land: 37.8 sq. mi.; Water: 0.0 sq. mi.

Dallas City City
ZIP: 62330 Lat: 40-37-51 N Long: 91-09-56 W
Pop: 840 (1990); 1,107 (1980) Pop Density: 466.7
Land: 1.8 sq. mi.; Water: 0.1 sq. mi.
Settled 1836; platted 1848; incorporated 1859. Part of the city is in Henderson County. Not coextensive with the township of the same name.
Name origin: For George M. Dallas (1792–1864), vice president under James K. Polk (1845–1849).

*Dallas City Township
Lat: 40-35-43 N Long: 91-09-41 W
Pop: 1,082 (1990); 1,395 (1980) Pop Density: 70.3
Land: 15.4 sq. mi.; Water: 0.1 sq. mi.

Durham Township
Lat: 40-35-41 N Long: 91-04-23 W
Pop: 333 (1990); 420 (1980) Pop Density: 9.0
Land: 36.9 sq. mi.; Water: 0.0 sq. mi.

Elvaston Village
ZIP: 62334 Lat: 40-23-39 N Long: 91-14-54 W
Pop: 198 (1990); 231 (1980) Pop Density: 247.5
Land: 0.8 sq. mi.; Water: 0.0 sq. mi.

Ferris Village
ZIP: 62336 Lat: 40-28-10 N Long: 91-10-09 W
Pop: 177 (1990); 202 (1980) Pop Density: 88.5
Land: 2.0 sq. mi.; Water: 0.0 sq. mi.

Fountain Green Township
Lat: 40-30-19 N Long: 90-58-25 W
Pop: 381 (1990); 414 (1980) Pop Density: 10.2
Land: 37.4 sq. mi.; Water: 0.0 sq. mi.

Hamilton City
ZIP: 62341 Lat: 40-23-20 N Long: 91-21-47 W
Pop: 3,281 (1990); 3,509 (1980) Pop Density: 911.4
Land: 3.6 sq. mi.; Water: 1.6 sq. mi.

Hancock Township
Lat: 40-24-59 N Long: 90-57-57 W
Pop: 255 (1990); 302 (1980) Pop Density: 6.7
Land: 38.1 sq. mi.; Water: 0.0 sq. mi.

ILLINOIS, Hancock County

Harmony — Township
Lat: 40-19-48 N Long: 91-04-52 W
Pop: 413 (1990); 485 (1980) Pop Density: 11.0
Land: 37.6 sq. mi.; Water: 0.0 sq. mi.

La Harpe — Town
ZIP: 61450 Lat: 40-35-02 N Long: 90-58-12 W
Pop: 1,407 (1990); 1,471 (1980) Pop Density: 1005.0
Land: 1.4 sq. mi.; Water: 0.0 sq. mi. Elev: 697 ft.
Not coextensive with the town of the same name.
Name origin: For founder Benard de la Harpe, who, with a band of French explorers, tried to cross the 100 mi. of trail from Fort Creve Coeur at Peoria to the Mississippi River and was stopped here by storms in the mid 1700s.

*La Harpe — Township
Lat: 40-35-33 N Long: 90-57-48 W
Pop: 1,686 (1990); 1,821 (1980) Pop Density: 45.2
Land: 37.3 sq. mi.; Water: 0.0 sq. mi.

Montebello — Township
Lat: 40-25-00 N Long: 91-18-48 W
Pop: 3,929 (1990); 4,141 (1980) Pop Density: 106.2
Land: 37.0 sq. mi.; Water: 4.2 sq. mi.

Nauvoo — Town
ZIP: 62354 Lat: 40-32-51 N Long: 91-23-05 W
Pop: 1,108 (1990); 1,133 (1980) Pop Density: 325.9
Land: 3.4 sq. mi.; Water: 1.4 sq. mi.
In western IL on the Mississippi River, 45 mi. north of Quincy. Partly coextensive with the township.

*Nauvoo — Township
Lat: 40-33-10 N Long: 91-22-51 W
Pop: 1,108 (1990); 1,260 (1980) Pop Density: 284.1
Land: 3.9 sq. mi.; Water: 2.5 sq. mi.

Pilot Grove — Township
Lat: 40-30-09 N Long: 91-04-45 W
Pop: 339 (1990); 397 (1980) Pop Density: 9.2
Land: 36.9 sq. mi.; Water: 0.1 sq. mi.

Plymouth — Village
ZIP: 62367 Lat: 40-17-28 N Long: 90-55-01 W
Pop: 518 (1990); 649 (1980) Pop Density: 863.3
Land: 0.6 sq. mi.; Water: 0.0 sq. mi. Elev: 656 ft.
Part of the town is in McDonough County.

Pontoosuc — Village
ZIP: 62330 Lat: 40-37-42 N Long: 91-12-41 W
Pop: 264 (1990); 261 (1980) Pop Density: 188.6
Land: 1.4 sq. mi.; Water: 0.7 sq. mi.
Not coextensive with the town of the same name.

*Pontoosuc — Township
Lat: 40-35-46 N Long: 91-13-21 W
Pop: 473 (1990); 556 (1980) Pop Density: 25.6
Land: 18.5 sq. mi.; Water: 1.4 sq. mi.

Prairie — Township
Lat: 40-25-27 N Long: 91-12-24 W
Pop: 449 (1990); 536 (1980) Pop Density: 13.6
Land: 33.1 sq. mi.; Water: 0.0 sq. mi.

Rock Creek — Township
Lat: 40-29-54 N Long: 91-11-13 W
Pop: 431 (1990); 525 (1980) Pop Density: 12.0
Land: 35.9 sq. mi.; Water: 0.0 sq. mi.

Rocky Run — Township
Lat: 40-14-43 N Long: 91-26-17 W
Pop: 202 (1990); 241 (1980) Pop Density: 5.5
Land: 36.9 sq. mi.; Water: 3.0 sq. mi.

St. Albans — Township
Lat: 40-14-52 N Long: 91-12-05 W
Pop: 503 (1990); 575 (1980) Pop Density: 13.9
Land: 36.2 sq. mi.; Water: 0.0 sq. mi.

St. Mary — Township
Lat: 40-19-37 N Long: 90-58-03 W
Pop: 701 (1990); 902 (1980) Pop Density: 19.0
Land: 36.9 sq. mi.; Water: 0.0 sq. mi.

Sonora — Township
Lat: 40-30-12 N Long: 91-18-08 W
Pop: 537 (1990); 626 (1980) Pop Density: 15.0
Land: 35.8 sq. mi.; Water: 1.7 sq. mi.

Walker — Township
Lat: 40-14-32 N Long: 91-18-46 W
Pop: 371 (1990); 481 (1980) Pop Density: 9.7
Land: 38.1 sq. mi.; Water: 0.0 sq. mi.

Warsaw — Town
ZIP: 62379 Lat: 40-21-10 N Long: 91-25-36 W
Pop: 1,882 (1990); 1,842 (1980) Pop Density: 285.2
Land: 6.6 sq. mi.; Water: 0.9 sq. mi. Elev: 577 ft.
Coextensive with the township of the same name.

*Warsaw — Township
Lat: 40-21-10 N Long: 91-25-36 W
Pop: 1,882 (1990); 1,842 (1980) Pop Density: 285.2
Land: 6.6 sq. mi.; Water: 0.9 sq. mi.

West Point — Village
ZIP: 62380 Lat: 40-15-20 N Long: 91-10-59 W
Pop: 214 (1990); 223 (1980) Pop Density: 1070.0
Land: 0.2 sq. mi.; Water: 0.0 sq. mi.

Wilcox — Township
Lat: 40-19-12 N Long: 91-25-17 W
Pop: 263 (1990); 195 (1980) Pop Density: 13.0
Land: 20.2 sq. mi.; Water: 0.9 sq. mi.

Wythe — Township
Lat: 40-19-23 N Long: 91-18-11 W
Pop: 282 (1990); 314 (1980) Pop Density: 7.4
Land: 38.1 sq. mi.; Water: 0.0 sq. mi.

Hardin County
County Seat: Elizabethtown (ZIP: 62931)

Pop: 5,189 (1990); 5,383 (1980)
Land: 178.3 sq. mi.; **Water:** 3.2 sq. mi.
Pop Density: 29.1
Area Code: 618

On the southeastern border of IL; organized Mar 2, 1839 from Pope County.
Name origin: For the county in KY, former home of many settlers.

Cave-In-Rock — Village
Lat: 37-28-12 N **Long:** 88-09-55 W
Pop: 381 (1990); 468 (1980) **Pop Density:** 1270.0
Land: 0.3 sq. mi.; **Water:** 0.0 sq. mi.

Elizabethtown — Village
ZIP: 62931 **Lat:** 37-27-02 N **Long:** 88-18-15 W
Pop: 427 (1990); 478 (1980) **Pop Density:** 610.0
Land: 0.7 sq. mi.; **Water:** 0.0 sq. mi.

Rosiclare — Town
ZIP: 62982 **Lat:** 37-25-20 N **Long:** 88-21-02 W
Pop: 1,378 (1990); 1,441 (1980) **Pop Density:** 626.4
Land: 2.2 sq. mi.; **Water:** 0.1 sq. mi.
In southeastern IL on the Ohio River, northeast of Paducah, KY.
Name origin: For Rose and Clair, daughters of an early settler.

Henderson County
County Seat: Oquawka (ZIP: 61469)

Pop: 8,096 (1990); 9,114 (1980)
Land: 378.8 sq. mi.; **Water:** 16.3 sq. mi.
Pop Density: 21.4
Area Code: 309

On the northwestern border of IL west of Galesburg; organized Jan 20, 1841 from Warren County.
Name origin: For either the county in KY, former home of many settlers, or the Henderson River, which flows through the county.

Bald Bluff — Township
Lat: 41-02-12 N **Long:** 90-51-14 W
Pop: 317 (1990); 434 (1980) **Pop Density:** 7.6
Land: 41.9 sq. mi.; **Water:** 0.8 sq. mi.

Biggsville — Village
ZIP: 61418 **Lat:** 40-51-12 N **Long:** 90-51-40 W
Pop: 349 (1990); 411 (1980) **Pop Density:** 1163.3
Land: 0.3 sq. mi.; **Water:** 0.0 sq. mi. **Elev:** 650 ft.
Incorporated as village 1879. Not coextensive with the town of the same name.
Name origin: Originally known as Grove Farm.

*Biggsville — Township
Lat: 40-51-05 N **Long:** 90-50-39 W
Pop: 627 (1990); 702 (1980) **Pop Density:** 17.1
Land: 36.7 sq. mi.; **Water:** 0.1 sq. mi.

Carman — Township
Lat: 40-45-45 N **Long:** 91-03-41 W
Pop: 398 (1990); 473 (1980) **Pop Density:** 18.1
Land: 22.0 sq. mi.; **Water:** 4.4 sq. mi.

Dallas City — City
ZIP: 62330 **Lat:** 40-38-25 N **Long:** 91-09-38 W
Pop: 197 (1990); 301 (1980) **Pop Density:** 394.0
Land: 0.5 sq. mi.; **Water:** 0.8 sq. mi.
Settled 1836; platted 1848; incorporated 1859. Part of the city is in Hancock County.
Name origin: For George M. Dallas (1792–1864), vice president under James K. Polk (1845–1849).

Gladstone — Village
ZIP: 61437 **Lat:** 40-51-49 N **Long:** 90-57-26 W
Pop: 270 (1990); 354 (1980) **Pop Density:** 675.0
Land: 0.4 sq. mi.; **Water:** 0.0 sq. mi.
Not coextensive with the town of the same name.

*Gladstone — Township
Lat: 40-50-40 N **Long:** 90-58-38 W
Pop: 1,166 (1990); 1,423 (1980) **Pop Density:** 24.9
Land: 46.8 sq. mi.; **Water:** 2.3 sq. mi.

Gulf Port — Village
Lat: 40-48-32 N **Long:** 91-05-00 W
Pop: 209 (1990); 224 (1980) **Pop Density:** 139.3
Land: 1.5 sq. mi.; **Water:** 0.9 sq. mi.

Lomax — Town
ZIP: 61454 **Lat:** 40-40-39 N **Long:** 91-04-34 W
Pop: 473 (1990); 601 (1980) **Pop Density:** 473.0
Land: 1.0 sq. mi.; **Water:** 0.0 sq. mi.
Incorporated Nov 4, 1913. Not coextensive with the town of the same name.

*Lomax — Township
Lat: 40-40-26 N **Long:** 91-04-45 W
Pop: 989 (1990); 1,142 (1980) **Pop Density:** 34.3
Land: 28.8 sq. mi.; **Water:** 4.5 sq. mi.

Media — Village
ZIP: 61460 **Lat:** 40-46-21 N **Long:** 90-50-02 W
Pop: 146 (1990); 179 (1980) **Pop Density:** 85.9
Land: 1.7 sq. mi.; **Water:** 0.0 sq. mi.
Not coextensive with the town of the same name.

ILLINOIS, Henderson County

*Media — Township
Lat: 40-45-56 N Long: 90-50-20 W
Pop: 484 (1990); 557 (1980) Pop Density: 13.3
Land: 36.4 sq. mi.; Water: 0.0 sq. mi.

Oquawka — Town
ZIP: 61469 Lat: 40-56-15 N Long: 90-56-58 W
Pop: 1,442 (1990); 1,533 (1980) Pop Density: 961.3
Land: 1.5 sq. mi.; Water: 0.4 sq. mi. Elev: 562 ft.
In northwestern IL on the Mississippi River, west of Galesburg. Not coextensive with the town of the same name.
Name origin: From either a Sac Indian term for 'yellow banks,' or an Indian personal name.

*Oquawka — Township
Lat: 40-57-21 N Long: 90-56-11 W
Pop: 2,100 (1990); 2,095 (1980) Pop Density: 86.8
Land: 24.2 sq. mi.; Water: 4.2 sq. mi.

Raritan — Village
ZIP: 61471 Lat: 40-41-43 N Long: 90-49-29 W
Pop: 146 (1990); 177 (1980) Pop Density: 1460.0
Land: 0.1 sq. mi.; Water: 0.0 sq. mi.
Not coextensive with the town of the same name.

*Raritan — Township
Lat: 40-40-44 N Long: 90-50-51 W
Pop: 345 (1990); 403 (1980) Pop Density: 10.1
Land: 34.1 sq. mi.; Water: 0.0 sq. mi.

Rozetta — Township
Lat: 40-56-25 N Long: 90-50-32 W
Pop: 310 (1990); 365 (1980) Pop Density: 8.5
Land: 36.4 sq. mi.; Water: 0.0 sq. mi.

Stronghurst — Village
ZIP: 61480 Lat: 40-44-47 N Long: 90-54-33 W
Pop: 799 (1990); 865 (1980) Pop Density: 887.8
Land: 0.9 sq. mi.; Water: 0.0 sq. mi.
Not coextensive with the town of the same name.

*Stronghurst — Township
Lat: 40-45-48 N Long: 90-57-48 W
Pop: 1,055 (1990); 1,147 (1980) Pop Density: 29.4
Land: 35.9 sq. mi.; Water: 0.0 sq. mi.

Terre Haute — Township
Lat: 40-40-27 N Long: 90-57-40 W
Pop: 305 (1990); 373 (1980) Pop Density: 8.6
Land: 35.6 sq. mi.; Water: 0.0 sq. mi.

Henry County
County Seat: Cambridge (ZIP: 61238)

Pop: 51,159 (1990); 57,968 (1980) Pop Density: 62.1
Land: 823.3 sq. mi.; Water: 2.4 sq. mi. Area Code: 309
In northwestern IL, southeast of Davenport; organized Jan 13, 1825 from Fulton County.
Name origin: For Patrick Henry (1736–99), patriot, governor of VA (1776–79; 1784–86), and statesman, famous for proclaiming, "Give me liberty or give me death."

Alba — Township
Lat: 41-27-22 N Long: 89-54-46 W
Pop: 268 (1990); 321 (1980) Pop Density: 7.4
Land: 36.0 sq. mi.; Water: 0.1 sq. mi.

Alpha — Village
ZIP: 61413 Lat: 41-11-31 N Long: 90-22-50 W
Pop: 753 (1990); 815 (1980) Pop Density: 2510.0
Land: 0.3 sq. mi.; Water: 0.0 sq. mi. Elev: 803 ft.
Founded 1871; incorporated as village 1894.
Name origin: For the first letter of the Greek alphabet.

Andover — Village
ZIP: 61233 Lat: 41-17-41 N Long: 90-17-25 W
Pop: 579 (1990); 612 (1980) Pop Density: 579.0
Land: 1.0 sq. mi.; Water: 0.0 sq. mi. Elev: 776 ft.
Not coextensive with the town of the same name.

*Andover — Township
Lat: 41-17-14 N Long: 90-15-42 W
Pop: 1,003 (1990); 1,180 (1980) Pop Density: 27.4
Land: 36.6 sq. mi.; Water: 0.0 sq. mi.

Annawan — Village
ZIP: 61234 Lat: 41-23-55 N Long: 89-54-25 W
Pop: 802 (1990); 908 (1980) Pop Density: 1145.7
Land: 0.7 sq. mi.; Water: 0.0 sq. mi. Elev: 625 ft.
Not coextensive with the town of the same name.
Name origin: For the 17th-century chief of the Wampanoag Indians of MA.

*Annawan — Township
Lat: 41-22-20 N Long: 89-55-18 W
Pop: 1,164 (1990); 1,334 (1980) Pop Density: 32.1
Land: 36.3 sq. mi.; Water: 0.2 sq. mi.

Atkinson — Village
ZIP: 61235 Lat: 41-25-07 N Long: 90-00-52 W
Pop: 950 (1990); 1,138 (1980) Pop Density: 950.0
Land: 1.0 sq. mi.; Water: 0.0 sq. mi.
Founded 1856. Not coextensive with the town of the same name.

*Atkinson — Township
Lat: 41-27-09 N Long: 90-01-29 W
Pop: 1,296 (1990); 1,603 (1980) Pop Density: 36.9
Land: 35.1 sq. mi.; Water: 0.1 sq. mi.

ILLINOIS, Henry County

Bishop Hill — Village
ZIP: 61419 Lat: 41-11-58 N Long: 90-07-02 W
Pop: 131 (1990); 166 (1980) Pop Density: 262.0
Land: 0.5 sq. mi.; Water: 0.0 sq. mi.
A restored Swedish village; IL's first commune (1846).
Name origin: A translation of Biskopskulla, Sweden, the birthplace of Erik Jansson, founder and religious communal leader.

Burns — Township
Lat: 41-16-40 N Long: 90-01-37 W
Pop: 353 (1990); 467 (1980) Pop Density: 9.7
Land: 36.4 sq. mi.; Water: 0.0 sq. mi.

Cambridge — Village
ZIP: 61238 Lat: 41-18-11 N Long: 90-11-35 W
Pop: 2,124 (1990); 2,217 (1980) Pop Density: 2124.0
Land: 1.0 sq. mi.; Water: 0.0 sq. mi.
Incorporated 1861. Not coextensive with the town of the same name.
Name origin: For the English university town.

*Cambridge — Township
Lat: 41-16-45 N Long: 90-08-50 W
Pop: 2,601 (1990); 2,926 (1980) Pop Density: 70.5
Land: 36.9 sq. mi.; Water: 0.0 sq. mi.

Cleveland — Village
ZIP: 61241 Lat: 41-30-10 N Long: 90-18-59 W
Pop: 283 (1990); 338 (1980) Pop Density: 707.5
Land: 0.4 sq. mi.; Water: 0.0 sq. mi.

Clover — Township
Lat: 41-11-43 N Long: 90-16-05 W
Pop: 1,027 (1990); 1,195 (1980) Pop Density: 29.4
Land: 34.9 sq. mi.; Water: 0.0 sq. mi.

Coal Valley — Village
ZIP: 61240 Lat: 41-26-47 N Long: 90-24-59 W
Pop: 51 (1990); 30 (1980) Pop Density: 63.8
Land: 0.8 sq. mi.; Water: 0.0 sq. mi.
Part of the town is also in Rock Island.

Colona — Village
ZIP: 61241 Lat: 41-28-14 N Long: 90-20-25 W
Pop: 2,237 (1990); 2,172 (1980) Pop Density: 798.9
Land: 2.8 sq. mi.; Water: 0.1 sq. mi.
Not coextensive with the town of the same name.

*Colona — Township
ZIP: 61241 Lat: 41-27-13 N Long: 90-22-06 W
Pop: 6,728 (1990); 7,616 (1980) Pop Density: 228.8
Land: 29.4 sq. mi.; Water: 0.8 sq. mi.

Cornwall — Township
Lat: 41-21-59 N Long: 90-01-46 W
Pop: 323 (1990); 362 (1980) Pop Density: 9.1
Land: 35.5 sq. mi.; Water: 0.1 sq. mi.

Edford — Township
Lat: 41-26-52 N Long: 90-15-33 W
Pop: 664 (1990); 811 (1980) Pop Density: 24.4
Land: 27.2 sq. mi.; Water: 0.1 sq. mi.

Galva — City
ZIP: 61434 Lat: 41-09-59 N Long: 90-02-20 W
Pop: 2,742 (1990); 3,185 (1980) Pop Density: 1612.9
Land: 1.7 sq. mi.; Water: 0.0 sq. mi.
Not coextensive with the town of the same name.
Name origin: For Gefle, a Swedish seaport, with spelling altered to reflect pronunciation.

*Galva — Township
Lat: 41-11-35 N Long: 90-02-25 W
Pop: 3,118 (1990); 3,683 (1980) Pop Density: 90.9
Land: 34.3 sq. mi.; Water: 0.0 sq. mi.

Geneseo — City
ZIP: 61254 Lat: 41-26-49 N Long: 90-09-16 W
Pop: 5,990 (1990); 6,373 (1980) Pop Density: 1711.4
Land: 3.5 sq. mi.; Water: 0.0 sq. mi.
Settled 1836 by colonists from Bergen and Geneseo, NY; incorporated Feb 14, 1855. Not coextensive with the town of the same name.
Name origin: For Geneseo, NY.

*Geneseo — Township
ZIP: 61254 Lat: 41-27-18 N Long: 90-08-40 W
Pop: 6,804 (1990); 7,357 (1980) Pop Density: 187.4
Land: 36.3 sq. mi.; Water: 0.1 sq. mi.

Green Rock — City
ZIP: 61241 Lat: 41-28-29 N Long: 90-21-49 W
Pop: 2,615 (1990); 3,324 (1980) Pop Density: 4358.3
Land: 0.6 sq. mi.; Water: 0.0 sq. mi.
In northwestern IL on the Rock River, just east of Moline.

Hanna — Township
Lat: 41-30-02 N Long: 90-14-41 W
Pop: 2,134 (1990); 2,402 (1980) Pop Density: 110.6
Land: 19.3 sq. mi.; Water: 0.6 sq. mi.

Hooppole — Town
ZIP: 61258 Lat: 41-31-15 N Long: 89-54-47 W
Pop: 196 (1990); 235 (1980) Pop Density: 653.3
Land: 0.3 sq. mi.; Water: 0.0 sq. mi.
In northwestern IL on the Green River, 22 mi. northeast of Geneseo.
Name origin: Because coopers cut hickory bands for their barrels in a nearby grove.

Kewanee — City
ZIP: 61443 Lat: 41-14-28 N Long: 89-55-32 W
Pop: 12,969 (1990); 14,508 (1980) Pop Density: 2236.0
Land: 5.8 sq. mi.; Water: 0.0 sq. mi. Elev: 820 ft.
In northwestern IL, 37 mi. north of Peoria. Incorporated Feb 14, 1855. Not coextensive with the town of the same name.
Name origin: From an Ottawa term *ke-won-nee* meaning 'prairie hen,' probably derived from an Indian personal name. Previously called Berrian.

*Kewanee — Township
ZIP: 61443 Lat: 41-16-50 N Long: 89-54-59 W
Pop: 10,536 (1990); 11,951 (1980) Pop Density: 291.0
Land: 36.2 sq. mi.; Water: 0.0 sq. mi.

Loraine — Township
Lat: 41-32-25 N Long: 90-02-09 W
Pop: 364 (1990); 428 (1980) Pop Density: 10.5
Land: 34.6 sq. mi.; Water: 0.0 sq. mi.

ILLINOIS, Henry County

Lynn
Township
Lat: 41-16-36 N Long: 90-22-18 W
Pop: 789 (1990); 837 (1980) Pop Density: 21.7
Land: 36.3 sq. mi.; Water: 0.0 sq. mi.

Munson
Township
Lat: 41-21-57 N Long: 90-08-48 W
Pop: 566 (1990); 626 (1980) Pop Density: 15.8
Land: 35.9 sq. mi.; Water: 0.0 sq. mi.

Orion
Town
ZIP: 61273 Lat: 41-21-04 N Long: 90-22-26 W
Pop: 1,821 (1990); 2,013 (1980) Pop Density: 2601.4
Land: 0.7 sq. mi.; Water: 0.0 sq. mi.
Name origin: For the constellation.

Osco
Township
Lat: 41-22-20 N Long: 90-15-24 W
Pop: 538 (1990); 601 (1980) Pop Density: 14.7
Land: 36.5 sq. mi.; Water: 0.0 sq. mi.

Oxford
Township
Lat: 41-11-40 N Long: 90-22-42 W
Pop: 1,290 (1990); 1,397 (1980) Pop Density: 36.2
Land: 35.6 sq. mi.; Water: 0.0 sq. mi.

Phenix
Township
Lat: 41-32-29 N Long: 90-08-54 W
Pop: 1,502 (1990); 1,704 (1980) Pop Density: 45.8
Land: 32.8 sq. mi.; Water: 0.2 sq. mi.

Weller
Township
Lat: 41-11-42 N Long: 90-09-17 W
Pop: 492 (1990); 630 (1980) Pop Density: 14.3
Land: 34.3 sq. mi.; Water: 0.0 sq. mi.

Western
Township
Lat: 41-22-21 N Long: 90-22-37 W
Pop: 3,121 (1990); 3,411 (1980) Pop Density: 87.9
Land: 35.5 sq. mi.; Water: 0.0 sq. mi.

Wethersfield
Township
Lat: 41-11-32 N Long: 89-55-25 W
Pop: 3,972 (1990); 4,484 (1980) Pop Density: 111.6
Land: 35.6 sq. mi.; Water: 0.0 sq. mi.

Woodhull
Village
ZIP: 61490 Lat: 41-10-42 N Long: 90-19-18 W
Pop: 808 (1990); 901 (1980) Pop Density: 1010.0
Land: 0.8 sq. mi.; Water: 0.0 sq. mi.

Yorktown
Township
Lat: 41-32-15 N Long: 89-54-59 W
Pop: 506 (1990); 642 (1980) Pop Density: 14.2
Land: 35.7 sq. mi.; Water: 0.0 sq. mi.

Iroquois County
County Seat: Watseka (ZIP: 60970)

Pop: 30,787 (1990); 32,976 (1980) Pop Density: 27.6
Land: 1116.5 sq. mi.; Water: 1.6 sq. mi. Area Code: 815
On the east-central border of IL south of Kankakee; organized Feb 26, 1833 from Vermilion County.
Name origin: For the Indian tribe; a French transliteration of the Algonquian name 'real adders.'

Artesia
Township
Lat: 40-36-25 N Long: 88-01-03 W
Pop: 977 (1990); 1,068 (1980) Pop Density: 17.1
Land: 57.2 sq. mi.; Water: 0.1 sq. mi.

Ash Grove
Township
Lat: 40-37-05 N Long: 87-50-36 W
Pop: 793 (1990); 853 (1980) Pop Density: 13.0
Land: 61.2 sq. mi.; Water: 0.1 sq. mi.

Ashkum
Village
ZIP: 60911 Lat: 40-52-42 N Long: 87-57-12 W
Pop: 650 (1990); 735 (1980) Pop Density: 812.5
Land: 0.8 sq. mi.; Water: 0.0 sq. mi.
Not coextensive with the town of the same name.

*Ashkum
Township
Lat: 40-52-50 N Long: 87-58-33 W
Pop: 1,484 (1990); 1,535 (1980) Pop Density: 23.7
Land: 62.6 sq. mi.; Water: 0.1 sq. mi.

Beaver
Township
Lat: 40-54-00 N Long: 87-35-18 W
Pop: 613 (1990); 581 (1980) Pop Density: 18.2
Land: 33.6 sq. mi.; Water: 0.0 sq. mi.

Beaverville
Village
ZIP: 60912 Lat: 40-57-12 N Long: 87-39-18 W
Pop: 278 (1990); 377 (1980) Pop Density: 1390.0
Land: 0.2 sq. mi.; Water: 0.0 sq. mi.
Not coextensive with the town of the same name.

*Beaverville
Township
Lat: 40-58-24 N Long: 87-36-12 W
Pop: 672 (1990); 764 (1980) Pop Density: 17.9
Land: 37.6 sq. mi.; Water: 0.0 sq. mi.

Belmont
Township
Lat: 40-43-52 N Long: 87-42-07 W
Pop: 2,439 (1990); 2,682 (1980) Pop Density: 67.0
Land: 36.4 sq. mi.; Water: 0.0 sq. mi.

Buckley
Village
ZIP: 60918 Lat: 40-35-49 N Long: 88-02-13 W
Pop: 557 (1990); 604 (1980) Pop Density: 1856.7
Land: 0.3 sq. mi.; Water: 0.0 sq. mi. Elev: 699 ft.

Chebanse — Village
ZIP: 60922　　Lat: 40-59-57 N　Long: 87-54-43 W
Pop: 657 (1990); 730 (1980)　　Pop Density: 2190.0
Land: 0.3 sq. mi.; Water: 0.0 sq. mi.

Part of the town is also in Kankakee County. Not coextensive with the township of the same name.
Name origin: From an Indian term probably meaning 'little duck.'

*Chebanse — Township
Lat: 40-57-33 N　Long: 87-55-03 W
Pop: 3,074 (1990); 3,298 (1980)　　Pop Density: 48.5
Land: 63.4 sq. mi.; Water: 0.2 sq. mi.

Cissna Park — Village
ZIP: 60924　　Lat: 40-34-00 N　Long: 87-53-33 W
Pop: 805 (1990); 825 (1980)　　Pop Density: 1150.0
Land: 0.7 sq. mi.; Water: 0.0 sq. mi.　　Elev: 666 ft.

Name origin: For pioneer Stephen Cissna.

Clifton — Village
ZIP: 60927　　Lat: 40-56-07 N　Long: 87-56-00 W
Pop: 1,347 (1990); 1,390 (1980)　　Pop Density: 1924.3
Land: 0.7 sq. mi.; Water: 0.0 sq. mi.　　Elev: 661 ft.

Concord — Township
Lat: 40-49-00 N　Long: 87-35-19 W
Pop: 524 (1990); 594 (1980)　　Pop Density: 12.9
Land: 40.5 sq. mi.; Water: 0.0 sq. mi.

Crescent — Township
Lat: 40-43-39 N　Long: 87-49-18 W
Pop: 680 (1990); 714 (1980)　　Pop Density: 18.7
Land: 36.3 sq. mi.; Water: 0.0 sq. mi.

Crescent City — Village
Lat: 40-46-17 N　Long: 87-51-23 W
Pop: 541 (1990); 641 (1980)　　Pop Density: 1082.0
Land: 0.5 sq. mi.; Water: 0.0 sq. mi.

Danforth — Village
ZIP: 60930　　Lat: 40-49-16 N　Long: 87-58-40 W
Pop: 457 (1990); 554 (1980)　　Pop Density: 914.0
Land: 0.5 sq. mi.; Water: 0.0 sq. mi.

Not coextensive with the town of the same name.
Name origin: For A. H. Danforth, who purchased land here in 1850 and induced 30 families from the Netherlands to emigrate here.

*Danforth — Township
Lat: 40-49-02 N　Long: 88-00-22 W
Pop: 972 (1990); 959 (1980)　　Pop Density: 18.8
Land: 51.7 sq. mi.; Water: 0.0 sq. mi.

Donovan — Village
ZIP: 60931　　Lat: 40-53-07 N　Long: 87-36-52 W
Pop: 361 (1990); 301 (1980)　　Pop Density: 1203.3
Land: 0.3 sq. mi.; Water: 0.0 sq. mi.　　Elev: 673 ft.

Douglas — Township
Lat: 40-46-13 N　Long: 88-00-14 W
Pop: 2,112 (1990); 2,334 (1980)　　Pop Density: 47.4
Land: 44.6 sq. mi.; Water: 0.1 sq. mi.

Fountain Creek — Township
Lat: 40-32-15 N　Long: 87-49-00 W
Pop: 414 (1990); 481 (1980)　　Pop Density: 11.5
Land: 36.1 sq. mi.; Water: 0.0 sq. mi.

Gilman — City
ZIP: 60938　　Lat: 40-45-57 N　Long: 87-59-46 W
Pop: 1,816 (1990); 1,913 (1980)　　Pop Density: 908.0
Land: 2.0 sq. mi.; Water: 0.0 sq. mi.　　Elev: 646 ft.

Iroquois — Town
ZIP: 60945　　Lat: 40-49-43 N　Long: 87-35-05 W
Pop: 199 (1990); 227 (1980)　　Pop Density: 331.7
Land: 0.6 sq. mi.; Water: 0.0 sq. mi.

In eastern IL on the Iroquois River south of Kankakee.
Name origin: From the river, which runs through the county, itself so named for a battle there between the Iroquois and Illinois Indians.

*Iroquois — Township
Lat: 40-48-55 N　Long: 87-49-20 W
Pop: 591 (1990); 706 (1980)　　Pop Density: 16.3
Land: 36.3 sq. mi.; Water: 0.4 sq. mi.

Loda — Village
ZIP: 60948　　Lat: 40-31-00 N　Long: 88-04-31 W
Pop: 390 (1990); 486 (1980)　　Pop Density: 278.6
Land: 1.4 sq. mi.; Water: 0.0 sq. mi.　　Elev: 781 ft.

Not coextensive with the town of the same name.

*Loda — Township
Lat: 40-31-46 N　Long: 88-03-09 W
Pop: 1,254 (1990); 1,306 (1980)　　Pop Density: 32.6
Land: 38.5 sq. mi.; Water: 0.3 sq. mi.

Lovejoy — Township
Lat: 40-32-12 N　Long: 87-42-14 W
Pop: 514 (1990); 629 (1980)　　Pop Density: 14.9
Land: 34.6 sq. mi.; Water: 0.0 sq. mi.

Martinton — Village
ZIP: 60951　　Lat: 40-54-55 N　Long: 87-43-34 W
Pop: 299 (1990); 363 (1980)　　Pop Density: 996.7
Land: 0.3 sq. mi.; Water: 0.0 sq. mi.

Not coextensive with the town of the same name.

*Martinton — Township
Lat: 40-54-04 N　Long: 87-44-17 W
Pop: 1,004 (1990); 1,111 (1980)　　Pop Density: 18.5
Land: 54.2 sq. mi.; Water: 0.2 sq. mi.

Middleport — Township
Lat: 40-49-00 N　Long: 87-42-28 W
Pop: 4,653 (1990); 4,645 (1980)　　Pop Density: 127.8
Land: 36.4 sq. mi.; Water: 0.1 sq. mi.

Milford — Town
ZIP: 60953　　Lat: 40-37-39 N　Long: 87-41-49 W
Pop: 1,512 (1990); 1,716 (1980)　　Pop Density: 2520.0
Land: 0.6 sq. mi.; Water: 0.0 sq. mi.

Not coextensive with the town of the same name.
Name origin: For a mill near the ford at the Hubbard Trail crossing of Sugar Creek.

*Milford — Township
Lat: 40-37-39 N　Long: 87-42-41 W
Pop: 2,026 (1990); 2,192 (1980)　　Pop Density: 45.5
Land: 44.5 sq. mi.; Water: 0.0 sq. mi.

Milks Grove — Township
Lat: 40-57-12 N　Long: 88-04-35 W
Pop: 221 (1990); 305 (1980)　　Pop Density: 6.1
Land: 36.4 sq. mi.; Water: 0.0 sq. mi.

ILLINOIS, Iroquois County

Onarga — Town
ZIP: 60955 Lat: 40-42-47 N Long: 88-00-47 W
Pop: 1,281 (1990); 1,269 (1980) Pop Density: 753.5
Land: 1.7 sq. mi.; Water: 0.0 sq. mi. Elev: 667 ft.
Not coextensive with the town of the same name.
Name origin: From an Iroquois term probably meaning 'place of rocky hills.'

*Onarga — Township
Lat: 40-42-29 N Long: 87-57-43 W
Pop: 1,678 (1990); 1,661 (1980) Pop Density: 34.7
Land: 48.4 sq. mi.; Water: 0.0 sq. mi.

Papineau — Village
ZIP: 60956 Lat: 40-58-03 N Long: 87-42-57 W
Pop: 142 (1990); 179 (1980) Pop Density: 710.0
Land: 0.2 sq. mi.; Water: 0.0 sq. mi.
Not coextensive with the town of the same name.

*Papineau — Township
Lat: 40-58-39 N Long: 87-44-41 W
Pop: 565 (1990); 585 (1980) Pop Density: 19.2
Land: 29.4 sq. mi.; Water: 0.1 sq. mi.

Pigeon Grove — Township
Lat: 40-32-01 N Long: 87-56-26 W
Pop: 1,122 (1990); 1,212 (1980) Pop Density: 31.3
Land: 35.9 sq. mi.; Water: 0.0 sq. mi.

Prairie Green — Township
Lat: 40-32-14 N Long: 87-35-35 W
Pop: 268 (1990); 310 (1980) Pop Density: 6.6
Land: 40.5 sq. mi.; Water: 0.0 sq. mi.

Ridgeland — Township
Lat: 40-42-01 N Long: 88-05-03 W
Pop: 374 (1990); 463 (1980) Pop Density: 13.9
Land: 26.9 sq. mi.; Water: 0.0 sq. mi.

Sheldon — Town
ZIP: 60966 Lat: 40-46-15 N Long: 87-33-59 W
Pop: 1,109 (1990); 1,215 (1980) Pop Density: 1386.3
Land: 0.8 sq. mi.; Water: 0.0 sq. mi. Elev: 687 ft.
Not coextensive with the town of the same name.

*Sheldon — Township
Lat: 40-43-49 N Long: 87-35-16 W
Pop: 1,422 (1990); 1,542 (1980) Pop Density: 35.8
Land: 39.7 sq. mi.; Water: 0.0 sq. mi.

Stockland — Township
Lat: 40-38-07 N Long: 87-35-36 W
Pop: 341 (1990); 446 (1980) Pop Density: 6.4
Land: 53.5 sq. mi.; Water: 0.0 sq. mi.

Thawville — Village
ZIP: 60968 Lat: 40-40-25 N Long: 88-06-47 W
Pop: 241 (1990); 275 (1980) Pop Density: 803.3
Land: 0.3 sq. mi.; Water: 0.0 sq. mi.

Watseka — City
ZIP: 60970 Lat: 40-46-33 N Long: 87-43-55 W
Pop: 5,424 (1990); 5,543 (1980) Pop Density: 2169.6
Land: 2.5 sq. mi.; Water: 0.0 sq. mi. Elev: 637 ft.
Incorporated Feb 19, 1867.
Name origin: Named in 1865 for *Watch-e-kee*, thought to mean 'pretty woman,' the name of the Potawatomi wife of early settler Gurdon Hubbard.

Wellington — Village
ZIP: 60973 Lat: 40-32-25 N Long: 87-40-41 W
Pop: 294 (1990); 370 (1980) Pop Density: 980.0
Land: 0.3 sq. mi.; Water: 0.0 sq. mi.

Woodland — Village
ZIP: 60974 Lat: 40-42-46 N Long: 87-43-50 W
Pop: 313 (1990); 333 (1980) Pop Density: 782.5
Land: 0.4 sq. mi.; Water: 0.0 sq. mi.

Jackson County
County Seat: Murphysboro (ZIP: 62966)

Pop: 61,067 (1990); 61,649 (1980) Pop Density: 103.8
Land: 588.1 sq. mi.; Water: 14.4 sq. mi. Area Code: 618
On the southwest border of IL southeast of St. Louis, MO; organized Jan 10, 1816 (prior to statehood) from Randolph and Johnson counties.
Name origin: For Andrew Jackson (1767–1845), seventh U.S. president.

Ava — City
ZIP: 62907 Lat: 37-53-18 N Long: 89-29-46 W
Pop: 674 (1990); 811 (1980) Pop Density: 612.7
Land: 1.1 sq. mi.; Water: 0.0 sq. mi.

Bradley — Township
Lat: 37-54-38 N Long: 89-32-39 W
Pop: 1,659 (1990); 1,808 (1980) Pop Density: 36.9
Land: 45.0 sq. mi.; Water: 0.0 sq. mi.

Campbell Hill — Village
ZIP: 62916 Lat: 37-55-48 N Long: 89-33-03 W
Pop: 351 (1990); 389 (1980) Pop Density: 877.5
Land: 0.4 sq. mi.; Water: 0.0 sq. mi.

Carbondale — City
ZIP: 62902 Lat: 37-43-28 N Long: 89-13-02 W
Pop: 27,033 (1990); 26,414 (1980) Pop Density: 2650.3
Land: 10.2 sq. mi.; Water: 0.2 sq. mi. Elev: 415 ft.
In southwestern IL, 40 mi. southwest of Mount Vernon. Founded 1852 after the arrival of the Illinois Central Railroad. Coal mining area. Incorporated Apr 15, 1869. Not coextensive with the town of the same name.
Name origin: For the huge coalfields upon which it is built.

*Carbondale — Township
ZIP: 62901 Lat: 37-43-48 N Long: 89-12-34 W
Pop: 31,252 (1990); 31,797 (1980) Pop Density: 824.6
Land: 37.9 sq. mi.; Water: 0.3 sq. mi.

Degognia
Township
Lat: 37-48-51 N Long: 89-38-15 W
Pop: 174 (1990); 218 (1980) Pop Density: 5.9
Land: 29.6 sq. mi.; Water: 1.1 sq. mi.

De Soto
Village
ZIP: 62924 Lat: 37-48-57 N Long: 89-13-37 W
Pop: 1,500 (1990); 1,589 (1980) Pop Density: 1666.7
Land: 0.9 sq. mi.; Water: 0.0 sq. mi.
Not coextensive with the town of the same name.
Name origin: For Spanish explorer Hernando de Soto (c. 1500–42).

*De Soto
Township
Lat: 37-49-06 N Long: 89-12-49 W
Pop: 2,073 (1990); 2,011 (1980) Pop Density: 55.3
Land: 37.5 sq. mi.; Water: 0.4 sq. mi.

Dowell
Village
ZIP: 62927 Lat: 37-56-22 N Long: 89-14-22 W
Pop: 465 (1990); 480 (1980) Pop Density: 1162.5
Land: 0.4 sq. mi.; Water: 0.0 sq. mi.

Elk
Township
Lat: 37-54-10 N Long: 89-12-18 W
Pop: 2,091 (1990); 2,003 (1980) Pop Density: 57.8
Land: 36.2 sq. mi.; Water: 1.0 sq. mi.

Elkville
Village
ZIP: 62932 Lat: 37-54-34 N Long: 89-14-11 W
Pop: 958 (1990); 973 (1980) Pop Density: 1197.5
Land: 0.8 sq. mi.; Water: 0.0 sq. mi. Elev: 401 ft.

Fountain Bluff
Township
Lat: 37-44-41 N Long: 89-32-10 W
Pop: 304 (1990); 380 (1980) Pop Density: 10.1
Land: 30.0 sq. mi.; Water: 1.2 sq. mi.

Gorham
Village
ZIP: 62940 Lat: 37-43-04 N Long: 89-28-57 W
Pop: 290 (1990); 381 (1980) Pop Density: 241.7
Land: 1.2 sq. mi.; Water: 0.0 sq. mi. Elev: 364 ft.

Grand Tower
Town
ZIP: 62942 Lat: 37-38-22 N Long: 89-30-11 W
Pop: 775 (1990); 748 (1980) Pop Density: 596.2
Land: 1.3 sq. mi.; Water: 0.0 sq. mi. Elev: 361 ft.
In southwestern IL on the Mississippi River, west of Carbondale. Not coextensive with the town of the same name.
Name origin: For Tower Rock, a 60-ft.-high natural stone in the river.

*Grand Tower
Township
Lat: 37-38-13 N Long: 89-28-23 W
Pop: 903 (1990); 897 (1980) Pop Density: 28.6
Land: 31.6 sq. mi.; Water: 1.8 sq. mi.

Kinkaid
Township
Lat: 37-49-25 N Long: 89-32-49 W
Pop: 365 (1990); 340 (1980) Pop Density: 10.3
Land: 35.6 sq. mi.; Water: 0.7 sq. mi.

Levan
Township
Lat: 37-49-03 N Long: 89-25-51 W
Pop: 596 (1990); 533 (1980) Pop Density: 17.8
Land: 33.5 sq. mi.; Water: 3.2 sq. mi.

Makanda
Town
ZIP: 62958 Lat: 37-37-08 N Long: 89-14-14 W
Pop: 404 (1990); 402 (1980) Pop Density: 94.0
Land: 4.3 sq. mi.; Water: 0.0 sq. mi. Elev: 437 ft.
In southern IL, within Shawnee National Forest, 17 mi. east of the MO border. Incorporated February 7, 1888. Not coextensive with the town of the same name.

*Makanda
Township
Lat: 37-37-57 N Long: 89-12-50 W
Pop: 3,700 (1990); 3,391 (1980) Pop Density: 98.9
Land: 37.4 sq. mi.; Water: 0.4 sq. mi.

Murphysboro
City
ZIP: 62966 Lat: 37-46-05 N Long: 89-20-14 W
Pop: 9,176 (1990); 9,866 (1980) Pop Density: 1994.8
Land: 4.6 sq. mi.; Water: 0.0 sq. mi.
In southwestern IL, 25 mi. west of Marion. County seat. Settled 1850; incorporated Mar 5, 1867. Not coextensive with the town of the same name.
Name origin: For William C. Murphy, a commissioner when the town was selected county seat.

*Murphysboro
Township
ZIP: 62966 Lat: 37-44-14 N Long: 89-19-33 W
Pop: 11,316 (1990); 11,712 (1980) Pop Density: 307.5
Land: 36.8 sq. mi.; Water: 0.2 sq. mi.

Ora
Township
Lat: 37-54-39 N Long: 89-25-30 W
Pop: 365 (1990); 434 (1980) Pop Density: 9.9
Land: 36.7 sq. mi.; Water: 0.0 sq. mi.

Pomona
Township
Lat: 37-38-32 N Long: 89-20-52 W
Pop: 769 (1990); 634 (1980) Pop Density: 15.4
Land: 50.0 sq. mi.; Water: 2.8 sq. mi.

Sand Ridge
Township
Lat: 37-44-20 N Long: 89-26-18 W
Pop: 800 (1990); 968 (1980) Pop Density: 22.5
Land: 35.6 sq. mi.; Water: 0.7 sq. mi.

Somerset
Township
Lat: 37-48-35 N Long: 89-19-22 W
Pop: 4,021 (1990); 3,796 (1980) Pop Density: 106.9
Land: 37.6 sq. mi.; Water: 0.1 sq. mi.

Vergennes
Village
ZIP: 62994 Lat: 37-54-07 N Long: 89-20-23 W
Pop: 314 (1990); 360 (1980) Pop Density: 785.0
Land: 0.4 sq. mi.; Water: 0.0 sq. mi.
Not coextensive with the town of the same name.

*Vergennes
Township
Lat: 37-54-21 N Long: 89-19-03 W
Pop: 679 (1990); 727 (1980) Pop Density: 18.4
Land: 37.0 sq. mi.; Water: 0.3 sq. mi.

ILLINOIS, Jasper County *American Places Dictionary*

Jasper County
County Seat: Newton (ZIP: 62448)

Pop: 10,609 (1990); 11,318 (1980) **Pop Density:** 21.5
Land: 494.4 sq. mi.; **Water:** 3.6 sq. mi. **Area Code:** 618

In east-central IL south of Urbana; organized Feb 15, 1831 from Crawford and Clay counties.

Name origin: For Sgt. William Jasper (1750–79), Revolutionary War soldier from SC.

Crooked Creek — Township
Lat: 39-07-05 N Long: 88-07-54 W
Pop: 820 (1990); 914 (1980) **Pop Density:** 14.6
Land: 56.3 sq. mi.; **Water:** 0.0 sq. mi.

Fox — Township
Lat: 38-54-34 N Long: 88-06-00 W
Pop: 593 (1990); 680 (1980) **Pop Density:** 14.6
Land: 40.6 sq. mi.; **Water:** 0.1 sq. mi.

Grandville — Township
Lat: 39-07-34 N Long: 88-00-06 W
Pop: 410 (1990); 440 (1980) **Pop Density:** 11.2
Land: 36.6 sq. mi.; **Water:** 0.0 sq. mi.

Grove — Township
Lat: 39-07-41 N Long: 88-16-39 W
Pop: 608 (1990); 641 (1980) **Pop Density:** 12.3
Land: 49.4 sq. mi.; **Water:** 0.0 sq. mi.

Hidalgo — Village
ZIP: 62432 Lat: 39-09-23 N Long: 88-09-02 W
Pop: 122 (1990); 161 (1980) **Pop Density:** 406.7
Land: 0.3 sq. mi.; **Water:** 0.0 sq. mi. **Elev:** 583 ft.

Hunt City — Township
Lat: 39-02-55 N Long: 88-01-13 W
Pop: 444 (1990); 418 (1980) **Pop Density:** 11.1
Land: 39.9 sq. mi.; **Water:** 0.0 sq. mi. **Elev:** 516 ft.

Newton — Town
ZIP: 62448 Lat: 38-59-17 N Long: 88-09-48 W
Pop: 3,154 (1990); 3,186 (1980) **Pop Density:** 1752.2
Land: 1.8 sq. mi.; **Water:** 0.0 sq. mi. **Elev:** 535 ft.
Name origin: For Revolutionary War hero Sgt. John Newton.

North Muddy — Township
Lat: 39-01-10 N Long: 88-18-42 W
Pop: 809 (1990); 827 (1980) **Pop Density:** 15.9
Land: 50.8 sq. mi.; **Water:** 0.0 sq. mi.

Rose Hill — Village
ZIP: 62432 Lat: 39-06-14 N Long: 88-09-04 W
Pop: 78 (1990); 121 (1980) **Pop Density:** 130.0
Land: 0.6 sq. mi.; **Water:** 0.0 sq. mi.

Ste. Marie — Village
Lat: 38-55-55 N Long: 88-01-35 W
Pop: 281 (1990); 312 (1980) **Pop Density:** 255.5
Land: 1.1 sq. mi.; **Water:** 0.0 sq. mi.

*Ste. Marie — Township
Lat: 38-54-01 N Long: 87-59-42 W
Pop: 659 (1990); 789 (1980) **Pop Density:** 15.3
Land: 43.0 sq. mi.; **Water:** 0.1 sq. mi.

Smallwood — Township
Lat: 38-54-13 N Long: 88-12-21 W
Pop: 461 (1990); 495 (1980) **Pop Density:** 11.1
Land: 41.7 sq. mi.; **Water:** 0.1 sq. mi.

South Muddy — Township
Lat: 38-54-03 N Long: 88-18-49 W
Pop: 365 (1990); 337 (1980) **Pop Density:** 10.2
Land: 35.8 sq. mi.; **Water:** 2.9 sq. mi.

Wade — Township
Lat: 39-00-48 N Long: 88-10-51 W
Pop: 4,835 (1990); 4,919 (1980) **Pop Density:** 65.2
Land: 74.1 sq. mi.; **Water:** 0.4 sq. mi.

Wheeler — Village
ZIP: 62479 Lat: 39-02-34 N Long: 88-19-07 W
Pop: 161 (1990); 166 (1980) **Pop Density:** 268.3
Land: 0.6 sq. mi.; **Water:** 0.0 sq. mi. **Elev:** 573 ft.

Willow Hill — Village
ZIP: 62480 Lat: 38-59-46 N Long: 88-01-16 W
Pop: 268 (1990); 292 (1980) **Pop Density:** 268.0
Land: 1.0 sq. mi.; **Water:** 0.0 sq. mi. **Elev:** 502 ft.
Not coextensive with the town of the same name.

*Willow Hill — Township
Lat: 38-59-12 N Long: 88-00-44 W
Pop: 605 (1990); 858 (1980) **Pop Density:** 23.1
Land: 26.2 sq. mi.; **Water:** 0.0 sq. mi.

Yale — Village
ZIP: 62481 Lat: 39-07-12 N Long: 88-01-27 W
Pop: 94 (1990); 129 (1980) **Pop Density:** 156.7
Land: 0.6 sq. mi.; **Water:** 0.0 sq. mi. **Elev:** 555 ft.

Jefferson County
County Seat: Mount Vernon (ZIP: 62864)

Pop: 37,020 (1990); 36,558 (1980)   **Pop Density:** 64.8
Land: 571.1 sq. mi.; **Water:** 12.7 sq. mi.   **Area Code:** 618

In south-central IL northeast of Carbondale; organized Mar 26, 1819 from Edwards and White counties.

Name origin: For Thomas Jefferson (1743–1826), U.S. patriot and statesman; third U.S. president.

Bald Hill — Township
Lat: 38-10-07 N   Long: 89-05-32 W
Pop: 781 (1990); 769 (1980)   Pop Density: 21.8
Land: 35.9 sq. mi.; Water: 0.3 sq. mi.

Belle Rive — Village
Lat: 38-13-55 N   Long: 88-44-23 W
Pop: 396 (1990); 401 (1980)   Pop Density: 396.0
Land: 1.0 sq. mi.; Water: 0.0 sq. mi.   Elev: 478 ft.

Blissville — Township
Lat: 38-15-23 N   Long: 89-05-15 W
Pop: 355 (1990); 356 (1980)   Pop Density: 10.2
Land: 34.8 sq. mi.; Water: 0.0 sq. mi.

Bluford — Village
ZIP: 62814   Lat: 38-19-34 N   Long: 88-44-08 W
Pop: 747 (1990); 728 (1980)   Pop Density: 498.0
Land: 1.5 sq. mi.; Water: 0.0 sq. mi.

Bonnie — Village
ZIP: 62816   Lat: 38-12-05 N   Long: 88-54-26 W
Pop: 411 (1990); 452 (1980)   Pop Density: 316.2
Land: 1.3 sq. mi.; Water: 0.0 sq. mi.

Casner — Township
Lat: 38-20-55 N   Long: 89-05-15 W
Pop: 998 (1990); 799 (1980)   Pop Density: 27.7
Land: 36.0 sq. mi.; Water: 0.1 sq. mi.

Dix — Village
ZIP: 62830   Lat: 38-26-26 N   Long: 88-56-32 W
Pop: 456 (1990); 319 (1980)   Pop Density: 217.1
Land: 2.1 sq. mi.; Water: 0.0 sq. mi.

Dodds — Township
Lat: 38-15-16 N   Long: 88-52-29 W
Pop: 2,666 (1990); 2,576 (1980)   Pop Density: 72.4
Land: 36.8 sq. mi.; Water: 0.2 sq. mi.

Elk Prairie — Township
Lat: 38-10-10 N   Long: 88-59-12 W
Pop: 754 (1990); 838 (1980)   Pop Density: 27.5
Land: 27.4 sq. mi.; Water: 9.1 sq. mi.

Farrington — Township
Lat: 38-25-45 N   Long: 88-45-26 W
Pop: 538 (1990); 536 (1980)   Pop Density: 14.7
Land: 36.7 sq. mi.; Water: 0.1 sq. mi.

Field — Township
Lat: 38-25-56 N   Long: 88-52-02 W
Pop: 1,159 (1990); 1,146 (1980)   Pop Density: 31.5
Land: 36.8 sq. mi.; Water: 0.3 sq. mi.

Grand Prairie — Township
Lat: 38-25-42 N   Long: 89-05-21 W
Pop: 898 (1990); 738 (1980)   Pop Density: 24.8
Land: 36.2 sq. mi.; Water: 0.1 sq. mi.

Ina — Village
ZIP: 62846   Lat: 38-09-07 N   Long: 88-54-13 W
Pop: 489 (1990); 460 (1980)   Pop Density: 232.9
Land: 2.1 sq. mi.; Water: 0.0 sq. mi.

McClellan — Township
Lat: 38-15-28 N   Long: 88-59-10 W
Pop: 1,183 (1990); 1,175 (1980)   Pop Density: 33.2
Land: 35.6 sq. mi.; Water: 0.1 sq. mi.

Moores Prairie — Township
Lat: 38-10-08 N   Long: 88-45-15 W
Pop: 371 (1990); 316 (1980)   Pop Density: 10.2
Land: 36.3 sq. mi.; Water: 0.2 sq. mi.

Mount Vernon — City
ZIP: 62864   Lat: 38-19-03 N   Long: 88-54-39 W
Pop: 16,988 (1990); 17,193 (1980)   Pop Density: 1573.0
Land: 10.8 sq. mi.; Water: 0.1 sq. mi.

In south-central IL, northeast of Carbondale. County seat. Settled 1819; incorporated Feb 10, 1837. Not coextensive with the town of the same name.

Name origin: For George Washington's (1732–99) VA estate.

*Mount Vernon — Township
ZIP: 62864   Lat: 38-20-54 N   Long: 88-51-33 W
Pop: 15,059 (1990); 16,282 (1980)   Pop Density: 408.1
Land: 36.9 sq. mi.; Water: 0.3 sq. mi.

Nason — City
ZIP: 62866   Lat: 38-10-34 N   Long: 88-57-57 W
Pop: 235 (1990); 272 (1980)   Pop Density: 261.1
Land: 0.9 sq. mi.; Water: 0.0 sq. mi.

Pendleton — Township
Lat: 38-15-31 N   Long: 88-45-17 W
Pop: 1,062 (1990); 1,064 (1980)   Pop Density: 29.8
Land: 35.6 sq. mi.; Water: 0.2 sq. mi.

Rome — Township
Lat: 38-25-49 N   Long: 88-58-33 W
Pop: 1,552 (1990); 1,312 (1980)   Pop Density: 42.9
Land: 36.2 sq. mi.; Water: 0.1 sq. mi.

Shiloh — Township
ZIP: 62864   Lat: 38-20-37 N   Long: 88-58-57 W
Pop: 6,119 (1990); 5,290 (1980)   Pop Density: 169.0
Land: 36.2 sq. mi.; Water: 0.1 sq. mi.

Spring Garden — Township
Lat: 38-10-24 N   Long: 88-52-36 W
Pop: 1,441 (1990); 1,430 (1980)   Pop Density: 39.3
Land: 36.7 sq. mi.; Water: 1.3 sq. mi.

Waltonville — Village
ZIP: 62894   Lat: 38-12-47 N   Long: 89-02-20 W
Pop: 396 (1990); 414 (1980)   Pop Density: 396.0
Land: 1.0 sq. mi.; Water: 0.0 sq. mi.

ILLINOIS, Jefferson County | *American Places Dictionary*

Webber
Township
Lat: 38-20-29 N **Long:** 88-45-23 W
Pop: 2,084 (1990); 1,931 (1980) **Pop Density:** 56.3
Land: 37.0 sq. mi.; **Water:** 0.2 sq. mi.

Woodlawn
Village
ZIP: 62898 **Lat:** 38-19-49 N **Long:** 89-02-06 W
Pop: 582 (1990); 471 (1980) **Pop Density:** 831.4
Land: 0.7 sq. mi.; **Water:** 0.0 sq. mi.

Jersey County
County Seat: Jerseyville (ZIP: 62052)

Pop: 20,539 (1990); 20,538 (1980) **Pop Density:** 55.6
Land: 369.2 sq. mi.; **Water:** 7.8 sq. mi. **Area Code:** 618
In west-central IL northwest of Alton; organized Feb 28, 1839 from Greene County.
Name origin: For the state of NJ.

Brighton
Village
ZIP: 62012 **Lat:** 39-02-16 N **Long:** 90-08-46 W
Pop: 303 (1990); 359 (1980) **Pop Density:** 1010.0
Land: 0.3 sq. mi.; **Water:** 0.0 sq. mi. **Elev:** 653 ft.
Part of the town is also in Macoupin County.

Elsah
Town
ZIP: 62028 **Lat:** 38-57-13 N **Long:** 90-21-16 W
Pop: 851 (1990); 990 (1980) **Pop Density:** 773.6
Land: 1.1 sq. mi.; **Water:** 0.0 sq. mi.
In southwestern IL, northwest of Alton. Founded in 1847 by a woodchopper who settled here in hopes of selling wood to the steamboats. Not coextensive with the town of the same name.
Name origin: The tiny settlement which attracted woodchoppers was first known as Jersey Landing, but the name was changed in 1853 (when it was platted as a town) by the first postmaster and later U.S. senator, James Semple. Semple named the town, a derivation of Ailsea, after his ancestral home in Scotland.

*Elsah
Township
Lat: 38-57-48 N **Long:** 90-19-38 W
Pop: 2,553 (1990); 2,570 (1980) **Pop Density:** 107.3
Land: 23.8 sq. mi.; **Water:** 2.7 sq. mi.

English
Township
Lat: 39-07-19 N **Long:** 90-25-42 W
Pop: 417 (1990); 461 (1980) **Pop Density:** 11.3
Land: 37.0 sq. mi.; **Water:** 0.0 sq. mi.

Fidelity
Village
ZIP: 62030 **Lat:** 39-09-16 N **Long:** 90-09-48 W
Pop: 66 (1990); 98 (1980) **Pop Density:** 660.0
Land: 0.1 sq. mi.; **Water:** 0.0 sq. mi. **Elev:** 630 ft.
Not coextensive with the town of the same name.

*Fidelity
Township
Lat: 39-08-09 N **Long:** 90-11-38 W
Pop: 655 (1990); 600 (1980) **Pop Density:** 18.1
Land: 36.2 sq. mi.; **Water:** 0.1 sq. mi.

Fieldon
Village
ZIP: 62031 **Lat:** 39-06-29 N **Long:** 90-29-59 W
Pop: 277 (1990); 299 (1980) **Pop Density:** 1385.0
Land: 0.2 sq. mi.; **Water:** 0.0 sq. mi. **Elev:** 700 ft.

Grafton
Town
ZIP: 62037 **Lat:** 38-58-21 N **Long:** 90-25-37 W
Pop: 918 (1990); 1,024 (1980) **Pop Density:** 270.0
Land: 3.4 sq. mi.; **Water:** 0.0 sq. mi.
In southwestern IL at the confluence of the Mississippi and Illinois rivers, northwest of Alton.

Jersey
Township
ZIP: 62052 **Lat:** 39-08-48 N **Long:** 90-18-15 W
Pop: 9,022 (1990); 8,835 (1980) **Pop Density:** 192.4
Land: 46.9 sq. mi.; **Water:** 0.0 sq. mi.

Jerseyville
City
ZIP: 62052 **Lat:** 39-07-10 N **Long:** 90-19-40 W
Pop: 7,382 (1990); 7,506 (1980) **Pop Density:** 1892.8
Land: 3.9 sq. mi.; **Water:** 0.0 sq. mi. **Elev:** 663 ft.
Incorporated Feb 14, 1855.

Mississippi
Township
Lat: 39-02-28 N **Long:** 90-18-38 W
Pop: 1,758 (1990); 1,609 (1980) **Pop Density:** 48.4
Land: 36.3 sq. mi.; **Water:** 0.0 sq. mi.
Name origin: For the Mississippi River, which forms the entire western border of IL.

Otter Creek
Township
Lat: 39-02-34 N **Long:** 90-25-42 W
Pop: 742 (1990); 728 (1980) **Pop Density:** 20.3
Land: 36.5 sq. mi.; **Water:** 0.1 sq. mi.

Otterville
Town
Lat: 39-03-03 N **Long:** 90-23-50 W
Pop: 115 (1990); 146 (1980) **Pop Density:** 115.0
Land: 1.0 sq. mi.; **Water:** 0.0 sq. mi.

Piasa
Township
Lat: 39-02-55 N **Long:** 90-12-30 W
Pop: 2,660 (1990); 2,737 (1980) **Pop Density:** 73.9
Land: 36.0 sq. mi.; **Water:** 0.1 sq. mi.

Quarry
Township
Lat: 38-59-08 N **Long:** 90-28-34 W
Pop: 1,294 (1990); 1,427 (1980) **Pop Density:** 63.1
Land: 20.5 sq. mi.; **Water:** 2.6 sq. mi.

Richwood
Township
Lat: 39-08-12 N **Long:** 90-33-00 W
Pop: 644 (1990); 711 (1980) **Pop Density:** 17.1
Land: 37.6 sq. mi.; **Water:** 0.2 sq. mi.

Rosedale
Township
Lat: 39-02-38 N **Long:** 90-32-05 W
Pop: 497 (1990); 510 (1980) **Pop Density:** 16.4
Land: 30.3 sq. mi.; **Water:** 1.9 sq. mi.

Ruyle
Township
Lat: 39-12-42 N **Long:** 90-11-32 W
Pop: 297 (1990); 350 (1980) **Pop Density:** 10.5
Land: 28.3 sq. mi.; **Water:** 0.0 sq. mi.

Jo Daviess County
County Seat: Galena (ZIP: 61036)

Pop: 21,821 (1990); 23,520 (1980) **Pop Density:** 36.3
Land: 601.2 sq. mi.; **Water:** 17.6 sq. mi. **Area Code:** 815

On the northwestern border of IL; organized Feb 17, 1827 from Mercer, Henry, and Putnam counties.

Name origin: For Col. Joseph Hamilton Daviess (1774–1811), VA soldier and jurist who unsuccessfully attempted to indict Aaron Burr (1756–1836) for treason (1807). According to Jacob Piatt Dunn, "The Colonel's name was Daveiss and he always wrote it that way"; however, the name is sometimes spelled 'Daviess' in biographical entries and in places named for him.

Apple River — Village
ZIP: 61001 **Lat:** 42-30-06 N **Long:** 90-05-40 W
Pop: 414 (1990); 472 (1980) **Pop Density:** 517.5
Land: 0.8 sq. mi.; **Water:** 0.0 sq. mi.

In northwestern IL on the WI border. Not coextensive with the town of the same name.
Name origin: For the river, which runs through the county.

*Apple River — Township
Lat: 42-28-44 N **Long:** 90-08-15 W
Pop: 535 (1990); 649 (1980) **Pop Density:** 28.9
Land: 18.5 sq. mi.; **Water:** 0.0 sq. mi.

Berreman — Township
Lat: 42-14-25 N **Long:** 89-56-22 W
Pop: 161 (1990); 182 (1980) **Pop Density:** 8.9
Land: 18.0 sq. mi.; **Water:** 0.0 sq. mi.

Council Hill — Township
Lat: 42-28-38 N **Long:** 90-21-02 W
Pop: 181 (1990); 202 (1980) **Pop Density:** 11.0
Land: 16.4 sq. mi.; **Water:** 0.0 sq. mi.

Derinda — Township
Lat: 42-14-22 N **Long:** 90-09-24 W
Pop: 328 (1990); 368 (1980) **Pop Density:** 8.9
Land: 37.0 sq. mi.; **Water:** 0.1 sq. mi.

Dunleith — Township
Lat: 42-28-42 N **Long:** 90-36-47 W
Pop: 3,877 (1990); 4,883 (1980) **Pop Density:** 416.9
Land: 9.3 sq. mi.; **Water:** 2.3 sq. mi.

East Dubuque — City
ZIP: 61025 **Lat:** 42-29-29 N **Long:** 90-38-19 W
Pop: 1,914 (1990); 2,194 (1980) **Pop Density:** 1595.0
Land: 1.2 sq. mi.; **Water:** 0.1 sq. mi.

In northwestern IL; opposite Dubuque, IA, on the east bank of the Mississippi River.
Name origin: For early French settler Julien Dubuque (1762–1810).

East Galena — Township
Lat: 42-24-40 N **Long:** 90-23-30 W
Pop: 1,063 (1990); 1,070 (1980) **Pop Density:** 45.6
Land: 23.3 sq. mi.; **Water:** 0.2 sq. mi.

Elizabeth — Village
ZIP: 61028 **Lat:** 42-18-58 N **Long:** 90-13-28 W
Pop: 641 (1990); 772 (1980) **Pop Density:** 1282.0
Land: 0.5 sq. mi.; **Water:** 0.0 sq. mi.

In northwestern IL on the banks of the Apple River; founded in 1832. Not coextensive with the town of the same name.
Name origin: Named in honor of Elizabeth Armstrong, the woman who rallied the residents of the fort to a successful defense against a hostile Indian attack.

*Elizabeth — Township
Lat: 42-20-01 N **Long:** 90-16-28 W
Pop: 1,050 (1990); 1,171 (1980) **Pop Density:** 28.5
Land: 36.8 sq. mi.; **Water:** 0.0 sq. mi.

Galena — City
ZIP: 61036 **Lat:** 42-25-14 N **Long:** 90-25-38 W
Pop: 3,647 (1990); 3,876 (1980) **Pop Density:** 1215.7
Land: 3.0 sq. mi.; **Water:** 0.0 sq. mi.

In northwestern IL, southeast of Dubuque, IA. Laid out 1826.
Name origin: Named in 1826 for the sulphide lead ore (galena) extracted from the area's bedrock.

Guilford — Township
Lat: 42-24-50 N **Long:** 90-17-23 W
Pop: 411 (1990); 369 (1980) **Pop Density:** 11.0
Land: 37.2 sq. mi.; **Water:** 0.2 sq. mi.

Hanover — Town
ZIP: 61041 **Lat:** 42-15-15 N **Long:** 90-16-43 W
Pop: 908 (1990); 1,069 (1980) **Pop Density:** 1513.3
Land: 0.6 sq. mi.; **Water:** 0.0 sq. mi.

In northwestern IL, southeast of Dubuque, IA. Founded 1828 by Daniel Fowler and Charles Ames. Not coextensive with the town of the same name.
Name origin: For Hanover, NH.

*Hanover — Township
Lat: 42-14-38 N **Long:** 90-18-04 W
Pop: 1,394 (1990); 1,537 (1980) **Pop Density:** 26.8
Land: 52.1 sq. mi.; **Water:** 4.7 sq. mi.

Menominee — Village
ZIP: 61025 **Lat:** 42-28-28 N **Long:** 90-32-31 W
Pop: 187 (1990); 231 (1980) **Pop Density:** 116.9
Land: 1.6 sq. mi.; **Water:** 0.0 sq. mi.

Not coextensive with the town of the same name.

*Menominee — Township
Lat: 42-27-51 N **Long:** 90-32-08 W
Pop: 998 (1990); 1,071 (1980) **Pop Density:** 35.5
Land: 28.1 sq. mi.; **Water:** 2.5 sq. mi.

Nora — Village
ZIP: 61059 **Lat:** 42-27-26 N **Long:** 89-56-40 W
Pop: 162 (1990); 185 (1980) **Pop Density:** 180.0
Land: 0.9 sq. mi.; **Water:** 0.0 sq. mi.

Not coextensive with the town of the same name.

ILLINOIS, Jo Daviess County

*Nora — Township
Lat: 42-26-07 N Long: 89-57-21 W
Pop: 443 (1990); 493 (1980) Pop Density: 17.5
Land: 25.3 sq. mi.; Water: 0.0 sq. mi.

Pleasant Valley — Township
Lat: 42-14-35 N Long: 90-02-17 W
Pop: 291 (1990); 352 (1980) Pop Density: 7.9
Land: 36.7 sq. mi.; Water: 0.0 sq. mi.

Rawlins — Township
Lat: 42-26-45 N Long: 90-26-31 W
Pop: 344 (1990); 310 (1980) Pop Density: 29.4
Land: 11.7 sq. mi.; Water: 0.0 sq. mi.

Rice — Township
Lat: 42-19-51 N Long: 90-22-55 W
Pop: 296 (1990); 256 (1980) Pop Density: 12.1
Land: 24.4 sq. mi.; Water: 5.3 sq. mi.

Rush — Township
Lat: 42-24-39 N Long: 90-02-19 W
Pop: 428 (1990); 487 (1980) Pop Density: 11.6
Land: 36.8 sq. mi.; Water: 0.0 sq. mi.

Scales Mound — Village
ZIP: 61075 Lat: 42-28-38 N Long: 90-15-07 W
Pop: 388 (1990); 347 (1980) Pop Density: 1940.0
Land: 0.2 sq. mi.; Water: 0.0 sq. mi. Elev: 950 ft.
Not coextensive with the town of the same name.

*Scales Mound — Township
Lat: 42-28-53 N Long: 90-14-54 W
Pop: 619 (1990); 606 (1980) Pop Density: 33.3
Land: 18.6 sq. mi.; Water: 0.0 sq. mi.

Stockton — Village
ZIP: 61085 Lat: 42-21-05 N Long: 90-00-21 W
Pop: 1,871 (1990); 1,872 (1980) Pop Density: 2672.9
Land: 0.7 sq. mi.; Water: 0.0 sq. mi.
Not coextensive with the town of the same name.

*Stockton — Township
Lat: 42-19-45 N Long: 90-02-23 W
Pop: 2,485 (1990); 2,471 (1980) Pop Density: 67.0
Land: 37.1 sq. mi.; Water: 0.0 sq. mi.

Thompson — Township
Lat: 42-24-51 N Long: 90-09-47 W
Pop: 585 (1990); 464 (1980) Pop Density: 16.2
Land: 36.2 sq. mi.; Water: 0.7 sq. mi.

Vinegar Hill — Township
Lat: 42-28-39 N Long: 90-27-00 W
Pop: 267 (1990); 249 (1980) Pop Density: 19.2
Land: 13.9 sq. mi.; Water: 0.0 sq. mi.

Wards Grove — Township
Lat: 42-20-06 N Long: 89-57-40 W
Pop: 282 (1990); 299 (1980) Pop Density: 15.8
Land: 17.8 sq. mi.; Water: 0.0 sq. mi.

Warren — Town
ZIP: 61087 Lat: 42-29-41 N Long: 89-59-24 W
Pop: 1,550 (1990); 1,595 (1980) Pop Density: 1722.2
Land: 0.9 sq. mi.; Water: 0.0 sq. mi. Elev: 1012 ft.
Organized 1850. Not coextensive with the town of the same name.
Name origin: Named in 1853 for the founder's son; changed from Courtland.

*Warren — Township
Lat: 42-28-57 N Long: 90-01-15 W
Pop: 1,760 (1990); 1,853 (1980) Pop Density: 89.3
Land: 19.7 sq. mi.; Water: 0.0 sq. mi.

West Galena — Township
Lat: 42-24-16 N Long: 90-27-32 W
Pop: 3,362 (1990); 3,505 (1980) Pop Density: 353.9
Land: 9.5 sq. mi.; Water: 1.7 sq. mi.

Woodbine — Township
Lat: 42-19-32 N Long: 90-10-02 W
Pop: 661 (1990); 673 (1980) Pop Density: 18.0
Land: 36.8 sq. mi.; Water: 0.0 sq. mi.

Johnson County
County Seat: Vienna (ZIP: 62995)

Pop: 11,347 (1990); 9,624 (1980) **Pop Density:** 32.8
Land: 346.0 sq. mi.; **Water:** 2.8 sq. mi. **Area Code:** 618

In south-central IL; organized Sep 14, 1812 (prior to statehood) from Randolph County.

Name origin: For Col. Richard Mentor Johnson (1781–1850), officer in War of 1812, U.S. senator from KY (1819–29), and U.S. vice president (1837–41).

Belknap — Village
ZIP: 62908 **Lat:** 37-19-20 N **Long:** 88-56-24 W
Pop: 125 (1990); 172 (1980) **Pop Density:** 125.0
Land: 1.0 sq. mi.; **Water:** 0.0 sq. mi. **Elev:** 341 ft.

Buncombe — Village
ZIP: 62912 **Lat:** 37-28-15 N **Long:** 88-58-29 W
Pop: 208 (1990); 231 (1980) **Pop Density:** 173.3
Land: 1.2 sq. mi.; **Water:** 0.0 sq. mi.

Cypress — Village
ZIP: 62923 **Lat:** 37-21-55 N **Long:** 89-01-08 W
Pop: 275 (1990); 271 (1980) **Pop Density:** 392.9
Land: 0.7 sq. mi.; **Water:** 0.0 sq. mi. **Elev:** 432 ft.

Goreville — Village
ZIP: 62939 **Lat:** 37-33-18 N **Long:** 88-58-25 W
Pop: 872 (1990); 978 (1980) **Pop Density:** 545.0
Land: 1.6 sq. mi.; **Water:** 0.0 sq. mi.

New Burnside — Village
ZIP: 62967 **Lat:** 37-34-42 N **Long:** 88-46-23 W
Pop: 259 (1990); 276 (1980) **Pop Density:** 235.5
Land: 1.1 sq. mi.; **Water:** 0.0 sq. mi.

Simpson — Village
ZIP: 62985 **Lat:** 37-28-03 N **Long:** 88-45-17 W
Pop: 61 (1990); 67 (1980) **Pop Density:** 122.0
Land: 0.5 sq. mi.; **Water:** 0.0 sq. mi.

Vienna — Town
ZIP: 62995 **Lat:** 37-24-51 N **Long:** 88-53-33 W
Pop: 1,446 (1990); 1,420 (1980) **Pop Density:** 688.6
Land: 2.1 sq. mi.; **Water:** 0.0 sq. mi. **Elev:** 404 ft.
Name origin: For Vienna, Austria.

Kane County
County Seat: Geneva (ZIP: 60134)

Pop: 317,471 (1990); 278,405 (1980) **Pop Density:** 609.7
Land: 520.7 sq. mi.; **Water:** 3.4 sq. mi. **Area Code:** 312

In northeastern IL, west of Chicago; organized Jan 16, 1836 from La Salle County.

Name origin: For Elisha Kent Kane (1796–1835), IL legislator, jurist, and U.S. senator (1825–35).

Algonquin — Village
ZIP: 60102 **Lat:** 42-09-13 N **Long:** 88-17-37 W
Pop: 1,469 (1990); 258 (1980) **Pop Density:** 3672.5
Land: 0.4 sq. mi.; **Water:** 0.0 sq. mi.

In northeastern IL, 40 mi. northwest of Chicago. Incorporated 1890. Part of the town is also in McHenry County.

Name origin: Probably for a ship that one of the town trustees had sailed on. Previously called Cornish's Ferry, Cornishville, Dennys Ferry, Osceola.

Aurora — Industrial city
ZIP: 60507 **Lat:** 41-45-56 N **Long:** 88-19-23 W
Pop: 84,770 (1990); 79,610 (1980) **Pop Density:** 3870.8
Land: 21.9 sq. mi.; **Water:** 0.4 sq. mi. **Elev:** 676 ft.

In northeastern IL on the Fox River, an industrial suburb 35 mi. west of Chicago. Town incorporated Feb 8, 1853. Part of the town is also in DuPage County. Not coextensive with the town of the same name.

Name origin: For the Roman goddess of dawn.

*Aurora — Township
ZIP: 60505 **Lat:** 41-46-07 N **Long:** 88-19-07 W
Pop: 101,769 (1990); 99,162 (1980) **Pop Density:** 2932.8
Land: 34.7 sq. mi.; **Water:** 0.6 sq. mi.

Barrington Hills — Village
ZIP: 60010 **Lat:** 42-08-35 N **Long:** 88-14-54 W
Pop: 151 (1990); 105 (1980) **Pop Density:** 88.8
Land: 1.7 sq. mi.; **Water:** 0.0 sq. mi. **Elev:** 877 ft.

Incorporated 1959. Part of the town is also in Cook, Lake, and McHenry counties.

Name origin: From nearby Barrington.

Bartlett — Village
ZIP: 60103 **Lat:** 41-59-23 N **Long:** 88-15-55 W
Pop: 11 (1990) **Pop Density:** 27.5
Land: 0.4 sq. mi.; **Water:** 0.0 sq. mi.

In northeastern IL, 30 mi. northwest of Chicago; a manufacturing and residential suburb. Founded 1873; incorporated 1891. Part of the town is also in Cook and DuPage counties.

Name origin: For founder Luther Bartlett, its first postmaster, who bought the site in 1844.

ILLINOIS, Kane County

Batavia
Industrial city
ZIP: 60510 **Lat:** 41-51-02 N **Long:** 88-18-01 W
Pop: 17,076 (1990); 12,574 (1980) **Pop Density:** 2474.8
Land: 6.9 sq. mi.; **Water:** 0.1 sq. mi. **Elev:** 716 ft.

In northeastern IL on the Fox River, 35 mi. west of Chicago. Founded 1834. Incorporated Jul 27, 1872. Part of the town is also in DuPage County. Not coextensive with the township of the same name.

Name origin: Possibly for Batavia, NY.

*Batavia
Township
ZIP: 60510 **Lat:** 41-49-58 N **Long:** 88-18-58 W
Pop: 20,306 (1990); 16,200 (1980) **Pop Density:** 1103.6
Land: 18.4 sq. mi.; **Water:** 0.3 sq. mi.

Big Rock
Township
Lat: 41-45-49 N **Long:** 88-32-47 W
Pop: 1,948 (1990); 1,924 (1980) **Pop Density:** 55.3
Land: 35.2 sq. mi.; **Water:** 0.0 sq. mi.

Blackberry
Township
Lat: 41-51-12 N **Long:** 88-25-52 W
Pop: 3,658 (1990); 3,121 (1980) **Pop Density:** 104.8
Land: 34.9 sq. mi.; **Water:** 0.1 sq. mi.

Burlington
Village
ZIP: 60109 **Lat:** 42-03-01 N **Long:** 88-32-50 W
Pop: 400 (1990); 442 (1980) **Pop Density:** 1333.3
Land: 0.3 sq. mi.; **Water:** 0.0 sq. mi.

In northeastern IL, 13 mi. west of Elgin. Dairy, livestock, and farming area. Not coextensive with the town of the same name.

*Burlington
Township
Lat: 42-01-47 N **Long:** 88-32-58 W
Pop: 1,555 (1990); 1,422 (1980) **Pop Density:** 46.0
Land: 33.8 sq. mi.; **Water:** 0.0 sq. mi.

Campton
Township
ZIP: 60183 **Lat:** 41-56-29 N **Long:** 88-26-08 W
Pop: 9,473 (1990); 5,928 (1980) **Pop Density:** 274.6
Land: 34.5 sq. mi.; **Water:** 0.1 sq. mi.

Carpentersville
Village
ZIP: 60110 **Lat:** 42-07-16 N **Long:** 88-16-17 W
Pop: 23,049 (1990); 23,272 (1980) **Pop Density:** 4268.3
Land: 5.4 sq. mi.; **Water:** 0.1 sq. mi.

In northeastern IL on the east bank of the Fox River, 35 mi. northwest of Chicago. Settled 1834; incorporated 1887.

Name origin: For either first settler, Angelo Carpenter of MA, or early settler D. G. Carpenter.

Dundee
Township
ZIP: 60118 **Lat:** 42-06-32 N **Long:** 88-17-50 W
Pop: 39,070 (1990); 35,662 (1980) **Pop Density:** 1109.9
Land: 35.2 sq. mi.; **Water:** 0.8 sq. mi.

East Dundee
Village
ZIP: 60118 **Lat:** 42-05-44 N **Long:** 88-15-20 W
Pop: 2,718 (1990); 2,618 (1980) **Pop Density:** 1132.5
Land: 2.4 sq. mi.; **Water:** 0.2 sq. mi.

Part of the town is also in Cook County.

Elburn
Village
ZIP: 60119 **Lat:** 41-53-24 N **Long:** 88-28-18 W
Pop: 1,275 (1990); 1,224 (1980) **Pop Density:** 1416.7
Land: 0.9 sq. mi.; **Water:** 0.0 sq. mi.

Elgin
City
ZIP: 60120 **Lat:** 42-02-33 N **Long:** 88-18-08 W
Pop: 61,610 (1990); 52,648 (1980) **Pop Density:** 3826.7
Land: 16.1 sq. mi.; **Water:** 0.3 sq. mi.

Founded in 1835 by James and Hezekiah Gifford, two settlers from New York. Incorporated 1854. Part of the town is also in Cook County. Not coextensive with the township of the same name.

*Elgin
Township
ZIP: 60120 **Lat:** 42-01-32 N **Long:** 88-19-14 W
Pop: 72,355 (1990); 61,576 (1980) **Pop Density:** 2247.0
Land: 32.2 sq. mi.; **Water:** 0.5 sq. mi.

Geneva
City
ZIP: 60134 **Lat:** 41-52-56 N **Long:** 88-18-52 W
Pop: 12,617 (1990); 9,881 (1980) **Pop Density:** 1911.7
Land: 6.6 sq. mi.; **Water:** 0.2 sq. mi.

In northeastern IL, 35 mi. west of Chicago. County seat. Incorporated Feb 25, 1867. Not coextensive with the town of the same name.

Name origin: For Geneva, NY.

*Geneva
Township
ZIP: 60134 **Lat:** 41-52-34 N **Long:** 88-19-19 W
Pop: 16,025 (1990); 12,371 (1980) **Pop Density:** 989.2
Land: 16.2 sq. mi.; **Water:** 0.2 sq. mi.

Gilberts
Village
ZIP: 60136 **Lat:** 42-06-05 N **Long:** 88-22-01 W
Pop: 987 (1990); 405 (1980) **Pop Density:** 448.6
Land: 2.2 sq. mi.; **Water:** 0.0 sq. mi.

Hampshire
Town
ZIP: 60140 **Lat:** 42-05-44 N **Long:** 88-31-18 W
Pop: 1,843 (1990); 1,735 (1980) **Pop Density:** 708.8
Land: 2.6 sq. mi.; **Water:** 0.0 sq. mi.

In northeastern IL, west of Chicago. Founded 1875 when the Chicago, Milwaukee, St. Paul, & Pacific Railroad reached here. Not coextensive with the town of the same name.

Name origin: Once called Henpeck.

*Hampshire
Township
Lat: 42-06-29 N **Long:** 88-31-49 W
Pop: 3,398 (1990); 2,991 (1980) **Pop Density:** 94.7
Land: 35.9 sq. mi.; **Water:** 0.0 sq. mi.

Hoffman Estates
Village
ZIP: 60196 **Lat:** 42-04-06 N **Long:** 88-14-25 W
Pop: 0 (1990)
Land: 0.1 sq. mi.; **Water:** 0.0 sq. mi.

Incorporated 1959. Part of the town is also in Cook County.

Kaneville
Township
Lat: 41-51-05 N **Long:** 88-33-11 W
Pop: 1,367 (1990); 1,259 (1980) **Pop Density:** 38.9
Land: 35.1 sq. mi.; **Water:** 0.0 sq. mi.

Maple Park
Village
ZIP: 60151 **Lat:** 41-54-25 N **Long:** 88-35-37 W
Pop: 637 (1990); 637 (1980) **Pop Density:** 1274.0
Land: 0.5 sq. mi.; **Water:** 0.0 sq. mi.

Part of the town is also in DeKalb County.

Montgomery
Town
ZIP: 60538 **Lat:** 41-43-51 N **Long:** 88-20-31 W
Pop: 3,675 (1990); 3,329 (1980) **Pop Density:** 1267.2
Land: 2.9 sq. mi.; **Water:** 0.1 sq. mi. **Elev:** 642 ft.
Settled 1840. Part of the town is also in Kendall County.
Name origin: For Montgomery County, NY, former home of the first settler.

North Aurora
Village
ZIP: 60542 **Lat:** 41-48-13 N **Long:** 88-19-49 W
Pop: 5,940 (1990); 5,205 (1980) **Pop Density:** 1605.4
Land: 3.7 sq. mi.; **Water:** 0.1 sq. mi.

Pingree Grove
Village
Lat: 42-04-06 N **Long:** 88-24-52 W
Pop: 138 (1990); 183 (1980) **Pop Density:** 172.5
Land: 0.8 sq. mi.; **Water:** 0.0 sq. mi. **Elev:** 912 ft.

Plato
Township
Lat: 42-01-33 N **Long:** 88-25-51 W
Pop: 3,469 (1990); 2,143 (1980) **Pop Density:** 103.6
Land: 33.5 sq. mi.; **Water:** 0.0 sq. mi.

Rutland
Township
Lat: 42-06-32 N **Long:** 88-25-18 W
Pop: 2,549 (1990); 1,850 (1980) **Pop Density:** 70.2
Land: 36.3 sq. mi.; **Water:** 0.1 sq. mi.

St. Charles
Town
ZIP: 60174 **Lat:** 41-55-14 N **Long:** 88-18-06 W
Pop: 22,491 (1990); 17,471 (1980) **Pop Density:** 2249.1
Land: 10.0 sq. mi.; **Water:** 0.2 sq. mi.
In northeastern IL on the Fox River, 33 mi. northwest of Chicago. Incorporated Feb 9, 1839. Part of the town is also in DuPage County. Not coextensive with the township of the same name.
Name origin: For Charlestown, NH. Name was changed to avoid confusion with Charleston, IL.

*St. Charles
Township
ZIP: 60174 **Lat:** 41-56-33 N **Long:** 88-19-12 W
Pop: 33,112 (1990); 27,319 (1980) **Pop Density:** 954.2
Land: 34.7 sq. mi.; **Water:** 0.6 sq. mi.

Sleepy Hollow
Village
ZIP: 60118 **Lat:** 42-05-36 N **Long:** 88-18-50 W
Pop: 3,241 (1990); 2,000 (1980) **Pop Density:** 1705.8
Land: 1.9 sq. mi.; **Water:** 0.0 sq. mi.

South Elgin
Town
ZIP: 60177 **Lat:** 41-59-46 N **Long:** 88-17-52 W
Pop: 7,474 (1990); 5,970 (1980) **Pop Density:** 2669.3
Land: 2.8 sq. mi.; **Water:** 0.1 sq. mi.
In northeastern IL, a suburb of Elgin.

Sugar Grove
Village
ZIP: 60554 **Lat:** 41-46-10 N **Long:** 88-27-31 W
Pop: 2,005 (1990); 1,366 (1980) **Pop Density:** 417.7
Land: 4.8 sq. mi.; **Water:** 0.0 sq. mi.
Not coextensive with the town of the same name.

*Sugar Grove
Township
ZIP: 60554 **Lat:** 41-46-09 N **Long:** 88-25-47 W
Pop: 5,514 (1990); 3,588 (1980) **Pop Density:** 157.1
Land: 35.1 sq. mi.; **Water:** 0.1 sq. mi.

Virgil
Township
Lat: 41-56-09 N **Long:** 88-32-48 W
Pop: 1,903 (1990); 1,889 (1980) **Pop Density:** 54.4
Land: 35.0 sq. mi.; **Water:** 0.0 sq. mi.

Wayne
Town
ZIP: 60184 **Lat:** 41-57-13 N **Long:** 88-16-31 W
Pop: 823 (1990); 480 (1980) **Pop Density:** 283.8
Land: 2.9 sq. mi.; **Water:** 0.0 sq. mi.
Part of the town is in DuPage County.
Name origin: For Gen. "Mad Anthony" Wayne (1745–96) of Revolutionary War fame.

West Dundee
Village
ZIP: 60118 **Lat:** 42-05-53 N **Long:** 88-17-31 W
Pop: 3,728 (1990); 3,551 (1980) **Pop Density:** 2867.7
Land: 1.3 sq. mi.; **Water:** 0.0 sq. mi.

Kankakee County
County Seat: Kankakee (ZIP: 60901)

Pop: 96,255 (1990); 102,926 (1980) **Pop Density:** 142.1
Land: 677.5 sq. mi.; **Water:** 4.0 sq. mi. **Area Code:** 815
On the northeastern border of IL, south of Chicago; organized Feb 11, 1853 from Iroquois and Will counties.
Name origin: For the Kankakee Indian tribe, possibly from Mohegan 'wolf' or 'wolf-place,' but meaning is unclear.

Aroma
Township
ZIP: 60901 **Lat:** 41-04-33 N **Long:** 87-46-46 W
Pop: 5,565 (1990); 6,107 (1980) **Pop Density:** 149.2
Land: 37.3 sq. mi.; **Water:** 0.8 sq. mi.

Aroma Park
Village
ZIP: 60910 **Lat:** 41-04-47 N **Long:** 87-48-19 W
Pop: 690 (1990); 673 (1980) **Pop Density:** 575.0
Land: 1.2 sq. mi.; **Water:** 0.2 sq. mi.

Bonfield
Village
ZIP: 60913 **Lat:** 41-08-49 N **Long:** 88-03-24 W
Pop: 299 (1990); 294 (1980) **Pop Density:** 996.7
Land: 0.3 sq. mi.; **Water:** 0.0 sq. mi.

Bourbonnais
Town
ZIP: 60914 **Lat:** 41-09-47 N **Long:** 87-52-49 W
Pop: 13,934 (1990); 13,280 (1980) **Pop Density:** 3765.9
Land: 3.7 sq. mi.; **Water:** 0.0 sq. mi. **Elev:** 663 ft.
In northeastern IL on the Kankakee River, 50 mi. southwest of Chicago. First settlement on the river; established as a

trading post 1832. Incorporated 1875. Not coextensive with the town of the same name.
Name origin: For Francois Bourbonnais, French fur trader who helped start the post and became historian of the area.

*Bourbonnais — Township
ZIP: 60914 Lat: 41-10-29 N Long: 87-51-36 W
Pop: 29,129 (1990); 29,316 (1980) Pop Density: 690.3
Land: 42.2 sq. mi.; Water: 0.4 sq. mi.

Bradley — Village
ZIP: 60915 Lat: 41-08-49 N Long: 87-51-20 W
Pop: 10,792 (1990); 11,015 (1980) Pop Density: 3481.3
Land: 3.1 sq. mi.; Water: 0.0 sq. mi. Elev: 632 ft.

In northeastern IL, 50 mi. southwest of Chicago. Founded 1892. Incorporated 1896.
Name origin: For David Bradley, who started an agricultural implement factory (the Bradley Manufacturing Company) here. Originally known as North Kankakee.

Buckingham — Village
ZIP: 60917 Lat: 41-02-48 N Long: 88-10-33 W
Pop: 340 (1990); 330 (1980) Pop Density: 1133.3
Land: 0.3 sq. mi.; Water: 0.0 sq. mi.

Cabery — Village
ZIP: 60919 Lat: 40-59-50 N Long: 88-12-14 W
Pop: 85 (1990); 108 (1980) Pop Density: 425.0
Land: 0.2 sq. mi.; Water: 0.0 sq. mi. Elev: 698 ft.

Part of the town is also in Ford County.

Chebanse — Village
ZIP: 60922 Lat: 41-00-17 N Long: 87-54-51 W
Pop: 425 (1990); 461 (1980) Pop Density: 2125.0
Land: 0.2 sq. mi.; Water: 0.0 sq. mi.

Part of the town is also in Iroquois County.
Name origin: From an Indian term probably meaning 'little duck.'

Essex — Village
ZIP: 60935 Lat: 41-10-42 N Long: 88-11-41 W
Pop: 482 (1990); 463 (1980) Pop Density: 283.5
Land: 1.7 sq. mi.; Water: 0.0 sq. mi. Elev: 590 ft.

Not coextensive with the town of the same name.

*Essex — Township
Lat: 41-09-31 N Long: 88-11-18 W
Pop: 994 (1990); 995 (1980) Pop Density: 27.9
Land: 35.6 sq. mi.; Water: 0.6 sq. mi.

Ganeer — Township
Lat: 41-09-19 N Long: 87-42-41 W
Pop: 3,146 (1990); 3,490 (1980) Pop Density: 78.8
Land: 39.9 sq. mi.; Water: 0.3 sq. mi.

Grant Park — Village
ZIP: 60940 Lat: 41-14-21 N Long: 87-38-40 W
Pop: 1,024 (1990); 1,038 (1980) Pop Density: 2048.0
Land: 0.5 sq. mi.; Water: 0.0 sq. mi.

Herscher — Village
ZIP: 60941 Lat: 41-02-56 N Long: 88-06-02 W
Pop: 1,278 (1990); 1,214 (1980) Pop Density: 751.8
Land: 1.7 sq. mi.; Water: 0.0 sq. mi.

Hopkins Park — Village
ZIP: 60944 Lat: 41-04-20 N Long: 87-36-53 W
Pop: 601 (1990); 673 (1980) Pop Density: 182.1
Land: 3.3 sq. mi.; Water: 0.0 sq. mi.

Irwin — Village
Lat: 41-03-09 N Long: 87-59-02 W
Pop: 50 (1990); 112 (1980) Pop Density: 500.0
Land: 0.1 sq. mi.; Water: 0.0 sq. mi. Elev: 662 ft.

Kankakee — City
ZIP: 60901 Lat: 41-06-55 N Long: 87-51-40 W
Pop: 27,575 (1990); 29,633 (1980) Pop Density: 2703.4
Land: 10.2 sq. mi.; Water: 0.5 sq. mi.

In northeastern IL on the Kankakee River, 50 mi. southwest of Chicago. County seat. Incorporated Feb 15, 1855. Not coextensive with the town of the same name.
Name origin: For the river, itself probably named from a Mohegan term for 'wolf' or 'wolf place,' but the meaning is unclear.

*Kankakee — Township
ZIP: 60901 Lat: 41-06-27 N Long: 87-51-27 W
Pop: 28,502 (1990); 31,081 (1980) Pop Density: 1592.3
Land: 17.9 sq. mi.; Water: 0.5 sq. mi.

Limestone — Township
Lat: 41-07-45 N Long: 87-57-43 W
Pop: 4,358 (1990); 4,627 (1980) Pop Density: 106.3
Land: 41.0 sq. mi.; Water: 0.4 sq. mi.

Manteno — Town
ZIP: 60950 Lat: 41-15-04 N Long: 87-50-12 W
Pop: 3,488 (1990); 3,155 (1980) Pop Density: 3170.9
Land: 1.1 sq. mi.; Water: 0.0 sq. mi.

Incorporated Apr 20, 1878. Not coextensive with the town of the same name.
Name origin: For the half-Indian daughter of 19th-century French scout Francois Bourbonnais, Jr.

*Manteno — Township
ZIP: 60950 Lat: 41-15-00 N Long: 87-50-17 W
Pop: 5,059 (1990); 4,951 (1980) Pop Density: 137.8
Land: 36.7 sq. mi.; Water: 0.1 sq. mi.

Momence — City
ZIP: 60954 Lat: 41-09-48 N Long: 87-39-48 W
Pop: 2,968 (1990); 3,297 (1980) Pop Density: 2283.1
Land: 1.3 sq. mi.; Water: 0.1 sq. mi. Elev: 626 ft.

Not coextensive with the town of the same name.

*Momence — Township
Lat: 41-09-44 N Long: 87-35-45 W
Pop: 3,570 (1990); 4,383 (1980) Pop Density: 84.0
Land: 42.5 sq. mi.; Water: 0.4 sq. mi.

Norton — Township
Lat: 41-03-32 N Long: 88-11-08 W
Pop: 1,129 (1990); 1,239 (1980) Pop Density: 22.7
Land: 49.8 sq. mi.; Water: 0.0 sq. mi.

Otto — Township
Lat: 41-02-21 N Long: 87-54-56 W
Pop: 2,558 (1990); 2,714 (1980) Pop Density: 53.1
Land: 48.2 sq. mi.; Water: 0.2 sq. mi.

Pembroke — Township
Lat: 41-03-49 N Long: 87-35-37 W
Pop: 3,320 (1990); 4,693 (1980) Pop Density: 63.2
Land: 52.5 sq. mi.; Water: 0.0 sq. mi.

Pilot — Township
Lat: 41-03-31 N Long: 88-04-21 W
Pop: 1,917 (1990); 1,868 (1980) Pop Density: 38.7
Land: 49.8 sq. mi.; Water: 0.0 sq. mi.

Reddick
Village
ZIP: 60961 **Lat:** 41-05-50 N **Long:** 88-14-55 W
Pop: 182 (1990); 203 (1980) **Pop Density:** 910.0
Land: 0.2 sq. mi.; **Water:** 0.0 sq. mi.
Part of the town is also in Livingston County.

Rockville
Township
Lat: 41-15-08 N **Long:** 87-56-51 W
Pop: 614 (1990); 612 (1980) **Pop Density:** 16.9
Land: 36.4 sq. mi.; **Water:** 0.2 sq. mi.

St. Anne
Town
ZIP: 60964 **Lat:** 41-01-23 N **Long:** 87-43-01 W
Pop: 1,153 (1990); 1,421 (1980) **Pop Density:** 2306.0
Land: 0.5 sq. mi.; **Water:** 0.0 sq. mi.
Not coextensive with the town of the same name.

*St. Anne
Township
Lat: 41-02-37 N **Long:** 87-42-57 W
Pop: 2,196 (1990); 2,547 (1980) **Pop Density:** 72.5
Land: 30.3 sq. mi.; **Water:** 0.0 sq. mi.

Salina
Township
Lat: 41-09-43 N **Long:** 88-03-53 W
Pop: 1,189 (1990); 1,218 (1980) **Pop Density:** 32.4
Land: 36.7 sq. mi.; **Water:** 0.0 sq. mi.

Sumner
Township
Lat: 41-14-59 N **Long:** 87-43-27 W
Pop: 799 (1990); 815 (1980) **Pop Density:** 21.5
Land: 37.2 sq. mi.; **Water:** 0.0 sq. mi.

Sun River Terrace
Village
Lat: 41-07-35 N **Long:** 87-44-04 W
Pop: 532 (1990) **Pop Density:** 1064.0
Land: 0.5 sq. mi.; **Water:** 0.0 sq. mi.

Union Hill
Village
ZIP: 60969 **Lat:** 41-06-33 N **Long:** 88-08-43 W
Pop: 37 (1990); 82 (1980) **Pop Density:** 740.0
Land: 0.05 sq. mi.; **Water:** 0.0 sq. mi.

Yellowhead
Township
Lat: 41-15-07 N **Long:** 87-35-46 W
Pop: 2,210 (1990); 2,270 (1980) **Pop Density:** 50.3
Land: 43.9 sq. mi.; **Water:** 0.0 sq. mi.

Kendall County
County Seat: Yorkville (ZIP: 60560)

Pop: 39,413 (1990); 37,202 (1980) **Pop Density:** 122.9
Land: 320.7 sq. mi.; **Water:** 2.0 sq. mi. **Area Code:** 312
In northeastern IL, southwest of Chicago; organized Feb 19, 1841 from La Salle and Kane counties.
Name origin: For Amos Kendall (1789–1869), U.S. postmaster general (1835–40) and publisher of the Washington *Evening Star*.

Big Grove
Township
Lat: 41-29-36 N **Long:** 88-32-55 W
Pop: 1,430 (1990); 1,448 (1980) **Pop Density:** 40.1
Land: 35.7 sq. mi.; **Water:** 0.0 sq. mi.

Boulder Hill
CDP
ZIP: 60538 **Lat:** 41-42-45 N **Long:** 88-20-09 W
Pop: 8,894 (1990); 9,333 (1980) **Pop Density:** 5929.3
Land: 1.5 sq. mi.; **Water:** 0.0 sq. mi.

Bristol
Township
ZIP: 60512 **Lat:** 41-41-14 N **Long:** 88-26-19 W
Pop: 5,598 (1990); 5,209 (1980) **Pop Density:** 195.7
Land: 28.6 sq. mi.; **Water:** 0.4 sq. mi.

Fox
Township
Lat: 41-35-22 N **Long:** 88-32-28 W
Pop: 1,146 (1990); 1,056 (1980) **Pop Density:** 31.7
Land: 36.2 sq. mi.; **Water:** 0.5 sq. mi.

Kendall
Township
Lat: 41-35-16 N **Long:** 88-25-50 W
Pop: 3,417 (1990); 3,321 (1980) **Pop Density:** 87.2
Land: 39.2 sq. mi.; **Water:** 0.1 sq. mi.

Lisbon
Village
ZIP: 60541 **Lat:** 41-28-50 N **Long:** 88-28-57 W
Pop: 216 (1990); 259 (1980) **Pop Density:** 720.0
Land: 0.3 sq. mi.; **Water:** 0.0 sq. mi.
Not coextensive with the town of the same name.

*Lisbon
Township
Lat: 41-30-23 N **Long:** 88-25-11 W
Pop: 784 (1990); 759 (1980) **Pop Density:** 21.4
Land: 36.6 sq. mi.; **Water:** 0.0 sq. mi.

Little Rock
Township
ZIP: 60545 **Lat:** 41-40-33 N **Long:** 88-32-46 W
Pop: 7,081 (1990); 6,945 (1980) **Pop Density:** 200.0
Land: 35.4 sq. mi.; **Water:** 0.2 sq. mi.

Millington
Village
ZIP: 60537 **Lat:** 41-33-39 N **Long:** 88-35-45 W
Pop: 258 (1990); 219 (1980) **Pop Density:** 1290.0
Land: 0.2 sq. mi.; **Water:** 0.0 sq. mi.
Part of the town is also in La Salle County.

Montgomery
Town
ZIP: 60538 **Lat:** 41-43-16 N **Long:** 88-20-10 W
Pop: 592 (1990); 40 (1980) **Pop Density:** 986.7
Land: 0.6 sq. mi.; **Water:** 0.0 sq. mi. **Elev:** 642 ft.
Settled 1840. Part of the town is also in Kane County.
Name origin: For Montgomery County, NY, former home of the first settler.

Naausay
Township
Lat: 41-35-25 N **Long:** 88-18-45 W
Pop: 1,067 (1990); 906 (1980) **Pop Density:** 31.2
Land: 34.2 sq. mi.; **Water:** 0.0 sq. mi.

ILLINOIS, Kendall County

Newark
Village
ZIP: 60541 Lat: 41-32-13 N Long: 88-34-50 W
Pop: 840 (1990); 798 (1980) Pop Density: 840.0
Land: 1.0 sq. mi.; Water: 0.0 sq. mi.

Oswego
Village
ZIP: 60543 Lat: 41-41-52 N Long: 88-19-57 W
Pop: 3,876 (1990); 3,021 (1980) Pop Density: 1020.0
Land: 3.8 sq. mi.; Water: 0.0 sq. mi. Elev: 646 ft.
In northeastern IL on the Fox River, 40 mi. southwest of Chicago. Not coextensive with the town of the same name.
Name origin: For Oswego, NY.

*Oswego
Township
ZIP: 60543 Lat: 41-40-53 N Long: 88-19-20 W
Pop: 18,078 (1990); 16,772 (1980) Pop Density: 453.1
Land: 39.9 sq. mi.; Water: 0.6 sq. mi.

Plano
Town
ZIP: 60545 Lat: 41-39-47 N Long: 88-32-05 W
Pop: 5,104 (1990); 4,875 (1980) Pop Density: 2430.5
Land: 2.1 sq. mi.; Water: 0.0 sq. mi. Elev: 650 ft.
In northeastern IL, 50 mi. southeast of Chicago. Settled 1835; incorporated Feb 16, 1865.

Sandwich
Town
ZIP: 60548 Lat: 41-38-49 N Long: 88-35-29 W
Pop: 1 (1990); 3 (1980) Pop Density: 10.0
Land: 0.1 sq. mi.; Water: 0.0 sq. mi.
Incorporated Feb 21, 1859. In northeastern IL, 55 mi. west of Chicago. Part of the town is also in DeKalb County.
Name origin: Named by early settlers, for Sandwich, MA.

Seward
Township
Lat: 41-30-27 N Long: 88-18-32 W
Pop: 812 (1990); 786 (1980) Pop Density: 23.2
Land: 35.0 sq. mi.; Water: 0.2 sq. mi.

Yorkville
Town
ZIP: 60560 Lat: 41-38-32 N Long: 88-26-51 W
Pop: 3,925 (1990); 3,422 (1980) Pop Density: 1266.1
Land: 3.1 sq. mi.; Water: 0.1 sq. mi.
In northeastern IL on the Fox River, southwest of Chicago.

Knox County
County Seat: Galesburg (ZIP: 61401)

Pop: 56,393 (1990); 61,607 (1980) Pop Density: 78.7
Land: 716.3 sq. mi.; Water: 3.4 sq. mi. Area Code: 309
In northwestern IL south of Moline; organized Jan 13, 1825 from Fulton County.
Name origin: For Gen. Henry Knox (1750–1806), Revolutionary War officer and first U.S. secretary of war (1785–95).

Abingdon
City
ZIP: 61410 Lat: 40-48-09 N Long: 90-24-02 W
Pop: 3,597 (1990); 4,210 (1980) Pop Density: 2569.3
Land: 1.4 sq. mi.; Water: 0.0 sq. mi. Elev: 753 ft.
In west-central IL, 10 mi. south of Galesburg. Incorporated 1857.

Altona
Village
ZIP: 61414 Lat: 41-06-54 N Long: 90-09-52 W
Pop: 559 (1990); 610 (1980) Pop Density: 559.0
Land: 1.0 sq. mi.; Water: 0.0 sq. mi.
Founded 1868; incorporated 1857.

Cedar
Township
Lat: 40-50-36 N Long: 90-23-24 W
Pop: 3,589 (1990); 4,098 (1980) Pop Density: 99.7
Land: 36.0 sq. mi.; Water: 0.2 sq. mi.

Chestnut
Township
Lat: 40-45-12 N Long: 90-16-27 W
Pop: 335 (1990); 438 (1980) Pop Density: 9.3
Land: 36.2 sq. mi.; Water: 0.0 sq. mi.

Copley
Township
Lat: 41-01-08 N Long: 90-09-20 W
Pop: 388 (1990); 441 (1980) Pop Density: 11.1
Land: 35.0 sq. mi.; Water: 0.4 sq. mi.

East Galesburg
Village
ZIP: 61430 Lat: 40-56-34 N Long: 90-18-40 W
Pop: 813 (1990); 928 (1980) Pop Density: 625.4
Land: 1.3 sq. mi.; Water: 0.1 sq. mi.

Elba
Township
Lat: 40-50-21 N Long: 90-02-44 W
Pop: 281 (1990); 373 (1980) Pop Density: 7.7
Land: 36.3 sq. mi.; Water: 0.0 sq. mi.

Galesburg
City
ZIP: 61401 Lat: 40-57-00 N Long: 90-22-40 W
Pop: 33,530 (1990); 35,305 (1980) Pop Density: 1984.0
Land: 16.9 sq. mi.; Water: 0.2 sq. mi. Elev: 773 ft.
In western IL, 40 mi. northwest of Peoria. County seat; founded 1836; coextensive with township at Galesburg City. Incorporated Jan 27, 1841.
Name origin: For the Rev. George Washington Gale, leader of the founding Presbyterian parishioners.

*Galesburg
Township
Lat: 40-55-19 N Long: 90-23-27 W
Pop: 526 (1990); 666 (1980) Pop Density: 24.7
Land: 21.3 sq. mi.; Water: 0.0 sq. mi.

Haw Creek
Township
Lat: 40-50-28 N Long: 90-09-11 W
Pop: 561 (1990); 608 (1980) Pop Density: 15.7
Land: 35.8 sq. mi.; Water: 0.0 sq. mi.

Henderson
Village
ZIP: 61439 Lat: 41-01-28 N Long: 90-21-10 W
Pop: 290 (1990); 369 (1980) Pop Density: 966.7
Land: 0.3 sq. mi.; Water: 0.0 sq. mi. Elev: 815 ft.
Not coextensive with the town of the same name.

*Henderson — Township
Lat: 41-01-16 N Long: 90-23-10 W
Pop: 1,290 (1990); 1,914 (1980) Pop Density: 37.8
Land: 34.1 sq. mi.; Water: 0.0 sq. mi.

Indian Point — Township
Lat: 40-45-31 N Long: 90-23-34 W
Pop: 1,781 (1990); 2,204 (1980) Pop Density: 49.5
Land: 36.0 sq. mi.; Water: 0.0 sq. mi.

Knox — Township
ZIP: 61448 Lat: 40-56-04 N Long: 90-16-31 W
Pop: 5,463 (1990); 5,942 (1980) Pop Density: 151.8
Land: 36.0 sq. mi.; Water: 0.1 sq. mi.

Knoxville — Town
ZIP: 61448 Lat: 40-54-22 N Long: 90-17-07 W
Pop: 3,243 (1990); 3,432 (1980) Pop Density: 1474.1
Land: 2.2 sq. mi.; Water: 0.0 sq. mi.
Name origin: For Gen. Henry Knox (1750–1806), Revolutionary War officer and first U.S. secretary of war.

London Mills — Town
ZIP: 61544 Lat: 40-42-56 N Long: 90-15-27 W
Pop: 12 (1990); 18 (1980) Pop Density: 120.0
Land: 0.1 sq. mi.; Water: 0.0 sq. mi. Elev: 533 ft.
Incorporated November 27, 1883. Part of the town is also in Fulton County.

Lynn — Township
Lat: 41-06-21 N Long: 90-02-28 W
Pop: 340 (1990); 433 (1980) Pop Density: 9.6
Land: 35.3 sq. mi.; Water: 0.0 sq. mi.

Maquon — Village
ZIP: 61458 Lat: 40-47-53 N Long: 90-09-45 W
Pop: 331 (1990); 350 (1980) Pop Density: 1655.0
Land: 0.2 sq. mi.; Water: 0.0 sq. mi.
Not coextensive with the town of the same name.

*Maquon — Township
Lat: 40-45-09 N Long: 90-08-52 W
Pop: 647 (1990); 705 (1980) Pop Density: 18.0
Land: 35.9 sq. mi.; Water: 0.2 sq. mi.

Oneida — City
ZIP: 61467 Lat: 41-04-20 N Long: 90-13-31 W
Pop: 723 (1990); 765 (1980) Pop Density: 1032.9
Land: 0.7 sq. mi.; Water: 0.0 sq. mi.

Ontario — Township
Lat: 41-06-27 N Long: 90-16-08 W
Pop: 1,044 (1990); 1,129 (1980) Pop Density: 28.8
Land: 36.2 sq. mi.; Water: 0.0 sq. mi.

Orange — Township
Lat: 40-50-25 N Long: 90-16-40 W
Pop: 650 (1990); 702 (1980) Pop Density: 17.9
Land: 36.4 sq. mi.; Water: 0.0 sq. mi.

Persifer — Township
Lat: 40-55-58 N Long: 90-09-20 W
Pop: 892 (1990); 822 (1980) Pop Density: 25.7
Land: 34.7 sq. mi.; Water: 0.9 sq. mi.

Rio — Village
ZIP: 61472 Lat: 41-06-31 N Long: 90-23-56 W
Pop: 260 (1990); 282 (1980) Pop Density: 866.7
Land: 0.3 sq. mi.; Water: 0.0 sq. mi. Elev: 778 ft.
Not coextensive with the town of the same name.

*Rio — Township
Lat: 41-06-19 N Long: 90-23-13 W
Pop: 622 (1990); 693 (1980) Pop Density: 17.2
Land: 36.2 sq. mi.; Water: 0.0 sq. mi.

St. Augustine — Village
ZIP: 61474 Lat: 40-43-11 N Long: 90-24-31 W
Pop: 151 (1990); 204 (1980) Pop Density: 251.7
Land: 0.6 sq. mi.; Water: 0.0 sq. mi.

Salem — Township
Lat: 40-45-13 N Long: 90-02-34 W
Pop: 1,129 (1990); 1,268 (1980) Pop Density: 31.6
Land: 35.7 sq. mi.; Water: 0.6 sq. mi.

Sparta — Township
Lat: 41-01-13 N Long: 90-16-03 W
Pop: 1,226 (1990); 1,441 (1980) Pop Density: 34.0
Land: 36.1 sq. mi.; Water: 0.0 sq. mi.

Truro — Township
Lat: 40-55-50 N Long: 90-02-22 W
Pop: 897 (1990); 972 (1980) Pop Density: 25.1
Land: 35.7 sq. mi.; Water: 0.1 sq. mi.

Victoria — Village
ZIP: 61485 Lat: 41-01-58 N Long: 90-05-43 W
Pop: 299 (1990); 389 (1980) Pop Density: 427.1
Land: 0.7 sq. mi.; Water: 0.0 sq. mi.
Not coextensive with the town of the same name.

*Victoria — Township
Lat: 41-01-19 N Long: 90-02-20 W
Pop: 376 (1990); 482 (1980) Pop Density: 10.7
Land: 35.0 sq. mi.; Water: 0.5 sq. mi.

Walnut Grove — Township
Lat: 41-06-30 N Long: 90-09-14 W
Pop: 826 (1990); 971 (1980) Pop Density: 23.3
Land: 35.5 sq. mi.; Water: 0.1 sq. mi.

Wataga — Town
ZIP: 61488 Lat: 41-01-30 N Long: 90-16-30 W
Pop: 879 (1990); 996 (1980) Pop Density: 976.7
Land: 0.9 sq. mi.; Water: 0.0 sq. mi.
Name origin: From a Cherokee Indian term probably meaning 'river of islands.'

Williamsfield — Village
ZIP: 61489 Lat: 40-55-34 N Long: 90-01-02 W
Pop: 571 (1990); 585 (1980) Pop Density: 439.2
Land: 1.3 sq. mi.; Water: 0.0 sq. mi. Elev: 711 ft.

Yates City — Town
ZIP: 61572 Lat: 40-46-40 N Long: 90-00-48 W
Pop: 760 (1990); 860 (1980) Pop Density: 1266.7
Land: 0.6 sq. mi.; Water: 0.0 sq. mi. Elev: 673 ft.
Name origin: For Gov. Richard Yates (1815–73).

ILLINOIS, Lake County — *American Places Dictionary*

Lake County
County Seat: Waukegan (ZIP: 60085)

Pop: 516,418 (1990); 440,388 (1980)   **Pop Density:** 1153.3
Land: 447.8 sq. mi.; **Water:** 920.3 sq. mi.   **Area Code:** 312
On the northeastern border of IL; organized Mar 1, 1839 from McHenry County.
Name origin: For Lake Michigan, which forms its eastern boundary.

Antioch — Lake resort village
ZIP: 60002   **Lat:** 42-28-29 N   **Long:** 88-04-46 W
Pop: 6,105 (1990); 4,419 (1980)   **Pop Density:** 911.2
Land: 6.7 sq. mi.; **Water:** 0.3 sq. mi.
In northeastern IL on the WI border, 45 mi. north of Chicago. Settled 1836; incorporated 1857.
Name origin: For the biblical city in Asia Minor.

*Antioch — Township
ZIP: 60002   **Lat:** 42-27-51 N   **Long:** 88-06-41 W
Pop: 18,046 (1990); 15,118 (1980)   **Pop Density:** 505.5
Land: 35.7 sq. mi.; **Water:** 6.7 sq. mi.

Arlington Heights — Residential village
ZIP: 60005
Pop: 0 (1990)
In northeastern IL, 20 mi. northwest of Chicago. Settled 1830s; incorporated 1887. Site of Arlington Park Race Track. Part of the town is also in Cook County.
Name origin: For Arlington, VA.

Avon — Township
ZIP: 60030   **Lat:** 42-21-24 N   **Long:** 88-03-50 W
Pop: 35,989 (1990); 29,963 (1980)   **Pop Density:** 1585.4
Land: 22.7 sq. mi.; **Water:** 1.1 sq. mi.
In northeastern IL.

Bannockburn — Village
ZIP: 60015   **Lat:** 42-11-33 N   **Long:** 87-52-06 W
Pop: 1,388 (1990); 1,316 (1980)   **Pop Density:** 694.0
Land: 2.0 sq. mi.; **Water:** 0.0 sq. mi.   **Elev:** 685 ft.
Incorporated 1929.
Name origin: For Bannockburn, Scotland, former home of early settlers.

Barrington — Village
ZIP: 60010   **Lat:** 42-09-38 N   **Long:** 88-07-48 W
Pop: 4,345 (1990); 4,074 (1980)   **Pop Density:** 2172.5
Land: 2.0 sq. mi.; **Water:** 0.1 sq. mi.
Incorporated 1959. In northeastern IL, a residential suburb 30 mi. northwest of Chicago. Founded 1845. Part of the town is also in Cook County.
Name origin: For Great Barrington, MA.

Barrington Hills — Village
ZIP: 60010   **Lat:** 42-10-04 N   **Long:** 88-10-49 W
Pop: 698 (1990); 524 (1980)   **Pop Density:** 225.2
Land: 3.1 sq. mi.; **Water:** 0.0 sq. mi.   **Elev:** 877 ft.
Part of the town is also in Cook, McHenry, and Kane counties.
Name origin: From nearby Barrington.

Beach Park — Village
ZIP: 60099   **Lat:** 42-25-29 N   **Long:** 87-51-22 W
Pop: 9,513 (1990); 8,468 (1980)   **Pop Density:** 1463.5
Land: 6.5 sq. mi.; **Water:** 0.0 sq. mi.

Benton — Township
ZIP: 60096   **Lat:** 42-27-49 N   **Long:** 87-50-34 W
Pop: 15,815 (1990); 14,534 (1980)   **Pop Density:** 1033.7
Land: 15.3 sq. mi.; **Water:** 0.1 sq. mi.

Buffalo Grove — Residential suburb
ZIP: 60089   **Lat:** 42-10-16 N   **Long:** 87-57-36 W
Pop: 21,930 (1990); 9,086 (1980)   **Pop Density:** 3781.0
Land: 5.8 sq. mi.; **Water:** 0.0 sq. mi.
In northeastern IL, 25 mi. northwest of Chicago. Incorporated 1958. Part of the town is also in Cook County.
Name origin: For the once-present American bison.

Channel Lake — CDP
Lat: 42-29-03 N   **Long:** 88-09-01 W
Pop: 1,660 (1990); 1,613 (1980)   **Pop Density:** 873.7
Land: 1.9 sq. mi.; **Water:** 0.3 sq. mi.

Cuba — Township
ZIP: 60010   **Lat:** 42-11-56 N   **Long:** 88-09-46 W
Pop: 14,118 (1990); 11,826 (1980)   **Pop Density:** 611.2
Land: 23.1 sq. mi.; **Water:** 1.1 sq. mi.

Deerfield — Village
ZIP: 60015   **Lat:** 42-10-05 N   **Long:** 87-51-04 W
Pop: 17,327 (1990); 17,430 (1980)   **Pop Density:** 3465.4
Land: 5.0 sq. mi.; **Water:** 0.0 sq. mi.
In northeastern IL, 25 mi. northwest of Chicago. Founded 1836 on the site of a Potawatomi Indian village; incorporated 1903. Part of the town is also in Cook County. Not coextensive with the township of the same name.
Name origin: For its descriptive connotations.

*Deerfield — Township
ZIP: 60035   **Lat:** 42-11-11 N   **Long:** 87-48-17 W
Pop: 34,814 (1990); 35,211 (1980)   **Pop Density:** 2901.2
Land: 12.0 sq. mi.; **Water:** 0.4 sq. mi.

Deer Park — Village
ZIP: 60010   **Lat:** 42-10-05 N   **Long:** 88-05-17 W
Pop: 2,887 (1990); 1,368 (1980)   **Pop Density:** 801.9
Land: 3.6 sq. mi.; **Water:** 0.1 sq. mi.

Ela — Township
ZIP: 60047   **Lat:** 42-11-51 N   **Long:** 88-03-48 W
Pop: 32,433 (1990); 19,969 (1980)   **Pop Density:** 929.3
Land: 34.9 sq. mi.; **Water:** 1.1 sq. mi.

Forest Lake — CDP
Lat: 42-12-20 N   **Long:** 88-03-07 W
Pop: 1,371 (1990); 1,148 (1980)   **Pop Density:** 1958.6
Land: 0.7 sq. mi.; **Water:** 0.1 sq. mi.

Fox Lake — Village
ZIP: 60020   **Lat:** 42-24-24 N   **Long:** 88-10-37 W
Pop: 7,430 (1990); 6,624 (1980)   **Pop Density:** 1688.6
Land: 4.4 sq. mi.; **Water:** 1.6 sq. mi.
Founded 1839; incorporated 1906. Part of the town is also in McHenry County.
Name origin: For the nearby lake.

Fox Lake Hills
CDP
Lat: 42-24-25 N **Long:** 88-07-24 W
Pop: 2,681 (1990); 2,199 (1980) **Pop Density:** 1577.1
Land: 1.7 sq. mi.; **Water:** 0.5 sq. mi.

Fox River Valley Gardens
Village
Lat: 42-14-29 N **Long:** 88-11-13 W
Pop: 665 (1990); 520 (1980) **Pop Density:** 198.0
Land: 0.5 sq. mi.; **Water:** 0.0 sq. mi.

Part of the town is also in McHenry County.

Fremont
Township
ZIP: 60060 **Lat:** 42-16-55 N **Long:** 88-03-31 W
Pop: 14,280 (1990); 12,234 (1980) **Pop Density:** 411.5
Land: 34.7 sq. mi.; **Water:** 1.0 sq. mi.

Gages Lake
CDP
ZIP: 60030 **Lat:** 42-21-05 N **Long:** 87-58-56 W
Pop: 8,349 (1990); 3,814 (1980) **Pop Density:** 2783.0
Land: 3.0 sq. mi.; **Water:** 0.2 sq. mi.

Grandwood Park
CDP
Lat: 42-23-35 N **Long:** 87-59-12 W
Pop: 2,470 (1990) **Pop Density:** 1235.0
Land: 2.0 sq. mi.; **Water:** 0.0 sq. mi.

Grant
Township
ZIP: 60041 **Lat:** 42-22-08 N **Long:** 88-09-35 W
Pop: 14,423 (1990); 12,868 (1980) **Pop Density:** 796.9
Land: 18.1 sq. mi.; **Water:** 5.2 sq. mi.

Grayslake
City
ZIP: 60030 **Lat:** 42-20-59 N **Long:** 88-02-18 W
Pop: 7,388 (1990); 5,260 (1980) **Pop Density:** 1802.0
Land: 4.1 sq. mi.; **Water:** 0.1 sq. mi.

Name origin: For the lake in the western corner of the county.

Green Oaks
Village
ZIP: 60048 **Lat:** 42-18-06 N **Long:** 87-54-54 W
Pop: 2,101 (1990); 1,415 (1980) **Pop Density:** 656.6
Land: 3.2 sq. mi.; **Water:** 0.1 sq. mi. **Elev:** 690 ft.

In northeastern IL, east of Libertyville.

Gurnee
City
ZIP: 60031 **Lat:** 42-22-37 N **Long:** 87-56-09 W
Pop: 13,701 (1990); 7,179 (1980) **Pop Density:** 1234.3
Land: 11.1 sq. mi.; **Water:** 0.0 sq. mi.

In northeastern IL on Lake Michigan, just north of Waukegan. Incorporated 1928.

Name origin: For either Louis J. Gurnee, railroad surveyor, or Walter S. Gurnee, founding landowner, political leader, and mayor of Chicago.

Hainesville
Village
Lat: 42-20-22 N **Long:** 88-03-52 W
Pop: 134 (1990); 187 (1980) **Pop Density:** 78.8
Land: 1.7 sq. mi.; **Water:** 0.0 sq. mi.

Hawthorn Woods
Village
ZIP: 60047 **Lat:** 42-13-24 N **Long:** 88-03-26 W
Pop: 4,423 (1990); 1,658 (1980) **Pop Density:** 804.2
Land: 5.5 sq. mi.; **Water:** 0.1 sq. mi.

Highland Park
City
ZIP: 60035 **Lat:** 42-10-57 N **Long:** 87-48-34 W
Pop: 30,575 (1990); 30,599 (1980) **Pop Density:** 2547.9
Land: 12.0 sq. mi.; **Water:** 0.4 sq. mi.

In northeastern IL on Lake Michigan, 25 mi. north of Chicago. Settled 1847. Incorporated Mar 11, 1869.

Name origin: Named in 1854 by Walter Gurnee, Chicago mayor (1852–53), when he bought the site. Previously known as Port Clinton and Saint Johns.

Highwood
City
ZIP: 60040 **Lat:** 42-12-41 N **Long:** 87-48-42 W
Pop: 5,331 (1990); 5,455 (1980) **Pop Density:** 4846.4
Land: 1.1 sq. mi.; **Water:** 0.0 sq. mi.

Incorporated Nov 27, 1886.

Indian Creek
Town
Lat: 42-13-33 N **Long:** 87-58-36 W
Pop: 247 (1990); 236 (1980) **Pop Density:** 823.3
Land: 0.3 sq. mi.; **Water:** 0.0 sq. mi. **Elev:** 741 ft.

In northeastern IL on Indian Creek, a tributary of the Des Plaines River, northwest of Chicago.

Name origin: For its location.

Island Lake
Town
ZIP: 60042 **Lat:** 42-16-39 N **Long:** 88-11-25 W
Pop: 1,983 (1990); 1,569 (1980) **Pop Density:** 1983.0
Land: 1.0 sq. mi.; **Water:** 0.1 sq. mi.

In northeastern IL on a small lake created by damming Cotton Creek in 1936. Incorporated 1954. Part of the town is also in McHenry County.

Kildeer
Town
ZIP: 60047 **Lat:** 42-10-45 N **Long:** 88-02-56 W
Pop: 2,257 (1990); 1,609 (1980) **Pop Density:** 752.3
Land: 3.0 sq. mi.; **Water:** 0.0 sq. mi.

Lake Barrington
Village
ZIP: 60010 **Lat:** 42-12-38 N **Long:** 88-09-54 W
Pop: 3,855 (1990); 2,320 (1980) **Pop Density:** 741.3
Land: 5.2 sq. mi.; **Water:** 0.2 sq. mi.

Lake Bluff
City
ZIP: 60044 **Lat:** 42-16-57 N **Long:** 87-51-01 W
Pop: 5,513 (1990); 4,434 (1980) **Pop Density:** 1378.3
Land: 4.0 sq. mi.; **Water:** 0.0 sq. mi.

Name origin: Descriptively named for its location on a bluff overlooking Lake Michigan.

Lake Catherine
CDP
Lat: 42-29-25 N **Long:** 88-07-32 W
Pop: 1,515 (1990); 1,335 (1980) **Pop Density:** 1377.3
Land: 1.1 sq. mi.; **Water:** 0.5 sq. mi.

Lake Forest
City
ZIP: 60045 **Lat:** 42-14-10 N **Long:** 87-51-27 W
Pop: 17,836 (1990); 15,245 (1980) **Pop Density:** 1087.6
Land: 16.4 sq. mi.; **Water:** 0.0 sq. mi.

In northeastern IL on Lake Michigan, 28 mi. north of Chicago. Incorporated Feb 21, 1861.

Name origin: Descriptive and promotional.

Lakemoor
Village
Lat: 42-20-05 N **Long:** 88-11-12 W
Pop: 261 (1990); 723 (1980) **Pop Density:** 261.0
Land: 1.0 sq. mi.; **Water:** 0.1 sq. mi.

Part of the town is also in McHenry County.

Lake Villa
Town
ZIP: 60046 **Lat:** 42-25-03 N **Long:** 88-04-56 W
Pop: 2,857 (1990); 1,462 (1980) **Pop Density:** 649.3
Land: 4.4 sq. mi.; **Water:** 0.8 sq. mi.

Not coextensive with the town of the same name.

Name origin: For the many nearby lakes.

ILLINOIS, Lake County

*Lake Villa — Township
ZIP: 60046   Lat: 42-24-59 N   Long: 88-04-05 W
Pop: 20,764 (1990); 16,114 (1980)   Pop Density: 898.9
Land: 23.1 sq. mi.; Water: 2.9 sq. mi.

Lake Zurich — City
ZIP: 60047   Lat: 42-11-32 N   Long: 88-05-16 W
Pop: 14,947 (1990); 8,225 (1980)   Pop Density: 2622.3
Land: 5.7 sq. mi.; Water: 0.4 sq. mi.

In northeastern IL, a resort area north of Chicago. Settled 1836 by Daniel Wright, veteran of the War of 1812; incorporated 1896.

Name origin: For the Swiss city and its lake.

Libertyville — City
ZIP: 60048   Lat: 42-17-02 N   Long: 87-57-57 W
Pop: 19,174 (1990); 16,520 (1980)   Pop Density: 2338.3
Land: 8.2 sq. mi.; Water: 0.3 sq. mi.

In northeastern IL on the Des Plaines River, 30 mi. northwest of Chicago. Not coextensive with the town of the same name.

Name origin: Patriotically renamed on Apr 16, 1838, upon establishment of the post office; formerly called Independence Grove, the name of a nearby settlement.

*Libertyville — Township
ZIP: 60048   Lat: 42-17-02 N   Long: 87-56-42 W
Pop: 42,436 (1990); 34,071 (1980)   Pop Density: 1192.0
Land: 35.6 sq. mi.; Water: 0.9 sq. mi.

Lincolnshire — Town
ZIP: 60069   Lat: 42-11-44 N   Long: 87-54-57 W
Pop: 4,931 (1990); 4,151 (1980)   Pop Density: 1369.7
Land: 3.6 sq. mi.; Water: 0.0 sq. mi.   Elev: 670 ft.

In northeastern IL on the Des Plaines River, 25 mi. northwest of Chicago.

Name origin: For Abraham Lincoln (1809–65), sixteenth U.S. president.

Lindenhurst — City
ZIP: 60046   Lat: 42-25-02 N   Long: 88-01-47 W
Pop: 8,038 (1990); 6,220 (1980)   Pop Density: 3091.5
Land: 2.6 sq. mi.; Water: 0.2 sq. mi.

Name origin: For the name of the farm on which the subdivision was built that created the city.

Long Grove — Village
ZIP: 60047   Lat: 42-11-43 N   Long: 88-00-10 W
Pop: 4,740 (1990); 2,013 (1980)   Pop Density: 388.5
Land: 12.2 sq. mi.; Water: 0.2 sq. mi.

Long Lake — CDP
Lat: 42-22-36 N   Long: 88-07-34 W
Pop: 2,888 (1990); 1,202 (1980)   Pop Density: 2221.5
Land: 1.3 sq. mi.; Water: 0.6 sq. mi.

Mettawa — Town
Lat: 42-14-37 N   Long: 87-54-55 W
Pop: 348 (1990); 330 (1980)   Pop Density: 82.9
Land: 4.2 sq. mi.; Water: 0.0 sq. mi.

Incorporated Jan 25, 1960.

Name origin: For Potawatomi chief Mettawa.

Mundelein — City
ZIP: 60060   Lat: 42-16-01 N   Long: 88-00-11 W
Pop: 21,215 (1990); 17,053 (1980)   Pop Density: 2828.7
Land: 7.5 sq. mi.; Water: 0.3 sq. mi.

In northeastern IL, 35 mi. northwest of Chicago.

Name origin: For Cardinal George William Mundelein (1872–1939), former archbishop of Chicago. Previously called Area.

Newport — Township
Lat: 42-27-11 N   Long: 87-56-27 W
Pop: 3,561 (1990); 3,042 (1980)   Pop Density: 107.9
Land: 33.0 sq. mi.; Water: 0.3 sq. mi.

North Barrington — Town
ZIP: 60010   Lat: 42-12-25 N   Long: 88-07-53 W
Pop: 1,787 (1990); 1,475 (1980)   Pop Density: 435.9
Land: 4.1 sq. mi.; Water: 0.2 sq. mi.

Incorporated November 2, 1959.

North Chicago — City
ZIP: 60064   Lat: 42-19-07 N   Long: 87-51-33 W
Pop: 34,978 (1990); 38,774 (1980)   Pop Density: 4726.8
Land: 7.4 sq. mi.; Water: 0.0 sq. mi.

In northeastern IL on Lake Michigan, 30 mi. north of Chicago. Incorporated May 7, 1895.

Name origin: Descriptive of its location in relation to Chicago.

Old Mill Creek — Village
Lat: 42-25-59 N   Long: 87-58-55 W
Pop: 73 (1990); 84 (1980)   Pop Density: 12.4
Land: 5.9 sq. mi.; Water: 0.0 sq. mi.   Elev: 709 ft.

Park City — City
ZIP: 60085   Lat: 42-21-02 N   Long: 87-53-27 W
Pop: 4,677 (1990); 3,673 (1980)   Pop Density: 4251.8
Land: 1.1 sq. mi.; Water: 0.0 sq. mi.

Riverwoods — Village
ZIP: 60015   Lat: 42-10-15 N   Long: 87-53-45 W
Pop: 2,868 (1990); 2,804 (1980)   Pop Density: 796.7
Land: 3.6 sq. mi.; Water: 0.0 sq. mi.

Round Lake — Town
ZIP: 60073   Lat: 42-20-59 N   Long: 88-06-37 W
Pop: 3,550 (1990); 3,175 (1980)   Pop Density: 1044.1
Land: 3.4 sq. mi.; Water: 0.1 sq. mi.

Round Lake Beach — Village
ZIP: 60073   Lat: 42-22-39 N   Long: 88-04-54 W
Pop: 16,434 (1990); 12,921 (1980)   Pop Density: 4213.8
Land: 3.9 sq. mi.; Water: 0.0 sq. mi.

In northeastern IL, 38 mi. northwest of Chicago. Incorporated 1937.

Name origin: For its descriptive connotations.

Round Lake Heights — Village
ZIP: 60073   Lat: 42-23-02 N   Long: 88-06-14 W
Pop: 1,251 (1990); 1,192 (1980)   Pop Density: 2085.0
Land: 0.6 sq. mi.; Water: 0.0 sq. mi.

Round Lake Park — Village
ZIP: 60073   Lat: 42-19-23 N   Long: 88-03-30 W
Pop: 4,045 (1990); 4,032 (1980)   Pop Density: 1225.8
Land: 3.3 sq. mi.; Water: 0.0 sq. mi.

Shields — Township
ZIP: 60045   Lat: 42-16-43 N   Long: 87-51-21 W
Pop: 43,414 (1990); 45,132 (1980)   Pop Density: 2452.8
Land: 17.7 sq. mi.; Water: 0.0 sq. mi.

Third Lake — Village
ZIP: 60046   Lat: 42-22-03 N   Long: 88-00-30 W
Pop: 1,248 (1990); 222 (1980)   Pop Density: 2496.0
Land: 0.5 sq. mi.; Water: 0.3 sq. mi.

Tower Lakes
Village
ZIP: 60010   **Lat:** 42-13-48 N   **Long:** 88-09-20 W
Pop: 1,333 (1990); 1,177 (1980)   **Pop Density:** 1333.0
Land: 1.0 sq. mi.; **Water:** 0.1 sq. mi.

Venetian Village
CDP
Lat: 42-23-59 N   **Long:** 88-02-46 W
Pop: 3,133 (1990); 2,817 (1980)   **Pop Density:** 870.3
Land: 3.6 sq. mi.; **Water:** 0.8 sq. mi.

Vernon
Township
ZIP: 60069   **Lat:** 42-11-49 N   **Long:** 87-56-33 W
Pop: 51,141 (1990); 32,285 (1980)   **Pop Density:** 1416.6
Land: 36.1 sq. mi.; **Water:** 0.1 sq. mi.

Vernon Hills
Village
ZIP: 60061   **Lat:** 42-14-09 N   **Long:** 87-57-45 W
Pop: 15,319 (1990); 9,827 (1980)   **Pop Density:** 2220.1
Land: 6.9 sq. mi.; **Water:** 0.2 sq. mi.

In northeastern IL, near Waukegan. Incorporated 1958.

Wadsworth
Town
ZIP: 60083   **Lat:** 42-26-12 N   **Long:** 87-55-24 W
Pop: 1,826 (1990); 1,104 (1980)   **Pop Density:** 268.5
Land: 6.8 sq. mi.; **Water:** 0.0 sq. mi.

In northeastern IL on the Des Plaines River, a suburb of Chicago.

Warren
Township
ZIP: 60031   **Lat:** 42-22-19 N   **Long:** 87-56-54 W
Pop: 34,785 (1990); 22,591 (1980)   **Pop Density:** 960.9
Land: 36.2 sq. mi.; **Water:** 0.6 sq. mi.

Wauconda
City
ZIP: 60084   **Lat:** 42-15-59 N   **Long:** 88-08-22 W
Pop: 6,294 (1990); 5,688 (1980)   **Pop Density:** 1966.9
Land: 3.2 sq. mi.; **Water:** 0.4 sq. mi.

In northeastern IL on Bangs Lake, 25 mi. northwest of Chicago. Settled 1836. Not coextensive with the town of the same name.

Name origin: Named by first settler Justus Bangs, for a fictional Indian character, from an Indian word thought to mean 'spirit.'

*Wauconda
Township
ZIP: 60084   **Lat:** 42-17-02 N   **Long:** 88-09-19 W
Pop: 12,859 (1990); 11,708 (1980)   **Pop Density:** 559.1
Land: 23.0 sq. mi.; **Water:** 1.0 sq. mi.

Waukegan
City
ZIP: 60085   **Lat:** 42-22-15 N   **Long:** 87-52-04 W
Pop: 69,392 (1990); 67,653 (1980)   **Pop Density:** 3125.8
Land: 22.2 sq. mi.; **Water:** 0.1 sq. mi.

In northeastern IL on Lake Michigan, 38 mi. northwest of Chicago. County seat. Settled 1835; incorporated Jun 15, 1852. Not coextensive with the town of the same name.

Name origin: For nearby Waukegan Creek, itself named from an Indian term probably meaning 'sheltering place.' Previously called Little Fort.

*Waukegan
Township
ZIP: 60085   **Lat:** 42-22-23 N   **Long:** 87-51-00 W
Pop: 78,185 (1990); 78,471 (1980)   **Pop Density:** 3705.5
Land: 21.1 sq. mi.; **Water:** 0.1 sq. mi.

West Deerfield
Township
ZIP: 60015   **Lat:** 42-11-42 N   **Long:** 87-51-33 W
Pop: 29,580 (1990); 27,386 (1980)   **Pop Density:** 1661.8
Land: 17.8 sq. mi.; **Water:** 0.1 sq. mi.

Wheeling
City
ZIP: 60090   **Lat:** 42-09-13 N   **Long:** 87-57-44 W
Pop: 0 (1990); 24 (1980)
Land: 0.001 sq. mi.; **Water:** 0.0 sq. mi.

In northeastern IL, 20 mi. northwest of Chicago. Settled 1830 as a country store. Incorporated 1894. Part of the town is also in Cook County.

Name origin: For Wheeling, WV.

Winthrop Harbor
Town
ZIP: 60096   **Lat:** 42-28-47 N   **Long:** 87-49-41 W
Pop: 6,240 (1990); 5,427 (1980)   **Pop Density:** 1485.7
Land: 4.2 sq. mi.; **Water:** 0.1 sq. mi.

Name origin: For the company that platted the town.

Zion
City
ZIP: 60099   **Lat:** 42-27-23 N   **Long:** 87-50-35 W
Pop: 19,775 (1990); 17,865 (1980)   **Pop Density:** 2602.0
Land: 7.6 sq. mi.; **Water:** 0.0 sq. mi.

In northeastern IL on Lake Michigan, 40 mi. north of Chicago. Incorporated Mar 31, 1902. Coextensive with the township.

Name origin: For Mount Zion in Palestine.

*Zion
Township
Lat: 42-27-23 N   **Long:** 87-50-35 W
Pop: 19,775 (1990); 17,865 (1980)   **Pop Density:** 2602.0
Land: 7.6 sq. mi.; **Water:** 0.0 sq. mi.

La Salle County
County Seat: Ottawa (ZIP: 61350)

Pop: 106,913 (1990); 112,033 (1980)   **Pop Density:** 94.2
Land: 1135.0 sq. mi.; **Water:** 13.1 sq. mi.   **Area Code:** 815

In north-central IL southwest of Chicago; organized Jan 15, 1831 from Putnam and Vermilion counties.

Name origin: For Robert Cavelier (1643-87), Sieur de La Salle, French adventurer and explorer who claimed the land west of the Mississippi River for France.

Adams
Township
Lat: 41-35-09 N   **Long:** 88-45-53 W
Pop: 1,353 (1990); 1,296 (1980)   **Pop Density:** 40.9
Land: 33.1 sq. mi.; **Water:** 0.0 sq. mi.

Allen
Township
Lat: 41-09-15 N   **Long:** 88-38-41 W
Pop: 690 (1990); 748 (1980)   **Pop Density:** 19.0
Land: 36.3 sq. mi.; **Water:** 0.0 sq. mi.

ILLINOIS, La Salle County

Brookfield
Township
Lat: 41-15-08 N **Long:** 88-38-55 W
Pop: 823 (1990); 797 (1980) **Pop Density:** 18.6
Land: 44.3 sq. mi.; **Water:** 3.5 sq. mi.

Bruce
Township
ZIP: 61364 **Lat:** 41-09-57 N **Long:** 88-50-44 W
Pop: 14,070 (1990); 15,639 (1980) **Pop Density:** 827.6
Land: 17.0 sq. mi.; **Water:** 0.0 sq. mi.

Cedar Point
Village
ZIP: 61316 **Lat:** 41-15-52 N **Long:** 89-07-30 W
Pop: 275 (1990); 344 (1980) **Pop Density:** 275.0
Land: 1.0 sq. mi.; **Water:** 0.0 sq. mi.

Dalzell
Village
ZIP: 61320 **Lat:** 41-21-22 N **Long:** 89-09-33 W
Pop: 0 (1990); 145 (1980)
Land: 0.3 sq. mi.; **Water:** 0.0 sq. mi.
Part of the town is also in Bureau County.

Dana
Village
ZIP: 61321 **Lat:** 40-57-22 N **Long:** 88-56-59 W
Pop: 165 (1990); 243 (1980) **Pop Density:** 825.0
Land: 0.2 sq. mi.; **Water:** 0.0 sq. mi.

Dayton
Township
Lat: 41-25-19 N **Long:** 88-48-37 W
Pop: 1,453 (1990); 1,287 (1980) **Pop Density:** 69.2
Land: 21.0 sq. mi.; **Water:** 0.2 sq. mi.

Deer Park
Township
Lat: 41-17-13 N **Long:** 88-59-35 W
Pop: 548 (1990); 616 (1980) **Pop Density:** 17.5
Land: 31.3 sq. mi.; **Water:** 1.7 sq. mi.

Dimmick
Township
Lat: 41-24-21 N **Long:** 89-06-31 W
Pop: 611 (1990); 654 (1980) **Pop Density:** 16.7
Land: 36.5 sq. mi.; **Water:** 0.0 sq. mi.

Eagle
Township
Lat: 41-08-38 N **Long:** 88-55-13 W
Pop: 1,854 (1990); 2,095 (1980) **Pop Density:** 59.2
Land: 31.3 sq. mi.; **Water:** 0.0 sq. mi.

Earl
Township
Lat: 41-35-33 N **Long:** 88-52-54 W
Pop: 2,305 (1990); 2,233 (1980) **Pop Density:** 61.5
Land: 37.5 sq. mi.; **Water:** 0.0 sq. mi.

Earlville
City
ZIP: 60518 **Lat:** 41-35-18 N **Long:** 88-55-25 W
Pop: 1,435 (1990); 1,382 (1980) **Pop Density:** 1304.5
Land: 1.1 sq. mi.; **Water:** 0.0 sq. mi. **Elev:** 705 ft.
Name origin: For the nephew of the first postmaster.

Eden
Township
Lat: 41-14-17 N **Long:** 89-06-50 W
Pop: 1,409 (1990); 1,579 (1980) **Pop Density:** 38.9
Land: 36.2 sq. mi.; **Water:** 0.0 sq. mi.

Fall River
Township
Lat: 41-18-36 N **Long:** 88-46-20 W
Pop: 885 (1990); 776 (1980) **Pop Density:** 43.8
Land: 20.2 sq. mi.; **Water:** 0.7 sq. mi.

Farm Ridge
Township
Lat: 41-14-12 N **Long:** 88-51-55 W
Pop: 971 (1990); 1,097 (1980) **Pop Density:** 27.9
Land: 34.8 sq. mi.; **Water:** 0.0 sq. mi.

Freedom
Township
Lat: 41-30-15 N **Long:** 88-52-04 W
Pop: 635 (1990); 652 (1980) **Pop Density:** 17.0
Land: 37.4 sq. mi.; **Water:** 0.0 sq. mi.

Grand Rapids
Township
Lat: 41-14-04 N **Long:** 88-45-53 W
Pop: 361 (1990); 400 (1980) **Pop Density:** 10.1
Land: 35.6 sq. mi.; **Water:** 0.0 sq. mi.

Grand Ridge
Village
ZIP: 61325 **Lat:** 41-14-10 N **Long:** 88-49-53 W
Pop: 560 (1990); 684 (1980) **Pop Density:** 1120.0
Land: 0.5 sq. mi.; **Water:** 0.0 sq. mi.
In northern IL, northwest of Kankakee.

Groveland
Township
Lat: 40-58-08 N **Long:** 88-59-13 W
Pop: 739 (1990); 978 (1980) **Pop Density:** 20.2
Land: 36.6 sq. mi.; **Water:** 0.0 sq. mi.

Hope
Township
Lat: 41-08-30 N **Long:** 89-06-03 W
Pop: 747 (1990); 818 (1980) **Pop Density:** 20.5
Land: 36.4 sq. mi.; **Water:** 0.0 sq. mi.

Kangley
Village
ZIP: 61364 **Lat:** 41-08-51 N **Long:** 88-52-21 W
Pop: 250 (1990); 280 (1980) **Pop Density:** 833.3
Land: 0.3 sq. mi.; **Water:** 0.0 sq. mi.

La Salle
City
ZIP: 61301 **Lat:** 41-20-23 N **Long:** 89-05-36 W
Pop: 9,717 (1990); 10,347 (1980) **Pop Density:** 3239.0
Land: 3.0 sq. mi.; **Water:** 0.1 sq. mi.
In north-central IL on the Utica River, 50 mi. northeast of Peoria. Incorporated Jun 23, 1852. Not coextensive with the town of the same name.
Name origin: For French adventurer and explorer Robert Cavelier (1643–87), Sieur de la Salle.

*La Salle
Township
ZIP: 61301 **Lat:** 41-19-30 N **Long:** 89-04-43 W
Pop: 13,768 (1990); 15,276 (1980) **Pop Density:** 814.7
Land: 16.9 sq. mi.; **Water:** 0.7 sq. mi.

Leland
Village
ZIP: 60531 **Lat:** 41-36-52 N **Long:** 88-47-52 W
Pop: 862 (1990); 775 (1980) **Pop Density:** 1436.7
Land: 0.6 sq. mi.; **Water:** 0.0 sq. mi.

Leonore
Village
ZIP: 61332 **Lat:** 41-11-21 N **Long:** 88-58-57 W
Pop: 134 (1990); 196 (1980) **Pop Density:** 1340.0
Land: 0.1 sq. mi.; **Water:** 0.0 sq. mi. **Elev:** 682 ft.

Lostant
Town
ZIP: 61334 **Lat:** 41-08-25 N **Long:** 89-03-40 W
Pop: 510 (1990); 539 (1980) **Pop Density:** 1275.0
Land: 0.4 sq. mi.; **Water:** 0.0 sq. mi. **Elev:** 703 ft.
Incorporated February 16, 1865.

Manlius
Township
ZIP: 61360 **Lat:** 41-20-06 N **Long:** 88-38-32 W
Pop: 5,267 (1990); 5,630 (1980) **Pop Density:** 221.3
Land: 23.8 sq. mi.; **Water:** 0.4 sq. mi.

Marseilles — Town
ZIP: 61341 Lat: 41-19-39 N Long: 88-41-16 W
Pop: 4,811 (1990); 4,766 (1980) Pop Density: 1202.8
Land: 4.0 sq. mi.; **Water:** 0.0 sq. mi. **Elev:** 504 ft.
Incorporated February 21, 1861.
Name origin: For the city in France.

Mendota — City
ZIP: 61342 Lat: 41-33-03 N Long: 89-07-12 W
Pop: 7,018 (1990); 7,134 (1980) Pop Density: 2263.9
Land: 3.1 sq. mi.; **Water:** 0.0 sq. mi. **Elev:** 740 ft.
Incorporated Feb 19, 1859. Not coextensive with the town of the same name.
Name origin: From the Dakota term *mdote* probably meaning 'coming together.' In IL the word has come to mean the junction of two railways.

*Mendota — Township
ZIP: 61342 Lat: 41-35-00 N Long: 89-06-33 W
Pop: 7,217 (1990); 7,372 (1980) Pop Density: 200.5
Land: 36.0 sq. mi.; **Water:** 0.1 sq. mi.

Meriden — Township
Lat: 41-34-55 N Long: 88-59-48 W
Pop: 338 (1990); 385 (1980) Pop Density: 9.6
Land: 35.3 sq. mi.; **Water:** 0.0 sq. mi.

Miller — Township
Lat: 41-24-32 N Long: 88-38-35 W
Pop: 522 (1990); 569 (1980) Pop Density: 14.7
Land: 35.4 sq. mi.; **Water:** 0.0 sq. mi.

Millington — Village
ZIP: 60537 Lat: 41-33-36 N Long: 88-36-03 W
Pop: 212 (1990); 220 (1980) Pop Density: 2120.0
Land: 0.1 sq. mi.; **Water:** 0.0 sq. mi.
Part of the town is also in Kendall County.

Mission — Township
Lat: 41-30-30 N Long: 88-38-49 W
Pop: 3,160 (1990); 2,431 (1980) Pop Density: 100.0
Land: 31.6 sq. mi.; **Water:** 0.5 sq. mi.

Naplate — Village
ZIP: 61350 Lat: 41-19-52 N Long: 88-52-41 W
Pop: 609 (1990); 581 (1980) Pop Density: 6090.0
Land: 0.1 sq. mi.; **Water:** 0.0 sq. mi.

North Utica — Village
Lat: 41-20-23 N Long: 89-00-40 W
Pop: 848 (1990); 1,067 (1980) Pop Density: 770.9
Land: 1.1 sq. mi.; **Water:** 0.0 sq. mi.

Northville — Township
Lat: 41-34-51 N Long: 88-39-49 W
Pop: 4,393 (1990); 2,614 (1980) Pop Density: 134.8
Land: 32.6 sq. mi.; **Water:** 0.7 sq. mi.

Oglesby — Town
ZIP: 61348 Lat: 41-17-40 N Long: 89-03-52 W
Pop: 3,619 (1990); 3,979 (1980) Pop Density: 1034.0
Land: 3.5 sq. mi.; **Water:** 0.0 sq. mi.
Name origin: For Gov. Richard J. Oglesby (1824–99).

Ophir — Township
Lat: 41-30-08 N Long: 88-59-48 W
Pop: 555 (1990); 659 (1980) Pop Density: 15.9
Land: 34.9 sq. mi.; **Water:** 0.0 sq. mi.

Osage — Township
Lat: 41-03-26 N Long: 88-59-49 W
Pop: 328 (1990); 410 (1980) Pop Density: 8.6
Land: 38.2 sq. mi.; **Water:** 0.0 sq. mi.

Ottawa — City
ZIP: 61350 Lat: 41-21-00 N Long: 88-50-21 W
Pop: 17,451 (1990); 18,166 (1980) Pop Density: 2908.5
Land: 6.0 sq. mi.; **Water:** 0.3 sq. mi.
In north-central IL at the confluence of the Illinois and Fox rivers, 75 mi. southwest of Chicago. County seat. Incorporated Jul 21, 1837. Not coextensive with the town of the same name.
Name origin: For the Ottawa Indians.

*Ottawa — Township
ZIP: 61350 Lat: 41-20-53 N Long: 88-52-50 W
Pop: 12,271 (1990); 13,301 (1980) Pop Density: 807.3
Land: 15.2 sq. mi.; **Water:** 0.9 sq. mi.

Otter Creek — Township
Lat: 41-09-15 N Long: 88-45-40 W
Pop: 3,003 (1990); 3,346 (1980) Pop Density: 83.6
Land: 35.9 sq. mi.; **Water:** 0.0 sq. mi.

Peru — City
ZIP: 61354 Lat: 41-20-30 N Long: 89-07-41 W
Pop: 9,302 (1990); 10,886 (1980) Pop Density: 1898.4
Land: 4.9 sq. mi.; **Water:** 0.1 sq. mi.
In north-central IL on the Illinois River, 85 mi. southwest of Chicago. Founded 1835; incorporated Feb 25, 1845. Not coextensive with the town of the same name.
Name origin: For the South American country.

*Peru — Township
ZIP: 61354 Lat: 41-19-28 N Long: 89-08-05 W
Pop: 10,326 (1990); 11,432 (1980) Pop Density: 590.1
Land: 17.5 sq. mi.; **Water:** 0.5 sq. mi.

Ransom — Village
ZIP: 60470 Lat: 41-09-29 N Long: 88-39-18 W
Pop: 438 (1990); 456 (1980) Pop Density: 438.0
Land: 1.0 sq. mi.; **Water:** 0.0 sq. mi.

Richland — Township
Lat: 41-08-41 N Long: 89-01-06 W
Pop: 437 (1990); 545 (1980) Pop Density: 18.0
Land: 24.3 sq. mi.; **Water:** 0.0 sq. mi.

Rutland — Village
ZIP: 61358 Lat: 40-59-02 N Long: 89-02-21 W
Pop: 391 (1990); 487 (1980) Pop Density: 488.8
Land: 0.8 sq. mi.; **Water:** 0.0 sq. mi.

*Rutland — Township
Lat: 41-22-59 N Long: 88-44-33 W
Pop: 3,292 (1990); 3,546 (1980) Pop Density: 94.1
Land: 35.0 sq. mi.; **Water:** 0.7 sq. mi.

Seneca — Town
ZIP: 61360 Lat: 41-18-12 N Long: 88-36-48 W
Pop: 1,878 (1990); 2,098 (1980) Pop Density: 647.6
Land: 2.9 sq. mi.; **Water:** 0.1 sq. mi.
Part of the town is also in Grundy County.
Name origin: For the Seneca Indians.

Serena — Township
Lat: 41-30-33 N Long: 88-45-37 W
Pop: 846 (1990); 862 (1980) Pop Density: 22.8
Land: 37.1 sq. mi.; **Water:** 0.2 sq. mi.

ILLINOIS, La Salle County

Sheridan
Town
ZIP: 60551 Lat: 41-31-33 N Long: 88-41-12 W
Pop: 1,288 (1990); 719 (1980) Pop Density: 1073.3
Land: 1.2 sq. mi.; Water: 0.0 sq. mi.

Somonauk
Town
ZIP: 60552 Lat: 41-37-44 N Long: 88-40-59 W
Pop: 232 (1990); 237 (1980) Pop Density: 1160.0
Land: 0.2 sq. mi.; Water: 0.0 sq. mi.
Part of the town is also in DeKalb County.
Name origin: From a Potawatomi term probably meaning 'pawpaw,' a fruit-bearing tree *Asimina triloba*.

South Ottawa
Township
ZIP: 61350 Lat: 41-18-29 N Long: 88-52-26 W
Pop: 7,684 (1990); 7,698 (1980) Pop Density: 390.1
Land: 19.7 sq. mi.; Water: 1.4 sq. mi.

Streator
City
ZIP: 61364 Lat: 41-07-31 N Long: 88-49-54 W
Pop: 14,028 (1990); 14,718 (1980) Pop Density: 2984.7
Land: 4.7 sq. mi.; Water: 0.0 sq. mi. Elev: 626 ft.
In north-central IL, 50 mi. northeast of Peoria. Incorporated Apr 6, 1874. Part of the town is also in Livingston County.
Name origin: For W. S. Streator of Cleveland, OH. Previously called Hardscrabble and Unionville.

Tonica
Village
ZIP: 61370 Lat: 41-12-50 N Long: 89-04-04 W
Pop: 715 (1990); 695 (1980) Pop Density: 715.0
Land: 1.0 sq. mi.; Water: 0.0 sq. mi.

Troy Grove
Village
ZIP: 61372 Lat: 41-27-55 N Long: 89-04-52 W
Pop: 259 (1990); 297 (1980) Pop Density: 370.0
Land: 0.7 sq. mi.; Water: 0.0 sq. mi.
Not coextensive with the town of the same name.

*Troy Grove
Township
Lat: 41-29-28 N Long: 89-06-45 W
Pop: 1,316 (1990); 1,345 (1980) Pop Density: 37.0
Land: 35.6 sq. mi.; Water: 0.0 sq. mi.

Utica
Township
Lat: 41-20-42 N Long: 88-59-02 W
Pop: 1,414 (1990); 1,601 (1980) Pop Density: 78.1
Land: 18.1 sq. mi.; Water: 0.7 sq. mi.

Vermillion
Township
Lat: 41-13-26 N Long: 88-59-56 W
Pop: 313 (1990); 351 (1980) Pop Density: 13.5
Land: 23.1 sq. mi.; Water: 0.0 sq. mi.

Wallace
Township
Lat: 41-24-14 N Long: 88-53-01 W
Pop: 489 (1990); 420 (1980) Pop Density: 17.7
Land: 27.6 sq. mi.; Water: 0.0 sq. mi.

Waltham
Township
Lat: 41-24-43 N Long: 88-59-23 W
Pop: 520 (1990); 575 (1980) Pop Density: 14.5
Land: 35.9 sq. mi.; Water: 0.0 sq. mi.

Wenona
City
Lat: 41-03-03 N Long: 89-02-46 W
Pop: 11 (1990); 1,025 (1980) Pop Density: 0.25
Land: 44.6 sq. mi.; Water: 0.0 sq. mi.
In north-central IL, northeast of Peoria. Part of the town is also in Marshall County.
Name origin: For Hiawatha's mother in Henry Wadsworth Longfellow's (1807–82) poem "The Song of Hiawatha."

Lawrence County
County Seat: Lawrenceville (ZIP: 62439)

Pop: 15,972 (1990); 17,807 (1980) Pop Density: 42.9
Land: 372.0 sq. mi.; Water: 2.0 sq. mi. Area Code: 618
On the east-central border of IL east of Olney; organized Jan 16, 1821 from Crawford and Edwards counties.
Name origin: For Capt. James Lawrence (1781–1813), U.S. naval officer in the war with Barbary pirates near Tripoli and commander of the U.S.S. *Chesapeake* in the War of 1812, who said, "Don't give up the ship!"

Allison
Township
Lat: 38-43-00 N Long: 87-34-53 W
Pop: 308 (1990); 381 (1980) Pop Density: 6.9
Land: 44.6 sq. mi.; Water: 0.8 sq. mi.

Birds
Village
ZIP: 62415 Lat: 38-50-14 N Long: 87-40-14 W
Pop: 160 (1990); 193 (1980) Pop Density: 800.0
Land: 0.2 sq. mi.; Water: 0.0 sq. mi.

Bond
Township
Lat: 38-48-55 N Long: 87-41-45 W
Pop: 844 (1990); 951 (1980) Pop Density: 23.8
Land: 35.4 sq. mi.; Water: 0.0 sq. mi.

Bridgeport
City
ZIP: 62417 Lat: 38-42-35 N Long: 87-45-30 W
Pop: 2,118 (1990); 2,281 (1980) Pop Density: 2118.0
Land: 1.0 sq. mi.; Water: 0.0 sq. mi. Elev: 446 ft.
Incorporated as a city 1865. Not coextensive with the town of the same name.
Name origin: For Bridgeport, CT.

*Bridgeport
Township
Lat: 38-42-03 N Long: 87-46-48 W
Pop: 2,588 (1990); 2,799 (1980) Pop Density: 161.8
Land: 16.0 sq. mi.; Water: 0.0 sq. mi.

American Places Dictionary   ILLINOIS, Lee County

Christy   Township
Lat: 38-41-54 N   Long: 87-51-34 W
Pop: 1,679 (1990); 1,914 (1980)   **Pop Density:** 49.8
Land: 33.7 sq. mi.; **Water:** 0.1 sq. mi.

Denison   Township
Lat: 38-37-43 N   Long: 87-41-39 W
Pop: 1,806 (1990); 2,054 (1980)   **Pop Density:** 31.2
Land: 57.9 sq. mi.; **Water:** 0.5 sq. mi.

Lawrence   Township
ZIP: 62439   Lat: 38-43-55 N   Long: 87-41-40 W
Pop: 7,041 (1990); 7,830 (1980)   **Pop Density:** 168.4
Land: 41.8 sq. mi.; **Water:** 0.2 sq. mi.

Lawrenceville   City
ZIP: 62439   Lat: 38-43-35 N   Long: 87-41-16 W
Pop: 4,897 (1990); 5,652 (1980)   **Pop Density:** 2880.6
Land: 1.7 sq. mi.; **Water:** 0.0 sq. mi.

Lukin   Township
Lat: 38-36-58 N   Long: 87-49-32 W
Pop: 397 (1990); 466 (1980)   **Pop Density:** 8.0
Land: 49.5 sq. mi.; **Water:** 0.0 sq. mi.

Petty   Township
Lat: 38-47-56 N   Long: 87-49-39 W
Pop: 827 (1990); 839 (1980)   **Pop Density:** 14.4
Land: 57.3 sq. mi.; **Water:** 0.0 sq. mi.

Russell   Township
Lat: 38-48-22 N   Long: 87-34-19 W
Pop: 482 (1990); 573 (1980)   **Pop Density:** 13.4
Land: 35.9 sq. mi.; **Water:** 0.4 sq. mi.

Russellville   Village
Lat: 38-49-11 N   Long: 87-31-45 W
Pop: 133 (1990); 171 (1980)   **Pop Density:** 266.0
Land: 0.5 sq. mi.; **Water:** 0.0 sq. mi.   **Elev:** 425 ft.

St. Francisville   Town
ZIP: 62460   Lat: 38-35-30 N   Long: 87-38-51 W
Pop: 851 (1990); 1,040 (1980)   **Pop Density:** 1215.7
Land: 0.7 sq. mi.; **Water:** 0.0 sq. mi.
Name origin: For St. Francis Xavier (1506–52).

Sumner   City
ZIP: 62466   Lat: 38-43-01 N   Long: 87-51-44 W
Pop: 1,083 (1990); 1,238 (1980)   **Pop Density:** 1083.0
Land: 1.0 sq. mi.; **Water:** 0.0 sq. mi.

Lee County
County Seat: Dixon (ZIP: 61021)

Pop: 34,392 (1990); 36,328 (1980)   **Pop Density:** 47.4
Land: 725.4 sq. mi.; **Water:** 3.9 sq. mi.   **Area Code:** 815
In north-central IL south of Rockford; organized Feb 27, 1839 from Ogle County.
Name origin: For Richard Henry Lee (1732–1794), VA statesman, a signer of the Declaration of Independence, and U.S. senator from VA (1789–92).

Alto   Township
Lat: 41-50-26 N   Long: 88-59-50 W
Pop: 568 (1990); 599 (1980)   **Pop Density:** 16.3
Land: 34.8 sq. mi.; **Water:** 0.0 sq. mi.

Amboy   City
ZIP: 61310   Lat: 41-42-59 N   Long: 89-20-00 W
Pop: 2,377 (1990); 2,377 (1980)   **Pop Density:** 1828.5
Land: 1.3 sq. mi.; **Water:** 0.0 sq. mi.   **Elev:** 743 ft.
Not coextensive with the town of the same name.
Name origin: For Amboy, NJ.

*Amboy   Township
Lat: 41-42-55 N   Long: 89-20-32 W
Pop: 3,047 (1990); 3,080 (1980)   **Pop Density:** 86.3
Land: 35.3 sq. mi.; **Water:** 0.2 sq. mi.

Ashton   Village
ZIP: 61006   Lat: 41-52-05 N   Long: 89-13-17 W
Pop: 1,042 (1990); 1,140 (1980)   **Pop Density:** 1488.6
Land: 0.7 sq. mi.; **Water:** 0.0 sq. mi.
Not coextensive with the town of the same name.
Name origin: For a banker who contributed a community center to the town.

*Ashton   Township
Lat: 41-52-04 N   Long: 89-13-30 W
Pop: 1,260 (1990); 1,375 (1980)   **Pop Density:** 70.8
Land: 17.8 sq. mi.; **Water:** 0.0 sq. mi.
Name origin: Previously called Ogle.

Bradford   Township
Lat: 41-47-39 N   Long: 89-13-09 W
Pop: 332 (1990); 387 (1980)   **Pop Density:** 9.2
Land: 36.0 sq. mi.; **Water:** 0.0 sq. mi.

Brooklyn   Township
Lat: 41-40-19 N   Long: 89-06-31 W
Pop: 886 (1990); 1,024 (1980)   **Pop Density:** 24.4
Land: 36.3 sq. mi.; **Water:** 0.0 sq. mi.

China   Township
Lat: 41-49-25 N   Long: 89-18-45 W
Pop: 1,389 (1990); 1,466 (1980)   **Pop Density:** 51.8
Land: 26.8 sq. mi.; **Water:** 0.0 sq. mi.

Compton   Village
ZIP: 61318   Lat: 41-41-39 N   Long: 89-05-09 W
Pop: 343 (1990); 376 (1980)   **Pop Density:** 1715.0
Land: 0.2 sq. mi.; **Water:** 0.0 sq. mi.

Dixon   City
ZIP: 61021   Lat: 41-50-58 N   Long: 89-28-43 W
Pop: 15,144 (1990); 15,710 (1980)   **Pop Density:** 2611.0
Land: 5.8 sq. mi.; **Water:** 0.4 sq. mi.   **Elev:** 659 ft.
In northwestern IL on the Rock River, 90 mi. west of Chicago. Founded 1830; incorporated 1853. Not coextensive with the town of the same name.
Name origin: For its founder, John Dixon, a trader who opened a tavern here.

ILLINOIS, Lee County

*Dixon
Township
ZIP: 61021   Lat: 41-52-03 N   Long: 89-27-33 W
Pop: 17,166 (1990); 17,903 (1980)   Pop Density: 589.9
Land: 29.1 sq. mi.; Water: 1.1 sq. mi.

East Grove
Township
Lat: 41-38-06 N   Long: 89-27-08 W
Pop: 292 (1990); 330 (1980)   Pop Density: 8.2
Land: 35.6 sq. mi.; Water: 0.1 sq. mi.

Franklin Grove
Village
ZIP: 61031   Lat: 41-50-27 N   Long: 89-18-00 W
Pop: 968 (1990); 965 (1980)   Pop Density: 2420.0
Land: 0.4 sq. mi.; Water: 0.0 sq. mi.

Hamilton
Township
Lat: 41-37-24 N   Long: 89-34-55 W
Pop: 224 (1990); 269 (1980)   Pop Density: 6.3
Land: 35.8 sq. mi.; Water: 0.0 sq. mi.

Harmon
Village
ZIP: 61042   Lat: 41-43-10 N   Long: 89-33-23 W
Pop: 186 (1990); 193 (1980)   Pop Density: 1860.0
Land: 0.1 sq. mi.; Water: 0.0 sq. mi.   Elev: 675 ft.
Not coextensive with the town of the same name.

*Harmon
Township
Lat: 41-43-07 N   Long: 89-34-32 W
Pop: 510 (1990); 588 (1980)   Pop Density: 14.2
Land: 35.8 sq. mi.; Water: 0.0 sq. mi.

Lee
Village
ZIP: 60530   Lat: 41-47-47 N   Long: 88-56-36 W
Pop: 176 (1990); 159 (1980)   Pop Density: 1760.0
Land: 0.1 sq. mi.; Water: 0.0 sq. mi.
Part of the town is also in DeKalb County.

Lee Center
Township
Lat: 41-43-09 N   Long: 89-13-52 W
Pop: 537 (1990); 561 (1980)   Pop Density: 14.8
Land: 36.3 sq. mi.; Water: 0.2 sq. mi.

Marion
Township
Lat: 41-42-52 N   Long: 89-27-46 W
Pop: 301 (1990); 396 (1980)   Pop Density: 8.4
Land: 35.7 sq. mi.; Water: 0.0 sq. mi.

May
Township
Lat: 41-37-54 N   Long: 89-20-34 W
Pop: 344 (1990); 350 (1980)   Pop Density: 9.7
Land: 35.6 sq. mi.; Water: 0.2 sq. mi.

Nachusa
Township
Lat: 41-49-41 N   Long: 89-22-26 W
Pop: 584 (1990); 619 (1980)   Pop Density: 20.2
Land: 28.9 sq. mi.; Water: 0.0 sq. mi.

Nelson
Village
ZIP: 61058   Lat: 41-47-43 N   Long: 89-36-09 W
Pop: 200 (1990); 215 (1980)   Pop Density: 1000.0
Land: 0.2 sq. mi.; Water: 0.0 sq. mi.
Not coextensive with the town of the same name.

*Nelson
Township
Lat: 41-47-20 N   Long: 89-34-22 W
Pop: 881 (1990); 884 (1980)   Pop Density: 39.2
Land: 22.5 sq. mi.; Water: 1.2 sq. mi.

Palmyra
Township
Lat: 41-51-31 N   Long: 89-34-45 W
Pop: 2,188 (1990); 2,275 (1980)   Pop Density: 62.7
Land: 34.9 sq. mi.; Water: 0.6 sq. mi.

Paw Paw
Town
Lat: 41-41-16 N   Long: 88-58-49 W
Pop: 791 (1990); 839 (1980)   Pop Density: 1977.5
Land: 0.4 sq. mi.; Water: 0.0 sq. mi.

Reynolds
Township
Lat: 41-51-14 N   Long: 89-06-43 W
Pop: 345 (1990); 359 (1980)   Pop Density: 9.7
Land: 35.5 sq. mi.; Water: 0.0 sq. mi.

South Dixon
Township
Lat: 41-47-42 N   Long: 89-27-51 W
Pop: 820 (1990); 970 (1980)   Pop Density: 27.7
Land: 29.6 sq. mi.; Water: 0.0 sq. mi.

Steward
Village
ZIP: 60553   Lat: 41-50-54 N   Long: 89-01-14 W
Pop: 282 (1990); 298 (1980)   Pop Density: 2820.0
Land: 0.1 sq. mi.; Water: 0.0 sq. mi.

Sublette
Village
ZIP: 61367   Lat: 41-38-36 N   Long: 89-13-54 W
Pop: 394 (1990); 442 (1980)   Pop Density: 1313.3
Land: 0.3 sq. mi.; Water: 0.0 sq. mi.   Elev: 927 ft.
Not coextensive with the town of the same name.

*Sublette
Township
Lat: 41-37-56 N   Long: 89-13-15 W
Pop: 745 (1990); 839 (1980)   Pop Density: 20.4
Land: 36.5 sq. mi.; Water: 0.0 sq. mi.

Viola
Township
Lat: 41-45-22 N   Long: 89-06-48 W
Pop: 300 (1990); 304 (1980)   Pop Density: 8.5
Land: 35.4 sq. mi.; Water: 0.0 sq. mi.

West Brooklyn
Village
ZIP: 61378   Lat: 41-41-35 N   Long: 89-08-49 W
Pop: 164 (1990); 210 (1980)   Pop Density: 1640.0
Land: 0.1 sq. mi.; Water: 0.0 sq. mi.

Willow Creek
Township
Lat: 41-45-31 N   Long: 88-59-38 W
Pop: 550 (1990); 554 (1980)   Pop Density: 15.7
Land: 35.0 sq. mi.; Water: 0.0 sq. mi.

Wyoming
Township
Lat: 41-40-45 N   Long: 88-59-27 W
Pop: 1,123 (1990); 1,196 (1980)   Pop Density: 31.2
Land: 36.0 sq. mi.; Water: 0.0 sq. mi.

American Places Dictionary   ILLINOIS, Livingston County

Livingston County
County Seat: Pontiac (ZIP: 61764)

Pop: 39,301 (1990); 41,381 (1980)   **Pop Density:** 37.7
Land: 1043.8 sq. mi.; **Water:** 1.7 sq. mi.   **Area Code:** 815
In east-central IL northeast of Peoria; organized Feb 27, 1837 from La Salle and McLean counties.
Name origin: For Edward Livingston (1764–1836), NY legislator, LA legislator and U.S. senator (1829–31), and U.S. secretary of state (1831–33).

Amity
Township
Lat: 40-58-15 N **Long:** 88-45-55 W
Pop: 968 (1990); 1,039 (1980)   **Pop Density:** 26.8
Land: 36.1 sq. mi.; **Water:** 0.2 sq. mi.

Avoca
Township
Lat: 40-48-28 N **Long:** 88-31-54 W
Pop: 406 (1990); 388 (1980)   **Pop Density:** 11.2
Land: 36.4 sq. mi.; **Water:** 0.1 sq. mi.

Belle Prairie
Township
Lat: 40-38-50 N **Long:** 88-31-22 W
Pop: 161 (1990); 190 (1980)   **Pop Density:** 7.1
Land: 22.8 sq. mi.; **Water:** 0.0 sq. mi.

Broughton
Township
Lat: 40-58-47 N **Long:** 88-18-20 W
Pop: 330 (1990); 368 (1980)   **Pop Density:** 9.4
Land: 35.2 sq. mi.; **Water:** 0.0 sq. mi.

Campus
Village
ZIP: 60920 **Lat:** 41-01-29 N **Long:** 88-18-28 W
Pop: 137 (1990); 224 (1980)   **Pop Density:** 1370.0
Land: 0.1 sq. mi.; **Water:** 0.0 sq. mi.   **Elev:** 658 ft.

Charlotte
Township
Lat: 40-47-50 N **Long:** 88-17-34 W
Pop: 168 (1990); 209 (1980)   **Pop Density:** 5.6
Land: 30.1 sq. mi.; **Water:** 0.0 sq. mi.

Chatsworth
Town
ZIP: 60921 **Lat:** 40-45-10 N **Long:** 88-17-37 W
Pop: 1,186 (1990); 1,187 (1980)   **Pop Density:** 1317.8
Land: 0.9 sq. mi.; **Water:** 0.0 sq. mi.   **Elev:** 735 ft.
Not coextensive with the town of the same name.

*Chatsworth
Township
Lat: 40-43-29 N **Long:** 88-17-32 W
Pop: 1,444 (1990); 1,431 (1980)   **Pop Density:** 40.2
Land: 35.9 sq. mi.; **Water:** 0.1 sq. mi.

Cornell
Village
ZIP: 61319 **Lat:** 40-59-32 N **Long:** 88-43-47 W
Pop: 556 (1990); 603 (1980)   **Pop Density:** 926.7
Land: 0.6 sq. mi.; **Water:** 0.0 sq. mi.   **Elev:** 638 ft.
Name origin: For NY philanthropist Ezra Cornell (1807–74).

Cullom
Village
ZIP: 60929 **Lat:** 40-52-40 N **Long:** 88-16-10 W
Pop: 568 (1990); 608 (1980)   **Pop Density:** 1893.3
Land: 0.3 sq. mi.; **Water:** 0.0 sq. mi.   **Elev:** 689 ft.

Dwight
Village
ZIP: 60420 **Lat:** 41-05-40 N **Long:** 88-25-38 W
Pop: 4,230 (1990); 4,117 (1980)   **Pop Density:** 2115.0
Land: 2.0 sq. mi.; **Water:** 0.0 sq. mi.   **Elev:** 640 ft.
Founded in 1854. Not coextensive with the town of the same name. Part of the town is also in Grundy County.
Name origin: Named for a civil engineer who worked on the nearby railroad.

*Dwight
Township
Lat: 41-03-56 N **Long:** 88-25-12 W
Pop: 4,511 (1990); 4,434 (1980)   **Pop Density:** 129.6
Land: 34.8 sq. mi.; **Water:** 0.0 sq. mi.

Emington
Village
ZIP: 60934 **Lat:** 40-58-12 N **Long:** 88-21-26 W
Pop: 135 (1990); 119 (1980)   **Pop Density:** 1350.0
Land: 0.1 sq. mi.; **Water:** 0.0 sq. mi.

Eppards Point
Township
Lat: 40-48-00 N **Long:** 88-38-27 W
Pop: 508 (1990); 539 (1980)   **Pop Density:** 14.1
Land: 36.1 sq. mi.; **Water:** 0.3 sq. mi.

Esmen
Township
Lat: 40-58-51 N **Long:** 88-38-39 W
Pop: 360 (1990); 424 (1980)   **Pop Density:** 10.0
Land: 36.1 sq. mi.; **Water:** 0.0 sq. mi.

Fairbury
City
ZIP: 61739 **Lat:** 40-44-47 N **Long:** 88-30-44 W
Pop: 3,643 (1990); 3,544 (1980)   **Pop Density:** 3035.8
Land: 1.2 sq. mi.; **Water:** 0.0 sq. mi.

Fayette
Township
Lat: 40-38-53 N **Long:** 88-24-00 W
Pop: 322 (1990); 335 (1980)   **Pop Density:** 14.2
Land: 22.6 sq. mi.; **Water:** 0.1 sq. mi.

Flanagan
Village
ZIP: 61740 **Lat:** 40-52-38 N **Long:** 88-51-38 W
Pop: 987 (1990); 978 (1980)   **Pop Density:** 1974.0
Land: 0.5 sq. mi.; **Water:** 0.0 sq. mi.   **Elev:** 666 ft.

Forrest
Village
ZIP: 61741 **Lat:** 40-44-59 N **Long:** 88-24-35 W
Pop: 1,124 (1990); 1,246 (1980)   **Pop Density:** 2248.0
Land: 0.5 sq. mi.; **Water:** 0.0 sq. mi.   **Elev:** 688 ft.
Not coextensive with the town of the same name.
Name origin: For a banker who was a friend of the first railroad company in the area.

*Forrest
Township
Lat: 40-43-25 N **Long:** 88-24-19 W
Pop: 1,521 (1990); 1,756 (1980)   **Pop Density:** 41.8
Land: 36.4 sq. mi.; **Water:** 0.0 sq. mi.

ILLINOIS, Livingston County

Germanville
Township
Lat: 40-38-59 N Long: 88-17-58 W
Pop: 91 (1990); 137 (1980) Pop Density: 4.0
Land: 22.9 sq. mi.; Water: 0.0 sq. mi.

Indian Grove
Township
Lat: 40-43-02 N Long: 88-31-44 W
Pop: 4,139 (1990); 4,045 (1980) Pop Density: 114.0
Land: 36.3 sq. mi.; Water: 0.1 sq. mi.

Long Point
Village
ZIP: 61333 Lat: 41-00-16 N Long: 88-53-37 W
Pop: 208 (1990); 313 (1980) Pop Density: 1040.0
Land: 0.2 sq. mi.; Water: 0.0 sq. mi.
Not coextensive with the town of the same name.

*Long Point
Township
Lat: 40-58-21 N Long: 88-52-19 W
Pop: 541 (1990); 652 (1980) Pop Density: 14.9
Land: 36.3 sq. mi.; Water: 0.0 sq. mi.

Nebraska
Township
Lat: 40-53-05 N Long: 88-52-35 W
Pop: 1,424 (1990); 1,343 (1980) Pop Density: 39.0
Land: 36.5 sq. mi.; Water: 0.0 sq. mi.

Nevada
Township
Lat: 41-03-41 N Long: 88-31-07 W
Pop: 930 (1990); 712 (1980) Pop Density: 25.4
Land: 36.6 sq. mi.; Water: 0.0 sq. mi.

Newtown
Township
Lat: 41-03-50 N Long: 88-45-44 W
Pop: 805 (1990); 897 (1980) Pop Density: 22.4
Land: 36.0 sq. mi.; Water: 0.3 sq. mi.

Odell
Village
ZIP: 60460 Lat: 41-00-10 N Long: 88-31-22 W
Pop: 1,030 (1990); 1,083 (1980) Pop Density: 936.4
Land: 1.1 sq. mi.; Water: 0.0 sq. mi.
Not coextensive with the town of the same name.

*Odell
Township
Lat: 40-58-10 N Long: 88-31-44 W
Pop: 1,234 (1990); 1,366 (1980) Pop Density: 34.3
Land: 36.0 sq. mi.; Water: 0.0 sq. mi.

Owego
Township
Lat: 40-53-25 N Long: 88-31-58 W
Pop: 302 (1990); 386 (1980) Pop Density: 8.3
Land: 36.2 sq. mi.; Water: 0.0 sq. mi.

Pike
Township
Lat: 40-47-55 N Long: 88-45-26 W
Pop: 295 (1990); 320 (1980) Pop Density: 8.1
Land: 36.4 sq. mi.; Water: 0.0 sq. mi.

Pleasant Ridge
Township
Lat: 40-47-52 N Long: 88-24-36 W
Pop: 288 (1990); 386 (1980) Pop Density: 9.8
Land: 29.3 sq. mi.; Water: 0.0 sq. mi.

Pontiac
City
ZIP: 61764 Lat: 40-52-35 N Long: 88-38-30 W
Pop: 11,428 (1990); 11,227 (1980) Pop Density: 2484.3
Land: 4.6 sq. mi.; Water: 0.0 sq. mi. Elev: 642 ft.
In northeast-central IL on the Vermilion River, 57 mi. southwest of Joliet. County seat. Founded 1837; incorporated Feb 10, 1857. Not coextensive with the town of the same name.
Name origin: For the Ottawa chief (c. 1720–69) who fought against the British in the French and Indian Wars.

*Pontiac
Township
ZIP: 61764 Lat: 40-53-16 N Long: 88-38-35 W
Pop: 12,923 (1990); 13,083 (1980) Pop Density: 358.0
Land: 36.1 sq. mi.; Water: 0.2 sq. mi.

Reading
Township
Lat: 41-04-03 N Long: 88-52-30 W
Pop: 2,379 (1990); 3,039 (1980) Pop Density: 63.3
Land: 37.6 sq. mi.; Water: 0.1 sq. mi.

Reddick
Village
ZIP: 60961 Lat: 41-05-51 N Long: 88-15-06 W
Pop: 26 (1990); 40 (1980) Pop Density: 260.0
Land: 0.1 sq. mi.; Water: 0.0 sq. mi.
Part of the town is also in Kankakee County.

Rooks Creek
Township
Lat: 40-53-21 N Long: 88-45-13 W
Pop: 483 (1990); 580 (1980) Pop Density: 13.2
Land: 36.5 sq. mi.; Water: 0.0 sq. mi.

Round Grove
Township
Lat: 41-04-05 N Long: 88-18-36 W
Pop: 445 (1990); 597 (1980) Pop Density: 12.3
Land: 36.2 sq. mi.; Water: 0.0 sq. mi.

Saunemin
Village
ZIP: 61769 Lat: 40-53-34 N Long: 88-24-23 W
Pop: 399 (1990); 463 (1980) Pop Density: 1995.0
Land: 0.2 sq. mi.; Water: 0.0 sq. mi. Elev: 690 ft.
Not coextensive with the town of the same name.

*Saunemin
Township
Lat: 40-53-00 N Long: 88-24-40 W
Pop: 683 (1990); 799 (1980) Pop Density: 15.8
Land: 43.2 sq. mi.; Water: 0.0 sq. mi.

Strawn
Village
ZIP: 61775 Lat: 40-39-09 N Long: 88-23-56 W
Pop: 132 (1990); 143 (1980) Pop Density: 264.0
Land: 0.5 sq. mi.; Water: 0.0 sq. mi. Elev: 767 ft.

Streator
City
ZIP: 61364 Lat: 41-06-19 N Long: 88-49-25 W
Pop: 93 (1990); 77 (1980) Pop Density: 930.0
Land: 0.1 sq. mi.; Water: 0.0 sq. mi. Elev: 626 ft.
In north-central IL, 50 mi. northeast of Peoria. Incorporated Apr 6, 1874. Part of the town is also in La Salle County.
Name origin: For W. S. Streator of Cleveland, OH. Previously called Hardscrabble and Unionville.

Sullivan
Township
Lat: 40-53-06 N Long: 88-17-27 W
Pop: 782 (1990); 877 (1980) Pop Density: 19.0
Land: 41.2 sq. mi.; Water: 0.0 sq. mi.

Sunbury
Township
Lat: 41-04-10 N Long: 88-38-00 W
Pop: 258 (1990); 332 (1980) Pop Density: 7.1
Land: 36.4 sq. mi.; Water: 0.0 sq. mi.

Union
Township
Lat: 40-58-44 N Long: 88-25-09 W
Pop: 271 (1990); 302 (1980) Pop Density: 7.7
Land: 35.2 sq. mi.; Water: 0.0 sq. mi.

Waldo
Township
Lat: 40-47-25 N Long: 88-52-37 W
Pop: 329 (1990); 415 (1980) Pop Density: 9.0
Land: 36.5 sq. mi.; Water: 0.0 sq. mi.

Logan County
County Seat: Lincoln (ZIP: 62656)

Pop: 30,798 (1990); 31,802 (1980)   **Pop Density:** 49.8
Land: 618.2 sq. mi.; **Water:** 0.9 sq. mi.   **Area Code:** 217
In central IL northeast of Springfield; organized Feb 15, 1839 from Sangamon County.
Name origin: For Dr. John Logan, an immigrant from Ireland in 1823, IL legislator, and father of John Alexander Logan (1826–86), U.S. general and statesman.

Aetna   Township
Lat: 40-05-21 N   **Long:** 89-11-41 W
Pop: 540 (1990); 579 (1980)   **Pop Density:** 15.6
Land: 34.6 sq. mi.; **Water:** 0.0 sq. mi.

Atlanta   City
ZIP: 61723   **Lat:** 40-15-43 N   **Long:** 89-13-55 W
Pop: 1,616 (1990); 1,807 (1980)   **Pop Density:** 1469.1
Land: 1.1 sq. mi.; **Water:** 0.0 sq. mi.
In central IL, 18 mi. southwest of Bloomington. Founded 1853. Not coextensive with the town of the same name.
Name origin: For Atlanta, GA. Previously named Xenia, Atalanta, and New Castle.

*Atlanta   Township
Lat: 40-14-55 N   **Long:** 89-12-34 W
Pop: 1,884 (1990); 2,048 (1980)   **Pop Density:** 77.9
Land: 24.2 sq. mi.; **Water:** 0.0 sq. mi.

Broadwell   Village
Lat: 40-04-02 N   **Long:** 89-26-33 W
Pop: 146 (1990); 183 (1980)   **Pop Density:** 730.0
Land: 0.2 sq. mi.; **Water:** 0.0 sq. mi.
Not coextensive with the town of the same name.

*Broadwell   Township
Lat: 40-05-30 N   **Long:** 89-25-20 W
Pop: 2,200 (1990); 1,359 (1980)   **Pop Density:** 66.9
Land: 32.9 sq. mi.; **Water:** 0.5 sq. mi.

Chester   Township
Lat: 40-05-33 N   **Long:** 89-18-47 W
Pop: 680 (1990); 773 (1980)   **Pop Density:** 17.8
Land: 38.3 sq. mi.; **Water:** 0.0 sq. mi.

Corwin   Township
Lat: 40-05-58 N   **Long:** 89-32-13 W
Pop: 727 (1990); 747 (1980)   **Pop Density:** 21.6
Land: 33.6 sq. mi.; **Water:** 0.0 sq. mi.

East Lincoln   Township
ZIP: 62656   **Lat:** 40-10-52 N   **Long:** 89-18-45 W
Pop: 8,887 (1990); 9,302 (1980)   **Pop Density:** 246.2
Land: 36.1 sq. mi.; **Water:** 0.0 sq. mi.

Elkhart   Village
ZIP: 62634   **Lat:** 40-01-09 N   **Long:** 89-28-54 W
Pop: 475 (1990); 493 (1980)   **Pop Density:** 316.7
Land: 1.5 sq. mi.; **Water:** 0.0 sq. mi.   **Elev:** 592 ft.
Not coextensive with the town of the same name.

*Elkhart   Township
Lat: 39-59-18 N   **Long:** 89-25-15 W
Pop: 656 (1990); 703 (1980)   **Pop Density:** 12.7
Land: 51.7 sq. mi.; **Water:** 0.0 sq. mi.

Emden   Village
ZIP: 62635   **Lat:** 40-17-51 N   **Long:** 89-29-06 W
Pop: 459 (1990); 527 (1980)   **Pop Density:** 2295.0
Land: 0.2 sq. mi.; **Water:** 0.0 sq. mi.

Eminence   Township
Lat: 40-16-02 N   **Long:** 89-19-07 W
Pop: 506 (1990); 618 (1980)   **Pop Density:** 11.9
Land: 42.5 sq. mi.; **Water:** 0.0 sq. mi.

Hartsburg   Village
ZIP: 62643   **Lat:** 40-15-02 N   **Long:** 89-26-26 W
Pop: 306 (1990); 379 (1980)   **Pop Density:** 3060.0
Land: 0.1 sq. mi.; **Water:** 0.0 sq. mi.

Hurlbut   Township
Lat: 40-00-45 N   **Long:** 89-32-10 W
Pop: 363 (1990); 389 (1980)   **Pop Density:** 14.4
Land: 25.2 sq. mi.; **Water:** 0.0 sq. mi.

Laenna   Township
Lat: 40-00-41 N   **Long:** 89-12-00 W
Pop: 810 (1990); 870 (1980)   **Pop Density:** 23.1
Land: 35.1 sq. mi.; **Water:** 0.0 sq. mi.

Lake Fork   Township
Lat: 39-56-13 N   **Long:** 89-11-28 W
Pop: 173 (1990); 187 (1980)   **Pop Density:** 9.7
Land: 17.8 sq. mi.; **Water:** 0.0 sq. mi.

Latham   Village
ZIP: 62543   **Lat:** 39-58-00 N   **Long:** 89-09-42 W
Pop: 482 (1990); 564 (1980)   **Pop Density:** 1606.7
Land: 0.3 sq. mi.; **Water:** 0.0 sq. mi.

Lincoln   City
ZIP: 62656   **Lat:** 40-09-02 N   **Long:** 89-22-00 W
Pop: 15,418 (1990); 16,327 (1980)   **Pop Density:** 2803.3
Land: 5.5 sq. mi.; **Water:** 0.0 sq. mi.   **Elev:** 591 ft.
In central IL, 30 mi. northeast of Springfield. Founded 1853; incorporated Feb 18, 1857.
Name origin: For Abraham Lincoln (1809–65), sixteenth U.S. president.

Middletown   Village
ZIP: 62666   **Lat:** 40-06-02 N   **Long:** 89-35-28 W
Pop: 436 (1990); 503 (1980)   **Pop Density:** 2180.0
Land: 0.2 sq. mi.; **Water:** 0.0 sq. mi.

Mount Pulaski   Town
ZIP: 62548   **Lat:** 40-00-36 N   **Long:** 89-16-59 W
Pop: 1,610 (1990); 1,783 (1980)   **Pop Density:** 1463.6
Land: 1.1 sq. mi.; **Water:** 0.0 sq. mi.
Not coextensive with the town of the same name.
Name origin: For Casimir Pulaski (1747–79), Polish soldier who fought with the Americans in the American Revolution.

ILLINOIS, Logan County

*Mount Pulaski
Township
Lat: 39-58-59 N Long: 89-18-43 W
Pop: 2,256 (1990); 2,404 (1980) Pop Density: 41.7
Land: 54.1 sq. mi.; Water: 0.0 sq. mi.

New Holland
Village
ZIP: 62671 Lat: 40-11-03 N Long: 89-34-56 W
Pop: 330 (1990); 295 (1980) Pop Density: 1100.0
Land: 0.3 sq. mi.; Water: 0.0 sq. mi.

Oran
Township
Lat: 40-10-59 N Long: 89-12-19 W
Pop: 437 (1990); 508 (1980) Pop Density: 12.7
Land: 34.3 sq. mi.; Water: 0.0 sq. mi.

Orvil
Township
Lat: 40-16-21 N Long: 89-25-37 W
Pop: 1,155 (1990); 1,294 (1980) Pop Density: 27.5
Land: 42.0 sq. mi.; Water: 0.0 sq. mi.

Prairie Creek
Township
Lat: 40-16-30 N Long: 89-33-00 W
Pop: 556 (1990); 641 (1980) Pop Density: 13.1
Land: 42.3 sq. mi.; Water: 0.0 sq. mi.

San Jose
Village
Lat: 40-18-24 N Long: 89-36-02 W
Pop: 159 (1990); 268 (1980) Pop Density: 795.0
Land: 0.2 sq. mi.; Water: 0.0 sq. mi. Elev: 573 ft.
Part of the town is also in Mason County.

Sheridan
Township
Lat: 40-10-41 N Long: 89-32-26 W
Pop: 593 (1990); 592 (1980) Pop Density: 16.7
Land: 35.5 sq. mi.; Water: 0.0 sq. mi.

West Lincoln
Township
ZIP: 62656 Lat: 40-10-37 N Long: 89-25-23 W
Pop: 8,375 (1990); 8,788 (1980) Pop Density: 219.8
Land: 38.1 sq. mi.; Water: 0.2 sq. mi.

Macon County
County Seat: Decatur (ZIP: 62523)

Pop: 117,206 (1990); 131,375 (1980) Pop Density: 201.9
Land: 580.6 sq. mi.; Water: 4.8 sq. mi. Area Code: 217
In central IL east of Springfield; organized Jan 19, 1829 from Shelby County.
Name origin: For Nathaniel Macon (1757–1837), NC legislator, U.S. representative (1791–1815), U.S. senator (1815–28), and president of the NC constitutional convention (1835).

Argenta
Village
ZIP: 62501 Lat: 39-59-05 N Long: 88-49-07 W
Pop: 940 (1990); 994 (1980) Pop Density: 1880.0
Land: 0.5 sq. mi.; Water: 0.0 sq. mi. Elev: 610 ft.
Founded 1874; incorporated as village 1891.
Name origin: Probably from the Latin for 'silver.' Previously called Friends Creek.

Austin
Township
Lat: 39-59-59 N Long: 89-05-42 W
Pop: 263 (1990); 300 (1980) Pop Density: 7.1
Land: 36.9 sq. mi.; Water: 0.0 sq. mi.

Blue Mound
Village
ZIP: 62513 Lat: 39-42-02 N Long: 89-07-07 W
Pop: 1,161 (1990); 1,338 (1980) Pop Density: 1935.0
Land: 0.6 sq. mi.; Water: 0.0 sq. mi.
Name origin: Descriptively named for a large glacial deposit, or mound, in the area covered with blue flowers in the spring.

*Blue Mound
Township
Lat: 39-46-20 N Long: 89-05-06 W
Pop: 916 (1990); 1,040 (1980) Pop Density: 28.1
Land: 32.6 sq. mi.; Water: 0.0 sq. mi.

Decatur
City
ZIP: 62523 Lat: 39-51-08 N Long: 88-56-01 W
Pop: 83,885 (1990); 93,939 (1980) Pop Density: 2261.1
Land: 37.1 sq. mi.; Water: 4.3 sq. mi. Elev: 670 ft.
In central IL on the Sangamon River, 35 mi. east of Springfield. County seat (1829); founded 1829; incorporated Mar 2, 1839. Not coextensive with the town of the same name.
Name origin: For Stephen Decatur (1779–1820), U.S. naval hero of the War of 1812.

*Decatur
Township
ZIP: 62521 Lat: 39-50-49 N Long: 88-57-34 W
Pop: 61,907 (1990); 71,849 (1980) Pop Density: 2127.4
Land: 29.1 sq. mi.; Water: 1.9 sq. mi.

Forsyth
Village
ZIP: 62535 Lat: 39-55-24 N Long: 88-57-21 W
Pop: 1,275 (1990); 1,029 (1980) Pop Density: 850.0
Land: 1.5 sq. mi.; Water: 0.0 sq. mi.

Friends Creek
Township
Lat: 40-00-24 N Long: 88-49-25 W
Pop: 1,429 (1990); 1,554 (1980) Pop Density: 29.0
Land: 49.2 sq. mi.; Water: 0.0 sq. mi.

Harristown
Village
ZIP: 62537 Lat: 39-50-29 N Long: 89-03-34 W
Pop: 1,319 (1990); 1,456 (1980) Pop Density: 732.8
Land: 1.8 sq. mi.; Water: 0.0 sq. mi.
Not coextensive with the town of the same name.

*Harristown
Township
Lat: 39-50-23 N Long: 89-05-07 W
Pop: 1,956 (1990); 2,209 (1980) Pop Density: 69.6
Land: 28.1 sq. mi.; Water: 0.2 sq. mi.

Hickory Point
Township
ZIP: 62526 Lat: 39-55-19 N Long: 88-58-19 W
Pop: 16,556 (1990); 16,596 (1980) Pop Density: 466.4
Land: 35.5 sq. mi.; Water: 0.0 sq. mi.

Illini
Township
Lat: 39-55-04 N **Long:** 89-05-23 W
Pop: 1,517 (1990); 1,656 (1980) **Pop Density:** 41.3
Land: 36.7 sq. mi.; **Water:** 0.0 sq. mi.

Long Creek
Village
ZIP: 62521 **Lat:** 39-48-15 N **Long:** 88-50-50 W
Pop: 1,250 (1990) **Pop Density:** 480.8
Land: 2.6 sq. mi.; **Water:** 0.0 sq. mi.

In central IL, 10 mi. south of Decatur. Not coextensive with the town of the same name.

*Long Creek
Township
ZIP: 62521 **Lat:** 39-49-15 N **Long:** 88-49-20 W
Pop: 10,628 (1990); 11,957 (1980) **Pop Density:** 279.7
Land: 38.0 sq. mi.; **Water:** 0.8 sq. mi.

Macon
Town
ZIP: 62544 **Lat:** 39-42-32 N **Long:** 88-59-57 W
Pop: 1,282 (1990); 1,300 (1980) **Pop Density:** 2136.7
Land: 0.6 sq. mi.; **Water:** 0.0 sq. mi. **Elev:** 714 ft.

In central IL, 10 mi. south of Decatur. Founded 1835; incorporated Apr 15, 1869.
Name origin: For the county.

Maroa
Town
ZIP: 61756 **Lat:** 40-02-17 N **Long:** 88-57-17 W
Pop: 1,602 (1990); 1,760 (1980) **Pop Density:** 2670.0
Land: 0.6 sq. mi.; **Water:** 0.0 sq. mi.

Incorporated March 7, 1867. Not coextensive with the town of the same name.
Name origin: Name formed by town council members pulling letters from a hat.

*Maroa
Township
Lat: 40-01-03 N **Long:** 88-57-56 W
Pop: 1,898 (1990); 2,116 (1980) **Pop Density:** 45.6
Land: 41.6 sq. mi.; **Water:** 0.0 sq. mi.

Milam
Township
Lat: 39-41-21 N **Long:** 88-52-05 W
Pop: 104 (1990); 138 (1980) **Pop Density:** 4.4
Land: 23.8 sq. mi.; **Water:** 0.0 sq. mi.

Mount Zion
City
ZIP: 62549 **Lat:** 39-46-40 N **Long:** 88-52-42 W
Pop: 4,522 (1990); 4,563 (1980) **Pop Density:** 1739.2
Land: 2.6 sq. mi.; **Water:** 0.0 sq. mi.

In central IL on the Saugamon River across from Decatur. Not coextensive with the town of the same name.
Name origin: Named by its founders for the biblical site.

*Mount Zion
Township
ZIP: 62549 **Lat:** 39-45-08 N **Long:** 88-51-00 W
Pop: 5,922 (1990); 6,097 (1980) **Pop Density:** 138.4
Land: 42.8 sq. mi.; **Water:** 0.0 sq. mi.

Niantic
Village
ZIP: 62551 **Lat:** 39-51-13 N **Long:** 89-09-55 W
Pop: 647 (1990); 761 (1980) **Pop Density:** 647.0
Land: 1.0 sq. mi.; **Water:** 0.0 sq. mi.

Not coextensive with the town of the same name.

*Niantic
Township
Lat: 39-51-58 N **Long:** 89-10-55 W
Pop: 850 (1990); 1,019 (1980) **Pop Density:** 29.1
Land: 29.2 sq. mi.; **Water:** 0.1 sq. mi.

Oakley
Township
Lat: 39-53-48 N **Long:** 88-47-37 W
Pop: 1,060 (1990); 1,023 (1980) **Pop Density:** 36.8
Land: 28.8 sq. mi.; **Water:** 0.6 sq. mi.

Oreana
Village
ZIP: 62554 **Lat:** 39-56-16 N **Long:** 88-52-09 W
Pop: 847 (1990); 999 (1980) **Pop Density:** 1694.0
Land: 0.5 sq. mi.; **Water:** 0.0 sq. mi. **Elev:** 688 ft.

Pleasant View
Township
Lat: 39-41-29 N **Long:** 89-04-50 W
Pop: 1,486 (1990); 1,656 (1980) **Pop Density:** 48.6
Land: 30.6 sq. mi.; **Water:** 0.0 sq. mi.

South Macon
Township
Lat: 39-41-47 N **Long:** 88-58-23 W
Pop: 1,633 (1990); 1,697 (1980) **Pop Density:** 48.6
Land: 33.6 sq. mi.; **Water:** 0.0 sq. mi.

South Wheatland
Township
Lat: 39-46-44 N **Long:** 88-58-43 W
Pop: 4,340 (1990); 5,219 (1980) **Pop Density:** 156.1
Land: 27.8 sq. mi.; **Water:** 0.4 sq. mi.

Warrensburg
Town
ZIP: 62573 **Lat:** 39-55-56 N **Long:** 89-03-40 W
Pop: 1,274 (1990); 1,372 (1980) **Pop Density:** 1820.0
Land: 0.7 sq. mi.; **Water:** 0.0 sq. mi.

In central IL, just northwest of Decatur.

Whitmore
Township
Lat: 39-55-53 N **Long:** 88-51-05 W
Pop: 4,741 (1990); 5,249 (1980) **Pop Density:** 131.3
Land: 36.1 sq. mi.; **Water:** 0.8 sq. mi.

ILLINOIS, Macoupin County

Macoupin County
County Seat: Carlinville (ZIP: 62626)

Pop: 47,679 (1990); 49,384 (1980) **Pop Density:** 55.2
Land: 863.7 sq. mi.; **Water:** 4.0 sq. mi. **Area Code:** 217

In west-central IL southwest of Springfield; organized Jan 17, 1829 from Madison and Greene counties.

Name origin: From an Algonquian Indian word probably meaning 'white potato.'

Barr
Township
Lat: 39-23-15 N **Long:** 90-05-22 W
Pop: 395 (1990); 437 (1980) **Pop Density:** 10.8
Land: 36.7 sq. mi.; **Water:** 0.2 sq. mi.

Benld
City
ZIP: 62009 **Lat:** 39-05-35 N **Long:** 89-48-06 W
Pop: 1,604 (1990); 1,638 (1980) **Pop Density:** 1458.2
Land: 1.1 sq. mi.; **Water:** 0.0 sq. mi.

Established and incorporated as a village 1900.
Name origin: For Ben L. Dorsey, an early settler.

Bird
Township
Lat: 39-17-54 N **Long:** 89-58-49 W
Pop: 323 (1990); 363 (1980) **Pop Density:** 8.9
Land: 36.1 sq. mi.; **Water:** 0.0 sq. mi.

Brighton
Village
ZIP: 62012 **Lat:** 39-02-28 N **Long:** 90-08-15 W
Pop: 1,967 (1990); 2,005 (1980) **Pop Density:** 1639.2
Land: 1.2 sq. mi.; **Water:** 0.0 sq. mi. **Elev:** 653 ft.

Not coextensive with the township of the same name. Part of the town is also in Jersey County.

*Brighton
Township
Lat: 39-02-30 N **Long:** 90-05-09 W
Pop: 3,814 (1990); 3,830 (1980) **Pop Density:** 105.1
Land: 36.3 sq. mi.; **Water:** 0.2 sq. mi.

Brushy Mound
Township
Lat: 39-12-59 N **Long:** 89-51-48 W
Pop: 697 (1990); 544 (1980) **Pop Density:** 19.8
Land: 35.2 sq. mi.; **Water:** 0.5 sq. mi.

Bunker Hill
City
ZIP: 62014 **Lat:** 39-02-25 N **Long:** 89-57-02 W
Pop: 1,722 (1990); 1,700 (1980) **Pop Density:** 1435.0
Land: 1.2 sq. mi.; **Water:** 0.0 sq. mi. **Elev:** 668 ft.

Incorporated as city 1857. Not coextensive with the town of the same name.
Name origin: For the famous battle of the American Revolution.

*Bunker Hill
Township
Lat: 39-02-36 N **Long:** 89-58-47 W
Pop: 3,052 (1990); 3,114 (1980) **Pop Density:** 84.1
Land: 36.3 sq. mi.; **Water:** 0.1 sq. mi.

Cahokia
Township
Lat: 39-07-46 N **Long:** 89-45-19 W
Pop: 3,266 (1990); 3,515 (1980) **Pop Density:** 89.0
Land: 36.7 sq. mi.; **Water:** 0.2 sq. mi.

Carlinville
City
ZIP: 62626 **Lat:** 39-16-49 N **Long:** 89-52-51 W
Pop: 5,416 (1990); 5,439 (1980) **Pop Density:** 2461.8
Land: 2.2 sq. mi.; **Water:** 0.0 sq. mi.

In southwest-central IL. City incorporated Mar 4, 1837. Not coextensive with the town of the same name.

*Carlinville
Township
ZIP: 62626 **Lat:** 39-18-16 N **Long:** 89-52-20 W
Pop: 6,553 (1990); 6,714 (1980) **Pop Density:** 185.1
Land: 35.4 sq. mi.; **Water:** 0.0 sq. mi.

Chesterfield
Village
ZIP: 62630 **Lat:** 39-15-20 N **Long:** 90-04-03 W
Pop: 230 (1990); 280 (1980) **Pop Density:** 460.0
Land: 0.5 sq. mi.; **Water:** 0.0 sq. mi.

Not coextensive with the town of the same name.

*Chesterfield
Township
Lat: 39-12-57 N **Long:** 90-05-24 W
Pop: 951 (1990); 1,095 (1980) **Pop Density:** 26.6
Land: 35.7 sq. mi.; **Water:** 0.0 sq. mi.

Dorchester
Village
ZIP: 62020 **Lat:** 39-05-10 N **Long:** 89-53-17 W
Pop: 145 (1990); 155 (1980) **Pop Density:** 207.1
Land: 0.7 sq. mi.; **Water:** 0.0 sq. mi.

Not coextensive with the town of the same name.

*Dorchester
Township
Lat: 39-02-26 N **Long:** 89-51-56 W
Pop: 1,517 (1990); 1,551 (1980) **Pop Density:** 42.0
Land: 36.1 sq. mi.; **Water:** 0.0 sq. mi.

Eagarville
Village
Lat: 39-06-37 N **Long:** 89-47-03 W
Pop: 127 (1990); 148 (1980) **Pop Density:** 127.0
Land: 1.0 sq. mi.; **Water:** 0.0 sq. mi.

East Gillespie
Village
ZIP: 62033 **Lat:** 39-08-17 N **Long:** 89-48-46 W
Pop: 205 (1990); 197 (1980) **Pop Density:** 683.3
Land: 0.3 sq. mi.; **Water:** 0.0 sq. mi.

Gillespie
City
ZIP: 62033 **Lat:** 39-07-31 N **Long:** 89-49-01 W
Pop: 3,645 (1990); 3,740 (1980) **Pop Density:** 2603.6
Land: 1.4 sq. mi.; **Water:** 0.0 sq. mi.

Not coextensive with the town of the same name.

*Gillespie
Township
Lat: 39-08-01 N **Long:** 89-52-17 W
Pop: 4,159 (1990); 4,111 (1980) **Pop Density:** 116.5
Land: 35.7 sq. mi.; **Water:** 0.5 sq. mi.

Girard
City
ZIP: 62640 **Lat:** 39-26-48 N **Long:** 89-46-56 W
Pop: 2,164 (1990); 2,246 (1980) **Pop Density:** 2404.4
Land: 0.9 sq. mi.; **Water:** 0.0 sq. mi.

Not coextensive with the town of the same name.

*Girard
Township
Lat: 39-26-58 N **Long:** 89-45-29 W
Pop: 2,454 (1990); 2,557 (1980) **Pop Density:** 135.6
Land: 18.1 sq. mi.; **Water:** 0.0 sq. mi.

Hettick
Village
ZIP: 62649 Lat: 39-21-18 N Long: 90-02-13 W
Pop: 211 (1990); 262 (1980) Pop Density: 703.3
Land: 0.3 sq. mi.; **Water:** 0.0 sq. mi.

Hillyard
Township
Lat: 39-07-46 N Long: 89-58-17 W
Pop: 792 (1990); 892 (1980) Pop Density: 21.9
Land: 36.1 sq. mi.; **Water:** 0.1 sq. mi.

Honey Point
Township
Lat: 39-13-04 N Long: 89-45-26 W
Pop: 290 (1990); 308 (1980) Pop Density: 7.8
Land: 37.0 sq. mi.; **Water:** 0.0 sq. mi.

Medora
Village
Lat: 39-10-33 N Long: 90-08-30 W
Pop: 420 (1990); 532 (1980) Pop Density: 1400.0
Land: 0.3 sq. mi.; **Water:** 0.0 sq. mi.

Modesto
Village
ZIP: 62667 Lat: 39-28-44 N Long: 89-58-48 W
Pop: 240 (1990); 260 (1980) Pop Density: 400.0
Land: 0.6 sq. mi.; **Water:** 0.0 sq. mi. Elev: 685 ft.

Mount Clare
Village
ZIP: 62033 Lat: 39-05-55 N Long: 89-49-29 W
Pop: 297 (1990); 300 (1980) Pop Density: 198.0
Land: 1.5 sq. mi.; **Water:** 0.0 sq. mi.

Mount Olive
Town
ZIP: 62069 Lat: 39-04-21 N Long: 89-43-40 W
Pop: 2,126 (1990); 2,357 (1980) Pop Density: 1932.7
Land: 1.1 sq. mi.; **Water:** 0.0 sq. mi. Elev: 684 ft.
Incorporated 1874. Not coextensive with the town of the same name.
Name origin: For the biblical site.

*Mount Olive
Township
Lat: 39-03-55 N Long: 89-45-10 W
Pop: 3,443 (1990); 3,561 (1980) Pop Density: 190.2
Land: 18.1 sq. mi.; **Water:** 0.2 sq. mi.

Nilwood
Town
ZIP: 62672 Lat: 39-23-58 N Long: 89-48-26 W
Pop: 238 (1990); 278 (1980) Pop Density: 476.0
Land: 0.5 sq. mi.; **Water:** 0.0 sq. mi.
Not coextensive with the town of the same name.

*Nilwood
Township
Lat: 39-23-38 N Long: 89-45-07 W
Pop: 633 (1990); 781 (1980) Pop Density: 17.3
Land: 36.5 sq. mi.; **Water:** 0.0 sq. mi.

North Otter
Township
Lat: 39-28-43 N Long: 89-52-10 W
Pop: 721 (1990); 852 (1980) Pop Density: 20.2
Land: 35.7 sq. mi.; **Water:** 0.7 sq. mi.

North Palmyra
Township
Lat: 39-28-39 N Long: 89-58-52 W
Pop: 905 (1990); 1,060 (1980) Pop Density: 25.1
Land: 36.1 sq. mi.; **Water:** 0.1 sq. mi.

Palmyra
Village
ZIP: 62674 Lat: 39-26-05 N Long: 89-59-46 W
Pop: 722 (1990); 864 (1980) Pop Density: 722.0
Land: 1.0 sq. mi.; **Water:** 0.0 sq. mi.

Polk
Township
Lat: 39-12-52 N Long: 89-58-38 W
Pop: 467 (1990); 441 (1980) Pop Density: 12.9
Land: 36.2 sq. mi.; **Water:** 0.2 sq. mi.

Royal Lakes
Village
ZIP: 62685 Lat: 39-06-44 N Long: 89-57-42 W
Pop: 272 (1990); 270 (1980) Pop Density: 544.0
Land: 0.5 sq. mi.; **Water:** 0.0 sq. mi.

Sawyerville
Village
ZIP: 62085 Lat: 39-04-35 N Long: 89-48-10 W
Pop: 312 (1990); 381 (1980) Pop Density: 312.0
Land: 1.0 sq. mi.; **Water:** 0.0 sq. mi.

Scottville
Village
ZIP: 62683 Lat: 39-28-38 N Long: 90-06-11 W
Pop: 165 (1990); 214 (1980) Pop Density: 165.0
Land: 1.0 sq. mi.; **Water:** 0.0 sq. mi.
Not coextensive with the town of the same name.

*Scottville
Township
Lat: 39-28-38 N Long: 90-05-47 W
Pop: 387 (1990); 490 (1980) Pop Density: 10.5
Land: 36.7 sq. mi.; **Water:** 0.0 sq. mi.

Shaws Point
Township
Lat: 39-18-01 N Long: 89-45-44 W
Pop: 489 (1990); 529 (1980) Pop Density: 14.3
Land: 34.1 sq. mi.; **Water:** 0.1 sq. mi.

Shipman
Town
ZIP: 62685 Lat: 39-07-14 N Long: 90-02-42 W
Pop: 624 (1990); 581 (1980) Pop Density: 480.0
Land: 1.3 sq. mi.; **Water:** 0.0 sq. mi.
Not coextensive with the town of the same name.

*Shipman
Township
Lat: 39-07-56 N Long: 90-05-49 W
Pop: 1,407 (1990); 1,437 (1980) Pop Density: 39.2
Land: 35.9 sq. mi.; **Water:** 0.1 sq. mi.

South Otter
Township
Lat: 39-23-28 N Long: 89-51-51 W
Pop: 426 (1990); 510 (1980) Pop Density: 11.9
Land: 35.8 sq. mi.; **Water:** 0.6 sq. mi.

South Palmyra
Township
Lat: 39-23-26 N Long: 89-58-25 W
Pop: 846 (1990); 957 (1980) Pop Density: 23.4
Land: 36.1 sq. mi.; **Water:** 0.0 sq. mi.

Standard City
Village
Lat: 39-21-01 N Long: 89-47-01 W
Pop: 128 (1990); 148 (1980) Pop Density: 213.3
Land: 0.6 sq. mi.; **Water:** 0.0 sq. mi.

Staunton
Town
ZIP: 62088 Lat: 39-00-45 N Long: 89-47-18 W
Pop: 4,806 (1990); 4,744 (1980) Pop Density: 2089.6
Land: 2.3 sq. mi.; **Water:** 0.0 sq. mi. Elev: 622 ft.
Founded 1817. Not coextensive with the town of the same name.

*Staunton
Township
ZIP: 62088 Lat: 39-01-08 N Long: 89-45-07 W
Pop: 5,482 (1990); 5,223 (1980) Pop Density: 301.2
Land: 18.2 sq. mi.; **Water:** 0.1 sq. mi.

Virden — City
ZIP: 62690   Lat: 39-30-13 N   Long: 89-46-11 W
Pop: 3,614 (1990); 3,885 (1980)   Pop Density: 2258.8
Land: 1.6 sq. mi.; Water: 0.0 sq. mi.

In southwest-central IL, 30 mi. south of Springfield. Part of the town is also in Sangamon County. Not coextensive with the town of the same name.
Name origin: For the Virden Mine Company.

*Virden — Township
Lat: 39-30-00 N   Long: 89-45-30 W
Pop: 3,944 (1990); 4,225 (1980)   Pop Density: 219.1
Land: 18.0 sq. mi.; Water: 0.0 sq. mi.

Western Mound — Township
Lat: 39-18-24 N   Long: 90-05-23 W
Pop: 266 (1990); 287 (1980)   Pop Density: 7.6
Land: 35.0 sq. mi.; Water: 0.1 sq. mi.

White City — Village
ZIP: 62069   Lat: 39-04-20 N   Long: 89-45-50 W
Pop: 229 (1990); 214 (1980)   Pop Density: 190.8
Land: 1.2 sq. mi.; Water: 0.0 sq. mi.   Elev: 652 ft.

Wilsonville — Village
ZIP: 62093   Lat: 39-04-07 N   Long: 89-51-19 W
Pop: 609 (1990); 608 (1980)   Pop Density: 609.0
Land: 1.0 sq. mi.; Water: 0.0 sq. mi.

Madison County
County Seat: Edwardsville (ZIP: 62025)

Pop: 249,238 (1990); 247,661 (1980)   Pop Density: 343.7
Land: 725.1 sq. mi.; Water: 15.3 sq. mi.   Area Code: 618

On the west-central border of IL, north of St. Louis; organized Sep 14, 1812 (prior to statehood) from Saint Clair County.
Name origin: For James Madison (1751–1836), fourth U.S. president.

Alhambra — Village
ZIP: 62001   Lat: 38-53-15 N   Long: 89-44-05 W
Pop: 709 (1990); 643 (1980)   Pop Density: 886.3
Land: 0.8 sq. mi.; Water: 0.0 sq. mi.

Name origin: For the famous Moorish palace and fortifications in Spain.

*Alhambra — Township
Lat: 38-52-17 N   Long: 89-46-00 W
Pop: 1,445 (1990); 1,322 (1980)   Pop Density: 41.3
Land: 35.0 sq. mi.; Water: 0.0 sq. mi.

Alton — City
ZIP: 62002   Lat: 38-54-14 N   Long: 90-09-14 W
Pop: 32,905 (1990); 34,171 (1980)   Pop Density: 2193.7
Land: 15.0 sq. mi.; Water: 0.8 sq. mi.

In southwestern IL on bluffs overlooking the Mississippi River, 20 mi. north of St. Louis, MO. Incorporated Jan 30, 1821. Coextensive with the township.
Name origin: Either for its height above the river or for Alton, NH.

*Alton — Township
ZIP: 62002   Lat: 38-54-14 N   Long: 90-09-14 W
Pop: 32,905 (1990); 34,171 (1980)   Pop Density: 2193.7
Land: 15.0 sq. mi.; Water: 0.8 sq. mi.

Bethalto — Village
ZIP: 62010   Lat: 38-54-02 N   Long: 90-02-48 W
Pop: 9,507 (1990); 8,630 (1980)   Pop Density: 1584.5
Land: 6.0 sq. mi.; Water: 0.0 sq. mi.

Name origin: From combining its former name *Bethel* (a church name) and *alto* from the nearby town of Alton.

Chouteau — Township
ZIP: 62040   Lat: 38-47-16 N   Long: 90-05-45 W
Pop: 7,792 (1990); 8,627 (1980)   Pop Density: 259.7
Land: 30.0 sq. mi.; Water: 2.4 sq. mi.

Collinsville — City
ZIP: 62234   Lat: 38-40-42 N   Long: 89-59-46 W
Pop: 20,100 (1990); 17,481 (1980)   Pop Density: 2051.0
Land: 9.8 sq. mi.; Water: 0.0 sq. mi.

In southwestern IL, 13 mi. east of St. Louis, MO. Incorporated Feb 15, 1855. Part of the town is also in St. Clair County.
Name origin: For the Collins family, founders, especially William Collins.

*Collinsville — Township
ZIP: 62234   Lat: 38-42-00 N   Long: 89-58-54 W
Pop: 29,842 (1990); 27,158 (1980)   Pop Density: 838.3
Land: 35.6 sq. mi.; Water: 0.1 sq. mi.

East Alton — Village
ZIP: 62024   Lat: 38-52-59 N   Long: 90-06-28 W
Pop: 7,063 (1990); 7,096 (1980)   Pop Density: 1358.3
Land: 5.2 sq. mi.; Water: 0.1 sq. mi.

Settled in 1800, East Alton developed as a river port. It was incorporated in 1894.

Edwardsville — City
ZIP: 62025   Lat: 38-47-46 N   Long: 89-57-53 W
Pop: 14,579 (1990); 12,480 (1980)   Pop Density: 1675.7
Land: 8.7 sq. mi.; Water: 0.2 sq. mi.

Founded in 1813; incorporated Feb 23, 1819.
Name origin: For Ninian Edwards (1775–1833), governor of Illinois Territory from 1809 to 1818 and one of the local landowners.

*Edwardsville — Township
ZIP: 62025   Lat: 38-47-12 N   Long: 89-58-48 W
Pop: 26,665 (1990); 23,249 (1980)   Pop Density: 751.1
Land: 35.5 sq. mi.; Water: 0.4 sq. mi.

Fairmont City — Village
ZIP: 62201   Lat: 38-39-41 N   Long: 90-05-41 W
Pop: 39 (1990); 2,313 (1980)   Pop Density: 195.0
Land: 0.2 sq. mi.; Water: 0.0 sq. mi.

Part of the town is also in St. Clair County.

ILLINOIS, Madison County

Fort Russell
Township
ZIP: 62010 Lat: 38-52-33 N Long: 89-59-21 W
Pop: 6,534 (1990); 5,912 (1980) Pop Density: 171.0
Land: 38.2 sq. mi.; Water: 0.3 sq. mi.

Foster
Township
Lat: 38-57-46 N Long: 90-05-59 W
Pop: 3,719 (1990); 3,502 (1980) Pop Density: 116.9
Land: 31.8 sq. mi.; Water: 0.1 sq. mi.

Glen Carbon
Village
ZIP: 62034 Lat: 38-45-37 N Long: 89-58-22 W
Pop: 7,731 (1990); 5,197 (1980) Pop Density: 1267.4
Land: 6.1 sq. mi.; Water: 0.0 sq. mi.

Godfrey
Township
ZIP: 62035 Lat: 38-57-37 N Long: 90-13-23 W
Pop: 15,785 (1990); 15,860 (1980) Pop Density: 457.5
Land: 34.5 sq. mi.; Water: 1.7 sq. mi.
Founded 1835.
Name origin: For retired Cape Cod sea captain Benjamin Godfrey.

Granite City
City
ZIP: 62040 Lat: 38-42-51 N Long: 90-07-46 W
Pop: 32,862 (1990); 36,815 (1980) Pop Density: 2629.0
Land: 12.5 sq. mi.; Water: 0.4 sq. mi.
In southwestern IL on the Mississippi River, 75 mi. southwest of Springfield. Incorporated Mar 9, 1896. Coextensive with the township of the same name.
Name origin: For granite ware, its first product.

*Granite City
Township
ZIP: 62040 Lat: 38-42-51 N Long: 90-07-46 W
Pop: 32,862 (1990); 36,815 (1980) Pop Density: 2629.0
Land: 12.5 sq. mi.; Water: 0.4 sq. mi.

Grantfork
Village
ZIP: 62249 Lat: 38-49-51 N Long: 89-40-04 W
Pop: 273 (1990); 268 (1980) Pop Density: 1365.0
Land: 0.2 sq. mi.; Water: 0.0 sq. mi.

Hamel
Village
ZIP: 62046 Lat: 38-53-18 N Long: 89-50-33 W
Pop: 530 (1990); 537 (1980) Pop Density: 441.7
Land: 1.2 sq. mi.; Water: 0.0 sq. mi.
Not coextensive with the town of the same name.

*Hamel
Township
Lat: 38-52-26 N Long: 89-52-10 W
Pop: 1,685 (1990); 1,744 (1980) Pop Density: 45.9
Land: 36.7 sq. mi.; Water: 0.0 sq. mi.

Hartford
Town
ZIP: 62048 Lat: 38-49-40 N Long: 90-05-30 W
Pop: 1,676 (1990); 1,887 (1980) Pop Density: 478.9
Land: 3.5 sq. mi.; Water: 0.0 sq. mi.

Helvetia
Township
ZIP: 62249 Lat: 38-41-55 N Long: 89-39-33 W
Pop: 7,238 (1990); 6,898 (1980) Pop Density: 200.5
Land: 36.1 sq. mi.; Water: 0.1 sq. mi.

Highland
City
ZIP: 62249 Lat: 38-44-27 N Long: 89-40-32 W
Pop: 7,525 (1990); 7,122 (1980) Pop Density: 2427.4
Land: 3.1 sq. mi.; Water: 0.0 sq. mi.
Incorporated Feb 14, 1863.
Name origin: For its descriptive connotations.

Jarvis
Township
ZIP: 62294 Lat: 38-42-26 N Long: 89-52-13 W
Pop: 9,360 (1990); 6,322 (1980) Pop Density: 261.5
Land: 35.8 sq. mi.; Water: 0.0 sq. mi.

Leef
Township
Lat: 38-51-50 N Long: 89-39-35 W
Pop: 488 (1990); 524 (1980) Pop Density: 16.6
Land: 29.4 sq. mi.; Water: 0.0 sq. mi.

Livingston
Village
ZIP: 62058 Lat: 38-58-03 N Long: 89-45-49 W
Pop: 928 (1990); 949 (1980) Pop Density: 843.6
Land: 1.1 sq. mi.; Water: 0.0 sq. mi.

Madison
City
ZIP: 62060 Lat: 38-40-46 N Long: 90-09-08 W
Pop: 4,623 (1990); 5,301 (1980) Pop Density: 1594.1
Land: 2.9 sq. mi.; Water: 0.0 sq. mi.
Part of the town is also in St. Clair County.
Name origin: For James Madison (1751–1836), fourth U.S. president.

Marine
Town
ZIP: 62061 Lat: 38-47-08 N Long: 89-46-44 W
Pop: 972 (1990); 957 (1980) Pop Density: 1215.0
Land: 0.8 sq. mi.; Water: 0.0 sq. mi.
Incorporated March 8, 1867.

*Marine
Township
Lat: 38-47-17 N Long: 89-45-37 W
Pop: 1,852 (1990); 1,871 (1980) Pop Density: 52.2
Land: 35.5 sq. mi.; Water: 0.0 sq. mi.

Maryville
Town
ZIP: 62062 Lat: 38-43-34 N Long: 89-57-53 W
Pop: 2,576 (1990); 1,949 (1980) Pop Density: 1030.4
Land: 2.5 sq. mi.; Water: 0.0 sq. mi.

Moro
Township
Lat: 38-57-34 N Long: 89-58-52 W
Pop: 2,768 (1990); 2,135 (1980) Pop Density: 86.2
Land: 32.1 sq. mi.; Water: 0.4 sq. mi.

Nameoki
Township
ZIP: 62040 Lat: 38-42-08 N Long: 90-05-05 W
Pop: 12,492 (1990); 13,594 (1980) Pop Density: 538.4
Land: 23.2 sq. mi.; Water: 2.7 sq. mi.
Name origin: Possibly for Nahmeokee, a character in a J. A. Stone play.

New Douglas
Village
ZIP: 62074 Lat: 38-58-12 N Long: 89-39-57 W
Pop: 387 (1990); 389 (1980) Pop Density: 351.8
Land: 1.1 sq. mi.; Water: 0.0 sq. mi. Elev: 619 ft.
Not coextensive with the town of the same name.

*New Douglas
Township
Lat: 38-57-26 N Long: 89-40-34 W
Pop: 644 (1990); 632 (1980) Pop Density: 30.7
Land: 21.0 sq. mi.; Water: 0.0 sq. mi.

Olive
Township
Lat: 38-57-34 N Long: 89-45-40 W
Pop: 1,820 (1990); 1,950 (1980) Pop Density: 58.0
Land: 31.4 sq. mi.; Water: 0.1 sq. mi.

Omphghent
Township
Lat: 38-57-30 N Long: 89-52-17 W
Pop: 1,995 (1990); 1,964 (1980) Pop Density: 58.7
Land: 34.0 sq. mi.; Water: 0.0 sq. mi.

ILLINOIS, Madison County

Pierron
Village
Lat: 38-46-31 N Long: 89-35-57 W
Pop: 21 (1990); 53 (1980) Pop Density: 105.0
Land: 0.2 sq. mi.; Water: 0.0 sq. mi.
Part of the town is also in Bond County.

Pin Oak
Township
Lat: 38-47-23 N Long: 89-52-29 W
Pop: 2,007 (1990); 1,593 (1980) Pop Density: 55.8
Land: 36.0 sq. mi.; Water: 0.1 sq. mi.

Pontoon Beach
Village
ZIP: 62040 Lat: 38-43-35 N Long: 90-03-04 W
Pop: 4,013 (1990); 3,336 (1980) Pop Density: 608.0
Land: 6.6 sq. mi.; Water: 0.2 sq. mi.

Rosewood Heights
CDP
Lat: 38-53-08 N Long: 90-04-12 W
Pop: 4,821 (1990); 5,085 (1980) Pop Density: 1928.4
Land: 2.5 sq. mi.; Water: 0.0 sq. mi.

Roxana
Town
ZIP: 62084 Lat: 38-50-11 N Long: 90-03-09 W
Pop: 1,562 (1990); 1,587 (1980) Pop Density: 332.3
Land: 4.7 sq. mi.; Water: 0.0 sq. mi.
In southwestern IL near the confluence of the Mississippi and Missouri rivers, 20 mi. northeast of St. Louis, MO.

St. Jacob
Village
Lat: 38-43-00 N Long: 89-46-07 W
Pop: 752 (1990); 792 (1980) Pop Density: 1504.0
Land: 0.5 sq. mi.; Water: 0.0 sq. mi. Elev: 518 ft.
Not coextensive with the town of the same name.

*St. Jacob
Township
Lat: 38-41-47 N Long: 89-46-04 W
Pop: 1,756 (1990); 1,735 (1980) Pop Density: 48.9
Land: 35.9 sq. mi.; Water: 0.0 sq. mi.

Saline
Township
Lat: 38-47-12 N Long: 89-39-23 W
Pop: 3,421 (1990); 2,979 (1980) Pop Density: 98.9
Land: 34.6 sq. mi.; Water: 1.0 sq. mi.

South Roxana
Town
ZIP: 62087 Lat: 38-49-19 N Long: 90-03-33 W
Pop: 1,961 (1990); 2,286 (1980) Pop Density: 1782.7
Land: 1.1 sq. mi.; Water: 0.0 sq. mi.

Troy
City
ZIP: 62294 Lat: 38-43-52 N Long: 89-53-37 W
Pop: 6,046 (1990); 3,772 (1980) Pop Density: 2418.4
Land: 2.5 sq. mi.; Water: 0.0 sq. mi.
Established 1819; incorporated Feb 18, 1857.
Name origin: Named by land speculators for Troy, NY.

Venice
City
ZIP: 62090 Lat: 38-40-19 N Long: 90-10-07 W
Pop: 3,571 (1990); 3,480 (1980) Pop Density: 1879.5
Land: 1.9 sq. mi.; Water: 0.0 sq. mi.
In southwestern IL on the Mississippi River, north of St. Louis, MO. Settled 1804; incorporated 1873. Not coextensive with the town of the same name.
Name origin: For Venice, Italy, because the streets here often flooded before levees were constructed.

*Venice
Township
ZIP: 62090 Lat: 38-42-01 N Long: 90-10-57 W
Pop: 8,657 (1990); 9,134 (1980) Pop Density: 832.4
Land: 10.4 sq. mi.; Water: 3.7 sq. mi.

Williamson
Village
Lat: 38-59-14 N Long: 89-45-50 W
Pop: 278 (1990); 319 (1980) Pop Density: 185.3
Land: 1.5 sq. mi.; Water: 0.0 sq. mi.

Wood River
City
ZIP: 62095 Lat: 38-51-43 N Long: 90-05-05 W
Pop: 11,490 (1990); 12,446 (1980) Pop Density: 2167.9
Land: 5.3 sq. mi.; Water: 0.0 sq. mi.
In southwestern IL near Mississippi River and MO border. Incorporated Sep 16, 1908. Not coextensive with the town of the same name.
Name origin: For the nearby Wood River.

*Wood River
Township
ZIP: 62095 Lat: 38-52-33 N Long: 90-05-01 W
Pop: 35,506 (1990); 37,970 (1980) Pop Density: 1420.2
Land: 25.0 sq. mi.; Water: 0.8 sq. mi.

Worden
Town
ZIP: 62097 Lat: 38-55-55 N Long: 89-50-18 W
Pop: 896 (1990); 953 (1980) Pop Density: 1493.3
Land: 0.6 sq. mi.; Water: 0.0 sq. mi.

Marion County
County Seat: Salem (ZIP: 62881)

Pop: 41,561 (1990); 43,523 (1980) Pop Density: 72.6
Land: 572.3 sq. mi.; Water: 3.4 sq. mi. Area Code: 618
In south-central IL west of Olney; organized Jan 24, 1823 from Fayette and Jefferson counties.
Name origin: For Gen. Francis Marion (c. 1732–95), SC soldier and legislator, known as "The Swamp Fox" for his tactics during the Revolutionary War.

Alma
Village
ZIP: 62807 Lat: 38-43-22 N Long: 88-54-36 W
Pop: 388 (1990); 428 (1980) Pop Density: 431.1
Land: 0.9 sq. mi.; Water: 0.0 sq. mi.
In south-central IL, 18 mi. northeast of Centralia. Founded 1855. Not coextensive with the town of the same name.
Name origin: For an early settler's wife.

*Alma
Township
Lat: 38-41-22 N Long: 88-51-55 W
Pop: 845 (1990); 893 (1980) Pop Density: 23.0
Land: 36.8 sq. mi.; Water: 0.1 sq. mi.

ILLINOIS, Marion County

Carrigan
Township
Lat: 38-41-18 N Long: 89-04-56 W
Pop: 437 (1990); 442 (1980) **Pop Density:** 12.5
Land: 35.1 sq. mi.; **Water:** 0.0 sq. mi.

Central City
Village
ZIP: 62801 Lat: 38-32-52 N Long: 89-07-43 W
Pop: 1,390 (1990); 1,505 (1980) **Pop Density:** 2316.7
Land: 0.6 sq. mi.; **Water:** 0.0 sq. mi.
Settled by German immigrants; incorporated as village 1857.
Name origin: For the Illinois Central Railroad.

Centralia
City
ZIP: 62801 Lat: 38-31-18 N Long: 89-07-16 W
Pop: 11,487 (1990); 12,353 (1980) **Pop Density:** 2167.4
Land: 5.3 sq. mi.; **Water:** 0.1 sq. mi.
In south-central IL, 20 mi. northwest of Mount Vernon, 60 mi. east of St. Louis, MO. Founded 1853 by members of the Illinois Central Railroad System; incorporated Feb 18, 1859. Not coextensive with the township of the same name. Part of the town is also in Clinton County.
Name origin: For either the railroad or its central location; (Latinized suffixes were common in the 1800s).

*Centralia
Township
ZIP: 62801 Lat: 38-31-03 N Long: 89-05-17 W
Pop: 16,834 (1990); 17,954 (1980) **Pop Density:** 482.3
Land: 34.9 sq. mi.; **Water:** 1.1 sq. mi.

Farina
Village
Lat: 38-48-51 N Long: 88-47-35 W
Pop: 0 (1990)
Land: 0.2 sq. mi.; **Water:** 0.0 sq. mi.
Part of the town is also in Fayette County.

Foster
Township
Lat: 38-47-00 N Long: 88-58-50 W
Pop: 342 (1990); 350 (1980) **Pop Density:** 9.6
Land: 35.5 sq. mi.; **Water:** 0.0 sq. mi.

Haines
Township
Lat: 38-31-09 N Long: 88-52-07 W
Pop: 852 (1990); 843 (1980) **Pop Density:** 23.7
Land: 36.0 sq. mi.; **Water:** 0.0 sq. mi.

Iuka
Town
ZIP: 62849 Lat: 38-36-52 N Long: 88-47-23 W
Pop: 388 (1990); 353 (1980) **Pop Density:** 970.0
Land: 0.4 sq. mi.; **Water:** 0.0 sq. mi. **Elev:** 518 ft.
Not coextensive with the town of the same name.
Name origin: Originally Middleton. Renamed in 1867 by the legislature at the request of Civil War veterans of the Battle of Iuka (MS).

*Iuka
Township
Lat: 38-36-15 N Long: 88-45-12 W
Pop: 965 (1990); 884 (1980) **Pop Density:** 26.8
Land: 36.0 sq. mi.; **Water:** 0.1 sq. mi.

Junction City
Village
Lat: 38-34-38 N Long: 89-07-31 W
Pop: 539 (1990); 456 (1980) **Pop Density:** 770.0
Land: 0.7 sq. mi.; **Water:** 0.0 sq. mi.

Kell
Village
ZIP: 62853 Lat: 38-29-26 N Long: 88-54-14 W
Pop: 213 (1990); 283 (1980) **Pop Density:** 213.0
Land: 1.0 sq. mi.; **Water:** 0.0 sq. mi.

Kinmundy
City
ZIP: 62854 Lat: 38-46-26 N Long: 88-50-58 W
Pop: 879 (1990); 945 (1980) **Pop Density:** 879.0
Land: 1.0 sq. mi.; **Water:** 0.0 sq. mi. **Elev:** 619 ft.
Not coextensive with the town of the same name.

*Kinmundy
Township
Lat: 38-46-41 N Long: 88-51-57 W
Pop: 1,306 (1990); 1,379 (1980) **Pop Density:** 35.4
Land: 36.9 sq. mi.; **Water:** 0.1 sq. mi.

Meacham
Township
Lat: 38-46-27 N Long: 88-45-12 W
Pop: 374 (1990); 421 (1980) **Pop Density:** 10.2
Land: 36.6 sq. mi.; **Water:** 0.1 sq. mi.

Odin
Town
ZIP: 62870 Lat: 38-36-58 N Long: 89-03-14 W
Pop: 1,150 (1990); 1,285 (1980) **Pop Density:** 1150.0
Land: 1.0 sq. mi.; **Water:** 0.0 sq. mi.
Not coextensive with the town of the same name.
Name origin: For the chief god of Norse mythology.

*Odin
Township
Lat: 38-36-24 N Long: 89-03-30 W
Pop: 1,758 (1990); 1,839 (1980) **Pop Density:** 97.1
Land: 18.1 sq. mi.; **Water:** 0.0 sq. mi.

Omega
Township
Lat: 38-41-54 N Long: 88-45-23 W
Pop: 472 (1990); 497 (1980) **Pop Density:** 13.3
Land: 35.4 sq. mi.; **Water:** 0.8 sq. mi.

Patoka
Town
ZIP: 62875 Lat: 38-45-12 N Long: 89-05-45 W
Pop: 656 (1990); 662 (1980) **Pop Density:** 596.4
Land: 1.1 sq. mi.; **Water:** 0.0 sq. mi. **Elev:** 507 ft.
In south-central IL, 17 mi. north of Centralia. Not coextensive with the town of the same name.
Name origin: For an Indian chief.

*Patoka
Township
Lat: 38-46-47 N Long: 89-05-08 W
Pop: 1,228 (1990); 1,187 (1980) **Pop Density:** 35.2
Land: 34.9 sq. mi.; **Water:** 0.0 sq. mi.

Raccoon
Township
Lat: 38-31-08 N Long: 88-58-35 W
Pop: 1,386 (1990); 1,384 (1980) **Pop Density:** 39.4
Land: 35.2 sq. mi.; **Water:** 0.5 sq. mi.

Romine
Township
Lat: 38-30-56 N Long: 88-45-08 W
Pop: 409 (1990); 489 (1980) **Pop Density:** 11.4
Land: 35.9 sq. mi.; **Water:** 0.1 sq. mi.

Salem
Town
ZIP: 62881 Lat: 38-37-41 N Long: 88-57-06 W
Pop: 7,470 (1990); 7,813 (1980) **Pop Density:** 1409.4
Land: 5.3 sq. mi.; **Water:** 0.1 sq. mi. **Elev:** 544 ft.
In south-central IL, east of E. St. Louis. Founded 1813; incorporated Feb 10, 1837. Not coextensive with the town of the same name.
Name origin: For the biblical city.

*Salem
Township
ZIP: 62881 Lat: 38-36-09 N Long: 88-58-46 W
Pop: 9,614 (1990); 10,055 (1980) **Pop Density:** 272.4
Land: 35.3 sq. mi.; **Water:** 0.3 sq. mi.

Sandoval
Town
ZIP: 62882 Lat: 38-36-40 N Long: 89-07-09 W
Pop: 1,535 (1990); 1,734 (1980) Pop Density: 1535.0
Land: 1.0 sq. mi.; Water: 0.0 sq. mi.
Not coextensive with the town of the same name.

*Sandoval
Township
Lat: 38-36-15 N Long: 89-06-48 W
Pop: 2,708 (1990); 2,861 (1980) Pop Density: 153.9
Land: 17.6 sq. mi.; Water: 0.1 sq. mi.

Stevenson
Township
Lat: 38-36-14 N Long: 88-51-48 W
Pop: 1,090 (1990); 1,089 (1980) Pop Density: 29.7
Land: 36.7 sq. mi.; Water: 0.0 sq. mi.

Tonti
Township
Lat: 38-41-25 N Long: 88-58-30 W
Pop: 941 (1990); 956 (1980) Pop Density: 26.6
Land: 35.4 sq. mi.; Water: 0.1 sq. mi.

Vernon
Village
ZIP: 62892 Lat: 38-48-07 N Long: 89-05-20 W
Pop: 207 (1990); 199 (1980) Pop Density: 230.0
Land: 0.9 sq. mi.; Water: 0.0 sq. mi. Elev: 515 ft.

Walnut Hill
Village
ZIP: 62893 Lat: 38-28-38 N Long: 89-02-39 W
Pop: 133 (1990); 223 (1980) Pop Density: 332.5
Land: 0.4 sq. mi.; Water: 0.0 sq. mi.

Wamac
Town
ZIP: 62801 Lat: 38-30-10 N Long: 89-08-24 W
Pop: 730 (1990); 767 (1980) Pop Density: 1460.0
Land: 0.5 sq. mi.; Water: 0.0 sq. mi.
In southern IL, east of St. Louis, MO. Part of the town is also in Clinton and Washington counties.
Name origin: An acronym for Washington, Marion, and Clinton counties, which converge here.

Marshall County
County Seat: Lacon (ZIP: 61540)

Pop: 12,846 (1990); 14,479 (1980) **Pop Density:** 33.3
Land: 386.1 sq. mi.; **Water:** 12.4 sq. mi. **Area Code:** 309
In north-central IL north of Peoria; organized Jan 19, 1839 from Putnam County.
Name origin: For John Marshall (1755–1835), American jurist and fourth Chief Justice of the U.S. Supreme Court (1801–35).

Bell Plain
Township
Lat: 40-58-33 N Long: 89-13-21 W
Pop: 459 (1990); 510 (1980) Pop Density: 12.5
Land: 36.8 sq. mi.; Water: 0.1 sq. mi.

Bennington
Township
Lat: 40-58-11 N Long: 89-06-23 W
Pop: 1,633 (1990); 1,876 (1980) Pop Density: 45.4
Land: 36.0 sq. mi.; Water: 0.0 sq. mi.

Evans
Township
Lat: 41-03-23 N Long: 89-06-44 W
Pop: 1,219 (1990); 1,376 (1980) Pop Density: 32.9
Land: 37.1 sq. mi.; Water: 0.0 sq. mi.

Henry
Town
ZIP: 61537 Lat: 41-06-44 N Long: 89-21-42 W
Pop: 2,591 (1990); 2,740 (1980) Pop Density: 2159.2
Land: 1.2 sq. mi.; Water: 0.1 sq. mi.
Settled 1833. Not coextensive with the town of the same name.
Name origin: For Gen. James D. Henry of Black Hawk War fame.

*Henry
Township
Lat: 41-07-09 N Long: 89-22-36 W
Pop: 2,877 (1990); 3,242 (1980) Pop Density: 201.2
Land: 14.3 sq. mi.; Water: 2.1 sq. mi.

Hopewell
Village
ZIP: 61565 Lat: 40-58-59 N Long: 89-27-22 W
Pop: 343 (1990) Pop Density: 311.8
Land: 1.1 sq. mi.; Water: 0.0 sq. mi.
Not coextensive with the town of the same name.

*Hopewell
Township
Lat: 41-03-01 N Long: 89-19-58 W
Pop: 511 (1990); 586 (1980) Pop Density: 15.2
Land: 33.7 sq. mi.; Water: 2.3 sq. mi.

Lacon
City
ZIP: 61540 Lat: 41-01-18 N Long: 89-24-24 W
Pop: 1,986 (1990); 2,135 (1980) Pop Density: 1324.0
Land: 1.5 sq. mi.; Water: 0.0 sq. mi. Elev: 495 ft.
Not coextensive with the town of the same name.

*Lacon
Township
Lat: 40-58-42 N Long: 89-25-35 W
Pop: 2,442 (1990); 2,691 (1980) Pop Density: 142.0
Land: 17.2 sq. mi.; Water: 4.8 sq. mi.

La Prairie
Township
Lat: 41-01-10 N Long: 89-34-59 W
Pop: 381 (1990); 471 (1980) Pop Density: 10.6
Land: 36.0 sq. mi.; Water: 0.0 sq. mi.

La Rose
Village
ZIP: 61541 Lat: 40-58-38 N Long: 89-14-04 W
Pop: 130 (1990); 173 (1980) Pop Density: 650.0
Land: 0.2 sq. mi.; Water: 0.0 sq. mi.

Richland
Township
Lat: 40-58-20 N Long: 89-19-27 W
Pop: 493 (1990); 553 (1980) Pop Density: 13.7
Land: 36.0 sq. mi.; Water: 0.0 sq. mi.

Roberts
Township
Lat: 41-03-28 N Long: 89-13-04 W
Pop: 910 (1990); 961 (1980) Pop Density: 24.1
Land: 37.7 sq. mi.; Water: 0.1 sq. mi.

Saratoga
Township
Lat: 41-06-03 N **Long:** 89-34-56 W
Pop: 353 (1990); 419 (1980) **Pop Density:** 9.8
Land: 36.0 sq. mi.; **Water:** 0.0 sq. mi.

Sparland
Village
ZIP: 61565 **Lat:** 41-01-49 N **Long:** 89-26-27 W
Pop: 412 (1990); 624 (1980) **Pop Density:** 686.7
Land: 0.6 sq. mi.; **Water:** 0.0 sq. mi.

Steuben
Township
Lat: 41-01-20 N **Long:** 89-28-21 W
Pop: 1,190 (1990); 1,357 (1980) **Pop Density:** 41.8
Land: 28.5 sq. mi.; **Water:** 3.0 sq. mi.

Toluca
Town
ZIP: 61369 **Lat:** 41-00-19 N **Long:** 89-07-59 W
Pop: 1,315 (1990); 1,471 (1980) **Pop Density:** 1315.0
Land: 1.0 sq. mi.; **Water:** 0.0 sq. mi.
Name origin: For Toluca, Mexico.

Varna
Village
ZIP: 61375 **Lat:** 41-02-08 N **Long:** 89-13-28 W
Pop: 405 (1990); 441 (1980) **Pop Density:** 1350.0
Land: 0.3 sq. mi.; **Water:** 0.0 sq. mi. **Elev:** 729 ft.

Washburn
Village
Lat: 40-55-30 N **Long:** 89-17-43 W
Pop: 35 (1990); 84 (1980) **Pop Density:** 350.0
Land: 0.1 sq. mi.; **Water:** 0.0 sq. mi.
Not coextensive with the town of the same name. Part of the town is also in Woodford County.

Wenona
Town
ZIP: 61377 **Lat:** 41-03-10 N **Long:** 89-03-12 W
Pop: 939 (1990); 1,025 (1980) **Pop Density:** 1878.0
Land: 0.5 sq. mi.; **Water:** 0.0 sq. mi. **Elev:** 699 ft.
In north-central IL, northeast of Peoria. Part of the town is also in La Salle County.
Name origin: For Hiawatha's mother in Henry Wadsworth Longfellow's (1807–82) poem "The Song of Hiawatha."

Whitefield
Township
Lat: 41-06-33 N **Long:** 89-28-02 W
Pop: 378 (1990); 437 (1980) **Pop Density:** 10.3
Land: 36.8 sq. mi.; **Water:** 0.0 sq. mi.

Mason County
County Seat: Havana (ZIP: 62644)

Pop: 16,269 (1990); 19,492 (1980) **Pop Density:** 30.2
Land: 539.0 sq. mi.; **Water:** 24.4 sq. mi. **Area Code:** 309
In central IL southwest of Peoria; organized Jan 20, 1841 from Tazewell County.
Name origin: For the county in KY, former home of many of the settlers.

Allen Grove
Township
Lat: 40-16-14 N **Long:** 89-39-47 W
Pop: 669 (1990); 859 (1980) **Pop Density:** 18.7
Land: 35.7 sq. mi.; **Water:** 0.0 sq. mi.

Bath
Village
ZIP: 62617 **Lat:** 40-11-28 N **Long:** 90-08-32 W
Pop: 388 (1990); 475 (1980) **Pop Density:** 970.0
Land: 0.4 sq. mi.; **Water:** 0.0 sq. mi. **Elev:** 462 ft.
Founded 1834; mapped out 1837 by then-surveyor Abraham Lincoln (1809–65), sixteenth U.S. president. Not coextensive with the town of the same name.
Name origin: For Bath, England.

*Bath
Township
Lat: 40-09-20 N **Long:** 90-06-52 W
Pop: 864 (1990); 1,076 (1980) **Pop Density:** 12.9
Land: 66.8 sq. mi.; **Water:** 5.1 sq. mi.

Crane Creek
Township
Lat: 40-10-08 N **Long:** 89-52-35 W
Pop: 195 (1990); 219 (1980) **Pop Density:** 5.7
Land: 34.0 sq. mi.; **Water:** 0.2 sq. mi.

Easton
Village
ZIP: 62633 **Lat:** 40-13-55 N **Long:** 89-50-31 W
Pop: 351 (1990); 392 (1980) **Pop Density:** 1755.0
Land: 0.2 sq. mi.; **Water:** 0.0 sq. mi.
Incorporated 1896.

Forest City
Village
ZIP: 61532 **Lat:** 40-22-15 N **Long:** 89-49-54 W
Pop: 321 (1990); 298 (1980) **Pop Density:** 642.0
Land: 0.5 sq. mi.; **Water:** 0.0 sq. mi.
Not coextensive with the town of the same name.

*Forest City
Township
Lat: 40-20-22 N **Long:** 89-49-09 W
Pop: 670 (1990); 828 (1980) **Pop Density:** 20.1
Land: 33.3 sq. mi.; **Water:** 0.0 sq. mi.

Havana
City
ZIP: 62644 **Lat:** 40-17-54 N **Long:** 90-03-24 W
Pop: 3,610 (1990); 4,277 (1980) **Pop Density:** 1719.0
Land: 2.1 sq. mi.; **Water:** 0.2 sq. mi.
Founded 1822 by Maj. Ossian M. Ross, veteran of the War of 1812. Not coextensive with the town of the same name.
Name origin: For Havana, Cuba.

*Havana
Township
ZIP: 62644 **Lat:** 40-16-24 N **Long:** 90-00-38 W
Pop: 5,593 (1990); 6,660 (1980) **Pop Density:** 96.8
Land: 57.8 sq. mi.; **Water:** 1.3 sq. mi.

Kilbourne
Town
ZIP: 62655 **Lat:** 40-09-05 N **Long:** 90-00-34 W
Pop: 350 (1990); 382 (1980) **Pop Density:** 350.0
Land: 1.0 sq. mi.; **Water:** 0.0 sq. mi.
Not coextensive with the town of the same name.

ILLINOIS, Mason County   *American Places Dictionary*

*Kilbourne   Township
Lat: 40-09-26 N   **Long:** 90-00-08 W
Pop: 633 (1990); 732 (1980)   **Pop Density:** 15.8
Land: 40.0 sq. mi.; **Water:** 0.3 sq. mi.

Lynchburg   Township
Lat: 40-05-52 N   **Long:** 90-13-44 W
Pop: 254 (1990); 378 (1980)   **Pop Density:** 6.0
Land: 42.0 sq. mi.; **Water:** 7.7 sq. mi.

Manito   Town
ZIP: 61546   **Lat:** 40-25-18 N   **Long:** 89-46-50 W
Pop: 1,711 (1990); 1,869 (1980)   **Pop Density:** 1140.7
Land: 1.5 sq. mi.; **Water:** 0.0 sq. mi.

In central IL near the confluence of the Illinois and Mackinaw rivers, 22 mi. southwest of Peoria. Not coextensive with the town of the same name.

Name origin: Possibly a spelling variation of the Algonquian term *manitou* meaning 'the Great Spirit.'

*Manito   Township
Lat: 40-23-27 N   **Long:** 89-46-14 W
Pop: 2,593 (1990); 3,099 (1980)   **Pop Density:** 59.2
Land: 43.8 sq. mi.; **Water:** 0.0 sq. mi.

Mason City   Town
ZIP: 62664   **Lat:** 40-12-06 N   **Long:** 89-41-46 W
Pop: 2,323 (1990); 2,719 (1980)   **Pop Density:** 2323.0
Land: 1.0 sq. mi.; **Water:** 0.0 sq. mi.

In central IL, 28 mi. north of Springfield. Platted 1857.

*Mason City   Township
Lat: 40-11-10 N   **Long:** 89-39-37 W
Pop: 2,729 (1990); 3,003 (1980)   **Pop Density:** 77.3
Land: 35.3 sq. mi.; **Water:** 0.1 sq. mi.

Pennsylvania   Township
Lat: 40-16-20 N   **Long:** 89-45-55 W
Pop: 238 (1990); 322 (1980)   **Pop Density:** 6.6
Land: 35.8 sq. mi.; **Water:** 0.0 sq. mi.

Quiver   Township
Lat: 40-22-40 N   **Long:** 89-56-14 W
Pop: 969 (1990); 1,342 (1980)   **Pop Density:** 22.9
Land: 42.4 sq. mi.; **Water:** 9.5 sq. mi.

Salt Creek   Township
Lat: 40-10-36 N   **Long:** 89-46-08 W
Pop: 239 (1990); 281 (1980)   **Pop Density:** 6.7
Land: 35.8 sq. mi.; **Water:** 0.2 sq. mi.

San Jose   Village
Lat: 40-18-21 N   **Long:** 89-36-21 W
Pop: 360 (1990); 516 (1980)   **Pop Density:** 1200.0
Land: 0.3 sq. mi.; **Water:** 0.0 sq. mi.

Part of the town is also in Logan County.

Sherman   Township
Lat: 40-15-38 N   **Long:** 89-53-39 W
Pop: 623 (1990); 693 (1980)   **Pop Density:** 17.3
Land: 36.0 sq. mi.; **Water:** 0.0 sq. mi.

Topeka   Town
ZIP: 61567   **Lat:** 40-19-47 N   **Long:** 89-55-51 W
Pop: 93 (1990); 140 (1980)   **Pop Density:** 930.0
Land: 0.1 sq. mi.; **Water:** 0.0 sq. mi.

Massac County
County Seat: Metropolis (ZIP: 62960)

Pop: 14,752 (1990); 14,990 (1980)   **Pop Density:** 61.7
Land: 239.1 sq. mi.; **Water:** 3.1 sq. mi.   **Area Code:** 618

On the southern border of IL; organized Feb 8, 1843 from Pope and Johnson counties.

Name origin: For Fort Massac, originally named Ft. Ascension and then renamed to honor Massiac, a French naval minister. The 'i' was dropped to form the current spelling.

Brookport   City
ZIP: 62910   **Lat:** 37-07-30 N   **Long:** 88-37-37 W
Pop: 1,070 (1990); 1,128 (1980)   **Pop Density:** 1337.5
Land: 0.8 sq. mi.; **Water:** 0.0 sq. mi.   **Elev:** 340 ft.

In southern IL on the Ohio River, opposite Paducah, KY. Incorporated 1888.

Joppa   Village
ZIP: 62953   **Lat:** 37-12-20 N   **Long:** 88-50-39 W
Pop: 492 (1990); 535 (1980)   **Pop Density:** 984.0
Land: 0.5 sq. mi.; **Water:** 0.0 sq. mi.

Metropolis   City
ZIP: 62960   **Lat:** 37-09-07 N   **Long:** 88-42-43 W
Pop: 6,734 (1990); 7,171 (1980)   **Pop Density:** 1374.3
Land: 4.9 sq. mi.; **Water:** 0.1 sq. mi.

In southeastern IL on the Ohio River, 8 mi. northwest of Paducah, KY. Founded in the 1830s; incorporated Feb 18, 1859.

Name origin: Named by its founder, developer William McBane, with high hopes for the future.

McDonough County
County Seat: Macomb (ZIP: 61455)

Pop: 35,244 (1990); 37,467 (1980)   **Pop Density:** 59.8
Land: 589.3 sq. mi.; **Water:** 0.8 sq. mi.   **Area Code:** 309

In west-central IL southwest of Peoria; organized Jan 25, 1826 from Schuyler County.

Name origin: For Capt. Thomas McDonough (1783–1825), naval officer in the war against Barbary pirates near Tripoli and in the War of 1812.

Bardolph — Village
ZIP: 61416   **Lat:** 40-29-48 N   **Long:** 90-33-47 W
Pop: 301 (1990); 294 (1980)   **Pop Density:** 501.7
Land: 0.6 sq. mi.; **Water:** 0.0 sq. mi.

Bethel — Township
Lat: 40-19-34 N   **Long:** 90-44-12 W
Pop: 302 (1990); 363 (1980)   **Pop Density:** 8.3
Land: 36.6 sq. mi.; **Water:** 0.0 sq. mi.

Blandinsville — Village
ZIP: 61420   **Lat:** 40-33-17 N   **Long:** 90-52-09 W
Pop: 762 (1990); 886 (1980)   **Pop Density:** 846.7
Land: 0.9 sq. mi.; **Water:** 0.0 sq. mi.   **Elev:** 729 ft.

Not coextensive with the town of the same name.

*Blandinsville — Township
Lat: 40-35-29 N   **Long:** 90-51-23 W
Pop: 1,003 (1990); 1,149 (1980)   **Pop Density:** 26.7
Land: 37.5 sq. mi.; **Water:** 0.0 sq. mi.

Bushnell — City
ZIP: 61422   **Lat:** 40-33-05 N   **Long:** 90-30-16 W
Pop: 3,288 (1990); 3,811 (1980)   **Pop Density:** 1644.0
Land: 2.0 sq. mi.; **Water:** 0.0 sq. mi.   **Elev:** 661 ft.

Incorporated 1865. Not coextensive with the town of the same name.

Name origin: For I.N. Bushnell, president of the Northern Cross Railroad.

*Bushnell — Township
Lat: 40-33-45 N   **Long:** 90-30-16 W
Pop: 3,511 (1990); 4,015 (1980)   **Pop Density:** 191.9
Land: 18.3 sq. mi.; **Water:** 0.0 sq. mi.

Chalmers — Township
Lat: 40-24-32 N   **Long:** 90-43-22 W
Pop: 804 (1990); 806 (1980)   **Pop Density:** 30.2
Land: 26.6 sq. mi.; **Water:** 0.0 sq. mi.

Colchester — City
ZIP: 62326   **Lat:** 40-25-36 N   **Long:** 90-47-34 W
Pop: 1,645 (1990); 1,729 (1980)   **Pop Density:** 1645.0
Land: 1.0 sq. mi.; **Water:** 0.0 sq. mi.   **Elev:** 697 ft.

In western IL, 6 mi. west-southwest of Macomb. Incorporated 1867. Not coextensive with the town of the same name.

Name origin: For Colchester, England, a coal town.

*Colchester — Township
Lat: 40-24-48 N   **Long:** 90-47-23 W
Pop: 2,168 (1990); 2,218 (1980)   **Pop Density:** 119.8
Land: 18.1 sq. mi.; **Water:** 0.1 sq. mi.

Eldorado — Township
Lat: 40-19-19 N   **Long:** 90-30-18 W
Pop: 250 (1990); 326 (1980)   **Pop Density:** 6.8
Land: 36.5 sq. mi.; **Water:** 0.1 sq. mi.

Emmet — Township
Lat: 40-29-52 N   **Long:** 90-44-10 W
Pop: 1,497 (1990); 2,108 (1980)   **Pop Density:** 45.9
Land: 32.6 sq. mi.; **Water:** 0.0 sq. mi.

Good Hope — Town
ZIP: 61438   **Lat:** 40-33-27 N   **Long:** 90-40-29 W
Pop: 416 (1990); 457 (1980)   **Pop Density:** 1386.7
Land: 0.3 sq. mi.; **Water:** 0.0 sq. mi.

In western IL, southwest of Peoria.

Name origin: Name finally agreed upon after years of confusion. Platted as Sheridan in 1866 by J. E. Morris. Rival town Milan built to its west in 1867 by W. F. Blandin. Railway tickets used name "Sheridan," conductors called out "Milan," and all mail was addressed to "Good Hope," name of the local post office. Also, some residents still used "Clarkesville," the town's original name.

Hire — Township
Lat: 40-30-10 N   **Long:** 90-50-45 W
Pop: 269 (1990); 369 (1980)   **Pop Density:** 7.1
Land: 37.7 sq. mi.; **Water:** 0.0 sq. mi.

Industry — Town
ZIP: 61440   **Lat:** 40-19-38 N   **Long:** 90-36-28 W
Pop: 571 (1990); 600 (1980)   **Pop Density:** 1142.0
Land: 0.5 sq. mi.; **Water:** 0.0 sq. mi.

In western IL, southwest of Peoria. Not coextensive with the town of the same name.

*Industry — Township
Lat: 40-19-28 N   **Long:** 90-37-06 W
Pop: 885 (1990); 984 (1980)   **Pop Density:** 23.8
Land: 37.2 sq. mi.; **Water:** 0.0 sq. mi.

Lamoine — Township
Lat: 40-19-32 N   **Long:** 90-51-15 W
Pop: 321 (1990); 334 (1980)   **Pop Density:** 8.7
Land: 37.0 sq. mi.; **Water:** 0.0 sq. mi.

Macomb — City
ZIP: 61455   **Lat:** 40-28-13 N   **Long:** 90-40-53 W
Pop: 19,952 (1990); 19,863 (1980)   **Pop Density:** 2168.7
Land: 9.2 sq. mi.; **Water:** 0.4 sq. mi.

In west-central IL, 70 mi. northwest of Springfield. County seat. Settled 1830; incorporated Jan 27, 1841. Site of Western Illinois University.

Name origin: For Gen. Alexander Macomb (1782–1841), commander-in-chief of the U.S. Army (1828–41). Previously called Washington.

*Macomb — Township
Lat: 40-29-58 N   **Long:** 90-36-43 W
Pop: 729 (1990); 867 (1980)   **Pop Density:** 21.8
Land: 33.5 sq. mi.; **Water:** 0.0 sq. mi.

ILLINOIS, McDonough County

Macomb City
Township
ZIP: 61455 Lat: 40-28-13 N Long: 90-40-53 W
Pop: 19,952 (1990); 19,863 (1980) Pop Density: 2168.7
Land: 9.2 sq. mi.; Water: 0.4 sq. mi.

Mound
Township
Lat: 40-29-53 N Long: 90-30-04 W
Pop: 365 (1990); 396 (1980) Pop Density: 10.1
Land: 36.1 sq. mi.; Water: 0.0 sq. mi.

New Salem
Township
Lat: 40-25-03 N Long: 90-30-07 W
Pop: 481 (1990); 530 (1980) Pop Density: 13.3
Land: 36.1 sq. mi.; Water: 0.0 sq. mi.

Plymouth
Village
Lat: 40-17-28 N Long: 90-54-27 W
Pop: 3 (1990) Pop Density: 150.0
Land: 0.02 sq. mi.; Water: 0.0 sq. mi.
Part of the town is also in Hancock County.

Prairie City
Town
ZIP: 61470 Lat: 40-37-14 N Long: 90-27-52 W
Pop: 497 (1990); 580 (1980) Pop Density: 497.0
Land: 1.0 sq. mi.; Water: 0.0 sq. mi. Elev: 667 ft.
In northwestern IL, 21 mi. northeast of Canton. Not coextensive with the town of the same name.
Name origin: For its descriptive connotations.

*Prairie City
Township
Lat: 40-36-13 N Long: 90-30-33 W
Pop: 651 (1990); 738 (1980) Pop Density: 36.2
Land: 18.0 sq. mi.; Water: 0.0 sq. mi.

Sciota
Village
ZIP: 61475 Lat: 40-33-43 N Long: 90-44-56 W
Pop: 68 (1990); 81 (1980) Pop Density: 226.7
Land: 0.3 sq. mi.; Water: 0.0 sq. mi. Elev: 753 ft.
Not coextensive with the town of the same name.

*Sciota
Township
Lat: 40-35-13 N Long: 90-44-06 W
Pop: 622 (1990); 720 (1980) Pop Density: 16.5
Land: 37.7 sq. mi.; Water: 0.0 sq. mi.

Scotland
Township
Lat: 40-24-41 N Long: 90-36-51 W
Pop: 521 (1990); 648 (1980) Pop Density: 14.6
Land: 35.7 sq. mi.; Water: 0.1 sq. mi.

Tennessee
Village
ZIP: 62374 Lat: 40-24-42 N Long: 90-50-09 W
Pop: 127 (1990); 175 (1980) Pop Density: 317.5
Land: 0.4 sq. mi.; Water: 0.0 sq. mi.
Not coextensive with the town of the same name.

*Tennessee
Township
Lat: 40-25-10 N Long: 90-51-39 W
Pop: 414 (1990); 465 (1980) Pop Density: 14.5
Land: 28.6 sq. mi.; Water: 0.0 sq. mi.

Walnut Grove
Township
Lat: 40-35-15 N Long: 90-36-38 W
Pop: 499 (1990); 568 (1980) Pop Density: 13.8
Land: 36.2 sq. mi.; Water: 0.0 sq. mi.

McHenry County
County Seat: Woodstock (ZIP: 60098)

Pop: 183,241 (1990); 147,897 (1980) Pop Density: 303.3
Land: 604.1 sq. mi.; Water: 7.0 sq. mi. Area Code: 815
On the northern border of IL, northwest of Chicago; organized Jan 16, 1836 from Cook county.

Name origin: For Maj. William McHenry (1774–1839), officer in the War of 1812 and the Black Hawk War (1832).

Alden
Township
Lat: 42-26-52 N Long: 88-31-50 W
Pop: 1,457 (1990); 1,304 (1980) Pop Density: 43.8
Land: 33.3 sq. mi.; Water: 0.1 sq. mi.

Algonquin
Village
ZIP: 60102 Lat: 42-09-50 N Long: 88-18-10 W
Pop: 10,194 (1990); 5,576 (1980) Pop Density: 2080.4
Land: 4.9 sq. mi.; Water: 0.1 sq. mi.
In northeastern IL, 40 mi. northwest of Chicago. Incorporated 1890. Part of the town is also in Kane County.
Name origin: Probably for a ship that one of the town trustees had sailed on. Previously called Cornish's Ferry, Cornishville, Dennys Ferry, Osceola.

*Algonquin
Township
ZIP: 60102 Lat: 42-11-48 N Long: 88-16-40 W
Pop: 57,746 (1990); 44,287 (1980) Pop Density: 1231.3
Land: 46.9 sq. mi.; Water: 1.1 sq. mi.

Barrington Hills
Village
ZIP: 60010 Lat: 42-10-19 N Long: 88-14-02 W
Pop: 1,223 (1990); 1,022 (1980) Pop Density: 207.3
Land: 5.9 sq. mi.; Water: 0.0 sq. mi. Elev: 877 ft.
Incorporated 1959. Part of the town is also in Lake, Cook, and Kane counties.
Name origin: From nearby Barrington.

Bull Valley
Village
Lat: 42-18-40 N Long: 88-20-59 W
Pop: 574 (1990); 509 (1980) Pop Density: 140.0
Land: 4.1 sq. mi.; Water: 0.0 sq. mi.

Burton
Township
Lat: 42-27-27 N Long: 88-13-12 W
Pop: 2,144 (1990); 1,768 (1980) Pop Density: 198.5
Land: 10.8 sq. mi.; Water: 0.1 sq. mi.

Cary
Village
ZIP: 60013　　**Lat:** 42-12-32 N　**Long:** 88-14-59 W
Pop: 10,043 (1990); 6,640 (1980)　　**Pop Density:** 2183.3
Land: 4.6 sq. mi.; **Water:** 0.0 sq. mi.　　**Elev:** 825 ft.
Incorporated 1893.

Chemung
Township
ZIP: 60033　　**Lat:** 42-27-15 N　**Long:** 88-39-13 W
Pop: 6,660 (1990); 5,884 (1980)　　**Pop Density:** 201.8
Land: 33.0 sq. mi.; **Water:** 0.0 sq. mi.

Coral
Township
Lat: 42-11-52 N　**Long:** 88-32-09 W
Pop: 2,549 (1990); 2,303 (1980)　　**Pop Density:** 70.8
Land: 36.0 sq. mi.; **Water:** 0.0 sq. mi.

Crystal Lake
City
ZIP: 60014　　**Lat:** 42-13-54 N　**Long:** 88-19-49 W
Pop: 24,512 (1990); 18,590 (1980)　　**Pop Density:** 1738.4
Land: 14.1 sq. mi.; **Water:** 0.2 sq. mi.
In northeastern IL, 40 mi. northwest of Chicago. Resort area. Incorporated Sep 23, 1914.
Name origin: For the small lake around which the town developed.

Dorr
Township
ZIP: 60098　　**Lat:** 42-17-07 N　**Long:** 88-25-00 W
Pop: 14,231 (1990); 12,199 (1980)　　**Pop Density:** 394.2
Land: 36.1 sq. mi.; **Water:** 0.0 sq. mi.

Dunham
Township
Lat: 42-21-59 N　**Long:** 88-39-07 W
Pop: 2,001 (1990); 1,755 (1980)　　**Pop Density:** 55.6
Land: 36.0 sq. mi.; **Water:** 0.0 sq. mi.

Fox Lake
Village
ZIP: 60020　　**Lat:** 42-27-38 N　**Long:** 88-12-38 W
Pop: 48 (1990); 207 (1980)　　**Pop Density:** 30.0
Land: 1.6 sq. mi.; **Water:** 0.0 sq. mi.
Founded 1839; incorporated 1906. Part of the town is also in Lake County.
Name origin: For the nearby lake.

Fox River Grove
Village
ZIP: 60021　　**Lat:** 42-11-49 N　**Long:** 88-13-08 W
Pop: 3,551 (1990); 2,515 (1980)　　**Pop Density:** 2536.4
Land: 1.4 sq. mi.; **Water:** 0.1 sq. mi.

Fox River Valley Gardens
Village
Lat: 42-14-41 N　**Long:** 88-12-10 W
Pop: 566 (1990); 520 (1980)　　**Pop Density:** 1132.0
Land: 0.5 sq. mi.; **Water:** 0.1 sq. mi.
Part of the town is also in Lake County.

Grafton
Township
ZIP: 60142　　**Lat:** 42-11-31 N　**Long:** 88-24-46 W
Pop: 9,946 (1990); 6,837 (1980)　　**Pop Density:** 277.0
Land: 35.9 sq. mi.; **Water:** 0.3 sq. mi.

Greenwood
Township
ZIP: 60098　　**Lat:** 42-21-57 N　**Long:** 88-25-14 W
Pop: 8,317 (1990); 6,965 (1980)　　**Pop Density:** 233.6
Land: 35.6 sq. mi.; **Water:** 0.5 sq. mi.

Hartland
Township
Lat: 42-22-23 N　**Long:** 88-31-58 W
Pop: 1,911 (1990); 1,523 (1980)　　**Pop Density:** 53.2
Land: 35.9 sq. mi.; **Water:** 0.2 sq. mi.

Harvard
City
ZIP: 60033　　**Lat:** 42-25-16 N　**Long:** 88-36-55 W
Pop: 5,975 (1990); 5,126 (1980)　　**Pop Density:** 2298.1
Land: 2.6 sq. mi.; **Water:** 0.0 sq. mi.　　**Elev:** 966 ft.
In northeastern IL, 28 mi. east-northeast of Rockford. Incorporated Feb 26, 1867.
Name origin: For Harvard University in MA.

Hebron
Town
ZIP: 60034　　**Lat:** 42-28-15 N　**Long:** 88-25-47 W
Pop: 809 (1990); 786 (1980)　　**Pop Density:** 1618.0
Land: 0.5 sq. mi.; **Water:** 0.0 sq. mi.
Not coextensive with the town of the same name.
Name origin: For the biblical city.

*Hebron
Township
Lat: 42-26-56 N　**Long:** 88-25-20 W
Pop: 1,817 (1990); 1,780 (1980)　　**Pop Density:** 55.9
Land: 32.5 sq. mi.; **Water:** 0.0 sq. mi.

Holiday Hills
Village
Lat: 42-17-28 N　**Long:** 88-13-36 W
Pop: 807 (1990); 802 (1980)　　**Pop Density:** 2690.0
Land: 0.3 sq. mi.; **Water:** 0.0 sq. mi.

Huntley
Town
ZIP: 60142　　**Lat:** 42-10-05 N　**Long:** 88-25-27 W
Pop: 2,453 (1990); 1,646 (1980)　　**Pop Density:** 1226.5
Land: 2.0 sq. mi.; **Water:** 0.0 sq. mi.
In northeastern IL, northwest of Chicago. Founded 1851 as a New Chicago & Northwestern Railway station.
Name origin: For its founder, Thomas Stilwell Huntley.

Island Lake
Town
ZIP: 60042　　**Lat:** 42-16-40 N　**Long:** 88-12-43 W
Pop: 2,466 (1990); 724 (1980)　　**Pop Density:** 1644.0
Land: 1.5 sq. mi.; **Water:** 0.1 sq. mi.
In northeastern IL on a small lake created by damming Cotton Creek in 1936. Incorporated 1954. Part of the town is also in Lake County.

Lake in the Hills
Village
ZIP: 60102　　**Lat:** 42-11-34 N　**Long:** 88-19-17 W
Pop: 5,866 (1990); 5,651 (1980)　　**Pop Density:** 1150.2
Land: 5.1 sq. mi.; **Water:** 0.1 sq. mi.

Lakemoor
Village
ZIP: 60050　　**Lat:** 42-20-30 N　**Long:** 88-12-56 W
Pop: 1,061 (1990); 723 (1980)　　**Pop Density:** 505.2
Land: 2.1 sq. mi.; **Water:** 0.1 sq. mi.
Part of the town is also in Lake County.

Lakewood
Town
ZIP: 60014　　**Lat:** 42-13-12 N　**Long:** 88-22-41 W
Pop: 1,609 (1990); 1,254 (1980)　　**Pop Density:** 618.8
Land: 2.6 sq. mi.; **Water:** 0.3 sq. mi.
In northeastern IL, northwest of Chicago, near Crystal Lake.

Marengo
City
ZIP: 60152　　**Lat:** 42-14-52 N　**Long:** 88-36-01 W
Pop: 4,768 (1990); 4,361 (1980)　　**Pop Density:** 1402.4
Land: 3.4 sq. mi.; **Water:** 0.0 sq. mi.　　**Elev:** 837 ft.
Not coextensive with the town of the same name.

*Marengo
Township
ZIP: 60152　　**Lat:** 42-17-24 N　**Long:** 88-38-28 W
Pop: 5,723 (1990); 5,319 (1980)　　**Pop Density:** 159.4
Land: 35.9 sq. mi.; **Water:** 0.0 sq. mi.

ILLINOIS, McHenry County

McCullom Lake — Village
ZIP: 60050 Lat: 42-22-07 N Long: 88-17-37 W
Pop: 1,033 (1990); 947 (1980) Pop Density: 5165.0
Land: 0.2 sq. mi.; Water: 0.0 sq. mi.

McHenry — City
ZIP: 60050 Lat: 42-20-26 N Long: 88-17-28 W
Pop: 16,177 (1990); 10,737 (1980) Pop Density: 1797.4
Land: 9.0 sq. mi.; Water: 0.4 sq. mi. Elev: 761 ft.
In northeastern IL on the Fox River, 45 mi. northwest of Chicago. Incorporated Feb 15, 1855. Not coextensive with the town of the same name.
Name origin: For Maj. William McHenry (1774–1839), officer in the War of 1812 and the Black Hawk War of 1832.

*McHenry — Township
ZIP: 60050 Lat: 42-22-28 N Long: 88-16-38 W
Pop: 37,034 (1990); 31,611 (1980) Pop Density: 824.8
Land: 44.9 sq. mi.; Water: 3.3 sq. mi.

Nunda — Township
ZIP: 60012 Lat: 42-17-00 N Long: 88-16-42 W
Pop: 24,759 (1990); 18,102 (1980) Pop Density: 526.8
Land: 47.0 sq. mi.; Water: 1.3 sq. mi.

Oakwood Hills — Village
ZIP: 60013 Lat: 42-14-50 N Long: 88-14-39 W
Pop: 1,498 (1990); 1,255 (1980) Pop Density: 2496.7
Land: 0.6 sq. mi.; Water: 0.1 sq. mi.

Pistakee Highlands — CDP
Lat: 42-24-11 N Long: 88-12-43 W
Pop: 3,848 (1990); 3,623 (1980) Pop Density: 2565.3
Land: 1.5 sq. mi.; Water: 0.3 sq. mi.

Prairie Grove — Village
Lat: 42-16-49 N Long: 88-15-59 W
Pop: 654 (1990); 680 (1980) Pop Density: 155.7
Land: 4.2 sq. mi.; Water: 0.1 sq. mi.

Richmond — Town
ZIP: 60071 Lat: 42-28-52 N Long: 88-18-26 W
Pop: 1,016 (1990); 1,068 (1980) Pop Density: 1016.0
Land: 1.0 sq. mi.; Water: 0.0 sq. mi.
In northern IL, 80 mi. northwest of Chicago. Not coextensive with the town of the same name.
Name origin: For Richmond, VA.

*Richmond — Township
Lat: 42-27-06 N Long: 88-17-51 W
Pop: 3,286 (1990); 2,839 (1980) Pop Density: 100.8
Land: 32.6 sq. mi.; Water: 0.1 sq. mi.

Riley — Township
Lat: 42-11-30 N Long: 88-38-50 W
Pop: 1,431 (1990); 1,356 (1980) Pop Density: 39.8
Land: 36.0 sq. mi.; Water: 0.1 sq. mi.

Seneca — Township
Lat: 42-16-43 N Long: 88-31-37 W
Pop: 2,229 (1990); 2,065 (1980) Pop Density: 62.1
Land: 35.9 sq. mi.; Water: 0.0 sq. mi.

Spring Grove — Village
ZIP: 60081 Lat: 42-26-41 N Long: 88-14-37 W
Pop: 1,066 (1990); 571 (1980) Pop Density: 304.6
Land: 3.5 sq. mi.; Water: 0.0 sq. mi.

Sunnyside — Village
ZIP: 60050 Lat: 42-23-44 N Long: 88-14-01 W
Pop: 1,529 (1990); 1,432 (1980) Pop Density: 1390.0
Land: 1.1 sq. mi.; Water: 0.0 sq. mi.

Union — Town
ZIP: 60180 Lat: 42-14-03 N Long: 88-32-36 W
Pop: 542 (1990); 622 (1980) Pop Density: 903.3
Land: 0.6 sq. mi.; Water: 0.0 sq. mi.

Wonder Lake — Village
ZIP: 60097 Lat: 42-23-03 N Long: 88-22-03 W
Pop: 1,024 (1990); 752 (1980) Pop Density: 2048.0
Land: 0.5 sq. mi.; Water: 0.0 sq. mi.

Woodstock — City
ZIP: 60098 Lat: 42-18-38 N Long: 88-26-12 W
Pop: 14,353 (1990); 11,725 (1980) Pop Density: 1435.3
Land: 10.0 sq. mi.; Water: 0.0 sq. mi. Elev: 942 ft.
In northeastern IL, 30 mi. east of Rockford. County seat. Incorporated Jun 22, 1852.
Name origin: Named by state legislator Joel Johnson for Woodstock, VT, his former home.

McLean County
County Seat: Bloomington (ZIP: 61701)

Pop: 129,180 (1990); 119,149 (1980) Pop Density: 109.1
Land: 1183.6 sq. mi.; Water: 2.7 sq. mi. Area Code: 309
In central IL southeast of Peoria; organized Dec 25, 1830 from Tazewell County.
Name origin: For John McLean (1791–1830), first U.S. representative from IL (1818–19) and U.S. senator (1824–25; 1829–30).

Allin — Township
Lat: 40-26-19 N Long: 89-12-30 W
Pop: 996 (1990); 1,057 (1980) Pop Density: 27.4
Land: 36.3 sq. mi.; Water: 0.0 sq. mi.

Anchor — Village
ZIP: 61720 Lat: 40-34-07 N Long: 88-32-19 W
Pop: 178 (1990); 192 (1980) Pop Density: 890.0
Land: 0.2 sq. mi.; Water: 0.0 sq. mi.
Not coextensive with the town of the same name.

ILLINOIS, McLean County

*Anchor — Township
Lat: 40-31-19 N   Long: 88-31-32 W
Pop: 393 (1990); 441 (1980)   Pop Density: 10.8
Land: 36.5 sq. mi.; Water: 0.0 sq. mi.

Arrowsmith — Village
Lat: 40-26-55 N   Long: 88-37-53 W
Pop: 313 (1990); 292 (1980)   Pop Density: 1565.0
Land: 0.2 sq. mi.; Water: 0.0 sq. mi.

*Arrowsmith — Township
Lat: 40-26-47 N   Long: 88-37-53 W
Pop: 549 (1990); 566 (1980)   Pop Density: 15.2
Land: 36.2 sq. mi.; Water: 0.0 sq. mi.

Bellflower — Village
ZIP: 61724   Lat: 40-20-25 N   Long: 88-31-36 W
Pop: 405 (1990); 421 (1980)   Pop Density: 1012.5
Land: 0.4 sq. mi.; Water: 0.0 sq. mi.
Not coextensive with the town of the same name.

*Bellflower — Township
Lat: 40-20-26 N   Long: 88-31-05 W
Pop: 702 (1990); 794 (1980)   Pop Density: 14.3
Land: 49.1 sq. mi.; Water: 0.0 sq. mi.

Bloomington — City
ZIP: 61701   Lat: 40-28-44 N   Long: 88-58-24 W
Pop: 51,972 (1990); 44,189 (1980)   Pop Density: 3112.1
Land: 16.7 sq. mi.; Water: 0.0 sq. mi.   Elev: 829 ft.
In central IL, 35 mi. southeast of Peoria. County seat. Settled 1822 at a crossroads of several Indian trails; incorporated Mar 2, 1839. Not coextensive with the town of the same name.
Name origin: Changed from Blooming Grove, so named for the profusion of wildflowers in its forest glades. Previously called Keg Grove, supposedly for a keg of liquor found here by local Indians.

*Bloomington — Township
Lat: 40-25-57 N   Long: 88-59-03 W
Pop: 3,835 (1990); 4,945 (1980)   Pop Density: 151.0
Land: 25.4 sq. mi.; Water: 0.0 sq. mi.

Bloomington City — Township
ZIP: 61701   Lat: 40-28-44 N   Long: 88-58-24 W
Pop: 51,972 (1990); 44,189 (1980)   Pop Density: 3112.1
Land: 16.7 sq. mi.; Water: 0.0 sq. mi.

Blue Mound — Township
Lat: 40-31-55 N   Long: 88-45-06 W
Pop: 478 (1990); 616 (1980)   Pop Density: 12.7
Land: 37.6 sq. mi.; Water: 0.0 sq. mi.

Carlock — Village
ZIP: 61725   Lat: 40-34-55 N   Long: 89-07-57 W
Pop: 418 (1990); 410 (1980)   Pop Density: 2090.0
Land: 0.2 sq. mi.; Water: 0.0 sq. mi.

Cheney's Grove — Township
Lat: 40-26-18 N   Long: 88-30-45 W
Pop: 1,051 (1990); 1,223 (1980)   Pop Density: 28.8
Land: 36.5 sq. mi.; Water: 0.0 sq. mi.

Chenoa — City
ZIP: 61726   Lat: 40-44-39 N   Long: 88-43-05 W
Pop: 1,732 (1990); 1,847 (1980)   Pop Density: 1574.5
Land: 1.1 sq. mi.; Water: 0.0 sq. mi.
Platted 1856 by Matthew T. Scott. Not coextensive with the town of the same name.
Name origin: From an Indian term meaning 'white dove.'

*Chenoa — Township
Lat: 40-42-34 N   Long: 88-45-01 W
Pop: 2,228 (1990); 2,368 (1980)   Pop Density: 61.2
Land: 36.4 sq. mi.; Water: 0.1 sq. mi.

Colfax — Village
ZIP: 61728   Lat: 40-34-00 N   Long: 88-36-59 W
Pop: 854 (1990); 920 (1980)   Pop Density: 1708.0
Land: 0.5 sq. mi.; Water: 0.0 sq. mi.

Cooksville — Village
ZIP: 61730   Lat: 40-32-33 N   Long: 88-42-54 W
Pop: 211 (1990); 259 (1980)   Pop Density: 1055.0
Land: 0.2 sq. mi.; Water: 0.0 sq. mi.

Cropsey — Township
Lat: 40-35-32 N   Long: 88-30-51 W
Pop: 240 (1990); 288 (1980)   Pop Density: 13.1
Land: 18.3 sq. mi.; Water: 0.0 sq. mi.

Dale — Township
Lat: 40-26-32 N   Long: 89-06-04 W
Pop: 1,192 (1990); 1,018 (1980)   Pop Density: 33.3
Land: 35.8 sq. mi.; Water: 0.0 sq. mi.

Danvers — Village
ZIP: 61732   Lat: 40-31-44 N   Long: 89-10-23 W
Pop: 981 (1990); 921 (1980)   Pop Density: 1090.0
Land: 0.9 sq. mi.; Water: 0.0 sq. mi.
Not coextensive with the town of the same name.

*Danvers — Township
Lat: 40-32-37 N   Long: 89-12-39 W
Pop: 1,692 (1990); 1,595 (1980)   Pop Density: 37.5
Land: 45.1 sq. mi.; Water: 0.1 sq. mi.

Dawson — Township
Lat: 40-26-13 N   Long: 88-45-09 W
Pop: 649 (1990); 688 (1980)   Pop Density: 17.4
Land: 37.3 sq. mi.; Water: 0.3 sq. mi.

Downs — Village
ZIP: 61736   Lat: 40-23-45 N   Long: 88-52-18 W
Pop: 620 (1990); 561 (1980)   Pop Density: 1240.0
Land: 0.5 sq. mi.; Water: 0.0 sq. mi.   Elev: 795 ft.
Not coextensive with the town of the same name.

*Downs — Township
Lat: 40-20-19 N   Long: 88-51-56 W
Pop: 992 (1990); 1,014 (1980)   Pop Density: 20.0
Land: 49.5 sq. mi.; Water: 0.0 sq. mi.

Dry Grove — Township
Lat: 40-31-37 N   Long: 89-05-27 W
Pop: 1,494 (1990); 1,501 (1980)   Pop Density: 41.5
Land: 36.0 sq. mi.; Water: 0.0 sq. mi.

Ellsworth — Village
ZIP: 61737   Lat: 40-26-58 N   Long: 88-42-59 W
Pop: 224 (1990); 244 (1980)   Pop Density: 1120.0
Land: 0.2 sq. mi.; Water: 0.0 sq. mi.   Elev: 874 ft.

Empire — Township
Lat: 40-20-40 N   Long: 88-45-00 W
Pop: 3,379 (1990); 3,473 (1980)   Pop Density: 68.3
Land: 49.5 sq. mi.; Water: 0.0 sq. mi.

Funks Grove — Township
Lat: 40-20-08 N   Long: 89-05-42 W
Pop: 302 (1990); 358 (1980)   Pop Density: 6.3
Land: 48.2 sq. mi.; Water: 0.0 sq. mi.

ILLINOIS, McLean County

Gridley
Town
ZIP: 61744   **Lat:** 40-44-38 N   **Long:** 88-52-49 W
Pop: 1,304 (1990); 1,246 (1980)   **Pop Density:** 1185.5
Land: 1.1 sq. mi.; **Water:** 0.0 sq. mi.

In central IL, 20 mi. north of Bloomington. Not coextensive with the town of the same name.

Name origin: For Brig. Gen. Asahel Gridley (1810–81), a Civil War officer from NY.

*Gridley
Township
Lat: 40-43-01 N   **Long:** 88-54-34 W
Pop: 1,813 (1990); 1,805 (1980)   **Pop Density:** 33.3
Land: 54.5 sq. mi.; **Water:** 0.0 sq. mi.

Heyworth
Town
ZIP: 61745   **Lat:** 40-18-49 N   **Long:** 88-58-43 W
Pop: 1,627 (1990); 1,598 (1980)   **Pop Density:** 1162.1
Land: 1.4 sq. mi.; **Water:** 0.0 sq. mi.   **Elev:** 749 ft.

Name origin: For Laurence Heyworth, former member of British Parliament and one of a group of English stockholders in the railroad here.

Hudson
Village
ZIP: 61748   **Lat:** 40-36-25 N   **Long:** 88-59-18 W
Pop: 1,006 (1990); 929 (1980)   **Pop Density:** 1676.7
Land: 0.6 sq. mi.; **Water:** 0.0 sq. mi.   **Elev:** 765 ft.

Not coextensive with the town of the same name.

*Hudson
Township
Lat: 40-37-02 N   **Long:** 88-59-09 W
Pop: 1,853 (1990); 1,766 (1980)   **Pop Density:** 51.3
Land: 36.1 sq. mi.; **Water:** 1.5 sq. mi.

Lawndale
Township
Lat: 40-37-14 N   **Long:** 88-37-32 W
Pop: 237 (1990); 273 (1980)   **Pop Density:** 6.0
Land: 39.7 sq. mi.; **Water:** 0.0 sq. mi.

Le Roy
City
ZIP: 61752   **Lat:** 40-20-29 N   **Long:** 88-45-52 W
Pop: 2,777 (1990); 2,870 (1980)   **Pop Density:** 1461.6
Land: 1.9 sq. mi.; **Water:** 0.0 sq. mi.

Lexington
Town
ZIP: 61753   **Lat:** 40-38-37 N   **Long:** 88-46-57 W
Pop: 1,809 (1990); 1,806 (1980)   **Pop Density:** 2010.0
Land: 0.9 sq. mi.; **Water:** 0.0 sq. mi.   **Elev:** 754 ft.

In central IL, east of Peoria, on the Mackinaw River. Not coextensive with the town of the same name.

Name origin: For the opening battle of the American Revolution at Lexington, MA.

*Lexington
Township
Lat: 40-37-19 N   **Long:** 88-44-25 W
Pop: 2,271 (1990); 2,441 (1980)   **Pop Density:** 55.4
Land: 41.0 sq. mi.; **Water:** 0.0 sq. mi.

Martin
Township
Lat: 40-31-37 N   **Long:** 88-37-31 W
Pop: 1,154 (1990); 1,180 (1980)   **Pop Density:** 31.9
Land: 36.2 sq. mi.; **Water:** 0.0 sq. mi.

McLean
Town
ZIP: 61754   **Lat:** 40-18-56 N   **Long:** 89-10-13 W
Pop: 797 (1990); 836 (1980)   **Pop Density:** 1992.5
Land: 0.4 sq. mi.; **Water:** 0.0 sq. mi.

Incorporated January 23, 1873.

Money Creek
Township
Lat: 40-36-47 N   **Long:** 88-51-28 W
Pop: 824 (1990); 780 (1980)   **Pop Density:** 21.1
Land: 39.0 sq. mi.; **Water:** 0.4 sq. mi.

Mount Hope
Township
Lat: 40-20-35 N   **Long:** 89-11-59 W
Pop: 1,130 (1990); 1,170 (1980)   **Pop Density:** 23.1
Land: 48.9 sq. mi.; **Water:** 0.0 sq. mi.

Normal
City
ZIP: 61761   **Lat:** 40-31-02 N   **Long:** 88-59-57 W
Pop: 40,023 (1990); 35,672 (1980)   **Pop Density:** 3280.6
Land: 12.2 sq. mi.; **Water:** 0.0 sq. mi.

In central IL, just north of Bloomington. Incorporated 1867. Not coextensive with the town of the same name. Site of Illinois State University.

Name origin: For the state's first normal school (teachers' college), opened here 1857.

*Normal
Township
ZIP: 61761   **Lat:** 40-32-07 N   **Long:** 88-59-05 W
Pop: 40,449 (1990); 36,157 (1980)   **Pop Density:** 1244.6
Land: 32.5 sq. mi.; **Water:** 0.0 sq. mi.

Oldtown
Township
Lat: 40-26-41 N   **Long:** 88-51-39 W
Pop: 1,738 (1990); 1,570 (1980)   **Pop Density:** 46.6
Land: 37.3 sq. mi.; **Water:** 0.0 sq. mi.

Randolph
Township
Lat: 40-20-28 N   **Long:** 88-58-55 W
Pop: 2,934 (1990); 3,010 (1980)   **Pop Density:** 59.4
Land: 49.4 sq. mi.; **Water:** 0.1 sq. mi.

Saybrook
Village
ZIP: 61770   **Lat:** 40-25-41 N   **Long:** 88-31-35 W
Pop: 767 (1990); 882 (1980)   **Pop Density:** 958.8
Land: 0.8 sq. mi.; **Water:** 0.0 sq. mi.   **Elev:** 790 ft.

Stanford
Village
ZIP: 61774   **Lat:** 40-26-02 N   **Long:** 89-13-12 W
Pop: 620 (1990); 720 (1980)   **Pop Density:** 1550.0
Land: 0.4 sq. mi.; **Water:** 0.0 sq. mi.

Towanda
Town
ZIP: 61776   **Lat:** 40-33-47 N   **Long:** 88-54-01 W
Pop: 856 (1990); 630 (1980)   **Pop Density:** 1222.9
Land: 0.7 sq. mi.; **Water:** 0.0 sq. mi.   **Elev:** 776 ft.

Not coextensive with the town of the same name.

Name origin: From an Indian term probably meaning 'place of burial.'

*Towanda
Township
Lat: 40-32-04 N   **Long:** 88-51-50 W
Pop: 1,191 (1990); 1,375 (1980)   **Pop Density:** 32.0
Land: 37.2 sq. mi.; **Water:** 0.0 sq. mi.

West
Township
Lat: 40-20-23 N   **Long:** 88-37-59 W
Pop: 264 (1990); 318 (1980)   **Pop Density:** 5.4
Land: 48.5 sq. mi.; **Water:** 0.0 sq. mi.

White Oak
Township
Lat: 40-35-58 N   **Long:** 89-05-49 W
Pop: 803 (1990); 761 (1980)   **Pop Density:** 48.4
Land: 16.6 sq. mi.; **Water:** 0.0 sq. mi.

Yates — Township
Lat: 40-43-12 N **Long:** 88-38-53 W
Pop: 375 (1990); 409 (1980) **Pop Density:** 10.3
Land: 36.5 sq. mi.; **Water:** 0.0 sq. mi.

Menard County
County Seat: Petersburg (ZIP: 62675)

Pop: 11,164 (1990); 11,700 (1980) **Pop Density:** 35.5
Land: 314.3 sq. mi.; **Water:** 1.1 sq. mi. **Area Code:** 217
In central Illinois, north of Springfield; organized Feb 15, 1839 from Sangamon County.
Name origin: For Lt. Col. Pierre Menard (1766–1844), jurist, first presiding officer of IL Territorial legislature (1812), and first lieutenant governor (1818–22).

Athens — City
ZIP: 62613 **Lat:** 39-57-39 N **Long:** 89-43-29 W
Pop: 1,404 (1990); 1,371 (1980) **Pop Density:** 1560.0
Land: 0.9 sq. mi.; **Water:** 0.0 sq. mi. **Elev:** 606 ft.
In central IL, 10 mi. north of Springfield. Founded 1831; incorporated 1859.
Name origin: For the classical Greek city.

Greenview — Village
ZIP: 62642 **Lat:** 40-05-05 N **Long:** 89-44-24 W
Pop: 848 (1990); 830 (1980) **Pop Density:** 1060.0
Land: 0.8 sq. mi.; **Water:** 0.0 sq. mi.
In central IL, 20 mi. northwest of Springfield.

Oakford — Village
ZIP: 62673 **Lat:** 40-06-03 N **Long:** 89-57-55 W
Pop: 246 (1990); 351 (1980) **Pop Density:** 1230.0
Land: 0.2 sq. mi.; **Water:** 0.0 sq. mi. **Elev:** 495 ft.

Petersburg — Town
ZIP: 62675 **Lat:** 40-00-44 N **Long:** 89-51-05 W
Pop: 2,261 (1990); 2,419 (1980) **Pop Density:** 2055.5
Land: 1.1 sq. mi.; **Water:** 0.0 sq. mi. **Elev:** 524 ft.

Tallula — Village
ZIP: 62688 **Lat:** 39-56-44 N **Long:** 89-56-10 W
Pop: 598 (1990); 681 (1980) **Pop Density:** 1196.0
Land: 0.5 sq. mi.; **Water:** 0.0 sq. mi.

Mercer County
County Seat: Aledo (ZIP: 61231)

Pop: 17,290 (1990); 19,286 (1980) **Pop Density:** 30.8
Land: 561.0 sq. mi.; **Water:** 7.9 sq. mi. **Area Code:** 309
On the western border of IL, south of Davenport, IA; organized Jan 13, 1825 from Pike County.
Name origin: For Gen. Hugh Mercer (1721–77), Revolutionary War officer and physician.

Abington — Township
Lat: 41-06-46 N **Long:** 90-50-03 W
Pop: 468 (1990); 533 (1980) **Pop Density:** 12.8
Land: 36.6 sq. mi.; **Water:** 0.0 sq. mi.

Aledo — City
ZIP: 61231 **Lat:** 41-11-53 N **Long:** 90-44-50 W
Pop: 3,681 (1990); 3,881 (1980) **Pop Density:** 1840.5
Land: 2.0 sq. mi.; **Water:** 0.0 sq. mi. **Elev:** 731 ft.
In northwestern IL, southwest of Moline. Settled 1832; incorporated 1885.

Alexis — Village
Lat: 41-03-59 N **Long:** 90-33-12 W
Pop: 382 (1990); 450 (1980) **Pop Density:** 1910.0
Land: 0.2 sq. mi.; **Water:** 0.0 sq. mi.
In northwestern IL on the Mercer-Warren county line. Part of the town is also in Warren County.

Duncan — Township
Lat: 41-17-01 N **Long:** 90-50-45 W
Pop: 337 (1990); 365 (1980) **Pop Density:** 9.2
Land: 36.6 sq. mi.; **Water:** 0.0 sq. mi.

Eliza — Township
Lat: 41-17-17 N **Long:** 90-59-29 W
Pop: 438 (1990); 480 (1980) **Pop Density:** 7.7
Land: 57.1 sq. mi.; **Water:** 2.5 sq. mi.

Greene — Township
Lat: 41-12-08 N **Long:** 90-36-39 W
Pop: 1,651 (1990); 1,944 (1980) **Pop Density:** 45.0
Land: 36.7 sq. mi.; **Water:** 0.0 sq. mi.

Joy — Village
ZIP: 61260 **Lat:** 41-11-48 N **Long:** 90-52-46 W
Pop: 452 (1990); 506 (1980) **Pop Density:** 1130.0
Land: 0.4 sq. mi.; **Water:** 0.0 sq. mi. **Elev:** 688 ft.

ILLINOIS, Mercer County

Keithsburg
Town
ZIP: 61442　　Lat: 41-06-03 N　Long: 90-56-09 W
Pop: 747 (1990); 936 (1980)　　Pop Density: 287.3
Land: 2.6 sq. mi.; Water: 0.6 sq. mi.　　Elev: 549 ft.
Not coextensive with the town of the same name.

*Keithsburg
Township
Lat: 41-07-17 N　Long: 90-56-09 W
Pop: 885 (1990); 1,058 (1980)　　Pop Density: 49.4
Land: 17.9 sq. mi.; Water: 1.9 sq. mi.

Matherville
Village
ZIP: 61263　　Lat: 41-15-32 N　Long: 90-36-20 W
Pop: 708 (1990); 793 (1980)　　Pop Density: 1770.0
Land: 0.4 sq. mi.; Water: 0.0 sq. mi.

Mercer
Township
Lat: 41-11-50 N　Long: 90-43-23 W
Pop: 4,227 (1990); 4,458 (1980)　　Pop Density: 119.4
Land: 35.4 sq. mi.; Water: 0.0 sq. mi.

Millersburg
Township
Lat: 41-11-56 N　Long: 90-50-23 W
Pop: 848 (1990); 972 (1980)　　Pop Density: 23.4
Land: 36.3 sq. mi.; Water: 0.0 sq. mi.

New Boston
Town
ZIP: 61272　　Lat: 41-10-09 N　Long: 91-00-01 W
Pop: 620 (1990); 731 (1980)　　Pop Density: 688.9
Land: 0.9 sq. mi.; Water: 0.5 sq. mi.
Incorporated February 21, 1859. Not coextensive with the town of the same name.
Name origin: Previously called Dennison's Landing and Upper Yellow Banks.

*New Boston
Township
Lat: 41-12-06 N　Long: 90-59-39 W
Pop: 1,225 (1990); 1,319 (1980)　　Pop Density: 24.2
Land: 50.7 sq. mi.; Water: 3.0 sq. mi.

North Henderson
Village
ZIP: 61466　　Lat: 41-05-26 N　Long: 90-28-30 W
Pop: 184 (1990); 234 (1980)　　Pop Density: 920.0
Land: 0.2 sq. mi.; Water: 0.0 sq. mi.　　Elev: 774 ft.
Not coextensive with the town of the same name.

*North Henderson
Township
Lat: 41-06-50 N　Long: 90-29-23 W
Pop: 472 (1990); 595 (1980)　　Pop Density: 13.5
Land: 35.0 sq. mi.; Water: 0.0 sq. mi.

Ohio Grove
Township
Lat: 41-07-08 N　Long: 90-43-22 W
Pop: 337 (1990); 364 (1980)　　Pop Density: 9.1
Land: 36.9 sq. mi.; Water: 0.0 sq. mi.

Perryton
Township
Lat: 41-16-37 N　Long: 90-43-16 W
Pop: 513 (1990); 560 (1980)　　Pop Density: 14.1
Land: 36.4 sq. mi.; Water: 0.0 sq. mi.

Preemption
Township
Lat: 41-17-03 N　Long: 90-36-36 W
Pop: 1,796 (1990); 1,997 (1980)　　Pop Density: 48.5
Land: 37.0 sq. mi.; Water: 0.0 sq. mi.

Reynolds
Village
ZIP: 61279　　Lat: 41-19-41 N　Long: 90-40-09 W
Pop: 77 (1990); 35 (1980)　　Pop Density: 1540.0
Land: 0.05 sq. mi.; Water: 0.0 sq. mi.
Part of the town is also in Rock Island County.

Richland Grove
Township
Lat: 41-16-36 N　Long: 90-29-37 W
Pop: 2,192 (1990); 2,410 (1980)　　Pop Density: 60.4
Land: 36.3 sq. mi.; Water: 0.3 sq. mi.

Rivoli
Township
Lat: 41-11-33 N　Long: 90-29-47 W
Pop: 1,171 (1990); 1,350 (1980)　　Pop Density: 33.5
Land: 35.0 sq. mi.; Water: 0.0 sq. mi.

Seaton
Village
ZIP: 61476　　Lat: 41-06-06 N　Long: 90-47-57 W
Pop: 221 (1990); 255 (1980)　　Pop Density: 138.1
Land: 1.6 sq. mi.; Water: 0.0 sq. mi.

Sherrard
Village
ZIP: 61281　　Lat: 41-19-06 N　Long: 90-30-18 W
Pop: 697 (1990); 811 (1980)　　Pop Density: 1742.5
Land: 0.4 sq. mi.; Water: 0.0 sq. mi.

Suez
Township
Lat: 41-06-43 N　Long: 90-36-29 W
Pop: 730 (1990); 881 (1980)　　Pop Density: 19.6
Land: 37.2 sq. mi.; Water: 0.0 sq. mi.

Viola
Town
ZIP: 61486　　Lat: 41-12-18 N　Long: 90-35-14 W
Pop: 964 (1990); 1,144 (1980)　　Pop Density: 1205.0
Land: 0.8 sq. mi.; Water: 0.0 sq. mi.
In northwestern IL, near the Iowa River, south of Moline.

Windsor
Village
Lat: 41-12-05 N　Long: 90-26-37 W
Pop: 774 (1990); 863 (1980)　　Pop Density: 1935.0
Land: 0.4 sq. mi.; Water: 0.0 sq. mi.

American Places Dictionary   ILLINOIS, Montgomery County

Monroe County
County Seat: Waterloo (ZIP: 62298)

Pop: 22,422 (1990); 20,117 (1980)   **Pop Density:** 57.7
Land: 388.3 sq. mi.; **Water:** 9.4 sq. mi.   **Area Code:** 618
On the southwest border of IL, south of St. Louis, MO; organized Jan 6, 1816 (prior to statehood) from Randolph and Saint Clair counties.
Name origin: For James Monroe (1758–1831), fifth U.S. president.

Columbia   City
ZIP: 62236   **Lat:** 38-27-18 N **Long:** 90-13-34 W
Pop: 5,524 (1990); 4,269 (1980)   **Pop Density:** 789.1
Land: 7.0 sq. mi.; **Water:** 0.0 sq. mi.
In southwestern IL. Founded early 1800s; incorporated Feb 19, 1859.
Name origin: Feminine form of Columbus, a poetic and honorific reference to Christopher Columbus (1451–1506) and America.

Fults   Village
ZIP: 62244   **Lat:** 38-09-49 N **Long:** 90-12-45 W
Pop: 45 (1990); 78 (1980)   **Pop Density:** 450.0
Land: 0.1 sq. mi.; **Water:** 0.0 sq. mi.

Hecker   Village
ZIP: 62248   **Lat:** 38-18-16 N **Long:** 89-59-38 W
Pop: 534 (1990); 531 (1980)   **Pop Density:** 2670.0
Land: 0.2 sq. mi.; **Water:** 0.0 sq. mi.

Maeystown   Village
ZIP: 62256   **Lat:** 38-13-35 N **Long:** 90-13-53 W
Pop: 116 (1990); 143 (1980)   **Pop Density:** 386.7
Land: 0.3 sq. mi.; **Water:** 0.0 sq. mi.

Valmeyer   Town
ZIP: 62295   **Lat:** 38-18-14 N **Long:** 90-18-46 W
Pop: 897 (1990); 898 (1980)   **Pop Density:** 690.0
Land: 1.3 sq. mi.; **Water:** 0.0 sq. mi.   **Elev:** 401 ft.

Waterloo   City
ZIP: 62298   **Lat:** 38-19-53 N **Long:** 90-09-20 W
Pop: 5,072 (1990); 4,646 (1980)   **Pop Density:** 1878.5
Land: 2.7 sq. mi.; **Water:** 0.1 sq. mi.   **Elev:** 717 ft.
Incorporated Feb 12, 1849.
Name origin: For the famous Flemish battlesite of Napoleon's (1769–1821) defeat.

Montgomery County
County Seat: Hillsboro (ZIP: 62049)

Pop: 30,728 (1990); 31,686 (1980)   **Pop Density:** 43.7
Land: 703.8 sq. mi.; **Water:** 5.9 sq. mi.   **Area Code:** 217
In central IL south of Springfield; organized Feb 12, 1821 from Bond and Madison counties.
Name origin: For Gen. Richard Montgomery (1736–75), American Revolutionary War officer who captured Montreal, Canada.

Audubon   Township
                              Lat: 39-16-48 N **Long:** 89-11-53 W
Pop: 627 (1990); 718 (1980)   **Pop Density:** 11.6
Land: 53.9 sq. mi.; **Water:** 0.0 sq. mi.

Bois D'Arc   Township
                              Lat: 39-28-40 N **Long:** 89-36-46 W
Pop: 1,047 (1990); 1,048 (1980)   **Pop Density:** 19.2
Land: 54.6 sq. mi.; **Water:** 0.1 sq. mi.

Butler   Village
ZIP: 62015   **Lat:** 39-11-52 N **Long:** 89-32-02 W
Pop: 156 (1990); 225 (1980)   **Pop Density:** 312.0
Land: 0.5 sq. mi.; **Water:** 0.0 sq. mi.

Butler Grove   Township
                              Lat: 39-12-41 N **Long:** 89-31-45 W
Pop: 723 (1990); 801 (1980)   **Pop Density:** 20.3
Land: 35.7 sq. mi.; **Water:** 0.3 sq. mi.

Coalton   Village
ZIP: 62075   **Lat:** 39-17-04 N **Long:** 89-18-16 W
Pop: 359 (1990); 406 (1980)   **Pop Density:** 718.0
Land: 0.5 sq. mi.; **Water:** 0.0 sq. mi.   **Elev:** 660 ft.

Coffeen   City
ZIP: 62017   **Lat:** 39-05-19 N **Long:** 89-23-25 W
Pop: 736 (1990); 842 (1980)   **Pop Density:** 736.0
Land: 1.0 sq. mi.; **Water:** 0.0 sq. mi.

Donnellson   Village
                              Lat: 39-01-52 N **Long:** 89-28-26 W
Pop: 167 (1990); 231 (1980)   **Pop Density:** 835.0
Land: 0.2 sq. mi.; **Water:** 0.0 sq. mi.   **Elev:** 611 ft.
Part of the town is also in Bond County.

East Fork   Township
                              Lat: 39-06-00 N **Long:** 89-25-07 W
Pop: 2,228 (1990); 2,533 (1980)   **Pop Density:** 38.4
Land: 58.0 sq. mi.; **Water:** 1.7 sq. mi.

Farmersville   Village
ZIP: 62533   **Lat:** 39-26-38 N **Long:** 89-39-10 W
Pop: 698 (1990); 686 (1980)   **Pop Density:** 698.0
Land: 1.0 sq. mi.; **Water:** 0.0 sq. mi.   **Elev:** 643 ft.

ILLINOIS, Montgomery County

Fillmore — Village
ZIP: 62032 Lat: 39-06-56 N Long: 89-16-45 W
Pop: 326 (1990); 350 (1980) Pop Density: 407.5
Land: 0.8 sq. mi.; Water: 0.0 sq. mi.
Not coextensive with the town of the same name.

*Fillmore — Township
Lat: 39-07-37 N Long: 89-18-15 W
Pop: 739 (1990); 778 (1980) Pop Density: 20.3
Land: 36.4 sq. mi.; Water: 0.0 sq. mi.

Grisham — Township
Lat: 39-03-08 N Long: 89-32-11 W
Pop: 648 (1990); 744 (1980) Pop Density: 26.6
Land: 24.4 sq. mi.; Water: 0.0 sq. mi.

Harvel — Village
ZIP: 62538 Lat: 39-21-25 N Long: 89-32-03 W
Pop: 148 (1990); 203 (1980) Pop Density: 370.0
Land: 0.4 sq. mi.; Water: 0.0 sq. mi.
Part of the town is also in Christian County. Not coextensive with the township of the same name.

*Harvel — Township
Lat: 39-23-52 N Long: 89-33-35 W
Pop: 272 (1990); 337 (1980) Pop Density: 15.1
Land: 18.0 sq. mi.; Water: 0.0 sq. mi.

Hillsboro — City
ZIP: 62049 Lat: 39-09-47 N Long: 89-29-03 W
Pop: 4,400 (1990); 4,408 (1980) Pop Density: 1692.3
Land: 2.6 sq. mi.; Water: 0.3 sq. mi.
Not coextensive with the town of the same name.

*Hillsboro — Township
ZIP: 62049 Lat: 39-07-29 N Long: 89-31-26 W
Pop: 6,726 (1990); 5,933 (1980) Pop Density: 185.8
Land: 36.2 sq. mi.; Water: 0.1 sq. mi.

Irving — Town
ZIP: 62051 Lat: 39-12-17 N Long: 89-24-21 W
Pop: 516 (1990); 612 (1980) Pop Density: 645.0
Land: 0.8 sq. mi.; Water: 0.0 sq. mi.
Not coextensive with the town of the same name.

*Irving — Township
Lat: 39-12-53 N Long: 89-24-55 W
Pop: 1,074 (1990); 1,079 (1980) Pop Density: 31.3
Land: 34.3 sq. mi.; Water: 1.4 sq. mi.

Litchfield — City
ZIP: 62056 Lat: 39-10-33 N Long: 89-39-21 W
Pop: 6,883 (1990); 7,204 (1980) Pop Density: 2294.3
Land: 3.0 sq. mi.; Water: 0.0 sq. mi.
Founded 1813 by Electus Bachus Litchfield from Delphi, NY. Incorporated Feb 16, 1859.
Name origin: For its founder.

Nokomis — Town
ZIP: 62075 Lat: 39-18-01 N Long: 89-17-07 W
Pop: 2,534 (1990); 2,656 (1980) Pop Density: 1949.2
Land: 1.3 sq. mi.; Water: 0.0 sq. mi. Elev: 670 ft.
Not coextensive with the town of the same name.
Name origin: For the grandmother of Hiawatha, legendary Indian chief made famous by Henry Wadsworth Longfellow's (1807–82) poem, "The Song of Hiawatha."

*Nokomis — Township
Lat: 39-18-17 N Long: 89-18-02 W
Pop: 3,372 (1990); 3,695 (1980) Pop Density: 92.4
Land: 36.5 sq. mi.; Water: 0.0 sq. mi.

North Litchfield — Township
ZIP: 62056 Lat: 39-13-17 N Long: 89-38-37 W
Pop: 5,240 (1990); 5,436 (1980) Pop Density: 145.2
Land: 36.1 sq. mi.; Water: 2.0 sq. mi.

Ohlman — Village
ZIP: 62076 Lat: 39-20-43 N Long: 89-13-05 W
Pop: 82 (1990); 178 (1980) Pop Density: 273.3
Land: 0.3 sq. mi.; Water: 0.0 sq. mi.

Panama — Village
Lat: 39-01-49 N Long: 89-31-24 W
Pop: 157 (1990); 243 (1980) Pop Density: 785.0
Land: 0.2 sq. mi.; Water: 0.0 sq. mi. Elev: 596 ft.
Part of the town is also in Bond County.

Pitman — Township
Lat: 39-23-21 N Long: 89-38-33 W
Pop: 547 (1990); 652 (1980) Pop Density: 15.0
Land: 36.4 sq. mi.; Water: 0.0 sq. mi.

Raymond — Town
ZIP: 62560 Lat: 39-19-12 N Long: 89-34-25 W
Pop: 820 (1990); 957 (1980) Pop Density: 745.5
Land: 1.1 sq. mi.; Water: 0.0 sq. mi.
Not coextensive with the town of the same name.

*Raymond — Township
Lat: 39-18-10 N Long: 89-31-51 W
Pop: 1,179 (1990); 1,295 (1980) Pop Density: 32.7
Land: 36.1 sq. mi.; Water: 0.0 sq. mi.

Rountree — Township
Lat: 39-18-19 N Long: 89-25-14 W
Pop: 335 (1990); 370 (1980) Pop Density: 9.4
Land: 35.8 sq. mi.; Water: 0.0 sq. mi.

Schram City — Village
ZIP: 62049 Lat: 39-09-45 N Long: 89-27-38 W
Pop: 692 (1990); 708 (1980) Pop Density: 865.0
Land: 0.8 sq. mi.; Water: 0.0 sq. mi.

South Fillmore — Township
Lat: 39-03-23 N Long: 89-18-32 W
Pop: 238 (1990); 286 (1980) Pop Density: 9.9
Land: 24.1 sq. mi.; Water: 0.0 sq. mi.

South Litchfield — Township
Lat: 39-07-49 N Long: 89-38-37 W
Pop: 3,678 (1990); 3,478 (1980) Pop Density: 98.9
Land: 37.2 sq. mi.; Water: 0.1 sq. mi.

Taylor Springs — Village
Lat: 39-07-50 N Long: 89-29-42 W
Pop: 670 (1990); 671 (1980) Pop Density: 744.4
Land: 0.9 sq. mi.; Water: 0.0 sq. mi.

Waggoner — Village
ZIP: 62572 Lat: 39-22-41 N Long: 89-39-08 W
Pop: 221 (1990); 277 (1980) Pop Density: 736.7
Land: 0.3 sq. mi.; Water: 0.0 sq. mi.

Walshville — Village
ZIP: 62091 Lat: 39-04-09 N Long: 89-37-10 W
Pop: 44 (1990); 106 (1980) Pop Density: 146.7
Land: 0.3 sq. mi.; Water: 0.0 sq. mi.
Not coextensive with the town of the same name.

American Places Dictionary   ILLINOIS, Morgan County

*Walshville — Township
Lat: 39-02-34 N Long: 89-38-15 W
Pop: 359 (1990); 412 (1980) Pop Density: 9.8
Land: 36.8 sq. mi.; Water: 0.0 sq. mi.

Wenonah — Village
ZIP: 62075 Lat: 39-19-12 N Long: 89-17-21 W
Pop: 40 (1990); 70 (1980) Pop Density: 26.7
Land: 1.5 sq. mi.; Water: 0.0 sq. mi.

Witt — Town
ZIP: 62094 Lat: 39-15-20 N Long: 89-20-56 W
Pop: 866 (1990); 1,205 (1980) Pop Density: 618.6
Land: 1.4 sq. mi.; Water: 0.0 sq. mi. Elev: 666 ft.
Not coextensive with the town of the same name.

*Witt — Township
Lat: 39-12-43 N Long: 89-18-28 W
Pop: 1,251 (1990); 1,549 (1980) Pop Density: 34.0
Land: 36.8 sq. mi.; Water: 0.0 sq. mi.

Zanesville — Township
Lat: 39-18-20 N Long: 89-38-33 W
Pop: 445 (1990); 542 (1980) Pop Density: 12.1
Land: 36.7 sq. mi.; Water: 0.2 sq. mi.

Morgan County
County Seat: Jacksonville (ZIP: 62650)

Pop: 36,397 (1990); 37,502 (1980) Pop Density: 64.0
Land: 568.8 sq. mi.; Water: 3.5 sq. mi. Area Code: 217

In west-central IL west of Springfield; organized Jan 31, 1823 from Sangamon County.

Name origin: For Gen. Daniel Morgan (1736–1802), an officer in the Revolutionary War and U.S. representative from VA (1797–99).

Chapin — Village
ZIP: 62628 Lat: 39-46-02 N Long: 90-24-11 W
Pop: 632 (1990); 648 (1980) Pop Density: 632.0
Land: 1.0 sq. mi.; Water: 0.0 sq. mi. Elev: 628 ft.

Concord — Village
ZIP: 62631 Lat: 39-48-58 N Long: 90-22-17 W
Pop: 172 (1990); 205 (1980) Pop Density: 573.3
Land: 0.3 sq. mi.; Water: 0.0 sq. mi. Elev: 595 ft.

Franklin — Village
ZIP: 62638 Lat: 39-37-13 N Long: 90-02-49 W
Pop: 634 (1990); 645 (1980) Pop Density: 1056.7
Land: 0.6 sq. mi.; Water: 0.0 sq. mi.

Jacksonville — City
ZIP: 62650 Lat: 39-43-46 N Long: 90-14-03 W
Pop: 19,324 (1990); 20,284 (1980) Pop Density: 2300.5
Land: 8.4 sq. mi.; Water: 0.2 sq. mi. Elev: 613 ft.
In west-central IL, 30 mi. west of Springfield. Settled 1819 by brothers Seymour and Elisha Kellogg, War of 1812 veterans; incorporated Feb 3, 1840.
Name origin: For Andrew Jackson (1767–1845), seventh U.S. president.

Lynnville — Village
ZIP: 62650 Lat: 39-41-06 N Long: 90-20-46 W
Pop: 125 (1990); 159 (1980) Pop Density: 1250.0
Land: 0.1 sq. mi.; Water: 0.0 sq. mi. Elev: 618 ft.

Meredosia — Town
ZIP: 62665 Lat: 39-49-53 N Long: 90-33-29 W
Pop: 1,134 (1990); 1,272 (1980) Pop Density: 1417.5
Land: 0.8 sq. mi.; Water: 0.1 sq. mi.
In west-central IL at the mouth of Meredosia Lake, west of Springfield. Not coextensive with the town of the same name.
Name origin: Possibly a corruption of the French *marais d'osier* meaning 'swamp of basket reeds.'

Murrayville — Village
ZIP: 62668 Lat: 39-34-56 N Long: 90-15-03 W
Pop: 673 (1990); 712 (1980) Pop Density: 1346.0
Land: 0.5 sq. mi.; Water: 0.0 sq. mi. Elev: 687 ft.

South Jacksonville — Village
ZIP: 62650 Lat: 39-42-26 N Long: 90-13-48 W
Pop: 3,187 (1990); 3,382 (1980) Pop Density: 2451.5
Land: 1.3 sq. mi.; Water: 0.1 sq. mi. Elev: 621 ft.

Waverly — Town
ZIP: 62692 Lat: 39-35-33 N Long: 89-57-08 W
Pop: 1,402 (1990); 1,537 (1980) Pop Density: 1402.0
Land: 1.0 sq. mi.; Water: 0.0 sq. mi.
Name origin: For novel *Waverly*, by Sir Walter Scott (1771–1832).

Woodson — Village
ZIP: 62695 Lat: 39-37-39 N Long: 90-13-22 W
Pop: 472 (1990); 503 (1980) Pop Density: 1573.3
Land: 0.3 sq. mi.; Water: 0.0 sq. mi. Elev: 677 ft.

Moultrie County
County Seat: Sullivan (ZIP: 61951)

Pop: 13,930 (1990); 14,546 (1980)   **Pop Density:** 41.5
Land: 335.6 sq. mi.; **Water:** 8.9 sq. mi.   **Area Code:** 217

In central IL southwest of Decatur; organized Feb 16, 1843 from Macon and Shelby counties.

Name origin: For Gen. William Moultrie (1731–1805), an officer in the Revolutionary War and governor of SC (1785–87; 1792–94).

Allenville — Village
Lat: 39-33-28 N **Long:** 88-32-18 W
Pop: 166 (1990); 203 (1980)   **Pop Density:** 276.7
Land: 0.6 sq. mi.; **Water:** 0.0 sq. mi.

Arthur — Village
ZIP: 61911   **Lat:** 39-43-04 N **Long:** 88-28-33 W
Pop: 747 (1990); 790 (1980)   **Pop Density:** 1867.5
Land: 0.4 sq. mi.; **Water:** 0.0 sq. mi.   **Elev:** 662 ft.

In east-central IL, 32 mi. southwest of Urbana. Village platted 1873; incorporated 1877. Originally an Amish colony. Part of the town is also in Douglas County.

Name origin: For either a prominent early settler or Chester A. Arthur (1829–86), twenty-first U.S. president.

Bethany — Village
ZIP: 61914   **Lat:** 39-38-39 N **Long:** 88-44-27 W
Pop: 1,369 (1990); 1,550 (1980)   **Pop Density:** 1521.1
Land: 0.9 sq. mi.; **Water:** 0.0 sq. mi.

Name origin: Named in 1831 by missionaries from the Bethany Cumberland Presbyterians of Tennessee. Previously called Marrowbone by two trappers who ate leftover venison here.

Dalton City — Village
ZIP: 61925   **Lat:** 39-42-50 N **Long:** 88-48-25 W
Pop: 573 (1990); 574 (1980)   **Pop Density:** 955.0
Land: 0.6 sq. mi.; **Water:** 0.0 sq. mi.

Dora — Township
Lat: 39-43-56 N **Long:** 88-44-53 W
Pop: 911 (1990); 932 (1980)   **Pop Density:** 26.0
Land: 35.0 sq. mi.; **Water:** 0.0 sq. mi.

East Nelson — Township
Lat: 39-33-58 N **Long:** 88-32-02 W
Pop: 997 (1990); 1,013 (1980)   **Pop Density:** 27.7
Land: 36.0 sq. mi.; **Water:** 0.8 sq. mi.

Gays — Village
ZIP: 61928   **Lat:** 39-27-28 N **Long:** 88-29-45 W
Pop: 237 (1990); 290 (1980)   **Pop Density:** 592.5
Land: 0.4 sq. mi.; **Water:** 0.0 sq. mi.   **Elev:** 755 ft.

Jonathan Creek — Township
Lat: 39-39-02 N **Long:** 88-31-45 W
Pop: 676 (1990); 599 (1980)   **Pop Density:** 18.4
Land: 36.8 sq. mi.; **Water:** 0.0 sq. mi.

Lovington — Village
ZIP: 61937   **Lat:** 39-42-52 N **Long:** 88-37-51 W
Pop: 1,143 (1990); 1,313 (1980)   **Pop Density:** 1428.8
Land: 0.8 sq. mi.; **Water:** 0.0 sq. mi.   **Elev:** 679 ft.

Not coextensive with the town of the same name.

*Lovington — Township
Lat: 39-43-47 N **Long:** 88-38-38 W
Pop: 1,671 (1990); 1,906 (1980)   **Pop Density:** 31.9
Land: 52.4 sq. mi.; **Water:** 0.0 sq. mi.

Lowe — Township
Lat: 39-44-24 N **Long:** 88-31-41 W
Pop: 1,523 (1990); 1,590 (1980)   **Pop Density:** 37.5
Land: 40.6 sq. mi.; **Water:** 0.0 sq. mi.

Marrowbone — Township
Lat: 39-38-12 N **Long:** 88-45-29 W
Pop: 1,784 (1990); 1,973 (1980)   **Pop Density:** 45.7
Land: 39.0 sq. mi.; **Water:** 0.6 sq. mi.

Sullivan — City
ZIP: 61951   **Lat:** 39-35-50 N **Long:** 88-36-25 W
Pop: 4,354 (1990); 4,526 (1980)   **Pop Density:** 2418.9
Land: 1.8 sq. mi.; **Water:** 0.0 sq. mi.

Not coextensive with the town of the same name.

*Sullivan — Township
ZIP: 61951   **Lat:** 39-35-10 N **Long:** 88-39-17 W
Pop: 5,690 (1990); 5,777 (1980)   **Pop Density:** 96.0
Land: 59.3 sq. mi.; **Water:** 7.4 sq. mi.

Whitley — Township
Lat: 39-29-17 N **Long:** 88-32-38 W
Pop: 678 (1990); 756 (1980)   **Pop Density:** 18.5
Land: 36.6 sq. mi.; **Water:** 0.0 sq. mi.

Ogle County
County Seat: Oregon (ZIP: 61061)

Pop: 45,957 (1990); 46,338 (1980) **Pop Density:** 60.6
Land: 758.9 sq. mi.; **Water:** 4.4 sq. mi. **Area Code:** 815
In north-central IL south of Rockford; organized Jan 16, 1836 from Jo Daviess County.
Name origin: For Lt. Joseph Ogle, first Methodist layman in IL and captain of the territorial militia.

Adeline — Village
ZIP: 61047 **Lat:** 42-08-26 N **Long:** 89-29-25 W
Pop: 141 (1990); 163 (1980) **Pop Density:** 705.0
Land: 0.2 sq. mi.; **Water:** 0.0 sq. mi. **Elev:** 796 ft.

Brookville — Township
Lat: 42-04-16 N **Long:** 89-39-10 W
Pop: 286 (1990); 317 (1980) **Pop Density:** 15.9
Land: 18.0 sq. mi.; **Water:** 0.0 sq. mi.

Buffalo — Township
Lat: 41-59-08 N **Long:** 89-34-11 W
Pop: 3,003 (1990); 3,179 (1980) **Pop Density:** 88.8
Land: 33.8 sq. mi.; **Water:** 0.0 sq. mi.

Byron — City
ZIP: 61010 **Lat:** 42-07-42 N **Long:** 89-15-29 W
Pop: 2,284 (1990); 2,035 (1980) **Pop Density:** 2537.8
Land: 0.9 sq. mi.; **Water:** 0.0 sq. mi. **Elev:** 729 ft.
Founded 1835 by New Englanders. Not coextensive with the town of the same name.
Name origin: For English poet George Gordon, Lord Byron (1788–1824).

*Byron — Township
Lat: 42-10-09 N **Long:** 89-16-29 W
Pop: 4,221 (1990); 3,541 (1980) **Pop Density:** 115.3
Land: 36.6 sq. mi.; **Water:** 0.6 sq. mi.

Creston — Village
ZIP: 60113 **Lat:** 41-55-50 N **Long:** 88-57-55 W
Pop: 535 (1990); 527 (1980) **Pop Density:** 2675.0
Land: 0.2 sq. mi.; **Water:** 0.0 sq. mi.

Davis Junction — Village
ZIP: 61020 **Lat:** 42-06-06 N **Long:** 89-05-31 W
Pop: 246 (1990); 289 (1980) **Pop Density:** 123.0
Land: 2.0 sq. mi.; **Water:** 0.0 sq. mi. **Elev:** 789 ft.

Dement — Township
Lat: 41-55-56 N **Long:** 88-59-48 W
Pop: 956 (1990); 972 (1980) **Pop Density:** 27.4
Land: 34.9 sq. mi.; **Water:** 0.1 sq. mi.

Eagle Point — Township
Lat: 41-58-37 N **Long:** 89-39-27 W
Pop: 288 (1990); 341 (1980) **Pop Density:** 14.7
Land: 19.6 sq. mi.; **Water:** 0.0 sq. mi.

Flagg — Township
ZIP: 61068 **Lat:** 41-56-14 N **Long:** 89-06-38 W
Pop: 11,841 (1990); 12,170 (1980) **Pop Density:** 332.6
Land: 35.6 sq. mi.; **Water:** 0.1 sq. mi.

Forreston — Village
ZIP: 61030 **Lat:** 42-07-34 N **Long:** 89-34-43 W
Pop: 1,361 (1990); 1,384 (1980) **Pop Density:** 1701.3
Land: 0.8 sq. mi.; **Water:** 0.0 sq. mi. **Elev:** 937 ft.
Not coextensive with the town of the same name.
Name origin: Descriptively named for the area's once-forested hills.

*Forreston — Township
Lat: 42-09-07 N **Long:** 89-37-18 W
Pop: 2,032 (1990); 2,149 (1980) **Pop Density:** 56.0
Land: 36.3 sq. mi.; **Water:** 0.0 sq. mi.

Grand Detour — Township
Lat: 41-54-42 N **Long:** 89-27-20 W
Pop: 771 (1990); 781 (1980) **Pop Density:** 70.7
Land: 10.9 sq. mi.; **Water:** 0.7 sq. mi.

Hillcrest — Village
ZIP: 61068 **Lat:** 41-57-08 N **Long:** 89-04-13 W
Pop: 828 (1990); 818 (1980) **Pop Density:** 2760.0
Land: 0.3 sq. mi.; **Water:** 0.0 sq. mi.

Lafayette — Township
Lat: 41-54-30 N **Long:** 89-13-37 W
Pop: 206 (1990); 226 (1980) **Pop Density:** 11.8
Land: 17.5 sq. mi.; **Water:** 0.0 sq. mi.

Leaf River — Village
ZIP: 61047 **Lat:** 42-07-23 N **Long:** 89-24-10 W
Pop: 546 (1990); 637 (1980) **Pop Density:** 606.7
Land: 0.9 sq. mi.; **Water:** 0.0 sq. mi. **Elev:** 709 ft.
Not coextensive with the town of the same name.

*Leaf River — Township
Lat: 42-09-30 N **Long:** 89-23-23 W
Pop: 1,282 (1990); 1,420 (1980) **Pop Density:** 35.9
Land: 35.7 sq. mi.; **Water:** 0.0 sq. mi.

Lincoln — Township
Lat: 42-03-58 N **Long:** 89-34-15 W
Pop: 526 (1990); 558 (1980) **Pop Density:** 14.6
Land: 36.0 sq. mi.; **Water:** 0.0 sq. mi.

Lynnville — Township
Lat: 42-01-14 N **Long:** 89-00-08 W
Pop: 552 (1990); 595 (1980) **Pop Density:** 15.8
Land: 34.9 sq. mi.; **Water:** 0.0 sq. mi.

Marion — Township
Lat: 42-05-24 N **Long:** 89-13-04 W
Pop: 2,740 (1990); 2,793 (1980) **Pop Density:** 61.2
Land: 44.8 sq. mi.; **Water:** 0.5 sq. mi.

Maryland — Township
Lat: 42-09-10 N **Long:** 89-30-26 W
Pop: 670 (1990); 678 (1980) **Pop Density:** 18.5
Land: 36.2 sq. mi.; **Water:** 0.0 sq. mi.

ILLINOIS, Ogle County

Monroe
Township
Lat: 42-05-58 N **Long:** 88-59-56 W
Pop: 1,378 (1990); 1,355 (1980) **Pop Density:** 38.1
Land: 36.2 sq. mi.; **Water:** 0.0 sq. mi.

Mount Morris
Town
ZIP: 61054 **Lat:** 42-02-56 N **Long:** 89-25-55 W
Pop: 2,919 (1990); 2,989 (1980) **Pop Density:** 2653.6
Land: 1.1 sq. mi.; **Water:** 0.0 sq. mi. **Elev:** 916 ft.
Not coextensive with the town of the same name.

*Mount Morris
Township
Lat: 42-04-09 N **Long:** 89-27-28 W
Pop: 4,042 (1990); 4,043 (1980) **Pop Density:** 111.7
Land: 36.2 sq. mi.; **Water:** 0.0 sq. mi.

Nashua
Township
Lat: 41-57-46 N **Long:** 89-19-11 W
Pop: 431 (1990); 406 (1980) **Pop Density:** 23.0
Land: 18.7 sq. mi.; **Water:** 0.4 sq. mi.

Oregon
Town
ZIP: 61061 **Lat:** 42-00-46 N **Long:** 89-20-07 W
Pop: 3,891 (1990); 3,559 (1980) **Pop Density:** 2288.8
Land: 1.7 sq. mi.; **Water:** 0.1 sq. mi.
In northwestern IL on the Rock River, 26 mi. southwest of Rockford. Not coextensive with the town of the same name.

*Oregon
Township
Lat: 42-00-09 N **Long:** 89-20-48 W
Pop: 4,760 (1990); 4,731 (1980) **Pop Density:** 241.6
Land: 19.7 sq. mi.; **Water:** 0.9 sq. mi.

Pine Creek
Township
Lat: 41-58-34 N **Long:** 89-27-31 W
Pop: 726 (1990); 732 (1980) **Pop Density:** 18.3
Land: 39.7 sq. mi.; **Water:** 0.0 sq. mi.

Pine Rock
Township
Lat: 41-58-51 N **Long:** 89-13-24 W
Pop: 883 (1990); 1,002 (1980) **Pop Density:** 23.1
Land: 38.2 sq. mi.; **Water:** 0.0 sq. mi.

Polo
Town
ZIP: 61064 **Lat:** 41-59-04 N **Long:** 89-34-41 W
Pop: 2,514 (1990); 2,643 (1980) **Pop Density:** 1933.8
Land: 1.3 sq. mi.; **Water:** 0.0 sq. mi. **Elev:** 874 ft.
In northwestern IL, 30 mi. southwest of Rockford.
Name origin: For explorer Marco Polo (1254–1324).

Rochelle
Town
ZIP: 61068 **Lat:** 41-55-06 N **Long:** 89-03-45 W
Pop: 8,769 (1990); 8,982 (1980) **Pop Density:** 2087.9
Land: 4.2 sq. mi.; **Water:** 0.0 sq. mi.
In northern IL, 27 mi. south of Rockford. Incorporated Feb 22, 1861.
Name origin: For La Rochelle, France.

Rockvale
Township
Lat: 42-04-16 N **Long:** 89-20-15 W
Pop: 1,336 (1990); 1,279 (1980) **Pop Density:** 38.3
Land: 34.9 sq. mi.; **Water:** 1.0 sq. mi.

Scott
Township
Lat: 42-06-24 N **Long:** 89-06-51 W
Pop: 1,418 (1990); 1,414 (1980) **Pop Density:** 39.5
Land: 35.9 sq. mi.; **Water:** 0.0 sq. mi.

Stillman Valley
Village
ZIP: 61084 **Lat:** 42-06-14 N **Long:** 89-10-41 W
Pop: 848 (1990); 961 (1980) **Pop Density:** 1696.0
Land: 0.5 sq. mi.; **Water:** 0.0 sq. mi.

Taylor
Township
Lat: 41-54-35 N **Long:** 89-20-09 W
Pop: 547 (1990); 512 (1980) **Pop Density:** 35.8
Land: 15.3 sq. mi.; **Water:** 0.2 sq. mi.

White Rock
Township
Lat: 42-00-48 N **Long:** 89-06-34 W
Pop: 717 (1990); 769 (1980) **Pop Density:** 20.1
Land: 35.6 sq. mi.; **Water:** 0.0 sq. mi.

Woosung
Township
Lat: 41-55-24 N **Long:** 89-34-27 W
Pop: 345 (1990); 375 (1980) **Pop Density:** 19.5
Land: 17.7 sq. mi.; **Water:** 0.0 sq. mi.

Peoria County
County Seat: Peoria (ZIP: 61602)

Pop: 182,827 (1990); 200,466 (1980) **Pop Density:** 295.1
Land: 619.6 sq. mi.; **Water:** 11.4 sq. mi. **Area Code:** 309
In central IL east of Galesburg; organized Jan 13, 1825 from Fulton County.
Name origin: For the Peoria tribe of the Illinois nation; anglicized from French *peouarea*, a transliteration of an Illinois word. Meaning of name is in dispute: possibly 'carriers' or 'ones who are carrying packs.'

Akron
Township
Lat: 40-55-43 N **Long:** 89-41-15 W
Pop: 859 (1990); 986 (1980) **Pop Density:** 23.6
Land: 36.4 sq. mi.; **Water:** 0.1 sq. mi.

Bartonville
Village
ZIP: 61607 **Lat:** 40-38-15 N **Long:** 89-39-50 W
Pop: 5,643 (1990); 6,137 (1980) **Pop Density:** 723.5
Land: 7.8 sq. mi.; **Water:** 0.4 sq. mi.
Founded 1881; incorporated 1903.

Bellevue
Village
ZIP: 61604 **Lat:** 40-41-10 N **Long:** 89-40-25 W
Pop: 1,491 (1990); 2,045 (1980) **Pop Density:** 1065.0
Land: 1.4 sq. mi.; **Water:** 0.0 sq. mi.
In north-central IL; a subdivision of Peoria until 1941.
Name origin: From French 'beautiful view.'

ILLINOIS, Peoria County

Brimfield
Village
ZIP: 61517 Lat: 40-50-17 N Long: 89-53-02 W
Pop: 797 (1990); 890 (1980) Pop Density: 1138.6
Land: 0.7 sq. mi.; Water: 0.0 sq. mi. Elev: 707 ft.
Not coextensive with the town of the same name.

*Brimfield
Township
Lat: 40-50-48 N Long: 89-55-22 W
Pop: 1,177 (1990); 1,420 (1980) Pop Density: 32.2
Land: 36.5 sq. mi.; Water: 0.0 sq. mi.

Chillicothe
City
ZIP: 61523 Lat: 40-55-05 N Long: 89-29-57 W
Pop: 5,959 (1990); 6,176 (1980) Pop Density: 1702.6
Land: 3.5 sq. mi.; Water: 0.3 sq. mi.
Incorporated 1861. Not coextensive with the town of the same name.
Name origin: For Chillicothe, OH.

*Chillicothe
Township
ZIP: 61523 Lat: 40-55-45 N Long: 89-29-41 W
Pop: 8,254 (1990); 9,283 (1980) Pop Density: 461.1
Land: 17.9 sq. mi.; Water: 2.5 sq. mi.

Dunlap
Village
ZIP: 61525 Lat: 40-51-38 N Long: 89-40-35 W
Pop: 851 (1990); 824 (1980) Pop Density: 2836.7
Land: 0.3 sq. mi.; Water: 0.0 sq. mi.

Elmwood
City
ZIP: 61529 Lat: 40-46-44 N Long: 89-58-00 W
Pop: 1,841 (1990); 2,117 (1980) Pop Density: 1673.6
Land: 1.1 sq. mi.; Water: 0.0 sq. mi. Elev: 643 ft.
In central IL, 19 miles west-northwest of Peoria. Founded in 1864 after the discovery of a rich coal deposit on the site of the present city. Not coextensive with the town of the same name.

*Elmwood
Township
Lat: 40-45-25 N Long: 89-55-39 W
Pop: 2,284 (1990); 2,637 (1980) Pop Density: 63.3
Land: 36.1 sq. mi.; Water: 0.5 sq. mi.

Glasford
Town
ZIP: 61533 Lat: 40-34-20 N Long: 89-48-47 W
Pop: 1,115 (1990); 1,201 (1980) Pop Density: 1238.9
Land: 0.9 sq. mi.; Water: 0.0 sq. mi.
Name origin: For 19th-century farmer Samuel Glasford.

Hallock
Township
Lat: 40-55-40 N Long: 89-35-17 W
Pop: 1,485 (1990); 1,308 (1980) Pop Density: 41.0
Land: 36.2 sq. mi.; Water: 0.0 sq. mi.

Hanna City
Village
ZIP: 61536 Lat: 40-41-32 N Long: 89-47-34 W
Pop: 1,205 (1990); 1,361 (1980) Pop Density: 2410.0
Land: 0.5 sq. mi.; Water: 0.0 sq. mi.

Hollis
Township
Lat: 40-35-15 N Long: 89-42-12 W
Pop: 1,603 (1990); 1,985 (1980) Pop Density: 67.1
Land: 23.9 sq. mi.; Water: 1.1 sq. mi.

Jubilee
Township
Lat: 40-50-31 N Long: 89-48-35 W
Pop: 1,187 (1990); 1,314 (1980) Pop Density: 32.7
Land: 36.3 sq. mi.; Water: 0.0 sq. mi.

Kickapoo
Township
Lat: 40-44-44 N Long: 89-41-51 W
Pop: 3,207 (1990); 3,833 (1980) Pop Density: 101.8
Land: 31.5 sq. mi.; Water: 0.1 sq. mi.

Kingston Mines
Village
ZIP: 61539 Lat: 40-33-29 N Long: 89-46-14 W
Pop: 293 (1990); 340 (1980) Pop Density: 225.4
Land: 1.3 sq. mi.; Water: 0.1 sq. mi.

Limestone
Township
ZIP: 61604 Lat: 40-40-22 N Long: 89-42-08 W
Pop: 19,072 (1990); 20,925 (1980) Pop Density: 534.2
Land: 35.7 sq. mi.; Water: 0.3 sq. mi.

Logan
Township
Lat: 40-40-04 N Long: 89-48-59 W
Pop: 3,041 (1990); 3,310 (1980) Pop Density: 83.1
Land: 36.6 sq. mi.; Water: 0.0 sq. mi.

Mapleton
Village
ZIP: 61547 Lat: 40-34-11 N Long: 89-43-17 W
Pop: 216 (1990); 255 (1980) Pop Density: 360.0
Land: 0.6 sq. mi.; Water: 0.0 sq. mi.

Medina
Township
ZIP: 61523 Lat: 40-50-55 N Long: 89-34-48 W
Pop: 6,124 (1990); 5,972 (1980) Pop Density: 228.5
Land: 26.8 sq. mi.; Water: 2.9 sq. mi.

Millbrook
Township
Lat: 40-55-58 N Long: 89-55-46 W
Pop: 500 (1990); 594 (1980) Pop Density: 13.7
Land: 36.5 sq. mi.; Water: 0.1 sq. mi.

Norwood
Village
ZIP: 61604 Lat: 40-42-24 N Long: 89-41-58 W
Pop: 495 (1990); 612 (1980) Pop Density: 1650.0
Land: 0.3 sq. mi.; Water: 0.0 sq. mi.

Pekin
City
ZIP: 61554 Lat: 40-34-26 N Long: 89-39-29 W
Pop: 0 (1990); 4 (1980)
Land: 0.1 sq. mi.; Water: 0.0 sq. mi.
In north-central IL on the Illinois River, 10 mi. south of Peoria. County seat. Settled 1824; incorporated Feb 23, 1839. Part of the town is in Tazewell County.
Name origin: For Peking, China.

Peoria
City
ZIP: 61602 Lat: 40-44-41 N Long: 89-36-33 W
Pop: 113,504 (1990); 124,160 (1980) Pop Density: 2775.2
Land: 40.9 sq. mi.; Water: 2.2 sq. mi.
In north-central IL on the Illinois River, 60 mi. north of Springfield. County seat. Incorporated Feb 21, 1837. Headquarters of Caterpillar Inc., the earthmoving equipment manufacturer, and the Peoria Union Stock Yards (cattle and hogs).
Name origin: Anglicization of the French name *peouarea* for an Illinois tribe. Meaning of Indian name is debatable, possibly 'carriers' or 'ones who are carrying packs.' Previously known as Fort Clark; called Fort le Pe until c. 1790, when it was first referred to as Piorias.

Peoria City
Township
ZIP: 61601 Lat: 40-44-41 N Long: 89-36-33 W
Pop: 113,504 (1990); 124,160 (1980) Pop Density: 2775.2
Land: 40.9 sq. mi.; Water: 2.2 sq. mi.

ILLINOIS, Peoria County

Peoria Heights — Village
ZIP: 61614 Lat: 40-44-47 N Long: 89-34-17 W
Pop: 6,887 (1990); 7,453 (1980) Pop Density: 2754.8
Land: 2.5 sq. mi.; Water: 0.1 sq. mi. Elev: 789 ft.
Part of the town is also in Tazewell and Woodford counties.

Princeville — Town
ZIP: 61559 Lat: 40-55-53 N Long: 89-45-20 W
Pop: 1,421 (1990); 1,712 (1980) Pop Density: 1093.1
Land: 1.3 sq. mi.; Water: 0.0 sq. mi.
Not coextensive with the town of the same name.
Name origin: For pioneer Daniel Prince, its first settler.

*Princeville — Township
Lat: 40-55-48 N Long: 89-48-44 W
Pop: 1,564 (1990); 1,911 (1980) Pop Density: 43.0
Land: 36.4 sq. mi.; Water: 0.0 sq. mi.

Radnor — Township
Lat: 40-50-25 N Long: 89-41-26 W
Pop: 2,044 (1990); 2,113 (1980) Pop Density: 55.1
Land: 37.1 sq. mi.; Water: 0.0 sq. mi.

Richwoods — Township
ZIP: 61614 Lat: 40-45-13 N Long: 89-34-59 W
Pop: 6,890 (1990); 8,081 (1980) Pop Density: 2222.6
Land: 3.1 sq. mi.; Water: 0.1 sq. mi.

Rome — CDP
Lat: 40-52-42 N Long: 89-30-42 W
Pop: 1,902 (1990); 2,744 (1980) Pop Density: 864.5
Land: 2.2 sq. mi.; Water: 0.0 sq. mi.

Rosefield — Township
Lat: 40-44-57 N Long: 89-49-04 W
Pop: 1,021 (1990); 980 (1980) Pop Density: 28.0
Land: 36.4 sq. mi.; Water: 0.2 sq. mi.

Timber — Township
Lat: 40-34-39 N Long: 89-49-06 W
Pop: 2,531 (1990); 2,731 (1980) Pop Density: 70.7
Land: 35.8 sq. mi.; Water: 1.0 sq. mi.

Trivoli — Township
Lat: 40-40-02 N Long: 89-55-57 W
Pop: 1,166 (1990); 1,165 (1980) Pop Density: 32.4
Land: 36.0 sq. mi.; Water: 0.1 sq. mi.

West Peoria — Township
ZIP: 61604 Lat: 40-39-04 N Long: 89-37-28 W
Pop: 5,314 (1990); 5,758 (1980) Pop Density: 1562.9
Land: 3.4 sq. mi.; Water: 0.2 sq. mi.

Perry County
County Seat: Pinckneyville (ZIP: 62274)

Pop: 21,412 (1990); 21,714 (1980) Pop Density: 48.6
Land: 441.0 sq. mi.; Water: 5.8 sq. mi. Area Code: 618
In south-central IL north of Carbondale; organized Jan 29, 1827 from Randolph and Jackson counties.
Name origin: For Oliver Hazard Perry (1785–1819), U.S. naval officer during the War of 1812, famous for the message, "We have met the enemy and they are ours."

Cutler — Village
ZIP: 62238 Lat: 38-01-57 N Long: 89-33-59 W
Pop: 523 (1990); 495 (1980) Pop Density: 1046.0
Land: 0.5 sq. mi.; Water: 0.0 sq. mi.

Du Quoin — City
ZIP: 62832 Lat: 38-00-15 N Long: 89-14-07 W
Pop: 6,697 (1990); 6,594 (1980) Pop Density: 1174.9
Land: 5.7 sq. mi.; Water: 0.1 sq. mi.
In southwestern IL, north of Carbondale. Du Quoin, although settled at an earlier time, was actually founded in 1853 when the first settlement was moved to the site of a new railroad. Incorporated Feb 22, 1861.
Name origin: Named for Jean Baptiste du Quoigne, a French-Indian chief of the Kaskaskia Indians whose village was nearby; spelling altered to reflect pronunciation.

Pinckneyville — Town
ZIP: 62274 Lat: 38-04-41 N Long: 89-23-03 W
Pop: 3,372 (1990); 3,319 (1980) Pop Density: 1983.5
Land: 1.7 sq. mi.; Water: 0.0 sq. mi. Elev: 439 ft.
Name origin: For Revolutionary War veteran Charles Pinckney (1757–1824), a Constitutional Convention delegate from SC.

St. Johns — Village
Lat: 38-01-52 N Long: 89-14-25 W
Pop: 262 (1990); 284 (1980) Pop Density: 327.5
Land: 0.8 sq. mi.; Water: 0.0 sq. mi.

Tamaroa — Village
ZIP: 62888 Lat: 38-08-07 N Long: 89-13-43 W
Pop: 780 (1990); 885 (1980) Pop Density: 866.7
Land: 0.9 sq. mi.; Water: 0.0 sq. mi.

Willisville — Village
ZIP: 62997 Lat: 37-58-58 N Long: 89-35-26 W
Pop: 577 (1990); 628 (1980) Pop Density: 1442.5
Land: 0.4 sq. mi.; Water: 0.0 sq. mi.

Piatt County
County Seat: Monticello (ZIP: 61856)

Pop: 15,548 (1990); 16,581 (1980) **Pop Density:** 35.3
Land: 440.0 sq. mi.; **Water:** 0.3 sq. mi. **Area Code:** 217
In central IL west of Urbana; organized Jan 27, 1841 from De Witt and Macon counties.
Name origin: For either James A. Piatt, Sr. (1789–1838), an early settler, or Benjamin Piatt, attorney general of IL Territory (1810–13).

Atwood — Village
ZIP: 61913 **Lat:** 39-48-06 N **Long:** 88-27-58 W
Pop: 651 (1990); 832 (1980) **Pop Density:** 2170.0
Land: 0.3 sq. mi.; **Water:** 0.0 sq. mi.
Established 1874; incorporated 1884. Not coextensive with the town of the same name. Part of this town is also in Douglas County.
Name origin: The name recalls a dense woods once found on the site: "at-wood."

Bement — Village
ZIP: 61813 **Lat:** 39-55-22 N **Long:** 88-34-17 W
Pop: 1,668 (1990); 1,770 (1980) **Pop Density:** 2085.0
Land: 0.8 sq. mi.; **Water:** 0.0 sq. mi.
In central IL, 22 mi. southwest of Champaign. Founded 1855. Not coextensive with the town of the same name.
Name origin: For an official of the Great Western Railroad.

*Bement — Township
Lat: 39-55-34 N **Long:** 88-32-28 W
Pop: 1,928 (1990); 2,067 (1980) **Pop Density:** 39.8
Land: 48.4 sq. mi.; **Water:** 0.0 sq. mi.

Blue Ridge — Township
Lat: 40-13-18 N **Long:** 88-32-42 W
Pop: 1,407 (1990); 1,418 (1980) **Pop Density:** 22.0
Land: 63.9 sq. mi.; **Water:** 0.1 sq. mi.

Cerro Gordo — Village
ZIP: 61818 **Lat:** 39-53-24 N **Long:** 88-44-04 W
Pop: 1,436 (1990); 1,553 (1980) **Pop Density:** 2051.4
Land: 0.7 sq. mi.; **Water:** 0.0 sq. mi.
Village incorporated 1873. Not coextensive with the town of the same name.
Name origin: For the Battle of Cerro Gordo (1847) in the Mexican War.

*Cerro Gordo — Township
Lat: 39-51-27 N **Long:** 88-40-45 W
Pop: 2,208 (1990); 2,474 (1980) **Pop Density:** 36.5
Land: 60.5 sq. mi.; **Water:** 0.0 sq. mi.

Cisco — Village
ZIP: 61830 **Lat:** 40-00-49 N **Long:** 88-43-24 W
Pop: 282 (1990); 333 (1980) **Pop Density:** 705.0
Land: 0.4 sq. mi.; **Water:** 0.0 sq. mi.

De Land — Village
Lat: 40-07-17 N **Long:** 88-38-37 W
Pop: 458 (1990); 509 (1980) **Pop Density:** 1145.0
Land: 0.4 sq. mi.; **Water:** 0.0 sq. mi.

Goose Creek — Township
Lat: 40-06-16 N **Long:** 88-38-21 W
Pop: 848 (1990); 985 (1980) **Pop Density:** 15.0
Land: 56.4 sq. mi.; **Water:** 0.0 sq. mi.

Hammond — Town
ZIP: 61929 **Lat:** 39-47-54 N **Long:** 88-35-29 W
Pop: 527 (1990); 556 (1980) **Pop Density:** 658.8
Land: 0.8 sq. mi.; **Water:** 0.0 sq. mi. **Elev:** 678 ft.
Settled 1855.

Ivesdale — Village
ZIP: 61851 **Lat:** 39-56-40 N **Long:** 88-27-46 W
Pop: 0 (1990); 2 (1980)
Land: 0.1 sq. mi.; **Water:** 0.0 sq. mi.
Part of the town is also in Champaign County.

Mansfield — Town
ZIP: 61854 **Lat:** 40-12-43 N **Long:** 88-30-32 W
Pop: 929 (1990); 921 (1980) **Pop Density:** 1858.0
Land: 0.5 sq. mi.; **Water:** 0.0 sq. mi. **Elev:** 730 ft.
Incorporated March 3, 1876.

Monticello — City
ZIP: 61856 **Lat:** 40-01-32 N **Long:** 88-34-28 W
Pop: 4,549 (1990); 4,753 (1980) **Pop Density:** 2394.2
Land: 1.9 sq. mi.; **Water:** 0.0 sq. mi. **Elev:** 675 ft.
In east-central IL, 25 mi. northeast of Decatur. Not coextensive with the town of the same name.
Name origin: Named by land promoters for third U.S. President Thomas Jefferson's (1743–1826) VA estate.

*Monticello — Township
ZIP: 61856 **Lat:** 40-00-34 N **Long:** 88-32-17 W
Pop: 5,339 (1990); 5,275 (1980) **Pop Density:** 111.5
Land: 47.9 sq. mi.; **Water:** 0.1 sq. mi.

Sangamon — Township
Lat: 40-06-40 N **Long:** 88-30-51 W
Pop: 1,481 (1990); 1,585 (1980) **Pop Density:** 31.2
Land: 47.4 sq. mi.; **Water:** 0.1 sq. mi.

Unity — Township
Lat: 39-49-40 N **Long:** 88-31-41 W
Pop: 1,605 (1990); 1,906 (1980) **Pop Density:** 33.3
Land: 48.2 sq. mi.; **Water:** 0.0 sq. mi.

Willow Branch — Township
Lat: 39-59-05 N **Long:** 88-40-47 W
Pop: 732 (1990); 871 (1980) **Pop Density:** 10.9
Land: 67.3 sq. mi.; **Water:** 0.1 sq. mi.

ILLINOIS, Pike County — *American Places Dictionary*

Pike County
County Seat: Pittsfield (ZIP: 62363)

Pop: 17,577 (1990); 18,896 (1980) **Pop Density:** 21.2
Land: 830.3 sq. mi.; **Water:** 18.6 sq. mi. **Area Code:** 217

On the west-central border of IL, south of Quincy; organized Jan 31, 1821 from Madison, Bond, and Clark counties.

Name origin: For Zebulon Montgomery Pike (1779–1813), U.S. army officer and discoverer of Pikes Peak in CO.

Atlas *Township*
Lat: 39-32-09 N **Long:** 91-01-05 W
Pop: 641 (1990); 733 (1980) **Pop Density:** 10.1
Land: 63.4 sq. mi.; **Water:** 4.4 sq. mi.

Barry *City*
ZIP: 62312 **Lat:** 39-41-44 N **Long:** 91-02-23 W
Pop: 1,391 (1990); 1,487 (1980) **Pop Density:** 1391.0
Land: 1.0 sq. mi.; **Water:** 0.0 sq. mi.

Founded 1836 by veterans of the War of 1812; incorporated as city 1859. Not coextensive with the town of the same name.

Name origin: For Barre, VT, with spelling altered to reflect pronunciation.

*Barry *Township*
Lat: 39-42-39 N **Long:** 91-05-25 W
Pop: 1,800 (1990); 1,931 (1980) **Pop Density:** 46.8
Land: 38.5 sq. mi.; **Water:** 0.0 sq. mi.

Baylis *Village*
ZIP: 62314 **Lat:** 39-43-44 N **Long:** 90-54-33 W
Pop: 257 (1990); 299 (1980) **Pop Density:** 514.0
Land: 0.5 sq. mi.; **Water:** 0.0 sq. mi.

Chambersburg *Township*
Lat: 39-47-55 N **Long:** 90-38-08 W
Pop: 203 (1990); 195 (1980) **Pop Density:** 7.0
Land: 29.0 sq. mi.; **Water:** 0.6 sq. mi.

Cincinnati *Township*
Lat: 39-37-45 N **Long:** 91-11-24 W
Pop: 73 (1990); 85 (1980) **Pop Density:** 3.1
Land: 23.5 sq. mi.; **Water:** 3.1 sq. mi.

Derry *Township*
Lat: 39-37-28 N **Long:** 90-58-14 W
Pop: 292 (1990); 296 (1980) **Pop Density:** 7.8
Land: 37.3 sq. mi.; **Water:** 0.0 sq. mi.

Detroit *Village*
ZIP: 62332 **Lat:** 39-37-11 N **Long:** 90-40-34 W
Pop: 126 (1990); 156 (1980) **Pop Density:** 630.0
Land: 0.2 sq. mi.; **Water:** 0.0 sq. mi. **Elev:** 639 ft.

Not coextensive with the town of the same name.

*Detroit *Township*
Lat: 39-37-15 N **Long:** 90-38-30 W
Pop: 353 (1990); 441 (1980) **Pop Density:** 13.4
Land: 26.3 sq. mi.; **Water:** 0.7 sq. mi.

El Dara *Village*
Lat: 39-37-19 N **Long:** 90-59-28 W
Pop: 94 (1990); 87 (1980) **Pop Density:** 94.0
Land: 1.0 sq. mi.; **Water:** 0.0 sq. mi. **Elev:** 741 ft.

Fairmount *Township*
Lat: 39-48-06 N **Long:** 90-51-40 W
Pop: 265 (1990); 279 (1980) **Pop Density:** 7.0
Land: 37.6 sq. mi.; **Water:** 0.0 sq. mi.

Flint *Township*
Lat: 39-42-29 N **Long:** 90-39-15 W
Pop: 118 (1990); 129 (1980) **Pop Density:** 7.7
Land: 15.3 sq. mi.; **Water:** 0.9 sq. mi.

Florence *Village*
Lat: 39-37-41 N **Long:** 90-36-36 W
Pop: 45 (1990); 59 (1980) **Pop Density:** 225.0
Land: 0.2 sq. mi.; **Water:** 0.0 sq. mi.

Griggsville *Town*
ZIP: 62340 **Lat:** 39-42-28 N **Long:** 90-43-37 W
Pop: 1,218 (1990); 1,301 (1980) **Pop Density:** 1218.0
Land: 1.0 sq. mi.; **Water:** 0.0 sq. mi.

In western IL, 5 mi. west of the Illinois River and southwest of Springfield. Not coextensive with the town of the same name.

Name origin: For 1833 settler Richard Griggs.

*Griggsville *Township*
Lat: 39-42-29 N **Long:** 90-44-29 W
Pop: 1,497 (1990); 1,603 (1980) **Pop Density:** 39.7
Land: 37.7 sq. mi.; **Water:** 0.0 sq. mi.

Hadley *Township*
Lat: 39-42-24 N **Long:** 90-58-02 W
Pop: 242 (1990); 304 (1980) **Pop Density:** 6.6
Land: 36.8 sq. mi.; **Water:** 0.0 sq. mi.

Hardin *Township*
Lat: 39-31-41 N **Long:** 90-44-49 W
Pop: 254 (1990); 274 (1980) **Pop Density:** 6.8
Land: 37.4 sq. mi.; **Water:** 0.0 sq. mi.

Hull *Village*
Lat: 39-42-32 N **Long:** 91-12-17 W
Pop: 514 (1990); 529 (1980) **Pop Density:** 285.6
Land: 1.8 sq. mi.; **Water:** 0.0 sq. mi.

Kinderhook *Village*
ZIP: 62345 **Lat:** 39-42-17 N **Long:** 91-09-17 W
Pop: 257 (1990); 259 (1980) **Pop Density:** 856.7
Land: 0.3 sq. mi.; **Water:** 0.0 sq. mi. **Elev:** 478 ft.

Not coextensive with the town of the same name.

*Kinderhook *Township*
Lat: 39-42-44 N **Long:** 91-12-27 W
Pop: 1,071 (1990); 1,084 (1980) **Pop Density:** 28.3
Land: 37.9 sq. mi.; **Water:** 0.1 sq. mi.

Levee *Township*
Lat: 39-43-33 N **Long:** 91-18-20 W
Pop: 175 (1990); 181 (1980) **Pop Density:** 8.0
Land: 22.0 sq. mi.; **Water:** 3.1 sq. mi.

ILLINOIS, Pike County

Martinsburg — Township
Lat: 39-31-56 N Long: 90-51-21 W
Pop: 380 (1990); 397 (1980) **Pop Density:** 10.1
Land: 37.7 sq. mi.; **Water:** 0.0 sq. mi.

Milton — Village
ZIP: 62352 Lat: 39-33-51 N Long: 90-38-59 W
Pop: 270 (1990); 349 (1980) **Pop Density:** 675.0
Land: 0.4 sq. mi.; **Water:** 0.0 sq. mi.

Montezuma — Township
Lat: 39-32-00 N Long: 90-37-48 W
Pop: 548 (1990); 618 (1980) **Pop Density:** 16.3
Land: 33.7 sq. mi.; **Water:** 0.7 sq. mi.

Nebo — Town
ZIP: 62355 Lat: 39-26-29 N Long: 90-47-25 W
Pop: 402 (1990); 487 (1980) **Pop Density:** 574.3
Land: 0.7 sq. mi.; **Water:** 0.0 sq. mi. **Elev:** 483 ft.
Name origin: From an Iroquois term probably meaning 'supreme being.'

Newburg — Township
Lat: 39-37-04 N Long: 90-44-13 W
Pop: 944 (1990); 838 (1980) **Pop Density:** 25.3
Land: 37.3 sq. mi.; **Water:** 0.4 sq. mi.

New Canton — Town
ZIP: 62356 Lat: 39-38-17 N Long: 91-05-52 W
Pop: 405 (1990); 420 (1980) **Pop Density:** 506.3
Land: 0.8 sq. mi.; **Water:** 0.0 sq. mi.

New Salem — Village
ZIP: 62357 Lat: 39-42-28 N Long: 90-50-50 W
Pop: 147 (1990); 170 (1980) **Pop Density:** 147.0
Land: 1.0 sq. mi.; **Water:** 0.0 sq. mi.
Not coextensive with the town of the same name.

*New Salem — Township
Lat: 39-42-35 N Long: 90-51-30 W
Pop: 651 (1990); 787 (1980) **Pop Density:** 17.0
Land: 38.3 sq. mi.; **Water:** 0.0 sq. mi.

Pearl — Village
ZIP: 62361 Lat: 39-27-30 N Long: 90-37-27 W
Pop: 177 (1990); 322 (1980) **Pop Density:** 118.0
Land: 1.5 sq. mi.; **Water:** 0.1 sq. mi.
Not coextensive with the town of the same name.

*Pearl — Township
Lat: 39-26-28 N Long: 90-39-00 W
Pop: 372 (1990); 478 (1980) **Pop Density:** 15.1
Land: 24.7 sq. mi.; **Water:** 0.6 sq. mi.

Perry — Village
ZIP: 62362 Lat: 39-46-56 N Long: 90-44-50 W
Pop: 491 (1990); 487 (1980) **Pop Density:** 1227.5
Land: 0.4 sq. mi.; **Water:** 0.0 sq. mi.
Not coextensive with the town of the same name.

*Perry — Township
Lat: 39-47-26 N Long: 90-44-20 W
Pop: 703 (1990); 806 (1980) **Pop Density:** 18.9
Land: 37.2 sq. mi.; **Water:** 0.0 sq. mi.

Pittsfield — Town
ZIP: 62363 Lat: 39-36-38 N Long: 90-48-33 W
Pop: 4,231 (1990); 4,170 (1980) **Pop Density:** 1839.6
Land: 2.3 sq. mi.; **Water:** 0.0 sq. mi.
In western IL between the Mississippi and Illinois rivers, southwest of Springfield. Not coextensive with the town of the same name.
Name origin: For Pittsfield, MA.

*Pittsfield — Township
Lat: 39-37-14 N Long: 90-51-40 W
Pop: 4,100 (1990); 4,344 (1980) **Pop Density:** 108.5
Land: 37.8 sq. mi.; **Water:** 0.1 sq. mi.

Pleasant Hill — Town
ZIP: 62366 Lat: 39-26-40 N Long: 90-52-22 W
Pop: 1,030 (1990); 1,112 (1980) **Pop Density:** 1716.7
Land: 0.6 sq. mi.; **Water:** 0.0 sq. mi.
Not coextensive with the town of the same name.

*Pleasant Hill — Township
Lat: 39-26-47 N Long: 90-51-18 W
Pop: 1,387 (1990); 1,467 (1980) **Pop Density:** 37.0
Land: 37.5 sq. mi.; **Water:** 0.1 sq. mi.

Pleasant Vale — Township
Lat: 39-37-20 N Long: 91-05-27 W
Pop: 658 (1990); 698 (1980) **Pop Density:** 16.9
Land: 39.0 sq. mi.; **Water:** 0.0 sq. mi.

Ross — Township
Lat: 39-27-05 N Long: 90-58-39 W
Pop: 134 (1990); 119 (1980) **Pop Density:** 4.9
Land: 27.1 sq. mi.; **Water:** 3.7 sq. mi.

Spring Creek — Township
Lat: 39-26-36 N Long: 90-44-42 W
Pop: 716 (1990); 809 (1980) **Pop Density:** 19.1
Land: 37.4 sq. mi.; **Water:** 0.0 sq. mi.

Time — Village
Lat: 39-33-40 N Long: 90-43-22 W
Pop: 36 (1990); 27 (1980) **Pop Density:** 90.0
Land: 0.4 sq. mi.; **Water:** 0.0 sq. mi. **Elev:** 692 ft.

Valley City — Village
Lat: 39-42-31 N Long: 90-38-56 W
Pop: 23 (1990); 60 (1980) **Pop Density:** 115.0
Land: 0.2 sq. mi.; **Water:** 0.0 sq. mi.

ILLINOIS, Pope County

Pope County
County Seat: Golconda (ZIP: 62938)

Pop: 4,373 (1990); 4,404 (1980)
Land: 370.9 sq. mi.; **Water:** 3.8 sq. mi.
Pop Density: 11.8
Area Code: 618

On the southeastern border of IL; organized Jan 10, 1816 (prior to statehood) from Johnson and Gallatin counties.

Name origin: For Nathaniel Pope (1784–1850), first territorial secretary of IL Territory (1809–16) and U.S. district judge for IL (1819–50).

Eddyville
Village
ZIP: 62928   **Lat:** 37-30-01 N   **Long:** 88-35-06 W
Pop: 151 (1990); 143 (1980)   **Pop Density:** 503.3
Land: 0.3 sq. mi.; **Water:** 0.0 sq. mi.   **Elev:** 662 ft.

Golconda
City
ZIP: 62938   **Lat:** 37-21-45 N   **Long:** 88-29-12 W
Pop: 823 (1990); 960 (1980)   **Pop Density:** 1646.0
Land: 0.5 sq. mi.; **Water:** 0.0 sq. mi.   **Elev:** 352 ft.

Hamletsburg
Village
ZIP: 62944   **Lat:** 37-08-26 N   **Long:** 88-26-45 W
Pop: 85 (1990); 93 (1980)   **Pop Density:** 47.2
Land: 1.8 sq. mi.; **Water:** 0.0 sq. mi.   **Elev:** 394 ft.

Pulaski County
County Seat: Mound City (ZIP: 62963)

Pop: 7,523 (1990); 8,840 (1980)
Land: 200.8 sq. mi.; **Water:** 2.5 sq. mi.
Pop Density: 37.5
Area Code: 618

On the southern border of IL; organized Mar 3, 1843 from Johnson County.

Name origin: For Count Casimir Pulaski (1747–79), Polish soldier who fought for America during the Revolutionary War.

Karnak
Village
ZIP: 62956   **Lat:** 37-17-38 N   **Long:** 88-58-33 W
Pop: 581 (1990); 646 (1980)   **Pop Density:** 322.8
Land: 1.8 sq. mi.; **Water:** 0.0 sq. mi.

Mound City
City
ZIP: 62963   **Lat:** 37-05-08 N   **Long:** 89-09-46 W
Pop: 765 (1990); 1,102 (1980)   **Pop Density:** 1092.9
Land: 0.7 sq. mi.; **Water:** 0.0 sq. mi.   **Elev:** 320 ft.
Name origin: For the area's ancient Indian burial mounds.

Mounds
Town
ZIP: 62964   **Lat:** 37-06-53 N   **Long:** 89-12-04 W
Pop: 1,407 (1990); 1,669 (1980)   **Pop Density:** 1172.5
Land: 1.2 sq. mi.; **Water:** 0.0 sq. mi.
Name origin: For nearby Indian burial mounds. Previously called Beechwood Junction and Mound City Junction.

New Grand Chain
Village
Lat: 37-15-11 N   **Long:** 89-01-01 W
Pop: 273 (1990); 232 (1980)   **Pop Density:** 248.2
Land: 1.1 sq. mi.; **Water:** 0.0 sq. mi.   **Elev:** 404 ft.

Olmsted
Village
ZIP: 62970   **Lat:** 37-10-53 N   **Long:** 89-05-01 W
Pop: 358 (1990); 439 (1980)   **Pop Density:** 210.6
Land: 1.7 sq. mi.; **Water:** 0.0 sq. mi.

Pulaski
Village
ZIP: 62976   **Lat:** 37-12-57 N   **Long:** 89-12-25 W
Pop: 361 (1990); 477 (1980)   **Pop Density:** 277.7
Land: 1.3 sq. mi.; **Water:** 0.0 sq. mi.   **Elev:** 343 ft.

Ullin
Town
ZIP: 62992   **Lat:** 37-16-53 N   **Long:** 89-11-01 W
Pop: 402 (1990); 550 (1980)   **Pop Density:** 446.7
Land: 0.9 sq. mi.; **Water:** 0.0 sq. mi.

Putnam County
County Seat: Hennepin (ZIP: 61327)

Pop: 5,730 (1990); 6,085 (1980)   **Pop Density:** 35.9
Land: 159.8 sq. mi.; **Water:** 12.4 sq. mi.   **Area Code:** 815
In north-central IL, northeast of Peoria; organized Jan 13, 1825 from Fulton County.
Name origin: For Gen. Israel Putnam (1718–90), Revolutionary War officer and American commander at Battle of Bunker Hill.

Granville   City
ZIP: 61326   **Lat:** 41-15-51 N   **Long:** 89-13-47 W
Pop: 1,407 (1990); 1,537 (1980)   **Pop Density:** 1407.0
Land: 1.0 sq. mi.; **Water:** 0.0 sq. mi.
Not coextensive with the town of the same name.

*Granville   Township
Lat: 41-15-30 N   **Long:** 89-13-06 W
Pop: 2,835 (1990); 3,070 (1980)   **Pop Density:** 63.6
Land: 44.6 sq. mi.; **Water:** 0.9 sq. mi.

Hennepin   Town
ZIP: 61327   **Lat:** 41-15-21 N   **Long:** 89-19-10 W
Pop: 669 (1990); 716 (1980)   **Pop Density:** 128.7
Land: 5.2 sq. mi.; **Water:** 0.4 sq. mi.
Not coextensive with the town of the same name.
Name origin: For Belgian missionary Father Louis Hennepin (1860–1701), one of the first Europeans to explore the region.

*Hennepin   Township
Lat: 41-12-54 N   **Long:** 89-18-13 W
Pop: 1,111 (1990); 1,166 (1980)   **Pop Density:** 26.8
Land: 41.4 sq. mi.; **Water:** 1.8 sq. mi.

Magnolia   Village
ZIP: 61336   **Lat:** 41-06-50 N   **Long:** 89-11-42 W
Pop: 261 (1990); 308 (1980)   **Pop Density:** 870.0
Land: 0.3 sq. mi.; **Water:** 0.0 sq. mi.   **Elev:** 673 ft.
Not coextensive with the town of the same name.

*Magnolia   Township
Lat: 41-08-30 N   **Long:** 89-13-40 W
Pop: 1,215 (1990); 1,254 (1980)   **Pop Density:** 28.7
Land: 42.3 sq. mi.; **Water:** 1.2 sq. mi.

Mark   Village
ZIP: 61340   **Lat:** 41-15-50 N   **Long:** 89-14-54 W
Pop: 391 (1990); 424 (1980)   **Pop Density:** 651.7
Land: 0.6 sq. mi.; **Water:** 0.0 sq. mi.

McNabb   Village
ZIP: 61335   **Lat:** 41-10-38 N   **Long:** 89-12-35 W
Pop: 310 (1990); 342 (1980)   **Pop Density:** 1550.0
Land: 0.2 sq. mi.; **Water:** 0.0 sq. mi.

Senachwine   Township
Lat: 41-11-27 N   **Long:** 89-23-59 W
Pop: 569 (1990); 595 (1980)   **Pop Density:** 18.1
Land: 31.5 sq. mi.; **Water:** 8.6 sq. mi.

Standard   Village
ZIP: 61363   **Lat:** 41-15-23 N   **Long:** 89-10-49 W
Pop: 260 (1990); 277 (1980)   **Pop Density:** 433.3
Land: 0.6 sq. mi.; **Water:** 0.0 sq. mi.

Randolph County
County Seat: Chester (ZIP: 62233)

Pop: 34,583 (1990); 35,652 (1980)   **Pop Density:** 59.8
Land: 578.4 sq. mi.; **Water:** 18.8 sq. mi.   **Area Code:** 618
On the southwestern border of IL; organized Oct 5, 1795 (prior to statehood) from Saint Clair County.
Name origin: For Edmund Jennings Randolph (1753–1813), governor of VA (1786–88), first U.S. Attorney General (1789), and U.S. secretary of state (1794–95).

Baldwin   Village
ZIP: 62217   **Lat:** 38-11-01 N   **Long:** 89-50-40 W
Pop: 426 (1990); 474 (1980)   **Pop Density:** 608.6
Land: 0.7 sq. mi.; **Water:** 0.0 sq. mi.

Chester   City
ZIP: 62233   **Lat:** 37-55-10 N   **Long:** 89-49-30 W
Pop: 8,194 (1990); 8,401 (1980)   **Pop Density:** 1388.8
Land: 5.9 sq. mi.; **Water:** 0.0 sq. mi.
In southwestern IL on the Mississippi River near the mouth of the Kaskaskia River. Founded 1819 by an Ohio land company; incorporated Jan 7, 1835.
Name origin: For Chester, England.

Coulterville   Village
ZIP: 62237   **Lat:** 38-11-05 N   **Long:** 89-36-15 W
Pop: 984 (1990); 1,118 (1980)   **Pop Density:** 1640.0
Land: 0.6 sq. mi.; **Water:** 0.0 sq. mi.
Name origin: For the Coulter brothers, early settlers from TN.

ILLINOIS, Randolph County

Ellis Grove
Village
Lat: 38-00-33 N Long: 89-54-31 W
Pop: 353 (1990); 296 (1980)   Pop Density: 706.0
Land: 0.5 sq. mi.; Water: 0.0 sq. mi.

Evansville
Village
ZIP: 62242   Lat: 38-05-19 N Long: 89-55-58 W
Pop: 844 (1990); 863 (1980)   Pop Density: 1205.7
Land: 0.7 sq. mi.; Water: 0.0 sq. mi.

Kaskaskia
Village
Lat: 37-55-16 N Long: 89-54-58 W
Pop: 32 (1990); 33 (1980)   Pop Density: 320.0
Land: 0.1 sq. mi.; Water: 0.0 sq. mi.

Percy
Village
ZIP: 62272   Lat: 38-00-57 N Long: 89-37-00 W
Pop: 925 (1990); 1,053 (1980)   Pop Density: 1156.3
Land: 0.8 sq. mi.; Water: 0.0 sq. mi.

Prairie du Rocher
Town
Lat: 38-04-52 N Long: 90-05-51 W
Pop: 540 (1990); 701 (1980)   Pop Density: 900.0
Land: 0.6 sq. mi.; Water: 0.0 sq. mi.   Elev: 396 ft.
In southern IL on bluffs overlooking the Mississippi River. Founded 1722 as a French settlement.

Red Bud
Town
ZIP: 62278   Lat: 38-12-36 N Long: 89-59-46 W
Pop: 2,918 (1990); 2,850 (1980)   Pop Density: 1716.5
Land: 1.7 sq. mi.; Water: 0.0 sq. mi.   Elev: 479 ft.
Name origin: For the redbud trees that once grew near the village site.

Rockwood
Village
ZIP: 62280   Lat: 37-50-16 N Long: 89-41-50 W
Pop: 45 (1990); 59 (1980)   Pop Density: 450.0
Land: 0.1 sq. mi.; Water: 0.0 sq. mi.

Ruma
Village
ZIP: 62278   Lat: 38-08-03 N Long: 89-59-54 W
Pop: 256 (1990); 254 (1980)   Pop Density: 853.3
Land: 0.3 sq. mi.; Water: 0.0 sq. mi.   Elev: 442 ft.

Sparta
Town
ZIP: 62286   Lat: 38-09-10 N Long: 89-42-55 W
Pop: 4,853 (1990); 4,957 (1980)   Pop Density: 510.8
Land: 9.5 sq. mi.; Water: 0.1 sq. mi.
Name origin: For the ancient Greek city.

Steeleville
Town
ZIP: 62288   Lat: 38-00-27 N Long: 89-39-38 W
Pop: 2,059 (1990); 2,240 (1980)   Pop Density: 1583.8
Land: 1.3 sq. mi.; Water: 0.0 sq. mi.
Name origin: For early settler John Steele.

Tilden
Village
ZIP: 62292   Lat: 38-12-42 N Long: 89-40-59 W
Pop: 919 (1990); 1,025 (1980)   Pop Density: 919.0
Land: 1.0 sq. mi.; Water: 0.0 sq. mi.   Elev: 522 ft.

Richland County
County Seat: Olney (ZIP: 62450)

Pop: 16,545 (1990); 17,587 (1980)   Pop Density: 45.9
Land: 360.2 sq. mi.; Water: 1.9 sq. mi.   Area Code: 618
In southeastern IL; organized Feb 24, 1841 from Clay and Lawrence counties.
Name origin: For the county in OH.

Bonpas
Township
Lat: 38-36-47 N Long: 87-57-52 W
Pop: 404 (1990); 424 (1980)   Pop Density: 10.8
Land: 37.5 sq. mi.; Water: 0.0 sq. mi.

Calhoun
Village
ZIP: 62419   Lat: 38-39-05 N Long: 88-02-34 W
Pop: 232 (1990); 267 (1980)   Pop Density: 232.0
Land: 1.0 sq. mi.; Water: 0.0 sq. mi.

Claremont
Village
ZIP: 62421   Lat: 38-43-08 N Long: 87-58-28 W
Pop: 256 (1990); 255 (1980)   Pop Density: 232.7
Land: 1.1 sq. mi.; Water: 0.0 sq. mi.
Not coextensive with the town of the same name.

*Claremont
Township
Lat: 38-42-23 N Long: 87-58-12 W
Pop: 914 (1990); 986 (1980)   Pop Density: 20.8
Land: 44.0 sq. mi.; Water: 0.0 sq. mi.

Decker
Township
Lat: 38-38-05 N Long: 88-12-49 W
Pop: 415 (1990); 426 (1980)   Pop Density: 11.8
Land: 35.3 sq. mi.; Water: 0.0 sq. mi.

Denver
Township
Lat: 38-48-10 N Long: 88-12-15 W
Pop: 428 (1990); 473 (1980)   Pop Density: 12.1
Land: 35.4 sq. mi.; Water: 0.0 sq. mi.

German
Township
Lat: 38-48-35 N Long: 87-58-16 W
Pop: 406 (1990); 471 (1980)   Pop Density: 10.7
Land: 37.9 sq. mi.; Water: 0.0 sq. mi.

Madison
Township
Lat: 38-36-45 N Long: 88-05-01 W
Pop: 920 (1990); 1,089 (1980)   Pop Density: 22.5
Land: 40.9 sq. mi.; Water: 0.0 sq. mi.

Noble
Town
ZIP: 62868   Lat: 38-41-49 N Long: 88-13-28 W
Pop: 756 (1990); 832 (1980)   Pop Density: 756.0
Land: 1.0 sq. mi.; Water: 0.0 sq. mi.   Elev: 478 ft.
Incorporated March 27, 1869. Not coextensive with the town of the same name.

*Noble
Township
Lat: 38-43-00 N **Long:** 88-12-52 W
Pop: 1,582 (1990); 1,613 (1980) **Pop Density:** 38.4
Land: 41.2 sq. mi.; **Water:** 0.0 sq. mi.

Olney
Town
ZIP: 62450 **Lat:** 38-43-53 N **Long:** 88-05-07 W
Pop: 8,664 (1990); 9,026 (1980) **Pop Density:** 1805.0
Land: 4.8 sq. mi.; **Water:** 0.0 sq. mi.
In southeastern IL, 55 mi. northeast of Mount Vernon. County seat. Incorporated Feb 24, 1841. Not coextensive with the town of the same name.
Name origin: For banker Nathan Olney.

*Olney
Township
ZIP: 62450 **Lat:** 38-42-33 N **Long:** 88-05-06 W
Pop: 10,170 (1990); 10,702 (1980) **Pop Density:** 215.5
Land: 47.2 sq. mi.; **Water:** 1.0 sq. mi.

Parkersburg
Village
Lat: 38-35-19 N **Long:** 88-03-20 W
Pop: 211 (1990); 268 (1980) **Pop Density:** 301.4
Land: 0.7 sq. mi.; **Water:** 0.0 sq. mi.

Preston
Township
Lat: 38-48-12 N **Long:** 88-05-23 W
Pop: 1,306 (1990); 1,403 (1980) **Pop Density:** 32.1
Land: 40.7 sq. mi.; **Water:** 0.8 sq. mi.

Rock Island County
County Seat: Rock Island (ZIP: 61201)

Pop: 148,723 (1990); 166,759 (1980) **Pop Density:** 348.5
Land: 426.8 sq. mi.; **Water:** 24.4 sq. mi. **Area Code:** 309
On the northwestern border of IL; organized Feb 9, 1831 from Jo Daviess County.
Name origin: For an island in the Mississippi River near the mouth of the Rock River.

Andalusia
Village
ZIP: 61232 **Lat:** 41-26-16 N **Long:** 90-43-31 W
Pop: 1,052 (1990); 1,238 (1980) **Pop Density:** 1052.0
Land: 1.0 sq. mi.; **Water:** 0.0 sq. mi.
In northwestern IL on the Mississippi River. Not coextensive with the town of the same name.
Name origin: For the region in Spain.

*Andalusia
Township
Lat: 41-26-11 N **Long:** 90-43-15 W
Pop: 1,899 (1990); 2,261 (1980) **Pop Density:** 149.5
Land: 12.7 sq. mi.; **Water:** 2.8 sq. mi.

Blackhawk
Township
ZIP: 61264 **Lat:** 41-26-28 N **Long:** 90-35-35 W
Pop: 10,991 (1990); 12,520 (1980) **Pop Density:** 393.9
Land: 27.9 sq. mi.; **Water:** 1.9 sq. mi.
Name origin: Probably for the Sauk and Fox Indian warrior and chief (1767–1838). Formerly called Camden.

Bowling
Township
Lat: 41-22-22 N **Long:** 90-36-32 W
Pop: 3,135 (1990); 3,655 (1980) **Pop Density:** 85.0
Land: 36.9 sq. mi.; **Water:** 0.0 sq. mi.

Buffalo Prairie
Township
Lat: 41-23-05 N **Long:** 90-50-10 W
Pop: 838 (1990); 953 (1980) **Pop Density:** 18.2
Land: 46.0 sq. mi.; **Water:** 4.1 sq. mi.

Canoe Creek
Township
Lat: 41-36-38 N **Long:** 90-11-23 W
Pop: 761 (1990); 962 (1980) **Pop Density:** 52.8
Land: 14.4 sq. mi.; **Water:** 0.5 sq. mi.

Carbon Cliff
Town
ZIP: 61239 **Lat:** 41-29-51 N **Long:** 90-23-25 W
Pop: 1,492 (1990); 1,578 (1980) **Pop Density:** 828.9
Land: 1.8 sq. mi.; **Water:** 0.0 sq. mi.
Name origin: For the coal deposits found in the area.

Coal Valley
Village
ZIP: 61240 **Lat:** 41-26-24 N **Long:** 90-27-29 W
Pop: 2,632 (1990); 3,770 (1980) **Pop Density:** 1754.7
Land: 1.5 sq. mi.; **Water:** 0.0 sq. mi.
Part of the town is in Henry County. Not coextensive with the township of the same name.

*Coal Valley
Township
Lat: 41-26-00 N **Long:** 90-28-31 W
Pop: 4,695 (1990); 5,460 (1980) **Pop Density:** 394.5
Land: 11.9 sq. mi.; **Water:** 0.2 sq. mi.

Coe
Township
Lat: 41-37-04 N **Long:** 90-16-04 W
Pop: 1,538 (1990); 1,343 (1980) **Pop Density:** 43.1
Land: 35.7 sq. mi.; **Water:** 0.0 sq. mi.

Cordova
Village
ZIP: 61242 **Lat:** 41-40-40 N **Long:** 90-19-19 W
Pop: 638 (1990); 697 (1980) **Pop Density:** 1276.0
Land: 0.5 sq. mi.; **Water:** 0.0 sq. mi.
Not coextensive with the town of the same name.

*Cordova
Township
Lat: 41-42-53 N **Long:** 90-16-58 W
Pop: 944 (1990); 1,050 (1980) **Pop Density:** 38.1
Land: 24.8 sq. mi.; **Water:** 2.3 sq. mi.

Drury
Township
Lat: 41-22-34 N **Long:** 90-58-36 W
Pop: 715 (1990); 836 (1980) **Pop Density:** 14.6
Land: 49.1 sq. mi.; **Water:** 4.4 sq. mi.

East Moline
City
ZIP: 61244 **Lat:** 41-30-51 N **Long:** 90-25-38 W
Pop: 20,147 (1990); 20,907 (1980) **Pop Density:** 2370.2
Land: 8.5 sq. mi.; **Water:** 0.0 sq. mi.
Incorporated Dec 20, 1902.

Edgington
Township
Lat: 41-22-32 N **Long:** 90-43-32 W
Pop: 1,619 (1990); 1,900 (1980) **Pop Density:** 45.4
Land: 35.7 sq. mi.; **Water:** 0.0 sq. mi.

ILLINOIS, Rock Island County

Hampton — Village
ZIP: 61256　　Lat: 41-33-11 N　**Long:** 90-24-20 W
Pop: 1,601 (1990); 1,873 (1980)　**Pop Density:** 1067.3
Land: 1.5 sq. mi.; **Water:** 0.0 sq. mi.　**Elev:** 580 ft.

In northwestern IL near the Mississippi River and the IA border. Not coextensive with the town of the same name.
Name origin: Perhaps from a shortening of Southhampton, England.

*Hampton — Township
ZIP: 61256　　Lat: 41-31-46 N　**Long:** 90-22-43 W
Pop: 20,498 (1990); 21,902 (1980)　**Pop Density:** 592.4
Land: 34.6 sq. mi.; **Water:** 2.2 sq. mi.

Hillsdale — Village
ZIP: 61257　　Lat: 41-36-42 N　**Long:** 90-10-30 W
Pop: 489 (1990); 731 (1980)　**Pop Density:** 698.6
Land: 0.7 sq. mi.; **Water:** 0.0 sq. mi.

Milan — Town
ZIP: 61264　　Lat: 41-26-38 N　**Long:** 90-33-40 W
Pop: 5,831 (1990); 6,371 (1980)　**Pop Density:** 1060.2
Land: 5.5 sq. mi.; **Water:** 0.5 sq. mi.

In northwestern IL on the Mississippi River across from Davenport, IA.
Name origin: For Milan, Italy.

Moline — City
ZIP: 61265　　Lat: 41-29-06 N　**Long:** 90-29-19 W
Pop: 43,202 (1990); 46,407 (1980)　**Pop Density:** 2880.1
Land: 15.0 sq. mi.; **Water:** 0.2 sq. mi.

In northwestern IL on the Mississippi River at the IA border, just east of Rock Island. Incorporated Feb 14, 1855. Not coextensive with the town of the same name.
Name origin: From either French *moulin* or Spanish *molino*, both meaning 'mill.'

*Moline — Township
ZIP: 61265　　Lat: 41-30-13 N　**Long:** 90-30-24 W
Pop: 23,484 (1990); 27,144 (1980)　**Pop Density:** 3669.4
Land: 6.4 sq. mi.; **Water:** 1.3 sq. mi.

Oak Grove — Village
ZIP: 61264　　Lat: 41-24-50 N　**Long:** 90-34-23 W
Pop: 626 (1990); 695 (1980)　**Pop Density:** 1043.3
Land: 0.6 sq. mi.; **Water:** 0.0 sq. mi.

Port Byron — Village
ZIP: 61275　　Lat: 41-37-16 N　**Long:** 90-19-25 W
Pop: 1,002 (1990); 1,289 (1980)　**Pop Density:** 385.4
Land: 2.6 sq. mi.; **Water:** 0.0 sq. mi.

Not coextensive with the town of the same name.

*Port Byron — Township
　　Lat: 41-37-41 N　**Long:** 90-20-06 W
Pop: 1,114 (1990); 1,409 (1980)　**Pop Density:** 318.3
Land: 3.5 sq. mi.; **Water:** 1.4 sq. mi.

Rapids City — Town
ZIP: 61278　　Lat: 41-34-54 N　**Long:** 90-20-29 W
Pop: 932 (1990); 1,058 (1980)　**Pop Density:** 621.3
Land: 1.5 sq. mi.; **Water:** 0.0 sq. mi.

Reynolds — Village
ZIP: 61279　　Lat: 41-19-57 N　**Long:** 90-40-22 W
Pop: 506 (1990); 666 (1980)　**Pop Density:** 1686.7
Land: 0.3 sq. mi.; **Water:** 0.0 sq. mi.

Part of the town is also in Mercer County.

Rock Island — City
ZIP: 61201　　Lat: 41-28-28 N　**Long:** 90-34-49 W
Pop: 40,552 (1990); 46,821 (1980)　**Pop Density:** 2685.6
Land: 15.1 sq. mi.; **Water:** 1.2 sq. mi.

In northwestern IL on the Mississippi and Rock rivers, 75 mi. northwest of Peoria. County seat. Incorporated Feb 27, 1841. Not coextensive with the town of the same name.
Name origin: For an island in the Mississippi River near the mouth of the Rock River.

*Rock Island — Township
ZIP: 61201　　Lat: 41-30-23 N　**Long:** 90-33-53 W
Pop: 18,140 (1990); 23,155 (1980)　**Pop Density:** 3779.2
Land: 4.8 sq. mi.; **Water:** 1.0 sq. mi.

Rural — Township
　　Lat: 41-22-09 N　**Long:** 90-29-27 W
Pop: 1,207 (1990); 1,276 (1980)　**Pop Density:** 33.4
Land: 36.1 sq. mi.; **Water:** 0.0 sq. mi.

Silvis — Town
ZIP: 61282　　Lat: 41-30-22 N　**Long:** 90-24-45 W
Pop: 6,926 (1990); 7,130 (1980)　**Pop Density:** 2473.6
Land: 2.8 sq. mi.; **Water:** 0.0 sq. mi.

In northwestern IL near the Mississippi River, just east of East Moline. Incorporated Dec 19, 1906.
Name origin: For 19th-century settler R. S. Silvis.

South Moline — Township
ZIP: 61244　　Lat: 41-29-13 N　**Long:** 90-28-13 W
Pop: 36,781 (1990); 39,014 (1980)　**Pop Density:** 2298.8
Land: 16.0 sq. mi.; **Water:** 1.0 sq. mi.

South Rock Island — Township
ZIP: 61201　　Lat: 41-28-34 N　**Long:** 90-34-10 W
Pop: 19,678 (1990); 21,111 (1980)　**Pop Density:** 2937.0
Land: 6.7 sq. mi.; **Water:** 0.7 sq. mi.

Zuma — Township
　　Lat: 41-33-20 N　**Long:** 90-15-48 W
Pop: 686 (1990); 808 (1980)　**Pop Density:** 29.1
Land: 23.6 sq. mi.; **Water:** 0.6 sq. mi.

St. Clair County
County Seat: Belleville (ZIP: 62220)

Pop: 262,852 (1990); 267,531 (1980) **Pop Density:** 395.9
Land: 663.9 sq. mi.; **Water:** 10.1 sq. mi. **Area Code:** 618

On the west-central border of IL, east of St. Louis, MO; organized Apr 27, 1790 (prior to statehood) from Northwest Territory.

Name origin: For Gen. Arthur St. Clair (1736?–1818), an officer in the French and Indian War and the Revolutionary War, president of the Continental Congress (1787), and governor of the Northwest Territory (1788–1802).

Alorton Village
ZIP: 62207 **Lat:** 38-35-08 N **Long:** 90-06-54 W
Pop: 2,960 (1990); 2,237 (1980) **Pop Density:** 1644.4
Land: 1.8 sq. mi.; **Water:** 0.0 sq. mi.

Belleville City
ZIP: 62220 **Lat:** 38-31-47 N **Long:** 90-00-11 W
Pop: 42,785 (1990); 41,580 (1980) **Pop Density:** 3056.1
Land: 14.0 sq. mi.; **Water:** 0.0 sq. mi. **Elev:** 529 ft.

In southwestern IL, 12 mi. southeast of St. Louis, MO; an industrial and manufacturing city. County seat; incorporated Mar 27, 1819.

Name origin: Named by George Blair from the French 'beautiful city,' because he wanted it to become one. Previously called Compton Hill.

*Belleville Township
ZIP: 62221 **Lat:** 38-31-47 N **Long:** 90-00-11 W
Pop: 42,785 (1990); 41,580 (1980) **Pop Density:** 3056.1
Land: 14.0 sq. mi.; **Water:** 0.0 sq. mi.

Brooklyn Village
ZIP: 62059 **Lat:** 38-39-05 N **Long:** 90-10-02 W
Pop: 1,144 (1990); 1,233 (1980) **Pop Density:** 1430.0
Land: 0.8 sq. mi.; **Water:** 0.0 sq. mi.

Cahokia Village
ZIP: 62206 **Lat:** 38-33-53 N **Long:** 90-10-39 W
Pop: 17,550 (1990); 18,904 (1980) **Pop Density:** 1828.1
Land: 9.6 sq. mi.; **Water:** 0.4 sq. mi.

In southwestern IL on the Mississippi River across from St. Louis, MO. Originally an Indian village; became French missionary post 1699. Incorporated 1927.

Name origin: For an Indian tribe of the Illinois Confederacy; meaning of name is unknown.

Canteen Township
ZIP: 62204 **Lat:** 38-38-00 N **Long:** 90-04-41 W
Pop: 15,029 (1990); 16,593 (1980) **Pop Density:** 863.7
Land: 17.4 sq. mi.; **Water:** 0.0 sq. mi.

Caseyville Village
ZIP: 62232 **Lat:** 38-37-58 N **Long:** 90-01-57 W
Pop: 4,419 (1990); 4,308 (1980) **Pop Density:** 960.7
Land: 4.6 sq. mi.; **Water:** 0.0 sq. mi.

In southwestern IL, 13 mi. east of St. Louis, MO. Not coextensive with the town of the same name.

Name origin: For Zadoc Casey, 19th-century IL lieutenant governor, U.S. representative, and state legislator.

*Caseyville Township
ZIP: 62232 **Lat:** 38-37-05 N **Long:** 89-59-08 W
Pop: 24,981 (1990); 24,274 (1980) **Pop Density:** 713.7
Land: 35.0 sq. mi.; **Water:** 0.1 sq. mi.

Centreville City
ZIP: 62207 **Lat:** 38-34-37 N **Long:** 90-06-05 W
Pop: 7,489 (1990); 9,747 (1980) **Pop Density:** 1783.1
Land: 4.2 sq. mi.; **Water:** 0.0 sq. mi.

In southwestern IL, 6 mi. southeast of St. Louis, MO. Incorporated Oct 9, 1957. Not coextensive with the town of the same name.

*Centreville Township
ZIP: 62207 **Lat:** 38-34-08 N **Long:** 90-08-29 W
Pop: 32,425 (1990); 35,568 (1980) **Pop Density:** 1149.8
Land: 28.2 sq. mi.; **Water:** 1.3 sq. mi.

Collinsville City
ZIP: 62234 **Lat:** 38-39-13 N **Long:** 90-00-37 W
Pop: 2,346 (1990); 1,994 (1980) **Pop Density:** 1675.7
Land: 1.4 sq. mi.; **Water:** 0.0 sq. mi.

In southwestern IL, 13 mi. east of St. Louis, MO. Incorporated Feb 15, 1855. Part of the town is also in Madison County.

Name origin: For the Collins family, founders, especially William Collins.

Dupo Village
ZIP: 62239 **Lat:** 38-31-02 N **Long:** 90-12-34 W
Pop: 3,164 (1990); 3,039 (1980) **Pop Density:** 1054.7
Land: 3.0 sq. mi.; **Water:** 0.0 sq. mi.

In southwestern IL on the Mississippi River, east of St. Louis, MO.

Name origin: A contraction of *Prairie du Pont*, French for 'meadow of the bridge,' referring to a nearby bridged creek.

East Carondelet Village
ZIP: 62240 **Lat:** 38-32-18 N **Long:** 90-14-13 W
Pop: 630 (1990); 628 (1980) **Pop Density:** 525.0
Land: 1.2 sq. mi.; **Water:** 0.0 sq. mi.

East St. Louis City
ZIP: 62201 **Lat:** 38-36-52 N **Long:** 90-07-51 W
Pop: 40,944 (1990); 55,200 (1980) **Pop Density:** 2903.8
Land: 14.1 sq. mi.; **Water:** 0.4 sq. mi.

In southwest IL on the Mississippi River east of St. Louis, MO. Incorporated Feb 16, 1865.

Name origin: A village, known as Cahokia, was established as early as 1699 by French missionaries who hoped to convert local Indian tribes. A new village was platted in 1818, and named Illinoistown. In 1859 the state legislature presented Illinoistown with a new charter incorporating it as a city and renaming it East Saint Louis.

*East St. Louis Township
ZIP: 62201 **Lat:** 38-36-52 N **Long:** 90-07-51 W
Pop: 40,944 (1990); 55,200 (1980) **Pop Density:** 2903.8
Land: 14.1 sq. mi.; **Water:** 0.4 sq. mi.

ILLINOIS, St. Clair County

Engelmann
Township
Lat: 38-26-14 N **Long:** 89-46-01 W
Pop: 576 (1990); 545 (1980) **Pop Density:** 19.4
Land: 29.7 sq. mi.; **Water:** 0.0 sq. mi.

Fairmont City
Village
ZIP: 62201 **Lat:** 38-39-03 N **Long:** 90-06-05 W
Pop: 2,101 (1990); 2,313 (1980) **Pop Density:** 955.0
Land: 2.2 sq. mi.; **Water:** 0.0 sq. mi.

Part of the town is also in Madison County.

Fairview Heights
City
ZIP: 62208 **Lat:** 38-35-48 N **Long:** 90-00-17 W
Pop: 14,351 (1990); 12,111 (1980) **Pop Density:** 1420.9
Land: 10.1 sq. mi.; **Water:** 0.1 sq. mi.

In southwestern IL, a residential suburb of East St. Louis. Incorporated Oct 2, 1969.

Name origin: Descriptively named to promote settlement.

Fayetteville
Village
ZIP: 62258 **Lat:** 38-22-40 N **Long:** 89-47-46 W
Pop: 371 (1990); 385 (1980) **Pop Density:** 1855.0
Land: 0.2 sq. mi.; **Water:** 0.0 sq. mi.

Not coextensive with the town of the same name.

*Fayetteville
Township
Lat: 38-21-27 N **Long:** 89-45-18 W
Pop: 1,599 (1990); 1,555 (1980) **Pop Density:** 36.8
Land: 43.4 sq. mi.; **Water:** 0.5 sq. mi.

Freeburg
Village
ZIP: 62243 **Lat:** 38-25-40 N **Long:** 89-54-29 W
Pop: 3,115 (1990); 2,989 (1980) **Pop Density:** 1832.4
Land: 1.7 sq. mi.; **Water:** 0.0 sq. mi. **Elev:** 518 ft.

Not coextensive with the town of the same name.

*Freeburg
Township
Lat: 38-26-33 N **Long:** 89-52-22 W
Pop: 4,710 (1990); 4,395 (1980) **Pop Density:** 133.4
Land: 35.3 sq. mi.; **Water:** 0.7 sq. mi.

Lebanon
City
ZIP: 62254 **Lat:** 38-36-10 N **Long:** 89-48-53 W
Pop: 3,688 (1990); 3,245 (1980) **Pop Density:** 1844.0
Land: 2.0 sq. mi.; **Water:** 0.0 sq. mi. **Elev:** 515 ft.

Not coextensive with the town of the same name.

*Lebanon
Township
Lat: 38-36-34 N **Long:** 89-45-56 W
Pop: 4,381 (1990); 4,179 (1980) **Pop Density:** 119.7
Land: 36.6 sq. mi.; **Water:** 0.0 sq. mi.

Lenzburg
Village
ZIP: 62255 **Lat:** 38-17-06 N **Long:** 89-49-07 W
Pop: 510 (1990); 435 (1980) **Pop Density:** 425.0
Land: 1.2 sq. mi.; **Water:** 0.1 sq. mi.

Not coextensive with the town of the same name.

*Lenzburg
Township
Lat: 38-15-51 N **Long:** 89-51-40 W
Pop: 1,053 (1990); 888 (1980) **Pop Density:** 36.1
Land: 29.2 sq. mi.; **Water:** 2.2 sq. mi.

Madison
City
ZIP: 62060 **Lat:** 38-39-07 N **Long:** 90-07-51 W
Pop: 6 (1990) **Pop Density:** 15.0
Land: 0.4 sq. mi.; **Water:** 0.0 sq. mi.

Part of the town is also in Madison County.

Name origin: For James Madison (1751–1836), fourth U.S. president.

Marissa
Town
ZIP: 62257 **Lat:** 38-15-18 N **Long:** 89-45-13 W
Pop: 2,375 (1990); 2,568 (1980) **Pop Density:** 742.2
Land: 3.2 sq. mi.; **Water:** 0.0 sq. mi.

Incorporated May 26, 1882. Not coextensive with the town of the same name.

Name origin: Named by an early settler from SC, James Wilson, who took it from Jewish historian Flavius Josephus's (c. 37–c. 100) *Antiquities of the Jews*.

*Marissa
Township
Lat: 38-15-58 N **Long:** 89-45-40 W
Pop: 2,875 (1990); 3,080 (1980) **Pop Density:** 83.3
Land: 34.5 sq. mi.; **Water:** 1.4 sq. mi.

Mascoutah
City
ZIP: 62258 **Lat:** 38-30-32 N **Long:** 89-48-19 W
Pop: 5,511 (1990); 4,962 (1980) **Pop Density:** 1312.1
Land: 4.2 sq. mi.; **Water:** 0.0 sq. mi. **Elev:** 424 ft.

Incorporated Feb 16, 1839. Not coextensive with the town of the same name.

Name origin: From an Algonquian term probably meaning 'prairie.'

*Mascoutah
Township
ZIP: 62258 **Lat:** 38-31-42 N **Long:** 89-45-55 W
Pop: 6,340 (1990); 5,698 (1980) **Pop Density:** 161.7
Land: 39.2 sq. mi.; **Water:** 0.1 sq. mi.

Millstadt
Town
ZIP: 62260 **Lat:** 38-27-33 N **Long:** 90-05-35 W
Pop: 2,566 (1990); 2,736 (1980) **Pop Density:** 2566.0
Land: 1.0 sq. mi.; **Water:** 0.0 sq. mi.

Platted 1836; incorporated 1878. Not coextensive with the town of the same name.

Name origin: A semi-German form of *Centerville*, the town's original name, changed to avoid postal confusion with another Centerville in IL.

*Millstadt
Township
Lat: 38-25-04 N **Long:** 90-05-04 W
Pop: 4,979 (1990); 4,674 (1980) **Pop Density:** 104.4
Land: 47.7 sq. mi.; **Water:** 0.2 sq. mi.

National City
Village
Lat: 38-38-54 N **Long:** 90-08-59 W
Pop: 57 (1990); 70 (1980) **Pop Density:** 57.0
Land: 1.0 sq. mi.; **Water:** 0.0 sq. mi.

New Athens
Town
ZIP: 62264 **Lat:** 38-19-08 N **Long:** 89-52-38 W
Pop: 2,010 (1990); 1,937 (1980) **Pop Density:** 1182.4
Land: 1.7 sq. mi.; **Water:** 0.1 sq. mi.

In southwestern IL on the Kaskaskia River, southeast of E. St. Louis. Settled 1836. Not coextensive with the town of the same name.

Name origin: For Athens, Greece.

*New Athens
Township
Lat: 38-20-54 N **Long:** 89-52-08 W
Pop: 2,588 (1990); 2,490 (1980) **Pop Density:** 74.2
Land: 34.9 sq. mi.; **Water:** 1.1 sq. mi.

New Baden — Town
ZIP: 62265 Lat: 38-32-04 N Long: 89-42-30 W
Pop: 73 (1990); 39 (1980) Pop Density: 730.0
Land: 0.1 sq. mi.; Water: 0.0 sq. mi. Elev: 462 ft.
Part of the town is also in Clinton County.
Name origin: Named in 1855 by German immigrants for the German spa.

O'Fallon — Town
ZIP: 62269 Lat: 38-35-31 N Long: 89-54-47 W
Pop: 16,073 (1990); 12,173 (1980) Pop Density: 2634.9
Land: 6.1 sq. mi.; Water: 0.0 sq. mi. Elev: 550 ft.
In southwestern IL, 15 mi. east of St. Louis, MO. Settled 1854; incorporated Feb 15, 1865. Not coextensive with the town of the same name.
Name origin: For John O'Fallon, prominent citizen of St. Louis and a merchant on the east bank of the Mississippi.

*O'Fallon — Township
ZIP: 62269 Lat: 38-36-58 N Long: 89-52-30 W
Pop: 16,660 (1990); 12,254 (1980) Pop Density: 470.6
Land: 35.4 sq. mi.; Water: 0.3 sq. mi.

Prairie Du Long — Township
Lat: 38-20-52 N Long: 89-58-58 W
Pop: 1,025 (1990); 853 (1980) Pop Density: 28.6
Land: 35.8 sq. mi.; Water: 0.2 sq. mi.

St. Clair — Township
ZIP: 62221 Lat: 38-31-44 N Long: 89-58-49 W
Pop: 27,024 (1990); 21,774 (1980) Pop Density: 1103.0
Land: 24.5 sq. mi.; Water: 0.0 sq. mi.

St. Libory — Village
ZIP: 62282 Lat: 38-21-52 N Long: 89-42-50 W
Pop: 525 (1990); 549 (1980) Pop Density: 656.3
Land: 0.8 sq. mi.; Water: 0.0 sq. mi.

Sauget — Village
Lat: 38-35-21 N Long: 90-10-10 W
Pop: 197 (1990); 205 (1980) Pop Density: 57.9
Land: 3.4 sq. mi.; Water: 0.3 sq. mi.

Shiloh — Village
ZIP: 62269 Lat: 38-33-12 N Long: 89-54-18 W
Pop: 2,655 (1990); 1,045 (1980) Pop Density: 1264.3
Land: 2.1 sq. mi.; Water: 0.0 sq. mi.

Shiloh Valley — Township
ZIP: 62221 Lat: 38-31-34 N Long: 89-52-24 W
Pop: 10,984 (1990); 11,245 (1980) Pop Density: 333.9
Land: 32.9 sq. mi.; Water: 0.0 sq. mi.

Smithton — Village
ZIP: 62285 Lat: 38-24-29 N Long: 89-59-24 W
Pop: 1,587 (1990); 1,447 (1980) Pop Density: 2267.1
Land: 0.7 sq. mi.; Water: 0.0 sq. mi.
Not coextensive with the town of the same name.

*Smithton — Township
Lat: 38-26-32 N Long: 89-59-15 W
Pop: 2,883 (1990); 2,661 (1980) Pop Density: 81.7
Land: 35.3 sq. mi.; Water: 0.4 sq. mi.

Stites — Township
Lat: 38-39-00 N Long: 90-09-45 W
Pop: 1,201 (1990); 1,303 (1980) Pop Density: 571.9
Land: 2.1 sq. mi.; Water: 0.2 sq. mi.

Stookey — Township
ZIP: 62221 Lat: 38-31-10 N Long: 90-05-24 W
Pop: 10,737 (1990); 9,726 (1980) Pop Density: 383.5
Land: 28.0 sq. mi.; Water: 0.0 sq. mi.

Sugar Loaf — Township
ZIP: 62240 Lat: 38-30-00 N Long: 90-11-49 W
Pop: 7,073 (1990); 6,996 (1980) Pop Density: 229.6
Land: 30.8 sq. mi.; Water: 0.9 sq. mi.

Summerfield — Village
ZIP: 62289 Lat: 38-35-44 N Long: 89-44-50 W
Pop: 509 (1990); 487 (1980) Pop Density: 1272.5
Land: 0.4 sq. mi.; Water: 0.0 sq. mi. Elev: 478 ft.

Swansea — Village
ZIP: 62220 Lat: 38-32-31 N Long: 89-59-18 W
Pop: 8,201 (1990); 5,529 (1980) Pop Density: 2645.5
Land: 3.1 sq. mi.; Water: 0.0 sq. mi.

Washington Park — Village
ZIP: 62204 Lat: 38-37-47 N Long: 90-05-31 W
Pop: 7,431 (1990); 8,223 (1980) Pop Density: 2972.4
Land: 2.5 sq. mi.; Water: 0.0 sq. mi.

Saline County
County Seat: Harrisburg (ZIP: 62946)

Pop: 26,551 (1990); 28,448 (1980) Pop Density: 69.3
Land: 383.3 sq. mi.; Water: 3.7 sq. mi. Area Code: 618
In southeastern IL, east of Carbondale; organized Feb 25, 1847 from Gallatin County.
Name origin: For the Saline River, which traverses the county.

Brushy — Township
Lat: 37-46-33 N Long: 88-39-10 W
Pop: 795 (1990); 928 (1980) Pop Density: 23.5
Land: 33.8 sq. mi.; Water: 0.5 sq. mi.

Carriers Mills — Village
ZIP: 62917 Lat: 37-41-18 N Long: 88-37-44 W
Pop: 1,991 (1990); 2,268 (1980) Pop Density: 1659.2
Land: 1.2 sq. mi.; Water: 0.0 sq. mi.

*Carriers Mills — Township
Lat: 37-41-34 N Long: 88-39-10 W
Pop: 2,732 (1990); 2,950 (1980) Pop Density: 71.9
Land: 38.0 sq. mi.; Water: 1.1 sq. mi.

Cottage — Township
Lat: 37-44-01 N Long: 88-25-52 W
Pop: 254 (1990); 243 (1980) Pop Density: 8.2
Land: 30.9 sq. mi.; Water: 0.2 sq. mi.

ILLINOIS, Saline County

East Eldorado
Township
ZIP: 62930   **Lat:** 37-49-13 N   **Long:** 88-25-46 W
Pop: 6,526 (1990); 7,155 (1980)   **Pop Density:** 178.3
Land: 36.6 sq. mi.; **Water:** 0.1 sq. mi.

Eldorado
City
ZIP: 62930   **Lat:** 37-48-42 N   **Long:** 88-26-30 W
Pop: 4,536 (1990); 5,198 (1980)   **Pop Density:** 2061.8
Land: 2.2 sq. mi.; **Water:** 0.0 sq. mi.   **Elev** 389 ft.

Galatia
Village
ZIP: 62935   **Lat:** 37-50-27 N   **Long:** 88-36-49 W
Pop: 983 (1990); 1,042 (1980)   **Pop Density:** 491.5
Land: 2.0 sq. mi.; **Water:** 0.0 sq. mi.   **Elev** 397 ft.
Not coextensive with the town of the same name.

*Galatia
Township
Lat: 37-50-31 N   **Long:** 88-38-59 W
Pop: 1,345 (1990); 1,398 (1980)   **Pop Density:** 72.3
Land: 18.6 sq. mi.; **Water:** 0.1 sq. mi.

Harrisburg
City
ZIP: 62946   **Lat:** 37-44-11 N   **Long:** 88-32-57 W
Pop: 9,289 (1990); 10,410 (1980)   **Pop Density:** 1857.8
Land: 5.0 sq. mi.; **Water:** 0.0 sq. mi.   **Elev** 403 ft.
In southeastern IL, 40 mi. southeast of Mount Vernon. County seat. Incorporated Feb 21, 1861. Not coextensive with the town of the same name.
Name origin: For sawmill proprietor James Harris, its first settler.

*Harrisburg
Township
ZIP: 62946   **Lat:** 37-43-53 N   **Long:** 88-32-28 W
Pop: 11,375 (1990); 12,418 (1980)   **Pop Density:** 308.3
Land: 36.9 sq. mi.; **Water:** 0.4 sq. mi.

Independence
Township
Lat: 37-38-19 N   **Long:** 88-32-43 W
Pop: 1,100 (1990); 961 (1980)   **Pop Density:** 29.5
Land: 37.3 sq. mi.; **Water:** 0.0 sq. mi.

Long Branch
Township
Lat: 37-53-10 N   **Long:** 88-32-19 W
Pop: 265 (1990); 256 (1980)   **Pop Density:** 14.6
Land: 18.2 sq. mi.; **Water:** 0.0 sq. mi.

Mountain
Township
Lat: 37-39-20 N   **Long:** 88-26-03 W
Pop: 349 (1990); 284 (1980)   **Pop Density:** 8.2
Land: 42.4 sq. mi.; **Water:** 0.5 sq. mi.

Muddy
Village
ZIP: 62965   **Lat:** 37-45-53 N   **Long:** 88-31-00 W
Pop: 87 (1990); 88 (1980)   **Pop Density:** 870.0
Land: 0.1 sq. mi.; **Water:** 0.0 sq. mi.

Raleigh
Village
ZIP: 62977   **Lat:** 37-49-31 N   **Long:** 88-31-53 W
Pop: 305 (1990); 352 (1980)   **Pop Density:** 152.5
Land: 2.0 sq. mi.; **Water:** 0.0 sq. mi.
Not coextensive with the town of the same name.

*Raleigh
Township
Lat: 37-49-04 N   **Long:** 88-32-17 W
Pop: 1,150 (1990); 1,111 (1980)   **Pop Density:** 31.8
Land: 36.2 sq. mi.; **Water:** 0.6 sq. mi.

Rector
Township
Lat: 37-53-11 N   **Long:** 88-25-51 W
Pop: 76 (1990); 100 (1980)   **Pop Density:** 4.2
Land: 18.2 sq. mi.; **Water:** 0.0 sq. mi.

Stonefort
Village
Lat: 37-37-05 N   **Long:** 88-42-03 W
Pop: 133 (1990); 140 (1980)   **Pop Density:** 147.8
Land: 0.9 sq. mi.; **Water:** 0.0 sq. mi.
Part of the town is also in Williamson County. Not coextensive with the township of the same name.

*Stonefort
Township
Lat: 37-36-49 N   **Long:** 88-39-04 W
Pop: 346 (1990); 380 (1980)   **Pop Density:** 19.5
Land: 17.7 sq. mi.; **Water:** 0.0 sq. mi.

Tate
Township
Lat: 37-53-03 N   **Long:** 88-38-58 W
Pop: 238 (1990); 264 (1980)   **Pop Density:** 13.1
Land: 18.2 sq. mi.; **Water:** 0.0 sq. mi.

Sangamon County
County Seat: Springfield (ZIP: 62701)

Pop: 178,386 (1990); 176,070 (1980)   **Pop Density:** 205.4
Land: 868.3 sq. mi.; **Water:** 8.8 sq. mi.   **Area Code:** 217
In central IL, east of Decatur; organized Jan 30, 1821 from Bond and Madison counties.
Name origin: For the Sangamon River, which flows through the county; from Ojibway, possibly 'the outlet' or 'the land of plenty to eat.'

Auburn
City
ZIP: 62615   **Lat:** 39-34-38 N   **Long:** 89-44-44 W
Pop: 3,724 (1990); 3,616 (1980)   **Pop Density:** 1379.3
Land: 2.7 sq. mi.; **Water:** 0.0 sq. mi.   **Elev** 626 ft.
Incorporated 1865. Not coextensive with the town of the same name.
Name origin: For the mythical village in the poem "The Deserted Village," by English poet Oliver Goldsmith (1730–74).

*Auburn
Township
ZIP: 62615   **Lat:** 39-34-02 N   **Long:** 89-45-38 W
Pop: 5,208 (1990); 5,082 (1980)   **Pop Density:** 145.5
Land: 35.8 sq. mi.; **Water:** 0.0 sq. mi.

Ball
Township
Lat: 39-38-50 N   **Long:** 89-38-56 W
Pop: 3,475 (1990); 3,280 (1980)   **Pop Density:** 108.9
Land: 31.9 sq. mi.; **Water:** 0.1 sq. mi.

American Places Dictionary — ILLINOIS, Sangamon County

Berlin — Village
ZIP: 62670 Lat: 39-45-27 N Long: 89-54-09 W
Pop: 180 (1990); 210 (1980) Pop Density: 180.0
Land: 1.0 sq. mi.; Water: 0.0 sq. mi.

Buffalo — Village
ZIP: 62515 Lat: 39-50-58 N Long: 89-24-32 W
Pop: 503 (1990); 514 (1980) Pop Density: 1257.5
Land: 0.4 sq. mi.; Water: 0.0 sq. mi. Elev: 611 ft.
Name origin: For the American bison once found in the area.

Buffalo Hart — Township
Lat: 39-53-58 N Long: 89-25-41 W
Pop: 226 (1990); 231 (1980) Pop Density: 10.0
Land: 22.7 sq. mi.; Water: 0.0 sq. mi.

Cantrall — Village
ZIP: 62625 Lat: 39-56-03 N Long: 89-40-48 W
Pop: 123 (1990); 141 (1980) Pop Density: 410.0
Land: 0.3 sq. mi.; Water: 0.0 sq. mi.

Capital — Township
Lat: 39-46-53 N Long: 89-38-40 W
Pop: 104,126 (1990); 100,054 (1980) Pop Density: 2509.1
Land: 41.5 sq. mi.; Water: 6.3 sq. mi.
Coextensive with the city of Springfield.
Name origin: Probably for its location/coextension with the state capital.

Cartwright — Township
Lat: 39-50-19 N Long: 89-54-33 W
Pop: 1,381 (1990); 1,414 (1980) Pop Density: 19.2
Land: 72.0 sq. mi.; Water: 0.0 sq. mi.

Chatham — Village
ZIP: 62629 Lat: 39-40-22 N Long: 89-41-49 W
Pop: 6,074 (1990); 5,597 (1980) Pop Density: 2169.3
Land: 2.8 sq. mi.; Water: 0.0 sq. mi. Elev: 606 ft.
Not coextensive with the town of the same name.
Name origin: For England's prime minister William Pitt (1708–78), the Earl of Chatham.

*Chatham — Township
Lat: 39-39-13 N Long: 89-45-20 W
Pop: 4,961 (1990); 4,736 (1980) Pop Density: 132.3
Land: 37.5 sq. mi.; Water: 0.0 sq. mi.

Clear Lake — Village
Lat: 39-48-50 N Long: 89-34-00 W
Pop: 193 (1990); 236 (1980) Pop Density: 1930.0
Land: 0.1 sq. mi.; Water: 0.0 sq. mi.
Not coextensive with the town of the same name.

*Clear Lake — Township
ZIP: 62707 Lat: 39-49-48 N Long: 89-32-34 W
Pop: 7,780 (1990); 7,587 (1980) Pop Density: 227.5
Land: 34.2 sq. mi.; Water: 0.7 sq. mi.

Cooper — Township
Lat: 39-44-37 N Long: 89-26-23 W
Pop: 771 (1990); 748 (1980) Pop Density: 27.1
Land: 28.5 sq. mi.; Water: 0.2 sq. mi.

Cotton Hill — Township
Lat: 39-39-33 N Long: 89-32-40 W
Pop: 954 (1990); 939 (1980) Pop Density: 32.0
Land: 29.8 sq. mi.; Water: 0.4 sq. mi.

Curran — Township
Lat: 39-44-31 N Long: 89-45-55 W
Pop: 1,505 (1990); 1,537 (1980) Pop Density: 44.4
Land: 33.9 sq. mi.; Water: 0.0 sq. mi.

Dawson — Village
ZIP: 62520 Lat: 39-51-13 N Long: 89-27-45 W
Pop: 536 (1990); 532 (1980) Pop Density: 595.6
Land: 0.9 sq. mi.; Water: 0.0 sq. mi. Elev: 599 ft.

Divernon — Village
ZIP: 62530 Lat: 39-34-09 N Long: 89-39-14 W
Pop: 1,178 (1990); 1,081 (1980) Pop Density: 1682.9
Land: 0.7 sq. mi.; Water: 0.0 sq. mi. Elev: 617 ft.
Not coextensive with the town of the same name.

*Divernon — Township
Lat: 39-34-05 N Long: 89-39-33 W
Pop: 1,484 (1990); 1,370 (1980) Pop Density: 54.6
Land: 27.2 sq. mi.; Water: 0.0 sq. mi.

Fancy Creek — Township
Lat: 39-55-06 N Long: 89-39-35 W
Pop: 3,293 (1990); 2,630 (1980) Pop Density: 72.7
Land: 45.3 sq. mi.; Water: 0.0 sq. mi.

Gardner — Township
Lat: 39-50-36 N Long: 89-46-13 W
Pop: 3,870 (1990); 3,037 (1980) Pop Density: 85.8
Land: 45.1 sq. mi.; Water: 0.2 sq. mi.

Grandview — Village
ZIP: 62702 Lat: 39-49-04 N Long: 89-37-01 W
Pop: 1,647 (1990); 1,794 (1980) Pop Density: 5490.0
Land: 0.3 sq. mi.; Water: 0.0 sq. mi.

Illiopolis — Town
ZIP: 62539 Lat: 39-51-04 N Long: 89-14-49 W
Pop: 934 (1990); 1,118 (1980) Pop Density: 2335.0
Land: 0.4 sq. mi.; Water: 0.0 sq. mi. Elev: 602 ft.
Not coextensive with the town of the same name.

*Illiopolis — Township
Lat: 39-51-49 N Long: 89-15-34 W
Pop: 1,366 (1990); 1,629 (1980) Pop Density: 40.1
Land: 34.1 sq. mi.; Water: 0.0 sq. mi.

Island Grove — Township
Lat: 39-45-42 N Long: 89-53-59 W
Pop: 494 (1990); 565 (1980) Pop Density: 17.5
Land: 28.2 sq. mi.; Water: 0.0 sq. mi.

Jerome — Village
ZIP: 62704 Lat: 39-46-00 N Long: 89-40-54 W
Pop: 1,206 (1990); 1,374 (1980) Pop Density: 4020.0
Land: 0.3 sq. mi.; Water: 0.0 sq. mi.

Lanesville — Township
Lat: 39-50-25 N Long: 89-20-09 W
Pop: 225 (1990); 280 (1980) Pop Density: 6.2
Land: 36.2 sq. mi.; Water: 0.0 sq. mi.

Leland Grove — City
ZIP: 62705 Lat: 39-46-44 N Long: 89-41-04 W
Pop: 1,679 (1990); 1,864 (1980) Pop Density: 2798.3
Land: 0.6 sq. mi.; Water: 0.0 sq. mi.

ILLINOIS, Sangamon County

Loami — Town
ZIP: 62661 Lat: 39-40-27 N Long: 89-50-52 W
Pop: 802 (1990); 770 (1980) Pop Density: 891.1
Land: 0.9 sq. mi.; Water: 0.0 sq. mi.

Incorporated July 29, 1875. Not coextensive with the town of the same name.

*Loami — Township
Lat: 39-39-02 N Long: 89-50-50 W
Pop: 1,071 (1990); 1,095 (1980) Pop Density: 50.8
Land: 21.1 sq. mi.; Water: 0.0 sq. mi.

Maxwell — Township
Lat: 39-39-11 N Long: 89-54-56 W
Pop: 215 (1990); 224 (1980) Pop Density: 10.2
Land: 21.0 sq. mi.; Water: 0.0 sq. mi.

Mechanicsburg — Town
ZIP: 62545 Lat: 39-48-36 N Long: 89-23-53 W
Pop: 538 (1990); 515 (1980) Pop Density: 1345.0
Land: 0.4 sq. mi.; Water: 0.0 sq. mi.

In central IL, 13 mi. east of Springfield. Incorporated Mar 26, 1869. Not coextensive with the town of the same name.

Name origin: For the fact that most of the male settlers were mechanics. Previously called Clear Creek.

*Mechanicsburg — Township
Lat: 39-49-47 N Long: 89-25-49 W
Pop: 2,261 (1990); 2,112 (1980) Pop Density: 62.1
Land: 36.4 sq. mi.; Water: 0.0 sq. mi.

New Berlin — Village
ZIP: 62670 Lat: 39-43-30 N Long: 89-54-42 W
Pop: 797 (1990); 834 (1980) Pop Density: 885.6
Land: 0.9 sq. mi.; Water: 0.0 sq. mi. Elev: 654 ft.

Not coextensive with the town of the same name.

*New Berlin — Township
Lat: 39-43-16 N Long: 89-54-19 W
Pop: 990 (1990); 1,069 (1980) Pop Density: 31.8
Land: 31.1 sq. mi.; Water: 0.1 sq. mi.

Pawnee — Town
ZIP: 62558 Lat: 39-35-31 N Long: 89-34-51 W
Pop: 2,384 (1990); 2,577 (1980) Pop Density: 2167.3
Land: 1.1 sq. mi.; Water: 0.0 sq. mi.

In west-central IL, 13 mi. south of Springfield. Not coextensive with the town of the same name.

Name origin: For the Pawnee Indians.

*Pawnee — Township
Lat: 39-34-08 N Long: 89-34-12 W
Pop: 2,775 (1990); 2,878 (1980) Pop Density: 102.8
Land: 27.0 sq. mi.; Water: 0.0 sq. mi.

Pleasant Plains — Village
ZIP: 62677 Lat: 39-52-23 N Long: 89-55-12 W
Pop: 701 (1990); 688 (1980) Pop Density: 637.3
Land: 1.1 sq. mi.; Water: 0.0 sq. mi. Elev: 615 ft.

Riverton — Town
ZIP: 62561 Lat: 39-50-57 N Long: 89-32-24 W
Pop: 2,638 (1990); 2,783 (1980) Pop Density: 1648.8
Land: 1.6 sq. mi.; Water: 0.0 sq. mi. Elev: 552 ft.

In central IL on the Sangamon River, a suburb of Springfield.

Name origin: For its descriptive connotations.

Rochester — Town
ZIP: 62563 Lat: 39-45-02 N Long: 89-32-29 W
Pop: 2,676 (1990); 2,488 (1980) Pop Density: 1574.1
Land: 1.7 sq. mi.; Water: 0.0 sq. mi. Elev: 577 ft.

In central IL, a suburb of Springfield. Not coextensive with the town of the same name.

Name origin: For Rochester, NY.

*Rochester — Township
Lat: 39-44-45 N Long: 89-31-59 W
Pop: 4,432 (1990); 4,120 (1980) Pop Density: 129.6
Land: 34.2 sq. mi.; Water: 0.2 sq. mi.

Sherman — Village
ZIP: 62684 Lat: 39-53-11 N Long: 89-36-32 W
Pop: 2,080 (1990); 1,501 (1980) Pop Density: 770.4
Land: 2.7 sq. mi.; Water: 0.0 sq. mi.

Southern View — Village
ZIP: 62703 Lat: 39-45-29 N Long: 89-39-07 W
Pop: 1,906 (1990); 1,306 (1980) Pop Density: 4765.0
Land: 0.4 sq. mi.; Water: 0.0 sq. mi.

Spaulding — Village
ZIP: 62561 Lat: 39-52-00 N Long: 89-32-31 W
Pop: 440 (1990); 428 (1980) Pop Density: 1466.7
Land: 0.3 sq. mi.; Water: 0.0 sq. mi.

Springfield — City
ZIP: 62701 Lat: 39-46-53 N Long: 89-38-40 W
Pop: 105,227 (1990); 100,054 (1980) Pop Density: 2475.9
Land: 42.5 sq. mi.; Water: 6.3 sq. mi.

In central IL on the Sangamon River, 60 mi. south of Peoria. Settled 1818; incorporated Feb 3, 1840. County seat (1821); designated state capital in 1837 but offices not moved from Vandalia until 1839. Transfer of capital from Vandalia was led by county representative Abraham Lincoln (1809–65), who lived here until his presidency (1861–65). Site of Lincoln's burial.

*Springfield — Township
ZIP: 62702 Lat: 39-50-35 N Long: 89-39-39 W
Pop: 7,857 (1990); 9,407 (1980) Pop Density: 523.8
Land: 15.0 sq. mi.; Water: 0.2 sq. mi.

Talkington — Township
Lat: 39-33-57 N Long: 89-52-22 W
Pop: 257 (1990); 319 (1980) Pop Density: 6.9
Land: 37.4 sq. mi.; Water: 0.0 sq. mi.

Thayer — Village
ZIP: 62689 Lat: 39-32-23 N Long: 89-45-30 W
Pop: 730 (1990); 759 (1980) Pop Density: 1216.7
Land: 0.6 sq. mi.; Water: 0.0 sq. mi.

Virden — City
ZIP: 62690 Lat: 39-31-29 N Long: 89-45-52 W
Pop: 21 (1990); 14 (1980) Pop Density: 210.0
Land: 0.1 sq. mi.; Water: 0.0 sq. mi.

In southwest-central IL, 30 mi. south of Springfield. Part of the town is also in Macoupin County.

Name origin: For the Virden Mine Company.

Williams — Township
Lat: 39-55-30 N Long: 89-32-41 W
Pop: 2,797 (1990); 2,482 (1980) Pop Density: 65.4
Land: 42.8 sq. mi.; Water: 0.1 sq. mi.

American Places Dictionary   ILLINOIS, Schuyler County

Williamsville — Town
ZIP: 62693   **Lat:** 39-57-10 N   **Long:** 89-33-22 W
Pop: 1,140 (1990); 996 (1980)   **Pop Density:** 1266.7
Land: 0.9 sq. mi.; **Water:** 0.0 sq. mi.

Woodside — Township
ZIP: 62703   **Lat:** 39-44-32 N   **Long:** 89-39-30 W
Pop: 14,612 (1990); 16,654 (1980)   **Pop Density:** 807.3
Land: 18.1 sq. mi.; **Water:** 0.0 sq. mi.

Schuyler County
County Seat: Rushville (ZIP: 62681)

Pop: 7,498 (1990); 8,365 (1980)   **Pop Density:** 17.1
Land: 437.4 sq. mi.; **Water:** 4.1 sq. mi.   **Area Code:** 217

In west-central IL, northeast of Quincy; organized Jan 13, 1825 from Pike and Fulton counties.

Name origin: For Gen. Philip John Schuyler (1733–1804), an officer in the Revolutionary War, member of the Continental Congress (1775–77; 1778–81), and U.S. senator from NY (1789–91; 1797–98).

Bainbridge — Township
Lat: 40-03-01 N   **Long:** 90-31-18 W
Pop: 526 (1990); 633 (1980)   **Pop Density:** 12.0
Land: 43.8 sq. mi.; **Water:** 1.3 sq. mi.

Birmingham — Township
Lat: 40-14-36 N   **Long:** 90-51-24 W
Pop: 169 (1990); 210 (1980)   **Pop Density:** 4.4
Land: 38.1 sq. mi.; **Water:** 0.0 sq. mi.

Brooklyn — Township
Lat: 40-13-57 N   **Long:** 90-44-03 W
Pop: 234 (1990); 272 (1980)   **Pop Density:** 6.3
Land: 37.1 sq. mi.; **Water:** 0.0 sq. mi.

Browning — Village
ZIP: 62624   **Lat:** 40-07-41 N   **Long:** 90-22-22 W
Pop: 193 (1990); 246 (1980)   **Pop Density:** 643.3
Land: 0.3 sq. mi.; **Water:** 0.0 sq. mi.
Not coextensive with the town of the same name.

*Browning — Township
Lat: 40-08-42 N   **Long:** 90-23-52 W
Pop: 556 (1990); 682 (1980)   **Pop Density:** 19.3
Land: 28.8 sq. mi.; **Water:** 0.4 sq. mi.

Buena Vista — Township
Lat: 40-08-21 N   **Long:** 90-37-08 W
Pop: 1,433 (1990); 1,479 (1980)   **Pop Density:** 39.3
Land: 36.5 sq. mi.; **Water:** 0.0 sq. mi.

Camden — Village
ZIP: 62319   **Lat:** 40-09-10 N   **Long:** 90-46-20 W
Pop: 115 (1990); 120 (1980)   **Pop Density:** 143.8
Land: 0.8 sq. mi.; **Water:** 0.0 sq. mi.
Not coextensive with the town of the same name.

*Camden — Township
Lat: 40-08-51 N   **Long:** 90-44-32 W
Pop: 317 (1990); 345 (1980)   **Pop Density:** 8.6
Land: 36.9 sq. mi.; **Water:** 0.0 sq. mi.

Frederick — Township
Lat: 40-04-53 N   **Long:** 90-26-21 W
Pop: 164 (1990); 248 (1980)   **Pop Density:** 11.9
Land: 13.8 sq. mi.; **Water:** 1.3 sq. mi.

Hickory — Township
Lat: 40-10-11 N   **Long:** 90-16-17 W
Pop: 210 (1990); 224 (1980)   **Pop Density:** 11.9
Land: 17.7 sq. mi.; **Water:** 0.9 sq. mi.

Huntsville — Township
Lat: 40-08-54 N   **Long:** 90-51-01 W
Pop: 189 (1990); 274 (1980)   **Pop Density:** 5.0
Land: 37.9 sq. mi.; **Water:** 0.0 sq. mi.

Littleton — Village
Lat: 40-14-04 N   **Long:** 90-37-23 W
Pop: 181 (1990); 168 (1980)   **Pop Density:** 150.8
Land: 1.2 sq. mi.; **Water:** 0.0 sq. mi.
Not coextensive with the town of the same name.

*Littleton — Township
Lat: 40-14-04 N   **Long:** 90-37-23 W
Pop: 386 (1990); 454 (1980)   **Pop Density:** 10.6
Land: 36.5 sq. mi.; **Water:** 0.0 sq. mi.

Oakland — Township
Lat: 40-13-34 N   **Long:** 90-30-37 W
Pop: 201 (1990); 240 (1980)   **Pop Density:** 5.5
Land: 36.4 sq. mi.; **Water:** 0.0 sq. mi.

Rushville — Town
ZIP: 62681   **Lat:** 40-07-11 N   **Long:** 90-33-56 W
Pop: 3,229 (1990); 3,348 (1980)   **Pop Density:** 2152.7
Land: 1.5 sq. mi.; **Water:** 0.0 sq. mi.   **Elev:** 676 ft.
In western IL on the La Moine River, southwest of Peoria. Not coextensive with the town of the same name.
Name origin: For Philadelphia physician William Rush.

*Rushville — Township
Lat: 40-08-52 N   **Long:** 90-30-31 W
Pop: 2,776 (1990); 2,874 (1980)   **Pop Density:** 76.3
Land: 36.4 sq. mi.; **Water:** 0.2 sq. mi.

Woodstock — Township
Lat: 40-03-35 N   **Long:** 90-37-03 W
Pop: 337 (1990); 430 (1980)   **Pop Density:** 9.0
Land: 37.3 sq. mi.; **Water:** 0.0 sq. mi.

ILLINOIS, Scott County — *American Places Dictionary*

Scott County
County Seat: Winchester (ZIP: 62694)

Pop: 5,644 (1990); 6,142 (1980)   **Pop Density:** 22.5
Land: 251.0 sq. mi.; **Water:** 1.8 sq. mi.   **Area Code:** 217

In west-central IL, southwest of Springfield; organized Feb 16, 1839 from Morgan County.

Name origin: For the county in KY.

Alsey — Village
ZIP: 62610   **Lat:** 39-33-33 N   **Long:** 90-26-00 W
Pop: 253 (1990); 318 (1980)   **Pop Density:** 421.7
Land: 0.6 sq. mi.; **Water:** 0.0 sq. mi.

Bluffs — Village
ZIP: 62621   **Lat:** 39-44-59 N   **Long:** 90-32-03 W
Pop: 774 (1990); 821 (1980)   **Pop Density:** 774.0
Land: 1.0 sq. mi.; **Water:** 0.0 sq. mi.   **Elev:** 474 ft.

Exeter — Village
ZIP: 62621   **Lat:** 39-43-08 N   **Long:** 90-29-45 W
Pop: 59 (1990); 73 (1980)   **Pop Density:** 84.3
Land: 0.7 sq. mi.; **Water:** 0.0 sq. mi.

Glasgow — Village
ZIP: 62694   **Lat:** 39-32-58 N   **Long:** 90-28-46 W
Pop: 163 (1990); 171 (1980)   **Pop Density:** 163.0
Land: 1.0 sq. mi.; **Water:** 0.0 sq. mi.   **Elev:** 587 ft.

Manchester — Town
ZIP: 62663   **Lat:** 39-32-31 N   **Long:** 90-19-49 W
Pop: 347 (1990); 387 (1980)   **Pop Density:** 347.0
Land: 1.0 sq. mi.; **Water:** 0.0 sq. mi.

In west-central IL, 40 mi. southwest of Springfield. Incorporated Feb 21, 1861.

Name origin: For Manchester, England.

Naples — Town
Lat: 39-45-14 N   **Long:** 90-36-28 W
Pop: 130 (1990); 128 (1980)   **Pop Density:** 216.7
Land: 0.6 sq. mi.; **Water:** 0.0 sq. mi.

Winchester — City
ZIP: 62694   **Lat:** 39-37-45 N   **Long:** 90-27-23 W
Pop: 1,769 (1990); 1,716 (1980)   **Pop Density:** 1608.2
Land: 1.1 sq. mi.; **Water:** 0.0 sq. mi.   **Elev:** 546 ft.

In western IL, 42 mi. southwest of Springfield. Founded 1830.

Name origin: Chosen by a KY settler when surveyors let him name the city in exchange for a jug of whiskey.

Shelby County
County Seat: Shelbyville (ZIP: 62565)

Pop: 22,261 (1990); 23,923 (1980)   **Pop Density:** 29.3
Land: 758.6 sq. mi.; **Water:** 9.5 sq. mi.   **Area Code:** 217

In central IL, south of Decatur; organized Jan 23, 1827 from Fayette County.

Name origin: For Gen. Isaac Shelby (1750–1826), officer in the Revolutionary War, NC legislator, and governor of KY (1792–96; 1812–16).

Ash Grove — Township
Lat: 39-23-40 N   **Long:** 88-31-48 W
Pop: 502 (1990); 519 (1980)   **Pop Density:** 11.9
Land: 42.1 sq. mi.; **Water:** 0.3 sq. mi.

Big Spring — Township
Lat: 39-18-28 N   **Long:** 88-31-28 W
Pop: 658 (1990); 682 (1980)   **Pop Density:** 22.4
Land: 29.4 sq. mi.; **Water:** 0.3 sq. mi.

Clarksburg — Township
Lat: 39-18-57 N   **Long:** 88-45-11 W
Pop: 371 (1990); 367 (1980)   **Pop Density:** 13.7
Land: 27.1 sq. mi.; **Water:** 0.0 sq. mi.

Cold Spring — Township
Lat: 39-18-04 N   **Long:** 88-57-51 W
Pop: 372 (1990); 390 (1980)   **Pop Density:** 10.7
Land: 34.9 sq. mi.; **Water:** 0.0 sq. mi.

Cowden — Village
ZIP: 62422   **Lat:** 39-14-56 N   **Long:** 88-51-31 W
Pop: 599 (1990); 623 (1980)   **Pop Density:** 1497.5
Land: 0.4 sq. mi.; **Water:** 0.0 sq. mi.

Dry Point — Township
Lat: 39-14-42 N   **Long:** 88-51-40 W
Pop: 1,096 (1990); 1,130 (1980)   **Pop Density:** 45.5
Land: 24.1 sq. mi.; **Water:** 0.0 sq. mi.

Findlay — Village
ZIP: 62534   **Lat:** 39-31-15 N   **Long:** 88-45-15 W
Pop: 787 (1990); 868 (1980)   **Pop Density:** 715.5
Land: 1.1 sq. mi.; **Water:** 0.0 sq. mi.

Flat Branch — Township
Lat: 39-33-58 N   **Long:** 88-58-24 W
Pop: 438 (1990); 510 (1980)   **Pop Density:** 13.0
Land: 33.8 sq. mi.; **Water:** 0.0 sq. mi.

Herrick
Village
ZIP: 62431 **Lat:** 39-13-08 N **Long:** 88-59-07 W
Pop: 466 (1990); 470 (1980) **Pop Density:** 1165.0
Land: 0.4 sq. mi.; **Water:** 0.0 sq. mi.
Not coextensive with the town of the same name.

*Herrick
Township
Lat: 39-14-40 N **Long:** 88-58-08 W
Pop: 628 (1990); 664 (1980) **Pop Density:** 36.1
Land: 17.4 sq. mi.; **Water:** 0.0 sq. mi.

Holland
Township
Lat: 39-14-37 N **Long:** 88-44-45 W
Pop: 408 (1990); 453 (1980) **Pop Density:** 15.1
Land: 27.0 sq. mi.; **Water:** 0.0 sq. mi.

Lakewood
Township
Lat: 39-18-39 N **Long:** 88-51-19 W
Pop: 415 (1990); 507 (1980) **Pop Density:** 13.8
Land: 30.1 sq. mi.; **Water:** 0.0 sq. mi.

Moweaqua
Town
ZIP: 62550 **Lat:** 39-37-31 N **Long:** 89-01-03 W
Pop: 1,785 (1990); 1,922 (1980) **Pop Density:** 2231.3
Land: 0.8 sq. mi.; **Water:** 0.0 sq. mi.
Part of the town is also in Christian County. Town and township are not coextensive.
Name origin: From the Potawatomi term probably meaning 'weeping woman' or 'wolf woman.'

*Moweaqua
Township
Lat: 39-38-13 N **Long:** 88-58-45 W
Pop: 2,001 (1990); 2,130 (1980) **Pop Density:** 119.1
Land: 16.8 sq. mi.; **Water:** 0.0 sq. mi.

Oconee
Village
ZIP: 62553 **Lat:** 39-17-11 N **Long:** 89-06-22 W
Pop: 201 (1990); 240 (1980) **Pop Density:** 502.5
Land: 0.4 sq. mi.; **Water:** 0.0 sq. mi.
Not coextensive with the town of the same name.

*Oconee
Township
Lat: 39-17-14 N **Long:** 89-04-51 W
Pop: 796 (1990); 872 (1980) **Pop Density:** 14.4
Land: 55.1 sq. mi.; **Water:** 0.1 sq. mi.

Okaw
Township
Lat: 39-28-13 N **Long:** 88-45-02 W
Pop: 914 (1990); 888 (1980) **Pop Density:** 29.5
Land: 31.0 sq. mi.; **Water:** 4.6 sq. mi.

Penn
Township
Lat: 39-37-10 N **Long:** 88-51-24 W
Pop: 136 (1990); 176 (1980) **Pop Density:** 5.7
Land: 23.8 sq. mi.; **Water:** 0.0 sq. mi.

Pickaway
Township
Lat: 39-33-46 N **Long:** 88-52-08 W
Pop: 203 (1990); 252 (1980) **Pop Density:** 6.8
Land: 29.7 sq. mi.; **Water:** 0.0 sq. mi.

Prairie
Township
Lat: 39-16-56 N **Long:** 88-38-17 W
Pop: 1,219 (1990); 1,349 (1980) **Pop Density:** 22.5
Land: 54.2 sq. mi.; **Water:** 0.0 sq. mi.

Richland
Township
Lat: 39-23-26 N **Long:** 88-38-32 W
Pop: 777 (1990); 817 (1980) **Pop Density:** 21.4
Land: 36.3 sq. mi.; **Water:** 0.0 sq. mi.

Ridge
Township
Lat: 39-28-42 N **Long:** 88-51-46 W
Pop: 512 (1990); 542 (1980) **Pop Density:** 14.5
Land: 35.3 sq. mi.; **Water:** 0.0 sq. mi.

Rose
Township
Lat: 39-23-28 N **Long:** 88-51-43 W
Pop: 1,799 (1990); 1,812 (1980) **Pop Density:** 50.7
Land: 35.5 sq. mi.; **Water:** 0.1 sq. mi.

Rural
Township
Lat: 39-28-44 N **Long:** 88-58-13 W
Pop: 354 (1990); 363 (1980) **Pop Density:** 10.3
Land: 34.5 sq. mi.; **Water:** 0.0 sq. mi.

Shelbyville
City
ZIP: 62565 **Lat:** 39-24-25 N **Long:** 88-48-14 W
Pop: 4,943 (1990); 5,259 (1980) **Pop Density:** 1977.2
Land: 2.5 sq. mi.; **Water:** 0.0 sq. mi. **Elev:** 650 ft.
Not coextensive with the town of the same name.

*Shelbyville
Township
Lat: 39-23-21 N **Long:** 88-44-52 W
Pop: 4,797 (1990); 5,152 (1980) **Pop Density:** 140.7
Land: 34.1 sq. mi.; **Water:** 1.8 sq. mi.

Sigel
Town
ZIP: 62462 **Lat:** 39-13-34 N **Long:** 88-29-42 W
Pop: 344 (1990); 360 (1980) **Pop Density:** 1146.7
Land: 0.3 sq. mi.; **Water:** 0.0 sq. mi.
Not coextensive with the town of the same name.

*Sigel
Township
Lat: 39-15-04 N **Long:** 88-31-27 W
Pop: 738 (1990); 781 (1980) **Pop Density:** 31.0
Land: 23.8 sq. mi.; **Water:** 0.0 sq. mi.

Stewardson
Village
ZIP: 62463 **Lat:** 39-15-51 N **Long:** 88-37-47 W
Pop: 660 (1990); 745 (1980) **Pop Density:** 1100.0
Land: 0.6 sq. mi.; **Water:** 0.0 sq. mi.

Strasburg
Village
ZIP: 62465 **Lat:** 39-21-01 N **Long:** 88-37-23 W
Pop: 473 (1990); 488 (1980) **Pop Density:** 946.0
Land: 0.5 sq. mi.; **Water:** 0.0 sq. mi. **Elev:** 642 ft.

Todds Point
Township
Lat: 39-32-36 N **Long:** 88-45-34 W
Pop: 496 (1990); 561 (1980) **Pop Density:** 26.0
Land: 19.1 sq. mi.; **Water:** 0.6 sq. mi.

Tower Hill
Village
ZIP: 62571 **Lat:** 39-23-12 N **Long:** 88-57-34 W
Pop: 601 (1990); 715 (1980) **Pop Density:** 601.0
Land: 1.0 sq. mi.; **Water:** 0.0 sq. mi. **Elev:** 658 ft.
Not coextensive with the town of the same name.

*Tower Hill
Township
Lat: 39-23-24 N **Long:** 88-58-07 W
Pop: 1,133 (1990); 1,449 (1980) **Pop Density:** 32.6
Land: 34.8 sq. mi.; **Water:** 0.2 sq. mi.

Windsor
City
ZIP: 61957 **Lat:** 39-26-17 N **Long:** 88-35-44 W
Pop: 1,143 (1990); 1,228 (1980) **Pop Density:** 1905.0
Land: 0.6 sq. mi.; **Water:** 0.0 sq. mi. **Elev:** 711 ft.
Not coextensive with the town of the same name.

ILLINOIS, Shelby County

*Windsor   Township
Lat: 39-28-17 N   **Long:** 88-39-09 W
Pop: 1,498 (1990); 1,557 (1980)   **Pop Density:** 52.4
Land: 28.6 sq. mi.; **Water:** 1.5 sq. mi.

Stark County
County Seat: Toulon (ZIP: 61483)

Pop: 6,534 (1990); 7,389 (1980)   **Pop Density:** 22.7
Land: 287.9 sq. mi.; **Water:** 0.3 sq. mi.   **Area Code:** 309
In central IL, north of Peoria; organized Mar 2, 1839 from Knox and Putnam counties.
Name origin: For Gen. John Stark (1728–1822), officer in the French and Indian War and the Revolutionary War.

Bradford   Town
ZIP: 61421   **Lat:** 41-10-36 N   **Long:** 89-39-25 W
Pop: 678 (1990); 924 (1980)   **Pop Density:** 1695.0
Land: 0.4 sq. mi.; **Water:** 0.0 sq. mi.   **Elev:** 810 ft.

Elmira   Township
Lat: 41-11-34 N   **Long:** 89-48-26 W
Pop: 412 (1990); 526 (1980)   **Pop Density:** 11.7
Land: 35.3 sq. mi.; **Water:** 0.0 sq. mi.

Essex   Township
Lat: 41-01-19 N   **Long:** 89-48-26 W
Pop: 672 (1990); 802 (1980)   **Pop Density:** 18.6
Land: 36.1 sq. mi.; **Water:** 0.0 sq. mi.

Goshen   Township
Lat: 41-06-10 N   **Long:** 89-55-55 W
Pop: 760 (1990); 851 (1980)   **Pop Density:** 20.8
Land: 36.5 sq. mi.; **Water:** 0.0 sq. mi.

La Fayette   Village
Lat: 41-06-35 N   **Long:** 89-58-24 W
Pop: 231 (1990); 281 (1980)   **Pop Density:** 1155.0
Land: 0.2 sq. mi.; **Water:** 0.0 sq. mi.

Osceola   Township
Lat: 41-11-11 N   **Long:** 89-41-31 W
Pop: 1,084 (1990); 1,304 (1980)   **Pop Density:** 30.5
Land: 35.5 sq. mi.; **Water:** 0.0 sq. mi.

Penn   Township
Lat: 41-06-04 N   **Long:** 89-41-12 W
Pop: 402 (1990); 391 (1980)   **Pop Density:** 11.2
Land: 36.0 sq. mi.; **Water:** 0.0 sq. mi.

Toulon   City
ZIP: 61483   **Lat:** 41-05-40 N   **Long:** 89-51-49 W
Pop: 1,328 (1990); 1,390 (1980)   **Pop Density:** 1475.6
Land: 0.9 sq. mi.; **Water:** 0.0 sq. mi.
Not coextensive with the town of the same name.
Name origin: For Toulon, France.

*Toulon   Township
Lat: 41-06-00 N   **Long:** 89-48-54 W
Pop: 2,464 (1990); 2,632 (1980)   **Pop Density:** 69.4
Land: 35.5 sq. mi.; **Water:** 0.2 sq. mi.

Valley   Township
Lat: 41-00-58 N   **Long:** 89-41-39 W
Pop: 398 (1990); 493 (1980)   **Pop Density:** 10.9
Land: 36.5 sq. mi.; **Water:** 0.0 sq. mi.

West Jersey   Township
Lat: 41-01-11 N   **Long:** 89-55-40 W
Pop: 342 (1990); 390 (1980)   **Pop Density:** 9.3
Land: 36.6 sq. mi.; **Water:** 0.0 sq. mi.

Wyoming   Town
ZIP: 61491   **Lat:** 41-03-52 N   **Long:** 89-46-20 W
Pop: 1,462 (1990); 1,614 (1980)   **Pop Density:** 2088.6
Land: 0.7 sq. mi.; **Water:** 0.0 sq. mi.   **Elev:** 707 ft.

Stephenson County
County Seat: Freeport (ZIP: 61032)

Pop: 48,052 (1990); 49,536 (1980)   **Pop Density:** 85.2
Land: 564.3 sq. mi.; **Water:** 0.5 sq. mi.   **Area Code:** 815
Located on northern border of Illinois; organized on Mar 4, 1837 from Winnebago and Jo Daviess counties
Name origin: For Benjamin Stephenson (?–1821), adjutant general of IL Territory (1813), IL legislator, and prominent banker.

Buckeye — Township
Lat: 42-25-18 N   Long: 89-38-18 W
Pop: 1,458 (1990); 1,646 (1980)   **Pop Density:** 40.5
Land: 36.0 sq. mi.; **Water:** 0.0 sq. mi.

Cedarville — Village
ZIP: 61013   Lat: 42-22-30 N   Long: 89-38-11 W
Pop: 751 (1990); 766 (1980)   **Pop Density:** 1877.5
Land: 0.4 sq. mi.; **Water:** 0.0 sq. mi.
Birthplace of Jane Addams (1860–1935), founder of Chicago's social settlement, Hull House (1889).

Dakota — Town
ZIP: 61018   Lat: 42-23-14 N   Long: 89-31-37 W
Pop: 549 (1990); 571 (1980)   **Pop Density:** 1830.0
Land: 0.3 sq. mi.; **Water:** 0.0 sq. mi.
Not coextensive with the town of the same name.

*Dakota — Township
Lat: 42-24-55 N   Long: 89-32-45 W
Pop: 914 (1990); 932 (1980)   **Pop Density:** 50.8
Land: 18.0 sq. mi.; **Water:** 0.0 sq. mi.

Davis — Village
ZIP: 61019   Lat: 42-25-19 N   Long: 89-24-56 W
Pop: 541 (1990); 560 (1980)   **Pop Density:** 1352.5
Land: 0.4 sq. mi.; **Water:** 0.0 sq. mi.

Erin — Township
Lat: 42-19-58 N   Long: 89-46-36 W
Pop: 482 (1990); 524 (1980)   **Pop Density:** 26.5
Land: 18.2 sq. mi.; **Water:** 0.0 sq. mi.

Florence — Township
Lat: 42-14-34 N   Long: 89-41-02 W
Pop: 1,332 (1990); 1,556 (1980)   **Pop Density:** 39.1
Land: 34.1 sq. mi.; **Water:** 0.0 sq. mi.

Freeport — City
ZIP: 61032   Lat: 42-17-24 N   Long: 89-38-04 W
Pop: 25,840 (1990); 26,266 (1980)   **Pop Density:** 2508.7
Land: 10.3 sq. mi.; **Water:** 0.0 sq. mi.
In northern IL on the Pecatonica River, 25 mi. west of Rockford. Incorporated Feb 14, 1855.
Name origin: Named by first settler William Baker's wife, who complained of her household being a "free port" to numerous visitors.

*Freeport — Township
ZIP: 61032   Lat: 42-17-24 N   Long: 89-38-04 W
Pop: 25,840 (1990); 26,266 (1980)   **Pop Density:** 2508.7
Land: 10.3 sq. mi.; **Water:** 0.0 sq. mi.

German Valley — Village
ZIP: 61039   Lat: 42-12-57 N   Long: 89-29-01 W
Pop: 480 (1990); 414 (1980)   **Pop Density:** 1200.0
Land: 0.4 sq. mi.; **Water:** 0.0 sq. mi.

Harlem — Township
Lat: 42-20-14 N   Long: 89-41-48 W
Pop: 2,344 (1990); 2,920 (1980)   **Pop Density:** 73.5
Land: 31.9 sq. mi.; **Water:** 0.1 sq. mi.

Jefferson — Township
Lat: 42-14-11 N   Long: 89-53-34 W
Pop: 277 (1990); 303 (1980)   **Pop Density:** 15.1
Land: 18.3 sq. mi.; **Water:** 0.0 sq. mi.

Kent — Township
Lat: 42-19-33 N   Long: 89-51-44 W
Pop: 763 (1990); 799 (1980)   **Pop Density:** 21.5
Land: 35.5 sq. mi.; **Water:** 0.0 sq. mi.

Lake Summerset — CDP
Lat: 42-27-20 N   Long: 89-24-29 W
Pop: 609 (1990)   **Pop Density:** 676.7
Land: 0.9 sq. mi.; **Water:** 0.1 sq. mi.
Part of the town is also in Winnebago County.

Lancaster — Township
Lat: 42-19-59 N   Long: 89-34-04 W
Pop: 1,643 (1990); 1,851 (1980)   **Pop Density:** 51.3
Land: 32.0 sq. mi.; **Water:** 0.1 sq. mi.

Lena — Town
ZIP: 61048   Lat: 42-22-51 N   Long: 89-49-32 W
Pop: 2,605 (1990); 2,295 (1980)   **Pop Density:** 1860.7
Land: 1.4 sq. mi.; **Water:** 0.0 sq. mi.
In northern IL, 10 mi. south of the WI border.

Loran — Township
Lat: 42-14-30 N   Long: 89-48-18 W
Pop: 1,276 (1990); 1,338 (1980)   **Pop Density:** 36.5
Land: 35.0 sq. mi.; **Water:** 0.0 sq. mi.

Oneco — Township
Lat: 42-29-07 N   Long: 89-39-47 W
Pop: 1,200 (1990); 1,325 (1980)   **Pop Density:** 43.6
Land: 27.5 sq. mi.; **Water:** 0.0 sq. mi.

Orangeville — Village
ZIP: 61060   Lat: 42-28-05 N   Long: 89-38-40 W
Pop: 451 (1990); 598 (1980)   **Pop Density:** 2255.0
Land: 0.2 sq. mi.; **Water:** 0.0 sq. mi.

Pearl City — Town
ZIP: 61062   Lat: 42-16-03 N   Long: 89-49-31 W
Pop: 670 (1990); 661 (1980)   **Pop Density:** 1340.0
Land: 0.5 sq. mi.; **Water:** 0.0 sq. mi.

Ridott — Village
ZIP: 61067   Lat: 42-17-51 N   Long: 89-28-38 W
Pop: 156 (1990); 194 (1980)   **Pop Density:** 1560.0
Land: 0.1 sq. mi.; **Water:** 0.0 sq. mi.
Not coextensive with the town of the same name.

ILLINOIS, Stephenson County

*Ridott
Township
Lat: 42-15-51 N Long: 89-27-42 W
Pop: 1,656 (1990); 1,535 (1980) Pop Density: 31.0
Land: 53.5 sq. mi.; Water: 0.0 sq. mi.

Rock City
Village
ZIP: 61070 Lat: 42-24-45 N Long: 89-28-14 W
Pop: 286 (1990); 293 (1980) Pop Density: 2860.0
Land: 0.1 sq. mi.; Water: 0.0 sq. mi.

Rock Grove
Township
Lat: 42-28-43 N Long: 89-29-10 W
Pop: 1,134 (1990); 957 (1980) Pop Density: 37.5
Land: 30.2 sq. mi.; Water: 0.1 sq. mi.

Rock Run
Township
Lat: 42-23-28 N Long: 89-27-49 W
Pop: 1,936 (1990); 1,767 (1980) Pop Density: 40.5
Land: 47.8 sq. mi.; Water: 0.0 sq. mi.

Silver Creek
Township
Lat: 42-14-48 N Long: 89-34-01 W
Pop: 1,027 (1990); 1,208 (1980) Pop Density: 28.8
Land: 35.7 sq. mi.; Water: 0.0 sq. mi.

Waddams
Township
Lat: 42-25-03 N Long: 89-45-10 W
Pop: 892 (1990); 931 (1980) Pop Density: 24.9
Land: 35.8 sq. mi.; Water: 0.0 sq. mi.

West Point
Township
Lat: 42-25-01 N Long: 89-52-09 W
Pop: 3,156 (1990); 2,881 (1980) Pop Density: 88.4
Land: 35.7 sq. mi.; Water: 0.1 sq. mi.

Winslow
Village
ZIP: 61089 Lat: 42-29-32 N Long: 89-47-46 W
Pop: 317 (1990); 361 (1980) Pop Density: 792.5
Land: 0.4 sq. mi.; Water: 0.0 sq. mi.
Not coextensive with the town of the same name.

*Winslow
Township
Lat: 42-29-05 N Long: 89-50-19 W
Pop: 722 (1990); 797 (1980) Pop Density: 25.2
Land: 28.7 sq. mi.; Water: 0.0 sq. mi.

Tazewell County
County Seat: Pekin (ZIP: 61554)

Pop: 123,692 (1990); 132,078 (1980) Pop Density: 190.6
Land: 648.9 sq. mi.; Water: 9.0 sq. mi. Area Code: 309
In central IL, south of Peoria; organized Jan 31, 1827 from Fayette County.
Name origin: For Littleton Waller Tazewell (1774–1860), VA legislator, U.S. senator (1824–32), and governor (1834–36).

Armington
Village
ZIP: 61721 Lat: 40-20-23 N Long: 89-18-49 W
Pop: 348 (1990); 297 (1980) Pop Density: 1160.0
Land: 0.3 sq. mi.; Water: 0.0 sq. mi.

Boynton
Township
Lat: 40-21-34 N Long: 89-25-33 W
Pop: 266 (1990); 277 (1980) Pop Density: 9.0
Land: 29.6 sq. mi.; Water: 0.0 sq. mi.

Cincinnati
Township
ZIP: 61554 Lat: 40-31-03 N Long: 89-39-46 W
Pop: 6,722 (1990); 6,964 (1980) Pop Density: 224.1
Land: 30.0 sq. mi.; Water: 0.4 sq. mi.

Creve Coeur
Village
ZIP: 61611 Lat: 40-38-28 N Long: 89-35-58 W
Pop: 5,938 (1990); 6,851 (1980) Pop Density: 1237.1
Land: 4.8 sq. mi.; Water: 0.4 sq. mi.
In central IL on the Illinois River, a suburb south of Peoria.
Name origin: For the first French fort built in the West and in IL (1680–1682).

Deer Creek
Village
ZIP: 61733 Lat: 40-37-45 N Long: 89-19-59 W
Pop: 630 (1990); 683 (1980) Pop Density: 2100.0
Land: 0.3 sq. mi.; Water: 0.0 sq. mi.
Part of the town is also in Woodford County. Not coextensive with the township of the same name.

*Deer Creek
Township
Lat: 40-36-29 N Long: 89-20-11 W
Pop: 1,098 (1990); 1,184 (1980) Pop Density: 39.8
Land: 27.6 sq. mi.; Water: 0.0 sq. mi.

Delavan
City
ZIP: 61734 Lat: 40-22-17 N Long: 89-32-41 W
Pop: 1,642 (1990); 1,973 (1980) Pop Density: 2345.7
Land: 0.7 sq. mi.; Water: 0.0 sq. mi. Elev: 609 ft.
Founded in 1863 by Edward Cornelius Delavan of RI, who auctioned off parcels of land on IL's wild prairie; incorporated 1888. Not coextensive with the town of the same name.
Name origin: For its founder.

*Delavan
Township
Lat: 40-21-32 N Long: 89-32-59 W
Pop: 2,019 (1990); 2,408 (1980) Pop Density: 66.9
Land: 30.2 sq. mi.; Water: 0.0 sq. mi.

Dillon
Township
Lat: 40-26-15 N Long: 89-32-18 W
Pop: 916 (1990); 980 (1980) Pop Density: 25.5
Land: 35.9 sq. mi.; Water: 0.0 sq. mi.

East Peoria
City
ZIP: 61611 Lat: 40-40-17 N Long: 89-32-52 W
Pop: 21,378 (1990); 22,385 (1980) Pop Density: 1250.2
Land: 17.1 sq. mi.; Water: 2.2 sq. mi.
In central IL, near Peoria. East Peoria was settled in 1884; incorporated Jul 1, 1884.
Name origin: Originally named Blue Town because many of the residents wore blue smocks, which were unique to their

native Alsace-Lorraine. Also called Hilton. The name was changed to East Peoria in 1889.

Elm Grove
Township
Lat: 40-31-26 N **Long:** 89-33-24 W
Pop: 2,675 (1990); 2,946 (1980) **Pop Density:** 74.3
Land: 36.0 sq. mi.; **Water:** 0.0 sq. mi.

Fondulac
Township
ZIP: 61611 **Lat:** 40-41-35 N **Long:** 89-32-13 W
Pop: 12,821 (1990); 13,574 (1980) **Pop Density:** 724.4
Land: 17.7 sq. mi.; **Water:** 3.7 sq. mi.

Goodfield
Village
ZIP: 61742 **Lat:** 40-36-32 N **Long:** 89-16-44 W
Pop: 1 (1990); 500 (1980) **Pop Density:** 3.3
Land: 0.3 sq. mi.; **Water:** 0.0 sq. mi.

Part of the town is also in Woodford County.

Green Valley
Village
ZIP: 61534 **Lat:** 40-24-23 N **Long:** 89-38-32 W
Pop: 745 (1990); 768 (1980) **Pop Density:** 2483.3
Land: 0.3 sq. mi.; **Water:** 0.0 sq. mi.

Groveland
Township
ZIP: 61535 **Lat:** 40-36-33 N **Long:** 89-33-19 W
Pop: 19,608 (1990); 20,849 (1980) **Pop Density:** 516.0
Land: 38.0 sq. mi.; **Water:** 0.2 sq. mi.

Hittle
Township
Lat: 40-22-06 N **Long:** 89-19-19 W
Pop: 650 (1990); 680 (1980) **Pop Density:** 21.5
Land: 30.3 sq. mi.; **Water:** 0.0 sq. mi.

Hopedale
Town
ZIP: 61747 **Lat:** 40-25-18 N **Long:** 89-24-58 W
Pop: 805 (1990); 913 (1980) **Pop Density:** 2012.5
Land: 0.4 sq. mi.; **Water:** 0.0 sq. mi.

*Hopedale
Township
Lat: 40-26-23 N **Long:** 89-26-04 W
Pop: 1,679 (1990); 1,885 (1980) **Pop Density:** 47.7
Land: 35.2 sq. mi.; **Water:** 0.0 sq. mi.

Little Mackinaw
Township
Lat: 40-26-31 N **Long:** 89-19-34 W
Pop: 1,483 (1990); 1,689 (1980) **Pop Density:** 40.7
Land: 36.4 sq. mi.; **Water:** 0.0 sq. mi.

Mackinaw
Town
ZIP: 61755 **Lat:** 40-32-06 N **Long:** 89-21-30 W
Pop: 1,331 (1990); 1,354 (1980) **Pop Density:** 1331.0
Land: 1.0 sq. mi.; **Water:** 0.0 sq. mi.

Incorporated January 21, 1840. Not coextensive with the town of the same name.
Name origin: From an Ojibway Indian term possibly meaning 'turtle.'

*Mackinaw
Township
Lat: 40-31-53 N **Long:** 89-19-40 W
Pop: 2,772 (1990); 2,813 (1980) **Pop Density:** 76.8
Land: 36.1 sq. mi.; **Water:** 0.2 sq. mi.

Malone
Township
Lat: 40-21-34 N **Long:** 89-39-19 W
Pop: 285 (1990); 294 (1980) **Pop Density:** 9.6
Land: 29.7 sq. mi.; **Water:** 0.0 sq. mi.

Marquette Heights
City
ZIP: 61554 **Lat:** 40-37-01 N **Long:** 89-36-13 W
Pop: 3,077 (1990); 3,386 (1980) **Pop Density:** 3418.9
Land: 0.9 sq. mi.; **Water:** 0.0 sq. mi.

Minier
Town
ZIP: 61759 **Lat:** 40-26-01 N **Long:** 89-18-50 W
Pop: 1,155 (1990); 1,261 (1980) **Pop Density:** 1925.0
Land: 0.6 sq. mi.; **Water:** 0.0 sq. mi.

Incorporated July 17, 1872.

Morton
City
ZIP: 61550 **Lat:** 40-36-40 N **Long:** 89-28-04 W
Pop: 13,799 (1990); 14,178 (1980) **Pop Density:** 1149.9
Land: 12.0 sq. mi.; **Water:** 0.0 sq. mi.

In central IL, 10 mi. southeast of Peoria. Incorporated 1877. Not coextensive with the town of the same name.
Name origin: For Marcus Morton, MA governor (1840–44).

*Morton
Township
ZIP: 61550 **Lat:** 40-36-51 N **Long:** 89-26-24 W
Pop: 14,975 (1990); 15,725 (1980) **Pop Density:** 420.6
Land: 35.6 sq. mi.; **Water:** 0.1 sq. mi.

North Pekin
Village
ZIP: 61554 **Lat:** 40-36-48 N **Long:** 89-37-13 W
Pop: 1,556 (1990); 1,824 (1980) **Pop Density:** 1556.0
Land: 1.0 sq. mi.; **Water:** 0.0 sq. mi.

Pekin
City
ZIP: 61554 **Lat:** 40-34-02 N **Long:** 89-37-38 W
Pop: 32,254 (1990); 33,963 (1980) **Pop Density:** 2986.5
Land: 10.8 sq. mi.; **Water:** 0.5 sq. mi.

In north-central IL on the Illinois River, 10 mi. south of Peoria. County seat. Settled 1824; incorporated Feb 23, 1839. Part of the town is in Peoria County. Not coextensive with the township of the same name.
Name origin: For Peking, China.

*Pekin
Township
ZIP: 61554 **Lat:** 40-35-24 N **Long:** 89-37-48 W
Pop: 31,135 (1990); 33,738 (1980) **Pop Density:** 2490.8
Land: 12.5 sq. mi.; **Water:** 1.4 sq. mi.

In north-central IL.

Peoria Heights
Village
ZIP: 61614 **Lat:** 40-44-46 N **Long:** 89-32-53 W
Pop: 0 (1990)
Land: 0.1 sq. mi.; **Water:** 0.2 sq. mi. **Elev:** 789 ft.

Part of the town is also in Woodford and Peoria counties.

Sand Prairie
Township
Lat: 40-26-04 N **Long:** 89-39-26 W
Pop: 1,515 (1990); 1,596 (1980) **Pop Density:** 42.7
Land: 35.5 sq. mi.; **Water:** 0.0 sq. mi.

South Pekin
Town
ZIP: 61564 **Lat:** 40-29-48 N **Long:** 89-39-06 W
Pop: 1,184 (1990); 1,243 (1980) **Pop Density:** 2960.0
Land: 0.4 sq. mi.; **Water:** 0.0 sq. mi. **Elev:** 514 ft.

Spring Lake
Township
Lat: 40-29-08 N **Long:** 89-47-30 W
Pop: 1,745 (1990); 1,968 (1980) **Pop Density:** 27.8
Land: 62.7 sq. mi.; **Water:** 2.9 sq. mi.

Tremont
Town
ZIP: 61568 **Lat:** 40-31-33 N **Long:** 89-29-25 W
Pop: 2,088 (1990); 2,096 (1980) **Pop Density:** 2088.0
Land: 1.0 sq. mi.; **Water:** 0.0 sq. mi.

Not coextensive with the town of the same name.
Name origin: Descriptively named for three local hills; possibly from Spanish *tres montes*.

ILLINOIS, Tazewell County

*Tremont Township
Lat: 40-31-15 N Long: 89-25-50 W
Pop: 2,421 (1990); 2,553 (1980)   **Pop Density:** 69.4
Land: 34.9 sq. mi.; **Water:** 0.1 sq. mi.

Washington City
ZIP: 61571   **Lat:** 40-41-53 N **Long:** 89-26-06 W
Pop: 10,099 (1990); 10,364 (1980)   **Pop Density:** 1578.0
Land: 6.4 sq. mi.; **Water:** 0.0 sq. mi.
In central IL, 12 mi. east of Peoria. Incorporated Feb 10, 1857. Not coextensive with the town of the same name.
Name origin: For George Washington (1732–99), first U.S. president.

*Washington Township
ZIP: 61571   **Lat:** 40-42-14 N **Long:** 89-25-03 W
Pop: 18,907 (1990); 19,955 (1980)   **Pop Density:** 344.4
Land: 54.9 sq. mi.; **Water:** 0.0 sq. mi.

Union County
County Seat: Jonesboro (ZIP: 62952)

Pop: 17,619 (1990); 17,765 (1980)   **Pop Density:** 42.3
Land: 416.2 sq. mi.; **Water:** 6.0 sq. mi.   **Area Code:** 618
On the southwest border of IL, south of Carbondale; organized Jan 2, 1818 (prior to statehood) from Johnson County.
Name origin: For the temporary union of the Baptists and Dunkards.

Alto Pass Village
ZIP: 62905   **Lat:** 37-34-22 N **Long:** 89-19-09 W
Pop: 417 (1990); 369 (1980)   **Pop Density:** 189.5
Land: 2.2 sq. mi.; **Water:** 0.0 sq. mi.   **Elev:** 757 ft.

Anna City
ZIP: 62906   **Lat:** 37-27-35 N **Long:** 89-14-28 W
Pop: 4,805 (1990); 5,408 (1980)   **Pop Density:** 1601.7
Land: 3.0 sq. mi.; **Water:** 0.0 sq. mi.   **Elev:** 631 ft.
In southwestern IL, south of Carbondale. Incorporated 1865.

Cobden Village
ZIP: 62920   **Lat:** 37-32-00 N **Long:** 89-15-15 W
Pop: 1,090 (1990); 1,210 (1980)   **Pop Density:** 908.3
Land: 1.2 sq. mi.; **Water:** 0.0 sq. mi.   **Elev:** 616 ft.
Incorporated 1875.
Name origin: For English investor Sir Richard Cobden.

Dongola Village
ZIP: 62926   **Lat:** 37-21-36 N **Long:** 89-09-49 W
Pop: 728 (1990); 886 (1980)   **Pop Density:** 661.8
Land: 1.1 sq. mi.; **Water:** 0.0 sq. mi.

Jonesboro Town
ZIP: 62952   **Lat:** 37-27-15 N **Long:** 89-16-10 W
Pop: 1,728 (1990); 1,842 (1980)   **Pop Density:** 1080.0
Land: 1.6 sq. mi.; **Water:** 0.0 sq. mi.   **Elev:** 568 ft.
In southeastern IL, 30 mi. southwest of Marion. First settled 1803.

Mill Creek Village
Lat: 37-20-29 N Long: 89-15-15 W
Pop: 87 (1990); 97 (1980)   **Pop Density:** 217.5
Land: 0.4 sq. mi.; **Water:** 0.0 sq. mi.   **Elev:** 374 ft.

Vermilion County
County Seat: Danville (ZIP: 61832)

Pop: 88,257 (1990); 95,222 (1980)   **Pop Density:** 98.2
Land: 899.1 sq. mi.; **Water:** 3.1 sq. mi.   **Area Code:** 217
On the east-central border of IL, east of Urbana; organized Jan 18, 1826 from Edgar County.
Name origin: For the Vermilion River, which runs through the county and is colored by the red soil.

Allerton Village
Lat: 39-54-54 N Long: 87-56-01 W
Pop: 274 (1990); 295 (1980)   **Pop Density:** 548.0
Land: 0.5 sq. mi.; **Water:** 0.0 sq. mi.
Part of the town is also in Champaign County.

Alvin Village
Lat: 40-18-27 N Long: 87-36-24 W
Pop: 339 (1990); 378 (1980)   **Pop Density:** 423.8
Land: 0.8 sq. mi.; **Water:** 0.0 sq. mi.

Belgium Village
Lat: 40-03-41 N Long: 87-37-50 W
Pop: 511 (1990); 568 (1980)   **Pop Density:** 1277.5
Land: 0.4 sq. mi.; **Water:** 0.0 sq. mi.   **Elev:** 652 ft.
Name origin: For the European country.

Blount Township
Lat: 40-12-50 N Long: 87-42-08 W
Pop: 3,122 (1990); 3,026 (1980)   **Pop Density:** 60.7
Land: 51.4 sq. mi.; **Water:** 0.4 sq. mi.

Butler — Township
Lat: 40-25-48 N Long: 87-50-51 W
Pop: 1,249 (1990); 1,447 (1980) **Pop Density:** 17.3
Land: 72.2 sq. mi.; **Water:** 0.0 sq. mi.

Carroll — Township
Lat: 39-55-41 N Long: 87-44-37 W
Pop: 715 (1990); 828 (1980) **Pop Density:** 19.2
Land: 37.3 sq. mi.; **Water:** 0.0 sq. mi.

Catlin — Village
ZIP: 61817 Lat: 40-04-06 N Long: 87-42-28 W
Pop: 2,173 (1990); 2,226 (1980) **Pop Density:** 2716.3
Land: 0.8 sq. mi.; **Water:** 0.0 sq. mi. **Elev:** 657 ft.
Not coextensive with the town of the same name.
Name origin: For J. M. Catlin, once president of the Great Western Railway Company.

*Catlin — Township
Lat: 40-03-38 N Long: 87-43-28 W
Pop: 3,402 (1990); 3,567 (1980) **Pop Density:** 68.5
Land: 49.7 sq. mi.; **Water:** 0.3 sq. mi.

Danville — City
ZIP: 61832 Lat: 40-08-38 N Long: 87-37-09 W
Pop: 33,828 (1990); 38,985 (1980) **Pop Density:** 2225.5
Land: 15.2 sq. mi.; **Water:** 0.1 sq. mi. **Elev:** 597 ft.
In east-central IL, 30 mi. east of Champaign/Urbana. Founded 1765 on the site of a Piankashaw Indian village next to the Vermilion River; incorporated Feb 3, 1839. Not coextensive with the town of the same name.
Name origin: Named in the 1800s for Dan Beckwith, its founder and surveyor. Previously called Salt Works for salt deposits.

*Danville — Township
ZIP: 61832 Lat: 40-06-37 N Long: 87-36-38 W
Pop: 37,025 (1990); 40,935 (1980) **Pop Density:** 749.5
Land: 49.4 sq. mi.; **Water:** 0.7 sq. mi.

Elwood — Township
Lat: 39-54-19 N Long: 87-38-39 W
Pop: 1,773 (1990); 2,012 (1980) **Pop Density:** 71.5
Land: 24.8 sq. mi.; **Water:** 0.1 sq. mi.

Fairmount — Village
ZIP: 61841 Lat: 40-02-45 N Long: 87-49-42 W
Pop: 678 (1990); 851 (1980) **Pop Density:** 2260.0
Land: 0.3 sq. mi.; **Water:** 0.0 sq. mi. **Elev:** 665 ft.

Fithian — Village
ZIP: 61844 Lat: 40-06-50 N Long: 87-52-28 W
Pop: 512 (1990); 540 (1980) **Pop Density:** 1280.0
Land: 0.4 sq. mi.; **Water:** 0.0 sq. mi. **Elev:** 659 ft.
Name origin: For Dr. William Fithian, an early settler and friend of sixteenth U.S. President Abraham Lincoln (1809–65).

Georgetown — City
ZIP: 61846 Lat: 39-58-35 N Long: 87-38-05 W
Pop: 3,678 (1990); 4,220 (1980) **Pop Density:** 2298.8
Land: 1.6 sq. mi.; **Water:** 0.0 sq. mi.
Founded 1827.

*Georgetown — Township
ZIP: 61846 Lat: 40-00-17 N Long: 87-38-23 W
Pop: 8,286 (1990); 8,887 (1980) **Pop Density:** 323.7
Land: 25.6 sq. mi.; **Water:** 0.0 sq. mi.

Grant — Township
ZIP: 60942 Lat: 40-26-50 N Long: 87-38-44 W
Pop: 6,673 (1990); 7,387 (1980) **Pop Density:** 76.7
Land: 87.0 sq. mi.; **Water:** 0.0 sq. mi.

Henning — Village
ZIP: 61848 Lat: 40-18-22 N Long: 87-42-02 W
Pop: 273 (1990); 317 (1980) **Pop Density:** 182.0
Land: 1.5 sq. mi.; **Water:** 0.0 sq. mi. **Elev:** 685 ft.

Hoopeston — City
ZIP: 60942 Lat: 40-27-54 N Long: 87-40-15 W
Pop: 5,871 (1990); 6,411 (1980) **Pop Density:** 2552.6
Land: 2.3 sq. mi.; **Water:** 0.0 sq. mi. **Elev:** 718 ft.
In eastern IL. Platted 1871 by three land companies. Incorporated Apr 17, 1877.
Name origin: For Thomas Hoopes, on whose farmland it was created.

Indianola — Village
ZIP: 61850 Lat: 39-55-37 N Long: 87-44-24 W
Pop: 336 (1990); 370 (1980) **Pop Density:** 840.0
Land: 0.4 sq. mi.; **Water:** 0.0 sq. mi. **Elev:** 674 ft.

Jamaica — Township
Lat: 39-58-46 N Long: 87-48-26 W
Pop: 229 (1990); 281 (1980) **Pop Density:** 7.4
Land: 31.1 sq. mi.; **Water:** 0.2 sq. mi.
Name origin: For the Caribbean island.

Love — Township
Lat: 39-55-36 N Long: 87-34-37 W
Pop: 321 (1990); 333 (1980) **Pop Density:** 15.7
Land: 20.4 sq. mi.; **Water:** 0.0 sq. mi.

McKendree — Township
Lat: 40-00-11 N Long: 87-34-36 W
Pop: 791 (1990); 772 (1980) **Pop Density:** 27.1
Land: 29.2 sq. mi.; **Water:** 0.1 sq. mi.

Middlefork — Township
Lat: 40-19-12 N Long: 87-50-17 W
Pop: 1,543 (1990); 1,634 (1980) **Pop Density:** 24.2
Land: 63.7 sq. mi.; **Water:** 0.0 sq. mi.

Muncie — Village
ZIP: 61857 Lat: 40-06-57 N Long: 87-50-33 W
Pop: 182 (1990); 201 (1980) **Pop Density:** 910.0
Land: 0.2 sq. mi.; **Water:** 0.0 sq. mi. **Elev:** 659 ft.

Newell — Township
ZIP: 61832 Lat: 40-12-36 N Long: 87-35-00 W
Pop: 13,930 (1990); 14,396 (1980) **Pop Density:** 278.6
Land: 50.0 sq. mi.; **Water:** 0.7 sq. mi.

Oakwood — Village
ZIP: 61858 Lat: 40-06-32 N Long: 87-46-35 W
Pop: 1,533 (1990); 1,627 (1980) **Pop Density:** 1703.3
Land: 0.9 sq. mi.; **Water:** 0.0 sq. mi. **Elev:** 645 ft.
Not coextensive with the town of the same name.

*Oakwood — Township
Lat: 40-07-56 N Long: 87-50-20 W
Pop: 3,538 (1990); 3,585 (1980) **Pop Density:** 54.9
Land: 64.5 sq. mi.; **Water:** 0.4 sq. mi.

Pilot — Township
Lat: 40-13-00 N Long: 87-51-03 W
Pop: 668 (1990); 712 (1980) **Pop Density:** 10.7
Land: 62.3 sq. mi.; **Water:** 0.0 sq. mi.

ILLINOIS, Vermilion County

Potomac — Town
ZIP: 61865 Lat: 40-18-23 N Long: 87-47-50 W
Pop: 753 (1990); 874 (1980) Pop Density: 1506.0
Land: 0.5 sq. mi.; Water: 0.0 sq. mi. Elev: 670 ft.
In east-central IL on the Vermilion River, 13 mi. west of the IN border.
Name origin: For the Potomac River.

Rankin — Town
ZIP: 60960 Lat: 40-27-53 N Long: 87-53-45 W
Pop: 619 (1990); 727 (1980) Pop Density: 1031.7
Land: 0.6 sq. mi.; Water: 0.0 sq. mi. Elev: 710 ft.

Ridge Farm — Town
ZIP: 61870 Lat: 39-53-43 N Long: 87-39-08 W
Pop: 939 (1990); 1,096 (1980) Pop Density: 302.9
Land: 3.1 sq. mi.; Water: 0.0 sq. mi. Elev: 700 ft.

Ross — Township
Lat: 40-21-24 N Long: 87-38-04 W
Pop: 1,601 (1990); 1,649 (1980) Pop Density: 36.9
Land: 43.4 sq. mi.; Water: 0.0 sq. mi.

Rossville — Town
ZIP: 60963 Lat: 40-22-54 N Long: 87-40-08 W
Pop: 1,334 (1990); 1,363 (1980) Pop Density: 1026.2
Land: 1.3 sq. mi.; Water: 0.0 sq. mi. Elev: 706 ft.
In eastern IL near the IN border. Founded 1857.
Name origin: For early settler Jacob Ross.

Sidell — Town
ZIP: 61876 Lat: 39-54-36 N Long: 87-49-19 W
Pop: 584 (1990); 625 (1980) Pop Density: 648.9
Land: 0.9 sq. mi.; Water: 0.0 sq. mi. Elev: 685 ft.
Not coextensive with the town of the same name.

*Sidell — Township
Lat: 39-55-51 N Long: 87-52-37 W
Pop: 1,077 (1990); 1,200 (1980) Pop Density: 24.8
Land: 43.4 sq. mi.; Water: 0.0 sq. mi.

South Ross — Township
Lat: 40-18-04 N Long: 87-39-23 W
Pop: 1,226 (1990); 1,303 (1980) Pop Density: 22.7
Land: 53.9 sq. mi.; Water: 0.0 sq. mi.

Tilton — Village
ZIP: 61833 Lat: 40-05-39 N Long: 87-38-18 W
Pop: 2,729 (1990); 2,405 (1980) Pop Density: 1049.6
Land: 2.6 sq. mi.; Water: 0.0 sq. mi. Elev: 648 ft.

Vance — Township
Lat: 40-02-41 N Long: 87-52-47 W
Pop: 1,088 (1990); 1,268 (1980) Pop Density: 27.2
Land: 40.0 sq. mi.; Water: 0.1 sq. mi.

Westville — City
ZIP: 61883 Lat: 40-02-41 N Long: 87-38-16 W
Pop: 3,387 (1990); 3,573 (1980) Pop Density: 2116.9
Land: 1.6 sq. mi.; Water: 0.0 sq. mi. Elev: 671 ft.
Settled 1873.
Name origin: For first settlers, W. P. and E. A. West.

Wabash County
County Seat: Mt. Carmel (ZIP: 62863)

Pop: 13,111 (1990); 13,713 (1980) Pop Density: 58.7
Land: 223.5 sq. mi.; Water: 4.3 sq. mi. Area Code: 618
On the southeastern border of IL, southeast of Olney; organized Dec 27, 1824 from Edwards County.
Name origin: For the Wabath River, from Miami Indian *wahba* 'white' and *shik-ki* 'color-bright', usually translated as 'white water.'

Allendale — Village
ZIP: 62410 Lat: 38-31-39 N Long: 87-42-37 W
Pop: 476 (1990); 613 (1980) Pop Density: 1586.7
Land: 0.3 sq. mi.; Water: 0.0 sq. mi.

Bellmont — Village
ZIP: 62811 Lat: 38-22-57 N Long: 87-54-34 W
Pop: 271 (1990); 307 (1980) Pop Density: 677.5
Land: 0.4 sq. mi.; Water: 0.0 sq. mi. Elev: 430 ft.

Keensburg — Village
ZIP: 62852 Lat: 38-21-07 N Long: 87-52-01 W
Pop: 238 (1990); 244 (1980) Pop Density: 793.3
Land: 0.3 sq. mi.; Water: 0.0 sq. mi. Elev: 425 ft.

Mount Carmel — City
ZIP: 62863 Lat: 38-25-01 N Long: 87-46-12 W
Pop: 8,287 (1990); 8,908 (1980) Pop Density: 1973.1
Land: 4.2 sq. mi.; Water: 0.2 sq. mi. Elev: 450 ft.
Incorporated Jan 10, 1825.

> **Warren County**
> **County Seat: Monmouth (ZIP: 61462)**
>
> **Pop:** 19,181 (1990); 21,943 (1980)   **Pop Density:** 35.4
> **Land:** 542.6 sq. mi.; **Water:** 0.6 sq. mi.   **Area Code:** 309
> In northwest IL, west of Galesburg; organized Jan 13, 1825 from Pike County.
> **Name origin:** For Gen. Joseph Warren (1741–75), Revolutionary War patriot and member of the Committee of Safety who dispatched Paul Revere (1735–1818) on his famous ride.

Alexis — Village
Lat: 41-03-38 N   **Long:** 90-33-16 W
Pop: 526 (1990); 626 (1980)   **Pop Density:** 1753.3
Land: 0.3 sq. mi.; **Water:** 0.0 sq. mi.

In northwestern IL on the Mercer-Warren county line. Part of the town is also in Mercer County.

Berwick — Township
Lat: 40-44-59 N   **Long:** 90-30-05 W
Pop: 435 (1990); 583 (1980)   **Pop Density:** 12.1
Land: 35.9 sq. mi.; **Water:** 0.0 sq. mi.

Coldbrook — Township
Lat: 40-56-02 N   **Long:** 90-29-48 W
Pop: 516 (1990); 650 (1980)   **Pop Density:** 14.5
Land: 35.7 sq. mi.; **Water:** 0.0 sq. mi.

Ellison — Township
Lat: 40-45-44 N   **Long:** 90-44-02 W
Pop: 360 (1990); 470 (1980)   **Pop Density:** 9.9
Land: 36.4 sq. mi.; **Water:** 0.0 sq. mi.

Floyd — Township
Lat: 40-50-42 N   **Long:** 90-29-58 W
Pop: 535 (1990); 646 (1980)   **Pop Density:** 14.9
Land: 35.8 sq. mi.; **Water:** 0.0 sq. mi.

Greenbush — Township
Lat: 40-40-33 N   **Long:** 90-30-42 W
Pop: 610 (1990); 688 (1980)   **Pop Density:** 17.2
Land: 35.5 sq. mi.; **Water:** 0.4 sq. mi.

Hale — Township
Lat: 40-56-22 N   **Long:** 90-43-47 W
Pop: 381 (1990); 455 (1980)   **Pop Density:** 10.4
Land: 36.6 sq. mi.; **Water:** 0.0 sq. mi.

Kelly — Township
Lat: 41-01-02 N   **Long:** 90-30-06 W
Pop: 491 (1990); 580 (1980)   **Pop Density:** 14.0
Land: 35.1 sq. mi.; **Water:** 0.0 sq. mi.

Kirkwood — Town
ZIP: 61447   **Lat:** 40-52-03 N   **Long:** 90-44-53 W
Pop: 884 (1990); 1,008 (1980)   **Pop Density:** 982.2
Land: 0.9 sq. mi.; **Water:** 0.0 sq. mi.

In northwestern IL, 20 mi. northeast of Burlington, IA.

Lenox — Township
Lat: 40-51-11 N   **Long:** 90-36-53 W
Pop: 354 (1990); 418 (1980)   **Pop Density:** 9.7
Land: 36.4 sq. mi.; **Water:** 0.0 sq. mi.

Little York — Village
ZIP: 61453   **Lat:** 41-00-37 N   **Long:** 90-44-48 W
Pop: 349 (1990); 347 (1980)   **Pop Density:** 1163.3
Land: 0.3 sq. mi.; **Water:** 0.0 sq. mi.

Monmouth — City
ZIP: 61462   **Lat:** 40-54-48 N   **Long:** 90-38-34 W
Pop: 9,489 (1990); 10,706 (1980)   **Pop Density:** 2497.1
Land: 3.8 sq. mi.; **Water:** 0.0 sq. mi.   **Elev:** 770 ft.

In western IL, 55 mi. northwest of Peoria. Settled 1836; incorporated Jun 21, 1852. Not coextensive with the town of the same name.
Name origin: Probably for the Revolutionary War Battle of Monmouth, NJ (1778).

*Monmouth — Township
ZIP: 61462   **Lat:** 40-55-59 N   **Long:** 90-36-27 W
Pop: 10,546 (1990); 11,758 (1980)   **Pop Density:** 285.8
Land: 36.9 sq. mi.; **Water:** 0.1 sq. mi.

Point Pleasant — Township
Lat: 40-40-12 N   **Long:** 90-44-23 W
Pop: 193 (1990); 250 (1980)   **Pop Density:** 5.4
Land: 36.0 sq. mi.; **Water:** 0.0 sq. mi.

Roseville — Town
ZIP: 61473   **Lat:** 40-43-50 N   **Long:** 90-39-45 W
Pop: 1,151 (1990); 1,254 (1980)   **Pop Density:** 1438.8
Land: 0.8 sq. mi.; **Water:** 0.0 sq. mi.

Not coextensive with the town of the same name.
Name origin: For its famous flowers.

*Roseville — Township
Lat: 40-45-31 N   **Long:** 90-37-14 W
Pop: 1,453 (1990); 1,617 (1980)   **Pop Density:** 39.6
Land: 36.7 sq. mi.; **Water:** 0.0 sq. mi.

Spring Grove — Township
Lat: 41-01-33 N   **Long:** 90-36-24 W
Pop: 1,133 (1990); 1,312 (1980)   **Pop Density:** 30.8
Land: 36.8 sq. mi.; **Water:** 0.1 sq. mi.

Sumner — Township
Lat: 41-01-26 N   **Long:** 90-43-34 W
Pop: 673 (1990); 726 (1980)   **Pop Density:** 18.1
Land: 37.1 sq. mi.; **Water:** 0.0 sq. mi.

Swan — Township
Lat: 40-40-11 N   **Long:** 90-36-42 W
Pop: 324 (1990); 431 (1980)   **Pop Density:** 9.2
Land: 35.2 sq. mi.; **Water:** 0.0 sq. mi.

Tompkins — Township
Lat: 40-50-59 N   **Long:** 90-43-50 W
Pop: 1,177 (1990); 1,359 (1980)   **Pop Density:** 32.2
Land: 36.5 sq. mi.; **Water:** 0.0 sq. mi.

ILLINOIS, Washington County *American Places Dictionary*

> ## Washington County
> **County Seat: Nashville (ZIP: 62263)**
>
> **Pop:** 14,965 (1990); 15,472 (1980) **Pop Density:** 26.6
> **Land:** 562.7 sq. mi.; **Water:** 1.5 sq. mi. **Area Code:** 618
> In south-central IL, southeast of Belleville; organized Jan 2, 1818 (prior to statehood) from Saint Clair County.
> **Name origin:** For George Washington (1732–99), American patriot and first U.S. president.

Addieville
Village
ZIP: 62214 **Lat:** 38-23-30 N **Long:** 89-29-14 W
Pop: 257 (1990); 286 (1980) **Pop Density:** 233.6
Land: 1.1 sq. mi.; **Water:** 0.0 sq. mi.

Ashley
City
ZIP: 62808 **Lat:** 38-19-44 N **Long:** 89-11-21 W
Pop: 583 (1990); 658 (1980) **Pop Density:** 530.0
Land: 1.1 sq. mi.; **Water:** 0.0 sq. mi.
Not coextensive with the town of the same name.
Name origin: For early settler John Ashley.

*Ashley
Township
Lat: 38-19-54 N **Long:** 89-12-07 W
Pop: 847 (1990); 986 (1980) **Pop Density:** 34.7
Land: 24.4 sq. mi.; **Water:** 0.1 sq. mi.

Beaucoup
Township
Lat: 38-20-45 N **Long:** 89-19-01 W
Pop: 493 (1990); 500 (1980) **Pop Density:** 13.0
Land: 37.8 sq. mi.; **Water:** 0.1 sq. mi.

Bolo
Township
Lat: 38-15-32 N **Long:** 89-19-01 W
Pop: 396 (1990); 394 (1980) **Pop Density:** 10.8
Land: 36.7 sq. mi.; **Water:** 0.6 sq. mi.

Covington
Township
Lat: 38-26-21 N **Long:** 89-25-20 W
Pop: 437 (1990); 425 (1980) **Pop Density:** 11.0
Land: 39.7 sq. mi.; **Water:** 0.1 sq. mi.

Du Bois
Township
Lat: 38-15-41 N **Long:** 89-11-43 W
Pop: 732 (1990); 830 (1980) **Pop Density:** 19.9
Land: 36.8 sq. mi.; **Water:** 0.0 sq. mi.

*Du Bois
Village
Lat: 38-13-18 N **Long:** 89-12-46 W
Pop: 216 (1990); 241 (1980) **Pop Density:** 196.4
Land: 1.1 sq. mi.; **Water:** 0.0 sq. mi.
Not coextensive with the town of the same name.

Hoyleton
Village
ZIP: 62803 **Lat:** 38-26-43 N **Long:** 89-16-17 W
Pop: 508 (1990); 542 (1980) **Pop Density:** 635.0
Land: 0.8 sq. mi.; **Water:** 0.0 sq. mi.
Not coextensive with the town of the same name.

*Hoyleton
Township
Lat: 38-27-06 N **Long:** 89-18-56 W
Pop: 1,214 (1990); 1,212 (1980) **Pop Density:** 23.8
Land: 51.0 sq. mi.; **Water:** 0.0 sq. mi.

Irvington
Town
ZIP: 62848 **Lat:** 38-26-13 N **Long:** 89-09-44 W
Pop: 827 (1990); 789 (1980) **Pop Density:** 1033.8
Land: 0.8 sq. mi.; **Water:** 0.0 sq. mi. **Elev:** 530 ft.
Not coextensive with the town of the same name.

*Irvington
Township
Lat: 38-27-02 N **Long:** 89-11-55 W
Pop: 1,624 (1990); 1,626 (1980) **Pop Density:** 33.6
Land: 48.4 sq. mi.; **Water:** 0.1 sq. mi.

Johannisburg
Township
Lat: 38-20-48 N **Long:** 89-39-29 W
Pop: 572 (1990); 583 (1980) **Pop Density:** 15.8
Land: 36.1 sq. mi.; **Water:** 0.0 sq. mi.

Lively Grove
Township
Lat: 38-15-48 N **Long:** 89-39-13 W
Pop: 728 (1990); 741 (1980) **Pop Density:** 20.2
Land: 36.0 sq. mi.; **Water:** 0.0 sq. mi.

Nashville
Town
ZIP: 62263 **Lat:** 38-20-53 N **Long:** 89-22-39 W
Pop: 3,202 (1990); 3,186 (1980) **Pop Density:** 1392.2
Land: 2.3 sq. mi.; **Water:** 0.1 sq. mi.
In south-central IL, 20 mi. southwest of Centralia. Not coextensive with the town of the same name.
Name origin: For Nashville, TN; named by Tennesseans who platted the town in 1830.

*Nashville
Township
Lat: 38-20-49 N **Long:** 89-25-27 W
Pop: 3,675 (1990); 3,697 (1980) **Pop Density:** 105.9
Land: 34.7 sq. mi.; **Water:** 0.1 sq. mi.

New Minden
Village
ZIP: 62263 **Lat:** 38-26-14 N **Long:** 89-22-15 W
Pop: 219 (1990); 223 (1980) **Pop Density:** 730.0
Land: 0.3 sq. mi.; **Water:** 0.0 sq. mi.

Oakdale
Village
ZIP: 62268 **Lat:** 38-15-49 N **Long:** 89-30-17 W
Pop: 179 (1990); 198 (1980) **Pop Density:** 111.9
Land: 1.6 sq. mi.; **Water:** 0.0 sq. mi.
Not coextensive with the town of the same name.

*Oakdale
Township
Lat: 38-15-55 N **Long:** 89-32-02 W
Pop: 620 (1990); 615 (1980) **Pop Density:** 16.6
Land: 37.4 sq. mi.; **Water:** 0.1 sq. mi.

Okawville
Village
ZIP: 62271 **Lat:** 38-26-03 N **Long:** 89-32-53 W
Pop: 1,274 (1990); 1,337 (1980) **Pop Density:** 670.5
Land: 1.9 sq. mi.; **Water:** 0.0 sq. mi.
Not coextensive with the town of the same name.

*Okawville
Township
Lat: 38-26-14 N **Long:** 89-32-00 W
Pop: 1,831 (1990); 1,976 (1980) **Pop Density:** 50.6
Land: 36.2 sq. mi.; **Water:** 0.1 sq. mi.

Pilot Knob
Township
Lat: 38-15-51 N **Long:** 89-25-41 W
Pop: 395 (1990); 431 (1980) **Pop Density:** 11.2
Land: 35.2 sq. mi.; **Water:** 0.1 sq. mi.

Plum Hill
Township
Lat: 38-20-48 N **Long:** 89-32-29 W
Pop: 539 (1990); 548 (1980) **Pop Density:** 14.2
Land: 37.9 sq. mi.; **Water:** 0.0 sq. mi.

Radom
Village
ZIP: 62876 **Lat:** 38-16-50 N **Long:** 89-11-30 W
Pop: 174 (1990); 174 (1980) **Pop Density:** 174.0
Land: 1.0 sq. mi.; **Water:** 0.0 sq. mi.

Richview
Village
ZIP: 62877 **Lat:** 38-22-32 N **Long:** 89-11-01 W
Pop: 307 (1990); 299 (1980) **Pop Density:** 383.8
Land: 0.8 sq. mi.; **Water:** 0.0 sq. mi.

Not coextensive with the town of the same name.

*Richview
Township
Lat: 38-22-18 N **Long:** 89-11-54 W
Pop: 428 (1990); 465 (1980) **Pop Density:** 35.7
Land: 12.0 sq. mi.; **Water:** 0.0 sq. mi.

Venedy
Village
ZIP: 62296 **Lat:** 38-23-45 N **Long:** 89-38-45 W
Pop: 158 (1990); 147 (1980) **Pop Density:** 526.7
Land: 0.3 sq. mi.; **Water:** 0.0 sq. mi.

Not coextensive with the town of the same name.

*Venedy
Township
Lat: 38-25-15 N **Long:** 89-38-01 W
Pop: 434 (1990); 443 (1980) **Pop Density:** 19.5
Land: 22.3 sq. mi.; **Water:** 0.1 sq. mi.

Wamac
Town
ZIP: 62801 **Lat:** 38-29-40 N **Long:** 89-09-02 W
Pop: 130 (1990); 145 (1980) **Pop Density:** 216.7
Land: 0.6 sq. mi.; **Water:** 0.0 sq. mi.

In southern IL, east of St. Louis, MO. Part of the town is also in Clinton and Marion counties.

Name origin: An acronym for Washington, Marion, and Clinton counties, which converge here.

Wayne County
County Seat: Fairfield (ZIP: 62837)

Pop: 17,241 (1990); 18,059 (1980) **Pop Density:** 24.1
Land: 713.9 sq. mi.; **Water:** 1.7 sq. mi. **Area Code:** 618

In southeastern IL, southwest of Olney; organized Mar 26, 1819 from Edwards County.

Name origin: For Gen. Anthony Wayne (1745–96), PA soldier and statesman, nicknamed "Mad Anthony" for his daring during the Revolutionary War.

Arrington
Township
Lat: 38-21-44 N **Long:** 88-31-43 W
Pop: 519 (1990); 572 (1980) **Pop Density:** 30.5
Land: 17.0 sq. mi.; **Water:** 0.0 sq. mi.

Barnhill
Township
Lat: 38-17-59 N **Long:** 88-19-01 W
Pop: 493 (1990); 410 (1980) **Pop Density:** 14.6
Land: 33.7 sq. mi.; **Water:** 0.2 sq. mi.

Bedford
Township
Lat: 38-31-20 N **Long:** 88-24-57 W
Pop: 1,063 (1990); 1,205 (1980) **Pop Density:** 30.9
Land: 34.4 sq. mi.; **Water:** 0.0 sq. mi.

Berry
Township
Lat: 38-25-41 N **Long:** 88-31-41 W
Pop: 349 (1990); 413 (1980) **Pop Density:** 9.3
Land: 37.5 sq. mi.; **Water:** 0.0 sq. mi.

Big Mound
Township
Lat: 38-19-12 N **Long:** 88-25-39 W
Pop: 1,825 (1990); 1,837 (1980) **Pop Density:** 35.3
Land: 51.7 sq. mi.; **Water:** 0.2 sq. mi.

Cisne
Village
ZIP: 62823 **Lat:** 38-30-50 N **Long:** 88-26-13 W
Pop: 645 (1990); 705 (1980) **Pop Density:** 1075.0
Land: 0.6 sq. mi.; **Water:** 0.0 sq. mi.

Elm River
Township
Lat: 38-30-30 N **Long:** 88-18-42 W
Pop: 340 (1990); 351 (1980) **Pop Density:** 9.4
Land: 36.0 sq. mi.; **Water:** 0.1 sq. mi.

Fairfield
City
ZIP: 62837 **Lat:** 38-22-49 N **Long:** 88-22-08 W
Pop: 5,439 (1990); 5,944 (1980) **Pop Density:** 1813.0
Land: 3.0 sq. mi.; **Water:** 0.0 sq. mi. **Elev:** 441 ft.

Settled 1819; incorporated Jan 31, 1840.

Name origin: Named by the settlers who declared that there was "no fairer field" for farms.

Four Mile
Township
Lat: 38-18-41 N **Long:** 88-39-18 W
Pop: 551 (1990); 613 (1980) **Pop Density:** 13.7
Land: 40.1 sq. mi.; **Water:** 0.0 sq. mi.

Garden Hill
Township
Lat: 38-35-11 N **Long:** 88-38-18 W
Pop: 138 (1990); 158 (1980) **Pop Density:** 7.4
Land: 18.6 sq. mi.; **Water:** 0.0 sq. mi.

Golden Gate
Village
Lat: 38-21-31 N **Long:** 88-12-19 W
Pop: 71 (1990); 126 (1980) **Pop Density:** 710.0
Land: 0.1 sq. mi.; **Water:** 0.0 sq. mi.

ILLINOIS, Wayne County

Grover
Township
Lat: 38-21-47 N **Long:** 88-18-27 W
Pop: 4,113 (1990); 4,398 (1980) **Pop Density:** 209.8
Land: 19.6 sq. mi.; **Water:** 0.0 sq. mi.

Hickory Hill
Township
Lat: 38-25-09 N **Long:** 88-38-50 W
Pop: 417 (1990); 421 (1980) **Pop Density:** 9.8
Land: 42.6 sq. mi.; **Water:** 0.1 sq. mi.

Indian Prairie
Township
Lat: 38-31-08 N **Long:** 88-31-33 W
Pop: 571 (1990); 555 (1980) **Pop Density:** 15.3
Land: 37.3 sq. mi.; **Water:** 0.2 sq. mi.

Jasper
Township
Lat: 38-25-47 N **Long:** 88-18-46 W
Pop: 1,746 (1990); 1,766 (1980) **Pop Density:** 52.6
Land: 33.2 sq. mi.; **Water:** 0.1 sq. mi.

Jeffersonville
Village
ZIP: 62842 **Lat:** 38-26-34 N **Long:** 88-24-16 W
Pop: 311 (1990); 340 (1980) **Pop Density:** 311.0
Land: 1.0 sq. mi.; **Water:** 0.0 sq. mi.

Johnsonville
Village
ZIP: 62850 **Lat:** 38-31-14 N **Long:** 88-32-13 W
Pop: 68 (1990); 71 (1980) **Pop Density:** 340.0
Land: 0.2 sq. mi.; **Water:** 0.0 sq. mi. **Elev:** 548 ft.

Keenes
Village
ZIP: 62851 **Lat:** 38-20-16 N **Long:** 88-38-28 W
Pop: 62 (1990); 123 (1980) **Pop Density:** 620.0
Land: 0.1 sq. mi.; **Water:** 0.0 sq. mi.

Keith
Township
Lat: 38-34-58 N **Long:** 88-28-44 W
Pop: 379 (1990); 390 (1980) **Pop Density:** 10.5
Land: 36.1 sq. mi.; **Water:** 0.0 sq. mi.

Lamard
Township
Lat: 38-25-30 N **Long:** 88-25-17 W
Pop: 1,343 (1990); 1,424 (1980) **Pop Density:** 39.0
Land: 34.4 sq. mi.; **Water:** 0.0 sq. mi.

Leech
Township
Lat: 38-19-23 N **Long:** 88-12-23 W
Pop: 538 (1990); 559 (1980) **Pop Density:** 10.1
Land: 53.5 sq. mi.; **Water:** 0.3 sq. mi.

Massilon
Township
Lat: 38-25-51 N **Long:** 88-12-44 W
Pop: 195 (1990); 197 (1980) **Pop Density:** 5.8
Land: 33.4 sq. mi.; **Water:** 0.0 sq. mi.

Mill Shoals
Village
ZIP: 62862 **Lat:** 38-15-43 N **Long:** 88-20-59 W
Pop: 0 (1990); 333 (1980)
Land: 0.1 sq. mi.; **Water:** 0.0 sq. mi. **Elev:** 380 ft.
Part of the town is also in White County.

Mount Erie
Village
ZIP: 62446 **Lat:** 38-30-52 N **Long:** 88-13-57 W
Pop: 137 (1990); 135 (1980) **Pop Density:** 342.5
Land: 0.4 sq. mi.; **Water:** 0.0 sq. mi.
Not coextensive with the town of the same name.

*Mount Erie
Township
Lat: 38-32-13 N **Long:** 88-12-17 W
Pop: 463 (1990); 486 (1980) **Pop Density:** 8.7
Land: 53.4 sq. mi.; **Water:** 0.1 sq. mi.

Orchard
Township
Lat: 38-31-00 N **Long:** 88-38-29 W
Pop: 555 (1990); 584 (1980) **Pop Density:** 15.1
Land: 36.8 sq. mi.; **Water:** 0.2 sq. mi.

Orel
Township
Lat: 38-18-23 N **Long:** 88-33-09 W
Pop: 1,523 (1990); 1,588 (1980) **Pop Density:** 32.3
Land: 47.2 sq. mi.; **Water:** 0.0 sq. mi.

Sims
Village
ZIP: 62886 **Lat:** 38-21-40 N **Long:** 88-32-05 W
Pop: 338 (1990); 355 (1980) **Pop Density:** 281.7
Land: 1.2 sq. mi.; **Water:** 0.0 sq. mi.

Wayne City
Town
ZIP: 62895 **Lat:** 38-20-55 N **Long:** 88-35-14 W
Pop: 1,099 (1990); 1,132 (1980) **Pop Density:** 732.7
Land: 1.5 sq. mi.; **Water:** 0.0 sq. mi. **Elev:** 437 ft.
Name origin: For Gen. "Mad Anthony" Wayne (1745–96) of Revolutionary War fame.

Zif
Township
Lat: 38-35-11 N **Long:** 88-18-59 W
Pop: 120 (1990); 132 (1980) **Pop Density:** 6.9
Land: 17.4 sq. mi.; **Water:** 0.0 sq. mi.

White County
County Seat: Carmi (ZIP: 62821)

Pop: 16,522 (1990); 17,864 (1980) **Pop Density:** 33.4
Land: 494.9 sq. mi.; **Water:** 6.8 sq. mi. **Area Code:** 618
On the southeastern border of IL; organized Dec 9, 1815 (prior to statehood) from Gallatin County.
Name origin: For Leonard White, a delegate to the IL Constitutional Convention (1818) and state legislator.

Burnt Prairie
Village
Lat: 38-15-01 N **Long:** 88-15-27 W
Pop: 71 (1990); 114 (1980) **Pop Density:** 710.0
Land: 0.1 sq. mi.; **Water:** 0.0 sq. mi.
Not coextensive with the town of the same name.

*Burnt Prairie
Township
Lat: 38-11-45 N **Long:** 88-12-17 W
Pop: 473 (1990); 565 (1980) **Pop Density:** 8.8
Land: 54.0 sq. mi.; **Water:** 0.0 sq. mi.

Carmi — City
ZIP: 62821   **Lat:** 38-05-11 N   **Long:** 88-10-16 W
Pop: 5,564 (1990); 6,107 (1980)   **Pop Density:** 2529.1
Land: 2.2 sq. mi.; **Water:** 0.0 sq. mi.   **Elev:** 383 ft.
In southeastern IL. Settled 1816; incorporated Mar 24, 1819. Not coextensive with the town of the same name.
Name origin: For a biblical character (Jacob's grandson).

*Carmi — Township
ZIP: 62821   **Lat:** 38-04-58 N   **Long:** 88-12-28 W
Pop: 7,327 (1990); 7,684 (1980)   **Pop Density:** 203.5
Land: 36.0 sq. mi.; **Water:** 0.5 sq. mi.

Crossville — Village
ZIP: 62827   **Lat:** 38-09-45 N   **Long:** 88-03-52 W
Pop: 805 (1990); 944 (1980)   **Pop Density:** 1341.7
Land: 0.6 sq. mi.; **Water:** 0.0 sq. mi.

Emma — Township
Lat: 37-58-31 N   **Long:** 88-05-06 W
Pop: 507 (1990); 575 (1980)   **Pop Density:** 8.0
Land: 63.2 sq. mi.; **Water:** 2.7 sq. mi.

Enfield — Village
ZIP: 62835   **Lat:** 38-06-05 N   **Long:** 88-20-14 W
Pop: 683 (1990); 890 (1980)   **Pop Density:** 569.2
Land: 1.2 sq. mi.; **Water:** 0.0 sq. mi.
Settled 1813. Not coextensive with the town of the same name.

*Enfield — Township
Lat: 38-04-31 N   **Long:** 88-18-57 W
Pop: 1,145 (1990); 1,294 (1980)   **Pop Density:** 32.3
Land: 35.5 sq. mi.; **Water:** 0.0 sq. mi.

Gray — Township
Lat: 38-14-29 N   **Long:** 88-04-12 W
Pop: 1,362 (1990); 1,484 (1980)   **Pop Density:** 50.4
Land: 27.0 sq. mi.; **Water:** 0.5 sq. mi.

Grayville — City
ZIP: 62844   **Lat:** 38-15-09 N   **Long:** 87-59-49 W
Pop: 1,133 (1990); 1,249 (1980)   **Pop Density:** 1618.6
Land: 0.7 sq. mi.; **Water:** 0.0 sq. mi.
Part of the town is also in Edwards County.

Hawthorne — Township
Lat: 38-05-19 N   **Long:** 88-04-10 W
Pop: 413 (1990); 630 (1980)   **Pop Density:** 7.8
Land: 52.8 sq. mi.; **Water:** 1.2 sq. mi.

Heralds Prairie — Township
Lat: 37-58-31 N   **Long:** 88-12-06 W
Pop: 641 (1990); 646 (1980)   **Pop Density:** 11.8
Land: 54.3 sq. mi.; **Water:** 0.4 sq. mi.

Indian Creek — Township
Lat: 37-58-26 N   **Long:** 88-19-10 W
Pop: 2,373 (1990); 2,502 (1980)   **Pop Density:** 44.1
Land: 53.8 sq. mi.; **Water:** 0.2 sq. mi.

Maunie — Village
ZIP: 62861   **Lat:** 38-02-06 N   **Long:** 88-02-43 W
Pop: 119 (1990); 225 (1980)   **Pop Density:** 595.0
Land: 0.2 sq. mi.; **Water:** 0.0 sq. mi.   **Elev:** 374 ft.

Mill Shoals — Village
ZIP: 62862   **Lat:** 38-14-46 N   **Long:** 88-20-37 W
Pop: 247 (1990); 333 (1980)   **Pop Density:** 823.3
Land: 0.3 sq. mi.; **Water:** 0.0 sq. mi.   **Elev:** 380 ft.
Part of the town is also in Wayne County. Not coextensive with the township of the same name.

*Mill Shoals — Township
Lat: 38-11-09 N   **Long:** 88-19-15 W
Pop: 893 (1990); 927 (1980)   **Pop Density:** 16.8
Land: 53.2 sq. mi.; **Water:** 0.0 sq. mi.

Norris City — Town
ZIP: 62869   **Lat:** 37-58-46 N   **Long:** 88-19-41 W
Pop: 1,341 (1990); 1,515 (1980)   **Pop Density:** 1117.5
Land: 1.2 sq. mi.; **Water:** 0.0 sq. mi.   **Elev:** 443 ft.

Phillips — Township
Lat: 38-10-08 N   **Long:** 88-02-58 W
Pop: 1,388 (1990); 1,557 (1980)   **Pop Density:** 21.3
Land: 65.1 sq. mi.; **Water:** 1.3 sq. mi.

Phillipstown — Village
Lat: 38-08-26 N   **Long:** 88-01-08 W
Pop: 48 (1990); 37 (1980)   **Pop Density:** 160.0
Land: 0.3 sq. mi.; **Water:** 0.0 sq. mi.

Springerton — Village
Lat: 38-10-43 N   **Long:** 88-21-17 W
Pop: 166 (1990); 154 (1980)   **Pop Density:** 1660.0
Land: 0.1 sq. mi.; **Water:** 0.0 sq. mi.

ILLINOIS, Whiteside County   *American Places Dictionary*

> ## Whiteside County
> **County Seat: Morrison (ZIP: 61270)**
>
> **Pop:** 60,186 (1990); 65,970 (1980)   **Pop Density:** 87.9
> **Land:** 684.8 sq. mi.; **Water:** 12.2 sq. mi.   **Area Code:** 815
> On the northwestern border of IL, northeast of Moline; organized Jan 16, 1836 from Jo Daviess and Henry counties.
> **Name origin:** For Gen. Samuel Whiteside, officer in the War of 1812 and the Black Hawk War; IL legislator.

Albany — Village
Lat: 41-47-08 N Long: 90-13-10 W
Pop: 835 (1990); 1,014 (1980)   **Pop Density:** 835.0
Land: 1.0 sq. mi.; **Water:** 0.0 sq. mi.
In northwestern IL on the Mississippi River. Not coextensive with the town of the same name.
Name origin: For Albany, NY.

*Albany — Township
Lat: 41-43-59 N Long: 90-13-29 W
Pop: 994 (1990); 1,254 (1980)   **Pop Density:** 80.2
Land: 12.4 sq. mi.; **Water:** 0.4 sq. mi.

Clyde — Township
Lat: 41-53-38 N Long: 89-55-11 W
Pop: 454 (1990); 503 (1980)   **Pop Density:** 12.7
Land: 35.8 sq. mi.; **Water:** 0.1 sq. mi.

Coleta — Village
ZIP: 61017   Lat: 41-54-19 N Long: 89-47-56 W
Pop: 154 (1990); 219 (1980)   **Pop Density:** 308.0
Land: 0.5 sq. mi.; **Water:** 0.0 sq. mi.   **Elev:** 815 ft.

Coloma — Township
ZIP: 61071   Lat: 41-46-16 N Long: 89-41-25 W
Pop: 12,083 (1990); 13,327 (1980)   **Pop Density:** 1196.3
Land: 10.1 sq. mi.; **Water:** 1.1 sq. mi.

Deer Grove — Village
ZIP: 61243   Lat: 41-36-36 N Long: 89-41-04 W
Pop: 44 (1990); 77 (1980)   **Pop Density:** 88.0
Land: 0.5 sq. mi.; **Water:** 0.0 sq. mi.

Erie — Village
ZIP: 61250   Lat: 41-39-31 N Long: 90-04-52 W
Pop: 1,572 (1990); 1,725 (1980)   **Pop Density:** 1122.9
Land: 1.4 sq. mi.; **Water:** 0.0 sq. mi.
In northwestern IL, northeast of Moline on the site of an old Indian crossroad. Village incorporated 1872. Not coextensive with the town of the same name.
Name origin: For Lake Erie.

*Erie — Township
Lat: 41-38-21 N Long: 90-07-01 W
Pop: 2,032 (1990); 2,270 (1980)   **Pop Density:** 84.7
Land: 24.0 sq. mi.; **Water:** 0.7 sq. mi.

Fenton — Township
Lat: 41-42-35 N Long: 90-02-12 W
Pop: 557 (1990); 673 (1980)   **Pop Density:** 16.0
Land: 34.9 sq. mi.; **Water:** 0.4 sq. mi.

Fulton — City
ZIP: 61252   Lat: 41-51-54 N Long: 90-09-31 W
Pop: 3,698 (1990); 3,936 (1980)   **Pop Density:** 1680.9
Land: 2.2 sq. mi.; **Water:** 0.1 sq. mi.
In northwestern IL on the Mississippi River. Founded 1839. Not coextensive with the town of the same name.
Name origin: For Robert Fulton (1765–1815), builder of the *Clermont*, the first commercially successful steamboat.

*Fulton — Township
Lat: 41-52-59 N Long: 90-08-04 W
Pop: 4,373 (1990); 4,707 (1980)   **Pop Density:** 251.3
Land: 17.4 sq. mi.; **Water:** 4.1 sq. mi.

Garden Plain — Township
Lat: 41-47-59 N Long: 90-08-16 W
Pop: 1,048 (1990); 1,119 (1980)   **Pop Density:** 34.1
Land: 30.7 sq. mi.; **Water:** 0.9 sq. mi.

Genesee — Township
Lat: 41-52-55 N Long: 89-47-57 W
Pop: 856 (1990); 1,005 (1980)   **Pop Density:** 24.0
Land: 35.7 sq. mi.; **Water:** 0.0 sq. mi.

Hahnaman — Township
Lat: 41-37-39 N Long: 89-41-19 W
Pop: 393 (1990); 468 (1980)   **Pop Density:** 11.0
Land: 35.8 sq. mi.; **Water:** 0.0 sq. mi.

Hopkins — Township
Lat: 41-47-51 N Long: 89-48-32 W
Pop: 2,308 (1990); 2,527 (1980)   **Pop Density:** 64.8
Land: 35.6 sq. mi.; **Water:** 0.4 sq. mi.

Hume — Township
Lat: 41-43-04 N Long: 89-47-50 W
Pop: 514 (1990); 563 (1980)   **Pop Density:** 17.4
Land: 29.5 sq. mi.; **Water:** 0.6 sq. mi.

Jordan — Township
Lat: 41-53-17 N Long: 89-41-31 W
Pop: 860 (1990); 987 (1980)   **Pop Density:** 24.0
Land: 35.8 sq. mi.; **Water:** 0.0 sq. mi.

Lyndon — Town
ZIP: 61261   Lat: 41-43-02 N Long: 89-55-30 W
Pop: 615 (1990); 777 (1980)   **Pop Density:** 768.8
Land: 0.8 sq. mi.; **Water:** 0.0 sq. mi.
Incorporated March 3, 1874. Not coextensive with the town of the same name.

*Lyndon — Township
Lat: 41-43-44 N Long: 89-54-54 W
Pop: 1,004 (1990); 1,254 (1980)   **Pop Density:** 36.8
Land: 27.3 sq. mi.; **Water:** 0.9 sq. mi.

Montmorency
Township
Lat: 41-42-22 N Long: 89-41-12 W
Pop: 2,451 (1990); 2,510 (1980)   **Pop Density:** 68.5
Land: 35.8 sq. mi.; **Water:** 0.1 sq. mi.

Morrison
Town
ZIP: 61270   Lat: 41-48-30 N Long: 89-57-55 W
Pop: 4,363 (1990); 4,605 (1980)   **Pop Density:** 2296.3
Land: 1.9 sq. mi.; **Water:** 0.0 sq. mi.

Mount Pleasant
Township
ZIP: 61270   Lat: 41-47-59 N Long: 89-55-32 W
Pop: 5,371 (1990); 5,569 (1980)   **Pop Density:** 150.4
Land: 35.7 sq. mi.; **Water:** 0.0 sq. mi.

Newton
Township
Lat: 41-42-55 N Long: 90-09-00 W
Pop: 476 (1990); 545 (1980)   **Pop Density:** 13.3
Land: 35.9 sq. mi.; **Water:** 0.0 sq. mi.

Portland
Township
Lat: 41-36-39 N Long: 90-03-18 W
Pop: 471 (1990); 626 (1980)   **Pop Density:** 13.5
Land: 34.8 sq. mi.; **Water:** 0.8 sq. mi.

Prophetstown
Town
ZIP: 61277   Lat: 41-40-10 N Long: 89-56-04 W
Pop: 1,749 (1990); 2,141 (1980)   **Pop Density:** 1345.4
Land: 1.3 sq. mi.; **Water:** 0.0 sq. mi.   **Elev:** 618 ft.
In northwestern IL near Rock Falls on the Rock River, northeast of Moline. Not coextensive with the town of the same name.
Name origin: For its being the site of the village of White Cloud (c. 1794–c. 1841), an Indian known as the Prophet.

*Prophetstown
Township
Lat: 41-38-22 N Long: 89-54-40 W
Pop: 2,569 (1990); 2,882 (1980)   **Pop Density:** 53.6
Land: 47.9 sq. mi.; **Water:** 0.5 sq. mi.

Rock Falls
Town
ZIP: 61071   Lat: 41-46-27 N Long: 89-41-28 W
Pop: 9,654 (1990); 10,633 (1980)   **Pop Density:** 3218.0
Land: 3.0 sq. mi.; **Water:** 0.1 sq. mi.   **Elev:** 641 ft.
In northwestern IL on the Rock River, 45 mi. southwest of Rockford. Settled 1837; incorporated Jun 21, 1889.
Name origin: Descriptively named for its location near the falls on the river.

Sterling
City
ZIP: 61081   Lat: 41-47-53 N Long: 89-41-29 W
Pop: 15,132 (1990); 16,281 (1980)   **Pop Density:** 3690.7
Land: 4.1 sq. mi.; **Water:** 0.2 sq. mi.
In northwestern IL on the Rock River, 45 mi. southwest of Rockford. Incorporated Feb 17, 1841. Not coextensive with the town of the same name.
Name origin: For Samuel Sterling, an early settler.

*Sterling
Township
ZIP: 61081   Lat: 41-48-49 N Long: 89-41-19 W
Pop: 18,329 (1990); 19,827 (1980)   **Pop Density:** 780.0
Land: 23.5 sq. mi.; **Water:** 1.1 sq. mi.

Tampico
Village
ZIP: 61283   Lat: 41-37-49 N Long: 89-47-07 W
Pop: 833 (1990); 966 (1980)   **Pop Density:** 2082.5
Land: 0.4 sq. mi.; **Water:** 0.0 sq. mi.
Not coextensive with the town of the same name.

*Tampico
Township
Lat: 41-37-43 N Long: 89-48-22 W
Pop: 1,253 (1990); 1,379 (1980)   **Pop Density:** 35.0
Land: 35.8 sq. mi.; **Water:** 0.0 sq. mi.

Union Grove
Township
Lat: 41-48-53 N Long: 90-02-01 W
Pop: 1,146 (1990); 1,300 (1980)   **Pop Density:** 32.7
Land: 35.0 sq. mi.; **Water:** 0.0 sq. mi.

Ustick
Township
Lat: 41-53-20 N Long: 90-02-03 W
Pop: 644 (1990); 675 (1980)   **Pop Density:** 18.2
Land: 35.4 sq. mi.; **Water:** 0.0 sq. mi.

Will County
County Seat: Joliet (ZIP: 60431)

Pop: 357,313 (1990); 324,460 (1980)   **Pop Density:** 426.8
Land: 837.3 sq. mi.; **Water:** 12.2 sq. mi.   **Area Code:** 815
On the northeastern border of IL, south of Chicago; organized Jan 12, 1836 from Cook and Iroquois counties.
Name origin: For Dr. Conrad Will (1779–1835), physician and IL legislator.

Beecher
Village
ZIP: 60401   Lat: 41-20-51 N Long: 87-36-53 W
Pop: 2,032 (1990); 2,024 (1980)   **Pop Density:** 1128.9
Land: 1.8 sq. mi.; **Water:** 0.0 sq. mi.   **Elev:** 736 ft.

Bolingbrook
Village
ZIP: 60440   Lat: 41-41-51 N Long: 88-04-38 W
Pop: 39,371 (1990); 36,107 (1980)   **Pop Density:** 3612.0
Land: 10.9 sq. mi.; **Water:** 0.0 sq. mi.   **Elev:** 703 ft.
In northeastern IL, 25 mi. southwest of Chicago. Incorporated 1965. Part of the town is also in DuPage County.
Name origin: For Bolingbroke, Lincolnshire, England, and for the Bolingbroke family; spelling change reflects pronunciation.

Braidwood
City
ZIP: 60408   Lat: 41-16-05 N Long: 88-13-23 W
Pop: 3,584 (1990); 3,429 (1980)   **Pop Density:** 1086.1
Land: 3.3 sq. mi.; **Water:** 0.0 sq. mi.
Settled 1865 when coal was found by a local resident drilling a well.

ILLINOIS, Will County

Channahon
Village
ZIP: 60410 Lat: 41-26-05 N Long: 88-12-38 W
Pop: 4,266 (1990); 3,788 (1980) Pop Density: 992.1
Land: 4.3 sq. mi.; Water: 0.4 sq. mi.
Not coextensive with the town of the same name. Part of the town is also in Grundy County.
Name origin: From an Indian term probably meaning 'meeting of the waters,' referring to the confluence of the Illinois and Kankakee rivers.

*Channahon
Township
ZIP: 60410 Lat: 41-25-06 N Long: 88-11-35 W
Pop: 5,386 (1990); 4,420 (1980) Pop Density: 161.3
Land: 33.4 sq. mi.; Water: 2.3 sq. mi.

Crest Hill
Village
ZIP: 60435 Lat: 41-33-58 N Long: 88-06-18 W
Pop: 10,643 (1990); 9,252 (1980) Pop Density: 1478.2
Land: 7.2 sq. mi.; Water: 0.1 sq. mi.
Incorporated Jan 22, 1960.

Crete
Village
ZIP: 60417 Lat: 41-27-11 N Long: 87-36-54 W
Pop: 6,773 (1990); 5,417 (1980) Pop Density: 1472.4
Land: 4.6 sq. mi.; Water: 0.0 sq. mi.
In northeastern IL near the IN border, 30 mi. south of Chicago. Not coextensive with the town of the same name.
Name origin: For the Mediterranean island.

*Crete
Township
ZIP: 60417 Lat: 41-25-53 N Long: 87-36-02 W
Pop: 21,512 (1990); 20,416 (1980) Pop Density: 482.3
Land: 44.6 sq. mi.; Water: 0.1 sq. mi.

Crystal Lawns
CDP
Lat: 41-34-12 N Long: 88-09-28 W
Pop: 3,037 (1990) Pop Density: 3037.0
Land: 1.0 sq. mi.; Water: 0.0 sq. mi.

Custer
Township
Lat: 41-13-55 N Long: 88-08-11 W
Pop: 1,110 (1990); 1,101 (1980) Pop Density: 43.4
Land: 25.6 sq. mi.; Water: 0.9 sq. mi.

Diamond
Village
Lat: 41-17-20 N Long: 88-14-30 W
Pop: 0 (1990)
Land: 0.1 sq. mi.; Water: 0.0 sq. mi.
Part of the town is also in Grundy County.

Du Page
Township
ZIP: 60441 Lat: 41-40-57 N Long: 88-05-01 W
Pop: 55,444 (1990); 47,088 (1980) Pop Density: 1527.4
Land: 36.3 sq. mi.; Water: 0.5 sq. mi.

Elwood
Village
ZIP: 60421 Lat: 41-24-43 N Long: 88-06-32 W
Pop: 951 (1990); 814 (1980) Pop Density: 951.0
Land: 1.0 sq. mi.; Water: 0.0 sq. mi.

Fairmont
CDP
Lat: 41-33-42 N Long: 88-03-35 W
Pop: 2,894 (1990) Pop Density: 1607.8
Land: 1.8 sq. mi.; Water: 0.0 sq. mi.

Florence
Township
Lat: 41-20-11 N Long: 88-04-19 W
Pop: 720 (1990); 931 (1980) Pop Density: 19.7
Land: 36.5 sq. mi.; Water: 0.0 sq. mi.

Frankfort
Village
ZIP: 60423 Lat: 41-29-49 N Long: 87-50-09 W
Pop: 7,180 (1990); 4,357 (1980) Pop Density: 865.1
Land: 8.3 sq. mi.; Water: 0.0 sq. mi. Elev: 767 ft.
In northeastern IL, 25 mi. southwest of Chicago. Not coextensive with the town of the same name.
Name origin: For Frankfort-am-Main, Germany.

*Frankfort
Township
ZIP: 60423 Lat: 41-30-41 N Long: 87-51-08 W
Pop: 25,755 (1990); 20,335 (1980) Pop Density: 698.0
Land: 36.9 sq. mi.; Water: 0.0 sq. mi.

Frankfort Square
CDP
Lat: 41-31-08 N Long: 87-48-11 W
Pop: 6,227 (1990) Pop Density: 3113.5
Land: 2.0 sq. mi.; Water: 0.0 sq. mi.

Godley
Village
Lat: 41-14-12 N Long: 88-14-31 W
Pop: 272 (1990); 322 (1980) Pop Density: 453.3
Land: 0.6 sq. mi.; Water: 0.0 sq. mi.
Part of the town is also in Grundy County.

Goodings Grove
CDP
Lat: 41-37-17 N Long: 87-56-26 W
Pop: 14,054 (1990) Pop Density: 1495.1
Land: 9.4 sq. mi.; Water: 0.0 sq. mi.

Green Garden
Township
Lat: 41-25-58 N Long: 87-51-17 W
Pop: 1,722 (1990); 1,420 (1980) Pop Density: 46.7
Land: 36.9 sq. mi.; Water: 0.0 sq. mi.

Homer
Township
ZIP: 60441 Lat: 41-36-23 N Long: 87-57-51 W
Pop: 21,464 (1990); 13,441 (1980) Pop Density: 596.2
Land: 36.0 sq. mi.; Water: 0.0 sq. mi.

Ingalls Park
CDP
Lat: 41-31-16 N Long: 88-02-01 W
Pop: 3,173 (1990) Pop Density: 2884.5
Land: 1.1 sq. mi.; Water: 0.0 sq. mi.

Jackson
Township
Lat: 41-25-40 N Long: 88-04-39 W
Pop: 2,700 (1990); 2,473 (1980) Pop Density: 74.2
Land: 36.4 sq. mi.; Water: 0.0 sq. mi.

Joliet
City
ZIP: 60431 Lat: 41-31-36 N Long: 88-07-20 W
Pop: 76,836 (1990); 77,956 (1980) Pop Density: 2763.9
Land: 27.8 sq. mi.; Water: 0.3 sq. mi.
In northeastern IL, 30 mi. southwest of Chicago. County seat. Discovered in 1673 by Father Marquette (1637–75) and Louis Joliet (or Jolliet). Incorporated Feb 26, 1845. Not coextensive with the town of the same name.
Name origin: Renamed in 1845 by the legislature, for Louis Joliet (1645–1700). Previous PO name was Juliet.

*Joliet
Township
ZIP: 60431 Lat: 41-30-34 N Long: 88-04-54 W
Pop: 84,243 (1990); 89,566 (1980) Pop Density: 2386.5
Land: 35.3 sq. mi.; Water: 0.8 sq. mi.

Lakewood Shores
CDP
Lat: 41-16-14 N Long: 88-08-10 W
Pop: 1,606 (1990) Pop Density: 669.2
Land: 2.4 sq. mi.; Water: 0.1 sq. mi.

ILLINOIS, Will County

Lockport — City
ZIP: 60441 **Lat:** 41-35-21 N **Long:** 88-02-52 W
Pop: 9,401 (1990); 9,192 (1980) **Pop Density:** 2292.9
Land: 4.1 sq. mi.; **Water:** 0.0 sq. mi.

In northeastern IL on the Illinois and Michigan Canal, 30 mi. southwest of Chicago. Incorporated Feb 12, 1853. Not coextensive with the town of the same name.

Name origin: For its descriptive connotations.

*Lockport — Township
ZIP: 60441 **Lat:** 41-35-46 N **Long:** 88-05-03 W
Pop: 32,336 (1990); 34,641 (1980) **Pop Density:** 900.7
Land: 35.9 sq. mi.; **Water:** 0.7 sq. mi.

Manhattan — Town
ZIP: 60442 **Lat:** 41-25-33 N **Long:** 87-59-19 W
Pop: 2,059 (1990); 1,944 (1980) **Pop Density:** 1583.8
Land: 1.3 sq. mi.; **Water:** 0.0 sq. mi.

Incorporated Dec 20, 1886. Not coextensive with the town of the same name.

Name origin: For Manhattan Island in New York Bay, NY.

*Manhattan — Township
Lat: 41-25-57 N **Long:** 87-57-13 W
Pop: 3,963 (1990); 3,386 (1980) **Pop Density:** 107.4
Land: 36.9 sq. mi.; **Water:** 0.0 sq. mi.

Minooka — Town
ZIP: 60447 **Lat:** 41-26-26 N **Long:** 88-14-33 W
Pop: 804 (1990); 138 (1980) **Pop Density:** 1340.0
Land: 0.6 sq. mi.; **Water:** 0.1 sq. mi.

Incorporated Mar 27, 1869. Part of the town is also in Grundy County.

Name origin: From the Delaware term *mino* meaning 'good' and *oki* meaning 'land.'

Mokena — Town
ZIP: 60448 **Lat:** 41-31-55 N **Long:** 87-52-32 W
Pop: 6,128 (1990); 4,578 (1980) **Pop Density:** 1332.2
Land: 4.6 sq. mi.; **Water:** 0.0 sq. mi. **Elev:** 706 ft.
Incorporated 1880.

Name origin: A variation of the Algonquian term for 'turtle.'

Monee — Town
ZIP: 60449 **Lat:** 41-25-19 N **Long:** 87-45-14 W
Pop: 1,044 (1990); 993 (1980) **Pop Density:** 497.1
Land: 2.1 sq. mi.; **Water:** 0.0 sq. mi.

In northeastern IL, 30 mi. south of Chicago. Incorporated 1874. Not coextensive with the town of the same name.

Name origin: From the Indian pronunciation of Marie Lefevre (1793–1866), Indian wife of French trader Joseph Baily.

*Monee — Township
ZIP: 60449 **Lat:** 41-25-27 N **Long:** 87-43-25 W
Pop: 10,765 (1990); 10,996 (1980) **Pop Density:** 299.9
Land: 35.9 sq. mi.; **Water:** 0.1 sq. mi.

Naperville — City
ZIP: 60566 **Lat:** 41-42-58 N **Long:** 88-08-41 W
Pop: 12,420 (1990); 901 (1980) **Pop Density:** 2435.3
Land: 5.1 sq. mi.; **Water:** 0.0 sq. mi.

In northeastern IL, 30 mi. west of Chicago. Incorporated Feb 7, 1857. Part of the town is also in DuPage County.

Name origin: For its founder, Capt. Joseph Naper, who built a sawmill and platted the townsite in 1832.

New Lenox — City
ZIP: 60451 **Lat:** 41-31-07 N **Long:** 87-59-02 W
Pop: 9,627 (1990); 5,792 (1980) **Pop Density:** 1631.7
Land: 5.9 sq. mi.; **Water:** 0.0 sq. mi.

In northeastern IL, 30 mi. southwest of Chicago. Not coextensive with the town of the same name.

*New Lenox — Township
ZIP: 60451 **Lat:** 41-30-40 N **Long:** 87-57-51 W
Pop: 20,716 (1990); 16,574 (1980) **Pop Density:** 580.3
Land: 35.7 sq. mi.; **Water:** 0.1 sq. mi.

Park Forest — Village
ZIP: 60466 **Lat:** 41-27-38 N **Long:** 87-41-30 W
Pop: 3,309 (1990); 3,311 (1980) **Pop Density:** 3008.2
Land: 1.1 sq. mi.; **Water:** 0.0 sq. mi.

In northeastern IL, 28 mi. south of Chicago. Incorporated 1949. Part of the town is also in Cook County.

Peotone — Town
ZIP: 60468 **Lat:** 41-19-53 N **Long:** 87-47-46 W
Pop: 2,947 (1990); 2,832 (1980) **Pop Density:** 2266.9
Land: 1.3 sq. mi.; **Water:** 0.0 sq. mi. **Elev:** 702 ft.

In northeastern IL, 20 mi. southeast of Joliet. Not coextensive with the town of the same name.

Name origin: From a Potawatomi term probably meaning 'bring to this place.'

*Peotone — Township
Lat: 41-20-24 N **Long:** 87-50-20 W
Pop: 3,613 (1990); 3,319 (1980) **Pop Density:** 100.1
Land: 36.1 sq. mi.; **Water:** 0.1 sq. mi.

Plainfield — Town
ZIP: 60544 **Lat:** 41-36-57 N **Long:** 88-12-14 W
Pop: 4,557 (1990); 3,777 (1980) **Pop Density:** 1168.5
Land: 3.9 sq. mi.; **Water:** 0.3 sq. mi.

In northeastern IL on the Du Page River, 35 mi. southwest of Chicago. Not coextensive with the town of the same name.

Name origin: Descriptively named for its prairie topography. Previously called Walker's Grove.

*Plainfield — Township
ZIP: 60544 **Lat:** 41-35-39 N **Long:** 88-12-01 W
Pop: 15,392 (1990); 14,685 (1980) **Pop Density:** 459.5
Land: 33.5 sq. mi.; **Water:** 1.7 sq. mi.

Preston Heights — CDP
Lat: 41-29-34 N **Long:** 88-04-23 W
Pop: 2,750 (1990) **Pop Density:** 1617.6
Land: 1.7 sq. mi.; **Water:** 0.0 sq. mi.

Reed — Township
Lat: 41-14-37 N **Long:** 88-13-01 W
Pop: 4,086 (1990); 3,944 (1980) **Pop Density:** 233.5
Land: 17.5 sq. mi.; **Water:** 0.6 sq. mi.

Rockdale — Village
ZIP: 60436 **Lat:** 41-30-19 N **Long:** 88-07-05 W
Pop: 1,709 (1990); 1,913 (1980) **Pop Density:** 2136.3
Land: 0.8 sq. mi.; **Water:** 0.0 sq. mi.

Romeoville — Village
ZIP: 60441 **Lat:** 41-38-45 N **Long:** 88-05-10 W
Pop: 14,074 (1990); 15,519 (1980) **Pop Density:** 1781.5
Land: 7.9 sq. mi.; **Water:** 0.1 sq. mi.

In northeastern IL on the Des Plaines River, 25 mi. southwest of Chicago. Incorporated 1895.

Name origin: For the hero of Shakespeare's *Romeo and Juliet.*

Sauk Village — Village
ZIP: 60411 Lat: 41-28-08 N Long: 87-34-33 W
Pop: 0 (1990)
Land: 0.01 sq. mi.; Water: 0.0 sq. mi.

In northeastern IL near the IN border, 28 mi. south of Chicago. Part of the town is also in Cook County.

Name origin: For the Sauk Indians.

Shorewood — Village
ZIP: 60435 Lat: 41-31-23 N Long: 88-12-08 W
Pop: 6,264 (1990); 4,714 (1980) Pop Density: 2320.0
Land: 2.7 sq. mi.; Water: 0.1 sq. mi. Elev: 581 ft.

Steger — Village
ZIP: 60475 Lat: 41-27-54 N Long: 87-38-10 W
Pop: 5,576 (1990); 5,855 (1980) Pop Density: 5069.1
Land: 1.1 sq. mi.; Water: 0.0 sq. mi. Elev: 715 ft.

Part of the town is also in Cook County.

Name origin: For piano maker John Steger.

Symerton — Village
ZIP: 60481 Lat: 41-19-41 N Long: 88-03-16 W
Pop: 110 (1990); 120 (1980) Pop Density: 1100.0
Land: 0.1 sq. mi.; Water: 0.0 sq. mi.

Tinley Park — Village
ZIP: 60477 Lat: 41-33-28 N Long: 87-48-33 W
Pop: 81 (1990); 20 (1980) Pop Density: 81.0
Land: 1.0 sq. mi.; Water: 0.0 sq. mi. Elev: 698 ft.

In northeastern IL, a residential suburb 20 mi. southwest of Chicago. Incorporated 1892. Part of the town is also in Cook County.

Name origin: For the Tinley brothers, Rock Island Railroad executives.

Troy — Township
ZIP: 60435 Lat: 41-30-27 N Long: 88-11-48 W
Pop: 21,642 (1990); 17,939 (1980) Pop Density: 621.9
Land: 34.8 sq. mi.; Water: 0.6 sq. mi.

University Park — Village
ZIP: 60466 Lat: 41-26-32 N Long: 87-42-34 W
Pop: 6,204 (1990); 6,243 (1980) Pop Density: 785.3
Land: 7.9 sq. mi.; Water: 0.0 sq. mi.

Part of the town is also in Cook County.

Washington — Township
Lat: 41-20-32 N Long: 87-36-05 W
Pop: 3,724 (1990); 3,536 (1980) Pop Density: 83.7
Land: 44.5 sq. mi.; Water: 0.0 sq. mi.

Wesley — Township
Lat: 41-15-20 N Long: 88-04-09 W
Pop: 2,540 (1990); 2,397 (1980) Pop Density: 90.7
Land: 28.0 sq. mi.; Water: 0.4 sq. mi.

Wheatland — Township
ZIP: 60544 Lat: 41-40-44 N Long: 88-12-40 W
Pop: 10,746 (1990); 4,491 (1980) Pop Density: 302.7
Land: 35.5 sq. mi.; Water: 0.3 sq. mi.

Will — Township
Lat: 41-19-58 N Long: 87-43-13 W
Pop: 1,323 (1990); 1,136 (1980) Pop Density: 36.6
Land: 36.1 sq. mi.; Water: 0.0 sq. mi.

Willowbrook — CDP
Lat: 41-27-27 N Long: 87-32-10 W
Pop: 1,808 (1990) Pop Density: 531.8
Land: 3.4 sq. mi.; Water: 0.0 sq. mi.

Wilmington — City
ZIP: 60481 Lat: 41-17-51 N Long: 88-09-34 W
Pop: 4,743 (1990); 4,424 (1980) Pop Density: 1009.1
Land: 4.7 sq. mi.; Water: 0.3 sq. mi.

Not coextensive with the town of the same name.

*Wilmington — Township
ZIP: 60481 Lat: 41-20-00 N Long: 88-11-19 W
Pop: 5,736 (1990); 5,538 (1980) Pop Density: 173.3
Land: 33.1 sq. mi.; Water: 2.9 sq. mi.

Wilton — Township
Lat: 41-20-17 N Long: 87-57-38 W
Pop: 675 (1990); 687 (1980) Pop Density: 18.8
Land: 36.0 sq. mi.; Water: 0.0 sq. mi.

Part of the town is also in DuPage County.

Woodridge — Village
ZIP: 60517 Lat: 41-41-33 N Long: 88-02-17 W
Pop: 24 (1990) Pop Density: 40.0
Land: 0.6 sq. mi.; Water: 0.0 sq. mi.

In northeastern IL, 24 mi. southwest of Chicago. Incorporated 1959. Part of the town is also in DuPage County.

Name origin: Descriptive and promotional.

Williamson County
County Seat: Marion (ZIP: 62959)

Pop: 57,733 (1990); 56,538 (1980) **Pop Density:** 136.1
Land: 424.2 sq. mi.; **Water:** 20.2 sq. mi. **Area Code:** 618
In south-central IL, east of Carbondale; organized Feb 28, 1839 from Franklin County.
Name origin: For Williamson County, TN, former home of many early settlers.

Bush   Village
Lat: 37-50-30 N **Long:** 89-07-47 W
Pop: 351 (1990); 368 (1980) **Pop Density:** 702.0
Land: 0.5 sq. mi.; **Water:** 0.0 sq. mi.

Cambria   Village
ZIP: 62915 **Lat:** 37-46-43 N **Long:** 89-06-51 W
Pop: 1,230 (1990); 1,090 (1980) **Pop Density:** 1118.2
Land: 1.1 sq. mi.; **Water:** 0.0 sq. mi.

Carterville   City
ZIP: 62918 **Lat:** 37-45-42 N **Long:** 89-04-57 W
Pop: 3,630 (1990); 3,445 (1980) **Pop Density:** 1251.7
Land: 2.9 sq. mi.; **Water:** 0.0 sq. mi. **Elev:** 457 ft.
In southern IL, 5 mi. southwest of Herrin. Incorporated 1892.
Name origin: For early farmer Laban Carter.

Colp   Village
ZIP: 62921 **Lat:** 37-48-26 N **Long:** 89-04-40 W
Pop: 235 (1990); 278 (1980) **Pop Density:** 2350.0
Land: 0.1 sq. mi.; **Water:** 0.0 sq. mi.

Crainville   Village
ZIP: 62918 **Lat:** 37-45-01 N **Long:** 89-03-36 W
Pop: 1,019 (1990); 910 (1980) **Pop Density:** 783.8
Land: 1.3 sq. mi.; **Water:** 0.0 sq. mi. **Elev:** 473 ft.

Creal Springs   City
ZIP: 62922 **Lat:** 37-37-06 N **Long:** 88-50-15 W
Pop: 791 (1990); 845 (1980) **Pop Density:** 878.9
Land: 0.9 sq. mi.; **Water:** 0.0 sq. mi.

Energy   Village
ZIP: 62933 **Lat:** 37-46-31 N **Long:** 89-01-32 W
Pop: 1,106 (1990); 1,138 (1980) **Pop Density:** 850.8
Land: 1.3 sq. mi.; **Water:** 0.0 sq. mi.

Freeman Spur   Village
Lat: 37-51-26 N **Long:** 88-59-58 W
Pop: 137 (1990); 199 (1980) **Pop Density:** 685.0
Land: 0.2 sq. mi.; **Water:** 0.0 sq. mi.
Part of the town is also in Franklin County.

Herrin   City
ZIP: 62948 **Lat:** 37-48-05 N **Long:** 89-01-53 W
Pop: 10,857 (1990); 10,708 (1980) **Pop Density:** 1529.2
Land: 7.1 sq. mi.; **Water:** 0.1 sq. mi.
In south-central IL, 35 mi. south of Mount Vernon; coal-mining center. Site of the Herrin Massacre during the 1922 miners' strike. Incorporated Mar 21, 1898.
Name origin: For Isaac Herrin, its first settler.

Hurst   City
Lat: 37-50-08 N **Long:** 89-08-36 W
Pop: 842 (1990); 938 (1980) **Pop Density:** 1052.5
Land: 0.8 sq. mi.; **Water:** 0.0 sq. mi.

Johnston City   Town
ZIP: 62951 **Lat:** 37-49-17 N **Long:** 88-55-31 W
Pop: 3,706 (1990); 3,873 (1980) **Pop Density:** 2180.0
Land: 1.7 sq. mi.; **Water:** 0.1 sq. mi.

Marion   City
ZIP: 62959 **Lat:** 37-43-58 N **Long:** 88-56-28 W
Pop: 14,545 (1990); 14,031 (1980) **Pop Density:** 1359.3
Land: 10.7 sq. mi.; **Water:** 0.1 sq. mi.
In southern IL on Crab Orchard Lake, 45 mi. south of Mount Vernon. County seat. Incorporated Feb 24, 1841.
Name origin: For Francis Marion (c. 1732–95), SC soldier and legislator known as "The Swamp Fox" for his tactics during the American Revolution.

Pittsburg   Town
ZIP: 62974 **Lat:** 37-46-36 N **Long:** 88-51-00 W
Pop: 602 (1990); 605 (1980) **Pop Density:** 286.7
Land: 2.1 sq. mi.; **Water:** 0.0 sq. mi. **Elev:** 466 ft.
Name origin: For Pittsburg, PA.

Spillertown   Village
Lat: 37-45-57 N **Long:** 88-55-15 W
Pop: 249 (1990); 206 (1980) **Pop Density:** 830.0
Land: 0.3 sq. mi.; **Water:** 0.0 sq. mi. **Elev:** 483 ft.

Stonefort   Village
Lat: 37-36-56 N **Long:** 88-42-44 W
Pop: 178 (1990); 176 (1980) **Pop Density:** 296.7
Land: 0.6 sq. mi.; **Water:** 0.0 sq. mi.
Part of the town is also in Saline County.

Whiteash   Village
Lat: 37-47-06 N **Long:** 88-55-49 W
Pop: 249 (1990); 268 (1980) **Pop Density:** 276.7
Land: 0.9 sq. mi.; **Water:** 0.0 sq. mi.

Winnebago County
County Seat: Rockford (ZIP: 61101)

Pop: 252,913 (1990); 250,884 (1980)
Land: 513.8 sq. mi.; **Water:** 5.5 sq. mi.
Pop Density: 492.2
Area Code: 815

On the northern border of IL; organized Jan 16, 1836 from Jo Daviess County.

Name origin: For the Indian tribe of Siouan linguistic stock; their name is thought to mean 'fish eaters.'

Burritt
Township
Lat: 42-19-55 N **Long:** 89-13-47 W
Pop: 932 (1990); 956 (1980) **Pop Density:** 28.9
Land: 32.3 sq. mi.; **Water:** 0.1 sq. mi.

Cherry Valley
Village
ZIP: 61016 **Lat:** 42-14-24 N **Long:** 88-57-42 W
Pop: 1,615 (1990); 946 (1980) **Pop Density:** 576.8
Land: 2.8 sq. mi.; **Water:** 0.0 sq. mi.

Not coextensive with the town of the same name.

*Cherry Valley
Township
ZIP: 61016 **Lat:** 42-12-14 N **Long:** 88-59-20 W
Pop: 15,828 (1990); 13,608 (1980) **Pop Density:** 520.7
Land: 30.4 sq. mi.; **Water:** 0.3 sq. mi.

Durand
Village
ZIP: 61024 **Lat:** 42-26-08 N **Long:** 89-19-43 W
Pop: 1,100 (1990); 1,073 (1980) **Pop Density:** 1833.3
Land: 0.6 sq. mi.; **Water:** 0.0 sq. mi.

Not coextensive with the town of the same name.

*Durand
Township
Lat: 42-24-41 N **Long:** 89-20-09 W
Pop: 1,910 (1990); 1,649 (1980) **Pop Density:** 64.5
Land: 29.6 sq. mi.; **Water:** 0.0 sq. mi.

Harlem
Township
ZIP: 61111 **Lat:** 42-22-26 N **Long:** 89-00-08 W
Pop: 28,453 (1990); 26,473 (1980) **Pop Density:** 867.5
Land: 32.8 sq. mi.; **Water:** 0.6 sq. mi.

Harrison
Township
Lat: 42-24-25 N **Long:** 89-14-09 W
Pop: 697 (1990); 735 (1980) **Pop Density:** 28.3
Land: 24.6 sq. mi.; **Water:** 0.1 sq. mi.

Lake Summerset
CDP
Lat: 42-27-14 N **Long:** 89-23-23 W
Pop: 687 (1990) **Pop Density:** 624.5
Land: 1.1 sq. mi.; **Water:** 0.3 sq. mi.

Part of the town is also in Stephenson County.

Laona
Township
Lat: 42-28-08 N **Long:** 89-19-26 W
Pop: 912 (1990); 825 (1980) **Pop Density:** 33.7
Land: 27.1 sq. mi.; **Water:** 0.3 sq. mi.

Loves Park
City
ZIP: 61111 **Lat:** 42-20-09 N **Long:** 89-00-35 W
Pop: 15,462 (1990); 13,192 (1980) **Pop Density:** 1310.3
Land: 11.8 sq. mi.; **Water:** 0.4 sq. mi.

In north-central IL on the Rock River, just north of Rockford. Incorporated April 30, 1947.

Name origin: For Malcolm Love, who bought a 9,236-acre farm.

Machesney Park
Village
ZIP: 61111 **Lat:** 42-21-37 N **Long:** 89-02-16 W
Pop: 19,033 (1990); 19,514 (1980) **Pop Density:** 2162.8
Land: 8.8 sq. mi.; **Water:** 0.3 sq. mi. **Elev:** 741 ft.

In north-central IL on the Rock River, 5 mi. north of Rockford. Incorporated Feb 24, 1981.

New Millford
Village
Lat: 42-10-28 N **Long:** 89-03-55 W
Pop: 463 (1990); 687 (1980) **Pop Density:** 926.0
Land: 0.5 sq. mi.; **Water:** 0.0 sq. mi.

Owen
Township
Lat: 42-22-00 N **Long:** 89-06-21 W
Pop: 2,995 (1990); 3,024 (1980) **Pop Density:** 84.6
Land: 35.4 sq. mi.; **Water:** 0.3 sq. mi.

Pecatonica
Town
ZIP: 61063 **Lat:** 42-18-35 N **Long:** 89-21-30 W
Pop: 1,760 (1990); 1,732 (1980) **Pop Density:** 1600.0
Land: 1.1 sq. mi.; **Water:** 0.0 sq. mi. **Elev:** 759 ft.

In northern IL on the Pecatonica River, 13 mi. northwest of Rockford. Not coextensive with the town of the same name.

Name origin: For the river, itself named from a Sac term probably meaning 'muddy.'

*Pecatonica
Township
Lat: 42-19-16 N **Long:** 89-20-11 W
Pop: 2,592 (1990); 2,592 (1980) **Pop Density:** 73.6
Land: 35.2 sq. mi.; **Water:** 0.4 sq. mi.

Rockford
City
ZIP: 61125 **Lat:** 42-16-13 N **Long:** 89-03-47 W
Pop: 139,426 (1990); 139,712 (1980) **Pop Density:** 3098.4
Land: 45.0 sq. mi.; **Water:** 0.6 sq. mi.

In north-central IL on the Rock River, 80 mi. northwest of Chicago. County seat. Founded 1834; incorporated Jan 3, 1852. Not coextensive with the town of the same name. Manufacturing city: screw products, machine-tool center, furniture.

Name origin: For the ford across the river's shallow, rock-bottom, used by travelers on the Chicago-Galena line before a settlement existed here.

*Rockford
Township
ZIP: 61101 **Lat:** 42-14-53 N **Long:** 89-04-27 W
Pop: 173,645 (1990); 178,858 (1980) **Pop Density:** 1563.0
Land: 111.1 sq. mi.; **Water:** 1.7 sq. mi.

Rockton
Town
ZIP: 61072 **Lat:** 42-26-57 N **Long:** 89-04-11 W
Pop: 2,928 (1990); 2,313 (1980) **Pop Density:** 1045.7
Land: 2.8 sq. mi.; **Water:** 0.2 sq. mi.

In north-central IL on the Rock River, 12 mi. north of Rockford. Not coextensive with the town of the same name.

American Places Dictionary ILLINOIS, Woodford County

*Rockton Township
ZIP: 61072 Lat: 42-27-11 N Long: 89-05-52 W
Pop: 10,470 (1990); 9,163 (1980) **Pop Density:** 288.4
Land: 36.3 sq. mi.; **Water:** 1.1 sq. mi.

Roscoe Town
ZIP: 61073 Lat: 42-25-00 N Long: 89-00-25 W
Pop: 2,079 (1990); 1,388 (1980) **Pop Density:** 483.5
Land: 4.3 sq. mi.; **Water:** 0.0 sq. mi. **Elev:** 741 ft.
In north-central IL, near Rockford. Not coextensive with the town of the same name.

*Roscoe Township
ZIP: 61073 Lat: 42-27-06 N Long: 88-59-35 W
Pop: 9,230 (1990); 7,754 (1980) **Pop Density:** 299.7
Land: 30.8 sq. mi.; **Water:** 0.6 sq. mi.

Seward Township
Lat: 42-15-11 N Long: 89-20-28 W
Pop: 1,001 (1990); 1,043 (1980) **Pop Density:** 28.0
Land: 35.8 sq. mi.; **Water:** 0.0 sq. mi.

Shirland Township
Lat: 42-27-46 N Long: 89-12-11 W
Pop: 1,011 (1990); 1,035 (1980) **Pop Density:** 52.7
Land: 19.2 sq. mi.; **Water:** 0.1 sq. mi.

South Beloit Town
ZIP: 61080 Lat: 42-29-04 N Long: 89-02-00 W
Pop: 4,072 (1990); 4,088 (1980) **Pop Density:** 1313.5
Land: 3.1 sq. mi.; **Water:** 0.1 sq. mi.
In northern IL on the WI border; a suburb of Beloit, WI.

Winnebago Town
ZIP: 61088 Lat: 42-16-04 N Long: 89-14-25 W
Pop: 1,840 (1990); 1,644 (1980) **Pop Density:** 1840.0
Land: 1.0 sq. mi.; **Water:** 0.0 sq. mi. **Elev:** 869 ft.
Not coextensive with the town of the same name.
Name origin: For the Winnebago Indians.

*Winnebago Township
Lat: 42-14-49 N Long: 89-13-51 W
Pop: 3,237 (1990); 3,169 (1980) **Pop Density:** 97.2
Land: 33.3 sq. mi.; **Water:** 0.0 sq. mi.

Woodford County
County Seat: Eureka (ZIP: 61530)

Pop: 32,653 (1990); 33,320 (1980) **Pop Density:** 61.8
Land: 528.0 sq. mi.; **Water:** 14.7 sq. mi. **Area Code:** 309
In central IL; organized Feb 27, 1841 from Tazewell and McLean counties.
Name origin: For Woodford County, KY, former home of many early settlers.

Bay View Gardens Village
Lat: 40-48-35 N Long: 89-31-08 W
Pop: 418 (1990); 417 (1980) **Pop Density:** 2090.0
Land: 0.2 sq. mi.; **Water:** 0.0 sq. mi.

Benson Village
ZIP: 61516 Lat: 40-51-02 N Long: 89-07-13 W
Pop: 410 (1990); 460 (1980) **Pop Density:** 2050.0
Land: 0.2 sq. mi.; **Water:** 0.0 sq. mi.

Cazenovia Township
Lat: 40-52-26 N Long: 89-20-03 W
Pop: 1,841 (1990); 1,932 (1980) **Pop Density:** 51.0
Land: 36.1 sq. mi.; **Water:** 0.0 sq. mi.

Clayton Township
Lat: 40-53-20 N Long: 89-05-42 W
Pop: 701 (1990); 808 (1980) **Pop Density:** 19.5
Land: 35.9 sq. mi.; **Water:** 0.0 sq. mi.

Congerville Village
ZIP: 61729 Lat: 40-37-00 N Long: 89-12-30 W
Pop: 397 (1990); 373 (1980) **Pop Density:** 496.3
Land: 0.8 sq. mi.; **Water:** 0.0 sq. mi.

Cruger Township
Lat: 40-42-17 N Long: 89-18-40 W
Pop: 1,125 (1990); 1,188 (1980) **Pop Density:** 65.8
Land: 17.1 sq. mi.; **Water:** 0.0 sq. mi.

Deer Creek Village
ZIP: 61733 Lat: 40-37-35 N Long: 89-19-30 W
Pop: 0 (1990); 5 (1980)
Land: 0.01 sq. mi.; **Water:** 0.0 sq. mi.
Part of the town is also in Tazewell County.

El Paso City
ZIP: 61738 Lat: 40-44-23 N Long: 89-00-53 W
Pop: 2,499 (1990); 2,676 (1980) **Pop Density:** 2082.5
Land: 1.2 sq. mi.; **Water:** 0.0 sq. mi. **Elev:** 752 ft.
In north-central IL, east of Peoria. Founded 1854. Not coextensive with the town of the same name.
Name origin: For the city in TX.

*El Paso Township
Lat: 40-42-41 N Long: 89-01-06 W
Pop: 2,985 (1990); 3,191 (1980) **Pop Density:** 123.3
Land: 24.2 sq. mi.; **Water:** 0.0 sq. mi.

Eureka City
ZIP: 61530 Lat: 40-42-56 N Long: 89-16-30 W
Pop: 4,435 (1990); 4,306 (1980) **Pop Density:** 2015.9
Land: 2.2 sq. mi.; **Water:** 0.0 sq. mi.
Founded 1830.
Name origin: From the Greek 'I have found it.'

Germantown Hills Village
ZIP: 61548 Lat: 40-46-08 N Long: 89-28-04 W
Pop: 1,195 (1990); 524 (1980) **Pop Density:** 1195.0
Land: 1.0 sq. mi.; **Water:** 0.0 sq. mi.

Goodfield Village
ZIP: 61742 Lat: 40-37-50 N Long: 89-16-03 W
Pop: 453 (1990); 500 (1980) **Pop Density:** 453.0
Land: 1.0 sq. mi.; **Water:** 0.0 sq. mi.
Part of the town is also in Tazewell County.

Greene
Township
Lat: 40-47-52 N **Long:** 89-05-52 W
Pop: 390 (1990); 367 (1980) **Pop Density:** 10.9
Land: 35.8 sq. mi.; **Water:** 0.0 sq. mi.

Kansas
Township
Lat: 40-38-14 N **Long:** 89-06-31 W
Pop: 319 (1990); 329 (1980) **Pop Density:** 17.3
Land: 18.4 sq. mi.; **Water:** 0.3 sq. mi.

Kappa
Village
ZIP: 61738 **Lat:** 40-40-29 N **Long:** 89-00-29 W
Pop: 134 (1990); 170 (1980) **Pop Density:** 670.0
Land: 0.2 sq. mi.; **Water:** 0.0 sq. mi.

Linn
Township
Lat: 40-52-39 N **Long:** 89-13-29 W
Pop: 375 (1990); 394 (1980) **Pop Density:** 10.2
Land: 36.7 sq. mi.; **Water:** 0.0 sq. mi.

Metamora
Town
ZIP: 61548 **Lat:** 40-47-31 N **Long:** 89-21-49 W
Pop: 2,520 (1990); 2,482 (1980) **Pop Density:** 2100.0
Land: 1.2 sq. mi.; **Water:** 0.0 sq. mi. **Elev:** 821 ft.

Not coextensive with the town of the same name.

Name origin: From the title character in John Stone's *Metamora, or the Last of the Wampanoags*, a popular play about Chief Metacomet ("King Philip"). Previously called Black Partridge and Hanover.

*Metamora
Township
Lat: 40-47-34 N **Long:** 89-20-10 W
Pop: 3,320 (1990); 3,338 (1980) **Pop Density:** 91.0
Land: 36.5 sq. mi.; **Water:** 0.0 sq. mi.

Minonk
Town
ZIP: 61760 **Lat:** 40-54-13 N **Long:** 89-02-14 W
Pop: 1,982 (1990); 2,039 (1980) **Pop Density:** 1524.6
Land: 1.3 sq. mi.; **Water:** 0.0 sq. mi.

Not coextensive with the town of the same name.

Name origin: From the Algonquian term *mino* probably meaning 'good' and *onk* 'place.'

*Minonk
Township
Lat: 40-53-03 N **Long:** 88-59-48 W
Pop: 2,334 (1990); 2,406 (1980) **Pop Density:** 63.6
Land: 36.7 sq. mi.; **Water:** 0.1 sq. mi.

Montgomery
Township
Lat: 40-37-36 N **Long:** 89-14-24 W
Pop: 1,863 (1990); 2,012 (1980) **Pop Density:** 50.5
Land: 36.9 sq. mi.; **Water:** 0.1 sq. mi.

Olio
Township
Lat: 40-42-17 N **Long:** 89-13-30 W
Pop: 4,630 (1990); 4,416 (1980) **Pop Density:** 148.4
Land: 31.2 sq. mi.; **Water:** 0.0 sq. mi.

Palestine
Township
Lat: 40-42-28 N **Long:** 89-06-57 W
Pop: 892 (1990); 979 (1980) **Pop Density:** 24.2
Land: 36.8 sq. mi.; **Water:** 0.0 sq. mi.

Panola
Village
ZIP: 61738 **Lat:** 40-47-06 N **Long:** 89-01-13 W
Pop: 43 (1990); 31 (1980) **Pop Density:** 215.0
Land: 0.2 sq. mi.; **Water:** 0.0 sq. mi. **Elev:** 734 ft.

Not coextensive with the town of the same name.

*Panola
Township
Lat: 40-47-55 N **Long:** 88-59-49 W
Pop: 366 (1990); 409 (1980) **Pop Density:** 10.1
Land: 36.3 sq. mi.; **Water:** 0.0 sq. mi.

Partridge
Township
Lat: 40-52-55 N **Long:** 89-26-53 W
Pop: 472 (1990); 503 (1980) **Pop Density:** 18.0
Land: 26.2 sq. mi.; **Water:** 7.5 sq. mi.

Peoria Heights
Village
ZIP: 61614 **Lat:** 40-46-39 N **Long:** 89-32-58 W
Pop: 43 (1990) **Pop Density:** 430.0
Land: 0.1 sq. mi.; **Water:** 3.9 sq. mi. **Elev:** 789 ft.

Part of the town is also in Tazewell and Peoria counties.

Roanoke
Town
ZIP: 61561 **Lat:** 40-47-46 N **Long:** 89-12-06 W
Pop: 1,910 (1990); 2,001 (1980) **Pop Density:** 2122.2
Land: 0.9 sq. mi.; **Water:** 0.0 sq. mi.

In central IL, 25 mi. northwest of Bloomington. Not coextensive with the town of the same name.

Name origin: For Roanoke, VA.

*Roanoke
Township
Lat: 40-47-41 N **Long:** 89-12-52 W
Pop: 2,500 (1990); 2,614 (1980) **Pop Density:** 67.9
Land: 36.8 sq. mi.; **Water:** 0.0 sq. mi.

Secor
Village
Lat: 40-44-25 N **Long:** 89-08-08 W
Pop: 389 (1990); 488 (1980) **Pop Density:** 1296.7
Land: 0.3 sq. mi.; **Water:** 0.0 sq. mi.

Spring Bay
Village
Lat: 40-49-24 N **Long:** 89-31-32 W
Pop: 439 (1990); 496 (1980) **Pop Density:** 1463.3
Land: 0.3 sq. mi.; **Water:** 0.2 sq. mi. **Elev:** 471 ft.

Not coextensive with the town of the same name.

*Spring Bay
Township
Lat: 40-47-35 N **Long:** 89-31-37 W
Pop: 2,658 (1990); 2,655 (1980) **Pop Density:** 258.1
Land: 10.3 sq. mi.; **Water:** 6.6 sq. mi.

Washburn
Village
ZIP: 61570 **Lat:** 40-55-11 N **Long:** 89-17-29 W
Pop: 1,040 (1990); 1,122 (1980) **Pop Density:** 1733.3
Land: 0.6 sq. mi.; **Water:** 0.0 sq. mi.

Part of the town is also in Marshall County.

Worth
Township
ZIP: 61548 **Lat:** 40-47-08 N **Long:** 89-27-15 W
Pop: 5,882 (1990); 5,779 (1980) **Pop Density:** 162.0
Land: 36.3 sq. mi.; **Water:** 0.0 sq. mi.

Index to Places and Counties in Illinois

Abingdon (Knox) City 76
Abington (Mercer) Township 107
Adams (La Salle) Township 81
Adams County 8
Addieville (Washington) Village 142
Addison (DuPage) Township 40
Addison (DuPage) Village 40
Adeline (Ogle) Village 113
Aetna (Logan) Township 89
Afton (DeKalb) Township 37
Akron (Peoria) Township 114
Alba (Henry) Township 60
Albany (Whiteside) Township 146
Albany (Whiteside) Village 146
Albers (Clinton) Village 23
Albion (Edwards) City 45
Alden (McHenry) Township 102
Aledo (Mercer) City 107
Alexander County 9
Alexis (Mercer) Village 107
Alexis (Warren) Village 141
Algonquin (Kane) Village 71
Algonquin (McHenry) Township 102
Algonquin (McHenry) Village 102
Alhambra (Madison) Township 94
Alhambra (Madison) Village 94
Allen (La Salle) Township 81
Allendale (Wabash) Village 140
Allen Grove (Mason) Township 99
Allenville (Moultrie) Village 112
Allerton (Champaign) Village 17
Allerton (Vermilion) Village 138
Allin (McLean) Township 104
Allison (Lawrence) Township 84
Alma (Marion) Township 96
Alma (Marion) Village 96
Alorton (St. Clair) Village 125
Alpha (Henry) Village 60
Alsey (Scott) Village 132
Alsip (Cook) Suburban village 25
Altamont (Effingham) City 45
Alto (Lee) Township 85
Alton (Madison) City 94
Alton (Madison) Township 94
Altona (Knox) Village 76
Alto Pass (Union) Village 138
Alvin (Vermilion) Village 138
Amboy (Lee) City 85
Amboy (Lee) Township 85
Amity (Livingston) Township 87
Anchor (McLean) Township 105
Anchor (McLean) Village 104
Andalusia (Rock Island) Township ... 123
Andalusia (Rock Island) Village 123
Anderson (Clark) Township 21
Andover (Henry) Township 60
Andover (Henry) Village 60
Anna (Union) City 138
Annawan (Henry) Township 60
Annawan (Henry) Village 60
Antioch (Lake) Lake resort village 78
Antioch (Lake) Township 78
Appanoose (Hancock) Township 57
Apple River (Jo Daviess) Township ... 69
Apple River (Jo Daviess) Village 69
Arcola (Douglas) City 39
Arcola (Douglas) Township 39
Arenzville (Cass) Township 16
Arenzville (Cass) Village 16
Argenta (Macon) Village 90

Arispie (Bureau) Township 12
Arlington (Bureau) Village 12
Arlington Heights (Cook) Residential village 25
Arlington Heights (Lake) Residential village 78
Armington (Tazewell) Village 136
Aroma (Kankakee) Township 73
Aroma Park (Kankakee) Village 73
Arrington (Wayne) Township 143
Arrowsmith (McLean) Township 105
Arrowsmith (McLean) Village 105
Artesia (Iroquois) Township 62
Arthur (Douglas) Village 39
Arthur (Moultrie) Village 112
Asbury (Gallatin) Township 52
Ash Grove (Iroquois) Township 62
Ash Grove (Shelby) Township 132
Ashkum (Iroquois) Township 62
Ashkum (Iroquois) Village 62
Ashland (Cass) Township 16
Ashland (Cass) Village 16
Ashley (Washington) City 142
Ashley (Washington) Township 142
Ashmore (Coles) Township 24
Ashmore (Coles) Village 24
Ashton (Lee) Township 85
Ashton (Lee) Village 85
Assumption (Christian) City 19
Assumption (Christian) Township 19
Astoria (Fulton) Town 50
Astoria (Fulton) Township 50
Athens (Menard) City 107
Athensville (Greene) Township 53
Atkinson (Henry) Township 60
Atkinson (Henry) Village 60
Atlanta (Logan) City 89
Atlanta (Logan) Township 89
Atlas (Pike) Township 118
Atwood (Douglas) Village 40
Atwood (Piatt) Village 117
Auburn (Clark) Township 21
Auburn (Sangamon) City 128
Auburn (Sangamon) Township 128
Audubon (Montgomery) Township ... 109
Augusta (Hancock) Township 57
Augusta (Hancock) Village 57
Aurora (DuPage) Industrial city 40
Aurora (Kane) Industrial city 71
Aurora (Kane) Township 71
Austin (Macon) Township 90
Aux Sable (Grundy) Township 54
Ava (Jackson) City 64
Avena (Fayette) Township 47
Aviston (Clinton) Village 23
Avoca (Livingston) Township 87
Avon (Fulton) Village 50
Avon (Lake) Township 78
Ayers (Champaign) Township 17
Bainbridge (Schuyler) Township 131
Bald Bluff (Henderson) Township 59
Bald Hill (Jefferson) Township 67
Baldwin (Randolph) Village 121
Ball (Sangamon) Township 128
Banner (Effingham) Township 45
Banner (Fulton) Township 50
Banner (Fulton) Village 50
Bannockburn (Lake) Village 78
Bardolph (McDonough) Village 101
Barnett (De Witt) Township 38

Barnhill (Wayne) Township 143
Barr (Macoupin) Township 92
Barren (Franklin) Township 49
Barrington (Cook) Township 26
Barrington (Cook) Village 26
Barrington (Lake) Village 78
Barrington Hills (Cook) Village 26
Barrington Hills (Kane) Village 71
Barrington Hills (Lake) Village 78
Barrington Hills (McHenry) Village .. 102
Barry (Pike) City 118
Barry (Pike) Township 118
Bartelso (Clinton) Village 23
Bartlett (Cook) Village 26
Bartlett (DuPage) Village 41
Bartlett (Kane) Village 71
Bartonville (Peoria) Village 114
Basco (Hancock) Village 57
Batavia (DuPage) Industrial city 41
Batavia (Kane) Industrial city 72
Batavia (Kane) Township 72
Batchtown (Calhoun) Village 15
Bath (Mason) Township 99
Bath (Mason) Village 99
Baylis (Pike) Village 118
Bay View Gardens (Woodford) Village 153
Beach Park (Lake) Village 78
Bear Creek (Christian) Township 20
Bear Creek (Hancock) Township 57
Beardstown (Cass) City 16
Beardstown (Cass) Township 16
Bear Grove (Fayette) Township 47
Beaucoup (Washington) Township ... 142
Beaver (Iroquois) Township 62
Beaver Creek (Hamilton) Township ... 56
Beaverville (Iroquois) Township 62
Beaverville (Iroquois) Village 62
Beckemeyer (Clinton) Village 23
Bedford (Wayne) Township 143
Bedford Park (Cook) Village 26
Beecher (Will) Village 147
Beecher City (Effingham) Village 45
Belgium (Vermilion) Village 138
Belknap (Johnson) Village 71
Belle Prairie (Livingston) Township ... 87
Belle Prairie City (Hamilton) Town 56
Belle Rive (Jefferson) Village 67
Belleville (St. Clair) City 125
Belleville (St. Clair) Township 125
Bellevue (Peoria) Village 114
Bellflower (McLean) Township 105
Bellflower (McLean) Village 105
Bellmont (Wabash) Village 140
Bell Plain (Marshall) Township 98
Bellwood (Cook) Industrial village 26
Belmont (Iroquois) Township 62
Belvidere (Boone) City 11
Belvidere (Boone) Township 11
Bement (Piatt) Township 117
Bement (Piatt) Village 117
Benld (Macoupin) City 92
Bennington (Marshall) Township 98
Bensenville (Cook) Village 26
Bensenville (DuPage) Village 41
Benson (Woodford) Village 153
Bentley (Hancock) Town 57
Benton (Franklin) City 49
Benton (Franklin) Township 49
Benton (Lake) Township 78

Berkeley (Cook) Village..................26
Berlin (Bureau) Township..............13
Berlin (Sangamon) Village............129
Bernadotte (Fulton) Township.........50
Berreman (Jo Daviess) Township......69
Berry (Wayne) Township................143
Berwick (Warren) Township.............141
Berwyn (Cook) Residential city........26
Berwyn (Cook) Township................26
Bethalto (Madison) Village.............94
Bethany (Moultrie) Village..............112
Bethel (McDonough) Township........101
Beverly (Adams) Township................8
Bible Grove (Clay) Township...........22
Big Grove (Kendall) Township.........75
Biggsville (Henderson) Township......59
Biggsville (Henderson) Village.........59
Big Mound (Wayne) Township........143
Big Rock (Kane) Township..............72
Big Spring (Shelby) Township.........132
Bingham (Fayette) Village...............47
Bird (Macoupin) Township..............92
Birds (Lawrence) Village...................84
Birmingham (Schuyler) Township....131
Bishop (Effingham) Township..........45
Bishop Hill (Henry) Village..............61
Blackberry (Kane) Township............72
Blackhawk (Rock Island) Township..123
Blair (Clay) Township......................22
Blandinsville (McDonough)
  Township................................ 101
Blandinsville (McDonough) Village..101
Blissville (Jefferson) Township...........67
Bloom (Cook) Township...................26
Bloomingdale (DuPage) Township......41
Bloomingdale (DuPage) Village 41
Bloomington (McLean) City 105
Bloomington (McLean) Township.....105
Bloomington City (McLean)
  Township................................ 105
Blount (Vermilion) Township...........138
Blue Island (Cook) City....................26
Blue Mound (Macon) Township.........90
Blue Mound (Macon) Village.............90
Blue Mound (McLean) Township......105
Blue Ridge (Piatt) Township............117
Bluffdale (Greene) Township............53
Bluffs (Scott) Village......................132
Bluff Springs (Cass) Township..........16
Bluford (Jefferson) Village.................67
Bois D'Arc (Montgomery) Township 109
Bolingbrook (DuPage) Village............41
Bolingbrook (Will) Village...............147
Bolo (Washington) Township..........142
Bond (Lawrence) Township...............84
Bond County................................10
Bondville (Champaign) Village.........17
Bone Gap (Edwards) Village............45
Bonfield (Kankakee) Village.............73
Bonnie (Jefferson) Village.................67
Bonpas (Richland) Township...........122
Bonus (Boone) Township.................11
Boone (Boone) Township..................11
Boone County..............................11
Boulder Hill (Kendall) CDP..............75
Bourbon (Douglas) Township............40
Bourbonnais (Kankakee) Town..........73
Bourbonnais (Kankakee) Township....74
Bowdre (Douglas) Township............40
Bowen (Hancock) Village.................57
Bowlesville (Gallatin) Township.......52
Bowling (Rock Island) Township.....123
Bowling Green (Fayette) Township....47
Boynton (Tazewell) Township.........136
Braceville (Grundy) Township..........54

Braceville (Grundy) Village.............54
Bradford (Lee) Township..................85
Bradford (Stark) Town....................134
Bradley (Jackson) Township.............64
Bradley (Kankakee) Village..............74
Braidwood (Will) City....................147
Breese (Clinton) City.......................23
Breese (Clinton) Township...............23
Bremen (Cook) Township................26
Brenton (Ford) Township.................48
Bridgeport (Lawrence) City..............84
Bridgeport (Lawrence) Township......84
Bridgeview (Cook) Village................26
Brighton (Jersey) Village.................68
Brighton (Macoupin) Township.........92
Brighton (Macoupin) Village.............92
Brimfield (Peoria) Township...........115
Brimfield (Peoria) Village...............115
Bristol (Kendall) Township..............75
Broadlands (Champaign) Village......17
Broadview (Cook) Residential suburb 26
Broadwell (Logan) Township............89
Broadwell (Logan) Village................89
Brocton (Edgar) Village...................44
Brookfield (Cook) Residential village.26
Brookfield (La Salle) Township.........82
Brooklyn (Lee) Township.................85
Brooklyn (Schuyler) Township........131
Brooklyn (St. Clair) Village............125
Brookport (Massac) City................100
Brookside (Clinton) Township..........23
Brookville (Ogle) Township.............113
Broughton (Hamilton) Village..........56
Broughton (Livingston) Township.....87
Brouilletts Creek (Edgar) Township....44
Brown (Champaign) Township.........17
Brown County..............................12
Browning (Franklin) Township.........49
Browning (Schuyler) Township........131
Browning (Schuyler) Village............131
Browns (Edwards) Village................45
Brownstown (Fayette) Village...........47
Bruce (La Salle) Township...............82
Brushy (Saline) Township...............127
Brushy Mound (Macoupin) Township 92
Brussels (Calhoun) Village...............15
Bryant (Fulton) Village....................50
Buck (Edgar) Township...................44
Buckeye (Stephenson) Township.....135
Buckhart (Christian) Township........20
Buckheart (Fulton) Township..........51
Buckhorn (Brown) Township...........12
Buckingham (Kankakee) Village.......74
Buckley (Iroquois) Village................62
Buckner (Franklin) Village...............49
Buda (Bureau) Village......................13
Buena Vista (Schuyler) Township....131
Buffalo (Ogle) Township.................113
Buffalo (Sangamon) Village............129
Buffalo Grove (Cook) Residential
  suburb..................................... 26
Buffalo Grove (Lake) Residential
  suburb..................................... 78
Buffalo Hart (Sangamon) Township .129
Buffalo Prairie (Rock Island)
  Township................................ 123
Bull Valley (McHenry) Village..........102
Bulpitt (Christian) Village................20
Buncombe (Johnson) Village............71
Bunker Hill (Macoupin) City............92
Bunker Hill (Macoupin) Township....92
Burbank (Cook) City.......................27
Bureau (Bureau) Township...............13
Bureau County..............................12
Bureau Junction (Bureau) Village......13

Burgess (Bond) Township................10
Burlington (Kane) Township............72
Burlington (Kane) Village................72
Burnham (Cook) Village..................27
Burns (Henry) Township..................61
Burnt Prairie (White) Township......144
Burnt Prairie (White) Village..........144
Burritt (Winnebago) Township.......152
Burr Ridge (Cook) Village................27
Burr Ridge (DuPage) Village.............41
Burton (Adams) Township.................8
Burton (McHenry) Township..........102
Bush (Williamson) Village..............151
Bushnell (McDonough) City............101
Bushnell (McDonough) Township....101
Butler (Montgomery) Village...........109
Butler (Vermilion) Township..........139
Butler Grove (Montgomery)
  Township................................ 109
Button (Ford) Township..................48
Byron (Ogle) City...........................113
Byron (Ogle) Township..................113
Cabery (Ford) Village.......................48
Cabery (Kankakee) Village...............74
Cahokia (Macoupin) Township.........92
Cahokia (St. Clair) Village..............125
Cairo (Alexander) City......................9
Caledonia (Boone) Township............11
Calhoun (Richland) Village............122
Calhoun County...........................15
Calumet (Cook) Township................27
Calumet City (Cook) City................27
Calumet Park (Cook) Village............27
Camargo (Douglas) Township..........40
Camargo (Douglas) Village..............40
Cambria (Williamson) Village........151
Cambridge (Henry) Township..........61
Cambridge (Henry) Village..............61
Camden (Schuyler) Township.........131
Camden (Schuyler) Village.............131
Campbell Hill (Jackson) Village........64
Camp Point (Adams) Town................8
Camp Point (Adams) Township.........8
Campton (Kane) Township..............72
Campus (Livingston) Village............87
Canoe Creek (Rock Island)
  Township................................ 123
Canteen (St. Clair) Township..........125
Canton (Fulton) City.......................51
Canton (Fulton) Township...............51
Cantrall (Sangamon) Village...........129
Capital (Sangamon) Township........129
Capron (Boone) Village....................11
Carbon Cliff (Rock Island) Town.....123
Carbondale (Jackson) City...............64
Carbondale (Jackson) Township.......64
Carbon Hill (Grundy) Village...........54
Carlinville (Macoupin) City..............92
Carlinville (Macoupin) Township......92
Carlock (McLean) Village...............105
Carlyle (Clinton) Town....................23
Carlyle (Clinton) Township..............23
Carman (Henderson) Township........59
Carmi (White) City........................145
Carmi (White) Township................145
Carol Stream (DuPage) Residential
  suburb..................................... 41
Carpentersville (Kane) Village..........72
Carriers Mills (Saline) Township......127
Carriers Mills (Saline) Village........127
Carrigan (Marion) Township............97
Carroll (Vermilion) Township..........139
Carroll County.............................15
Carrollton (Greene) City..................53
Carrollton (Greene) Township..........53

Carson (Fayette) Township..................47
Carterville (Williamson) City......151
Carthage (Hancock) City.................57
Carthage (Hancock) Township............57
Cartwright (Sangamon) Township.....129
Cary (McHenry) Village.................103
Casey (Clark) City..........................21
Casey (Clark) Township...................21
Casey (Cumberland) City..................36
Caseyville (St. Clair) Township.......125
Caseyville (St. Clair) Village..........125
Casner (Jefferson) Township.............67
Cass (Fulton) Township...................51
Cass County...............................16
Catlin (Vermilion) Township............139
Catlin (Vermilion) Village.............139
Cave (Franklin) Township................49
Cave-In-Rock (Hardin) Village..........59
Cazenovia (Woodford) Township......153
Cedar (Knox) Township....................76
Cedar Point (La Salle) Village.........82
Cedarville (Stephenson) Village.......135
Central (Bond) Township.................10
Central City (Marion) Village..........97
Centralia (Clinton) City.................23
Centralia (Marion) City..................97
Centralia (Marion) Township.............97
Centreville (St. Clair) City............125
Centreville (St. Clair) Township.......125
Cerro Gordo (Piatt) Township...........117
Cerro Gordo (Piatt) Village............117
Chadwick (Carroll) Village..............15
Chalmers (McDonough) Township...101
Chambersburg (Pike) Township........118
Champaign (Champaign) City...........17
Champaign (Champaign) Township....17
Champaign County.........................17
Chandlerville (Cass) Township..........17
Chandlerville (Cass) Village............16
Channahon (Grundy) Village............54
Channahon (Will) Township............148
Channahon (Will) Village..............148
Channel Lake (Lake) CDP.................78
Chapin (Morgan) Village...............111
Charleston (Coles) City..................25
Charleston (Coles) Township............25
Charlotte (Livingston) Township........87
Chatham (Sangamon) Township......129
Chatham (Sangamon) Village..........129
Chatsworth (Livingston) Town...........87
Chatsworth (Livingston) Township......87
Chebanse (Iroquois) Township...........63
Chebanse (Iroquois) Village.............63
Chebanse (Kankakee) Village............74
Chemung (McHenry) Township.........103
Cheney's Grove (McLean) Township 105
Chenoa (McLean) City....................105
Chenoa (McLean) Township.............105
Cherry (Bureau) Village..................13
Cherry Grove-Shannon (Carroll)
  Township..................................15
Cherry Valley (Winnebago)
  Township.................................152
Cherry Valley (Winnebago) Village...152
Chester (Logan) Township................89
Chester (Randolph) City................121
Chesterfield (Macoupin) Township......92
Chesterfield (Macoupin) Village........92
Chestnut (Knox) Township................76
Chicago (Cook) City......................27
Chicago (DuPage) City...................41
Chicago Heights (Cook) City............27
Chicago Ridge (Cook) Village...........27
Chili (Hancock) Township................57
Chillicothe (Peoria) City...............115

Chillicothe (Peoria) Township..........115
China (Lee) Township....................85
Chouteau (Madison) Township...........94
Chrisman (Edgar) City...................44
Christian County..........................19
Christopher (Franklin) City.............49
Christy (Lawrence) Township............85
Cicero (Cook) Town......................27
Cicero (Cook) Township..................27
Cincinnati (Pike) Township............118
Cincinnati (Tazewell) Township.......136
Cisco (Piatt) Village..................117
Cisne (Wayne) Village..................143
Cissna Park (Iroquois) Village.........63
Claremont (Richland) Township........122
Claremont (Richland) Village.........122
Clarendon Hills (DuPage) Village......41
Clarion (Bureau) Township..............13
Clark County..............................21
Clarksburg (Shelby) Township.........132
Clay City (Clay) Township...............22
Clay City (Clay) Village................22
Clay County...............................22
Clayton (Adams) Township................8
Clayton (Adams) Village..................8
Clayton (Woodford) Township..........153
Clear Lake (Sangamon) Township....129
Clear Lake (Sangamon) Village.......129
Clement (Clinton) Township.............23
Cleveland (Henry) Village...............61
Clifton (Iroquois) Village..............63
Clinton (De Witt) City...................38
Clinton (DeKalb) Township..............37
Clinton County............................23
Clintonia (De Witt) Township...........38
Clover (Henry) Township.................61
Clyde (Whiteside) Township...........146
Coal City (Grundy) City.................55
Coalton (Montgomery) Village.........109
Coal Valley (Henry) Village.............61
Coal Valley (Rock Island) Township.123
Coal Valley (Rock Island) Village...123
Coatsburg (Adams) Village................8
Cobden (Union) Village................138
Coe (Rock Island) Township............123
Coffeen (Montgomery) City............109
Colchester (McDonough) City..........101
Colchester (McDonough) Township..101
Coldbrook (Warren) Township.........141
Cold Spring (Shelby) Township.......132
Coles County..............................24
Coleta (Whiteside) Village............146
Colfax (Champaign) Township...........17
Colfax (McLean) Village...............105
Collinsville (Madison) City..............94
Collinsville (Madison) Township........94
Collinsville (St. Clair) City...........125
Coloma (Whiteside) Township.........146
Colona (Henry) Township................61
Colona (Henry) Village..................61
Colp (Williamson) Village.............151
Columbia (Monroe) City................109
Columbus (Adams) Township..............8
Columbus (Adams) Village................8
Compromise (Champaign) Township.17
Compton (Lee) Village...................85
Concord (Adams) Township................8
Concord (Bureau) Township..............13
Concord (Iroquois) Township............63
Concord (Morgan) Village..............111
Condit (Champaign) Township...........17
Congerville (Woodford) Village.......153
Cook County...............................25
Cooksville (McLean) Village..........105
Cooper (Sangamon) Township..........129

Cooperstown (Brown) Township.........12
Copley (Knox) Township..................76
Coral (McHenry) Township..............103
Cordova (Rock Island) Township......123
Cordova (Rock Island) Village........123
Cornell (Livingston) Village............87
Cornwall (Henry) Township..............61
Cortland (DeKalb) Town..................37
Cortland (DeKalb) Township.............37
Corwin (Logan) Township.................89
Cottage (Saline) Township.............127
Cotton Hill (Sangamon) Township....129
Cottonwood (Cumberland) Township.36
Coulterville (Randolph) Village......121
Council Hill (Jo Daviess) Township...69
Country Club Hills (Cook) Village......27
Countryside (Cook) Village..............27
Covington (Washington) Township....142
Cowden (Shelby) Village...............132
Crainville (Williamson) Village......151
Crane Creek (Mason) Township.........99
Crawford County..........................35
Creal Springs (Williamson) City......151
Creek (De Witt) Township................38
Crescent (Iroquois) Township...........63
Crescent City (Iroquois) Village........63
Crest Hill (Will) Village..............148
Creston (Ogle) Village................113
Crestwood (Cook) Village................27
Crete (Will) Township..................148
Crete (Will) Village...................148
Creve Coeur (Tazewell) Village.......136
Crittenden (Champaign) Township.....17
Crook (Hamilton) Township..............56
Crooked Creek (Cumberland)
  Township..................................36
Crooked Creek (Jasper) Township......66
Cropsey (McLean) Township............105
Crossville (White) Village.............145
Crouch (Hamilton) Township.............56
Cruger (Woodford) Township...........153
Crystal Lake (McHenry) City..........103
Crystal Lawns (Will) CDP..............148
Cuba (Fulton) City.......................51
Cuba (Lake) Township....................78
Cullom (Livingston) Village............87
Cumberland County.......................36
Cunningham (Champaign) Township.17
Curran (Sangamon) Township..........129
Custer (Will) Township.................148
Cutler (Perry) Village..................116
Cypress (Johnson) Village...............71
Dahlgren (Hamilton) Township..........56
Dahlgren (Hamilton) Village............56
Dakota (Stephenson) Town.............135
Dakota (Stephenson) Township........135
Dale (McLean) Township................105
Dallas City (Hancock) City..............57
Dallas City (Hancock) Township........57
Dallas City (Henderson) City...........59
Dalton City (Moultrie) Village.......112
Dalzell (Bureau) Village................13
Dalzell (La Salle) Village..............82
Damiansville (Clinton) Village.........23
Dana (La Salle) Village.................82
Danforth (Iroquois) Township...........63
Danforth (Iroquois) Village............63
Danvers (McLean) Township...........105
Danvers (McLean) Village.............105
Danville (Vermilion) City.............139
Danville (Vermilion) Township........139
Darien (DuPage) City....................41
Darwin (Clark) Township................21
Davis (Stephenson) Village............135
Davis Junction (Ogle) Village........113

ILLINOIS

Dawson (McLean) Township............105
Dawson (Sangamon) Village............129
Dayton (La Salle) Township............82
Decatur (Macon) City............90
Decatur (Macon) Township............90
Decker (Richland) Township............122
Deer Creek (Tazewell) Township......136
Deer Creek (Tazewell) Village............136
Deer Creek (Woodford) Village............153
Deerfield (Cook) Village............27
Deerfield (Fulton) Township............51
Deerfield (Lake) Township............78
Deerfield (Lake) Village............78
Deer Grove (Whiteside) Village............146
Deer Park (La Salle) Township............82
Deer Park (Lake) Village............78
Degognia (Jackson) Township............65
De Kalb (DeKalb) City............37
De Kalb (DeKalb) Township............37
DeKalb County............37
De Land (Piatt) Village............117
Delavan (Tazewell) City............136
Delavan (Tazewell) Township............136
Dement (Ogle) Township............113
Denison (Lawrence) Township............85
Denning (Franklin) Township............49
Denver (Richland) Township............122
De Pue (Bureau) Town............13
Derinda (Jo Daviess) Township............69
Derry (Pike) Township............118
De Soto (Jackson) Township............65
De Soto (Jackson) Village............65
Des Plaines (Cook) City............27
Detroit (Pike) Township............118
Detroit (Pike) Village............118
De Witt (De Witt) Township............38
De Witt (De Witt) Village............39
De Witt County............38
Diamond (Grundy) Village............55
Diamond (Will) Village............148
Dieterich (Effingham) Village............45
Dillon (Tazewell) Township............136
Dimmick (La Salle) Township............82
Divernon (Sangamon) Township............129
Divernon (Sangamon) Village............129
Dix (Ford) Township............48
Dix (Jefferson) Village............67
Dixmoor (Cook) Village............28
Dixon (Lee) City............85
Dixon (Lee) Township............86
Dodds (Jefferson) Township............67
Dolson (Clark) Township............21
Dolton (Cook) Village............28
Dongola (Union) Village............138
Donnellson (Bond) Village............10
Donnellson (Montgomery) Village............109
Donovan (Iroquois) Village............63
Dora (Moultrie) Township............112
Dorchester (Macoupin) Township............92
Dorchester (Macoupin) Village............92
Dorr (McHenry) Township............103
Douglas (Clark) Township............21
Douglas (Effingham) Township............46
Douglas (Iroquois) Township............63
Douglas County............39
Dover (Bureau) Township............13
Dover (Bureau) Village............13
Dowell (Jackson) Village............65
Downers Grove (DuPage) Township..41
Downers Grove (DuPage) Village............41
Downs (McLean) Township............105
Downs (McLean) Village............105
Drummer (Ford) Township............48
Drury (Rock Island) Township............123
Dry Grove (McLean) Township............105

Dry Point (Shelby) Township............132
Du Bois (Washington) Township......142
Du Bois (Washington) Village............142
Duncan (Mercer) Township............107
Dundee (Kane) Township............72
Dunfermline (Fulton) Village............51
Dunham (McHenry) Township............103
Dunlap (Peoria) Village............115
Dunleith (Jo Daviess) Township............69
Du Page (Will) Township............148
DuPage County............40
Dupo (St. Clair) Village............125
Du Quoin (Perry) City............116
Durand (Winnebago) Township............152
Durand (Winnebago) Village............152
Durham (Hancock) Township............57
Dwight (Grundy) Village............55
Dwight (Livingston) Township............87
Dwight (Livingston) Village............87
Eagarville (Macoupin) Village............92
Eagle (La Salle) Township............82
Eagle Creek (Gallatin) Township............52
Eagle Point (Ogle) Township............113
Earl (La Salle) Township............82
Earlville (La Salle) City............82
East Alton (Madison) Village............94
East Bend (Champaign) Township......17
East Brooklyn (Grundy) Village............55
East Cape Girardeau (Alexander) Village............9
East Carondelet (St. Clair) Village....125
East Dubuque (Jo Daviess) City............69
East Dundee (Cook) Village............28
East Dundee (Kane) Village............72
East Eldorado (Saline) Township............128
Eastern (Franklin) Township............49
East Fork (Clinton) Township............23
East Fork (Montgomery) Township..109
East Galena (Jo Daviess) Township....69
East Galesburg (Knox) Village............76
East Gillespie (Macoupin) Village............92
East Grove (Lee) Township............86
East Hazel Crest (Cook) Village............28
East Lincoln (Logan) Township............89
East Moline (Rock Island) City............123
East Nelson (Moultrie) Township............112
East Oakland (Coles) Township............25
Easton (Mason) Village............99
East Peoria (Tazewell) City............136
East St. Louis (St. Clair) City............125
East St. Louis (St. Clair) Township............125
Eddyville (Pope) Village............120
Eden (La Salle) Township............82
Edford (Henry) Township............61
Edgar (Edgar) Township............44
Edgar County............44
Edgewood (Effingham) Village............46
Edgington (Rock Island) Township............123
Edinburg (Christian) Village............20
Edwards County............45
Edwardsville (Madison) City............94
Edwardsville (Madison) Township............94
Effingham (Effingham) City............46
Effingham County............45
Ela (Lake) Township............78
Elba (Knox) Township............76
Elbridge (Edgar) Township............44
Elburn (Kane) Village............72
El Dara (Pike) Village............118
Eldorado (McDonough) Township............101
Eldorado (Saline) City............128
Eldred (Greene) Village............53
Elgin (Cook) City............28
Elgin (Kane) City............72
Elgin (Kane) Township............72

Eliza (Mercer) Township............107
Elizabeth (Jo Daviess) Township............69
Elizabeth (Jo Daviess) Village............69
Elizabethtown (Hardin) Village............59
Elk (Jackson) Township............65
Elk Grove (Cook) Township............28
Elk Grove Village (Cook) Village............28
Elk Grove Village (DuPage) Village...41
Elkhart (Logan) Township............89
Elkhart (Logan) Village............89
Elkhorn (Brown) Township............12
Elkhorn Grove (Carroll) Township......15
Elk Prairie (Jefferson) Township............67
Elkville (Jackson) Village............65
Ellington (Adams) Township............8
Elliott (Ford) Village............48
Ellis Grove (Randolph) Village............122
Ellison (Warren) Township............141
Ellisville (Fulton) Township............51
Ellisville (Fulton) Village............51
Ellsworth (McLean) Village............105
Elm Grove (Tazewell) Township............137
Elmhurst (DuPage) City............42
Elmira (Stark) Township............134
Elm River (Wayne) Township............143
Elmwood (Peoria) City............115
Elmwood (Peoria) Township............115
Elmwood Park (Cook) Village............28
El Paso (Woodford) City............153
El Paso (Woodford) Township............153
Elsah (Jersey) Town............68
Elsah (Jersey) Township............68
Elvaston (Hancock) Village............57
Elwood (Vermilion) Township............139
Elwood (Will) Village............148
Embarrass (Edgar) Township............44
Emden (Logan) Village............89
Eminence (Logan) Township............89
Emington (Livingston) Village............87
Emma (White) Township............145
Emmet (McDonough) Township............101
Empire (McLean) Township............105
Energy (Williamson) Village............151
Enfield (White) Township............145
Enfield (White) Village............145
Engelmann (St. Clair) Township............126
English (Jersey) Township............68
Eppards Point (Livingston) Township 87
Equality (Gallatin) Township............52
Equality (Gallatin) Village............52
Erie (Whiteside) Township............146
Erie (Whiteside) Village............146
Erienna (Grundy) Township............55
Erin (Stephenson) Township............135
Esmen (Livingston) Township............87
Essex (Kankakee) Township............74
Essex (Kankakee) Village............74
Essex (Stark) Township............134
Eureka (Woodford) City............153
Evans (Marshall) Township............98
Evanston (Cook) City............28
Evanston (Cook) Township............28
Evansville (Randolph) Village............122
Evergreen Park (Cook) Village............28
Ewing (Franklin) Township............49
Ewing (Franklin) Village............49
Exeter (Scott) Village............132
Fairbury (Livingston) City............87
Fairfield (Bureau) Township............13
Fairfield (Wayne) City............143
Fairhaven (Carroll) Township............15
Fairmont (Will) CDP............148
Fairmont City (Madison) Village............94
Fairmont City (St. Clair) Village............126
Fairmount (Pike) Township............118

Name	Page
Fairmount (Vermilion) Village	139
Fairview (Fulton) Township	51
Fairview (Fulton) Village	51
Fairview Heights (St. Clair) City	126
Fall Creek (Adams) Township	8
Fall River (La Salle) Township	82
Fancy Creek (Sangamon) Township	129
Farina (Fayette) Village	47
Farina (Marion) Village	97
Farmer City (De Witt) City	39
Farmers (Fulton) Township	51
Farmersville (Montgomery) Village	109
Farmington (Fulton) City	51
Farmington (Fulton) Township	51
Farm Ridge (La Salle) Township	82
Farrington (Jefferson) Township	67
Fayette (Livingston) Township	87
Fayette County	47
Fayetteville (St. Clair) Township	126
Fayetteville (St. Clair) Village	126
Felix (Grundy) Township	55
Fenton (Whiteside) Township	146
Ferris (Hancock) Village	57
Fidelity (Jersey) Township	68
Fidelity (Jersey) Village	68
Field (Jefferson) Township	67
Fieldon (Jersey) Village	68
Fillmore (Montgomery) Township	110
Fillmore (Montgomery) Village	110
Findlay (Shelby) Village	132
Fisher (Champaign) Village	18
Fithian (Vermilion) Village	139
Flagg (Ogle) Township	113
Flanagan (Livingston) Village	87
Flannigan (Hamilton) Township	56
Flat Branch (Shelby) Township	132
Flat Rock (Crawford) Village	35
Flint (Pike) Township	118
Flora (Boone) Township	11
Flora (Clay) City	22
Florence (Pike) Village	118
Florence (Stephenson) Township	135
Florence (Will) Township	148
Flossmoor (Cook) Village	28
Floyd (Warren) Township	141
Fondulac (Tazewell) Township	137
Foosland (Champaign) Village	18
Ford County	48
Ford Heights (Cook) Village	28
Forest City (Mason) Township	99
Forest City (Mason) Village	99
Forest Lake (Lake) CDP	78
Forest Park (Cook) Village	28
Forest View (Cook) Village	28
Forrest (Livingston) Township	87
Forrest (Livingston) Village	87
Forreston (Ogle) Township	113
Forreston (Ogle) Village	113
Forsyth (Macon) Village	90
Fort Russell (Madison) Township	95
Foster (Madison) Township	95
Foster (Marion) Township	97
Fountain Bluff (Jackson) Township	65
Fountain Creek (Iroquois) Township	63
Fountain Green (Hancock) Township	57
Four Mile (Wayne) Township	143
Fox (Jasper) Township	66
Fox (Kendall) Township	75
Fox Lake (Lake) Village	78
Fox Lake (McHenry) Village	103
Fox Lake Hills (Lake) CDP	79
Fox River Grove (McHenry) Village	103
Fox River Valley Gardens (Lake) Village	79
Fox River Valley Gardens (McHenry) Village	103
Frankfort (Franklin) Township	49
Frankfort (Will) Township	148
Frankfort (Will) Village	148
Frankfort Square (Will) CDP	148
Franklin (DeKalb) Township	37
Franklin (Morgan) Village	111
Franklin County	49
Franklin Grove (Lee) Village	86
Franklin Park (Cook) Village	28
Frederick (Schuyler) Township	131
Freeburg (St. Clair) Township	126
Freeburg (St. Clair) Village	126
Freedom (Carroll) Township	15
Freedom (La Salle) Township	82
Freeman Spur (Franklin) Village	49
Freeman Spur (Williamson) Village	151
Freeport (Stephenson) City	135
Freeport (Stephenson) Township	135
Fremont (Lake) Township	79
Friends Creek (Macon) Township	90
Fulton (Whiteside) City	146
Fulton (Whiteside) Township	146
Fulton County	50
Fults (Monroe) Village	109
Funks Grove (McLean) Township	105
Gages Lake (Lake) CDP	79
Galatia (Saline) Township	128
Galatia (Saline) Village	128
Galena (Jo Daviess) City	69
Galesburg (Knox) City	76
Galesburg (Knox) Township	76
Gallatin County	52
Galva (Henry) City	61
Galva (Henry) Township	61
Ganeer (Kankakee) Township	74
Garden Hill (Wayne) Township	143
Garden Plain (Whiteside) Township	146
Gardner (Grundy) Town	55
Gardner (Sangamon) Township	129
Garfield (Grundy) Township	55
Garrett (Douglas) Township	40
Garrett (Douglas) Village	40
Gays (Moultrie) Village	112
Genesee (Whiteside) Township	146
Geneseo (Henry) City	61
Geneseo (Henry) Township	61
Geneva (Kane) City	72
Geneva (Kane) Township	72
Genoa (DeKalb) City	37
Genoa (DeKalb) Township	37
Georgetown (Vermilion) City	139
Georgetown (Vermilion) Township	139
German (Richland) Township	122
Germantown (Clinton) Township	24
Germantown (Clinton) Village	24
Germantown Hills (Woodford) Village	153
German Valley (Stephenson) Village	135
Germanville (Livingston) Township	88
Gibson City (Ford) City	48
Gifford (Champaign) Village	18
Gilberts (Kane) Village	72
Gillespie (Macoupin) City	92
Gillespie (Macoupin) Township	92
Gilman (Iroquois) City	63
Gilmer (Adams) Township	8
Girard (Macoupin) City	92
Girard (Macoupin) Township	92
Gladstone (Henderson) Township	59
Gladstone (Henderson) Village	59
Glasford (Peoria) Town	115
Glasgow (Scott) Village	132
Glenbard South (DuPage) CDP	42
Glen Carbon (Madison) Village	95
Glencoe (Cook) Village	28
Glendale Heights (DuPage) City	42
Glen Ellyn (DuPage) Village	42
Glenview (Cook) Village	29
Glenwood (Cook) Village	29
Godfrey (Madison) Township	95
Godley (Grundy) Village	55
Godley (Will) Village	148
Golconda (Pope) City	120
Gold (Bureau) Township	13
Golden (Adams) Village	8
Golden Gate (Wayne) Village	143
Gold Hill (Gallatin) Township	52
Golf (Cook) Village	29
Goode (Franklin) Township	49
Goodfarm (Grundy) Township	55
Goodfield (Tazewell) Village	137
Goodfield (Woodford) Village	153
Good Hope (McDonough) Town	101
Goodings Grove (Will) CDP	148
Goose Creek (Piatt) Township	117
Goose Lake (Grundy) Township	55
Goreville (Johnson) Village	71
Gorham (Jackson) Village	65
Goshen (Stark) Township	134
Grafton (Jersey) Town	68
Grafton (McHenry) Township	103
Grand Detour (Ogle) Township	113
Grand Prairie (Jefferson) Township	67
Grand Rapids (La Salle) Township	82
Grand Ridge (La Salle) Village	82
Grand Tower (Jackson) Town	65
Grand Tower (Jackson) Township	65
Grandview (Edgar) Township	44
Grandview (Sangamon) Village	129
Grandville (Jasper) Township	66
Grandwood Park (Lake) CDP	79
Granite City (Madison) City	95
Granite City (Madison) Township	95
Grant (Lake) Township	79
Grant (Vermilion) Township	139
Grantfork (Madison) Village	95
Grant Park (Kankakee) Village	74
Granville (Putnam) City	121
Granville (Putnam) Township	121
Gray (White) Township	145
Grayslake (Lake) City	79
Grayville (Edwards) City	45
Grayville (White) City	145
Greenbush (Warren) Township	141
Greene (Mercer) Township	107
Greene (Woodford) Township	154
Greene County	53
Greenfield (Greene) City	53
Greenfield (Grundy) Township	55
Green Garden (Will) Township	148
Green Oaks (Lake) Village	79
Green Rock (Henry) City	61
Greenup (Cumberland) City	36
Greenup (Cumberland) Township	36
Green Valley (Tazewell) Village	137
Greenview (Menard) Village	107
Greenville (Bond) City	10
Greenville (Bureau) Township	13
Greenwood (Christian) Township	20
Greenwood (McHenry) Township	103
Gridley (McLean) Town	106
Gridley (McLean) Township	106
Griggsville (Pike) Town	118
Griggsville (Pike) Township	118
Grisham (Montgomery) Township	110
Grove (Jasper) Township	66
Groveland (La Salle) Township	82
Groveland (Tazewell) Township	137

ILLINOIS

Grover (Wayne) Township *144*
Grundy County *54*
Guilford (Jo Daviess) Township *69*
Gulf Port (Henderson) Village *59*
Gurnee (Lake) City *79*
Hadley (Pike) Township *118*
Hagener (Cass) Township *17*
Hahnaman (Whiteside) Township.....*146*
Haines (Marion) Township....................*97*
Hainesville (Lake) Village *79*
Hale (Warren) Township *141*
Hall (Bureau) Township *13*
Hallock (Peoria) Township *115*
Hamburg (Calhoun) Town *15*
Hamel (Madison) Township...................*95*
Hamel (Madison) Village *95*
Hamilton (Hancock) City *57*
Hamilton (Lee) Township *86*
Hamilton County...............................*56*
Hamletsburg (Pope) Village................*120*
Hammond (Piatt) Town *117*
Hampshire (Kane) Town *72*
Hampshire (Kane) Township *72*
Hampton (Rock Island) Township....*124*
Hampton (Rock Island) Village *124*
Hanaford (Franklin) Village *49*
Hancock (Hancock) Township *57*
Hancock County................................*57*
Hanna (Henry) Township *61*
Hanna City (Peoria) Village *115*
Hanover (Cook) Township *29*
Hanover (Jo Daviess) Town *69*
Hanover (Jo Daviess) Township *69*
Hanover Park (Cook) City *29*
Hanover Park (DuPage) City *42*
Hardin (Calhoun) Town *15*
Hardin (Pike) Township *118*
Hardin County....................................*59*
Harlem (Stephenson) Township *135*
Harlem (Winnebago) Township *152*
Harmon (Lee) Township *86*
Harmon (Lee) Village *86*
Harmony (Hancock) Township *58*
Harp (De Witt) Township *39*
Harris (Fulton) Township *51*
Harrisburg (Saline) City *128*
Harrisburg (Saline) Township *128*
Harrison (Winnebago) Township *152*
Harristown (Macon) Township *90*
Harristown (Macon) Village *90*
Harter (Clay) Township *22*
Hartford (Madison) Town *95*
Hartland (McHenry) Township *103*
Hartsburg (Logan) Village *89*
Harvard (McHenry) City *103*
Harvel (Christian) Village *20*
Harvel (Montgomery) Township *110*
Harvel (Montgomery) Village *110*
Harvey (Cook) City *29*
Harwood (Champaign) Township *18*
Harwood Heights (Cook) City *29*
Havana (Mason) City *99*
Havana (Mason) Township *99*
Haw Creek (Knox) Township *76*
Hawthorne (White) Township *145*
Hawthorn Woods (Lake) Village *79*
Hazel Crest (Cook) City *29*
Hebron (McHenry) Town *103*
Hebron (McHenry) Township *103*
Hecker (Monroe) Village *109*
Helvetia (Madison) Township *95*
Henderson (Knox) Township *77*
Henderson (Knox) Village *76*
Henderson County............................*59*
Hennepin (Putnam) Town *121*

Hennepin (Putnam) Township *121*
Henning (Vermilion) Village *139*
Henry (Marshall) Town *98*
Henry (Marshall) Township *98*
Henry County....................................*60*
Hensley (Champaign) Township *18*
Heralds Prairie (White) Township *145*
Herrick (Shelby) Township *133*
Herrick (Shelby) Village *133*
Herrin (Williamson) City *151*
Herscher (Kankakee) Village...............*74*
Hettick (Macoupin) Village *93*
Heyworth (McLean) Town *106*
Hickory (Schuyler) Township *131*
Hickory Hill (Wayne) Township *144*
Hickory Hills (Cook) City *29*
Hickory Point (Macon) Township *90*
Hidalgo (Jasper) Village *66*
Highland (Grundy) Township *55*
Highland (Madison) City *95*
Highland Park (Lake) City *79*
Highwood (Lake) City *79*
Hillcrest (Ogle) Village *113*
Hillsboro (Montgomery) City *110*
Hillsboro (Montgomery) Township ...*110*
Hillsdale (Rock Island) Village *124*
Hillside (Cook) City *29*
Hillview (Greene) Village *53*
Hillyard (Macoupin) Township *93*
Hinckley (DeKalb) Town *37*
Hindsboro (Douglas) Village *40*
Hinsdale (Cook) City *29*
Hinsdale (DuPage) City *42*
Hire (McDonough) Township *101*
Hittle (Tazewell) Township *137*
Hodgkins (Cook) Town *29*
Hoffman (Clinton) Village *24*
Hoffman Estates (Cook) Village *29*
Hoffman Estates (Kane) Village............*72*
Holiday Hills (McHenry) Village *103*
Holland (Shelby) Township *133*
Hollis (Peoria) Township *115*
Hollowayville (Bureau) Village *13*
Homer (Champaign) Village *18*
Homer (Will) Township *148*
Hometown (Cook) City *29*
Homewood (Cook) City *29*
Honey Creek (Adams) Township *8*
Honey Creek (Crawford) Township *35*
Honey Point (Macoupin) Township *93*
Hoopeston (Vermilion) City *139*
Hooppole (Henry) Town *61*
Hoosier (Clay) Township *22*
Hope (La Salle) Township *82*
Hopedale (Tazewell) Town *137*
Hopedale (Tazewell) Township *137*
Hopewell (Marshall) Township *98*
Hopewell (Marshall) Village *98*
Hopkins (Whiteside) Township *146*
Hopkins Park (Kankakee) Village *74*
Houston (Adams) Township *8*
Hoyleton (Washington) Township *142*
Hoyleton (Washington) Village *142*
Hudson (McLean) Township *106*
Hudson (McLean) Village *106*
Huey (Clinton) Village *24*
Hull (Pike) Village *118*
Humboldt (Coles) Township *25*
Humboldt (Coles) Village *25*
Hume (Edgar) Village *44*
Hume (Whiteside) Township *146*
Hunt City (Jasper) Township *66*
Hunter (Edgar) Township *44*
Huntley (McHenry) Town *103*
Huntsville (Schuyler) Township *131*

American Places Dictionary

Hurlbut (Logan) Township *89*
Hurricane (Fayette) Township *47*
Hurst (Williamson) City *151*
Hutsonville (Crawford) Township *35*
Hutsonville (Crawford) Village *35*
Hutton (Coles) Township *25*
Illini (Macon) Township *91*
Illiopolis (Sangamon) Town *129*
Illiopolis (Sangamon) Township *129*
Ina (Jefferson) Village *67*
Independence (Saline) Township *128*
Indian Creek (Lake) Town *79*
Indian Creek (White) Township *145*
Indian Grove (Livingston) Township .*88*
Indian Head Park (Cook) Village *29*
Indianola (Vermilion) Village *139*
Indian Point (Knox) Township *77*
Indian Prairie (Wayne) Township *144*
Indiantown (Bureau) Township *13*
Industry (McDonough) Town.............*101*
Industry (McDonough) Township *101*
Ingalls Park (Will) CDP *148*
Inverness (Cook) Town *29*
Iola (Clay) Village *22*
Ipava (Fulton) Village *51*
Irishtown (Clinton) Township *24*
Iroquois (Iroquois) Town *63*
Iroquois (Iroquois) Township *63*
Iroquois County.................................*62*
Irving (Montgomery) Town *110*
Irving (Montgomery) Township *110*
Irvington (Washington) Town *142*
Irvington (Washington) Township.....*142*
Irwin (Kankakee) Village *74*
Isabel (Fulton) Township *51*
Island Grove (Sangamon) Township.*129*
Island Lake (Lake) Town *79*
Island Lake (McHenry) Town *103*
Itasca (DuPage) City *42*
Iuka (Marion) Town *97*
Iuka (Marion) Township *97*
Ivesdale (Champaign) Village *18*
Ivesdale (Piatt) Village *117*
Jackson (Effingham) Township *46*
Jackson (Will) Township *148*
Jackson County..................................*64*
Jacksonville (Morgan) City *111*
Jamaica (Vermilion) Township *139*
Jarvis (Madison) Township *95*
Jasper (Wayne) Township *144*
Jasper County....................................*66*
Jefferson (Stephenson) Township.......*135*
Jefferson County *67*
Jeffersonville (Wayne) Village *144*
Jeiseyville (Christian) Village *20*
Jerome (Sangamon) Village *129*
Jersey (Jersey) Township *68*
Jersey County *68*
Jerseyville (Jersey) City *68*
Jewett (Cumberland) Village *36*
Jo Daviess County *69*
Johannisburg (Washington)
  Township *142*
Johnson (Christian) Township *20*
Johnson (Clark) Township.....................*21*
Johnson County.................................*71*
Johnsonville (Wayne) Village *144*
Johnston City (Williamson) Town *151*
Joliet (Will) City *148*
Joliet (Will) Township *148*
Jonathan Creek (Moultrie)
  Township *112*
Jonesboro (Union) Town *138*
Joppa (Massac) Village *100*
Jordan (Whiteside) Township *146*

Joshua (Fulton) Township 51
Joy (Mercer) Village 107
Jubilee (Peoria) Township 115
Junction (Gallatin) Village 53
Junction City (Marion) Village 97
Justice (Cook) Village 29
Kampsville (Calhoun) Village 15
Kane (Greene) Township 54
Kane (Greene) Village 53
Kane County 71
Kaneville (Kane) Township 72
Kangley (La Salle) Village 82
Kankakee (Kankakee) City 74
Kankakee (Kankakee) Township 74
Kankakee County 73
Kansas (Edgar) Town 44
Kansas (Edgar) Township 44
Kansas (Woodford) Township 154
Kappa (Woodford) Village 154
Karnak (Pulaski) Village 120
Kaskaskia (Fayette) Township 47
Kaskaskia (Randolph) Village 122
Keene (Adams) Township 8
Keenes (Wayne) Village 144
Keensburg (Wabash) Village 140
Keith (Wayne) Township 144
Keithsburg (Mercer) Town 108
Keithsburg (Mercer) Township 108
Kell (Marion) Village 97
Kelly (Warren) Township 141
Kempton (Ford) Village 48
Kendall (Kendall) Township 75
Kendall County 75
Kenilworth (Cook) Town 29
Kenney (De Witt) Village 39
Kent (Stephenson) Township 135
Kerr (Champaign) Township 18
Kerton (Fulton) Township 51
Kewanee (Henry) City 61
Kewanee (Henry) Township 61
Keyesport (Bond) Village 10
Keyesport (Clinton) Village 24
Kickapoo (Peoria) Township 115
Kilbourne (Mason) Town 99
Kilbourne (Mason) Township 100
Kildeer (Lake) Town 79
Kincaid (Christian) Town 20
Kinderhook (Pike) Township 118
Kinderhook (Pike) Village 118
King (Christian) Township 20
Kingston (DeKalb) Township 37
Kingston (DeKalb) Village 37
Kingston Mines (Peoria) Village 115
Kinkaid (Jackson) Township 65
Kinmundy (Marion) City 97
Kinmundy (Marion) Township 97
Kinsman (Grundy) Village 55
Kirkland (DeKalb) Town 37
Kirkwood (Warren) Town 141
Knight Prairie (Hamilton) Township 56
Knox (Knox) Township 77
Knox County 76
Knoxville (Knox) Town 77
La Clede (Fayette) Township 47
Lacon (Marshall) City 98
Lacon (Marshall) Township 98
Ladd (Bureau) Town 13
Laenna (Logan) Township 89
Lafayette (Coles) Township 25
Lafayette (Ogle) Township 113
La Fayette (Stark) Village 134
Lagrange (Bond) Township 10
La Grange (Cook) City 30
La Grange Park (Cook) City 30
La Harpe (Hancock) Town 58

La Harpe (Hancock) Township 58
Lake (Clinton) Township 24
Lake Barrington (Lake) Village 79
Lake Bluff (Lake) City 79
Lake Catherine (Lake) CDP 79
Lake County 78
Lake Forest (Lake) City 79
Lake Fork (Logan) Township 89
Lake in the Hills (McHenry) Village 103
Lakemoor (Lake) Village 79
Lakemoor (McHenry) Village 103
Lake of the Woods (Champaign)
    CDP 18
Lake Summerset (Stephenson) CDP.135
Lake Summerset (Winnebago) CDP .152
Lake Villa (Lake) Town 79
Lake Villa (Lake) Township 80
Lakewood (McHenry) Town 103
Lakewood (Shelby) Township 133
Lakewood Shores (Will) CDP 148
Lake Zurich (Lake) City 80
Lamard (Wayne) Township 144
La Moille (Bureau) Township 13
La Moille (Bureau) Village 13
Lamoine (McDonough) Township 101
Lamotte (Crawford) Township 35
Lanark (Carroll) Town 15
Lancaster (Stephenson) Township.....135
Lanesville (Sangamon) Township 129
Lansing (Cook) City 30
Laona (Winnebago) Township 152
La Prairie (Adams) Village 8
La Prairie (Marshall) Township 98
Larkinsburg (Clay) Township 22
La Rose (Marshall) Village 98
La Salle (La Salle) City 82
La Salle (La Salle) Township 82
La Salle County 81
Latham (Logan) Village 89
Lawndale (McLean) Township 106
Lawrence (Lawrence) Township 85
Lawrence County 84
Lawrenceville (Lawrence) City............85
Leaf River (Ogle) Township 113
Leaf River (Ogle) Village 113
Lebanon (St. Clair) City 126
Lebanon (St. Clair) Township 126
Lee (Brown) Township 12
Lee (DeKalb) Village 37
Lee (Fulton) Township 51
Lee (Lee) Village 86
Lee Center (Lee) Township 86
Leech (Wayne) Township 144
Lee County 85
Leef (Madison) Township 95
Leepertown (Bureau) Township 13
Leland (La Salle) Village 82
Leland Grove (Sangamon) City 129
Lemont (Cook) City 30
Lemont (Cook) Township 30
Lena (Stephenson) Town 135
Lenox (Warren) Township 141
Lenzburg (St. Clair) Township 126
Lenzburg (St. Clair) Village 126
Leonore (La Salle) Village 82
Lerna (Coles) Village 25
LeRoy (Boone) Township 11
Le Roy (McLean) City 106
Levan (Jackson) Township 65
Levee (Pike) Township 118
Lewistown (Fulton) City 51
Lewistown (Fulton) Township 51
Lexington (McLean) Town 106
Lexington (McLean) Township 106
Leyden (Cook) Township 30

Liberty (Adams) Township 8
Liberty (Adams) Village 8
Liberty (Effingham) Township 46
Libertyville (Lake) City 80
Libertyville (Lake) Township 80
Licking (Crawford) Township 35
Lima (Adams) Township 9
Lima (Adams) Village 8
Limestone (Kankakee) Township 74
Limestone (Peoria) Township 115
Lincoln (Logan) City 89
Lincoln (Ogle) Township 113
Lincolnshire (Lake) Town 80
Lincolnwood (Cook) City 30
Lindenhurst (Lake) City 80
Linder (Greene) Township 54
Linn (Woodford) Township 154
Lisbon (Kendall) Township 75
Lisbon (Kendall) Village 75
Lisle (DuPage) City 42
Lisle (DuPage) Township 42
Litchfield (Montgomery) City 110
Little Mackinaw (Tazewell)
    Township 137
Little Rock (Kendall) Township 75
Littleton (Schuyler) Township 131
Littleton (Schuyler) Village 131
Little York (Warren) Village 141
Lively Grove (Washington)
    Township 142
Liverpool (Fulton) Township 51
Liverpool (Fulton) Village 51
Livingston (Madison) Village 95
Livingston County 87
Loami (Sangamon) Town 130
Loami (Sangamon) Township 130
Lockport (Will) City 149
Lockport (Will) Township 149
Locust (Christian) Township 20
Loda (Iroquois) Township 63
Loda (Iroquois) Village 63
Logan (Peoria) Township 115
Logan County 89
Lomax (Henderson) Town 59
Lomax (Henderson) Township 59
Lombard (DuPage) City 42
London Mills (Fulton) Town 51
London Mills (Knox) Town 77
Lone Grove (Fayette) Township 47
Long Branch (Saline) Township 128
Long Creek (Macon) Township 91
Long Creek (Macon) Village 91
Long Grove (Lake) Village 80
Long Lake (Lake) CDP 80
Long Point (Livingston) Township 88
Long Point (Livingston) Village 88
Longview (Champaign) Village 18
Looking Glass (Clinton) Township 24
Loraine (Adams) Village 9
Loraine (Henry) Township 61
Loran (Stephenson) Township 135
Lostant (La Salle) Town 82
Loudon (Fayette) Township 47
Louisville (Clay) Town 22
Louisville (Clay) Township 22
Love (Vermilion) Township 139
Lovejoy (Iroquois) Township 63
Loves Park (Winnebago) City 152
Lovington (Moultrie) Township 112
Lovington (Moultrie) Village 112
Lowe (Moultrie) Township 112
Lucas (Effingham) Township 46
Ludlow (Champaign) Township 18
Ludlow (Champaign) Village 18
Lukin (Lawrence) Township 85

ILLINOIS · *American Places Dictionary*

Entry	Page
Lyman (Ford) Township	48
Lynchburg (Mason) Township	100
Lyndon (Whiteside) Town	146
Lyndon (Whiteside) Township	146
Lynn (Henry) Township	62
Lynn (Knox) Township	77
Lynnville (Morgan) Village	111
Lynnville (Ogle) Township	113
Lynwood (Cook) Town	30
Lyons (Cook) City	30
Lyons (Cook) Township	30
Macedonia (Franklin) Village	50
Macedonia (Hamilton) Village	56
Machesney Park (Winnebago) Village	152
Mackinaw (Tazewell) Town	137
Mackinaw (Tazewell) Township	137
Macomb (McDonough) City	101
Macomb (McDonough) Township	101
Macomb City (McDonough) Township	102
Macon (Bureau) Township	13
Macon (Macon) Town	91
Macon County	90
Macoupin County	92
Madison (Madison) City	95
Madison (Richland) Township	122
Madison (St. Clair) City	126
Madison County	94
Maeystown (Monroe) Village	109
Magnolia (Putnam) Township	121
Magnolia (Putnam) Village	121
Mahomet (Champaign) Township	18
Mahomet (Champaign) Village	18
Maine (Cook) Township	30
Maine (Grundy) Township	55
Makanda (Jackson) Town	65
Makanda (Jackson) Township	65
Malden (Bureau) Village	13
Malone (Tazewell) Township	137
Malta (DeKalb) Township	37
Malta (DeKalb) Village	37
Manchester (Boone) Township	11
Manchester (Scott) Town	132
Manhattan (Will) Town	149
Manhattan (Will) Township	149
Manito (Mason) Town	100
Manito (Mason) Township	100
Manlius (Bureau) Township	13
Manlius (Bureau) Village	13
Manlius (La Salle) Township	82
Mansfield (Piatt) Town	117
Manteno (Kankakee) Town	74
Manteno (Kankakee) Township	74
Maple Park (DeKalb) Village	37
Maple Park (Kane) Village	72
Mapleton (Peoria) Village	115
Maquon (Knox) Township	77
Maquon (Knox) Village	77
Marengo (McHenry) City	103
Marengo (McHenry) Township	103
Marietta (Fulton) Village	52
Marine (Madison) Town	95
Marine (Madison) Township	95
Marion (Lee) Township	86
Marion (Ogle) Township	113
Marion (Williamson) City	151
Marion County	96
Marissa (St. Clair) Town	126
Marissa (St. Clair) Township	126
Mark (Putnam) Village	121
Markham (Cook) City	30
Maroa (Macon) Town	91
Maroa (Macon) Township	91
Marquette Heights (Tazewell) City	137
Marrowbone (Moultrie) Township	112
Marseilles (La Salle) Town	83
Marshall (Clark) Town	21
Marshall (Clark) Township	21
Marshall County	98
Martin (Crawford) Township	35
Martin (McLean) Township	106
Martinsburg (Pike) Township	119
Martinsville (Clark) Town	21
Martinsville (Clark) Township	21
Martinton (Iroquois) Township	63
Martinton (Iroquois) Village	63
Maryland (Ogle) Township	113
Maryville (Madison) Town	95
Mascoutah (St. Clair) City	126
Mascoutah (St. Clair) Township	126
Mason (Effingham) Town	46
Mason (Effingham) Township	46
Mason City (Mason) Town	100
Mason City (Mason) Township	100
Mason County	99
Massac County	100
Massilon (Wayne) Township	144
Matherville (Mercer) Village	108
Matteson (Cook) City	30
Mattoon (Coles) City	25
Mattoon (Coles) Township	25
Maunie (White) Village	145
Maxwell (Sangamon) Township	130
May (Christian) Township	20
May (Lee) Township	86
Mayberry (Hamilton) Township	56
Mayfield (DeKalb) Township	37
Maywood (Cook) City	30
Mazon (Grundy) Town	55
Mazon (Grundy) Township	55
McClellan (Jefferson) Township	67
McCook (Cook) Village	30
McCullom Lake (McHenry) Village	104
McDonough County	101
McHenry (McHenry) City	104
McHenry (McHenry) Township	104
McHenry County	102
McKee (Adams) Township	9
McKendree (Vermilion) Township	139
McLean (McLean) Town	106
McLean County	104
McLeansboro (Hamilton) City	56
McLeansboro (Hamilton) Township	56
McNabb (Putnam) Village	121
Meacham (Marion) Township	97
Mechanicsburg (Sangamon) Town	130
Mechanicsburg (Sangamon) Township	130
Media (Henderson) Township	60
Media (Henderson) Village	59
Medina (Peoria) Township	115
Medinah (DuPage) CDP	42
Medora (Macoupin) Village	93
Melrose (Adams) Township	9
Melrose (Clark) Township	21
Melrose Park (Cook) City	30
Melvin (Ford) Village	48
Menard County	107
Mendon (Adams) Township	9
Mendon (Adams) Village	9
Mendota (La Salle) City	83
Mendota (La Salle) Township	83
Menominee (Jo Daviess) Township	69
Menominee (Jo Daviess) Village	69
Mercer (Mercer) Township	108
Mercer County	107
Meredosia (Morgan) Town	111
Meriden (La Salle) Township	83
Meridian (Clinton) Township	24
Merrionette Park (Cook) Town	30
Metamora (Woodford) Town	154
Metamora (Woodford) Township	154
Metcalf (Edgar) Village	44
Metropolis (Massac) City	100
Mettawa (Lake) Town	80
Middlefork (Vermilion) Township	139
Middleport (Iroquois) Township	63
Middletown (Logan) Village	89
Midlothian (Cook) City	31
Milam (Macon) Township	91
Milan (DeKalb) Township	37
Milan (Rock Island) Town	124
Milford (Iroquois) Town	63
Milford (Iroquois) Township	63
Milks Grove (Iroquois) Township	63
Millbrook (Peoria) Township	115
Mill Creek (Union) Village	138
Milledgeville (Carroll) Town	15
Miller (La Salle) Township	83
Millersburg (Mercer) Township	108
Millington (Kendall) Village	75
Millington (La Salle) Village	83
Mills (Bond) Township	10
Mill Shoals (Wayne) Village	144
Mill Shoals (White) Township	145
Mill Shoals (White) Village	145
Millstadt (St. Clair) Town	126
Millstadt (St. Clair) Township	126
Milo (Bureau) Township	13
Milton (DuPage) Township	42
Milton (Pike) Village	119
Mineral (Bureau) Township	14
Mineral (Bureau) Village	14
Minier (Tazewell) Town	137
Minonk (Woodford) Town	154
Minonk (Woodford) Township	154
Minooka (Grundy) Town	55
Minooka (Will) Town	149
Mission (La Salle) Township	83
Mississippi (Jersey) Township	68
Missouri (Brown) Township	12
Moccasin (Effingham) Township	46
Modesto (Macoupin) Village	93
Mokena (Will) Town	149
Moline (Rock Island) City	124
Moline (Rock Island) Township	124
Momence (Kankakee) City	74
Momence (Kankakee) Township	74
Mona (Ford) Township	48
Monee (Will) Town	149
Monee (Will) Township	149
Money Creek (McLean) Township	106
Monmouth (Warren) City	141
Monmouth (Warren) Township	141
Monroe (Ogle) Township	114
Monroe County	109
Montebello (Hancock) Township	58
Montezuma (Pike) Township	119
Montgomery (Crawford) Township	35
Montgomery (Kane) Town	73
Montgomery (Kendall) Town	75
Montgomery (Woodford) Township	154
Montgomery County	109
Monticello (Piatt) City	117
Monticello (Piatt) Township	117
Montmorency (Whiteside) Township	147
Montrose (Cumberland) Village	36
Montrose (Effingham) Village	46
Moores Prairie (Jefferson) Township	67
Morgan (Coles) Township	25
Morgan County	111
Moro (Madison) Township	95
Morris (Grundy) City	55
Morris (Grundy) Township	55

Place	Page
Morrison (Whiteside) Town	147
Morrisonville (Christian) Town	20
Morton (Tazewell) City	137
Morton (Tazewell) Township	137
Morton Grove (Cook) City	31
Mosquito (Christian) Township	20
Moultrie County	112
Mound (Effingham) Township	46
Mound (McDonough) Township	102
Mound City (Pulaski) City	120
Mounds (Pulaski) Town	120
Mound Station (Brown) Village	12
Mountain (Saline) Township	128
Mount Auburn (Christian) Township	20
Mount Auburn (Christian) Village	20
Mount Carmel (Wabash) City	140
Mount Carroll (Carroll) City	15
Mount Carroll (Carroll) Township	15
Mount Clare (Macoupin) Village	93
Mount Erie (Wayne) Township	144
Mount Erie (Wayne) Village	144
Mount Hope (McLean) Township	106
Mount Morris (Ogle) Town	114
Mount Morris (Ogle) Township	114
Mount Olive (Macoupin) Town	93
Mount Olive (Macoupin) Township	93
Mount Pleasant (Whiteside) Township	147
Mount Prospect (Cook) City	31
Mount Pulaski (Logan) Town	89
Mount Pulaski (Logan) Township	90
Mount Sterling (Brown) Town	12
Mount Sterling (Brown) Township	12
Mount Vernon (Jefferson) City	67
Mount Vernon (Jefferson) Township	67
Mount Zion (Macon) City	91
Mount Zion (Macon) Township	91
Moweaqua (Christian) Village	20
Moweaqua (Shelby) Town	133
Moweaqua (Shelby) Township	133
Muddy (Saline) Village	128
Mulberry Grove (Bond) Town	10
Mulberry Grove (Bond) Township	10
Muncie (Vermilion) Village	139
Mundelein (Lake) City	80
Munson (Henry) Township	62
Murdock (Douglas) Township	40
Murphysboro (Jackson) City	65
Murphysboro (Jackson) Township	65
Murrayville (Morgan) Village	111
Naausay (Kendall) Township	75
Nachusa (Lee) Township	86
Nameoki (Madison) Township	95
Naperville (DuPage) City	42
Naperville (DuPage) Township	42
Naperville (Will) City	149
Naplate (La Salle) Village	83
Naples (Scott) Town	132
Nashua (Ogle) Township	114
Nashville (Washington) Town	142
Nashville (Washington) Township	142
Nason (Jefferson) Town	67
National City (St. Clair) Village	126
Nauvoo (Hancock) Town	58
Nauvoo (Hancock) Township	58
Nebo (Pike) Town	119
Nebraska (Livingston) Township	88
Nelson (Lee) Township	86
Nelson (Lee) Village	86
Neoga (Cumberland) City	36
Neoga (Cumberland) Township	36
Neponset (Bureau) Township	14
Neponset (Bureau) Village	14
Nettle Creek (Grundy) Township	55
Nevada (Livingston) Township	88
Newark (Kendall) Village	76
New Athens (St. Clair) Town	126
New Athens (St. Clair) Township	126
New Baden (Clinton) Town	24
New Baden (St. Clair) Town	127
New Bedford (Bureau) Village	14
New Berlin (Sangamon) Township	130
New Berlin (Sangamon) Village	130
New Boston (Mercer) Town	108
New Boston (Mercer) Township	108
Newburg (Pike) Township	119
New Burnside (Johnson) Village	71
New Canton (Pike) Town	119
Newcomb (Champaign) Township	18
New Douglas (Madison) Township	95
New Douglas (Madison) Village	95
Newell (Vermilion) Township	139
New Grand Chain (Pulaski) Village	120
New Haven (Gallatin) Township	53
New Haven (Gallatin) Village	53
New Holland (Logan) Village	90
New Lenox (Will) City	149
New Lenox (Will) Township	149
Newman (Douglas) Town	40
Newman (Douglas) Township	40
Newmansville (Cass) Township	17
New Millford (Winnebago) Village	152
New Minden (Washington) Village	142
Newport (Lake) Township	80
New Salem (McDonough) Township	102
New Salem (Pike) Township	119
New Salem (Pike) Village	119
Newton (Jasper) Town	66
Newton (Whiteside) Township	147
Newtown (Livingston) Township	88
New Trier (Cook) Township	31
Niantic (Macon) Township	91
Niantic (Macon) Village	91
Niles (Cook) City	31
Niles (Cook) Township	31
Nilwood (Macoupin) Town	93
Nilwood (Macoupin) Township	93
Nixon (De Witt) Township	39
Noble (Richland) Town	122
Noble (Richland) Township	123
Nokomis (Montgomery) Town	110
Nokomis (Montgomery) Township	110
Nora (Jo Daviess) Township	70
Nora (Jo Daviess) Village	69
Normal (McLean) City	106
Normal (McLean) Township	106
Norman (Grundy) Township	55
Norridge (Cook) Village	31
Norris (Fulton) Village	52
Norris City (White) Village	145
North Aurora (Kane) Village	73
North Barrington (Lake) Town	80
Northbrook (Cook) City	31
North Chicago (Lake) City	80
North City (Franklin) Village	50
Northeast (Adams) Township	9
Northern (Franklin) Township	50
Northfield (Cook) Township	31
Northfield (Cook) Village	31
North Fork (Gallatin) Township	53
North Henderson (Mercer) Township	108
North Henderson (Mercer) Village	108
Northlake (Cook) City	31
North Litchfield (Montgomery) Township	110
North Muddy (Jasper) Township	66
North Okaw (Coles) Township	25
North Otter (Macoupin) Township	93
North Palmyra (Macoupin) Township	93
North Pekin (Tazewell) Village	137
North Riverside (Cook) Village	31
North Utica (La Salle) Village	83
Northville (La Salle) Township	83
Norton (Kankakee) Township	74
Norwood (Peoria) Village	115
Norwood Park (Cook) Township	31
Nunda (McHenry) Township	104
Oak Brook (Cook) Town	31
Oak Brook (DuPage) Town	42
Oakbrook Terrace (DuPage) City	42
Oakdale (Washington) Township	142
Oakdale (Washington) Village	142
Oakford (Menard) Village	107
Oak Forest (Cook) City	31
Oak Grove (Rock Island) Village	124
Oakland (Coles) Town	25
Oakland (Schuyler) Township	131
Oak Lawn (Cook) City	31
Oakley (Macon) Township	91
Oak Park (Cook) City	31
Oak Park (Cook) Township	31
Oakwood (Vermilion) Township	139
Oakwood (Vermilion) Village	139
Oakwood Hills (McHenry) Village	104
Oblong (Crawford) Town	35
Oblong (Crawford) Township	35
Oconee (Shelby) Township	133
Oconee (Shelby) Village	133
Odell (Livingston) Township	88
Odell (Livingston) Village	88
Odin (Marion) Town	97
Odin (Marion) Township	97
O'Fallon (St. Clair) Town	127
O'Fallon (St. Clair) Township	127
Ogden (Champaign) Township	18
Ogden (Champaign) Village	18
Ogle County	113
Oglesby (La Salle) Town	83
Ohio (Bureau) Township	14
Ohio (Bureau) Village	14
Ohio Grove (Mercer) Township	108
Ohlman (Montgomery) Village	110
Okaw (Shelby) Township	133
Okawville (Washington) Township	143
Okawville (Washington) Village	142
Old Mill Creek (Lake) Village	80
Old Ripley (Bond) Township	10
Old Ripley (Bond) Village	10
Old Shawneetown (Gallatin) Village	53
Oldtown (McLean) Township	106
Olio (Woodford) Township	154
Olive (Madison) Township	95
Olmsted (Pulaski) Village	120
Olney (Richland) Town	123
Olney (Richland) Township	123
Olympia Fields (Cook) Town	32
Omaha (Gallatin) Township	53
Omaha (Gallatin) Village	53
Omega (Marion) Township	97
Omphghent (Madison) Township	95
Onarga (Iroquois) Town	64
Onarga (Iroquois) Township	64
Oneco (Stephenson) Township	135
Oneida (Knox) City	77
Ontario (Knox) Township	77
Ophir (La Salle) Township	83
Oquawka (Henderson) Town	60
Oquawka (Henderson) Township	60
Ora (Jackson) Township	65
Oran (Logan) Township	90
Orange (Clark) Township	22
Orange (Knox) Township	77
Orangeville (Stephenson) Village	135
Orchard (Wayne) Township	144

Oreana (Macon) Village 91	Pecatonica (Winnebago) Township ... 152	Pleasant Vale (Pike) Township 119
Oregon (Ogle) Town 114	Pekin (Peoria) City 115	Pleasant Valley (Jo Daviess) Township 70
Oregon (Ogle) Township 114	Pekin (Tazewell) City 137	
Orel (Wayne) Township 144	Pekin (Tazewell) Township 137	Pleasant View (Macon) Township 91
Orient (Franklin) City 50	Pella (Ford) Township 48	Plum Hill (Washington) Township 143
Orion (Fulton) Township 52	Pembroke (Kankakee) Township 74	Plymouth (Hancock) Village 58
Orion (Henry) Town 62	Pendleton (Jefferson) Township 67	Plymouth (McDonough) Village 102
Orland (Cook) Township 32	Penn (Shelby) Township 133	Pocahontas (Bond) Town 10
Orland Hills (Cook) Village 32	Penn (Stark) Township 134	Point Pleasant (Warren) Township ... 141
Orland Park (Cook) Village 32	Pennsylvania (Mason) Township 100	Polk (Macoupin) Township 93
Orvil (Logan) Township 90	Peoria (Peoria) City 115	Polo (Ogle) Town 114
Osage (La Salle) Township 83	Peoria City (Peoria) Township 115	Pomona (Jackson) Township 65
Osceola (Stark) Township 134	**Peoria County** 114	Pontiac (Livingston) City 88
Osco (Henry) Township 62	Peoria Heights (Peoria) Village 116	Pontiac (Livingston) Township 88
Oskaloosa (Clay) Township 22	Peoria Heights (Tazewell) Village 137	Pontoon Beach (Madison) Village 96
Oswego (Kendall) Township 76	Peoria Heights (Woodford) Village ... 154	Pontoosuc (Hancock) Township 58
Oswego (Kendall) Village 76	Peotone (Will) Town 149	Pontoosuc (Hancock) Village 58
Otego (Fayette) Township 47	Peotone (Will) Township 149	Pope (Fayette) Township 47
Ottawa (La Salle) City 83	Percy (Randolph) Village 122	**Pope County** 120
Ottawa (La Salle) Township 83	Perry (Pike) Township 119	Poplar Grove (Boone) Town 11
Otter Creek (Jersey) Township 68	Perry (Pike) Village 119	Poplar Grove (Boone) Township 11
Otter Creek (La Salle) Township 83	**Perry County** 116	Port Byron (Rock Island) Township . 124
Otterville (Jersey) Town 68	Perryton (Mercer) Township 108	Port Byron (Rock Island) Village 124
Otto (Kankakee) Township 74	Persifer (Knox) Township 77	Portland (Whiteside) Township 147
Owaneco (Christian) Village 20	Peru (La Salle) City 83	Posen (Cook) Town 32
Owego (Livingston) Township 88	Peru (La Salle) Township 83	Potomac (Vermilion) Town 140
Owen (Winnebago) Township 152	Pesotum (Champaign) Town 18	Prairie (Crawford) Township 35
Oxford (Henry) Township 62	Pesotum (Champaign) Township 18	Prairie (Edgar) Township 44
Palatine (Cook) Town 32	Petersburg (Menard) Town 107	Prairie (Hancock) Township 58
Palatine (Cook) Township 32	Petty (Lawrence) Township 85	Prairie (Shelby) Township 133
Palestine (Crawford) Town 35	Phenix (Henry) Township 62	Prairie City (McDonough) Town 102
Palestine (Woodford) Township 154	Philadelphia (Cass) Township 17	Prairie City (McDonough) Township 102
Palmer (Christian) Village 20	Phillips (White) Township 145	
Palmyra (Lee) Township 86	Phillipstown (White) Village 145	Prairie Creek (Logan) Township 90
Palmyra (Macoupin) Village 93	Philo (Champaign) Town 18	Prairie Du Long (St. Clair) Township 127
Palos (Cook) Township 32	Philo (Champaign) Township 18	
Palos Heights (Cook) Town 32	Phoenix (Cook) Village 32	Prairie du Rocher (Randolph) Town 122
Palos Hills (Cook) City 32	Piasa (Jersey) Township 68	Prairie Green (Iroquois) Township 64
Palos Park (Cook) Village 32	**Piatt County** 117	Prairie Grove (McHenry) Village 104
Pana (Christian) City 20	Pickaway (Shelby) Township 133	Prairieton (Christian) Township 20
Pana (Christian) Township 20	Pierce (DeKalb) Township 38	Preemption (Mercer) Township 108
Panama (Bond) Village 10	Pierron (Bond) Village 10	Preston (Richland) Township 123
Panama (Montgomery) Village 110	Pierron (Madison) Village 96	Preston Heights (Will) CDP 149
Panola (Woodford) Township 154	Pigeon Grove (Iroquois) Township 64	Princeton (Bureau) Town 14
Panola (Woodford) Village 154	Pike (Livingston) Township 88	Princeton (Bureau) Township 14
Panther Creek (Cass) Township 17	**Pike County** 118	Princeville (Peoria) Town 116
Papineau (Iroquois) Township 64	Pilot (Kankakee) Township 74	Princeville (Peoria) Township 116
Papineau (Iroquois) Village 64	Pilot (Vermilion) Township 139	Prophetstown (Whiteside) Town 147
Paradise (Coles) Township 25	Pilot Grove (Hancock) Township 58	Prophetstown (Whiteside) Township 147
Paris (Edgar) City 44	Pilot Knob (Washington) Township .. 143	Prospect Heights (Cook) City 32
Paris (Edgar) Township 44	Pinckneyville (Perry) Town 116	Proviso (Cook) Township 32
Park City (Lake) City 80	Pine Creek (Ogle) Township 114	Pulaski (Pulaski) Village 120
Parker (Clark) Township 22	Pine Rock (Ogle) Township 114	**Pulaski County** 120
Parkersburg (Richland) Village 123	Pingree Grove (Kane) Village 73	Putnam (Fulton) Township 52
Park Forest (Cook) Village 32	Pin Oak (Madison) Township 96	**Putnam County** 121
Park Forest (Will) Village 149	Piper City (Ford) Village 48	Quarry (Jersey) Township 68
Park Ridge (Cook) City 32	Pistakee Highlands (McHenry) CDP 104	Quincy (Adams) City 9
Partridge (Woodford) Township 154	Pitman (Montgomery) Township 110	Quincy (Adams) Township 9
Patoka (Marion) Town 97	Pittsburg (Williamson) Town 151	Quiver (Mason) Township 100
Patoka (Marion) Township 97	Pittsfield (Pike) Town 119	Raccoon (Marion) Township 97
Patterson (Greene) Township 54	Pittsfield (Pike) Township 119	Radnor (Peoria) Township 116
Patton (Ford) Township 48	Pixley (Clay) Township 22	Radom (Washington) Village 143
Pawnee (Sangamon) Town 130	Plainfield (Will) Town 149	Raleigh (Saline) Township 128
Pawnee (Sangamon) Township 130	Plainfield (Will) Township 149	Raleigh (Saline) Village 128
Paw Paw (DeKalb) Township 37	Plainville (Adams) Village 9	Ramsey (Fayette) Town 47
Paw Paw (Lee) Town 86	Plano (Kendall) Town 76	Ramsey (Fayette) Township 47
Paxton (Ford) Town 48	Plato (Kane) Township 73	Randolph (McLean) Township 106
Payson (Adams) Town 9	Pleasant (Fulton) Township 52	**Randolph County** 121
Payson (Adams) Township 9	Pleasant Grove (Coles) Township 25	Rankin (Vermilion) Town 140
Peach Orchard (Ford) Township 48	Pleasant Hill (Pike) Town 119	Ransom (La Salle) Village 83
Pea Ridge (Brown) Township 12	Pleasant Hill (Pike) Township 119	Rantoul (Champaign) City 18
Pearl (Pike) Township 119	Pleasant Mound (Bond) Township 10	Rantoul (Champaign) Township 18
Pearl (Pike) Village 119	Pleasant Plains (Sangamon) Village .. 130	Rapids City (Rock Island) Town 124
Pearl City (Stephenson) Town 135	Pleasant Ridge (Livingston) Township 88	Raritan (Henderson) Township 60
Pecatonica (Winnebago) Town 152		Raritan (Henderson) Village 60

ILLINOIS

Entry	Page
Rawlins (Jo Daviess) Township	70
Raymond (Champaign) Township	18
Raymond (Montgomery) Town	110
Raymond (Montgomery) Township	110
Reading (Livingston) Township	88
Rector (Saline) Township	128
Red Bud (Randolph) Town	122
Reddick (Kankakee) Village	75
Reddick (Livingston) Village	88
Redmon (Edgar) Village	44
Reed (Will) Township	149
Reynolds (Lee) Township	86
Reynolds (Mercer) Village	108
Reynolds (Rock Island) Village	124
Rice (Jo Daviess) Township	70
Rich (Cook) Township	32
Richfield (Adams) Township	9
Richland (La Salle) Township	83
Richland (Marshall) Township	98
Richland (Shelby) Township	133
Richland County	122
Richland Grove (Mercer) Township	108
Richmond (McHenry) Town	104
Richmond (McHenry) Township	104
Richton Park (Cook) Village	32
Richview (Washington) Township	143
Richview (Washington) Village	143
Richwood (Jersey) Township	68
Richwoods (Peoria) Township	116
Ricks (Christian) Township	20
Ridge (Shelby) Township	133
Ridge Farm (Vermilion) Town	140
Ridgeland (Iroquois) Township	64
Ridgway (Gallatin) Town	53
Ridgway (Gallatin) Township	53
Ridott (Stephenson) Township	136
Ridott (Stephenson) Village	135
Riley (McHenry) Township	104
Rio (Knox) Township	77
Rio (Knox) Village	77
Ripley (Brown) Township	12
Ripley (Brown) Village	12
Riverdale (Cook) Village	32
River Forest (Cook) Township	33
River Forest (Cook) Village	32
River Grove (Cook) City	33
Riverside (Adams) Township	9
Riverside (Cook) City	33
Riverside (Cook) Township	33
Riverton (Sangamon) Town	130
Riverwoods (Lake) Village	80
Rivoli (Mercer) Township	108
Roanoke (Woodford) Town	154
Roanoke (Woodford) Township	154
Robbins (Cook) City	33
Roberts (Ford) Village	49
Roberts (Marshall) Township	98
Robinson (Crawford) Town	35
Robinson (Crawford) Township	35
Rochelle (Ogle) Town	114
Rochester (Sangamon) Town	130
Rochester (Sangamon) Township	130
Rockbridge (Greene) Township	54
Rockbridge (Greene) Village	54
Rock City (Stephenson) Village	136
Rock Creek (Hancock) Township	58
Rock Creek-Lima (Carroll) Township	16
Rockdale (Will) Village	149
Rock Falls (Whiteside) Town	147
Rockford (Winnebago) City	152
Rockford (Winnebago) Township	152
Rock Grove (Stephenson) Township	136
Rock Island (Rock Island) City	124
Rock Island (Rock Island) Township	124
Rock Island County	123
Rock Run (Stephenson) Township	136
Rockton (Winnebago) Town	152
Rockton (Winnebago) Township	153
Rockvale (Ogle) Township	114
Rockville (Kankakee) Township	75
Rockwood (Randolph) Village	122
Rocky Run (Hancock) Township	58
Rogers (Ford) Township	49
Rolling Meadows (Cook) City	33
Rome (Jefferson) Township	67
Rome (Peoria) CDP	116
Romeoville (Will) Village	149
Romine (Marion) Township	97
Roodhouse (Greene) Town	54
Roodhouse (Greene) Township	54
Rooks Creek (Livingston) Township	88
Rosamond (Christian) Township	20
Roscoe (Winnebago) Town	153
Roscoe (Winnebago) Township	153
Rose (Shelby) Township	133
Rosedale (Jersey) Township	68
Rosefield (Peoria) Township	116
Rose Hill (Jasper) Village	66
Roselle (Cook) Village	33
Roselle (DuPage) Village	42
Rosemont (Cook) Village	33
Roseville (Warren) Town	141
Roseville (Warren) Township	141
Rosewood Heights (Madison) CDP	96
Rosiclare (Hardin) Town	59
Ross (Edgar) Township	44
Ross (Pike) Township	119
Ross (Vermilion) Township	140
Rossville (Vermilion) Town	140
Round Grove (Livingston) Township	88
Round Lake (Lake) Town	80
Round Lake Beach (Lake) Village	80
Round Lake Heights (Lake) Village	80
Round Lake Park (Lake) Village	80
Rountree (Montgomery) Township	110
Roxana (Madison) Town	96
Royal (Champaign) Village	18
Royal Lakes (Macoupin) Village	93
Royalton (Franklin) Town	50
Rozetta (Henderson) Township	60
Rubicon (Greene) Township	54
Ruma (Randolph) Village	122
Rural (Rock Island) Township	124
Rural (Shelby) Township	133
Rush (Jo Daviess) Township	70
Rushville (Schuyler) Town	131
Rushville (Schuyler) Township	131
Russell (Lawrence) Township	85
Russellville (Lawrence) Village	85
Rutland (Kane) Township	73
Rutland (La Salle) Township	83
Rutland (La Salle) Village	83
Rutledge (De Witt) Township	39
Ruyle (Jersey) Township	68
Sadorus (Champaign) Township	19
Sadorus (Champaign) Village	19
Sailor Springs (Clay) Village	22
St. Albans (Hancock) Township	58
St. Anne (Kankakee) Town	75
St. Anne (Kankakee) Township	75
St. Augustine (Knox) Village	77
St. Charles (DuPage) Town	42
St. Charles (Kane) Town	73
St. Charles (Kane) Township	73
St. Clair (St. Clair) Township	127
St. Clair County	125
St. David (Fulton) Village	52
St. Elmo (Fayette) City	47
Ste. Marie (Jasper) Township	66
Ste. Marie (Jasper) Village	66
St. Francis (Effingham) Township	46
St. Francisville (Lawrence) Town	85
St. Jacob (Madison) Township	96
St. Jacob (Madison) Village	96
St. Johns (Perry) Village	116
St. Joseph (Champaign) Township	19
St. Joseph (Champaign) Village	19
St. Libory (St. Clair) Village	127
St. Mary (Hancock) Township	58
St. Peter (Fayette) Village	47
St. Rose (Clinton) Township	24
Salem (Carroll) Township	16
Salem (Knox) Township	77
Salem (Marion) Town	97
Salem (Marion) Township	97
Salina (Kankakee) Township	75
Saline (Madison) Township	96
Saline County	127
Salt Creek (Mason) Township	100
Sandoval (Marion) Town	98
Sandoval (Marion) Township	98
Sand Prairie (Tazewell) Township	137
Sand Ridge (Jackson) Township	65
Sandwich (DeKalb) Town	38
Sandwich (DeKalb) Township	38
Sandwich (Kendall) Town	76
Sangamon (Piatt) Township	117
Sangamon County	128
Sangamon Valley (Cass) Township	17
San Jose (Logan) Village	90
San Jose (Mason) Village	100
Santa Anna (De Witt) Township	39
Santa Fe (Clinton) Township	24
Saratoga (Grundy) Township	55
Saratoga (Marshall) Township	99
Sargent (Douglas) Township	40
Sauget (St. Clair) Village	127
Sauk Village (Cook) Village	33
Sauk Village (Will) Village	150
Saunemin (Livingston) Township	88
Saunemin (Livingston) Village	88
Savanna (Carroll) Town	16
Savanna (Carroll) Township	16
Savoy (Champaign) Town	19
Sawyerville (Macoupin) Village	93
Saybrook (McLean) Village	106
Scales Mound (Jo Daviess) Township	70
Scales Mound (Jo Daviess) Village	70
Schaumburg (Cook) Township	33
Schaumburg (Cook) Village	33
Schaumburg (DuPage) Village	43
Schiller Park (Cook) Village	33
Schram City (Montgomery) Village	110
Schuyler County	131
Sciota (McDonough) Township	102
Sciota (McDonough) Village	102
Scotland (McDonough) Township	102
Scott (Champaign) Township	19
Scott (Ogle) Township	114
Scott County	132
Scottville (Macoupin) Township	93
Scottville (Macoupin) Village	93
Seaton (Mercer) Village	108
Seatonville (Bureau) Village	14
Secor (Woodford) Village	154
Sefton (Fayette) Township	47
Selby (Bureau) Township	14
Seminary (Fayette) Township	47
Senachwine (Putnam) Township	121
Seneca (Grundy) Town	56
Seneca (La Salle) Town	83
Seneca (McHenry) Township	104
Serena (La Salle) Township	83
Sesser (Franklin) Town	50
Seven Hickory (Coles) Township	25

ILLINOIS

Seward (Kendall) Township 76
Seward (Winnebago) Township 153
Shabbona (DeKalb) Town 38
Shabbona (DeKalb) Township 38
Shafter (Fayette) Township.................47
Shannon (Carroll) Village....................16
Sharon (Fayette) Township..................47
Shawnee (Gallatin) Village 53
Shawneetown (Gallatin) City 53
Shaws Point (Macoupin) Township 93
Sheffield (Bureau) Village...................14
Shelby County 132
Shelbyville (Shelby) City 133
Shelbyville (Shelby) Township 133
Sheldon (Iroquois) Town 64
Sheldon (Iroquois) Township 64
Sheridan (La Salle) Town 84
Sheridan (Logan) Township 90
Sherman (Mason) Township................100
Sherman (Sangamon) Village 130
Sherrard (Mercer) Village...................108
Shields (Lake) Township 80
Shiloh (Edgar) Township 44
Shiloh (Jefferson) Township 67
Shiloh (St. Clair) Village 127
Shiloh Valley (St. Clair) Township....127
Shipman (Macoupin) Town 93
Shipman (Macoupin) Township 93
Shirland (Winnebago) Township........153
Shoal Creek (Bond) Township 10
Shorewood (Will) Village...................150
Shumway (Effingham) Village 46
Sibley (Ford) Village 49
Sidell (Vermilion) Town 140
Sidell (Vermilion) Township..............140
Sidney (Champaign) Town 19
Sidney (Champaign) Township 19
Sigel (Shelby) Town 133
Sigel (Shelby) Township 133
Silver Creek (Stephenson) Township 136
Silvis (Rock Island) Town 124
Simpson (Johnson) Village 71
Sims (Wayne) Village........................144
Six Mile (Franklin) Township.............50
Skokie (Cook) City..............................33
Sleepy Hollow (Kane) Village 73
Smallwood (Jasper) Township.............66
Smithboro (Bond) Village....................10
Smithfield (Fulton) Village..................52
Smithton (St. Clair) Township...........127
Smithton (St. Clair) Village................127
Somer (Champaign) Township 19
Somerset (Jackson) Township 65
Somonauk (DeKalb) Town 38
Somonauk (DeKalb) Township 38
Somonauk (La Salle) Town 84
Songer (Clay) Township......................23
Sonora (Hancock) Township 58
Sorento (Bond) Town 11
South Barrington (Cook) Village.........33
South Beloit (Winnebago) Town 153
South Chicago Heights (Cook)
   Village 33
South Crouch (Hamilton) Township...56
South Dixon (Lee) Township 86
South Elgin (Kane) Town 73
Southern View (Sangamon) Village ..130
South Fillmore (Montgomery)
   Township....................................... 110
South Flannigan (Hamilton)
   Township... 56
South Fork (Christian) Township........20
South Grove (DeKalb) Township 38
South Holland (Cook) City 33
South Homer (Champaign) Township 19

South Hurricane (Fayette) Township ..48
South Jacksonville (Morgan) Village 111
South Litchfield (Montgomery)
   Township....................................... 110
South Macon (Macon) Township........91
South Moline (Rock Island)
   Township....................................... 124
South Muddy (Jasper) Township 66
South Ottawa (La Salle) Township 84
South Otter (Macoupin) Township 93
South Palmyra (Macoupin) Township 93
South Pekin (Tazewell) Town............137
South Rock Island (Rock Island)
   Township....................................... 124
South Ross (Vermilion) Township 140
South Roxana (Madison) Town 96
South Twigg (Hamilton) Township.....57
Southwest (Crawford) Township.........35
South Wheatland (Macon) Township .91
South Wilmington (Grundy) Village...56
Sparland (Marshall) Village.................99
Sparta (Knox) Township......................77
Sparta (Randolph) Town 122
Spaulding (Sangamon) Village...........130
Spillertown (Williamson) Village 151
Spring (Boone) Township 11
Spring Bay (Woodford) Township.....154
Spring Bay (Woodford) Village.........154
Spring Creek (Pike) Township 119
Springerton (White) Village 145
Springfield (Sangamon) City 130
Springfield (Sangamon) Township 130
Spring Garden (Jefferson) Township ..67
Spring Grove (McHenry) Village 104
Spring Grove (Warren) Township 141
Spring Lake (Tazewell) Township 137
Spring Point (Cumberland) Township 36
Spring Valley (Bureau) Town 14
Squaw Grove (DeKalb) Township 38
Standard (Putnam) Village 121
Standard City (Macoupin) Village......93
Stanford (Clay) Township....................23
Stanford (McLean) Village 106
Stanton (Champaign) Township..........19
Stark County 134
Staunton (Macoupin) Town 93
Staunton (Macoupin) Township..........93
Steeleville (Randolph) Town 122
Steger (Cook) Village 33
Steger (Will) Village..........................150
Stephenson County................................135
Sterling (Whiteside) City 147
Sterling (Whiteside) Township 147
Steuben (Marshall) Township..............99
Stevenson (Marion) Township 98
Steward (Lee) Village..........................86
Stewardson (Shelby) Village 133
Stickney (Cook) Township 33
Stickney (Cook) Village 33
Stillman Valley (Ogle) Village 114
Stites (St. Clair) Township 127
Stockland (Iroquois) Township 64
Stockton (Jo Daviess) Township.........70
Stockton (Jo Daviess) Village.............70
Stonefort (Saline) Township 128
Stonefort (Saline) Village...................128
Stonefort (Williamson) Village..........151
Stone Park (Cook) Village...................33
Stonington (Christian) Township........21
Stonington (Christian) Village............21
Stookey (St. Clair) Township.............127
Stoy (Crawford) Village 35
Strasburg (Shelby) Village 133
Stratton (Edgar) Township 44
Strawn (Livingston) Village................88

American Places Dictionary

Streamwood (Cook) Village.................34
Streator (La Salle) City........................84
Streator (Livingston) City....................88
Stronghurst (Henderson) Township 60
Stronghurst (Henderson) Village........60
Sublette (Lee) Township 86
Sublette (Lee) Village..........................86
Suez (Mercer) Township....................108
Sugar Creek (Clinton) Township........24
Sugar Grove (Kane) Township............73
Sugar Grove (Kane) Village.................73
Sugar Loaf (St. Clair) Township......127
Sullivan (Livingston) Township 88
Sullivan (Moultrie) City 112
Sullivan (Moultrie) Township............112
Sullivant (Ford) Township...................49
Summerfield (St. Clair) Village.........127
Summit (Cook) Village........................34
Summit (Effingham) Township 46
Sumner (Kankakee) Township 75
Sumner (Lawrence) City......................85
Sumner (Warren) Township 141
Sumpter (Cumberland) Township 36
Sunbury (Livingston) Township 88
Sunnyside (McHenry) Village 104
Sun River Terrace (Kankakee) Village 75
Swan (Warren) Township 141
Swansea (St. Clair) Village 127
Sycamore (DeKalb) City 38
Sycamore (DeKalb) Township 38
Symerton (Will) Village.....................150
Symmes (Edgar) Township..................44
Table Grove (Fulton) Village..............52
Talkington (Sangamon) Township.....130
Tallula (Menard) Village...................107
Tamalco (Bond) Township 11
Tamaroa (Perry) Village 116
Tamms (Alexander) Village 9
Tampico (Whiteside) Township 147
Tampico (Whiteside) Village.............147
Tate (Saline) Township 128
Taylor (Ogle) Township 114
Taylor Springs (Montgomery)
   Village 110
Taylorville (Christian) City..................21
Taylorville (Christian) Township 21
Tazewell County 136
Tennessee (McDonough) Township ..102
Tennessee (McDonough) Village 102
Terre Haute (Henderson) Township...60
Teutopolis (Effingham) Town.............46
Teutopolis (Effingham) Township 46
Texas (De Witt) Township 39
Thawville (Iroquois) Village 64
Thayer (Sangamon) Village 130
Thebes (Alexander) Village 10
Third Lake (Lake) Village...................80
Thomasboro (Champaign) Town 19
Thompson (Jo Daviess) Township......70
Thompsonville (Franklin) Village 50
Thomson (Carroll) Village...................16
Thornton (Cook) Town........................34
Thornton (Cook) Township 34
Tilden (Randolph) Village 122
Tilton (Vermilion) Village 140
Timber (Peoria) Township 116
Time (Pike) Village............................119
Tinley Park (Cook) Village..................34
Tinley Park (Will) Village 150
Tiskilwa (Bureau) Village 14
Todds Point (Shelby) Township 133
Toledo (Cumberland) Town 36
Tolono (Champaign) Town 19
Tolono (Champaign) Township 19
Toluca (Marshall) Town......................99

Tompkins (Warren) Township............*141*	Villa Grove (Douglas) Town *40*	Webber (Jefferson) Township...............*68*
Tonica (La Salle) Village.......................*84*	Villa Park (DuPage) City *43*	Weldon (De Witt) Village........................*39*
Tonti (Marion) Township.......................*98*	Vinegar Hill (Jo Daviess) Township...*70*	Weller (Henry) Township........................*62*
Topeka (Mason) Town..........................*100*	Viola (Lee) Township..............................*86*	Wellington (Iroquois) Village *64*
Toulon (Stark) City................................*134*	Viola (Mercer) Town.............................*108*	Wenona (La Salle) City...........................*84*
Toulon (Stark) Township......................*134*	Virden (Macoupin) City *94*	Wenona (Marshall) Town *99*
Tovey (Christian) Village........................*21*	Virden (Macoupin) Township................*94*	Wenonah (Montgomery) Village *111*
Towanda (McLean) Town......................*106*	Virden (Sangamon) City.......................*130*	Wesley (Will) Township.........................*150*
Towanda (McLean) Township..............*106*	Virgil (Kane) Township *73*	West (Effingham) Township...................*46*
Tower Hill (Shelby) Township...............*133*	Virginia (Cass) City..................................*17*	West (McLean) Township.....................*106*
Tower Hill (Shelby) Village...................*133*	Virginia (Cass) Township........................*17*	West Brooklyn (Lee) Village..................*86*
Tower Lakes (Lake) Village....................*81*	Wabash (Clark) Township.......................*22*	Westchester (Cook) Village....................*34*
Tremont (Tazewell) Town.....................*137*	**Wabash County**..................................*140*	West Chicago (DuPage) City..................*43*
Tremont (Tazewell) Township...............*138*	Waddams (Stephenson) Township *136*	West City (Franklin) Village...................*50*
Trenton (Clinton) Town..........................*24*	Wade (Clinton) Township.......................*24*	West Deerfield (Lake) Township............*81*
Trivoli (Peoria) Township......................*116*	Wade (Jasper) Township.........................*66*	West Dundee (Kane) Village..................*73*
Troy (Madison) City................................*96*	Wadsworth (Lake) Town.........................*81*	Western (Henry) Township....................*62*
Troy (Will) Township..............................*150*	Waggoner (Montgomery) Village........*110*	Western Mound (Macoupin)
Troy Grove (La Salle) Township.............*84*	Waldo (Livingston) Township.................*88*	Township..................................... *94*
Troy Grove (La Salle) Village *84*	Walker (Hancock) Township...................*58*	Western Springs (Cook) City..................*34*
Truro (Knox) Township...........................*77*	Walkerville (Greene) Township...............*54*	Westfield (Bureau) Township.................*14*
Tunbridge (De Witt) Township...............*39*	Wall (Ford) Township..............................*49*	Westfield (Clark) Township....................*22*
Tuscola (Douglas) City............................*40*	Wallace (La Salle) Township...................*84*	Westfield (Clark) Village *22*
Tuscola (Douglas) Township...................*40*	Walnut (Bureau) Township.....................*14*	West Frankfort (Franklin) City *50*
Twigg (Hamilton) Township....................*57*	Walnut (Bureau) Village *14*	West Galena (Jo Daviess) Township...*70*
Tyrone (Franklin) Township....................*50*	Walnut Grove (Knox) Township...........*77*	West Jersey (Stark) Township *134*
Ullin (Pulaski) Town *120*	Walnut Grove (McDonough)	West Lincoln (Logan) Township *90*
Union (Cumberland) Township *36*	Township................................. *102*	Westmont (DuPage) City........................*43*
Union (Effingham) Township..................*46*	Walnut Hill (Marion) Village..................*98*	West Peoria (Peoria) Township............*116*
Union (Fulton) Township........................*52*	Walshville (Montgomery) Township.*111*	West Point (Hancock) Village *58*
Union (Livingston) Township.................*88*	Walshville (Montgomery) Village.......*110*	West Point (Stephenson) Township ..*136*
Union (McHenry) Town........................*104*	Waltham (La Salle) Township *84*	West Salem (Edwards) Village.............*45*
Union County....................................*138*	Waltonville (Jefferson) Village................*67*	Westville (Vermilion) City....................*140*
Union Grove (Whiteside) Township.*147*	Wamac (Clinton) Town *24*	Wethersfield (Henry) Township............*62*
Union Hill (Kankakee) Village *75*	Wamac (Marion) Town...........................*98*	Wheatfield (Clinton) Township...........*24*
Unity (Piatt) Township..........................*117*	Wamac (Washington) Town.................*143*	Wheatland (Bureau) Township..............*14*
University Park (Cook) Village................*34*	Wapella (De Witt) Township..................*39*	Wheatland (Fayette) Township..............*48*
University Park (Will) Village...............*150*	Wapella (De Witt) Village........................*39*	Wheatland (Will) Township *150*
Urbana (Champaign) City.......................*19*	Wards Grove (Jo Daviess) Township..*70*	Wheaton (DuPage) City *43*
Urbana (Champaign) Township..........*19*	Warren (Jo Daviess) Town *70*	Wheeler (Jasper) Village.........................*66*
Ursa (Adams) Township...........................*9*	Warren (Jo Daviess) Township...............*70*	Wheeling (Cook) City.............................*34*
Ursa (Adams) Village................................*9*	Warren (Lake) Township........................*81*	Wheeling (Cook) Township....................*34*
Ustick (Whiteside) Township................*147*	**Warren County**...................................*141*	Wheeling (Lake) City...............................*81*
Utica (La Salle) Township.......................*84*	Warrensburg (Macon) Town...................*91*	Whiteash (Williamson) Village............*151*
Valier (Franklin) Town............................*50*	Warrenville (DuPage) Town *43*	White City (Macoupin) Village *94*
Valley (Stark) Township........................*134*	Warsaw (Hancock) Town......................*58*	**White County**....................................*144*
Valley City (Pike) Village.....................*119*	Warsaw (Hancock) Township.................*58*	Whitefield (Marshall) Township............*99*
Valmeyer (Monroe) Town......................*109*	Washburn (Marshall) Village...................*99*	White Hall (Greene) Town *54*
Vance (Vermilion) Township................*140*	Washburn (Woodford) Village..............*154*	White Hall (Greene) Township..............*54*
Vandalia (Fayette) City............................*48*	Washington (Carroll) Township..............*16*	White Oak (McLean) Township...........*106*
Vandalia (Fayette) Township..................*48*	Washington (Tazewell) City.................*138*	White Rock (Ogle) Township...............*114*
Varna (Marshall) Village.........................*99*	Washington (Tazewell) Township.......*138*	**Whiteside County**..............................*146*
Venedy (Washington) Township...........*143*	Washington (Will) Township..............*150*	Whitley (Moultrie) Township................*112*
Venedy (Washington) Village *143*	**Washington County**..........................*142*	Whitmore (Macon) Township................*91*
Venetian Village (Lake) CDP...................*81*	Washington Park (St. Clair) Village..*127*	Wilberton (Fayette) Township...............*48*
Venice (Madison) City.............................*96*	Wataga (Knox) Town.............................*77*	Wilcox (Hancock) Township...................*58*
Venice (Madison) Township...................*96*	Waterford (Fulton) Township..................*52*	Will (Will) Township.............................*150*
Vergennes (Jackson) Township...............*65*	Waterloo (Monroe) City........................*109*	**Will County**..*147*
Vergennes (Jackson) Village....................*65*	Waterman (DeKalb) Village *38*	Williams (Sangamon) Township..........*130*
Vermilion (Edgar) Village.......................*44*	Watseka (Iroquois) City...........................*64*	Williamsfield (Knox) Village..................*77*
Vermilion County *138*	Watson (Effingham) Township...............*46*	Williamson (Madison) Village...............*96*
Vermillion (La Salle) Township.............*84*	Watson (Effingham) Village....................*46*	**Williamson County**...........................*151*
Vermont (Fulton) Town..........................*52*	Wauconda (Lake) City.............................*81*	Williamsville (Sangamon) Town *131*
Vermont (Fulton) Township....................*52*	Wauconda (Lake) Township....................*81*	Willisville (Perry) Village......................*116*
Vernon (Lake) Township........................*81*	Waukegan (Lake) City.............................*81*	Willow Branch (Piatt) Township........*117*
Vernon (Marion) Village.........................*98*	Waukegan (Lake) Township....................*81*	Willowbrook (DuPage) Village.............*43*
Vernon Hills (Lake) Village....................*81*	Wauponsee (Grundy) Township............*56*	Willowbrook (Will) CDP......................*150*
Verona (Grundy) Village.........................*56*	Waverly (Morgan) Town.......................*111*	Willow Creek (Lee) Township...............*86*
Versailles (Brown) Township..................*12*	Wayne (DuPage) Town *43*	Willow Hill (Jasper) Township..............*66*
Versailles (Brown) Village *12*	Wayne (DuPage) Township....................*43*	Willow Hill (Jasper) Village *66*
Victor (DeKalb) Township......................*38*	Wayne (Kane) Town................................*73*	Willow Springs (Cook) Town *34*
Victoria (Knox) Township......................*77*	Wayne City (Wayne) Town...................*144*	Willow Springs (DuPage) Village *43*
Victoria (Knox) Village..........................*77*	**Wayne County**...................................*143*	Wilmette (Cook) Residential village...*34*
Vienna (Grundy) Township....................*56*	Waynesville (De Witt) Township *39*	Wilmington (Greene) Village *54*
Vienna (Johnson) Town..........................*71*	Waynesville (De Witt) Village..............*39*	Wilmington (Will) City *150*

ILLINOIS

Wilmington (Will) Township............150	Woodford County...............................153	Wyoming (Lee) Township 86
Wilson (De Witt) Township 39	Woodhull (Henry) Village..................62	Wyoming (Stark) Town 134
Wilsonville (Macoupin) Village...........94	Woodland (Carroll) Township............16	Wysox (Carroll) Township...................16
Wilton (Will) Township.....................150	Woodland (Fulton) Township.............52	Wythe (Hancock) Township................58
Winchester (Scott) City 132	Woodland (Iroquois) Village 64	Xenia (Clay) Township.......................23
Windsor (Mercer) Village 108	Woodlawn (Jefferson) Village.............68	Xenia (Clay) Village...........................23
Windsor (Shelby) City 133	Woodridge (DuPage) Village..............43	Yale (Jasper) Village...........................66
Windsor (Shelby) Township 134	Woodridge (Will) Village..................150	Yates (McLean) Township................107
Winfield (DuPage) Town.....................43	Wood River (Madison) City...............96	Yates City (Knox) Town.....................77
Winfield (DuPage) Township..............43	Wood River (Madison) Township.......96	Yellowhead (Kankakee) Township 75
Winnebago (Winnebago) Town 153	Woodside (Sangamon) Township 131	York (Carroll) Township.....................16
Winnebago (Winnebago) Township ..153	Woodson (Morgan) Village................111	York (Clark) Township 22
Winnebago County 152	Woodstock (McHenry) City..............104	York (DuPage) Township 43
Winnetka (Cook) Village 34	Woodstock (Schuyler) Township 131	Yorktown (Henry) Township..............62
Winslow (Stephenson) Township 136	Woodville (Greene) Township.............54	Yorkville (Kendall) Town 76
Winslow (Stephenson) Village............136	Woosung (Ogle) Township................114	Young America (Edgar) Township 45
Winthrop Harbor (Lake) Town 81	Worden (Madison) Town....................96	Young Hickory (Fulton) Township......52
Witt (Montgomery) Town 111	Worth (Cook) Residential Village 34	Zanesville (Montgomery) Township..111
Witt (Montgomery) Township............111	Worth (Cook) Township 34	Zeigler (Franklin) Town 50
Wonder Lake (McHenry) Village 104	Worth (Woodford) Township 154	Zif (Wayne) Township 144
Woodbine (Jo Daviess) Township........70	Wrights (Greene) Township 54	Zion (Lake) City 81
Woodbury (Cumberland) Township....36	Wyanet (Bureau) Town........................14	Zion (Lake) Township 81
Wood Dale (DuPage) Town..................43	Wyanet (Bureau) Township.................14	Zuma (Rock Island) Township..........124

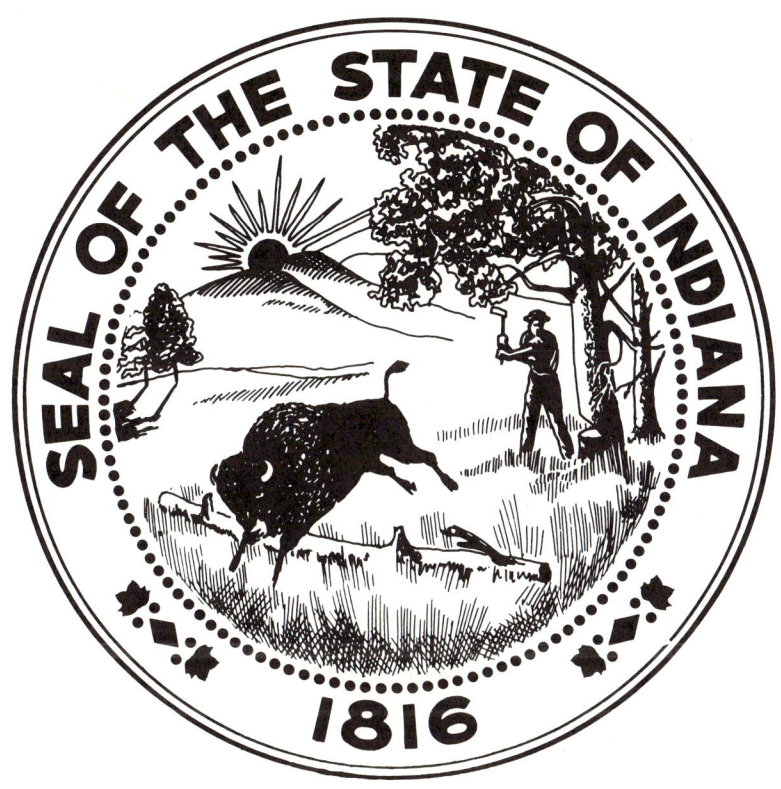

Indiana

INDIANA

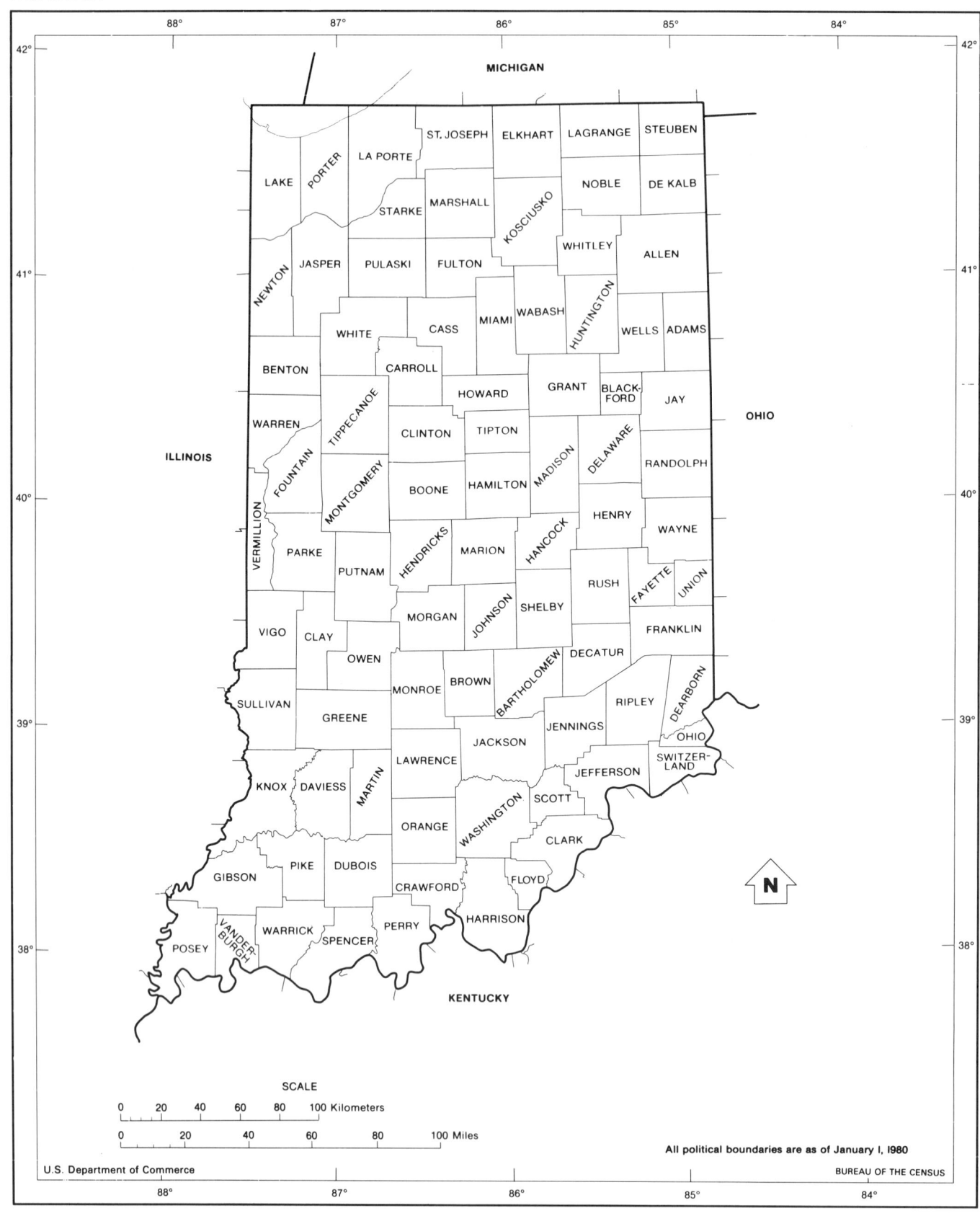

Indiana

Population: 5,544,159 (1990); 5,490,224 (1980)
Population rank (1990): 14
Percent population change (1980-1990): 1.0
Population projection: 5,738,000 (1995); 5,831,000 (2000)

Area: total 36,420 sq. mi.; 35,870 sq. mi. land, 550 sq. mi. water
Area rank: 38
Highest elevation: 1,257 ft. (Wayne County)
Lowest point: 320 ft. (Posey County)

State capital: Indianapolis (Marion County)
Largest city: Indianapolis (741,952)
Second largest city: Fort Wayne (173,072)
Largest county: Marion (797,159)

Total housing units: 2,246,046
No. of occupied housing units: 2,065,355
Vacant housing units (%): 8.0
Distribution of population by race and Hispanic origin (%):
 White: 90.6
 Black: 7.8
 Hispanic (any race): 1.8
 Native American: 0.2
 Asian/Pacific: 0.7
 Other: 0.7

Admission date: December 11, 1816 (19th state).

Location: In the east-central United States, bordering Kentucky, Illinois, Lake Michigan, Michigan, and Ohio.

Name Origin: A Latinized or Spanish form meaning 'land of the Indians'; used in 1768 by the Philadelphus Trading Company, land developers, for territory ceded to them by the Iroquois.

State bird: cardinal *(Cardinalis cardinalis)*
State flower: peony
State poem: "Indiana"
State song: "On the Banks of the Wabash, Far Away"
State stone: Indiana limestone
State tree: tulip tree (yellow poplar; *Liriodendron tulipifera*)
State motto: The Crossroads of America
State nickname: Hoosier State

Area codes: 219 (north of Indianapolis), 317 (Indianapolis and environs), 812 (south of Indianapolis)
Time zones: Eastern, Central
Abbreviations: IN (postal); Ind. (traditional)

Part of (region): Great Lakes, Midwest

Local Government

Counties

Indiana has 92 counties, each governed by a board of commissioners. In 1984, when counties were given the power to impose local income taxes, six counties, representing 20% of the state's population, chose to do so. In 1970, Marion County and Indianapolis were consolidated and are governed by an elected mayor and council.

Municipalities

There are 1,008 townships, 115 cities, and 450 incorporated towns. Indiana is the only state with townships throughout its entire area. The cities cannot adopt their own charters and must operate within state guidelines.

Settlement History and Early Development

It is not known when the first humans inhabited present-day Indiana, but evidence of the Mound Builders (c. 1000 B.C.) may be found in many places. The first Europeans, who arrived in the 1670s, were probably the French Jesuit missionary Fr. Jacques Marquette and the explorer Robert Cavelier, Sieur de La Salle, and they encountered the Miami, Potawatomi, Wea, and Kickapoo Indians. French fur traders from Canada established trading posts in the 1720s near present-day Fort Wayne and Lafayette. A fort on the Wabash River, constructed in 1732, later became Vincennes. At the close of the French and Indian Wars in 1763, France ceded its claims to present-day Indiana, among other regions, to Britain.

The American Revolution

The Revolution, which began in 1775, was hardly felt in Indiana until 1777 when British troops moved into the area around Vincennes and captured Fort Sackville. A band of Virginia frontiersmen, led by George Rogers Clark, recaptured Vincennes in 1779, thus giving the Americans control over the Northwest. The first U.S. settlement in Indiana, Clarksville, was established in 1784 on land across the Ohio River from Louisville, Kentucky, granted to Clark's veterans. In 1787 Indiana was included as part of the Northwest Territory. Indians continued to fight white settlers until 1794 when Gen. Anthony Wayne defeated the Miami and other tribes in the Battle of Fallen Timbers near present-day Toledo, Ohio.

In 1800, as Ohio was preparing to become a state, the rest of the Northwest Territory was set off and called Indiana Territory. It included the present states of Indiana, Illinois, and Wisconsin, and parts of Michigan and Minnesota. When Michigan Territory was detached in 1805 and

Illinois Territory in 1809, Indiana assumed its present boundaries. Its first territorial governor was Gen. William Henry Harrison, who negotiated with the Indians for the purchase of 2,900,000 acres of Indian land in southern Indiana. Many Indians objected strenuously and gathered under the Shawnee chief, Tecumseh. He obtained guns and powder from the British, but lost to Harrison in the Battle of Tippecanoe in 1811. The Indians continued to fight by siding with the British in the War of 1812.

Statehood

The treaty that ended the War of 1812 put a halt to British influence in the Territory. After the death of Tecumseh at the Battle of the Thames in 1813, Indian resistance to white settlement in the Northwest Territory also ceased, opening the way for development of the area. Settlers from the upper South began pouring in, as well as from Ohio, Pennsylvania, New York, and New England. In 1816 the settlers adopted a constitution excluding slavery, and Indiana became the nineteenth state on December 11. The same year, the Lincoln family moved to Indiana from Kentucky. Abraham Lincoln lived in southern Indiana between the ages of 7 and 21. Unlike most other states, Indiana was settled from the south to the north; central and northern Indiana was settled as land was bought from the Indians, the last Indian being transferred west by 1846. Privately financed railroads offered new Eastern markets for local crops. Irish immigrants came to dig canals and lay the rails; Germans came to do woodworking and farming; and Levi Coffin, a Quaker, began the Underground Railroad in the state to assist escaping Southern slaves.

The Civil War

Indiana remained with the Union and sent some 200,000 men to fight. No battles were fought in its territory but John Hunt Morgan's Confederate cavalrymen, called Morgan's Raiders, crossed the Ohio River from Kentucky, raided Corydon in the southeast in July 1863, then continued into Ohio.

Business and Industry

In 1852 the Studebaker brothers, Clement and Henry, opened a blacksmith and wagon shop in South Bend, which became the largest wagon manufacturer in the country, and eventually an automobile company. Richard Gatling invented the first practical machine gun in Indianapolis in 1862. During the 1860s James Oliver invented the hard-steel plow that could cut through the tough prairie sod.

After the Civil War industries developed rapidly throughout the state. Studebaker's wagons had won fame during the war, as had Van Camp's canned pork and beans from Indianapolis. Natural gas was discovered near Portland in 1886 and the resultant low fuel prices attracted out-of-state industries and spurred the growth of glass factories. In 1889 Standard Oil built one of the world's largest refineries at Whiting on Lake Michigan. In 1894 Elwood Haynes of Kokomo designed and drove one of the first successful gasoline-powered cars, and eventually there were 375 Indiana factories producing automobiles. A testing racetrack was built outside Indianapolis in 1908, and the famous 500-mile race was first run in 1911. The U.S. Steel Corporation set up a huge facility in Gary in 1906, which eventually grew into one of the greatest steel-producing areas in the world. Small local industries were also started: gristmills, sawmills, meat-packing plants, distilleries and breweries, leatherworking shops, furniture factories, and steamboat and carriage makers.

Many residents of Indiana favored neutrality when World War I began, but the state's economy benefited from the war. After the Great Depression of the 1930s, the state continued its shift from agriculture to manufacturing. During and after World War II the manufacture of farm implements, auto parts, furniture, and pharmaceuticals, as well as the meat-packing, coal mining, and limestone industries, all were important in Indiana's economy.

Indiana has been a leader in conservation because of the work of Richard Lieber, a state official from 1933 to 1944, who urged the preservation of land for state and federal parks and forests.

The state's economic growth was spurred by the 1970 opening of a port on Lake Michigan. The port serves international shipping via the Saint Lawrence Seaway. Indiana produces steel products, electrical machinery, chemicals, and such agricultural goods as corn, soybeans, wheat, hogs, and cattle.

State Boundaries

In 1800, as Ohio prepared to become a state, the rest of the Northwestern Territory was set off and called Indiana Territory. The Michigan Territory was detached in 1805 and Illinois Territory in 1809, leaving Indiana with the borders it had when it became a state.

Indiana Counties

Adams	Elkhart	Jefferson	Noble	Starke
Allen	Fayette	Jennings	Ohio	Steuben
Bartholomew	Floyd	Johnson	Orange	Sullivan
Benton	Fountain	Knox	Owen	Switzerland
Blackford	Franklin	Kosciusko	Parke	Tippecanoe
Boone	Fulton	Lagrange	Perry	Tipton
Brown	Gibson	Lake	Pike	Union
Carroll	Grant	La Porte	Porter	Vanderburgh
Cass	Greene	Lawrence	Posey	Vermillion
Clark	Hamilton	Madison	Pulaski	Vigo
Clay	Hancock	Marion	Putnam	Wabash
Clinton	Harrison	Marshall	Randolph	Warren
Crawford	Hendricks	Martin	Ripley	Warrick
Daviess	Henry	Miami	Rush	Washington
Dearborn	Howard	Monroe	St. Joseph	Wayne
Decatur	Huntington	Montgomery	Scott	Wells
Dekalb	Jackson	Morgan	Shelby	White
Delaware	Jasper	Newton	Spencer	Whitley
Dubois	Jay			

Multi-County Places

The following Indiana places are in more than one county. Given here is the total population for each multi-county place, and the names of the counties it is in.

Albany, pop. 2,357; Delaware (2,151), Randolph (206)
Ashley, pop. 767; Dekalb (488), Steuben (279)
Batesville, pop. 4,720; Ripley (3,869), Franklin (851)
Chesterfield, pop. 2,730; Madison (2,721), Delaware (9)
Converse, pop. 1,144; Miami (965), Grant (179)
Cumberland, pop. 4,557; Marion (2,933), Hancock (1,624)
Dunkirk, pop. 2,739; Jay (2,587), Blackford (152)
Edinburgh, pop. 4,536; Johnson (4,131), Bartholomew (405)
Elwood, pop. 9,494; Madison (9,490), Tipton (4)
Glenwood, pop. 285; Rush (175), Fayette (110)
Grissom AFB, pop. 4,271; Miami (4,271), Cass (0)
Hamilton, pop. 684; Steuben (590), Dekalb (94)
Jamestown, pop. 764; Boone (764), Hendricks (0)
Koontz Lake, pop. 1,615; Starke (1,450), Marshall (165)
Lakes of the Four Seasons, pop. 6,556; Lake (3,724), Porter (2,832)
Markle, pop. 1,208; Huntington (789), Wells (419)
Milltown, pop. 917; Crawford (489), Harrison (428)
Nappanee, pop. 5,510; Elkhart (5,510), Kosciusko (0)
Otterbein, pop. 1,291; Benton (910), Tippecanoe (381)
St. Paul, pop. 1,032; Decatur (576), Shelby (456)
Shirley, pop. 817; Hancock (678), Henry (139)
Wolcottville, pop. 879; Noble (483), Lagrange (396)

INDIANA, Adams County — *American Places Dictionary*

Adams County
County Seat: Decatur (ZIP: 46733)

Pop: 31,095 (1990); 29,619 (1980)   **Pop Density:** 91.6
Land: 339.4 sq. mi.; **Water:** 0.6 sq. mi.   **Area Code:** 219
On the east-central border of IN, south of Ft. Wayne; organized Jan 23, 1836 from Warren County.
Name origin: For John Quincy Adams (1767–1848), sixth U.S. president.

Berne   City
ZIP: 46711   **Lat:** 40-39-25 N **Long:** 84-57-15 W
Pop: 3,559 (1990); 3,300 (1980)   **Pop Density:** 2224.4
Land: 1.6 sq. mi.; **Water:** 0.0 sq. mi.   **Elev:** 861 ft.
Platted by Swiss settlers 1871.
Name origin: For the capital of Switzerland.

Blue Creek   Township
ZIP: 46772   **Lat:** 40-41-58 N **Long:** 84-50-12 W
Pop: 873 (1990); 813 (1980)   **Pop Density:** 35.9
Land: 24.3 sq. mi.; **Water:** 0.0 sq. mi.

Decatur   City
ZIP: 46733   **Lat:** 40-49-48 N **Long:** 84-55-41 W
Pop: 8,644 (1990); 8,649 (1980)   **Pop Density:** 2161.0
Land: 4.0 sq. mi.; **Water:** 0.0 sq. mi.   **Elev:** 794 ft.
In eastern IN, 20 mi. south-southeast of Fort Wayne. County seat.
Name origin: For U.S. naval officer Stephen Decatur (1779–1820), famous for proclaiming: "our country, right or wrong!"

French   Township
Lat: 40-42-03 N **Long:** 85-01-48 W
Pop: 888 (1990); 834 (1980)   **Pop Density:** 37.2
Land: 23.9 sq. mi.; **Water:** 0.0 sq. mi.

Geneva   Town
ZIP: 46740   **Lat:** 40-35-49 N **Long:** 84-57-25 W
Pop: 1,280 (1990); 1,430 (1980)   **Pop Density:** 1280.0
Land: 1.0 sq. mi.; **Water:** 0.1 sq. mi.   **Elev:** 849 ft.
Founded 1853.
Name origin: For Geneva, Switzerland.

Hartford   Township
Lat: 40-36-57 N **Long:** 85-01-40 W
Pop: 816 (1990); 775 (1980)   **Pop Density:** 33.9
Land: 24.1 sq. mi.; **Water:** 0.0 sq. mi.

Jefferson   Township
Lat: 40-36-47 N **Long:** 84-50-39 W
Pop: 848 (1990); 735 (1980)   **Pop Density:** 35.0
Land: 24.2 sq. mi.; **Water:** 0.0 sq. mi.

Kirkland   Township
Lat: 40-47-09 N **Long:** 85-01-45 W
Pop: 845 (1990); 814 (1980)   **Pop Density:** 34.9
Land: 24.2 sq. mi.; **Water:** 0.0 sq. mi.

Monroe   Town
ZIP: 46772   **Lat:** 40-44-40 N **Long:** 84-56-25 W
Pop: 788 (1990); 739 (1980)   **Pop Density:** 1576.0
Land: 0.5 sq. mi.; **Water:** 0.0 sq. mi.   **Elev:** 825 ft.
Founded 1832. Not coextensive with the town of the same name.
Name origin: Named in 1832 for James Monroe (1758–1831), fifth U.S. president.

*Monroe   Township
ZIP: 46772   **Lat:** 40-42-10 N **Long:** 84-56-03 W
Pop: 4,174 (1990); 3,902 (1980)   **Pop Density:** 114.7
Land: 36.4 sq. mi.; **Water:** 0.0 sq. mi.

Preble   Township
Lat: 40-52-33 N **Long:** 85-01-58 W
Pop: 1,047 (1990); 1,026 (1980)   **Pop Density:** 43.8
Land: 23.9 sq. mi.; **Water:** 0.1 sq. mi.

Root   Township
Lat: 40-52-43 N **Long:** 84-56-31 W
Pop: 3,922 (1990); 3,365 (1980)   **Pop Density:** 110.8
Land: 35.4 sq. mi.; **Water:** 0.1 sq. mi.

St. Marys   Township
Lat: 40-47-20 N **Long:** 84-50-41 W
Pop: 1,213 (1990); 1,198 (1980)   **Pop Density:** 49.3
Land: 24.6 sq. mi.; **Water:** 0.0 sq. mi.

Union   Township
Lat: 40-52-32 N **Long:** 84-50-29 W
Pop: 978 (1990); 1,013 (1980)   **Pop Density:** 39.6
Land: 24.7 sq. mi.; **Water:** 0.0 sq. mi.

Wabash   Township
ZIP: 46740   **Lat:** 40-36-51 N **Long:** 84-56-14 W
Pop: 5,394 (1990); 4,782 (1980)   **Pop Density:** 148.6
Land: 36.3 sq. mi.; **Water:** 0.3 sq. mi.

Washington   Township
ZIP: 46733   **Lat:** 40-47-26 N **Long:** 84-56-07 W
Pop: 10,097 (1990); 10,362 (1980)   **Pop Density:** 269.3
Land: 37.5 sq. mi.; **Water:** 0.0 sq. mi.

Allen County
County Seat: Fort Wayne (ZIP: 46802)

Pop: 300,836 (1990); 294,335 (1980)
Land: 657.3 sq. mi.; **Water:** 2.9 sq. mi.
Pop Density: 457.7
Area Code: 219
On the northeastern border of IN, northeast of Marion; organized Apr 1, 1824 from Indian lands.
Name origin: For Col. John Allen (?–1813), KY lawyer and army officer.

Aboite — Township
ZIP: 46804　**Lat:** 41-03-07 N **Long:** 85-17-07 W
Pop: 18,490 (1990); 11,663 (1980)　**Pop Density:** 555.3
Land: 33.3 sq. mi.; **Water:** 0.0 sq. mi.

Adams — Township
ZIP: 46774　**Lat:** 41-02-44 N **Long:** 85-03-01 W
Pop: 31,023 (1990); 31,897 (1980)　**Pop Density:** 948.7
Land: 32.7 sq. mi.; **Water:** 0.0 sq. mi.
In northeastern IN, east of Fort Wayne.

Cedar Creek — Township
ZIP: 46741　**Lat:** 41-13-28 N **Long:** 85-01-00 W
Pop: 6,688 (1990); 5,864 (1980)　**Pop Density:** 193.9
Land: 34.5 sq. mi.; **Water:** 1.2 sq. mi.

Eel River — Township
Lat: 41-13-39 N **Long:** 85-15-23 W
Pop: 2,576 (1990); 2,423 (1980)　**Pop Density:** 70.6
Land: 36.5 sq. mi.; **Water:** 0.1 sq. mi.

Fort Wayne — City
ZIP: 46802　**Lat:** 41-04-25 N **Long:** 85-08-20 W
Pop: 173,072 (1990); 172,391 (1980)　**Pop Density:** 2760.3
Land: 62.7 sq. mi.; **Water:** 0.2 sq. mi.　**Elev:** 781 ft.
In northeastern IN, 105 mi. northeast of Indianapolis. County seat. Commercial and industrial city: machinery, electronic parts and equipment, and transportation equipment.
Name origin: For Gen. Anthony Wayne (1745–96), PA soldier and statesman, nicknamed "Mad Anthony" for his daring during the Revolutionary War.

Grabill — Town
ZIP: 46741　**Lat:** 41-12-38 N **Long:** 84-58-04 W
Pop: 751 (1990); 658 (1980)　**Pop Density:** 1502.0
Land: 0.5 sq. mi.; **Water:** 0.0 sq. mi.　**Elev:** 825 ft.
Settled 1902.
Name origin: For local resident Joseph Grabill.

Huntertown — Town
ZIP: 46748　**Lat:** 41-13-52 N **Long:** 85-10-11 W
Pop: 1,330 (1990); 1,265 (1980)　**Pop Density:** 1330.0
Land: 1.0 sq. mi.; **Water:** 0.0 sq. mi.　**Elev:** 838 ft.
Settled 1836.
Name origin: For founder William T. Hunter.

Jackson — Township
ZIP: 46773　**Lat:** 41-03-18 N **Long:** 84-50-18 W
Pop: 561 (1990); 602 (1980)　**Pop Density:** 22.0
Land: 25.5 sq. mi.; **Water:** 0.0 sq. mi.

Jefferson — Township
Lat: 41-03-02 N **Long:** 84-56-28 W
Pop: 1,882 (1990); 2,142 (1980)　**Pop Density:** 51.7
Land: 36.4 sq. mi.; **Water:** 0.0 sq. mi.

Lafayette — Township
Lat: 40-57-45 N **Long:** 85-17-08 W
Pop: 2,530 (1990); 2,389 (1980)　**Pop Density:** 73.1
Land: 34.6 sq. mi.; **Water:** 0.0 sq. mi.

Lake — Township
Lat: 41-07-44 N **Long:** 85-16-30 W
Pop: 1,914 (1990); 2,184 (1980)　**Pop Density:** 53.5
Land: 35.8 sq. mi.; **Water:** 0.1 sq. mi.

Madison — Township
Lat: 40-57-32 N **Long:** 84-56-28 W
Pop: 1,615 (1990); 1,729 (1980)　**Pop Density:** 44.0
Land: 36.7 sq. mi.; **Water:** 0.0 sq. mi.

Marion — Township
Lat: 40-57-42 N **Long:** 85-03-23 W
Pop: 3,529 (1990); 3,600 (1980)　**Pop Density:** 101.4
Land: 34.8 sq. mi.; **Water:** 0.2 sq. mi.

Maumee — Township
ZIP: 46797　**Lat:** 41-08-13 N **Long:** 84-50-22 W
Pop: 2,459 (1990); 2,408 (1980)　**Pop Density:** 93.5
Land: 26.3 sq. mi.; **Water:** 0.4 sq. mi.

Milan — Township
Lat: 41-08-17 N **Long:** 84-56-53 W
Pop: 3,165 (1990); 3,178 (1980)　**Pop Density:** 85.1
Land: 37.2 sq. mi.; **Water:** 0.4 sq. mi.

Monroe — Township
Lat: 40-57-59 N **Long:** 84-50-38 W
Pop: 1,969 (1990); 2,174 (1980)　**Pop Density:** 79.4
Land: 24.8 sq. mi.; **Water:** 0.0 sq. mi.

Monroeville — Town
ZIP: 46773　**Lat:** 40-58-20 N **Long:** 84-52-03 W
Pop: 1,232 (1990); 1,372 (1980)　**Pop Density:** 3080.0
Land: 0.4 sq. mi.; **Water:** 0.0 sq. mi.　**Elev:** 810 ft.
Name origin: For Monroe Township.

New Haven — City
ZIP: 46774　**Lat:** 41-04-08 N **Long:** 85-01-30 W
Pop: 9,320 (1990); 6,714 (1980)　**Pop Density:** 1606.9
Land: 5.8 sq. mi.; **Water:** 0.0 sq. mi.　**Elev:** 758 ft.
Name origin: For New Haven, CT.

Perry — Township
ZIP: 46748　**Lat:** 41-13-10 N **Long:** 85-07-35 W
Pop: 10,909 (1990); 8,299 (1980)　**Pop Density:** 307.3
Land: 35.5 sq. mi.; **Water:** 0.1 sq. mi.

Pleasant — Township
Lat: 40-57-34 N **Long:** 85-10-07 W
Pop: 3,355 (1990); 3,472 (1980)　**Pop Density:** 95.6
Land: 35.1 sq. mi.; **Water:** 0.0 sq. mi.

INDIANA, Allen County
American Places Dictionary

St. Joseph
Township
ZIP: 46805 **Lat:** 41-08-18 N **Long:** 85-03-49 W
Pop: 61,167 (1990); 55,348 (1980) **Pop Density:** 1732.8
Land: 35.3 sq. mi.; **Water:** 0.0 sq. mi.

Scipio
Township
Lat: 41-13-36 N **Long:** 84-49-36 W
Pop: 414 (1990); 396 (1980) **Pop Density:** 31.4
Land: 13.2 sq. mi.; **Water:** 0.0 sq. mi.

Springfield
Township
ZIP: 46743 **Lat:** 41-13-39 N **Long:** 84-54-30 W
Pop: 3,169 (1990); 2,987 (1980) **Pop Density:** 89.5
Land: 35.4 sq. mi.; **Water:** 0.1 sq. mi.

Washington
Township
ZIP: 46808 **Lat:** 41-08-08 N **Long:** 85-10-27 W
Pop: 27,416 (1990); 23,851 (1980) **Pop Density:** 867.6
Land: 31.6 sq. mi.; **Water:** 0.1 sq. mi.

Wayne
Township
ZIP: 46806 **Lat:** 41-02-58 N **Long:** 85-09-52 W
Pop: 116,005 (1990); 127,729 (1980) **Pop Density:** 2748.9
Land: 42.2 sq. mi.; **Water:** 0.1 sq. mi.

Woodburn
City
ZIP: 46797 **Lat:** 41-07-33 N **Long:** 84-51-09 W
Pop: 1,321 (1990); 1,002 (1980) **Pop Density:** 2201.7
Land: 0.6 sq. mi.; **Water:** 0.0 sq. mi. **Elev:** 756 ft.
Founded 1865.
Name origin: For settler John Woodburn.

Bartholomew County
County Seat: Columbus (ZIP: 47202)

Pop: 63,657 (1990); 65,088 (1980) **Pop Density:** 156.5
Land: 406.9 sq. mi.; **Water:** 2.5 sq. mi. **Area Code:** 812
In south-central IN, south of Indianapolis; organized 1821 from Indian lands.
Name origin: For Gen. Joseph Bartholomew (?–1840), officer wounded at the Battle of Tippecanoe (1811) and IN state senator (1821–24).

Clay
Township
Lat: 39-13-26 N **Long:** 85-49-02 W
Pop: 2,421 (1990); 2,647 (1980) **Pop Density:** 104.4
Land: 23.2 sq. mi.; **Water:** 0.0 sq. mi.

Clifford
Town
ZIP: 47226 **Lat:** 39-16-58 N **Long:** 85-52-10 W
Pop: 308 (1990); 310 (1980) **Pop Density:** 3080.0
Land: 0.1 sq. mi.; **Water:** 0.0 sq. mi. **Elev:** 662 ft.
Founded 1853.
Name origin: Named in 1853 for a local settler.

Clifty
Township
Lat: 39-13-34 N **Long:** 85-43-57 W
Pop: 1,003 (1990); 905 (1980) **Pop Density:** 44.0
Land: 22.8 sq. mi.; **Water:** 0.0 sq. mi.

Columbus
City
ZIP: 47201 **Lat:** 39-12-38 N **Long:** 85-54-48 W
Pop: 31,802 (1990); 30,614 (1980) **Pop Density:** 1574.4
Land: 20.2 sq. mi.; **Water:** 0.3 sq. mi. **Elev:** 640 ft.
In central IN, 34 mi. east of Bloomington. County seat. Incorporated 1839. Not coextensive with the town of the same name.
Name origin: Previously called Tiptonia; given present name in 1821 when it became the county seat.

*Columbus
Township
ZIP: 47201 **Lat:** 39-12-42 N **Long:** 85-56-05 W
Pop: 37,466 (1990); 37,012 (1980) **Pop Density:** 592.8
Land: 63.2 sq. mi.; **Water:** 0.7 sq. mi.

Edinburgh
Town
Lat: 39-20-41 N **Long:** 85-58-06 W
Pop: 405 (1990); 4,856 (1980) **Pop Density:** 1350.0
Land: 0.3 sq. mi.; **Water:** 0.0 sq. mi. **Elev:** 670 ft.
Part of the town is also in Johnson County.
Name origin: For Edinburgh, Scotland.

Elizabethtown
Town
ZIP: 47232 **Lat:** 39-08-07 N **Long:** 85-48-45 W
Pop: 495 (1990); 603 (1980) **Pop Density:** 1650.0
Land: 0.3 sq. mi.; **Water:** 0.0 sq. mi. **Elev:** 644 ft.
Name origin: For the wife of George W. Branham, who laid out the town in 1845.

Flat Rock
Township
Lat: 39-17-49 N **Long:** 85-51-07 W
Pop: 1,468 (1990); 1,719 (1980) **Pop Density:** 47.1
Land: 31.2 sq. mi.; **Water:** 0.0 sq. mi.

German
Township
ZIP: 47201 **Lat:** 39-18-09 N **Long:** 85-59-19 W
Pop: 5,507 (1990); 5,631 (1980) **Pop Density:** 88.7
Land: 62.1 sq. mi.; **Water:** 0.1 sq. mi.

Harrison
Township
Lat: 39-11-19 N **Long:** 86-01-42 W
Pop: 2,769 (1990); 2,520 (1980) **Pop Density:** 109.0
Land: 25.4 sq. mi.; **Water:** 0.3 sq. mi.

Hartsville
Town
ZIP: 47244 **Lat:** 39-16-01 N **Long:** 85-41-55 W
Pop: 391 (1990); 379 (1980) **Pop Density:** 1303.3
Land: 0.3 sq. mi.; **Water:** 0.0 sq. mi. **Elev:** 761 ft.
Name origin: For pioneer Gideon B. Hart.

Haw Creek
Township
Lat: 39-18-28 N **Long:** 85-44-51 W
Pop: 3,914 (1990); 4,517 (1980) **Pop Density:** 105.5
Land: 37.1 sq. mi.; **Water:** 0.1 sq. mi.

Hope
Town
ZIP: 47246 **Lat:** 39-17-59 N **Long:** 85-46-05 W
Pop: 2,171 (1990); 2,185 (1980) **Pop Density:** 2713.8
Land: 0.8 sq. mi.; **Water:** 0.0 sq. mi. **Elev:** 723 ft.
Settled in 1830 and platted in 1836 by a Moravian congregation from NC.
Name origin: For an earlier Moravian settlement in NC.

Jackson
Township
Lat: 39-03-53 N **Long:** 86-02-13 W
Pop: 750 (1990); 760 (1980) **Pop Density:** 36.4
Land: 20.6 sq. mi.; **Water:** 0.2 sq. mi.

Jonesville
Town
ZIP: 47247 **Lat:** 39-03-36 N **Long:** 85-53-19 W
Pop: 221 (1990); 213 (1980) **Pop Density:** 2210.0
Land: 0.1 sq. mi.; **Water:** 0.0 sq. mi. **Elev:** 595 ft.
Founded 1851.
Name origin: For its founder, Benjamin Jones.

Ohio
Township
Lat: 39-07-30 N **Long:** 86-01-39 W
Pop: 1,557 (1990); 1,964 (1980) **Pop Density:** 78.6
Land: 19.8 sq. mi.; **Water:** 0.4 sq. mi.

Rock Creek
Township
Lat: 39-09-57 N **Long:** 85-45-21 W
Pop: 1,261 (1990); 1,361 (1980) **Pop Density:** 47.6
Land: 26.5 sq. mi.; **Water:** 0.0 sq. mi.

Sand Creek
Township
Lat: 39-07-17 N **Long:** 85-50-27 W
Pop: 2,104 (1990); 2,370 (1980) **Pop Density:** 80.6
Land: 26.1 sq. mi.; **Water:** 0.2 sq. mi.

Taylorsville
CDP
Lat: 39-17-46 N **Long:** 85-56-57 W
Pop: 1,044 (1990); 1,247 (1980) **Pop Density:** 1160.0
Land: 0.9 sq. mi.; **Water:** 0.0 sq. mi.

Wayne
Township
Lat: 39-05-43 N **Long:** 85-56-08 W
Pop: 3,437 (1990); 3,682 (1980) **Pop Density:** 70.0
Land: 49.1 sq. mi.; **Water:** 0.4 sq. mi.

Benton County
County Seat: Fowler (ZIP: 47944)

Pop: 9,441 (1990); 10,218 (1980) **Pop Density:** 23.2
Land: 406.3 sq. mi.; **Water:** 0.1 sq. mi. **Area Code:** 317
On the northwest border of IN, northwest of Lafayette; organized Feb 18, 1840 from Indian lands.

Name origin: For Thomas Hart Benton (1782–1858), U.S. journalist and statesman; nicknamed "Old Bullion" for championing the use of gold and silver currency rather than paper money.

Ambia
Town
ZIP: 47917 **Lat:** 40-29-19 N **Long:** 87-30-58 W
Pop: 249 (1990); 274 (1980) **Pop Density:** 830.0
Land: 0.3 sq. mi.; **Water:** 0.0 sq. mi. **Elev:** 731 ft.
Name origin: Possibly for Ambialet, France.

Bolivar
Township
Lat: 40-31-34 N **Long:** 87-09-54 W
Pop: 1,277 (1990); 1,235 (1980) **Pop Density:** 35.4
Land: 36.1 sq. mi.; **Water:** 0.0 sq. mi.

Boswell
Town
ZIP: 47921 **Lat:** 40-31-08 N **Long:** 87-22-57 W
Pop: 767 (1990); 810 (1980) **Pop Density:** 1534.0
Land: 0.5 sq. mi.; **Water:** 0.0 sq. mi. **Elev:** 760 ft.
Name origin: For Charles Boswell, who settled here in 1872.

Center
Township
Lat: 40-36-15 N **Long:** 87-17-42 W
Pop: 2,875 (1990); 3,062 (1980) **Pop Density:** 53.3
Land: 53.9 sq. mi.; **Water:** 0.0 sq. mi.

Earl Park
Town
ZIP: 47942 **Lat:** 40-41-08 N **Long:** 87-25-13 W
Pop: 443 (1990); 469 (1980) **Pop Density:** 492.2
Land: 0.9 sq. mi.; **Water:** 0.0 sq. mi. **Elev:** 780 ft.
Name origin: For prominent landowner Adam Earl, who helped lay out the town in 1872.

Fowler
Town
ZIP: 47944 **Lat:** 40-37-01 N **Long:** 87-19-01 W
Pop: 2,333 (1990); 2,319 (1980) **Pop Density:** 1944.2
Land: 1.2 sq. mi.; **Water:** 0.0 sq. mi. **Elev:** 826 ft.

Gilboa
Township
Lat: 40-41-36 N **Long:** 87-09-30 W
Pop: 281 (1990); 311 (1980) **Pop Density:** 7.8
Land: 35.9 sq. mi.; **Water:** 0.0 sq. mi.

Grant
Township
Lat: 40-31-12 N **Long:** 87-22-40 W
Pop: 1,118 (1990); 1,202 (1980) **Pop Density:** 31.1
Land: 35.9 sq. mi.; **Water:** 0.0 sq. mi.

Hickory Grove
Township
Lat: 40-31-06 N **Long:** 87-28-47 W
Pop: 476 (1990); 560 (1980) **Pop Density:** 16.5
Land: 28.8 sq. mi.; **Water:** 0.0 sq. mi.

Oak Grove
Township
Lat: 40-31-09 N **Long:** 87-15-54 W
Pop: 1,641 (1990); 1,810 (1980) **Pop Density:** 46.2
Land: 35.5 sq. mi.; **Water:** 0.0 sq. mi.

INDIANA, Benton County

Otterbein
Town
ZIP: 47970 **Lat:** 40-29-18 N **Long:** 87-05-50 W
Pop: 910 (1990); 1,118 (1980) **Pop Density:** 3033.3
Land: 0.3 sq. mi.; **Water:** 0.0 sq. mi. **Elev:** 706 ft.
Part of the town is also in Tippecanoe County.
Name origin: For pioneer settler Otterbein Brown.

Oxford
Town
ZIP: 47971 **Lat:** 40-31-16 N **Long:** 87-14-54 W
Pop: 1,273 (1990); 1,327 (1980) **Pop Density:** 2546.0
Land: 0.5 sq. mi.; **Water:** 0.0 sq. mi. **Elev:** 732 ft.
Name origin: For Oxford, England.

Parish Grove
Township
Lat: 40-36-27 N **Long:** 87-27-25 W
Pop: 312 (1990); 395 (1980) **Pop Density:** 6.9
Land: 45.4 sq. mi.; **Water:** 0.0 sq. mi.

Pine
Township
Lat: 40-35-55 N **Long:** 87-09-03 W
Pop: 264 (1990); 264 (1980) **Pop Density:** 7.4
Land: 35.7 sq. mi.; **Water:** 0.0 sq. mi.

Richland
Township
Lat: 40-41-17 N **Long:** 87-22-36 W
Pop: 679 (1990); 767 (1980) **Pop Density:** 18.9
Land: 35.9 sq. mi.; **Water:** 0.0 sq. mi.

Union
Township
Lat: 40-41-27 N **Long:** 87-15-49 W
Pop: 294 (1990); 367 (1980) **Pop Density:** 8.2
Land: 35.8 sq. mi.; **Water:** 0.0 sq. mi.

York
Township
Lat: 40-42-02 N **Long:** 87-29-03 W
Pop: 224 (1990); 245 (1980) **Pop Density:** 8.1
Land: 27.5 sq. mi.; **Water:** 0.0 sq. mi.

Blackford County
County Seat: Hartford City (ZIP: 47348)

Pop: 14,067 (1990); 15,570 (1980) **Pop Density:** 85.2
Land: 165.1 sq. mi.; **Water:** 0.3 sq. mi. **Area Code:** 317
In east-central IN, north of Muncie; organized Feb 15, 1838 from Jay County.
Name origin: For Isaac Newton Blackford (1786–1859), IN legislator and justice of the IN Supreme Court (1817–52).

Dunkirk
City
ZIP: 47336 **Lat:** 40-22-50 N **Long:** 85-12-30 W
Pop: 152 (1990); 3,180 (1980) **Pop Density:** 3800.0
Land: 0.04 sq. mi.; **Water:** 0.0 sq. mi. **Elev:** 954 ft.
Part of the town is also in Jay County.
Name origin: For Dunkirk, NY. Previously called Quincy.

Harrison
Township
Lat: 40-31-48 N **Long:** 85-16-06 W
Pop: 2,911 (1990); 3,103 (1980) **Pop Density:** 69.3
Land: 42.0 sq. mi.; **Water:** 0.1 sq. mi.

Hartford City
City
ZIP: 47348 **Lat:** 40-27-09 N **Long:** 85-22-18 W
Pop: 6,960 (1990); 7,622 (1980) **Pop Density:** 2047.1
Land: 3.4 sq. mi.; **Water:** 0.0 sq. mi. **Elev:** 922 ft.
Name origin: Named in 1854 for Hartford, CT. Previously called Blackford.

Jackson
Township
ZIP: 47348 **Lat:** 40-25-49 N **Long:** 85-16-01 W
Pop: 1,394 (1990); 1,723 (1980) **Pop Density:** 30.6
Land: 45.6 sq. mi.; **Water:** 0.1 sq. mi.

Licking
Township
ZIP: 47348 **Lat:** 40-26-00 N **Long:** 85-23-14 W
Pop: 8,825 (1990); 9,670 (1980) **Pop Density:** 213.7
Land: 41.3 sq. mi.; **Water:** 0.1 sq. mi.

Montpelier
City
ZIP: 47359 **Lat:** 40-33-10 N **Long:** 85-16-54 W
Pop: 1,880 (1990); 1,995 (1980) **Pop Density:** 2088.9
Land: 0.9 sq. mi.; **Water:** 0.0 sq. mi. **Elev:** 870 ft.
Name origin: For Montpelier, VT, former home of early settlers.

Shamrock Lakes
Town
ZIP: 47348 **Lat:** 40-24-39 N **Long:** 85-25-34 W
Pop: 207 (1990); 206 (1980) **Pop Density:** 690.0
Land: 0.3 sq. mi.; **Water:** 0.0 sq. mi.
Name origin: For the trifoliate plant.

Washington
Township
ZIP: 47348 **Lat:** 40-31-04 N **Long:** 85-23-40 W
Pop: 937 (1990); 1,074 (1980) **Pop Density:** 25.9
Land: 36.2 sq. mi.; **Water:** 0.0 sq. mi.

Boone County
County Seat: Lebanon (ZIP: 46052)

Pop: 38,147 (1990); 36,446 (1980)
Land: 422.7 sq. mi.; **Water:** 0.6 sq. mi.
Pop Density: 90.2
Area Code: 317
In central IN, northwest of Indianapolis; organized Jan 29, 1830 from Indian lands.
Name origin: For Daniel Boone (1734?–1820), U.S. frontiersman and KY pioneer.

Advance — Town
ZIP: 46102 **Lat:** 39-59-42 N **Long:** 86-37-13 W
Pop: 520 (1990); 559 (1980) **Pop Density:** 866.7
Land: 0.6 sq. mi.; **Water:** 0.0 sq. mi. **Elev:** 934 ft.
Settled 1820s.
Name origin: For the progress the Midland Railway would bring to the community.

Center — Township
ZIP: 46052 **Lat:** 40-02-48 N **Long:** 86-27-27 W
Pop: 14,538 (1990); 14,376 (1980) **Pop Density:** 224.4
Land: 64.8 sq. mi.; **Water:** 0.0 sq. mi.

Clinton — Township
Lat: 40-08-01 N **Long:** 86-24-21 W
Pop: 786 (1990); 856 (1980) **Pop Density:** 24.3
Land: 32.4 sq. mi.; **Water:** 0.0 sq. mi.

Eagle — Township
ZIP: 46077 **Lat:** 39-57-26 N **Long:** 86-17-43 W
Pop: 9,864 (1990); 7,995 (1980) **Pop Density:** 373.6
Land: 26.4 sq. mi.; **Water:** 0.3 sq. mi.

Harrison — Township
Lat: 39-57-38 N **Long:** 86-29-32 W
Pop: 700 (1990); 682 (1980) **Pop Density:** 28.7
Land: 24.4 sq. mi.; **Water:** 0.0 sq. mi.

Jackson — Township
Lat: 39-57-48 N **Long:** 86-37-02 W
Pop: 2,526 (1990); 2,725 (1980) **Pop Density:** 53.1
Land: 47.6 sq. mi.; **Water:** 0.0 sq. mi.

Jamestown — Town
ZIP: 46147 **Lat:** 39-55-38 N **Long:** 86-37-42 W
Pop: 764 (1990); 924 (1980) **Pop Density:** 1910.0
Land: 0.4 sq. mi.; **Water:** 0.0 sq. mi. **Elev:** 946 ft.
Founded 1832. Part of the town is also in Hendricks County.

Jefferson — Township
Lat: 40-03-10 N **Long:** 86-37-17 W
Pop: 969 (1990); 1,090 (1980) **Pop Density:** 20.8
Land: 46.5 sq. mi.; **Water:** 0.0 sq. mi.

Lebanon — City
ZIP: 46052 **Lat:** 40-03-05 N **Long:** 86-28-24 W
Pop: 12,059 (1990); 11,456 (1980) **Pop Density:** 2009.8
Land: 6.0 sq. mi.; **Water:** 0.0 sq. mi. **Elev:** 948 ft.
In central IN, 24 mi. northwest of Indianapolis.
Name origin: For the biblical mountain known for its tall cedar trees.

Marion — Township
Lat: 40-07-16 N **Long:** 86-17-32 W
Pop: 1,191 (1990); 1,214 (1980) **Pop Density:** 25.9
Land: 46.0 sq. mi.; **Water:** 0.0 sq. mi.

Perry — Township
Lat: 39-56-57 N **Long:** 86-24-27 W
Pop: 1,162 (1990); 1,144 (1980) **Pop Density:** 55.9
Land: 20.8 sq. mi.; **Water:** 0.0 sq. mi.

Sugar Creek — Township
Lat: 40-08-08 N **Long:** 86-38-22 W
Pop: 2,231 (1990); 2,188 (1980) **Pop Density:** 66.4
Land: 33.6 sq. mi.; **Water:** 0.0 sq. mi.

Thorntown — Town
ZIP: 46071 **Lat:** 40-07-43 N **Long:** 86-36-36 W
Pop: 1,506 (1990); 1,468 (1980) **Pop Density:** 2510.0
Land: 0.6 sq. mi.; **Water:** 0.0 sq. mi. **Elev:** 861 ft.
Name origin: An English translation of an Indian term meaning 'place of thorns.'

Ulen — Town
Lat: 40-03-51 N **Long:** 86-27-48 W
Pop: 50 (1990); 193 (1980) **Pop Density:** 500.0
Land: 0.1 sq. mi.; **Water:** 0.0 sq. mi. **Elev:** 940 ft.

Union — Township
Lat: 40-01-56 N **Long:** 86-17-30 W
Pop: 1,707 (1990); 1,634 (1980) **Pop Density:** 68.0
Land: 25.1 sq. mi.; **Water:** 0.1 sq. mi.

Washington — Township
Lat: 40-07-52 N **Long:** 86-31-36 W
Pop: 1,095 (1990); 1,164 (1980) **Pop Density:** 30.5
Land: 35.9 sq. mi.; **Water:** 0.1 sq. mi.

Whitestown — Town
ZIP: 46075 **Lat:** 39-59-44 N **Long:** 86-20-46 W
Pop: 476 (1990); 497 (1980) **Pop Density:** 1586.7
Land: 0.3 sq. mi.; **Water:** 0.0 sq. mi. **Elev:** 940 ft.
Name origin: For Albert White, railroad president and local congressman.

Worth — Township
Lat: 39-59-54 N **Long:** 86-21-24 W
Pop: 1,378 (1990); 1,378 (1980) **Pop Density:** 72.1
Land: 19.1 sq. mi.; **Water:** 0.0 sq. mi.

Zionsville — Town
ZIP: 46077 **Lat:** 39-57-08 N **Long:** 86-16-21 W
Pop: 5,281 (1990); 3,948 (1980) **Pop Density:** 2112.4
Land: 2.5 sq. mi.; **Water:** 0.1 sq. mi. **Elev:** 849 ft.
Settled 1830.
Name origin: For pioneer William Zion.

Brown County
County Seat: Nashville (ZIP: 47448)

Pop: 14,080 (1990); 12,377 (1980)　　**Pop Density:** 45.1
Land: 312.3 sq. mi.; **Water:** 4.4 sq. mi.　　**Area Code:** 812
In central IN, west of Columbus; organized Feb 4, 1836 from Monroe, Jackson, and Bartholomew counties.
Name origin: For Gen. Jacob Jennings Brown (1775–1828), an officer in the War of 1812 and commander of the U.S. Army (1821–28).

Hamblen — Township
Lat: 39-16-57 N **Long:** 86-09-33 W
Pop: 4,032 (1990); 3,365 (1980)　**Pop Density:** 63.0
Land: 64.0 sq. mi.; **Water:** 0.9 sq. mi.

Jackson — Township
ZIP: 47448　**Lat:** 39-17-01 N **Long:** 86-18-02 W
Pop: 4,151 (1990); 3,774 (1980)　**Pop Density:** 67.6
Land: 61.4 sq. mi.; **Water:** 1.0 sq. mi.

Nashville — Town
ZIP: 47448　**Lat:** 39-12-13 N **Long:** 86-14-09 W
Pop: 873 (1990); 705 (1980)　**Pop Density:** 970.0
Land: 0.9 sq. mi.; **Water:** 0.0 sq. mi.　**Elev:** 629 ft.
Founded 1834.
Name origin: For Nashville, TN.

Van Buren — Township
ZIP: 47448　**Lat:** 39-05-39 N **Long:** 86-10-26 W
Pop: 1,419 (1990); 1,207 (1980)　**Pop Density:** 16.3
Land: 87.2 sq. mi.; **Water:** 0.1 sq. mi.

Washington — Township
ZIP: 47448　**Lat:** 39-10-02 N **Long:** 86-15-47 W
Pop: 4,478 (1990); 4,031 (1980)　**Pop Density:** 45.0
Land: 99.6 sq. mi.; **Water:** 2.4 sq. mi.

Carroll County
County Seat: Delphi (ZIP: 46923)

Pop: 18,809 (1990); 19,722 (1980)　　**Pop Density:** 50.5
Land: 372.3 sq. mi.; **Water:** 2.8 sq. mi.　　**Area Code:** 317
In west-central IN, west of Kokoma; organized Jan 7, 1828 from Indian lands.
Name origin: For Charles Carroll (1737–1832), a signer of the Declaration of Independence, U.S. senator from MD (1789–92), and founder of the Baltimore and Ohio Railroad.

Adams — Township
Lat: 40-42-12 N **Long:** 86-36-38 W
Pop: 461 (1990); 567 (1980)　**Pop Density:** 17.9
Land: 25.7 sq. mi.; **Water:** 0.3 sq. mi.

Burlington — Town
ZIP: 46915　**Lat:** 40-28-52 N **Long:** 86-23-40 W
Pop: 568 (1990); 680 (1980)　**Pop Density:** 1136.0
Land: 0.5 sq. mi.; **Water:** 0.0 sq. mi.　**Elev:** 780 ft.
Not coextensive with the town of the same name.
Name origin: For Burlington, a Wyandotte Indian chief.

*Burlington — Township
Lat: 40-28-10 N **Long:** 86-25-15 W
Pop: 1,686 (1990); 1,933 (1980)　**Pop Density:** 57.7
Land: 29.2 sq. mi.; **Water:** 0.0 sq. mi.

Camden — Town
ZIP: 46917　**Lat:** 40-36-36 N **Long:** 86-32-19 W
Pop: 607 (1990); 618 (1980)　**Pop Density:** 2023.3
Land: 0.3 sq. mi.; **Water:** 0.0 sq. mi.　**Elev:** 670 ft.
Settled 1833.
Name origin: For Camden, NJ.

Carrollton — Township
Lat: 40-33-36 N **Long:** 86-25-11 W
Pop: 593 (1990); 637 (1980)　**Pop Density:** 20.0
Land: 29.6 sq. mi.; **Water:** 0.0 sq. mi.

Clay — Township
Lat: 40-27-27 N **Long:** 86-37-57 W
Pop: 882 (1990); 787 (1980)　**Pop Density:** 42.4
Land: 20.8 sq. mi.; **Water:** 0.0 sq. mi.

Deer Creek — Township
ZIP: 46917　**Lat:** 40-35-14 N **Long:** 86-37-59 W
Pop: 4,258 (1990); 4,458 (1980)　**Pop Density:** 97.4
Land: 43.7 sq. mi.; **Water:** 0.2 sq. mi.

Delphi — City
ZIP: 46923　**Lat:** 40-35-04 N **Long:** 86-40-13 W
Pop: 2,531 (1990); 3,042 (1980)　**Pop Density:** 1687.3
Land: 1.5 sq. mi.; **Water:** 0.0 sq. mi.　**Elev:** 580 ft.
Incorporated 1838.
Name origin: For the famous Greek shrine. Previously called Carrollton for the county.

INDIANA, Cass County

Democrat
Township
Lat: 40-28-03 N Long: 86-31-31 W
Pop: 809 (1990); 805 (1980) Pop Density: 27.2
Land: 29.7 sq. mi.; Water: 0.0 sq. mi.

Flora
Town
ZIP: 46929 Lat: 40-32-41 N Long: 86-31-24 W
Pop: 2,179 (1990); 2,303 (1980) Pop Density: 2179.0
Land: 1.0 sq. mi.; Water: 0.0 sq. mi. Elev: 710 ft.
Established 1872.
Name origin: For its founder, John Flora.

Jackson
Township
Lat: 40-35-50 N Long: 86-31-42 W
Pop: 1,285 (1990); 1,269 (1980) Pop Density: 42.7
Land: 30.1 sq. mi.; Water: 0.0 sq. mi.

Jefferson
Township
Lat: 40-41-44 N Long: 86-42-40 W
Pop: 1,937 (1990); 1,908 (1980) Pop Density: 63.3
Land: 30.6 sq. mi.; Water: 1.0 sq. mi.

Liberty
Township
Lat: 40-40-00 N Long: 86-30-04 W
Pop: 487 (1990); 523 (1980) Pop Density: 28.0
Land: 17.4 sq. mi.; Water: 0.1 sq. mi.

Madison
Township
Lat: 40-30-25 N Long: 86-38-12 W
Pop: 479 (1990); 580 (1980) Pop Density: 22.9
Land: 20.9 sq. mi.; Water: 0.0 sq. mi.

Monroe
Township
Lat: 40-32-00 N Long: 86-31-30 W
Pop: 2,916 (1990); 3,108 (1980) Pop Density: 121.0
Land: 24.1 sq. mi.; Water: 0.0 sq. mi.

Rock Creek
Township
Lat: 40-39-51 N Long: 86-35-08 W
Pop: 409 (1990); 457 (1980) Pop Density: 30.3
Land: 13.5 sq. mi.; Water: 0.3 sq. mi.

Tippecanoe
Township
Lat: 40-36-44 N Long: 86-43-35 W
Pop: 1,957 (1990); 1,982 (1980) Pop Density: 71.9
Land: 27.2 sq. mi.; Water: 0.8 sq. mi.

Washington
Township
Lat: 40-39-08 N Long: 86-25-12 W
Pop: 650 (1990); 708 (1980) Pop Density: 21.8
Land: 29.8 sq. mi.; Water: 0.0 sq. mi.

Yeoman
Town
ZIP: 47997 Lat: 40-40-01 N Long: 86-43-24 W
Pop: 131 (1990); 154 (1980) Pop Density: 1310.0
Land: 0.1 sq. mi.; Water: 0.0 sq. mi. Elev: 663 ft.
Name origin: For railroad official Col. Yeoman.

Cass County
County Seat: Logansport (ZIP: 46947)

Pop: 38,413 (1990); 40,936 (1980) Pop Density: 93.0
Land: 412.9 sq. mi.; Water: 2.1 sq. mi. Area Code: 219
In west-central IN, northwest of Kokomo; established Dec 18, 1828 from Indian lands.
Name origin: For Gen. Lewis Cass (1782-1866), OH legislator, governor of MI Territory (1813-31), U.S. secretary of war (1831-36), and U.S. secretary of state (1857-60).

Adams
Township
Lat: 40-51-32 N Long: 86-12-51 W
Pop: 873 (1990); 969 (1980) Pop Density: 30.2
Land: 28.9 sq. mi.; Water: 0.0 sq. mi.

Bethlehem
Township
Lat: 40-52-03 N Long: 86-18-12 W
Pop: 838 (1990); 941 (1980) Pop Density: 23.7
Land: 35.3 sq. mi.; Water: 0.0 sq. mi.

Boone
Township
Lat: 40-52-03 N Long: 86-31-34 W
Pop: 1,558 (1990); 1,627 (1980) Pop Density: 44.3
Land: 35.2 sq. mi.; Water: 0.0 sq. mi.

Clay
Township
Lat: 40-48-03 N Long: 86-18-02 W
Pop: 2,878 (1990); 2,779 (1980) Pop Density: 143.2
Land: 20.1 sq. mi.; Water: 0.1 sq. mi.

Clinton
Township
Lat: 40-43-28 N Long: 86-27-21 W
Pop: 1,014 (1990); 1,249 (1980) Pop Density: 41.1
Land: 24.7 sq. mi.; Water: 0.4 sq. mi.

Deer Creek
Township
Lat: 40-36-13 N Long: 86-18-38 W
Pop: 925 (1990); 1,069 (1980) Pop Density: 25.6
Land: 36.1 sq. mi.; Water: 0.0 sq. mi.

Eel
Township
ZIP: 46947 Lat: 40-45-13 N Long: 86-21-22 W
Pop: 17,746 (1990); 18,890 (1980) Pop Density: 1848.5
Land: 9.6 sq. mi.; Water: 0.4 sq. mi.
Name origin: For the Eel River, which flows through the county.

Galveston
Town
ZIP: 46932 Lat: 40-34-35 N Long: 86-11-30 W
Pop: 1,609 (1990); 1,822 (1980) Pop Density: 3218.0
Land: 0.5 sq. mi.; Water: 0.0 sq. mi.
Name origin: For Galveston, TX.

Grissom Air Force Base
Military Facility
Lat: 40-38-00 N Long: 86-10-11 W
Pop: 0 (1990)
Land: 0.2 sq. mi.; Water: 0.0 sq. mi.
Part of the facility is also in Miami County.

Harrison
Township
Lat: 40-51-58 N Long: 86-24-17 W
Pop: 809 (1990); 908 (1980)   Pop Density: 22.8
Land: 35.5 sq. mi.; Water: 0.0 sq. mi.

Jackson
Township
Lat: 40-36-29 N Long: 86-12-52 W
Pop: 3,059 (1990); 3,325 (1980)   Pop Density: 102.0
Land: 30.0 sq. mi.; Water: 0.0 sq. mi.

Jefferson
Township
Lat: 40-46-43 N Long: 86-31-29 W
Pop: 1,432 (1990); 1,326 (1980)   Pop Density: 40.0
Land: 35.8 sq. mi.; Water: 0.3 sq. mi.

Logansport
City
ZIP: 46947   Lat: 40-45-13 N Long: 86-21-26 W
Pop: 16,812 (1990); 17,731 (1980)   Pop Density: 2626.9
Land: 6.4 sq. mi.; Water: 0.1 sq. mi.   Elev: 602 ft.
In north-central IN, 22 mi. northwest of Kokomo.
Name origin: For Shawnee Capt. John Logan (1786–1812), who was killed during the War of 1812.

Miami
Township
Lat: 40-46-23 N Long: 86-13-08 W
Pop: 1,158 (1990); 1,306 (1980)   Pop Density: 57.6
Land: 20.1 sq. mi.; Water: 0.3 sq. mi.

Noble
Township
Lat: 40-47-19 N Long: 86-25-06 W
Pop: 1,942 (1990); 2,052 (1980)   Pop Density: 75.3
Land: 25.8 sq. mi.; Water: 0.2 sq. mi.

Onward
Town
ZIP: 46967   Lat: 40-41-38 N Long: 86-11-43 W
Pop: 63 (1990); 121 (1980)   Pop Density: 630.0
Land: 0.1 sq. mi.; Water: 0.0 sq. mi.   Elev: 765 ft.

Royal Center
Town
ZIP: 46978   Lat: 40-51-52 N Long: 86-30-01 W
Pop: 859 (1990); 908 (1980)   Pop Density: 1718.0
Land: 0.5 sq. mi.; Water: 0.0 sq. mi.   Elev: 740 ft.

Tipton
Township
Lat: 40-41-54 N Long: 86-13-06 W
Pop: 2,439 (1990); 2,684 (1980)   Pop Density: 60.1
Land: 40.6 sq. mi.; Water: 0.1 sq. mi.

Walton
Town
ZIP: 46994   Lat: 40-39-44 N Long: 86-14-41 W
Pop: 1,053 (1990); 1,202 (1980)   Pop Density: 2632.5
Land: 0.4 sq. mi.; Water: 0.0 sq. mi.   Elev: 765 ft.
Name origin: For its founder, Gilber Wall.

Washington
Township
Lat: 40-41-46 N Long: 86-19-54 W
Pop: 1,742 (1990); 1,811 (1980)   Pop Density: 49.5
Land: 35.2 sq. mi.; Water: 0.2 sq. mi.

Clark County
County Seat: Jeffersonville (ZIP: 47130)

Pop: 87,777 (1990); 88,838 (1980)   Pop Density: 234.0
Land: 375.2 sq. mi.; Water: 1.1 sq. mi.   Area Code: 812
On the southeast border of IN, north of Louisville, KY; organized Feb 3, 1801 (prior to statehood) from Knox County.
Name origin: For Gen. George Rogers Clark (1752–1818), officer in the Revolutionary War and frontiersman in the Northwest Territory.

Bethlehem
Township
Lat: 38-32-48 N Long: 85-27-25 W
Pop: 363 (1990); 359 (1980)   Pop Density: 19.6
Land: 18.5 sq. mi.; Water: 0.2 sq. mi.

Carr
Township
Lat: 38-26-46 N Long: 85-50-11 W
Pop: 1,640 (1990); 1,660 (1980)   Pop Density: 61.9
Land: 26.5 sq. mi.; Water: 0.3 sq. mi.

Charlestown
City
ZIP: 47111   Lat: 38-27-13 N Long: 85-40-05 W
Pop: 5,889 (1990); 5,596 (1980)   Pop Density: 2804.3
Land: 2.1 sq. mi.; Water: 0.0 sq. mi.   Elev: 590 ft.
Incorporated 1813. Not coextensive with the town of the same name.

*Charlestown
Township
ZIP: 47111   Lat: 38-27-34 N Long: 85-39-46 W
Pop: 9,933 (1990); 9,196 (1980)   Pop Density: 154.0
Land: 64.5 sq. mi.; Water: 0.1 sq. mi.

Clarksville
Town
ZIP: 47129   Lat: 38-18-59 N Long: 85-45-55 W
Pop: 19,833 (1990); 15,164 (1980)   Pop Density: 2333.3
Land: 8.5 sq. mi.; Water: 0.1 sq. mi.   Elev: 455 ft.
Name origin: For Gen. George Rogers Clark (1752–1818), officer in the Revolutionary War and frontiersman in the Northwest Territory.

Jeffersonville
City
ZIP: 47130   Lat: 38-18-03 N Long: 85-43-35 W
Pop: 21,841 (1990); 21,220 (1980)   Pop Density: 2299.1
Land: 9.5 sq. mi.; Water: 0.0 sq. mi.   Elev: 450 ft.
In southern IN across from Louisville, KY, on the Ohio River. Not coextensive with the town of the same name.
Name origin: For Thomas Jefferson (1743–1826), third U.S. president.

*Jeffersonville
Township
ZIP: 47129   Lat: 38-18-57 N Long: 85-44-18 W
Pop: 53,449 (1990); 55,831 (1980)   Pop Density: 1994.4
Land: 26.8 sq. mi.; Water: 0.1 sq. mi.

Monroe Township
Lat: 38-32-40 N Long: 85-46-25 W
Pop: 3,917 (1990); 3,966 (1980) Pop Density: 69.9
Land: 56.0 sq. mi.; Water: 0.1 sq. mi.

New Providence Town
Lat: 38-27-28 N Long: 85-55-14 W
Pop: 270 (1990); 384 (1980) Pop Density: 207.7
Land: 1.3 sq. mi.; Water: 0.0 sq. mi. Elev: 562 ft.
Founded 1817.
Name origin: For divine providence.

Oak Park CDP
ZIP: 47130 Lat: 38-18-14 N Long: 85-41-26 W
Pop: 5,630 (1990); 5,457 (1980) Pop Density: 2165.4
Land: 2.6 sq. mi.; Water: 0.0 sq. mi.

Oregon Township
Lat: 38-33-02 N Long: 85-38-28 W
Pop: 1,212 (1990); 1,147 (1980) Pop Density: 38.8
Land: 31.2 sq. mi.; Water: 0.0 sq. mi.

Owen Township
Lat: 38-30-01 N Long: 85-31-29 W
Pop: 646 (1990); 690 (1980) Pop Density: 37.3
Land: 17.3 sq. mi.; Water: 0.1 sq. mi.

Sellersburg Town
ZIP: 47172 Lat: 38-23-27 N Long: 85-45-25 W
Pop: 5,745 (1990); 3,211 (1980) Pop Density: 2497.8
Land: 2.3 sq. mi.; Water: 0.0 sq. mi. Elev: 500 ft.
Founded 1846.
Name origin: For cofounder Moses Sellers.

Silver Creek Township
ZIP: 47172 Lat: 38-23-40 N Long: 85-45-42 W
Pop: 8,014 (1990); 7,887 (1980) Pop Density: 471.4
Land: 17.0 sq. mi.; Water: 0.1 sq. mi.

Union Township
Lat: 38-28-25 N Long: 85-46-01 W
Pop: 1,837 (1990); 1,805 (1980) Pop Density: 86.7
Land: 21.2 sq. mi.; Water: 0.0 sq. mi.

Utica Town
ZIP: 47130 Lat: 38-19-58 N Long: 85-39-17 W
Pop: 411 (1990); 501 (1980) Pop Density: 1370.0
Land: 0.3 sq. mi.; Water: 0.0 sq. mi. Elev: 450 ft.
Not coextensive with the town of the same name.
Name origin: Named in 1816 for Utica, NY.

***Utica** Township
Lat: 38-21-29 N Long: 85-40-28 W
Pop: 3,124 (1990); 2,704 (1980) Pop Density: 142.6
Land: 21.9 sq. mi.; Water: 0.0 sq. mi.

Washington Township
ZIP: 47162 Lat: 38-33-57 N Long: 85-33-27 W
Pop: 1,534 (1990); 1,566 (1980) Pop Density: 43.5
Land: 35.3 sq. mi.; Water: 0.0 sq. mi.

Wood Township
Lat: 38-27-25 N Long: 85-55-45 W
Pop: 2,108 (1990); 2,027 (1980) Pop Density: 54.2
Land: 38.9 sq. mi.; Water: 0.0 sq. mi.

Clay County
County Seat: Brazil (ZIP: 47834)

Pop: 24,705 (1990); 24,862 (1980) Pop Density: 69.1
Land: 357.6 sq. mi.; Water: 2.8 sq. mi. Area Code: 812
In southwest IN, east of Terre Haute; organized Feb 12, 1825 from Indian lands.
Name origin: For Henry Clay (1777–1852), U.S. senator from KY, known as the "Great Pacificator" for his advocacy of compromise to avert national crises.

Brazil City
ZIP: 47834 Lat: 39-31-24 N Long: 87-07-24 W
Pop: 7,640 (1990); 7,852 (1980) Pop Density: 2829.6
Land: 2.7 sq. mi.; Water: 0.0 sq. mi. Elev: 659 ft.
Not coextensive with the town of the same name.
Name origin: For the South American country.

***Brazil** Township
ZIP: 47834 Lat: 39-32-07 N Long: 87-07-21 W
Pop: 8,216 (1990); 8,422 (1980) Pop Density: 1264.0
Land: 6.5 sq. mi.; Water: 0.1 sq. mi.

Carbon Town
ZIP: 47837 Lat: 39-35-56 N Long: 87-06-26 W
Pop: 350 (1990); 307 (1980) Pop Density: 1750.0
Land: 0.2 sq. mi.; Water: 0.0 sq. mi. Elev: 687 ft.
Name origin: For the coal, or carbon, deposits nearby.

Cass Township
ZIP: 47868 Lat: 39-26-58 N Long: 86-58-49 W
Pop: 310 (1990); 267 (1980) Pop Density: 25.8
Land: 12.0 sq. mi.; Water: 0.0 sq. mi.

Center Point Town
Lat: 39-24-53 N Long: 87-04-28 W
Pop: 278 (1990); 242 (1980) Pop Density: 397.1
Land: 0.7 sq. mi.; Water: 0.0 sq. mi. Elev: 671 ft.

Clay City Town
ZIP: 47841 Lat: 39-16-37 N Long: 87-06-43 W
Pop: 929 (1990); 883 (1980) Pop Density: 1858.0
Land: 0.5 sq. mi.; Water: 0.0 sq. mi. Elev: 587 ft.
Established 1873.
Name origin: For its county.

Dick Johnson Township
ZIP: 47834 Lat: 39-33-52 N Long: 87-09-49 W
Pop: 1,147 (1990); 1,125 (1980) Pop Density: 53.3
Land: 21.5 sq. mi.; Water: 0.1 sq. mi.

Harmony Town
ZIP: 47853 Lat: 39-32-02 N Long: 87-04-24 W
Pop: 645 (1990); 613 (1980) Pop Density: 806.3
Land: 0.8 sq. mi.; Water: 0.0 sq. mi. Elev: 673 ft.
Settled 1839.

INDIANA, Clay County

Harrison
Township
ZIP: 47841 **Lat:** 39-16-10 N **Long:** 87-06-36 W
Pop: 2,275 (1990); 2,220 (1980) **Pop Density:** 36.5
Land: 62.3 sq. mi.; **Water:** 0.4 sq. mi.

Jackson
Township
ZIP: 47834 **Lat:** 39-28-50 N **Long:** 87-04-24 W
Pop: 2,126 (1990); 2,022 (1980) **Pop Density:** 60.7
Land: 35.0 sq. mi.; **Water:** 0.6 sq. mi.

Knightsville
Town
ZIP: 47857 **Lat:** 39-31-34 N **Long:** 87-05-23 W
Pop: 740 (1990); 763 (1980) **Pop Density:** 740.0
Land: 1.0 sq. mi.; **Water:** 0.0 sq. mi. **Elev:** 680 ft.
Founded 1867.
Name origin: For its founder, A. W. Knight.

Lewis
Township
Lat: 39-13-21 N **Long:** 87-11-22 W
Pop: 1,310 (1990); 1,502 (1980) **Pop Density:** 29.7
Land: 44.1 sq. mi.; **Water:** 0.2 sq. mi.

Perry
Township
ZIP: 47846 **Lat:** 39-22-32 N **Long:** 87-11-39 W
Pop: 874 (1990); 971 (1980) **Pop Density:** 19.6
Land: 44.6 sq. mi.; **Water:** 0.1 sq. mi.

Posey
Township
ZIP: 47834 **Lat:** 39-28-26 N **Long:** 87-11-01 W
Pop: 3,347 (1990); 3,459 (1980) **Pop Density:** 95.6
Land: 35.0 sq. mi.; **Water:** 0.7 sq. mi.

Staunton
Town
ZIP: 47881 **Lat:** 39-29-09 N **Long:** 87-11-21 W
Pop: 592 (1990); 607 (1980) **Pop Density:** 1973.3
Land: 0.3 sq. mi.; **Water:** 0.0 sq. mi. **Elev:** 646 ft.
Founded 1851.
Name origin: For Staunton, VA.

Sugar Ridge
Township
ZIP: 47840 **Lat:** 39-22-35 N **Long:** 87-06-04 W
Pop: 955 (1990); 956 (1980) **Pop Density:** 33.7
Land: 28.3 sq. mi.; **Water:** 0.5 sq. mi.

Van Buren
Township
ZIP: 47837 **Lat:** 39-33-46 N **Long:** 87-03-37 W
Pop: 3,411 (1990); 3,168 (1980) **Pop Density:** 105.9
Land: 32.2 sq. mi.; **Water:** 0.1 sq. mi.

Washington
Township
ZIP: 47833 **Lat:** 39-23-08 N **Long:** 86-59-42 W
Pop: 734 (1990); 750 (1980) **Pop Density:** 20.3
Land: 36.2 sq. mi.; **Water:** 0.0 sq. mi.

Clinton County
County Seat: Frankfort (ZIP: 46041)

Pop: 30,974 (1990); 31,545 (1980) **Pop Density:** 76.5
Land: 405.1 sq. mi.; **Water:** 0.2 sq. mi. **Area Code:** 317
In central IN, east of Lafayette; organized Jan 29, 1830 from Indian lands.
Name origin: For DeWitt Clinton (1769–1828), governor of NY (1817–21; 1825–28) and supporter of the Erie Canal.

Center
Township
ZIP: 46041 **Lat:** 40-16-45 N **Long:** 86-29-52 W
Pop: 15,845 (1990); 16,338 (1980) **Pop Density:** 769.2
Land: 20.6 sq. mi.; **Water:** 0.0 sq. mi.

Colfax
Town
ZIP: 46035 **Lat:** 40-11-39 N **Long:** 86-40-02 W
Pop: 727 (1990); 823 (1980) **Pop Density:** 2423.3
Land: 0.3 sq. mi.; **Water:** 0.0 sq. mi. **Elev:** 845 ft.
Name origin: For Indianan Schuyler Colfax (1823–85), U.S. legislator and vice president (1869–73).

Forest
Township
ZIP: 46039 **Lat:** 40-22-16 N **Long:** 86-18-50 W
Pop: 890 (1990); 935 (1980) **Pop Density:** 33.6
Land: 26.5 sq. mi.; **Water:** 0.0 sq. mi.

Frankfort
City
ZIP: 46041 **Lat:** 40-16-51 N **Long:** 86-30-37 W
Pop: 14,754 (1990); 15,168 (1980) **Pop Density:** 3207.4
Land: 4.6 sq. mi.; **Water:** 0.0 sq. mi. **Elev:** 855 ft.
In central IN, 46 mi. north-northwest of Indianapolis. County seat.
Name origin: For Frankfurt am Main, Germany, home of the landowner's ancestors.

Jackson
Township
Lat: 40-13-12 N **Long:** 86-30-12 W
Pop: 1,199 (1990); 1,200 (1980) **Pop Density:** 27.6
Land: 43.5 sq. mi.; **Water:** 0.0 sq. mi.

Johnson
Township
Lat: 40-18-18 N **Long:** 86-18-32 W
Pop: 641 (1990); 679 (1980) **Pop Density:** 24.0
Land: 26.7 sq. mi.; **Water:** 0.0 sq. mi.

Kirklin
Town
ZIP: 46050 **Lat:** 40-11-34 N **Long:** 86-21-34 W
Pop: 707 (1990); 662 (1980) **Pop Density:** 2356.7
Land: 0.3 sq. mi.; **Water:** 0.0 sq. mi. **Elev:** 919 ft.
Not coextensive with the town of the same name.
Name origin: For 1830s taverner Nathan Kirk.

*Kirklin
Township
ZIP: 46050 **Lat:** 40-12-57 N **Long:** 86-22-38 W
Pop: 1,314 (1990); 1,279 (1980) **Pop Density:** 37.5
Land: 35.0 sq. mi.; **Water:** 0.0 sq. mi.

Madison
Township
Lat: 40-20-30 N **Long:** 86-39-03 W
Pop: 1,938 (1990); 1,847 (1980) **Pop Density:** 76.0
Land: 25.5 sq. mi.; **Water:** 0.0 sq. mi.

Michigan
Township
Lat: 40-19-06 N **Long:** 86-24-17 W
Pop: 1,566 (1990); 1,585 (1980) **Pop Density:** 43.7
Land: 35.8 sq. mi.; **Water:** 0.0 sq. mi.

Michigantown
Town
ZIP: 46057   **Lat:** 40-19-40 N   **Long:** 86-23-27 W
Pop: 472 (1990); 453 (1980)   **Pop Density:** 1573.3
Land: 0.3 sq. mi.; **Water:** 0.0 sq. mi.   **Elev:** 872 ft.
Name origin: For the north-south Michigan Road that passes through the town.

Mulberry
Town
ZIP: 46058   **Lat:** 40-20-44 N   **Long:** 86-40-04 W
Pop: 1,262 (1990); 1,225 (1980)   **Pop Density:** 2103.3
Land: 0.6 sq. mi.; **Water:** 0.0 sq. mi.   **Elev:** 770 ft.

Owen
Township
Lat: 40-23-25 N   **Long:** 86-30-55 W
Pop: 838 (1990); 886 (1980)   **Pop Density:** 33.5
Land: 25.0 sq. mi.; **Water:** 0.0 sq. mi.

Perry
Township
Lat: 40-13-17 N   **Long:** 86-38-24 W
Pop: 1,396 (1990); 1,462 (1980)   **Pop Density:** 42.2
Land: 33.1 sq. mi.; **Water:** 0.0 sq. mi.

Ross
Township
Lat: 40-23-45 N   **Long:** 86-36-47 W
Pop: 2,217 (1990); 2,182 (1980)   **Pop Density:** 74.9
Land: 29.6 sq. mi.; **Water:** 0.0 sq. mi.

Rossville
Town
ZIP: 46065   **Lat:** 40-25-16 N   **Long:** 86-35-44 W
Pop: 1,175 (1990); 1,148 (1980)   **Pop Density:** 2350.0
Land: 0.5 sq. mi.; **Water:** 0.0 sq. mi.   **Elev:** 722 ft.

Sugar Creek
Township
Lat: 40-13-53 N   **Long:** 86-17-11 W
Pop: 485 (1990); 508 (1980)   **Pop Density:** 18.8
Land: 25.8 sq. mi.; **Water:** 0.0 sq. mi.

Union
Township
Lat: 40-19-28 N   **Long:** 86-30-48 W
Pop: 905 (1990); 850 (1980)   **Pop Density:** 45.7
Land: 19.8 sq. mi.; **Water:** 0.1 sq. mi.

Warren
Township
Lat: 40-23-42 N   **Long:** 86-25-08 W
Pop: 689 (1990); 722 (1980)   **Pop Density:** 23.4
Land: 29.4 sq. mi.; **Water:** 0.0 sq. mi.

Washington
Township
Lat: 40-17-16 N   **Long:** 86-36-42 W
Pop: 1,051 (1990); 1,072 (1980)   **Pop Density:** 36.6
Land: 28.7 sq. mi.; **Water:** 0.0 sq. mi.

Crawford County
County Seat: English (ZIP: 47118)

Pop: 9,914 (1990); 9,820 (1980)   **Pop Density:** 32.4
Land: 305.7 sq. mi.; **Water:** 3.2 sq. mi.   **Area Code:** 812
On the south-central border of IN; organized Jan 19, 1818 from Harrison County.
Name origin: For either Col. William Crawford (1732–82), VA officer in the Revolutionary War, Indian fighter, and surveyor; or William Harris Crawford (1772–1834), senator from GA (1807–13), U.S. secretary of war (1815–16), and U.S. secretary of the treasury (1816–25).

Alton
Town
Lat: 38-07-20 N   **Long:** 86-25-16 W
Pop: 57 (1990); 64 (1980)   **Pop Density:** 285.0
Land: 0.2 sq. mi.; **Water:** 0.0 sq. mi.   **Elev:** 425 ft.
Settled 1838.
Name origin: For Alton, England.

Boone
Township
Lat: 38-09-22 N   **Long:** 86-26-27 W
Pop: 153 (1990); 200 (1980)   **Pop Density:** 12.8
Land: 12.0 sq. mi.; **Water:** 0.2 sq. mi.

Carefree
Town
ZIP: 47137   **Lat:** 38-14-35 N   **Long:** 86-21-28 W
Pop: 26 (1990); 41 (1980)   **Pop Density:** 28.9
Land: 0.9 sq. mi.; **Water:** 0.0 sq. mi.
Name origin: Named by its founders to express their feelings about the community.

English
Town
ZIP: 47118   **Lat:** 38-19-58 N   **Long:** 86-27-47 W
Pop: 614 (1990); 633 (1980)   **Pop Density:** 511.7
Land: 1.2 sq. mi.; **Water:** 0.0 sq. mi.   **Elev:** 512 ft.
Founded 1839.
Name origin: For Indiana statesman William English.

Jennings
Township
Lat: 38-14-06 N   **Long:** 86-21-03 W
Pop: 1,235 (1990); 1,285 (1980)   **Pop Density:** 27.5
Land: 44.9 sq. mi.; **Water:** 0.2 sq. mi.

Johnson
Township
ZIP: 47116   **Lat:** 38-17-42 N   **Long:** 86-37-24 W
Pop: 526 (1990); 453 (1980)   **Pop Density:** 21.7
Land: 24.2 sq. mi.; **Water:** 0.0 sq. mi.

Leavenworth
Town
ZIP: 47137   **Lat:** 38-12-01 N   **Long:** 86-20-47 W
Pop: 320 (1990); 356 (1980)   **Pop Density:** 400.0
Land: 0.8 sq. mi.; **Water:** 0.0 sq. mi.   **Elev:** 668 ft.
Settled 1818.
Name origin: For the Leavenworths, early landowners.

Liberty
Township
Lat: 38-21-48 N   **Long:** 86-21-46 W
Pop: 1,835 (1990); 1,760 (1980)   **Pop Density:** 85.3
Land: 21.5 sq. mi.; **Water:** 0.0 sq. mi.

Marengo
Town
ZIP: 47140   **Lat:** 38-22-17 N   **Long:** 86-20-37 W
Pop: 856 (1990); 892 (1980)   **Pop Density:** 1070.0
Land: 0.8 sq. mi.; **Water:** 0.0 sq. mi.   **Elev:** 620 ft.
Name origin: For Marengo, Italy, site of Napoleon I's (1769–1821) victory over the Austrians (Jun 14, 1800).

INDIANA, Crawford County

Milltown
Town
ZIP: 47145 **Lat:** 38-20-31 N **Long:** 86-16-50 W
Pop: 489 (1990); 620 (1980) **Pop Density:** 698.6
Land: 0.7 sq. mi.; **Water:** 0.0 sq. mi. **Elev:** 600 ft.
Settled 1827. Part of the town is also in Harrison County.
Name origin: Originally called Leavenworth's Mill for Zebulon Leavenworth; name altered later.

Ohio
Township
Lat: 38-11-56 N **Long:** 86-24-56 W
Pop: 568 (1990); 508 (1980) **Pop Density:** 18.8
Land: 30.2 sq. mi.; **Water:** 0.7 sq. mi.

Patoka
Township
Lat: 38-21-18 N **Long:** 86-36-22 W
Pop: 1,262 (1990); 1,185 (1980) **Pop Density:** 28.9
Land: 43.7 sq. mi.; **Water:** 2.0 sq. mi.

Sterling
Township
Lat: 38-20-12 N **Long:** 86-27-13 W
Pop: 1,743 (1990); 1,799 (1980) **Pop Density:** 36.0
Land: 48.4 sq. mi.; **Water:** 0.1 sq. mi.

Union
Township
Lat: 38-14-58 N **Long:** 86-31-24 W
Pop: 863 (1990); 861 (1980) **Pop Density:** 20.4
Land: 42.4 sq. mi.; **Water:** 0.0 sq. mi.

Whiskey Run
Township
Lat: 38-20-10 N **Long:** 86-18-26 W
Pop: 1,729 (1990); 1,769 (1980) **Pop Density:** 44.9
Land: 38.5 sq. mi.; **Water:** 0.0 sq. mi.

Daviess County
County Seat: Washington (ZIP: 47501)

Pop: 27,533 (1990); 27,836 (1980) **Pop Density:** 63.9
Land: 430.7 sq. mi.; **Water:** 6.1 sq. mi. **Area Code:** 812
In southwestern IN, east of Vincennes; established Dec 24, 1816 from Indian lands.
Name origin: For Col. Joseph Hamilton Daviess (1774–1811), VA soldier and jurist who unsuccessfully attempted to indict Aaron Burr for treason (1806). According to Jacob Piatt Dunn, "the Colonel's name was Daveiss and he always wrote it that way"; however, the name is sometimes spelled 'Daviess' in biographical entries and in places named for him.

Alfordsville
Town
Lat: 38-33-36 N **Long:** 86-56-55 W
Pop: 74 (1990); 132 (1980) **Pop Density:** 740.0
Land: 0.1 sq. mi.; **Water:** 0.0 sq. mi. **Elev:** 520 ft.
Name origin: For early settler James Alford.

Barr
Township
ZIP: 47519 **Lat:** 38-40-10 N **Long:** 87-00-36 W
Pop: 3,396 (1990); 3,205 (1980) **Pop Density:** 47.0
Land: 72.2 sq. mi.; **Water:** 1.0 sq. mi.

Bogard
Township
ZIP: 47568 **Lat:** 38-46-08 N **Long:** 87-04-25 W
Pop: 1,068 (1990); 940 (1980) **Pop Density:** 29.1
Land: 36.7 sq. mi.; **Water:** 0.1 sq. mi.

Cannelburg
Town
ZIP: 47519 **Lat:** 38-40-08 N **Long:** 86-59-52 W
Pop: 97 (1990); 152 (1980) **Pop Density:** 485.0
Land: 0.2 sq. mi.; **Water:** 0.0 sq. mi. **Elev:** 524 ft.
Settled 1844.
Name origin: For the cannel coal mined nearby.

Elmore
Township
ZIP: 47529 **Lat:** 38-51-44 N **Long:** 87-04-16 W
Pop: 1,305 (1990); 1,376 (1980) **Pop Density:** 37.4
Land: 34.9 sq. mi.; **Water:** 0.3 sq. mi.

Elnora
Town
ZIP: 47529 **Lat:** 38-52-38 N **Long:** 87-05-05 W
Pop: 679 (1990); 756 (1980) **Pop Density:** 1131.7
Land: 0.6 sq. mi.; **Water:** 0.0 sq. mi. **Elev:** 476 ft.
Founded 1885.
Name origin: For Elnora Griffith, wife of a local merchant.

Harrison
Township
ZIP: 47501 **Lat:** 38-34-05 N **Long:** 87-04-52 W
Pop: 544 (1990); 600 (1980) **Pop Density:** 17.8
Land: 30.5 sq. mi.; **Water:** 1.6 sq. mi.

Madison
Township
ZIP: 47562 **Lat:** 38-51-33 N **Long:** 86-58-00 W
Pop: 2,609 (1990); 2,788 (1980) **Pop Density:** 71.1
Land: 36.7 sq. mi.; **Water:** 0.1 sq. mi.

Montgomery
Town
ZIP: 47558 **Lat:** 38-39-54 N **Long:** 87-02-49 W
Pop: 351 (1990); 390 (1980) **Pop Density:** 1170.0
Land: 0.3 sq. mi.; **Water:** 0.0 sq. mi. **Elev:** 533 ft.
Name origin: For Revolutionary War hero Gen. Richard Montgomery (1736–75).

Odon
Town
ZIP: 47562 **Lat:** 38-50-32 N **Long:** 86-59-19 W
Pop: 1,475 (1990); 1,463 (1980) **Pop Density:** 1638.9
Land: 0.9 sq. mi.; **Water:** 0.0 sq. mi. **Elev:** 535 ft.

Plainville
Town
ZIP: 47568 **Lat:** 38-48-15 N **Long:** 87-09-06 W
Pop: 444 (1990); 556 (1980) **Pop Density:** 1480.0
Land: 0.3 sq. mi.; **Water:** 0.0 sq. mi. **Elev:** 475 ft.

Reeve
Township
Lat: 38-33-47 N **Long:** 86-58-31 W
Pop: 632 (1990); 723 (1980) **Pop Density:** 14.3
Land: 44.1 sq. mi.; **Water:** 0.8 sq. mi.

Steele
Township
ZIP: 47501 **Lat:** 38-46-26 N **Long:** 87-11-05 W
Pop: 895 (1990); 981 (1980) **Pop Density:** 20.9
Land: 42.9 sq. mi.; **Water:** 0.6 sq. mi.

Van Buren Township
Lat: 38-46-26 N Long: 86-58-18 W
Pop: 1,589 (1990); 1,333 (1980) **Pop Density:** 52.6
Land: 30.2 sq. mi.; **Water:** 0.7 sq. mi.

Veale Township
ZIP: 47501 Lat: 38-33-59 N Long: 87-11-04 W
Pop: 779 (1990); 682 (1980) **Pop Density:** 26.7
Land: 29.2 sq. mi.; **Water:** 0.5 sq. mi.

Washington City
ZIP: 47501 Lat: 38-39-29 N Long: 87-10-22 W
Pop: 10,838 (1990); 11,325 (1980) **Pop Density:** 2520.5
Land: 4.3 sq. mi.; **Water:** 0.0 sq. mi. **Elev:** 504 ft.

In southwestern IN, 17 mi. east of Vincennes. Not coextensive with the town of the same name.
Name origin: For George Washington (1732–99), American patriot and first U.S. president.

***Washington** Township
ZIP: 47501 Lat: 38-40-10 N Long: 87-10-32 W
Pop: 14,716 (1990); 15,208 (1980) **Pop Density:** 200.8
Land: 73.3 sq. mi.; **Water:** 0.5 sq. mi.

Dearborn County
County Seat: Lawrenceburg (ZIP: 47025)

Pop: 38,835 (1990); 34,291 (1980) **Pop Density:** 127.2
Land: 305.2 sq. mi.; **Water:** 1.8 sq. mi. **Area Code:** 812

On the southeastern border of IN, east of Columbus; organized Mar 7, 1803 (prior to statehood).
Name origin: For Gen. Henry Dearborn (1751–1829), an officer in the Revolutionary War, MA legislator, U.S. secretary of war (1801–09), and Minister to Portugal (1822–24).

Aurora City
ZIP: 47001 Lat: 39-03-59 N Long: 84-54-11 W
Pop: 3,825 (1990); 3,816 (1980) **Pop Density:** 1366.1
Land: 2.8 sq. mi.; **Water:** 0.1 sq. mi. **Elev:** 501 ft.
Founded 1819; incorporated 1839; granted city charter 1848.
Name origin: For the Roman goddess of the dawn.

Bright CDP
Lat: 39-12-09 N Long: 84-51-27 W
Pop: 3,945 (1990) **Pop Density:** 270.2
Land: 14.6 sq. mi.; **Water:** 0.0 sq. mi.

Caesar Creek Township
Lat: 38-58-10 N Long: 85-05-55 W
Pop: 310 (1990); 275 (1980) **Pop Density:** 26.1
Land: 11.9 sq. mi.; **Water:** 0.0 sq. mi.

Center Township
ZIP: 47001 Lat: 39-03-18 N Long: 84-54-48 W
Pop: 5,182 (1990); 5,157 (1980) **Pop Density:** 479.8
Land: 10.8 sq. mi.; **Water:** 0.4 sq. mi.

Clay Township
Lat: 39-00-43 N Long: 85-03-34 W
Pop: 2,813 (1990); 2,444 (1980) **Pop Density:** 111.2
Land: 25.3 sq. mi.; **Water:** 0.0 sq. mi.

Dillsboro Town
Lat: 39-01-07 N Long: 85-03-42 W
Pop: 1,200 (1990); 1,038 (1980) **Pop Density:** 1714.3
Land: 0.7 sq. mi.; **Water:** 0.0 sq. mi. **Elev:** 615 ft.

Greendale Town
ZIP: 47025 Lat: 39-07-03 N Long: 84-51-36 W
Pop: 3,881 (1990); 3,795 (1980) **Pop Density:** 1848.1
Land: 2.1 sq. mi.; **Water:** 0.0 sq. mi. **Elev:** 528 ft.
Name origin: Descriptive of its verdant surroundings.

Harrison Township
Lat: 39-16-06 N Long: 84-51-19 W
Pop: 2,421 (1990); 1,801 (1980) **Pop Density:** 142.4
Land: 17.0 sq. mi.; **Water:** 0.3 sq. mi.

Hidden Valley CDP
Lat: 39-09-44 N Long: 84-50-35 W
Pop: 2,116 (1990) **Pop Density:** 431.8
Land: 4.9 sq. mi.; **Water:** 0.3 sq. mi.

Hogan Township
Lat: 39-03-45 N Long: 84-58-37 W
Pop: 936 (1990); 932 (1980) **Pop Density:** 60.8
Land: 15.4 sq. mi.; **Water:** 0.1 sq. mi.

Jackson Township
Lat: 39-15-17 N Long: 85-03-09 W
Pop: 1,184 (1990); 1,124 (1980) **Pop Density:** 47.9
Land: 24.7 sq. mi.; **Water:** 0.0 sq. mi.

Kelso Township
Lat: 39-15-19 N Long: 84-58-17 W
Pop: 1,819 (1990); 1,706 (1980) **Pop Density:** 71.1
Land: 25.6 sq. mi.; **Water:** 0.0 sq. mi.

Lawrenceburg City
ZIP: 47025 Lat: 39-06-01 N Long: 84-52-10 W
Pop: 4,375 (1990); 4,403 (1980) **Pop Density:** 1041.7
Land: 4.2 sq. mi.; **Water:** 0.1 sq. mi. **Elev:** 478 ft.
Not coextensive with the town of the same name.
Name origin: Named by founder Samuel C. Vance for his wife's maiden name (Lawrence).

***Lawrenceburg** Township
ZIP: 47025 Lat: 39-07-03 N Long: 84-52-14 W
Pop: 9,923 (1990); 9,647 (1980) **Pop Density:** 418.7
Land: 23.7 sq. mi.; **Water:** 0.6 sq. mi.

INDIANA, Dearborn County

Logan
Township
Lat: 39-15-03 N **Long:** 84-54-12 W
Pop: 2,129 (1990); 1,657 (1980) **Pop Density:** 119.6
Land: 17.8 sq. mi.; **Water:** 0.1 sq. mi.

Manchester
Township
ZIP: 47001 **Lat:** 39-08-53 N **Long:** 85-00-39 W
Pop: 2,571 (1990); 2,342 (1980) **Pop Density:** 56.4
Land: 45.6 sq. mi.; **Water:** 0.0 sq. mi.

Miller
Township
Lat: 39-10-48 N **Long:** 84-52-27 W
Pop: 4,761 (1990); 2,903 (1980) **Pop Density:** 182.4
Land: 26.1 sq. mi.; **Water:** 0.2 sq. mi.

Moores Hill
Town
ZIP: 47032 **Lat:** 39-06-48 N **Long:** 85-05-20 W
Pop: 649 (1990); 566 (1980) **Pop Density:** 1622.5
Land: 0.4 sq. mi.; **Water:** 0.0 sq. mi. **Elev:** 994 ft.
Founded 1828.
Name origin: For mill owner Adam Moore.

St. Leon
Town
Lat: 39-17-14 N **Long:** 84-58-01 W
Pop: 493 (1990); 515 (1980) **Pop Density:** 69.4
Land: 7.1 sq. mi.; **Water:** 0.0 sq. mi. **Elev:** 1016 ft.

Sparta
Township
Lat: 39-04-58 N **Long:** 85-03-35 W
Pop: 2,531 (1990); 2,314 (1980) **Pop Density:** 86.1
Land: 29.4 sq. mi.; **Water:** 0.0 sq. mi.

Washington
Township
Lat: 39-01-40 N **Long:** 84-58-03 W
Pop: 1,387 (1990); 1,210 (1980) **Pop Density:** 102.7
Land: 13.5 sq. mi.; **Water:** 0.0 sq. mi.

West Harrison
Town
ZIP: 47060 **Lat:** 39-15-40 N **Long:** 84-49-15 W
Pop: 318 (1990); 328 (1980) **Pop Density:** 3180.0
Land: 0.1 sq. mi.; **Water:** 0.0 sq. mi. **Elev:** 520 ft.
Settled 1812.
Name origin: For Harrison Township.

York
Township
ZIP: 47022 **Lat:** 39-11-14 N **Long:** 84-57-17 W
Pop: 868 (1990); 779 (1980) **Pop Density:** 46.9
Land: 18.5 sq. mi.; **Water:** 0.0 sq. mi.

Decatur County
County Seat: Greensburg (ZIP: 47240)

Pop: 23,645 (1990); 23,841 (1980) **Pop Density:** 63.5
Land: 372.6 sq. mi.; **Water:** 0.8 sq. mi. **Area Code:** 812
In southeast IN, east of Columbus; established Dec 31, 1821 from Indian lands.
Name origin: For Stephen Decatur (1779–1820), U.S. naval officer during the War of 1812 and in actions against the Barbary pirates near Tripoli, who said, "... may she always be in the right; but our country, right or wrong!"

Adams
Township
Lat: 39-24-52 N **Long:** 85-33-55 W
Pop: 1,889 (1990); 1,903 (1980) **Pop Density:** 57.2
Land: 33.0 sq. mi.; **Water:** 0.0 sq. mi.

Clay
Township
Lat: 39-18-45 N **Long:** 85-37-08 W
Pop: 1,413 (1990); 1,507 (1980) **Pop Density:** 27.9
Land: 50.7 sq. mi.; **Water:** 0.1 sq. mi.

Clinton
Township
Lat: 39-25-18 N **Long:** 85-28-03 W
Pop: 494 (1990); 497 (1980) **Pop Density:** 22.1
Land: 22.4 sq. mi.; **Water:** 0.0 sq. mi.

Fugit
Township
Lat: 39-24-00 N **Long:** 85-21-09 W
Pop: 1,639 (1990); 1,520 (1980) **Pop Density:** 38.5
Land: 42.6 sq. mi.; **Water:** 0.4 sq. mi.

Greensburg
City
ZIP: 47240 **Lat:** 39-20-28 N **Long:** 85-28-49 W
Pop: 9,286 (1990); 9,254 (1980) **Pop Density:** 2579.4
Land: 3.6 sq. mi.; **Water:** 0.0 sq. mi. **Elev:** 971 ft.
Name origin: For Greensburg, PA.

Jackson
Township
Lat: 39-11-54 N **Long:** 85-38-29 W
Pop: 1,000 (1990); 1,092 (1980) **Pop Density:** 24.8
Land: 40.4 sq. mi.; **Water:** 0.0 sq. mi.

Marion
Township
Lat: 39-14-30 N **Long:** 85-27-08 W
Pop: 1,653 (1990); 1,651 (1980) **Pop Density:** 29.8
Land: 55.4 sq. mi.; **Water:** 0.1 sq. mi.

Milford
Town
ZIP: 47240 **Lat:** 39-21-00 N **Long:** 85-37-10 W
Pop: 126 (1990); 177 (1980) **Pop Density:** 1260.0
Land: 0.1 sq. mi.; **Water:** 0.0 sq. mi. **Elev:** 843 ft.

Millhousen
Town
ZIP: 47261 **Lat:** 39-12-38 N **Long:** 85-26-07 W
Pop: 151 (1990); 214 (1980) **Pop Density:** 151.0
Land: 1.0 sq. mi.; **Water:** 0.0 sq. mi. **Elev:** 904 ft.
Settled 1838.
Name origin: For a town in Germany.

Newpoint
Town
Lat: 39-18-32 N **Long:** 85-19-48 W
Pop: 296 (1990); 296 (1980) **Pop Density:** 986.7
Land: 0.3 sq. mi.; **Water:** 0.0 sq. mi.
Name origin: Previously called Crackway and Rossburg.

American Places Dictionary — INDIANA, Dekalb County

St. Paul — Town
Lat: 39-25-37 N **Long:** 85-37-39 W
Pop: 576 (1990); 976 (1980) **Pop Density:** 2880.0
Land: 0.2 sq. mi.; **Water:** 0.0 sq. mi. **Elev:** 858 ft.
Settled 1853. Part of the town is also in Shelby County.
Name origin: For early settler Jonathan Paul, with 'saint' added for euphony.

Salt Creek — Township
Lat: 39-18-34 N **Long:** 85-20-31 W
Pop: 1,187 (1990); 1,119 (1980) **Pop Density:** 39.8
Land: 29.8 sq. mi.; **Water:** 0.0 sq. mi.

Sand Creek — Township
Lat: 39-12-24 N **Long:** 85-33-11 W
Pop: 3,040 (1990); 3,206 (1980) **Pop Density:** 70.5
Land: 43.1 sq. mi.; **Water:** 0.0 sq. mi.

Washington — Township
ZIP: 47240 **Lat:** 39-20-13 N **Long:** 85-28-22 W
Pop: 11,330 (1990); 11,346 (1980) **Pop Density:** 205.6
Land: 55.1 sq. mi.; **Water:** 0.2 sq. mi.

Westport — Town
ZIP: 47283 **Lat:** 39-10-33 N **Long:** 85-34-30 W
Pop: 1,478 (1990); 1,450 (1980) **Pop Density:** 1136.9
Land: 1.3 sq. mi.; **Water:** 0.0 sq. mi. **Elev:** 806 ft.
Settled 1836.

Dekalb County
County Seat: Auburn (ZIP: 46706)

Pop: 35,324 (1990); 33,606 (1980) **Pop Density:** 97.3
Land: 362.9 sq. mi.; **Water:** 1.0 sq. mi. **Area Code:** 219
On the northeastern border of IN. north of Ft. Wayne; established Feb 7, 1835 from Allen County.
Name origin: For Johann (1721–80), Baron de Kalb, German-born French soldier who fought with the Americans during the Revolutionary War.

Altona — Town
ZIP: 46738 **Lat:** 41-21-03 N **Long:** 85-09-10 W
Pop: 156 (1990); 263 (1980) **Pop Density:** 520.0
Land: 0.3 sq. mi.; **Water:** 0.0 sq. mi. **Elev:** 890 ft.
Name origin: For Altona, Germany.

Ashley — Town
ZIP: 46705 **Lat:** 41-31-27 N **Long:** 85-04-04 W
Pop: 488 (1990); 528 (1980) **Pop Density:** 976.0
Land: 0.5 sq. mi.; **Water:** 0.0 sq. mi. **Elev:** 1000 ft.
Part of the town is also in Steuben County.
Name origin: Named in 1892 for Ashley, PA.

Auburn — City
ZIP: 46706 **Lat:** 41-21-47 N **Long:** 85-03-27 W
Pop: 9,379 (1990); 8,122 (1980) **Pop Density:** 2084.2
Land: 4.5 sq. mi.; **Water:** 0.0 sq. mi. **Elev:** 869 ft.
Founded 1836.
Name origin: For Auburn, England.

Butler — City
ZIP: 46721 **Lat:** 41-25-45 N **Long:** 84-52-14 W
Pop: 2,601 (1990); 2,509 (1980) **Pop Density:** 1734.0
Land: 1.5 sq. mi.; **Water:** 0.0 sq. mi. **Elev:** 876 ft.
Name origin: For pioneer David Butler. Previously called Norristown.

*Butler — Township
ZIP: 46721 **Lat:** 41-17-34 N **Long:** 85-08-15 W
Pop: 1,606 (1990); 1,612 (1980) **Pop Density:** 67.8
Land: 23.7 sq. mi.; **Water:** 0.1 sq. mi.

Concord — Township
ZIP: 46785 **Lat:** 41-20-08 N **Long:** 84-54-39 W
Pop: 1,166 (1990); 1,195 (1980) **Pop Density:** 65.1
Land: 17.9 sq. mi.; **Water:** 0.0 sq. mi.

Corunna — Town
ZIP: 46730 **Lat:** 41-26-08 N **Long:** 85-08-39 W
Pop: 241 (1990); 304 (1980) **Pop Density:** 1205.0
Land: 0.2 sq. mi.; **Water:** 0.0 sq. mi. **Elev:** 980 ft.
Settled 1855.
Name origin: For Corunna, MI.

Fairfield — Township
ZIP: 46730 **Lat:** 41-28-44 N **Long:** 85-07-57 W
Pop: 1,220 (1990); 1,119 (1980) **Pop Density:** 34.2
Land: 35.7 sq. mi.; **Water:** 0.3 sq. mi.

Franklin — Township
Lat: 41-28-53 N **Long:** 84-54-21 W
Pop: 1,087 (1990); 1,050 (1980) **Pop Density:** 31.1
Land: 35.0 sq. mi.; **Water:** 0.1 sq. mi.

Garrett — City
ZIP: 46738 **Lat:** 41-20-59 N **Long:** 85-07-39 W
Pop: 5,349 (1990); 4,751 (1980) **Pop Density:** 2325.7
Land: 2.3 sq. mi.; **Water:** 0.0 sq. mi. **Elev:** 880 ft.
Name origin: For B & O Railroad president John W. Garrett.

Grant — Township
Lat: 41-25-15 N **Long:** 85-01-11 W
Pop: 2,801 (1990); 2,769 (1980) **Pop Density:** 161.0
Land: 17.4 sq. mi.; **Water:** 0.0 sq. mi.

Hamilton — Town
ZIP: 46742 **Lat:** 41-31-27 N **Long:** 84-54-57 W
Pop: 94 (1990); 121 (1980) **Pop Density:** 235.0
Land: 0.4 sq. mi.; **Water:** 0.0 sq. mi. **Elev:** 900 ft.
Founded 1823. Part of the town is also in Steuben County.
Name origin: For Alexander Hamilton (1755–1804), first U.S. secretary of the treasury (1789–95).

INDIANA, Dekalb County

Jackson
Township
Lat: 41-18-29 N Long: 85-01-00 W
Pop: 2,099 (1990); 1,899 (1980)   Pop Density: 59.1
Land: 35.5 sq. mi.; Water: 0.1 sq. mi.

Keyser
Township
ZIP: 46738   Lat: 41-21-03 N Long: 85-08-06 W
Pop: 6,459 (1990); 6,148 (1980)   Pop Density: 269.1
Land: 24.0 sq. mi.; Water: 0.0 sq. mi.

Newville
Township
ZIP: 46721   Lat: 41-18-50 N Long: 84-49-30 W
Pop: 500 (1990); 430 (1980)   Pop Density: 36.2
Land: 13.8 sq. mi.; Water: 0.0 sq. mi.

Richland
Township
Lat: 41-24-43 N Long: 85-08-31 W
Pop: 1,153 (1990); 1,201 (1980)   Pop Density: 49.1
Land: 23.5 sq. mi.; Water: 0.1 sq. mi.

St. Joe
Town
Lat: 41-18-53 N Long: 84-54-12 W
Pop: 452 (1990); 546 (1980)   Pop Density: 1506.7
Land: 0.3 sq. mi.; Water: 0.0 sq. mi.   Elev: 825 ft.
Name origin: From a nickname for the St. Joseph River, which crosses the southeastern corner of the county.

Smithfield
Township
Lat: 41-29-01 N Long: 85-01-29 W
Pop: 1,520 (1990); 1,590 (1980)   Pop Density: 43.6
Land: 34.9 sq. mi.; Water: 0.1 sq. mi.

Spencer
Township
Lat: 41-17-32 N Long: 84-54-16 W
Pop: 923 (1990); 1,016 (1980)   Pop Density: 51.3
Land: 18.0 sq. mi.; Water: 0.1 sq. mi.

Stafford
Township
ZIP: 46721   Lat: 41-23-50 N Long: 84-49-19 W
Pop: 275 (1990); 239 (1980)   Pop Density: 18.6
Land: 14.8 sq. mi.; Water: 0.0 sq. mi.

Troy
Township
Lat: 41-28-50 N Long: 84-49-51 W
Pop: 302 (1990); 311 (1980)   Pop Density: 20.3
Land: 14.9 sq. mi.; Water: 0.0 sq. mi.

Union
Township
ZIP: 46706   Lat: 41-22-24 N Long: 85-01-22 W
Pop: 10,404 (1990); 9,293 (1980)   Pop Density: 587.8
Land: 17.7 sq. mi.; Water: 0.0 sq. mi.

Waterloo
Town
ZIP: 46793   Lat: 41-26-00 N Long: 85-01-35 W
Pop: 2,040 (1990); 1,951 (1980)   Pop Density: 1457.1
Land: 1.4 sq. mi.; Water: 0.0 sq. mi.   Elev: 904 ft.
Settled 1841.
Name origin: For the Battle of Waterloo, site of Napoleon I's (1769–1821) defeat.

Wilmington
Township
ZIP: 46721   Lat: 41-23-56 N Long: 84-54-27 W
Pop: 3,809 (1990); 3,734 (1980)   Pop Density: 105.8
Land: 36.0 sq. mi.; Water: 0.0 sq. mi.

Delaware County
County Seat: Muncie (ZIP: 47305)

Pop: 119,659 (1990); 128,587 (1980)   Pop Density: 304.2
Land: 393.3 sq. mi.; Water: 2.6 sq. mi.   Area Code: 317
In east-central IN.; organized Jan 26, 1827 from Indian lands.
Name origin: For the Delaware Indians (also called Leni or Leni-Lenape), in turn named for Thomas West (1577–1618), Lord Delaware (or De La Warr).

Albany
Town
ZIP: 47320   Lat: 40-18-06 N Long: 85-14-11 W
Pop: 2,151 (1990); 2,625 (1980)   Pop Density: 2151.0
Land: 1.0 sq. mi.; Water: 0.0 sq. mi.   Elev: 954 ft.
Founded 1833. Part of the town is in Randolph County.
Name origin: For Albany, NY.

Center
Township
ZIP: 47302   Lat: 40-11-29 N Long: 85-23-09 W
Pop: 74,656 (1990); 80,012 (1980)   Pop Density: 2151.5
Land: 34.7 sq. mi.; Water: 0.0 sq. mi.

Chesterfield
Town
ZIP: 46017   Lat: 40-06-48 N Long: 85-34-24 W
Pop: 9 (1990); 2,701 (1980)   Pop Density: 90.0
Land: 0.1 sq. mi.; Water: 0.0 sq. mi.   Elev: 908 ft.
Part of the town is also in Madison County.

Daleville
Town
ZIP: 47334   Lat: 40-07-07 N Long: 85-33-22 W
Pop: 1,681 (1990)   Pop Density: 933.9
Land: 1.8 sq. mi.; Water: 0.0 sq. mi.   Elev: 912 ft.

Delaware
Township
Lat: 40-16-08 N Long: 85-16-20 W
Pop: 3,781 (1990); 4,267 (1980)   Pop Density: 128.6
Land: 29.4 sq. mi.; Water: 0.1 sq. mi.

Eaton
Town
ZIP: 47338   Lat: 40-20-25 N Long: 85-21-17 W
Pop: 1,614 (1990); 1,804 (1980)   Pop Density: 1467.3
Land: 1.1 sq. mi.; Water: 0.0 sq. mi.   Elev: 914 ft.
Founded 1854.
Name origin: Named in 1854 for an early settler.

Gaston
Town
ZIP: 47342   Lat: 40-18-48 N Long: 85-30-04 W
Pop: 979 (1990); 1,150 (1980)   Pop Density: 3263.3
Land: 0.3 sq. mi.; Water: 0.0 sq. mi.   Elev: 890 ft.
Name origin: Named in 1880s when natural gas was discovered. Previously called New Corner.

Hamilton
Township
ZIP: 47302   Lat: 40-16-11 N Long: 85-23-19 W
Pop: 7,052 (1990); 7,525 (1980)   Pop Density: 236.6
Land: 29.8 sq. mi.; Water: 0.0 sq. mi.

Harrison
Township
Lat: 40-15-36 N **Long:** 85-30-34 W
Pop: 3,336 (1990); 3,585 (1980) **Pop Density:** 78.7
Land: 42.4 sq. mi.; **Water:** 0.0 sq. mi.

Liberty
Township
ZIP: 47383 **Lat:** 40-11-27 N **Long:** 85-16-20 W
Pop: 4,917 (1990); 5,487 (1980) **Pop Density:** 140.9
Land: 34.9 sq. mi.; **Water:** 0.1 sq. mi.

Monroe
Township
Lat: 40-06-49 N **Long:** 85-23-15 W
Pop: 3,458 (1990); 3,839 (1980) **Pop Density:** 114.5
Land: 30.2 sq. mi.; **Water:** 0.0 sq. mi.

Mount Pleasant
Township
ZIP: 47396 **Lat:** 40-11-11 N **Long:** 85-30-20 W
Pop: 10,711 (1990); 10,812 (1980) **Pop Density:** 316.9
Land: 33.8 sq. mi.; **Water:** 0.2 sq. mi.

Muncie
City
ZIP: 47302 **Lat:** 40-11-50 N **Long:** 85-23-26 W
Pop: 71,035 (1990); 77,216 (1980) **Pop Density:** 3115.6
Land: 22.8 sq. mi.; **Water:** 0.0 sq. mi. **Elev:** 952 ft.
In east-central IN, 48 mi. northeast of Indianapolis. Founded 1824; incorporated as town 1854, as city 1865.
Name origin: Named in 1845 because so many of the Delaware Indians of the Munsee clan lived here. Previously called Munseetown or Muncey Town; sometimes spelled Monsy or Monthee.

Niles
Township
ZIP: 47338 **Lat:** 40-20-31 N **Long:** 85-16-52 W
Pop: 1,217 (1990); 1,333 (1980) **Pop Density:** 41.1
Land: 29.6 sq. mi.; **Water:** 0.1 sq. mi.

Perry
Township
Lat: 40-06-52 N **Long:** 85-16-36 W
Pop: 1,377 (1990); 1,528 (1980) **Pop Density:** 48.8
Land: 28.2 sq. mi.; **Water:** 1.9 sq. mi.

Salem
Township
ZIP: 47334 **Lat:** 40-07-01 N **Long:** 85-30-33 W
Pop: 3,899 (1990); 4,303 (1980) **Pop Density:** 110.8
Land: 35.2 sq. mi.; **Water:** 0.1 sq. mi.

Selma
Town
ZIP: 47383 **Lat:** 40-11-18 N **Long:** 85-16-27 W
Pop: 800 (1990); 1,056 (1980) **Pop Density:** 1000.0
Land: 0.8 sq. mi.; **Water:** 0.0 sq. mi. **Elev:** 1009 ft.
Settled 1852.

Union
Township
Lat: 40-20-52 N **Long:** 85-23-02 W
Pop: 3,054 (1990); 3,428 (1980) **Pop Density:** 103.2
Land: 29.6 sq. mi.; **Water:** 0.1 sq. mi.

Washington
Township
Lat: 40-20-59 N **Long:** 85-31-00 W
Pop: 2,201 (1990); 2,468 (1980) **Pop Density:** 62.2
Land: 35.4 sq. mi.; **Water:** 0.0 sq. mi.

Yorktown
Town
ZIP: 47396 **Lat:** 40-10-23 N **Long:** 85-28-42 W
Pop: 4,106 (1990); 3,945 (1980) **Pop Density:** 1415.9
Land: 2.9 sq. mi.; **Water:** 0.1 sq. mi. **Elev:** 907 ft.
Established 1836.
Name origin: For the York tribe of the Delaware Indians.

Dubois County
County Seat: Jasper (ZIP: 47546)

Pop: 36,616 (1990); 34,238 (1980) **Pop Density:** 85.1
Land: 430.1 sq. mi.; **Water:** 5.1 sq. mi. **Area Code:** 812
In south-central IN, northeast of Evansville; established Dec 20, 1817 from Orange and Perry counties.
Name origin: For Toussaint Dubois, a French immigrant who fought with the Americans at the Battle of Tippecanoe (1811).

Bainbridge
Township
ZIP: 47546 **Lat:** 38-23-10 N **Long:** 86-55-57 W
Pop: 13,125 (1990); 12,036 (1980) **Pop Density:** 370.8
Land: 35.4 sq. mi.; **Water:** 0.1 sq. mi.
Name origin: For naval hero William Bainbridge (1774–1833).

Birdseye
Town
ZIP: 47513 **Lat:** 38-18-48 N **Long:** 86-41-45 W
Pop: 472 (1990); 533 (1980) **Pop Density:** 674.3
Land: 0.7 sq. mi.; **Water:** 0.0 sq. mi. **Elev:** 719 ft.
Name origin: Named by a local postmaster, the Rev. 'Bird' Johnson, who helped select site.

Boone
Township
Lat: 38-28-23 N **Long:** 87-00-44 W
Pop: 763 (1990); 741 (1980) **Pop Density:** 23.0
Land: 33.2 sq. mi.; **Water:** 0.3 sq. mi.

Cass
Township
ZIP: 47541 **Lat:** 38-14-31 N **Long:** 87-00-19 W
Pop: 2,072 (1990); 1,911 (1980) **Pop Density:** 53.5
Land: 38.7 sq. mi.; **Water:** 0.2 sq. mi.

Columbia
Township
ZIP: 47527 **Lat:** 38-28-52 N **Long:** 86-44-00 W
Pop: 952 (1990); 840 (1980) **Pop Density:** 26.1
Land: 36.5 sq. mi.; **Water:** 0.1 sq. mi.

Ferdinand
Town
ZIP: 47532 **Lat:** 38-13-41 N **Long:** 86-51-43 W
Pop: 2,318 (1990); 2,192 (1980) **Pop Density:** 1287.8
Land: 1.8 sq. mi.; **Water:** 0.0 sq. mi. **Elev:** 541 ft.
Not coextensive with the town of the same name.
Name origin: For Emperor Ferdinand I (1793–1875) of Austria.

INDIANA, Dubois County

*Ferdinand
Township
ZIP: 47532 Lat: 38-14-32 N Long: 86-51-07 W
Pop: 3,725 (1990); 3,431 (1980) Pop Density: 100.1
Land: 37.2 sq. mi.; Water: 0.1 sq. mi.

Hall
Township
Lat: 38-23-49 N Long: 86-44-15 W
Pop: 927 (1990); 841 (1980) Pop Density: 27.7
Land: 33.5 sq. mi.; Water: 3.1 sq. mi.

Harbison
Township
ZIP: 47527 Lat: 38-28-14 N Long: 86-51-30 W
Pop: 1,510 (1990); 1,524 (1980) Pop Density: 40.1
Land: 37.7 sq. mi.; Water: 0.3 sq. mi.

Holland
Town
ZIP: 47541 Lat: 38-14-45 N Long: 87-02-18 W
Pop: 675 (1990); 683 (1980) Pop Density: 2250.0
Land: 0.3 sq. mi.; Water: 0.0 sq. mi. Elev: 544 ft.
Laid out 1859 by Dutch settler Henry Kunz.
Name origin: Named by Kunz for his native country.

Huntingburg
City
ZIP: 47542 Lat: 38-17-53 N Long: 86-57-31 W
Pop: 5,242 (1990); 5,376 (1980) Pop Density: 1638.1
Land: 3.2 sq. mi.; Water: 0.0 sq. mi. Elev: 475 ft.
Name origin: Descriptively named by its founder, Joseph Geiger, who hunted in the area before settling here.

Jackson
Township
ZIP: 47542 Lat: 38-18-48 N Long: 86-50-02 W
Pop: 1,919 (1990); 1,729 (1980) Pop Density: 55.1
Land: 34.8 sq. mi.; Water: 0.0 sq. mi.

Jasper
City
ZIP: 47546 Lat: 38-23-35 N Long: 86-56-06 W
Pop: 10,030 (1990); 9,097 (1980) Pop Density: 1208.4
Land: 8.3 sq. mi.; Water: 0.0 sq. mi. Elev: 472 ft.
Name origin: For Sgt. William Jasper (1750–79), a Revolutionary War soldier from SC.

Jefferson
Township
Lat: 38-18-07 N Long: 86-43-17 W
Pop: 1,538 (1990); 1,377 (1980) Pop Density: 43.0
Land: 35.8 sq. mi.; Water: 0.0 sq. mi.

Madison
Township
Lat: 38-22-57 N Long: 87-01-46 W
Pop: 1,692 (1990); 1,492 (1980) Pop Density: 47.8
Land: 35.4 sq. mi.; Water: 0.3 sq. mi.

Marion
Township
Lat: 38-24-02 N Long: 86-50-14 W
Pop: 1,646 (1990); 1,567 (1980) Pop Density: 51.0
Land: 32.3 sq. mi.; Water: 0.4 sq. mi.

Patoka
Township
ZIP: 47542 Lat: 38-18-08 N Long: 86-58-50 W
Pop: 6,747 (1990); 6,749 (1980) Pop Density: 170.4
Land: 39.6 sq. mi.; Water: 0.3 sq. mi.

Elkhart County
County Seat: Goshen (ZIP: 46526)

Pop: 156,198 (1990); 137,330 (1980) Pop Density: 336.8
Land: 463.8 sq. mi.; Water: 4.0 sq. mi. Area Code: 219
On the north-central border of IN; organized Jan 29, 1830 from Indian lands.
Name origin: For the Elkhart River, named for the Elkhart Indians. Name is probably a translation of either a Potawatomi or Kickapoo term for 'elk's heart'; early English spelling was Elksheart.

Baugo
Township
ZIP: 46514 Lat: 41-38-35 N Long: 86-01-48 W
Pop: 6,640 (1990); 6,097 (1980) Pop Density: 451.7
Land: 14.7 sq. mi.; Water: 0.3 sq. mi.

Benton
Township
Lat: 41-28-54 N Long: 85-42-26 W
Pop: 1,762 (1990); 1,479 (1980) Pop Density: 49.2
Land: 35.8 sq. mi.; Water: 0.1 sq. mi.

Bristol
Town
ZIP: 46507 Lat: 41-43-15 N Long: 85-49-09 W
Pop: 1,133 (1990); 1,203 (1980) Pop Density: 472.1
Land: 2.4 sq. mi.; Water: 0.1 sq. mi. Elev: 772 ft.
Settled 1830.
Name origin: For Bristol, England.

Cleveland
Township
ZIP: 46514 Lat: 41-43-20 N Long: 86-01-52 W
Pop: 7,843 (1990); 6,547 (1980) Pop Density: 487.1
Land: 16.1 sq. mi.; Water: 0.5 sq. mi.

Clinton
Township
Lat: 41-34-05 N Long: 85-42-28 W
Pop: 3,735 (1990); 2,918 (1980) Pop Density: 104.6
Land: 35.7 sq. mi.; Water: 0.1 sq. mi.

Concord
Township
ZIP: 46514 Lat: 41-39-09 N Long: 85-56-37 W
Pop: 49,126 (1990); 46,214 (1980) Pop Density: 1368.4
Land: 35.9 sq. mi.; Water: 0.7 sq. mi.

Dunlap
CDP
ZIP: 46514 Lat: 41-38-07 N Long: 85-55-09 W
Pop: 5,705 (1990); 5,397 (1980) Pop Density: 1213.8
Land: 4.7 sq. mi.; Water: 0.0 sq. mi.

Elkhart
City
ZIP: 46515 Lat: 41-41-12 N Long: 85-58-07 W
Pop: 43,627 (1990); 41,305 (1980) Pop Density: 2551.3
Land: 17.1 sq. mi.; Water: 0.8 sq. mi. Elev: 750 ft.
In northern IN, 15 mi. east of South Bend.
Name origin: For the Elkhart River, which traverses the county.

INDIANA, Elkhart County

*Elkhart
Township
ZIP: 46526 Lat: 41-33-59 N Long: 85-49-41 W
Pop: 27,995 (1990); 23,202 (1980) Pop Density: 795.3
Land: 35.2 sq. mi.; Water: 0.4 sq. mi.

Goshen
City
ZIP: 46526 Lat: 41-34-42 N Long: 85-50-06 W
Pop: 23,797 (1990); 19,665 (1980) Pop Density: 2105.9
Land: 11.3 sq. mi.; Water: 0.2 sq. mi. Elev: 806 ft.
In northern IN, 22 mi. east-southeast of South Bend. County seat.
Name origin: For the biblical land of plenty, reflecting the rich farmland in the area.

Harrison
Township
Lat: 41-33-56 N Long: 85-56-40 W
Pop: 2,693 (1990); 2,421 (1980) Pop Density: 75.4
Land: 35.7 sq. mi.; Water: 0.0 sq. mi.

Jackson
Township
Lat: 41-28-51 N Long: 85-49-34 W
Pop: 3,232 (1990); 2,642 (1980) Pop Density: 88.8
Land: 36.4 sq. mi.; Water: 0.0 sq. mi.

Jefferson
Township
Lat: 41-38-56 N Long: 85-49-39 W
Pop: 4,604 (1990); 3,687 (1980) Pop Density: 130.8
Land: 35.2 sq. mi.; Water: 0.1 sq. mi.

Locke
Township
Lat: 41-28-48 N Long: 86-01-52 W
Pop: 3,881 (1990); 3,137 (1980) Pop Density: 218.0
Land: 17.8 sq. mi.; Water: 0.0 sq. mi.

Middlebury
Town
ZIP: 46540 Lat: 41-40-23 N Long: 85-42-34 W
Pop: 2,004 (1990); 1,665 (1980) Pop Density: 835.0
Land: 2.4 sq. mi.; Water: 0.0 sq. mi. Elev: 837 ft.
Founded 1835. Not coextensive with the town of the same name.
Name origin: For Middlebury, VT.

*Middlebury
Township
ZIP: 46540 Lat: 41-39-10 N Long: 85-43-04 W
Pop: 5,770 (1990); 4,604 (1980) Pop Density: 162.1
Land: 35.6 sq. mi.; Water: 0.1 sq. mi.

Millersburg
Town
ZIP: 46543 Lat: 41-31-34 N Long: 85-41-44 W
Pop: 854 (1990); 809 (1980) Pop Density: 1708.0
Land: 0.5 sq. mi.; Water: 0.0 sq. mi. Elev: 880 ft.
Name origin: For Solomon Miller, who owned the site.

Nappanee
City
ZIP: 46550 Lat: 41-26-45 N Long: 85-59-04 W
Pop: 5,510 (1990); 4,694 (1980) Pop Density: 1574.3
Land: 3.5 sq. mi.; Water: 0.0 sq. mi. Elev: 878 ft.
Part of the town is also in Kosciusko County.

New Paris
CDP
ZIP: 46553 Lat: 41-30-17 N Long: 85-49-35 W
Pop: 1,007 (1990); 1,062 (1980) Pop Density: 1258.8
Land: 0.8 sq. mi.; Water: 0.0 sq. mi.

Olive
Township
Lat: 41-33-36 N Long: 86-01-52 W
Pop: 2,895 (1990); 2,398 (1980) Pop Density: 159.9
Land: 18.1 sq. mi.; Water: 0.0 sq. mi.

Osolo
Township
ZIP: 46514 Lat: 41-43-27 N Long: 85-56-46 W
Pop: 22,452 (1990); 20,115 (1980) Pop Density: 898.1
Land: 25.0 sq. mi.; Water: 1.0 sq. mi.

Simonton Lake
CDP
Lat: 41-44-51 N Long: 85-58-06 W
Pop: 3,554 (1990); 3,276 (1980) Pop Density: 1015.4
Land: 3.5 sq. mi.; Water: 0.4 sq. mi.

Union
Township
ZIP: 46550 Lat: 41-28-32 N Long: 85-56-20 W
Pop: 5,487 (1990); 4,872 (1980) Pop Density: 153.3
Land: 35.8 sq. mi.; Water: 0.0 sq. mi.

Wakarusa
Town
ZIP: 46573 Lat: 41-32-04 N Long: 86-00-45 W
Pop: 1,667 (1990); 1,281 (1980) Pop Density: 980.6
Land: 1.7 sq. mi.; Water: 0.0 sq. mi. Elev: 847 ft.
Name origin: For the Wakarusa River in KS.

Washington
Township
ZIP: 46507 Lat: 41-43-53 N Long: 85-49-54 W
Pop: 5,136 (1990); 4,681 (1980) Pop Density: 202.2
Land: 25.4 sq. mi.; Water: 0.7 sq. mi.

York
Township
Lat: 41-43-38 N Long: 85-43-06 W
Pop: 2,947 (1990); 2,316 (1980) Pop Density: 116.5
Land: 25.3 sq. mi.; Water: 0.2 sq. mi.

INDIANA, Fayette County

Fayette County
County Seat: Connersville (ZIP: 47331)

Pop: 26,015 (1990); 28,272 (1980) **Pop Density:** 121.0
Land: 215.0 sq. mi.; **Water:** 0.2 sq. mi. **Area Code:** 317

In east-central IN, southwest of Richmond; established Dec 28, 1818 from Wayne County.

Name origin: For the Marquis de Lafayette (1757–1834), French statesman and soldier who fought with Americans during the Revolutionary War.

Columbia Township
ZIP: 47331 Lat: 39-33-36 N Long: 85-12-12 W
Pop: 1,128 (1990); 1,078 (1980) **Pop Density:** 52.5
Land: 21.5 sq. mi.; **Water:** 0.0 sq. mi.

Connersville City
ZIP: 47331 Lat: 39-39-20 N Long: 85-08-26 W
Pop: 15,550 (1990); 17,023 (1980) **Pop Density:** 2073.3
Land: 7.5 sq. mi.; **Water:** 0.0 sq. mi. **Elev:** 828 ft.

In eastern IN, 58 mi. east-southeast of Indianapolis. County seat. Founded 1813; incorporated 1841.

Name origin: For founder John Conner, an Indian trader, entrepreneur, and state senator.

*Connersville Township
ZIP: 47331 Lat: 39-37-49 N Long: 85-10-11 W
Pop: 13,421 (1990); 14,479 (1980) **Pop Density:** 410.4
Land: 32.7 sq. mi.; **Water:** 0.1 sq. mi.

Fairview Township
ZIP: 47331 Lat: 39-39-54 N Long: 85-16-06 W
Pop: 333 (1990); 397 (1980) **Pop Density:** 17.9
Land: 18.6 sq. mi.; **Water:** 0.0 sq. mi.

Glenwood Town
ZIP: 46133 Lat: 39-37-35 N Long: 85-17-59 W
Pop: 110 (1990); 124 (1980) **Pop Density:** 2750.0
Land: 0.04 sq. mi.; **Water:** 0.0 sq. mi. **Elev:** 1082 ft.

Part of the town is also in Rush County.

Harrison Township
ZIP: 47331 Lat: 39-41-09 N Long: 85-10-19 W
Pop: 7,084 (1990); 7,797 (1980) **Pop Density:** 258.5
Land: 27.4 sq. mi.; **Water:** 0.0 sq. mi.

Jackson Township
ZIP: 47331 Lat: 39-33-29 N Long: 85-06-26 W
Pop: 1,387 (1990); 1,582 (1980) **Pop Density:** 50.6
Land: 27.4 sq. mi.; **Water:** 0.0 sq. mi.

Jennings Township
ZIP: 47331 Lat: 39-36-28 N Long: 85-03-50 W
Pop: 752 (1990); 803 (1980) **Pop Density:** 41.3
Land: 18.2 sq. mi.; **Water:** 0.0 sq. mi.

Orange Township
ZIP: 47331 Lat: 39-34-23 N Long: 85-16-33 W
Pop: 770 (1990); 840 (1980) **Pop Density:** 36.3
Land: 21.2 sq. mi.; **Water:** 0.0 sq. mi.

Posey Township
ZIP: 47331 Lat: 39-44-42 N Long: 85-14-33 W
Pop: 545 (1990); 607 (1980) **Pop Density:** 17.5
Land: 31.1 sq. mi.; **Water:** 0.0 sq. mi.

Waterloo Township
ZIP: 47331 Lat: 39-41-41 N Long: 85-04-42 W
Pop: 595 (1990); 689 (1980) **Pop Density:** 34.8
Land: 17.1 sq. mi.; **Water:** 0.0 sq. mi.

Floyd County
County Seat: New Albany (ZIP: 47150)

Pop: 64,404 (1990); 61,205 (1980) **Pop Density:** 435.1
Land: 148.0 sq. mi.; **Water:** 0.3 sq. mi. **Area Code:** 812

On the southeast border of IN, northwest of Louisville, KY; organized Jan 2, 1819 from Harrison and Clark counties.

Name origin: According to most sources, for Gen. John Floyd (1783–1837), VA jurist, U.S. congressman from VA (1817–29), and governor (1830–34). Others claim Col. Davis Floyd, an associate of Aaron Burr and an important member of the IN General Assembly.

Franklin Township
Lat: 38-14-06 N Long: 85-54-50 W
Pop: 1,307 (1990); 1,213 (1980) **Pop Density:** 56.6
Land: 23.1 sq. mi.; **Water:** 0.0 sq. mi.

Galena CDP
ZIP: 47119 Lat: 38-21-01 N Long: 85-56-21 W
Pop: 1,231 (1990); 1,186 (1980) **Pop Density:** 473.5
Land: 2.6 sq. mi.; **Water:** 0.0 sq. mi.

Georgetown Town
ZIP: 47122 Lat: 38-17-57 N Long: 85-58-14 W
Pop: 2,092 (1990); 1,494 (1980) **Pop Density:** 1394.7
Land: 1.5 sq. mi.; **Water:** 0.0 sq. mi. **Elev:** 714 ft.

Founded 1833. Not coextensive with the town of the same name.

Name origin: For town father George Waltz.

*Georgetown — Township
ZIP: 47122 Lat: 38-18-02 N Long: 85-56-56 W
Pop: 7,053 (1990); 6,110 (1980) Pop Density: 264.2
Land: 26.7 sq. mi.; Water: 0.0 sq. mi.

Greenville — Town
ZIP: 47124 Lat: 38-22-15 N Long: 85-59-04 W
Pop: 508 (1990); 537 (1980) Pop Density: 846.7
Land: 0.6 sq. mi.; Water: 0.0 sq. mi. Elev: 808 ft.
Settled 1807. Not coextensive with the town of the same name.
Name origin: For Greenville Township.

*Greenville — Township
ZIP: 47124 Lat: 38-22-06 N Long: 85-58-42 W
Pop: 5,190 (1990); 4,729 (1980) Pop Density: 155.4
Land: 33.4 sq. mi.; Water: 0.0 sq. mi.

Lafayette — Township
ZIP: 47119 Lat: 38-21-37 N Long: 85-52-53 W
Pop: 5,896 (1990); 5,273 (1980) Pop Density: 225.9
Land: 26.1 sq. mi.; Water: 0.0 sq. mi.

New Albany — City
ZIP: 47150 Lat: 38-18-14 N Long: 85-49-32 W
Pop: 36,322 (1990); 37,103 (1980) Pop Density: 2710.6
Land: 13.4 sq. mi.; Water: 0.2 sq. mi. Elev: 467 ft.
In southern IN on the Ohio River, across from Louisville, KY. Founded 1813 by three Scibner brothers from NY. Not coextensive with the town of the same name.
Name origin: For Albany, NY.

*New Albany — Township
ZIP: 47150 Lat: 38-18-45 N Long: 85-49-56 W
Pop: 44,958 (1990); 43,880 (1980) Pop Density: 1161.7
Land: 38.7 sq. mi.; Water: 0.2 sq. mi.

Fountain County
County Seat: Covington (ZIP: 47932)

Pop: 17,808 (1990); 19,033 (1980) Pop Density: 45.0
Land: 395.7 sq. mi.; Water: 2.2 sq. mi. Area Code: 317
On the central western border of IN, north of Terre Haute; established Dec 20, 1825 from Montgomery County.
Name origin: For Maj. James Fountain (originally Fontaine) (?–1790), KY army officer killed near Ft. Wayne in the Battle of Maumee.

Attica — City
ZIP: 47918 Lat: 40-17-15 N Long: 87-14-47 W
Pop: 3,457 (1990); 3,841 (1980) Pop Density: 2304.7
Land: 1.5 sq. mi.; Water: 0.0 sq. mi. Elev: 547 ft.
Established 1825.
Name origin: For the ancient Greek province.

Cain — Township
Lat: 40-04-58 N Long: 87-09-05 W
Pop: 1,160 (1990); 1,242 (1980) Pop Density: 29.0
Land: 40.0 sq. mi.; Water: 0.0 sq. mi.

Covington — City
ZIP: 47932 Lat: 40-08-23 N Long: 87-23-28 W
Pop: 2,747 (1990); 2,883 (1980) Pop Density: 2289.2
Land: 1.2 sq. mi.; Water: 0.0 sq. mi. Elev: 560 ft.
Incorporated 1851.
Name origin: For Covington, VA, home of the first settlers.

Davis — Township
Lat: 40-18-26 N Long: 87-07-41 W
Pop: 527 (1990); 571 (1980) Pop Density: 22.3
Land: 23.6 sq. mi.; Water: 0.2 sq. mi.

Fulton — Township
Lat: 39-59-05 N Long: 87-22-16 W
Pop: 725 (1990); 731 (1980) Pop Density: 23.8
Land: 30.4 sq. mi.; Water: 0.3 sq. mi.

Hillsboro — Town
ZIP: 47949 Lat: 40-06-34 N Long: 87-09-25 W
Pop: 499 (1990); 561 (1980) Pop Density: 1663.3
Land: 0.3 sq. mi.; Water: 0.0 sq. mi. Elev: 715 ft.
Settled 1826.
Name origin: For its descriptive connotations.

Jackson — Township
Lat: 39-59-45 N Long: 87-08-51 W
Pop: 635 (1990); 662 (1980) Pop Density: 17.6
Land: 36.0 sq. mi.; Water: 0.1 sq. mi.

Kingman — Town
ZIP: 47952 Lat: 39-57-56 N Long: 87-16-41 W
Pop: 561 (1990); 566 (1980) Pop Density: 701.3
Land: 0.8 sq. mi.; Water: 0.0 sq. mi. Elev: 705 ft.

Logan — Township
Lat: 40-17-14 N Long: 87-12-38 W
Pop: 4,064 (1990); 4,456 (1980) Pop Density: 183.1
Land: 22.2 sq. mi.; Water: 0.4 sq. mi.

Mellott — Town
ZIP: 47958 Lat: 40-09-50 N Long: 87-08-57 W
Pop: 222 (1990); 294 (1980) Pop Density: 1110.0
Land: 0.2 sq. mi.; Water: 0.0 sq. mi. Elev: 712 ft.
Founded 1882.
Name origin: For its founders, John and Syrena Mellott.

Millcreek — Township
Lat: 40-00-32 N Long: 87-15-29 W
Pop: 1,450 (1990); 1,475 (1980) Pop Density: 34.0
Land: 42.7 sq. mi.; Water: 0.2 sq. mi.

Newtown — Town
ZIP: 47969 Lat: 40-12-15 N Long: 87-08-52 W
Pop: 243 (1990); 277 (1980) Pop Density: 486.0
Land: 0.5 sq. mi.; Water: 0.0 sq. mi. Elev: 711 ft.
Name origin: For Sgt. John Newton, a Revolutionary War hero.

Richland
Township
Lat: 40-12-06 N **Long:** 87-08-41 W
Pop: 1,015 (1990); 1,149 (1980) **Pop Density:** 19.5
Land: 52.0 sq. mi.; **Water:** 0.0 sq. mi.

Shawnee
Township
Lat: 40-13-17 N **Long:** 87-15-37 W
Pop: 585 (1990); 657 (1980) **Pop Density:** 16.9
Land: 34.7 sq. mi.; **Water:** 0.1 sq. mi.

Troy
Township
Lat: 40-09-25 N **Long:** 87-21-00 W
Pop: 3,840 (1990); 4,019 (1980) **Pop Density:** 87.7
Land: 43.8 sq. mi.; **Water:** 0.6 sq. mi.

Van Buren
Township
Lat: 40-07-48 N **Long:** 87-15-16 W
Pop: 3,081 (1990); 3,266 (1980) **Pop Density:** 82.2
Land: 37.5 sq. mi.; **Water:** 0.0 sq. mi.

Veedersburg
Town
ZIP: 47987 **Lat:** 40-06-45 N **Long:** 87-15-33 W
Pop: 2,192 (1990); 2,261 (1980) **Pop Density:** 913.3
Land: 2.4 sq. mi.; **Water:** 0.0 sq. mi. **Elev:** 612 ft.
Founded 1872.
Name origin: For its founder, Peter S. Veeder.

Wabash
Township
Lat: 40-03-30 N **Long:** 87-21-25 W
Pop: 726 (1990); 805 (1980) **Pop Density:** 22.0
Land: 33.0 sq. mi.; **Water:** 0.3 sq. mi.

Wallace
Town
ZIP: 47988 **Lat:** 39-59-16 N **Long:** 87-08-51 W
Pop: 89 (1990); 88 (1980) **Pop Density:** 890.0
Land: 0.1 sq. mi.; **Water:** 0.0 sq. mi. **Elev:** 708 ft.
Settled 1832.
Name origin: For Gov. David Wallace.

Franklin County
County Seat: Brookville (ZIP: 47012)

Pop: 19,580 (1990); 19,612 (1980) **Pop Density:** 50.7
Land: 386.0 sq. mi.; **Water:** 5.3 sq. mi. **Area Code:** 317
On southeastern border of IN, south of Richmond; established Nov 27, 1810 (prior to statehood) from Wayne and Ripley counties.
Name origin: For Benjamin Franklin (1706–90), patriot, diplomat, and statesman.

Batesville
City
ZIP: 47006 **Lat:** 39-18-18 N **Long:** 85-14-10 W
Pop: 851 (1990); 683 (1980) **Pop Density:** 709.2
Land: 1.2 sq. mi.; **Water:** 0.0 sq. mi. **Elev:** 983 ft.
Part of the town is also in Ripley County.
Name origin: For the pioneer Bates family.

Bath
Township
ZIP: 47010 **Lat:** 39-30-06 N **Long:** 84-52-38 W
Pop: 405 (1990); 453 (1980) **Pop Density:** 21.9
Land: 18.5 sq. mi.; **Water:** 0.0 sq. mi.

Blooming Grove
Township
ZIP: 47012 **Lat:** 39-30-01 N **Long:** 85-04-46 W
Pop: 924 (1990); 877 (1980) **Pop Density:** 43.0
Land: 21.5 sq. mi.; **Water:** 0.0 sq. mi.

Brookville
Town
ZIP: 47012 **Lat:** 39-25-24 N **Long:** 85-00-30 W
Pop: 2,529 (1990); 2,980 (1980) **Pop Density:** 2529.0
Land: 1.0 sq. mi.; **Water:** 0.0 sq. mi. **Elev:** 671 ft.
Settled 1808. Not coextensive with the town of the same name.
Name origin: From the maiden name of the mother of Jesse Brooks Thomas, one of the town founders. Shortened from Brooksville to its present form in 1811.

*Brookville
Township
ZIP: 47012 **Lat:** 39-25-16 N **Long:** 85-00-24 W
Pop: 5,565 (1990); 5,294 (1980) **Pop Density:** 86.1
Land: 64.6 sq. mi.; **Water:** 2.4 sq. mi.

Butler
Township
Lat: 39-20-55 N **Long:** 85-07-24 W
Pop: 992 (1990); 942 (1980) **Pop Density:** 32.6
Land: 30.4 sq. mi.; **Water:** 0.0 sq. mi.

Cedar Grove
Town
ZIP: 47016 **Lat:** 39-21-20 N **Long:** 84-56-13 W
Pop: 246 (1990); 217 (1980) **Pop Density:** 2460.0
Land: 0.1 sq. mi.; **Water:** 0.0 sq. mi. **Elev:** 609 ft.
Founded 1837.

Fairfield
Township
ZIP: 47012 **Lat:** 39-30-17 N **Long:** 84-58-20 W
Pop: 276 (1990); 236 (1980) **Pop Density:** 20.8
Land: 13.3 sq. mi.; **Water:** 2.5 sq. mi.

Highland
Township
Lat: 39-20-21 N **Long:** 84-59-47 W
Pop: 1,226 (1990); 1,273 (1980) **Pop Density:** 40.1
Land: 30.6 sq. mi.; **Water:** 0.1 sq. mi.

Laurel
Town
ZIP: 47024 **Lat:** 39-30-05 N **Long:** 85-11-18 W
Pop: 544 (1990); 819 (1980) **Pop Density:** 2720.0
Land: 0.2 sq. mi.; **Water:** 0.0 sq. mi. **Elev:** 809 ft.
Founded 1836. Not coextensive with the town of the same name.
Name origin: For Laurel, DE.

*Laurel
Township
ZIP: 47024 **Lat:** 39-29-03 N **Long:** 85-11-28 W
Pop: 1,462 (1990); 1,739 (1980) **Pop Density:** 46.1
Land: 31.7 sq. mi.; **Water:** 0.0 sq. mi.

Metamora
Township
ZIP: 47030 **Lat:** 39-25-43 N **Long:** 85-07-53 W
Pop: 866 (1990); 977 (1980) **Pop Density:** 44.2
Land: 19.6 sq. mi.; **Water:** 0.0 sq. mi.

Mount Carmel
Town
ZIP: 47012 **Lat:** 39-24-26 N **Long:** 84-52-32 W
Pop: 108 (1990); 151 (1980) **Pop Density:** 2700.0
Land: 0.04 sq. mi.; **Water:** 0.0 sq. mi. **Elev:** 1023 ft.

American Places Dictionary — INDIANA, Fulton County

Oldenburg — Town
ZIP: 47036 Lat: 39-20-18 N Long: 85-12-10 W
Pop: 715 (1990); 770 (1980) Pop Density: 1787.5
Land: 0.4 sq. mi.; Water: 0.0 sq. mi. Elev: 881 ft.

Posey — Township
Lat: 39-28-41 N Long: 85-16-12 W
Pop: 930 (1990); 1,124 (1980) Pop Density: 51.1
Land: 18.2 sq. mi.; Water: 0.0 sq. mi.

Ray — Township
Lat: 39-19-40 N Long: 85-14-29 W
Pop: 3,098 (1990); 2,999 (1980) Pop Density: 77.8
Land: 39.8 sq. mi.; Water: 0.0 sq. mi.

Salt Creek — Township
ZIP: 47024 Lat: 39-24-58 N Long: 85-14-11 W
Pop: 868 (1990); 821 (1980) Pop Density: 31.9
Land: 27.2 sq. mi.; Water: 0.0 sq. mi.

Springfield — Township
Lat: 39-25-44 N Long: 84-52-15 W
Pop: 1,078 (1990); 952 (1980) Pop Density: 30.2
Land: 35.7 sq. mi.; Water: 0.0 sq. mi.

Whitewater — Township
Lat: 39-20-54 N Long: 84-52-18 W
Pop: 1,890 (1990); 1,925 (1980) Pop Density: 54.0
Land: 35.0 sq. mi.; Water: 0.2 sq. mi.

Fulton County
County Seat: Rochester (ZIP: 46975)

Pop: 18,840 (1990); 19,335 (1980) Pop Density: 51.1
Land: 368.5 sq. mi.; Water: 2.9 sq. mi. Area Code: 219
In north-central IN, west of Ft. Wayne; established Feb 7, 1835 from Indian lands.
Name origin: For Robert Fulton (1765–1815), builder of the *Clermont*, the first commercially successful steamboat.

Akron — Town
ZIP: 46910 Lat: 41-02-19 N Long: 86-01-29 W
Pop: 1,001 (1990); 1,045 (1980) Pop Density: 2002.0
Land: 0.5 sq. mi.; Water: 0.0 sq. mi. Elev: 859 ft.
Laid out 1838.
Name origin: For Akron, OH.

Aubbeenaubbee — Township
Lat: 41-07-41 N Long: 86-24-58 W
Pop: 1,262 (1990); 1,306 (1980) Pop Density: 36.6
Land: 34.5 sq. mi.; Water: 0.2 sq. mi.

Fulton — Town
ZIP: 46931 Lat: 40-56-47 N Long: 86-15-50 W
Pop: 371 (1990); 393 (1980) Pop Density: 1855.0
Land: 0.2 sq. mi.; Water: 0.0 sq. mi. Elev: 787 ft.
Name origin: For its county.

Henry — Township
Lat: 41-02-23 N Long: 86-03-12 W
Pop: 2,615 (1990); 2,698 (1980) Pop Density: 56.4
Land: 46.4 sq. mi.; Water: 0.3 sq. mi.

Kewanna — Town
ZIP: 46939 Lat: 41-01-08 N Long: 86-24-45 W
Pop: 542 (1990); 711 (1980) Pop Density: 1084.0
Land: 0.5 sq. mi.; Water: 0.0 sq. mi. Elev: 773 ft.

Liberty — Township
Lat: 40-57-07 N Long: 86-14-57 W
Pop: 1,764 (1990); 1,827 (1980) Pop Density: 37.5
Land: 47.0 sq. mi.; Water: 0.3 sq. mi.

Newcastle — Township
Lat: 41-07-40 N Long: 86-07-45 W
Pop: 1,153 (1990); 1,180 (1980) Pop Density: 34.7
Land: 33.2 sq. mi.; Water: 0.1 sq. mi.

Richland — Township
Lat: 41-08-06 N Long: 86-16-13 W
Pop: 970 (1990); 945 (1980) Pop Density: 25.8
Land: 37.6 sq. mi.; Water: 0.1 sq. mi.

Rochester — City
ZIP: 46975 Lat: 41-03-41 N Long: 86-11-43 W
Pop: 5,969 (1990); 5,050 (1980) Pop Density: 1455.9
Land: 4.1 sq. mi.; Water: 1.1 sq. mi. Elev: 779 ft.
Founded 1835. Not coextensive with the town of the same name.
Name origin: For Rochester, NY.

*Rochester — Township
ZIP: 46975 Lat: 41-03-10 N Long: 86-14-25 W
Pop: 9,110 (1990); 9,057 (1980) Pop Density: 110.4
Land: 82.5 sq. mi.; Water: 1.4 sq. mi.

Union — Township
Lat: 41-02-10 N Long: 86-23-52 W
Pop: 1,355 (1990); 1,588 (1980) Pop Density: 33.4
Land: 40.6 sq. mi.; Water: 0.4 sq. mi.

Wayne — Township
Lat: 40-57-11 N Long: 86-23-41 W
Pop: 611 (1990); 734 (1980) Pop Density: 13.1
Land: 46.7 sq. mi.; Water: 0.1 sq. mi.

INDIANA, Gibson County *American Places Dictionary*

Gibson County
County Seat: Princeton (ZIP: 47670)

Pop: 31,913 (1990); 33,156 (1980)   **Pop Density:** 65.3
Land: 488.9 sq. mi.; **Water:** 10.2 sq. mi.   **Area Code:** 812

On the southwest border of IN, north of Evansville; organized Mar 9, 1813 (prior to statehood) from Knox County.

Name origin: For Gen. John Gibson (1740–1822), an officer in the French and Indian War and the Revolutionary War, jurist, and secretary of IN Territory (1801–16).

Barton   Township
Lat: 38-14-46 N   **Long:** 87-23-26 W
Pop: 1,650 (1990); 1,921 (1980)   **Pop Density:** 33.5
Land: 49.2 sq. mi.; **Water:** 0.1 sq. mi.

Center   Township
Lat: 38-20-31 N   **Long:** 87-27-16 W
Pop: 1,503 (1990); 1,563 (1980)   **Pop Density:** 39.9
Land: 37.7 sq. mi.; **Water:** 0.0 sq. mi.

Columbia   Township
Lat: 38-20-06 N   **Long:** 87-21-41 W
Pop: 4,244 (1990); 4,717 (1980)   **Pop Density:** 138.2
Land: 30.7 sq. mi.; **Water:** 0.4 sq. mi.

Fort Branch   Town
ZIP: 47648   **Lat:** 38-14-48 N   **Long:** 87-34-29 W
Pop: 2,447 (1990); 2,504 (1980)   **Pop Density:** 3495.7
Land: 0.7 sq. mi.; **Water:** 0.0 sq. mi.   **Elev:** 450 ft.

Name origin: For the early military outpost, which was near the present town.

Francisco   Town
ZIP: 47649   **Lat:** 38-20-02 N   **Long:** 87-26-55 W
Pop: 560 (1990); 612 (1980)   **Pop Density:** 1120.0
Land: 0.5 sq. mi.; **Water:** 0.0 sq. mi.   **Elev:** 470 ft.

Haubstadt   Town
ZIP: 47639   **Lat:** 38-12-11 N   **Long:** 87-34-29 W
Pop: 1,455 (1990); 1,389 (1980)   **Pop Density:** 2425.0
Land: 0.6 sq. mi.; **Water:** 0.0 sq. mi.   **Elev:** 473 ft.

Name origin: For pioneer merchant Henry Haub plus German *stadt* 'town, city.' Previously called Haub's City.

Hazleton   Town
ZIP: 47640   **Lat:** 38-29-20 N   **Long:** 87-32-25 W
Pop: 357 (1990); 368 (1980)   **Pop Density:** 1190.0
Land: 0.3 sq. mi.; **Water:** 0.0 sq. mi.   **Elev:** 423 ft.
Founded 1856.

Name origin: For its founder, Gervas Hazelton.

Johnson   Township
Lat: 38-11-39 N   **Long:** 87-34-31 W
Pop: 3,099 (1990); 2,882 (1980)   **Pop Density:** 76.3
Land: 40.6 sq. mi.; **Water:** 0.0 sq. mi.

Mackey   Town
ZIP: 47654   **Lat:** 38-14-59 N   **Long:** 87-23-26 W
Pop: 89 (1990); 165 (1980)   **Pop Density:** 890.0
Land: 0.1 sq. mi.; **Water:** 0.0 sq. mi.   **Elev:** 450 ft.
Founded 1882.

Name origin: For its founder, railroad entrepreneur O. J. Mackey.

Montgomery   Township
Lat: 38-17-14 N   **Long:** 87-43-46 W
Pop: 3,133 (1990); 3,112 (1980)   **Pop Density:** 34.2
Land: 91.6 sq. mi.; **Water:** 5.6 sq. mi.

Oakland City   City
ZIP: 47660   **Lat:** 38-20-24 N   **Long:** 87-20-52 W
Pop: 2,810 (1990); 3,301 (1980)   **Pop Density:** 2554.5
Land: 1.1 sq. mi.; **Water:** 0.0 sq. mi.   **Elev:** 461 ft.

Name origin: Descriptively named in 1856 for its many oak groves.

Owensville   Town
ZIP: 47665   **Lat:** 38-16-18 N   **Long:** 87-41-26 W
Pop: 1,053 (1990); 1,261 (1980)   **Pop Density:** 2106.0
Land: 0.5 sq. mi.; **Water:** 0.0 sq. mi.   **Elev:** 510 ft.
Founded 1817.

Name origin: For Thomas Owen of KY.

Patoka   Town
ZIP: 47666   **Lat:** 38-24-20 N   **Long:** 87-35-15 W
Pop: 704 (1990); 832 (1980)   **Pop Density:** 1005.7
Land: 0.7 sq. mi.; **Water:** 0.0 sq. mi.   **Elev:** 440 ft.

In southwestern IN, 30 mi. north of Evansville. Settled early 1800s. Not coextensive with the town of the same name.

Name origin: For the Patoka River, which traverses the county.

*Patoka   Township
ZIP: 47666   **Lat:** 38-21-02 N   **Long:** 87-35-27 W
Pop: 11,582 (1990); 11,999 (1980)   **Pop Density:** 168.1
Land: 68.9 sq. mi.; **Water:** 0.1 sq. mi.

Princeton   City
ZIP: 47670   **Lat:** 38-21-20 N   **Long:** 87-34-09 W
Pop: 8,127 (1990); 8,976 (1980)   **Pop Density:** 2322.0
Land: 3.5 sq. mi.; **Water:** 0.0 sq. mi.

Name origin: For Capt. William Prince, who arrived in the area in the early 1800s.

Somerville   Town
ZIP: 47683   **Lat:** 38-16-39 N   **Long:** 87-22-36 W
Pop: 223 (1990); 340 (1980)   **Pop Density:** 743.3
Land: 0.3 sq. mi.; **Water:** 0.0 sq. mi.   **Elev:** 480 ft.

Name origin: Named by the post office. Originally known as Summitville.

Union   Township
Lat: 38-14-46 N   **Long:** 87-33-18 W
Pop: 4,031 (1990); 4,197 (1980)   **Pop Density:** 80.0
Land: 50.4 sq. mi.; **Water:** 0.0 sq. mi.

Wabash   Township
Lat: 38-16-14 N   **Long:** 87-52-16 W
Pop: 55 (1990); 88 (1980)   **Pop Density:** 1.5
Land: 35.5 sq. mi.; **Water:** 2.4 sq. mi.

Washington
Township
Lat: 38-26-40 N Long: 87-28-21 W
Pop: 714 (1990); 718 (1980) **Pop Density:** 19.5
Land: 36.6 sq. mi.; **Water:** 0.2 sq. mi.

White River
Township
Lat: 38-26-10 N Long: 87-36-37 W
Pop: 1,902 (1990); 1,959 (1980) **Pop Density:** 40.0
Land: 47.6 sq. mi.; **Water:** 1.4 sq. mi. **Elev:** 397 ft.

Grant County
County Seat: Marion (ZIP: 46953)

Pop: 74,169 (1990); 80,934 (1980) **Pop Density:** 179.1
Land: 414.0 sq. mi.; **Water:** 0.8 sq. mi. **Area Code:** 317
In central IN, northwest of Muncie; organized Feb 10, 1831 from Delaware County.
Name origin: For Samuel and Moses Grant, killed in 1790 in Indian battles in southern IL.

Center
Township
ZIP: 46952 Lat: 40-32-18 N Long: 85-37-15 W
Pop: 25,894 (1990); 28,703 (1980) **Pop Density:** 1035.8
Land: 25.0 sq. mi.; **Water:** 0.1 sq. mi.

Converse
Town
ZIP: 46919 Lat: 40-34-36 N Long: 85-51-24 W
Pop: 179 (1990); 1,279 (1980) **Pop Density:** 895.0
Land: 0.2 sq. mi.; **Water:** 0.0 sq. mi. **Elev:** 832 ft.
Platted 1849. Part of the town is also in Miami County.
Name origin: For a prominent landowner in the area.

Fairmount
Town
ZIP: 46928 Lat: 40-25-00 N Long: 85-38-52 W
Pop: 3,130 (1990); 3,286 (1980) **Pop Density:** 2407.7
Land: 1.3 sq. mi.; **Water:** 0.0 sq. mi. **Elev:** 870 ft.
Founded 1850. Not coextensive with the town of the same name.
Name origin: Named in 1850 for Fairmont Waterworks in Philadelphia, IN.

*Fairmount
Township
ZIP: 46928 Lat: 40-24-51 N Long: 85-36-48 W
Pop: 4,571 (1990); 4,868 (1980) **Pop Density:** 150.4
Land: 30.4 sq. mi.; **Water:** 0.1 sq. mi.

Fowlerton
Town
ZIP: 46930 Lat: 40-24-34 N Long: 85-34-22 W
Pop: 306 (1990); 300 (1980) **Pop Density:** 1530.0
Land: 0.2 sq. mi.; **Water:** 0.0 sq. mi. **Elev:** 883 ft.

Franklin
Township
ZIP: 46952 Lat: 40-31-22 N Long: 85-43-50 W
Pop: 8,245 (1990); 9,405 (1980) **Pop Density:** 228.4
Land: 36.1 sq. mi.; **Water:** 0.0 sq. mi.

Gas City
City
ZIP: 46933 Lat: 40-29-20 N Long: 85-36-27 W
Pop: 6,296 (1990); 6,370 (1980) **Pop Density:** 2518.4
Land: 2.5 sq. mi.; **Water:** 0.0 sq. mi. **Elev:** 853 ft.
Name origin: For natural gas deposits found here in 1887.

Green
Township
Lat: 40-25-22 N Long: 85-49-30 W
Pop: 636 (1990); 715 (1980) **Pop Density:** 22.9
Land: 27.8 sq. mi.; **Water:** 0.0 sq. mi.

Jefferson
Township
ZIP: 46989 Lat: 40-25-54 N Long: 85-30-13 W
Pop: 5,230 (1990); 5,516 (1980) **Pop Density:** 125.1
Land: 41.8 sq. mi.; **Water:** 0.2 sq. mi.

Jonesboro
Town
ZIP: 46938 Lat: 40-28-45 N Long: 85-37-47 W
Pop: 2,073 (1990); 2,279 (1980) **Pop Density:** 2591.3
Land: 0.8 sq. mi.; **Water:** 0.0 sq. mi. **Elev:** 850 ft.
Name origin: For early settler Obediah Jones. Formerly spelled Jonesborough.

Liberty
Township
Lat: 40-25-46 N Long: 85-43-34 W
Pop: 1,003 (1990); 1,418 (1980) **Pop Density:** 23.8
Land: 42.2 sq. mi.; **Water:** 0.0 sq. mi.

Marion
City
ZIP: 46952 Lat: 40-32-56 N Long: 85-40-01 W
Pop: 32,618 (1990); 35,874 (1980) **Pop Density:** 2609.4
Land: 12.5 sq. mi.; **Water:** 0.0 sq. mi. **Elev:** 815 ft.
In north-central IN, 27 mi. northwest of Muncie.
Name origin: For Gen. Francis Marion (c. 1732–95), known as the "Swamp Fox" for his daring exploits during the American Revolution.

Matthews
Town
ZIP: 46957 Lat: 40-23-14 N Long: 85-29-53 W
Pop: 571 (1990); 745 (1980) **Pop Density:** 1903.3
Land: 0.3 sq. mi.; **Water:** 0.0 sq. mi. **Elev:** 870 ft.
Settled 1833.

Mill
Township
ZIP: 46933 Lat: 40-28-52 N Long: 85-37-04 W
Pop: 11,522 (1990); 11,976 (1980) **Pop Density:** 498.8
Land: 23.1 sq. mi.; **Water:** 0.0 sq. mi.

Monroe
Township
Lat: 40-31-51 N Long: 85-29-59 W
Pop: 1,448 (1990); 1,520 (1980) **Pop Density:** 40.9
Land: 35.4 sq. mi.; **Water:** 0.0 sq. mi.

Pleasant
Township
ZIP: 46952 Lat: 40-36-42 N Long: 85-44-00 W
Pop: 6,677 (1990); 7,005 (1980) **Pop Density:** 191.3
Land: 34.9 sq. mi.; **Water:** 0.3 sq. mi.

Richland
Township
Lat: 40-36-08 N Long: 85-49-07 W
Pop: 946 (1990); 979 (1980) **Pop Density:** 39.7
Land: 23.8 sq. mi.; **Water:** 0.0 sq. mi.

Sims
Township
Lat: 40-31-08 N Long: 85-49-42 W
Pop: 1,891 (1990); 2,035 (1980) **Pop Density:** 78.5
Land: 24.1 sq. mi.; **Water:** 0.0 sq. mi.

INDIANA, Grant County

Swayzee
Town
ZIP: 46986 **Lat:** 40-30-24 N **Long:** 85-49-26 W
Pop: 1,059 (1990); 1,127 (1980) **Pop Density:** 2647.5
Land: 0.4 sq. mi.; **Water:** 0.0 sq. mi. **Elev:** 866 ft.
Founded 1881.
Name origin: For landowner James Swayzee.

Sweetser
Town
ZIP: 46987 **Lat:** 40-34-10 N **Long:** 85-46-01 W
Pop: 924 (1990); 944 (1980) **Pop Density:** 1026.7
Land: 0.9 sq. mi.; **Water:** 0.0 sq. mi. **Elev:** 847 ft.
Name origin: For James Sweetser, a local landowner in the 1870s.

Upland
Town
ZIP: 46989 **Lat:** 40-27-46 N **Long:** 85-30-47 W
Pop: 3,295 (1990); 3,335 (1980) **Pop Density:** 890.5
Land: 3.7 sq. mi.; **Water:** 0.0 sq. mi. **Elev:** 932 ft.
Name origin: Named in 1867 by the railroad because it was the highest point between Union City and Logansport.

Van Buren
Town
ZIP: 46991 **Lat:** 40-36-58 N **Long:** 85-30-19 W
Pop: 934 (1990); 935 (1980) **Pop Density:** 2335.0
Land: 0.4 sq. mi.; **Water:** 0.0 sq. mi. **Elev:** 850 ft.
Not coextensive with the town of the same name.
Name origin: For its township. Originally known as Rood's Corner.

*Van Buren
Township
ZIP: 46991 **Lat:** 40-36-30 N **Long:** 85-30-17 W
Pop: 2,012 (1990); 2,055 (1980) **Pop Density:** 56.7
Land: 35.5 sq. mi.; **Water:** 0.0 sq. mi.

Washington
Township
Lat: 40-37-01 N **Long:** 85-37-01 W
Pop: 4,094 (1990); 4,739 (1980) **Pop Density:** 120.1
Land: 34.1 sq. mi.; **Water:** 0.1 sq. mi.

Greene County
County Seat: Bloomfield (ZIP: 47424)

Pop: 30,410 (1990); 30,416 (1980) **Pop Density:** 56.1
Land: 542.1 sq. mi.; **Water:** 3.8 sq. mi. **Area Code:** 812
In southwest IN, southwest of Bloomington; organized Jan 5, 1821 from Knox County.
Name origin: For Gen. Nathanael Greene (1742–86), hero of the Revolutionary War, quartermaster general (1778–80), and commander of the army in the South (1780).

Beech Creek
Township
Lat: 39-07-21 N **Long:** 86-45-10 W
Pop: 1,832 (1990); 1,464 (1980) **Pop Density:** 38.6
Land: 47.4 sq. mi.; **Water:** 0.0 sq. mi.

Bloomfield
Town
ZIP: 47424 **Lat:** 39-01-34 N **Long:** 86-56-13 W
Pop: 2,592 (1990); 2,705 (1980) **Pop Density:** 1851.4
Land: 1.4 sq. mi.; **Water:** 0.0 sq. mi. **Elev:** 605 ft.
Founded 1824.
Name origin: Named by its founder, Hallet Dean, for his birthplace, Bloomfield, NJ.

Cass
Township
ZIP: 47449 **Lat:** 38-55-38 N **Long:** 87-00-36 W
Pop: 386 (1990); 418 (1980) **Pop Density:** 21.9
Land: 17.6 sq. mi.; **Water:** 0.5 sq. mi.

Center
Township
ZIP: 47424 **Lat:** 39-02-05 N **Long:** 86-45-13 W
Pop: 2,439 (1990); 1,912 (1980) **Pop Density:** 50.6
Land: 48.2 sq. mi.; **Water:** 0.0 sq. mi.

Fairplay
Township
ZIP: 47465 **Lat:** 39-02-31 N **Long:** 87-00-15 W
Pop: 643 (1990); 645 (1980) **Pop Density:** 24.9
Land: 25.8 sq. mi.; **Water:** 0.5 sq. mi.

Grant
Township
ZIP: 47465 **Lat:** 39-02-08 N **Long:** 87-05-09 W
Pop: 704 (1990); 764 (1980) **Pop Density:** 28.6
Land: 24.6 sq. mi.; **Water:** 0.0 sq. mi.

Highland
Township
ZIP: 47424 **Lat:** 39-07-17 N **Long:** 86-53-13 W
Pop: 583 (1990); 581 (1980) **Pop Density:** 18.0
Land: 32.4 sq. mi.; **Water:** 0.3 sq. mi.

Jackson
Township
Lat: 38-57-02 N **Long:** 86-45-21 W
Pop: 1,499 (1990); 1,328 (1980) **Pop Density:** 30.6
Land: 49.0 sq. mi.; **Water:** 0.1 sq. mi.

Jasonville
City
ZIP: 47438 **Lat:** 39-09-45 N **Long:** 87-11-58 W
Pop: 2,200 (1990); 2,497 (1980) **Pop Density:** 1692.3
Land: 1.3 sq. mi.; **Water:** 0.0 sq. mi. **Elev:** 640 ft.
Name origin: For Jason Rogers, who purchased the land in 1853.

Jefferson
Township
ZIP: 47471 **Lat:** 39-08-00 N **Long:** 86-58-56 W
Pop: 1,964 (1990); 2,041 (1980) **Pop Density:** 60.8
Land: 32.3 sq. mi.; **Water:** 0.2 sq. mi.

Linton
City
ZIP: 47441 **Lat:** 39-02-09 N **Long:** 87-09-33 W
Pop: 5,814 (1990); 6,315 (1980) **Pop Density:** 1938.0
Land: 3.0 sq. mi.; **Water:** 0.0 sq. mi. **Elev:** 531 ft.
Settled 1816.
Name origin: For congressional candidate, Col. William Linton. Previously called New Jerusalem.

Lyons
Town
ZIP: 47443 **Lat:** 38-59-17 N **Long:** 87-04-53 W
Pop: 753 (1990); 782 (1980) **Pop Density:** 836.7
Land: 0.9 sq. mi.; **Water:** 0.0 sq. mi. **Elev:** 521 ft.
Name origin: For county auditor Joe Lyon, who promoted the use of his name; the *s* was added at a later date.

Newberry
Town
ZIP: 47449 **Lat:** 38-55-25 N **Long:** 87-01-08 W
Pop: 207 (1990); 246 (1980) **Pop Density:** 414.0
Land: 0.5 sq. mi.; **Water:** 0.0 sq. mi. **Elev:** 554 ft.
Founded 1830.
Name origin: Named in 1830 for Newberry, SC.

Richland
Township
ZIP: 47424 **Lat:** 39-02-05 N **Long:** 86-54-00 W
Pop: 4,904 (1990); 4,882 (1980) **Pop Density:** 114.8
Land: 42.7 sq. mi.; **Water:** 0.4 sq. mi.

Smith
Township
ZIP: 47471 **Lat:** 39-07-51 N **Long:** 87-04-47 W
Pop: 401 (1990); 440 (1980) **Pop Density:** 13.5
Land: 29.8 sq. mi.; **Water:** 0.0 sq. mi.

Stafford
Township
Lat: 38-56-55 N **Long:** 87-10-36 W
Pop: 493 (1990); 590 (1980) **Pop Density:** 13.8
Land: 35.8 sq. mi.; **Water:** 0.2 sq. mi.

Stockton
Township
ZIP: 47441 **Lat:** 39-02-20 N **Long:** 87-11-02 W
Pop: 8,313 (1990); 8,658 (1980) **Pop Density:** 229.0
Land: 36.3 sq. mi.; **Water:** 0.5 sq. mi.

Switz City
Town
ZIP: 47465 **Lat:** 39-02-04 N **Long:** 87-03-12 W
Pop: 257 (1990); 300 (1980) **Pop Density:** 1285.0
Land: 0.2 sq. mi.; **Water:** 0.0 sq. mi. **Elev:** 523 ft.
Name origin: For John Switz, a local landowner in the 1860s.

Taylor
Township
ZIP: 47424 **Lat:** 38-56-50 N **Long:** 86-53-56 W
Pop: 1,086 (1990); 1,107 (1980) **Pop Density:** 25.7
Land: 42.3 sq. mi.; **Water:** 0.1 sq. mi.

Washington
Township
ZIP: 47443 **Lat:** 38-57-48 N **Long:** 87-03-31 W
Pop: 1,213 (1990); 1,366 (1980) **Pop Density:** 28.6
Land: 42.4 sq. mi.; **Water:** 0.5 sq. mi.

Worthington
Town
ZIP: 47471 **Lat:** 39-07-06 N **Long:** 86-58-47 W
Pop: 1,473 (1990); 1,574 (1980) **Pop Density:** 1841.3
Land: 0.8 sq. mi.; **Water:** 0.0 sq. mi. **Elev:** 523 ft.
Name origin: For Worthington, OH.

Wright
Township
ZIP: 47441 **Lat:** 39-07-31 N **Long:** 87-11-11 W
Pop: 3,950 (1990); 4,220 (1980) **Pop Density:** 110.6
Land: 35.7 sq. mi.; **Water:** 0.5 sq. mi.

Hamilton County
County Seat: Noblesville (ZIP: 46060)

Pop: 108,936 (1990); 82,027 (1980) **Pop Density:** 273.7
Land: 398.0 sq. mi.; **Water:** 4.7 sq. mi. **Area Code:** 317
In central IN, north of Indianapolis; organized Jan 8, 1823 from Hancock and Marion counties.
Name origin: For Alexander Hamilton (1755–1804), U.S. statesman and first secretary of the treasury (1789–95).

Adams
Township
Lat: 40-09-25 N **Long:** 86-11-07 W
Pop: 4,504 (1990); 4,307 (1980) **Pop Density:** 93.1
Land: 48.4 sq. mi.; **Water:** 0.0 sq. mi.

Arcadia
Town
ZIP: 46030 **Lat:** 40-10-26 N **Long:** 86-01-16 W
Pop: 1,468 (1990); 1,801 (1980) **Pop Density:** 2446.7
Land: 0.6 sq. mi.; **Water:** 0.0 sq. mi. **Elev:** 863 ft.
Settled 1849.
Name origin: For the ancient Greek province noted for its pastoral beauty.

Atlanta
Town
ZIP: 46031 **Lat:** 40-12-53 N **Long:** 86-01-37 W
Pop: 703 (1990); 657 (1980) **Pop Density:** 2343.3
Land: 0.3 sq. mi.; **Water:** 0.0 sq. mi. **Elev:** 862 ft.
Settled 1839.
Name origin: For Atlanta, GA.

Carmel
City
ZIP: 46032 **Lat:** 39-58-09 N **Long:** 86-06-34 W
Pop: 25,380 (1990); 18,272 (1980) **Pop Density:** 2014.3
Land: 12.6 sq. mi.; **Water:** 0.1 sq. mi. **Elev:** 829 ft.
In central IN, 15 mi. north of Indianapolis.
Name origin: For the biblical mountain.

Cicero
Town
ZIP: 46034 **Lat:** 40-07-28 N **Long:** 86-01-21 W
Pop: 3,268 (1990); 2,557 (1980) **Pop Density:** 2513.8
Land: 1.3 sq. mi.; **Water:** 0.1 sq. mi. **Elev:** 838 ft.

Clay
Township
ZIP: 46032 **Lat:** 39-57-48 N **Long:** 86-08-53 W
Pop: 43,007 (1990); 32,606 (1980) **Pop Density:** 858.4
Land: 50.1 sq. mi.; **Water:** 0.1 sq. mi.

Delaware
Township
ZIP: 46060 **Lat:** 39-57-24 N **Long:** 86-01-37 W
Pop: 10,524 (1990); 4,660 (1980) **Pop Density:** 674.6
Land: 15.6 sq. mi.; **Water:** 0.2 sq. mi.

Fall Creek
Township
Lat: 39-57-35 N **Long:** 85-55-49 W
Pop: 4,415 (1990); 2,757 (1980) **Pop Density:** 128.3
Land: 34.4 sq. mi.; **Water:** 1.5 sq. mi.

Fishers
Town
ZIP: 46038 **Lat:** 39-57-14 N **Long:** 86-01-24 W
Pop: 7,508 (1990); 2,008 (1980) **Pop Density:** 904.6
Land: 8.3 sq. mi.; **Water:** 0.0 sq. mi. **Elev:** 824 ft.
Founded 1872.
Name origin: For its founder, Salathel Fisher.

Jackson
Township
ZIP: 47030 **Lat:** 40-09-21 N **Long:** 86-03-36 W
Pop: 8,446 (1990); 7,435 (1980) **Pop Density:** 153.6
Land: 55.0 sq. mi.; **Water:** 1.2 sq. mi.

Noblesville
City
ZIP: 46060 **Lat:** 40-03-23 N **Long:** 86-01-54 W
Pop: 17,655 (1990); 12,253 (1980) **Pop Density:** 2052.9
Land: 8.6 sq. mi.; **Water:** 1.2 sq. mi. **Elev:** 772 ft.
In central IN, 21 mi. northeast of Indianapolis. Not coextensive with the town of the same name.
Name origin: For Lavinia Noble, fiancee of founder Josiah Polk.

*Noblesville
Township
ZIP: 46060 **Lat:** 40-03-08 N **Long:** 86-01-30 W
Pop: 24,247 (1990); 18,894 (1980) **Pop Density:** 510.5
Land: 47.5 sq. mi.; **Water:** 1.6 sq. mi.

Sheridan
Town
ZIP: 46069 **Lat:** 40-08-04 N **Long:** 86-13-07 W
Pop: 2,046 (1990); 2,200 (1980) **Pop Density:** 2922.9
Land: 0.7 sq. mi.; **Water:** 0.0 sq. mi. **Elev:** 949 ft.
Name origin: For Gen. Philip H. Sheridan (1831–88) of Civil War fame.

Washington
Township
ZIP: 46074 **Lat:** 40-02-58 N **Long:** 86-10-21 W
Pop: 9,272 (1990); 7,425 (1980) **Pop Density:** 165.9
Land: 55.9 sq. mi.; **Water:** 0.1 sq. mi.

Wayne
Township
Lat: 40-03-22 N **Long:** 85-54-29 W
Pop: 2,071 (1990); 1,898 (1980) **Pop Density:** 59.0
Land: 35.1 sq. mi.; **Water:** 0.0 sq. mi.

Westfield
Town
ZIP: 46074 **Lat:** 40-02-49 N **Long:** 86-07-51 W
Pop: 3,304 (1990); 2,783 (1980) **Pop Density:** 1376.7
Land: 2.4 sq. mi.; **Water:** 0.0 sq. mi. **Elev:** 899 ft.
Name origin: Named by Quaker settlers in 1834, for a former home.

White River
Township
Lat: 40-09-21 N **Long:** 85-55-48 W
Pop: 2,450 (1990); 2,045 (1980) **Pop Density:** 43.8
Land: 56.0 sq. mi.; **Water:** 0.1 sq. mi.

Hancock County
County Seat: Greenfield (ZIP: 46140)

Pop: 45,527 (1990); 43,939 (1980) **Pop Density:** 148.7
Land: 306.2 sq. mi.; **Water:** 0.6 sq. mi. **Area Code:** 317
In central IN, east of Indianapolis; established Jan 26, 1827 from Madison County.
Name origin: For John Hancock (1737–93), noted signer of the Declaration of Independence and governor of MA (1780–85; 1787–93).

Blue River
Township
Lat: 39-44-41 N **Long:** 85-40-41 W
Pop: 1,033 (1990); 1,201 (1980) **Pop Density:** 34.7
Land: 29.8 sq. mi.; **Water:** 0.0 sq. mi.

Brandywine
Township
Lat: 39-43-33 N **Long:** 85-46-29 W
Pop: 1,646 (1990); 1,658 (1980) **Pop Density:** 68.0
Land: 24.2 sq. mi.; **Water:** 0.0 sq. mi.

Brown
Township
Lat: 39-54-23 N **Long:** 85-38-02 W
Pop: 2,573 (1990); 2,703 (1980) **Pop Density:** 83.5
Land: 30.8 sq. mi.; **Water:** 0.0 sq. mi.

Buck Creek
Township
ZIP: 46140 **Lat:** 39-49-37 N **Long:** 85-53-54 W
Pop: 5,435 (1990); 4,675 (1980) **Pop Density:** 151.4
Land: 35.9 sq. mi.; **Water:** 0.0 sq. mi.

Center
Township
ZIP: 46140 **Lat:** 39-48-58 N **Long:** 85-46-30 W
Pop: 16,578 (1990); 16,135 (1980) **Pop Density:** 312.2
Land: 53.1 sq. mi.; **Water:** 0.3 sq. mi.

Cumberland
Town
Lat: 39-47-11 N **Long:** 85-56-40 W
Pop: 1,624 (1990); 3,375 (1980) **Pop Density:** 1804.4
Land: 0.9 sq. mi.; **Water:** 0.0 sq. mi.
Part of the town is also in Marion County.

Fortville
Town
ZIP: 46040 **Lat:** 39-56-09 N **Long:** 85-50-49 W
Pop: 2,690 (1990); 2,787 (1980) **Pop Density:** 2690.0
Land: 1.0 sq. mi.; **Water:** 0.0 sq. mi. **Elev:** 859 ft.

Green
Township
Lat: 39-54-16 N **Long:** 85-44-44 W
Pop: 1,609 (1990); 1,686 (1980) **Pop Density:** 53.3
Land: 30.2 sq. mi.; **Water:** 0.2 sq. mi.

Greenfield
City
ZIP: 46140 **Lat:** 39-47-34 N **Long:** 85-46-12 W
Pop: 11,657 (1990); 11,288 (1980) **Pop Density:** 1911.0
Land: 6.1 sq. mi.; **Water:** 0.0 sq. mi. **Elev:** 888 ft.
In central IN, 19 mi. east of Indianapolis. Founded 1828.
Name origin: For pioneer settler John Green.

Jackson
Township
Lat: 39-49-44 N **Long:** 85-38-59 W
Pop: 1,762 (1990); 1,884 (1980) **Pop Density:** 49.5
Land: 35.6 sq. mi.; **Water:** 0.0 sq. mi.

McCordsville
Town
ZIP: 46055 **Lat:** 39-54-29 N **Long:** 85-55-52 W
Pop: 684 (1990) **Pop Density:** 213.8
Land: 3.2 sq. mi.; **Water:** 0.0 sq. mi.

New Palestine
Town
ZIP: 46163 **Lat:** 39-43-15 N **Long:** 85-53-29 W
Pop: 671 (1990); 749 (1980) **Pop Density:** 2236.7
Land: 0.3 sq. mi.; **Water:** 0.0 sq. mi. **Elev:** 827 ft.
Founded 1838.
Name origin: Named in 1838 for the biblical place.

Shirley
Town
ZIP: 47384 **Lat:** 39-53-29 N **Long:** 85-34-54 W
Pop: 678 (1990); 742 (1980) **Pop Density:** 2260.0
Land: 0.3 sq. mi.; **Water:** 0.0 sq. mi. **Elev:** 1029 ft.
Settled 1890. Part of the town is also in Henry County.
Name origin: For railroad superintendent Joseph Shirley.

Spring Lake
Town
Lat: 39-46-36 N **Long:** 85-51-15 W
Pop: 216 (1990); 236 (1980) **Pop Density:** 1080.0
Land: 0.2 sq. mi.; **Water:** 0.0 sq. mi. **Elev:** 845 ft.
Name origin: For the spring-fed artificial lake created by William Dye in 1884.

Sugar Creek
Township
ZIP: 46163 **Lat:** 39-44-21 N **Long:** 85-53-41 W
Pop: 9,163 (1990); 8,114 (1980) **Pop Density:** 259.6
Land: 35.3 sq. mi.; **Water:** 0.0 sq. mi.

Vernon
Township
ZIP: 46040 **Lat:** 39-54-24 N **Long:** 85-52-17 W
Pop: 5,728 (1990); 5,883 (1980) **Pop Density:** 183.0
Land: 31.3 sq. mi.; **Water:** 0.0 sq. mi.

Wilkinson
Town
ZIP: 46186 **Lat:** 39-53-05 N **Long:** 85-36-29 W
Pop: 446 (1990); 493 (1980) **Pop Density:** 2230.0
Land: 0.2 sq. mi.; **Water:** 0.0 sq. mi. **Elev:** 1009 ft.
Name origin: For the surveyors who measured the area in 1883.

Harrison County
County Seat: Corydon (ZIP: 47112)

Pop: 29,890 (1990); 27,276 (1980) **Pop Density:** 61.6
Land: 485.3 sq. mi.; **Water:** 1.7 sq. mi. **Area Code:** 812
On the southern border of IN; organized Oct 11, 1808 (prior to statehood) from Northwest Territory.
Name origin: For William Henry Harrison (1773–1841), first territorial governor of IN (1800–11) and ninth U.S. president.

Blue River
Township
Lat: 38-22-39 N **Long:** 86-12-50 W
Pop: 1,867 (1990); 1,471 (1980) **Pop Density:** 48.2
Land: 38.7 sq. mi.; **Water:** 0.0 sq. mi.

Boone
Township
Lat: 38-02-56 N **Long:** 86-04-25 W
Pop: 1,161 (1990); 1,065 (1980) **Pop Density:** 24.5
Land: 47.4 sq. mi.; **Water:** 0.4 sq. mi.

Corydon
Town
ZIP: 47112 **Lat:** 38-12-45 N **Long:** 86-07-31 W
Pop: 2,661 (1990); 2,724 (1980) **Pop Density:** 1663.1
Land: 1.6 sq. mi.; **Water:** 0.0 sq. mi. **Elev:** 549 ft.
Name origin: Named by William Henry Harrison (1773–1841), first territorial governor of IN (1800–11) and ninth U.S. president, for the shepherd in the song "Pastoral Elegy."

Crandall
Town
ZIP: 47114 **Lat:** 38-17-16 N **Long:** 86-03-56 W
Pop: 147 (1990); 176 (1980) **Pop Density:** 1470.0
Land: 0.1 sq. mi.; **Water:** 0.0 sq. mi. **Elev:** 659 ft.
Name origin: For its founder Cornelius F. Crandall.

Elizabeth
Town
ZIP: 47117 **Lat:** 38-07-31 N **Long:** 85-58-29 W
Pop: 153 (1990); 178 (1980) **Pop Density:** 1530.0
Land: 0.1 sq. mi.; **Water:** 0.0 sq. mi. **Elev:** 750 ft.
Name origin: For Elizabeth Veach, whose husband donated its site in 1812.

Franklin
Township
Lat: 38-14-22 N **Long:** 86-00-20 W
Pop: 3,087 (1990); 2,872 (1980) **Pop Density:** 89.5
Land: 34.5 sq. mi.; **Water:** 0.0 sq. mi.

Harrison
Township
ZIP: 47122 **Lat:** 38-11-02 N **Long:** 86-10-32 W
Pop: 8,239 (1990); 7,727 (1980) **Pop Density:** 81.3
Land: 101.3 sq. mi.; **Water:** 0.3 sq. mi.

Heth
Township
Lat: 38-03-39 N **Long:** 86-10-56 W
Pop: 961 (1990); 880 (1980) **Pop Density:** 28.4
Land: 33.8 sq. mi.; **Water:** 0.5 sq. mi.

Jackson
Township
Lat: 38-17-54 N **Long:** 86-05-35 W
Pop: 4,627 (1990); 3,977 (1980) **Pop Density:** 127.8
Land: 36.2 sq. mi.; **Water:** 0.0 sq. mi.

Laconia
Town
ZIP: 47135 **Lat:** 38-01-55 N **Long:** 86-05-07 W
Pop: 75 (1990); 58 (1980) **Pop Density:** 1500.0
Land: 0.05 sq. mi.; **Water:** 0.0 sq. mi. **Elev:** 667 ft.
Founded 1816.
Name origin: For the ancient Greek city.

Lanesville
Town
ZIP: 47136 **Lat:** 38-14-17 N **Long:** 85-59-05 W
Pop: 512 (1990); 570 (1980) **Pop Density:** 1706.7
Land: 0.3 sq. mi.; **Water:** 0.0 sq. mi. **Elev:** 730 ft.

Mauckport
Town
ZIP: 47142 **Lat:** 38-01-27 N **Long:** 86-12-05 W
Pop: 95 (1990); 109 (1980) **Pop Density:** 950.0
Land: 0.1 sq. mi.; **Water:** 0.0 sq. mi. **Elev:** 423 ft.
Founded 1827.
Name origin: For its founder, Frederick Mauck.

Milltown
Town
ZIP: 47145 **Lat:** 38-20-32 N **Long:** 86-15-59 W
Pop: 428 (1990); 386 (1980) **Pop Density:** 611.4
Land: 0.7 sq. mi.; **Water:** 0.0 sq. mi. **Elev:** 600 ft.
Settled 1827. Part of the town is also in Crawford County.
Name origin: Originally called Leavenworth's Mill for Zebulon Leavenworth; name altered later.

Morgan
Township
ZIP: 47164 **Lat:** 38-22-11 N **Long:** 86-05-13 W
Pop: 3,250 (1990); 2,965 (1980) **Pop Density:** 91.0
Land: 35.7 sq. mi.; **Water:** 0.1 sq. mi.

New Amsterdam
Town
ZIP: 47110 **Lat:** 38-06-10 N **Long:** 86-16-36 W
Pop: 30 (1990); 31 (1980) **Pop Density:** 300.0
Land: 0.1 sq. mi.; **Water:** 0.0 sq. mi. **Elev:** 430 ft.
Settled 1815.
Name origin: From the former Dutch name for New York City.

New Middletown
Town
ZIP: 47160 **Lat:** 38-09-48 N **Long:** 86-03-00 W
Pop: 82 (1990); 115 (1980) **Pop Density:** 1640.0
Land: 0.05 sq. mi.; **Water:** 0.0 sq. mi. **Elev:** 700 ft.
Name origin: Originally Middletown, 'new' was added in 1860.

Palmyra
Town
ZIP: 47164 **Lat:** 38-24-29 N **Long:** 86-06-51 W
Pop: 621 (1990); 692 (1980) **Pop Density:** 887.1
Land: 0.7 sq. mi.; **Water:** 0.0 sq. mi. **Elev:** 770 ft.
Settled 1810.
Name origin: For the ancient Syrian city.

Posey
Township
Lat: 38-07-55 N **Long:** 85-57-21 W
Pop: 2,553 (1990); 2,203 (1980) **Pop Density:** 64.5
Land: 39.6 sq. mi.; **Water:** 0.0 sq. mi.

Spencer
Township
Lat: 38-17-18 N **Long:** 86-13-46 W
Pop: 1,687 (1990); 1,625 (1980) **Pop Density:** 44.0
Land: 38.3 sq. mi.; **Water:** 0.0 sq. mi.

Taylor
Township
Lat: 38-03-13 N **Long:** 85-57-36 W
Pop: 576 (1990); 611 (1980) **Pop Density:** 20.2
Land: 28.5 sq. mi.; **Water:** 0.1 sq. mi.

Washington
Township
Lat: 38-06-37 N **Long:** 86-14-29 W
Pop: 392 (1990); 387 (1980) **Pop Density:** 18.8
Land: 20.9 sq. mi.; **Water:** 0.2 sq. mi.

Webster
Township
Lat: 38-08-36 N **Long:** 86-03-19 W
Pop: 1,490 (1990); 1,493 (1980) **Pop Density:** 49.0
Land: 30.4 sq. mi.; **Water:** 0.0 sq. mi.

Hendricks County
County Seat: Danville (ZIP: 46122)

Pop: 75,717 (1990); 69,804 (1980) **Pop Density:** 185.4
Land: 408.4 sq. mi.; **Water:** 0.5 sq. mi. **Area Code:** 317
In central IN, west of Indianapolis; established Dec 20, 1823 from Indian lands.
Name origin: For William Hendricks (1782–1850), IN legislator, governor (1822–25), and U.S. senator (1825–37).

Amo
Town
ZIP: 46103 **Lat:** 39-41-21 N **Long:** 86-36-50 W
Pop: 380 (1990); 444 (1980) **Pop Density:** 950.0
Land: 0.4 sq. mi.; **Water:** 0.0 sq. mi. **Elev:** 822 ft.
Settled 1850.
Name origin: From the Latin *amo* meaning 'I love.'

Brown
Township
Lat: 39-53-17 N **Long:** 86-22-44 W
Pop: 4,617 (1990); 4,176 (1980) **Pop Density:** 182.5
Land: 25.3 sq. mi.; **Water:** 0.0 sq. mi.

Brownsburg
Town
ZIP: 46112 **Lat:** 39-50-29 N **Long:** 86-23-39 W
Pop: 7,628 (1990); 6,242 (1980) **Pop Density:** 2118.9
Land: 3.6 sq. mi.; **Water:** 0.0 sq. mi. **Elev:** 884 ft.
Founded 1835.

Center
Township
ZIP: 46122 **Lat:** 39-46-08 N **Long:** 86-31-17 W
Pop: 7,359 (1990); 7,057 (1980) **Pop Density:** 159.6
Land: 46.1 sq. mi.; **Water:** 0.1 sq. mi.

Clay
Township
Lat: 39-41-48 N **Long:** 86-37-03 W
Pop: 1,992 (1990); 2,030 (1980) **Pop Density:** 75.2
Land: 26.5 sq. mi.; **Water:** 0.0 sq. mi.

Clayton
Town
ZIP: 46118 **Lat:** 39-41-21 N **Long:** 86-31-24 W
Pop: 610 (1990); 703 (1980) **Pop Density:** 1220.0
Land: 0.5 sq. mi.; **Water:** 0.0 sq. mi. **Elev:** 872 ft.
Name origin: For Henry Clay (1777–1852), U.S. senator from KY and U.S. secretary of state (1825–29), known as the "Great Pacificator" for his advocacy of compromise to avert national crises.

INDIANA, Hendricks County

Coatesville — Town
ZIP: 46121 Lat: 39-41-14 N Long: 86-40-09 W
Pop: 469 (1990); 474 (1980) Pop Density: 781.7
Land: 0.6 sq. mi.; Water: 0.0 sq. mi. Elev: 873 ft.
Settled 1830s.

Danville — Town
ZIP: 46122 Lat: 39-45-43 N Long: 86-31-11 W
Pop: 4,345 (1990); 4,220 (1980) Pop Density: 1551.8
Land: 2.8 sq. mi.; Water: 0.0 sq. mi. Elev: 954 ft.
Settled 1824; incorporated 1839.
Name origin: Named by the local circuit judge for his brother Dan.

Eel River — Township
Lat: 39-52-19 N Long: 86-37-49 W
Pop: 1,541 (1990); 1,595 (1980) Pop Density: 36.3
Land: 42.5 sq. mi.; Water: 0.0 sq. mi.

Franklin — Township
Lat: 39-38-35 N Long: 86-37-21 W
Pop: 1,135 (1990); 1,261 (1980) Pop Density: 43.0
Land: 26.4 sq. mi.; Water: 0.0 sq. mi.

Guilford — Township
ZIP: 46168 Lat: 39-40-27 N Long: 86-22-56 W
Pop: 19,468 (1990); 17,052 (1980) Pop Density: 543.8
Land: 35.8 sq. mi.; Water: 0.1 sq. mi.
In southeastern IN, 45 mi. south of Richmond.

Jamestown — Town
ZIP: 46147 Lat: 39-55-20 N Long: 86-37-27 W
Pop: 0 (1990)
Land: 0.003 sq. mi.; Water: 0.0 sq. mi. Elev: 946 ft.
Founded 1832. Part of the town is also in Boone County.

Liberty — Township
Lat: 39-40-13 N Long: 86-29-52 W
Pop: 4,566 (1990); 4,719 (1980) Pop Density: 92.2
Land: 49.5 sq. mi.; Water: 0.0 sq. mi.

Lincoln — Township
ZIP: 46112 Lat: 39-49-47 N Long: 86-22-55 W
Pop: 14,008 (1990); 13,351 (1980) Pop Density: 588.6
Land: 23.8 sq. mi.; Water: 0.1 sq. mi.

Lizton — Town
ZIP: 46149 Lat: 39-53-08 N Long: 86-32-33 W
Pop: 410 (1990); 456 (1980) Pop Density: 2050.0
Land: 0.2 sq. mi.; Water: 0.0 sq. mi. Elev: 958 ft.
Founded 1851.
Name origin: Shortened by the railroad from its original name of New Elizabeth.

Marion — Township
Lat: 39-46-05 N Long: 86-38-13 W
Pop: 1,273 (1990); 1,289 (1980) Pop Density: 33.0
Land: 38.6 sq. mi.; Water: 0.0 sq. mi.

Middle — Township
Lat: 39-51-53 N Long: 86-28-10 W
Pop: 3,466 (1990); 3,189 (1980) Pop Density: 111.4
Land: 31.1 sq. mi.; Water: 0.0 sq. mi.

North Salem — Town
ZIP: 46165 Lat: 39-51-33 N Long: 86-38-40 W
Pop: 499 (1990); 581 (1980) Pop Density: 1663.3
Land: 0.3 sq. mi.; Water: 0.0 sq. mi. Elev: 879 ft.
Founded 1839.
Name origin: For a town in KY.

Pittsboro — Town
ZIP: 46167 Lat: 39-52-02 N Long: 86-27-53 W
Pop: 815 (1990); 891 (1980) Pop Density: 1018.8
Land: 0.8 sq. mi.; Water: 0.0 sq. mi. Elev: 940 ft.

Plainfield — Town
ZIP: 46168 Lat: 39-42-01 N Long: 86-23-16 W
Pop: 10,433 (1990); 9,191 (1980) Pop Density: 2819.7
Land: 3.7 sq. mi.; Water: 0.0 sq. mi. Elev: 739 ft.
In central IN, 15 mi. west of Indianapolis.
Name origin: For its descriptive connotations.

Stilesville — Town
ZIP: 46180 Lat: 39-38-17 N Long: 86-37-56 W
Pop: 298 (1990); 350 (1980) Pop Density: 993.3
Land: 0.3 sq. mi.; Water: 0.0 sq. mi. Elev: 795 ft.
Established 1828.
Name origin: For landowner Jeremiah Stiles.

Union — Township
Lat: 39-52-45 N Long: 86-32-35 W
Pop: 1,586 (1990); 1,579 (1980) Pop Density: 66.1
Land: 24.0 sq. mi.; Water: 0.0 sq. mi.

Washington — Township
ZIP: 46122 Lat: 39-45-34 N Long: 86-23-41 W
Pop: 14,706 (1990); 12,506 (1980) Pop Density: 380.0
Land: 38.7 sq. mi.; Water: 0.0 sq. mi.

Henry County
County Seat: New Castle (ZIP: 47362)

Pop: 48,139 (1990); 53,336 (1980)   **Pop Density:** 122.5
Land: 393.0 sq. mi.; **Water:** 2.0 sq. mi.   **Area Code:** 317

In east-central IN, south of Muncie; established Dec 31, 1821 from Delaware County.

Name origin: For Patrick Henry (1736–99), patriot, governor of VA (1776–79; 1784–86), and statesman, famous for proclaiming, "Give me liberty or give me death."

Blountsville — Town
Lat: 40-03-34 N   **Long:** 85-14-19 W
Pop: 155 (1990); 213 (1980)   **Pop Density:** 1550.0
Land: 0.1 sq. mi.; **Water:** 0.0 sq. mi.   **Elev:** 1096 ft.
Name origin: For its original landowner, Andrew Blount.

Blue River — Township
Lat: 39-59-25 N   **Long:** 85-15-25 W
Pop: 1,265 (1990); 1,351 (1980)   **Pop Density:** 57.5
Land: 22.0 sq. mi.; **Water:** 0.0 sq. mi.

Cadi — Town
ZIP: 47362   **Lat:** 39-57-01 N   **Long:** 85-29-11 W
Pop: 202 (1990); 180 (1980)   **Pop Density:** 2020.0
Land: 0.1 sq. mi.; **Water:** 0.0 sq. mi.   **Elev:** 1074 ft.

Dudley — Township
ZIP: 47387   **Lat:** 39-49-54 N   **Long:** 85-16-38 W
Pop: 1,300 (1990); 1,401 (1980)   **Pop Density:** 42.1
Land: 30.9 sq. mi.; **Water:** 0.0 sq. mi.

Dunreith — Town
ZIP: 47337   **Lat:** 39-48-10 N   **Long:** 85-26-12 W
Pop: 205 (1990); 184 (1980)   **Pop Density:** 2050.0
Land: 0.1 sq. mi.; **Water:** 0.0 sq. mi.   **Elev:** 1036 ft.
Name origin: For early settler Emery Dunreith Coffin.

Fall Creek — Township
Lat: 40-02-14 N   **Long:** 85-31-29 W
Pop: 4,613 (1990); 5,094 (1980)   **Pop Density:** 152.7
Land: 30.2 sq. mi.; **Water:** 0.0 sq. mi.

Franklin — Township
Lat: 39-50-18 N   **Long:** 85-21-54 W
Pop: 1,219 (1990); 1,457 (1980)   **Pop Density:** 42.6
Land: 28.6 sq. mi.; **Water:** 0.0 sq. mi.

Greensboro — Town
ZIP: 47344   **Lat:** 39-52-41 N   **Long:** 85-27-46 W
Pop: 204 (1990); 175 (1980)   **Pop Density:** 2040.0
Land: 0.1 sq. mi.; **Water:** 0.0 sq. mi.   **Elev:** 1000 ft.
Not coextensive with the town of the same name. Settled 1830.
Name origin: For Greensboro, NC, former home of early settlers.

*Greensboro — Township
Lat: 39-53-07 N   **Long:** 85-30-29 W
Pop: 1,483 (1990); 1,503 (1980)   **Pop Density:** 57.9
Land: 25.6 sq. mi.; **Water:** 0.0 sq. mi.

Harrison — Township
Lat: 39-57-07 N   **Long:** 85-30-17 W
Pop: 1,379 (1990); 1,560 (1980)   **Pop Density:** 38.6
Land: 35.7 sq. mi.; **Water:** 0.0 sq. mi.

Henry — Township
ZIP: 47362   **Lat:** 39-55-01 N   **Long:** 85-23-08 W
Pop: 23,814 (1990); 26,730 (1980)   **Pop Density:** 650.7
Land: 36.6 sq. mi.; **Water:** 0.3 sq. mi.
In east-central IN, near New Castle.

Jefferson — Township
Lat: 40-01-23 N   **Long:** 85-26-36 W
Pop: 1,242 (1990); 1,340 (1980)   **Pop Density:** 43.3
Land: 28.7 sq. mi.; **Water:** 0.0 sq. mi.

Kennard — Town
ZIP: 47351   **Lat:** 39-54-15 N   **Long:** 85-31-11 W
Pop: 382 (1990); 441 (1980)   **Pop Density:** 1273.3
Land: 0.3 sq. mi.; **Water:** 0.0 sq. mi.   **Elev:** 1041 ft.
Name origin: Named in 1882 for Jenkins Kennard, a prominent citizen who promoted his name.

Knightstown — Town
ZIP: 46148   **Lat:** 39-47-44 N   **Long:** 85-31-41 W
Pop: 2,048 (1990); 2,325 (1980)   **Pop Density:** 2925.7
Land: 0.7 sq. mi.; **Water:** 0.0 sq. mi.   **Elev:** 938 ft.
Name origin: For John Knight, a construction engineer on the National Railroad.

Lewisville — Town
ZIP: 47352   **Lat:** 39-48-21 N   **Long:** 85-21-11 W
Pop: 437 (1990); 577 (1980)   **Pop Density:** 1456.7
Land: 0.3 sq. mi.; **Water:** 0.0 sq. mi.   **Elev:** 1050 ft.
Name origin: For founder Lewis Freeman.

Liberty — Township
ZIP: 47362   **Lat:** 39-55-15 N   **Long:** 85-15-41 W
Pop: 1,504 (1990); 1,652 (1980)   **Pop Density:** 36.9
Land: 40.8 sq. mi.; **Water:** 0.0 sq. mi.

Middletown — Town
ZIP: 47356   **Lat:** 40-03-34 N   **Long:** 85-32-33 W
Pop: 2,333 (1990); 2,978 (1980)   **Pop Density:** 2120.9
Land: 1.1 sq. mi.; **Water:** 0.0 sq. mi.   **Elev:** 965 ft.
Name origin: For its location between Ft. Wayne and Decatur.

Mooreland — Town
ZIP: 47360   **Lat:** 39-59-51 N   **Long:** 85-15-06 W
Pop: 465 (1990); 479 (1980)   **Pop Density:** 4650.0
Land: 0.1 sq. mi.; **Water:** 0.0 sq. mi.   **Elev:** 1124 ft.
Name origin: Named in 1882 for original landowner Miles Moore.

Mount Summit — Town
ZIP: 47361   **Lat:** 40-00-11 N   **Long:** 85-23-12 W
Pop: 238 (1990); 357 (1980)   **Pop Density:** 1190.0
Land: 0.2 sq. mi.; **Water:** 0.0 sq. mi.   **Elev:** 1097 ft.

New Castle — City
ZIP: 47362 **Lat:** 39-55-15 N **Long:** 85-21-53 W
Pop: 17,753 (1990); 20,056 (1980) **Pop Density:** 3114.6
Land: 5.7 sq. mi.; **Water:** 0.0 sq. mi. **Elev:** 1058 ft.
In east-central IN, 17 mi. south of Muncie. Founded 1820.
Name origin: For Newcastle, Northumberland, England.

Prairie — Township
Lat: 40-01-01 N **Long:** 85-21-16 W
Pop: 3,393 (1990); 3,769 (1980) **Pop Density:** 85.5
Land: 39.7 sq. mi.; **Water:** 0.9 sq. mi.

Shirley — Town
ZIP: 47384 **Lat:** 39-53-28 N **Long:** 85-34-29 W
Pop: 139 (1990); 177 (1980) **Pop Density:** 1390.0
Land: 0.1 sq. mi.; **Water:** 0.0 sq. mi. **Elev:** 1029 ft.
Settled 1890. Part of the town is also in Hancock County.
Name origin: For railroad superintendent Joseph Shirley.

Spiceland — Town
ZIP: 47385 **Lat:** 39-50-17 N **Long:** 85-26-17 W
Pop: 757 (1990); 940 (1980) **Pop Density:** 1892.5
Land: 0.4 sq. mi.; **Water:** 0.0 sq. mi. **Elev:** 1050 ft.
Not coextensive with the town of the same name.
Name origin: Descriptive of the area's abundant spicebush, either *Lindera benzoin* or *Calycanthus occidentalis*.

*Spiceland — Township
ZIP: 47385 **Lat:** 39-49-12 N **Long:** 85-27-11 W
Pop: 2,270 (1990); 2,365 (1980) **Pop Density:** 101.8
Land: 22.3 sq. mi.; **Water:** 0.1 sq. mi.

Springport — Town
ZIP: 47386 **Lat:** 40-02-48 N **Long:** 85-23-34 W
Pop: 194 (1990); 221 (1980) **Pop Density:** 1940.0
Land: 0.1 sq. mi.; **Water:** 0.0 sq. mi. **Elev:** 1050 ft.
Founded 1868.
Name origin: For a local spring.

Stoney Creek — Township
Lat: 40-02-45 N **Long:** 85-15-18 W
Pop: 815 (1990); 989 (1980) **Pop Density:** 42.2
Land: 19.3 sq. mi.; **Water:** 0.6 sq. mi.

Straughn — Town
ZIP: 47387 **Lat:** 39-48-29 N **Long:** 85-17-25 W
Pop: 318 (1990); 331 (1980) **Pop Density:** 3180.0
Land: 0.1 sq. mi.; **Water:** 0.0 sq. mi. **Elev:** 1080 ft.
Name origin: For pioneer settler Merriman Straughn.

Sulphur Springs — Town
Lat: 40-00-20 N **Long:** 85-26-36 W
Pop: 257 (1990); 345 (1980) **Pop Density:** 856.7
Land: 0.3 sq. mi.; **Water:** 0.0 sq. mi. **Elev:** 1055 ft.
Name origin: For its descriptive connotations.

Wayne — Township
Lat: 39-49-48 N **Long:** 85-32-46 W
Pop: 3,842 (1990); 4,125 (1980) **Pop Density:** 118.6
Land: 32.4 sq. mi.; **Water:** 0.1 sq. mi.

Howard County
County Seat: Kokomo (ZIP: 46901)

Pop: 80,827 (1990); 86,896 (1980) **Pop Density:** 275.8
Land: 293.1 sq. mi.; **Water:** 0.9 sq. mi. **Area Code:** 317
In central IN, east of Marion; organized as Richardville County Jan 15, 1844 from Indian lands; name changed 1846.
Name origin: For Tilghman Ashurst Howard (1797–1844), TN legislator, U.S. representative from IN (1839–40), and chargé d'affaires to the Republic of TX (1844).

Center — Township
ZIP: 46902 **Lat:** 40-29-00 N **Long:** 86-08-08 W
Pop: 47,354 (1990); 52,504 (1980) **Pop Density:** 1842.6
Land: 25.7 sq. mi.; **Water:** 0.1 sq. mi.

Clay — Township
Lat: 40-31-21 N **Long:** 86-11-37 W
Pop: 3,707 (1990); 3,970 (1980) **Pop Density:** 129.2
Land: 28.7 sq. mi.; **Water:** 0.0 sq. mi.

Ervin — Township
Lat: 40-31-19 N **Long:** 86-18-33 W
Pop: 2,178 (1990); 1,966 (1980) **Pop Density:** 51.6
Land: 42.2 sq. mi.; **Water:** 0.0 sq. mi.

Greentown — Town
ZIP: 46936 **Lat:** 40-28-42 N **Long:** 85-57-52 W
Pop: 2,172 (1990); 2,265 (1980) **Pop Density:** 2715.0
Land: 0.8 sq. mi.; **Water:** 0.0 sq. mi. **Elev:** 844 ft.
Platted in 1848.
Name origin: For Chief Green, a Miami Indian, on the site of whose village the town was platted.

Harrison — Township
ZIP: 46979 **Lat:** 40-26-12 N **Long:** 86-11-12 W
Pop: 6,960 (1990); 6,960 (1980) **Pop Density:** 320.7
Land: 21.7 sq. mi.; **Water:** 0.1 sq. mi.

Honey Creek — Township
Lat: 40-24-50 N **Long:** 86-16-12 W
Pop: 1,724 (1990); 1,794 (1980) **Pop Density:** 117.3
Land: 14.7 sq. mi.; **Water:** 0.0 sq. mi.

Howard — Township
Lat: 40-31-44 N **Long:** 86-03-30 W
Pop: 2,694 (1990); 2,884 (1980) **Pop Density:** 90.7
Land: 29.7 sq. mi.; **Water:** 0.4 sq. mi.

Indian Heights — CDP
Lat: 40-25-29 N **Long:** 86-06-59 W
Pop: 3,669 (1990); 4,277 (1980) **Pop Density:** 3335.5
Land: 1.1 sq. mi.; **Water:** 0.0 sq. mi.

INDIANA, Howard County

Jackson
Township
Lat: 40-31-26 N **Long:** 85-54-29 W
Pop: 595 (1990); 617 (1980) **Pop Density:** 25.3
Land: 23.5 sq. mi.; **Water:** 0.0 sq. mi.

Kokomo
City
ZIP: 46902 **Lat:** 40-28-31 N **Long:** 86-07-59 W
Pop: 44,962 (1990); 47,808 (1980) **Pop Density:** 3122.4
Land: 14.4 sq. mi.; **Water:** 0.1 sq. mi. **Elev:** 810 ft.
In north-central IN, 48 mi. north of Indianapolis. Founded c. 1843.
Name origin: For a Miami Indian chief, name meaning 'black walnuts.'

Liberty
Township
Lat: 40-29-58 N **Long:** 85-58-51 W
Pop: 4,387 (1990); 4,371 (1980) **Pop Density:** 139.3
Land: 31.5 sq. mi.; **Water:** 0.2 sq. mi.

Monroe
Township
Lat: 40-27-05 N **Long:** 86-18-58 W
Pop: 1,397 (1990); 1,241 (1980) **Pop Density:** 72.8
Land: 19.2 sq. mi.; **Water:** 0.0 sq. mi.

Russiaville
Town
ZIP: 46979 **Lat:** 40-25-07 N **Long:** 86-16-13 W
Pop: 988 (1990); 973 (1980) **Pop Density:** 1976.0
Land: 0.5 sq. mi.; **Water:** 0.0 sq. mi. **Elev:** 850 ft.
Name origin: A corruption of *Richardsville*, the French name for a Miami Indian chief. Generally pronounced as Rusherville and sometimes so written.

Taylor
Township
ZIP: 46901 **Lat:** 40-26-03 N **Long:** 86-03-07 W
Pop: 8,877 (1990); 9,628 (1980) **Pop Density:** 291.0
Land: 30.5 sq. mi.; **Water:** 0.0 sq. mi.

Union
Township
Lat: 40-26-24 N **Long:** 85-54-46 W
Pop: 954 (1990); 961 (1980) **Pop Density:** 37.0
Land: 25.8 sq. mi.; **Water:** 0.0 sq. mi.

Huntington County
County Seat: Huntington (ZIP: 46750)

Pop: 35,427 (1990); 35,596 (1980) **Pop Density:** 92.6
Land: 382.6 sq. mi.; **Water:** 5.3 sq. mi. **Area Code:** 219
In northeastern IN, southwest of Ft. Wayne; established Feb 2, 1832 from Grant County.
Name origin: For Samuel Huntington (1731–96), a signer of the Declaration of Independence, president of the Continental Congress (1779–81; 1783), chief justice of CT Superior Court (1784), and governor of CT (1786–96).

Andrews
Town
ZIP: 46702 **Lat:** 40-51-34 N **Long:** 85-36-03 W
Pop: 1,118 (1990); 1,243 (1980) **Pop Density:** 2236.0
Land: 0.5 sq. mi.; **Water:** 0.0 sq. mi. **Elev:** 737 ft.
Name origin: For a local railroad official. Previously named Antioch.

Clear Creek
Township
Lat: 40-57-27 N **Long:** 85-30-44 W
Pop: 1,306 (1990); 1,286 (1980) **Pop Density:** 36.5
Land: 35.8 sq. mi.; **Water:** 0.0 sq. mi.

Dallas
Township
ZIP: 46702 **Lat:** 40-52-05 N **Long:** 85-36-06 W
Pop: 1,982 (1990); 2,072 (1980) **Pop Density:** 86.9
Land: 22.8 sq. mi.; **Water:** 0.2 sq. mi.

Huntington
City
ZIP: 46750 **Lat:** 40-52-50 N **Long:** 85-30-20 W
Pop: 16,389 (1990); 16,202 (1980) **Pop Density:** 2214.7
Land: 7.4 sq. mi.; **Water:** 0.1 sq. mi. **Elev:** 743 ft.
In northeastern IN, 21 mi. southwest of Fort Wayne. Not coextensive with the town of the same name.
Name origin: For Samuel Huntington (1731–96), a signer of the Declaration of Independence, president of the Continental Congress (1779–81; 1783), chief justice of CT Superior Court (1784), and governor of CT (1786–96).

*Huntington
Township
ZIP: 46750 **Lat:** 40-52-22 N **Long:** 85-30-45 W
Pop: 20,236 (1990); 20,032 (1980) **Pop Density:** 554.4
Land: 36.5 sq. mi.; **Water:** 0.8 sq. mi.

Jackson
Township
Lat: 40-57-38 N **Long:** 85-23-49 W
Pop: 3,297 (1990); 3,325 (1980) **Pop Density:** 89.6
Land: 36.8 sq. mi.; **Water:** 0.2 sq. mi.

Jefferson
Township
Lat: 40-42-13 N **Long:** 85-30-42 W
Pop: 834 (1990); 1,306 (1980) **Pop Density:** 23.0
Land: 36.2 sq. mi.; **Water:** 0.0 sq. mi.

Lancaster
Township
ZIP: 46750 **Lat:** 40-46-36 N **Long:** 85-30-18 W
Pop: 1,058 (1990); 1,185 (1980) **Pop Density:** 29.9
Land: 35.4 sq. mi.; **Water:** 0.5 sq. mi.

Markle
Town
ZIP: 46770 **Lat:** 40-49-32 N **Long:** 85-20-36 W
Pop: 789 (1990); 755 (1980) **Pop Density:** 1578.0
Land: 0.5 sq. mi.; **Water:** 0.0 sq. mi. **Elev:** 780 ft.
Settled 1836. Part of the town is also in Wells County.

Mount Etna
Town
ZIP: 46750 **Lat:** 40-44-30 N **Long:** 85-33-45 W
Pop: 111 (1990); 122 (1980) **Pop Density:** 1110.0
Land: 0.1 sq. mi.; **Water:** 0.0 sq. mi. **Elev:** 813 ft.

American Places Dictionary   INDIANA, Jackson County

Polk   Township
ZIP: 46750   **Lat:** 40-47-09 N   **Long:** 85-36-09 W
Pop: 399 (1990); 409 (1980)   **Pop Density:** 18.2
Land: 21.9 sq. mi.; **Water:** 2.3 sq. mi.

Roanoke   Town
ZIP: 46783   **Lat:** 40-57-51 N   **Long:** 85-22-30 W
Pop: 1,018 (1990); 891 (1980)   **Pop Density:** 1696.7
Land: 0.6 sq. mi.; **Water:** 0.0 sq. mi.   **Elev:** 780 ft.
Name origin: For the Roanoke Indians of VA.

Rock Creek   Township
ZIP: 46750   **Lat:** 40-47-03 N   **Long:** 85-23-48 W
Pop: 1,471 (1990); 1,463 (1980)   **Pop Density:** 40.3
Land: 36.5 sq. mi.; **Water:** 0.4 sq. mi.

Salamonie   Township
ZIP: 46792   **Lat:** 40-41-26 N   **Long:** 85-23-23 W
Pop: 2,404 (1990); 2,018 (1980)   **Pop Density:** 65.9
Land: 36.5 sq. mi.; **Water:** 0.0 sq. mi.

Union   Township
Lat: 40-52-26 N   **Long:** 85-23-32 W
Pop: 1,174 (1990); 1,120 (1980)   **Pop Density:** 33.1
Land: 35.5 sq. mi.; **Water:** 0.9 sq. mi.

Warren   Town
ZIP: 46792   **Lat:** 40-41-12 N   **Long:** 85-25-24 W
Pop: 1,185 (1990); 1,254 (1980)   **Pop Density:** 1481.3
Land: 0.8 sq. mi.; **Water:** 0.0 sq. mi.   **Elev:** 830 ft.
Not coextensive with the town of the same name.
Name origin: For Revolutionary War figure Dr. Joseph Warren (1741–75), most noted for having sent Paul Revere (1735–1818) and William Dawes (1745–99) on their famous "midnight ride."

*****Warren**   Township
ZIP: 46792   **Lat:** 40-57-35 N   **Long:** 85-36-34 W
Pop: 717 (1990); 759 (1980)   **Pop Density:** 29.4
Land: 24.4 sq. mi.; **Water:** 0.0 sq. mi.

Wayne   Township
Lat: 40-41-48 N   **Long:** 85-36-10 W
Pop: 549 (1990); 621 (1980)   **Pop Density:** 22.5
Land: 24.4 sq. mi.; **Water:** 0.0 sq. mi.

Jackson County
County Seat: Brownstown (ZIP: 47220)

Pop: 37,730 (1990); 36,523 (1980)   **Pop Density:** 74.1
Land: 509.3 sq. mi.; **Water:** 4.4 sq. mi.   **Area Code:** 812
In south-central IN, south of Columbus; established Dec 18, 1815 (prior to statehood) from Washington County.
Name origin: For Andrew Jackson (1767–1845), seventh U.S. president.

Brownstown   Town
ZIP: 47220   **Lat:** 38-52-49 N   **Long:** 86-02-46 W
Pop: 2,872 (1990); 2,704 (1980)   **Pop Density:** 2209.2
Land: 1.3 sq. mi.; **Water:** 0.0 sq. mi.   **Elev:** 627 ft.
Not coextensive with the town of the same name.
Name origin: For Gen. Jacob Jennings Brown (1775–1828), hero of the War of 1812.

*****Brownstown**   Township
ZIP: 47220   **Lat:** 38-53-26 N   **Long:** 86-02-48 W
Pop: 4,963 (1990); 4,650 (1980)   **Pop Density:** 79.3
Land: 62.6 sq. mi.; **Water:** 1.0 sq. mi.

Carr   Township
Lat: 38-48-44 N   **Long:** 86-12-54 W
Pop: 1,576 (1990); 1,554 (1980)   **Pop Density:** 38.1
Land: 41.4 sq. mi.; **Water:** 0.7 sq. mi.

Crothersville   Town
ZIP: 47229   **Lat:** 38-47-47 N   **Long:** 85-50-23 W
Pop: 1,687 (1990); 1,747 (1980)   **Pop Density:** 2410.0
Land: 0.7 sq. mi.; **Water:** 0.0 sq. mi.   **Elev:** 565 ft.
Established 1835.
Name origin: For a railroad superintendent named Crothers.

Driftwood   Township
Lat: 38-48-42 N   **Long:** 86-06-53 W
Pop: 959 (1990); 937 (1980)   **Pop Density:** 35.0
Land: 27.4 sq. mi.; **Water:** 0.8 sq. mi.

Grassy Fork   Township
Lat: 38-47-22 N   **Long:** 85-57-54 W
Pop: 732 (1990); 792 (1980)   **Pop Density:** 18.4
Land: 39.7 sq. mi.; **Water:** 0.1 sq. mi.

Hamilton   Township
Lat: 38-58-46 N   **Long:** 86-00-06 W
Pop: 1,680 (1990); 1,509 (1980)   **Pop Density:** 26.8
Land: 62.7 sq. mi.; **Water:** 0.5 sq. mi.

Jackson   Township
ZIP: 47274   **Lat:** 38-56-26 N   **Long:** 85-52-46 W
Pop: 16,369 (1990); 15,784 (1980)   **Pop Density:** 475.8
Land: 34.4 sq. mi.; **Water:** 0.4 sq. mi.

Medora   Town
ZIP: 47260   **Lat:** 38-49-28 N   **Long:** 86-10-14 W
Pop: 805 (1990); 853 (1980)   **Pop Density:** 2683.3
Land: 0.3 sq. mi.; **Water:** 0.0 sq. mi.   **Elev:** 526 ft.
Founded 1853.
Name origin: From George Gordon, Lord Byron's (1788–1824) poem *The Corsair* (1813).

Owen   Township
Lat: 38-54-36 N   **Long:** 86-12-01 W
Pop: 1,525 (1990); 1,380 (1980)   **Pop Density:** 28.0
Land: 54.5 sq. mi.; **Water:** 0.2 sq. mi.

Pershing   Township
Lat: 39-00-00 N   **Long:** 86-07-29 W
Pop: 1,380 (1990); 1,296 (1980)   **Pop Density:** 44.8
Land: 30.8 sq. mi.; **Water:** 0.1 sq. mi.

INDIANA, Jackson County

Redding
Township
Lat: 39-00-29 N **Long:** 85-50-59 W
Pop: 3,758 (1990); 3,786 (1980) **Pop Density:** 110.5
Land: 34.0 sq. mi.; **Water:** 0.5 sq. mi.

Salt Creek
Township
Lat: 39-00-59 N **Long:** 86-14-10 W
Pop: 309 (1990); 314 (1980) **Pop Density:** 7.2
Land: 43.0 sq. mi.; **Water:** 0.1 sq. mi.

Seymour
City
ZIP: 47274 **Lat:** 38-57-30 N **Long:** 85-53-10 W
Pop: 15,576 (1990); 15,050 (1980) **Pop Density:** 2781.4
Land: 5.6 sq. mi.; **Water:** 0.0 sq. mi. **Elev:** 605 ft.
In southern IN, 37 mi. southeast of Bloomington.
Name origin: For railroad superintendent Henry Seymour.

Vernon
Township
Lat: 38-48-47 N **Long:** 85-50-39 W
Pop: 3,512 (1990); 3,613 (1980) **Pop Density:** 81.7
Land: 43.0 sq. mi.; **Water:** 0.0 sq. mi.

Washington
Township
Lat: 38-52-11 N **Long:** 85-54-05 W
Pop: 967 (1990); 908 (1980) **Pop Density:** 26.9
Land: 35.9 sq. mi.; **Water:** 0.0 sq. mi.

Jasper County
County Seat: Rensselaer (ZIP: 47978)

Pop: 24,960 (1990); 26,138 (1980) **Pop Density:** 44.6
Land: 559.9 sq. mi.; **Water:** 1.4 sq. mi. **Area Code:** 219
In northwestern IN, southeast of Gary; established Feb 7, 1835 from Indian lands.
Name origin: For Sgt. William Jasper (1750–79), Revolutionary War soldier from SC.

Barkley
Township
Lat: 41-01-32 N **Long:** 87-04-19 W
Pop: 789 (1990); 909 (1980) **Pop Density:** 13.2
Land: 59.9 sq. mi.; **Water:** 0.0 sq. mi.

Carpenter
Township
Lat: 40-46-40 N **Long:** 87-10-57 W
Pop: 1,937 (1990); 2,038 (1980) **Pop Density:** 37.0
Land: 52.4 sq. mi.; **Water:** 0.1 sq. mi.

Collegeville
CDP
Lat: 40-54-29 N **Long:** 87-09-50 W
Pop: 993 (1990); 1,059 (1980) **Pop Density:** 763.8
Land: 1.3 sq. mi.; **Water:** 0.0 sq. mi.

De Motte
Town
Lat: 41-11-58 N **Long:** 87-11-57 W
Pop: 2,482 (1990); 2,559 (1980) **Pop Density:** 689.4
Land: 3.6 sq. mi.; **Water:** 0.0 sq. mi.

Gillam
Township
Lat: 41-03-23 N **Long:** 86-57-51 W
Pop: 662 (1990); 818 (1980) **Pop Density:** 17.4
Land: 38.1 sq. mi.; **Water:** 0.0 sq. mi.

Hanging Grove
Township
Lat: 40-56-16 N **Long:** 86-59-35 W
Pop: 230 (1990); 313 (1980) **Pop Density:** 7.7
Land: 29.9 sq. mi.; **Water:** 0.0 sq. mi. **Elev:** 697 ft.

Jordan
Township
Lat: 40-51-24 N **Long:** 87-11-58 W
Pop: 297 (1990); 374 (1980) **Pop Density:** 7.9
Land: 37.4 sq. mi.; **Water:** 0.1 sq. mi.

Kankakee
Township
Lat: 41-12-17 N **Long:** 86-59-52 W
Pop: 853 (1990); 1,054 (1980) **Pop Density:** 33.6
Land: 25.4 sq. mi.; **Water:** 0.6 sq. mi.

Keener
Township
ZIP: 46310 **Lat:** 41-11-23 N **Long:** 87-12-45 W
Pop: 6,495 (1990); 6,578 (1980) **Pop Density:** 134.5
Land: 48.3 sq. mi.; **Water:** 0.0 sq. mi.

Marion
Township
ZIP: 47978 **Lat:** 40-55-59 N **Long:** 87-07-50 W
Pop: 6,913 (1990); 7,150 (1980) **Pop Density:** 131.7
Land: 52.5 sq. mi.; **Water:** 0.1 sq. mi.

Milroy
Township
Lat: 40-51-48 N **Long:** 87-02-36 W
Pop: 227 (1990); 237 (1980) **Pop Density:** 9.6
Land: 23.7 sq. mi.; **Water:** 0.0 sq. mi.

Newton
Township
Lat: 40-57-29 N **Long:** 87-13-48 W
Pop: 658 (1990); 715 (1980) **Pop Density:** 19.2
Land: 34.3 sq. mi.; **Water:** 0.0 sq. mi.

Remington
Town
ZIP: 47977 **Lat:** 40-45-45 N **Long:** 87-09-05 W
Pop: 1,247 (1990); 1,268 (1980) **Pop Density:** 1781.4
Land: 0.7 sq. mi.; **Water:** 0.0 sq. mi. **Elev:** 724 ft.
Name origin: For a pioneer merchant. Originally called Carpenter's Creek and Carpenter's Station.

Rensselaer
City
ZIP: 47978 **Lat:** 40-56-07 N **Long:** 87-08-56 W
Pop: 5,045 (1990); 4,944 (1980) **Pop Density:** 2102.1
Land: 2.4 sq. mi.; **Water:** 0.0 sq. mi. **Elev:** 657 ft.
Founded 1837.
Name origin: For its founder, NY merchant James Van Rensselaer.

Union
Township
Lat: 41-04-42 N **Long:** 87-12-31 W
Pop: 1,254 (1990); 1,260 (1980) **Pop Density:** 22.2
Land: 56.4 sq. mi.; **Water:** 0.2 sq. mi.

Walker
Township
Lat: 41-08-12 N **Long:** 87-03-18 W
Pop: 2,098 (1990); 2,250 (1980) **Pop Density:** 36.1
Land: 58.1 sq. mi.; **Water:** 0.4 sq. mi.

Wheatfield — Town
ZIP: 46392 Lat: 41-11-28 N Long: 87-03-08 W
Pop: 621 (1990); 755 (1980) Pop Density: 1035.0
Land: 0.6 sq. mi.; Water: 0.0 sq. mi. Elev: 663 ft.
Founded 1870s. Not coextensive with the town of the same name.
Name origin: For its chief agricultural crop.

*Wheatfield — Township
ZIP: 46392 Lat: 41-13-35 N Long: 87-06-07 W
Pop: 2,547 (1990); 2,442 (1980) Pop Density: 58.7
Land: 43.4 sq. mi.; Water: 0.0 sq. mi.

Jay County
County Seat: Portland (ZIP: 47371)

Pop: 21,512 (1990); 23,239 (1980) Pop Density: 56.1
Land: 383.7 sq. mi.; Water: 0.2 sq. mi. Area Code: 219
On central eastern border of IN, northeast of Muncie; established Feb 7, 1835 from Randolph County.
Name origin: For John Jay (1745–1829), first Chief Justice of the U.S. Supreme Court (1789–95), and governor of NY (1795–1801).

Bearcreek — Township
Lat: 40-31-35 N Long: 84-55-51 W
Pop: 1,228 (1990); 1,162 (1980) Pop Density: 33.9
Land: 36.2 sq. mi.; Water: 0.0 sq. mi.

Bryant — Town
ZIP: 47326 Lat: 40-32-03 N Long: 84-57-46 W
Pop: 273 (1990); 277 (1980) Pop Density: 1365.0
Land: 0.2 sq. mi.; Water: 0.0 sq. mi. Elev: 875 ft.
Established 1872.
Name origin: For a railroad construction boss named Bryan.

Dunkirk — City
ZIP: 47336 Lat: 40-22-22 N Long: 85-12-30 W
Pop: 2,587 (1990); 3,017 (1980) Pop Density: 2874.4
Land: 0.9 sq. mi.; Water: 0.0 sq. mi. Elev: 954 ft.
Part of the town is also in Blackford County.
Name origin: For Dunkirk, NY. Previously called Quincy.

Greene — Township
Lat: 40-25-58 N Long: 85-04-10 W
Pop: 982 (1990); 1,066 (1980) Pop Density: 27.9
Land: 35.2 sq. mi.; Water: 0.0 sq. mi.

Jackson — Township
Lat: 40-31-35 N Long: 85-03-09 W
Pop: 814 (1990); 829 (1980) Pop Density: 22.4
Land: 36.4 sq. mi.; Water: 0.0 sq. mi.

Jefferson — Township
Lat: 40-21-00 N Long: 85-04-30 W
Pop: 859 (1990); 945 (1980) Pop Density: 24.5
Land: 35.1 sq. mi.; Water: 0.0 sq. mi.

Knox — Township
Lat: 40-26-13 N Long: 85-10-17 W
Pop: 474 (1990); 602 (1980) Pop Density: 20.1
Land: 23.6 sq. mi.; Water: 0.0 sq. mi.

Madison — Township
Lat: 40-21-18 N Long: 84-51-35 W
Pop: 741 (1990); 693 (1980) Pop Density: 24.1
Land: 30.8 sq. mi.; Water: 0.0 sq. mi.

Noble — Township
Lat: 40-26-26 N Long: 84-51-16 W
Pop: 688 (1990); 732 (1980) Pop Density: 22.1
Land: 31.1 sq. mi.; Water: 0.0 sq. mi. Elev: 925 ft.

Penn — Township
ZIP: 47369 Lat: 40-31-45 N Long: 85-09-29 W
Pop: 1,236 (1990); 1,362 (1980) Pop Density: 40.9
Land: 30.2 sq. mi.; Water: 0.0 sq. mi.

Pennville — Town
ZIP: 47369 Lat: 40-29-35 N Long: 85-08-50 W
Pop: 637 (1990); 805 (1980) Pop Density: 1592.5
Land: 0.4 sq. mi.; Water: 0.0 sq. mi. Elev: 885 ft.
Settled 1836.
Name origin: For William Penn (1644–1718), founder of PA.

Pike — Township
Lat: 40-20-54 N Long: 84-57-41 W
Pop: 904 (1990); 955 (1980) Pop Density: 24.3
Land: 37.2 sq. mi.; Water: 0.0 sq. mi.

Portland — City
ZIP: 47371 Lat: 40-25-59 N Long: 84-58-51 W
Pop: 6,483 (1990); 7,074 (1980) Pop Density: 2025.9
Land: 3.2 sq. mi.; Water: 0.0 sq. mi. Elev: 908 ft.
Name origin: For Portland, ME, home of many early settlers.

Redkey — Town
ZIP: 47373 Lat: 40-20-52 N Long: 85-09-09 W
Pop: 1,383 (1990); 1,537 (1980) Pop Density: 1536.7
Land: 0.9 sq. mi.; Water: 0.0 sq. mi. Elev: 964 ft.
Name origin: For James Redkey, who settled here in the mid 1800s.

Richland — Township
Lat: 40-20-36 N Long: 85-10-36 W
Pop: 4,999 (1990); 5,668 (1980) Pop Density: 183.1
Land: 27.3 sq. mi.; Water: 0.0 sq. mi.

Salamonia — Town
ZIP: 47381 Lat: 40-22-55 N Long: 84-51-57 W
Pop: 138 (1990); 147 (1980) Pop Density: 345.0
Land: 0.4 sq. mi.; Water: 0.0 sq. mi. Elev: 970 ft.
Founded 1839.
Name origin: For the Salamonia River, which traverses the county.

Wabash
Township
Lat: 40-31-57 N Long: 84-50-34 W
Pop: 541 (1990); 594 (1980)   **Pop Density:** 23.0
Land: 23.5 sq. mi.; **Water:** 0.0 sq. mi.

Wayne
Township
ZIP: 47371   Lat: 40-26-10 N Long: 84-57-35 W
Pop: 8,046 (1990); 8,631 (1980)   **Pop Density:** 216.9
Land: 37.1 sq. mi.; **Water:** 0.0 sq. mi.

Jefferson County
County Seat: Madison (ZIP: 47250)

Pop: 29,797 (1990); 30,419 (1980)   **Pop Density:** 82.5
Land: 361.4 sq. mi.; **Water:** 1.6 sq. mi.   **Area Code:** 812
On southeastern border of IN, southeast of Columbus; established Nov 23, 1810 (prior to statehood) from Indian lands.
Name origin: For Thomas Jefferson (1743–1826), U.S. patriot and statesman; third U.S. president.

Brooksburg
Town
Lat: 38-44-06 N Long: 85-14-37 W
Pop: 79 (1990); 132 (1980)   **Pop Density:** 790.0
Land: 0.1 sq. mi.; **Water:** 0.0 sq. mi.   **Elev:** 470 ft.
Laid out 1840s.
Name origin: For Noah Brooks, who platted the town.

Dupont
Town
ZIP: 47231   Lat: 38-53-28 N Long: 85-31-00 W
Pop: 391 (1990); 392 (1980)   **Pop Density:** 391.0
Land: 1.0 sq. mi.; **Water:** 0.0 sq. mi.   **Elev:** 783 ft.
Name origin: For the Du Pont family, chemists and industrialists of DE.

Graham
Township
Lat: 38-46-53 N Long: 85-37-52 W
Pop: 1,448 (1990); 1,446 (1980)   **Pop Density:** 34.4
Land: 42.1 sq. mi.; **Water:** 0.2 sq. mi.

Hanover
Town
ZIP: 47243   Lat: 38-42-57 N Long: 85-28-19 W
Pop: 3,610 (1990); 4,054 (1980)   **Pop Density:** 2123.5
Land: 1.7 sq. mi.; **Water:** 0.0 sq. mi.   **Elev:** 780 ft.
Founded 1832. Not coextensive with the town of the same name.
Name origin: For Hanover, NH.

*Hanover
Township
ZIP: 47243   Lat: 38-42-13 N Long: 85-29-30 W
Pop: 4,898 (1990); 5,162 (1980)   **Pop Density:** 261.9
Land: 18.7 sq. mi.; **Water:** 0.2 sq. mi.

Lancaster
Township
Lat: 38-52-07 N Long: 85-30-27 W
Pop: 1,534 (1990); 1,484 (1980)   **Pop Density:** 47.6
Land: 32.2 sq. mi.; **Water:** 0.1 sq. mi.

Madison
City
ZIP: 47250   Lat: 38-45-19 N Long: 85-23-56 W
Pop: 12,006 (1990); 12,472 (1980) **Pop Density:** 1500.8
Land: 8.0 sq. mi.; **Water:** 0.3 sq. mi.   **Elev:** 497 ft.
In southeastern IN, 37 mi. northeast of New Albany on the Ohio River. Settled 1805. Not coextensive with the town of the same name.
Name origin: For James Madison (1751–1836), fourth U.S. president.

*Madison
Township
ZIP: 47250   Lat: 38-46-44 N Long: 85-23-05 W
Pop: 16,117 (1990); 16,225 (1980) **Pop Density:** 280.3
Land: 57.5 sq. mi.; **Water:** 0.5 sq. mi.

Milton
Township
Lat: 38-46-00 N Long: 85-14-15 W
Pop: 879 (1990); 1,204 (1980)   **Pop Density:** 25.2
Land: 34.9 sq. mi.; **Water:** 0.2 sq. mi.

Monroe
Township
Lat: 38-52-16 N Long: 85-24-57 W
Pop: 391 (1990); 357 (1980)   **Pop Density:** 10.7
Land: 36.6 sq. mi.; **Water:** 0.0 sq. mi.

Republican
Township
Lat: 38-43-48 N Long: 85-33-32 W
Pop: 1,468 (1990); 1,447 (1980)   **Pop Density:** 53.4
Land: 27.5 sq. mi.; **Water:** 0.1 sq. mi.

Saluda
Township
Lat: 38-37-37 N Long: 85-30-09 W
Pop: 1,305 (1990); 1,358 (1980)   **Pop Density:** 34.8
Land: 37.5 sq. mi.; **Water:** 0.2 sq. mi.

Shelby
Township
Lat: 38-52-42 N Long: 85-16-33 W
Pop: 827 (1990); 850 (1980)   **Pop Density:** 17.1
Land: 48.5 sq. mi.; **Water:** 0.0 sq. mi.

Smyrna
Township
Lat: 38-47-35 N Long: 85-30-33 W
Pop: 930 (1990); 886 (1980)   **Pop Density:** 35.9
Land: 25.9 sq. mi.; **Water:** 0.0 sq. mi.

Jennings County
County Seat: Vernon (ZIP: 47282)

Pop: 23,661 (1990); 22,854 (1980)
Land: 377.3 sq. mi.; **Water:** 1.1 sq. mi.
Pop Density: 62.7
Area Code: 812

In southeastern IN, southeast of Columbus; established Dec 27, 1816 from Indian lands.

Name origin: For Jonathan Jennings (1784–1834), U.S. representative from IN (1809–16; 1822–31) and first governor (1816–22).

Bigger — Township
ZIP: 47265 **Lat:** 38-57-22 N **Long:** 85-29-40 W
Pop: 611 (1990); 574 (1980) **Pop Density:** 19.9
Land: 30.7 sq. mi.; **Water:** 0.1 sq. mi.

Campbell — Township
Lat: 39-02-14 N **Long:** 85-30-01 W
Pop: 1,790 (1990); 2,164 (1980) **Pop Density:** 58.5
Land: 30.6 sq. mi.; **Water:** 0.3 sq. mi.

Center — Township
ZIP: 47265 **Lat:** 39-00-51 N **Long:** 85-37-10 W
Pop: 7,800 (1990); 7,806 (1980) **Pop Density:** 293.2
Land: 26.6 sq. mi.; **Water:** 0.0 sq. mi.

Columbia — Township
Lat: 39-07-02 N **Long:** 85-29-34 W
Pop: 813 (1990); 774 (1980) **Pop Density:** 20.6
Land: 39.5 sq. mi.; **Water:** 0.0 sq. mi.

Geneva — Township
ZIP: 47273 **Lat:** 39-04-51 N **Long:** 85-43-15 W
Pop: 5,040 (1990); 3,849 (1980) **Pop Density:** 89.4
Land: 56.4 sq. mi.; **Water:** 0.2 sq. mi.

Lovett — Township
Lat: 38-54-15 N **Long:** 85-38-29 W
Pop: 768 (1990); 809 (1980) **Pop Density:** 26.0
Land: 29.5 sq. mi.; **Water:** 0.1 sq. mi.

Marion — Township
Lat: 38-51-09 N **Long:** 85-44-57 W
Pop: 972 (1990); 984 (1980) **Pop Density:** 29.5
Land: 33.0 sq. mi.; **Water:** 0.0 sq. mi.

Montgomery — Township
Lat: 38-51-29 N **Long:** 85-38-24 W
Pop: 896 (1990); 941 (1980) **Pop Density:** 44.4
Land: 20.2 sq. mi.; **Water:** 0.0 sq. mi.

North Vernon — City
ZIP: 47265 **Lat:** 39-00-28 N **Long:** 85-37-52 W
Pop: 5,311 (1990); 5,768 (1980) **Pop Density:** 1659.7
Land: 3.2 sq. mi.; **Water:** 0.0 sq. mi. **Elev:** 725 ft.

Name origin: For its location north of Vernon.

Sand Creek — Township
Lat: 39-05-15 N **Long:** 85-36-24 W
Pop: 714 (1990); 803 (1980) **Pop Density:** 25.5
Land: 28.0 sq. mi.; **Water:** 0.0 sq. mi.

Spencer — Township
Lat: 38-58-24 N **Long:** 85-44-41 W
Pop: 1,980 (1990); 2,093 (1980) **Pop Density:** 40.6
Land: 48.8 sq. mi.; **Water:** 0.3 sq. mi.

Vernon — Town
ZIP: 47282 **Lat:** 38-59-06 N **Long:** 85-36-39 W
Pop: 370 (1990); 329 (1980) **Pop Density:** 1850.0
Land: 0.2 sq. mi.; **Water:** 0.0 sq. mi. **Elev:** 665 ft.

Founded 1815. Not coextensive with the town of the same name.

Name origin: Named in 1815 for Mount Vernon, first U.S. president George Washington's (1732–99) VA estate.

*Vernon — Township
Lat: 38-57-17 N **Long:** 85-35-55 W
Pop: 2,277 (1990); 2,057 (1980) **Pop Density:** 67.0
Land: 34.0 sq. mi.; **Water:** 0.1 sq. mi.

INDIANA, Johnson County   *American Places Dictionary*

> ## Johnson County
> **County Seat: Franklin (ZIP: 46131)**
>
> **Pop:** 88,109 (1990); 77,240 (1980) **Pop Density:** 275.2
> **Land:** 320.2 sq. mi.; **Water:** 1.4 sq. mi. **Area Code:** 317
> In central IN, south of Indianapolis; established Dec 31, 1822 from Indian lands.
> **Name origin:** For John Johnson, a judge of the first IN supreme court.

Bargersville Town
ZIP: 46106 **Lat:** 39-31-11 N **Long:** 86-09-56 W
Pop: 1,681 (1990); 1,647 (1980) **Pop Density:** 2401.4
Land: 0.7 sq. mi.; **Water:** 0.0 sq. mi. **Elev:** 819 ft.
Settled 1850.
Name origin: For Jefferson Barger, who laid out the town.

Blue River Township
ZIP: 46124 **Lat:** 39-23-25 N **Long:** 85-59-29 W
Pop: 5,115 (1990); 5,319 (1980) **Pop Density:** 211.4
Land: 24.2 sq. mi.; **Water:** 0.1 sq. mi.

Clark Township
Lat: 39-35-05 N **Long:** 85-59-45 W
Pop: 1,632 (1990); 1,690 (1980) **Pop Density:** 47.4
Land: 34.4 sq. mi.; **Water:** 0.0 sq. mi.

Edinburgh Town
ZIP: 46124 **Lat:** 39-21-13 N **Long:** 85-58-03 W
Pop: 4,131 (1990); 4,395 (1980) **Pop Density:** 2581.9
Land: 1.6 sq. mi.; **Water:** 0.0 sq. mi. **Elev:** 670 ft.
Part of the town is also in Bartholomew County.
Name origin: For Edinburgh, Scotland.

Franklin City
ZIP: 46131 **Lat:** 39-29-31 N **Long:** 86-03-23 W
Pop: 12,907 (1990); 11,563 (1980) **Pop Density:** 1792.6
Land: 7.2 sq. mi.; **Water:** 0.0 sq. mi. **Elev:** 728 ft.
In central IN, 20 mi. south of Indianapolis. County seat. Founded 1811. Not coextensive with the town of the same name.
Name origin: For Benjamin Franklin (1706–90), patriot, diplomat, and statesman.

*Franklin Township
ZIP: 46131 **Lat:** 39-29-04 N **Long:** 86-05-29 W
Pop: 13,774 (1990); 12,972 (1980) **Pop Density:** 388.0
Land: 35.5 sq. mi.; **Water:** 0.0 sq. mi.

Greenwood City
ZIP: 46142 **Lat:** 39-36-55 N **Long:** 86-06-49 W
Pop: 26,265 (1990); 19,327 (1980) **Pop Density:** 2431.9
Land: 10.8 sq. mi.; **Water:** 0.0 sq. mi. **Elev:** 812 ft.
In central IN, 9 mi. south of Indianapolis. Founded 1864.
Name origin: For a local church.

Hensley Township
Lat: 39-23-29 N **Long:** 86-11-28 W
Pop: 2,500 (1990); 2,265 (1980) **Pop Density:** 68.5
Land: 36.5 sq. mi.; **Water:** 0.4 sq. mi.

Needham Township
ZIP: 46162 **Lat:** 39-29-13 N **Long:** 85-59-58 W
Pop: 3,538 (1990); 3,339 (1980) **Pop Density:** 101.1
Land: 35.0 sq. mi.; **Water:** 0.0 sq. mi.

New Whiteland Town
ZIP: 46184 **Lat:** 39-33-43 N **Long:** 86-05-48 W
Pop: 4,097 (1990); 4,502 (1980) **Pop Density:** 3724.5
Land: 1.1 sq. mi.; **Water:** 0.0 sq. mi. **Elev:** 806 ft.
Founded mid 1700s.
Name origin: For its founder Joel White.

Nineveh Township
ZIP: 46164 **Lat:** 39-22-58 N **Long:** 86-04-56 W
Pop: 3,278 (1990); 2,999 (1980) **Pop Density:** 90.6
Land: 36.2 sq. mi.; **Water:** 0.4 sq. mi.

Pleasant Township
ZIP: 46131 **Lat:** 39-35-03 N **Long:** 86-05-13 W
Pop: 28,094 (1990); 26,106 (1980) **Pop Density:** 872.5
Land: 32.2 sq. mi.; **Water:** 0.0 sq. mi.

Princes Lakes Town
Lat: 39-21-02 N **Long:** 86-06-32 W
Pop: 1,055 (1990); 937 (1980) **Pop Density:** 879.2
Land: 1.2 sq. mi.; **Water:** 0.2 sq. mi.

Trafalgar Town
ZIP: 46181 **Lat:** 39-24-53 N **Long:** 86-08-58 W
Pop: 531 (1990); 466 (1980) **Pop Density:** 482.7
Land: 1.1 sq. mi.; **Water:** 0.0 sq. mi. **Elev:** 828 ft.
Founded 1851.
Name origin: For the great English naval victory in 1805.

Union Township
Lat: 39-29-01 N **Long:** 86-11-29 W
Pop: 1,946 (1990); 2,023 (1980) **Pop Density:** 53.9
Land: 36.1 sq. mi.; **Water:** 0.0 sq. mi.

Whiteland Town
ZIP: 46184 **Lat:** 39-33-01 N **Long:** 86-05-19 W
Pop: 2,446 (1990); 1,956 (1980) **Pop Density:** 1063.5
Land: 2.3 sq. mi.; **Water:** 0.0 sq. mi. **Elev:** 800 ft.
Founded 1863.
Name origin: For pioneer Joel White.

White River Township
ZIP: 46142 **Lat:** 39-34-39 N **Long:** 86-11-34 W
Pop: 28,232 (1990); 20,527 (1980) **Pop Density:** 562.4
Land: 50.2 sq. mi.; **Water:** 0.3 sq. mi.

Knox County
County Seat: Vincennes (ZIP: 47591)

Pop: 39,884 (1990); 41,838 (1980) **Pop Density:** 77.3
Land: 515.9 sq. mi.; **Water:** 8.2 sq. mi. **Area Code:** 812
On the southwest border of IN; organized Jun 20, 1790 (prior to statehood) from Northwest Territory.
Name origin: For Gen. Henry Knox (1750–1806), Revolutionary War officer and first U.S. secretary of war (1785–94).

Bicknell — City
ZIP: 47512 **Lat:** 38-46-30 N **Long:** 87-18-30 W
Pop: 3,357 (1990); 4,713 (1980) **Pop Density:** 2238.0
Land: 1.5 sq. mi.; **Water:** 0.0 sq. mi. **Elev:** 530 ft.
Name origin: Named in 1869 for pioneer John Bicknell.

Bruceville — Town
ZIP: 47516 **Lat:** 38-45-29 N **Long:** 87-24-51 W
Pop: 471 (1990); 646 (1980) **Pop Density:** 1570.0
Land: 0.3 sq. mi.; **Water:** 0.0 sq. mi. **Elev:** 513 ft.
Name origin: For its first settler, Maj. William Bruce.

Busseron — Township
ZIP: 47561 **Lat:** 38-50-51 N **Long:** 87-28-14 W
Pop: 1,372 (1990); 1,485 (1980) **Pop Density:** 26.5
Land: 51.8 sq. mi.; **Water:** 0.9 sq. mi.

Decker — Town
ZIP: 47524 **Lat:** 38-31-06 N **Long:** 87-31-25 W
Pop: 281 (1990); 256 (1980) **Pop Density:** 936.7
Land: 0.3 sq. mi.; **Water:** 0.0 sq. mi. **Elev:** 450 ft.
Not coextensive with the town of the same name.
Name origin: For its founder, Issac Decker.

*Decker — Township
ZIP: 47524 **Lat:** 38-28-31 N **Long:** 87-38-00 W
Pop: 251 (1990); 270 (1980) **Pop Density:** 5.7
Land: 44.4 sq. mi.; **Water:** 2.2 sq. mi.

Edwardsport — Town
ZIP: 47528 **Lat:** 38-48-44 N **Long:** 87-15-05 W
Pop: 380 (1990); 459 (1980) **Pop Density:** 1266.7
Land: 0.3 sq. mi.; **Water:** 0.0 sq. mi. **Elev:** 512 ft.
Name origin: For its founder, Henry Edwards.

Harrison — Township
Lat: 38-35-21 N **Long:** 87-21-09 W
Pop: 1,911 (1990); 1,872 (1980) **Pop Density:** 24.2
Land: 79.0 sq. mi.; **Water:** 1.3 sq. mi.

Johnson — Township
Lat: 38-34-07 N **Long:** 87-30-36 W
Pop: 1,449 (1990); 1,501 (1980) **Pop Density:** 28.7
Land: 50.5 sq. mi.; **Water:** 0.5 sq. mi.

Monroe City — Town
ZIP: 47557 **Lat:** 38-36-50 N **Long:** 87-21-12 W
Pop: 538 (1990); 569 (1980) **Pop Density:** 1793.3
Land: 0.3 sq. mi.; **Water:** 0.0 sq. mi. **Elev:** 520 ft.
Name origin: For early landowner Monroe Alton.

Oaktown — Town
ZIP: 47561 **Lat:** 38-52-17 N **Long:** 87-26-28 W
Pop: 655 (1990); 776 (1980) **Pop Density:** 2183.3
Land: 0.3 sq. mi.; **Water:** 0.0 sq. mi. **Elev:** 475 ft.
Settled 1867.
Name origin: For its many oak trees.

Palmyra — Township
Lat: 38-40-48 N **Long:** 87-24-33 W
Pop: 1,401 (1990); 1,578 (1980) **Pop Density:** 37.4
Land: 37.5 sq. mi.; **Water:** 0.0 sq. mi.

Sandborn — Town
ZIP: 47578 **Lat:** 38-53-48 N **Long:** 87-11-04 W
Pop: 455 (1990); 576 (1980) **Pop Density:** 1137.5
Land: 0.4 sq. mi.; **Water:** 0.0 sq. mi. **Elev:** 480 ft.
Name origin: For a civil engineer on the Indianapolis & Vincennes Railroad.

Steen — Township
ZIP: 47597 **Lat:** 38-40-01 N **Long:** 87-17-58 W
Pop: 885 (1990); 1,071 (1980) **Pop Density:** 24.3
Land: 36.4 sq. mi.; **Water:** 0.5 sq. mi.

Vigo — Township
ZIP: 47512 **Lat:** 38-50-17 N **Long:** 87-14-16 W
Pop: 4,666 (1990); 5,513 (1980) **Pop Density:** 70.6
Land: 66.1 sq. mi.; **Water:** 1.0 sq. mi.

Vincennes — City
ZIP: 47591 **Lat:** 38-40-34 N **Long:** 87-30-39 W
Pop: 19,859 (1990); 20,857 (1980) **Pop Density:** 3103.0
Land: 6.4 sq. mi.; **Water:** 0.1 sq. mi. **Elev:** 429 ft.
In southwestern IN on the Wabash River, 54 mi. south of Terre Haute. Oldest town in IN and former capital of the Old Northwest Territory. Not coextensive with the town of the same name.
Name origin: For French commander François-Marie Bissot (1700–1736), sieur de Vincennes, who was killed by Indians near here in 1736.

*Vincennes — Township
ZIP: 47591 **Lat:** 38-37-59 N **Long:** 87-33-35 W
Pop: 24,365 (1990); 24,945 (1980) **Pop Density:** 405.4
Land: 60.1 sq. mi.; **Water:** 1.7 sq. mi.

Washington — Township
ZIP: 47516 **Lat:** 38-45-48 N **Long:** 87-23-49 W
Pop: 2,387 (1990); 2,316 (1980) **Pop Density:** 48.9
Land: 48.8 sq. mi.; **Water:** 0.2 sq. mi.

Wheatland — Town
ZIP: 47597 **Lat:** 38-39-50 N **Long:** 87-18-23 W
Pop: 439 (1990); 532 (1980) **Pop Density:** 1463.3
Land: 0.3 sq. mi.; **Water:** 0.0 sq. mi. **Elev:** 490 ft.
Name origin: For the area's good wheat production.

Widner — Township
ZIP: 47561 **Lat:** 38-51-51 N **Long:** 87-20-33 W
Pop: 1,197 (1990); 1,287 (1980) **Pop Density:** 29.1
Land: 41.2 sq. mi.; **Water:** 0.0 sq. mi.

INDIANA, Kosciusko County — *American Places Dictionary*

Kosciusko County
County Seat: Warsaw (ZIP: 46580)

Pop: 65,294 (1990); 59,555 (1980) **Pop Density:** 121.5
Land: 537.5 sq. mi.; **Water:** 16.8 sq. mi. **Area Code:** 219
In north-central IN, south of Elkhart; established Feb 7, 1835 from Indian lands.
Name origin: For Thaddeus Kosciusko (1746–1817), Polish soldier who fought with the Americans during the Revolutionary War.

Burket — Town
ZIP: 46508 **Lat:** 41-09-15 N **Long:** 85-58-08 W
Pop: 200 (1990); 260 (1980) **Pop Density:** 2000.0
Land: 0.1 sq. mi.; **Water:** 0.0 sq. mi. **Elev:** 860 ft.
Name origin: For its founder.

Clay — Township
Lat: 41-07-58 N **Long:** 85-50-44 W
Pop: 1,625 (1990); 1,621 (1980) **Pop Density:** 55.3
Land: 29.4 sq. mi.; **Water:** 0.4 sq. mi.

Claypool — Town
ZIP: 46510 **Lat:** 41-07-40 N **Long:** 85-52-46 W
Pop: 411 (1990); 464 (1980) **Pop Density:** 2055.0
Land: 0.2 sq. mi.; **Water:** 0.0 sq. mi. **Elev:** 900 ft.
Settled 1841.
Name origin: For a local settler.

Etna — Township
Lat: 41-18-00 N **Long:** 86-02-00 W
Pop: 1,290 (1990); 1,150 (1980) **Pop Density:** 63.9
Land: 20.2 sq. mi.; **Water:** 0.1 sq. mi.

Etna Green — Town
ZIP: 46524 **Lat:** 41-16-41 N **Long:** 86-02-46 W
Pop: 578 (1990); 522 (1980) **Pop Density:** 1926.7
Land: 0.3 sq. mi.; **Water:** 0.0 sq. mi. **Elev:** 820 ft.
Established 1849.
Name origin: Named in 1954 to parody the name of the Scottish village Gretna Green; first part of the name comes from the county. Previously called Camp Creek.

Franklin — Township
Lat: 41-07-19 N **Long:** 86-01-42 W
Pop: 985 (1990); 1,019 (1980) **Pop Density:** 28.7
Land: 34.3 sq. mi.; **Water:** 0.0 sq. mi.

Harrison — Township
Lat: 41-12-54 N **Long:** 85-58-51 W
Pop: 3,377 (1990); 3,226 (1980) **Pop Density:** 79.1
Land: 42.7 sq. mi.; **Water:** 0.3 sq. mi.

Jackson — Township
Lat: 41-04-43 N **Long:** 85-44-09 W
Pop: 1,225 (1990); 1,251 (1980) **Pop Density:** 42.2
Land: 29.0 sq. mi.; **Water:** 0.0 sq. mi.

Jefferson — Township
Lat: 41-23-27 N **Long:** 85-56-02 W
Pop: 1,201 (1990); 1,089 (1980) **Pop Density:** 38.2
Land: 31.4 sq. mi.; **Water:** 0.0 sq. mi.

Lake — Township
Lat: 41-04-17 N **Long:** 85-50-53 W
Pop: 1,566 (1990); 1,661 (1980) **Pop Density:** 67.8
Land: 23.1 sq. mi.; **Water:** 0.2 sq. mi.

Leesburg — Town
ZIP: 46538 **Lat:** 41-19-46 N **Long:** 85-50-54 W
Pop: 584 (1990); 629 (1980) **Pop Density:** 2920.0
Land: 0.2 sq. mi.; **Water:** 0.0 sq. mi. **Elev:** 853 ft.
Founded 1835.
Name origin: For its founder, Levi Lee.

Mentone — Town
ZIP: 46539 **Lat:** 41-10-25 N **Long:** 86-02-12 W
Pop: 912 (1990); 973 (1980) **Pop Density:** 1520.0
Land: 0.6 sq. mi.; **Water:** 0.0 sq. mi. **Elev:** 839 ft.
Founded 1882.
Name origin: Named in 1882 for Menton, France, with a spelling variation.

Milford — Town
ZIP: 46542 **Lat:** 41-24-37 N **Long:** 85-50-54 W
Pop: 1,388 (1990); 1,153 (1980) **Pop Density:** 1388.0
Land: 1.0 sq. mi.; **Water:** 0.0 sq. mi. **Elev:** 835 ft.
Name origin: For a mill built here on Turkey Creek ford.

Monroe — Township
Lat: 41-08-46 N **Long:** 85-44-35 W
Pop: 1,088 (1990); 932 (1980) **Pop Density:** 45.0
Land: 24.2 sq. mi.; **Water:** 0.1 sq. mi.

Nappanee — City
ZIP: 46550 **Lat:** 41-26-02 N **Long:** 85-58-39 W
Pop: 0 (1990)
Land: 0.2 sq. mi.; **Water:** 0.0 sq. mi. **Elev:** 878 ft.
Part of the town is also in Elkhart County.

North Webster — Town
ZIP: 46555 **Lat:** 41-19-31 N **Long:** 85-41-49 W
Pop: 881 (1990); 709 (1980) **Pop Density:** 1468.3
Land: 0.6 sq. mi.; **Water:** 0.0 sq. mi. **Elev:** 880 ft.
Name origin: For pioneer Malcolm Webster, who settled here 1841.

Pierceton — Town
ZIP: 46562 **Lat:** 41-11-58 N **Long:** 85-42-27 W
Pop: 1,030 (1990); 1,086 (1980) **Pop Density:** 1471.4
Land: 0.7 sq. mi.; **Water:** 0.0 sq. mi. **Elev:** 928 ft.

Plain — Township
ZIP: 46538 **Lat:** 41-17-59 N **Long:** 85-49-37 W
Pop: 5,211 (1990); 4,968 (1980) **Pop Density:** 151.9
Land: 34.3 sq. mi.; **Water:** 1.6 sq. mi.

Prairie — Township
Lat: 41-17-51 N **Long:** 85-56-11 W
Pop: 1,279 (1990); 1,188 (1980) **Pop Density:** 35.9
Land: 35.6 sq. mi.; **Water:** 0.3 sq. mi.

Scott — Township
Lat: 41-23-08 N **Long:** 86-01-22 W
Pop: 1,272 (1990); 1,190 (1980) **Pop Density:** 54.4
Land: 23.4 sq. mi.; **Water:** 0.0 sq. mi.

Seward
Township
Lat: 41-06-29 N Long: 85-56-45 W
Pop: 2,039 (1990); 1,921 (1980) **Pop Density:** 57.8
Land: 35.3 sq. mi.; **Water:** 1.0 sq. mi.

Sidney
Town
ZIP: 46566 Lat: 41-06-18 N Long: 85-44-34 W
Pop: 167 (1990); 194 (1980) **Pop Density:** 1670.0
Land: 0.1 sq. mi.; **Water:** 0.0 sq. mi. **Elev:** 976 ft.
Founded 1834.
Name origin: For the Sidneys, local landowners.

Silver Lake
Town
ZIP: 46982 Lat: 41-04-20 N Long: 85-53-30 W
Pop: 528 (1990); 576 (1980) **Pop Density:** 1760.0
Land: 0.3 sq. mi.; **Water:** 0.0 sq. mi. **Elev:** 912 ft.
Settled 1860.
Name origin: For nearby Silver Lake.

Syracuse
Town
ZIP: 46567 Lat: 41-25-23 N Long: 85-44-56 W
Pop: 2,729 (1990); 2,579 (1980) **Pop Density:** 1705.6
Land: 1.6 sq. mi.; **Water:** 0.3 sq. mi. **Elev:** 870 ft.
Name origin: For Syracuse, NY.

Tippecanoe
Township
ZIP: 46555 Lat: 41-18-45 N Long: 85-42-30 W
Pop: 6,197 (1990); 5,340 (1980) **Pop Density:** 198.6
Land: 31.2 sq. mi.; **Water:** 3.9 sq. mi.

Turkey Creek
Township
ZIP: 46567 Lat: 41-23-42 N Long: 85-42-42 W
Pop: 7,695 (1990); 6,587 (1980) **Pop Density:** 262.6
Land: 29.3 sq. mi.; **Water:** 6.1 sq. mi.

Van Buren
Township
Lat: 41-23-30 N Long: 85-49-32 W
Pop: 3,660 (1990); 3,118 (1980) **Pop Density:** 103.4
Land: 35.4 sq. mi.; **Water:** 1.1 sq. mi.

Warsaw
City
ZIP: 46580 Lat: 41-14-22 N Long: 85-50-51 W
Pop: 10,968 (1990); 10,647 (1980) **Pop Density:** 1166.8
Land: 9.4 sq. mi.; **Water:** 1.0 sq. mi. **Elev:** 826 ft.
In northern IN, 35 mi. southeast of South Bend. Founded 1836.
Name origin: For the capital of Poland.

Washington
Township
Lat: 41-12-59 N Long: 85-42-30 W
Pop: 3,128 (1990); 2,847 (1980) **Pop Density:** 88.9
Land: 35.2 sq. mi.; **Water:** 0.2 sq. mi.

Wayne
Township
ZIP: 46590 Lat: 41-13-10 N Long: 85-50-15 W
Pop: 22,456 (1990); 20,447 (1980) **Pop Density:** 516.2
Land: 43.5 sq. mi.; **Water:** 1.5 sq. mi.
In north-central IN.

Winona Lake
Town
ZIP: 46590 Lat: 41-13-07 N Long: 85-48-55 W
Pop: 4,053 (1990); 2,827 (1980) **Pop Density:** 1762.2
Land: 2.3 sq. mi.; **Water:** 0.4 sq. mi. **Elev:** 830 ft.
Name origin: For the lake, itself probably named for a local woman. Formerly Eagle Lake.

Lagrange County
County Seat: Lagrange (ZIP: 46761)

Pop: 29,477 (1990); 25,550 (1980) **Pop Density:** 77.7
Land: 379.6 sq. mi.; **Water:** 7.2 sq. mi. **Area Code:** 219
On the northeastern border of IN, east of Elkhart; organized Feb 2, 1832 from unorganized territory in Elkhart County.
Name origin: For the country home near Paris of the Marquis de Lafayette (1757–1834), who fought with the Americans during the Revolutionary War; from French 'the barn.'

Bloomfield
Township
Lat: 41-38-56 N Long: 85-21-31 W
Pop: 4,737 (1990); 4,159 (1980) **Pop Density:** 133.4
Land: 35.5 sq. mi.; **Water:** 0.3 sq. mi.

Clay
Township
Lat: 41-39-03 N Long: 85-28-41 W
Pop: 2,485 (1990); 2,213 (1980) **Pop Density:** 68.8
Land: 36.1 sq. mi.; **Water:** 0.1 sq. mi.

Clearspring
Township
Lat: 41-34-08 N Long: 85-28-57 W
Pop: 3,248 (1990); 2,778 (1980) **Pop Density:** 91.0
Land: 35.7 sq. mi.; **Water:** 0.3 sq. mi.

Eden
Township
Lat: 41-34-12 N Long: 85-35-34 W
Pop: 2,501 (1990); 2,067 (1980) **Pop Density:** 69.7
Land: 35.9 sq. mi.; **Water:** 0.1 sq. mi.

Greenfield
Township
Lat: 41-43-32 N Long: 85-16-59 W
Pop: 1,135 (1990); 1,088 (1980) **Pop Density:** 31.2
Land: 36.4 sq. mi.; **Water:** 0.4 sq. mi.

Johnson
Township
Lat: 41-34-23 N Long: 85-22-10 W
Pop: 2,880 (1990); 2,593 (1980) **Pop Density:** 86.5
Land: 33.3 sq. mi.; **Water:** 2.4 sq. mi.

Lagrange
Town
ZIP: 46761 Lat: 41-38-36 N Long: 85-25-02 W
Pop: 2,382 (1990); 2,164 (1980) **Pop Density:** 2382.0
Land: 1.0 sq. mi.; **Water:** 0.0 sq. mi.
Name origin: For the country home near Paris of the Marquis de Lafayette (1757–1834), who fought with the Americans during the Revolutionary War; from French 'the barn.'

Lima
Township
ZIP: 46746 Lat: 41-43-47 N Long: 85-25-31 W
Pop: 2,294 (1990); 1,889 (1980) Pop Density: 94.0
Land: 24.4 sq. mi.; Water: 0.7 sq. mi.

Milford
Township
Lat: 41-34-14 N Long: 85-15-05 W
Pop: 2,548 (1990); 2,297 (1980) Pop Density: 75.4
Land: 33.8 sq. mi.; Water: 1.7 sq. mi.

Newbury
Township
Lat: 41-39-03 N Long: 85-35-41 W
Pop: 3,850 (1990); 3,168 (1980) Pop Density: 109.4
Land: 35.2 sq. mi.; Water: 0.5 sq. mi.

Shipshewana
Town
ZIP: 46565 Lat: 41-40-29 N Long: 85-34-45 W
Pop: 524 (1990); 466 (1980) Pop Density: 1310.0
Land: 0.4 sq. mi.; Water: 0.0 sq. mi. Elev: 900 ft.
Name origin: For a nearby lake, so named from an Indian term meaning 'vision of a lion.'

Springfield
Township
Lat: 41-39-35 N Long: 85-15-33 W
Pop: 1,188 (1990); 1,094 (1980) Pop Density: 33.4
Land: 35.6 sq. mi.; Water: 0.3 sq. mi.

Topeka
Town
ZIP: 46571 Lat: 41-32-18 N Long: 85-32-31 W
Pop: 912 (1990); 876 (1980) Pop Density: 701.5
Land: 1.3 sq. mi.; Water: 0.0 sq. mi. Elev: 925 ft.
Name origin: From a Shawnee Indian term for the Jerusalem artichoke.

Van Buren
Township
Lat: 41-43-50 N Long: 85-34-20 W
Pop: 2,611 (1990); 2,204 (1980) Pop Density: 69.4
Land: 37.6 sq. mi.; Water: 0.5 sq. mi.

Wolcottville
Town
ZIP: 46795 Lat: 41-31-45 N Long: 85-21-56 W
Pop: 396 (1990); 890 (1980) Pop Density: 792.0
Land: 0.5 sq. mi.; Water: 0.0 sq. mi. Elev: 934 ft.
Part of the town is also in Noble County.
Name origin: For prominent businessman George Wolcott.

Lake County
County Seat: Crown Point (ZIP: 46307)

Pop: 475,594 (1990); 522,917 (1980) Pop Density: 956.9
Land: 497.0 sq. mi.; Water: 129.4 sq. mi. Area Code: 219
In the northwest corner of IN; established Jan 28, 1836 from Porter and Newton counties.
Name origin: For its location on the southern shore of Lake Michigan.

Calumet
Township
ZIP: 46402 Lat: 41-35-07 N Long: 87-21-14 W
Pop: 141,875 (1990); 176,916 (1980) Pop Density: 2295.7
Land: 61.8 sq. mi.; Water: 7.0 sq. mi.

Cedar Creek
Township
ZIP: 46356 Lat: 41-15-17 N Long: 87-22-43 W
Pop: 9,009 (1990); 8,704 (1980) Pop Density: 150.1
Land: 60.0 sq. mi.; Water: 0.6 sq. mi.

Cedar Lake
Town
ZIP: 46303 Lat: 41-22-23 N Long: 87-26-10 W
Pop: 8,885 (1990); 8,754 (1980) Pop Density: 1326.1
Land: 6.7 sq. mi.; Water: 1.3 sq. mi. Elev: 725 ft.
Name origin: Named for the red cedars along the shore of the nearby lake.

Center
Township
ZIP: 46307 Lat: 41-23-36 N Long: 87-22-01 W
Pop: 24,369 (1990); 24,017 (1980) Pop Density: 620.1
Land: 39.3 sq. mi.; Water: 0.6 sq. mi.

Crown Point
City
ZIP: 46307 Lat: 41-25-27 N Long: 87-21-27 W
Pop: 17,728 (1990); 16,455 (1980) Pop Density: 2244.1
Land: 7.9 sq. mi.; Water: 0.0 sq. mi. Elev: 735 ft.
In northwestern IN, 13 mi. south of Lake Michigan. County seat. Established 1834.
Name origin: For a high point of land upon which the courthouse stood. Previously called Liverpool.

Dyer
Town
ZIP: 46311 Lat: 41-30-12 N Long: 87-30-18 W
Pop: 10,923 (1990); 9,555 (1980) Pop Density: 1950.5
Land: 5.6 sq. mi.; Water: 0.0 sq. mi. Elev: 630 ft.
Settled 1850s.

Eagle Creek
Township
Lat: 41-16-55 N Long: 87-16-56 W
Pop: 1,431 (1990); 1,421 (1980) Pop Density: 25.6
Land: 55.8 sq. mi.; Water: 0.2 sq. mi.

East Chicago
City
ZIP: 46312 Lat: 41-38-55 N Long: 87-27-06 W
Pop: 33,892 (1990); 39,786 (1980) Pop Density: 2824.3
Land: 12.0 sq. mi.; Water: 3.7 sq. mi. Elev: 592 ft.
In northwestern IN on Lake Michigan, 18 mi. southeast of Chicago.
Name origin: For its location east of Chicago.

Gary
City
ZIP: 46401 Lat: 41-35-44 N Long: 87-20-38 W
Pop: 116,646 (1990); 151,968 (1980) Pop Density: 2323.6
Land: 50.2 sq. mi.; Water: 7.0 sq. mi. Elev: 600 ft.
In northwestern IN on Lake Michigan. Established 1906.
Name origin: For Elbert Henry Gary (1846–1927), board chairman of U.S. Steel.

INDIANA, Lake County

Griffith
Town
ZIP: 46319 **Lat:** 41-31-20 N **Long:** 87-25-25 W
Pop: 17,916 (1990); 17,026 (1980) **Pop Density:** 2059.3
Land: 8.7 sq. mi.; **Water:** 0.0 sq. mi. **Elev:** 625 ft.
In northwestern IN, 7 mi. south of Gary.
Name origin: For railroad civil engineer Benjamin Griffith.

Hammond
City
ZIP: 46320 **Lat:** 41-37-15 N **Long:** 87-29-25 W
Pop: 84,236 (1990); 93,714 (1980) **Pop Density:** 3678.4
Land: 22.9 sq. mi.; **Water:** 1.9 sq. mi. **Elev:** 585 ft.
In northwestern IN on the IL border. Incorporated 1884.
Name origin: For prominent meat packer George Hammond (1838–86).

Hanover
Township
ZIP: 46303 **Lat:** 41-23-24 N **Long:** 87-28-41 W
Pop: 7,365 (1990); 7,101 (1980) **Pop Density:** 257.5
Land: 28.6 sq. mi.; **Water:** 0.9 sq. mi.

Highland
Town
ZIP: 46322 **Lat:** 41-32-56 N **Long:** 87-27-27 W
Pop: 23,696 (1990); 25,935 (1980) **Pop Density:** 3484.7
Land: 6.8 sq. mi.; **Water:** 0.0 sq. mi. **Elev:** 620 ft.
In northwestern IN, 6 mi. south of Lake Michigan.
Name origin: For its location on ground higher than the surrounding area.

Hobart
City
ZIP: 46342 **Lat:** 41-31-53 N **Long:** 87-16-02 W
Pop: 21,822 (1990); 22,987 (1980) **Pop Density:** 1417.0
Land: 15.4 sq. mi.; **Water:** 0.5 sq. mi. **Elev:** 632 ft.
In northwestern IN, 7 mi. south of Lake Michigan. Founded 1849. Not coextensive with the town of the same name.
Name origin: For Hobart Earle, the brother of George Earle, the town's founder.

*Hobart
Township
ZIP: 46342 **Lat:** 41-32-48 N **Long:** 87-15-53 W
Pop: 38,942 (1990); 42,485 (1980) **Pop Density:** 1533.1
Land: 25.4 sq. mi.; **Water:** 0.7 sq. mi.

Lake Dalecarlia
CDP
Lat: 41-20-20 N **Long:** 87-24-11 W
Pop: 1,276 (1990) **Pop Density:** 911.4
Land: 1.4 sq. mi.; **Water:** 0.3 sq. mi.

Lakes of the Four Seasons
CDP
Lat: 41-24-40 N **Long:** 87-13-41 W
Pop: 3,724 (1990) **Pop Density:** 2482.7
Land: 1.5 sq. mi.; **Water:** 0.3 sq. mi.
Part of the town is also in Porter County.

Lake Station
City
ZIP: 46405 **Lat:** 41-34-21 N **Long:** 87-15-41 W
Pop: 13,899 (1990); 15,087 (1980) **Pop Density:** 1674.6
Land: 8.3 sq. mi.; **Water:** 0.2 sq. mi.
Name origin: Descriptively named by its founders.

Lowell
Town
ZIP: 46356 **Lat:** 41-17-41 N **Long:** 87-24-47 W
Pop: 6,430 (1990); 5,827 (1980) **Pop Density:** 1648.7
Land: 3.9 sq. mi.; **Water:** 0.1 sq. mi. **Elev:** 684 ft.
Name origin: For Lowell, MA.

Merrillville
Town
ZIP: 46410 **Lat:** 41-28-17 N **Long:** 87-19-32 W
Pop: 27,257 (1990); 27,677 (1980) **Pop Density:** 879.3
Land: 31.0 sq. mi.; **Water:** 0.0 sq. mi. **Elev:** 650 ft.
In northwestern IN, 9 mi. south of Gary.
Name origin: For storekeeper Dudley Merrill.

Munster
Town
ZIP: 46321 **Lat:** 41-32-48 N **Long:** 87-30-13 W
Pop: 19,949 (1990); 20,671 (1980) **Pop Density:** 2659.9
Land: 7.5 sq. mi.; **Water:** 0.1 sq. mi. **Elev:** 600 ft.
In northwestern IN, 9 mi. south of Lake Michigan.
Name origin: For early settler Jacob Munster.

New Chicago
Town
ZIP: 46342 **Lat:** 41-33-31 N **Long:** 87-16-19 W
Pop: 2,066 (1990); 2,581 (1980) **Pop Density:** 2951.4
Land: 0.7 sq. mi.; **Water:** 0.0 sq. mi. **Elev:** 630 ft.
Founded 1907.
Name origin: For Chicago, IL.

North
Township
ZIP: 46312 **Lat:** 41-36-39 N **Long:** 87-28-51 W
Pop: 166,928 (1990); 185,736 (1980) **Pop Density:** 3273.1
Land: 51.0 sq. mi.; **Water:** 7.2 sq. mi.

Ross
Township
ZIP: 46410 **Lat:** 41-28-18 N **Long:** 87-18-40 W
Pop: 34,683 (1990); 34,842 (1980) **Pop Density:** 706.4
Land: 49.1 sq. mi.; **Water:** 0.0 sq. mi.

St. John
Town
Lat: 41-26-49 N **Long:** 87-28-33 W
Pop: 4,921 (1990); 3,974 (1980) **Pop Density:** 806.7
Land: 6.1 sq. mi.; **Water:** 0.0 sq. mi. **Elev:** 750 ft.
In northwestern IN, 12 mi. southwest of Gary. Founded 1830s. Not coextensive with the town of the same name.
Name origin: For early settler John Hack. 'Saint' was added for euphony.

*St. John
Township
ZIP: 46373 **Lat:** 41-28-36 N **Long:** 87-27-44 W
Pop: 41,782 (1990); 33,718 (1980) **Pop Density:** 1065.9
Land: 39.2 sq. mi.; **Water:** 0.2 sq. mi.

Schererville
Town
ZIP: 46375 **Lat:** 41-29-21 N **Long:** 87-26-53 W
Pop: 19,926 (1990); 13,209 (1980) **Pop Density:** 1532.8
Land: 13.0 sq. mi.; **Water:** 0.0 sq. mi. **Elev:** 626 ft.
In northwestern IN, 9 mi. south of Hammond. Platted 1866.
Name origin: For founder Scherer Wright.

Schneider
Town
ZIP: 46376 **Lat:** 41-11-31 N **Long:** 87-26-51 W
Pop: 310 (1990); 364 (1980) **Pop Density:** 344.4
Land: 0.9 sq. mi.; **Water:** 0.0 sq. mi. **Elev:** 636 ft.
Name origin: For a landowner of the 1900s.

West Creek
Township
Lat: 41-15-28 N **Long:** 87-28-56 W
Pop: 4,223 (1990); 4,316 (1980) **Pop Density:** 68.2
Land: 61.9 sq. mi.; **Water:** 0.1 sq. mi.

Whiting
City
ZIP: 46394 **Lat:** 41-40-41 N **Long:** 87-29-12 W
Pop: 5,155 (1990); 5,630 (1980) **Pop Density:** 2863.9
Land: 1.8 sq. mi.; **Water:** 1.5 sq. mi. **Elev:** 585 ft.
Name origin: For a railroad conductor involved in a nearby train wreck.

INDIANA, Lake County

Winfield
Township
Lat: 41-23-14 N **Long:** 87-15-12 W
Pop: 4,987 (1990); 3,661 (1980) **Pop Density:** 201.1
Land: 24.8 sq. mi.; **Water:** 0.3 sq. mi.

La Porte County
County Seat: La Porte (ZIP: 46350)

Pop: 107,066 (1990); 108,632 (1980) **Pop Density:** 179.0
Land: 598.3 sq. mi.; **Water:** 14.8 sq. mi. **Area Code:** 219

On the northwestern border of IN, west of South Bend; organized Jan 9, 1832 from Indian lands.

Name origin: French 'the port' or 'the door,' referring to a natural opening through the forest that served as a gateway to the north.

Cass
Township
Lat: 41-23-10 N **Long:** 86-52-04 W
Pop: 1,690 (1990); 1,772 (1980) **Pop Density:** 46.7
Land: 36.2 sq. mi.; **Water:** 0.0 sq. mi.

Center
Township
ZIP: 46350 **Lat:** 41-38-23 N **Long:** 86-45-24 W
Pop: 23,438 (1990); 23,140 (1980) **Pop Density:** 753.6
Land: 31.1 sq. mi.; **Water:** 1.9 sq. mi.

Clinton
Township
Lat: 41-28-43 N **Long:** 86-52-31 W
Pop: 1,034 (1990); 969 (1980) **Pop Density:** 30.1
Land: 34.3 sq. mi.; **Water:** 0.0 sq. mi.

Coolspring
Township
ZIP: 46360 **Lat:** 41-39-17 N **Long:** 86-52-23 W
Pop: 14,492 (1990); 14,679 (1980) **Pop Density:** 402.6
Land: 36.0 sq. mi.; **Water:** 0.1 sq. mi.

Dewey
Township
Lat: 41-18-01 N **Long:** 86-52-54 W
Pop: 1,179 (1990); 1,260 (1980) **Pop Density:** 32.8
Land: 35.9 sq. mi.; **Water:** 0.0 sq. mi.

Galena
Township
Lat: 41-43-45 N **Long:** 86-38-17 W
Pop: 1,543 (1990); 1,553 (1980) **Pop Density:** 57.4
Land: 26.9 sq. mi.; **Water:** 0.3 sq. mi.

Hanna
Township
ZIP: 46340 **Lat:** 41-24-25 N **Long:** 86-44-50 W
Pop: 930 (1990); 858 (1980) **Pop Density:** 35.2
Land: 26.4 sq. mi.; **Water:** 0.2 sq. mi.

Hudson
Township
Lat: 41-43-25 N **Long:** 86-33-13 W
Pop: 2,151 (1990); 1,682 (1980) **Pop Density:** 169.4
Land: 12.7 sq. mi.; **Water:** 0.9 sq. mi.

Johnson
Township
Lat: 41-28-37 N **Long:** 86-33-19 W
Pop: 229 (1990); 228 (1980) **Pop Density:** 12.9
Land: 17.8 sq. mi.; **Water:** 0.0 sq. mi.

Kankakee
Township
Lat: 41-38-54 N **Long:** 86-39-01 W
Pop: 3,361 (1990); 3,483 (1980) **Pop Density:** 109.8
Land: 30.6 sq. mi.; **Water:** 0.2 sq. mi.

Kingsbury
Town
ZIP: 46345 **Lat:** 41-31-52 N **Long:** 86-41-44 W
Pop: 258 (1990); 329 (1980) **Pop Density:** 430.0
Land: 0.6 sq. mi.; **Water:** 0.0 sq. mi. **Elev:** 750 ft.

Kingsford Heights
Town
ZIP: 46346 **Lat:** 41-28-47 N **Long:** 86-41-28 W
Pop: 1,486 (1990); 1,618 (1980) **Pop Density:** 1486.0
Land: 1.0 sq. mi.; **Water:** 0.0 sq. mi. **Elev:** 717 ft.

La Crosse
Town
ZIP: 46348 **Lat:** 41-19-04 N **Long:** 86-53-23 W
Pop: 677 (1990); 713 (1980) **Pop Density:** 1354.0
Land: 0.5 sq. mi.; **Water:** 0.0 sq. mi. **Elev:** 678 ft.

Name origin: French for 'club'; probably a reference to the game (now called lacrosse) played by the Indians of the region with a stick the French thought resembled a bishop's crozier or cross.

La Porte
City
ZIP: 46350 **Lat:** 41-36-26 N **Long:** 86-42-53 W
Pop: 21,507 (1990); 21,796 (1980) **Pop Density:** 1903.3
Land: 11.3 sq. mi.; **Water:** 0.7 sq. mi. **Elev:** 817 ft.

In northern IN, 24 mi. west of South Bend. Settled 1832; chartered 1852.

Name origin: From French meaning 'the door,' describing a natural opening in the forest which served as a gateway to the north.

Lincoln
Township
Lat: 41-33-54 N **Long:** 86-32-31 W
Pop: 1,862 (1990); 1,739 (1980) **Pop Density:** 68.2
Land: 27.3 sq. mi.; **Water:** 0.5 sq. mi.

Long Beach
Town
Lat: 41-44-47 N **Long:** 86-51-07 W
Pop: 2,044 (1990); 2,262 (1980) **Pop Density:** 2044.0
Land: 1.0 sq. mi.; **Water:** 2.1 sq. mi. **Elev:** 610 ft.

Michiana Shores
Town
Lat: 41-45-22 N **Long:** 86-49-06 W
Pop: 378 (1990); 464 (1980) **Pop Density:** 1260.0
Land: 0.3 sq. mi.; **Water:** 0.0 sq. mi. **Elev:** 610 ft.

On the southeastern shore of Lake Michigan.

Name origin: From the first syllable of Michigan and the last three of Indiana; descriptive of its location.

Michigan
Township
ZIP: 46360 **Lat:** 41-43-33 N **Long:** 86-52-32 W
Pop: 31,196 (1990); 34,653 (1980) **Pop Density:** 1742.8
Land: 17.9 sq. mi.; **Water:** 9.5 sq. mi.

Michigan City
City
ZIP: 46360 **Lat:** 41-42-45 N **Long:** 86-52-33 W
Pop: 33,822 (1990); 36,850 (1980) **Pop Density:** 1725.6
Land: 19.6 sq. mi.; **Water:** 3.5 sq. mi. **Elev:** 625 ft.
In northern IN on Lake Michigan. Founded 1832.
Name origin: For its location.

New Durham
Township
ZIP: 46350 **Lat:** 41-33-58 N **Long:** 86-52-20 W
Pop: 6,695 (1990); 4,413 (1980) **Pop Density:** 185.5
Land: 36.1 sq. mi.; **Water:** 0.1 sq. mi.

Noble
Township
Lat: 41-28-22 N **Long:** 86-45-44 W
Pop: 1,333 (1990); 1,350 (1980) **Pop Density:** 42.9
Land: 31.1 sq. mi.; **Water:** 0.0 sq. mi.

Pleasant
Township
Lat: 41-34-52 N **Long:** 86-38-34 W
Pop: 2,897 (1990); 3,098 (1980) **Pop Density:** 116.8
Land: 24.8 sq. mi.; **Water:** 0.1 sq. mi.

Pottawattomie Park
Town
Lat: 41-43-21 N **Long:** 86-52-01 W
Pop: 281 (1990); 284 (1980) **Pop Density:** 936.7
Land: 0.3 sq. mi.; **Water:** 0.0 sq. mi.
Name origin: For one of the area's original Indian tribes.

Prairie
Township
Lat: 41-20-07 N **Long:** 86-46-35 W
Pop: 224 (1990); 194 (1980) **Pop Density:** 9.3
Land: 24.0 sq. mi.; **Water:** 0.0 sq. mi.

Scipio
Township
Lat: 41-33-59 N **Long:** 86-45-51 W
Pop: 3,490 (1990); 3,631 (1980) **Pop Density:** 108.4
Land: 32.2 sq. mi.; **Water:** 0.2 sq. mi.

Springfield
Township
Lat: 41-43-09 N **Long:** 86-45-38 W
Pop: 4,600 (1990); 4,968 (1980) **Pop Density:** 138.6
Land: 33.2 sq. mi.; **Water:** 0.1 sq. mi.

Trail Creek
Town
Lat: 41-41-47 N **Long:** 86-51-22 W
Pop: 2,463 (1990); 2,581 (1980) **Pop Density:** 2052.5
Land: 1.2 sq. mi.; **Water:** 0.0 sq. mi. **Elev:** 632 ft.
Name origin: From an Indian term meaning 'river road.'

Union
Township
Lat: 41-27-55 N **Long:** 86-38-34 W
Pop: 2,505 (1990); 2,757 (1980) **Pop Density:** 90.1
Land: 27.8 sq. mi.; **Water:** 0.0 sq. mi.

Wanatah
Town
ZIP: 46390 **Lat:** 41-25-50 N **Long:** 86-53-19 W
Pop: 852 (1990); 879 (1980) **Pop Density:** 710.0
Land: 1.2 sq. mi.; **Water:** 0.0 sq. mi. **Elev:** 725 ft.
Name origin: From an Indian term meaning 'he who attacks his enemies.'

Washington
Township
Lat: 41-31-14 N **Long:** 86-38-55 W
Pop: 926 (1990); 942 (1980) **Pop Density:** 34.8
Land: 26.6 sq. mi.; **Water:** 0.0 sq. mi.

Westville
Town
ZIP: 46391 **Lat:** 41-32-22 N **Long:** 86-54-21 W
Pop: 5,255 (1990); 2,887 (1980) **Pop Density:** 1751.7
Land: 3.0 sq. mi.; **Water:** 0.0 sq. mi. **Elev:** 805 ft.
Founded 1852.
Name origin: Descriptively named in 1852.

Wills
Township
Lat: 41-38-59 N **Long:** 86-33-21 W
Pop: 1,291 (1990); 1,263 (1980) **Pop Density:** 43.9
Land: 29.4 sq. mi.; **Water:** 0.5 sq. mi.

Lawrence County
County Seat: Bedford (ZIP: 47421)

Pop: 42,836 (1990); 42,472 (1980) **Pop Density:** 95.4
Land: 448.9 sq. mi.; **Water:** 3.2 sq. mi. **Area Code:** 812
In south-central IN, south of Bloomington; organized Jan 7, 1818 from Orange County.
Name origin: For Capt. James Lawrence (1781–1813), U.S. naval officer in the war with Barbary pirates near Tripoli and commander of the U.S.S. *Chesapeake* in the War of 1812, who said, "Don't give up the ship!"

Bedford
City
ZIP: 47421 **Lat:** 38-51-37 N **Long:** 86-29-26 W
Pop: 13,817 (1990); 14,410 (1980) **Pop Density:** 1161.1
Land: 11.9 sq. mi.; **Water:** 0.0 sq. mi. **Elev:** 710 ft.
In southern IN, 20 mi. south of Bloomington. Platted 1825. County seat.
Name origin: For Bedford County, TN.

Bono
Township
ZIP: 47446 **Lat:** 38-43-19 N **Long:** 86-21-32 W
Pop: 668 (1990); 721 (1980) **Pop Density:** 25.7
Land: 26.0 sq. mi.; **Water:** 0.4 sq. mi.

Guthrie
Township
ZIP: 47467 **Lat:** 38-48-38 N **Long:** 86-20-13 W
Pop: 1,358 (1990); 1,275 (1980) **Pop Density:** 32.2
Land: 42.2 sq. mi.; **Water:** 0.6 sq. mi.

Indian Creek
Township
ZIP: 47421 **Lat:** 38-51-59 N **Long:** 86-36-09 W
Pop: 2,528 (1990); 2,296 (1980) **Pop Density:** 66.5
Land: 38.0 sq. mi.; **Water:** 0.2 sq. mi.

INDIANA, Lawrence County

Marion
Township
ZIP: 47446 Lat: 38-44-59 N Long: 86-28-50 W
Pop: 8,983 (1990); 8,913 (1980) Pop Density: 135.7
Land: 66.2 sq. mi.; Water: 0.6 sq. mi.

Marshall
Township
ZIP: 47421 Lat: 38-56-33 N Long: 86-30-53 W
Pop: 3,800 (1990); 3,509 (1980) Pop Density: 104.7
Land: 36.3 sq. mi.; Water: 0.0 sq. mi.

Mitchell
City
ZIP: 47446 Lat: 38-44-11 N Long: 86-28-31 W
Pop: 4,669 (1990); 4,641 (1980) Pop Density: 1459.1
Land: 3.2 sq. mi.; Water: 0.0 sq. mi. Elev: 687 ft.
Name origin: For railroad engineer O. M. Mitchell.

Oolitic
Town
ZIP: 47451 Lat: 38-53-29 N Long: 86-31-34 W
Pop: 1,424 (1990); 1,495 (1980) Pop Density: 1780.0
Land: 0.8 sq. mi.; Water: 0.0 sq. mi. Elev: 589 ft.
Established 1888.
Name origin: Descriptive of the oolitic texture of the area's limestone.

Perry
Township
ZIP: 47462 Lat: 38-56-58 N Long: 86-38-12 W
Pop: 1,726 (1990); 1,533 (1980) Pop Density: 48.3
Land: 35.7 sq. mi.; Water: 0.0 sq. mi.

Pleasant Run
Township
ZIP: 47436 Lat: 38-56-30 N Long: 86-21-58 W
Pop: 1,649 (1990); 1,579 (1980) Pop Density: 25.4
Land: 64.8 sq. mi.; Water: 0.0 sq. mi.

Shawswick
Township
ZIP: 47421 Lat: 38-51-21 N Long: 86-26-07 W
Pop: 20,136 (1990); 20,569 (1980) Pop Density: 289.7
Land: 69.5 sq. mi.; Water: 0.4 sq. mi.

Spice Valley
Township
Lat: 38-45-11 N Long: 86-37-28 W
Pop: 1,988 (1990); 2,077 (1980) Pop Density: 28.3
Land: 70.2 sq. mi.; Water: 1.0 sq. mi.

Madison County
County Seat: Anderson (ZIP: 46016)

Pop: 130,669 (1990); 139,336 (1980) Pop Density: 289.0
Land: 452.2 sq. mi.; Water: 0.8 sq. mi. Area Code: 317
In central IN, west of Muncie; organized Jan 4, 1823 from Fayette County.
Name origin: For James Madison (1751–1836), fourth U.S. president.

Adams
Township
Lat: 39-59-40 N Long: 85-37-10 W
Pop: 3,688 (1990); 3,795 (1980) Pop Density: 102.4
Land: 36.0 sq. mi.; Water: 0.0 sq. mi.

Alexandria
City
ZIP: 46001 Lat: 40-15-29 N Long: 85-40-34 W
Pop: 5,709 (1990); 6,028 (1980) Pop Density: 2195.8
Land: 2.6 sq. mi.; Water: 0.0 sq. mi. Elev: 866 ft.
Established 1836.
Name origin: For Alexandria, Egypt.

Anderson
City
ZIP: 46011 Lat: 40-05-34 N Long: 85-41-16 W
Pop: 59,459 (1990); 64,695 (1980) Pop Density: 1568.8
Land: 37.9 sq. mi.; Water: 0.1 sq. mi. Elev: 887 ft.
In central IN, 40 mi. north-northeast of Indianapolis. Platted 1823. Incorporated 1849. Not coextensive with the town of the same name.
Name origin: For a local Delaware Indian chief whose English name was William Anderson. Previously called Andersonville.

*Anderson
Township
ZIP: 46016 Lat: 40-05-29 N Long: 85-41-32 W
Pop: 59,892 (1990); 65,134 (1980) Pop Density: 1601.4
Land: 37.4 sq. mi.; Water: 0.1 sq. mi.

Boone
Township
Lat: 40-20-27 N Long: 85-43-35 W
Pop: 681 (1990); 734 (1980) Pop Density: 22.6
Land: 30.1 sq. mi.; Water: 0.0 sq. mi.

Chesterfield
Town
ZIP: 46017 Lat: 40-06-42 N Long: 85-35-34 W
Pop: 2,721 (1990); 2,701 (1980) Pop Density: 2473.6
Land: 1.1 sq. mi.; Water: 0.0 sq. mi. Elev: 908 ft.
Part of the town is also in Delaware County.

Country Club Heights
Town
Lat: 40-07-31 N Long: 85-41-15 W
Pop: 112 (1990); 97 (1980) Pop Density: 373.3
Land: 0.3 sq. mi.; Water: 0.0 sq. mi. Elev: 860 ft.
Name origin: Named by its developers for its descriptive connotations.

Duck Creek
Township
ZIP: 46036 Lat: 40-19-59 N Long: 85-49-17 W
Pop: 547 (1990); 572 (1980) Pop Density: 22.8
Land: 24.0 sq. mi.; Water: 0.0 sq. mi.

Edgewood
Town
Lat: 40-06-09 N Long: 85-44-15 W
Pop: 2,057 (1990); 2,215 (1980) Pop Density: 2571.3
Land: 0.8 sq. mi.; Water: 0.0 sq. mi. Elev: 876 ft.
Name origin: Descriptive of its location at the edge of a large forest.

Elwood
City
ZIP: 46036 Lat: 40-16-32 N Long: 85-50-20 W
Pop: 9,490 (1990); 10,867 (1980) Pop Density: 2965.6
Land: 3.2 sq. mi.; Water: 0.0 sq. mi. Elev: 865 ft.
Part of the town is also in Tipton County.
Name origin: For resident, Elwood Frazier. Previously called Quincy.

Fall Creek
Township
ZIP: 46011 **Lat:** 39-59-53 N **Long:** 85-43-49 W
Pop: 12,054 (1990); 10,854 (1980) **Pop Density:** 286.3
Land: 42.1 sq. mi.; **Water:** 0.1 sq. mi.

Frankton
Town
ZIP: 46044 **Lat:** 40-13-13 N **Long:** 85-46-20 W
Pop: 1,736 (1990); 2,080 (1980) **Pop Density:** 1928.9
Land: 0.9 sq. mi.; **Water:** 0.0 sq. mi. **Elev:** 862 ft.
Laid out 1853.
Name origin: For Francis 'Frank' Sigler, one of the founders.

Green
Township
Lat: 39-59-22 N **Long:** 85-49-10 W
Pop: 2,863 (1990); 2,732 (1980) **Pop Density:** 119.3
Land: 24.0 sq. mi.; **Water:** 0.1 sq. mi.

Ingalls
Town
ZIP: 46048 **Lat:** 39-57-36 N **Long:** 85-47-55 W
Pop: 889 (1990); 909 (1980) **Pop Density:** 1270.0
Land: 0.7 sq. mi.; **Water:** 0.0 sq. mi. **Elev:** 869 ft.
Name origin: For M. E. Ingalls, a railroad president.

Jackson
Township
Lat: 40-08-44 N **Long:** 85-49-42 W
Pop: 1,910 (1990); 2,159 (1980) **Pop Density:** 66.1
Land: 28.9 sq. mi.; **Water:** 0.1 sq. mi.

Lafayette
Township
ZIP: 46011 **Lat:** 40-10-42 N **Long:** 85-43-45 W
Pop: 5,408 (1990); 6,166 (1980) **Pop Density:** 153.2
Land: 35.3 sq. mi.; **Water:** 0.0 sq. mi.

Lapel
Town
ZIP: 46051 **Lat:** 40-04-07 N **Long:** 85-50-51 W
Pop: 1,742 (1990); 1,881 (1980) **Pop Density:** 4355.0
Land: 0.4 sq. mi.; **Water:** 0.0 sq. mi. **Elev:** 858 ft.
Name origin: Descriptive of a nearby railroad right-of-way that resembled a lapel.

Markleville
Town
ZIP: 46056 **Lat:** 39-58-38 N **Long:** 85-36-58 W
Pop: 412 (1990); 427 (1980) **Pop Density:** 1030.0
Land: 0.4 sq. mi.; **Water:** 0.0 sq. mi. **Elev:** 954 ft.
Founded 1852.
Name origin: For its founder, John Markle.

Monroe
Township
ZIP: 46001 **Lat:** 40-15-51 N **Long:** 85-39-28 W
Pop: 10,057 (1990); 10,832 (1980) **Pop Density:** 196.0
Land: 51.3 sq. mi.; **Water:** 0.0 sq. mi.

Orestes
Town
ZIP: 46063 **Lat:** 40-16-14 N **Long:** 85-43-30 W
Pop: 458 (1990); 539 (1980) **Pop Density:** 1526.7
Land: 0.3 sq. mi.; **Water:** 0.0 sq. mi. **Elev:** 874 ft.
Name origin: For Orestes McMahan, son of its first postmaster.

Pendleton
Town
ZIP: 46064 **Lat:** 40-00-00 N **Long:** 85-44-31 W
Pop: 2,309 (1990); 2,130 (1980) **Pop Density:** 1924.2
Land: 1.2 sq. mi.; **Water:** 0.0 sq. mi. **Elev:** 860 ft.
Name origin: For its founder, Thomas Pendleton.

Pipe Creek
Township
ZIP: 46036 **Lat:** 40-14-40 N **Long:** 85-48-02 W
Pop: 13,795 (1990); 15,411 (1980) **Pop Density:** 324.6
Land: 42.5 sq. mi.; **Water:** 0.1 sq. mi.

Richland
Township
ZIP: 46011 **Lat:** 40-10-31 N **Long:** 85-37-21 W
Pop: 5,494 (1990); 5,634 (1980) **Pop Density:** 199.1
Land: 27.6 sq. mi.; **Water:** 0.2 sq. mi.

River Forest
Town
Lat: 40-06-34 N **Long:** 85-43-45 W
Pop: 16 (1990); 29 (1980) **Pop Density:** 800.0
Land: 0.02 sq. mi.; **Water:** 0.0 sq. mi. **Elev:** 850 ft.
Name origin: For its descriptive connotations.

Stony Creek
Township
Lat: 40-04-30 N **Long:** 85-48-32 W
Pop: 3,588 (1990); 3,890 (1980) **Pop Density:** 126.8
Land: 28.3 sq. mi.; **Water:** 0.0 sq. mi.

Summitville
Town
ZIP: 46070 **Lat:** 40-20-14 N **Long:** 85-38-34 W
Pop: 1,010 (1990); 1,085 (1980) **Pop Density:** 2020.0
Land: 0.5 sq. mi.; **Water:** 0.0 sq. mi. **Elev:** 883 ft.
Name origin: For its high-altitude location.

Union
Township
ZIP: 46017 **Lat:** 40-05-39 N **Long:** 85-36-19 W
Pop: 8,790 (1990); 9,288 (1980) **Pop Density:** 446.2
Land: 19.7 sq. mi.; **Water:** 0.1 sq. mi.

Van Buren
Township
Lat: 40-20-34 N **Long:** 85-37-31 W
Pop: 1,902 (1990); 2,135 (1980) **Pop Density:** 76.4
Land: 24.9 sq. mi.; **Water:** 0.0 sq. mi.

Woodlawn Heights
Town
Lat: 40-07-01 N **Long:** 85-41-48 W
Pop: 109 (1990); 109 (1980) **Pop Density:** 1090.0
Land: 0.1 sq. mi.; **Water:** 0.0 sq. mi. **Elev:** 880 ft.
Name origin: Euphoniously named by its incorporators.

INDIANA, Marion County — *American Places Dictionary*

> ## Marion County
> **County Seat: Indianapolis (ZIP: 46204)**
>
> **Pop:** 797,159 (1990); 765,233 (1980) **Pop Density:** 2011.0
> **Land:** 396.4 sq. mi.; **Water:** 6.7 sq. mi. **Area Code:** 317
> In central IN, southwest of Muncie; established Dec 31, 1821 from Ohio County.
> **Name origin:** For Gen. Francis Marion (c. 1732–95), SC soldier and legislator, known as "The Swamp Fox" for his tactics during the Revolutionary War.

Beech Grove — City
ZIP: 46107 **Lat:** 39-42-53 N **Long:** 86-05-14 W
Pop: 13,383 (1990); 13,196 (1980) **Pop Density:** 3264.1
Land: 4.1 sq. mi.; **Water:** 0.0 sq. mi. **Elev:** 800 ft.
In central IN, 7 mi. southeast of Indianapolis.
Name origin: For a nearby farm called Beech Grove Farm.

Castleton — Town
ZIP: 46250 **Lat:** 39-54-17 N **Long:** 86-03-00 W
Pop: 37 (1990); 80 (1980) **Pop Density:** 185.0
Land: 0.2 sq. mi.; **Water:** 0.0 sq. mi. **Elev:** 820 ft.
Name origin: Named by founder Thomas Gentry for Castleton, NC, his former home.

Center — Township
ZIP: 46204 **Lat:** 39-46-25 N **Long:** 86-08-21 W
Pop: 182,140 (1990); 208,624 (1980) **Pop Density:** 4347.0
Land: 41.9 sq. mi.; **Water:** 0.9 sq. mi.

Clermont — Town
ZIP: 46234 **Lat:** 39-49-02 N **Long:** 86-19-13 W
Pop: 1,678 (1990); 1,671 (1980) **Pop Density:** 2397.1
Land: 0.7 sq. mi.; **Water:** 0.0 sq. mi. **Elev:** 833 ft.
Name origin: Changed from Mechanicsburg to its present name in 1855 to avoid confusion with other cities in IN with the same name.

Crows Nest — Town
Lat: 39-51-07 N **Long:** 86-10-22 W
Pop: 114 (1990); 106 (1980) **Pop Density:** 285.0
Land: 0.4 sq. mi.; **Water:** 0.0 sq. mi. **Elev:** 750 ft.
Name origin: Descriptively named by its settlers.

Cumberland — Town
Lat: 39-46-40 N **Long:** 85-57-43 W
Pop: 2,933 (1990); 2,246 (1980) **Pop Density:** 4190.0
Land: 0.7 sq. mi.; **Water:** 0.0 sq. mi.
Part of the town is also in Hancock County.

Decatur — Township
ZIP: 46241 **Lat:** 39-40-54 N **Long:** 86-16-38 W
Pop: 21,092 (1990); 19,426 (1980) **Pop Density:** 653.0
Land: 32.3 sq. mi.; **Water:** 0.1 sq. mi.

Franklin — Township
ZIP: 46239 **Lat:** 39-40-56 N **Long:** 86-01-02 W
Pop: 21,458 (1990); 16,477 (1980) **Pop Density:** 509.7
Land: 42.1 sq. mi.; **Water:** 0.0 sq. mi.

Homecroft — Town
Lat: 39-40-12 N **Long:** 86-07-48 W
Pop: 758 (1990); 831 (1980) **Pop Density:** 3790.0
Land: 0.2 sq. mi.; **Water:** 0.0 sq. mi. **Elev:** 764 ft.

Indianapolis — City
ZIP: 46206 **Lat:** 39-46-35 N **Long:** 86-08-46 W
Pop: 731,327 (1990); 700,807 (1980) **Pop Density:** 2021.9
Land: 361.7 sq. mi.; **Water:** 6.6 sq. mi.
In central IN. Settled Feb 1820; state capital 1825. Indianapolis and Marion County governments are consolidated. Diverse manufacturing city: transportation equipment, chemical and pharmaceutical products; food processing; and printing; major Midwestern distribution center. Site of the Indianapolis 500 automobile race.
Name origin: Coined by adding Greek *polis* 'city' to the state name.

Lawrence — City
ZIP: 46226 **Lat:** 39-52-06 N **Long:** 85-59-13 W
Pop: 26,763 (1990); 25,591 (1980) **Pop Density:** 1331.5
Land: 20.1 sq. mi.; **Water:** 0.1 sq. mi. **Elev:** 860 ft.
In central IN, 10 mi. northeast of Indianapolis. Not coextensive with the town of the same name.
Name origin: For U.S. Navy hero of the War of 1812, Capt. James Lawrence (1781–1813), who is famous for saying "Don't give up the ship!"

*Lawrence — Township
ZIP: 46226 **Lat:** 39-52-47 N **Long:** 86-00-37 W
Pop: 94,548 (1990); 75,860 (1980) **Pop Density:** 2015.9
Land: 46.9 sq. mi.; **Water:** 1.6 sq. mi.

Meridian Hills — Town
Lat: 39-53-10 N **Long:** 86-09-23 W
Pop: 1,728 (1990); 1,801 (1980) **Pop Density:** 1152.0
Land: 1.5 sq. mi.; **Water:** 0.0 sq. mi. **Elev:** 800 ft.
Name origin: Descriptively named by its developers.

North Crows Nest — Town
Lat: 39-51-54 N **Long:** 86-09-43 W
Pop: 57 (1990); 82 (1980) **Pop Density:** 570.0
Land: 0.1 sq. mi.; **Water:** 0.0 sq. mi. **Elev:** 775 ft.

Perry — Township
ZIP: 46227 **Lat:** 39-40-34 N **Long:** 86-09-21 W
Pop: 85,060 (1990); 78,485 (1980) **Pop Density:** 1857.2
Land: 45.8 sq. mi.; **Water:** 0.1 sq. mi.

Pike — Township
ZIP: 46254 **Lat:** 39-52-39 N **Long:** 86-16-02 W
Pop: 45,204 (1990); 25,336 (1980) **Pop Density:** 1089.3
Land: 41.5 sq. mi.; **Water:** 2.6 sq. mi.

Rocky Ripple — Town
Lat: 39-50-56 N **Long:** 86-10-23 W
Pop: 751 (1990); 778 (1980) **Pop Density:** 2503.3
Land: 0.3 sq. mi.; **Water:** 0.0 sq. mi. **Elev:** 705 ft.

Southport — City
ZIP: 46227 **Lat:** 39-39-34 N **Long:** 86-06-59 W
Pop: 1,969 (1990); 2,266 (1980) **Pop Density:** 3281.7
Land: 0.6 sq. mi.; **Water:** 0.0 sq. mi. **Elev:** 775 ft.
Founded 1852.
Name origin: Named in 1852 for its descriptive connotations.

Speedway — Town
ZIP: 46224 **Lat:** 39-47-36 N **Long:** 86-14-50 W
Pop: 13,092 (1990); 12,641 (1980) **Pop Density:** 2727.5
Land: 4.8 sq. mi.; **Water:** 0.0 sq. mi. **Elev:** 744 ft.
In central IN, 4 mi. west of Indianapolis.
Name origin: For the Indianapolis Motor Speedway, which is located here.

Spring Hill — Town
Lat: 39-50-00 N **Long:** 86-11-33 W
Pop: 112 (1990); 27 (1980) **Pop Density:** 1120.0
Land: 0.1 sq. mi.; **Water:** 0.0 sq. mi. **Elev:** 757 ft.
Name origin: For a large spring on a nearby hill.

Warren — Township
ZIP: 46219 **Lat:** 39-46-29 N **Long:** 86-01-01 W
Pop: 87,989 (1990); 89,208 (1980) **Pop Density:** 1818.0
Land: 48.4 sq. mi.; **Water:** 0.0 sq. mi.

Warren Park — Town
Lat: 39-46-56 N **Long:** 86-03-08 W
Pop: 1,763 (1990); 1,803 (1980) **Pop Density:** 3526.0
Land: 0.5 sq. mi.; **Water:** 0.0 sq. mi. **Elev:** 814 ft.
Name origin: Probably for Revolutionary War patriot Dr. Joseph Warren (1741–75), most noted for having sent Paul Revere (1735–1818) and William Dawes (1745–99) on their famous "midnight ride."

Washington — Township
ZIP: 46220 **Lat:** 39-52-33 N **Long:** 86-08-30 W
Pop: 133,969 (1990); 129,008 (1980) **Pop Density:** 2756.6
Land: 48.6 sq. mi.; **Water:** 1.1 sq. mi.

Wayne — Township
ZIP: 46241 **Lat:** 39-46-15 N **Long:** 86-15-40 W
Pop: 125,699 (1990); 122,809 (1980) **Pop Density:** 2570.5
Land: 48.9 sq. mi.; **Water:** 0.4 sq. mi.

Williams Creek — Town
Lat: 39-54-01 N **Long:** 86-08-59 W
Pop: 425 (1990); 427 (1980) **Pop Density:** 1416.7
Land: 0.3 sq. mi.; **Water:** 0.0 sq. mi. **Elev:** 775 ft.
Name origin: For a local pioneer family.

Wynnedale — Town
Lat: 39-49-57 N **Long:** 86-11-55 W
Pop: 269 (1990); 289 (1980) **Pop Density:** 1345.0
Land: 0.2 sq. mi.; **Water:** 0.0 sq. mi. **Elev:** 750 ft.

Marshall County
County Seat: Plymouth (ZIP: 46563)

Pop: 42,182 (1990); 39,155 (1980) **Pop Density:** 94.9
Land: 444.3 sq. mi.; **Water:** 5.6 sq. mi. **Area Code:** 219
In north-central IN, south of South Bend; established Feb 7, 1835 from Indian lands.
Name origin: For John Marshall (1755–1835), fourth Chief Justice of the U.S. Supreme Court (1801–35).

Argos — Town
ZIP: 46501 **Lat:** 41-14-15 N **Long:** 86-14-51 W
Pop: 1,642 (1990); 1,547 (1980) **Pop Density:** 2345.7
Land: 0.7 sq. mi.; **Water:** 0.0 sq. mi. **Elev:** 828 ft.
Name origin: Named in 1859 for the ancient Greek city.

Bourbon — Town
ZIP: 46504 **Lat:** 41-17-51 N **Long:** 86-07-00 W
Pop: 1,672 (1990); 1,522 (1980) **Pop Density:** 1857.8
Land: 0.9 sq. mi.; **Water:** 0.0 sq. mi. **Elev:** 850 ft.
Not coextensive with the town of the same name.
Name origin: For Bourbon County, KY, former home of early settlers..

*Bourbon — Township
ZIP: 46504 **Lat:** 41-19-41 N **Long:** 86-07-34 W
Pop: 2,976 (1990); 2,708 (1980) **Pop Density:** 59.9
Land: 49.7 sq. mi.; **Water:** 0.0 sq. mi.

Bremen — Town
ZIP: 46506 **Lat:** 41-26-49 N **Long:** 86-09-15 W
Pop: 4,725 (1990); 3,565 (1980) **Pop Density:** 2362.5
Land: 2.0 sq. mi.; **Water:** 0.0 sq. mi. **Elev:** 854 ft.
Name origin: Named by German settlers for the city in Germany.

Center — Township
ZIP: 46563 **Lat:** 41-19-52 N **Long:** 86-16-06 W
Pop: 12,501 (1990); 11,377 (1980) **Pop Density:** 210.1
Land: 59.5 sq. mi.; **Water:** 0.3 sq. mi.

Culver — Town
ZIP: 46511 **Lat:** 41-13-04 N **Long:** 86-25-21 W
Pop: 1,404 (1990); 1,601 (1980) **Pop Density:** 2005.7
Land: 0.7 sq. mi.; **Water:** 0.0 sq. mi. **Elev:** 754 ft.
Name origin: For Henry H. Culver, founder of Culver Military Academy. Previously called Union Town and Marmount.

German — Township
ZIP: 46506 **Lat:** 41-26-11 N **Long:** 86-08-37 W
Pop: 8,427 (1990); 7,166 (1980) **Pop Density:** 136.8
Land: 61.6 sq. mi.; **Water:** 0.6 sq. mi.

Green — Township
Lat: 41-13-14 N **Long:** 86-18-27 W
Pop: 970 (1990); 963 (1980) **Pop Density:** 29.8
Land: 32.6 sq. mi.; **Water:** 0.1 sq. mi.

INDIANA, Marshall County

Koontz Lake
CDP
Lat: 41-24-30 N **Long:** 86-27-43 W
Pop: 165 (1990); 166 (1980) **Pop Density:** 825.0
Land: 0.2 sq. mi.; **Water:** 0.1 sq. mi.
Part of the town is also in Starke County.

La Paz
Town
Lat: 41-27-33 N **Long:** 86-18-35 W
Pop: 562 (1990); 651 (1980) **Pop Density:** 1405.0
Land: 0.4 sq. mi.; **Water:** 0.0 sq. mi. **Elev:** 879 ft.
Founded 1873.
Name origin: For La Paz, Bolivia.

North
Township
Lat: 41-25-59 N **Long:** 86-17-30 W
Pop: 4,088 (1990); 3,913 (1980) **Pop Density:** 97.8
Land: 41.8 sq. mi.; **Water:** 0.2 sq. mi.

Plymouth
City
ZIP: 46563 **Lat:** 41-20-49 N **Long:** 86-18-52 W
Pop: 8,303 (1990); 7,693 (1980) **Pop Density:** 1537.6
Land: 5.4 sq. mi.; **Water:** 0.0 sq. mi. **Elev:** 799 ft.

Polk
Township
Lat: 41-25-43 N **Long:** 86-24-39 W
Pop: 2,497 (1990); 2,527 (1980) **Pop Density:** 59.2
Land: 42.2 sq. mi.; **Water:** 0.1 sq. mi.

Tippecanoe
Township
ZIP: 46570 **Lat:** 41-13-07 N **Long:** 86-06-14 W
Pop: 1,188 (1990); 1,244 (1980) **Pop Density:** 33.2
Land: 35.8 sq. mi.; **Water:** 0.0 sq. mi.

Union
Township
Lat: 41-13-24 N **Long:** 86-24-24 W
Pop: 3,289 (1990); 3,604 (1980) **Pop Density:** 80.6
Land: 40.8 sq. mi.; **Water:** 3.1 sq. mi.

Walnut
Township
Lat: 41-13-30 N **Long:** 86-12-24 W
Pop: 2,660 (1990); 2,486 (1980) **Pop Density:** 69.6
Land: 38.2 sq. mi.; **Water:** 0.0 sq. mi.

West
Township
Lat: 41-19-30 N **Long:** 86-24-18 W
Pop: 3,586 (1990); 3,167 (1980) **Pop Density:** 85.0
Land: 42.2 sq. mi.; **Water:** 1.2 sq. mi.

Martin County
County Seat: Shoals (**ZIP:** 47581)

Pop: 10,369 (1990); 11,001 (1980) **Pop Density:** 30.8
Land: 336.2 sq. mi.; **Water:** 4.4 sq. mi. **Area Code:** 812
In southwestern IN, southwest of Bloomington; organized Jan 17, 1820 from Indian lands.
Name origin: For Maj. John Preston Martin (1811-62), U.S. representative from KY (1845-47).

Center
Township
ZIP: 47553 **Lat:** 38-40-52 N **Long:** 86-48-59 W
Pop: 1,820 (1990); 1,761 (1980) **Pop Density:** 46.1
Land: 39.5 sq. mi.; **Water:** 0.8 sq. mi.

Crane
Town
ZIP: 47522 **Lat:** 38-53-42 N **Long:** 86-54-01 W
Pop: 216 (1990); 297 (1980) **Pop Density:** 2160.0
Land: 0.1 sq. mi.; **Water:** 0.0 sq. mi. **Elev:** 545 ft.
Name origin: For an early settler.

Halbert
Township
ZIP: 47581 **Lat:** 38-39-39 N **Long:** 86-44-17 W
Pop: 1,587 (1990); 1,646 (1980) **Pop Density:** 30.6
Land: 51.9 sq. mi.; **Water:** 0.4 sq. mi.

Loogootee
City
ZIP: 47553 **Lat:** 38-40-31 N **Long:** 86-54-51 W
Pop: 2,884 (1990); 3,100 (1980) **Pop Density:** 1802.5
Land: 1.6 sq. mi.; **Water:** 0.0 sq. mi. **Elev:** 537 ft.
Platted in 1853.
Name origin: A combination of the names Lowe, engineer of the first railroad through town, and Gootee, owner of the land on which the town was built.

Lost River
Township
Lat: 38-33-14 N **Long:** 86-45-51 W
Pop: 449 (1990); 524 (1980) **Pop Density:** 10.5
Land: 42.6 sq. mi.; **Water:** 0.2 sq. mi.

Mitcheltree
Township
Lat: 38-49-00 N **Long:** 86-44-24 W
Pop: 706 (1990); 792 (1980) **Pop Density:** 10.0
Land: 70.9 sq. mi.; **Water:** 0.5 sq. mi.

Perry
Township
ZIP: 47553 **Lat:** 38-46-37 N **Long:** 86-51-39 W
Pop: 5,126 (1990); 5,624 (1980) **Pop Density:** 53.1
Land: 96.5 sq. mi.; **Water:** 1.8 sq. mi.

Rutherford
Township
ZIP: 47553 **Lat:** 38-33-33 N **Long:** 86-52-56 W
Pop: 681 (1990); 654 (1980) **Pop Density:** 19.6
Land: 34.8 sq. mi.; **Water:** 0.6 sq. mi.

Shoals
Town
ZIP: 47581 **Lat:** 38-40-01 N **Long:** 86-47-36 W
Pop: 853 (1990); 967 (1980) **Pop Density:** 473.9
Land: 1.8 sq. mi.; **Water:** 0.1 sq. mi. **Elev:** 450 ft.
Name origin: Descriptive of its location on the shoals of the White River.

Miami County
County Seat: Peru (ZIP: 46970)

Pop: 36,897 (1990); 39,820 (1980) **Pop Density:** 98.2
Land: 375.8 sq. mi.; **Water:** 1.6 sq. mi. **Area Code:** 317
In north-central IN, north of Kokomo; established Feb 2, 1832 from Cass County.
Name origin: For the Miami Indians, an Algonquin tribe. Origin of the name is uncertain: probably from Ojibway *oumaumeg* 'people of the peninsula' or Delaware *we-mi-a-mik* 'all friends.'

Allen — Township
Lat: 40-57-57 N Long: 86-07-04 W
Pop: 697 (1990); 695 (1980) Pop Density: 32.3
Land: 21.6 sq. mi.; Water: 0.0 sq. mi.

Amboy — Town
ZIP: 46911 Lat: 40-36-05 N Long: 85-55-38 W
Pop: 370 (1990); 450 (1980) Pop Density: 925.0
Land: 0.4 sq. mi.; Water: 0.0 sq. mi. Elev: 815 ft.
Founded 1873.

Bunker Hill — Town
ZIP: 46914 Lat: 40-39-37 N Long: 86-06-06 W
Pop: 1,010 (1990); 984 (1980) Pop Density: 2525.0
Land: 0.4 sq. mi.; Water: 0.0 sq. mi. Elev: 810 ft.
Name origin: For the famous Revolutionary War battle in MA.

Butler — Township
Lat: 40-42-02 N Long: 85-58-48 W
Pop: 791 (1990); 828 (1980) Pop Density: 27.3
Land: 29.0 sq. mi.; Water: 0.8 sq. mi.

Clay — Township
Lat: 40-36-19 N Long: 86-03-01 W
Pop: 847 (1990); 811 (1980) Pop Density: 35.4
Land: 23.9 sq. mi.; Water: 0.0 sq. mi.

Converse — Town
ZIP: 46919 Lat: 40-34-47 N Long: 85-52-40 W
Pop: 965 (1990); 1,155 (1980) Pop Density: 1378.6
Land: 0.7 sq. mi.; Water: 0.0 sq. mi. Elev: 832 ft.
Platted 1849. Part of the town is also in Grant County.
Name origin: For a prominent landowner in the area.

Deer Creek — Township
Lat: 40-36-33 N Long: 86-07-51 W
Pop: 1,656 (1990); 1,809 (1980) Pop Density: 69.9
Land: 23.7 sq. mi.; Water: 0.0 sq. mi.

Denver — Town
ZIP: 46926 Lat: 40-51-51 N Long: 86-04-35 W
Pop: 504 (1990); 589 (1980) Pop Density: 2520.0
Land: 0.2 sq. mi.; Water: 0.0 sq. mi. Elev: 709 ft.
Name origin: Probably for Denver, CO.

Erie — Township
Lat: 40-47-50 N Long: 85-58-55 W
Pop: 451 (1990); 498 (1980) Pop Density: 27.0
Land: 16.7 sq. mi.; Water: 0.2 sq. mi.

Grissom Air Force Base — Military Facility
Lat: 40-39-33 N Long: 86-08-51 W
Pop: 4,271 (1990) Pop Density: 1067.8
Land: 4.0 sq. mi.; Water: 0.0 sq. mi.
Part of the facility is also in Cass County.

Harrison — Township
Lat: 40-36-41 N Long: 85-58-38 W
Pop: 748 (1990); 722 (1980) Pop Density: 32.0
Land: 23.4 sq. mi.; Water: 0.0 sq. mi.

Jackson — Township
Lat: 40-36-13 N Long: 85-54-13 W
Pop: 2,021 (1990); 2,231 (1980) Pop Density: 86.4
Land: 23.4 sq. mi.; Water: 0.0 sq. mi.

Jefferson — Township
Lat: 40-49-30 N Long: 86-06-55 W
Pop: 2,630 (1990); 2,702 (1980) Pop Density: 80.7
Land: 32.6 sq. mi.; Water: 0.0 sq. mi.

Macy — Town
ZIP: 46951 Lat: 40-57-27 N Long: 86-07-44 W
Pop: 218 (1990); 282 (1980) Pop Density: 2180.0
Land: 0.1 sq. mi.; Water: 0.0 sq. mi. Elev: 882 ft.
Name origin: Previously called Lincoln.

Mexico — CDP
Lat: 40-48-46 N Long: 86-06-39 W
Pop: 1,003 (1990) Pop Density: 185.7
Land: 5.4 sq. mi.; Water: 0.0 sq. mi.

Perry — Township
Lat: 40-57-24 N Long: 86-00-47 W
Pop: 836 (1990); 905 (1980) Pop Density: 20.7
Land: 40.4 sq. mi.; Water: 0.1 sq. mi.

Peru — City
ZIP: 46970 Lat: 40-45-13 N Long: 86-04-04 W
Pop: 12,843 (1990); 13,764 (1980) Pop Density: 3293.1
Land: 3.9 sq. mi.; Water: 0.0 sq. mi. Elev: 656 ft.
In north-central IN, 17 mi. north of Kokomo. Established 1838. Not coextensive with the town of the same name.
Name origin: For the South American country.

*Peru — Township
ZIP: 46970 Lat: 40-46-25 N Long: 86-05-14 W
Pop: 12,730 (1990); 13,798 (1980) Pop Density: 505.2
Land: 25.2 sq. mi.; Water: 0.3 sq. mi.

Pipe Creek — Township
ZIP: 46914 Lat: 40-41-46 N Long: 86-07-57 W
Pop: 8,074 (1990); 8,901 (1980) Pop Density: 315.4
Land: 25.6 sq. mi.; Water: 0.1 sq. mi.

Richland — Township
Lat: 40-52-18 N Long: 86-00-26 W
Pop: 1,000 (1990); 1,115 (1980) Pop Density: 24.9
Land: 40.1 sq. mi.; Water: 0.0 sq. mi.

Union — Township
Lat: 40-53-59 N Long: 86-07-27 W
Pop: 813 (1990); 967 (1980) Pop Density: 37.3
Land: 21.8 sq. mi.; Water: 0.0 sq. mi.

INDIANA, Miami County — American Places Dictionary

Washington
Township
Lat: 40-41-51 N Long: 86-03-11 W
Pop: 3,603 (1990); 3,838 (1980) **Pop Density:** 127.3
Land: 28.3 sq. mi.; **Water:** 0.1 sq. mi.

Monroe County
County Seat: Bloomington (ZIP: 47402)

Pop: 108,978 (1990); 98,787 (1980) **Pop Density:** 276.3
Land: 394.4 sq. mi.; **Water:** 17.0 sq. mi. **Area Code:** 812
In central IN, west of Columbus; organized Jan 14, 1818 from Orange County.
Name origin: For James Monroe (1758–1831), fifth U.S. president.

Bean Blossom
Township
ZIP: 47429 Lat: 39-17-46 N Long: 86-37-18 W
Pop: 2,358 (1990); 2,168 (1980) **Pop Density:** 64.8
Land: 36.4 sq. mi.; **Water:** 0.0 sq. mi.

Benton
Township
Lat: 39-14-45 N Long: 86-25-29 W
Pop: 3,116 (1990); 2,892 (1980) **Pop Density:** 56.8
Land: 54.9 sq. mi.; **Water:** 1.7 sq. mi.

Bloomington
City
ZIP: 47408 Lat: 39-09-59 N Long: 86-31-17 W
Pop: 60,633 (1990); 52,663 (1980) **Pop Density:** 4015.4
Land: 15.1 sq. mi.; **Water:** 0.2 sq. mi. **Elev:** 745 ft.
In south-central IN, 45 mi. southwest of Indianapolis. Settled early 1800s; incorporated 1845. Not coextensive with the town of the same name.
Name origin: For local settler William Bloom or for wild roses that grew on original site.

*Bloomington
Township
ZIP: 47401 Lat: 39-12-24 N Long: 86-31-10 W
Pop: 42,156 (1990); 39,877 (1980) **Pop Density:** 1151.8
Land: 36.6 sq. mi.; **Water:** 0.2 sq. mi.

Clear Creek
Township
ZIP: 47426 Lat: 39-02-01 N Long: 86-30-56 W
Pop: 3,883 (1990); 3,089 (1980) **Pop Density:** 128.2
Land: 30.3 sq. mi.; **Water:** 5.6 sq. mi.

Ellettsville
Town
ZIP: 47429 Lat: 39-13-53 N Long: 86-37-19 W
Pop: 3,275 (1990); 3,328 (1980) **Pop Density:** 2729.2
Land: 1.2 sq. mi.; **Water:** 0.0 sq. mi. **Elev:** 722 ft.
Name origin: For early-19th-century tavern owner Edward Elletts.

Indian Creek
Township
Lat: 39-02-11 N Long: 86-38-20 W
Pop: 1,429 (1990); 1,281 (1980) **Pop Density:** 40.7
Land: 35.1 sq. mi.; **Water:** 0.0 sq. mi.

Perry
Township
ZIP: 47401 Lat: 39-07-21 N Long: 86-31-08 W
Pop: 31,985 (1990); 26,634 (1980) **Pop Density:** 906.1
Land: 35.3 sq. mi.; **Water:** 0.1 sq. mi.

Polk
Township
Lat: 39-01-24 N Long: 86-24-16 W
Pop: 332 (1990); 373 (1980) **Pop Density:** 9.6
Land: 34.7 sq. mi.; **Water:** 6.1 sq. mi.

Richland
Township
ZIP: 47429 Lat: 39-12-52 N Long: 86-37-37 W
Pop: 10,156 (1990); 9,763 (1980) **Pop Density:** 286.9
Land: 35.4 sq. mi.; **Water:** 0.0 sq. mi.

Salt Creek
Township
Lat: 39-07-24 N Long: 86-24-36 W
Pop: 1,316 (1990); 1,157 (1980) **Pop Density:** 49.5
Land: 26.6 sq. mi.; **Water:** 3.2 sq. mi.

Stinesville
Town
ZIP: 47464 Lat: 39-18-01 N Long: 86-38-57 W
Pop: 204 (1990); 227 (1980) **Pop Density:** 2040.0
Land: 0.1 sq. mi.; **Water:** 0.0 sq. mi. **Elev:** 610 ft.
Name origin: For prominent landowner Eusebius Stine, who helped lay out the town in 1855.

Van Buren
Township
ZIP: 47401 Lat: 39-07-23 N Long: 86-37-58 W
Pop: 10,470 (1990); 9,839 (1980) **Pop Density:** 300.0
Land: 34.9 sq. mi.; **Water:** 0.0 sq. mi.

Washington
Township
Lat: 39-17-45 N Long: 86-31-08 W
Pop: 1,777 (1990); 1,710 (1980) **Pop Density:** 52.0
Land: 34.2 sq. mi.; **Water:** 0.0 sq. mi.

Montgomery County
County Seat: Crawfordsville (ZIP: 47933)

Pop: 34,436 (1990); 35,501 (1980)   **Pop Density:** 68.2
Land: 504.6 sq. mi.; **Water:** 0.8 sq. mi.   **Area Code:** 317
In west-central IN, south of Lafayette; organized Mar 1, 1823 from Indian lands.
Name origin: For Gen. Richard Montgomery (1738–75), American Revolutionary War officer who captured Montreal, Canada.

Alamo — Town
ZIP: 47916   **Lat:** 39-59-01 N   **Long:** 87-03-18 W
Pop: 112 (1990); 178 (1980)   **Pop Density:** 1120.0
Land: 0.1 sq. mi.; **Water:** 0.0 sq. mi.   **Elev:** 811 ft.
Founded 1837.
Name origin: For the historic fort in San Antonio, TX.

Brown — Township
Lat: 39-54-33 N   **Long:** 87-00-22 W
Pop: 1,660 (1990); 1,764 (1980)   **Pop Density:** 30.9
Land: 53.8 sq. mi.; **Water:** 0.5 sq. mi.

Clark — Township
Lat: 39-54-20 N   **Long:** 86-45-29 W
Pop: 1,843 (1990); 1,972 (1980)   **Pop Density:** 50.8
Land: 36.3 sq. mi.; **Water:** 0.0 sq. mi.

Coal Creek — Township
Lat: 40-10-04 N   **Long:** 87-00-30 W
Pop: 1,461 (1990); 1,541 (1980)   **Pop Density:** 27.2
Land: 53.8 sq. mi.; **Water:** 0.0 sq. mi.

Crawfordsville — City
ZIP: 47933   **Lat:** 40-02-39 N   **Long:** 86-53-47 W
Pop: 13,584 (1990); 13,325 (1980)   **Pop Density:** 1787.4
Land: 7.6 sq. mi.; **Water:** 0.0 sq. mi.   **Elev:** 769 ft.
In west-central IN, 43 mi. west-northwest of Indianapolis. County seat. Settled 1823.
Name origin: For William Harris Crawford (1772–1834), senator from GA (1807–13), U.S. secretary of war (1815–16), and U.S. secretary of the treasury (1816–25).

Darlington — Town
ZIP: 47940   **Lat:** 40-06-29 N   **Long:** 86-46-35 W
Pop: 740 (1990); 811 (1980)   **Pop Density:** 2466.7
Land: 0.3 sq. mi.; **Water:** 0.0 sq. mi.   **Elev:** 765 ft.
Name origin: Named by Quaker settlers for Darlington, England.

Franklin — Township
Lat: 40-05-23 N   **Long:** 86-45-02 W
Pop: 1,569 (1990); 1,700 (1980)   **Pop Density:** 40.3
Land: 38.9 sq. mi.; **Water:** 0.0 sq. mi.

Ladoga — Town
ZIP: 47954   **Lat:** 39-55-00 N   **Long:** 86-47-55 W
Pop: 1,124 (1990); 1,151 (1980)   **Pop Density:** 2248.0
Land: 0.5 sq. mi.; **Water:** 0.0 sq. mi.   **Elev:** 826 ft.
Name origin: For Lake Ladoga in Russia, Europe's largest lake.

Linden — Town
ZIP: 47955   **Lat:** 40-11-26 N   **Long:** 86-54-07 W
Pop: 718 (1990); 700 (1980)   **Pop Density:** 2393.3
Land: 0.3 sq. mi.; **Water:** 0.0 sq. mi.   **Elev:** 787 ft.
Founded 1852.
Name origin: Named in 1852 for the many linden trees in the area.

Madison — Township
Lat: 40-10-25 N   **Long:** 86-51-56 W
Pop: 1,274 (1990); 1,158 (1980)   **Pop Density:** 35.1
Land: 36.3 sq. mi.; **Water:** 0.0 sq. mi.

New Market — Town
ZIP: 47965   **Lat:** 39-57-06 N   **Long:** 86-55-19 W
Pop: 614 (1990); 608 (1980)   **Pop Density:** 2046.7
Land: 0.3 sq. mi.; **Water:** 0.0 sq. mi.   **Elev:** 810 ft.
Name origin: Founded after a fire; new businesses sprang up and suggested the name.

New Richmond — Town
ZIP: 47967   **Lat:** 40-11-38 N   **Long:** 86-58-42 W
Pop: 312 (1990); 403 (1980)   **Pop Density:** 1560.0
Land: 0.2 sq. mi.; **Water:** 0.0 sq. mi.   **Elev:** 782 ft.
Name origin: Named by pioneer Samuel Kincaid for New Richmond, OH, his former home.

New Ross — Town
ZIP: 47968   **Lat:** 39-57-49 N   **Long:** 86-42-49 W
Pop: 331 (1990); 306 (1980)   **Pop Density:** 1103.3
Land: 0.3 sq. mi.; **Water:** 0.0 sq. mi.   **Elev:** 890 ft.
Name origin: Named by innkeeper George Dorsey for Ross, England.

Ripley — Township
Lat: 39-59-44 N   **Long:** 87-02-41 W
Pop: 887 (1990); 1,032 (1980)   **Pop Density:** 28.2
Land: 31.5 sq. mi.; **Water:** 0.0 sq. mi.

Scott — Township
Lat: 39-54-39 N   **Long:** 86-52-13 W
Pop: 738 (1990); 826 (1980)   **Pop Density:** 20.6
Land: 35.9 sq. mi.; **Water:** 0.0 sq. mi.

Sugar Creek — Township
Lat: 40-10-43 N   **Long:** 86-45-42 W
Pop: 372 (1990); 447 (1980)   **Pop Density:** 11.0
Land: 33.8 sq. mi.; **Water:** 0.0 sq. mi.

Union — Township
ZIP: 47933   **Lat:** 40-02-15 N   **Long:** 86-53-51 W
Pop: 21,663 (1990); 21,992 (1980)   **Pop Density:** 194.3
Land: 111.5 sq. mi.; **Water:** 0.3 sq. mi.

Walnut — Township
Lat: 39-59-38 N   **Long:** 86-45-06 W
Pop: 1,440 (1990); 1,475 (1980)   **Pop Density:** 39.6
Land: 36.4 sq. mi.; **Water:** 0.0 sq. mi.

Waveland — Town
ZIP: 47989   **Lat:** 39-52-37 N   **Long:** 87-02-46 W
Pop: 474 (1990); 559 (1980)   **Pop Density:** 1185.0
Land: 0.4 sq. mi.; **Water:** 0.0 sq. mi.   **Elev:** 731 ft.
Name origin: Named by pioneer John Milligan for a KY estate he liked.

Wayne
Township
Lat: 40-05-15 N **Long:** 87-02-09 W
Pop: 1,529 (1990); 1,594 (1980) **Pop Density:** 42.0
Land: 36.4 sq. mi.; **Water:** 0.0 sq. mi.

Waynetown
Town
ZIP: 47990 **Lat:** 40-05-15 N **Long:** 87-03-55 W
Pop: 911 (1990); 915 (1980) **Pop Density:** 2277.5
Land: 0.4 sq. mi.; **Water:** 0.0 sq. mi. **Elev:** 750 ft.
Name origin: For Gen. Anthony Wayne (1745–96), PA soldier and statesman, nicknamed "Mad Anthony" for his daring during the Revolutionary War.

Wingate
Town
ZIP: 47994 **Lat:** 40-10-13 N **Long:** 87-04-24 W
Pop: 275 (1990); 373 (1980) **Pop Density:** 916.7
Land: 0.3 sq. mi.; **Water:** 0.0 sq. mi. **Elev:** 769 ft.
Name origin: For pioneer John Wingate, who helped bring the railroad to the area.

Morgan County
County Seat: Martinsville (ZIP: 46151)

Pop: 55,920 (1990); 51,999 (1980) **Pop Density:** 137.6
Land: 406.5 sq. mi.; **Water:** 2.9 sq. mi. **Area Code:** 317
In central IN, southwest of Indianapolis; organized Feb 15, 1823 from Indian lands.
Name origin: For Gen. Daniel Morgan (1736–1802), an officer in the Revolutionary War and U.S. representative from VA (1797–99).

Adams
Township
Lat: 39-33-33 N **Long:** 86-37-13 W
Pop: 972 (1990); 970 (1980) **Pop Density:** 32.6
Land: 29.8 sq. mi.; **Water:** 0.0 sq. mi.

Ashland
Township
ZIP: 46151 **Lat:** 39-28-38 N **Long:** 86-36-21 W
Pop: 1,212 (1990); 1,098 (1980) **Pop Density:** 38.2
Land: 31.7 sq. mi.; **Water:** 0.1 sq. mi.

Baker
Township
Lat: 39-21-22 N **Long:** 86-32-51 W
Pop: 540 (1990); 549 (1980) **Pop Density:** 34.6
Land: 15.6 sq. mi.; **Water:** 0.0 sq. mi.

Bethany
Town
Lat: 39-32-01 N **Long:** 86-22-43 W
Pop: 90 (1990); 127 (1980) **Pop Density:** 900.0
Land: 0.1 sq. mi.; **Water:** 0.0 sq. mi. **Elev:** 648 ft.
Name origin: Named by its settlers for the biblical village.

Brooklyn
Town
ZIP: 46111 **Lat:** 39-32-33 N **Long:** 86-22-17 W
Pop: 1,162 (1990); 888 (1980) **Pop Density:** 2324.0
Land: 0.5 sq. mi.; **Water:** 0.0 sq. mi. **Elev:** 646 ft.
Name origin: For Brooklyn, NY.

Brown
Township
ZIP: 46158 **Lat:** 39-35-55 N **Long:** 86-22-30 W
Pop: 10,049 (1990); 9,285 (1980) **Pop Density:** 446.6
Land: 22.5 sq. mi.; **Water:** 0.1 sq. mi.

Clay
Township
Lat: 39-31-44 N **Long:** 86-24-12 W
Pop: 3,745 (1990); 3,381 (1980) **Pop Density:** 124.0
Land: 30.2 sq. mi.; **Water:** 0.5 sq. mi.

Green
Township
Lat: 39-28-25 N **Long:** 86-18-19 W
Pop: 2,419 (1990); 1,968 (1980) **Pop Density:** 72.6
Land: 33.3 sq. mi.; **Water:** 0.1 sq. mi.

Gregg
Township
Lat: 39-31-43 N **Long:** 86-31-27 W
Pop: 2,530 (1990); 2,315 (1980) **Pop Density:** 99.2
Land: 25.5 sq. mi.; **Water:** 0.1 sq. mi.

Harrison
Township
Lat: 39-32-28 N **Long:** 86-16-23 W
Pop: 1,538 (1990); 1,501 (1980) **Pop Density:** 178.8
Land: 8.6 sq. mi.; **Water:** 0.2 sq. mi.

Jackson
Township
Lat: 39-23-10 N **Long:** 86-18-15 W
Pop: 3,057 (1990); 2,668 (1980) **Pop Density:** 85.9
Land: 35.6 sq. mi.; **Water:** 0.3 sq. mi.

Jefferson
Township
Lat: 39-27-06 N **Long:** 86-29-40 W
Pop: 2,867 (1990); 2,617 (1980) **Pop Density:** 80.8
Land: 35.5 sq. mi.; **Water:** 0.2 sq. mi.

Lake Hart
Town
Lat: 39-34-06 N **Long:** 86-25-48 W
Pop: 213 (1990); 231 (1980) **Pop Density:** 2130.0
Land: 0.1 sq. mi.; **Water:** 0.0 sq. mi.

Madison
Township
ZIP: 46158 **Lat:** 39-34-57 N **Long:** 86-18-09 W
Pop: 5,408 (1990); 5,290 (1980) **Pop Density:** 195.9
Land: 27.6 sq. mi.; **Water:** 0.3 sq. mi.

Martinsville
City
ZIP: 46151 **Lat:** 39-25-22 N **Long:** 86-25-17 W
Pop: 11,677 (1990); 11,311 (1980) **Pop Density:** 2919.3
Land: 4.0 sq. mi.; **Water:** 0.0 sq. mi. **Elev:** 607 ft.
In central IN, 27 mi. southwest of Indianapolis. Founded 1822.
Name origin: For county commissioner Gen. John Martin (1740–1808).

Monroe
Township
Lat: 39-34-58 N **Long:** 86-28-49 W
Pop: 4,351 (1990); 3,813 (1980) **Pop Density:** 164.2
Land: 26.5 sq. mi.; **Water:** 0.1 sq. mi.

Mooresville
Town
ZIP: 46158 **Lat:** 39-36-57 N **Long:** 86-22-12 W
Pop: 5,541 (1990); 5,349 (1980) **Pop Density:** 2308.8
Land: 2.4 sq. mi.; **Water:** 0.0 sq. mi. **Elev:** 690 ft.
Founded 1824.
Name origin: For its founder, Samuel Moore.

American Places Dictionary   INDIANA, Newton County

Morgantown   Town
Lat: 39-22-25 N   **Long:** 86-15-33 W
Pop: 978 (1990); 897 (1980)   **Pop Density:** 2445.0
Land: 0.4 sq. mi.; **Water:** 0.0 sq. mi.   **Elev:** 680 ft.
Settled 1831.
Name origin: For its county.

Paragon   Town
ZIP: 46166   **Lat:** 39-23-41 N   **Long:** 86-33-46 W
Pop: 515 (1990); 538 (1980)   **Pop Density:** 2575.0
Land: 0.2 sq. mi.; **Water:** 0.0 sq. mi.   **Elev:** 580 ft.
In central IN, 18 mi. north of Bloomington. Settled 1852.

Ray   Township
Lat: 39-24-32 N   **Long:** 86-35-12 W
Pop: 1,255 (1990); 1,286 (1980)   **Pop Density:** 48.6
Land: 25.8 sq. mi.; **Water:** 0.0 sq. mi.

Washington   Township
ZIP: 46151   **Lat:** 39-24-21 N   **Long:** 86-24-53 W
Pop: 15,977 (1990); 15,258 (1980)   **Pop Density:** 275.0
Land: 58.1 sq. mi.; **Water:** 0.8 sq. mi.

Newton County
County Seat: Kentland (ZIP: 47951)

Pop: 13,551 (1990); 14,844 (1980)   **Pop Density:** 33.7
Land: 401.9 sq. mi.; **Water:** 1.7 sq. mi.   **Area Code:** 219
In northwestern IN, south of Gary; organized Feb 7, 1857 from Jasper County.
Name origin: For Sgt. John Newton (1752–80), a soldier under Gen. Francis Marion (1732?–95) in the Revolutionary War, who saved several colonial patriots from execution by surprising and capturing the British soldiers guarding them.

Beaver   Township
Lat: 40-57-33 N   **Long:** 87-27-24 W
Pop: 1,547 (1990); 1,863 (1980)   **Pop Density:** 37.8
Land: 40.9 sq. mi.; **Water:** 1.4 sq. mi.

Brook   Town
ZIP: 47922   **Lat:** 40-51-57 N   **Long:** 87-21-56 W
Pop: 899 (1990); 926 (1980)   **Pop Density:** 1284.3
Land: 0.7 sq. mi.; **Water:** 0.0 sq. mi.   **Elev:** 646 ft.
Name origin: Descriptive of a small stream that runs through the area.

Colfax   Township
Lat: 41-02-09 N   **Long:** 87-20-34 W
Pop: 197 (1990); 213 (1980)   **Pop Density:** 5.4
Land: 36.5 sq. mi.; **Water:** 0.0 sq. mi.

Goodland   Town
ZIP: 47948   **Lat:** 40-45-51 N   **Long:** 87-17-41 W
Pop: 1,033 (1990); 1,200 (1980)   **Pop Density:** 1475.7
Land: 0.7 sq. mi.; **Water:** 0.0 sq. mi.   **Elev:** 727 ft.
Name origin: Descriptively named in 1861 for the surrounding fertile farmland.

Grant   Township
Lat: 40-47-01 N   **Long:** 87-19-29 W
Pop: 1,341 (1990); 1,567 (1980)   **Pop Density:** 37.7
Land: 35.6 sq. mi.; **Water:** 0.0 sq. mi.

Iroquois   Township
Lat: 40-52-08 N   **Long:** 87-19-41 W
Pop: 1,341 (1990); 1,359 (1980)   **Pop Density:** 36.5
Land: 36.7 sq. mi.; **Water:** 0.1 sq. mi.

Jackson   Township
Lat: 40-57-11 N   **Long:** 87-20-36 W
Pop: 480 (1990); 578 (1980)   **Pop Density:** 13.1
Land: 36.7 sq. mi.; **Water:** 0.0 sq. mi.

Jefferson   Township
Lat: 40-46-47 N   **Long:** 87-26-55 W
Pop: 2,224 (1990); 2,384 (1980)   **Pop Density:** 49.3
Land: 45.1 sq. mi.; **Water:** 0.0 sq. mi.

Kentland   Town
ZIP: 47951   **Lat:** 40-46-21 N   **Long:** 87-26-45 W
Pop: 1,798 (1990); 1,936 (1980)   **Pop Density:** 1284.3
Land: 1.4 sq. mi.; **Water:** 0.0 sq. mi.   **Elev:** 680 ft.
Name origin: For its founder, A. J. Kent. Originally called Kent; changed to present name to avoid confusion with another IN town.

Lake   Township
Lat: 41-07-49 N   **Long:** 87-27-46 W
Pop: 2,208 (1990); 2,311 (1980)   **Pop Density:** 55.5
Land: 39.8 sq. mi.; **Water:** 0.0 sq. mi.

Lincoln   Township
Lat: 41-08-06 N   **Long:** 87-19-27 W
Pop: 3,591 (1990); 3,753 (1980)   **Pop Density:** 84.7
Land: 42.4 sq. mi.; **Water:** 0.2 sq. mi.

McClellan   Township
Lat: 41-02-40 N   **Long:** 87-27-31 W
Pop: 237 (1990); 280 (1980)   **Pop Density:** 5.6
Land: 42.3 sq. mi.; **Water:** 0.0 sq. mi.

Morocco   Town
ZIP: 47963   **Lat:** 40-56-44 N   **Long:** 87-27-09 W
Pop: 1,044 (1990); 1,348 (1980)   **Pop Density:** 1740.0
Land: 0.6 sq. mi.; **Water:** 0.0 sq. mi.   **Elev:** 698 ft.
Founded 1851.
Name origin: Named in 1851 for the North African country.

Mount Ayr   Town
ZIP: 47964   **Lat:** 40-57-05 N   **Long:** 87-17-53 W
Pop: 151 (1990); 207 (1980)   **Pop Density:** 1510.0
Land: 0.1 sq. mi.; **Water:** 0.0 sq. mi.   **Elev:** 699 ft.
Name origin: Named in 1882 by settler Louis Marion for his former home in NC.

Washington   Township
Lat: 40-52-15 N   **Long:** 87-27-12 W
Pop: 385 (1990); 536 (1980)   **Pop Density:** 8.4
Land: 45.9 sq. mi.; **Water:** 0.0 sq. mi.

INDIANA, Noble County   American Places Dictionary

Noble County
County Seat: Albion (ZIP: 46701)

Pop: 37,877 (1990); 35,443 (1980) **Pop Density:** 92.1
Land: 411.1 sq. mi.; **Water:** 6.5 sq. mi. **Area Code:** 219

In northeastern IN, southeast of Elkhart; established Feb 7, 1835 from Elkhart County.

Name origin: For either James Noble (1785–1831), U.S. senator from IN (1816–31), or for Moah Noble, governor of IN (1831–37) when the county was established.

Albion   Town
ZIP: 46701   **Lat:** 41-23-42 N **Long:** 85-25-10 W
Pop: 1,823 (1990); 1,637 (1980)   **Pop Density:** 1519.2
Land: 1.2 sq. mi.; **Water:** 0.0 sq. mi.   **Elev:** 963 ft.
Platted 1846. Not coextensive with the town of the same name.
Name origin: For the ancient and literary name of Britain.

*Albion   Township
ZIP: 46701   **Lat:** 41-23-45 N **Long:** 85-25-28 W
Pop: 1,951 (1990); 1,732 (1980)   **Pop Density:** 513.4
Land: 3.8 sq. mi.; **Water:** 0.1 sq. mi.

Allen   Township
ZIP: 46755   **Lat:** 41-23-32 N **Long:** 85-14-51 W
Pop: 5,132 (1990); 4,798 (1980)   **Pop Density:** 143.4
Land: 35.8 sq. mi.; **Water:** 0.1 sq. mi.

Avilla   Town
ZIP: 46710   **Lat:** 41-21-54 N **Long:** 85-14-16 W
Pop: 1,366 (1990); 1,272 (1980)   **Pop Density:** 1707.5
Land: 0.8 sq. mi.; **Water:** 0.0 sq. mi.   **Elev:** 972 ft.
Settled 1819.
Name origin: For Avila, Spain, with a spelling variation.

Cromwell   Town
ZIP: 46732   **Lat:** 41-24-12 N **Long:** 85-36-51 W
Pop: 520 (1990); 458 (1980)   **Pop Density:** 1733.3
Land: 0.3 sq. mi.; **Water:** 0.0 sq. mi.   **Elev:** 953 ft.
Founded 1853.
Name origin: For British statesman Oliver Cromwell (1599–1658).

Elkhart   Township
                  Lat: 41-28-53 N **Long:** 85-28-42 W
Pop: 1,545 (1990); 1,501 (1980)   **Pop Density:** 43.8
Land: 35.3 sq. mi.; **Water:** 0.5 sq. mi.

Green   Township
                  Lat: 41-18-53 N **Long:** 85-22-30 W
Pop: 1,482 (1990); 1,301 (1980)   **Pop Density:** 41.5
Land: 35.7 sq. mi.; **Water:** 0.3 sq. mi.

Jefferson   Township
ZIP: 46701   **Lat:** 41-23-55 N **Long:** 85-21-41 W
Pop: 1,230 (1990); 1,189 (1980)   **Pop Density:** 36.8
Land: 33.4 sq. mi.; **Water:** 0.3 sq. mi.

Kendallville   City
ZIP: 46755   **Lat:** 41-26-36 N **Long:** 85-15-29 W
Pop: 7,773 (1990); 7,299 (1980)   **Pop Density:** 1766.6
Land: 4.4 sq. mi.; **Water:** 0.2 sq. mi.   **Elev:** 982 ft.
Name origin: For Amos Kendall (1789–1869), U.S. postmaster general (1835–40).

Ligonier   City
ZIP: 46767   **Lat:** 41-27-50 N **Long:** 85-35-41 W
Pop: 3,443 (1990); 3,134 (1980)   **Pop Density:** 1721.5
Land: 2.0 sq. mi.; **Water:** 0.0 sq. mi.   **Elev:** 880 ft.
Settled 1835.
Name origin: For Ligonier, PA.

Noble   Township
                  Lat: 41-18-47 N **Long:** 85-28-41 W
Pop: 2,724 (1990); 2,490 (1980)   **Pop Density:** 80.6
Land: 33.8 sq. mi.; **Water:** 1.4 sq. mi.

Orange   Township
                  Lat: 41-28-55 N **Long:** 85-21-43 W
Pop: 3,703 (1990); 4,016 (1980)   **Pop Density:** 106.7
Land: 34.7 sq. mi.; **Water:** 1.5 sq. mi.

Perry   Township
ZIP: 46767   **Lat:** 41-29-03 N **Long:** 85-35-44 W
Pop: 5,110 (1990); 4,436 (1980)   **Pop Density:** 143.1
Land: 35.7 sq. mi.; **Water:** 0.1 sq. mi.

Rome City   Town
ZIP: 46784   **Lat:** 41-29-18 N **Long:** 85-21-20 W
Pop: 1,138 (1990); 1,319 (1980)   **Pop Density:** 1625.7
Land: 0.7 sq. mi.; **Water:** 1.0 sq. mi.   **Elev:** 930 ft.
Settled 1837.
Name origin: For Rome, Italy.

Sparta   Township
ZIP: 46760   **Lat:** 41-23-44 N **Long:** 85-35-35 W
Pop: 2,497 (1990); 1,867 (1980)   **Pop Density:** 71.3
Land: 35.0 sq. mi.; **Water:** 0.3 sq. mi.

Swan   Township
ZIP: 46763   **Lat:** 41-18-17 N **Long:** 85-14-50 W
Pop: 1,877 (1990); 1,861 (1980)   **Pop Density:** 51.9
Land: 36.2 sq. mi.; **Water:** 0.0 sq. mi.

Washington   Township
ZIP: 46760   **Lat:** 41-19-24 N **Long:** 85-35-28 W
Pop: 979 (1990); 979 (1980)   **Pop Density:** 42.4
Land: 23.1 sq. mi.; **Water:** 0.6 sq. mi.

Wayne   Township
ZIP: 46755   **Lat:** 41-28-47 N **Long:** 85-15-19 W
Pop: 8,636 (1990); 8,274 (1980)   **Pop Density:** 243.3
Land: 35.5 sq. mi.; **Water:** 0.9 sq. mi.

Wolcottville   Town
                  Lat: 41-31-21 N **Long:** 85-21-57 W
Pop: 483 (1990); 520 (1980)   **Pop Density:** 966.0
Land: 0.5 sq. mi.; **Water:** 0.0 sq. mi.   **Elev:** 934 ft.
Part of the town is also in Lagrange County.
Name origin: For prominent businessman George Wolcott.

American Places Dictionary | INDIANA, Orange County

York — Township
Lat: 41-24-04 N Long: 85-28-51 W
Pop: 1,011 (1990); 999 (1980) Pop Density: 30.5
Land: 33.1 sq. mi.; Water: 0.4 sq. mi.

Ohio County
County Seat: Rising Sun (ZIP: 47040)

Pop: 5,315 (1990); 5,114 (1980) Pop Density: 61.3
Land: 86.7 sq. mi.; Water: 0.7 sq. mi. Area Code: 812
On the southeastern border of IN, southwest of Cincinnati, OH; organized Jan 4, 1844 from Dearborn county.
Name origin: For the Ohio River, which forms the eastern border of the county.

Cass — Township
Lat: 38-55-52 N Long: 84-59-22 W
Pop: 546 (1990); 481 (1980) Pop Density: 29.5
Land: 18.5 sq. mi.; Water: 0.0 sq. mi.

Pike — Township
Lat: 38-56-00 N Long: 85-04-57 W
Pop: 303 (1990); 332 (1980) Pop Density: 16.2
Land: 18.7 sq. mi.; Water: 0.0 sq. mi.

Randolph — Township
Lat: 38-56-46 N Long: 84-53-44 W
Pop: 4,023 (1990); 4,034 (1980) Pop Density: 106.4
Land: 37.8 sq. mi.; Water: 0.7 sq. mi.

Rising Sun — City
ZIP: 47040 Lat: 38-57-05 N Long: 84-51-25 W
Pop: 2,311 (1990); 2,478 (1980) Pop Density: 2100.9
Land: 1.1 sq. mi.; Water: 0.1 sq. mi. Elev: 520 ft.

Union — Township
Lat: 38-59-15 N Long: 84-58-01 W
Pop: 443 (1990); 267 (1980) Pop Density: 38.2
Land: 11.6 sq. mi.; Water: 0.0 sq. mi.

Orange County
County Seat: Paoli (ZIP: 47454)

Pop: 18,409 (1990); 18,677 (1980) Pop Density: 46.1
Land: 399.6 sq. mi.; Water: 8.7 sq. mi. Area Code: 812
In south-central IN, south of Bloomington; established Dec 26, 1815 (prior to statehood) from Crawford and Washington counties.
Name origin: For Orange County, NC, former home of many early settlers.

French Lick — Town
ZIP: 47432 Lat: 38-32-50 N Long: 86-37-12 W
Pop: 2,087 (1990); 2,265 (1980) Pop Density: 1304.4
Land: 1.6 sq. mi.; Water: 0.0 sq. mi. Elev: 511 ft.
In south-central IN, south of Bloomington. Not coextensive with the town of the same name.
Name origin: Local wildlife came to the salt springs, so pioneers named the trading post The Lick. In the early 1800s the French built a fort and it became French Lick.

***French Lick** — Township
ZIP: 47432 Lat: 38-32-40 N Long: 86-36-40 W
Pop: 4,902 (1990); 5,184 (1980) Pop Density: 90.8
Land: 54.0 sq. mi.; Water: 0.1 sq. mi.

Greenfield — Township
Lat: 38-26-45 N Long: 86-30-38 W
Pop: 418 (1990); 469 (1980) Pop Density: 10.1
Land: 41.4 sq. mi.; Water: 1.8 sq. mi.

Jackson — Township
ZIP: 47432 Lat: 38-26-58 N Long: 86-37-09 W
Pop: 416 (1990); 346 (1980) Pop Density: 11.6
Land: 35.9 sq. mi.; Water: 6.7 sq. mi.

Northeast — Township
ZIP: 47452 Lat: 38-38-12 N Long: 86-20-46 W
Pop: 548 (1990); 594 (1980) Pop Density: 19.1
Land: 28.7 sq. mi.; Water: 0.0 sq. mi.

Northwest — Township
ZIP: 47469 Lat: 38-38-42 N Long: 86-38-20 W
Pop: 359 (1990); 343 (1980) Pop Density: 11.8
Land: 30.4 sq. mi.; Water: 0.0 sq. mi.

Orangeville — Township
ZIP: 47452 Lat: 38-38-13 N Long: 86-33-13 W
Pop: 559 (1990); 521 (1980) Pop Density: 19.9
Land: 28.1 sq. mi.; Water: 0.0 sq. mi.

Orleans — Town
ZIP: 47452 Lat: 38-39-43 N Long: 86-27-10 W
Pop: 2,083 (1990); 2,161 (1980) Pop Density: 1388.7
Land: 1.5 sq. mi.; Water: 0.0 sq. mi. Elev: 635 ft.
Not coextensive with the town of the same name.
Name origin: In commemoration of seventh U.S. President Andrew Jackson's (1767–1845) victory at the Battle of New Orleans.

*Orleans
Township
ZIP: 47452 **Lat:** 38-39-14 N **Long:** 86-26-57 W
Pop: 3,202 (1990); 3,210 (1980) **Pop Density:** 88.9
Land: 36.0 sq. mi.; **Water:** 0.1 sq. mi.

Paoli
Town
ZIP: 47454 **Lat:** 38-33-27 N **Long:** 86-28-09 W
Pop: 3,542 (1990); 3,637 (1980) **Pop Density:** 932.1
Land: 3.8 sq. mi.; **Water:** 0.0 sq. mi. **Elev:** 615 ft.
Not coextensive with the town of the same name.
Name origin: For Corsican revolutionary and statesman Pasquale Paoli (1725–1807).

*Paoli
Township
ZIP: 47454 **Lat:** 38-33-21 N **Long:** 86-27-30 W
Pop: 5,624 (1990); 5,780 (1980) **Pop Density:** 88.8
Land: 63.3 sq. mi.; **Water:** 0.0 sq. mi.

Southeast
Township
Lat: 38-26-39 N **Long:** 86-22-59 W
Pop: 1,536 (1990); 1,435 (1980) **Pop Density:** 28.8
Land: 53.3 sq. mi.; **Water:** 0.0 sq. mi.

Stampers Creek
Township
ZIP: 47454 **Lat:** 38-32-20 N **Long:** 86-20-59 W
Pop: 845 (1990); 795 (1980) **Pop Density:** 29.6
Land: 28.5 sq. mi.; **Water:** 0.0 sq. mi. **Elev:** 699 ft.

West Baden Springs
Town
ZIP: 47469 **Lat:** 38-34-03 N **Long:** 86-36-44 W
Pop: 675 (1990); 796 (1980) **Pop Density:** 613.6
Land: 1.1 sq. mi.; **Water:** 0.0 sq. mi. **Elev:** 500 ft.
Name origin: Named by Dr. John R. Lane, an itinerant medicine peddler who built the first resort here in 1851, for the famous West Baden spa in Germany.

Owen County
County Seat: Spencer (ZIP: 47460)

Pop: 17,281 (1990); 15,841 (1980) **Pop Density:** 44.9
Land: 385.2 sq. mi.; **Water:** 2.6 sq. mi. **Area Code:** 812
In west-central IN, northwest of Bloomington; established Dec 21, 1818 from Indian lands.
Name origin: For Col. Abraham Owen (?–1811), killed in the Battle of Tippecanoe.

Clay
Township
ZIP: 47460 **Lat:** 39-12-31 N **Long:** 86-43-47 W
Pop: 1,931 (1990); 1,823 (1980) **Pop Density:** 53.6
Land: 36.0 sq. mi.; **Water:** 0.0 sq. mi.

Franklin
Township
ZIP: 47431 **Lat:** 39-12-37 N **Long:** 86-51-00 W
Pop: 1,003 (1990); 791 (1980) **Pop Density:** 28.6
Land: 35.1 sq. mi.; **Water:** 0.0 sq. mi.

Gosport
Town
ZIP: 47433 **Lat:** 39-21-01 N **Long:** 86-39-56 W
Pop: 764 (1990); 729 (1980) **Pop Density:** 1910.0
Land: 0.4 sq. mi.; **Water:** 0.0 sq. mi. **Elev:** 650 ft.
Founded 1829.
Name origin: For its founders, the Goss brothers.

Harrison
Township
ZIP: 47433 **Lat:** 39-26-19 N **Long:** 86-40-16 W
Pop: 355 (1990); 355 (1980) **Pop Density:** 20.2
Land: 17.6 sq. mi.; **Water:** 0.0 sq. mi.

Jackson
Township
Lat: 39-26-18 N **Long:** 86-53-56 W
Pop: 1,103 (1990); 1,248 (1980) **Pop Density:** 50.4
Land: 21.9 sq. mi.; **Water:** 1.3 sq. mi.

Jefferson
Township
ZIP: 47427 **Lat:** 39-12-33 N **Long:** 86-58-48 W
Pop: 849 (1990); 853 (1980) **Pop Density:** 17.8
Land: 47.8 sq. mi.; **Water:** 0.1 sq. mi.

Jennings
Township
Lat: 39-26-01 N **Long:** 86-48-53 W
Pop: 706 (1990); 640 (1980) **Pop Density:** 36.2
Land: 19.5 sq. mi.; **Water:** 0.5 sq. mi.

Lafayette
Township
ZIP: 47460 **Lat:** 39-17-28 N **Long:** 86-53-06 W
Pop: 912 (1990); 589 (1980) **Pop Density:** 31.4
Land: 29.0 sq. mi.; **Water:** 0.1 sq. mi.

Marion
Township
ZIP: 47455 **Lat:** 39-18-19 N **Long:** 86-59-58 W
Pop: 798 (1990); 723 (1980) **Pop Density:** 22.2
Land: 35.9 sq. mi.; **Water:** 0.1 sq. mi.

Montgomery
Township
ZIP: 47460 **Lat:** 39-22-00 N **Long:** 86-46-22 W
Pop: 872 (1990); 718 (1980) **Pop Density:** 37.1
Land: 23.5 sq. mi.; **Water:** 0.1 sq. mi.

Morgan
Township
Lat: 39-21-51 N **Long:** 86-53-15 W
Pop: 885 (1990); 677 (1980) **Pop Density:** 29.9
Land: 29.6 sq. mi.; **Water:** 0.1 sq. mi.

Spencer
Town
ZIP: 47460 **Lat:** 39-17-13 N **Long:** 86-46-08 W
Pop: 2,609 (1990); 2,732 (1980) **Pop Density:** 2174.2
Land: 1.2 sq. mi.; **Water:** 0.0 sq. mi. **Elev:** 566 ft.
Name origin: For Capt. Spier Spencer, killed in the Battle of Tippecanoe (1811).

Taylor
Township
ZIP: 47460 **Lat:** 39-25-59 N **Long:** 86-44-39 W
Pop: 795 (1990); 922 (1980) **Pop Density:** 40.2
Land: 19.8 sq. mi.; **Water:** 0.1 sq. mi.

Washington
Township
ZIP: 47460 **Lat:** 39-17-34 N **Long:** 86-45-25 W
Pop: 5,570 (1990); 5,070 (1980) **Pop Density:** 117.5
Land: 47.4 sq. mi.; **Water:** 0.2 sq. mi.

Wayne   Township
ZIP: 47433   **Lat:** 39-22-37 N   **Long:** 86-40-29 W
Pop: 1,502 (1990); 1,432 (1980)   **Pop Density:** 68.0
Land: 22.1 sq. mi.; **Water:** 0.0 sq. mi.

Parke County
County Seat: Rockville (ZIP: 47872)

Pop: 15,410 (1990); 16,372 (1980)   **Pop Density:** 34.6
Land: 444.8 sq. mi.; **Water:** 5.3 sq. mi.   **Area Code:** 317
In west-central IN, north of Terre Haute; organized Jan 9, 1821 from Indian lands.
Name origin: For Benjamin Parke (1777–1835), attorney general of IN Territory (1804–08), IN legislator, and judge of the U.S. District Court of IN (1817–35).

Adams   Township
ZIP: 47872   **Lat:** 39-44-25 N   **Long:** 87-12-31 W
Pop: 4,628 (1990); 4,535 (1980)   **Pop Density:** 82.9
Land: 55.8 sq. mi.; **Water:** 0.3 sq. mi.

Bloomingdale   Town
ZIP: 47832   **Lat:** 39-49-53 N   **Long:** 87-14-58 W
Pop: 341 (1990); 409 (1980)   **Pop Density:** 568.3
Land: 0.6 sq. mi.; **Water:** 0.0 sq. mi.   **Elev:** 650 ft.
Name origin: Previously called Elevatis for the elevation on which the Quaker meeting house was built.

Florida   Township
ZIP: 47874   **Lat:** 39-39-02 N   **Long:** 87-18-59 W
Pop: 2,480 (1990); 2,632 (1980)   **Pop Density:** 51.5
Land: 48.2 sq. mi.; **Water:** 0.3 sq. mi.

Greene   Township
                     Lat: 39-49-11 N   **Long:** 87-04-06 W
Pop: 416 (1990); 524 (1980)   **Pop Density:** 11.7
Land: 35.6 sq. mi.; **Water:** 0.1 sq. mi.

Howard   Township
ZIP: 47859   **Lat:** 39-54-10 N   **Long:** 87-07-58 W
Pop: 244 (1990); 226 (1980)   **Pop Density:** 10.3
Land: 23.7 sq. mi.; **Water:** 0.1 sq. mi.

Jackson   Township
                     Lat: 39-38-57 N   **Long:** 87-03-38 W
Pop: 667 (1990); 669 (1980)   **Pop Density:** 18.7
Land: 35.6 sq. mi.; **Water:** 0.2 sq. mi.

Judson   Town
ZIP: 47856   **Lat:** 39-48-48 N   **Long:** 87-08-06 W
Pop: 61 (1990); 80 (1980)   **Pop Density:** 610.0
Land: 0.1 sq. mi.; **Water:** 0.0 sq. mi.   **Elev:** 607 ft.
Settled 1872.
Name origin: For KY missionary Adoniram Judson (d. 1850). Originally called Buchanan's Springs.

Liberty   Township
                     Lat: 39-54-45 N   **Long:** 87-19-58 W
Pop: 719 (1990); 889 (1980)   **Pop Density:** 18.5
Land: 38.9 sq. mi.; **Water:** 0.4 sq. mi.

Marshall   Town
ZIP: 47859   **Lat:** 39-50-49 N   **Long:** 87-11-08 W
Pop: 379 (1990); 413 (1980)   **Pop Density:** 1895.0
Land: 0.2 sq. mi.; **Water:** 0.0 sq. mi.   **Elev:** 700 ft.
Name origin: For Mahlon Marshall, who donated the land for the town.

Mecca   Town
ZIP: 47860   **Lat:** 39-43-37 N   **Long:** 87-19-53 W
Pop: 331 (1990); 482 (1980)   **Pop Density:** 827.5
Land: 0.4 sq. mi.; **Water:** 0.0 sq. mi.   **Elev:** 495 ft.
Settled 1840s.
Name origin: For the holy Moslem city.

Montezuma   Town
ZIP: 47862   **Lat:** 39-47-27 N   **Long:** 87-22-08 W
Pop: 1,134 (1990); 1,352 (1980)   **Pop Density:** 1890.0
Land: 0.6 sq. mi.; **Water:** 0.0 sq. mi.   **Elev:** 501 ft.
Name origin: For the last Aztec emperor of Mexico (1466–1520).

Penn   Township
ZIP: 47832   **Lat:** 39-51-09 N   **Long:** 87-15-30 W
Pop: 843 (1990); 897 (1980)   **Pop Density:** 35.6
Land: 23.7 sq. mi.; **Water:** 0.0 sq. mi.

Raccoon   Township
ZIP: 47874   **Lat:** 39-39-00 N   **Long:** 87-10-55 W
Pop: 818 (1990); 856 (1980)   **Pop Density:** 22.1
Land: 37.0 sq. mi.; **Water:** 0.0 sq. mi.

Reserve   Township
ZIP: 47862   **Lat:** 39-49-35 N   **Long:** 87-20-17 W
Pop: 1,444 (1990); 1,635 (1980)   **Pop Density:** 57.5
Land: 25.1 sq. mi.; **Water:** 0.3 sq. mi.

Rockville   Town
ZIP: 47872   **Lat:** 39-46-00 N   **Long:** 87-13-51 W
Pop: 2,706 (1990); 2,785 (1980)   **Pop Density:** 1932.9
Land: 1.4 sq. mi.; **Water:** 0.0 sq. mi.   **Elev:** 711 ft.
Name origin: Descriptive of a large rock now on the courthouse lawn.

Rosedale   Town
ZIP: 47874   **Lat:** 39-37-23 N   **Long:** 87-16-55 W
Pop: 783 (1990); 744 (1980)   **Pop Density:** 1957.5
Land: 0.4 sq. mi.; **Water:** 0.0 sq. mi.   **Elev:** 542 ft.
Name origin: For Chauncey Rose, prominent early settler.

Sugar Creek   Township
ZIP: 47859   **Lat:** 39-55-32 N   **Long:** 87-12-29 W
Pop: 300 (1990); 292 (1980)   **Pop Density:** 12.0
Land: 24.9 sq. mi.; **Water:** 0.0 sq. mi.

Union   Township
ZIP: 47872   **Lat:** 39-44-05 N   **Long:** 87-03-42 W
Pop: 1,169 (1990); 1,172 (1980)   **Pop Density:** 35.7
Land: 32.7 sq. mi.; **Water:** 3.1 sq. mi.

INDIANA, Parke County   *American Places Dictionary*

Wabash Township
ZIP: 47860   Lat: 39-43-56 N   Long: 87-20-00 W
Pop: 778 (1990); 1,028 (1980)   Pop Density: 28.3
Land: 27.5 sq. mi.; Water: 0.3 sq. mi.

Washington Township
ZIP: 47859   Lat: 39-49-42 N   Long: 87-10-38 W
Pop: 904 (1990); 1,017 (1980)   Pop Density: 25.1
Land: 36.0 sq. mi.; Water: 0.2 sq. mi.

Perry County
County Seat: Cannelton (ZIP: 47520)

Pop: 19,107 (1990); 19,346 (1980)   Pop Density: 50.1
Land: 381.4 sq. mi.; Water: 4.9 sq. mi.   Area Code: 812

On the south-central border of IN; organized Sep 7, 1814 (prior to statehood) from Harrison and Warrick counties.

Name origin: For Oliver Hazard Perry (1785–1819), U.S. naval officer during the War of 1812, famous for the message, "We have met the enemy and they are ours."

Anderson Township
ZIP: 47586   Lat: 38-02-47 N   Long: 86-42-22 W
Pop: 1,340 (1990); 1,359 (1980)   Pop Density: 22.6
Land: 59.4 sq. mi.; Water: 0.1 sq. mi.

Cannelton City
ZIP: 47520   Lat: 37-54-36 N   Long: 86-44-12 W
Pop: 1,786 (1990); 2,373 (1980)   Pop Density: 1190.7
Land: 1.5 sq. mi.; Water: 0.1 sq. mi.   Elev: 426 ft.
Name origin: For the cannel coal mined nearby.

Clark Township
Lat: 38-11-02 N   Long: 86-43-01 W
Pop: 1,136 (1990); 1,111 (1980)   Pop Density: 15.2
Land: 74.6 sq. mi.; Water: 0.3 sq. mi.

Leopold Township
ZIP: 47551   Lat: 38-06-13 N   Long: 86-36-22 W
Pop: 623 (1990); 619 (1980)   Pop Density: 19.4
Land: 32.1 sq. mi.; Water: 0.3 sq. mi.

Oil Township
ZIP: 47576   Lat: 38-10-46 N   Long: 86-33-49 W
Pop: 1,639 (1990); 894 (1980)   Pop Density: 24.7
Land: 66.3 sq. mi.; Water: 0.2 sq. mi.

Tell City City
ZIP: 47586   Lat: 37-56-59 N   Long: 86-45-26 W
Pop: 8,088 (1990); 8,704 (1980)   Pop Density: 2185.9
Land: 3.7 sq. mi.; Water: 0.1 sq. mi.   Elev: 436 ft.
Name origin: For legendary Swiss hero William Tell.

Tobin Township
ZIP: 47574   Lat: 37-57-16 N   Long: 86-35-37 W
Pop: 684 (1990); 901 (1980)   Pop Density: 10.7
Land: 63.7 sq. mi.; Water: 1.9 sq. mi.

Troy Town
Lat: 37-59-45 N   Long: 86-48-05 W
Pop: 465 (1990); 550 (1980)   Pop Density: 1550.0
Land: 0.3 sq. mi.; Water: 0.0 sq. mi.   Elev: 430 ft.
In south-central IN on the Ohio River. Settled 1809. Not coextensive with the town of the same name.
Name origin: For the ancient city in Asia Minor.

*Troy Township
ZIP: 47588   Lat: 37-57-37 N   Long: 86-42-52 W
Pop: 13,173 (1990); 13,921 (1980)   Pop Density: 306.3
Land: 43.0 sq. mi.; Water: 1.3 sq. mi.

Union Township
ZIP: 47555   Lat: 38-04-05 N   Long: 86-30-38 W
Pop: 512 (1990); 541 (1980)   Pop Density: 12.1
Land: 42.3 sq. mi.; Water: 0.9 sq. mi.

Pike County
County Seat: Petersburg (ZIP: 47567)

Pop: 12,509 (1990); 13,465 (1980)   Pop Density: 37.2
Land: 336.2 sq. mi.; Water: 4.9 sq. mi.   Area Code: 812

In southwestern IN, northeast of Evansville; established Dec 21, 1816 from Indian lands.

Name origin: For Zebulon Montgomery Pike (1779–1813), U.S. army officer and discoverer of Pikes Peak in CO.

Clay Township
Lat: 38-29-24 N   Long: 87-25-30 W
Pop: 358 (1990); 374 (1980)   Pop Density: 15.2
Land: 23.6 sq. mi.; Water: 0.3 sq. mi.

Jefferson Township
ZIP: 47564   Lat: 38-29-01 N   Long: 87-08-42 W
Pop: 1,626 (1990); 1,657 (1980)   Pop Density: 30.9
Land: 52.6 sq. mi.; Water: 0.5 sq. mi.

American Places Dictionary INDIANA, Porter County

Lockhart — Township
ZIP: 47585 **Lat:** 38-16-41 N **Long:** 87-08-07 W
Pop: 724 (1990); 681 (1980) **Pop Density:** 14.9
Land: 48.5 sq. mi.; **Water:** 0.5 sq. mi.

Logan — Township
ZIP: 47567 **Lat:** 38-25-01 N **Long:** 87-21-32 W
Pop: 379 (1990); 380 (1980) **Pop Density:** 15.8
Land: 24.0 sq. mi.; **Water:** 0.3 sq. mi.

Madison — Township
ZIP: 47567 **Lat:** 38-29-28 N **Long:** 87-21-36 W
Pop: 443 (1990); 472 (1980) **Pop Density:** 20.4
Land: 21.7 sq. mi.; **Water:** 0.4 sq. mi.

Marion — Township
ZIP: 47590 **Lat:** 38-22-53 N **Long:** 87-07-47 W
Pop: 580 (1990); 587 (1980) **Pop Density:** 16.3
Land: 35.6 sq. mi.; **Water:** 0.5 sq. mi.

Monroe — Township
ZIP: 47584 **Lat:** 38-17-15 N **Long:** 87-15-27 W
Pop: 733 (1990); 839 (1980) **Pop Density:** 17.1
Land: 42.8 sq. mi.; **Water:** 0.9 sq. mi.

Patoka — Township
ZIP: 47598 **Lat:** 38-22-42 N **Long:** 87-14-48 W
Pop: 2,935 (1990); 3,213 (1980) **Pop Density:** 68.1
Land: 43.1 sq. mi.; **Water:** 0.7 sq. mi.

Petersburg — City
ZIP: 47567 **Lat:** 38-29-30 N **Long:** 87-16-54 W
Pop: 2,449 (1990); 2,987 (1980) **Pop Density:** 1749.3
Land: 1.4 sq. mi.; **Water:** 0.0 sq. mi. **Elev:** 439 ft.

Spurgeon — Town
ZIP: 47584 **Lat:** 38-15-20 N **Long:** 87-15-33 W
Pop: 149 (1990); 250 (1980) **Pop Density:** 745.0
Land: 0.2 sq. mi.; **Water:** 0.0 sq. mi. **Elev:** 509 ft.

Washington — Township
ZIP: 47567 **Lat:** 38-28-35 N **Long:** 87-15-22 W
Pop: 4,731 (1990); 5,262 (1980) **Pop Density:** 106.8
Land: 44.3 sq. mi.; **Water:** 0.8 sq. mi.

Winslow — Town
ZIP: 47598 **Lat:** 38-23-01 N **Long:** 87-12-45 W
Pop: 875 (1990); 1,017 (1980) **Pop Density:** 1458.3
Land: 0.6 sq. mi.; **Water:** 0.0 sq. mi. **Elev:** 440 ft.

Porter County
County Seat: Valparaiso (ZIP: 46383)

Pop: 128,932 (1990); 119,816 (1980) **Pop Density:** 308.3
Land: 418.2 sq. mi.; **Water:** 103.4 sq. mi. **Area Code:** 219

On the northwestern border of IN, east of Gary, bordered on north by Lake Michigan; established Feb 7, 1835 from Indian lands.

Name origin: For Commodore David Porter (1780–1843), naval hero in the War of 1812 and U.S. minister to Turkey (1839).

Beverly Shores — Town
ZIP: 46301 **Lat:** 41-41-07 N **Long:** 86-58-43 W
Pop: 622 (1990); 864 (1980) **Pop Density:** 172.8
Land: 3.6 sq. mi.; **Water:** 0.0 sq. mi. **Elev:** 650 ft.
Name origin: Euphoniously named by its developer.

Boone — Township
Lat: 41-18-35 N **Long:** 87-09-05 W
Pop: 4,909 (1990); 4,492 (1980) **Pop Density:** 135.6
Land: 36.2 sq. mi.; **Water:** 0.0 sq. mi.

Burns Harbor — Town
Lat: 41-36-50 N **Long:** 87-07-31 W
Pop: 788 (1990); 920 (1980) **Pop Density:** 160.8
Land: 4.9 sq. mi.; **Water:** 0.0 sq. mi. **Elev:** 620 ft.

Center — Township
ZIP: 46383 **Lat:** 41-28-39 N **Long:** 87-04-28 W
Pop: 32,603 (1990); 29,392 (1980) **Pop Density:** 1105.2
Land: 29.5 sq. mi.; **Water:** 0.3 sq. mi.

Chesterton — Town
ZIP: 46304 **Lat:** 41-36-03 N **Long:** 87-03-25 W
Pop: 9,124 (1990); 8,531 (1980) **Pop Density:** 1285.1
Land: 7.1 sq. mi.; **Water:** 0.1 sq. mi. **Elev:** 640 ft.

Dune Acres — Town
Lat: 41-38-37 N **Long:** 87-06-11 W
Pop: 263 (1990); 291 (1980) **Pop Density:** 131.5
Land: 2.0 sq. mi.; **Water:** 0.0 sq. mi. **Elev:** 621 ft.
Name origin: Descriptively named for the famous Indiana Dunes along the shore of Lake Michigan.

Hebron — Town
ZIP: 46341 **Lat:** 41-19-20 N **Long:** 87-12-10 W
Pop: 3,183 (1990); 2,696 (1980) **Pop Density:** 2273.6
Land: 1.4 sq. mi.; **Water:** 0.0 sq. mi. **Elev:** 703 ft.
Laid out 1844.
Name origin: Named in 1844 by the Rev. Hannan for the biblical place. Formerly called The Corners.

Jackson — Township
Lat: 41-33-31 N **Long:** 86-58-46 W
Pop: 3,473 (1990); 2,983 (1980) **Pop Density:** 129.1
Land: 26.9 sq. mi.; **Water:** 0.1 sq. mi.

Kouts — Town
ZIP: 46347 **Lat:** 41-19-00 N **Long:** 87-01-34 W
Pop: 1,603 (1990); 1,619 (1980) **Pop Density:** 1457.3
Land: 1.1 sq. mi.; **Water:** 0.0 sq. mi. **Elev:** 684 ft.
Name origin: For settler Barnardt Kouts with whom railroad surveyors boarded in 1865.

Lakes of the Four Seasons — CDP
Lat: 41-24-20 N **Long:** 87-12-44 W
Pop: 2,832 (1990) **Pop Density:** 2360.0
Land: 1.2 sq. mi.; **Water:** 0.2 sq. mi.
Part of the town is also in Lake County.

Liberty — Township
ZIP: 46383 **Lat:** 41-33-37 N **Long:** 87-04-32 W
Pop: 5,740 (1990); 5,367 (1980) **Pop Density:** 231.5
Land: 24.8 sq. mi.; **Water:** 0.3 sq. mi.

INDIANA, Porter County   *American Places Dictionary*

Morgan
Township
Lat: 41-23-53 N **Long:** 86-59-44 W
Pop: 2,102 (1990); 1,769 (1980)   **Pop Density:** 45.9
Land: 45.8 sq. mi.; **Water:** 0.0 sq. mi.

Ogden Dunes
Town
ZIP: 46368   **Lat:** 41-37-22 N **Long:** 87-11-36 W
Pop: 1,499 (1990); 1,489 (1980)   **Pop Density:** 2141.4
Land: 0.7 sq. mi.; **Water:** 0.0 sq. mi.   **Elev:** 700 ft.

Pine
Township
Lat: 41-39-16 N **Long:** 86-58-13 W
Pop: 2,779 (1990); 3,311 (1980)   **Pop Density:** 103.7
Land: 26.8 sq. mi.; **Water:** 2.3 sq. mi.

Pleasant
Township
Lat: 41-17-46 N **Long:** 86-59-39 W
Pop: 3,266 (1990); 3,172 (1980)   **Pop Density:** 57.6
Land: 56.7 sq. mi.; **Water:** 0.0 sq. mi.

Portage
City
ZIP: 46368   **Lat:** 41-35-12 N **Long:** 87-10-53 W
Pop: 29,060 (1990); 27,409 (1980)   **Pop Density:** 1397.1
Land: 20.8 sq. mi.; **Water:** 0.2 sq. mi.   **Elev:** 644 ft.

In northwestern IN, 11 mi. northwest of Valparaiso. Not coextensive with the town of the same name.

Name origin: For the township, itself named for Portage County, OH.

*Portage
Township
ZIP: 46368   **Lat:** 41-34-41 N **Long:** 87-10-33 W
Pop: 40,929 (1990); 39,765 (1980)   **Pop Density:** 1152.9
Land: 35.5 sq. mi.; **Water:** 2.0 sq. mi.

Porter
Town
ZIP: 46304   **Lat:** 41-37-38 N **Long:** 87-04-54 W
Pop: 3,118 (1990); 2,988 (1980)   **Pop Density:** 494.9
Land: 6.3 sq. mi.; **Water:** 0.0 sq. mi.   **Elev:** 640 ft.

Name origin: For David Porter (1780–1843), naval hero in the War of 1812 and U.S. minister to Turkey (1839).

*Porter
Township
ZIP: 46383   **Lat:** 41-23-27 N **Long:** 87-09-09 W
Pop: 7,300 (1990); 6,493 (1980)   **Pop Density:** 162.6
Land: 44.9 sq. mi.; **Water:** 0.3 sq. mi.

South Haven
CDP
ZIP: 46383   **Lat:** 41-32-36 N **Long:** 87-08-02 W
Pop: 6,112 (1990); 6,679 (1980)   **Pop Density:** 6112.0
Land: 1.0 sq. mi.; **Water:** 0.0 sq. mi.

Town of Pines
Town
Lat: 41-41-18 N **Long:** 86-57-05 W
Pop: 789 (1990); 962 (1980)   **Pop Density:** 343.0
Land: 2.3 sq. mi.; **Water:** 0.0 sq. mi.   **Elev:** 620 ft.

Name origin: For its descriptive connotations.

Union
Township
ZIP: 46342   **Lat:** 41-28-41 N **Long:** 87-10-19 W
Pop: 7,167 (1990); 5,337 (1980)   **Pop Density:** 242.9
Land: 29.5 sq. mi.; **Water:** 0.4 sq. mi.

Valparaiso
City
ZIP: 46383   **Lat:** 41-28-38 N **Long:** 87-03-03 W
Pop: 24,414 (1990); 22,247 (1980)   **Pop Density:** 2417.2
Land: 10.1 sq. mi.; **Water:** 0.0 sq. mi.   **Elev:** 738 ft.

In northwestern IN, 11 mi. south of Lake Michigan. Settled 1836.

Name origin: For the city in Chile, South America.

Washington
Township
Lat: 41-28-44 N **Long:** 86-58-59 W
Pop: 3,113 (1990); 2,424 (1980)   **Pop Density:** 105.5
Land: 29.5 sq. mi.; **Water:** 0.0 sq. mi.

Westchester
Township
ZIP: 46304   **Lat:** 41-37-33 N **Long:** 87-04-18 W
Pop: 15,551 (1990); 15,311 (1980)   **Pop Density:** 484.5
Land: 32.1 sq. mi.; **Water:** 0.3 sq. mi.

Posey County
County Seat: Mount Vernon (ZIP: 47620)

Pop: 25,968 (1990); 26,414 (1980)   **Pop Density:** 63.6
Land: 408.5 sq. mi.; **Water:** 10.9 sq. mi.   **Area Code:** 812

In the southwestern corner of IN, west of Evansville; organized Sep 7, 1814 (prior to statehood) from Knox County.

Name origin: For Gen. Thomas Posey (1750–1818), officer in the American Revolution, LA legislator (1805–06), U.S. senator from LA (1812–13), and IN territorial governor (1813–16).

Bethel
Township
Lat: 38-12-18 N **Long:** 87-55-36 W
Pop: 329 (1990); 386 (1980)   **Pop Density:** 17.2
Land: 19.1 sq. mi.; **Water:** 0.7 sq. mi.

Black
Township
ZIP: 47620   **Lat:** 37-56-58 N **Long:** 87-55-04 W
Pop: 9,962 (1990); 10,429 (1980)   **Pop Density:** 114.5
Land: 87.0 sq. mi.; **Water:** 1.9 sq. mi.

In southwestern IN on the Black River, northwest of Evansville.

Center
Township
Lat: 38-05-41 N **Long:** 87-48-29 W
Pop: 1,166 (1990); 1,151 (1980)   **Pop Density:** 46.5
Land: 25.1 sq. mi.; **Water:** 0.0 sq. mi.

Cynthiana
Town
ZIP: 47612   **Lat:** 38-11-12 N **Long:** 87-42-31 W
Pop: 669 (1990); 874 (1980)   **Pop Density:** 1672.5
Land: 0.4 sq. mi.; **Water:** 0.0 sq. mi.   **Elev:** 440 ft.

Name origin: For Cynthiana, KY, former home of early settlers.

Griffin
Town
ZIP: 47616 **Lat:** 38-12-15 N **Long:** 87-54-55 W
Pop: 171 (1990); 192 (1980) **Pop Density:** 1710.0
Land: 0.1 sq. mi.; **Water:** 0.0 sq. mi. **Elev:** 385 ft.
Name origin: For its first postmaster, Samuel Griffin.

Harmony
Township
Lat: 38-07-18 N **Long:** 87-54-23 W
Pop: 1,432 (1990); 1,536 (1980) **Pop Density:** 40.7
Land: 35.2 sq. mi.; **Water:** 0.7 sq. mi.

Lynn
Township
Lat: 38-02-48 N **Long:** 87-55-33 W
Pop: 991 (1990); 891 (1980) **Pop Density:** 22.7
Land: 43.6 sq. mi.; **Water:** 1.1 sq. mi.

Marrs
Township
Lat: 37-56-46 N **Long:** 87-45-20 W
Pop: 4,462 (1990); 4,182 (1980) **Pop Density:** 86.6
Land: 51.5 sq. mi.; **Water:** 0.6 sq. mi.

Mount Vernon
City
ZIP: 47620 **Lat:** 37-56-09 N **Long:** 87-53-55 W
Pop: 7,217 (1990); 7,656 (1980) **Pop Density:** 3007.1
Land: 2.4 sq. mi.; **Water:** 0.1 sq. mi. **Elev:** 398 ft.

New Harmony
Town
ZIP: 47631 **Lat:** 38-07-42 N **Long:** 87-55-56 W
Pop: 846 (1990); 945 (1980) **Pop Density:** 1410.0
Land: 0.6 sq. mi.; **Water:** 0.0 sq. mi. **Elev:** 384 ft.
Settled 1814.
Name origin: For Harmonie, PA.

Point
Township
Lat: 37-50-17 N **Long:** 87-59-36 W
Pop: 477 (1990); 443 (1980) **Pop Density:** 9.7
Land: 49.2 sq. mi.; **Water:** 5.9 sq. mi.

Poseyville
Town
ZIP: 47633 **Lat:** 38-10-12 N **Long:** 87-46-58 W
Pop: 1,089 (1990); 1,247 (1980) **Pop Density:** 1815.0
Land: 0.6 sq. mi.; **Water:** 0.0 sq. mi. **Elev:** 434 ft.
Name origin: For Gen. Thomas Posey (1750–1818), officer in the American Revolution, LA legislator, U.S. senator from LA (1812–13), and IN territorial governor (1813–16).

Robb
Township
Lat: 38-10-39 N **Long:** 87-49-38 W
Pop: 2,009 (1990); 2,167 (1980) **Pop Density:** 53.9
Land: 37.3 sq. mi.; **Water:** 0.0 sq. mi.

Robinson
Township
Lat: 38-03-00 N **Long:** 87-45-03 W
Pop: 3,863 (1990); 3,750 (1980) **Pop Density:** 98.8
Land: 39.1 sq. mi.; **Water:** 0.0 sq. mi.

Smith
Township
Lat: 38-09-46 N **Long:** 87-43-13 W
Pop: 1,277 (1990); 1,479 (1980) **Pop Density:** 60.2
Land: 21.2 sq. mi.; **Water:** 0.0 sq. mi.

Pulaski County
County Seat: Winamac (ZIP: 46996)

Pop: 12,643 (1990); 13,258 (1980) **Pop Density:** 29.2
Land: 433.7 sq. mi.; **Water:** 0.9 sq. mi. **Area Code:** 219
In northwestern IN, southwest of South Bend; established Feb 7, 1835 from Cass County.
Name origin: For Count Casimir Pulaski (1747–79), Polish soldier who fought for America during the Revolutionary War.

Beaver
Township
Lat: 40-57-21 N **Long:** 86-45-24 W
Pop: 379 (1990); 439 (1980) **Pop Density:** 10.6
Land: 35.6 sq. mi.; **Water:** 0.0 sq. mi.

Cass
Township
Lat: 41-07-43 N **Long:** 86-52-03 W
Pop: 788 (1990); 913 (1980) **Pop Density:** 21.8
Land: 36.2 sq. mi.; **Water:** 0.0 sq. mi.

Francesville
Town
ZIP: 47946 **Lat:** 40-59-08 N **Long:** 86-53-01 W
Pop: 969 (1990); 944 (1980) **Pop Density:** 3230.0
Land: 0.3 sq. mi.; **Water:** 0.0 sq. mi. **Elev:** 681 ft.

Franklin
Township
Lat: 41-07-38 N **Long:** 86-38-27 W
Pop: 637 (1990); 644 (1980) **Pop Density:** 17.5
Land: 36.4 sq. mi.; **Water:** 0.0 sq. mi.

Harrison
Township
Lat: 41-02-15 N **Long:** 86-30-57 W
Pop: 650 (1990); 725 (1980) **Pop Density:** 20.6
Land: 31.5 sq. mi.; **Water:** 0.1 sq. mi.

Indian Creek
Township
Lat: 40-57-06 N **Long:** 86-38-11 W
Pop: 632 (1990); 645 (1980) **Pop Density:** 17.8
Land: 35.5 sq. mi.; **Water:** 0.3 sq. mi.

Jefferson
Township
Lat: 41-02-34 N **Long:** 86-45-44 W
Pop: 414 (1990); 482 (1980) **Pop Density:** 11.4
Land: 36.4 sq. mi.; **Water:** 0.0 sq. mi.

Medaryville
Town
ZIP: 47957 **Lat:** 41-04-48 N **Long:** 86-53-24 W
Pop: 689 (1990); 731 (1980) **Pop Density:** 1378.0
Land: 0.5 sq. mi.; **Water:** 0.0 sq. mi. **Elev:** 685 ft.
Name origin: For OH statesman Joseph Medary.

Monroe
Township
Lat: 41-02-52 N **Long:** 86-37-56 W
Pop: 3,802 (1990); 3,833 (1980) **Pop Density:** 92.7
Land: 41.0 sq. mi.; **Water:** 0.4 sq. mi.

INDIANA, Pulaski County

Monterey — Town
ZIP: 46960 Lat: 41-09-22 N Long: 86-28-54 W
Pop: 230 (1990); 236 (1980) Pop Density: 1150.0
Land: 0.2 sq. mi.; Water: 0.0 sq. mi. Elev: 725 ft.
Settled 1849.
Name origin: For Monterrey, Mexico, site of twelfth U.S. President Gen. Zachary Taylor's (1784–1850) famous Mexican War victory (Sep 23, 1846); with a spelling variation.

Rich Grove — Township
Lat: 41-07-41 N Long: 86-45-23 W
Pop: 722 (1990); 811 (1980) Pop Density: 19.9
Land: 36.2 sq. mi.; Water: 0.0 sq. mi.

Salem — Township
Lat: 40-57-25 N Long: 86-52-32 W
Pop: 1,429 (1990); 1,459 (1980) Pop Density: 40.0
Land: 35.7 sq. mi.; Water: 0.0 sq. mi.

Tippecanoe — Township
Lat: 41-07-37 N Long: 86-31-32 W
Pop: 997 (1990); 1,041 (1980) Pop Density: 27.4
Land: 36.4 sq. mi.; Water: 0.1 sq. mi.

Van Buren — Township
Lat: 40-57-21 N Long: 86-31-48 W
Pop: 951 (1990); 1,014 (1980) Pop Density: 26.3
Land: 36.2 sq. mi.; Water: 0.0 sq. mi.

White Post — Township
Lat: 41-02-21 N Long: 86-52-23 W
Pop: 1,242 (1990); 1,252 (1980) Pop Density: 34.0
Land: 36.5 sq. mi.; Water: 0.0 sq. mi.

Winamac — Town
ZIP: 46996 Lat: 41-03-10 N Long: 86-36-11 W
Pop: 2,262 (1990); 2,370 (1980) Pop Density: 1740.0
Land: 1.3 sq. mi.; Water: 0.0 sq. mi. Elev: 710 ft.
Name origin: From a Potawatomi Indian term meaning 'catfish.'

Putnam County
County Seat: Greencastle (ZIP: 46135)

Pop: 30,315 (1990); 29,163 (1980) Pop Density: 63.1
Land: 480.3 sq. mi.; Water: 2.3 sq. mi. Area Code: 317
In west-central IN, west of Indianapolis; established Dec 31, 1821 from Indian lands.
Name origin: For Gen. Israel Putnam (1718–90), Revolutionary War officer and American commander at the Battle of Bunker Hill.

Bainbridge — Town
ZIP: 46105 Lat: 39-45-37 N Long: 86-48-39 W
Pop: 682 (1990); 644 (1980) Pop Density: 1705.0
Land: 0.4 sq. mi.; Water: 0.0 sq. mi. Elev: 929 ft.
Founded 1824.
Name origin: For U.S. naval hero William Bainbridge (1774–1833).

Clinton — Township
Lat: 39-44-14 N Long: 86-56-45 W
Pop: 989 (1990); 1,144 (1980) Pop Density: 28.2
Land: 35.1 sq. mi.; Water: 0.5 sq. mi.

Cloverdale — City
ZIP: 46120 Lat: 39-31-16 N Long: 86-47-55 W
Pop: 1,681 (1990); 1,357 (1980) Pop Density: 525.3
Land: 3.2 sq. mi.; Water: 0.0 sq. mi. Elev: 779 ft.
Not coextensive with the town of the same name.
Name origin: Descriptively named for the area's clover fields.

*Cloverdale — Township
ZIP: 46120 Lat: 39-30-01 N Long: 86-47-41 W
Pop: 3,079 (1990); 2,584 (1980) Pop Density: 67.4
Land: 45.7 sq. mi.; Water: 0.5 sq. mi.

Fillmore — Town
ZIP: 46128 Lat: 39-40-15 N Long: 86-45-12 W
Pop: 497 (1990) Pop Density: 261.6
Land: 1.9 sq. mi.; Water: 0.0 sq. mi.

Floyd — Township
Lat: 39-43-39 N Long: 86-44-16 W
Pop: 1,754 (1990); 1,487 (1980) Pop Density: 51.9
Land: 33.8 sq. mi.; Water: 0.5 sq. mi.

Franklin — Township
Lat: 39-49-10 N Long: 86-50-40 W
Pop: 1,495 (1990); 1,699 (1980) Pop Density: 43.5
Land: 34.4 sq. mi.; Water: 0.0 sq. mi.

Greencastle — City
ZIP: 46135 Lat: 39-38-31 N Long: 86-50-26 W
Pop: 8,984 (1990); 8,403 (1980) Pop Density: 1761.6
Land: 5.1 sq. mi.; Water: 0.0 sq. mi. Elev: 849 ft.
In west-central IN, 31 mi. northeast of Terre Haute. Not coextensive with the town of the same name.
Name origin: For Greencastle, PA.

*Greencastle — Township
ZIP: 46135 Lat: 39-38-36 N Long: 86-50-48 W
Pop: 11,416 (1990); 10,986 (1980) Pop Density: 331.9
Land: 34.4 sq. mi.; Water: 0.1 sq. mi.

Jackson — Township
Lat: 39-48-47 N Long: 86-44-25 W
Pop: 798 (1990); 797 (1980) Pop Density: 23.1
Land: 34.6 sq. mi.; Water: 0.0 sq. mi.

Jefferson — Township
Lat: 39-34-02 N Long: 86-42-50 W
Pop: 1,073 (1990); 1,008 (1980) Pop Density: 26.1
Land: 41.1 sq. mi.; Water: 0.0 sq. mi.

American Places Dictionary — INDIANA, Randolph County

Madison
Township
Lat: 39-39-07 N **Long:** 86-57-32 W
Pop: 895 (1990); 1,040 (1980)   **Pop Density:** 25.4
Land: 35.2 sq. mi.; **Water:** 0.2 sq. mi.

Marion
Township
Lat: 39-38-22 N **Long:** 86-44-29 W
Pop: 1,844 (1990); 1,974 (1980)   **Pop Density:** 54.1
Land: 34.1 sq. mi.; **Water:** 0.0 sq. mi.

Monroe
Township
Lat: 39-43-19 N **Long:** 86-50-33 W
Pop: 1,393 (1990); 1,442 (1980)   **Pop Density:** 40.3
Land: 34.6 sq. mi.; **Water:** 0.0 sq. mi.

Roachdale
Town
ZIP: 46172   **Lat:** 39-50-55 N **Long:** 86-48-01 W
Pop: 902 (1990); 958 (1980)   **Pop Density:** 1804.0
Land: 0.5 sq. mi.; **Water:** 0.0 sq. mi.   **Elev:** 846 ft.
Name origin: For Judge Roach, a director of the local railroad.

Russell
Township
Lat: 39-48-46 N **Long:** 86-57-04 W
Pop: 775 (1990); 876 (1980)   **Pop Density:** 21.8
Land: 35.5 sq. mi.; **Water:** 0.0 sq. mi.

Russellville
Town
ZIP: 46175   **Lat:** 39-51-25 N **Long:** 86-59-00 W
Pop: 336 (1990); 376 (1980)   **Pop Density:** 1680.0
Land: 0.2 sq. mi.; **Water:** 0.0 sq. mi.   **Elev:** 831 ft.
Name origin: For its township.

Warren
Township
Lat: 39-34-07 N **Long:** 86-51-01 W
Pop: 2,777 (1990); 2,174 (1980)   **Pop Density:** 95.8
Land: 29.0 sq. mi.; **Water:** 0.0 sq. mi.

Washington
Township
Lat: 39-32-35 N **Long:** 86-57-18 W
Pop: 2,027 (1990); 1,952 (1980)   **Pop Density:** 38.3
Land: 52.9 sq. mi.; **Water:** 0.3 sq. mi.

Randolph County
County Seat: Winchester (ZIP: 47394)

Pop: 27,148 (1990); 29,997 (1980)   **Pop Density:** 59.9
Land: 452.9 sq. mi.; **Water:** 0.4 sq. mi.   **Area Code:** 317
On the east-central border of IN, east of Muncie; organized Jan 10, 1818 from Wayne County.
Name origin: For either Thomas Randolph (?–1811), attorney-general of IN Territory killed at the Battle of Tippecanoe, or for Randolph County, NC, former home of many early settlers.

Albany
Town
ZIP: 47320   **Lat:** 40-18-09 N **Long:** 85-13-01 W
Pop: 206 (1990); 245 (1980)   **Pop Density:** 2060.0
Land: 0.1 sq. mi.; **Water:** 0.0 sq. mi.   **Elev:** 954 ft.
Founded 1833. Part of the town is in Delaware County.
Name origin: For Albany, NY.

Farmland
Town
ZIP: 47340   **Lat:** 40-11-20 N **Long:** 85-07-37 W
Pop: 1,412 (1990); 1,560 (1980)   **Pop Density:** 2824.0
Land: 0.5 sq. mi.; **Water:** 0.0 sq. mi.   **Elev:** 1039 ft.
Name origin: Descriptively named for the area's rich farmland.

Franklin
Township
Lat: 40-15-52 N **Long:** 85-03-21 W
Pop: 1,343 (1990); 1,578 (1980)   **Pop Density:** 56.0
Land: 24.0 sq. mi.; **Water:** 0.0 sq. mi.

Green
Township
Lat: 40-16-17 N **Long:** 85-09-27 W
Pop: 991 (1990); 1,119 (1980)   **Pop Density:** 33.6
Land: 29.5 sq. mi.; **Water:** 0.0 sq. mi.

Greensfork
Township
Lat: 40-03-28 N **Long:** 84-52-00 W
Pop: 1,219 (1990); 1,360 (1980)   **Pop Density:** 26.4
Land: 46.1 sq. mi.; **Water:** 0.0 sq. mi.

Jackson
Township
Lat: 40-15-51 N **Long:** 84-51-19 W
Pop: 613 (1990); 736 (1980)   **Pop Density:** 20.2
Land: 30.4 sq. mi.; **Water:** 0.0 sq. mi.

Losantville
Town
ZIP: 47354   **Lat:** 40-01-23 N **Long:** 85-10-59 W
Pop: 253 (1990); 306 (1980)   **Pop Density:** 1265.0
Land: 0.2 sq. mi.; **Water:** 0.0 sq. mi.   **Elev:** 1138 ft.
Name origin: A corruption of Losantiville, the original coined name of Cincinnati. *L* for Licking Creek, Latin *os* 'mouth,' plus Greek *anti* 'opposite,' combined with *-ville* thus 'the town opposite the mouth of Licking creek.' Originally called Hunt's Cross Roads and Bronson.

Lynn
Town
ZIP: 47355   **Lat:** 40-02-55 N **Long:** 84-56-32 W
Pop: 1,183 (1990); 1,250 (1980)   **Pop Density:** 2366.0
Land: 0.5 sq. mi.; **Water:** 0.0 sq. mi.   **Elev:** 1180 ft.
Founded 1847.

Modoc
Town
ZIP: 47358   **Lat:** 40-02-40 N **Long:** 85-07-34 W
Pop: 218 (1990); 243 (1980)   **Pop Density:** 2180.0
Land: 0.1 sq. mi.; **Water:** 0.0 sq. mi.   **Elev:** 1177 ft.
Settled 1882.
Name origin: For the Modoc Indians.

Monroe
Township
Lat: 40-12-43 N **Long:** 85-09-20 W
Pop: 3,602 (1990); 3,916 (1980)   **Pop Density:** 123.4
Land: 29.2 sq. mi.; **Water:** 0.0 sq. mi.

INDIANA, Randolph County   *American Places Dictionary*

Parker City — Town
ZIP: 47368   Lat: 40-11-22 N   Long: 85-12-12 W
Pop: 1,323 (1990); 1,414 (1980)   Pop Density: 2205.0
Land: 0.6 sq. mi.; Water: 0.0 sq. mi.   Elev: 1025 ft.
Name origin: For early settler Thomas Parker. Previously called Morristown.

Ridgeville — Town
ZIP: 47380   Lat: 40-17-22 N   Long: 85-01-47 W
Pop: 808 (1990); 933 (1980)   Pop Density: 1616.0
Land: 0.5 sq. mi.; Water: 0.0 sq. mi.   Elev: 1000 ft.
Founded 1837.
Name origin: Descriptive of its location on a ridge.

Saratoga — Town
ZIP: 47382   Lat: 40-14-12 N   Long: 84-54-55 W
Pop: 266 (1990); 338 (1980)   Pop Density: 886.7
Land: 0.3 sq. mi.; Water: 0.0 sq. mi.   Elev: 1050 ft.
Established 1875.
Name origin: For Saratoga, NY.

Stoney Creek — Township
Lat: 40-08-18 N   Long: 85-09-21 W
Pop: 1,032 (1990); 1,113 (1980)   Pop Density: 38.5
Land: 26.8 sq. mi.; Water: 0.0 sq. mi.

Union — Township
Lat: 40-03-49 N   Long: 85-07-30 W
Pop: 2,201 (1990); 2,628 (1980)   Pop Density: 30.8
Land: 71.5 sq. mi.; Water: 0.1 sq. mi.

Union City — City
ZIP: 47390   Lat: 40-12-05 N   Long: 84-49-02 W
Pop: 3,612 (1990); 3,908 (1980)   Pop Density: 2408.0
Land: 1.5 sq. mi.; Water: 0.0 sq. mi.   Elev: 1114 ft.
Founded 1849.
Name origin: Patriotically named in 1849.

Ward — Township
Lat: 40-15-35 N   Long: 84-57-37 W
Pop: 1,244 (1990); 1,370 (1980)   Pop Density: 33.8
Land: 36.8 sq. mi.; Water: 0.0 sq. mi.

Washington — Township
Lat: 40-03-33 N   Long: 84-59-01 W
Pop: 2,325 (1990); 2,596 (1980)   Pop Density: 52.2
Land: 44.5 sq. mi.; Water: 0.0 sq. mi.

Wayne — Township
Lat: 40-09-51 N   Long: 84-51-22 W
Pop: 4,780 (1990); 5,160 (1980)   Pop Density: 120.4
Land: 39.7 sq. mi.; Water: 0.0 sq. mi.

White River — Township
ZIP: 47394   Lat: 40-10-30 N   Long: 85-00-21 W
Pop: 7,798 (1990); 8,421 (1980)   Pop Density: 104.7
Land: 74.5 sq. mi.; Water: 0.1 sq. mi.

Winchester — City
ZIP: 47394   Lat: 40-10-18 N   Long: 84-58-37 W
Pop: 5,095 (1990); 5,659 (1980)   Pop Density: 2122.9
Land: 2.4 sq. mi.; Water: 0.0 sq. mi.   Elev: 1097 ft.
Settled 1818.
Name origin: For Winchester, England.

Ripley County
County Seat: Versailles (ZIP: 47042)

Pop: 24,616 (1990); 24,398 (1980)   Pop Density: 55.1
Land: 446.4 sq. mi.; Water: 1.6 sq. mi.   Area Code: 812
In southeastern IN, east of Columbus; established Dec 27, 1816 from Indian lands.
Name origin: For Gen. Eleazar Wheelock Ripley (1782–1839), officer in the War of 1812, MA legislator, and U.S. representative from LA (1835–39).

Adams — Township
Lat: 39-16-01 N   Long: 85-08-33 W
Pop: 3,553 (1990); 3,385 (1980)   Pop Density: 81.9
Land: 43.4 sq. mi.; Water: 0.5 sq. mi.

Batesville — City
Lat: 39-17-40 N   Long: 85-12-42 W
Pop: 3,869 (1990); 3,469 (1980)   Pop Density: 1334.1
Land: 2.9 sq. mi.; Water: 0.0 sq. mi.   Elev: 983 ft.
Part of the town is also in Franklin County.
Name origin: For the pioneer Bates family.

Brown — Township
Lat: 38-57-56 N   Long: 85-13-06 W
Pop: 1,418 (1990); 1,461 (1980)   Pop Density: 26.5
Land: 53.6 sq. mi.; Water: 0.1 sq. mi.

Center — Township
Lat: 39-08-16 N   Long: 85-18-16 W
Pop: 2,579 (1990); 2,498 (1980)   Pop Density: 87.4
Land: 29.5 sq. mi.; Water: 0.1 sq. mi.

Delaware — Township
Lat: 39-10-49 N   Long: 85-14-51 W
Pop: 1,250 (1990); 1,181 (1980)   Pop Density: 37.5
Land: 33.3 sq. mi.; Water: 0.1 sq. mi.

Franklin — Township
Lat: 39-10-13 N   Long: 85-08-28 W
Pop: 3,053 (1990); 3,434 (1980)   Pop Density: 83.9
Land: 36.4 sq. mi.; Water: 0.1 sq. mi.

Holton — Town
ZIP: 47023   Lat: 39-04-32 N   Long: 85-23-04 W
Pop: 451 (1990); 487 (1980)   Pop Density: 250.6
Land: 1.8 sq. mi.; Water: 0.0 sq. mi.   Elev: 911 ft.
Founded 1854.
Name origin: For its founder, Jesse Holman.

Jackson — Township
Lat: 39-12-00 N   Long: 85-22-27 W
Pop: 956 (1990); 1,033 (1980)   Pop Density: 32.1
Land: 29.8 sq. mi.; Water: 0.0 sq. mi.   Elev: 810 ft.

American Places Dictionary   INDIANA, Rush County

Johnson
Township
Lat: 39-03-31 N   **Long:** 85-14-59 W
Pop: 3,190 (1990); 2,960 (1980)   **Pop Density:** 58.4
Land: 54.6 sq. mi.; **Water:** 0.4 sq. mi.

Laughery
Township
Lat: 39-15-07 N   **Long:** 85-15-13 W
Pop: 4,441 (1990); 4,357 (1980)   **Pop Density:** 172.1
Land: 25.8 sq. mi.; **Water:** 0.1 sq. mi.

Milan
Town
ZIP: 47031   **Lat:** 39-07-30 N   **Long:** 85-07-50 W
Pop: 1,529 (1990); 1,566 (1980)   **Pop Density:** 955.6
Land: 1.6 sq. mi.; **Water:** 0.0 sq. mi.   **Elev:** 990 ft.
Name origin: Named in 1831 for Milan, Italy.

Napoleon
Town
ZIP: 47034   **Lat:** 39-12-19 N   **Long:** 85-19-38 W
Pop: 238 (1990); 246 (1980)   **Pop Density:** 1190.0
Land: 0.2 sq. mi.; **Water:** 0.0 sq. mi.   **Elev:** 970 ft.

Osgood
Town
ZIP: 47037   **Lat:** 39-07-41 N   **Long:** 85-17-30 W
Pop: 1,688 (1990); 1,554 (1980)   **Pop Density:** 1406.7
Land: 1.2 sq. mi.; **Water:** 0.0 sq. mi.   **Elev:** 990 ft.
Name origin: For a railroad surveyor who came through in 1857.

Otter Creek
Township
ZIP: 47023   **Lat:** 39-05-41 N   **Long:** 85-23-27 W
Pop: 1,334 (1990); 1,377 (1980)   **Pop Density:** 32.0
Land: 41.7 sq. mi.; **Water:** 0.0 sq. mi.

Shelby
Township
Lat: 38-58-19 N   **Long:** 85-22-33 W
Pop: 853 (1990); 901 (1980)   **Pop Density:** 12.4
Land: 69.0 sq. mi.; **Water:** 0.2 sq. mi.

Sunman
Town
ZIP: 47041   **Lat:** 39-14-02 N   **Long:** 85-05-46 W
Pop: 623 (1990); 924 (1980)   **Pop Density:** 1557.5
Land: 0.4 sq. mi.; **Water:** 0.0 sq. mi.   **Elev:** 1021 ft.
Settled 1856.
Name origin: For prominent citizen Thomas Sunman.

Versailles
Town
ZIP: 47042   **Lat:** 39-03-51 N   **Long:** 85-15-27 W
Pop: 1,791 (1990); 1,560 (1980)   **Pop Density:** 1194.0
Land: 1.5 sq. mi.; **Water:** 0.0 sq. mi.   **Elev:** 968 ft.
Name origin: For Versailles, France.

Washington
Township
Lat: 39-04-13 N   **Long:** 85-08-29 W
Pop: 1,989 (1990); 1,811 (1980)   **Pop Density:** 67.7
Land: 29.4 sq. mi.; **Water:** 0.0 sq. mi.

Rush County
County Seat: Rushville (ZIP: 46173)

Pop: 18,129 (1990); 19,604 (1980)   **Pop Density:** 44.4
Land: 408.3 sq. mi.; **Water:** 0.3 sq. mi.   **Area Code:** 317
In east-central IN, southeast of Indianapolis; established Dec 31, 1821 from Franklin County.
Name origin: For Benjamin Rush (1745–1813), surgeon general in the Continental Army and a signer of the Declaration of Independence.

Anderson
Township
Lat: 39-29-50 N   **Long:** 85-27-42 W
Pop: 1,342 (1990); 1,487 (1980)   **Pop Density:** 37.9
Land: 35.4 sq. mi.; **Water:** 0.0 sq. mi.

Carthage
Town
ZIP: 46115   **Lat:** 39-44-13 N   **Long:** 85-34-17 W
Pop: 887 (1990); 886 (1980)   **Pop Density:** 1478.3
Land: 0.6 sq. mi.; **Water:** 0.0 sq. mi.   **Elev:** 886 ft.
First settled 1834.
Name origin: For Carthage, NC.

Center
Township
Lat: 39-44-44 N   **Long:** 85-28-17 W
Pop: 1,025 (1990); 1,177 (1980)   **Pop Density:** 28.0
Land: 36.6 sq. mi.; **Water:** 0.0 sq. mi.

Glenwood
Town
Lat: 39-37-29 N   **Long:** 85-18-04 W
Pop: 175 (1990); 246 (1980)   **Pop Density:** 1750.0
Land: 0.1 sq. mi.; **Water:** 0.0 sq. mi.   **Elev:** 1082 ft.
Part of the town is also in Fayette County.

Jackson
Township
Lat: 39-39-51 N   **Long:** 85-28-32 W
Pop: 381 (1990); 435 (1980)   **Pop Density:** 16.9
Land: 22.6 sq. mi.; **Water:** 0.0 sq. mi.

Noble
Township
Lat: 39-34-08 N   **Long:** 85-20-51 W
Pop: 658 (1990); 817 (1980)   **Pop Density:** 19.8
Land: 33.2 sq. mi.; **Water:** 0.0 sq. mi.

Orange
Township
Lat: 39-29-57 N   **Long:** 85-34-15 W
Pop: 811 (1990); 828 (1980)   **Pop Density:** 22.3
Land: 36.3 sq. mi.; **Water:** 0.0 sq. mi.

Posey
Township
Lat: 39-39-17 N   **Long:** 85-34-16 W
Pop: 1,194 (1990); 1,271 (1980)   **Pop Density:** 33.0
Land: 36.2 sq. mi.; **Water:** 0.0 sq. mi.

Richland
Township
Lat: 39-29-23 N   **Long:** 85-21-45 W
Pop: 397 (1990); 460 (1980)   **Pop Density:** 13.9
Land: 28.6 sq. mi.; **Water:** 0.0 sq. mi.

Ripley
Township
Lat: 39-44-32 N   **Long:** 85-34-42 W
Pop: 1,910 (1990); 1,988 (1980)   **Pop Density:** 53.5
Land: 35.7 sq. mi.; **Water:** 0.2 sq. mi.

Rushville
City
ZIP: 46173   **Lat:** 39-36-52 N   **Long:** 85-26-49 W
Pop: 5,533 (1990); 6,113 (1980)   **Pop Density:** 2912.1
Land: 1.9 sq. mi.; **Water:** 0.0 sq. mi.   **Elev:** 966 ft.

*Rushville — Township
ZIP: 46173 Lat: 39-35-29 N Long: 85-27-24 W
Pop: 7,996 (1990); 8,596 (1980) Pop Density: 181.7
Land: 44.0 sq. mi.; Water: 0.0 sq. mi.

Union — Township
Lat: 39-39-43 N Long: 85-21-51 W
Pop: 918 (1990); 920 (1980) Pop Density: 25.9
Land: 35.5 sq. mi.; Water: 0.0 sq. mi.

Walker — Township
Lat: 39-34-22 N Long: 85-34-35 W
Pop: 966 (1990); 1,057 (1980) Pop Density: 32.2
Land: 30.0 sq. mi.; Water: 0.0 sq. mi.

Washington — Township
Lat: 39-44-56 N Long: 85-21-09 W
Pop: 531 (1990); 568 (1980) Pop Density: 15.5
Land: 34.3 sq. mi.; Water: 0.0 sq. mi.

St. Joseph County
County Seat: South Bend (ZIP: 46601)

Pop: 247,052 (1990); 241,617 (1980) Pop Density: 540.2
Land: 457.3 sq. mi.; Water: 3.6 sq. mi. Area Code: 219
On the central northern border of IN; organized Jan 29, 1830 from Indian lands.
Name origin: For the St. Joseph River, which runs through the county.

Centre — Township
ZIP: 46614 Lat: 41-35-41 N Long: 86-15-09 W
Pop: 13,031 (1990); 12,402 (1980) Pop Density: 675.2
Land: 19.3 sq. mi.; Water: 0.0 sq. mi.

Clay — Township
ZIP: 46637 Lat: 41-43-45 N Long: 86-13-20 W
Pop: 31,033 (1990); 28,147 (1980) Pop Density: 1575.3
Land: 19.7 sq. mi.; Water: 0.1 sq. mi.

Georgetown — CDP
Lat: 41-43-45 N Long: 86-13-41 W
Pop: 3,993 (1990) Pop Density: 2101.6
Land: 1.9 sq. mi.; Water: 0.0 sq. mi.

German — Township
ZIP: 46628 Lat: 41-43-50 N Long: 86-19-01 W
Pop: 7,222 (1990); 6,826 (1980) Pop Density: 429.9
Land: 16.8 sq. mi.; Water: 0.1 sq. mi.

Granger — CDP
ZIP: 46530 Lat: 41-44-07 N Long: 86-08-22 W
Pop: 20,241 (1990) Pop Density: 760.9
Land: 26.6 sq. mi.; Water: 0.0 sq. mi.

Greene — Township
Lat: 41-35-43 N Long: 86-22-05 W
Pop: 3,037 (1990); 3,036 (1980) Pop Density: 88.5
Land: 34.3 sq. mi.; Water: 0.3 sq. mi.

Gulivoire Park — CDP
Lat: 41-36-47 N Long: 86-14-42 W
Pop: 2,788 (1990) Pop Density: 1858.7
Land: 1.5 sq. mi.; Water: 0.0 sq. mi.

Harris — Township
ZIP: 46530 Lat: 41-44-04 N Long: 86-07-27 W
Pop: 11,543 (1990); 5,265 (1980) Pop Density: 547.1
Land: 21.1 sq. mi.; Water: 0.0 sq. mi.

Indian Village — Town
Lat: 41-42-52 N Long: 86-13-54 W
Pop: 142 (1990); 151 (1980) Pop Density: 1420.0
Land: 0.1 sq. mi.; Water: 0.0 sq. mi. Elev: 730 ft.
Name origin: For an Indian village that once occupied the site.

Lakeville — Town
ZIP: 46536 Lat: 41-31-32 N Long: 86-16-28 W
Pop: 655 (1990); 629 (1980) Pop Density: 1637.5
Land: 0.4 sq. mi.; Water: 0.0 sq. mi. Elev: 833 ft.

Liberty — Township
Lat: 41-31-35 N Long: 86-24-12 W
Pop: 3,011 (1990); 2,922 (1980) Pop Density: 70.8
Land: 42.5 sq. mi.; Water: 0.4 sq. mi.

Lincoln — Township
Lat: 41-28-54 N Long: 86-29-08 W
Pop: 2,782 (1990); 2,875 (1980) Pop Density: 125.3
Land: 22.2 sq. mi.; Water: 0.0 sq. mi.

Madison — Township
Lat: 41-31-55 N Long: 86-07-24 W
Pop: 1,798 (1990); 1,860 (1980) Pop Density: 34.5
Land: 52.1 sq. mi.; Water: 0.0 sq. mi.

Mishawaka — City
ZIP: 46544 Lat: 41-40-09 N Long: 86-10-06 W
Pop: 42,608 (1990); 40,201 (1980) Pop Density: 3065.3
Land: 13.9 sq. mi.; Water: 0.3 sq. mi. Elev: 722 ft.
In northern IN, 4 mi. southeast of South Bend. Laid out 1833.
Name origin: From a Potawatomi Indian term *M'seh-wah-keeoki* meaning 'country of dead trees,' referring to a tract of dead timber near here.

New Carlisle — Town
ZIP: 46552 Lat: 41-42-16 N Long: 86-30-39 W
Pop: 1,446 (1990); 1,439 (1980) Pop Density: 1807.5
Land: 0.8 sq. mi.; Water: 0.0 sq. mi. Elev: 780 ft.
Founded 1835.
Name origin: For its founder Richard Carlisle.

North Liberty — Town
ZIP: 46554 Lat: 41-31-58 N Long: 86-25-49 W
Pop: 1,366 (1990); 1,211 (1980) Pop Density: 2276.7
Land: 0.6 sq. mi.; Water: 0.0 sq. mi. Elev: 733 ft.
Name origin: For North Liberty Township.

Olive — Township
Lat: 41-41-07 N Long: 86-28-16 W
Pop: 3,573 (1990); 3,418 (1980) Pop Density: 62.2
Land: 57.4 sq. mi.; Water: 0.1 sq. mi.

American Places Dictionary   INDIANA, Scott County

Osceola
Town
ZIP: 46561   **Lat:** 41-39-54 N   **Long:** 86-04-42 W
Pop: 1,999 (1990); 1,990 (1980)   **Pop Density:** 1537.7
Land: 1.3 sq. mi.; **Water:** 0.0 sq. mi.   **Elev:** 735 ft.
Founded 1837.
Name origin: For Osceola (c. 1804–38), the famous Seminole Indian chief.

Penn
Township
ZIP: 46544   **Lat:** 41-38-44 N   **Long:** 86-08-03 W
Pop: 59,879 (1990); 56,471 (1980)   **Pop Density:** 958.1
Land: 62.5 sq. mi.; **Water:** 1.1 sq. mi.

Portage
Township
ZIP: 46601   **Lat:** 41-40-08 N   **Long:** 86-16-32 W
Pop: 101,791 (1990); 109,694 (1980)   **Pop Density:** 2950.5
Land: 34.5 sq. mi.; **Water:** 0.4 sq. mi.

Roseland
Town
Lat: 41-43-00 N   **Long:** 86-15-05 W
Pop: 706 (1990); 832 (1980)   **Pop Density:** 1765.0
Land: 0.4 sq. mi.; **Water:** 0.0 sq. mi.   **Elev:** 725 ft.
Name origin: Descriptive of the area's many wild roses.

South Bend
City
ZIP: 46624   **Lat:** 41-40-31 N   **Long:** 86-15-56 W
Pop: 105,511 (1990); 109,727 (1980)   **Pop Density:** 2898.7
Land: 36.4 sq. mi.; **Water:** 0.4 sq. mi.   **Elev:** 725 ft.
In north-central IN, 67 mi. northwest of Fort Wayne. Established 1820; incorporated as town 1835, as city 1865. Site of the University of Notre Dame; a regional commercial, retail, and medical center.
Name origin: For its location on a bend in the St. Joseph's River. Originally called Big St. Joseph Station.

Union
Township
Lat: 41-31-07 N   **Long:** 86-15-39 W
Pop: 3,355 (1990); 3,374 (1980)   **Pop Density:** 78.2
Land: 42.9 sq. mi.; **Water:** 0.2 sq. mi.

Walkerton
Town
ZIP: 46574   **Lat:** 41-27-50 N   **Long:** 86-28-56 W
Pop: 2,061 (1990); 2,051 (1980)   **Pop Density:** 1374.0
Land: 1.5 sq. mi.; **Water:** 0.0 sq. mi.   **Elev:** 707 ft.
Name origin: For 1850s railroad promoter John Walker.

Warren
Township
Lat: 41-41-28 N   **Long:** 86-22-59 W
Pop: 4,997 (1990); 5,327 (1980)   **Pop Density:** 155.7
Land: 32.1 sq. mi.; **Water:** 0.8 sq. mi.

Scott County
County Seat: Scottsburg (ZIP: 47170)

Pop: 20,991 (1990); 20,422 (1980)   **Pop Density:** 110.2
Land: 190.4 sq. mi.; **Water:** 2.3 sq. mi.   **Area Code:** 812
On the southeastern border of IN, north of Louisville, KY; organized Jan 12, 1820 from Clark and Jackson counties.
Name origin: For Gen. Charles Scott (1739–1813), an officer in the Revolutionary War; governor of KY (1808–12).

Austin
Town
ZIP: 47102   **Lat:** 38-44-36 N   **Long:** 85-48-36 W
Pop: 4,310 (1990); 4,857 (1980)   **Pop Density:** 2052.4
Land: 2.1 sq. mi.; **Water:** 0.0 sq. mi.   **Elev:** 575 ft.
Name origin: Named in 1850s by Mexican War veterans, for Austin, TX.

Finley
Township
Lat: 38-38-53 N   **Long:** 85-51-07 W
Pop: 1,123 (1990); 1,048 (1980)   **Pop Density:** 28.6
Land: 39.3 sq. mi.; **Water:** 0.3 sq. mi.

Jennings
Township
ZIP: 47102   **Lat:** 38-45-53 N   **Long:** 85-46-52 W
Pop: 6,713 (1990); 7,091 (1980)   **Pop Density:** 219.4
Land: 30.6 sq. mi.; **Water:** 0.1 sq. mi.

Johnson
Township
Lat: 38-44-54 N   **Long:** 85-42-24 W
Pop: 2,181 (1990); 1,989 (1980)   **Pop Density:** 70.8
Land: 30.8 sq. mi.; **Water:** 1.2 sq. mi.

Lexington
Township
ZIP: 47138   **Lat:** 38-39-15 N   **Long:** 85-38-42 W
Pop: 2,803 (1990); 2,605 (1980)   **Pop Density:** 56.6
Land: 49.5 sq. mi.; **Water:** 0.5 sq. mi.

Scottsburg
City
ZIP: 47170   **Lat:** 38-41-09 N   **Long:** 85-46-51 W
Pop: 5,334 (1990); 5,068 (1980)   **Pop Density:** 1333.5
Land: 4.0 sq. mi.; **Water:** 0.0 sq. mi.   **Elev:** 570 ft.
Founded 1871.
Name origin: Named in 1871 for railroad president Thomas Scott.

Vienna
Township
ZIP: 47170   **Lat:** 38-39-23 N   **Long:** 85-46-28 W
Pop: 8,171 (1990); 7,689 (1980)   **Pop Density:** 203.8
Land: 40.1 sq. mi.; **Water:** 0.4 sq. mi.

Shelby County
County Seat: Shelbyville (ZIP: 46176)

Pop: 40,307 (1990); 39,887 (1980)   **Pop Density:** 97.7
Land: 412.7 sq. mi.; **Water:** 0.5 sq. mi.   **Area Code:** 317
In central IN, southeast of Indianapolis; established Dec 31, 1821 from Indian lands.
Name origin: For Gen. Isaac Shelby (1750–1826), officer in the Revolutionary War, NC legislator, and first governor of KY (1792–96; 1812–16).

Addison — Township
ZIP: 46176   Lat: 39-31-32 N   Long: 85-46-09 W
Pop: 17,577 (1990); 17,334 (1980)   **Pop Density:** 630.0
Land: 27.9 sq. mi.; **Water:** 0.3 sq. mi.

Brandywine — Township
Lat: 39-34-55 N   Long: 85-50-19 W
Pop: 2,115 (1990); 2,167 (1980)   **Pop Density:** 94.8
Land: 22.3 sq. mi.; **Water:** 0.1 sq. mi.

Fairland — CDP
ZIP: 46126   Lat: 39-35-55 N   Long: 85-51-29 W
Pop: 1,348 (1990)   **Pop Density:** 385.1
Land: 3.5 sq. mi.; **Water:** 0.0 sq. mi.

Hanover — Township
Lat: 39-40-09 N   Long: 85-40-43 W
Pop: 2,215 (1990); 2,134 (1980)   **Pop Density:** 81.1
Land: 27.3 sq. mi.; **Water:** 0.0 sq. mi.

Hendricks — Township
Lat: 39-29-05 N   Long: 85-53-38 W
Pop: 1,219 (1990); 1,244 (1980)   **Pop Density:** 33.3
Land: 36.6 sq. mi.; **Water:** 0.0 sq. mi.

Jackson — Township
Lat: 39-23-49 N   Long: 85-53-56 W
Pop: 1,180 (1990); 1,196 (1980)   **Pop Density:** 34.4
Land: 34.3 sq. mi.; **Water:** 0.0 sq. mi.

Liberty — Township
Lat: 39-28-59 N   Long: 85-39-51 W
Pop: 1,878 (1990); 1,844 (1980)   **Pop Density:** 79.6
Land: 23.6 sq. mi.; **Water:** 0.0 sq. mi.

Marion — Township
Lat: 39-35-29 N   Long: 85-45-18 W
Pop: 1,384 (1990); 1,326 (1980)   **Pop Density:** 55.4
Land: 25.0 sq. mi.; **Water:** 0.0 sq. mi.

Moral — Township
Lat: 39-38-56 N   Long: 85-53-31 W
Pop: 4,567 (1990); 4,565 (1980)   **Pop Density:** 124.4
Land: 36.7 sq. mi.; **Water:** 0.0 sq. mi.

Morristown — Town
ZIP: 46161   Lat: 39-40-20 N   Long: 85-41-59 W
Pop: 980 (1990); 989 (1980)   **Pop Density:** 1633.3
Land: 0.6 sq. mi.; **Water:** 0.0 sq. mi.   **Elev:** 830 ft.
Founded 1828.
Name origin: For cofounder Samuel Morris.

Noble — Township
Lat: 39-23-24 N   Long: 85-40-43 W
Pop: 1,469 (1990); 1,345 (1980)   **Pop Density:** 40.4
Land: 36.4 sq. mi.; **Water:** 0.0 sq. mi.

St. Paul — Town
Lat: 39-25-41 N   Long: 85-37-54 W
Pop: 456 (1990); 326 (1980)   **Pop Density:** 4560.0
Land: 0.1 sq. mi.; **Water:** 0.0 sq. mi.
Settled 1853. Part of the town is also in Decatur County.
Name origin: For early settler Jonathan Paul, with 'saint' added for euphony.

Shelby — Township
Lat: 39-28-03 N   Long: 85-46-07 W
Pop: 1,991 (1990); 2,122 (1980)   **Pop Density:** 68.7
Land: 29.0 sq. mi.; **Water:** 0.0 sq. mi.

Shelbyville — City
ZIP: 46176   Lat: 39-31-23 N   Long: 85-46-32 W
Pop: 15,336 (1990); 14,989 (1980)   **Pop Density:** 2396.3
Land: 6.4 sq. mi.; **Water:** 0.1 sq. mi.   **Elev:** 764 ft.
In central IN, 26 mi. southeast of Indianapolis.
Name origin: For Gen. Isaac Shelby (1750–1826), officer in the Revolutionary War, NC legislator, and first governor of KY (1792–96; 1812–16).

Sugar Creek — Township
Lat: 39-33-49 N   Long: 85-54-54 W
Pop: 958 (1990); 928 (1980)   **Pop Density:** 39.9
Land: 24.0 sq. mi.; **Water:** 0.0 sq. mi.

Union — Township
Lat: 39-34-40 N   Long: 85-40-11 W
Pop: 859 (1990); 782 (1980)   **Pop Density:** 31.9
Land: 26.9 sq. mi.; **Water:** 0.0 sq. mi.

Van Buren — Township
Lat: 39-39-42 N   Long: 85-47-30 W
Pop: 1,555 (1990); 1,488 (1980)   **Pop Density:** 55.7
Land: 27.9 sq. mi.; **Water:** 0.0 sq. mi.

Washington — Township
Lat: 39-24-05 N   Long: 85-47-39 W
Pop: 1,340 (1990); 1,412 (1980)   **Pop Density:** 38.5
Land: 34.8 sq. mi.; **Water:** 0.0 sq. mi.

Spencer County
County Seat: Rockport (ZIP: 47635)

Pop: 19,490 (1990); 19,361 (1980) **Pop Density:** 48.9
Land: 398.7 sq. mi.; **Water:** 2.5 sq. mi. **Area Code:** 812

On the southwestern border of IN, east of Evansville; organized Jan 10, 1818 from Warrick County.

Name origin: For Captain Spier (Spear?) Spencer (?–1811), a KY officer killed at the Battle of Tippecanoe.

Carter   Township
ZIP: 47523   **Lat:** 38-09-21 N **Long:** 86-57-32 W
Pop: 3,032 (1990); 3,160 (1980)   **Pop Density:** 84.2
Land: 36.0 sq. mi.; **Water:** 0.1 sq. mi.

Chrisney   Town
ZIP: 47611   **Lat:** 38-00-44 N **Long:** 87-02-02 W
Pop: 511 (1990); 537 (1980)   **Pop Density:** 1277.5
Land: 0.4 sq. mi.; **Water:** 0.0 sq. mi.   **Elev:** 441 ft.

Clay   Township
Lat: 38-04-25 N **Long:** 86-57-16 W
Pop: 1,467 (1990); 996 (1980)   **Pop Density:** 40.0
Land: 36.7 sq. mi.; **Water:** 0.6 sq. mi.

Dale   Town
ZIP: 47523   **Lat:** 38-10-01 N **Long:** 86-59-11 W
Pop: 1,553 (1990); 1,693 (1980)   **Pop Density:** 1725.6
Land: 0.9 sq. mi.; **Water:** 0.0 sq. mi.   **Elev:** 470 ft.
Founded 1843.
Name origin: For U.S. Congressman Robert Dale Owen (1801–77).

Gentryville   Town
ZIP: 47537   **Lat:** 38-06-31 N **Long:** 87-01-49 W
Pop: 277 (1990); 299 (1980)   **Pop Density:** 692.5
Land: 0.4 sq. mi.; **Water:** 0.0 sq. mi.   **Elev:** 405 ft.
Name origin: For merchant James Gentry, who lived here in the 1850s.

Grandview   Town
ZIP: 47615   **Lat:** 37-56-16 N **Long:** 86-58-59 W
Pop: 761 (1990); 670 (1980)   **Pop Density:** 845.6
Land: 0.9 sq. mi.; **Water:** 0.0 sq. mi.   **Elev:** 390 ft.
Established 1851.
Name origin: For its bluff-top location, which allows a view of the Ohio River in both directions.

Grass   Township
Lat: 38-00-08 N **Long:** 87-06-00 W
Pop: 1,456 (1990); 1,387 (1980)   **Pop Density:** 31.9
Land: 45.6 sq. mi.; **Water:** 0.1 sq. mi.

Hammond   Township
Lat: 37-58-46 N **Long:** 86-57-35 W
Pop: 1,667 (1990); 1,653 (1980)   **Pop Density:** 40.5
Land: 41.2 sq. mi.; **Water:** 0.9 sq. mi.

Harrison   Township
Lat: 38-08-05 N **Long:** 86-50-26 W
Pop: 2,286 (1990); 2,234 (1980)   **Pop Density:** 41.5
Land: 55.1 sq. mi.; **Water:** 0.1 sq. mi.

Huff   Township
Lat: 38-01-56 N **Long:** 86-51-02 W
Pop: 1,047 (1990); 1,034 (1980)   **Pop Density:** 24.6
Land: 42.6 sq. mi.; **Water:** 0.5 sq. mi.

Jackson   Township
ZIP: 47537   **Lat:** 38-04-30 N **Long:** 87-02-54 W
Pop: 824 (1990); 848 (1980)   **Pop Density:** 40.4
Land: 20.4 sq. mi.; **Water:** 0.1 sq. mi.

Luce   Township
Lat: 37-54-46 N **Long:** 87-12-04 W
Pop: 2,862 (1990); 2,981 (1980)   **Pop Density:** 53.7
Land: 53.3 sq. mi.; **Water:** 0.1 sq. mi.

Ohio   Township
Lat: 37-53-00 N **Long:** 87-05-51 W
Pop: 4,849 (1990); 5,068 (1980)   **Pop Density:** 71.5
Land: 67.8 sq. mi.; **Water:** 0.2 sq. mi.

Rockport   City
ZIP: 47635   **Lat:** 37-53-01 N **Long:** 87-03-03 W
Pop: 2,315 (1990); 2,590 (1980)   **Pop Density:** 2572.2
Land: 0.9 sq. mi.; **Water:** 0.0 sq. mi.   **Elev:** 445 ft.
Name origin: Euphoniously named. Previously called Hanging Rock.

Santa Claus   Town
ZIP: 47579   **Lat:** 38-06-55 N **Long:** 86-55-30 W
Pop: 927 (1990); 514 (1980)   **Pop Density:** 178.3
Land: 5.2 sq. mi.; **Water:** 0.4 sq. mi.   **Elev:** 510 ft.
In south-central IN, northeast of Evansville.
Name origin: For the legendary Christmas figure. On Christmas Eve, 1852, the locals were trying to find a name for their town, when the local Santa Claus walked in, laden with gifts, and they unanimously agreed upon the name.

Starke County
County Seat: Knox (ZIP: 46534)

Pop: 22,747 (1990); 21,997 (1980)   **Pop Density:** 73.5
Land: 309.3 sq. mi.; **Water:** 3.0 sq. mi.   **Area Code:** 219

In northwestern IN, southwest of South Bend; established Feb 7, 1835 from Marshall County.

Name origin: For Gen. John Stark (1728–1822), an officer in the French and Indian Wars and the American Revolution; no reason known why spelling was altered.

California — Township
Lat: 41-13-02 N   Long: 86-38-43 W
Pop: 2,077 (1990); 2,041 (1980)   **Pop Density:** 59.9
Land: 34.7 sq. mi.; **Water:** 1.6 sq. mi.

Center — Township
ZIP: 46534   Lat: 41-18-11 N   Long: 86-38-20 W
Pop: 6,270 (1990); 6,195 (1980)   **Pop Density:** 172.3
Land: 36.4 sq. mi.; **Water:** 0.0 sq. mi.

Davis — Township
Lat: 41-23-11 N   Long: 86-38-41 W
Pop: 1,170 (1990); 1,123 (1980)   **Pop Density:** 32.6
Land: 35.9 sq. mi.; **Water:** 0.1 sq. mi.

Hamlet — Town
ZIP: 46532   Lat: 41-22-42 N   Long: 86-34-59 W
Pop: 789 (1990); 738 (1980)   **Pop Density:** 789.0
Land: 1.0 sq. mi.; **Water:** 0.0 sq. mi.   **Elev:** 697 ft.
Founded 1863.
Name origin: For its founder, John Hamlet.

Jackson — Township
Lat: 41-17-48 N   Long: 86-44-43 W
Pop: 482 (1990); 465 (1980)   **Pop Density:** 21.8
Land: 22.1 sq. mi.; **Water:** 0.0 sq. mi.

Knox — City
ZIP: 46534   Lat: 41-17-30 N   Long: 86-37-16 W
Pop: 3,705 (1990); 3,674 (1980)   **Pop Density:** 1089.7
Land: 3.4 sq. mi.; **Water:** 0.0 sq. mi.   **Elev:** 702 ft.
Settled 1851.
Name origin: For Gen. Henry Knox (1750–1806), officer in the Revolutionary War and first U.S. secretary of war (1785–94).

Koontz Lake — CDP
Lat: 41-25-05 N   Long: 86-29-02 W
Pop: 1,450 (1990); 1,270 (1980)   **Pop Density:** 453.1
Land: 3.2 sq. mi.; **Water:** 0.4 sq. mi.
Part of the town is also in Marshall County.

North Bend — Township
Lat: 41-12-49 N   Long: 86-31-38 W
Pop: 1,214 (1990); 1,153 (1980)   **Pop Density:** 34.2
Land: 35.5 sq. mi.; **Water:** 0.7 sq. mi.

North Judson — Town
ZIP: 46366   Lat: 41-13-01 N   Long: 86-46-33 W
Pop: 1,582 (1990); 1,653 (1980)   **Pop Density:** 1757.8
Land: 0.9 sq. mi.; **Water:** 0.0 sq. mi.   **Elev:** 700 ft.
Name origin: For an early KY missionary named Judson.

Oregon — Township
Lat: 41-23-23 N   Long: 86-31-40 W
Pop: 3,144 (1990); 2,826 (1980)   **Pop Density:** 88.3
Land: 35.6 sq. mi.; **Water:** 0.5 sq. mi.

Railroad — Township
Lat: 41-12-59 N   Long: 86-51-58 W
Pop: 1,493 (1990); 1,495 (1980)   **Pop Density:** 40.8
Land: 36.6 sq. mi.; **Water:** 0.0 sq. mi.

Washington — Township
Lat: 41-17-55 N   Long: 86-31-19 W
Pop: 2,244 (1990); 2,112 (1980)   **Pop Density:** 62.2
Land: 36.1 sq. mi.; **Water:** 0.1 sq. mi.

Wayne — Township
Lat: 41-12-55 N   Long: 86-45-21 W
Pop: 4,653 (1990); 4,587 (1980)   **Pop Density:** 127.8
Land: 36.4 sq. mi.; **Water:** 0.1 sq. mi.

Steuben County
County Seat: Angola (ZIP: 46703)

Pop: 27,446 (1990); 24,694 (1980)   **Pop Density:** 88.9
Land: 308.7 sq. mi.; **Water:** 13.8 sq. mi.   **Area Code:** 219

In the northeastern corner of IN; established Feb 7, 1835 from Indian lands.
Name origin: For Friedrich Wilhelm, Baron von Steuben (1730–94), Prussian soldier named inspector general of the U.S. Continental Army (1778).

Angola — City
ZIP: 46703   Lat: 41-38-34 N   Long: 85-00-00 W
Pop: 5,824 (1990); 5,486 (1980)   **Pop Density:** 2008.3
Land: 2.9 sq. mi.; **Water:** 0.0 sq. mi.   **Elev:** 950 ft.
Settled 1837.
Name origin: For Angola, NY.

Ashley — Town
Lat: 41-31-43 N   Long: 85-03-52 W
Pop: 279 (1990); 313 (1980)   **Pop Density:** 930.0
Land: 0.3 sq. mi.; **Water:** 0.0 sq. mi.   **Elev:** 1000 ft.
Part of the town is also in Dekalb County.
Name origin: Named in 1892 for Ashley, PA.

INDIANA, Steuben County

Clear Lake — Town
ZIP: 46737 **Lat:** 41-44-08 N **Long:** 84-50-18 W
Pop: 272 (1990); 301 (1980) **Pop Density:** 272.0
Land: 1.0 sq. mi.; **Water:** 1.3 sq. mi. **Elev:** 1050 ft.
Incorporated 1933.
Name origin: For nearby Clear Lake.

*Clear Lake — Township
ZIP: 46737 **Lat:** 41-43-46 N **Long:** 84-50-09 W
Pop: 635 (1990); 576 (1980) **Pop Density:** 66.1
Land: 9.6 sq. mi.; **Water:** 1.5 sq. mi.

Fremont — Town
ZIP: 46737 **Lat:** 41-43-52 N **Long:** 84-56-01 W
Pop: 1,407 (1990); 1,180 (1980) **Pop Density:** 879.4
Land: 1.6 sq. mi.; **Water:** 0.0 sq. mi. **Elev:** 1030 ft.
Founded 1837. Not coextensive with the town of the same name.
Name origin: For John Charles Frémont (1813–90), soldier and explorer who led five expeditions to the West, U.S. senator from CA (1850–51), and governor of the AZ Territory (1878–83).

*Fremont — Township
ZIP: 46737 **Lat:** 41-44-01 N **Long:** 84-55-02 W
Pop: 2,016 (1990); 1,730 (1980) **Pop Density:** 87.7
Land: 23.0 sq. mi.; **Water:** 0.2 sq. mi.

Hamilton — Town
ZIP: 46742 **Lat:** 41-32-07 N **Long:** 84-55-14 W
Pop: 590 (1990); 466 (1980) **Pop Density:** 590.0
Land: 1.0 sq. mi.; **Water:** 0.0 sq. mi. **Elev:** 900 ft.
Founded 1823. Part of the town is also in Dekalb County.
Name origin: For Alexander Hamilton (1755–1804), first U.S. secretary of the treasury (1789–95).

Hudson — Town
ZIP: 46747 **Lat:** 41-32-00 N **Long:** 85-04-53 W
Pop: 438 (1990); 447 (1980) **Pop Density:** 730.0
Land: 0.6 sq. mi.; **Water:** 0.0 sq. mi. **Elev:** 990 ft.
Name origin: Named in 1875 for a local resident. Previously called Benton.

Jackson — Township
Lat: 41-39-22 N **Long:** 85-08-36 W
Pop: 1,425 (1990); 1,157 (1980) **Pop Density:** 41.9
Land: 34.0 sq. mi.; **Water:** 1.1 sq. mi.

Jamestown — Township
ZIP: 46737 **Lat:** 41-43-50 N **Long:** 85-01-42 W
Pop: 3,018 (1990); 2,051 (1980) **Pop Density:** 146.5
Land: 20.6 sq. mi.; **Water:** 3.0 sq. mi.

Millgrove — Township
Lat: 41-44-04 N **Long:** 85-08-12 W
Pop: 1,326 (1990); 1,295 (1980) **Pop Density:** 60.3
Land: 22.0 sq. mi.; **Water:** 1.7 sq. mi.

Orland — Town
ZIP: 46776 **Lat:** 41-43-51 N **Long:** 85-10-16 W
Pop: 361 (1990); 424 (1980) **Pop Density:** 515.7
Land: 0.7 sq. mi.; **Water:** 0.0 sq. mi. **Elev:** 962 ft.
Founded 1834.
Name origin: Supposedly from the name of a popular hymn. Originally known as the Vermont Settlement, then Millgrove.

Otsego — Township
ZIP: 46742 **Lat:** 41-34-13 N **Long:** 84-54-40 W
Pop: 1,977 (1990); 2,296 (1980) **Pop Density:** 59.2
Land: 33.4 sq. mi.; **Water:** 1.5 sq. mi.

Pleasant — Township
ZIP: 46703 **Lat:** 41-39-28 N **Long:** 85-01-35 W
Pop: 10,874 (1990); 9,387 (1980) **Pop Density:** 339.8
Land: 32.0 sq. mi.; **Water:** 3.2 sq. mi.

Richland — Township
Lat: 41-34-15 N **Long:** 84-49-54 W
Pop: 515 (1990); 480 (1980) **Pop Density:** 33.0
Land: 15.6 sq. mi.; **Water:** 0.0 sq. mi.

Salem — Township
Lat: 41-34-15 N **Long:** 85-08-23 W
Pop: 1,848 (1990); 1,945 (1980) **Pop Density:** 54.7
Land: 33.8 sq. mi.; **Water:** 0.7 sq. mi.

Scott — Township
ZIP: 46703 **Lat:** 41-39-10 N **Long:** 84-55-16 W
Pop: 865 (1990); 831 (1980) **Pop Density:** 30.1
Land: 28.7 sq. mi.; **Water:** 0.2 sq. mi.

Steuben — Township
Lat: 41-34-22 N **Long:** 85-01-30 W
Pop: 2,456 (1990); 2,352 (1980) **Pop Density:** 72.9
Land: 33.7 sq. mi.; **Water:** 0.7 sq. mi.

York — Township
ZIP: 46703 **Lat:** 41-39-27 N **Long:** 84-50-36 W
Pop: 491 (1990); 594 (1980) **Pop Density:** 22.0
Land: 22.3 sq. mi.; **Water:** 0.0 sq. mi.

Sullivan County
County Seat: Sullivan (ZIP: 47882)

Pop: 18,993 (1990); 21,107 (1980) **Pop Density:** 42.5
Land: 447.2 sq. mi.; **Water:** 6.9 sq. mi. **Area Code:** 812
On the west-central border of IN, south of Terre Haute; established Dec 30, 1816 from Knox County.
Name origin: For Gen. Daniel Sullivan (?–1779), killed during the Revolutionary War.

Carlisle   Town
ZIP: 47838 **Lat:** 38-57-43 N **Long:** 87-24-02 W
Pop: 613 (1990); 717 (1980) **Pop Density:** 1532.5
Land: 0.4 sq. mi.; **Water:** 0.0 sq. mi. **Elev:** 504 ft.
Settled 1803.
Name origin: For Carlisle, PA.

Cass   Township
ZIP: 47882 **Lat:** 39-05-07 N **Long:** 87-17-40 W
Pop: 1,912 (1990); 2,454 (1980) **Pop Density:** 50.3
Land: 38.0 sq. mi.; **Water:** 1.5 sq. mi.

Curry   Township
ZIP: 47879 **Lat:** 39-12-51 N **Long:** 87-23-55 W
Pop: 3,633 (1990); 3,988 (1980) **Pop Density:** 104.1
Land: 34.9 sq. mi.; **Water:** 0.2 sq. mi.

Dugger   Town
ZIP: 47848 **Lat:** 39-04-06 N **Long:** 87-15-37 W
Pop: 936 (1990); 1,118 (1980) **Pop Density:** 1337.1
Land: 0.7 sq. mi.; **Water:** 0.0 sq. mi. **Elev:** 684 ft.
Founded 1879.
Name origin: For its founder, F.M. Dugger.

Fairbanks   Township
ZIP: 47849 **Lat:** 39-12-36 N **Long:** 87-31-49 W
Pop: 655 (1990); 864 (1980) **Pop Density:** 16.0
Land: 40.9 sq. mi.; **Water:** 0.6 sq. mi.

Farmersburg   Town
ZIP: 47850 **Lat:** 39-15-08 N **Long:** 87-22-49 W
Pop: 1,159 (1990); 1,240 (1980) **Pop Density:** 1931.7
Land: 0.6 sq. mi.; **Water:** 0.0 sq. mi. **Elev:** 559 ft.
Name origin: Named in 1875 for the area's many farmers.

Gill   Township
ZIP: 47861 **Lat:** 39-01-23 N **Long:** 87-30-13 W
Pop: 959 (1990); 1,089 (1980) **Pop Density:** 16.0
Land: 60.0 sq. mi.; **Water:** 1.0 sq. mi.

Haddon   Township
ZIP: 47838 **Lat:** 38-57-43 N **Long:** 87-24-02 W
Pop: 1,780 (1990); 1,817 (1980) **Pop Density:** 24.9
Land: 71.4 sq. mi.; **Water:** 0.3 sq. mi.

Hamilton   Township
ZIP: 47882 **Lat:** 39-06-47 N **Long:** 87-23-38 W
Pop: 6,899 (1990); 6,945 (1980) **Pop Density:** 115.8
Land: 59.6 sq. mi.; **Water:** 1.4 sq. mi.

Hymera   Town
ZIP: 47855 **Lat:** 39-11-08 N **Long:** 87-17-55 W
Pop: 771 (1990); 1,054 (1980) **Pop Density:** 1101.4
Land: 0.7 sq. mi.; **Water:** 0.0 sq. mi. **Elev:** 524 ft.
Founded 1870.
Name origin: For the ancient Sicilian city of Himera, with a spelling alteration.

Jackson   Township
ZIP: 47855 **Lat:** 39-12-21 N **Long:** 87-17-48 W
Pop: 1,667 (1990); 2,099 (1980) **Pop Density:** 38.5
Land: 43.3 sq. mi.; **Water:** 0.8 sq. mi.

Jefferson   Township
ZIP: 47838 **Lat:** 38-57-43 N **Long:** 87-17-18 W
Pop: 544 (1990); 887 (1980) **Pop Density:** 12.8
Land: 42.5 sq. mi.; **Water:** 0.5 sq. mi.

Merom   Town
ZIP: 47861 **Lat:** 39-03-24 N **Long:** 87-34-04 W
Pop: 257 (1990); 360 (1980) **Pop Density:** 642.5
Land: 0.4 sq. mi.; **Water:** 0.0 sq. mi.
Founded 1817.
Name origin: For the biblical lake.

Shelburn   Town
ZIP: 47879 **Lat:** 39-10-46 N **Long:** 87-23-48 W
Pop: 1,147 (1990); 1,259 (1980) **Pop Density:** 1638.6
Land: 0.7 sq. mi.; **Water:** 0.0 sq. mi. **Elev:** 540 ft.
Founded 1855.
Name origin: For its founder, Paschal Shelburne, with a spelling variation.

Sullivan   City
ZIP: 47882 **Lat:** 39-05-48 N **Long:** 87-24-27 W
Pop: 4,663 (1990); 4,774 (1980) **Pop Density:** 2454.2
Land: 1.9 sq. mi.; **Water:** 0.0 sq. mi. **Elev:** 532 ft.
Name origin: For Revolutionary War hero Gen. Daniel Sullivan (?–1779).

Turman   Township
ZIP: 47882 **Lat:** 39-07-38 N **Long:** 87-33-10 W
Pop: 944 (1990); 964 (1980) **Pop Density:** 16.6
Land: 56.7 sq. mi.; **Water:** 0.6 sq. mi.

Switzerland County
County Seat: Vevay (ZIP: 47043)

Pop: 7,738 (1990); 7,153 (1980)   **Pop Density:** 35.0
Land: 221.2 sq. mi.; **Water:** 2.3 sq. mi.   **Area Code:** 812
In the southeastern corner of IN, southeast of Columbus; organized Sep 7, 1814 (prior to statehood) from Indian lands.
Name origin: For the European country, named by Swiss settlers.

Cotton
Township
Lat: 38-52-17 N   **Long:** 85-00-57 W
Pop: 1,214 (1990); 1,009 (1980)   **Pop Density:** 33.7
Land: 36.0 sq. mi.; **Water:** 0.1 sq. mi.

Craig
Township
Lat: 38-44-48 N   **Long:** 85-08-52 W
Pop: 695 (1990); 761 (1980)   **Pop Density:** 17.9
Land: 38.9 sq. mi.; **Water:** 0.2 sq. mi.

Jefferson
Township
Lat: 38-47-47 N   **Long:** 85-03-07 W
Pop: 2,657 (1990); 2,487 (1980)   **Pop Density:** 71.6
Land: 37.1 sq. mi.; **Water:** 0.1 sq. mi.

Patriot
Town
ZIP: 47038   **Lat:** 38-50-17 N   **Long:** 84-49-40 W
Pop: 190 (1990); 265 (1980)   **Pop Density:** 950.0
Land: 0.2 sq. mi.; **Water:** 0.0 sq. mi.   **Elev:** 466 ft.
Name origin: When town was renamed, the settlers wanted to call it Washington for George (1732–99), the first U.S. president, but since there were already several towns of that name in the state, they settled on the present name. Previously called Troy.

Pleasant
Township
Lat: 38-51-33 N   **Long:** 85-09-11 W
Pop: 1,076 (1990); 1,039 (1980)   **Pop Density:** 23.4
Land: 46.0 sq. mi.; **Water:** 0.0 sq. mi.

Posey
Township
Lat: 38-51-17 N   **Long:** 84-52-15 W
Pop: 1,323 (1990); 1,149 (1980)   **Pop Density:** 33.7
Land: 39.3 sq. mi.; **Water:** 1.5 sq. mi.

Vevay
Town
ZIP: 47043   **Lat:** 38-44-39 N   **Long:** 85-04-16 W
Pop: 1,393 (1990); 1,343 (1980)   **Pop Density:** 1990.0
Land: 0.7 sq. mi.; **Water:** 0.0 sq. mi.   **Elev:** 489 ft.
Name origin: Named in 1813 by Swiss settlers, for the commune in Switzerland.

York
Township
Lat: 38-48-48 N   **Long:** 84-56-16 W
Pop: 773 (1990); 708 (1980)   **Pop Density:** 32.5
Land: 23.8 sq. mi.; **Water:** 0.5 sq. mi.

Tippecanoe County
County Seat: Lafayette (ZIP: 47901)

Pop: 130,598 (1990); 121,702 (1980)   **Pop Density:** 261.3
Land: 499.8 sq. mi.; **Water:** 3.3 sq. mi.   **Area Code:** 317
In west-central IN, west of Kokomo; organized Jan 20, 1826 from Montgomery County.
Name origin: For the Tippecanoe River, itself named from Potawatomi *quit-te-pe-con-nac* 'buffalo fish,' which were plentiful in the river.

Battle Ground
Town
ZIP: 47920   **Lat:** 40-30-35 N   **Long:** 86-50-18 W
Pop: 806 (1990); 812 (1980)   **Pop Density:** 2686.7
Land: 0.3 sq. mi.; **Water:** 0.0 sq. mi.   **Elev:** 575 ft.
In west-central Indiana near the junction of the Wabash and Tippecanoe rivers, north of Lafayette.
Name origin: For the site of the Battle of Tippecanoe (Nov. 7, 1811), where Gen. William H. Harrison (1773–1841) defeated the Shawnee Indian chief Tecumseh (1768–1813).

Clarks Hill
Town
ZIP: 47930   **Lat:** 40-14-48 N   **Long:** 86-43-28 W
Pop: 716 (1990); 653 (1980)   **Pop Density:** 2386.7
Land: 0.3 sq. mi.; **Water:** 0.0 sq. mi.   **Elev:** 826 ft.
Settled 1850s.
Name origin: For its first settler, Daniel Clark.

Dayton
Town
ZIP: 47941   **Lat:** 40-22-39 N   **Long:** 86-46-36 W
Pop: 996 (1990); 781 (1980)   **Pop Density:** 996.0
Land: 1.0 sq. mi.; **Water:** 0.0 sq. mi.   **Elev:** 673 ft.
Established 1827.
Name origin: For Dayton, OH.

Fairfield
Township
ZIP: 47904   **Lat:** 40-25-35 N   **Long:** 86-51-18 W
Pop: 46,166 (1990); 44,533 (1980)   **Pop Density:** 1672.7
Land: 27.6 sq. mi.; **Water:** 0.5 sq. mi.

Jackson
Township
Lat: 40-15-33 N   **Long:** 87-02-06 W
Pop: 512 (1990); 520 (1980)   **Pop Density:** 12.4
Land: 41.4 sq. mi.; **Water:** 0.0 sq. mi.

INDIANA, Tippecanoe County

Lafayette
City
ZIP: 47901   **Lat:** 40-24-39 N   **Long:** 86-52-14 W
Pop: 43,764 (1990); 43,011 (1980)   **Pop Density:** 3266.0
Land: 13.4 sq. mi.; **Water:** 0.0 sq. mi.   **Elev:** 567 ft.
In west-central IN on the Wabash River, 57 mi. northwest of Indianapolis. Settled 1824.
Name origin: For the Marquis de Lafayette (1757–1834), French statesman and soldier who fought with the Americans during the Revolutionary War.

Lauramie
Township
Lat: 40-15-03 N   **Long:** 86-46-59 W
Pop: 2,119 (1990); 2,125 (1980)   **Pop Density:** 39.2
Land: 54.0 sq. mi.; **Water:** 0.0 sq. mi.

Otterbein
Town
Lat: 40-29-16 N   **Long:** 87-05-26 W
Pop: 381 (1990); 300 (1980)   **Pop Density:** 1270.0
Land: 0.3 sq. mi.; **Water:** 0.0 sq. mi.   **Elev:** 706 ft.
Part of the town is also in Benton County.
Name origin: Named in honor of pioneer settler Otterbein Brown.

Perry
Township
Lat: 40-25-53 N   **Long:** 86-45-06 W
Pop: 2,990 (1990); 2,720 (1980)   **Pop Density:** 82.8
Land: 36.1 sq. mi.; **Water:** 0.2 sq. mi.

Randolph
Township
Lat: 40-15-26 N   **Long:** 86-54-39 W
Pop: 694 (1990); 754 (1980)   **Pop Density:** 23.2
Land: 29.9 sq. mi.; **Water:** 0.0 sq. mi.

Shadeland
Town
Lat: 40-20-40 N   **Long:** 86-57-49 W
Pop: 1,674 (1990)   **Pop Density:** 61.8
Land: 27.1 sq. mi.; **Water:** 0.2 sq. mi.   **Elev:** 622 ft.

Sheffield
Township
Lat: 40-20-37 N   **Long:** 86-45-19 W
Pop: 2,454 (1990); 2,254 (1980)   **Pop Density:** 67.6
Land: 36.3 sq. mi.; **Water:** 0.0 sq. mi.

Shelby
Township
Lat: 40-28-51 N   **Long:** 87-03-01 W
Pop: 1,974 (1990); 1,855 (1980)   **Pop Density:** 36.8
Land: 53.6 sq. mi.; **Water:** 0.5 sq. mi.

Tippecanoe
Township
ZIP: 47906   **Lat:** 40-31-33 N   **Long:** 86-50-54 W
Pop: 5,012 (1990); 4,636 (1980)   **Pop Density:** 104.0
Land: 48.2 sq. mi.; **Water:** 0.7 sq. mi.

Union
Township
Lat: 40-20-40 N   **Long:** 86-57-49 W
Pop: 1,674 (1990); 1,713 (1980)   **Pop Density:** 61.5
Land: 27.2 sq. mi.; **Water:** 0.2 sq. mi.

Wabash
Township
ZIP: 47906   **Lat:** 40-28-20 N   **Long:** 86-57-14 W
Pop: 49,348 (1990); 44,267 (1980)   **Pop Density:** 1015.4
Land: 48.6 sq. mi.; **Water:** 0.5 sq. mi.

Washington
Township
Lat: 40-30-28 N   **Long:** 86-44-43 W
Pop: 2,393 (1990); 2,394 (1980)   **Pop Density:** 89.6
Land: 26.7 sq. mi.; **Water:** 0.3 sq. mi.

Wayne
Township
Lat: 40-21-15 N   **Long:** 87-02-27 W
Pop: 1,184 (1990); 1,233 (1980)   **Pop Density:** 34.5
Land: 34.3 sq. mi.; **Water:** 0.3 sq. mi.

Wea
Township
ZIP: 47901   **Lat:** 40-20-34 N   **Long:** 86-52-02 W
Pop: 14,078 (1990); 12,698 (1980)   **Pop Density:** 391.1
Land: 36.0 sq. mi.; **Water:** 0.0 sq. mi.

West Lafayette
City
ZIP: 47906   **Lat:** 40-26-40 N   **Long:** 86-54-42 W
Pop: 25,907 (1990); 21,247 (1980)   **Pop Density:** 5287.1
Land: 4.9 sq. mi.; **Water:** 0.0 sq. mi.   **Elev:** 617 ft.
In west-central IN, a suburb of Lafayette across the Wabash River. Site of Purdue University.
Name origin: For its location west of Lafayette. Originally known as Kingston.

Tipton County
County Seat: Tipton (ZIP: 46072)

Pop: 16,119 (1990); 16,819 (1980)   **Pop Density:** 61.9
Land: 260.4 sq. mi.; **Water:** 0.0 sq. mi.   **Area Code:** 317
In central IN, south of Kokomo; organized Jan 15, 1844 from Hamilton County.
Name origin: For Gen. John Tipton (1786–1839), IN legislator (1819–23), and U.S. senator (1832–39).

Cicero
Township
ZIP: 46031   **Lat:** 40-16-34 N   **Long:** 86-02-47 W
Pop: 8,060 (1990); 8,374 (1980)   **Pop Density:** 119.2
Land: 67.6 sq. mi.; **Water:** 0.0 sq. mi.

Elwood
City
ZIP: 46036   **Lat:** 40-16-39 N   **Long:** 85-51-39 W
Pop: 4 (1990); 259 (1980)   **Pop Density:** 1000.0
Land: 0.004 sq. mi.; **Water:** 0.0 sq. mi.   **Elev:** 865 ft.
Part of the town is also in Madison County.
Name origin: For resident, Elwood Frazier. Previously called Quincy.

Jefferson
Township
Lat: 40-15-35 N   **Long:** 86-11-29 W
Pop: 1,501 (1990); 1,550 (1980)   **Pop Density:** 38.5
Land: 39.0 sq. mi.; **Water:** 0.0 sq. mi.

Kempton
Town
ZIP: 46049   **Lat:** 40-17-15 N   **Long:** 86-13-48 W
Pop: 362 (1990); 410 (1980)   **Pop Density:** 1810.0
Land: 0.2 sq. mi.; **Water:** 0.0 sq. mi.   **Elev:** 928 ft.
Name origin: For David Kemp, on whose land it was founded.

Liberty
Township
Lat: 40-22-07 N **Long:** 86-03-47 W
Pop: 2,445 (1990); 2,455 (1980) **Pop Density:** 70.1
Land: 34.9 sq. mi.; **Water:** 0.0 sq. mi.

Madison
Township
Lat: 40-16-34 N **Long:** 85-54-38 W
Pop: 1,465 (1990); 1,602 (1980) **Pop Density:** 32.9
Land: 44.5 sq. mi.; **Water:** 0.0 sq. mi.

Prairie
Township
Lat: 40-21-10 N **Long:** 86-11-36 W
Pop: 1,125 (1990); 1,141 (1980) **Pop Density:** 28.4
Land: 39.6 sq. mi.; **Water:** 0.0 sq. mi.

Sharpsville
Town
ZIP: 46068 **Lat:** 40-22-47 N **Long:** 86-05-14 W
Pop: 769 (1990); 617 (1980) **Pop Density:** 3845.0
Land: 0.2 sq. mi.; **Water:** 0.0 sq. mi. **Elev:** 881 ft.
Name origin: For early settler E. M. Sharp.

Tipton
City
ZIP: 46072 **Lat:** 40-16-58 N **Long:** 86-02-25 W
Pop: 4,751 (1990); 5,004 (1980) **Pop Density:** 3167.3
Land: 1.5 sq. mi.; **Water:** 0.0 sq. mi. **Elev:** 864 ft.
Name origin: For Gen. John Tipton (1786–1839), IN legislator (1819–23) and U.S. senator (1832–39).

Wildcat
Township
Lat: 40-22-17 N **Long:** 85-55-33 W
Pop: 1,523 (1990); 1,697 (1980) **Pop Density:** 43.8
Land: 34.8 sq. mi.; **Water:** 0.0 sq. mi.

Windfall City
Town
Lat: 40-21-46 N **Long:** 85-57-27 W
Pop: 779 (1990); 911 (1980) **Pop Density:** 2596.7
Land: 0.3 sq. mi.; **Water:** 0.0 sq. mi.
Founded 1853.

Union County
County Seat: Liberty (ZIP: 47353)

Pop: 6,976 (1990); 6,860 (1980) **Pop Density:** 43.2
Land: 161.6 sq. mi.; **Water:** 3.7 sq. mi. **Area Code:** 317
On the southeastern border of IN, south of Richmond; organized Jan 15, 1821 from Wayne County.
Name origin: As an expression of belief in the federal union of the states.

Brownsville
Township
ZIP: 47325 **Lat:** 39-41-34 N **Long:** 84-58-50 W
Pop: 850 (1990); 921 (1980) **Pop Density:** 29.7
Land: 28.6 sq. mi.; **Water:** 0.0 sq. mi.

Center
Township
Lat: 39-37-39 N **Long:** 84-53-00 W
Pop: 2,816 (1990); 2,754 (1980) **Pop Density:** 100.6
Land: 28.0 sq. mi.; **Water:** 0.1 sq. mi.

Harmony
Township
Lat: 39-33-16 N **Long:** 84-59-06 W
Pop: 419 (1990); 377 (1980) **Pop Density:** 20.2
Land: 20.7 sq. mi.; **Water:** 2.3 sq. mi.

Harrison
Township
Lat: 39-41-15 N **Long:** 84-51-58 W
Pop: 481 (1990); 538 (1980) **Pop Density:** 16.0
Land: 30.1 sq. mi.; **Water:** 0.0 sq. mi.

Liberty
Town
ZIP: 47353 **Lat:** 39-38-04 N **Long:** 84-55-37 W
Pop: 2,051 (1990); 1,844 (1980) **Pop Density:** 2563.8
Land: 0.8 sq. mi.; **Water:** 0.0 sq. mi. **Elev:** 992 ft.
Not coextensive with the town of the same name.
Name origin: For Liberty, VA, former home of early settlers.

*Liberty
Township
ZIP: 47353 **Lat:** 39-37-07 N **Long:** 84-59-41 W
Pop: 910 (1990); 873 (1980) **Pop Density:** 38.2
Land: 23.8 sq. mi.; **Water:** 1.2 sq. mi.

Union
Township
Lat: 39-33-52 N **Long:** 84-52-30 W
Pop: 1,500 (1990); 1,397 (1980) **Pop Density:** 49.2
Land: 30.5 sq. mi.; **Water:** 0.1 sq. mi.

West College Corner
Town
Lat: 39-34-10 N **Long:** 84-49-09 W
Pop: 686 (1990); 614 (1980) **Pop Density:** 2286.7
Land: 0.3 sq. mi.; **Water:** 0.0 sq. mi. **Elev:** 989 ft.
Name origin: For its location west of College Corner, OH.

INDIANA, Vanderburgh County

Vanderburgh County
County Seat: Evansville (ZIP: 47708)

Pop: 165,058 (1990); 167,515 (1980)
Land: 234.6 sq. mi.; **Water:** 1.2 sq. mi.
Pop Density: 703.6
Area Code: 812

On the southwestern border of IN; organized Jan 7, 1818 from Indian lands.

Name origin: For Henry Vanderburgh, officer in the Revolutionary War and judge of the first court in the IN Territory.

Armstrong
Township
Lat: 38-07-09 N Long: 87-38-46 W
Pop: 1,694 (1990); 1,665 (1980) **Pop Density:** 57.4
Land: 29.5 sq. mi.; **Water:** 0.0 sq. mi.

Center
Township
ZIP: 47710 Lat: 38-02-26 N Long: 87-32-21 W
Pop: 27,185 (1990); 23,839 (1980) **Pop Density:** 799.6
Land: 34.0 sq. mi.; **Water:** 0.2 sq. mi.

Darmstadt
Town
ZIP: 47711 Lat: 38-05-27 N Long: 87-34-34 W
Pop: 1,346 (1990); 1,280 (1980) **Pop Density:** 286.4
Land: 4.7 sq. mi.; **Water:** 0.0 sq. mi. **Elev:** 483 ft.

Name origin: Named in 1860 by German settlers for Darmstadt, Germany.

Evansville
City
ZIP: 47708 Lat: 37-59-02 N Long: 87-32-35 W
Pop: 126,272 (1990); 130,496 (1980) **Pop Density:** 3102.5
Land: 40.7 sq. mi.; **Water:** 0.1 sq. mi. **Elev:** 388 ft.

In southwestern IN on the Ohio River, on the KY border. County seat.

Name origin: For Gen. Robert Evans, who settled here in 1817.

German
Township
ZIP: 47712 Lat: 38-02-35 N Long: 87-38-37 W
Pop: 7,063 (1990); 6,718 (1980) **Pop Density:** 246.1
Land: 28.7 sq. mi.; **Water:** 0.1 sq. mi.

Highland
CDP
Lat: 38-02-53 N Long: 87-33-43 W
Pop: 3,508 (1990) **Pop Density:** 1525.2
Land: 2.3 sq. mi.; **Water:** 0.0 sq. mi.

Knight
Township
ZIP: 47711 Lat: 37-58-02 N Long: 87-29-47 W
Pop: 65,522 (1990); 63,515 (1980) **Pop Density:** 1893.7
Land: 34.6 sq. mi.; **Water:** 0.0 sq. mi.

Name origin: In southwestern IN, near Evansville.

Melody Hill
CDP
Lat: 38-01-27 N Long: 87-30-47 W
Pop: 2,932 (1990) **Pop Density:** 2094.3
Land: 1.4 sq. mi.; **Water:** 0.0 sq. mi.

Perry
Township
ZIP: 47712 Lat: 37-58-16 N Long: 87-39-25 W
Pop: 20,615 (1990); 19,815 (1980) **Pop Density:** 738.9
Land: 27.9 sq. mi.; **Water:** 0.1 sq. mi.

Pigeon
Township
ZIP: 47708 Lat: 37-58-27 N Long: 87-34-09 W
Pop: 37,856 (1990); 46,866 (1980) **Pop Density:** 3473.0
Land: 10.9 sq. mi.; **Water:** 0.0 sq. mi.

Scott
Township
Lat: 38-06-59 N Long: 87-32-14 W
Pop: 4,731 (1990); 4,674 (1980) **Pop Density:** 113.5
Land: 41.7 sq. mi.; **Water:** 0.1 sq. mi.

Union
Township
Lat: 37-52-31 N Long: 87-37-49 W
Pop: 392 (1990); 423 (1980) **Pop Density:** 14.4
Land: 27.3 sq. mi.; **Water:** 0.5 sq. mi.

Vermillion County
County Seat: Newport (ZIP: 47966)

Pop: 16,773 (1990); 18,229 (1980)
Land: 256.9 sq. mi.; **Water:** 3.0 sq. mi.
Pop Density: 65.3
Area Code: 317

On the central western border of IN, north of Terre Haute; organized Jan 2, 1824 from Parke County.

Name origin: For the Big Vermillion River, which runs across the northern part of the county. Shortened French literal transliteration *Vermillion Jaune* 'yellow red' of the Indian name *Osanamon*, suggesting vermilion paint, probably from the soil that colored the river.

Cayuga
Town
ZIP: 47928 Lat: 39-56-49 N Long: 87-27-53 W
Pop: 1,083 (1990); 1,258 (1980) **Pop Density:** 1547.1
Land: 0.7 sq. mi.; **Water:** 0.0 sq. mi. **Elev:** 511 ft.

Name origin: For Cayuga Lake and Cayuga, NY, former home of early settlers.

Clinton
City
ZIP: 47842 Lat: 39-39-39 N Long: 87-24-16 W
Pop: 5,040 (1990); 5,267 (1980) **Pop Density:** 2290.9
Land: 2.2 sq. mi.; **Water:** 0.0 sq. mi. **Elev:** 498 ft.

Not coextensive with the town of the same name.

Name origin: For DeWitt Clinton (1769–1828), governor of NY (1817–23; 1825–28) and supporter of the Erie Canal.

*Clinton   Township
ZIP: 47842   **Lat:** 39-38-56 N   **Long:** 87-27-26 W
Pop: 9,250 (1990); 9,781 (1980)   **Pop Density:** 204.2
Land: 45.3 sq. mi.; **Water:** 1.1 sq. mi.

Dana   Town
ZIP: 47847   **Lat:** 39-48-24 N   **Long:** 87-29-39 W
Pop: 612 (1990); 803 (1980)   **Pop Density:** 2040.0
Land: 0.3 sq. mi.; **Water:** 0.0 sq. mi.   **Elev:** 637 ft.
Name origin: Named by and for railroad stockholder Charles Dana.

Eugene   Township
                        Lat: 39-57-32 N   **Long:** 87-28-25 W
Pop: 2,138 (1990); 2,407 (1980)   **Pop Density:** 54.8
Land: 39.0 sq. mi.; **Water:** 0.6 sq. mi.

Fairview Park   Town
ZIP: 47842   **Lat:** 39-40-54 N   **Long:** 87-24-48 W
Pop: 1,446 (1990); 1,545 (1980)   **Pop Density:** 1606.7
Land: 0.9 sq. mi.; **Water:** 0.0 sq. mi.   **Elev:** 572 ft.
Name origin: For its descriptive connotations.

Helt   Township
ZIP: 47847   **Lat:** 39-45-31 N   **Long:** 87-27-21 W
Pop: 2,691 (1990); 3,102 (1980)   **Pop Density:** 37.6
Land: 71.6 sq. mi.; **Water:** 0.5 sq. mi.

Highland   Township
ZIP: 47854   **Lat:** 40-04-46 N   **Long:** 87-28-31 W
Pop: 1,672 (1990); 1,854 (1980)   **Pop Density:** 33.0
Land: 50.6 sq. mi.; **Water:** 0.4 sq. mi.

Newport   Town
ZIP: 47966   **Lat:** 39-53-05 N   **Long:** 87-24-22 W
Pop: 627 (1990); 704 (1980)   **Pop Density:** 783.8
Land: 0.8 sq. mi.; **Water:** 0.0 sq. mi.   **Elev:** 498 ft.
Name origin: For Newport, DE.

Perrysville   Town
ZIP: 47974   **Lat:** 40-03-12 N   **Long:** 87-26-08 W
Pop: 443 (1990); 532 (1980)   **Pop Density:** 1476.7
Land: 0.3 sq. mi.; **Water:** 0.0 sq. mi.   **Elev:** 542 ft.
Founded 1826.
Name origin: For Commodore Oliver Hazard Perry (1785–1819), hero of the War of 1812, famous for the message, "We have met the enemy and they are ours."

Universal   Town
ZIP: 47884   **Lat:** 39-37-17 N   **Long:** 87-27-10 W
Pop: 392 (1990); 428 (1980)   **Pop Density:** 1306.7
Land: 0.3 sq. mi.; **Water:** 0.0 sq. mi.   **Elev:** 482 ft.
Settled 1911.
Name origin: For the local Universal Mines.

Vermillion   Township
                        Lat: 39-52-15 N   **Long:** 87-27-19 W
Pop: 1,022 (1990); 1,085 (1980)   **Pop Density:** 20.2
Land: 50.5 sq. mi.; **Water:** 0.5 sq. mi.

Vigo County
County Seat: Terre Haute (ZIP: 47807)

Pop: 106,107 (1990); 112,385 (1980)   **Pop Density:** 263.1
Land: 403.3 sq. mi.; **Water:** 7.2 sq. mi.   **Area Code:** 812
On the central western border of IN, northwest of Bloomington; organized Jan 21, 1818 from Indian lands.
Name origin: For Giuseppe Maria Francesco Vigo (1747–1836), also known as Col. Francis Vigo, a Mondovian-born fur trader who furnished funds and assistance to Revolutionary soldier George Rogers Clark (1752–1818).

Fayette   Township
ZIP: 47885   **Lat:** 39-33-36 N   **Long:** 87-27-54 W
Pop: 2,787 (1990); 3,095 (1980)   **Pop Density:** 69.7
Land: 40.0 sq. mi.; **Water:** 0.6 sq. mi.

Harrison   Township
ZIP: 47807   **Lat:** 39-28-32 N   **Long:** 87-23-19 W
Pop: 53,810 (1990); 60,462 (1980)   **Pop Density:** 2349.8
Land: 22.9 sq. mi.; **Water:** 0.6 sq. mi.

Honey Creek   Township
ZIP: 47802   **Lat:** 39-23-35 N   **Long:** 87-24-25 W
Pop: 13,559 (1990); 11,533 (1980)   **Pop Density:** 402.3
Land: 33.7 sq. mi.; **Water:** 0.4 sq. mi.
In west-central IN, near Terre Haute.

Linton   Township
                        Lat: 39-18-22 N   **Long:** 87-24-42 W
Pop: 1,308 (1990); 1,451 (1980)   **Pop Density:** 37.4
Land: 35.0 sq. mi.; **Water:** 0.5 sq. mi.

Lost Creek   Township
ZIP: 47803   **Lat:** 39-28-38 N   **Long:** 87-17-40 W
Pop: 8,633 (1990); 7,753 (1980)   **Pop Density:** 244.6
Land: 35.3 sq. mi.; **Water:** 0.5 sq. mi.

Nevins   Township
ZIP: 47851   **Lat:** 39-33-51 N   **Long:** 87-14-53 W
Pop: 2,196 (1990); 2,306 (1980)   **Pop Density:** 71.8
Land: 30.6 sq. mi.; **Water:** 0.2 sq. mi.

North Terre Haute   CDP
                        Lat: 39-32-23 N   **Long:** 87-21-36 W
Pop: 4,331 (1990)   **Pop Density:** 1312.4
Land: 3.3 sq. mi.; **Water:** 0.0 sq. mi.

Otter Creek   Township
ZIP: 47805   **Lat:** 39-33-43 N   **Long:** 87-20-52 W
Pop: 8,792 (1990); 9,485 (1980)   **Pop Density:** 249.1
Land: 35.3 sq. mi.; **Water:** 0.4 sq. mi.

INDIANA, Vigo County

Pierson
Township
Lat: 39-18-11 N **Long:** 87-17-35 W
Pop: 1,339 (1990); 1,469 (1980) **Pop Density:** 38.0
Land: 35.2 sq. mi.; **Water:** 0.7 sq. mi.

Prairie Creek
Township
ZIP: 47869 **Lat:** 39-17-52 N **Long:** 87-31-52 W
Pop: 1,299 (1990); 1,339 (1980) **Pop Density:** 34.2
Land: 38.0 sq. mi.; **Water:** 0.6 sq. mi.

Prairieton
Township
ZIP: 47870 **Lat:** 39-21-33 N **Long:** 87-30-11 W
Pop: 1,277 (1990); 1,766 (1980) **Pop Density:** 71.7
Land: 17.8 sq. mi.; **Water:** 0.7 sq. mi.

Riley
Town
ZIP: 47871 **Lat:** 39-23-23 N **Long:** 87-18-01 W
Pop: 232 (1990); 269 (1980) **Pop Density:** 2320.0
Land: 0.1 sq. mi.; **Water:** 0.0 sq. mi. **Elev:** 568 ft.
Not coextensive with the town of the same name.
Name origin: Named by the U. S. Post Office for the local township.

*Riley
Township
ZIP: 47871 **Lat:** 39-23-22 N **Long:** 87-17-44 W
Pop: 2,435 (1990); 2,224 (1980) **Pop Density:** 69.0
Land: 35.3 sq. mi.; **Water:** 0.6 sq. mi.

Seelyville
Town
ZIP: 47878 **Lat:** 39-29-38 N **Long:** 87-16-01 W
Pop: 1,090 (1990); 1,374 (1980) **Pop Density:** 1211.1
Land: 0.9 sq. mi.; **Water:** 0.0 sq. mi. **Elev:** 588 ft.
Name origin: For its first postmaster, Jonas Seely.

Sugar Creek
Township
ZIP: 47885 **Lat:** 39-27-34 N **Long:** 87-28-49 W
Pop: 8,672 (1990); 9,502 (1980) **Pop Density:** 196.2
Land: 44.2 sq. mi.; **Water:** 1.4 sq. mi.

Terre Haute
City
ZIP: 47808 **Lat:** 39-28-13 N **Long:** 87-23-00 W
Pop: 57,483 (1990); 61,125 (1980) **Pop Density:** 2075.2
Land: 27.7 sq. mi.; **Water:** 0.7 sq. mi. **Elev:** 501 ft.
In western IN on the Wabash River, 66 mi. southwest of Indianapolis. Platted 1816; incorporated as town 1832, as city 1853. Site of Indiana State University.
Name origin: French 'high land,' for its location on a 60-ft.-high plateau on the east bank of the Wabash River.

West Terre Haute
Town
ZIP: 47885 **Lat:** 39-27-51 N **Long:** 87-26-56 W
Pop: 2,495 (1990); 2,806 (1980) **Pop Density:** 4158.3
Land: 0.6 sq. mi.; **Water:** 0.0 sq. mi. **Elev:** 476 ft.
Founded 1836.
Name origin: For its relation to Terre Haute.

Wabash County
County Seat: Wabash (ZIP: 46992)

Pop: 35,069 (1990); 36,640 (1980)
Land: 413.2 sq. mi.; **Water:** 7.9 sq. mi. **Pop Density:** 84.9
Area Code: 219
In north-central IN, southwest of Ft. Wayne; established Feb 2, 1832 from Huntington County.
Name origin: For the Wabash River, which runs across the center of the county itself named from a Miami Indian word probably meaning 'pure white,' referring to a limestone bed in the river.

Chester
Township
ZIP: 46962 **Lat:** 40-58-13 N **Long:** 85-43-43 W
Pop: 8,303 (1990); 8,334 (1980) **Pop Density:** 127.2
Land: 65.3 sq. mi.; **Water:** 0.0 sq. mi.

La Fontaine
Town
ZIP: 46940 **Lat:** 40-40-25 N **Long:** 85-43-18 W
Pop: 909 (1990); 946 (1980) **Pop Density:** 1515.0
Land: 0.6 sq. mi.; **Water:** 0.0 sq. mi. **Elev:** 808 ft.
Incorporated 1862.
Name origin: For Chief La Fontaine, a Miami Indian.

Lagro
Town
ZIP: 46941 **Lat:** 40-50-17 N **Long:** 85-43-42 W
Pop: 496 (1990); 549 (1980) **Pop Density:** 826.7
Land: 0.6 sq. mi.; **Water:** 0.0 sq. mi. **Elev:** 681 ft.
Not coextensive with the town of the same name.
Name origin: For Chief LeGros (fl. 1820s), French nickname for a local Miami Indian chief.

*Lagro
Township
ZIP: 46941 **Lat:** 40-49-49 N **Long:** 85-42-29 W
Pop: 2,916 (1990); 2,990 (1980) **Pop Density:** 35.9
Land: 81.2 sq. mi.; **Water:** 2.1 sq. mi.

Liberty
Township
Lat: 40-41-44 N **Long:** 85-43-03 W
Pop: 2,398 (1990); 2,506 (1980) **Pop Density:** 51.7
Land: 46.4 sq. mi.; **Water:** 0.7 sq. mi.

Noble
Township
ZIP: 46992 **Lat:** 40-47-53 N **Long:** 85-51-08 W
Pop: 16,066 (1990); 17,314 (1980) **Pop Density:** 195.7
Land: 82.1 sq. mi.; **Water:** 0.5 sq. mi.

North Manchester
Town
ZIP: 46962 **Lat:** 41-00-17 N **Long:** 85-46-26 W
Pop: 6,383 (1990); 5,998 (1980) **Pop Density:** 2059.0
Land: 3.1 sq. mi.; **Water:** 0.0 sq. mi. **Elev:** 773 ft.
Settled 1837.
Name origin: For Manchester, England.

Paw Paw
Township
Lat: 40-53-54 N **Long:** 85-51-51 W
Pop: 1,612 (1990); 1,674 (1980) **Pop Density:** 39.9
Land: 40.4 sq. mi.; **Water:** 0.0 sq. mi.

Pleasant
Township
Lat: 40-59-41 N **Long:** 85-51-45 W
Pop: 2,469 (1990); 2,456 (1980) **Pop Density:** 45.2
Land: 54.6 sq. mi.; **Water:** 0.4 sq. mi.

American Places Dictionary   INDIANA, Warren County

Roann   Town
ZIP: 46974   **Lat:** 40-54-40 N   **Long:** 85-55-25 W
Pop: 447 (1990); 548 (1980)   **Pop Density:** 2235.0
Land: 0.2 sq. mi.; **Water:** 0.0 sq. mi.   **Elev:** 750 ft.
Name origin: For Roanne, France, with a spelling variation.

Wabash   City
ZIP: 46992   **Lat:** 40-47-57 N   **Long:** 85-49-30 W
Pop: 12,127 (1990); 12,985 (1980)   **Pop Density:** 2288.1
Land: 5.3 sq. mi.; **Water:** 0.1 sq. mi.   **Elev:** 984 ft.

In northern IN, 19 mi. northwest of Marion.
Name origin: For the Wabash River, which traverses the county, itself named from a Miami Indian word meaning 'pure white,' referring to a limestone bed in the river.

Walt   Township
Lat: 40-41-39 N   **Long:** 85-51-22 W
Pop: 1,305 (1990); 1,366 (1980)   **Pop Density:** 30.2
Land: 43.2 sq. mi.; **Water:** 4.1 sq. mi.

Warren County
County Seat: Williamsport (ZIP: 47993)

Pop: 8,176 (1990); 8,976 (1980)   **Pop Density:** 22.4
Land: 364.9 sq. mi.; **Water:** 1.7 sq. mi.   **Area Code:** 317
On the west-central border of IN, southwest of Lafayette; organized Jan 19, 1827 from Indian lands.
Name origin: For Dr. Joseph Warren (1741–75), Revolutionary War general and member of the Committee of Safety who dispatched Paul Revere (1735–1818) on his famous ride.

Adams   Township
Lat: 40-26-27 N   **Long:** 87-13-14 W
Pop: 493 (1990); 578 (1980)   **Pop Density:** 18.3
Land: 27.0 sq. mi.; **Water:** 0.0 sq. mi.

Jordan   Township
Lat: 40-21-00 N   **Long:** 87-27-49 W
Pop: 313 (1990); 364 (1980)   **Pop Density:** 7.7
Land: 40.5 sq. mi.; **Water:** 0.0 sq. mi.

Kent   Township
Lat: 40-11-44 N   **Long:** 87-28-32 W
Pop: 467 (1990); 504 (1980)   **Pop Density:** 33.4
Land: 14.0 sq. mi.; **Water:** 0.1 sq. mi.

Liberty   Township
Lat: 40-20-36 N   **Long:** 87-19-40 W
Pop: 680 (1990); 811 (1980)   **Pop Density:** 15.5
Land: 44.0 sq. mi.; **Water:** 0.0 sq. mi.

Medina   Township
Lat: 40-26-11 N   **Long:** 87-08-26 W
Pop: 371 (1990); 381 (1980)   **Pop Density:** 13.8
Land: 26.9 sq. mi.; **Water:** 0.2 sq. mi.

Mound   Township
Lat: 40-08-52 N   **Long:** 87-28-11 W
Pop: 448 (1990); 483 (1980)   **Pop Density:** 27.0
Land: 16.6 sq. mi.; **Water:** 0.2 sq. mi.

Pike   Township
Lat: 40-15-20 N   **Long:** 87-23-19 W
Pop: 1,234 (1990); 1,480 (1980)   **Pop Density:** 70.9
Land: 17.4 sq. mi.; **Water:** 0.2 sq. mi.

Pine   Township
Lat: 40-25-40 N   **Long:** 87-19-12 W
Pop: 446 (1990); 442 (1980)   **Pop Density:** 12.4
Land: 36.1 sq. mi.; **Water:** 0.0 sq. mi.

Pine Village   Town
ZIP: 47975   **Lat:** 40-26-59 N   **Long:** 87-15-08 W
Pop: 134 (1990); 257 (1980)   **Pop Density:** 670.0
Land: 0.2 sq. mi.; **Water:** 0.0 sq. mi.   **Elev:** 667 ft.

Prairie   Township
Lat: 40-26-27 N   **Long:** 87-27-22 W
Pop: 318 (1990); 396 (1980)   **Pop Density:** 6.7
Land: 47.8 sq. mi.; **Water:** 0.0 sq. mi.

State Line City   Town
Lat: 40-11-49 N   **Long:** 87-31-38 W
Pop: 182 (1990); 233 (1980)   **Pop Density:** 1820.0
Land: 0.1 sq. mi.; **Water:** 0.0 sq. mi.
Name origin: For its location on the IL border.

Steuben   Township
Lat: 40-14-57 N   **Long:** 87-27-40 W
Pop: 495 (1990); 575 (1980)   **Pop Density:** 12.5
Land: 39.6 sq. mi.; **Water:** 0.0 sq. mi.

Warren   Township
Lat: 40-20-56 N   **Long:** 87-11-21 W
Pop: 699 (1990); 711 (1980)   **Pop Density:** 19.5
Land: 35.9 sq. mi.; **Water:** 0.5 sq. mi.

Washington   Township
Lat: 40-16-36 N   **Long:** 87-19-41 W
Pop: 2,212 (1990); 2,251 (1980)   **Pop Density:** 115.8
Land: 19.1 sq. mi.; **Water:** 0.4 sq. mi.

West Lebanon   Town
ZIP: 47991   **Lat:** 40-16-16 N   **Long:** 87-23-00 W
Pop: 760 (1990); 946 (1980)   **Pop Density:** 1085.7
Land: 0.7 sq. mi.; **Water:** 0.0 sq. mi.   **Elev:** 714 ft.
Founded 1830.
Name origin: Named Lebanon in 1830; "West" added to distinguish it from another Lebanon, IN.

Williamsport   Town
ZIP: 47993   **Lat:** 40-17-13 N   **Long:** 87-17-36 W
Pop: 1,798 (1990); 1,747 (1980)   **Pop Density:** 1798.0
Land: 1.0 sq. mi.; **Water:** 0.0 sq. mi.   **Elev:** 630 ft.
Name origin: For its original landowner, William Harrison.

INDIANA, Warrick County

Warrick County
County Seat: Boonville (ZIP: 47601)

Pop: 44,920 (1990); 41,474 (1980)   **Pop Density:** 117.0
Land: 384.1 sq. mi.; **Water:** 6.8 sq. mi.   **Area Code:** 812
On the southwestern border of IN, east of Evansville; organized Mar 9, 1813 (prior to statehood) from Indian lands.
Name origin: For Capt. Jacob Warrick (1773–1811), distinguished early settler and officer who died at the Battle of Tippecanoe.

Anderson   Township
ZIP: 47630   **Lat:** 37-56-00 N   **Long:** 87-18-08 W
Pop: 1,056 (1990); 999 (1980)   **Pop Density:** 51.0
Land: 20.7 sq. mi.; **Water:** 1.4 sq. mi.

Boon   Township
ZIP: 47601   **Lat:** 38-02-23 N   **Long:** 87-16-37 W
Pop: 11,708 (1990); 11,420 (1980)   **Pop Density:** 141.2
Land: 82.9 sq. mi.; **Water:** 2.1 sq. mi.
In southwestern IL.

Boonville   City
ZIP: 47601   **Lat:** 38-02-42 N   **Long:** 87-16-25 W
Pop: 6,724 (1990); 6,300 (1980)   **Pop Density:** 2241.3
Land: 3.0 sq. mi.; **Water:** 0.0 sq. mi.   **Elev:** 430 ft.

Campbell   Township
Lat: 38-05-30 N   **Long:** 87-25-03 W
Pop: 620 (1990); 1,001 (1980)   **Pop Density:** 15.7
Land: 39.6 sq. mi.; **Water:** 0.5 sq. mi.

Chandler   Town
ZIP: 47610   **Lat:** 38-02-31 N   **Long:** 87-22-08 W
Pop: 3,099 (1990); 3,043 (1980)   **Pop Density:** 2817.3
Land: 1.1 sq. mi.; **Water:** 0.0 sq. mi.   **Elev:** 421 ft.

Elberfeld   Town
ZIP: 47613   **Lat:** 38-09-40 N   **Long:** 87-26-53 W
Pop: 635 (1990); 640 (1980)   **Pop Density:** 2116.7
Land: 0.3 sq. mi.; **Water:** 0.0 sq. mi.   **Elev:** 445 ft.
Founded 1885.
Name origin: Named by German settlers for Elberfeld, Germany.

Greer   Township
Lat: 38-10-24 N   **Long:** 87-24-45 W
Pop: 1,888 (1990); 1,935 (1980)   **Pop Density:** 69.7
Land: 27.1 sq. mi.; **Water:** 0.4 sq. mi.

Hart   Township
Lat: 38-10-21 N   **Long:** 87-17-48 W
Pop: 1,329 (1990); 1,360 (1980)   **Pop Density:** 32.4
Land: 41.0 sq. mi.; **Water:** 1.0 sq. mi.

Lane   Township
Lat: 38-12-18 N   **Long:** 87-10-54 W
Pop: 279 (1990); 302 (1980)   **Pop Density:** 11.9
Land: 23.5 sq. mi.; **Water:** 0.5 sq. mi.

Lynnville   Town
ZIP: 47619   **Lat:** 38-11-56 N   **Long:** 87-19-02 W
Pop: 640 (1990); 566 (1980)   **Pop Density:** 376.5
Land: 1.7 sq. mi.; **Water:** 0.2 sq. mi.   **Elev:** 497 ft.
Founded 1839.
Name origin: For its founder, John Lynn.

Newburgh   Town
ZIP: 47630   **Lat:** 37-56-47 N   **Long:** 87-24-13 W
Pop: 2,880 (1990); 2,906 (1980)   **Pop Density:** 2618.2
Land: 1.1 sq. mi.; **Water:** 0.0 sq. mi.   **Elev:** 393 ft.
Name origin: Originally Sprinklesburg, it combined with a nearby village named Newburgh and took its name.

Ohio   Township
ZIP: 47610   **Lat:** 37-59-36 N   **Long:** 87-23-31 W
Pop: 24,933 (1990); 21,318 (1980)   **Pop Density:** 564.1
Land: 44.2 sq. mi.; **Water:** 0.2 sq. mi.

Owen   Township
Lat: 38-09-08 N   **Long:** 87-11-14 W
Pop: 628 (1990); 576 (1980)   **Pop Density:** 25.1
Land: 25.0 sq. mi.; **Water:** 0.5 sq. mi.

Pigeon   Township
Lat: 38-10-01 N   **Long:** 87-04-52 W
Pop: 927 (1990); 992 (1980)   **Pop Density:** 22.9
Land: 40.4 sq. mi.; **Water:** 0.1 sq. mi.

Skelton   Township
Lat: 38-04-41 N   **Long:** 87-09-07 W
Pop: 1,552 (1990); 1,571 (1980)   **Pop Density:** 39.1
Land: 39.7 sq. mi.; **Water:** 0.2 sq. mi.

Tennyson   Town
ZIP: 47637   **Lat:** 38-04-53 N   **Long:** 87-07-08 W
Pop: 267 (1990); 331 (1980)   **Pop Density:** 890.0
Land: 0.3 sq. mi.; **Water:** 0.0 sq. mi.   **Elev:** 435 ft.
Settled 1882.
Name origin: For British poet laureate Alfred, Lord Tennyson (1809–92).

Washington County
County Seat: Salem (ZIP: 47167)

Pop: 23,717 (1990); 21,932 (1980)   **Pop Density:** 46.1
Land: 514.5 sq. mi.; **Water:** 2.1 sq. mi.   **Area Code:** 812
In south-central IN, northwest of Louisville, KY; established Dec 21, 1813 (prior to statehood) from Indian lands.
Name origin: For George Washington (1732–99), American patriot and first U.S. president.

Brown   Township
ZIP: 47108   **Lat:** 38-42-23 N   **Long:** 86-15-50 W
Pop: 1,229 (1990); 1,336 (1980)   **Pop Density:** 40.2
Land: 30.6 sq. mi.; **Water:** 0.3 sq. mi.

Campbellsburg   Town
ZIP: 47108   **Lat:** 38-39-04 N   **Long:** 86-15-39 W
Pop: 606 (1990); 695 (1980)   **Pop Density:** 606.0
Land: 1.0 sq. mi.; **Water:** 0.0 sq. mi.   **Elev:** 830 ft.
Established 1851 by Robert Campbell.
Name origin: For its founder.

Franklin   Township
Lat: 38-36-04 N   **Long:** 85-56-38 W
Pop: 1,601 (1990); 1,290 (1980)   **Pop Density:** 36.1
Land: 44.3 sq. mi.; **Water:** 0.0 sq. mi.

Fredericksburg   Town
ZIP: 47120   **Lat:** 38-25-58 N   **Long:** 86-11-18 W
Pop: 155 (1990); 233 (1980)   **Pop Density:** 387.5
Land: 0.4 sq. mi.; **Water:** 0.0 sq. mi.   **Elev:** 615 ft.
Founded 1815.
Name origin: For its founder, Frederick Royse.

Gibson   Township
Lat: 38-42-25 N   **Long:** 85-57-02 W
Pop: 967 (1990); 917 (1980)   **Pop Density:** 19.0
Land: 51.0 sq. mi.; **Water:** 0.2 sq. mi.

Hardinsburg   Town
ZIP: 47125   **Lat:** 38-27-37 N   **Long:** 86-16-21 W
Pop: 322 (1990); 298 (1980)   **Pop Density:** 161.0
Land: 2.0 sq. mi.; **Water:** 0.0 sq. mi.   **Elev:** 700 ft.
Name origin: For Aaron Hardin, who laid out the town in 1838.

Howard   Township
Lat: 38-31-11 N   **Long:** 86-10-12 W
Pop: 1,084 (1990); 1,079 (1980)   **Pop Density:** 30.1
Land: 36.0 sq. mi.; **Water:** 0.1 sq. mi.

Jackson   Township
Lat: 38-26-22 N   **Long:** 86-03-17 W
Pop: 1,247 (1990); 972 (1980)   **Pop Density:** 48.9
Land: 25.5 sq. mi.; **Water:** 0.0 sq. mi.

Jefferson   Township
ZIP: 47108   **Lat:** 38-42-55 N   **Long:** 86-11-43 W
Pop: 944 (1990); 836 (1980)   **Pop Density:** 19.7
Land: 48.0 sq. mi.; **Water:** 0.8 sq. mi.

Little York   Town
ZIP: 47139   **Lat:** 38-41-58 N   **Long:** 85-54-14 W
Pop: 155 (1990); 150 (1980)   **Pop Density:** 155.0
Land: 1.0 sq. mi.; **Water:** 0.0 sq. mi.   **Elev:** 563 ft.
Name origin: Named by settlers from NY for their home state.

Livonia   Town
ZIP: 47108   **Lat:** 38-33-25 N   **Long:** 86-16-44 W
Pop: 136 (1990); 120 (1980)   **Pop Density:** 170.0
Land: 0.8 sq. mi.; **Water:** 0.0 sq. mi.   **Elev:** 780 ft.
Name origin: Named by its early pioneers for a former Baltic province in Russia. Previously called Bethel for a local church.

Madison   Township
ZIP: 47108   **Lat:** 38-31-15 N   **Long:** 86-16-36 W
Pop: 607 (1990); 555 (1980)   **Pop Density:** 23.3
Land: 26.1 sq. mi.; **Water:** 0.0 sq. mi.

Monroe   Township
Lat: 38-43-23 N   **Long:** 86-04-16 W
Pop: 525 (1990); 460 (1980)   **Pop Density:** 13.7
Land: 38.4 sq. mi.; **Water:** 0.4 sq. mi.

New Pekin   Town
Lat: 38-30-09 N   **Long:** 86-00-55 W
Pop: 1,095 (1990); 1,125 (1980)   **Pop Density:** 476.1
Land: 2.3 sq. mi.; **Water:** 0.0 sq. mi.   **Elev:** 703 ft.
Settled 1852.
Name origin: For nearby Pekin.

Pierce   Township
Lat: 38-30-40 N   **Long:** 86-03-46 W
Pop: 1,948 (1990); 1,738 (1980)   **Pop Density:** 54.6
Land: 35.7 sq. mi.; **Water:** 0.0 sq. mi.

Polk   Township
Lat: 38-31-43 N   **Long:** 85-56-38 W
Pop: 1,863 (1990); 1,682 (1980)   **Pop Density:** 51.9
Land: 35.9 sq. mi.; **Water:** 0.1 sq. mi.

Posey   Township
Lat: 38-26-45 N   **Long:** 86-12-52 W
Pop: 1,480 (1990); 1,525 (1980)   **Pop Density:** 43.8
Land: 33.8 sq. mi.; **Water:** 0.0 sq. mi.

Salem   City
ZIP: 47167   **Lat:** 38-36-14 N   **Long:** 86-05-55 W
Pop: 5,619 (1990); 5,290 (1980)   **Pop Density:** 1478.7
Land: 3.8 sq. mi.; **Water:** 0.0 sq. mi.   **Elev:** 747 ft.
Settled 1866.
Name origin: For Salem, MA.

Saltillo   Town
ZIP: 47108   **Lat:** 38-39-56 N   **Long:** 86-17-53 W
Pop: 117 (1990); 134 (1980)   **Pop Density:** 97.5
Land: 1.2 sq. mi.; **Water:** 0.0 sq. mi.   **Elev:** 800 ft.
Founded 1849.
Name origin: For Saltillo, Mexico.

INDIANA, Washington County

Vernon Township
ZIP: 47108 Lat: 38-36-23 N Long: 86-15-13 W
Pop: 727 (1990); 659 (1980) Pop Density: 21.3
Land: 34.1 sq. mi.; Water: 0.0 sq. mi.

Washington Township
ZIP: 47167 Lat: 38-36-49 N Long: 86-06-07 W
Pop: 9,495 (1990); 8,883 (1980) Pop Density: 126.4
Land: 75.1 sq. mi.; Water: 0.2 sq. mi.

Wayne County
County Seat: Richmond (ZIP: 47374)

Pop: 71,951 (1990); 76,058 (1980) Pop Density: 178.3
Land: 403.6 sq. mi.; Water: 0.8 sq. mi. Area Code: 317
On the central-eastern border of IN, southeast of Muncie; established Nov 27, 1810 (prior to statehood) from Indian lands.
Name origin: For Gen. Anthony Wayne (1745–96), PA soldier and statesman, nicknamed "Mad Anthony" for his daring during the Revolutionary War, but honored here mostly for his defeat of Miami Indian chief Little Turtle (c. 1752–1812) in the Battle of Fallen Timbers (1794).

Abington Township
ZIP: 47330 Lat: 39-45-15 N Long: 84-59-27 W
Pop: 865 (1990); 793 (1980) Pop Density: 40.8
Land: 21.2 sq. mi.; Water: 0.0 sq. mi.

Boston Town
ZIP: 47324 Lat: 39-44-29 N Long: 84-51-04 W
Pop: 159 (1990); 189 (1980) Pop Density: 795.0
Land: 0.2 sq. mi.; Water: 0.0 sq. mi. Elev: 1136 ft.
Settled 1832. Not coextensive with the town of the same name.
Name origin: For Boston, MA.

*Boston Township
Lat: 39-45-29 N Long: 84-52-22 W
Pop: 917 (1990); 1,029 (1980) Pop Density: 37.0
Land: 24.8 sq. mi.; Water: 0.0 sq. mi.

Cambridge City Town
ZIP: 47327 Lat: 39-48-43 N Long: 85-10-14 W
Pop: 2,091 (1990); 2,407 (1980) Pop Density: 2091.0
Land: 1.0 sq. mi.; Water: 0.0 sq. mi. Elev: 937 ft.
Originally a depot on the Whitewater Canal. Incorporated 1841.
Name origin: For Cambridge, England.

Center Township
ZIP: 47330 Lat: 39-49-21 N Long: 84-59-50 W
Pop: 7,345 (1990); 7,315 (1980) Pop Density: 173.6
Land: 42.3 sq. mi.; Water: 0.1 sq. mi.

Centerville City
ZIP: 47330 Lat: 39-49-01 N Long: 84-59-43 W
Pop: 2,398 (1990); 2,284 (1980) Pop Density: 2664.4
Land: 0.9 sq. mi.; Water: 0.0 sq. mi. Elev: 1002 ft.
Incorporated 1815.

Clay Township
ZIP: 47345 Lat: 39-53-28 N Long: 85-02-38 W
Pop: 1,042 (1990); 1,061 (1980) Pop Density: 52.4
Land: 19.9 sq. mi.; Water: 0.0 sq. mi.

Dalton Township
ZIP: 47346 Lat: 39-58-39 N Long: 85-09-33 W
Pop: 580 (1990); 612 (1980) Pop Density: 36.7
Land: 15.8 sq. mi.; Water: 0.0 sq. mi.

Dublin Town
ZIP: 47335 Lat: 39-48-44 N Long: 85-12-18 W
Pop: 805 (1990); 979 (1980) Pop Density: 1610.0
Land: 0.5 sq. mi.; Water: 0.0 sq. mi.
Founded 1820s.
Name origin: For Dublin, Ireland.

East Germantown Town
Lat: 39-48-45 N Long: 85-08-12 W
Pop: 372 (1990); 438 (1980) Pop Density: 3720.0
Land: 0.1 sq. mi.; Water: 0.0 sq. mi. Elev: 1050 ft.
Name origin: For German settlers from PA who came here in the 1830s. Previously called Pershing.

Economy Town
ZIP: 47339 Lat: 39-58-38 N Long: 85-05-13 W
Pop: 151 (1990); 237 (1980) Pop Density: 1510.0
Land: 0.1 sq. mi.; Water: 0.0 sq. mi. Elev: 1146 ft.
Name origin: Named in 1825 at the suggestion of the original landowner, who subdivided his land to raise money.

Fountain City Town
ZIP: 47341 Lat: 39-57-21 N Long: 84-55-04 W
Pop: 766 (1990); 839 (1980) Pop Density: 1915.0
Land: 0.4 sq. mi.; Water: 0.0 sq. mi. Elev: 1114 ft.

Franklin Township
ZIP: 47346 Lat: 39-57-20 N Long: 84-50-35 W
Pop: 1,306 (1990); 1,450 (1980) Pop Density: 46.0
Land: 28.4 sq. mi.; Water: 0.0 sq. mi.

Greene Township
ZIP: 47393 Lat: 39-57-43 N Long: 85-00-18 W
Pop: 1,249 (1990); 1,326 (1980) Pop Density: 43.5
Land: 28.7 sq. mi.; Water: 0.0 sq. mi.

Greens Fork Town
ZIP: 47345 Lat: 39-53-29 N Long: 85-02-32 W
Pop: 416 (1990); 426 (1980) Pop Density: 4160.0
Land: 0.1 sq. mi.; Water: 0.0 sq. mi. Elev: 1010 ft.
Founded 1818.
Name origin: Named in 1818 for nearby Green's Fork Stream.

American Places Dictionary   INDIANA, Wells County

Hagerstown — Town
ZIP: 47346   **Lat:** 39-54-42 N   **Long:** 85-09-24 W
Pop: 1,835 (1990); 1,950 (1980)   **Pop Density:** 1310.7
Land: 1.4 sq. mi.; **Water:** 0.0 sq. mi.
Settled 1830.
Name origin: For Hagerstown, MD.

Harrison — Township
ZIP: 47327   **Lat:** 39-51-11 N   **Long:** 85-06-07 W
Pop: 363 (1990); 333 (1980)   **Pop Density:** 22.0
Land: 16.5 sq. mi.; **Water:** 0.0 sq. mi.

Jackson — Township
ZIP: 47327   **Lat:** 39-49-17 N   **Long:** 85-09-58 W
Pop: 4,803 (1990); 5,588 (1980)   **Pop Density:** 170.3
Land: 28.2 sq. mi.; **Water:** 0.2 sq. mi.

Jefferson — Township
ZIP: 47346   **Lat:** 39-54-39 N   **Long:** 85-08-50 W
Pop: 3,331 (1990); 3,479 (1980)   **Pop Density:** 120.3
Land: 27.7 sq. mi.; **Water:** 0.0 sq. mi.

Milton — Town
ZIP: 47357   **Lat:** 39-47-11 N   **Long:** 85-09-22 W
Pop: 634 (1990); 729 (1980)   **Pop Density:** 2113.3
Land: 0.3 sq. mi.; **Water:** 0.0 sq. mi.   **Elev:** 929 ft.
Name origin: Descriptively named by its founders for being the location of several watermills.

Mount Auburn — Town
ZIP: 47327   **Lat:** 39-48-46 N   **Long:** 85-11-25 W
Pop: 138 (1990); 192 (1980)   **Pop Density:** 690.0
Land: 0.2 sq. mi.; **Water:** 0.0 sq. mi.   **Elev:** 995 ft.
Name origin: Originally called Black Hawk.

New Garden — Township
Lat: 39-57-38 N   **Long:** 84-55-11 W
Pop: 1,847 (1990); 1,924 (1980)   **Pop Density:** 79.3
Land: 23.3 sq. mi.; **Water:** 0.0 sq. mi.

Perry — Township
ZIP: 47339   **Lat:** 39-58-29 N   **Long:** 85-05-14 W
Pop: 700 (1990); 762 (1980)   **Pop Density:** 40.0
Land: 17.5 sq. mi.; **Water:** 0.0 sq. mi.

Richmond — City
ZIP: 47374   **Lat:** 39-49-46 N   **Long:** 84-53-07 W
Pop: 38,705 (1990); 41,349 (1980)   **Pop Density:** 2103.5
Land: 18.4 sq. mi.; **Water:** 0.1 sq. mi.   **Elev:** 966 ft.
In eastern IN, 36 mi. southeast of Muncie. County seat. Incorporated 1840.
Name origin: Originally called Smithville, but when it incorporated with the adjoining town of Coxborough, the present name was chosen for the richness of the soil.

Spring Grove — Town
ZIP: 47374   **Lat:** 39-50-50 N   **Long:** 84-53-25 W
Pop: 420 (1990); 469 (1980)   **Pop Density:** 1400.0
Land: 0.3 sq. mi.; **Water:** 0.0 sq. mi.   **Elev:** 1010 ft.
Name origin: For its descriptive connotations.

Washington — Township
Lat: 39-45-15 N   **Long:** 85-06-51 W
Pop: 1,539 (1990); 1,706 (1980)   **Pop Density:** 36.6
Land: 42.0 sq. mi.; **Water:** 0.1 sq. mi.

Wayne — Township
ZIP: 47374   **Lat:** 39-50-27 N   **Long:** 84-52-32 W
Pop: 44,743 (1990); 47,236 (1980)   **Pop Density:** 852.2
Land: 52.5 sq. mi.; **Water:** 0.4 sq. mi.

Webster — Township
ZIP: 47392   **Lat:** 39-53-53 N   **Long:** 84-57-18 W
Pop: 1,321 (1990); 1,444 (1980)   **Pop Density:** 88.7
Land: 14.9 sq. mi.; **Water:** 0.0 sq. mi.

Whitewater — Town
ZIP: 47374   **Lat:** 39-56-39 N   **Long:** 84-49-50 W
Pop: 111 (1990); 107 (1980)   **Pop Density:** 1110.0
Land: 0.1 sq. mi.; **Water:** 0.0 sq. mi.   **Elev:** 1127 ft.
Settled 1828.
Name origin: For the Whitewater River, which traverses the county.

Wells County
County Seat: Bluffton (ZIP: 46714)

Pop: 25,948 (1990); 25,401 (1980)   **Pop Density:** 70.1
Land: 370.0 sq. mi.; **Water:** 0.4 sq. mi.   **Area Code:** 219
In northeastern IN, south of Ft. Wayne; established Feb 7, 1835 from Indian lands.
Name origin: For Capt. William Wells (1770?–1812), a white man adopted by Miami Indian Chief Little Turtle (c. 1752–1812), who served with the Indians; he returned to the white men and served as Indian agent, then fought the Indians at the Battle of Tippecanoe (1811).

Bluffton — City
ZIP: 46714   **Lat:** 40-44-29 N   **Long:** 85-10-15 W
Pop: 9,020 (1990); 8,705 (1980)   **Pop Density:** 1610.7
Land: 5.6 sq. mi.; **Water:** 0.0 sq. mi.   **Elev:** 828 ft.
In eastern IN on the Wabash River, 23 mi. south of Fort Wayne. Incorporated 1851.
Name origin: For its location on the river's bluffs.

Chester — Township
ZIP: 46781   **Lat:** 40-36-24 N   **Long:** 85-16-07 W
Pop: 981 (1990); 1,085 (1980)   **Pop Density:** 27.4
Land: 35.8 sq. mi.; **Water:** 0.0 sq. mi.

Harrison — Township
ZIP: 46714   **Lat:** 40-41-34 N   **Long:** 85-08-51 W
Pop: 8,836 (1990); 8,957 (1980)   **Pop Density:** 183.3
Land: 48.2 sq. mi.; **Water:** 0.1 sq. mi.

INDIANA, Wells County

Jackson
Township
Lat: 40-36-37 N **Long:** 85-23-29 W
Pop: 824 (1990); 864 (1980) **Pop Density:** 22.9
Land: 36.0 sq. mi.; **Water:** 0.0 sq. mi.

Jefferson
Township
Lat: 40-52-16 N **Long:** 85-09-06 W
Pop: 4,961 (1990); 4,637 (1980) **Pop Density:** 105.3
Land: 47.1 sq. mi.; **Water:** 0.0 sq. mi.

Lancaster
Township
Lat: 40-47-08 N **Long:** 85-08-19 W
Pop: 4,625 (1990); 4,259 (1980) **Pop Density:** 96.6
Land: 47.9 sq. mi.; **Water:** 0.1 sq. mi.

Liberty
Township
ZIP: 46766 **Lat:** 40-41-53 N **Long:** 85-16-42 W
Pop: 1,166 (1990); 1,264 (1980) **Pop Density:** 32.6
Land: 35.8 sq. mi.; **Water:** 0.0 sq. mi.

Markle
Town
Lat: 40-49-38 N **Long:** 85-19-56 W
Pop: 419 (1990); 220 (1980) **Pop Density:** 1396.7
Land: 0.3 sq. mi.; **Water:** 0.0 sq. mi. **Elev:** 780 ft.
Settled 1836. Part of the town is also in Huntington County.

Nottingham
Township
Lat: 40-36-52 N **Long:** 85-08-41 W
Pop: 1,086 (1990); 1,132 (1980) **Pop Density:** 22.5
Land: 48.2 sq. mi.; **Water:** 0.0 sq. mi.

Ossian
Town
ZIP: 46777 **Lat:** 40-52-42 N **Long:** 85-10-06 W
Pop: 2,428 (1990); 1,945 (1980) **Pop Density:** 1734.3
Land: 1.4 sq. mi.; **Water:** 0.0 sq. mi. **Elev:** 830 ft.
Name origin: Named in 1846 by Scottish settlers for Ossian Hall, County Old, Scotland.

Poneto
Town
ZIP: 46781 **Lat:** 40-39-22 N **Long:** 85-13-19 W
Pop: 236 (1990); 250 (1980) **Pop Density:** 2360.0
Land: 0.1 sq. mi.; **Water:** 0.0 sq. mi. **Elev:** 852 ft.

Rockcreek
Township
Lat: 40-46-47 N **Long:** 85-16-42 W
Pop: 1,541 (1990); 1,323 (1980) **Pop Density:** 42.9
Land: 35.9 sq. mi.; **Water:** 0.1 sq. mi.

Union
Township
Lat: 40-52-25 N **Long:** 85-16-50 W
Pop: 1,928 (1990); 1,880 (1980) **Pop Density:** 54.9
Land: 35.1 sq. mi.; **Water:** 0.1 sq. mi.

Uniondale
Town
ZIP: 46791 **Lat:** 40-49-42 N **Long:** 85-14-28 W
Pop: 289 (1990); 303 (1980) **Pop Density:** 2890.0
Land: 0.1 sq. mi.; **Water:** 0.0 sq. mi. **Elev:** 817 ft.
Name origin: For its township.

Vera Cruz
Town
ZIP: 46714 **Lat:** 40-42-03 N **Long:** 85-04-46 W
Pop: 83 (1990); 117 (1980) **Pop Density:** 830.0
Land: 0.1 sq. mi.; **Water:** 0.0 sq. mi. **Elev:** 825 ft.
Founded 1848.
Name origin: For Vera Cruz, Mexico, captured by U.S. soldiers in 1847 during the Mexican War.

White County
County Seat: Monticello (ZIP: 47960)

Pop: 23,265 (1990); 23,867 (1980) **Pop Density:** 46.0
Land: 505.3 sq. mi.; **Water:** 3.6 sq. mi. **Area Code:** 219
In northwestern IN, north of Lafayette; organized Feb 1, 1834 from Carroll County.
Name origin: For Col. Isaac White (?–1811), killed at the Battle of Tippecanoe.

Big Creek
Township
Lat: 40-41-15 N **Long:** 86-51-39 W
Pop: 835 (1990); 911 (1980) **Pop Density:** 25.2
Land: 33.1 sq. mi.; **Water:** 0.0 sq. mi.

Brookston
Town
ZIP: 47923 **Lat:** 40-36-00 N **Long:** 86-51-56 W
Pop: 1,804 (1990); 1,701 (1980) **Pop Density:** 3006.7
Land: 0.6 sq. mi.; **Water:** 0.0 sq. mi. **Elev:** 674 ft.
Name origin: For railroad resident James Brooks.

Burnettsville
Town
ZIP: 47926 **Lat:** 40-45-41 N **Long:** 86-35-41 W
Pop: 401 (1990); 496 (1980) **Pop Density:** 572.9
Land: 0.7 sq. mi.; **Water:** 0.0 sq. mi. **Elev:** 710 ft.
Name origin: For nearby Burnetts Stream.

Cass
Township
Lat: 40-52-11 N **Long:** 86-38-19 W
Pop: 569 (1990); 570 (1980) **Pop Density:** 15.7
Land: 36.2 sq. mi.; **Water:** 0.0 sq. mi.

Chalmers
Town
ZIP: 47929 **Lat:** 40-39-45 N **Long:** 86-52-03 W
Pop: 525 (1990); 554 (1980) **Pop Density:** 2625.0
Land: 0.2 sq. mi.; **Water:** 0.0 sq. mi. **Elev:** 705 ft.

Honey Creek
Township
Lat: 40-46-20 N **Long:** 86-52-21 W
Pop: 1,148 (1990); 1,296 (1980) **Pop Density:** 27.1
Land: 42.4 sq. mi.; **Water:** 0.0 sq. mi.

Jackson
Township
Lat: 40-47-20 N **Long:** 86-36-11 W
Pop: 745 (1990); 862 (1980) **Pop Density:** 47.8
Land: 15.6 sq. mi.; **Water:** 0.0 sq. mi.

Liberty
Township
Lat: 40-51-02 N **Long:** 86-44-26 W
Pop: 1,777 (1990); 1,733 (1980) **Pop Density:** 53.5
Land: 33.2 sq. mi.; **Water:** 0.8 sq. mi.

Lincoln
Township
Lat: 40-47-03 N Long: 86-39-46 W
Pop: 673 (1990); 714 (1980) **Pop Density:** 31.2
Land: 21.6 sq. mi.; **Water:** 0.0 sq. mi.

Monon
Town
ZIP: 47959 Lat: 40-51-49 N Long: 86-52-43 W
Pop: 1,585 (1990); 1,540 (1980) **Pop Density:** 3170.0
Land: 0.5 sq. mi.; **Water:** 0.0 sq. mi. **Elev:** 668 ft.
Not coextensive with the town of the same name.
Name origin: From a Potawatomi Indian term meaning 'to carry.'

*Monon
Township
ZIP: 47959 Lat: 40-52-16 N Long: 86-52-45 W
Pop: 3,140 (1990); 3,389 (1980) **Pop Density:** 49.5
Land: 63.4 sq. mi.; **Water:** 0.5 sq. mi.

Monticello
City
ZIP: 47960 Lat: 40-44-48 N Long: 86-45-50 W
Pop: 5,237 (1990); 5,162 (1980) **Pop Density:** 1870.4
Land: 2.8 sq. mi.; **Water:** 0.2 sq. mi. **Elev:** 682 ft.
Name origin: For third U.S. President Thomas Jefferson's (1743–1826) VA estate.

Prairie
Township
Lat: 40-36-14 N Long: 86-52-50 W
Pop: 2,950 (1990); 2,788 (1980) **Pop Density:** 44.4
Land: 66.5 sq. mi.; **Water:** 0.0 sq. mi.

Princeton
Township
Lat: 40-47-12 N Long: 87-00-53 W
Pop: 1,495 (1990); 1,535 (1980) **Pop Density:** 23.9
Land: 62.5 sq. mi.; **Water:** 0.0 sq. mi.

Reynolds
Town
ZIP: 47980 Lat: 40-44-55 N Long: 86-52-25 W
Pop: 528 (1990); 632 (1980) **Pop Density:** 1056.0
Land: 0.5 sq. mi.; **Water:** 0.0 sq. mi. **Elev:** 700 ft.
Name origin: For its founder, Benjamin Reynolds.

Round Grove
Township
Lat: 40-36-15 N Long: 87-02-12 W
Pop: 250 (1990); 282 (1980) **Pop Density:** 7.1
Land: 35.4 sq. mi.; **Water:** 0.0 sq. mi.

Union
Township
ZIP: 47960 Lat: 40-44-55 N Long: 86-46-14 W
Pop: 9,265 (1990); 9,357 (1980) **Pop Density:** 222.2
Land: 41.7 sq. mi.; **Water:** 2.1 sq. mi.

West Point
Township
Lat: 40-41-26 N Long: 87-01-01 W
Pop: 418 (1990); 430 (1980) **Pop Density:** 7.8
Land: 53.5 sq. mi.; **Water:** 0.1 sq. mi.

Wolcott
Town
ZIP: 47995 Lat: 40-45-29 N Long: 87-02-36 W
Pop: 886 (1990); 923 (1980) **Pop Density:** 1772.0
Land: 0.5 sq. mi.; **Water:** 0.0 sq. mi. **Elev:** 718 ft.
Founded 1861.
Name origin: Named in 1861 by and for its founders, the Wolcott family.

Whitley County
County Seat: Columbia City (ZIP: 46725)

Pop: 27,651 (1990); 26,215 (1980) **Pop Density:** 82.4
Land: 335.5 sq. mi.; **Water:** 2.4 sq. mi. **Area Code:** 219
In northeastern IN, west of Ft. Wayne; established Feb 7, 1835 from Huntington County.
Name origin: For Col. William Whitley (1749–1813), soldier in the War of 1812 who enlisted at the age of 63.

Churubusco
Town
ZIP: 46723 Lat: 41-13-56 N Long: 85-19-17 W
Pop: 1,781 (1990); 1,638 (1980) **Pop Density:** 2226.3
Land: 0.8 sq. mi.; **Water:** 0.0 sq. mi. **Elev:** 909 ft.

Cleveland
Township
Lat: 41-03-58 N Long: 85-37-33 W
Pop: 3,215 (1990); 3,071 (1980) **Pop Density:** 65.5
Land: 49.1 sq. mi.; **Water:** 0.0 sq. mi.

Columbia
Township
ZIP: 46725 Lat: 41-08-05 N Long: 85-30-44 W
Pop: 8,134 (1990); 7,694 (1980) **Pop Density:** 221.6
Land: 36.7 sq. mi.; **Water:** 0.0 sq. mi.

Columbia City
City
ZIP: 46725 Lat: 41-09-30 N Long: 85-29-05 W
Pop: 5,706 (1990); 5,091 (1980) **Pop Density:** 2037.9
Land: 2.8 sq. mi.; **Water:** 0.0 sq. mi. **Elev:** 861 ft.
Established 1839.
Name origin: Feminine form of Columbus, a poetic and honorific reference to Christopher Columbus (1451–1506) and America.

Etna-Troy
Township
ZIP: 46764 Lat: 41-15-37 N Long: 85-35-30 W
Pop: 1,564 (1990); 1,453 (1980) **Pop Density:** 44.4
Land: 35.2 sq. mi.; **Water:** 0.9 sq. mi.

Jefferson
Township
ZIP: 46725 Lat: 41-02-40 N Long: 85-24-11 W
Pop: 1,855 (1990); 1,697 (1980) **Pop Density:** 52.8
Land: 35.1 sq. mi.; **Water:** 0.0 sq. mi.

Larwill
Town
ZIP: 46764 Lat: 41-10-43 N Long: 85-37-27 W
Pop: 219 (1990); 286 (1980) **Pop Density:** 1095.0
Land: 0.2 sq. mi.; **Water:** 0.0 sq. mi. **Elev:** 940 ft.
Name origin: For engineers William and Joseph Larwill, who supervised the construction of the railroad through town.

INDIANA, Whitley County

Richland
Township
ZIP: 46764 **Lat:** 41-09-24 N **Long:** 85-36-55 W
Pop: 1,492 (1990); 1,452 (1980) **Pop Density:** 40.3
Land: 37.0 sq. mi.; **Water:** 0.1 sq. mi.

Smith
Township
ZIP: 46723 **Lat:** 41-13-21 N **Long:** 85-22-04 W
Pop: 5,082 (1990); 4,821 (1980) **Pop Density:** 145.6
Land: 34.9 sq. mi.; **Water:** 0.4 sq. mi.

South Whitley
Town
ZIP: 46787 **Lat:** 41-05-08 N **Long:** 85-37-43 W
Pop: 1,482 (1990); 1,575 (1980) **Pop Density:** 2470.0
Land: 0.6 sq. mi.; **Water:** 0.0 sq. mi. **Elev:** 808 ft.
Founded 1838.
Name origin: For its county.

Thorncreek
Township
ZIP: 46725 **Lat:** 41-13-15 N **Long:** 85-29-03 W
Pop: 3,299 (1990); 3,036 (1980) **Pop Density:** 93.7
Land: 35.2 sq. mi.; **Water:** 0.9 sq. mi.

Tri-Lakes
CDP
Lat: 41-13-15 N **Long:** 85-29-03 W
Pop: 3,299 (1990); 1,356 (1980) **Pop Density:** 93.7
Land: 35.2 sq. mi.; **Water:** 0.9 sq. mi.

Union
Township
ZIP: 46725 **Lat:** 41-07-58 N **Long:** 85-23-43 W
Pop: 1,898 (1990); 1,801 (1980) **Pop Density:** 51.4
Land: 36.9 sq. mi.; **Water:** 0.1 sq. mi.

Washington
Township
ZIP: 46725 **Lat:** 41-02-58 N **Long:** 85-30-21 W
Pop: 1,112 (1990); 1,190 (1980) **Pop Density:** 31.4
Land: 35.4 sq. mi.; **Water:** 0.0 sq. mi.

Index to Places and Counties in Indiana

Abington (Wayne) Township............*260*
Aboite (Allen) Township....................*175*
Adams (Allen) Township...................*175*
Adams (Carroll) Township................*180*
Adams (Cass) Township....................*181*
Adams (Decatur) Township...............*188*
Adams (Hamilton) Township.............*201*
Adams (Madison) Township...............*222*
Adams (Morgan) Township................*230*
Adams (Parke) Township...................*235*
Adams (Ripley) Township..................*242*
Adams (Warren) Township................*257*
Adams County..................................*174*
Addison (Shelby) Township...............*246*
Advance (Boone) Town.....................*179*
Akron (Fulton) Town.........................*197*
Alamo (Montgomery) Town...............*229*
Albany (Delaware) Town...................*190*
Albany (Randolph) Town...................*241*
Albion (Noble) Town.........................*232*
Albion (Noble) Township...................*232*
Alexandria (Madison) City................*222*
Alfordsville (Daviess) Town...............*186*
Allen (Miami) Township....................*227*
Allen (Noble) Township.....................*232*
Allen County....................................*175*
Alton (Crawford) Town.....................*185*
Altona (Dekalb) Town.......................*189*
Ambia (Benton) Town........................*177*
Amboy (Miami) Town........................*227*
Amo (Hendricks) Town......................*204*
Anderson (Madison) City..................*222*
Anderson (Madison) Township..........*222*
Anderson (Perry) Township...............*236*
Anderson (Rush) Township................*243*
Anderson (Warrick) Township...........*258*
Andrews (Huntington) Town.............*208*
Angola (Steuben) City.......................*248*
Arcadia (Hamilton) Town..................*201*
Argos (Marshall) Town......................*225*
Armstrong (Vanderburgh) Township.*254*
Ashland (Morgan) Township..............*230*
Ashley (Dekalb) Town.......................*189*
Ashley (Steuben) Town.....................*248*
Atlanta (Hamilton) Town...................*201*
Attica (Fountain) City.......................*195*
Aubbeenaubbee (Fulton) Township ..*197*
Auburn (Dekalb) City........................*189*
Aurora (Dearborn) City.....................*187*
Austin (Scott) Town...........................*245*
Avilla (Noble) Town...........................*232*
Bainbridge (Dubois) Township..........*191*
Bainbridge (Putnam) Town................*240*
Baker (Morgan) Township.................*230*
Bargersville (Johnson) Town.............*214*
Barkley (Jasper) Township................*210*
Barr (Daviess) Township...................*186*
Bartholomew County.......................*176*
Barton (Gibson) Township................*198*
Batesville (Franklin) City..................*196*
Batesville (Ripley) City.....................*242*
Bath (Franklin) Township..................*196*
Battle Ground (Tippecanoe) Town ...*251*
Baugo (Elkhart) Township.................*192*
Bean Blossom (Monroe) Township...*228*
Bearcreek (Jay) Township.................*211*
Beaver (Newton) Township...............*231*
Beaver (Pulaski) Township................*239*
Bedford (Lawrence) City...................*221*
Beech Creek (Greene) Township.......*200*

Beech Grove (Marion) City..............*224*
Benton (Elkhart) Township...............*192*
Benton (Monroe) Township...............*228*
Benton County...................................*177*
Berne (Adams) City..........................*174*
Bethany (Morgan) Town...................*230*
Bethel (Posey) Township...................*238*
Bethlehem (Cass) Township..............*181*
Bethlehem (Clark) Township.............*182*
Beverly Shores (Porter) Town..........*237*
Bicknell (Knox) City..........................*215*
Big Creek (White) Township.............*262*
Bigger (Jennings) Township..............*213*
Birdseye (Dubois) Town....................*191*
Black (Posey) Township....................*238*
Blackford County............................*178*
Bloomfield (Greene) Town................*200*
Bloomfield (Lagrange) Township......*217*
Bloomingdale (Parke) Town..............*235*
Blooming Grove (Franklin)
  Township.......................................*196*
Bloomington (Monroe) City..............*228*
Bloomington (Monroe) Township.....*228*
Blountsville (Henry) Town................*206*
Blue Creek (Adams) Township..........*174*
Blue River (Hancock) Township.......*202*
Blue River (Harrison) Township.......*203*
Blue River (Henry) Township...........*206*
Blue River (Johnson) Township........*214*
Bluffton (Wells) City.........................*261*
Bogard (Daviess) Township..............*186*
Bolivar (Benton) Township...............*177*
Bono (Lawrence) Township..............*221*
Boon (Warrick) Township.................*258*
Boone (Cass) Township....................*181*
Boone (Crawford) Township............*185*
Boone (Dubois) Township................*191*
Boone (Harrison) Township..............*203*
Boone (Madison) Township..............*222*
Boone (Porter) Township..................*237*
Boone County..................................*179*
Boonville (Warrick) City..................*258*
Boston (Wayne) Town......................*260*
Boston (Wayne) Township................*260*
Boswell (Benton) Town.....................*177*
Bourbon (Marshall) Town.................*225*
Bourbon (Marshall) Township..........*225*
Brandywine (Hancock) Township.....*202*
Brandywine (Shelby) Township........*246*
Brazil (Clay) City..............................*183*
Brazil (Clay) Township.....................*183*
Bremen (Marshall) Town..................*225*
Bright (Dearborn) CDP.....................*187*
Bristol (Elkhart) Town......................*192*
Brook (Newton) Town.......................*231*
Brooklyn (Morgan) Town..................*230*
Brooksburg (Jefferson) Town...........*212*
Brookston (White) Town...................*262*
Brookville (Franklin) Town...............*196*
Brookville (Franklin) Township........*196*
Brown (Hancock) Township.............*202*
Brown (Hendricks) Township...........*204*
Brown (Montgomery) Township.......*229*
Brown (Morgan) Township...............*230*
Brown (Ripley) Township.................*242*
Brown (Washington) Township........*259*
Brown County..................................*180*
Brownsburg (Hendricks) Town.........*204*
Brownstown (Jackson) Town............*209*
Brownstown (Jackson) Township.....*209*

Brownsville (Union) Township.........*253*
Bruceville (Knox) Town....................*215*
Bryant (Jay) Town.............................*211*
Buck Creek (Hancock) Township.....*202*
Bunker Hill (Miami) Town................*227*
Burket (Kosciusko) Town..................*216*
Burlington (Carroll) Town................*180*
Burlington (Carroll) Township..........*180*
Burnettsville (White) Town...............*262*
Burns Harbor (Porter) Town............*237*
Busseron (Knox) Township...............*215*
Butler (Dekalb) City..........................*189*
Butler (Dekalb) Township.................*189*
Butler (Franklin) Township...............*196*
Butler (Miami) Township..................*227*
Cadi (Henry) Town............................*206*
Caesar Creek (Dearborn) Township..*187*
Cain (Fountain) Township.................*195*
California (Starke) Township............*248*
Calumet (Lake) Township.................*218*
Cambridge City (Wayne) Town........*260*
Camden (Carroll) Town....................*180*
Campbell (Jennings) Township.........*213*
Campbell (Warrick) Township..........*258*
Campbellsburg (Washington) Town ..*259*
Cannelburg (Daviess) Town..............*186*
Cannelton (Perry) City......................*236*
Carbon (Clay) Town..........................*183*
Carefree (Crawford) Town................*185*
Carlisle (Sullivan) Town...................*250*
Carmel (Hamilton) City....................*201*
Carpenter (Jasper) Township............*210*
Carr (Clark) Township......................*182*
Carr (Jackson) Township..................*209*
Carroll County................................*180*
Carrollton (Carroll) Township..........*180*
Carter (Spencer) Township...............*247*
Carthage (Rush) Town......................*243*
Cass (Clay) Township.......................*183*
Cass (Dubois) Township...................*191*
Cass (Greene) Township...................*200*
Cass (La Porte) Township.................*220*
Cass (Ohio) Township.......................*233*
Cass (Pulaski) Township...................*239*
Cass (Sullivan) Township..................*250*
Cass (White) Township.....................*262*
Cass County....................................*181*
Castleton (Marion) Town..................*224*
Cayuga (Vermillion) Town................*254*
Cedar Creek (Allen) Township..........*175*
Cedar Creek (Lake) Township..........*218*
Cedar Grove (Franklin) Town...........*196*
Cedar Lake (Lake) Town..................*218*
Center (Benton) Township................*177*
Center (Boone) Township.................*179*
Center (Clinton) Township...............*184*
Center (Dearborn) Township............*187*
Center (Delaware) Township............*190*
Center (Gibson) Township................*198*
Center (Grant) Township..................*199*
Center (Greene) Township................*200*
Center (Hancock) Township.............*202*
Center (Hendricks) Township...........*204*
Center (Howard) Township...............*207*
Center (Jennings) Township.............*213*
Center (La Porte) Township.............*220*
Center (Lake) Township....................*218*
Center (Marion) Township................*224*
Center (Marshall) Township.............*225*
Center (Martin) Township.................*226*

INDIANA

Center (Porter) Township 237
Center (Posey) Township 238
Center (Ripley) Township 242
Center (Rush) Township 243
Center (Starke) Township 248
Center (Union) Township 253
Center (Vanderburgh) Township 254
Center (Wayne) Township 260
Center Point (Clay) Town 183
Centerville (Wayne) City 260
Centre (St. Joseph) Township 244
Chalmers (White) Town 262
Chandler (Warrick) Town 258
Charlestown (Clark) City 182
Charlestown (Clark) Township 182
Chester (Wabash) Township 256
Chester (Wells) Township 261
Chesterfield (Delaware) Town 190
Chesterfield (Madison) Town 222
Chesterton (Porter) Town 237
Chrisney (Spencer) Town 247
Churubusco (Whitley) Town 263
Cicero (Hamilton) Town 201
Cicero (Tipton) Township 252
Clark (Johnson) Township 214
Clark (Montgomery) Township 229
Clark (Perry) Township 236
Clark County 182
Clarks Hill (Tippecanoe) Town 251
Clarksville (Clark) Town 182
Clay (Bartholomew) Township 176
Clay (Carroll) Township 180
Clay (Cass) Township 181
Clay (Dearborn) Township 187
Clay (Decatur) Township 188
Clay (Hamilton) Township 201
Clay (Hendricks) Township 204
Clay (Howard) Township 207
Clay (Kosciusko) Township 216
Clay (Lagrange) Township 217
Clay (Miami) Township 227
Clay (Morgan) Township 230
Clay (Owen) Township 234
Clay (Pike) Township 236
Clay (Spencer) Township 247
Clay (St. Joseph) Township 244
Clay (Wayne) Township 260
Clay City (Clay) Town 183
Clay County 183
Claypool (Kosciusko) Town 216
Clayton (Hendricks) Town 204
Clear Creek (Huntington) Township .208
Clear Creek (Monroe) Township 228
Clear Lake (Steuben) Town 249
Clear Lake (Steuben) Township 249
Clearspring (Lagrange) Township 217
Clermont (Marion) Town 224
Cleveland (Elkhart) Township 192
Cleveland (Whitley) Township 263
Clifford (Bartholomew) Town 176
Clifty (Bartholomew) Township 176
Clinton (Boone) Township 179
Clinton (Cass) Township 181
Clinton (Decatur) Township 188
Clinton (Elkhart) Township 192
Clinton (La Porte) Township 220
Clinton (Putnam) Township 240
Clinton (Vermillion) City 254
Clinton (Vermillion) Township 255
Clinton County 184
Cloverdale (Putnam) City 240
Cloverdale (Putnam) Township 240
Coal Creek (Montgomery) Township 229
Coatesville (Hendricks) Town 205
Colfax (Clinton) Town 184

Colfax (Newton) Township 231
Collegeville (Jasper) CDP 210
Columbia (Dubois) Township 191
Columbia (Fayette) Township 194
Columbia (Gibson) Township 198
Columbia (Jennings) Township 213
Columbia (Whitley) Township 263
Columbia City (Whitley) City 263
Columbus (Bartholomew) City 176
Columbus (Bartholomew) Township.176
Concord (Dekalb) Township 189
Concord (Elkhart) Township 192
Connersville (Fayette) City 194
Connersville (Fayette) Township 194
Converse (Grant) Town 199
Converse (Miami) Town 227
Coolspring (La Porte) Township 220
Corunna (Dekalb) Town 189
Corydon (Harrison) Town 203
Cotton (Switzerland) Township 251
Country Club Heights (Madison)
   Town 222
Covington (Fountain) City 195
Craig (Switzerland) Township 251
Crandall (Harrison) Town 203
Crane (Martin) Town 226
Crawford County 185
Crawfordsville (Montgomery) City ...229
Cromwell (Noble) Town 232
Crothersville (Jackson) Town 209
Crown Point (Lake) City 218
Crows Nest (Marion) Town 224
Culver (Marshall) Town 225
Cumberland (Hancock) Town 202
Cumberland (Marion) Town 224
Curry (Sullivan) Township 250
Cynthiana (Posey) Town 238
Dale (Spencer) Town 247
Daleville (Delaware) Town 190
Dallas (Huntington) Township 208
Dalton (Wayne) Township 260
Dana (Vermillion) Town 255
Danville (Hendricks) Town 205
Darlington (Montgomery) Town 229
Darmstadt (Vanderburgh) Town 254
Daviess County 186
Davis (Fountain) Township 195
Davis (Starke) Township 248
Dayton (Tippecanoe) Town 251
Dearborn County 187
Decatur (Adams) City 174
Decatur (Marion) Township 224
Decatur County 188
Decker (Knox) Town 215
Decker (Knox) Township 215
Deer Creek (Carroll) Township 180
Deer Creek (Cass) Township 181
Deer Creek (Miami) Township 227
Dekalb County 189
Delaware (Delaware) Township 190
Delaware (Hamilton) Township 201
Delaware (Ripley) Township 242
Delaware County 190
Delphi (Carroll) City 180
Democrat (Carroll) Township 181
De Motte (Jasper) Town 210
Denver (Miami) Town 227
Dewey (La Porte) Township 220
Dick Johnson (Clay) Township 183
Dillsboro (Dearborn) Town 187
Driftwood (Jackson) Township 209
Dublin (Wayne) Town 260
Dubois County 191
Duck Creek (Madison) Township 222
Dudley (Henry) Township 206

American Places Dictionary

Dugger (Sullivan) Town 250
Dune Acres (Porter) Town 237
Dunkirk (Blackford) City 178
Dunkirk (Jay) City 211
Dunlap (Elkhart) CDP 192
Dunreith (Henry) Town 206
Dupont (Jefferson) Town 212
Dyer (Lake) Town 218
Eagle (Boone) Township 179
Eagle Creek (Lake) Township 218
Earl Park (Benton) Town 177
East Chicago (Lake) City 218
East Germantown (Wayne) Town 260
Eaton (Delaware) Town 190
Economy (Wayne) Town 260
Eden (Lagrange) Township 217
Edgewood (Madison) Town 222
Edinburgh (Bartholomew) Town 176
Edinburgh (Johnson) Town 214
Edwardsport (Knox) Town 215
Eel (Cass) Township 181
Eel River (Allen) Township 175
Eel River (Hendricks) Township 205
Elberfeld (Warrick) Town 258
Elizabeth (Harrison) Town 203
Elizabethtown (Bartholomew) Town.176
Elkhart (Elkhart) City 192
Elkhart (Elkhart) Township 193
Elkhart (Noble) Township 232
Elkhart County 192
Ellettsville (Monroe) Town 228
Elmore (Daviess) Township 186
Elnora (Daviess) Town 186
Elwood (Madison) City 222
Elwood (Tipton) City 252
English (Crawford) Town 185
Erie (Miami) Township 227
Ervin (Howard) Township 207
Etna (Kosciusko) Township 216
Etna Green (Kosciusko) Town 216
Etna-Troy (Whitley) Township 263
Eugene (Vermillion) Township 255
Evansville (Vanderburgh) City 254
Fairbanks (Sullivan) Township 250
Fairfield (Dekalb) Township 189
Fairfield (Franklin) Township 196
Fairfield (Tippecanoe) Township 251
Fairland (Shelby) CDP 246
Fairmount (Grant) Town 199
Fairmount (Grant) Township 199
Fairplay (Greene) Township 200
Fairview (Fayette) Township 194
Fairview Park (Vermillion) Town 255
Fall Creek (Hamilton) Township 202
Fall Creek (Henry) Township 206
Fall Creek (Madison) Township 223
Farmersburg (Sullivan) Township 250
Farmland (Randolph) Town 241
Fayette (Vigo) Township 255
Fayette County 194
Ferdinand (Dubois) Town 191
Ferdinand (Dubois) Township 192
Fillmore (Putnam) Town 240
Finley (Scott) Township 245
Fishers (Hamilton) Town 202
Flat Rock (Bartholomew) Township .176
Flora (Carroll) Town 181
Florida (Parke) Township 235
Floyd (Putnam) Township 240
Floyd County 194
Forest (Clinton) Township 184
Fort Branch (Gibson) Town 198
Fortville (Hancock) Town 202
Fort Wayne (Allen) City 175
Fountain City (Wayne) Town 260

Fountain County *195*	Green (Hancock) Township *202*	Harrison (Henry) Township *206*
Fowler (Benton) Town *177*	Green (Madison) Township *223*	Harrison (Howard) Township *207*
Fowlerton (Grant) Town *199*	Green (Marshall) Township *225*	Harrison (Knox) Township *215*
Francesville (Pulaski) Town *239*	Green (Morgan) Township *230*	Harrison (Kosciusko) Township *216*
Francisco (Gibson) Town *198*	Green (Noble) Township *232*	Harrison (Miami) Township *227*
Frankfort (Clinton) City *184*	Green (Randolph) Township *241*	Harrison (Morgan) Township *230*
Franklin (Dekalb) Township *189*	Greencastle (Putnam) City *240*	Harrison (Owen) Township *234*
Franklin (Floyd) Township *194*	Greencastle (Putnam) Township *240*	Harrison (Pulaski) Township *239*
Franklin (Grant) Township *199*	Greendale (Dearborn) Town *187*	Harrison (Spencer) Township *247*
Franklin (Harrison) Township *203*	Greene (Jay) Township *211*	Harrison (Union) Township *253*
Franklin (Hendricks) Township *205*	Greene (Parke) Township *235*	Harrison (Vigo) Township *255*
Franklin (Henry) Township *206*	Greene (St. Joseph) Township *244*	Harrison (Wayne) Township *261*
Franklin (Johnson) City *214*	Greene (Wayne) Township *260*	Harrison (Wells) Township *261*
Franklin (Johnson) Township *214*	**Greene County** *200*	**Harrison County** *203*
Franklin (Kosciusko) Township *216*	Greenfield (Hancock) City *202*	Hart (Warrick) Township *258*
Franklin (Marion) Township *224*	Greenfield (Lagrange) Township *217*	Hartford (Adams) Township *174*
Franklin (Montgomery) Township *229*	Greenfield (Orange) Township *233*	Hartford City (Blackford) City *178*
Franklin (Owen) Township *234*	Greensboro (Henry) Town *206*	Hartsville (Bartholomew) Town *176*
Franklin (Pulaski) Township *239*	Greensboro (Henry) Township *206*	Haubstadt (Gibson) Town *198*
Franklin (Putnam) Township *240*	Greensburg (Decatur) City *188*	Haw Creek (Bartholomew)
Franklin (Randolph) Township *241*	Greensfork (Randolph) Township *241*	Township *177*
Franklin (Ripley) Township *242*	Greens Fork (Wayne) Town *260*	Hazleton (Gibson) Town *198*
Franklin (Washington) Township *259*	Greentown (Howard) Town *207*	Hebron (Porter) Town *237*
Franklin (Wayne) Township *260*	Greenville (Floyd) Town *195*	Helt (Vermillion) Township *255*
Franklin County *196*	Greenville (Floyd) Township *195*	Hendricks (Shelby) Township *246*
Frankton (Madison) Town *223*	Greenwood (Johnson) City *214*	**Hendricks County** *204*
Fredericksburg (Washington) Town .. *259*	Greer (Warrick) Township *258*	Henry (Fulton) Township *197*
Fremont (Steuben) Town *249*	Gregg (Morgan) Township *230*	Henry (Henry) Township *206*
Fremont (Steuben) Township *249*	Griffin (Posey) Town *239*	**Henry County** *206*
French (Adams) Township *174*	Griffith (Lake) Town *219*	Hensley (Johnson) Township *214*
French Lick (Orange) Town *233*	Grissom Air Force Base (Cass) Military	Heth (Harrison) Township *203*
French Lick (Orange) Township *233*	Facility *181*	Hickory Grove (Benton) Township ... *177*
Fugit (Decatur) Township *188*	Grissom Air Force Base (Miami) Mili-	Hidden Valley (Dearborn) CDP *187*
Fulton (Fountain) Township *195*	tary Facility *227*	Highland (Franklin) Township *196*
Fulton (Fulton) Town *197*	Guilford (Hendricks) Township *205*	Highland (Greene) Township *200*
Fulton County *197*	Gulivoire Park (St. Joseph) CDP *244*	Highland (Lake) Town *219*
Galena (Floyd) CDP *194*	Guthrie (Lawrence) Township *221*	Highland (Vanderburgh) CDP *254*
Galena (La Porte) Township *220*	Haddon (Sullivan) Township *250*	Highland (Vermillion) Township *255*
Galveston (Cass) Town *181*	Hagerstown (Wayne) Town *261*	Hillsboro (Fountain) Town *195*
Garrett (Dekalb) City *189*	Halbert (Martin) Township *226*	Hobart (Lake) City *219*
Gary (Lake) City *218*	Hall (Dubois) Township *192*	Hobart (Lake) Township *219*
Gas City (Grant) City *199*	Hamblen (Brown) Township *180*	Hogan (Dearborn) Township *187*
Gaston (Delaware) Town *190*	Hamilton (Dekalb) Town *189*	Holland (Dubois) Town *192*
Geneva (Adams) Town *174*	Hamilton (Delaware) Township *190*	Holton (Ripley) Town *242*
Geneva (Jennings) Township *213*	Hamilton (Jackson) Township *209*	Homecroft (Marion) Town *224*
Gentryville (Spencer) Town *247*	Hamilton (Steuben) Town *249*	Honey Creek (Howard) Township ... *207*
Georgetown (Floyd) Town *194*	Hamilton (Sullivan) Township *250*	Honey Creek (Vigo) Township *255*
Georgetown (Floyd) Township *195*	**Hamilton County** *201*	Honey Creek (White) Township *262*
Georgetown (St. Joseph) CDP *244*	Hamlet (Starke) Town *248*	Hope (Bartholomew) Town *177*
German (Bartholomew) Township *176*	Hammond (Lake) City *219*	Howard (Howard) Township *207*
German (Marshall) Township *225*	Hammond (Spencer) Township *247*	Howard (Parke) Township *235*
German (St. Joseph) Township *244*	**Hancock County** *202*	Howard (Washington) Township *259*
German (Vanderburgh) Township *254*	Hanging Grove (Jasper) Township ... *210*	**Howard County** *207*
Gibson (Washington) Township *259*	Hanna (La Porte) Township *220*	Hudson (La Porte) Township *220*
Gibson County *198*	Hanover (Jefferson) Town *212*	Hudson (Steuben) Town *249*
Gilboa (Benton) Township *177*	Hanover (Jefferson) Township *212*	Huff (Spencer) Township *247*
Gill (Sullivan) Township *250*	Hanover (Lake) Township *219*	Huntertown (Allen) Town *175*
Gillam (Jasper) Township *210*	Hanover (Shelby) Township *246*	Huntingburg (Dubois) City *192*
Glenwood (Fayette) Town *194*	Harbison (Dubois) Township *192*	Huntington (Huntington) City *208*
Glenwood (Rush) Town *243*	Hardinsburg (Washington) Town *259*	Huntington (Huntington) Township . *208*
Goodland (Newton) Town *231*	Harmony (Clay) Town *183*	**Huntington County** *208*
Goshen (Elkhart) City *193*	Harmony (Posey) Township *239*	Hymera (Sullivan) Town *250*
Gosport (Owen) Town *234*	Harmony (Union) Township *253*	Indianapolis (Marion) City *224*
Grabill (Allen) Town *175*	Harris (St. Joseph) Township *244*	Indian Creek (Lawrence) Township .. *221*
Graham (Jefferson) Township *212*	Harrison (Bartholomew) Township ... *176*	Indian Creek (Monroe) Township *228*
Grandview (Spencer) Town *247*	Harrison (Blackford) Township *178*	Indian Creek (Pulaski) Township *239*
Granger (St. Joseph) CDP *244*	Harrison (Boone) Township *179*	Indian Heights (Howard) CDP *207*
Grant (Benton) Township *177*	Harrison (Cass) Township *182*	Indian Village (St. Joseph) Town *244*
Grant (Dekalb) Township *189*	Harrison (Clay) Township *184*	Ingalls (Madison) Town *223*
Grant (Greene) Township *200*	Harrison (Daviess) Township *186*	Iroquois (Newton) Township *231*
Grant (Newton) Township *231*	Harrison (Dearborn) Township *187*	Jackson (Allen) Township *175*
Grant County *199*	Harrison (Delaware) Township *191*	Jackson (Bartholomew) Township ... *177*
Grass (Spencer) Township *247*	Harrison (Elkhart) Township *193*	Jackson (Blackford) Township *178*
Grassy Fork (Jackson) Township *209*	Harrison (Fayette) Township *194*	Jackson (Boone) Township *179*
Green (Grant) Township *199*	Harrison (Harrison) Township *203*	Jackson (Brown) Township *180*

INDIANA

American Places Dictionary

Jackson (Carroll) Township...........181	Jefferson (Wayne) Township...........261	Lakes of the Four Seasons (Porter)
Jackson (Cass) Township...............182	Jefferson (Wells) Township............262	CDP.....................................237
Jackson (Clay) Township................184	Jefferson (Whitley) Township..........263	Lake Station (Lake) City................219
Jackson (Clinton) Township............184	**Jefferson County**........................212	Lakeville (St. Joseph) Town...........244
Jackson (Dearborn) Township.........187	Jeffersonville (Clark) City...............182	Lancaster (Huntington) Township....208
Jackson (Decatur) Township..........188	Jeffersonville (Clark) Township........182	Lancaster (Jefferson) Township.......212
Jackson (Dekalb) Township............190	Jennings (Crawford) Township........185	Lancaster (Wells) Township............262
Jackson (Dubois) Township............192	Jennings (Fayette) Township..........194	Lane (Warrick) Township...............258
Jackson (Elkhart) Township............193	Jennings (Owen) Township.............234	Lanesville (Harrison) Town.............203
Jackson (Fayette) Township............194	Jennings (Scott) Township..............245	La Paz (Marshall) Town..................226
Jackson (Fountain) Township..........195	**Jennings County**.........................213	Lapel (Madison) Town...................223
Jackson (Greene) Township............200	Johnson (Clinton) Township...........184	La Porte (La Porte) City.................220
Jackson (Hamilton) Township..........202	Johnson (Crawford) Township........185	**La Porte County**.........................220
Jackson (Hancock) Township..........203	Johnson (Gibson) Township...........198	Larwill (Whitley) Town....................263
Jackson (Harrison) Township..........203	Johnson (Knox) Township..............215	Laughery (Ripley) Township...........243
Jackson (Howard) Township...........208	Johnson (La Porte) Township.........220	Lauramie (Tippecanoe) Township....252
Jackson (Huntington) Township.......208	Johnson (Lagrange) Township.......217	Laurel (Franklin) Town....................196
Jackson (Jackson) Township...........209	Johnson (Ripley) Township............243	Laurel (Franklin) Township..............196
Jackson (Jay) Township.................211	Johnson (Scott) Township..............245	Lawrence (Marion) City..................224
Jackson (Kosciusko) Township........216	**Johnson County**.........................214	Lawrence (Marion) Township..........224
Jackson (Madison) Township..........223	Jonesboro (Grant) Town................199	Lawrenceburg (Dearborn) City........187
Jackson (Miami) Township.............227	Jonesville (Bartholomew) Town.......177	Lawrenceburg (Dearborn) Township.187
Jackson (Morgan) Township...........230	Jordan (Jasper) Township..............210	**Lawrence County**........................221
Jackson (Newton) Township...........231	Jordan (Warren) Township.............257	Leavenworth (Crawford) Town........185
Jackson (Orange) Township...........233	Judson (Parke) Town....................235	Lebanon (Boone) City...................179
Jackson (Owen) Township..............234	Kankakee (Jasper) Township..........210	Leesburg (Kosciusko) Town............216
Jackson (Parke) Township..............235	Kankakee (La Porte) Township........220	Leopold (Perry) Township..............236
Jackson (Porter) Township.............237	Keener (Jasper) Township..............210	Lewis (Clay) Township...................184
Jackson (Putnam) Township...........240	Kelso (Dearborn) Township............187	Lewisville (Henry) Town..................206
Jackson (Randolph) Township.........241	Kempton (Tipton) Town..................252	Lexington (Scott) Township.............245
Jackson (Ripley) Township..............242	Kendallville (Noble) City.................232	Liberty (Carroll) Township...............181
Jackson (Rush) Township..............243	Kennard (Henry) Town..................206	Liberty (Crawford) Township...........185
Jackson (Shelby) Township.............246	Kent (Warren) Township.................257	Liberty (Delaware) Township...........191
Jackson (Spencer) Township..........247	Kentland (Newton) Town................231	Liberty (Fulton) Township...............197
Jackson (Starke) Township.............248	Kewanna (Fulton) Town..................197	Liberty (Grant) Township................199
Jackson (Steuben) Township..........249	Keyser (Dekalb) Township..............190	Liberty (Hendricks) Township..........205
Jackson (Sullivan) Township...........250	Kingman (Fountain) Town..............195	Liberty (Henry) Township...............206
Jackson (Tippecanoe) Township......251	Kingsbury (La Porte) Town.............220	Liberty (Howard) Township.............208
Jackson (Washington) Township......259	Kingsford Heights (La Porte) Town..220	Liberty (Parke) Township................235
Jackson (Wayne) Township............261	Kirkland (Adams) Township............174	Liberty (Porter) Township...............237
Jackson (Wells) Township..............262	Kirklin (Clinton) Town....................184	Liberty (Shelby) Township..............246
Jackson (White) Township..............262	Kirklin (Clinton) Township..............184	Liberty (St. Joseph) Township.........244
Jackson County..........................209	Knight (Vanderburgh) Township......254	Liberty (Tipton) Township...............253
Jamestown (Boone) Town.............179	Knightstown (Henry) Town.............206	Liberty (Union) Town.....................253
Jamestown (Hendricks) Town........205	Knightsville (Clay) Town.................184	Liberty (Union) Township...............253
Jamestown (Steuben) Township.....249	Knox (Jay) Township.....................211	Liberty (Wabash) Township............256
Jasonville (Greene) City.................200	Knox (Starke) City........................248	Liberty (Warren) Township.............257
Jasper (Dubois) City.....................192	**Knox County**..............................215	Liberty (Wells) Township................262
Jasper County............................210	Kokomo (Howard) City..................208	Liberty (White) Township...............262
Jay County................................211	Koontz Lake (Marshall) CDP..........226	Licking (Blackford) Township..........178
Jefferson (Adams) Township..........174	Koontz Lake (Starke) CDP.............248	Ligonier (Noble) City.....................232
Jefferson (Allen) Township.............175	**Kosciusko County**.......................216	Lima (Lagrange) Township.............218
Jefferson (Boone) Township..........179	Kouts (Porter) Town.....................237	Lincoln (Hendricks) Township.........205
Jefferson (Carroll) Township..........181	Laconia (Harrison) Town...............203	Lincoln (La Porte) Township...........220
Jefferson (Cass) Township.............182	La Crosse (La Porte) Town.............220	Lincoln (Newton) Township............231
Jefferson (Dubois) Township..........192	Ladoga (Montgomery) Town...........229	Lincoln (St. Joseph) Township........244
Jefferson (Elkhart) Township..........193	Lafayette (Allen) Township.............175	Lincoln (White) Township...............263
Jefferson (Grant) Township...........199	Lafayette (Floyd) Township............195	Linden (Montgomery) Town............229
Jefferson (Greene) Township.........200	Lafayette (Madison) Township........223	Linton (Greene) City.....................200
Jefferson (Henry) Township...........206	Lafayette (Owen) Township............234	Linton (Vigo) Township..................255
Jefferson (Huntington) Township.....208	Lafayette (Tippecanoe) City...........252	Little York (Washington) Town........259
Jefferson (Jay) Township...............211	La Fontaine (Wabash) Town..........256	Livonia (Washington) Town............259
Jefferson (Kosciusko) Township.....216	Lagrange (Lagrange) Town............217	Lizton (Hendricks) Town................205
Jefferson (Miami) Township...........227	**Lagrange County**........................217	Locke (Elkhart) Township...............193
Jefferson (Morgan) Township.........230	Lagro (Wabash) Town..................256	Lockhart (Pike) Township...............237
Jefferson (Newton) Township.........231	Lagro (Wabash) Township.............256	Logan (Dearborn) Township...........188
Jefferson (Noble) Township...........232	Lake (Allen) Township...................175	Logan (Fountain) Township............195
Jefferson (Owen) Township...........234	Lake (Kosciusko) Township............216	Logan (Pike) Township..................237
Jefferson (Pike) Township.............236	Lake (Newton) Township...............231	Logansport (Cass) City.................182
Jefferson (Pulaski) Township.........239	**Lake County**..............................218	Long Beach (La Porte) Town..........220
Jefferson (Putnam) Township........240	Lake Dalecarlia (Lake) CDP............219	Loogootee (Martin) City................226
Jefferson (Sullivan) Township........250	Lake Hart (Morgan) Town..............230	Losantville (Randolph) Town..........241
Jefferson (Switzerland) Township....251	Lakes of the Four Seasons (Lake)	Lost Creek (Vigo) Township...........255
Jefferson (Tipton) Township..........252	CDP.....................................219	Lost River (Martin) Township..........226
Jefferson (Washington) Township...259		Lovett (Jennings) Township............213

268

Lowell (Lake) Town 219	Middlebury (Elkhart) Township........193	Munster (Lake) Town 219
Luce (Spencer) Township 247	Middletown (Henry) Town 206	Napoleon (Ripley) Town 243
Lynn (Posey) Township 239	Milan (Allen) Township.....................175	Nappanee (Elkhart) City 193
Lynn (Randolph) Town 241	Milan (Ripley) Town 243	Nappanee (Kosciusko) City.............216
Lynnville (Warrick) Town...................258	Milford (Decatur) Town 188	Nashville (Brown) Town 180
Lyons (Greene) Town 201	Milford (Kosciusko) Town 216	Needham (Johnson) Township.........214
Mackey (Gibson) Town 198	Milford (Lagrange) Township............218	Nevins (Vigo) Township...................255
Macy (Miami) Town..........................227	Mill (Grant) Township 199	New Albany (Floyd) City 195
Madison (Allen) Township 175	Millcreek (Fountain) Township..........195	New Albany (Floyd) Township 195
Madison (Carroll) Township 181	Miller (Dearborn) Township 188	New Amsterdam (Harrison) Town....204
Madison (Clinton) Township.............184	Millersburg (Elkhart) Town 193	Newberry (Greene) Town 201
Madison (Daviess) Township 186	Millgrove (Steuben) Township 249	Newburgh (Warrick) Town................258
Madison (Dubois) Township 192	Millhousen (Decatur) Town 188	Newbury (Lagrange) Township 218
Madison (Jay) Township 211	Milltown (Crawford) Town 186	New Carlisle (St. Joseph) Town 244
Madison (Jefferson) City 212	Milltown (Harrison) Town 204	Newcastle (Fulton) Township...........197
Madison (Jefferson) Township 212	Milroy (Jasper) Township.................210	New Castle (Henry) City 207
Madison (Montgomery) Township...229	Milton (Jefferson) Township 212	New Chicago (Lake) Town 219
Madison (Morgan) Township 230	Milton (Wayne) Town 261	New Durham (La Porte) Township ..221
Madison (Pike) Township 237	Mishawaka (St. Joseph) City............244	New Garden (Wayne) Township 261
Madison (Putnam) Township 241	Mitchell (Lawrence) City..................222	New Harmony (Posey) Town 239
Madison (St. Joseph) Township 244	Mitcheltree (Martin) Township 226	New Haven (Allen) City....................175
Madison (Tipton) Township..............253	Modoc (Randolph) Town 241	New Market (Montgomery) Town 229
Madison (Washington) Township.....259	Monon (White) Town........................263	New Middletown (Harrison) Town....204
Madison County..............................222	Monon (White) Township.................263	New Palestine (Hancock) Town 203
Manchester (Dearborn) Township ...188	Monroe (Adams) Town.....................174	New Paris (Elkhart) CDP 193
Marengo (Crawford) Town 185	Monroe (Adams) Township..............174	New Pekin (Washington) Town........259
Marion (Allen) Township...................175	Monroe (Allen) Township 175	Newpoint (Decatur) Town................188
Marion (Boone) Township 179	Monroe (Carroll) Township...............181	Newport (Vermillion) Town 255
Marion (Decatur) Township..............188	Monroe (Clark) Township 183	New Providence (Clark) Town..........183
Marion (Dubois) Township 192	Monroe (Delaware) Township 191	New Richmond (Montgomery)
Marion (Grant) City...........................199	Monroe (Grant) Township 199	Town 229
Marion (Hendricks) Township 205	Monroe (Howard) Township 208	New Ross (Montgomery) Town 229
Marion (Jasper) Township................210	Monroe (Jefferson) Township 212	Newton (Jasper) Township 210
Marion (Jennings) Township............213	Monroe (Kosciusko) Township.........216	**Newton County**...............................231
Marion (Lawrence) Township 222	Monroe (Madison) Township...........223	Newtown (Fountain) Town...............195
Marion (Owen) Township 234	Monroe (Morgan) Township 230	Newville (Dekalb) Township............190
Marion (Pike) Township 237	Monroe (Pike) Township..................237	New Whiteland (Johnson) Town......214
Marion (Putnam) Township 241	Monroe (Pulaski) Township 239	Niles (Delaware) Township..............191
Marion (Shelby) Township................246	Monroe (Putnam) Township 241	Nineveh (Johnson) Township 214
Marion County................................224	Monroe (Randolph) Township 241	Noble (Cass) Township....................182
Markle (Huntington) Town 208	Monroe (Washington) Township......259	Noble (Jay) Township......................211
Markle (Wells) Town 262	Monroe City (Knox) Town.................215	Noble (La Porte) Township..............221
Markleville (Madison) Town.............223	**Monroe County**...............................228	Noble (Noble) Township..................232
Marrs (Posey) Township...................239	Monroeville (Allen) Town 175	Noble (Rush) Township 243
Marshall (Lawrence) Township........222	Monterey (Pulaski) Town 240	Noble (Shelby) Township.................246
Marshall (Parke) Town 235	Montezuma (Parke) Town................235	Noble (Wabash) Township 256
Marshall County.............................225	Montgomery (Daviess) Town 186	**Noble County**..................................232
Martin County.................................226	Montgomery (Gibson) Township 198	Noblesville (Hamilton) City..............202
Martinsville (Morgan) City 230	Montgomery (Jennings) Township....213	Noblesville (Hamilton) Township 202
Matthews (Grant) Town 199	Montgomery (Owen) Township 234	North (Lake) Township 219
Mauckport (Harrison) Town 204	**Montgomery County**.......................229	North (Marshall) Township 226
Maumee (Allen) Township................175	Monticello (White) City 263	North Bend (Starke) Township 248
McClellan (Newton) Township..........231	Montpelier (Blackford) City 178	North Crows Nest (Marion) Town....224
McCordsville (Hancock) Town..........203	Mooreland (Henry) Town 206	Northeast (Orange) Township 233
Mecca (Parke) Town 235	Moores Hill (Dearborn) Town 188	North Judson (Starke) Town 248
Medaryville (Pulaski) Town 239	Mooresville (Morgan) Town 230	North Liberty (St. Joseph) Town 244
Medina (Warren) Township..............257	Moral (Shelby) Township 246	North Manchester (Wabash) Town ...256
Medora (Jackson) Town 209	Morgan (Harrison) Township 204	North Salem (Hendricks) Town 205
Mellott (Fountain) Town 195	Morgan (Owen) Township 234	North Terre Haute (Vigo) CDP 255
Melody Hill (Vanderburgh) CDP 254	Morgan (Porter) Township 238	North Vernon (Jennings) City...........213
Mentone (Kosciusko) Town 216	**Morgan County** 230	North Webster (Kosciusko) Town....216
Meridian Hills (Marion) Town...........224	Morgantown (Morgan) Town 231	Northwest (Orange) Township 233
Merom (Sullivan) Town 250	Morocco (Newton) Town..................231	Nottingham (Wells) Township.........262
Merrillville (Lake) Town 219	Morristown (Shelby) Town...............246	Oak Grove (Benton) Township 177
Metamora (Franklin) Township 196	Mound (Warren) Township 257	Oakland City (Gibson) City..............198
Mexico (Miami) CDP.........................227	Mount Auburn (Wayne) Town 261	Oak Park (Clark) CDP 183
Miami (Cass) Township....................182	Mount Ayr (Newton) Town................231	Oaktown (Knox) Town 215
Miami County.................................227	Mount Carmel (Franklin) Town........196	Odon (Daviess) Town 186
Michiana Shores (La Porte) Town 220	Mount Etna (Huntington) Town 208	Ogden Dunes (Porter) Town 238
Michigan (Clinton) Township............184	Mount Pleasant (Delaware)	Ohio (Bartholomew) Township 177
Michigan (La Porte) Township..........220	Township 191	Ohio (Crawford) Township 186
Michigan City (La Porte) City 221	Mount Summit (Henry) Town 206	Ohio (Spencer) Township.................247
Michigantown (Clinton) Town...........185	Mount Vernon (Posey) City 239	Ohio (Warrick) Township..................258
Middle (Hendricks) Township...........205	Mulberry (Clinton) Town 185	**Ohio County**....................................233
Middlebury (Elkhart) Town................193	Muncie (Delaware) City 191	Oil (Perry) Township 236

INDIANA

Oldenburg (Franklin) Town...............197
Olive (Elkhart) Township................193
Olive (St. Joseph) Township...........244
Onward (Cass) Town......................182
Oolitic (Lawrence) Town.................222
Orange (Fayette) Township.............194
Orange (Noble) Township................232
Orange (Rush) Township.................243
Orange County............................233
Orangeville (Orange) Township........233
Oregon (Clark) Township................183
Oregon (Starke) Township...............248
Orestes (Madison) Town.................223
Orland (Steuben) Town..................249
Orleans (Orange) Town..................233
Orleans (Orange) Township.............234
Osceola (St. Joseph) Town..............245
Osgood (Ripley) Town....................243
Osolo (Elkhart) Township................193
Ossian (Wells) Town......................262
Otsego (Steuben) Township.............249
Otterbein (Benton) Town.................178
Otterbein (Tippecanoe) Town...........252
Otter Creek (Ripley) Township.........243
Otter Creek (Vigo) Township............255
Owen (Clark) Township..................183
Owen (Clinton) Township................185
Owen (Jackson) Township...............209
Owen (Warrick) Township................258
Owen County..............................234
Owensville (Gibson) Town..............198
Oxford (Benton) Town....................178
Palmyra (Harrison) Town................204
Palmyra (Knox) Township...............215
Paoli (Orange) Town......................234
Paoli (Orange) Township.................234
Paragon (Morgan) Town.................231
Parish Grove (Benton) Township......178
Parke County..............................235
Parker City (Randolph) Town..........242
Patoka (Crawford) Township...........186
Patoka (Dubois) Township..............192
Patoka (Gibson) Town....................198
Patoka (Gibson) Township...............198
Patoka (Pike) Township..................237
Patriot (Switzerland) Town..............251
Paw Paw (Wabash) Township..........256
Pendleton (Madison) Town.............223
Penn (Jay) Township.....................211
Penn (Parke) Township..................235
Penn (St. Joseph) Township............245
Pennville (Jay) Town.....................211
Perry (Allen) Township...................175
Perry (Boone) Township.................179
Perry (Clay) Township....................184
Perry (Clinton) Township.................185
Perry (Delaware) Township..............191
Perry (Lawrence) Township..............222
Perry (Marion) Township.................224
Perry (Martin) Township..................226
Perry (Miami) Township..................227
Perry (Monroe) Township................228
Perry (Noble) Township...................232
Perry (Tippecanoe) Township..........252
Perry (Vanderburgh) Township........254
Perry (Wayne) Township................261
Perry County...............................236
Perrysville (Vermillion) Town...........255
Pershing (Jackson) Township..........209
Peru (Miami) City..........................227
Peru (Miami) Township..................227
Petersburg (Pike) City...................237
Pierce (Washington) Township........259
Pierceton (Kosciusko) Town............216
Pierson (Vigo) Township................256

Pigeon (Vanderburgh) Township......254
Pigeon (Warrick) Township.............258
Pike (Jay) Township......................211
Pike (Marion) Township..................224
Pike (Ohio) Township....................233
Pike (Warren) Township.................257
Pike County................................236
Pine (Benton) Township.................178
Pine (Porter) Township...................238
Pine (Warren) Township.................257
Pine Village (Warren) Town............257
Pipe Creek (Madison) Township......223
Pipe Creek (Miami) Township.........227
Pittsboro (Hendricks) Town.............205
Plain (Kosciusko) Township............216
Plainfield (Hendricks) Town............205
Plainville (Daviess) Town...............186
Pleasant (Allen) Township...............175
Pleasant (Grant) Township..............199
Pleasant (Johnson) Township..........214
Pleasant (La Porte) Township.........221
Pleasant (Porter) Township.............238
Pleasant (Steuben) Township..........249
Pleasant (Switzerland) Township.....251
Pleasant (Wabash) Township..........256
Pleasant Run (Lawrence) Township..222
Plymouth (Marshall) City................226
Point (Posey) Township.................239
Polk (Huntington) Township............209
Polk (Marshall) Township...............226
Polk (Monroe) Township................228
Polk (Washington) Township..........259
Poneto (Wells) Town.....................262
Portage (Porter) City.....................238
Portage (Porter) Township.............238
Portage (St. Joseph) Township.......245
Porter (Porter) Town......................238
Porter (Porter) Township................238
Porter County..............................237
Portland (Jay) City........................211
Posey (Clay) Township..................184
Posey (Fayette) Township..............194
Posey (Franklin) Township..............197
Posey (Harrison) Township.............204
Posey (Rush) Township.................243
Posey (Switzerland) Township........251
Posey (Washington) Township........259
Posey County..............................238
Poseyville (Posey) Town................239
Pottawattomie Park (La Porte) Town...............................221
Prairie (Henry) Township................207
Prairie (Kosciusko) Township.........216
Prairie (La Porte) Township............221
Prairie (Tipton) Township...............253
Prairie (Warren) Township..............257
Prairie (White) Township................263
Prairie Creek (Vigo) Township........256
Prairieton (Vigo) Township.............256
Preble (Adams) Township..............174
Princes Lakes (Johnson) Town......214
Princeton (Gibson) City..................198
Princeton (White) Township............263
Pulaski County.............................239
Putnam County............................240
Raccoon (Parke) Township............235
Railroad (Starke) Township............248
Randolph (Ohio) Township.............233
Randolph (Tippecanoe) Township...252
Randolph County.........................241
Ray (Franklin) Township................197
Ray (Morgan) Township.................231
Redding (Jackson) Township.........210
Redkey (Jay) Town.......................211
Reeve (Daviess) Township............186

American Places Dictionary

Remington (Jasper) Town...............210
Rensselaer (Jasper) City................210
Republican (Jefferson) Township....212
Reserve (Parke) Township.............235
Reynolds (White) Town..................263
Rich Grove (Pulaski) Township......240
Richland (Benton) Township..........178
Richland (Dekalb) Township..........190
Richland (Fountain) Township........196
Richland (Fulton) Township............197
Richland (Grant) Township.............199
Richland (Greene) Township..........201
Richland (Jay) Township................211
Richland (Madison) Township........223
Richland (Miami) Township............227
Richland (Monroe) Township..........228
Richland (Rush) Township.............243
Richland (Steuben) Township........249
Richland (Whitley) Township..........264
Richmond (Wayne) City..................261
Ridgeville (Randolph) Town...........242
Riley (Vigo) Town.........................256
Riley (Vigo) Township...................256
Ripley (Montgomery) Township......229
Ripley (Rush) Township.................243
Ripley County..............................242
Rising Sun (Ohio) City...................233
River Forest (Madison) Town.........223
Roachdale (Putnam) Town.............241
Roann (Wabash) Town..................257
Roanoke (Huntington) Town..........209
Robb (Posey) Township................239
Robinson (Posey) Township..........239
Rochester (Fulton) City..................197
Rochester (Fulton) Township.........197
Rock Creek (Bartholomew) Township...............................177
Rock Creek (Carroll) Township......181
Rock Creek (Huntington) Township.209
Rockcreek (Wells) Township..........262
Rockport (Spencer) City................247
Rockville (Parke) Town..................235
Rocky Ripple (Marion) Town.........224
Rome City (Noble) Town...............232
Root (Adams) Township................174
Rosedale (Parke) Town.................235
Roseland (St. Joseph) Town.........245
Ross (Clinton) Township...............185
Ross (Lake) Township..................219
Rossville (Clinton) Township..........185
Round Grove (White) Township.....263
Royal Center (Cass) Town............182
Rush County...............................243
Rushville (Rush) City....................243
Rushville (Rush) Township............244
Russell (Putnam) Township...........241
Russellville (Putnam) Town............241
Russiaville (Howard) Town............208
Rutherford (Martin) Township.........226
St. Joe (Dekalb) Town...................190
St. John (Lake) Town....................219
St. John (Lake) Township..............219
St. Joseph (Allen) Township..........176
St. Joseph County........................244
St. Leon (Dearborn) Town.............188
St. Marys (Adams) Township.........174
St. Paul (Decatur) Town................189
St. Paul (Shelby) Town..................246
Salamonia (Jay) Town...................211
Salamonie (Huntington) Township..209
Salem (Delaware) Township..........191
Salem (Pulaski) Township..............240
Salem (Steuben) Township............249
Salem (Washington) City...............259
Salt Creek (Decatur) Township......189

Salt Creek (Franklin) Township 197
Salt Creek (Jackson) Township 210
Salt Creek (Monroe) Township 228
Saltillo (Washington) Town 259
Saluda (Jefferson) Township 212
Sandborn (Knox) Town 215
Sand Creek (Bartholomew)
  Township 177
Sand Creek (Decatur) Township 189
Sand Creek (Jennings) Township 213
Santa Claus (Spencer) Town 247
Saratoga (Randolph) Town 242
Schererville (Lake) Town 219
Schneider (Lake) Town 219
Scipio (Allen) Township 176
Scipio (La Porte) Township 221
Scott (Kosciusko) Township 216
Scott (Montgomery) Township 229
Scott (Steuben) Township 249
Scott (Vanderburgh) Township 254
Scott County 245
Scottsburg (Scott) City 245
Seelyville (Vigo) Town 256
Sellersburg (Clark) Town 183
Selma (Delaware) Town 191
Seward (Kosciusko) Township 217
Seymour (Jackson) City 210
Shadeland (Tippecanoe) Town 252
Shamrock Lakes (Blackford) Town ... 178
Sharpsville (Tipton) Town 253
Shawnee (Fountain) Township 196
Shawswick (Lawrence) Township 222
Sheffield (Tippecanoe) Township 252
Shelburn (Sullivan) Town 250
Shelby (Jefferson) Township 212
Shelby (Ripley) Township 243
Shelby (Shelby) Township 246
Shelby (Tippecanoe) Township 252
Shelby County 246
Shelbyville (Shelby) City 246
Sheridan (Hamilton) Town 202
Shipshewana (Lagrange) Town 218
Shirley (Hancock) Town 203
Shirley (Henry) Town 207
Shoals (Martin) Town 226
Sidney (Kosciusko) Town 217
Silver Creek (Clark) Township 183
Silver Lake (Kosciusko) Town 217
Simonton Lake (Elkhart) CDP 193
Sims (Grant) Township 199
Skelton (Warrick) Township 258
Smith (Greene) Township 201
Smith (Posey) Township 239
Smith (Whitley) Township 264
Smithfield (Dekalb) Township 190
Smyrna (Jefferson) Township 212
Somerville (Gibson) Town 198
South Bend (St. Joseph) City 245
Southeast (Orange) Township 234
South Haven (Porter) CDP 238
Southport (Marion) City 225
South Whitley (Whitley) Town 264
Sparta (Dearborn) Township 188
Sparta (Noble) Township 232
Speedway (Marion) Town 225
Spencer (Dekalb) Township 190
Spencer (Harrison) Township 204
Spencer (Jennings) Township 213
Spencer (Owen) Town 234
Spencer County 247
Spiceland (Henry) Town 207
Spiceland (Henry) Township 207
Spice Valley (Lawrence) Township 222
Springfield (Allen) Township 176
Springfield (Franklin) Township 197

Springfield (La Porte) Township 221
Springfield (Lagrange) Township 218
Spring Grove (Wayne) Town 261
Spring Hill (Marion) Town 225
Spring Lake (Hancock) Town 203
Springport (Henry) Town 207
Spurgeon (Pike) Town 237
Stafford (Dekalb) Township 190
Stafford (Greene) Township 201
Stampers Creek (Orange) Township .. 234
Starke County 248
State Line City (Warren) Town 257
Staunton (Clay) Town 184
Steele (Daviess) Township 186
Steen (Knox) Township 215
Sterling (Crawford) Township 186
Steuben (Steuben) Township 249
Steuben (Warren) Township 257
Steuben County 248
Stilesville (Hendricks) Town 205
Stinesville (Monroe) Town 228
Stockton (Greene) Township 201
Stoney Creek (Henry) Township 207
Stoney Creek (Randolph) Township .. 242
Stony Creek (Madison) Township 223
Straughn (Henry) Town 207
Sugar Creek (Boone) Township 179
Sugar Creek (Clinton) Township 185
Sugar Creek (Hancock) Township 203
Sugar Creek (Montgomery)
  Township 229
Sugar Creek (Parke) Township 235
Sugar Creek (Shelby) Township 246
Sugar Creek (Vigo) Township 256
Sugar Ridge (Clay) Township 184
Sullivan (Sullivan) City 250
Sullivan County 250
Sulphur Springs (Henry) Town 207
Summitville (Madison) Town 223
Sunman (Ripley) Town 243
Swan (Noble) Township 232
Swayzee (Grant) Town 200
Sweetser (Grant) Town 200
Switz City (Greene) Town 201
Switzerland County 251
Syracuse (Kosciusko) Town 217
Taylor (Greene) Township 201
Taylor (Harrison) Township 204
Taylor (Howard) Township 208
Taylor (Owen) Township 234
Taylorsville (Bartholomew) CDP 177
Tell City (Perry) City 236
Tennyson (Warrick) Town 258
Terre Haute (Vigo) City 256
Thorncreek (Whitley) Township 264
Thorntown (Boone) Town 179
Tippecanoe (Carroll) Township 181
Tippecanoe (Kosciusko) Township ... 217
Tippecanoe (Marshall) Township 226
Tippecanoe (Pulaski) Township 240
Tippecanoe (Tippecanoe) Township .. 252
Tippecanoe County 251
Tipton (Cass) Township 182
Tipton (Tipton) City 253
Tipton County 252
Tobin (Perry) Township 236
Topeka (Lagrange) Town 218
Town of Pines (Porter) Town 238
Trafalgar (Johnson) Town 214
Trail Creek (La Porte) Town 221
Tri-Lakes (Whitley) CDP 264
Troy (Dekalb) Township 190
Troy (Fountain) Township 196
Troy (Perry) Town 236
Troy (Perry) Township 236

Turkey Creek (Kosciusko) Township 217
Turman (Sullivan) Township 250
Ulen (Boone) Town 179
Union (Adams) Township 174
Union (Benton) Township 178
Union (Boone) Township 179
Union (Clark) Township 183
Union (Clinton) Township 185
Union (Crawford) Township 186
Union (Dekalb) Township 190
Union (Delaware) Township 191
Union (Elkhart) Township 193
Union (Fulton) Township 197
Union (Gibson) Township 198
Union (Hendricks) Township 205
Union (Howard) Township 208
Union (Huntington) Township 209
Union (Jasper) Township 210
Union (Johnson) Township 214
Union (La Porte) Township 221
Union (Madison) Township 223
Union (Marshall) Township 226
Union (Miami) Township 227
Union (Montgomery) Township 229
Union (Ohio) Township 233
Union (Parke) Township 235
Union (Perry) Township 236
Union (Porter) Township 238
Union (Randolph) Township 242
Union (Rush) Township 244
Union (Shelby) Township 246
Union (St. Joseph) Township 245
Union (Tippecanoe) Township 252
Union (Union) Township 253
Union (Vanderburgh) Township 254
Union (Wells) Township 262
Union (White) Township 263
Union (Whitley) Township 264
Union City (Randolph) City 242
Union County 253
Uniondale (Wells) Town 262
Universal (Vermillion) Town 255
Upland (Grant) Town 200
Utica (Clark) Town 183
Utica (Clark) Township 183
Valparaiso (Porter) City 238
Van Buren (Brown) Township 180
Van Buren (Clay) Township 184
Van Buren (Daviess) Township 187
Van Buren (Fountain) Township 196
Van Buren (Grant) Town 200
Van Buren (Grant) Township 200
Van Buren (Kosciusko) Township 217
Van Buren (Lagrange) Township 218
Van Buren (Madison) Township 223
Van Buren (Monroe) Township 228
Van Buren (Pulaski) Township 240
Van Buren (Shelby) Township 246
Vanderburgh County 254
Veale (Daviess) Township 187
Veedersburg (Fountain) Town 196
Vera Cruz (Wells) Town 262
Vermillion (Vermillion) Township 255
Vermillion County 254
Vernon (Hancock) Township 203
Vernon (Jackson) Township 210
Vernon (Jennings) Town 213
Vernon (Jennings) Township 213
Vernon (Washington) Township 260
Versailles (Ripley) Town 243
Vevay (Switzerland) Town 251
Vienna (Scott) Township 245
Vigo (Knox) Township 215
Vigo County 255
Vincennes (Knox) City 215

INDIANA

Vincennes (Knox) Township 215
Wabash (Adams) Township 174
Wabash (Fountain) Township............196
Wabash (Gibson) Township 198
Wabash (Jay) Township 212
Wabash (Parke) Township 236
Wabash (Tippecanoe) Township 252
Wabash (Wabash) City.......................257
Wabash County 256
Wakarusa (Elkhart) Town 193
Walker (Jasper) Township 210
Walker (Rush) Township 244
Walkerton (St. Joseph) Town 245
Wallace (Fountain) Town...................196
Walnut (Marshall) Township 226
Walnut (Montgomery) Township 229
Walt (Wabash) Township...................257
Walton (Cass) Town...........................182
Wanatah (La Porte) Town 221
Ward (Randolph) Township 242
Warren (Clinton) Township...............185
Warren (Huntington) Town 209
Warren (Huntington) Township 209
Warren (Marion) Township................225
Warren (Putnam) Township 241
Warren (St. Joseph) Township 245
Warren (Warren) Township 257
Warren County 257
Warren Park (Marion) Town 225
Warrick County 258
Warsaw (Kosciusko) City 217
Washington (Adams) Township.........174
Washington (Allen) Township...........176
Washington (Blackford) Township 178
Washington (Boone) Township..........179
Washington (Brown) Township 180
Washington (Carroll) Township 181
Washington (Cass) Township 182
Washington (Clark) Township...........183
Washington (Clay) Township 184
Washington (Clinton) Township........185
Washington (Daviess) City 187
Washington (Daviess) Township 187
Washington (Dearborn) Township 188
Washington (Decatur) Township.......189
Washington (Delaware) Township.....191
Washington (Elkhart) Township........193
Washington (Gibson) Township........199
Washington (Grant) Township 200
Washington (Greene) Township 201
Washington (Hamilton) Township 202
Washington (Harrison) Township 204
Washington (Hendricks) Township ...205
Washington (Jackson) Township 210
Washington (Knox) Township 215
Washington (Kosciusko) Township ...217
Washington (La Porte) Township......221
Washington (Marion) Township........225
Washington (Miami) Township 228
Washington (Monroe) Township 228
Washington (Morgan) Township 231
Washington (Newton) Township 231
Washington (Noble) Township 232
Washington (Owen) Township 234
Washington (Parke) Township 236
Washington (Pike) Township.............237
Washington (Porter) Township..........238
Washington (Putnam) Township 241
Washington (Randolph) Township 242
Washington (Ripley) Township 243
Washington (Rush) Township 244
Washington (Shelby) Township 246
Washington (Starke) Township..........248
Washington (Tippecanoe) Township .252
Washington (Warren) Township 257
Washington (Washington) Township.260
Washington (Wayne) Township 261
Washington (Whitley) Township 264
Washington County 259
Waterloo (Dekalb) Town 190
Waterloo (Fayette) Township............194
Waveland (Montgomery) Town.........229
Wayne (Allen) Township 176
Wayne (Bartholomew) Township 177
Wayne (Fulton) Township 197
Wayne (Hamilton) Township 202
Wayne (Henry) Township..................207
Wayne (Huntington) Township 209
Wayne (Jay) Township 212
Wayne (Kosciusko) Township 217
Wayne (Marion) Township 225
Wayne (Montgomery) Township 230
Wayne (Noble) Township 232
Wayne (Owen) Township...................235
Wayne (Randolph) Township 242
Wayne (Starke) Township..................248
Wayne (Tippecanoe) Township 252
Wayne (Wayne) Township 261
Wayne County 260
Waynetown (Montgomery) Town......230
Wea (Tippecanoe) Township 252
Webster (Harrison) Township 204
Webster (Wayne) Township 261
Wells County 261
West (Marshall) Township.................226
West Baden Springs (Orange) Town .234
Westchester (Porter) Township..........238
West College Corner (Union) Town..253
West Creek (Lake) Township 219
Westfield (Hamilton) Town 202
West Harrison (Dearborn) Town.......188
West Lafayette (Tippecanoe) City.....252
West Lebanon (Warren) Town...........257
West Point (White) Township............263
Westport (Decatur) Town 189
West Terre Haute (Vigo) Town 256
Westville (La Porte) Town.................221
Wheatfield (Jasper) Town..................211
Wheatfield (Jasper) Township...........211
Wheatland (Knox) Town 215
Whiskey Run (Crawford) Township .186
White County 262
Whiteland (Johnson) Town 214
White Post (Pulaski) Township..........240
White River (Gibson) Township 199
White River (Hamilton) Township ...202
White River (Johnson) Township 214
White River (Randolph) Township...242
Whitestown (Boone) Town 179
Whitewater (Franklin) Township 197
Whitewater (Wayne) Town 261
Whiting (Lake) City...........................219
Whitley County 263
Widner (Knox) Township..................215
Wildcat (Tipton) Township 253
Wilkinson (Hancock) Town...............203
Williams Creek (Marion) Town 225
Williamsport (Warren) Town 257
Wills (La Porte) Township 221
Wilmington (Dekalb) Township........190
Winamac (Pulaski) Town 240
Winchester (Randolph) City..............242
Windfall City (Tipton) Town 253
Winfield (Lake) Township.................220
Wingate (Montgomery) Town 230
Winona Lake (Kosciusko) Town.......217
Winslow (Pike) Town 237
Wolcott (White) Town 263
Wolcottville (Lagrange) Town 218
Wolcottville (Noble) Town 232
Wood (Clark) Township 183
Woodburn (Allen) City......................176
Woodlawn Heights (Madison) Town.223
Worth (Boone) Township 179
Worthington (Greene) Town 201
Wright (Greene) Township................201
Wynnedale (Marion) Town 225
Yeoman (Carroll) Town.....................181
York (Benton) Township 178
York (Dearborn) Township 188
York (Elkhart) Township 193
York (Noble) Township 233
York (Steuben) Township 249
York (Switzerland) Township............251
Yorktown (Delaware) Town 191
Zionsville (Boone) Town 179

Iowa

IOWA

Iowa

Population: 2,776,755 (1990); 2,913,808 (1980)
Population rank (1990): 30
Percent population change (1980-1990): - 4.7
Population projection: 2,741,000 (1995); 2,671,000 (2000)

Area: total: 56,276 sq. mi.; 55,875 sq. mi. land, 401 sq. mi. water
Area rank: 26
Highest elevation: 1,670 ft. along the northern boundary of Osceola County
Lowest point: 480 ft. at the junction of the Mississippi and Des Moines rivers (Lee County)

State capital: Des Moines (Polk County)
Largest city: Des Moines (193,187)
Second largest city: Cedar Rapids (108,751)
Largest county: Polk (327,140)

Total housing units: 1,143,669
No. of occupied housing units: 1,064,325
Vacant housing units (%): 6.9
Distribution of population by race and Hispanic origin (%):
  White: 96.6
  Black: 1.7
  Hispanic (any race): 1.2
  Native American: 0.3
  Asian/Pacific: 0.9
  Other: 0.5

Admission date: December 28, 1846 (29th state).

Location: In the central United States, bordering Missouri, Nebraska, South Dakota, Minnesota, Wisconsin, and Illinois.

Name Origin: For the Iowa River, itself named for the Iowa Indians of Siouan linguistic stock. The name is a French version of the Dakota name for the tribe, variously *Ayuhwa, Ouaouia, Aiouez,* or *Ioways* 'the sleepy ones.' The tribal name *Ouaouiatonon* appears on a 1673 French map, near the Iowa River.

State bird: eastern goldfinch *(Carduelis tristis)*
State flower: wild rose *(Rosa pratincola)*
State song: "The Song of Iowa"
State stone: geode
State tree: oak *(Quercus)*

State motto: Our Liberties We Prize and Our Rights We Will Maintain
State nickname: The Hawkeye State; the Corn State

Area codes: 319 (east), 515 (central), 712 (west)

Time zone: Central
Abbreviations: IA (postal); Ia. (traditional)
Part of (region): Plains, Midwest

Local Government

Counties
Iowa has 99 counties, which were granted home rule in 1978.

Municipalities
There are 955 municipal units.

Settlement History and Early Development

Indians hunted in the land of present-day Iowa about 12,000 years ago. When the first white men arrived in June 1673, they found Sioux, Illinois, and Iowa Indians. A French Jesuit missionary, Fr. Jacques Marquette, and a trapper, Louis Jolliet, were the first explorers to arrive, followed in 1680 by Robert Cavelier, Sieur de La Salle, Michel Aco, and Fr. Louis Hennepin. La Salle claimed all of the region drained by the Mississippi for France and named it Louisiana in honor of King Louis XIV. More trappers, traders, and missionaries visited the Iowa region, but no permanent white settlements were made.

In 1762 France ceded to Spain all of Louisiana west of the Mississippi River. In 1788 Julien Dubuque, a French-Canadian, received sole permission from the Fox Indians to mine lead west of the Mississippi. He became Iowa's first, and for 20 years only white settler. In 1800 Spain agreed to return its part of Louisiana, which included the Iowa region, to France. Then in 1803 Iowa became part of the U.S. under the terms of the Louisiana Purchase. The Territory of Louisiana, which included the Iowa region, was created by the federal government in 1805. When Louisiana became a state in 1812, the Iowa region was reorganized as part of the Territory of Missouri. Trading posts were established on the Des Moines, Mississippi, and Missouri rivers during the early 1800s, but President Andrew Jackson intended the region to remain Indian land, closed to white settlement. When Missouri became a state in 1821, Iowa became part of the unorganized territory of the U.S.

Statehood

The Sauk and Fox Indians were driven from Illinois and eastern Iowa in 1832, and the first whites began to settle in Iowa. In 1834 Iowa was placed under the jurisdiction of Michigan, then in 1836 under that of the Territory of Wisconsin; it became a separate territory in 1838. After a prolonged dispute about its borders, Iowa was admitted to the Union as the twenty-ninth state on December 28, 1846, with its present boundaries.

The new state offered large expanses of fertile topsoil and thus drew thousands of farmers from Indiana, Ohio, Tennessee, Virginia, the Carolinas, New York, and New England. The settlers were primarily Anglo-Americans and overwhelmingly Protestant. The New Englanders had a cultural influence that far exceeded their five percent of the population, and the small Iowa towns with large frame houses, elm-lined streets, and Congregational churches looked like faithful reproductions of New England villages.

The Civil War

Iowa supported the Union and fought not only for the abolition of slavery and preservation of the Union, but also to keep open the Mississippi River, the main artery for the transport of its agricultural products. No battles were fought in its territory.

Business and Commerce

The first railroad to cross Iowa from the Mississippi River to Council Bluffs was completed in 1867. By 1870 four railroads crossed the state. Farmers believed the freight rates to be unfair and there ensued eight years of legislative battling before rates acceptable to both sides were finally set. By the 1900s the railroads had created new markets for industries, and dam construction provided a power source that helped them develop.

Between 1850 and 1870 steamboating on the Mississippi River flourished. Also, lumber companies in Wisconsin and Minnesota sent logs downriver, furnishing a ready supply for building.

Iowa farmland sold well during and just after World War I, but during the 1920s and early 1930s more than half of the state's farmers lost their land because they failed to pay their mortgages. Many farmers managed to protect their farms by joining farm cooperatives to buy supplies and sell their products. The demand for Iowa's farm products rose sharply during World War II. After the war Iowa's economy became more industrialized with the growth of farm machinery and food processing industries, but agriculture, especially growing corn and soybeans and raising hogs and cattle, is still very important in Iowa's economy.

State Boundaries

The first territorial governor, Robert Lucas, extended Iowa's northern boundary up to present-day Minneapolis, but when the territory sought to become a state, a dispute arose over its size. Eventually Iowa kept all the land from the Mississippi River on the east to the Missouri River on the west, but had to abandon its northern claim and was admitted as a state with its present boundaries.

Iowa Counties

Adair	Clay	Hancock	Madison	Sac
Adams	Clayton	Hardin	Mahaska	Scott
Allamakee	Clinton	Harrison	Marion	Shelby
Appanoose	Crawford	Henry	Marshall	Sioux
Audubon	Dallas	Howard	Mills	Story
Benton	Davis	Humboldt	Mitchell	Tama
Black Hawk	Decatur	Ida	Monona	Taylor
Boone	Delaware	Iowa	Monroe	Union
Bremer	Des Moines	Jackson	Montgomery	Van Buren
Buchanan	Dickinson	Jasper	Muscatine	Wapello
Buena Vista	Dubuque	Jefferson	O'Brien	Warren
Butler	Emmet	Johnson	Osceola	Washington
Calhoun	Fayette	Jones	Page	Wayne
Carroll	Floyd	Keokuk	Palo Alto	Webster
Cass	Franklin	Kossuth	Plymouth	Winnebago
Cedar	Fremont	Lee	Pocahontas	Winneshiek
Cerro Gordo	Greene	Linn	Polk	Woodbury
Cherokee	Grundy	Louisa	Pottawattamie	Worth
Chickasaw	Guthrie	Lucas	Poweshiek	Wright
Clarke	Hamilton	Lyon	Ringgold	

Multi-County Places

The following Iowa places are in more than one county. Given here is the total population for each multi-county place, and the names of the counties it is in.

Ackley, pop. 1,696; Hardin (1,642), Franklin (54)
Adair, pop. 894; Adair (830), Guthrie (64)
Barnes City, pop. 221; Mahaska (198), Poweshiek (23)
Bevington, pop. 67; Madison (44), Warren (23)
Carlisle, pop. 3,241; Warren (3,236), Polk (5)
Cascade, pop. 1,812; Dubuque (1,430), Jones (382)
Casey, pop. 441; Guthrie (426), Adair (15)
Clearfield, pop. 417; Taylor (407), Ringgold (10)
Coppock, pop. 50; Henry (33), Washington (12), Jefferson (5)
Dows, pop. 660; Wright (560), Franklin (100)
Durant, pop. 1,549; Cedar (1,540), Muscatine (7), Scott (2)
Dyersville, pop. 3,703; Dubuque (3,666), Delaware (37)
Eddyville, pop. 1,010; Wapello (837), Mahaska (173), Monroe (0)
Edgewood, pop. 776; Delaware (460), Clayton (316)
Fairbank, pop. 1,018; Buchanan (851), Fayette (167)
Farnhamville, pop. 414; Calhoun (414), Webster (0)
Forest City, pop. 4,430; Winnebago (4,075), Hancock (355)
Gilmore City, pop. 560; Humboldt (319), Pocahontas (241)
Janesville, pop. 822; Bremer (689), Black Hawk (133)
Lenox, pop. 1,303; Taylor (1,303), Adams (0)
Lu Verne, pop. 328; Kossuth (274), Humboldt (54)
Lytton, pop. 320; Sac (278), Calhoun (42)
North English, pop. 944; Iowa (932), Keokuk (12)
Postville, pop. 1,472; Allamakee (1,465), Clayton (7)
Ralston, pop. 119; Carroll (111), Greene (8)
Riceville, pop. 827; Mitchell (493), Howard (334)
Shannon City, pop. 97; Union (92), Ringgold (5)
Shelby, pop. 637; Shelby (570), Pottawattamie (67)
Sheldahl, pop. 315; Story (171), Polk (122), Boone (22)
Sheldon, pop. 4,937; O'Brien (4,866), Sioux (71)
Shenandoah, pop. 5,572; Page (5,572), Fremont (0)
Stanley, pop. 116; Buchanan (116), Fayette (0)
Stratford, pop. 715; Hamilton (679), Webster (36)
Stuart, pop. 1,522; Guthrie (993), Adair (529)
Tabor, pop. 957; Fremont (901), Mills (56)
Victor, pop. 966; Iowa (842), Poweshiek (124)
Walcott, pop. 1,356; Scott (1,356), Muscatine (0)
Walford, pop. 303; Benton (290), Linn (13)
West Bend, pop. 862; Palo Alto (856), Kossuth (6)
West Des Moines, pop. 31,702; Polk (31,695), Dallas (7)
Wilton, pop. 2,577; Muscatine (2,573), Cedar (4)
Zwingle, pop. 94; Dubuque (84), Jackson (10)

Adair County
County Seat: Greenfield (ZIP: 50849)

Pop: 8,409 (1990); 9,509 (1980) **Pop Density:** 14.8
Land: 569.3 sq. mi.; **Water:** 1.0 sq. mi. **Area Code:** 515

In south-central IA, east of Council Bluffs; established Jan 15, 1851 from Cass County.

Name origin: For John Adair (1757–1840), governor of KY (1820–24).

Adair City
Lat: 41-29-49 N **Long:** 94-38-37 W
Pop: 830 (1990); 817 (1980) **Pop Density:** 553.3
Land: 1.5 sq. mi.; **Water:** 0.0 sq. mi.

Incorporated Feb 23, 1884. Part of the town is also in Guthrie County.

Name origin: For John Adair (1757–1840), governor of KY (1820–24).

Bridgewater City
ZIP: 50837 **Lat:** 41-14-48 N **Long:** 94-40-02 W
Pop: 209 (1990); 233 (1980) **Pop Density:** 696.7
Land: 0.3 sq. mi.; **Water:** 0.0 sq. mi.

Incorporated Apr 1, 1905.

Casey City
Lat: 41-30-11 N **Long:** 94-31-16 W
Pop: 15 (1990); 14 (1980) **Pop Density:** 75.0
Land: 0.2 sq. mi.; **Water:** 0.0 sq. mi.

Incorporated Jun 29, 1880. Part of the town is also in Guthrie County.

Fontanelle City
ZIP: 50846 **Lat:** 41-17-23 N **Long:** 94-33-38 W
Pop: 712 (1990); 805 (1980) **Pop Density:** 791.1
Land: 0.9 sq. mi.; **Water:** 0.0 sq. mi.

Incorporated Aug 23, 1871.

Name origin: For Louis Fontanelle, a trapper who worked for the American Fur Company, or for his son, Omaha Chief Logan Fontanelle.

Greenfield City
ZIP: 50849 **Lat:** 41-18-19 N **Long:** 94-27-30 W
Pop: 2,074 (1990); 2,243 (1980) **Pop Density:** 1152.2
Land: 1.8 sq. mi.; **Water:** 0.0 sq. mi.

Incorporated May 22, 1876.

Name origin: For Greenfield, MA.

Orient City
ZIP: 50858 **Lat:** 41-12-10 N **Long:** 94-25-04 W
Pop: 376 (1990); 416 (1980) **Pop Density:** 940.0
Land: 0.4 sq. mi.; **Water:** 0.0 sq. mi.

Incorporated Mar 21, 1882.

Stuart City
Lat: 41-29-50 N **Long:** 94-19-02 W
Pop: 529 (1990); 523 (1980) **Pop Density:** 587.8
Land: 0.9 sq. mi.; **Water:** 0.0 sq. mi. **Elev:** 1210 ft.

Incorporated Feb 6, 1877. Part of the town is also in Guthrie County.

Adams County
County Seat: Corning (ZIP: 50841)

Pop: 4,866 (1990); 5,731 (1980) **Pop Density:** 11.5
Land: 423.6 sq. mi.; **Water:** 1.9 sq. mi. **Area Code:** 515

In southwestern IA, southeast of Council Bluffs; established Jan 15, 1851 from Taylor County.

Name origin: For John Adams (1735–1826), second U.S. president.

Carbon City
ZIP: 50839 **Lat:** 41-02-57 N **Long:** 94-49-24 W
Pop: 60 (1990); 110 (1980) **Pop Density:** 85.7
Land: 0.7 sq. mi.; **Water:** 0.0 sq. mi.

Incorporated Jul 18, 1903.

Name origin: For the presence of coal deposits.

Corning City
ZIP: 50841 **Lat:** 40-59-38 N **Long:** 94-44-21 W
Pop: 1,806 (1990); 1,939 (1980) **Pop Density:** 1290.0
Land: 1.4 sq. mi.; **Water:** 0.0 sq. mi.

Incorporated Dec 13, 1871.

Name origin: For merchant Erastus Corning.

Lenox City
Lat: 40-54-08 N **Long:** 94-33-11 W
Pop: 0 (1990); 2 (1980)
Land: 0.1 sq. mi.; **Water:** 0.0 sq. mi.

Incorporated Jul 2, 1875. Part of the town is also in Taylor County.

Nodaway City
ZIP: 50857 **Lat:** 40-56-11 N **Long:** 94-53-42 W
Pop: 153 (1990); 185 (1980) **Pop Density:** 306.0
Land: 0.5 sq. mi.; **Water:** 0.0 sq. mi.

Incorporated May 28, 1900.

Name origin: For the Nodaway River. Algonquian term for shake, referring to their enemies.

Prescott — City
ZIP: 50859 **Lat:** 41-01-24 N **Long:** 94-36-44 W
Pop: 287 (1990); 349 (1980) **Pop Density:** 717.5
Land: 0.4 sq. mi.; **Water:** 0.0 sq. mi.
Incorporated Nov 26, 1890.

Allamakee County
County Seat: Waukon (ZIP: 52172)

Pop: 13,855 (1990); 15,108 (1980) **Pop Density:** 21.7
Land: 639.6 sq. mi.; **Water:** 19.1 sq. mi. **Area Code:** 319
On the northeastern border of IA; county established Feb 20, 1847 from Clayton County.
Name origin: Combined form of an Indian trader's name, Allan Makee.

Harpers Ferry — City
ZIP: 52146 **Lat:** 43-12-03 N **Long:** 91-09-04 W
Pop: 284 (1990); 258 (1980) **Pop Density:** 473.3
Land: 0.6 sq. mi.; **Water:** 0.0 sq. mi.
Incorporated Dec 24, 1901.

Lansing — City
ZIP: 52151 **Lat:** 43-21-42 N **Long:** 91-13-32 W
Pop: 1,007 (1990); 1,181 (1980) **Pop Density:** 1007.0
Land: 1.0 sq. mi.; **Water:** 0.1 sq. mi.
Incorporated Jul 1, 1867.
Name origin: For Lansing, MI.

New Albin — City
ZIP: 52160 **Lat:** 43-29-49 N **Long:** 91-17-18 W
Pop: 534 (1990); 609 (1980) **Pop Density:** 2670.0
Land: 0.2 sq. mi.; **Water:** 0.0 sq. mi.
Incorporated May 20, 1895.

Postville — City
ZIP: 52162 **Lat:** 43-05-06 N **Long:** 91-34-09 W
Pop: 1,465 (1990); 1,475 (1980) **Pop Density:** 2092.9
Land: 0.7 sq. mi.; **Water:** 0.0 sq. mi.
Incorporated Mar 17, 1873. Part of the town is also in Clayton County.
Name origin: For settler Joel Post, who arrived here in 1841.

Waterville — City
ZIP: 52170 **Lat:** 43-12-29 N **Long:** 91-17-41 W
Pop: 140 (1990); 157 (1980) **Pop Density:** 350.0
Land: 0.4 sq. mi.; **Water:** 0.0 sq. mi.
Incorporated Jun 18, 1912.

Waukon — City
ZIP: 52172 **Lat:** 43-16-11 N **Long:** 91-28-34 W
Pop: 4,019 (1990); 3,983 (1980) **Pop Density:** 1607.6
Land: 2.5 sq. mi.; **Water:** 0.0 sq. mi.
Incorporated Apr 4, 1883.
Name origin: For the Winnebago Chief, Waukon Decorah (1775–1868).

Appanoose County
County Seat: Centerville (ZIP: 52544)

Pop: 13,743 (1990); 15,511 (1980) **Pop Density:** 27.7
Land: 496.3 sq. mi.; **Water:** 20.1 sq. mi. **Area Code:** 515
On the central-southern border of IA; established Feb 17, 1843 (prior to statehood) from Davis County.
Name origin: For a respected chief of the Sac and Fox tribes, prominent in IA and KS in the 1830s and 1840s. His name means 'chief when a child; prince.'

Centerville — City
ZIP: 52544 **Lat:** 40-43-50 N **Long:** 92-52-27 W
Pop: 5,936 (1990); 6,558 (1980) **Pop Density:** 1447.8
Land: 4.1 sq. mi.; **Water:** 0.0 sq. mi.
Incorporated Jan 23, 1857.
Name origin: For its location in the center of the county.

Cincinnati — City
ZIP: 52549 **Lat:** 40-37-54 N **Long:** 92-55-18 W
Pop: 363 (1990); 598 (1980) **Pop Density:** 213.5
Land: 1.7 sq. mi.; **Water:** 0.0 sq. mi.
Incorporated Feb 13, 1875.

Exline — City
ZIP: 52555 **Lat:** 40-38-55 N **Long:** 92-50-30 W
Pop: 187 (1990); 217 (1980) **Pop Density:** 187.0
Land: 1.0 sq. mi.; **Water:** 0.0 sq. mi.
Incorporated Jun 20, 1904.

Moravia — City
ZIP: 52571 **Lat:** 40-53-31 N **Long:** 92-49-05 W
Pop: 679 (1990); 706 (1980) **Pop Density:** 565.8
Land: 1.2 sq. mi.; **Water:** 0.0 sq. mi.
Incorporated Sep 26, 1881.

Moulton
City
ZIP: 52572   **Lat:** 40-41-06 N **Long:** 92-40-44 W
Pop: 613 (1990); 762 (1980)   **Pop Density:** 471.5
Land: 1.3 sq. mi.; **Water:** 0.0 sq. mi.
Incorporated Feb 24, 1869.
Name origin: For an engineer of the Chicago, Burlington and Quincy Railroad.

Mystic
City
ZIP: 52574   **Lat:** 40-46-44 N **Long:** 92-56-37 W
Pop: 545 (1990); 665 (1980)   **Pop Density:** 187.9
Land: 2.9 sq. mi.; **Water:** 0.0 sq. mi.
Incorporated Oct 29, 1889.

Numa
City
ZIP: 52575   **Lat:** 40-41-07 N **Long:** 92-58-49 W
Pop: 151 (1990); 205 (1980)   **Pop Density:** 377.5
Land: 0.4 sq. mi.; **Water:** 0.0 sq. mi.
Incorporated Nov 9, 1909.

Plano
City
ZIP: 52581   **Lat:** 40-45-19 N **Long:** 93-02-45 W
Pop: 75 (1990); 111 (1980)   **Pop Density:** 125.0
Land: 0.6 sq. mi.; **Water:** 0.0 sq. mi.
Incorporated Oct 5, 1916.
Name origin: For Plano, IL.

Rathbun
City
    Lat: 40-48-07 N **Long:** 92-53-16 W
Pop: 89 (1990); 93 (1980)   **Pop Density:** 445.0
Land: 0.2 sq. mi.; **Water:** 0.0 sq. mi.
Incorporated Mar 1, 1894.

Udell
City
ZIP: 52593   **Lat:** 40-46-48 N **Long:** 92-44-33 W
Pop: 76 (1990); 75 (1980)   **Pop Density:** 253.3
Land: 0.3 sq. mi.; **Water:** 0.0 sq. mi.
Incorporated Apr 9, 1903.

Unionville
City
ZIP: 52594   **Lat:** 40-49-08 N **Long:** 92-41-48 W
Pop: 133 (1990); 150 (1980)   **Pop Density:** 190.0
Land: 0.7 sq. mi.; **Water:** 0.0 sq. mi.
Incorporated Jul 1, 1922.

Audubon County
County Seat: Audubon (ZIP: 50025)

Pop: 7,334 (1990); 8,559 (1980)   **Pop Density:** 16.5
Land: 443.2 sq. mi.; **Water:** 0.4 sq. mi.   **Area Code:** 712
In west-central IA, east of Council Bluffs; established Jan 15, 1851 from Cass and Black Hawk counties.
Name origin: For John James Audubon (1785–1851), ornithologist and artist.

Audubon
City
ZIP: 50025   **Lat:** 41-43-05 N **Long:** 94-55-47 W
Pop: 2,524 (1990); 2,841 (1980)   **Pop Density:** 1484.7
Land: 1.7 sq. mi.; **Water:** 0.0 sq. mi.   **Elev:** 1373 ft.
Incorporated Dec 2, 1880.
Name origin: For John James Audubon (1785–1851), ornithologist and artist.

Brayton
City
ZIP: 50042   **Lat:** 41-32-33 N **Long:** 94-55-32 W
Pop: 148 (1990); 170 (1980)   **Pop Density:** 92.5
Land: 1.6 sq. mi.; **Water:** 0.0 sq. mi.
Incorporated May 17, 1899.
Name origin: For the civil engineer who surveyed here for the railroad.

Exira
City
ZIP: 50076   **Lat:** 41-35-29 N **Long:** 94-52-45 W
Pop: 955 (1990); 978 (1980)   **Pop Density:** 1061.1
Land: 0.9 sq. mi.; **Water:** 0.0 sq. mi.
Incorporated Dec 13, 1880.
Name origin: For Exira Eckman, the daughter of a local judge.

Gray
City
ZIP: 50110   **Lat:** 41-50-28 N **Long:** 94-59-02 W
Pop: 83 (1990); 108 (1980)   **Pop Density:** 83.0
Land: 1.0 sq. mi.; **Water:** 0.0 sq. mi.   **Elev:** 1374 ft.
Incorporated Nov 10, 1894.

Kimballton
City
ZIP: 51543   **Lat:** 41-37-41 N **Long:** 95-04-27 W
Pop: 289 (1990); 362 (1980)   **Pop Density:** 361.3
Land: 0.8 sq. mi.; **Water:** 0.0 sq. mi.   **Elev:** 1290 ft.
Incorporated Jun 5, 1908.

Benton County
County Seat: Vinton (ZIP: 52349)

Pop: 22,429 (1990); 23,649 (1980)
Land: 716.5 sq. mi.; **Water:** 2.1 sq. mi.
Pop Density: 31.3
Area Code: 319

In east-central IA, west of Grand Rapids; established Dec 21, 1837 (prior to statehood), from Indian lands.

Name origin: For Thomas Hart Benton (1782–1858), U.S. journalist and statesman; nicknamed "Old Bullion" for championing the use of gold and silver currency rather than paper money.

Atkins — City
ZIP: 52206   Lat: 41-59-50 N   Long: 91-51-33 W
Pop: 637 (1990); 678 (1980)   Pop Density: 910.0
Land: 0.7 sq. mi.; Water: 0.0 sq. mi.
Incorporated May 15, 1917.

Belle Plaine — City
ZIP: 52208   Lat: 41-53-47 N   Long: 92-16-26 W
Pop: 2,834 (1990); 2,903 (1980)   Pop Density: 914.2
Land: 3.1 sq. mi.; Water: 0.0 sq. mi.
Incorporated May 26, 1868.
Name origin: From French meaning 'beautiful plain.'

Blairstown — City
ZIP: 52209   Lat: 41-54-21 N   Long: 92-04-54 W
Pop: 672 (1990); 695 (1980)   Pop Density: 1344.0
Land: 0.5 sq. mi.; Water: 0.0 sq. mi.
Incorporated Oct 15, 1868.

Garrison — City
ZIP: 52229   Lat: 42-08-36 N   Long: 92-08-34 W
Pop: 320 (1990); 411 (1980)   Pop Density: 1600.0
Land: 0.2 sq. mi.; Water: 0.0 sq. mi.
Incorporated Jun 9, 1883.

Keystone — City
ZIP: 52249   Lat: 41-59-59 N   Long: 92-11-54 W
Pop: 568 (1990); 618 (1980)   Pop Density: 1420.0
Land: 0.4 sq. mi.; Water: 0.0 sq. mi.
Incorporated Dec 15, 1893.

Luzerne — City
ZIP: 52257   Lat: 41-54-22 N   Long: 92-10-48 W
Pop: 110 (1990); 114 (1980)   Pop Density: 1100.0
Land: 0.1 sq. mi.; Water: 0.0 sq. mi.
Incorporated Oct 24, 1895.

Mount Auburn — City
ZIP: 52313   Lat: 42-15-24 N   Long: 92-05-35 W
Pop: 134 (1990); 188 (1980)   Pop Density: 446.7
Land: 0.3 sq. mi.; Water: 0.0 sq. mi.
Incorporated Nov 19, 1906.

Newhall — City
ZIP: 52315   Lat: 41-59-34 N   Long: 91-58-00 W
Pop: 854 (1990); 899 (1980)   Pop Density: 2846.7
Land: 0.3 sq. mi.; Water: 0.0 sq. mi.   Elev: 899 ft.
Incorporated Jun 3, 1912.

Norway — City
ZIP: 52318   Lat: 41-54-10 N   Long: 91-55-18 W
Pop: 583 (1990); 633 (1980)   Pop Density: 1457.5
Land: 0.4 sq. mi.; Water: 0.0 sq. mi.   Elev: 796 ft.
Incorporated Dec 20, 1894.
Name origin: Named by Norwegian settlers for their former home.

Shellsburg — City
ZIP: 52332   Lat: 42-05-35 N   Long: 91-52-09 W
Pop: 765 (1990); 771 (1980)   Pop Density: 1275.0
Land: 0.6 sq. mi.; Water: 0.0 sq. mi.
Incorporated Feb 19, 1874.

Urbana — City
ZIP: 52345   Lat: 42-13-23 N   Long: 91-52-29 W
Pop: 595 (1990); 574 (1980)   Pop Density: 1983.3
Land: 0.3 sq. mi.; Water: 0.0 sq. mi.
Incorporated Nov 4, 1892.

Van Horne — City
ZIP: 52346   Lat: 42-00-36 N   Long: 92-05-24 W
Pop: 695 (1990); 682 (1980)   Pop Density: 992.9
Land: 0.7 sq. mi.; Water: 0.0 sq. mi.
Incorporated Jun 12, 1883.

Vinton — City
ZIP: 52349   Lat: 42-09-50 N   Long: 92-01-37 W
Pop: 5,103 (1990); 5,040 (1980)   Pop Density: 1215.0
Land: 4.2 sq. mi.; Water: 0.0 sq. mi.
Incorporated Jul 17, 1869.
Name origin: For the Hon. Plynn Vinton.

Walford — City
ZIP: 52351   Lat: 41-52-36 N   Long: 91-50-06 W
Pop: 290 (1990); 266 (1980)   Pop Density: 1450.0
Land: 0.2 sq. mi.; Water: 0.0 sq. mi.
Incorporated Apr 15, 1954. Part of the town is also in Linn County.

Black Hawk County
County Seat: Waterloo (ZIP: 50703)

Pop: 123,798 (1990); 137,961 (1980)   **Pop Density:** 218.2
Land: 567.4 sq. mi.; **Water:** 4.6 sq. mi.   **Area Code:** 319

In east-central IA, northwest of Cedar Rapids; established Feb 17, 1843 (prior to statehood) from Delaware County.

Name origin: For Black Hawk (1767–1838), famous Indian warrior and chief of the Sac and Fox tribes.

Cedar Falls   City
ZIP: 50613   **Lat:** 42-31-14 N **Long:** 92-27-10 W
Pop: 34,298 (1990); 36,322 (1980)   **Pop Density:** 1207.7
Land: 28.4 sq. mi.; **Water:** 0.4 sq. mi.

In northeast-central IA, 5 mi. west of Waterloo. Incorporated Feb 24, 1858.

Name origin: For its proximity to the falls in the Cedar River.

Dunkerton   City
ZIP: 50626   **Lat:** 42-34-06 N **Long:** 92-09-35 W
Pop: 746 (1990); 718 (1980)   **Pop Density:** 828.9
Land: 0.9 sq. mi.; **Water:** 0.0 sq. mi.

Incorporated Mar 18, 1899.

Elk Run Heights   City
Lat: 42-28-01 N **Long:** 92-14-57 W
Pop: 1,088 (1990); 1,186 (1980)   **Pop Density:** 1088.0
Land: 1.0 sq. mi.; **Water:** 0.0 sq. mi.

Incorporated May 31, 1951.

Evansdale   City
ZIP: 50707   **Lat:** 42-27-42 N **Long:** 92-16-32 W
Pop: 4,638 (1990); 4,798 (1980)   **Pop Density:** 1104.3
Land: 4.2 sq. mi.; **Water:** 0.0 sq. mi.

Incorporated Nov 13, 1947.

Gilbertville   City
ZIP: 50634   **Lat:** 42-25-07 N **Long:** 92-12-49 W
Pop: 748 (1990); 740 (1980)   **Pop Density:** 1870.0
Land: 0.4 sq. mi.; **Water:** 0.0 sq. mi.

Incorporated Apr 9, 1917.

Hudson   City
ZIP: 50643   **Lat:** 42-25-23 N **Long:** 92-27-16 W
Pop: 2,037 (1990); 2,267 (1980)   **Pop Density:** 261.2
Land: 7.8 sq. mi.; **Water:** 0.0 sq. mi.

Incorporated Jul 1, 1893.

Janesville   City
Lat: 42-38-24 N **Long:** 92-27-45 W
Pop: 133 (1990); 112 (1980)   **Pop Density:** 332.5
Land: 0.4 sq. mi.; **Water:** 0.0 sq. mi.

Incorporated Oct 29, 1895. Part of the town is also in Bremer County.

Name origin: For the wife of founder John T. Barrick.

La Porte City   City
ZIP: 50651   **Lat:** 42-18-47 N **Long:** 92-11-28 W
Pop: 2,128 (1990); 2,324 (1980)   **Pop Density:** 818.5
Land: 2.6 sq. mi.; **Water:** 0.0 sq. mi.

Incorporated Jan 31, 1871.

Name origin: From French term meaning 'door' or 'opening,' or from the La Porte family.

Raymond   City
ZIP: 50667   **Lat:** 42-28-00 N **Long:** 92-13-41 W
Pop: 619 (1990); 655 (1980)   **Pop Density:** 412.7
Land: 1.5 sq. mi.; **Water:** 0.0 sq. mi.

Incorporated May 31, 1956.

Waterloo   City
ZIP: 50701   **Lat:** 42-29-29 N **Long:** 92-21-03 W
Pop: 66,467 (1990); 75,985 (1980)   **Pop Density:** 1096.8
Land: 60.6 sq. mi.; **Water:** 1.3 sq. mi.

In northeast-central IA on Cedar River, 50 mi. northwest of Cedar Rapids. Incorporated Jul 1, 1868.

Name origin: For the great battle at which Napoleon I (1769–1821) was decisively defeated.

Boone County
County Seat: Boone (ZIP: 50036)

Pop: 25,186 (1990); 26,184 (1980) **Pop Density:** 44.1
Land: 571.5 sq. mi.; **Water:** 2.1 sq. mi. **Area Code:** 515
In central IA, northwest of Des Moines; established Jan 13, 1846 from Polk County.
Name origin: For Capt. Nathan Boone (1782–1863), son of Daniel; officer in the U.S. Dragoons and early explorer of IA.

Beaver — City
ZIP: 50031 **Lat:** 42-02-16 N **Long:** 94-08-27 W
Pop: 46 (1990); 85 (1980) **Pop Density:** 153.3
Land: 0.3 sq. mi.; **Water:** 0.0 sq. mi.
Incorporated Oct 5, 1912.
Name origin: For the once-abundant beaver in the area.

Berkley — City
Lat: 41-56-46 N **Long:** 94-06-48 W
Pop: 39 (1990); 49 (1980) **Pop Density:** 195.0
Land: 0.2 sq. mi.; **Water:** 0.0 sq. mi. **Elev:** 973 ft.
Incorporated Oct 11, 1912.

Boone — City
ZIP: 50036 **Lat:** 42-03-08 N **Long:** 93-52-45 W
Pop: 12,392 (1990); 12,602 (1980) **Pop Density:** 1408.2
Land: 8.8 sq. mi.; **Water:** 0.0 sq. mi.
In central IA, 36 mi. north-northwest of Des Moines. Incorporated Oct 24, 1876.
Name origin: For Capt. Nathan Boone (1782–1863), son of Daniel; officer in the U.S. Dragoons and early explorer of IA.

Boxholm — City
ZIP: 50040 **Lat:** 42-10-23 N **Long:** 94-06-22 W
Pop: 214 (1990); 267 (1980) **Pop Density:** 214.0
Land: 1.0 sq. mi.; **Water:** 0.0 sq. mi.
Incorporated Sep 29, 1913.

Fraser — City
ZIP: 50036 **Lat:** 42-07-36 N **Long:** 93-58-25 W
Pop: 120 (1990); 139 (1980) **Pop Density:** 150.0
Land: 0.8 sq. mi.; **Water:** 0.1 sq. mi.
Incorporated Feb 8, 1904.

Luther — City
ZIP: 50152 **Lat:** 41-58-01 N **Long:** 93-49-10 W
Pop: 154 (1990); 155 (1980) **Pop Density:** 192.5
Land: 0.8 sq. mi.; **Water:** 0.0 sq. mi.
Incorporated Dec 29, 1903.

Madrid — City
ZIP: 50156 **Lat:** 41-52-31 N **Long:** 93-49-10 W
Pop: 2,395 (1990); 2,281 (1980) **Pop Density:** 2177.3
Land: 1.1 sq. mi.; **Water:** 0.0 sq. mi.
Incorporated Jun 9, 1883.

Ogden — City
ZIP: 50212 **Lat:** 42-02-21 N **Long:** 94-01-42 W
Pop: 1,909 (1990); 1,953 (1980) **Pop Density:** 1468.5
Land: 1.3 sq. mi.; **Water:** 0.0 sq. mi. **Elev:** 1092 ft.
Incorporated Apr 29, 1878.

Pilot Mound — Township
ZIP: 50223 **Lat:** 42-09-32 N **Long:** 94-01-07 W
Pop: 199 (1990); 223 (1980) **Pop Density:** 221.1
Land: 0.9 sq. mi.; **Water:** 0.0 sq. mi.
Incorporated Jun 23, 1897.

Sheldahl — City
Lat: 41-52-01 N **Long:** 93-42-10 W
Pop: 22 (1990); 25 (1980) **Pop Density:** 110.0
Land: 0.2 sq. mi.; **Water:** 0.0 sq. mi.
Incorporated Jan 18, 1882. Part of the town is also in Polk and Story counties.

Bremer County
County Seat: Waverly (ZIP: 50677)

Pop: 22,813 (1990); 24,820 (1980) **Pop Density:** 52.1
Land: 437.9 sq. mi.; **Water:** 1.7 sq. mi. **Area Code:** 319
In east-central IA, north of Waterloo; established Apr 29, 1851 from Winnebago Indian Reserve.
Name origin: For Frederika Bremer (1801–65), Swedish novelist, traveler, and early feminist.

Denver — City
ZIP: 50622 **Lat:** 42-40-16 N **Long:** 92-20-02 W
Pop: 1,600 (1990); 1,647 (1980) **Pop Density:** 1142.9
Land: 1.4 sq. mi.; **Water:** 0.0 sq. mi.
Incorporated Jun 30, 1896.

Frederika — City
ZIP: 50631 **Lat:** 42-53-00 N **Long:** 92-18-21 W
Pop: 188 (1990); 223 (1980) **Pop Density:** 940.0
Land: 0.2 sq. mi.; **Water:** 0.0 sq. mi.
Incorporated Mar 28, 1896.
Name origin: For Frederika Bremer (1801–65), Swedish novelist, traveler, and early feminist.

Janesville
City
Lat: 42-38-56 N **Long:** 92-27-54 W
Pop: 689 (1990); 728 (1980)   **Pop Density:** 984.3
Land: 0.7 sq. mi.; **Water:** 0.0 sq. mi.
Incorporated Oct 29, 1895. Part of the town is also in Black Hawk County.
Name origin: For the wife of founder John T. Barrick.

Plainfield
City
ZIP: 50666   **Lat:** 42-50-38 N **Long:** 92-32-07 W
Pop: 455 (1990); 469 (1980)   **Pop Density:** 1516.7
Land: 0.3 sq. mi.; **Water:** 0.0 sq. mi.
Incorporated Oct 17, 1895.

Readlyn
City
ZIP: 50668   **Lat:** 42-42-12 N **Long:** 92-13-29 W
Pop: 773 (1990); 858 (1980)   **Pop Density:** 2576.7
Land: 0.3 sq. mi.; **Water:** 0.0 sq. mi.
Incorporated Feb 1, 1905.

Sumner
City
ZIP: 50674   **Lat:** 42-50-59 N **Long:** 92-05-45 W
Pop: 2,078 (1990); 2,335 (1980)   **Pop Density:** 944.5
Land: 2.2 sq. mi.; **Water:** 0.0 sq. mi.
Incorporated Jun 1, 1894.
Name origin: For U.S. Senator Charles Sumner (1811–74).

Tripoli
City
ZIP: 50676   **Lat:** 42-48-35 N **Long:** 92-15-27 W
Pop: 1,188 (1990); 1,280 (1980)   **Pop Density:** 848.6
Land: 1.4 sq. mi.; **Water:** 0.0 sq. mi.
Incorporated Oct 16, 1894.

Waverly
City
ZIP: 50677   **Lat:** 42-43-31 N **Long:** 92-28-11 W
Pop: 8,539 (1990); 8,444 (1980)   **Pop Density:** 776.3
Land: 11.0 sq. mi.; **Water:** 0.3 sq. mi.
Incorporated Mar 2, 1859.
Name origin: For Sir Walter Scott's (1771–1832) novel, *Waverley* (1814).

Buchanan County
County Seat: Independence (ZIP: 50644)

Pop: 20,844 (1990); 22,900 (1980)   **Pop Density:** 36.5
Land: 571.3 sq. mi.; **Water:** 2.1 sq. mi.   **Area Code:** 319
In east-central IA, north of Cedar Rapids; established Dec 21, 1837 (prior to statehood), from Delaware County.
Name origin: For James Buchanan (1791–1868), fifteenth U.S. president.

Aurora
City
ZIP: 50607   **Lat:** 42-37-09 N **Long:** 91-43-47 W
Pop: 196 (1990); 248 (1980)   **Pop Density:** 326.7
Land: 0.6 sq. mi.; **Water:** 0.0 sq. mi.
Incorporated Aug 26, 1899.
Name origin: From Latin term meaning 'morning' or 'dawn.'

Brandon
City
ZIP: 52210   **Lat:** 42-18-50 N **Long:** 92-00-08 W
Pop: 320 (1990); 337 (1980)   **Pop Density:** 1066.7
Land: 0.3 sq. mi.; **Water:** 0.0 sq. mi.
Incorporated Apr 14, 1905.

Fairbank
City
ZIP: 50629   **Lat:** 42-38-19 N **Long:** 92-03-00 W
Pop: 851 (1990); 837 (1980)   **Pop Density:** 2127.5
Land: 0.4 sq. mi.; **Water:** 0.0 sq. mi.
Incorporated May 12, 1891. Part of the town is also in Fayette County.

Hazleton
City
ZIP: 50641   **Lat:** 42-37-05 N **Long:** 91-54-19 W
Pop: 733 (1990); 877 (1980)   **Pop Density:** 1047.1
Land: 0.7 sq. mi.; **Water:** 0.0 sq. mi.
Incorporated Jun 22, 1892.

Independence
City
ZIP: 50644   **Lat:** 42-28-04 N **Long:** 91-53-27 W
Pop: 5,972 (1990); 6,392 (1980)   **Pop Density:** 1809.7
Land: 3.3 sq. mi.; **Water:** 0.1 sq. mi.
Incorporated Oct 15, 1864.

Jesup
City
ZIP: 50648   **Lat:** 42-28-33 N **Long:** 92-04-00 W
Pop: 2,121 (1990); 2,343 (1980)   **Pop Density:** 1325.6
Land: 1.6 sq. mi.; **Water:** 0.0 sq. mi.
Incorporated Dec 21, 1875.
Name origin: For banker Morris K. Jesup of NY (1830–1908).

Lamont
City
ZIP: 50650   **Lat:** 42-35-55 N **Long:** 91-38-26 W
Pop: 471 (1990); 554 (1980)   **Pop Density:** 785.0
Land: 0.6 sq. mi.; **Water:** 0.0 sq. mi.
Incorporated Dec 10, 1892.

Quasqueton
City
ZIP: 52326   **Lat:** 42-23-43 N **Long:** 91-45-23 W
Pop: 579 (1990); 599 (1980)   **Pop Density:** 526.4
Land: 1.1 sq. mi.; **Water:** 0.0 sq. mi.
Settled 1842; incorporated Jul 1, 1902.
Name origin: From the Fox term for 'swiftly running water.'

Rowley
City
ZIP: 52329   **Lat:** 42-22-06 N **Long:** 91-50-41 W
Pop: 272 (1990); 275 (1980)   **Pop Density:** 680.0
Land: 0.4 sq. mi.; **Water:** 0.0 sq. mi.
Incorporated Apr 20, 1920.

Stanley
City
ZIP: 50671   **Lat:** 42-38-28 N **Long:** 91-48-42 W
Pop: 116 (1990); 154 (1980)   **Pop Density:** 580.0
Land: 0.2 sq. mi.; **Water:** 0.0 sq. mi.
Incorporated Mar 23, 1914. Part of the town is also in Fayette County.

Winthrop
City
ZIP: 50682 **Lat:** 42-28-23 N **Long:** 91-44-01 W
Pop: 742 (1990); 767 (1980) **Pop Density:** 1484.0
Land: 0.5 sq. mi.; **Water:** 0.0 sq. mi.
Incorporated Jun 7, 1886.

Buena Vista County
County Seat: Storm Lake (ZIP: 50588)

Pop: 19,965 (1990); 20,774 (1980) **Pop Density:** 34.7
Land: 574.8 sq. mi.; **Water:** 5.3 sq. mi. **Area Code:** 712
In west-central IA, northwest of Fort Dodge; established Jan 15, 1851 from Sac and Clay counties.
Name origin: For the Mexican town in Coahuila, site of Gen. Zachary Taylor's (1784–1850; twelfth U.S. president) final victory in the Mexican War (1847); Spanish for 'good view.'

Albert City
City
ZIP: 50510 **Lat:** 42-46-52 N **Long:** 94-56-56 W
Pop: 779 (1990); 818 (1980) **Pop Density:** 1558.0
Land: 0.5 sq. mi.; **Water:** 0.0 sq. mi.
Incorporated Dec 10, 1900.

Alta
City
ZIP: 51002 **Lat:** 42-40-19 N **Long:** 95-18-16 W
Pop: 1,820 (1990); 1,720 (1980) **Pop Density:** 1820.0
Land: 1.0 sq. mi.; **Water:** 0.0 sq. mi.
Incorporated Nov 11, 1878.
Name origin: From Spanish for a high point along a railroad.

Lakeside
City
ZIP: 50588 **Lat:** 42-37-10 N **Long:** 95-10-25 W
Pop: 522 (1990); 589 (1980) **Pop Density:** 2610.0
Land: 0.2 sq. mi.; **Water:** 0.0 sq. mi.
Incorporated Jul 15, 1933.

Linn Grove
City
ZIP: 51033 **Lat:** 42-53-33 N **Long:** 95-14-30 W
Pop: 194 (1990); 205 (1980) **Pop Density:** 323.3
Land: 0.6 sq. mi.; **Water:** 0.0 sq. mi.
Incorporated Mar 4, 1912.
Name origin: For the Hon. Lewis F. Linn, U.S. senator from MO.

Marathon
City
ZIP: 50565 **Lat:** 42-51-39 N **Long:** 94-58-58 W
Pop: 320 (1990); 442 (1980) **Pop Density:** 457.1
Land: 0.7 sq. mi.; **Water:** 0.0 sq. mi.
Incorporated Oct 31, 1892.

Newell
City
ZIP: 50568 **Lat:** 42-36-38 N **Long:** 95-00-13 W
Pop: 1,089 (1990); 913 (1980) **Pop Density:** 837.7
Land: 1.3 sq. mi.; **Water:** 0.0 sq. mi.
Incorporated Sep 30, 1876.

Rembrandt
City
ZIP: 50576 **Lat:** 42-49-35 N **Long:** 95-09-56 W
Pop: 229 (1990); 291 (1980) **Pop Density:** 1145.0
Land: 0.2 sq. mi.; **Water:** 0.0 sq. mi.
Incorporated Aug 12, 1901.

Sioux Rapids
City
ZIP: 50585 **Lat:** 42-53-30 N **Long:** 95-08-53 W
Pop: 761 (1990); 897 (1980) **Pop Density:** 1268.3
Land: 0.6 sq. mi.; **Water:** 0.0 sq. mi.
Incorporated Apr 6, 1882.
Name origin: For the falls on the nearby Little Sioux River.

Storm Lake
City
ZIP: 50588 **Lat:** 42-38-42 N **Long:** 95-11-59 W
Pop: 8,769 (1990); 8,814 (1980) **Pop Density:** 2435.8
Land: 3.6 sq. mi.; **Water:** 0.0 sq. mi.
Incorporated Feb 28, 1873.

Truesdale
City
ZIP: 50592 **Lat:** 42-43-46 N **Long:** 95-10-57 W
Pop: 132 (1990); 128 (1980) **Pop Density:** 1320.0
Land: 0.1 sq. mi.; **Water:** 0.0 sq. mi.
Incorporated May 15, 1917.
Name origin: For railroad official W.H. Truesdale.

Butler County
County Seat: Allison (ZIP: 50602)

Pop: 15,731 (1990); 17,668 (1980)　**Pop Density:** 27.1
Land: 580.4 sq. mi.; **Water:** 1.2 sq. mi.　**Area Code:** 319
In north-central IA, northwest of Waterloo; established Jan 15, 1851 from Buchanan and Black Hawk counties.
Name origin: For Maj. William Orlando Butler (1791–1880), officer in the War of 1812 and Mexican-American War; U.S. representative from KY (1839–43).

Allison　City
ZIP: 50602　**Lat:** 42-45-08 N　**Long:** 92-47-44 W
Pop: 1,000 (1990); 1,132 (1980)　**Pop Density:** 333.3
Land: 3.0 sq. mi.; **Water:** 0.0 sq. mi.
Incorporated Jul 25, 1881.

Aplington　City
ZIP: 50604　**Lat:** 42-34-53 N　**Long:** 92-52-51 W
Pop: 1,034 (1990); 1,027 (1980)　**Pop Density:** 1723.3
Land: 0.6 sq. mi.; **Water:** 0.0 sq. mi.
Incorporated Nov 9, 1877.

Aredale　City
ZIP: 50605　**Lat:** 42-50-00 N　**Long:** 93-00-16 W
Pop: 88 (1990); 88 (1980)　**Pop Density:** 88.0
Land: 1.0 sq. mi.; **Water:** 0.0 sq. mi.
Incorporated Jun 5, 1920.

Bristow　City
ZIP: 50611　**Lat:** 42-46-24 N　**Long:** 92-54-24 W
Pop: 197 (1990); 252 (1980)　**Pop Density:** 218.9
Land: 0.9 sq. mi.; **Water:** 0.0 sq. mi.
Incorporated Dec 15, 1881.

Clarksville　City
ZIP: 50619　**Lat:** 42-46-48 N　**Long:** 92-40-05 W
Pop: 1,382 (1990); 1,424 (1980)　**Pop Density:** 1151.7
Land: 1.2 sq. mi.; **Water:** 0.0 sq. mi.
Incorporated May 11, 1874.

Dumont　City
ZIP: 50625　**Lat:** 42-45-05 N　**Long:** 92-58-24 W
Pop: 705 (1990); 815 (1980)　**Pop Density:** 391.7
Land: 1.8 sq. mi.; **Water:** 0.0 sq. mi.
Incorporated Jan 24, 1896.

Greene　City
ZIP: 50636　**Lat:** 42-53-48 N　**Long:** 92-48-14 W
Pop: 1,142 (1990); 1,332 (1980)　**Pop Density:** 1038.2
Land: 1.1 sq. mi.; **Water:** 0.1 sq. mi.
Incorporated Jul 15, 1879.
Name origin: For Judge George Green of Linn County.

New Hartford　City
ZIP: 50660　**Lat:** 42-34-01 N　**Long:** 92-37-20 W
Pop: 683 (1990); 764 (1980)　**Pop Density:** 1366.0
Land: 0.5 sq. mi.; **Water:** 0.0 sq. mi.
Incorporated Dec 7, 1883.
Name origin: For Hartford, CT.

Parkersburg　City
ZIP: 50665　**Lat:** 42-34-24 N　**Long:** 92-46-57 W
Pop: 1,804 (1990); 1,968 (1980)　**Pop Density:** 1640.0
Land: 1.1 sq. mi.; **Water:** 0.0 sq. mi.
Incorporated Dec 7, 1874.

Shell Rock　City
ZIP: 50670　**Lat:** 42-42-45 N　**Long:** 92-34-53 W
Pop: 1,385 (1990); 1,478 (1980)　**Pop Density:** 923.3
Land: 1.5 sq. mi.; **Water:** 0.1 sq. mi.
Incorporated Jun 1, 1875.

Calhoun County
County Seat: Rockwell City (ZIP: 50579)

Pop: 11,508 (1990); 13,542 (1980)　**Pop Density:** 20.2
Land: 570.2 sq. mi.; **Water:** 2.1 sq. mi.　**Area Code:** 712
In central IA, west of Fort Dodge; established as Fox County Jan 15, 1851 from Greene County; name changed Jan 12, 1853.
Name origin: For John Caldwell Calhoun (1782–1850), U.S. statesman and proponent of Southern causes.

Farnhamville　City
ZIP: 50538　**Lat:** 42-16-38 N　**Long:** 94-24-28 W
Pop: 414 (1990); 461 (1980)　**Pop Density:** 690.0
Land: 0.6 sq. mi.; **Water:** 0.0 sq. mi.
Incorporated Apr 1, 1893. Part of the town is also in Webster County.

Jolley　City
ZIP: 50551　**Lat:** 42-28-45 N　**Long:** 94-43-04 W
Pop: 68 (1990); 91 (1980)　**Pop Density:** 680.0
Land: 0.1 sq. mi.; **Water:** 0.0 sq. mi.
Incorporated Nov 16, 1895.

Knierim City
ZIP: 50552   **Lat:** 42-27-21 N **Long:** 94-27-22 W
Pop: 71 (1990); 125 (1980)   **Pop Density:** 71.0
Land: 1.0 sq. mi.; **Water:** 0.0 sq. mi.   **Elev:** 1175 ft.
Incorporated Jun 13, 1901.

Lake City City
ZIP: 51449   **Lat:** 42-16-03 N **Long:** 94-43-50 W
Pop: 1,841 (1990); 2,006 (1980)   **Pop Density:** 383.5
Land: 4.8 sq. mi.; **Water:** 0.0 sq. mi.
Incorporated Mar 13, 1887.

Lohrville City
ZIP: 51453   **Lat:** 42-16-04 N **Long:** 94-33-03 W
Pop: 453 (1990); 521 (1980)   **Pop Density:** 116.2
Land: 3.9 sq. mi.; **Water:** 0.0 sq. mi.
Incorporated Dec 14, 1882.

Lytton City
ZIP: 50561   **Lat:** 42-25-24 N **Long:** 94-51-21 W
Pop: 42 (1990); 43 (1980)   **Pop Density:** 2100.0
Land: 0.02 sq. mi.; **Water:** 0.0 sq. mi.
Incorporated Jul 21, 1911. Part of the town is also in Sac County.

Manson City
Lat: 42-31-43 N **Long:** 94-32-21 W
Pop: 1,844 (1990); 1,924 (1980)   **Pop Density:** 576.3
Land: 3.2 sq. mi.; **Water:** 0.0 sq. mi.   **Elev:** 1221 ft.
Incorporated May 5, 1877.
Name origin: For one of the town's residents.

Pomeroy City
ZIP: 50575   **Lat:** 42-33-12 N **Long:** 94-40-42 W
Pop: 762 (1990); 895 (1980)   **Pop Density:** 381.0
Land: 2.0 sq. mi.; **Water:** 0.0 sq. mi.
Incorporated Apr 22, 1880.

Rinard City
ZIP: 50587   **Lat:** 42-20-22 N **Long:** 94-29-11 W
Pop: 71 (1990); 97 (1980)   **Pop Density:** 71.0
Land: 1.0 sq. mi.; **Water:** 0.0 sq. mi.
Incorporated Dec 29, 1914.

Rockwell City City
ZIP: 50579   **Lat:** 42-23-54 N **Long:** 94-37-51 W
Pop: 1,981 (1990); 2,276 (1980)   **Pop Density:** 507.9
Land: 3.9 sq. mi.; **Water:** 0.0 sq. mi.
Incorporated May 2, 1882.

Somers City
ZIP: 50586   **Lat:** 42-22-40 N **Long:** 94-25-50 W
Pop: 161 (1990); 220 (1980)   **Pop Density:** 536.7
Land: 0.3 sq. mi.; **Water:** 0.0 sq. mi.
Incorporated Apr 26, 1902.

Yetter City
Lat: 42-18-59 N **Long:** 94-50-36 W
Pop: 49 (1990); 52 (1980)   **Pop Density:** 490.0
Land: 0.1 sq. mi.; **Water:** 0.0 sq. mi.   **Elev:** 1216 ft.
Incorporated Jan 11, 1904.

Carroll County
County Seat: Carroll (ZIP: 51401)

Pop: 21,423 (1990); 22,951 (1980)   **Pop Density:** 37.6
Land: 569.3 sq. mi.; **Water:** 0.9 sq. mi.   **Area Code:** 712
In west-central IA, west of Ames; established Jan 15, 1851 from Guthrie County.
Name origin: For Charles Carroll (1737–1832), a signer of the Declaration of Independence and U.S. senator from MD (1789–92).

Arcadia City
ZIP: 51430   **Lat:** 42-05-13 N **Long:** 95-02-36 W
Pop: 485 (1990); 454 (1980)   **Pop Density:** 485.0
Land: 1.0 sq. mi.; **Water:** 0.0 sq. mi.
Incorporated Nov 3, 1881.
Name origin: For a region in ancient Greece, said to be noted for its pastoral simplicity and contentment.

Breda City
ZIP: 51436   **Lat:** 42-10-59 N **Long:** 94-58-39 W
Pop: 467 (1990); 502 (1980)   **Pop Density:** 934.0
Land: 0.5 sq. mi.; **Water:** 0.0 sq. mi.
Incorporated Oct 30, 1883.

Carroll City
ZIP: 51401   **Lat:** 42-04-09 N **Long:** 94-51-52 W
Pop: 9,579 (1990); 9,705 (1980)   **Pop Density:** 1842.1
Land: 5.2 sq. mi.; **Water:** 0.0 sq. mi.
Incorporated Sep 27, 1869.
Name origin: For Charles Carroll, (1737–1832), a signer of the Declaration of Independence and U.S. senator from MD (1789–92).

Coon Rapids City
ZIP: 50058   **Lat:** 41-52-20 N **Long:** 94-40-35 W
Pop: 1,266 (1990); 1,448 (1980)   **Pop Density:** 973.8
Land: 1.3 sq. mi.; **Water:** 0.0 sq. mi.
Incorporated Nov 2, 1882.
Name origin: For the rapids on Middle Raccoon River, on which the town is located..

Dedham City
ZIP: 51440   **Lat:** 41-54-31 N **Long:** 94-49-21 W
Pop: 264 (1990); 321 (1980)   **Pop Density:** 440.0
Land: 0.6 sq. mi.; **Water:** 0.0 sq. mi.
Incorporated Apr 2, 1884.

Glidden City
ZIP: 51443   **Lat:** 42-03-26 N **Long:** 94-43-30 W
Pop: 1,099 (1990); 1,076 (1980)   **Pop Density:** 1099.0
Land: 1.0 sq. mi.; **Water:** 0.0 sq. mi.
Incorporated Aug 22, 1873.

IOWA, Carroll County

Halbur
City
ZIP: 51444 Lat: 42-00-19 N Long: 94-58-17 W
Pop: 215 (1990); 229 (1980) Pop Density: 716.7
Land: 0.3 sq. mi.; Water: 0.0 sq. mi.
Incorporated Apr 22, 1902.

Lanesboro
City
ZIP: 51451 Lat: 42-11-00 N Long: 94-41-27 W
Pop: 182 (1990); 196 (1980) Pop Density: 260.0
Land: 0.7 sq. mi.; Water: 0.0 sq. mi. Elev: 1149 ft.
Incorporated Apr 30, 1903.

Lidderdale
City
ZIP: 51452 Lat: 42-07-26 N Long: 94-47-03 W
Pop: 202 (1990); 197 (1980) Pop Density: 84.2
Land: 2.4 sq. mi.; Water: 0.0 sq. mi.
Incorporated Nov 27, 1905.

Manning
City
ZIP: 51455 Lat: 41-54-34 N Long: 95-03-51 W
Pop: 1,484 (1990); 1,609 (1980) Pop Density: 618.3
Land: 2.4 sq. mi.; Water: 0.0 sq. mi. Elev: 1355 ft.
Incorporated Feb 17, 1882.
Name origin: For a local merchant.

Ralston
City
ZIP: 51459 Lat: 42-02-27 N Long: 94-38-02 W
Pop: 111 (1990); 102 (1980) Pop Density: 222.0
Land: 0.5 sq. mi.; Water: 0.0 sq. mi.
Incorporated Oct 31, 1903. Part of the town is also in Greene County.
Name origin: For an officer of the American Express Company.

Templeton
City
ZIP: 51463 Lat: 41-55-05 N Long: 94-56-32 W
Pop: 321 (1990); 319 (1980) Pop Density: 1070.0
Land: 0.3 sq. mi.; Water: 0.0 sq. mi.
Incorporated Sep 28, 1883.

Willey
City
ZIP: 51401 Lat: 41-58-42 N Long: 94-49-14 W
Pop: 78 (1990); 94 (1980) Pop Density: 390.0
Land: 0.2 sq. mi.; Water: 0.0 sq. mi.
Incorporated Feb 29, 1912.

Cass County
County Seat: Atlantic (ZIP: 50022)

Pop: 15,128 (1990); 16,932 (1980) Pop Density: 26.8
Land: 564.3 sq. mi.; Water: 0.7 sq. mi. Area Code: 712
In southwestern IA, east of Council Bluffs; established Jan 15, 1851 from Pottawattamie County.
Name origin: For Lewis Cass (1782–1866), OH legislator, governor of MI Territory (1813–31), U.S. secretary of war (1831–36), and U.S. secretary of state (1857–60).

Anita
City
ZIP: 50020 Lat: 41-26-36 N Long: 94-45-55 W
Pop: 1,068 (1990); 1,153 (1980) Pop Density: 667.5
Land: 1.6 sq. mi.; Water: 0.0 sq. mi.
Incorporated May 19, 1875.
Name origin: For the niece of the surveyor who laid out the town.

Atlantic
City
ZIP: 50022 Lat: 41-23-53 N Long: 95-00-53 W
Pop: 7,432 (1990); 7,789 (1980) Pop Density: 917.5
Land: 8.1 sq. mi.; Water: 0.0 sq. mi. Elev: 1215 ft.
Incorporated Nov 26, 1869.

Cumberland
City
ZIP: 50843 Lat: 41-16-25 N Long: 94-52-10 W
Pop: 295 (1990); 351 (1980) Pop Density: 491.7
Land: 0.6 sq. mi.; Water: 0.0 sq. mi.
Incorporated May 2, 1893.

Griswold
City
ZIP: 51535 Lat: 41-14-02 N Long: 95-08-19 W
Pop: 1,049 (1990); 1,176 (1980) Pop Density: 1748.3
Land: 0.6 sq. mi.; Water: 0.0 sq. mi.
Incorporated Dec 13, 1885.
Name origin: For railroad official, J.N.A. Griswold.

Lewis
City
ZIP: 51544 Lat: 41-18-22 N Long: 95-05-03 W
Pop: 433 (1990); 497 (1980) Pop Density: 866.0
Land: 0.5 sq. mi.; Water: 0.0 sq. mi.
Incorporated May 14, 1874.
Name origin: For Lewis Cass (1782–1866), OH legislator, governor of MI Territory (1813–31), U.S. secretary of war (1831–36), and U.S. secretary of state (1857–60).

Marne
City
ZIP: 51552 Lat: 41-26-54 N Long: 95-06-37 W
Pop: 149 (1990); 162 (1980) Pop Density: 248.3
Land: 0.6 sq. mi.; Water: 0.0 sq. mi.
Incorporated May 10, 1892.

Massena
City
ZIP: 50853 Lat: 41-15-04 N Long: 94-46-09 W
Pop: 372 (1990); 518 (1980) Pop Density: 531.4
Land: 0.7 sq. mi.; Water: 0.0 sq. mi.
Incorporated Jan 18, 1887.
Name origin: For André Masséna (1758–1817), French marshall under Napoleon (1769–1821).

Wiota
City
ZIP: 50274 **Lat:** 41-24-02 N **Long:** 94-53-14 W
Pop: 160 (1990); 181 (1980) **Pop Density:** 533.3
Land: 0.3 sq. mi.; **Water:** 0.0 sq. mi.
Incorporated Jan 16, 1884.
Name origin: From Sioux term for 'many moons'; from Winnebago term for 'much water.'

Cedar County
County Seat: Tipton (ZIP: 52772)

Pop: 17,381 (1990); 18,635 (1980) **Pop Density:** 30.0
Land: 579.6 sq. mi.; **Water:** 2.4 sq. mi. **Area Code:** 319
In central-eastern IA, east of Iowa City; established Dec 21, 1837 (prior to statehood) from Wisconsin Territory.
Name origin: For the Red Cedar River that runs through the county.

Bennett
City
ZIP: 52721 **Lat:** 41-44-23 N **Long:** 90-58-27 W
Pop: 395 (1990); 458 (1980) **Pop Density:** 1975.0
Land: 0.2 sq. mi.; **Water:** 0.0 sq. mi.
Incorporated Dec 26, 1896.
Name origin: For railroad man Chet Bennett.

Clarence
City
ZIP: 52216 **Lat:** 41-53-09 N **Long:** 91-03-29 W
Pop: 936 (1990); 1,001 (1980) **Pop Density:** 1560.0
Land: 0.6 sq. mi.; **Water:** 0.0 sq. mi.
Incorporated Feb 26, 1866.

Durant
City
ZIP: 52747 **Lat:** 41-36-03 N **Long:** 90-54-32 W
Pop: 1,540 (1990); 1,579 (1980) **Pop Density:** 2566.7
Land: 0.6 sq. mi.; **Water:** 0.0 sq. mi.
Incorporated Jul 1, 1867. Part of the town is also in Muscatine and Scott counties.

Lowden
City
ZIP: 52255 **Lat:** 41-51-30 N **Long:** 90-55-22 W
Pop: 726 (1990); 717 (1980) **Pop Density:** 726.0
Land: 1.0 sq. mi.; **Water:** 0.0 sq. mi.
Incorporated Mar 12, 1869.

Mechanicsville
City
ZIP: 52306 **Lat:** 41-54-17 N **Long:** 91-15-11 W
Pop: 1,012 (1990); 1,166 (1980) **Pop Density:** 1445.7
Land: 0.7 sq. mi.; **Water:** 0.0 sq. mi.
Incorporated Nov 25, 1867.
Name origin: For the first settlers, who were mechanics.

Stanwood
City
ZIP: 52337 **Lat:** 41-53-37 N **Long:** 91-08-59 W
Pop: 646 (1990); 705 (1980) **Pop Density:** 1076.7
Land: 0.6 sq. mi.; **Water:** 0.0 sq. mi.
Incorporated Mar 29, 1887.

Tipton
City
ZIP: 52772 **Lat:** 41-46-13 N **Long:** 91-07-44 W
Pop: 2,998 (1990); 3,055 (1980) **Pop Density:** 1665.6
Land: 1.8 sq. mi.; **Water:** 0.0 sq. mi.
Incorporated Jan 27, 1857.

West Branch
City
ZIP: 52358 **Lat:** 41-40-12 N **Long:** 91-20-57 W
Pop: 1,908 (1990); 1,867 (1980) **Pop Density:** 1004.2
Land: 1.9 sq. mi.; **Water:** 0.0 sq. mi.
Incorporated Apr 12, 1875.

Wilton
City
Lat: 41-35-53 N **Long:** 91-01-10 W
Pop: 4 (1990); 9 (1980) **Pop Density:** 133.3
Land: 0.035 sq. mi.; **Water:** 0.0 sq. mi.
Incorporated Feb 12, 1878. Part of the town is also in Muscatine County.

IOWA, Cerro Gordo County *American Places Dictionary*

Cerro Gordo County
County Seat: Mason City (ZIP: 50401)

Pop: 46,733 (1990); 48,458 (1980) **Pop Density:** 82.2
Land: 568.4 sq. mi.; **Water:** 6.8 sq. mi. **Area Code:** 515

In north-central IA, northeast of Fort Dodge; established Jan 15, 1851 from Floyd County.

Name origin: For the city in Mexico, site of a Mexican War battle on Apr 18, 1847. Spanish 'fat hill' or 'big hill.'

Clear Lake City
ZIP: 50428 Lat: 43-08-06 N Long: 93-22-24 W
Pop: 8,183 (1990); 7,458 (1980) Pop Density: 802.3
Land: 10.2 sq. mi.; Water: 2.6 sq. mi.

In north-central IA, east of Mason City. Incorporated May 26, 1871.

Name origin: For its location at the northern end of Clear Lake.

Dougherty City
ZIP: 50433 Lat: 42-55-21 N Long: 93-02-10 W
Pop: 107 (1990); 128 (1980) Pop Density: 178.3
Land: 0.6 sq. mi.; Water: 0.0 sq. mi.

Incorporated Dec 29, 1900.

Name origin: For prominent resident, Daniel Dougherty.

Mason City City
ZIP: 50401 Lat: 43-09-04 N Long: 93-11-54 W
Pop: 29,040 (1990); 30,144 (1980) Pop Density: 1134.4
Land: 25.6 sq. mi.; Water: 0.3 sq. mi.

In northern IA, 60 mi. northwest of Waterloo. Settled 1853; incorporated as a city Dec 21, 1869.

Name origin: Named by members of the local Masonic lodge for the town's large brick and tile industry. Previously called Masonville.

Meservey City
ZIP: 50457 Lat: 42-54-54 N Long: 93-28-23 W
Pop: 292 (1990); 324 (1980) Pop Density: 194.7
Land: 1.5 sq. mi.; Water: 0.0 sq. mi.

Incorporated Aug 24, 1893.

Plymouth City
ZIP: 50464 Lat: 43-14-48 N Long: 93-07-20 W
Pop: 453 (1990); 463 (1980) Pop Density: 1132.5
Land: 0.4 sq. mi.; Water: 0.0 sq. mi. Elev: 1128 ft.

Incorporated Oct 18, 1900.

Rock Falls City
ZIP: 50467 Lat: 43-12-25 N Long: 93-05-13 W
Pop: 130 (1990); 148 (1980) Pop Density: 650.0
Land: 0.2 sq. mi.; Water: 0.0 sq. mi.

Incorporated Jul 17, 1882.

Rockwell City
ZIP: 50469 Lat: 42-58-47 N Long: 93-11-12 W
Pop: 1,008 (1990); 1,039 (1980) Pop Density: 336.0
Land: 3.0 sq. mi.; Water: 0.0 sq. mi.

Incorporated Jul 9, 1881.

Swaledale City
ZIP: 50477 Lat: 42-58-36 N Long: 93-18-55 W
Pop: 190 (1990); 186 (1980) Pop Density: 633.3
Land: 0.3 sq. mi.; Water: 0.0 sq. mi.

Incorporated Mar 31, 1892.

Thornton City
ZIP: 50479 Lat: 42-56-38 N Long: 93-23-15 W
Pop: 431 (1990); 442 (1980) Pop Density: 359.2
Land: 1.2 sq. mi.; Water: 0.0 sq. mi.

Incorporated Aug 22, 1892.

Ventura City
ZIP: 50482 Lat: 43-07-35 N Long: 93-27-35 W
Pop: 590 (1990); 614 (1980) Pop Density: 347.1
Land: 1.7 sq. mi.; Water: 0.6 sq. mi.

Incorporated May 28, 1960.

Cherokee County
County Seat: Cherokee (ZIP: 51012)

Pop: 14,098 (1990); 16,238 (1980) **Pop Density:** 24.4
Land: 577.2 sq. mi.; **Water:** 0.2 sq. mi. **Area Code:** 712

In northwestern IA, northeast of Sioux City; established Jan 15, 1851 from Crawford County.

Name origin: For the Indian tribe of Iroquoian linguistic stock. Name may derive from Creek *tciloki* 'people of a different speech.'

Aurelia City
ZIP: 51005 Lat: 42-42-46 N Long: 95-26-12 W
Pop: 1,034 (1990); 1,143 (1980) Pop Density: 1034.0
Land: 1.0 sq. mi.; Water: 0.0 sq. mi.

Incorporated Dec 27, 1879.

Cherokee City
ZIP: 51012 Lat: 42-45-02 N Long: 95-33-08 W
Pop: 6,026 (1990); 7,004 (1980) Pop Density: 987.9
Land: 6.1 sq. mi.; Water: 0.0 sq. mi.

Incorporated Apr 5, 1873.

Name origin: For the Indian tribe of Iroquoian linguistic stock. Name may derive from Creek *tciloki* 'people of a different speech.'

Cleghorn — City
ZIP: 51014   Lat: 42-48-41 N   Long: 95-42-48 W
Pop: 275 (1990); 275 (1980)   Pop Density: 916.7
Land: 0.3 sq. mi.; Water: 0.0 sq. mi.
Incorporated Jan 25, 1901.
Name origin: For Dr. Cleghorn, who donated the land to the town in 1901.

Larrabee — City
ZIP: 51029   Lat: 42-51-40 N   Long: 95-32-41 W
Pop: 175 (1990); 169 (1980)   Pop Density: 1750.0
Land: 0.1 sq. mi.; Water: 0.0 sq. mi.
Incorporated Jul 25, 1896.
Name origin: For William Larrabee, who was governor of IA at the time of naming in 1886.

Marcus — City
ZIP: 51035   Lat: 42-49-26 N   Long: 95-48-25 W
Pop: 1,171 (1990); 1,206 (1980)   Pop Density: 688.8
Land: 1.7 sq. mi.; Water: 0.0 sq. mi.
Incorporated May 15, 1882.

Meriden — City
ZIP: 51037   Lat: 42-47-39 N   Long: 95-37-57 W
Pop: 193 (1990); 233 (1980)   Pop Density: 1930.0
Land: 0.1 sq. mi.; Water: 0.0 sq. mi.
Incorporated Dec 24, 1881.
Name origin: Renamed by the post office. Previously called Hazzard.

Quimby — City
ZIP: 51049   Lat: 42-37-45 N   Long: 95-38-33 W
Pop: 334 (1990); 424 (1980)   Pop Density: 1113.3
Land: 0.3 sq. mi.; Water: 0.0 sq. mi.
Incorporated Jun 7, 1906.

Washta — City
ZIP: 51061   Lat: 42-34-33 N   Long: 95-43-09 W
Pop: 284 (1990); 320 (1980)   Pop Density: 258.2
Land: 1.1 sq. mi.; Water: 0.0 sq. mi.
Incorporated Jun 6, 1890.
Name origin: A phonetic spelling of the Dakota term *waste* meaning 'good.'

Chickasaw County
County Seat: New Hampton (ZIP: 50659)

Pop: 13,295 (1990); 15,437 (1980)   Pop Density: 26.3
Land: 504.7 sq. mi.; Water: 0.8 sq. mi.   Area Code: 515
In northeastern IA, north of Waterloo; established Jan 15, 1851 from Fayette County.
Name origin: For the Indian tribe, closely connected with the Choctaw, and of Muskhogean linguistic stock; meaning of name unknown.

Alta Vista — City
ZIP: 50603   Lat: 43-11-44 N   Long: 92-25-01 W
Pop: 246 (1990); 314 (1980)   Pop Density: 307.5
Land: 0.8 sq. mi.; Water: 0.0 sq. mi.
Incorporated Sep 18, 1894.

Bassett — City
ZIP: 50645   Lat: 43-03-44 N   Long: 92-30-56 W
Pop: 74 (1990); 128 (1980)   Pop Density: 185.0
Land: 0.4 sq. mi.; Water: 0.0 sq. mi.
Incorporated Nov 7, 1896.

Fredericksburg — City
Lat: 42-57-52 N   Long: 92-11-53 W
Pop: 1,011 (1990); 1,075 (1980)   Pop Density: 1444.3
Land: 0.7 sq. mi.; Water: 0.0 sq. mi.
Founded 1856; incorporated Dec 18, 1894.
Name origin: For founder Frederick Padden.

Ionia — City
ZIP: 50645   Lat: 43-02-10 N   Long: 92-27-27 W
Pop: 304 (1990); 350 (1980)   Pop Density: 506.7
Land: 0.6 sq. mi.; Water: 0.0 sq. mi.
Incorporated Apr 23, 1891.

Lawler — City
ZIP: 52154   Lat: 43-04-18 N   Long: 92-09-13 W
Pop: 517 (1990); 534 (1980)   Pop Density: 574.4
Land: 0.9 sq. mi.; Water: 0.0 sq. mi.
Incorporated Apr 28, 1873.

Nashua — City
ZIP: 50658   Lat: 42-57-01 N   Long: 92-32-20 W
Pop: 1,476 (1990); 1,846 (1980)   Pop Density: 615.0
Land: 2.4 sq. mi.; Water: 0.2 sq. mi.
Incorporated Jan 29, 1857.
Name origin: For Nashua, NY, former home of early settlers.

New Hampton — City
ZIP: 50659   Lat: 43-03-35 N   Long: 92-18-52 W
Pop: 3,660 (1990); 3,940 (1980)   Pop Density: 1464.0
Land: 2.5 sq. mi.; Water: 0.0 sq. mi.
Incorporated Apr 26, 1873.

North Washington — City
ZIP: 50661   Lat: 43-06-58 N   Long: 92-24-53 W
Pop: 107 (1990); 142 (1980)   Pop Density: 535.0
Land: 0.2 sq. mi.; Water: 0.0 sq. mi.
Incorporated Apr 16, 1904.

IOWA, Clarke County   *American Places Dictionary*

> ## Clarke County
> **County Seat: Osceola (ZIP: 50213)**
>
> **Pop:** 8,287 (1990); 8,612 (1980)   **Pop Density:** 19.2
> **Land:** 431.2 sq. mi.; **Water:** 0.6 sq. mi.   **Area Code:** 515
>
> In south-central IA, south of Des Moines; established Jan 13, 1846 from Lucas County.
>
> **Name origin:** For James Clarke (1811–50), publisher of Burlington, IA, *Gazette* (1837), and last governor of IA Territory (1845–46).

Murray   City
ZIP: 50174   **Lat:** 41-02-28 N **Long:** 93-56-54 W
Pop: 731 (1990); 703 (1980)   **Pop Density:** 913.8
Land: 0.8 sq. mi.; **Water:** 0.0 sq. mi.
Incorporated Oct 21, 1880.

Osceola   City
ZIP: 50213   **Lat:** 41-01-52 N **Long:** 93-46-25 W
Pop: 4,164 (1990); 3,750 (1980)   **Pop Density:** 832.8
Land: 5.0 sq. mi.; **Water:** 0.1 sq. mi.
Incorporated Dec 24, 1866.
Name origin: For Osceola (c. 1804–38), the famous chief of the Florida Seminole Indians.

Woodburn   City
ZIP: 50275   **Lat:** 41-00-37 N **Long:** 93-35-47 W
Pop: 240 (1990); 207 (1980)   **Pop Density:** 400.0
Land: 0.6 sq. mi.; **Water:** 0.0 sq. mi.
Incorporated Feb 12, 1878.

> ## Clay County
> **County Seat: Spencer (ZIP: 51301)**
>
> **Pop:** 17,585 (1990); 19,576 (1980)   **Pop Density:** 30.9
> **Land:** 568.9 sq. mi.; **Water:** 3.6 sq. mi.   **Area Code:** 712
>
> In north-central IA, northwest of Fort Dodge; established Jan 15, 1851 from Indian lands.
>
> **Name origin:** For Lt. Col. Henry Clay, Jr. (1807–47), son of the statesman (1777–1852); killed at the Battle of Buena Vista during the Mexican-American War.

Dickens   City
ZIP: 51333   **Lat:** 43-08-00 N **Long:** 95-01-19 W
Pop: 214 (1990); 289 (1980)   **Pop Density:** 267.5
Land: 0.8 sq. mi.; **Water:** 0.0 sq. mi.
Incorporated Apr 7, 1909.

Everly   City
ZIP: 51338   **Lat:** 43-09-37 N **Long:** 95-19-17 W
Pop: 706 (1990); 796 (1980)   **Pop Density:** 706.0
Land: 1.0 sq. mi.; **Water:** 0.0 sq. mi.
Incorporated Apr 7, 1902.

Fostoria   City
ZIP: 51340   **Lat:** 43-14-29 N **Long:** 95-09-17 W
Pop: 205 (1990); 261 (1980)   **Pop Density:** 410.0
Land: 0.5 sq. mi.; **Water:** 0.0 sq. mi.
Incorporated Jan 30, 1912.

Gillett Grove   City
ZIP: 51341   **Lat:** 43-00-55 N **Long:** 95-02-06 W
Pop: 67 (1990); 93 (1980)   **Pop Density:** 335.0
Land: 0.2 sq. mi.; **Water:** 0.0 sq. mi.
Incorporated Aug 29, 1974.

Greenville   City
ZIP: 51343   **Lat:** 43-01-01 N **Long:** 95-08-42 W
Pop: 84 (1990); 122 (1980)   **Pop Density:** 420.0
Land: 0.2 sq. mi.; **Water:** 0.0 sq. mi.
Incorporated Dec 30, 1916.

Peterson   City
ZIP: 51047   **Lat:** 42-55-06 N **Long:** 95-20-28 W
Pop: 390 (1990); 470 (1980)   **Pop Density:** 1300.0
Land: 0.3 sq. mi.; **Water:** 0.0 sq. mi.
Incorporated Nov 12, 1886.

Rossie   City
ZIP: 51357   **Lat:** 43-00-47 N **Long:** 95-11-19 W
Pop: 68 (1990); 72 (1980)   **Pop Density:** 340.0
Land: 0.2 sq. mi.; **Water:** 0.0 sq. mi.
Incorporated Aug 30, 1922.

Royal   City
ZIP: 51357   **Lat:** 43-03-50 N **Long:** 95-16-59 W
Pop: 466 (1990); 522 (1980)   **Pop Density:** 1553.3
Land: 0.3 sq. mi.; **Water:** 0.0 sq. mi.
Incorporated Aug 30, 1910.

Spencer   City
ZIP: 51301   **Lat:** 43-08-45 N **Long:** 95-09-04 W
Pop: 11,066 (1990); 11,726 (1980)   **Pop Density:** 1106.6
Land: 10.0 sq. mi.; **Water:** 0.0 sq. mi.   **Elev:** 1321 ft.
Incorporated Mar 9, 1880.
Name origin: For U.S. senator George E. Spencer from AL.

Webb   City
ZIP: 51366   **Lat:** 42-56-57 N **Long:** 95-00-43 W
Pop: 167 (1990); 222 (1980)   **Pop Density:** 334.0
Land: 0.5 sq. mi.; **Water:** 0.0 sq. mi.
Incorporated Apr 9, 1901.

Clayton County
County Seat: Elkader (ZIP: 52043)

Pop: 19,054 (1990); 21,098 (1980) **Pop Density:** 24.5
Land: 778.8 sq. mi.; **Water:** 14.0 sq. mi. **Area Code:** 319

On northeastern border of IA, north of Dubuque; established Dec 21, 1837 (prior to statehood) from Dubuque County.

Name origin: For John Middleton Clayton (1796–1856), U.S. senator from DE and U.S. secretary of state (1849–50).

Clayton City
ZIP: 52049 **Lat:** 42-54-08 N **Long:** 91-09-00 W
Pop: 41 (1990); 68 (1980) **Pop Density:** 68.3
Land: 0.6 sq. mi.; **Water:** 0.0 sq. mi.

Incorporated Nov 23, 1901.

Name origin: For John Middleton Clayton (1796–1856), U.S. senator from DE and U.S. secretary of state (1849–50).

Edgewood City
ZIP: 52042 **Lat:** 42-38-54 N **Long:** 91-24-06 W
Pop: 316 (1990); 372 (1980) **Pop Density:** 790.0
Land: 0.4 sq. mi.; **Water:** 0.0 sq. mi.

Incorporated Apr 6, 1899. Part of the town is also in Delaware County.

Elkader City
ZIP: 52043 **Lat:** 42-51-21 N **Long:** 91-24-10 W
Pop: 1,510 (1990); 1,688 (1980) **Pop Density:** 1258.3
Land: 1.2 sq. mi.; **Water:** 0.0 sq. mi.

Incorporated May 1, 1891.

Name origin: Named in 1845 for Abd el Kader (1808–83), Algerian revolutionary leader.

Elkport City
ZIP: 52044 **Lat:** 42-44-27 N **Long:** 91-16-31 W
Pop: 82 (1990); 98 (1980) **Pop Density:** 410.0
Land: 0.2 sq. mi.; **Water:** 0.0 sq. mi.

Incorporated Feb 24, 1896.

Farmersburg City
ZIP: 52047 **Lat:** 42-57-30 N **Long:** 91-22-02 W
Pop: 291 (1990); 276 (1980) **Pop Density:** 727.5
Land: 0.4 sq. mi.; **Water:** 0.0 sq. mi.

Incorporated Jun 1, 1902.

Garber City
ZIP: 52048 **Lat:** 42-44-38 N **Long:** 91-15-46 W
Pop: 118 (1990); 140 (1980) **Pop Density:** 590.0
Land: 0.2 sq. mi.; **Water:** 0.0 sq. mi.

Incorporated Nov 18, 1907.

Garnavillo City
ZIP: 52049 **Lat:** 42-52-04 N **Long:** 91-14-11 W
Pop: 727 (1990); 723 (1980) **Pop Density:** 807.8
Land: 0.9 sq. mi.; **Water:** 0.0 sq. mi.

Incorporated Nov 21, 1907.

Guttenberg City
ZIP: 52052 **Lat:** 42-47-16 N **Long:** 91-06-14 W
Pop: 2,257 (1990); 2,428 (1980) **Pop Density:** 1074.8
Land: 2.1 sq. mi.; **Water:** 0.0 sq. mi. **Elev:** 625 ft.

Incorporated Jan 27, 1857.

Littleport City
ZIP: 52055 **Lat:** 42-45-11 N **Long:** 91-22-08 W
Pop: 88 (1990); 106 (1980) **Pop Density:** 293.3
Land: 0.3 sq. mi.; **Water:** 0.0 sq. mi. **Elev:** 708 ft.

Incorporated Nov 21, 1907.

Luana City
ZIP: 52156 **Lat:** 43-03-39 N **Long:** 91-27-17 W
Pop: 190 (1990); 246 (1980) **Pop Density:** 172.7
Land: 1.1 sq. mi.; **Water:** 0.0 sq. mi.

Incorporated May 29, 1911.

Marquette City
ZIP: 52158 **Lat:** 43-02-34 N **Long:** 91-11-02 W
Pop: 479 (1990); 528 (1980) **Pop Density:** 435.5
Land: 1.1 sq. mi.; **Water:** 0.1 sq. mi.

Incorporated Jun 2, 1874.

Name origin: For French explorer and missionary Jacques Marquette (1637–75), known as Père Marquette.

McGregor City
ZIP: 52157 **Lat:** 43-01-22 N **Long:** 91-10-50 W
Pop: 797 (1990); 945 (1980) **Pop Density:** 569.3
Land: 1.4 sq. mi.; **Water:** 0.0 sq. mi.

Incorporated Mar 7, 1859.

Name origin: For early proprietor, Alexander McGregor.

Millville City
ZIP: 52052 **Lat:** 42-42-17 N **Long:** 91-04-37 W
Pop: 20 (1990); 50 (1980) **Pop Density:** 200.0
Land: 0.1 sq. mi.; **Water:** 0.0 sq. mi.

Incorporated Apr 27, 1967.

Monona City
ZIP: 52159 **Lat:** 43-03-04 N **Long:** 91-23-25 W
Pop: 1,520 (1990); 1,530 (1980) **Pop Density:** 1381.8
Land: 1.1 sq. mi.; **Water:** 0.0 sq. mi.

Incorporated May 11, 1897.

Name origin: Origin and meaning of the name is unclear: possibly the name of a legendary Indian girl or an Indian divinity, or an Ottawa Indian term for 'beautiful land.'

North Buena Vista City
ZIP: 52066 **Lat:** 42-40-56 N **Long:** 90-57-22 W
Pop: 145 (1990); 155 (1980) **Pop Density:** 207.1
Land: 0.7 sq. mi.; **Water:** 0.0 sq. mi.

Incorporated Oct 25, 1907.

Osterdock City
Lat: 42-43-56 N **Long:** 91-09-30 W
Pop: 49 (1990); 35 (1980) **Pop Density:** 98.0
Land: 0.5 sq. mi.; **Water:** 0.0 sq. mi.

Incorporated Apr 16, 1904.

IOWA, Clayton County

Postville
City
Lat: 43-04-42 N Long: 91-34-22 W
Pop: 7 (1990) **Pop Density:** 70.0
Land: 0.1 sq. mi.; **Water:** 0.0 sq. mi.
Incorporated Mar 17, 1873. Part of the town is also in Allamakee County.
Name origin: For settler Joel Post, who arrived here in 1841.

St. Olaf
City
Lat: 42-55-39 N Long: 91-23-13 W
Pop: 111 (1990); 138 (1980) **Pop Density:** 555.0
Land: 0.2 sq. mi.; **Water:** 0.0 sq. mi.
Incorporated May 31, 1900.

Strawberry Point
City
ZIP: 52076 Lat: 42-40-58 N Long: 91-32-07 W
Pop: 1,357 (1990); 1,463 (1980) **Pop Density:** 753.9
Land: 1.8 sq. mi.; **Water:** 0.0 sq. mi.
Platted 1853; incorporated Dec 19, 1887.
Name origin: Named by soldiers for the abundance of wild strawberries in the area.

Volga
City
Lat: 42-48-09 N Long: 91-32-34 W
Pop: 306 (1990); 310 (1980) **Pop Density:** 382.5
Land: 0.8 sq. mi.; **Water:** 0.0 sq. mi.
Incorporated Oct 16, 1895.
Name origin: For the Volga River in Russia.

Clinton County
County Seat: Clinton (ZIP: 52732)

Pop: 51,040 (1990); 57,122 (1980) **Pop Density:** 73.4
Land: 695.0 sq. mi.; **Water:** 15.2 sq. mi. **Area Code:** 319
On central eastern border, north of Davenport; established Dec 21, 1837 (prior to statehood) from Dubuque County.
Name origin: For DeWitt Clinton (1769–1828), governor of NY (1817–23; 1825–28) and supporter of the Erie Canal.

Andover
City
ZIP: 52701 Lat: 41-58-43 N Long: 90-15-05 W
Pop: 99 (1990); 107 (1980) **Pop Density:** 495.0
Land: 0.2 sq. mi.; **Water:** 0.0 sq. mi.
Incorporated Jan 12, 1910.

Calamus
City
ZIP: 52729 Lat: 41-49-35 N Long: 90-45-34 W
Pop: 379 (1990); 452 (1980) **Pop Density:** 758.0
Land: 0.5 sq. mi.; **Water:** 0.0 sq. mi.
Incorporated Oct 6, 1875.
Name origin: For the wild marsh plant, sweet flag, found in the area.

Camanche
City
ZIP: 52730 Lat: 41-47-38 N Long: 90-16-30 W
Pop: 4,436 (1990); 4,725 (1980) **Pop Density:** 515.8
Land: 8.6 sq. mi.; **Water:** 0.7 sq. mi.
Incorporated Jan 28, 1857.
Name origin: For the Comanche Indians, a Shoshone Indian tribe; with a spelling alteration.

Charlotte
City
ZIP: 52731 Lat: 41-57-42 N Long: 90-28-03 W
Pop: 359 (1990); 442 (1980) **Pop Density:** 598.3
Land: 0.6 sq. mi.; **Water:** 0.0 sq. mi.
Incorporated Dec 5, 1904.

Clinton
City
ZIP: 52732 Lat: 41-50-35 N Long: 90-13-58 W
Pop: 29,201 (1990); 32,828 (1980) **Pop Density:** 822.6
Land: 35.5 sq. mi.; **Water:** 2.7 sq. mi.
In eastern IA on the Mississippi River, 28 mi. northeast of Davenport. Incorporated Jan 26, 1857.
Name origin: For DeWitt Clinton (1769–1828), governor of NY (1817–23; 1825–28) and supporter of the Erie Canal. Previously called New York.

Delmar
City
ZIP: 52037 Lat: 41-59-58 N Long: 90-36-28 W
Pop: 517 (1990); 633 (1980) **Pop Density:** 646.3
Land: 0.8 sq. mi.; **Water:** 0.0 sq. mi.
Incorporated Jun 10, 1876.

De Witt
City
ZIP: 52742 Lat: 41-49-17 N Long: 90-32-48 W
Pop: 4,514 (1990); 4,512 (1980) **Pop Density:** 940.4
Land: 4.8 sq. mi.; **Water:** 0.0 sq. mi.
Incorporated Sep 20, 1858.

Goose Lake
City
ZIP: 52750 Lat: 41-58-05 N Long: 90-22-55 W
Pop: 221 (1990); 274 (1980) **Pop Density:** 1105.0
Land: 0.2 sq. mi.; **Water:** 0.0 sq. mi.
Incorporated Dec 26, 1908.

Grand Mound
City
ZIP: 52751 Lat: 41-49-24 N Long: 90-38-56 W
Pop: 619 (1990); 674 (1980) **Pop Density:** 343.9
Land: 1.8 sq. mi.; **Water:** 0.0 sq. mi.
Incorporated Feb 11, 1884.
Name origin: For an eroded glacial terminal moraine nearby.

Lost Nation
City
ZIP: 52254 Lat: 41-57-57 N Long: 90-49-02 W
Pop: 467 (1990); 524 (1980) **Pop Density:** 778.3
Land: 0.6 sq. mi.; **Water:** 0.0 sq. mi.
Incorporated Jun 9, 1903.

Low Moor
City
ZIP: 52757 Lat: 41-48-08 N Long: 90-21-15 W
Pop: 280 (1990); 346 (1980) **Pop Density:** 560.0
Land: 0.5 sq. mi.; **Water:** 0.0 sq. mi.
Incorporated Feb 10, 1897.

American Places Dictionary   IOWA, Crawford County

Toronto — City
ZIP: 52343   **Lat:** 41-54-11 N   **Long:** 90-51-46 W
Pop: 132 (1990); 172 (1980)   **Pop Density:** 660.0
Land: 0.2 sq. mi.; **Water:** 0.0 sq. mi.
Incorporated Jul 26, 1909.
Name origin: Named in 1844 by George W. Thorn, for his former home of Toronto, Ontario, Canada.

Welton — City
ZIP: 52774   **Lat:** 41-54-42 N   **Long:** 90-35-52 W
Pop: 177 (1990); 119 (1980)   **Pop Density:** 1770.0
Land: 0.1 sq. mi.; **Water:** 0.0 sq. mi.
Incorporated Apr 25, 1908.

Wheatland — City
ZIP: 52777   **Lat:** 41-49-58 N   **Long:** 90-50-14 W
Pop: 723 (1990); 840 (1980)   **Pop Density:** 1205.0
Land: 0.6 sq. mi.; **Water:** 0.0 sq. mi.
Incorporated Jul 13, 1869.
Name origin: Named for the PA estate of James Buchanan (1791–1868), fifteenth U.S. president.

Crawford County
County Seat: Denison (ZIP: 51442)

Pop: 16,775 (1990); 18,935 (1980)   **Pop Density:** 23.5
Land: 714.4 sq. mi.; **Water:** 0.6 sq. mi.   **Area Code:** 712
In west-central IA, northeast of Council Bluffs; established Jan 15, 1851 from Shelby County.
Name origin: For William Harris Crawford (1772–1834), U.S. senator from GA (1807–13), U.S. secretary of war (1815–16), and U.S. secretary of treasury (1816–25).

Arion — City
ZIP: 51520   **Lat:** 41-56-54 N   **Long:** 95-27-44 W
Pop: 148 (1990); 207 (1980)   **Pop Density:** 296.0
Land: 0.5 sq. mi.; **Water:** 0.0 sq. mi.
Incorporated May 31, 1894.

Aspinwall — City
ZIP: 51432   **Lat:** 41-54-41 N   **Long:** 95-08-05 W
Pop: 52 (1990); 65 (1980)   **Pop Density:** 520.0
Land: 0.1 sq. mi.; **Water:** 0.0 sq. mi.   **Elev:** 1381 ft.
Incorporated Nov 10, 1914.

Buck Grove — City
Lat: 41-55-07 N   **Long:** 95-23-49 W
Pop: 20 (1990); 84 (1980)   **Pop Density:** 100.0
Land: 0.2 sq. mi.; **Water:** 0.0 sq. mi.   **Elev:** 1302 ft.
Incorporated Jun 29, 1906.

Charter Oak — City
ZIP: 51439   **Lat:** 42-04-04 N   **Long:** 95-35-20 W
Pop: 497 (1990); 615 (1980)   **Pop Density:** 994.0
Land: 0.5 sq. mi.; **Water:** 0.0 sq. mi.
Incorporated Feb 6, 1891.

Deloit — City
ZIP: 51441   **Lat:** 42-05-49 N   **Long:** 95-19-03 W
Pop: 296 (1990); 345 (1980)   **Pop Density:** 740.0
Land: 0.4 sq. mi.; **Water:** 0.0 sq. mi.   **Elev:** 1202 ft.
Incorporated May 15, 1900.

Denison — City
ZIP: 51442   **Lat:** 42-01-05 N   **Long:** 95-20-56 W
Pop: 6,604 (1990); 6,675 (1980)   **Pop Density:** 1223.0
Land: 5.4 sq. mi.; **Water:** 0.0 sq. mi.
Incorporated Oct 2, 1875.
Name origin: For Baptist minister J.W. Denison.

Dow City — City
ZIP: 51528   **Lat:** 41-55-41 N   **Long:** 95-29-39 W
Pop: 439 (1990); 616 (1980)   **Pop Density:** 1463.3
Land: 0.3 sq. mi.; **Water:** 0.0 sq. mi.   **Elev:** 1131 ft.
Incorporated Feb 22, 1884.
Name origin: For an early settler, S.E. Dow.

Kiron — City
ZIP: 51448   **Lat:** 42-11-37 N   **Long:** 95-19-36 W
Pop: 301 (1990); 317 (1980)   **Pop Density:** 1505.0
Land: 0.2 sq. mi.; **Water:** 0.0 sq. mi.   **Elev:** 1341 ft.
Incorporated Jun 22, 1900.

Manilla — City
ZIP: 51454   **Lat:** 41-53-20 N   **Long:** 95-14-06 W
Pop: 898 (1990); 1,020 (1980)   **Pop Density:** 1122.5
Land: 0.8 sq. mi.; **Water:** 0.0 sq. mi.   **Elev:** 1317 ft.
Incorporated Oct 3, 1887.

Ricketts — City
ZIP: 51460   **Lat:** 42-07-38 N   **Long:** 95-34-27 W
Pop: 105 (1990); 143 (1980)   **Pop Density:** 350.0
Land: 0.3 sq. mi.; **Water:** 0.0 sq. mi.   **Elev:** 1366 ft.
Incorporated Mar 19, 1902.

Schleswig — City
ZIP: 51461   **Lat:** 42-09-42 N   **Long:** 95-26-04 W
Pop: 851 (1990); 868 (1980)   **Pop Density:** 709.2
Land: 1.2 sq. mi.; **Water:** 0.0 sq. mi.   **Elev:** 1497 ft.
Incorporated Feb 15, 1900.

Vail — City
ZIP: 51465   **Lat:** 42-03-35 N   **Long:** 95-12-02 W
Pop: 388 (1990); 490 (1980)   **Pop Density:** 646.7
Land: 0.6 sq. mi.; **Water:** 0.0 sq. mi.
Incorporated Oct 1, 1875.

IOWA, Crawford County

Westside City
Lat: 42-04-30 N **Long:** 95-05-59 W
Pop: 348 (1990); 387 (1980) **Pop Density:** 232.0
Land: 1.5 sq. mi.; **Water:** 0.0 sq. mi.
Incorporated 1871.
Name origin: For its location on the western side of the Chicago and Northwestern Transportation roadbed.

Dallas County
County Seat: Adel (ZIP: 50003)

Pop: 29,755 (1990); 29,513 (1980) **Pop Density:** 50.7
Land: 586.5 sq. mi.; **Water:** 5.3 sq. mi. **Area Code:** 515
In central IA, west of Des Moines; organized 1846 from Polk County.
Name origin: For George Mifflin Dallas (1792–1864), U.S. Minister to Great Britain (1856–61).

Adel City
ZIP: 50003 **Lat:** 41-36-45 N **Long:** 94-01-37 W
Pop: 3,304 (1990); 2,846 (1980) **Pop Density:** 1032.5
Land: 3.2 sq. mi.; **Water:** 0.0 sq. mi. **Elev:** 930 ft.
Incorporated Jun 27, 1877.
Name origin: For the location in a dell of the North Raccoon River. Previously called Adell.

Bouton City
ZIP: 50039 **Lat:** 41-51-06 N **Long:** 94-00-38 W
Pop: 149 (1990); 139 (1980) **Pop Density:** 1490.0
Land: 0.1 sq. mi.; **Water:** 0.0 sq. mi. **Elev:** 938 ft.
Incorporated Sep 27, 1911

Dallas Center City
ZIP: 50063 **Lat:** 41-41-04 N **Long:** 93-59-02 W
Pop: 1,454 (1990); 1,360 (1980) **Pop Density:** 346.2
Land: 4.2 sq. mi.; **Water:** 0.0 sq. mi. **Elev:** 1072 ft.
Incorporated Mar 22, 1880.

Dawson City
ZIP: 50066 **Lat:** 41-50-35 N **Long:** 94-13-11 W
Pop: 174 (1990); 229 (1980) **Pop Density:** 348.0
Land: 0.5 sq. mi.; **Water:** 0.0 sq. mi. **Elev:** 948 ft.
Incorporated Apr 25, 1908.

De Soto City
ZIP: 50069 **Lat:** 41-32-04 N **Long:** 94-00-30 W
Pop: 1,033 (1990); 1,035 (1980) **Pop Density:** 794.6
Land: 1.3 sq. mi.; **Water:** 0.0 sq. mi. **Elev:** 975 ft.
Incorporated Apr 28, 1875.

Dexter City
ZIP: 50070 **Lat:** 41-30-56 N **Long:** 94-13-36 W
Pop: 628 (1990); 678 (1980) **Pop Density:** 523.3
Land: 1.2 sq. mi.; **Water:** 0.0 sq. mi. **Elev:** 1150 ft.
Founded 1865; incorporated Jan 7, 1871.
Name origin: For a racehorse.

Granger City
ZIP: 50109 **Lat:** 41-45-37 N **Long:** 93-49-25 W
Pop: 624 (1990); 619 (1980) **Pop Density:** 2080.0
Land: 0.3 sq. mi.; **Water:** 0.0 sq. mi.
Incorporated Sep 6, 1905.
Name origin: For railroad official Ben Granger.

Linden City
ZIP: 50146 **Lat:** 41-38-34 N **Long:** 94-16-12 W
Pop: 201 (1990); 264 (1980) **Pop Density:** 251.3
Land: 0.8 sq. mi.; **Water:** 0.0 sq. mi. **Elev:** 1120 ft.
Incorporated Jan 12, 1893.
Name origin: For the linden tree, which grew abundantly in the area.

Minburn City
ZIP: 50167 **Lat:** 41-45-28 N **Long:** 94-01-39 W
Pop: 346 (1990); 390 (1980) **Pop Density:** 1730.0
Land: 0.2 sq. mi.; **Water:** 0.0 sq. mi. **Elev:** 1042 ft.
Incorporated May 24, 1892.

Perry City
ZIP: 50220 **Lat:** 41-50-31 N **Long:** 94-05-59 W
Pop: 6,652 (1990); 7,053 (1980) **Pop Density:** 1956.5
Land: 3.4 sq. mi.; **Water:** 0.0 sq. mi. **Elev:** 998 ft.
Incorporated May 18, 1875.
Name origin: For Col. Perry, one of the owners of the Des Moines Valley Railroad.

Redfield City
ZIP: 50233 **Lat:** 41-35-24 N **Long:** 94-11-51 W
Pop: 883 (1990); 959 (1980) **Pop Density:** 802.7
Land: 1.1 sq. mi.; **Water:** 0.0 sq. mi.
Incorporated Mar 21, 1881.
Name origin: For Civil War soldier, Col. James Redfield.

Van Meter City
ZIP: 50261 **Lat:** 41-31-49 N **Long:** 93-57-20 W
Pop: 751 (1990); 747 (1980) **Pop Density:** 1251.7
Land: 0.6 sq. mi.; **Water:** 0.0 sq. mi.
Incorporated Dec 29, 1877.

Waukee City
ZIP: 50263 **Lat:** 41-36-27 N **Long:** 93-51-44 W
Pop: 2,512 (1990); 2,227 (1980) **Pop Density:** 717.7
Land: 3.5 sq. mi.; **Water:** 0.0 sq. mi.
Incorporated Dec 23, 1878.
Name origin: Located on the Milwaukee and Northwestern railroads, it was given its present name by the Northwestern Railroad because it was believed that this name had a religious meaning to the local Indians. Previously named Shirley.

West Des Moines City
  Lat: 41-35-46 N Long: 93-47-46 W
Pop: 7 (1990); 21,894 (1980)   **Pop Density:** 7.8
Land: 0.9 sq. mi.; **Water:** 0.0 sq. mi.
In south-central IA, 8 mi. west of Des Moines. Incorporated Aug 15, 1893. Part of the town is also in Polk County.
Name origin: Previously called Valley Junction.

Woodward City
ZIP: 50276   Lat: 41-51-22 N Long: 93-55-16 W
Pop: 1,197 (1990); 1,212 (1980)   **Pop Density:** 1330.0
Land: 0.9 sq. mi.; **Water:** 0.0 sq. mi.
Incorporated Oct 13, 1883.

Davis County
County Seat: Bloomfield (ZIP: 52537)

Pop: 8,312 (1990); 9,104 (1980)   **Pop Density:** 16.5
Land: 503.3 sq. mi.; **Water:** 1.6 sq. mi.   **Area Code:** 515
On southern border of IA, west of Burlington; established Feb 17, 1843 (prior to statehood) from Van Buren County.
Name origin: For Garrett Davis (1801–72), KY legislator and U.S. senator (1861–72).

Bloomfield City
ZIP: 52537   Lat: 40-44-53 N Long: 92-25-05 W
Pop: 2,580 (1990); 2,849 (1980)   **Pop Density:** 1228.6
Land: 2.1 sq. mi.; **Water:** 0.0 sq. mi.
Incorporated Jan 13, 1855.
Name origin: Named by county commissioners for its descriptive connotations.

Drakesville City
ZIP: 52552   Lat: 40-47-52 N Long: 92-28-51 W
Pop: 172 (1990); 212 (1980)   **Pop Density:** 860.0
Land: 0.2 sq. mi.; **Water:** 0.0 sq. mi.
Incorporated May 5, 1866.
Name origin: For John A. Drake, who laid out the town.

Floris City
ZIP: 52560   Lat: 40-51-50 N Long: 92-19-55 W
Pop: 172 (1990); 187 (1980)   **Pop Density:** 344.0
Land: 0.5 sq. mi.; **Water:** 0.0 sq. mi.
Incorporated May 12, 1913.

Pulaski City
ZIP: 52584   Lat: 40-41-50 N Long: 92-16-26 W
Pop: 221 (1990); 267 (1980)   **Pop Density:** 1105.0
Land: 0.2 sq. mi.; **Water:** 0.0 sq. mi.
Incorporated May 3, 1893.
Name origin: For Count Casimir Pulaski (1747–79), Polish soldier who fought with the Americans during the Revolutionary War.

Decatur County
County Seat: Leon (ZIP: 50144)

Pop: 8,338 (1990); 9,794 (1980)   **Pop Density:** 15.7
Land: 532.3 sq. mi.; **Water:** 1.1 sq. mi.   **Area Code:** 515
On central southern border of IA, south of Des Moines; organized 1846 from Appanoose County.
Name origin: For Stephen Decatur (1779–1820), U.S. naval officer during the War of 1812 and in actions against the Barbary pirates near Tripoli, who said, ". . . may she always be in the right; but our country, right or wrong!"

Davis City Township
ZIP: 50065   Lat: 40-38-24 N Long: 93-48-42 W
Pop: 257 (1990); 327 (1980)   **Pop Density:** 428.3
Land: 0.6 sq. mi.; **Water:** 0.0 sq. mi.
Incorporated May 19, 1877.

Decatur City City
  Lat: 40-44-32 N Long: 93-49-57 W
Pop: 177 (1990); 199 (1980)   **Pop Density:** 442.5
Land: 0.4 sq. mi.; **Water:** 0.0 sq. mi.
Incorporated Jan 8, 1875.
Name origin: For Stephen Decatur (1779–1820), U.S. naval officer during the War of 1812 and in actions against the Barbary pirates near Tripoli, who said, ". . . may she always be in the right; but our country, right or wrong!"

Garden Grove City
ZIP: 50103   Lat: 40-49-35 N Long: 93-36-27 W
Pop: 229 (1990); 297 (1980)   **Pop Density:** 327.1
Land: 0.7 sq. mi.; **Water:** 0.0 sq. mi.
Incorporated Nov 14, 1879.

Grand River City
ZIP: 50108   Lat: 40-49-08 N Long: 93-57-45 W
Pop: 171 (1990); 188 (1980)   **Pop Density:** 855.0
Land: 0.2 sq. mi.; **Water:** 0.0 sq. mi.
Incorporated Dec 21, 1899.

Lamoni City
ZIP: 50140 **Lat:** 40-37-14 N **Long:** 93-56-14 W
Pop: 2,319 (1990); 2,705 (1980) **Pop Density:** 748.1
Land: 3.1 sq. mi.; **Water:** 0.1 sq. mi.
Incorporated Oct 15, 1885.

Leon City
ZIP: 50144 **Lat:** 40-44-28 N **Long:** 93-45-11 W
Pop: 2,047 (1990); 2,094 (1980) **Pop Density:** 660.3
Land: 3.1 sq. mi.; **Water:** 0.0 sq. mi.
Incorporated May 2, 1867.
Name origin: Chosen by the town's officials in an 1854 petition to the legislature.

Le Roy City
Lat: 40-52-44 N **Long:** 93-35-31 W
Pop: 34 (1990); 31 (1980) **Pop Density:** 113.3
Land: 0.3 sq. mi.; **Water:** 0.0 sq. mi.
Incorporated May 6, 1904.

Pleasanton City
Lat: 40-34-56 N **Long:** 93-44-34 W
Pop: 58 (1990); 75 (1980) **Pop Density:** 193.3
Land: 0.3 sq. mi.; **Water:** 0.0 sq. mi.
Incorporated Feb 21, 1884.

Van Wert City
ZIP: 50262 **Lat:** 40-52-14 N **Long:** 93-47-30 W
Pop: 249 (1990); 245 (1980) **Pop Density:** 830.0
Land: 0.3 sq. mi.; **Water:** 0.0 sq. mi.
Incorporated Mar 4, 1891.

Weldon City
ZIP: 50264 **Lat:** 40-53-52 N **Long:** 93-44-06 W
Pop: 151 (1990); 187 (1980) **Pop Density:** 755.0
Land: 0.2 sq. mi.; **Water:** 0.0 sq. mi.
Incorporated Oct 20, 1902.

Delaware County
County Seat: Manchester (ZIP: 52057)

Pop: 18,035 (1990); 18,933 (1980) **Pop Density:** 31.2
Land: 577.9 sq. mi.; **Water:** 1.2 sq. mi. **Area Code:** 319

In eastern IA, west of Dubuque; established Dec 21, 1837 (prior to statehood) from Dubuque County.

Name origin: For the state, in appreciation of the services of John Middleton Clayton (1796–1856), U.S. senator from DE (1829–36; 1845–49; 1853–56) and U.S. secretary of state (1849–50).

Colesburg City
ZIP: 52035 **Lat:** 42-38-18 N **Long:** 91-12-03 W
Pop: 439 (1990); 463 (1980) **Pop Density:** 1463.3
Land: 0.3 sq. mi.; **Water:** 0.0 sq. mi.
Incorporated Feb 21, 1893.

Delaware City
ZIP: 52036 **Lat:** 42-28-18 N **Long:** 91-20-24 W
Pop: 176 (1990); 170 (1980) **Pop Density:** 220.0
Land: 0.8 sq. mi.; **Water:** 0.0 sq. mi.
Incorporated Jul 22, 1915.
Name origin: For Thomas West, Baron De La Warre (1577–1618), governor of VA (1610).

Delhi City
ZIP: 52223 **Lat:** 42-25-48 N **Long:** 91-19-53 W
Pop: 485 (1990); 511 (1980) **Pop Density:** 485.0
Land: 1.0 sq. mi.; **Water:** 0.1 sq. mi.
Incorporated Apr 26, 1909.
Name origin: Probably for Delhi, India.

Dundee City
ZIP: 52038 **Lat:** 42-34-46 N **Long:** 91-32-49 W
Pop: 174 (1990); 164 (1980) **Pop Density:** 435.0
Land: 0.4 sq. mi.; **Water:** 0.0 sq. mi. **Elev:** 998 ft.
Incorporated Aug 30, 1917.

Dyersville City
Lat: 42-28-58 N **Long:** 91-08-12 W
Pop: 37 (1990); 45 (1980) **Pop Density:** 46.3
Land: 0.8 sq. mi.; **Water:** 0.0 sq. mi.
Incorporated Nov 9, 1872. Part of the town is also in Dubuque County.

Earlville City
ZIP: 52041 **Lat:** 42-28-58 N **Long:** 91-16-10 W
Pop: 822 (1990); 844 (1980) **Pop Density:** 1644.0
Land: 0.5 sq. mi.; **Water:** 0.0 sq. mi.
Incorporated Jun 12, 1882.
Name origin: For first settler G. M. Earl.

Edgewood City
ZIP: 52042 **Lat:** 42-38-24 N **Long:** 91-24-01 W
Pop: 460 (1990); 528 (1980) **Pop Density:** 1150.0
Land: 0.4 sq. mi.; **Water:** 0.0 sq. mi.
Incorporated Apr 6, 1899. Part of the town is also in Clayton County.

Greeley City
ZIP: 52050 **Lat:** 42-35-06 N **Long:** 91-20-30 W
Pop: 263 (1990); 313 (1980) **Pop Density:** 657.5
Land: 0.4 sq. mi.; **Water:** 0.0 sq. mi.
Incorporated Jul 8, 1892.
Name origin: For newspaper publisher Horace Greeley (1811–72).

Hopkinton City
ZIP: 52237 **Lat:** 42-20-36 N **Long:** 91-14-55 W
Pop: 695 (1990); 774 (1980) **Pop Density:** 1158.3
Land: 0.6 sq. mi.; **Water:** 0.0 sq. mi.
Incorporated Mar 3, 1874.

American Places Dictionary   IOWA, Des Moines County

Manchester   City
ZIP: 52057   **Lat:** 42-29-06 N   **Long:** 91-27-20 W
Pop: 5,137 (1990); 4,942 (1980)   **Pop Density:** 1252.9
Land: 4.1 sq. mi.; **Water:** 0.0 sq. mi.
Incorporated Mar 19, 1864.
Name origin: An inversion of Chesterman, the surname of the city's original proprietor.

Masonville   City
ZIP: 50654   **Lat:** 42-28-47 N   **Long:** 91-35-30 W
Pop: 129 (1990); 150 (1980)   **Pop Density:** 430.0
Land: 0.3 sq. mi.; **Water:** 0.0 sq. mi.
Incorporated Jun 28, 1901.

Oneida   City
ZIP: 52057   **Lat:** 42-32-28 N   **Long:** 91-21-10 W
Pop: 49 (1990); 61 (1980)   **Pop Density:** 61.3
Land: 0.8 sq. mi.; **Water:** 0.0 sq. mi.
Incorporated May 29, 1912.
Name origin: Named by settlers from NY for the Oneida Indians, whose name means 'standing stone,' with reference to a large stone at one of their villages.

Ryan   City
ZIP: 52330   **Lat:** 42-21-09 N   **Long:** 91-28-58 W
Pop: 382 (1990); 390 (1980)   **Pop Density:** 955.0
Land: 0.4 sq. mi.; **Water:** 0.0 sq. mi.
Incorporated May 6, 1901.

Des Moines County
County Seat: Burlington (ZIP: 52601)

Pop: 42,614 (1990); 46,203 (1980)   **Pop Density:** 102.4
Land: 416.2 sq. mi.; **Water:** 13.6 sq. mi.   **Area Code:** 319
On southeastern border of IA; established Sep 6, 1834 (prior to statehood) from Wisconsin Territory.
Name origin: For the Des Moines River, which runs through the southeastern part of the state. From French *des* 'of the,' and *moines,* a form of the Indian tribal name *Moingona* 'river of the mounds.' French name became *Rivière des Moines* 'river of the monks,' because the area was explored by Catholic missionaries. Also spelled De Moin, De Moyen, and Demoine.

Burlington   City
ZIP: 52601   **Lat:** 40-48-31 N   **Long:** 91-07-22 W
Pop: 27,208 (1990); 29,529 (1980)   **Pop Density:** 2061.2
Land: 13.2 sq. mi.; **Water:** 0.8 sq. mi.
In southeastern IA on the Mississippi River. Settled 1832; incorporated as town 1836, as a city Jun 10, 1845.
Name origin: For Burlington, VT. Previously called Flint Hills.

Danville   City
ZIP: 52623   **Lat:** 40-51-40 N   **Long:** 91-18-50 W
Pop: 926 (1990); 994 (1980)   **Pop Density:** 1157.5
Land: 0.8 sq. mi.; **Water:** 0.0 sq. mi.
Incorporated Sep 27, 1902.

Mediapolis   City
ZIP: 52637   **Lat:** 41-00-29 N   **Long:** 91-09-52 W
Pop: 1,637 (1990); 1,685 (1980)   **Pop Density:** 1488.2
Land: 1.1 sq. mi.; **Water:** 0.0 sq. mi.
Incorporated Jun 14, 1875.
Name origin: For its location halfway between Burlington and Washington.

Middletown   City
ZIP: 52638   **Lat:** 40-49-45 N   **Long:** 91-15-38 W
Pop: 386 (1990); 487 (1980)   **Pop Density:** 965.0
Land: 0.4 sq. mi.; **Water:** 0.0 sq. mi.
Incorporated May 11, 1914.

West Burlington   City
ZIP: 52655   **Lat:** 40-49-24 N   **Long:** 91-10-42 W
Pop: 3,083 (1990); 3,371 (1980)   **Pop Density:** 629.2
Land: 4.9 sq. mi.; **Water:** 0.0 sq. mi.
Incorporated Dec 15, 1883.

IOWA, Dickinson County   *American Places Dictionary*

> ## Dickinson County
> **County Seat: Spirit Lake (ZIP: 51360)**
>
> **Pop:** 14,909 (1990); 15,629 (1980)   **Pop Density:** 39.1
> **Land:** 381.1 sq. mi.; **Water:** 22.6 sq. mi.   **Area Code:** 712
>
> On the northern border of IA; established Jan 15, 1851 from Kossuth County.
>
> **Name origin:** For Daniel Stevens Dickinson (1800–66), U.S. senator from NY (1844–51).

Arnolds Park   City
ZIP: 51331   **Lat:** 43-21-46 N **Long:** 95-07-54 W
Pop: 953 (1990); 1,051 (1980)   **Pop Density:** 1058.9
Land: 0.9 sq. mi.; **Water:** 0.0 sq. mi.
Incorporated Mar 30, 1897.

Lake Park   City
ZIP: 51347   **Lat:** 43-26-54 N **Long:** 95-19-29 W
Pop: 996 (1990); 1,123 (1980)   **Pop Density:** 664.0
Land: 1.5 sq. mi.; **Water:** 0.0 sq. mi.
Incorporated Jul 1, 1892.

Milford   City
ZIP: 51351   **Lat:** 43-19-37 N **Long:** 95-09-06 W
Pop: 2,170 (1990); 2,076 (1980)   **Pop Density:** 1808.3
Land: 1.2 sq. mi.; **Water:** 0.0 sq. mi.
Incorporated Jan 12, 1892.

Okoboji   City
ZIP: 51355   **Lat:** 43-23-31 N **Long:** 95-08-10 W
Pop: 775 (1990); 559 (1980)   **Pop Density:** 455.9
Land: 1.7 sq. mi.; **Water:** 0.0 sq. mi.
Incorporated Jul 28, 1922. IA's most popular summer resort area.

Name origin: From a Sioux term, the meaning of which is in debate. The common interpretations—'place of rest,' 'rushes,' 'a field of swamp grass,' or 'blue waters'—are not sustained by the Dakota language.

Orleans   City
ZIP: 51360   **Lat:** 43-26-42 N **Long:** 95-05-55 W
Pop: 560 (1990); 546 (1980)   **Pop Density:** 560.0
Land: 1.0 sq. mi.; **Water:** 0.0 sq. mi.
Incorporated Jul 3, 1895.

Spirit Lake   City
ZIP: 51360   **Lat:** 43-25-21 N **Long:** 95-06-41 W
Pop: 3,871 (1990); 3,976 (1980)   **Pop Density:** 1548.4
Land: 2.5 sq. mi.; **Water:** 0.0 sq. mi.
Incorporated Oct 14, 1878.

Name origin: For nearby Spirit Lake. The Indians called the lake *Minnewauken* 'spirit water,' because they believed its waters were haunted by spirits.

Superior   City
ZIP: 51363   **Lat:** 43-25-57 N **Long:** 94-56-49 W
Pop: 128 (1990); 188 (1980)   **Pop Density:** 320.0
Land: 0.4 sq. mi.; **Water:** 0.0 sq. mi.
Incorporated Dec 11, 1895.

Terril   City
ZIP: 51364   **Lat:** 43-18-30 N **Long:** 94-58-07 W
Pop: 383 (1990); 420 (1980)   **Pop Density:** 766.0
Land: 0.5 sq. mi.; **Water:** 0.0 sq. mi.
Incorporated Dec 20, 1899.

Wahpeton   City
ZIP: 51351   **Lat:** 43-22-28 N **Long:** 95-10-28 W
Pop: 484 (1990); 372 (1980)   **Pop Density:** 372.3
Land: 1.3 sq. mi.; **Water:** 0.0 sq. mi.
Incorporated Jun 24, 1933.

Name origin: From Sioux term *Wakhpetonwan* meaning 'dwellers among the leaves.'

West Okoboji   City
ZIP: 51351   **Lat:** 43-20-57 N **Long:** 95-09-55 W
Pop: 263 (1990); 435 (1980)   **Pop Density:** 219.2
Land: 1.2 sq. mi.; **Water:** 0.1 sq. mi.
Incorporated Dec 17, 1924.

> ## Dubuque County
> **County Seat: Dubuque (ZIP: 52001)**
>
> **Pop:** 86,403 (1990); 93,745 (1980)   **Pop Density:** 142.1
> **Land:** 608.2 sq. mi.; **Water:** 8.4 sq. mi.   **Area Code:** 319
>
> On the eastern border of IA, northeast of Cedar Rapids; established Sep 6, 1834 (prior to statehood) from Wisconsin Territory. The present boundaries were established in 1837.
>
> **Name origin:** For Julien Dubuque (1762–1810), a French-Canadian and the first permanent white settler in Iowa (1785); he negotiated an agreement in 1788 with the Fox Indians so he could work lead mines in the IA region.

Asbury   City
ZIP: 52001   **Lat:** 42-30-53 N **Long:** 90-45-30 W
Pop: 2,013 (1990); 2,017 (1980)   **Pop Density:** 2875.7
Land: 0.7 sq. mi.; **Water:** 0.0 sq. mi.
Incorporated Sep 7, 1933.

Balltown   City
ZIP: 52073   **Lat:** 42-38-15 N **Long:** 90-52-06 W
Pop: 64 (1990); 106 (1980)   **Pop Density:** 640.0
Land: 0.1 sq. mi.; **Water:** 0.0 sq. mi.
Incorporated Jul 22, 1933.

IOWA, Dubuque County

Bankston — City
ZIP: 52045 Lat: 42-30-31 N Long: 90-57-36 W
Pop: 35 (1990); 40 (1980) Pop Density: 116.7
Land: 0.3 sq. mi.; Water: 0.0 sq. mi.
Incorporated Sep 8, 1933.

Bernard — City
ZIP: 52032 Lat: 42-18-45 N Long: 90-49-51 W
Pop: 123 (1990); 130 (1980) Pop Density: 1230.0
Land: 0.1 sq. mi.; Water: 0.0 sq. mi.
Incorporated Jun 8, 1897.

Cascade — City
ZIP: 52033 Lat: 42-17-58 N Long: 91-00-32 W
Pop: 1,430 (1990); 1,512 (1980) Pop Density: 2042.9
Land: 0.7 sq. mi.; Water: 0.0 sq. mi.
Incorporated Dec 14, 1880. Part of the town is also in Jones County.

Centralia — City
ZIP: 52068 Lat: 42-28-20 N Long: 90-50-12 W
Pop: 123 (1990); 106 (1980) Pop Density: 246.0
Land: 0.5 sq. mi.; Water: 0.0 sq. mi.
Platted 1850, incorporated Jun 3, 1933.
Name origin: Previously called Dakotah.

Dubuque — City
ZIP: 52001 Lat: 42-30-16 N Long: 90-41-24 W
Pop: 57,546 (1990); 62,374 (1980) Pop Density: 2491.2
Land: 23.1 sq. mi.; Water: 1.2 sq. mi.
In eastern IA on the Mississippi River. Incorporated Jan 28, 1857.
Name origin: For Julien Dubuque (1762–1810), a French-Canadian and the first permanent white settler in Iowa (1785); he negotiated an agreement in 1788 with the Fox Indians so he could work lead mines in the IA region. Previously called Dubuque's Lead Mines.

Durango — City
ZIP: 52039 Lat: 42-33-41 N Long: 90-46-24 W
Pop: 34 (1990); 41 (1980) Pop Density: 1133.3
Land: 0.03 sq. mi.; Water: 0.0 sq. mi.
Incorporated Jun 5, 1933.

Dyersville — City
Lat: 42-28-48 N Long: 91-06-48 W
Pop: 3,666 (1990); 3,780 (1980) Pop Density: 940.0
Land: 3.9 sq. mi.; Water: 0.0 sq. mi.
Incorporated Nov 9, 1872. Part of the town is also in Delaware County.

Epworth — City
ZIP: 52045 Lat: 42-26-48 N Long: 90-56-02 W
Pop: 1,297 (1990); 1,380 (1980) Pop Density: 1080.8
Land: 1.2 sq. mi.; Water: 0.0 sq. mi.
Incorporated Oct 20, 1879.
Name origin: For the parish in Lincolnshire, England, birthplace of Methodist leader John Wesley (1703–91).

Farley — City
ZIP: 52046 Lat: 42-26-38 N Long: 91-00-24 W
Pop: 1,354 (1990); 1,287 (1980) Pop Density: 1041.5
Land: 1.3 sq. mi.; Water: 0.0 sq. mi.
Incorporated Mar 1, 1879.
Name origin: For railroad man J.P. Farley.

Graf — City
ZIP: 52039 Lat: 42-29-40 N Long: 90-52-08 W
Pop: 78 (1990); 98 (1980) Pop Density: 260.0
Land: 0.3 sq. mi.; Water: 0.0 sq. mi.
Incorporated Aug 30, 1933.

Holy Cross — City
ZIP: 52053 Lat: 42-36-05 N Long: 90-59-46 W
Pop: 304 (1990); 310 (1980) Pop Density: 1013.3
Land: 0.3 sq. mi.; Water: 0.0 sq. mi.
Incorporated Aug 20, 1898.

Luxemburg — City
ZIP: 52056 Lat: 42-36-10 N Long: 91-04-22 W
Pop: 257 (1990); 271 (1980) Pop Density: 856.7
Land: 0.3 sq. mi.; Water: 0.0 sq. mi. Elev: 1180 ft.
Incorporated Jan 2, 1912.

New Vienna — City
ZIP: 52065 Lat: 42-32-52 N Long: 91-06-48 W
Pop: 376 (1990); 430 (1980) Pop Density: 940.0
Land: 0.4 sq. mi.; Water: 0.0 sq. mi.
Incorporated Jul 17, 1895.

Peosta — City
ZIP: 52068 Lat: 42-26-55 N Long: 90-51-02 W
Pop: 128 (1990); 120 (1980) Pop Density: 256.0
Land: 0.5 sq. mi.; Water: 0.0 sq. mi.
Incorporated Jun 16, 1933.
Name origin: For the Indian warrior, Peosta, whose wife discovered lead in this area c. 1780.

Rickardsville — City
ZIP: 52039 Lat: 42-35-01 N Long: 90-52-31 W
Pop: 171 (1990); 215 (1980) Pop Density: 213.8
Land: 0.8 sq. mi.; Water: 0.0 sq. mi.
Incorporated Nov 17, 1964.

Sageville — City
ZIP: 52001 Lat: 42-32-55 N Long: 90-42-13 W
Pop: 288 (1990); 291 (1980) Pop Density: 480.0
Land: 0.6 sq. mi.; Water: 0.0 sq. mi.
Incorporated Jun 2, 1933.

Sherrill — City
ZIP: 52073 Lat: 42-36-10 N Long: 90-46-55 W
Pop: 148 (1990); 208 (1980) Pop Density: 1480.0
Land: 0.1 sq. mi.; Water: 0.0 sq. mi.
Incorporated Jun 29, 1933.

Worthington — City
ZIP: 52078 Lat: 42-23-47 N Long: 91-07-14 W
Pop: 439 (1990); 432 (1980) Pop Density: 878.0
Land: 0.5 sq. mi.; Water: 0.0 sq. mi.
Incorporated Jan 10, 1893.

Zwingle — City
ZIP: 52079 Lat: 42-17-52 N Long: 90-41-12 W
Pop: 84 (1990); 89 (1980) Pop Density: 840.0
Land: 0.1 sq. mi.; Water: 0.0 sq. mi.
Incorporated Dec 17, 1900. Part of the town is also in Jackson County.
Name origin: For Swiss reformer Ulrich or Huldrych Zwingli (1484–1531).

IOWA, Emmet County

Emmet County
County Seat: Estherville (ZIP: 51334)

Pop: 11,569 (1990); 13,336 (1980)
Land: 395.8 sq. mi.; **Water:** 6.6 sq. mi.
Pop Density: 29.2
Area Code: 712

On central northern border of IA, northwest of Fort Dodge; established Jan 15, 1851 from Kossuth and Dickinson counties.

Name origin: For Robert W. Emmet (1778–1803), Irish patriot executed by the English for revolutionary acts. Places were named for him during a time when leaders of rebellions were honored by Americans.

Armstrong   City
ZIP: 50514   **Lat:** 43-23-36 N   **Long:** 94-28-44 W
Pop: 1,025 (1990); 1,153 (1980)   **Pop Density:** 1464.3
Land: 0.7 sq. mi.; **Water:** 0.0 sq. mi.
Incorporated Mar 30, 1893.

Dolliver   City
ZIP: 50531   **Lat:** 43-27-53 N   **Long:** 94-36-52 W
Pop: 103 (1990); 125 (1980)   **Pop Density:** 257.5
Land: 0.4 sq. mi.; **Water:** 0.0 sq. mi.
Incorporated Apr 16, 1902.

Estherville   City
ZIP: 51334   **Lat:** 43-23-57 N   **Long:** 94-49-59 W
Pop: 6,720 (1990); 7,518 (1980)   **Pop Density:** 1292.3
Land: 5.2 sq. mi.; **Water:** 0.0 sq. mi.
Incorporated Oct 4, 1881.
Name origin: For Esther A. Ridley, wife of one of the original proprietors.

Gruver   City
ZIP: 51344   **Lat:** 43-23-35 N   **Long:** 94-42-11 W
Pop: 102 (1990); 145 (1980)   **Pop Density:** 1020.0
Land: 0.1 sq. mi.; **Water:** 0.0 sq. mi.
Incorporated Feb 4, 1913.

Ringsted   City
ZIP: 50578   **Lat:** 43-17-47 N   **Long:** 94-30-23 W
Pop: 481 (1990); 557 (1980)   **Pop Density:** 437.3
Land: 1.1 sq. mi.; **Water:** 0.0 sq. mi.
Incorporated Mar 29, 1900.

Wallingford   City
ZIP: 51365   **Lat:** 43-19-12 N   **Long:** 94-47-31 W
Pop: 196 (1990); 256 (1980)   **Pop Density:** 196.0
Land: 1.0 sq. mi.; **Water:** 0.0 sq. mi.
Incorporated Nov 4, 1913.

Fayette County
County Seat: West Union (ZIP: 52175)

Pop: 21,843 (1990); 25,488 (1980)
Land: 731.0 sq. mi.; **Water:** 0.5 sq. mi.
Pop Density: 29.9
Area Code: 319

In northeastern IA, northeast of Waterloo; established Dec 21, 1837 (prior to statehood) from Clayton County.

Name origin: For the Marquis de Lafayette (1757–1834), French statesman and soldier who fought with the Americans during the Revolutionary War.

Arlington   City
ZIP: 50606   **Lat:** 42-44-55 N   **Long:** 91-40-13 W
Pop: 465 (1990); 498 (1980)   **Pop Density:** 465.0
Land: 1.0 sq. mi.; **Water:** 0.0 sq. mi.
Incorporated Apr 30, 1895.

Clermont   City
ZIP: 52135   **Lat:** 43-00-01 N   **Long:** 91-39-11 W
Pop: 523 (1990); 602 (1980)   **Pop Density:** 475.5
Land: 1.1 sq. mi.; **Water:** 0.0 sq. mi.
Incorporated Jun 15, 1875.

Donnan   City
ZIP: 52142   **Lat:** 42-54-03 N   **Long:** 91-52-09 W
Pop: 7 (1990); 10 (1980)   **Pop Density:** 6.4
Land: 1.1 sq. mi.; **Water:** 0.0 sq. mi.
Incorporated Sep 5, 1922; disincorporated Mar 1991.

Elgin   City
ZIP: 52141   **Lat:** 42-57-21 N   **Long:** 91-38-03 W
Pop: 637 (1990); 702 (1980)   **Pop Density:** 1061.7
Land: 0.6 sq. mi.; **Water:** 0.0 sq. mi.
Incorporated Mar 14, 1892.
Name origin: For Elgin, IL.

Fairbank   City
ZIP: 50629   **Lat:** 42-38-33 N   **Long:** 92-02-46 W
Pop: 167 (1990); 143 (1980)   **Pop Density:** 1670.0
Land: 0.1 sq. mi.; **Water:** 0.0 sq. mi.
Incorporated May 12, 1891. Part of the town is also in Buchanan County.

Fayette   City
ZIP: 52142   **Lat:** 42-50-25 N   **Long:** 91-48-09 W
Pop: 1,317 (1990); 1,515 (1980)   **Pop Density:** 940.7
Land: 1.4 sq. mi.; **Water:** 0.0 sq. mi.
Incorporated Mar 14, 1874.
Name origin: For the Marquis de Lafayette (1757–1834),

French officer who fought with the Americans during the Revolutionary War.

Hawkeye
City
ZIP: 52147 **Lat:** 42-56-16 N **Long:** 91-57-03 W
Pop: 460 (1990); 512 (1980) **Pop Density:** 657.1
Land: 0.7 sq. mi.; **Water:** 0.0 sq. mi.

Incorporated Apr 9, 1895.

Name origin: For either Sauk Chief Black Hawk or the character 'Hawkeye' in James Fenimore Cooper's (1789-1851) novel *The Last of the Mohicans* (1826).

Maynard
City
ZIP: 50655 **Lat:** 42-46-27 N **Long:** 91-52-36 W
Pop: 513 (1990); 561 (1980) **Pop Density:** 513.0
Land: 1.0 sq. mi.; **Water:** 0.0 sq. mi.

Incorporated Jun 9, 1887.

Oelwein
City
ZIP: 50662 **Lat:** 42-40-34 N **Long:** 91-54-50 W
Pop: 6,493 (1990); 7,564 (1980) **Pop Density:** 1803.6
Land: 3.6 sq. mi.; **Water:** 0.0 sq. mi.

Incorporated Nov 29, 1887.

Name origin: For a German settler who donated land to the railroad.

Randalia
City
ZIP: 52164 **Lat:** 42-51-47 N **Long:** 91-53-10 W
Pop: 88 (1990); 101 (1980) **Pop Density:** 440.0
Land: 0.2 sq. mi.; **Water:** 0.0 sq. mi.

Incorporated Apr 30, 1896.

St. Lucas
City
Lat: 43-03-59 N **Long:** 91-56-02 W
Pop: 174 (1990); 194 (1980) **Pop Density:** 580.0
Land: 0.3 sq. mi.; **Water:** 0.0 sq. mi.

Incorporated Mar 6, 1900.

Stanley
City
Lat: 42-38-41 N **Long:** 91-48-48 W
Pop: 0 (1990)
Land: 0.02 sq. mi.; **Water:** 0.0 sq. mi.

Incorporated Mar 23, 1914. Part of the town is also in Buchanan County.

Wadena
City
ZIP: 52169 **Lat:** 42-50-22 N **Long:** 91-39-28 W
Pop: 236 (1990); 230 (1980) **Pop Density:** 337.1
Land: 0.7 sq. mi.; **Water:** 0.0 sq. mi.

Incorporated Jul 11, 1895.

Name origin: For Ojibway Chief Wadena, who was wounded in the last battle between the Ojibway and the Sioux in 1858.

Waucoma
City
ZIP: 52171 **Lat:** 43-03-19 N **Long:** 92-02-04 W
Pop: 277 (1990); 308 (1980) **Pop Density:** 692.5
Land: 0.4 sq. mi.; **Water:** 0.0 sq. mi.

Incorporated Jun 5, 1883.

Name origin: Probably named by settlers from WI for Waucoma Creek (now known as Badfish Creek) in WI.

Westgate
City
ZIP: 50681 **Lat:** 42-46-06 N **Long:** 91-59-42 W
Pop: 207 (1990); 263 (1980) **Pop Density:** 517.5
Land: 0.4 sq. mi.; **Water:** 0.0 sq. mi.

Incorporated Jul 6, 1896.

West Union
City
ZIP: 52175 **Lat:** 42-57-31 N **Long:** 91-48-45 W
Pop: 2,490 (1990); 2,783 (1980) **Pop Density:** 922.2
Land: 2.7 sq. mi.; **Water:** 0.0 sq. mi.

Incorporated Dec 9, 1879.

Floyd County
County Seat: Charles City (ZIP: 50616)

Pop: 17,058 (1990); 19,597 (1980) **Pop Density:** 34.1
Land: 500.6 sq. mi.; **Water:** 0.7 sq. mi. **Area Code:** 515

In north-central IA, northwest of Waterloo; established Jan 15, 1851 from Chickasaw County.

Name origin: For Sgt. Charles Floyd (?-1804), a member of the Lewis and Clark expedition (1803-6). He is buried on the banks of the Missouri River; his is the first recorded death and burial of a white man in IA. Some claim for William Floyd (1734-1821), a signer of the Declaration of Independence.

Charles City
City
ZIP: 50616 **Lat:** 43-04-02 N **Long:** 92-40-30 W
Pop: 7,878 (1990); 8,778 (1980) **Pop Density:** 1432.4
Land: 5.5 sq. mi.; **Water:** 0.1 sq. mi.

Incorporated May 1, 1869.

Name origin: For Charles Kelly, son of the town's founder.

Colwell
City
ZIP: 50620 **Lat:** 43-09-29 N **Long:** 92-35-29 W
Pop: 94 (1990); 91 (1980) **Pop Density:** 470.0
Land: 0.2 sq. mi.; **Water:** 0.0 sq. mi.

Incorporated Sep 27, 1921.

Floyd
City
ZIP: 50435 **Lat:** 43-07-42 N **Long:** 92-44-21 W
Pop: 359 (1990); 408 (1980) **Pop Density:** 512.9
Land: 0.7 sq. mi.; **Water:** 0.0 sq. mi.

Incorporated Feb 26, 1899.

Name origin: For Sgt. Charles Floyd (?-1804), a member of the Lewis and Clark expedition (1803-6). He is buried on the banks of the Missouri River; his is the first recorded death and burial of a white man in IA.

IOWA, Floyd County

Marble Rock
City
ZIP: 50653   Lat: 42-57-53 N   Long: 92-52-03 W
Pop: 361 (1990); 419 (1980)   Pop Density: 451.3
Land: 0.8 sq. mi.; Water: 0.0 sq. mi.
Incorporated Feb 8, 1881.

Nora Springs
City
ZIP: 50458   Lat: 43-08-38 N   Long: 93-00-31 W
Pop: 1,505 (1990); 1,572 (1980)   Pop Density: 684.1
Land: 2.2 sq. mi.; Water: 0.0 sq. mi.
Incorporated Sep 17, 1874.

Rockford
City
ZIP: 50468   Lat: 43-03-10 N   Long: 92-56-50 W
Pop: 863 (1990); 1,012 (1980)   Pop Density: 1438.3
Land: 0.6 sq. mi.; Water: 0.0 sq. mi.
Incorporated Mar 19, 1878.

Rudd
City
ZIP: 50471   Lat: 43-07-36 N   Long: 92-54-17 W
Pop: 429 (1990); 460 (1980)   Pop Density: 429.0
Land: 1.0 sq. mi.; Water: 0.0 sq. mi.
Incorporated Feb 7, 1900.

Franklin County
County Seat: Hampton (ZIP: 50441)

Pop: 11,364 (1990); 13,036 (1980)   Pop Density: 19.5
Land: 582.5 sq. mi.; Water: 0.6 sq. mi.   Area Code: 515
In central IA, northwest of Waterloo; established Jan 15, 1851 from Chickasaw County.
Name origin: For Benjamin Franklin (1706–90), U.S. patriot, diplomat, and statesman.

Ackley
City
Lat: 42-33-48 N   Long: 93-02-57 W
Pop: 54 (1990); 69 (1980)   Pop Density: 67.5
Land: 0.8 sq. mi.; Water: 0.0 sq. mi.
Founded 1857; incorporated Aug 28, 1869. Part of the town is in Hardin County.
Name origin: For J. W. Ackley.

Alexander
City
ZIP: 50420   Lat: 42-48-17 N   Long: 93-28-37 W
Pop: 170 (1990); 190 (1980)   Pop Density: 39.5
Land: 4.3 sq. mi.; Water: 0.0 sq. mi.
Incorporated Mar 25, 1902.

Coulter
City
ZIP: 50431   Lat: 42-43-59 N   Long: 93-22-13 W
Pop: 252 (1990); 264 (1980)   Pop Density: 100.8
Land: 2.5 sq. mi.; Water: 0.0 sq. mi.
Incorporated Apr 24, 1909.

Dows
City
Lat: 42-39-31 N   Long: 93-29-45 W
Pop: 100 (1990); 136 (1980)   Pop Density: 333.3
Land: 0.3 sq. mi.; Water: 0.0 sq. mi.
Incorporated May 3, 1892. Part of the town is also in Wright County.

Geneva
City
ZIP: 50633   Lat: 42-40-33 N   Long: 93-07-47 W
Pop: 169 (1990); 218 (1980)   Pop Density: 422.5
Land: 0.4 sq. mi.; Water: 0.0 sq. mi.
Incorporated Apr 7, 1903.

Hampton
City
ZIP: 50441   Lat: 42-44-42 N   Long: 93-12-03 W
Pop: 4,133 (1990); 4,630 (1980)   Pop Density: 1087.6
Land: 3.8 sq. mi.; Water: 0.0 sq. mi.
Incorporated Nov 19, 1870.

Hansell
City
ZIP: 50640   Lat: 42-45-26 N   Long: 93-06-12 W
Pop: 83 (1990); 138 (1980)   Pop Density: 415.0
Land: 0.2 sq. mi.; Water: 0.0 sq. mi.
Incorporated May 7, 1918.

Latimer
City
ZIP: 50452   Lat: 42-45-47 N   Long: 93-21-53 W
Pop: 430 (1990); 441 (1980)   Pop Density: 187.0
Land: 2.3 sq. mi.; Water: 0.0 sq. mi.
Incorporated Apr 17, 1901.

Popejoy
City
ZIP: 50227   Lat: 42-35-38 N   Long: 93-25-36 W
Pop: 92 (1990); 112 (1980)   Pop Density: 131.4
Land: 0.7 sq. mi.; Water: 0.0 sq. mi.
Incorporated Jul 24, 1908.

Sheffield
City
ZIP: 50475   Lat: 42-53-39 N   Long: 93-12-37 W
Pop: 1,174 (1990); 1,224 (1980)   Pop Density: 209.6
Land: 5.6 sq. mi.; Water: 0.0 sq. mi.
Incorporated Apr 8, 1876.
Name origin: For railroad contractor James Sheffield.

Fremont County
County Seat: Sidney (ZIP: 51652)

Pop: 8,226 (1990); 9,401 (1980)　　　**Pop Density:** 16.1
Land: 511.3 sq. mi.; **Water:** 5.5 sq. mi.　　　**Area Code:** 712

On southwestern border of IA, south of Council Bluffs; established Feb 24, 1847 from Pottawattamie County.

Name origin: For John Charles Frémont (1813–90), soldier and explorer who led five expeditions to the West, U.S. senator from CA (1850–51), and governor of the AZ Territory (1878–83).

Farragut　　　City
ZIP: 51639　　　**Lat:** 40-43-11 N **Long:** 95-28-48 W
Pop: 498 (1990); 603 (1980)　　　**Pop Density:** 1245.0
Land: 0.4 sq. mi.; **Water:** 0.0 sq. mi.
Incorporated Jan 21, 1878.
Name origin: For Adm. David Farragut (1801–70), famous for saying "Damn the torpedoes! Full speed ahead!"

Hamburg　　　City
ZIP: 51640　　　**Lat:** 40-36-20 N **Long:** 95-39-17 W
Pop: 1,248 (1990); 1,597 (1980)　　　**Pop Density:** 1040.0
Land: 1.2 sq. mi.; **Water:** 0.0 sq. mi.　　　**Elev:** 914 ft.
Incorporated Apr 1, 1867.
Name origin: Probably for Hamburg, Germany.

Imogene　　　City
ZIP: 51645　　　**Lat:** 40-52-43 N **Long:** 95-25-38 W
Pop: 88 (1990); 188 (1980)　　　**Pop Density:** 293.3
Land: 0.3 sq. mi.; **Water:** 0.0 sq. mi.
Incorporated Feb 18, 1881.

Randolph　　　City
ZIP: 51649　　　**Lat:** 40-52-22 N **Long:** 95-33-51 W
Pop: 243 (1990); 223 (1980)　　　**Pop Density:** 810.0
Land: 0.3 sq. mi.; **Water:** 0.0 sq. mi.　　　**Elev:** 977 ft.
Incorporated Jul 6, 1881.

Riverton　　　City
ZIP: 51650　　　**Lat:** 40-41-14 N **Long:** 95-34-07 W
Pop: 333 (1990); 342 (1980)　　　**Pop Density:** 555.0
Land: 0.6 sq. mi.; **Water:** 0.0 sq. mi.
Incorporated Jun 22, 1876.

Shenandoah　　　City
　　　Lat: 40-45-48 N **Long:** 95-23-08 W
Pop: 0 (1990); 6,274 (1980)
Land: 0.03 sq. mi.; **Water:** 0.0 sq. mi.
Incorporated Jun 20, 1871. Part of the town is also in Page County.
Name origin: For the Shenandoah Valley in VA, which resembles the Nishnabotna River Valley in which the town is located.

Sidney　　　City
ZIP: 51652　　　**Lat:** 40-44-45 N **Long:** 95-38-39 W
Pop: 1,253 (1990); 1,308 (1980)　　　**Pop Density:** 895.0
Land: 1.4 sq. mi.; **Water:** 0.0 sq. mi.
Incorporated May 7, 1870.
Name origin: For Sidney, OH.

Tabor　　　City
ZIP: 51653　　　**Lat:** 40-53-37 N **Long:** 95-40-19 W
Pop: 901 (1990); 967 (1980)　　　**Pop Density:** 750.8
Land: 1.2 sq. mi.; **Water:** 0.0 sq. mi.
Incorporated Oct 5, 1868. Part of the town is also in Mills County.

Thurman　　　City
ZIP: 51654　　　**Lat:** 40-49-09 N **Long:** 95-44-54 W
Pop: 239 (1990); 221 (1980)　　　**Pop Density:** 398.3
Land: 0.6 sq. mi.; **Water:** 0.0 sq. mi.
Incorporated Feb 10, 1879.

IOWA, Greene County   *American Places Dictionary*

Greene County
County Seat: Jefferson (ZIP: 50129)

Pop: 10,045 (1990); 12,119 (1980)   **Pop Density:** 17.7
Land: 568.4 sq. mi.; **Water:** 2.7 sq. mi.   **Area Code:** 515

In central IA, west of Ames; established Jan 15, 1851 from Dallas County.

Name origin: For Gen. Nathanael Greene (1742–86), hero of the Revolutionary War, quartermaster general (1778–80), and commander of the Army of the South (1780).

Churdan   City
ZIP: 50050   **Lat:** 42-09-16 N **Long:** 94-28-39 W
Pop: 423 (1990); 540 (1980)   **Pop Density:** 235.0
Land: 1.8 sq. mi.; **Water:** 0.0 sq. mi.   **Elev:** 1110 ft.
Incorporated Mar 25, 1884.

Dana   City
ZIP: 50064   **Lat:** 42-06-24 N **Long:** 94-14-24 W
Pop: 71 (1990); 110 (1980)   **Pop Density:** 236.7
Land: 0.3 sq. mi.; **Water:** 0.0 sq. mi.
Incorporated Jul 22, 1907.

Grand Junction   City
Lat: 42-01-55 N **Long:** 94-14-11 W
Pop: 808 (1990); 970 (1980)   **Pop Density:** 808.0
Land: 1.0 sq. mi.; **Water:** 0.0 sq. mi.
Incorporated May 6, 1872.

Name origin: For its location at the junction of the Keokuk and Des Moines and the Chicago and Northwestern Railroads.

Jefferson   City
ZIP: 50129   **Lat:** 42-01-07 N **Long:** 94-22-35 W
Pop: 4,292 (1990); 4,854 (1980)   **Pop Density:** 841.6
Land: 5.1 sq. mi.; **Water:** 0.0 sq. mi.   **Elev:** 1078 ft.
Incorporated Nov 20, 1871.

Name origin: For Thomas Jefferson (1743–1826), third U.S. president.

Paton   City
ZIP: 50217   **Lat:** 42-09-50 N **Long:** 94-15-17 W
Pop: 255 (1990); 291 (1980)   **Pop Density:** 425.0
Land: 0.6 sq. mi.; **Water:** 0.0 sq. mi.
Incorporated Feb 20, 1884.

Ralston   City
ZIP: 51459   **Lat:** 42-02-16 N **Long:** 94-37-04 W
Pop: 8 (1990); 6 (1980)   **Pop Density:** 8.0
Land: 1.0 sq. mi.; **Water:** 0.0 sq. mi.
Incorporated Oct 31, 1903. Part of the town is also in Carroll County.

Name origin: For an officer of the American Express Company.

Rippey   City
ZIP: 50235   **Lat:** 41-56-04 N **Long:** 94-11-59 W
Pop: 275 (1990); 304 (1980)   **Pop Density:** 343.8
Land: 0.8 sq. mi.; **Water:** 0.0 sq. mi.   **Elev:** 1077 ft.
Incorporated Apr 14, 1896. Changed to present name Nov 5, 1957.

Name origin: For early settler Capt. C. M. Rippey. Previously called New Rippey.

Scranton   City
ZIP: 51462   **Lat:** 42-01-13 N **Long:** 94-32-53 W
Pop: 583 (1990); 748 (1980)   **Pop Density:** 306.8
Land: 1.9 sq. mi.; **Water:** 0.0 sq. mi.   **Elev:** 1185 ft.
Incorporated May 18, 1880.

Grundy County
County Seat: Grundy Center (ZIP: 50638)

Pop: 12,029 (1990); 14,366 (1980)   **Pop Density:** 23.9
Land: 502.6 sq. mi.; **Water:** 0.0 sq. mi.   **Area Code:** 319

In central IA, west of Waterloo; established Jan 15, 1851 from Black Hawk County.

Name origin: For Felix Grundy (1777–1840) of KY, U.S. senator from TN (1829–38; 1839–40) and U.S. attorney general (1838–39).

Beaman   City
ZIP: 50609   **Lat:** 42-13-12 N **Long:** 92-49-22 W
Pop: 183 (1990); 219 (1980)   **Pop Density:** 915.0
Land: 0.2 sq. mi.; **Water:** 0.0 sq. mi.
Incorporated Apr 26, 1884.

Conrad   City
ZIP: 50621   **Lat:** 42-13-26 N **Long:** 92-52-24 W
Pop: 964 (1990); 1,133 (1980)   **Pop Density:** 803.3
Land: 1.2 sq. mi.; **Water:** 0.0 sq. mi.
Incorporated Nov 15, 1886.

Dike   City
ZIP: 50624   **Lat:** 42-27-47 N **Long:** 92-37-48 W
Pop: 875 (1990); 987 (1980)   **Pop Density:** 875.0
Land: 1.0 sq. mi.; **Water:** 0.0 sq. mi.
Incorporated Jan 16, 1901.

Grundy Center   City
ZIP: 50638   **Lat:** 42-21-46 N **Long:** 92-46-28 W
Pop: 2,491 (1990); 2,880 (1980)   **Pop Density:** 996.4
Land: 2.5 sq. mi.; **Water:** 0.0 sq. mi.   **Elev:** 1026 ft.
Incorporated Apr 17, 1877.

Name origin: For Felix Grundy (1777–1840) of KY, U.S.

senator from TN (1829–38; 1839–40) and U.S. attorney general (1838–39).

Holland
City
ZIP: 50642 Lat: 42-23-59 N Long: 92-47-57 W
Pop: 215 (1990); 278 (1980) Pop Density: 1075.0
Land: 0.2 sq. mi.; Water: 0.0 sq. mi.
Incorporated Jun 29, 1897.

Morrison
City
ZIP: 50657 Lat: 42-20-36 N Long: 92-40-22 W
Pop: 113 (1990); 146 (1980) Pop Density: 1130.0
Land: 0.1 sq. mi.; Water: 0.0 sq. mi.
Incorporated Apr 24, 1884.

Reinbeck
City
ZIP: 50669 Lat: 42-19-20 N Long: 92-35-54 W
Pop: 1,605 (1990); 1,808 (1980) Pop Density: 944.1
Land: 1.7 sq. mi.; Water: 0.0 sq. mi.
Incorporated May 13, 1878.

Stout
City
ZIP: 50673 Lat: 42-31-37 N Long: 92-42-40 W
Pop: 192 (1990); 190 (1980) Pop Density: 640.0
Land: 0.3 sq. mi.; Water: 0.0 sq. mi.
Incorporated Jun 25, 1909.

Wellsburg
City
ZIP: 50680 Lat: 42-26-01 N Long: 92-55-27 W
Pop: 682 (1990); 761 (1980) Pop Density: 682.0
Land: 1.0 sq. mi.; Water: 0.0 sq. mi.
Incorporated Mar 28, 1896.

Guthrie County
County Seat: Guthrie Center (ZIP: 50115)

Pop: 10,935 (1990); 11,983 (1980) Pop Density: 18.5
Land: 590.6 sq. mi.; Water: 2.5 sq. mi. Area Code: 515
In west-central IA, west of Des Moines; established Jan 15, 1851 from Jackson County.
Name origin: For Capt. Edwin Guthrie (?–1847), army officer from IA killed during the Mexican War.

Adair
City
Lat: 41-30-38 N Long: 94-38-31 W
Pop: 64 (1990); 66 (1980) Pop Density: 91.4
Land: 0.7 sq. mi.; Water: 0.0 sq. mi.
Incorporated Feb 23, 1884. Part of the town is also in Adair County.
Name origin: For John Adair (1757–1840), governor of KY (1820–24).

Bagley
City
ZIP: 50026 Lat: 41-50-44 N Long: 94-25-47 W
Pop: 303 (1990); 370 (1980) Pop Density: 1010.0
Land: 0.3 sq. mi.; Water: 0.0 sq. mi. Elev: 1106 ft.
Incorporated Jun 16, 1891.

Bayard
City
ZIP: 50029 Lat: 41-51-08 N Long: 94-33-30 W
Pop: 511 (1990); 637 (1980) Pop Density: 1277.5
Land: 0.4 sq. mi.; Water: 0.0 sq. mi. Elev: 1135 ft.
Incorporated Jun 14, 1883.

Casey
City
Lat: 41-30-33 N Long: 94-31-17 W
Pop: 426 (1990); 459 (1980) Pop Density: 710.0
Land: 0.6 sq. mi.; Water: 0.0 sq. mi.
Incorporated Jun 29, 1880. Part of the town is also in Adair County.

Guthrie Center
City
ZIP: 50115 Lat: 41-40-43 N Long: 94-29-53 W
Pop: 1,614 (1990); 1,713 (1980) Pop Density: 645.6
Land: 2.5 sq. mi.; Water: 0.0 sq. mi. Elev: 1150 ft.
Incorporated Jun 25, 1880.
Name origin: For Capt. Edwin Guthrie (?–1847), army officer from IA killed during the Mexican War.

Jamaica
City
ZIP: 50128 Lat: 41-50-43 N Long: 94-18-25 W
Pop: 232 (1990); 275 (1980) Pop Density: 464.0
Land: 0.5 sq. mi.; Water: 0.0 sq. mi. Elev: 1048 ft.
Incorporated Jan 4, 1901.
Name origin: Possibly because a name could not be agreed upon, so the mayor was blindfolded and faced toward a map. His finger landed on the island of Jamaica in the West Indies. Previously called Van Ness.

Menlo
City
ZIP: 50164 Lat: 41-31-19 N Long: 94-24-12 W
Pop: 356 (1990); 410 (1980) Pop Density: 712.0
Land: 0.5 sq. mi.; Water: 0.0 sq. mi. Elev: 1265 ft.
Incorporated Feb 2, 1881.

Panora
City
ZIP: 50216 Lat: 41-41-27 N Long: 94-21-53 W
Pop: 1,100 (1990); 1,211 (1980) Pop Density: 647.1
Land: 1.7 sq. mi.; Water: 0.0 sq. mi. Elev: 1071 ft.
Incorporated Jul 6, 1872.
Name origin: From a contraction of *panorama*.

Stuart
City
Lat: 41-30-30 N Long: 94-19-02 W
Pop: 993 (1990); 1,127 (1980) Pop Density: 1241.3
Land: 0.8 sq. mi.; Water: 0.0 sq. mi. Elev: 1210 ft.
Incorporated Feb. 6, 1877. Part of the town is also in Adair County.

Yale
City
ZIP: 50277 Lat: 41-46-31 N Long: 94-21-24 W
Pop: 220 (1990); 299 (1980) Pop Density: 733.3
Land: 0.3 sq. mi.; Water: 0.0 sq. mi.
Incorporated Nov 27, 1901.

Hamilton County
County Seat: Webster City (ZIP: 50595)

Pop: 16,071 (1990); 17,862 (1980) **Pop Density:** 27.9
Land: 576.7 sq. mi.; **Water:** 0.8 sq. mi. **Area Code:** 515
In central IA, north of Ames; established Dec 22, 1856 from Webster County.
Name origin: For William H. Hamilton, president of the IA senate (1856–57) at the time the county was established.

Blairsburg   City
ZIP: 50034   **Lat:** 42-28-46 N **Long:** 93-38-33 W
Pop: 269 (1990); 288 (1980)   **Pop Density:** 448.3
Land: 0.6 sq. mi.; **Water:** 0.0 sq. mi.
Incorporated Dec 21, 1900.

Ellsworth   City
ZIP: 50075   **Lat:** 42-18-38 N **Long:** 93-34-54 W
Pop: 451 (1990); 480 (1980)   **Pop Density:** 501.1
Land: 0.9 sq. mi.; **Water:** 0.0 sq. mi.
Incorporated Oct 12, 1893.
Name origin: For a banker who lived in Iowa Falls.

Jewell Junction   City
Lat: 42-18-40 N **Long:** 93-38-18 W
Pop: 1,106 (1990); 1,145 (1980)   **Pop Density:** 283.6
Land: 3.9 sq. mi.; **Water:** 0.1 sq. mi.
Incorporated Oct 22, 1880.
Name origin: Named for founder David T. Jewell.

Kamrar   City
ZIP: 50132   **Lat:** 42-23-30 N **Long:** 93-43-38 W
Pop: 203 (1990); 225 (1980)   **Pop Density:** 253.8
Land: 0.8 sq. mi.; **Water:** 0.0 sq. mi.
Incorporated Jun 6, 1896.

Randall   City
ZIP: 50231   **Lat:** 42-14-14 N **Long:** 93-36-10 W
Pop: 161 (1990); 171 (1980)   **Pop Density:** 322.0
Land: 0.5 sq. mi.; **Water:** 0.0 sq. mi.
Incorporated Jul 15, 1940.

Stanhope   City
ZIP: 50246   **Lat:** 42-17-18 N **Long:** 93-47-42 W
Pop: 447 (1990); 492 (1980)   **Pop Density:** 447.0
Land: 1.0 sq. mi.; **Water:** 0.0 sq. mi.
Incorporated Dec 3, 1897.

Stratford   City
ZIP: 50249   **Lat:** 42-16-15 N **Long:** 93-55-25 W
Pop: 679 (1990); 775 (1980)   **Pop Density:** 522.3
Land: 1.3 sq. mi.; **Water:** 0.0 sq. mi.
Incorporated Sep 27, 1883. Part of the town is also in Webster County.
Name origin: For Stratford, CT.

Webster City   City
ZIP: 50595   **Lat:** 42-27-48 N **Long:** 93-48-59 W
Pop: 7,894 (1990); 8,572 (1980)   **Pop Density:** 928.7
Land: 8.5 sq. mi.; **Water:** 0.0 sq. mi.
Incorporated Sep 16, 1874.
Name origin: Probably for Daniel Webster (1782–1852), U.S. congressman (1813–17; 1823–41; 1845–50) and secretary of state (1841–43; 1850–52).

Williams   City
ZIP: 50271   **Lat:** 42-29-24 N **Long:** 93-32-29 W
Pop: 368 (1990); 410 (1980)   **Pop Density:** 408.9
Land: 0.9 sq. mi.; **Water:** 0.0 sq. mi.
Incorporated Sep 13, 1883.

Hancock County
County Seat: Garner (ZIP: 50438)

Pop: 12,638 (1990); 13,833 (1980) **Pop Density:** 22.1
Land: 571.1 sq. mi.; **Water:** 2.0 sq. mi. **Area Code:** 515
In north-central IA, west of Mason City; established Jan 15, 1851 from Wright County.
Name origin: For John Hancock (1737–93), noted signer of the Declaration of Independence, governor of MA (1780–85; 1787–93), and statesman.

Britt   City
ZIP: 50423   **Lat:** 43-05-50 N **Long:** 93-48-11 W
Pop: 2,133 (1990); 2,185 (1980)   **Pop Density:** 1777.5
Land: 1.2 sq. mi.; **Water:** 0.0 sq. mi.
Incorporated Jun 23, 1881.
Name origin: For a local newspaper editor.

Corwith   City
ZIP: 50430   **Lat:** 42-59-21 N **Long:** 93-57-30 W
Pop: 354 (1990); 480 (1980)   **Pop Density:** 221.3
Land: 1.6 sq. mi.; **Water:** 0.0 sq. mi.
Incorporated Jun 1, 1886.

Crystal Lake   City
ZIP: 50432   **Lat:** 43-13-25 N **Long:** 93-47-33 W
Pop: 266 (1990); 314 (1980)   **Pop Density:** 1330.0
Land: 0.2 sq. mi.; **Water:** 0.0 sq. mi.
Incorporated Apr 19, 1898.

Forest City
Township
Lat: 43-14-56 N Long: 93-38-15 W
Pop: 355 (1990); 350 (1980) **Pop Density:** 221.9
Land: 1.6 sq. mi.; **Water:** 0.0 sq. mi.
Incorporated Jun 14, 1878. Part of the town is also in Winnebago County.

Garner
City
ZIP: 50438 Lat: 43-05-53 N Long: 93-36-08 W
Pop: 2,916 (1990); 2,908 (1980) **Pop Density:** 1534.7
Land: 1.9 sq. mi.; **Water:** 0.0 sq. mi.
Incorporated Nov 19, 1881.

Goodell
City
ZIP: 50439 Lat: 42-55-25 N Long: 93-36-49 W
Pop: 201 (1990); 220 (1980) **Pop Density:** 502.5
Land: 0.4 sq. mi.; **Water:** 0.0 sq. mi.
Incorporated Feb 3, 1893.

Kanawha
City
ZIP: 50447 Lat: 42-56-02 N Long: 93-47-38 W
Pop: 763 (1990); 756 (1980) **Pop Density:** 381.5
Land: 2.0 sq. mi.; **Water:** 0.0 sq. mi.
Incorporated Apr 18, 1902.
Name origin: For the Kanawha River in WV, named by settlers from there.

Klemme
City
ZIP: 50449 Lat: 43-00-32 N Long: 93-36-03 W
Pop: 587 (1990); 620 (1980) **Pop Density:** 1174.0
Land: 0.5 sq. mi.; **Water:** 0.0 sq. mi.
Incorporated Feb 9, 1899.

Woden
City
ZIP: 50484 Lat: 43-13-49 N Long: 93-54-37 W
Pop: 259 (1990); 287 (1980) **Pop Density:** 647.5
Land: 0.4 sq. mi.; **Water:** 0.0 sq. mi.
Incorporated Jan 7, 1904.

Hardin County
County Seat: Eldora (ZIP: 50627)

Pop: 19,094 (1990); 21,776 (1980) **Pop Density:** 33.5
Land: 569.3 sq. mi.; **Water:** 0.7 sq. mi. **Area Code:** 515
In central IA, east of Fort Dodge; established Jan 15, 1851 from Black Hawk County.
Name origin: For Gen. John J. Hardin (1810–47), officer in the Black Hawk War and U.S. representative from IL (1843–45). He was killed at the Battle of Buena Vista in the Mexican-American War.

Ackley
City
Lat: 42-32-50 N Long: 93-03-12 W
Pop: 1,642 (1990); 1,831 (1980) **Pop Density:** 1026.3
Land: 1.6 sq. mi.; **Water:** 0.0 sq. mi.
Founded 1857; incorporated Aug 28, 1869. Part of the town is in Franklin County.
Name origin: For J. W. Ackley.

Alden
City
ZIP: 50006 Lat: 42-30-44 N Long: 93-22-44 W
Pop: 855 (1990); 953 (1980) **Pop Density:** 502.9
Land: 1.7 sq. mi.; **Water:** 0.0 sq. mi.
Incorporated Feb 11, 1879.
Name origin: For Henry Alden, who settled here in 1854.

Buckeye
City
ZIP: 50043 Lat: 42-25-06 N Long: 93-22-33 W
Pop: 105 (1990); 154 (1980) **Pop Density:** 105.0
Land: 1.0 sq. mi.; **Water:** 0.0 sq. mi.
Incorporated 1901.

Eldora
City
ZIP: 50627 Lat: 42-21-36 N Long: 93-06-04 W
Pop: 3,038 (1990); 3,063 (1980) **Pop Density:** 706.5
Land: 4.3 sq. mi.; **Water:** 0.0 sq. mi. **Elev:** 1088 ft.
Incorporated Jul 1, 1895.
Name origin: For Eldora Edgington, deceased baby of Mrs. Samuel Edgington. Previously called Eldorado for the 1851 discovery of gold along the Iowa River.

Hubbard
City
ZIP: 50122 Lat: 42-18-22 N Long: 93-18-01 W
Pop: 814 (1990); 852 (1980) **Pop Density:** 452.2
Land: 1.8 sq. mi.; **Water:** 0.0 sq. mi.
Incorporated Nov 1, 1881.

Iowa Falls
City
ZIP: 50126 Lat: 42-31-15 N Long: 93-15-56 W
Pop: 5,424 (1990); 6,174 (1980) **Pop Density:** 1106.9
Land: 4.9 sq. mi.; **Water:** 0.1 sq. mi.
Incorporated May 4, 1869.
Name origin: For falls in the Iowa River, which runs through the town.

New Providence
City
ZIP: 50206 Lat: 42-16-54 N Long: 93-10-20 W
Pop: 240 (1990); 249 (1980) **Pop Density:** 240.0
Land: 1.0 sq. mi.; **Water:** 0.0 sq. mi. **Elev:** 1130 ft.
Incorporated Jan 30, 1893.

Owasa
City
ZIP: 50126 Lat: 42-25-52 N Long: 93-12-18 W
Pop: 37 (1990); 65 (1980) **Pop Density:** 61.7
Land: 0.6 sq. mi.; **Water:** 0.0 sq. mi. **Elev:** 1085 ft.
Incorporated Mar 18, 1920.
Name origin: Possibly for either a character in one of Henry Rowe Schoolcraft's (1793–1864) legends, or a misspelling of *Owaissa*, the bluebird in Henry Wadsworth Longfellow's (1807–82) poem "Hiawatha."

IOWA, Hardin County

Radcliffe — City
ZIP: 50230 Lat: 42-19-05 N Long: 93-26-04 W
Pop: 574 (1990); 593 (1980) Pop Density: 574.0
Land: 1.0 sq. mi.; Water: 0.0 sq. mi.
Incorporated Jul 8, 1891.

Steamboat Rock — City
ZIP: 50672 Lat: 42-24-28 N Long: 93-03-57 W
Pop: 335 (1990); 387 (1980) Pop Density: 670.0
Land: 0.5 sq. mi.; Water: 0.0 sq. mi.
Incorporated Oct 7, 1875.
Name origin: For a large rock that resembles a steamboat found in the Iowa River, on which the town is located.

Union — City
ZIP: 50258 Lat: 42-14-34 N Long: 93-03-45 W
Pop: 448 (1990); 515 (1980) Pop Density: 746.7
Land: 0.6 sq. mi.; Water: 0.0 sq. mi.
Incorporated Oct 26, 1874.
Name origin: For patriotic sentiment.

Whitten — City
ZIP: 50269 Lat: 42-15-53 N Long: 93-00-40 W
Pop: 137 (1990); 168 (1980) Pop Density: 274.0
Land: 0.5 sq. mi.; Water: 0.0 sq. mi.
Incorporated Mar 13, 1896.

Harrison County
County Seat: Logan (ZIP: 51546)

Pop: 14,730 (1990); 16,348 (1980) Pop Density: 21.1
Land: 696.9 sq. mi.; Water: 4.1 sq. mi. Area Code: 712
On central western border of IA, north of Council Bluffs; established Jan 15, 1851 from Pottawattamie County.
Name origin: For William Henry Harrison (1773–1841), ninth U.S. president.

Dunlap — City
ZIP: 51529 Lat: 41-51-10 N Long: 95-35-58 W
Pop: 1,251 (1990); 1,374 (1980) Pop Density: 1251.0
Land: 1.0 sq. mi.; Water: 0.0 sq. mi. Elev: 1158 ft.
Incorporated Jan 1871.

Little Sioux — City
ZIP: 51545 Lat: 41-48-29 N Long: 96-01-36 W
Pop: 205 (1990); 251 (1980) Pop Density: 512.5
Land: 0.4 sq. mi.; Water: 0.0 sq. mi. Elev: 1033 ft.
Incorporated Nov 26, 1883.
Name origin: For its location on the Little Sioux River.

Logan — City
ZIP: 51546 Lat: 41-38-40 N Long: 95-47-27 W
Pop: 1,401 (1990); 1,540 (1980) Pop Density: 1401.0
Land: 1.0 sq. mi.; Water: 0.0 sq. mi. Elev: 1104 ft.
Incorporated Apr 22, 1876.
Name origin: For Civil War General, U.S. Senator and Congressman John Alexander Logan (1826–86).

Magnolia — City
ZIP: 51550 Lat: 41-41-14 N Long: 95-52-27 W
Pop: 204 (1990); 207 (1980) Pop Density: 340.0
Land: 0.6 sq. mi.; Water: 0.0 sq. mi.
Incorporated Nov 30, 1909.
Name origin: For the magnolia trees growing abundantly in the area.

Missouri Valley — City
ZIP: 51555 Lat: 41-33-32 N Long: 95-53-42 W
Pop: 2,888 (1990); 3,107 (1980) Pop Density: 1255.7
Land: 2.3 sq. mi.; Water: 0.0 sq. mi. Elev: 1019 ft.
Incorporated Oct 30, 1871.
Name origin: For the Missouri Indians who lived along it. The name is from an Indian term meaning 'canoe men.'

Modale — City
ZIP: 51556 Lat: 41-37-09 N Long: 96-00-43 W
Pop: 289 (1990); 373 (1980) Pop Density: 262.7
Land: 1.1 sq. mi.; Water: 0.0 sq. mi. Elev: 1013 ft.
Incorporated Apr 22, 1882.
Name origin: For its location near the Missouri River; a combination of *Mo* for Missouri plus *dale*.

Mondamin — City
ZIP: 51557 Lat: 41-42-35 N Long: 96-01-14 W
Pop: 403 (1990); 423 (1980) Pop Density: 806.0
Land: 0.5 sq. mi.; Water: 0.0 sq. mi.
Incorporated Dec 23, 1881.
Name origin: From the Ojibway term for corn.

Persia — City
ZIP: 51563 Lat: 41-34-44 N Long: 95-34-12 W
Pop: 312 (1990); 355 (1980) Pop Density: 624.0
Land: 0.5 sq. mi.; Water: 0.0 sq. mi. Elev: 1273 ft.
Incorporated Apr 30, 1891.
Name origin: For the country now called Iran.

Pisgah — City
ZIP: 51564 Lat: 41-49-50 N Long: 95-55-36 W
Pop: 268 (1990); 307 (1980) Pop Density: 268.0
Land: 1.0 sq. mi.; Water: 0.0 sq. mi. Elev: 1060 ft.
Incorporated Jul 2, 1904.
Name origin: For the biblical mount from which Moses viewed the Promised Land.

Woodbine — City
ZIP: 51579 Lat: 41-44-11 N Long: 95-42-25 W
Pop: 1,500 (1990); 1,463 (1980) Pop Density: 1363.6
Land: 1.1 sq. mi.; Water: 0.0 sq. mi. Elev: 1078 ft.
Incorporated Nov 9, 1877.

Henry County
County Seat: Mount Pleasant (ZIP: 52641)

Pop: 19,226 (1990); 18,890 (1980)
Land: 434.5 sq. mi.; **Water:** 2.2 sq. mi.
Pop Density: 44.3
Area Code: 319

In southeastern IA, west of Burlington; established Dec 7, 1836 (prior to statehood) from Wisconsin Territory.

Name origin: For Col. Henry Dodge (1782–1867), officer in the Black Hawk War; governor of WI Territory (1836–41, 1845–48), and U.S. senator from WI (1848–57).

Coppock   City
ZIP: 52654 **Lat:** 41-09-38 N **Long:** 91-42-48 W
Pop: 33 (1990); 32 (1980) **Pop Density:** 330.0
Land: 0.1 sq. mi.; **Water:** 0.0 sq. mi.

Incorporated Aug 24, 1901. Part of the town is also in Washington and Jefferson counties.

Hillsboro   City
ZIP: 52630 **Lat:** 40-50-12 N **Long:** 91-42-48 W
Pop: 151 (1990); 208 (1980) **Pop Density:** 755.0
Land: 0.2 sq. mi.; **Water:** 0.0 sq. mi.

Incorporated Jul 19, 1916.

Mount Pleasant   City
ZIP: 52641 **Lat:** 40-57-47 N **Long:** 91-32-47 W
Pop: 8,027 (1990); 7,322 (1980) **Pop Density:** 1114.9
Land: 7.2 sq. mi.; **Water:** 0.0 sq. mi.

Incorporated Jul 15, 1856.

Mount Union   City
ZIP: 52644 **Lat:** 41-03-26 N **Long:** 91-23-26 W
Pop: 140 (1990); 145 (1980) **Pop Density:** 1400.0
Land: 0.1 sq. mi.; **Water:** 0.0 sq. mi.

Incorporated Aug 20, 1904.

New London   City
ZIP: 52645 **Lat:** 40-55-39 N **Long:** 91-24-26 W
Pop: 1,922 (1990); 2,043 (1980) **Pop Density:** 1922.0
Land: 1.0 sq. mi.; **Water:** 0.0 sq. mi.

Incorporated Oct 22, 1860.
Name origin: For New London, CT.

Olds   City
ZIP: 52647 **Lat:** 41-07-59 N **Long:** 91-32-43 W
Pop: 205 (1990); 225 (1980) **Pop Density:** 683.3
Land: 0.3 sq. mi.; **Water:** 0.0 sq. mi.

Incorporated Dec 12, 1900.

Rome   City
ZIP: 52642 **Lat:** 40-58-59 N **Long:** 91-40-50 W
Pop: 124 (1990); 113 (1980) **Pop Density:** 1240.0
Land: 0.1 sq. mi.; **Water:** 0.0 sq. mi.

Incorporated Jan 1, 1869.
Name origin: Probably for Rome, Italy.

Salem   City
Lat: 40-51-07 N **Long:** 91-37-14 W
Pop: 453 (1990); 463 (1980) **Pop Density:** 755.0
Land: 0.6 sq. mi.; **Water:** 0.0 sq. mi.

Incorporated Jan 24, 1855.

Wayland   City
ZIP: 52654 **Lat:** 41-08-51 N **Long:** 91-39-28 W
Pop: 838 (1990); 720 (1980) **Pop Density:** 1047.5
Land: 0.8 sq. mi.; **Water:** 0.0 sq. mi.

Incorporated Feb 5, 1890.

Westwood   City
Lat: 40-57-53 N **Long:** 91-37-37 W
Pop: 104 (1990) **Pop Density:** 520.0
Land: 0.2 sq. mi.; **Water:** 0.0 sq. mi.

Incorporated Jan 14, 1982.

Winfield   City
ZIP: 52659 **Lat:** 41-07-32 N **Long:** 91-26-13 W
Pop: 1,051 (1990); 1,042 (1980) **Pop Density:** 1051.0
Land: 1.0 sq. mi.; **Water:** 0.0 sq. mi.

Incorporated Mar 27, 1882.

Howard County
County Seat: Cresco (ZIP: 52136)

Pop: 9,809 (1990); 11,114 (1980)
Land: 473.4 sq. mi.; **Water:** 0.4 sq. mi.
Pop Density: 20.7
Area Code: 319

On northern border of IA, north of Waterloo; established Jan 15, 1851 from Chickasaw and Floyd counties.

Name origin: For Tilghman Ashurst Howard (1797–1844), TN legislator, U.S. representative from IN (1839–40), and TX patriot.

Chester
City
ZIP: 52134 **Lat:** 43-29-24 N **Long:** 92-21-48 W
Pop: 158 (1990); 175 (1980) **Pop Density:** 121.5
Land: 1.3 sq. mi.; **Water:** 0.0 sq. mi.
Incorporated Sep 22, 1900.

Cresco
City
ZIP: 52136 **Lat:** 43-22-18 N **Long:** 92-06-56 W
Pop: 3,669 (1990); 3,860 (1980) **Pop Density:** 1146.6
Land: 3.2 sq. mi.; **Water:** 0.0 sq. mi.
Incorporated Jun 6, 1868.
Name origin: From Latin meaning 'I grow.'

Elma
City
ZIP: 50628 **Lat:** 43-14-44 N **Long:** 92-26-23 W
Pop: 653 (1990); 714 (1980) **Pop Density:** 502.3
Land: 1.3 sq. mi.; **Water:** 0.0 sq. mi.
Incorporated Jul 11, 1891.

Lime Springs
City
Lat: 43-27-00 N **Long:** 92-16-52 W
Pop: 438 (1990); 476 (1980) **Pop Density:** 547.5
Land: 0.8 sq. mi.; **Water:** 0.0 sq. mi.
Incorporated Apr 17, 1876.
Name origin: For springs in the limestone rocks here.

Protivin
City
ZIP: 52163 **Lat:** 43-13-03 N **Long:** 92-05-17 W
Pop: 305 (1990); 368 (1980) **Pop Density:** 762.5
Land: 0.4 sq. mi.; **Water:** 0.0 sq. mi.
Incorporated Aug 1, 1894.

Riceville
City
ZIP: 50466 **Lat:** 43-21-45 N **Long:** 92-33-00 W
Pop: 334 (1990); 356 (1980) **Pop Density:** 556.7
Land: 0.6 sq. mi.; **Water:** 0.0 sq. mi.
Incorporated Nov 17, 1892. Part of the town is also in Mitchell County.
Name origin: For the three Rice brothers.

Humboldt County
County Seat: Dakota City (ZIP: 50529)

Pop: 10,756 (1990); 12,246 (1980)
Land: 434.4 sq. mi.; **Water:** 1.3 sq. mi.
Pop Density: 24.8
Area Code: 515

In north-central IA, north of Fort Dodge; established Jan 15, 1851 from Webster County.

Name origin: For Alexander von Humboldt (1769–1859), German explorer and naturalist.

Bode
City
ZIP: 50519 **Lat:** 42-52-05 N **Long:** 94-17-11 W
Pop: 335 (1990); 406 (1980) **Pop Density:** 837.5
Land: 0.4 sq. mi.; **Water:** 0.0 sq. mi.
Incorporated Feb 20, 1892.

Bradgate
City
ZIP: 50520 **Lat:** 42-48-09 N **Long:** 94-25-09 W
Pop: 124 (1990); 151 (1980) **Pop Density:** 413.3
Land: 0.3 sq. mi.; **Water:** 0.0 sq. mi.
Incorporated Jun 20, 1893.

Dakota City
City
ZIP: 50529 **Lat:** 42-43-19 N **Long:** 94-11-48 W
Pop: 1,024 (1990); 1,072 (1980) **Pop Density:** 1280.0
Land: 0.8 sq. mi.; **Water:** 0.0 sq. mi.
Incorporated Jun 22, 1878.
Name origin: Named in 1855 by Edward McKnight for the name of the alliance of Plains Indians, popularly known as the Sioux. The name means 'united' or 'allied,' because the whole nation consists of allied tribes.

Gilmore City
Township
ZIP: 50541 **Lat:** 42-43-21 N **Long:** 94-25-55 W
Pop: 319 (1990); 366 (1980) **Pop Density:** 319.0
Land: 1.0 sq. mi.; **Water:** 0.0 sq. mi.
Incorporated Apr 16, 1887. Part of the town is also in Pocahontas County.

Hardy
City
ZIP: 50545 **Lat:** 42-48-36 N **Long:** 94-03-05 W
Pop: 47 (1990); 72 (1980) **Pop Density:** 117.5
Land: 0.4 sq. mi.; **Water:** 0.0 sq. mi.
Incorporated Apr 13, 1915.

Humboldt   *City*
ZIP: 50548   **Lat:** 42-43-17 N   **Long:** 94-13-25 W
Pop: 4,438 (1990); 4,794 (1980)   **Pop Density:** 986.2
Land: 4.5 sq. mi.; **Water:** 0.1 sq. mi.
Incorporated Mar 22, 1874.
Name origin: For Alexander von Humboldt (1769–1859), German explorer and naturalist.

Livermore   *City*
ZIP: 50558   **Lat:** 42-52-04 N   **Long:** 94-11-01 W
Pop: 436 (1990); 490 (1980)   **Pop Density:** 622.9
Land: 0.7 sq. mi.; **Water:** 0.0 sq. mi.
Incorporated Mar 11, 1882.

Lu Verne   *City*
Lat: 42-54-13 N   **Long:** 94-05-13 W
Pop: 54 (1990); 68 (1980)   **Pop Density:** 45.0
Land: 1.2 sq. mi.; **Water:** 0.0 sq. mi.
Incorporated Jul 6, 1887. Part of the town is also in Kossuth County.

Ottosen   *City*
ZIP: 50570   **Lat:** 42-53-58 N   **Long:** 94-22-31 W
Pop: 72 (1990); 92 (1980)   **Pop Density:** 120.0
Land: 0.6 sq. mi.; **Water:** 0.0 sq. mi.
Incorporated Jul 16, 1909.

Pioneer   *City*
Lat: 42-39-12 N   **Long:** 94-23-28 W
Pop: 46 (1990); 40 (1980)   **Pop Density:** 460.0
Land: 0.1 sq. mi.; **Water:** 0.0 sq. mi.
Incorporated Feb 8, 1910.

Renwick   *City*
ZIP: 50577   **Lat:** 42-49-38 N   **Long:** 93-58-50 W
Pop: 287 (1990); 410 (1980)   **Pop Density:** 287.0
Land: 1.0 sq. mi.; **Water:** 0.0 sq. mi.
Incorporated Oct 17, 1891.

Rutland   *City*
ZIP: 50582   **Lat:** 42-45-40 N   **Long:** 94-17-33 W
Pop: 149 (1990); 163 (1980)   **Pop Density:** 165.6
Land: 0.9 sq. mi.; **Water:** 0.0 sq. mi.
Incorporated Jul 6, 1907.

Thor   *City*
ZIP: 50591   **Lat:** 42-41-19 N   **Long:** 94-02-59 W
Pop: 205 (1990); 200 (1980)   **Pop Density:** 205.0
Land: 1.0 sq. mi.; **Water:** 0.0 sq. mi.
Incorporated Apr 23, 1900.

Ida County
County Seat: Ida Grove (ZIP: 51445)

Pop: 8,365 (1990); 8,908 (1980)   **Pop Density:** 19.4
Land: 431.7 sq. mi.; **Water:** 0.5 sq. mi.   **Area Code:** 712
In western IA, east of Sioux City; established Jan 15, 1851 from Cherokee County.
Name origin: For Mt. Ida of Greek myth; either the one in Crete or the one near ancient Troy (in present-day Turkey). The name was suggested by Eliphalet Price to connect the old classic civilization of Europe with the new civilization of the plains. Other sources say the county is named for the first white child born in the community (July 19, 1856), Ida Smith, daughter of Edwin Smith, a trapper.

Arthur   *City*
ZIP: 51431   **Lat:** 42-20-06 N   **Long:** 95-20-46 W
Pop: 272 (1990); 288 (1980)   **Pop Density:** 1360.0
Land: 0.2 sq. mi.; **Water:** 0.0 sq. mi.
Incorporated Apr 21, 1897.

Battle Creek   *City*
ZIP: 51006   **Lat:** 42-19-00 N   **Long:** 95-35-57 W
Pop: 818 (1990); 919 (1980)   **Pop Density:** 1636.0
Land: 0.5 sq. mi.; **Water:** 0.0 sq. mi.   **Elev:** 1194 ft.
Incorporated Nov 13, 1880.
Name origin: For the creek, itself named in 1849 for a skirmish that took place here between a government survey party and Sioux Indians.

Galva   *City*
ZIP: 51020   **Lat:** 42-30-22 N   **Long:** 95-24-58 W
Pop: 398 (1990); 420 (1980)   **Pop Density:** 663.3
Land: 0.6 sq. mi.; **Water:** 0.0 sq. mi.
Incorporated Sep 26, 1889.

Holstein   *City*
ZIP: 51025   **Lat:** 42-29-12 N   **Long:** 95-32-32 W
Pop: 1,449 (1990); 1,477 (1980)   **Pop Density:** 1035.0
Land: 1.4 sq. mi.; **Water:** 0.0 sq. mi.   **Elev:** 1437 ft.
Incorporated Apr 25, 1883.

Ida Grove   *City*
ZIP: 51445   **Lat:** 42-20-39 N   **Long:** 95-28-22 W
Pop: 2,357 (1990); 2,285 (1980)   **Pop Density:** 1178.5
Land: 2.0 sq. mi.; **Water:** 0.0 sq. mi.   **Elev:** 1236 ft.
Incorporated May 31, 1878.
Name origin: Named by settlers for Ida Mountain of Greek myth.

IOWA, Iowa County

Iowa County
County Seat: Marengo (ZIP: 52301)

Pop: 14,630 (1990); 15,429 (1980)
Land: 586.5 sq. mi.; **Water:** 0.9 sq. mi.
Pop Density: 24.9
Area Code: 319

In east-central IA, west of Iowa City; established Feb 17, 1843 (prior to statehood) from Washington County.
Name origin: For the Iowa River.

Ladora   City
ZIP: 52251 **Lat:** 41-45-20 N **Long:** 92-11-07 W
Pop: 308 (1990); 289 (1980) **Pop Density:** 1026.7
Land: 0.3 sq. mi.; **Water:** 0.0 sq. mi.
Incorporated Dec 27, 1879.

Marengo   City
ZIP: 52301 **Lat:** 41-47-50 N **Long:** 92-04-09 W
Pop: 2,270 (1990); 2,308 (1980) **Pop Density:** 2522.2
Land: 0.9 sq. mi.; **Water:** 0.0 sq. mi.
Incorporated Jul 4, 1859.
Name origin: For the battlefield in Italy where Napoleon I (1769–1821) defeated the Austrians.

Millersburg   City
ZIP: 52308 **Lat:** 41-34-21 N **Long:** 92-09-32 W
Pop: 188 (1990); 184 (1980) **Pop Density:** 1880.0
Land: 0.1 sq. mi.; **Water:** 0.0 sq. mi.
Incorporated Jan 12, 1911.

North English   City
ZIP: 52316 **Lat:** 41-30-57 N **Long:** 92-04-41 W
Pop: 932 (1990); 972 (1980) **Pop Density:** 1864.0
Land: 0.5 sq. mi.; **Water:** 0.0 sq. mi. **Elev:** 815 ft.
Incorporated Mar 13, 1891. Part of the town is also in Keokuk County.

Parnell   City
ZIP: 52325 **Lat:** 41-35-00 N **Long:** 92-00-17 W
Pop: 209 (1990); 234 (1980) **Pop Density:** 1045.0
Land: 0.2 sq. mi.; **Water:** 0.0 sq. mi.
Incorporated Mar 24, 1891.

Victor   City
ZIP: 52347 **Lat:** 41-43-49 N **Long:** 92-17-39 W
Pop: 842 (1990); 897 (1980) **Pop Density:** 2105.0
Land: 0.4 sq. mi.; **Water:** 0.0 sq. mi.
Incorporated Nov 30, 1868. Part of the town is also in Poweshiek County.

Williamsburg   City
ZIP: 52361 **Lat:** 41-40-04 N **Long:** 92-00-30 W
Pop: 2,174 (1990); 2,033 (1980) **Pop Density:** 805.2
Land: 2.7 sq. mi.; **Water:** 0.0 sq. mi.
Incorporated Dec 3, 1884.

York   Township
Lat: 41-38-44 N **Long:** 91-53-19 W
Pop: 368 (1990); 404 (1980) **Pop Density:** 10.3
Land: 35.7 sq. mi.; **Water:** 0.0 sq. mi.

Jackson County
County Seat: Maquoketa (ZIP: 52060)

Pop: 19,950 (1990); 22,503 (1980)
Land: 636.1 sq. mi.; **Water:** 13.7 sq. mi.
Pop Density: 31.4
Area Code: 319

On central eastern border of IA, south of Dubuque; established Dec 21, 1837 (prior to statehood) from Wisconsin Territory.
Name origin: For Andrew Jackson (1767–1845), seventh U.S. president.

Andrew   City
ZIP: 52030 **Lat:** 42-09-11 N **Long:** 90-35-30 W
Pop: 319 (1990); 349 (1980) **Pop Density:** 1063.3
Land: 0.3 sq. mi.; **Water:** 0.0 sq. mi.
Incorporated Aug 4, 1863.

Baldwin   City
ZIP: 52207 **Lat:** 42-04-24 N **Long:** 90-50-20 W
Pop: 137 (1990); 198 (1980) **Pop Density:** 342.5
Land: 0.4 sq. mi.; **Water:** 0.0 sq. mi.
Incorporated Dec 8, 1881.

Bellevue   City
ZIP: 52031 **Lat:** 42-15-31 N **Long:** 90-25-42 W
Pop: 2,239 (1990); 2,450 (1980) **Pop Density:** 2487.8
Land: 0.9 sq. mi.; **Water:** 0.1 sq. mi.
Incorporated Feb 5, 1851.
Name origin: From French meaning 'beautiful view.'

Green Island   City
ZIP: 52051 **Lat:** 42-09-16 N **Long:** 90-19-20 W
Pop: 54 (1990); 103 (1980) **Pop Density:** 540.0
Land: 0.1 sq. mi.; **Water:** 0.0 sq. mi.
Incorporated Feb 8, 1904.

La Motte
City
ZIP: 52054 **Lat:** 42-17-41 N **Long:** 90-37-16 W
Pop: 219 (1990); 322 (1980) **Pop Density:** 547.5
Land: 0.4 sq. mi.; **Water:** 0.0 sq. mi. **Elev:** 915 ft.
Incorporated May 24, 1879.
Name origin: For Capt. Pierre Sieur de la Motte, French explorer.

Maquoketa
City
ZIP: 52060 **Lat:** 42-03-55 N **Long:** 90-39-57 W
Pop: 6,111 (1990); 6,313 (1980) **Pop Density:** 1797.4
Land: 3.4 sq. mi.; **Water:** 0.0 sq. mi.
Incorporated Jan 27, 1857.
Name origin: For the Maquoketa River, which got its name from an Indian term probably meaning 'there are bears' or 'abundance of bears.'

Miles
City
ZIP: 52064 **Lat:** 42-02-53 N **Long:** 90-19-02 W
Pop: 409 (1990); 398 (1980) **Pop Density:** 409.0
Land: 1.0 sq. mi.; **Water:** 0.0 sq. mi.
Incorporated May 4, 1893.

Monmouth
City
ZIP: 52309 **Lat:** 42-04-25 N **Long:** 90-52-54 W
Pop: 169 (1990); 210 (1980) **Pop Density:** 281.7
Land: 0.6 sq. mi.; **Water:** 0.0 sq. mi.
Incorporated Jul 12, 1894.

Preston
City
ZIP: 52069 **Lat:** 42-02-54 N **Long:** 90-23-57 W
Pop: 1,025 (1990); 1,120 (1980) **Pop Density:** 1138.9
Land: 0.9 sq. mi.; **Water:** 0.0 sq. mi.
Incorporated Nov 11, 1890.

Sabula
City
ZIP: 52070 **Lat:** 42-04-04 N **Long:** 90-10-26 W
Pop: 710 (1990); 824 (1980) **Pop Density:** 1775.0
Land: 0.4 sq. mi.; **Water:** 1.0 sq. mi.
Incorporated Sep 1864.

St. Donatus
City
Lat: 42-21-43 N **Long:** 90-32-35 W
Pop: 145 (1990); 197 (1980) **Pop Density:** 362.5
Land: 0.4 sq. mi.; **Water:** 0.0 sq. mi.
Incorporated Jun 8, 1964.

Spragueville
City
ZIP: 52074 **Lat:** 42-04-13 N **Long:** 90-25-51 W
Pop: 118 (1990); 149 (1980) **Pop Density:** 168.6
Land: 0.7 sq. mi.; **Water:** 0.0 sq. mi.
Incorporated May 18, 1912.

Springbrook
City
ZIP: 52075 **Lat:** 42-10-02 N **Long:** 90-28-54 W
Pop: 116 (1990); 209 (1980) **Pop Density:** 193.3
Land: 0.6 sq. mi.; **Water:** 0.0 sq. mi.
Incorporated Mar 2, 1897.

Zwingle
City
ZIP: 52079 **Lat:** 42-17-39 N **Long:** 90-41-17 W
Pop: 10 (1990); 30 (1980) **Pop Density:** 500.0
Land: 0.02 sq. mi.; **Water:** 0.0 sq. mi.
Incorporated Dec 17, 1900. Part of the town is also in Dubuque County.
Name origin: For Swiss reformer Ulrich or Huldrych Zwingli (1484–1531).

Jasper County
County Seat: Newton (ZIP: 50208)

Pop: 34,795 (1990); 36,425 (1980) **Pop Density:** 47.7
Land: 730.0 sq. mi.; **Water:** 2.9 sq. mi. **Area Code:** 515
In central IA, east of Des Moines; established Jan 13, 1846 from Mahaska County.
Name origin: For Sgt. William Jasper (1750–79), Revolutionary War soldier from SC.

Baxter
City
ZIP: 50028 **Lat:** 41-49-32 N **Long:** 93-09-02 W
Pop: 938 (1990); 951 (1980) **Pop Density:** 1876.0
Land: 0.5 sq. mi.; **Water:** 0.0 sq. mi.
Incorporated Dec 13, 1894.

Colfax
City
ZIP: 50054 **Lat:** 41-40-34 N **Long:** 93-14-24 W
Pop: 2,462 (1990); 2,234 (1980) **Pop Density:** 1758.6
Land: 1.4 sq. mi.; **Water:** 0.0 sq. mi.
Incorporated Aug 10, 1875.
Name origin: For Schuyler Colfax (1823–85), U.S. vice president (1869–73).

Kellogg
City
ZIP: 50135 **Lat:** 41-42-59 N **Long:** 92-54-26 W
Pop: 626 (1990); 654 (1980) **Pop Density:** 2086.7
Land: 0.3 sq. mi.; **Water:** 0.0 sq. mi.
Incorporated Feb 6, 1874.

Lambs Grove
City
ZIP: 50208 **Lat:** 41-42-01 N **Long:** 93-04-41 W
Pop: 212 (1990); 228 (1980) **Pop Density:** 2120.0
Land: 0.1 sq. mi.; **Water:** 0.0 sq. mi.
Incorporated Dec 29, 1952.

Lynnville
City
ZIP: 50153 **Lat:** 41-34-36 N **Long:** 92-47-10 W
Pop: 393 (1990); 406 (1980) **Pop Density:** 655.0
Land: 0.6 sq. mi.; **Water:** 0.0 sq. mi.
Incorporated Aug 9, 1875.

Mingo
City
ZIP: 50168 **Lat:** 41-46-02 N **Long:** 93-17-03 W
Pop: 252 (1990); 303 (1980) **Pop Density:** 504.0
Land: 0.5 sq. mi.; **Water:** 0.0 sq. mi.
Incorporated Feb 13, 1903.
Name origin: From either the name used by Lenape Indians for certain Iroquois-speaking Indians, derived from *mengwe* 'stealthy, treacherous'; or possibly from James Fenimore

IOWA, Jasper County

Cooper's (1789–1851) novels, in which the enemies of the Delaware Indians were called Mingos.

Monroe   City
ZIP: 50170   **Lat:** 41-31-12 N **Long:** 93-06-16 W
Pop: 1,739 (1990); 1,875 (1980)   **Pop Density:** 1159.3
Land: 1.5 sq. mi.; **Water:** 0.0 sq. mi.

Incorporated May 1, 1897.

Name origin: For James Monroe (1758–1831), fifth U.S. president.

Newton   City
ZIP: 50208   **Lat:** 41-41-42 N **Long:** 93-02-42 W
Pop: 14,789 (1990); 15,292 (1980) **Pop Density:** 1643.2
Land: 9.0 sq. mi.; **Water:** 0.0 sq. mi.

In south-central IA, 31 mi. east of Des Moines. Incorporated Jan 6, 1857.

Name origin: For Revolutionary War soldier John Newton.

Oakland Acres   City
                         Lat: 41-43-09 N **Long:** 92-49-11 W
Pop: 152 (1990); 139 (1980)   **Pop Density:** 506.7
Land: 0.3 sq. mi.; **Water:** 0.0 sq. mi.

Incorporated Jan 22, 1975.

Prairie City   City
ZIP: 50228   **Lat:** 41-35-53 N **Long:** 93-14-07 W
Pop: 1,360 (1990); 1,278 (1980)   **Pop Density:** 1942.9
Land: 0.7 sq. mi.; **Water:** 0.0 sq. mi.

Settled 1856; incorporated Aug 7, 1874.

Name origin: For the surrounding prairie.

Reasnor   City
ZIP: 50232   **Lat:** 41-34-42 N **Long:** 93-01-21 W
Pop: 191 (1990); 277 (1980)   **Pop Density:** 382.0
Land: 0.5 sq. mi.; **Water:** 0.0 sq. mi.

Sully   City
ZIP: 50251   **Lat:** 41-34-43 N **Long:** 92-50-47 W
Pop: 841 (1990); 828 (1980)   **Pop Density:** 2102.5
Land: 0.4 sq. mi.; **Water:** 0.0 sq. mi.

Incorporated Feb 23, 1901.

Valeria   City
ZIP: 50054   **Lat:** 41-43-46 N **Long:** 93-19-28 W
Pop: 69 (1990); 80 (1980)   **Pop Density:** 1725.0
Land: 0.04 sq. mi.; **Water:** 0.0 sq. mi.

Jefferson County
County Seat: Fairfield (ZIP: 52556)

Pop: 16,310 (1990); 16,316 (1980)   **Pop Density:** 37.5
Land: 435.4 sq. mi.; **Water:** 1.4 sq. mi.   **Area Code:** 515

In southeastern IA, east of Ottumwa; established Jan 21, 1839 (prior to statehood) from Indian lands.

Name origin: For Thomas Jefferson (1743–1826), U.S. patriot, statesman, and third U.S. president.

Batavia   City
ZIP: 52533   **Lat:** 40-59-41 N **Long:** 92-10-03 W
Pop: 520 (1990); 525 (1980)   **Pop Density:** 866.7
Land: 0.6 sq. mi.; **Water:** 0.0 sq. mi.

Incorporated Jan 6, 1868.

Coppock   City
ZIP: 52654   **Lat:** 41-09-43 N **Long:** 91-43-01 W
Pop: 5 (1990); 7 (1980)   **Pop Density:** 500.0
Land: 0.01 sq. mi.; **Water:** 0.0 sq. mi.

Incorporated Aug 24, 1901. Part of the town is also in Henry and Washington counties.

Fairfield   City
ZIP: 52556   **Lat:** 41-00-25 N **Long:** 91-58-01 W
Pop: 9,768 (1990); 9,428 (1980)   **Pop Density:** 1878.5
Land: 5.2 sq. mi.; **Water:** 0.1 sq. mi.   **Elev:** 778 ft.

Incorporated May 14, 1875.

Libertyville   City
ZIP: 52567   **Lat:** 40-57-30 N **Long:** 92-02-56 W
Pop: 264 (1990); 281 (1980)   **Pop Density:** 880.0
Land: 0.3 sq. mi.; **Water:** 0.0 sq. mi.

Incorporated Apr 15, 1916.

Lockridge   City
ZIP: 52635   **Lat:** 40-59-36 N **Long:** 91-44-51 W
Pop: 270 (1990); 271 (1980)   **Pop Density:** 385.7
Land: 0.7 sq. mi.; **Water:** 0.0 sq. mi.

Incorporated Jun 17, 1913.

Packwood   City
ZIP: 52580   **Lat:** 41-07-56 N **Long:** 92-04-54 W
Pop: 208 (1990); 210 (1980)   **Pop Density:** 260.0
Land: 0.8 sq. mi.; **Water:** 0.0 sq. mi.

Incorporated May 7, 1894.

Pleasant Plain   City
                         Lat: 41-08-50 N **Long:** 91-51-34 W
Pop: 128 (1990); 144 (1980)   **Pop Density:** 128.0
Land: 1.0 sq. mi.; **Water:** 0.0 sq. mi.

Incorporated Apr 12, 1900.

Johnson County
County Seat: Iowa City (ZIP: 52240)

Pop: 96,119 (1990); 81,717 (1980) **Pop Density:** 156.4
Land: 614.5 sq. mi.; **Water:** 8.9 sq. mi. **Area Code:** 319

In east-central IA, south of Cedar Rapids; established Dec 21, 1837 (prior to statehood) from Des Moines County.

Name origin: For Col. Richard Mentor Johnson (1780–1850), officer in the War of 1812, U.S. senator from KY (1819–29), and U.S. vice president (1837–41).

Coralville — City
ZIP: 52241 **Lat:** 41-41-27 N **Long:** 91-36-02 W
Pop: 10,347 (1990); 7,687 (1980) **Pop Density:** 1326.5
Land: 7.8 sq. mi.; **Water:** 0.0 sq. mi.

Incorporated Nov 22, 1873.

Name origin: For the abundant coral found along the banks of the Iowa River, which flows through the town.

Hills — City
Lat: 41-34-28 N **Long:** 91-32-13 W
Pop: 662 (1990); 547 (1980) **Pop Density:** 1103.3
Land: 0.6 sq. mi.; **Water:** 0.0 sq. mi.

Incorporated 1906.

Name origin: For its descriptive connotations.

Iowa City — City
ZIP: 52240 **Lat:** 41-39-29 N **Long:** 91-32-06 W
Pop: 59,738 (1990); 50,508 (1980) **Pop Density:** 2715.4
Land: 22.0 sq. mi.; **Water:** 0.3 sq. mi.

In eastern IA, 26 mi. south of Cedar Rapids. Settled 1838, incorporated Jan 24, 1853; former capital of IA (1841–57). Site of the University of Iowa.

Name origin: For the Iowa River, itself probably named for the Ioway Indians. Meaning of the name is unknown.

Lone Tree — City
ZIP: 52755 **Lat:** 41-29-09 N **Long:** 91-25-29 W
Pop: 979 (1990); 1,014 (1980) **Pop Density:** 979.0
Land: 1.0 sq. mi.; **Water:** 0.0 sq. mi.

Incorporated May 20, 1890.

Name origin: For a single tree which stood on the prairie.

North Liberty — City
ZIP: 52317 **Lat:** 41-44-29 N **Long:** 91-36-33 W
Pop: 2,926 (1990); 2,046 (1980) **Pop Density:** 609.6
Land: 4.8 sq. mi.; **Water:** 0.0 sq. mi.

Incorporated Nov 10, 1913.

Oxford — City
ZIP: 52322 **Lat:** 41-43-28 N **Long:** 91-47-22 W
Pop: 663 (1990); 676 (1980) **Pop Density:** 1657.5
Land: 0.4 sq. mi.; **Water:** 0.0 sq. mi.

Incorporated Apr 8, 1881.

Shueyville — City
Lat: 41-50-53 N **Long:** 91-38-54 W
Pop: 223 (1990); 287 (1980) **Pop Density:** 159.3
Land: 1.4 sq. mi.; **Water:** 0.0 sq. mi.

Incorporated Mar 8, 1968.

Solon — City
ZIP: 52333 **Lat:** 41-48-17 N **Long:** 91-29-40 W
Pop: 1,050 (1990); 969 (1980) **Pop Density:** 2100.0
Land: 0.5 sq. mi.; **Water:** 0.0 sq. mi.

Incorporated Apr 28, 1877.

Swisher — City
ZIP: 52338 **Lat:** 41-50-36 N **Long:** 91-41-44 W
Pop: 645 (1990); 654 (1980) **Pop Density:** 1612.5
Land: 0.4 sq. mi.; **Water:** 0.0 sq. mi.

Incorporated Jul 25, 1933.

Tiffin — City
ZIP: 52340 **Lat:** 41-42-23 N **Long:** 91-40-38 W
Pop: 460 (1990); 413 (1980) **Pop Density:** 353.8
Land: 1.3 sq. mi.; **Water:** 0.0 sq. mi.

Incorporated Dec 27, 1906.

University Heights — City
ZIP: 52240 **Lat:** 41-39-16 N **Long:** 91-33-28 W
Pop: 1,042 (1990); 1,069 (1980) **Pop Density:** 3473.3
Land: 0.3 sq. mi.; **Water:** 0.0 sq. mi.

Incorporated Aug 13, 1935.

Name origin: For the University of IA.

IOWA, Jones County

Jones County
County Seat: Anamosa (ZIP: 52205)

Pop: 19,444 (1990); 20,401 (1980)
Land: 575.4 sq. mi.; **Water:** 1.4 sq. mi.
Pop Density: 33.8
Area Code: 319

In eastern IA, east of Cedar Rapids; established Dec 21, 1837 (prior to statehood) from Wisconsin Territory.

Name origin: For George Wallace Jones (1804–96), surveyor of public lands for WI and IA territories and U.S. senator from IA (1848–59).

Anamosa City
ZIP: 52205 **Lat:** 42-06-32 N **Long:** 91-16-52 W
Pop: 5,100 (1990); 4,958 (1980) **Pop Density:** 2833.3
Land: 1.8 sq. mi.; **Water:** 0.0 sq. mi.
Founded 1845; incorporated Dec 17, 1867.
Name origin: From an Algonquian term meaning 'little dog.' Previously called Lexington.

Cascade City
ZIP: 52033 **Lat:** 42-17-40 N **Long:** 91-01-04 W
Pop: 382 (1990); 400 (1980) **Pop Density:** 1910.0
Land: 0.2 sq. mi.; **Water:** 0.0 sq. mi.
Incorporated Dec 14, 1880. Part of the town is also in Dubuque County.

Center Junction City
Lat: 42-06-51 N **Long:** 91-05-21 W
Pop: 166 (1990); 182 (1980) **Pop Density:** 415.0
Land: 0.4 sq. mi.; **Water:** 0.0 sq. mi.
Incorporated Mar 26, 1885.

Martelle City
ZIP: 52305 **Lat:** 42-01-13 N **Long:** 91-21-27 W
Pop: 290 (1990); 316 (1980) **Pop Density:** 725.0
Land: 0.4 sq. mi.; **Water:** 0.0 sq. mi.
Incorporated Apr 28, 1899.

Monticello City
Lat: 42-14-15 N **Long:** 91-11-27 W
Pop: 3,522 (1990); 3,641 (1980) **Pop Density:** 1006.3
Land: 3.5 sq. mi.; **Water:** 0.0 sq. mi.

Morley City
ZIP: 52312 **Lat:** 42-00-23 N **Long:** 91-14-47 W
Pop: 85 (1990); 94 (1980) **Pop Density:** 850.0
Land: 0.1 sq. mi.; **Water:** 0.0 sq. mi.
Incorporated Jan 26, 1881.

Olin City
ZIP: 52320 **Lat:** 41-59-51 N **Long:** 91-08-27 W
Pop: 663 (1990); 735 (1980) **Pop Density:** 663.0
Land: 1.0 sq. mi.; **Water:** 0.0 sq. mi.
Incorporated Nov 14, 1879.

Onslow City
ZIP: 52321 **Lat:** 42-06-28 N **Long:** 91-00-49 W
Pop: 216 (1990); 218 (1980) **Pop Density:** 1080.0
Land: 0.2 sq. mi.; **Water:** 0.0 sq. mi.
Incorporated Jun 20, 1888.

Oxford Junction City
ZIP: 52323 **Lat:** 41-59-04 N **Long:** 90-57-15 W
Pop: 581 (1990); 600 (1980) **Pop Density:** 968.3
Land: 0.6 sq. mi.; **Water:** 0.0 sq. mi.
Incorporated Jan 15, 1884.

Wyoming City
ZIP: 52362 **Lat:** 42-03-36 N **Long:** 91-00-17 W
Pop: 659 (1990); 702 (1980) **Pop Density:** 1318.0
Land: 0.5 sq. mi.; **Water:** 0.0 sq. mi.
Incorporated Oct 21, 1873.
Name origin: For the Wyoming Valley in PA, the site of a famous massacre by British soldiers, Tories, and Iroquois Indians in 1778.

Keokuk County
County Seat: Sigourney (ZIP: 52591)

Pop: 11,624 (1990); 12,921 (1980)
Land: 579.2 sq. mi.; **Water:** 0.8 sq. mi.
Pop Density: 20.1
Area Code: 515

In south-central IA, north of Ottumwa; established Dec 21, 1837 (prior to statehood) from Washington County.

Name origin: For Keokuk (c. 1780–1848), the chief of the Sac and Fox Indians at the time the first settlers arrived. His name was originally *Kiyokaga* 'he who moves around alert.'

Delta City
ZIP: 52550 **Lat:** 41-19-23 N **Long:** 92-19-46 W
Pop: 409 (1990); 482 (1980) **Pop Density:** 409.0
Land: 1.0 sq. mi.; **Water:** 0.0 sq. mi.
Incorporated Mar 22, 1877.

Gibson City
ZIP: 50104 **Lat:** 41-28-50 N **Long:** 92-23-29 W
Pop: 63 (1990); 75 (1980) **Pop Density:** 630.0
Land: 0.1 sq. mi.; **Water:** 0.0 sq. mi.
Incorporated Dec 14, 1954.

Harper — City
ZIP: 52231 **Lat:** 41-21-48 N **Long:** 92-03-04 W
Pop: 147 (1990); 138 (1980) **Pop Density:** 1470.0
Land: 0.1 sq. mi.; **Water:** 0.0 sq. mi.
Incorporated Nov 17, 1879.

Hayesville — City
ZIP: 52562 **Lat:** 41-15-52 N **Long:** 92-14-49 W
Pop: 62 (1990); 93 (1980) **Pop Density:** 206.7
Land: 0.3 sq. mi.; **Water:** 0.0 sq. mi.
Incorporated Oct 13, 1916.

Hedrick — City
ZIP: 52563 **Lat:** 41-10-14 N **Long:** 92-18-27 W
Pop: 810 (1990); 847 (1980) **Pop Density:** 540.0
Land: 1.5 sq. mi.; **Water:** 0.0 sq. mi.
Incorporated Apr 23, 1883.

Keota — City
ZIP: 52248 **Lat:** 41-21-57 N **Long:** 91-57-19 W
Pop: 1,000 (1990); 1,034 (1980) **Pop Density:** 1666.7
Land: 0.6 sq. mi.; **Water:** 0.0 sq. mi.
Incorporated Dec 18, 1873.
Name origin: Originally called Keoton from a combination of the first three letters of Keokuk and the last three of Washington, when a railroad shipping point was established halfway between those two counties. Later shortened to present form.

Keswick — City
ZIP: 50136 **Lat:** 41-27-18 N **Long:** 92-14-14 W
Pop: 284 (1990); 300 (1980) **Pop Density:** 710.0
Land: 0.4 sq. mi.; **Water:** 0.0 sq. mi.
Incorporated Jul 5, 1912.

Kinross — City
ZIP: 52250 **Lat:** 41-27-33 N **Long:** 91-59-13 W
Pop: 89 (1990); 79 (1980) **Pop Density:** 445.0
Land: 0.2 sq. mi.; **Water:** 0.0 sq. mi.
Incorporated Sep 10, 1898.

Martinsburg — City
ZIP: 52568 **Lat:** 41-10-42 N **Long:** 92-15-08 W
Pop: 157 (1990); 174 (1980) **Pop Density:** 392.5
Land: 0.4 sq. mi.; **Water:** 0.0 sq. mi.
Incorporated Dec 30, 1887.

North English — City
ZIP: 52316 **Lat:** 41-30-34 N **Long:** 92-04-38 W
Pop: 12 (1990); 18 (1980) **Pop Density:** 1200.0
Land: 0.01 sq. mi.; **Water:** 0.0 sq. mi. **Elev:** 815 ft.
Incorporated Mar 13, 1891. Part of the town is also in Iowa County.

Ollie — City
ZIP: 52576 **Lat:** 41-11-55 N **Long:** 92-05-34 W
Pop: 207 (1990); 232 (1980) **Pop Density:** 207.0
Land: 1.0 sq. mi.; **Water:** 0.0 sq. mi.
Incorporated Mar 1, 1892.

Richland — City
ZIP: 52585 **Lat:** 41-11-09 N **Long:** 91-59-41 W
Pop: 522 (1990); 600 (1980) **Pop Density:** 652.5
Land: 0.8 sq. mi.; **Water:** 0.0 sq. mi.
Incorporated Dec 31, 1868.
Name origin: For the rich farm land.

Sigourney — City
ZIP: 52591 **Lat:** 41-20-02 N **Long:** 92-12-23 W
Pop: 2,111 (1990); 2,330 (1980) **Pop Density:** 1055.5
Land: 2.0 sq. mi.; **Water:** 0.0 sq. mi.
Incorporated Oct 4, 1858.
Name origin: For the poet Lydia Howard Sigourney (1791–1865).

South English — City
ZIP: 52335 **Lat:** 41-27-08 N **Long:** 92-05-26 W
Pop: 224 (1990); 211 (1980) **Pop Density:** 746.7
Land: 0.3 sq. mi.; **Water:** 0.0 sq. mi.
Incorporated Jul 13, 1892.

Thornburg — City
ZIP: 50255 **Lat:** 41-27-22 N **Long:** 92-19-57 W
Pop: 91 (1990); 103 (1980) **Pop Density:** 455.0
Land: 0.2 sq. mi.; **Water:** 0.0 sq. mi.
Incorporated Sep 25, 1883.

Webster — City
ZIP: 52355 **Lat:** 41-26-16 N **Long:** 92-10-15 W
Pop: 103 (1990); 124 (1980) **Pop Density:** 343.3
Land: 0.3 sq. mi.; **Water:** 0.0 sq. mi.
Incorporated Apr 13, 1909.
Name origin: For Daniel Webster (1782–1852), MA statesman.

What Cheer — City
ZIP: 50268 **Lat:** 41-24-00 N **Long:** 92-21-13 W
Pop: 762 (1990); 803 (1980) **Pop Density:** 635.0
Land: 1.2 sq. mi.; **Water:** 0.0 sq. mi.
Incorporated Feb 27, 1880.
Name origin: Named by a Scotch miner when he discovered coal in the area.

IOWA, Kossuth County

Kossuth County
County Seat: Algona (ZIP: 50511)

Pop: 18,591 (1990); 21,891 (1980) **Pop Density:** 19.1
Land: 973.1 sq. mi.; **Water:** 1.4 sq. mi. **Area Code:** 515

On central northern border of IA, north of Fort Dodge; established Jan 15, 1851 from Webster County.

Name origin: For Lajos Kossuth (1802–94), Hungarian resistance leader against Austrian domination who was enthusiastically acclaimed on a visit to the U.S. Named at a time when revolutionaries were celebrated in the U.S.

Algona City
ZIP: 50511 **Lat:** 43-04-26 N **Long:** 94-13-50 W
Pop: 6,015 (1990); 6,289 (1980) **Pop Density:** 1398.8
Land: 4.3 sq. mi.; **Water:** 0.0 sq. mi.

Incorporated Jan 31, 1872.

Name origin: One of several names extracted from the word *Algonquin* by Henry Rowe Schoolcraft (1793–1864)), author, explorer, MI legislator, and superintendent of Indian Affairs for MI (1836–41). Originally known as Call's Grove.

Bancroft City
ZIP: 50517 **Lat:** 43-17-33 N **Long:** 94-13-00 W
Pop: 857 (1990); 1,082 (1980) **Pop Density:** 1714.0
Land: 0.5 sq. mi.; **Water:** 0.0 sq. mi.

Incorporated Feb 16, 1884.

Burt City
ZIP: 50522 **Lat:** 43-11-57 N **Long:** 94-13-16 W
Pop: 575 (1990); 689 (1980) **Pop Density:** 1437.5
Land: 0.4 sq. mi.; **Water:** 0.0 sq. mi.

Incorporated Nov 28, 1893.

Name origin: For the president of the Union Pacific Railroad.

Fenton City
ZIP: 50539 **Lat:** 43-13-05 N **Long:** 94-25-39 W
Pop: 346 (1990); 394 (1980) **Pop Density:** 1153.3
Land: 0.3 sq. mi.; **Water:** 0.0 sq. mi.

Incorporated Jun 10, 1903.

Lakota City
ZIP: 50451 **Lat:** 43-22-40 N **Long:** 94-05-38 W
Pop: 281 (1990); 330 (1980) **Pop Density:** 1405.0
Land: 0.2 sq. mi.; **Water:** 0.0 sq. mi.

Incorporated Oct 1, 1918.

Name origin: The Santee dialect for Dakota, the name of the Sioux Indian nation; the name probably means 'allies.' Previously called Germania.

Ledyard City
ZIP: 50556 **Lat:** 43-25-12 N **Long:** 94-09-31 W
Pop: 164 (1990); 215 (1980) **Pop Density:** 546.7
Land: 0.3 sq. mi.; **Water:** 0.0 sq. mi.

Incorporated Apr 16, 1895.

Lone Rock City
ZIP: 50559 **Lat:** 43-13-13 N **Long:** 94-19-29 W
Pop: 185 (1990); 169 (1980) **Pop Density:** 1850.0
Land: 0.1 sq. mi.; **Water:** 0.0 sq. mi.

Incorporated Aug 5, 1915.

Lu Verne City
Lat: 42-54-54 N **Long:** 94-04-45 W
Pop: 274 (1990); 350 (1980) **Pop Density:** 249.1
Land: 1.1 sq. mi.; **Water:** 0.0 sq. mi.

Incorporated Jul 6, 1887. Part of the town is also in Humboldt County.

Swea City City
ZIP: 50590 **Lat:** 43-22-58 N **Long:** 94-18-36 W
Pop: 634 (1990); 813 (1980) **Pop Density:** 905.7
Land: 0.7 sq. mi.; **Water:** 0.0 sq. mi. **Elev:** 1181 ft.

Incorporated May 7, 1895.

Name origin: Named by Swedish emigrants for the Swedish name for their country.

Titonka City
ZIP: 50480 **Lat:** 43-14-11 N **Long:** 94-02-29 W
Pop: 612 (1990); 607 (1980) **Pop Density:** 2040.0
Land: 0.3 sq. mi.; **Water:** 0.0 sq. mi.

Incorporated Feb 1, 1900.

Name origin: From the Sioux term for 'big house.'

Wesley City
ZIP: 50483 **Lat:** 43-05-20 N **Long:** 93-59-34 W
Pop: 444 (1990); 598 (1980) **Pop Density:** 740.0
Land: 0.6 sq. mi.; **Water:** 0.0 sq. mi.

Incorporated Apr 13, 1892.

West Bend City
Lat: 42-57-09 N **Long:** 94-26-27 W
Pop: 6 (1990); 17 (1980) **Pop Density:** 200.0
Land: 0.03 sq. mi.; **Water:** 0.0 sq. mi.

Incorporated Feb 27, 1884. Part of the town is also in Palo Alto County.

Whittemore City
ZIP: 50598 **Lat:** 43-03-48 N **Long:** 94-25-26 W
Pop: 535 (1990); 647 (1980) **Pop Density:** 1337.5
Land: 0.4 sq. mi.; **Water:** 0.0 sq. mi.

Incorporated Nov 19, 1891.

Lee County
County Seat: Fort Madison (ZIP: 52627)

Pop: 38,687 (1990); 43,106 (1980) **Pop Density:** 74.8
Land: 517.4 sq. mi.; **Water:** 21.4 sq. mi. **Area Code:** 319

On southeasternmost border of IA; established Dec 7, 1836 (prior to statehood) from Des Moines County.

Name origin: Probably for Albert Miller Lea (1807–90), a surveyor of the Des Moines River who mapped the Iowa District, or for Charles Lee, an official of the New York Land Company, which had extensive landholdings in the area.

Donnellson City
ZIP: 52625 **Lat:** 40-38-36 N **Long:** 91-33-53 W
Pop: 940 (1990); 972 (1980) **Pop Density:** 1175.0
Land: 0.8 sq. mi.; **Water:** 0.0 sq. mi.

Incorporated Oct 25, 1892.

Fort Madison City
ZIP: 52627 **Lat:** 40-37-11 N **Long:** 91-21-07 W
Pop: 11,618 (1990); 13,520 (1980) **Pop Density:** 1249.2
Land: 9.3 sq. mi.; **Water:** 3.7 sq. mi.

In southeastern IA on the Mississippi River. Incorporated Feb 5, 1851.

Name origin: For James Madison (1751–1836), fifth U.S. president.

Franklin City
ZIP: 52625 **Lat:** 40-39-59 N **Long:** 91-30-42 W
Pop: 152 (1990); 142 (1980) **Pop Density:** 760.0
Land: 0.2 sq. mi.; **Water:** 0.0 sq. mi.

Incorporated Nov 14, 1874.

Name origin: For Benjamin Franklin (1706–90), U.S. statesman and patriot.

Houghton City
ZIP: 52631 **Lat:** 40-46-58 N **Long:** 91-36-44 W
Pop: 127 (1990); 124 (1980) **Pop Density:** 423.3
Land: 0.3 sq. mi.; **Water:** 0.0 sq. mi.

Incorporated Feb 19, 1962.

Keokuk City
ZIP: 52632 **Lat:** 40-24-34 N **Long:** 91-24-12 W
Pop: 12,451 (1990); 13,536 (1980) **Pop Density:** 1353.4
Land: 9.2 sq. mi.; **Water:** 1.5 sq. mi.

On the southeasternmost tip of IA that dips into MO, on the Mississippi River. Incorporated Dec 13, 1848.

Name origin: For Keokuk (c. 1780–1848), the chief of the Sac and Fox Indians at the time the first settlers arrived. His name was originally *Kiyokaga* 'he who moves around alert.'

Montrose City
ZIP: 52639 **Lat:** 40-31-31 N **Long:** 91-24-58 W
Pop: 957 (1990); 1,038 (1980) **Pop Density:** 870.0
Land: 1.1 sq. mi.; **Water:** 0.0 sq. mi. **Elev:** 530 ft.

Incorporated 1875.

Name origin: Previously called Mount of Roses.

St. Paul City
Lat: 40-46-00 N **Long:** 91-31-00 W
Pop: 120 (1990); 141 (1980) **Pop Density:** 300.0
Land: 0.4 sq. mi.; **Water:** 0.0 sq. mi.

Incorporated Apr 1, 1895.

West Point City
ZIP: 52656 **Lat:** 40-42-56 N **Long:** 91-27-05 W
Pop: 1,079 (1990); 1,132 (1980) **Pop Density:** 1798.3
Land: 0.6 sq. mi.; **Water:** 0.0 sq. mi.

Incorporated Mar 25, 1858.

Linn County
County Seat: Cedar Rapids (ZIP: 52401)

Pop: 168,767 (1990); 169,775 (1980) **Pop Density:** 235.2
Land: 717.5 sq. mi.; **Water:** 7.1 sq. mi. **Area Code:** 319

In east-central IA, north of Iowa City; established Dec 21, 1837 (prior to statehood) from Wisconsin Territory.

Name origin: For Lewis Fields Linn (1795–1843), U.S. senator from MO (1833–43).

Alburnett City
ZIP: 52202 **Lat:** 42-08-58 N **Long:** 91-37-05 W
Pop: 456 (1990); 411 (1980) **Pop Density:** 570.0
Land: 0.8 sq. mi.; **Water:** 0.0 sq. mi.

Incorporated Jun 29, 1912.

Bertram City
Lat: 41-57-17 N **Long:** 91-32-11 W
Pop: 201 (1990); 216 (1980) **Pop Density:** 167.5
Land: 1.2 sq. mi.; **Water:** 0.0 sq. mi.

Incorporated Jan 17, 1914.

Cedar Rapids City
ZIP: 52401 **Lat:** 41-58-22 N **Long:** 91-40-10 W
Pop: 108,751 (1990); 110,243 (1980) **Pop Density:** 2032.7
Land: 53.5 sq. mi.; **Water:** 1.2 sq. mi.

In eastern IA on the Cedar River, 100 mi. northeast of Des Moines. Settled 1838; incorporated Jan 15, 1849. Manufacturing (cereal, corn, soybean, meat processing, machinery, flight control equipment) and distributing city; surrounded by large farms and dairies.

Name origin: For the rapids in the Cedar River, itself originally called *Mosk-wah-wak-wah* 'red cedar' by the Sauk-Fox Indians. Previously called Rapids City.

IOWA, Linn County

Center Point   City
ZIP: 52213   **Lat:** 42-11-05 N **Long:** 91-46-36 W
Pop: 1,693 (1990); 1,591 (1980)   **Pop Density:** 806.2
Land: 2.1 sq. mi.; **Water:** 0.0 sq. mi.
Incorporated Feb 6, 1875.

Central City   City
ZIP: 52214   **Lat:** 42-12-12 N **Long:** 91-31-24 W
Pop: 1,063 (1990); 1,067 (1980)   **Pop Density:** 1518.6
Land: 0.7 sq. mi.; **Water:** 0.0 sq. mi.
Incorporated Jul 6, 1889.

Coggon   City
ZIP: 52218   **Lat:** 42-16-45 N **Long:** 91-31-51 W
Pop: 645 (1990); 639 (1980)   **Pop Density:** 1075.0
Land: 0.6 sq. mi.; **Water:** 0.0 sq. mi.
Incorporated Jun 14, 1892.

Ely   City
ZIP: 52227   **Lat:** 41-52-30 N **Long:** 91-35-14 W
Pop: 517 (1990); 425 (1980)   **Pop Density:** 517.0
Land: 1.0 sq. mi.; **Water:** 0.0 sq. mi.
Incorporated Aug 12, 1903.

Fairfax   City
ZIP: 52228   **Lat:** 41-55-17 N **Long:** 91-46-48 W
Pop: 780 (1990); 683 (1980)   **Pop Density:** 709.1
Land: 1.1 sq. mi.; **Water:** 0.0 sq. mi.
Incorporated Aug 11, 1930.

Hiawatha   City
ZIP: 52233   **Lat:** 42-02-47 N **Long:** 91-41-01 W
Pop: 4,986 (1990); 4,825 (1980)   **Pop Density:** 1662.0
Land: 3.0 sq. mi.; **Water:** 0.0 sq. mi.
Incorporated Jun 12, 1950.
Name origin: For the Indian hero in Henry Wadsworth Longfellow's (1807–82) poem, "The Song of Hiawatha."

Lisbon   City
ZIP: 52253   **Lat:** 41-55-16 N **Long:** 91-23-28 W
Pop: 1,452 (1990); 1,458 (1980)   **Pop Density:** 726.0
Land: 2.0 sq. mi.; **Water:** 0.0 sq. mi.
Incorporated Feb 10, 1875.
Name origin: For Lisbon, Portugal.

Marion   City
ZIP: 52302   **Lat:** 42-02-03 N **Long:** 91-35-22 W
Pop: 20,403 (1990); 19,474 (1980)   **Pop Density:** 2147.7
Land: 9.5 sq. mi.; **Water:** 0.0 sq. mi.
In eastern IA, 8 mi. north-northeast of Cedar Rapids. Incorporated Aug 10, 1865.
Name origin: For Gen. Francis Marion (c. 1732–1795), known as the "Swamp Fox" for his daring exploits during the American Revolution.

Mount Vernon   City
ZIP: 52314   **Lat:** 41-55-23 N **Long:** 91-25-25 W
Pop: 3,657 (1990); 3,325 (1980)   **Pop Density:** 1044.9
Land: 3.5 sq. mi.; **Water:** 0.0 sq. mi.
Incorporated Jul 7, 1869.
Name origin: Probably for the name of first U.S. President George Washington's (1732–99) estate in VA.

Palo   City
ZIP: 52324   **Lat:** 42-03-51 N **Long:** 91-47-45 W
Pop: 514 (1990); 529 (1980)   **Pop Density:** 1285.0
Land: 0.4 sq. mi.; **Water:** 0.0 sq. mi.
Incorporated Apr 25, 1905.
Name origin: From Spanish for 'stick,' probably used as a marker.

Prairieburg   City
ZIP: 52219   **Lat:** 42-14-16 N **Long:** 91-25-33 W
Pop: 213 (1990); 197 (1980)   **Pop Density:** 426.0
Land: 0.5 sq. mi.; **Water:** 0.0 sq. mi.
Incorporated Mar 30, 1905.

Robins   City
ZIP: 52328   **Lat:** 42-04-42 N **Long:** 91-40-09 W
Pop: 875 (1990); 726 (1980)   **Pop Density:** 324.1
Land: 2.7 sq. mi.; **Water:** 0.0 sq. mi.
Incorporated May 3, 1910.

Springville   City
ZIP: 52336   **Lat:** 42-03-20 N **Long:** 91-26-38 W
Pop: 1,068 (1990); 1,165 (1980)   **Pop Density:** 1780.0
Land: 0.6 sq. mi.; **Water:** 0.0 sq. mi.
Incorporated Jan 27, 1882.

Walford   City
ZIP: 52351   **Lat:** 41-52-50 N **Long:** 91-49-50 W
Pop: 13 (1990); 19 (1980)   **Pop Density:** 130.0
Land: 0.1 sq. mi.; **Water:** 0.0 sq. mi.
Incorporated Apr 15, 1954. Part of the town is also in Benton County.

Walker   City
ZIP: 52352   **Lat:** 42-17-10 N **Long:** 91-46-51 W
Pop: 673 (1990); 733 (1980)   **Pop Density:** 961.4
Land: 0.7 sq. mi.; **Water:** 0.0 sq. mi.
Incorporated Jun 13, 1891.

Louisa County
County Seat: Wapello (ZIP: 52653)

Pop: 11,592 (1990); 12,055 (1980) **Pop Density:** 28.8
Land: 401.9 sq. mi.; **Water:** 15.7 sq. mi. **Area Code:** 319

On southeastern border of IA, north of Burlington; established Dec 7, 1836 (prior to statehood) from Des Moines County.

Name origin: For Louisa Massey, pioneer heroine who shot and wounded her brother's murderer. Some sources claim Louisa, queen of Denmark (1724–51), youngest daughter of George II of England.

Columbus City — City
ZIP: 52737 **Lat:** 41-15-33 N **Long:** 91-22-30 W
Pop: 328 (1990); 367 (1980) **Pop Density:** 1640.0
Land: 0.2 sq. mi.; **Water:** 0.0 sq. mi.
Incorporated Nov 26, 1870.

Columbus Junction — City
ZIP: 52738 **Lat:** 41-16-45 N **Long:** 91-21-52 W
Pop: 1,616 (1990); 1,429 (1980) **Pop Density:** 808.0
Land: 2.0 sq. mi.; **Water:** 0.0 sq. mi.
Incorporated May 25, 1874.

Cotter — City
ZIP: 52738 **Lat:** 41-17-33 N **Long:** 91-28-13 W
Pop: 53 (1990); 60 (1980) **Pop Density:** 265.0
Land: 0.2 sq. mi.; **Water:** 0.0 sq. mi.
Incorporated Apr 1, 1912.

Fredonia — City
ZIP: 52738 **Lat:** 41-17-04 N **Long:** 91-20-20 W
Pop: 201 (1990); 224 (1980) **Pop Density:** 1005.0
Land: 0.2 sq. mi.; **Water:** 0.0 sq. mi.
Incorporated May 30, 1874.

Grandview — City
ZIP: 52752 **Lat:** 41-16-37 N **Long:** 91-11-14 W
Pop: 514 (1990); 473 (1980) **Pop Density:** 2570.0
Land: 0.2 sq. mi.; **Water:** 0.0 sq. mi.
Incorporated Feb 18, 1901.

Letts — City
ZIP: 52754 **Lat:** 41-19-48 N **Long:** 91-14-05 W
Pop: 390 (1990); 473 (1980) **Pop Density:** 650.0
Land: 0.6 sq. mi.; **Water:** 0.0 sq. mi.
Incorporated Jul 28, 1877.

Morning Sun — City
ZIP: 52640 **Lat:** 41-05-38 N **Long:** 91-15-05 W
Pop: 841 (1990); 959 (1980) **Pop Density:** 1051.3
Land: 0.8 sq. mi.; **Water:** 0.0 sq. mi.
Incorporated Jun 3, 1867.

Oakville — City
ZIP: 52646 **Lat:** 41-05-52 N **Long:** 91-02-36 W
Pop: 442 (1990); 470 (1980) **Pop Density:** 1105.0
Land: 0.4 sq. mi.; **Water:** 0.0 sq. mi.
Incorporated Oct 27, 1902.

Wapello — City
ZIP: 52653 **Lat:** 41-10-42 N **Long:** 91-11-19 W
Pop: 2,013 (1990); 2,011 (1980) **Pop Density:** 1830.0
Land: 1.1 sq. mi.; **Water:** 0.0 sq. mi.
Incorporated Jul 15, 1856.
Name origin: For Wapello, chief of the Fox Indians.

Lucas County
County Seat: Chariton (ZIP: 50049)

Pop: 9,070 (1990); 10,313 (1980) **Pop Density:** 21.1
Land: 430.6 sq. mi.; **Water:** 3.6 sq. mi. **Area Code:** 515

In south-central IA, southeast of Des Moines; established Jan 13, 1846 from Monroe County.

Name origin: For Col. Robert Lucas (1781–1853), governor of OH (1832–36) and first territorial governor of IA (1838–41).

Chariton — City
ZIP: 50049 **Lat:** 41-01-03 N **Long:** 93-18-35 W
Pop: 4,616 (1990); 5,116 (1980) **Pop Density:** 1318.9
Land: 3.5 sq. mi.; **Water:** 0.0 sq. mi.
Incorporated Dec 9, 1874.

Derby — City
ZIP: 50068 **Lat:** 40-55-47 N **Long:** 93-27-24 W
Pop: 135 (1990); 171 (1980) **Pop Density:** 450.0
Land: 0.3 sq. mi.; **Water:** 0.0 sq. mi.
Incorporated Feb 4, 1901.

Lucas — City
ZIP: 50151 **Lat:** 41-01-54 N **Long:** 93-27-36 W
Pop: 224 (1990); 292 (1980) **Pop Density:** 224.0
Land: 1.0 sq. mi.; **Water:** 0.0 sq. mi.
Incorporated Mar 18, 1887.

Russell — City
ZIP: 50238 **Lat:** 40-58-49 N **Long:** 93-12-02 W
Pop: 531 (1990); 593 (1980) **Pop Density:** 531.0
Land: 1.0 sq. mi.; **Water:** 0.0 sq. mi.
Incorporated Apr 25, 1887.

Williamson
City
ZIP: 50272 **Lat:** 41-05-16 N **Long:** 93-15-24 W
Pop: 166 (1990); 210 (1980) **Pop Density:** 553.3
Land: 0.3 sq. mi.; **Water:** 0.0 sq. mi.
Incorporated Jun 14, 1922.

Lyon County
County Seat: Rock Rapids (ZIP: 51246)

Pop: 11,952 (1990); 12,896 (1980) **Pop Density:** 20.3
Land: 587.6 sq. mi.; **Water:** 0.1 sq. mi. **Area Code:** 712

On northwestern border of IA; established as Buncombe County Jan 15, 1851 from Woodbury County; name changed Sep 11, 1862.

Name origin: For Gen. Nathaniel Lyon (1818–61), Union commander in the Civil War who helped preserve MO for the Union when it seemed likely to join the Confederacy. He was killed leading the First Iowa Infantry at the Battle of Wilson Creek, MO.

Alvord
City
ZIP: 51230 **Lat:** 43-20-31 N **Long:** 96-18-09 W
Pop: 204 (1990); 246 (1980) **Pop Density:** 680.0
Land: 0.3 sq. mi.; **Water:** 0.0 sq. mi.
Incorporated Sep 16, 1892.

Doon
City
ZIP: 51235 **Lat:** 43-16-43 N **Long:** 96-13-53 W
Pop: 476 (1990); 537 (1980) **Pop Density:** 793.3
Land: 0.6 sq. mi.; **Water:** 0.0 sq. mi.
Incorporated Mar 8, 1892.
Name origin: For the Doon River in Scotland.

George
City
ZIP: 51237 **Lat:** 43-20-30 N **Long:** 96-00-09 W
Pop: 1,066 (1990); 1,241 (1980) **Pop Density:** 444.2
Land: 2.4 sq. mi.; **Water:** 0.0 sq. mi.
Incorporated Mar 27, 1890.

Inwood
City
ZIP: 51240 **Lat:** 43-17-13 N **Long:** 96-26-24 W
Pop: 824 (1990); 755 (1980) **Pop Density:** 206.0
Land: 4.0 sq. mi.; **Water:** 0.0 sq. mi.
Incorporated Apr 25, 1893.

Larchwood
City
ZIP: 51241 **Lat:** 43-27-18 N **Long:** 96-26-14 W
Pop: 739 (1990); 701 (1980) **Pop Density:** 821.1
Land: 0.9 sq. mi.; **Water:** 0.0 sq. mi.
Incorporated Jan 6, 1892.
Name origin: For the many larch trees planted in the area by town founder J.W. Foll.

Lester
City
ZIP: 51242 **Lat:** 43-26-21 N **Long:** 96-19-48 W
Pop: 257 (1990); 274 (1980) **Pop Density:** 122.4
Land: 2.1 sq. mi.; **Water:** 0.0 sq. mi.
Incorporated Dec 26, 1892.

Little Rock
City
ZIP: 51243 **Lat:** 43-26-40 N **Long:** 95-52-51 W
Pop: 493 (1990); 490 (1980) **Pop Density:** 616.3
Land: 0.8 sq. mi.; **Water:** 0.0 sq. mi.
Incorporated Nov 26, 1894.
Name origin: From French *Petite Roche* or *Rochelle* 'little rock,' a small promontory on the Arkansas River. Previously called Arkopolis.

Rock Rapids
City
ZIP: 51246 **Lat:** 43-25-32 N **Long:** 96-09-57 W
Pop: 2,601 (1990); 2,693 (1980) **Pop Density:** 650.3
Land: 4.0 sq. mi.; **Water:** 0.0 sq. mi.
Incorporated Apr 8, 1885.
Name origin: For its location near the falls of the Rock River.

Madison County
County Seat: Winterset (ZIP: 50273)

Pop: 12,483 (1990); 12,597 (1980)   **Pop Density:** 22.2
Land: 561.2 sq. mi.; **Water:** 1.2 sq. mi.   **Area Code:** 515

In south-central IA, southwest of Des Moines; established Feb 14, 1844 (prior to statehood) from Polk County.

Name origin: For James Madison (1751–1836), fourth U.S. president.

Bevington   City
ZIP: 50033   **Lat:** 41-21-33 N **Long:** 93-47-32 W
Pop: 44 (1990); 55 (1980)   **Pop Density:** 440.0
Land: 0.1 sq. mi.; **Water:** 0.0 sq. mi.
Incorporated Feb 1, 1916. Part of the town is also in Warren County.

Earlham   City
ZIP: 50072   **Lat:** 41-29-31 N **Long:** 94-07-19 W
Pop: 1,157 (1990); 1,140 (1980)   **Pop Density:** 1652.9
Land: 0.7 sq. mi.; **Water:** 0.0 sq. mi.
Incorporated Apr 26, 1870.

East Peru   City
Lat: 41-13-38 N **Long:** 93-55-39 W
Pop: 132 (1990); 124 (1980)   **Pop Density:** 146.7
Land: 0.9 sq. mi.; **Water:** 0.0 sq. mi.
Incorporated Mar 31, 1897.

Macksburg   City
ZIP: 50155   **Lat:** 41-12-51 N **Long:** 94-11-07 W
Pop: 110 (1990); 132 (1980)   **Pop Density:** 55.0
Land: 2.0 sq. mi.; **Water:** 0.0 sq. mi.
Incorporated Dec 24, 1876.

Patterson   City
ZIP: 50218   **Lat:** 41-20-56 N **Long:** 93-52-45 W
Pop: 128 (1990); 138 (1980)   **Pop Density:** 640.0
Land: 0.2 sq. mi.; **Water:** 0.0 sq. mi.
Incorporated Dec 7, 1877.

St. Charles   City
Lat: 41-17-16 N **Long:** 93-48-22 W
Pop: 537 (1990); 507 (1980)   **Pop Density:** 1342.5
Land: 0.4 sq. mi.; **Water:** 0.0 sq. mi.
Incorporated May 15, 1876.

Truro   City
ZIP: 50257   **Lat:** 41-12-37 N **Long:** 93-50-44 W
Pop: 391 (1990); 407 (1980)   **Pop Density:** 391.0
Land: 1.0 sq. mi.; **Water:** 0.0 sq. mi.   **Elev:** 1082 ft.
Incorporated Feb 24, 1902.

Winterset   City
ZIP: 50273   **Lat:** 41-20-16 N **Long:** 94-01-06 W
Pop: 4,196 (1990); 4,021 (1980)   **Pop Density:** 1353.5
Land: 3.1 sq. mi.; **Water:** 0.0 sq. mi.
Incorporated Jan 16, 1857.

Mahaska County
County Seat: Oskaloosa (ZIP: 52577)

Pop: 21,522 (1990); 22,867 (1980)   **Pop Density:** 37.7
Land: 570.9 sq. mi.; **Water:** 2.5 sq. mi.   **Area Code:** 515

In south-central IA, northwest of Ottumwa; established Feb 17, 1843 (prior to statehood) from Indian lands.

Name origin: For Mahaska (1784–1834), a chief of the Iowa tribe, whose name means 'white cloud.' The county seat was named for one of his wives.

Barnes City   City
ZIP: 50027   **Lat:** 41-30-22 N **Long:** 92-28-07 W
Pop: 198 (1990); 244 (1980)   **Pop Density:** 396.0
Land: 0.5 sq. mi.; **Water:** 0.0 sq. mi.
Incorporated Apr 20, 1899. Part of the town is also in Poweshiek County.

Beacon   City
ZIP: 52534   **Lat:** 41-16-28 N **Long:** 92-40-52 W
Pop: 509 (1990); 530 (1980)   **Pop Density:** 509.0
Land: 1.0 sq. mi.; **Water:** 0.0 sq. mi.
Incorporated Feb 7, 1874.
Name origin: For Benjamin Disraeli, earl of Beaconsfield (1804–81), English author and prime minister (1868; 1874–80).

Eddyville   City
Lat: 41-09-51 N **Long:** 92-38-14 W
Pop: 173 (1990); 191 (1980)   **Pop Density:** 576.7
Land: 0.3 sq. mi.; **Water:** 0.0 sq. mi.
Incorporated Feb 22, 1900. Part of the town is also in Monroe and Wapello counties.

Fremont   City
ZIP: 52561   **Lat:** 41-12-43 N **Long:** 92-26-05 W
Pop: 701 (1990); 730 (1980)   **Pop Density:** 701.0
Land: 1.0 sq. mi.; **Water:** 0.0 sq. mi.
Incorporated Mar 14, 1883.
Name origin: For John Charles Frémont (1813–90), soldier and explorer who led five expeditions to the West, U.S. senator from CA (1850–51), and governor of the AZ Territory (1878–83).

IOWA, Mahaska County

Keomah Village — City
ZIP: 52577   **Lat:** 41-17-17 N **Long:** 92-32-10 W
Pop: 99 (1990); 99 (1980)   **Pop Density:** 3300.0
Land: 0.03 sq. mi.; **Water:** 0.0 sq. mi.
Incorporated Aug 3, 1973.
Name origin: A combination of the first syllables from Keokuk and Mahaska, the two adjoining counties that helped finance the Lake Keomah State Park. Formerly Keomah; changed to present name Jan 1, 1982.

Leighton — City
ZIP: 50143   **Lat:** 41-20-18 N **Long:** 92-47-11 W
Pop: 142 (1990); 137 (1980)   **Pop Density:** 1420.0
Land: 0.1 sq. mi.; **Water:** 0.0 sq. mi.
Incorporated Sep 21, 1909.

New Sharon — City
ZIP: 50207   **Lat:** 41-28-12 N **Long:** 92-39-02 W
Pop: 1,136 (1990); 1,225 (1980)   **Pop Density:** 1262.2
Land: 0.9 sq. mi.; **Water:** 0.0 sq. mi.
Incorporated 1871.

Oskaloosa — City
ZIP: 52577   **Lat:** 41-17-34 N **Long:** 92-38-22 W
Pop: 10,632 (1990); 10,989 (1980)   **Pop Density:** 1933.1
Land: 5.5 sq. mi.; **Water:** 0.0 sq. mi.
In southeastern-central IA, 56 mi. east-southeast of Des Moines. Incorporated Feb 4, 1875.
Name origin: There is no official mention of the origin of the name, so many myths have been invented to explain it. Possibly for Oskaloosa, a wife of the Indian leader in the book, *Osceola, or Fact and Fiction*. Previously called Mahaska.

Rose Hill — City
ZIP: 52586   **Lat:** 41-19-13 N **Long:** 92-27-45 W
Pop: 171 (1990); 214 (1980)   **Pop Density:** 1710.0
Land: 0.1 sq. mi.; **Water:** 0.0 sq. mi.
Incorporated Aug 22, 1876.

University Park — City
ZIP: 52595   **Lat:** 41-17-12 N **Long:** 92-36-56 W
Pop: 604 (1990); 645 (1980)   **Pop Density:** 755.0
Land: 0.8 sq. mi.; **Water:** 0.0 sq. mi.
Incorporated Apr 13, 1909.

Marion County
County Seat: Knoxville (ZIP: 50138)

Pop: 30,001 (1990); 29,669 (1980)   **Pop Density:** 54.1
Land: 554.3 sq. mi.; **Water:** 16.3 sq. mi.   **Area Code:** 515
In south-central IA, southeast of Des Moines; established Jun 10, 1845 (prior to statehood) from Washington County.
Name origin: For Gen. Francis Marion (c. 1732–95), SC soldier and legislator, known as "The Swamp Fox" for his tactics during the Revolutionary War.

Bussey — City
ZIP: 50044   **Lat:** 41-12-21 N **Long:** 92-53-02 W
Pop: 494 (1990); 579 (1980)   **Pop Density:** 1646.7
Land: 0.3 sq. mi.; **Water:** 0.0 sq. mi.
Incorporated Apr 9, 1895.

Hamilton — City
ZIP: 50116   **Lat:** 41-10-11 N **Long:** 92-54-14 W
Pop: 115 (1990); 163 (1980)   **Pop Density:** 230.0
Land: 0.5 sq. mi.; **Water:** 0.0 sq. mi.
Incorporated Apr 11, 1900.
Name origin: For William W. Hamilton, president of the senate in 1857.

Harvey — City
ZIP: 50119   **Lat:** 41-18-59 N **Long:** 92-55-24 W
Pop: 235 (1990); 275 (1980)   **Pop Density:** 335.7
Land: 0.7 sq. mi.; **Water:** 0.0 sq. mi.
Incorporated Dec 12, 1903.

Knoxville — City
ZIP: 50138   **Lat:** 41-19-08 N **Long:** 93-06-04 W
Pop: 8,232 (1990); 8,143 (1980)   **Pop Density:** 1960.0
Land: 4.2 sq. mi.; **Water:** 0.0 sq. mi.
Incorporated Jan 24, 1855.
Name origin: For Gen. Henry Knox (1750–1806), U.S. secretary of war (1785–94) under presidency of George Washington (1732–99).

Marysville — City
ZIP: 50116   **Lat:** 41-10-57 N **Long:** 92-57-12 W
Pop: 65 (1990); 84 (1980)   **Pop Density:** 162.5
Land: 0.4 sq. mi.; **Water:** 0.0 sq. mi.
Incorporated Jul 31, 1875.

Melcher-Dallas — City
Lat: 41-13-40 N **Long:** 93-14-27 W
Pop: 1,302 (1990)   **Pop Density:** 1302.0
Land: 1.0 sq. mi.; **Water:** 0.0 sq. mi.

Pella — City
ZIP: 50219   **Lat:** 41-24-31 N **Long:** 92-55-08 W
Pop: 9,270 (1990); 8,349 (1980)   **Pop Density:** 2155.8
Land: 4.3 sq. mi.; **Water:** 0.0 sq. mi.
Incorporated Apr 10, 1868.
Name origin: Named by settlers from the Netherlands; from Dutch 'city of refuge.'

Pleasantville — City
ZIP: 50225   **Lat:** 41-23-20 N **Long:** 93-16-02 W
Pop: 1,536 (1990); 1,531 (1980)   **Pop Density:** 1181.5
Land: 1.3 sq. mi.; **Water:** 0.0 sq. mi.
Incorporated Jun 11, 1872.

Swan — City
ZIP: 50252   **Lat:** 41-27-56 N **Long:** 93-18-33 W
Pop: 76 (1990); 102 (1980)   **Pop Density:** 126.7
Land: 0.6 sq. mi.; **Water:** 0.0 sq. mi.
Incorporated Jun 26, 1884.

Marshall County
County Seat: Marshalltown (ZIP: 50158)

Pop: 38,276 (1990); 41,652 (1980)   **Pop Density:** 66.9
Land: 572.4 sq. mi.; **Water:** 0.7 sq. mi.   **Area Code:** 515
In central IA, east of Ames; established Jan 13, 1846 from Jasper County.
Name origin: For John Marshall (1755–1835), Chief Justice of the U.S. Supreme Court (1801–35).

Albion   City
ZIP: 50005   **Lat:** 42-06-45 N   **Long:** 92-59-21 W
Pop: 585 (1990); 739 (1980)   **Pop Density:** 975.0
Land: 0.6 sq. mi.; **Water:** 0.0 sq. mi.
Incorporated Mar 8, 1870.
Name origin: Probably for the literary name for Britain.

Clemons   City
Lat: 42-06-47 N   **Long:** 93-09-29 W
Pop: 173 (1990); 175 (1980)   **Pop Density:** 576.7
Land: 0.3 sq. mi.; **Water:** 0.0 sq. mi.
Incorporated May 25, 1903.

Ferguson   City
ZIP: 50078   **Lat:** 41-56-18 N   **Long:** 92-51-48 W
Pop: 166 (1990); 173 (1980)   **Pop Density:** 830.0
Land: 0.2 sq. mi.; **Water:** 0.0 sq. mi.
Incorporated Dec 4, 1906.

Gilman   City
ZIP: 50106   **Lat:** 41-52-42 N   **Long:** 92-47-16 W
Pop: 586 (1990); 642 (1980)   **Pop Density:** 1172.0
Land: 0.5 sq. mi.; **Water:** 0.0 sq. mi.
Incorporated Apr 24, 1876.

Haverhill   City
ZIP: 50120   **Lat:** 41-56-38 N   **Long:** 92-57-40 W
Pop: 144 (1990); 173 (1980)   **Pop Density:** 1440.0
Land: 0.1 sq. mi.; **Water:** 0.0 sq. mi.
Incorporated Jul 12, 1968.

Laurel   City
ZIP: 50141   **Lat:** 41-53-01 N   **Long:** 92-55-16 W
Pop: 271 (1990); 278 (1980)   **Pop Density:** 903.3
Land: 0.3 sq. mi.; **Water:** 0.0 sq. mi.
Incorporated Apr 23, 1903.

Le Grand   City
ZIP: 50142   **Lat:** 42-00-25 N   **Long:** 92-46-30 W
Pop: 854 (1990); 921 (1980)   **Pop Density:** 854.0
Land: 1.0 sq. mi.; **Water:** 0.0 sq. mi.
Incorporated May 9, 1891.
Name origin: From French term for 'the big one.'

Liscomb   City
ZIP: 50148   **Lat:** 42-11-26 N   **Long:** 93-00-19 W
Pop: 258 (1990); 296 (1980)   **Pop Density:** 258.0
Land: 1.0 sq. mi.; **Water:** 0.0 sq. mi.
Incorporated Mar 23, 1874.

Marshalltown   City
ZIP: 50158   **Lat:** 42-02-07 N   **Long:** 92-54-42 W
Pop: 25,178 (1990); 26,938 (1980)   **Pop Density:** 1667.4
Land: 15.1 sq. mi.; **Water:** 0.0 sq. mi.
In central IA, 50 mi. northeast of Des Moines. Settled 1851; incorporated as a village 1863, as a city Mar 5, 1923.
Name origin: Named by founder Harry Anson for Marshall, MI.

Melbourne   City
ZIP: 50162   **Lat:** 41-56-30 N   **Long:** 93-06-07 W
Pop: 669 (1990); 732 (1980)   **Pop Density:** 1115.0
Land: 0.6 sq. mi.; **Water:** 0.0 sq. mi.
Incorporated Oct 29, 1895.

Rhodes   City
ZIP: 50234   **Lat:** 41-55-38 N   **Long:** 93-11-02 W
Pop: 272 (1990); 367 (1980)   **Pop Density:** 272.0
Land: 1.0 sq. mi.; **Water:** 0.0 sq. mi.
Incorporated May 12, 1882.

St. Anthony   City
Lat: 42-07-27 N   **Long:** 93-11-52 W
Pop: 112 (1990); 140 (1980)   **Pop Density:** 186.7
Land: 0.6 sq. mi.; **Water:** 0.0 sq. mi.
Incorporated Nov 6, 1897.

State Center   City
ZIP: 50247   **Lat:** 42-00-55 N   **Long:** 93-09-55 W
Pop: 1,248 (1990); 1,292 (1980)   **Pop Density:** 1248.0
Land: 1.0 sq. mi.; **Water:** 0.0 sq. mi.
Incorporated Aug 26, 1867.
Name origin: For its location at the center of the state.

IOWA, Mills County

Mills County
County Seat: Glenwood (ZIP: 51534)

Pop: 13,202 (1990); 13,406 (1980)
Land: 436.6 sq. mi.; **Water:** 3.1 sq. mi.
Pop Density: 30.2
Area Code: 712

On southwestern border of IA, south of Council Bluffs; established Jan 15, 1851 from Pottawattamie County.

Name origin: For Maj. Frederick D. Mills (?–1847), IA officer killed at San Antonio Garita during the Mexican-American War.

Emerson — City
ZIP: 51533 **Lat:** 41-01-06 N **Long:** 95-24-10 W
Pop: 476 (1990); 502 (1980) **Pop Density:** 1586.7
Land: 0.3 sq. mi.; **Water:** 0.0 sq. mi.
Incorporated Dec 2, 1875.

Glenwood — City
ZIP: 51534 **Lat:** 41-02-52 N **Long:** 95-44-31 W
Pop: 4,571 (1990); 5,280 (1980) **Pop Density:** 2285.5
Land: 2.0 sq. mi.; **Water:** 0.0 sq. mi.
Incorporated Jan 17, 1857.

Hastings — City
ZIP: 51540 **Lat:** 41-01-26 N **Long:** 95-29-44 W
Pop: 187 (1990); 215 (1980) **Pop Density:** 467.5
Land: 0.4 sq. mi.; **Water:** 0.0 sq. mi.
Incorporated May 26, 1879.

Henderson — City
ZIP: 51541 **Lat:** 41-08-20 N **Long:** 95-25-51 W
Pop: 206 (1990); 236 (1980) **Pop Density:** 1030.0
Land: 0.2 sq. mi.; **Water:** 0.0 sq. mi.
Incorporated May 18, 1893.

Malvern — City
ZIP: 51551 **Lat:** 41-00-27 N **Long:** 95-35-07 W
Pop: 1,210 (1990); 1,244 (1980) **Pop Density:** 1008.3
Land: 1.2 sq. mi.; **Water:** 0.0 sq. mi.
Incorporated Feb 24, 1872.

Pacific Junction — City
ZIP: 51561 **Lat:** 41-01-05 N **Long:** 95-47-58 W
Pop: 548 (1990); 511 (1980) **Pop Density:** 685.0
Land: 0.8 sq. mi.; **Water:** 0.0 sq. mi.
Incorporated Jan 11, 1882.
Name origin: A stopping place for emigrants bound for the west coast.

Silver City — City
ZIP: 51571 **Lat:** 41-06-39 N **Long:** 95-38-16 W
Pop: 252 (1990); 291 (1980) **Pop Density:** 1260.0
Land: 0.2 sq. mi.; **Water:** 0.0 sq. mi.
Incorporated Jun 23, 1883.

Tabor — City
ZIP: 51653 **Lat:** 40-54-08 N **Long:** 95-40-18 W
Pop: 56 (1990); 121 (1980) **Pop Density:** 560.0
Land: 0.1 sq. mi.; **Water:** 0.0 sq. mi.
Incorporated Oct 5, 1868. Part of the town is also in Fremont County.

Mitchell County
County Seat: Osage (ZIP: 50461)

Pop: 10,928 (1990); 12,329 (1980)
Land: 469.0 sq. mi.; **Water:** 0.5 sq. mi.
Pop Density: 23.3
Area Code: 515

On the central northern border of IA, northeast of Mason City; established Jan 15, 1851 from Chickasaw County.

Name origin: Named by Irish settlers for John Mitchel (1815–75), Irish journalist and nationalist who was imprisoned for helping to lead revolt against Britain and escaped to the U.S. in 1853.

Carpenter — City
ZIP: 50426 **Lat:** 43-24-53 N **Long:** 93-01-02 W
Pop: 102 (1990); 109 (1980) **Pop Density:** 510.0
Land: 0.2 sq. mi.; **Water:** 0.0 sq. mi.
Incorporated Apr 20, 1880.

McIntire — City
Lat: 43-26-13 N **Long:** 92-35-35 W
Pop: 147 (1990); 197 (1980) **Pop Density:** 147.0
Land: 1.0 sq. mi.; **Water:** 0.0 sq. mi.
Incorporated Jul 9, 1894.

Mitchell — City
ZIP: 50461 **Lat:** 43-19-16 N **Long:** 92-52-12 W
Pop: 170 (1990); 193 (1980) **Pop Density:** 340.0
Land: 0.5 sq. mi.; **Water:** 0.0 sq. mi.
Incorporated May 27, 1879.
Name origin: For John Mitchel (1815–75), Irish journalist and nationalist who was imprisoned for helping to lead revolt against Britain and escaped to the U.S. in 1853.

Orchard — City
ZIP: 50460 **Lat:** 43-13-37 N **Long:** 92-46-27 W
Pop: 93 (1990); 95 (1980) **Pop Density:** 930.0
Land: 0.1 sq. mi.; **Water:** 0.0 sq. mi.
Incorporated Jul 10, 1913.

American Places Dictionary   IOWA, Monona County

Osage
City
ZIP: 50461   **Lat:** 43-17-00 N **Long:** 92-48-42 W
Pop: 3,439 (1990); 3,718 (1980)   **Pop Density:** 1637.6
Land: 2.1 sq. mi.; **Water:** 0.0 sq. mi.
Incorporated Apr 14, 1871.
Name origin: For banker Orrin Sage, who signed his name O. Sage and was known for his generous donation to the town library.

Riceville
City
ZIP: 50466   **Lat:** 43-21-44 N **Long:** 92-33-30 W
Pop: 493 (1990); 563 (1980)   **Pop Density:** 986.0
Land: 0.5 sq. mi.; **Water:** 0.0 sq. mi.
Incorporated Nov 17, 1892. Part of the town is also in Howard County.
Name origin: For the three Rice brothers.

St. Ansgar
City
Lat: 43-22-41 N **Long:** 92-55-10 W
Pop: 1,063 (1990); 1,100 (1980)   **Pop Density:** 1771.7
Land: 0.6 sq. mi.; **Water:** 0.0 sq. mi.   **Elev:** 1171 ft.
Incorporated Feb 9, 1876.
Name origin: Name by Czech settlers.

Stacyville
City
ZIP: 50476   **Lat:** 43-26-18 N **Long:** 92-46-58 W
Pop: 481 (1990); 538 (1980)   **Pop Density:** 1202.5
Land: 0.4 sq. mi.; **Water:** 0.0 sq. mi.
Incorporated Mar 30, 1900.

Monona County
County Seat: Onawa (ZIP: 51040)

Pop: 10,034 (1990); 11,692 (1980)   **Pop Density:** 14.5
Land: 693.2 sq. mi.; **Water:** 5.7 sq. mi.   **Area Code:** 712
On central western border of IA, south of Sioux City; established Jan 15, 1851 from Harrison County.
Name origin: Possibly the name of a legendary Indian girl who leaped into the Mississippi River when she believed that her lover had been killed; or the name of an Indian divinity; or Ottawa for 'beautiful land.'

Blencoe
City
ZIP: 51523   **Lat:** 41-55-47 N **Long:** 96-04-51 W
Pop: 250 (1990); 247 (1980)   **Pop Density:** 357.1
Land: 0.7 sq. mi.; **Water:** 0.0 sq. mi.
Incorporated Oct 24, 1891.

Castana
City
ZIP: 51010   **Lat:** 42-04-24 N **Long:** 95-54-33 W
Pop: 159 (1990); 228 (1980)   **Pop Density:** 176.7
Land: 0.9 sq. mi.; **Water:** 0.0 sq. mi.   **Elev:** 1166 ft.
Incorporated Mar 3, 1891.

Mapleton
City
ZIP: 51034   **Lat:** 42-10-03 N **Long:** 95-47-26 W
Pop: 1,294 (1990); 1,495 (1980)   **Pop Density:** 862.7
Land: 1.5 sq. mi.; **Water:** 0.0 sq. mi.   **Elev:** 1157 ft.
Incorporated May 10, 1878.

Moorhead
City
ZIP: 51558   **Lat:** 41-55-27 N **Long:** 95-51-01 W
Pop: 259 (1990); 264 (1980)   **Pop Density:** 647.5
Land: 0.4 sq. mi.; **Water:** 0.0 sq. mi.   **Elev:** 1200 ft.
Incorporated Apr 9, 1900.

Onawa
City
ZIP: 51040   **Lat:** 42-01-38 N **Long:** 96-05-17 W
Pop: 2,936 (1990); 3,283 (1980)   **Pop Density:** 599.2
Land: 4.9 sq. mi.; **Water:** 0.0 sq. mi.   **Elev:** 1052 ft.
Platted 1857; incorporated Mar 22, 1859.
Name origin: From a name in Henry Wadsworth Longfellow's (1807–82) poem "The Song of Hiawatha" (1855).

Rodney
City
ZIP: 51051   **Lat:** 42-12-17 N **Long:** 95-57-04 W
Pop: 65 (1990); 82 (1980)   **Pop Density:** 325.0
Land: 0.2 sq. mi.; **Water:** 0.0 sq. mi.   **Elev:** 1122 ft.
Incorporated Feb 2, 1892.

Soldier
City
ZIP: 51572   **Lat:** 41-59-04 N **Long:** 95-46-46 W
Pop: 205 (1990); 257 (1980)   **Pop Density:** 683.3
Land: 0.3 sq. mi.; **Water:** 0.0 sq. mi.
Incorporated Apr 1, 1901.
Name origin: For the Soldier River which runs through this region.

Turin
City
ZIP: 51059   **Lat:** 42-01-13 N **Long:** 95-57-56 W
Pop: 95 (1990); 103 (1980)   **Pop Density:** 950.0
Land: 0.1 sq. mi.; **Water:** 0.0 sq. mi.
Incorporated Apr 6, 1900.
Name origin: For Turin, Italy.

Ute
City
ZIP: 51060   **Lat:** 42-02-59 N **Long:** 95-42-20 W
Pop: 395 (1990); 479 (1980)   **Pop Density:** 987.5
Land: 0.4 sq. mi.; **Water:** 0.0 sq. mi.
Incorporated Nov 4, 1891.
Name origin: Probably named by the Northwestern Railroad for the Ute Indians.

Whiting
City
ZIP: 51063   **Lat:** 42-07-34 N **Long:** 96-09-02 W
Pop: 683 (1990); 734 (1980)   **Pop Density:** 683.0
Land: 1.0 sq. mi.; **Water:** 0.0 sq. mi.
Incorporated May 15, 1883.
Name origin: For Sen. Whiting.

IOWA, Monroe County — *American Places Dictionary*

Monroe County
County Seat: Albia (ZIP: 52531)

Pop: 8,114 (1990); 9,209 (1980)   **Pop Density:** 18.7
Land: 433.4 sq. mi.; **Water:** 0.7 sq. mi.   **Area Code:** 515

In south-central IA, west of Ottumwa; established as Kishkekosh County Feb 17, 1843 (prior to statehood) from Wapello County. Name changed Jan 19, 1846.

Name origin: For James Monroe (1758–1831), fifth U.S. president.

Albia — City
ZIP: 52531   **Lat:** 41-01-35 N **Long:** 92-48-10 W
Pop: 3,870 (1990); 4,184 (1980)   **Pop Density:** 1248.4
Land: 3.1 sq. mi.; **Water:** 0.0 sq. mi.
Incorporated Jan 28, 1857.

Eddyville — City
Lat: 41-09-37 N **Long:** 92-38-30 W
Pop: 0 (1990); 5 (1980)
Land: 0.02 sq. mi.; **Water:** 0.0 sq. mi.
Incorporated Feb 22, 1900. Part of the town is also in Wapello and Mahaska counties.

Lovilia — City
ZIP: 50150   **Lat:** 41-08-07 N **Long:** 92-54-28 W
Pop: 551 (1990); 637 (1980)   **Pop Density:** 1102.0
Land: 0.5 sq. mi.; **Water:** 0.0 sq. mi.
Incorporated Apr 21, 1933.

Melrose — City
ZIP: 52569   **Lat:** 40-58-51 N **Long:** 93-02-57 W
Pop: 150 (1990); 218 (1980)   **Pop Density:** 136.4
Land: 1.1 sq. mi.; **Water:** 0.0 sq. mi.
Incorporated Mar 20, 1882.

Montgomery County
County Seat: Red Oak (ZIP: 51566)

Pop: 12,076 (1990); 13,413 (1980)   **Pop Density:** 28.5
Land: 423.9 sq. mi.; **Water:** 0.9 sq. mi.   **Area Code:** 712

In southwestern IA, southeast of Council Bluffs; established Jan 15, 1851 from Polk County.

Name origin: For Gen. Richard Montgomery (1736–75), American Revolutionary War officer who captured Montreal, Canada.

Coburg — City
Lat: 40-55-04 N **Long:** 95-15-56 W
Pop: 58 (1990); 52 (1980)   **Pop Density:** 193.3
Land: 0.3 sq. mi.; **Water:** 0.0 sq. mi.

Elliott — City
ZIP: 51532   **Lat:** 41-08-59 N **Long:** 95-09-46 W
Pop: 399 (1990); 493 (1980)   **Pop Density:** 997.5
Land: 0.4 sq. mi.; **Water:** 0.0 sq. mi.
Incorporated Mar 14, 1882.

Grant — City
ZIP: 50847   **Lat:** 41-08-31 N **Long:** 94-59-06 W
Pop: 123 (1990); 143 (1980)   **Pop Density:** 175.7
Land: 0.7 sq. mi.; **Water:** 0.0 sq. mi.
Incorporated Feb 27, 1912.
Name origin: For Ulysses S. Grant (1822–85), eighteenth U.S. president.

Red Oak — City
ZIP: 51566   **Lat:** 41-00-44 N **Long:** 95-13-28 W
Pop: 6,264 (1990); 6,810 (1980)   **Pop Density:** 1693.0
Land: 3.7 sq. mi.; **Water:** 0.1 sq. mi.
Incorporated Jun 28, 1869.
Name origin: For a nearby grove of red oak trees.

Stanton — City
ZIP: 51573   **Lat:** 40-58-51 N **Long:** 95-06-11 W
Pop: 692 (1990); 747 (1980)   **Pop Density:** 768.9
Land: 0.9 sq. mi.; **Water:** 0.0 sq. mi.
Incorporated Mar 12, 1883.
Name origin: For Edwin Stanton (1814–69), U.S. attorney general (1860–61) and U.S. secretary of war (1862–68).

Villisca — City
ZIP: 50864   **Lat:** 40-55-51 N **Long:** 94-58-40 W
Pop: 1,332 (1990); 1,434 (1980)   **Pop Density:** 832.5
Land: 1.6 sq. mi.; **Water:** 0.0 sq. mi.
Incorporated Sep 3, 1869.
Name origin: A spelling variant of the Sauk and Fox term *Waliska* meaning 'evil spirit.' Previously called Valiska.

Muscatine County
County Seat: Muscatine (ZIP: 52761)

Pop: 39,907 (1990); 40,436 (1980)   **Pop Density:** 91.0
Land: 438.7 sq. mi.; **Water:** 10.4 sq. mi.   **Area Code:** 319

On eastern border of IA, west of Davenport; established Dec 7, 1836 (prior to statehood) from Des Moines County.

Name origin: Variant name for the Mascouten tribe of the Potawatomie Indians. Meaning of the name is uncertain, but locally believed to be 'burning island.'

Atalissa   City
ZIP: 52720   **Lat:** 41-34-17 N **Long:** 91-09-59 W
Pop: 357 (1990); 360 (1980)   **Pop Density:** 3570.0
Land: 0.1 sq. mi.; **Water:** 0.0 sq. mi.

Established 1848; incorporated Mar 26, 1900.

Name origin: Probably from Thomas Campbell's (1777–1844) famous poem "Gertrude of Wyoming," which names a fictional Oneida chief, Outalissi.

Conesville   City
   Lat: 41-22-49 N **Long:** 91-20-52 W
Pop: 334 (1990); 301 (1980)   **Pop Density:** 835.0
Land: 0.4 sq. mi.; **Water:** 0.0 sq. mi.

Incorporated Mar 21, 1874.

Durant   City
ZIP: 52747   **Lat:** 41-35-47 N **Long:** 90-54-48 W
Pop: 7 (1990)   **Pop Density:** 700.0
Land: 0.01 sq. mi.; **Water:** 0.0 sq. mi.

Incorporated Jul 1, 1867. Part of the town is also in Cedar and Scott counties.

Fruitland   City
ZIP: 52749   **Lat:** 41-20-48 N **Long:** 91-07-32 W
Pop: 511 (1990); 461 (1980)   **Pop Density:** 300.6
Land: 1.7 sq. mi.; **Water:** 0.0 sq. mi.

Incorporated Aug 24, 1972.

Muscatine   City
ZIP: 52761   **Lat:** 41-25-03 N **Long:** 91-04-18 W
Pop: 22,881 (1990); 23,467 (1980)   **Pop Density:** 1330.3
Land: 17.2 sq. mi.; **Water:** 1.0 sq. mi.

Incorporated Feb 1, 1851.

Nichols   City
ZIP: 52766   **Lat:** 41-28-44 N **Long:** 91-18-29 W
Pop: 366 (1990); 375 (1980)   **Pop Density:** 1830.0
Land: 0.2 sq. mi.; **Water:** 0.0 sq. mi.

Incorporated Mar 15, 1884.

Stockton   City
ZIP: 52769   **Lat:** 41-35-25 N **Long:** 90-51-18 W
Pop: 187 (1990); 240 (1980)   **Pop Density:** 1870.0
Land: 0.1 sq. mi.; **Water:** 0.0 sq. mi.

Incorporated Feb 11, 1902.

Walcott   City
   Lat: 41-35-32 N **Long:** 90-47-13 W
Pop: 0 (1990); 1,425 (1980)
Land: 0.05 sq. mi.; **Water:** 0.0 sq. mi.

Incorporated Jul 10, 1894. Part of the town is also in Scott County.

West Liberty   City
ZIP: 52776   **Lat:** 41-34-21 N **Long:** 91-15-49 W
Pop: 2,935 (1990); 2,723 (1980)   **Pop Density:** 1956.7
Land: 1.5 sq. mi.; **Water:** 0.0 sq. mi.

Incorporated Jul 1, 1867.

Wilton   City
   Lat: 41-35-20 N **Long:** 91-01-28 W
Pop: 2,573 (1990); 2,493 (1980)   **Pop Density:** 1429.4
Land: 1.8 sq. mi.; **Water:** 0.0 sq. mi.

Incorporated Feb 12, 1878. Part of the town is also in Cedar County.

O'Brien County
County Seat: Primghar (ZIP: 51245)

Pop: 15,444 (1990); 16,972 (1980)   **Pop Density:** 26.9
Land: 573.1 sq. mi.; **Water:** 0.2 sq. mi.   **Area Code:** 712

In northwestern IA; established Jan 15, 1851 from Cherokee County.

Name origin: For William Smith O'Brien (1803–64), leader of the Irish rebellion of 1848.

Archer   City
ZIP: 51231   **Lat:** 43-06-52 N **Long:** 95-44-38 W
Pop: 131 (1990); 134 (1980)   **Pop Density:** 1310.0
Land: 0.1 sq. mi.; **Water:** 0.0 sq. mi.

Incorporated May 5, 1902.

Calumet   City
ZIP: 51009   **Lat:** 42-56-41 N **Long:** 95-33-01 W
Pop: 160 (1990); 212 (1980)   **Pop Density:** 533.3
Land: 0.3 sq. mi.; **Water:** 0.0 sq. mi.

Incorporated Jan 31, 1895.

Name origin: From French term for the Indian peace pipe.

Hartley City
ZIP: 51346 **Lat:** 43-10-45 N **Long:** 95-28-39 W
Pop: 1,632 (1990); 1,700 (1980) **Pop Density:** 1255.4
Land: 1.3 sq. mi.; **Water:** 0.0 sq. mi.
Incorporated Jul 24, 1888.

Moneta City
ZIP: 51346 **Lat:** 43-07-56 N **Long:** 95-23-32 W
Pop: 29 (1990); 43 (1980) **Pop Density:** 96.7
Land: 0.3 sq. mi.; **Water:** 0.0 sq. mi.
Incorporated Feb 16, 1903.

Paullina City
ZIP: 51046 **Lat:** 42-58-47 N **Long:** 95-41-12 W
Pop: 1,134 (1990); 1,224 (1980) **Pop Density:** 2268.0
Land: 0.5 sq. mi.; **Water:** 0.0 sq. mi.
Incorporated Oct 30, 1883.

Primghar City
ZIP: 51245 **Lat:** 43-05-15 N **Long:** 95-37-34 W
Pop: 950 (1990); 1,050 (1980) **Pop Density:** 1583.3
Land: 0.6 sq. mi.; **Water:** 0.0 sq. mi.
Incorporated Feb 15, 1888.
Name origin: From a combination of the initials of the eight men active in platting the town: Pumphrey, Roberts, Inman, McCormack, Green, Hayes, Albright, and Rerick.

Sanborn City
ZIP: 51248 **Lat:** 43-10-51 N **Long:** 95-39-22 W
Pop: 1,345 (1990); 1,398 (1980) **Pop Density:** 747.2
Land: 1.8 sq. mi.; **Water:** 0.0 sq. mi.
Incorporated Mar 15, 1880.

Sheldon City
ZIP: 51201 **Lat:** 43-10-47 N **Long:** 95-50-26 W
Pop: 4,866 (1990); 4,988 (1980) **Pop Density:** 1315.1
Land: 3.7 sq. mi.; **Water:** 0.0 sq. mi.
Incorporated Apr 24, 1876. Part of the town is also in Sioux County.
Name origin: For Israel Sheldon, a stockholder in the first railroad to pass through town.

Sutherland City
ZIP: 51058 **Lat:** 42-58-20 N **Long:** 95-29-42 W
Pop: 714 (1990); 897 (1980) **Pop Density:** 793.3
Land: 0.9 sq. mi.; **Water:** 0.0 sq. mi.
Incorporated Oct 29, 1883.

Osceola County
County Seat: Sibley (ZIP: 51249)

Pop: 7,267 (1990); 8,371 (1980) **Pop Density:** 18.2
Land: 398.8 sq. mi.; **Water:** 0.7 sq. mi. **Area Code:** 712

On the northwestern border of IA; established Jan 15, 1851 from Woodbury County.

Name origin: For Osceola (c. 1804–38), Seminole leader during the early years of the Second Seminole War (1835–37). Name, also spelled *Ashi Vaholo Yahola*, means 'black drink hallower.'

Ashton City
ZIP: 51232 **Lat:** 43-18-35 N **Long:** 95-47-31 W
Pop: 462 (1990); 441 (1980) **Pop Density:** 462.0
Land: 1.0 sq. mi.; **Water:** 0.0 sq. mi.
Incorporated Mar 28, 1885.

Harris City
ZIP: 51345 **Lat:** 43-26-51 N **Long:** 95-25-58 W
Pop: 170 (1990); 228 (1980) **Pop Density:** 1700.0
Land: 0.1 sq. mi.; **Water:** 0.0 sq. mi.
Incorporated 1903.

Melvin City
ZIP: 51350 **Lat:** 43-17-12 N **Long:** 95-36-30 W
Pop: 250 (1990); 277 (1980) **Pop Density:** 1250.0
Land: 0.2 sq. mi.; **Water:** 0.0 sq. mi.
Incorporated 1901.

Ocheyedan City
ZIP: 51354 **Lat:** 43-25-05 N **Long:** 95-32-11 W
Pop: 539 (1990); 599 (1980) **Pop Density:** 449.2
Land: 1.2 sq. mi.; **Water:** 0.0 sq. mi.
Incorporated Feb 20, 1891.
Name origin: For the Ocheyedan River, which traverses the county, and Ocheyedan Mound; from Dakota term for 'little hill where they mourn.'

Sibley City
ZIP: 51249 **Lat:** 43-24-05 N **Long:** 95-44-41 W
Pop: 2,815 (1990); 3,051 (1980) **Pop Density:** 2010.7
Land: 1.4 sq. mi.; **Water:** 0.0 sq. mi.
Incorporated Apr 5, 1876.

Page County
County Seat: Clarinda (ZIP: 51632)

Pop: 16,870 (1990); 19,063 (1980) **Pop Density:** 31.5
Land: 534.9 sq. mi.; **Water:** 0.5 sq. mi. **Area Code:** 712

On southwestern border of IA; established Feb 14, 1847 from Pottawattamie County.

Name origin: For Capt. John Page (?–1846), killed at the Battle of Palo Alto during the Mexican-American War.

Blanchard   City
ZIP: 51630   **Lat:** 40-34-50 N **Long:** 95-13-14 W
Pop: 67 (1990); 101 (1980)   **Pop Density:** 335.0
Land: 0.2 sq. mi.; **Water:** 0.0 sq. mi.
Incorporated Jun 11, 1880.

Braddyville   City
Lat: 40-34-40 N **Long:** 95-02-39 W
Pop: 219 (1990); 199 (1980)   **Pop Density:** 81.1
Land: 2.7 sq. mi.; **Water:** 0.0 sq. mi.
Incorporated Feb 9, 1880.

Clarinda   City
ZIP: 51632   **Lat:** 40-44-19 N **Long:** 95-02-08 W
Pop: 5,104 (1990); 5,458 (1980)   **Pop Density:** 945.2
Land: 5.4 sq. mi.; **Water:** 0.0 sq. mi.
Incorporated Dec 8, 1866.
Name origin: For Clarinda Buck, the niece of the city founder.

Coin   City
ZIP: 51636   **Lat:** 40-39-21 N **Long:** 95-14-06 W
Pop: 278 (1990); 316 (1980)   **Pop Density:** 347.5
Land: 0.8 sq. mi.; **Water:** 0.0 sq. mi.
Incorporated Jul 20, 1881.

College Springs   City
ZIP: 51637   **Lat:** 40-37-15 N **Long:** 95-07-18 W
Pop: 230 (1990); 307 (1980)   **Pop Density:** 209.1
Land: 1.1 sq. mi.; **Water:** 0.0 sq. mi.
Incorporated Jan 19, 1875.

Essex   City
ZIP: 51638   **Lat:** 40-49-58 N **Long:** 95-18-12 W
Pop: 916 (1990); 1,001 (1980)   **Pop Density:** 610.7
Land: 1.5 sq. mi.; **Water:** 0.0 sq. mi.
Incorporated Jan 20, 1876.

Hepburn   City
Lat: 40-50-53 N **Long:** 95-00-59 W
Pop: 41 (1990); 42 (1980)   **Pop Density:** 410.0
Land: 0.1 sq. mi.; **Water:** 0.0 sq. mi.
Incorporated Jan 13, 1883.
Name origin: For William Peters Hepburn (1833–1916), U.S. legislator.

Northboro   City
ZIP: 51647   **Lat:** 40-36-31 N **Long:** 95-17-35 W
Pop: 78 (1990); 115 (1980)   **Pop Density:** 260.0
Land: 0.3 sq. mi.; **Water:** 0.0 sq. mi.
Incorporated Oct 14, 1902.

Shambaugh   City
ZIP: 51651   **Lat:** 40-39-25 N **Long:** 95-02-09 W
Pop: 190 (1990); 197 (1980)   **Pop Density:** 633.3
Land: 0.3 sq. mi.; **Water:** 0.0 sq. mi.
Incorporated Apr 21, 1903.

Shenandoah   City
ZIP: 51601   **Lat:** 40-45-33 N **Long:** 95-22-01 W
Pop: 5,572 (1990); 6,274 (1980)   **Pop Density:** 1797.4
Land: 3.1 sq. mi.; **Water:** 0.0 sq. mi.
Incorporated Jun 20, 1871. Part of the town is also in Fremont County.
Name origin: For the Shenandoah Valley in VA, which resembles the Nishnabotna River Valley in which the town is located.

Yorktown   City
ZIP: 51656   **Lat:** 40-44-11 N **Long:** 95-09-17 W
Pop: 100 (1990); 123 (1980)   **Pop Density:** 333.3
Land: 0.3 sq. mi.; **Water:** 0.0 sq. mi.
Incorporated Mar 25, 1899.
Name origin: For the final battle of the American Revolution.

IOWA, Palo Alto County American Places Dictionary

Palo Alto County
County Seat: Emmetsburg (ZIP: 50536)

Pop: 10,669 (1990); 12,721 (1980) **Pop Density:** 18.9
Land: 563.9 sq. mi.; **Water:** 5.6 sq. mi. **Area Code:** 712

In north-central IA, northwest of Fort Dodge; established Jan 15, 1851 from Kossuth County.

Name origin: From Spanish *palo* 'stick,' and *alto* 'tall' or 'high.' For a small town in Texas, the scene of the first battle (1846) of the Mexican War.

Ayrshire City
ZIP: 50515 **Lat:** 43-02-25 N **Long:** 94-50-00 W
Pop: 195 (1990); 243 (1980) **Pop Density:** 975.0
Land: 0.2 sq. mi.; **Water:** 0.0 sq. mi.
Incorporated Sep 20, 1895.
Name origin: For Ayrshire, Scotland.

Curlew City
ZIP: 50527 **Lat:** 42-58-46 N **Long:** 94-44-13 W
Pop: 56 (1990); 85 (1980) **Pop Density:** 70.0
Land: 0.8 sq. mi.; **Water:** 0.0 sq. mi.
Incorporated May 22, 1902.

Cylinder City
ZIP: 50528 **Lat:** 43-05-25 N **Long:** 94-33-04 W
Pop: 112 (1990); 119 (1980) **Pop Density:** 1120.0
Land: 0.1 sq. mi.; **Water:** 0.0 sq. mi.
Incorporated Apr 5, 1900.

Emmetsburg City
ZIP: 50536 **Lat:** 43-06-48 N **Long:** 94-40-49 W
Pop: 3,940 (1990); 4,621 (1980) **Pop Density:** 1094.4
Land: 3.6 sq. mi.; **Water:** 0.2 sq. mi.
Incorporated Nov 17, 1877.
Name origin: For Irish nationalist Robert Emmet (1778–1803).

Graettinger City
ZIP: 51342 **Lat:** 43-14-11 N **Long:** 94-45-03 W
Pop: 813 (1990); 923 (1980) **Pop Density:** 1161.4
Land: 0.7 sq. mi.; **Water:** 0.0 sq. mi.
Incorporated Sep 30, 1893.

Mallard City
ZIP: 50562 **Lat:** 42-56-23 N **Long:** 94-41-02 W
Pop: 360 (1990); 407 (1980) **Pop Density:** 900.0
Land: 0.4 sq. mi.; **Water:** 0.0 sq. mi.
Incorporated Jun 25, 1895.

Rodman City
ZIP: 50580 **Lat:** 43-01-33 N **Long:** 94-31-34 W
Pop: 56 (1990); 86 (1980) **Pop Density:** 280.0
Land: 0.2 sq. mi.; **Water:** 0.0 sq. mi.
Incorporated Jun 17, 1899.

Ruthven City
ZIP: 51358 **Lat:** 43-07-46 N **Long:** 94-53-57 W
Pop: 707 (1990); 769 (1980) **Pop Density:** 1767.5
Land: 0.4 sq. mi.; **Water:** 0.0 sq. mi.
Incorporated Mar 12, 1885.
Name origin: For the three Ruthven brothers.

West Bend City
 Lat: 42-57-36 N **Long:** 94-26-52 W
Pop: 856 (1990); 924 (1980) **Pop Density:** 1426.7
Land: 0.6 sq. mi.; **Water:** 0.0 sq. mi.
Incorporated Feb 27, 1884. Part of the town is also in Kossuth County.

Plymouth County
County Seat: Le Mars (ZIP: 51031)

Pop: 23,388 (1990); 24,743 (1980) **Pop Density:** 27.1
Land: 863.6 sq. mi.; **Water:** 0.4 sq. mi. **Area Code:** 712

On northwestern border of IA, north of Sioux City; established Jan 15, 1851 from Woodbury County.

Name origin: For Plymouth, Devonshire, England, from which the *Mayflower* sailed for America in 1620, or to honor Plymouth, MA, the landing site of the pilgrims.

Akron City
ZIP: 51001 **Lat:** 42-49-38 N **Long:** 96-33-22 W
Pop: 1,450 (1990); 1,517 (1980) **Pop Density:** 1208.3
Land: 1.2 sq. mi.; **Water:** 0.0 sq. mi.
Incorporated Sep 7, 1882.
Name origin: Possibly named for Akron, OH; from Greek for 'summit' or 'peak.'

Brunsville City
ZIP: 51008 **Lat:** 42-48-40 N **Long:** 96-15-58 W
Pop: 137 (1990); 140 (1980) **Pop Density:** 685.0
Land: 0.2 sq. mi.; **Water:** 0.0 sq. mi.
Incorporated Jul 18, 1911.

Craig City
ZIP: 51017 Lat: 42-53-43 N Long: 96-18-36 W
Pop: 116 (1990); 105 (1980) Pop Density: 1160.0
Land: 0.1 sq. mi.; Water: 0.0 sq. mi.
Incorporated Apr 6, 1911.

Hinton City
ZIP: 51024 Lat: 42-37-29 N Long: 96-17-38 W
Pop: 697 (1990); 659 (1980) Pop Density: 1394.0
Land: 0.5 sq. mi.; Water: 0.0 sq. mi.
Incorporated Jun 6, 1908.

Kingsley City
ZIP: 51028 Lat: 42-35-15 N Long: 95-58-04 W
Pop: 1,129 (1990); 1,209 (1980) Pop Density: 705.6
Land: 1.6 sq. mi.; Water: 0.0 sq. mi.
Incorporated Jan 15, 1884.
Name origin: For railroad official J. T. Kingsley.

Le Mars City
ZIP: 51031 Lat: 42-47-15 N Long: 96-10-11 W
Pop: 8,454 (1990); 8,276 (1980) Pop Density: 1595.1
Land: 5.3 sq. mi.; Water: 0.0 sq. mi. Elev: 1231 ft.
Incorporated May 25, 1881.
Name origin: From the initials of the ladies who accompanied the city's founder on his first visit to the site.

Merrill City
ZIP: 51038 Lat: 42-43-15 N Long: 96-14-56 W
Pop: 729 (1990); 737 (1980) Pop Density: 1822.5
Land: 0.4 sq. mi.; Water: 0.0 sq. mi.
Incorporated Apr 24, 1894.

Oyens City
ZIP: 51045 Lat: 42-49-09 N Long: 96-03-26 W
Pop: 113 (1990); 146 (1980) Pop Density: 1130.0
Land: 0.1 sq. mi.; Water: 0.0 sq. mi.
Incorporated Jan 29, 1909.

Remsen City
ZIP: 51050 Lat: 42-48-47 N Long: 95-58-21 W
Pop: 1,513 (1990); 1,592 (1980) Pop Density: 1375.5
Land: 1.1 sq. mi.; Water: 0.0 sq. mi.
Incorporated 1889.
Name origin: For landowner Remsen Smith.

Struble City
ZIP: 51057 Lat: 42-53-41 N Long: 96-11-38 W
Pop: 67 (1990); 70 (1980) Pop Density: 335.0
Land: 0.2 sq. mi.; Water: 0.0 sq. mi.
Incorporated Aug 17, 1895.

Westfield City
ZIP: 51062 Lat: 42-45-24 N Long: 96-36-19 W
Pop: 160 (1990); 199 (1980) Pop Density: 1600.0
Land: 0.1 sq. mi.; Water: 0.0 sq. mi.
Incorporated May 27, 1903.

Pocahontas County
County Seat: Pocahontas (ZIP: 50574)

Pop: 9,525 (1990); 11,369 (1980) Pop Density: 16.5
Land: 577.7 sq. mi.; Water: 1.4 sq. mi. Area Code: 712
In north-central IA, northwest of Fort Dodge; established Jan 15, 1851 from Humboldt and Greene counties.
Name origin: For Pocahontas (Matoaka, c. 1595–1617), daughter of Chief Powhatan, who prevented the execution of Capt. John Smith (c. 1580–1631).

Fonda City
ZIP: 50540 Lat: 42-34-54 N Long: 94-50-43 W
Pop: 731 (1990); 863 (1980) Pop Density: 731.0
Land: 1.0 sq. mi.; Water: 0.0 sq. mi.
Incorporated Mar 21, 1884.

Gilmore City Township
ZIP: 50541 Lat: 42-43-49 N Long: 94-26-47 W
Pop: 241 (1990); 260 (1980) Pop Density: 803.3
Land: 0.3 sq. mi.; Water: 0.0 sq. mi.
Incorporated Apr 16, 1887. Part of the town is also in Humboldt County.

Havelock City
ZIP: 50546 Lat: 42-50-01 N Long: 94-42-00 W
Pop: 217 (1990); 279 (1980) Pop Density: 361.7
Land: 0.6 sq. mi.; Water: 0.0 sq. mi.
Incorporated Feb 16, 1892.

Laurens City
ZIP: 50554 Lat: 42-50-51 N Long: 94-50-52 W
Pop: 1,550 (1990); 1,606 (1980) Pop Density: 2214.3
Land: 0.7 sq. mi.; Water: 0.0 sq. mi.
Incorporated Apr 30, 1890.

Palmer City
Lat: 42-37-43 N Long: 94-35-53 W
Pop: 230 (1990); 288 (1980) Pop Density: 575.0
Land: 0.4 sq. mi.; Water: 0.0 sq. mi.
Incorporated May 21, 1901.

Plover City
ZIP: 50573 Lat: 42-52-37 N Long: 94-37-20 W
Pop: 101 (1990); 135 (1980) Pop Density: 202.0
Land: 0.5 sq. mi.; Water: 0.0 sq. mi.
Incorporated Oct 13, 1916.

Pocahontas City
ZIP: 50574 Lat: 42-44-10 N Long: 94-40-00 W
Pop: 2,085 (1990); 2,352 (1980) Pop Density: 1097.4
Land: 1.9 sq. mi.; Water: 0.0 sq. mi.
Incorporated May 16, 1892.
Name origin: For Pocahontas (Matoaka, c. 1595–1617), daughter of Chief Powhatan, who prevented the execution of Capt. John Smith (c. 1580–1631).

IOWA, Pocahontas County

Rolfe — City
ZIP: 50581 **Lat:** 42-48-46 N **Long:** 94-31-49 W
Pop: 721 (1990); 796 (1980) **Pop Density:** 721.0
Land: 1.0 sq. mi.; **Water:** 0.0 sq. mi.
Incorporated Jan 4, 1884.
Name origin: For either John Rolfe who married Pocahontas (c. 1595–1617) in 1614, or for the man who previously owned the townsite.

Varina — City
ZIP: 50593 **Lat:** 42-39-30 N **Long:** 94-53-54 W
Pop: 102 (1990); 122 (1980) **Pop Density:** 510.0
Land: 0.2 sq. mi.; **Water:** 0.0 sq. mi.
Incorporated Mar 29, 1901.

Polk County
County Seat: Des Moines (ZIP: 50309)

Pop: 327,140 (1990); 303,170 (1980) **Pop Density:** 574.5
Land: 569.5 sq. mi.; **Water:** 22.5 sq. mi. **Area Code:** 512
In south-central IA, south of Ames; established Jan 17, 1846 from Indian lands.
Name origin: For James Knox Polk (1795–1849), eleventh U.S. president.

Alleman — City
ZIP: 50007 **Lat:** 41-49-01 N **Long:** 93-36-37 W
Pop: 340 (1990); 307 (1980) **Pop Density:** 141.7
Land: 2.4 sq. mi.; **Water:** 0.0 sq. mi.
Incorporated May 18, 1973.

Altoona — City
ZIP: 50009 **Lat:** 41-39-03 N **Long:** 93-28-34 W
Pop: 7,191 (1990); 5,764 (1980) **Pop Density:** 1634.3
Land: 4.4 sq. mi.; **Water:** 0.0 sq. mi.
Incorporated Mar 11, 1876.
Name origin: For its location at the highest elevation between the Des Moines and Mississippi rivers. Possibly from Latin *altus* meaning 'high.'

Ankeny — City
ZIP: 50021 **Lat:** 41-43-29 N **Long:** 93-36-19 W
Pop: 18,482 (1990); 15,429 (1980) **Pop Density:** 1400.2
Land: 13.2 sq. mi.; **Water:** 0.0 sq. mi.
Incorporated Feb 27, 1903.
Name origin: For founder J.F. Ankeney.

Bondurant — City
ZIP: 50035 **Lat:** 41-41-18 N **Long:** 93-27-43 W
Pop: 1,584 (1990); 1,283 (1980) **Pop Density:** 360.0
Land: 4.4 sq. mi.; **Water:** 0.0 sq. mi.
Incorporated Dec 23, 1897.

Carlisle — City
Lat: 41-31-07 N **Long:** 93-29-07 W
Pop: 5 (1990); 3,073 (1980) **Pop Density:** 2.9
Land: 1.7 sq. mi.; **Water:** 0.0 sq. mi.
Incorporated May 19, 1870. Part of the town is also in Warren County.

Clive — City
ZIP: 50322 **Lat:** 41-36-27 N **Long:** 93-46-10 W
Pop: 7,462 (1990); 6,064 (1980) **Pop Density:** 1554.6
Land: 4.8 sq. mi.; **Water:** 0.0 sq. mi.
Incorporated Oct 9, 1956.

Des Moines — City
ZIP: 50318 **Lat:** 41-34-36 N **Long:** 93-37-02 W
Pop: 193,187 (1990); 191,003 (1980) **Pop Density:** 2565.6
Land: 75.3 sq. mi.; **Water:** 1.5 sq. mi.
In south-central IA at the confluence of the Des Moines and Raccoon rivers. Incorporated Oct 18, 1851; capital and largest city. Diverse manufacturing city: printing and publishing, nonelectrical machinery, food products.
Name origin: For the Des Moines River, which French explorers called *Riviere des Moines* a form of the name of a now-lost Indian tribe *Moingwenas*. The name probably refers to the tribe's totemic bird or a clan totem.

Elkhart — City
ZIP: 50073 **Lat:** 41-47-38 N **Long:** 93-30-52 W
Pop: 388 (1990); 256 (1980) **Pop Density:** 168.7
Land: 2.3 sq. mi.; **Water:** 0.0 sq. mi.
Incorporated Jul 27, 1904.
Name origin: Probably a translation of a Potawatomi or Kickapoo term for 'elk's heart.'

Grimes — City
ZIP: 50111 **Lat:** 41-39-38 N **Long:** 93-47-21 W
Pop: 2,653 (1990); 1,973 (1980) **Pop Density:** 379.0
Land: 7.0 sq. mi.; **Water:** 0.0 sq. mi.
Incorporated May 7, 1894.
Name origin: For James Wilson Grimes (1816–72), U.S. senator (1859–69) and governor of IA (1854–58).

Johnston — City
ZIP: 50131 **Lat:** 41-41-09 N **Long:** 93-42-08 W
Pop: 4,702 (1990); 2,526 (1980) **Pop Density:** 338.3
Land: 13.9 sq. mi.; **Water:** 1.1 sq. mi.
Incorporated Sep 19, 1969.

Mitchellville — City
ZIP: 50169 **Lat:** 41-39-41 N **Long:** 93-21-39 W
Pop: 1,670 (1990); 1,530 (1980) **Pop Density:** 1192.9
Land: 1.4 sq. mi.; **Water:** 0.0 sq. mi.
Incorporated Sep 30, 1875.
Name origin: For one Thomas Mitchell.

Pleasant Hill — City
Lat: 41-35-08 N **Long:** 93-30-52 W
Pop: 3,671 (1990); 3,493 (1980) **Pop Density:** 749.2
Land: 4.9 sq. mi.; **Water:** 0.1 sq. mi.
Incorporated May 12, 1956.

Polk City — Township
ZIP: 50226 **Lat:** 41-46-23 N **Long:** 93-42-59 W
Pop: 1,908 (1990); 1,658 (1980) **Pop Density:** 706.7
Land: 2.7 sq. mi.; **Water:** 0.0 sq. mi. **Elev:** 889 ft.
Incorporated Mar 13, 1875.

Runnells   City
ZIP: 50237   **Lat:** 41-30-44 N **Long:** 93-21-28 W
Pop: 306 (1990); 377 (1980)   **Pop Density:** 1020.0
Land: 0.3 sq. mi.; **Water:** 0.0 sq. mi.
Incorporated May 21, 1903.

Saylorville   CDP
Lat: 41-41-04 N **Long:** 93-37-32 W
Pop: 2,709 (1990)   **Pop Density:** 285.2
Land: 9.5 sq. mi.; **Water:** 0.0 sq. mi.

Sheldahl   City
Lat: 41-51-38 N **Long:** 93-41-37 W
Pop: 122 (1990); 132 (1980)   **Pop Density:** 406.7
Land: 0.3 sq. mi.; **Water:** 0.0 sq. mi.
Incorporated Jan 18, 1882. Part of the town is also in Story and Boone counties.

Urbandale   City
ZIP: 50322   **Lat:** 41-38-11 N **Long:** 93-44-27 W
Pop: 23,500 (1990); 17,869 (1980)   **Pop Density:** 2196.3
Land: 10.7 sq. mi.; **Water:** 0.0 sq. mi.
Incorporated May 3, 1917.

West Des Moines   City
ZIP: 50265   **Lat:** 41-34-14 N **Long:** 93-45-10 W
Pop: 31,695 (1990); 21,894 (1980)   **Pop Density:** 1864.4
Land: 17.0 sq. mi.; **Water:** 0.7 sq. mi.
In south-central IA, 8 mi. west of Des Moines. Incorporated Aug 15, 1893. Part of the town is also in Dallas county.
Name origin: Previously called Valley Junction.

Windsor Heights   City
ZIP: 50311   **Lat:** 41-36-17 N **Long:** 93-42-42 W
Pop: 5,190 (1990); 5,474 (1980)   **Pop Density:** 3707.1
Land: 1.4 sq. mi.; **Water:** 0.0 sq. mi.
Incorporated Jul 19, 1941.

Pottawattamie County
County Seat: Council Bluffs (ZIP: 51501)

Pop: 82,628 (1990); 86,561 (1980)   **Pop Density:** 86.6
Land: 954.3 sq. mi.; **Water:** 5.7 sq. mi.   **Area Code:** 712
On southwestern border of IA; established Jan 15, 1848 from Indian lands.
Name origin: For the Potawatomie Indian tribe of Algonquian linguistic stock; name means 'people of the place of fire.'

Avoca   City
ZIP: 51521   **Lat:** 41-28-50 N **Long:** 95-20-07 W
Pop: 1,497 (1990); 1,650 (1980)   **Pop Density:** 935.6
Land: 1.6 sq. mi.; **Water:** 0.0 sq. mi.
Incorporated Dec 2, 1874.

Carson   City
ZIP: 51525   **Lat:** 41-14-11 N **Long:** 95-24-58 W
Pop: 705 (1990); 716 (1980)   **Pop Density:** 1410.0
Land: 0.5 sq. mi.; **Water:** 0.0 sq. mi.
Incorporated Mar 28, 1881.

Carter Lake   City
ZIP: 51510   **Lat:** 41-17-19 N **Long:** 95-54-57 W
Pop: 3,200 (1990); 3,438 (1980)   **Pop Density:** 1777.8
Land: 1.8 sq. mi.; **Water:** 0.2 sq. mi.
Incorporated Jul 5, 1930.

Council Bluffs   City
ZIP: 51501   **Lat:** 41-14-23 N **Long:** 95-51-34 W
Pop: 54,315 (1990); 56,449 (1980)   **Pop Density:** 1476.0
Land: 36.8 sq. mi.; **Water:** 2.3 sq. mi.   **Elev:** 986 ft.
In southwestern IA on the Missouri River across from Omaha, NE. Incorporated Jan 19, 1853.
Name origin: For bluffs on the Missouri River, 15 miles upstream from the present location of the city where, in 1804, explorers Meriwether Lewis (1774–1809) and William Clark (1770–1838) held a conference with Oto and Missouri Indians. Previously called Kanesville.

Crescent   City
ZIP: 51526   **Lat:** 41-21-58 N **Long:** 95-51-31 W
Pop: 113 (1990); 547 (1980)   **Pop Density:** 188.3
Land: 0.6 sq. mi.; **Water:** 0.0 sq. mi.
Incorporated Oct 16, 1959.
Name origin: For the bluffs rising in a crescent above the town.

Hancock   City
ZIP: 51536   **Lat:** 41-23-35 N **Long:** 95-21-53 W
Pop: 201 (1990); 254 (1980)   **Pop Density:** 287.1
Land: 0.7 sq. mi.; **Water:** 0.0 sq. mi.
Incorporated May 16, 1891.
Name origin: For John Hancock (1737–93), signer of the Declaration of Independence.

Macedonia   City
ZIP: 51549   **Lat:** 41-11-31 N **Long:** 95-25-29 W
Pop: 262 (1990); 279 (1980)   **Pop Density:** 873.3
Land: 0.3 sq. mi.; **Water:** 0.0 sq. mi.
Incorporated Jun 21, 1892.
Name origin: For area in ancient Greece.

McClelland   City
Lat: 41-19-39 N **Long:** 95-41-01 W
Pop: 139 (1990); 177 (1980)   **Pop Density:** 695.0
Land: 0.2 sq. mi.; **Water:** 0.0 sq. mi.
Incorporated Dec 14, 1904.

Minden   City
ZIP: 51553   **Lat:** 41-28-01 N **Long:** 95-32-31 W
Pop: 498 (1990); 483 (1980)   **Pop Density:** 1245.0
Land: 0.4 sq. mi.; **Water:** 0.0 sq. mi.
Incorporated Oct 6, 1880.

Neola — City
ZIP: 51559 **Lat:** 41-27-03 N **Long:** 95-37-02 W
Pop: 894 (1990); 839 (1980) **Pop Density:** 2235.0
Land: 0.4 sq. mi.; **Water:** 0.0 sq. mi.
Incorporated Mar 7, 1882.

Oakland — City
ZIP: 51560 **Lat:** 41-18-30 N **Long:** 95-23-48 W
Pop: 1,496 (1990); 1,552 (1980) **Pop Density:** 997.3
Land: 1.5 sq. mi.; **Water:** 0.0 sq. mi. **Elev:** 1103 ft.
Incorporated Mar 14, 1882.

Shelby — City
Lat: 41-29-48 N **Long:** 95-27-00 W
Pop: 67 (1990); 58 (1980) **Pop Density:** 95.7
Land: 0.7 sq. mi.; **Water:** 0.0 sq. mi. **Elev:** 1338 ft.
Incorporated Nov 24, 1877. Part of the town is also in Shelby County.
Name origin: For Isaac Shelby (1750–1826), first governor of KY (1792–96).

Treynor — City
ZIP: 51575 **Lat:** 41-13-51 N **Long:** 95-36-22 W
Pop: 897 (1990); 981 (1980) **Pop Density:** 1495.0
Land: 0.6 sq. mi.; **Water:** 0.0 sq. mi.
Incorporated Aug 24, 1904.

Underwood — City
ZIP: 51576 **Lat:** 41-23-08 N **Long:** 95-40-45 W
Pop: 515 (1990); 448 (1980) **Pop Density:** 1716.7
Land: 0.3 sq. mi.; **Water:** 0.0 sq. mi.
Incorporated Jan 28, 1902.

Walnut — City
ZIP: 51577 **Lat:** 41-28-44 N **Long:** 95-13-21 W
Pop: 857 (1990); 897 (1980) **Pop Density:** 1071.3
Land: 0.8 sq. mi.; **Water:** 0.0 sq. mi.
Incorporated Oct 2, 1877.

Poweshiek County
County Seat: Montezuma (ZIP: 50171)

Pop: 19,033 (1990); 19,306 (1980) **Pop Density:** 32.5
Land: 585.1 sq. mi.; **Water:** 1.1 sq. mi. **Area Code:** 515

In central IA, east of Iowa City; established Feb 17, 1843 (prior to statehood) from Keokuk, Iowa, Johnson, and Mahaska counties.

Name origin: For a Sac and Fox chief, properly *Pawishika* 'he who shakes (something off himself).' He was chief during the Black Hawk War (1832); on behalf of his tribe he signed the Treaty of Fort Armstrong at Rock Island, IL.

Barnes City — City
ZIP: 50027 **Lat:** 41-30-34 N **Long:** 92-28-07 W
Pop: 23 (1990); 22 (1980) **Pop Density:** 230.0
Land: 0.1 sq. mi.; **Water:** 0.0 sq. mi.
Incorporated Apr 20, 1899. Part of the town is also in Mahaska County.

Brooklyn — City
ZIP: 52211 **Lat:** 41-43-52 N **Long:** 92-26-40 W
Pop: 1,439 (1990); 1,509 (1980) **Pop Density:** 1199.2
Land: 1.2 sq. mi.; **Water:** 0.0 sq. mi.
Incorporated May 3, 1869.

Deep River — City
ZIP: 52222 **Lat:** 41-34-53 N **Long:** 92-22-20 W
Pop: 345 (1990); 323 (1980) **Pop Density:** 862.5
Land: 0.4 sq. mi.; **Water:** 0.0 sq. mi.
Incorporated Jun 15, 1887.
Name origin: For the South Fork of the English River, at whose head the town is located.

Grinnell — City
ZIP: 50112 **Lat:** 41-44-26 N **Long:** 92-43-21 W
Pop: 8,902 (1990); 8,868 (1980) **Pop Density:** 2342.6
Land: 3.8 sq. mi.; **Water:** 0.0 sq. mi.
Incorporated Apr 28, 1865.
Name origin: For the Hon. W. H. Grinnell, a local resident.

Guernsey — City
ZIP: 50172 **Lat:** 41-38-57 N **Long:** 92-20-35 W
Pop: 70 (1990); 83 (1980) **Pop Density:** 350.0
Land: 0.2 sq. mi.; **Water:** 0.0 sq. mi.
Incorporated Sep 4, 1906.

Hartwick — City
ZIP: 52232 **Lat:** 41-47-02 N **Long:** 92-20-45 W
Pop: 115 (1990); 92 (1980) **Pop Density:** 1150.0
Land: 0.1 sq. mi.; **Water:** 0.0 sq. mi.
Incorporated 1912.

Malcom — City
ZIP: 50157 **Lat:** 41-42-27 N **Long:** 92-33-28 W
Pop: 447 (1990); 418 (1980) **Pop Density:** 745.0
Land: 0.6 sq. mi.; **Water:** 0.0 sq. mi.
Incorporated Apr 23, 1872.
Name origin: For an early Scotch settler.

Montezuma — City
ZIP: 50171 **Lat:** 41-34-58 N **Long:** 92-31-38 W
Pop: 1,651 (1990); 1,485 (1980) **Pop Density:** 687.9
Land: 2.4 sq. mi.; **Water:** 0.0 sq. mi.
Incorporated Feb 21, 1868.
Name origin: For the Aztec ruler Montezuma II (1466–1520).

Searsboro — City
ZIP: 50242 **Lat:** 41-34-47 N **Long:** 92-42-17 W
Pop: 164 (1990); 134 (1980) **Pop Density:** 410.0
Land: 0.4 sq. mi.; **Water:** 0.0 sq. mi.
Incorporated Aug 3, 1876.

Victor — City
ZIP: 52347 **Lat:** 41-43-47 N **Long:** 92-18-05 W
Pop: 124 (1990); 149 (1980) **Pop Density:** 3100.0
Land: 0.04 sq. mi.; **Water:** 0.0 sq. mi.
Incorporated Nov 30, 1868. Part of the town is alo in Iowa County.

Ringgold County
County Seat: Mount Ayr (ZIP: 50854)

Pop: 5,420 (1990); 6,112 (1980) **Pop Density:** 10.1
Land: 537.7 sq. mi.; **Water:** 1.2 sq. mi. **Area Code:** 515
On central-southern border of IA, southwest of Des Moines; established Feb 24, 1847 from Taylor County.
Name origin: For Maj. Samuel Ringgold (1800–1846), officer in the Seminole War and the Mexican-American War; he died at the Battle of Palo Alto.

Beaconsfield — City
ZIP: 50030 **Lat:** 40-48-25 N **Long:** 94-03-01 W
Pop: 27 (1990); 39 (1980) **Pop Density:** 38.6
Land: 0.7 sq. mi.; **Water:** 0.0 sq. mi.
Incorporated Jan 18, 1900.
Name origin: For Benjamin Disraeli, earl of Beaconsfield (1804–81), English author and prime minister (1868; 1874–80).

Benton — City
ZIP: 50835 **Lat:** 40-42-06 N **Long:** 94-21-33 W
Pop: 39 (1990); 33 (1980) **Pop Density:** 65.0
Land: 0.6 sq. mi.; **Water:** 0.0 sq. mi.
Incorporated Jul 3, 1900.

Clearfield — City
Lat: 40-48-15 N **Long:** 94-28-14 W
Pop: 10 (1990); 15 (1980) **Pop Density:** 100.0
Land: 0.1 sq. mi.; **Water:** 0.0 sq. mi.
Incorporated Dec 16, 1882. Part of the town is also in Taylor County.

Delphos — City
ZIP: 50844 **Lat:** 40-39-47 N **Long:** 94-20-21 W
Pop: 23 (1990); 45 (1980) **Pop Density:** 115.0
Land: 0.2 sq. mi.; **Water:** 0.0 sq. mi.
Incorporated Apr 3, 1920.

Diagonal — City
ZIP: 50845 **Lat:** 40-48-38 N **Long:** 94-20-28 W
Pop: 298 (1990); 362 (1980) **Pop Density:** 331.1
Land: 0.9 sq. mi.; **Water:** 0.0 sq. mi.
Incorporated Mar 6, 1896.

Ellston — City
ZIP: 50074 **Lat:** 40-50-25 N **Long:** 94-06-29 W
Pop: 44 (1990); 60 (1980) **Pop Density:** 220.0
Land: 0.2 sq. mi.; **Water:** 0.0 sq. mi.

Kellerton — City
ZIP: 50133 **Lat:** 40-42-36 N **Long:** 94-02-55 W
Pop: 314 (1990); 278 (1980) **Pop Density:** 523.3
Land: 0.6 sq. mi.; **Water:** 0.0 sq. mi.
Incorporated Dec 3, 1881.

Maloy — City
ZIP: 50852 **Lat:** 40-40-27 N **Long:** 94-24-40 W
Pop: 36 (1990); 38 (1980) **Pop Density:** 60.0
Land: 0.6 sq. mi.; **Water:** 0.0 sq. mi.
Incorporated Jun 18, 1901.

Mount Ayr — City
ZIP: 50854 **Lat:** 40-42-51 N **Long:** 94-14-16 W
Pop: 1,796 (1990); 1,938 (1980) **Pop Density:** 748.3
Land: 2.4 sq. mi.; **Water:** 0.0 sq. mi.
Incorporated Jun 8, 1875.
Name origin: For its location on a high rolling prairie.

Redding — City
ZIP: 50860 **Lat:** 40-36-21 N **Long:** 94-23-12 W
Pop: 119 (1990); 91 (1980) **Pop Density:** 119.0
Land: 1.0 sq. mi.; **Water:** 0.0 sq. mi.
Incorporated Apr 10, 1882.

Shannon City — City
Lat: 40-53-52 N **Long:** 94-15-58 W
Pop: 5 (1990); 14 (1980) **Pop Density:** 166.7
Land: 0.03 sq. mi.; **Water:** 0.0 sq. mi.
Incorporated Dec 26, 1892. Part of the town is also in Union County.

Tingley — City
ZIP: 50863 **Lat:** 40-51-09 N **Long:** 94-11-43 W
Pop: 179 (1990); 210 (1980) **Pop Density:** 255.7
Land: 0.7 sq. mi.; **Water:** 0.0 sq. mi.
Incorporated Jun 17, 1884.

Sac County
County Seat: Sac City (ZIP: 50583)

Pop: 12,324 (1990); 14,118 (1980)　　　　**Pop Density:** 21.4
Land: 575.8 sq. mi.; **Water:** 2.6 sq. mi.　　**Area Code:** 712

In west-central IA, southwest of Fort Dodge; established Jan 15, 1851 from Greene County.

Name origin: An Indian tribal name meaning 'outlet.' Also spelled *Sauk*.

Auburn　　　　　　　　　　　　　　City
ZIP: 51433　　　　**Lat:** 42-14-59 N　**Long:** 94-52-36 W
Pop: 283 (1990); 320 (1980)　　**Pop Density:** 566.0
Land: 0.5 sq. mi.; **Water:** 0.0 sq. mi.　　**Elev:** 1220 ft.
Incorporated Jan 10, 1887.

Name origin: For the name of the village in Oliver Goldsmith's (1730–74) poem "The Deserted Village."

Early　　　　　　　　　　　　　　City
ZIP: 50535　　　　**Lat:** 42-27-39 N　**Long:** 95-09-09 W
Pop: 649 (1990); 670 (1980)　　**Pop Density:** 1622.5
Land: 0.4 sq. mi.; **Water:** 0.0 sq. mi.
Incorporated May 22, 1883.

Name origin: For pioneer D.C. Early, who settled here in the 1870s.

Lake View　　　　　　　　　　　　City
　　　　　　　　　Lat: 42-18-22 N　**Long:** 95-02-47 W
Pop: 1,303 (1990); 1,291 (1980)　　**Pop Density:** 723.9
Land: 1.8 sq. mi.; **Water:** 0.3 sq. mi.
Incorporated Oct 29, 1887.

Lytton　　　　　　　　　　　　　　City
ZIP: 50561　　　　**Lat:** 42-25-24 N　**Long:** 94-51-37 W
Pop: 278 (1990); 334 (1980)　　**Pop Density:** 1390.0
Land: 0.2 sq. mi.; **Water:** 0.0 sq. mi.
Incorporated Jul 21, 1911. Part of the town is also in Calhoun County.

Nemaha　　　　　　　　　　　　　City
ZIP: 50567　　　　**Lat:** 42-30-54 N　**Long:** 95-05-15 W
Pop: 112 (1990); 120 (1980)　　**Pop Density:** 560.0
Land: 0.2 sq. mi.; **Water:** 0.0 sq. mi.
Incorporated Jan 27, 1915.

Name origin: For either the Nemaha or the Little Nemaha River, itself named either for the Maha Indians or an Indian term for 'water of cultivation' or 'muddy water.'

Odebolt　　　　　　　　　　　　　City
ZIP: 51458　　　　**Lat:** 42-18-41 N　**Long:** 95-15-13 W
Pop: 1,158 (1990); 1,299 (1980)　　**Pop Density:** 1158.0
Land: 1.0 sq. mi.; **Water:** 0.0 sq. mi.　　**Elev:** 1377 ft.
Incorporated Jun 17, 1878.

Name origin: For Odebeau, a French trapper who lived alone by the creek here.

Sac City　　　　　　　　　　　　　City
ZIP: 50583　　　　**Lat:** 42-25-19 N　**Long:** 94-59-50 W
Pop: 2,492 (1990); 3,000 (1980)　　**Pop Density:** 508.6
Land: 4.9 sq. mi.; **Water:** 0.0 sq. mi.
Incorporated Dec 22, 1874.

Name origin: For the Sac or Sauk Indian tribe.

Schaller　　　　　　　　　　　　　City
ZIP: 51053　　　　**Lat:** 42-29-44 N　**Long:** 95-17-43 W
Pop: 768 (1990); 832 (1980)　　**Pop Density:** 590.8
Land: 1.3 sq. mi.; **Water:** 0.0 sq. mi.　　**Elev:** 1439 ft.
Incorporated May 25, 1883.

Wall Lake　　　　　　　　　　　　City
ZIP: 51466　　　　**Lat:** 42-16-10 N　**Long:** 95-05-34 W
Pop: 875 (1990); 892 (1980)　　**Pop Density:** 795.5
Land: 1.1 sq. mi.; **Water:** 0.0 sq. mi.
Incorporated Dec 7, 1880.

Scott County
County Seat: Davenport (ZIP: 52801)

Pop: 150,979 (1990); 160,022 (1980)   **Pop Density:** 329.7
Land: 457.9 sq. mi.; **Water:** 10.3 sq. mi.   **Area Code:** 319
On central eastern border of IA; established Dec 21, 1837 (prior to statehood) from Wisconsin Territory.
Name origin: For Gen. Winfield Scott (1786–1866), officer in the War of 1812 and the Mexican-American War; general in chief of the U.S. Army (1841–61).

Bettendorf   City
ZIP: 52722   **Lat:** 41-33-51 N   **Long:** 90-28-34 W
Pop: 28,132 (1990); 27,381 (1980)   **Pop Density:** 1327.0
Land: 21.2 sq. mi.; **Water:** 1.1 sq. mi.
In eastern IA on the Mississippi River, 6 mi. east of Davenport. Incorporated Jun 5, 1903.
Name origin: For the Bettendorf family.

Blue Grass   City
ZIP: 52726   **Lat:** 41-30-30 N   **Long:** 90-45-49 W
Pop: 1,214 (1990); 1,377 (1980)   **Pop Density:** 505.8
Land: 2.4 sq. mi.; **Water:** 0.0 sq. mi.
Incorporated Dec 10, 1903.
Name origin: For a variety of grass that grows in KY.

Buffalo   City
ZIP: 52728   **Lat:** 41-27-36 N   **Long:** 90-43-05 W
Pop: 1,260 (1990); 1,569 (1980)   **Pop Density:** 229.1
Land: 5.5 sq. mi.; **Water:** 0.0 sq. mi.
Incorporated Jul 15, 1875.

Davenport   City
ZIP: 52802   **Lat:** 41-33-24 N   **Long:** 90-36-15 W
Pop: 95,333 (1990); 103,264 (1980)   **Pop Density:** 1552.7
Land: 61.4 sq. mi.; **Water:** 2.1 sq. mi.
In eastern IA on the Mississippi River opposite Rock Island, IL. Founded 1835, county seat 1838, incorporated Feb 5, 1851. Site of the first railroad bridge across the Mississippi River (1856). Largest of the Quad Cities: Rock Island, Moline, and East Moline, IL, and Davenport. Manufacturing and transportation center amid rich farmland.
Name origin: For George Davenport (1785–1845), fur trader who had great influence with the Sac and Fox tribes.

Dixon   City
ZIP: 52745   **Lat:** 41-44-33 N   **Long:** 90-46-53 W
Pop: 202 (1990); 312 (1980)   **Pop Density:** 2020.0
Land: 0.1 sq. mi.; **Water:** 0.0 sq. mi.
Incorporated May 12, 1909.

Donahue   City
ZIP: 52746   **Lat:** 41-41-30 N   **Long:** 90-40-30 W
Pop: 316 (1990); 289 (1980)   **Pop Density:** 1053.3
Land: 0.3 sq. mi.; **Water:** 0.0 sq. mi.
Incorporated May 1, 1909.

Durant   City
ZIP: 52747   **Lat:** 41-36-04 N   **Long:** 90-53-54 W
Pop: 2 (1990); 4 (1980)   **Pop Density:** 20.0
Land: 0.1 sq. mi.; **Water:** 0.0 sq. mi.
Incorporated Jul 1, 1867. Part of the town is also in Cedar and Muscatine counties.

Eldridge   City
ZIP: 52748   **Lat:** 41-38-08 N   **Long:** 90-34-24 W
Pop: 3,378 (1990); 3,279 (1980)   **Pop Density:** 359.4
Land: 9.4 sq. mi.; **Water:** 0.0 sq. mi.
Incorporated May 1, 1900.

Le Claire   City
ZIP: 52753   **Lat:** 41-35-55 N   **Long:** 90-21-52 W
Pop: 2,734 (1990); 2,899 (1980)   **Pop Density:** 651.0
Land: 4.2 sq. mi.; **Water:** 0.2 sq. mi.
Incorporated Jan 13, 1855.
Name origin: For Antoine Le Clair, the founder of Davenport.

Long Grove   City
ZIP: 52756   **Lat:** 41-41-40 N   **Long:** 90-34-49 W
Pop: 605 (1990); 596 (1980)   **Pop Density:** 756.3
Land: 0.8 sq. mi.; **Water:** 0.0 sq. mi.
Incorporated Aug 1, 1912.

Maysville   City
Lat: 41-38-56 N   **Long:** 90-43-05 W
Pop: 170 (1990); 151 (1980)   **Pop Density:** 566.7
Land: 0.3 sq. mi.; **Water:** 0.0 sq. mi.
Incorporated Jun 21, 1909.

McCausland   City
ZIP: 52758   **Lat:** 41-44-36 N   **Long:** 90-26-42 W
Pop: 308 (1990); 381 (1980)   **Pop Density:** 616.0
Land: 0.5 sq. mi.; **Water:** 0.0 sq. mi.
Incorporated May 28, 1909.

New Liberty   City
ZIP: 52765   **Lat:** 41-42-59 N   **Long:** 90-52-42 W
Pop: 139 (1990); 136 (1980)   **Pop Density:** 1390.0
Land: 0.1 sq. mi.; **Water:** 0.0 sq. mi.
Incorporated Jul 26, 1909.

Panorama Park   City
Lat: 41-33-18 N   **Long:** 90-27-16 W
Pop: 127 (1990); 145 (1980)   **Pop Density:** 1270.0
Land: 0.1 sq. mi.; **Water:** 0.0 sq. mi.
Incorporated Jul 6, 1953.

Park View   CDP
ZIP: 52748   **Lat:** 41-41-22 N   **Long:** 90-32-26 W
Pop: 2,192 (1990); 2,140 (1980)   **Pop Density:** 1992.7
Land: 1.1 sq. mi.; **Water:** 0.0 sq. mi.

Princeton   City
ZIP: 52768   **Lat:** 41-40-15 N   **Long:** 90-21-34 W
Pop: 806 (1990); 965 (1980)   **Pop Density:** 310.0
Land: 2.6 sq. mi.; **Water:** 0.0 sq. mi.
Incorporated Jan 29, 1857.

IOWA, Scott County

Riverdale — City
ZIP: 52722 Lat: 41-32-07 N Long: 90-28-01 W
Pop: 433 (1990); 462 (1980) Pop Density: 240.6
Land: 1.8 sq. mi.; Water: 0.4 sq. mi.
Incorporated Dec 27, 1950.

Walcott — City
Lat: 41-35-40 N Long: 90-46-30 W
Pop: 1,356 (1990); 1,425 (1980) Pop Density: 616.4
Land: 2.2 sq. mi.; Water: 0.0 sq. mi.
Incorporated Jul 10, 1894. Part of the town is also in Muscatine County.

Shelby County
County Seat: Harlan (ZIP: 51537)

Pop: 13,230 (1990); 15,043 (1980) Pop Density: 22.4
Land: 590.9 sq. mi.; Water: 0.5 sq. mi. Area Code: 712
In western IA, northeast of Council Bluffs; established Jan 15, 1851 from Cass County.

Name origin: For Gen. Isaac Shelby (1750–1826), officer in the Revolutionary War, NC legislator, and governor of KY (1792–96; 1812–16).

Defiance — City
ZIP: 51527 Lat: 41-49-31 N Long: 95-20-21 W
Pop: 312 (1990); 383 (1980) Pop Density: 780.0
Land: 0.4 sq. mi.; Water: 0.0 sq. mi. Elev: 1283 ft.
Incorporated Dec 4, 1882.

Earling — City
ZIP: 51530 Lat: 41-46-33 N Long: 95-25-10 W
Pop: 466 (1990); 520 (1980) Pop Density: 776.7
Land: 0.6 sq. mi.; Water: 0.0 sq. mi. Elev: 1408 ft.
Incorporated Jun 1, 1892.

Elk Horn — City
ZIP: 51531 Lat: 41-35-33 N Long: 95-03-37 W
Pop: 672 (1990); 746 (1980) Pop Density: 840.0
Land: 0.8 sq. mi.; Water: 0.0 sq. mi. Elev: 1363 ft.
Incorporated Feb 28, 1910.

Harlan — City
ZIP: 51537 Lat: 41-38-56 N Long: 95-19-34 W
Pop: 5,148 (1990); 5,357 (1980) Pop Density: 1170.0
Land: 4.4 sq. mi.; Water: 0.0 sq. mi. Elev: 1250 ft.
Incorporated Apr 25, 1879.
Name origin: For James Harlan, U.S. senator from IA.

Irwin — City
ZIP: 51446 Lat: 41-47-24 N Long: 95-12-24 W
Pop: 394 (1990); 427 (1980) Pop Density: 656.7
Land: 0.6 sq. mi.; Water: 0.0 sq. mi. Elev: 1264 ft.
Incorporated May 20, 1892.

Kirkman — City
ZIP: 51447 Lat: 41-43-44 N Long: 95-15-58 W
Pop: 98 (1990); 95 (1980) Pop Density: 326.7
Land: 0.3 sq. mi.; Water: 0.0 sq. mi.
Incorporated Jul 6, 1892.

Panama — City
ZIP: 51562 Lat: 41-43-36 N Long: 95-28-30 W
Pop: 201 (1990); 229 (1980) Pop Density: 670.0
Land: 0.3 sq. mi.; Water: 0.0 sq. mi. Elev: 1325 ft.
Incorporated May 17, 1886.
Name origin: Probably for Pan-America.

Portsmouth — City
ZIP: 51565 Lat: 41-39-02 N Long: 95-31-09 W
Pop: 209 (1990); 240 (1980) Pop Density: 696.7
Land: 0.3 sq. mi.; Water: 0.0 sq. mi. Elev: 1237 ft.
Incorporated 1883.

Shelby — City
Lat: 41-30-48 N Long: 95-27-00 W
Pop: 570 (1990); 607 (1980) Pop Density: 570.0
Land: 1.0 sq. mi.; Water: 0.0 sq. mi. Elev: 1338 ft.
Incorporated Nov 24, 1877. Part of the town is also in Pottawattamie County.
Name origin: For Isaac Shelby (1750–1826), first governor of KY (1792–96).

Tennant — City
ZIP: 51574 Lat: 41-35-43 N Long: 95-26-34 W
Pop: 78 (1990); 77 (1980) Pop Density: 111.4
Land: 0.7 sq. mi.; Water: 0.0 sq. mi. Elev: 1382 ft.
Incorporated Apr 23, 1915.

Westphalia — City
ZIP: 51578 Lat: 41-43-09 N Long: 95-23-35 W
Pop: 144 (1990); 169 (1980) Pop Density: 1440.0
Land: 0.1 sq. mi.; Water: 0.0 sq. mi. Elev: 1402 ft.
Incorporated Nov 7, 1919.

> ## Sioux County
> **County Seat: Orange City (ZIP: 51041)**
>
> **Pop:** 29,903 (1990); 30,813 (1980) **Pop Density:** 38.9
> **Land:** 767.9 sq. mi.; **Water:** 0.7 sq. mi. **Area Code:** 712
> On the northwestern border of IA, north of Sioux City; established Jan 13, 1851 from Plymouth County.
> **Name origin:** For the Indian tribe, sometimes known as the Dakotas. Name is French form of Ojibway *nadouessioux* 'snakes' or 'enemies.'

Alton City
ZIP: 51003 **Lat:** 42-59-10 N **Long:** 96-00-27 W
Pop: 1,063 (1990); 986 (1980) **Pop Density:** 708.7
Land: 1.5 sq. mi.; **Water:** 0.0 sq. mi.
Incorporated Mar 8, 1883.

Boyden City
ZIP: 51234 **Lat:** 43-11-24 N **Long:** 96-00-07 W
Pop: 651 (1990); 708 (1980) **Pop Density:** 2170.0
Land: 0.3 sq. mi.; **Water:** 0.0 sq. mi.
Incorporated May 24, 1889.

Chatsworth City
ZIP: 51011 **Lat:** 42-54-59 N **Long:** 96-30-52 W
Pop: 103 (1990); 110 (1980) **Pop Density:** 206.0
Land: 0.5 sq. mi.; **Water:** 0.0 sq. mi.
Incorporated Dec 31, 1900.

Granville City
ZIP: 51022 **Lat:** 42-59-05 N **Long:** 95-52-29 W
Pop: 298 (1990); 336 (1980) **Pop Density:** 993.3
Land: 0.3 sq. mi.; **Water:** 0.0 sq. mi.
Incorporated Jun 22, 1891.
Name origin: From French 'large town.'

Hawarden City
ZIP: 51023 **Lat:** 43-00-07 N **Long:** 96-28-56 W
Pop: 2,439 (1990); 2,722 (1980) **Pop Density:** 841.0
Land: 2.9 sq. mi.; **Water:** 0.1 sq. mi.
Incorporated Mar 18, 1887.

Hospers City
ZIP: 51238 **Lat:** 43-04-19 N **Long:** 95-54-12 W
Pop: 643 (1990); 655 (1980) **Pop Density:** 1286.0
Land: 0.5 sq. mi.; **Water:** 0.0 sq. mi.
Incorporated Dec 6, 1890.

Hull City
ZIP: 51239 **Lat:** 43-11-24 N **Long:** 96-07-57 W
Pop: 1,724 (1990); 1,714 (1980) **Pop Density:** 1567.3
Land: 1.1 sq. mi.; **Water:** 0.0 sq. mi.
Incorporated May 15, 1886.
Name origin: For John Hull.

Ireton City
ZIP: 51027 **Lat:** 42-58-31 N **Long:** 96-19-17 W
Pop: 597 (1990); 588 (1980) **Pop Density:** 597.0
Land: 1.0 sq. mi.; **Water:** 0.0 sq. mi.
Incorporated Oct 13, 1890.

Matlock City
ZIP: 51244 **Lat:** 43-14-40 N **Long:** 95-56-03 W
Pop: 92 (1990); 109 (1980) **Pop Density:** 230.0
Land: 0.4 sq. mi.; **Water:** 0.0 sq. mi.
Incorporated Jul 5, 1897.

Maurice City
ZIP: 51036 **Lat:** 42-57-58 N **Long:** 96-10-58 W
Pop: 243 (1990); 288 (1980) **Pop Density:** 486.0
Land: 0.5 sq. mi.; **Water:** 0.0 sq. mi.
Incorporated May 23, 1891.

Orange City City
ZIP: 51041 **Lat:** 43-00-11 N **Long:** 96-03-30 W
Pop: 4,940 (1990); 4,588 (1980) **Pop Density:** 2058.3
Land: 2.4 sq. mi.; **Water:** 0.0 sq. mi.
Incorporated Feb 29, 1884.

Rock Valley City
ZIP: 51247 **Lat:** 43-12-16 N **Long:** 96-17-49 W
Pop: 2,540 (1990); 2,706 (1980) **Pop Density:** 1693.3
Land: 1.5 sq. mi.; **Water:** 0.1 sq. mi.
Incorporated Nov 26, 1886.
Name origin: For the Rock River.

Sheldon City
ZIP: 51201 **Lat:** 43-10-49 N **Long:** 95-52-05 W
Pop: 71 (1990); 15 (1980) **Pop Density:** 142.0
Land: 0.5 sq. mi.; **Water:** 0.0 sq. mi.
Incorporated Apr 24, 1876. Part of the town is also in O'Brien County.
Name origin: For Israel Sheldon, a stockholder in the first railroad to pass through town.

Sioux Center City
ZIP: 51250 **Lat:** 43-04-35 N **Long:** 96-10-17 W
Pop: 5,074 (1990); 4,588 (1980) **Pop Density:** 975.8
Land: 5.2 sq. mi.; **Water:** 0.0 sq. mi.
Incorporated Oct 1, 1891.
Name origin: For the Sioux Indians.

Story County
County Seat: Nevada (ZIP: 50201)

Pop: 74,252 (1990); 72,326 (1980)
Land: 572.9 sq. mi.; **Water:** 0.8 sq. mi.
Pop Density: 129.6
Area Code: 515
In central IA, north of Des Moines; established Jan 13, 1846 from Jasper, Polk, and Boone counties.
Name origin: For Joseph Story (1779–1845), MA legislator and associate justice of the U.S. Supreme Court (1811–45).

Ames City
ZIP: 50010 **Lat:** 42-01-24 N **Long:** 93-37-32 W
Pop: 47,198 (1990); 45,775 (1980) **Pop Density:** 2395.8
Land: 19.7 sq. mi.; **Water:** 0.0 sq. mi.
In central IA, 30 mi. north of Des Moines. Incorporated Dec 20, 1869. Site of Iowa State University.
Name origin: For Oakes Ames (1804–73), U.S. representative from MA.

Cambridge City
ZIP: 50046 **Lat:** 41-53-58 N **Long:** 93-31-51 W
Pop: 714 (1990); 732 (1980) **Pop Density:** 714.0
Land: 1.0 sq. mi.; **Water:** 0.0 sq. mi.
Incorporated Dec 6, 1881.

Collins City
ZIP: 50055 **Lat:** 41-54-08 N **Long:** 93-18-19 W
Pop: 455 (1990); 451 (1980) **Pop Density:** 1137.5
Land: 0.4 sq. mi.; **Water:** 0.0 sq. mi.
Incorporated Dec 28, 1894.

Colo City
ZIP: 50056 **Lat:** 42-00-57 N **Long:** 93-19-06 W
Pop: 771 (1990); 808 (1980) **Pop Density:** 963.8
Land: 0.8 sq. mi.; **Water:** 0.0 sq. mi.
Incorporated Apr 26, 1876.
Name origin: For the favorite dog of railroad official John Blair.

Gilbert City
ZIP: 50105 **Lat:** 42-06-26 N **Long:** 93-38-51 W
Pop: 796 (1990); 805 (1980) **Pop Density:** 995.0
Land: 0.8 sq. mi.; **Water:** 0.0 sq. mi.
Incorporated Jul 15, 1882.

Huxley City
ZIP: 50124 **Lat:** 41-53-45 N **Long:** 93-36-08 W
Pop: 2,047 (1990); 1,884 (1980) **Pop Density:** 2047.0
Land: 1.0 sq. mi.; **Water:** 0.0 sq. mi.
Incorporated Aug 27, 1902.

Kelley City
ZIP: 50134 **Lat:** 41-57-03 N **Long:** 93-39-52 W
Pop: 246 (1990); 237 (1980) **Pop Density:** 820.0
Land: 0.3 sq. mi.; **Water:** 0.0 sq. mi.
Incorporated Jan 31, 1900.

Maxwell City
ZIP: 50161 **Lat:** 41-53-29 N **Long:** 93-23-55 W
Pop: 788 (1990); 783 (1980) **Pop Density:** 985.0
Land: 0.8 sq. mi.; **Water:** 0.0 sq. mi.
Incorporated Dec 17, 1883.

McCallsburg City
ZIP: 50154 **Lat:** 42-09-55 N **Long:** 93-23-25 W
Pop: 292 (1990); 304 (1980) **Pop Density:** 584.0
Land: 0.5 sq. mi.; **Water:** 0.0 sq. mi.
Incorporated Feb 25, 1901.

Nevada City
ZIP: 50201 **Lat:** 42-01-05 N **Long:** 93-27-00 W
Pop: 6,009 (1990); 5,912 (1980) **Pop Density:** 1820.9
Land: 3.3 sq. mi.; **Water:** 0.0 sq. mi. **Elev:** 1003 ft.
Incorporated Oct 4, 1869.
Name origin: Named by settlers from the state of NV; from Spanish for 'snow-covered,' referring to snow-capped peaks.

Roland City
ZIP: 50236 **Lat:** 42-10-01 N **Long:** 93-30-04 W
Pop: 1,035 (1990); 1,005 (1980) **Pop Density:** 1035.0
Land: 1.0 sq. mi.; **Water:** 0.0 sq. mi.
Incorporated Dec 29, 1891.

Sheldahl City
Lat: 41-51-57 N **Long:** 93-41-27 W
Pop: 171 (1990); 158 (1980) **Pop Density:** 570.0
Land: 0.3 sq. mi.; **Water:** 0.0 sq. mi.
Incorporated Jan 18, 1882. Part of the town is also in Boone and Polk counties.

Slater City
ZIP: 50244 **Lat:** 41-52-49 N **Long:** 93-41-02 W
Pop: 1,268 (1990); 1,312 (1980) **Pop Density:** 1152.7
Land: 1.1 sq. mi.; **Water:** 0.0 sq. mi.
Incorporated May 5, 1890.

Story City City
ZIP: 50248 **Lat:** 42-11-11 N **Long:** 93-35-29 W
Pop: 2,959 (1990); 2,762 (1980) **Pop Density:** 1409.0
Land: 2.1 sq. mi.; **Water:** 0.0 sq. mi.
Platted 1855; incorporated Dec 12, 1881.
Name origin: For Joseph Story (1779–1845), MA legislator and associate justice of the U.S. Supreme Court (1811–45). Previously called Fairview.

Zearing City
ZIP: 50278 **Lat:** 42-09-31 N **Long:** 93-17-47 W
Pop: 614 (1990); 630 (1980) **Pop Density:** 877.1
Land: 0.7 sq. mi.; **Water:** 0.0 sq. mi.
Incorporated Feb 6, 1883.
Name origin: For Doctor Zearing, who promised the town a church if the town was named for him.

Tama County
County Seat: Toledo (ZIP: 52342)

Pop: 17,419 (1990); 19,533 (1980)
Land: 721.4 sq. mi.; **Water:** 1.1 sq. mi.
Pop Density: 24.1
Area Code: 515

In central IA, west of Cedar Rapids; established Feb 17, 1843 (prior to statehood) from Boone and Benton counties.

Name origin: For either a Fox Indian chief or for the wife of Chief Poweshiek. Meaning is uncertain; has been interpreted as 'beautiful,' 'lovely' or 'pleasant,' when referring to a woman, or 'a bear with a voice that makes the rocks tremble' when applied to a man. A nearby Mesquaki Indian suggested that the name derives from *tewaime*, associated with the sound of thunder.

Chelsea — City
ZIP: 52215 **Lat:** 41-55-14 N **Long:** 92-23-42 W
Pop: 336 (1990); 376 (1980) **Pop Density:** 336.0
Land: 1.0 sq. mi.; **Water:** 0.0 sq. mi. **Elev:** 792 ft.
Incorporated Mar 4, 1878.

Clutier — City
ZIP: 52217 **Lat:** 42-04-43 N **Long:** 92-24-10 W
Pop: 219 (1990); 249 (1980) **Pop Density:** 273.8
Land: 0.8 sq. mi.; **Water:** 0.0 sq. mi.
Incorporated Jan 16, 1901.

Dysart — City
ZIP: 52224 **Lat:** 42-10-19 N **Long:** 92-18-33 W
Pop: 1,230 (1990); 1,355 (1980) **Pop Density:** 946.2
Land: 1.3 sq. mi.; **Water:** 0.0 sq. mi.
Incorporated May 30, 1881.

Elberon — City
ZIP: 52225 **Lat:** 42-00-19 N **Long:** 92-18-56 W
Pop: 203 (1990); 194 (1980) **Pop Density:** 290.0
Land: 0.7 sq. mi.; **Water:** 0.0 sq. mi.
Incorporated Oct 28, 1893.

Garwin — City
ZIP: 50632 **Lat:** 42-05-38 N **Long:** 92-40-41 W
Pop: 533 (1990); 626 (1980) **Pop Density:** 533.0
Land: 1.0 sq. mi.; **Water:** 0.0 sq. mi.
Incorporated Jun 5, 1890.

Gladbrook — City
ZIP: 50635 **Lat:** 42-11-09 N **Long:** 92-42-51 W
Pop: 881 (1990); 970 (1980) **Pop Density:** 1258.6
Land: 0.7 sq. mi.; **Water:** 0.0 sq. mi.
Incorporated Dec 20, 1880.

Lincoln — City
ZIP: 50652 **Lat:** 42-15-47 N **Long:** 92-41-27 W
Pop: 173 (1990); 202 (1980) **Pop Density:** 432.5
Land: 0.4 sq. mi.; **Water:** 0.0 sq. mi.
Incorporated Sep 10, 1913.
Name origin: Originally named Berlin by German settlers, but anti-German feeling during World War I resulted in the renaming, probably for Abraham Lincoln (1809–65), sixteenth U.S. president.

Montour — City
ZIP: 50173 **Lat:** 41-58-49 N **Long:** 92-42-55 W
Pop: 312 (1990); 387 (1980) **Pop Density:** 624.0
Land: 0.5 sq. mi.; **Water:** 0.0 sq. mi.
Incorporated May 4, 1883.
Name origin: For an early settler from Quebec, Canada.

Tama — City
ZIP: 52339 **Lat:** 41-57-48 N **Long:** 92-34-29 W
Pop: 2,697 (1990); 2,968 (1980) **Pop Density:** 870.0
Land: 3.1 sq. mi.; **Water:** 0.1 sq. mi.
Incorporated Mat 16, 1887.
Name origin: For Tama, a famous chief of the Fox Indians. Meaning is uncertain; has been interpreted as 'beautiful,' 'lovely' or 'pleasant,' when referring to a woman, or 'a bear with a voice that makes the rocks tremble' when applied to a man.

Toledo — City
ZIP: 52342 **Lat:** 41-59-25 N **Long:** 92-34-49 W
Pop: 2,380 (1990); 2,445 (1980) **Pop Density:** 1034.8
Land: 2.3 sq. mi.; **Water:** 0.0 sq. mi.
Incorporated Jan 1, 1866.
Name origin: For Toledo, OH.

Traer — City
ZIP: 50675 **Lat:** 42-11-32 N **Long:** 92-27-53 W
Pop: 1,552 (1990); 1,703 (1980) **Pop Density:** 1410.9
Land: 1.1 sq. mi.; **Water:** 0.0 sq. mi.
Incorporated Jan 18, 1875.

Vining — City
ZIP: 52348 **Lat:** 41-59-24 N **Long:** 92-23-07 W
Pop: 78 (1990); 96 (1980) **Pop Density:** 130.0
Land: 0.6 sq. mi.; **Water:** 0.0 sq. mi.
Incorporated May 26, 1913.

IOWA, Taylor County   *American Places Dictionary*

Taylor County
County Seat: Bedford (ZIP: 50833)

Pop: 7,114 (1990); 8,353 (1980)   **Pop Density:** 13.3
Land: 534.0 sq. mi.; **Water:** 0.9 sq. mi.   **Area Code:** 712
On southern border of IA; established Feb 24, 1847 from Page County.
Name origin: For Zachary Taylor (1784–1850), twelfth U.S. president.

Athelstan   City
Lat: 40-34-21 N **Long:** 94-32-32 W
Pop: 31 (1990); 45 (1980)   **Pop Density:** 310.0
Land: 0.1 sq. mi.; **Water:** 0.0 sq. mi.
Incorporated Oct 28, 1895.

Bedford   City
ZIP: 50833   **Lat:** 40-40-15 N **Long:** 94-43-26 W
Pop: 1,528 (1990); 1,692 (1980)   **Pop Density:** 955.0
Land: 1.6 sq. mi.; **Water:** 0.0 sq. mi.
Incorporated Jul 28, 1866.

Blockton   City
ZIP: 50836   **Lat:** 40-37-00 N **Long:** 94-28-39 W
Pop: 213 (1990); 280 (1980)   **Pop Density:** 355.0
Land: 0.6 sq. mi.; **Water:** 0.0 sq. mi.
Incorporated Mar 28, 1890.

Clearfield   City
Lat: 40-48-07 N **Long:** 94-28-37 W
Pop: 407 (1990); 418 (1980)   **Pop Density:** 581.4
Land: 0.7 sq. mi.; **Water:** 0.0 sq. mi.
Incorporated Dec 16, 1882. Part of the town is also in Ringgold County.

Conway   City
Lat: 40-44-59 N **Long:** 94-37-10 W
Pop: 57 (1990); 93 (1980)   **Pop Density:** 285.0
Land: 0.2 sq. mi.; **Water:** 0.0 sq. mi.
Incorporated Dec 27, 1878.

Gravity   City
ZIP: 50848   **Lat:** 40-45-36 N **Long:** 94-44-34 W
Pop: 218 (1990); 245 (1980)   **Pop Density:** 726.7
Land: 0.3 sq. mi.; **Water:** 0.0 sq. mi.
Settled 1881, incorporated May 26, 1882.
Name origin: Named by early resident Sara Cox for being the main attraction in the area.

Lenox   City
Lat: 40-52-55 N **Long:** 94-33-29 W
Pop: 1,303 (1990); 1,336 (1980)   **Pop Density:** 685.8
Land: 1.9 sq. mi.; **Water:** 0.0 sq. mi.
Incorporated Jul 2, 1875. Part of the town is also in Adams County.

New Market   City
ZIP: 51646   **Lat:** 40-43-56 N **Long:** 94-54-00 W
Pop: 454 (1990); 554 (1980)   **Pop Density:** 1135.0
Land: 0.4 sq. mi.; **Water:** 0.0 sq. mi.
Incorporated Dec 9, 1882.

Sharpsburg   City
ZIP: 50862   **Lat:** 40-48-10 N **Long:** 94-38-27 W
Pop: 116 (1990); 114 (1980)   **Pop Density:** 290.0
Land: 0.4 sq. mi.; **Water:** 0.0 sq. mi.
Incorporated Apr 25, 1905.

Union County
County Seat: Creston (ZIP: 50801)

Pop: 12,750 (1990); 13,858 (1980)   **Pop Density:** 30.0
Land: 424.4 sq. mi.; **Water:** 1.6 sq. mi.   **Area Code:** 515
In south-central IA, southwest of Des Moines; established Jan 15, 1851 from Clarke County.
Name origin: Probably for the union of the states.

Afton   City
ZIP: 50830   **Lat:** 41-01-40 N **Long:** 94-11-44 W
Pop: 953 (1990); 985 (1980)   **Pop Density:** 953.0
Land: 1.0 sq. mi.; **Water:** 0.0 sq. mi.
Founded 1854; incorporated Nov 30, 1868.
Name origin: Named by Mrs. Baker, wife of one of the proprietors, for the Afton River in Scotland.

Arispe   City
ZIP: 50831   **Lat:** 40-56-56 N **Long:** 94-13-07 W
Pop: 92 (1990); 89 (1980)   **Pop Density:** 184.0
Land: 0.5 sq. mi.; **Water:** 0.0 sq. mi.
Incorporated Oct 21, 1904.

Creston   City
ZIP: 50801   **Lat:** 41-03-32 N **Long:** 94-21-50 W
Pop: 7,911 (1990); 8,429 (1980)   **Pop Density:** 1551.2
Land: 5.1 sq. mi.; **Water:** 0.1 sq. mi.
Incorporated Apr 22, 1871.
Name origin: For its location on a crest, the highest point on the Chicago, Burlington and Quincy Railroad line.

Cromwell   City
ZIP: 50842   **Lat:** 41-02-23 N **Long:** 94-27-42 W
Pop: 120 (1990); 157 (1980)   **Pop Density:** 400.0
Land: 0.3 sq. mi.; **Water:** 0.0 sq. mi.
Incorporated Nov 24, 1893.

Kent　　　　　　　　　　　　　　　　　　　City
ZIP: 50850　　　　**Lat:** 40-57-11 N **Long:** 94-27-22 W
Pop: 65 (1990); 70 (1980)　　**Pop Density:** 216.7
Land: 0.3 sq. mi.; **Water:** 0.0 sq. mi.
Incorporated Aug 5, 1903.

Lorimor　　　　　　　　　　　　　　　　　City
ZIP: 50149　　　　**Lat:** 41-07-39 N **Long:** 94-03-25 W
Pop: 377 (1990); 405 (1980)　　**Pop Density:** 942.5
Land: 0.4 sq. mi.; **Water:** 0.0 sq. mi.
Incorporated Dec 16, 1892.
Name origin: For founder Josiah Lorimar.

Shannon City　　　　　　　　　　　　　　City
　　　　　　　　　　　　Lat: 40-54-03 N **Long:** 94-15-49 W
Pop: 92 (1990); 79 (1980)　　**Pop Density:** 920.0
Land: 0.1 sq. mi.; **Water:** 0.0 sq. mi.
Incorporated Dec 26, 1892. Part of the town is also in Ringgold County.

Thayer　　　　　　　　　　　　　　　　　　City
ZIP: 50254　　　　**Lat:** 41-01-45 N **Long:** 94-02-58 W
Pop: 79 (1990); 87 (1980)　　**Pop Density:** 790.0
Land: 0.1 sq. mi.; **Water:** 0.0 sq. mi.　　**Elev:** 1107 ft.
Incorporated May 11, 1894.

Van Buren County
County Seat: Keosauqua (ZIP: 52565)

Pop: 7,676 (1990); 8,626 (1980)　　**Pop Density:** 15.8
Land: 485.3 sq. mi.; **Water:** 5.3 sq. mi.　　**Area Code:** 319
On the southeastern border of IA, west of Burlington; established Dec 7, 1836 (prior to statehood) from Des Moines County.
Name origin: For Martin Van Buren (1782–1862), eighth U.S. president.

Birmingham　　　　　　　　　　　　　　City
ZIP: 52535　　　　**Lat:** 40-52-42 N **Long:** 91-56-51 W
Pop: 386 (1990); 410 (1980)　　**Pop Density:** 350.9
Land: 1.1 sq. mi.; **Water:** 0.0 sq. mi.
Incorporated May 20, 1856.

Bonaparte　　　　　　　　　　　　　　　City
ZIP: 52620　　　　**Lat:** 40-42-03 N **Long:** 91-48-01 W
Pop: 465 (1990); 489 (1980)　　**Pop Density:** 1162.5
Land: 0.4 sq. mi.; **Water:** 0.0 sq. mi.
Incorporated Jan 31, 1899.
Name origin: For Napoléon Bonaparte (1769–1821), emperor of France, who sold the Louisiana Territory to the United States, from which IA was formed.

Cantril　　　　　　　　　　　　　　　　　City
ZIP: 52542　　　　**Lat:** 40-38-35 N **Long:** 92-04-07 W
Pop: 262 (1990); 299 (1980)　　**Pop Density:** 524.0
Land: 0.5 sq. mi.; **Water:** 0.0 sq. mi.
Incorporated Jun 4, 1874.

Farmington　　　　　　　　　　　　　　City
ZIP: 52626　　　　**Lat:** 40-38-19 N **Long:** 91-44-19 W
Pop: 655 (1990); 869 (1980)　　**Pop Density:** 1310.0
Land: 0.5 sq. mi.; **Water:** 0.0 sq. mi.　　**Elev:** 569 ft.
Incorporated Jan 11, 1841.
Name origin: For area's main economic activity.

Keosauqua　　　　　　　　　　　　　　　City
ZIP: 52565　　　　**Lat:** 40-44-04 N **Long:** 91-57-37 W
Pop: 1,020 (1990); 1,003 (1980)　　**Pop Density:** 680.0
Land: 1.5 sq. mi.; **Water:** 0.1 sq. mi.
Incorporated Feb 5, 1851.
Name origin: Meaning of the name in doubt; possibly 'great bend,' referring to a great horseshoe bend in the Des Moines River here.

Milton　　　　　　　　　　　　　　　　　　City
ZIP: 52570　　　　**Lat:** 40-40-16 N **Long:** 92-09-45 W
Pop: 506 (1990); 567 (1980)　　**Pop Density:** 202.4
Land: 2.5 sq. mi.; **Water:** 0.0 sq. mi.
Incorporated May 20, 1878.

Mount Sterling　　　　　　　　　　　　City
ZIP: 52573　　　　**Lat:** 40-37-08 N **Long:** 91-56-20 W
Pop: 53 (1990); 96 (1980)　　**Pop Density:** 132.5
Land: 0.4 sq. mi.; **Water:** 0.0 sq. mi.
Incorporated Oct 29, 1907.

Stockport　　　　　　　　　　　　　　　　City
ZIP: 52651　　　　**Lat:** 40-51-25 N **Long:** 91-49-59 W
Pop: 260 (1990); 272 (1980)　　**Pop Density:** 260.0
Land: 1.0 sq. mi.; **Water:** 0.0 sq. mi.
Incorporated Jan 9, 1903.

IOWA, Wapello County

Wapello County
County Seat: Ottumwa (ZIP: 52501)

Pop: 35,687 (1990); 40,241 (1980)
Land: 431.8 sq. mi.; **Water:** 4.2 sq. mi.
Pop Density: 82.6
Area Code: 515

In south-central IA; established Feb 17, 1843 (prior to statehood) from Indian lands.

Name origin: For Wapello (1787–1842), a Fox Indian chief who figured prominently in the signing of several treaties. Variously translated as 'light,' 'dawn,' and 'he of the morning.' It may be just a birth-time designation, for which the last translation would be correct.

Agency   City
Lat: 40-59-48 N **Long:** 92-18-26 W
Pop: 616 (1990); 657 (1980)   **Pop Density:** 1026.7
Land: 0.6 sq. mi.; **Water:** 0.0 sq. mi.
Incorporated Jan 6, 1859.

Name origin: Named in 1838 for the Sac and Fox Indian Agency established here.

Blakesburg   City
ZIP: 52536   **Lat:** 40-57-42 N **Long:** 92-38-07 W
Pop: 333 (1990); 404 (1980)   **Pop Density:** 1110.0
Land: 0.3 sq. mi.; **Water:** 0.0 sq. mi.
Incorporated Dec 31, 1900.

Chillicothe   City
ZIP: 52548   **Lat:** 41-05-09 N **Long:** 92-31-46 W
Pop: 119 (1990); 131 (1980)   **Pop Density:** 595.0
Land: 0.2 sq. mi.; **Water:** 0.0 sq. mi.
Incorporated Dec 22, 1881.

Name origin: From Shawnee *chilakatha*, the name of one of the four principal divisions of the Shawnee tribe, whose main village always bore this name. Meaning is unsure, possibly 'village.'

Eddyville   City
Lat: 41-09-31 N **Long:** 92-37-34 W
Pop: 837 (1990); 920 (1980)   **Pop Density:** 930.0
Land: 0.9 sq. mi.; **Water:** 0.0 sq. mi.
Incorporated Feb 22, 1900. Part of the town is also in Mahaska and Monroe counties.

Eldon   City
ZIP: 52554   **Lat:** 40-55-03 N **Long:** 92-13-05 W
Pop: 1,070 (1990); 1,255 (1980)   **Pop Density:** 972.7
Land: 1.1 sq. mi.; **Water:** 0.0 sq. mi.
Incorporated Apr 29, 1872.

Kirkville   City
ZIP: 52566   **Lat:** 41-08-34 N **Long:** 92-30-08 W
Pop: 177 (1990); 220 (1980)   **Pop Density:** 295.0
Land: 0.6 sq. mi.; **Water:** 0.0 sq. mi.
Incorporated Dec 2, 1883.

Ottumwa   City
ZIP: 52501   **Lat:** 41-01-11 N **Long:** 92-25-05 W
Pop: 24,488 (1990); 27,381 (1980)   **Pop Density:** 1559.7
Land: 15.7 sq. mi.; **Water:** 0.7 sq. mi.

In southeastern IA on the Des Moines River, 74 mi. southeast of Des Moines. Incorporated Feb 2, 1888.

Name origin: For the former Fox village of Ottumwah. Possible meanings of the name are 'place of the lone chief' or 'tumbling water.'

Warren County
County Seat: Indianola (ZIP: 50125)

Pop: 36,033 (1990); 34,878 (1980)
Land: 571.7 sq. mi.; **Water:** 1.6 sq. mi.
Pop Density: 63.0
Area Code: 515

In south-central IA, south of Des Moines; established Jan 13, 1846 from Polk County.

Name origin: For Dr. Joseph Warren (1741–75), Revolutionary War patriot and member of the Committee of Safety who sent Paul Revere (1735–1818) on his famous ride.

Ackworth   City
ZIP: 50001   **Lat:** 41-21-54 N **Long:** 93-28-22 W
Pop: 66 (1990); 83 (1980)   **Pop Density:** 330.0
Land: 0.2 sq. mi.; **Water:** 0.0 sq. mi.
Incorporated May 9, 1881.

Bevington   City
ZIP: 50033   **Lat:** 41-21-36 N **Long:** 93-47-11 W
Pop: 23 (1990); 5 (1980)   **Pop Density:** 230.0
Land: 0.1 sq. mi.; **Water:** 0.0 sq. mi.
Incorporated Feb 1, 1916. Part of the town is also in Madison County.

Carlisle — City
Lat: 41-29-56 N Long: 93-29-24 W
Pop: 3,236 (1990); 3,073 (1980)   Pop Density: 2489.2
Land: 1.3 sq. mi.; Water: 0.0 sq. mi.
Incorporated May 19, 1870. Part of the town is also in Polk County.

Cumming — City
ZIP: 50061   Lat: 41-29-04 N Long: 93-45-42 W
Pop: 132 (1990); 151 (1980)   Pop Density: 264.0
Land: 0.5 sq. mi.; Water: 0.0 sq. mi.
Incorporated Oct 21, 1924.

Hartford — City
ZIP: 50118   Lat: 41-27-27 N Long: 93-24-13 W
Pop: 768 (1990); 761 (1980)   Pop Density: 768.0
Land: 1.0 sq. mi.; Water: 0.0 sq. mi.
Incorporated Jun 29, 1913.

Indianola — City
ZIP: 50125   Lat: 41-21-38 N Long: 93-33-55 W
Pop: 11,340 (1990); 10,843 (1980)   Pop Density: 1350.0
Land: 8.4 sq. mi.; Water: 0.0 sq. mi.
In south-central IA, 15 mi. south of Des Moines. Incorporated Oct 5, 1863.
Name origin: From *Indian* plus either a pseudo-Latin ending or from Choctaw term *-olah* meaning 'this side of.'

Lacona — City
ZIP: 50139   Lat: 41-11-23 N Long: 93-23-03 W
Pop: 357 (1990); 376 (1980)   Pop Density: 1190.0
Land: 0.3 sq. mi.; Water: 0.0 sq. mi.
Incorporated Nov 25, 1881.

Martensdale — City
ZIP: 50160   Lat: 41-22-26 N Long: 93-44-17 W
Pop: 491 (1990); 438 (1980)   Pop Density: 1227.5
Land: 0.4 sq. mi.; Water: 0.0 sq. mi.
Incorporated Oct 29, 1920.

Milo — City
ZIP: 50166   Lat: 41-17-21 N Long: 93-26-18 W
Pop: 864 (1990); 778 (1980)   Pop Density: 1440.0
Land: 0.6 sq. mi.; Water: 0.0 sq. mi.
Incorporated Nov 4, 1880.

New Virginia — City
ZIP: 50210   Lat: 41-10-51 N Long: 93-43-49 W
Pop: 433 (1990); 512 (1980)   Pop Density: 866.0
Land: 0.5 sq. mi.; Water: 0.0 sq. mi.
Incorporated Apr 27, 1901.

Norwalk — City
ZIP: 50211   Lat: 41-29-52 N Long: 93-40-51 W
Pop: 5,726 (1990); 2,676 (1980)   Pop Density: 1122.7
Land: 5.1 sq. mi.; Water: 0.2 sq. mi.
Incorporated Jun 15, 1901.
Name origin: For Norwalk, CT.

St. Marys — City
Lat: 41-18-31 N Long: 93-43-59 W
Pop: 113 (1990); 111 (1980)   Pop Density: 1130.0
Land: 0.1 sq. mi.; Water: 0.0 sq. mi.   Elev: 1033 ft.
Incorporated Apr 5, 1923.

Sandyville — City
ZIP: 50001   Lat: 41-22-12 N Long: 93-23-07 W
Pop: 59 (1990); 86 (1980)   Pop Density: 118.0
Land: 0.5 sq. mi.; Water: 0.0 sq. mi.

Spring Hill — City
Lat: 41-24-43 N Long: 93-38-56 W
Pop: 86 (1990); 95 (1980)   Pop Density: 860.0
Land: 0.1 sq. mi.; Water: 0.0 sq. mi.
Incorporated Nov 22, 1881.

Washington County
County Seat: Washington (ZIP: 52353)

Pop: 19,612 (1990); 20,141 (1980)   Pop Density: 34.5
Land: 568.8 sq. mi.; Water: 2.0 sq. mi.   Area Code: 319
In southeastern IA, south of Iowa City; established Jan 16, 1837 (prior to statehood) from Wisconsin Territory.
Name origin: For George Washington (1732–1799), American patriot and first U.S. president.

Ainsworth — City
ZIP: 52201   Lat: 41-17-24 N Long: 91-33-14 W
Pop: 506 (1990); 547 (1980)   Pop Density: 1265.0
Land: 0.4 sq. mi.; Water: 0.0 sq. mi.
Incorporated Jun 18, 1892.
Name origin: For D. H. Ainsworth, a civil engineer.

Brighton — City
ZIP: 52540   Lat: 41-10-27 N Long: 91-49-14 W
Pop: 684 (1990); 804 (1980)   Pop Density: 977.1
Land: 0.7 sq. mi.; Water: 0.0 sq. mi.
Incorporated Jul 26, 1870.
Name origin: Probably for Brighton, England.

Coppock — City
ZIP: 52654   Lat: 41-09-51 N Long: 91-42-52 W
Pop: 12 (1990); 8 (1980)   Pop Density: 120.0
Land: 0.1 sq. mi.; Water: 0.0 sq. mi.
Incorporated Aug 24, 1901. Part of the town is also in Jefferson and Henry counties.

Crawfordsville — City
ZIP: 52621   Lat: 41-12-51 N Long: 91-32-09 W
Pop: 265 (1990); 290 (1980)   Pop Density: 662.5
Land: 0.4 sq. mi.; Water: 0.0 sq. mi.
Incorporated Mar 26, 1891.

IOWA, Washington County

Kalona
City
ZIP: 52247 **Lat:** 41-29-15 N **Long:** 91-42-01 W
Pop: 1,942 (1990); 1,862 (1980) **Pop Density:** 1022.1
Land: 1.9 sq. mi.; **Water:** 0.0 sq. mi.
Incorporated May 22, 1890.

Riverside
City
ZIP: 52327 **Lat:** 41-28-56 N **Long:** 91-34-23 W
Pop: 824 (1990); 826 (1980) **Pop Density:** 824.0
Land: 1.0 sq. mi.; **Water:** 0.0 sq. mi.
Incorporated Mar 22, 1882.
Name origin: For its location.

Washington
City
ZIP: 52353 **Lat:** 41-17-55 N **Long:** 91-41-27 W
Pop: 7,074 (1990); 6,584 (1980) **Pop Density:** 1537.8
Land: 4.6 sq. mi.; **Water:** 0.0 sq. mi.
Incorporated Jun 6, 1864.
Name origin: For George Washington (1732–99), first U.S. president.

Wellman
City
ZIP: 52356 **Lat:** 41-28-04 N **Long:** 91-50-13 W
Pop: 1,085 (1990); 1,125 (1980) **Pop Density:** 1356.3
Land: 0.8 sq. mi.; **Water:** 0.0 sq. mi.
Incorporated Oct 28, 1885.

West Chester
City
ZIP: 52359 **Lat:** 41-20-24 N **Long:** 91-48-58 W
Pop: 178 (1990); 191 (1980) **Pop Density:** 593.3
Land: 0.3 sq. mi.; **Water:** 0.0 sq. mi.
Incorporated Apr 17, 1899.

Wayne County
County Seat: Corydon (ZIP: 50060)

Pop: 7,067 (1990); 8,199 (1980) **Pop Density:** 13.4
Land: 525.6 sq. mi.; **Water:** 1.5 sq. mi. **Area Code:** 515
On the central southern border of IA; established Jan 16, 1846 from Appanoose County.
Name origin: For Gen. Anthony Wayne (1745–96), PA soldier and statesman, nicknamed "Mad Anthony" for his daring during the Revolutionary War.

Allerton
City
ZIP: 50008 **Lat:** 40-42-29 N **Long:** 93-22-01 W
Pop: 599 (1990); 670 (1980) **Pop Density:** 599.0
Land: 1.0 sq. mi.; **Water:** 0.0 sq. mi.
Incorporated Oct 1, 1874.

Clio
City
ZIP: 50052 **Lat:** 40-38-04 N **Long:** 93-27-06 W
Pop: 103 (1990); 106 (1980) **Pop Density:** 147.1
Land: 0.7 sq. mi.; **Water:** 0.0 sq. mi.
Incorporated Feb 20, 1882.

Corydon
City
ZIP: 50060 **Lat:** 40-45-32 N **Long:** 93-19-03 W
Pop: 1,675 (1990); 1,818 (1980) **Pop Density:** 1395.8
Land: 1.2 sq. mi.; **Water:** 0.0 sq. mi.
Incorporated Apr 27, 1867.

Humeston
City
ZIP: 50123 **Lat:** 40-51-37 N **Long:** 93-29-48 W
Pop: 553 (1990); 671 (1980) **Pop Density:** 921.7
Land: 0.6 sq. mi.; **Water:** 0.0 sq. mi.
Incorporated Mar 4, 1881.

Lineville
City
ZIP: 50147 **Lat:** 40-35-09 N **Long:** 93-31-25 W
Pop: 289 (1990); 319 (1980) **Pop Density:** 321.1
Land: 0.9 sq. mi.; **Water:** 0.0 sq. mi.
Incorporated Nov 6, 1871.
Name origin: Named in 1871 for its location on the IA-MO state line. Originally known as Grand River.

Millerton
City
ZIP: 50165 **Lat:** 40-50-57 N **Long:** 93-18-24 W
Pop: 44 (1990); 72 (1980) **Pop Density:** 440.0
Land: 0.1 sq. mi.; **Water:** 0.0 sq. mi.
Incorporated Apr 26, 1915.

Promise City
City
ZIP: 52583 **Lat:** 40-44-48 N **Long:** 93-09-03 W
Pop: 132 (1990); 149 (1980) **Pop Density:** 660.0
Land: 0.2 sq. mi.; **Water:** 0.0 sq. mi.
Platted 1855; incorporated Aug 23, 1901.
Name origin: For the hope of early settlers, that this would become an important center.

Seymour
City
ZIP: 52590 **Lat:** 40-40-58 N **Long:** 93-07-18 W
Pop: 869 (1990); 1,036 (1980) **Pop Density:** 362.1
Land: 2.4 sq. mi.; **Water:** 0.0 sq. mi.
Incorporated Feb 28, 1874.

Webster County
County Seat: Fort Dodge (ZIP: 50501)

Pop: 40,342 (1990); 45,953 (1980) **Pop Density:** 56.4
Land: 715.3 sq. mi.; **Water:** 2.8 sq. mi. **Area Code:** 515
In central IA, northwest of Ames; established Jan 12, 1853 from Yell and Risley counties, both of which were organized in 1851 and abolished in 1853.
Name origin: For Daniel Webster (1782–1852), U.S. statesman and orator from MA.

Badger City
ZIP: 50516 **Lat:** 42-36-44 N **Long:** 94-08-33 W
Pop: 569 (1990); 653 (1980) **Pop Density:** 334.7
Land: 1.7 sq. mi.; **Water:** 0.0 sq. mi.
Incorporated Dec 28, 1899.

Barnum City
ZIP: 50518 **Lat:** 42-30-24 N **Long:** 94-21-51 W
Pop: 174 (1990); 198 (1980) **Pop Density:** 580.0
Land: 0.3 sq. mi.; **Water:** 0.0 sq. mi.
Incorporated May 29, 1894.

Callender City
ZIP: 50523 **Lat:** 42-21-43 N **Long:** 94-17-44 W
Pop: 384 (1990); 446 (1980) **Pop Density:** 768.0
Land: 0.5 sq. mi.; **Water:** 0.0 sq. mi.
Incorporated Nov 17, 1893.

Clare City
ZIP: 50524 **Lat:** 42-35-15 N **Long:** 94-20-40 W
Pop: 161 (1990); 229 (1980) **Pop Density:** 536.7
Land: 0.3 sq. mi.; **Water:** 0.0 sq. mi.
Incorporated Mar 29, 1892.

Dayton City
ZIP: 50530 **Lat:** 42-15-42 N **Long:** 94-04-17 W
Pop: 818 (1990); 941 (1980) **Pop Density:** 1022.5
Land: 0.8 sq. mi.; **Water:** 0.0 sq. mi.
Incorporated Jul 8, 1881.

Duncombe City
ZIP: 50532 **Lat:** 42-28-11 N **Long:** 93-59-45 W
Pop: 488 (1990); 504 (1980) **Pop Density:** 244.0
Land: 2.0 sq. mi.; **Water:** 0.0 sq. mi.
Incorporated Jan 25, 1893.
Name origin: For Hon. J. F. Duncombe.

Farnhamville City
ZIP: 50538 **Lat:** 42-16-47 N **Long:** 94-23-42 W
Pop: 0 (1990)
Land: 0.02 sq. mi.; **Water:** 0.0 sq. mi.
Incorporated Apr 1, 1893. Part of the town is also in Calhoun County.

Fort Dodge City
ZIP: 50501 **Lat:** 42-30-28 N **Long:** 94-10-36 W
Pop: 25,894 (1990); 29,423 (1980) **Pop Density:** 1798.2
Land: 14.4 sq. mi.; **Water:** 0.3 sq. mi.
In north-central IA, 70 mi. northwest of Des Moines. Incorporated Oct 26, 1869.
Name origin: For Henry Dodge (1782–1867), U.S. legislator and governor of WI (1836–41; 1845–48).

Gowrie City
ZIP: 50543 **Lat:** 42-16-36 N **Long:** 94-17-18 W
Pop: 1,028 (1990); 1,089 (1980) **Pop Density:** 642.5
Land: 1.6 sq. mi.; **Water:** 0.0 sq. mi. **Elev:** 1137 ft.
Incorporated Mar 18, 1881.

Harcourt City
ZIP: 50544 **Lat:** 42-15-39 N **Long:** 94-10-29 W
Pop: 306 (1990); 347 (1980) **Pop Density:** 306.0
Land: 1.0 sq. mi.; **Water:** 0.0 sq. mi.
Incorporated Feb 11, 1896.

Lehigh City
ZIP: 50557 **Lat:** 42-21-21 N **Long:** 94-03-11 W
Pop: 536 (1990); 654 (1980) **Pop Density:** 255.2
Land: 2.1 sq. mi.; **Water:** 0.1 sq. mi.
Incorporated Feb 10, 1883.
Name origin: For the Lehigh River, a tributary of the Delaware in PA; from a Delaware Indian term meaning 'forked stream'; so-named by settlers from the region.

Moorland City
ZIP: 50566 **Lat:** 42-26-27 N **Long:** 94-17-38 W
Pop: 209 (1990); 257 (1980) **Pop Density:** 209.0
Land: 1.0 sq. mi.; **Water:** 0.0 sq. mi.
Incorporated Oct 6, 1902.
Name origin: Descriptive of the land encountered by the first settlers.

Otho City
ZIP: 50569 **Lat:** 42-25-15 N **Long:** 94-08-51 W
Pop: 529 (1990); 692 (1980) **Pop Density:** 1322.5
Land: 0.4 sq. mi.; **Water:** 0.0 sq. mi.
Incorporated Jun 3, 1954.

Stratford City
ZIP: 50249 **Lat:** 42-16-10 N **Long:** 93-56-11 W
Pop: 36 (1990); 31 (1980) **Pop Density:** 51.4
Land: 0.7 sq. mi.; **Water:** 0.0 sq. mi.
Incorporated Sep 27, 1883. Part of the town is also in Hamilton County.
Name origin: For Stratford, CT.

Vincent City
ZIP: 50594 **Lat:** 42-35-28 N **Long:** 94-01-04 W
Pop: 185 (1990); 207 (1980) **Pop Density:** 925.0
Land: 0.2 sq. mi.; **Water:** 0.0 sq. mi.
Incorporated May 27, 1898.

IOWA, Winnebago County

Winnebago County
County Seat: Forest City (ZIP: 50436)

Pop: 12,122 (1990); 13,010 (1980) **Pop Density:** 30.3
Land: 400.5 sq. mi.; **Water:** 1.1 sq. mi. **Area Code:** 515

On the central northern border of IA, northwest of Mason City; established Feb 20, 1847 from Kossuth County.

Name origin: For the Indian tribe of Siouan linguistic stock; their name is thought to mean 'fish eaters.'

Buffalo Center City
ZIP: 50424 **Lat:** 43-23-23 N **Long:** 93-56-35 W
Pop: 1,081 (1990); 1,233 (1980) **Pop Density:** 982.7
Land: 1.1 sq. mi.; **Water:** 0.0 sq. mi.
Incorporated Feb 17, 1894.
Name origin: For the large herds of buffalo the first settlers found.

Forest City Township
ZIP: 50436 **Lat:** 43-15-54 N **Long:** 93-38-18 W
Pop: 4,075 (1990); 3,920 (1980) **Pop Density:** 1771.7
Land: 2.3 sq. mi.; **Water:** 0.0 sq. mi.
Incorporated Jun 14, 1878. Part of the town is also in Hancock County.

Lake Mills City
ZIP: 50450 **Lat:** 43-24-58 N **Long:** 93-31-55 W
Pop: 2,143 (1990); 2,281 (1980) **Pop Density:** 824.2
Land: 2.6 sq. mi.; **Water:** 0.0 sq. mi.
Incorporated Jun 7, 1880.

Leland City
ZIP: 50453 **Lat:** 43-20-01 N **Long:** 93-38-13 W
Pop: 311 (1990); 274 (1980) **Pop Density:** 207.3
Land: 1.5 sq. mi.; **Water:** 0.0 sq. mi.
Incorporated Feb 28, 1895.

Rake City
ZIP: 50465 **Lat:** 43-28-52 N **Long:** 93-55-15 W
Pop: 238 (1990); 283 (1980) **Pop Density:** 238.0
Land: 1.0 sq. mi.; **Water:** 0.0 sq. mi.
Incorporated Jan 20, 1908.

Scarville City
ZIP: 50473 **Lat:** 43-28-14 N **Long:** 93-36-58 W
Pop: 92 (1990); 82 (1980) **Pop Density:** 920.0
Land: 0.1 sq. mi.; **Water:** 0.0 sq. mi.
Incorporated Apr 11, 1904.

Thompson City
ZIP: 50478 **Lat:** 43-22-10 N **Long:** 93-46-27 W
Pop: 498 (1990); 668 (1980) **Pop Density:** 622.5
Land: 0.8 sq. mi.; **Water:** 0.0 sq. mi.
Incorporated Feb 24, 1894.

Winneshiek County
County Seat: Decorah (ZIP: 52101)

Pop: 20,847 (1990); 21,876 (1980) **Pop Density:** 30.2
Land: 689.7 sq. mi.; **Water:** 0.3 sq. mi. **Area Code:** 319

On the central northern border of IA, northwest of Mason City; established Feb 20, 1847 from Indian lands.

Name origin: For the younger (1812–72?) of two chiefs of the Winnebago tribe with the same name; he took part in the Black Hawk War. Name probably formed from *Winne* for Winnebago and *shiek* 'leader.'

Calmar City
ZIP: 52132 **Lat:** 43-10-45 N **Long:** 91-52-00 W
Pop: 1,026 (1990); 1,053 (1980) **Pop Density:** 1026.0
Land: 1.0 sq. mi.; **Water:** 0.0 sq. mi.
Incorporated Jul 14, 1869.

Castalia City
ZIP: 52133 **Lat:** 43-06-42 N **Long:** 91-40-35 W
Pop: 177 (1990); 188 (1980) **Pop Density:** 252.9
Land: 0.7 sq. mi.; **Water:** 0.0 sq. mi.
Incorporated Aug 16, 1901.

Decorah City
ZIP: 52101 **Lat:** 43-18-18 N **Long:** 91-47-35 W
Pop: 8,063 (1990); 7,991 (1980) **Pop Density:** 1366.6
Land: 5.9 sq. mi.; **Water:** 0.0 sq. mi.
Incorporated Jun 30, 1857.
Name origin: For a noted line of Winnebago Indians descended from Waukon, who was born in 1729, the son of Hopoekaw and a French officer, Sabrevoir de Carrie, whose last name was corrupted to Decorah.

Fort Atkinson City
ZIP: 52144 **Lat:** 43-08-38 N **Long:** 91-56-04 W
Pop: 367 (1990); 374 (1980) **Pop Density:** 1223.3
Land: 0.3 sq. mi.; **Water:** 0.0 sq. mi.
Incorporated Jun 5, 1895.

Jackson Junction City
Lat: 43-06-11 N **Long:** 92-02-52 W
Pop: 87 (1990); 94 (1980) **Pop Density:** 14.5
Land: 6.0 sq. mi.; **Water:** 0.0 sq. mi.
Incorporated Jan 9, 1897.

Ossian   City
ZIP: 52161   **Lat:** 43-08-48 N **Long:** 91-45-52 W
Pop: 810 (1990); 829 (1980)   **Pop Density:** 810.0
Land: 1.0 sq. mi.; **Water:** 0.0 sq. mi.
Incorporated Feb 10, 1876.

Ridgeway   City
ZIP: 52165   **Lat:** 43-17-49 N **Long:** 91-59-27 W
Pop: 295 (1990); 308 (1980)   **Pop Density:** 268.2
Land: 1.1 sq. mi.; **Water:** 0.0 sq. mi.
Incorporated Mar 15, 1894.

Spillville   City
ZIP: 52168   **Lat:** 43-12-14 N **Long:** 91-57-06 W
Pop: 387 (1990); 415 (1980)   **Pop Density:** 967.5
Land: 0.4 sq. mi.; **Water:** 0.0 sq. mi.
Incorporated Dec 5, 1894.

Woodbury County
County Seat: Sioux City (ZIP: 51101)

Pop: 98,276 (1990); 100,884 (1980)   **Pop Density:** 112.6
Land: 872.7 sq. mi.; **Water:** 4.8 sq. mi.   **Area Code:** 712
On the western border of IA; established Jan 15, 1851 from Indian lands.
Name origin: For Levi Woodbury (1789–1851), governor of NH (1823–24), U.S. senator (1825–31; 1841–45), U.S. secretary of the navy (1831–34), U.S. secretary of the treasury (1834–41), and U.S. Supreme Court Justice (1845–51).

Anthon   City
ZIP: 51004   **Lat:** 42-23-15 N **Long:** 95-51-57 W
Pop: 638 (1990); 687 (1980)   **Pop Density:** 911.4
Land: 0.7 sq. mi.; **Water:** 0.0 sq. mi.
Incorporated Jul 25, 1890.

Bronson   City
ZIP: 51007   **Lat:** 42-24-34 N **Long:** 96-12-40 W
Pop: 209 (1990); 289 (1980)   **Pop Density:** 696.7
Land: 0.3 sq. mi.; **Water:** 0.0 sq. mi.
Incorporated Jun 8, 1967.

Correctionville   City
ZIP: 51016   **Lat:** 42-28-41 N **Long:** 95-47-00 W
Pop: 897 (1990); 935 (1980)   **Pop Density:** 1495.0
Land: 0.6 sq. mi.; **Water:** 0.0 sq. mi.
Incorporated Oct 3, 1882.
Name origin: For its location on a surveying correction line.

Cushing   City
ZIP: 51018   **Lat:** 42-27-54 N **Long:** 95-40-33 W
Pop: 220 (1990); 270 (1980)   **Pop Density:** 733.3
Land: 0.3 sq. mi.; **Water:** 0.0 sq. mi.   **Elev:** 1327 ft.
Incorporated Nov 21, 1892.

Danbury   City
ZIP: 51019   **Lat:** 42-14-13 N **Long:** 95-43-17 W
Pop: 430 (1990); 492 (1980)   **Pop Density:** 1075.0
Land: 0.4 sq. mi.; **Water:** 0.0 sq. mi.
Incorporated Oct 1, 1881.
Name origin: Probably for Danbury in Essex, England.

Hornick   City
ZIP: 51026   **Lat:** 42-13-51 N **Long:** 96-05-46 W
Pop: 222 (1990); 239 (1980)   **Pop Density:** 740.0
Land: 0.3 sq. mi.; **Water:** 0.0 sq. mi.   **Elev:** 1067 ft.
Incorporated Jun 23, 1896.

Lawton   City
ZIP: 51030   **Lat:** 42-28-43 N **Long:** 96-11-03 W
Pop: 482 (1990); 447 (1980)   **Pop Density:** 964.0
Land: 0.5 sq. mi.; **Water:** 0.0 sq. mi.   **Elev:** 1179 ft.
Incorporated 1906.

Moville   City
ZIP: 51039   **Lat:** 42-29-22 N **Long:** 96-04-00 W
Pop: 1,306 (1990); 1,273 (1980)   **Pop Density:** 1632.5
Land: 0.8 sq. mi.; **Water:** 0.0 sq. mi.
Incorporated Aug 13, 1889.
Name origin: For a combination of *Mo* for Missouri and the French term *ville* 'town.'

Oto   City
ZIP: 51044   **Lat:** 42-16-53 N **Long:** 95-53-37 W
Pop: 118 (1990); 172 (1980)   **Pop Density:** 393.3
Land: 0.3 sq. mi.; **Water:** 0.0 sq. mi.
Incorporated Jul 10, 1888.
Name origin: For the Oto(e) Indian tribe.

Pierson   City
ZIP: 51048   **Lat:** 42-32-37 N **Long:** 95-52-00 W
Pop: 341 (1990); 408 (1980)   **Pop Density:** 682.0
Land: 0.5 sq. mi.; **Water:** 0.0 sq. mi.
Incorporated Nov 27, 1891.

Salix   City
ZIP: 51052   **Lat:** 42-18-34 N **Long:** 96-17-11 W
Pop: 367 (1990); 429 (1980)   **Pop Density:** 611.7
Land: 0.6 sq. mi.; **Water:** 0.0 sq. mi.   **Elev:** 1083 ft.
Incorporated Apr 19, 1893.

Sergeant Bluff   City
ZIP: 51054   **Lat:** 42-24-02 N **Long:** 96-21-20 W
Pop: 2,772 (1990); 2,416 (1980)   **Pop Density:** 1260.0
Land: 2.2 sq. mi.; **Water:** 0.0 sq. mi.   **Elev:** 1092 ft.
Established 1854; incorporated May 1, 1904.
Name origin: For Sgt. Charles Floyd (?–1804), the only man to die on the Lewis and Clark expedition (1803–6). He was buried on a bluff on the IA side of the Missouri River.

IOWA, Woodbury County　　　　　　　　　　　　　　　　　　　　　　　　　　　*American Places Dictionary*

Sioux City　　　　　　　　　　　　　City
ZIP: 51101　　　　　　　**Lat:** 42-30-00 N **Long:** 96-23-38 W
Pop: 80,505 (1990); 82,003 (1980)　　**Pop Density:** 1482.6
Land: 54.3 sq. mi.; **Water:** 1.1 sq. mi.　　**Elev:** 1117 ft.
In western IA on the Missouri River where the Big Sioux and Floyd rivers join. Platted 1854; incorporated Jan 16, 1857.
Name origin: For the Indians, sometimes known as the Dakotas. The name is from Ojibway *nadouessioux* 'snakes' or 'enemies,' a designation rival tribes applied to each other.

Sloan　　　　　　　　　　　　　City
ZIP: 51055　　　　　　　**Lat:** 42-14-03 N **Long:** 96-13-26 W
Pop: 938 (1990); 978 (1980)　　**Pop Density:** 2345.0
Land: 0.4 sq. mi.; **Water:** 0.0 sq. mi.
Incorporated Oct 16, 1883.

Smithland　　　　　　　　　　　　　City
ZIP: 51056　　　　　　　**Lat:** 42-13-44 N **Long:** 95-55-53 W
Pop: 235 (1990); 282 (1980)　　**Pop Density:** 587.5
Land: 0.4 sq. mi.; **Water:** 0.0 sq. mi.　　**Elev:** 1090 ft.
Incorporated May 6, 1889.

Worth County
County Seat: Northwood (ZIP: 50459)

Pop: 7,991 (1990); 9,075 (1980)　　**Pop Density:** 20.0
Land: 400.0 sq. mi.; **Water:** 1.7 sq. mi.　　**Area Code:** 515
On the central northern border of IA, north of Mason City; established Jan 15, 1851 from Mitchell County.
Name origin: For Gen. William Jenkins Worth (1794–1849), officer in the War of 1812, Seminole War, and Mexican-American War; cited by Congress for bravery.

Fertile　　　　　　　　　　　　　City
ZIP: 50434　　　　　　　**Lat:** 43-15-53 N **Long:** 93-25-21 W
Pop: 382 (1990); 372 (1980)　　**Pop Density:** 424.4
Land: 0.9 sq. mi.; **Water:** 0.0 sq. mi.
Incorporated Apr 10, 1908.

Grafton　　　　　　　　　　　　　City
ZIP: 50440　　　　　　　**Lat:** 43-19-48 N **Long:** 93-04-11 W
Pop: 282 (1990); 255 (1980)　　**Pop Density:** 940.0
Land: 0.3 sq. mi.; **Water:** 0.0 sq. mi.
Incorporated Apr 10, 1896.

Hanlontown　　　　　　　　　　　　　City
ZIP: 50444　　　　　　　**Lat:** 43-16-51 N **Long:** 93-22-44 W
Pop: 193 (1990); 213 (1980)　　**Pop Density:** 193.0
Land: 1.0 sq. mi.; **Water:** 0.0 sq. mi.
Incorporated Jan 18, 1902.

Joice　　　　　　　　　　　　　City
ZIP: 50446　　　　　　　**Lat:** 43-21-51 N **Long:** 93-27-25 W
Pop: 245 (1990); 223 (1980)　　**Pop Density:** 245.0
Land: 1.0 sq. mi.; **Water:** 0.0 sq. mi.
Incorporated Jun 4, 1913.

Kensett　　　　　　　　　　　　　City
ZIP: 50448　　　　　　　**Lat:** 43-21-14 N **Long:** 93-12-39 W
Pop: 298 (1990); 360 (1980)　　**Pop Density:** 198.7
Land: 1.5 sq. mi.; **Water:** 0.0 sq. mi.　　**Elev:** 1225 ft.
Incorporated Feb 10, 1894.

Manly　　　　　　　　　　　　　City
ZIP: 50456　　　　　　　**Lat:** 43-17-17 N **Long:** 93-12-06 W
Pop: 1,349 (1990); 1,496 (1980)　　**Pop Density:** 899.3
Land: 1.5 sq. mi.; **Water:** 0.0 sq. mi.　　**Elev:** 1198 ft.
Incorporated Nov 19, 1898.

Northwood　　　　　　　　　　　　　City
ZIP: 50459　　　　　　　**Lat:** 43-26-40 N **Long:** 93-12-58 W
Pop: 1,940 (1990); 2,193 (1980)　　**Pop Density:** 510.5
Land: 3.8 sq. mi.; **Water:** 0.0 sq. mi.
Incorporated Jun 7, 1875.

Wright County
County Seat: Clarion (ZIP: 50525)

Pop: 14,269 (1990); 16,319 (1980)   **Pop Density:** 24.6
Land: 580.8 sq. mi.; **Water:** 1.8 sq. mi.   **Area Code:** 515

In north-central IA, northeast of Fort Dodge; established Jan 15, 1851 from Webster County.

Name origin: For Joseph Albert Wright (1810–67), IN legislator, governor (1849–57), and U.S. senator (1862–63). Also for Silas Wright (1795–1847), U.S. senator from NY (1833–44) and governor (1844–46).

Belmond   City
ZIP: 50421   **Lat:** 42-50-57 N   **Long:** 93-36-34 W
Pop: 2,500 (1990); 2,505 (1980)   **Pop Density:** 1315.8
Land: 1.9 sq. mi.; **Water:** 0.0 sq. mi.
Incorporated Oct 21, 1881.
Name origin: For settler Belle Dumond.

Clarion   City
ZIP: 50525   **Lat:** 42-43-55 N   **Long:** 93-43-55 W
Pop: 2,703 (1990); 3,060 (1980)   **Pop Density:** 1001.1
Land: 2.7 sq. mi.; **Water:** 0.0 sq. mi.
Incorporated Oct 15, 1881.

Dows   City
Lat: 42-39-29 N   **Long:** 93-30-13 W
Pop: 560 (1990); 635 (1980)   **Pop Density:** 1120.0
Land: 0.5 sq. mi.; **Water:** 0.0 sq. mi.
Incorporated May 3, 1892. Part of the town is also in Franklin County.

Eagle Grove   City
ZIP: 50533   **Lat:** 42-40-02 N   **Long:** 93-54-04 W
Pop: 3,671 (1990); 4,324 (1980)   **Pop Density:** 917.8
Land: 4.0 sq. mi.; **Water:** 0.0 sq. mi.
Incorporated Oct 16, 1882.
Name origin: For the many eagles that built nests in a local grove of tall trees.

Galt   City
ZIP: 50101   **Lat:** 42-41-38 N   **Long:** 93-36-17 W
Pop: 43 (1990); 60 (1980)   **Pop Density:** 86.0
Land: 0.5 sq. mi.; **Water:** 0.0 sq. mi.
Incorporated Jan 2, 1913.

Goldfield   City
Lat: 42-44-08 N   **Long:** 93-55-16 W
Pop: 710 (1990); 789 (1980)   **Pop Density:** 710.0
Land: 1.0 sq. mi.; **Water:** 0.0 sq. mi.   **Elev:** 1130 ft.
Incorporated Mar 19, 1885.

Rowan   City
ZIP: 50470   **Lat:** 42-44-24 N   **Long:** 93-32-58 W
Pop: 189 (1990); 259 (1980)   **Pop Density:** 315.0
Land: 0.6 sq. mi.; **Water:** 0.0 sq. mi.
Incorporated Dec 21, 1901.

Woolstock   City
ZIP: 50599   **Lat:** 42-33-55 N   **Long:** 93-50-36 W
Pop: 212 (1990); 235 (1980)   **Pop Density:** 212.0
Land: 1.0 sq. mi.; **Water:** 0.0 sq. mi.
Incorporated Apr 19, 1895.

Index to Places and Counties in Iowa

Ackley (Franklin) City ... 304
Ackley (Hardin) City ... 309
Ackworth (Warren) City ... 348
Adair (Adair) City ... 278
Adair (Guthrie) City ... 307
Adair County ... 278
Adams County ... 278
Adel (Dallas) City ... 296
Afton (Union) City ... 346
Agency (Wapello) City ... 348
Ainsworth (Washington) City ... 349
Akron (Plymouth) City ... 334
Albert City (Buena Vista) City ... 285
Albia (Monroe) City ... 330
Albion (Marshall) City ... 327
Alburnett (Linn) City ... 321
Alden (Hardin) City ... 309
Alexander (Franklin) City ... 304
Algona (Kossuth) City ... 320
Allamakee County ... 279
Alleman (Polk) City ... 336
Allerton (Wayne) City ... 350
Allison (Butler) City ... 286
Alta (Buena Vista) City ... 285
Alta Vista (Chickasaw) City ... 291
Alton (Sioux) City ... 343
Altoona (Polk) City ... 336
Alvord (Lyon) City ... 324
Ames (Story) City ... 344
Anamosa (Jones) City ... 318
Andover (Clinton) City ... 294
Andrew (Jackson) City ... 314
Anita (Cass) City ... 288
Ankeny (Polk) City ... 336
Anthon (Woodbury) City ... 353
Aplington (Butler) City ... 286
Appanoose County ... 279
Arcadia (Carroll) City ... 287
Archer (O'Brien) City ... 331
Aredale (Butler) City ... 286
Arion (Crawford) City ... 295
Arispe (Union) City ... 346
Arlington (Fayette) City ... 302
Armstrong (Emmet) City ... 302
Arnolds Park (Dickinson) City ... 300
Arthur (Ida) City ... 313
Asbury (Dubuque) City ... 300
Ashton (Osceola) City ... 332
Aspinwall (Crawford) City ... 295
Atalissa (Muscatine) City ... 331
Athelstan (Taylor) City ... 346
Atkins (Benton) City ... 281
Atlantic (Cass) City ... 288
Auburn (Sac) City ... 340
Audubon (Audubon) City ... 280
Audubon County ... 280
Aurelia (Cherokee) City ... 290
Aurora (Buchanan) City ... 284
Avoca (Pottawattamie) City ... 337
Ayrshire (Palo Alto) City ... 334
Badger (Webster) City ... 351
Bagley (Guthrie) City ... 307
Baldwin (Jackson) City ... 314
Balltown (Dubuque) City ... 300
Bancroft (Kossuth) City ... 320
Bankston (Dubuque) City ... 301
Barnes City (Mahaska) City ... 325
Barnes City (Poweshiek) City ... 338
Barnum (Webster) City ... 351
Bassett (Chickasaw) City ... 291

Batavia (Jefferson) City ... 316
Battle Creek (Ida) City ... 313
Baxter (Jasper) City ... 315
Bayard (Guthrie) City ... 307
Beacon (Mahaska) City ... 325
Beaconsfield (Ringgold) City ... 339
Beaman (Grundy) City ... 306
Beaver (Boone) City ... 283
Bedford (Taylor) City ... 346
Belle Plaine (Benton) City ... 281
Bellevue (Jackson) City ... 314
Belmond (Wright) City ... 355
Bennett (Cedar) City ... 289
Benton (Ringgold) City ... 339
Benton County ... 281
Berkley (Boone) City ... 283
Bernard (Dubuque) City ... 301
Bertram (Linn) City ... 321
Bettendorf (Scott) City ... 341
Bevington (Madison) City ... 325
Bevington (Warren) City ... 348
Birmingham (Van Buren) City ... 347
Black Hawk County ... 282
Blairsburg (Hamilton) City ... 308
Blairstown (Benton) City ... 281
Blakesburg (Wapello) City ... 348
Blanchard (Page) City ... 333
Blencoe (Monona) City ... 329
Blockton (Taylor) City ... 346
Bloomfield (Davis) City ... 297
Blue Grass (Scott) City ... 341
Bode (Humboldt) City ... 312
Bonaparte (Van Buren) City ... 347
Bondurant (Polk) City ... 336
Boone (Boone) City ... 283
Boone County ... 283
Bouton (Dallas) City ... 296
Boxholm (Boone) City ... 283
Boyden (Sioux) City ... 343
Braddyville (Page) City ... 333
Bradgate (Humboldt) City ... 312
Brandon (Buchanan) City ... 284
Brayton (Audubon) City ... 280
Breda (Carroll) City ... 287
Bremer County ... 283
Bridgewater (Adair) City ... 278
Brighton (Washington) City ... 349
Bristow (Butler) City ... 286
Britt (Hancock) City ... 308
Bronson (Woodbury) City ... 353
Brooklyn (Poweshiek) City ... 338
Brunsville (Plymouth) City ... 334
Buchanan County ... 284
Buckeye (Hardin) City ... 309
Buck Grove (Crawford) City ... 295
Buena Vista County ... 285
Buffalo (Scott) City ... 341
Buffalo Center (Winnebago) City ... 352
Burlington (Des Moines) City ... 299
Burt (Kossuth) City ... 320
Bussey (Marion) City ... 326
Butler County ... 286
Calamus (Clinton) City ... 294
Calhoun County ... 286
Callender (Webster) City ... 351
Calmar (Winneshiek) City ... 352
Calumet (O'Brien) City ... 331
Camanche (Clinton) City ... 294
Cambridge (Story) City ... 344
Cantril (Van Buren) City ... 347

Carbon (Adams) City ... 278
Carlisle (Polk) City ... 336
Carlisle (Warren) City ... 349
Carpenter (Mitchell) City ... 328
Carroll (Carroll) City ... 287
Carroll County ... 287
Carson (Pottawattamie) City ... 337
Carter Lake (Pottawattamie) City ... 337
Cascade (Dubuque) City ... 301
Cascade (Jones) City ... 318
Casey (Adair) City ... 278
Casey (Guthrie) City ... 307
Cass County ... 288
Castalia (Winneshiek) City ... 352
Castana (Monona) City ... 329
Cedar County ... 289
Cedar Falls (Black Hawk) City ... 282
Cedar Rapids (Linn) City ... 321
Center Junction (Jones) City ... 318
Center Point (Linn) City ... 322
Centerville (Appanoose) City ... 279
Central City (Linn) City ... 322
Centralia (Dubuque) City ... 301
Cerro Gordo County ... 290
Chariton (Lucas) City ... 323
Charles City (Floyd) City ... 303
Charlotte (Clinton) City ... 294
Charter Oak (Crawford) City ... 295
Chatsworth (Sioux) City ... 343
Chelsea (Tama) City ... 345
Cherokee (Cherokee) City ... 290
Cherokee County ... 290
Chester (Howard) City ... 312
Chickasaw County ... 291
Chillicothe (Wapello) City ... 348
Churdan (Greene) City ... 306
Cincinnati (Appanoose) City ... 279
Clare (Webster) City ... 351
Clarence (Cedar) City ... 289
Clarinda (Page) City ... 333
Clarion (Wright) City ... 355
Clarke County ... 292
Clarksville (Butler) City ... 286
Clay County ... 292
Clayton (Clayton) City ... 293
Clayton County ... 293
Clearfield (Ringgold) City ... 339
Clearfield (Taylor) City ... 346
Clear Lake (Cerro Gordo) City ... 290
Cleghorn (Cherokee) City ... 291
Clemons (Marshall) City ... 327
Clermont (Fayette) City ... 302
Clinton (Clinton) City ... 294
Clinton County ... 294
Clio (Wayne) City ... 350
Clive (Polk) City ... 336
Clutier (Tama) City ... 345
Coburg (Montgomery) City ... 330
Coggon (Linn) City ... 322
Coin (Page) City ... 333
Colesburg (Delaware) City ... 298
Colfax (Jasper) City ... 315
College Springs (Page) City ... 333
Collins (Story) City ... 344
Colo (Story) City ... 344
Columbus City (Louisa) City ... 323
Columbus Junction (Louisa) City ... 323
Colwell (Floyd) City ... 303
Conesville (Muscatine) City ... 331
Conrad (Grundy) City ... 306

Name	Page
Conway (Taylor) City	346
Coon Rapids (Carroll) City	287
Coppock (Henry) City	311
Coppock (Jefferson) City	316
Coppock (Washington) City	349
Coralville (Johnson) City	317
Corning (Adams) City	278
Correctionville (Woodbury) City	353
Corwith (Hancock) City	308
Corydon (Wayne) City	350
Cotter (Louisa) City	323
Coulter (Franklin) City	304
Council Bluffs (Pottawattamie) City	337
Craig (Plymouth) City	335
Crawford County	295
Crawfordsville (Washington) City	349
Crescent (Pottawattamie) City	337
Cresco (Howard) City	312
Creston (Union) City	346
Cromwell (Union) City	346
Crystal Lake (Hancock) City	308
Cumberland (Cass) City	288
Cumming (Warren) City	349
Curlew (Palo Alto) City	334
Cushing (Woodbury) City	353
Cylinder (Palo Alto) City	334
Dakota City (Humboldt) City	312
Dallas Center (Dallas) City	296
Dallas County	296
Dana (Greene) City	306
Danbury (Woodbury) City	353
Danville (Des Moines) City	299
Davenport (Scott) City	341
Davis City (Decatur) Township	297
Davis County	297
Dawson (Dallas) City	296
Dayton (Webster) City	351
Decatur City (Decatur) City	297
Decatur County	297
Decorah (Winneshiek) City	352
Dedham (Carroll) City	287
Deep River (Poweshiek) City	338
Defiance (Shelby) City	342
Delaware (Delaware) City	298
Delaware County	298
Delhi (Delaware) City	298
Delmar (Clinton) City	294
Deloit (Crawford) City	295
Delphos (Ringgold) City	339
Delta (Keokuk) City	318
Denison (Crawford) City	295
Denver (Bremer) City	283
Derby (Lucas) City	323
Des Moines (Polk) City	336
Des Moines County	299
De Soto (Dallas) City	296
De Witt (Clinton) City	294
Dexter (Dallas) City	296
Diagonal (Ringgold) City	339
Dickens (Clay) City	292
Dickinson County	300
Dike (Grundy) City	306
Dixon (Scott) City	341
Dolliver (Emmet) City	302
Donahue (Scott) City	341
Donnan (Fayette) City	302
Donnellson (Lee) City	321
Doon (Lyon) City	324
Dougherty (Cerro Gordo) City	290
Dow City (Crawford) City	295
Dows (Franklin) City	304
Dows (Wright) City	355
Drakesville (Davis) City	297
Dubuque (Dubuque) City	301
Dubuque County	300
Dumont (Butler) City	286
Duncombe (Webster) City	351
Dundee (Delaware) City	298
Dunkerton (Black Hawk) City	282
Dunlap (Harrison) City	310
Durango (Dubuque) City	301
Durant (Cedar) City	289
Durant (Muscatine) City	331
Durant (Scott) City	341
Dyersville (Delaware) City	298
Dyersville (Dubuque) City	301
Dysart (Tama) City	345
Eagle Grove (Wright) City	355
Earlham (Madison) City	325
Earling (Shelby) City	342
Earlville (Delaware) City	298
Early (Sac) City	340
East Peru (Madison) City	325
Eddyville (Mahaska) City	325
Eddyville (Monroe) City	330
Eddyville (Wapello) City	348
Edgewood (Clayton) City	293
Edgewood (Delaware) City	298
Elberon (Tama) City	345
Eldon (Wapello) City	348
Eldora (Hardin) City	309
Eldridge (Scott) City	341
Elgin (Fayette) City	302
Elkader (Clayton) City	293
Elkhart (Polk) City	336
Elk Horn (Shelby) City	342
Elkport (Clayton) City	293
Elk Run Heights (Black Hawk) City	282
Elliott (Montgomery) City	330
Ellston (Ringgold) City	339
Ellsworth (Hamilton) City	308
Elma (Howard) City	312
Ely (Linn) City	322
Emerson (Mills) City	328
Emmet County	302
Emmetsburg (Palo Alto) City	334
Epworth (Dubuque) City	301
Essex (Page) City	333
Estherville (Emmet) City	302
Evansdale (Black Hawk) City	282
Everly (Clay) City	292
Exira (Audubon) City	280
Exline (Appanoose) City	279
Fairbank (Buchanan) City	284
Fairbank (Fayette) City	302
Fairfax (Linn) City	322
Fairfield (Jefferson) City	316
Farley (Dubuque) City	301
Farmersburg (Clayton) City	293
Farmington (Van Buren) City	347
Farnhamville (Calhoun) City	286
Farnhamville (Webster) City	351
Farragut (Fremont) City	305
Fayette (Fayette) City	302
Fayette County	302
Fenton (Kossuth) City	320
Ferguson (Marshall) City	327
Fertile (Worth) City	354
Floris (Davis) City	297
Floyd (Floyd) City	303
Floyd County	303
Fonda (Pocahontas) City	335
Fontanelle (Adair) City	278
Forest City (Hancock) Township	309
Forest City (Winnebago) Township	352
Fort Atkinson (Winneshiek) City	352
Fort Dodge (Webster) City	351
Fort Madison (Lee) City	321
Fostoria (Clay) City	292
Franklin (Lee) City	321
Franklin County	304
Fraser (Boone) City	283
Fredericksburg (Chickasaw) City	291
Frederika (Bremer) City	283
Fredonia (Louisa) City	323
Fremont (Mahaska) City	325
Fremont County	305
Fruitland (Muscatine) City	331
Galt (Wright) City	355
Galva (Ida) City	313
Garber (Clayton) City	293
Garden Grove (Decatur) City	297
Garnavillo (Clayton) City	293
Garner (Hancock) City	309
Garrison (Benton) City	281
Garwin (Tama) City	345
Geneva (Franklin) City	304
George (Lyon) City	324
Gibson (Keokuk) City	318
Gilbert (Story) City	344
Gilbertville (Black Hawk) City	282
Gillett Grove (Clay) City	292
Gilman (Marshall) City	327
Gilmore City (Humboldt) Township	312
Gilmore City (Pocahontas) Township	335
Gladbrook (Tama) City	345
Glenwood (Mills) City	328
Glidden (Carroll) City	287
Goldfield (Wright) City	355
Goodell (Hancock) City	309
Goose Lake (Clinton) City	294
Gowrie (Webster) City	351
Graettinger (Palo Alto) City	334
Graf (Dubuque) City	301
Grafton (Worth) City	354
Grand Junction (Greene) City	306
Grand Mound (Clinton) City	294
Grand River (Decatur) City	297
Grandview (Louisa) City	323
Granger (Dallas) City	296
Grant (Montgomery) City	330
Granville (Sioux) City	343
Gravity (Taylor) City	346
Gray (Audubon) City	280
Greeley (Delaware) City	298
Greene (Butler) City	286
Greene County	306
Greenfield (Adair) City	278
Green Island (Jackson) City	314
Greenville (Clay) City	292
Grimes (Polk) City	336
Grinnell (Poweshiek) City	338
Griswold (Cass) City	288
Grundy Center (Grundy) City	306
Grundy County	306
Gruver (Emmet) City	302
Guernsey (Poweshiek) City	338
Guthrie Center (Guthrie) City	307
Guthrie County	307
Guttenberg (Clayton) City	293
Halbur (Carroll) City	288
Hamburg (Fremont) City	305
Hamilton (Marion) City	326
Hamilton County	308
Hampton (Franklin) City	304
Hancock (Pottawattamie) City	337
Hancock County	308
Hanlontown (Worth) City	354
Hansell (Franklin) City	304
Harcourt (Webster) City	351
Hardin County	309
Hardy (Humboldt) City	312
Harlan (Shelby) City	342
Harper (Keokuk) City	319

IOWA

Harpers Ferry (Allamakee) City 279
Harris (Osceola) City 332
Harrison County 310
Hartford (Warren) City 349
Hartley (O'Brien) City 332
Hartwick (Poweshiek) City 338
Harvey (Marion) City 326
Hastings (Mills) City 328
Havelock (Pocahontas) City 335
Haverhill (Marshall) City 327
Hawarden (Sioux) City 343
Hawkeye (Fayette) City 303
Hayesville (Keokuk) City 319
Hazleton (Buchanan) City 284
Hedrick (Keokuk) City 319
Henderson (Mills) City 328
Henry County 311
Hepburn (Page) City 333
Hiawatha (Linn) City 322
Hills (Johnson) City 317
Hillsboro (Henry) City 311
Hinton (Plymouth) City 335
Holland (Grundy) City 307
Holstein (Ida) City 313
Holy Cross (Dubuque) City 301
Hopkinton (Delaware) City 298
Hornick (Woodbury) City 353
Hospers (Sioux) City 343
Houghton (Lee) City 321
Howard County 312
Hubbard (Hardin) City 309
Hudson (Black Hawk) City 282
Hull (Sioux) City 343
Humboldt (Humboldt) City 313
Humboldt County 312
Humeston (Wayne) City 350
Huxley (Story) City 344
Ida County 313
Ida Grove (Ida) City 313
Imogene (Fremont) City 305
Independence (Buchanan) City 284
Indianola (Warren) City 349
Inwood (Lyon) City 324
Ionia (Chickasaw) City 291
Iowa City (Johnson) City 317
Iowa County 314
Iowa Falls (Hardin) City 309
Ireton (Sioux) City 343
Irwin (Shelby) City 342
Jackson County 314
Jackson Junction (Winneshiek) City . 352
Jamaica (Guthrie) City 307
Janesville (Black Hawk) City 282
Janesville (Bremer) City 284
Jasper County 315
Jefferson (Greene) City 306
Jefferson County 316
Jesup (Buchanan) City 284
Jewell Junction (Hamilton) City 308
Johnson County 317
Johnston (Polk) City 336
Joice (Worth) City 354
Jolley (Calhoun) City 286
Jones County 318
Kalona (Washington) City 350
Kamrar (Hamilton) City 308
Kanawha (Hancock) City 309
Kellerton (Ringgold) City 339
Kelley (Story) City 344
Kellogg (Jasper) City 315
Kensett (Worth) City 354
Kent (Union) City 347
Keokuk (Lee) City 321
Keokuk County 318
Keomah Village (Mahaska) City 326

Keosauqua (Van Buren) City 347
Keota (Keokuk) City 319
Keswick (Keokuk) City 319
Keystone (Benton) City 281
Kimballton (Audubon) City 280
Kingsley (Plymouth) City 335
Kinross (Keokuk) City 319
Kirkman (Shelby) City 342
Kirkville (Wapello) City 348
Kiron (Crawford) City 295
Klemme (Hancock) City 309
Knierim (Calhoun) City 287
Knoxville (Marion) City 326
Kossuth County 320
Lacona (Warren) City 349
Ladora (Iowa) City 314
Lake City (Calhoun) City 287
Lake Mills (Winnebago) City 352
Lake Park (Dickinson) City 300
Lakeside (Buena Vista) City 285
Lake View (Sac) City 340
Lakota (Kossuth) City 320
Lambs Grove (Jasper) City 315
Lamoni (Decatur) City 298
Lamont (Buchanan) City 284
La Motte (Jackson) City 315
Lanesboro (Carroll) City 288
Lansing (Allamakee) City 279
La Porte City (Black Hawk) City 282
Larchwood (Lyon) City 324
Larrabee (Cherokee) City 291
Latimer (Franklin) City 304
Laurel (Marshall) City 327
Laurens (Pocahontas) City 335
Lawler (Chickasaw) City 291
Lawton (Woodbury) City 353
Le Claire (Scott) City 341
Ledyard (Kossuth) City 320
Lee County 321
Le Grand (Marshall) City 327
Lehigh (Webster) City 351
Leighton (Mahaska) City 326
Leland (Winnebago) City 352
Le Mars (Plymouth) City 335
Lenox (Adams) City 278
Lenox (Taylor) City 346
Leon (Decatur) City 298
Le Roy (Decatur) City 298
Lester (Lyon) City 324
Letts (Louisa) City 323
Lewis (Cass) City 288
Libertyville (Jefferson) City 316
Lidderdale (Carroll) City 288
Lime Springs (Howard) City 312
Lincoln (Tama) City 345
Linden (Dallas) City 296
Lineville (Wayne) City 350
Linn County 321
Linn Grove (Buena Vista) City 285
Lisbon (Linn) City 322
Liscomb (Marshall) City 327
Littleport (Clayton) City 293
Little Rock (Lyon) City 324
Little Sioux (Harrison) City 310
Livermore (Humboldt) City 313
Lockridge (Jefferson) City 316
Logan (Harrison) City 310
Lohrville (Calhoun) City 287
Lone Rock (Kossuth) City 320
Lone Tree (Johnson) City 317
Long Grove (Scott) City 341
Lorimor (Union) City 347
Lost Nation (Clinton) City 294
Louisa County 323
Lovilia (Monroe) City 330

Lowden (Cedar) City 289
Low Moor (Clinton) City 294
Luana (Clayton) City 293
Lucas (Lucas) City 323
Lucas County 323
Luther (Boone) City 283
Lu Verne (Humboldt) City 313
Lu Verne (Kossuth) City 320
Luxemburg (Dubuque) City 301
Luzerne (Benton) City 281
Lynnville (Jasper) City 315
Lyon County 324
Lytton (Calhoun) City 287
Lytton (Sac) City 340
Macedonia (Pottawattamie) City 337
Macksburg (Madison) City 325
Madison County 325
Madrid (Boone) City 283
Magnolia (Harrison) City 310
Mahaska County 325
Malcom (Poweshiek) City 338
Mallard (Palo Alto) City 334
Maloy (Ringgold) City 339
Malvern (Mills) City 328
Manchester (Delaware) City 299
Manilla (Crawford) City 295
Manly (Worth) City 354
Manning (Carroll) City 288
Manson (Calhoun) City 287
Mapleton (Monona) City 329
Maquoketa (Jackson) City 315
Marathon (Buena Vista) City 285
Marble Rock (Floyd) City 304
Marcus (Cherokee) City 291
Marengo (Iowa) City 314
Marion (Linn) City 322
Marion County 326
Marne (Cass) City 288
Marquette (Clayton) City 293
Marshall County 327
Marshalltown (Marshall) City 327
Martelle (Jones) City 318
Martensdale (Warren) City 349
Martinsburg (Keokuk) City 319
Marysville (Marion) City 326
Mason City (Cerro Gordo) City 290
Masonville (Delaware) City 299
Massena (Cass) City 288
Matlock (Sioux) City 343
Maurice (Sioux) City 343
Maxwell (Story) City 344
Maynard (Fayette) City 303
Maysville (Scott) City 341
McCallsburg (Story) City 344
McCausland (Scott) City 341
McClelland (Pottawattamie) City 337
McGregor (Clayton) City 293
McIntire (Mitchell) City 328
Mechanicsville (Cedar) City 289
Mediapolis (Des Moines) City 299
Melbourne (Marshall) City 327
Melcher-Dallas (Marion) City 326
Melrose (Monroe) City 330
Melvin (Osceola) City 332
Menlo (Guthrie) City 307
Meriden (Cherokee) City 291
Merrill (Plymouth) City 335
Meservey (Cerro Gordo) City 290
Middletown (Des Moines) City 299
Miles (Jackson) City 315
Milford (Dickinson) City 300
Millersburg (Iowa) City 314
Millerton (Wayne) City 350
Mills County 328
Millville (Clayton) City 293

Milo (Warren) City 349
Milton (Van Buren) City 347
Minburn (Dallas) City 296
Minden (Pottawattamie) City 337
Mingo (Jasper) City 315
Missouri Valley (Harrison) City 310
Mitchell (Mitchell) City 328
Mitchell County 328
Mitchellville (Polk) City 336
Modale (Harrison) City 310
Mondamin (Harrison) City 310
Moneta (O'Brien) City 332
Monmouth (Jackson) City 315
Monona (Clayton) City 293
Monona County 329
Monroe (Jasper) City 316
Monroe County 330
Montezuma (Poweshiek) City 338
Montgomery County 330
Monticello (Jones) City 318
Montour (Tama) City 345
Montrose (Lee) City 321
Moorhead (Monona) City 329
Moorland (Webster) City 351
Moravia (Appanoose) City 279
Morley (Jones) City 318
Morning Sun (Louisa) City 323
Morrison (Grundy) City 307
Moulton (Appanoose) City 280
Mount Auburn (Benton) City 281
Mount Ayr (Ringgold) City 339
Mount Pleasant (Henry) City 311
Mount Sterling (Van Buren) City 347
Mount Union (Henry) City 311
Mount Vernon (Linn) City 322
Moville (Woodbury) City 353
Murray (Clarke) City 292
Muscatine (Muscatine) City 331
Muscatine County 331
Mystic (Appanoose) City 280
Nashua (Chickasaw) City 291
Nemaha (Sac) City 340
Neola (Pottawattamie) City 338
Nevada (Story) City 344
New Albin (Allamakee) City 279
Newell (Buena Vista) City 285
Newhall (Benton) City 281
New Hampton (Chickasaw) City 291
New Hartford (Butler) City 286
New Liberty (Scott) City 341
New London (Henry) City 311
New Market (Taylor) City 346
New Providence (Hardin) City 309
New Sharon (Mahaska) City 326
Newton (Jasper) City 316
New Vienna (Dubuque) City 301
New Virginia (Warren) City 349
Nichols (Muscatine) City 331
Nodaway (Adams) City 278
Nora Springs (Floyd) City 304
Northboro (Page) City 333
North Buena Vista (Clayton) City 293
North English (Iowa) City 314
North English (Keokuk) City 319
North Liberty (Johnson) City 317
North Washington (Chickasaw) City 291
Northwood (Worth) City 354
Norwalk (Warren) City 349
Norway (Benton) City 281
Numa (Appanoose) City 280
Oakland (Pottawattamie) City 338
Oakland Acres (Jasper) City 316
Oakville (Louisa) City 323
O'Brien County 331
Ocheyedan (Osceola) City 332

Odebolt (Sac) City 340
Oelwein (Fayette) City 303
Ogden (Boone) City 283
Okoboji (Dickinson) City 300
Olds (Henry) City 311
Olin (Jones) City 318
Ollie (Keokuk) City 319
Onawa (Monona) City 329
Oneida (Delaware) City 299
Onslow (Jones) City 318
Orange City (Sioux) City 343
Orchard (Mitchell) City 328
Orient (Adair) City 278
Orleans (Dickinson) City 300
Osage (Mitchell) City 329
Osceola (Clarke) City 292
Osceola County 332
Oskaloosa (Mahaska) City 326
Ossian (Winneshiek) City 353
Osterdock (Clayton) City 293
Otho (Webster) City 351
Oto (Woodbury) City 353
Ottosen (Humboldt) City 313
Ottumwa (Wapello) City 348
Owasa (Hardin) City 309
Oxford (Johnson) City 317
Oxford Junction (Jones) City 318
Oyens (Plymouth) City 335
Pacific Junction (Mills) City 328
Packwood (Jefferson) City 316
Page County 333
Palmer (Pocahontas) City 335
Palo (Linn) City 322
Palo Alto County 334
Panama (Shelby) City 342
Panora (Guthrie) City 307
Panorama Park (Scott) City 341
Parkersburg (Butler) City 286
Park View (Scott) CDP 341
Parnell (Iowa) City 314
Paton (Greene) City 306
Patterson (Madison) City 325
Paullina (O'Brien) City 332
Pella (Marion) City 326
Peosta (Dubuque) City 301
Perry (Dallas) City 296
Persia (Harrison) City 310
Peterson (Clay) City 292
Pierson (Woodbury) City 353
Pilot Mound (Boone) Township 283
Pioneer (Humboldt) City 313
Pisgah (Harrison) City 310
Plainfield (Bremer) City 284
Plano (Appanoose) City 280
Pleasant Hill (Polk) City 336
Pleasanton (Decatur) City 298
Pleasant Plain (Jefferson) City 316
Pleasantville (Marion) City 326
Plover (Pocahontas) City 335
Plymouth (Cerro Gordo) City 290
Plymouth County 334
Pocahontas (Pocahontas) City 335
Pocahontas County 335
Polk City (Polk) Township 336
Polk County 336
Pomeroy (Calhoun) City 287
Popejoy (Franklin) City 304
Portsmouth (Shelby) City 342
Postville (Allamakee) City 279
Postville (Clayton) City 294
Pottawattamie County 337
Poweshiek County 338
Prairieburg (Linn) City 322
Prairie City (Jasper) City 316
Prescott (Adams) City 279

Preston (Jackson) City 315
Primghar (O'Brien) City 332
Princeton (Scott) City 341
Promise City (Wayne) City 350
Protivin (Howard) City 312
Pulaski (Davis) City 297
Quasqueton (Buchanan) City 284
Quimby (Cherokee) City 291
Radcliffe (Hardin) City 310
Rake (Winnebago) City 352
Ralston (Carroll) City 288
Ralston (Greene) City 306
Randalia (Fayette) City 303
Randall (Hamilton) City 308
Randolph (Fremont) City 305
Rathbun (Appanoose) City 280
Raymond (Black Hawk) City 282
Readlyn (Bremer) City 284
Reasnor (Jasper) City 316
Redding (Ringgold) City 339
Redfield (Dallas) City 296
Red Oak (Montgomery) City 330
Reinbeck (Grundy) City 307
Rembrandt (Buena Vista) City 285
Remsen (Plymouth) City 335
Renwick (Humboldt) City 313
Rhodes (Marshall) City 327
Riceville (Howard) City 312
Riceville (Mitchell) City 329
Richland (Keokuk) City 319
Rickardsville (Dubuque) City 301
Ricketts (Crawford) City 295
Ridgeway (Winneshiek) City 353
Rinard (Calhoun) City 287
Ringgold County 339
Ringsted (Emmet) City 302
Rippey (Greene) City 306
Riverdale (Scott) City 342
Riverside (Washington) City 350
Riverton (Fremont) City 305
Robins (Linn) City 322
Rock Falls (Cerro Gordo) City 290
Rockford (Floyd) City 304
Rock Rapids (Lyon) City 324
Rock Valley (Sioux) City 343
Rockwell (Cerro Gordo) City 290
Rockwell City (Calhoun) City 287
Rodman (Palo Alto) City 334
Rodney (Monona) City 329
Roland (Story) City 344
Rolfe (Pocahontas) City 336
Rome (Henry) City 311
Rose Hill (Mahaska) City 326
Rossie (Clay) City 292
Rowan (Wright) City 355
Rowley (Buchanan) City 284
Royal (Clay) City 292
Rudd (Floyd) City 304
Runnells (Polk) City 337
Russell (Lucas) City 323
Ruthven (Palo Alto) City 334
Rutland (Humboldt) City 313
Ryan (Delaware) City 299
Sabula (Jackson) City 315
Sac City (Sac) City 340
Sac County 340
Sageville (Dubuque) City 301
St. Ansgar (Mitchell) City 329
St. Anthony (Marshall) City 327
St. Charles (Madison) City 325
St. Donatus (Jackson) City 315
St. Lucas (Fayette) City 303
St. Marys (Warren) City 349
St. Olaf (Clayton) City 294
St. Paul (Lee) City 321

IOWA

Place	Page
Salem (Henry) City	311
Salix (Woodbury) City	353
Sanborn (O'Brien) City	332
Sandyville (Warren) City	349
Saylorville (Polk) CDP	337
Scarville (Winnebago) City	352
Schaller (Sac) City	340
Schleswig (Crawford) City	295
Scott County	341
Scranton (Greene) City	306
Searsboro (Poweshiek) City	338
Sergeant Bluff (Woodbury) City	353
Seymour (Wayne) City	350
Shambaugh (Page) City	333
Shannon City (Ringgold) City	339
Shannon City (Union) City	347
Sharpsburg (Taylor) City	346
Sheffield (Franklin) City	304
Shelby (Pottawattamie) City	338
Shelby (Shelby) City	342
Shelby County	342
Sheldahl (Boone) City	283
Sheldahl (Polk) City	337
Sheldahl (Story) City	344
Sheldon (O'Brien) City	332
Sheldon (Sioux) City	343
Shell Rock (Butler) City	286
Shellsburg (Benton) City	281
Shenandoah (Fremont) City	305
Shenandoah (Page) City	333
Sherrill (Dubuque) City	301
Shueyville (Johnson) City	317
Sibley (Osceola) City	332
Sidney (Fremont) City	305
Sigourney (Keokuk) City	319
Silver City (Mills) City	328
Sioux Center (Sioux) City	343
Sioux City (Woodbury) City	354
Sioux County	343
Sioux Rapids (Buena Vista) City	285
Slater (Story) City	344
Sloan (Woodbury) City	354
Smithland (Woodbury) City	354
Soldier (Monona) City	329
Solon (Johnson) City	317
Somers (Calhoun) City	287
South English (Keokuk) City	319
Spencer (Clay) City	292
Spillville (Winneshiek) City	353
Spirit Lake (Dickinson) City	300
Spragueville (Jackson) City	315
Springbrook (Jackson) City	315
Spring Hill (Warren) City	349
Springville (Linn) City	322
Stacyville (Mitchell) City	329
Stanhope (Hamilton) City	308
Stanley (Buchanan) City	284
Stanley (Fayette) City	303
Stanton (Montgomery) City	330
Stanwood (Cedar) City	289
State Center (Marshall) City	327
Steamboat Rock (Hardin) City	310
Stockport (Van Buren) City	347
Stockton (Muscatine) City	331
Storm Lake (Buena Vista) City	285
Story City (Story) City	344
Story County	344
Stout (Grundy) City	307
Stratford (Hamilton) City	308
Stratford (Webster) City	351
Strawberry Point (Clayton) City	294
Struble (Plymouth) City	335
Stuart (Adair) City	278
Stuart (Guthrie) City	307
Sully (Jasper) City	316
Sumner (Bremer) City	284
Superior (Dickinson) City	300
Sutherland (O'Brien) City	332
Swaledale (Cerro Gordo) City	290
Swan (Marion) City	326
Swea City (Kossuth) City	320
Swisher (Johnson) City	317
Tabor (Fremont) City	305
Tabor (Mills) City	328
Tama (Tama) City	345
Tama County	345
Taylor County	346
Templeton (Carroll) City	288
Tennant (Shelby) City	342
Terril (Dickinson) City	300
Thayer (Union) City	347
Thompson (Winnebago) City	352
Thor (Humboldt) City	313
Thornburg (Keokuk) City	319
Thornton (Cerro Gordo) City	290
Thurman (Fremont) City	305
Tiffin (Johnson) City	317
Tingley (Ringgold) City	339
Tipton (Cedar) City	289
Titonka (Kossuth) City	320
Toledo (Tama) City	345
Toronto (Clinton) City	295
Traer (Tama) City	345
Treynor (Pottawattamie) City	338
Tripoli (Bremer) City	284
Truesdale (Buena Vista) City	285
Truro (Madison) City	325
Turin (Monona) City	329
Udell (Appanoose) City	280
Underwood (Pottawattamie) City	338
Union (Hardin) City	310
Union County	346
Unionville (Appanoose) City	280
University Heights (Johnson) City	317
University Park (Mahaska) City	326
Urbana (Benton) City	281
Urbandale (Polk) City	337
Ute (Monona) City	329
Vail (Crawford) City	295
Valeria (Jasper) City	316
Van Buren County	347
Van Horne (Benton) City	281
Van Meter (Dallas) City	296
Van Wert (Decatur) City	298
Varina (Pocahontas) City	336
Ventura (Cerro Gordo) City	290
Victor (Iowa) City	314
Victor (Poweshiek) City	339
Villisca (Montgomery) City	330
Vincent (Webster) City	351
Vining (Tama) City	345
Vinton (Benton) City	281
Volga (Clayton) City	294
Wadena (Fayette) City	303
Wahpeton (Dickinson) City	300
Walcott (Muscatine) City	331
Walcott (Scott) City	342
Walford (Benton) City	281
Walford (Linn) City	322
Walker (Linn) City	322
Wallingford (Emmet) City	302
Wall Lake (Sac) City	340
Walnut (Pottawattamie) City	338
Wapello (Louisa) City	323
Wapello County	348
Warren County	348
Washington (Washington) City	350
Washington County	349
Washta (Cherokee) City	291
Waterloo (Black Hawk) City	282
Waterville (Allamakee) City	279
Waucoma (Fayette) City	303
Waukee (Dallas) City	296
Waukon (Allamakee) City	279
Waverly (Bremer) City	284
Wayland (Henry) City	311
Wayne County	350
Webb (Clay) City	292
Webster (Keokuk) City	319
Webster City (Hamilton) City	308
Webster County	351
Weldon (Decatur) City	298
Wellman (Washington) City	350
Wellsburg (Grundy) City	307
Welton (Clinton) City	295
Wesley (Kossuth) City	320
West Bend (Kossuth) City	320
West Bend (Palo Alto) City	334
West Branch (Cedar) City	289
West Burlington (Des Moines) City	299
West Chester (Washington) City	350
West Des Moines (Dallas) City	297
West Des Moines (Polk) City	337
Westfield (Plymouth) City	335
Westgate (Fayette) City	303
West Liberty (Muscatine) City	331
West Okoboji (Dickinson) City	300
Westphalia (Shelby) City	342
West Point (Lee) City	321
Westside (Crawford) City	296
West Union (Fayette) City	303
Westwood (Henry) City	311
What Cheer (Keokuk) City	319
Wheatland (Clinton) City	295
Whiting (Monona) City	329
Whittemore (Kossuth) City	320
Whitten (Hardin) City	310
Willey (Carroll) City	288
Williams (Hamilton) City	308
Williamsburg (Iowa) City	314
Williamson (Lucas) City	324
Wilton (Cedar) City	289
Wilton (Muscatine) City	331
Windsor Heights (Polk) City	337
Winfield (Henry) City	311
Winnebago County	352
Winneshiek County	352
Winterset (Madison) City	325
Winthrop (Buchanan) City	285
Wiota (Cass) City	289
Woden (Hancock) City	309
Woodbine (Harrison) City	310
Woodburn (Clarke) City	292
Woodbury County	353
Woodward (Dallas) City	297
Woolstock (Wright) City	355
Worth County	354
Worthington (Dubuque) City	301
Wright County	355
Wyoming (Jones) City	318
Yale (Guthrie) City	307
Yetter (Calhoun) City	287
York (Iowa) Township	314
Yorktown (Page) City	333
Zearing (Story) City	344
Zwingle (Dubuque) City	301
Zwingle (Jackson) City	315

Michigan

MICHIGAN

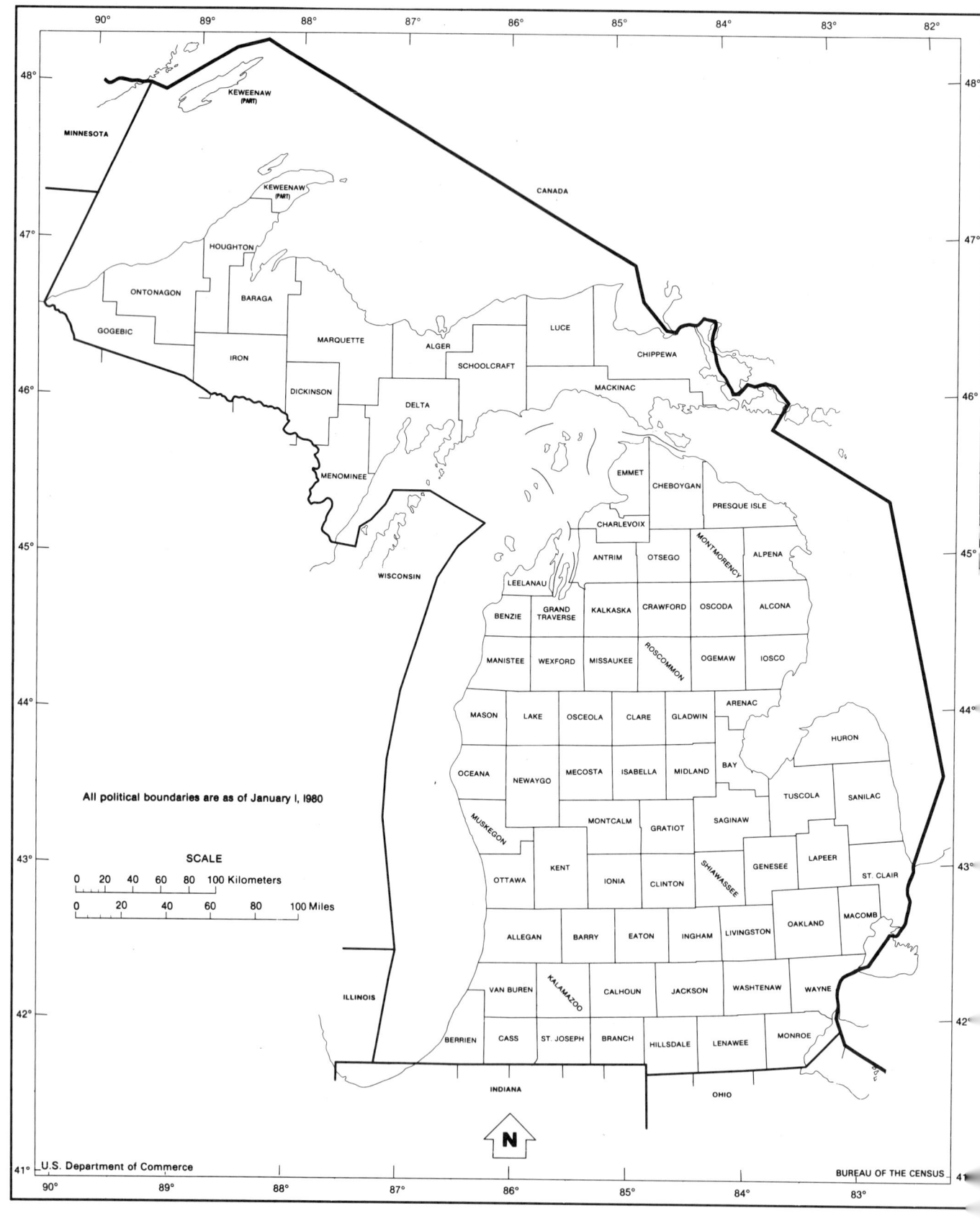

Michigan

Population: 9,295,297 (1990); 9,262,078 (1980)
Population rank (1990): 8
Percent population change (1980-1990): 0.4
Population projection: 9,534,000 (1995); 9,692,000 (2000)

Area: total 96,810 sq. mi.; 56,809 sq. mi. land, 40,001 sq. mi. water
Area rank: 11
Highest elevation: 1,980 ft., Mount Curwood (Baraga County)
Lowest point: 572 ft. along Lake Erie

State capital: Lansing (Clinton, Eaton, and Ingham counties)
Largest city: Detroit (1,027,974)
Second largest city: Grand Rapids (189,126)
Largest county: Wayne (2,111,687)

Total housing units: 3,847,926
No. of occupied housing units: 3,419,331
Vacant housing units (%): 11.1
Distribution of population by race and Hispanic origin (%):
 White: 83.4
 Black: 13.9
 Hispanic (any race): 2.2
 Native American: 0.6
 Asian/Pacific: 1.1
 Other: 0.9

Admission date: January 26, 1837 (26th state).

Location: In the Great Lakes region of the United States, bordering Ohio, Indiana, Wisconsin, Lake Superior, Lake Michigan, Lake Huron, Ontario (Canada), and Lake Erie.

Name Origin: Named in 1805, apparently for Lake Michigan; itself named from an Indian word, possibly Chippewa *Michigama* 'great lake', or possibly from *mishi-maikin-nac* 'swimming turtle,' descriptive of Mackinac Island. Early 18th century maps of North America vary, some labeling present-day Lake Huron as Lake Michigan (and labeling the latter as Lake Illinois), but present naming practice is seen on maps regularly after 1757.

State bird: robin *(Turdus migratorius)*
State fish: brook trout *(Salvelinus fontinalis)*
State flower: apple blossom *(Malus sylvestris)*
State gem: chlorastrolite
State soil: Kalkaska Soil Series
State song: "Michigan, My Michigan"
State stone: Petoskey stone

State tree: white pine *(Pinus strobus)*

State motto: *Si quaeris peninsulam amoenam, circumspice* (Latin, 'If you seek a pleasant peninsula, look about you')
State nicknames: The Wolverine State; The Water Wonderland; Upper Peninsula often referred to as the Land of Hiawatha

Area codes: 313 (Detroit and southeast), 810 (eastern counties north of Detroit), 517 (central), 616 (west), 906 (Upper Peninsula)
Time zones: Eastern, Central (western counties of Upper Peninsula)
Abbreviations: MI (postal); Mich. (traditional)
Part of (region): Great Lakes, Midwest

Local Government

Counties

Michigan has 83 counties, divided into a total of 1,241 townships.

Municipalities

There are 534 municipal governments (271 cities and 263 villages) and hundreds of school and other special districts. Additionally, counties are divided into two types of townships: geographical (or congressional) and political. A geographical township has an area of 36 sq. mi.; in sparsely populated areas, two or more geographical townships may be combined into one political township.

Settlement History and Early Development

Indians inhabited present-day Michigan about 11,000 years ago. By 5,000 B.C. they were making use of copper found in the Upper Peninsula—the first known use of a metal by peoples anywhere in the western hemisphere. When the first whites arrived in the early seventeenth century, the lower peninsula was virtually uninhabited. The upper peninsula was only sparsely populated with Ojibway, Menominee, Winnebago, Potawatomi, Miami, and Huron Indians.

Étienne Brulé was probably the first European to reach present-day Michigan. He was a Frenchman who explored the Upper Peninsula around 1620; he was followed in 1634 by Jean Nicolet. Fr. Jacques Marquette established missions and fur-trading posts at Sault Ste. Marie in 1668 and St. Ignace in 1671. In 1701 Antoine Laumet de la Mothe Cadillac founded a permanent settlement at the site of present-day Detroit. There was little development of the area, though, because the French were primarily interested in converting the Indians to

Christianity and in developing a fur trade, neither of which attracted many settlers.

After France's defeat in the French and Indian Wars, the Indians feared that the British would bring farmers from their eastern colonies to settle, with a subsequent destruction of their way of life. They banded together under the Ottawa chief Pontiac, who led an uprising in 1763, attacking the British at Fort Michilimackinac and settlers at other forts. The Indians laid siege to Detroit for about five months but were finally repelled. In 1774 Michigan became part of the province of British-controlled Quebec. The British, like the French, were more interested in the fur trade than in settlement.

The American Revolution

Most of the people in Michigan supported the British during the Revolution, since if the rebels won, it was expected they would migrate west and convert fur-trapping wilderness into croplands. Even though the Treaty of Paris in 1783 assigned these territories to the United States, Britain did not surrender Detroit or Fort Mackinac to the U.S. until the summer of 1796.

In 1787 the Michigan region became part of the Northwest Territory. In 1800 the Indiana Territory, including part of Michigan, was created by Congress; in 1803 the rest of Michigan was included. In 1805 Congress established the Territory of Michigan, which included the Lower Peninsula and the eastern part of the Upper Peninsula.

War of 1812

The British captured Detroit on August 16, 1812, and although the Americans recaptured it in September 1813, the British continued to occupy the fort on Mackinac Island, which enabled them to control most of Michigan. It was not until the end of the war in 1814 that the area was returned to the Americans.

Until the War of 1812, the Indians traded with the Europeans and were respected as potential allies when the rival colonial powers threatened war. But after the war Indian lands in Michigan were ceded to the federal government and most of the tribes removed from the area. Some Potawatomi remained on reservations and most of the Ojibway and Ottawa Indians remained in the north.

Statehood

The Erie Canal opened in 1825, linking the Great Lakes with the Atlantic Ocean and providing a transportation route between the eastern states and the western territories. Settlers began moving into southern Michigan, and it was admitted to the Union as the 26th state on January 26, 1837, with its present-day boundaries.

The Civil War

Michigan sent about 90,000 men to serve in the Union armies; the Michigan cavalry was led by General George A. Custer. On May 10, 1865, the Fourth Michigan Cavalry captured Jefferson Davis, president of the Confederacy. No battles were fought within the state.

Business and Industry

Agriculture was responsible for the initial growth of the new state and the rapid increase in population. In the late 1840s mining in the Upper Peninsula attracted large numbers of miners and prospectors, and the need to ship the iron ore from western Michigan to the iron and steel centers on the Great Lakes led to the construction of the Soo Canals. After the Civil War lumbering in the northern pine forests made Michigan the top lumber producer in the U.S. Construction of saw mills helped develop the furniture industry, which started in Grand Rapids in the 1830s.

In 1899 Ransom Olds founded Michigan's first automobile factory in Detroit, and in 1903 Henry Ford organized the Ford Motor Company. Detroit was soon the center of the nation's automobile industry, earning it the nicknames "Automobile Capital of the World" and "the Motor City" or "Motown."

During World War I Michigan's factories built trucks, armored vehicles, and other military products. The state suffered greatly during the depression of the 1930s, when federal efforts such as the Civilian Conservation Corps and Works Progress Administration tried to counter the state's massive unemployment. The late 1930s saw the growth of union representation in Michigan's factories. The state's factories were devoted to military production during World War II and the state continued to prosper in the decades following the war with automotive and related industries. Nationwide economic woes and the gas shortages of the 1970s led to problems for the automotive industry and the highest unemployment rates in the nation by 1980. Sales of American-made automobiles began to rebound somewhat during the 1980s and early 1990s, but with the national economy still flagging, Michigan still faces the challenge of further diversifying its industrial base.

State Boundaries

In 1805 the southern boundary of the Michigan Territory was a line due east from the southernmost point of Lake Michigan to Lake Erie. On the north, only the eastern tip of the Upper Peninsula was included. Congress denied Michigan's petition for statehood in 1834 because of a dispute over its southern boundary. When Indiana became a state in 1816, it had been given a strip of land in southwestern Michigan. In 1834 the state of Ohio claimed it had rights to this land, including the present site of Toledo. In the so-called Toledo War of 1835, during which no one was killed, Michigan's militia held off the Ohioans in their bid to take over the area. Ohio's political power in Congress, however, enabled them to prevail, and Michigan was granted the entire Upper Peninsula as compensation for the loss.

American Places Dictionary MICHIGAN

Michigan Counties

Alcona	Clare	Iosco	Marquette	Oscoda
Alger	Clinton	Iron	Mason	Otsego
Allegan	Crawford	Isabella	Mecosta	Ottawa
Alpena	Delta	Jackson	Menominee	Presque Isle
Antrim	Dickinson	Kalamazoo	Midland	Roscommon
Arenac	Eaton	Kalkaska	Missaukee	Saginaw
Baraga	Emmet	Kent	Monroe	St. Clair
Barry	Genesee	Keweenaw	Montcalm	St. Joseph
Bay	Gladwin	Lake	Montmorency	Sanilac
Benzie	Gogebic	Lapeer	Muskegon	Schoolcraft
Berrien	Grand Traverse	Leelanau	Newaygo	Shiawassee
Branch	Gratiot	Lenawee	Oakland	Tuscola
Calhoun	Hillsdale	Livingston	Oceana	Van Buren
Cass	Houghton	Luce	Ogemaw	Washtenaw
Charlevoix	Huron	Mackinac	Ontonagon	Wayne
Cheboygan	Ingham	Macomb	Osceola	Wexford
Chippewa	Ionia	Manistee		

Multi-County Places

The following Michigan places are in more than one county. Given here is the total population for each multi-county place, and the names of the counties it is in.

Brown City, pop. 1,244; Sanilac (1,235), Lapeer (9)
Casnovia, pop. 376; Kent (189), Muskegon (187)
Cement City, pop. 493; Lenawee (465), Jackson (28)
Clare, pop. 3,021; Clare (3,013), Isabella (8)
Grosse Pointe Shores, pop. 2,955; Wayne (2,850), Macomb (105)
Hesperia, pop. 846; Oceana (586), Newaygo (260)
Holland, pop. 30,745; Ottawa (25,086), Allegan (5,659)
Hubbardston, pop. 404; Ionia (385), Clinton (19)
Lansing, pop. 127,321; Ingham (122,700), Eaton (4,621)
Lennon, pop. 534; Shiawassee (450), Genesee (84)
Mackinaw City, pop. 875; Emmet (467), Cheboygan (408)
Memphis, pop. 1,221; Macomb (896), St. Clair (325)
Midland, pop. 38,053; Midland (37,819), Bay (234)
Milan, pop. 4,040; Washtenaw (3,060), Monroe (980)
Niles, pop. 12,458; Berrien (12,456), Cass (2)
Northville, pop. 6,226; Oakland (3,367), Wayne (2,859)
Otter Lake, pop. 474; Lapeer (419), Genesee (55)
Ovid, pop. 1,442; Clinton (1,442), Shiawassee (0)
South Haven, pop. 5,563; Van Buren (5,563), Allegan (0)
Traverse City, pop. 15,155; Grand Traverse (15,116), Leelanau (39)
Union City, pop. 1,767; Branch (1,760), Calhoun (7)
Whitmore Lake, pop. 3,251; Livingston (1,694), Washtenaw (1,557)

MICHIGAN, Alcona County　　　　　　　　　　　　　　　　　　　　　　　　*American Places Dictionary*

Alcona County
County Seat: Harrisville (ZIP: 48740)

Pop: 10,145 (1990); 9,740 (1980)　　　　　　　　　　**Pop Density:** 15.0
Land: 674.5 sq. mi.; **Water:** 1116.1 sq. mi.　　　　　**Area Code:** 517

On the northeastern coast of MI on Lake Huron; established as Neewaygo County Apr 1, 1840 from Alpena County; name changed Mar 8, 1843.

Name origin: A local coinage, said to mean 'beautiful plains.'

Alcona　　　　　　　　　　　　　　　Township
　　　　　　　　　Lat: 44-48-18 N **Long:** 83-26-53 W
Pop: 906 (1990); 811 (1980)　　　　　　**Pop Density:** 15.7
Land: 57.6 sq. mi.; **Water:** 8.8 sq. mi.

Caledonia　　　　　　　　　　　　Township
　　　　　　　　　Lat: 44-49-38 N **Long:** 83-36-49 W
Pop: 987 (1990); 1,065 (1980)　　　　　**Pop Density:** 14.6
Land: 67.4 sq. mi.; **Water:** 5.1 sq. mi.

Curtis　　　　　　　　　　　　　　　Township
　　　　　　　　　Lat: 44-33-31 N **Long:** 83-45-51 W
Pop: 1,128 (1990); 1,082 (1980)　　　　**Pop Density:** 16.5
Land: 68.3 sq. mi.; **Water:** 2.4 sq. mi.

Greenbush　　　　　　　　　　　　Township
ZIP: 48738　　**Lat:** 44-34-01 N **Long:** 83-21-06 W
Pop: 1,373 (1990); 1,292 (1980)　　　　**Pop Density:** 55.1
Land: 24.9 sq. mi.; **Water:** 1.2 sq. mi.

Gustin　　　　　　　　　　　　　　　Township
　　　　　　　　　Lat: 44-38-28 N **Long:** 83-28-10 W
Pop: 823 (1990); 796 (1980)　　　　　　**Pop Density:** 23.1
Land: 35.7 sq. mi.; **Water:** 0.1 sq. mi.

Harrisville　　　　　　　　　　　　　　　City
ZIP: 48740　　**Lat:** 44-39-23 N **Long:** 83-17-39 W
Pop: 470 (1990); 559 (1980)　　　　　　**Pop Density:** 783.3
Land: 0.6 sq. mi.; **Water:** 0.0 sq. mi.

Not coextensive with the town of the same name.

Name origin: For early settlers Benjamin Harris and his sons, Levi and Henry.

*Harrisville　　　　　　　　　　　Township
ZIP: 48740　　**Lat:** 44-38-31 N **Long:** 83-21-07 W
Pop: 1,315 (1990); 1,093 (1980)　　　　**Pop Density:** 43.5
Land: 30.2 sq. mi.; **Water:** 0.0 sq. mi.

Hawes　　　　　　　　　　　　　　Township
　　　　　　　　　Lat: 44-43-57 N **Long:** 83-31-27 W
Pop: 1,035 (1990); 996 (1980)　　　　　**Pop Density:** 14.8
Land: 70.0 sq. mi.; **Water:** 1.4 sq. mi.

Haynes　　　　　　　　　　　　　　Township
　　　　　　　　　Lat: 44-43-35 N **Long:** 83-21-03 W
Pop: 549 (1990); 569 (1980)　　　　　　**Pop Density:** 15.7
Land: 35.0 sq. mi.; **Water:** 0.1 sq. mi.

Lincoln　　　　　　　　　　　　　　　Village
ZIP: 48742　　**Lat:** 44-41-06 N **Long:** 83-24-45 W
Pop: 337 (1990); 361 (1980)　　　　　　**Pop Density:** 421.3
Land: 0.8 sq. mi.; **Water:** 0.2 sq. mi.

Name origin: For Abraham Lincoln (1809–65), sixteenth U.S. president.

Mikado　　　　　　　　　　　　　　Township
ZIP: 48745　　**Lat:** 44-33-31 N **Long:** 83-31-07 W
Pop: 852 (1990); 865 (1980)　　　　　　**Pop Density:** 11.9
Land: 71.3 sq. mi.; **Water:** 0.1 sq. mi.

Millen　　　　　　　　　　　　　　　Township
　　　　　　　　　Lat: 44-38-33 N **Long:** 83-38-54 W
Pop: 417 (1990); 364 (1980)　　　　　　**Pop Density:** 5.9
Land: 70.6 sq. mi.; **Water:** 0.6 sq. mi.

Mitchell　　　　　　　　　　　　　　Township
　　　　　　　　　Lat: 44-43-27 N **Long:** 83-47-54 W
Pop: 290 (1990); 248 (1980)　　　　　　**Pop Density:** 2.0
Land: 142.8 sq. mi.; **Water:** 0.9 sq. mi.

Alger County
County Seat: Munising (ZIP: 49862)

Pop: 8,972 (1990); 9,225 (1980)　　　　　　　　　　**Pop Density:** 9.8
Land: 917.9 sq. mi.; **Water:** 4126.4 sq. mi.　　　　**Area Code:** 906

On the north-central coast of the Upper Peninsula of MI, on Lake Superior; established Mar 17, 1885, from Schoolcraft County.

Name origin: For Gen. Russell Alexander Alger (1836–1907), governor of MI (1885–87), U.S. secretary of war (1897–99), and U.S. senator from MI (1902–07).

Au Train　　　　　　　　　　　　Township
ZIP: 49806　　**Lat:** 46-21-21 N **Long:** 86-45-50 W
Pop: 1,047 (1990); 928 (1980)　　　　　**Pop Density:** 7.4
Land: 142.1 sq. mi.; **Water:** 23.5 sq. mi.

Burt　　　　　　　　　　　　　　　Township
　　　　　　　　　Lat: 46-35-23 N **Long:** 86-05-24 W
Pop: 508 (1990); 539 (1980)　　　　　　**Pop Density:** 2.2
Land: 231.0 sq. mi.; **Water:** 25.5 sq. mi.

American Places Dictionary   MICHIGAN, Allegan County

Chatham   Village
ZIP: 49816   **Lat:** 46-20-39 N   **Long:** 86-55-50 W
Pop: 268 (1990); 315 (1980)   **Pop Density:** 103.1
Land: 2.6 sq. mi.; **Water:** 0.0 sq. mi.
Founded 1897.
Name origin: For Chatham, Ontario, Canada.

Grand Island   Township
Lat: 46-29-19 N   **Long:** 86-40-40 W
Pop: 21 (1990); 23 (1980)   **Pop Density:** 0.9
Land: 22.4 sq. mi.; **Water:** 26.6 sq. mi.

Limestone   Township
Lat: 46-13-45 N   **Long:** 87-01-01 W
Pop: 334 (1990); 373 (1980)   **Pop Density:** 4.5
Land: 74.6 sq. mi.; **Water:** 0.5 sq. mi.

Mathias   Township
Lat: 46-12-50 N   **Long:** 86-52-17 W
Pop: 563 (1990); 680 (1980)   **Pop Density:** 7.9
Land: 71.0 sq. mi.; **Water:** 1.1 sq. mi.

Munising   City
ZIP: 49862   **Lat:** 46-25-01 N   **Long:** 86-38-28 W
Pop: 2,783 (1990); 3,083 (1980)   **Pop Density:** 515.4
Land: 5.4 sq. mi.; **Water:** 3.8 sq. mi.
Name origin: From the Indian term *minissing* meaning 'island in a lake' or 'near the island.'

*Munising   Township
ZIP: 49862   **Lat:** 46-23-40 N   **Long:** 86-31-26 W
Pop: 2,193 (1990); 1,963 (1980)   **Pop Density:** 10.8
Land: 202.6 sq. mi.; **Water:** 10.4 sq. mi.

Onota   Township
Lat: 46-28-15 N   **Long:** 86-59-52 W
Pop: 244 (1990); 228 (1980)   **Pop Density:** 2.8
Land: 88.0 sq. mi.; **Water:** 8.1 sq. mi.

Rock River   Township
Lat: 46-21-12 N   **Long:** 86-59-16 W
Pop: 1,279 (1990); 1,408 (1980)   **Pop Density:** 15.8
Land: 80.9 sq. mi.; **Water:** 0.1 sq. mi.   **Elev:** 614 ft.

Allegan County
County Seat: Allegan (ZIP: 49010)

Pop: 90,509 (1990); 81,555 (1980)   **Pop Density:** 109.4
Land: 827.5 sq. mi.; **Water:** 1006.0 sq. mi.   **Area Code:** 616

On the southwestern coast of MI, bordered on the west by Lake Michigan; established Mar 2, 1831 (prior to statehood) from Kalamazoo County.

Name origin: Named for the Allegan (Alleghen) Indian tribe by Henry Rowe Schoolcraft (1793–1864), explorer, MI legislator, author, and superintendent of Indian Affairs for MI (1836–41).

Allegan   City
ZIP: 49010   **Lat:** 42-31-41 N   **Long:** 85-50-43 W
Pop: 4,547 (1990); 4,576 (1980)   **Pop Density:** 1228.9
Land: 3.7 sq. mi.; **Water:** 0.5 sq. mi.   **Elev:** 658 ft.
Incorporated 1838.
Name origin: For the Allegan Indians.

*Allegan   Township
ZIP: 49010   **Lat:** 42-33-00 N   **Long:** 85-50-12 W
Pop: 3,976 (1990); 3,464 (1980)   **Pop Density:** 129.9
Land: 30.6 sq. mi.; **Water:** 1.4 sq. mi.

Casco   Township
Lat: 42-27-27 N   **Long:** 86-11-50 W
Pop: 2,856 (1990); 2,839 (1980)   **Pop Density:** 73.4
Land: 38.9 sq. mi.; **Water:** 0.0 sq. mi.

Cheshire   Township
Lat: 42-27-30 N   **Long:** 85-57-20 W
Pop: 1,967 (1990); 1,797 (1980)   **Pop Density:** 56.2
Land: 35.0 sq. mi.; **Water:** 1.1 sq. mi.

Clyde   Township
Lat: 42-33-13 N   **Long:** 86-04-49 W
Pop: 2,001 (1990); 2,099 (1980)   **Pop Density:** 57.2
Land: 35.0 sq. mi.; **Water:** 0.6 sq. mi.

Dorr   Township
ZIP: 49323   **Lat:** 42-43-28 N   **Long:** 85-43-20 W
Pop: 5,453 (1990); 5,014 (1980)   **Pop Density:** 150.6
Land: 36.2 sq. mi.; **Water:** 0.0 sq. mi.

Douglas   Village
ZIP: 49406   **Lat:** 42-38-30 N   **Long:** 86-12-37 W
Pop: 1,040 (1990); 948 (1980)   **Pop Density:** 577.8
Land: 1.8 sq. mi.; **Water:** 0.1 sq. mi.
Settled 1851.
Name origin: For either U.S. statesman Stephen Douglas (1813–61), or the town of Douglas on the Isle of Man, former home of an early settler.

Fennville   City
ZIP: 49408   **Lat:** 42-35-41 N   **Long:** 86-06-18 W
Pop: 1,023 (1990); 934 (1980)   **Pop Density:** 930.0
Land: 1.1 sq. mi.; **Water:** 0.0 sq. mi.
Name origin: For pioneer Elam Fenn, who built a sawmill here in 1862.

Fillmore   Township
Lat: 42-43-04 N   **Long:** 86-04-25 W
Pop: 2,710 (1990); 2,307 (1980)   **Pop Density:** 87.7
Land: 30.9 sq. mi.; **Water:** 0.1 sq. mi.

Ganges   Township
Lat: 42-32-48 N   **Long:** 86-11-11 W
Pop: 2,124 (1990); 2,009 (1980)   **Pop Density:** 65.4
Land: 32.5 sq. mi.; **Water:** 0.2 sq. mi.

Gunplain   Township
Lat: 42-28-32 N   **Long:** 85-35-57 W
Pop: 4,754 (1990); 4,298 (1980)   **Pop Density:** 139.0
Land: 34.2 sq. mi.; **Water:** 0.3 sq. mi.

Heath
Township
Lat: 42-38-05 N **Long:** 85-57-29 W
Pop: 2,297 (1990); 1,962 (1980) **Pop Density:** 64.7
Land: 35.5 sq. mi.; **Water:** 0.4 sq. mi.

Holland
City
ZIP: 49423 **Lat:** 42-45-27 N **Long:** 86-06-06 W
Pop: 5,659 (1990); 4,514 (1980) **Pop Density:** 992.8
Land: 5.7 sq. mi.; **Water:** 0.0 sq. mi.

In southwestern MI on Lake Michigan. Settled 1847 by Dutch. Part of the town is also in Ottawa County.
Name origin: Named by settlers for their former home.

Hopkins
Village
ZIP: 49328 **Lat:** 42-37-31 N **Long:** 85-45-49 W
Pop: 546 (1990); 536 (1980) **Pop Density:** 1092.0
Land: 0.5 sq. mi.; **Water:** 0.0 sq. mi. **Elev:** 704 ft.

Not coextensive with the town of the same name.
Name origin: For Stephen Hopkins (1707–85), a signer of the Declaration of Independence and governor of RI.

*Hopkins
Township
ZIP: 49328 **Lat:** 42-38-20 N **Long:** 85-43-27 W
Pop: 2,350 (1990); 2,109 (1980) **Pop Density:** 65.6
Land: 35.8 sq. mi.; **Water:** 0.2 sq. mi.

Laketown
Township
Lat: 42-43-21 N **Long:** 86-10-07 W
Pop: 4,888 (1990); 4,332 (1980) **Pop Density:** 226.3
Land: 21.6 sq. mi.; **Water:** 0.1 sq. mi.

Lee
Township
Lat: 42-27-43 N **Long:** 86-04-32 W
Pop: 2,672 (1990); 2,249 (1980) **Pop Density:** 75.7
Land: 35.3 sq. mi.; **Water:** 0.8 sq. mi.

Leighton
Township
Lat: 42-43-42 N **Long:** 85-36-49 W
Pop: 3,069 (1990); 2,772 (1980) **Pop Density:** 87.7
Land: 35.0 sq. mi.; **Water:** 0.6 sq. mi.

Manlius
Township
Lat: 42-38-39 N **Long:** 86-04-32 W
Pop: 1,776 (1990); 1,458 (1980) **Pop Density:** 50.2
Land: 35.4 sq. mi.; **Water:** 0.6 sq. mi.

Martin
Village
ZIP: 49070 **Lat:** 42-32-13 N **Long:** 85-38-14 W
Pop: 462 (1990); 447 (1980) **Pop Density:** 513.3
Land: 0.9 sq. mi.; **Water:** 0.0 sq. mi. **Elev:** 832 ft.

Not coextensive with the town of the same name.
Name origin: For Martin Van Buren (1782–1862), eighth U.S. president.

*Martin
Township
ZIP: 49070 **Lat:** 42-33-10 N **Long:** 85-36-26 W
Pop: 2,487 (1990); 2,331 (1980) **Pop Density:** 69.7
Land: 35.7 sq. mi.; **Water:** 0.3 sq. mi.

Monterey
Township
Lat: 42-38-18 N **Long:** 85-50-31 W
Pop: 1,534 (1990); 1,320 (1980) **Pop Density:** 43.0
Land: 35.7 sq. mi.; **Water:** 0.2 sq. mi.

Otsego
City
ZIP: 49078 **Lat:** 42-27-27 N **Long:** 85-41-49 W
Pop: 3,937 (1990); 3,802 (1980) **Pop Density:** 2187.2
Land: 1.8 sq. mi.; **Water:** 0.1 sq. mi.

Settled 1831 by pioneer Samuel Foster.
Name origin: For Otsego County, NY.

*Otsego
Township
ZIP: 49078 **Lat:** 42-27-45 N **Long:** 85-43-04 W
Pop: 4,780 (1990); 4,479 (1980) **Pop Density:** 143.1
Land: 33.4 sq. mi.; **Water:** 0.6 sq. mi.

Overisel
Township
Lat: 42-43-29 N **Long:** 85-57-30 W
Pop: 2,324 (1990); 2,248 (1980) **Pop Density:** 64.9
Land: 35.8 sq. mi.; **Water:** 0.0 sq. mi.

Plainwell
City
ZIP: 49080 **Lat:** 42-26-42 N **Long:** 85-38-38 W
Pop: 4,057 (1990); 3,751 (1980) **Pop Density:** 1931.9
Land: 2.1 sq. mi.; **Water:** 0.1 sq. mi.

Settled 1833.

Salem
Township
Lat: 42-43-27 N **Long:** 85-50-19 W
Pop: 2,708 (1990); 2,183 (1980) **Pop Density:** 75.6
Land: 35.8 sq. mi.; **Water:** 0.3 sq. mi.

Saugatuck
Village
ZIP: 49453 **Lat:** 42-39-21 N **Long:** 86-12-20 W
Pop: 954 (1990); 1,079 (1980) **Pop Density:** 795.0
Land: 1.2 sq. mi.; **Water:** 0.3 sq. mi.

Settled 1830. Not coextensive with the town of the same name.
Name origin: From the Potawatomi Indian term for 'river's mouth,' referring to the Kalamazoo River, which empties into Lake Michigan near here.

*Saugatuck
Township
ZIP: 49453 **Lat:** 42-37-45 N **Long:** 86-10-49 W
Pop: 2,916 (1990); 3,780 (1980) **Pop Density:** 115.3
Land: 25.3 sq. mi.; **Water:** 0.9 sq. mi.

South Haven
City
Lat: 42-25-10 N **Long:** 86-16-21 W
Pop: 0 (1990); 5,943 (1980)
Land: 0.01 sq. mi.; **Water:** 0.0 sq. mi.

First settlers arrived 1831. Part of the town is also in Van Buren County.
Name origin: For its location south of Grand Haven.

Trowbridge
Township
Lat: 42-27-59 N **Long:** 85-50-37 W
Pop: 2,328 (1990); 2,210 (1980) **Pop Density:** 67.1
Land: 34.7 sq. mi.; **Water:** 1.1 sq. mi.

Valley
Township
Lat: 42-33-06 N **Long:** 85-57-20 W
Pop: 1,145 (1990); 906 (1980) **Pop Density:** 34.7
Land: 33.0 sq. mi.; **Water:** 3.0 sq. mi.

Watson
Township
Lat: 42-33-19 N **Long:** 85-43-32 W
Pop: 1,897 (1990); 1,658 (1980) **Pop Density:** 53.6
Land: 35.4 sq. mi.; **Water:** 0.7 sq. mi.

Wayland
City
ZIP: 49348 **Lat:** 42-40-18 N **Long:** 85-38-29 W
Pop: 2,751 (1990); 2,023 (1980) **Pop Density:** 1058.1
Land: 2.6 sq. mi.; **Water:** 0.0 sq. mi.

Settled 1837 by Col. Isaac Barnes.
Name origin: For Wayland, NY.

Alpena County
County Seat: Alpena (ZIP: 49707)

Pop: 30,605 (1990); 32,315 (1980)   **Pop Density:** 53.3
Land: 574.2 sq. mi.; **Water:** 1120.9 sq. mi.   **Area Code:** 517

On the northeastern coast of MI, bordered on the east by Lake Huron; established as Anamickee County Apr 1, 1840 from Presque Isle County; name changed Mar 8, 1843.

Name origin: From an Indian word probably meaning 'partridge' or 'partridge country.' Originally named for the Chippewa chief.

Alpena   City
ZIP: 49707   **Lat:** 45-04-22 N   **Long:** 83-26-15 W
Pop: 11,354 (1990); 12,214 (1980)   **Pop Density:** 1335.8
Land: 8.5 sq. mi.; **Water:** 0.7 sq. mi.

In northeastern MI on the Lower Peninsula at the north end of Thunder Bay on Lake Huron, 100 mi. northeast of Saginaw. County seat. Established as a city 1871.

Name origin: From an Indian word probably meaning 'partridge' or 'partridge country.' Previously named Anamickee.

*Alpena   Township
ZIP: 49707   **Lat:** 45-05-22 N   **Long:** 83-24-42 W
Pop: 9,602 (1990); 10,152 (1980)   **Pop Density:** 91.5
Land: 104.9 sq. mi.; **Water:** 36.4 sq. mi.

Green   Township
Lat: 45-00-28 N   **Long:** 83-48-23 W
Pop: 1,095 (1990); 1,083 (1980)   **Pop Density:** 15.3
Land: 71.4 sq. mi.; **Water:** 8.7 sq. mi.

Long Rapids   Township
Lat: 45-07-55 N   **Long:** 83-41-45 W
Pop: 1,021 (1990); 1,006 (1980)   **Pop Density:** 18.7
Land: 54.7 sq. mi.; **Water:** 0.0 sq. mi.

Maple Ridge   Township
Lat: 45-08-22 N   **Long:** 83-34-47 W
Pop: 1,514 (1990); 1,572 (1980)   **Pop Density:** 29.2
Land: 51.9 sq. mi.; **Water:** 1.9 sq. mi.

Ossineke   Township
ZIP: 49766   **Lat:** 44-53-33 N   **Long:** 83-42-28 W
Pop: 1,652 (1990); 1,607 (1980)   **Pop Density:** 15.6
Land: 106.0 sq. mi.; **Water:** 1.2 sq. mi.

Sanborn   Township
Lat: 44-53-31 N   **Long:** 83-26-05 W
Pop: 2,196 (1990); 2,297 (1980)   **Pop Density:** 50.1
Land: 43.8 sq. mi.; **Water:** 5.9 sq. mi.

Wellington   Township
Lat: 45-08-21 N   **Long:** 83-49-08 W
Pop: 269 (1990); 286 (1980)   **Pop Density:** 5.0
Land: 53.4 sq. mi.; **Water:** 0.0 sq. mi.

Wilson   Township
Lat: 45-00-19 N   **Long:** 83-36-48 W
Pop: 1,902 (1990); 2,098 (1980)   **Pop Density:** 23.9
Land: 79.5 sq. mi.; **Water:** 0.2 sq. mi.

Antrim County
County Seat: Bellaire (ZIP: 49615)

Pop: 18,185 (1990); 16,194 (1980)   **Pop Density:** 38.1
Land: 476.9 sq. mi.; **Water:** 125.0 sq. mi.   **Area Code:** 616

On the northwest coast of MI; established as Meegisee County Apr 1, 1840 from Mackinac County; name changed Mar 8, 1843.

Name origin: For the county in Ireland.

Banks   Township
Lat: 45-09-39 N   **Long:** 85-18-22 W
Pop: 1,513 (1990); 1,515 (1980)   **Pop Density:** 33.6
Land: 45.0 sq. mi.; **Water:** 6.2 sq. mi.

Bellaire   Village
ZIP: 49615   **Lat:** 44-58-33 N   **Long:** 85-12-24 W
Pop: 1,104 (1990); 1,063 (1980)   **Pop Density:** 849.2
Land: 1.3 sq. mi.; **Water:** 0.1 sq. mi.   **Elev:** 616 ft.

Founded on the property of Ambrose Palmer in northern MI, east of Grand Traverse Bay. Established 1879.

Name origin: For its descriptive connotations.

Central Lake   Village
ZIP: 49622   **Lat:** 45-04-11 N   **Long:** 85-15-47 W
Pop: 954 (1990); 895 (1980)   **Pop Density:** 795.0
Land: 1.2 sq. mi.; **Water:** 0.2 sq. mi.   **Elev:** 635 ft.

Not coextensive with the town of the same name.

Name origin: For its location on Central Lake.

*Central Lake   Township
ZIP: 49622   **Lat:** 45-04-38 N   **Long:** 85-16-54 W
Pop: 1,919 (1990); 1,766 (1980)   **Pop Density:** 69.5
Land: 27.6 sq. mi.; **Water:** 3.7 sq. mi.

Chestonia   Township
Lat: 44-59-09 N   **Long:** 85-01-38 W
Pop: 401 (1990); 433 (1980)   **Pop Density:** 11.3
Land: 35.5 sq. mi.; **Water:** 0.0 sq. mi.

MICHIGAN, Antrim County

Custer — Township
Lat: 44-53-45 N **Long:** 85-09-15 W
Pop: 630 (1990); 490 (1980) **Pop Density:** 18.2
Land: 34.7 sq. mi.; **Water:** 0.4 sq. mi.

Echo — Township
Lat: 45-04-58 N **Long:** 85-09-29 W
Pop: 766 (1990); 723 (1980) **Pop Density:** 21.9
Land: 34.9 sq. mi.; **Water:** 0.5 sq. mi.

Elk Rapids — Village
ZIP: 49629 **Lat:** 44-53-41 N **Long:** 85-24-15 W
Pop: 1,626 (1990); 1,504 (1980) **Pop Density:** 1016.3
Land: 1.6 sq. mi.; **Water:** 0.3 sq. mi. **Elev:** 587 ft.
Platted 1852. Not coextensive with the town of the same name.
Name origin: Named by an early settler for a pair of elk horns found in a nearby stream.

*Elk Rapids — Township
ZIP: 49629 **Lat:** 44-53-43 N **Long:** 85-23-55 W
Pop: 2,374 (1990); 2,086 (1980) **Pop Density:** 334.4
Land: 7.1 sq. mi.; **Water:** 3.8 sq. mi.

Ellsworth — Village
ZIP: 49729 **Lat:** 45-09-58 N **Long:** 85-14-39 W
Pop: 418 (1990); 436 (1980) **Pop Density:** 597.1
Land: 0.7 sq. mi.; **Water:** 0.1 sq. mi. **Elev:** 621 ft.
Name origin: For Civil War hero Elmer Ephraim Ellsworth (1837–61).

Forest Home — Township
Lat: 44-58-47 N **Long:** 85-15-09 W
Pop: 1,410 (1990); 1,333 (1980) **Pop Density:** 58.0
Land: 24.3 sq. mi.; **Water:** 9.3 sq. mi.

Helena — Township
Lat: 44-53-44 N **Long:** 85-15-42 W
Pop: 837 (1990); 781 (1980) **Pop Density:** 51.3
Land: 16.3 sq. mi.; **Water:** 6.9 sq. mi.

Jordan — Township
Lat: 45-04-31 N **Long:** 85-02-31 W
Pop: 583 (1990); 410 (1980) **Pop Density:** 16.5
Land: 35.3 sq. mi.; **Water:** 0.1 sq. mi.

Kearney — Township
Lat: 44-58-46 N **Long:** 85-09-28 W
Pop: 1,487 (1990); 1,241 (1980) **Pop Density:** 43.5
Land: 34.2 sq. mi.; **Water:** 0.9 sq. mi.

Mancelona — Village
ZIP: 49659 **Lat:** 44-54-07 N **Long:** 85-03-39 W
Pop: 1,370 (1990); 1,432 (1980) **Pop Density:** 1370.0
Land: 1.0 sq. mi.; **Water:** 0.0 sq. mi.
Established 1889. Not coextensive with the town of the same name.
Name origin: For the youngest daughter of Perry Andress, first settler and postmaster.

*Mancelona — Township
ZIP: 49659 **Lat:** 44-54-20 N **Long:** 84-57-33 W
Pop: 3,173 (1990); 2,720 (1980) **Pop Density:** 44.4
Land: 71.4 sq. mi.; **Water:** 0.3 sq. mi.

Milton — Township
Lat: 44-55-13 N **Long:** 85-20-13 W
Pop: 1,468 (1990); 1,271 (1980) **Pop Density:** 56.9
Land: 25.8 sq. mi.; **Water:** 19.1 sq. mi.

Star — Township
Lat: 44-59-55 N **Long:** 84-54-33 W
Pop: 575 (1990); 453 (1980) **Pop Density:** 16.8
Land: 34.2 sq. mi.; **Water:** 0.1 sq. mi.

Torch Lake — Township
Lat: 45-02-47 N **Long:** 85-20-56 W
Pop: 762 (1990); 711 (1980) **Pop Density:** 50.1
Land: 15.2 sq. mi.; **Water:** 5.9 sq. mi.

Warner — Township
Lat: 45-04-10 N **Long:** 84-54-27 W
Pop: 287 (1990); 261 (1980) **Pop Density:** 8.1
Land: 35.4 sq. mi.; **Water:** 0.2 sq. mi.

Arenac County
County Seat: Standish (ZIP: 48658)

Pop: 14,931 (1990); 14,706 (1980) **Pop Density:** 40.7
Land: 366.9 sq. mi.; **Water:** 313.9 sq. mi. **Area Code:** 517
On the east coast of MI on Saginaw Bay; established Mar 2, 1831 (prior to statehood).
Name origin: Name coined by Henry Rowe Schoolcraft (1793–1864), author, explorer, MI legislator, and superintendent of Indian Affairs for MI (1836–41), meaning 'sandy place' from Spanish *arena* 'sand' and *-ac* 'place of.'

Adams — Township
Lat: 44-02-22 N **Long:** 84-06-00 W
Pop: 417 (1990); 457 (1980) **Pop Density:** 11.7
Land: 35.7 sq. mi.; **Water:** 0.1 sq. mi.

Arenac — Township
Lat: 44-02-20 N **Long:** 83-51-48 W
Pop: 921 (1990); 892 (1980) **Pop Density:** 25.2
Land: 36.6 sq. mi.; **Water:** 1.4 sq. mi.

Au Gres — City
ZIP: 48703 **Lat:** 44-02-39 N **Long:** 83-41-34 W
Pop: 838 (1990); 768 (1980) **Pop Density:** 380.9
Land: 2.2 sq. mi.; **Water:** 0.1 sq. mi. **Elev:** 589 ft.
Name origin: From French 'gritty stone' in the region.

American Places Dictionary MICHIGAN, Baraga County

*Au Gres — Township
ZIP: 48703 Lat: 44-02-15 N Long: 83-44-30 W
Pop: 1,007 (1990); 907 (1980) Pop Density: 29.6
Land: 34.0 sq. mi.; Water: 5.0 sq. mi.

Clayton — Township
 Lat: 44-07-28 N Long: 83-59-07 W
Pop: 908 (1990); 967 (1980) Pop Density: 28.3
Land: 32.1 sq. mi.; Water: 0.0 sq. mi.

Deep River — Township
 Lat: 44-02-28 N Long: 83-59-12 W
Pop: 2,074 (1990); 1,874 (1980) Pop Density: 58.6
Land: 35.4 sq. mi.; Water: 0.1 sq. mi.

Lincoln — Township
 Lat: 43-57-30 N Long: 84-00-39 W
Pop: 969 (1990); 1,090 (1980) Pop Density: 46.1
Land: 21.0 sq. mi.; Water: 0.1 sq. mi.

Mason — Township
 Lat: 44-07-26 N Long: 83-52-07 W
Pop: 865 (1990); 852 (1980) Pop Density: 26.9
Land: 32.1 sq. mi.; Water: 0.0 sq. mi.

Moffatt — Township
 Lat: 44-07-16 N Long: 84-06-28 W
Pop: 780 (1990); 657 (1980) Pop Density: 24.6
Land: 31.7 sq. mi.; Water: 0.4 sq. mi.

Omer — City
ZIP: 48749 Lat: 44-02-58 N Long: 83-51-25 W
Pop: 385 (1990); 403 (1980) Pop Density: 320.8
Land: 1.2 sq. mi.; Water: 0.0 sq. mi.
Settled 1860s.
Name origin: Called Homer until a postal conflict led to its shortening.

Sims — Township
 Lat: 44-03-03 N Long: 83-34-58 W
Pop: 836 (1990); 695 (1980) Pop Density: 72.7
Land: 11.5 sq. mi.; Water: 32.2 sq. mi.

Standish — City
ZIP: 48658 Lat: 43-58-50 N Long: 83-57-48 W
Pop: 1,377 (1990); 1,264 (1980) Pop Density: 655.7
Land: 2.1 sq. mi.; Water: 0.0 sq. mi. Elev: 631 ft.
Name origin: For pioneer John Standish, who built a mill here in 1871.

*Standish — Township
ZIP: 48658 Lat: 43-57-12 N Long: 83-55-08 W
Pop: 1,945 (1990); 2,011 (1980) Pop Density: 70.2
Land: 27.7 sq. mi.; Water: 2.9 sq. mi.

Sterling — Village
ZIP: 48659 Lat: 44-01-55 N Long: 84-01-13 W
Pop: 520 (1990); 457 (1980) Pop Density: 520.0
Land: 1.0 sq. mi.; Water: 0.0 sq. mi. Elev: 759 ft.
Incorporated 1917.
Name origin: For lumberman William C. Sterling.

Turner — Village
ZIP: 48765 Lat: 44-08-30 N Long: 83-47-17 W
Pop: 158 (1990); 187 (1980) Pop Density: 158.0
Land: 1.0 sq. mi.; Water: 0.0 sq. mi.
Founded by Joseph Turner. Not coextensive with the town of the same name.
Name origin: For its founder.

*Turner — Township
ZIP: 48765 Lat: 44-07-27 N Long: 83-45-06 W
Pop: 628 (1990); 791 (1980) Pop Density: 19.4
Land: 32.4 sq. mi.; Water: 0.0 sq. mi.

Twining — Village
ZIP: 48766 Lat: 44-06-45 N Long: 83-48-28 W
Pop: 169 (1990); 196 (1980) Pop Density: 169.0
Land: 1.0 sq. mi.; Water: 0.0 sq. mi.
Name origin: For lumberman Frederick Twining.

Whitney — Township
 Lat: 44-05-49 N Long: 83-34-44 W
Pop: 981 (1990); 1,078 (1980) Pop Density: 31.3
Land: 31.3 sq. mi.; Water: 16.3 sq. mi.

Baraga County
County Seat: L'Anse (ZIP: 49946)

Pop: 7,954 (1990); 8,484 (1980) Pop Density: 8.8
Land: 904.2 sq. mi.; Water: 165.0 sq. mi. Area Code: 906
On the north coast of the Upper Peninsula of MI on Keweenaw Bay; established Feb 19, 1875 from Houghton County.
Name origin: For the Rev. Frederic Baraga (1797–1868), Slovenian-born Roman Catholic missionary to the Ojibways who became a bishop in 1853. He established schools for the Chippewa and Ottawa (1830–68).

Arvon — Township
 Lat: 46-50-45 N Long: 88-10-20 W
Pop: 422 (1990); 439 (1980) Pop Density: 3.4
Land: 124.6 sq. mi.; Water: 6.7 sq. mi.

Baraga — Village
ZIP: 49908 Lat: 46-46-38 N Long: 88-29-36 W
Pop: 1,231 (1990); 1,055 (1980) Pop Density: 586.2
Land: 2.1 sq. mi.; Water: 0.5 sq. mi. Elev: 614 ft.
Not coextensive with the town of the same name.
Name origin: For the Rev. Frederic Baraga (1797–1868), Slovenian-born Roman Catholic missionary to the Ojibways who became a bishop in 1853. He established schools for the Chippewa and Ottawa (1830–68).

*Baraga — Township
ZIP: 49908 Lat: 46-44-19 N Long: 88-34-19 W
Pop: 2,832 (1990); 2,717 (1980) Pop Density: 15.3
Land: 185.7 sq. mi.; Water: 1.7 sq. mi.

MICHIGAN, Baraga County

Covington
Township
ZIP: 49919 **Lat:** 46-30-53 N **Long:** 88-30-37 W
Pop: 651 (1990); 734 (1980) **Pop Density:** 3.4
Land: 193.2 sq. mi.; **Water:** 3.2 sq. mi.

L'Anse
Village
ZIP: 49946 **Lat:** 46-45-12 N **Long:** 88-26-57 W
Pop: 2,151 (1990); 2,500 (1980) **Pop Density:** 896.2
Land: 2.4 sq. mi.; **Water:** 0.0 sq. mi. **Elev:** 682 ft.
On the northwestern coast of the Upper Peninsula of MI at the southern end of Keweenaw Bay. Not coextensive with the town of the same name.

Name origin: For a French Indian mission established here 1660 and given the French name for 'the bay.'

*L'Anse
Township
Lat: 46-42-58 N **Long:** 88-18-25 W
Pop: 3,818 (1990); 4,316 (1980) **Pop Density:** 15.4
Land: 248.7 sq. mi.; **Water:** 20.3 sq. mi.

Spurr
Township
Lat: 46-31-46 N **Long:** 88-12-49 W
Pop: 231 (1990); 278 (1980) **Pop Density:** 1.5
Land: 151.9 sq. mi.; **Water:** 7.3 sq. mi.

Barry County
County Seat: Hastings (ZIP: 49058)

Pop: 50,057 (1990); 45,781 (1980) **Pop Density:** 90.0
Land: 556.2 sq. mi.; **Water:** 20.8 sq. mi. **Area Code:** 616
In southwestern MI, northeast of Kalamazoo; established Oct 29, 1829 (prior to statehood) from Eaton County.

Name origin: For William Taylor Barry (1784-1835), KY legislator, U.S. senator (1814-16), and U.S. Postmaster General (1829-35).

Assyria
Township
Lat: 42-27-23 N **Long:** 85-08-01 W
Pop: 1,799 (1990); 1,714 (1980) **Pop Density:** 49.8
Land: 36.1 sq. mi.; **Water:** 0.3 sq. mi.

Baltimore
Township
Lat: 42-32-52 N **Long:** 85-14-40 W
Pop: 1,701 (1990); 1,697 (1980) **Pop Density:** 48.1
Land: 35.4 sq. mi.; **Water:** 0.7 sq. mi.

Barry
Township
Lat: 42-27-51 N **Long:** 85-22-17 W
Pop: 3,190 (1990); 3,146 (1980) **Pop Density:** 91.7
Land: 34.8 sq. mi.; **Water:** 1.7 sq. mi.

Carlton
Township
Lat: 42-43-25 N **Long:** 85-15-13 W
Pop: 2,067 (1990); 1,981 (1980) **Pop Density:** 58.7
Land: 35.2 sq. mi.; **Water:** 0.5 sq. mi. **Elev:** 832 ft.

Castleton
Township
Lat: 42-38-34 N **Long:** 85-07-45 W
Pop: 3,379 (1990); 3,290 (1980) **Pop Density:** 96.3
Land: 35.1 sq. mi.; **Water:** 0.6 sq. mi.

Freeport
Village
ZIP: 49325 **Lat:** 42-45-48 N **Long:** 85-18-52 W
Pop: 458 (1990); 479 (1980) **Pop Density:** 572.5
Land: 0.8 sq. mi.; **Water:** 0.0 sq. mi.

Name origin: Named by founders, the Rousch brothers, for Freeport, OH, their former home.

Hastings
City
ZIP: 49058 **Lat:** 42-39-00 N **Long:** 85-17-18 W
Pop: 6,549 (1990); 6,418 (1980) **Pop Density:** 1259.4
Land: 5.2 sq. mi.; **Water:** 0.0 sq. mi. **Elev:** 810 ft.
Settled 1836.

Name origin: For bank president E. P. Hastings, who owned the townsite.

*Hastings
Township
ZIP: 49058 **Lat:** 42-37-45 N **Long:** 85-14-33 W
Pop: 2,830 (1990); 2,638 (1980) **Pop Density:** 93.7
Land: 30.2 sq. mi.; **Water:** 0.4 sq. mi.

Hope
Township
Lat: 42-33-09 N **Long:** 85-22-09 W
Pop: 2,993 (1990); 2,599 (1980) **Pop Density:** 91.8
Land: 32.6 sq. mi.; **Water:** 3.5 sq. mi.

Irving
Township
Lat: 42-43-05 N **Long:** 85-21-48 W
Pop: 1,905 (1990); 1,608 (1980) **Pop Density:** 53.1
Land: 35.9 sq. mi.; **Water:** 0.2 sq. mi.

Johnstown
Township
Lat: 42-27-40 N **Long:** 85-15-16 W
Pop: 2,932 (1990); 2,895 (1980) **Pop Density:** 83.3
Land: 35.2 sq. mi.; **Water:** 1.4 sq. mi.

Maple Grove
Township
Lat: 42-33-07 N **Long:** 85-07-54 W
Pop: 1,398 (1990); 1,358 (1980) **Pop Density:** 38.9
Land: 35.9 sq. mi.; **Water:** 0.0 sq. mi.

Middleville
Village
ZIP: 49333 **Lat:** 42-42-48 N **Long:** 85-27-55 W
Pop: 1,966 (1990); 1,797 (1980) **Pop Density:** 1156.5
Land: 1.7 sq. mi.; **Water:** 0.1 sq. mi. **Elev:** 726 ft.

Name origin: For its proximity to Middle Village. Previously called Thornapple.

Nashville
Village
ZIP: 49073 **Lat:** 42-36-10 N **Long:** 85-05-37 W
Pop: 1,654 (1990); 1,628 (1980) **Pop Density:** 787.6
Land: 2.1 sq. mi.; **Water:** 0.1 sq. mi.
Founded 1865.

Name origin: For railroad engineer George Nash.

Orangeville
Township
Lat: 42-33-13 N **Long:** 85-29-24 W
Pop: 2,880 (1990); 2,533 (1980) **Pop Density:** 85.7
Land: 33.6 sq. mi.; **Water:** 2.0 sq. mi.

American Places Dictionary   MICHIGAN, Bay County

Prairieville   Township
Lat: 42-27-28 N   **Long:** 85-28-47 W
Pop: 3,409 (1990); 3,031 (1980)   **Pop Density:** 102.4
Land: 33.3 sq. mi.; **Water:** 3.3 sq. mi.

Rutland   Township
Lat: 42-38-01 N   **Long:** 85-22-22 W
Pop: 2,797 (1990); 2,444 (1980)   **Pop Density:** 79.5
Land: 35.2 sq. mi.; **Water:** 1.0 sq. mi.

Thornapple   Township
ZIP: 49333   **Lat:** 42-43-46 N   **Long:** 85-29-24 W
Pop: 5,226 (1990); 4,298 (1980)   **Pop Density:** 147.2
Land: 35.5 sq. mi.; **Water:** 0.4 sq. mi.

Woodland   Village
ZIP: 48897   **Lat:** 42-43-35 N   **Long:** 85-08-05 W
Pop: 466 (1990); 431 (1980)   **Pop Density:** 582.5
Land: 0.8 sq. mi.; **Water:** 0.0 sq. mi.   **Elev:** 875 ft.
Settled 1837. Not coextensive with the town of the same name.
Name origin: Descriptively named for its location in thick woods.

*Woodland   Township
ZIP: 48897   **Lat:** 42-43-35 N   **Long:** 85-07-59 W
Pop: 2,025 (1990); 1,880 (1980)   **Pop Density:** 57.2
Land: 35.4 sq. mi.; **Water:** 0.5 sq. mi.

Yankee Springs   Township
ZIP: 49333   **Lat:** 42-38-44 N   **Long:** 85-29-00 W
Pop: 2,977 (1990); 2,251 (1980)   **Pop Density:** 94.5
Land: 31.5 sq. mi.; **Water:** 4.3 sq. mi.

Bay County
County Seat: Bay City (ZIP: 48704)

Pop: 111,723 (1990); 119,881 (1980)   **Pop Density:** 251.5
Land: 444.3 sq. mi.; **Water:** 186.7 sq. mi.   **Area Code:** 517
On the east coast of MI, north of Saginaw; established Feb 17, 1857 from Saginaw and Midland counties.
Name origin: For its location at the head of Saginaw Bay.

Auburn   City
ZIP: 48611   **Lat:** 43-36-06 N   **Long:** 84-04-37 W
Pop: 1,855 (1990); 1,921 (1980)   **Pop Density:** 1855.0
Land: 1.0 sq. mi.; **Water:** 0.0 sq. mi.
Name origin: Named in 1877 for the town in "The Deserted Village" by English poet Oliver Goldsmith (1730-74).

Bangor   Township
ZIP: 48706   **Lat:** 43-39-03 N   **Long:** 83-53-43 W
Pop: 16,028 (1990); 17,494 (1980)   **Pop Density:** 1153.1
Land: 13.9 sq. mi.; **Water:** 7.2 sq. mi.

Bay City   City
ZIP: 48707   **Lat:** 43-35-24 N   **Long:** 83-53-19 W
Pop: 38,936 (1990); 41,593 (1980)   **Pop Density:** 3743.8
Land: 10.4 sq. mi.; **Water:** 0.9 sq. mi.
In east-central MI on Lake Huron's Saginaw Bay, 15 mi. north of Saginaw. Established 1865.
Name origin: Descriptive of its location.

Beaver   Township
Lat: 43-41-49 N   **Long:** 84-06-27 W
Pop: 2,810 (1990); 3,027 (1980)   **Pop Density:** 79.4
Land: 35.4 sq. mi.; **Water:** 0.0 sq. mi.

Essexville   City
ZIP: 48732   **Lat:** 43-36-40 N   **Long:** 83-50-36 W
Pop: 4,088 (1990); 4,378 (1980)   **Pop Density:** 3406.7
Land: 1.2 sq. mi.; **Water:** 0.2 sq. mi.
Settled 1850 by Ransom Essex.
Name origin: For the first settler.

Frankenlust   Township
Lat: 43-32-23 N   **Long:** 83-58-19 W
Pop: 2,281 (1990); 2,525 (1980)   **Pop Density:** 100.0
Land: 22.8 sq. mi.; **Water:** 0.3 sq. mi.

Fraser   Township
Lat: 43-47-06 N   **Long:** 83-59-09 W
Pop: 3,680 (1990); 3,954 (1980)   **Pop Density:** 113.9
Land: 32.3 sq. mi.; **Water:** 5.9 sq. mi.

Garfield   Township
Lat: 43-46-37 N   **Long:** 84-05-48 W
Pop: 1,736 (1990); 1,810 (1980)   **Pop Density:** 48.6
Land: 35.7 sq. mi.; **Water:** 0.0 sq. mi.

Gibson   Township
Lat: 43-57-27 N   **Long:** 84-05-57 W
Pop: 1,090 (1990); 1,068 (1980)   **Pop Density:** 30.5
Land: 35.7 sq. mi.; **Water:** 0.0 sq. mi.

Hampton   Township
ZIP: 48732   **Lat:** 43-36-18 N   **Long:** 83-46-11 W
Pop: 9,520 (1990); 10,418 (1980)   **Pop Density:** 351.3
Land: 27.1 sq. mi.; **Water:** 5.5 sq. mi.
In east-central MI on Lake Huron's Saginaw Bay

Kawkawlin   Township
ZIP: 48631   **Lat:** 43-41-57 N   **Long:** 83-58-41 W
Pop: 4,852 (1990); 5,077 (1980)   **Pop Density:** 148.4
Land: 32.7 sq. mi.; **Water:** 9.7 sq. mi.

Merritt   Township
Lat: 43-31-06 N   **Long:** 83-44-55 W
Pop: 1,510 (1990); 1,676 (1980)   **Pop Density:** 47.6
Land: 31.7 sq. mi.; **Water:** 0.0 sq. mi.

Midland   City
ZIP: 48640   **Lat:** 43-36-09 N   **Long:** 84-09-47 W
Pop: 234 (1990); 234 (1980)   **Pop Density:** 585.0
Land: 0.4 sq. mi.; **Water:** 0.0 sq. mi.   **Elev:** 629 ft.
In east-central MI on the Tittabawassee River, 50 mi. north-

west of Flint. County seat; settled 1836; became village 1869; city 1887. Part of the town is also in Midland County.
Name origin: For its county, located in the middle of the state and near Saginaw Bay.

Monitor
Township
ZIP: 48706 Lat: 43-36-29 N Long: 83-58-55 W
Pop: 9,512 (1990); 10,143 (1980) Pop Density: 257.8
Land: 36.9 sq. mi.; Water: 0.0 sq. mi.

Mount Forest
Township
Lat: 43-52-10 N Long: 84-06-35 W
Pop: 1,457 (1990); 1,444 (1980) Pop Density: 40.5
Land: 36.0 sq. mi.; Water: 0.0 sq. mi.

Pinconning
City
ZIP: 48650 Lat: 43-51-28 N Long: 83-57-52 W
Pop: 1,291 (1990); 1,430 (1980) Pop Density: 1434.4
Land: 0.9 sq. mi.; Water: 0.0 sq. mi.
Name origin: For the nearby Pinconning River.

*Pinconning
Township
ZIP: 48650 Lat: 43-52-27 N Long: 83-58-34 W
Pop: 2,647 (1990); 2,984 (1980) Pop Density: 72.3
Land: 36.6 sq. mi.; Water: 5.4 sq. mi.

Portsmouth
Township
Lat: 43-33-29 N Long: 83-49-45 W
Pop: 3,918 (1990); 4,291 (1980) Pop Density: 195.9
Land: 20.0 sq. mi.; Water: 0.1 sq. mi.

Williams
Township
Lat: 43-36-20 N Long: 84-06-14 W
Pop: 4,278 (1990); 4,414 (1980) Pop Density: 127.3
Land: 33.6 sq. mi.; Water: 0.0 sq. mi.

Benzie County
County Seat: Beulah (ZIP: 49617)

Pop: 12,200 (1990); 11,205 (1980) Pop Density: 38.0
Land: 321.3 sq. mi.; Water: 538.4 sq. mi. Area Code: 616

On the northwestern coast of MI, bordered on west by Lake Michigan; established Feb 27, 1863 from Manistee and Grand Traverse counties.

Name origin: Origin uncertain; perhaps a variant of the French name for the Betsie River, *Aux Bec Scies* 'sawbill,' a species of duck. Americans corrupted it to *Betsie*, then to *Benzie* for the county.

Almira
Township
Lat: 44-43-41 N Long: 85-52-21 W
Pop: 1,449 (1990); 1,078 (1980) Pop Density: 42.9
Land: 33.8 sq. mi.; Water: 2.2 sq. mi.

Benzonia
Village
ZIP: 49616 Lat: 44-36-59 N Long: 86-05-52 W
Pop: 449 (1990); 466 (1980) Pop Density: 449.0
Land: 1.0 sq. mi.; Water: 0.0 sq. mi.
Not coextensive with the town of the same name.
Name origin: The French term for the local river was *Aux Bec Scies* meaning 'sawbill,' a species of duck. American sailors corrupted it into the Betsie River, which in turn became Benzie when the county was formed, then into the present town name.

*Benzonia
Township
ZIP: 49616 Lat: 44-38-18 N Long: 86-05-17 W
Pop: 2,405 (1990); 2,461 (1980) Pop Density: 85.0
Land: 28.3 sq. mi.; Water: 5.7 sq. mi.

Beulah
Village
ZIP: 49617 Lat: 44-37-46 N Long: 86-05-43 W
Pop: 421 (1990); 454 (1980) Pop Density: 1052.5
Land: 0.4 sq. mi.; Water: 0.0 sq. mi.
Settled 1880s.
Name origin: For the biblical name prophesied for Israel by Isaiah.

Blaine
Township
Lat: 44-33-00 N Long: 86-10-52 W
Pop: 424 (1990); 449 (1980) Pop Density: 21.9
Land: 19.4 sq. mi.; Water: 1.6 sq. mi.

Colfax
Township
Lat: 44-33-21 N Long: 85-52-33 W
Pop: 415 (1990); 340 (1980) Pop Density: 11.6
Land: 35.8 sq. mi.; Water: 0.1 sq. mi.

Crystal Lake
Township
Lat: 44-38-12 N Long: 86-12-25 W
Pop: 759 (1990); 753 (1980) Pop Density: 59.3
Land: 12.8 sq. mi.; Water: 4.2 sq. mi.

Elberta
Village
ZIP: 49628 Lat: 44-37-17 N Long: 86-13-46 W
Pop: 478 (1990); 556 (1980) Pop Density: 682.9
Land: 0.7 sq. mi.; Water: 0.2 sq. mi.
Name origin: Named in 1911 for the locally grown Elberta peach. Previously called Frankfort.

Frankfort
City
ZIP: 49635 Lat: 44-38-12 N Long: 86-14-02 W
Pop: 1,546 (1990); 1,603 (1980) Pop Density: 1104.3
Land: 1.4 sq. mi.; Water: 0.2 sq. mi. Elev: 600 ft.
Settled 1850.
Name origin: For Frankfurt, Germany, with spelling altered to reflect pronunciation.

Gilmore
Township
Lat: 44-36-19 N Long: 86-11-24 W
Pop: 794 (1990); 794 (1980) Pop Density: 108.8
Land: 7.3 sq. mi.; Water: 0.2 sq. mi.

Homestead
Township
Lat: 44-38-47 N Long: 85-59-23 W
Pop: 1,477 (1990); 1,290 (1980) Pop Density: 48.9
Land: 30.2 sq. mi.; Water: 0.0 sq. mi.

Honor — Village
ZIP: 49640 Lat: 44-40-00 N Long: 86-01-12 W
Pop: 292 (1990); 281 (1980) Pop Density: 584.0
Land: 0.5 sq. mi.; Water: 0.0 sq. mi.
Founded 1895.
Name origin: For the baby daughter of local business executive J.A. Gifford.

Inland — Township
Lat: 44-38-41 N Long: 85-52-03 W
Pop: 1,096 (1990); 843 (1980) Pop Density: 30.6
Land: 35.8 sq. mi.; Water: 0.4 sq. mi.

Joyfield — Township
Lat: 44-33-04 N Long: 86-06-20 W
Pop: 626 (1990); 573 (1980) Pop Density: 31.3
Land: 20.0 sq. mi.; Water: 0.0 sq. mi.

Lake — Township
Lat: 44-41-46 N Long: 86-09-06 W
Pop: 508 (1990); 387 (1980) Pop Density: 21.4
Land: 23.7 sq. mi.; Water: 11.5 sq. mi.

Lake Ann — Village
ZIP: 49650 Lat: 44-43-32 N Long: 85-50-40 W
Pop: 217 (1990); 235 (1980) Pop Density: 542.5
Land: 0.4 sq. mi.; Water: 0.0 sq. mi.
Name origin: For Lake Ann, named for the wife of A.P. Wheelock, the first settler.

Platte — Township
Lat: 44-43-54 N Long: 86-00-11 W
Pop: 253 (1990); 256 (1980) Pop Density: 7.0
Land: 36.2 sq. mi.; Water: 0.2 sq. mi.

Thompsonville — Village
ZIP: 49683 Lat: 44-31-14 N Long: 85-56-19 W
Pop: 416 (1990); 331 (1980) Pop Density: 416.0
Land: 1.0 sq. mi.; Water: 0.0 sq. mi. Elev: 793 ft.
Incorporated 1892.
Name origin: For lumberman Sumner Thompson.

Weldon — Township
Lat: 44-33-32 N Long: 85-59-31 W
Pop: 448 (1990); 378 (1980) Pop Density: 12.2
Land: 36.6 sq. mi.; Water: 0.0 sq. mi.

Berrien County
County Seat: St. Joseph (ZIP: 49085)

Pop: 161,378 (1990); 171,276 (1980) Pop Density: 282.6
Land: 571.0 sq. mi.; Water: 1010.4 sq. mi. Area Code: 616
In the southwestern corner of MI, bordered on west by Lake Michigan; established Oct 29, 1829 (prior to statehood) from Indian lands.
Name origin: For Col. John Macpherson Berrien (1781–1856), U.S. senator from GA (1825–29; 1841–52) and U.S. attorney general (1829–31).

Bainbridge — Township
Lat: 42-06-56 N Long: 86-17-20 W
Pop: 2,865 (1990); 2,879 (1980) Pop Density: 81.4
Land: 35.2 sq. mi.; Water: 0.3 sq. mi.

Baroda — Village
ZIP: 49101 Lat: 41-57-16 N Long: 86-29-15 W
Pop: 657 (1990); 627 (1980) Pop Density: 1095.0
Land: 0.6 sq. mi.; Water: 0.0 sq. mi.
Not coextensive with the town of the same name.

*Baroda — Township
ZIP: 49101 Lat: 41-56-41 N Long: 86-29-17 W
Pop: 2,731 (1990); 2,666 (1980) Pop Density: 153.4
Land: 17.8 sq. mi.; Water: 0.0 sq. mi.

Benton Charter — Township
ZIP: 49022 Lat: 42-06-55 N Long: 86-23-47 W
Pop: 17,163 (1990); 19,120 (1980) Pop Density: 526.5
Land: 32.6 sq. mi.; Water: 0.1 sq. mi.

Benton Harbor — City
ZIP: 49022 Lat: 42-06-59 N Long: 86-26-46 W
Pop: 12,818 (1990); 14,707 (1980) Pop Density: 2913.2
Land: 4.4 sq. mi.; Water: 0.1 sq. mi.
In southwestern MI on Lake Michigan, 50 mi. southwest of Kalamazoo. Founded 1863.
Name origin: For U.S. Senator and Representative Thomas Hart Benton (1782–1858).

Benton Heights — CDP
ZIP: 49022 Lat: 42-07-15 N Long: 86-24-54 W
Pop: 5,465 (1990); 6,787 (1980) Pop Density: 1438.2
Land: 3.8 sq. mi.; Water: 0.0 sq. mi.

Berrien — Township
Lat: 41-56-15 N Long: 86-17-18 W
Pop: 4,697 (1990); 4,302 (1980) Pop Density: 133.1
Land: 35.3 sq. mi.; Water: 1.4 sq. mi.

Berrien Springs — Village
ZIP: 49103 Lat: 41-56-50 N Long: 86-20-24 W
Pop: 1,927 (1990); 2,042 (1980) Pop Density: 2141.1
Land: 0.9 sq. mi.; Water: 0.1 sq. mi.
Settled 1830s.
Name origin: For Col. John Macpherson Berrien (1781–1856), U.S. senator from GA (1825–29; 1841–52) and U.S. attorney general (1829–31).

Bertrand — Township
Lat: 41-47-07 N Long: 86-22-29 W
Pop: 2,228 (1990); 2,369 (1980) Pop Density: 64.6
Land: 34.5 sq. mi.; Water: 0.5 sq. mi.

Bridgman — City
ZIP: 49106 Lat: 41-56-26 N Long: 86-33-48 W
Pop: 2,140 (1990); 2,235 (1980) Pop Density: 737.9
Land: 2.9 sq. mi.; Water: 0.0 sq. mi.
Name origin: For a local lumber company owner. Previously called Charlotteville.

MICHIGAN, Berrien County

Buchanan
City
ZIP: 49107   **Lat:** 41-49-40 N   **Long:** 86-22-00 W
Pop: 4,992 (1990); 5,142 (1980)   **Pop Density:** 2080.0
Land: 2.4 sq. mi.; **Water:** 0.0 sq. mi.
Settled 1833.
Name origin: For James Buchanan (1791–1868), U.S. senator and fifteenth U.S. president.

*Buchanan
Township
ZIP: 49107   **Lat:** 41-51-33 N   **Long:** 86-24-29 W
Pop: 3,402 (1990); 3,571 (1980)   **Pop Density:** 105.7
Land: 32.2 sq. mi.; **Water:** 1.0 sq. mi.

Chikaming
Township
         Lat: 41-51-46 N   **Long:** 86-37-11 W
Pop: 3,717 (1990); 4,302 (1980)   **Pop Density:** 168.2
Land: 22.1 sq. mi.; **Water:** 0.1 sq. mi.

Coloma
City
ZIP: 49038   **Lat:** 42-11-11 N   **Long:** 86-18-27 W
Pop: 1,679 (1990); 1,833 (1980)   **Pop Density:** 1865.6
Land: 0.9 sq. mi.; **Water:** 0.0 sq. mi.   **Elev:** 649 ft.
Settled 1834.
Name origin: For Coloma, CA. Previously called Dickerville.

*Coloma
Township
ZIP: 49038   **Lat:** 42-12-27 N   **Long:** 86-18-21 W
Pop: 5,123 (1990); 5,345 (1980)   **Pop Density:** 281.5
Land: 18.2 sq. mi.; **Water:** 0.8 sq. mi.

Eau Claire
Village
ZIP: 49111   **Lat:** 41-59-02 N   **Long:** 86-18-13 W
Pop: 494 (1990); 573 (1980)   **Pop Density:** 705.7
Land: 0.7 sq. mi.; **Water:** 0.0 sq. mi.
Name origin: Named by early settlers for a sparkling creek. From French 'clear water.'

Fair Plain
CDP
ZIP: 49022   **Lat:** 42-04-54 N   **Long:** 86-27-12 W
Pop: 8,051 (1990); 5,057 (1980)   **Pop Density:** 1916.9
Land: 4.2 sq. mi.; **Water:** 0.2 sq. mi.

Galien
Village
ZIP: 49113   **Lat:** 41-48-05 N   **Long:** 86-29-58 W
Pop: 596 (1990); 692 (1980)   **Pop Density:** 1490.0
Land: 0.4 sq. mi.; **Water:** 0.0 sq. mi.   **Elev:** 679 ft.
Not coextensive with the town of the same name.
Name origin: For French explorer Reno De Galien.

*Galien
Township
ZIP: 49113   **Lat:** 41-47-26 N   **Long:** 86-30-52 W
Pop: 1,591 (1990); 1,786 (1980)   **Pop Density:** 72.0
Land: 22.1 sq. mi.; **Water:** 0.0 sq. mi.

Grand Beach
Village
         Lat: 41-46-28 N   **Long:** 86-47-17 W
Pop: 146 (1990); 227 (1980)   **Pop Density:** 162.2
Land: 0.9 sq. mi.; **Water:** 0.0 sq. mi.
Name origin: Descriptively named for its location on the shores of Lake Michigan.

Hagar
Township
         Lat: 42-11-27 N   **Long:** 86-22-36 W
Pop: 4,113 (1990); 4,943 (1980)   **Pop Density:** 221.1
Land: 18.6 sq. mi.; **Water:** 0.1 sq. mi.

Lake Charter
Township
         Lat: 41-56-15 N   **Long:** 86-32-36 W
Pop: 2,487 (1990); 2,212 (1980)   **Pop Density:** 133.0
Land: 18.7 sq. mi.; **Water:** 0.0 sq. mi.

Lake Michigan Beach
CDP
         Lat: 42-12-51 N   **Long:** 86-22-56 W
Pop: 1,694 (1990); 2,001 (1980)   **Pop Density:** 445.8
Land: 3.8 sq. mi.; **Water:** 2.3 sq. mi.

Lincoln
Township
ZIP: 49127   **Lat:** 42-00-55 N   **Long:** 86-30-21 W
Pop: 13,604 (1990); 13,520 (1980)   **Pop Density:** 760.0
Land: 17.9 sq. mi.; **Water:** 0.5 sq. mi.

Michiana
Village
         Lat: 41-45-48 N   **Long:** 86-48-40 W
Pop: 164 (1990); 333 (1980)   **Pop Density:** 410.0
Land: 0.4 sq. mi.; **Water:** 0.0 sq. mi.
Name origin: Coined from the first syllable of MI and the last three of IN; for its location on the MI-IN border.

New Buffalo
City
ZIP: 49117   **Lat:** 41-47-25 N   **Long:** 86-44-42 W
Pop: 2,317 (1990); 2,821 (1980)   **Pop Density:** 1103.3
Land: 2.1 sq. mi.; **Water:** 0.1 sq. mi.
Name origin: For Buffalo, NY.

*New Buffalo
Township
ZIP: 49117   **Lat:** 41-47-15 N   **Long:** 86-43-18 W
Pop: 2,419 (1990); 2,878 (1980)   **Pop Density:** 118.0
Land: 20.5 sq. mi.; **Water:** 0.0 sq. mi.

Niles
City
ZIP: 49120   **Lat:** 41-49-52 N   **Long:** 86-15-07 W
Pop: 12,456 (1990); 13,115 (1980)   **Pop Density:** 2442.4
Land: 5.1 sq. mi.; **Water:** 0.1 sq. mi.   **Elev:** 658 ft.
In southwestern MI, 25 mi. southeast of Benton Harbor. Settled 1829. Part of the town is also in Cass County.
Name origin: For editor, publisher, and author Hezekiah Niles (1777–1830).

*Niles
Township
ZIP: 49120   **Lat:** 41-50-58 N   **Long:** 86-16-27 W
Pop: 12,828 (1990); 13,165 (1980)   **Pop Density:** 340.3
Land: 37.7 sq. mi.; **Water:** 0.8 sq. mi.

Oronoko
Township
ZIP: 49103   **Lat:** 41-56-44 N   **Long:** 86-24-27 W
Pop: 9,819 (1990); 10,761 (1980)   **Pop Density:** 302.1
Land: 32.5 sq. mi.; **Water:** 0.8 sq. mi.

Paw Paw Lake
CDP
         Lat: 42-12-40 N   **Long:** 86-16-32 W
Pop: 3,782 (1990); 2,720 (1980)   **Pop Density:** 727.3
Land: 5.2 sq. mi.; **Water:** 1.5 sq. mi.

Pipestone
Township
         Lat: 42-01-51 N   **Long:** 86-17-26 W
Pop: 2,303 (1990); 2,364 (1980)   **Pop Density:** 64.5
Land: 35.7 sq. mi.; **Water:** 0.2 sq. mi.

Royalton
Township
         Lat: 42-01-01 N   **Long:** 86-25-31 W
Pop: 3,135 (1990); 3,046 (1980)   **Pop Density:** 173.2
Land: 18.1 sq. mi.; **Water:** 0.4 sq. mi.

St. Joseph
City
ZIP: 49085   **Lat:** 42-05-48 N   **Long:** 86-29-28 W
Pop: 9,214 (1990); 9,622 (1980)   **Pop Density:** 2710.0
Land: 3.4 sq. mi.; **Water:** 2.5 sq. mi.
Name origin: For the St. Joseph River, which traverses the town.

St. Joseph Charter Township
ZIP: 49022　　**Lat:** 42-04-07 N **Long:** 86-28-47 W
Pop: 9,613 (1990); 9,961 (1980)　　**Pop Density:** 1434.8
Land: 6.7 sq. mi.; **Water:** 0.3 sq. mi.

Shoreham Village
　　　　　　　Lat: 42-03-27 N **Long:** 86-30-41 W
Pop: 737 (1990); 742 (1980)　　**Pop Density:** 1228.3
Land: 0.6 sq. mi.; **Water:** 0.0 sq. mi.　　**Elev:** 605 ft.
Incorporated 1930.
Name origin: For its location along Lake Michigan.

Shorewood-Tower Hills-Harbert CDP
　　　　　　　Lat: 41-53-04 N **Long:** 86-37-13 W
Pop: 1,636 (1990); 1,720 (1980)　　**Pop Density:** 363.6
Land: 4.5 sq. mi.; **Water:** 2.1 sq. mi.

Sodus Township
ZIP: 49126　　**Lat:** 42-01-44 N **Long:** 86-21-48 W
Pop: 2,065 (1990); 2,260 (1980)　　**Pop Density:** 105.9
Land: 19.5 sq. mi.; **Water:** 0.5 sq. mi.

Stevensville Village
ZIP: 49127　　**Lat:** 42-00-49 N **Long:** 86-31-30 W
Pop: 1,230 (1990); 1,268 (1980)　　**Pop Density:** 1230.0
Land: 1.0 sq. mi.; **Water:** 0.0 sq. mi.　　**Elev:** 635 ft.
Name origin: For landowner Thomas Stevens, who platted the village in the 1870s.

Three Oaks Village
ZIP: 49128　　**Lat:** 41-47-57 N **Long:** 86-36-45 W
Pop: 1,786 (1990); 1,774 (1980)　　**Pop Density:** 1786.0
Land: 1.0 sq. mi.; **Water:** 0.0 sq. mi.　　**Elev:** 679 ft.
Settled 1850. Not coextensive with the town of the same name.
Name origin: For three white-oak trees growing on the town site.

*Three Oaks Township
ZIP: 49128　　**Lat:** 41-47-42 N **Long:** 86-37-18 W
Pop: 2,952 (1990); 3,045 (1980)　　**Pop Density:** 126.2
Land: 23.4 sq. mi.; **Water:** 0.1 sq. mi.

Watervliet City
ZIP: 49098　　**Lat:** 42-11-11 N **Long:** 86-15-25 W
Pop: 1,867 (1990); 1,867 (1980)　　**Pop Density:** 1555.8
Land: 1.2 sq. mi.; **Water:** 0.0 sq. mi.
Founded 1833.
Name origin: For Watervliet, NY.

*Watervliet Township
ZIP: 49098　　**Lat:** 42-11-52 N **Long:** 86-15-01 W
Pop: 2,926 (1990); 3,275 (1980)　　**Pop Density:** 215.1
Land: 13.6 sq. mi.; **Water:** 0.8 sq. mi.

Weesaw Township
　　　　　　　Lat: 41-51-21 N **Long:** 86-30-48 W
Pop: 2,114 (1990); 2,164 (1980)　　**Pop Density:** 59.5
Land: 35.5 sq. mi.; **Water:** 0.1 sq. mi.

Branch County
County Seat: Coldwater (ZIP: 49036)

Pop: 41,502 (1990); 40,188 (1980)　　**Pop Density:** 81.8
Land: 507.4 sq. mi.; **Water:** 12.1 sq. mi.　　**Area Code:** 517
On the south-central border of MI; established Oct 29, 1829 (prior to statehood) from St. Joseph County.
Name origin: For John Branch (1782–1863), NC governor (1817–20), U.S. secretary of the navy (1829–31), and governor of FL Territory (1844–45).

Algansee Township
　　　　　　　Lat: 41-51-25 N **Long:** 84-52-22 W
Pop: 1,859 (1990); 1,775 (1980)　　**Pop Density:** 52.2
Land: 35.6 sq. mi.; **Water:** 0.5 sq. mi.

Batavia Township
　　　　　　　Lat: 41-56-31 N **Long:** 85-07-07 W
Pop: 1,522 (1990); 1,572 (1980)　　**Pop Density:** 42.6
Land: 35.7 sq. mi.; **Water:** 0.4 sq. mi.

Bethel Township
　　　　　　　Lat: 41-51-10 N **Long:** 85-06-42 W
Pop: 1,279 (1990); 1,311 (1980)　　**Pop Density:** 35.6
Land: 35.9 sq. mi.; **Water:** 0.2 sq. mi.

Bronson City
ZIP: 49028　　**Lat:** 41-52-25 N **Long:** 85-11-29 W
Pop: 2,342 (1990); 2,271 (1980)　　**Pop Density:** 1801.5
Land: 1.3 sq. mi.; **Water:** 0.0 sq. mi.
Settled 1828.
Name origin: For Jebez Bronson, first settler.

*Bronson Township
ZIP: 49028　　**Lat:** 41-51-32 N **Long:** 85-14-11 W
Pop: 1,228 (1990); 1,331 (1980)　　**Pop Density:** 35.3
Land: 34.8 sq. mi.; **Water:** 0.0 sq. mi.

Butler Township
　　　　　　　Lat: 42-01-45 N **Long:** 84-52-30 W
Pop: 1,191 (1990); 1,060 (1980)　　**Pop Density:** 33.5
Land: 35.6 sq. mi.; **Water:** 0.1 sq. mi.

California Township
　　　　　　　Lat: 41-47-07 N **Long:** 84-53-19 W
Pop: 797 (1990); 713 (1980)　　**Pop Density:** 37.4
Land: 21.3 sq. mi.; **Water:** 0.0 sq. mi.

Coldwater City
ZIP: 49036　　**Lat:** 41-56-26 N **Long:** 85-00-16 W
Pop: 9,607 (1990); 9,461 (1980)　　**Pop Density:** 1412.8
Land: 6.8 sq. mi.; **Water:** 0.2 sq. mi.　　**Elev:** 969 ft.
Founded 1832; incorporated 1861. County seat. Not coextensive with the town of the same name.
Name origin: For the Coldwater River on which it is located.

MICHIGAN, Branch County

*Coldwater
Township
ZIP: 49036   Lat: 41-57-24 N   Long: 84-59-53 W
Pop: 4,795 (1990); 4,246 (1980)   Pop Density: 168.8
Land: 28.4 sq. mi.; Water: 1.1 sq. mi.

Gilead
Township
Lat: 41-47-08 N   Long: 85-06-54 W
Pop: 688 (1990); 704 (1980)   Pop Density: 32.6
Land: 21.1 sq. mi.; Water: 0.3 sq. mi.

Girard
Township
Lat: 42-01-46 N   Long: 85-00-01 W
Pop: 1,800 (1990); 1,890 (1980)   Pop Density: 50.6
Land: 35.6 sq. mi.; Water: 1.0 sq. mi.

Kinderhook
Township
Lat: 41-47-13 N   Long: 84-59-59 W
Pop: 1,292 (1990); 1,024 (1980)   Pop Density: 66.3
Land: 19.5 sq. mi.; Water: 1.8 sq. mi.

Matteson
Township
Lat: 41-56-21 N   Long: 85-14-03 W
Pop: 1,231 (1990); 1,284 (1980)   Pop Density: 34.4
Land: 35.8 sq. mi.; Water: 0.5 sq. mi.

Noble
Township
Lat: 41-47-15 N   Long: 85-13-51 W
Pop: 479 (1990); 508 (1980)   Pop Density: 22.8
Land: 21.0 sq. mi.; Water: 0.3 sq. mi.

Ovid
Township
Lat: 41-51-19 N   Long: 84-59-50 W
Pop: 2,103 (1990); 2,065 (1980)   Pop Density: 63.2
Land: 33.3 sq. mi.; Water: 2.9 sq. mi.

Quincy
Village
ZIP: 49082   Lat: 41-56-38 N   Long: 84-52-58 W
Pop: 1,680 (1990); 1,569 (1980)   Pop Density: 1292.3
Land: 1.3 sq. mi.; Water: 0.0 sq. mi.   Elev: 1017 ft.
Established 1833. Not coextensive with the town of the same name.
Name origin: For Quincy, MA.

*Quincy
Township
ZIP: 49082   Lat: 41-56-28 N   Long: 84-53-01 W
Pop: 4,003 (1990); 3,929 (1980)   Pop Density: 113.4
Land: 35.3 sq. mi.; Water: 1.0 sq. mi.

Sherwood
Village
ZIP: 49089   Lat: 41-59-59 N   Long: 85-14-23 W
Pop: 320 (1990); 353 (1980)   Pop Density: 320.0
Land: 1.0 sq. mi.; Water: 0.0 sq. mi.   Elev: 883 ft.
Not coextensive with the town of the same name.
Name origin: For England's Sherwood Forest.

*Sherwood
Township
ZIP: 49089   Lat: 42-01-33 N   Long: 85-14-00 W
Pop: 2,310 (1990); 2,126 (1980)   Pop Density: 66.2
Land: 34.9 sq. mi.; Water: 1.2 sq. mi.

Union
Township
Lat: 42-01-54 N   Long: 85-07-09 W
Pop: 2,976 (1990); 2,918 (1980)   Pop Density: 83.4
Land: 35.7 sq. mi.; Water: 0.3 sq. mi.

Union City
Village
ZIP: 49094   Lat: 42-03-58 N   Long: 85-08-25 W
Pop: 1,760 (1990); 1,646 (1980)   Pop Density: 1353.8
Land: 1.3 sq. mi.; Water: 0.0 sq. mi.
Incorporated 1866. Part of the town is also in Calhoun County.
Name origin: Possibly because the St. Joseph and Coldwater rivers unite here.

Calhoun County
County Seat: Marshall (ZIP: 49068)

Pop: 135,982 (1990); 141,579 (1980)   Pop Density: 191.8
Land: 708.9 sq. mi.; Water: 9.6 sq. mi.   Area Code: 616
In south-central MI, east of Kalamazoo; established Oct 29, 1829 (prior to statehood) from Indian lands.
Name origin: For John Caldwell Calhoun (1782–1850), U.S. statesman and proponent of Southern causes.

Albion
City
ZIP: 49224   Lat: 42-14-46 N   Long: 84-45-24 W
Pop: 10,066 (1990); 11,059 (1980)   Pop Density: 2396.7
Land: 4.2 sq. mi.; Water: 0.0 sq. mi.   Elev: 959 ft.
In south-central MI, 40 mi. west of Ann Arbor. Settled 1835.
Name origin: For Albion, NY.

*Albion
Township
ZIP: 49224   Lat: 42-12-28 N   Long: 84-46-15 W
Pop: 1,256 (1990); 1,413 (1980)   Pop Density: 38.3
Land: 32.8 sq. mi.; Water: 0.3 sq. mi.

Athens
Village
ZIP: 49011   Lat: 42-05-09 N   Long: 85-14-10 W
Pop: 990 (1990); 960 (1980)   Pop Density: 990.0
Land: 1.0 sq. mi.; Water: 0.0 sq. mi.   Elev: 896 ft.
Settled 1831. Not coextensive with the town of the same name.
Name origin: For Athens, NY, former home of early settlers.

*Athens
Township
ZIP: 49011   Lat: 42-06-52 N   Long: 85-14-21 W
Pop: 2,515 (1990); 2,294 (1980)   Pop Density: 69.7
Land: 36.1 sq. mi.; Water: 0.0 sq. mi.

MICHIGAN, Calhoun County

Battle Creek — City
ZIP: 49016 Lat: 42-17-55 N Long: 85-13-44 W
Pop: 53,540 (1990); 35,724 (1980) Pop Density: 1250.9
Land: 42.8 sq. mi.; Water: 0.8 sq. mi.
In south-central MI on the Kalamazoo River, 20 mi. east of Kalamazoo. Home of Kellogg's cereals. Settled 1831; incorporated as a village 1850; as a city 1859.
Name origin: For a nearby stream, so named for an 1824 fight there between two Indians and two surveyors.

Bedford — Township
ZIP: 49017 Lat: 42-23-07 N Long: 85-14-10 W
Pop: 9,810 (1990); 10,157 (1980) Pop Density: 332.5
Land: 29.5 sq. mi.; Water: 0.3 sq. mi.
Name origin: Possibly for Bedford or Bedfordshire, England, or for one of the Dukes of Bedford.

Brownlee Park — CDP
Lat: 42-19-27 N Long: 85-08-01 W
Pop: 2,536 (1990); 2,370 (1980) Pop Density: 1268.0
Land: 2.0 sq. mi.; Water: 0.0 sq. mi.

Burlington — Village
ZIP: 49029 Lat: 42-06-17 N Long: 85-04-44 W
Pop: 294 (1990); 367 (1980) Pop Density: 420.0
Land: 0.7 sq. mi.; Water: 0.0 sq. mi. Elev: 923 ft.
Not coextensive with the town of the same name.
Name origin: For the War of 1812 gunboat, *Burlington*, on which a number of settlers had served.

*Burlington — Township
ZIP: 49029 Lat: 42-06-50 N Long: 85-07-06 W
Pop: 1,773 (1990); 1,909 (1980) Pop Density: 49.4
Land: 35.9 sq. mi.; Water: 0.3 sq. mi.

Clarence — Township
Lat: 42-22-49 N Long: 84-46-29 W
Pop: 2,051 (1990); 1,916 (1980) Pop Density: 62.7
Land: 32.7 sq. mi.; Water: 1.5 sq. mi.

Clarendon — Township
Lat: 42-07-19 N Long: 84-53-01 W
Pop: 1,100 (1990); 1,176 (1980) Pop Density: 30.9
Land: 35.6 sq. mi.; Water: 0.1 sq. mi.

Convis — Township
Lat: 42-22-21 N Long: 84-59-44 W
Pop: 1,739 (1990); 1,734 (1980) Pop Density: 49.3
Land: 35.3 sq. mi.; Water: 1.1 sq. mi.

Eckford — Township
Lat: 42-12-25 N Long: 84-52-49 W
Pop: 1,217 (1990); 1,273 (1980) Pop Density: 34.4
Land: 35.4 sq. mi.; Water: 0.2 sq. mi.

Emmett — Township
ZIP: 49017 Lat: 42-17-17 N Long: 85-07-02 W
Pop: 10,764 (1990); 11,155 (1980) Pop Density: 334.3
Land: 32.2 sq. mi.; Water: 0.2 sq. mi.

Fredonia — Township
Lat: 42-11-38 N Long: 85-00-05 W
Pop: 1,741 (1990); 1,755 (1980) Pop Density: 50.9
Land: 34.2 sq. mi.; Water: 0.9 sq. mi.

Homer — Village
ZIP: 49245 Lat: 42-08-43 N Long: 84-48-35 W
Pop: 1,758 (1990); 1,791 (1980) Pop Density: 1352.3
Land: 1.3 sq. mi.; Water: 0.0 sq. mi. Elev: 994 ft.
Not coextensive with the town of the same name.
Name origin: For Homer, NY, the area from which the early settlers came.

*Homer — Township
ZIP: 49245 Lat: 42-06-55 N Long: 84-46-26 W
Pop: 2,875 (1990); 3,041 (1980) Pop Density: 80.5
Land: 35.7 sq. mi.; Water: 0.4 sq. mi.

Lee — Township
Lat: 42-22-15 N Long: 84-53-00 W
Pop: 1,281 (1990); 1,186 (1980) Pop Density: 35.3
Land: 36.3 sq. mi.; Water: 0.1 sq. mi.

Leroy — Township
Lat: 42-12-09 N Long: 85-13-57 W
Pop: 3,026 (1990); 2,929 (1980) Pop Density: 84.3
Land: 35.9 sq. mi.; Water: 0.4 sq. mi.

Level Park-Oak Park — CDP
Lat: 42-21-48 N Long: 85-16-09 W
Pop: 3,502 (1990); 3,210 (1980) Pop Density: 660.8
Land: 5.3 sq. mi.; Water: 0.0 sq. mi.

Marengo — Township
Lat: 42-17-11 N Long: 84-52-47 W
Pop: 1,801 (1990); 1,811 (1980) Pop Density: 51.2
Land: 35.2 sq. mi.; Water: 0.5 sq. mi.

Marshall — City
ZIP: 49068 Lat: 42-15-42 N Long: 84-57-30 W
Pop: 6,891 (1990); 7,201 (1980) Pop Density: 1230.5
Land: 5.6 sq. mi.; Water: 0.2 sq. mi. Elev: 916 ft.
Settled 1830.
Name origin: For John Marshall (1755–1835), fourth Chief Justice of the U.S. Supreme Court.

*Marshall — Township
ZIP: 49068 Lat: 42-17-29 N Long: 85-00-47 W
Pop: 2,655 (1990); 2,564 (1980) Pop Density: 84.3
Land: 31.5 sq. mi.; Water: 0.4 sq. mi.

Newton — Township
Lat: 42-12-40 N Long: 85-07-08 W
Pop: 2,025 (1990); 1,979 (1980) Pop Density: 56.4
Land: 35.9 sq. mi.; Water: 0.3 sq. mi.

Pennfield — Township
ZIP: 49017 Lat: 42-22-31 N Long: 85-06-56 W
Pop: 8,386 (1990); 8,743 (1980) Pop Density: 241.0
Land: 34.8 sq. mi.; Water: 0.3 sq. mi.

Sheridan — Township
Lat: 42-17-14 N Long: 84-45-59 W
Pop: 2,139 (1990); 2,257 (1980) Pop Density: 67.5
Land: 31.7 sq. mi.; Water: 0.4 sq. mi.

Springfield — City
ZIP: 49015 Lat: 42-19-26 N Long: 85-14-15 W
Pop: 5,582 (1990); 5,917 (1980) Pop Density: 1468.9
Land: 3.8 sq. mi.; Water: 0.0 sq. mi.
Established 1904.
Name origin: For Springfield, IL.

MICHIGAN, Calhoun County

Tekonsha
Village
ZIP: 49092 Lat: 42-05-40 N Long: 84-59-21 W
Pop: 722 (1990); 755 (1980) Pop Density: 1203.3
Land: 0.6 sq. mi.; Water: 0.0 sq. mi.

Settled 1830s. Not coextensive with the town of the same name.

Name origin: For a local Potawatomi chief, Tekon-qua-sha.

*Tekonsha
Township
ZIP: 49092 Lat: 42-06-40 N Long: 85-00-02 W
Pop: 1,749 (1990); 1,771 (1980) Pop Density: 49.0
Land: 35.7 sq. mi.; Water: 0.7 sq. mi.

Union City
Village
Lat: 42-04-26 N Long: 85-08-03 W
Pop: 7 (1990); 21 (1980) Pop Density: 175.0
Land: 0.04 sq. mi.; Water: 0.0 sq. mi.

Incorporated 1866. Part of the town is also in Branch County.

Name origin: Possibly because the St. Joseph and Coldwater rivers unite here.

Cass County
County Seat: Cassopolis (ZIP: 49031)

Pop: 49,477 (1990); 49,499 (1980) Pop Density: 100.5
Land: 492.2 sq. mi.; Water: 16.3 sq. mi. Area Code: 616

On the southwestern border of MI, southwest of Kalamazoo; established Oct 29, 1829 (prior to statehood) from Indian lands.

Name origin: For Gen. Lewis Cass (1782–1866), OH legislator, governor of MI Territory (1813–31), U.S. secretary of war (1831–36), and U.S. secretary of state (1857–60).

Calvin
Township
Lat: 41-51-05 N Long: 85-55-39 W
Pop: 1,813 (1990); 1,643 (1980) Pop Density: 52.7
Land: 34.4 sq. mi.; Water: 1.1 sq. mi.

Cassopolis
Village
ZIP: 49031 Lat: 41-54-44 N Long: 86-00-28 W
Pop: 1,822 (1990); 1,933 (1980) Pop Density: 1138.8
Land: 1.6 sq. mi.; Water: 0.2 sq. mi. Elev: 902 ft.
Settled 1829, incorporated 1863.

Name origin: For Lewis Cass (1782–1866), OH legislator, governor of MI Territory (1813–31), U.S. secretary of war (1831–36), and U.S. secretary of state (1857–60).

Dowagiac
City
ZIP: 49047 Lat: 41-59-01 N Long: 86-06-38 W
Pop: 6,409 (1990); 6,307 (1980) Pop Density: 1643.3
Land: 3.9 sq. mi.; Water: 0.0 sq. mi. Elev: 772 ft.
Platted 1848.

Name origin: From an Indian term meaning 'foraging ground.'

Edwardsburg
Village
ZIP: 49112 Lat: 41-47-48 N Long: 86-05-00 W
Pop: 1,142 (1990); 1,135 (1980) Pop Density: 1268.9
Land: 0.9 sq. mi.; Water: 0.1 sq. mi. Elev: 829 ft.
Settled 1828.

Name origin: Named by and for the town's first merchant, Thomas Edwards.

Howard
Township
ZIP: 49120 Lat: 41-51-18 N Long: 86-09-59 W
Pop: 6,378 (1990); 6,524 (1980) Pop Density: 182.2
Land: 35.0 sq. mi.; Water: 0.6 sq. mi.

Jefferson
Township
Lat: 41-51-11 N Long: 86-02-49 W
Pop: 2,112 (1990); 1,963 (1980) Pop Density: 60.3
Land: 35.0 sq. mi.; Water: 1.0 sq. mi.

La Grange
Township
Lat: 41-56-49 N Long: 86-02-48 W
Pop: 3,406 (1990); 3,526 (1980) Pop Density: 101.7
Land: 33.5 sq. mi.; Water: 1.2 sq. mi.

Marcellus
Village
ZIP: 49067 Lat: 42-01-33 N Long: 85-48-47 W
Pop: 1,193 (1990); 1,134 (1980) Pop Density: 1704.3
Land: 0.7 sq. mi.; Water: 0.0 sq. mi.

Platted 1870. Not coextensive with the town of the same name.

Name origin: For the ancient Roman general Marcus Claudius Marcellus (268?–208 B.C.).

*Marcellus
Township
ZIP: 49067 Lat: 42-01-35 N Long: 85-49-06 W
Pop: 2,569 (1990); 2,463 (1980) Pop Density: 77.1
Land: 33.3 sq. mi.; Water: 1.5 sq. mi.

Mason
Township
Lat: 41-47-05 N Long: 85-56-34 W
Pop: 2,450 (1990); 2,132 (1980) Pop Density: 120.7
Land: 20.3 sq. mi.; Water: 0.3 sq. mi.

Milton
Township
Lat: 41-47-21 N Long: 86-10-35 W
Pop: 2,284 (1990); 2,235 (1980) Pop Density: 107.2
Land: 21.3 sq. mi.; Water: 0.2 sq. mi.

Newberg
Township
Lat: 41-56-50 N Long: 85-48-33 W
Pop: 1,627 (1990); 1,382 (1980) Pop Density: 47.0
Land: 34.6 sq. mi.; Water: 0.9 sq. mi.

Niles
City
ZIP: 49120-21 **Lat:** 41-52-34 N **Long:** 86-12-21 W
Pop: 2 (1990) **Pop Density:** 4.0
Land: 0.5 sq. mi.; **Water:** 0.0 sq. mi. **Elev:** 658 ft.
In southwestern MI, 25 mi. southeast of Benton Harbor. Settled 1829. Part of the town is also in Berrien County.
Name origin: For editor, publisher, and author Hezekiah Niles (1777–1830).

Ontwa
Township
ZIP: 49112 **Lat:** 41-46-55 N **Long:** 86-02-58 W
Pop: 5,592 (1990); 5,787 (1980) **Pop Density:** 286.8
Land: 19.5 sq. mi.; **Water:** 1.5 sq. mi.

Penn
Township
Lat: 41-56-28 N **Long:** 85-56-18 W
Pop: 1,877 (1990); 2,044 (1980) **Pop Density:** 55.7
Land: 33.7 sq. mi.; **Water:** 1.8 sq. mi.

Pokagon
Township
Lat: 41-56-26 N **Long:** 86-10-14 W
Pop: 2,188 (1990); 2,394 (1980) **Pop Density:** 63.2
Land: 34.6 sq. mi.; **Water:** 0.1 sq. mi.

Porter
Township
Lat: 41-50-00 N **Long:** 85-49-23 W
Pop: 3,857 (1990); 3,857 (1980) **Pop Density:** 74.6
Land: 51.7 sq. mi.; **Water:** 2.9 sq. mi.

Silver Creek
Township
Lat: 42-01-39 N **Long:** 86-10-31 W
Pop: 3,101 (1990); 3,361 (1980) **Pop Density:** 96.3
Land: 32.2 sq. mi.; **Water:** 2.1 sq. mi.

Vandalia
Village
ZIP: 49095 **Lat:** 41-55-06 N **Long:** 85-54-53 W
Pop: 357 (1990); 447 (1980) **Pop Density:** 357.0
Land: 1.0 sq. mi.; **Water:** 0.0 sq. mi. **Elev:** 877 ft.
Laid out 1851.
Name origin: For Vandalia, NY.

Volinia
Township
Lat: 42-01-22 N **Long:** 85-56-20 W
Pop: 1,032 (1990); 1,182 (1980) **Pop Density:** 30.0
Land: 34.4 sq. mi.; **Water:** 0.7 sq. mi.

Wayne
Township
Lat: 42-01-44 N **Long:** 86-02-56 W
Pop: 2,780 (1990); 2,699 (1980) **Pop Density:** 81.0
Land: 34.3 sq. mi.; **Water:** 0.5 sq. mi.

Charlevoix County
County Seat: Charlevoix (ZIP: 49720)

Pop: 21,468 (1990); 19,907 (1980) **Pop Density:** 51.5
Land: 416.9 sq. mi.; **Water:** 974.0 sq. mi. **Area Code:** 616
On the northwestern coast of MI, bordered on west by Lake Michigan; established as Reshkauko County Apr 1, 1840; name changed Mar 8, 1843.
Name origin: For Pierre François Xavier de Charlevoix (1682–1761), French Jesuit explorer and writer who traveled from the Great Lakes down the Illinois and Mississippi rivers to New Orleans (1720–22).

Bay
Township
Lat: 45-17-30 N **Long:** 85-04-09 W
Pop: 825 (1990); 599 (1980) **Pop Density:** 47.4
Land: 17.4 sq. mi.; **Water:** 3.3 sq. mi.

Boyne City
City
ZIP: 49712 **Lat:** 45-12-47 N **Long:** 85-00-49 W
Pop: 3,478 (1990); 3,348 (1980) **Pop Density:** 891.8
Land: 3.9 sq. mi.; **Water:** 1.3 sq. mi.
Settled 1856.
Name origin: For the nearby Boyne River, itself named for a river in Ireland.

Boyne Falls
Village
ZIP: 49713 **Lat:** 45-10-01 N **Long:** 84-54-48 W
Pop: 369 (1990); 378 (1980) **Pop Density:** 738.0
Land: 0.5 sq. mi.; **Water:** 0.0 sq. mi.

Boyne Valley
Township
Lat: 45-09-43 N **Long:** 84-55-06 W
Pop: 1,102 (1990); 948 (1980) **Pop Density:** 31.4
Land: 35.1 sq. mi.; **Water:** 0.5 sq. mi.

Chandler
Township
Lat: 45-14-45 N **Long:** 84-47-42 W
Pop: 182 (1990); 132 (1980) **Pop Density:** 5.1
Land: 35.6 sq. mi.; **Water:** 0.0 sq. mi.

Charlevoix
City
ZIP: 49720 **Lat:** 45-18-50 N **Long:** 85-15-14 W
Pop: 3,116 (1990); 3,296 (1980) **Pop Density:** 1558.0
Land: 2.0 sq. mi.; **Water:** 0.1 sq. mi.
Incorporated as a village 1879; as a city 1905.
Name origin: For Pierre François Xavier de Charlevoix (1682–1761), French Jesuit explorer and writer who traveled from the Great Lakes down the Illinois and Mississippi rivers to New Orleans (1720–22).

*Charlevoix
Township
ZIP: 49720 **Lat:** 45-20-10 N **Long:** 85-14-48 W
Pop: 1,016 (1990); 993 (1980) **Pop Density:** 169.3
Land: 6.0 sq. mi.; **Water:** 13.2 sq. mi.

East Jordan
City
ZIP: 49727 **Lat:** 45-09-28 N **Long:** 85-07-48 W
Pop: 2,240 (1990); 2,185 (1980) **Pop Density:** 829.6
Land: 2.7 sq. mi.; **Water:** 0.9 sq. mi.
Name origin: For its location on the east side of the Jordan River.

MICHIGAN, Charlevoix County

Evangeline
Township
Lat: 45-15-08 N Long: 85-01-28 W
Pop: 646 (1990); 538 (1980) **Pop Density:** 58.7
Land: 11.0 sq. mi.; **Water:** 3.7 sq. mi.

Eveline
Township
Lat: 45-14-41 N Long: 85-08-40 W
Pop: 1,100 (1990); 1,061 (1980) **Pop Density:** 42.3
Land: 26.0 sq. mi.; **Water:** 10.7 sq. mi.

Hayes
Township
Lat: 45-19-29 N Long: 85-08-51 W
Pop: 1,317 (1990); 1,274 (1980) **Pop Density:** 46.5
Land: 28.3 sq. mi.; **Water:** 13.1 sq. mi.

Hudson
Township
Lat: 45-09-10 N Long: 84-47-47 W
Pop: 481 (1990); 343 (1980) **Pop Density:** 14.0
Land: 34.4 sq. mi.; **Water:** 1.1 sq. mi.

Marion
Township
Lat: 45-15-06 N Long: 85-15-58 W
Pop: 1,130 (1990); 946 (1980) **Pop Density:** 44.1
Land: 25.6 sq. mi.; **Water:** 0.9 sq. mi.

Melrose
Township
Lat: 45-15-03 N Long: 84-54-57 W
Pop: 1,106 (1990); 947 (1980) **Pop Density:** 33.6
Land: 32.9 sq. mi.; **Water:** 2.0 sq. mi.

Norwood
Township
Lat: 45-15-14 N Long: 85-21-11 W
Pop: 516 (1990); 540 (1980) **Pop Density:** 28.4
Land: 18.2 sq. mi.; **Water:** 6.2 sq. mi.

Peaine
Township
Lat: 45-40-23 N Long: 85-32-33 W
Pop: 128 (1990); 81 (1980) **Pop Density:** 2.4
Land: 52.5 sq. mi.; **Water:** 22.6 sq. mi.

St. James
Township
Lat: 45-45-30 N Long: 85-34-02 W
Pop: 276 (1990); 240 (1980) **Pop Density:** 13.8
Land: 20.0 sq. mi.; **Water:** 296.0 sq. mi.

South Arm
Township
Lat: 45-09-43 N Long: 85-10-00 W
Pop: 1,418 (1990); 1,237 (1980) **Pop Density:** 45.6
Land: 31.1 sq. mi.; **Water:** 1.9 sq. mi.

Wilson
Township
Lat: 45-09-45 N Long: 85-02-47 W
Pop: 1,391 (1990); 1,199 (1980) **Pop Density:** 40.8
Land: 34.1 sq. mi.; **Water:** 0.4 sq. mi.

Cheboygan County
County Seat: Cheboygan (ZIP: 49721)

Pop: 21,398 (1990); 20,649 (1980) **Pop Density:** 29.9
Land: 715.6 sq. mi.; **Water:** 169.7 sq. mi. **Area Code:** 616

On the north coast of MI; established Apr 1, 1840 from Antrim County.

Name origin: For the Cheboygan River; the name is Algonquian but the meaning is in dispute.

Aloha
Township
Lat: 45-29-48 N Long: 84-25-11 W
Pop: 707 (1990); 726 (1980) **Pop Density:** 24.0
Land: 29.4 sq. mi.; **Water:** 2.9 sq. mi.

Beaugrand
Township
Lat: 45-39-52 N Long: 84-33-20 W
Pop: 1,004 (1990); 1,023 (1980) **Pop Density:** 42.0
Land: 23.9 sq. mi.; **Water:** 0.1 sq. mi.

Benton
Township
Lat: 45-36-21 N Long: 84-22-15 W
Pop: 2,388 (1990); 2,017 (1980) **Pop Density:** 40.7
Land: 58.7 sq. mi.; **Water:** 3.8 sq. mi.

Burt
Township
Lat: 45-30-48 N Long: 84-40-00 W
Pop: 533 (1990); 520 (1980) **Pop Density:** 27.1
Land: 19.7 sq. mi.; **Water:** 15.4 sq. mi.

Cheboygan
City
ZIP: 49721 Lat: 45-38-30 N Long: 84-28-07 W
Pop: 4,999 (1990); 5,106 (1980) **Pop Density:** 757.4
Land: 6.6 sq. mi.; **Water:** 0.2 sq. mi.
Settled 1846. Established 1853.

Name origin: From an obscure Algonquian word; the meaning is in dispute.

Ellis
Township
Lat: 45-19-23 N Long: 84-33-06 W
Pop: 345 (1990); 298 (1980) **Pop Density:** 9.7
Land: 35.6 sq. mi.; **Water:** 0.1 sq. mi.

Forest
Township
Lat: 45-17-00 N Long: 84-18-24 W
Pop: 929 (1990); 971 (1980) **Pop Density:** 13.5
Land: 68.7 sq. mi.; **Water:** 0.9 sq. mi.

Grant
Township
Lat: 45-31-43 N Long: 84-18-51 W
Pop: 686 (1990); 579 (1980) **Pop Density:** 14.1
Land: 48.8 sq. mi.; **Water:** 9.2 sq. mi.

Hebron
Township
Lat: 45-40-46 N Long: 84-39-29 W
Pop: 202 (1990); 188 (1980) **Pop Density:** 5.9
Land: 34.1 sq. mi.; **Water:** 0.7 sq. mi.

Inverness
Township
Lat: 45-35-19 N Long: 84-32-37 W
Pop: 1,952 (1990); 2,179 (1980) **Pop Density:** 57.2
Land: 34.1 sq. mi.; **Water:** 3.3 sq. mi.

Koehler
Township
Lat: 45-25-03 N Long: 84-30-51 W
Pop: 722 (1990); 755 (1980) **Pop Density:** 16.6
Land: 43.5 sq. mi.; **Water:** 2.2 sq. mi.

Mackinaw
Township
Lat: 45-44-27 N **Long:** 84-41-29 W
Pop: 604 (1990); 550 (1980)   **Pop Density:** 53.0
Land: 11.4 sq. mi.; **Water:** 0.4 sq. mi.

Mackinaw City
Village
ZIP: 49701   **Lat:** 45-46-46 N **Long:** 84-43-43 W
Pop: 408 (1990); 392 (1980)   **Pop Density:** 680.0
Land: 0.6 sq. mi.; **Water:** 0.1 sq. mi.
Part of the town is also in Emmet County.
Name origin: A shortened version of Fort Michilimackinac, the latter an Indian term meaning 'island of the large turtle.'

Mentor
Township
Lat: 45-19-45 N **Long:** 84-40-01 W
Pop: 518 (1990); 462 (1980)   **Pop Density:** 14.5
Land: 35.8 sq. mi.; **Water:** 0.1 sq. mi.

Mullett
Township
Lat: 45-30-41 N **Long:** 84-33-27 W
Pop: 1,056 (1990); 934 (1980)   **Pop Density:** 55.6
Land: 19.0 sq. mi.; **Water:** 16.7 sq. mi.

Munro
Township
Lat: 45-35-32 N **Long:** 84-40-23 W
Pop: 512 (1990); 459 (1980)   **Pop Density:** 18.0
Land: 28.5 sq. mi.; **Water:** 6.7 sq. mi.

Nunda
Township
Lat: 45-14-37 N **Long:** 84-29-44 W
Pop: 725 (1990); 690 (1980)   **Pop Density:** 10.3
Land: 70.2 sq. mi.; **Water:** 1.1 sq. mi.

Tuscarora
Township
Lat: 45-24-56 N **Long:** 84-38-44 W
Pop: 2,297 (1990); 1,952 (1980)   **Pop Density:** 77.9
Land: 29.5 sq. mi.; **Water:** 12.5 sq. mi.

Walker
Township
Lat: 45-19-47 N **Long:** 84-26-08 W
Pop: 256 (1990); 260 (1980)   **Pop Density:** 7.5
Land: 34.3 sq. mi.; **Water:** 0.3 sq. mi.

Waverly
Township
Lat: 45-25-01 N **Long:** 84-20-34 W
Pop: 371 (1990); 456 (1980)   **Pop Density:** 7.7
Land: 48.1 sq. mi.; **Water:** 5.1 sq. mi.

Wilmot
Township
Lat: 45-14-44 N **Long:** 84-40-01 W
Pop: 592 (1990); 524 (1980)   **Pop Density:** 16.6
Land: 35.7 sq. mi.; **Water:** 0.1 sq. mi.

Wolverine
Village
ZIP: 49799   **Lat:** 45-16-24 N **Long:** 84-36-19 W
Pop: 283 (1990); 364 (1980)   **Pop Density:** 314.4
Land: 0.9 sq. mi.; **Water:** 0.0 sq. mi.
Name origin: For the once-abundant state animal.

Chippewa County
County Seat: Sault Ste. Marie (ZIP: 49783)

Pop: 34,604 (1990); 29,029 (1980)   **Pop Density:** 22.2
Land: 1561.1 sq. mi.; **Water:** 1136.9 sq. mi.   **Area Code:** 906
On the northeast coast of the Upper Peninsula of MI on Whitefish Bay; established Dec 22, 1826 (prior to statehood) from Mackinac County.
Name origin: For the Ojibway Indians of Algonquian linguistic stock. The name means 'puckered' and probably refers to the seam in their moccasins.

Bay Mills
Township
Lat: 46-27-06 N **Long:** 84-46-18 W
Pop: 787 (1990); 695 (1980)   **Pop Density:** 12.2
Land: 64.7 sq. mi.; **Water:** 41.1 sq. mi.

Bruce
Township
Lat: 46-19-17 N **Long:** 84-17-32 W
Pop: 1,610 (1990); 1,449 (1980)   **Pop Density:** 18.5
Land: 87.1 sq. mi.; **Water:** 3.2 sq. mi.

Chippewa
Township
Lat: 46-21-44 N **Long:** 85-00-11 W
Pop: 279 (1990); 291 (1980)   **Pop Density:** 2.9
Land: 94.9 sq. mi.; **Water:** 0.6 sq. mi.

Dafter
Township
ZIP: 49724   **Lat:** 46-21-37 N **Long:** 84-26-29 W
Pop: 1,083 (1990); 1,037 (1980)   **Pop Density:** 22.7
Land: 47.8 sq. mi.; **Water:** 0.1 sq. mi.

Detour
Township
Lat: 46-00-30 N **Long:** 84-00-08 W
Pop: 806 (1990); 794 (1980)   **Pop Density:** 16.5
Land: 48.9 sq. mi.; **Water:** 18.8 sq. mi.

De Tour Village
Village
ZIP: 49725   **Lat:** 45-59-09 N **Long:** 83-54-08 W
Pop: 407 (1990); 466 (1980)   **Pop Density:** 113.1
Land: 3.6 sq. mi.; **Water:** 4.8 sq. mi.   **Elev:** 613 ft.

Drummond
Township
Lat: 46-00-23 N **Long:** 83-42-00 W
Pop: 835 (1990); 746 (1980)   **Pop Density:** 6.5
Land: 129.1 sq. mi.; **Water:** 119.9 sq. mi.

Hulbert
Township
Lat: 46-19-13 N **Long:** 85-09-57 W
Pop: 208 (1990); 251 (1980)   **Pop Density:** 2.9
Land: 71.1 sq. mi.; **Water:** 0.7 sq. mi.

Kinross
Township
ZIP: 49752   **Lat:** 46-18-05 N **Long:** 84-41-14 W
Pop: 6,566 (1990); 1,891 (1980)   **Pop Density:** 54.7
Land: 120.1 sq. mi.; **Water:** 0.9 sq. mi.

Pickford
Township
ZIP: 49774   **Lat:** 46-10-55 N **Long:** 84-19-38 W
Pop: 1,360 (1990); 1,264 (1980)   **Pop Density:** 12.5
Land: 108.7 sq. mi.; **Water:** 11.1 sq. mi.

MICHIGAN, Chippewa County

Raber
Township
Lat: 46-07-25 N **Long:** 84-07-07 W
Pop: 569 (1990); 543 (1980) **Pop Density:** 5.8
Land: 98.1 sq. mi.; **Water:** 45.0 sq. mi.

Rudyard
Township
ZIP: 49780 **Lat:** 46-13-34 N **Long:** 84-36-46 W
Pop: 1,270 (1990); 1,260 (1980) **Pop Density:** 14.1
Land: 89.9 sq. mi.; **Water:** 0.2 sq. mi.

Sault Ste. Marie
City
ZIP: 49783 **Lat:** 46-29-04 N **Long:** 84-21-55 W
Pop: 14,689 (1990); 14,448 (1980) **Pop Density:** 992.5
Land: 14.8 sq. mi.; **Water:** 5.4 sq. mi. **Elev:** 613 ft.
On the north coast of the Upper Peninsula of MI on the St. Mary's River between Lakes Superior and Huron, across from Sault Ste. Marie, Ontario, Canada. County seat. Established 1668 (oldest city in Michigan).
Name origin: From French 'the rapids of Saint Mary's,' descriptive of its location on the heights overlooking the river.

Soo
Township
Lat: 46-22-29 N **Long:** 84-13-45 W
Pop: 2,165 (1990); 2,179 (1980) **Pop Density:** 43.1
Land: 50.2 sq. mi.; **Water:** 17.7 sq. mi.

Sugar Island
Township
Lat: 46-26-25 N **Long:** 84-11-11 W
Pop: 441 (1990); 400 (1980) **Pop Density:** 8.9
Land: 49.4 sq. mi.; **Water:** 27.0 sq. mi.

Superior
Township
Lat: 46-22-36 N **Long:** 84-40-58 W
Pop: 990 (1990); 923 (1980) **Pop Density:** 9.6
Land: 103.2 sq. mi.; **Water:** 1.5 sq. mi.

Trout Lake
Township
Lat: 46-12-54 N **Long:** 84-55-11 W
Pop: 429 (1990); 386 (1980) **Pop Density:** 3.0
Land: 141.7 sq. mi.; **Water:** 1.9 sq. mi.

Whitefish
Township
Lat: 46-35-51 N **Long:** 85-07-10 W
Pop: 517 (1990); 472 (1980) **Pop Density:** 2.1
Land: 241.5 sq. mi.; **Water:** 35.8 sq. mi.

Clare County
County Seat: Harrison (ZIP: 48625)

Pop: 24,952 (1990); 23,822 (1980) **Pop Density:** 44.0
Land: 566.9 sq. mi.; **Water:** 8.4 sq. mi. **Area Code:** 517
In central MI, northwest of Midland; established as Kaykakee County Apr 1, 1840 from Isabella County; name changed Mar 8, 1843.
Name origin: For the county in Ireland. Originally for the Indian chief, Kaykakee 'pigeon hawk,' who had signed the Treaty of 1826.

Arthur
Township
Lat: 43-57-06 N **Long:** 84-39-56 W
Pop: 544 (1990); 562 (1980) **Pop Density:** 15.1
Land: 36.1 sq. mi.; **Water:** 0.1 sq. mi.

Clare
City
ZIP: 48617 **Lat:** 43-49-38 N **Long:** 84-45-58 W
Pop: 3,013 (1990); 3,300 (1980) **Pop Density:** 1205.2
Land: 2.5 sq. mi.; **Water:** 0.1 sq. mi. **Elev:** 841 ft.
Established 1940. Part of the town is also in Isabella County.
Name origin: For its county, itself named for County Clare, Ireland.

Farwell
Village
ZIP: 48622 **Lat:** 43-50-08 N **Long:** 84-52-03 W
Pop: 851 (1990); 804 (1980) **Pop Density:** 654.6
Land: 1.3 sq. mi.; **Water:** 0.0 sq. mi.
Founded 1870.
Name origin: For railroad investor Samuel Farwell.

Franklin
Township
Lat: 44-06-50 N **Long:** 84-40-12 W
Pop: 600 (1990); 631 (1980) **Pop Density:** 16.9
Land: 35.4 sq. mi.; **Water:** 0.1 sq. mi.

Freeman
Township
Lat: 43-56-32 N **Long:** 85-01-28 W
Pop: 613 (1990); 437 (1980) **Pop Density:** 17.7
Land: 34.6 sq. mi.; **Water:** 1.1 sq. mi.

Frost
Township
Lat: 44-07-05 N **Long:** 84-47-48 W
Pop: 826 (1990); 852 (1980) **Pop Density:** 23.6
Land: 35.0 sq. mi.; **Water:** 0.4 sq. mi.

Garfield
Township
Lat: 43-51-36 N **Long:** 85-01-33 W
Pop: 1,477 (1990); 1,416 (1980) **Pop Density:** 44.2
Land: 33.4 sq. mi.; **Water:** 2.3 sq. mi.

Grant
Township
Lat: 43-51-55 N **Long:** 84-47-51 W
Pop: 2,636 (1990); 2,227 (1980) **Pop Density:** 79.2
Land: 33.3 sq. mi.; **Water:** 0.4 sq. mi.

Greenwood
Township
Lat: 44-01-53 N **Long:** 84-54-30 W
Pop: 718 (1990); 649 (1980) **Pop Density:** 20.4
Land: 35.2 sq. mi.; **Water:** 0.3 sq. mi.

Hamilton
Township
Lat: 44-01-59 N **Long:** 84-39-37 W
Pop: 1,546 (1990); 1,595 (1980) **Pop Density:** 43.1
Land: 35.9 sq. mi.; **Water:** 0.5 sq. mi.

Harrison
City
ZIP: 48625 **Lat:** 44-01-02 N **Long:** 84-48-26 W
Pop: 1,835 (1990); 1,700 (1980) **Pop Density:** 495.9
Land: 3.7 sq. mi.; **Water:** 0.3 sq. mi. **Elev:** 1186 ft.
Incorporated 1885.
Name origin: For William Henry Harrison (1773–1841), ninth U.S. president.

Hatton
Township
Lat: 43-56-02 N **Long:** 84-47-24 W
Pop: 673 (1990); 638 (1980) **Pop Density:** 18.7
Land: 36.0 sq. mi.; **Water:** 0.2 sq. mi.

Hayes
Township
Lat: 44-01-48 N **Long:** 84-47-12 W
Pop: 3,811 (1990); 3,609 (1980) **Pop Density:** 121.4
Land: 31.4 sq. mi.; **Water:** 0.7 sq. mi.

Lincoln
Township
Lat: 43-56-26 N **Long:** 84-54-34 W
Pop: 1,253 (1990); 974 (1980) **Pop Density:** 35.6
Land: 35.2 sq. mi.; **Water:** 0.7 sq. mi.

Redding
Township
Lat: 44-01-52 N **Long:** 85-01-38 W
Pop: 448 (1990); 401 (1980) **Pop Density:** 12.7
Land: 35.3 sq. mi.; **Water:** 0.0 sq. mi.

Sheridan
Township
Lat: 43-51-44 N **Long:** 84-39-50 W
Pop: 1,051 (1990); 1,033 (1980) **Pop Density:** 29.0
Land: 36.3 sq. mi.; **Water:** 0.2 sq. mi.

Summerfield
Township
Lat: 44-07-11 N **Long:** 84-54-32 W
Pop: 316 (1990); 279 (1980) **Pop Density:** 8.9
Land: 35.6 sq. mi.; **Water:** 0.3 sq. mi.

Surrey
Township
Lat: 43-51-25 N **Long:** 84-54-41 W
Pop: 3,221 (1990); 3,101 (1980) **Pop Density:** 91.2
Land: 35.3 sq. mi.; **Water:** 0.6 sq. mi.

Winterfield
Township
Lat: 44-06-49 N **Long:** 85-01-51 W
Pop: 371 (1990); 418 (1980) **Pop Density:** 10.1
Land: 36.6 sq. mi.; **Water:** 0.1 sq. mi.

Clinton County
County Seat: St. Johns (ZIP: 48879)

Pop: 57,883 (1990); 55,893 (1980) **Pop Density:** 101.3
Land: 571.5 sq. mi.; **Water:** 3.1 sq. mi. **Area Code:** 517
In central MI, north of Lansing; established Mar 2, 1831 (prior to statehood) from Shiawassee County.
Name origin: For DeWitt Clinton (1769–1828), governor of NY (1817–21; 1825–28) and supporter of the Erie Canal.

Bath
Township
ZIP: 48808 **Lat:** 42-48-21 N **Long:** 84-25-05 W
Pop: 6,387 (1990); 5,746 (1980) **Pop Density:** 177.4
Land: 36.0 sq. mi.; **Water:** 0.5 sq. mi.

Bengal
Township
Lat: 42-59-16 N **Long:** 84-39-14 W
Pop: 989 (1990); 1,067 (1980) **Pop Density:** 27.1
Land: 36.5 sq. mi.; **Water:** 0.0 sq. mi.

Bingham
Township
Lat: 42-59-06 N **Long:** 84-32-32 W
Pop: 2,546 (1990); 2,371 (1980) **Pop Density:** 76.9
Land: 33.1 sq. mi.; **Water:** 0.0 sq. mi.

Dallas
Township
Lat: 42-59-14 N **Long:** 84-46-46 W
Pop: 2,146 (1990); 2,288 (1980) **Pop Density:** 58.6
Land: 36.6 sq. mi.; **Water:** 0.0 sq. mi.

De Witt
City
ZIP: 48820 **Lat:** 42-50-09 N **Long:** 84-34-32 W
Pop: 3,964 (1990); 3,165 (1980) **Pop Density:** 1366.9
Land: 2.9 sq. mi.; **Water:** 0.1 sq. mi.
Charter township in central MI, 12 mi. north of Lansing. Settled 1830s; founded 1833.
Name origin: For DeWitt Clinton (1769–1828), NY governor and supporter of the Erie Canal.

*De Witt
Township
ZIP: 48820 **Lat:** 42-48-40 N **Long:** 84-32-21 W
Pop: 10,448 (1990); 10,038 (1980) **Pop Density:** 313.8
Land: 33.3 sq. mi.; **Water:** 0.0 sq. mi.

Duplain
Township
Lat: 43-04-21 N **Long:** 84-25-11 W
Pop: 2,235 (1990); 2,330 (1980) **Pop Density:** 63.3
Land: 35.3 sq. mi.; **Water:** 0.1 sq. mi.

Eagle
Village
ZIP: 48822 **Lat:** 42-48-35 N **Long:** 84-47-25 W
Pop: 120 (1990); 155 (1980) **Pop Density:** 1200.0
Land: 0.1 sq. mi.; **Water:** 0.0 sq. mi.
Established 1834. Not coextensive with the town of the same name.
Name origin: For its township.

*Eagle
Township
ZIP: 48822 **Lat:** 42-48-34 N **Long:** 84-47-01 W
Pop: 2,151 (1990); 2,060 (1980) **Pop Density:** 60.8
Land: 35.4 sq. mi.; **Water:** 0.4 sq. mi.

Elsie
Village
ZIP: 48831 **Lat:** 43-05-20 N **Long:** 84-23-26 W
Pop: 957 (1990); 1,022 (1980) **Pop Density:** 797.5
Land: 1.2 sq. mi.; **Water:** 0.0 sq. mi.
Founded 1857.
Name origin: For postmaster Frank Tillotson's baby daughter.

Essex
Township
Lat: 43-04-43 N **Long:** 84-39-05 W
Pop: 1,677 (1990); 1,688 (1980) **Pop Density:** 47.1
Land: 35.6 sq. mi.; **Water:** 0.0 sq. mi.

MICHIGAN, Clinton County   *American Places Dictionary*

Fowler
Village
ZIP: 48835   Lat: 43-00-14 N Long: 84-44-24 W
Pop: 912 (1990); 1,021 (1980)   Pop Density: 701.5
Land: 1.3 sq. mi.; Water: 0.0 sq. mi.   Elev: 743 ft.
Name origin: Named in 1867 for local landowner J.N. Fowler. Previously called Dalles.

Greenbush
Township
Lat: 43-04-30 N Long: 84-32-41 W
Pop: 2,028 (1990); 1,929 (1980)   Pop Density: 57.6
Land: 35.2 sq. mi.; Water: 0.2 sq. mi.

Hubbardston
Village
ZIP: 48845   Lat: 43-05-33 N Long: 84-50-12 W
Pop: 19 (1990); 41 (1980)   Pop Density: 38.0
Land: 0.5 sq. mi.; Water: 0.0 sq. mi.
Incorporated 1867. Part of the town is also in Ionia County.
Name origin: For founder Thomas Hubbard.

Lebanon
Township
Lat: 43-04-58 N Long: 84-46-20 W
Pop: 644 (1990); 697 (1980)   Pop Density: 18.2
Land: 35.4 sq. mi.; Water: 0.0 sq. mi.

Maple Rapids
Village
ZIP: 48853   Lat: 43-06-23 N Long: 84-41-24 W
Pop: 680 (1990); 683 (1980)   Pop Density: 485.7
Land: 1.4 sq. mi.; Water: 0.0 sq. mi.
Name origin: For its location near rapids on the Maple River.

Olive
Township
Lat: 42-54-13 N Long: 84-32-49 W
Pop: 2,122 (1990); 2,111 (1980)   Pop Density: 59.4
Land: 35.7 sq. mi.; Water: 0.1 sq. mi.

Ovid
Village
ZIP: 48866   Lat: 43-00-09 N Long: 84-22-28 W
Pop: 1,442 (1990); 1,712 (1980)   Pop Density: 1602.2
Land: 0.9 sq. mi.; Water: 0.0 sq. mi.
Settled 1834. Not coextensive with the town of the same name. Part of the town is also in Shiawassee County.
Name origin: For Ovid, NY.

*Ovid
Township
ZIP: 48866   Lat: 42-59-33 N Long: 84-25-20 W
Pop: 3,105 (1990); 3,241 (1980)   Pop Density: 86.7
Land: 35.8 sq. mi.; Water: 0.1 sq. mi.

Riley
Township
Lat: 42-53-43 N Long: 84-39-56 W
Pop: 1,543 (1990); 1,547 (1980)   Pop Density: 43.2
Land: 35.7 sq. mi.; Water: 0.0 sq. mi.

St. Johns
City
ZIP: 48879   Lat: 43-00-00 N Long: 84-33-27 W
Pop: 7,284 (1990); 7,376 (1980)   Pop Density: 2349.7
Land: 3.1 sq. mi.; Water: 0.0 sq. mi.   Elev: 794 ft.
Laid out by state official John Swegles.
Name origin: For Swegles, dubbed "Saint John" by a Baptist minister.

Victor
Township
Lat: 42-53-54 N Long: 84-25-20 W
Pop: 2,784 (1990); 2,287 (1980)   Pop Density: 80.5
Land: 34.6 sq. mi.; Water: 1.4 sq. mi.

Watertown
Township
Lat: 42-48-30 N Long: 84-39-17 W
Pop: 3,731 (1990); 3,602 (1980)   Pop Density: 104.5
Land: 35.7 sq. mi.; Water: 0.0 sq. mi.

Westphalia
Village
ZIP: 48894   Lat: 42-55-46 N Long: 84-47-52 W
Pop: 780 (1990); 896 (1980)   Pop Density: 709.1
Land: 1.1 sq. mi.; Water: 0.0 sq. mi.   Elev: 761 ft.
Not coextensive with the town of the same name.
Name origin: For Westphalia, Germany, homeland of farmers who came to the area in 1836.

*Westphalia
Township
Lat: 42-53-54 N Long: 84-46-40 W
Pop: 2,099 (1990); 2,350 (1980)   Pop Density: 59.1
Land: 35.5 sq. mi.; Water: 0.0 sq. mi.

Crawford County
County Seat: Grayling (ZIP: 49738)

Pop: 12,260 (1990); 9,465 (1980)   Pop Density: 22.0
Land: 558.2 sq. mi.; Water: 5.2 sq. mi.   Area Code: 517
In north-central MI; established Apr 1, 1840 as Shawano County; name changed Mar 8, 1843.
Name origin: For Col. William Crawford (1732–82), VA officer in the Revolutionary War, Indian fighter, and surveyor.

Beaver Creek
Township
Lat: 44-33-15 N Long: 84-43-49 W
Pop: 1,175 (1990); 745 (1980)   Pop Density: 16.5
Land: 71.4 sq. mi.; Water: 0.1 sq. mi.

Frederic
Township
ZIP: 49733   Lat: 44-46-31 N Long: 84-47-34 W
Pop: 1,287 (1990); 1,142 (1980)   Pop Density: 17.9
Land: 72.0 sq. mi.; Water: 0.1 sq. mi.

Grayling
City
ZIP: 49738   Lat: 44-39-26 N Long: 84-42-34 W
Pop: 1,944 (1990); 1,792 (1980)   Pop Density: 972.0
Land: 2.0 sq. mi.; Water: 0.0 sq. mi.   Elev: 1137 ft.
Name origin: For the area's once-plentiful grayling trout.

*Grayling
Township
ZIP: 49738   Lat: 44-40-40 N Long: 84-38-33 W
Pop: 5,647 (1990); 4,019 (1980)   Pop Density: 33.0
Land: 171.1 sq. mi.; Water: 3.7 sq. mi.

Lovells
Township
Lat: 44-47-06 N **Long:** 84-28-41 W
Pop: 420 (1990); 316 (1980) **Pop Density:** 4.2
Land: 101.0 sq. mi.; **Water:** 0.8 sq. mi.

Maple Forest
Township
Lat: 44-48-34 N **Long:** 84-39-17 W
Pop: 407 (1990); 355 (1980) **Pop Density:** 11.5
Land: 35.3 sq. mi.; **Water:** 0.3 sq. mi.

South Branch
Township
Lat: 44-35-19 N **Long:** 84-28-27 W
Pop: 1,380 (1990); 1,096 (1980) **Pop Density:** 13.1
Land: 105.4 sq. mi.; **Water:** 0.2 sq. mi.

Delta County
County Seat: Escanaba (ZIP: 49829)

Pop: 37,780 (1990); 38,947 (1980) **Pop Density:** 32.3
Land: 1170.2 sq. mi.; **Water:** 821.6 sq. mi. **Area Code:** 906
On the Upper Peninsula of MI on Green Bay; established Mar 9, 1843 from Schoolcraft County.
Name origin: For the Greek letter, which the shape of the county resembles.

Baldwin
Township
Lat: 45-58-36 N **Long:** 87-05-48 W
Pop: 726 (1990); 769 (1980) **Pop Density:** 8.7
Land: 83.8 sq. mi.; **Water:** 0.4 sq. mi.

Bark River
Township
ZIP: 49807 **Lat:** 45-42-36 N **Long:** 87-17-38 W
Pop: 1,548 (1990); 1,571 (1980) **Pop Density:** 33.9
Land: 45.6 sq. mi.; **Water:** 0.1 sq. mi.

Bay de Noc
Township
Lat: 45-46-31 N **Long:** 86-53-52 W
Pop: 320 (1990); 343 (1980) **Pop Density:** 4.7
Land: 67.5 sq. mi.; **Water:** 23.6 sq. mi.

Brampton
Township
Lat: 45-54-08 N **Long:** 87-02-48 W
Pop: 1,142 (1990); 1,113 (1980) **Pop Density:** 48.2
Land: 23.7 sq. mi.; **Water:** 1.9 sq. mi.

Cornell
Township
ZIP: 49818 **Lat:** 45-55-40 N **Long:** 87-16-08 W
Pop: 529 (1990); 531 (1980) **Pop Density:** 8.8
Land: 59.8 sq. mi.; **Water:** 0.4 sq. mi.

Ensign
Township
Lat: 45-52-15 N **Long:** 86-52-02 W
Pop: 669 (1990); 746 (1980) **Pop Density:** 11.3
Land: 59.0 sq. mi.; **Water:** 6.8 sq. mi.

Escanaba
City
ZIP: 49829 **Lat:** 45-44-46 N **Long:** 87-04-50 W
Pop: 13,659 (1990); 14,355 (1980) **Pop Density:** 1167.4
Land: 11.7 sq. mi.; **Water:** 3.9 sq. mi. **Elev:** 598 ft.
On the south coast of MI's Upper Peninsula at the mouth of the Escanaba River. Incorporated 1863 as a village; 1883 as a city.
Name origin: For the Escanaba River, which flows over a bed of flat rock; itself named from an Ojibway term meaning 'flat rock.' Previously called Sandy Point.

*Escanaba
Township
ZIP: 49829 **Lat:** 45-50-28 N **Long:** 87-10-26 W
Pop: 3,340 (1990); 3,229 (1980) **Pop Density:** 55.7
Land: 60.0 sq. mi.; **Water:** 0.7 sq. mi.

Fairbanks
Township
Lat: 45-31-17 N **Long:** 86-43-26 W
Pop: 309 (1990); 358 (1980) **Pop Density:** 6.5
Land: 47.2 sq. mi.; **Water:** 252.0 sq. mi.

Ford River
Township
Lat: 45-40-32 N **Long:** 87-12-42 W
Pop: 2,002 (1990); 2,136 (1980) **Pop Density:** 30.9
Land: 64.8 sq. mi.; **Water:** 0.5 sq. mi.

Garden
Village
ZIP: 49835 **Lat:** 45-46-31 N **Long:** 86-33-08 W
Pop: 268 (1990); 296 (1980) **Pop Density:** 335.0
Land: 0.8 sq. mi.; **Water:** 0.2 sq. mi. **Elev:** 618 ft.
Not coextensive with the town of the same name.
Name origin: Descriptively named for the fertile soil.

*Garden
Township
ZIP: 49835 **Lat:** 45-55-43 N **Long:** 86-32-58 W
Pop: 783 (1990); 812 (1980) **Pop Density:** 4.9
Land: 159.9 sq. mi.; **Water:** 24.5 sq. mi.

Gladstone
City
ZIP: 49837 **Lat:** 45-51-07 N **Long:** 87-01-29 W
Pop: 4,565 (1990); 4,533 (1980) **Pop Density:** 1014.4
Land: 4.5 sq. mi.; **Water:** 2.9 sq. mi. **Elev:** 601 ft.
Founded 1887.
Name origin: For British Prime Minister William E. Gladstone (1809–98).

Maple Ridge
Township
Lat: 46-04-41 N **Long:** 87-08-14 W
Pop: 829 (1990); 946 (1980) **Pop Density:** 7.7
Land: 108.2 sq. mi.; **Water:** 0.0 sq. mi.

Masonville
Township
Lat: 46-02-20 N **Long:** 86-53-09 W
Pop: 1,709 (1990); 1,807 (1980) **Pop Density:** 10.2
Land: 167.7 sq. mi.; **Water:** 2.7 sq. mi.

Nahma
Township
Lat: 45-59-41 N **Long:** 86-42-20 W
Pop: 491 (1990); 517 (1980) **Pop Density:** 3.0
Land: 166.3 sq. mi.; **Water:** 22.6 sq. mi.

MICHIGAN, Delta County

Wells
Township
ZIP: 49894 Lat: 45-46-12 N Long: 87-09-26 W
Pop: 5,159 (1990); 5,181 (1980) Pop Density: 127.4
Land: 40.5 sq. mi.; Water: 0.3 sq. mi.

Dickinson County
County Seat: Iron Mountain (ZIP: 49801)

Pop: 26,831 (1990); 25,341 (1980) Pop Density: 35.0
Land: 766.4 sq. mi.; Water: 10.8 sq. mi. Area Code: 906

On the south-central border of the Upper Peninsula of MI, south of Ishpeming; established May 21, 1891 from Marquette County.

Name origin: For Donald McDonald Dickinson (1846–1917), U.S. postmaster-general (1887–89).

Breen
Township
Lat: 45-58-32 N Long: 87-42-37 W
Pop: 464 (1990); 471 (1980) Pop Density: 5.3
Land: 87.9 sq. mi.; Water: 0.4 sq. mi.

Breitung
Township
ZIP: 49876 Lat: 45-50-37 N Long: 88-01-20 W
Pop: 5,483 (1990); 4,669 (1980) Pop Density: 84.2
Land: 65.1 sq. mi.; Water: 3.2 sq. mi.

Felch
Township
Lat: 46-04-35 N Long: 87-53-26 W
Pop: 705 (1990); 615 (1980) Pop Density: 4.9
Land: 143.1 sq. mi.; Water: 0.7 sq. mi.

Iron Mountain
City
ZIP: 49801 Lat: 45-49-39 N Long: 88-03-41 W
Pop: 8,525 (1990); 8,341 (1980) Pop Density: 1184.0
Land: 7.2 sq. mi.; Water: 0.6 sq. mi. Elev: 1138 ft.

Name origin: For the nearby iron ore mine.

Kingsford
City
ZIP: 49801 Lat: 45-48-28 N Long: 88-05-56 W
Pop: 5,480 (1990); 5,290 (1980) Pop Density: 1274.4
Land: 4.3 sq. mi.; Water: 0.2 sq. mi.

Name origin: For Ford executive Edward G. Kingsford.

Norway
City
ZIP: 49870 Lat: 45-48-09 N Long: 87-54-52 W
Pop: 2,910 (1990); 2,919 (1980) Pop Density: 330.7
Land: 8.8 sq. mi.; Water: 0.1 sq. mi.

Settled 1877 by Norwegian miner Anton Odell.

Name origin: Named by Odell for his home country.

*Norway
Township
ZIP: 49870 Lat: 45-52-14 N Long: 87-53-30 W
Pop: 1,325 (1990); 1,257 (1980) Pop Density: 14.8
Land: 89.3 sq. mi.; Water: 1.6 sq. mi.

Quinnesec
CDP
ZIP: 49876 Lat: 45-48-05 N Long: 87-59-54 W
Pop: 1,254 (1990) Pop Density: 1140.0
Land: 1.1 sq. mi.; Water: 0.1 sq. mi.

Sagola
Township
ZIP: 49881 Lat: 46-06-32 N Long: 88-02-02 W
Pop: 1,166 (1990); 1,146 (1980) Pop Density: 7.3
Land: 160.3 sq. mi.; Water: 2.5 sq. mi.

Waucedah
Township
Lat: 45-49-47 N Long: 87-45-41 W
Pop: 693 (1990); 577 (1980) Pop Density: 7.8
Land: 89.0 sq. mi.; Water: 1.1 sq. mi.

West Branch
Township
Lat: 46-08-54 N Long: 87-43-29 W
Pop: 80 (1990); 56 (1980) Pop Density: 0.7
Land: 111.5 sq. mi.; Water: 0.4 sq. mi.

Eaton County
County Seat: Charlotte (ZIP: 48813)

Pop: 92,879 (1990); 88,337 (1980) **Pop Density:** 161.1
Land: 576.5 sq. mi.; **Water:** 2.5 sq. mi. **Area Code:** 517
In south-central MI, east of Lansing; established Oct 29, 1829.
Name origin: For John Henry Eaton (1790–1856), U.S. senator from TN (1818–29), U.S. secretary of war (1829–31), and governor of FL Territory (1834–36).

Bellevue — Village
ZIP: 49021 Lat: 42-26-38 N Long: 85-01-07 W
Pop: 1,401 (1990); 1,289 (1980) Pop Density: 1401.0
Land: 1.0 sq. mi.; Water: 0.1 sq. mi.
Not coextensive with the town of the same name.
Name origin: Descriptively named for its pleasant surroundings.

*Bellevue — Township
ZIP: 49021 Lat: 42-28-09 N Long: 85-00-24 W
Pop: 2,938 (1990); 2,725 (1980) Pop Density: 80.7
Land: 36.4 sq. mi.; Water: 0.2 sq. mi.

Benton — Township
Lat: 42-38-42 N Long: 84-47-07 W
Pop: 2,528 (1990); 2,405 (1980) Pop Density: 74.1
Land: 34.1 sq. mi.; Water: 0.0 sq. mi.

Brookfield — Township
Lat: 42-27-41 N Long: 84-46-05 W
Pop: 1,331 (1990); 1,380 (1980) Pop Density: 37.1
Land: 35.9 sq. mi.; Water: 0.3 sq. mi.

Carmel — Township
Lat: 42-33-20 N Long: 84-54-03 W
Pop: 2,433 (1990); 2,168 (1980) Pop Density: 71.3
Land: 34.1 sq. mi.; Water: 0.0 sq. mi.

Charlotte — City
ZIP: 48813 Lat: 42-33-51 N Long: 84-49-56 W
Pop: 8,083 (1990); 8,251 (1980) Pop Density: 1418.1
Land: 5.7 sq. mi.; Water: 0.0 sq. mi. Elev: 917 ft.
Established October 10, 1863, as a village; March 29, 1871, as a city.
Name origin: For the wife of early landowner Edmond Bostwick.

Chester — Township
Lat: 42-38-30 N Long: 84-53-28 W
Pop: 1,602 (1990); 1,622 (1980) Pop Density: 44.4
Land: 36.1 sq. mi.; Water: 0.0 sq. mi.

Delta — Township
ZIP: 48917 Lat: 42-43-37 N Long: 84-39-37 W
Pop: 26,129 (1990); 23,822 (1980) Pop Density: 757.4
Land: 34.5 sq. mi.; Water: 0.5 sq. mi.
Name origin: For the shape of a bend in the Grand River, which resembled the Greek letter, which has the form of a triangle.

Dimondale — Village
ZIP: 48821 Lat: 42-38-55 N Long: 84-38-56 W
Pop: 1,247 (1990); 1,008 (1980) Pop Density: 1247.0
Land: 1.0 sq. mi.; Water: 0.0 sq. mi.
Name origin: For Isaac Dimond, who built a sawmill here in 1856.

Eaton — Township
Lat: 42-32-57 N Long: 84-46-57 W
Pop: 3,492 (1990); 3,315 (1980) Pop Density: 106.5
Land: 32.8 sq. mi.; Water: 0.0 sq. mi.

Eaton Rapids — City
ZIP: 48827 Lat: 42-30-36 N Long: 84-39-14 W
Pop: 4,695 (1990); 4,510 (1980) Pop Density: 1565.0
Land: 3.0 sq. mi.; Water: 0.1 sq. mi. Elev: 871 ft.
Name origin: For John Henry Eaton (1790–1856), U.S. senator from TN (1818–29), U.S. secretary of war (1829–31), and governor of FL Territory (1834–36), and for the nearby Grand River rapids.

*Eaton Rapids — Township
ZIP: 48827 Lat: 42-33-01 N Long: 84-39-15 W
Pop: 3,003 (1990); 2,823 (1980) Pop Density: 87.6
Land: 34.3 sq. mi.; Water: 0.2 sq. mi.

Grand Ledge — City
ZIP: 48837 Lat: 42-45-09 N Long: 84-44-54 W
Pop: 7,579 (1990); 6,920 (1980) Pop Density: 3445.0
Land: 2.2 sq. mi.; Water: 0.1 sq. mi.
Name origin: Descriptive of its location on the Grand River and of the great ledge nearby.

Hamlin — Township
Lat: 42-28-10 N Long: 84-39-45 W
Pop: 2,351 (1990); 2,195 (1980) Pop Density: 68.3
Land: 34.4 sq. mi.; Water: 0.2 sq. mi.

Kalamo — Township
Lat: 42-33-06 N Long: 85-00-41 W
Pop: 1,665 (1990); 1,683 (1980) Pop Density: 45.5
Land: 36.6 sq. mi.; Water: 0.1 sq. mi.

Lansing — City
ZIP: 48901-99 Lat: 42-41-19 N Long: 84-36-27 W
Pop: 4,621 (1990); 4,440 (1980) Pop Density: 4200.9
Land: 1.1 sq. mi.; Water: 0.0 sq. mi.
In south-central MI, 80 mi. northwest of Detroit. Settled 1830s; state capital since 1847; incorporated 1859. Automobile manufacturing city; trade center for the surrounding agricultural area. Part of the town is also in Ingham County.
Name origin: For Lansing, NY.

Mulliken — Village
ZIP: 48861 Lat: 42-45-46 N Long: 84-53-42 W
Pop: 590 (1990); 550 (1980) Pop Density: 590.0
Land: 1.0 sq. mi.; Water: 0.0 sq. mi.
Name origin: For the contractor who built the railroad here.

MICHIGAN, Eaton County

Olivet
City
ZIP: 49076 **Lat:** 42-26-45 N **Long:** 84-55-24 W
Pop: 1,604 (1990); 1,604 (1980) **Pop Density:** 1604.0
Land: 1.0 sq. mi.; **Water:** 0.0 sq. mi.
Colony founded here in 1844 by the Rev. John Shipherd.
Name origin: Named by Shipherd for the biblical Mount Olivet.

Oneida Charter
Township
Lat: 42-43-17 N **Long:** 84-46-10 W
Pop: 3,228 (1990); 3,378 (1980) **Pop Density:** 96.4
Land: 33.5 sq. mi.; **Water:** 0.1 sq. mi.

Potterville
City
ZIP: 48876 **Lat:** 42-37-40 N **Long:** 84-44-44 W
Pop: 1,523 (1990); 1,502 (1980) **Pop Density:** 1087.9
Land: 1.4 sq. mi.; **Water:** 0.0 sq. mi.
Settled 1844 by Linus Potter.
Name origin: For Linus Potter, the first settler.

Roxand
Township
Lat: 42-44-01 N **Long:** 84-53-12 W
Pop: 1,903 (1990); 1,975 (1980) **Pop Density:** 52.1
Land: 36.5 sq. mi.; **Water:** 0.0 sq. mi.

Sunfield
Village
ZIP: 48890 **Lat:** 42-45-42 N **Long:** 84-59-30 W
Pop: 610 (1990); 591 (1980) **Pop Density:** 1016.7
Land: 0.6 sq. mi.; **Water:** 0.0 sq. mi. **Elev:** 866 ft.
Settled 1830s.
Name origin: For its township.

*Sunfield
Township
ZIP: 48890 **Lat:** 42-43-40 N **Long:** 85-00-37 W
Pop: 2,086 (1990); 1,998 (1980) **Pop Density:** 57.9
Land: 36.0 sq. mi.; **Water:** 0.3 sq. mi.

Vermontville
Village
ZIP: 49096 **Lat:** 42-37-33 N **Long:** 85-01-33 W
Pop: 776 (1990); 832 (1980) **Pop Density:** 646.7
Land: 1.2 sq. mi.; **Water:** 0.0 sq. mi. **Elev:** 928 ft.
Settled 1836 as a Congregationalist colony of Vermonters, organized by the Rev. Sylvester Cochrane. Not coextensive with the town of the same name.
Name origin: For the settlers' former home.

*Vermontville
Township
ZIP: 49096 **Lat:** 42-38-11 N **Long:** 85-01-11 W
Pop: 1,896 (1990); 1,942 (1980) **Pop Density:** 52.2
Land: 36.3 sq. mi.; **Water:** 0.1 sq. mi.

Walton
Township
Lat: 42-28-07 N **Long:** 84-53-41 W
Pop: 1,729 (1990); 1,601 (1980) **Pop Density:** 49.1
Land: 35.2 sq. mi.; **Water:** 0.2 sq. mi.

Waverly
CDP
Lat: 42-44-21 N **Long:** 84-37-14 W
Pop: 15,614 (1990) **Pop Density:** 2739.3
Land: 5.7 sq. mi.; **Water:** 0.0 sq. mi.

Windsor
Township
ZIP: 48821 **Lat:** 42-38-28 N **Long:** 84-39-43 W
Pop: 6,460 (1990); 6,078 (1980) **Pop Density:** 184.6
Land: 35.0 sq. mi.; **Water:** 0.1 sq. mi.

Emmet County
County Seat: Petoskey (ZIP: 49770)

Pop: 25,040 (1990); 22,992 (1980) **Pop Density:** 53.5
Land: 468.0 sq. mi.; **Water:** 414.4 sq. mi. **Area Code:** 616

On the northwest coast of MI, bordered on west by Lake Michigan; established as Tonedagana County Apr 1, 1840 from Mackinac County; name changed Mar 8, 1843.

Name origin: For Robert W. Emmet (1778–1803), Irish rebel executed by the British; named for him during a time when rebel leaders were honored by Americans.

Alanson
Village
ZIP: 49706 **Lat:** 45-26-28 N **Long:** 84-47-14 W
Pop: 677 (1990); 508 (1980) **Pop Density:** 677.0
Land: 1.0 sq. mi.; **Water:** 0.0 sq. mi. **Elev:** 615 ft.
Name origin: Named in 1882 for railroad official Alanson Cook, when the railroad came through the area.

Bear Creek
Township
Lat: 45-20-55 N **Long:** 84-54-48 W
Pop: 3,469 (1990); 3,287 (1980) **Pop Density:** 87.6
Land: 39.6 sq. mi.; **Water:** 6.2 sq. mi.

Bliss
Township
Lat: 45-41-46 N **Long:** 84-55-11 W
Pop: 483 (1990); 441 (1980) **Pop Density:** 11.0
Land: 43.9 sq. mi.; **Water:** 2.3 sq. mi.

Carp Lake
Township
ZIP: 49718 **Lat:** 45-40-44 N **Long:** 84-47-22 W
Pop: 597 (1990); 637 (1980) **Pop Density:** 18.4
Land: 32.4 sq. mi.; **Water:** 2.8 sq. mi.

Center
Township
Lat: 45-35-49 N **Long:** 84-55-12 W
Pop: 517 (1990); 435 (1980) **Pop Density:** 15.0
Land: 34.4 sq. mi.; **Water:** 0.9 sq. mi.

Cross Village
Township
Lat: 45-38-38 N **Long:** 85-00-51 W
Pop: 201 (1990); 215 (1980) **Pop Density:** 20.1
Land: 10.0 sq. mi.; **Water:** 0.2 sq. mi.

Friendship
Township
Lat: 45-30-56 N **Long:** 85-02-05 W
Pop: 591 (1990); 467 (1980) **Pop Density:** 18.8
Land: 31.4 sq. mi.; **Water:** 0.0 sq. mi.

Harbor Springs City
ZIP: 49740 **Lat:** 45-25-55 N **Long:** 84-59-22 W
Pop: 1,540 (1990); 1,567 (1980) **Pop Density:** 1184.6
Land: 1.3 sq. mi.; **Water:** 0.0 sq. mi.
Incorporated 1881.
Name origin: For its natural harbor and abundant local springs.

Littlefield Township
Lat: 45-26-01 N **Long:** 84-47-19 W
Pop: 2,310 (1990); 1,822 (1980) **Pop Density:** 106.5
Land: 21.7 sq. mi.; **Water:** 2.8 sq. mi.

Little Traverse Township
Lat: 45-26-20 N **Long:** 84-54-34 W
Pop: 1,805 (1990); 1,574 (1980) **Pop Density:** 100.3
Land: 18.0 sq. mi.; **Water:** 2.4 sq. mi.

Mackinaw City Village
ZIP: 49701 **Lat:** 45-46-44 N **Long:** 84-44-59 W
Pop: 467 (1990); 428 (1980) **Pop Density:** 179.6
Land: 2.6 sq. mi.; **Water:** 0.6 sq. mi.
Part of the town is also in Cheboygan County.
Name origin: A shortened version of Fort Michilimackinac, the latter an Indian term meaning 'island of the large turtle.'

Maple River Township
Lat: 45-30-25 N **Long:** 84-47-33 W
Pop: 743 (1990); 654 (1980) **Pop Density:** 21.0
Land: 35.3 sq. mi.; **Water:** 0.2 sq. mi.

McKinley Township
Lat: 45-35-36 N **Long:** 84-47-37 W
Pop: 1,080 (1990); 961 (1980) **Pop Density:** 30.7
Land: 35.2 sq. mi.; **Water:** 0.1 sq. mi.

Pellston Village
ZIP: 49769 **Lat:** 45-33-05 N **Long:** 84-46-59 W
Pop: 583 (1990); 565 (1980) **Pop Density:** 306.8
Land: 1.9 sq. mi.; **Water:** 0.0 sq. mi. **Elev:** 702 ft.
Founded by William Pells 1876.
Name origin: For the founder.

Petoskey City
ZIP: 49770 **Lat:** 45-21-58 N **Long:** 84-57-18 W
Pop: 6,056 (1990); 6,097 (1980) **Pop Density:** 1835.2
Land: 3.3 sq. mi.; **Water:** 0.1 sq. mi. **Elev:** 786 ft.
Founded as an Indian mission 1852.
Name origin: For Chippewa Chief Petoskey, whose name is a corrupt version of *Petosega* meaning 'rising sun.'

Pleasant View Township
Lat: 45-30-02 N **Long:** 84-55-28 W
Pop: 375 (1990); 212 (1980) **Pop Density:** 10.5
Land: 35.7 sq. mi.; **Water:** 0.0 sq. mi.

Readmond Township
Lat: 45-35-13 N **Long:** 85-02-02 W
Pop: 374 (1990); 356 (1980) **Pop Density:** 12.1
Land: 31.0 sq. mi.; **Water:** 0.0 sq. mi.

Resort Township
Lat: 45-20-15 N **Long:** 85-00-59 W
Pop: 2,068 (1990); 1,687 (1980) **Pop Density:** 98.5
Land: 21.0 sq. mi.; **Water:** 2.4 sq. mi.

Springvale Township
Lat: 45-21-09 N **Long:** 84-47-29 W
Pop: 1,300 (1990); 1,073 (1980) **Pop Density:** 29.1
Land: 44.7 sq. mi.; **Water:** 2.4 sq. mi.

Wawatam Township
Lat: 45-44-45 N **Long:** 84-47-22 W
Pop: 563 (1990); 510 (1980) **Pop Density:** 35.9
Land: 15.7 sq. mi.; **Water:** 1.7 sq. mi.

West Traverse Township
Lat: 45-27-28 N **Long:** 85-01-19 W
Pop: 968 (1990); 997 (1980) **Pop Density:** 72.8
Land: 13.3 sq. mi.; **Water:** 0.0 sq. mi.

Genesee County
County Seat: Flint (ZIP: 48502)

Pop: 430,459 (1990); 450,449 (1980) **Pop Density:** 672.9
Land: 639.7 sq. mi.; **Water:** 9.7 sq. mi. **Area Code:** 313
In east-central MI, northeast of Lansing; organized Mar 28, 1835 (prior to statehood) from Oakland County.
Name origin: For Genesee County, NY, former home of many early settlers; from Iroquoian 'beautiful valley.'

Argentine Township
Lat: 42-49-21 N **Long:** 83-52-06 W
Pop: 4,651 (1990); 4,180 (1980) **Pop Density:** 132.5
Land: 35.1 sq. mi.; **Water:** 1.2 sq. mi.

Atlas Township
ZIP: 48438 **Lat:** 42-55-05 N **Long:** 83-31-00 W
Pop: 5,551 (1990); 4,891 (1980) **Pop Density:** 156.8
Land: 35.4 sq. mi.; **Water:** 0.6 sq. mi.

Beecher CDP
ZIP: 48458 **Lat:** 43-05-26 N **Long:** 83-42-17 W
Pop: 14,465 (1990); 3,907 (1980) **Pop Density:** 2451.7
Land: 5.9 sq. mi.; **Water:** 0.0 sq. mi.

Burton City
ZIP: 48509 **Lat:** 42-59-48 N **Long:** 83-37-10 W
Pop: 27,617 (1990); 29,976 (1980) **Pop Density:** 1175.2
Land: 23.5 sq. mi.; **Water:** 0.0 sq. mi.
In south-central MI, just southeast of Flint.

MICHIGAN, Genesee County

Clayton — Township
ZIP: 48473 Lat: 43-00-28 N Long: 83-52-06 W
Pop: 7,368 (1990); 7,269 (1980) Pop Density: 214.8
Land: 34.3 sq. mi.; Water: 0.0 sq. mi.

Clio — City
ZIP: 48420 Lat: 43-10-37 N Long: 83-44-10 W
Pop: 2,629 (1990); 2,669 (1980) Pop Density: 2190.8
Land: 1.2 sq. mi.; Water: 0.0 sq. mi.
Name origin: Named in 1866 for the Muse of history. Previously called Varna.

Davison — City
ZIP: 48423 Lat: 43-01-55 N Long: 83-31-05 W
Pop: 5,693 (1990); 6,087 (1980) Pop Density: 3162.8
Land: 1.8 sq. mi.; Water: 0.0 sq. mi. Elev: 799 ft.
In southeastern MI, 8 mi. east of Flint.
Name origin: Named by the legislature for Norman Davison, whose village of Davisonville had been renamed Atlas.

*Davison — Township
ZIP: 48423 Lat: 43-00-20 N Long: 83-30-59 W
Pop: 14,671 (1990); 13,708 (1980) Pop Density: 437.9
Land: 33.5 sq. mi.; Water: 0.2 sq. mi.

Fenton — City
ZIP: 48430 Lat: 42-48-00 N Long: 83-42-51 W
Pop: 8,444 (1990); 8,098 (1980) Pop Density: 1279.4
Land: 6.6 sq. mi.; Water: 0.3 sq. mi.
In southeastern MI, 15 mi. south of Flint.
Name origin: For William M. Fenton, who platted the town in 1837.

*Fenton — Township
ZIP: 48430 Lat: 42-50-04 N Long: 83-45-10 W
Pop: 10,055 (1990); 11,744 (1980) Pop Density: 420.7
Land: 23.9 sq. mi.; Water: 3.7 sq. mi.

Flint — City
ZIP: 48501 Lat: 43-01-22 N Long: 83-41-34 W
Pop: 140,761 (1990); 159,611 (1980) Pop Density: 4164.5
Land: 33.8 sq. mi.; Water: 0.4 sq. mi.
In south-central MI on the Flint River, 25 mi. northwest of Pontiac. Settled 1819; incorporated as city 1855. Largest manufacturing center of General Motors Corp.
Name origin: For the river.

*Flint — Township
ZIP: 48532 Lat: 43-00-22 N Long: 83-46-08 W
Pop: 34,081 (1990); 35,405 (1980) Pop Density: 1438.0
Land: 23.7 sq. mi.; Water: 0.0 sq. mi.

Flushing — City
ZIP: 48433 Lat: 43-03-53 N Long: 83-50-29 W
Pop: 8,542 (1990); 8,624 (1980) Pop Density: 1986.5
Land: 4.3 sq. mi.; Water: 0.0 sq. mi.
Settled 1830s.
Name origin: For its township.

*Flushing — Township
ZIP: 48433 Lat: 43-05-46 N Long: 83-52-27 W
Pop: 9,223 (1990); 9,246 (1980) Pop Density: 298.5
Land: 30.9 sq. mi.; Water: 0.2 sq. mi.

Forest — Township
Lat: 43-10-24 N Long: 83-31-16 W
Pop: 4,409 (1990); 4,255 (1980) Pop Density: 123.2
Land: 35.8 sq. mi.; Water: 0.3 sq. mi.

Gaines — Village
ZIP: 48436 Lat: 42-52-20 N Long: 83-54-42 W
Pop: 427 (1990); 440 (1980) Pop Density: 1423.3
Land: 0.3 sq. mi.; Water: 0.0 sq. mi.
Not coextensive with the town of the same name.
Name origin: For Gen. Edmund P. Gaines (1777–1849), defender of Fort Erie during the War of 1812.

*Gaines — Township
ZIP: 48436 Lat: 42-54-44 N Long: 83-52-35 W
Pop: 5,391 (1990); 5,209 (1980) Pop Density: 153.2
Land: 35.2 sq. mi.; Water: 0.1 sq. mi.

Genesee — Township
ZIP: 48437 Lat: 43-05-44 N Long: 83-37-45 W
Pop: 24,093 (1990); 25,065 (1980) Pop Density: 819.5
Land: 29.4 sq. mi.; Water: 1.0 sq. mi.
Charter township in east-central MI, northeast of Flint. Established 1836.
Name origin: For Genesee County, NY, former home of many early settlers; from Iroquoian 'beautiful valley.'

Goodrich — Village
ZIP: 48438 Lat: 42-54-59 N Long: 83-30-29 W
Pop: 916 (1990); 795 (1980) Pop Density: 398.3
Land: 2.3 sq. mi.; Water: 0.0 sq. mi. Elev: 894 ft.
Settled 1835.
Name origin: For the Goodrich brothers, the first settlers.

Grand Blanc — City
ZIP: 48439 Lat: 42-55-32 N Long: 83-37-07 W
Pop: 7,760 (1990); 6,848 (1980) Pop Density: 2097.3
Land: 3.7 sq. mi.; Water: 0.0 sq. mi.
In southeastern MI, 8 mi. south of Flint. Not coextensive with the town of the same name.
Name origin: Named in 1823 for a husky French trader nicknamed by the Indians *Grand Blanc* (French for 'Big White'). Previously called Grumlaw.

*Grand Blanc — Township
ZIP: 48439 Lat: 42-54-41 N Long: 83-37-39 W
Pop: 25,392 (1990); 24,413 (1980) Pop Density: 776.5
Land: 32.7 sq. mi.; Water: 0.1 sq. mi.

Lake Fenton — CDP
ZIP: 48430 Lat: 42-50-45 N Long: 83-42-28 W
Pop: 4,091 (1990); 3,154 (1980) Pop Density: 743.8
Land: 5.5 sq. mi.; Water: 1.7 sq. mi.

Lennon — Village
ZIP: 48449 Lat: 42-59-08 N Long: 83-55-35 W
Pop: 84 (1990); 114 (1980) Pop Density: 420.0
Land: 0.2 sq. mi.; Water: 0.0 sq. mi.
Part of the town is also in Shiawassee County.
Name origin: For railroad builder Peter Lennon.

Linden — Village
ZIP: 48451 Lat: 42-49-09 N Long: 83-46-53 W
Pop: 2,415 (1990); 2,174 (1980) Pop Density: 1006.2
Land: 2.4 sq. mi.; Water: 0.0 sq. mi.
Settled 1835.
Name origin: For the area's linden trees.

Montrose
Village
ZIP: 48457   **Lat:** 43-10-32 N   **Long:** 83-53-33 W
Pop: 1,811 (1990); 1,706 (1980)   **Pop Density:** 2012.2
Land: 0.9 sq. mi.; **Water:** 0.0 sq. mi.
Not coextensive with the town of the same name.
Name origin: Named by Scottish pioneer John Farquharson for Montrose, Scotland.

*Montrose
Township
ZIP: 48457   **Lat:** 43-10-35 N   **Long:** 83-52-24 W
Pop: 6,236 (1990); 7,870 (1980)   **Pop Density:** 181.3
Land: 34.4 sq. mi.; **Water:** 0.2 sq. mi.

Mount Morris
City
ZIP: 48458   **Lat:** 43-06-58 N   **Long:** 83-41-56 W
Pop: 3,292 (1990); 3,246 (1980)   **Pop Density:** 2743.3
Land: 1.2 sq. mi.; **Water:** 0.0 sq. mi.   **Elev:** 794 ft.
Name origin: For Mount Morris, NY.

*Mount Morris
Township
ZIP: 48458   **Lat:** 43-05-26 N   **Long:** 83-45-35 W
Pop: 25,198 (1990); 27,928 (1980)   **Pop Density:** 802.5
Land: 31.4 sq. mi.; **Water:** 0.0 sq. mi.

Mundy
Township
ZIP: 48507   **Lat:** 42-54-53 N   **Long:** 83-44-55 W
Pop: 11,511 (1990); 10,786 (1980)   **Pop Density:** 322.4
Land: 35.7 sq. mi.; **Water:** 0.1 sq. mi.
In southeastern MI, south of Flint.
Name origin: For Lt.-Gov. Edward S. Mundy. Previously called Independence.

Otisville
Village
ZIP: 48463   **Lat:** 43-09-54 N   **Long:** 83-31-27 W
Pop: 724 (1990); 682 (1980)   **Pop Density:** 804.4
Land: 0.9 sq. mi.; **Water:** 0.1 sq. mi.

Otter Lake
Village
ZIP: 48464   **Lat:** 43-12-45 N   **Long:** 83-28-00 W
Pop: 55 (1990); 14 (1980)   **Pop Density:** 137.5
Land: 0.4 sq. mi.; **Water:** 0.0 sq. mi.
Part of the town is also in Lapeer County.
Name origin: For the nearby lake, which once had an abundant otter population.

Richfield
Township
ZIP: 48423   **Lat:** 43-05-46 N   **Long:** 83-31-21 W
Pop: 7,271 (1990); 6,895 (1980)   **Pop Density:** 206.0
Land: 35.3 sq. mi.; **Water:** 1.1 sq. mi.

Swartz Creek
City
ZIP: 48473   **Lat:** 42-57-43 N   **Long:** 83-49-35 W
Pop: 4,851 (1990); 5,013 (1980)   **Pop Density:** 1212.8
Land: 4.0 sq. mi.; **Water:** 0.0 sq. mi.
Settled 1836.
Name origin: For nearby Swartz (German for 'black') Creek.

Thetford
Township
ZIP: 48420   **Lat:** 43-11-02 N   **Long:** 83-38-06 W
Pop: 8,333 (1990); 8,499 (1980)   **Pop Density:** 240.1
Land: 34.7 sq. mi.; **Water:** 0.1 sq. mi.

Vienna
Township
ZIP: 48420   **Lat:** 43-10-48 N   **Long:** 83-45-17 W
Pop: 13,210 (1990); 12,914 (1980)   **Pop Density:** 377.4
Land: 35.0 sq. mi.; **Water:** 0.0 sq. mi.
In southeastern MI, north of Flint.
Name origin: For Vienna, Austria.

Gladwin County
County Seat: Gladwin (ZIP: 48624)

Pop: 21,896 (1990); 19,957 (1980)   **Pop Density:** 43.2
Land: 506.8 sq. mi.; **Water:** 9.6 sq. mi.   **Area Code:** 517
In east-central MI, north of Midland; established Mar 2, 1831 (prior to statehood) from unorganized territory.
Name origin: For Gen. Henry Gladwin (1729–91), British soldier during the French and Indian War and defender of Detroit against Chief Pontiac.

Beaverton
City
ZIP: 48612   **Lat:** 43-52-54 N   **Long:** 84-29-15 W
Pop: 1,150 (1990); 1,025 (1980)   **Pop Density:** 1150.0
Land: 1.0 sq. mi.; **Water:** 0.2 sq. mi.
A town since 1875.
Name origin: For Beaverton, Ontario, Canada.

*Beaverton
Township
ZIP: 48612   **Lat:** 43-51-24 N   **Long:** 84-32-32 W
Pop: 1,671 (1990); 1,612 (1980)   **Pop Density:** 47.1
Land: 35.5 sq. mi.; **Water:** 0.1 sq. mi.

Bentley
Township
Lat: 43-52-15 N   **Long:** 84-14-16 W
Pop: 751 (1990); 771 (1980)   **Pop Density:** 21.0
Land: 35.7 sq. mi.; **Water:** 0.1 sq. mi.

Billings
Township
Lat: 43-52-19 N   **Long:** 84-19-34 W
Pop: 2,305 (1990); 2,076 (1980)   **Pop Density:** 106.2
Land: 21.7 sq. mi.; **Water:** 1.4 sq. mi.

Bourret
Township
Lat: 44-07-36 N   **Long:** 84-13-57 W
Pop: 400 (1990); 315 (1980)   **Pop Density:** 12.3
Land: 32.4 sq. mi.; **Water:** 0.4 sq. mi.

Buckeye
Township
Lat: 43-56-47 N   **Long:** 84-25-28 W
Pop: 996 (1990); 970 (1980)   **Pop Density:** 28.4
Land: 35.1 sq. mi.; **Water:** 0.0 sq. mi.

Butman
Township
Lat: 44-07-05 N   **Long:** 84-25-27 W
Pop: 1,188 (1990); 834 (1980)   **Pop Density:** 34.8
Land: 34.1 sq. mi.; **Water:** 1.6 sq. mi.

Clement
Township
Lat: 44-07-23 N **Long:** 84-19-29 W
Pop: 822 (1990); 781 (1980) **Pop Density:** 40.7
Land: 20.2 sq. mi.; **Water:** 0.8 sq. mi.

Gladwin
City
ZIP: 48624 **Lat:** 43-59-02 N **Long:** 84-29-29 W
Pop: 2,682 (1990); 2,479 (1980) **Pop Density:** 1219.1
Land: 2.2 sq. mi.; **Water:** 0.0 sq. mi. **Elev:** 786 ft.
Not coextensive with the town of the same name.
Name origin: For Henry Gladwin (1729–91), British officer during the French and Indian War and defender of Detroit against Chief Pontiac.

*Gladwin
Township
ZIP: 48624 **Lat:** 44-01-33 N **Long:** 84-26-05 W
Pop: 916 (1990); 743 (1980) **Pop Density:** 25.9
Land: 35.3 sq. mi.; **Water:** 0.0 sq. mi.

Grim
Township
Lat: 44-00-17 N **Long:** 84-12-54 W
Pop: 100 (1990); 115 (1980) **Pop Density:** 1.4
Land: 70.7 sq. mi.; **Water:** 0.7 sq. mi.

Grout
Township
Lat: 43-56-23 N **Long:** 84-32-44 W
Pop: 1,626 (1990); 1,542 (1980) **Pop Density:** 46.9
Land: 34.7 sq. mi.; **Water:** 0.1 sq. mi.

Hay
Township
Lat: 43-57-18 N **Long:** 84-19-18 W
Pop: 1,173 (1990); 1,056 (1980) **Pop Density:** 52.8
Land: 22.2 sq. mi.; **Water:** 0.4 sq. mi.

Sage
Township
Lat: 44-01-50 N **Long:** 84-32-46 W
Pop: 2,177 (1990); 2,049 (1980) **Pop Density:** 62.9
Land: 34.6 sq. mi.; **Water:** 0.9 sq. mi.

Secord
Township
Lat: 44-01-42 N **Long:** 84-19-48 W
Pop: 914 (1990); 850 (1980) **Pop Density:** 40.6
Land: 22.5 sq. mi.; **Water:** 0.9 sq. mi.

Sherman
Township
Lat: 44-07-05 N **Long:** 84-32-32 W
Pop: 796 (1990); 773 (1980) **Pop Density:** 22.8
Land: 34.9 sq. mi.; **Water:** 0.5 sq. mi.

Tobacco
Township
Lat: 43-51-25 N **Long:** 84-25-31 W
Pop: 2,229 (1990); 1,966 (1980) **Pop Density:** 65.6
Land: 34.0 sq. mi.; **Water:** 1.3 sq. mi.

Gogebic County
County Seat: Bessemer (ZIP: 49911)

Pop: 18,052 (1990); 19,686 (1980) **Pop Density:** 16.4
Land: 1101.9 sq. mi.; **Water:** 374.6 sq. mi. **Area Code:** 906
On the southwest border of the Upper Peninsula of MI; organized Feb 7, 1887 from Ontonagon County.

Name origin: From Ojibway *agogebic*, of uncertain origin, though *bic* translates to 'lake'; also possibly 'trembling ground.'

Bessemer
City
ZIP: 49911 **Lat:** 46-28-39 N **Long:** 90-02-58 W
Pop: 2,272 (1990); 2,553 (1980) **Pop Density:** 413.1
Land: 5.5 sq. mi.; **Water:** 0.0 sq. mi. **Elev:** 1432 ft.
Established 1884 as a mining town; formally organized as a city in 1889.
Name origin: For Sir Henry Bessemer (1813–98), inventor of the Bessemer smelting process.

*Bessemer
Township
ZIP: 49911 **Lat:** 46-23-46 N **Long:** 89-55-08 W
Pop: 1,374 (1990); 1,560 (1980) **Pop Density:** 12.1
Land: 113.9 sq. mi.; **Water:** 1.6 sq. mi.

Erwin
Township
Lat: 46-21-34 N **Long:** 90-04-17 W
Pop: 477 (1990); 527 (1980) **Pop Density:** 10.0
Land: 47.8 sq. mi.; **Water:** 0.9 sq. mi.

Ironwood
City
ZIP: 49938 **Lat:** 46-27-16 N **Long:** 90-09-09 W
Pop: 6,849 (1990); 7,741 (1980) **Pop Density:** 1180.9
Land: 5.8 sq. mi.; **Water:** 0.0 sq. mi. **Elev:** 1503 ft.
Settled 1885.
Name origin: For prominent mining organizer James Wood.

*Ironwood
Township
ZIP: 49938 **Lat:** 46-34-39 N **Long:** 90-09-38 W
Pop: 2,303 (1990); 2,331 (1980) **Pop Density:** 13.1
Land: 175.5 sq. mi.; **Water:** 13.4 sq. mi.

Marenisco
Township
ZIP: 49947 **Lat:** 46-23-07 N **Long:** 89-34-57 W
Pop: 959 (1990); 824 (1980) **Pop Density:** 3.1
Land: 310.9 sq. mi.; **Water:** 15.0 sq. mi.

Wakefield
City
ZIP: 49968 **Lat:** 46-28-36 N **Long:** 89-56-00 W
Pop: 2,318 (1990); 2,591 (1980) **Pop Density:** 293.4
Land: 7.9 sq. mi.; **Water:** 0.5 sq. mi. **Elev:** 1550 ft.
Settled 1884.
Name origin: For pioneer George Wakefield, who platted the town in 1885.

*Wakefield
Township
ZIP: 49968 **Lat:** 46-33-09 N **Long:** 89-51-43 W
Pop: 452 (1990); 465 (1980) **Pop Density:** 2.5
Land: 179.9 sq. mi.; **Water:** 1.0 sq. mi.

Watersmeet
Township
ZIP: 49969 **Lat:** 46-14-57 N **Long:** 89-12-44 W
Pop: 1,048 (1990); 1,094 (1980) **Pop Density:** 4.1
Land: 254.8 sq. mi.; **Water:** 23.1 sq. mi.

Grand Traverse County
County Seat: Traverse City (ZIP: 49684)

Pop: 64,273 (1990); 54,899 (1980)   **Pop Density:** 138.2
Land: 465.1 sq. mi.; **Water:** 136.1 sq. mi.   **Area Code:** 616

On the northwest coast of MI on Grand Traverse Bay; organized as Omeena County Apr 1, 1840; name changed Apr 17, 1851.

Name origin: From French *Le Grand Traverse* 'the long crossing,' for the trail across the foot of Traverse Bay.

Acme   Township
Lat: 44-47-40 N   **Long:** 85-27-09 W
Pop: 3,447 (1990); 2,909 (1980)   **Pop Density:** 136.8
Land: 25.2 sq. mi.; **Water:** 0.2 sq. mi.

Blair   Township
ZIP: 49684   **Lat:** 44-38-47 N   **Long:** 85-38-07 W
Pop: 5,249 (1990); 4,613 (1980)   **Pop Density:** 147.4
Land: 35.6 sq. mi.; **Water:** 0.3 sq. mi.

East Bay   Township
ZIP: 49684   **Lat:** 44-41-43 N   **Long:** 85-30-40 W
Pop: 8,307 (1990); 6,212 (1980)   **Pop Density:** 208.2
Land: 39.9 sq. mi.; **Water:** 2.4 sq. mi.

Fife Lake   Village
ZIP: 49633   **Lat:** 44-34-25 N   **Long:** 85-21-11 W
Pop: 394 (1990); 402 (1980)   **Pop Density:** 562.9
Land: 0.7 sq. mi.; **Water:** 0.5 sq. mi.   **Elev:** 1038 ft.
Not coextensive with the town of the same name.
Name origin: For state highway commissioner William Fife.

*Fife Lake   Township
ZIP: 49633   **Lat:** 44-33-18 N   **Long:** 85-23-43 W
Pop: 1,344 (1990); 1,056 (1980)   **Pop Density:** 39.1
Land: 34.4 sq. mi.; **Water:** 1.6 sq. mi.

Garfield   Township
ZIP: 49684   **Lat:** 44-43-16 N   **Long:** 85-38-27 W
Pop: 10,516 (1990); 8,747 (1980)   **Pop Density:** 392.4
Land: 26.8 sq. mi.; **Water:** 1.0 sq. mi.

Grant   Township
Lat: 44-33-54 N   **Long:** 85-45-34 W
Pop: 745 (1990); 676 (1980)   **Pop Density:** 21.0
Land: 35.4 sq. mi.; **Water:** 0.6 sq. mi.

Green Lake   Township
Lat: 44-38-39 N   **Long:** 85-45-24 W
Pop: 3,677 (1990); 2,997 (1980)   **Pop Density:** 125.1
Land: 29.4 sq. mi.; **Water:** 6.9 sq. mi.

Kingsley   Village
ZIP: 49649   **Lat:** 44-35-03 N   **Long:** 85-32-07 W
Pop: 738 (1990); 664 (1980)   **Pop Density:** 820.0
Land: 0.9 sq. mi.; **Water:** 0.0 sq. mi.   **Elev:** 996 ft.
Incorporated 1890.
Name origin: For Judson L.W. Kingsley, who first platted the town on part of his homestead.

Long Lake   Township
ZIP: 49684   **Lat:** 44-43-50 N   **Long:** 85-45-35 W
Pop: 5,977 (1990); 3,823 (1980)   **Pop Density:** 198.6
Land: 30.1 sq. mi.; **Water:** 5.5 sq. mi.

Mayfield   Township
Lat: 44-33-15 N   **Long:** 85-38-37 W
Pop: 967 (1990); 806 (1980)   **Pop Density:** 26.9
Land: 35.9 sq. mi.; **Water:** 0.2 sq. mi.

Paradise   Township
Lat: 44-34-45 N   **Long:** 85-31-19 W
Pop: 2,508 (1990); 2,117 (1980)   **Pop Density:** 47.4
Land: 52.9 sq. mi.; **Water:** 0.1 sq. mi.

Peninsula   Township
Lat: 44-53-39 N   **Long:** 85-31-22 W
Pop: 4,340 (1990); 3,833 (1980)   **Pop Density:** 155.6
Land: 27.9 sq. mi.; **Water:** 1.2 sq. mi.

Traverse City   City
ZIP: 49684   **Lat:** 44-45-15 N   **Long:** 85-36-04 W
Pop: 15,116 (1990); 15,516 (1980)   **Pop Density:** 1913.4
Land: 7.9 sq. mi.; **Water:** 0.3 sq. mi.   **Elev:** 599 ft.
In northwestern MI at the southern end of the West Arm of Lake Michigan's Grand Traverse Bay. Established 1847. Part of the town is also in Leelanau County.
Name origin: From French *lac travers*, a translation of the Siouxan term *mdehdakinyan* meaning 'lake lying crosswise.'

Union   Township
Lat: 44-38-45 N   **Long:** 85-24-05 W
Pop: 255 (1990); 185 (1980)   **Pop Density:** 7.1
Land: 35.8 sq. mi.; **Water:** 0.2 sq. mi.

Whitewater   Township
Lat: 44-45-18 N   **Long:** 85-23-24 W
Pop: 1,825 (1990); 1,409 (1980)   **Pop Density:** 38.2
Land: 47.8 sq. mi.; **Water:** 5.8 sq. mi.

Gratiot County
County Seat: Ithaca (ZIP: 48847)

Pop: 38,982 (1990); 40,448 (1980)
Land: 570.2 sq. mi.; **Water:** 1.5 sq. mi.
Pop Density: 68.4
Area Code: 517

In central MI, north of Lansing; established Mar 2, 1831 from Saginaw County.
Name origin: For Gen. Charles Gratiot (1786–1855), U.S. army officer who built Ft. Gratiot at Port Huron (1814); chief engineer of U.S. Army (1828–38).

Alma
City
ZIP: 48801 **Lat:** 43-22-45 N **Long:** 84-39-17 W
Pop: 9,034 (1990); 9,652 (1980) **Pop Density:** 1673.0
Land: 5.4 sq. mi.; **Water:** 0.1 sq. mi. **Elev:** 736 ft.
Settled 1853.
Name origin: For Alma Gargett, daughter of the town founder.

Arcada
Township
Lat: 43-20-06 N **Long:** 84-40-02 W
Pop: 1,660 (1990); 1,784 (1980) **Pop Density:** 51.1
Land: 32.5 sq. mi.; **Water:** 0.2 sq. mi.

Ashley
Village
ZIP: 48806 **Lat:** 43-11-15 N **Long:** 84-28-34 W
Pop: 518 (1990); 570 (1980) **Pop Density:** 863.3
Land: 0.6 sq. mi.; **Water:** 0.0 sq. mi. **Elev:** 671 ft.
Founded 1884.
Name origin: For railroad builder John M. Ashley.

Bethany
Township
Lat: 43-25-09 N **Long:** 84-32-35 W
Pop: 1,814 (1990); 1,526 (1980) **Pop Density:** 51.5
Land: 35.2 sq. mi.; **Water:** 0.0 sq. mi.

Breckenridge
Village
ZIP: 48615 **Lat:** 43-24-27 N **Long:** 84-28-42 W
Pop: 1,301 (1990); 1,495 (1980) **Pop Density:** 1301.0
Land: 1.0 sq. mi.; **Water:** 0.0 sq. mi.
Settled 1872.
Name origin: For an early mill owner.

Elba
Township
Lat: 43-09-39 N **Long:** 84-25-30 W
Pop: 1,390 (1990); 1,537 (1980) **Pop Density:** 39.6
Land: 35.1 sq. mi.; **Water:** 0.0 sq. mi.

Emerson
Township
Lat: 43-20-18 N **Long:** 84-32-16 W
Pop: 1,003 (1990); 1,092 (1980) **Pop Density:** 28.5
Land: 35.2 sq. mi.; **Water:** 0.0 sq. mi.

Fulton
Township
Lat: 43-09-46 N **Long:** 84-39-52 W
Pop: 2,114 (1990); 2,165 (1980) **Pop Density:** 60.1
Land: 35.2 sq. mi.; **Water:** 0.6 sq. mi.

Hamilton
Township
Lat: 43-15-03 N **Long:** 84-25-25 W
Pop: 489 (1990); 530 (1980) **Pop Density:** 14.0
Land: 34.9 sq. mi.; **Water:** 0.1 sq. mi.

Ithaca
City
ZIP: 48847 **Lat:** 43-17-32 N **Long:** 84-36-17 W
Pop: 3,009 (1990); 2,950 (1980) **Pop Density:** 771.5
Land: 3.9 sq. mi.; **Water:** 0.0 sq. mi.
Name origin: For Ithaca, NY, an area from which some early settlers came.

Lafayette
Township
Lat: 43-20-16 N **Long:** 84-25-04 W
Pop: 683 (1990); 776 (1980) **Pop Density:** 19.0
Land: 36.0 sq. mi.; **Water:** 0.0 sq. mi.

Newark
Township
Lat: 43-14-56 N **Long:** 84-39-43 W
Pop: 1,138 (1990); 1,097 (1980) **Pop Density:** 32.8
Land: 34.7 sq. mi.; **Water:** 0.0 sq. mi.

New Haven
Township
Lat: 43-14-55 N **Long:** 84-46-36 W
Pop: 972 (1990); 1,021 (1980) **Pop Density:** 27.4
Land: 35.5 sq. mi.; **Water:** 0.1 sq. mi.

North Shade
Township
Lat: 43-09-50 N **Long:** 84-46-22 W
Pop: 758 (1990); 815 (1980) **Pop Density:** 21.3
Land: 35.6 sq. mi.; **Water:** 0.0 sq. mi.

North Star
Township
Lat: 43-14-53 N **Long:** 84-32-28 W
Pop: 1,055 (1990); 1,171 (1980) **Pop Density:** 30.6
Land: 34.5 sq. mi.; **Water:** 0.0 sq. mi.

Perrinton
Village
ZIP: 48871 **Lat:** 43-10-54 N **Long:** 84-40-42 W
Pop: 393 (1990); 448 (1980) **Pop Density:** 655.0
Land: 0.6 sq. mi.; **Water:** 0.0 sq. mi.
Founded 1886.
Name origin: For a lawyer from St. Johns with large local land interests.

Pine River
Township
Lat: 43-25-46 N **Long:** 84-40-18 W
Pop: 2,064 (1990); 1,939 (1980) **Pop Density:** 67.0
Land: 30.8 sq. mi.; **Water:** 0.1 sq. mi.

St. Louis
City
Lat: 43-24-33 N **Long:** 84-36-56 W
Pop: 3,828 (1990); 4,107 (1980) **Pop Density:** 1367.1
Land: 2.8 sq. mi.; **Water:** 0.2 sq. mi.
Platted 1855.
Name origin: For St. Louis, MO.

Seville
Township
Lat: 43-25-22 N **Long:** 84-47-08 W
Pop: 2,217 (1990); 2,091 (1980) **Pop Density:** 62.1
Land: 35.7 sq. mi.; **Water:** 0.1 sq. mi.

Sumner
Township
ZIP: 48889 **Lat:** 43-20-07 N **Long:** 84-47-07 W
Pop: 1,799 (1990); 1,897 (1980) **Pop Density:** 50.1
Land: 35.9 sq. mi.; **Water:** 0.0 sq. mi.

Washington
Township
Lat: 43-09-31 N **Long:** 84-32-18 W
Pop: 1,029 (1990); 1,079 (1980) **Pop Density:** 29.1
Land: 35.4 sq. mi.; **Water:** 0.0 sq. mi.

Wheeler   Township
ZIP: 48662   **Lat:** 43-25-25 N   **Long:** 84-25-45 W
Pop: 2,926 (1990); 3,219 (1980)   **Pop Density:** 81.7
Land: 35.8 sq. mi.; **Water:** 0.0 sq. mi.

Hillsdale County
County Seat: Hillsdale (ZIP: 49242)

Pop: 43,431 (1990); 42,071 (1980)   **Pop Density:** 72.5
Land: 598.9 sq. mi.; **Water:** 8.3 sq. mi.   **Area Code:** 517
On the south-central border of MI, southeast of Kalamazoo; established Oct 29, 1829 (prior to statehood) from Lenawee County.
Name origin: For its topography of hills and dales.

Adams   Township
Lat: 41-56-29 N   **Long:** 84-32-04 W
Pop: 2,339 (1990); 2,260 (1980)   **Pop Density:** 65.5
Land: 35.7 sq. mi.; **Water:** 0.4 sq. mi.

Allen   Village
ZIP: 49227   **Lat:** 41-57-28 N   **Long:** 84-46-02 W
Pop: 201 (1990); 266 (1980)   **Pop Density:** 1005.0
Land: 0.2 sq. mi.; **Water:** 0.0 sq. mi.
Name origin: For Capt. Moses Allen, who arrived in 1827. Not coextensive with the town of the same name.

*Allen   Township
ZIP: 49227   **Lat:** 41-56-25 N   **Long:** 84-46-22 W
Pop: 1,412 (1990); 1,501 (1980)   **Pop Density:** 39.1
Land: 36.1 sq. mi.; **Water:** 0.2 sq. mi.

Amboy   Township
Lat: 41-43-23 N   **Long:** 84-35-37 W
Pop: 978 (1990); 936 (1980)   **Pop Density:** 32.6
Land: 30.0 sq. mi.; **Water:** 0.7 sq. mi.

Cambria   Township
Lat: 41-51-34 N   **Long:** 84-39-22 W
Pop: 2,372 (1990); 2,326 (1980)   **Pop Density:** 68.0
Land: 34.9 sq. mi.; **Water:** 1.3 sq. mi.

Camden   Village
ZIP: 49232   **Lat:** 41-45-22 N   **Long:** 84-45-25 W
Pop: 482 (1990); 420 (1980)   **Pop Density:** 535.6
Land: 0.9 sq. mi.; **Water:** 0.0 sq. mi.
Not coextensive with the town of the same name.
Name origin: Named by Easton Chester, the village's second postmaster, for Camden, NY.

*Camden   Township
ZIP: 49232   **Lat:** 41-45-19 N   **Long:** 84-45-48 W
Pop: 1,984 (1990); 1,848 (1980)   **Pop Density:** 46.8
Land: 42.4 sq. mi.; **Water:** 0.2 sq. mi.

Fayette   Township
Lat: 41-58-37 N   **Long:** 84-39-14 W
Pop: 3,190 (1990); 3,115 (1980)   **Pop Density:** 137.5
Land: 23.2 sq. mi.; **Water:** 0.2 sq. mi.

Hillsdale   City
ZIP: 49242   **Lat:** 41-55-32 N   **Long:** 84-38-08 W
Pop: 8,170 (1990); 7,432 (1980)   **Pop Density:** 1602.0
Land: 5.1 sq. mi.; **Water:** 0.2 sq. mi.
Incorporated 1847.
Name origin: For its descriptive connotations.

*Hillsdale   Township
ZIP: 49242   **Lat:** 41-54-58 N   **Long:** 84-39-39 W
Pop: 1,786 (1990); 1,873 (1980)   **Pop Density:** 139.5
Land: 12.8 sq. mi.; **Water:** 0.6 sq. mi.

Jefferson   Township
Lat: 41-51-11 N   **Long:** 84-31-29 W
Pop: 3,083 (1990); 2,920 (1980)   **Pop Density:** 86.6
Land: 35.6 sq. mi.; **Water:** 0.5 sq. mi.

Jonesville   Village
ZIP: 49250   **Lat:** 41-58-51 N   **Long:** 84-39-59 W
Pop: 2,283 (1990); 2,172 (1980)   **Pop Density:** 951.2
Land: 2.4 sq. mi.; **Water:** 0.0 sq. mi.
Name origin: For pioneer Benaiah Jones, who arrived in 1829.

Litchfield   City
ZIP: 49252   **Lat:** 42-02-35 N   **Long:** 84-45-27 W
Pop: 1,317 (1990); 1,353 (1980)   **Pop Density:** 598.6
Land: 2.2 sq. mi.; **Water:** 0.0 sq. mi.
Founded 1834.
Name origin: For Litchfield, CT.

*Litchfield   Township
ZIP: 49252   **Lat:** 42-01-36 N   **Long:** 84-46-05 W
Pop: 957 (1990); 1,027 (1980)   **Pop Density:** 28.7
Land: 33.3 sq. mi.; **Water:** 0.0 sq. mi.

Montgomery   Village
Lat: 41-46-36 N   **Long:** 84-48-21 W
Pop: 388 (1990); 408 (1980)   **Pop Density:** 388.0
Land: 1.0 sq. mi.; **Water:** 0.0 sq. mi.

Moscow   Township
Lat: 42-01-46 N   **Long:** 84-32-43 W
Pop: 1,353 (1990); 1,396 (1980)   **Pop Density:** 38.4
Land: 35.2 sq. mi.; **Water:** 0.3 sq. mi.

North Adams   Village
ZIP: 49262   **Lat:** 41-58-18 N   **Long:** 84-31-27 W
Pop: 512 (1990); 565 (1980)   **Pop Density:** 1024.0
Land: 0.5 sq. mi.; **Water:** 0.0 sq. mi.
Began around a tavern in 1835.
Name origin: For its location within Adams Township.

Pittsford   Township
ZIP: 49271   **Lat:** 41-51-24 N   **Long:** 84-25-14 W
Pop: 1,595 (1990); 1,550 (1980)   **Pop Density:** 44.9
Land: 35.5 sq. mi.; **Water:** 0.2 sq. mi.

MICHIGAN, Hillsdale County

Ransom
Township
Lat: 41-46-30 N **Long:** 84-32-06 W
Pop: 911 (1990); 949 (1980) **Pop Density:** 30.3
Land: 30.1 sq. mi.; **Water:** 0.1 sq. mi.

Reading
City
ZIP: 49274 **Lat:** 41-50-21 N **Long:** 84-44-50 W
Pop: 1,127 (1990); 1,203 (1980) **Pop Density:** 1127.0
Land: 1.0 sq. mi.; **Water:** 0.0 sq. mi.
Settled by a group in the township in 1840. Incorporated as a village in 1873; as a city in 1934.
Name origin: For its township, itself named for Reading, PA.

*Reading
Township
ZIP: 49274 **Lat:** 41-51-17 N **Long:** 84-45-49 W
Pop: 1,768 (1990); 1,653 (1980) **Pop Density:** 51.8
Land: 34.1 sq. mi.; **Water:** 1.0 sq. mi.

Scipio
Township
Lat: 42-02-02 N **Long:** 84-38-32 W
Pop: 1,479 (1990); 1,352 (1980) **Pop Density:** 50.5
Land: 29.3 sq. mi.; **Water:** 0.2 sq. mi.

Somerset
Township
Lat: 42-01-52 N **Long:** 84-25-45 W
Pop: 3,416 (1990); 3,142 (1980) **Pop Density:** 102.3
Land: 33.4 sq. mi.; **Water:** 2.2 sq. mi.

Waldron
Village
ZIP: 49288 **Lat:** 41-43-28 N **Long:** 84-25-05 W
Pop: 581 (1990); 570 (1980) **Pop Density:** 581.0
Land: 1.0 sq. mi.; **Water:** 0.0 sq. mi. **Elev:** 900 ft.
Settlers from NY arrived in 1835.
Name origin: For U.S. Congressman Henry Waldron.

Wheatland
Township
Lat: 41-56-17 N **Long:** 84-24-56 W
Pop: 1,225 (1990); 1,255 (1980) **Pop Density:** 34.4
Land: 35.6 sq. mi.; **Water:** 0.0 sq. mi.

Woodbridge
Township
Lat: 41-46-24 N **Long:** 84-39-10 W
Pop: 1,160 (1990); 1,115 (1980) **Pop Density:** 38.5
Land: 30.1 sq. mi.; **Water:** 0.0 sq. mi.

Wright
Township
Lat: 41-45-46 N **Long:** 84-24-47 W
Pop: 1,809 (1990); 1,865 (1980) **Pop Density:** 41.8
Land: 43.3 sq. mi.; **Water:** 0.2 sq. mi.

Houghton County
County Seat: Houghton (ZIP: 49931)

Pop: 35,446 (1990); 37,872 (1980) **Pop Density:** 35.0
Land: 1011.7 sq. mi.; **Water:** 489.9 sq. mi. **Area Code:** 906
On the northwest coast of the Upper Peninsula of MI; organized Mar 19, 1845 from Marquette, Schoolcraft, and Ontonagon counties.
Name origin: For Douglas Houghton (1809–45), professor and pioneer state geologist (1834–41).

Adams
Township
Lat: 47-02-15 N **Long:** 88-41-41 W
Pop: 2,388 (1990); 2,461 (1980) **Pop Density:** 50.5
Land: 47.3 sq. mi.; **Water:** 0.4 sq. mi.

Calumet
Village
ZIP: 49913 **Lat:** 47-14-50 N **Long:** 88-27-11 W
Pop: 818 (1990); 1,013 (1980) **Pop Density:** 4090.0
Land: 0.2 sq. mi.; **Water:** 0.0 sq. mi. **Elev:** 1208 ft.
Founded 1860s. Not coextensive with the town of the same name.
Name origin: For the long-stemmed pipe used by Indians on ceremonial occasions; the peace pipe.

*Calumet
Township
ZIP: 49913 **Lat:** 47-15-30 N **Long:** 88-26-32 W
Pop: 7,015 (1990); 7,965 (1980) **Pop Density:** 210.0
Land: 33.4 sq. mi.; **Water:** 0.1 sq. mi.

Chassell
Township
ZIP: 49916 **Lat:** 46-59-34 N **Long:** 88-31-39 W
Pop: 1,686 (1990); 1,738 (1980) **Pop Density:** 34.6
Land: 48.7 sq. mi.; **Water:** 3.2 sq. mi.

Copper City
Village
ZIP: 49917 **Lat:** 47-17-04 N **Long:** 88-23-12 W
Pop: 198 (1990); 244 (1980) **Pop Density:** 1980.0
Land: 0.1 sq. mi.; **Water:** 0.0 sq. mi. **Elev:** 877 ft.
Incorporated 1917.
Name origin: For the mineral mined there.

Duncan
Township
Lat: 46-30-27 N **Long:** 88-49-43 W
Pop: 304 (1990); 344 (1980) **Pop Density:** 1.7
Land: 176.5 sq. mi.; **Water:** 1.1 sq. mi.

Elm River
Township
Lat: 46-53-35 N **Long:** 88-50-34 W
Pop: 159 (1990); 184 (1980) **Pop Density:** 1.7
Land: 91.4 sq. mi.; **Water:** 1.9 sq. mi.

Franklin
Township
Lat: 47-09-39 N **Long:** 88-32-14 W
Pop: 1,164 (1990); 1,303 (1980) **Pop Density:** 58.2
Land: 20.0 sq. mi.; **Water:** 0.7 sq. mi.

Hancock
City
ZIP: 49930 **Lat:** 47-07-56 N **Long:** 88-36-02 W
Pop: 4,547 (1990); 5,122 (1980) **Pop Density:** 2526.1
Land: 1.8 sq. mi.; **Water:** 0.0 sq. mi. **Elev:** 686 ft.
Incorporated 1875.
Name origin: For U.S. statesman John Hancock (1737–93),

first signer of the Declaration of Independence and governor of MA.

*Hancock — Township
ZIP: 49930 **Lat:** 47-12-23 N **Long:** 88-35-19 W
Pop: 287 (1990); 288 (1980) **Pop Density:** 18.2
Land: 15.8 sq. mi.; **Water:** 0.3 sq. mi.

Houghton — City
ZIP: 49931 **Lat:** 47-06-48 N **Long:** 88-33-42 W
Pop: 7,498 (1990); 7,512 (1980) **Pop Density:** 2343.1
Land: 3.2 sq. mi.; **Water:** 0.2 sq. mi. **Elev:** 607 ft.
Settled 1852.
Name origin: For Douglas Houghton (1809–45), professor and pioneer state geologist (1834–41).

Hubbell — CDP
Lat: 47-10-45 N **Long:** 88-26-11 W
Pop: 1,174 (1990); 394 (1980) **Pop Density:** 617.9
Land: 1.9 sq. mi.; **Water:** 0.0 sq. mi.

Laird — Township
Lat: 46-42-41 N **Long:** 88-47-54 W
Pop: 582 (1990); 646 (1980) **Pop Density:** 3.1
Land: 188.0 sq. mi.; **Water:** 1.3 sq. mi.

Lake Linden — Village
ZIP: 49945 **Lat:** 47-11-42 N **Long:** 88-24-12 W
Pop: 1,203 (1990); 1,181 (1980) **Pop Density:** 1718.6
Land: 0.7 sq. mi.; **Water:** 0.1 sq. mi.
Name origin: Descriptively named for its location near Torch Lake and for the linden trees that grow there.

Laurium — Village
ZIP: 49913 **Lat:** 47-14-11 N **Long:** 88-26-15 W
Pop: 2,268 (1990); 2,678 (1980) **Pop Density:** 3240.0
Land: 0.7 sq. mi.; **Water:** 0.0 sq. mi. **Elev:** 1246 ft.
Once a prominent copper-mining site.
Name origin: For Mount Laurium, Greece, an ancient silver-mining district.

Osceola — Township
Lat: 47-11-15 N **Long:** 88-29-07 W
Pop: 1,878 (1990); 2,074 (1980) **Pop Density:** 75.7
Land: 24.8 sq. mi.; **Water:** 1.1 sq. mi.

Portage — Township
Lat: 46-57-37 N **Long:** 88-38-05 W
Pop: 2,941 (1990); 3,244 (1980) **Pop Density:** 25.9
Land: 113.7 sq. mi.; **Water:** 4.1 sq. mi.

Quincy — Township
Lat: 47-09-23 N **Long:** 88-35-24 W
Pop: 223 (1990); 256 (1980) **Pop Density:** 50.7
Land: 4.4 sq. mi.; **Water:** 0.0 sq. mi.

Schoolcraft — Township
Lat: 47-12-27 N **Long:** 88-21-10 W
Pop: 2,037 (1990); 2,071 (1980) **Pop Density:** 50.8
Land: 40.1 sq. mi.; **Water:** 0.7 sq. mi.

South Range — Village
ZIP: 49963 **Lat:** 47-04-13 N **Long:** 88-38-40 W
Pop: 745 (1990); 861 (1980) **Pop Density:** 2483.3
Land: 0.3 sq. mi.; **Water:** 0.0 sq. mi. **Elev:** 1140 ft.
Founded 1902.
Name origin: For its location at the south end of the county.

Stanton — Township
Lat: 47-04-54 N **Long:** 88-47-21 W
Pop: 1,184 (1990); 1,063 (1980) **Pop Density:** 9.7
Land: 122.3 sq. mi.; **Water:** 0.9 sq. mi.

Torch Lake — Township
Lat: 47-05-54 N **Long:** 88-23-12 W
Pop: 1,553 (1990); 1,601 (1980) **Pop Density:** 19.4
Land: 80.2 sq. mi.; **Water:** 12.9 sq. mi.

Huron County
County Seat: Bad Axe (ZIP: 48413)

Pop: 34,951 (1990); 36,459 (1980) **Pop Density:** 41.8
Land: 836.6 sq. mi.; **Water:** 1300.7 sq. mi. **Area Code:** 517
On the east coast of MI on Saginaw Bay; organized Apr 1, 1840 from Sanilac and Tuscola counties.
Name origin: For the Huron Indians (later known as Wyandots), a tribe of Iroquoian linguistic stock; from a French word for 'rough,' probably because they were formidable opponents.

Bad Axe — City
ZIP: 48413 **Lat:** 43-48-10 N **Long:** 82-59-48 W
Pop: 3,484 (1990); 3,184 (1980) **Pop Density:** 1833.7
Land: 1.9 sq. mi.; **Water:** 0.0 sq. mi. **Elev:** 765 ft.
Name origin: For a much-used axe that an early surveyor found at his campsite here.

Bingham — Township
Lat: 43-43-27 N **Long:** 82-56-23 W
Pop: 1,617 (1990); 1,679 (1980) **Pop Density:** 45.0
Land: 35.9 sq. mi.; **Water:** 0.0 sq. mi.

Bloomfield — Township
Lat: 43-54-02 N **Long:** 82-49-38 W
Pop: 563 (1990); 632 (1980) **Pop Density:** 15.6
Land: 36.0 sq. mi.; **Water:** 0.0 sq. mi.

Brookfield — Township
Lat: 43-42-50 N **Long:** 83-17-48 W
Pop: 947 (1990); 998 (1980) **Pop Density:** 26.7
Land: 35.5 sq. mi.; **Water:** 0.0 sq. mi.

MICHIGAN, Huron County

Caseville — Village
ZIP: 48725 Lat: 43-56-31 N Long: 83-16-28 W
Pop: 857 (1990); 851 (1980) Pop Density: 779.1
Land: 1.1 sq. mi.; Water: 0.0 sq. mi.
Settled by Ruben Dodge in 1836. Not coextensive with the town of the same name.
Name origin: Originally called Pigeon River Settlement. Renamed in 1859 for prominent landowner Leonard Case.

*Caseville — Township
ZIP: 48725 Lat: 43-55-31 N Long: 83-17-10 W
Pop: 2,139 (1990); 2,067 (1980) Pop Density: 153.9
Land: 13.9 sq. mi.; Water: 0.3 sq. mi.

Chandler — Township
Lat: 43-53-17 N Long: 83-10-20 W
Pop: 509 (1990); 555 (1980) Pop Density: 14.4
Land: 35.3 sq. mi.; Water: 0.0 sq. mi.

Colfax — Township
Lat: 43-48-21 N Long: 83-03-57 W
Pop: 1,936 (1990); 1,907 (1980) Pop Density: 55.2
Land: 35.1 sq. mi.; Water: 0.0 sq. mi.

Dwight — Township
Lat: 43-59-10 N Long: 82-56-26 W
Pop: 917 (1990); 1,145 (1980) Pop Density: 25.7
Land: 35.7 sq. mi.; Water: 0.0 sq. mi.

Elkton — Village
ZIP: 48731 Lat: 43-49-07 N Long: 83-10-50 W
Pop: 958 (1990); 953 (1980) Pop Density: 958.0
Land: 1.0 sq. mi.; Water: 0.0 sq. mi. Elev: 647 ft.
Name origin: Named by an early blacksmith who killed a large elk nearby.

Fairhaven — Township
Lat: 43-48-01 N Long: 83-25-15 W
Pop: 1,250 (1990); 1,292 (1980) Pop Density: 59.2
Land: 21.1 sq. mi.; Water: 36.9 sq. mi.

Gore — Township
Lat: 43-58-13 N Long: 82-44-44 W
Pop: 125 (1990); 175 (1980) Pop Density: 18.4
Land: 6.8 sq. mi.; Water: 0.1 sq. mi.

Grant — Township
Lat: 43-42-44 N Long: 83-10-17 W
Pop: 778 (1990); 819 (1980) Pop Density: 22.0
Land: 35.4 sq. mi.; Water: 0.0 sq. mi.

Harbor Beach — City
ZIP: 48441 Lat: 43-50-47 N Long: 82-39-17 W
Pop: 2,089 (1990); 2,000 (1980) Pop Density: 1228.8
Land: 1.7 sq. mi.; Water: 0.1 sq. mi. Elev: 610 ft.
In central-eastern MI on Lake Huron. Founded 1837.
Name origin: Name changed in 1889 from Sand Beach to better describe the area.

Hume — Township
Lat: 43-58-24 N Long: 83-03-43 W
Pop: 714 (1990); 753 (1980) Pop Density: 23.8
Land: 30.0 sq. mi.; Water: 0.0 sq. mi.

Huron — Township
Lat: 43-58-50 N Long: 82-49-56 W
Pop: 376 (1990); 433 (1980) Pop Density: 11.2
Land: 33.6 sq. mi.; Water: 0.0 sq. mi.

Kinde — Village
ZIP: 48445 Lat: 43-56-23 N Long: 82-59-41 W
Pop: 473 (1990); 600 (1980) Pop Density: 473.0
Land: 1.0 sq. mi.; Water: 0.0 sq. mi.
Incorporated 1903.
Name origin: For storekeeper John Kinde.

Lake — Township
Lat: 43-57-52 N Long: 83-10-33 W
Pop: 800 (1990); 822 (1980) Pop Density: 41.7
Land: 19.2 sq. mi.; Water: 1.5 sq. mi.

Lincoln — Township
Lat: 43-53-40 N Long: 82-56-18 W
Pop: 868 (1990); 1,042 (1980) Pop Density: 24.2
Land: 35.8 sq. mi.; Water: 0.0 sq. mi.

McKinley — Township
Lat: 43-52-09 N Long: 83-17-40 W
Pop: 527 (1990); 555 (1980) Pop Density: 26.0
Land: 20.3 sq. mi.; Water: 0.3 sq. mi.

Meade — Township
Lat: 43-53-38 N Long: 83-03-38 W
Pop: 777 (1990); 789 (1980) Pop Density: 21.8
Land: 35.7 sq. mi.; Water: 0.0 sq. mi.

Oliver — Township
Lat: 43-48-17 N Long: 83-10-28 W
Pop: 1,685 (1990); 1,756 (1980) Pop Density: 47.7
Land: 35.3 sq. mi.; Water: 0.0 sq. mi.

Owendale — Village
ZIP: 48754 Lat: 43-43-37 N Long: 83-16-03 W
Pop: 285 (1990); 308 (1980) Pop Density: 407.1
Land: 0.7 sq. mi.; Water: 0.0 sq. mi. Elev: 643 ft.
Name origin: For early sawmill operator John Owen.

Paris — Township
Lat: 43-43-35 N Long: 82-49-03 W
Pop: 624 (1990); 732 (1980) Pop Density: 17.3
Land: 36.1 sq. mi.; Water: 0.0 sq. mi.

Pigeon — Village
ZIP: 48755 Lat: 43-49-46 N Long: 83-16-11 W
Pop: 1,207 (1990); 1,247 (1980) Pop Density: 1508.8
Land: 0.8 sq. mi.; Water: 0.0 sq. mi.
Incorporated 1902.
Name origin: For the nearby Pigeon River.

Pointe Aux Barques — Township
ZIP: 48467 Lat: 44-03-35 N Long: 82-57-12 W
Pop: 15 (1990); 6 (1980) Pop Density: 11.5
Land: 1.3 sq. mi.; Water: 0.3 sq. mi.

Port Austin — Village
ZIP: 48467 Lat: 44-02-33 N Long: 82-59-43 W
Pop: 815 (1990); 839 (1980) Pop Density: 815.0
Land: 1.0 sq. mi.; Water: 0.0 sq. mi.
Not coextensive with the town of the same name.
Name origin: For lumber mill owner P. C. Austin. Previously called Byrd's Creek.

*Port Austin — Township
ZIP: 48467 Lat: 44-02-24 N Long: 82-56-14 W
Pop: 1,474 (1990); 1,570 (1980) Pop Density: 89.9
Land: 16.4 sq. mi.; Water: 0.3 sq. mi.

Port Hope — Village
ZIP: 48468　　Lat: 43-56-22 N　Long: 82-42-54 W
Pop: 313 (1990); 369 (1980)　　Pop Density: 313.0
Land: 1.0 sq. mi.; Water: 0.0 sq. mi.
Name origin: Named by two early residents who landed here after going adrift in a small skiff.

Rubicon — Township
Lat: 43-54-11 N　Long: 82-43-06 W
Pop: 766 (1990); 892 (1980)　　Pop Density: 32.3
Land: 23.7 sq. mi.; Water: 0.0 sq. mi.

Sand Beach — Township
ZIP: 48441　　Lat: 43-49-00 N　Long: 82-41-52 W
Pop: 1,358 (1990); 1,399 (1980)　　Pop Density: 37.2
Land: 36.5 sq. mi.; Water: 0.2 sq. mi.

Sebewaing — Village
ZIP: 48759　　Lat: 43-43-54 N　Long: 83-27-03 W
Pop: 1,923 (1990); 2,046 (1980)　　Pop Density: 1201.9
Land: 1.6 sq. mi.; Water: 0.1 sq. mi.　　Elev: 585 ft.
Settled 1845. Not coextensive with the town of the same name.
Name origin: From an Indian term meaning 'crooked creek,' referring to the one flowing nearby.

***Sebewaing** — Township
ZIP: 48759　　Lat: 43-42-43 N　Long: 83-24-30 W
Pop: 2,937 (1990); 3,259 (1980)　　Pop Density: 90.1
Land: 32.6 sq. mi.; Water: 0.2 sq. mi.

Sheridan — Township
Lat: 43-42-56 N　Long: 83-04-07 W
Pop: 694 (1990); 812 (1980)　　Pop Density: 19.2
Land: 36.2 sq. mi.; Water: 0.0 sq. mi.

Sherman — Township
Lat: 43-43-47 N　Long: 82-41-27 W
Pop: 1,155 (1990); 1,251 (1980)　　Pop Density: 26.2
Land: 44.1 sq. mi.; Water: 0.0 sq. mi.

Sigel — Township
ZIP: 48441　　Lat: 43-48-39 N　Long: 82-49-14 W
Pop: 599 (1990); 673 (1980)　　Pop Density: 16.7
Land: 35.8 sq. mi.; Water: 0.0 sq. mi.

Ubly — Village
ZIP: 48475　　Lat: 43-42-39 N　Long: 82-56-04 W
Pop: 821 (1990); 862 (1980)　　Pop Density: 912.2
Land: 0.9 sq. mi.; Water: 0.0 sq. mi.　　Elev: 789 ft.
Name origin: For Ubly, England. Previously called Pagett's Corners.

Verona — Township
Lat: 43-48-49 N　Long: 82-55-59 W
Pop: 1,196 (1990); 1,122 (1980)　　Pop Density: 35.0
Land: 34.2 sq. mi.; Water: 0.0 sq. mi.　　Elev: 803 ft.

Winsor — Township
Lat: 43-47-57 N　Long: 83-17-43 W
Pop: 2,032 (1990); 2,140 (1980)　　Pop Density: 57.4
Land: 35.4 sq. mi.; Water: 0.0 sq. mi.

Ingham County
County Seat: Mason (ZIP: 48854)

Pop: 281,912 (1990); 275,520 (1980)　　Pop Density: 504.1
Land: 559.2 sq. mi.; Water: 1.8 sq. mi.　　Area Code: 517
In south-central MI; established Oct 29, 1829 (prior to statehood) from unorganized territory.
Name origin: For Samuel Delucenna Ingham (1779–1860), U.S. representative from PA (1813–18; 1822–29) and U.S. secretary of the treasury (1829–31).

Alaiedon — Township
Lat: 42-38-43 N　Long: 84-25-23 W
Pop: 3,173 (1990); 2,845 (1980)　　Pop Density: 87.7
Land: 36.2 sq. mi.; Water: 0.0 sq. mi.

Aurelius — Township
Lat: 42-33-12 N　Long: 84-32-28 W
Pop: 2,686 (1990); 2,460 (1980)　　Pop Density: 73.6
Land: 36.5 sq. mi.; Water: 0.0 sq. mi.

Bunker Hill — Township
Lat: 42-28-13 N　Long: 84-18-34 W
Pop: 1,888 (1990); 1,794 (1980)　　Pop Density: 57.2
Land: 33.0 sq. mi.; Water: 0.0 sq. mi.

Dansville — Village
ZIP: 48819　　Lat: 42-33-19 N　Long: 84-18-08 W
Pop: 437 (1990); 479 (1980)　　Pop Density: 437.0
Land: 1.0 sq. mi.; Water: 0.0 sq. mi.
Name origin: For pioneer Daniel Crossman, who platted the village in 1857.

Delhi Charter — Township
ZIP: 48842　　Lat: 42-38-00 N　Long: 84-32-17 W
Pop: 19,190 (1990); 17,144 (1980)　　Pop Density: 666.3
Land: 28.8 sq. mi.; Water: 0.1 sq. mi.
In south-central MI, south of Lansing.
Name origin: Probably for Delhi, NY, former home of many early settlers.

East Lansing — City
ZIP: 48826　　Lat: 42-44-09 N　Long: 84-29-03 W
Pop: 50,677 (1990); 51,392 (1980)　　Pop Density: 5334.4
Land: 9.5 sq. mi.; Water: 0.0 sq. mi.
In south-central MI, northeast of Lansing. Settled 1849; incorporated May 8, 1907. Site of Michigan State University.
Name origin: For its location.

Edgemont Park — CDP
Lat: 42-44-48 N　Long: 84-35-37 W
Pop: 2,532 (1990)　　Pop Density: 3165.0
Land: 0.8 sq. mi.; Water: 0.0 sq. mi.

MICHIGAN, Ingham County

Haslett
CDP
ZIP: 48840 Lat: 42-45-09 N Long: 84-24-20 W
Pop: 10,230 (1990); 7,025 (1980) Pop Density: 1232.5
Land: 8.3 sq. mi.; Water: 0.7 sq. mi.

Holt
CDP
ZIP: 48842 Lat: 42-38-14 N Long: 84-31-32 W
Pop: 11,744 (1990); 10,097 (1980) Pop Density: 2731.2
Land: 4.3 sq. mi.; Water: 0.0 sq. mi.

Ingham
Township
Lat: 42-33-34 N Long: 84-18-28 W
Pop: 1,942 (1990); 1,974 (1980) Pop Density: 59.4
Land: 32.7 sq. mi.; Water: 0.0 sq. mi.

Lansing
City
ZIP: 48901 Lat: 42-42-37 N Long: 84-33-11 W
Pop: 122,700 (1990); 125,974 (1980) Pop Density: 3740.9
Land: 32.8 sq. mi.; Water: 0.2 sq. mi.
In south-central MI, 80 mi. northwest of Detroit. Settled 1830s; state capital since 1847; incorporated 1859. Automobile manufacturing city; trade center for the surrounding agricultural area. Part of the town is also in Eaton County.
Name origin: For Lansing, NY.

*Lansing
Township
ZIP: 48912 Lat: 42-43-52 N Long: 84-34-56 W
Pop: 8,919 (1990); 10,097 (1980) Pop Density: 1820.2
Land: 4.9 sq. mi.; Water: 0.1 sq. mi.
Charter township in south-central MI.
Name origin: For Lansing, NY.

Leroy
Township
Lat: 42-38-56 N Long: 84-12-17 W
Pop: 3,561 (1990); 3,413 (1980) Pop Density: 104.1
Land: 34.2 sq. mi.; Water: 0.0 sq. mi.

Leslie
City
ZIP: 49251 Lat: 42-27-00 N Long: 84-25-50 W
Pop: 1,872 (1990); 2,110 (1980) Pop Density: 1701.8
Land: 1.1 sq. mi.; Water: 0.0 sq. mi. Elev: 935 ft.
Name origin: For the Leslie family from NY. Previously called Meekersville.

*Leslie
Township
ZIP: 49251 Lat: 42-27-56 N Long: 84-25-25 W
Pop: 2,436 (1990); 2,190 (1980) Pop Density: 69.2
Land: 35.2 sq. mi.; Water: 0.1 sq. mi.

Locke
Township
Lat: 42-44-10 N Long: 84-12-13 W
Pop: 1,521 (1990); 1,456 (1980) Pop Density: 42.1
Land: 36.1 sq. mi.; Water: 0.0 sq. mi.

Mason
City
ZIP: 48854 Lat: 42-34-54 N Long: 84-26-38 W
Pop: 6,768 (1990); 6,019 (1980) Pop Density: 1538.2
Land: 4.4 sq. mi.; Water: 0.0 sq. mi.
Founded 1836.
Name origin: For Gov. Steven T. Mason.

Meridian
Township
ZIP: 48823 Lat: 42-43-37 N Long: 84-24-54 W
Pop: 35,644 (1990); 28,754 (1980) Pop Density: 1120.9
Land: 31.8 sq. mi.; Water: 0.8 sq. mi.
In south-central MI south of Lansing.
Name origin: For the township, itself named because the principal meridian forms its eastern boundary.

Okemos
CDP
ZIP: 48864 Lat: 42-42-29 N Long: 84-24-52 W
Pop: 20,216 (1990); 8,882 (1980) Pop Density: 1168.6
Land: 17.3 sq. mi.; Water: 0.0 sq. mi.

Onondaga
Township
ZIP: 49264 Lat: 42-27-37 N Long: 84-32-46 W
Pop: 2,444 (1990); 2,299 (1980) Pop Density: 67.0
Land: 36.5 sq. mi.; Water: 0.0 sq. mi.

Stockbridge
Village
ZIP: 49285 Lat: 42-27-02 N Long: 84-10-41 W
Pop: 1,202 (1990); 1,213 (1980) Pop Density: 1202.0
Land: 1.0 sq. mi.; Water: 0.0 sq. mi.
Platted by settler Silas Beebe. Not coextensive with the town of the same name.
Name origin: For its township.

*Stockbridge
Township
ZIP: 49285 Lat: 42-27-49 N Long: 84-12-03 W
Pop: 2,971 (1990); 2,914 (1980) Pop Density: 83.5
Land: 35.6 sq. mi.; Water: 0.3 sq. mi.

Vevay
Township
Lat: 42-33-02 N Long: 84-25-34 W
Pop: 3,668 (1990); 3,113 (1980) Pop Density: 113.6
Land: 32.3 sq. mi.; Water: 0.0 sq. mi.

Webberville
Village
ZIP: 48892 Lat: 42-40-02 N Long: 84-10-48 W
Pop: 1,698 (1990); 1,535 (1980) Pop Density: 1415.0
Land: 1.2 sq. mi.; Water: 0.0 sq. mi.
Settled 1837.
Name origin: For postmaster Hubert Webber.

Wheatfield
Township
Lat: 42-38-45 N Long: 84-18-43 W
Pop: 1,571 (1990); 1,523 (1980) Pop Density: 52.2
Land: 30.1 sq. mi.; Water: 0.0 sq. mi.

White Oak
Township
Lat: 42-33-21 N Long: 84-12-29 W
Pop: 1,074 (1990); 1,096 (1980) Pop Density: 29.4
Land: 36.5 sq. mi.; Water: 0.0 sq. mi.

Williamston
City
ZIP: 48895 Lat: 42-41-23 N Long: 84-16-55 W
Pop: 2,922 (1990); 2,981 (1980) Pop Density: 1948.0
Land: 1.5 sq. mi.; Water: 0.0 sq. mi.
Settled 1834.
Name origin: For lumberman O. B. Williams.

Williamstown
Township
Lat: 42-44-12 N Long: 84-18-43 W
Pop: 4,285 (1990); 3,972 (1980) Pop Density: 145.3
Land: 29.5 sq. mi.; Water: 0.0 sq. mi.

Ionia County
County Seat: Ionia (ZIP: 48846)

Pop: 57,024 (1990); 51,815 (1980) **Pop Density:** 99.5
Land: 573.2 sq. mi.; **Water:** 7.0 sq. mi. **Area Code:** 616
In central MI, east of Grand Rapids; established Mar 2, 1831 (prior to statehood) from unorganized territory.
Name origin: For the ancient province in Greece.

Belding City
ZIP: 48809   **Lat:** 43-05-47 N **Long:** 85-13-58 W
Pop: 5,969 (1990); 5,634 (1980)   **Pop Density:** 1243.5
Land: 4.8 sq. mi.; **Water:** 0.2 sq. mi.
Name origin: For Hiram Belding, founder of a local silk-goods business (1855).

Berlin Township
Lat: 42-54-27 N **Long:** 85-07-27 W
Pop: 3,610 (1990); 2,660 (1980)   **Pop Density:** 85.7
Land: 42.1 sq. mi.; **Water:** 0.3 sq. mi.

Boston Township
Lat: 42-54-19 N **Long:** 85-15-36 W
Pop: 4,313 (1990); 3,681 (1980)   **Pop Density:** 123.2
Land: 35.0 sq. mi.; **Water:** 0.9 sq. mi.

Campbell Township
Lat: 42-49-12 N **Long:** 85-15-07 W
Pop: 1,814 (1990); 1,692 (1980)   **Pop Density:** 50.7
Land: 35.8 sq. mi.; **Water:** 0.1 sq. mi.

Clarksville Village
ZIP: 48815   **Lat:** 42-50-29 N **Long:** 85-14-31 W
Pop: 360 (1990); 348 (1980)   **Pop Density:** 720.0
Land: 0.5 sq. mi.; **Water:** 0.0 sq. mi.   **Elev:** 826 ft.
Name origin: Named by and for the first postmaster, Clark L. Howard.

Danby Township
Lat: 42-48-43 N **Long:** 84-54-02 W
Pop: 2,371 (1990); 2,082 (1980)   **Pop Density:** 67.2
Land: 35.3 sq. mi.; **Water:** 0.8 sq. mi.

Easton Township
ZIP: 48846   **Lat:** 42-59-33 N **Long:** 85-08-30 W
Pop: 5,384 (1990); 4,501 (1980)   **Pop Density:** 179.5
Land: 30.0 sq. mi.; **Water:** 0.2 sq. mi.

Hubbardston Village
ZIP: 48845   **Lat:** 43-05-42 N **Long:** 84-50-37 W
Pop: 385 (1990); 380 (1980)   **Pop Density:** 350.0
Land: 1.1 sq. mi.; **Water:** 0.1 sq. mi.
Incorporated 1867. Part of the town is also in Clinton County.
Name origin: For founder Thomas Hubbard.

Ionia City
ZIP: 48846   **Lat:** 42-59-06 N **Long:** 85-03-28 W
Pop: 5,935 (1990); 5,920 (1980)   **Pop Density:** 2119.6
Land: 2.8 sq. mi.; **Water:** 0.1 sq. mi.   **Elev:** 660 ft.
Settled 1830s.
Name origin: For the ancient province in Greece.

***Ionia** Township
ZIP: 48846   **Lat:** 42-59-15 N **Long:** 85-01-02 W
Pop: 3,153 (1990); 2,842 (1980)   **Pop Density:** 93.0
Land: 33.9 sq. mi.; **Water:** 0.4 sq. mi.

Keene Township
Lat: 42-59-00 N **Long:** 85-15-01 W
Pop: 1,376 (1990); 1,085 (1980)   **Pop Density:** 38.5
Land: 35.7 sq. mi.; **Water:** 0.3 sq. mi.

Lake Odessa Village
ZIP: 48849   **Lat:** 42-46-58 N **Long:** 85-08-14 W
Pop: 2,256 (1990); 2,171 (1980)   **Pop Density:** 2820.0
Land: 0.8 sq. mi.; **Water:** 0.0 sq. mi.
Name origin: For Odessa Township and its nearby lakes.

Lyons Village
ZIP: 48851   **Lat:** 42-58-59 N **Long:** 84-56-43 W
Pop: 824 (1990); 708 (1980)   **Pop Density:** 686.7
Land: 1.2 sq. mi.; **Water:** 0.1 sq. mi.
Not coextensive with the town of the same name.

***Lyons** Township
ZIP: 48851   **Lat:** 42-59-05 N **Long:** 84-54-01 W
Pop: 3,276 (1990); 3,126 (1980)   **Pop Density:** 90.5
Land: 36.2 sq. mi.; **Water:** 0.7 sq. mi.

Muir Village
ZIP: 48860   **Lat:** 42-59-50 N **Long:** 84-56-07 W
Pop: 667 (1990); 698 (1980)   **Pop Density:** 833.8
Land: 0.8 sq. mi.; **Water:** 0.0 sq. mi.   **Elev:** 655 ft.

North Plains Township
Lat: 43-05-00 N **Long:** 84-53-57 W
Pop: 1,333 (1990); 1,345 (1980)   **Pop Density:** 37.1
Land: 35.9 sq. mi.; **Water:** 0.1 sq. mi.

Odessa Township
Lat: 42-49-06 N **Long:** 85-08-36 W
Pop: 3,885 (1990); 3,531 (1980)   **Pop Density:** 108.5
Land: 35.8 sq. mi.; **Water:** 0.4 sq. mi.

Orange Township
Lat: 42-54-09 N **Long:** 85-01-18 W
Pop: 1,047 (1990); 994 (1980)   **Pop Density:** 29.1
Land: 36.0 sq. mi.; **Water:** 0.0 sq. mi.

Orleans Township
ZIP: 48865   **Lat:** 43-04-35 N **Long:** 85-08-04 W
Pop: 2,548 (1990); 2,230 (1980)   **Pop Density:** 71.8
Land: 35.5 sq. mi.; **Water:** 0.7 sq. mi.

Otisco Township
Lat: 43-04-21 N **Long:** 85-15-28 W
Pop: 1,863 (1990); 1,826 (1980)   **Pop Density:** 59.1
Land: 31.5 sq. mi.; **Water:** 0.4 sq. mi.

Pewamo Village
ZIP: 48873   **Lat:** 43-00-04 N **Long:** 84-50-47 W
Pop: 520 (1990); 488 (1980)   **Pop Density:** 520.0
Land: 1.0 sq. mi.; **Water:** 0.0 sq. mi.
Began 1859.
Name origin: Named by early settler J.C. Blanchard for the Indian chief who hunted with him.

MICHIGAN, Ionia County

Portland
City
ZIP: 48875 **Lat:** 42-52-16 N **Long:** 84-54-03 W
Pop: 3,889 (1990); 3,963 (1980) **Pop Density:** 1620.4
Land: 2.4 sq. mi.; **Water:** 0.1 sq. mi.
Incorporated 1869.

Name origin: For its excellent boat-loading facilities on the Grand River.

*Portland
Township
ZIP: 48875 **Lat:** 42-54-27 N **Long:** 84-54-06 W
Pop: 2,383 (1990); 2,245 (1980) **Pop Density:** 73.5
Land: 32.4 sq. mi.; **Water:** 1.1 sq. mi.

Ronald
Township
Lat: 43-04-44 N **Long:** 85-01-13 W
Pop: 1,715 (1990); 1,353 (1980) **Pop Density:** 47.2
Land: 36.3 sq. mi.; **Water:** 0.2 sq. mi.

Saranac
Village
ZIP: 48881 **Lat:** 42-55-47 N **Long:** 85-12-33 W
Pop: 1,461 (1990); 1,421 (1980) **Pop Density:** 1217.5
Land: 1.2 sq. mi.; **Water:** 0.1 sq. mi. **Elev:** 644 ft.
Incorporated 1869.

Name origin: For Saranac Lake, NY.

Sebewa
Township
Lat: 42-49-09 N **Long:** 85-00-38 W
Pop: 1,160 (1990); 1,105 (1980) **Pop Density:** 32.4
Land: 35.8 sq. mi.; **Water:** 0.0 sq. mi.

Iosco County
County Seat: Tawas City (ZIP: 48764)

Pop: 30,209 (1990); 28,349 (1980) **Pop Density:** 55.0
Land: 549.1 sq. mi.; **Water:** 1341.6 sq. mi. **Area Code:** 517

On the east-central coast of MI bordered on east by Lake Huron; organized as Kanotin County Apr 1, 1840 from unorganized territory; name changed Mar 8, 1843.

Name origin: From an Indian word meaning 'shining water' or 'water of light.'

Alabaster
Township
Lat: 44-11-32 N **Long:** 83-36-06 W
Pop: 394 (1990); 371 (1980) **Pop Density:** 17.8
Land: 22.1 sq. mi.; **Water:** 0.0 sq. mi.

Au Sable
Township
Lat: 44-22-50 N **Long:** 83-22-02 W
Pop: 2,312 (1990); 2,198 (1980) **Pop Density:** 112.2
Land: 20.6 sq. mi.; **Water:** 0.5 sq. mi.

Baldwin
Township
Lat: 44-19-16 N **Long:** 83-28-23 W
Pop: 1,670 (1990); 1,393 (1980) **Pop Density:** 58.8
Land: 28.4 sq. mi.; **Water:** 2.9 sq. mi.

Burleigh
Township
Lat: 44-12-00 N **Long:** 83-49-16 W
Pop: 695 (1990); 761 (1980) **Pop Density:** 20.0
Land: 34.7 sq. mi.; **Water:** 0.0 sq. mi.

East Tawas
City
ZIP: 48730 **Lat:** 44-17-10 N **Long:** 83-29-02 W
Pop: 2,887 (1990); 2,584 (1980) **Pop Density:** 995.5
Land: 2.9 sq. mi.; **Water:** 0.5 sq. mi. **Elev:** 689 ft.
Incorporated 1895.

Name origin: For its location east of Tawas City.

Grant
Township
Lat: 44-17-35 N **Long:** 83-41-37 W
Pop: 1,154 (1990); 1,043 (1980) **Pop Density:** 33.1
Land: 34.9 sq. mi.; **Water:** 0.6 sq. mi.

Oscoda
Township
ZIP: 48750 **Lat:** 44-28-20 N **Long:** 83-32-43 W
Pop: 11,958 (1990); 11,386 (1980) **Pop Density:** 98.2
Land: 121.8 sq. mi.; **Water:** 9.4 sq. mi.

In central eastern MI on Lake Huron, northeast of Bay City.

Name origin: Coined by 19th-century explorer-ethnographer Henry Rowe Schoolcraft (1793–1864), by combining the Algonquian Indian terms *ossin* meaning 'stone' and *muskoda* meaning 'prairie.'

Plainfield
Township
Lat: 44-24-14 N **Long:** 83-47-11 W
Pop: 3,490 (1990); 3,160 (1980) **Pop Density:** 33.6
Land: 103.8 sq. mi.; **Water:** 3.8 sq. mi.

Reno
Township
Lat: 44-17-21 N **Long:** 83-49-13 W
Pop: 572 (1990); 566 (1980) **Pop Density:** 16.2
Land: 35.4 sq. mi.; **Water:** 0.1 sq. mi.

Sherman
Township
Lat: 44-12-03 N **Long:** 83-41-50 W
Pop: 502 (1990); 465 (1980) **Pop Density:** 14.0
Land: 35.9 sq. mi.; **Water:** 0.0 sq. mi.

Tawas
Township
Lat: 44-16-51 N **Long:** 83-35-51 W
Pop: 1,465 (1990); 1,463 (1980) **Pop Density:** 43.9
Land: 33.4 sq. mi.; **Water:** 0.0 sq. mi.

Tawas City
City
ZIP: 48764 **Lat:** 44-16-02 N **Long:** 83-31-19 W
Pop: 2,009 (1990); 1,967 (1980) **Pop Density:** 1181.8
Land: 1.7 sq. mi.; **Water:** 0.4 sq. mi. **Elev:** 587 ft.
Platted 1855.

Name origin: For either the Ottawa Indians or Otawas, a local Chippewa Indian chief.

Wilber
Township
Lat: 44-22-59 N **Long:** 83-31-05 W
Pop: 638 (1990); 554 (1980) **Pop Density:** 8.8
Land: 72.5 sq. mi.; **Water:** 0.2 sq. mi.

Wurtsmith Air Force Base Military Facility
ZIP: 48753　　　　Lat: 44-27-40 N　**Long:** 83-23-04 W
Pop: 5,080 (1990); 5,166 (1980)　**Pop Density:** 695.9
Land: 7.3 sq. mi.; **Water:** 0.0 sq. mi.

Iron County
County Seat: Crystal Falls (ZIP: 49920)

Pop: 13,175 (1990); 13,635 (1980)　　　**Pop Density:** 11.3
Land: 1166.5 sq. mi.; **Water:** 44.7 sq. mi.　　**Area Code:** 906
On the southwest border of the Upper Peninsula of MI; established Apr 3, 1885 from Marquette and Menominee counties.
Name origin: For the iron mines in the area.

Alpha　　　　　　　　　　　　　　　Village
ZIP: 49902　　　Lat: 46-02-38 N　**Long:** 88-22-41 W
Pop: 219 (1990); 229 (1980)　**Pop Density:** 243.3
Land: 0.9 sq. mi.; **Water:** 0.1 sq. mi.
An iron-mining settlement organized in 1885. Originally called Mastodon
Name origin: For the first letter of the Greek alphabet.

Bates　　　　　　　　　　　　　Township
　　　　　　　　Lat: 46-14-39 N　**Long:** 88-36-54 W
Pop: 966 (1990); 1,003 (1980)　**Pop Density:** 7.7
Land: 125.4 sq. mi.; **Water:** 5.9 sq. mi.

Caspian　　　　　　　　　　　　　　City
ZIP: 49915　　　Lat: 46-03-54 N　**Long:** 88-37-32 W
Pop: 1,031 (1990); 1,038 (1980)　**Pop Density:** 736.4
Land: 1.4 sq. mi.; **Water:** 0.0 sq. mi.　**Elev:** 1492 ft.
Name origin: For the nearby Caspian, Baltic, and Fogarty mines.

Crystal Falls　　　　　　　　　　　　City
ZIP: 49920　　　Lat: 46-05-50 N　**Long:** 88-19-39 W
Pop: 1,922 (1990); 1,965 (1980)　**Pop Density:** 582.4
Land: 3.3 sq. mi.; **Water:** 0.2 sq. mi.　**Elev:** 1517 ft.
Established 1880.
Name origin: For its location at the falls on the nearby Paint River.

*Crystal Falls　　　　　　　　　　Township
ZIP: 49920　　　Lat: 46-14-17 N　**Long:** 88-19-24 W
Pop: 1,614 (1990); 1,648 (1980)　**Pop Density:** 7.1
Land: 228.8 sq. mi.; **Water:** 6.4 sq. mi.

Gaastra　　　　　　　　　　　　　　City
ZIP: 49927　　　Lat: 46-03-31 N　**Long:** 88-36-19 W
Pop: 376 (1990); 404 (1980)　**Pop Density:** 235.0
Land: 1.6 sq. mi.; **Water:** 0.0 sq. mi.
Name origin: For building contractor Douwe Gaastra, who platted the village in 1908.

Hematite　　　　　　　　　　　Township
　　　　　　　　Lat: 46-19-02 N　**Long:** 88-29-35 W
Pop: 366 (1990); 404 (1980)　**Pop Density:** 2.4
Land: 153.5 sq. mi.; **Water:** 2.3 sq. mi.

Iron River　　　　　　　　　　　　　City
ZIP: 49935　　　Lat: 46-05-55 N　**Long:** 88-38-17 W
Pop: 2,095 (1990); 2,426 (1980)　**Pop Density:** 598.6
Land: 3.5 sq. mi.; **Water:** 0.0 sq. mi.　**Elev:** 1510 ft.
In western Upper Peninsula of MI. Established 1885.
Name origin: For its location near the Nanaimo iron mine, for which it was previously named.

*Iron River　　　　　　　　　　　Township
ZIP: 49935　　　Lat: 46-14-29 N　**Long:** 88-47-17 W
Pop: 1,398 (1990); 1,445 (1980)　**Pop Density:** 5.8
Land: 239.6 sq. mi.; **Water:** 4.4 sq. mi.

Mansfield　　　　　　　　　　　Township
　　　　　　　　Lat: 46-11-45 N　**Long:** 88-11-19 W
Pop: 248 (1990); 222 (1980)　**Pop Density:** 2.5
Land: 99.3 sq. mi.; **Water:** 8.4 sq. mi.

Mastodon　　　　　　　　　　　Township
　　　　　　　　Lat: 46-01-09 N　**Long:** 88-16-54 W
Pop: 654 (1990); 621 (1980)　**Pop Density:** 5.2
Land: 126.6 sq. mi.; **Water:** 8.7 sq. mi.

Mineral Hills　　　　　　　　　　　Village
　　　　　　　　Lat: 46-06-44 N　**Long:** 88-38-40 W
Pop: 200 (1990); 257 (1980)　**Pop Density:** 153.8
Land: 1.3 sq. mi.; **Water:** 0.0 sq. mi.
Name origin: For the area's rich iron-bearing hills.

Stambaugh　　　　　　　　　　　　　City
ZIP: 49964　　　Lat: 46-04-45 N　**Long:** 88-38-00 W
Pop: 1,281 (1990); 1,442 (1980)　**Pop Density:** 800.6
Land: 1.6 sq. mi.; **Water:** 0.0 sq. mi.　**Elev:** 1539 ft.
Founded 1882.
Name origin: For prominent businessman John Stambaugh.

*Stambaugh　　　　　　　　　　Township
　　　　　　　　Lat: 46-05-05 N　**Long:** 88-50-07 W
Pop: 1,224 (1990); 1,017 (1980)　**Pop Density:** 6.7
Land: 181.8 sq. mi.; **Water:** 8.3 sq. mi.

Isabella County
County Seat: Mount Pleasant (ZIP: 48858)

Pop: 54,624 (1990); 54,110 (1980) **Pop Density:** 95.1
Land: 574.3 sq. mi.; **Water:** 3.5 sq. mi. **Area Code:** 517

In central MI, west of Midland; organized Mar 2, 1831 (prior to statehood) from unorganized territory.

Name origin: For Isabella (1451–1504), queen of Spain who financed Christopher Columbus's expeditions.

Beal City   CDP
Lat: 43-40-11 N Long: 84-54-35 W
Pop: 345 (1990) **Pop Density:** 86.3
Land: 4.0 sq. mi.; **Water:** 0.0 sq. mi.

Broomfield   Township
Lat: 43-35-48 N Long: 85-01-34 W
Pop: 1,266 (1990); 1,246 (1980) **Pop Density:** 36.3
Land: 34.9 sq. mi.; **Water:** 0.8 sq. mi.

Chippewa   Township
Lat: 43-35-52 N Long: 84-40-26 W
Pop: 4,130 (1990); 3,784 (1980) **Pop Density:** 114.1
Land: 36.2 sq. mi.; **Water:** 0.1 sq. mi.

Clare   City
ZIP: 48617 Lat: 43-48-52 N Long: 84-45-28 W
Pop: 8 (1990) **Pop Density:** 80.0
Land: 0.1 sq. mi.; **Water:** 0.0 sq. mi. **Elev:** 841 ft.

Established 1940. Part of the town is also in Clare County.
Name origin: For its county, itself named for County Clare, Ireland.

Coe   Township
Lat: 43-30-17 N Long: 84-40-20 W
Pop: 2,967 (1990); 3,141 (1980) **Pop Density:** 82.0
Land: 36.2 sq. mi.; **Water:** 0.0 sq. mi.

Coldwater   Township
Lat: 43-46-24 N Long: 85-02-11 W
Pop: 732 (1990); 714 (1980) **Pop Density:** 20.4
Land: 35.9 sq. mi.; **Water:** 0.1 sq. mi.

Deerfield   Township
Lat: 43-35-38 N Long: 84-54-11 W
Pop: 2,598 (1990); 2,160 (1980) **Pop Density:** 72.6
Land: 35.8 sq. mi.; **Water:** 0.1 sq. mi.

Denver   Township
Lat: 43-41-00 N Long: 84-40-12 W
Pop: 1,019 (1990); 1,059 (1980) **Pop Density:** 27.9
Land: 36.5 sq. mi.; **Water:** 0.0 sq. mi.

Fremont   Township
Lat: 43-30-38 N Long: 84-54-29 W
Pop: 1,217 (1990); 1,215 (1980) **Pop Density:** 34.0
Land: 35.8 sq. mi.; **Water:** 0.0 sq. mi.

Gilmore   Township
Lat: 43-46-29 N Long: 84-54-39 W
Pop: 1,072 (1990); 966 (1980) **Pop Density:** 30.0
Land: 35.7 sq. mi.; **Water:** 0.3 sq. mi.

Isabella   Township
Lat: 43-41-01 N Long: 84-47-11 W
Pop: 2,025 (1990); 1,916 (1980) **Pop Density:** 55.6
Land: 36.4 sq. mi.; **Water:** 0.0 sq. mi.

Lincoln   Township
Lat: 43-30-36 N Long: 84-47-07 W
Pop: 1,794 (1990); 1,698 (1980) **Pop Density:** 49.7
Land: 36.1 sq. mi.; **Water:** 0.1 sq. mi.

Mount Pleasant   City
ZIP: 48804 Lat: 43-35-47 N Long: 84-46-41 W
Pop: 23,285 (1990); 23,746 (1980) **Pop Density:** 3234.0
Land: 7.2 sq. mi.; **Water:** 0.0 sq. mi.

In central MI, 65 mi. north of Lansing. County seat; incorporated as a village 1875; as city 1889.
Name origin: Named by founder, David Ward, for his hometown in OH.

Nottawa   Township
Lat: 43-40-33 N Long: 84-54-29 W
Pop: 1,968 (1990); 2,042 (1980) **Pop Density:** 55.6
Land: 35.4 sq. mi.; **Water:** 0.6 sq. mi.

Rolland   Township
Lat: 43-30-34 N Long: 85-01-34 W
Pop: 1,138 (1990); 1,105 (1980) **Pop Density:** 31.9
Land: 35.7 sq. mi.; **Water:** 0.1 sq. mi.

Rosebush   Village
ZIP: 48878 Lat: 43-41-58 N Long: 84-45-56 W
Pop: 333 (1990); 336 (1980) **Pop Density:** 370.0
Land: 0.9 sq. mi.; **Water:** 0.0 sq. mi.

Name origin: For Rose Bush, wife of pioneer James Bush, who platted the town.

Shepherd   Village
ZIP: 48883 Lat: 43-31-28 N Long: 84-41-37 W
Pop: 1,413 (1990); 1,534 (1980) **Pop Density:** 1766.3
Land: 0.8 sq. mi.; **Water:** 0.0 sq. mi.

Founded in the 1850s by lumberman Isaac Shepherd.
Name origin: For its founder.

Sherman   Township
Lat: 43-41-07 N Long: 85-01-40 W
Pop: 1,725 (1990); 1,405 (1980) **Pop Density:** 49.6
Land: 34.8 sq. mi.; **Water:** 0.8 sq. mi.

Union   Township
ZIP: 48858 Lat: 43-35-39 N Long: 84-47-51 W
Pop: 5,139 (1990); 5,306 (1980) **Pop Density:** 177.2
Land: 29.0 sq. mi.; **Water:** 0.1 sq. mi.

Vernon   Township
Lat: 43-45-54 N Long: 84-46-58 W
Pop: 1,308 (1990); 1,389 (1980) **Pop Density:** 36.4
Land: 35.9 sq. mi.; **Water:** 0.2 sq. mi.

Weidman   CDP
ZIP: 48893 Lat: 43-41-38 N Long: 84-58-22 W
Pop: 696 (1990) **Pop Density:** 165.7
Land: 4.2 sq. mi.; **Water:** 0.3 sq. mi.

Wise — Township
Lat: 43-46-17 N Long: 84-40-29 W
Pop: 1,233 (1990); 1,218 (1980) **Pop Density:** 33.7
Land: 36.6 sq. mi.; **Water:** 0.0 sq. mi.

Jackson County
County Seat: Jackson (ZIP: 49201)

Pop: 149,756 (1990); 151,495 (1980) **Pop Density:** 211.9
Land: 706.6 sq. mi.; **Water:** 17.2 sq. mi. **Area Code:** 517
In south-central MI, west of Ann Arbor; established Oct 29, 1829 (prior to statehood) from Washtenaw County.
Name origin: For Andrew Jackson (1767–1845), seventh U.S. president.

Blackman — Township
ZIP: 49202 Lat: 42-17-42 N Long: 84-25-45 W
Pop: 20,492 (1990); 19,741 (1980) **Pop Density:** 644.4
Land: 31.8 sq. mi.; **Water:** 0.0 sq. mi.

Brooklyn — Village
ZIP: 49230 Lat: 42-06-19 N Long: 84-14-55 W
Pop: 1,027 (1990); 1,110 (1980) **Pop Density:** 1027.0
Land: 1.0 sq. mi.; **Water:** 0.0 sq. mi. **Elev:** 992 ft.
Settled 1833.
Name origin: For Brooklyn, NY.

Cement City — Village
Lat: 42-04-30 N Long: 84-19-36 W
Pop: 28 (1990); 38 (1980) **Pop Density:** 140.0
Land: 0.2 sq. mi.; **Water:** 0.0 sq. mi.
Part of the town is also in Lenawee County.
Name origin: Named 1901 upon the arrival of a cement company.

Columbia — Township
ZIP: 49230 Lat: 42-06-27 N Long: 84-17-10 W
Pop: 6,308 (1990); 6,019 (1980) **Pop Density:** 171.9
Land: 36.7 sq. mi.; **Water:** 2.7 sq. mi.

Concord — Village
ZIP: 49237 Lat: 42-10-30 N Long: 84-38-38 W
Pop: 944 (1990); 900 (1980) **Pop Density:** 674.3
Land: 1.4 sq. mi.; **Water:** 0.1 sq. mi.
Settled 1832. Not coextensive with the town of the same name.
Name origin: For the community's quality.

***Concord** — Township
ZIP: 49237 Lat: 42-12-27 N Long: 84-39-20 W
Pop: 2,408 (1990); 2,320 (1980) **Pop Density:** 67.1
Land: 35.9 sq. mi.; **Water:** 0.4 sq. mi.

Grass Lake — Village
ZIP: 49240 Lat: 42-15-03 N Long: 84-12-21 W
Pop: 903 (1990); 962 (1980) **Pop Density:** 1003.3
Land: 0.9 sq. mi.; **Water:** 0.0 sq. mi. **Elev:** 996 ft.
Settled 1829. Not coextensive with the town of the same name.
Name origin: For a nearby grassy lake.

***Grass Lake** — Township
ZIP: 49240 Lat: 42-14-56 N Long: 84-11-23 W
Pop: 3,774 (1990); 3,685 (1980) **Pop Density:** 80.0
Land: 47.2 sq. mi.; **Water:** 1.3 sq. mi.

Hanover — Village
ZIP: 49241 Lat: 42-06-02 N Long: 84-33-09 W
Pop: 481 (1990); 490 (1980) **Pop Density:** 1202.5
Land: 0.4 sq. mi.; **Water:** 0.0 sq. mi. **Elev:** 1117 ft.
Not coextensive with the town of the same name.

***Hanover** — Township
ZIP: 49241 Lat: 42-07-00 N Long: 84-32-25 W
Pop: 3,710 (1990); 3,650 (1980) **Pop Density:** 106.0
Land: 35.0 sq. mi.; **Water:** 0.8 sq. mi.

Henrietta — Township
Lat: 42-22-27 N Long: 84-18-50 W
Pop: 3,858 (1990); 3,814 (1980) **Pop Density:** 106.6
Land: 36.2 sq. mi.; **Water:** 0.9 sq. mi.

Jackson — City
ZIP: 49204 Lat: 42-14-35 N Long: 84-24-17 W
Pop: 37,446 (1990); 39,739 (1980) **Pop Density:** 3404.2
Land: 11.0 sq. mi.; **Water:** 0.0 sq. mi.
In south-central MI, 35 mi. south of Lansing. Settled 1829; incorporated as city 1857.
Name origin: For Andrew Jackson (1767–1845), seventh U.S. president.

Leoni — Township
ZIP: 49201 Lat: 42-16-13 N Long: 84-18-19 W
Pop: 13,435 (1990); 14,259 (1980) **Pop Density:** 273.6
Land: 49.1 sq. mi.; **Water:** 2.1 sq. mi.
In south-central MI, southeast of Jackson.

Liberty — Township
Lat: 42-07-15 N Long: 84-25-27 W
Pop: 2,452 (1990); 2,312 (1980) **Pop Density:** 70.9
Land: 34.6 sq. mi.; **Water:** 1.0 sq. mi.

Michigan Center — CDP
ZIP: 49254 Lat: 42-13-36 N Long: 84-19-21 W
Pop: 4,863 (1990); 5,244 (1980) **Pop Density:** 935.2
Land: 5.2 sq. mi.; **Water:** 0.5 sq. mi.

Napoleon — Township
ZIP: 49261 Lat: 42-10-35 N Long: 84-17-49 W
Pop: 6,273 (1990); 6,141 (1980) **Pop Density:** 212.6
Land: 29.5 sq. mi.; **Water:** 2.0 sq. mi.

Norvell — Township
Lat: 42-07-25 N Long: 84-10-15 W
Pop: 2,657 (1990); 2,418 (1980) **Pop Density:** 88.6
Land: 30.0 sq. mi.; **Water:** 2.0 sq. mi.

MICHIGAN, Jackson County

Parma
Village
ZIP: 49269 Lat: 42-15-26 N Long: 84-35-54 W
Pop: 809 (1990); 873 (1980) Pop Density: 2022.5
Land: 0.4 sq. mi.; Water: 0.0 sq. mi. Elev: 992 ft.
Settled 1833. Not coextensive with the town of the same name.
Name origin: For Parma, NY.

*Parma
Township
ZIP: 49269 Lat: 42-17-21 N Long: 84-39-41 W
Pop: 2,491 (1990); 2,715 (1980) Pop Density: 68.6
Land: 36.3 sq. mi.; Water: 0.1 sq. mi.

Pulaski
Township
Lat: 42-07-18 N Long: 84-39-25 W
Pop: 1,816 (1990); 1,725 (1980) Pop Density: 50.2
Land: 36.2 sq. mi.; Water: 0.4 sq. mi.

Rives
Township
Lat: 42-22-44 N Long: 84-25-40 W
Pop: 4,026 (1990); 4,081 (1980) Pop Density: 112.1
Land: 35.9 sq. mi.; Water: 0.3 sq. mi.

Sandstone
Township
Lat: 42-17-11 N Long: 84-32-35 W
Pop: 3,300 (1990); 3,300 (1980) Pop Density: 90.9
Land: 36.3 sq. mi.; Water: 0.0 sq. mi.

Spring Arbor
Township
ZIP: 49283 Lat: 42-12-22 N Long: 84-32-20 W
Pop: 6,939 (1990); 6,868 (1980) Pop Density: 196.0
Land: 35.4 sq. mi.; Water: 0.4 sq. mi.

Springport
Village
ZIP: 49284 Lat: 42-22-40 N Long: 84-41-50 W
Pop: 707 (1990); 675 (1980) Pop Density: 543.8
Land: 1.3 sq. mi.; Water: 0.0 sq. mi.
Founded 1836 by John Oyer. Not coextensive with the town of the same name.
Name origin: Named in 1838 for the area's many springs.

*Springport
Township
ZIP: 49284 Lat: 42-23-03 N Long: 84-39-04 W
Pop: 2,090 (1990); 1,999 (1980) Pop Density: 57.9
Land: 36.1 sq. mi.; Water: 0.2 sq. mi.

Summit
Township
ZIP: 49203 Lat: 42-12-01 N Long: 84-25-48 W
Pop: 21,130 (1990); 22,113 (1980) Pop Density: 721.2
Land: 29.3 sq. mi.; Water: 0.6 sq. mi.
In south-central MI, south of Jackson. Formed from Old Jackson township 1857.
Name origin: For having the highest elevations in the county.

Tompkins
Township
Lat: 42-22-40 N Long: 84-32-23 W
Pop: 2,321 (1990); 2,152 (1980) Pop Density: 64.3
Land: 36.1 sq. mi.; Water: 0.3 sq. mi.

Vandercook Lake
CDP
Lat: 42-11-29 N Long: 84-23-07 W
Pop: 4,642 (1990); 4,975 (1980) Pop Density: 1031.6
Land: 4.5 sq. mi.; Water: 0.2 sq. mi.

Waterloo
Township
Lat: 42-22-04 N Long: 84-10-52 W
Pop: 2,830 (1990); 2,444 (1980) Pop Density: 59.1
Land: 47.9 sq. mi.; Water: 1.6 sq. mi.

Kalamazoo County
County Seat: Kalamazoo (ZIP: 49007)

Pop: 223,411 (1990); 212,378 (1980) Pop Density: 397.6
Land: 561.9 sq. mi.; Water: 18.3 sq. mi. Area Code: 616

In southwest MI, south of Grand Rapids; organized Oct 29, 1829 (prior to statehood) from St. Joseph County.
Name origin: From Algonquian, *ke-kala-mazoo*, meaning uncertain, interpreted as connected with 'smoke,' 'beautiful water,' 'otters,' or 'boiling water.'

Alamo
Township
Lat: 42-22-08 N Long: 85-42-21 W
Pop: 3,276 (1990); 2,909 (1980) Pop Density: 90.2
Land: 36.3 sq. mi.; Water: 0.2 sq. mi.

Augusta
Village
ZIP: 49012 Lat: 42-20-15 N Long: 85-21-04 W
Pop: 927 (1990); 913 (1980) Pop Density: 1030.0
Land: 0.9 sq. mi.; Water: 0.0 sq. mi.
Settled 1832. Established 1836.
Name origin: For Augusta, ME.

Brady
Township
Lat: 42-07-20 N Long: 85-27-56 W
Pop: 3,857 (1990); 3,852 (1980) Pop Density: 110.5
Land: 34.9 sq. mi.; Water: 1.2 sq. mi.

Charleston
Township
Lat: 42-16-54 N Long: 85-21-30 W
Pop: 1,776 (1990); 1,748 (1980) Pop Density: 50.9
Land: 34.9 sq. mi.; Water: 0.7 sq. mi.

Climax
Village
ZIP: 49034 Lat: 42-14-22 N Long: 85-20-13 W
Pop: 677 (1990); 619 (1980) Pop Density: 677.0
Land: 1.0 sq. mi.; Water: 0.0 sq. mi.
Settled 1835. Not coextensive with the town of the same name.
Name origin: Originally called Climax Prairie because it climaxed the end of settlers' search for a good place to settle; shortened in 1874.

*Climax
Township
ZIP: 49034 Lat: 42-12-32 N Long: 85-21-43 W
Pop: 2,221 (1990); 1,978 (1980) Pop Density: 61.5
Land: 36.1 sq. mi.; Water: 0.2 sq. mi.

Comstock — Township
ZIP: 49041 Lat: 42-17-24 N Long: 85-28-18 W
Pop: 11,834 (1990); 11,162 (1980) Pop Density: 358.6
Land: 33.0 sq. mi.; Water: 2.0 sq. mi.
In southwestern MI, an eastern suburb of Kalamazoo.
Name origin: For early settler Horace H. Comstock.

Comstock Northwest — CDP
Lat: 42-19-20 N Long: 85-31-01 W
Pop: 3,402 (1990) Pop Density: 1063.1
Land: 3.2 sq. mi.; Water: 0.0 sq. mi.

Cooper — Township
ZIP: 49007 Lat: 42-22-34 N Long: 85-35-14 W
Pop: 8,442 (1990); 8,434 (1980) Pop Density: 232.6
Land: 36.3 sq. mi.; Water: 0.4 sq. mi.

Eastwood — CDP
ZIP: 49001 Lat: 42-18-07 N Long: 85-32-38 W
Pop: 6,340 (1990); 7,186 (1980) Pop Density: 3170.0
Land: 2.0 sq. mi.; Water: 0.0 sq. mi.

Galesburg — City
ZIP: 49053 Lat: 42-17-26 N Long: 85-25-03 W
Pop: 1,863 (1990); 1,822 (1980) Pop Density: 1330.7
Land: 1.4 sq. mi.; Water: 0.1 sq. mi.
Founded 1835 by pioneer George Gale.
Name origin: For its founder.

Kalamazoo — City
ZIP: 49001 Lat: 42-16-28 N Long: 85-35-17 W
Pop: 80,277 (1990); 79,722 (1980) Pop Density: 3263.3
Land: 24.6 sq. mi.; Water: 0.5 sq. mi.
In southwestern MI on the Kalamazoo River, 65 mi. southwest of Lansing. Settled as Bronson in 1829; name changed in 1836, incorporated as city in 1884. Site of Western Michigan University.
Name origin: For the river, itself named from Algonquian Indian *ke-kala-mazoo* of disputed meaning, possibly 'smoke', 'beautiful water', 'otters', or 'boiling water.'

*Kalamazoo — Township
ZIP: 49004 Lat: 42-18-41 N Long: 85-35-35 W
Pop: 20,976 (1990); 20,942 (1980) Pop Density: 1777.6
Land: 11.8 sq. mi.; Water: 0.1 sq. mi.

Oshtemo — Township
ZIP: 49077 Lat: 42-17-08 N Long: 85-42-23 W
Pop: 13,401 (1990); 10,958 (1980) Pop Density: 372.3
Land: 36.0 sq. mi.; Water: 0.1 sq. mi.
Charter township in southwestern MI, south of Grand Rapids. Established 1838 or 1839.
Name origin: From an Indian term meaning 'headwaters.'

Parchment — City
ZIP: 49004 Lat: 42-19-37 N Long: 85-33-55 W
Pop: 1,958 (1990); 1,817 (1980) Pop Density: 2175.6
Land: 0.9 sq. mi.; Water: 0.0 sq. mi.

Pavilion — Township
ZIP: 49088 Lat: 42-12-14 N Long: 85-27-53 W
Pop: 5,500 (1990); 4,811 (1980) Pop Density: 157.6
Land: 34.9 sq. mi.; Water: 1.4 sq. mi.

Portage — City
ZIP: 49081 Lat: 42-12-04 N Long: 85-35-25 W
Pop: 41,042 (1990); 38,157 (1980) Pop Density: 1274.6
Land: 32.2 sq. mi.; Water: 2.8 sq. mi.
In southwestern MI, 10 mi. south of Kalamazoo. First European settler arrived 1830; incorporated as city 1963.
Name origin: For its chief stream, Portage Creek, used to portage water-craft between the Kalamazoo and St. Joseph rivers.

Prairie Ronde — Township
Lat: 42-06-30 N Long: 85-42-09 W
Pop: 1,365 (1990); 1,189 (1980) Pop Density: 38.1
Land: 35.8 sq. mi.; Water: 0.6 sq. mi.

Richland — Village
ZIP: 49083 Lat: 42-22-32 N Long: 85-27-22 W
Pop: 465 (1990); 486 (1980) Pop Density: 387.5
Land: 1.2 sq. mi.; Water: 0.0 sq. mi.
Organized 1832. Not coextensive with the town of the same name.
Name origin: For its township.

*Richland — Township
ZIP: 49083 Lat: 42-22-35 N Long: 85-28-27 W
Pop: 5,099 (1990); 4,677 (1980) Pop Density: 146.5
Land: 34.8 sq. mi.; Water: 1.7 sq. mi.

Ross — Township
Lat: 42-22-44 N Long: 85-21-08 W
Pop: 4,730 (1990); 4,747 (1980) Pop Density: 142.0
Land: 33.3 sq. mi.; Water: 2.7 sq. mi.

Schoolcraft — Village
ZIP: 49087 Lat: 42-06-54 N Long: 85-38-00 W
Pop: 1,517 (1990); 1,359 (1980) Pop Density: 1896.3
Land: 0.8 sq. mi.; Water: 0.0 sq. mi.
Platted 1831. Not coextensive with the town of the same name.
Name origin: For Henry Rowe Schoolcraft (1793–1864), author, explorer, MI legislator, and superintendent of Indian Affairs for MI (1836–41).

*Schoolcraft — Township
ZIP: 49087 Lat: 42-06-59 N Long: 85-35-04 W
Pop: 6,705 (1990); 6,435 (1980) Pop Density: 194.9
Land: 34.4 sq. mi.; Water: 1.7 sq. mi.

South Gull Lake — CDP
Lat: 42-23-15 N Long: 85-23-48 W
Pop: 1,453 (1990) Pop Density: 1117.7
Land: 1.3 sq. mi.; Water: 1.8 sq. mi.

Texas — Township
ZIP: 49009 Lat: 42-12-07 N Long: 85-42-11 W
Pop: 7,711 (1990); 5,643 (1980) Pop Density: 223.5
Land: 34.5 sq. mi.; Water: 1.9 sq. mi.

Vicksburg — Village
ZIP: 49097 Lat: 42-07-13 N Long: 85-32-03 W
Pop: 2,216 (1990); 2,224 (1980) Pop Density: 1704.6
Land: 1.3 sq. mi.; Water: 0.1 sq. mi. Elev: 860 ft.
Name origin: Named in 1871, possibly after the great Civil War battle. Previously called Brady.

Wakeshma — Township
Lat: 42-06-56 N Long: 85-21-12 W
Pop: 1,378 (1990); 1,375 (1980) Pop Density: 38.2
Land: 36.1 sq. mi.; Water: 0.0 sq. mi.

MICHIGAN, Kalamazoo County

Westwood CDP
ZIP: 49007 Lat: 42-18-12 N **Long:** 85-37-48 W
Pop: 8,957 (1990); 8,519 (1980) **Pop Density:** 3198.9
Land: 2.8 sq. mi.; **Water:** 0.0 sq. mi.

Kalkaska County
County Seat: Kalkaska (ZIP: 49646)

Pop: 13,497 (1990); 10,952 (1980) **Pop Density:** 24.1
Land: 561.0 sq. mi.; **Water:** 9.7 sq. mi. **Area Code:** 616

In north-central MI, east of Traverse City; established as Wabassee County Apr 1, 1840 from Crawford County; name changed Mar 8, 1843.

Name origin: From an Indian word of uncertain origin and meaning, although some sources suggest that it is from a Chippewa word meaning 'burned over.'

Bear Lake Township
Lat: 44-40-24 N **Long:** 84-54-29 W
Pop: 639 (1990); 433 (1980) **Pop Density:** 8.9
Land: 71.5 sq. mi.; **Water:** 0.9 sq. mi.

Blue Lake Township
Lat: 44-48-44 N **Long:** 84-54-30 W
Pop: 378 (1990); 300 (1980) **Pop Density:** 10.9
Land: 34.7 sq. mi.; **Water:** 1.6 sq. mi.

Boardman Township
Lat: 44-38-23 N **Long:** 85-16-43 W
Pop: 1,076 (1990); 903 (1980) **Pop Density:** 30.0
Land: 35.9 sq. mi.; **Water:** 0.2 sq. mi.

Clearwater Township
Lat: 44-48-37 N **Long:** 85-16-16 W
Pop: 1,959 (1990); 1,531 (1980) **Pop Density:** 63.0
Land: 31.1 sq. mi.; **Water:** 2.6 sq. mi.

Cold Springs Township
Lat: 44-49-21 N **Long:** 85-02-26 W
Pop: 1,073 (1990); 942 (1980) **Pop Density:** 31.2
Land: 34.4 sq. mi.; **Water:** 1.8 sq. mi.

Excelsior Township
Lat: 44-43-14 N **Long:** 85-01-57 W
Pop: 714 (1990); 580 (1980) **Pop Density:** 20.1
Land: 35.6 sq. mi.; **Water:** 0.6 sq. mi.

Garfield Township
Lat: 44-33-18 N **Long:** 85-01-51 W
Pop: 596 (1990); 366 (1980) **Pop Density:** 5.6
Land: 106.7 sq. mi.; **Water:** 0.0 sq. mi.

Kalkaska Village
ZIP: 49646 Lat: 44-44-04 N **Long:** 85-10-47 W
Pop: 1,952 (1990); 1,654 (1980) **Pop Density:** 1148.2
Land: 1.7 sq. mi.; **Water:** 0.0 sq. mi. **Elev:** 1035 ft.
Established 1873. Not coextensive with the town of the same name.

Name origin: From an Indian term of uncertain origin and meaning though some sources suggest that it is from a Chippewa word meaning 'burned over.'

*Kalkaska Township
ZIP: 49646 Lat: 44-43-36 N **Long:** 85-12-25 W
Pop: 4,269 (1990); 3,544 (1980) **Pop Density:** 60.6
Land: 70.4 sq. mi.; **Water:** 0.8 sq. mi.

Oliver Township
Lat: 44-38-53 N **Long:** 85-02-46 W
Pop: 291 (1990); 241 (1980) **Pop Density:** 8.1
Land: 36.1 sq. mi.; **Water:** 0.1 sq. mi.

Orange Township
Lat: 44-38-25 N **Long:** 85-09-15 W
Pop: 885 (1990); 792 (1980) **Pop Density:** 25.9
Land: 34.2 sq. mi.; **Water:** 0.7 sq. mi.

Rapid River Township
Lat: 44-48-54 N **Long:** 85-09-26 W
Pop: 746 (1990); 581 (1980) **Pop Density:** 21.2
Land: 35.2 sq. mi.; **Water:** 0.1 sq. mi.

Springfield Township
Lat: 44-33-23 N **Long:** 85-16-16 W
Pop: 871 (1990); 739 (1980) **Pop Density:** 24.7
Land: 35.2 sq. mi.; **Water:** 0.3 sq. mi.

> ## Kent County
> **County Seat: Grand Rapids (ZIP: 49503)**
>
> **Pop:** 500,631 (1990); 444,506 (1980) **Pop Density:** 584.7
> **Land:** 856.2 sq. mi.; **Water:** 16.0 sq. mi. **Area Code:** 616
> In west-central MI, east of Muskegon; established Mar 2, 1831 (prior to statehood) from unorganized territory.
> **Name origin:** For James Kent (1763–1847), chief justice of the NY supreme court (1804–14).

Ada
Township
ZIP: 49301 **Lat:** 42-58-57 N **Long:** 85-28-52 W
Pop: 7,578 (1990); 6,472 (1980) **Pop Density:** 209.9
Land: 36.1 sq. mi.; **Water:** 1.0 sq. mi.

Algoma
Township
ZIP: 49341 **Lat:** 43-09-41 N **Long:** 85-36-34 W
Pop: 5,496 (1990); 4,411 (1980) **Pop Density:** 157.0
Land: 35.0 sq. mi.; **Water:** 0.4 sq. mi.

Alpine
Township
ZIP: 49321 **Lat:** 43-04-49 N **Long:** 85-43-28 W
Pop: 9,863 (1990); 8,934 (1980) **Pop Density:** 274.7
Land: 35.9 sq. mi.; **Water:** 0.1 sq. mi.

Bowne
Township
Lat: 42-48-19 N **Long:** 85-22-44 W
Pop: 1,907 (1990); 1,719 (1980) **Pop Density:** 53.1
Land: 35.9 sq. mi.; **Water:** 0.2 sq. mi.

Byron
Township
ZIP: 49315 **Lat:** 42-48-44 N **Long:** 85-43-26 W
Pop: 13,235 (1990); 10,104 (1980) **Pop Density:** 361.6
Land: 36.6 sq. mi.; **Water:** 0.0 sq. mi.

Caledonia
Village
ZIP: 49316 **Lat:** 42-47-37 N **Long:** 85-30-47 W
Pop: 885 (1990); 722 (1980) **Pop Density:** 737.5
Land: 1.2 sq. mi.; **Water:** 0.0 sq. mi.
Settled 1836. Not coextensive with the town of the same name.
Name origin: For Caledonia, NY.

*Caledonia
Township
ZIP: 49316 **Lat:** 42-48-47 N **Long:** 85-29-08 W
Pop: 6,254 (1990); 4,927 (1980) **Pop Density:** 177.7
Land: 35.2 sq. mi.; **Water:** 0.6 sq. mi.

Cannon
Township
ZIP: 49341 **Lat:** 43-04-43 N **Long:** 85-29-10 W
Pop: 7,928 (1990); 4,983 (1980) **Pop Density:** 220.8
Land: 35.9 sq. mi.; **Water:** 1.2 sq. mi.

Cascade
Township
ZIP: 49506 **Lat:** 42-53-44 N **Long:** 85-29-11 W
Pop: 12,869 (1990); 10,120 (1980) **Pop Density:** 379.6
Land: 33.9 sq. mi.; **Water:** 0.9 sq. mi.

Casnovia
Village
ZIP: 49318 **Lat:** 43-14-04 N **Long:** 85-47-18 W
Pop: 189 (1990); 167 (1980) **Pop Density:** 378.0
Land: 0.5 sq. mi.; **Water:** 0.0 sq. mi. **Elev:** 881 ft.
Founded 1850. Part of the town is also in Muskegon County.
Name origin: From the Latin *casa* 'home' and *nova* 'new.' Also spelled Casinova and Cazenovia.

Cedar Springs
City
ZIP: 49319 **Lat:** 43-13-17 N **Long:** 85-33-11 W
Pop: 2,600 (1990); 2,615 (1980) **Pop Density:** 1529.4
Land: 1.7 sq. mi.; **Water:** 0.0 sq. mi.

Comstock Park
CDP
ZIP: 49321 **Lat:** 43-02-41 N **Long:** 85-40-20 W
Pop: 6,530 (1990); 4,515 (1980) **Pop Density:** 2040.6
Land: 3.2 sq. mi.; **Water:** 0.0 sq. mi.

Courtland
Township
Lat: 43-09-57 N **Long:** 85-29-44 W
Pop: 3,950 (1990); 3,272 (1980) **Pop Density:** 111.3
Land: 35.5 sq. mi.; **Water:** 0.5 sq. mi.

Cutlerville
CDP
ZIP: 49508 **Lat:** 42-50-29 N **Long:** 85-39-41 W
Pop: 11,228 (1990); 3,091 (1980) **Pop Density:** 3208.0
Land: 3.5 sq. mi.; **Water:** 0.0 sq. mi.

East Grand Rapids
City
ZIP: 49506 **Lat:** 42-56-47 N **Long:** 85-36-26 W
Pop: 10,807 (1990); 10,914 (1980) **Pop Density:** 3726.6
Land: 2.9 sq. mi.; **Water:** 0.5 sq. mi. **Elev:** 756 ft.
In southwestern MI east of Grand Rapids. Incorporated as a village 1891; as a city 1926.
Name origin: For its location.

Forest Hills
CDP
Lat: 42-57-34 N **Long:** 85-29-22 W
Pop: 16,690 (1990) **Pop Density:** 337.9
Land: 49.4 sq. mi.; **Water:** 1.4 sq. mi.

Gaines
Township
ZIP: 49508 **Lat:** 42-48-16 N **Long:** 85-36-17 W
Pop: 14,533 (1990); 10,364 (1980) **Pop Density:** 404.8
Land: 35.9 sq. mi.; **Water:** 0.0 sq. mi.

Grand Rapids
City
ZIP: 49501 **Lat:** 42-57-40 N **Long:** 85-39-20 W
Pop: 189,126 (1990); 181,843 (1980) **Pop Density:** 4269.2
Land: 44.3 sq. mi.; **Water:** 0.7 sq. mi.
In southwestern MI, 50 mi. north of Kalamazoo. Second largest city, founded 1825, settled 1826, incorporated 1850. Nicknamed "the Rapids." Diverse manufacturing city: office and home furniture, automobile parts, machinery, aircraft equipment. Site of Gerald R. Ford Museum. Not coextensive with the township of the same name.
Name origin: For the big rapids of the Grand River.

*Grand Rapids
Township
ZIP: 49505 **Lat:** 42-59-10 N **Long:** 85-34-55 W
Pop: 10,760 (1990); 9,294 (1980) **Pop Density:** 681.0
Land: 15.8 sq. mi.; **Water:** 0.1 sq. mi.

MICHIGAN, Kent County

Grandville — City
ZIP: 49418 Lat: 42-54-13 N Long: 85-45-22 W
Pop: 15,624 (1990); 12,412 (1980) Pop Density: 2083.2
Land: 7.5 sq. mi.; Water: 0.2 sq. mi. Elev: 604 ft.
In southwestern MI, 5 mi. south of Grand Rapids. Established 1933.
Name origin: For the Grand River, which traverses the county.

Grattan — Township
Lat: 43-04-13 N Long: 85-22-01 W
Pop: 2,876 (1990); 2,575 (1980) Pop Density: 82.2
Land: 35.0 sq. mi.; Water: 1.9 sq. mi.

Kent City — Village
ZIP: 49330 Lat: 43-13-08 N Long: 85-45-07 W
Pop: 899 (1990); 860 (1980) Pop Density: 998.9
Land: 0.9 sq. mi.; Water: 0.0 sq. mi. Elev: 800 ft.
Name origin: For James Kent (1763–1847), Chief Justice of the NY supreme court (1804–14).

Kentwood — City
ZIP: 49508 Lat: 42-52-56 N Long: 85-35-31 W
Pop: 37,826 (1990); 30,438 (1980) Pop Density: 1801.2
Land: 21.0 sq. mi.; Water: 0.0 sq. mi. Elev: 689 ft.
In southwestern MI, 10 mi. west of Grand Rapids. Established 1967.
Name origin: For James Kent (1763–1847), Chief Justice of the NY supreme court (1804–14).

Lowell — City
ZIP: 49331 Lat: 42-55-59 N Long: 85-20-44 W
Pop: 3,983 (1990); 3,707 (1980) Pop Density: 1422.5
Land: 2.8 sq. mi.; Water: 0.2 sq. mi.
Incorporated 1863.
Name origin: For Lowell, MA.

*Lowell — Township
ZIP: 49331 Lat: 42-53-41 N Long: 85-22-25 W
Pop: 4,774 (1990); 3,972 (1980) Pop Density: 146.4
Land: 32.6 sq. mi.; Water: 0.7 sq. mi.

Nelson — Township
Lat: 43-15-24 N Long: 85-29-10 W
Pop: 3,406 (1990); 2,641 (1980) Pop Density: 94.3
Land: 36.1 sq. mi.; Water: 0.2 sq. mi.

Northview — City
ZIP: 49505 Lat: 43-02-44 N Long: 85-36-02 W
Pop: 13,712 (1990); 11,662 (1980) Pop Density: 1318.5
Land: 10.4 sq. mi.; Water: 0.6 sq. mi.

Oakfield — Township
Lat: 43-09-37 N Long: 85-22-19 W
Pop: 3,842 (1990); 2,983 (1980) Pop Density: 111.0
Land: 34.6 sq. mi.; Water: 1.8 sq. mi.

Plainfield — Township
ZIP: 49321 Lat: 43-04-27 N Long: 85-36-35 W
Pop: 24,946 (1990); 20,611 (1980) Pop Density: 710.7
Land: 35.1 sq. mi.; Water: 1.4 sq. mi.
In southwestern MI, north of Grand Rapids. Established 1838.
Name origin: For its descriptive connotations.

Rockford — City
ZIP: 49341 Lat: 43-07-34 N Long: 85-33-23 W
Pop: 3,750 (1990); 3,324 (1980) Pop Density: 1293.1
Land: 2.9 sq. mi.; Water: 0.0 sq. mi. Elev: 693 ft.
Settled by Smith Lapham in 1843.
Name origin: Named in 1865 for a crossing over the rocky bed of the Grand River. Previously called Laphamville.

Sand Lake — Village
ZIP: 49343 Lat: 43-17-27 N Long: 85-31-05 W
Pop: 456 (1990); 388 (1980) Pop Density: 651.4
Land: 0.7 sq. mi.; Water: 0.0 sq. mi.
Name origin: For its descriptive connotations.

Solon — Township
Lat: 43-14-50 N Long: 85-36-31 W
Pop: 3,648 (1990); 2,809 (1980) Pop Density: 101.6
Land: 35.9 sq. mi.; Water: 0.5 sq. mi.

Sparta — Village
ZIP: 49345 Lat: 43-09-28 N Long: 85-42-33 W
Pop: 3,968 (1990); 3,373 (1980) Pop Density: 2088.4
Land: 1.9 sq. mi.; Water: 0.0 sq. mi. Elev: 753 ft.
Founded 1848. Not coextensive with the town of the same name.
Name origin: For the ancient Greek city.

*Sparta — Township
ZIP: 49345 Lat: 43-09-41 N Long: 85-43-39 W
Pop: 8,447 (1990); 6,934 (1980) Pop Density: 231.4
Land: 36.5 sq. mi.; Water: 0.0 sq. mi.

Spencer — Township
Lat: 43-15-11 N Long: 85-22-37 W
Pop: 3,184 (1990); 2,385 (1980) Pop Density: 90.7
Land: 35.1 sq. mi.; Water: 1.6 sq. mi.

Tyrone — Township
Lat: 43-15-05 N Long: 85-43-36 W
Pop: 3,757 (1990); 3,220 (1980) Pop Density: 103.2
Land: 36.4 sq. mi.; Water: 0.1 sq. mi.

Vergennes — Township
Lat: 42-59-14 N Long: 85-22-04 W
Pop: 2,492 (1990); 1,819 (1980) Pop Density: 71.6
Land: 34.8 sq. mi.; Water: 0.7 sq. mi.

Walker — City
ZIP: 49504 Lat: 42-59-04 N Long: 85-44-51 W
Pop: 17,279 (1990); 15,088 (1980) Pop Density: 685.7
Land: 25.2 sq. mi.; Water: 0.3 sq. mi. Elev: 742 ft.
Walker Township organized in 1837; established as a city in 1962.
Name origin: Settled by Canadians and named for an early settler.

Wyoming — City
ZIP: 49509 Lat: 42-53-32 N Long: 85-42-09 W
Pop: 63,891 (1990); 59,616 (1980) Pop Density: 2629.3
Land: 24.3 sq. mi.; Water: 0.1 sq. mi. Elev: 646 ft.
In southwestern MI, a residential and commercial suburb directly south of Grand Rapids. Incorporated 1958.
Name origin: From the Delaware Indian term *maughwauwame* meaning 'large meadows' (referring to a valley in PA).

Keweenaw County
County Seat: Eagle River (ZIP: 49924)

Pop: 1,701 (1990); 1,963 (1980)   **Pop Density:** 3.1
Land: 541.2 sq. mi.; **Water:** 5519.3 sq. mi.   **Area Code:** 906
On northernmost tip of the Upper Peninsula of MI on Lake Superior; organized Mar 11, 1861 from Houghton County.
Name origin: From Ojibway (or Potawatomi), probably 'to cross a point,' or 'portage'; variant of Kewaunee.

Ahmeek   Village
ZIP: 49901   **Lat:** 47-17-52 N   **Long:** 88-23-49 W
Pop: 148 (1990); 210 (1980)   **Pop Density:** 1480.0
Land: 0.1 sq. mi.; **Water:** 0.0 sq. mi.
Name origin: From the Chippewa term for 'beaver,' an animal abundant here.

Alloue   Township
Lat: 47-19-46 N   **Long:** 88-21-59 W
Pop: 1,422 (1990); 1,508 (1980)   **Pop Density:** 26.0
Land: 54.7 sq. mi.; **Water:** 0.0 sq. mi.

Eagle Harbor   City
ZIP: 49950
Pop: 70 (1990)

Eagle Harbor   Township
Lat: 47-56-15 N   **Long:** 88-55-58 W
Pop: 82 (1990); 113 (1980)   **Pop Density:** 0.5
Land: 180.7 sq. mi.; **Water:** 362.4 sq. mi.

Eagle River   City
ZIP: 49924
Pop: 50 (1990)

Grant   Township
Lat: 47-23-48 N   **Long:** 87-52-31 W
Pop: 104 (1990); 118 (1980)   **Pop Density:** 0.9
Land: 119.3 sq. mi.; **Water:** 83.4 sq. mi.

Houghton   Township
Lat: 48-06-37 N   **Long:** 88-32-14 W
Pop: 54 (1990); 161 (1980)   **Pop Density:** 0.4
Land: 121.4 sq. mi.; **Water:** 396.3 sq. mi.

Sherman   Township
Lat: 47-15-53 N   **Long:** 88-13-00 W
Pop: 39 (1990); 63 (1980)   **Pop Density:** 0.6
Land: 65.1 sq. mi.; **Water:** 4.2 sq. mi.

Lake County
County Seat: Baldwin (ZIP: 49304)

Pop: 8,583 (1990); 7,711 (1980)   **Pop Density:** 15.1
Land: 567.6 sq. mi.; **Water:** 7.1 sq. mi.   **Area Code:** 616
In west-central MI, north of Grand Rapids; established as Aishcum County Apr 1, 1840; name changed Mar 8, 1843.
Name origin: Possibly for Lake Michigan.

Baldwin   Village
ZIP: 49304   **Lat:** 43-53-51 N   **Long:** 85-51-08 W
Pop: 821 (1990); 674 (1980)   **Pop Density:** 684.2
Land: 1.2 sq. mi.; **Water:** 0.0 sq. mi.   **Elev:** 838 ft.
Established 1870.
Name origin: For Henry Baldwin, governor of MI in 1872.

Chase   Township
ZIP: 49623   **Lat:** 43-51-55 N   **Long:** 85-37-31 W
Pop: 999 (1990); 858 (1980)   **Pop Density:** 28.1
Land: 35.5 sq. mi.; **Water:** 0.1 sq. mi.

Cherry Valley   Township
Lat: 43-56-10 N   **Long:** 85-44-49 W
Pop: 248 (1990); 272 (1980)   **Pop Density:** 7.0
Land: 35.6 sq. mi.; **Water:** 0.0 sq. mi.

Dover   Township
Lat: 44-07-08 N   **Long:** 85-37-25 W
Pop: 318 (1990); 293 (1980)   **Pop Density:** 8.6
Land: 36.8 sq. mi.; **Water:** 0.2 sq. mi.

Eden   Township
Lat: 44-07-15 N   **Long:** 85-51-30 W
Pop: 235 (1990); 174 (1980)   **Pop Density:** 6.5
Land: 36.4 sq. mi.; **Water:** 0.1 sq. mi.

Elk   Township
Lat: 44-07-10 N   **Long:** 85-58-50 W
Pop: 580 (1990); 538 (1980)   **Pop Density:** 16.3
Land: 35.6 sq. mi.; **Water:** 1.2 sq. mi.

Ellsworth   Township
Lat: 44-01-31 N   **Long:** 85-37-21 W
Pop: 622 (1990); 542 (1980)   **Pop Density:** 17.7
Land: 35.2 sq. mi.; **Water:** 0.2 sq. mi.

Lake   Township
Lat: 43-51-22 N   **Long:** 85-58-42 W
Pop: 700 (1990); 516 (1980)   **Pop Density:** 20.5
Land: 34.1 sq. mi.; **Water:** 1.9 sq. mi.

MICHIGAN, Lake County

Luther
Village
ZIP: 49656   Lat: 44-02-19 N   Long: 85-40-58 W
Pop: 343 (1990); 414 (1980)   Pop Density: 381.1
Land: 0.9 sq. mi.; Water: 0.0 sq. mi.
Name origin: For the lumber firm of Luther and Wilson. Previously called Wilson.

Newkirk
Township
Lat: 44-05-00 N   Long: 85-45-11 W
Pop: 586 (1990); 608 (1980)   Pop Density: 8.0
Land: 72.8 sq. mi.; Water: 0.1 sq. mi.

Peacock
Township
Lat: 44-01-43 N   Long: 85-51-45 W
Pop: 344 (1990); 278 (1980)   Pop Density: 9.9
Land: 34.8 sq. mi.; Water: 0.9 sq. mi.

Pinora
Township
Lat: 43-56-42 N   Long: 85-37-02 W
Pop: 414 (1990); 348 (1980)   Pop Density: 11.7
Land: 35.5 sq. mi.; Water: 0.0 sq. mi.

Pleasant Plains
Township
Lat: 43-51-27 N   Long: 85-51-37 W
Pop: 1,464 (1990); 1,401 (1980)   Pop Density: 42.2
Land: 34.7 sq. mi.; Water: 0.6 sq. mi.

Sauble
Township
Lat: 44-01-58 N   Long: 85-59-07 W
Pop: 297 (1990); 260 (1980)   Pop Density: 8.6
Land: 34.6 sq. mi.; Water: 0.7 sq. mi.

Sweetwater
Township
Lat: 43-57-02 N   Long: 85-58-38 W
Pop: 223 (1990); 206 (1980)   Pop Density: 6.2
Land: 35.7 sq. mi.; Water: 0.1 sq. mi.

Webber
Township
Lat: 43-56-35 N   Long: 85-51-31 W
Pop: 968 (1990); 865 (1980)   Pop Density: 27.7
Land: 34.9 sq. mi.; Water: 0.6 sq. mi.

Yates
Township
Lat: 43-51-15 N   Long: 85-44-50 W
Pop: 585 (1990); 552 (1980)   Pop Density: 16.5
Land: 35.4 sq. mi.; Water: 0.3 sq. mi.

Lapeer County
County Seat: Lapeer (ZIP: 48446)

Pop: 74,768 (1990); 70,038 (1980)   Pop Density: 114.3
Land: 654.3 sq. mi.; Water: 8.8 sq. mi.   Area Code: 313
In east-central MI, east of Flint; established Sep 10, 1822 (prior to statehood) from Oakland and Saint Clair counties.
Name origin: From the local spelling of French *la pierre* 'the stone' or 'flint'; probably a transliteration of an Indian name for the Flint River, for its rocky bed.

Almont
Village
ZIP: 48003   Lat: 42-55-16 N   Long: 83-02-40 W
Pop: 2,354 (1990); 1,857 (1980)   Pop Density: 1810.8
Land: 1.3 sq. mi.; Water: 0.0 sq. mi.
Incorporated 1855. Not coextensive with the town of the same name.
Name origin: For Mexican Gen. Juan N. Almonte (1804?–69), with a spelling variation.

*Almont
Township
ZIP: 48003   Lat: 42-56-04 N   Long: 83-02-41 W
Pop: 4,660 (1990); 4,124 (1980)   Pop Density: 125.9
Land: 37.0 sq. mi.; Water: 0.1 sq. mi.

Arcadia
Township
Lat: 43-06-28 N   Long: 83-09-57 W
Pop: 2,448 (1990); 2,347 (1980)   Pop Density: 69.3
Land: 35.3 sq. mi.; Water: 0.9 sq. mi.

Attica
Township
Lat: 43-01-29 N   Long: 83-09-39 W
Pop: 3,873 (1990); 3,642 (1980)   Pop Density: 108.2
Land: 35.8 sq. mi.; Water: 0.5 sq. mi.

Barnes Lake-Millers Lake
CDP
Lat: 43-10-41 N   Long: 83-18-37 W
Pop: 1,304 (1990); 1,172 (1980)   Pop Density: 420.6
Land: 3.1 sq. mi.; Water: 0.4 sq. mi.

Brown City
City
ZIP: 48416   Lat: 43-12-50 N   Long: 83-00-00 W
Pop: 9 (1990); 5 (1980)   Pop Density: 450.0
Land: 0.02 sq. mi.; Water: 0.0 sq. mi.   Elev: 813 ft.
Founded 1879. Part of the town is also in Sanilac County.
Name origin: For the founding Brown brothers.

Burlington
Township
Lat: 43-16-41 N   Long: 83-10-51 W
Pop: 1,495 (1990); 1,562 (1980)   Pop Density: 42.0
Land: 35.6 sq. mi.; Water: 0.0 sq. mi.

Burnside
Township
Lat: 43-13-14 N   Long: 83-03-38 W
Pop: 1,753 (1990); 1,772 (1980)   Pop Density: 32.4
Land: 54.1 sq. mi.; Water: 0.0 sq. mi.

Clifford
Village
ZIP: 48727   Lat: 43-18-51 N   Long: 83-10-43 W
Pop: 354 (1990); 406 (1980)   Pop Density: 236.0
Land: 1.5 sq. mi.; Water: 0.0 sq. mi.
Founded 1862.
Name origin: For Clifford Lyman, the founder's son.

MICHIGAN, Lapeer County

Columbiaville
Village
ZIP: 48421 Lat: 43-09-28 N Long: 83-24-28 W
Pop: 934 (1990); 953 (1980) Pop Density: 1037.8
Land: 0.9 sq. mi.; Water: 0.3 sq. mi. Elev: 780 ft.
Name origin: For Columbia County, NY, an early settler's hometown.

Deerfield
Township
Lat: 43-11-12 N Long: 83-17-36 W
Pop: 4,903 (1990); 4,672 (1980) Pop Density: 136.6
Land: 35.9 sq. mi.; Water: 0.5 sq. mi.

Dryden
Village
ZIP: 48428 Lat: 42-56-43 N Long: 83-07-28 W
Pop: 628 (1990); 650 (1980) Pop Density: 628.0
Land: 1.0 sq. mi.; Water: 0.0 sq. mi. Elev: 919 ft.
Not coextensive with the town of the same name.
Name origin: For English poet John Dryden (1631–1700).

*Dryden
Township
ZIP: 48428 Lat: 42-55-52 N Long: 83-09-59 W
Pop: 3,399 (1990); 2,977 (1980) Pop Density: 94.7
Land: 35.9 sq. mi.; Water: 0.3 sq. mi.

Elba
Township
ZIP: 48446 Lat: 43-01-02 N Long: 83-23-43 W
Pop: 4,536 (1990); 4,604 (1980) Pop Density: 138.3
Land: 32.8 sq. mi.; Water: 1.2 sq. mi.

Goodland
Township
ZIP: 48444 Lat: 43-06-47 N Long: 83-03-03 W
Pop: 1,476 (1990); 1,534 (1980) Pop Density: 41.5
Land: 35.6 sq. mi.; Water: 0.0 sq. mi.

Hadley
Township
Lat: 42-55-32 N Long: 83-24-09 W
Pop: 3,830 (1990); 3,331 (1980) Pop Density: 108.5
Land: 35.3 sq. mi.; Water: 0.8 sq. mi.

Imlay
Township
ZIP: 48444 Lat: 43-01-28 N Long: 83-02-42 W
Pop: 2,143 (1990); 2,238 (1980) Pop Density: 63.8
Land: 33.6 sq. mi.; Water: 0.1 sq. mi.

Imlay City
City
ZIP: 48444 Lat: 43-00-58 N Long: 83-04-40 W
Pop: 2,921 (1990); 2,495 (1980) Pop Density: 1327.7
Land: 2.2 sq. mi.; Water: 0.0 sq. mi. Elev: 830 ft.
Organized 1850.
Name origin: For CT speculator William Imlay, who bought acreage here in 1836.

Lapeer
City
ZIP: 48446 Lat: 43-02-49 N Long: 83-19-29 W
Pop: 7,759 (1990); 6,198 (1980) Pop Density: 1410.7
Land: 5.5 sq. mi.; Water: 0.0 sq. mi.
Settled Nov 11, 1831, by Alvin N. Hart and his family.
Name origin: An anglicized version of the French name *La Pierre* 'the stone.'

*Lapeer
Township
ZIP: 48446 Lat: 43-00-51 N Long: 83-16-15 W
Pop: 4,519 (1990); 4,261 (1980) Pop Density: 141.2
Land: 32.0 sq. mi.; Water: 0.3 sq. mi.

Marathon
Township
Lat: 43-11-06 N Long: 83-24-39 W
Pop: 4,286 (1990); 4,336 (1980) Pop Density: 128.3
Land: 33.4 sq. mi.; Water: 1.0 sq. mi.

Mayfield
Township
ZIP: 48446 Lat: 43-06-17 N Long: 83-17-19 W
Pop: 7,133 (1990); 7,098 (1980) Pop Density: 205.0
Land: 34.8 sq. mi.; Water: 0.3 sq. mi.

Metamora
Village
ZIP: 48455 Lat: 42-56-28 N Long: 83-17-26 W
Pop: 447 (1990); 552 (1980) Pop Density: 638.6
Land: 0.7 sq. mi.; Water: 0.0 sq. mi.
Settled 1850. Not coextensive with the town of the same name.
Name origin: From an Indian term meaning 'hills.'

*Metamora
Township
ZIP: 48455 Lat: 42-55-36 N Long: 83-16-22 W
Pop: 3,544 (1990); 3,220 (1980) Pop Density: 101.8
Land: 34.8 sq. mi.; Water: 0.5 sq. mi.

North Branch
Village
ZIP: 48461 Lat: 43-13-47 N Long: 83-11-30 W
Pop: 1,023 (1990); 896 (1980) Pop Density: 1136.7
Land: 0.9 sq. mi.; Water: 0.0 sq. mi.
Founded 1856. Not coextensive with the town of the same name.
Name origin: For its location on the north branch of the Flint River.

*North Branch
Township
ZIP: 48461 Lat: 43-11-31 N Long: 83-10-47 W
Pop: 3,006 (1990); 2,721 (1980) Pop Density: 83.3
Land: 36.1 sq. mi.; Water: 0.2 sq. mi.

Oregon
Township
ZIP: 48446 Lat: 43-05-45 N Long: 83-24-10 W
Pop: 5,913 (1990); 5,652 (1980) Pop Density: 178.1
Land: 33.2 sq. mi.; Water: 2.1 sq. mi.

Otter Lake
Village
ZIP: 48464 Lat: 43-12-45 N Long: 83-27-20 W
Pop: 419 (1990); 442 (1980) Pop Density: 1396.7
Land: 0.3 sq. mi.; Water: 0.1 sq. mi.
Part of the town is also in Genesee County.
Name origin: For the nearby lake, which once had an abundant otter population.

Rich
Township
Lat: 43-16-45 N Long: 83-17-47 W
Pop: 1,162 (1990); 1,249 (1980) Pop Density: 33.0
Land: 35.2 sq. mi.; Water: 0.1 sq. mi.

Leelanau County
County Seat: Leland (ZIP: 49654)

Pop: 16,527 (1990); 14,007 (1980)　　**Pop Density:** 47.4
Land: 348.5 sq. mi.; **Water:** 2184.9 sq. mi.　　**Area Code:** 616
On the northwest coast of MI, bordered on west by Lake Michigan; established Apr 1, 1840.

Name origin: For an Indian maid, supposedly, whose name means 'delight of life.' Named at the suggestion of Henry Rowe Schoolcraft (1793–1864), author, explorer, MI legislator, and superintendent of Indian Affairs for MI (1836–41).

Bingham
Township
Lat: 44-54-15 N **Long:** 85-38-36 W
Pop: 2,051 (1990); 1,546 (1980)　**Pop Density:** 86.9
Land: 23.6 sq. mi.; **Water:** 15.7 sq. mi.

Centerville
Township
Lat: 44-54-28 N **Long:** 85-45-23 W
Pop: 836 (1990); 709 (1980)　**Pop Density:** 30.2
Land: 27.7 sq. mi.; **Water:** 2.7 sq. mi.

Cleveland
Township
Lat: 44-56-54 N **Long:** 85-54-00 W
Pop: 783 (1990); 654 (1980)　**Pop Density:** 25.3
Land: 31.0 sq. mi.; **Water:** 39.7 sq. mi.

Elmwood
Township
Lat: 44-49-13 N **Long:** 85-39-44 W
Pop: 3,427 (1990); 3,004 (1980)　**Pop Density:** 169.7
Land: 20.2 sq. mi.; **Water:** 10.8 sq. mi.

Empire
Village
ZIP: 49630　**Lat:** 44-48-47 N **Long:** 86-03-32 W
Pop: 355 (1990); 340 (1980)　**Pop Density:** 394.4
Land: 0.9 sq. mi.; **Water:** 0.1 sq. mi.　**Elev:** 619 ft.
Not coextensive with the town of the same name.

Name origin: For the schooner *Empire*, which became ice-bound here in 1863.

*Empire
Township
ZIP: 49630　**Lat:** 44-49-02 N **Long:** 86-00-31 W
Pop: 858 (1990); 797 (1980)　**Pop Density:** 24.3
Land: 35.3 sq. mi.; **Water:** 7.6 sq. mi.

Glen Arbor
Township
ZIP: 49636　**Lat:** 44-56-15 N **Long:** 86-03-44 W
Pop: 644 (1990); 578 (1980)　**Pop Density:** 22.5
Land: 28.6 sq. mi.; **Water:** 59.0 sq. mi.

Greilickville
CDP
Lat: 44-47-56 N **Long:** 85-38-44 W
Pop: 1,165 (1990)　**Pop Density:** 388.3
Land: 3.0 sq. mi.; **Water:** 2.4 sq. mi.

Kasson
Township
Lat: 44-49-44 N **Long:** 85-52-38 W
Pop: 1,135 (1990); 952 (1980)　**Pop Density:** 31.6
Land: 35.9 sq. mi.; **Water:** 0.3 sq. mi.

Leelanau
Township
Lat: 45-17-30 N **Long:** 85-47-43 W
Pop: 1,694 (1990); 1,560 (1980)　**Pop Density:** 34.4
Land: 49.2 sq. mi.; **Water:** 178.4 sq. mi.

Leland
Township
ZIP: 49654　**Lat:** 45-03-22 N **Long:** 85-52-03 W
Pop: 1,642 (1990); 1,446 (1980)　**Pop Density:** 36.0
Land: 45.6 sq. mi.; **Water:** 100.9 sq. mi.

Northport
Village
ZIP: 49670　**Lat:** 45-07-50 N **Long:** 85-37-00 W
Pop: 605 (1990); 611 (1980)　**Pop Density:** 355.9
Land: 1.7 sq. mi.; **Water:** 0.0 sq. mi.

Solon
Township
Lat: 44-48-42 N **Long:** 85-45-53 W
Pop: 1,268 (1990); 987 (1980)　**Pop Density:** 47.7
Land: 26.6 sq. mi.; **Water:** 3.1 sq. mi.

Suttons Bay
Village
ZIP: 49682　**Lat:** 44-58-44 N **Long:** 85-39-05 W
Pop: 561 (1990); 504 (1980)　**Pop Density:** 561.0
Land: 1.0 sq. mi.; **Water:** 0.0 sq. mi.
Not coextensive with the town of the same name.

Name origin: For Harry Sutton, on whose land it was created, and for its location on Grand Traverse Bay.

*Suttons Bay
Township
ZIP: 49682　**Lat:** 45-00-02 N **Long:** 85-37-58 W
Pop: 2,150 (1990); 1,774 (1980)　**Pop Density:** 87.4
Land: 24.6 sq. mi.; **Water:** 17.3 sq. mi.
Part of the town is also in Grand Traverse County.

Traverse City
City
Lat: 44-46-39 N **Long:** 85-38-52 W
Pop: 39 (1990)　**Pop Density:** 195.0
Land: 0.2 sq. mi.; **Water:** 0.0 sq. mi.

In northwestern MI at the southern end of the West Arm of Lake Michigan's Grand Traverse Bay. Established 1847. Part of the town is also in Grand Traverse County.

Name origin: From French *lac travers*, a translation of the Siouxan term *mdehdakinyan* meaning 'lake lying crosswise.'

Lenawee County
County Seat: Adrian (ZIP: 49221)

Pop: 91,476 (1990); 89,948 (1980) **Pop Density:** 121.9
Land: 750.6 sq. mi.; **Water:** 10.8 sq. mi. **Area Code:** 517
On the southern border of MI, southwest of Ann Arbor; established Sep 10, 1822 (prior to statehood) from Indian lands.
Name origin: Origin uncertain; perhaps from an Indian word meaning 'man.'

Addison — Village
ZIP: 49220 **Lat:** 41-59-09 N **Long:** 84-20-56 W
Pop: 632 (1990); 655 (1980) **Pop Density:** 632.0
Land: 1.0 sq. mi.; **Water:** 0.0 sq. mi.
Name origin: For banker Addison J. Comstock. Previously called Nanetall.

Adrian — City
ZIP: 49221 **Lat:** 41-53-53 N **Long:** 84-02-36 W
Pop: 22,097 (1990); 21,276 (1980) **Pop Density:** 3202.5
Land: 6.9 sq. mi.; **Water:** 0.0 sq. mi.
In southeastern MI, 25 mi. southwest of Ann Arbor. Settled 1825; incorporated 1853.
Name origin: Named by the wife of an early settler, for the Roman emperor Hadrian (Publius Aelius Hadrianus, 76–138); spelling changed when incorporated.

*Adrian — Township
ZIP: 49221 **Lat:** 41-56-56 N **Long:** 84-04-29 W
Pop: 4,336 (1990); 4,522 (1980) **Pop Density:** 125.0
Land: 34.7 sq. mi.; **Water:** 0.1 sq. mi.

Blissfield — Village
ZIP: 49228 **Lat:** 41-49-56 N **Long:** 83-51-51 W
Pop: 3,172 (1990); 3,107 (1980) **Pop Density:** 1669.5
Land: 1.9 sq. mi.; **Water:** 0.0 sq. mi. **Elev:** 694 ft.
Settled 1824. Not coextensive with the town of the same name.
Name origin: For Hervey Bliss, the first settler.

*Blissfield — Township
ZIP: 49228 **Lat:** 41-51-46 N **Long:** 83-51-10 W
Pop: 3,849 (1990); 3,744 (1980) **Pop Density:** 182.4
Land: 21.1 sq. mi.; **Water:** 0.0 sq. mi.

Britton — Village
ZIP: 49229 **Lat:** 41-59-10 N **Long:** 83-49-54 W
Pop: 694 (1990); 693 (1980) **Pop Density:** 771.1
Land: 0.9 sq. mi.; **Water:** 0.0 sq. mi.
Name origin: For storekeeper John Britton, who paid the Wabash Railroad $500 to have the station (and town) named for him.

Cambridge — Township
Lat: 42-01-39 N **Long:** 84-11-20 W
Pop: 4,429 (1990); 3,800 (1980) **Pop Density:** 138.4
Land: 32.0 sq. mi.; **Water:** 3.5 sq. mi.

Cement City — Village
Lat: 42-03-53 N **Long:** 84-19-39 W
Pop: 465 (1990); 501 (1980) **Pop Density:** 664.3
Land: 0.7 sq. mi.; **Water:** 0.0 sq. mi.
Part of the town is also in Jackson County.
Name origin: Named 1901 upon the arrival of a cement company.

Clayton — Village
ZIP: 49235 **Lat:** 41-51-51 N **Long:** 84-14-09 W
Pop: 384 (1990); 396 (1980) **Pop Density:** 548.6
Land: 0.7 sq. mi.; **Water:** 0.0 sq. mi. **Elev:** 891 ft.
Settled 1836.
Name origin: For the Rev. Clayton, a Presbyterian minister.

Clinton — Village
ZIP: 49236 **Lat:** 42-04-07 N **Long:** 83-58-20 W
Pop: 2,475 (1990); 2,342 (1980) **Pop Density:** 1903.8
Land: 1.3 sq. mi.; **Water:** 0.0 sq. mi.
Established 1831. Not coextensive with the town of the same name.
Name origin: For DeWitt Clinton (1769–1828), governor of NY and supporter of the Erie Canal.

*Clinton — Township
ZIP: 49236 **Lat:** 42-03-37 N **Long:** 83-56-49 W
Pop: 3,557 (1990); 3,413 (1980) **Pop Density:** 196.5
Land: 18.1 sq. mi.; **Water:** 0.1 sq. mi.

Deerfield — Village
ZIP: 49238 **Lat:** 41-53-24 N **Long:** 83-46-42 W
Pop: 922 (1990); 957 (1980) **Pop Density:** 1024.4
Land: 0.9 sq. mi.; **Water:** 0.0 sq. mi. **Elev:** 673 ft.
Settled 1826. Not coextensive with the town of the same name.
Name origin: For its descriptive connotations.

*Deerfield — Township
ZIP: 49238 **Lat:** 41-53-07 N **Long:** 83-48-03 W
Pop: 1,659 (1990); 1,729 (1980) **Pop Density:** 66.1
Land: 25.1 sq. mi.; **Water:** 0.0 sq. mi.

Dover — Township
Lat: 41-51-25 N **Long:** 84-10-36 W
Pop: 1,811 (1990); 1,933 (1980) **Pop Density:** 51.6
Land: 35.1 sq. mi.; **Water:** 0.1 sq. mi.

Fairfield — Township
Lat: 41-45-48 N **Long:** 84-04-06 W
Pop: 1,883 (1990); 1,986 (1980) **Pop Density:** 44.8
Land: 42.0 sq. mi.; **Water:** 0.0 sq. mi.

Franklin — Township
Lat: 42-01-53 N **Long:** 84-04-28 W
Pop: 2,473 (1990); 2,463 (1980) **Pop Density:** 64.2
Land: 38.5 sq. mi.; **Water:** 0.8 sq. mi.

Hudson — City
ZIP: 49247 **Lat:** 41-51-22 N **Long:** 84-20-44 W
Pop: 2,580 (1990); 2,545 (1980) **Pop Density:** 1228.6
Land: 2.1 sq. mi.; **Water:** 0.0 sq. mi. **Elev:** 918 ft.
First settler arrived 1833.
Name origin: For Dr. Daniel Hudson of Geneva, NY.

MICHIGAN, Lenawee County

*Hudson — Township
ZIP: 49247 Lat: 41-51-21 N Long: 84-18-04 W
Pop: 1,481 (1990); 1,550 (1980) Pop Density: 41.7
Land: 35.5 sq. mi.; Water: 1.1 sq. mi.

Macon — Township
Lat: 42-02-37 N Long: 83-49-48 W
Pop: 1,421 (1990); 1,480 (1980) Pop Density: 43.6
Land: 32.6 sq. mi.; Water: 0.0 sq. mi.

Madison Charter — Township
ZIP: 49221 Lat: 41-51-17 N Long: 84-04-04 W
Pop: 5,351 (1990); 5,035 (1980) Pop Density: 174.3
Land: 30.7 sq. mi.; Water: 0.2 sq. mi.

Manitou Beach-Devils Lake — CDP
Lat: 41-58-29 N Long: 84-16-47 W
Pop: 2,061 (1990); 1,633 (1980) Pop Density: 343.5
Land: 6.0 sq. mi.; Water: 2.7 sq. mi.

Medina — Township
Lat: 41-45-26 N Long: 84-17-25 W
Pop: 1,368 (1990); 1,455 (1980) Pop Density: 28.7
Land: 47.6 sq. mi.; Water: 0.1 sq. mi.

Morenci — City
ZIP: 49256 Lat: 41-43-17 N Long: 84-12-59 W
Pop: 2,342 (1990); 2,110 (1980) Pop Density: 1115.2
Land: 2.1 sq. mi.; Water: 0.0 sq. mi.
Settled 1835.

Ogden — Township
Lat: 41-46-20 N Long: 83-56-28 W
Pop: 1,146 (1990); 1,224 (1980) Pop Density: 27.3
Land: 42.0 sq. mi.; Water: 0.0 sq. mi.

Onsted — Village
ZIP: 49265 Lat: 42-00-27 N Long: 84-11-24 W
Pop: 801 (1990); 670 (1980) Pop Density: 801.0
Land: 1.0 sq. mi.; Water: 0.0 sq. mi. Elev: 989 ft.
Founded 1884 by William Onsted.
Name origin: For the founder's father.

Palmyra — Township
ZIP: 49268 Lat: 41-52-08 N Long: 83-56-19 W
Pop: 2,602 (1990); 2,476 (1980) Pop Density: 70.9
Land: 36.7 sq. mi.; Water: 0.0 sq. mi.

Raisin — Township
ZIP: 49221 Lat: 41-56-53 N Long: 83-56-38 W
Pop: 5,648 (1990); 5,499 (1980) Pop Density: 155.6
Land: 36.3 sq. mi.; Water: 0.2 sq. mi.

Ridgeway — Township
Lat: 41-57-54 N Long: 83-50-03 W
Pop: 1,572 (1990); 1,746 (1980) Pop Density: 54.8
Land: 28.7 sq. mi.; Water: 0.0 sq. mi.

Riga — Township
ZIP: 49276 Lat: 41-46-11 N Long: 83-49-24 W
Pop: 1,471 (1990); 1,671 (1980) Pop Density: 36.0
Land: 40.9 sq. mi.; Water: 0.0 sq. mi.

Rollin — Township
Lat: 41-56-16 N Long: 84-17-59 W
Pop: 3,323 (1990); 3,428 (1980) Pop Density: 98.0
Land: 33.9 sq. mi.; Water: 2.3 sq. mi.

Rome — Township
Lat: 41-56-36 N Long: 84-11-11 W
Pop: 1,632 (1990); 1,681 (1980) Pop Density: 45.5
Land: 35.9 sq. mi.; Water: 0.0 sq. mi.

Seneca — Township
Lat: 41-45-41 N Long: 84-10-04 W
Pop: 1,289 (1990); 1,377 (1980) Pop Density: 32.2
Land: 40.0 sq. mi.; Water: 0.1 sq. mi.

Tecumseh — City
ZIP: 49286 Lat: 42-00-21 N Long: 83-56-40 W
Pop: 7,462 (1990); 7,320 (1980) Pop Density: 1522.9
Land: 4.9 sq. mi.; Water: 0.2 sq. mi.
Founded 1824.
Name origin: For the famous Shawnee Indian chief (1768–1813).

*Tecumseh — Township
ZIP: 49286 Lat: 42-01-22 N Long: 83-57-03 W
Pop: 1,539 (1990); 1,480 (1980) Pop Density: 114.9
Land: 13.4 sq. mi.; Water: 0.1 sq. mi.

Woodstock — Township
Lat: 42-01-35 N Long: 84-18-19 W
Pop: 3,155 (1990); 3,005 (1980) Pop Density: 93.1
Land: 33.9 sq. mi.; Water: 1.8 sq. mi.

Livingston County
County Seat: Howell (ZIP: 48843)

Pop: 115,645 (1990); 100,289 (1980) Pop Density: 203.5
Land: 568.4 sq. mi.; Water: 17.1 sq. mi. Area Code: 517

In south-central MI, southwest of Flint; established Mar 21, 1833 (prior to statehood) from Shiawassee County.

Name origin: For Edward Livingston (1764–1836), NY legislator, LA legislator and U.S. senator (1829–31), and U.S. secretary of state (1831–33).

Brighton — City
ZIP: 48116 Lat: 42-31-48 N Long: 83-47-05 W
Pop: 5,686 (1990); 4,268 (1980) Pop Density: 1579.4
Land: 3.6 sq. mi.; Water: 0.1 sq. mi.
Founded 1832.
Name origin: For Brighton, NY, former home of early settlers.

*Brighton — Township
ZIP: 48116 Lat: 42-33-49 N Long: 83-44-11 W
Pop: 14,815 (1990); 11,222 (1980) Pop Density: 447.6
Land: 33.1 sq. mi.; Water: 1.4 sq. mi.

Cohoctah — Township
Lat: 42-43-47 N Long: 83-58-53 W
Pop: 2,693 (1990); 2,436 (1980) Pop Density: 70.7
Land: 38.1 sq. mi.; Water: 0.2 sq. mi.

MICHIGAN, Livingston County

Conway
Township
Lat: 42-44-06 N Long: 84-05-43 W
Pop: 1,818 (1990); 1,722 (1980) Pop Density: 48.1
Land: 37.8 sq. mi.; Water: 0.0 sq. mi.

Deerfield
Township
Lat: 42-44-12 N Long: 83-51-34 W
Pop: 3,000 (1990); 2,611 (1980) Pop Density: 82.4
Land: 36.4 sq. mi.; Water: 1.3 sq. mi.

Fowlerville
Village
ZIP: 48836 Lat: 42-39-36 N Long: 84-04-20 W
Pop: 2,648 (1990); 2,289 (1980) Pop Density: 1557.6
Land: 1.7 sq. mi.; Water: 0.0 sq. mi.
Settled 1836.
Name origin: For pioneer Ralph Fowler, first settler.

Genoa
Township
ZIP: 48116 Lat: 42-33-18 N Long: 83-51-30 W
Pop: 10,820 (1990); 9,261 (1980) Pop Density: 315.5
Land: 34.3 sq. mi.; Water: 2.1 sq. mi.
In southeastern MI. Established 1836.
Name origin: Probably for either Genoa, Italy, or Genoa, NY.

Green Oak
Township
ZIP: 48116 Lat: 42-28-12 N Long: 83-43-37 W
Pop: 11,604 (1990); 10,802 (1980) Pop Density: 334.4
Land: 34.7 sq. mi.; Water: 2.0 sq. mi.

Hamburg
Township
ZIP: 48169 Lat: 42-28-02 N Long: 83-50-53 W
Pop: 13,083 (1990); 11,318 (1980) Pop Density: 403.8
Land: 32.4 sq. mi.; Water: 3.6 sq. mi.
In southeastern MI, a northwestern suburb of Detroit.
Name origin: For Hamburg, Germany.

Handy
Township
ZIP: 48836 Lat: 42-38-40 N Long: 84-05-11 W
Pop: 5,488 (1990); 4,681 (1980) Pop Density: 159.1
Land: 34.5 sq. mi.; Water: 0.1 sq. mi.

Hartland
Township
ZIP: 48353 Lat: 42-39-15 N Long: 83-44-13 W
Pop: 6,860 (1990); 6,034 (1980) Pop Density: 188.5
Land: 36.4 sq. mi.; Water: 1.3 sq. mi.

Howell
City
ZIP: 48844 Lat: 42-36-33 N Long: 83-56-08 W
Pop: 8,184 (1990); 6,976 (1980) Pop Density: 2153.7
Land: 3.8 sq. mi.; Water: 0.2 sq. mi. Elev: 922 ft.
Settled 1834.
Name origin: For Thomas Howell, friend of one of the early settlers.

*Howell
Township
Lat: 42-38-36 N Long: 83-58-34 W
Pop: 4,298 (1990); 3,999 (1980) Pop Density: 133.9
Land: 32.1 sq. mi.; Water: 0.2 sq. mi.

Iosco
Township
Lat: 42-33-05 N Long: 84-04-45 W
Pop: 1,567 (1990); 1,436 (1980) Pop Density: 44.1
Land: 35.5 sq. mi.; Water: 0.1 sq. mi.

Marion
Township
Lat: 42-33-24 N Long: 83-58-25 W
Pop: 4,918 (1990); 4,754 (1980) Pop Density: 138.1
Land: 35.6 sq. mi.; Water: 0.8 sq. mi.

Oceola
Township
Lat: 42-38-51 N Long: 83-51-23 W
Pop: 4,825 (1990); 4,175 (1980) Pop Density: 132.9
Land: 36.3 sq. mi.; Water: 0.5 sq. mi.

Pinckney
Village
ZIP: 48169 Lat: 42-27-16 N Long: 83-56-43 W
Pop: 1,603 (1990); 1,390 (1980) Pop Density: 1068.7
Land: 1.5 sq. mi.; Water: 0.0 sq. mi.
Begun 1836 by William Kirkland.
Name origin: For Charles Pinckney Kirkland, the founder's brother.

Putnam
Township
ZIP: 48169 Lat: 42-27-47 N Long: 83-57-49 W
Pop: 6,183 (1990); 5,643 (1980) Pop Density: 179.7
Land: 34.4 sq. mi.; Water: 1.2 sq. mi.

Tyrone
Township
ZIP: 48430 Lat: 42-44-48 N Long: 83-44-37 W
Pop: 6,854 (1990); 6,077 (1980) Pop Density: 192.5
Land: 35.6 sq. mi.; Water: 1.1 sq. mi.

Unadilla
Township
ZIP: 48137 Lat: 42-28-04 N Long: 84-05-06 W
Pop: 2,949 (1990); 2,874 (1980) Pop Density: 86.7
Land: 34.0 sq. mi.; Water: 0.8 sq. mi.

Whitmore Lake
CDP
Lat: 42-26-26 N Long: 83-44-40 W
Pop: 1,694 (1990); 1,590 (1980) Pop Density: 1129.3
Land: 1.5 sq. mi.; Water: 0.4 sq. mi.
Part of the town is also in Washtenaw County.

Luce County
County Seat: Newberry (ZIP: 49868)

Pop: 5,763 (1990); 6,659 (1980) **Pop Density:** 6.4
Land: 903.1 sq. mi.; **Water:** 1008.8 sq. mi. **Area Code:** 906
On the northern coast of the Upper Peninsula of MI on Lake Superior; established Mar 1, 1887 from Chippewa County.
Name origin: For Cyrus Gray Luce (1824–1905), MI legislator, member of MI Constitutional Convention (1867), and governor (1887–96).

Columbus   Township
Lat: 46-24-54 N **Long:** 85-44-51 W
Pop: 218 (1990); 293 (1980) **Pop Density:** 1.5
Land: 140.8 sq. mi.; **Water:** 2.5 sq. mi.

Lakefield   Township
Lat: 46-17-17 N **Long:** 85-44-15 W
Pop: 869 (1990); 804 (1980) **Pop Density:** 13.7
Land: 63.4 sq. mi.; **Water:** 8.7 sq. mi.

McMillan   Township
ZIP: 49853 **Lat:** 46-31-43 N **Long:** 85-29-46 W
Pop: 2,961 (1990); 3,355 (1980) **Pop Density:** 5.0
Land: 592.0 sq. mi.; **Water:** 12.6 sq. mi.

Newberry   Village
ZIP: 49868 **Lat:** 46-21-11 N **Long:** 85-30-32 W
Pop: 1,873 (1990); 2,120 (1980) **Pop Density:** 1873.0
Land: 1.0 sq. mi.; **Water:** 0.0 sq. mi. **Elev:** 788 ft.
Name origin: For Detroit industrialist Truman Newberry. Previously called Grant Corner.

Pentland   Township
Lat: 46-17-01 N **Long:** 85-26-05 W
Pop: 1,715 (1990); 2,207 (1980) **Pop Density:** 16.0
Land: 106.9 sq. mi.; **Water:** 0.4 sq. mi.

Mackinac County
County Seat: St. Ignace (ZIP: 49781)

Pop: 10,674 (1990); 10,178 (1980) **Pop Density:** 10.4
Land: 1021.6 sq. mi.; **Water:** 1079.0 sq. mi. **Area Code:** 906
On the southeast coast of the Upper Peninsula of MI bordering Lakes Michigan and Huron; original county; established as Michilimackinac County Oct 26, 1818 (prior to statehood); name changed Mar 9, 1843.
Name origin: For Mackinac Island, from Ojibway *Michilimackinak* 'island of the large turtle.'

Bois Blanc   Township
Lat: 45-44-58 N **Long:** 84-27-54 W
Pop: 59 (1990); 62 (1980) **Pop Density:** 1.7
Land: 35.3 sq. mi.; **Water:** 13.7 sq. mi.

Brevort   Township
Lat: 46-03-44 N **Long:** 84-50-52 W
Pop: 484 (1990); 451 (1980) **Pop Density:** 5.2
Land: 92.5 sq. mi.; **Water:** 6.4 sq. mi.

Clark   Township
Lat: 46-00-54 N **Long:** 84-21-02 W
Pop: 2,012 (1990); 1,879 (1980) **Pop Density:** 25.4
Land: 79.1 sq. mi.; **Water:** 22.5 sq. mi.

Garfield   Township
Lat: 46-09-45 N **Long:** 85-29-43 W
Pop: 1,156 (1990); 1,206 (1980) **Pop Density:** 8.6
Land: 134.1 sq. mi.; **Water:** 3.2 sq. mi.

Hendricks   Township
Lat: 46-09-05 N **Long:** 85-10-34 W
Pop: 161 (1990); 166 (1980) **Pop Density:** 2.0
Land: 78.9 sq. mi.; **Water:** 2.2 sq. mi.

Hudson   Township
Lat: 46-09-31 N **Long:** 85-17-50 W
Pop: 197 (1990); 212 (1980) **Pop Density:** 2.9
Land: 68.7 sq. mi.; **Water:** 0.7 sq. mi.

Mackinac Island   City
Lat: 45-51-21 N **Long:** 84-37-18 W
Pop: 469 (1990); 479 (1980) **Pop Density:** 106.6
Land: 4.4 sq. mi.; **Water:** 1.2 sq. mi.
Settled by French 1780.
Name origin: A shortened version of the Ojibway place name *Michilimackinak* 'island of the large turtle.'

Marquette   Township
Lat: 46-02-08 N **Long:** 84-31-26 W
Pop: 550 (1990); 461 (1980) **Pop Density:** 5.7
Land: 97.2 sq. mi.; **Water:** 37.4 sq. mi.

Moran   Township
ZIP: 49760 **Lat:** 46-01-19 N **Long:** 84-57-40 W
Pop: 838 (1990); 823 (1980) **Pop Density:** 6.6
Land: 127.5 sq. mi.; **Water:** 6.9 sq. mi.

Newton   Township
Lat: 46-04-47 N **Long:** 85-44-19 W
Pop: 358 (1990); 354 (1980) **Pop Density:** 2.4
Land: 148.6 sq. mi.; **Water:** 6.3 sq. mi.

American Places Dictionary   MICHIGAN, Macomb County

Portage Township
Lat: 46-12-11 N **Long:** 85-44-10 W
Pop: 890 (1990); 747 (1980) **Pop Density:** 16.1
Land: 55.4 sq. mi.; **Water:** 16.8 sq. mi.

St. Ignace City
ZIP: 49781 **Lat:** 45-52-06 N **Long:** 84-43-32 W
Pop: 2,568 (1990); 2,632 (1980) **Pop Density:** 951.1
Land: 2.7 sq. mi.; **Water:** 0.0 sq. mi.
Name origin: For the St. Ignace mission founded here by French Jesuits in 1671.

*St. Ignace Township
Lat: 46-01-21 N **Long:** 84-41-50 W
Pop: 932 (1990); 706 (1980) **Pop Density:** 9.6
Land: 97.1 sq. mi.; **Water:** 46.7 sq. mi.

Macomb County
County Seat: Mount Clemens (ZIP: 48043)

Pop: 717,400 (1990); 694,600 (1980)   **Pop Density:** 1493.3
Land: 480.4 sq. mi.; **Water:** 89.4 sq. mi.   **Area Code:** 313
On the southeast coast of MI, north of Detroit; original county; established Jan 15, 1818 (prior to statehood).
Name origin: For Alexander Macomb (1782–1841), officer in the War of 1812 and commanding general of the U.S. army (1835–41).

Armada Village
ZIP: 48005 **Lat:** 42-50-27 N **Long:** 82-53-00 W
Pop: 1,548 (1990); 1,392 (1980) **Pop Density:** 2211.4
Land: 0.7 sq. mi.; **Water:** 0.0 sq. mi.
Incorporated 1867. Not coextensive with the town of the same name.
Name origin: Named by early settlers for the township.

*Armada Township
ZIP: 48005 **Lat:** 42-51-24 N **Long:** 82-55-27 W
Pop: 4,491 (1990); 3,887 (1980) **Pop Density:** 123.0
Land: 36.5 sq. mi.; **Water:** 0.0 sq. mi.

Bruce Township
ZIP: 48065 **Lat:** 42-51-05 N **Long:** 83-01-47 W
Pop: 6,012 (1990); 5,756 (1980) **Pop Density:** 165.2
Land: 36.4 sq. mi.; **Water:** 0.2 sq. mi.

Center Line City
ZIP: 48015 **Lat:** 42-28-52 N **Long:** 83-01-30 W
Pop: 9,026 (1990); 9,293 (1980) **Pop Density:** 5309.4
Land: 1.7 sq. mi.; **Water:** 0.0 sq. mi.
Name origin: Named by the French for its location on the middle Indian trail from the fort at Detroit to the northern trading posts.

Chesterfield Township
ZIP: 48047 **Lat:** 42-40-48 N **Long:** 82-48-22 W
Pop: 25,905 (1990); 18,276 (1980) **Pop Density:** 928.5
Land: 27.9 sq. mi.; **Water:** 2.8 sq. mi.

Clinton Township
ZIP: 48043 **Lat:** 42-35-12 N **Long:** 82-55-12 W
Pop: 85,866 (1990); 72,400 (1980) **Pop Density:** 3044.9
Land: 28.2 sq. mi.; **Water:** 0.0 sq. mi.

Eastpointe City
ZIP: 48021 **Lat:** 42-27-57 N **Long:** 82-56-47 W
Pop: 35,283 (1990); 38,280 (1980) **Pop Density:** 6918.2
Land: 5.1 sq. mi.; **Water:** 0.0 sq. mi.
In southeastern MI in the northeastern Detroit metropolitan area. Settled 1827; incorporated as city 1929. Changed name from East Detroit July 1992.

Fraser City
ZIP: 48026 **Lat:** 42-32-23 N **Long:** 82-56-54 W
Pop: 13,899 (1990); 14,560 (1980) **Pop Density:** 3309.3
Land: 4.2 sq. mi.; **Water:** 0.0 sq. mi.
Settled in 1850. Incorporated as Frazer village 1895; as Fraser city 1957. In east-central MI, 15 mi. north of Detroit.
Name origin: For attorney and landowner Alex Fraser (or Frazer), who founded the village in 1857.

Grosse Pointe Shores Village
Lat: 42-27-32 N **Long:** 82-52-05 W
Pop: 105 (1990); 110 (1980) **Pop Density:** 525.0
Land: 0.2 sq. mi.; **Water:** 0.5 sq. mi. **Elev:** 586 ft.
Incorporated 1911. Part of the town is also in Wayne County.

Harrison Township
ZIP: 48045 **Lat:** 42-35-10 N **Long:** 82-49-12 W
Pop: 24,685 (1990); 23,464 (1980) **Pop Density:** 1750.7
Land: 14.1 sq. mi.; **Water:** 9.6 sq. mi.
In southeastern MI, northeast of Detroit.
Name origin: Possibly for William Henry Harrison (1773–1841), ninth U.S. president.

Lake Township
Lat: 42-27-32 N **Long:** 82-52-05 W
Pop: 105 (1990); 110 (1980) **Pop Density:** 525.0
Land: 0.2 sq. mi.; **Water:** 0.5 sq. mi.

Lenox Township
ZIP: 48062 **Lat:** 42-45-42 N **Long:** 82-47-57 W
Pop: 5,400 (1990); 4,899 (1980) **Pop Density:** 139.2
Land: 38.8 sq. mi.; **Water:** 0.0 sq. mi.

Macomb Township
ZIP: 48044 **Lat:** 42-40-05 N **Long:** 82-54-36 W
Pop: 22,714 (1990); 14,230 (1980) **Pop Density:** 625.7
Land: 36.3 sq. mi.; **Water:** 0.0 sq. mi.
Name origin: For Alexander Macomb (1782–1841), officer in the War of 1812 and commanding general of the U.S. army (1835–41).

Memphis — City
ZIP: 48041 **Lat:** 42-53-33 N **Long:** 82-46-20 W
Pop: 896 (1990); 817 (1980) **Pop Density:** 1493.3
Land: 0.6 sq. mi.; **Water:** 0.0 sq. mi.

Part of the town is also in St. Clair County.

Name origin: For the ancient Egyptian city.

Mount Clemens — City
ZIP: 48046 **Lat:** 42-35-52 N **Long:** 82-52-54 W
Pop: 18,405 (1990); 18,991 (1980) **Pop Density:** 4382.1
Land: 4.2 sq. mi.; **Water:** 0.0 sq. mi. **Elev:** 614 ft.

In southeastern MI, 20 mi. northeast of Detroit. Settled 1818.

Name origin: For Christian Clemens (1768–1844), pioneer settler and founder. The *mount* was added for euphony.

New Baltimore — City
ZIP: 48047 **Lat:** 42-40-59 N **Long:** 82-44-17 W
Pop: 5,798 (1990); 5,439 (1980) **Pop Density:** 1260.4
Land: 4.6 sq. mi.; **Water:** 2.1 sq. mi.

First settlers arrived 1796; incorporated 1867.

New Haven — Village
ZIP: 48048 **Lat:** 42-43-57 N **Long:** 82-47-38 W
Pop: 2,331 (1990); 1,871 (1980) **Pop Density:** 971.2
Land: 2.4 sq. mi.; **Water:** 0.0 sq. mi.

Incorporated 1869.

Name origin: For New Haven, CT.

Ray — Township
Lat: 42-45-43 N **Long:** 82-55-13 W
Pop: 3,230 (1990); 3,121 (1980) **Pop Density:** 87.8
Land: 36.8 sq. mi.; **Water:** 0.0 sq. mi.

Richmond — City
ZIP: 48062 **Lat:** 42-48-32 N **Long:** 82-45-16 W
Pop: 4,141 (1990); 3,536 (1980) **Pop Density:** 1656.4
Land: 2.5 sq. mi.; **Water:** 0.0 sq. mi.

Founded 1830s.

Name origin: For Richmond, NY.

*Richmond — Township
Lat: 42-51-09 N **Long:** 82-47-51 W
Pop: 2,528 (1990); 2,453 (1980) **Pop Density:** 67.4
Land: 37.5 sq. mi.; **Water:** 0.0 sq. mi.

Romeo — Village
ZIP: 48065 **Lat:** 42-48-15 N **Long:** 83-00-19 W
Pop: 3,520 (1990); 3,509 (1980) **Pop Density:** 1760.0
Land: 2.0 sq. mi.; **Water:** 0.0 sq. mi.

Settled 1822 by pioneer Ashael Bailey.

Name origin: For the Shakespearean lover of Juliet.

Roseville — City
ZIP: 48066 **Lat:** 42-30-26 N **Long:** 82-56-11 W
Pop: 51,412 (1990); 54,311 (1980) **Pop Density:** 5246.1
Land: 9.8 sq. mi.; **Water:** 0.0 sq. mi.

In southeastern MI, a residential suburb 12 mi. northeast of Detroit. Established as unincorporated village in 1875, incorporated as a village in 1926; as a city in 1957.

Name origin: For William C. Rose, first postmaster.

St. Clair Shores — City
ZIP: 48080 **Lat:** 42-29-35 N **Long:** 82-53-28 W
Pop: 68,107 (1990); 76,210 (1980) **Pop Density:** 5922.3
Land: 11.5 sq. mi.; **Water:** 2.7 sq. mi. **Elev:** 585 ft.

In southeastern MI on Lake St. Clair, a residential suburb 15 mi. northeast of Detroit. Established as a township in 1837, as a village in 1925, as a city in 1951.

Name origin: For the lake, originally named by de La Salle (1643–87) for St. Clare but changed to honor Gen. Arthur St. Clair (1736–1818), first governor of the Northwest Territory (1787–1802).

Shelby — Township
ZIP: 48315 **Lat:** 42-40-14 N **Long:** 83-01-59 W
Pop: 48,655 (1990); 38,939 (1980) **Pop Density:** 1402.2
Land: 34.7 sq. mi.; **Water:** 0.5 sq. mi.

In southeastern MI, north of Detroit.

Sterling Heights — City
ZIP: 48311 **Lat:** 42-34-48 N **Long:** 83-01-49 W
Pop: 117,810 (1990); 108,999 (1980) **Pop Density:** 3218.9
Land: 36.6 sq. mi.; **Water:** 0.1 sq. mi.

In southeastern MI, 20 mi. north of Detroit. Established as Jefferson Township 1835; name changed to Sterling in 1838. Established as city in 1968.

Name origin: For pioneer Azariah Sterling.

Utica — City
ZIP: 48318 **Lat:** 42-37-42 N **Long:** 83-01-15 W
Pop: 5,081 (1990); 5,282 (1980) **Pop Density:** 2822.8
Land: 1.8 sq. mi.; **Water:** 0.0 sq. mi.

Platted 1829.

Name origin: For Utica, NY.

Warren — City
ZIP: 48090 **Lat:** 42-29-34 N **Long:** 83-01-41 W
Pop: 144,864 (1990); 161,134 (1980) **Pop Density:** 4223.4
Land: 34.3 sq. mi.; **Water:** 0.0 sq. mi.

In southeastern MI, 12 mi. north of Detroit. Settled 1835; incorporated as a village 1909, as a city 1957.

Name origin: Named in 1838 for Joseph Warren (1741–75), the Boston physician who sent Paul Revere (1735–1818) on his famous ride and who was killed at the Battle of Bunker Hill. Previously called Alba.

Washington — Township
ZIP: 48094 **Lat:** 42-45-18 N **Long:** 83-01-42 W
Pop: 13,087 (1990); 10,213 (1980) **Pop Density:** 363.5
Land: 36.0 sq. mi.; **Water:** 0.9 sq. mi.

In southeastern MI, north of Detroit.

Name origin: Probably for George Washington (1732–99), American patriot and first U.S. president.

> **Manistee County**
> **County Seat: Manistee (ZIP: 49660)**
>
> **Pop:** 21,265 (1990); 23,019 (1980) **Pop Density:** 39.1
> **Land:** 543.9 sq. mi.; **Water:** 737.0 sq. mi. **Area Code:** 616
>
> On the northwest coast of MI, bordered on west by Lake Michigan; established Apr 1, 1840.
>
> **Name origin:** For the Manistee River, which runs through it; from an Ojibway word possibly meaning 'sound of the winds,' 'lost river,' 'spirit of the woods,' 'crooked river,' or 'red river.'

Arcadia — Township
ZIP: 49613 **Lat:** 44-28-13 N **Long:** 86-12-48 W
Pop: 553 (1990); 641 (1980) **Pop Density:** 29.7
Land: 18.6 sq. mi.; **Water:** 0.3 sq. mi.

Bear Lake — Village
ZIP: 49614 **Lat:** 44-25-11 N **Long:** 86-08-44 W
Pop: 339 (1990); 388 (1980) **Pop Density:** 1130.0
Land: 0.3 sq. mi.; **Water:** 0.0 sq. mi.

Founded 1863. Not coextensive with the town of the same name.

Name origin: For nearby Bear Lake.

*Bear Lake — Township
ZIP: 49614 **Lat:** 44-22-40 N **Long:** 86-07-30 W
Pop: 1,419 (1990); 1,658 (1980) **Pop Density:** 40.9
Land: 34.7 sq. mi.; **Water:** 1.3 sq. mi.

Brown — Township
Lat: 44-17-32 N **Long:** 86-07-02 W
Pop: 588 (1990); 631 (1980) **Pop Density:** 16.5
Land: 35.7 sq. mi.; **Water:** 0.5 sq. mi.

Cleon — Township
Lat: 44-28-07 N **Long:** 85-52-35 W
Pop: 713 (1990); 764 (1980) **Pop Density:** 19.8
Land: 36.0 sq. mi.; **Water:** 0.1 sq. mi.

Copemish — Village
ZIP: 49625 **Lat:** 44-28-51 N **Long:** 85-55-26 W
Pop: 222 (1990); 287 (1980) **Pop Density:** 246.7
Land: 0.9 sq. mi.; **Water:** 0.1 sq. mi. **Elev:** 808 ft.

Name origin: From an Indian term meaning 'big beech tree.'

Dickson — Township
Lat: 44-17-57 N **Long:** 85-56-45 W
Pop: 735 (1990); 777 (1980) **Pop Density:** 10.5
Land: 70.1 sq. mi.; **Water:** 1.6 sq. mi.

Eastlake — Village
Lat: 44-14-43 N **Long:** 86-17-37 W
Pop: 473 (1990); 514 (1980) **Pop Density:** 394.2
Land: 1.2 sq. mi.; **Water:** 0.3 sq. mi. **Elev:** 660 ft.

Filer — Township
Lat: 44-12-23 N **Long:** 86-19-28 W
Pop: 1,966 (1990); 2,143 (1980) **Pop Density:** 124.4
Land: 15.8 sq. mi.; **Water:** 0.4 sq. mi.

Kaleva — Village
ZIP: 49645 **Lat:** 44-22-20 N **Long:** 86-00-46 W
Pop: 484 (1990); 445 (1980) **Pop Density:** 440.0
Land: 1.1 sq. mi.; **Water:** 0.0 sq. mi.

Settled by Finnish pioneers.

Name origin: For *Kalevala*, Finland's national epic.

Manistee — City
ZIP: 49660 **Lat:** 44-14-40 N **Long:** 86-19-35 W
Pop: 6,734 (1990); 7,665 (1980) **Pop Density:** 2040.6
Land: 3.3 sq. mi.; **Water:** 1.1 sq. mi.

In northwestern MI, on the eastern shore of Lake Michigan. Founded 1840s.

Name origin: For the county, itself named for the Manistee River, which traverses the county. An Ojibway word of disputed meaning; possibly 'spirit of the woods,' 'crooked river,' 'lost river,' 'red river,' or 'sound of the winds.'

*Manistee — Township
ZIP: 49660 **Lat:** 44-17-33 N **Long:** 86-14-45 W
Pop: 2,952 (1990); 3,209 (1980) **Pop Density:** 65.7
Land: 44.9 sq. mi.; **Water:** 3.3 sq. mi.

Maple Grove — Township
Lat: 44-23-05 N **Long:** 86-00-20 W
Pop: 1,123 (1990); 1,071 (1980) **Pop Density:** 31.5
Land: 35.7 sq. mi.; **Water:** 0.1 sq. mi.

Marilla — Township
Lat: 44-23-07 N **Long:** 85-52-12 W
Pop: 268 (1990); 266 (1980) **Pop Density:** 7.6
Land: 35.4 sq. mi.; **Water:** 0.0 sq. mi.

Norman — Township
Lat: 44-12-27 N **Long:** 85-56-40 W
Pop: 1,189 (1990); 944 (1980) **Pop Density:** 16.7
Land: 71.0 sq. mi.; **Water:** 1.2 sq. mi.

Onekama — Village
ZIP: 49675 **Lat:** 44-22-00 N **Long:** 86-12-11 W
Pop: 515 (1990); 582 (1980) **Pop Density:** 858.3
Land: 0.6 sq. mi.; **Water:** 0.0 sq. mi.

Settled 1845. Not coextensive with the town of the same name.

Name origin: From an Indian term meaning 'portage.'

*Onekama — Township
ZIP: 49675 **Lat:** 44-23-03 N **Long:** 86-13-46 W
Pop: 1,266 (1990); 1,444 (1980) **Pop Density:** 69.9
Land: 18.1 sq. mi.; **Water:** 5.3 sq. mi.

Pleasanton — Township
Lat: 44-28-49 N **Long:** 86-07-06 W
Pop: 573 (1990); 627 (1980) **Pop Density:** 17.1
Land: 33.6 sq. mi.; **Water:** 1.9 sq. mi.

Springdale — Township
Lat: 44-27-55 N **Long:** 85-59-40 W
Pop: 498 (1990); 452 (1980) **Pop Density:** 13.9
Land: 35.7 sq. mi.; **Water:** 0.1 sq. mi.

MICHIGAN, Manistee County

Stronach — Township
Lat: 44-12-35 N Long: 86-10-26 W
Pop: 688 (1990); 727 (1980) Pop Density: 12.4
Land: 55.4 sq. mi.; Water: 0.3 sq. mi.

Marquette County
County Seat: Marquette (ZIP: 49855)

Pop: 70,887 (1990); 74,101 (1980) Pop Density: 38.9
Land: 1821.3 sq. mi.; Water: 1605.6 sq. mi. Area Code: 906
On the north coast of the Upper Peninsula of MI on Lake Superior; organized Mar 9, 1843 from Schoolcraft County.
Name origin: For Jacques Marquette (1637–75), known as Père Marquette, French Jesuit missionary and explorer with Louis Joliet (1645–1700).

Champion — Township
ZIP: 49814 Lat: 46-38-33 N Long: 87-51-40 W
Pop: 346 (1990); 460 (1980) Pop Density: 2.9
Land: 120.9 sq. mi.; Water: 4.0 sq. mi.

Chocolay — Township
ZIP: 49855 Lat: 46-27-27 N Long: 87-14-26 W
Pop: 6,025 (1990); 5,685 (1980) Pop Density: 100.9
Land: 59.7 sq. mi.; Water: 1.2 sq. mi.

Ely — Township
Lat: 46-25-11 N Long: 87-48-05 W
Pop: 1,946 (1990); 1,955 (1980) Pop Density: 14.1
Land: 137.7 sq. mi.; Water: 2.9 sq. mi.

Ewing — Township
Lat: 46-06-03 N Long: 87-18-06 W
Pop: 156 (1990); 163 (1980) Pop Density: 3.2
Land: 48.4 sq. mi.; Water: 0.4 sq. mi.

Forsyth — Township
ZIP: 49833 Lat: 46-15-32 N Long: 87-27-28 W
Pop: 8,775 (1990); 9,679 (1980) Pop Density: 50.1
Land: 175.2 sq. mi.; Water: 3.9 sq. mi.

Gwinn — CDP
Lat: 46-17-27 N Long: 87-26-21 W
Pop: 2,370 (1990); 1,408 (1980) Pop Density: 464.7
Land: 5.1 sq. mi.; Water: 0.0 sq. mi.

Harvey — CDP
Lat: 46-29-34 N Long: 87-21-03 W
Pop: 1,377 (1990); 1,341 (1980) Pop Density: 688.5
Land: 2.0 sq. mi.; Water: 0.5 sq. mi.

Humboldt — Township
Lat: 46-22-26 N Long: 87-55-29 W
Pop: 500 (1990); 577 (1980) Pop Density: 5.3
Land: 93.8 sq. mi.; Water: 1.9 sq. mi.

Ishpeming — City
ZIP: 49849 Lat: 46-29-14 N Long: 87-39-49 W
Pop: 7,200 (1990); 7,538 (1980) Pop Density: 827.6
Land: 8.7 sq. mi.; Water: 0.6 sq. mi. Elev: 1411 ft.
Settled 1856.
Name origin: From a Chippewa Indian term meaning 'heaven; high place.'

***Ishpeming** — Township
Lat: 46-37-40 N Long: 87-41-24 W
Pop: 3,515 (1990); 3,612 (1980) Pop Density: 40.6
Land: 86.5 sq. mi.; Water: 5.0 sq. mi.

K. I. Sawyer Air Force Base — Military Facility
ZIP: 49843 Lat: 46-20-40 N Long: 87-22-56 W
Pop: 6,577 (1990); 4,837 (1980) Pop Density: 854.2
Land: 7.7 sq. mi.; Water: 0.0 sq. mi.

Marquette — City
ZIP: 49855 Lat: 46-33-02 N Long: 87-23-44 W
Pop: 21,977 (1990); 23,288 (1980) Pop Density: 1927.8
Land: 11.4 sq. mi.; Water: 8.0 sq. mi. Elev: 628 ft.
In north-central Upper Peninsula of MI on Lake Superior. Established 1850; incorporated 1871.
Name origin: For Jacques Marquette (1637–75), known as Père Marquette, French Jesuit missionary and explorer with Louis Joliet (1645–1700).

***Marquette** — Township
ZIP: 49855 Lat: 46-36-33 N Long: 87-30-53 W
Pop: 2,757 (1990); 2,669 (1980) Pop Density: 50.4
Land: 54.7 sq. mi.; Water: 5.4 sq. mi.

Michigamme — Township
ZIP: 49861 Lat: 46-38-58 N Long: 87-59-40 W
Pop: 339 (1990); 383 (1980) Pop Density: 2.5
Land: 133.7 sq. mi.; Water: 8.1 sq. mi.

Negaunee — City
ZIP: 49866 Lat: 46-29-59 N Long: 87-35-48 W
Pop: 4,741 (1990); 5,189 (1980) Pop Density: 343.6
Land: 13.8 sq. mi.; Water: 0.9 sq. mi. Elev: 1375 ft.
Settled 1846.
Name origin: From a Chippewa term meaning 'pioneer.'

***Negaunee** — Township
ZIP: 49866 Lat: 46-32-06 N Long: 87-33-09 W
Pop: 2,368 (1990); 2,443 (1980) Pop Density: 56.2
Land: 42.1 sq. mi.; Water: 1.6 sq. mi.

Powell — Township
Lat: 46-48-42 N Long: 87-48-44 W
Pop: 660 (1990); 667 (1980) Pop Density: 4.3
Land: 154.2 sq. mi.; Water: 8.1 sq. mi.

Republic — Township
ZIP: 49879 Lat: 46-22-28 N Long: 88-03-06 W
Pop: 1,170 (1990); 1,390 (1980) Pop Density: 10.3
Land: 113.2 sq. mi.; Water: 6.3 sq. mi.

Richmond — Township
Lat: 46-24-10 N Long: 87-33-07 W
Pop: 1,095 (1990); 1,246 (1980) Pop Density: 19.7
Land: 55.6 sq. mi.; Water: 1.9 sq. mi.

American Places Dictionary   MICHIGAN, Mason County

Sands
Township
Lat: 46-25-39 N **Long:** 87-25-54 W
Pop: 2,696 (1990); 2,437 (1980) **Pop Density:** 38.0
Land: 70.9 sq. mi.; **Water:** 0.3 sq. mi.

Skandia
Township
ZIP: 49885 **Lat:** 46-19-58 N **Long:** 87-10-20 W
Pop: 933 (1990); 999 (1980) **Pop Density:** 13.0
Land: 72.0 sq. mi.; **Water:** 0.1 sq. mi.

Tilden
Township
Lat: 46-21-39 N **Long:** 87-41-17 W
Pop: 1,010 (1990); 1,044 (1980) **Pop Density:** 10.7
Land: 94.3 sq. mi.; **Water:** 1.8 sq. mi.

Trowbridge Park
CDP
Lat: 46-33-20 N **Long:** 87-26-27 W
Pop: 1,831 (1990); 1,928 (1980) **Pop Density:** 1307.9
Land: 1.4 sq. mi.; **Water:** 0.0 sq. mi.

Turin
Township
Lat: 46-11-31 N **Long:** 87-15-00 W
Pop: 156 (1990); 160 (1980) **Pop Density:** 1.9
Land: 84.2 sq. mi.; **Water:** 0.0 sq. mi.

Wells
Township
Lat: 46-04-03 N **Long:** 87-28-37 W
Pop: 281 (1990); 351 (1980) **Pop Density:** 1.8
Land: 154.9 sq. mi.; **Water:** 0.3 sq. mi.

West Branch
Township
Lat: 46-22-48 N **Long:** 87-17-36 W
Pop: 2,241 (1990); 2,166 (1980) **Pop Density:** 63.1
Land: 35.5 sq. mi.; **Water:** 0.2 sq. mi.

Mason County
County Seat: Ludington (ZIP: 49431)

Pop: 25,537 (1990); 26,365 (1980) **Pop Density:** 51.6
Land: 495.2 sq. mi.; **Water:** 746.8 sq. mi. **Area Code:** 616

On the west-central coast of MI bordered on west by Lake Michigan; established as Notipekago County Apr 1, 1840 from Ionia County; name changed Mar 8, 1843.
Name origin: For Stevens Thomson Mason (1811–43), secretary and acting governor of MI Territory (1831–35) and first state governor (1835–38).

Amber
Township
Lat: 43-57-12 N **Long:** 86-20-04 W
Pop: 1,684 (1990); 1,556 (1980) **Pop Density:** 60.1
Land: 28.0 sq. mi.; **Water:** 0.2 sq. mi.

Branch
Township
Lat: 43-56-46 N **Long:** 86-05-53 W
Pop: 973 (1990); 1,021 (1980) **Pop Density:** 27.5
Land: 35.4 sq. mi.; **Water:** 0.5 sq. mi.

Custer
Village
ZIP: 49405 **Lat:** 43-57-00 N **Long:** 86-13-09 W
Pop: 312 (1990); 341 (1980) **Pop Density:** 312.0
Land: 1.0 sq. mi.; **Water:** 0.0 sq. mi. **Elev:** 698 ft.
Founded 1876. Not coextensive with the town of the same name.
Name origin: For Gen. George A. Custer (1839–76), Civil War officer and Indian fighter.

*Custer
Township
ZIP: 49405 **Lat:** 43-56-53 N **Long:** 86-13-03 W
Pop: 1,176 (1990); 1,338 (1980) **Pop Density:** 33.7
Land: 34.9 sq. mi.; **Water:** 0.1 sq. mi.

Eden
Township
Lat: 43-52-08 N **Long:** 86-13-27 W
Pop: 491 (1990); 511 (1980) **Pop Density:** 13.9
Land: 35.4 sq. mi.; **Water:** 0.4 sq. mi.

Fountain
Village
ZIP: 49410 **Lat:** 44-02-52 N **Long:** 86-10-46 W
Pop: 165 (1990); 195 (1980) **Pop Density:** 165.0
Land: 1.0 sq. mi.; **Water:** 0.0 sq. mi.
Established 1882.
Name origin: For a local spring.

Free Soil
Village
ZIP: 49411 **Lat:** 44-06-27 N **Long:** 86-12-49 W
Pop: 148 (1990); 212 (1980) **Pop Density:** 148.0
Land: 1.0 sq. mi.; **Water:** 0.0 sq. mi. **Elev:** 677 ft.
Not coextensive with the town of the same name.
Name origin: For the short-lived (1848–56) antislavery party.

*Free Soil
Township
ZIP: 49411 **Lat:** 44-07-39 N **Long:** 86-13-06 W
Pop: 860 (1990); 925 (1980) **Pop Density:** 22.2
Land: 38.7 sq. mi.; **Water:** 0.4 sq. mi.

Grant
Township
Lat: 44-07-05 N **Long:** 86-21-01 W
Pop: 749 (1990); 747 (1980) **Pop Density:** 15.4
Land: 48.7 sq. mi.; **Water:** 0.2 sq. mi.

Hamlin
Township
Lat: 44-02-12 N **Long:** 86-27-05 W
Pop: 2,597 (1990); 2,616 (1980) **Pop Density:** 94.4
Land: 27.5 sq. mi.; **Water:** 6.9 sq. mi.

Logan
Township
Lat: 43-51-27 N **Long:** 86-05-21 W
Pop: 203 (1990); 177 (1980) **Pop Density:** 5.7
Land: 35.9 sq. mi.; **Water:** 0.1 sq. mi.

Ludington
City
ZIP: 49431 **Lat:** 43-57-25 N **Long:** 86-26-34 W
Pop: 8,507 (1990); 8,937 (1980) **Pop Density:** 2577.9
Land: 3.3 sq. mi.; **Water:** 0.3 sq. mi. **Elev:** 584 ft.
Settled 1847.
Name origin: For timber investor James Ludington.

MICHIGAN, Mason County

Meade
Township
Lat: 44-07-24 N **Long:** 86-06-29 W
Pop: 142 (1990); 135 (1980) **Pop Density:** 3.8
Land: 37.6 sq. mi.; **Water:** 0.1 sq. mi.

Pere Marquetter Charter
Township
Lat: 43-55-50 N **Long:** 86-25-08 W
Pop: 2,065 (1990); 2,068 (1980) **Pop Density:** 146.5
Land: 14.1 sq. mi.; **Water:** 1.6 sq. mi.

Riverton
Township
Lat: 43-52-08 N **Long:** 86-19-41 W
Pop: 1,115 (1990); 1,177 (1980) **Pop Density:** 31.9
Land: 34.9 sq. mi.; **Water:** 0.4 sq. mi.

Scottville
City
ZIP: 49454 **Lat:** 43-57-01 N **Long:** 86-16-48 W
Pop: 1,287 (1990); 1,241 (1980) **Pop Density:** 858.0
Land: 1.5 sq. mi.; **Water:** 0.0 sq. mi. **Elev:** 678 ft.
Founded 1870.
Name origin: For Hiram E. Scott, a sawmill owner and one of the platters of the town.

Sheridan
Township
Lat: 44-01-57 N **Long:** 86-06-26 W
Pop: 837 (1990); 828 (1980) **Pop Density:** 24.3
Land: 34.4 sq. mi.; **Water:** 1.6 sq. mi.

Sherman
Township
Lat: 44-02-10 N **Long:** 86-12-45 W
Pop: 952 (1990); 996 (1980) **Pop Density:** 26.3
Land: 36.2 sq. mi.; **Water:** 0.1 sq. mi.

Summit
Township
Lat: 43-51-29 N **Long:** 86-24-32 W
Pop: 815 (1990); 922 (1980) **Pop Density:** 63.2
Land: 12.9 sq. mi.; **Water:** 1.4 sq. mi.

Victory
Township
Lat: 44-02-01 N **Long:** 86-20-18 W
Pop: 1,084 (1990); 1,170 (1980) **Pop Density:** 30.2
Land: 35.9 sq. mi.; **Water:** 0.6 sq. mi.

Mecosta County
County Seat: Big Rapids (ZIP: 49307)

Pop: 37,308 (1990); 36,961 (1980) **Pop Density:** 67.1
Land: 555.8 sq. mi.; **Water:** 15.4 sq. mi. **Area Code:** 616

In central MI, northeast of Grand Rapids; established Apr 1, 1840 from Newaygo and Osceola counties.
Name origin: For the Potawatomi chief whose name means 'bear cub.'

Aetna
Township
Lat: 43-30-35 N **Long:** 85-30-39 W
Pop: 1,622 (1990); 1,351 (1980) **Pop Density:** 45.6
Land: 35.6 sq. mi.; **Water:** 0.3 sq. mi.

Austin
Township
Lat: 43-35-53 N **Long:** 85-22-24 W
Pop: 1,102 (1990); 898 (1980) **Pop Density:** 30.9
Land: 35.7 sq. mi.; **Water:** 0.0 sq. mi.

Barryton
Village
ZIP: 49305 **Lat:** 43-44-58 N **Long:** 85-08-33 W
Pop: 393 (1990); 422 (1980) **Pop Density:** 436.7
Land: 0.9 sq. mi.; **Water:** 0.1 sq. mi. **Elev:** 976 ft.
Founded 1894.
Name origin: For founder Frank Barry.

Big Rapids
City
ZIP: 49307 **Lat:** 43-42-13 N **Long:** 85-29-10 W
Pop: 12,603 (1990); 14,361 (1980) **Pop Density:** 2136.1
Land: 5.9 sq. mi.; **Water:** 0.1 sq. mi.
In central-eastern MI on the Muskegon River, 50 mi. northeast of Grand Rapids.
Name origin: For its location at the river's biggest rapids.

*Big Rapids
Township
ZIP: 49307 **Lat:** 43-40-49 N **Long:** 85-30-12 W
Pop: 3,100 (1990); 2,471 (1980) **Pop Density:** 106.9
Land: 29.0 sq. mi.; **Water:** 0.4 sq. mi.

Chippewa
Township
Lat: 43-46-28 N **Long:** 85-16-09 W
Pop: 1,035 (1990); 1,009 (1980) **Pop Density:** 31.3
Land: 33.1 sq. mi.; **Water:** 2.4 sq. mi.

Colfax
Township
Lat: 43-40-46 N **Long:** 85-22-38 W
Pop: 1,915 (1990); 1,885 (1980) **Pop Density:** 54.6
Land: 35.1 sq. mi.; **Water:** 0.7 sq. mi.

Deerfield
Township
Lat: 43-30-39 N **Long:** 85-23-06 W
Pop: 1,231 (1990); 1,032 (1980) **Pop Density:** 34.4
Land: 35.8 sq. mi.; **Water:** 0.1 sq. mi.

Fork
Township
Lat: 43-45-53 N **Long:** 85-08-40 W
Pop: 1,395 (1990); 1,348 (1980) **Pop Density:** 39.9
Land: 35.0 sq. mi.; **Water:** 0.3 sq. mi.

Grant
Township
Lat: 43-46-14 N **Long:** 85-22-53 W
Pop: 644 (1990); 642 (1980) **Pop Density:** 19.8
Land: 32.6 sq. mi.; **Water:** 1.5 sq. mi.

Green
Township
Lat: 43-46-21 N **Long:** 85-30-13 W
Pop: 2,833 (1990); 2,847 (1980) **Pop Density:** 76.8
Land: 36.9 sq. mi.; **Water:** 0.7 sq. mi.

Hinton
Township
Lat: 43-31-05 N **Long:** 85-15-33 W
Pop: 995 (1990); 855 (1980) **Pop Density:** 27.9
Land: 35.7 sq. mi.; **Water:** 0.0 sq. mi.

Martiny
Township
Lat: 43-40-59 N **Long:** 85-16-10 W
Pop: 1,348 (1990); 1,210 (1980) **Pop Density:** 41.9
Land: 32.2 sq. mi.; **Water:** 3.2 sq. mi.

Mecosta Village
ZIP: 49332 Lat: 43-37-08 N Long: 85-13-49 W
Pop: 393 (1990); 428 (1980) Pop Density: 357.3
Land: 1.1 sq. mi.; Water: 0.0 sq. mi.
Settled by John Davis in 1851. Not coextensive with the town of the same name.
Name origin: For its county.

*Mecosta Township
ZIP: 49332 Lat: 43-36-16 N Long: 85-30-06 W
Pop: 1,966 (1990); 1,885 (1980) Pop Density: 58.0
Land: 33.9 sq. mi.; Water: 2.0 sq. mi.

Millbrook Township
Lat: 43-30-34 N Long: 85-08-58 W
Pop: 1,012 (1990); 947 (1980) Pop Density: 28.3
Land: 35.7 sq. mi.; Water: 0.1 sq. mi.

Morley Village
ZIP: 49336 Lat: 43-29-28 N Long: 85-26-45 W
Pop: 528 (1990); 507 (1980) Pop Density: 586.7
Land: 0.9 sq. mi.; Water: 0.1 sq. mi.
Incorporated 1870.

Morton Township
Lat: 43-35-48 N Long: 85-15-47 W
Pop: 2,122 (1990); 1,789 (1980) Pop Density: 63.9
Land: 33.2 sq. mi.; Water: 2.5 sq. mi.

Sheridan Township
Lat: 43-40-59 N Long: 85-08-31 W
Pop: 1,020 (1990); 1,007 (1980) Pop Density: 29.3
Land: 34.8 sq. mi.; Water: 1.0 sq. mi.

Stanwood Village
ZIP: 49346 Lat: 43-34-48 N Long: 85-26-52 W
Pop: 174 (1990); 209 (1980) Pop Density: 870.0
Land: 0.2 sq. mi.; Water: 0.0 sq. mi.
Name origin: For the area's large stand of timber.

Wheatland Township
Lat: 43-35-50 N Long: 85-08-47 W
Pop: 1,365 (1990); 1,424 (1980) Pop Density: 38.5
Land: 35.5 sq. mi.; Water: 0.2 sq. mi.

Menominee County
County Seat: Menominee (ZIP: 49858)

Pop: 24,920 (1990); 26,201 (1980) Pop Density: 23.9
Land: 1043.7 sq. mi.; Water: 294.5 sq. mi. Area Code: 906
On the south-central coast of the Upper Peninsula of MI on Green Bay; established as Bleecker County Mar 19, 1863 from Marquette County; name changed Mar 19, 1863.
Name origin: For the Menominee Indians, a tribe of Algonquian linguistic stock; name means 'wild rice people.'

Carney Village
ZIP: 49812 Lat: 45-35-20 N Long: 87-33-14 W
Pop: 197 (1990) Pop Density: 179.1
Land: 1.1 sq. mi.; Water: 0.0 sq. mi.

Cedarville Township
Lat: 45-28-31 N Long: 87-22-34 W
Pop: 185 (1990); 212 (1980) Pop Density: 2.3
Land: 79.0 sq. mi.; Water: 0.1 sq. mi.

Daggett Village
ZIP: 49821 Lat: 45-27-43 N Long: 87-36-16 W
Pop: 260 (1990); 274 (1980) Pop Density: 236.4
Land: 1.1 sq. mi.; Water: 0.0 sq. mi.
Not coextensive with the town of the same name.
Name origin: Named in 1876 by founder Thomas Faulkner for his wife's maiden name.

*Daggett Township
ZIP: 49821 Lat: 45-28-40 N Long: 87-33-05 W
Pop: 745 (1990); 803 (1980) Pop Density: 20.8
Land: 35.9 sq. mi.; Water: 0.2 sq. mi.

Faithorn Township
Lat: 45-39-01 N Long: 87-44-17 W
Pop: 213 (1990); 227 (1980) Pop Density: 4.0
Land: 53.6 sq. mi.; Water: 0.7 sq. mi.

Gourley Township
Lat: 45-35-37 N Long: 87-23-50 W
Pop: 362 (1990); 406 (1980) Pop Density: 10.1
Land: 35.7 sq. mi.; Water: 0.0 sq. mi.

Harris Township
Lat: 45-48-23 N Long: 87-23-38 W
Pop: 1,542 (1990); 1,563 (1980) Pop Density: 10.8
Land: 143.1 sq. mi.; Water: 0.1 sq. mi.

Holmes Township
Lat: 45-31-11 N Long: 87-43-13 W
Pop: 292 (1990); 253 (1980) Pop Density: 4.1
Land: 71.3 sq. mi.; Water: 1.2 sq. mi.

Ingallston Township
Lat: 45-18-10 N Long: 87-31-49 W
Pop: 1,055 (1990); 1,066 (1980) Pop Density: 14.9
Land: 70.8 sq. mi.; Water: 0.8 sq. mi.

Lake Township
Lat: 45-24-30 N Long: 87-45-31 W
Pop: 603 (1990); 622 (1980) Pop Density: 8.5
Land: 70.8 sq. mi.; Water: 2.0 sq. mi.

Mellen Township
Lat: 45-20-16 N Long: 87-37-00 W
Pop: 1,183 (1990); 1,159 (1980) Pop Density: 38.4
Land: 30.8 sq. mi.; Water: 0.6 sq. mi.

MICHIGAN, Menominee County

Menominee
City
ZIP: 49858 Lat: 45-07-16 N Long: 87-37-24 W
Pop: 9,398 (1990); 10,099 (1980) Pop Density: 1879.6
Land: 5.0 sq. mi.; Water: 0.3 sq. mi.
Settled 1836.
Name origin: For the Menominee Indians, a tribe of Algonquian linguistic stock; name means 'wild rice people.'

*Menominee
Township
ZIP: 49858 Lat: 45-12-51 N Long: 87-39-30 W
Pop: 3,956 (1990); 4,026 (1980) Pop Density: 54.3
Land: 72.8 sq. mi.; Water: 0.8 sq. mi.

Meyer
Township
Lat: 45-44-37 N Long: 87-38-27 W
Pop: 1,090 (1990); 1,004 (1980) Pop Density: 12.1
Land: 89.8 sq. mi.; Water: 0.4 sq. mi.

Nadeau
Township
Lat: 45-34-14 N Long: 87-32-34 W
Pop: 1,161 (1990); 1,219 (1980) Pop Density: 14.4
Land: 80.7 sq. mi.; Water: 0.1 sq. mi.

Powers
Village
ZIP: 49874 Lat: 45-41-15 N Long: 87-31-34 W
Pop: 271 (1990); 490 (1980) Pop Density: 271.0
Land: 1.0 sq. mi.; Water: 0.0 sq. mi. Elev: 869 ft.
Name origin: For pioneer settler L.K. Powers.

Spalding
Township
ZIP: 49886 Lat: 45-50-01 N Long: 87-30-48 W
Pop: 1,536 (1990); 1,842 (1980) Pop Density: 9.5
Land: 162.5 sq. mi.; Water: 0.4 sq. mi.

Stephenson
City
ZIP: 49813 Lat: 45-24-49 N Long: 87-36-32 W
Pop: 904 (1990); 967 (1980) Pop Density: 821.8
Land: 1.1 sq. mi.; Water: 0.0 sq. mi.
A station on the Chicago & Northwestern Railroad in 1872; incorporated as a village 1898.
Name origin: For U.S. Congressman Samuel Stephenson.

*Stephenson
Township
ZIP: 49813 Lat: 45-24-49 N Long: 87-32-16 W
Pop: 695 (1990); 733 (1980) Pop Density: 17.1
Land: 40.7 sq. mi.; Water: 0.5 sq. mi.

Midland County
County Seat: Midland (ZIP: 48640)

Pop: 75,651 (1990); 73,578 (1980) Pop Density: 145.1
Land: 521.2 sq. mi.; Water: 6.7 sq. mi. Area Code: 517
In central MI, east of Bay City; established Mar 2, 1831 (prior to statehood) from Saginaw County.
Name origin: For its location in the geographic center of the state.

Coleman
City
ZIP: 48618 Lat: 43-45-24 N Long: 84-35-12 W
Pop: 1,237 (1990); 1,429 (1980) Pop Density: 1237.0
Land: 1.0 sq. mi.; Water: 0.0 sq. mi. Elev: 757 ft.
Incorporated 1887.
Name origin: For early landowner Seymour Coleman.

Edenville
Township
ZIP: 48620 Lat: 43-45-45 N Long: 84-25-21 W
Pop: 2,367 (1990); 2,029 (1980) Pop Density: 68.0
Land: 34.8 sq. mi.; Water: 1.0 sq. mi.

Geneva
Township
Lat: 43-41-01 N Long: 84-32-53 W
Pop: 1,048 (1990); 1,157 (1980) Pop Density: 29.1
Land: 36.0 sq. mi.; Water: 0.0 sq. mi.

Greendale
Township
Lat: 43-35-55 N Long: 84-32-49 W
Pop: 1,495 (1990); 1,244 (1980) Pop Density: 41.4
Land: 36.1 sq. mi.; Water: 0.0 sq. mi.

Homer
Township
Lat: 43-36-42 N Long: 84-19-45 W
Pop: 4,235 (1990); 4,477 (1980) Pop Density: 181.8
Land: 23.3 sq. mi.; Water: 0.2 sq. mi.

Hope
Township
ZIP: 48628 Lat: 43-47-02 N Long: 84-19-37 W
Pop: 1,220 (1990); 1,249 (1980) Pop Density: 53.0
Land: 23.0 sq. mi.; Water: 0.4 sq. mi.

Ingersoll
Township
Lat: 43-31-29 N Long: 84-13-56 W
Pop: 2,788 (1990); 3,011 (1980) Pop Density: 76.6
Land: 36.4 sq. mi.; Water: 0.1 sq. mi.

Jasper
Township
Lat: 43-30-32 N Long: 84-32-53 W
Pop: 1,096 (1990); 1,129 (1980) Pop Density: 30.4
Land: 36.1 sq. mi.; Water: 0.0 sq. mi.

Jerome
Township
Lat: 43-40-40 N Long: 84-25-24 W
Pop: 4,470 (1990); 4,171 (1980) Pop Density: 131.5
Land: 34.0 sq. mi.; Water: 1.7 sq. mi.

Larkin
Township
Lat: 43-41-52 N Long: 84-13-16 W
Pop: 3,588 (1990); 3,284 (1980) Pop Density: 105.2
Land: 34.1 sq. mi.; Water: 0.0 sq. mi.

Lee
Township
Lat: 43-35-45 N Long: 84-25-38 W
Pop: 4,017 (1990); 3,325 (1980) Pop Density: 111.6
Land: 36.0 sq. mi.; Water: 0.0 sq. mi.

Lincoln
Township
Lat: 43-42-01 N Long: 84-19-28 W
Pop: 1,807 (1990); 1,643 (1980) Pop Density: 76.6
Land: 23.6 sq. mi.; Water: 0.1 sq. mi.

American Places Dictionary   MICHIGAN, Missaukee County

Midland — City
ZIP: 48640   Lat: 43-37-21 N   Long: 84-13-50 W
Pop: 37,819 (1990); 37,035 (1980)   Pop Density: 1390.4
Land: 27.2 sq. mi.; Water: 0.6 sq. mi.   Elev: 629 ft.
In east-central MI on the Tittabawassee River, 50 mi. northwest of Flint. County seat; settled 1836; became village 1869; city 1887. Part of the town is also in Bay County.
Name origin: For its county, located in the middle of the state and near Saginaw Bay.

*Midland — Township
Lat: 43-35-35 N   Long: 84-13-52 W
Pop: 2,221 (1990); 2,389 (1980)   Pop Density: 224.3
Land: 9.9 sq. mi.; Water: 1.6 sq. mi.

Mills — Township
Lat: 43-47-09 N   Long: 84-13-47 W
Pop: 1,635 (1990); 1,461 (1980)   Pop Density: 46.7
Land: 35.0 sq. mi.; Water: 1.0 sq. mi.

Mount Haley — Township
Lat: 43-31-02 N   Long: 84-19-53 W
Pop: 1,656 (1990); 1,586 (1980)   Pop Density: 69.6
Land: 23.8 sq. mi.; Water: 0.0 sq. mi.

Porter — Township
Lat: 43-30-42 N   Long: 84-25-46 W
Pop: 1,140 (1990); 1,113 (1980)   Pop Density: 31.9
Land: 35.7 sq. mi.; Water: 0.0 sq. mi.

Sanford — Village
ZIP: 48657   Lat: 43-40-32 N   Long: 84-22-50 W
Pop: 889 (1990); 864 (1980)   Pop Density: 683.8
Land: 1.3 sq. mi.; Water: 0.3 sq. mi.
Settled 1864 by pioneer Charles Sanford.
Name origin: For the first settler.

Warren — Township
Lat: 43-46-17 N   Long: 84-32-32 W
Pop: 1,812 (1990); 1,846 (1980)   Pop Density: 51.6
Land: 35.1 sq. mi.; Water: 0.0 sq. mi.

Missaukee County
County Seat: Lake City (ZIP: 49651)

Pop: 12,147 (1990); 10,009 (1980)   Pop Density: 21.4
Land: 566.8 sq. mi.; Water: 7.1 sq. mi.   Area Code: 616
In north-central MI, east of Cadillac; established Apr 1, 1840 from unorganized territory.
Name origin: For an Ottawa chief.

Aetna — Township
Lat: 44-17-04 N   Long: 85-02-15 W
Pop: 416 (1990); 437 (1980)   Pop Density: 11.6
Land: 35.9 sq. mi.; Water: 0.0 sq. mi.

Bloomfield — Township
Lat: 44-28-05 N   Long: 85-16-37 W
Pop: 390 (1990); 268 (1980)   Pop Density: 10.9
Land: 35.7 sq. mi.; Water: 0.0 sq. mi.

Butterfield — Township
Lat: 44-17-53 N   Long: 84-55-14 W
Pop: 452 (1990); 390 (1980)   Pop Density: 12.6
Land: 35.8 sq. mi.; Water: 0.2 sq. mi.

Caldwell — Township
Lat: 44-23-30 N   Long: 85-16-56 W
Pop: 1,104 (1990); 856 (1980)   Pop Density: 32.1
Land: 34.4 sq. mi.; Water: 1.2 sq. mi.

Clam Union — Township
Lat: 44-12-23 N   Long: 85-01-53 W
Pop: 854 (1990); 797 (1980)   Pop Density: 23.9
Land: 35.8 sq. mi.; Water: 0.2 sq. mi.

Enterprise — Township
Lat: 44-22-57 N   Long: 84-54-34 W
Pop: 127 (1990); 127 (1980)   Pop Density: 3.7
Land: 34.7 sq. mi.; Water: 0.3 sq. mi.

Forest — Township
Lat: 44-22-25 N   Long: 85-08-56 W
Pop: 878 (1990); 728 (1980)   Pop Density: 24.9
Land: 35.2 sq. mi.; Water: 0.0 sq. mi.

Holland — Township
Lat: 44-12-33 N   Long: 84-54-47 W
Pop: 169 (1990); 159 (1980)   Pop Density: 4.7
Land: 35.8 sq. mi.; Water: 0.1 sq. mi.

Lake — Township
Lat: 44-17-18 N   Long: 85-16-32 W
Pop: 1,980 (1990); 1,345 (1980)   Pop Density: 62.5
Land: 31.7 sq. mi.; Water: 4.4 sq. mi.

Lake City — City
ZIP: 49651   Lat: 44-19-49 N   Long: 85-12-30 W
Pop: 858 (1990); 843 (1980)   Pop Density: 780.0
Land: 1.1 sq. mi.; Water: 0.0 sq. mi.   Elev: 1260 ft.

McBain — City
Lat: 44-11-39 N   Long: 85-12-51 W
Pop: 692 (1990); 519 (1980)   Pop Density: 576.7
Land: 1.2 sq. mi.; Water: 0.0 sq. mi.

Norwich — Township
Lat: 44-27-55 N   Long: 84-58-22 W
Pop: 505 (1990); 418 (1980)   Pop Density: 7.0
Land: 71.9 sq. mi.; Water: 0.6 sq. mi.

Pioneer — Township
Lat: 44-27-44 N   Long: 85-09-01 W
Pop: 388 (1990); 323 (1980)   Pop Density: 10.8
Land: 35.9 sq. mi.; Water: 0.0 sq. mi.

Reeder — Township
Lat: 44-17-03 N   Long: 85-09-06 W
Pop: 772 (1990); 647 (1980)   Pop Density: 22.1
Land: 34.9 sq. mi.; Water: 0.0 sq. mi.

MICHIGAN, Missaukee County

Richland
Township
Lat: 44-12-34 N Long: 85-16-14 W
Pop: 1,236 (1990); 1,008 (1980) **Pop Density:** 34.6
Land: 35.7 sq. mi.; **Water:** 0.0 sq. mi.

Riverside
Township
Lat: 44-12-31 N Long: 85-09-16 W
Pop: 853 (1990); 773 (1980) **Pop Density:** 24.0
Land: 35.5 sq. mi.; **Water:** 0.0 sq. mi.

West Branch
Township
Lat: 44-22-45 N Long: 85-02-03 W
Pop: 473 (1990); 371 (1980) **Pop Density:** 13.2
Land: 35.7 sq. mi.; **Water:** 0.0 sq. mi.

Monroe County
County Seat: Monroe (ZIP: 48161)

Pop: 133,600 (1990); 134,659 (1980) **Pop Density:** 242.4
Land: 551.1 sq. mi.; **Water:** 129.0 sq. mi. **Area Code:** 313

In the southeast corner of MI bordered on east by Lake Erie; original county; established Jul 14, 1817 (prior to statehood).

Name origin: For James Monroe (1758–1831), fifth U.S. president.

Ash
Township
ZIP: 48117 Lat: 42-03-22 N Long: 83-21-56 W
Pop: 7,480 (1990); 7,688 (1980) **Pop Density:** 216.2
Land: 34.6 sq. mi.; **Water:** 0.2 sq. mi.

Bedford
Township
ZIP: 48182 Lat: 41-46-40 N Long: 83-35-20 W
Pop: 23,748 (1990); 22,902 (1980) **Pop Density:** 607.4
Land: 39.1 sq. mi.; **Water:** 0.2 sq. mi.

Berlin
Township
ZIP: 48166 Lat: 42-01-22 N Long: 83-15-21 W
Pop: 6,286 (1990); 6,488 (1980) **Pop Density:** 195.8
Land: 32.1 sq. mi.; **Water:** 5.1 sq. mi.

Carleton
Village
ZIP: 48117 Lat: 42-03-27 N Long: 83-23-23 W
Pop: 2,770 (1990); 2,786 (1980) **Pop Density:** 2770.0
Land: 1.0 sq. mi.; **Water:** 0.0 sq. mi.
Laid out 1872.

Name origin: For MI poet Will Carleton.

Detroit Beach
CDP
Lat: 41-55-53 N Long: 83-19-43 W
Pop: 2,113 (1990); 2,112 (1980) **Pop Density:** 3521.7
Land: 0.6 sq. mi.; **Water:** 0.0 sq. mi.

Dundee
Village
ZIP: 48131 Lat: 41-57-25 N Long: 83-39-37 W
Pop: 2,664 (1990); 2,575 (1980) **Pop Density:** 1776.0
Land: 1.5 sq. mi.; **Water:** 0.0 sq. mi.

First European settler arrived 1823. Not coextensive with the town of the same name.

Name origin: For Dundee, Scotland.

*Dundee
Township
ZIP: 48131 Lat: 41-57-26 N Long: 83-40-29 W
Pop: 5,376 (1990); 5,395 (1980) **Pop Density:** 111.1
Land: 48.4 sq. mi.; **Water:** 0.2 sq. mi.

Erie
Township
Lat: 41-46-41 N Long: 83-29-00 W
Pop: 4,492 (1990); 4,576 (1980) **Pop Density:** 186.4
Land: 24.1 sq. mi.; **Water:** 5.6 sq. mi.

Estral Beach
Village
ZIP: 48166 Lat: 41-59-09 N Long: 83-14-13 W
Pop: 430 (1990); 463 (1980) **Pop Density:** 860.0
Land: 0.5 sq. mi.; **Water:** 0.0 sq. mi.
Incorporated 1925.

Exeter
Township
Lat: 42-02-57 N Long: 83-28-38 W
Pop: 3,253 (1990); 3,236 (1980) **Pop Density:** 88.9
Land: 36.6 sq. mi.; **Water:** 0.1 sq. mi.

Frenchtown
Township
ZIP: 48161 Lat: 41-57-50 N Long: 83-21-31 W
Pop: 18,210 (1990); 18,204 (1980) **Pop Density:** 432.5
Land: 42.1 sq. mi.; **Water:** 1.1 sq. mi.

Ida
Township
ZIP: 48140 Lat: 41-51-55 N Long: 83-35-19 W
Pop: 4,554 (1990); 4,467 (1980) **Pop Density:** 124.1
Land: 36.7 sq. mi.; **Water:** 0.1 sq. mi.

Lambertville
CDP
ZIP: 48144 Lat: 41-44-50 N Long: 83-37-22 W
Pop: 7,860 (1990); 6,341 (1980) **Pop Density:** 1288.5
Land: 6.1 sq. mi.; **Water:** 0.0 sq. mi.

La Salle
Township
Lat: 41-51-14 N Long: 83-28-37 W
Pop: 4,985 (1990); 5,011 (1980) **Pop Density:** 186.7
Land: 26.7 sq. mi.; **Water:** 0.2 sq. mi.

London
Township
Lat: 42-02-31 N Long: 83-35-41 W
Pop: 2,915 (1990); 3,266 (1980) **Pop Density:** 81.7
Land: 35.7 sq. mi.; **Water:** 0.1 sq. mi.

Luna Pier
City
ZIP: 48157 Lat: 41-48-18 N Long: 83-26-32 W
Pop: 1,507 (1990); 1,443 (1980) **Pop Density:** 1004.7
Land: 1.5 sq. mi.; **Water:** 0.2 sq. mi.
Established 1929.

Name origin: From Latin *luna* 'moon' and for its Lake Erie pier.

Maybee
Village
ZIP: 48159 **Lat:** 42-00-20 N **Long:** 83-30-57 W
Pop: 500 (1990); 490 (1980) **Pop Density:** 416.7
Land: 1.2 sq. mi.; **Water:** 0.0 sq. mi.
Name origin: For sawmill owner Abram Maybee.

Milan
City
ZIP: 48160 **Lat:** 42-04-45 N **Long:** 83-41-04 W
Pop: 980 (1990); 922 (1980) **Pop Density:** 753.8
Land: 1.3 sq. mi.; **Water:** 0.0 sq. mi.
Part of the town is also in Washtenaw County.
Name origin: Named in 1836 for Milan, Italy. Previously called Tolanville.

*Milan
Township
Lat: 42-02-22 N **Long:** 83-42-57 W
Pop: 1,659 (1990); 2,021 (1980) **Pop Density:** 47.3
Land: 35.1 sq. mi.; **Water:** 0.0 sq. mi.

Monroe
City
ZIP: 48161 **Lat:** 41-55-00 N **Long:** 83-23-09 W
Pop: 22,902 (1990); 23,531 (1980) **Pop Density:** 2544.7
Land: 9.0 sq. mi.; **Water:** 1.0 sq. mi.
In southeastern MI, 38 mi. south of Detroit. Settled by the French in 1784, established as a city in 1837.
Name origin: Renamed in 1817 for James Monroe (1758–1831), fifth U.S. president. Previously called Frenchtown.

*Monroe
Township
ZIP: 48161 **Lat:** 41-53-31 N **Long:** 83-25-21 W
Pop: 11,909 (1990); 11,654 (1980) **Pop Density:** 684.4
Land: 17.4 sq. mi.; **Water:** 1.1 sq. mi.

Petersburg
City
ZIP: 49270 **Lat:** 41-53-58 N **Long:** 83-42-42 W
Pop: 1,201 (1990); 1,222 (1980) **Pop Density:** 3002.5
Land: 0.4 sq. mi.; **Water:** 0.0 sq. mi.
Incorporated 1869.
Name origin: For pioneer Richard Peters.

Raisinville
Township
Lat: 41-57-17 N **Long:** 83-30-25 W
Pop: 4,634 (1990); 4,797 (1980) **Pop Density:** 96.1
Land: 48.2 sq. mi.; **Water:** 0.4 sq. mi.

South Monroe
CDP
ZIP: 48161 **Lat:** 41-53-44 N **Long:** 83-25-03 W
Pop: 5,266 (1990); 4,232 (1980) **Pop Density:** 2194.2
Land: 2.4 sq. mi.; **Water:** 0.0 sq. mi.

South Rockwood
Village
ZIP: 48179 **Lat:** 42-03-43 N **Long:** 83-15-38 W
Pop: 1,221 (1990); 1,353 (1980) **Pop Density:** 508.7
Land: 2.4 sq. mi.; **Water:** 0.0 sq. mi.
Founded 1863.
Name origin: For Rockwood, Ontario, Canada.

Stony Point
CDP
Lat: 41-56-49 N **Long:** 83-16-17 W
Pop: 1,598 (1990); 1,650 (1980) **Pop Density:** 1452.7
Land: 1.1 sq. mi.; **Water:** 0.0 sq. mi.

Summerfield
Township
Lat: 41-52-04 N **Long:** 83-42-45 W
Pop: 3,076 (1990); 3,176 (1980) **Pop Density:** 72.9
Land: 42.2 sq. mi.; **Water:** 0.2 sq. mi.

Temperance
CDP
ZIP: 48182 **Lat:** 41-46-03 N **Long:** 83-34-20 W
Pop: 6,542 (1990) **Pop Density:** 1422.2
Land: 4.6 sq. mi.; **Water:** 0.1 sq. mi.

West Monroe
CDP
Lat: 41-54-49 N **Long:** 83-25-53 W
Pop: 3,919 (1990) **Pop Density:** 3014.6
Land: 1.3 sq. mi.; **Water:** 0.0 sq. mi.

Whiteford
Township
Lat: 41-46-19 N **Long:** 83-42-35 W
Pop: 4,433 (1990); 4,660 (1980) **Pop Density:** 111.4
Land: 39.8 sq. mi.; **Water:** 0.4 sq. mi.

Woodland Beach
CDP
Lat: 41-56-30 N **Long:** 83-18-51 W
Pop: 2,309 (1990); 2,383 (1980) **Pop Density:** 4618.0
Land: 0.5 sq. mi.; **Water:** 0.0 sq. mi.

Montcalm County
County Seat: Stanton (ZIP: 48888)

Pop: 53,059 (1990); 47,555 (1980) **Pop Density:** 74.9
Land: 708.1 sq. mi.; **Water:** 12.9 sq. mi. **Area Code:** 517
In central MI, northeast of Grand Rapids; established Mar 2, 1831 (prior to statehood) from Isabella County.
Name origin: For Louis Joseph de Montcalm (1712–59), commander of French troops against the British in Canada.

Belvidere
Township
Lat: 43-25-14 N **Long:** 85-08-38 W
Pop: 2,134 (1990); 1,955 (1980) **Pop Density:** 61.3
Land: 34.8 sq. mi.; **Water:** 1.2 sq. mi.

Bloomer
Township
Lat: 43-09-41 N **Long:** 84-53-53 W
Pop: 2,922 (1990); 1,226 (1980) **Pop Density:** 83.0
Land: 35.2 sq. mi.; **Water:** 0.0 sq. mi.

Bushnell
Township
Lat: 43-09-33 N **Long:** 85-00-35 W
Pop: 1,291 (1990); 1,270 (1980) **Pop Density:** 36.3
Land: 35.6 sq. mi.; **Water:** 0.1 sq. mi.

MICHIGAN, Montcalm County

Carson City
City
ZIP: 48811 Lat: 43-10-42 N Long: 84-50-48 W
Pop: 1,158 (1990); 1,229 (1980) Pop Density: 1654.3
Land: 0.7 sq. mi.; Water: 0.0 sq. mi.
Name origin: For explorer and frontiersman Christopher "Kit" Carson (1809–68).

Cato
Township
Lat: 43-25-54 N Long: 85-15-55 W
Pop: 2,500 (1990); 2,441 (1980) Pop Density: 70.8
Land: 35.3 sq. mi.; Water: 0.8 sq. mi.

Crystal
Township
ZIP: 48818 Lat: 43-15-01 N Long: 84-54-00 W
Pop: 2,541 (1990); 2,224 (1980) Pop Density: 74.5
Land: 34.1 sq. mi.; Water: 1.7 sq. mi.

Day
Township
Lat: 43-20-05 N Long: 85-01-18 W
Pop: 1,196 (1990); 1,234 (1980) Pop Density: 34.0
Land: 35.2 sq. mi.; Water: 0.1 sq. mi.

Douglass
Township
Lat: 43-19-56 N Long: 85-08-21 W
Pop: 1,944 (1990); 1,787 (1980) Pop Density: 55.5
Land: 35.0 sq. mi.; Water: 0.8 sq. mi.

Edmore
Village
ZIP: 48829 Lat: 43-24-27 N Long: 85-02-15 W
Pop: 1,126 (1990); 1,176 (1980) Pop Density: 804.3
Land: 1.4 sq. mi.; Water: 0.0 sq. mi. Elev: 965 ft.
Founded 1878 by Edwin Moore.
Name origin: From a contraction of the founder's name.

Eureka
Township
Lat: 43-09-29 N Long: 85-15-04 W
Pop: 2,594 (1990); 2,303 (1980) Pop Density: 87.3
Land: 29.7 sq. mi.; Water: 0.7 sq. mi.

Evergreen
Township
Lat: 43-14-54 N Long: 85-01-11 W
Pop: 2,531 (1990); 2,183 (1980) Pop Density: 72.9
Land: 34.7 sq. mi.; Water: 0.6 sq. mi.

Fairplain
Township
Lat: 43-09-44 N Long: 85-07-48 W
Pop: 1,575 (1990); 1,380 (1980) Pop Density: 44.4
Land: 35.5 sq. mi.; Water: 0.5 sq. mi.

Ferris
Township
Lat: 43-20-38 N Long: 84-54-22 W
Pop: 1,189 (1990); 1,133 (1980) Pop Density: 32.9
Land: 36.1 sq. mi.; Water: 0.0 sq. mi.

Greenville
City
ZIP: 48838 Lat: 43-10-40 N Long: 85-15-13 W
Pop: 8,101 (1990); 8,019 (1980) Pop Density: 1472.9
Land: 5.5 sq. mi.; Water: 0.2 sq. mi.
Founded 1844 by John Green.
Name origin: For its founder.

Home
Township
Lat: 43-25-28 N Long: 85-01-37 W
Pop: 2,513 (1990); 2,614 (1980) Pop Density: 69.8
Land: 36.0 sq. mi.; Water: 0.1 sq. mi.

Howard City
Village
ZIP: 49329 Lat: 43-23-42 N Long: 85-27-58 W
Pop: 1,351 (1990); 1,118 (1980) Pop Density: 562.9
Land: 2.4 sq. mi.; Water: 0.0 sq. mi.
Incorporated 1873.
Name origin: For Detroit railroad attorney William A. Howard.

Lakeview
Village
ZIP: 48850 Lat: 43-26-47 N Long: 85-16-31 W
Pop: 1,108 (1990); 1,139 (1980) Pop Density: 923.3
Land: 1.2 sq. mi.; Water: 0.3 sq. mi. Elev: 953 ft.
Settled 1858.
Name origin: Descriptively named for its location on Tamarack Lake.

Maple Valley
Township
Lat: 43-20-54 N Long: 85-22-40 W
Pop: 1,824 (1990); 1,815 (1980) Pop Density: 51.5
Land: 35.4 sq. mi.; Water: 0.7 sq. mi.

McBride
Village
Lat: 43-21-10 N Long: 85-02-35 W
Pop: 236 (1990); 252 (1980) Pop Density: 590.0
Land: 0.4 sq. mi.; Water: 0.0 sq. mi. Elev: 964 ft.
Name origin: For pioneer Alexander McBride, who built a sawmill here in 1874.

Montcalm
Township
Lat: 43-15-26 N Long: 85-14-36 W
Pop: 2,879 (1990); 2,521 (1980) Pop Density: 80.6
Land: 35.7 sq. mi.; Water: 0.7 sq. mi.

Pierson
Village
ZIP: 49339 Lat: 43-19-08 N Long: 85-29-51 W
Pop: 207 (1990); 216 (1980) Pop Density: 690.0
Land: 0.3 sq. mi.; Water: 0.0 sq. mi. Elev: 900 ft.
Founded 1856 by pioneer David Pierson. Not coextensive with the town of the same name.
Name origin: For the founder.

*Pierson
Township
ZIP: 49339 Lat: 43-20-18 N Long: 85-30-36 W
Pop: 2,177 (1990); 1,701 (1980) Pop Density: 62.7
Land: 34.7 sq. mi.; Water: 1.5 sq. mi.

Pine
Township
Lat: 43-19-57 N Long: 85-15-38 W
Pop: 1,392 (1990); 1,224 (1980) Pop Density: 39.5
Land: 35.2 sq. mi.; Water: 1.0 sq. mi.

Reynolds
Township
Lat: 43-25-24 N Long: 85-30-09 W
Pop: 3,028 (1990); 2,362 (1980) Pop Density: 84.1
Land: 36.0 sq. mi.; Water: 0.1 sq. mi.

Richland
Township
Lat: 43-25-37 N Long: 84-53-46 W
Pop: 2,355 (1990); 2,421 (1980) Pop Density: 65.6
Land: 35.9 sq. mi.; Water: 0.4 sq. mi.

Sheridan
Village
ZIP: 48884 Lat: 43-12-37 N Long: 85-04-21 W
Pop: 730 (1990); 664 (1980) Pop Density: 811.1
Land: 0.9 sq. mi.; Water: 0.1 sq. mi.
Settled 1851.
Name origin: For Gen. Phillip Sheridan (1831–88), commander in chief of Union forces in the Civil War.

Sidney
Township
ZIP: 48885   **Lat:** 43-14-51 N   **Long:** 85-07-52 W
Pop: 2,375 (1990); 2,053 (1980)   **Pop Density:** 69.6
Land: 34.1 sq. mi.; **Water:** 1.0 sq. mi.

Stanton
City
ZIP: 48888   **Lat:** 43-17-35 N   **Long:** 85-04-45 W
Pop: 1,504 (1990); 1,315 (1980)   **Pop Density:** 716.2
Land: 2.1 sq. mi.; **Water:** 0.0 sq. mi.   **Elev:** 919 ft.
Founded 1860.
Name origin: Named in 1863 for Edwin Stanton (1814–69), U.S. attorney general (1860–61) and secretary of war (1862–68).

Winfield
Township
Lat: 43-25-52 N   **Long:** 85-23-06 W
Pop: 1,336 (1990); 1,145 (1980)   **Pop Density:** 37.6
Land: 35.5 sq. mi.; **Water:** 0.7 sq. mi.

Montmorency County
County Seat: Atlanta (ZIP: 49709)

Pop: 8,936 (1990); 7,492 (1980)   **Pop Density:** 16.3
Land: 547.6 sq. mi.; **Water:** 14.8 sq. mi.   **Area Code:** 517

In northeast MI, west of Alpena; established as Chenoquet County Apr 1, 1840 from Alpena County; name changed Mar 8, 1843.
Name origin: For Count Raymond de Montmorency (1806–89), a French officer who helped the colonies against England during the Revolutionary War.

Albert
Township
Lat: 44-54-16 N   **Long:** 84-15-13 W
Pop: 2,097 (1990); 1,620 (1980)   **Pop Density:** 31.9
Land: 65.8 sq. mi.; **Water:** 4.7 sq. mi.

Avery
Township
Lat: 44-58-32 N   **Long:** 84-04-23 W
Pop: 579 (1990); 552 (1980)   **Pop Density:** 16.5
Land: 35.0 sq. mi.; **Water:** 0.3 sq. mi.   **Elev:** 799 ft.

Briley
Township
Lat: 45-01-46 N   **Long:** 84-10-51 W
Pop: 1,831 (1990); 1,699 (1980)   **Pop Density:** 26.8
Land: 68.3 sq. mi.; **Water:** 2.0 sq. mi.

Hillman
Village
ZIP: 49746   **Lat:** 45-03-57 N   **Long:** 83-54-02 W
Pop: 643 (1990); 373 (1980)   **Pop Density:** 584.5
Land: 1.1 sq. mi.; **Water:** 0.0 sq. mi.   **Elev:** 813 ft.
Established 1880 by John Hillman Stevens. Not coextensive with the town of the same name.
Name origin: For the establisher.

*Hillman
Township
ZIP: 49746   **Lat:** 45-04-37 N   **Long:** 83-59-53 W
Pop: 2,189 (1990); 1,650 (1980)   **Pop Density:** 32.4
Land: 67.6 sq. mi.; **Water:** 1.3 sq. mi.

Loud
Township
Lat: 44-53-46 N   **Long:** 84-04-07 W
Pop: 220 (1990); 224 (1980)   **Pop Density:** 6.1
Land: 35.8 sq. mi.; **Water:** 0.0 sq. mi.

Montmorency
Township
Lat: 45-09-45 N   **Long:** 84-08-10 W
Pop: 1,075 (1990); 884 (1980)   **Pop Density:** 7.8
Land: 137.4 sq. mi.; **Water:** 3.1 sq. mi.

Rust
Township
Lat: 44-57-07 N   **Long:** 83-57-24 W
Pop: 514 (1990); 502 (1980)   **Pop Density:** 7.5
Land: 68.6 sq. mi.; **Water:** 3.3 sq. mi.

Vienna
Township
Lat: 45-02-35 N   **Long:** 84-18-16 W
Pop: 431 (1990); 361 (1980)   **Pop Density:** 6.2
Land: 69.1 sq. mi.; **Water:** 0.3 sq. mi.

MICHIGAN, Muskegon County

Muskegon County
County Seat: Muskegon (ZIP: 49442)

Pop: 158,983 (1990); 157,589 (1980)   **Pop Density:** 312.2
Land: 509.2 sq. mi.; **Water:** 950.1 sq. mi.   **Area Code:** 616

On the west-central coast of MI, bordered on west by Lake Michigan; established Jan 7, 1859 from Newaygo County.

Name origin: For the Muskegon River, from an Ojibway word meaning 'marshy river.'

Blue Lake — Township
Lat: 43-25-42 N   Long: 86-13-07 W
Pop: 1,235 (1990); 1,101 (1980)   **Pop Density:** 35.9
Land: 34.4 sq. mi.; **Water:** 1.3 sq. mi.

Casnovia — Village
ZIP: 49318   Lat: 43-14-01 N   Long: 85-47-37 W
Pop: 187 (1990); 181 (1980)   **Pop Density:** 374.0
Land: 0.5 sq. mi.; **Water:** 0.0 sq. mi.   **Elev:** 881 ft.
Founded 1850. Part of the town is also in Kent County.
Name origin: From the Latin *casa* 'home' and *nova* 'new.' Also spelled Casinova and Cazenovia.

*Casnovia — Township
ZIP: 49318   Lat: 43-15-11 N   Long: 85-50-50 W
Pop: 2,361 (1990); 2,158 (1980)   **Pop Density:** 66.1
Land: 35.7 sq. mi.; **Water:** 0.1 sq. mi.

Cedar Creek — Township
Lat: 43-20-30 N   Long: 86-05-44 W
Pop: 2,846 (1990); 2,454 (1980)   **Pop Density:** 80.9
Land: 35.2 sq. mi.; **Water:** 1.0 sq. mi.

Dalton — Township
ZIP: 49445   Lat: 43-19-54 N   Long: 86-13-18 W
Pop: 6,276 (1990); 5,897 (1980)   **Pop Density:** 175.8
Land: 35.7 sq. mi.; **Water:** 0.8 sq. mi.

Egelston — Township
ZIP: 49442   Lat: 43-14-38 N   Long: 86-04-56 W
Pop: 7,640 (1990); 7,310 (1980)   **Pop Density:** 218.3
Land: 35.0 sq. mi.; **Water:** 0.6 sq. mi.

Fruitland — Township
Lat: 43-20-39 N   Long: 86-20-30 W
Pop: 4,391 (1990); 4,168 (1980)   **Pop Density:** 120.3
Land: 36.5 sq. mi.; **Water:** 3.2 sq. mi.

Fruitport — Village
ZIP: 49415   Lat: 43-07-32 N   Long: 86-09-21 W
Pop: 1,090 (1990); 1,143 (1980)   **Pop Density:** 1211.1
Land: 0.9 sq. mi.; **Water:** 0.1 sq. mi.
In southwestern MI on Spring Lake (a Lake Michigan inlet), 35 mi. northwest of Grand Rapids. Settled 1868. Not coextensive with the town of the same name.
Name origin: Descriptively named as a lake port in a fruit-growing region.

*Fruitport — Township
ZIP: 49415   Lat: 43-08-52 N   Long: 86-09-08 W
Pop: 11,485 (1990); 10,646 (1980)   **Pop Density:** 382.8
Land: 30.0 sq. mi.; **Water:** 0.1 sq. mi.

Holton — Township
ZIP: 49425   Lat: 43-25-14 N   Long: 86-06-13 W
Pop: 2,318 (1990); 2,022 (1980)   **Pop Density:** 65.9
Land: 35.2 sq. mi.; **Water:** 0.5 sq. mi.

Laketon — Township
ZIP: 49445   Lat: 43-16-14 N   Long: 86-19-00 W
Pop: 6,538 (1990); 6,327 (1980)   **Pop Density:** 377.9
Land: 17.3 sq. mi.; **Water:** 1.4 sq. mi.

Lakewood Club — Village
ZIP: 49457   Lat: 43-22-35 N   Long: 86-15-18 W
Pop: 659 (1990); 695 (1980)   **Pop Density:** 346.8
Land: 1.9 sq. mi.; **Water:** 0.1 sq. mi.

Montague — City
ZIP: 49437   Lat: 43-24-44 N   Long: 86-21-46 W
Pop: 2,276 (1990); 2,332 (1980)   **Pop Density:** 843.0
Land: 2.7 sq. mi.; **Water:** 0.5 sq. mi.
Founded 1874.
Name origin: For pioneer William Montague Ferry.

*Montague — Township
ZIP: 49437   Lat: 43-26-10 N   Long: 86-21-03 W
Pop: 1,429 (1990); 1,359 (1980)   **Pop Density:** 75.6
Land: 18.9 sq. mi.; **Water:** 0.4 sq. mi.

Moorland — Township
Lat: 43-14-53 N   Long: 85-57-52 W
Pop: 1,543 (1990); 1,521 (1980)   **Pop Density:** 42.4
Land: 36.4 sq. mi.; **Water:** 0.0 sq. mi.

Muskegon — City
ZIP: 49440   Lat: 43-13-39 N   Long: 86-15-19 W
Pop: 40,283 (1990); 40,823 (1980)   **Pop Density:** 2797.4
Land: 14.4 sq. mi.; **Water:** 3.7 sq. mi.
On the southwestern coast of MI on the Muskegon River and Lake Michigan, 35 mi. northwest of Grand Rapids. County seat; originally occupied by Potawatomi Indians; established as a trading post by Frenchman Baptiste Recollet 1810; incorporated 1869.
Name origin: From an Ojibway term meaning 'marshy river.'

*Muskegon — Township
ZIP: 49445   Lat: 43-15-38 N   Long: 86-11-00 W
Pop: 15,302 (1990); 14,557 (1980)   **Pop Density:** 642.9
Land: 23.8 sq. mi.; **Water:** 0.1 sq. mi.

Muskegon Heights — City
ZIP: 49444   Lat: 43-12-05 N   Long: 86-14-27 W
Pop: 13,176 (1990); 14,611 (1980)   **Pop Density:** 4117.5
Land: 3.2 sq. mi.; **Water:** 0.0 sq. mi.
In southwestern MI, directly south of Muskegon. Incorporated as a village 1891; as a city 1903.

North Muskegon — City
ZIP: 49445   Lat: 43-15-01 N   Long: 86-16-20 W
Pop: 3,919 (1990); 4,024 (1980)   **Pop Density:** 2177.2
Land: 1.8 sq. mi.; **Water:** 2.3 sq. mi.   **Elev:** 621 ft.
An old lumber boom town. Incorporated as a city 1891.
Name origin: For its location north of Muskegon.

Norton Shores — City
ZIP: 49441 Lat: 43-09-36 N Long: 86-15-09 W
Pop: 21,755 (1990); 22,025 (1980) Pop Density: 937.7
Land: 23.2 sq. mi.; Water: 1.2 sq. mi. Elev: 612 ft.

Ravenna — Village
ZIP: 49451 Lat: 43-11-22 N Long: 85-56-24 W
Pop: 919 (1990); 951 (1980) Pop Density: 835.5
Land: 1.1 sq. mi.; Water: 0.0 sq. mi.
Founded 1844. Not coextensive with the town of the same name.
Name origin: For Ravenna, OH.

*Ravenna — Township
ZIP: 49451 Lat: 43-09-22 N Long: 85-58-15 W
Pop: 2,354 (1990); 2,471 (1980) Pop Density: 64.8
Land: 36.3 sq. mi.; Water: 0.0 sq. mi.

Roosevelt Park — City
Lat: 43-11-51 N Long: 86-16-24 W
Pop: 3,885 (1990); 4,015 (1980) Pop Density: 3885.0
Land: 1.0 sq. mi.; Water: 0.0 sq. mi.
Incorporated 1946.
Name origin: For Franklin D. Roosevelt (1882–1945), thirty-second U.S. president.

Sullivan — Township
ZIP: 49451 Lat: 43-10-12 N Long: 86-04-30 W
Pop: 2,230 (1990); 2,356 (1980) Pop Density: 92.5
Land: 24.1 sq. mi.; Water: 0.0 sq. mi.

Twin Lake — CDP
ZIP: 49457 Lat: 43-22-08 N Long: 86-10-47 W
Pop: 1,328 (1990) Pop Density: 553.3
Land: 2.4 sq. mi.; Water: 0.5 sq. mi.

Whitehall — City
ZIP: 49461 Lat: 43-23-53 N Long: 86-20-28 W
Pop: 3,027 (1990); 2,856 (1980) Pop Density: 1043.8
Land: 2.9 sq. mi.; Water: 0.6 sq. mi. Elev: 593 ft.
Platted 1859.
Name origin: For its location on White Lake.

*Whitehall — Township
Lat: 43-24-45 N Long: 86-17-47 W
Pop: 1,464 (1990); 1,341 (1980) Pop Density: 154.1
Land: 9.5 sq. mi.; Water: 0.2 sq. mi.

White River — Township
Lat: 43-25-36 N Long: 86-25-15 W
Pop: 1,250 (1990); 1,215 (1980) Pop Density: 78.6
Land: 15.9 sq. mi.; Water: 0.0 sq. mi.

Wolf Lake — CDP
Lat: 43-14-43 N Long: 86-06-21 W
Pop: 4,110 (1990); 3,876 (1980) Pop Density: 1174.3
Land: 3.5 sq. mi.; Water: 0.4 sq. mi.

Newaygo County
County Seat: White Cloud (ZIP: 49349)

Pop: 38,202 (1990); 34,917 (1980) Pop Density: 45.3
Land: 842.4 sq. mi.; Water: 19.0 sq. mi. Area Code: 616
In west-central MI, north of Grand Rapids; established Apr 1, 1840 from unorganized territory.
Name origin: For the Ojibway Indian chief, signer of the Saginaw Treaty of 1819.

Ashland — Township
Lat: 43-20-12 N Long: 85-51-26 W
Pop: 1,997 (1990); 1,751 (1980) Pop Density: 57.2
Land: 34.9 sq. mi.; Water: 0.4 sq. mi. Elev: 784 ft.

Barton — Township
Lat: 43-46-33 N Long: 85-37-56 W
Pop: 624 (1990); 558 (1980) Pop Density: 17.4
Land: 35.8 sq. mi.; Water: 0.0 sq. mi.

Beaver — Township
Lat: 43-40-43 N Long: 85-58-28 W
Pop: 417 (1990); 443 (1980) Pop Density: 11.7
Land: 35.6 sq. mi.; Water: 0.2 sq. mi.

Big Prairie — Township
Lat: 43-31-07 N Long: 85-37-55 W
Pop: 1,731 (1990); 1,202 (1980) Pop Density: 55.0
Land: 31.5 sq. mi.; Water: 4.7 sq. mi.

Bridgeton — Township
ZIP: 49327 Lat: 43-20-05 N Long: 85-58-22 W
Pop: 1,574 (1990); 1,562 (1980) Pop Density: 44.3
Land: 35.5 sq. mi.; Water: 0.5 sq. mi.

Brooks — Township
Lat: 43-25-24 N Long: 85-44-23 W
Pop: 2,728 (1990); 2,349 (1980) Pop Density: 85.8
Land: 31.8 sq. mi.; Water: 2.3 sq. mi.

Croton — Township
ZIP: 49337 Lat: 43-25-03 N Long: 85-37-24 W
Pop: 1,965 (1990); 1,556 (1980) Pop Density: 57.8
Land: 34.0 sq. mi.; Water: 2.3 sq. mi.

Dayton — Township
Lat: 43-30-51 N Long: 85-59-21 W
Pop: 1,971 (1990); 1,938 (1980) Pop Density: 57.8
Land: 34.1 sq. mi.; Water: 0.4 sq. mi.

Denver — Township
Lat: 43-36-12 N Long: 85-59-06 W
Pop: 1,532 (1990); 1,422 (1980) Pop Density: 43.3
Land: 35.4 sq. mi.; Water: 0.4 sq. mi.

Ensley — Township
Lat: 43-20-32 N Long: 85-37-59 W
Pop: 1,984 (1990); 1,461 (1980) Pop Density: 55.6
Land: 35.7 sq. mi.; Water: 0.4 sq. mi.

MICHIGAN, Newaygo County

Everett
Township
Lat: 43-30-40 N **Long:** 85-43-56 W
Pop: 1,519 (1990); 1,360 (1980) **Pop Density:** 42.7
Land: 35.6 sq. mi.; **Water:** 0.2 sq. mi.

Fremont
City
ZIP: 49412 **Lat:** 43-27-41 N **Long:** 85-57-07 W
Pop: 3,875 (1990); 3,672 (1980) **Pop Density:** 1336.2
Land: 2.9 sq. mi.; **Water:** 1.3 sq. mi. **Elev:** 823 ft.

Garfield
Township
Lat: 43-25-29 N **Long:** 85-51-55 W
Pop: 2,067 (1990); 1,822 (1980) **Pop Density:** 61.9
Land: 33.4 sq. mi.; **Water:** 1.0 sq. mi.

Goodwell
Township
Lat: 43-36-03 N **Long:** 85-36-56 W
Pop: 358 (1990); 387 (1980) **Pop Density:** 10.1
Land: 35.6 sq. mi.; **Water:** 0.1 sq. mi.

Grant
City
ZIP: 49327 **Lat:** 43-20-02 N **Long:** 85-48-36 W
Pop: 764 (1990); 683 (1980) **Pop Density:** 1273.3
Land: 0.6 sq. mi.; **Water:** 0.0 sq. mi. **Elev:** 835 ft.
Name origin: For Gen. Ulysses S. Grant (1822–85), eighteenth U.S. president.

*Grant
Township
ZIP: 49327 **Lat:** 43-19-47 N **Long:** 85-44-46 W
Pop: 2,558 (1990); 2,274 (1980) **Pop Density:** 71.3
Land: 35.9 sq. mi.; **Water:** 0.2 sq. mi.

Hesperia
Village
ZIP: 49421 **Lat:** 43-34-10 N **Long:** 86-02-05 W
Pop: 260 (1990); 347 (1980) **Pop Density:** 866.7
Land: 0.3 sq. mi.; **Water:** 0.0 sq. mi.
Incorporated 1883. Part of the town is also in Oceana County.
Name origin: For the classical goddess of gardens.

Home
Township
Lat: 43-46-01 N **Long:** 85-44-37 W
Pop: 202 (1990); 185 (1980) **Pop Density:** 5.7
Land: 35.6 sq. mi.; **Water:** 0.0 sq. mi.

Lilley
Township
Lat: 43-46-27 N **Long:** 85-51-06 W
Pop: 565 (1990); 568 (1980) **Pop Density:** 16.4
Land: 34.5 sq. mi.; **Water:** 1.1 sq. mi.

Lincoln
Township
Lat: 43-36-14 N **Long:** 85-51-53 W
Pop: 969 (1990); 885 (1980) **Pop Density:** 27.6
Land: 35.1 sq. mi.; **Water:** 0.5 sq. mi.

Merrill
Township
Lat: 43-41-06 N **Long:** 85-51-41 W
Pop: 451 (1990); 508 (1980) **Pop Density:** 12.9
Land: 34.9 sq. mi.; **Water:** 0.9 sq. mi.

Monroe
Township
Lat: 43-40-31 N **Long:** 85-44-05 W
Pop: 247 (1990); 263 (1980) **Pop Density:** 6.9
Land: 35.8 sq. mi.; **Water:** 0.2 sq. mi.

Newaygo
City
ZIP: 49337 **Lat:** 43-25-12 N **Long:** 85-48-01 W
Pop: 1,336 (1990); 1,271 (1980) **Pop Density:** 477.1
Land: 2.8 sq. mi.; **Water:** 0.1 sq. mi. **Elev:** 633 ft.
Incorporated 1867.
Name origin: For the Ojibway Indian chief, signer of the Saginaw Treaty of 1819.

Norwich
Township
Lat: 43-41-28 N **Long:** 85-37-26 W
Pop: 499 (1990); 450 (1980) **Pop Density:** 14.1
Land: 35.3 sq. mi.; **Water:** 0.2 sq. mi.

Sheridan Charter
Township
Lat: 43-25-09 N **Long:** 85-59-10 W
Pop: 2,252 (1990); 2,465 (1980) **Pop Density:** 67.4
Land: 33.4 sq. mi.; **Water:** 0.0 sq. mi.

Sherman
Township
Lat: 43-30-32 N **Long:** 85-51-32 W
Pop: 1,866 (1990); 1,810 (1980) **Pop Density:** 53.9
Land: 34.6 sq. mi.; **Water:** 1.2 sq. mi.

Troy
Township
Lat: 43-47-01 N **Long:** 85-59-10 W
Pop: 173 (1990); 199 (1980) **Pop Density:** 4.8
Land: 36.2 sq. mi.; **Water:** 0.1 sq. mi.

White Cloud
City
ZIP: 49349 **Lat:** 43-33-10 N **Long:** 85-46-21 W
Pop: 1,147 (1990); 1,101 (1980) **Pop Density:** 603.7
Land: 1.9 sq. mi.; **Water:** 0.1 sq. mi. **Elev:** 871 ft.
Settled 1870s.
Name origin: Named in 1877. Previously called Morganville for one of the founders.

Wilcox
Township
Lat: 43-36-33 N **Long:** 85-44-50 W
Pop: 831 (1990); 772 (1980) **Pop Density:** 24.5
Land: 33.9 sq. mi.; **Water:** 0.1 sq. mi.

Oakland County
County Seat: Pontiac (ZIP: 48341)

Pop: 1,083,590 (1990); 1,011,790 (1980) **Pop Density:** 1241.6
Land: 872.7 sq. mi.; **Water:** 35.4 sq. mi. **Area Code:** 313

In southeast MI, northwest of Detroit; original county; established Jan 12, 1819 (prior to statehood).

Name origin: For the abundant oak trees in the area.

Addison   Township
ZIP: 48367   **Lat:** 42-50-30 N **Long:** 83-09-26 W
Pop: 5,142 (1990); 4,607 (1980)   **Pop Density:** 142.0
Land: 36.2 sq. mi.; **Water:** 0.9 sq. mi.

Auburn Hills   City
ZIP: 48321   **Lat:** 42-40-28 N **Long:** 83-14-36 W
Pop: 17,076 (1990)   **Pop Density:** 1028.7
Land: 16.6 sq. mi.; **Water:** 0.0 sq. mi.

In southeastern MI, just east of Pontiac, a suburb of Pontiac and Detroit. Established 1983 as a city.

Berkley   City
ZIP: 48072   **Lat:** 42-29-49 N **Long:** 83-11-07 W
Pop: 16,960 (1990); 18,637 (1980)   **Pop Density:** 6523.1
Land: 2.6 sq. mi.; **Water:** 0.0 sq. mi.

In southeastern MI, 15 mi. northwest of Detroit. Established 1829; incorporated as a village 1923; as a city 1932.

Name origin: For a local farm or school, possibly so named for its English-sounding quality.

Beverly Hills   Village
ZIP: 48009   **Lat:** 42-31-11 N **Long:** 83-14-29 W
Pop: 10,610 (1990); 11,598 (1980)   **Pop Density:** 2652.5
Land: 4.0 sq. mi.; **Water:** 0.0 sq. mi.

In southeastern MI, near Pontiac. Established 1958.

Name origin: For the Beverly Hills housing subdivision here.

Bingham Farms   Village
  Lat: 42-30-53 N **Long:** 83-16-40 W
Pop: 1,001 (1990); 529 (1980)   **Pop Density:** 834.2
Land: 1.2 sq. mi.; **Water:** 0.0 sq. mi.   **Elev:** 716 ft.

Incorporated 1955.

Name origin: For the Bingham family's farm.

Birmingham   City
ZIP: 48012   **Lat:** 42-32-41 N **Long:** 83-12-59 W
Pop: 19,997 (1990); 21,689 (1980)   **Pop Density:** 4166.0
Land: 4.8 sq. mi.; **Water:** 0.0 sq. mi.

In southeastern MI, 15 mi. northwest of Detroit, a suburb of Detroit and Pontiac. Founded 1819.

Name origin: For Birmingham, England.

Bloomfield   Township
ZIP: 48302   **Lat:** 42-34-32 N **Long:** 83-16-20 W
Pop: 42,473 (1990); 42,876 (1980)   **Pop Density:** 1698.9
Land: 25.0 sq. mi.; **Water:** 1.1 sq. mi.

Bloomfield Hills   City
ZIP: 48303   **Lat:** 42-34-43 N **Long:** 83-14-50 W
Pop: 4,288 (1990); 3,985 (1980)   **Pop Density:** 875.1
Land: 4.9 sq. mi.; **Water:** 0.0 sq. mi.

In southeastern MI, 19 mi. southwest of Detroit. Established 1932.

Name origin: From its township.

Bloomfield Township   CDP
ZIP: 48201   **Lat:** 42-34-32 N **Long:** 83-16-20 W
Pop: 42,137 (1990); 42,876 (1980)   **Pop Density:** 1692.2
Land: 24.9 sq. mi.; **Water:** 1.1 sq. mi.

Brandon   Township
ZIP: 48462   **Lat:** 42-50-07 N **Long:** 83-23-10 W
Pop: 12,051 (1990); 9,526 (1980)   **Pop Density:** 343.3
Land: 35.1 sq. mi.; **Water:** 0.8 sq. mi.

Clarkston   Village
ZIP: 48016   **Lat:** 42-44-07 N **Long:** 83-25-15 W
Pop: 1,005 (1990); 968 (1980)   **Pop Density:** 2010.0
Land: 0.5 sq. mi.; **Water:** 0.0 sq. mi.

Name origin: For the Clark brothers, who platted the town in 1840.

Clawson   City
ZIP: 48017   **Lat:** 42-32-13 N **Long:** 83-09-05 W
Pop: 13,874 (1990); 15,103 (1980)   **Pop Density:** 6306.4
Land: 2.2 sq. mi.; **Water:** 0.0 sq. mi.   **Elev:** 667 ft.

In southeastern MI, 10 mi. northwest of Detroit. Established 1920 as village; 1940 as city.

Name origin: For the local Lawson family, but a clerical error occurred and the post office approved the present name.

Commerce   Township
ZIP: 48382   **Lat:** 42-34-33 N **Long:** 83-29-39 W
Pop: 26,955 (1990); 23,757 (1980)   **Pop Density:** 976.6
Land: 27.6 sq. mi.; **Water:** 2.3 sq. mi.

Charter township in southeastern MI, 30 mi. northwest of Detroit.

Name origin: With high hopes for the future.

Farmington   City
ZIP: 48333   **Lat:** 42-27-47 N **Long:** 83-22-38 W
Pop: 10,132 (1990); 11,022 (1980)   **Pop Density:** 3752.6
Land: 2.7 sq. mi.; **Water:** 0.0 sq. mi.

In southeastern MI, midway between Flint and Pontiac. Established 1823.

Name origin: For Farmington, NY, home of the first settlers.

Farmington Hills   City
ZIP: 48331   **Lat:** 42-29-09 N **Long:** 83-22-32 W
Pop: 74,652 (1990); 58,056 (1980)   **Pop Density:** 2241.8
Land: 33.3 sq. mi.; **Water:** 0.0 sq. mi.   **Elev:** 800 ft.

In southeastern MI. Established as a city 1973.

Name origin: Former township name.

Ferndale   City
ZIP: 48220   **Lat:** 42-27-33 N **Long:** 83-07-51 W
Pop: 25,084 (1990); 26,227 (1980)   **Pop Density:** 6431.8
Land: 3.9 sq. mi.; **Water:** 0.0 sq. mi.   **Elev:** 649 ft.

In southeastern MI in Detroit's northwestern metropolitan area. Founded 1917. Incorporated as village 1918; as city 1927.

Name origin: For its descriptive connotations.

Franklin
Village
ZIP: 48025 **Lat:** 42-31-02 N **Long:** 83-18-07 W
Pop: 2,626 (1990); 2,864 (1980) **Pop Density:** 972.6
Land: 2.7 sq. mi.; **Water:** 0.0 sq. mi. **Elev:** 833 ft.
PA settlers arrived in the 1820s.
Name origin: For Benjamin Franklin (1706–90), U.S. patriot, diplomat, and statesman.

Groveland
Township
Lat: 42-50-24 N **Long:** 83-30-36 W
Pop: 4,705 (1990); 4,114 (1980) **Pop Density:** 132.2
Land: 35.6 sq. mi.; **Water:** 0.5 sq. mi.

Hazel Park
City
ZIP: 48030 **Lat:** 42-27-46 N **Long:** 83-05-53 W
Pop: 20,051 (1990); 20,914 (1980) **Pop Density:** 7161.1
Land: 2.8 sq. mi.; **Water:** 0.0 sq. mi.
In southeastern MI, 10 mi. north of Detroit. Incorporated 1942.
Name origin: For the area's many hazelnut bushes. Previously called Hazel Stump.

Highland
Township
ZIP: 48356 **Lat:** 42-39-12 N **Long:** 83-37-10 W
Pop: 17,941 (1990); 16,958 (1980) **Pop Density:** 532.4
Land: 33.7 sq. mi.; **Water:** 2.1 sq. mi.
Charter township in southeastern MI, 40 mi. north of Detroit. Established 1835.
Name origin: The site was supposed to be highest land in settled MI, with water running north and south.

Holly
Village
ZIP: 48442 **Lat:** 42-47-56 N **Long:** 83-37-21 W
Pop: 5,595 (1990); 4,874 (1980) **Pop Density:** 1998.2
Land: 2.8 sq. mi.; **Water:** 0.3 sq. mi. **Elev:** 937 ft.
Settled 1840s. Not coextensive with the town of the same name.
Name origin: For the abundant holly bushes.

*Holly
Township
ZIP: 48442 **Lat:** 42-49-35 N **Long:** 83-37-31 W
Pop: 8,852 (1990); 8,486 (1980) **Pop Density:** 254.4
Land: 34.8 sq. mi.; **Water:** 1.8 sq. mi.

Huntington Woods
City
ZIP: 48070 **Lat:** 42-28-53 N **Long:** 83-10-05 W
Pop: 6,419 (1990); 6,937 (1980) **Pop Density:** 4279.3
Land: 1.5 sq. mi.; **Water:** 0.0 sq. mi.
Name origin: Descriptively named for the area's small-game hunting locale.

Independence
Township
ZIP: 48346 **Lat:** 42-44-45 N **Long:** 83-23-23 W
Pop: 24,722 (1990); 21,537 (1980) **Pop Density:** 692.5
Land: 35.7 sq. mi.; **Water:** 1.2 sq. mi.

Keego Harbor
City
ZIP: 48320 **Lat:** 42-36-24 N **Long:** 83-20-39 W
Pop: 2,932 (1990); 3,083 (1980) **Pop Density:** 5864.0
Land: 0.5 sq. mi.; **Water:** 0.0 sq. mi.
Developed 1902.
Name origin: For the keego, a local, slender fish.

Lake Angelus
City
ZIP: 48055 **Lat:** 42-41-30 N **Long:** 83-19-31 W
Pop: 328 (1990); 397 (1980) **Pop Density:** 328.0
Land: 1.0 sq. mi.; **Water:** 0.6 sq. mi.

Lake Orion
Village
ZIP: 48035 **Lat:** 42-47-01 N **Long:** 83-14-39 W
Pop: 3,057 (1990); 2,907 (1980) **Pop Density:** 3821.3
Land: 0.8 sq. mi.; **Water:** 0.5 sq. mi.
Name origin: Named in 1859 for the lake formed by a power dam in 1828, and for the mythical hunter and the constellation named for him. Previously called Canandiagua City.

Lathrup Village
City
ZIP: 48076 **Lat:** 42-29-32 N **Long:** 83-13-38 W
Pop: 4,329 (1990); 4,639 (1980) **Pop Density:** 2886.0
Land: 1.5 sq. mi.; **Water:** 0.0 sq. mi. **Elev:** 703 ft.
Founded 1926 by real estate developer Louise Lathrup.
Name origin: For the founder.

Leonard
Village
ZIP: 48367 **Lat:** 42-51-57 N **Long:** 83-08-35 W
Pop: 357 (1990); 423 (1980) **Pop Density:** 357.0
Land: 1.0 sq. mi.; **Water:** 0.0 sq. mi. **Elev:** 1003 ft.
Founded 1882 by Leonard Rowland.
Name origin: For its founder.

Lyon
Township
ZIP: 48167 **Lat:** 42-28-53 N **Long:** 83-36-12 W
Pop: 9,450 (1990); 7,078 (1980) **Pop Density:** 295.3
Land: 32.0 sq. mi.; **Water:** 0.6 sq. mi.

Madison Heights
City
ZIP: 48071 **Lat:** 42-30-13 N **Long:** 83-06-09 W
Pop: 32,196 (1990); 35,375 (1980) **Pop Density:** 4471.7
Land: 7.2 sq. mi.; **Water:** 0.0 sq. mi.
In southeastern MI, in the Detroit metropolitan area, 12 mi. north of Detroit. Incorporated January 17, 1955.

Milford
Village
ZIP: 48380 **Lat:** 42-35-08 N **Long:** 83-36-04 W
Pop: 5,511 (1990); 5,041 (1980) **Pop Density:** 2204.4
Land: 2.5 sq. mi.; **Water:** 0.1 sq. mi. **Elev:** 945 ft.
In southeastern MI, 20 mi. northwest of Detroit. Charter township established 1831; incorporated as village 1869. Not coextensive with the town of the same name.
Name origin: For the water-mill resources of the nearby Huron River and Pettibone Creek.

*Milford
Township
ZIP: 48380 **Lat:** 42-33-57 N **Long:** 83-36-56 W
Pop: 12,121 (1990); 10,187 (1980) **Pop Density:** 364.0
Land: 33.3 sq. mi.; **Water:** 1.9 sq. mi.

Northville
City
ZIP: 48167 **Lat:** 42-26-23 N **Long:** 83-29-36 W
Pop: 3,367 (1990); 2,785 (1980) **Pop Density:** 3367.0
Land: 1.0 sq. mi.; **Water:** 0.0 sq. mi. **Elev:** 829 ft.
Settlers arrived 1825. Part of the town is also in Wayne County.

Novi
City
ZIP: 48376 **Lat:** 42-28-31 N **Long:** 83-29-25 W
Pop: 32,998 (1990); 22,525 (1980) **Pop Density:** 1081.9
Land: 30.5 sq. mi.; **Water:** 0.9 sq. mi. **Elev:** 909 ft.
In southeastern MI, 25 mi. northwest of Detroit. Settled 1825; incorporated as a city 1969.
Name origin: Perhaps a spelling of No. VI (the place being the sixth stopping point on an old toll road out of Detroit), or from the Latin meaning 'new,' implying a fresh start.

MICHIGAN, Oakland County

*Novi — Township
Lat: 42-27-21 N Long: 83-28-55 W
Pop: 150 (1990); 150 (1980) **Pop Density:** 1500.0
Land: 0.1 sq. mi.; **Water:** 0.0 sq. mi.

Oakland Charter — Township
ZIP: 48363 Lat: 42-45-17 N Long: 83-09-45 W
Pop: 8,227 (1990); 7,628 (1980) **Pop Density:** 226.0
Land: 36.4 sq. mi.; **Water:** 0.3 sq. mi.

Oak Park — City
ZIP: 48237 Lat: 42-27-47 N Long: 83-10-49 W
Pop: 30,462 (1990); 31,537 (1980) **Pop Density:** 6092.4
Land: 5.0 sq. mi.; **Water:** 0.0 sq. mi. **Elev:** 666 ft.
In southeastern MI in Detroit's northwestern metropolitan area. Incorporated 1927; chartered as a city 1945.
Name origin: For its descriptive connotations.

Orchard Lake Village — City
Lat: 42-34-56 N Long: 83-22-38 W
Pop: 2,286 (1990); 1,798 (1980) **Pop Density:** 879.2
Land: 2.6 sq. mi.; **Water:** 1.5 sq. mi.
Name origin: For its lake and apple orchards. Known to the Indians by a term meaning 'apple place.'

Orion — Township
ZIP: 48360 Lat: 42-45-07 N Long: 83-16-48 W
Pop: 24,076 (1990); 22,473 (1980) **Pop Density:** 720.8
Land: 33.4 sq. mi.; **Water:** 2.6 sq. mi.
Charter township in southeastern MI, northeast of Pontiac. Established 1835.
Name origin: Because "it was short, easy to write, and altogether lovely."

Ortonville — Village
ZIP: 48462 Lat: 42-51-05 N Long: 83-26-39 W
Pop: 1,252 (1990); 1,190 (1980) **Pop Density:** 1252.0
Land: 1.0 sq. mi.; **Water:** 0.0 sq. mi. **Elev:** 941 ft.
Name origin: For pioneer Amos Orton, who built a sawmill here in 1848.

Oxford — Village
ZIP: 48370 Lat: 42-49-15 N Long: 83-15-14 W
Pop: 2,929 (1990); 2,746 (1980) **Pop Density:** 2440.8
Land: 1.2 sq. mi.; **Water:** 0.2 sq. mi. **Elev:** 1057 ft.
In southeastern MI, 35 mi. northwest of Detroit. Founded 1836; chartered 1876. Not coextensive with the town of the same name.
Name origin: For the township, itself named because "most settlers had ox teams and would probably keep them for years to come."

*Oxford — Township
ZIP: 48370 Lat: 42-50-23 N Long: 83-16-41 W
Pop: 11,933 (1990); 10,569 (1980) **Pop Density:** 352.0
Land: 33.9 sq. mi.; **Water:** 1.3 sq. mi.

Pleasant Ridge — City
ZIP: 48069 Lat: 42-28-15 N Long: 83-08-41 W
Pop: 2,775 (1990); 3,217 (1980) **Pop Density:** 4625.0
Land: 0.6 sq. mi.; **Water:** 0.0 sq. mi.
Founded 1913.
Name origin: For a local thoroughfare, Ridge Road.

Pontiac — City
ZIP: 48343 Lat: 42-38-56 N Long: 83-17-13 W
Pop: 71,166 (1990); 76,715 (1980) **Pop Density:** 3558.3
Land: 20.0 sq. mi.; **Water:** 0.2 sq. mi. **Elev:** 943 ft.
In southeastern MI, 25 mi. northwest of Detroit. County seat; settled 1818; incorporated 1861.
Name origin: For Pontiac (c. 1720–69), an Ottawa Indian chief of French and Indian War fame.

Rochester — City
ZIP: 48308 Lat: 42-41-12 N Long: 83-07-25 W
Pop: 7,130 (1990); 7,203 (1980) **Pop Density:** 1828.2
Land: 3.9 sq. mi.; **Water:** 0.0 sq. mi. **Elev:** 749 ft.
Settled 1817. Incorporated as village in 1869, city in 1967.
Name origin: For Rochester, NY.

Rochester Hills — City
ZIP: 48309 Lat: 42-39-56 N Long: 83-09-29 W
Pop: 61,766 (1990) **Pop Density:** 1883.1
Land: 32.8 sq. mi.; **Water:** 0.1 sq. mi.
In southeastern MI, 20 mi. northwest of Detroit, a suburb of Pontiac. City formed 1984.
Name origin: Probably for Rochester, NY.

Rose — Township
ZIP: 48442 Lat: 42-44-23 N Long: 83-37-26 W
Pop: 4,926 (1990); 4,465 (1980) **Pop Density:** 140.7
Land: 35.0 sq. mi.; **Water:** 1.3 sq. mi.

Royal Oak — City
ZIP: 48068 Lat: 42-30-30 N Long: 83-09-16 W
Pop: 65,410 (1990); 70,893 (1980) **Pop Density:** 5543.2
Land: 11.8 sq. mi.; **Water:** 0.0 sq. mi.
In southeastern MI, 10 mi. north of Detroit. Organized as a township in 1832, incorporated as a village in 1891; as a city in 1921.
Name origin: Named by Gov. Lewis Cass (1782–1866) for a large oak tree that reminded him of the famous Royal Oak of Scotland.

*Royal Oak — Township
ZIP: 48220 Lat: 42-27-11 N Long: 83-10-12 W
Pop: 5,011 (1990); 5,784 (1980) **Pop Density:** 7158.6
Land: 0.7 sq. mi.; **Water:** 0.0 sq. mi.

Southfield — City
ZIP: 48037 Lat: 42-28-32 N Long: 83-15-33 W
Pop: 75,728 (1990); 75,568 (1980) **Pop Density:** 2890.4
Land: 26.2 sq. mi.; **Water:** 0.0 sq. mi. **Elev:** 684 ft.
In southeastern MI, 15 mi. northwest of Detroit. Settled 1823.
Name origin: For its township.

*Southfield — Township
ZIP: 48009 Lat: 42-31-14 N Long: 83-16-06 W
Pop: 14,255 (1990); 15,031 (1980) **Pop Density:** 1781.9
Land: 8.0 sq. mi.; **Water:** 0.0 sq. mi.

South Lyon — City
ZIP: 48178 Lat: 42-27-38 N Long: 83-39-04 W
Pop: 5,857 (1990); 5,214 (1980) **Pop Density:** 2169.3
Land: 2.7 sq. mi.; **Water:** 0.0 sq. mi. **Elev:** 919 ft.
Name origin: Descriptively named for its location in Lyon Township.

Springfield — Township
ZIP: 48346 Lat: 42-44-27 N Long: 83-30-20 W
Pop: 9,927 (1990); 8,295 (1980) **Pop Density:** 278.8
Land: 35.6 sq. mi.; **Water:** 1.2 sq. mi.

MICHIGAN, Oakland County

Sylvan Lake
City
ZIP: 48053 **Lat:** 42-37-01 N **Long:** 83-19-58 W
Pop: 1,884 (1990); 1,949 (1980) **Pop Density:** 3768.0
Land: 0.5 sq. mi.; **Water:** 0.3 sq. mi.
Organized 1921.
Name origin: For its location near Sylvan Lake.

Troy
City
ZIP: 48099 **Lat:** 42-34-48 N **Long:** 83-08-34 W
Pop: 72,884 (1990); 67,102 (1980) **Pop Density:** 2175.6
Land: 33.5 sq. mi.; **Water:** 0.1 sq. mi.
In southeastern MI, 20 mi. northwest of Detroit.
Name origin: For Troy, New York. First settled in 1822; established as a city in 1955.

Walled Lake
City
ZIP: 48390 **Lat:** 42-32-02 N **Long:** 83-28-42 W
Pop: 6,278 (1990); 4,748 (1980) **Pop Density:** 2729.6
Land: 2.3 sq. mi.; **Water:** 0.2 sq. mi. **Elev:** 939 ft.
Settled 1830s along Walled Lake.
Name origin: Descriptively named because the lake appeared to have been walled either by man, drift deposit, or by the action of water and ice.

Waterford
Township
ZIP: 48329 **Lat:** 42-39-46 N **Long:** 83-23-16 W
Pop: 66,692 (1990); 64,437 (1980) **Pop Density:** 2130.7
Land: 31.3 sq. mi.; **Water:** 4.0 sq. mi.
Charter township in southeastern MI, northwest of Pontiac. Established 1835.

West Bloomfield
Township
ZIP: 48323 **Lat:** 42-34-09 N **Long:** 83-22-55 W
Pop: 54,516 (1990); 41,962 (1980) **Pop Density:** 1996.9
Land: 27.3 sq. mi.; **Water:** 3.9 sq. mi.
Established 1833.

White Lake
Township
ZIP: 48383 **Lat:** 42-39-15 N **Long:** 83-30-04 W
Pop: 22,608 (1990); 21,870 (1980) **Pop Density:** 672.9
Land: 33.6 sq. mi.; **Water:** 3.5 sq. mi.
In southeastern MI, west of Pontiac.
Name origin: For the largest lake in the township.

Wixom
City
ZIP: 48393 **Lat:** 42-31-26 N **Long:** 83-32-07 W
Pop: 8,550 (1990); 6,705 (1980) **Pop Density:** 909.6
Land: 9.4 sq. mi.; **Water:** 0.1 sq. mi. **Elev:** 930 ft.
Settled 1830 by Lewis Norton.
Name origin: For early settler Willard Wixom.

Wolverine Lake
Village
ZIP: 48088 **Lat:** 42-33-24 N **Long:** 83-29-03 W
Pop: 4,727 (1990); 4,968 (1980) **Pop Density:** 3636.2
Land: 1.3 sq. mi.; **Water:** 0.4 sq. mi.
Platted 1881.
Name origin: For the man-made lake named for MI's state animal.

Oceana County
County Seat: Hart (ZIP: 49420)

Pop: 22,454 (1990); 22,002 (1980) **Pop Density:** 41.5
Land: 540.5 sq. mi.; **Water:** 766.3 sq. mi. **Area Code:** 616
On the west-central coast of MI, bordered on west by Lake Michigan; established Mar 2, 1831 (prior to statehood) from Newaygo County.
Name origin: For its long shoreline on the "fresh water ocean" of Lake Michigan.

Benona
Township
Lat: 43-36-13 N **Long:** 86-28-00 W
Pop: 1,133 (1990); 1,203 (1980) **Pop Density:** 27.8
Land: 40.8 sq. mi.; **Water:** 0.5 sq. mi.

Claybanks
Township
Lat: 43-31-22 N **Long:** 86-26-24 W
Pop: 679 (1990); 733 (1980) **Pop Density:** 28.4
Land: 23.9 sq. mi.; **Water:** 0.1 sq. mi.

Colfax
Township
Lat: 43-46-23 N **Long:** 86-05-52 W
Pop: 374 (1990); 328 (1980) **Pop Density:** 10.6
Land: 35.4 sq. mi.; **Water:** 0.6 sq. mi.

Crystal
Township
Lat: 43-46-30 N **Long:** 86-13-24 W
Pop: 658 (1990); 602 (1980) **Pop Density:** 18.3
Land: 36.0 sq. mi.; **Water:** 0.0 sq. mi.

Elbridge
Township
Lat: 43-41-06 N **Long:** 86-13-06 W
Pop: 820 (1990); 899 (1980) **Pop Density:** 22.7
Land: 36.2 sq. mi.; **Water:** 0.1 sq. mi.

Ferry
Township
Lat: 43-35-57 N **Long:** 86-13-10 W
Pop: 1,033 (1990); 898 (1980) **Pop Density:** 28.7
Land: 36.0 sq. mi.; **Water:** 0.1 sq. mi.

Golden
Township
Lat: 43-41-27 N **Long:** 86-27-07 W
Pop: 1,302 (1990); 1,358 (1980) **Pop Density:** 38.9
Land: 33.5 sq. mi.; **Water:** 1.5 sq. mi.

Grant
Township
Lat: 43-30-55 N **Long:** 86-20-23 W
Pop: 2,578 (1990); 2,366 (1980) **Pop Density:** 72.8
Land: 35.4 sq. mi.; **Water:** 0.4 sq. mi.

Greenwood
Township
Lat: 43-30-39 N **Long:** 86-05-49 W
Pop: 915 (1990); 815 (1980) **Pop Density:** 25.6
Land: 35.8 sq. mi.; **Water:** 0.2 sq. mi.

American Places Dictionary   **MICHIGAN, Ogemaw County**

Hart   City
ZIP: 49420   **Lat:** 43-41-49 N   **Long:** 86-21-47 W
Pop: 1,942 (1990); 1,888 (1980)   **Pop Density:** 1493.8
Land: 1.3 sq. mi.; **Water:** 0.1 sq. mi.
Settled 1856.
Name origin: For early pioneer Wellington Hart.

***Hart**   Township
ZIP: 49420   **Lat:** 43-41-12 N   **Long:** 86-19-56 W
Pop: 1,513 (1990); 1,801 (1980)   **Pop Density:** 43.9
Land: 34.5 sq. mi.; **Water:** 0.4 sq. mi.

Hesperia   Village
ZIP: 49421   **Lat:** 43-34-04 N   **Long:** 86-02-40 W
Pop: 586 (1990); 529 (1980)   **Pop Density:** 1172.0
Land: 0.5 sq. mi.; **Water:** 0.0 sq. mi.
Incorporated 1883. Part of the town is also in Newaygo County.
Name origin: For the classical goddess of gardens.

Leavitt   Township
Lat: 43-41-07 N   **Long:** 86-05-54 W
Pop: 804 (1990); 848 (1980)   **Pop Density:** 22.8
Land: 35.3 sq. mi.; **Water:** 0.6 sq. mi.

New Era   Village
ZIP: 49446   **Lat:** 43-33-34 N   **Long:** 86-20-48 W
Pop: 520 (1990); 534 (1980)   **Pop Density:** 650.0
Land: 0.8 sq. mi.; **Water:** 0.0 sq. mi.   **Elev:** 754 ft.
Name origin: Named by the early settlers for their new beginning.

Newfield   Township
Lat: 43-35-35 N   **Long:** 86-05-58 W
Pop: 2,144 (1990); 1,968 (1980)   **Pop Density:** 61.1
Land: 35.1 sq. mi.; **Water:** 0.7 sq. mi.

Otto   Township
Lat: 43-30-05 N   **Long:** 86-13-15 W
Pop: 404 (1990); 426 (1980)   **Pop Density:** 11.3
Land: 35.9 sq. mi.; **Water:** 0.1 sq. mi.

Pentwater   Village
ZIP: 49449   **Lat:** 43-46-45 N   **Long:** 86-25-51 W
Pop: 1,050 (1990); 1,165 (1980)   **Pop Density:** 807.7
Land: 1.3 sq. mi.; **Water:** 0.3 sq. mi.   **Elev:** 689 ft.
Settled 1850s. Not coextensive with the town of the same name.
Name origin: For nearby Pentwater Lake, itself named either because its small outlet made it 'pent-up water,' or else a corruption of *paint water* for its dark color.

***Pentwater**   Township
ZIP: 49449   **Lat:** 43-46-01 N   **Long:** 86-25-37 W
Pop: 1,422 (1990); 1,424 (1980)   **Pop Density:** 106.1
Land: 13.4 sq. mi.; **Water:** 0.7 sq. mi.

Rothbury   Village
ZIP: 49452   **Lat:** 43-30-26 N   **Long:** 86-20-54 W
Pop: 407 (1990); 522 (1980)   **Pop Density:** 407.0
Land: 1.0 sq. mi.; **Water:** 0.0 sq. mi.   **Elev:** 690 ft.

Shelby   Village
ZIP: 49455   **Lat:** 43-36-39 N   **Long:** 86-21-54 W
Pop: 1,871 (1990); 1,624 (1980)   **Pop Density:** 1169.4
Land: 1.6 sq. mi.; **Water:** 0.0 sq. mi.
Not coextensive with the town of the same name.
Name origin: For Isaac Shelby (1750–1826), first KY governor, whose volunteer force defeated the British at Detroit (Battle of the Thames) in the War of 1812.

***Shelby**   Township
ZIP: 49455   **Lat:** 43-36-10 N   **Long:** 86-20-21 W
Pop: 3,692 (1990); 3,506 (1980)   **Pop Density:** 102.6
Land: 36.0 sq. mi.; **Water:** 0.1 sq. mi.

Walkerville   Village
ZIP: 49459   **Lat:** 43-42-53 N   **Long:** 86-07-32 W
Pop: 262 (1990); 296 (1980)   **Pop Density:** 218.3
Land: 1.2 sq. mi.; **Water:** 0.0 sq. mi.   **Elev:** 870 ft.

Weare   Township
Lat: 43-46-20 N   **Long:** 86-20-28 W
Pop: 1,041 (1990); 939 (1980)   **Pop Density:** 28.8
Land: 36.1 sq. mi.; **Water:** 0.0 sq. mi.

Ogemaw County
County Seat: West Branch (ZIP: 48661)

Pop: 18,681 (1990); 16,436 (1980)   **Pop Density:** 33.1
Land: 564.4 sq. mi.; **Water:** 10.3 sq. mi.   **Area Code:** 517
In northeast MI, north of Bay City; established Apr 1, 1840.
Name origin: The Chippewa word for 'chief.'

Churchill   Township
Lat: 44-17-22 N   **Long:** 84-04-19 W
Pop: 1,130 (1990); 1,058 (1980)   **Pop Density:** 31.7
Land: 35.7 sq. mi.; **Water:** 0.3 sq. mi.

Cumming   Township
Lat: 44-23-31 N   **Long:** 84-03-50 W
Pop: 686 (1990); 675 (1980)   **Pop Density:** 19.8
Land: 34.7 sq. mi.; **Water:** 0.7 sq. mi.

Edwards   Township
Lat: 44-12-10 N   **Long:** 84-18-26 W
Pop: 1,210 (1990); 1,036 (1980)   **Pop Density:** 34.6
Land: 35.0 sq. mi.; **Water:** 0.7 sq. mi.   **Elev:** 847 ft.

Foster   Township
Lat: 44-25-57 N   **Long:** 84-17-45 W
Pop: 719 (1990); 463 (1980)   **Pop Density:** 8.1
Land: 89.3 sq. mi.; **Water:** 0.6 sq. mi.

Goodar   Township
Lat: 44-26-58 N   **Long:** 83-57-03 W
Pop: 381 (1990); 374 (1980)   **Pop Density:** 10.8
Land: 35.3 sq. mi.; **Water:** 0.6 sq. mi.   **Elev:** 1040 ft.

Hill   Township
Lat: 44-22-56 N   **Long:** 83-56-55 W
Pop: 1,546 (1990); 1,301 (1980)   **Pop Density:** 47.3
Land: 32.7 sq. mi.; **Water:** 3.4 sq. mi.

MICHIGAN, Ogemaw County

Horton
Township
Lat: 44-12-29 N **Long:** 84-11-10 W
Pop: 955 (1990); 729 (1980) **Pop Density:** 26.9
Land: 35.5 sq. mi.; **Water:** 0.3 sq. mi.

Klacking
Township
Lat: 44-22-50 N **Long:** 84-11-49 W
Pop: 430 (1990); 386 (1980) **Pop Density:** 12.0
Land: 35.8 sq. mi.; **Water:** 0.1 sq. mi.

Logan
Township
Lat: 44-17-15 N **Long:** 83-56-01 W
Pop: 547 (1990); 567 (1980) **Pop Density:** 15.5
Land: 35.3 sq. mi.; **Water:** 0.7 sq. mi.

Mills
Township
Lat: 44-12-16 N **Long:** 84-04-08 W
Pop: 3,174 (1990); 2,624 (1980) **Pop Density:** 92.0
Land: 34.5 sq. mi.; **Water:** 1.1 sq. mi.

Ogemaw
Township
Lat: 44-17-08 N **Long:** 84-18-24 W
Pop: 893 (1990); 814 (1980) **Pop Density:** 24.5
Land: 36.4 sq. mi.; **Water:** 0.1 sq. mi.

Prescott
Village
ZIP: 48756 **Lat:** 44-11-29 N **Long:** 83-55-54 W
Pop: 314 (1990); 332 (1980) **Pop Density:** 261.7
Land: 1.2 sq. mi.; **Water:** 0.0 sq. mi.
Name origin: For pioneer railroadman C. H. Prescott, who established a railroad here in 1880.

Richland
Township
Lat: 44-12-40 N **Long:** 83-56-52 W
Pop: 856 (1990); 803 (1980) **Pop Density:** 24.6
Land: 34.8 sq. mi.; **Water:** 0.9 sq. mi.

Rose
Township
Lat: 44-28-15 N **Long:** 84-05-58 W
Pop: 1,260 (1990); 1,085 (1980) **Pop Density:** 23.8
Land: 52.9 sq. mi.; **Water:** 0.3 sq. mi.

Rose City
City
ZIP: 48654 **Lat:** 44-25-15 N **Long:** 84-06-55 W
Pop: 686 (1990); 661 (1980) **Pop Density:** 623.6
Land: 1.1 sq. mi.; **Water:** 0.0 sq. mi.
Incorporated 1892.
Name origin: For pioneer storekeeper Allan S. Rose.

Skidway Lake
CDP
Lat: 44-11-38 N **Long:** 84-02-40 W
Pop: 2,569 (1990) **Pop Density:** 227.3
Land: 11.3 sq. mi.; **Water:** 0.3 sq. mi.

West Branch
City
ZIP: 48661 **Lat:** 44-16-32 N **Long:** 84-14-07 W
Pop: 1,914 (1990); 1,785 (1980) **Pop Density:** 1595.0
Land: 1.2 sq. mi.; **Water:** 0.0 sq. mi. **Elev:** 959 ft.
Railroad arrived 1871.
Name origin: For its location on the west branch of the Rifle River.

*West Branch
Township
ZIP: 48661 **Lat:** 44-17-33 N **Long:** 84-11-33 W
Pop: 2,294 (1990); 2,075 (1980) **Pop Density:** 66.9
Land: 34.3 sq. mi.; **Water:** 0.5 sq. mi.

Ontonagon County
County Seat: Ontonagon (ZIP: 49953)

Pop: 8,854 (1990); 9,861 (1980) **Pop Density:** 6.8
Land: 1311.6 sq. mi.; **Water:** 2429.7 sq. mi. **Area Code:** 906
On the northwest coast of the Upper Peninsula of MI; established Mar 9, 1843 from Michilimackinac and Chippewa counties.
Name origin: For the Ontonagon River, which runs through it; from Ojibway *onagan* 'dish' or 'bowl,' from the shape of the river's mouth.

Bergland
Township
ZIP: 49910 **Lat:** 46-34-29 N **Long:** 89-39-00 W
Pop: 618 (1990); 648 (1980) **Pop Density:** 6.3
Land: 98.5 sq. mi.; **Water:** 9.8 sq. mi.

Bohemia
Township
Lat: 46-50-19 N **Long:** 88-57-34 W
Pop: 90 (1990); 116 (1980) **Pop Density:** 1.0
Land: 91.9 sq. mi.; **Water:** 0.5 sq. mi.

Carp Lake
Township
Lat: 46-44-05 N **Long:** 89-40-44 W
Pop: 1,193 (1990); 1,434 (1980) **Pop Density:** 5.3
Land: 225.1 sq. mi.; **Water:** 0.8 sq. mi.

Greenland
Township
Lat: 46-48-08 N **Long:** 89-03-16 W
Pop: 1,001 (1990); 1,181 (1980) **Pop Density:** 8.8
Land: 113.2 sq. mi.; **Water:** 0.0 sq. mi.

Haight
Township
Lat: 46-24-07 N **Long:** 89-13-00 W
Pop: 218 (1990); 228 (1980) **Pop Density:** 2.1
Land: 105.8 sq. mi.; **Water:** 1.3 sq. mi.

Interior
Township
Lat: 46-26-37 N **Long:** 89-02-55 W
Pop: 480 (1990); 528 (1980) **Pop Density:** 5.5
Land: 86.5 sq. mi.; **Water:** 3.0 sq. mi.

Matchwood
Township
Lat: 46-34-35 N **Long:** 89-27-45 W
Pop: 122 (1990); 137 (1980) **Pop Density:** 1.1
Land: 109.5 sq. mi.; **Water:** 0.0 sq. mi.

McMillan
Township
Lat: 46-31-04 N **Long:** 89-18-05 W
Pop: 650 (1990); 688 (1980) **Pop Density:** 9.2
Land: 70.4 sq. mi.; **Water:** 0.1 sq. mi.

Ontonagon   Village
ZIP: 49953   **Lat:** 46-52-01 N   **Long:** 89-18-51 W
Pop: 2,040 (1990); 2,182 (1980)   **Pop Density:** 582.9
Land: 3.5 sq. mi.; **Water:** 0.1 sq. mi.   **Elev:** 642 ft.
Platted 1854. Not coextensive with the town of the same name.
Name origin: From Ojibway *onagan* 'dish' or 'bowl,' from the shape of the Ontonagon River's mouth.

*Ontonagon   Township
ZIP: 49953   **Lat:** 46-49-04 N   **Long:** 89-16-40 W
Pop: 3,238 (1990); 3,525 (1980)   **Pop Density:** 16.8
Land: 192.9 sq. mi.; **Water:** 0.8 sq. mi.

Rockland   Township
   Lat: 46-41-13 N   **Long:** 89-14-06 W
Pop: 371 (1990); 448 (1980)   **Pop Density:** 4.0
Land: 92.8 sq. mi.; **Water:** 1.0 sq. mi.

Stannard   Township
   Lat: 46-36-44 N   **Long:** 89-08-31 W
Pop: 873 (1990); 928 (1980)   **Pop Density:** 7.0
Land: 125.1 sq. mi.; **Water:** 0.0 sq. mi.

Osceola County
County Seat: Reed City (ZIP: 49677)

Pop: 20,146 (1990); 18,928 (1980)   **Pop Density:** 35.6
Land: 566.1 sq. mi.; **Water:** 7.0 sq. mi.   **Area Code:** 616
In central MI, south of Cadillac; established as Unwattin County Apr 1, 1840; name changed Mar 8, 1843.
Name origin: For the Seminole chief (c. 1804–38) who led the second Seminole War against the U.S.

Burdell   Township
   Lat: 44-07-02 N   **Long:** 85-30-10 W
Pop: 1,153 (1990); 1,067 (1980)   **Pop Density:** 30.8
Land: 37.4 sq. mi.; **Water:** 0.2 sq. mi.

Cedar   Township
   Lat: 43-56-52 N   **Long:** 85-22-53 W
Pop: 267 (1990); 235 (1980)   **Pop Density:** 7.7
Land: 34.5 sq. mi.; **Water:** 0.6 sq. mi.

Evart   City
ZIP: 49631   **Lat:** 43-54-08 N   **Long:** 85-16-25 W
Pop: 1,744 (1990); 1,945 (1980)   **Pop Density:** 872.0
Land: 2.0 sq. mi.; **Water:** 0.0 sq. mi.
Name origin: For Civil War veteran Perry Everts, who settled in the area.

*Evart   Township
ZIP: 49631   **Lat:** 43-51-33 N   **Long:** 85-16-05 W
Pop: 1,229 (1990); 1,029 (1980)   **Pop Density:** 37.5
Land: 32.8 sq. mi.; **Water:** 1.4 sq. mi.

Hartwick   Township
   Lat: 44-01-23 N   **Long:** 85-16-25 W
Pop: 456 (1990); 420 (1980)   **Pop Density:** 13.0
Land: 35.0 sq. mi.; **Water:** 0.5 sq. mi.

Hersey   Village
ZIP: 49639   **Lat:** 43-50-58 N   **Long:** 85-26-31 W
Pop: 354 (1990); 364 (1980)   **Pop Density:** 321.8
Land: 1.1 sq. mi.; **Water:** 0.0 sq. mi.
Not coextensive with the town of the same name.
Name origin: For trapper Nathan Hershey, who arrived in 1843.

*Hersey   Township
ZIP: 49639   **Lat:** 43-51-08 N   **Long:** 85-23-05 W
Pop: 1,455 (1990); 1,229 (1980)   **Pop Density:** 41.2
Land: 35.3 sq. mi.; **Water:** 0.6 sq. mi.

Highland   Township
   Lat: 44-06-58 N   **Long:** 85-16-05 W
Pop: 1,012 (1990); 1,063 (1980)   **Pop Density:** 27.1
Land: 37.4 sq. mi.; **Water:** 0.0 sq. mi.   **Elev:** 1336 ft.

Le Roy   Village
ZIP: 49655   **Lat:** 44-02-18 N   **Long:** 85-27-09 W
Pop: 251 (1990); 293 (1980)   **Pop Density:** 251.0
Land: 1.0 sq. mi.; **Water:** 0.0 sq. mi.
Settled 1872. Not coextensive with the town of the same name.
Name origin: For federal land agent Le Roy Carr.

*Le Roy   Township
ZIP: 49655   **Lat:** 44-02-04 N   **Long:** 85-29-59 W
Pop: 958 (1990); 858 (1980)   **Pop Density:** 27.4
Land: 34.9 sq. mi.; **Water:** 0.2 sq. mi.

Lincoln   Township
   Lat: 43-56-39 N   **Long:** 85-30-06 W
Pop: 1,228 (1990); 1,173 (1980)   **Pop Density:** 35.0
Land: 35.1 sq. mi.; **Water:** 0.4 sq. mi.

Marion   Village
ZIP: 49665   **Lat:** 44-06-09 N   **Long:** 85-08-49 W
Pop: 807 (1990); 816 (1980)   **Pop Density:** 807.0
Land: 1.0 sq. mi.; **Water:** 0.0 sq. mi.
Settled 1860s. Not coextensive with the town of the same name.
Name origin: For the wife of Christopher Clarke, the first postmaster.

*Marion   Township
ZIP: 49665   **Lat:** 44-06-56 N   **Long:** 85-08-58 W
Pop: 1,445 (1990); 1,491 (1980)   **Pop Density:** 39.1
Land: 37.0 sq. mi.; **Water:** 0.0 sq. mi.

Middle Branch   Township
   Lat: 44-01-49 N   **Long:** 85-08-48 W
Pop: 701 (1990); 642 (1980)   **Pop Density:** 19.7
Land: 35.5 sq. mi.; **Water:** 0.0 sq. mi.

Orient
Township
Lat: 43-51-22 N **Long:** 85-08-42 W
Pop: 692 (1990); 635 (1980) **Pop Density:** 19.9
Land: 34.8 sq. mi.; **Water:** 0.6 sq. mi.

Osceola
Township
Lat: 43-56-21 N **Long:** 85-16-18 W
Pop: 937 (1990); 920 (1980) **Pop Density:** 27.4
Land: 34.2 sq. mi.; **Water:** 0.2 sq. mi.

Reed City
City
ZIP: 49677 **Lat:** 43-52-21 N **Long:** 85-30-33 W
Pop: 2,379 (1990); 2,221 (1980) **Pop Density:** 1321.7
Land: 1.8 sq. mi.; **Water:** 0.0 sq. mi. **Elev:** 1039 ft.
Name origin: For founder James M. Reed.

Richmond
Township
Lat: 43-51-28 N **Long:** 85-30-14 W
Pop: 1,722 (1990); 1,649 (1980) **Pop Density:** 51.9
Land: 33.2 sq. mi.; **Water:** 0.1 sq. mi.

Rose Lake
Township
Lat: 44-01-27 N **Long:** 85-22-55 W
Pop: 968 (1990); 847 (1980) **Pop Density:** 28.8
Land: 33.6 sq. mi.; **Water:** 1.2 sq. mi.

Sherman
Township
Lat: 44-07-00 N **Long:** 85-23-08 W
Pop: 948 (1990); 847 (1980) **Pop Density:** 25.6
Land: 37.1 sq. mi.; **Water:** 0.2 sq. mi.

Sylvan
Township
Lat: 43-56-43 N **Long:** 85-08-51 W
Pop: 852 (1990); 657 (1980) **Pop Density:** 24.7
Land: 34.5 sq. mi.; **Water:** 0.7 sq. mi.

Tustin
Village
ZIP: 49688 **Lat:** 44-06-07 N **Long:** 85-27-29 W
Pop: 236 (1990); 264 (1980) **Pop Density:** 590.0
Land: 0.4 sq. mi.; **Water:** 0.0 sq. mi.
Settled 1872.
Name origin: For Dr. J. P. Tustin.

Oscoda County
County Seat: Mio (ZIP: 48647)

Pop: 7,842 (1990); 6,858 (1980) **Pop Density:** 13.9
Land: 565.0 sq. mi.; **Water:** 6.6 sq. mi. **Area Code:** 517
In northeast MI, southwest of Alpena; established Apr 1, 1840 from unorganized territory.

Name origin: 'Pebbly prairie' from *ossin* 'stone' and *muskoda* 'prairie,' coined by Henry Rowe Schoolcraft (1793–1864), author, explorer, MI legislator, and superintendent of Indian Affairs for MI (1836–41).

Big Creek
Township
Lat: 44-35-28 N **Long:** 84-15-07 W
Pop: 2,778 (1990); 2,392 (1980) **Pop Density:** 19.6
Land: 141.5 sq. mi.; **Water:** 1.7 sq. mi.

Clinton
Township
Lat: 44-49-01 N **Long:** 84-00-18 W
Pop: 447 (1990); 442 (1980) **Pop Density:** 6.4
Land: 70.3 sq. mi.; **Water:** 1.4 sq. mi.

Comins
Township
ZIP: 48619 **Lat:** 44-43-53 N **Long:** 84-00-36 W
Pop: 1,785 (1990); 1,583 (1980) **Pop Density:** 25.3
Land: 70.5 sq. mi.; **Water:** 1.3 sq. mi.

Elmer
Township
Lat: 44-46-08 N **Long:** 84-11-38 W
Pop: 854 (1990); 742 (1980) **Pop Density:** 12.1
Land: 70.8 sq. mi.; **Water:** 0.6 sq. mi.

Greenwood
Township
Lat: 44-46-12 N **Long:** 84-18-40 W
Pop: 880 (1990); 696 (1980) **Pop Density:** 12.6
Land: 69.9 sq. mi.; **Water:** 1.0 sq. mi.

Mentor
Township
Lat: 44-35-36 N **Long:** 84-00-24 W
Pop: 1,098 (1990); 1,003 (1980) **Pop Density:** 7.7
Land: 142.1 sq. mi.; **Water:** 0.7 sq. mi.

Mio
CDP
ZIP: 48647 **Lat:** 44-39-46 N **Long:** 84-08-40 W
Pop: 1,886 (1990) **Pop Density:** 251.5
Land: 7.5 sq. mi.; **Water:** 0.6 sq. mi.

Otsego County
County Seat: Gaylord (ZIP: 49735)

Pop: 17,957 (1990); 14,993 (1980)   **Pop Density:** 34.9
Land: 514.6 sq. mi.; **Water:** 11.4 sq. mi.   **Area Code:** 517
In north-central MI, southeast of Petoskey; established as Okkuddo County Apr 1, 1840; name changed Mar 8, 1843.
Name origin: Probably for Otsego County, NY, home of some early settlers; from Iroquoian 'rock site' or 'place of the rock.'

Bagley   Township
Lat: 44-58-58 N   Long: 84-39-33 W
Pop: 4,929 (1990); 4,106 (1980)   **Pop Density:** 167.1
Land: 29.5 sq. mi.; **Water:** 2.7 sq. mi.

Charlton   Township
Lat: 44-59-20 N   Long: 84-25-55 W
Pop: 913 (1990); 823 (1980)   **Pop Density:** 9.1
Land: 100.4 sq. mi.; **Water:** 1.9 sq. mi.

Chester   Township
Lat: 44-56-16 N   Long: 84-32-32 W
Pop: 934 (1990); 661 (1980)   **Pop Density:** 13.8
Land: 67.7 sq. mi.; **Water:** 1.1 sq. mi.

Corwith   Township
Lat: 45-09-31 N   Long: 84-33-00 W
Pop: 1,416 (1990); 1,313 (1980)   **Pop Density:** 13.2
Land: 107.5 sq. mi.; **Water:** 0.6 sq. mi.

Dover   Township
Lat: 45-04-26 N   Long: 84-33-30 W
Pop: 485 (1990); 432 (1980)   **Pop Density:** 13.8
Land: 35.2 sq. mi.; **Water:** 0.0 sq. mi.

Elmira   Township
ZIP: 49730   Lat: 45-04-01 N   Long: 84-47-46 W
Pop: 1,038 (1990); 899 (1980)   **Pop Density:** 29.1
Land: 35.7 sq. mi.; **Water:** 0.5 sq. mi.

Gaylord   City
ZIP: 49735   Lat: 45-01-24 N   Long: 84-40-41 W
Pop: 3,256 (1990); 3,011 (1980)   **Pop Density:** 1205.9
Land: 2.7 sq. mi.; **Water:** 0.0 sq. mi.   **Elev:** 1349 ft.
Name origin: Named in 1874 for railroad lawyer A. S. Gaylord. Previously called Barnes.

Hayes   Township
Lat: 44-56-31 N   Long: 84-47-22 W
Pop: 1,437 (1990); 888 (1980)   **Pop Density:** 20.9
Land: 68.8 sq. mi.; **Water:** 1.6 sq. mi.

Livingston   Township
Lat: 45-04-23 N   Long: 84-40-36 W
Pop: 1,755 (1990); 1,703 (1980)   **Pop Density:** 51.2
Land: 34.3 sq. mi.; **Water:** 0.3 sq. mi.

Otsego Lake   Township
Lat: 44-54-13 N   Long: 84-40-14 W
Pop: 1,794 (1990); 1,157 (1980)   **Pop Density:** 54.9
Land: 32.7 sq. mi.; **Water:** 2.7 sq. mi.

Vanderbilt   Village
ZIP: 49795   Lat: 45-08-36 N   Long: 84-39-48 W
Pop: 605 (1990); 525 (1980)   **Pop Density:** 550.0
Land: 1.1 sq. mi.; **Water:** 0.0 sq. mi.
Settled 1875.
Name origin: For the Vanderbilt family of NY.

Ottawa County
County Seat: Grand Haven (ZIP: 49417)

Pop: 187,768 (1990); 157,174 (1980)   **Pop Density:** 331.9
Land: 565.7 sq. mi.; **Water:** 1066.4 sq. mi.   **Area Code:** 616
On the west-central coast of MI bordered on west by Lake Michigan; established Mar 2, 1831 (prior to statehood).
Name origin: For the Ottawa Indians, a tribe of Algonquian linguistic stock whose name is derived from *adawe* 'to trade.'

Allendale   Township
ZIP: 49401   Lat: 42-58-39 N   Long: 85-57-31 W
Pop: 8,022 (1990); 6,080 (1980)   **Pop Density:** 256.3
Land: 31.3 sq. mi.; **Water:** 0.9 sq. mi.

Beechwood   CDP
Lat: 42-47-49 N   Long: 86-07-33 W
Pop: 2,676 (1990); 2,169 (1980)   **Pop Density:** 1408.4
Land: 1.9 sq. mi.; **Water:** 0.9 sq. mi.

Blendon   Township
Lat: 42-53-52 N   Long: 85-58-16 W
Pop: 4,740 (1990); 3,763 (1980)   **Pop Density:** 129.9
Land: 36.5 sq. mi.; **Water:** 0.0 sq. mi.

Chester   Township
Lat: 43-09-42 N   Long: 85-51-03 W
Pop: 2,133 (1990); 2,034 (1980)   **Pop Density:** 59.7
Land: 35.7 sq. mi.; **Water:** 0.2 sq. mi.

Coopersville   City
ZIP: 49404   Lat: 43-03-55 N   Long: 85-56-01 W
Pop: 3,421 (1990); 2,889 (1980)   **Pop Density:** 712.7
Land: 4.8 sq. mi.; **Water:** 0.0 sq. mi.
Name origin: Named by and for early settler Benjamin Cooper, who donated land to the railroad there.

Crockery
Township
Lat: 43-04-47 N **Long:** 86-05-11 W
Pop: 3,599 (1990); 3,536 (1980) **Pop Density:** 110.1
Land: 32.7 sq. mi.; **Water:** 0.7 sq. mi.

Ferrysburg
City
ZIP: 49409 **Lat:** 43-05-10 N **Long:** 86-13-09 W
Pop: 2,919 (1990); 2,440 (1980) **Pop Density:** 973.0
Land: 3.0 sq. mi.; **Water:** 0.6 sq. mi.
Established 1857 by brothers Col. William Montague and Thomas White Ferry.
Name origin: For their father, the Rev. William M. Ferry, founder of Grand Haven.

Georgetown
Township
ZIP: 49426 **Lat:** 42-54-17 N **Long:** 85-50-46 W
Pop: 32,672 (1990); 26,104 (1980) **Pop Density:** 975.3
Land: 33.5 sq. mi.; **Water:** 0.6 sq. mi.

Grand Haven
City
ZIP: 49417 **Lat:** 43-03-18 N **Long:** 86-13-27 W
Pop: 11,951 (1990); 11,763 (1980) **Pop Density:** 2060.5
Land: 5.8 sq. mi.; **Water:** 1.6 sq. mi.
In southwestern MI on Lake Michigan, at the mouth of the Grand River. Settled 1833; established 1834.
Name origin: For its descriptive connotations.

*Grand Haven
Township
ZIP: 49417 **Lat:** 42-59-47 N **Long:** 86-11-55 W
Pop: 9,710 (1990); 7,238 (1980) **Pop Density:** 338.3
Land: 28.7 sq. mi.; **Water:** 7.0 sq. mi.

Holland
City
ZIP: 49423 **Lat:** 42-46-57 N **Long:** 86-05-58 W
Pop: 25,086 (1990); 21,767 (1980) **Pop Density:** 2951.3
Land: 8.5 sq. mi.; **Water:** 0.6 sq. mi.
In southwestern MI on Lake Michigan. Settled 1847 by Dutch. Part of the town is also in Allegan County.
Name origin: Named by settlers for their former home.

*Holland
Township
ZIP: 49423 **Lat:** 42-49-16 N **Long:** 86-04-36 W
Pop: 17,523 (1990); 13,739 (1980) **Pop Density:** 641.9
Land: 27.3 sq. mi.; **Water:** 0.3 sq. mi.
Charter township in southwestern MI, southwest of Grand Rapids.
Name origin: Probably for the European country.

Hudsonville
City
ZIP: 49426 **Lat:** 42-51-54 N **Long:** 85-51-47 W
Pop: 6,170 (1990); 4,844 (1980) **Pop Density:** 1582.1
Land: 3.9 sq. mi.; **Water:** 0.0 sq. mi.
Name origin: For its first postmaster, Homer Hudson.

Jamestown
Township
Lat: 42-48-14 N **Long:** 85-49-56 W
Pop: 4,059 (1990); 3,546 (1980) **Pop Density:** 113.4
Land: 35.8 sq. mi.; **Water:** 0.0 sq. mi.

Jenison
CDP
ZIP: 49428 **Lat:** 42-54-31 N **Long:** 85-49-47 W
Pop: 17,882 (1990); 16,330 (1980) **Pop Density:** 3030.8
Land: 5.9 sq. mi.; **Water:** 0.0 sq. mi.

Olive
Township
Lat: 42-53-46 N **Long:** 86-05-09 W
Pop: 2,866 (1990); 2,449 (1980) **Pop Density:** 79.2
Land: 36.2 sq. mi.; **Water:** 0.0 sq. mi.

Park
Township
ZIP: 49423 **Lat:** 42-48-28 N **Long:** 86-10-25 W
Pop: 13,541 (1990); 10,354 (1980) **Pop Density:** 701.6
Land: 19.3 sq. mi.; **Water:** 2.0 sq. mi.
In southwestern MI on Lake Michigan. Established 1916.

Polkton
Township
Lat: 43-04-10 N **Long:** 85-58-26 W
Pop: 2,284 (1990); 2,027 (1980) **Pop Density:** 58.3
Land: 39.2 sq. mi.; **Water:** 0.4 sq. mi.

Port Sheldon
Township
ZIP: 49460 **Lat:** 42-53-59 N **Long:** 86-10-49 W
Pop: 2,929 (1990); 2,206 (1980) **Pop Density:** 130.8
Land: 22.4 sq. mi.; **Water:** 0.3 sq. mi.

Robinson
Township
Lat: 42-59-37 N **Long:** 86-05-07 W
Pop: 3,925 (1990); 3,018 (1980) **Pop Density:** 101.7
Land: 38.6 sq. mi.; **Water:** 0.8 sq. mi. **Elev:** 628 ft.

Spring Lake
Village
ZIP: 49456 **Lat:** 43-04-29 N **Long:** 86-11-25 W
Pop: 2,537 (1990); 2,731 (1980) **Pop Density:** 2306.4
Land: 1.1 sq. mi.; **Water:** 0.1 sq. mi. **Elev:** 594 ft.
In southwestern MI on the Grand River at Spring Lake (a Lake Michigan inlet), 30 mi. northwest of Grand Rapids. Not coextensive with the town of the same name.
Name origin: For its location.

*Spring Lake
Township
ZIP: 49456 **Lat:** 43-05-38 N **Long:** 86-11-52 W
Pop: 10,751 (1990); 9,588 (1980) **Pop Density:** 651.6
Land: 16.5 sq. mi.; **Water:** 3.4 sq. mi.

Tallmadge
Township
ZIP: 49504 **Lat:** 42-59-23 N **Long:** 85-50-18 W
Pop: 6,293 (1990); 5,927 (1980) **Pop Density:** 194.2
Land: 32.4 sq. mi.; **Water:** 0.6 sq. mi.

Wright
Township
Lat: 43-04-32 N **Long:** 85-50-35 W
Pop: 3,285 (1990); 3,387 (1980) **Pop Density:** 90.7
Land: 36.2 sq. mi.; **Water:** 0.1 sq. mi.

Zeeland
City
ZIP: 49464 **Lat:** 42-48-47 N **Long:** 86-00-47 W
Pop: 5,417 (1990); 4,764 (1980) **Pop Density:** 1805.7
Land: 3.0 sq. mi.; **Water:** 0.0 sq. mi. **Elev:** 646 ft.
Name origin: Named by Dutch colonists for the province in the Netherlands that had been their home.

*Zeeland
Township
ZIP: 49464 **Lat:** 42-48-54 N **Long:** 85-57-17 W
Pop: 4,472 (1990); 3,711 (1980) **Pop Density:** 130.0
Land: 34.4 sq. mi.; **Water:** 0.0 sq. mi.

Presque Isle County
County Seat: Rogers City (ZIP: 49779)

Pop: 13,743 (1990); 14,267 (1980)
Land: 660.1 sq. mi.; **Water:** 1913.2 sq. mi.
Pop Density: 20.8
Area Code: 517

On the northeast coast of MI, bordered on east by Lake Huron; established Apr 1, 1840 from unorganized territory.

Name origin: French 'almost an island,' i.e., a peninsula.

Allis — Township
Lat: 45-17-02 N Long: 84-10-45 W
Pop: 887 (1990); 834 (1980) Pop Density: 13.8
Land: 64.5 sq. mi.; Water: 1.4 sq. mi.

Bearinger — Township
Lat: 45-32-13 N Long: 84-12-20 W
Pop: 246 (1990); 217 (1980) Pop Density: 4.0
Land: 61.5 sq. mi.; Water: 2.1 sq. mi.

Belknap — Township
Lat: 45-20-49 N Long: 83-48-55 W
Pop: 920 (1990); 1,026 (1980) Pop Density: 25.7
Land: 35.8 sq. mi.; Water: 0.0 sq. mi. Elev: 824 ft.

Bismarck — Township
Lat: 45-17-18 N Long: 83-56-30 W
Pop: 319 (1990); 278 (1980) Pop Density: 4.7
Land: 67.6 sq. mi.; Water: 2.2 sq. mi.

Case — Township
Lat: 45-16-36 N Long: 84-04-27 W
Pop: 770 (1990); 830 (1980) Pop Density: 11.4
Land: 67.4 sq. mi.; Water: 0.9 sq. mi.

Krakow — Township
Lat: 45-17-55 N Long: 83-34-17 W
Pop: 617 (1990); 570 (1980) Pop Density: 11.1
Land: 55.8 sq. mi.; Water: 5.0 sq. mi.

Metz — Township
Lat: 45-15-13 N Long: 83-48-38 W
Pop: 403 (1990); 421 (1980) Pop Density: 11.3
Land: 35.8 sq. mi.; Water: 0.0 sq. mi.

Millersburg — Village
ZIP: 49759 Lat: 45-20-01 N Long: 84-03-38 W
Pop: 250 (1990); 231 (1980) Pop Density: 250.0
Land: 1.0 sq. mi.; Water: 0.0 sq. mi.

Name origin: For its founder, C.R. Miller.

Moltke — Township
Lat: 45-25-05 N Long: 83-56-58 W
Pop: 309 (1990); 326 (1980) Pop Density: 9.1
Land: 34.0 sq. mi.; Water: 0.0 sq. mi.

North Allis — Township
Lat: 45-24-53 N Long: 84-11-37 W
Pop: 502 (1990); 485 (1980) Pop Density: 15.4
Land: 32.7 sq. mi.; Water: 1.6 sq. mi.

Ocqueoc — Township
Lat: 45-26-17 N Long: 84-04-10 W
Pop: 521 (1990); 578 (1980) Pop Density: 10.0
Land: 52.3 sq. mi.; Water: 0.3 sq. mi.

Onaway — City
ZIP: 49765 Lat: 45-21-30 N Long: 84-13-41 W
Pop: 1,039 (1990); 1,084 (1980) Pop Density: 611.2
Land: 1.7 sq. mi.; Water: 0.0 sq. mi.

Platted 1886.

Name origin: Believed to be for an Indian maiden.

Posen — Village
ZIP: 49776 Lat: 45-15-43 N Long: 83-41-57 W
Pop: 263 (1990); 270 (1980) Pop Density: 263.0
Land: 1.0 sq. mi.; Water: 0.0 sq. mi.

Settled 1870. Not coextensive with the town of the same name.

Name origin: For the Polish province of Poznan, with spelling variation.

*Posen — Township
ZIP: 49776 Lat: 45-15-21 N Long: 83-41-42 W
Pop: 972 (1990); 1,082 (1980) Pop Density: 27.5
Land: 35.3 sq. mi.; Water: 0.2 sq. mi.

Presque Isle — Township
Lat: 45-16-19 N Long: 83-28-08 W
Pop: 1,312 (1990); 1,334 (1980) Pop Density: 36.9
Land: 35.6 sq. mi.; Water: 11.6 sq. mi.

Pulawski — Township
Lat: 45-20-16 N Long: 83-42-18 W
Pop: 427 (1990); 477 (1980) Pop Density: 10.2
Land: 41.9 sq. mi.; Water: 1.9 sq. mi.

Rogers — Township
Lat: 45-25-41 N Long: 83-52-12 W
Pop: 857 (1990); 802 (1980) Pop Density: 25.5
Land: 33.6 sq. mi.; Water: 0.1 sq. mi.

Rogers City — City
ZIP: 49779 Lat: 45-25-06 N Long: 83-48-23 W
Pop: 3,642 (1990); 3,923 (1980) Pop Density: 791.7
Land: 4.6 sq. mi.; Water: 3.9 sq. mi.

Roscommon County
County Seat: Roscommon (ZIP: 48653)

Pop: 19,776 (1990); 16,374 (1980)   **Pop Density:** 37.9
Land: 521.4 sq. mi.; **Water:** 58.4 sq. mi.   **Area Code:** 517
In central MI, east of Cadillac; established as Mikenauk County Apr 1, 1840; name changed Mar 8, 1843.
Name origin: For the county in Ireland.

Au Sable
Township
Lat: 44-28-12 N   **Long:** 84-25-38 W
Pop: 231 (1990); 229 (1980)   **Pop Density:** 6.5
Land: 35.8 sq. mi.; **Water:** 0.0 sq. mi.

Backus
Township
Lat: 44-17-45 N   **Long:** 84-33-22 W
Pop: 249 (1990); 213 (1980)   **Pop Density:** 7.3
Land: 34.3 sq. mi.; **Water:** 1.6 sq. mi.

Denton
Township
Lat: 44-17-33 N   **Long:** 84-40-32 W
Pop: 4,290 (1990); 3,555 (1980)   **Pop Density:** 162.5
Land: 26.4 sq. mi.; **Water:** 9.6 sq. mi.

Gerrish
Township
Lat: 44-27-54 N   **Long:** 84-40-23 W
Pop: 2,421 (1990); 1,629 (1980)   **Pop Density:** 87.7
Land: 27.6 sq. mi.; **Water:** 9.6 sq. mi.

Higgins
Township
Lat: 44-25-25 N   **Long:** 84-33-40 W
Pop: 1,685 (1990); 1,581 (1980)   **Pop Density:** 23.9
Land: 70.5 sq. mi.; **Water:** 2.8 sq. mi.

Houghton Lake
CDP
ZIP: 48629   **Lat:** 44-18-48 N   **Long:** 84-45-50 W
Pop: 3,353 (1990); 766 (1980)   **Pop Density:** 568.3
Land: 5.9 sq. mi.; **Water:** 1.6 sq. mi.

Lake
Township
Lat: 44-22-46 N   **Long:** 84-47-51 W
Pop: 1,234 (1990); 992 (1980)   **Pop Density:** 51.8
Land: 23.8 sq. mi.; **Water:** 11.8 sq. mi.

Lyon
Township
Lat: 44-27-59 N   **Long:** 84-47-30 W
Pop: 1,037 (1990); 910 (1980)   **Pop Density:** 34.6
Land: 30.0 sq. mi.; **Water:** 6.5 sq. mi.

Markey
Township
Lat: 44-22-29 N   **Long:** 84-40-22 W
Pop: 1,768 (1990); 1,335 (1980)   **Pop Density:** 61.2
Land: 28.9 sq. mi.; **Water:** 7.3 sq. mi.

Nester
Township
Lat: 44-12-17 N   **Long:** 84-29-36 W
Pop: 225 (1990); 245 (1980)   **Pop Density:** 3.2
Land: 71.3 sq. mi.; **Water:** 0.9 sq. mi.

Prudenville
CDP
ZIP: 48651   **Lat:** 44-18-04 N   **Long:** 84-39-52 W
Pop: 1,513 (1990)   **Pop Density:** 540.4
Land: 2.8 sq. mi.; **Water:** 0.8 sq. mi.

Richfield
Township
Lat: 44-19-23 N   **Long:** 84-25-12 W
Pop: 3,413 (1990); 2,926 (1980)   **Pop Density:** 49.5
Land: 68.9 sq. mi.; **Water:** 4.0 sq. mi.

Roscommon
Village
ZIP: 48653   **Lat:** 44-29-26 N   **Long:** 84-35-20 W
Pop: 858 (1990); 834 (1980)   **Pop Density:** 536.3
Land: 1.6 sq. mi.; **Water:** 0.0 sq. mi.   **Elev:** 1130 ft.
Not coextensive with the town of the same name.
Name origin: For County Roscommon, Ireland.

*Roscommon
Township
ZIP: 48653   **Lat:** 44-13-40 N   **Long:** 84-45-08 W
Pop: 3,223 (1990); 2,759 (1980)   **Pop Density:** 31.0
Land: 103.9 sq. mi.; **Water:** 4.3 sq. mi.

St. Helen
CDP
Lat: 44-21-46 N   **Long:** 84-25-06 W
Pop: 2,390 (1990)   **Pop Density:** 682.9
Land: 3.5 sq. mi.; **Water:** 0.9 sq. mi.

MICHIGAN, Saginaw County

> ## Saginaw County
> **County Seat: Saginaw (ZIP: 48602)**
>
> **Pop:** 211,946 (1990); 228,059 (1980) **Pop Density:** 262.0
> **Land:** 809.0 sq. mi.; **Water:** 6.8 sq. mi. **Area Code:** 517
>
> In central MI, northwest of Flint; established Sep 10, 1822 (prior to statehood) from unorganized territory.
>
> **Name origin:** For the Saginaw River, which runs through it; from Ojibway 'the place of the Sac [Indians].'

Albee Township
Lat: 43-15-36 N Long: 83-59-35 W
Pop: 2,402 (1990); 2,642 (1980) **Pop Density:** 66.5
Land: 36.1 sq. mi.; **Water:** 0.0 sq. mi.

Birch Run Village
ZIP: 48415 Lat: 43-15-00 N Long: 83-47-24 W
Pop: 992 (1990); 1,196 (1980) **Pop Density:** 551.1
Land: 1.8 sq. mi.; **Water:** 0.0 sq. mi. **Elev** 635 ft.
Settled 1852. Not coextensive with the town of the same name.
Name origin: For nearby Birch Creek.

*Birch Run Township
ZIP: 48415 Lat: 43-15-47 N Long: 83-45-37 W
Pop: 5,354 (1990); 5,488 (1980) **Pop Density:** 150.4
Land: 35.6 sq. mi.; **Water:** 0.0 sq. mi.

Blumfield Township
Lat: 43-26-26 N Long: 83-45-35 W
Pop: 1,999 (1990); 2,047 (1980) **Pop Density:** 56.2
Land: 35.6 sq. mi.; **Water:** 0.0 sq. mi.

Brady Township
Lat: 43-10-28 N Long: 84-13-18 W
Pop: 2,396 (1990); 2,498 (1980) **Pop Density:** 65.3
Land: 36.7 sq. mi.; **Water:** 0.0 sq. mi.

Brant Township
ZIP: 48614 Lat: 43-15-27 N Long: 84-13-53 W
Pop: 1,942 (1990); 1,849 (1980) **Pop Density:** 52.3
Land: 37.1 sq. mi.; **Water:** 0.0 sq. mi.

Bridgeport Township
ZIP: 48722 Lat: 43-20-53 N Long: 83-52-30 W
Pop: 12,747 (1990); 13,978 (1980) **Pop Density:** 368.4
Land: 34.6 sq. mi.; **Water:** 0.1 sq. mi.
In central MI, 6 mi. southeast of Saginaw.

Buena Vista Charter Township
ZIP: 48601 Lat: 43-27-04 N Long: 83-51-51 W
Pop: 10,900 (1990); 12,768 (1980) **Pop Density:** 302.8
Land: 36.0 sq. mi.; **Water:** 0.2 sq. mi.

Burt CDP
ZIP: 48417 Lat: 43-14-12 N Long: 83-54-22 W
Pop: 1,169 (1990) **Pop Density:** 259.8
Land: 4.5 sq. mi.; **Water:** 0.0 sq. mi.

Carrollton Township
ZIP: 48724 Lat: 43-27-34 N Long: 83-56-22 W
Pop: 6,521 (1990); 7,482 (1980) **Pop Density:** 2037.8
Land: 3.2 sq. mi.; **Water:** 0.2 sq. mi.

Chapin Township
Lat: 43-10-27 N Long: 84-19-20 W
Pop: 969 (1990); 1,054 (1980) **Pop Density:** 39.2
Land: 24.7 sq. mi.; **Water:** 0.0 sq. mi.

Chesaning Village
ZIP: 48616 Lat: 43-11-04 N Long: 84-07-11 W
Pop: 2,567 (1990); 2,656 (1980) **Pop Density:** 855.7
Land: 3.0 sq. mi.; **Water:** 0.0 sq. mi.
Settled 1839. Not coextensive with the town of the same name.
Name origin: From an Indian term for 'big rock.'

*Chesaning Township
ZIP: 48616 Lat: 43-10-36 N Long: 84-06-29 W
Pop: 4,904 (1990); 5,317 (1980) **Pop Density:** 141.3
Land: 34.7 sq. mi.; **Water:** 0.0 sq. mi.

Frankenmuth City
ZIP: 48734 Lat: 43-19-49 N Long: 83-44-24 W
Pop: 4,408 (1990); 3,753 (1980) **Pop Density:** 1763.2
Land: 2.5 sq. mi.; **Water:** 0.1 sq. mi.
German settlers arrived 1845. Established as village 1904; as city 1959.
Name origin: Its name combines Franconia, a district in Germany, and German *muth* 'courage.'

*Frankenmuth Township
ZIP: 48734 Lat: 43-20-52 N Long: 83-45-12 W
Pop: 2,122 (1990); 2,389 (1980) **Pop Density:** 64.9
Land: 32.7 sq. mi.; **Water:** 0.2 sq. mi.

Freeland CDP
ZIP: 48623 Lat: 43-31-15 N Long: 84-07-03 W
Pop: 1,421 (1990); 1,364 (1980) **Pop Density:** 947.3
Land: 1.5 sq. mi.; **Water:** 0.0 sq. mi.

Fremont Township
Lat: 43-20-54 N Long: 84-13-42 W
Pop: 2,137 (1990); 2,087 (1980) **Pop Density:** 58.1
Land: 36.8 sq. mi.; **Water:** 0.0 sq. mi.

Hemlock CDP
ZIP: 48626 Lat: 43-24-56 N Long: 84-13-53 W
Pop: 1,601 (1990); 1,362 (1980) **Pop Density:** 615.8
Land: 2.6 sq. mi.; **Water:** 0.0 sq. mi.

James Township
Lat: 43-21-33 N Long: 84-03-08 W
Pop: 2,005 (1990); 2,168 (1980) **Pop Density:** 110.2
Land: 18.2 sq. mi.; **Water:** 1.4 sq. mi.

Jonesfield Township
Lat: 43-26-07 N Long: 84-20-08 W
Pop: 1,740 (1990); 1,920 (1980) **Pop Density:** 69.0
Land: 25.2 sq. mi.; **Water:** 0.0 sq. mi.

Kochville Township
Lat: 43-30-04 N Long: 83-59-01 W
Pop: 2,740 (1990); 2,828 (1980) **Pop Density:** 145.7
Land: 18.8 sq. mi.; **Water:** 0.0 sq. mi.

MICHIGAN, Saginaw County

Lakefield
Township
Lat: 43-20-44 N **Long:** 84-19-55 W
Pop: 962 (1990); 960 (1980) **Pop Density:** 39.9
Land: 24.1 sq. mi.; **Water:** 0.0 sq. mi.

Maple Grove
Township
Lat: 43-10-43 N **Long:** 83-59-34 W
Pop: 2,830 (1990); 2,994 (1980) **Pop Density:** 79.5
Land: 35.6 sq. mi.; **Water:** 1.0 sq. mi.

Marion
Township
Lat: 43-15-13 N **Long:** 84-20-17 W
Pop: 928 (1990); 913 (1980) **Pop Density:** 37.7
Land: 24.6 sq. mi.; **Water:** 0.0 sq. mi.

Merrill
Village
ZIP: 48637 **Lat:** 43-24-33 N **Long:** 84-20-07 W
Pop: 755 (1990); 851 (1980) **Pop Density:** 1078.6
Land: 0.7 sq. mi.; **Water:** 0.0 sq. mi. **Elev:** 671 ft.
Settled 1870s.
Name origin: For railroadman N.W. Merrill.

Oakley
Village
ZIP: 48649 **Lat:** 43-08-35 N **Long:** 84-10-06 W
Pop: 362 (1990); 412 (1980) **Pop Density:** 362.0
Land: 1.0 sq. mi.; **Water:** 0.0 sq. mi.
Settled 1840s.
Name origin: For Judge Oakley of Dutchess County, NY, a relative of one of the founders.

Richland
Township
Lat: 43-26-11 N **Long:** 84-13-48 W
Pop: 4,177 (1990); 4,402 (1980) **Pop Density:** 112.6
Land: 37.1 sq. mi.; **Water:** 0.0 sq. mi.

Robin Glen-Indiantown
CDP
Lat: 43-27-38 N **Long:** 83-50-12 W
Pop: 1,395 (1990) **Pop Density:** 664.3
Land: 2.1 sq. mi.; **Water:** 0.0 sq. mi.

Saginaw
City
ZIP: 48605 **Lat:** 43-25-10 N **Long:** 83-56-58 W
Pop: 69,512 (1990); 77,508 (1980) **Pop Density:** 3994.9
Land: 17.4 sq. mi.; **Water:** 0.7 sq. mi.
In east-central MI on the Saginaw River, 30 mi. northwest of Flint. Settled 1816; chartered 1870; combined with East Saginaw to form Saginaw 1889.
Name origin: From Ojibway term meaning 'place of the Sac [Indians].'

*Saginaw
Township
ZIP: 48603 **Lat:** 43-26-52 N **Long:** 84-01-19 W
Pop: 37,684 (1990); 38,668 (1980) **Pop Density:** 1531.9
Land: 24.6 sq. mi.; **Water:** 0.1 sq. mi.

St. Charles
Village
Lat: 43-17-57 N **Long:** 84-08-58 W
Pop: 2,144 (1990); 2,276 (1980) **Pop Density:** 857.6
Land: 2.5 sq. mi.; **Water:** 0.0 sq. mi.
Not coextensive with the town of the same name.
Name origin: For its first storekeeper, Charles Kimberly, nicknamed 'St. Charles' by the area lumberjacks for his fastidious ways.

*St. Charles
Township
Lat: 43-15-42 N **Long:** 84-06-35 W
Pop: 3,505 (1990); 3,689 (1980) **Pop Density:** 94.7
Land: 37.0 sq. mi.; **Water:** 0.2 sq. mi. **Elev:** 593 ft.

Shields
CDP
ZIP: 48603 **Lat:** 43-25-03 N **Long:** 84-04-23 W
Pop: 6,634 (1990) **Pop Density:** 1020.6
Land: 6.5 sq. mi.; **Water:** 0.1 sq. mi.

Spaulding
Township
Lat: 43-20-23 N **Long:** 83-58-44 W
Pop: 2,662 (1990); 3,164 (1980) **Pop Density:** 100.1
Land: 26.6 sq. mi.; **Water:** 0.8 sq. mi.

Swan Creek
Township
Lat: 43-21-11 N **Long:** 84-07-58 W
Pop: 2,346 (1990); 2,530 (1980) **Pop Density:** 101.1
Land: 23.2 sq. mi.; **Water:** 0.5 sq. mi.

Taymouth
Township
Lat: 43-15-42 N **Long:** 83-52-01 W
Pop: 4,524 (1990); 4,581 (1980) **Pop Density:** 127.1
Land: 35.6 sq. mi.; **Water:** 0.1 sq. mi.

Thomas
Township
ZIP: 48603 **Lat:** 43-25-56 N **Long:** 84-06-54 W
Pop: 10,971 (1990); 11,184 (1980) **Pop Density:** 348.3
Land: 31.5 sq. mi.; **Water:** 0.4 sq. mi.
In east-central MI, north of Flint.

Tittabawassee
Township
Lat: 43-31-31 N **Long:** 84-06-34 W
Pop: 4,627 (1990); 4,908 (1980) **Pop Density:** 131.4
Land: 35.2 sq. mi.; **Water:** 0.3 sq. mi.

Zilwaukee
City
ZIP: 48604 **Lat:** 43-28-48 N **Long:** 83-55-18 W
Pop: 1,850 (1990); 2,201 (1980) **Pop Density:** 840.9
Land: 2.2 sq. mi.; **Water:** 0.1 sq. mi.
Name origin: Named by sawmill owners Daniel and Solomon Johnson, who hoped German immigrant workers would confuse the name with Milwaukee and so be lured to the town.

*Zilwaukee
Township
Lat: 43-30-11 N **Long:** 83-53-48 W
Pop: 82 (1990); 89 (1980) **Pop Density:** 14.4
Land: 5.7 sq. mi.; **Water:** 0.3 sq. mi.

> ## St. Clair County
> **County Seat: Port Huron (ZIP: 48060)**
>
> **Pop:** 145,607 (1990); 138,802 (1980)   **Pop Density:** 201.0
> **Land:** 724.5 sq. mi.; **Water:** 108.1 sq. mi.   **Area Code:** 313
> On the southeast coast of Michigan, northeast of Detroit, bordered on east by the St. Clair River; original county; established Mar 28, 1820 (prior to statehood).
> **Name origin:** For Gen. Arthur St. Clair (1736?–1818), an officer in the French and Indian War and the Revolutionary War, president of the Continental Congress (1787), and governor of the Northwest Territory (1788–1802).

Algonac   City
ZIP: 48001   **Lat:** 42-37-19 N   **Long:** 82-32-04 W
Pop: 4,551 (1990); 4,412 (1980)   **Pop Density:** 3250.7
Land: 1.4 sq. mi.; **Water:** 0.0 sq. mi.
Established early 1800s.
Name origin: For the Algonquin Indians.

Anchorville   CDP
Lat: 42-41-33 N   **Long:** 82-41-46 W
Pop: 3,202 (1990)   **Pop Density:** 1455.5
Land: 2.2 sq. mi.; **Water:** 2.7 sq. mi.

Berlin   Township
Lat: 42-56-41 N   **Long:** 82-55-36 W
Pop: 2,407 (1990); 2,160 (1980)   **Pop Density:** 64.9
Land: 37.1 sq. mi.; **Water:** 0.0 sq. mi.

Brockway   Township
Lat: 43-06-41 N   **Long:** 82-48-34 W
Pop: 1,609 (1990); 1,586 (1980)   **Pop Density:** 47.5
Land: 33.9 sq. mi.; **Water:** 0.0 sq. mi.

Burtchville   Township
Lat: 43-07-08 N   **Long:** 82-31-05 W
Pop: 3,559 (1990); 3,069 (1980)   **Pop Density:** 228.1
Land: 15.6 sq. mi.; **Water:** 0.0 sq. mi.

Capac   Village
ZIP: 48014   **Lat:** 43-00-47 N   **Long:** 82-55-45 W
Pop: 1,583 (1990); 1,377 (1980)   **Pop Density:** 1439.1
Land: 1.1 sq. mi.; **Water:** 0.0 sq. mi.
Founded 1857.
Name origin: For the last Inca emperor Huayna Capac (?–1525).

Casco   Township
Lat: 42-45-49 N   **Long:** 82-40-20 W
Pop: 4,552 (1990); 4,331 (1980)   **Pop Density:** 122.0
Land: 37.3 sq. mi.; **Water:** 0.0 sq. mi.

China   Township
Lat: 42-46-20 N   **Long:** 82-33-42 W
Pop: 2,644 (1990); 2,466 (1980)   **Pop Density:** 76.9
Land: 34.4 sq. mi.; **Water:** 0.0 sq. mi.

Clay   Township
ZIP: 48001   **Lat:** 42-35-48 N   **Long:** 82-38-42 W
Pop: 8,862 (1990); 8,518 (1980)   **Pop Density:** 249.6
Land: 35.5 sq. mi.; **Water:** 43.1 sq. mi.

Clyde   Township
ZIP: 48049   **Lat:** 43-02-06 N   **Long:** 82-34-21 W
Pop: 5,052 (1990); 4,632 (1980)   **Pop Density:** 140.7
Land: 35.9 sq. mi.; **Water:** 0.1 sq. mi.

Columbus   Township
Lat: 42-51-19 N   **Long:** 82-40-35 W
Pop: 3,235 (1990); 3,097 (1980)   **Pop Density:** 87.0
Land: 37.2 sq. mi.; **Water:** 0.1 sq. mi.

Cottrellville   Township
Lat: 42-41-39 N   **Long:** 82-33-37 W
Pop: 3,301 (1990); 3,075 (1980)   **Pop Density:** 155.7
Land: 21.2 sq. mi.; **Water:** 1.2 sq. mi.

East China   Township
Lat: 42-45-46 N   **Long:** 82-29-21 W
Pop: 3,216 (1990); 3,122 (1980)   **Pop Density:** 487.3
Land: 6.6 sq. mi.; **Water:** 1.1 sq. mi.

Emmett   Village
ZIP: 48022   **Lat:** 42-59-28 N   **Long:** 82-45-57 W
Pop: 297 (1990); 285 (1980)   **Pop Density:** 198.0
Land: 1.5 sq. mi.; **Water:** 0.0 sq. mi.   **Elev:** 775 ft.
Not coextensive with the town of the same name.
Name origin: For Robert W. Emmet (1778–1803), Irish patriot.

*Emmett   Township
ZIP: 48022   **Lat:** 43-01-31 N   **Long:** 82-49-13 W
Pop: 1,816 (1990); 1,698 (1980)   **Pop Density:** 51.4
Land: 35.3 sq. mi.; **Water:** 0.0 sq. mi.

Fair Haven   CDP
ZIP: 48023   **Lat:** 42-40-38 N   **Long:** 82-38-53 W
Pop: 1,505 (1990)   **Pop Density:** 752.5
Land: 2.0 sq. mi.; **Water:** 1.7 sq. mi.

Fort Gratiot   Township
ZIP: 48060   **Lat:** 43-02-25 N   **Long:** 82-29-04 W
Pop: 8,968 (1990); 8,496 (1980)   **Pop Density:** 553.6
Land: 16.2 sq. mi.; **Water:** 0.0 sq. mi.

Grant   Township
Lat: 43-07-18 N   **Long:** 82-35-19 W
Pop: 1,210 (1990); 1,119 (1980)   **Pop Density:** 40.6
Land: 29.8 sq. mi.; **Water:** 0.0 sq. mi.

Greenwood   Township
Lat: 43-07-04 N   **Long:** 82-41-37 W
Pop: 1,037 (1990); 1,046 (1980)   **Pop Density:** 29.0
Land: 35.8 sq. mi.; **Water:** 0.1 sq. mi.

Ira   Township
ZIP: 48023   **Lat:** 42-41-33 N   **Long:** 82-39-33 W
Pop: 5,587 (1990); 4,316 (1980)   **Pop Density:** 328.6
Land: 17.0 sq. mi.; **Water:** 4.5 sq. mi.

Kenockee   Township
Lat: 43-01-55 N   **Long:** 82-41-39 W
Pop: 1,854 (1990); 1,730 (1980)   **Pop Density:** 51.8
Land: 35.8 sq. mi.; **Water:** 0.0 sq. mi.

MICHIGAN, St. Clair County

Kimball
Township
ZIP: 48074   Lat: 42-56-46 N **Long:** 82-33-42 W
Pop: 7,247 (1990); 7,180 (1980)   **Pop Density:** 194.3
Land: 37.3 sq. mi.; **Water:** 0.2 sq. mi.

Lynn
Township
Lat: 43-06-42 N **Long:** 82-56-11 W
Pop: 921 (1990); 999 (1980)   **Pop Density:** 25.5
Land: 36.1 sq. mi.; **Water:** 0.0 sq. mi.

Marine City
City
ZIP: 48039   Lat: 42-42-51 N **Long:** 82-30-04 W
Pop: 4,556 (1990); 4,414 (1980)   **Pop Density:** 2070.9
Land: 2.2 sq. mi.; **Water:** 0.3 sq. mi.   **Elev:** 588 ft.
Name origin: Descriptively named for its location at the mouth of the Belle River. Previously called Yankee Point.

Marysville
City
ZIP: 48040   Lat: 42-54-36 N **Long:** 82-28-47 W
Pop: 8,515 (1990); 7,345 (1980)   **Pop Density:** 1234.1
Land: 6.9 sq. mi.; **Water:** 1.0 sq. mi.
Begun as a sawmill town 1843.
Name origin: For Mary Mills, wife of a local lumberman.

Memphis
City
ZIP: 48041   Lat: 42-54-01 N **Long:** 82-46-03 W
Pop: 325 (1990); 354 (1980)   **Pop Density:** 650.0
Land: 0.5 sq. mi.; **Water:** 0.0 sq. mi.
Part of the town is also in Macomb County.
Name origin: For the ancient Egyptian city.

Mussey
Township
Lat: 43-01-37 N **Long:** 82-55-45 W
Pop: 3,113 (1990); 2,768 (1980)   **Pop Density:** 86.5
Land: 36.0 sq. mi.; **Water:** 0.0 sq. mi.

Pearl Beach
CDP
Lat: 42-37-27 N **Long:** 82-35-27 W
Pop: 3,394 (1990); 3,430 (1980)   **Pop Density:** 1616.2
Land: 2.1 sq. mi.; **Water:** 1.0 sq. mi.

Port Huron
City
ZIP: 48061   Lat: 42-59-37 N **Long:** 82-26-01 W
Pop: 33,694 (1990); 33,981 (1980)   **Pop Density:** 4211.8
Land: 8.0 sq. mi.; **Water:** 4.2 sq. mi.
In southeastern MI on the St. Clair River at the south point of Lake Huron, 50 mi. northeast of Detroit. Founded 1828; incorporated as village 1849, as city 1857.
Name origin: For the Huron Indians. Originally known as Fort Gratiot.

*Port Huron
Township
ZIP: 48074   Lat: 42-58-32 N **Long:** 82-28-43 W
Pop: 7,621 (1990); 7,886 (1980)   **Pop Density:** 590.8
Land: 12.9 sq. mi.; **Water:** 0.2 sq. mi.

Riley
Township
Lat: 42-56-19 N **Long:** 82-48-22 W
Pop: 2,154 (1990); 2,075 (1980)   **Pop Density:** 56.2
Land: 38.3 sq. mi.; **Water:** 0.0 sq. mi.

St. Clair
City
ZIP: 48079   Lat: 42-49-29 N **Long:** 82-29-34 W
Pop: 5,116 (1990); 4,780 (1980)   **Pop Density:** 1827.1
Land: 2.8 sq. mi.; **Water:** 0.6 sq. mi.

*St. Clair
Township
Lat: 42-51-39 N **Long:** 82-33-15 W
Pop: 4,614 (1990); 3,965 (1980)   **Pop Density:** 118.6
Land: 38.9 sq. mi.; **Water:** 0.6 sq. mi.

Sparlingville
CDP
Lat: 42-57-37 N **Long:** 82-31-33 W
Pop: 1,974 (1990); 1,718 (1980)   **Pop Density:** 789.6
Land: 2.5 sq. mi.; **Water:** 0.0 sq. mi.

Wales
Township
Lat: 42-56-29 N **Long:** 82-40-45 W
Pop: 2,294 (1990); 2,368 (1980)   **Pop Density:** 61.3
Land: 37.4 sq. mi.; **Water:** 0.0 sq. mi.

Yale
City
ZIP: 48097   Lat: 43-07-40 N **Long:** 82-47-46 W
Pop: 1,977 (1990); 1,814 (1980)   **Pop Density:** 1520.8
Land: 1.3 sq. mi.; **Water:** 0.0 sq. mi.   **Elev:** 802 ft.

St. Joseph County
County Seat: Centreville (ZIP: 49032)

Pop: 58,913 (1990); 56,083 (1980)   **Pop Density:** 117.0
Land: 503.7 sq. mi.; **Water:** 17.4 sq. mi.   **Area Code:** 616
On the southern border of MI, south of Kalamazoo; established Oct 29, 1829 (prior to statehood) from Indian lands.
Name origin: For the spouse of the Virgin Mary.

Burr Oak
Village
ZIP: 49030   Lat: 41-50-53 N **Long:** 85-19-15 W
Pop: 882 (1990); 853 (1980)   **Pop Density:** 882.0
Land: 1.0 sq. mi.; **Water:** 0.0 sq. mi.   **Elev:** 883 ft.
Settled 1835. Not coextensive with the town of the same name.
Name origin: For the area's many burr oaks.

*Burr Oak
Township
ZIP: 49030   Lat: 41-51-23 N **Long:** 85-20-40 W
Pop: 2,542 (1990); 2,502 (1980)   **Pop Density:** 71.4
Land: 35.6 sq. mi.; **Water:** 0.5 sq. mi.

Centreville
Village
ZIP: 49032   Lat: 41-55-18 N **Long:** 85-31-38 W
Pop: 1,516 (1990); 1,202 (1980)   **Pop Density:** 1378.2
Land: 1.1 sq. mi.; **Water:** 0.0 sq. mi.   **Elev:** 826 ft.
Incorporated 1837.
Name origin: For its location in the center of the county.

MICHIGAN, St. Joseph County

Colon
Village
ZIP: 49040 **Lat:** 41-57-32 N **Long:** 85-19-24 W
Pop: 1,224 (1990); 1,190 (1980) **Pop Density:** 874.3
Land: 1.4 sq. mi.; **Water:** 0.3 sq. mi.

Not coextensive with the town of the same name.

Name origin: Because a broadening in the St. Joseph River and a lake resemble the shape of a colon, according to Lorensie Schellhouse, a founder.

*Colon
Township
ZIP: 49040 **Lat:** 41-56-21 N **Long:** 85-21-26 W
Pop: 3,217 (1990); 3,033 (1980) **Pop Density:** 93.0
Land: 34.6 sq. mi.; **Water:** 1.8 sq. mi.

Constantine
Village
ZIP: 49042 **Lat:** 41-50-16 N **Long:** 85-39-55 W
Pop: 2,032 (1990); 1,680 (1980) **Pop Density:** 1195.3
Land: 1.7 sq. mi.; **Water:** 0.1 sq. mi.

Not coextensive with the town of the same name.

Name origin: Named in 1835 for Constantine the Great (?–337), the first Christian Roman Emperor. Previously called Meek's Mill.

*Constantine
Township
ZIP: 49042 **Lat:** 41-50-50 N **Long:** 85-41-57 W
Pop: 4,152 (1990); 3,647 (1980) **Pop Density:** 120.0
Land: 34.6 sq. mi.; **Water:** 1.1 sq. mi.

Fabius
Township
Lat: 41-56-28 N **Long:** 85-42-15 W
Pop: 3,187 (1990); 3,153 (1980) **Pop Density:** 97.8
Land: 32.6 sq. mi.; **Water:** 3.0 sq. mi.

Fawn River
Township
Lat: 41-46-56 N **Long:** 85-20-50 W
Pop: 1,571 (1990); 1,639 (1980) **Pop Density:** 78.2
Land: 20.1 sq. mi.; **Water:** 0.4 sq. mi.

Florence
Township
Lat: 41-51-37 N **Long:** 85-35-40 W
Pop: 1,518 (1990); 1,403 (1980) **Pop Density:** 45.2
Land: 33.6 sq. mi.; **Water:** 0.2 sq. mi.

Flowerfield
Township
Lat: 42-01-20 N **Long:** 85-42-29 W
Pop: 1,418 (1990); 1,290 (1980) **Pop Density:** 39.6
Land: 35.8 sq. mi.; **Water:** 0.0 sq. mi.

Leonidas
Township
ZIP: 49066 **Lat:** 42-01-40 N **Long:** 85-21-12 W
Pop: 1,171 (1990); 1,249 (1980) **Pop Density:** 32.8
Land: 35.7 sq. mi.; **Water:** 0.5 sq. mi.

Lockport
Township
Lat: 41-56-26 N **Long:** 85-34-59 W
Pop: 3,395 (1990); 3,048 (1980) **Pop Density:** 113.2
Land: 30.0 sq. mi.; **Water:** 1.7 sq. mi.

Mendon
Village
ZIP: 49072 **Lat:** 42-00-30 N **Long:** 85-27-14 W
Pop: 920 (1990); 951 (1980) **Pop Density:** 1314.3
Land: 0.7 sq. mi.; **Water:** 0.0 sq. mi. **Elev:** 852 ft.

Not coextensive with the town of the same name.

Name origin: Named by the first settlers, for their hometown of Mendon, MA.

*Mendon
Township
ZIP: 49072 **Lat:** 42-01-48 N **Long:** 85-28-01 W
Pop: 2,695 (1990); 2,820 (1980) **Pop Density:** 77.0
Land: 35.0 sq. mi.; **Water:** 1.2 sq. mi.

Mottville
Township
Lat: 41-47-19 N **Long:** 85-42-40 W
Pop: 1,501 (1990); 1,490 (1980) **Pop Density:** 76.6
Land: 19.6 sq. mi.; **Water:** 0.4 sq. mi.

Nottawa
Township
Lat: 41-56-25 N **Long:** 85-28-14 W
Pop: 3,637 (1990); 3,324 (1980) **Pop Density:** 101.6
Land: 35.8 sq. mi.; **Water:** 1.8 sq. mi.

Park
Township
Lat: 42-01-48 N **Long:** 85-35-26 W
Pop: 2,769 (1990); 2,772 (1980) **Pop Density:** 78.9
Land: 35.1 sq. mi.; **Water:** 0.7 sq. mi.

Sherman
Township
Lat: 41-51-39 N **Long:** 85-28-39 W
Pop: 2,978 (1990); 2,756 (1980) **Pop Density:** 89.4
Land: 33.3 sq. mi.; **Water:** 1.9 sq. mi.

Sturgis
City
ZIP: 49091 **Lat:** 41-48-05 N **Long:** 85-25-16 W
Pop: 10,130 (1990); 9,468 (1980) **Pop Density:** 1986.3
Land: 5.1 sq. mi.; **Water:** 0.0 sq. mi.

Name origin: Named in 1857 for Judge John Sturgis, who arrived 1827.

*Sturgis
Township
ZIP: 49091 **Lat:** 41-47-17 N **Long:** 85-28-36 W
Pop: 1,965 (1990); 1,871 (1980) **Pop Density:** 109.2
Land: 18.0 sq. mi.; **Water:** 0.1 sq. mi.

Three Rivers
City
ZIP: 49093 **Lat:** 41-56-38 N **Long:** 85-37-55 W
Pop: 7,413 (1990); 7,015 (1980) **Pop Density:** 1950.8
Land: 3.8 sq. mi.; **Water:** 0.2 sq. mi.

Platted 1830s.

Name origin: For its location at the confluence of the St. Joseph, Rocky, and Portage rivers.

White Pigeon
Village
ZIP: 49099 **Lat:** 41-47-54 N **Long:** 85-38-34 W
Pop: 1,458 (1990); 1,478 (1980) **Pop Density:** 1620.0
Land: 0.9 sq. mi.; **Water:** 0.0 sq. mi.

Settled 1827. Not coextensive with the town of the same name.

Name origin: For Indian chief White Pigeon.

*White Pigeon
Township
ZIP: 49099 **Lat:** 41-47-05 N **Long:** 85-35-38 W
Pop: 3,654 (1990); 3,603 (1980) **Pop Density:** 143.3
Land: 25.5 sq. mi.; **Water:** 2.0 sq. mi.

Sanilac County
County Seat: Sandusky (ZIP: 48471)

Pop: 39,928 (1990); 40,789 (1980)
Land: 963.9 sq. mi.; **Water:** 626.8 sq. mi.
Pop Density: 41.4
Area Code: 313

On the east-central coast of MI bordered on the east by Lake Huron; established Sep 10, 1822 (prior to statehood).

Name origin: For the Wyandot chief who is the main character in Henry Whiting's poem "Sannilac." The name was spelled with only one 'n' in the proclamation by Gov. Lewis Cass (1782–1866) that announced the formation of the county.

Applegate — Village
ZIP: 48401 **Lat:** 43-21-17 N **Long:** 82-38-11 W
Pop: 297 (1990); 257 (1980) **Pop Density:** 297.0
Land: 1.0 sq. mi.; **Water:** 0.0 sq. mi.
Settled 1856.
Name origin: For Oregon Trail pioneer Jesse Applegate (1811–88).

Argyle — Township
Lat: 43-32-31 N **Long:** 82-56-02 W
Pop: 820 (1990); 912 (1980) **Pop Density:** 22.6
Land: 36.3 sq. mi.; **Water:** 0.0 sq. mi.

Austin — Township
Lat: 43-38-17 N **Long:** 82-55-57 W
Pop: 639 (1990); 802 (1980) **Pop Density:** 17.7
Land: 36.2 sq. mi.; **Water:** 0.0 sq. mi.

Bridgehampton — Township
Lat: 43-28-19 N **Long:** 82-41-53 W
Pop: 845 (1990); 974 (1980) **Pop Density:** 23.3
Land: 36.2 sq. mi.; **Water:** 0.0 sq. mi.

Brown City — City
ZIP: 48416 **Lat:** 43-12-44 N **Long:** 82-59-15 W
Pop: 1,235 (1990); 1,158 (1980) **Pop Density:** 1122.7
Land: 1.1 sq. mi.; **Water:** 0.0 sq. mi. **Elev:** 813 ft.
Founded 1879. Part of the town is also in Lapeer County.
Name origin: For the founding Brown brothers.

Buel — Township
Lat: 43-16-58 N **Long:** 82-42-54 W
Pop: 844 (1990); 890 (1980) **Pop Density:** 22.4
Land: 37.7 sq. mi.; **Water:** 0.0 sq. mi.

Carsonville — Village
ZIP: 48419 **Lat:** 43-25-32 N **Long:** 82-40-21 W
Pop: 583 (1990); 622 (1980) **Pop Density:** 530.0
Land: 1.1 sq. mi.; **Water:** 0.0 sq. mi. **Elev:** 823 ft.
Name origin: For Arthur Carson, who built a store here in 1864.

Croswell — City
ZIP: 48422 **Lat:** 43-16-25 N **Long:** 82-37-07 W
Pop: 2,174 (1990); 2,073 (1980) **Pop Density:** 988.2
Land: 2.2 sq. mi.; **Water:** 0.0 sq. mi. **Elev:** 736 ft.
Name origin: Renamed in 1877 for Gov. Charles Croswell. Previously called Davisville.

Custer — Township
Lat: 43-27-56 N **Long:** 82-48-41 W
Pop: 1,018 (1990); 1,122 (1980) **Pop Density:** 28.8
Land: 35.4 sq. mi.; **Water:** 0.0 sq. mi.

Deckerville — Village
ZIP: 48427 **Lat:** 43-31-32 N **Long:** 82-44-31 W
Pop: 1,015 (1990); 887 (1980) **Pop Density:** 780.8
Land: 1.3 sq. mi.; **Water:** 0.0 sq. mi.
Name origin: For prominent lumberman Charles Decker.

Delaware — Township
Lat: 43-38-41 N **Long:** 82-40-58 W
Pop: 961 (1990); 1,071 (1980) **Pop Density:** 20.6
Land: 46.6 sq. mi.; **Water:** 0.0 sq. mi.

Elk — Township
Lat: 43-17-00 N **Long:** 82-49-41 W
Pop: 1,465 (1990); 1,535 (1980) **Pop Density:** 41.0
Land: 35.7 sq. mi.; **Water:** 0.0 sq. mi.

Elmer — Township
Lat: 43-22-56 N **Long:** 82-55-30 W
Pop: 774 (1990); 829 (1980) **Pop Density:** 21.3
Land: 36.3 sq. mi.; **Water:** 0.0 sq. mi.

Evergreen — Township
Lat: 43-32-48 N **Long:** 83-03-00 W
Pop: 907 (1990); 1,042 (1980) **Pop Density:** 25.6
Land: 35.4 sq. mi.; **Water:** 0.0 sq. mi.

Flynn — Township
Lat: 43-17-25 N **Long:** 82-56-10 W
Pop: 914 (1990); 963 (1980) **Pop Density:** 25.5
Land: 35.8 sq. mi.; **Water:** 0.0 sq. mi.

Forester — Township
Lat: 43-31-51 N **Long:** 82-36-18 W
Pop: 919 (1990); 958 (1980) **Pop Density:** 36.3
Land: 25.3 sq. mi.; **Water:** 0.0 sq. mi.

Forestville — Village
ZIP: 48434 **Lat:** 43-39-38 N **Long:** 82-36-47 W
Pop: 153 (1990); 159 (1980) **Pop Density:** 191.3
Land: 0.8 sq. mi.; **Water:** 0.0 sq. mi. **Elev:** 635 ft.

Fremont — Township
Lat: 43-12-47 N **Long:** 82-42-23 W
Pop: 787 (1990); 847 (1980) **Pop Density:** 22.5
Land: 35.0 sq. mi.; **Water:** 0.0 sq. mi.

Greenleaf — Township
Lat: 43-37-59 N **Long:** 83-03-38 W
Pop: 667 (1990); 746 (1980) **Pop Density:** 18.6
Land: 35.9 sq. mi.; **Water:** 0.0 sq. mi.

Lamotte — Township
Lat: 43-27-30 N **Long:** 83-02-59 W
Pop: 949 (1990); 1,065 (1980) **Pop Density:** 26.7
Land: 35.5 sq. mi.; **Water:** 0.0 sq. mi.

Lexington
Village
ZIP: 48450 **Lat:** 43-16-06 N **Long:** 82-32-01 W
Pop: 779 (1990); 765 (1980) **Pop Density:** 1112.9
Land: 0.7 sq. mi.; **Water:** 0.0 sq. mi. **Elev:** 623 ft.
Founded in the 1840s. Not coextensive with the town of the same name.
Name origin: For Lexington, MA, in honor of the Revolutionary War battle fought there.

*Lexington
Township
ZIP: 48450 **Lat:** 43-17-36 N **Long:** 82-35-36 W
Pop: 3,028 (1990); 2,958 (1980) **Pop Density:** 83.4
Land: 36.3 sq. mi.; **Water:** 0.0 sq. mi.

Maple Valley
Township
Lat: 43-11-56 N **Long:** 82-56-21 W
Pop: 1,022 (1990); 1,009 (1980) **Pop Density:** 29.6
Land: 34.5 sq. mi.; **Water:** 0.0 sq. mi.

Marion
Township
Lat: 43-33-17 N **Long:** 82-41-21 W
Pop: 1,831 (1990); 1,741 (1980) **Pop Density:** 50.7
Land: 36.1 sq. mi.; **Water:** 0.0 sq. mi.

Marlette
Village
ZIP: 48453 **Lat:** 43-19-35 N **Long:** 83-04-50 W
Pop: 1,924 (1990); 1,761 (1980) **Pop Density:** 1202.5
Land: 1.6 sq. mi.; **Water:** 0.0 sq. mi.
Incorporated 1881.
Name origin: For the maiden name of two early Irish settlers who carved their name on a log. The *e* was added when the name was suggested for the town.

*Marlette
Township
ZIP: 48453 **Lat:** 43-21-01 N **Long:** 83-03-17 W
Pop: 1,910 (1990); 3,790 (1980) **Pop Density:** 36.3
Land: 52.6 sq. mi.; **Water:** 0.0 sq. mi.

Melvin
Village
ZIP: 48454 **Lat:** 43-11-04 N **Long:** 82-51-48 W
Pop: 148 (1990); 171 (1980) **Pop Density:** 148.0
Land: 1.0 sq. mi.; **Water:** 0.0 sq. mi.
Began around a saloon; incorporated as a village 1907.

Minden
Township
Lat: 43-38-17 N **Long:** 82-49-03 W
Pop: 670 (1990); 710 (1980) **Pop Density:** 18.6
Land: 36.1 sq. mi.; **Water:** 0.0 sq. mi.

Minden City
Village
ZIP: 48456 **Lat:** 43-40-15 N **Long:** 82-46-30 W
Pop: 233 (1990); 284 (1980) **Pop Density:** 233.0
Land: 1.0 sq. mi.; **Water:** 0.0 sq. mi.

Moore
Township
Lat: 43-27-46 N **Long:** 82-55-44 W
Pop: 1,238 (1990); 1,318 (1980) **Pop Density:** 34.1
Land: 36.3 sq. mi.; **Water:** 0.0 sq. mi.

Peck
Village
ZIP: 48466 **Lat:** 43-15-32 N **Long:** 82-48-59 W
Pop: 558 (1990); 606 (1980) **Pop Density:** 558.0
Land: 1.0 sq. mi.; **Water:** 0.0 sq. mi.
Incorporated 1903.

Port Sanilac
Village
ZIP: 48469 **Lat:** 43-25-48 N **Long:** 82-32-45 W
Pop: 656 (1990); 598 (1980) **Pop Density:** 937.1
Land: 0.7 sq. mi.; **Water:** 0.0 sq. mi.
Settled 1840s.
Name origin: For its county.

Sandusky
City
ZIP: 48471 **Lat:** 43-25-22 N **Long:** 82-49-54 W
Pop: 2,403 (1990); 2,216 (1980) **Pop Density:** 1501.9
Land: 1.6 sq. mi.; **Water:** 0.0 sq. mi. **Elev:** 774 ft.
Founded 1870 by Wildman Mills.
Name origin: For Sandusky, OH.

Sanilac
Township
Lat: 43-24-25 N **Long:** 82-35-00 W
Pop: 2,362 (1990); 2,284 (1980) **Pop Density:** 57.8
Land: 40.9 sq. mi.; **Water:** 0.0 sq. mi.

Speaker
Township
Lat: 43-12-35 N **Long:** 82-49-17 W
Pop: 1,171 (1990); 1,265 (1980) **Pop Density:** 33.8
Land: 34.6 sq. mi.; **Water:** 0.0 sq. mi.

Washington
Township
Lat: 43-23-12 N **Long:** 82-41-57 W
Pop: 1,557 (1990); 1,525 (1980) **Pop Density:** 43.1
Land: 36.1 sq. mi.; **Water:** 0.0 sq. mi.

Watertown
Township
Lat: 43-22-48 N **Long:** 82-48-04 W
Pop: 1,235 (1990); 1,346 (1980) **Pop Density:** 34.8
Land: 35.5 sq. mi.; **Water:** 0.0 sq. mi.

Wheatland
Township
Lat: 43-32-52 N **Long:** 82-49-14 W
Pop: 513 (1990); 582 (1980) **Pop Density:** 14.1
Land: 36.4 sq. mi.; **Water:** 0.0 sq. mi.

Worth
Township
Lat: 43-12-20 N **Long:** 82-34-48 W
Pop: 3,146 (1990); 3,058 (1980) **Pop Density:** 81.1
Land: 38.8 sq. mi.; **Water:** 0.0 sq. mi.

MICHIGAN, Schoolcraft County   *American Places Dictionary*

Schoolcraft County
County Seat: Manistique (ZIP: 49854)

Pop: 8,302 (1990); 8,575 (1980) **Pop Density:** 7.0
Land: 1178.2 sq. mi.; **Water:** 705.6 sq. mi. **Area Code:** 906
On the south-central coast of the Upper Peninsula of MI, on Lake Michigan; established Mar 9, 1843 from Michilimackinac and Chippewa counties.
Name origin: For Henry Rowe Schoolcraft (1793–1864), explorer, MI legislator, author, and superintendent of Indian Affairs for MI (1836–41).

Doyle   Township
Lat: 46-10-10 N **Long:** 86-03-34 W
Pop: 616 (1990); 629 (1980) **Pop Density:** 4.2
Land: 147.4 sq. mi.; **Water:** 6.7 sq. mi.

Germfask   Township
ZIP: 49836 **Lat:** 46-14-44 N **Long:** 85-55-36 W
Pop: 542 (1990); 607 (1980) **Pop Density:** 8.0
Land: 67.8 sq. mi.; **Water:** 3.9 sq. mi.
Settled 1881.
Name origin: Named by Dr. W.W. French from the surname initials of the eight founders: John Grant, Matthew Edge, George Robinson, Thaddeus Mead, Dr. W.W. French, Ezekiel Ackley, Oscar Shepard, and Hezekiah Knaggs.

Hiawatha   Township
Lat: 46-13-58 N **Long:** 86-19-33 W
Pop: 1,279 (1990); 1,096 (1980) **Pop Density:** 4.6
Land: 278.5 sq. mi.; **Water:** 12.3 sq. mi.

Inwood   Township
Lat: 46-05-12 N **Long:** 86-28-41 W
Pop: 638 (1990); 592 (1980) **Pop Density:** 5.3
Land: 120.3 sq. mi.; **Water:** 6.2 sq. mi.

Manistique   City
ZIP: 49854 **Lat:** 45-57-31 N **Long:** 86-15-00 W
Pop: 3,456 (1990); 3,962 (1980) **Pop Density:** 1080.0
Land: 3.2 sq. mi.; **Water:** 0.3 sq. mi.
Founded 1871.
Name origin: For the Monistique River, which flows across the southeastern part of the county; itself named from an Ojibway Indian term meaning 'vermillion river.' Clerical error in the spelling was allowed to stand.

*Manistique   Township
ZIP: 49854 **Lat:** 46-08-26 N **Long:** 86-10-59 W
Pop: 916 (1990); 862 (1980) **Pop Density:** 6.1
Land: 150.3 sq. mi.; **Water:** 3.4 sq. mi.

Mueller   Township
Lat: 46-03-31 N **Long:** 85-55-13 W
Pop: 206 (1990); 255 (1980) **Pop Density:** 2.5
Land: 83.9 sq. mi.; **Water:** 4.1 sq. mi.

Seney   Township
ZIP: 49883 **Lat:** 46-24-31 N **Long:** 86-02-58 W
Pop: 185 (1990); 174 (1980) **Pop Density:** 0.9
Land: 213.9 sq. mi.; **Water:** 1.7 sq. mi.

Thompson   Township
Lat: 45-59-07 N **Long:** 86-22-43 W
Pop: 464 (1990); 398 (1980) **Pop Density:** 4.1
Land: 113.0 sq. mi.; **Water:** 5.4 sq. mi.

Shiawassee County
County Seat: Corunna (ZIP: 48817)

Pop: 69,770 (1990); 71,140 (1980) **Pop Density:** 129.5
Land: 538.8 sq. mi.; **Water:** 1.9 sq. mi. **Area Code:** 517
In south-central MI, west of Flint; established Sep 10, 1822 (prior to statehood) from Indian lands,
Name origin: For the Shiawassee River, which runs through it; from Algonquian 'the water straight ahead' or 'river that twists about.'

Antrim   Township
ZIP: 48418 **Lat:** 42-49-32 N **Long:** 84-06-22 W
Pop: 1,679 (1990); 1,752 (1980) **Pop Density:** 46.0
Land: 36.5 sq. mi.; **Water:** 0.2 sq. mi.

Bancroft   Village
ZIP: 48414 **Lat:** 42-52-36 N **Long:** 84-03-55 W
Pop: 599 (1990); 618 (1980) **Pop Density:** 1198.0
Land: 0.5 sq. mi.; **Water:** 0.0 sq. mi. **Elev:** 854 ft.
Settled 1877.
Name origin: For the Bancroft Mining Company.

Bennington   Township
Lat: 42-54-31 N **Long:** 84-13-24 W
Pop: 2,726 (1990); 2,758 (1980) **Pop Density:** 74.7
Land: 36.5 sq. mi.; **Water:** 0.3 sq. mi.

Burns   Township
ZIP: 48418 **Lat:** 42-49-39 N **Long:** 83-58-55 W
Pop: 3,019 (1990); 3,273 (1980) **Pop Density:** 85.0
Land: 35.5 sq. mi.; **Water:** 0.2 sq. mi.

Byron
Village
ZIP: 48418   **Lat:** 42-49-31 N   **Long:** 83-56-56 W
Pop: 573 (1990); 689 (1980)   **Pop Density:** 818.6
Land: 0.7 sq. mi.; **Water:** 0.0 sq. mi.
Name origin: For its township.

Caledonia
Township
Lat: 43-00-01 N   **Long:** 84-06-10 W
Pop: 4,514 (1990); 4,785 (1980)   **Pop Density:** 142.4
Land: 31.7 sq. mi.; **Water:** 0.1 sq. mi.

Corunna
City
ZIP: 48817   **Lat:** 42-59-02 N   **Long:** 84-07-00 W
Pop: 3,091 (1990); 3,206 (1980)   **Pop Density:** 997.1
Land: 3.1 sq. mi.; **Water:** 0.0 sq. mi.
Settled 1836. Established 1869.
Name origin: For La Coruña, Spain, with a spelling variation.

Durand
City
ZIP: 48429   **Lat:** 42-54-46 N   **Long:** 83-59-17 W
Pop: 4,283 (1990); 4,206 (1980)   **Pop Density:** 2519.4
Land: 1.7 sq. mi.; **Water:** 0.0 sq. mi.   **Elev:** 796 ft.
Name origin: For U.S. Rep. George Durand.

Fairfield
Township
Lat: 43-04-54 N   **Long:** 84-19-00 W
Pop: 790 (1990); 904 (1980)   **Pop Density:** 31.5
Land: 25.1 sq. mi.; **Water:** 0.0 sq. mi.

Hazelton
Township
Lat: 43-05-07 N   **Long:** 83-59-12 W
Pop: 2,294 (1990); 2,411 (1980)   **Pop Density:** 61.5
Land: 37.3 sq. mi.; **Water:** 0.0 sq. mi.

Laingsburg
City
ZIP: 48848   **Lat:** 42-53-23 N   **Long:** 84-20-55 W
Pop: 1,148 (1990); 1,145 (1980)   **Pop Density:** 717.5
Land: 1.6 sq. mi.; **Water:** 0.0 sq. mi.
Founded 1836.
Name origin: For founder Dr. Peter Laing.

Lennon
Village
ZIP: 48449   **Lat:** 42-59-02 N   **Long:** 83-55-56 W
Pop: 450 (1990); 486 (1980)   **Pop Density:** 642.9
Land: 0.7 sq. mi.; **Water:** 0.0 sq. mi.
Part of the town is also in Genesee County.
Name origin: For railroad builder Peter Lennon.

Middlebury
Township
Lat: 43-00-00 N   **Long:** 84-19-27 W
Pop: 1,536 (1990); 1,574 (1980)   **Pop Density:** 62.2
Land: 24.7 sq. mi.; **Water:** 0.0 sq. mi.

Middletown
CDP
Lat: 42-59-08 N   **Long:** 84-08-41 W
Pop: 1,010 (1990)   **Pop Density:** 2020.0
Land: 0.5 sq. mi.; **Water:** 0.0 sq. mi.

Morrice
Village
ZIP: 48857   **Lat:** 42-50-16 N   **Long:** 84-10-46 W
Pop: 630 (1990); 733 (1980)   **Pop Density:** 572.7
Land: 1.1 sq. mi.; **Water:** 0.0 sq. mi.
Name origin: For the Morrice brothers, who settled here in the 1830s.

New Haven
Township
Lat: 43-04-46 N   **Long:** 84-06-21 W
Pop: 1,286 (1990); 1,425 (1980)   **Pop Density:** 36.0
Land: 35.7 sq. mi.; **Water:** 0.0 sq. mi.

New Lothrop
Village
ZIP: 48460   **Lat:** 43-06-57 N   **Long:** 83-58-08 W
Pop: 596 (1990); 646 (1980)   **Pop Density:** 745.0
Land: 0.8 sq. mi.; **Water:** 0.0 sq. mi.
Settled in the 1830s.
Name origin: For William Lothrop, who gave bells to the Methodist Church.

Ovid
Village
Lat: 43-00-27 N   **Long:** 84-21-58 W
Pop: 0 (1990)
Land: 0.002 sq. mi.; **Water:** 0.0 sq. mi.
Settled 1834. Part of the town is also in Clinton County.
Name origin: For Ovid, NY.

Owosso
City
ZIP: 48867   **Lat:** 42-59-42 N   **Long:** 84-10-32 W
Pop: 16,322 (1990); 16,455 (1980)   **Pop Density:** 3331.0
Land: 4.9 sq. mi.; **Water:** 0.0 sq. mi.
In south-central MI on the Shiawassee River, 25 mi. northeast of Lansing. Settled 1833; incorporated as a city 1859.
Name origin: For Chief Owasso (or Wassa or Wasso), of the Shiawassee Ojibway. From the term *wasso* meaning 'one bright spot.'

*Owosso
Township
ZIP: 48867   **Lat:** 42-59-49 N   **Long:** 84-13-58 W
Pop: 4,121 (1990); 4,530 (1980)   **Pop Density:** 126.8
Land: 32.5 sq. mi.; **Water:** 0.0 sq. mi.

Perry
City
ZIP: 48872   **Lat:** 42-49-15 N   **Long:** 84-13-41 W
Pop: 2,163 (1990); 2,051 (1980)   **Pop Density:** 801.1
Land: 2.7 sq. mi.; **Water:** 0.0 sq. mi.   **Elev:** 889 ft.
Established 1850.
Name origin: For its township.

*Perry
Township
ZIP: 48872   **Lat:** 42-48-52 N   **Long:** 84-13-13 W
Pop: 3,698 (1990); 3,467 (1980)   **Pop Density:** 115.6
Land: 32.0 sq. mi.; **Water:** 0.0 sq. mi.

Rush
Township
Lat: 43-05-04 N   **Long:** 84-13-06 W
Pop: 1,405 (1990); 1,500 (1980)   **Pop Density:** 39.9
Land: 35.2 sq. mi.; **Water:** 0.0 sq. mi.

Sciota
Township
Lat: 42-54-23 N   **Long:** 84-19-24 W
Pop: 1,578 (1990); 1,527 (1980)   **Pop Density:** 58.9
Land: 26.8 sq. mi.; **Water:** 0.1 sq. mi.

Shiawassee
Township
Lat: 42-54-49 N   **Long:** 84-06-33 W
Pop: 2,731 (1990); 2,709 (1980)   **Pop Density:** 74.4
Land: 36.7 sq. mi.; **Water:** 0.2 sq. mi.

Venice
Township
Lat: 42-59-31 N   **Long:** 83-59-30 W
Pop: 2,812 (1990); 3,063 (1980)   **Pop Density:** 75.0
Land: 37.5 sq. mi.; **Water:** 0.0 sq. mi.

Vernon — Village
ZIP: 48476 Lat: 42-56-22 N Long: 84-01-47 W
Pop: 913 (1990); 1,008 (1980) Pop Density: 1304.3
Land: 0.7 sq. mi.; Water: 0.0 sq. mi.
Settled 1833. Not coextensive with the town of the same name.
Name origin: For first U.S. President George Washington's (1732–99) VA estate, Mount Vernon.

*Vernon — Township
Lat: 42-55-05 N Long: 83-59-16 W
Pop: 4,989 (1990); 5,038 (1980) Pop Density: 145.9
Land: 34.2 sq. mi.; Water: 0.2 sq. mi.

Woodhull — Township
Lat: 42-48-55 N Long: 84-19-05 W
Pop: 3,585 (1990); 3,361 (1980) Pop Density: 132.3
Land: 27.1 sq. mi.; Water: 0.3 sq. mi.

Tuscola County
County Seat: Caro (ZIP: 48723)

Pop: 55,498 (1990); 56,961 (1980) Pop Density: 68.3
Land: 812.6 sq. mi.; Water: 101.2 sq. mi. Area Code: 517
In east MI, northeast of Flint; established Apr 1, 1840 from Sanilac County.
Name origin: Name coined by Henry Rowe Schoolcraft (1793–1864), author, explorer, MI legislator, and superintendent of Indian Affairs for MI (1836–41); means either 'warrior prairie' or 'level lands.'

Akron — Village
ZIP: 48701 Lat: 43-34-01 N Long: 83-30-51 W
Pop: 421 (1990); 538 (1980) Pop Density: 421.0
Land: 1.0 sq. mi.; Water: 0.0 sq. mi. Elev: 646 ft.
Incorporated 1910. Not coextensive with the town of the same name.
Name origin: For Akron, OH.

*Akron — Township
ZIP: 48701 Lat: 43-38-31 N Long: 83-31-33 W
Pop: 1,609 (1990); 1,811 (1980) Pop Density: 30.4
Land: 52.9 sq. mi.; Water: 4.0 sq. mi.

Almer — Township
Lat: 43-32-05 N Long: 83-24-40 W
Pop: 2,628 (1990); 2,720 (1980) Pop Density: 76.0
Land: 34.6 sq. mi.; Water: 0.0 sq. mi.

Arbela — Township
Lat: 43-15-31 N Long: 83-38-14 W
Pop: 3,182 (1990); 3,192 (1980) Pop Density: 95.3
Land: 33.4 sq. mi.; Water: 0.0 sq. mi.

Caro — Village
ZIP: 48723 Lat: 43-29-16 N Long: 83-24-07 W
Pop: 4,054 (1990); 4,317 (1980) Pop Density: 1842.7
Land: 2.2 sq. mi.; Water: 0.0 sq. mi.
Settled 1850s.
Name origin: For Cairo, Egypt, with spelling altered to reflect pronunciation.

Cass City — Village
ZIP: 48726 Lat: 43-36-08 N Long: 83-10-30 W
Pop: 2,276 (1990); 2,258 (1980) Pop Density: 1625.7
Land: 1.4 sq. mi.; Water: 0.0 sq. mi. Elev: 743 ft.
Incorporated 1863.
Name origin: For the Cass River, on which it is situated and which traverses the county.

Columbia — Township
Lat: 43-37-28 N Long: 83-24-52 W
Pop: 1,383 (1990); 1,428 (1980) Pop Density: 38.3
Land: 36.1 sq. mi.; Water: 0.0 sq. mi.

Dayton — Township
Lat: 43-22-01 N Long: 83-17-02 W
Pop: 1,706 (1990); 1,728 (1980) Pop Density: 47.5
Land: 35.9 sq. mi.; Water: 0.3 sq. mi.

Denmark — Township
Lat: 43-26-10 N Long: 83-38-26 W
Pop: 3,369 (1990); 3,615 (1980) Pop Density: 95.4
Land: 35.3 sq. mi.; Water: 0.0 sq. mi.

Elkland — Township
Lat: 43-37-51 N Long: 83-10-24 W
Pop: 3,430 (1990); 3,449 (1980) Pop Density: 96.3
Land: 35.6 sq. mi.; Water: 0.0 sq. mi.

Ellington — Township
Lat: 43-32-13 N Long: 83-16-49 W
Pop: 1,215 (1990); 1,214 (1980) Pop Density: 34.0
Land: 35.7 sq. mi.; Water: 0.0 sq. mi.

Elmwood — Township
Lat: 43-37-53 N Long: 83-17-37 W
Pop: 1,260 (1990); 1,337 (1980) Pop Density: 35.5
Land: 35.5 sq. mi.; Water: 0.0 sq. mi.

Fairgrove — Village
ZIP: 48733 Lat: 43-31-26 N Long: 83-32-29 W
Pop: 592 (1990); 691 (1980) Pop Density: 538.2
Land: 1.1 sq. mi.; Water: 0.0 sq. mi.
Settled 1852. Not coextensive with the town of the same name.
Name origin: For its descriptive connotations.

*Fairgrove — Township
ZIP: 48733 Lat: 43-31-27 N Long: 83-31-26 W
Pop: 1,743 (1990); 1,946 (1980) Pop Density: 49.4
Land: 35.3 sq. mi.; Water: 0.0 sq. mi.

Fremont — Township
Lat: 43-21-37 N Long: 83-24-15 W
Pop: 3,153 (1990); 2,871 (1980) Pop Density: 87.8
Land: 35.9 sq. mi.; Water: 0.2 sq. mi.

Gagetown — Village
ZIP: 48735 Lat: 43-39-24 N Long: 83-14-42 W
Pop: 337 (1990); 428 (1980) Pop Density: 337.0
Land: 1.0 sq. mi.; Water: 0.0 sq. mi.
Name origin: For its first postmaster, James Gage.

Gilford — Township
Lat: 43-31-21 N Long: 83-38-30 W
Pop: 824 (1990); 915 (1980) Pop Density: 23.7
Land: 34.8 sq. mi.; Water: 0.0 sq. mi.

Indianfields — Township
ZIP: 48723 Lat: 43-27-10 N Long: 83-24-11 W
Pop: 6,699 (1990); 7,037 (1980) Pop Density: 193.1
Land: 34.7 sq. mi.; Water: 0.5 sq. mi.

Juniata — Township
Lat: 43-26-11 N Long: 83-31-06 W
Pop: 1,666 (1990); 1,619 (1980) Pop Density: 47.2
Land: 35.3 sq. mi.; Water: 0.0 sq. mi.

Kingston — Village
ZIP: 48741 Lat: 43-24-48 N Long: 83-11-12 W
Pop: 439 (1990); 417 (1980) Pop Density: 548.8
Land: 0.8 sq. mi.; Water: 0.0 sq. mi.
Not coextensive with the town of the same name.
Name origin: For first settler Alanson K. King.

*Kingston — Township
ZIP: 48741 Lat: 43-26-57 N Long: 83-09-52 W
Pop: 1,498 (1990); 1,539 (1980) Pop Density: 41.7
Land: 35.9 sq. mi.; Water: 0.0 sq. mi.

Koylton — Township
Lat: 43-22-12 N Long: 83-10-12 W
Pop: 1,446 (1990); 1,399 (1980) Pop Density: 40.1
Land: 36.1 sq. mi.; Water: 0.1 sq. mi.

Mayville — Village
ZIP: 48744 Lat: 43-20-09 N Long: 83-21-11 W
Pop: 1,010 (1990); 958 (1980) Pop Density: 1010.0
Land: 1.0 sq. mi.; Water: 0.0 sq. mi.

Millington — Village
ZIP: 48746 Lat: 43-16-49 N Long: 83-31-43 W
Pop: 1,114 (1990); 1,237 (1980) Pop Density: 1114.0
Land: 1.0 sq. mi.; Water: 0.0 sq. mi.
Incorporated 1877. Not coextensive with the town of the same name.
Name origin: For Millington Creek, so named for the many mills along it.

*Millington — Township
ZIP: 48746 Lat: 43-16-06 N Long: 83-31-37 W
Pop: 4,199 (1990); 4,429 (1980) Pop Density: 117.3
Land: 35.8 sq. mi.; Water: 0.2 sq. mi.

Novesta — Township
Lat: 43-32-36 N Long: 83-10-17 W
Pop: 1,464 (1990); 1,482 (1980) Pop Density: 40.8
Land: 35.9 sq. mi.; Water: 0.0 sq. mi.

Reese — Village
ZIP: 48757 Lat: 43-27-06 N Long: 83-41-18 W
Pop: 1,414 (1990); 1,645 (1980) Pop Density: 1285.5
Land: 1.1 sq. mi.; Water: 0.0 sq. mi. Elev: 628 ft.
Name origin: For railroad superintendent G. W. Reese.

Tuscola — Township
Lat: 43-20-52 N Long: 83-38-12 W
Pop: 2,144 (1990); 2,255 (1980) Pop Density: 64.2
Land: 33.4 sq. mi.; Water: 0.1 sq. mi.

Unionville — Village
ZIP: 48767 Lat: 43-39-14 N Long: 83-28-00 W
Pop: 590 (1990); 578 (1980) Pop Density: 655.6
Land: 0.9 sq. mi.; Water: 0.0 sq. mi.
Settled 1850s.
Name origin: For Union, OH.

Vassar — City
ZIP: 48768 Lat: 43-22-17 N Long: 83-34-43 W
Pop: 2,559 (1990); 2,727 (1980) Pop Density: 1218.6
Land: 2.1 sq. mi.; Water: 0.0 sq. mi.
Founded 1849.
Name origin: For Matthew Vassar (1792–1868), founder of Vassar College, Poughkeepsie, NY.

*Vassar — Township
ZIP: 48768 Lat: 43-20-57 N Long: 83-31-13 W
Pop: 3,866 (1990); 3,709 (1980) Pop Density: 110.8
Land: 34.9 sq. mi.; Water: 0.1 sq. mi.

Watertown — Township
Lat: 43-16-44 N Long: 83-24-33 W
Pop: 2,132 (1990); 2,122 (1980) Pop Density: 65.2
Land: 32.7 sq. mi.; Water: 0.2 sq. mi.

Wells — Township
Lat: 43-27-11 N Long: 83-17-21 W
Pop: 1,528 (1990); 1,501 (1980) Pop Density: 43.2
Land: 35.4 sq. mi.; Water: 0.0 sq. mi.

Wisner — Township
Lat: 43-35-59 N Long: 83-38-01 W
Pop: 795 (1990); 916 (1980) Pop Density: 41.0
Land: 19.4 sq. mi.; Water: 5.8 sq. mi.

MICHIGAN, Van Buren County

Van Buren County
County Seat: Paw Paw (ZIP: 49079)

Pop: 70,060 (1990); 66,814 (1980)   **Pop Density:** 114.7
Land: 611.0 sq. mi.; **Water:** 479.3 sq. mi.   **Area Code:** 616

On the southwest coast of MI, bordered on west by Lake Michigan; established Oct 29, 1829 (prior to statehood) from unorganized territory.

Name origin: For Martin Van Buren (1782–1862), eighth U.S. president.

Almena — Township
Lat: 42-17-05 N   Long: 85-49-15 W
Pop: 3,581 (1990); 2,956 (1980)   **Pop Density:** 103.8
Land: 34.5 sq. mi.; **Water:** 0.3 sq. mi.

Antwerp — Township
ZIP: 49065   Lat: 42-12-05 N   Long: 85-49-36 W
Pop: 9,293 (1990); 7,744 (1980)   **Pop Density:** 266.3
Land: 34.9 sq. mi.; **Water:** 0.2 sq. mi.

Arlington — Township
Lat: 42-16-59 N   Long: 86-02-47 W
Pop: 1,929 (1990); 1,884 (1980)   **Pop Density:** 55.6
Land: 34.7 sq. mi.; **Water:** 0.4 sq. mi.

Bangor — City
ZIP: 49013   Lat: 42-18-41 N   Long: 86-06-52 W
Pop: 1,922 (1990); 2,001 (1980)   **Pop Density:** 1067.8
Land: 1.8 sq. mi.; **Water:** 0.0 sq. mi.   **Elev:** 658 ft.

In southwestern MI, 25 mi. west of Kalamazoo. First settled 1837. Incorporated as a village 1877.

Name origin: For Bangor, ME.

*Bangor — Township
ZIP: 49013   Lat: 42-17-17 N   Long: 86-10-12 W
Pop: 1,948 (1990); 1,993 (1980)   **Pop Density:** 57.8
Land: 33.7 sq. mi.; **Water:** 0.7 sq. mi.

Bloomingdale — Village
ZIP: 49026   Lat: 42-23-00 N   Long: 85-57-27 W
Pop: 503 (1990); 537 (1980)   **Pop Density:** 457.3
Land: 1.1 sq. mi.; **Water:** 0.0 sq. mi.

Incorporated 1881. Not coextensive with the town of the same name.

Name origin: For its location in a 'blooming valley.'

*Bloomingdale — Township
ZIP: 49026   Lat: 42-22-23 N   Long: 85-56-14 W
Pop: 2,854 (1990); 2,490 (1980)   **Pop Density:** 83.7
Land: 34.1 sq. mi.; **Water:** 1.0 sq. mi.

Breedsville — Village
ZIP: 49027   Lat: 42-20-49 N   Long: 86-04-15 W
Pop: 213 (1990); 244 (1980)   **Pop Density:** 304.3
Land: 0.7 sq. mi.; **Water:** 0.0 sq. mi.

Name origin: For Silas Breed, who built the first sawmill here.

Columbia — Township
Lat: 42-22-35 N   Long: 86-03-00 W
Pop: 2,552 (1990); 2,248 (1980)   **Pop Density:** 74.8
Land: 34.1 sq. mi.; **Water:** 1.3 sq. mi.

Covert — Township
ZIP: 49043   Lat: 42-16-42 N   Long: 86-17-16 W
Pop: 2,855 (1990); 2,706 (1980)   **Pop Density:** 81.6
Land: 35.0 sq. mi.; **Water:** 0.0 sq. mi.

Decatur — Village
ZIP: 49045   Lat: 42-06-34 N   Long: 85-58-24 W
Pop: 1,760 (1990); 1,915 (1980)   **Pop Density:** 1600.0
Land: 1.1 sq. mi.; **Water:** 0.0 sq. mi.

Settled 1847. Not coextensive with the town of the same name.

Name origin: For U.S. naval hero Stephen Decatur (1779–1820), famous for proclaiming: " . . . may she always be in the right; but our country, right or wrong!"

*Decatur — Township
ZIP: 49045   Lat: 42-07-05 N   Long: 85-56-17 W
Pop: 3,616 (1990); 3,599 (1980)   **Pop Density:** 102.7
Land: 35.2 sq. mi.; **Water:** 0.3 sq. mi.

Geneva — Township
Lat: 42-22-30 N   Long: 86-10-03 W
Pop: 3,162 (1990); 2,984 (1980)   **Pop Density:** 89.6
Land: 35.3 sq. mi.; **Water:** 0.0 sq. mi.

Gobles — City
ZIP: 49055   Lat: 42-21-42 N   Long: 85-52-36 W
Pop: 769 (1990); 816 (1980)   **Pop Density:** 769.0
Land: 1.0 sq. mi.; **Water:** 0.0 sq. mi.   **Elev:** 815 ft.

Settled 1864.

Name origin: For the Goble family, the first settlers.

Hamilton — Township
Lat: 42-06-57 N   Long: 86-03-25 W
Pop: 1,515 (1990); 1,586 (1980)   **Pop Density:** 43.9
Land: 34.5 sq. mi.; **Water:** 1.1 sq. mi.

Hartford — City
ZIP: 49057   Lat: 42-12-27 N   Long: 86-09-58 W
Pop: 2,341 (1990); 2,493 (1980)   **Pop Density:** 2341.0
Land: 1.0 sq. mi.; **Water:** 0.0 sq. mi.

Name origin: Name changed from Hartland in 1837 because there was already another MI town of the same name. Previously called Bloody Corners.

*Hartford — Township
ZIP: 49057   Lat: 42-12-00 N   Long: 86-09-48 W
Pop: 3,032 (1990); 2,707 (1980)   **Pop Density:** 88.9
Land: 34.1 sq. mi.; **Water:** 0.1 sq. mi.

Keeler — Township
Lat: 42-06-48 N   Long: 86-10-01 W
Pop: 2,344 (1990); 2,638 (1980)   **Pop Density:** 68.9
Land: 34.0 sq. mi.; **Water:** 1.0 sq. mi.

Lawrence — Village
ZIP: 49064   Lat: 42-13-07 N   Long: 86-03-10 W
Pop: 915 (1990); 903 (1980)   **Pop Density:** 653.6
Land: 1.4 sq. mi.; **Water:** 0.0 sq. mi.

Not coextensive with the town of the same name.

MICHIGAN, Washtenaw County

*Lawrence — Township
ZIP: 49064　　Lat: 42-11-50 N　Long: 86-03-07 W
Pop: 3,030 (1990); 3,017 (1980)　Pop Density: 86.6
Land: 35.0 sq. mi.; **Water:** 0.9 sq. mi.

Lawton — Village
ZIP: 49065　　Lat: 42-10-01 N　Long: 85-50-47 W
Pop: 1,685 (1990); 1,558 (1980)　Pop Density: 732.6
Land: 2.3 sq. mi.; **Water:** 0.0 sq. mi.
Name origin: For pioneer Nathan Lawton, who donated 10 acres to the Michigan Central Railroad in 1849.

Mattawan — Village
ZIP: 49071　　Lat: 42-12-50 N　Long: 85-47-15 W
Pop: 2,456 (1990); 2,143 (1980)　Pop Density: 599.0
Land: 4.1 sq. mi.; **Water:** 0.0 sq. mi.
Platted by railroad attorney Nathaniel L. Chesbrough in 1845.
Name origin: Named by Chesbrough for Mattawan, NY.

Paw Paw — Village
ZIP: 49079　　Lat: 42-13-04 N　Long: 85-53-23 W
Pop: 3,169 (1990); 3,211 (1980)　Pop Density: 1667.9
Land: 1.9 sq. mi.; **Water:** 0.2 sq. mi.
First settler arrived 1832. Not coextensive with the town of the same name.
Name origin: For the Paw Paw River, itself named for the paw paw fruit trees growing on its banks.

*Paw Paw — Township
ZIP: 49079　　Lat: 42-11-56 N　Long: 85-56-29 W
Pop: 6,701 (1990); 6,285 (1980)　Pop Density: 190.9
Land: 35.1 sq. mi.; **Water:** 1.8 sq. mi.

Pine Grove — Township
Lat: 42-22-44 N　Long: 85-48-58 W
Pop: 2,594 (1990); 2,379 (1980)　Pop Density: 75.4
Land: 34.4 sq. mi.; **Water:** 0.6 sq. mi.

Porter — Township
Lat: 42-06-33 N　Long: 85-48-55 W
Pop: 2,086 (1990); 2,041 (1980)　Pop Density: 62.6
Land: 33.3 sq. mi.; **Water:** 2.1 sq. mi.

South Haven — City
ZIP: 49090　　Lat: 42-24-01 N　Long: 86-16-21 W
Pop: 5,563 (1990); 5,943 (1980)　Pop Density: 2139.6
Land: 2.6 sq. mi.; **Water:** 0.0 sq. mi.　Elev: 618 ft.
First settlers arrived 1831. Part of the town is also in Allegan County.
Name origin: For its location south of Grand Haven.

*South Haven — Township
ZIP: 49090　　Lat: 42-22-11 N　Long: 86-15-32 W
Pop: 4,185 (1990); 4,174 (1980)　Pop Density: 228.7
Land: 18.3 sq. mi.; **Water:** 0.0 sq. mi.

Waverly — Township
Lat: 42-17-21 N　Long: 85-56-07 W
Pop: 2,188 (1990); 2,130 (1980)　Pop Density: 63.8
Land: 34.3 sq. mi.; **Water:** 0.2 sq. mi.

Washtenaw County
County Seat: Ann Arbor (ZIP: 48107)

Pop: 282,937 (1990); 264,740 (1980)　Pop Density: 398.5
Land: 710.1 sq. mi.; **Water:** 12.5 sq. mi.　Area Code: 313
In southeast MI, west of Detroit; original county; established Sep 10, 1822 (prior to statehood).
Name origin: For the small stream running through the county; from an Ojibway word meaning 'on the river' or 'far off.'

Ann Arbor — City
ZIP: 48106　　Lat: 42-16-31 N　Long: 83-43-51 W
Pop: 109,592 (1990); 107,969 (1980)　Pop Density: 4231.4
Land: 25.9 sq. mi.; **Water:** 0.7 sq. mi.
In southeastern MI on the Huron River, 35 mi. west of Detroit. Settled 1825. Incorporated 1833 as a village, 1851 as a city. Site of the University of Michigan.
Name origin: For the wives of the first two settlers (both named Ann) and for the area's abundant groves of trees. Possibly first known as Anns' Arbor.

*Ann Arbor — Township
Lat: 42-18-52 N　Long: 83-42-32 W
Pop: 3,793 (1990); 3,090 (1980)　Pop Density: 206.1
Land: 18.4 sq. mi.; **Water:** 0.1 sq. mi.

Augusta — Township
Lat: 42-07-42 N　Long: 83-36-06 W
Pop: 4,415 (1990); 4,643 (1980)　Pop Density: 120.3
Land: 36.7 sq. mi.; **Water:** 0.0 sq. mi.

Barton Hills — Village
ZIP: 48105　　Lat: 42-19-03 N　Long: 83-45-19 W
Pop: 320 (1990); 357 (1980)　Pop Density: 400.0
Land: 0.8 sq. mi.; **Water:** 0.0 sq. mi.

Bridgewater — Township
Lat: 42-07-03 N　Long: 83-57-30 W
Pop: 1,304 (1990); 1,371 (1980)　Pop Density: 35.6
Land: 36.6 sq. mi.; **Water:** 0.3 sq. mi.

Chelsea — Village
ZIP: 48118　　Lat: 42-18-51 N　Long: 84-01-19 W
Pop: 3,772 (1990); 3,816 (1980)　Pop Density: 1571.7
Land: 2.4 sq. mi.; **Water:** 0.0 sq. mi.
Established April 7, 1834.
Name origin: For Chelsea, MA.

Dexter — Village
ZIP: 48130   **Lat:** 42-19-53 N   **Long:** 83-52-47 W
Pop: 1,497 (1990); 1,524 (1980)   **Pop Density:** 998.0
Land: 1.5 sq. mi.; **Water:** 0.0 sq. mi.   **Elev:** 862 ft.
Not coextensive with the town of the same name.
Name origin: For Judge Samuel Dexter, who settled here in 1824.

*Dexter — Township
ZIP: 48130   **Lat:** 42-22-49 N   **Long:** 83-57-18 W
Pop: 4,407 (1990); 3,872 (1980)   **Pop Density:** 143.1
Land: 30.8 sq. mi.; **Water:** 2.5 sq. mi.

Freedom — Township
Lat: 42-12-24 N   **Long:** 83-57-14 W
Pop: 1,486 (1990); 1,436 (1980)   **Pop Density:** 41.9
Land: 35.5 sq. mi.; **Water:** 0.3 sq. mi.

Lima — Township
Lat: 42-17-44 N   **Long:** 83-57-29 W
Pop: 2,585 (1990); 2,544 (1980)   **Pop Density:** 71.4
Land: 36.2 sq. mi.; **Water:** 0.5 sq. mi.

Lodi — Township
Lat: 42-13-09 N   **Long:** 83-51-05 W
Pop: 3,902 (1990); 2,773 (1980)   **Pop Density:** 115.8
Land: 33.7 sq. mi.; **Water:** 0.1 sq. mi.

Lyndon — Township
Lat: 42-22-43 N   **Long:** 84-04-51 W
Pop: 2,228 (1990); 2,057 (1980)   **Pop Density:** 69.4
Land: 32.1 sq. mi.; **Water:** 2.9 sq. mi.

Manchester — Village
ZIP: 48158   **Lat:** 42-08-56 N   **Long:** 84-02-07 W
Pop: 1,753 (1990); 1,686 (1980)   **Pop Density:** 973.9
Land: 1.8 sq. mi.; **Water:** 0.1 sq. mi.
Settled 1833, incorporated as village 1867. Not coextensive with the town of the same name.
Name origin: For Manchester, Ontario County, NY.

*Manchester — Township
ZIP: 48158   **Lat:** 42-06-48 N   **Long:** 84-04-23 W
Pop: 3,492 (1990); 3,226 (1980)   **Pop Density:** 91.9
Land: 38.0 sq. mi.; **Water:** 0.6 sq. mi.

Milan — City
ZIP: 48160   **Lat:** 42-05-19 N   **Long:** 83-40-54 W
Pop: 3,060 (1990); 3,260 (1980)   **Pop Density:** 3400.0
Land: 0.9 sq. mi.; **Water:** 0.0 sq. mi.
Part of the town is also in Monroe County.
Name origin: Named in 1836 for Milan, Italy. Previously called Tolanville.

Northfield — Township
ZIP: 48189   **Lat:** 42-23-41 N   **Long:** 83-43-44 W
Pop: 6,732 (1990); 4,672 (1980)   **Pop Density:** 185.5
Land: 36.3 sq. mi.; **Water:** 0.8 sq. mi.

Pittsfield — Township
ZIP: 48108   **Lat:** 42-12-27 N   **Long:** 83-42-59 W
Pop: 17,668 (1990); 12,986 (1980)   **Pop Density:** 628.8
Land: 28.1 sq. mi.; **Water:** 0.0 sq. mi.
In southeastern MI, south of Ann Arbor.
Name origin: For William Pitt (1708–78), English statesman who supported the American colonies.

Salem — Township
Lat: 42-23-24 N   **Long:** 83-36-11 W
Pop: 3,734 (1990); 3,342 (1980)   **Pop Density:** 108.9
Land: 34.3 sq. mi.; **Water:** 0.0 sq. mi.

Saline — City
ZIP: 48176   **Lat:** 42-10-32 N   **Long:** 83-46-47 W
Pop: 6,660 (1990); 6,483 (1980)   **Pop Density:** 1585.7
Land: 4.2 sq. mi.; **Water:** 0.0 sq. mi.
Platted 1832.
Name origin: For the Saline River, which flows through the southern part of the county.

*Saline — Township
ZIP: 48176   **Lat:** 42-07-03 N   **Long:** 83-50-26 W
Pop: 1,276 (1990); 1,221 (1980)   **Pop Density:** 36.6
Land: 34.9 sq. mi.; **Water:** 0.0 sq. mi.

Scio — Township
ZIP: 48130   **Lat:** 42-17-48 N   **Long:** 83-50-13 W
Pop: 11,077 (1990); 8,029 (1980)   **Pop Density:** 323.9
Land: 34.2 sq. mi.; **Water:** 0.3 sq. mi.

Sharon — Township
ZIP: 48158   **Lat:** 42-12-05 N   **Long:** 84-03-55 W
Pop: 1,366 (1990); 1,363 (1980)   **Pop Density:** 36.3
Land: 37.6 sq. mi.; **Water:** 0.0 sq. mi.

Superior — Township
ZIP: 48197   **Lat:** 42-18-17 N   **Long:** 83-36-16 W
Pop: 8,720 (1990); 8,060 (1980)   **Pop Density:** 246.3
Land: 35.4 sq. mi.; **Water:** 0.2 sq. mi.

Sylvan — Township
ZIP: 48118   **Lat:** 42-17-43 N   **Long:** 84-04-33 W
Pop: 5,827 (1990); 5,524 (1980)   **Pop Density:** 165.5
Land: 35.2 sq. mi.; **Water:** 0.8 sq. mi.

Webster — Township
ZIP: 48130   **Lat:** 42-22-39 N   **Long:** 83-50-17 W
Pop: 3,235 (1990); 2,760 (1980)   **Pop Density:** 91.6
Land: 35.3 sq. mi.; **Water:** 0.6 sq. mi.

Whitmore Lake — CDP
ZIP: 48189   **Lat:** 42-25-04 N   **Long:** 83-45-16 W
Pop: 1,557 (1990); 1,330 (1980)   **Pop Density:** 973.1
Land: 1.6 sq. mi.; **Water:** 0.5 sq. mi.
Part of the town is also in Livingston County.

York — Township
ZIP: 48160   **Lat:** 42-07-19 N   **Long:** 83-42-39 W
Pop: 6,225 (1990); 5,517 (1980)   **Pop Density:** 176.8
Land: 35.2 sq. mi.; **Water:** 0.0 sq. mi.

Ypsilanti — City
ZIP: 48197   **Lat:** 42-14-39 N   **Long:** 83-37-15 W
Pop: 24,846 (1990); 24,031 (1980)   **Pop Density:** 5646.8
Land: 4.4 sq. mi.; **Water:** 0.1 sq. mi.
In southeastern MI on the Huron River, 7 mi. southeast of Ann Arbor. Established 1823; incorporated as a village in 1832; as a city in 1858. Site of Eastern Michigan University.
Name origin: For Demetrius Ypsilanti (1793–1832), a hero of the Greek war of independence.

*Ypsilanti — Township
ZIP: 48197   **Lat:** 42-12-48 N   **Long:** 83-35-54 W
Pop: 45,307 (1990); 44,511 (1980)   **Pop Density:** 1500.2
Land: 30.2 sq. mi.; **Water:** 1.6 sq. mi.

> **Wayne County**
> **County Seat: Detroit (ZIP: 48226)**
>
> **Pop:** 2,111,690 (1990); 2,337,840 (1980)   **Pop Density:** 3438.4
> **Land:** 614.1 sq. mi.; **Water:** 58.1 sq. mi.   **Area Code:** 313
> In southeastern MI bordered on the east by the Detroit River and Lake St. Clair; original colony; established Nov 21, 1815 (prior to statehood).
> **Name origin:** For Gen. Anthony Wayne (1745–96), PA soldier and statesman, nicknamed "Mad Anthony" for his daring during the Revolutionary War.

Allen Park   City
ZIP: 48101   **Lat:** 42-15-34 N   **Long:** 83-12-37 W
Pop: 31,092 (1990); 34,196 (1980)   **Pop Density:** 4441.7
Land: 7.0 sq. mi.; **Water:** 0.0 sq. mi.

In southeastern MI, a suburb of Detroit. Incorporated 1957.
Name origin: For prominent nineteenth-century attorney and landowner Lewis Allen.

Belleville   City
ZIP: 48111   **Lat:** 42-12-12 N   **Long:** 83-28-56 W
Pop: 3,270 (1990); 3,366 (1980)   **Pop Density:** 2972.7
Land: 1.1 sq. mi.; **Water:** 0.0 sq. mi.

Name origin: From French meaning 'beautiful town.'

Brownstown   Township
ZIP: 48134   **Lat:** 42-06-33 N   **Long:** 83-13-44 W
Pop: 18,811 (1990); 18,302 (1980)   **Pop Density:** 836.0
Land: 22.5 sq. mi.; **Water:** 8.1 sq. mi.

Canton   Township
ZIP: 48184   **Lat:** 42-18-30 N   **Long:** 83-28-55 W
Pop: 57,040 (1990); 48,616 (1980)   **Pop Density:** 1584.4
Land: 36.0 sq. mi.; **Water:** 0.0 sq. mi.

Established March 7, 1834.

Dearborn   City
ZIP: 48120   **Lat:** 42-18-40 N   **Long:** 83-12-48 W
Pop: 89,286 (1990); 90,660 (1980)   **Pop Density:** 3659.3
Land: 24.4 sq. mi.; **Water:** 0.1 sq. mi.

In southeastern MI, due west of Detroit. Settled 1795; incorporated 1929.
Name origin: For Gen. Henry Dearborn (1751–1829), Revolutionary War soldier and U.S. secretary of war (1801–09).

Dearborn Heights   City
ZIP: 48125   **Lat:** 42-19-37 N   **Long:** 83-16-22 W
Pop: 60,838 (1990); 67,706 (1980)   **Pop Density:** 5199.8
Land: 11.7 sq. mi.; **Water:** 0.0 sq. mi.

In southeastern MI, west of Detroit and Dearborn. Once part of Dearborn. Established April 8, 1963.
Name origin: For the city.

Detroit   City
ZIP: 48231   **Lat:** 42-22-59 N   **Long:** 83-06-07 W
Pop: 1,027,974 (1990); 1,203,368 (1980)
   Pop Density: 7411.5
Land: 138.7 sq. mi.; **Water:** 4.2 sq. mi.

In southeastern MI on the Detroit River between Lakes St. Clair and Erie, across from Windsor, Ontario, Canada; 30 mi. east of Ann Arbor. Largest city and port; county seat. Founded 1701 by French explorer Antoine de la Mothe Cadillac (1658–1730); incorporated as city 1815. Nicknamed "Motor City" and "Motown." Diverse industrial and manufacturing city (automobile and truck parts and assembly; business machines, chemicals, hardware); local shipping between Great Lakes ports and internationally via the St. Lawrence Seaway. The Detroit River is one of world's busiest inland waterways. Site of Wayne State University and the University of Detroit.
Name origin: From French term meaning 'strait.'

Ecorse   City
ZIP: 48229   **Lat:** 42-14-59 N   **Long:** 83-08-25 W
Pop: 12,180 (1990); 14,447 (1980)   **Pop Density:** 4511.1
Land: 2.7 sq. mi.; **Water:** 0.9 sq. mi.

In southeastern MI on the Detroit River, in the Detroit metropolitan area.
Name origin: From French *Riviere aux Ecorses* 'Bark River,' for the trees on the bank whose bark was used by the Indians for their canoes; probably translated from an Indian term. Previously called Grand Port for its location on the river.

Flat Rock   City
ZIP: 48134   **Lat:** 42-06-06 N   **Long:** 83-16-22 W
Pop: 7,290 (1990); 6,853 (1980)   **Pop Density:** 1088.1
Land: 6.7 sq. mi.; **Water:** 0.1 sq. mi.

Settled 1821.
Name origin: Descriptively named for the smooth rock bed of the nearby Huron River.

Garden City   City
ZIP: 48135   **Lat:** 42-19-25 N   **Long:** 83-20-32 W
Pop: 31,846 (1990); 35,640 (1980)   **Pop Density:** 5397.6
Land: 5.9 sq. mi.; **Water:** 0.0 sq. mi.   **Elev:** 636 ft.

In southeastern MI in the Detroit metropolitan area, 15 mi. west of Detroit. Founded during the Great Depression. Established as a city December, 1933.
Name origin: For having been platted into lots large enough for vegetable gardens.

Gibraltar   City
ZIP: 48173   **Lat:** 42-05-41 N   **Long:** 83-12-09 W
Pop: 4,297 (1990); 4,458 (1980)   **Pop Density:** 1130.8
Land: 3.8 sq. mi.; **Water:** 0.5 sq. mi.   **Elev:** 584 ft.

Settled 1811.
Name origin: For the Gibraltar and Flat Rock Company.

Grosse Ile   Township
ZIP: 48138   **Lat:** 42-07-42 N   **Long:** 83-08-57 W
Pop: 9,781 (1990); 9,320 (1980)   **Pop Density:** 1018.9
Land: 9.6 sq. mi.; **Water:** 8.7 sq. mi.

Established 1914.
Name origin: From French for the 'large island' in the Detroit River

MICHIGAN, Wayne County

Grosse Pointe — City
ZIP: 48236 **Lat:** 42-22-59 N **Long:** 82-54-21 W
Pop: 5,681 (1990); 5,901 (1980) **Pop Density:** 5164.5
Land: 1.1 sq. mi.; **Water:** 1.2 sq. mi.
Incorporated 1911. Part of the town is also in Macomb County.
Name origin: From French for the 'large point' that projects into Lake St. Clair and forms the township's eastern boundary.

Grosse Pointe Farms — City
ZIP: 48236 **Lat:** 42-22-59 N **Long:** 82-51-32 W
Pop: 10,092 (1990); 10,551 (1980) **Pop Density:** 3737.8
Land: 2.7 sq. mi.; **Water:** 9.6 sq. mi.
Name origin: Once part of Grosse Pointe; became independent 1893.

Grosse Pointe Park — City
ZIP: 48230 **Lat:** 42-22-25 N **Long:** 82-55-24 W
Pop: 12,857 (1990); 13,562 (1980) **Pop Density:** 5844.1
Land: 2.2 sq. mi.; **Water:** 1.5 sq. mi.
In southeastern MI on Lake St. Clair and the Detroit River, 8 mi. northeast of Detroit. Incorporated as a village in 1907; as a city in 1950.
Name origin: For nearby Grosse Pointe.

Grosse Pointe Shores — Village
Lat: 42-26-22 N **Long:** 82-52-43 W
Pop: 2,850 (1990); 3,012 (1980) **Pop Density:** 2850.0
Land: 1.0 sq. mi.; **Water:** 0.6 sq. mi.
Incorporated 1911. Part of the town is also in Macomb County.

Grosse Pointe Woods — City
ZIP: 48225 **Lat:** 42-26-08 N **Long:** 82-53-54 W
Pop: 17,715 (1990); 18,886 (1980) **Pop Density:** 5368.2
Land: 3.3 sq. mi.; **Water:** 0.0 sq. mi. **Elev:** 587 ft.
In southeastern MI, 12 mi. northeast of Detroit. Established 1927 as Village of Lochmoor; renamed in 1939; incorporated 1950 as a city.
Name origin: For its descriptive connotations.

Hamtramck — City
ZIP: 48212 **Lat:** 42-23-45 N **Long:** 83-03-19 W
Pop: 18,372 (1990); 21,300 (1980) **Pop Density:** 8748.6
Land: 2.1 sq. mi.; **Water:** 0.0 sq. mi.
In southeastern MI, entirely within the city of Detroit.
Name origin: For Col. John F. Hamtramck, who occupied Detroit after the British left during the Revolutionary War.

Harper Woods — City
ZIP: 48225 **Lat:** 42-26-17 N **Long:** 82-55-42 W
Pop: 14,903 (1990); 16,361 (1980) **Pop Density:** 5731.9
Land: 2.6 sq. mi.; **Water:** 0.0 sq. mi.
In southeastern MI, 10 mi. northeast of Detroit. Settled 1850s; incorporated 1951.
Name origin: Named in 1949 for Walter Harper, prominent Detroit citizen, and for the surrounding woods.

Highland Park — City
ZIP: 48203 **Lat:** 42-24-17 N **Long:** 83-05-55 W
Pop: 20,121 (1990); 27,909 (1980) **Pop Density:** 6707.0
Land: 3.0 sq. mi.; **Water:** 0.0 sq. mi. **Elev:** 636 ft.
In southeastern MI in the west Detroit metropolitan area, completely surrounded by Detroit. Established as a village in 1884, as a city in 1918.
Name origin: The cabin of Richard Ford, first known settler, was built on a highland. The ridge was later leveled when Woodward Avenue was put through from Detroit.

Huron — Township
ZIP: 48164 **Lat:** 42-08-00 N **Long:** 83-21-43 W
Pop: 10,447 (1990); 9,849 (1980) **Pop Density:** 293.5
Land: 35.6 sq. mi.; **Water:** 0.5 sq. mi.

Inkster — City
ZIP: 48141 **Lat:** 42-17-36 N **Long:** 83-18-59 W
Pop: 30,772 (1990); 35,190 (1980) **Pop Density:** 4884.4
Land: 6.3 sq. mi.; **Water:** 0.0 sq. mi. **Elev:** 628 ft.
In southeastern MI, 20 mi. southwest of Detroit. Settled 1825, incorporated as village 1926; as city 1964.
Name origin: For first postmaster, Robert Inkster.

Lincoln Park — City
ZIP: 48146 **Lat:** 42-14-36 N **Long:** 83-10-51 W
Pop: 41,832 (1990); 45,105 (1980) **Pop Density:** 7212.4
Land: 5.8 sq. mi.; **Water:** 0.0 sq. mi. **Elev:** 587 ft.
In southeastern MI, 10 mi. south of Detroit. Laid out 1906; incorporated as a village in 1921; as a city in 1925.
Name origin: Named by a developer for a community in IL.

Livonia — City
ZIP: 48150 **Lat:** 42-23-53 N **Long:** 83-22-21 W
Pop: 100,850 (1990); 104,814 (1980) **Pop Density:** 2824.9
Land: 35.7 sq. mi.; **Water:** 0.1 sq. mi. **Elev:** 638 ft.
In southeastern MI, 15 mi. northwest of Detroit. Township organized in 1835, incorporated as a city in 1950.
Name origin: For a western province of Russia, to ensure no duplication of the name elsewhere in MI.

Melvindale — City
ZIP: 48122 **Lat:** 42-16-52 N **Long:** 83-10-44 W
Pop: 11,216 (1990); 12,322 (1980) **Pop Density:** 4005.7
Land: 2.8 sq. mi.; **Water:** 0.0 sq. mi.
In southeastern MI, 10 mi. southwest of Detroit. Settled 1870; incorporated as a village 1927; as a city 1932.
Name origin: For Melvin Wilkinson, local philantropist. Previously called Oakwood Heights.

Northville — City
ZIP: 48167 **Lat:** 42-25-53 N **Long:** 83-29-06 W
Pop: 2,859 (1990); 2,913 (1980) **Pop Density:** 2859.0
Land: 1.0 sq. mi.; **Water:** 0.0 sq. mi. **Elev:** 829 ft.
Settlers arrived 1825. Part of the town is also in Oakland County.

*Northville — Township
ZIP: 48167 **Lat:** 42-25-04 N **Long:** 83-29-33 W
Pop: 17,313 (1990); 12,987 (1980) **Pop Density:** 1049.3
Land: 16.5 sq. mi.; **Water:** 0.2 sq. mi.

Plymouth — City
ZIP: 48170 **Lat:** 42-22-16 N **Long:** 83-28-02 W
Pop: 9,560 (1990); 9,986 (1980) **Pop Density:** 4345.5
Land: 2.2 sq. mi.; **Water:** 0.0 sq. mi.
In southeastern MI, 20 mi. northwest of Detroit. Manufacturing city; settled 1825; incorporated as a village in 1867; as a city in 1932.
Name origin: For Plymouth, MA, previous home of early settlers; suggested by local resident William Bartow.

*Plymouth — Township
ZIP: 48170 **Lat:** 42-22-16 N **Long:** 83-29-39 W
Pop: 23,648 (1990); 23,028 (1980) **Pop Density:** 1487.3
Land: 15.9 sq. mi.; **Water:** 0.0 sq. mi.

Redford
Township
ZIP: 48239 **Lat:** 42-23-41 N **Long:** 83-17-39 W
Pop: 54,387 (1990); 58,441 (1980) **Pop Density:** 4856.0
Land: 11.2 sq. mi.; **Water:** 0.0 sq. mi.

River Rouge
City
ZIP: 48218 **Lat:** 42-16-27 N **Long:** 83-07-24 W
Pop: 11,314 (1990); 12,912 (1980) **Pop Density:** 4190.4
Land: 2.7 sq. mi.; **Water:** 0.7 sq. mi. **Elev:** 584 ft.

In southeastern MI on the Rouge River in the southwestern Detroit metropolitan area. Established 1927, incorporated as village in 1899; as city in 1922. Originally a French settlement.

Name origin: For the Rouge [French 'red'] River, which flows through the county.

Riverview
City
ZIP: 48192 **Lat:** 42-10-16 N **Long:** 83-11-31 W
Pop: 13,894 (1990); 14,569 (1980) **Pop Density:** 3157.7
Land: 4.4 sq. mi.; **Water:** 0.1 sq. mi.

In southeastern MI on the Lake Erie end of the Detroit River, 15 mi. south of Detroit. Founded 1906; incorporated as village in 1922; incorporated as city 1959.

Name origin: For its descriptive connotations.

Rockwood
City
ZIP: 48173 **Lat:** 42-04-13 N **Long:** 83-14-39 W
Pop: 3,141 (1990); 3,346 (1980) **Pop Density:** 1163.3
Land: 2.7 sq. mi.; **Water:** 0.0 sq. mi.

First settlers arrived 1834.

Name origin: Named in 1872.

Romulus
City
ZIP: 48174 **Lat:** 42-13-25 N **Long:** 83-21-58 W
Pop: 22,897 (1990); 24,857 (1980) **Pop Density:** 637.8
Land: 35.9 sq. mi.; **Water:** 0.0 sq. mi.

In southeastern MI, 20 mi. southwest of Detroit. Settled 1827; incorporated as city 1970.

Name origin: Named by first settlers for their hometown in NY.

Southgate
City
ZIP: 48195 **Lat:** 42-12-12 N **Long:** 83-12-22 W
Pop: 30,771 (1990); 32,058 (1980) **Pop Density:** 4459.6
Land: 6.9 sq. mi.; **Water:** 0.0 sq. mi. **Elev:** 591 ft.

In southeastern MI in the southern Detroit metropolitan area. Incorporated as a city 1958.

Name origin: For its location on the southern boundary of Metro Detroit.

Sumpter
Township
ZIP: 48111 **Lat:** 42-07-40 N **Long:** 83-29-08 W
Pop: 10,891 (1990); 11,112 (1980) **Pop Density:** 289.7
Land: 37.6 sq. mi.; **Water:** 0.0 sq. mi.

In southeastern MI, southwest of Detroit.

Taylor
City
ZIP: 48180 **Lat:** 42-13-30 N **Long:** 83-16-06 W
Pop: 70,811 (1990); 77,568 (1980) **Pop Density:** 3000.5
Land: 23.6 sq. mi.; **Water:** 0.0 sq. mi. **Elev:** 615 ft.

In southeastern MI, 20 mi. southwest of Detroit. Incorporated as a township in 1847; as a city in 1968.

Name origin: For Zachary Taylor (1784–1850), twelfth U.S. president.

Trenton
City
ZIP: 48183 **Lat:** 42-08-23 N **Long:** 83-11-34 W
Pop: 20,586 (1990); 22,762 (1980) **Pop Density:** 2820.0
Land: 7.3 sq. mi.; **Water:** 0.2 sq. mi.

In southeastern MI on the Detroit River near Lake Erie, 15 mi. southwest of Detroit. Established 1827; incorporated as a village in 1855; as a city in 1957.

Name origin: Named in 1847 for the geologic Trentonian rocks in the limestone strata under the town. Previously called Truaxton.

Van Buren
Township
ZIP: 48111 **Lat:** 42-13-12 N **Long:** 83-29-02 W
Pop: 21,010 (1990); 18,940 (1980) **Pop Density:** 619.8
Land: 33.9 sq. mi.; **Water:** 1.9 sq. mi.

Charter township in southeastern MI. Established 1827 as part of Huron Township.

Name origin: Township became independent in 1835 and was renamed for Martin Van Buren (1782–1862), then vice president and a year later eighth U.S. president.

Wayne
City
ZIP: 48184 **Lat:** 42-16-36 N **Long:** 83-23-17 W
Pop: 19,899 (1990); 21,159 (1980) **Pop Density:** 3316.5
Land: 6.0 sq. mi.; **Water:** 0.0 sq. mi. **Elev:** 658 ft.

In southeastern MI, 18 mi. southwest of Detroit. Organized 1835; incorporated as a village 1869; as a city 1960.

Name origin: For Gen. "Mad Anthony" Wayne (1745–96), of Revolutionary War fame.

Westland
City
ZIP: 48185 **Lat:** 42-19-08 N **Long:** 83-22-51 W
Pop: 84,724 (1990); 84,603 (1980) **Pop Density:** 4132.9
Land: 20.5 sq. mi.; **Water:** 0.0 sq. mi.

In southeastern MI, west of Detroit. Incorporated 1966.

Name origin: For its location relative to Detroit.

Woodhaven
City
ZIP: 48183 **Lat:** 42-07-56 N **Long:** 83-14-12 W
Pop: 11,631 (1990); 10,902 (1980) **Pop Density:** 1789.4
Land: 6.5 sq. mi.; **Water:** 0.0 sq. mi.

In southeastern MI, 18 mi. southwest of Detroit. Incorporated as a village 1961; as a city 1965.

Name origin: For Woodhaven, NY.

Wyandotte
City
ZIP: 48192 **Lat:** 42-12-41 N **Long:** 83-09-23 W
Pop: 30,938 (1990); 34,006 (1980) **Pop Density:** 5837.4
Land: 5.3 sq. mi.; **Water:** 1.7 sq. mi.

In southeastern MI, 15 mi. south of Detroit. Established 1854; incorporated as a city in 1867; annexed the village of Ford City in 1923.

Name origin: For the Indian tribe; the name is thought to mean 'islanders' or 'those who live on a peninsula.'

MICHIGAN, Wexford County

Wexford County
County Seat: Cadillac (ZIP: 49601)

Pop: 26,360 (1990); 25,102 (1980)
Land: 565.5 sq. mi.; **Water:** 10.3 sq. mi.
Pop Density: 46.6
Area Code: 616

In northwest MI, south of Traverse City; established as Kautawaubet County Apr 1, 1840 from unorganized territory; name changed Mar 8, 1843.
Name origin: For the county in Ireland.

Antioch
Township
Lat: 44-22-55 N **Long:** 85-38-10 W
Pop: 671 (1990); 618 (1980) **Pop Density:** 19.1
Land: 35.2 sq. mi.; **Water:** 0.1 sq. mi.

Boon
Township
ZIP: 49618 **Lat:** 44-17-46 N **Long:** 85-38-28 W
Pop: 562 (1990); 500 (1980) **Pop Density:** 15.6
Land: 36.0 sq. mi.; **Water:** 0.0 sq. mi.

Buckley
Village
ZIP: 49620 **Lat:** 44-30-14 N **Long:** 85-40-18 W
Pop: 402 (1990); 357 (1980) **Pop Density:** 223.3
Land: 1.8 sq. mi.; **Water:** 0.1 sq. mi.
Founded 1905.
Name origin: For the local Buckley and Douglas Lumber Company.

Cadillac
City
ZIP: 49601 **Lat:** 44-14-53 N **Long:** 85-24-57 W
Pop: 10,104 (1990); 10,199 (1980) **Pop Density:** 1508.1
Land: 6.7 sq. mi.; **Water:** 1.8 sq. mi. **Elev:** 1328 ft.
In northwestern MI on Lake Mitchell, 35 mi. north of Big Rapids. County seat. Established 1877.
Name origin: Named in 1877 for Antoine de La Mothe Cadillac (1658–1730), French founder of Detroit. Previously called Clam Lake.

Cedar Creek
Township
Lat: 44-22-42 N **Long:** 85-24-10 W
Pop: 1,013 (1990); 1,010 (1980) **Pop Density:** 29.6
Land: 34.2 sq. mi.; **Water:** 0.0 sq. mi.

Cherry Grove
Township
Lat: 44-12-21 N **Long:** 85-31-11 W
Pop: 1,763 (1990); 1,517 (1980) **Pop Density:** 52.8
Land: 33.4 sq. mi.; **Water:** 2.8 sq. mi.

Clam Lake
Township
Lat: 44-12-36 N **Long:** 85-23-32 W
Pop: 1,739 (1990); 1,658 (1980) **Pop Density:** 56.3
Land: 30.9 sq. mi.; **Water:** 0.3 sq. mi.

Colfax
Township
Lat: 44-22-31 N **Long:** 85-31-12 W
Pop: 556 (1990); 602 (1980) **Pop Density:** 15.8
Land: 35.3 sq. mi.; **Water:** 0.1 sq. mi.

Greenwood
Township
Lat: 44-28-05 N **Long:** 85-31-36 W
Pop: 372 (1990); 297 (1980) **Pop Density:** 10.5
Land: 35.3 sq. mi.; **Water:** 0.0 sq. mi.

Hanover
Township
Lat: 44-28-00 N **Long:** 85-38-32 W
Pop: 826 (1990); 665 (1980) **Pop Density:** 22.9
Land: 36.0 sq. mi.; **Water:** 0.2 sq. mi.

Haring
Township
Lat: 44-18-24 N **Long:** 85-23-48 W
Pop: 2,501 (1990); 2,523 (1980) **Pop Density:** 76.7
Land: 32.6 sq. mi.; **Water:** 0.4 sq. mi.

Harrietta
Village
ZIP: 49638 **Lat:** 44-18-34 N **Long:** 85-42-01 W
Pop: 157 (1990); 139 (1980) **Pop Density:** 174.4
Land: 0.9 sq. mi.; **Water:** 0.0 sq. mi. **Elev:** 1112 ft.
Name origin: Named in 1889 by a railroad builder by combining the names of his father, Harry, and his fiancee, Henrietta.

Henderson
Township
Lat: 44-12-31 N **Long:** 85-37-51 W
Pop: 162 (1990); 140 (1980) **Pop Density:** 4.5
Land: 36.2 sq. mi.; **Water:** 0.0 sq. mi.

Liberty
Township
Lat: 44-28-08 N **Long:** 85-23-49 W
Pop: 641 (1990); 542 (1980) **Pop Density:** 17.6
Land: 36.5 sq. mi.; **Water:** 0.0 sq. mi.

Manton
City
ZIP: 49663 **Lat:** 44-24-41 N **Long:** 85-24-01 W
Pop: 1,161 (1990); 1,212 (1980) **Pop Density:** 725.6
Land: 1.6 sq. mi.; **Water:** 0.1 sq. mi.
Settled 1874.
Name origin: Named by and for George Manton, first settler and postmaster.

Mesick
Village
ZIP: 49668 **Lat:** 44-24-12 N **Long:** 85-43-09 W
Pop: 406 (1990); 374 (1980) **Pop Density:** 406.0
Land: 1.0 sq. mi.; **Water:** 0.0 sq. mi.
Founded and platted in 1890 by Howard Mesick.
Name origin: For the founder.

Selma
Township
Lat: 44-17-42 N **Long:** 85-31-13 W
Pop: 1,607 (1990); 1,289 (1980) **Pop Density:** 46.7
Land: 34.4 sq. mi.; **Water:** 1.6 sq. mi.

Slagle
Township
Lat: 44-17-40 N **Long:** 85-45-35 W
Pop: 470 (1990); 406 (1980) **Pop Density:** 13.1
Land: 35.8 sq. mi.; **Water:** 0.0 sq. mi.

South Branch
Township
Lat: 44-12-43 N **Long:** 85-45-31 W
Pop: 306 (1990); 276 (1980) **Pop Density:** 8.5
Land: 36.1 sq. mi.; **Water:** 0.0 sq. mi.

Springville
Township
Lat: 44-23-01 N **Long:** 85-45-40 W
Pop: 1,339 (1990); 1,191 (1980) **Pop Density:** 40.9
Land: 32.7 sq. mi.; **Water:** 2.9 sq. mi.

Wexford Township
Lat: 44-28-09 N **Long:** 85-45-44 W
Pop: 567 (1990); 457 (1980) **Pop Density:** 15.5
Land: 36.5 sq. mi.; **Water:** 0.0 sq. mi.

MICHIGAN

Index to Places and Counties in Michigan

Acme (Grand Traverse) Township....395
Ada (Kent) Township........................411
Adams (Arenac) Township................370
Adams (Hillsdale) Township.............397
Adams (Houghton) Township............398
Addison (Lenawee) Village...............417
Addison (Oakland) Township............437
Adrian (Lenawee) City.....................417
Adrian (Lenawee) Township.............417
Aetna (Mecosta) Township................426
Aetna (Missaukee) Township............429
Ahmeek (Keweenaw) Village............413
Akron (Tuscola) Township................458
Akron (Tuscola) Village....................458
Alabaster (Iosco) Township..............404
Alaiedon (Ingham) Township............401
Alamo (Kalamazoo) Township..........408
Alanson (Emmet) Village..................390
Albee (Saginaw) Township................449
Albert (Montmorency) Township......433
Albion (Calhoun) City.......................378
Albion (Calhoun) Township..............378
Alcona (Alcona) Township................366
Alcona County....................................366
Algansee (Branch) Township............377
Alger County.....................................366
Algoma (Kent) Township.................411
Algonac (St. Clair) City....................451
Allegan (Allegan) City......................367
Allegan (Allegan) Township.............367
Allegan County.................................367
Allen (Hillsdale) Township...............397
Allen (Hillsdale) Village...................397
Allendale (Ottawa) Township...........445
Allen Park (Wayne) City..................463
Allis (Presque Isle) Township...........447
Alloue (Keweenaw) Township..........413
Alma (Gratiot) City..........................396
Almena (Van Buren) Township........460
Almer (Tuscola) Township................458
Almira (Benzie) Township................374
Almont (Lapeer) Township...............414
Almont (Lapeer) Village...................414
Aloha (Cheboygan) Township..........382
Alpena (Alpena) City........................369
Alpena (Alpena) Township...............369
Alpena County.................................369
Alpha (Iron) Village.........................405
Alpine (Kent) Township...................411
Amber (Mason) Township................425
Amboy (Hillsdale) Township............397
Anchorville (St. Clair) CDP..............451
Ann Arbor (Washtenaw) City...........461
Ann Arbor (Washtenaw) Township...461
Antioch (Wexford) Township...........466
Antrim (Shiawassee) Township........456
Antrim County.................................369
Antwerp (Van Buren) Township......460
Applegate (Sanilac) Village..............454
Arbela (Tuscola) Township...............458
Arcada (Gratiot) Township...............396
Arcadia (Lapeer) Township..............414
Arcadia (Manistee) Township...........423
Arenac (Arenac) Township...............370
Arenac County.................................370
Argentine (Genesee) Township........391
Argyle (Sanilac) Township...............454
Arlington (Van Buren) Township.....460
Armada (Macomb) Township...........421
Armada (Macomb) Village...............421

Arthur (Clare) Township..................384
Arvon (Baraga) Township................371
Ash (Monroe) Township..................430
Ashland (Newaygo) Township.........435
Ashley (Gratiot) Village...................396
Assyria (Barry) Township................372
Athens (Calhoun) Township.............378
Athens (Calhoun) Village.................378
Atlas (Genesee) Township................391
Attica (Lapeer) Township.................414
Auburn (Bay) City...........................373
Auburn Hills (Oakland) City............437
Au Gres (Arenac) City.....................370
Au Gres (Arenac) Township.............371
Augusta (Kalamazoo) Village...........408
Augusta (Washtenaw) Township......461
Aurelius (Ingham) Township............401
Au Sable (Iosco) Township...............404
Au Sable (Roscommon) Township....448
Austin (Mecosta) Township..............426
Austin (Sanilac) Township................454
Au Train (Alger) Township...............366
Avery (Montmorency) Township......433
Backus (Roscommon) Township......448
Bad Axe (Huron) City......................399
Bagley (Otsego) Township...............445
Bainbridge (Berrien) Township........375
Baldwin (Delta) Township................387
Baldwin (Iosco) Township................404
Baldwin (Lake) Village.....................413
Baltimore (Barry) Township.............372
Bancroft (Shiawassee) Village..........456
Bangor (Bay) Township....................373
Bangor (Van Buren) City..................460
Bangor (Van Buren) Township........460
Banks (Antrim) Township.................369
Baraga (Baraga) Township................371
Baraga (Baraga) Village....................371
Baraga County.................................371
Bark River (Delta) Township............387
Barnes Lake-Millers Lake (Lapeer)
  CDP 414
Baroda (Berrien) Township...............375
Baroda (Berrien) Village...................375
Barry (Barry) Township....................372
Barry County...................................372
Barryton (Mecosta) Village...............426
Barton (Newaygo) Township............435
Barton Hills (Washtenaw) Village.....461
Batavia (Branch) Township..............377
Bates (Iron) Township......................405
Bath (Clinton) Township..................385
Battle Creek (Calhoun) City.............379
Bay (Charlevoix) Township..............381
Bay City (Bay) City..........................373
Bay County......................................373
Bay de Noc (Delta) Township...........387
Bay Mills (Chippewa) Township......383
Beal City (Isabella) CDP..................406
Bear Creek (Emmet) Township........390
Bearinger (Presque Isle) Township...447
Bear Lake (Kalkaska) Township.......410
Bear Lake (Manistee) Township.......423
Bear Lake (Manistee) Village...........423
Beaugrand (Cheboygan) Township...382
Beaver (Bay) Township....................373
Beaver (Newaygo) Township...........435
Beaver Creek (Crawford) Township..386
Beaverton (Gladwin) City.................393
Beaverton (Gladwin) Township........393

Bedford (Calhoun) Township...........379
Bedford (Monroe) Township............430
Beecher (Genesee) CDP...................391
Beechwood (Ottawa) CDP................445
Belding (Ionia) City..........................403
Belknap (Presque Isle) Township.....447
Bellaire (Antrim) Village..................369
Belleville (Wayne) City....................463
Bellevue (Eaton) Township...............389
Bellevue (Eaton) Village...................389
Belvidere (Montcalm) Township......431
Bengal (Clinton) Township...............385
Bennington (Shiawassee) Township ..456
Benona (Oceana) Township..............440
Bentley (Gladwin) Township............393
Benton (Cheboygan) Township.........382
Benton (Eaton) Township.................389
Benton Charter (Berrien) Township..375
Benton Harbor (Berrien) City...........375
Benton Heights (Berrien) CDP.........375
Benzie County..................................374
Benzonia (Benzie) Township............374
Benzonia (Benzie) Village................374
Bergland (Ontonagon) Township......442
Berkley (Oakland) City....................437
Berlin (Ionia) Township....................403
Berlin (Monroe) Township...............430
Berlin (St. Clair) Township..............451
Berrien (Berrien) Township..............375
Berrien County................................375
Berrien Springs (Berrien) Village.....375
Bertrand (Berrien) Township...........375
Bessemer (Gogebic) City..................394
Bessemer (Gogebic) Township........394
Bethany (Gratiot) Township.............396
Bethel (Branch) Township................377
Beulah (Benzie) Village....................374
Beverly Hills (Oakland) Village........437
Big Creek (Oscoda) Township..........444
Big Prairie (Newaygo) Township......435
Big Rapids (Mecosta) City...............426
Big Rapids (Mecosta) Township.......426
Billings (Gladwin) Township............393
Bingham (Clinton) Township...........385
Bingham (Huron) Township.............399
Bingham (Leelanau) Township........416
Bingham Farms (Oakland) Village...437
Birch Run (Saginaw) Township........449
Birch Run (Saginaw) Village............449
Birmingham (Oakland) City............437
Bismarck (Presque Isle) Township....447
Blackman (Jackson) Township.........407
Blaine (Benzie) Township.................374
Blair (Grand Traverse) Township.....395
Blendon (Ottawa) Township.............445
Bliss (Emmet) Township..................390
Blissfield (Lenawee) Township........417
Blissfield (Lenawee) Village.............417
Bloomer (Montcalm) Township.......431
Bloomfield (Huron) Township.........399
Bloomfield (Missaukee) Township....429
Bloomfield (Oakland) Township......437
Bloomfield Hills (Oakland) City......437
Bloomfield Township (Oakland)
  CDP 437
Bloomingdale (Van Buren)
  Township 460
Bloomingdale (Van Buren) Village....460
Blue Lake (Kalkaska) Township.......410
Blue Lake (Muskegon) Township......434

468

Blumfield (Saginaw) Township..........*449*
Boardman (Kalkaska) Township......*410*
Bohemia (Ontonagon) Township......*442*
Bois Blanc (Mackinac) Township......*420*
Boon (Wexford) Township..................*466*
Boston (Ionia) Township....................*403*
Bourret (Gladwin) Township.............*393*
Bowne (Kent) Township.....................*411*
Boyne City (Charlevoix) City............*381*
Boyne Falls (Charlevoix) Village.......*381*
Boyne Valley (Charlevoix) Township*381*
Brady (Kalamazoo) Township............*408*
Brady (Saginaw) Township................*449*
Brampton (Delta) Township...............*387*
Branch (Mason) Township.................*425*
Branch County.....................................*377*
Brandon (Oakland) Township............*437*
Brant (Saginaw) Township.................*449*
Breckenridge (Gratiot) Village..........*396*
Breedsville (Van Buren) Village........*460*
Breen (Dickinson) Township..............*388*
Breitung (Dickinson) Township..........*388*
Brevort (Mackinac) Township............*420*
Bridgehampton (Sanilac) Township ..*454*
Bridgeport (Saginaw) Township........*449*
Bridgeton (Newaygo) Township........*435*
Bridgewater (Washtenaw) Township.*461*
Bridgman (Berrien) City....................*375*
Brighton (Livingston) City *418*
Brighton (Livingston) Township *418*
Briley (Montmorency) Township *433*
Britton (Lenawee) Village.................*417*
Brockway (St. Clair) Township *451*
Bronson (Branch) City........................*377*
Bronson (Branch) Township...............*377*
Brookfield (Eaton) Township *389*
Brookfield (Huron) Township *399*
Brooklyn (Jackson) Village................*407*
Brooks (Newaygo) Township.............*435*
Broomfield (Isabella) Township *406*
Brown (Manistee) Township *423*
Brown City (Lapeer) City..................*414*
Brown City (Sanilac) City..................*454*
Brownlee Park (Calhoun) CDP..........*379*
Brownstown (Wayne) Township........*463*
Bruce (Chippewa) Township *383*
Bruce (Macomb) Township *421*
Buchanan (Berrien) City....................*376*
Buchanan (Berrien) Township...........*376*
Buckeye (Gladwin) Township *393*
Buckley (Wexford) Village................*466*
Buel (Sanilac) Township....................*454*
Buena Vista Charter (Saginaw) Township...*449*
Bunker Hill (Ingham) Township *401*
Burdell (Osceola) Township *443*
Burleigh (Iosco) Township.................*404*
Burlington (Calhoun) Township........*379*
Burlington (Calhoun) Village............*379*
Burlington (Lapeer) Township *414*
Burns (Shiawassee) Township *456*
Burnside (Lapeer) Township *414*
Burr Oak (St. Joseph) Township.......*452*
Burr Oak (St. Joseph) Village...........*452*
Burt (Alger) Township *366*
Burt (Cheboygan) Township..............*382*
Burt (Saginaw) CDP *449*
Burtchville (St. Clair) Township *451*
Burton (Genesee) City........................*391*
Bushnell (Montcalm) Township.........*431*
Butler (Branch) Township..................*377*
Butman (Gladwin) Township.............*393*
Butterfield (Missaukee) Township.....*429*
Byron (Kent) Township......................*411*
Byron (Shiawassee) Village................*457*

Cadillac (Wexford) City.....................*466*
Caldwell (Missaukee) Township........*429*
Caledonia (Alcona) Township...........*366*
Caledonia (Kent) Township *411*
Caledonia (Kent) Village....................*411*
Caledonia (Shiawassee) Township....*457*
Calhoun County..................................*378*
California (Branch) Township..........*377*
Calumet (Houghton) Township.........*398*
Calumet (Houghton) Village.............*398*
Calvin (Cass) Township.....................*380*
Cambria (Hillsdale) Township *397*
Cambridge (Lenawee) Township.......*417*
Camden (Hillsdale) Township...........*397*
Camden (Hillsdale) Village................*397*
Campbell (Ionia) Township...............*403*
Cannon (Kent) Township....................*411*
Canton (Wayne) Township................*463*
Capac (St. Clair) Village....................*451*
Carleton (Monroe) Village.................*430*
Carlton (Barry) Township..................*372*
Carmel (Eaton) Township *389*
Carney (Menominee) Village.............*427*
Caro (Tuscola) Village.......................*458*
Carp Lake (Emmet) Township *390*
Carp Lake (Ontonagon) Township....*442*
Carrollton (Saginaw) Township........*449*
Carson City (Montcalm) City *432*
Carsonville (Sanilac) Village.............*454*
Cascade (Kent) Township..................*411*
Casco (Allegan) Township.................*367*
Casco (St. Clair) Township................*451*
Case (Presque Isle) Township...........*447*
Caseville (Huron) Township *400*
Caseville (Huron) Village..................*400*
Casnovia (Kent) Village.....................*411*
Casnovia (Muskegon) Township........*434*
Casnovia (Muskegon) Village............*434*
Caspian (Iron) City............................*405*
Cass City (Tuscola) Village...............*458*
Cass County *380*
Cassopolis (Cass) Village *380*
Castleton (Barry) Township..............*372*
Cato (Montcalm) Township *432*
Cedar (Osceola) Township.................*443*
Cedar Creek (Muskegon) Township..*434*
Cedar Creek (Wexford) Township.....*466*
Cedar Springs (Kent) City.................*411*
Cedarville (Menominee) Township...*427*
Cement City (Jackson) Village..........*407*
Cement City (Lenawee) Village.........*417*
Center (Emmet) Township *390*
Center Line (Macomb) City..............*421*
Centerville (Leelanau) Township......*416*
Central Lake (Antrim) Township......*369*
Central Lake (Antrim) Village..........*369*
Centreville (St. Joseph) Village.........*452*
Champion (Marquette) Township.....*424*
Chandler (Charlevoix) Township......*381*
Chandler (Huron) Township *400*
Chapin (Saginaw) Township..............*449*
Charleston (Kalamazoo) Township....*408*
Charlevoix (Charlevoix) City............*381*
Charlevoix (Charlevoix) Township ...*381*
Charlevoix County.............................*381*
Charlotte (Eaton) City.......................*389*
Charlton (Otsego) Township.............*445*
Chase (Lake) Township *413*
Chassell (Houghton) Township..........*398*
Chatham (Alger) Village....................*367*
Cheboygan (Cheboygan) City............*382*
Cheboygan County............................*382*
Chelsea (Washtenaw) Village.............*461*
Cherry Grove (Wexford) Township...*466*
Cherry Valley (Lake) Township.........*413*

Chesaning (Saginaw) Township........*449*
Chesaning (Saginaw) Village............*449*
Cheshire (Allegan) Township............*367*
Chester (Eaton) Township *389*
Chester (Otsego) Township................*445*
Chester (Ottawa) Township *445*
Chesterfield (Macomb) Township.....*421*
Chestonia (Antrim) Township...........*369*
Chikaming (Berrien) Township.........*376*
China (St. Clair) Township *451*
Chippewa (Chippewa) Township *383*
Chippewa (Isabella) Township..........*406*
Chippewa (Mecosta) Township.........*426*
Chippewa County *383*
Chocolay (Marquette) Township.......*424*
Churchill (Ogemaw) Township.........*441*
Clam Lake (Wexford) Township *466*
Clam Union (Missaukee) Township..*429*
Clare (Clare) City..............................*384*
Clare (Isabella) City..........................*406*
Clare County *384*
Clarence (Calhoun) Township...........*379*
Clarendon (Calhoun) Township........*379*
Clark (Mackinac) Township *420*
Clarkston (Oakland) Village..............*437*
Clarksville (Ionia) Village..................*403*
Clawson (Oakland) City....................*437*
Clay (St. Clair) Township..................*451*
Claybanks (Oceana) Township..........*440*
Clayton (Arenac) Township...............*371*
Clayton (Genesee) Township *392*
Clayton (Lenawee) Village................*417*
Clearwater (Kalkaska) Township......*410*
Clement (Gladwin) Township *394*
Cleon (Manistee) Township *423*
Cleveland (Leelanau) Township........*416*
Clifford (Lapeer) Village *414*
Climax (Kalamazoo) Township.........*408*
Climax (Kalamazoo) Village.............*408*
Clinton (Lenawee) Township *417*
Clinton (Lenawee) Village.................*417*
Clinton (Macomb) Township.............*421*
Clinton (Oscoda) Township...............*444*
Clinton County *385*
Clio (Genesee) City *392*
Clyde (Allegan) Township *367*
Clyde (St. Clair) Township................*451*
Coe (Isabella) Township *406*
Cohoctah (Livingston) Township......*418*
Cold Springs (Kalkaska) Township...*410*
Coldwater (Branch) City....................*377*
Coldwater (Branch) Township...........*378*
Coldwater (Isabella) Township..........*406*
Coleman (Midland) City....................*428*
Colfax (Benzie) Township *374*
Colfax (Huron) Township..................*400*
Colfax (Mecosta) Township...............*426*
Colfax (Oceana) Township *440*
Colfax (Wexford) Township *466*
Coloma (Berrien) City.......................*376*
Coloma (Berrien) Township...............*376*
Colon (St. Joseph) Township.............*453*
Colon (St. Joseph) Village.................*453*
Columbia (Jackson) Township..........*407*
Columbia (Tuscola) Township...........*458*
Columbia (Van Buren) Township *460*
Columbiaville (Lapeer) Village *415*
Columbus (Luce) Township...............*420*
Columbus (St. Clair) Township.........*451*
Comins (Oscoda) Township *444*
Commerce (Oakland) Township........*437*
Comstock (Kalamazoo) Township *409*
Comstock Northwest (Kalamazoo) CDP *409*
Comstock Park (Kent) CDP..............*411*

MICHIGAN

American Places Dictionary

Concord (Jackson) Township *407*
Concord (Jackson) Village *407*
Constantine (St. Joseph) Township ... *453*
Constantine (St. Joseph) Village *453*
Convis (Calhoun) Township *379*
Conway (Livingston) Township *419*
Cooper (Kalamazoo) Township *409*
Coopersville (Ottawa) City *445*
Copemish (Manistee) Village *423*
Copper City (Houghton) Village *398*
Cornell (Delta) Township *387*
Corunna (Shiawassee) City *457*
Corwith (Otsego) Township *445*
Cottrellville (St. Clair) Township *451*
Courtland (Kent) Township *411*
Covert (Van Buren) Township *460*
Covington (Baraga) Township *372*
Crawford County **386**
Crockery (Ottawa) Township *446*
Cross Village (Emmet) Township *390*
Croswell (Sanilac) City *454*
Croton (Newaygo) Township *435*
Crystal (Montcalm) Township *432*
Crystal (Oceana) Township *440*
Crystal Falls (Iron) City *405*
Crystal Falls (Iron) Township *405*
Crystal Lake (Benzie) Township *374*
Cumming (Ogemaw) Township *441*
Curtis (Alcona) Township *366*
Custer (Antrim) Township *370*
Custer (Mason) Township *425*
Custer (Mason) Village *425*
Custer (Sanilac) Township *454*
Cutlerville (Kent) CDP *411*
Dafter (Chippewa) Township *383*
Daggett (Menominee) Township *427*
Daggett (Menominee) Village *427*
Dallas (Clinton) Township *385*
Dalton (Muskegon) Township *434*
Danby (Ionia) Township *403*
Dansville (Ingham) Village *401*
Davison (Genesee) City *392*
Davison (Genesee) Township *392*
Day (Montcalm) Township *432*
Dayton (Newaygo) Township *435*
Dayton (Tuscola) Township *458*
Dearborn (Wayne) City *463*
Dearborn Heights (Wayne) City *463*
Decatur (Van Buren) Township *460*
Decatur (Van Buren) Village *460*
Deckerville (Sanilac) Village *454*
Deep River (Arenac) Township *371*
Deerfield (Isabella) Township *406*
Deerfield (Lapeer) Township *415*
Deerfield (Lenawee) Township *417*
Deerfield (Lenawee) Village *417*
Deerfield (Livingston) Township *419*
Deerfield (Mecosta) Township *426*
Delaware (Sanilac) Township *454*
Delhi Charter (Ingham) Township *401*
Delta (Eaton) Township *389*
Delta County **387**
Denmark (Tuscola) Township *458*
Denton (Roscommon) Township *448*
Denver (Isabella) Township *406*
Denver (Newaygo) Township *435*
Detour (Chippewa) Township *383*
De Tour Village (Chippewa) Village . *383*
Detroit (Wayne) City *463*
Detroit Beach (Monroe) CDP *430*
De Witt (Clinton) City *385*
De Witt (Clinton) Township *385*
Dexter (Washtenaw) Township *462*
Dexter (Washtenaw) Village *462*
Dickinson County **388**

Dickson (Manistee) Township *423*
Dimondale (Eaton) Village *389*
Dorr (Allegan) Township *367*
Douglas (Allegan) Village *367*
Douglass (Montcalm) Township *432*
Dover (Lake) Township *413*
Dover (Lenawee) Township *417*
Dover (Otsego) Township *445*
Dowagiac (Cass) City *380*
Doyle (Schoolcraft) Township *456*
Drummond (Chippewa) Township ... *383*
Dryden (Lapeer) Township *415*
Dryden (Lapeer) Village *415*
Duncan (Houghton) Township *398*
Dundee (Monroe) Township *430*
Dundee (Monroe) Village *430*
Duplain (Clinton) Township *385*
Durand (Shiawassee) City *457*
Dwight (Huron) Township *400*
Eagle (Clinton) Township *385*
Eagle (Clinton) Village *385*
Eagle Harbor (Keweenaw) City *413*
Eagle Harbor (Keweenaw) Township *413*
Eagle River (Keweenaw) City *413*
East Bay (Grand Traverse)
  Township *395*
East China (St. Clair) Township *451*
East Grand Rapids (Kent) City *411*
East Jordan (Charlevoix) City *381*
Eastlake (Manistee) Village *423*
East Lansing (Ingham) City *401*
Easton (Ionia) Township *403*
Eastpointe (Macomb) City *421*
East Tawas (Iosco) City *404*
Eastwood (Kalamazoo) CDP *409*
Eaton (Eaton) Township *389*
Eaton County **389**
Eaton Rapids (Eaton) City *389*
Eaton Rapids (Eaton) Township *389*
Eau Claire (Berrien) Village *376*
Echo (Antrim) Township *370*
Eckford (Calhoun) Township *379*
Ecorse (Wayne) City *463*
Eden (Lake) Township *413*
Eden (Mason) Township *425*
Edenville (Midland) Township *428*
Edgemont Park (Ingham) CDP *401*
Edmore (Montcalm) Village *432*
Edwards (Ogemaw) Township *441*
Edwardsburg (Cass) Village *380*
Egelston (Muskegon) Township *434*
Elba (Gratiot) Township *396*
Elba (Lapeer) Township *415*
Elberta (Benzie) Village *374*
Elbridge (Oceana) Township *440*
Elk (Lake) Township *413*
Elk (Sanilac) Township *454*
Elkland (Tuscola) Township *458*
Elk Rapids (Antrim) Township *370*
Elk Rapids (Antrim) Village *370*
Elkton (Huron) Village *400*
Ellington (Tuscola) Township *458*
Ellis (Cheboygan) Township *382*
Ellsworth (Antrim) Village *370*
Ellsworth (Lake) Township *413*
Elmer (Oscoda) Township *444*
Elmer (Sanilac) Township *454*
Elmira (Otsego) Township *445*
Elm River (Houghton) Township *398*
Elmwood (Leelanau) Township *416*
Elmwood (Tuscola) Township *458*
Elsie (Clinton) Village *385*
Ely (Marquette) Township *424*
Emerson (Gratiot) Township *396*
Emmet County **390**

Emmett (Calhoun) Township *379*
Emmett (St. Clair) Township *451*
Emmett (St. Clair) Village *451*
Empire (Leelanau) Township *416*
Empire (Leelanau) Village *416*
Ensign (Delta) Township *387*
Ensley (Newaygo) Township *435*
Enterprise (Missaukee) Township *429*
Erie (Monroe) Township *430*
Erwin (Gogebic) Township *394*
Escanaba (Delta) City *387*
Escanaba (Delta) Township *387*
Essex (Clinton) Township *385*
Essexville (Bay) City *373*
Estral Beach (Monroe) Village *430*
Eureka (Montcalm) Township *432*
Evangeline (Charlevoix) Township ... *382*
Evart (Osceola) City *443*
Evart (Osceola) Township *443*
Eveline (Charlevoix) Township *382*
Everett (Newaygo) Township *436*
Evergreen (Montcalm) Township *432*
Evergreen (Sanilac) Township *454*
Ewing (Marquette) Township *424*
Excelsior (Kalkaska) Township *410*
Exeter (Monroe) Township *430*
Fabius (St. Joseph) Township *453*
Fairbanks (Delta) Township *387*
Fairfield (Lenawee) Township *417*
Fairfield (Shiawassee) Township *457*
Fairgrove (Tuscola) Township *458*
Fairgrove (Tuscola) Village *458*
Fairhaven (Huron) Township *400*
Fair Haven (St. Clair) CDP *451*
Fair Plain (Berrien) CDP *376*
Fairplain (Montcalm) Township *432*
Faithorn (Menominee) Township *427*
Farmington (Oakland) City *437*
Farmington Hills (Oakland) City *437*
Farwell (Clare) Village *384*
Fawn River (St. Joseph) Township ... *453*
Fayette (Hillsdale) Township *397*
Felch (Dickinson) Township *388*
Fennville (Allegan) City *367*
Fenton (Genesee) City *392*
Fenton (Genesee) Township *392*
Ferndale (Oakland) City *437*
Ferris (Montcalm) Township *432*
Ferry (Oceana) Township *440*
Ferrysburg (Ottawa) City *446*
Fife Lake (Grand Traverse)
  Township *395*
Fife Lake (Grand Traverse) Village .. *395*
Filer (Manistee) Township *423*
Fillmore (Allegan) Township *367*
Flat Rock (Wayne) City *463*
Flint (Genesee) City *392*
Flint (Genesee) Township *392*
Florence (St. Joseph) Township *453*
Flowerfield (St. Joseph) Township ... *453*
Flushing (Genesee) City *392*
Flushing (Genesee) Township *392*
Flynn (Sanilac) Township *454*
Ford River (Delta) Township *387*
Forest (Cheboygan) Township *382*
Forest (Genesee) Township *392*
Forest (Missaukee) Township *429*
Forester (Sanilac) Township *454*
Forest Hills (Kent) CDP *411*
Forest Home (Antrim) Township *370*
Forestville (Sanilac) Village *454*
Fork (Mecosta) Township *426*
Forsyth (Marquette) Township *424*
Fort Gratiot (St. Clair) Township *451*
Foster (Ogemaw) Township *441*

470

MICHIGAN

Fountain (Mason) Village 425
Fowler (Clinton) Village 386
Fowlerville (Livingston) Village 419
Frankenlust (Bay) Township 373
Frankenmuth (Saginaw) City 449
Frankenmuth (Saginaw) Township ..449
Frankfort (Benzie) City 374
Franklin (Clare) Township 384
Franklin (Houghton) Township 398
Franklin (Lenawee) Township 417
Franklin (Oakland) Village 438
Fraser (Bay) Township 373
Fraser (Macomb) City 421
Frederic (Crawford) Township 386
Fredonia (Calhoun) Township 379
Freedom (Washtenaw) Township 462
Freeland (Saginaw) CDP 449
Freeman (Clare) Township 384
Freeport (Barry) Village 372
Free Soil (Mason) Township 425
Free Soil (Mason) Village 425
Fremont (Isabella) Township 406
Fremont (Newaygo) City 436
Fremont (Saginaw) Township 449
Fremont (Sanilac) Township 454
Fremont (Tuscola) Township 458
Frenchtown (Monroe) Township 430
Friendship (Emmet) Township 390
Frost (Clare) Township 384
Fruitland (Muskegon) Township 434
Fruitport (Muskegon) Township 434
Fruitport (Muskegon) Village 434
Fulton (Gratiot) Township 396
Gaastra (Iron) City 405
Gagetown (Tuscola) Village 459
Gaines (Genesee) Township 392
Gaines (Genesee) Village 392
Gaines (Kent) Township 411
Galesburg (Kalamazoo) City 409
Galien (Berrien) Township 376
Galien (Berrien) Village 376
Ganges (Allegan) Township 367
Garden (Delta) Township 387
Garden (Delta) Village 387
Garden City (Wayne) City 463
Garfield (Bay) Township 373
Garfield (Clare) Township 384
Garfield (Grand Traverse) Township 395
Garfield (Kalkaska) Township 410
Garfield (Mackinac) Township 420
Garfield (Newaygo) Township 436
Gaylord (Otsego) City 445
Genesee (Genesee) Township 392
Genesee County 391
Geneva (Midland) Township 428
Geneva (Van Buren) Township 460
Genoa (Livingston) Township 419
Georgetown (Ottawa) Township 446
Germfask (Schoolcraft) Township 456
Gerrish (Roscommon) Township 448
Gibraltar (Wayne) City 463
Gibson (Bay) Township 373
Gilead (Branch) Township 378
Gilford (Tuscola) Township 459
Gilmore (Benzie) Township 374
Gilmore (Isabella) Township 406
Girard (Branch) Township 378
Gladstone (Delta) City 387
Gladwin (Gladwin) City 394
Gladwin (Gladwin) Township 394
Gladwin County 393
Glen Arbor (Leelanau) Township 416
Gobles (Van Buren) City 460
Gogebic County 394
Golden (Oceana) Township 440

Goodar (Ogemaw) Township 441
Goodland (Lapeer) Township 415
Goodrich (Genesee) Village 392
Goodwell (Newaygo) Township 436
Gore (Huron) Township 400
Gourley (Menominee) Township 427
Grand Beach (Berrien) Village 376
Grand Blanc (Genesee) City 392
Grand Blanc (Genesee) Township 392
Grand Haven (Ottawa) City 446
Grand Haven (Ottawa) Township 446
Grand Island (Alger) Township 367
Grand Ledge (Eaton) City 389
Grand Rapids (Kent) City 411
Grand Rapids (Kent) Township 411
Grand Traverse County 395
Grandville (Kent) City 412
Grant (Cheboygan) Township 382
Grant (Clare) Township 384
Grant (Grand Traverse) Township ... 395
Grant (Huron) Township 400
Grant (Iosco) Township 404
Grant (Keweenaw) Township 413
Grant (Mason) Township 425
Grant (Mecosta) Township 426
Grant (Newaygo) City 436
Grant (Newaygo) Township 436
Grant (Oceana) Township 440
Grant (St. Clair) Township 451
Grass Lake (Jackson) Township 407
Grass Lake (Jackson) Village 407
Gratiot County 396
Grattan (Kent) Township 412
Grayling (Crawford) City 386
Grayling (Crawford) Township 386
Green (Alpena) Township 369
Green (Mecosta) Township 426
Greenbush (Alcona) Township 366
Greenbush (Clinton) Township 386
Greendale (Midland) Township 428
Green Lake (Grand Traverse)
  Township 395
Greenland (Ontonagon) Township ... 442
Greenleaf (Sanilac) Township 454
Green Oak (Livingston) Township ... 419
Greenville (Montcalm) City 432
Greenwood (Clare) Township 384
Greenwood (Oceana) Township 440
Greenwood (Oscoda) Township 444
Greenwood (St. Clair) Township 451
Greenwood (Wexford) Township 466
Greilickville (Leelanau) CDP 416
Grim (Gladwin) Township 394
Grosse Ile (Wayne) Township 463
Grosse Pointe (Wayne) City 464
Grosse Pointe Farms (Wayne) City ... 464
Grosse Pointe Park (Wayne) City 464
Grosse Pointe Shores (Macomb)
  Village 421
Grosse Pointe Shores (Wayne)
  Village 464
Grosse Pointe Woods (Wayne) City ..464
Grout (Gladwin) Township 394
Groveland (Oakland) Township 438
Gunplain (Allegan) Township 367
Gustin (Alcona) Township 366
Gwinn (Marquette) CDP 424
Hadley (Lapeer) Township 415
Hagar (Berrien) Township 376
Haight (Ontonagon) Township 442
Hamburg (Livingston) Township 419
Hamilton (Clare) Township 384
Hamilton (Gratiot) Township 396
Hamilton (Van Buren) Township 460
Hamlin (Eaton) Township 389

Hamlin (Mason) Township 425
Hampton (Bay) Township 373
Hamtramck (Wayne) City 464
Hancock (Houghton) City 398
Hancock (Houghton) Township 399
Handy (Livingston) Township 419
Hanover (Jackson) Township 407
Hanover (Jackson) Village 407
Hanover (Wexford) Township 466
Harbor Beach (Huron) City 400
Harbor Springs (Emmet) City 391
Haring (Wexford) Township 466
Harper Woods (Wayne) City 464
Harrietta (Wexford) Village 466
Harris (Menominee) Township 427
Harrison (Clare) City 384
Harrison (Macomb) Township 421
Harrisville (Alcona) City 366
Harrisville (Alcona) Township 366
Hart (Oceana) City 441
Hart (Oceana) Township 441
Hartford (Van Buren) City 460
Hartford (Van Buren) Township 460
Hartland (Livingston) Township 419
Hartwick (Osceola) Township 443
Harvey (Marquette) CDP 424
Haslett (Ingham) CDP 402
Hastings (Barry) City 372
Hastings (Barry) Township 372
Hatton (Clare) Township 385
Hawes (Alcona) Township 366
Hay (Gladwin) Township 394
Hayes (Charlevoix) Township 382
Hayes (Clare) Township 385
Hayes (Otsego) Township 445
Haynes (Alcona) Township 366
Hazel Park (Oakland) City 438
Hazelton (Shiawassee) Township 457
Heath (Allegan) Township 368
Hebron (Cheboygan) Township 382
Helena (Antrim) Township 370
Hematite (Iron) Township 405
Hemlock (Saginaw) CDP 449
Henderson (Wexford) Township 466
Hendricks (Mackinac) Township 420
Henrietta (Jackson) Township 407
Hersey (Osceola) Township 443
Hersey (Osceola) Village 443
Hesperia (Newaygo) Village 436
Hesperia (Oceana) Village 441
Hiawatha (Schoolcraft) Township 456
Higgins (Roscommon) Township 448
Highland (Oakland) Township 438
Highland (Osceola) Township 443
Highland Park (Wayne) City 464
Hill (Ogemaw) Township 441
Hillman (Montmorency) Township ..433
Hillman (Montmorency) Village 433
Hillsdale (Hillsdale) City 397
Hillsdale (Hillsdale) Township 397
Hillsdale County 397
Hinton (Mecosta) Township 426
Holland (Allegan) City 368
Holland (Missaukee) Township 429
Holland (Ottawa) City 446
Holland (Ottawa) Township 446
Holly (Oakland) Township 438
Holly (Oakland) Village 438
Holmes (Menominee) Township 427
Holt (Ingham) CDP 402
Holton (Muskegon) Township 434
Home (Montcalm) Township 432
Home (Newaygo) Township 436
Homer (Calhoun) Township 379
Homer (Calhoun) Village 379

471

MICHIGAN

Homer (Midland) Township............*428*	Jordan (Antrim) Township................*370*	Larkin (Midland) Township..............*428*
Homestead (Benzie) Township..........*374*	Joyfield (Benzie) Township *375*	La Salle (Monroe) Township.............*430*
Honor (Benzie) Village.....................*375*	Juniata (Tuscola) Township...............*459*	Lathrup Village (Oakland) City *438*
Hope (Barry) Township....................*372*	Kalamazoo (Kalamazoo) City...........*409*	Laurium (Houghton) Village..............*399*
Hope (Midland) Township *428*	Kalamazoo (Kalamazoo) Township ..*409*	Lawrence (Van Buren) Township......*461*
Hopkins (Allegan) Township.............*368*	**Kalamazoo County**............................*408*	Lawrence (Van Buren) Village...........*460*
Hopkins (Allegan) Village..................*368*	Kalamo (Eaton) Township.................*389*	Lawton (Van Buren) Village..............*461*
Horton (Ogemaw) Township.............*442*	Kaleva (Manistee) Village *423*	Leavitt (Oceana) Township *441*
Houghton (Houghton) City................*399*	Kalkaska (Kalkaska) Township *410*	Lebanon (Clinton) Township..............*386*
Houghton (Keweenaw) Township......*413*	Kalkaska (Kalkaska) Village..............*410*	Lee (Allegan) Township.....................*368*
Houghton County..............................*398*	**Kalkaska County**................................*410*	Lee (Calhoun) Township *379*
Houghton Lake (Roscommon) CDP .*448*	Kasson (Leelanau) Township *416*	Lee (Midland) Township *428*
Howard (Cass) Township *380*	Kawkawlin (Bay) Township...............*373*	Leelanau (Leelanau) Township..........*416*
Howard City (Montcalm) Village......*432*	Kearney (Antrim) Township *370*	**Leelanau County**................................*416*
Howell (Livingston) City....................*419*	Keego Harbor (Oakland) City...........*438*	Leighton (Allegan) Township *368*
Howell (Livingston) Township...........*419*	Keeler (Van Buren) Township............*460*	Leland (Leelanau) Township *416*
Hubbardston (Clinton) Village...........*386*	Keene (Ionia) Township *403*	**Lenawee County**.................................*417*
Hubbardston (Ionia) Village..............*403*	Kenockee (St. Clair) Township..........*451*	Lennon (Genesee) Village..................*392*
Hubbell (Houghton) CDP *399*	Kent City (Kent) Village *412*	Lennon (Shiawassee) Village.............*457*
Hudson (Charlevoix) Township *382*	**Kent County** *411*	Lenox (Macomb) Township *421*
Hudson (Lenawee) City.....................*417*	Kentwood (Kent) City........................*412*	Leonard (Oakland) Village *438*
Hudson (Lenawee) Township *418*	**Keweenaw County** *413*	Leoni (Jackson) Township..................*407*
Hudson (Mackinac) Township *420*	Kimball (St. Clair) Township..............*452*	Leonidas (St. Joseph) Township.........*453*
Hudsonville (Ottawa) City *446*	Kinde (Huron) Village.......................*400*	Leroy (Calhoun) Township *379*
Hulbert (Chippewa) Township *383*	Kinderhook (Branch) Township.........*378*	Leroy (Ingham) Township..................*402*
Humboldt (Marquette) Township *424*	Kingsford (Dickinson) City................*388*	Le Roy (Osceola) Township *443*
Hume (Huron) Township *400*	Kingsley (Grand Traverse) Village....*395*	Le Roy (Osceola) Village *443*
Huntington Woods (Oakland) City ...*438*	Kingston (Tuscola) Township............*459*	Leslie (Ingham) City..........................*402*
Huron (Huron) Township..................*400*	Kingston (Tuscola) Village *459*	Leslie (Ingham) Township *402*
Huron (Wayne) Township *464*	Kinross (Chippewa) Township...........*383*	Level Park-Oak Park (Calhoun)
Huron County....................................*399*	K. I. Sawyer Air Force Base (Mar-	CDP *379*
Ida (Monroe) Township.....................*430*	quette) Military Facility *424*	Lexington (Sanilac) Township...........*455*
Imlay (Lapeer) Township *415*	Klacking (Ogemaw) Township *442*	Lexington (Sanilac) Village................*455*
Imlay City (Lapeer) City *415*	Kochville (Saginaw) Township..........*449*	Liberty (Jackson) Township *407*
Independence (Oakland) Township...*438*	Koehler (Cheboygan) Township........*382*	Liberty (Wexford) Township *466*
Indianfields (Tuscola) Township *459*	Koylton (Tuscola) Township..............*459*	Lilley (Newaygo) Township *436*
Ingallston (Menominee) Township....*427*	Krakow (Presque Isle) Township *447*	Lima (Washtenaw) Township *462*
Ingersoll (Midland) Township............*428*	Lafayette (Gratiot) Township............*396*	Limestone (Alger) Township *367*
Ingham (Ingham) Township *402*	La Grange (Cass) Township..............*380*	Lincoln (Alcona) Village....................*366*
Ingham County..................................*401*	Laingsburg (Shiawassee) City............*457*	Lincoln (Arenac) Township *371*
Inkster (Wayne) City..........................*464*	Laird (Houghton) Township...............*399*	Lincoln (Berrien) Township *376*
Inland (Benzie) Township..................*375*	Lake (Benzie) Township *375*	Lincoln (Clare) Township..................*385*
Interior (Ontonagon) Township.........*442*	Lake (Huron) Township *400*	Lincoln (Huron) Township.................*400*
Inverness (Cheboygan) Township.......*382*	Lake (Lake) Township *413*	Lincoln (Isabella) Township *406*
Inwood (Schoolcraft) Township *456*	Lake (Macomb) Township.................*421*	Lincoln (Midland) Township *428*
Ionia (Ionia) City...............................*403*	Lake (Menominee) Township *427*	Lincoln (Newaygo) Township *436*
Ionia (Ionia) Township......................*403*	Lake (Missaukee) Township..............*429*	Lincoln (Osceola) Township..............*443*
Ionia County......................................*403*	Lake (Roscommon) Township...........*448*	Lincoln Park (Wayne) City................*464*
Iosco (Livingston) Township *419*	Lake Angelus (Oakland) City *438*	Linden (Genesee) Village *392*
Iosco County.....................................*404*	Lake Ann (Benzie) Village................*375*	Litchfield (Hillsdale) City...................*397*
Ira (St. Clair) Township.....................*451*	Lake Charter (Berrien) Township *376*	Litchfield (Hillsdale) Township..........*397*
Iron County *405*	Lake City (Missaukee) City...............*429*	Littlefield (Emmet) Township *391*
Iron Mountain (Dickinson) City........*388*	**Lake County**......................................*413*	Little Traverse (Emmet) Township ...*391*
Iron River (Iron) City........................*405*	Lake Fenton (Genesee) CDP.............*392*	Livingston (Otsego) Township...........*445*
Iron River (Iron) Township................*405*	Lakefield (Luce) Township................*420*	**Livingston County**..............................*418*
Ironwood (Gogebic) City...................*394*	Lakefield (Saginaw) Township *450*	Livonia (Wayne) City *464*
Ironwood (Gogebic) Township..........*394*	Lake Linden (Houghton) Village.......*399*	Locke (Ingham) Township.................*402*
Irving (Barry) Township....................*372*	Lake Michigan Beach (Berrien)	Lockport (St. Joseph) Township........*453*
Isabella (Isabella) Township *406*	CDP *376*	Lodi (Washtenaw) Township.............*462*
Isabella County *406*	Lake Odessa (Ionia) Village *403*	Logan (Mason) Township..................*425*
Ishpeming (Marquette) City..............*424*	Lake Orion (Oakland) Village...........*438*	Logan (Ogemaw) Township...............*442*
Ishpeming (Marquette) Township *424*	Laketon (Muskegon) Township.........*434*	London (Monroe) Township *430*
Ithaca (Gratiot) City..........................*396*	Laketown (Allegan) Township...........*368*	Long Lake (Grand Traverse)
Jackson (Jackson) City......................*407*	Lakeview (Montcalm) Village...........*432*	Township..*395*
Jackson County.................................*407*	Lakewood Club (Muskegon) Village .*434*	Long Rapids (Alpena) Township........*369*
James (Saginaw) Township................*449*	Lambertville (Monroe) CDP..............*430*	Loud (Montmorency) Township *433*
Jamestown (Ottawa) Township *446*	Lamotte (Sanilac) Township..............*454*	Lovells (Crawford) Township............*387*
Jasper (Midland) Township...............*428*	L'Anse (Baraga) Township *372*	Lowell (Kent) City.............................*412*
Jefferson (Cass) Township.................*380*	L'Anse (Baraga) Village *372*	Lowell (Kent) Township....................*412*
Jefferson (Hillsdale) Township...........*397*	Lansing (Eaton) Township.................*389*	**Luce County** *420*
Jenison (Ottawa) CDP.......................*446*	Lansing (Ingham) City.......................*402*	Ludington (Mason) City....................*425*
Jerome (Midland) Township.............*428*	Lansing (Ingham) Township..............*402*	Luna Pier (Monroe) City...................*430*
Johnstown (Barry) Township.............*372*	Lapeer (Lapeer) City.........................*415*	Luther (Lake) Village........................*414*
Jonesfield (Saginaw) Township *449*	Lapeer (Lapeer) Township.................*415*	Lyndon (Washtenaw) Township *462*
Jonesville (Hillsdale) Village..............*397*	**Lapeer County** *414*	Lynn (St. Clair) Township..................*452*

Lyon (Oakland) Township 438	Maybee (Monroe) Village................431	Monroe (Monroe) Township 431
Lyon (Roscommon) Township 448	Mayfield (Grand Traverse)	Monroe (Newaygo) Township 436
Lyons (Ionia) Township.....................403	Township......................................395	**Monroe County** 430
Lyons (Ionia) Village 403	Mayfield (Lapeer) Township 415	Montague (Muskegon) City 434
Mackinac County 420	Mayville (Tuscola) Village.................459	Montague (Muskegon) Township......434
Mackinac Island (Mackinac) City 420	McBain (Missaukee) City..................429	Montcalm (Montcalm) Township......432
Mackinaw (Cheboygan) Township 383	McBride (Montcalm) Village............432	**Montcalm County** 431
Mackinaw City (Cheboygan) Village.383	McKinley (Emmet) Township...........391	Monterey (Allegan) Township 368
Mackinaw City (Emmet) Village.......391	McKinley (Huron) Township............400	Montgomery (Hillsdale) Village 397
Macomb (Macomb) Township 421	McMillan (Luce) Township 420	Montmorency (Montmorency)
Macomb County..............................421	McMillan (Ontonagon) Township.....442	Township......................................433
Macon (Lenawee) Township..............418	Meade (Huron) Township 400	**Montmorency County**....................433
Madison Charter (Lenawee)	Meade (Mason) Township.................426	Montrose (Genesee) Township.........393
Township......................................418	Mecosta (Mecosta) Township 427	Montrose (Genesee) Village.............393
Madison Heights (Oakland) City 438	Mecosta (Mecosta) Village................427	Moore (Sanilac) Township................455
Mancelona (Antrim) Township 370	**Mecosta County** 426	Moorland (Muskegon) Township 434
Mancelona (Antrim) Village..............370	Medina (Lenawee) Township............418	Moran (Mackinac) Township...........420
Manchester (Washtenaw) Township..462	Mellen (Menominee) Township 427	Morenci (Lenawee) City 418
Manchester (Washtenaw) Village 462	Melrose (Charlevoix) Township 382	Morley (Mecosta) Village 427
Manistee (Manistee) City 423	Melvin (Sanilac) Village 455	Morrice (Shiawassee) Village............457
Manistee (Manistee) Township 423	Melvindale (Wayne) City..................464	Morton (Mecosta) Township............427
Manistee County 423	Memphis (Macomb) City..................422	Moscow (Hillsdale) Township..........397
Manistique (Schoolcraft) City 456	Memphis (St. Clair) City...................452	Mottville (St. Joseph) Township.......453
Manistique (Schoolcraft) Township ..456	Mendon (St. Joseph) Township........453	Mount Clemens (Macomb) City 422
Manitou Beach-Devils Lake (Lenawee)	Mendon (St. Joseph) Village.............453	Mount Forest (Bay) Township..........374
CDP 418	Menominee (Menominee) City 428	Mount Haley (Midland) Township ...429
Manlius (Allegan) Township..............368	Menominee (Menominee) Township 428	Mount Morris (Genesee) City 393
Mansfield (Iron) Township................405	**Menominee County** 427	Mount Morris (Genesee) Township..393
Manton (Wexford) City 466	Mentor (Cheboygan) Township........383	Mount Pleasant (Isabella) City..........406
Maple Forest (Crawford) Township..387	Mentor (Oscoda) Township..............444	Mueller (Schoolcraft) Township 456
Maple Grove (Barry) Township 372	Meridian (Ingham) Township...........402	Muir (Ionia) Village..........................403
Maple Grove (Manistee) Township ..423	Merrill (Newaygo) Township............436	Mullett (Cheboygan) Township 383
Maple Grove (Saginaw) Township....450	Merrill (Saginaw) Village..................450	Mulliken (Eaton) Village 389
Maple Rapids (Clinton) Village 386	Merritt (Bay) Township 373	Mundy (Genesee) Township 393
Maple Ridge (Alpena) Township......369	Mesick (Wexford) Village 466	Munising (Alger) City.......................367
Maple Ridge (Delta) Township.........387	Metamora (Lapeer) Township 415	Munising (Alger) Township..............367
Maple River (Emmet) Township.......391	Metamora (Lapeer) Village...............415	Munro (Cheboygan) Township.........383
Maple Valley (Montcalm) Township.432	Metz (Presque Isle) Township 447	Muskegon (Muskegon) City.............434
Maple Valley (Sanilac) Township 455	Meyer (Menominee) Township 428	Muskegon (Muskegon) Township....434
Marathon (Lapeer) Township............415	Michiana (Berrien) Village 376	**Muskegon County**..........................434
Marcellus (Cass) Township................380	Michigamme (Marquette) Township.424	Muskegon Heights (Muskegon) City.434
Marcellus (Cass) Village 380	Michigan Center (Jackson) CDP.......407	Mussey (St. Clair) Township 452
Marengo (Calhoun) Township 379	Middle Branch (Osceola) Township..443	Nadeau (Menominee) Township 428
Marenisco (Gogebic) Township........394	Middlebury (Shiawassee) Township..457	Nahma (Delta) Township 387
Marilla (Manistee) Township 423	Middletown (Shiawassee) CDP.........457	Napoleon (Jackson) Township 407
Marine City (St. Clair) City 452	Middleville (Barry) Village................372	Nashville (Barry) Village 372
Marion (Charlevoix) Township.........382	Midland (Bay) City...........................373	Negaunee (Marquette) City..............424
Marion (Livingston) Township..........419	Midland (Midland) City 429	Negaunee (Marquette) Township 424
Marion (Osceola) Township 443	Midland (Midland) Township...........429	Nelson (Kent) Township 412
Marion (Osceola) Village 443	**Midland County** 428	Nester (Roscommon) Township........448
Marion (Saginaw) Township.............450	Mikado (Alcona) Township 366	Newark (Gratiot) Township 396
Marion (Sanilac) Township 455	Milan (Monroe) City 431	Newaygo (Newaygo) City 436
Markey (Roscommon) Township 448	Milan (Monroe) Township................431	**Newaygo County**............................435
Marlette (Sanilac) Township 455	Milan (Washtenaw) City...................462	New Baltimore (Macomb) City.........422
Marlette (Sanilac) Village 455	Milford (Oakland) Township............438	Newberg (Cass) Township 380
Marquette (Mackinac) Township 420	Milford (Oakland) Village 438	Newberry (Luce) Village...................420
Marquette (Marquette) City..............424	Millbrook (Mecosta) Township 427	New Buffalo (Berrien) City 376
Marquette (Marquette) Township.....424	Millen (Alcona) Township 366	New Buffalo (Berrien) Township 376
Marquette County 424	Millersburg (Presque Isle) Village 447	New Era (Oceana) Village 441
Marshall (Calhoun) City....................379	Millington (Tuscola) Township 459	Newfield (Oceana) Township 441
Marshall (Calhoun) Township 379	Millington (Tuscola) Village..............459	New Haven (Gratiot) Township.......396
Martin (Allegan) Township 368	Mills (Midland) Township 429	New Haven (Macomb) Village.........422
Martin (Allegan) Village....................368	Mills (Ogemaw) Township 442	New Haven (Shiawassee) Township..457
Martiny (Mecosta) Township 426	Milton (Antrim) Township................370	Newkirk (Lake) Township 414
Marysville (St. Clair) City 452	Milton (Cass) Township 380	New Lothrop (Shiawassee) Village....457
Mason (Arenac) Township 371	Minden (Sanilac) Township..............455	Newton (Calhoun) Township 379
Mason (Cass) Township.....................380	Minden City (Sanilac) Village 455	Newton (Mackinac) Township 420
Mason (Ingham) City 402	Mineral Hills (Iron) Village...............405	Niles (Berrien) City 376
Mason County 425	Mio (Oscoda) CDP 444	Niles (Berrien) Township 376
Masonville (Delta) Township 387	**Missaukee County**..........................429	Niles (Cass) City 381
Mastodon (Iron) Township 405	Mitchell (Alcona) Township 366	Noble (Branch) Township 378
Matchwood (Ontonagon) Township..442	Moffatt (Arenac) Township 371	Norman (Manistee) Township...........423
Mathias (Alger) Township 367	Moltke (Presque Isle) Township 447	North Adams (Hillsdale) Village.......397
Mattawan (Van Buren) Village..........461	Monitor (Bay) Township...................374	North Allis (Presque Isle) Township.447
Matteson (Branch) Township 378	Monroe (Monroe) City 431	North Branch (Lapeer) Township 415

MICHIGAN

American Places Dictionary

North Branch (Lapeer) Village..........415
Northfield (Washtenaw) Township....462
North Muskegon (Muskegon) City....434
North Plains (Ionia) Township.........403
Northport (Leelanau) Village 416
North Shade (Gratiot) Township......396
North Star (Gratiot) Township 396
Northview (Kent) City......................412
Northville (Oakland) City.................438
Northville (Wayne) City 464
Northville (Wayne) Township..........464
Norton Shores (Muskegon) City 435
Norvell (Jackson) Township.............407
Norway (Dickinson) City..................388
Norway (Dickinson) Township 388
Norwich (Missaukee) Township......429
Norwich (Newaygo) Township.........436
Norwood (Charlevoix) Township......382
Nottawa (Isabella) Township.............406
Nottawa (St. Joseph) Township........453
Novesta (Tuscola) Township 459
Novi (Oakland) City.........................438
Novi (Oakland) Township.................439
Nunda (Cheboygan) Township.........383
Oakfield (Kent) Township................412
Oakland Charter (Oakland)
Township..439
Oakland County................................437
Oakley (Saginaw) Village.................450
Oak Park (Oakland) City..................439
Oceana County..................................440
Oceola (Livingston) Township 419
Ocqueoc (Presque Isle) Township.....447
Odessa (Ionia) Township..................403
Ogden (Lenawee) Township.............418
Ogemaw (Ogemaw) Township.........442
Ogemaw County................................441
Okemos (Ingham) CDP.....................402
Olive (Clinton) Township.................386
Olive (Ottawa) Township..................446
Oliver (Huron) Township..................400
Oliver (Kalkaska) Township..............410
Olivet (Eaton) City...........................390
Omer (Arenac) City...........................371
Onaway (Presque Isle) City...............447
Oneida Charter (Eaton) Township....390
Onekama (Manistee) Township.......423
Onekama (Manistee) Village 423
Onondaga (Ingham) Township.........402
Onota (Alger) Township...................367
Onsted (Lenawee) Village.................418
Ontonagon (Ontonagon) Township...443
Ontonagon (Ontonagon) Village 443
Ontonagon County 442
Ontwa (Cass) Township....................381
Orange (Ionia) Township..................403
Orange (Kalkaska) Township 410
Orangeville (Barry) Township 372
Orchard Lake Village (Oakland)
City..439
Oregon (Lapeer) Township...............415
Orient (Osceola) Township...............444
Orion (Oakland) Township...............439
Orleans (Ionia) Township.................403
Oronoko (Berrien) Township 376
Ortonville (Oakland) Village.............439
Osceola (Houghton) Township.........399
Osceola (Osceola) Township.............444
Osceola County 443
Oscoda (Iosco) Township 404
Oscoda County 444
Oshtemo (Kalamazoo) Township......409
Ossineke (Alpena) Township............369
Otisco (Ionia) Township...................403
Otisville (Genesee) Village 393

Otsego (Allegan) City........................368
Otsego (Allegan) City........................368
Otsego County..................................445
Otsego Lake (Otsego) Township.......445
Ottawa County..................................445
Otter Lake (Genesee) Village 393
Otter Lake (Lapeer) Village...............415
Otto (Oceana) Township...................441
Overisel (Allegan) Township............368
Ovid (Branch) Township..................378
Ovid (Clinton) Township..................386
Ovid (Clinton) Village......................386
Ovid (Shiawassee) Village 457
Owendale (Huron) Village................400
Owosso (Shiawassee) City................457
Owosso (Shiawassee) Township 457
Oxford (Oakland) Township............439
Oxford (Oakland) Village 439
Palmyra (Lenawee) Township 418
Paradise (Grand Traverse)
Township....................................... 395
Parchment (Kalamazoo) City...........409
Paris (Huron) Township...................400
Park (Ottawa) Township...................446
Park (St. Joseph) Township..............453
Parma (Jackson) Township...............408
Parma (Jackson) Village...................408
Pavilion (Kalamazoo) Township......409
Paw Paw (Van Buren) Township 461
Paw Paw (Van Buren) Village..........461
Paw Paw Lake (Berrien) CDP...........376
Peacock (Lake) Township................414
Peaine (Charlevoix) Township.........382
Pearl Beach (St. Clair) CDP.............452
Peck (Sanilac) Village......................455
Pellston (Emmet) Village 391
Peninsula (Grand Traverse)
Township....................................... 395
Penn (Cass) Township 381
Pennfield (Calhoun) Township.........379
Pentland (Luce) Township................420
Pentwater (Oceana) Township.........441
Pentwater (Oceana) Village 441
Pere Marquetter Charter (Mason)
Township....................................... 426
Perrinton (Gratiot) Village................396
Perry (Shiawassee) City....................457
Perry (Shiawassee) Township 457
Petersburg (Monroe) City.................431
Petoskey (Emmet) City.....................391
Pewamo (Ionia) Village....................403
Pickford (Chippewa) Township........383
Pierson (Montcalm) Township.........432
Pierson (Montcalm) Village..............432
Pigeon (Huron) Village....................400
Pinckney (Livingston) Village..........419
Pinconning (Bay) City......................374
Pinconning (Bay) Township.............374
Pine (Montcalm) Township..............432
Pine Grove (Van Buren) Township...461
Pine River (Gratiot) Township..........396
Pinora (Lake) Township...................414
Pioneer (Missaukee) Township........429
Pipestone (Berrien) Township..........376
Pittsfield (Washtenaw) Township......462
Pittsford (Hillsdale) Township 397
Plainfield (Iosco) Township..............404
Plainfield (Kent) Township...............412
Plainwell (Allegan) City...................368
Platte (Benzie) Township..................375
Pleasanton (Manistee) Township......423
Pleasant Plains (Lake) Township 414
Pleasant Ridge (Oakland) City..........439
Pleasant View (Emmet) Township....391
Plymouth (Wayne) City....................464

Plymouth (Wayne) Township 464
Pointe Aux Barques (Huron)
Township....................................... 400
Pokagon (Cass) Township.................381
Polkton (Ottawa) Township..............446
Pontiac (Oakland) City.....................439
Portage (Houghton) Township 399
Portage (Kalamazoo) City 409
Portage (Mackinac) Township..........421
Port Austin (Huron) Township 400
Port Austin (Huron) Village.............400
Porter (Cass) Township 381
Porter (Midland) Township..............429
Porter (Van Buren) Township 461
Port Hope (Huron) Village...............401
Port Huron (St. Clair) City 452
Port Huron (St. Clair) Township 452
Portland (Ionia) City.........................404
Portland (Ionia) Township 404
Port Sanilac (Sanilac) Village...........455
Port Sheldon (Ottawa) Township......446
Portsmouth (Bay) Township.............374
Posen (Presque Isle) Township.........447
Posen (Presque Isle) Village..............447
Potterville (Eaton) City 390
Powell (Marquette) Township..........424
Powers (Menominee) Village...........428
Prairie Ronde (Kalamazoo)
Township....................................... 409
Prairieville (Barry) Township............373
Prescott (Ogemaw) Village 442
Presque Isle (Presque Isle) Township447
Presque Isle County 447
Prudenville (Roscommon) CDP 448
Pulaski (Jackson) Township 408
Pulaski (Presque Isle) Township......447
Putnam (Livingston) Township........419
Quincy (Branch) Township 378
Quincy (Branch) Village 378
Quincy (Houghton) Township..........399
Quinnesec (Dickinson) CDP............388
Raber (Chippewa) Township............384
Raisin (Lenawee) Township 418
Raisinville (Monroe) Township........431
Ransom (Hillsdale) Township..........398
Rapid River (Kalkaska) Township....410
Ravenna (Muskegon) Township 435
Ravenna (Muskegon) Village 435
Ray (Macomb) Township 422
Reading (Hillsdale) City...................398
Reading (Hillsdale) Township..........398
Readmond (Emmet) Township 391
Redding (Clare) Township................385
Redford (Wayne) Township..............465
Reed City (Osceola) City..................444
Reeder (Missaukee) Township.........429
Reese (Tuscola) Village....................459
Reno (Iosco) Township.....................404
Republic (Marquette) Township 424
Resort (Emmet) Township 391
Reynolds (Montcalm) Township 432
Rich (Lapeer) Township 415
Richfield (Genesee) Township..........393
Richfield (Roscommon) Township ...448
Richland (Kalamazoo) Township.....409
Richland (Kalamazoo) Village..........409
Richland (Missaukee) Township 430
Richland (Montcalm) Township 432
Richland (Ogemaw) Township.........442
Richland (Saginaw) Township..........450
Richmond (Macomb) City...............422
Richmond (Macomb) Township 422
Richmond (Marquette) Township....424
Richmond (Osceola) Township 444
Ridgeway (Lenawee) Township........418

Entry	Page
Riga (Lenawee) Township	418
Riley (Clinton) Township	386
Riley (St. Clair) Township	452
River Rouge (Wayne) City	465
Riverside (Missaukee) Township	430
Riverton (Mason) Township	426
Riverview (Wayne) City	465
Rives (Jackson) Township	408
Robin Glen-Indiantown (Saginaw) CDP	450
Robinson (Ottawa) Township	446
Rochester (Oakland) City	439
Rochester Hills (Oakland) City	439
Rockford (Kent) City	412
Rockland (Ontonagon) Township	443
Rock River (Alger) Township	367
Rockwood (Wayne) City	465
Rogers (Presque Isle) Township	447
Rogers City (Presque Isle) City	447
Rolland (Isabella) Township	406
Rollin (Lenawee) Township	418
Rome (Lenawee) Township	418
Romeo (Macomb) Village	422
Romulus (Wayne) City	465
Ronald (Ionia) Township	404
Roosevelt Park (Muskegon) City	435
Roscommon (Roscommon) Township	448
Roscommon (Roscommon) Village	448
Roscommon County	448
Rose (Oakland) Township	439
Rose (Ogemaw) Township	442
Rosebush (Isabella) Village	406
Rose City (Ogemaw) City	442
Rose Lake (Osceola) Township	444
Roseville (Macomb) City	422
Ross (Kalamazoo) Township	409
Rothbury (Oceana) Village	441
Roxand (Eaton) Township	390
Royal Oak (Oakland) City	439
Royal Oak (Oakland) Township	439
Royalton (Berrien) Township	376
Rubicon (Huron) Township	401
Rudyard (Chippewa) Township	384
Rush (Shiawassee) Township	457
Rust (Montmorency) Township	433
Rutland (Barry) Township	373
Sage (Gladwin) Township	394
Saginaw (Saginaw) City	450
Saginaw (Saginaw) Township	450
Saginaw County	449
Sagola (Dickinson) Township	388
St. Charles (Saginaw) Township	450
St. Charles (Saginaw) Village	450
St. Clair (St. Clair) City	452
St. Clair (St. Clair) Township	452
St. Clair County	451
St. Clair Shores (Macomb) City	422
St. Helen (Roscommon) CDP	448
St. Ignace (Mackinac) City	421
St. Ignace (Mackinac) Township	421
St. James (Charlevoix) Township	382
St. Johns (Clinton) City	386
St. Joseph (Berrien) City	376
St. Joseph Charter (Berrien) Township	377
St. Joseph County	452
St. Louis (Gratiot) City	396
Salem (Allegan) Township	368
Salem (Washtenaw) Township	462
Saline (Washtenaw) City	462
Saline (Washtenaw) Township	462
Sanborn (Alpena) Township	369
Sand Beach (Huron) Township	401
Sand Lake (Kent) Village	412
Sands (Marquette) Township	425
Sandstone (Jackson) Township	408
Sandusky (Sanilac) City	455
Sanford (Midland) Village	429
Sanilac (Sanilac) Township	455
Sanilac County	454
Saranac (Ionia) Village	404
Sauble (Lake) Township	414
Saugatuck (Allegan) Township	368
Saugatuck (Allegan) Village	368
Sault Ste. Marie (Chippewa) City	384
Schoolcraft (Houghton) Township	399
Schoolcraft (Kalamazoo) Township	409
Schoolcraft (Kalamazoo) Village	409
Schoolcraft County	456
Scio (Washtenaw) Township	462
Sciota (Shiawassee) Township	457
Scipio (Hillsdale) Township	398
Scottville (Mason) City	426
Sebewa (Ionia) Township	404
Sebewaing (Huron) Township	401
Sebewaing (Huron) Village	401
Secord (Gladwin) Township	394
Selma (Wexford) Township	466
Seneca (Lenawee) Township	418
Seney (Schoolcraft) Township	456
Seville (Gratiot) Township	396
Sharon (Washtenaw) Township	462
Shelby (Macomb) Township	422
Shelby (Oceana) Township	441
Shelby (Oceana) Village	441
Shepherd (Isabella) Village	406
Sheridan (Calhoun) Township	379
Sheridan (Clare) Township	385
Sheridan (Huron) Township	401
Sheridan (Mason) Township	426
Sheridan (Mecosta) Township	427
Sheridan (Montcalm) Village	432
Sheridan Charter (Newaygo) Township	436
Sherman (Gladwin) Township	394
Sherman (Huron) Township	401
Sherman (Iosco) Township	404
Sherman (Isabella) Township	406
Sherman (Keweenaw) Township	413
Sherman (Mason) Township	426
Sherman (Newaygo) Township	436
Sherman (Osceola) Township	444
Sherman (St. Joseph) Township	453
Sherwood (Branch) Township	378
Sherwood (Branch) Village	378
Shiawassee (Shiawassee) Township	457
Shiawassee County	456
Shields (Saginaw) CDP	450
Shoreham (Berrien) Village	377
Shorewood-Tower Hills-Harbert (Berrien) CDP	377
Sidney (Montcalm) Township	433
Sigel (Huron) Township	401
Silver Creek (Cass) Township	381
Sims (Arenac) Township	371
Skandia (Marquette) Township	425
Skidway Lake (Ogemaw) CDP	442
Slagle (Wexford) Township	466
Sodus (Berrien) Township	377
Solon (Kent) Township	412
Solon (Leelanau) Township	416
Somerset (Hillsdale) Township	398
Soo (Chippewa) Township	384
South Arm (Charlevoix) Township	382
South Branch (Crawford) Township	387
South Branch (Wexford) Township	466
Southfield (Oakland) City	439
Southfield (Oakland) Township	439
Southgate (Wayne) City	465
South Gull Lake (Kalamazoo) CDP	409
South Haven (Allegan) City	368
South Haven (Van Buren) City	461
South Haven (Van Buren) Township	461
South Lyon (Oakland) City	439
South Monroe (Monroe) CDP	431
South Range (Houghton) Village	399
South Rockwood (Monroe) Village	431
Spalding (Menominee) Township	428
Sparlingville (St. Clair) CDP	452
Sparta (Kent) Township	412
Sparta (Kent) Village	412
Spaulding (Saginaw) Township	450
Speaker (Sanilac) Township	455
Spencer (Kent) Township	412
Spring Arbor (Jackson) Township	408
Springdale (Manistee) Township	423
Springfield (Calhoun) City	379
Springfield (Kalkaska) Township	410
Springfield (Oakland) Township	439
Spring Lake (Ottawa) Township	446
Spring Lake (Ottawa) Village	446
Springport (Jackson) Township	408
Springport (Jackson) Village	408
Springvale (Emmet) Township	391
Springville (Wexford) Township	466
Spurr (Baraga) Township	372
Stambaugh (Iron) City	405
Stambaugh (Iron) Township	405
Standish (Arenac) City	371
Standish (Arenac) Township	371
Stannard (Ontonagon) Township	443
Stanton (Houghton) Township	399
Stanton (Montcalm) City	433
Stanwood (Mecosta) Village	427
Star (Antrim) Township	370
Stephenson (Menominee) City	428
Stephenson (Menominee) Township	428
Sterling (Arenac) Village	371
Sterling Heights (Macomb) City	422
Stevensville (Berrien) Village	377
Stockbridge (Ingham) Township	402
Stockbridge (Ingham) Village	402
Stony Point (Monroe) CDP	431
Stronach (Manistee) Township	424
Sturgis (St. Joseph) City	453
Sturgis (St. Joseph) Township	453
Sugar Island (Chippewa) Township	384
Sullivan (Muskegon) Township	435
Summerfield (Clare) Township	385
Summerfield (Monroe) Township	431
Summit (Jackson) Township	408
Summit (Mason) Township	426
Sumner (Gratiot) Township	396
Sumpter (Wayne) Township	465
Sunfield (Eaton) Township	390
Sunfield (Eaton) Village	390
Superior (Chippewa) Township	384
Superior (Washtenaw) Township	462
Surrey (Clare) Township	385
Suttons Bay (Leelanau) Township	416
Suttons Bay (Leelanau) Village	416
Swan Creek (Saginaw) Township	450
Swartz Creek (Genesee) City	393
Sweetwater (Lake) Township	414
Sylvan (Osceola) Township	444
Sylvan (Washtenaw) Township	462
Sylvan Lake (Oakland) City	440
Tallmadge (Ottawa) Township	446
Tawas (Iosco) Township	404
Tawas City (Iosco) City	404
Taylor (Wayne) City	465
Taymouth (Saginaw) Township	450
Tecumseh (Lenawee) City	418
Tecumseh (Lenawee) Township	418

MICHIGAN

Tekonsha (Calhoun) Township..........*380*
Tekonsha (Calhoun) Village..............*380*
Temperance (Monroe) CDP................*431*
Texas (Kalamazoo) Township..........*409*
Thetford (Genesee) Township..........*393*
Thomas (Saginaw) Township *450*
Thompson (Schoolcraft) Township...*456*
Thompsonville (Benzie) Village *375*
Thornapple (Barry) Township............*373*
Three Oaks (Berrien) Township........*377*
Three Oaks (Berrien) Village............*377*
Three Rivers (St. Joseph) City..........*453*
Tilden (Marquette) Township *425*
Tittabawassee (Saginaw) Township...*450*
Tobacco (Gladwin) Township *394*
Tompkins (Jackson) Township..........*408*
Torch Lake (Antrim) Township........*370*
Torch Lake (Houghton) Township....*399*
Traverse City (Grand Traverse) City *395*
Traverse City (Leelanau) City *416*
Trenton (Wayne) City *465*
Trout Lake (Chippewa) Township....*384*
Trowbridge (Allegan) Township *368*
Trowbridge Park (Marquette) CDP ..*425*
Troy (Newayo) Township *436*
Troy (Oakland) City *440*
Turin (Marquette) Township *425*
Turner (Arenac) Township *371*
Turner (Arenac) Village....................*371*
Tuscarora (Cheboygan) Township.....*383*
Tuscola (Tuscola) Township *459*
Tuscola County................................*458*
Tustin (Osceola) Village...................*444*
Twining (Arenac) Township............*371*
Twin Lake (Muskegon) CDP............*435*
Tyrone (Kent) Township..................*412*
Tyrone (Livingston) Township *419*
Ubly (Huron) Village........................*401*
Unadilla (Livingston) Township *419*
Union (Branch) Township................*378*
Union (Grand Traverse) Township...*395*
Union (Isabella) Township *406*
Union City (Branch) Village............*378*
Union City (Calhoun) Village..........*380*
Unionville (Tuscola) Village............*459*
Utica (Macomb) City *422*
Valley (Allegan) Township *368*
Van Buren (Wayne) Township..........*465*
Van Buren County *460*
Vandalia (Cass) Village....................*381*
Vanderbilt (Otsego) Village..............*445*
Vandercook Lake (Jackson) CDP......*408*
Vassar (Tuscola) City.......................*459*
Vassar (Tuscola) Township...............*459*
Venice (Shiawassee) Township........*457*
Vergennes (Kent) Township *412*
Vermontville (Eaton) Township.......*390*
Vermontville (Eaton) Village............*390*
Vernon (Isabella) Township..............*406*
Vernon (Shiawassee) Township........*458*
Vernon (Shiawassee) Village............*458*
Verona (Huron) Township.................*401*
Vevay (Ingham) Township................*402*
Vicksburg (Kalamazoo) Village........*409*

Victor (Clinton) Township *386*
Victory (Mason) Township................*426*
Vienna (Genesee) Township.............*393*
Vienna (Montmorency) Township *433*
Volinia (Cass) Township...................*381*
Wakefield (Gogebic) City *394*
Wakefield (Gogebic) Township *394*
Wakeshma (Kalamazoo) Township ...*409*
Waldron (Hillsdale) Village *398*
Wales (St. Clair) Township *452*
Walker (Cheboygan) Township.........*383*
Walker (Kent) City *412*
Walkerville (Oceana) Village *441*
Walled Lake (Oakland) City.............*440*
Walton (Eaton) Township.................*390*
Warner (Antrim) Township *370*
Warren (Macomb) City.....................*422*
Warren (Midland) Township *429*
Washington (Gratiot) Township........*396*
Washington (Macomb) Township *422*
Washington (Sanilac) Township *455*
Washtenaw County.............................*461*
Waterford (Oakland) Township........*440*
Waterloo (Jackson) Township...........*408*
Watersmeet (Gogebic) Township......*394*
Watertown (Clinton) Township.........*386*
Watertown (Sanilac) Township..........*455*
Watertown (Tuscola) Township *459*
Watervliet (Berrien) City *377*
Watervliet (Berrien) Township *377*
Watson (Allegan) Township..............*368*
Waucedah (Dickinson) Township......*388*
Waverly (Cheboygan) Township.......*383*
Waverly (Eaton) CDP.......................*390*
Waverly (Van Buren) Township *461*
Wawatam (Emmet) Township *391*
Wayland (Allegan) City.....................*368*
Wayne (Cass) Township....................*381*
Wayne (Wayne) City *465*
Wayne County *463*
Weare (Oceana) Township................*441*
Webber (Lake) Township..................*414*
Webberville (Ingham) Village..........*402*
Webster (Washtenaw) Township.......*462*
Weesaw (Berrien) Township.............*377*
Weidman (Isabella) CDP..................*406*
Weldon (Benzie) Township...............*375*
Wellington (Alpena) Township *369*
Wells (Delta) Township *388*
Wells (Marquette) Township *425*
Wells (Tuscola) Township *459*
West Bloomfield (Oakland)
  Township..*440*
West Branch (Dickinson) Township..*388*
West Branch (Marquette) Township .*425*
West Branch (Missaukee) Township.*430*
West Branch (Ogemaw) City *442*
West Branch (Ogemaw) Township ...*442*
Westland (Wayne) City.....................*465*
West Monroe (Monroe) CDP............*431*
Westphalia (Clinton) Township........*386*
Westphalia (Clinton) Village *386*
West Traverse (Emmet) Township *391*
Westwood (Kalamazoo) CDP............*410*

Wexford (Wexford) Township *467*
Wexford County *466*
Wheatfield (Ingham) Township........*402*
Wheatland (Hillsdale) Township......*398*
Wheatland (Mecosta) Township.......*427*
Wheatland (Sanilac) Township.........*455*
Wheeler (Gratiot) Township.............*397*
White Cloud (Newaygo) City...........*436*
Whitefish (Chippewa) Township......*384*
Whiteford (Monroe) Township *431*
Whitehall (Muskegon) City *435*
Whitehall (Muskegon) Township.....*435*
White Lake (Oakland) Township *440*
White Oak (Ingham) Township.........*402*
White Pigeon (St. Joseph) Township *453*
White Pigeon (St. Joseph) Village.....*453*
White River (Muskegon) Township ..*435*
Whitewater (Grand Traverse)
  Township..*395*
Whitmore Lake (Livingston) CDP....*419*
Whitmore Lake (Washtenaw) CDP...*462*
Whitney (Arenac) Township.............*371*
Wilber (Iosco) Township *404*
Wilcox (Newaygo) Township...........*436*
Williams (Bay) Township..................*374*
Williamston (Ingham) City...............*402*
Williamstown (Ingham) Township....*402*
Wilmot (Cheboygan) Township........*383*
Wilson (Alpena) Township *369*
Wilson (Charlevoix) Township.........*382*
Windsor (Eaton) Township *390*
Winfield (Montcalm) Township........*433*
Winsor (Huron) Township *401*
Winterfield (Clare) Township............*385*
Wise (Isabella) Township..................*407*
Wisner (Tuscola) Township...............*459*
Wixom (Oakland) City......................*440*
Wolf Lake (Muskegon) CDP *435*
Wolverine (Cheboygan) Village.........*383*
Wolverine Lake (Oakland) Village....*440*
Woodbridge (Hillsdale) Township.....*398*
Woodhaven (Wayne) City.................*465*
Woodhull (Shiawassee) Township *458*
Woodland (Barry) Township *373*
Woodland (Barry) Village..................*373*
Woodland Beach (Monroe) CDP *431*
Woodstock (Lenawee) Township.......*418*
Worth (Sanilac) Township *455*
Wright (Hillsdale) Township *398*
Wright (Ottawa) Township................*446*
Wurtsmith Air Force Base (Iosco) Military Facility...............................*405*
Wyandotte (Wayne) City *465*
Wyoming (Kent) City *412*
Yale (St. Clair) City *452*
Yankee Springs (Barry) Township.....*373*
Yates (Lake) Township *414*
York (Washtenaw) Township............*462*
Ypsilanti (Washtenaw) City...............*462*
Ypsilanti (Washtenaw) Township......*462*
Zeeland (Ottawa) City.......................*446*
Zeeland (Ottawa) Township *446*
Zilwaukee (Saginaw) City.................*450*
Zilwaukee (Saginaw) Township.........*450*

Minnesota

MINNESOTA

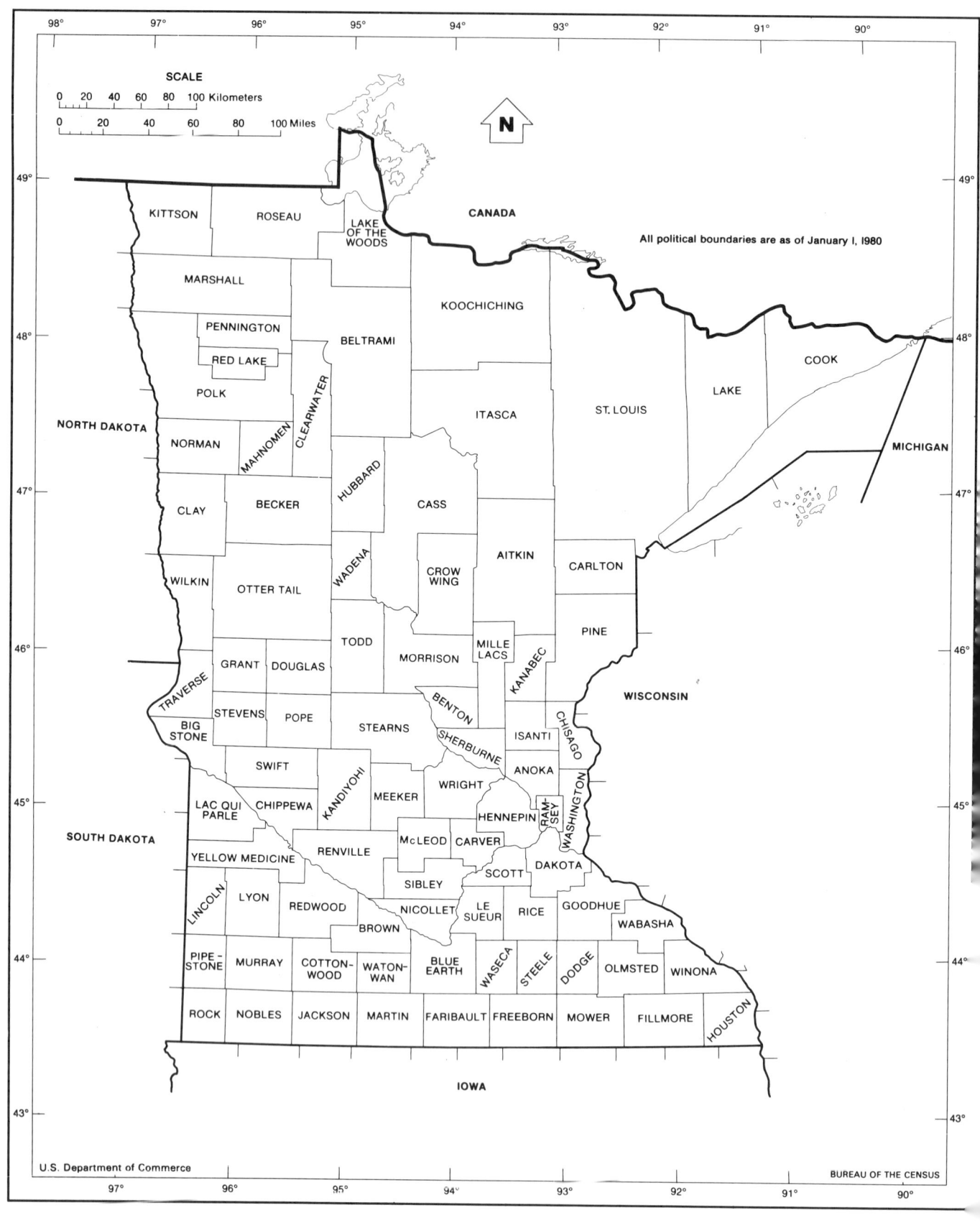

Minnesota

Population: 4,375,099 (1990); 4,075,970 (1980)
Population rank (1990): 20
Percent population change (1980-1990): 7.3
Population projection: 4,513,000 (1995); 4,615,000 (2000)

Area: total 86,943 sq. mi.; 79,617 sq. mi. land, 7,326 sq. mi. water
Area rank: 12
Highest elevation: 2,301 ft., Eagle Mountain (Cook County)
Lowest point: 602 ft., surface of Lake Superior

State capital: St. Paul (Ramsey County)
Largest city: Minneapolis (368,383)
Second largest city: St. Paul (272,235)
Largest county: Hennepin (1,032,431)

Total housing units: 1,848,445
No. of occupied housing units: 1,647,853
Vacant housing units (%): 10.9
Distribution of population by race and Hispanic origin (%):
  White: 94.4
  Black: 2.2
  Hispanic (any race): 1.2
  Native American: 1.1
  Asian/Pacific: 1.8
  Other: 0.5

Admission date: May 11, 1858 (32nd state).

Location: In the north-central United States bordering Iowa, South Dakota, North Dakota, the Canadian provinces of Manitoba and Ontario, Lake Superior, and Wisconsin.

Name Origin: For the Minnesota River, which flows east across the southern portion of the state, joining the Mississippi River at St. Paul. The name is from a Siouan word *Menesota* 'cloudy water,' or possibly 'water reflecting cloudy skies.'

State bird: common loon (*Gavia immer*)
State drink: milk
State fish: walleye (*Stizostedion vitreum*)
State flower: pink and white lady's-slipper (*Cypripedium reginae*)
State gem: Lake Superior agate
State grain: wild rice or manomin (*Zizania aquatica*)
State muffin: blueberry muffin
State mushroom: morel or sponge mushroom (*Morchella esculenta*)
State song: "Hail! Minnesota"
State tree: Norway (red) pine (*Pinus resinosa*)

State motto: L'Etoile du Nord (French 'The North Star')
State nicknames: North Star State; Gopher State; Bread and Butter State

Area codes: 218 (northern half), 507 (Rochester and south), 612 (Minneapolis and central)
Time zone: Central
Abbreviations: MN (postal); Minn. (traditional)
Part of (region): Great Lakes, Midwest

Local Government

Counties

Minnesota has 87 counties, each governed by a board of commissioners, and 13 regional development commissions (RDCs).

Municipalities

Minnesota has 855 cities, of which 108 operate under home rule charters, 747 being statutory cities. There are 1,803 townships, more than any other state.

Settlement History and Early Development

Indians occupied the area of present-day Minnesota 10,000 years ago. When the first Europeans arrived in the seventeenth and early eighteenth centuries, they found Dakota, or Minnesota Sioux, and Ojibwa, or Chippewa. In 1736 the Dakota attacked a party of French missionaries and traders, allies of the Ojibwa, and their Cree Indian guides at the Lake of the Woods. The Ojibwa took this as a declaration of war and thus began more than 100 years of fighting between them, with the Dakota eventually being pressed to the south and west and the Ojibwa becoming established in the north.

Few scholars accept the authenticity of the Kensington Rune Stone, found in 1898, leading to claims that the Vikings were in present-day Minnesota in 1362. The first documented Europeans to travel through the region were the French fur traders Pierre Esprit Radisson and Medart Chouart, Sieur de Groseilliers, his brother-in-law, who arrived about 1660. In 1679, Daniel Greysolon, Sieur Duluth (Du Lhut), arrived and claimed the land for Louis XIV of France. In 1763, after the French and Indian Wars, the part of Minnesota east of the Mississippi was given to the British and the lands west of the Mississippi, then known as Louisiana, to Spain. The latter ignored its territory, but the British sent in fur traders and explorers.

The American Revolution and War of 1812

There was little activity in the area during the Revolution, but at its close Britain ceded its territories south of the Great Lakes and east of the Mississippi River (including part of present-day Minnesota) to the United States.

This area became part of the Northwest Territory created by Congress in 1787, but British fur companies, notably the North West Company, continued to trade in the region. The North West Company commissioned David Thompson to map the territory, which was done by 1797. In 1800 Spain ceded Louisiana back to the French, and in 1803 it was purchased by the United States under the terms of the Louisiana Purchase.

In 1805 Zebulon Pike was sent to explore the upper Mississippi River and the Minnesota wilderness. He failed to find the source of the river, but gained two parcels of land along the river by a treaty with the Dakota. The United States did not gain full control of the area until after the War of 1812, when John Jacob Astor's American Fur Company replaced the British trading companies. No permanent settlement was made until the establishment of Fort St. Anthony in 1819 by Swiss refugees from Lord Selkirk's colony, Pembina, in present-day North Dakota. Fort St. Anthony was renamed Fort Snelling in 1826. The fort was built on the land at the confluence of the Minnesota and Missouri rivers, and it served for thirty years as the center of Minnesota civilization and the major outpost in the northwest.

Treaties in 1837 with the Dakota and Ojibwa transferred large portions of Indian land to the U.S. government, thus curtailing the profitable relationship between fur traders and Indians. Lumberers, farmers, and settlers soon arrived and permanent settlements were established, including St. Anthony (later Minneapolis) and St. Paul (originally Pig's Eye) in 1838.

Statehood, the Civil War, and the Dakota War of 1862

In 1849 Minnesota Territory was established. The population boomed as further Indian treaties opened up more land for settlement and lumbering prospered. On May 11, 1858, Minnesota became the 32nd state. In its first presidential election Abraham Lincoln carried the state, and Minnesota was the first state to answer his call for troops when the Civil War broke out. More than 20,000 Minnesota men fought with the Union.

The Indians mourned the loss of their land, disliked reservation life, and were ultimately near starvation; their appeals to the U.S. Indian agencies were unsuccessful. In 1862, four young Dakota Indians murdered five whites and started a bloody uprising in which more than 300 whites and an unknown number of Indians were killed. The remaining Dakota were removed to reservations in Nebraska, and the Ojibwa were confined to the remnants of their former lands.

Business and Industry

The end of the Civil War brought about rapid development. Railroads expanded across the state, the old Sioux hunting ground became wheat lands, and flour mills sprang up, especially around Minneapolis, giving it by 1880 the nickname "Mill City." The state government and the railroads sent pamphlets to Europe to attract immigrants, and during the period 1870–90 thousands of Germans, Norwegians, and Swedes settled in the state.

In 1884 the first iron ore was shipped from the Vermilion Range, and in 1890 the ore in the great Mesabi Range was discovered, which became the major supplier for steel mills in the early 1900s. In 1889 William W. Mayo and his sons, William and Charles, established the Mayo Clinic in Rochester.

During World War I Minnesota supplied both agricultural products—wheat and other grains—and iron ore for the war effort. During the Great Depression of the 1930s, Minnesota was hit hard by unemployment, and the state did not recover until the advent of World War II, when Minnesota supplied food, lumber, and minerals to the military.

During the 1950s the iron ore industry started to slump, and the state turned to the mining of taconite, which contains iron ore in the form of iron oxide. Many taconite plants were built, but the air and water pollution caused by them became a matter of great concern. During the 1970s and 1980s pollution control standards were instituted to control the waste products from taconite processing. The state still faces the challenge of trying to develop its copper-nickel ore and its logging operations while maintaining its natural beauty. Additionally, falling farm prices have led to economic woes for many in Minnesota's rural areas.

State Boundaries

When the Minnesota Territory was established its northern, eastern, and southern boundaries were as they are at present, but on the west it extended to the Missouri River and included parts of present-day North and South Dakota. At the time of statehood, the western border was fixed at the Red River.

About 20 acres of land along the Red River near Fargo was transferred from Minnesota to North Dakota on August 25, 1961. Access to this parcel from Minnesota had become difficult after the river's channel had been moved to provide flood control.

Minnesota's Lake of the Woods County includes an area of about 124 square miles, the Northwest Angle, that is non-contiguous with the rest of the state. This area can only be reached from the rest of Minnesota by boat or by traveling through part of Canada (Manitoba or Ontario). Excepting Alaska, it is the northernmost tract of the United States, wholly above the forty-ninth parallel. The inclusion of this area in the United States resulted from the use of inaccurate maps during treaty negotiations with the British in 1783 and 1818. In 1917 the International Joint Commission, United States and Canada, described the situation as a "politico-geographical curiosity of a boundary."

Minnesota Counties

Aitkin	Dakota	Lac qui Parle	Norman	Sibley
Anoka	Dodge	Lake	Olmsted	Stearns
Becker	Douglas	Lake of the	Otter Tail	Steele
Beltrami	Faribault	Woods	Pennington	Stevens
Benton	Fillmore	Le Sueur	Pine	Swift
Big Stone	Freeborn	Lincoln	Pipestone	Todd
Blue Earth	Goodhue	Lyon	Polk	Traverse
Brown	Grant	Mahnomen	Pope	Wabasha
Carlton	Hennepin	Marshall	Ramsey	Wadena
Carver	Houston	Martin	Red Lake	Waseca
Cass	Hubbard	McLeod	Redwood	Washington
Chippewa	Isanti	Meeker	Renville	Watonwan
Chisago	Itasca	Mille Lacs	Rice	Wilkin
Clay	Jackson	Morrison	Rock	Winona
Clearwater	Kanabec	Mower	Roseau	Wright
Cook	Kandiyohi	Murray	St. Louis	Yellow Medi-
Cottonwood	Kittson	Nicollet	Scott	cine
Crow Wing	Koochiching	Nobles	Sherburne	

Multi-County Places

The following Minnesota places are in more than one county. Given here is the total population for each multi-county place, and the names of the counties it is in.

Bellechester, pop. 110; Goodhue (110), Wabasha (0)
Blaine, pop. 38,975; Anoka (38,975), Ramsey (0)
Blooming Prairie, pop. 2,043; Steele (2,043), Dodge (0)
Braham, pop. 1,139; Isanti (1,139), Kanabec (0)
Brooten, pop. 589; Stearns (589), Pope (0)
Chanhassen, pop. 11,732; Carver (11,732), Hennepin (0)
Chatfield, pop. 2,226; Fillmore (1,249), Olmsted (977)
Comfrey, pop. 433; Brown (430), Cottonwood (3)
Dayton, pop. 4,443; Hennepin (4,392), Wright (51)
Dennison, pop. 152; Goodhue (152), Rice (0)
Eden Valley, pop. 732; Meeker (417), Stearns (315)
Elysian, pop. 445; Le Sueur (443), Waseca (2)
Granite Falls, pop. 3,083; Yellow Medicine (2,346), Chippewa (737)
Hanover, pop. 787; Wright (518), Hennepin (269)
Hastings, pop. 15,445; Dakota (15,440), Washington (5)
Jasper, pop. 599; Pipestone (524), Rock (75)
Lake City, pop. 4,391; Wabasha (3,889), Goodhue (502)
Mankato, pop. 31,477; Blue Earth (31,468), Nicollet (9)
Minneiska, pop. 127; Wabasha (66), Winona (61)
Motley, pop. 441; Morrison (441), Cass (0)
New Prague, pop. 3,569; Scott (2,356), Le Sueur (1,213)
Northfield, pop. 14,684; Rice (14,514), Dakota (170)
North Mankato, pop. 10,164; Nicollet (10,164), Blue Earth (0)
Ormsby, pop. 159; Watonwan (107), Martin (52)
Ortonville, pop. 2,205; Big Stone (2,205), Lac qui Parle (0)
Osakis, pop. 1,256; Douglas (1,198), Todd (58)
Pine Island, pop. 2,125; Goodhue (2,125), Olmsted (0)
Princeton, pop. 3,719; Mille Lacs (3,717), Sherburne (2)
Rockford, pop. 2,665; Wright (2,225), Hennepin (440)

Roosevelt, pop. 180; Roseau (170), Lake of the Woods (10)
Rothsay, pop. 443; Wilkin (253), Otter Tail (190)
St. Anthony, pop. 7,727; Hennepin (5,278), Ramsey (2,449)
St. Cloud, pop. 48,812; Stearns (37,616), Benton (5,950), Sherburne (5,246)
Sartell, pop. 5,393; Stearns (3,549), Benton (1,844)
Spring Lake Park, pop. 6,532; Anoka (6,429), Ramsey (103)
Staples, pop. 2,754; Todd (2,357), Wadena (397)
Wadena, pop. 4,131; Wadena (4,109), Otter Tail (22)
White Bear Lake, pop. 24,704; Ramsey (24,288), Washington (416)

Aitkin County
County Seat: Aitkin (ZIP: 56431)

Pop: 12,425 (1990); 13,404 (1980)
Land: 1819.4 sq. mi.; **Water:** 176.0 sq. mi.
Pop Density: 6.8
Area Code: 218
In east-central MN, west of Duluth; established May 23, 1857 (prior to statehood) from Cass and Itasca counties.
Name origin: For William Alexander Aitkin (c. 1787–1851), a local fur trader.

Aitkin — City
ZIP: 56431 Lat: 46-31-48 N Long: 93-42-37 W
Pop: 1,698 (1990); 1,770 (1980) Pop Density: 1415.0
Land: 1.2 sq. mi.; Water: 0.0 sq. mi. Elev: 1217 ft.
City and township not coextensive.
Name origin: Named by and for fur trader William Aitkin (c. 1787–1851).

*Aitkin — Township
ZIP: 56431 Lat: 46-33-27 N Long: 93-45-05 W
Pop: 856 (1990); 917 (1980) Pop Density: 26.1
Land: 32.8 sq. mi.; Water: 2.3 sq. mi.

Ball Bluff — Township
ZIP: 55752 Lat: 46-58-39 N Long: 93-14-54 W
Pop: 257 (1990); 335 (1980) Pop Density: 7.6
Land: 33.9 sq. mi.; Water: 1.4 sq. mi.

Balsam — Township
ZIP: 55787 Lat: 46-48-18 N Long: 93-07-13 W
Pop: 23 (1990); 43 (1980) Pop Density: 0.6
Land: 36.1 sq. mi.; Water: 0.8 sq. mi.

Beaver — Township
ZIP: 56350 Lat: 46-28-35 N Long: 93-06-25 W
Pop: 88 (1990); 61 (1980) Pop Density: 2.5
Land: 35.3 sq. mi.; Water: 0.0 sq. mi.

Clark — Township
ZIP: 55787 Lat: 46-37-28 N Long: 93-07-56 W
Pop: 149 (1990); 148 (1980) Pop Density: 4.6
Land: 32.4 sq. mi.; Water: 0.5 sq. mi.

Cornish — Township
ZIP: 55752 Lat: 46-54-08 N Long: 93-14-53 W
Pop: 19 (1990); 27 (1980) Pop Density: 0.6
Land: 34.3 sq. mi.; Water: 1.5 sq. mi.

Davidson — Pop. Place
Lat: 46-33-25 N Long: 93-21-42 W
Pop: 54 (1990); 62 (1980) Pop Density: 1.7
Land: 31.8 sq. mi.; Water: 5.6 sq. mi.

Farm Island — Township
ZIP: 56431 Lat: 46-27-52 N Long: 93-45-03 W
Pop: 692 (1990); 613 (1980) Pop Density: 24.7
Land: 28.0 sq. mi.; Water: 7.6 sq. mi.

Fleming — Township
Lat: 46-38-17 N Long: 93-30-39 W
Pop: 283 (1990); 289 (1980) Pop Density: 8.4
Land: 33.5 sq. mi.; Water: 2.6 sq. mi.

Glen — Township
ZIP: 56431 Lat: 46-27-13 N Long: 93-29-31 W
Pop: 295 (1990); 343 (1980) Pop Density: 8.7
Land: 33.8 sq. mi.; Water: 2.8 sq. mi.

Haugen — Township
ZIP: 55787 Lat: 46-43-42 N Long: 93-08-23 W
Pop: 145 (1990); 150 (1980) Pop Density: 4.1
Land: 35.7 sq. mi.; Water: 0.6 sq. mi.

Hazelton — Township
ZIP: 56431 Lat: 46-20-12 N Long: 93-45-17 W
Pop: 440 (1990); 467 (1980) Pop Density: 15.7
Land: 28.1 sq. mi.; Water: 42.7 sq. mi.

Hill City — City
ZIP: 55748 Lat: 46-59-09 N Long: 93-35-47 W
Pop: 469 (1990); 533 (1980) Pop Density: 426.4
Land: 1.1 sq. mi.; Water: 0.2 sq. mi. Elev: 1357 ft.
Name origin: For the glacial moraine, which dominates the immediate vicinity.

Hill Lake — Township
Lat: 46-59-17 N Long: 93-37-55 W
Pop: 377 (1990); 429 (1980) Pop Density: 11.3
Land: 33.4 sq. mi.; Water: 1.2 sq. mi.

Idun — Township
ZIP: 56350 Lat: 46-12-30 N Long: 93-22-03 W
Pop: 182 (1990); 202 (1980) Pop Density: 5.0
Land: 36.6 sq. mi.; Water: 0.6 sq. mi.

Jevne — Township
ZIP: 55760 Lat: 46-38-28 N Long: 93-22-30 W
Pop: 290 (1990); 261 (1980) Pop Density: 8.5
Land: 34.1 sq. mi.; Water: 1.7 sq. mi.

Jewett — Pop. Place
Lat: 46-22-33 N Long: 93-22-23 W
Pop: 24 (1990); 22 (1980) Pop Density: 0.7
Land: 35.2 sq. mi.; Water: 0.1 sq. mi.

Kimberly — Township
ZIP: 56431 Lat: 46-33-15 N Long: 93-29-43 W
Pop: 185 (1990); 220 (1980) Pop Density: 5.2
Land: 35.9 sq. mi.; Water: 1.1 sq. mi.

Lakeside — Township
ZIP: 56431 Lat: 46-17-35 N Long: 93-29-41 W
Pop: 337 (1990); 320 (1980) Pop Density: 11.6
Land: 29.1 sq. mi.; Water: 7.8 sq. mi.

Lee — Township
ZIP: 56431 Lat: 46-28-21 N Long: 93-21-35 W
Pop: 40 (1990); 60 (1980) Pop Density: 1.2
Land: 34.5 sq. mi.; Water: 1.2 sq. mi.

Libby — Township
ZIP: 56469 Lat: 46-48-42 N Long: 93-23-35 W
Pop: 22 (1990); 64 (1980) Pop Density: 0.6
Land: 34.7 sq. mi.; Water: 1.4 sq. mi.

MINNESOTA, Aitkin County

Logan
Township
ZIP: 56469   **Lat:** 46-43-27 N   **Long:** 93-30-32 W
Pop: 210 (1990); 246 (1980)   **Pop Density:** 5.9
Land: 35.3 sq. mi.; **Water:** 0.6 sq. mi.

Macville
Township
Lat: 46-54-04 N   **Long:** 93-38-05 W
Pop: 184 (1990); 242 (1980)   **Pop Density:** 5.1
Land: 36.2 sq. mi.; **Water:** 0.3 sq. mi.

Malmo
Township
ZIP: 56431   **Lat:** 46-23-25 N   **Long:** 93-30-34 W
Pop: 214 (1990); 218 (1980)   **Pop Density:** 6.5
Land: 33.0 sq. mi.; **Water:** 2.7 sq. mi.

McGrath
City
ZIP: 56350   **Lat:** 46-14-34 N   **Long:** 93-16-27 W
Pop: 62 (1990); 81 (1980)   **Pop Density:** 155.0
Land: 0.4 sq. mi.; **Water:** 0.0 sq. mi.

McGregor
City
Lat: 46-36-29 N   **Long:** 93-18-21 W
Pop: 376 (1990); 447 (1980)   **Pop Density:** 188.0
Land: 2.0 sq. mi.; **Water:** 0.1 sq. mi.   **Elev:** 1233 ft.
City and township not coextensive.

*McGregor
Township
Lat: 46-37-59 N   **Long:** 93-15-01 W
Pop: 121 (1990); 106 (1980)   **Pop Density:** 3.7
Land: 32.7 sq. mi.; **Water:** 1.5 sq. mi.

Millward
Township
Lat: 46-22-33 N   **Long:** 93-08-11 W
Pop: 41 (1990)   **Pop Density:** 1.2
Land: 35.5 sq. mi.; **Water:** 0.0 sq. mi.

Morrison
Township
ZIP: 56469   **Lat:** 46-38-20 N   **Long:** 93-37-47 W
Pop: 159 (1990); 210 (1980)   **Pop Density:** 4.4
Land: 36.0 sq. mi.; **Water:** 0.7 sq. mi.

Nordland
Township
ZIP: 56431   **Lat:** 46-27-40 N   **Long:** 93-37-14 W
Pop: 622 (1990); 642 (1980)   **Pop Density:** 19.9
Land: 31.3 sq. mi.; **Water:** 5.4 sq. mi.

Northeast Aitkin
Pop. Place
Lat: 46-56-48 N   **Long:** 93-08-11 W
Pop: 15 (1990); 14 (1980)   **Pop Density:** 0.2
Land: 74.2 sq. mi.; **Water:** 0.1 sq. mi.

Northwest Aitkin
Pop. Place
Lat: 46-50-28 N   **Long:** 93-36-11 W
Pop: 266 (1990); 335 (1980)   **Pop Density:** 0.9
Land: 287.7 sq. mi.; **Water:** 5.4 sq. mi.

Palisade
City
ZIP: 56469   **Lat:** 46-42-47 N   **Long:** 93-29-26 W
Pop: 144 (1990); 155 (1980)   **Pop Density:** 480.0
Land: 0.3 sq. mi.; **Water:** 0.0 sq. mi.
Name origin: For a geological feature.

Pliny
Township
ZIP: 56350   **Lat:** 46-16-32 N   **Long:** 93-14-17 W
Pop: 117 (1990); 124 (1980)   **Pop Density:** 3.2
Land: 36.4 sq. mi.; **Water:** 0.0 sq. mi.

Rice River
Township
ZIP: 55760   **Lat:** 46-28-08 N   **Long:** 93-13-50 W
Pop: 130 (1990); 151 (1980)   **Pop Density:** 3.6
Land: 36.1 sq. mi.; **Water:** 0.0 sq. mi.

Salo
Township
ZIP: 55760   **Lat:** 46-33-44 N   **Long:** 93-06-27 W
Pop: 101 (1990); 126 (1980)   **Pop Density:** 2.8
Land: 35.5 sq. mi.; **Water:** 0.1 sq. mi.

Seavey
Township
ZIP: 56350   **Lat:** 46-18-15 N   **Long:** 93-22-05 W
Pop: 64 (1990); 70 (1980)   **Pop Density:** 1.8
Land: 36.3 sq. mi.; **Water:** 0.1 sq. mi.

Shamrock
Township
ZIP: 55760   **Lat:** 46-43-22 N   **Long:** 93-15-12 W
Pop: 793 (1990); 820 (1980)   **Pop Density:** 32.4
Land: 24.5 sq. mi.; **Water:** 11.1 sq. mi.

Southeast Aitkin
Pop. Place
Lat: 46-17-19 N   **Long:** 93-06-20 W
Pop: 0 (1990); 53 (1980)
Land: 35.9 sq. mi.; **Water:** 0.0 sq. mi.

Spalding
Township
ZIP: 55760   **Lat:** 46-32-55 N   **Long:** 93-14-00 W
Pop: 183 (1990); 216 (1980)   **Pop Density:** 5.0
Land: 36.8 sq. mi.; **Water:** 0.4 sq. mi.

Spencer
Township
Lat: 46-33-08 N   **Long:** 93-37-43 W
Pop: 479 (1990); 458 (1980)   **Pop Density:** 12.9
Land: 37.0 sq. mi.; **Water:** 0.8 sq. mi.

Tamarack
City
ZIP: 55787   **Lat:** 46-39-06 N   **Long:** 93-07-08 W
Pop: 53 (1990); 83 (1980)   **Pop Density:** 18.3
Land: 2.9 sq. mi.; **Water:** 0.0 sq. mi.   **Elev:** 1269 ft.

Turner
Township
ZIP: 55760   **Lat:** 46-48-21 N   **Long:** 93-15-04 W
Pop: 164 (1990); 122 (1980)   **Pop Density:** 5.5
Land: 29.8 sq. mi.; **Water:** 6.0 sq. mi.

Verdon
Township
ZIP: 56469   **Lat:** 46-54-01 N   **Long:** 93-22-32 W
Pop: 36 (1990); 54 (1980)   **Pop Density:** 1.0
Land: 35.7 sq. mi.; **Water:** 0.5 sq. mi.

Wagner
Township
Lat: 46-12-09 N   **Long:** 93-06-59 W
Pop: 276 (1990); 300 (1980)   **Pop Density:** 7.9
Land: 35.0 sq. mi.; **Water:** 0.8 sq. mi.

Waukenabo
Township
ZIP: 56469   **Lat:** 46-43-51 N   **Long:** 93-37-59 W
Pop: 229 (1990); 272 (1980)   **Pop Density:** 7.0
Land: 32.9 sq. mi.; **Water:** 3.2 sq. mi.

Wealthwood
Township
ZIP: 56431   **Lat:** 46-21-59 N   **Long:** 93-37-09 W
Pop: 163 (1990); 196 (1980)   **Pop Density:** 7.0
Land: 23.2 sq. mi.; **Water:** 49.4 sq. mi.

White Pine
Township
ZIP: 56350   **Lat:** 46-22-26 N   **Long:** 93-14-59 W
Pop: 43 (1990); 49 (1980)   **Pop Density:** 1.2
Land: 36.6 sq. mi.; **Water:** 0.0 sq. mi.

Williams
Township
Lat: 46-12-08 N   **Long:** 93-13-59 W
Pop: 124 (1990); 126 (1980)   **Pop Density:** 3.5
Land: 35.9 sq. mi.; **Water:** 0.0 sq. mi.

Workman Township
ZIP: 56469　　Lat: 46-43-54 N　Long: 93-22-23 W
Pop: 131 (1990); 152 (1980)　　Pop Density: 4.0
Land: 32.8 sq. mi.; Water: 2.9 sq. mi.

Anoka County
County Seat: Anoka (ZIP: 55303)

Pop: 243,641 (1990); 195,998 (1980)　　Pop Density: 574.6
Land: 424.0 sq. mi.; Water: 22.3 sq. mi.　　Area Code: 612

In east-central MN, north of Minneapolis; established May 23, 1857 (prior to statehood) from Hennepin County; annexed Manomin County in 1869.

Name origin: For the town of the same name; from Siouan 'the other side' or 'both sides': the town is on both sides of the Rum River.

Andover City
ZIP: 55304　　Lat: 45-15-27 N　Long: 93-19-52 W
Pop: 15,216 (1990); 9,387 (1980)　　Pop Density: 446.2
Land: 34.1 sq. mi.; Water: 0.9 sq. mi.　　Elev: 891 ft.
Name origin: For Andover, MA.

Anoka City
ZIP: 55303　　Lat: 45-12-37 N　Long: 93-23-24 W
Pop: 17,192 (1990); 15,634 (1980)　　Pop Density: 2604.8
Land: 6.6 sq. mi.; Water: 0.5 sq. mi.
In eastern MN on the Mississippi River, 17 mi. northwest of Minneapolis.
Name origin: From the Sioux term probably meaning 'the other side,' or 'both sides': the town is on both sides of the Rum River.

Bethel City
ZIP: 55005　　Lat: 45-24-02 N　Long: 93-16-09 W
Pop: 394 (1990); 272 (1980)　　Pop Density: 437.8
Land: 0.9 sq. mi.; Water: 0.1 sq. mi.
Name origin: For early settler Moses Twitchell's hometown of Bethel, ME.

Blaine City
ZIP: 55014　　Lat: 45-09-58 N　Long: 93-12-30 W
Pop: 38,975 (1990); 28,558 (1980)　　Pop Density: 1153.1
Land: 33.8 sq. mi.; Water: 0.1 sq. mi.
In eastern MN, northwest of Minneapolis. Founded 1862. Part of the town is also in Ramsey County.
Name origin: For James Blaine, prominent Republican senator from ME and presidential candidate.

Burns Township
　　Lat: 45-20-15 N　Long: 93-26-52 W
Pop: 2,401 (1990); 1,976 (1980)　　Pop Density: 71.0
Land: 33.8 sq. mi.; Water: 1.4 sq. mi.

Centerville City
　　Lat: 45-09-53 N　Long: 93-03-10 W
Pop: 1,633 (1990); 734 (1980)　　Pop Density: 742.3
Land: 2.2 sq. mi.; Water: 0.3 sq. mi.

Circle Pines City
ZIP: 55014　　Lat: 45-08-18 N　Long: 93-09-08 W
Pop: 4,704 (1990); 3,321 (1980)　　Pop Density: 2613.3
Land: 1.8 sq. mi.; Water: 0.2 sq. mi.

Columbia Heights City
ZIP: 55421　　Lat: 45-02-56 N　Long: 93-14-47 W
Pop: 18,910 (1990); 20,029 (1980)　　Pop Density: 5561.8
Land: 3.4 sq. mi.; Water: 0.1 sq. mi.
In eastern MN on the Mississippi River, 5 mi. north of Minneapolis.
Name origin: Euphoniously named by early settler Thomas Lowry.

Columbus Township
ZIP: 55011　　Lat: 45-15-58 N　Long: 93-04-29 W
Pop: 3,690 (1990); 3,232 (1980)　　Pop Density: 82.2
Land: 44.9 sq. mi.; Water: 2.9 sq. mi.

Coon Rapids City
ZIP: 55433　　Lat: 45-10-26 N　Long: 93-18-39 W
Pop: 52,978 (1990); 35,826 (1980)　　Pop Density: 2323.6
Land: 22.8 sq. mi.; Water: 0.7 sq. mi.
In southeastern MN, a northern suburb of Minneapolis.
Name origin: For its descriptive connotations.

East Bethel City
ZIP: 55005　　Lat: 45-20-38 N　Long: 93-12-05 W
Pop: 8,050 (1990); 6,626 (1980)　　Pop Density: 179.3
Land: 44.9 sq. mi.; Water: 3.2 sq. mi.
Name origin: Named by early settler, Moses Twitchell, for his former home in Bethel, ME.

Fridley City
ZIP: 55432　　Lat: 45-05-05 N　Long: 93-15-32 W
Pop: 28,335 (1990); 30,228 (1980)　　Pop Density: 2805.4
Land: 10.1 sq. mi.; Water: 0.7 sq. mi.
In eastern MN, a northern suburb of Minneapolis.
Name origin: For Abram Fridley, who was a prosperous farmer and member of the state legislature.

Ham Lake City
ZIP: 55304　　Lat: 45-15-35 N　Long: 93-12-02 W
Pop: 8,924 (1990); 7,832 (1980)　　Pop Density: 259.4
Land: 34.4 sq. mi.; Water: 1.3 sq. mi.　　Elev: 911 ft.

Hilltop City
　　Lat: 45-03-12 N　Long: 93-14-55 W
Pop: 749 (1990); 817 (1980)　　Pop Density: 7490.0
Land: 0.1 sq. mi.; Water: 0.0 sq. mi.

Lexington City
ZIP: 55014　　Lat: 45-08-19 N　Long: 93-10-15 W
Pop: 2,279 (1990); 2,150 (1980)　　Pop Density: 3255.7
Land: 0.7 sq. mi.; Water: 0.0 sq. mi.

MINNESOTA, Anoka County

Lino Lakes — City
ZIP: 55014 Lat: 45-09-42 N Long: 93-04-57 W
Pop: 8,807 (1990); 4,966 (1980) Pop Density: 311.2
Land: 28.3 sq. mi.; Water: 4.9 sq. mi.

Linwood — Township
ZIP: 55005 Lat: 45-22-21 N Long: 93-04-48 W
Pop: 3,588 (1990); 2,839 (1980) Pop Density: 107.4
Land: 33.4 sq. mi.; Water: 2.5 sq. mi.

Oak Grove — Township
ZIP: 55011 Lat: 45-20-41 N Long: 93-19-35 W
Pop: 5,441 (1990); 3,926 (1980) Pop Density: 161.5
Land: 33.7 sq. mi.; Water: 1.3 sq. mi.

Ramsey — City
ZIP: 55303 Lat: 45-15-48 N Long: 93-26-51 W
Pop: 12,408 (1990); 10,093 (1980) Pop Density: 430.8
Land: 28.8 sq. mi.; Water: 1.0 sq. mi.

Name origin: For Alexander Ramsey, the first governor of the MN territory, 1849–53.

St. Francis — City
Lat: 45-23-59 N Long: 93-23-22 W
Pop: 2,538 (1990); 1,184 (1980) Pop Density: 108.0
Land: 23.5 sq. mi.; Water: 0.2 sq. mi. Elev: 918 ft.

Name origin: For St. Francis of Assisi (1181?–1226), who founded the Franciscan order.

Spring Lake Park — City
ZIP: 55432 Lat: 45-06-57 N Long: 93-14-46 W
Pop: 6,429 (1990); 6,368 (1980) Pop Density: 3383.7
Land: 1.9 sq. mi.; Water: 0.1 sq. mi.

Part of the town is also in Ramsey County.

Becker County
County Seat: Detroit Lakes (ZIP: 56501)

Pop: 27,881 (1990); 29,336 (1980) Pop Density: 21.3
Land: 1310.5 sq. mi.; Water: 134.7 sq. mi. Area Code: 218

In west-central MN, east of Fargo, ND; established Mar 18, 1858 from Indian lands.

Name origin: For Gen. George Loomis Becker (1829–1904), lawyer, MN legislator, and land commissioner of the St. Paul and Pacific Railroad.

Atlanta — Township
Lat: 47-01-18 N Long: 96-07-37 W
Pop: 141 (1990); 162 (1980) Pop Density: 4.0
Land: 35.6 sq. mi.; Water: 0.5 sq. mi.

Audubon — City
ZIP: 56511 Lat: 46-51-51 N Long: 95-58-51 W
Pop: 411 (1990); 383 (1980) Pop Density: 822.0
Land: 0.5 sq. mi.; Water: 0.0 sq. mi.

City and township not coextensive.

Name origin: For ornithologist and artist John Audubon (1785–1851).

*Audubon — Township
ZIP: 56511 Lat: 46-51-09 N Long: 95-59-07 W
Pop: 420 (1990); 453 (1980) Pop Density: 13.0
Land: 32.4 sq. mi.; Water: 3.0 sq. mi.

Burlington — Township
Lat: 46-45-49 N Long: 95-43-59 W
Pop: 1,146 (1990); 1,149 (1980) Pop Density: 34.3
Land: 33.4 sq. mi.; Water: 2.2 sq. mi.

Callaway — City
ZIP: 56521 Lat: 46-58-58 N Long: 95-54-40 W
Pop: 212 (1990); 238 (1980) Pop Density: 353.3
Land: 0.6 sq. mi.; Water: 0.0 sq. mi. Elev: 1370 ft.

City and township not coextensive.

Name origin: For William Callaway, general agent for the Soo Railway in 1906.

*Callaway — Township
ZIP: 56521 Lat: 47-01-30 N Long: 95-51-46 W
Pop: 305 (1990); 355 (1980) Pop Density: 9.0
Land: 33.9 sq. mi.; Water: 1.4 sq. mi.

Carsonville — Township
Lat: 46-55-59 N Long: 95-21-28 W
Pop: 227 (1990); 292 (1980) Pop Density: 6.5
Land: 35.1 sq. mi.; Water: 0.7 sq. mi.

Cormorant — Township
Lat: 46-45-49 N Long: 96-06-40 W
Pop: 738 (1990); 688 (1980) Pop Density: 28.1
Land: 26.3 sq. mi.; Water: 9.9 sq. mi.

Cuba — Township
Lat: 46-56-03 N Long: 96-06-33 W
Pop: 238 (1990); 273 (1980) Pop Density: 7.0
Land: 34.2 sq. mi.; Water: 1.4 sq. mi.

Detroit — Township
Lat: 46-51-07 N Long: 95-51-49 W
Pop: 2,348 (1990); 2,472 (1980) Pop Density: 83.9
Land: 28.0 sq. mi.; Water: 4.9 sq. mi.

Detroit Lakes — City
ZIP: 56501 Lat: 46-48-47 N Long: 95-50-31 W
Pop: 6,635 (1990); 7,106 (1980) Pop Density: 1618.3
Land: 4.1 sq. mi.; Water: 0.0 sq. mi.

Name origin: Named by an early French explorer who noticed that a long sand bar bifurcated part of Detroit Lake and created a strait, *detroit* in French.

Eagle View — Township
Lat: 47-06-25 N Long: 95-36-15 W
Pop: 128 (1990) Pop Density: 4.1
Land: 31.3 sq. mi.; Water: 4.9 sq. mi.

MINNESOTA, Becker County

Erie — Township
Lat: 46-50-49 N Long: 95-44-05 W
Pop: 1,496 (1990); 1,290 (1980) Pop Density: 46.6
Land: 32.1 sq. mi.; Water: 4.3 sq. mi.

Evergreen — Township
Lat: 46-45-46 N Long: 95-28-12 W
Pop: 298 (1990); 348 (1980) Pop Density: 8.2
Land: 36.2 sq. mi.; Water: 0.1 sq. mi.

Forest — Township
Lat: 47-06-40 N Long: 95-21-26 W
Pop: 54 (1990); 53 (1980) Pop Density: 1.7
Land: 32.4 sq. mi.; Water: 3.6 sq. mi.

Frazee — City
ZIP: 56544 Lat: 46-43-37 N Long: 95-41-58 W
Pop: 1,176 (1990); 1,284 (1980) Pop Density: 1470.0
Land: 0.8 sq. mi.; Water: 0.1 sq. mi.
Name origin: For Randoph Frazee, who served in the MN state legislature in 1875 and ran a local lumber mill.

Green Valley — Township
Lat: 46-50-47 N Long: 95-13-16 W
Pop: 318 (1990); 312 (1980) Pop Density: 9.0
Land: 35.4 sq. mi.; Water: 0.5 sq. mi.

Hamden — Township
Lat: 46-55-58 N Long: 95-58-59 W
Pop: 252 (1990); 274 (1980) Pop Density: 7.4
Land: 34.0 sq. mi.; Water: 1.5 sq. mi.

Height of Land — Township
Lat: 46-53-32 N Long: 95-36-36 W
Pop: 688 (1990); 681 (1980) Pop Density: 11.9
Land: 58.0 sq. mi.; Water: 13.5 sq. mi.

Holmesville — Township
Lat: 46-56-06 N Long: 95-43-40 W
Pop: 393 (1990); 460 (1980) Pop Density: 14.0
Land: 28.1 sq. mi.; Water: 8.1 sq. mi.

Lake Eunice — Township
Lat: 46-45-45 N Long: 95-59-12 W
Pop: 955 (1990); 1,021 (1980) Pop Density: 31.8
Land: 30.0 sq. mi.; Water: 6.0 sq. mi.

Lake Park — City
ZIP: 56554 Lat: 46-53-00 N Long: 96-05-47 W
Pop: 638 (1990); 716 (1980) Pop Density: 638.0
Land: 1.0 sq. mi.; Water: 0.0 sq. mi.
City and village not coextensive. Founded 1841.
Name origin: From an Indian collective term for the many local lakes meaning 'the lakes with the beautiful parks.'

***Lake Park** — Township
ZIP: 56554 Lat: 46-50-23 N Long: 96-06-41 W
Pop: 432 (1990); 500 (1980) Pop Density: 14.1
Land: 30.7 sq. mi.; Water: 4.3 sq. mi.

Lake View — Township
Lat: 46-45-22 N Long: 95-51-30 W
Pop: 1,949 (1990); 1,915 (1980) Pop Density: 84.7
Land: 23.0 sq. mi.; Water: 12.6 sq. mi.

Maple Grove — Township
Lat: 47-06-14 N Long: 95-44-52 W
Pop: 330 (1990); 425 (1980) Pop Density: 11.9
Land: 27.7 sq. mi.; Water: 8.0 sq. mi.

Ogema — City
ZIP: 56569 Lat: 47-06-05 N Long: 95-55-20 W
Pop: 164 (1990); 215 (1980) Pop Density: 136.7
Land: 1.2 sq. mi.; Water: 0.1 sq. mi.
Name origin: From an Ojibway Indian term meaning 'chief.'

Osage — Township
ZIP: 56570 Lat: 46-56-01 N Long: 95-13-24 W
Pop: 626 (1990); 583 (1980) Pop Density: 17.9
Land: 34.9 sq. mi.; Water: 0.9 sq. mi.

Pine Point — Township
Lat: 47-00-49 N Long: 95-20-57 W
Pop: 405 (1990); 446 (1980) Pop Density: 11.8
Land: 34.4 sq. mi.; Water: 1.4 sq. mi. Elev: 1538 ft.

Riceville — Township
Lat: 47-01-18 N Long: 95-59-50 W
Pop: 103 (1990); 143 (1980) Pop Density: 2.8
Land: 37.0 sq. mi.; Water: 0.5 sq. mi.

Richwood — Township
Lat: 46-56-06 N Long: 95-51-49 W
Pop: 594 (1990); 596 (1980) Pop Density: 17.4
Land: 34.1 sq. mi.; Water: 1.9 sq. mi.

Round Lake — Township
Lat: 47-04-14 N Long: 95-29-02 W
Pop: 116 (1990); 169 (1980) Pop Density: 1.8
Land: 64.1 sq. mi.; Water: 8.5 sq. mi.

Runeberg — Township
Lat: 46-45-47 N Long: 95-13-47 W
Pop: 372 (1990); 392 (1980) Pop Density: 10.4
Land: 35.7 sq. mi.; Water: 0.0 sq. mi.

Savannah — Township
Lat: 47-06-35 N Long: 95-14-05 W
Pop: 150 (1990); 121 (1980) Pop Density: 4.4
Land: 34.3 sq. mi.; Water: 2.2 sq. mi.

Shell Lake — Township
Lat: 46-56-24 N Long: 95-29-07 W
Pop: 299 (1990); 300 (1980) Pop Density: 10.5
Land: 28.5 sq. mi.; Water: 7.4 sq. mi.

Silver Leaf — Township
Lat: 46-45-35 N Long: 95-36-09 W
Pop: 459 (1990); 541 (1980) Pop Density: 13.1
Land: 35.0 sq. mi.; Water: 1.2 sq. mi.

Spring Creek — Township
Lat: 47-06-08 N Long: 96-00-01 W
Pop: 135 (1990); 161 (1980) Pop Density: 3.6
Land: 37.2 sq. mi.; Water: 0.6 sq. mi.

Spruce Grove — Township
Lat: 46-45-47 N Long: 95-20-31 W
Pop: 369 (1990); 454 (1980) Pop Density: 10.4
Land: 35.6 sq. mi.; Water: 0.1 sq. mi.

Sugar Bush — Township
Lat: 47-01-04 N Long: 95-40-55 W
Pop: 440 (1990); 392 (1980) Pop Density: 6.7
Land: 65.3 sq. mi.; Water: 7.3 sq. mi.

Toad Lake — Township
Lat: 46-51-04 N Long: 95-28-55 W
Pop: 381 (1990); 500 (1980) Pop Density: 11.7
Land: 32.6 sq. mi.; Water: 3.7 sq. mi.

MINNESOTA, Becker County

Two Inlets
Township
Lat: 47-00-25 N **Long:** 95-14-04 W
Pop: 236 (1990); 219 (1980) **Pop Density:** 6.9
Land: 34.1 sq. mi.; **Water:** 1.9 sq. mi.

Walworth
Township
Lat: 47-06-32 N **Long:** 96-07-48 W
Pop: 132 (1990); 195 (1980) **Pop Density:** 3.7
Land: 36.1 sq. mi.; **Water:** 0.1 sq. mi.

White Earth
Township
Lat: 47-06-19 N **Long:** 95-52-38 W
Pop: 698 (1990); 668 (1980) **Pop Density:** 21.6
Land: 32.3 sq. mi.; **Water:** 2.6 sq. mi.

Wolf Lake
City
ZIP: 56593 **Lat:** 46-48-10 N **Long:** 95-21-18 W
Pop: 35 (1990); 67 (1980) **Pop Density:** 350.0
Land: 0.1 sq. mi.; **Water:** 0.0 sq. mi.
Name origin: Named by early settlers for the nearby large lake.

*Wolf Lake
Township
Lat: 46-50-21 N **Long:** 95-21-38 W
Pop: 239 (1990); 324 (1980) **Pop Density:** 7.2
Land: 33.1 sq. mi.; **Water:** 2.8 sq. mi.

Beltrami County
County Seat: Bemidji (ZIP: 56601)

Pop: 34,384 (1990); 30,982 (1980) **Pop Density:** 13.7
Land: 2505.4 sq. mi.; **Water:** 550.3 sq. mi. **Area Code:** 218

In north-central MN, east of Grand Forks, ND; established Feb 28, 1866 from unorganized territory.

Name origin: For Giacomo Constantino Beltrami (1779–1855), an Italian who, under the anglicized name James Constantine, explored the sources of the Mississippi River and wrote *A Pilgrimage in Europe and America, Leading to the Discovery of the Sources of the Mississippi and Bloody River.*

Alaska
Township
ZIP: 56667 **Lat:** 47-47-10 N **Long:** 95-04-00 W
Pop: 256 (1990); 171 (1980) **Pop Density:** 8.0
Land: 32.2 sq. mi.; **Water:** 3.2 sq. mi.

Battle
Township
ZIP: 56674 **Lat:** 47-58-40 N **Long:** 94-41-51 W
Pop: 53 (1990); 67 (1980) **Pop Density:** 3.9
Land: 13.7 sq. mi.; **Water:** 0.0 sq. mi.

Bemidji
City
ZIP: 56601 **Lat:** 47-28-56 N **Long:** 94-52-42 W
Pop: 11,245 (1990); 10,949 (1980) **Pop Density:** 1013.1
Land: 11.1 sq. mi.; **Water:** 1.2 sq. mi.

In northern MN, 28 mi. south of Lower Red Lake.
Name origin: For the Ojibway chief.

*Bemidji
Township
Lat: 47-26-32 N **Long:** 94-51-41 W
Pop: 2,660 (1990); 2,270 (1980) **Pop Density:** 124.3
Land: 21.4 sq. mi.; **Water:** 4.5 sq. mi.

Benville
Township
Lat: 48-18-53 N **Long:** 95-31-27 W
Pop: 98 (1990); 150 (1980) **Pop Density:** 2.8
Land: 34.5 sq. mi.; **Water:** 0.0 sq. mi.

Birch
Township
ZIP: 56630 **Lat:** 47-37-39 N **Long:** 94-28-39 W
Pop: 85 (1990); 71 (1980) **Pop Density:** 2.5
Land: 34.1 sq. mi.; **Water:** 2.0 sq. mi.

Blackduck
City
ZIP: 56630 **Lat:** 47-43-35 N **Long:** 94-32-53 W
Pop: 718 (1990); 653 (1980) **Pop Density:** 478.7
Land: 1.5 sq. mi.; **Water:** 0.0 sq. mi. **Elev:** 1383 ft.
Name origin: For nearby Black Duck Lake, which was named for the common ring-necked duck.

Brook Lake
Pop. Place
Lat: 47-27-21 N **Long:** 94-28-39 W
Pop: 176 (1990); 183 (1980) **Pop Density:** 7.0
Land: 25.3 sq. mi.; **Water:** 11.0 sq. mi.

Buzzle
Township
Lat: 47-37-42 N **Long:** 95-06-49 W
Pop: 277 (1990); 213 (1980) **Pop Density:** 7.9
Land: 34.9 sq. mi.; **Water:** 1.3 sq. mi.

Cormant
Township
ZIP: 56630 **Lat:** 47-52-39 N **Long:** 94-36-36 W
Pop: 199 (1990); 220 (1980) **Pop Density:** 5.5
Land: 36.4 sq. mi.; **Water:** 0.0 sq. mi.

Durand
Township
ZIP: 56667 **Lat:** 47-41-32 N **Long:** 94-52-52 W
Pop: 135 (1990); 158 (1980) **Pop Density:** 8.9
Land: 15.1 sq. mi.; **Water:** 3.2 sq. mi.

Eckles
Township
Lat: 47-32-44 N **Long:** 95-00-09 W
Pop: 805 (1990); 607 (1980) **Pop Density:** 25.4
Land: 31.7 sq. mi.; **Water:** 0.6 sq. mi.

Frohn
Township
Lat: 47-27-20 N **Long:** 94-44-06 W
Pop: 1,151 (1990); 918 (1980) **Pop Density:** 35.4
Land: 32.5 sq. mi.; **Water:** 3.9 sq. mi.

Funkley
City
ZIP: 56630 **Lat:** 47-47-11 N **Long:** 94-25-38 W
Pop: 15 (1990); 18 (1980) **Pop Density:** 37.5
Land: 0.4 sq. mi.; **Water:** 0.0 sq. mi.

Grant Valley
Township
Lat: 47-27-02 N **Long:** 94-59-21 W
Pop: 1,040 (1990); 868 (1980) **Pop Density:** 30.5
Land: 34.1 sq. mi.; **Water:** 1.8 sq. mi.

MINNESOTA, Beltrami County

Hagali   Township
ZIP: 56647   **Lat:** 47-43-36 N   **Long:** 94-44-11 W
Pop: 255 (1990); 256 (1980)   **Pop Density:** 7.7
Land: 33.3 sq. mi.; **Water:** 3.1 sq. mi.

Hamre   Township
Lat: 48-14-16 N   **Long:** 95-24-39 W
Pop: 27 (1990); 31 (1980)   **Pop Density:** 0.8
Land: 35.9 sq. mi.; **Water:** 0.0 sq. mi.

Hines   Township
ZIP: 56647   **Lat:** 47-42-19 N   **Long:** 94-36-46 W
Pop: 556 (1990); 575 (1980)   **Pop Density:** 18.2
Land: 30.5 sq. mi.; **Water:** 4.7 sq. mi.

Hornet   Township
ZIP: 56630   **Lat:** 47-49-00 N   **Long:** 94-29-50 W
Pop: 225 (1990); 219 (1980)   **Pop Density:** 6.3
Land: 35.8 sq. mi.; **Water:** 0.0 sq. mi.

Jones   Township
Lat: 47-27-35 N   **Long:** 95-07-38 W
Pop: 230 (1990); 219 (1980)   **Pop Density:** 6.5
Land: 35.4 sq. mi.; **Water:** 0.6 sq. mi.

Kelliher   City
ZIP: 56650   **Lat:** 47-56-34 N   **Long:** 94-26-45 W
Pop: 348 (1990); 324 (1980)   **Pop Density:** 174.0
Land: 2.0 sq. mi.; **Water:** 0.1 sq. mi.   **Elev:** 1361 ft.
City and township not coextensive.
Name origin: For lumber agent A. O. Kelliher.

*Kelliher   Township
ZIP: 56650   **Lat:** 47-58-19 N   **Long:** 94-28-07 W
Pop: 100 (1990); 160 (1980)   **Pop Density:** 3.0
Land: 33.6 sq. mi.; **Water:** 0.0 sq. mi.

Lammers   Township
ZIP: 56678   **Lat:** 47-32-33 N   **Long:** 95-06-34 W
Pop: 390 (1990); 386 (1980)   **Pop Density:** 11.2
Land: 34.8 sq. mi.; **Water:** 0.3 sq. mi.

Langor   Township
ZIP: 56630   **Lat:** 47-48-46 N   **Long:** 94-36-43 W
Pop: 186 (1990); 182 (1980)   **Pop Density:** 5.1
Land: 36.2 sq. mi.; **Water:** 0.0 sq. mi.

Lee   Township
Lat: 48-14-43 N   **Long:** 95-31-05 W
Pop: 50 (1990); 54 (1980)   **Pop Density:** 1.4
Land: 36.2 sq. mi.; **Water:** 0.2 sq. mi.

Liberty   Township
ZIP: 56667   **Lat:** 47-38-08 N   **Long:** 95-00-12 W
Pop: 473 (1990); 342 (1980)   **Pop Density:** 14.4
Land: 32.9 sq. mi.; **Water:** 3.4 sq. mi.

Little Rock   CDP
Lat: 47-52-04 N   **Long:** 95-06-37 W
Pop: 714 (1990)   **Pop Density:** 54.9
Land: 13.0 sq. mi.; **Water:** 0.7 sq. mi.

Lower Red Lake   Pop. Place
Lat: 47-55-08 N   **Long:** 94-59-26 W
Pop: 3,621 (1990); 2,855 (1980)   **Pop Density:** 25.6
Land: 141.2 sq. mi.; **Water:** 279.6 sq. mi.

Maple Ridge   Township
ZIP: 56667   **Lat:** 47-43-22 N   **Long:** 95-00-09 W
Pop: 95 (1990); 117 (1980)   **Pop Density:** 2.4
Land: 39.9 sq. mi.; **Water:** 2.5 sq. mi.

Minnie   Township
Lat: 48-19-00 N   **Long:** 95-16-56 W
Pop: 9 (1990); 15 (1980)   **Pop Density:** 0.3
Land: 34.9 sq. mi.; **Water:** 0.0 sq. mi.

Moose Lake   Township
Lat: 47-32-27 N   **Long:** 94-28-38 W
Pop: 166 (1990); 167 (1980)   **Pop Density:** 5.4
Land: 30.9 sq. mi.; **Water:** 5.3 sq. mi.

Nebish   Township
ZIP: 56667   **Lat:** 47-45-18 N   **Long:** 94-52-30 W
Pop: 301 (1990); 292 (1980)   **Pop Density:** 8.8
Land: 34.3 sq. mi.; **Water:** 1.6 sq. mi.

North Beltrami   Pop. Place
Lat: 48-27-22 N   **Long:** 95-24-39 W
Pop: 42 (1990); 40 (1980)   **Pop Density:** 0.2
Land: 215.6 sq. mi.; **Water:** 0.2 sq. mi.

Northern   Township
Lat: 47-32-39 N   **Long:** 94-51-30 W
Pop: 3,638 (1990); 3,211 (1980)   **Pop Density:** 130.4
Land: 27.9 sq. mi.; **Water:** 7.3 sq. mi.

O'Brien   Township
Lat: 47-48-34 N   **Long:** 94-44-00 W
Pop: 80 (1990); 85 (1980)   **Pop Density:** 2.2
Land: 35.9 sq. mi.; **Water:** 0.0 sq. mi.

Ponemah   CDP
Lat: 48-02-32 N   **Long:** 94-54-28 W
Pop: 704 (1990)   **Pop Density:** 35.9
Land: 19.6 sq. mi.; **Water:** 0.0 sq. mi.

Port Hope   Township
Lat: 47-37-37 N   **Long:** 94-44-32 W
Pop: 505 (1990); 388 (1980)   **Pop Density:** 17.8
Land: 28.4 sq. mi.; **Water:** 4.1 sq. mi.

Quiring   Township
ZIP: 56630   **Lat:** 47-53-02 N   **Long:** 94-43-05 W
Pop: 75 (1990); 67 (1980)   **Pop Density:** 3.1
Land: 23.9 sq. mi.; **Water:** 0.0 sq. mi.

Redby   CDP
Lat: 47-50-39 N   **Long:** 94-55-49 W
Pop: 787 (1990)   **Pop Density:** 67.3
Land: 11.7 sq. mi.; **Water:** 0.5 sq. mi.

Red Lake   CDP
Lat: 47-51-34 N   **Long:** 95-00-05 W
Pop: 1,068 (1990)   **Pop Density:** 106.8
Land: 10.0 sq. mi.; **Water:** 0.4 sq. mi.

Roosevelt   Township
Lat: 47-42-37 N   **Long:** 95-08-57 W
Pop: 180 (1990); 165 (1980)   **Pop Density:** 6.4
Land: 28.3 sq. mi.; **Water:** 1.7 sq. mi.

Shooks   Township
Lat: 47-53-04 N   **Long:** 94-28-45 W
Pop: 217 (1990); 228 (1980)   **Pop Density:** 5.9
Land: 36.5 sq. mi.; **Water:** 0.0 sq. mi.

Shotley   Township
ZIP: 56650   **Lat:** 48-03-51 N   **Long:** 94-38-18 W
Pop: 57 (1990); 64 (1980)   **Pop Density:** 1.7
Land: 32.8 sq. mi.; **Water:** 14.0 sq. mi.

MINNESOTA, Beltrami County

Shotley Brook
Pop. Place
Lat: 48-04-04 N Long: 94-29-19 W
Pop: 23 (1990); 18 (1980) Pop Density: 0.6
Land: 35.9 sq. mi.; Water: 0.0 sq. mi.

Solway
City
ZIP: 56678 Lat: 47-31-14 N Long: 95-07-47 W
Pop: 74 (1990); 89 (1980) Pop Density: 74.0
Land: 1.0 sq. mi.; Water: 0.0 sq. mi.

Spruce Grove
Township
Lat: 48-19-04 N Long: 95-24-01 W
Pop: 81 (1990); 64 (1980) Pop Density: 2.3
Land: 34.6 sq. mi.; Water: 0.0 sq. mi.

Steenerson
Township
Lat: 48-14-49 N Long: 95-16-35 W
Pop: 44 (1990); 52 (1980) Pop Density: 1.2
Land: 36.3 sq. mi.; Water: 0.0 sq. mi.

Sugar Bush
Township
Lat: 47-32-30 N Long: 94-36-23 W
Pop: 113 (1990); 121 (1980) Pop Density: 3.8
Land: 29.6 sq. mi.; Water: 5.5 sq. mi.

Summit
Township
ZIP: 56630 Lat: 47-42-38 N Long: 94-28-59 W
Pop: 237 (1990); 205 (1980) Pop Density: 6.8
Land: 35.0 sq. mi.; Water: 0.2 sq. mi.

Taylor
Township
Lat: 47-37-29 N Long: 94-36-02 W
Pop: 133 (1990); 92 (1980) Pop Density: 4.1
Land: 32.2 sq. mi.; Water: 2.1 sq. mi.

Ten Lake
Township
Lat: 47-26-56 N Long: 94-36-03 W
Pop: 651 (1990); 496 (1980) Pop Density: 28.7
Land: 22.7 sq. mi.; Water: 13.3 sq. mi.

Tenstrike
City
ZIP: 56683 Lat: 47-39-38 N Long: 94-41-04 W
Pop: 184 (1990); 159 (1980) Pop Density: 55.8
Land: 3.3 sq. mi.; Water: 1.2 sq. mi. Elev: 1403 ft.

Turtle Lake
Township
ZIP: 56667 Lat: 47-37-31 N Long: 94-51-37 W
Pop: 838 (1990); 713 (1980) Pop Density: 29.2
Land: 28.7 sq. mi.; Water: 7.5 sq. mi.

Turtle River
City
ZIP: 56601 Lat: 47-35-18 N Long: 94-45-36 W
Pop: 62 (1990); 60 (1980) Pop Density: 56.4
Land: 1.1 sq. mi.; Water: 0.0 sq. mi.

*Turtle River
Township
Lat: 47-32-20 N Long: 94-44-21 W
Pop: 799 (1990); 526 (1980) Pop Density: 25.4
Land: 31.5 sq. mi.; Water: 4.4 sq. mi.

Upper Red Lake
Pop. Place
Lat: 48-16-15 N Long: 95-00-40 W
Pop: 27 (1990); 37 (1980) Pop Density: 0.0
Land: 694.3 sq. mi.; Water: 147.6 sq. mi.

Waskish
Township
ZIP: 56685 Lat: 48-10-50 N Long: 94-29-36 W
Pop: 111 (1990); 133 (1980) Pop Density: 1.7
Land: 65.0 sq. mi.; Water: 7.0 sq. mi.

Wilton
City
ZIP: 56687 Lat: 47-30-18 N Long: 94-59-28 W
Pop: 171 (1990); 176 (1980) Pop Density: 74.3
Land: 2.3 sq. mi.; Water: 0.0 sq. mi.
Name origin: For a common English place name, already used in the east and Canada.

Woodrow
Township
ZIP: 56674 Lat: 47-58-42 N Long: 94-36-53 W
Pop: 97 (1990); 83 (1980) Pop Density: 2.7
Land: 35.9 sq. mi.; Water: 0.0 sq. mi.

Benton County
County Seat: Foley (ZIP: 56329)

Pop: 30,185 (1990); 25,187 (1980) Pop Density: 73.9
Land: 408.3 sq. mi.; Water: 4.7 sq. mi. Area Code: 612
In east-central MN, northeast of St. Cloud; original county; established Oct 27, 1849 (prior to statehood).
Name origin: For Thomas Hart Benton (1782–1858), U.S. journalist and statesman; nicknamed "Old Bullion" for championing the use of gold and silver currency rather than paper money.

Alberta
Township
Lat: 45-46-28 N Long: 93-56-21 W
Pop: 760 (1990); 757 (1980) Pop Density: 20.9
Land: 36.3 sq. mi.; Water: 0.0 sq. mi.

Foley
City
ZIP: 56329 Lat: 45-39-47 N Long: 93-54-33 W
Pop: 1,854 (1990); 1,606 (1980) Pop Density: 1158.8
Land: 1.6 sq. mi.; Water: 0.0 sq. mi.
Name origin: For John Foley, one of its founders.

Gilman
City
ZIP: 56333 Lat: 45-44-06 N Long: 93-57-00 W
Pop: 192 (1990); 156 (1980) Pop Density: 384.0
Land: 0.5 sq. mi.; Water: 0.0 sq. mi.
Name origin: For Charles Gilman, who served MN in the state legislature and as the register of the U.S. Land Office in St. Cloud. He was both lieutenant governor and state librarian in the 1880s and 1890s.

Gilmanton
Township
Lat: 45-41-23 N Long: 93-56-52 W
Pop: 775 (1990); 861 (1980)   **Pop Density:** 22.4
Land: 34.6 sq. mi.; **Water:** 0.0 sq. mi.

Glendorado
Township
Lat: 45-36-47 N Long: 93-49-06 W
Pop: 762 (1990); 765 (1980)   **Pop Density:** 20.9
Land: 36.4 sq. mi.; **Water:** 0.1 sq. mi.

Graham
Township
Lat: 45-46-46 N Long: 94-04-07 W
Pop: 549 (1990); 579 (1980)   **Pop Density:** 15.0
Land: 36.7 sq. mi.; **Water:** 0.0 sq. mi.

Granite Ledge
Township
Lat: 45-46-42 N Long: 93-48-57 W
Pop: 615 (1990); 581 (1980)   **Pop Density:** 17.5
Land: 35.2 sq. mi.; **Water:** 0.0 sq. mi.

Langola
Township
ZIP: 56367   Lat: 45-47-10 N Long: 94-13-21 W
Pop: 795 (1990); 714 (1980)   **Pop Density:** 20.0
Land: 39.8 sq. mi.; **Water:** 1.5 sq. mi.

Mayhew Lake
Township
Lat: 45-41-42 N Long: 94-04-37 W
Pop: 751 (1990); 743 (1980)   **Pop Density:** 20.4
Land: 36.9 sq. mi.; **Water:** 0.2 sq. mi.

Maywood
Township
Lat: 45-41-49 N Long: 93-49-18 W
Pop: 845 (1990); 817 (1980)   **Pop Density:** 23.9
Land: 35.3 sq. mi.; **Water:** 0.0 sq. mi.

Minden
Township
Lat: 45-35-54 N Long: 94-04-17 W
Pop: 1,900 (1990); 1,828 (1980)   **Pop Density:** 51.9
Land: 36.6 sq. mi.; **Water:** 0.1 sq. mi.

Rice
City
ZIP: 56367   Lat: 45-44-55 N Long: 94-13-43 W
Pop: 610 (1990); 499 (1980)   **Pop Density:** 101.7
Land: 6.0 sq. mi.; **Water:** 0.1 sq. mi.

Ronneby
City
ZIP: 56329   Lat: 45-40-56 N Long: 93-51-56 W
Pop: 58 (1990); 56 (1980)   **Pop Density:** 290.0
Land: 0.2 sq. mi.; **Water:** 0.0 sq. mi.

St. Cloud
City
ZIP: 56301   Lat: 45-34-04 N Long: 94-08-36 W
Pop: 5,950 (1990); 4,645 (1980)   **Pop Density:** 3305.6
Land: 1.8 sq. mi.; **Water:** 0.1 sq. mi.
In central MN on the Mississippi River, 58 mi. northwest of Minneapolis. Part of the town is also in Sherburne and Stearns counties.
Name origin: Named by town founder John Wilson for Napoleon I's (1769–1821) palace of St. Cloud outside Paris.

St. George
Township
Lat: 45-35-48 N Long: 93-57-16 W
Pop: 856 (1990); 959 (1980)   **Pop Density:** 23.3
Land: 36.7 sq. mi.; **Water:** 0.1 sq. mi.

Sartell
City
ZIP: 56377   Lat: 45-37-08 N Long: 94-11-26 W
Pop: 1,844 (1990); 1,227 (1980)   **Pop Density:** 2305.0
Land: 0.8 sq. mi.; **Water:** 0.1 sq. mi.
Part of the town is also in Stearns County.
Name origin: For Joseph Sartell, who settled here in 1854 and established a sawmill.

Sauk Rapids
City
ZIP: 56379   Lat: 45-35-39 N Long: 94-09-57 W
Pop: 7,825 (1990); 5,793 (1980)   **Pop Density:** 2445.3
Land: 3.2 sq. mi.; **Water:** 0.2 sq. mi.
Organized 1854. City and township not coextensive.
Name origin: For the nearby rapids in the Sauk River.

*Sauk Rapids
Township
Lat: 45-37-56 N Long: 94-09-54 W
Pop: 850 (1990); 758 (1980)   **Pop Density:** 90.4
Land: 9.4 sq. mi.; **Water:** 0.2 sq. mi.

Watab
Township
Lat: 45-41-51 N Long: 94-10-21 W
Pop: 2,394 (1990); 1,843 (1980)   **Pop Density:** 117.9
Land: 20.3 sq. mi.; **Water:** 2.1 sq. mi.

Big Stone County
County Seat: Ortonville (ZIP: 56278)

Pop: 6,285 (1990); 7,716 (1980)   **Pop Density:** 12.6
Land: 497.0 sq. mi.; **Water:** 30.9 sq. mi.   **Area Code:** 612
On central western border of MN; established Feb 20, 1862 from Pierce County (which was abolished the same year).
Name origin: For Big Stone Lake in the western part of the county.

Akron
Township
Lat: 45-15-48 N Long: 96-10-09 W
Pop: 233 (1990); 306 (1980)   **Pop Density:** 4.8
Land: 48.6 sq. mi.; **Water:** 4.7 sq. mi.

Almond
Township
Lat: 45-27-19 N Long: 96-25-41 W
Pop: 157 (1990); 238 (1980)   **Pop Density:** 4.7
Land: 33.2 sq. mi.; **Water:** 1.6 sq. mi.

Artichoke
Township
Lat: 45-22-03 N Long: 96-10-31 W
Pop: 104 (1990); 137 (1980)   **Pop Density:** 3.2
Land: 32.2 sq. mi.; **Water:** 3.3 sq. mi.

MINNESOTA, Big Stone County

Barry
City
ZIP: 56210 Lat: 45-33-30 N Long: 96-33-35 W
Pop: 40 (1990); 43 (1980) Pop Density: 200.0
Land: 0.2 sq. mi.; Water: 0.0 sq. mi.
Name origin: For the Barry brothers, early settlers from MA.

Beardsley
City
ZIP: 56211 Lat: 45-33-28 N Long: 96-42-51 W
Pop: 297 (1990); 344 (1980) Pop Density: 594.0
Land: 0.5 sq. mi.; Water: 0.0 sq. mi. Elev: 1098 ft.
Name origin: The town is located on the former farm of early settler, W. W. Beardsley.

Big Stone
Township
Lat: 45-21-44 N Long: 96-25-56 W
Pop: 269 (1990); 395 (1980) Pop Density: 8.9
Land: 30.3 sq. mi.; Water: 4.1 sq. mi.

Browns Valley
Township
Lat: 45-32-55 N Long: 96-42-17 W
Pop: 494 (1990); 565 (1980) Pop Density: 10.4
Land: 47.6 sq. mi.; Water: 1.3 sq. mi.

Clinton
City
ZIP: 56225 Lat: 45-27-43 N Long: 96-26-35 W
Pop: 574 (1990); 622 (1980) Pop Density: 574.0
Land: 1.0 sq. mi.; Water: 0.1 sq. mi.
Name origin: For DeWitt Clinton (1769–1828), governor of NY and supporter of the Erie Canal.

Correll
City
ZIP: 56227 Lat: 45-13-54 N Long: 96-09-45 W
Pop: 60 (1990); 83 (1980) Pop Density: 150.0
Land: 0.4 sq. mi.; Water: 0.0 sq. mi.
Name origin: Named by officers of the Chicago, Milwaukee, & St. Paul Railroad for an employee.

Foster
Township
Lat: 45-27-54 N Long: 96-40-11 W
Pop: 132 (1990); 233 (1980) Pop Density: 4.4
Land: 30.1 sq. mi.; Water: 3.1 sq. mi.

Graceville
City
ZIP: 56240 Lat: 45-34-06 N Long: 96-26-14 W
Pop: 671 (1990); 780 (1980) Pop Density: 1342.0
Land: 0.5 sq. mi.; Water: 0.0 sq. mi. Elev: 1116 ft.
Settled late 1870s. City and township not coextensive.
Name origin: Named by Roman Catholic settlers for Thomas Grace, Bishop of St. Paul.

*Graceville
Township
ZIP: 56240 Lat: 45-32-50 N Long: 96-26-09 W
Pop: 199 (1990); 211 (1980) Pop Density: 6.0
Land: 33.0 sq. mi.; Water: 2.0 sq. mi.

Johnson
City
ZIP: 56250 Lat: 45-34-18 N Long: 96-17-37 W
Pop: 46 (1990); 57 (1980) Pop Density: 153.3
Land: 0.3 sq. mi.; Water: 0.0 sq. mi.

Malta
Township
Lat: 45-27-23 N Long: 96-18-25 W
Pop: 112 (1990); 145 (1980) Pop Density: 3.1
Land: 36.3 sq. mi.; Water: 0.9 sq. mi.

Moonshine
Township
Lat: 45-32-57 N Long: 96-18-45 W
Pop: 161 (1990); 226 (1980) Pop Density: 4.3
Land: 37.5 sq. mi.; Water: 0.0 sq. mi.

Odessa
City
ZIP: 56276 Lat: 45-15-40 N Long: 96-19-52 W
Pop: 155 (1990); 177 (1980) Pop Density: 193.8
Land: 0.8 sq. mi.; Water: 0.0 sq. mi.
City and township not coextensive.
Name origin: For Odessa, Russia.

*Odessa
Township
ZIP: 56276 Lat: 45-17-11 N Long: 96-17-47 W
Pop: 183 (1990); 209 (1980) Pop Density: 5.1
Land: 35.6 sq. mi.; Water: 0.8 sq. mi.

Ortonville
City
ZIP: 56278 Lat: 45-18-13 N Long: 96-26-27 W
Pop: 2,205 (1990); 2,550 (1980) Pop Density: 648.5
Land: 3.4 sq. mi.; Water: 0.0 sq. mi.
Founded 1870s. Part of the town is also in Lac qui Parle County.
Name origin: For founder Cornelius Knute Orton, who was a prominent local businessman.

*Ortonville
Township
ZIP: 56278 Lat: 45-17-13 N Long: 96-24-57 W
Pop: 2,326 (1990); 2,745 (1980) Pop Density: 133.7
Land: 17.4 sq. mi.; Water: 1.1 sq. mi.

Otrey
Township
Lat: 45-22-11 N Long: 96-17-59 W
Pop: 119 (1990); 147 (1980) Pop Density: 3.5
Land: 34.1 sq. mi.; Water: 3.1 sq. mi.

Prior
Township
Lat: 45-26-24 N Long: 96-32-42 W
Pop: 201 (1990); 332 (1980) Pop Density: 4.5
Land: 44.5 sq. mi.; Water: 3.4 sq. mi.

Toqua
Township
Lat: 45-32-00 N Long: 96-33-22 W
Pop: 95 (1990); 122 (1980) Pop Density: 2.8
Land: 33.8 sq. mi.; Water: 1.3 sq. mi.

Blue Earth County
County Seat: Mankato (ZIP: 56001)

Pop: 54,044 (1990); 52,314 (1980) **Pop Density:** 71.8
Land: 752.4 sq. mi.; **Water:** 13.5 sq. mi. **Area Code:** 507

In south-central MN, west of Rochester; established Mar 5, 1853 (prior to statehood) from unorganized territory.

Name origin: For the Blue Earth River, which runs through it; a transliteration of the Nankato name for the color of the earth in the river, used as a pigment by the Sisseton Sioux.

Amboy — City
ZIP: 56010 **Lat:** 43-53-18 N **Long:** 94-09-26 W
Pop: 517 (1990); 606 (1980) **Pop Density:** 1723.3
Land: 0.3 sq. mi.; **Water:** 0.0 sq. mi. **Elev:** 1044 ft.
Name origin: For the former IL hometown of the city's first postmaster, Robert Richardson.

Beauford — Township
Lat: 43-58-42 N **Long:** 93-56-53 W
Pop: 432 (1990); 509 (1980) **Pop Density:** 12.1
Land: 35.6 sq. mi.; **Water:** 0.3 sq. mi.

Butternut Valley — Township
Lat: 44-09-03 N **Long:** 94-18-35 W
Pop: 359 (1990); 398 (1980) **Pop Density:** 10.1
Land: 35.4 sq. mi.; **Water:** 0.6 sq. mi.

Cambria — Township
Lat: 44-13-23 N **Long:** 94-19-06 W
Pop: 293 (1990); 319 (1980) **Pop Density:** 14.9
Land: 19.7 sq. mi.; **Water:** 0.0 sq. mi.

Ceresco — Township
Lat: 43-58-27 N **Long:** 94-18-39 W
Pop: 266 (1990); 315 (1980) **Pop Density:** 7.4
Land: 35.8 sq. mi.; **Water:** 0.1 sq. mi.

Danville — Township
Lat: 43-53-31 N **Long:** 93-49-29 W
Pop: 272 (1990); 332 (1980) **Pop Density:** 7.6
Land: 35.9 sq. mi.; **Water:** 0.3 sq. mi.

Decoria — Township
Lat: 44-04-21 N **Long:** 93-56-53 W
Pop: 807 (1990); 864 (1980) **Pop Density:** 22.5
Land: 35.8 sq. mi.; **Water:** 0.0 sq. mi.

Eagle Lake — City
ZIP: 56024 **Lat:** 44-09-33 N **Long:** 93-52-57 W
Pop: 1,703 (1990); 1,470 (1980) **Pop Density:** 1419.2
Land: 1.2 sq. mi.; **Water:** 0.0 sq. mi. **Elev:** 1014 ft.
Name origin: For nearby Eagle Lake, which was named for the many bald eagles nesting around it.

Garden City — Township
ZIP: 56034 **Lat:** 44-04-11 N **Long:** 94-11-13 W
Pop: 716 (1990); 788 (1980) **Pop Density:** 21.6
Land: 33.2 sq. mi.; **Water:** 1.8 sq. mi.

Good Thunder — City
ZIP: 56037 **Lat:** 44-00-24 N **Long:** 94-04-12 W
Pop: 561 (1990); 560 (1980) **Pop Density:** 935.0
Land: 0.6 sq. mi.; **Water:** 0.0 sq. mi.
Name origin: For Winnebago chief, Good Thunder, whose village was nearby.

Jamestown — Township
Lat: 44-13-04 N **Long:** 93-49-51 W
Pop: 547 (1990); 448 (1980) **Pop Density:** 35.8
Land: 15.3 sq. mi.; **Water:** 2.2 sq. mi.

Judson — Township
Lat: 44-09-07 N **Long:** 94-11-27 W
Pop: 651 (1990); 727 (1980) **Pop Density:** 17.5
Land: 37.1 sq. mi.; **Water:** 0.6 sq. mi.

Lake Crystal — City
ZIP: 56055 **Lat:** 44-06-12 N **Long:** 94-13-04 W
Pop: 2,084 (1990); 2,078 (1980) **Pop Density:** 1603.1
Land: 1.3 sq. mi.; **Water:** 0.0 sq. mi. **Elev:** 1000 ft.
Name origin: For the nearby lake, which was named by explorers Jean Nicolet (1786–1843) and John C. Frémont (1813–90) for its crystal waters.

Le Ray — Township
Lat: 44-09-10 N **Long:** 93-49-42 W
Pop: 753 (1990); 722 (1980) **Pop Density:** 23.0
Land: 32.7 sq. mi.; **Water:** 2.5 sq. mi.

Lime — Township
Lat: 44-12-58 N **Long:** 93-57-09 W
Pop: 1,156 (1990); 1,101 (1980) **Pop Density:** 65.7
Land: 17.6 sq. mi.; **Water:** 1.0 sq. mi.

Lincoln — Township
Lat: 44-03-41 N **Long:** 94-18-59 W
Pop: 229 (1990); 305 (1980) **Pop Density:** 6.4
Land: 36.0 sq. mi.; **Water:** 0.0 sq. mi.

Lyra — Township
Lat: 43-59-13 N **Long:** 94-04-01 W
Pop: 382 (1990); 405 (1980) **Pop Density:** 10.7
Land: 35.6 sq. mi.; **Water:** 0.0 sq. mi.

Madison Lake — City
ZIP: 56063 **Lat:** 44-12-07 N **Long:** 93-48-51 W
Pop: 643 (1990); 592 (1980) **Pop Density:** 1607.5
Land: 0.4 sq. mi.; **Water:** 0.0 sq. mi.
Name origin: For adjoining Madison Lake, itself named for James Madison (1751–1836), fourth U.S. president.

Mankato — City
ZIP: 56001 **Lat:** 44-09-54 N **Long:** 93-59-28 W
Pop: 31,468 (1990); 28,637 (1980) **Pop Density:** 2784.8
Land: 11.3 sq. mi.; **Water:** 0.2 sq. mi.
In southern MN on the Minnesota River, 65 mi. southwest of Minneapolis. Part of the town is also in Nicollet County.
Name origin: For the Sioux name for the Blue Earth River.

*Mankato — Township
Lat: 44-08-41 N **Long:** 93-57-00 W
Pop: 2,135 (1990); 2,757 (1980) **Pop Density:** 69.3
Land: 30.8 sq. mi.; **Water:** 0.6 sq. mi.

MINNESOTA, Blue Earth County

Mapleton
City
ZIP: 56065　　Lat: 43-55-33 N　Long: 93-57-14 W
Pop: 1,526 (1990); 1,516 (1980)　　Pop Density: 1017.3
Land: 1.5 sq. mi.; Water: 0.0 sq. mi.
City and township not coextensive.
Name origin: For the Maple River, which was named for the many maple trees along it.

*Mapleton
Township
ZIP: 56065　　Lat: 43-53-30 N　Long: 93-57-13 W
Pop: 341 (1990); 378 (1980)　　Pop Density: 10.0
Land: 34.1 sq. mi.; Water: 0.3 sq. mi.

McPherson
Township
Lat: 44-03-43 N　Long: 93-49-59 W
Pop: 450 (1990); 476 (1980)　　Pop Density: 12.9
Land: 35.0 sq. mi.; Water: 0.4 sq. mi.

Medo
Township
Lat: 43-59-16 N　Long: 93-49-37 W
Pop: 380 (1990); 426 (1980)　　Pop Density: 10.9
Land: 35.0 sq. mi.; Water: 0.7 sq. mi.

North Mankato
City
Lat: 44-11-03 N　Long: 94-00-54 W
Pop: 0 (1990); 9,145 (1980)
Land: 0.007 sq. mi.; Water: 0.0 sq. mi.
In southern MN, across the Minnesota River from Mankato. Part of the town is also in Nicollet County.
Name origin: For its location.

Pemberton
City
ZIP: 56078　　Lat: 44-00-32 N　Long: 93-47-01 W
Pop: 228 (1990); 208 (1980)　　Pop Density: 1140.0
Land: 0.2 sq. mi.; Water: 0.0 sq. mi.

Pleasant Mound
Township
Lat: 43-53-29 N　Long: 94-18-31 W
Pop: 304 (1990); 335 (1980)　　Pop Density: 8.4
Land: 36.0 sq. mi.; Water: 0.0 sq. mi.

Rapidan
Township
Lat: 44-03-42 N　Long: 94-03-50 W
Pop: 1,117 (1990); 1,060 (1980)　　Pop Density: 31.5
Land: 35.5 sq. mi.; Water: 0.0 sq. mi.

St. Clair
City
Lat: 44-04-51 N　Long: 93-51-27 W
Pop: 633 (1990); 655 (1980)　　Pop Density: 1055.0
Land: 0.6 sq. mi.; Water: 0.0 sq. mi.
Name origin: Named by officers of the Chicago, Milwaukee & St. Paul Railway. Previously called Hilton.

Shelby
Township
Lat: 43-53-44 N　Long: 94-11-43 W
Pop: 351 (1990); 357 (1980)　　Pop Density: 9.9
Land: 35.6 sq. mi.; Water: 0.2 sq. mi.

Skyline
City
Lat: 44-08-24 N　Long: 94-02-06 W
Pop: 272 (1990); 399 (1980)　　Pop Density: 1360.0
Land: 0.2 sq. mi.; Water: 0.0 sq. mi.

South Bend
Township
Lat: 44-08-26 N　Long: 94-05-06 W
Pop: 1,515 (1990); 1,514 (1980)　　Pop Density: 89.6
Land: 16.9 sq. mi.; Water: 0.0 sq. mi.

Sterling
Township
Lat: 43-53-42 N　Long: 94-04-08 W
Pop: 277 (1990); 315 (1980)　　Pop Density: 8.1
Land: 34.4 sq. mi.; Water: 1.6 sq. mi.

Vernon Center
City
ZIP: 56090　　Lat: 43-57-48 N　Long: 94-10-00 W
Pop: 339 (1990); 365 (1980)　　Pop Density: 678.0
Land: 0.5 sq. mi.; Water: 0.0 sq. mi.
Settled 1855.
Name origin: For Mount Vernon, OH.

*Vernon Center
Township
ZIP: 56090　　Lat: 43-58-29 N　Long: 94-10-43 W
Pop: 337 (1990); 377 (1980)　　Pop Density: 9.5
Land: 35.6 sq. mi.; Water: 0.0 sq. mi.

Brown County
County Seat: New Ulm (ZIP: 56073)

Pop: 26,984 (1990); 28,645 (1980)　　Pop Density: 44.2
Land: 610.9 sq. mi.; Water: 7.7 sq. mi.　　Area Code: 507
In south-central MN, west of Mankato; established Feb 20, 1855 (prior to statehood) from Nicollet County.
Name origin: For Joseph Renshaw Brown (1805–70), a trader with the Sioux Indians, publisher, and MN legislator.

Albin
Township
Lat: 44-08-48 N　Long: 94-41-06 W
Pop: 361 (1990); 444 (1980)　　Pop Density: 10.5
Land: 34.4 sq. mi.; Water: 1.2 sq. mi.

Bashaw
Township
Lat: 44-09-08 N　Long: 94-55-08 W
Pop: 273 (1990); 356 (1980)　　Pop Density: 7.6
Land: 35.8 sq. mi.; Water: 0.0 sq. mi.

Burnstown
Township
Lat: 44-14-39 N　Long: 94-55-26 W
Pop: 322 (1990); 350 (1980)　　Pop Density: 9.3
Land: 34.7 sq. mi.; Water: 0.2 sq. mi.

Cobden
City
ZIP: 56085　　Lat: 44-17-01 N　Long: 94-50-51 W
Pop: 62 (1990); 72 (1980)　　Pop Density: 62.0
Land: 1.0 sq. mi.; Water: 0.0 sq. mi.

Comfrey
City
ZIP: 56019 Lat: 44-06-39 N Long: 94-54-09 W
Pop: 430 (1990); 508 (1980) Pop Density: 1075.0
Land: 0.4 sq. mi.; Water: 0.0 sq. mi. Elev: 1301 ft.
Part of the town is also in Cottonwood County.
Name origin: For a nearby post office named for the famous medicinal plant.

Cottonwood
Township
Lat: 44-14-19 N Long: 94-26-34 W
Pop: 923 (1990); 946 (1980) Pop Density: 26.1
Land: 35.4 sq. mi.; Water: 0.0 sq. mi.

Eden
Township
Lat: 44-25-11 N Long: 94-48-55 W
Pop: 378 (1990); 416 (1980) Pop Density: 9.2
Land: 41.3 sq. mi.; Water: 0.2 sq. mi.

Evan
City
ZIP: 56238 Lat: 44-21-09 N Long: 94-50-12 W
Pop: 83 (1990); 90 (1980) Pop Density: 83.0
Land: 1.0 sq. mi.; Water: 0.0 sq. mi.
Name origin: For Eva Norseth, the wife of the town's first postmaster, Martin Norseth; with a spelling variation.

Hanska
City
ZIP: 56041 Lat: 44-08-53 N Long: 94-29-40 W
Pop: 443 (1990); 429 (1980) Pop Density: 2215.0
Land: 0.2 sq. mi.; Water: 0.0 sq. mi.
Name origin: From a Sioux Indian term meaning 'one,' their name for the adjacent lake.

Home
Township
Lat: 44-21-28 N Long: 94-40-58 W
Pop: 712 (1990); 792 (1980) Pop Density: 13.5
Land: 52.6 sq. mi.; Water: 0.1 sq. mi.

Lake Hanska
Township
Lat: 44-08-30 N Long: 94-32-52 W
Pop: 378 (1990); 474 (1980) Pop Density: 10.3
Land: 36.7 sq. mi.; Water: 2.1 sq. mi.

Leavenworth
Township
Lat: 44-14-34 N Long: 94-47-54 W
Pop: 400 (1990); 509 (1980) Pop Density: 11.4
Land: 35.1 sq. mi.; Water: 0.3 sq. mi.

Linden
Township
Lat: 44-08-48 N Long: 94-25-53 W
Pop: 363 (1990); 436 (1980) Pop Density: 10.3
Land: 35.2 sq. mi.; Water: 0.8 sq. mi.

Milford
Township
Lat: 44-19-45 N Long: 94-34-08 W
Pop: 711 (1990); 754 (1980) Pop Density: 18.0
Land: 39.4 sq. mi.; Water: 0.4 sq. mi.

Mulligan
Township
Lat: 44-09-27 N Long: 94-48-31 W
Pop: 274 (1990); 369 (1980) Pop Density: 7.6
Land: 35.9 sq. mi.; Water: 0.4 sq. mi.

New Ulm
City
ZIP: 56073 Lat: 44-18-47 N Long: 94-27-49 W
Pop: 13,132 (1990); 13,755 (1980) Pop Density: 1527.0
Land: 8.6 sq. mi.; Water: 0.2 sq. mi.
In southern MN on the Minnesota River, 24 mi. northwest of Mankato.
Name origin: For Ulm, Germany.

North Star
Township
Lat: 44-14-17 N Long: 95-02-51 W
Pop: 365 (1990); 395 (1980) Pop Density: 10.2
Land: 35.8 sq. mi.; Water: 0.0 sq. mi.

Prairieville
Township
Lat: 44-19-37 N Long: 94-48-10 W
Pop: 378 (1990); 401 (1980) Pop Density: 11.0
Land: 34.4 sq. mi.; Water: 0.0 sq. mi.

Sigel
Township
Lat: 44-14-35 N Long: 94-33-38 W
Pop: 478 (1990); 527 (1980) Pop Density: 12.3
Land: 38.8 sq. mi.; Water: 0.8 sq. mi.

Sleepy Eye
City
ZIP: 56085 Lat: 44-17-59 N Long: 94-43-29 W
Pop: 3,694 (1990); 3,581 (1980) Pop Density: 2638.6
Land: 1.4 sq. mi.; Water: 0.3 sq. mi. Elev: 1030 ft.
Name origin: For a chief of the Lower Sisseton Sioux Indians.

Springfield
City
ZIP: 56087 Lat: 44-14-16 N Long: 94-58-36 W
Pop: 2,173 (1990); 2,303 (1980) Pop Density: 1552.1
Land: 1.4 sq. mi.; Water: 0.0 sq. mi. Elev: 1026 ft.
Name origin: For either Springfield, MA, or a large spring nearby.

Stark
Township
Lat: 44-14-27 N Long: 94-41-15 W
Pop: 423 (1990); 462 (1980) Pop Density: 11.9
Land: 35.6 sq. mi.; Water: 0.5 sq. mi.

Stately
Township
Lat: 44-08-43 N Long: 95-02-06 W
Pop: 228 (1990); 276 (1980) Pop Density: 6.3
Land: 36.0 sq. mi.; Water: 0.1 sq. mi.

MINNESOTA, Carlton County   *American Places Dictionary*

Carlton County
County Seat: Carlton (ZIP: 55718)

Pop: 29,259 (1990); 29,936 (1980)   **Pop Density:** 34.0
Land: 860.4 sq. mi.; **Water:** 14.9 sq. mi.   **Area Code:** 218
On central-eastern border of MN, south of Duluth; established May 23, 1857 (prior to statehood) from Pine County.
Name origin: For Reuben B. Carlton (1812–62), farmer and blacksmith for Ojibway Indians and MN state legislator.

Atkinson   Township
ZIP: 55718   **Lat:** 46-36-51 N **Long:** 92-36-40 W
Pop: 259 (1990); 302 (1980)   **Pop Density:** 14.9
Land: 17.4 sq. mi.; **Water:** 0.8 sq. mi.

Automba   Township
ZIP: 55757   **Lat:** 46-33-48 N **Long:** 92-59-30 W
Pop: 156 (1990); 204 (1980)   **Pop Density:** 4.3
Land: 36.4 sq. mi.; **Water:** 0.0 sq. mi.

Barnum   City
ZIP: 55707   **Lat:** 46-30-17 N **Long:** 92-41-21 W
Pop: 482 (1990); 464 (1980)   **Pop Density:** 482.0
Land: 1.0 sq. mi.; **Water:** 0.0 sq. mi.   **Elev:** 1103 ft.
City and township not coextensive.
Name origin: For George Barnum, an official of the St. Paul & Duluth railway.

*Barnum   Township
ZIP: 55707   **Lat:** 46-29-53 N **Long:** 92-38-59 W
Pop: 767 (1990); 756 (1980)   **Pop Density:** 17.0
Land: 45.0 sq. mi.; **Water:** 1.2 sq. mi.

Beseman   Township
ZIP: 55798   **Lat:** 46-43-23 N **Long:** 92-59-43 W
Pop: 130 (1990); 106 (1980)   **Pop Density:** 3.6
Land: 36.0 sq. mi.; **Water:** 0.0 sq. mi.

Blackhoof   Township
ZIP: 55718   **Lat:** 46-33-02 N **Long:** 92-30-02 W
Pop: 578 (1990); 573 (1980)   **Pop Density:** 16.1
Land: 36.0 sq. mi.; **Water:** 0.5 sq. mi.

Carlton   City
ZIP: 55718   **Lat:** 46-39-36 N **Long:** 92-25-23 W
Pop: 923 (1990); 862 (1980)   **Pop Density:** 439.5
Land: 2.1 sq. mi.; **Water:** 0.2 sq. mi.   **Elev:** 1091 ft.
Name origin: For Reuben B. Carlton (1812–62), farmer and blacksmith for the Ojibway Indians and MN state legislator, who settled in the area in 1847.

Clear Creek   Pop. Place
                          Lat: 46-27-42 N **Long:** 92-29-30 W
Pop: 128 (1990); 134 (1980)   **Pop Density:** 3.5
Land: 36.5 sq. mi.; **Water:** 0.2 sq. mi.

Cloquet   City
ZIP: 55720   **Lat:** 46-43-44 N **Long:** 92-29-39 W
Pop: 10,885 (1990); 11,142 (1980) **Pop Density:** 309.2
Land: 35.2 sq. mi.; **Water:** 0.7 sq. mi.   **Elev:** 1204 ft.
In eastern MN, 17 mi. southwest of Duluth.
Name origin: For the nearby Cloquet River.

Cromwell   City
ZIP: 55726   **Lat:** 46-40-46 N **Long:** 92-52-14 W
Pop: 221 (1990); 229 (1980)   **Pop Density:** 130.0
Land: 1.7 sq. mi.; **Water:** 0.2 sq. mi.   **Elev:** 1311 ft.
Name origin: Named by Northern Pacific Railway officials for English Prime Minister Oliver Cromwell (1599–1658).

Eagle   Township
                          Lat: 46-37-48 N **Long:** 92-52-02 W
Pop: 529 (1990)   **Pop Density:** 15.2
Land: 34.7 sq. mi.; **Water:** 1.1 sq. mi.

Holyoke   Township
ZIP: 55797   **Lat:** 46-27-54 N **Long:** 92-22-17 W
Pop: 160 (1990); 226 (1980)   **Pop Density:** 4.2
Land: 37.9 sq. mi.; **Water:** 0.1 sq. mi.

Kalevala   Township
ZIP: 55757   **Lat:** 46-32-30 N **Long:** 92-51-21 W
Pop: 285 (1990); 312 (1980)   **Pop Density:** 8.0
Land: 35.8 sq. mi.; **Water:** 0.0 sq. mi.

Kettle River   City
ZIP: 55757   **Lat:** 46-29-11 N **Long:** 92-52-40 W
Pop: 190 (1990); 174 (1980)   **Pop Density:** 475.0
Land: 0.4 sq. mi.; **Water:** 0.0 sq. mi.   **Elev:** 1182 ft.
Name origin: For the river, whose name is a transliteration of the Ojibway Indian name.

Lakeview   Township
ZIP: 55798   **Lat:** 46-37-49 N **Long:** 92-59-34 W
Pop: 167 (1990); 169 (1980)   **Pop Density:** 5.0
Land: 33.4 sq. mi.; **Water:** 1.0 sq. mi.

Mahtowa   Township
ZIP: 55762   **Lat:** 46-33-26 N **Long:** 92-37-15 W
Pop: 504 (1990); 511 (1980)   **Pop Density:** 21.2
Land: 23.8 sq. mi.; **Water:** 0.3 sq. mi.

Moose Lake   City
ZIP: 55767   **Lat:** 46-26-45 N **Long:** 92-46-06 W
Pop: 1,206 (1990); 1,408 (1980)   **Pop Density:** 524.3
Land: 2.3 sq. mi.; **Water:** 0.4 sq. mi.   **Elev:** 1062 ft.
City and township not coextensive.
Name origin: For the nearby lake, named by the Ojibway for the abundant moose in the area.

*Moose Lake   Township
ZIP: 55767   **Lat:** 46-27-13 N **Long:** 92-42-06 W
Pop: 1,239 (1990); 1,237 (1980)   **Pop Density:** 37.4
Land: 33.1 sq. mi.; **Water:** 0.8 sq. mi.

North Carlton   Pop. Place
                          Lat: 46-40-50 N **Long:** 92-45-31 W
Pop: 807 (1990); 1,362 (1980)   **Pop Density:** 6.5
Land: 124.3 sq. mi.; **Water:** 2.8 sq. mi.

Perch Lake — Township
Lat: 46-43-19 N Long: 92-37-00 W
Pop: 833 (1990); 730 (1980) Pop Density: 24.1
Land: 34.6 sq. mi.; Water: 1.9 sq. mi.

Scanlon — City
ZIP: 55720 Lat: 46-42-26 N Long: 92-25-44 W
Pop: 878 (1990); 1,050 (1980) Pop Density: 1097.5
Land: 0.8 sq. mi.; Water: 0.0 sq. mi.

Silver — Township
ZIP: 55757 Lat: 46-27-44 N Long: 92-52-09 W
Pop: 373 (1990); 411 (1980) Pop Density: 10.6
Land: 35.1 sq. mi.; Water: 0.0 sq. mi.

Silver Brook — Township
ZIP: 55718 Lat: 46-36-31 N Long: 92-21-18 W
Pop: 535 (1990); 511 (1980) Pop Density: 29.9
Land: 17.9 sq. mi.; Water: 0.0 sq. mi.

Skelton — Township
ZIP: 55707 Lat: 46-33-01 N Long: 92-44-17 W
Pop: 364 (1990); 355 (1980) Pop Density: 10.4
Land: 35.0 sq. mi.; Water: 0.0 sq. mi.

Split Rock — Township
ZIP: 55757 Lat: 46-26-59 N Long: 92-59-14 W
Pop: 141 (1990); 182 (1980) Pop Density: 3.9
Land: 36.6 sq. mi.; Water: 0.0 sq. mi.

Thomson — City
ZIP: 55718 Lat: 46-39-50 N Long: 92-23-23 W
Pop: 132 (1990); 152 (1980) Pop Density: 69.5
Land: 1.9 sq. mi.; Water: 0.3 sq. mi.
City and township not coextensive.

*Thomson — Township
ZIP: 55718 Lat: 46-42-45 N Long: 92-21-45 W
Pop: 3,970 (1990); 3,962 (1980) Pop Density: 100.0
Land: 39.7 sq. mi.; Water: 0.2 sq. mi.

Twin Lakes — Township
ZIP: 55718 Lat: 46-38-22 N Long: 92-27-49 W
Pop: 1,673 (1990); 1,595 (1980) Pop Density: 37.3
Land: 44.9 sq. mi.; Water: 2.0 sq. mi.

Wrenshall — City
ZIP: 55749 Lat: 46-37-05 N Long: 92-23-00 W
Pop: 296 (1990); 333 (1980) Pop Density: 197.3
Land: 1.5 sq. mi.; Water: 0.0 sq. mi. Elev: 1041 ft.
Name origin: For Northern Pacific Railway Company supervisor, C. C. Wrenshall.

*Wrenshall — Township
ZIP: 55749 Lat: 46-32-45 N Long: 92-21-32 W
Pop: 304 (1990); 322 (1980) Pop Density: 8.0
Land: 37.9 sq. mi.; Water: 0.0 sq. mi.

Wright — City
ZIP: 55798 Lat: 46-40-19 N Long: 93-00-23 W
Pop: 144 (1990); 162 (1980) Pop Density: 96.0
Land: 1.5 sq. mi.; Water: 0.0 sq. mi. Elev: 1303 ft.
Name origin: For pioneer developer and land surveyor George B. Wright.

Carver County
County Seat: Chaska (ZIP: 55318)

Pop: 47,915 (1990); 37,046 (1980) Pop Density: 134.2
Land: 357.1 sq. mi.; Water: 19.1 sq. mi. Area Code: 612
In south-central MN, east of Minneapolis; established Feb 20, 1855 (prior to statehood) from Hennepin County.
Name origin: For Capt. Jonathan Carver (1710–80), an officer in the French and Indian War, explorer, and author.

Benton — Township
Lat: 44-45-35 N Long: 93-50-15 W
Pop: 895 (1990); 939 (1980) Pop Density: 26.2
Land: 34.1 sq. mi.; Water: 0.9 sq. mi.

Camden — Township
Lat: 44-50-41 N Long: 93-57-05 W
Pop: 910 (1990); 898 (1980) Pop Density: 26.3
Land: 34.6 sq. mi.; Water: 0.6 sq. mi.

Carver — City
ZIP: 55315 Lat: 44-45-37 N Long: 93-37-38 W
Pop: 744 (1990); 642 (1980) Pop Density: 190.8
Land: 3.9 sq. mi.; Water: 0.2 sq. mi.
Name origin: For Capt. Johnathan Carver, who explored the area in 1847.

Chanhassen — City
ZIP: 55317 Lat: 44-51-25 N Long: 93-33-28 W
Pop: 11,732 (1990); 6,351 (1980) Pop Density: 569.5
Land: 20.6 sq. mi.; Water: 2.1 sq. mi. Elev: 976 ft.
Settled 1852. Part of the town is also in Hennepin County.
Name origin: From the Sioux Indian term meaning 'sugar maple,' or 'the tree of sweet juice.'

Chaska — City
ZIP: 55318 Lat: 44-49-15 N Long: 93-36-18 W
Pop: 11,339 (1990); 8,346 (1980) Pop Density: 827.7
Land: 13.7 sq. mi.; Water: 0.6 sq. mi. Elev: 728 ft.
In southeast-central MN on the Minnesota River, 20 mi. southwest of Minneapolis. Founded in 1854 by the Shaska Co. City and township not coextensive.
Name origin: From the Sioux Indian name usually given to the first-born boy.

MINNESOTA, Carver County

*Chaska
Township
ZIP: 55318   Lat: 44-47-48 N **Long:** 93-37-38 W
Pop: 174 (1990); 205 (1980)   **Pop Density:** 60.0
Land: 2.9 sq. mi.; **Water:** 0.0 sq. mi.

Cologne
City
ZIP: 55322   Lat: 44-46-17 N **Long:** 93-47-16 W
Pop: 563 (1990); 545 (1980)   **Pop Density:** 938.3
Land: 0.6 sq. mi.; **Water:** 0.1 sq. mi.   **Elev:** 948 ft.
Name origin: For Cologne, Germany, former homeland of German settlers.

Dahlgren
Township
Lat: 44-46-05 N **Long:** 93-42-34 W
Pop: 1,296 (1990); 1,225 (1980)   **Pop Density:** 36.5
Land: 35.5 sq. mi.; **Water:** 0.4 sq. mi.

Hamburg
City
ZIP: 55339   Lat: 44-43-53 N **Long:** 93-57-47 W
Pop: 492 (1990); 475 (1980)   **Pop Density:** 2460.0
Land: 0.2 sq. mi.; **Water:** 0.0 sq. mi.
For Hamburg, Germany.

Hancock
Township
Lat: 44-41-39 N **Long:** 93-49-44 W
Pop: 364 (1990); 391 (1980)   **Pop Density:** 20.6
Land: 17.7 sq. mi.; **Water:** 0.2 sq. mi.

Hollywood
Township
Lat: 44-55-53 N **Long:** 93-56-43 W
Pop: 1,060 (1990); 1,100 (1980)   **Pop Density:** 29.4
Land: 36.0 sq. mi.; **Water:** 0.1 sq. mi.

Laketown
Township
Lat: 44-51-01 N **Long:** 93-42-59 W
Pop: 2,232 (1990); 2,424 (1980)   **Pop Density:** 80.6
Land: 27.7 sq. mi.; **Water:** 2.7 sq. mi.

Mayer
City
ZIP: 55360   Lat: 44-53-03 N **Long:** 93-53-18 W
Pop: 471 (1990); 388 (1980)   **Pop Density:** 1177.5
Land: 0.4 sq. mi.; **Water:** 0.0 sq. mi.   **Elev:** 979 ft.
Name origin: Named by Great Northern Railway officials for a company officer.

New Germany
City
ZIP: 55367   Lat: 44-53-01 N **Long:** 93-58-15 W
Pop: 353 (1990); 347 (1980)   **Pop Density:** 706.0
Land: 0.5 sq. mi.; **Water:** 0.0 sq. mi.
Name origin: For the many German settlers in the area.

Norwood
City
ZIP: 55368   Lat: 44-46-06 N **Long:** 93-55-33 W
Pop: 1,351 (1990); 1,219 (1980)   **Pop Density:** 1688.8
Land: 0.8 sq. mi.; **Water:** 0.0 sq. mi.
Founded 1870s.
Name origin: Named by an early pioneer for a personal friend.

San Francisco
Township
Lat: 44-41-52 N **Long:** 93-42-06 W
Pop: 773 (1990); 650 (1980)   **Pop Density:** 33.3
Land: 23.2 sq. mi.; **Water:** 0.9 sq. mi.

Victoria
City
ZIP: 55386   Lat: 44-51-57 N **Long:** 93-39-30 W
Pop: 2,354 (1990); 1,425 (1980)   **Pop Density:** 336.3
Land: 7.0 sq. mi.; **Water:** 1.5 sq. mi.
Name origin: For Britain's Queen Victoria (1819–1901).

Waconia
City
ZIP: 55387   Lat: 44-50-52 N **Long:** 93-47-38 W
Pop: 3,498 (1990); 2,638 (1980)   **Pop Density:** 1943.3
Land: 1.8 sq. mi.; **Water:** 0.0 sq. mi.   **Elev:** 991 ft.
City and township not coextensive.
Name origin: From the Sioux Indian term meaning 'spring' or 'fountain.'

*Waconia
Township
ZIP: 55387   Lat: 44-51-08 N **Long:** 93-49-22 W
Pop: 1,287 (1990); 1,402 (1980)   **Pop Density:** 45.6
Land: 28.2 sq. mi.; **Water:** 5.4 sq. mi.

Watertown
City
ZIP: 55388   Lat: 44-57-47 N **Long:** 93-50-44 W
Pop: 2,408 (1990); 1,818 (1980)   **Pop Density:** 2189.1
Land: 1.1 sq. mi.; **Water:** 0.0 sq. mi.
Settled 1856. City and township not coextensive.
Name origin: For the town's good water supply from six lakes and a river.

*Watertown
Township
ZIP: 55388   Lat: 44-55-49 N **Long:** 93-49-06 W
Pop: 1,349 (1990); 1,429 (1980)   **Pop Density:** 40.8
Land: 33.1 sq. mi.; **Water:** 2.0 sq. mi.

Young America
City
ZIP: 55397   Lat: 44-46-50 N **Long:** 93-54-55 W
Pop: 1,354 (1990); 1,237 (1980)   **Pop Density:** 1934.3
Land: 0.7 sq. mi.; **Water:** 0.1 sq. mi.
Incorporated 1879.
Name origin: Named by its early settlers to signify the vigor and progressiveness of American youth. Formerly called Farmington and Florence.

*Young America
Township
Lat: 44-46-09 N **Long:** 93-56-47 W
Pop: 916 (1990); 952 (1980)   **Pop Density:** 27.8
Land: 33.0 sq. mi.; **Water:** 1.2 sq. mi.

Cass County
County Seat: Walker (ZIP: 56484)

Pop: 21,791 (1990); 21,050 (1980) **Pop Density:** 10.8
Land: 2017.7 sq. mi.; **Water:** 396.6 sq. mi. **Area Code:** 218
In central MN, northwest of Duluth; original county; established Mar 31, 1851 (prior to statehood).
Name origin: For Gen. Lewis Cass (1782–1866), OH legislator, governor of MI Territory (1813–31), U.S. secretary of war (1831–36), and U.S. secretary of state (1857–60). Formerly called Van Buren.

Ansel Township
Lat: 46-40-10 N **Long:** 94-43-03 W
Pop: 104 (1990); 116 (1980) **Pop Density:** 2.9
Land: 35.3 sq. mi.; **Water:** 0.4 sq. mi.

Backus City
ZIP: 56435 **Lat:** 46-49-15 N **Long:** 94-30-50 W
Pop: 240 (1990); 255 (1980) **Pop Density:** 400.0
Land: 0.6 sq. mi.; **Water:** 0.0 sq. mi.
Name origin: For well-known Minneapolis lumberman, Edward Backus.

Barclay Township
ZIP: 56474 **Lat:** 46-46-19 N **Long:** 94-22-04 W
Pop: 396 (1990); 440 (1980) **Pop Density:** 28.3
Land: 14.0 sq. mi.; **Water:** 1.1 sq. mi.

Becker Township
Lat: 46-24-53 N **Long:** 94-43-18 W
Pop: 414 (1990); 355 (1980) **Pop Density:** 11.4
Land: 36.3 sq. mi.; **Water:** 1.0 sq. mi.

Bena City
ZIP: 56626 **Lat:** 47-20-27 N **Long:** 94-12-22 W
Pop: 147 (1990); 153 (1980) **Pop Density:** 294.0
Land: 0.5 sq. mi.; **Water:** 0.0 sq. mi.
Name origin: From an Ojibway Indian term meaning 'partridge.'

Beulah Township
ZIP: 56662 **Lat:** 46-51-04 N **Long:** 93-50-57 W
Pop: 30 (1990); 42 (1980) **Pop Density:** 0.9
Land: 34.6 sq. mi.; **Water:** 1.1 sq. mi.

Birch Lake Township
ZIP: 56452 **Lat:** 46-56-38 N **Long:** 94-28-20 W
Pop: 426 (1990); 388 (1980) **Pop Density:** 14.8
Land: 28.7 sq. mi.; **Water:** 6.6 sq. mi.

Blind Lake Township
ZIP: 56474 **Lat:** 46-50-50 N **Long:** 94-13-14 W
Pop: 78 (1990); 75 (1980) **Pop Density:** 2.3
Land: 34.0 sq. mi.; **Water:** 1.3 sq. mi.

Boy Lake Township
ZIP: 56655 **Lat:** 47-06-26 N **Long:** 94-13-52 W
Pop: 116 (1990); 117 (1980) **Pop Density:** 4.2
Land: 27.6 sq. mi.; **Water:** 8.7 sq. mi.

Boy River City
ZIP: 56632 **Lat:** 47-10-00 N **Long:** 94-07-20 W
Pop: 43 (1990); 50 (1980) **Pop Density:** 107.5
Land: 0.4 sq. mi.; **Water:** 0.0 sq. mi. **Elev:** 1329 ft.
City and township not coextensive.

*Boy River Township
ZIP: 56632 **Lat:** 47-10-55 N **Long:** 94-04-54 W
Pop: 89 (1990); 111 (1980) **Pop Density:** 2.5
Land: 35.6 sq. mi.; **Water:** 0.3 sq. mi.

Bull Moose Township
Lat: 46-46-12 N **Long:** 94-35-43 W
Pop: 87 (1990); 90 (1980) **Pop Density:** 2.5
Land: 34.3 sq. mi.; **Water:** 1.7 sq. mi.

Bungo Township
Lat: 46-39-55 N **Long:** 94-35-17 W
Pop: 105 (1990); 98 (1980) **Pop Density:** 3.0
Land: 34.6 sq. mi.; **Water:** 1.3 sq. mi.

Byron Township
Lat: 46-30-08 N **Long:** 94-42-55 W
Pop: 140 (1990); 164 (1980) **Pop Density:** 3.9
Land: 35.7 sq. mi.; **Water:** 0.2 sq. mi.

Cass Lake City
ZIP: 56633 **Lat:** 47-22-43 N **Long:** 94-36-02 W
Pop: 923 (1990); 1,001 (1980) **Pop Density:** 923.0
Land: 1.0 sq. mi.; **Water:** 0.0 sq. mi.
Name origin: For Lewis Cass (1782–1866), OH legislator, governor of MI Territory (1813–31), U.S. secretary of war (1831–36), and U.S. secretary of state (1857–60).

Chickamaw Beach City
ZIP: 56474 **Lat:** 46-44-55 N **Long:** 94-23-23 W
Pop: 132 (1990); 124 (1980) **Pop Density:** 60.0
Land: 2.2 sq. mi.; **Water:** 0.4 sq. mi.

Crooked Lake Township
ZIP: 56662 **Lat:** 46-50-43 N **Long:** 93-58-03 W
Pop: 318 (1990); 346 (1980) **Pop Density:** 10.6
Land: 30.0 sq. mi.; **Water:** 6.0 sq. mi.

Deerfield Township
ZIP: 56435 **Lat:** 46-51-04 N **Long:** 94-36-11 W
Pop: 114 (1990); 91 (1980) **Pop Density:** 3.5
Land: 32.4 sq. mi.; **Water:** 3.5 sq. mi.

East Cass Pop. Place
Lat: 47-06-15 N **Long:** 93-50-07 W
Pop: 14 (1990); 62 (1980) **Pop Density:** 0.4
Land: 33.1 sq. mi.; **Water:** 3.0 sq. mi.

East Gull Lake City
Lat: 46-24-38 N **Long:** 94-21-07 W
Pop: 687 (1990); 586 (1980) **Pop Density:** 87.0
Land: 7.9 sq. mi.; **Water:** 6.9 sq. mi. **Elev:** 1252 ft.

Fairview Township
Lat: 46-24-42 N **Long:** 94-27-08 W
Pop: 354 (1990); 311 (1980) **Pop Density:** 9.9
Land: 35.7 sq. mi.; **Water:** 4.1 sq. mi.

MINNESOTA, Cass County

Federal Dam
City
ZIP: 56641　　Lat: 47-14-18 N　Long: 94-13-07 W
Pop: 118 (1990); 192 (1980)　　Pop Density: 62.1
Land: 1.9 sq. mi.; Water: 0.0 sq. mi.
Name origin: For the reservoir dam on nearby Leech Lake River.

Gould
Township
　　Lat: 47-11-49 N　Long: 94-13-47 W
Pop: 229 (1990); 189 (1980)　　Pop Density: 6.9
Land: 33.4 sq. mi.; Water: 10.8 sq. mi.

Hackensack
City
ZIP: 56452　　Lat: 46-55-40 N　Long: 94-31-06 W
Pop: 245 (1990); 285 (1980)　　Pop Density: 350.0
Land: 0.7 sq. mi.; Water: 0.0 sq. mi.
Name origin: For Hackensack, NJ.

Hiram
Township
ZIP: 56452　　Lat: 46-56-03 N　Long: 94-35-52 W
Pop: 205 (1990); 186 (1980)　　Pop Density: 7.6
Land: 27.1 sq. mi.; Water: 8.5 sq. mi.

Home Brook
Township
　　Lat: 46-29-49 N　Long: 94-27-23 W
Pop: 173 (1990); 168 (1980)　　Pop Density: 4.8
Land: 36.0 sq. mi.; Water: 0.2 sq. mi.

Inguadona
Township
ZIP: 56655　　Lat: 47-01-33 N　Long: 94-05-33 W
Pop: 135 (1990); 124 (1980)　　Pop Density: 3.9
Land: 34.6 sq. mi.; Water: 3.5 sq. mi.

Kego
Township
ZIP: 56655　　Lat: 47-01-37 N　Long: 94-12-43 W
Pop: 297 (1990); 321 (1980)　　Pop Density: 9.4
Land: 31.6 sq. mi.; Water: 4.6 sq. mi.

Lake Shore
City
　　Lat: 46-29-43 N　Long: 94-21-39 W
Pop: 693 (1990); 583 (1980)　　Pop Density: 54.1
Land: 12.8 sq. mi.; Water: 5.4 sq. mi.　Elev: 1242 ft.

Leech Lake
Township
ZIP: 56484　　Lat: 47-11-51 N　Long: 94-36-25 W
Pop: 279 (1990); 264 (1980)　　Pop Density: 12.0
Land: 23.2 sq. mi.; Water: 12.1 sq. mi.

Lima
Township
ZIP: 56672　　Lat: 47-01-06 N　Long: 93-50-35 W
Pop: 118 (1990); 98 (1980)　　Pop Density: 3.3
Land: 35.4 sq. mi.; Water: 0.6 sq. mi.

Longville
City
ZIP: 56655　　Lat: 46-59-12 N　Long: 94-12-54 W
Pop: 224 (1990); 191 (1980)　　Pop Density: 373.3
Land: 0.6 sq. mi.; Water: 0.0 sq. mi.

Loon Lake
Township
　　Lat: 46-35-29 N　Long: 94-21-43 W
Pop: 264 (1990); 209 (1980)　　Pop Density: 15.2
Land: 17.4 sq. mi.; Water: 0.6 sq. mi.

Maple
Township
　　Lat: 46-36-00 N　Long: 94-27-58 W
Pop: 257 (1990); 251 (1980)　　Pop Density: 7.1
Land: 36.2 sq. mi.; Water: 0.3 sq. mi.

May
Township
　　Lat: 46-23-25 N　Long: 94-34-50 W
Pop: 599 (1990); 520 (1980)　　Pop Density: 10.0
Land: 60.0 sq. mi.; Water: 0.6 sq. mi.

McKinley
Township
　　Lat: 46-45-32 N　Long: 94-43-54 W
Pop: 121 (1990); 144 (1980)　　Pop Density: 3.4
Land: 36.1 sq. mi.; Water: 0.3 sq. mi.

Meadow Brook
Township
　　Lat: 46-30-06 N　Long: 94-36-25 W
Pop: 140 (1990); 155 (1980)　　Pop Density: 3.6
Land: 38.6 sq. mi.; Water: 0.4 sq. mi.

Moose Lake
Township
　　Lat: 46-34-48 N　Long: 94-35-50 W
Pop: 153 (1990); 123 (1980)　　Pop Density: 4.1
Land: 37.5 sq. mi.; Water: 1.2 sq. mi.

Motley
City
ZIP: 56466　　Lat: 46-20-30 N　Long: 94-38-02 W
Pop: 0 (1990); 2 (1980)
Land: 0.1 sq. mi.; Water: 0.0 sq. mi.　Elev: 1229 ft.
Settled 1870s. Part of the town is also in Morrison County.
Name origin: Named by officers of the Northern Pacific Railway Company.

North Cass
Pop. Place
　　Lat: 47-20-43 N　Long: 94-12-51 W
Pop: 299 (1990); 407 (1980)　　Pop Density: 1.4
Land: 207.3 sq. mi.; Water: 74.0 sq. mi.

North Central Cass
Pop. Place
　　Lat: 47-10-12 N　Long: 94-22-27 W
Pop: 12 (1990)　　Pop Density: 1.5
Land: 8.2 sq. mi.; Water: 80.9 sq. mi.

Otter Tail Peninsula
Township
　　Lat: 47-15-58 N　Long: 94-24-15 W
Pop: 40 (1990)　　Pop Density: 0.6
Land: 64.3 sq. mi.; Water: 10.8 sq. mi.

Pike Bay
Township
ZIP: 56633　　Lat: 47-21-56 N　Long: 94-36-27 W
Pop: 1,420 (1990); 1,211 (1980)　　Pop Density: 63.1
Land: 22.5 sq. mi.; Water: 12.4 sq. mi.

Pillager
City
ZIP: 56473　　Lat: 46-19-36 N　Long: 94-28-35 W
Pop: 306 (1990); 341 (1980)　　Pop Density: 510.0
Land: 0.6 sq. mi.; Water: 0.0 sq. mi.　Elev: 1209 ft.
Name origin: For an early trader who, being robbed in the mid-1760s by Ojibways, called them 'pillagers.'

Pine Lake
Township
ZIP: 56485　　Lat: 47-01-02 N　Long: 94-20-39 W
Pop: 138 (1990); 168 (1980)　　Pop Density: 4.9
Land: 28.4 sq. mi.; Water: 6.0 sq. mi.

Pine River
City
ZIP: 56474　　Lat: 46-43-21 N　Long: 94-23-53 W
Pop: 871 (1990); 881 (1980)　　Pop Density: 791.8
Land: 1.1 sq. mi.; Water: 0.0 sq. mi.
Name origin: For the river, which is named for the abundant pine stands once in the area.

*Pine River
Township
ZIP: 56474　　Lat: 46-45-47 N　Long: 94-28-20 W
Pop: 838 (1990); 637 (1980)　　Pop Density: 24.0
Land: 34.9 sq. mi.; Water: 1.1 sq. mi.

Ponto Lake
Township
ZIP: 56474　　Lat: 46-50-55 N　Long: 94-20-23 W
Pop: 453 (1990); 384 (1980)　　Pop Density: 15.3
Land: 29.6 sq. mi.; Water: 6.8 sq. mi.

MINNESOTA, Cass County

Poplar — Township
Lat: 46-35-21 N Long: 94-43-24 W
Pop: 201 (1990); 217 (1980) Pop Density: 5.7
Land: 35.5 sq. mi.; Water: 0.0 sq. mi.

Powers — Township
ZIP: 56435 Lat: 46-51-03 N Long: 94-28-33 W
Pop: 603 (1990); 542 (1980) Pop Density: 21.0
Land: 28.7 sq. mi.; Water: 6.6 sq. mi.

Remer — City
ZIP: 56672 Lat: 47-03-28 N Long: 93-54-49 W
Pop: 342 (1990); 396 (1980) Pop Density: 263.1
Land: 1.3 sq. mi.; Water: 0.0 sq. mi. Elev: 1340 ft.
Name origin: For the Remer brothers, who were prominent in the founding of the town.

*Remer — Township
ZIP: 56672 Lat: 47-02-34 N Long: 93-58-37 W
Pop: 156 (1990); 190 (1980) Pop Density: 5.3
Land: 29.2 sq. mi.; Water: 5.9 sq. mi.

Rogers — Township
Lat: 47-05-50 N Long: 94-05-38 W
Pop: 33 (1990); 57 (1980) Pop Density: 1.1
Land: 30.8 sq. mi.; Water: 5.5 sq. mi.

Salem — Township
ZIP: 56632 Lat: 47-10-26 N Long: 93-57-37 W
Pop: 106 (1990); 86 (1980) Pop Density: 3.0
Land: 35.1 sq. mi.; Water: 1.3 sq. mi.

Shingobee — Township
ZIP: 56484 Lat: 47-04-25 N Long: 94-35-42 W
Pop: 1,481 (1990); 1,472 (1980) Pop Density: 27.5
Land: 53.8 sq. mi.; Water: 18.1 sq. mi.

Slater — Township
ZIP: 56672 Lat: 47-07-16 N Long: 93-58-26 W
Pop: 204 (1990); 201 (1980) Pop Density: 6.1
Land: 33.7 sq. mi.; Water: 2.8 sq. mi.

Smoky Hollow — Township
ZIP: 56672 Lat: 46-55-55 N Long: 93-50-50 W
Pop: 51 (1990); 79 (1980) Pop Density: 1.5
Land: 34.8 sq. mi.; Water: 1.3 sq. mi.

Sylvan — Township
ZIP: 56473 Lat: 46-20-10 N Long: 94-24-38 W
Pop: 1,268 (1990); 846 (1980) Pop Density: 41.0
Land: 30.9 sq. mi.; Water: 3.9 sq. mi.

Thunder Lake — Township
ZIP: 56672 Lat: 46-56-02 N Long: 93-57-37 W
Pop: 178 (1990); 194 (1980) Pop Density: 5.5
Land: 32.2 sq. mi.; Water: 4.2 sq. mi.

Torrey — Township
ZIP: 56632 Lat: 47-11-03 N Long: 93-50-16 W
Pop: 113 (1990); 146 (1980) Pop Density: 3.6
Land: 31.8 sq. mi.; Water: 2.4 sq. mi.

Trelipe — Township
ZIP: 56662 Lat: 46-53-42 N Long: 94-04-43 W
Pop: 119 (1990); 144 (1980) Pop Density: 1.8
Land: 66.8 sq. mi.; Water: 4.1 sq. mi.

Turtle Lake — Township
ZIP: 56484 Lat: 47-03-37 N Long: 94-28-09 W
Pop: 506 (1990); 469 (1980) Pop Density: 10.4
Land: 48.7 sq. mi.; Water: 23.3 sq. mi.

Wabedo — Township
ZIP: 56655 Lat: 46-55-51 N Long: 94-13-18 W
Pop: 269 (1990); 273 (1980) Pop Density: 10.9
Land: 24.6 sq. mi.; Water: 10.7 sq. mi. Elev: 1316 ft.

Wahnena — Township
ZIP: 56632 Lat: 47-17-09 N Long: 93-51-01 W
Pop: 187 (1990); 190 (1980) Pop Density: 5.5
Land: 34.0 sq. mi.; Water: 0.5 sq. mi.

Walden — Township
ZIP: 56474 Lat: 46-40-45 N Long: 94-28-16 W
Pop: 348 (1990); 374 (1980) Pop Density: 9.6
Land: 36.1 sq. mi.; Water: 0.0 sq. mi.

Walker — City
ZIP: 56484 Lat: 47-05-23 N Long: 94-34-44 W
Pop: 950 (1990); 970 (1980) Pop Density: 678.6
Land: 1.4 sq. mi.; Water: 0.0 sq. mi.
Name origin: For Thomas B. Walker, who held extensive lumber and land interests in Cass County.

Wilkinson — Township
ZIP: 56633 Lat: 47-16-50 N Long: 94-36-10 W
Pop: 207 (1990); 277 (1980) Pop Density: 6.7
Land: 30.7 sq. mi.; Water: 5.3 sq. mi.

Wilson — Township
ZIP: 56474 Lat: 46-40-49 N Long: 94-22-41 W
Pop: 426 (1990); 469 (1980) Pop Density: 24.1
Land: 17.7 sq. mi.; Water: 0.1 sq. mi.

Woodrow — Township
ZIP: 56474 Lat: 46-56-04 N Long: 94-20-43 W
Pop: 459 (1990); 449 (1980) Pop Density: 18.3
Land: 25.1 sq. mi.; Water: 11.7 sq. mi.

Chippewa County
County Seat: Montevideo (ZIP: 56265)

Pop: 13,228 (1990); 14,941 (1980)   **Pop Density:** 22.7
Land: 582.8 sq. mi.; **Water:** 5.0 sq. mi.   **Area Code:** 612

In west-central MN, southwest of St. Cloud; established Feb 20, 1862 from Pierce County, which was abolished in 1862.

Name origin: For the Chippewa (more properly Ojibway) Indians, a tribe of Algonquian linguistic stock. The name probably means 'puckered,' and refers to the seam in their moccasins.

Big Bend — Township
Lat: 45-06-24 N   Long: 95-47-56 W
Pop: 321 (1990); 378 (1980)   **Pop Density:** 9.0
Land: 35.7 sq. mi.; **Water:** 0.0 sq. mi.

Clara City — City
ZIP: 56222   Lat: 44-57-28 N   Long: 95-21-57 W
Pop: 1,307 (1990); 1,574 (1980)   **Pop Density:** 687.9
Land: 1.9 sq. mi.; **Water:** 0.0 sq. mi.   **Elev:** 1062 ft.
Name origin: For the wife of Theodor Koch, who helped settle the area.

Crate — Township
Lat: 45-01-17 N   Long: 95-26-12 W
Pop: 279 (1990); 310 (1980)   **Pop Density:** 7.8
Land: 35.9 sq. mi.; **Water:** 0.0 sq. mi.

Grace — Township
Lat: 45-06-03 N   Long: 95-32-35 W
Pop: 150 (1990); 257 (1980)   **Pop Density:** 4.2
Land: 35.9 sq. mi.; **Water:** 0.0 sq. mi.

Granite Falls — City
ZIP: 56241   Lat: 44-48-41 N   Long: 95-31-36 W
Pop: 737 (1990); 785 (1980)   **Pop Density:** 433.5
Land: 1.7 sq. mi.; **Water:** 0.1 sq. mi.   **Elev:** 920 ft.
Part of the town is also in Yellow Medicine County.
Name origin: For the falls over large granite outcrops in the Minnesota River.

*Granite Falls — Township
Lat: 44-50-17 N   Long: 95-31-36 W
Pop: 255 (1990); 299 (1980)   **Pop Density:** 8.1
Land: 31.5 sq. mi.; **Water:** 0.3 sq. mi.

Havelock — Township
Lat: 45-01-14 N   Long: 95-33-09 W
Pop: 197 (1990); 249 (1980)   **Pop Density:** 5.5
Land: 35.8 sq. mi.; **Water:** 0.0 sq. mi.

Kragero — Township
Lat: 45-06-15 N   Long: 95-55-16 W
Pop: 190 (1990); 244 (1980)   **Pop Density:** 4.6
Land: 41.5 sq. mi.; **Water:** 3.2 sq. mi.

Leenthrop — Township
Lat: 44-56-30 N   Long: 95-33-41 W
Pop: 298 (1990); 334 (1980)   **Pop Density:** 8.3
Land: 35.7 sq. mi.; **Water:** 0.0 sq. mi.

Lone Tree — Township
Lat: 45-01-26 N   Long: 95-18-39 W
Pop: 256 (1990); 321 (1980)   **Pop Density:** 7.1
Land: 36.2 sq. mi.; **Water:** 0.0 sq. mi.

Louriston — Township
Lat: 45-06-36 N   Long: 95-25-36 W
Pop: 240 (1990); 278 (1980)   **Pop Density:** 6.7
Land: 35.6 sq. mi.; **Water:** 0.5 sq. mi.

Mandt — Township
Lat: 45-06-56 N   Long: 95-40-56 W
Pop: 204 (1990); 251 (1980)   **Pop Density:** 5.7
Land: 35.5 sq. mi.; **Water:** 0.0 sq. mi.

Maynard — City
ZIP: 56260   Lat: 44-54-17 N   Long: 95-28-01 W
Pop: 419 (1990); 428 (1980)   **Pop Density:** 698.3
Land: 0.6 sq. mi.; **Water:** 0.0 sq. mi.   **Elev:** 1029 ft.
Name origin: For the brother-in-law of Great Northern Railway superintendent John Spicer.

Milan — City
ZIP: 56262   Lat: 45-06-50 N   Long: 95-54-48 W
Pop: 353 (1990); 417 (1980)   **Pop Density:** 353.0
Land: 1.0 sq. mi.; **Water:** 0.0 sq. mi.   **Elev:** 1005 ft.
Founded 1880s.
Name origin: For Milan, Italy.

Montevideo — City
ZIP: 56265   Lat: 44-57-04 N   Long: 95-43-06 W
Pop: 5,499 (1990); 5,845 (1980)   **Pop Density:** 1410.0
Land: 3.9 sq. mi.; **Water:** 0.0 sq. mi.
Name origin: For the capital of Uruguay.

Rheiderland — Township
Lat: 44-56-17 N   Long: 95-17-58 W
Pop: 316 (1990); 382 (1980)   **Pop Density:** 9.1
Land: 34.8 sq. mi.; **Water:** 0.0 sq. mi.

Rosewood — Township
Lat: 45-01-24 N   Long: 95-40-30 W
Pop: 351 (1990); 379 (1980)   **Pop Density:** 9.8
Land: 35.7 sq. mi.; **Water:** 0.1 sq. mi.

Sparta — Township
Lat: 44-56-01 N   Long: 95-41-02 W
Pop: 866 (1990); 1,060 (1980)   **Pop Density:** 21.7
Land: 39.9 sq. mi.; **Water:** 0.4 sq. mi.

Stoneham — Township
Lat: 44-55-35 N   Long: 95-25-36 W
Pop: 287 (1990); 360 (1980)   **Pop Density:** 8.2
Land: 34.8 sq. mi.; **Water:** 0.0 sq. mi.

Tunsberg — Township
Lat: 45-01-20 N   Long: 95-47-42 W
Pop: 225 (1990); 226 (1980)   **Pop Density:** 6.8
Land: 33.0 sq. mi.; **Water:** 0.3 sq. mi.

Watson City
ZIP: 56295 Lat: 45-00-37 N Long: 95-47-59 W
Pop: 211 (1990); 238 (1980) Pop Density: 1055.0
Land: 0.2 sq. mi.; Water: 0.0 sq. mi. Elev: 1031 ft.
Name origin: Named by Chicago, Milwaukee, & St. Paul Railway officers for one of their employees.

Woods Township
Lat: 45-06-39 N Long: 95-18-16 W
Pop: 267 (1990); 326 (1980) Pop Density: 7.4
Land: 36.2 sq. mi.; Water: 0.0 sq. mi.

Chisago County
County Seat: Center City (ZIP: 55012)

Pop: 30,521 (1990); 25,717 (1980) Pop Density: 73.1
Land: 417.7 sq. mi.; Water: 24.9 sq. mi. Area Code: 612

On the central eastern border of MN, northeast of Minneapolis; established Sep 1, 1851 (prior to statehood) from Washington County.
Name origin: For Chisago Lake, largest in the county; from Ojibway *kichi* 'large' and *saga* 'fair' or 'beautiful.' The first syllable was omitted and a clerical error changed *a* to *o*.

Amador Township
Lat: 45-30-10 N Long: 92-46-01 W
Pop: 632 (1990); 593 (1980) Pop Density: 21.1
Land: 29.9 sq. mi.; Water: 0.6 sq. mi.

Branch City
ZIP: 55056 Lat: 45-30-52 N Long: 92-57-27 W
Pop: 2,400 (1990); 1,866 (1980) Pop Density: 70.4
Land: 34.1 sq. mi.; Water: 0.3 sq. mi.
Settled 1872.
Name origin: For the north branch of the Sunrise River, which flows through the town.

Center City City
ZIP: 55012 Lat: 45-23-27 N Long: 92-49-05 W
Pop: 451 (1990); 458 (1980) Pop Density: 1503.3
Land: 0.3 sq. mi.; Water: 0.0 sq. mi.
Name origin: For its central location between Chisago City and Taylor's Fall.

Chisago City City
ZIP: 55013 Lat: 45-22-13 N Long: 92-53-16 W
Pop: 2,009 (1990); 1,634 (1980) Pop Density: 1057.4
Land: 1.9 sq. mi.; Water: 0.0 sq. mi.
Name origin: For Chisago Lake; from Ojibway *kichi* 'large' and *saga* 'fair' or 'beautiful.' The first syllable was omitted and a clerical error changed *a* to *o*.

Chisago Lake Township
ZIP: 55012 Lat: 45-23-38 N Long: 92-50-59 W
Pop: 3,057 (1990); 2,629 (1980) Pop Density: 64.8
Land: 47.2 sq. mi.; Water: 8.3 sq. mi.

Fish Lake Township
ZIP: 55032 Lat: 45-36-01 N Long: 93-04-54 W
Pop: 1,183 (1990); 1,074 (1980) Pop Density: 36.6
Land: 32.3 sq. mi.; Water: 2.3 sq. mi.

Franconia Township
ZIP: 55074 Lat: 45-20-43 N Long: 92-45-46 W
Pop: 1,151 (1990); 1,007 (1980) Pop Density: 37.7
Land: 30.5 sq. mi.; Water: 1.4 sq. mi.

Harris City
ZIP: 55032 Lat: 45-36-10 N Long: 92-59-20 W
Pop: 843 (1990); 678 (1980) Pop Density: 42.6
Land: 19.8 sq. mi.; Water: 0.1 sq. mi. Elev: 902 ft.
Incorporated 1884.
Name origin: For Phillip Harris, an officer of St. Paul & Duluth Railway Company.

Lent Township
Lat: 45-25-43 N Long: 92-57-24 W
Pop: 1,797 (1990); 1,380 (1980) Pop Density: 53.8
Land: 33.4 sq. mi.; Water: 2.2 sq. mi.

Lindstrom City
ZIP: 55045 Lat: 45-23-09 N Long: 92-50-25 W
Pop: 2,461 (1990); 1,972 (1980) Pop Density: 1538.1
Land: 1.6 sq. mi.; Water: 0.0 sq. mi.
Name origin: For Swedish farmer and pioneer Daniel Lindstrom, who came to the region in the mid 1800s.

Nessel Township
Lat: 45-41-11 N Long: 93-04-15 W
Pop: 1,354 (1990); 1,460 (1980) Pop Density: 35.5
Land: 38.1 sq. mi.; Water: 5.1 sq. mi.

North Branch City
ZIP: 55056 Lat: 45-30-51 N Long: 92-58-42 W
Pop: 1,867 (1990); 1,597 (1980) Pop Density: 1166.9
Land: 1.6 sq. mi.; Water: 0.0 sq. mi. Elev: 896 ft.
Founded 1870s.
Name origin: For the north branch of the Sunrise River, which traverses the county.

Rush City City
ZIP: 55069 Lat: 45-40-54 N Long: 92-57-56 W
Pop: 1,497 (1990); 1,198 (1980) Pop Density: 935.6
Land: 1.6 sq. mi.; Water: 0.0 sq. mi. Elev: 917 ft.
Founded 1868.
Name origin: For the Rush River.

Rushseba Township
ZIP: 55069 Lat: 45-41-17 N Long: 92-55-54 W
Pop: 715 (1990); 732 (1980) Pop Density: 22.2
Land: 32.2 sq. mi.; Water: 0.4 sq. mi.

Shafer
City
ZIP: 55074 Lat: 45-23-15 N Long: 92-44-45 W
Pop: 368 (1990); 180 (1980) Pop Density: 736.0
Land: 0.5 sq. mi.; Water: 0.0 sq. mi.

*Shafer
Township
ZIP: 55074 Lat: 45-25-13 N Long: 92-43-33 W
Pop: 727 (1990); 768 (1980) Pop Density: 24.2
Land: 30.1 sq. mi.; Water: 0.3 sq. mi.

Stacy
City
Lat: 45-23-52 N Long: 92-59-15 W
Pop: 1,081 (1990); 996 (1980) Pop Density: 1081.0
Land: 1.0 sq. mi.; Water: 0.0 sq. mi.
Established 1875.
Name origin: For pioneer Dr. Stacy Collins.

Sunrise
Township
ZIP: 55032 Lat: 45-33-25 N Long: 92-53-18 W
Pop: 1,125 (1990); 1,001 (1980) Pop Density: 24.8
Land: 45.3 sq. mi.; Water: 0.6 sq. mi.

Taylors Falls
City
ZIP: 55084 Lat: 45-24-41 N Long: 92-39-42 W
Pop: 694 (1990); 623 (1980) Pop Density: 187.6
Land: 3.7 sq. mi.; Water: 0.3 sq. mi. Elev: 744 ft.
Founded 1850.
Name origin: For pioneer Jesse Taylor.

Wyoming
City
Lat: 45-20-00 N Long: 92-59-45 W
Pop: 2,142 (1990); 1,559 (1980) Pop Density: 823.8
Land: 2.6 sq. mi.; Water: 0.0 sq. mi.
City and township not coextensive.
Name origin: For the Wyoming Valley in Luzerne County, PA.

*Wyoming
Township
Lat: 45-20-15 N Long: 92-57-48 W
Pop: 2,967 (1990); 2,312 (1980) Pop Density: 99.2
Land: 29.9 sq. mi.; Water: 2.6 sq. mi.

Clay County
County Seat: Moorhead (ZIP: 56560)

Pop: 50,422 (1990); 49,327 (1980) Pop Density: 48.2
Land: 1045.3 sq. mi.; Water: 7.5 sq. mi. Area Code: 218

On the central western border of MN; established as Breckenridge County Mar 9, 1862; name changed later in 1862.

Name origin: For Henry Clay (1777–1852), U.S. senator from KY, known as the "Great Pacificator" for his advocacy of compromise to avert national crises.

Alliance
Township
Lat: 46-40-01 N Long: 96-36-52 W
Pop: 267 (1990); 308 (1980) Pop Density: 7.4
Land: 36.3 sq. mi.; Water: 0.0 sq. mi.

Barnesville
City
ZIP: 56514 Lat: 46-38-55 N Long: 96-25-03 W
Pop: 2,066 (1990); 2,207 (1980) Pop Density: 983.8
Land: 2.1 sq. mi.; Water: 0.0 sq. mi.
Incorporated as a village in 1881; as a city in 1889.
Name origin: For founder and farmer, George Barnes.

*Barnesville
Township
ZIP: 56514 Lat: 46-40-32 N Long: 96-29-12 W
Pop: 180 (1990); 203 (1980) Pop Density: 5.1
Land: 35.5 sq. mi.; Water: 0.0 sq. mi.

Comstock
City
ZIP: 56525 Lat: 46-39-35 N Long: 96-44-47 W
Pop: 123 (1990); 110 (1980) Pop Density: 615.0
Land: 0.2 sq. mi.; Water: 0.0 sq. mi.
Name origin: For Solomon Comstock, both a state and U.S. congressional representative for the area.

Cromwell
Township
Lat: 46-56-31 N Long: 96-21-11 W
Pop: 310 (1990); 307 (1980) Pop Density: 9.3
Land: 33.3 sq. mi.; Water: 0.4 sq. mi.

Dilworth
City
ZIP: 56529 Lat: 46-52-31 N Long: 96-41-55 W
Pop: 2,562 (1990); 2,585 (1980) Pop Density: 1507.1
Land: 1.7 sq. mi.; Water: 0.0 sq. mi.
Name origin: Named by Northern Pacific Railway officials for one of their employees.

Eglon
Township
Lat: 46-50-29 N Long: 96-14-19 W
Pop: 419 (1990); 461 (1980) Pop Density: 12.3
Land: 34.0 sq. mi.; Water: 1.9 sq. mi.

Elkton
Township
Lat: 46-45-41 N Long: 96-29-24 W
Pop: 338 (1990); 324 (1980) Pop Density: 9.4
Land: 36.1 sq. mi.; Water: 0.1 sq. mi.

Elmwood
Township
Lat: 46-45-45 N Long: 96-36-26 W
Pop: 392 (1990); 459 (1980) Pop Density: 11.0
Land: 35.7 sq. mi.; Water: 0.0 sq. mi.

Felton
City
ZIP: 56536 Lat: 47-04-35 N Long: 96-30-17 W
Pop: 211 (1990); 264 (1980) Pop Density: 211.0
Land: 1.0 sq. mi.; Water: 0.0 sq. mi. Elev: 910 ft.
City and township not coextensive.
Name origin: For S.M. Felton, a Great Northern Railroad officer.

*Felton
Township
ZIP: 56536 Lat: 47-06-53 N Long: 96-30-13 W
Pop: 106 (1990); 140 (1980) Pop Density: 3.0
Land: 35.3 sq. mi.; Water: 0.0 sq. mi.

Flowing
Township
Lat: 47-01-13 N **Long:** 96-29-39 W
Pop: 114 (1990); 111 (1980) **Pop Density:** 3.2
Land: 35.9 sq. mi.; **Water:** 0.0 sq. mi.

Georgetown
City
ZIP: 56546 **Lat:** 47-04-41 N **Long:** 96-47-41 W
Pop: 107 (1990); 124 (1980) **Pop Density:** 107.0
Land: 1.0 sq. mi.; **Water:** 0.0 sq. mi.
Founded 1859 as Hudson Bay Trading Post.
Name origin: For one of the trading post's employees.

*Georgetown
Township
ZIP: 56546 **Lat:** 47-06-52 N **Long:** 96-45-50 W
Pop: 179 (1990); 237 (1980) **Pop Density:** 4.9
Land: 36.9 sq. mi.; **Water:** 0.0 sq. mi.

Glyndon
City
ZIP: 56547 **Lat:** 46-52-21 N **Long:** 96-34-45 W
Pop: 862 (1990); 882 (1980) **Pop Density:** 615.7
Land: 1.4 sq. mi.; **Water:** 0.0 sq. mi. **Elev:** 922 ft.
Founded 1872. City and township not coextensive.
Name origin: Named by officials of the Northern Pacific Railroad Company for poet, Mrs. Edward W. Searing, whose pen name was Howard Glyndon.

*Glyndon
Township
ZIP: 56547 **Lat:** 46-51-10 N **Long:** 96-37-03 W
Pop: 314 (1990); 356 (1980) **Pop Density:** 9.2
Land: 34.1 sq. mi.; **Water:** 0.0 sq. mi.

Goose Prairie
Township
Lat: 47-01-01 N **Long:** 96-15-25 W
Pop: 206 (1990); 221 (1980) **Pop Density:** 5.9
Land: 34.8 sq. mi.; **Water:** 0.8 sq. mi.

Hagen
Township
Lat: 47-06-37 N **Long:** 96-22-48 W
Pop: 200 (1990); 225 (1980) **Pop Density:** 6.2
Land: 32.5 sq. mi.; **Water:** 0.0 sq. mi.

Hawley
City
ZIP: 56549 **Lat:** 46-52-41 N **Long:** 96-18-58 W
Pop: 1,655 (1990); 1,634 (1980) **Pop Density:** 1034.4
Land: 1.6 sq. mi.; **Water:** 0.0 sq. mi.
City and township not coextensive.
Name origin: For Gov. Joseph Hawley, Civil War hero and U.S. senator. Originally known as Bethel.

*Hawley
Township
ZIP: 56549 **Lat:** 46-50-34 N **Long:** 96-22-16 W
Pop: 421 (1990); 379 (1980) **Pop Density:** 13.4
Land: 31.5 sq. mi.; **Water:** 0.5 sq. mi.

Highland Grove
Township
Lat: 46-55-48 N **Long:** 96-14-26 W
Pop: 300 (1990); 343 (1980) **Pop Density:** 8.7
Land: 34.3 sq. mi.; **Water:** 0.6 sq. mi.

Hitterdal
City
ZIP: 56552 **Lat:** 46-58-42 N **Long:** 96-15-29 W
Pop: 242 (1990); 253 (1980) **Pop Density:** 302.5
Land: 0.8 sq. mi.; **Water:** 0.1 sq. mi.

Holy Cross
Township
Lat: 46-40-12 N **Long:** 96-44-06 W
Pop: 137 (1990); 160 (1980) **Pop Density:** 4.1
Land: 33.3 sq. mi.; **Water:** 0.0 sq. mi.

Humboldt
Township
Lat: 46-40-30 N **Long:** 96-20-48 W
Pop: 260 (1990); 273 (1980) **Pop Density:** 7.9
Land: 33.1 sq. mi.; **Water:** 0.0 sq. mi.

Keene
Township
Lat: 47-01-00 N **Long:** 96-22-27 W
Pop: 165 (1990); 161 (1980) **Pop Density:** 5.1
Land: 32.4 sq. mi.; **Water:** 0.2 sq. mi.

Kragnes
Township
Lat: 47-01-05 N **Long:** 96-45-36 W
Pop: 346 (1990); 406 (1980) **Pop Density:** 9.1
Land: 38.2 sq. mi.; **Water:** 0.0 sq. mi.

Kurtz
Township
Lat: 46-45-37 N **Long:** 96-44-01 W
Pop: 322 (1990); 318 (1980) **Pop Density:** 9.9
Land: 32.5 sq. mi.; **Water:** 0.0 sq. mi.

Moland
Township
Lat: 46-56-21 N **Long:** 96-36-54 W
Pop: 310 (1990); 360 (1980) **Pop Density:** 8.8
Land: 35.1 sq. mi.; **Water:** 0.0 sq. mi.

Moorhead
City
ZIP: 56560 **Lat:** 46-51-52 N **Long:** 96-45-20 W
Pop: 32,295 (1990); 29,998 (1980) **Pop Density:** 3197.5
Land: 10.1 sq. mi.; **Water:** 0.0 sq. mi.
In western MN on the Red River, opposite Fargo, ND. Settled 1870s. City and township not coextensive.
Name origin: For William G. Moorhead, who was a Great Northern Railroad director of that time.

*Moorhead
Township
Lat: 46-50-11 N **Long:** 96-43-30 W
Pop: 501 (1990); 702 (1980) **Pop Density:** 23.6
Land: 21.2 sq. mi.; **Water:** 0.0 sq. mi.

Morken
Township
Lat: 47-01-38 N **Long:** 96-37-34 W
Pop: 190 (1990); 203 (1980) **Pop Density:** 5.3
Land: 35.9 sq. mi.; **Water:** 0.0 sq. mi.

Oakport
Township
Lat: 46-56-29 N **Long:** 96-43-31 W
Pop: 1,386 (1990); 1,714 (1980) **Pop Density:** 45.4
Land: 30.5 sq. mi.; **Water:** 0.0 sq. mi.

Parke
Township
Lat: 46-45-31 N **Long:** 96-14-29 W
Pop: 468 (1990); 368 (1980) **Pop Density:** 13.7
Land: 34.1 sq. mi.; **Water:** 1.9 sq. mi.

Riverton
Township
Lat: 46-51-06 N **Long:** 96-29-00 W
Pop: 401 (1990); 466 (1980) **Pop Density:** 11.2
Land: 35.8 sq. mi.; **Water:** 0.0 sq. mi.

Sabin
City
ZIP: 56580 **Lat:** 46-46-49 N **Long:** 96-39-10 W
Pop: 495 (1990); 446 (1980) **Pop Density:** 1650.0
Land: 0.3 sq. mi.; **Water:** 0.0 sq. mi.
Name origin: For Dwight Sabin, a prominent MN businessman and U.S. senator (1883–89).

Skree
Township
Lat: 46-45-47 N **Long:** 96-21-22 W
Pop: 157 (1990); 174 (1980) **Pop Density:** 4.7
Land: 33.6 sq. mi.; **Water:** 0.3 sq. mi.

Spring Prairie
Township
Lat: 46-56-22 N Long: 96-28-29 W
Pop: 311 (1990); 313 (1980) **Pop Density:** 8.7
Land: 35.6 sq. mi.; **Water:** 0.0 sq. mi.

Tansem
Township
Lat: 46-40-06 N Long: 96-13-32 W
Pop: 226 (1990); 229 (1980) **Pop Density:** 6.3
Land: 35.6 sq. mi.; **Water:** 0.5 sq. mi.

Ulen
City
ZIP: 56585 Lat: 47-04-45 N Long: 96-15-34 W
Pop: 547 (1990); 514 (1980) **Pop Density:** 497.3
Land: 1.1 sq. mi.; **Water:** 0.0 sq. mi.
City and township not coextensive.
Name origin: For the town's first settler Ole Ulen.

*Ulen
Township
ZIP: 56585 Lat: 47-06-39 N Long: 96-15-12 W
Pop: 192 (1990); 240 (1980) **Pop Density:** 5.5
Land: 35.2 sq. mi.; **Water:** 0.0 sq. mi.

Viding
Township
Lat: 47-06-36 N Long: 96-38-18 W
Pop: 139 (1990); 149 (1980) **Pop Density:** 3.9
Land: 35.7 sq. mi.; **Water:** 0.0 sq. mi.

Clearwater County
County Seat: Bagley (ZIP: 56621)

Pop: 8,309 (1990); 8,761 (1980) **Pop Density:** 8.4
Land: 994.8 sq. mi.; **Water:** 35.1 sq. mi. **Area Code:** 218
In north-central MN, east of Grand Forks, ND; established Dec 2, 1902 from Beltrami County.
Name origin: For Clearwater River and Lake, which are partly within the county.

Bagley
City
ZIP: 56621 Lat: 47-31-24 N Long: 95-24-13 W
Pop: 1,388 (1990); 1,335 (1980) **Pop Density:** 771.1
Land: 1.8 sq. mi.; **Water:** 0.1 sq. mi. **Elev** 1441 ft.
Name origin: Named by the town's settlers for Sumner Bagley, a pioneer lumberman.

Bear Creek
Township
ZIP: 56676 Lat: 47-22-26 N Long: 95-14-10 W
Pop: 124 (1990); 152 (1980) **Pop Density:** 4.1
Land: 30.3 sq. mi.; **Water:** 1.7 sq. mi.

Clearbrook
City
ZIP: 56634 Lat: 47-41-40 N Long: 95-25-42 W
Pop: 560 (1990); 579 (1980) **Pop Density:** 1400.0
Land: 0.4 sq. mi.; **Water:** 0.0 sq. mi.
Name origin: For the nearby brook.

Clover
Township
ZIP: 56652 Lat: 47-46-47 N Long: 95-15-45 W
Pop: 119 (1990); 111 (1980) **Pop Density:** 7.0
Land: 17.1 sq. mi.; **Water:** 0.6 sq. mi.

Copley
Township
ZIP: 56621 Lat: 47-32-13 N Long: 95-21-16 W
Pop: 798 (1990); 907 (1980) **Pop Density:** 23.5
Land: 33.9 sq. mi.; **Water:** 0.2 sq. mi.

Dudley
Township
ZIP: 56652 Lat: 47-38-01 N Long: 95-14-52 W
Pop: 313 (1990); 306 (1980) **Pop Density:** 10.6
Land: 29.6 sq. mi.; **Water:** 1.7 sq. mi.

Eddy
Township
ZIP: 56634 Lat: 47-37-44 N Long: 95-28-48 W
Pop: 366 (1990); 350 (1980) **Pop Density:** 10.5
Land: 34.8 sq. mi.; **Water:** 0.8 sq. mi.

Falk
Township
ZIP: 56621 Lat: 47-27-51 N Long: 95-29-30 W
Pop: 282 (1990); 323 (1980) **Pop Density:** 7.8
Land: 36.3 sq. mi.; **Water:** 0.3 sq. mi.

Gonvick
City
ZIP: 56644 Lat: 47-44-17 N Long: 95-30-45 W
Pop: 302 (1990); 362 (1980) **Pop Density:** 232.3
Land: 1.3 sq. mi.; **Water:** 0.0 sq. mi.
Name origin: For early Norwegian pioneer, Martin Gonvick.

Greenwood
Township
ZIP: 56634 Lat: 47-47-23 N Long: 95-24-30 W
Pop: 83 (1990); 102 (1980) **Pop Density:** 3.5
Land: 23.7 sq. mi.; **Water:** 0.0 sq. mi.

Hangaard
Township
ZIP: 56644 Lat: 47-52-33 N Long: 95-31-35 W
Pop: 17 (1990); 22 (1980) **Pop Density:** 0.8
Land: 22.0 sq. mi.; **Water:** 0.0 sq. mi.

Holst
Township
ZIP: 56652 Lat: 47-37-50 N Long: 95-22-20 W
Pop: 326 (1990); 333 (1980) **Pop Density:** 9.3
Land: 35.1 sq. mi.; **Water:** 0.5 sq. mi.

Itasca
Township
ZIP: 56460 Lat: 47-17-06 N Long: 95-14-26 W
Pop: 150 (1990); 159 (1980) **Pop Density:** 4.4
Land: 34.4 sq. mi.; **Water:** 1.5 sq. mi.

La Prairie
Township
Lat: 47-17-18 N Long: 95-29-01 W
Pop: 353 (1990); 363 (1980) **Pop Density:** 3.5
Land: 99.6 sq. mi.; **Water:** 7.5 sq. mi.

Leon
Township
ZIP: 56634 Lat: 47-43-06 N Long: 95-22-53 W
Pop: 323 (1990); 365 (1980) **Pop Density:** 9.1
Land: 35.4 sq. mi.; **Water:** 0.4 sq. mi.

American Places Dictionary — MINNESOTA, Cook County

Leonard — City
ZIP: 56652 Lat: 47-39-08 N Long: 95-15-58 W
Pop: 26 (1990); 50 (1980) Pop Density: 52.0
Land: 0.5 sq. mi.; Water: 0.0 sq. mi.

Minerva — Township
ZIP: 56621 Lat: 47-22-14 N Long: 95-21-46 W
Pop: 262 (1990); 289 (1980) Pop Density: 7.6
Land: 34.5 sq. mi.; Water: 1.6 sq. mi.

Moose Creek — Township
ZIP: 56676 Lat: 47-27-03 N Long: 95-14-47 W
Pop: 202 (1990); 211 (1980) Pop Density: 6.4
Land: 31.7 sq. mi.; Water: 0.5 sq. mi.

Nora — Township
ZIP: 56621 Lat: 47-26-54 N Long: 95-21-36 W
Pop: 426 (1990); 407 (1980) Pop Density: 11.9
Land: 35.8 sq. mi.; Water: 0.3 sq. mi.

North Clearwater — Pop. Place
Lat: 47-55-32 N Long: 95-23-12 W
Pop: 37 (1990); 65 (1980) Pop Density: 0.2
Land: 187.2 sq. mi.; Water: 4.8 sq. mi.

Pine Lake — Township
ZIP: 56644 Lat: 47-43-03 N Long: 95-31-03 W
Pop: 359 (1990); 370 (1980) Pop Density: 11.3
Land: 31.8 sq. mi.; Water: 2.5 sq. mi.

Popple — Township
ZIP: 56621 Lat: 47-32-32 N Long: 95-29-10 W
Pop: 435 (1990); 469 (1980) Pop Density: 12.5
Land: 34.9 sq. mi.; Water: 0.9 sq. mi.

Rice — Township
Lat: 47-16-29 N Long: 95-21-39 W
Pop: 110 (1990); 136 (1980) Pop Density: 3.2
Land: 34.9 sq. mi.; Water: 1.1 sq. mi.

Shevlin — City
ZIP: 56676 Lat: 47-31-50 N Long: 95-15-33 W
Pop: 157 (1990); 193 (1980) Pop Density: 196.3
Land: 0.8 sq. mi.; Water: 0.0 sq. mi.
City and township not coextensive.

*Shevlin — Township
ZIP: 56676 Lat: 47-32-42 N Long: 95-14-17 W
Pop: 404 (1990); 367 (1980) Pop Density: 13.0
Land: 31.0 sq. mi.; Water: 0.0 sq. mi.

Sinclair — Township
ZIP: 56652 Lat: 47-43-02 N Long: 95-15-25 W
Pop: 181 (1990); 204 (1980) Pop Density: 5.2
Land: 34.5 sq. mi.; Water: 1.7 sq. mi.

South Clearwater — Pop. Place
Lat: 47-11-43 N Long: 95-17-50 W
Pop: 50 (1990); 36 (1980) Pop Density: 0.8
Land: 65.8 sq. mi.; Water: 6.4 sq. mi.

Winsor — Township
ZIP: 56644 Lat: 47-48-40 N Long: 95-30-17 W
Pop: 156 (1990); 195 (1980) Pop Density: 4.4
Land: 35.7 sq. mi.; Water: 0.1 sq. mi.

Cook County
County Seat: Grand Marais (ZIP: 55604)

Pop: 3,868 (1990); 4,092 (1980) Pop Density: 2.7
Land: 1450.7 sq. mi.; Water: 1888.5 sq. mi. Area Code: 218
On the northeastern border of MN; established Mar 9, 1874 from Lake County.
Name origin: For Maj. Michael Cook (1828–64), an officer in the Civil War and MN legislator. Some claim John Cook (?–1872), killed by Ojibway Indians.

East Cook — Pop. Place
Lat: 47-58-20 N Long: 90-10-15 W
Pop: 483 (1990); 475 (1980) Pop Density: 1.2
Land: 395.3 sq. mi.; Water: 42.3 sq. mi.

Grand Marais — City
ZIP: 55604 Lat: 47-45-18 N Long: 90-20-41 W
Pop: 1,171 (1990); 1,289 (1980) Pop Density: 433.7
Land: 2.7 sq. mi.; Water: 0.0 sq. mi. Elev: 688 ft.
Name origin: Named by early French trappers for its original feature, a 'Great Marsh.'

Grand Portage — Pop. Place
Lat: 47-56-38 N Long: 89-43-09 W
Pop: 321 (1990); 324 (1980) Pop Density: 4.3
Land: 74.4 sq. mi.; Water: 118.4 sq. mi.

Lutsen — Township
ZIP: 55612 Lat: 47-46-11 N Long: 90-42-01 W
Pop: 240 (1990) Pop Density: 2.5
Land: 97.9 sq. mi.; Water: 7.9 sq. mi.

Schroeder — Township
ZIP: 55613 Lat: 47-41-43 N Long: 90-57-48 W
Pop: 174 (1990); 325 (1980) Pop Density: 1.2
Land: 149.9 sq. mi.; Water: 9.1 sq. mi.

Tofte — Township
ZIP: 55615 Lat: 47-45-55 N Long: 90-50-27 W
Pop: 231 (1990); 275 (1980) Pop Density: 1.5
Land: 154.6 sq. mi.; Water: 8.0 sq. mi.

West Cook — Pop. Place
Lat: 47-58-07 N Long: 90-38-46 W
Pop: 1,248 (1990); 1,404 (1980) Pop Density: 2.2
Land: 575.9 sq. mi.; Water: 87.2 sq. mi.

Cottonwood County
County Seat: Windom (ZIP: 56101)

Pop: 12,694 (1990); 14,854 (1980) **Pop Density:** 19.8
Land: 640.0 sq. mi.; **Water:** 8.9 sq. mi. **Area Code:** 507

In southwestern MN, southwest of Mankato; established May 23, 1857 (prior to statehood) from Brown County.

Name origin: For the Cottonwood River, which runs through the county; itself named for the poplar trees along its banks, which have cotton-like tufts on the seeds.

Amboy
Township
Lat: 44-03-27 N **Long:** 95-08-59 W
Pop: 227 (1990); 296 (1980) **Pop Density:** 6.4
Land: 35.6 sq. mi.; **Water:** 0.0 sq. mi.

Amo
Township
Lat: 43-58-50 N **Long:** 95-17-09 W
Pop: 184 (1990); 281 (1980) **Pop Density:** 5.2
Land: 35.1 sq. mi.; **Water:** 0.7 sq. mi.

Ann
Township
Lat: 44-09-12 N **Long:** 95-24-30 W
Pop: 231 (1990); 321 (1980) **Pop Density:** 6.4
Land: 36.2 sq. mi.; **Water:** 0.0 sq. mi.

Bingham Lake
City
ZIP: 56118 **Lat:** 43-54-33 N **Long:** 95-02-43 W
Pop: 155 (1990); 222 (1980) **Pop Density:** 221.4
Land: 0.7 sq. mi.; **Water:** 0.0 sq. mi.
Incorporated 1900.
Name origin: For K. S. Bingham, U.S. senator and MI governor in the pre-Civil War era.

Carson
Township
Lat: 43-58-42 N **Long:** 95-02-15 W
Pop: 363 (1990); 437 (1980) **Pop Density:** 10.3
Land: 35.2 sq. mi.; **Water:** 0.6 sq. mi.

Comfrey
City
ZIP: 56019 **Lat:** 44-06-27 N **Long:** 94-54-10 W
Pop: 3 (1990); 40 (1980) **Pop Density:** 1500.0
Land: 0.002 sq. mi.; **Water:** 0.0 sq. mi. **Elev:** 1301 ft.
Part of the town is also in Brown County.
Name origin: For a nearby post office named for the famous medicinal plant.

Dale
Township
Lat: 43-58-49 N **Long:** 95-09-57 W
Pop: 182 (1990); 260 (1980) **Pop Density:** 5.1
Land: 35.6 sq. mi.; **Water:** 0.5 sq. mi.

Delton
Township
Lat: 44-03-52 N **Long:** 95-02-16 W
Pop: 173 (1990); 215 (1980) **Pop Density:** 4.8
Land: 35.7 sq. mi.; **Water:** 0.0 sq. mi.

Germantown
Township
Lat: 44-08-46 N **Long:** 95-09-43 W
Pop: 274 (1990); 344 (1980) **Pop Density:** 7.7
Land: 35.8 sq. mi.; **Water:** 0.0 sq. mi.

Great Bend
Township
Lat: 43-53-52 N **Long:** 95-09-42 W
Pop: 665 (1990); 708 (1980) **Pop Density:** 20.7
Land: 32.2 sq. mi.; **Water:** 0.7 sq. mi.

Highwater
Township
Lat: 44-09-09 N **Long:** 95-16-33 W
Pop: 213 (1990); 276 (1980) **Pop Density:** 5.9
Land: 35.9 sq. mi.; **Water:** 0.2 sq. mi.

Jeffers
City
ZIP: 56145 **Lat:** 44-03-19 N **Long:** 95-11-43 W
Pop: 443 (1990); 437 (1980) **Pop Density:** 1107.5
Land: 0.4 sq. mi.; **Water:** 0.0 sq. mi.
Name origin: For George Jeffers, on whose land the town was built.

Lakeside
Township
Lat: 43-53-03 N **Long:** 95-02-55 W
Pop: 277 (1990); 372 (1980) **Pop Density:** 8.3
Land: 33.5 sq. mi.; **Water:** 1.8 sq. mi.

Midway
Township
Lat: 43-59-01 N **Long:** 94-55-03 W
Pop: 307 (1990); 395 (1980) **Pop Density:** 9.0
Land: 34.3 sq. mi.; **Water:** 0.4 sq. mi.

Mountain Lake
City
ZIP: 56159 **Lat:** 43-56-25 N **Long:** 94-55-34 W
Pop: 1,906 (1990); 2,277 (1980) **Pop Density:** 1466.2
Land: 1.3 sq. mi.; **Water:** 0.0 sq. mi. **Elev:** 1305 ft.
Name origin: For a former lake, which had a large mountain-like island rising from it.

*Mountain Lake
Township
ZIP: 56159 **Lat:** 43-53-02 N **Long:** 94-55-08 W
Pop: 293 (1990); 284 (1980) **Pop Density:** 8.2
Land: 35.7 sq. mi.; **Water:** 0.1 sq. mi.

Rose Hill
Township
Lat: 43-58-34 N **Long:** 95-24-11 W
Pop: 211 (1990); 277 (1980) **Pop Density:** 5.9
Land: 35.7 sq. mi.; **Water:** 0.8 sq. mi.

Selma
Township
Lat: 44-03-51 N **Long:** 94-55-46 W
Pop: 275 (1990); 290 (1980) **Pop Density:** 7.6
Land: 36.1 sq. mi.; **Water:** 0.0 sq. mi.

Southbrook
Township
Lat: 43-53-02 N **Long:** 95-23-28 W
Pop: 145 (1990); 177 (1980) **Pop Density:** 4.2
Land: 34.3 sq. mi.; **Water:** 2.1 sq. mi.

Springfield
Township
Lat: 43-53-55 N **Long:** 95-17-07 W
Pop: 216 (1990); 264 (1980) **Pop Density:** 6.0
Land: 36.1 sq. mi.; **Water:** 0.0 sq. mi.

Storden
City
ZIP: 56174 **Lat:** 44-02-22 N **Long:** 95-19-11 W
Pop: 283 (1990); 341 (1980) **Pop Density:** 1415.0
Land: 0.2 sq. mi.; **Water:** 0.0 sq. mi.
City and township not coextensive.

American Places Dictionary | MINNESOTA, Crow Wing County

*Storden — Township
ZIP: 56174   Lat: 44-03-45 N   Long: 95-16-36 W
Pop: 254 (1990); 343 (1980)   Pop Density: 7.1
Land: 35.7 sq. mi.; Water: 0.1 sq. mi.

Westbrook — City
ZIP: 56183   Lat: 44-02-33 N   Long: 95-26-05 W
Pop: 853 (1990); 978 (1980)   Pop Density: 1066.3
Land: 0.8 sq. mi.; Water: 0.0 sq. mi.   Elev: 1422 ft.
Founded 1878. City and township not coextensive.
Name origin: For the west branch of Highwater Creek.

*Westbrook — Township
ZIP: 56183   Lat: 44-04-21 N   Long: 95-23-27 W
Pop: 278 (1990); 353 (1980)   Pop Density: 8.0
Land: 34.7 sq. mi.; Water: 0.7 sq. mi.

Windom — City
ZIP: 56101   Lat: 43-52-10 N   Long: 95-07-05 W
Pop: 4,283 (1990); 4,666 (1980)   Pop Density: 1476.9
Land: 2.9 sq. mi.; Water: 0.2 sq. mi.   Elev: 1364 ft.
Name origin: For William Windom, U.S. senator and cabinet officer in the late 1800s.

Crow Wing County
County Seat: Brainerd (ZIP: 56401)

Pop: 44,249 (1990); 41,722 (1980)   Pop Density: 44.4
Land: 996.7 sq. mi.; Water: 159.9 sq. mi.   Area Code: 218
In central MN, north of St. Cloud; established May 23, 1857 (prior to statehood) from Cass and Aitkin counties.
Name origin: For the Crow Wing River, which forms the southwestern border of the county; the Ojibway called the river *Kagiwigwan* or *Gagagiwigwuni* 'crow wing' or 'raven feather.'

Baxter — City
ZIP: 56401   Lat: 46-20-28 N   Long: 94-16-56 W
Pop: 3,695 (1990); 2,625 (1980)   Pop Density: 213.6
Land: 17.3 sq. mi.; Water: 2.4 sq. mi.   Elev: 1208 ft.
Name origin: For Luther Baxter, soldier, attorney, and state representative in the 1870s.

Bay Lake — Township
ZIP: 56444   Lat: 46-22-35 N   Long: 93-52-19 W
Pop: 657 (1990); 719 (1980)   Pop Density: 24.3
Land: 27.0 sq. mi.; Water: 9.2 sq. mi.

Brainerd — City
ZIP: 56401   Lat: 46-21-15 N   Long: 94-11-38 W
Pop: 12,353 (1990); 11,489 (1980)   Pop Density: 1790.3
Land: 6.9 sq. mi.; Water: 0.5 sq. mi.
In central MN on the Mississippi River, 53 mi. north of St. Cloud. Founded 1870.
Name origin: For the wife of the president of the Northern Pacific Railway.

Breezy Point — City
ZIP: 56472   Lat: 46-36-05 N   Long: 94-13-09 W
Pop: 432 (1990); 384 (1980)   Pop Density: 33.8
Land: 12.8 sq. mi.; Water: 1.2 sq. mi.

Center — Township
Lat: 46-29-43 N   Long: 94-06-36 W
Pop: 517 (1990); 470 (1980)   Pop Density: 29.0
Land: 17.8 sq. mi.; Water: 4.0 sq. mi.

Crosby — City
ZIP: 56441   Lat: 46-29-23 N   Long: 93-57-23 W
Pop: 2,073 (1990); 2,218 (1980)   Pop Density: 691.0
Land: 3.0 sq. mi.; Water: 0.6 sq. mi.   Elev: 1261 ft.
Name origin: For George Crosby, former manager of the local iron mines.

Crosslake — City
ZIP: 56442   Lat: 46-40-56 N   Long: 94-05-41 W
Pop: 1,132 (1990); 1,064 (1980)   Pop Density: 44.2
Land: 25.6 sq. mi.; Water: 11.3 sq. mi.

Crow Wing — Township
Lat: 46-17-01 N   Long: 94-14-26 W
Pop: 914 (1990); 687 (1980)   Pop Density: 29.5
Land: 31.0 sq. mi.; Water: 0.3 sq. mi.

Cuyuna — City
ZIP: 56444   Lat: 46-30-42 N   Long: 93-55-44 W
Pop: 172 (1990); 157 (1980)   Pop Density: 52.1
Land: 3.3 sq. mi.; Water: 0.2 sq. mi.
Name origin: For Cuyler Adams, who discovered and owned the iron mine in the area, and his dog Una.

Daggett Brook — Township
Lat: 46-12-12 N   Long: 94-07-40 W
Pop: 396 (1990); 458 (1980)   Pop Density: 10.9
Land: 36.3 sq. mi.; Water: 0.1 sq. mi.

Dean Lake — Township
ZIP: 56441   Lat: 46-36-03 N   Long: 93-50-37 W
Pop: 59 (1990); 72 (1980)   Pop Density: 3.5
Land: 16.8 sq. mi.; Water: 1.3 sq. mi.

Deerwood — City
ZIP: 56444   Lat: 46-28-23 N   Long: 93-53-56 W
Pop: 524 (1990); 580 (1980)   Pop Density: 374.3
Land: 1.4 sq. mi.; Water: 0.7 sq. mi.   Elev: 1277 ft.
City and township not coextensive.
Name origin: Named by early settlers for the plentiful deer in the nearby woods.

*Deerwood — Township
ZIP: 56444   Lat: 46-27-44 N   Long: 93-52-33 W
Pop: 859 (1990); 952 (1980)   Pop Density: 30.1
Land: 28.5 sq. mi.; Water: 5.1 sq. mi.

Emily — City
ZIP: 56447   Lat: 46-45-24 N   Long: 93-57-41 W
Pop: 613 (1990); 588 (1980)   Pop Density: 20.4
Land: 30.0 sq. mi.; Water: 6.1 sq. mi.
Name origin: For Emily Lake, itself believed to be named for the wife of an early lumberman.

Fairfield
Township
ZIP: 56447   **Lat:** 46-40-25 N   **Long:** 93-57-48 W
Pop: 244 (1990); 267 (1980)   **Pop Density:** 7.3
Land: 33.6 sq. mi.; **Water:** 2.4 sq. mi.

Fifty Lakes
City
ZIP: 56448   **Lat:** 46-44-55 N   **Long:** 94-05-45 W
Pop: 299 (1990); 263 (1980)   **Pop Density:** 10.3
Land: 29.0 sq. mi.; **Water:** 4.4 sq. mi.
Name origin: For the many lakes in the area.

Fort Ripley
City
ZIP: 56449   **Lat:** 46-09-59 N   **Long:** 94-21-41 W
Pop: 92 (1990); 83 (1980)   **Pop Density:** 65.7
Land: 1.4 sq. mi.; **Water:** 0.0 sq. mi.
City and township not coextensive.

*Fort Ripley
Township
ZIP: 56449   **Lat:** 46-13-13 N   **Long:** 94-20-37 W
Pop: 448 (1990); 450 (1980)   **Pop Density:** 20.2
Land: 22.2 sq. mi.; **Water:** 1.7 sq. mi.

Gail Lake
Township
ZIP: 56463   **Lat:** 46-46-45 N   **Long:** 94-19-01 W
Pop: 87 (1990); 106 (1980)   **Pop Density:** 5.2
Land: 16.7 sq. mi.; **Water:** 1.4 sq. mi.

Garrison
City
ZIP: 56450   **Lat:** 46-18-09 N   **Long:** 93-49-24 W
Pop: 138 (1990); 174 (1980)   **Pop Density:** 138.0
Land: 1.0 sq. mi.; **Water:** 0.0 sq. mi.
City and township not coextensive.

*Garrison
Township
ZIP: 56450   **Lat:** 46-17-16 N   **Long:** 93-52-58 W
Pop: 488 (1990); 498 (1980)   **Pop Density:** 16.6
Land: 29.4 sq. mi.; **Water:** 6.1 sq. mi.

Ideal
Township
Lat: 46-40-16 N   **Long:** 94-13-07 W
Pop: 724 (1990); 760 (1980)   **Pop Density:** 36.9
Land: 19.6 sq. mi.; **Water:** 15.4 sq. mi.

Irondale
Township
Lat: 46-26-53 N   **Long:** 94-00-52 W
Pop: 993 (1990); 949 (1980)   **Pop Density:** 34.8
Land: 28.5 sq. mi.; **Water:** 3.3 sq. mi.

Ironton
City
ZIP: 56455   **Lat:** 46-28-51 N   **Long:** 93-59-47 W
Pop: 553 (1990); 537 (1980)   **Pop Density:** 368.7
Land: 1.5 sq. mi.; **Water:** 0.5 sq. mi.
Name origin: For the large U.S. Steel camp mill in the town.

Jenkins
City
ZIP: 56456   **Lat:** 46-39-08 N   **Long:** 94-19-44 W
Pop: 262 (1990); 219 (1980)   **Pop Density:** 65.5
Land: 4.0 sq. mi.; **Water:** 0.0 sq. mi.
City and township not coextensive.
Name origin: For lumberman and founder George Jenkins.

*Jenkins
Township
Lat: 46-40-37 N   **Long:** 94-18-42 W
Pop: 280 (1990); 317 (1980)   **Pop Density:** 23.5
Land: 11.9 sq. mi.; **Water:** 2.1 sq. mi.

Lake Edwards
Township
ZIP: 56468   **Lat:** 46-29-52 N   **Long:** 94-12-12 W
Pop: 1,528 (1990); 1,442 (1980)   **Pop Density:** 60.2
Land: 25.4 sq. mi.; **Water:** 10.8 sq. mi.

Little Pine
Township
Lat: 46-45-21 N   **Long:** 93-50-33 W
Pop: 86 (1990); 103 (1980)   **Pop Density:** 2.5
Land: 34.5 sq. mi.; **Water:** 1.3 sq. mi.

Long Lake
Township
Lat: 46-17-27 N   **Long:** 94-07-20 W
Pop: 855 (1990); 877 (1980)   **Pop Density:** 25.0
Land: 34.2 sq. mi.; **Water:** 2.2 sq. mi.

Manhattan Beach
City
ZIP: 56463   **Lat:** 46-44-03 N   **Long:** 94-08-39 W
Pop: 61 (1990); 60 (1980)   **Pop Density:** 40.7
Land: 1.5 sq. mi.; **Water:** 0.0 sq. mi.

Maple Grove
Township
ZIP: 56450   **Lat:** 46-17-30 N   **Long:** 94-01-04 W
Pop: 543 (1990); 459 (1980)   **Pop Density:** 15.8
Land: 34.3 sq. mi.; **Water:** 1.6 sq. mi.

Mission
Township
ZIP: 56441   **Lat:** 46-35-04 N   **Long:** 94-04-34 W
Pop: 514 (1990); 527 (1980)   **Pop Density:** 17.4
Land: 29.6 sq. mi.; **Water:** 5.1 sq. mi.

Nisswa
City
ZIP: 56468   **Lat:** 46-30-00 N   **Long:** 94-17-50 W
Pop: 1,391 (1990); 1,407 (1980)   **Pop Density:** 127.6
Land: 10.9 sq. mi.; **Water:** 7.5 sq. mi.   **Elev:** 1231 ft.
Name origin: From an Ojibway Indian term meaning 'in the middle'; reference is unknown.

Nokay Lake
Township
Lat: 46-22-56 N   **Long:** 93-59-37 W
Pop: 567 (1990); 530 (1980)   **Pop Density:** 17.1
Land: 33.1 sq. mi.; **Water:** 2.8 sq. mi.

Oak Lawn
Township
Lat: 46-23-20 N   **Long:** 94-06-43 W
Pop: 1,950 (1990); 2,093 (1980)   **Pop Density:** 54.8
Land: 35.6 sq. mi.; **Water:** 2.4 sq. mi.

Pelican
Township
Lat: 46-33-48 N   **Long:** 94-11-51 W
Pop: 245 (1990); 267 (1980)   **Pop Density:** 29.9
Land: 8.2 sq. mi.; **Water:** 13.6 sq. mi.

Pequot Lakes
City
ZIP: 56472   **Lat:** 46-36-07 N   **Long:** 94-19-14 W
Pop: 843 (1990); 681 (1980)   **Pop Density:** 936.7
Land: 0.9 sq. mi.; **Water:** 0.2 sq. mi.   **Elev:** 1280 ft.
Name origin: For an Algonquian Indian tribe in eastern CT.

Perry Lake
Township
ZIP: 56441   **Lat:** 46-35-51 N   **Long:** 93-57-25 W
Pop: 201 (1990); 186 (1980)   **Pop Density:** 6.5
Land: 30.9 sq. mi.; **Water:** 1.7 sq. mi.

Platte Lake
Township
Lat: 46-11-33 N   **Long:** 94-00-33 W
Pop: 260 (1990); 277 (1980)   **Pop Density:** 7.3
Land: 35.7 sq. mi.; **Water:** 0.3 sq. mi.

Rabbit Lake
Township
Lat: 46-32-29 N   **Long:** 93-52-24 W
Pop: 189 (1990); 184 (1980)   **Pop Density:** 8.6
Land: 22.0 sq. mi.; **Water:** 2.1 sq. mi.

Riverton
City
ZIP: 56455   **Lat:** 46-27-39 N   **Long:** 94-02-55 W
Pop: 122 (1990); 112 (1980)   **Pop Density:** 152.5
Land: 0.8 sq. mi.; **Water:** 0.1 sq. mi.   **Elev:** 1228 ft.

Roosevelt
Township
Lat: 46-12-27 N **Long:** 93-52-40 W
Pop: 342 (1990); 404 (1980) **Pop Density:** 11.0
Land: 31.1 sq. mi.; **Water:** 5.2 sq. mi.

Ross Lake
Township
Lat: 46-40-27 N **Long:** 93-50-17 W
Pop: 116 (1990); 109 (1980) **Pop Density:** 3.5
Land: 33.4 sq. mi.; **Water:** 2.8 sq. mi.

St. Mathias
Township
Lat: 46-11-43 N **Long:** 94-15-06 W
Pop: 441 (1990); 440 (1980) **Pop Density:** 12.5
Land: 35.4 sq. mi.; **Water:** 0.5 sq. mi.

Sibley
Township
ZIP: 56472 **Lat:** 46-35-34 N **Long:** 94-18-02 W
Pop: 697 (1990); 557 (1980) **Pop Density:** 44.7
Land: 15.6 sq. mi.; **Water:** 1.6 sq. mi.

Timothy
Township
ZIP: 56463 **Lat:** 46-45-31 N **Long:** 94-13-05 W
Pop: 129 (1990); 119 (1980) **Pop Density:** 3.8
Land: 34.1 sq. mi.; **Water:** 1.5 sq. mi.

Trommald
City
ZIP: 56441 **Lat:** 46-30-16 N **Long:** 94-01-00 W
Pop: 80 (1990); 84 (1980) **Pop Density:** 21.6
Land: 3.7 sq. mi.; **Water:** 0.2 sq. mi.

West Crow Wing
Pop. Place
Lat: 46-24-44 N **Long:** 94-14-09 W
Pop: 3,987 (1990); 3,655 (1980) **Pop Density:** 112.6
Land: 35.4 sq. mi.; **Water:** 13.7 sq. mi.

Wolford
Township
ZIP: 56441 **Lat:** 46-31-38 N **Long:** 94-00-36 W
Pop: 220 (1990); 175 (1980) **Pop Density:** 15.1
Land: 14.6 sq. mi.; **Water:** 2.4 sq. mi.

Dakota County
County Seat: Hastings (ZIP: 55033)

Pop: 275,227 (1990); 194,279 (1980) **Pop Density:** 483.1
Land: 569.7 sq. mi.; **Water:** 16.6 sq. mi. **Area Code:** 612

On the southeastern border of MN, south of St. Paul; original county; established Oct 27, 1849 (prior to statehood); originally spelled Dakotah.

Name origin: For the Dakota (also known as Sioux) Indians of Siouan linguistic stock.

Apple Valley
City
ZIP: 55124 **Lat:** 44-44-56 N **Long:** 93-11-50 W
Pop: 34,598 (1990); 21,818 (1980) **Pop Density:** 1999.9
Land: 17.3 sq. mi.; **Water:** 0.4 sq. mi. **Elev:** 955 ft.
In southeastern MN, near St. Paul.
Name origin: For local fruit production.

Burnsville
City
ZIP: 55337 **Lat:** 44-45-52 N **Long:** 93-16-47 W
Pop: 51,288 (1990); 35,674 (1980) **Pop Density:** 2059.8
Land: 24.9 sq. mi.; **Water:** 1.9 sq. mi. **Elev:** 975 ft.
Name origin: For Canadian emigrant William Burns, who arrived in 1853.

Castle Rock
Township
ZIP: 55010 **Lat:** 44-35-27 N **Long:** 93-05-25 W
Pop: 1,480 (1990); 1,340 (1980) **Pop Density:** 41.3
Land: 35.8 sq. mi.; **Water:** 0.0 sq. mi.

Coates
City
ZIP: 55068 **Lat:** 44-42-56 N **Long:** 93-02-06 W
Pop: 186 (1990); 207 (1980) **Pop Density:** 132.9
Land: 1.4 sq. mi.; **Water:** 0.0 sq. mi.

Douglas
Township
Lat: 44-35-28 N **Long:** 92-50-52 W
Pop: 670 (1990); 614 (1980) **Pop Density:** 20.0
Land: 33.5 sq. mi.; **Water:** 0.0 sq. mi.

Eagan
City
ZIP: 55121 **Lat:** 44-49-09 N **Long:** 93-09-46 W
Pop: 47,409 (1990); 20,700 (1980) **Pop Density:** 1472.3
Land: 32.2 sq. mi.; **Water:** 1.1 sq. mi. **Elev:** 955 ft.
Founded 1861.
Name origin: For one of the first settlers, Patrick Eagan.

Empire
Township
ZIP: 55024 **Lat:** 44-40-17 N **Long:** 93-05-07 W
Pop: 1,340 (1990); 1,224 (1980) **Pop Density:** 39.0
Land: 34.4 sq. mi.; **Water:** 0.0 sq. mi.

Eureka
Township
Lat: 44-34-53 N **Long:** 93-13-41 W
Pop: 1,405 (1990); 1,268 (1980) **Pop Density:** 39.7
Land: 35.4 sq. mi.; **Water:** 0.5 sq. mi.

Farmington
City
ZIP: 55024 **Lat:** 44-39-25 N **Long:** 93-10-42 W
Pop: 5,940 (1990); 4,370 (1980) **Pop Density:** 503.4
Land: 11.8 sq. mi.; **Water:** 0.0 sq. mi. **Elev:** 904 ft.
Name origin: For the many farms originally in the area.

Greenvale
Township
Lat: 44-30-49 N **Long:** 93-12-57 W
Pop: 685 (1990); 641 (1980) **Pop Density:** 22.9
Land: 29.9 sq. mi.; **Water:** 0.0 sq. mi.

Hampton
City
ZIP: 55031 **Lat:** 44-36-33 N **Long:** 93-00-08 W
Pop: 363 (1990); 299 (1980) **Pop Density:** 279.2
Land: 1.3 sq. mi.; **Water:** 0.0 sq. mi. **Elev:** 980 ft.
Founded 1858. City and township not coextensive.
Name origin: For Hampton, CT.

*Hampton
Township
ZIP: 55031 **Lat:** 44-35-39 N **Long:** 92-57-39 W
Pop: 866 (1990); 848 (1980) **Pop Density:** 25.2
Land: 34.3 sq. mi.; **Water:** 0.0 sq. mi.

MINNESOTA, Dakota County

Hastings — City
ZIP: 55033 Lat: 44-43-58 N Long: 92-51-09 W
Pop: 15,440 (1990); 12,811 (1980) Pop Density: 1696.7
Land: 9.1 sq. mi.; Water: 0.7 sq. mi. Elev: 730 ft.

In southeastern MN on the Mississippi River, 20 mi. southeast of St. Paul. Part of the town is also in Washington County.

Name origin: For pioneer and first governor of MN Henry Hastings Sibley (1811–91), who defended the state during the 1862 Sioux uprising.

Inver Grove Heights — City
ZIP: 55076 Lat: 44-49-30 N Long: 93-03-27 W
Pop: 22,477 (1990); 17,171 (1980) Pop Density: 783.2
Land: 28.7 sq. mi.; Water: 1.5 sq. mi.

In southeastern MN, 3 mi. southeast of St. Paul.

Name origin: Named by Irish settler, John McGroartt, for a town in Ireland.

Lakeville — City
ZIP: 55024 Lat: 44-40-45 N Long: 93-14-41 W
Pop: 24,854 (1990); 14,790 (1980) Pop Density: 686.6
Land: 36.2 sq. mi.; Water: 1.3 sq. mi. Elev: 974 ft.

In southeastern MN, 26 mi. southeast of Minneapolis.

Name origin: For adjacent Lake Marion.

Lilydale — City
ZIP: 55118 Lat: 44-54-50 N Long: 93-07-48 W
Pop: 506 (1990); 417 (1980) Pop Density: 722.9
Land: 0.7 sq. mi.; Water: 0.2 sq. mi.

Marshan — Township
Lat: 44-40-21 N Long: 92-51-24 W
Pop: 1,286 (1990); 1,655 (1980) Pop Density: 37.0
Land: 34.8 sq. mi.; Water: 0.0 sq. mi.

Mendota — City
ZIP: 55150 Lat: 44-53-12 N Long: 93-09-33 W
Pop: 164 (1990); 219 (1980) Pop Density: 820.0
Land: 0.2 sq. mi.; Water: 0.0 sq. mi.

Mendota Heights — City
ZIP: 55118 Lat: 44-52-55 N Long: 93-08-25 W
Pop: 9,431 (1990); 7,288 (1980) Pop Density: 992.7
Land: 9.5 sq. mi.; Water: 0.7 sq. mi.

Name origin: For an elevated part of the Mendota area.

Miesville — City
Lat: 44-36-00 N Long: 92-48-36 W
Pop: 135 (1990); 179 (1980) Pop Density: 61.4
Land: 2.2 sq. mi.; Water: 0.0 sq. mi.

New Trier — City
ZIP: 55031 Lat: 44-36-14 N Long: 92-55-59 W
Pop: 96 (1990); 115 (1980) Pop Density: 480.0
Land: 0.2 sq. mi.; Water: 0.0 sq. mi. Elev: 980 ft.

Nininger — Township
Lat: 44-44-39 N Long: 92-55-22 W
Pop: 805 (1990); 774 (1980) Pop Density: 58.3
Land: 13.8 sq. mi.; Water: 3.9 sq. mi.

Northfield — City
ZIP: 55057 Lat: 44-28-22 N Long: 93-09-28 W
Pop: 170 (1990); 13 (1980) Pop Density: 850.0
Land: 0.2 sq. mi.; Water: 0.0 sq. mi.

In southern MN, south of Minneapolis. Part of the town is also in Rice County.

Name origin: For founder John North, who later became a U.S. judge in CA.

Randolph — City
ZIP: 55065 Lat: 44-31-34 N Long: 93-01-06 W
Pop: 331 (1990); 351 (1980) Pop Density: 331.0
Land: 1.0 sq. mi.; Water: 0.0 sq. mi.

City and township not coextensive.

Name origin: For a local railway official.

*Randolph — Township
ZIP: 55065 Lat: 44-31-54 N Long: 92-58-04 W
Pop: 448 (1990); 385 (1980) Pop Density: 47.7
Land: 9.4 sq. mi.; Water: 1.2 sq. mi.

Ravenna — Township
Lat: 44-41-14 N Long: 92-45-42 W
Pop: 1,926 (1990); 1,683 (1980) Pop Density: 93.5
Land: 20.6 sq. mi.; Water: 1.3 sq. mi.

Rosemount — City
ZIP: 55068 Lat: 44-44-51 N Long: 93-04-14 W
Pop: 8,622 (1990); 5,083 (1980) Pop Density: 255.8
Land: 33.7 sq. mi.; Water: 1.4 sq. mi. Elev: 970 ft.

Name origin: For the village of Rosemount, Ireland.

Sciota — Township
Lat: 44-30-25 N Long: 93-04-33 W
Pop: 252 (1990); 242 (1980) Pop Density: 16.8
Land: 15.0 sq. mi.; Water: 0.0 sq. mi.

South St. Paul — City
ZIP: 55075 Lat: 44-53-16 N Long: 93-02-24 W
Pop: 20,197 (1990); 21,235 (1980) Pop Density: 3543.3
Land: 5.7 sq. mi.; Water: 0.4 sq. mi.

In southeastern MN on the Mississippi River, 4 mi. southeast of St. Paul.

Name origin: For its location in relation to St. Paul.

Sunfish Lake — City
ZIP: 55118 Lat: 44-52-29 N Long: 93-05-48 W
Pop: 413 (1990); 344 (1980) Pop Density: 258.1
Land: 1.6 sq. mi.; Water: 0.1 sq. mi.

Vermillion — City
ZIP: 55085 Lat: 44-40-28 N Long: 92-57-50 W
Pop: 510 (1990); 438 (1980) Pop Density: 510.0
Land: 1.0 sq. mi.; Water: 0.0 sq. mi.

City and township not coextensive.

Name origin: For the bright red sandstone found on the banks of the Vermillion River.

*Vermillion — Township
ZIP: 55085 Lat: 44-39-34 N Long: 92-58-30 W
Pop: 1,201 (1990); 1,070 (1980) Pop Density: 35.2
Land: 34.1 sq. mi.; Water: 0.0 sq. mi.

Waterford — Township
Lat: 44-30-45 N Long: 93-08-16 W
Pop: 485 (1990); 486 (1980) Pop Density: 32.8
Land: 14.8 sq. mi.; Water: 0.0 sq. mi.

West St. Paul — City
ZIP: 55118 Lat: 44-54-09 N Long: 93-05-08 W
Pop: 19,248 (1990); 18,527 (1980) Pop Density: 3849.6
Land: 5.0 sq. mi.; Water: 0.0 sq. mi.

In southeastern MN, a suburb of St. Paul.

Name origin: For its location in relation to St. Paul.

MINNESOTA, Dodge County

> ## Dodge County
> **County Seat: Mantorville (ZIP: 55955)**
>
> **Pop:** 15,731 (1990); 14,773 (1980) **Pop Density:** 35.8
> **Land:** 439.5 sq. mi.; **Water:** 0.1 sq. mi. **Area Code:** 507
> In southeastern MN, west of Rochester; established Feb 20, 1855 (prior to statehood) from Olmstead County.
> **Name origin:** For Gen. Henry Dodge (1782–1867), officer in the War of 1812 and the Black Hawk War, governor of WI Territory (1836–41; 1845–48), and U.S. senator (1848–57); also for his son, Augustus Caesar Dodge (1812–83), U.S. senator from IA (1848–55) and U.S. Minister to Spain (1855–59).

Ashland — Township
Lat: 43-58-51 N **Long:** 92-52-04 W
Pop: 420 (1990); 421 (1980) **Pop Density:** 11.2
Land: 37.4 sq. mi.; **Water:** 0.0 sq. mi.

Blooming Prairie — City
Lat: 43-52-07 N **Long:** 93-02-33 W
Pop: 0 (1990); 1,969 (1980)
Land: 0.1 sq. mi.; **Water:** 0.0 sq. mi.
Settled 1856. Part of the town is also in Steele County.
Name origin: For the abundant spring prairie flowers.

Canisteo — Township
ZIP: 55944 **Lat:** 43-58-54 N **Long:** 92-44-02 W
Pop: 599 (1990); 608 (1980) **Pop Density:** 16.7
Land: 35.9 sq. mi.; **Water:** 0.0 sq. mi.

Claremont — City
ZIP: 55924 **Lat:** 44-02-40 N **Long:** 92-59-46 W
Pop: 530 (1990); 591 (1980) **Pop Density:** 530.0
Land: 1.0 sq. mi.; **Water:** 0.0 sq. mi.
Settled 1858. City and township not coextensive.
Name origin: For Claremont, NH, former hometown of settlers.

*Claremont — Township
ZIP: 55924 **Lat:** 44-03-54 N **Long:** 92-59-03 W
Pop: 449 (1990); 449 (1980) **Pop Density:** 12.9
Land: 34.9 sq. mi.; **Water:** 0.1 sq. mi.

Concord — Township
ZIP: 55985 **Lat:** 44-08-59 N **Long:** 92-52-07 W
Pop: 557 (1990); 659 (1980) **Pop Density:** 15.1
Land: 36.9 sq. mi.; **Water:** 0.0 sq. mi.

Dodge Center — City
ZIP: 55927 **Lat:** 44-01-42 N **Long:** 92-50-56 W
Pop: 1,954 (1990); 1,816 (1980) **Pop Density:** 1149.4
Land: 1.7 sq. mi.; **Water:** 0.0 sq. mi. **Elev:** 1293 ft.
Incorporated 1872.
Name origin: For its central position in the county.

Ellington — Township
ZIP: 55985 **Lat:** 44-09-28 N **Long:** 92-59-35 W
Pop: 313 (1990); 363 (1980) **Pop Density:** 8.7
Land: 36.0 sq. mi.; **Water:** 0.0 sq. mi.

Hayfield — City
ZIP: 55940 **Lat:** 43-53-24 N **Long:** 92-50-49 W
Pop: 1,283 (1990); 1,243 (1980) **Pop Density:** 986.9
Land: 1.3 sq. mi.; **Water:** 0.0 sq. mi.
City and township not coextensive.

*Hayfield — Township
ZIP: 55940 **Lat:** 43-53-27 N **Long:** 92-51-40 W
Pop: 371 (1990); 380 (1980) **Pop Density:** 10.1
Land: 36.6 sq. mi.; **Water:** 0.0 sq. mi.

Kasson — City
ZIP: 55944 **Lat:** 44-01-45 N **Long:** 92-45-10 W
Pop: 3,514 (1990); 2,827 (1980) **Pop Density:** 2342.7
Land: 1.5 sq. mi.; **Water:** 0.0 sq. mi. **Elev:** 1242 ft.
Name origin: For original landowner J. H. Kasson.

Mantorville — City
ZIP: 55955 **Lat:** 44-03-57 N **Long:** 92-45-12 W
Pop: 874 (1990); 705 (1980) **Pop Density:** 582.7
Land: 1.5 sq. mi.; **Water:** 0.0 sq. mi.
City and township not coextensive.
Name origin: For lumber businessman C. Peter Mantor, who was a leading force in the establishment of the town.

*Mantorville — Township
ZIP: 55955 **Lat:** 44-04-04 N **Long:** 92-44-02 W
Pop: 1,158 (1990); 1,013 (1980) **Pop Density:** 35.2
Land: 32.9 sq. mi.; **Water:** 0.0 sq. mi.

Milton — Township
ZIP: 55985 **Lat:** 44-08-29 N **Long:** 92-43-54 W
Pop: 671 (1990); 720 (1980) **Pop Density:** 18.6
Land: 36.0 sq. mi.; **Water:** 0.1 sq. mi.

Ripley — Township
Lat: 43-58-47 N **Long:** 92-59-00 W
Pop: 200 (1990); 230 (1980) **Pop Density:** 5.5
Land: 36.2 sq. mi.; **Water:** 0.0 sq. mi.

Vernon — Township
Lat: 43-53-07 N **Long:** 92-43-42 W
Pop: 600 (1990); 631 (1980) **Pop Density:** 16.6
Land: 36.2 sq. mi.; **Water:** 0.0 sq. mi.

Wasioja — Township
ZIP: 55927 **Lat:** 44-04-04 N **Long:** 92-51-49 W
Pop: 945 (1990); 859 (1980) **Pop Density:** 26.0
Land: 36.3 sq. mi.; **Water:** 0.0 sq. mi.

West Concord — City
ZIP: 55985 **Lat:** 44-09-10 N **Long:** 92-53-58 W
Pop: 871 (1990); 762 (1980) **Pop Density:** 791.8
Land: 1.1 sq. mi.; **Water:** 0.0 sq. mi.
Founded 1885.
Name origin: Euphoniously named by officials of the Chicago Great Western Railway.

Westfield — Township
Lat: 43-53-31 N **Long:** 92-59-04 W
Pop: 422 (1990); 496 (1980) **Pop Density:** 11.7
Land: 36.2 sq. mi.; **Water:** 0.0 sq. mi.

MINNESOTA, Douglas County   *American Places Dictionary*

Douglas County
County Seat: Alexandria (ZIP: 56308)

Pop: 28,674 (1990); 27,839 (1980)   **Pop Density:** 45.2
Land: 634.3 sq. mi.; **Water:** 85.6 sq. mi.   **Area Code:** 612
In west-central MN, northwest of St. Cloud; established Mar 8, 1858 from Todd County.
Name origin: For Stephen Arnold Douglas (1813–61), U.S. orator and statesman.

Alexandria   City
ZIP: 56308   **Lat:** 45-52-26 N **Long:** 95-22-30 W
Pop: 7,838 (1990); 7,608 (1980)   **Pop Density:** 967.7
Land: 8.1 sq. mi.; **Water:** 0.4 sq. mi.
City and township not coextensive.
Name origin: For Alexander Kinkaid, the first settler in the area.

*Alexandria   Township
ZIP: 56308   **Lat:** 45-53-30 N **Long:** 95-19-03 W
Pop: 4,014 (1990); 3,521 (1980)   **Pop Density:** 161.9
Land: 24.8 sq. mi.; **Water:** 4.6 sq. mi.

Belle River   Township
ZIP: 56319   **Lat:** 45-59-01 N **Long:** 95-12-57 W
Pop: 373 (1990); 432 (1980)   **Pop Density:** 10.4
Land: 35.8 sq. mi.; **Water:** 0.2 sq. mi.

Brandon   City
ZIP: 56315   **Lat:** 45-57-55 N **Long:** 95-35-49 W
Pop: 441 (1990); 473 (1980)   **Pop Density:** 1470.0
Land: 0.3 sq. mi.; **Water:** 0.0 sq. mi.
City and township not coextensive.

*Brandon   Township
ZIP: 56315   **Lat:** 45-58-47 N **Long:** 95-34-48 W
Pop: 586 (1990); 555 (1980)   **Pop Density:** 19.2
Land: 30.5 sq. mi.; **Water:** 5.2 sq. mi.

Carlos   City
ZIP: 56319   **Lat:** 45-58-26 N **Long:** 95-17-34 W
Pop: 361 (1990); 364 (1980)   **Pop Density:** 902.5
Land: 0.4 sq. mi.; **Water:** 0.0 sq. mi.
City and township not coextensive.
Name origin: For nearby Lake Carlos.

*Carlos   Township
ZIP: 56319   **Lat:** 45-58-45 N **Long:** 95-20-12 W
Pop: 1,402 (1990); 1,354 (1980)   **Pop Density:** 46.4
Land: 30.2 sq. mi.; **Water:** 5.3 sq. mi.

Evansville   City
ZIP: 56326   **Lat:** 46-00-26 N **Long:** 95-41-01 W
Pop: 566 (1990); 571 (1980)   **Pop Density:** 943.3
Land: 0.6 sq. mi.; **Water:** 0.0 sq. mi.   **Elev:** 1359 ft.
City and township not coextensive.
Name origin: For the first mail carrier in the area who was killed in the Sioux outbreak of 1862.

*Evansville   Township
ZIP: 56326   **Lat:** 45-58-05 N **Long:** 95-42-24 W
Pop: 265 (1990); 270 (1980)   **Pop Density:** 8.1
Land: 32.7 sq. mi.; **Water:** 2.7 sq. mi.

Forada   City
ZIP: 56308   **Lat:** 45-47-22 N **Long:** 95-21-19 W
Pop: 171 (1990); 191 (1980)   **Pop Density:** 342.0
Land: 0.5 sq. mi.; **Water:** 0.0 sq. mi.   **Elev:** 1414 ft.

Garfield   City
ZIP: 56332   **Lat:** 45-56-25 N **Long:** 95-29-39 W
Pop: 203 (1990); 284 (1980)   **Pop Density:** 290.0
Land: 0.7 sq. mi.; **Water:** 0.0 sq. mi.

Holmes City   Township
     Lat: 45-48-31 N **Long:** 95-34-30 W
Pop: 614 (1990); 595 (1980)   **Pop Density:** 20.2
Land: 30.4 sq. mi.; **Water:** 6.0 sq. mi.

Hudson   Township
ZIP: 56308   **Lat:** 45-48-48 N **Long:** 95-19-19 W
Pop: 632 (1990); 585 (1980)   **Pop Density:** 19.0
Land: 33.2 sq. mi.; **Water:** 2.0 sq. mi.

Ida   Township
ZIP: 56332   **Lat:** 45-58-24 N **Long:** 95-26-59 W
Pop: 789 (1990); 720 (1980)   **Pop Density:** 28.3
Land: 27.9 sq. mi.; **Water:** 7.6 sq. mi.

Kensington   City
ZIP: 56343   **Lat:** 45-46-40 N **Long:** 95-41-43 W
Pop: 295 (1990); 331 (1980)   **Pop Density:** 983.3
Land: 0.3 sq. mi.; **Water:** 0.0 sq. mi.
Incorporated 1891.
Name origin: For a borough of London, England.

La Grand   Township
ZIP: 56308   **Lat:** 45-53-21 N **Long:** 95-27-27 W
Pop: 3,550 (1990); 3,080 (1980)   **Pop Density:** 132.0
Land: 26.9 sq. mi.; **Water:** 6.6 sq. mi.

Lake Mary   Township
ZIP: 56308   **Lat:** 45-48-20 N **Long:** 95-26-59 W
Pop: 848 (1990); 880 (1980)   **Pop Density:** 29.4
Land: 28.8 sq. mi.; **Water:** 6.5 sq. mi.

Leaf Valley   Township
ZIP: 56332   **Lat:** 46-03-25 N **Long:** 95-26-42 W
Pop: 438 (1990); 541 (1980)   **Pop Density:** 13.1
Land: 33.4 sq. mi.; **Water:** 2.8 sq. mi.

Lund   Township
     Lat: 46-04-16 N **Long:** 95-42-18 W
Pop: 318 (1990); 323 (1980)   **Pop Density:** 11.3
Land: 28.2 sq. mi.; **Water:** 7.8 sq. mi.

Millerville   City
ZIP: 56315   **Lat:** 46-04-15 N **Long:** 95-33-09 W
Pop: 104 (1990); 124 (1980)   **Pop Density:** 115.6
Land: 0.9 sq. mi.; **Water:** 0.0 sq. mi.   **Elev:** 1392 ft.
City and township not coextensive.

*Millerville   Township
ZIP: 56315   **Lat:** 46-03-55 N **Long:** 95-35-17 W
Pop: 322 (1990); 376 (1980)   **Pop Density:** 10.1
Land: 31.9 sq. mi.; **Water:** 3.4 sq. mi.

American Places Dictionary   MINNESOTA, Faribault County

Miltona   City
ZIP: 56354   **Lat:** 46-02-41 N   **Long:** 95-17-31 W
Pop: 181 (1990); 187 (1980)   **Pop Density:** 362.0
Land: 0.5 sq. mi.; **Water:** 0.0 sq. mi.
City and township not coextensive.

*Miltona   Township
ZIP: 56354   **Lat:** 46-03-59 N   **Long:** 95-20-12 W
Pop: 685 (1990); 617 (1980)   **Pop Density:** 25.3
Land: 27.1 sq. mi.; **Water:** 8.7 sq. mi.

Moe   Township
ZIP: 56315   **Lat:** 45-53-08 N   **Long:** 95-34-03 W
Pop: 495 (1990); 495 (1980)   **Pop Density:** 16.3
Land: 30.3 sq. mi.; **Water:** 5.6 sq. mi.

Nelson   City
ZIP: 56355   **Lat:** 45-53-06 N   **Long:** 95-15-56 W
Pop: 177 (1990); 209 (1980)   **Pop Density:** 252.9
Land: 0.7 sq. mi.; **Water:** 0.0 sq. mi.
Founded 1875.
Name origin: For U.S. senator from MN, Knute Nelson.

Orange   Township
ZIP: 56360   **Lat:** 45-48-27 N   **Long:** 95-11-28 W
Pop: 367 (1990); 355 (1980)   **Pop Density:** 10.6
Land: 34.5 sq. mi.; **Water:** 1.4 sq. mi.

Osakis   City
ZIP: 56360   **Lat:** 45-51-55 N   **Long:** 95-09-19 W
Pop: 1,198 (1990); 1,267 (1980)   **Pop Density:** 704.7
Land: 1.7 sq. mi.; **Water:** 0.1 sq. mi.
Part of the town is also in Todd County.
Name origin: For the lake, itself named for the Sauk Indians, who once lived in the area.

*Osakis   Township
ZIP: 56360   **Lat:** 45-53-17 N   **Long:** 95-12-44 W
Pop: 574 (1990); 555 (1980)   **Pop Density:** 18.3
Land: 31.4 sq. mi.; **Water:** 2.7 sq. mi.

Solem   Township
ZIP: 56343   **Lat:** 45-48-08 N   **Long:** 95-41-53 W
Pop: 242 (1990); 303 (1980)   **Pop Density:** 7.1
Land: 33.9 sq. mi.; **Water:** 1.9 sq. mi.

Spruce Hill   Township
ZIP: 56354   **Lat:** 46-03-47 N   **Long:** 95-12-53 W
Pop: 392 (1990); 433 (1980)   **Pop Density:** 10.9
Land: 35.8 sq. mi.; **Water:** 0.3 sq. mi.

Urness   Township
ZIP: 56326   **Lat:** 45-53-17 N   **Long:** 95-41-22 W
Pop: 233 (1990); 240 (1980)   **Pop Density:** 7.3
Land: 31.9 sq. mi.; **Water:** 3.8 sq. mi.

Faribault County
County Seat: Blue Earth (ZIP: 56013)

Pop: 16,937 (1990); 19,714 (1980)   **Pop Density:** 23.7
Land: 713.7 sq. mi.; **Water:** 8.0 sq. mi.   **Area Code:** 507
On the central southern border of MN, south of Mankato; established Feb 20, 1855 (prior to statehood) from Blue Earth County.
Name origin: For Jean Baptiste Faribault (1774–1860), a French-Canadian fur trader in the Northwest Territory who had great influence with the Sioux.

Barber   Township
Lat: 43-43-14 N   **Long:** 93-56-50 W
Pop: 321 (1990); 431 (1980)   **Pop Density:** 8.9
Land: 36.0 sq. mi.; **Water:** 0.0 sq. mi.

Blue Earth   City
ZIP: 56013   **Lat:** 43-38-20 N   **Long:** 94-05-59 W
Pop: 3,745 (1990); 4,132 (1980)   **Pop Density:** 1208.1
Land: 3.1 sq. mi.; **Water:** 0.0 sq. mi.
Name origin: For the Blue Earth River, so named because a blue-green clay was found in the shaly layer of the rock bluff near its mouth.

Blue Earth City   Township
Lat: 43-37-20 N   **Long:** 94-04-14 W
Pop: 476 (1990); 522 (1980)   **Pop Density:** 14.4
Land: 33.0 sq. mi.; **Water:** 0.0 sq. mi.

Bricelyn   City
ZIP: 56014   **Lat:** 43-33-38 N   **Long:** 93-48-46 W
Pop: 426 (1990); 487 (1980)   **Pop Density:** 1420.0
Land: 0.3 sq. mi.; **Water:** 0.0 sq. mi.
Name origin: For original landowner, John Brice.

Brush Creek   Township
Lat: 43-38-15 N   **Long:** 93-49-04 W
Pop: 239 (1990); 297 (1980)   **Pop Density:** 6.8
Land: 35.1 sq. mi.; **Water:** 1.0 sq. mi.

Clark   Township
Lat: 43-42-58 N   **Long:** 93-42-11 W
Pop: 459 (1990); 510 (1980)   **Pop Density:** 13.2
Land: 34.8 sq. mi.; **Water:** 0.0 sq. mi.

Delavan   City
ZIP: 56023   **Lat:** 43-46-02 N   **Long:** 94-01-06 W
Pop: 245 (1990); 262 (1980)   **Pop Density:** 222.7
Land: 1.1 sq. mi.; **Water:** 0.0 sq. mi.   **Elev:** 1063 ft.
Incorporated 1877. City and township not coextensive.
Name origin: For Oren Delavan Brown, a railroad official with the Southern Minnesota Railroad.

*Delavan   Township
ZIP: 56023   **Lat:** 43-48-33 N   **Long:** 94-04-43 W
Pop: 248 (1990); 339 (1980)   **Pop Density:** 7.4
Land: 33.3 sq. mi.; **Water:** 2.2 sq. mi.

Dunbar   Township
Lat: 43-47-54 N   **Long:** 93-43-05 W
Pop: 370 (1990); 422 (1980)   **Pop Density:** 10.3
Land: 35.9 sq. mi.; **Water:** 0.0 sq. mi.

Easton — City
ZIP: 56025   Lat: 43-45-57 N   Long: 93-54-00 W
Pop: 229 (1990); 283 (1980)   Pop Density: 254.4
Land: 0.9 sq. mi.; Water: 0.0 sq. mi.
Founded 1874.
Name origin: For one of the original landowners, Jason Easton.

Elmore — City
ZIP: 56027   Lat: 43-30-21 N   Long: 94-05-18 W
Pop: 709 (1990); 882 (1980)   Pop Density: 787.8
Land: 0.9 sq. mi.; Water: 0.0 sq. mi.
Founded 1855. City and township not coextensive.
Name origin: For Wisconsin civic leader Andrew Elmore. Previously called Dobson.

*Elmore — Township
ZIP: 56027   Lat: 43-32-09 N   Long: 94-04-34 W
Pop: 229 (1990); 311 (1980)   Pop Density: 6.5
Land: 35.0 sq. mi.; Water: 0.0 sq. mi.

Emerald — Township
Lat: 43-38-03 N   Long: 93-57-21 W
Pop: 258 (1990); 330 (1980)   Pop Density: 7.2
Land: 35.8 sq. mi.; Water: 0.0 sq. mi.

Foster — Township
Lat: 43-37-50 N   Long: 93-42-18 W
Pop: 314 (1990); 373 (1980)   Pop Density: 8.9
Land: 35.4 sq. mi.; Water: 0.4 sq. mi.

Frost — City
ZIP: 56033   Lat: 43-35-01 N   Long: 93-55-31 W
Pop: 236 (1990); 293 (1980)   Pop Density: 472.0
Land: 0.5 sq. mi.; Water: 0.0 sq. mi.

Jo Daviess — Township
Lat: 43-37-50 N   Long: 94-11-29 W
Pop: 310 (1990); 370 (1980)   Pop Density: 8.6
Land: 35.9 sq. mi.; Water: 0.0 sq. mi.

Kiester — City
ZIP: 56051   Lat: 43-32-11 N   Long: 93-42-41 W
Pop: 606 (1990); 670 (1980)   Pop Density: 1515.0
Land: 0.4 sq. mi.; Water: 0.0 sq. mi.
City and township not coextensive.
Name origin: For Jacob Kiester, who became historian of Faribault County.

*Kiester — Township
ZIP: 56051   Lat: 43-32-36 N   Long: 93-42-17 W
Pop: 317 (1990); 349 (1980)   Pop Density: 8.9
Land: 35.8 sq. mi.; Water: 0.0 sq. mi.

Lura — Township
Lat: 43-48-25 N   Long: 93-56-12 W
Pop: 243 (1990); 302 (1980)   Pop Density: 6.9
Land: 35.2 sq. mi.; Water: 0.0 sq. mi.

Minnesota Lake — City
ZIP: 56068   Lat: 43-50-25 N   Long: 93-49-43 W
Pop: 681 (1990); 744 (1980)   Pop Density: 425.6
Land: 1.6 sq. mi.; Water: 0.5 sq. mi.
City and township not coextensive.

*Minnesota Lake — Township
ZIP: 56068   Lat: 43-48-07 N   Long: 93-49-47 W
Pop: 263 (1990); 322 (1980)   Pop Density: 8.4
Land: 31.4 sq. mi.; Water: 2.6 sq. mi.

Pilot Grove — Township
Lat: 43-32-10 N   Long: 94-11-50 W
Pop: 187 (1990); 246 (1980)   Pop Density: 5.2
Land: 36.0 sq. mi.; Water: 0.0 sq. mi.

Prescott — Township
Lat: 43-43-14 N   Long: 94-04-20 W
Pop: 245 (1990); 308 (1980)   Pop Density: 6.8
Land: 35.9 sq. mi.; Water: 0.2 sq. mi.

Rome — Township
Lat: 43-32-58 N   Long: 93-56-42 W
Pop: 208 (1990); 284 (1980)   Pop Density: 5.8
Land: 35.7 sq. mi.; Water: 0.0 sq. mi.

Seely — Township
Lat: 43-32-36 N   Long: 93-49-41 W
Pop: 247 (1990); 297 (1980)   Pop Density: 6.8
Land: 36.1 sq. mi.; Water: 0.0 sq. mi.

Verona — Township
Lat: 43-43-14 N   Long: 94-11-31 W
Pop: 483 (1990); 476 (1980)   Pop Density: 13.6
Land: 35.5 sq. mi.; Water: 0.0 sq. mi.

Walnut Lake — Township
Lat: 43-43-16 N   Long: 93-49-03 W
Pop: 291 (1990); 362 (1980)   Pop Density: 8.3
Land: 34.9 sq. mi.; Water: 1.0 sq. mi.

Walters — City
ZIP: 56092   Lat: 43-36-18 N   Long: 93-40-24 W
Pop: 86 (1990); 118 (1980)   Pop Density: 430.0
Land: 0.2 sq. mi.; Water: 0.0 sq. mi.
Name origin: Named by officials of the Chicago, Rock Island, & Pacific Railway Company for one of their employees.

Wells — City
ZIP: 56097   Lat: 43-44-37 N   Long: 93-43-34 W
Pop: 2,465 (1990); 2,777 (1980)   Pop Density: 2054.2
Land: 1.2 sq. mi.; Water: 0.0 sq. mi.
Name origin: For the maiden name of settler Mrs. Clark W. Thompson.

Winnebago — City
ZIP: 56098   Lat: 43-45-57 N   Long: 94-10-05 W
Pop: 1,565 (1990); 1,869 (1980)   Pop Density: 745.2
Land: 2.1 sq. mi.; Water: 0.0 sq. mi.
Name origin: For the Winnebago Indian tribe.

Winnebago City — Township
Lat: 43-48-28 N   Long: 94-10-41 W
Pop: 236 (1990); 346 (1980)   Pop Density: 6.8
Land: 34.5 sq. mi.; Water: 0.0 sq. mi.

Fillmore County
County Seat: Preston (ZIP: 55965)

Pop: 20,777 (1990); 21,930 (1980)   **Pop Density:** 24.1
Land: 861.3 sq. mi.; **Water:** 0.9 sq. mi.   **Area Code:** 507
On the southeastern border of MN, southeast of Rochester; original county; established Mar 5, 1853 (prior to statehood).
Name origin: For Millard Fillmore (1800–74), thirteenth U.S. president.

Amherst   Township
Lat: 43-37-53 N   Long: 91-54-18 W
Pop: 416 (1990); 365 (1980)   **Pop Density:** 11.6
Land: 35.8 sq. mi.; **Water:** 0.0 sq. mi.

Arendahl   Township
ZIP: 55962   Lat: 43-48-12 N   Long: 91-54-30 W
Pop: 341 (1990); 366 (1980)   **Pop Density:** 9.6
Land: 35.7 sq. mi.; **Water:** 0.1 sq. mi.

Beaver   Township
Lat: 43-32-35 N   Long: 92-23-06 W
Pop: 239 (1990); 294 (1980)   **Pop Density:** 6.6
Land: 36.1 sq. mi.; **Water:** 0.0 sq. mi.

Bloomfield   Township
Lat: 43-37-40 N   Long: 92-23-19 W
Pop: 414 (1990); 454 (1980)   **Pop Density:** 11.6
Land: 35.7 sq. mi.; **Water:** 0.0 sq. mi.

Bristol   Township
ZIP: 55939   Lat: 43-32-39 N   Long: 92-08-47 W
Pop: 385 (1990); 455 (1980)   **Pop Density:** 10.7
Land: 36.0 sq. mi.; **Water:** 0.0 sq. mi.

Canton   City
ZIP: 55922   Lat: 43-31-48 N   Long: 91-55-45 W
Pop: 362 (1990); 386 (1980)   **Pop Density:** 362.0   **Elev:** 1345 ft.
Settled 1851. City and township not coextensive.
Name origin: For Canton, OH.

*****Canton**   Township
ZIP: 55922   Lat: 43-32-38 N   Long: 91-54-33 W
Pop: 612 (1990); 581 (1980)   **Pop Density:** 17.4
Land: 35.1 sq. mi.; **Water:** 0.0 sq. mi.

Carimona   Township
ZIP: 55965   Lat: 43-37-49 N   Long: 92-09-26 W
Pop: 336 (1990); 358 (1980)   **Pop Density:** 9.4
Land: 35.6 sq. mi.; **Water:** 0.0 sq. mi.

Carrolton   Township
Lat: 43-43-25 N   Long: 92-01-28 W
Pop: 333 (1990); 377 (1980)   **Pop Density:** 8.8
Land: 37.8 sq. mi.; **Water:** 0.1 sq. mi.

Chatfield   City
ZIP: 55923   Lat: 43-50-25 N   Long: 92-11-04 W
Pop: 1,249 (1990); 1,160 (1980)   **Pop Density:** 1040.8
Land: 1.2 sq. mi.; **Water:** 0.0 sq. mi.
Part of the town is also in Olmsted County.
Name origin: Named 1858 for Judge Andrew Chatfield, who presided over the first court held in the county.

*****Chatfield**   Township
ZIP: 55923   Lat: 43-48-28 N   Long: 92-09-14 W
Pop: 432 (1990); 479 (1980)   **Pop Density:** 12.5
Land: 34.6 sq. mi.; **Water:** 0.0 sq. mi.

Fillmore   Township
ZIP: 55990   Lat: 43-43-22 N   Long: 92-16-07 W
Pop: 461 (1990); 561 (1980)   **Pop Density:** 13.2
Land: 34.9 sq. mi.; **Water:** 0.0 sq. mi.

Forestville   Township
Lat: 43-38-04 N   Long: 92-16-42 W
Pop: 401 (1990); 478 (1980)   **Pop Density:** 11.1
Land: 36.2 sq. mi.; **Water:** 0.0 sq. mi.

Fountain   City
ZIP: 55935   Lat: 43-44-26 N   Long: 92-08-02 W
Pop: 327 (1990); 327 (1980)   **Pop Density:** 408.8
Land: 0.8 sq. mi.; **Water:** 0.0 sq. mi.   **Elev:** 1305 ft.
City and township not coextensive.
Name origin: For local water supply, "Fountain Spring."

*****Fountain**   Township
ZIP: 55935   Lat: 43-43-25 N   Long: 92-09-06 W
Pop: 335 (1990); 381 (1980)   **Pop Density:** 9.6
Land: 35.0 sq. mi.; **Water:** 0.0 sq. mi.

Harmony   City
ZIP: 55939   Lat: 43-33-19 N   Long: 92-00-33 W
Pop: 1,081 (1990); 1,133 (1980)   **Pop Density:** 982.7
Land: 1.1 sq. mi.; **Water:** 0.0 sq. mi.
City and township not coextensive.
Name origin: Euphoniously named by early pioneers.

*****Harmony**   Township
ZIP: 55939   Lat: 43-33-04 N   Long: 92-01-41 W
Pop: 431 (1990); 427 (1980)   **Pop Density:** 12.4
Land: 34.8 sq. mi.; **Water:** 0.0 sq. mi.

Holt   Township
Lat: 43-43-12 N   Long: 91-54-25 W
Pop: 239 (1990); 309 (1980)   **Pop Density:** 7.3
Land: 32.9 sq. mi.; **Water:** 0.2 sq. mi.

Jordan   Township
Lat: 43-48-06 N   Long: 92-15-44 W
Pop: 359 (1990); 371 (1980)   **Pop Density:** 10.0
Land: 36.0 sq. mi.; **Water:** 0.0 sq. mi.

Lanesboro   City
ZIP: 55949   Lat: 43-43-10 N   Long: 91-58-24 W
Pop: 858 (1990); 923 (1980)   **Pop Density:** 715.0
Land: 1.2 sq. mi.; **Water:** 0.0 sq. mi.   **Elev:** 846 ft.
Name origin: For Lanesboro, MA, the former home of settlers.

Mabel   City
ZIP: 55954   Lat: 43-31-13 N   Long: 91-46-05 W
Pop: 745 (1990); 861 (1980)   **Pop Density:** 1490.0
Land: 0.5 sq. mi.; **Water:** 0.0 sq. mi.   **Elev:** 1134 ft.
Name origin: For the deceased daughter of railroad engineer Frank Adams.

Newburg
Township
Lat: 43-32-34 N **Long:** 91-47-28 W
Pop: 482 (1990); 502 (1980) **Pop Density:** 13.6
Land: 35.4 sq. mi.; **Water:** 0.0 sq. mi.

Norway
Township
Lat: 43-43-14 N **Long:** 91-47-29 W
Pop: 316 (1990); 418 (1980) **Pop Density:** 8.8
Land: 35.8 sq. mi.; **Water:** 0.0 sq. mi.

Ostrander
City
ZIP: 55961 **Lat:** 43-36-50 N **Long:** 92-25-32 W
Pop: 276 (1990); 293 (1980) **Pop Density:** 690.0
Land: 0.4 sq. mi.; **Water:** 0.0 sq. mi.
Founded 1890s.
Name origin: For the Ostranders, two brothers who originally owned the land.

Peterson
City
ZIP: 55962 **Lat:** 43-47-09 N **Long:** 91-49-59 W
Pop: 259 (1990); 291 (1980) **Pop Density:** 518.0
Land: 0.5 sq. mi.; **Water:** 0.0 sq. mi.
Name origin: For Peter Peterson Haslerud, a Norwegian pioneer and member of the state legislature.

Pilot Mound
Township
ZIP: 55923 **Lat:** 43-48-31 N **Long:** 92-01-34 W
Pop: 367 (1990); 379 (1980) **Pop Density:** 10.7
Land: 34.2 sq. mi.; **Water:** 0.1 sq. mi.

Preble
Township
Lat: 43-38-02 N **Long:** 91-47-31 W
Pop: 243 (1990); 311 (1980) **Pop Density:** 6.8
Land: 35.8 sq. mi.; **Water:** 0.0 sq. mi.

Preston
City
ZIP: 55965 **Lat:** 43-40-17 N **Long:** 92-04-57 W
Pop: 1,530 (1990); 1,478 (1980) **Pop Density:** 665.2
Land: 2.3 sq. mi.; **Water:** 0.0 sq. mi.
Settled 1853.
Name origin: Named by a local millowner for his millwright, Luther Preston.

*Preston
Township
ZIP: 55965 **Lat:** 43-37-22 N **Long:** 92-02-19 W
Pop: 341 (1990); 340 (1980) **Pop Density:** 9.9
Land: 34.5 sq. mi.; **Water:** 0.0 sq. mi.

Rushford
City
ZIP: 55971 **Lat:** 43-48-44 N **Long:** 91-45-08 W
Pop: 1,485 (1990); 1,478 (1980) **Pop Density:** 928.1
Land: 1.6 sq. mi.; **Water:** 0.0 sq. mi. **Elev:** 726 ft.
Settled 1853.
Name origin: For nearby Rush Creek, a tributary of the Root River.

Rushford Village
City
Lat: 43-48-15 N **Long:** 91-47-14 W
Pop: 705 (1990); 688 (1980) **Pop Density:** 21.0
Land: 33.5 sq. mi.; **Water:** 0.2 sq. mi.

Spring Valley
City
ZIP: 55975 **Lat:** 43-41-09 N **Long:** 92-23-23 W
Pop: 2,461 (1990); 2,616 (1980) **Pop Density:** 984.4
Land: 2.5 sq. mi.; **Water:** 0.0 sq. mi.
City and township not coextensive.
Name origin: For several large springs within several miles of the city limits.

*Spring Valley
Township
ZIP: 55975 **Lat:** 43-43-16 N **Long:** 92-23-00 W
Pop: 557 (1990); 582 (1980) **Pop Density:** 17.4
Land: 32.1 sq. mi.; **Water:** 0.0 sq. mi.

Sumner
Township
Lat: 43-47-58 N **Long:** 92-23-48 W
Pop: 454 (1990); 499 (1980) **Pop Density:** 12.1
Land: 37.5 sq. mi.; **Water:** 0.0 sq. mi.

Whalan
City
ZIP: 55986 **Lat:** 43-43-58 N **Long:** 91-55-39 W
Pop: 94 (1990); 119 (1980) **Pop Density:** 313.3
Land: 0.3 sq. mi.; **Water:** 0.0 sq. mi. **Elev:** 793 ft.
Founded 1868.
Name origin: For the original landowner John Whaalahan, with spelling variation.

Wykoff
City
ZIP: 55990 **Lat:** 43-42-29 N **Long:** 92-16-02 W
Pop: 493 (1990); 482 (1980) **Pop Density:** 547.8
Land: 0.9 sq. mi.; **Water:** 0.0 sq. mi. **Elev:** 1322 ft.
Incorporated 1876.
Name origin: For railroad surveyor C. G. Wykoff.

York
Township
Lat: 43-32-42 N **Long:** 92-15-53 W
Pop: 358 (1990); 408 (1980) **Pop Density:** 9.9
Land: 36.1 sq. mi.; **Water:** 0.1 sq. mi.

Freeborn County
County Seat: Albert Lea (ZIP: 56007)

Pop: 33,060 (1990); 36,329 (1980)   **Pop Density:** 46.7
Land: 707.7 sq. mi.; **Water:** 15.0 sq. mi.   **Area Code:** 507
On the southern border of MN, southwest of Rochester; established Feb 20, 1855 (prior to statehood) from Blue Earth and Rice counties.
Name origin: For William Freeborn (1816–1900), MN territorial legislator (1854–57).

Albert Lea   City
ZIP: 56007   **Lat:** 43-39-18 N   **Long:** 93-21-59 W
Pop: 18,310 (1990); 19,200 (1980)   **Pop Density:** 1907.3
Land: 9.6 sq. mi.; **Water:** 1.6 sq. mi.
In southern MN, 20 mi. west of Austin. City and township not coextensive.
Name origin: For early explorer Albert Miller, who mapped the region in 1835.

*Albert Lea   Township
ZIP: 56007   **Lat:** 43-37-28 N   **Long:** 93-20-24 W
Pop: 964 (1990); 1,675 (1980)   **Pop Density:** 39.3
Land: 24.5 sq. mi.; **Water:** 3.0 sq. mi.

Alden   City
ZIP: 56009   **Lat:** 43-40-12 N   **Long:** 93-34-23 W
Pop: 623 (1990); 687 (1980)   **Pop Density:** 623.0
Land: 1.0 sq. mi.; **Water:** 0.0 sq. mi.
Incorporated 1879. City and township not coextensive.
Name origin: Probably for an early settler.

*Alden   Township
ZIP: 56009   **Lat:** 43-38-04 N   **Long:** 93-34-42 W
Pop: 359 (1990); 434 (1980)   **Pop Density:** 10.1
Land: 35.4 sq. mi.; **Water:** 0.0 sq. mi.

Bancroft   Township
Lat: 43-43-04 N   **Long:** 93-20-44 W
Pop: 1,086 (1990); 1,395 (1980)   **Pop Density:** 32.2
Land: 33.7 sq. mi.; **Water:** 0.0 sq. mi.

Bath   Township
Lat: 43-48-10 N   **Long:** 93-20-56 W
Pop: 489 (1990); 603 (1980)   **Pop Density:** 13.7
Land: 35.7 sq. mi.; **Water:** 0.1 sq. mi.

Carlston   Township
Lat: 43-43-00 N   **Long:** 93-35-52 W
Pop: 369 (1990); 417 (1980)   **Pop Density:** 11.1
Land: 33.1 sq. mi.; **Water:** 2.9 sq. mi.

Clarks Grove   City
ZIP: 56016   **Lat:** 43-45-51 N   **Long:** 93-19-40 W
Pop: 675 (1990); 620 (1980)   **Pop Density:** 1687.5
Land: 0.4 sq. mi.; **Water:** 0.0 sq. mi.
Settled 1890.
Name origin: For early pioneer, J. Mead Clark.

Conger   City
ZIP: 56020   **Lat:** 43-36-55 N   **Long:** 93-31-43 W
Pop: 143 (1990); 183 (1980)   **Pop Density:** 1430.0
Land: 0.1 sq. mi.; **Water:** 0.0 sq. mi.   **Elev:** 1289 ft.
Name origin: Named by Rock Island & Pacific Railroad officials for a company employee.

Emmons   City
ZIP: 56029   **Lat:** 43-30-26 N   **Long:** 93-29-01 W
Pop: 439 (1990); 465 (1980)   **Pop Density:** 548.8
Land: 0.8 sq. mi.; **Water:** 0.0 sq. mi.
Name origin: For Henry Emmons, a local merchant and later state legislator.

Freeborn   City
ZIP: 56032   **Lat:** 43-45-59 N   **Long:** 93-33-47 W
Pop: 301 (1990); 323 (1980)   **Pop Density:** 1505.0
Land: 0.2 sq. mi.; **Water:** 0.0 sq. mi.
City and township not coextensive.
Name origin: For the county.

*Freeborn   Township
Lat: 43-48-02 N   **Long:** 93-35-10 W
Pop: 331 (1990); 421 (1980)   **Pop Density:** 9.3
Land: 35.7 sq. mi.; **Water:** 0.5 sq. mi.

Freeman   Township
Lat: 43-32-34 N   **Long:** 93-20-45 W
Pop: 554 (1990); 588 (1980)   **Pop Density:** 15.4
Land: 35.9 sq. mi.; **Water:** 0.0 sq. mi.

Geneva   City
ZIP: 56035   **Lat:** 43-49-26 N   **Long:** 93-16-05 W
Pop: 444 (1990); 417 (1980)   **Pop Density:** 1110.0
Land: 0.4 sq. mi.; **Water:** 0.0 sq. mi.
City and township not coextensive.

*Geneva   Township
Lat: 43-47-49 N   **Long:** 93-14-02 W
Pop: 481 (1990); 574 (1980)   **Pop Density:** 14.6
Land: 33.0 sq. mi.; **Water:** 2.6 sq. mi.

Glenville   City
ZIP: 56036   **Lat:** 43-34-08 N   **Long:** 93-16-32 W
Pop: 778 (1990); 851 (1980)   **Pop Density:** 353.6
Land: 2.2 sq. mi.; **Water:** 0.0 sq. mi.
Name origin: Named by local railway officials in 1898. Previously called Shell Rock.

Hartland   City
ZIP: 56042   **Lat:** 43-48-15 N   **Long:** 93-29-08 W
Pop: 270 (1990); 322 (1980)   **Pop Density:** 900.0
Land: 0.3 sq. mi.; **Water:** 0.0 sq. mi.   **Elev:** 1252 ft.
City and township not coextensive.
Name origin: Named in 1857 for Hartland, VT, the former home of settlers.

*Hartland   Township
ZIP: 56042   **Lat:** 43-48-13 N   **Long:** 93-27-52 W
Pop: 342 (1990); 333 (1980)   **Pop Density:** 9.5
Land: 35.9 sq. mi.; **Water:** 0.0 sq. mi.

MINNESOTA, Freeborn County

Hayward City
ZIP: 56043 Lat: 43-38-57 N Long: 93-14-48 W
Pop: 246 (1990); 294 (1980) Pop Density: 410.0
Land: 0.6 sq. mi.; Water: 0.0 sq. mi.
City and township not coextensive.
Name origin: For early settler, David Hayward.

*Hayward Township
ZIP: 56043 Lat: 43-37-20 N Long: 93-13-45 W
Pop: 459 (1990); 491 (1980) Pop Density: 13.3
Land: 34.6 sq. mi.; Water: 1.0 sq. mi.

Hollandale City
ZIP: 56045 Lat: 43-45-35 N Long: 93-12-19 W
Pop: 289 (1990); 290 (1980) Pop Density: 722.5
Land: 0.4 sq. mi.; Water: 0.0 sq. mi.
Name origin: Named by Dutch settlers for their former country.

London Township
Lat: 43-32-34 N Long: 93-06-36 W
Pop: 365 (1990); 419 (1980) Pop Density: 10.1
Land: 36.1 sq. mi.; Water: 0.0 sq. mi.

Manchester City
ZIP: 56064 Lat: 43-43-29 N Long: 93-27-02 W
Pop: 69 (1990); 96 (1980) Pop Density: 690.0
Land: 0.1 sq. mi.; Water: 0.0 sq. mi. Elev: 1283 ft.
City and township not coextensive.

*Manchester Township
Lat: 43-43-13 N Long: 93-28-15 W
Pop: 483 (1990); 510 (1980) Pop Density: 13.5
Land: 35.7 sq. mi.; Water: 0.3 sq. mi.

Mansfield Township
Lat: 43-32-27 N Long: 93-35-27 W
Pop: 346 (1990); 412 (1980) Pop Density: 9.6
Land: 36.1 sq. mi.; Water: 0.0 sq. mi.

Moscow Township
Lat: 43-43-09 N Long: 93-06-14 W
Pop: 619 (1990); 661 (1980) Pop Density: 17.1
Land: 36.1 sq. mi.; Water: 0.1 sq. mi.

Myrtle City
ZIP: 56070 Lat: 43-33-47 N Long: 93-09-46 W
Pop: 72 (1990); 86 (1980) Pop Density: 720.0
Land: 0.1 sq. mi.; Water: 0.0 sq. mi.

Newry Township
Lat: 43-48-30 N Long: 93-06-55 W
Pop: 510 (1990); 601 (1980) Pop Density: 14.1
Land: 36.1 sq. mi.; Water: 0.0 sq. mi.

Nunda Township
Lat: 43-32-21 N Long: 93-28-17 W
Pop: 378 (1990); 414 (1980) Pop Density: 11.5
Land: 32.9 sq. mi.; Water: 1.9 sq. mi.

Oakland Township
ZIP: 56076 Lat: 43-37-44 N Long: 93-06-23 W
Pop: 426 (1990); 490 (1980) Pop Density: 11.8
Land: 36.0 sq. mi.; Water: 0.0 sq. mi.

Pickerel Lake Township
Lat: 43-37-48 N Long: 93-28-48 W
Pop: 715 (1990); 691 (1980) Pop Density: 20.5
Land: 34.8 sq. mi.; Water: 0.9 sq. mi.

Riceland Township
Lat: 43-43-21 N Long: 93-13-51 W
Pop: 495 (1990); 577 (1980) Pop Density: 13.7
Land: 36.1 sq. mi.; Water: 0.0 sq. mi.

Shell Rock Township
Lat: 43-32-09 N Long: 93-13-08 W
Pop: 476 (1990); 579 (1980) Pop Density: 14.1
Land: 33.7 sq. mi.; Water: 0.0 sq. mi.

Twin Lakes City
ZIP: 56089 Lat: 43-33-39 N Long: 93-25-24 W
Pop: 154 (1990); 210 (1980) Pop Density: 308.0
Land: 0.5 sq. mi.; Water: 0.0 sq. mi.
Name origin: For its descriptive connotations.

Goodhue County
County Seat: Red Wing (ZIP: 55066)

Pop: 40,690 (1990); 38,749 (1980) Pop Density: 53.6
Land: 758.6 sq. mi.; Water: 21.9 sq. mi. Area Code: 612

In southeastern MN, southeast of St. Paul; established Mar 5, 1853 (prior to statehood) from Wabasha County.

Name origin: For James Madison Goodhue (1810–52), lawyer and prominent editor of the first newspaper in the MN Territory.

Bellechester City
ZIP: 55027 Lat: 44-22-15 N Long: 92-30-42 W
Pop: 110 (1990); 157 (1980) Pop Density: 366.7
Land: 0.3 sq. mi.; Water: 0.0 sq. mi.
Part of the town is also in Wabasha County.

Belle Creek Township
ZIP: 55027 Lat: 44-24-29 N Long: 92-44-10 W
Pop: 403 (1990); 518 (1980) Pop Density: 11.3
Land: 35.6 sq. mi.; Water: 0.0 sq. mi.

Belvidere Township
ZIP: 55027 Lat: 44-24-53 N Long: 92-28-58 W
Pop: 477 (1990); 522 (1980) Pop Density: 13.4
Land: 35.6 sq. mi.; Water: 0.0 sq. mi.

Cannon Falls City
ZIP: 55009 Lat: 44-30-59 N Long: 92-54-09 W
Pop: 3,232 (1990); 2,653 (1980) Pop Density: 950.6
Land: 3.4 sq. mi.; Water: 0.1 sq. mi. Elev: 838 ft.
Settled 1854. City and township not coextensive.
Name origin: Named by early American explorers for the

falls in the Cannon River, which traverses the northern part of the county.

*Cannon Falls — Township
ZIP: 55009　**Lat:** 44-29-31 N　**Long:** 92-51-26 W
Pop: 1,369 (1990); 1,373 (1980)　**Pop Density:** 39.7
Land: 34.5 sq. mi.; **Water:** 0.0 sq. mi.

Cherry Grove — Township
Lat: 44-14-07 N　**Long:** 92-50-58 W
Pop: 396 (1990); 435 (1980)　**Pop Density:** 10.3
Land: 38.3 sq. mi.; **Water:** 0.0 sq. mi.

Dennison — City
ZIP: 55018　**Lat:** 44-24-12 N　**Long:** 93-01-43 W
Pop: 152 (1990); 176 (1980)　**Pop Density:** 126.7
Land: 1.2 sq. mi.; **Water:** 0.0 sq. mi.
Founded 1856. Part of the town is also in Rice County.
Name origin: For Morris Dennison, who owned the land upon which the city was founded.

Featherstone — Township
Lat: 44-30-24 N　**Long:** 92-37-16 W
Pop: 811 (1990); 800 (1980)　**Pop Density:** 22.6
Land: 35.9 sq. mi.; **Water:** 0.0 sq. mi.

Florence — Township
ZIP: 55026　**Lat:** 44-29-34 N　**Long:** 92-21-16 W
Pop: 1,196 (1990); 1,123 (1980)　**Pop Density:** 34.2
Land: 35.0 sq. mi.; **Water:** 5.6 sq. mi.

Goodhue — City
ZIP: 55027　**Lat:** 44-24-02 N　**Long:** 92-37-17 W
Pop: 533 (1990); 657 (1980)　**Pop Density:** 761.4
Land: 0.7 sq. mi.; **Water:** 0.0 sq. mi.
City and township not coextensive.
Name origin: For James Madison Goodhue (1810–52), lawyer and prominent editor of the first newspaper in the MN Territory.

*Goodhue — Township
ZIP: 55027　**Lat:** 44-24-20 N　**Long:** 92-36-39 W
Pop: 661 (1990); 576 (1980)　**Pop Density:** 18.8
Land: 35.2 sq. mi.; **Water:** 0.0 sq. mi.

Hay Creek — Township
Lat: 44-29-36 N　**Long:** 92-29-33 W
Pop: 690 (1990); 751 (1980)　**Pop Density:** 19.8
Land: 34.9 sq. mi.; **Water:** 0.0 sq. mi.

Holden — Township
Lat: 44-19-38 N　**Long:** 92-58-48 W
Pop: 445 (1990); 504 (1980)　**Pop Density:** 12.4
Land: 35.9 sq. mi.; **Water:** 0.0 sq. mi.

Kenyon — City
ZIP: 55946　**Lat:** 44-16-20 N　**Long:** 92-59-09 W
Pop: 1,552 (1990); 1,529 (1980)　**Pop Density:** 674.8
Land: 2.3 sq. mi.; **Water:** 0.0 sq. mi.
Settled 1858. City and township not coextensive.
Name origin: For a merchant who founded a general store.

*Kenyon — Township
ZIP: 55946　**Lat:** 44-13-58 N　**Long:** 92-58-12 W
Pop: 420 (1990); 472 (1980)　**Pop Density:** 12.5
Land: 33.7 sq. mi.; **Water:** 0.0 sq. mi.

Lake City — City
ZIP: 55041　**Lat:** 44-27-54 N　**Long:** 92-17-32 W
Pop: 502 (1990); 470 (1980)　**Pop Density:** 627.5
Land: 0.8 sq. mi.; **Water:** 0.0 sq. mi.　**Elev:** 701 ft.
Part of the town is also in Wabasha County.
Name origin: For its location next to Lake Popin.

Leon — Township
Lat: 44-25-04 N　**Long:** 92-51-36 W
Pop: 916 (1990); 902 (1980)　**Pop Density:** 24.2
Land: 37.8 sq. mi.; **Water:** 0.0 sq. mi.

Minneola — Township
Lat: 44-19-16 N　**Long:** 92-44-02 W
Pop: 614 (1990); 684 (1980)　**Pop Density:** 18.1
Land: 34.0 sq. mi.; **Water:** 0.0 sq. mi.

Pine Island — City
ZIP: 55963　**Lat:** 44-12-17 N　**Long:** 92-38-58 W
Pop: 2,125 (1990); 1,977 (1980)　**Pop Density:** 850.0
Land: 2.5 sq. mi.; **Water:** 0.0 sq. mi.
Settled 1854. Part of the town is also in Olmsted County.
Name origin: From an Indian term referring to a secure winter camp ground sheltered by the island's pines.

*Pine Island — Township
ZIP: 55963　**Lat:** 44-14-30 N　**Long:** 92-36-01 W
Pop: 673 (1990); 634 (1980)　**Pop Density:** 20.3
Land: 33.1 sq. mi.; **Water:** 0.0 sq. mi.

Red Wing — City
ZIP: 55066　**Lat:** 44-34-54 N　**Long:** 92-36-07 W
Pop: 15,134 (1990); 13,736 (1980)　**Pop Density:** 433.6
Land: 34.9 sq. mi.; **Water:** 5.9 sq. mi.　**Elev:** 750 ft.
In southeastern MN on the Mississippi River, 40 mi. southeast of St. Paul.
Name origin: For a great Dakota Indian chief of that era.

Roscoe — Township
ZIP: 55983　**Lat:** 44-14-34 N　**Long:** 92-43-23 W
Pop: 662 (1990); 735 (1980)　**Pop Density:** 18.5
Land: 35.8 sq. mi.; **Water:** 0.0 sq. mi.

Stanton — Township
Lat: 44-28-51 N　**Long:** 92-58-46 W
Pop: 838 (1990); 918 (1980)　**Pop Density:** 36.9
Land: 22.7 sq. mi.; **Water:** 1.1 sq. mi.

Vasa — Township
ZIP: 55089　**Lat:** 44-30-14 N　**Long:** 92-43-31 W
Pop: 889 (1990); 847 (1980)　**Pop Density:** 21.6
Land: 41.2 sq. mi.; **Water:** 0.0 sq. mi.

Wacouta — Township
Lat: 44-33-00 N　**Long:** 92-25-44 W
Pop: 398 (1990); 350 (1980)　**Pop Density:** 94.8
Land: 4.2 sq. mi.; **Water:** 5.6 sq. mi.

Wanamingo — City
ZIP: 55983　**Lat:** 44-18-18 N　**Long:** 92-47-29 W
Pop: 847 (1990); 717 (1980)　**Pop Density:** 941.1
Land: 0.9 sq. mi.; **Water:** 0.0 sq. mi.
Name origin: An Indian term of uncertain origin and meaning.

*Wanamingo — Township
ZIP: 55983　**Lat:** 44-19-30 N　**Long:** 92-51-15 W
Pop: 472 (1990); 511 (1980)　**Pop Density:** 12.6
Land: 37.6 sq. mi.; **Water:** 0.0 sq. mi.

MINNESOTA, Goodhue County

Warsaw — Township
Lat: 44-24-31 N Long: 92-59-13 W
Pop: 574 (1990); 591 (1980) **Pop Density:** 16.6
Land: 34.6 sq. mi.; **Water:** 0.0 sq. mi.

Welch — Township
ZIP: 55089 Lat: 44-36-57 N Long: 92-43-57 W
Pop: 678 (1990); 689 (1980) **Pop Density:** 17.3
Land: 39.3 sq. mi.; **Water:** 3.4 sq. mi.

Zumbrota — City
ZIP: 55992 Lat: 44-17-40 N Long: 92-40-21 W
Pop: 2,312 (1990); 2,129 (1980) **Pop Density:** 1156.0
Land: 2.0 sq. mi.; **Water:** 0.0 sq. mi. **Elev:** 1005 ft.
Name origin: From a mispronunciation of the French and Dakota names for the nearby Zumbro River, which flows through the southern part of the township.

*Zumbrota — Township
ZIP: 55992 Lat: 44-19-35 N Long: 92-37-05 W
Pop: 609 (1990); 613 (1980) **Pop Density:** 17.5
Land: 34.8 sq. mi.; **Water:** 0.0 sq. mi.

Grant County
County Seat: Elbow Lake (ZIP: 56531)

Pop: 6,246 (1990); 7,171 (1980) **Pop Density:** 11.4
Land: 546.5 sq. mi.; **Water:** 28.8 sq. mi. **Area Code:** 218

In west-central MN, southeast of Fargo, ND; established Mar 6, 1868 from Stearns County.

Name origin: For Ulysses S. Grant (1822–85), Civil War general and eighteenth U.S. president.

Ashby — City
ZIP: 56309 Lat: 46-05-35 N Long: 95-48-57 W
Pop: 469 (1990); 486 (1980) **Pop Density:** 938.0
Land: 0.5 sq. mi.; **Water:** 0.0 sq. mi.

Barrett — City
ZIP: 56311 Lat: 45-54-38 N Long: 95-53-28 W
Pop: 350 (1990); 388 (1980) **Pop Density:** 166.7
Land: 2.1 sq. mi.; **Water:** 0.0 sq. mi. **Elev:** 1166 ft.
Name origin: For Civil War hero and local farmer, Gen. Theodore H. Barrett.

Delaware — Township
Lat: 45-53-23 N Long: 96-04-02 W
Pop: 136 (1990); 172 (1980) **Pop Density:** 3.8
Land: 35.5 sq. mi.; **Water:** 0.9 sq. mi.

Elbow Lake — City
ZIP: 56531 Lat: 45-59-30 N Long: 95-58-38 W
Pop: 1,186 (1990); 1,358 (1980) **Pop Density:** 847.1
Land: 1.4 sq. mi.; **Water:** 0.4 sq. mi. **Elev:** 1222 ft.
Name origin: For the nearby lake, which resembles an arm bent at the elbow.

*Elbow Lake — Township
ZIP: 56531 Lat: 45-58-50 N Long: 96-05-11 W
Pop: 158 (1990); 198 (1980) **Pop Density:** 4.5
Land: 35.4 sq. mi.; **Water:** 0.3 sq. mi.

Elk Lake — Township
ZIP: 56311 Lat: 45-52-54 N Long: 95-49-26 W
Pop: 298 (1990); 302 (1980) **Pop Density:** 9.3
Land: 32.2 sq. mi.; **Water:** 3.3 sq. mi.

Erdahl — Township
ZIP: 56531 Lat: 45-58-45 N Long: 95-49-16 W
Pop: 307 (1990); 356 (1980) **Pop Density:** 9.1
Land: 33.9 sq. mi.; **Water:** 2.0 sq. mi.

Gorton — Township
Lat: 45-53-06 N Long: 96-11-27 W
Pop: 81 (1990); 115 (1980) **Pop Density:** 2.3
Land: 34.7 sq. mi.; **Water:** 0.0 sq. mi.

Herman — City
ZIP: 56248 Lat: 45-48-38 N Long: 96-08-23 W
Pop: 485 (1990); 600 (1980) **Pop Density:** 485.0
Land: 1.0 sq. mi.; **Water:** 0.0 sq. mi. **Elev:** 1073 ft.
Name origin: For Herman Trett, land agent of the St. Paul & Pacific Railway.

Hoffman — City
ZIP: 56339 Lat: 45-49-54 N Long: 95-47-09 W
Pop: 576 (1990); 631 (1980) **Pop Density:** 250.4
Land: 2.3 sq. mi.; **Water:** 0.0 sq. mi. **Elev:** 1254 ft.
Name origin: For Robert C. Hoffman, who was the chief engineer of the Minneapolis, St. Paul & South Ste. Marie Railway.

Land — Township
ZIP: 56339 Lat: 45-48-38 N Long: 95-49-14 W
Pop: 276 (1990); 272 (1980) **Pop Density:** 8.3
Land: 33.4 sq. mi.; **Water:** 0.3 sq. mi.

Lawrence — Township
Lat: 46-03-35 N Long: 96-12-13 W
Pop: 98 (1990); 127 (1980) **Pop Density:** 2.8
Land: 35.1 sq. mi.; **Water:** 0.8 sq. mi.

Lien — Township
ZIP: 56311 Lat: 45-53-33 N Long: 95-56-43 W
Pop: 151 (1990); 188 (1980) **Pop Density:** 4.7
Land: 32.2 sq. mi.; **Water:** 2.2 sq. mi.

Logan — Township
Lat: 45-48-12 N Long: 96-12-09 W
Pop: 128 (1990); 174 (1980) **Pop Density:** 3.7
Land: 34.8 sq. mi.; **Water:** 0.1 sq. mi.

Macsville — Township
Lat: 45-48-09 N Long: 96-03-57 W
Pop: 153 (1990); 194 (1980) **Pop Density:** 4.7
Land: 32.4 sq. mi.; **Water:** 3.8 sq. mi.

Norcross
City
ZIP: 56274   **Lat:** 45-52-06 N   **Long:** 96-11-45 W
Pop: 86 (1990); 124 (1980)   **Pop Density:** 53.8
Land: 1.6 sq. mi.; **Water:** 0.0 sq. mi.

North Ottawa
Township
Lat: 45-58-40 N   **Long:** 96-11-59 W
Pop: 93 (1990); 118 (1980)   **Pop Density:** 2.6
Land: 35.8 sq. mi.; **Water:** 0.0 sq. mi.

Pelican Lake
Township
Lat: 46-03-55 N   **Long:** 95-49-51 W
Pop: 400 (1990); 356 (1980)   **Pop Density:** 14.7
Land: 27.2 sq. mi.; **Water:** 8.2 sq. mi.

Pomme de Terre
Township
Lat: 46-03-51 N   **Long:** 95-57-21 W
Pop: 174 (1990); 212 (1980)   **Pop Density:** 5.1
Land: 34.1 sq. mi.; **Water:** 1.8 sq. mi.

Roseville
Township
Lat: 45-48-37 N   **Long:** 95-56-01 W
Pop: 162 (1990); 212 (1980)   **Pop Density:** 4.6
Land: 35.3 sq. mi.; **Water:** 0.7 sq. mi.

Sanford
Township
Lat: 45-58-32 N   **Long:** 95-57-08 W
Pop: 169 (1990); 191 (1980)   **Pop Density:** 5.3
Land: 32.1 sq. mi.; **Water:** 2.0 sq. mi.

Stony Brook
Township
Lat: 46-04-05 N   **Long:** 96-05-04 W
Pop: 151 (1990); 181 (1980)   **Pop Density:** 4.6
Land: 32.8 sq. mi.; **Water:** 1.8 sq. mi.

Wendell
City
ZIP: 56590   **Lat:** 46-02-07 N   **Long:** 96-06-03 W
Pop: 159 (1990); 216 (1980)   **Pop Density:** 144.5
Land: 1.1 sq. mi.; **Water:** 0.0 sq. mi.
Founded 1880s.
Name origin: For a town in MA.

Hennepin County
County Seat: Minneapolis (ZIP: 55487)

Pop: 1,032,430 (1990); 941,411 (1980)   **Pop Density:** 1854.8
Land: 556.6 sq. mi.; **Water:** 49.8 sq. mi.   **Area Code:** 612

In east-central MN, west of St. Paul; original county; established Mar 6, 1852 (prior to statehood).

Name origin: For Louis Hennepin (1640–1701), Franciscan missionary and explorer (with La Salle) who named the Falls of St. Anthony in the Mississippi River at present-day Minneapolis.

Bloomington
City
ZIP: 55420   **Lat:** 44-49-46 N   **Long:** 93-18-54 W
Pop: 86,335 (1990); 81,831 (1980)   **Pop Density:** 2432.0
Land: 35.5 sq. mi.; **Water:** 2.9 sq. mi.
In southeast-central MN, southwest of Minneapolis.
Name origin: For Bloomington, IL, the hometown of early settlers.

Brooklyn Center
City
ZIP: 55429   **Lat:** 45-04-07 N   **Long:** 93-19-04 W
Pop: 28,887 (1990); 31,230 (1980)   **Pop Density:** 3656.6
Land: 7.9 sq. mi.; **Water:** 0.4 sq. mi.
In southeast-central MN, 8 mi. northwest of Minneapolis.

Brooklyn Park
City
ZIP: 55443   **Lat:** 45-06-34 N   **Long:** 93-21-07 W
Pop: 56,381 (1990); 43,332 (1980)   **Pop Density:** 2168.5
Land: 26.0 sq. mi.; **Water:** 0.5 sq. mi.
In southeast-central MN, northwest of Minneapolis.
Name origin: For the NY borough.

Champlin
City
ZIP: 55316   **Lat:** 45-09-55 N   **Long:** 93-23-21 W
Pop: 16,849 (1990); 9,006 (1980)   **Pop Density:** 2054.8
Land: 8.2 sq. mi.; **Water:** 0.6 sq. mi.
Settled 1851.
Name origin: For Civil War soldier and state legislator, Ezra Champlin.

Chanhassen
City
ZIP: 55317   **Lat:** 44-51-49 N   **Long:** 93-30-56 W
Pop: 0 (1990); 8 (1980)
Land: 0.2 sq. mi.; **Water:** 0.0 sq. mi.   **Elev:** 976 ft.
Settled 1852. Part of the town is also in Carver County.
Name origin: From the Sioux Indian term meaning 'sugar maple,' or 'the tree of sweet juice.'

Corcoran
City
ZIP: 55340   **Lat:** 45-07-01 N   **Long:** 93-35-10 W
Pop: 5,199 (1990); 4,252 (1980)   **Pop Density:** 145.2
Land: 35.8 sq. mi.; **Water:** 0.1 sq. mi.
Name origin: Named in 1858 for Patrick Corcoran, the first school teacher and postmaster.

Crystal
City
ZIP: 55428   **Lat:** 45-02-14 N   **Long:** 93-21-33 W
Pop: 23,788 (1990); 25,543 (1980)   **Pop Density:** 4173.3
Land: 5.7 sq. mi.; **Water:** 0.1 sq. mi.
In southeast-central MN, 15 mi. west of Minneapolis.
Name origin: Named in 1887 for nearby Crystal Lake.

Dayton
City
ZIP: 55327   **Lat:** 45-11-23 N   **Long:** 93-28-18 W
Pop: 4,392 (1990); 4,000 (1980)   **Pop Density:** 187.7
Land: 23.4 sq. mi.; **Water:** 1.7 sq. mi.
Part of the town is also in Wright County.
Name origin: Named in the 1850s for Lyman Dayton, railroad president and local real estate investor.

MINNESOTA, Hennepin County

Deephaven   City
ZIP: 55331   Lat: 44-55-45 N Long: 93-31-22 W
Pop: 3,653 (1990); 3,716 (1980)   Pop Density: 1588.3
Land: 2.3 sq. mi.; Water: 0.1 sq. mi.
Name origin: For its excellent harbor on Lake Minnetonka.

Eden Prairie   City
ZIP: 55344   Lat: 44-50-57 N Long: 93-27-29 W
Pop: 39,311 (1990); 16,263 (1980)   Pop Density: 1213.3
Land: 32.4 sq. mi.; Water: 2.8 sq. mi.
In southeast-central MN, near Minneapolis.
Name origin: Named in 1852 by Governor Alexander Ramsey (1815–1903) for the beautiful natural prairie on the town's southern boundary.

Edina   City
ZIP: 55410   Lat: 44-53-27 N Long: 93-21-34 W
Pop: 46,070 (1990); 46,073 (1980)   Pop Density: 2934.4
Land: 15.7 sq. mi.; Water: 0.3 sq. mi.
In southeast-central MN, 8 mi. southwest of Minneapolis. Incorporated 1888.
Name origin: For a local flour mill, itself named for a place near Edinburgh, Scotland.

Excelsior   City
ZIP: 55331   Lat: 44-54-02 N Long: 93-33-59 W
Pop: 2,367 (1990); 2,523 (1980)   Pop Density: 3945.0
Land: 0.6 sq. mi.; Water: 0.0 sq. mi.
Established 1852 by the Excelsior Pioneer Association of NY.
Name origin: The Association was named for the poem by Henry Wadsworth Longfellow (1807–82).

Fort Snelling   Pop. Place
                    Lat: 44-52-56 N Long: 93-12-29 W
Pop: 97 (1990); 223 (1980)   Pop Density: 15.4
Land: 6.3 sq. mi.; Water: 0.3 sq. mi.

Golden Valley   City
ZIP: 55427   Lat: 44-59-23 N Long: 93-21-31 W
Pop: 20,971 (1990); 22,775 (1980)   Pop Density: 2056.0
Land: 10.2 sq. mi.; Water: 0.3 sq. mi.
In southeast-central MN, 5 mi. west of Minneapolis.
Name origin: For its small valley and lake.

Greenfield   City
                    Lat: 45-06-17 N Long: 93-41-46 W
Pop: 1,450 (1990); 1,391 (1980)   Pop Density: 71.1
Land: 20.4 sq. mi.; Water: 1.0 sq. mi.

Greenwood   City
ZIP: 55331   Lat: 44-54-29 N Long: 93-33-01 W
Pop: 614 (1990); 653 (1980)   Pop Density: 2046.7
Land: 0.3 sq. mi.; Water: 0.3 sq. mi.

Hanover   City
ZIP: 55341   Lat: 45-09-23 N Long: 93-39-05 W
Pop: 269 (1990); 248 (1980)   Pop Density: 128.1
Land: 2.1 sq. mi.; Water: 0.1 sq. mi.
Part of the town is also in Wright County.
Name origin: Named by German immigrants, the Vellbrecht brothers, for their birthplace in Germany.

Hassan   Township
ZIP: 55374   Lat: 45-11-07 N Long: 93-34-50 W
Pop: 1,951 (1990); 1,766 (1980)   Pop Density: 87.1
Land: 22.4 sq. mi.; Water: 0.9 sq. mi.

Hopkins   City
ZIP: 55343   Lat: 44-55-36 N Long: 93-24-19 W
Pop: 16,534 (1990); 15,336 (1980)   Pop Density: 4032.7
Land: 4.1 sq. mi.; Water: 0.0 sq. mi.
Name origin: For postmaster Harley Hopkins.

Independence   City
ZIP: 55359   Lat: 45-01-19 N Long: 93-42-18 W
Pop: 2,822 (1990); 2,640 (1980)   Pop Density: 86.6
Land: 32.6 sq. mi.; Water: 2.0 sq. mi.
Name origin: For the largest of the local lakes, itself named by 4th of July picnickers in honor of the national holiday.

Long Lake   City
ZIP: 55356   Lat: 44-59-07 N Long: 93-34-07 W
Pop: 1,984 (1990); 1,747 (1980)   Pop Density: 2480.0
Land: 0.8 sq. mi.; Water: 0.1 sq. mi.   Elev: 981 ft.

Loretto   City
ZIP: 55357   Lat: 45-03-19 N Long: 93-38-06 W
Pop: 404 (1990); 297 (1980)   Pop Density: 1346.7
Land: 0.3 sq. mi.; Water: 0.0 sq. mi.
Founded 1886.
Name origin: For a Roman Catholic men's society, named for a pilgrimage shrine in Italy.

Maple Grove   City
ZIP: 55369   Lat: 45-06-21 N Long: 93-27-35 W
Pop: 38,736 (1990); 20,525 (1980)   Pop Density: 1181.0
Land: 32.8 sq. mi.; Water: 2.1 sq. mi.
In southeast-central MN, 14 mi. northwest of Minneapolis.
Name origin: For its descriptive connotations.

Maple Plain   City
ZIP: 55359   Lat: 45-00-32 N Long: 93-39-41 W
Pop: 2,005 (1990); 1,421 (1980)   Pop Density: 1822.7
Land: 1.1 sq. mi.; Water: 0.0 sq. mi.
Founded 1868.
Name origin: For the many sugar maple groves in the area.

Medicine Lake   City
ZIP: 55441   Lat: 45-00-08 N Long: 93-25-22 W
Pop: 385 (1990); 419 (1980)   Pop Density: 1925.0
Land: 0.2 sq. mi.; Water: 0.2 sq. mi.

Medina   City
ZIP: 55340   Lat: 45-01-52 N Long: 93-35-43 W
Pop: 3,096 (1990); 2,623 (1980)   Pop Density: 120.9
Land: 25.6 sq. mi.; Water: 1.3 sq. mi.
Name origin: Named in 1858 for the holy Muslim city in Saudi Arabia. Previously called Hamburg.

Minneapolis   City
ZIP: 55440   Lat: 44-57-42 N Long: 93-16-00 W
Pop: 368,383 (1990); 370,951 (1980) Pop Density: 6710.1
Land: 54.9 sq. mi.; Water: 3.5 sq. mi.
In southeast-central MN on both sides of the Mississippi River, opposite its "twin city," St. Paul. Founded 1850; incorporated as a city March 2, 1866. A major Midwestern center of trade, finance, industry, and transportation; home of the University of Minnesota. Called "City of Lakes" for the 22 natural lakes within the city limits.
Name origin: A compound of Sioux *minne* 'water' and Greek *polis*, 'city.' In 1872, Minneapolis on the west side of the Falls of St. Anthony merged with the village of St. Anthony on the east side of the Falls under the name of Minneapolis.

Minnetonka — City
ZIP: 55345 **Lat:** 44-55-55 N **Long:** 93-27-40 W
Pop: 48,370 (1990); 38,683 (1980) **Pop Density:** 1784.9
Land: 27.1 sq. mi.; **Water:** 1.1 sq. mi.
In southeast-central MN, west of Minneapolis.
Name origin: For the lake.

Minnetonka Beach — City
ZIP: 55361 **Lat:** 44-56-23 N **Long:** 93-35-17 W
Pop: 573 (1990); 575 (1980) **Pop Density:** 1146.0
Land: 0.5 sq. mi.; **Water:** 0.0 sq. mi.

Minnetrista — City
ZIP: 55364 **Lat:** 44-56-33 N **Long:** 93-42-11 W
Pop: 3,439 (1990); 3,236 (1980) **Pop Density:** 131.8
Land: 26.1 sq. mi.; **Water:** 4.7 sq. mi.
Name origin: For a Sioux Indian term adopted by early settlers, meaning 'crooked waters' and referring to the shapes of the many lakes in the area.

Mound — City
ZIP: 55364 **Lat:** 44-56-01 N **Long:** 93-39-36 W
Pop: 9,634 (1990); 9,280 (1980) **Pop Density:** 3322.1
Land: 2.9 sq. mi.; **Water:** 2.0 sq. mi. **Elev:** 942 ft.
Name origin: For the numerous aboriginal mounds in the area.

New Hope — City
ZIP: 55428 **Lat:** 45-02-13 N **Long:** 93-23-13 W
Pop: 21,853 (1990); 23,087 (1980) **Pop Density:** 4284.9
Land: 5.1 sq. mi.; **Water:** 0.0 sq. mi.
In southeast-central MN, a suburb of Minneapolis.
Name origin: Descriptively named by early settlers embodying their wishes for the new city.

Orono — City
ZIP: 55331 **Lat:** 44-57-54 N **Long:** 93-35-12 W
Pop: 7,285 (1990); 6,845 (1980) **Pop Density:** 452.5
Land: 16.1 sq. mi.; **Water:** 8.9 sq. mi.
Name origin: For Orono, ME.

Osseo — City
ZIP: 55369 **Lat:** 45-07-04 N **Long:** 93-23-56 W
Pop: 2,704 (1990); 2,974 (1980) **Pop Density:** 3380.0
Land: 0.8 sq. mi.; **Water:** 0.0 sq. mi.
Name origin: For a character in "The Song of Hiawatha" by Henry Wadsworth Longfellow (1807–82).

Plymouth — City
ZIP: 55441 **Lat:** 45-01-27 N **Long:** 93-27-36 W
Pop: 50,889 (1990); 31,615 (1980) **Pop Density:** 1546.8
Land: 32.9 sq. mi.; **Water:** 2.4 sq. mi.
In southeastern MN, northwest of Minneapolis.
Name origin: For Plymouth, England, and Plymouth, MA, where the Pilgrams landed in 1620–21.

Richfield — City
ZIP: 55423 **Lat:** 44-52-37 N **Long:** 93-16-55 W
Pop: 35,710 (1990); 37,851 (1980) **Pop Density:** 5175.4
Land: 6.9 sq. mi.; **Water:** 0.2 sq. mi. **Elev:** 842 ft.
Settled 1849. In southeast-central MN, 7 mi. south of Minneapolis.
Name origin: For its descriptive connotations.

Robbinsdale — City
ZIP: 55422 **Lat:** 45-01-36 N **Long:** 93-19-59 W
Pop: 14,396 (1990); 14,422 (1980) **Pop Density:** 5141.4
Land: 2.8 sq. mi.; **Water:** 0.2 sq. mi.
In southeast-central MN, 5 mi. northwest of Minneapolis.
Name origin: For Andrew Robbins, one of the town's original landowners.

Rockford — City
Lat: 45-05-12 N **Long:** 93-43-40 W
Pop: 440 (1990); 380 (1980) **Pop Density:** 1466.7
Land: 0.3 sq. mi.; **Water:** 0.0 sq. mi. **Elev:** 916 ft.
Founded 1855. Part of the town is also in Wright County.
Name origin: For a rocky ford of the Crow River where a sawmill was built.

Rogers — City
ZIP: 55374 **Lat:** 45-11-38 N **Long:** 93-33-06 W
Pop: 698 (1990); 652 (1980) **Pop Density:** 232.7
Land: 3.0 sq. mi.; **Water:** 0.0 sq. mi.

St. Anthony — City
ZIP: 55418 **Lat:** 45-01-23 N **Long:** 93-12-57 W
Pop: 5,278 (1990); 5,619 (1980) **Pop Density:** 3104.7
Land: 1.7 sq. mi.; **Water:** 0.0 sq. mi. **Elev:** 920 ft.
Part of the town is also in Ramsey County.
Name origin: For an early church.

St. Bonifacius — City
Lat: 44-54-17 N **Long:** 93-44-49 W
Pop: 1,180 (1990); 857 (1980) **Pop Density:** 1072.7
Land: 1.1 sq. mi.; **Water:** 0.0 sq. mi. **Elev:** 970 ft.

St. Louis Park — City
ZIP: 55426 **Lat:** 44-56-54 N **Long:** 93-21-53 W
Pop: 43,787 (1990); 42,931 (1980) **Pop Density:** 4092.2
Land: 10.7 sq. mi.; **Water:** 0.2 sq. mi.
In southeast-central MN, 6 mi. southwest of Minneapolis.
Name origin: For the Minneapolis & St. Louis Railway.

Shorewood — City
ZIP: 55331 **Lat:** 44-55-11 N **Long:** 93-33-55 W
Pop: 5,917 (1990); 4,646 (1980) **Pop Density:** 1116.4
Land: 5.3 sq. mi.; **Water:** 8.0 sq. mi.
Name origin: A euphonious name decided upon by the town's incorporators.

Spring Park — City
ZIP: 55384 **Lat:** 44-56-08 N **Long:** 93-37-59 W
Pop: 1,571 (1990); 1,465 (1980) **Pop Density:** 3927.5
Land: 0.4 sq. mi.; **Water:** 0.3 sq. mi.
Name origin: For euphony.

Tonka Bay — City
ZIP: 55331 **Lat:** 44-54-56 N **Long:** 93-35-25 W
Pop: 1,472 (1990); 1,354 (1980) **Pop Density:** 1472.0
Land: 1.0 sq. mi.; **Water:** 0.0 sq. mi.
Name origin: From the Sioux Indian term meaning 'water.'

Wayzata — City
ZIP: 55391 **Lat:** 44-58-13 N **Long:** 93-30-49 W
Pop: 3,806 (1990); 3,621 (1980) **Pop Density:** 1189.4
Land: 3.2 sq. mi.; **Water:** 0.1 sq. mi.
Name origin: From the Dakota Sioux term meaning 'at the pines, the north,' used here to refer to a location at the north side of the east end of Lake Minnetonka.

Woodland
City
Lat: 44-57-02 N **Long:** 93-30-53 W
Pop: 496 (1990); 526 (1980) **Pop Density:** 826.7
Land: 0.6 sq. mi.; **Water:** 0.0 sq. mi.
Name origin: For its descriptive connotations.

Houston County
County Seat: Caledonia (ZIP: 55921)

Pop: 18,497 (1990); 18,382 (1980) **Pop Density:** 33.1
Land: 558.4 sq. mi.; **Water:** 10.5 sq. mi. **Area Code:** 507
In the southeastern corner of MN, southeast of Rochester; established Feb 23, 1854 (prior to statehood) from Fillmore County.
Name origin: For Samuel Houston (1793–1863), governor of TN (1827–29), president of the Republic of Texas (1836–38; 1841–44), U.S. senator from TX (1846–59), and TX governor (1859–61).

Black Hammer
Township
Lat: 43-37-50 N **Long:** 91-41-09 W
Pop: 318 (1990); 356 (1980) **Pop Density:** 8.9
Land: 35.7 sq. mi.; **Water:** 0.0 sq. mi.

Brownsville
City
ZIP: 55919 **Lat:** 43-41-55 N **Long:** 91-16-49 W
Pop: 415 (1990); 418 (1980) **Pop Density:** 230.6
Land: 1.8 sq. mi.; **Water:** 0.2 sq. mi.
City and township not coextensive.
Name origin: For Job and Charles Brown, who set up a steamboat landing and settled in MN in 1848.

*Brownsville
Township
ZIP: 55919 **Lat:** 43-41-35 N **Long:** 91-19-29 W
Pop: 408 (1990); 362 (1980) **Pop Density:** 14.3
Land: 28.5 sq. mi.; **Water:** 1.1 sq. mi.

Caledonia
City
ZIP: 55921 **Lat:** 43-38-02 N **Long:** 91-30-00 W
Pop: 2,846 (1990); 2,691 (1980) **Pop Density:** 981.4
Land: 2.9 sq. mi.; **Water:** 0.0 sq. mi. **Elev:** 1174 ft.
Name origin: From ancient Roman name for Scotland.

*Caledonia
Township
ZIP: 55921 **Lat:** 43-37-58 N **Long:** 91-33-10 W
Pop: 529 (1990); 528 (1980) **Pop Density:** 15.7
Land: 33.8 sq. mi.; **Water:** 0.0 sq. mi.

Crooked Creek
Township
Lat: 43-36-08 N **Long:** 91-19-36 W
Pop: 310 (1990); 327 (1980) **Pop Density:** 9.7
Land: 32.1 sq. mi.; **Water:** 1.8 sq. mi.

Eitzen
City
ZIP: 55931 **Lat:** 43-30-29 N **Long:** 91-27-52 W
Pop: 221 (1990); 226 (1980) **Pop Density:** 368.3
Land: 0.6 sq. mi.; **Water:** 0.0 sq. mi.
Name origin: Named by early settlers from Germany for their former home.

Hokah
City
ZIP: 55941 **Lat:** 43-45-36 N **Long:** 91-21-00 W
Pop: 687 (1990); 686 (1980) **Pop Density:** 981.4
Land: 0.7 sq. mi.; **Water:** 0.0 sq. mi.
City and township not coextensive.
Name origin: For Sioux Indian chief, Hokah, whose village formerly occupied part of the town.

*Hokah
Township
ZIP: 55941 **Lat:** 43-46-13 N **Long:** 91-19-06 W
Pop: 551 (1990); 562 (1980) **Pop Density:** 23.2
Land: 23.8 sq. mi.; **Water:** 1.7 sq. mi.

Houston
City
ZIP: 55943 **Lat:** 43-45-38 N **Long:** 91-34-20 W
Pop: 1,013 (1990); 1,057 (1980) **Pop Density:** 1125.6
Land: 0.9 sq. mi.; **Water:** 0.0 sq. mi. **Elev:** 684 ft.
Founded 1850s. City and township not coextensive.
Name origin: For Samuel Houston (1793–1863), governor of TN (1827–29), president of the Republic of Texas (1836–38; 1841–44), U.S. senator from TX (1846–59), and TX governor (1859–61).

*Houston
Township
ZIP: 55943 **Lat:** 43-47-15 N **Long:** 91-32-38 W
Pop: 423 (1990); 468 (1980) **Pop Density:** 12.7
Land: 33.3 sq. mi.; **Water:** 0.3 sq. mi.

Jefferson
Township
Lat: 43-32-46 N **Long:** 91-18-34 W
Pop: 136 (1990); 174 (1980) **Pop Density:** 4.3
Land: 32.0 sq. mi.; **Water:** 2.8 sq. mi.

La Crescent
City
ZIP: 55947 **Lat:** 43-49-45 N **Long:** 91-18-03 W
Pop: 4,311 (1990); 3,674 (1980) **Pop Density:** 1658.1
Land: 2.6 sq. mi.; **Water:** 0.3 sq. mi.
Settled 1851. City and township coextensive.
Name origin: For contrast to La Crosse, WI, across the Mississippi River. Mistakenly believing La Crosse to mean 'the cross' instead of a bat used in a ball game, it is a reference to the cross and crescent of the Crusaders and Saracens.

*La Crescent
Township
ZIP: 55947 **Lat:** 43-49-14 N **Long:** 91-21-07 W
Pop: 1,427 (1990); 1,441 (1980) **Pop Density:** 66.1
Land: 21.6 sq. mi.; **Water:** 1.5 sq. mi.

Mayville
Township
Lat: 43-37-56 N **Long:** 91-26-26 W
Pop: 436 (1990); 504 (1980) **Pop Density:** 14.3
Land: 30.5 sq. mi.; **Water:** 0.1 sq. mi.

Money Creek
Township
Lat: 43-49-36 N **Long:** 91-38-52 W
Pop: 429 (1990); 525 (1980) **Pop Density:** 12.1
Land: 35.6 sq. mi.; **Water:** 0.2 sq. mi.

Mound Prairie
Township
Lat: 43-47-14 N **Long:** 91-26-24 W
Pop: 581 (1990); 549 (1980) **Pop Density:** 16.0
Land: 36.2 sq. mi.; **Water:** 0.5 sq. mi.

Sheldon
Township
Lat: 43-42-37 N **Long:** 91-33-22 W
Pop: 276 (1990); 307 (1980) **Pop Density:** 9.3
Land: 29.8 sq. mi.; **Water:** 0.0 sq. mi.

Spring Grove
City
ZIP: 55974 **Lat:** 43-33-39 N **Long:** 91-38-22 W
Pop: 1,153 (1990); 1,275 (1980) **Pop Density:** 1441.3
Land: 0.8 sq. mi.; **Water:** 0.0 sq. mi.
City and township not coextensive.
Name origin: For its descriptive connotations.

*Spring Grove
Township
ZIP: 55974 **Lat:** 43-33-01 N **Long:** 91-40-07 W
Pop: 567 (1990); 566 (1980) **Pop Density:** 16.2
Land: 35.1 sq. mi.; **Water:** 0.0 sq. mi.

Union
Township
Lat: 43-42-52 N **Long:** 91-24-57 W
Pop: 334 (1990); 422 (1980) **Pop Density:** 12.7
Land: 26.2 sq. mi.; **Water:** 0.0 sq. mi.

Wilmington
Township
Lat: 43-32-40 N **Long:** 91-33-26 W
Pop: 520 (1990); 558 (1980) **Pop Density:** 14.4
Land: 36.0 sq. mi.; **Water:** 0.0 sq. mi.

Winnebago
Township
Lat: 43-32-54 N **Long:** 91-25-53 W
Pop: 271 (1990); 355 (1980) **Pop Density:** 7.7
Land: 35.2 sq. mi.; **Water:** 0.0 sq. mi.

Yucatan
Township
Lat: 43-43-50 N **Long:** 91-40-49 W
Pop: 335 (1990); 351 (1980) **Pop Density:** 7.8
Land: 42.8 sq. mi.; **Water:** 0.2 sq. mi.

Hubbard County
County Seat: Park Rapids (ZIP: 56470)

Pop: 14,939 (1990); 14,098 (1980) **Pop Density:** 16.2
Land: 922.6 sq. mi.; **Water:** 76.9 sq. mi. **Area Code:** 218
In north-central MN, northeast of Fargo, ND; established Feb 26, 1883 from Cass County.
Name origin: For Gen. Lucius Frederick Hubbard (1836–1913), an officer in the Civil War and the Spanish-American War; MN legislator and governor (1882–87).

Akeley
City
ZIP: 56433 **Lat:** 47-00-01 N **Long:** 94-43-39 W
Pop: 393 (1990); 486 (1980) **Pop Density:** 262.0
Land: 1.5 sq. mi.; **Water:** 0.0 sq. mi.
Name origin: For locally prominent 19th-century businessman, Healy Akeley.

*Akeley
Township
ZIP: 56433 **Lat:** 47-01-29 N **Long:** 94-44-00 W
Pop: 332 (1990); 339 (1980) **Pop Density:** 10.6
Land: 31.4 sq. mi.; **Water:** 3.1 sq. mi.

Arago
Township
ZIP: 56470 **Lat:** 47-00-54 N **Long:** 95-06-16 W
Pop: 485 (1990); 385 (1980) **Pop Density:** 15.7
Land: 30.9 sq. mi.; **Water:** 4.4 sq. mi.

Badoura
Township
ZIP: 56433 **Lat:** 46-51-09 N **Long:** 94-43-25 W
Pop: 87 (1990); 98 (1980) **Pop Density:** 2.5
Land: 35.5 sq. mi.; **Water:** 1.0 sq. mi.

Clay
Township
Lat: 47-06-33 N **Long:** 94-58-44 W
Pop: 58 (1990); 71 (1980) **Pop Density:** 1.7
Land: 33.4 sq. mi.; **Water:** 2.7 sq. mi.

Clover
Township
ZIP: 56458 **Lat:** 47-06-33 N **Long:** 95-07-17 W
Pop: 101 (1990); 97 (1980) **Pop Density:** 3.0
Land: 33.8 sq. mi.; **Water:** 1.8 sq. mi.

Crow Wing Lake
Township
Lat: 46-51-19 N **Long:** 94-51-04 W
Pop: 187 (1990); 191 (1980) **Pop Density:** 6.3
Land: 29.5 sq. mi.; **Water:** 5.8 sq. mi.

Farden
Township
Lat: 47-21-58 N **Long:** 94-43-36 W
Pop: 769 (1990); 651 (1980) **Pop Density:** 22.8
Land: 33.7 sq. mi.; **Water:** 2.5 sq. mi.

Fern
Township
ZIP: 56625 **Lat:** 47-22-34 N **Long:** 95-06-30 W
Pop: 196 (1990); 152 (1980) **Pop Density:** 5.5
Land: 35.5 sq. mi.; **Water:** 0.7 sq. mi.

Guthrie
Township
ZIP: 56461 **Lat:** 47-17-25 N **Long:** 94-51-08 W
Pop: 386 (1990); 404 (1980) **Pop Density:** 11.1
Land: 34.8 sq. mi.; **Water:** 0.5 sq. mi.

Hart Lake
Township
Lat: 47-16-23 N **Long:** 94-43-00 W
Pop: 343 (1990); 351 (1980) **Pop Density:** 10.1
Land: 33.8 sq. mi.; **Water:** 1.7 sq. mi.

Helga
Township
Lat: 47-21-57 N **Long:** 94-52-02 W
Pop: 950 (1990); 767 (1980) **Pop Density:** 28.6
Land: 33.2 sq. mi.; **Water:** 2.5 sq. mi.

Hendrickson
Township
ZIP: 56461 **Lat:** 47-12-20 N **Long:** 94-50-43 W
Pop: 246 (1990); 198 (1980) **Pop Density:** 7.0
Land: 35.1 sq. mi.; **Water:** 0.7 sq. mi.

MINNESOTA, Hubbard County

Henrietta
Township
Lat: 46-55-47 N **Long:** 94-58-28 W
Pop: 1,276 (1990); 1,194 (1980) **Pop Density:** 40.1
Land: 31.8 sq. mi.; **Water:** 3.4 sq. mi.

Hubbard
Township
ZIP: 56470 **Lat:** 46-50-30 N **Long:** 94-58-28 W
Pop: 631 (1990); 600 (1980) **Pop Density:** 19.2
Land: 32.8 sq. mi.; **Water:** 3.2 sq. mi.

Lake Alice
Township
ZIP: 56458 **Lat:** 47-12-11 N **Long:** 95-06-03 W
Pop: 90 (1990); 91 (1980) **Pop Density:** 2.7
Land: 33.9 sq. mi.; **Water:** 0.8 sq. mi.

Lake Emma
Township
ZIP: 56470 **Lat:** 47-01-11 N **Long:** 94-58-23 W
Pop: 631 (1990); 550 (1980) **Pop Density:** 23.1
Land: 27.3 sq. mi.; **Water:** 8.8 sq. mi.

Lake George
Township
ZIP: 56458 **Lat:** 47-11-46 N **Long:** 94-58-42 W
Pop: 320 (1990); 319 (1980) **Pop Density:** 9.5
Land: 33.8 sq. mi.; **Water:** 2.4 sq. mi.

Lake Hattie
Township
ZIP: 56625 **Lat:** 47-17-20 N **Long:** 95-06-22 W
Pop: 127 (1990); 84 (1980) **Pop Density:** 3.8
Land: 33.4 sq. mi.; **Water:** 1.0 sq. mi.

Lakeport
Township
ZIP: 56461 **Lat:** 47-11-32 N **Long:** 94-43-40 W
Pop: 548 (1990); 436 (1980) **Pop Density:** 18.6
Land: 29.5 sq. mi.; **Water:** 5.8 sq. mi.

Laporte
City
ZIP: 56461 **Lat:** 47-12-51 N **Long:** 94-45-26 W
Pop: 101 (1990); 160 (1980) **Pop Density:** 144.3
Land: 0.7 sq. mi.; **Water:** 0.0 sq. mi.
Name origin: From French 'the door,' probably referring to an early trade route through the area's lakes.

Mantrap
Township
ZIP: 56467 **Lat:** 47-01-24 N **Long:** 94-51-08 W
Pop: 275 (1990); 213 (1980) **Pop Density:** 8.9
Land: 30.8 sq. mi.; **Water:** 5.0 sq. mi.

Nevis
City
ZIP: 56467 **Lat:** 46-57-52 N **Long:** 94-50-30 W
Pop: 375 (1990); 332 (1980) **Pop Density:** 416.7
Land: 0.9 sq. mi.; **Water:** 0.1 sq. mi. **Elev:** 1470 ft.
City and township not coextensive.
Name origin: Named by Scottish settlers for Ben Nevis, a mountain in Scotland.

*Nevis
Township
ZIP: 56467 **Lat:** 46-56-14 N **Long:** 94-51-15 W
Pop: 603 (1990); 644 (1980) **Pop Density:** 21.7
Land: 27.8 sq. mi.; **Water:** 5.7 sq. mi.

Park Rapids
City
ZIP: 56470 **Lat:** 46-55-02 N **Long:** 95-03-36 W
Pop: 2,863 (1990); 2,976 (1980) **Pop Density:** 584.3
Land: 4.9 sq. mi.; **Water:** 0.1 sq. mi.
Name origin: Named by landowner Frank Rice for the park-like groves and the rapids on the nearby Fish Hook River.

Rockwood
Township
ZIP: 56625 **Lat:** 47-21-44 N **Long:** 94-58-47 W
Pop: 365 (1990); 269 (1980) **Pop Density:** 11.0
Land: 33.2 sq. mi.; **Water:** 2.9 sq. mi.

Schoolcraft
Township
ZIP: 56458 **Lat:** 47-17-29 N **Long:** 94-58-58 W
Pop: 75 (1990); 58 (1980) **Pop Density:** 2.2
Land: 34.5 sq. mi.; **Water:** 0.8 sq. mi.

Steamboat River
Township
Lat: 47-07-00 N **Long:** 94-43-42 W
Pop: 78 (1990); 74 (1980) **Pop Density:** 2.3
Land: 34.5 sq. mi.; **Water:** 1.5 sq. mi.

Straight River
Township
Lat: 46-51-26 N **Long:** 95-06-06 W
Pop: 481 (1990); 535 (1980) **Pop Density:** 13.9
Land: 34.5 sq. mi.; **Water:** 1.1 sq. mi.

Thorpe
Township
ZIP: 56433 **Lat:** 47-07-06 N **Long:** 94-50-32 W
Pop: 33 (1990); 24 (1980) **Pop Density:** 0.9
Land: 34.8 sq. mi.; **Water:** 1.2 sq. mi.

Todd
Township
ZIP: 56470 **Lat:** 46-56-36 N **Long:** 95-06-40 W
Pop: 1,240 (1990); 1,070 (1980) **Pop Density:** 46.1
Land: 26.9 sq. mi.; **Water:** 3.5 sq. mi.

White Oak
Township
ZIP: 56433 **Lat:** 46-56-30 N **Long:** 94-43-53 W
Pop: 294 (1990); 279 (1980) **Pop Density:** 8.5
Land: 34.4 sq. mi.; **Water:** 2.1 sq. mi.

Isanti County
County Seat: Cambridge (ZIP: 55008)

Pop: 25,921 (1990); 23,600 (1980)　　**Pop Density:** 59.0
Land: 439.1 sq. mi.; **Water:** 12.8 sq. mi.　　**Area Code:** 612

In central-eastern MN, north of Minneapolis; established Feb 13, 1857 (prior to statehood) from Anoka County.

Name origin: For the Izaty or Santee Indians, a tribe of the Dakotas who inhabited the area. Also spelled *Issati*. The name means 'knife' or perhaps 'ones who make knives.'

Athens — Township
Lat: 45-26-18 N　Long: 93-13-20 W
Pop: 2,062 (1990); 1,793 (1980)　**Pop Density:** 65.7
Land: 31.4 sq. mi.; **Water:** 0.4 sq. mi.

Bradford — Township
Lat: 45-30-44 N　Long: 93-19-50 W
Pop: 2,637 (1990); 2,370 (1980)　**Pop Density:** 76.4
Land: 34.5 sq. mi.; **Water:** 1.5 sq. mi.

Braham — City
ZIP: 55006　Lat: 45-43-20 N　Long: 93-10-18 W
Pop: 1,139 (1990); 1,015 (1980)　**Pop Density:** 949.2
Land: 1.2 sq. mi.; **Water:** 0.0 sq. mi.

Part of the town is also in Kanabec County.

Name origin: Named by the Great Northern Railway for one of its officers.

Cambridge — City
ZIP: 55008　Lat: 45-33-51 N　Long: 93-13-36 W
Pop: 5,094 (1990); 3,287 (1980)　**Pop Density:** 1340.5
Land: 3.8 sq. mi.; **Water:** 0.0 sq. mi.　**Elev:** 962 ft.

Name origin: For Cambridge, MA, former hometown of settlers.

*Cambridge — Township
ZIP: 55008　Lat: 45-36-10 N　Long: 93-12-20 W
Pop: 1,988 (1990); 2,300 (1980)　**Pop Density:** 62.9
Land: 31.6 sq. mi.; **Water:** 1.4 sq. mi.

Dalbo — Township
ZIP: 55017　Lat: 45-41-36 N　Long: 93-27-13 W
Pop: 616 (1990); 665 (1980)　**Pop Density:** 17.4
Land: 35.5 sq. mi.; **Water:** 0.8 sq. mi.

Isanti — City
ZIP: 55040　Lat: 45-29-23 N　Long: 93-15-09 W
Pop: 1,228 (1990); 858 (1980)　**Pop Density:** 944.6
Land: 1.3 sq. mi.; **Water:** 0.0 sq. mi.

City and township not coextensive.

Name origin: For the Izaty or Santee Indians, a tribe of the Dakotas who inhabited the area. Also spelled *Issati*. The name means 'knife' or perhaps 'ones who make knives.'

*Isanti — Township
ZIP: 55040　Lat: 45-30-40 N　Long: 93-11-18 W
Pop: 1,800 (1990); 2,239 (1980)　**Pop Density:** 55.0
Land: 32.7 sq. mi.; **Water:** 0.9 sq. mi.

Maple Ridge — Township
Lat: 45-40-53 N　Long: 93-19-48 W
Pop: 658 (1990); 722 (1980)　**Pop Density:** 18.8
Land: 35.0 sq. mi.; **Water:** 0.7 sq. mi.

North Branch — Township
Lat: 45-30-35 N　Long: 93-05-11 W
Pop: 1,486 (1990); 1,507 (1980)　**Pop Density:** 42.9
Land: 34.6 sq. mi.; **Water:** 0.3 sq. mi.

Oxford — Township
Lat: 45-26-16 N　Long: 93-04-37 W
Pop: 638 (1990); 554 (1980)　**Pop Density:** 28.2
Land: 22.6 sq. mi.; **Water:** 1.2 sq. mi.

Spencer Brook — Township
Lat: 45-30-54 N　Long: 93-26-57 W
Pop: 1,203 (1990); 1,146 (1980)　**Pop Density:** 35.1
Land: 34.3 sq. mi.; **Water:** 1.1 sq. mi.

Springvale — Township
Lat: 45-35-34 N　Long: 93-19-59 W
Pop: 1,113 (1990); 1,046 (1980)　**Pop Density:** 31.8
Land: 35.0 sq. mi.; **Water:** 0.5 sq. mi.

Stanchfield — Township
ZIP: 55080　Lat: 45-41-09 N　Long: 93-11-42 W
Pop: 1,060 (1990); 1,077 (1980)　**Pop Density:** 31.4
Land: 33.8 sq. mi.; **Water:** 0.8 sq. mi.

Stanford — Township
ZIP: 55080　Lat: 45-26-32 N　Long: 93-24-21 W
Pop: 1,822 (1990); 1,592 (1980)　**Pop Density:** 47.2
Land: 38.6 sq. mi.; **Water:** 0.8 sq. mi.

Wyanett — Township
Lat: 45-36-19 N　Long: 93-27-22 W
Pop: 1,377 (1990); 1,429 (1980)　**Pop Density:** 41.5
Land: 33.2 sq. mi.; **Water:** 2.5 sq. mi.

MINNESOTA, Itasca County

Itasca County
County Seat: Grand Rapids (ZIP: 55744)

Pop: 40,863 (1990); 43,069 (1980) **Pop Density:** 15.3
Land: 2665.3 sq. mi.; **Water:** 262.6 sq. mi. **Area Code:** 218

In north-central MN, west of Hibbing; original county; established Oct 27, 1850 (prior to statehood).

Name origin: For Itasca Lake; name coined by explorer and ethnologist Henry Rowe Schoolcraft (1793–1864), who thought the lake was the "true source" of the Mississippi River. From Latin: the last part of ver*itas* 'truth,' and first part of *ca*put 'head.'

Alvwood — Township
Lat: 47-42-59 N **Long:** 94-14-38 W
Pop: 57 (1990); 78 (1980) **Pop Density:** 1.6
Land: 35.1 sq. mi.; **Water:** 0.4 sq. mi.

Arbo — Township
Lat: 47-20-16 N **Long:** 93-31-00 W
Pop: 832 (1990); 784 (1980) **Pop Density:** 24.8
Land: 33.6 sq. mi.; **Water:** 3.2 sq. mi.

Ardenhurst — Township
Lat: 47-48-17 N **Long:** 94-13-12 W
Pop: 142 (1990); 160 (1980) **Pop Density:** 4.8
Land: 29.4 sq. mi.; **Water:** 5.6 sq. mi.

Balsam — Township
Lat: 47-29-40 N **Long:** 93-25-13 W
Pop: 502 (1990); 507 (1980) **Pop Density:** 6.9
Land: 73.1 sq. mi.; **Water:** 10.7 sq. mi.

Bass Brook — Township
ZIP: 55721 **Lat:** 47-14-07 N **Long:** 93-38-06 W
Pop: 1,970 (1990); 1,871 (1980) **Pop Density:** 74.3
Land: 26.5 sq. mi.; **Water:** 8.8 sq. mi.

Bearville — Township
Lat: 47-43-03 N **Long:** 93-08-00 W
Pop: 143 (1990); 115 (1980) **Pop Density:** 2.0
Land: 71.8 sq. mi.; **Water:** 1.1 sq. mi.

Bigfork — City
ZIP: 56628 **Lat:** 47-44-54 N **Long:** 93-39-12 W
Pop: 384 (1990); 457 (1980) **Pop Density:** 240.0
Land: 1.6 sq. mi.; **Water:** 0.0 sq. mi. **Elev:** 1318 ft.
City and township not coextensive.
Name origin: For the town's location on the Big Fork of the Rainy River.

*Bigfork — Township
ZIP: 56628 **Lat:** 47-45-13 N **Long:** 93-40-44 W
Pop: 333 (1990); 308 (1980) **Pop Density:** 7.0
Land: 47.8 sq. mi.; **Water:** 0.4 sq. mi.

Blackberry — Township
Lat: 47-09-13 N **Long:** 93-23-20 W
Pop: 698 (1990); 627 (1980) **Pop Density:** 19.9
Land: 35.1 sq. mi.; **Water:** 1.0 sq. mi.

Bovey — City
ZIP: 55709 **Lat:** 47-17-39 N **Long:** 93-24-08 W
Pop: 662 (1990); 813 (1980) **Pop Density:** 287.8
Land: 2.3 sq. mi.; **Water:** 0.0 sq. mi.

Bowstring — Township
Lat: 47-32-36 N **Long:** 93-50-21 W
Pop: 217 (1990); 283 (1980) **Pop Density:** 8.2
Land: 26.6 sq. mi.; **Water:** 9.4 sq. mi.

Bowstring Lake — Pop. Place
Lat: 47-30-01 N **Long:** 94-07-13 W
Pop: 972 (1990); 970 (1980) **Pop Density:** 4.5
Land: 215.4 sq. mi.; **Water:** 68.8 sq. mi.

Calumet — City
ZIP: 55716 **Lat:** 47-19-08 N **Long:** 93-16-10 W
Pop: 382 (1990); 469 (1980) **Pop Density:** 238.8
Land: 1.6 sq. mi.; **Water:** 0.0 sq. mi. **Elev:** 1392 ft.
Name origin: For the ceremonial smoking of the "peace" pipe used by the Sioux to solemnize special occasions.

Carpenter — Township
Lat: 47-51-15 N **Long:** 93-17-19 W
Pop: 178 (1990); 236 (1980) **Pop Density:** 1.8
Land: 100.9 sq. mi.; **Water:** 5.2 sq. mi.

Coleraine — City
ZIP: 55722 **Lat:** 47-18-22 N **Long:** 93-25-23 W
Pop: 1,041 (1990); 1,116 (1980) **Pop Density:** 179.5
Land: 5.8 sq. mi.; **Water:** 0.2 sq. mi.
Name origin: For Thomas Cole, who had an influential role in this Mesabi Range town.

Deer Lake — Pop. Place
Lat: 47-20-06 N **Long:** 93-40-16 W
Pop: 3,046 (1990); 2,733 (1980) **Pop Density:** 16.7
Land: 182.7 sq. mi.; **Water:** 33.3 sq. mi.

Deer River — City
ZIP: 56636 **Lat:** 47-20-09 N **Long:** 93-47-38 W
Pop: 838 (1990); 907 (1980) **Pop Density:** 1197.1
Land: 0.7 sq. mi.; **Water:** 0.0 sq. mi. **Elev:** 1291 ft.
Name origin: From *wawashkeshini,* the Ojibway Indian term meaning 'Deer River.'

*Deer River — Township
Lat: 47-23-19 N **Long:** 93-44-56 W
Pop: 621 (1990); 541 (1980) **Pop Density:** 18.6
Land: 33.3 sq. mi.; **Water:** 2.3 sq. mi.

Effie — City
ZIP: 56639 **Lat:** 47-50-26 N **Long:** 93-38-15 W
Pop: 130 (1990); 141 (1980) **Pop Density:** 23.2
Land: 5.6 sq. mi.; **Water:** 0.0 sq. mi. **Elev:** 1381 ft.
Name origin: For the daughter of its postmaster.

*Effie — Pop. Place
Lat: 47-51-44 N **Long:** 93-37-09 W
Pop: 216 (1990); 279 (1980) **Pop Density:** 2.7
Land: 79.7 sq. mi.; **Water:** 0.7 sq. mi.

Feeley — Township
ZIP: 55793 **Lat:** 47-09-34 N **Long:** 93-16-29 W
Pop: 294 (1990); 320 (1980) **Pop Density:** 9.3
Land: 31.6 sq. mi.; **Water:** 1.1 sq. mi.

MINNESOTA, Itasca County

Good Hope — Township
ZIP: 56681 Lat: 47-37-22 N Long: 94-13-31 W
Pop: 99 (1990); 136 (1980) Pop Density: 3.2
Land: 30.8 sq. mi.; Water: 3.8 sq. mi.

Goodland — Township
ZIP: 55742 Lat: 47-11-15 N Long: 93-07-38 W
Pop: 437 (1990); 526 (1980) Pop Density: 6.3
Land: 69.2 sq. mi.; Water: 3.1 sq. mi.

Grand Rapids — City
ZIP: 55744 Lat: 47-13-43 N Long: 93-31-28 W
Pop: 7,976 (1990); 7,934 (1980) Pop Density: 1307.5
Land: 6.1 sq. mi.; Water: 0.7 sq. mi. Elev: 1290 ft.
City and township not coextensive.
Name origin: For the adjacent rapids on the Mississippi River.

*Grand Rapids — Township
Lat: 47-14-18 N Long: 93-30-43 W
Pop: 11,613 (1990); 11,649 (1980) Pop Density: 344.6
Land: 33.7 sq. mi.; Water: 2.3 sq. mi.

Grattan — Township
Lat: 47-48-02 N Long: 94-06-27 W
Pop: 56 (1990); 50 (1980) Pop Density: 1.6
Land: 34.8 sq. mi.; Water: 0.9 sq. mi.

Greenway — Township
Lat: 47-19-35 N Long: 93-15-29 W
Pop: 1,936 (1990); 2,382 (1980) Pop Density: 57.8
Land: 33.5 sq. mi.; Water: 2.6 sq. mi.

Harris — Township
Lat: 47-08-36 N Long: 93-30-20 W
Pop: 2,888 (1990); 3,007 (1980) Pop Density: 90.5
Land: 31.9 sq. mi.; Water: 4.0 sq. mi.

Iron Range — Township
Lat: 47-20-00 N Long: 93-22-18 W
Pop: 590 (1990); 625 (1980) Pop Density: 21.7
Land: 27.2 sq. mi.; Water: 1.8 sq. mi.

Keewatin — City
ZIP: 55753 Lat: 47-24-14 N Long: 93-05-07 W
Pop: 1,118 (1990); 1,443 (1980) Pop Density: 657.6
Land: 1.7 sq. mi.; Water: 0.4 sq. mi. Elev: 1469 ft.
Name origin: From the Ojibway Indian term meaning 'the northwest wind.'

Kinghurst — Township
Lat: 47-43-19 N Long: 94-05-25 W
Pop: 121 (1990); 151 (1980) Pop Density: 3.6
Land: 33.2 sq. mi.; Water: 2.1 sq. mi.

Lake Jessie — Township
Lat: 47-38-05 N Long: 93-50-21 W
Pop: 252 (1990); 278 (1980) Pop Density: 7.5
Land: 33.4 sq. mi.; Water: 3.3 sq. mi.

La Prairie — City
ZIP: 55744 Lat: 47-13-38 N Long: 93-29-24 W
Pop: 438 (1990); 536 (1980) Pop Density: 398.2
Land: 1.1 sq. mi.; Water: 0.0 sq. mi.

Lawrence — Township
Lat: 47-24-54 N Long: 93-23-12 W
Pop: 442 (1990); 487 (1980) Pop Density: 13.1
Land: 33.7 sq. mi.; Water: 2.3 sq. mi.

Liberty — Township
Lat: 47-45-42 N Long: 93-49-41 W
Pop: 66 (1990); 59 (1980) Pop Density: 0.9
Land: 70.7 sq. mi.; Water: 1.7 sq. mi.

Little Sand Lake — Pop. Place
Lat: 47-14-59 N Long: 93-15-07 W
Pop: 401 (1990); 438 (1980) Pop Density: 11.6
Land: 34.7 sq. mi.; Water: 1.1 sq. mi.

Lone Pine — Township
ZIP: 55769 Lat: 47-19-09 N Long: 93-07-40 W
Pop: 472 (1990); 592 (1980) Pop Density: 14.4
Land: 32.8 sq. mi.; Water: 4.1 sq. mi.

Marble — City
ZIP: 55764 Lat: 47-19-42 N Long: 93-17-36 W
Pop: 618 (1990); 757 (1980) Pop Density: 143.7
Land: 4.3 sq. mi.; Water: 0.1 sq. mi.

Marcell — Township
ZIP: 56657 Lat: 47-35-35 N Long: 93-40-20 W
Pop: 309 (1990); 353 (1980) Pop Density: 6.5
Land: 47.9 sq. mi.; Water: 9.3 sq. mi.

Max — Township
ZIP: 56659 Lat: 47-36-50 N Long: 94-05-44 W
Pop: 116 (1990); 155 (1980) Pop Density: 4.0
Land: 28.7 sq. mi.; Water: 5.5 sq. mi.

Moose Park — Township
Lat: 47-43-47 N Long: 94-21-15 W
Pop: 83 (1990); 86 (1980) Pop Density: 2.3
Land: 36.5 sq. mi.; Water: 0.0 sq. mi.

Morse — Township
Lat: 47-20-31 N Long: 93-50-19 W
Pop: 573 (1990); 606 (1980) Pop Density: 15.7
Land: 36.6 sq. mi.; Water: 0.9 sq. mi.

Nashwauk — City
ZIP: 55769 Lat: 47-23-03 N Long: 93-10-03 W
Pop: 1,026 (1990); 1,419 (1980) Pop Density: 256.5
Land: 4.0 sq. mi.; Water: 0.3 sq. mi.
City and township not coextensive.
Name origin: For the Nashauk River, near Fredericton, New Brunswick, Canada.

*Nashwauk — Township
ZIP: 55769 Lat: 47-24-32 N Long: 93-11-42 W
Pop: 1,809 (1990); 2,231 (1980) Pop Density: 27.2
Land: 66.6 sq. mi.; Water: 2.5 sq. mi.

Nore — Township
Lat: 47-47-08 N Long: 94-21-12 W
Pop: 37 (1990); 77 (1980) Pop Density: 1.0
Land: 36.3 sq. mi.; Water: 0.1 sq. mi.

Northeast Itasca — Pop. Place
Lat: 47-38-27 N Long: 93-20-01 W
Pop: 1,047 (1990); 1,176 (1980) Pop Density: 2.6
Land: 398.6 sq. mi.; Water: 25.7 sq. mi.

Oteneagen — Township
Lat: 47-27-28 N Long: 93-50-05 W
Pop: 218 (1990); 206 (1980) Pop Density: 6.0
Land: 36.1 sq. mi.; Water: 0.2 sq. mi.

Pomroy — Township
Lat: 47-48-09 N Long: 93-58-18 W
Pop: 31 (1990); 54 (1980) Pop Density: 0.8
Land: 36.8 sq. mi.; Water: 0.3 sq. mi.

MINNESOTA, Itasca County

Sago
Township
ZIP: 55784 Lat: 47-03-25 N Long: 93-15-23 W
Pop: 158 (1990); 174 (1980) Pop Density: 4.7
Land: 33.8 sq. mi.; Water: 0.6 sq. mi.

Sand Lake
Township
ZIP: 56680 Lat: 47-37-57 N Long: 93-57-41 W
Pop: 123 (1990); 158 (1980) Pop Density: 4.2
Land: 29.5 sq. mi.; Water: 8.0 sq. mi.

Spang
Township
Lat: 47-04-27 N Long: 93-40-04 W
Pop: 229 (1990); 203 (1980) Pop Density: 4.4
Land: 52.2 sq. mi.; Water: 0.6 sq. mi.

Splithand
Township
Lat: 47-03-36 N Long: 93-22-48 W
Pop: 247 (1990) Pop Density: 7.6
Land: 32.6 sq. mi.; Water: 0.7 sq. mi.

Squaw Lake
City
ZIP: 56681 Lat: 47-37-36 N Long: 94-08-27 W
Pop: 139 (1990); 162 (1980) Pop Density: 173.8
Land: 0.8 sq. mi.; Water: 0.0 sq. mi. Elev: 1360 ft.

Stokes
Township
ZIP: 56628 Lat: 47-40-51 N Long: 93-40-14 W
Pop: 209 (1990); 265 (1980) Pop Density: 4.0
Land: 52.5 sq. mi.; Water: 4.8 sq. mi.

Taconite
City
ZIP: 55786 Lat: 47-19-23 N Long: 93-21-36 W
Pop: 310 (1990); 331 (1980) Pop Density: 63.3
Land: 4.9 sq. mi.; Water: 0.4 sq. mi.
Name origin: For the local deposits of the mineral.

Third River
Township
Lat: 47-38-04 N Long: 94-21-49 W
Pop: 56 (1990); 56 (1980) Pop Density: 1.6
Land: 34.9 sq. mi.; Water: 1.4 sq. mi.

Trout Lake
Township
Lat: 47-14-31 N Long: 93-22-38 W
Pop: 810 (1990); 836 (1980) Pop Density: 26.2
Land: 30.9 sq. mi.; Water: 4.1 sq. mi.

Wabana
Township
Lat: 47-24-59 N Long: 93-30-51 W
Pop: 401 (1990); 354 (1980) Pop Density: 13.8
Land: 29.1 sq. mi.; Water: 6.9 sq. mi.

Warba
City
ZIP: 55793 Lat: 47-08-08 N Long: 93-16-15 W
Pop: 137 (1990); 150 (1980) Pop Density: 42.8
Land: 3.2 sq. mi.; Water: 0.1 sq. mi.
Name origin: From an Ojibway Indian term meaning 'soon.'

Wawina
Township
Lat: 47-03-58 N Long: 93-06-50 W
Pop: 73 (1990); 128 (1980) Pop Density: 2.0
Land: 36.5 sq. mi.; Water: 0.0 sq. mi.

Wildwood
Township
Lat: 47-03-48 N Long: 93-30-09 W
Pop: 144 (1990) Pop Density: 4.8
Land: 30.2 sq. mi.; Water: 3.2 sq. mi.

Wirt
Township
Lat: 47-42-29 N Long: 93-57-44 W
Pop: 84 (1990); 82 (1980) Pop Density: 2.5
Land: 34.1 sq. mi.; Water: 2.1 sq. mi.

Zemple
City
ZIP: 56636 Lat: 47-19-24 N Long: 93-47-10 W
Pop: 63 (1990); 62 (1980) Pop Density: 90.0
Land: 0.7 sq. mi.; Water: 0.0 sq. mi.

Jackson County
County Seat: Jackson (ZIP: 56143)

Pop: 11,677 (1990); 13,690 (1980) Pop Density: 16.6
Land: 701.9 sq. mi.; Water: 17.6 sq. mi. Area Code: 507
On southern border of MN, southwest of Mankato; established May 23, 1857 (prior to statehood) from unorganized lands.
Name origin: For Henry Jackson (1811–57), an early merchant in St. Paul (1842), first postmaster (1846–49), and territorial legislator. There is also a debatable claim that the county was named for Andrew Jackson.

Alba
Township
Lat: 43-43-11 N Long: 95-23-14 W
Pop: 217 (1990); 279 (1980) Pop Density: 6.1
Land: 35.3 sq. mi.; Water: 0.0 sq. mi.

Alpha
City
ZIP: 56111 Lat: 43-38-21 N Long: 94-52-16 W
Pop: 105 (1990); 180 (1980) Pop Density: 525.0
Land: 0.2 sq. mi.; Water: 0.0 sq. mi. Elev: 1387 ft.
Founded 1895.
Name origin: For the first letter of the Greek alphabet.

Belmont
Township
Lat: 43-42-54 N Long: 95-01-56 W
Pop: 263 (1990); 317 (1980) Pop Density: 7.3
Land: 36.0 sq. mi.; Water: 0.2 sq. mi.

Christiania
Township
Lat: 43-48-21 N Long: 95-01-36 W
Pop: 329 (1990); 408 (1980) Pop Density: 9.3
Land: 35.4 sq. mi.; Water: 0.8 sq. mi.

Delafield
Township
Lat: 43-47-59 N Long: 95-08-42 W
Pop: 282 (1990); 333 (1980) Pop Density: 8.1
Land: 34.7 sq. mi.; Water: 0.4 sq. mi.

Des Moines
Township
Lat: 43-37-49 N **Long:** 95-01-56 W
Pop: 300 (1990); 429 (1980) **Pop Density:** 9.3
Land: 32.3 sq. mi.; **Water:** 0.7 sq. mi.

Enterprise
Township
Lat: 43-43-11 N **Long:** 94-55-28 W
Pop: 238 (1990); 328 (1980) **Pop Density:** 6.6
Land: 36.0 sq. mi.; **Water:** 0.1 sq. mi.

Ewington
Township
Lat: 43-37-48 N **Long:** 95-23-47 W
Pop: 286 (1990); 366 (1980) **Pop Density:** 8.0
Land: 35.7 sq. mi.; **Water:** 0.0 sq. mi.

Heron Lake
City
ZIP: 56137 **Lat:** 43-47-43 N **Long:** 95-19-25 W
Pop: 730 (1990); 783 (1980) **Pop Density:** 663.6
Land: 1.1 sq. mi.; **Water:** 0.0 sq. mi.
Name origin: For Heron Lake; a transliteration of the Sioux Indian name meaning 'nesting place of herons.'

*Heron Lake
Township
ZIP: 56137 **Lat:** 43-43-10 N **Long:** 95-10-18 W
Pop: 442 (1990); 512 (1980) **Pop Density:** 11.4
Land: 38.8 sq. mi.; **Water:** 5.1 sq. mi.

Hunter
Township
Lat: 43-37-53 N **Long:** 95-09-20 W
Pop: 309 (1990); 363 (1980) **Pop Density:** 8.7
Land: 35.7 sq. mi.; **Water:** 0.1 sq. mi.

Jackson
City
ZIP: 56143 **Lat:** 43-37-27 N **Long:** 94-59-20 W
Pop: 3,559 (1990); 3,797 (1980) **Pop Density:** 1016.9
Land: 3.5 sq. mi.; **Water:** 0.0 sq. mi.
Name origin: For Henry Jackson (1811–57), an early merchant in St. Paul (1842), first postmaster (1846–49), and territorial legislator.

Kimball
Township
Lat: 43-48-16 N **Long:** 94-54-44 W
Pop: 176 (1990); 223 (1980) **Pop Density:** 4.9
Land: 35.9 sq. mi.; **Water:** 0.0 sq. mi.

La Crosse
Township
Lat: 43-48-05 N **Long:** 95-23-28 W
Pop: 218 (1990); 295 (1980) **Pop Density:** 6.2
Land: 34.9 sq. mi.; **Water:** 0.1 sq. mi.

Lakefield
City
ZIP: 56150 **Lat:** 43-40-40 N **Long:** 95-10-15 W
Pop: 1,679 (1990); 1,845 (1980) **Pop Density:** 1526.4
Land: 1.1 sq. mi.; **Water:** 0.0 sq. mi. **Elev:** 1476 ft.
Name origin: For adjacent Heron Lake.

Middletown
Township
Lat: 43-32-09 N **Long:** 95-01-50 W
Pop: 254 (1990); 338 (1980) **Pop Density:** 7.1
Land: 35.7 sq. mi.; **Water:** 0.5 sq. mi.

Minneota
Township
Lat: 43-32-14 N **Long:** 95-08-56 W
Pop: 245 (1990); 350 (1980) **Pop Density:** 7.3
Land: 33.6 sq. mi.; **Water:** 2.6 sq. mi.

Okabena
City
ZIP: 56161 **Lat:** 43-44-18 N **Long:** 95-18-57 W
Pop: 223 (1990); 263 (1980) **Pop Density:** 1115.0
Land: 0.2 sq. mi.; **Water:** 0.0 sq. mi. **Elev:** 1424 ft.
Name origin: From a Sioux Indian term meaning 'the nesting place of the herons.'

Petersburg
Township
Lat: 43-32-59 N **Long:** 94-54-14 W
Pop: 288 (1990); 386 (1980) **Pop Density:** 8.0
Land: 36.1 sq. mi.; **Water:** 0.0 sq. mi.

Rost
Township
Lat: 43-38-03 N **Long:** 95-16-46 W
Pop: 271 (1990); 310 (1980) **Pop Density:** 7.5
Land: 36.1 sq. mi.; **Water:** 0.0 sq. mi.

Round Lake
Township
Lat: 43-32-49 N **Long:** 95-24-07 W
Pop: 204 (1990); 293 (1980) **Pop Density:** 6.0
Land: 33.8 sq. mi.; **Water:** 2.0 sq. mi.

Sioux Valley
Township
Lat: 43-32-25 N **Long:** 95-15-52 W
Pop: 287 (1990); 371 (1980) **Pop Density:** 8.0
Land: 35.7 sq. mi.; **Water:** 0.5 sq. mi.

Weimer
Township
Lat: 43-48-09 N **Long:** 95-16-18 W
Pop: 242 (1990); 288 (1980) **Pop Density:** 7.9
Land: 30.6 sq. mi.; **Water:** 4.3 sq. mi.

West Heron Lake
Township
Lat: 43-42-38 N **Long:** 95-17-06 W
Pop: 166 (1990); 196 (1980) **Pop Density:** 6.1
Land: 27.4 sq. mi.; **Water:** 0.1 sq. mi.

Wilder
City
ZIP: 56184 **Lat:** 43-49-31 N **Long:** 95-12-22 W
Pop: 83 (1990); 120 (1980) **Pop Density:** 103.8
Land: 0.8 sq. mi.; **Water:** 0.0 sq. mi.
Name origin: For 19th-century businessman and industrialist Amherst H. Wilder.

Wisconsin
Township
Lat: 43-37-50 N **Long:** 94-54-54 W
Pop: 281 (1990); 317 (1980) **Pop Density:** 7.9
Land: 35.5 sq. mi.; **Water:** 0.0 sq. mi.

Kanabec County
County Seat: Mora (ZIP: 55051)

Pop: 12,802 (1990); 12,161 (1980) **Pop Density:** 24.4
Land: 525.0 sq. mi.; **Water:** 8.5 sq. mi. **Area Code:** 612
In east-central MN, north of Minneapolis; established Mar 13, 1858 from Pine County.

Name origin: For the meandering Snake River, which flows through the county; from the Ojibway word for 'snake.'

Ann Lake — Township
ZIP: 56358 **Lat:** 45-55-56 N **Long:** 93-27-07 W
Pop: 264 (1990); 226 (1980) **Pop Density:** 8.4
Land: 31.6 sq. mi.; **Water:** 0.8 sq. mi.

Arthur — Township
Lat: 45-51-33 N **Long:** 93-19-52 W
Pop: 1,533 (1990); 1,435 (1980) **Pop Density:** 49.9
Land: 30.7 sq. mi.; **Water:** 1.0 sq. mi.

Braham — City
ZIP: 55006 **Lat:** 45-43-55 N **Long:** 93-10-12 W
Pop: 0 (1990)
Land: 0.1 sq. mi.; **Water:** 0.0 sq. mi.
Part of the town is also in Isanti County.
Name origin: Named by the Great Northern Railway for one of its officers.

Brunswick — Township
ZIP: 55051 **Lat:** 45-46-45 N **Long:** 93-19-56 W
Pop: 1,107 (1990); 978 (1980) **Pop Density:** 32.0
Land: 34.6 sq. mi.; **Water:** 0.7 sq. mi.

Comfort — Township
Lat: 45-51-25 N **Long:** 93-12-36 W
Pop: 819 (1990); 756 (1980) **Pop Density:** 23.1
Land: 35.5 sq. mi.; **Water:** 0.5 sq. mi.

Ford — Township
Lat: 46-06-28 N **Long:** 93-14-32 W
Pop: 150 (1990); 137 (1980) **Pop Density:** 4.1
Land: 36.2 sq. mi.; **Water:** 0.1 sq. mi.

Grass Lake — Township
Lat: 45-45-39 N **Long:** 93-11-51 W
Pop: 888 (1990); 944 (1980) **Pop Density:** 25.7
Land: 34.6 sq. mi.; **Water:** 0.3 sq. mi.

Grasston — City
ZIP: 55030 **Lat:** 45-47-40 N **Long:** 93-09-13 W
Pop: 119 (1990); 123 (1980) **Pop Density:** 119.0
Land: 1.0 sq. mi.; **Water:** 0.0 sq. mi.

Hay Brook — Township
Lat: 46-07-22 N **Long:** 93-22-38 W
Pop: 165 (1990); 206 (1980) **Pop Density:** 4.5
Land: 36.3 sq. mi.; **Water:** 0.2 sq. mi.

Hillman — Township
Lat: 46-01-28 N **Long:** 93-22-44 W
Pop: 335 (1990); 311 (1980) **Pop Density:** 9.1
Land: 36.8 sq. mi.; **Water:** 0.2 sq. mi.

Kanabec — Township
ZIP: 56358 **Lat:** 45-51-30 N **Long:** 93-27-21 W
Pop: 633 (1990); 656 (1980) **Pop Density:** 17.7
Land: 35.7 sq. mi.; **Water:** 0.4 sq. mi.

Knife Lake — Township
ZIP: 55051 **Lat:** 45-56-41 N **Long:** 93-20-03 W
Pop: 825 (1990); 727 (1980) **Pop Density:** 26.9
Land: 30.7 sq. mi.; **Water:** 1.1 sq. mi.

Kroschel — Township
Lat: 46-06-32 N **Long:** 93-07-37 W
Pop: 188 (1990); 216 (1980) **Pop Density:** 5.4
Land: 34.9 sq. mi.; **Water:** 1.2 sq. mi.

Mora — City
ZIP: 55051 **Lat:** 45-52-38 N **Long:** 93-17-35 W
Pop: 2,905 (1990); 2,890 (1980) **Pop Density:** 785.1
Land: 3.7 sq. mi.; **Water:** 0.1 sq. mi. **Elev:** 1010 ft.
Name origin: Named in the 1880s by landowner Myron Kent for Mora, Sweden.

Ogilvie — City
ZIP: 56358 **Lat:** 45-49-50 N **Long:** 93-25-11 W
Pop: 510 (1990); 423 (1980) **Pop Density:** 425.0
Land: 1.2 sq. mi.; **Water:** 0.0 sq. mi. **Elev:** 1047 ft.
Name origin: For Oric Ogilvie Whited, a prominent lawyer and landowner in the area.

Peace — Township
Lat: 46-01-31 N **Long:** 93-14-35 W
Pop: 609 (1990); 485 (1980) **Pop Density:** 16.7
Land: 36.4 sq. mi.; **Water:** 1.6 sq. mi.

Pomroy — Township
Lat: 46-00-55 N **Long:** 93-06-51 W
Pop: 321 (1990); 342 (1980) **Pop Density:** 8.5
Land: 37.6 sq. mi.; **Water:** 0.1 sq. mi.

Quamba — City
ZIP: 55051 **Lat:** 45-54-55 N **Long:** 93-10-28 W
Pop: 124 (1990); 122 (1980) **Pop Density:** 177.1
Land: 0.7 sq. mi.; **Water:** 0.0 sq. mi.
Name origin: Named by officials of the Great Northern Railway Company.

South Fork — Township
ZIP: 56358 **Lat:** 45-46-27 N **Long:** 93-26-53 W
Pop: 614 (1990); 568 (1980) **Pop Density:** 16.9
Land: 36.3 sq. mi.; **Water:** 0.0 sq. mi.

Whited — Township
Lat: 45-56-58 N **Long:** 93-11-55 W
Pop: 693 (1990); 616 (1980) **Pop Density:** 22.7
Land: 30.5 sq. mi.; **Water:** 0.2 sq. mi.

Kandiyohi County
County Seat: Willmar (ZIP: 56201)

Pop: 38,761 (1990); 36,763 (1980)   **Pop Density:** 48.7
Land: 796.2 sq. mi.; **Water:** 65.8 sq. mi.   **Area Code:** 612

In south-central MN, west of Minneapolis; established Mar 20, 1858 from Meeker County, annexed Monongalia County in Nov 1870.

Name origin: From Siouan 'place where the buffalo fish arrive,' the Indian name for several lakes at the source of the Crow River where the fish *Ictiobus cyprinella, I. urus,* and *I. bubalus* go to spawn.

Arctander   Township
Lat: 45-17-11 N   **Long:** 95-11-52 W
Pop: 431 (1990); 422 (1980)   **Pop Density:** 12.5
Land: 34.5 sq. mi.; **Water:** 1.6 sq. mi.

Atwater   City
ZIP: 56209   **Lat:** 45-08-07 N   **Long:** 94-46-36 W
Pop: 1,053 (1990); 1,128 (1980)   **Pop Density:** 1053.0
Land: 1.0 sq. mi.; **Water:** 0.0 sq. mi.   **Elev:** 1215 ft.
Founded 1869.
Name origin: For E. D. Atwater, an official of the St. Paul & Pacific Railway.

Blomkest   City
ZIP: 56216   **Lat:** 44-56-35 N   **Long:** 95-01-20 W
Pop: 183 (1990); 200 (1980)   **Pop Density:** 183.0
Land: 1.0 sq. mi.; **Water:** 0.0 sq. mi.

Burbank   Township
Lat: 45-21-58 N   **Long:** 94-57-14 W
Pop: 427 (1990); 406 (1980)   **Pop Density:** 12.9
Land: 33.0 sq. mi.; **Water:** 2.8 sq. mi.

Colfax   Township
Lat: 45-22-12 N   **Long:** 95-03-55 W
Pop: 496 (1990); 490 (1980)   **Pop Density:** 15.1
Land: 32.8 sq. mi.; **Water:** 3.1 sq. mi.

Dovre   Township
Lat: 45-11-38 N   **Long:** 95-04-04 W
Pop: 1,746 (1990); 1,450 (1980)   **Pop Density:** 63.7
Land: 27.4 sq. mi.; **Water:** 7.3 sq. mi.

East Lake Lillian   Township
Lat: 44-55-42 N   **Long:** 94-48-45 W
Pop: 285 (1990); 283 (1980)   **Pop Density:** 8.5
Land: 33.6 sq. mi.; **Water:** 2.2 sq. mi.

Edwards   Township
Lat: 45-01-27 N   **Long:** 95-10-44 W
Pop: 427 (1990); 368 (1980)   **Pop Density:** 12.0
Land: 35.5 sq. mi.; **Water:** 0.4 sq. mi.

Fahlun   Township
Lat: 45-01-39 N   **Long:** 94-56-10 W
Pop: 338 (1990); 358 (1980)   **Pop Density:** 11.5
Land: 29.5 sq. mi.; **Water:** 6.5 sq. mi.

Gennessee   Township
Lat: 45-06-52 N   **Long:** 94-49-06 W
Pop: 495 (1990); 430 (1980)   **Pop Density:** 15.3
Land: 32.4 sq. mi.; **Water:** 2.5 sq. mi.

Green Lake   Township
Lat: 45-11-40 N   **Long:** 94-56-17 W
Pop: 1,270 (1990); 1,287 (1980)   **Pop Density:** 41.5
Land: 30.6 sq. mi.; **Water:** 3.8 sq. mi.

Harrison   Township
Lat: 45-11-46 N   **Long:** 94-49-31 W
Pop: 579 (1990); 596 (1980)   **Pop Density:** 18.3
Land: 31.7 sq. mi.; **Water:** 3.5 sq. mi.

Holland   Township
Lat: 44-55-38 N   **Long:** 95-11-20 W
Pop: 429 (1990); 445 (1980)   **Pop Density:** 12.1
Land: 35.4 sq. mi.; **Water:** 0.0 sq. mi.

Irving   Township
Lat: 45-17-07 N   **Long:** 94-49-41 W
Pop: 571 (1990); 699 (1980)   **Pop Density:** 17.4
Land: 32.8 sq. mi.; **Water:** 3.3 sq. mi.

Kandiyohi   City
ZIP: 56251   **Lat:** 45-07-51 N   **Long:** 94-55-56 W
Pop: 506 (1990); 447 (1980)   **Pop Density:** 1686.7
Land: 0.3 sq. mi.; **Water:** 0.0 sq. mi.   **Elev:** 1223 ft.
City and township not coextensive.
Name origin: From Siouan 'place where the buffalo fish arrive,' the Indian name for several lakes at the source of the Crow River where the fish *Ictiobus cyprinella, I. urus,* and *I. bubalus* go to spawn.

*Kandiyohi   Township
ZIP: 56251   **Lat:** 45-06-18 N   **Long:** 94-56-22 W
Pop: 663 (1990); 702 (1980)   **Pop Density:** 19.9
Land: 33.3 sq. mi.; **Water:** 2.0 sq. mi.

Lake Andrew   Township
Lat: 45-16-30 N   **Long:** 95-04-24 W
Pop: 749 (1990); 656 (1980)   **Pop Density:** 25.5
Land: 29.4 sq. mi.; **Water:** 6.5 sq. mi.

Lake Elizabeth   Township
Lat: 45-01-24 N   **Long:** 94-49-09 W
Pop: 293 (1990); 320 (1980)   **Pop Density:** 8.5
Land: 34.4 sq. mi.; **Water:** 1.5 sq. mi.

Lake Lillian   City
ZIP: 56253   **Lat:** 44-56-44 N   **Long:** 94-52-49 W
Pop: 229 (1990); 329 (1980)   **Pop Density:** 458.0
Land: 0.5 sq. mi.; **Water:** 0.0 sq. mi.
Name origin: For the wife of artist and writer, Edwin Whitefield, who was part of the exploring party in 1856.

*Lake Lillian   Township
ZIP: 56253   **Lat:** 44-56-10 N   **Long:** 94-56-38 W
Pop: 254 (1990); 283 (1980)   **Pop Density:** 7.1
Land: 35.6 sq. mi.; **Water:** 0.6 sq. mi.

Mamre   Township
Lat: 45-12-15 N   **Long:** 95-11-05 W
Pop: 427 (1990); 402 (1980)   **Pop Density:** 12.6
Land: 33.9 sq. mi.; **Water:** 1.7 sq. mi.

New London — City
ZIP: 56273 Lat: 45-17-57 N Long: 94-56-44 W
Pop: 971 (1990); 812 (1980) Pop Density: 1387.1
Land: 0.7 sq. mi.; Water: 0.1 sq. mi.
City and township not coextensive.
Name origin: For New London, WI, former home of pioneer Louis Larson.

*New London — Township
ZIP: 56273 Lat: 45-16-49 N Long: 94-56-56 W
Pop: 2,679 (1990); 2,289 (1980) Pop Density: 107.2
Land: 25.0 sq. mi.; Water: 9.9 sq. mi.

Norway Lake — Township
Lat: 45-22-08 N Long: 95-11-55 W
Pop: 291 (1990); 360 (1980) Pop Density: 8.9
Land: 32.7 sq. mi.; Water: 2.7 sq. mi.

Pennock — City
ZIP: 56279 Lat: 45-08-46 N Long: 95-10-31 W
Pop: 476 (1990); 410 (1980) Pop Density: 476.0
Land: 1.0 sq. mi.; Water: 0.0 sq. mi. Elev: 1131 ft.
Name origin: For George Pennock, one-time superintendent of the Great Northern Railway.

Prinsburg — City
ZIP: 56281 Lat: 44-56-08 N Long: 95-11-08 W
Pop: 502 (1990); 557 (1980) Pop Density: 456.4
Land: 1.1 sq. mi.; Water: 0.0 sq. mi. Elev: 1104 ft.
Name origin: For Martin Prins, a landowner from Holland who came to the area in 1884.

Raymond — City
ZIP: 56282 Lat: 45-00-57 N Long: 95-14-13 W
Pop: 668 (1990); 723 (1980) Pop Density: 1336.0
Land: 0.5 sq. mi.; Water: 0.0 sq. mi.
Founded 1887.
Name origin: For Raymond Spicer, the son of a prominent pioneer.

Regal — City
Lat: 45-24-18 N Long: 94-50-24 W
Pop: 51 (1990); 70 (1980) Pop Density: 102.0
Land: 0.5 sq. mi.; Water: 0.0 sq. mi.

Roseland — Township
Lat: 44-56-19 N Long: 95-03-18 W
Pop: 485 (1990); 519 (1980) Pop Density: 13.8
Land: 35.1 sq. mi.; Water: 0.0 sq. mi.

Roseville — Township
Lat: 45-22-05 N Long: 94-49-23 W
Pop: 485 (1990); 541 (1980) Pop Density: 13.9
Land: 35.0 sq. mi.; Water: 0.4 sq. mi.

St. Johns — Township
Lat: 45-06-37 N Long: 95-11-05 W
Pop: 439 (1990); 499 (1980) Pop Density: 12.7
Land: 34.7 sq. mi.; Water: 0.3 sq. mi.

Spicer — City
ZIP: 56288 Lat: 45-13-57 N Long: 94-56-19 W
Pop: 1,020 (1990); 909 (1980) Pop Density: 1133.3
Land: 0.9 sq. mi.; Water: 0.0 sq. mi. Elev: 1171 ft.
Founded 1886.
Name origin: For John Spicer, who owned the town site.

Sunburg — City
ZIP: 56289 Lat: 45-20-52 N Long: 95-14-21 W
Pop: 117 (1990); 130 (1980) Pop Density: 234.0
Land: 0.5 sq. mi.; Water: 0.0 sq. mi.
Name origin: Named euphoniously and descriptively by the town's founders.

Whitefield — Township
Lat: 45-01-26 N Long: 95-03-37 W
Pop: 506 (1990); 531 (1980) Pop Density: 14.3
Land: 35.3 sq. mi.; Water: 0.9 sq. mi.

Willmar — City
ZIP: 56201 Lat: 45-07-28 N Long: 95-02-58 W
Pop: 17,531 (1990); 15,895 (1980) Pop Density: 1638.4
Land: 10.7 sq. mi.; Water: 1.3 sq. mi.
In southwest-central MN, 52 mi. southwest of St. Cloud.
Name origin: For a European stockholder of the St. Paul & Pacific Railroad Company.

*Willmar — Township
ZIP: 56201 Lat: 45-05-54 N Long: 95-04-30 W
Pop: 689 (1990); 817 (1980) Pop Density: 28.7
Land: 24.0 sq. mi.; Water: 0.5 sq. mi.

Kittson County
County Seat: Hallock (ZIP: 56728)

Pop: 5,767 (1990); 6,672 (1980) Pop Density: 5.3
Land: 1097.1 sq. mi.; Water: 6.4 sq. mi. Area Code: 218
In the northwestern corner of MN, north of Grand Forks, ND; established as Pembina County Apr 24, 1879 from unorganized lands; name changed Mar 9, 1878.
Name origin: For Norman Wolfred Kittson (1814–88), fur trader, territorial legislator (1851–55), and mayor of St. Paul (1858).

Arveson — Township
Lat: 48-34-21 N Long: 96-27-25 W
Pop: 103 (1990); 93 (1980) Pop Density: 3.3
Land: 31.3 sq. mi.; Water: 3.3 sq. mi.

Cannon — Township
Lat: 48-50-48 N Long: 96-35-26 W
Pop: 18 (1990); 30 (1980) Pop Density: 0.5
Land: 35.7 sq. mi.; Water: 0.0 sq. mi.

Caribou — Township
Lat: 48-56-26 N Long: 96-28-14 W
Pop: 49 (1990); 39 (1980) Pop Density: 1.1
Land: 44.2 sq. mi.; Water: 0.0 sq. mi.

Clow — Township
Lat: 48-56-53 N Long: 97-00-02 W
Pop: 33 (1990); 49 (1980) Pop Density: 0.7
Land: 45.5 sq. mi.; Water: 0.0 sq. mi.

MINNESOTA, Kittson County

Davis
Township
Lat: 48-35-09 N **Long:** 96-50-19 W
Pop: 60 (1990); 77 (1980) **Pop Density:** 1.7
Land: 35.3 sq. mi.; **Water:** 0.0 sq. mi.

Deerwood
Township
Lat: 48-35-13 N **Long:** 96-35-01 W
Pop: 167 (1990); 248 (1980) **Pop Density:** 4.7
Land: 35.6 sq. mi.; **Water:** 0.0 sq. mi.

Donaldson
City
ZIP: 56720 **Lat:** 48-34-29 N **Long:** 96-53-50 W
Pop: 57 (1990); 84 (1980) **Pop Density:** 71.3
Land: 0.8 sq. mi.; **Water:** 0.0 sq. mi.
Name origin: For Capt. Hugh Donaldson, who managed a large farm in the area.

East Kittson
Pop. Place
Lat: 48-49-13 N **Long:** 96-28-13 W
Pop: 7 (1990); 15 (1980) **Pop Density:** 0.1
Land: 72.3 sq. mi.; **Water:** 0.4 sq. mi.

Granville
Township
Lat: 48-50-37 N **Long:** 96-51-23 W
Pop: 97 (1990); 129 (1980) **Pop Density:** 2.8
Land: 34.5 sq. mi.; **Water:** 0.0 sq. mi.

Hallock
City
ZIP: 56728 **Lat:** 48-45-59 N **Long:** 96-56-36 W
Pop: 1,304 (1990); 1,405 (1980) **Pop Density:** 621.0
Land: 2.1 sq. mi.; **Water:** 0.0 sq. mi. **Elev:** 817 ft.
City and township not coextensive.
Name origin: For sportsman and journalist, Charles Hallock, who built a hotel in the city in 1890.

*Hallock
Township
ZIP: 56728 **Lat:** 48-45-57 N **Long:** 97-00-10 W
Pop: 114 (1990); 115 (1980) **Pop Density:** 3.4
Land: 33.9 sq. mi.; **Water:** 0.0 sq. mi.

Halma
City
ZIP: 56729 **Lat:** 48-39-38 N **Long:** 96-35-51 W
Pop: 73 (1990); 97 (1980) **Pop Density:** 81.1
Land: 0.9 sq. mi.; **Water:** 0.0 sq. mi. **Elev:** 1001 ft.
Name origin: Early Norwegian settlers named the town for a place in Norway.

Hampden
Township
Lat: 48-50-56 N **Long:** 96-59-45 W
Pop: 56 (1990); 64 (1980) **Pop Density:** 1.6
Land: 36.0 sq. mi.; **Water:** 0.0 sq. mi.

Hazelton
Township
Lat: 48-46-03 N **Long:** 96-44-18 W
Pop: 96 (1990); 111 (1980) **Pop Density:** 2.7
Land: 36.0 sq. mi.; **Water:** 0.0 sq. mi.

Hill
Township
Lat: 48-50-50 N **Long:** 97-07-01 W
Pop: 32 (1990); 41 (1980) **Pop Density:** 1.0
Land: 32.0 sq. mi.; **Water:** 0.3 sq. mi.

Humboldt
City
ZIP: 56731 **Lat:** 48-55-17 N **Long:** 97-05-39 W
Pop: 74 (1990); 111 (1980) **Pop Density:** 740.0
Land: 0.1 sq. mi.; **Water:** 0.0 sq. mi.
Name origin: For German scientist and naturalist, Baron Alexander von Humboldt (1769–1859).

Jupiter
Township
Lat: 48-40-00 N **Long:** 96-42-13 W
Pop: 148 (1990); 181 (1980) **Pop Density:** 4.1
Land: 35.7 sq. mi.; **Water:** 0.0 sq. mi.

Karlstad
City
ZIP: 56732 **Lat:** 48-34-41 N **Long:** 96-30-56 W
Pop: 881 (1990); 934 (1980) **Pop Density:** 587.3
Land: 1.5 sq. mi.; **Water:** 0.0 sq. mi. **Elev:** 1048 ft.
Name origin: Named by early Swedish settlers for Karlstad, Sweden.

Kennedy
City
ZIP: 56733 **Lat:** 48-38-36 N **Long:** 96-54-36 W
Pop: 337 (1990); 405 (1980) **Pop Density:** 842.5
Land: 0.4 sq. mi.; **Water:** 0.0 sq. mi.
Name origin: For railway director and banker, John Stewart Kennedy, who was well-known for his humanitarian work.

Lake Bronson
City
ZIP: 56734 **Lat:** 48-43-57 N **Long:** 96-39-45 W
Pop: 272 (1990); 298 (1980) **Pop Density:** 453.3
Land: 0.6 sq. mi.; **Water:** 0.0 sq. mi.
Name origin: For early farmer, Giles Bronson, a well-known sportsman.

Lancaster
City
ZIP: 56735 **Lat:** 48-51-28 N **Long:** 96-48-10 W
Pop: 342 (1990); 368 (1980) **Pop Density:** 155.5
Land: 2.2 sq. mi.; **Water:** 0.0 sq. mi.
Name origin: For the county in England.

McKinley
Township
Lat: 48-56-19 N **Long:** 96-36-46 W
Pop: 39 (1990); 36 (1980) **Pop Density:** 0.8
Land: 45.9 sq. mi.; **Water:** 0.0 sq. mi.

North Red River
Township
Lat: 48-46-04 N **Long:** 97-07-00 W
Pop: 24 (1990); 31 (1980) **Pop Density:** 1.0
Land: 23.4 sq. mi.; **Water:** 0.3 sq. mi.

Norway
Township
Lat: 48-40-05 N **Long:** 96-35-39 W
Pop: 73 (1990); 103 (1980) **Pop Density:** 2.1
Land: 35.1 sq. mi.; **Water:** 0.1 sq. mi.

Pelan
Township
Lat: 48-40-51 N **Long:** 96-28-15 W
Pop: 72 (1990); 58 (1980) **Pop Density:** 2.0
Land: 35.6 sq. mi.; **Water:** 0.0 sq. mi.

Percy
Township
Lat: 48-46-20 N **Long:** 96-36-05 W
Pop: 67 (1990); 69 (1980) **Pop Density:** 1.9
Land: 34.8 sq. mi.; **Water:** 0.5 sq. mi.

Poppleton
Township
Lat: 48-50-55 N **Long:** 96-43-58 W
Pop: 128 (1990); 167 (1980) **Pop Density:** 3.7
Land: 35.0 sq. mi.; **Water:** 0.0 sq. mi.

Richardville
Township
Lat: 48-56-49 N **Long:** 96-51-43 W
Pop: 126 (1990); 171 (1980) **Pop Density:** 2.8
Land: 45.2 sq. mi.; **Water:** 0.1 sq. mi.

St. Joseph
Township
Lat: 48-56-06 N **Long:** 96-43-53 W
Pop: 59 (1990); 90 (1980) **Pop Density:** 1.3
Land: 44.8 sq. mi.; **Water:** 0.2 sq. mi.

St. Vincent
City
Lat: 48-58-17 N **Long:** 97-13-31 W
Pop: 116 (1990); 141 (1980) **Pop Density:** 105.5
Land: 1.1 sq. mi.; **Water:** 0.1 sq. mi.
City and township not coextensive.

*St. Vincent
Township
Lat: 48-56-34 N **Long:** 97-08-15 W
Pop: 118 (1990); 127 (1980) **Pop Density:** 2.2
Land: 54.2 sq. mi.; **Water:** 0.3 sq. mi.

Skane
Township
Lat: 48-40-55 N **Long:** 96-58-50 W
Pop: 74 (1990); 76 (1980) **Pop Density:** 2.1
Land: 35.5 sq. mi.; **Water:** 0.0 sq. mi.

South Red River
Township
Lat: 48-40-07 N **Long:** 97-04-22 W
Pop: 14 (1990); 33 (1980) **Pop Density:** 0.8
Land: 17.6 sq. mi.; **Water:** 0.2 sq. mi.

Spring Brook
Township
Lat: 48-35-10 N **Long:** 96-42-14 W
Pop: 90 (1990); 117 (1980) **Pop Density:** 2.5
Land: 35.9 sq. mi.; **Water:** 0.0 sq. mi.

Svea
Township
Lat: 48-35-14 N **Long:** 96-57-55 W
Pop: 63 (1990); 72 (1980) **Pop Density:** 1.8
Land: 35.8 sq. mi.; **Water:** 0.0 sq. mi.

Tegner
Township
Lat: 48-40-15 N **Long:** 96-50-40 W
Pop: 56 (1990); 75 (1980) **Pop Density:** 1.6
Land: 35.7 sq. mi.; **Water:** 0.0 sq. mi.

Teien
Township
Lat: 48-35-06 N **Long:** 97-05-40 W
Pop: 130 (1990); 183 (1980) **Pop Density:** 4.5
Land: 28.8 sq. mi.; **Water:** 0.5 sq. mi.

Thompson
Township
Lat: 48-45-50 N **Long:** 96-51-13 W
Pop: 198 (1990); 229 (1980) **Pop Density:** 5.5
Land: 36.0 sq. mi.; **Water:** 0.0 sq. mi.

Koochiching County
County Seat: International Falls (ZIP: 56649)

Pop: 16,299 (1990); 17,571 (1980) **Pop Density:** 5.3
Land: 3102.4 sq. mi.; **Water:** 52.0 sq. mi. **Area Code:** 218
On the central-northern border of MN; established Dec 19, 1906 from Itasca County.

Name origin: Origin uncertain, but evidence points to a Cree Indian word meaning 'rainy lake,' descriptive of the mists from the nearby International Falls on Rainy River.

Big Falls
City
ZIP: 56627 **Lat:** 48-11-06 N **Long:** 93-48-29 W
Pop: 341 (1990); 490 (1980) **Pop Density:** 56.8
Land: 6.0 sq. mi.; **Water:** 0.0 sq. mi.
Name origin: For the large waterfall in the Big Fork River on the edge of the town.

East Koochiching
Pop. Place
Lat: 48-17-57 N **Long:** 93-21-31 W
Pop: 417 (1990); 498 (1980) **Pop Density:** 1.1
Land: 385.2 sq. mi.; **Water:** 0.9 sq. mi.

International Falls
City
ZIP: 56649 **Lat:** 48-35-15 N **Long:** 93-24-22 W
Pop: 8,325 (1990); 5,611 (1980) **Pop Density:** 1321.4
Land: 6.3 sq. mi.; **Water:** 0.1 sq. mi. **Elev:** 1128 ft.
Name origin: For the town's location on the international Canadian-American boundary at the Koochiching Falls of the Rainy River.

Island View
City
ZIP: 56649 **Lat:** 48-36-21 N **Long:** 93-11-26 W
Pop: 150 (1990); 101 (1980) **Pop Density:** 57.7
Land: 2.6 sq. mi.; **Water:** 5.0 sq. mi.

Littlefork
City
ZIP: 56653 **Lat:** 48-23-47 N **Long:** 93-33-24 W
Pop: 838 (1990); 918 (1980) **Pop Density:** 761.8
Land: 1.1 sq. mi.; **Water:** 0.0 sq. mi.
Name origin: For its location on the little fork of the Rainy River.

Mizpah
City
ZIP: 56660 **Lat:** 47-55-21 N **Long:** 94-12-55 W
Pop: 100 (1990); 129 (1980) **Pop Density:** 33.3
Land: 3.0 sq. mi.; **Water:** 0.0 sq. mi. **Elev:** 1385 ft.
Name origin: From the Old Testament Hebrew term meaning 'watchtower.' It is also a salutation meaning 'the Lord be with you.'

Nett Lake
Pop. Place
Lat: 48-05-06 N **Long:** 93-14-01 W
Pop: 69 (1990); 77 (1980) **Pop Density:** 0.5
Land: 131.4 sq. mi.; **Water:** 7.8 sq. mi.

Northome
City
ZIP: 56661 **Lat:** 47-52-28 N **Long:** 94-15-56 W
Pop: 283 (1990); 312 (1980) **Pop Density:** 188.7
Land: 1.5 sq. mi.; **Water:** 0.4 sq. mi. **Elev:** 1429 ft.

*Northome
Pop. Place
Lat: 47-57-17 N **Long:** 94-12-33 W
Pop: 496 (1990); 597 (1980) **Pop Density:** 1.7
Land: 296.0 sq. mi.; **Water:** 1.3 sq. mi.

Northwest Koochiching   Pop. Place
Lat: 48-21-36 N   Long: 94-09-17 W
Pop: 594 (1990); 639 (1980)   **Pop Density:** 0.6
Land: 1077.1 sq. mi.; **Water:** 3.4 sq. mi.

Rainy Lake   Pop. Place
Lat: 48-29-25 N   Long: 93-23-11 W
Pop: 4,198 (1990); 4,793 (1980)   **Pop Density:** 12.1
Land: 347.6 sq. mi.; **Water:** 32.0 sq. mi.

Ranier   City
ZIP: 56668   Lat: 48-36-47 N   Long: 93-20-47 W
Pop: 199 (1990); 237 (1980)   **Pop Density:** 1990.0
Land: 0.1 sq. mi.; **Water:** 0.0 sq. mi.

South Koochiching   Pop. Place
Lat: 48-03-18 N   Long: 93-39-27 W
Pop: 289 (1990); 363 (1980)   **Pop Density:** 0.3
Land: 844.3 sq. mi.; **Water:** 1.1 sq. mi.

Lac qui Parle County
County Seat: Madison (ZIP: 56256)

Pop: 8,924 (1990); 10,592 (1980)   **Pop Density:** 11.7
Land: 764.9 sq. mi.; **Water:** 13.2 sq. mi.   **Area Code:** 612

On the southwestern border of MN; organized 1863 north of the Minnesota River, disestablished in 1868, then recreated Mar 6, 1871 south of the river.

Name origin: French 'talking lake,' probably a transliteration of Siouan *mde* 'lake,' *iye* 'speaks,' and *dan*, a diminutive suffix. Origin uncertain, but possibly for echoes reflected from surrounding cliffs.

Agassiz   Township
Lat: 45-11-22 N   Long: 96-17-53 W
Pop: 127 (1990); 153 (1980)   **Pop Density:** 3.6
Land: 34.9 sq. mi.; **Water:** 2.4 sq. mi.

Arena   Township
Lat: 45-01-17 N   Long: 96-17-34 W
Pop: 182 (1990); 208 (1980)   **Pop Density:** 5.0
Land: 36.7 sq. mi.; **Water:** 0.4 sq. mi.

Augusta   Township
Lat: 45-01-06 N   Long: 96-24-11 W
Pop: 141 (1990); 177 (1980)   **Pop Density:** 4.9
Land: 28.5 sq. mi.; **Water:** 0.2 sq. mi.

Baxter   Township
Lat: 44-55-58 N   Long: 95-54-47 W
Pop: 234 (1990); 285 (1980)   **Pop Density:** 6.5
Land: 35.9 sq. mi.; **Water:** 0.1 sq. mi.

Bellingham   City
ZIP: 56212   Lat: 45-08-08 N   Long: 96-16-58 W
Pop: 247 (1990); 290 (1980)   **Pop Density:** 617.5
Land: 0.4 sq. mi.; **Water:** 0.0 sq. mi.
Name origin: For early settler, Robert Bellingham.

Boyd   City
ZIP: 56218   Lat: 44-51-03 N   Long: 95-54-02 W
Pop: 251 (1990); 329 (1980)   **Pop Density:** 502.0
Land: 0.5 sq. mi.; **Water:** 0.0 sq. mi.
Name origin: For an officer of the Minneapolis & St. Louis Railway Company.

Camp Release   Township
Lat: 44-55-55 N   Long: 95-48-29 W
Pop: 266 (1990); 285 (1980)   **Pop Density:** 9.1
Land: 29.3 sq. mi.; **Water:** 0.0 sq. mi.

Cerro Gordo   Township
Lat: 45-01-22 N   Long: 96-02-37 W
Pop: 303 (1990); 274 (1980)   **Pop Density:** 8.5
Land: 35.8 sq. mi.; **Water:** 0.1 sq. mi.

Dawson   City
ZIP: 56232   Lat: 44-55-43 N   Long: 96-02-56 W
Pop: 1,626 (1990); 1,901 (1980)   **Pop Density:** 1084.0
Land: 1.5 sq. mi.; **Water:** 0.0 sq. mi.   **Elev:** 1058 ft.
Founded 1885.
Name origin: For William Dawson, a banker who owned land in the area.

Freeland   Township
Lat: 44-50-56 N   Long: 96-16-32 W
Pop: 153 (1990); 200 (1980)   **Pop Density:** 4.2
Land: 36.4 sq. mi.; **Water:** 0.0 sq. mi.

Garfield   Township
Lat: 44-56-41 N   Long: 96-17-52 W
Pop: 196 (1990); 210 (1980)   **Pop Density:** 5.3
Land: 37.2 sq. mi.; **Water:** 0.0 sq. mi.

Hamlin   Township
Lat: 44-56-35 N   Long: 96-10-31 W
Pop: 215 (1990); 296 (1980)   **Pop Density:** 6.0
Land: 35.9 sq. mi.; **Water:** 0.2 sq. mi.

Hantho   Township
Lat: 45-06-17 N   Long: 96-03-07 W
Pop: 134 (1990); 152 (1980)   **Pop Density:** 4.5
Land: 30.1 sq. mi.; **Water:** 3.1 sq. mi.

Lac qui Parle   Township
Lat: 45-01-34 N   Long: 95-55-58 W
Pop: 231 (1990); 260 (1980)   **Pop Density:** 8.0
Land: 28.7 sq. mi.; **Water:** 2.8 sq. mi.

Lake Shore   Township
Lat: 45-07-57 N   Long: 96-09-55 W
Pop: 265 (1990); 336 (1980)   **Pop Density:** 5.1
Land: 51.7 sq. mi.; **Water:** 2.2 sq. mi.

Louisburg   City
ZIP: 56254   Lat: 45-09-58 N   Long: 96-10-12 W
Pop: 42 (1990); 52 (1980)   **Pop Density:** 140.0
Land: 0.3 sq. mi.; **Water:** 0.0 sq. mi.

MINNESOTA, Lac qui Parle County

Madison
City
ZIP: 56256 Lat: 45-00-49 N Long: 96-11-20 W
Pop: 1,951 (1990); 2,212 (1980) Pop Density: 1951.0
Land: 1.0 sq. mi.; Water: 0.0 sq. mi.
Settled 1877. City and township not coexistent.
Name origin: For Madison, WI, former home of a pioneer.

*Madison
Township
ZIP: 56256 Lat: 45-01-17 N Long: 96-10-30 W
Pop: 278 (1990); 370 (1980) Pop Density: 8.0
Land: 34.6 sq. mi.; Water: 0.4 sq. mi.

Manfred
Township
Lat: 44-51-02 N Long: 96-23-41 W
Pop: 132 (1990); 174 (1980) Pop Density: 4.0
Land: 33.1 sq. mi.; Water: 0.3 sq. mi.

Marietta
City
ZIP: 56257 Lat: 45-00-37 N Long: 96-25-04 W
Pop: 211 (1990); 279 (1980) Pop Density: 527.5
Land: 0.4 sq. mi.; Water: 0.0 sq. mi.
Founded 1880s by the Minneapolis & St. Louis Railway Company.
Name origin: For Marietta, OH, former home of settlers.

Maxwell
Township
Lat: 44-50-58 N Long: 96-02-12 W
Pop: 212 (1990); 242 (1980) Pop Density: 5.9
Land: 36.2 sq. mi.; Water: 0.1 sq. mi.

Mehurin
Township
Lat: 44-55-59 N Long: 96-24-12 W
Pop: 104 (1990); 164 (1980) Pop Density: 3.6
Land: 28.7 sq. mi.; Water: 0.4 sq. mi.

Nassau
City
ZIP: 56272 Lat: 45-04-04 N Long: 96-26-28 W
Pop: 83 (1990); 115 (1980) Pop Density: 415.0
Land: 0.2 sq. mi.; Water: 0.0 sq. mi.
Name origin: Named by German settlers for a duchy in Germany.

Ortonville
City
ZIP: 56278 Lat: 45-17-54 N Long: 96-27-04 W
Pop: 0 (1990)
Land: 0.03 sq. mi.; Water: 0.0 sq. mi.
Founded 1870s. Part of the town is also in Big Stone County.
Name origin: For founder Cornelius Knute Orton, who was a prominent local businessman.

Perry
Township
Lat: 45-07-03 N Long: 96-17-20 W
Pop: 142 (1990); 216 (1980) Pop Density: 3.8
Land: 36.9 sq. mi.; Water: 0.1 sq. mi.

Providence
Township
Lat: 44-50-59 N Long: 96-09-08 W
Pop: 214 (1990); 253 (1980) Pop Density: 5.9
Land: 36.1 sq. mi.; Water: 0.0 sq. mi.

Riverside
Township
Lat: 44-56-14 N Long: 96-02-33 W
Pop: 370 (1990); 359 (1980) Pop Density: 10.8
Land: 34.4 sq. mi.; Water: 0.1 sq. mi.

Ten Mile Lake
Township
Lat: 44-51-01 N Long: 95-54-46 W
Pop: 205 (1990); 253 (1980) Pop Density: 5.8
Land: 35.3 sq. mi.; Water: 0.3 sq. mi.

Walter
Township
Lat: 45-06-25 N Long: 96-24-12 W
Pop: 210 (1990); 266 (1980) Pop Density: 7.2
Land: 29.0 sq. mi.; Water: 0.0 sq. mi.

Yellow Bank
Township
Lat: 45-12-14 N Long: 96-24-15 W
Pop: 199 (1990); 281 (1980) Pop Density: 5.7
Land: 35.2 sq. mi.; Water: 0.1 sq. mi.

Lake County
County Seat: Two Harbors (ZIP: 55616)

Pop: 10,415 (1990); 13,043 (1980) Pop Density: 5.0
Land: 2099.4 sq. mi.; Water: 891.7 sq. mi. Area Code: 218
On the northeastern border of MN, northeast of Duluth; established Mar 1, 1856 (prior to statehood); name changed from Doty County.
Name origin: For Lake Superior, which forms its eastern border.

Beaver Bay
City
ZIP: 55601 Lat: 47-15-24 N Long: 91-17-55 W
Pop: 147 (1990); 283 (1980) Pop Density: 294.0
Land: 0.5 sq. mi.; Water: 0.5 sq. mi.
Name origin: For the once-plentiful beaver of the area.

*Beaver Bay
Township
ZIP: 55601 Lat: 47-21-59 N Long: 91-20-09 W
Pop: 511 (1990); 851 (1980) Pop Density: 3.7
Land: 138.5 sq. mi.; Water: 1.6 sq. mi.

Crystal Bay
Township
ZIP: 55614 Lat: 47-38-04 N Long: 91-13-02 W
Pop: 460 (1990); 760 (1980) Pop Density: 2.3
Land: 203.7 sq. mi.; Water: 6.6 sq. mi.

Fall Lake
Township
Lat: 47-59-19 N Long: 91-26-24 W
Pop: 475 (1990); 522 (1980) Pop Density: 1.0
Land: 456.9 sq. mi.; Water: 130.5 sq. mi.

Lake No. 1
Pop. Place
Lat: 47-39-32 N Long: 91-05-58 W
Pop: 105 (1990); 139 (1980) Pop Density: 0.6
Land: 177.8 sq. mi.; Water: 14.0 sq. mi.

Lake No. 2
Pop. Place
Lat: 47-18-21 N Long: 91-42-55 W
Pop: 1,856 (1990) Pop Density: 6.9
Land: 268.4 sq. mi.; Water: 3.9 sq. mi.

Silver Bay — City
ZIP: 55614 **Lat:** 47-17-30 N **Long:** 91-16-42 W
Pop: 1,894 (1990); 2,917 (1980) **Pop Density:** 242.8
Land: 7.8 sq. mi.; **Water:** 0.4 sq. mi.
Name origin: For the play of light on Lake Superior.

Silver Creek — Township
ZIP: 55616 **Lat:** 47-17-09 N **Long:** 91-32-09 W
Pop: 1,097 (1990); 1,175 (1980) **Pop Density:** 3.7
Land: 294.9 sq. mi.; **Water:** 1.8 sq. mi.

Stony River — Township
Lat: 47-41-21 N **Long:** 91-30-28 W
Pop: 219 (1990) **Pop Density:** 0.4
Land: 547.8 sq. mi.; **Water:** 31.2 sq. mi.

Two Harbors — City
ZIP: 55616 **Lat:** 47-01-49 N **Long:** 91-40-32 W
Pop: 3,651 (1990); 4,039 (1980) **Pop Density:** 1140.9
Land: 3.2 sq. mi.; **Water:** 0.0 sq. mi.
Name origin: For its location on two little bays, Agate and Burlington.

Lake of the Woods County
County Seat: Baudette (ZIP: 56623)

Pop: 4,076 (1990); 3,764 (1980) **Pop Density:** 3.1
Land: 1296.7 sq. mi.; **Water:** 478.4 sq. mi. **Area Code:** 218
On the central northern border of MN; established Nov 28, 1922 from Beltrami County; the latest county formed.
Name origin: For the Lake of the Woods in Canada, which forms its northern border.

Baudette — City
ZIP: 56623 **Lat:** 48-42-40 N **Long:** 94-35-13 W
Pop: 1,146 (1990); 1,170 (1980) **Pop Density:** 347.3
Land: 3.3 sq. mi.; **Water:** 0.4 sq. mi.
County seat.
Name origin: For an early French trapper.

Roosevelt — City
ZIP: 56673 **Lat:** 48-47-49 N **Long:** 95-05-13 W
Pop: 10 (1990); 6 (1980) **Pop Density:** 250.0
Land: 0.04 sq. mi.; **Water:** 0.0 sq. mi. **Elev:** 1163 ft.
Part of the town is also in Roseau County.
Name origin: For Theodore Roosevelt (1858–1919), twenty-sixth U.S. president.

Williams — City
ZIP: 56686 **Lat:** 48-46-06 N **Long:** 94-57-09 W
Pop: 212 (1990); 217 (1980) **Pop Density:** 212.0
Land: 1.0 sq. mi.; **Water:** 0.0 sq. mi.

Le Sueur County
County Seat: Le Center (ZIP: 56057)

Pop: 23,239 (1990); 23,434 (1980) **Pop Density:** 51.8
Land: 448.5 sq. mi.; **Water:** 25.4 sq. mi. **Area Code:** 612
In south-central MN, north of Mankato; established Mar 5, 1853 (prior to statehood) from unorganized lands.
Name origin: For Pierre Charles Le Sueur (1657–1702?), French-Canadian fur trader and explorer of the upper Mississippi River and its tributaries.

Cleveland — City
ZIP: 56017 **Lat:** 44-19-25 N **Long:** 93-50-06 W
Pop: 699 (1990); 699 (1980) **Pop Density:** 1165.0
Land: 0.6 sq. mi.; **Water:** 0.0 sq. mi. **Elev:** 1051 ft.
City and township not coextensive.
Name origin: Named in 1858 for Cleveland, OH, former hometown of settlers.

*Cleveland — Township
ZIP: 56017 **Lat:** 44-19-39 N **Long:** 93-49-25 W
Pop: 559 (1990); 569 (1980) **Pop Density:** 16.7
Land: 33.4 sq. mi.; **Water:** 3.7 sq. mi.

Cordova — Township
Lat: 44-19-56 N **Long:** 93-42-08 W
Pop: 533 (1990); 587 (1980) **Pop Density:** 15.4
Land: 34.7 sq. mi.; **Water:** 1.5 sq. mi.

Derrynane
Township
Lat: 44-29-50 N **Long:** 93-42-24 W
Pop: 600 (1990); 664 (1980) **Pop Density:** 16.8
Land: 35.8 sq. mi.; **Water:** 0.3 sq. mi.

Elysian
City
ZIP: 56028 **Lat:** 44-11-59 N **Long:** 93-40-37 W
Pop: 443 (1990); 450 (1980) **Pop Density:** 1107.5
Land: 0.4 sq. mi.; **Water:** 0.0 sq. mi.
Settled 1858. Part of the town is also in Waseca County.
Name origin: For the ancient Greek heaven, the Elysian Fields.

*Elysian
Township
ZIP: 56028 **Lat:** 44-14-23 N **Long:** 93-41-51 W
Pop: 860 (1990); 874 (1980) **Pop Density:** 28.0
Land: 30.7 sq. mi.; **Water:** 5.0 sq. mi.

Heidelberg
City
ZIP: 56071 **Lat:** 44-29-36 N **Long:** 93-37-24 W
Pop: 73 (1990); 102 (1980) **Pop Density:** 146.0
Land: 0.5 sq. mi.; **Water:** 0.0 sq. mi.

Kasota
City
ZIP: 56050 **Lat:** 44-17-24 N **Long:** 93-58-05 W
Pop: 655 (1990); 739 (1980) **Pop Density:** 655.0
Land: 1.0 sq. mi.; **Water:** 0.0 sq. mi.
City and township not coextensive.
Name origin: A Sioux Indian word meaning 'cleared off,' referring to the nearby prairie.

*Kasota
Township
ZIP: 56050 **Lat:** 44-17-22 N **Long:** 93-56-02 W
Pop: 1,303 (1990); 1,252 (1980) **Pop Density:** 34.7
Land: 37.6 sq. mi.; **Water:** 1.7 sq. mi.

Kilkenny
City
ZIP: 56052 **Lat:** 44-18-47 N **Long:** 93-34-27 W
Pop: 167 (1990); 177 (1980) **Pop Density:** 1670.0
Land: 0.1 sq. mi.; **Water:** 0.0 sq. mi.
City and township not coextensive.
Name origin: Named by Irish settlers for the county in Ireland.

*Kilkenny
Township
ZIP: 56052 **Lat:** 44-19-39 N **Long:** 93-35-31 W
Pop: 444 (1990); 569 (1980) **Pop Density:** 13.1
Land: 33.9 sq. mi.; **Water:** 2.2 sq. mi.

Lanesburgh
Township
Lat: 44-29-27 N **Long:** 93-34-57 W
Pop: 1,613 (1990); 1,433 (1980) **Pop Density:** 48.7
Land: 33.1 sq. mi.; **Water:** 1.5 sq. mi.

Le Center
City
ZIP: 56057 **Lat:** 44-23-15 N **Long:** 93-43-58 W
Pop: 2,006 (1990); 1,967 (1980) **Pop Density:** 1543.1
Land: 1.3 sq. mi.; **Water:** 0.0 sq. mi. **Elev:** 1052 ft.
Organized 1890.
Name origin: For its location at the exact geographic center of the county.

Le Sueur
City
ZIP: 56058 **Lat:** 44-27-47 N **Long:** 93-54-22 W
Pop: 3,714 (1990); 3,763 (1980) **Pop Density:** 1031.7
Land: 3.6 sq. mi.; **Water:** 0.1 sq. mi.
Name origin: For Pierre Charles Le Sueur (1657–1702?), French-Canadian fur trader and explorer of the Upper Mississippi River and its tributaries, who explored the region in 1689.

Lexington
Township
Lat: 44-24-42 N **Long:** 93-42-42 W
Pop: 745 (1990); 766 (1980) **Pop Density:** 21.7
Land: 34.3 sq. mi.; **Water:** 0.7 sq. mi.

Montgomery
City
ZIP: 56069 **Lat:** 44-26-21 N **Long:** 93-34-49 W
Pop: 2,399 (1990); 2,349 (1980) **Pop Density:** 1599.3
Land: 1.5 sq. mi.; **Water:** 0.0 sq. mi. **Elev:** 1065 ft.
Settled 1850s. City and township not coextensive.
Name origin: For Revolutionary War hero, General Richard Montgomery (1736–75).

*Montgomery
Township
ZIP: 56069 **Lat:** 44-24-49 N **Long:** 93-35-04 W
Pop: 627 (1990); 737 (1980) **Pop Density:** 18.6
Land: 33.7 sq. mi.; **Water:** 0.9 sq. mi.

New Prague
City
ZIP: 56071 **Lat:** 44-32-15 N **Long:** 93-34-34 W
Pop: 1,213 (1990); 1,054 (1980) **Pop Density:** 1347.8
Land: 0.9 sq. mi.; **Water:** 0.0 sq. mi.
Settled 1850s. Part of the town is also in Scott County.
Name origin: For the ancient European city of Prague.

Ottawa
Township
Lat: 44-24-22 N **Long:** 93-55-15 W
Pop: 323 (1990); 376 (1980) **Pop Density:** 21.3
Land: 15.2 sq. mi.; **Water:** 0.2 sq. mi.

Sharon
Township
Lat: 44-24-45 N **Long:** 93-49-08 W
Pop: 559 (1990); 660 (1980) **Pop Density:** 15.7
Land: 35.7 sq. mi.; **Water:** 0.1 sq. mi.

Tyrone
Township
Lat: 44-29-54 N **Long:** 93-49-36 W
Pop: 662 (1990); 715 (1980) **Pop Density:** 18.3
Land: 36.2 sq. mi.; **Water:** 0.1 sq. mi.

Washington
Township
Lat: 44-15-31 N **Long:** 93-49-28 W
Pop: 652 (1990); 616 (1980) **Pop Density:** 54.3
Land: 12.0 sq. mi.; **Water:** 3.2 sq. mi.

Waterville
City
ZIP: 56096 **Lat:** 44-13-21 N **Long:** 93-34-27 W
Pop: 1,771 (1990); 1,717 (1980) **Pop Density:** 1041.8
Land: 1.7 sq. mi.; **Water:** 0.6 sq. mi.
City and township not coextensive.
Name origin: For the nearby lakes and rivers.

*Waterville
Township
ZIP: 56096 **Lat:** 44-14-22 N **Long:** 93-35-07 W
Pop: 619 (1990); 599 (1980) **Pop Density:** 20.4
Land: 30.4 sq. mi.; **Water:** 3.4 sq. mi.

> ## Lincoln County
> **County Seat: Ivanhoe (ZIP: 56142)**
>
> **Pop:** 6,890 (1990); 8,207 (1980) **Pop Density:** 12.8
> **Land:** 537.1 sq. mi.; **Water:** 11.4 sq. mi. **Area Code:** 507
> On the southwestern border of MN; established Mar 1, 1866 from Lyon County.
> **Name origin:** For Abraham Lincoln (1809–65), sixteenth U.S. president.

Alta Vista
Township
Lat: 44-35-14 N **Long:** 96-09-19 W
Pop: 252 (1990); 289 (1980) **Pop Density:** 6.9
Land: 36.5 sq. mi.; **Water:** 0.0 sq. mi.

Arco
City
ZIP: 56113 **Lat:** 44-23-00 N **Long:** 96-10-50 W
Pop: 104 (1990); 96 (1980) **Pop Density:** 173.3
Land: 0.6 sq. mi.; **Water:** 0.1 sq. mi.
Name origin: Named in 1900 by local railroad officials for an ancient city in Italy.

Ash Lake
Township
Lat: 44-25-22 N **Long:** 96-16-17 W
Pop: 224 (1990); 294 (1980) **Pop Density:** 6.2
Land: 36.1 sq. mi.; **Water:** 0.6 sq. mi.

Diamond Lake
Township
Lat: 44-20-12 N **Long:** 96-16-17 W
Pop: 216 (1990); 319 (1980) **Pop Density:** 6.7
Land: 32.2 sq. mi.; **Water:** 2.8 sq. mi.

Drammen
Township
Lat: 44-19-30 N **Long:** 96-23-20 W
Pop: 180 (1990); 233 (1980) **Pop Density:** 4.7
Land: 38.6 sq. mi.; **Water:** 0.0 sq. mi.

Hansonville
Township
Lat: 44-35-05 N **Long:** 96-24-07 W
Pop: 150 (1990); 202 (1980) **Pop Density:** 4.5
Land: 33.5 sq. mi.; **Water:** 0.3 sq. mi.

Hendricks
City
ZIP: 56136 **Lat:** 44-30-31 N **Long:** 96-25-34 W
Pop: 684 (1990); 737 (1980) **Pop Density:** 684.0
Land: 1.0 sq. mi.; **Water:** 0.0 sq. mi.
City and township not coextensive.
Name origin: For nearby Lake Hendricks, which was named for Thomas A. Hendricks (1819–85), U.S. vice president in 1885.

*Hendricks
Township
ZIP: 56136 **Lat:** 44-29-58 N **Long:** 96-23-08 W
Pop: 255 (1990); 377 (1980) **Pop Density:** 7.2
Land: 35.2 sq. mi.; **Water:** 1.3 sq. mi.

Hope
Township
Lat: 44-14-39 N **Long:** 96-08-38 W
Pop: 331 (1990); 407 (1980) **Pop Density:** 9.5
Land: 34.8 sq. mi.; **Water:** 0.0 sq. mi.

Ivanhoe
City
ZIP: 56142 **Lat:** 44-27-50 N **Long:** 96-15-01 W
Pop: 751 (1990); 761 (1980) **Pop Density:** 834.4
Land: 0.9 sq. mi.; **Water:** 0.0 sq. mi.
Founded 1900.
Name origin: For the hero of Sir Walter Scott's novel (1819).

Lake Benton
City
ZIP: 56149 **Lat:** 44-15-45 N **Long:** 96-17-33 W
Pop: 693 (1990); 869 (1980) **Pop Density:** 192.5
Land: 3.6 sq. mi.; **Water:** 0.8 sq. mi.
City and township not coextensive.
Name origin: For Lake Benton, which was named by explorers J. N. Nicollet (1786–1843) and John C. Fremont (1813–90) for Frémont's father-in-law, U.S. senator Thomas Hart Benton (1782–1858).

*Lake Benton
Township
ZIP: 56149 **Lat:** 44-14-49 N **Long:** 96-15-13 W
Pop: 234 (1990); 238 (1980) **Pop Density:** 7.0
Land: 33.5 sq. mi.; **Water:** 0.5 sq. mi.

Lake Stay
Township
Lat: 44-24-42 N **Long:** 96-08-28 W
Pop: 187 (1990); 248 (1980) **Pop Density:** 5.3
Land: 35.0 sq. mi.; **Water:** 0.6 sq. mi.

Limestone
Township
Lat: 44-30-33 N **Long:** 96-08-40 W
Pop: 195 (1990); 233 (1980) **Pop Density:** 5.7
Land: 34.3 sq. mi.; **Water:** 0.3 sq. mi.

Marble
Township
Lat: 44-35-21 N **Long:** 96-16-49 W
Pop: 214 (1990); 297 (1980) **Pop Density:** 5.9
Land: 36.5 sq. mi.; **Water:** 0.1 sq. mi.

Marshfield
Township
Lat: 44-19-37 N **Long:** 96-07-59 W
Pop: 242 (1990); 312 (1980) **Pop Density:** 7.0
Land: 34.8 sq. mi.; **Water:** 1.2 sq. mi.

Royal
Township
Lat: 44-30-11 N **Long:** 96-15-33 W
Pop: 271 (1990); 357 (1980) **Pop Density:** 8.3
Land: 32.8 sq. mi.; **Water:** 1.1 sq. mi.

Shaokatan
Township
Lat: 44-25-16 N **Long:** 96-23-38 W
Pop: 216 (1990); 254 (1980) **Pop Density:** 5.9
Land: 36.7 sq. mi.; **Water:** 1.6 sq. mi.

Tyler
City
ZIP: 56178 **Lat:** 44-16-45 N **Long:** 96-08-06 W
Pop: 1,257 (1990); 1,353 (1980) **Pop Density:** 661.6
Land: 1.9 sq. mi.; **Water:** 0.0 sq. mi. **Elev:** 1733 ft.
Name origin: For local newspaperman and banker C. B. Tyler.

Verdi
Township
ZIP: 56179 **Lat:** 44-14-29 N **Long:** 96-23-26 W
Pop: 234 (1990); 331 (1980) **Pop Density:** 6.1
Land: 38.6 sq. mi.; **Water:** 0.0 sq. mi.

Lyon County
County Seat: Marshall (ZIP: 56258)

Pop: 24,789 (1990); 25,207 (1980)
Land: 714.2 sq. mi.; **Water:** 7.2 sq. mi.
Pop Density: 34.7
Area Code: 507

In southwestern MN; established Mar 6, 1868 from Yellow Medicine County.

Name origin: For Gen. Nathaniel Lyon (1818–61), officer in the Seminole War and the Mexican-American War; as a Union commander in the Civil War, he helped preserve MO for the Union.

Amiret
Township
ZIP: 56112 Lat: 44-19-06 N Long: 95-39-33 W
Pop: 285 (1990); 366 (1980) Pop Density: 7.9
Land: 36.3 sq. mi.; Water: 0.0 sq. mi.

Balaton
City
ZIP: 56115 Lat: 44-13-59 N Long: 95-52-15 W
Pop: 737 (1990); 752 (1980) Pop Density: 526.4
Land: 1.4 sq. mi.; Water: 0.1 sq. mi. Elev: 1523 ft.
Name origin: For Lake Balaton in western Hungary.

Clifton
Township
Lat: 44-25-04 N Long: 95-38-57 W
Pop: 291 (1990); 334 (1980) Pop Density: 8.1
Land: 36.1 sq. mi.; Water: 0.1 sq. mi.

Coon Creek
Township
Lat: 44-19-53 N Long: 96-00-32 W
Pop: 286 (1990); 306 (1980) Pop Density: 8.0
Land: 35.9 sq. mi.; Water: 0.5 sq. mi.

Cottonwood
City
ZIP: 56229 Lat: 44-36-35 N Long: 95-40-14 W
Pop: 982 (1990); 924 (1980) Pop Density: 1227.5
Land: 0.8 sq. mi.; Water: 0.0 sq. mi.
Name origin: For nearby Cottonwood Lake, which has cottonwood trees along the shore.

Custer
Township
Lat: 44-14-58 N Long: 95-46-04 W
Pop: 279 (1990); 340 (1980) Pop Density: 7.9
Land: 35.5 sq. mi.; Water: 0.4 sq. mi.

Eidsvold
Township
Lat: 44-35-00 N Long: 96-02-16 W
Pop: 229 (1990); 312 (1980) Pop Density: 6.8
Land: 33.5 sq. mi.; Water: 0.1 sq. mi.

Fairview
Township
Lat: 44-30-01 N Long: 95-46-01 W
Pop: 513 (1990); 561 (1980) Pop Density: 15.3
Land: 33.6 sq. mi.; Water: 0.0 sq. mi.

Florence
City
ZIP: 56130 Lat: 44-14-12 N Long: 96-03-05 W
Pop: 53 (1990); 55 (1980) Pop Density: 265.0
Land: 0.2 sq. mi.; Water: 0.0 sq. mi.

Garvin
City
ZIP: 56132 Lat: 44-12-53 N Long: 95-45-39 W
Pop: 149 (1990); 172 (1980) Pop Density: 496.7
Land: 0.3 sq. mi.; Water: 0.0 sq. mi.

Ghent
City
ZIP: 56239 Lat: 44-30-46 N Long: 95-53-32 W
Pop: 316 (1990); 356 (1980) Pop Density: 1053.3
Land: 0.3 sq. mi.; Water: 0.0 sq. mi. Elev: 1164 ft.
Name origin: Named in 1880 by Belgian colonists for Ghent, Belgium. Previously called Grandview.

Grandview
Township
Lat: 44-30-10 N Long: 95-53-58 W
Pop: 345 (1990); 332 (1980) Pop Density: 9.8
Land: 35.2 sq. mi.; Water: 0.0 sq. mi.

Island Lake
Township
Lat: 44-24-49 N Long: 96-01-34 W
Pop: 250 (1990); 286 (1980) Pop Density: 7.0
Land: 35.7 sq. mi.; Water: 0.5 sq. mi.

Lake Marshall
Township
Lat: 44-24-31 N Long: 95-46-11 W
Pop: 511 (1990); 570 (1980) Pop Density: 17.0
Land: 30.1 sq. mi.; Water: 0.4 sq. mi.

Lucas
Township
Lat: 44-34-46 N Long: 95-39-34 W
Pop: 281 (1990); 321 (1980) Pop Density: 8.3
Land: 33.9 sq. mi.; Water: 1.8 sq. mi.

Lynd
City
ZIP: 56157 Lat: 44-23-06 N Long: 95-53-44 W
Pop: 287 (1990); 304 (1980) Pop Density: 956.7
Land: 0.3 sq. mi.; Water: 0.0 sq. mi. Elev: 1320 ft.
City and township not coextensive.
Name origin: Named in 1873 for fur trader James Lynd, who was killed in the 1862 Sioux uprising.

*Lynd
Township
ZIP: 56157 Lat: 44-24-56 N Long: 95-53-59 W
Pop: 468 (1990); 458 (1980) Pop Density: 13.0
Land: 36.0 sq. mi.; Water: 0.0 sq. mi.

Lyons
Township
Lat: 44-19-18 N Long: 95-53-14 W
Pop: 211 (1990); 258 (1980) Pop Density: 6.0
Land: 35.2 sq. mi.; Water: 0.3 sq. mi.

Marshall
City
ZIP: 56258 Lat: 44-27-02 N Long: 95-47-22 W
Pop: 12,023 (1990); 11,161 (1980) Pop Density: 1647.0
Land: 7.3 sq. mi.; Water: 0.0 sq. mi.
In southwestern MN, southwest of Minneapolis. Incorporated 1876.
Name origin: For William Rainey Marshall (1825–96), MN businessman and governor (1866–70).

Minneota
City
ZIP: 56264 Lat: 44-33-49 N Long: 95-58-55 W
Pop: 1,417 (1990); 1,470 (1980) Pop Density: 1012.1
Land: 1.4 sq. mi.; Water: 0.0 sq. mi.

Monroe
Township
Lat: 44-14-28 N Long: 95-39-49 W
Pop: 259 (1990); 294 (1980) Pop Density: 7.6
Land: 33.9 sq. mi.; Water: 0.3 sq. mi.

Nordland
Township
Lat: 44-30-07 N **Long:** 96-01-02 W
Pop: 267 (1990); 267 (1980) **Pop Density:** 7.6
Land: 35.1 sq. mi.; **Water:** 0.0 sq. mi.

Rock Lake
Township
Lat: 44-13-57 N **Long:** 95-53-28 W
Pop: 324 (1990); 362 (1980) **Pop Density:** 9.8
Land: 33.1 sq. mi.; **Water:** 1.5 sq. mi.

Russell
City
ZIP: 56169 **Lat:** 44-19-08 N **Long:** 95-56-52 W
Pop: 394 (1990); 412 (1980) **Pop Density:** 437.8
Land: 0.9 sq. mi.; **Water:** 0.0 sq. mi. **Elev:** 1527 ft.
Name origin: For Russell Spicer, the son of the builder of the area's branch railway.

Shelburne
Township
Lat: 44-14-15 N **Long:** 96-01-20 W
Pop: 227 (1990); 285 (1980) **Pop Density:** 6.5
Land: 34.9 sq. mi.; **Water:** 1.0 sq. mi.

Sodus
Township
Lat: 44-19-38 N **Long:** 95-46-34 W
Pop: 271 (1990); 345 (1980) **Pop Density:** 7.5
Land: 36.3 sq. mi.; **Water:** 0.0 sq. mi.

Stanley
Township
Lat: 44-30-24 N **Long:** 95-39-20 W
Pop: 294 (1990); 299 (1980) **Pop Density:** 8.4
Land: 35.2 sq. mi.; **Water:** 0.0 sq. mi.

Taunton
City
ZIP: 56291 **Lat:** 44-35-35 N **Long:** 96-03-47 W
Pop: 175 (1990); 177 (1980) **Pop Density:** 175.0
Land: 1.0 sq. mi.; **Water:** 0.0 sq. mi. **Elev:** 1175 ft.
Name origin: Named by Chicago & Northwestern Railway official C. C. Wheeler for Taunton, MA.

Tracy
City
ZIP: 56175 **Lat:** 44-14-14 N **Long:** 95-37-00 W
Pop: 2,059 (1990); 2,478 (1980) **Pop Density:** 935.9
Land: 2.2 sq. mi.; **Water:** 0.1 sq. mi. **Elev:** 1398 ft.
Name origin: For John F. Tracy, a former president of the Chicago & Northwestern Railway.

Vallers
Township
Lat: 44-34-59 N **Long:** 95-47-13 W
Pop: 289 (1990); 313 (1980) **Pop Density:** 7.9
Land: 36.4 sq. mi.; **Water:** 0.0 sq. mi.

Westerheim
Township
Lat: 44-35-25 N **Long:** 95-53-59 W
Pop: 317 (1990); 337 (1980) **Pop Density:** 8.7
Land: 36.3 sq. mi.; **Water:** 0.0 sq. mi.

Mahnomen County
County Seat: Mahnomen (ZIP: 56557)

Pop: 5,044 (1990); 5,535 (1980) **Pop Density:** 9.1
Land: 556.2 sq. mi.; **Water:** 26.8 sq. mi. **Area Code:** 218
In west-central MN, northeast of Fargo, ND; established Dec 27, 1906 from Norman County.
Name origin: The Ojibway word meaning 'wild rice,' which grows abundantly in the region.

Beaulieu
Township
ZIP: 56557 **Lat:** 47-22-03 N **Long:** 95-44-15 W
Pop: 133 (1990); 175 (1980) **Pop Density:** 4.0
Land: 33.5 sq. mi.; **Water:** 2.1 sq. mi.

Bejou
City
ZIP: 56516 **Lat:** 47-26-30 N **Long:** 95-58-19 W
Pop: 110 (1990); 109 (1980) **Pop Density:** 275.0
Land: 0.4 sq. mi.; **Water:** 0.0 sq. mi. **Elev:** 1222 ft.
City and township not coextensive.
Name origin: From the French greeting *bonjour*, with altered spelling and pronunciation.

*Bejou
Township
ZIP: 56516 **Lat:** 47-27-21 N **Long:** 96-00-22 W
Pop: 119 (1990); 133 (1980) **Pop Density:** 3.2
Land: 37.3 sq. mi.; **Water:** 0.0 sq. mi.

Chief
Township
Lat: 47-21-29 N **Long:** 95-53-08 W
Pop: 159 (1990); 187 (1980) **Pop Density:** 4.6
Land: 34.6 sq. mi.; **Water:** 1.5 sq. mi.

Clover
Township
Lat: 47-22-06 N **Long:** 95-37-51 W
Pop: 131 (1990); 123 (1980) **Pop Density:** 3.8
Land: 34.7 sq. mi.; **Water:** 0.9 sq. mi.

Gregory
Township
Lat: 47-27-31 N **Long:** 95-52-16 W
Pop: 129 (1990); 150 (1980) **Pop Density:** 3.7
Land: 35.1 sq. mi.; **Water:** 1.1 sq. mi.

Heier
Township
Lat: 47-27-17 N **Long:** 95-44-34 W
Pop: 160 (1990); 155 (1980) **Pop Density:** 4.8
Land: 33.6 sq. mi.; **Water:** 2.6 sq. mi.

Island Lake
Township
Lat: 47-27-31 N **Long:** 95-37-10 W
Pop: 235 (1990); 274 (1980) **Pop Density:** 6.9
Land: 34.3 sq. mi.; **Water:** 2.3 sq. mi.

La Garde
Township
Lat: 47-17-01 N **Long:** 95-44-15 W
Pop: 142 (1990); 189 (1980) **Pop Density:** 4.2
Land: 33.6 sq. mi.; **Water:** 2.2 sq. mi.

Lake Grove
Township
Lat: 47-11-13 N **Long:** 95-52-15 W
Pop: 199 (1990); 251 (1980) **Pop Density:** 5.7
Land: 34.9 sq. mi.; **Water:** 1.4 sq. mi.

Mahnomen
City
ZIP: 56557 **Lat:** 47-18-53 N **Long:** 95-58-08 W
Pop: 1,154 (1990); 1,283 (1980) **Pop Density:** 1648.6
Land: 0.7 sq. mi.; **Water:** 0.0 sq. mi.
Name origin: From an Ojibway Indian term meaning 'wild rice.'

Marsh Creek
Township
Lat: 47-22-13 N **Long:** 96-00-12 W
Pop: 147 (1990); 168 (1980) **Pop Density:** 3.9
Land: 37.6 sq. mi.; **Water:** 0.0 sq. mi.

Naytahwaush
CDP
ZIP: 56566 **Lat:** 47-17-08 N **Long:** 95-37-51 W
Pop: 378 (1990) **Pop Density:** 87.9
Land: 4.3 sq. mi.; **Water:** 0.5 sq. mi.

Oakland
Township
Lat: 47-12-03 N **Long:** 95-44-46 W
Pop: 225 (1990); 252 (1980) **Pop Density:** 7.0
Land: 32.2 sq. mi.; **Water:** 3.2 sq. mi.

Pembina
Township
Lat: 47-16-48 N **Long:** 95-59-53 W
Pop: 517 (1990); 598 (1980) **Pop Density:** 14.1
Land: 36.7 sq. mi.; **Water:** 0.1 sq. mi.

Popple Grove
Township
Lat: 47-10-54 N **Long:** 96-00-20 W
Pop: 207 (1990); 203 (1980) **Pop Density:** 5.5
Land: 37.3 sq. mi.; **Water:** 0.1 sq. mi.

Rosedale
Township
Lat: 47-16-47 N **Long:** 95-52-35 W
Pop: 162 (1990); 202 (1980) **Pop Density:** 4.6
Land: 34.9 sq. mi.; **Water:** 1.4 sq. mi.

Southeast Mahnomen
Pop. Place
Lat: 47-11-28 N **Long:** 95-37-10 W
Pop: 168 (1990); 133 (1980) **Pop Density:** 5.4
Land: 31.3 sq. mi.; **Water:** 4.5 sq. mi.

Twin Lakes
Township
Lat: 47-17-05 N **Long:** 95-36-44 W
Pop: 617 (1990); 560 (1980) **Pop Density:** 18.8
Land: 32.8 sq. mi.; **Water:** 3.2 sq. mi.

Waubun
City
ZIP: 56589 **Lat:** 47-11-02 N **Long:** 95-56-22 W
Pop: 330 (1990); 390 (1980) **Pop Density:** 660.0
Land: 0.5 sq. mi.; **Water:** 0.0 sq. mi.
Name origin: From an Ojibway Indian term meaning 'east' or 'morning.'

Marshall County
County Seat: Warren (ZIP: 56762)

Pop: 10,993 (1990); 13,027 (1980) **Pop Density:** 6.2
Land: 1772.3 sq. mi.; **Water:** 40.6 sq. mi. **Area Code:** 218
In northwestern MN, north of Grand Forks, ND; established Feb 25, 1879 from Kittson County.
Name origin: For Gen. William Rainey Marshall (1825–96), MN businessman and governor (1866–70).

Agder
Township
Lat: 48-13-10 N **Long:** 96-03-06 W
Pop: 112 (1990); 141 (1980) **Pop Density:** 2.5
Land: 44.3 sq. mi.; **Water:** 0.0 sq. mi.

Alma
Township
Lat: 48-19-23 N **Long:** 96-41-51 W
Pop: 124 (1990); 149 (1980) **Pop Density:** 3.4
Land: 36.4 sq. mi.; **Water:** 0.0 sq. mi.

Alvarado
City
ZIP: 56710 **Lat:** 48-11-33 N **Long:** 96-59-53 W
Pop: 356 (1990); 385 (1980) **Pop Density:** 1780.0
Land: 0.2 sq. mi.; **Water:** 0.0 sq. mi. **Elev:** 812 ft.
Name origin: For a seaport in Mexico.

Argyle
City
ZIP: 56713 **Lat:** 48-20-14 N **Long:** 96-48-56 W
Pop: 636 (1990); 741 (1980) **Pop Density:** 424.0
Land: 1.5 sq. mi.; **Water:** 0.0 sq. mi. **Elev:** 847 ft.
Name origin: For the county in Scotland.

Augsburg
Township
Lat: 48-30-31 N **Long:** 96-43-05 W
Pop: 120 (1990); 156 (1980) **Pop Density:** 3.3
Land: 36.2 sq. mi.; **Water:** 0.0 sq. mi.

Big Woods
Township
Lat: 48-19-58 N **Long:** 97-04-31 W
Pop: 119 (1990); 157 (1980) **Pop Density:** 3.9
Land: 30.6 sq. mi.; **Water:** 0.4 sq. mi.

Bloomer
Township
Lat: 48-19-59 N **Long:** 96-56-45 W
Pop: 119 (1990); 111 (1980) **Pop Density:** 3.3
Land: 36.4 sq. mi.; **Water:** 0.0 sq. mi.

Boxville
Township
Lat: 48-10-58 N **Long:** 96-49-34 W
Pop: 47 (1990); 56 (1980) **Pop Density:** 5.5
Land: 8.6 sq. mi.; **Water:** 0.0 sq. mi.

Cedar
Township
Lat: 48-24-44 N **Long:** 96-03-37 W
Pop: 113 (1990); 140 (1980) **Pop Density:** 3.5
Land: 32.1 sq. mi.; **Water:** 4.1 sq. mi.

MINNESOTA, Marshall County

Como — Township
Lat: 48-30-13 N Long: 96-02-34 W
Pop: 70 (1990); 78 (1980) Pop Density: 1.9
Land: 36.3 sq. mi.; Water: 0.0 sq. mi.

Comstock — Township
Lat: 48-13-43 N Long: 96-33-47 W
Pop: 143 (1990); 184 (1980) Pop Density: 3.2
Land: 45.3 sq. mi.; Water: 0.0 sq. mi.

Donnelly — Township
Lat: 48-29-46 N Long: 96-58-35 W
Pop: 36 (1990); 30 (1980) Pop Density: 1.0
Land: 36.1 sq. mi.; Water: 0.0 sq. mi.

Eagle Point — Township
Lat: 48-30-01 N Long: 97-05-42 W
Pop: 82 (1990); 112 (1980) Pop Density: 2.9
Land: 27.9 sq. mi.; Water: 0.4 sq. mi.

East Park — Township
Lat: 48-29-53 N Long: 96-18-51 W
Pop: 16 (1990); 36 (1980) Pop Density: 0.5
Land: 33.8 sq. mi.; Water: 2.5 sq. mi.

East Valley — Township
Lat: 48-19-22 N Long: 96-02-51 W
Pop: 57 (1990); 79 (1980) Pop Density: 2.6
Land: 22.0 sq. mi.; Water: 12.9 sq. mi.

Eckvoll — Township
Lat: 48-19-28 N Long: 95-47-36 W
Pop: 130 (1990); 87 (1980) Pop Density: 3.7
Land: 35.5 sq. mi.; Water: 0.0 sq. mi.

Espelie — Township
Lat: 48-13-24 N Long: 95-38-52 W
Pop: 51 (1990); 66 (1980) Pop Density: 1.1
Land: 44.6 sq. mi.; Water: 0.0 sq. mi.

Excel — Township
Lat: 48-13-58 N Long: 96-09-44 W
Pop: 270 (1990); 307 (1980) Pop Density: 5.8
Land: 46.8 sq. mi.; Water: 0.0 sq. mi.

Foldahl — Township
Lat: 48-19-20 N Long: 96-34-04 W
Pop: 122 (1990); 123 (1980) Pop Density: 3.4
Land: 36.3 sq. mi.; Water: 0.0 sq. mi.

Fork — Township
Lat: 48-24-48 N Long: 97-05-43 W
Pop: 30 (1990); 50 (1980) Pop Density: 1.1
Land: 26.6 sq. mi.; Water: 0.5 sq. mi.

Grand Plain — Township
Lat: 48-13-46 N Long: 95-54-22 W
Pop: 75 (1990); 86 (1980) Pop Density: 1.7
Land: 44.9 sq. mi.; Water: 0.0 sq. mi.

Grygla — City
ZIP: 56727 Lat: 48-17-58 N Long: 95-37-10 W
Pop: 220 (1990); 216 (1980) Pop Density: 733.3
Land: 0.3 sq. mi.; Water: 0.0 sq. mi.
Name origin: For Frank Grygla, a Polish patriot and descendant of a noble Polish family.

Holt — City
ZIP: 56738 Lat: 48-17-31 N Long: 96-11-38 W
Pop: 88 (1990); 119 (1980) Pop Density: 88.0
Land: 1.0 sq. mi.; Water: 0.0 sq. mi. Elev: 1155 ft.
City and township not coextensive.

*Holt — Township
ZIP: 56738 Lat: 48-19-44 N Long: 96-09-36 W
Pop: 184 (1990); 162 (1980) Pop Density: 5.5
Land: 33.7 sq. mi.; Water: 0.0 sq. mi.

Huntly — Township
Lat: 48-30-32 N Long: 96-11-24 W
Pop: 90 (1990); 107 (1980) Pop Density: 2.5
Land: 36.0 sq. mi.; Water: 0.6 sq. mi.

Lincoln — Township
Lat: 48-30-01 N Long: 96-27-11 W
Pop: 143 (1990); 166 (1980) Pop Density: 4.0
Land: 35.6 sq. mi.; Water: 0.0 sq. mi.

Linsell — Township
Lat: 48-30-19 N Long: 95-39-55 W
Pop: 45 (1990); 60 (1980) Pop Density: 1.3
Land: 35.8 sq. mi.; Water: 0.0 sq. mi.

Marsh Grove — Township
Lat: 48-19-42 N Long: 96-25-45 W
Pop: 144 (1990); 162 (1980) Pop Density: 4.0
Land: 35.8 sq. mi.; Water: 0.0 sq. mi.

McCrea — Township
Lat: 48-13-26 N Long: 96-41-49 W
Pop: 282 (1990); 346 (1980) Pop Density: 6.3
Land: 45.0 sq. mi.; Water: 0.0 sq. mi.

Middle River — City
ZIP: 56737 Lat: 48-26-08 N Long: 96-09-42 W
Pop: 285 (1990); 349 (1980) Pop Density: 570.0
Land: 0.5 sq. mi.; Water: 0.0 sq. mi.
Name origin: For a tributary of the Snake River, which flows through the central part of the county.

*Middle River — Township
ZIP: 56737 Lat: 48-19-37 N Long: 96-50-07 W
Pop: 115 (1990); 162 (1980) Pop Density: 3.3
Land: 34.8 sq. mi.; Water: 0.0 sq. mi.

Moose River — Township
Lat: 48-29-48 N Long: 95-47-45 W
Pop: 49 (1990); 61 (1980) Pop Density: 1.5
Land: 33.6 sq. mi.; Water: 2.0 sq. mi.

Moylan — Township
Lat: 48-13-23 N Long: 95-47-12 W
Pop: 136 (1990); 159 (1980) Pop Density: 3.0
Land: 45.1 sq. mi.; Water: 0.0 sq. mi.

Mud Lake — Pop. Place
Lat: 48-19-26 N Long: 95-54-47 W
Pop: 0 (1990); 5 (1980)
Land: 31.3 sq. mi.; Water: 4.7 sq. mi.

Nelson Park — Township
Lat: 48-30-01 N Long: 96-34-47 W
Pop: 195 (1990); 195 (1980) Pop Density: 5.4
Land: 36.1 sq. mi.; Water: 0.1 sq. mi.

Newfolden — City
ZIP: 56738 Lat: 48-21-18 N Long: 96-19-47 W
Pop: 345 (1990); 384 (1980) Pop Density: 383.3
Land: 0.9 sq. mi.; Water: 0.0 sq. mi.
City and township not coextensive.

New Folden — Township
Lat: 48-19-38 N Long: 96-18-16 W
Pop: 207 (1990); 252 (1980) Pop Density: 5.9
Land: 35.0 sq. mi.; Water: 0.0 sq. mi.

MINNESOTA, Marshall County

New Maine Township
Lat: 48-24-48 N Long: 96-19-55 W
Pop: 212 (1990); 231 (1980) Pop Density: 5.7
Land: 36.9 sq. mi.; Water: 0.0 sq. mi.

New Solum Township
Lat: 48-13-40 N Long: 96-17-29 W
Pop: 304 (1990); 349 (1980) Pop Density: 6.6
Land: 46.3 sq. mi.; Water: 0.0 sq. mi.

Oak Park Township
Lat: 48-13-53 N Long: 97-04-28 W
Pop: 190 (1990); 205 (1980) Pop Density: 4.9
Land: 38.8 sq. mi.; Water: 0.4 sq. mi.

Oslo City
ZIP: 56744 Lat: 48-11-41 N Long: 97-07-40 W
Pop: 362 (1990); 379 (1980) Pop Density: 724.0
Land: 0.5 sq. mi.; Water: 0.0 sq. mi.
Name origin: For the capital of Norway.

Parker Township
Lat: 48-24-46 N Long: 96-57-55 W
Pop: 56 (1990); 54 (1980) Pop Density: 1.6
Land: 35.9 sq. mi.; Water: 0.0 sq. mi.

Rollis Township
Lat: 48-24-38 N Long: 95-48-08 W
Pop: 131 (1990); 212 (1980) Pop Density: 3.6
Land: 36.0 sq. mi.; Water: 0.0 sq. mi.

Sinnott Township
Lat: 48-29-58 N Long: 96-50-08 W
Pop: 62 (1990); 85 (1980) Pop Density: 1.7
Land: 36.2 sq. mi.; Water: 0.0 sq. mi.

Spruce Valley Township
Lat: 48-24-20 N Long: 96-11-14 W
Pop: 263 (1990); 326 (1980) Pop Density: 7.2
Land: 36.3 sq. mi.; Water: 0.0 sq. mi.

Stephen City
ZIP: 56757 Lat: 48-27-05 N Long: 96-52-37 W
Pop: 707 (1990); 898 (1980) Pop Density: 883.8
Land: 0.8 sq. mi.; Water: 0.0 sq. mi.
Name origin: For George Stephen, a prominent stockholder in the Great Northern Railway.

Strandquist City
ZIP: 56758 Lat: 48-29-23 N Long: 96-26-53 W
Pop: 98 (1990); 136 (1980) Pop Density: 326.7
Land: 0.3 sq. mi.; Water: 0.0 sq. mi.

Tamarac Township
Lat: 48-24-30 N Long: 96-51-14 W
Pop: 139 (1990); 185 (1980) Pop Density: 3.9
Land: 35.3 sq. mi.; Water: 0.0 sq. mi.

Thief Lake Township
Lat: 48-30-38 N Long: 95-56-10 W
Pop: 67 (1990); 103 (1980) Pop Density: 2.4
Land: 27.6 sq. mi.; Water: 8.9 sq. mi.

Valley Township
Lat: 48-18-51 N Long: 95-39-27 W
Pop: 213 (1990); 224 (1980) Pop Density: 6.2
Land: 34.3 sq. mi.; Water: 0.0 sq. mi.

Vega Township
Lat: 48-13-35 N Long: 96-57-21 W
Pop: 127 (1990); 167 (1980) Pop Density: 2.8
Land: 44.9 sq. mi.; Water: 0.0 sq. mi.

Veldt Township
Lat: 48-24-59 N Long: 95-40-01 W
Pop: 50 (1990); 67 (1980) Pop Density: 1.4
Land: 35.3 sq. mi.; Water: 0.1 sq. mi.

Viking City
ZIP: 56760 Lat: 48-13-04 N Long: 96-24-23 W
Pop: 103 (1990); 129 (1980) Pop Density: 206.0
Land: 0.5 sq. mi.; Water: 0.0 sq. mi.
City and township not coextensive.
Name origin: For the famous Scandinavian raiders of medieval Europe.

*Viking Township
ZIP: 56760 Lat: 48-13-30 N Long: 96-26-07 W
Pop: 178 (1990); 233 (1980) Pop Density: 4.0
Land: 44.9 sq. mi.; Water: 0.0 sq. mi.

Wanger Township
Lat: 48-24-27 N Long: 96-42-13 W
Pop: 108 (1990); 170 (1980) Pop Density: 3.0
Land: 36.0 sq. mi.; Water: 0.0 sq. mi.

Warren City
ZIP: 56762 Lat: 48-11-45 N Long: 96-46-11 W
Pop: 1,813 (1990); 2,105 (1980) Pop Density: 1510.8
Land: 1.2 sq. mi.; Water: 0.0 sq. mi. Elev: 854 ft.
Founded 1879.
Name origin: For Charles Warren, the general passenger agent of the St. Paul, Minneapolis, & Manitoba Railway Company.

Warrenton Township
Lat: 48-14-18 N Long: 96-49-13 W
Pop: 100 (1990); 112 (1980) Pop Density: 2.8
Land: 35.5 sq. mi.; Water: 0.0 sq. mi.

West Valley Township
Lat: 48-24-12 N Long: 96-27-21 W
Pop: 145 (1990); 180 (1980) Pop Density: 4.0
Land: 36.4 sq. mi.; Water: 0.0 sq. mi.

Whiteford Township
Lat: 48-25-02 N Long: 95-55-39 W
Pop: 49 (1990); 75 (1980) Pop Density: 1.5
Land: 33.5 sq. mi.; Water: 2.8 sq. mi.

Wright Township
Lat: 48-24-43 N Long: 96-35-01 W
Pop: 160 (1990); 223 (1980) Pop Density: 4.4
Land: 36.0 sq. mi.; Water: 0.1 sq. mi.

Martin County
County Seat: Fairmont (ZIP: 56031)

Pop: 22,914 (1990); 24,687 (1980)   **Pop Density:** 32.3
Land: 709.4 sq. mi.; **Water:** 20.2 sq. mi.   **Area Code:** 507

On the central southern border of MN, southwest of Mankato; established May 23, 1857 (prior to statehood) from Faribault County.

Name origin: Either for Henry Martin (1829–1908), CT speculator with large holdings in the area, or for Morgan Lewis Martin (1805–87), U.S. representative from WI Territory who introduced the bill for the organization of the Territory of MN.

Cedar   Township
Lat: 43-48-19 N   **Long:** 94-47-36 W
Pop: 268 (1990); 326 (1980)   **Pop Density:** 7.8
Land: 34.5 sq. mi.; **Water:** 1.3 sq. mi.

Center Creek   Township
Lat: 43-43-09 N   **Long:** 94-18-13 W
Pop: 307 (1990); 358 (1980)   **Pop Density:** 8.6
Land: 35.5 sq. mi.; **Water:** 0.0 sq. mi.

Ceylon   City
ZIP: 56121   **Lat:** 43-31-54 N   **Long:** 94-37-55 W
Pop: 461 (1990); 543 (1980)   **Pop Density:** 658.6
Land: 0.7 sq. mi.; **Water:** 0.0 sq. mi.

Name origin: For the island country of Ceylon (present-day Sri Lanka) in the Indian Ocean.

Dunnell   City
ZIP: 56127   **Lat:** 43-33-37 N   **Long:** 94-46-25 W
Pop: 187 (1990); 216 (1980)   **Pop Density:** 467.5
Land: 0.4 sq. mi.; **Water:** 0.0 sq. mi.

East Chain   Township
Lat: 43-32-34 N   **Long:** 94-18-28 W
Pop: 375 (1990); 425 (1980)   **Pop Density:** 10.7
Land: 35.2 sq. mi.; **Water:** 0.7 sq. mi.

Elm Creek   Township
Lat: 43-43-23 N   **Long:** 94-47-00 W
Pop: 217 (1990); 290 (1980)   **Pop Density:** 6.2
Land: 34.9 sq. mi.; **Water:** 1.3 sq. mi.

Fairmont   City
ZIP: 56031   **Lat:** 43-38-32 N   **Long:** 94-27-27 W
Pop: 11,265 (1990); 11,506 (1980)   **Pop Density:** 782.3
Land: 14.4 sq. mi.; **Water:** 2.0 sq. mi.

In southern MN, 41 mi. southwest of Mankato.

Name origin: For the city's position overlooking the central chain of lakes.

*Fairmont   Township
ZIP: 56031   **Lat:** 43-37-35 N   **Long:** 94-25-02 W
Pop: 277 (1990); 312 (1980)   **Pop Density:** 13.5
Land: 20.5 sq. mi.; **Water:** 1.3 sq. mi.

Fox Lake   Township
Lat: 43-42-54 N   **Long:** 94-40-43 W
Pop: 316 (1990); 334 (1980)   **Pop Density:** 9.3
Land: 34.1 sq. mi.; **Water:** 1.5 sq. mi.

Fraser   Township
Lat: 43-43-15 N   **Long:** 94-33-41 W
Pop: 331 (1990); 373 (1980)   **Pop Density:** 9.1
Land: 36.5 sq. mi.; **Water:** 0.3 sq. mi.

Galena   Township
Lat: 43-48-19 N   **Long:** 94-40-21 W
Pop: 284 (1990); 314 (1980)   **Pop Density:** 8.1
Land: 34.9 sq. mi.; **Water:** 0.5 sq. mi.

Granada   City
ZIP: 56039   **Lat:** 43-41-37 N   **Long:** 94-20-57 W
Pop: 374 (1990); 377 (1980)   **Pop Density:** 623.3
Land: 0.6 sq. mi.; **Water:** 0.0 sq. mi.

Name origin: For the city in Spain.

Jay   Township
Lat: 43-38-14 N   **Long:** 94-48-13 W
Pop: 290 (1990); 341 (1980)   **Pop Density:** 8.0
Land: 36.3 sq. mi.; **Water:** 0.0 sq. mi.

Lake Belt   Township
Lat: 43-32-33 N   **Long:** 94-40-43 W
Pop: 259 (1990); 362 (1980)   **Pop Density:** 7.5
Land: 34.5 sq. mi.; **Water:** 1.0 sq. mi.

Lake Fremont   Township
Lat: 43-32-41 N   **Long:** 94-47-38 W
Pop: 265 (1990); 282 (1980)   **Pop Density:** 7.4
Land: 36.0 sq. mi.; **Water:** 0.0 sq. mi.

Manyaska   Township
Lat: 43-38-00 N   **Long:** 94-41-02 W
Pop: 347 (1990); 356 (1980)   **Pop Density:** 10.3
Land: 33.8 sq. mi.; **Water:** 0.6 sq. mi.

Nashville   Township
ZIP: 56088   **Lat:** 43-48-34 N   **Long:** 94-18-08 W
Pop: 280 (1990); 354 (1980)   **Pop Density:** 7.7
Land: 36.5 sq. mi.; **Water:** 0.0 sq. mi.

Northrop   City
ZIP: 56075   **Lat:** 43-44-08 N   **Long:** 94-26-08 W
Pop: 276 (1990); 269 (1980)   **Pop Density:** 1380.0
Land: 0.2 sq. mi.; **Water:** 0.0 sq. mi.

Ormsby   City
ZIP: 56162   **Lat:** 43-50-49 N   **Long:** 94-41-46 W
Pop: 52 (1990); 65 (1980)   **Pop Density:** 520.0
Land: 0.1 sq. mi.; **Water:** 0.0 sq. mi.

Founded 1800s. Part of the town is also in Watonwan County.

Name origin: For Colonel Ormsby of IA.

Pleasant Prairie   Township
Lat: 43-37-58 N   **Long:** 94-19-01 W
Pop: 327 (1990); 385 (1980)   **Pop Density:** 9.1
Land: 35.8 sq. mi.; **Water:** 0.2 sq. mi.

Rolling Green   Township
Lat: 43-37-39 N   **Long:** 94-32-55 W
Pop: 314 (1990); 405 (1980)   **Pop Density:** 8.9
Land: 35.2 sq. mi.; **Water:** 0.7 sq. mi.

Rutland
Township
Lat: 43-43-03 N **Long:** 94-25-46 W
Pop: 448 (1990); 498 (1980) **Pop Density:** 12.6
Land: 35.5 sq. mi.; **Water:** 1.4 sq. mi.

Sherburn
City
ZIP: 56171 **Lat:** 43-39-13 N **Long:** 94-43-35 W
Pop: 1,105 (1990); 1,275 (1980) **Pop Density:** 1227.8
Land: 0.9 sq. mi.; **Water:** 0.0 sq. mi.

Silver Lake
Township
Lat: 43-32-50 N **Long:** 94-26-14 W
Pop: 488 (1990); 584 (1980) **Pop Density:** 14.0
Land: 34.9 sq. mi.; **Water:** 2.4 sq. mi.

Tenhassen
Township
Lat: 43-32-44 N **Long:** 94-33-33 W
Pop: 331 (1990); 395 (1980) **Pop Density:** 10.3
Land: 32.0 sq. mi.; **Water:** 4.6 sq. mi.

Trimont
City
ZIP: 56176 **Lat:** 43-45-41 N **Long:** 94-42-55 W
Pop: 745 (1990); 805 (1980) **Pop Density:** 931.3
Land: 0.8 sq. mi.; **Water:** 0.0 sq. mi.
Name origin: For three hills in the area.

Truman
City
ZIP: 56088 **Lat:** 43-49-40 N **Long:** 94-26-10 W
Pop: 1,292 (1990); 1,392 (1980) **Pop Density:** 1174.5
Land: 1.1 sq. mi.; **Water:** 0.0 sq. mi.
Name origin: For Truman Clark, the son of a railway vice-president.

Waverly
Township
Lat: 43-48-05 N **Long:** 94-32-58 W
Pop: 282 (1990); 301 (1980) **Pop Density:** 7.7
Land: 36.6 sq. mi.; **Water:** 0.2 sq. mi.

Welcome
City
ZIP: 56181 **Lat:** 43-40-06 N **Long:** 94-37-06 W
Pop: 790 (1990); 855 (1980) **Pop Density:** 877.8
Land: 0.9 sq. mi.; **Water:** 0.0 sq. mi. **Elev:** 1235 ft.
Name origin: For nearby farmer Alfred Welcome.

Westford
Township
Lat: 43-47-46 N **Long:** 94-26-00 W
Pop: 361 (1990); 389 (1980) **Pop Density:** 10.0
Land: 36.2 sq. mi.; **Water:** 0.4 sq. mi.

McLeod County
County Seat: Glencoe (ZIP: 55336)

Pop: 32,030 (1990); 29,657 (1980) **Pop Density:** 65.1
Land: 491.9 sq. mi.; **Water:** 13.8 sq. mi. **Area Code:** 612

In south-central MN, west of Minneapolis; established Mar 1, 1856 (prior to statehood) from Carver County.

Name origin: For Martin McLeod (1813–60), fur trader, MN territorial legislator (1849–53), and a founder of Glencoe.

Acoma
Township
Lat: 44-56-12 N **Long:** 94-26-48 W
Pop: 1,040 (1990); 881 (1980) **Pop Density:** 32.6
Land: 31.9 sq. mi.; **Water:** 3.3 sq. mi.

Bergen
Township
Lat: 44-50-33 N **Long:** 94-04-05 W
Pop: 844 (1990); 840 (1980) **Pop Density:** 23.8
Land: 35.5 sq. mi.; **Water:** 0.1 sq. mi.

Biscay
City
ZIP: 55336 **Lat:** 44-49-35 N **Long:** 94-16-26 W
Pop: 113 (1990); 114 (1980) **Pop Density:** 1130.0
Land: 0.1 sq. mi.; **Water:** 0.0 sq. mi.

Brownton
City
ZIP: 55312 **Lat:** 44-43-57 N **Long:** 94-21-04 W
Pop: 781 (1990); 697 (1980) **Pop Density:** 2603.3
Land: 0.3 sq. mi.; **Water:** 0.0 sq. mi. **Elev:** 1021 ft.
Name origin: For farmer and Civil War captain, Alonzo Brown.

Collins
Township
Lat: 44-46-19 N **Long:** 94-26-13 W
Pop: 495 (1990); 518 (1980) **Pop Density:** 14.6
Land: 33.9 sq. mi.; **Water:** 1.5 sq. mi.

Glencoe
City
ZIP: 55336 **Lat:** 44-46-10 N **Long:** 94-08-58 W
Pop: 4,648 (1990); 4,396 (1980) **Pop Density:** 2213.3
Land: 2.1 sq. mi.; **Water:** 0.0 sq. mi.
Founded 1855.
Name origin: For Glencoe, Scotland.

*Glencoe
Township
ZIP: 55336 **Lat:** 44-45-35 N **Long:** 94-11-38 W
Pop: 617 (1990); 661 (1980) **Pop Density:** 18.0
Land: 34.3 sq. mi.; **Water:** 0.1 sq. mi.

Hale
Township
Lat: 44-55-48 N **Long:** 94-12-01 W
Pop: 992 (1990); 1,004 (1980) **Pop Density:** 29.0
Land: 34.2 sq. mi.; **Water:** 1.4 sq. mi.

Hassan Valley
Township
Lat: 44-50-54 N **Long:** 94-18-39 W
Pop: 786 (1990); 926 (1980) **Pop Density:** 23.0
Land: 34.2 sq. mi.; **Water:** 0.0 sq. mi.

Helen
Township
Lat: 44-45-42 N **Long:** 94-04-03 W
Pop: 884 (1990); 868 (1980) **Pop Density:** 25.0
Land: 35.3 sq. mi.; **Water:** 0.0 sq. mi.

Hutchinson
City
ZIP: 55350 **Lat:** 44-53-19 N **Long:** 94-22-29 W
Pop: 11,523 (1990); 9,244 (1980) **Pop Density:** 2133.9
Land: 5.4 sq. mi.; **Water:** 0.3 sq. mi. **Elev:** 1056 ft.
In south-central MN, west of Minneapolis.
Name origin: For founders, the Hutchinson brothers.

*Hutchinson
Township
ZIP: 55350 **Lat:** 44-56-07 N **Long:** 94-19-17 W
Pop: 1,069 (1990); 1,090 (1980) **Pop Density:** 32.9
Land: 32.5 sq. mi.; **Water:** 2.2 sq. mi.

Lester Prairie
City
ZIP: 55354 **Lat:** 44-53-01 N **Long:** 94-02-23 W
Pop: 1,180 (1990); 1,229 (1980) **Pop Density:** 1966.7
Land: 0.6 sq. mi.; **Water:** 0.0 sq. mi. **Elev:** 1004 ft.
Founded 1888.
Name origin: For Mr. and Mrs. John Lester, the original landowners.

Lynn
Township
Lat: 44-50-59 N **Long:** 94-25-58 W
Pop: 734 (1990); 693 (1980) **Pop Density:** 22.1
Land: 33.2 sq. mi.; **Water:** 1.5 sq. mi.

Penn
Township
Lat: 44-40-55 N **Long:** 94-19-11 W
Pop: 390 (1990); 393 (1980) **Pop Density:** 11.1
Land: 35.2 sq. mi.; **Water:** 0.9 sq. mi.

Plato
City
ZIP: 55370 **Lat:** 44-46-20 N **Long:** 94-02-20 W
Pop: 355 (1990); 390 (1980) **Pop Density:** 1183.3
Land: 0.3 sq. mi.; **Water:** 0.0 sq. mi.
Name origin: For the Greek philosopher (c. 427–c. 347 B.C.).

Rich Valley
Township
Lat: 44-50-48 N **Long:** 94-11-21 W
Pop: 701 (1990); 817 (1980) **Pop Density:** 19.4
Land: 36.1 sq. mi.; **Water:** 0.1 sq. mi.

Round Grove
Township
Lat: 44-40-29 N **Long:** 94-25-36 W
Pop: 349 (1990); 374 (1980) **Pop Density:** 9.8
Land: 35.7 sq. mi.; **Water:** 0.4 sq. mi.

Silver Lake
City
ZIP: 55381 **Lat:** 44-54-13 N **Long:** 94-11-51 W
Pop: 764 (1990); 698 (1980) **Pop Density:** 2546.7
Land: 0.3 sq. mi.; **Water:** 0.0 sq. mi.
Name origin: For its location next to Silver Lake.

Stewart
City
ZIP: 55385 **Lat:** 44-43-30 N **Long:** 94-29-16 W
Pop: 566 (1990); 616 (1980) **Pop Density:** 566.0
Land: 1.0 sq. mi.; **Water:** 0.0 sq. mi. **Elev:** 1062 ft.
Incorporated 1888.
Name origin: For the town's founder, Dr. D. A. Stewart.

Sumter
Township
Lat: 44-46-06 N **Long:** 94-18-54 W
Pop: 515 (1990); 510 (1980) **Pop Density:** 14.7
Land: 35.0 sq. mi.; **Water:** 0.8 sq. mi.

Winsted
City
ZIP: 55395 **Lat:** 44-57-56 N **Long:** 94-02-55 W
Pop: 1,581 (1990); 1,522 (1980) **Pop Density:** 2258.6
Land: 0.7 sq. mi.; **Water:** 0.0 sq. mi.
City and township not coextensive.
Name origin: For Winsted, CT, former home of early settler Eli Lewis.

*Winsted
Township
ZIP: 55395 **Lat:** 44-56-01 N **Long:** 94-04-28 W
Pop: 1,103 (1990); 1,176 (1980) **Pop Density:** 32.3
Land: 34.2 sq. mi.; **Water:** 1.1 sq. mi.

Meeker County
County Seat: Litchfield (ZIP: 55355)

Pop: 20,846 (1990); 20,594 (1980) **Pop Density:** 34.3
Land: 608.6 sq. mi.; **Water:** 36.5 sq. mi. **Area Code:** 612
In south-central MN, northwest of Minneapolis; established Feb 23, 1856 (prior to statehood) from Wright County.
Name origin: For Bradley B. Meeker (1813–73), associate justice of the MN supreme court (1849–53).

Acton
Township
Lat: 45-07-04 N **Long:** 94-42-02 W
Pop: 460 (1990); 475 (1980) **Pop Density:** 13.8
Land: 33.3 sq. mi.; **Water:** 2.4 sq. mi.

Cedar Mills
City
Lat: 44-56-50 N **Long:** 94-31-02 W
Pop: 80 (1990); 73 (1980) **Pop Density:** 200.0
Land: 0.4 sq. mi.; **Water:** 0.0 sq. mi. **Elev:** 1091 ft.
City and township not coextensive.

*Cedar Mills
Township
Lat: 44-56-12 N **Long:** 94-34-24 W
Pop: 520 (1990); 569 (1980) **Pop Density:** 13.5
Land: 38.5 sq. mi.; **Water:** 0.5 sq. mi.

Collinwood
Township
Lat: 45-01-08 N **Long:** 94-19-20 W
Pop: 844 (1990); 735 (1980) **Pop Density:** 27.2
Land: 31.0 sq. mi.; **Water:** 5.0 sq. mi.

Cosmos
City
ZIP: 56228 **Lat:** 44-56-09 N **Long:** 94-41-50 W
Pop: 610 (1990); 571 (1980) **Pop Density:** 610.0
Land: 1.0 sq. mi.; **Water:** 0.0 sq. mi.
City and township not coextensive.
Name origin: Early settler, Daniel Hoyt, gave the town the Greek name meaning 'orderly universe.'

*Cosmos
Township
ZIP: 56228   Lat: 44-56-11 N   Long: 94-41-07 W
Pop: 269 (1990); 274 (1980)   Pop Density: 7.7
Land: 34.9 sq. mi.; Water: 0.4 sq. mi.

Danielson
Township
Lat: 45-01-13 N   Long: 94-41-28 W
Pop: 338 (1990); 357 (1980)   Pop Density: 9.8
Land: 34.5 sq. mi.; Water: 1.4 sq. mi.

Darwin
City
ZIP: 55324   Lat: 45-05-49 N   Long: 94-24-14 W
Pop: 252 (1990); 282 (1980)   Pop Density: 360.0
Land: 0.7 sq. mi.; Water: 0.1 sq. mi.   Elev: 1132 ft.
City and township not coextensive.
Name origin: For Darwin Litchfield, chief stockholder of the Great Northern Railway Company.

*Darwin
Township
ZIP: 55324   Lat: 45-06-29 N   Long: 94-26-46 W
Pop: 684 (1990); 606 (1980)   Pop Density: 21.1
Land: 32.4 sq. mi.; Water: 2.9 sq. mi.

Dassel
City
ZIP: 55325   Lat: 45-04-54 N   Long: 94-18-26 W
Pop: 1,082 (1990); 1,066 (1980)   Pop Density: 1082.0
Land: 1.0 sq. mi.; Water: 0.1 sq. mi.   Elev: 1091 ft.
City and township not coextensive.
Name origin: Named in 1871 for Bernard Dassel, who at that time was the secretary of the Great Northern Railroad.

*Dassel
Township
ZIP: 55325   Lat: 45-06-18 N   Long: 94-18-45 W
Pop: 1,000 (1990); 967 (1980)   Pop Density: 32.6
Land: 30.7 sq. mi.; Water: 4.1 sq. mi.

Eden Valley
City
ZIP: 55329   Lat: 45-19-19 N   Long: 94-32-44 W
Pop: 417 (1990); 472 (1980)   Pop Density: 595.7
Land: 0.7 sq. mi.; Water: 0.0 sq. mi.
Part of the town is also in Stearns County.
Name origin: Named euphoniously by St. Paul, Minneapolis, & Sault Ste. Marie Railway officers.

Ellsworth
Township
Lat: 45-01-46 N   Long: 94-26-49 W
Pop: 697 (1990); 632 (1980)   Pop Density: 23.7
Land: 29.4 sq. mi.; Water: 6.9 sq. mi.

Forest City
Township
Lat: 45-11-09 N   Long: 94-26-26 W
Pop: 617 (1990); 661 (1980)   Pop Density: 17.9
Land: 34.4 sq. mi.; Water: 1.4 sq. mi.

Forest Prairie
Township
Lat: 45-17-07 N   Long: 94-26-43 W
Pop: 833 (1990); 920 (1980)   Pop Density: 24.3
Land: 34.3 sq. mi.; Water: 1.1 sq. mi.

Greenleaf
Township
Lat: 45-01-24 N   Long: 94-34-24 W
Pop: 654 (1990); 664 (1980)   Pop Density: 18.3
Land: 35.8 sq. mi.; Water: 3.2 sq. mi.

Grove City
City
ZIP: 56243   Lat: 45-09-06 N   Long: 94-40-52 W
Pop: 547 (1990); 596 (1980)   Pop Density: 1823.3
Land: 0.3 sq. mi.; Water: 0.0 sq. mi.
Name origin: For the many original forest groves in the vicinity.

Harvey
Township
Lat: 45-11-51 N   Long: 94-34-07 W
Pop: 421 (1990); 431 (1980)   Pop Density: 10.9
Land: 38.6 sq. mi.; Water: 0.4 sq. mi.

Kingston
City
ZIP: 55326   Lat: 45-11-47 N   Long: 94-18-35 W
Pop: 131 (1990); 141 (1980)   Pop Density: 262.0
Land: 0.5 sq. mi.; Water: 0.0 sq. mi.   Elev: 1027 ft.
Settled 1856. City and township not coextensive.
Name origin: Named by lawyer George Nourse for a common English place name.

*Kingston
Township
Lat: 45-12-58 N   Long: 94-19-20 W
Pop: 1,064 (1990); 971 (1980)   Pop Density: 20.5
Land: 51.8 sq. mi.; Water: 1.8 sq. mi.

Litchfield
City
ZIP: 55355   Lat: 45-07-10 N   Long: 94-31-37 W
Pop: 6,041 (1990); 5,904 (1980)   Pop Density: 1678.1
Land: 3.6 sq. mi.; Water: 0.9 sq. mi.
City and township not coextensive.
Name origin: For the local Litchfield brothers, who were railroad contractors. Originally called Ness.

*Litchfield
Township
ZIP: 55355   Lat: 45-06-32 N   Long: 94-34-20 W
Pop: 792 (1990); 817 (1980)   Pop Density: 24.8
Land: 31.9 sq. mi.; Water: 2.2 sq. mi.

Manannah
Township
Lat: 45-16-38 N   Long: 94-34-17 W
Pop: 611 (1990); 628 (1980)   Pop Density: 15.9
Land: 38.5 sq. mi.; Water: 0.1 sq. mi.

Swede Grove
Township
Lat: 45-11-38 N   Long: 94-41-10 W
Pop: 421 (1990); 409 (1980)   Pop Density: 12.1
Land: 34.7 sq. mi.; Water: 0.9 sq. mi.

Union Grove
Township
Lat: 45-16-28 N   Long: 94-42-00 W
Pop: 612 (1990); 616 (1980)   Pop Density: 17.4
Land: 35.2 sq. mi.; Water: 0.8 sq. mi.

Watkins
City
ZIP: 55389   Lat: 45-18-53 N   Long: 94-24-28 W
Pop: 849 (1990); 757 (1980)   Pop Density: 1698.0
Land: 0.5 sq. mi.; Water: 0.0 sq. mi.
Name origin: Named by officers of the Soo Railway Company for a company employee.

American Places Dictionary

MINNESOTA, Mille Lacs County

> ## Mille Lacs County
> **County Seat:** Milaca (ZIP: 56353)
>
> **Pop:** 18,670 (1990); 18,430 (1980)   **Pop Density:** 32.5
> **Land:** 574.5 sq. mi.; **Water:** 107.3 sq. mi.   **Area Code:** 612
>
> In east-central MN, northeast of St. Cloud; established May 23, 1857 (prior to statehood) from Kanabec County.
>
> **Name origin:** For Mille Lacs Lake in the northern part of the county; French 'thousand lakes.'

Bock — City
ZIP: 56313   **Lat:** 45-47-05 N **Long:** 93-33-11 W
Pop: 115 (1990); 105 (1980)   **Pop Density:** 1150.0
Land: 0.1 sq. mi.; **Water:** 0.0 sq. mi.   **Elev:** 1105 ft.

Bogus Brook — Township
   Lat: 45-41-15 N **Long:** 93-34-28 W
Pop: 876 (1990); 860 (1980)   **Pop Density:** 24.2
Land: 36.2 sq. mi.; **Water:** 0.0 sq. mi.

Borgholm — Township
   Lat: 45-46-48 N **Long:** 93-34-34 W
Pop: 1,021 (1990); 1,042 (1980)   **Pop Density:** 28.9
Land: 35.3 sq. mi.; **Water:** 0.0 sq. mi.

Bradbury — Township
ZIP: 56359   **Lat:** 46-01-59 N **Long:** 93-44-29 W
Pop: 144 (1990); 157 (1980)   **Pop Density:** 3.9
Land: 36.7 sq. mi.; **Water:** 0.0 sq. mi.

Dailey — Township
ZIP: 56359   **Lat:** 45-57-07 N **Long:** 93-42-08 W
Pop: 193 (1990); 213 (1980)   **Pop Density:** 6.2
Land: 31.0 sq. mi.; **Water:** 0.0 sq. mi.

East Side — Township
   Lat: 46-12-03 N **Long:** 93-29-38 W
Pop: 543 (1990); 621 (1980)   **Pop Density:** 25.4
Land: 21.4 sq. mi.; **Water:** 16.7 sq. mi.

Foreston — City
ZIP: 56330   **Lat:** 45-43-59 N **Long:** 93-42-33 W
Pop: 354 (1990); 283 (1980)   **Pop Density:** 252.9
Land: 1.4 sq. mi.; **Water:** 0.0 sq. mi.

Greenbush — Township
   Lat: 45-36-19 N **Long:** 93-42-15 W
Pop: 1,027 (1990); 1,086 (1980)   **Pop Density:** 27.6
Land: 37.2 sq. mi.; **Water:** 0.1 sq. mi.

Hayland — Township
   Lat: 45-51-44 N **Long:** 93-35-37 W
Pop: 295 (1990); 354 (1980)   **Pop Density:** 8.2
Land: 35.9 sq. mi.; **Water:** 0.0 sq. mi.

Isle — City
ZIP: 56342   **Lat:** 46-08-31 N **Long:** 93-27-37 W
Pop: 566 (1990); 573 (1980)   **Pop Density:** 283.0
Land: 2.0 sq. mi.; **Water:** 0.4 sq. mi.
Name origin: For a port on Mille Lacs protected from storms by Great or Big Island.

Isle Harbor — Township
ZIP: 56386   **Lat:** 46-06-26 N **Long:** 93-29-56 W
Pop: 416 (1990); 445 (1980)   **Pop Density:** 15.3
Land: 27.2 sq. mi.; **Water:** 5.0 sq. mi.

Kathio — Township
ZIP: 56359   **Lat:** 46-10-16 N **Long:** 93-45-09 W
Pop: 930 (1990); 901 (1980)   **Pop Density:** 21.9
Land: 42.4 sq. mi.; **Water:** 30.2 sq. mi.

Lewis — Township
ZIP: 56386   **Lat:** 46-00-20 N **Long:** 93-28-44 W
Pop: 43 (1990); 60 (1980)   **Pop Density:** 1.2
Land: 35.7 sq. mi.; **Water:** 0.2 sq. mi.

Milaca — City
ZIP: 56353   **Lat:** 45-45-28 N **Long:** 93-39-10 W
Pop: 2,182 (1990); 2,104 (1980)   **Pop Density:** 779.3
Land: 2.8 sq. mi.; **Water:** 0.0 sq. mi.   **Elev:** 1079 ft.
City and township not coextensive.
Name origin: A revised version of the county name, Mille Lacs. Originally called Oak City

*Milaca — Township
ZIP: 56353   **Lat:** 45-46-53 N **Long:** 93-42-18 W
Pop: 989 (1990); 1,001 (1980)   **Pop Density:** 30.0
Land: 33.0 sq. mi.; **Water:** 0.0 sq. mi.

Milo — Township
ZIP: 56330   **Lat:** 45-41-07 N **Long:** 93-42-03 W
Pop: 999 (1990); 957 (1980)   **Pop Density:** 28.7
Land: 34.8 sq. mi.; **Water:** 0.0 sq. mi.

Mudgett — Township
ZIP: 56359   **Lat:** 45-56-26 N **Long:** 93-35-30 W
Pop: 88 (1990); 100 (1980)   **Pop Density:** 2.9
Land: 30.2 sq. mi.; **Water:** 0.1 sq. mi.

Onamia — City
ZIP: 56359   **Lat:** 46-04-09 N **Long:** 93-39-54 W
Pop: 676 (1990); 691 (1980)   **Pop Density:** 751.1
Land: 0.9 sq. mi.; **Water:** 0.0 sq. mi.
Name origin: From Ojibway term.

*Onamia — Township
ZIP: 56359   **Lat:** 46-01-30 N **Long:** 93-37-17 W
Pop: 517 (1990); 516 (1980)   **Pop Density:** 14.4
Land: 35.9 sq. mi.; **Water:** 0.2 sq. mi.

Page — Township
ZIP: 56353   **Lat:** 45-51-55 N **Long:** 93-41-49 W
Pop: 440 (1990); 456 (1980)   **Pop Density:** 12.3
Land: 35.8 sq. mi.; **Water:** 0.0 sq. mi.

Pease — City
ZIP: 56363   **Lat:** 45-41-53 N **Long:** 93-39-02 W
Pop: 178 (1990); 174 (1980)   **Pop Density:** 445.0
Land: 0.4 sq. mi.; **Water:** 0.0 sq. mi.

MINNESOTA, Mille Lacs County

Princeton — City
ZIP: 55371 **Lat:** 45-34-23 N **Long:** 93-35-22 W
Pop: 3,717 (1990); 3,144 (1980) **Pop Density:** 1161.6
Land: 3.2 sq. mi.; **Water:** 0.0 sq. mi. **Elev:** 983 ft.
Part of the town is also in Sherburne County.
Name origin: For John Prince, who helped lay out the town in 1855.

*Princeton — Township
ZIP: 55371 **Lat:** 45-36-23 N **Long:** 93-34-40 W
Pop: 1,601 (1990); 1,625 (1980) **Pop Density:** 49.1
Land: 32.6 sq. mi.; **Water:** 0.4 sq. mi.

South Harbor — Township
ZIP: 56359 **Lat:** 46-10-41 N **Long:** 93-36-19 W
Pop: 563 (1990); 691 (1980) **Pop Density:** 26.4
Land: 21.3 sq. mi.; **Water:** 53.8 sq. mi.

Vineland — CDP
ZIP: 56359 **Lat:** 46-10-57 N **Long:** 93-46-25 W
Pop: 438 (1990) **Pop Density:** 67.4
Land: 6.5 sq. mi.; **Water:** 0.1 sq. mi.

Wahkon — City
ZIP: 56386 **Lat:** 46-07-07 N **Long:** 93-31-25 W
Pop: 197 (1990); 271 (1980) **Pop Density:** 197.0
Land: 1.0 sq. mi.; **Water:** 0.0 sq. mi.
Name origin: From the Sioux Indian term meaning 'sacred' or 'holy.'

Morrison County
County Seat: Little Falls (ZIP: 56345)

Pop: 29,604 (1990); 29,311 (1980) **Pop Density:** 26.3
Land: 1124.5 sq. mi.; **Water:** 28.8 sq. mi. **Area Code:** 612

In central MN, north of St. Cloud; established Feb 25, 1856 (prior to statehood) from Benton and Stearns counties.

Name origin: For the Morrison brothers: William (1785–1866), fur trader and explorer, and Allen (1803–77), fur trader and representative in the first territorial legislature.

Agram — Township
ZIP: 56364 **Lat:** 45-56-26 N **Long:** 94-10-22 W
Pop: 444 (1990); 381 (1980) **Pop Density:** 22.5
Land: 19.7 sq. mi.; **Water:** 0.4 sq. mi.

Belle Prairie — Township
ZIP: 56345 **Lat:** 46-01-23 N **Long:** 94-15-56 W
Pop: 1,620 (1990); 1,597 (1980) **Pop Density:** 35.8
Land: 45.2 sq. mi.; **Water:** 1.0 sq. mi.

Bellevue — Township
ZIP: 56373 **Lat:** 45-51-45 N **Long:** 94-17-09 W
Pop: 852 (1990); 793 (1980) **Pop Density:** 18.9
Land: 45.0 sq. mi.; **Water:** 0.7 sq. mi.

Bowlus — City
ZIP: 56314 **Lat:** 45-49-12 N **Long:** 94-24-26 W
Pop: 260 (1990); 276 (1980) **Pop Density:** 216.7
Land: 1.2 sq. mi.; **Water:** 0.0 sq. mi. **Elev:** 1108 ft.

Buckman — City
ZIP: 56317 **Lat:** 45-53-52 N **Long:** 94-05-32 W
Pop: 201 (1990); 171 (1980) **Pop Density:** 201.0
Land: 1.0 sq. mi.; **Water:** 0.0 sq. mi.
City and township not coextensive.
Name origin: For one of the area's first settlers, Clarence Buckman.

*Buckman — Township
Lat: 45-52-08 N **Long:** 94-06-25 W
Pop: 716 (1990); 763 (1980) **Pop Density:** 13.1
Land: 54.5 sq. mi.; **Water:** 0.1 sq. mi.

Buh — Township
ZIP: 56364 **Lat:** 46-01-51 N **Long:** 94-07-29 W
Pop: 582 (1990); 604 (1980) **Pop Density:** 16.3
Land: 35.8 sq. mi.; **Water:** 0.1 sq. mi.

Culdrum — Township
Lat: 45-58-56 N **Long:** 94-35-14 W
Pop: 487 (1990); 528 (1980) **Pop Density:** 14.5
Land: 33.5 sq. mi.; **Water:** 0.2 sq. mi.

Cushing — Township
ZIP: 56443 **Lat:** 46-08-56 N **Long:** 94-30-29 W
Pop: 502 (1990); 337 (1980) **Pop Density:** 6.5
Land: 77.8 sq. mi.; **Water:** 2.1 sq. mi.

Darling — Township
ZIP: 56345 **Lat:** 46-03-23 N **Long:** 94-26-28 W
Pop: 597 (1990); 583 (1980) **Pop Density:** 17.6
Land: 34.0 sq. mi.; **Water:** 0.3 sq. mi.

Elmdale — City
ZIP: 56314 **Lat:** 45-50-14 N **Long:** 94-29-24 W
Pop: 130 (1990); 126 (1980) **Pop Density:** 38.2
Land: 3.4 sq. mi.; **Water:** 0.0 sq. mi. **Elev:** 1169 ft.
City and township not coextensive.

*Elmdale — Township
ZIP: 56314 **Lat:** 45-48-36 N **Long:** 94-32-42 W
Pop: 847 (1990); 872 (1980) **Pop Density:** 21.9
Land: 38.7 sq. mi.; **Water:** 1.0 sq. mi.

Flensburg — City
ZIP: 56328 **Lat:** 45-56-51 N **Long:** 94-31-48 W
Pop: 213 (1990); 256 (1980) **Pop Density:** 30.9
Land: 6.9 sq. mi.; **Water:** 0.1 sq. mi.
Name origin: Named by early settlers for their former home, a seaport in Prussia.

Genola — City
Lat: 45-58-07 N **Long:** 94-06-39 W
Pop: 85 (1990); 83 (1980) **Pop Density:** 283.3
Land: 0.3 sq. mi.; **Water:** 0.0 sq. mi. **Elev:** 1161 ft.

Granite
Township
Lat: 46-01-37 N **Long:** 93-59-57 W
Pop: 520 (1990); 524 (1980) **Pop Density:** 14.4
Land: 36.1 sq. mi.; **Water:** 0.0 sq. mi.

Green Prairie
Township
ZIP: 56345 **Lat:** 46-03-23 N **Long:** 94-22-15 W
Pop: 672 (1990); 650 (1980) **Pop Density:** 42.0
Land: 16.0 sq. mi.; **Water:** 0.7 sq. mi.

Harding
City
ZIP: 56364 **Lat:** 46-07-14 N **Long:** 94-02-37 W
Pop: 76 (1990); 93 (1980) **Pop Density:** 23.0
Land: 3.3 sq. mi.; **Water:** 0.0 sq. mi.

Hillman
City
ZIP: 56338 **Lat:** 46-00-32 N **Long:** 93-53-17 W
Pop: 45 (1990); 51 (1980) **Pop Density:** 90.0
Land: 0.5 sq. mi.; **Water:** 0.0 sq. mi. **Elev:** 1315 ft.

*Hillman
Township
ZIP: 56338 **Lat:** 45-56-22 N **Long:** 93-56-33 W
Pop: 167 (1990); 171 (1980) **Pop Density:** 5.9
Land: 28.2 sq. mi.; **Water:** 0.0 sq. mi.

Lakin
Township
Lat: 45-51-54 N **Long:** 93-49-28 W
Pop: 334 (1990); 408 (1980) **Pop Density:** 9.3
Land: 35.8 sq. mi.; **Water:** 0.0 sq. mi.

Lastrup
City
ZIP: 56344 **Lat:** 46-02-23 N **Long:** 94-03-40 W
Pop: 112 (1990); 150 (1980) **Pop Density:** 280.0
Land: 0.4 sq. mi.; **Water:** 0.0 sq. mi.

Leigh
Township
ZIP: 56338 **Lat:** 46-01-23 N **Long:** 93-52-20 W
Pop: 174 (1990); 192 (1980) **Pop Density:** 4.8
Land: 36.0 sq. mi.; **Water:** 0.1 sq. mi.

Little Falls
City
ZIP: 56345 **Lat:** 45-58-40 N **Long:** 94-21-39 W
Pop: 7,232 (1990); 7,250 (1980) **Pop Density:** 1506.7
Land: 4.8 sq. mi.; **Water:** 0.4 sq. mi.
Incorporated 1879.
Name origin: For the rapids of the adjacent Mississippi River.

*Little Falls
Township
ZIP: 56345 **Lat:** 45-56-47 N **Long:** 94-17-42 W
Pop: 1,532 (1990); 1,137 (1980) **Pop Density:** 43.8
Land: 35.0 sq. mi.; **Water:** 1.7 sq. mi.

Morrill
Township
Lat: 45-51-44 N **Long:** 93-57-11 W
Pop: 608 (1990); 575 (1980) **Pop Density:** 17.2
Land: 35.3 sq. mi.; **Water:** 0.0 sq. mi.

Motley
City
ZIP: 56466 **Lat:** 46-20-05 N **Long:** 94-38-39 W
Pop: 441 (1990); 442 (1980) **Pop Density:** 400.9
Land: 1.1 sq. mi.; **Water:** 0.1 sq. mi. **Elev:** 1229 ft.
Settled 1870s. Part of the town is also in Cass County.
Name origin: Named by officers of the Northern Pacific Railway Company.

*Motley
Township
ZIP: 56466 **Lat:** 46-18-21 N **Long:** 94-35-28 W
Pop: 179 (1990); 159 (1980) **Pop Density:** 11.6
Land: 15.4 sq. mi.; **Water:** 0.6 sq. mi.

Mount Morris
Township
ZIP: 56338 **Lat:** 45-56-17 N **Long:** 93-49-36 W
Pop: 93 (1990); 103 (1980) **Pop Density:** 3.1
Land: 30.0 sq. mi.; **Water:** 0.0 sq. mi.

Parker
Township
ZIP: 56475 **Lat:** 46-04-00 N **Long:** 94-34-58 W
Pop: 453 (1990); 483 (1980) **Pop Density:** 11.8
Land: 38.4 sq. mi.; **Water:** 0.0 sq. mi.

Pierz
City
ZIP: 56364 **Lat:** 45-58-42 N **Long:** 94-06-01 W
Pop: 1,014 (1990); 1,018 (1980) **Pop Density:** 1014.0
Land: 1.0 sq. mi.; **Water:** 0.0 sq. mi.
Name origin: For Francis Xavier Pierz, a Roman Catholic missionary to the Ojibway Indians in the mid 1850s.

*Pierz
Township
ZIP: 56364 **Lat:** 45-57-13 N **Long:** 94-04-17 W
Pop: 636 (1990); 612 (1980) **Pop Density:** 22.3
Land: 28.5 sq. mi.; **Water:** 0.0 sq. mi.

Pike Creek
Township
Lat: 45-58-44 N **Long:** 94-26-45 W
Pop: 937 (1990); 946 (1980) **Pop Density:** 27.5
Land: 34.1 sq. mi.; **Water:** 0.2 sq. mi.

Platte
Township
Lat: 46-06-51 N **Long:** 94-08-03 W
Pop: 369 (1990); 351 (1980) **Pop Density:** 10.3
Land: 35.8 sq. mi.; **Water:** 0.0 sq. mi.

Pulaski
Township
Lat: 46-07-40 N **Long:** 94-00-12 W
Pop: 295 (1990); 322 (1980) **Pop Density:** 9.5
Land: 31.0 sq. mi.; **Water:** 1.3 sq. mi.

Rail Prairie
Township
ZIP: 56443 **Lat:** 46-14-42 N **Long:** 94-26-28 W
Pop: 127 (1990); 130 (1980) **Pop Density:** 3.2
Land: 39.4 sq. mi.; **Water:** 2.0 sq. mi.

Randall
City
ZIP: 56475 **Lat:** 46-05-21 N **Long:** 94-29-58 W
Pop: 571 (1990); 527 (1980) **Pop Density:** 285.5
Land: 2.0 sq. mi.; **Water:** 0.0 sq. mi.
Incorporated 1900.
Name origin: For John H. Randall, an official of the Northern Pacific Railway Company.

Richardson
Township
ZIP: 56338 **Lat:** 46-07-01 N **Long:** 93-52-53 W
Pop: 412 (1990); 405 (1980) **Pop Density:** 12.1
Land: 34.1 sq. mi.; **Water:** 2.1 sq. mi.

Ripley
Township
Lat: 46-07-38 N **Long:** 94-16-17 W
Pop: 607 (1990); 615 (1980) **Pop Density:** 12.7
Land: 47.7 sq. mi.; **Water:** 0.7 sq. mi.

Rosing
Township
ZIP: 56466 **Lat:** 46-17-53 N **Long:** 94-26-32 W
Pop: 105 (1990); 103 (1980) **Pop Density:** 5.8
Land: 18.1 sq. mi.; **Water:** 1.1 sq. mi.

Royalton
City
ZIP: 56373 **Lat:** 45-49-54 N **Long:** 94-17-21 W
Pop: 802 (1990); 660 (1980) **Pop Density:** 445.6
Land: 1.8 sq. mi.; **Water:** 0.0 sq. mi.
Name origin: Named by early settlers for their former home in VT.

MINNESOTA, Morrison County   *American Places Dictionary*

Scandia Valley
Township
Lat: 46-14-31 N   **Long:** 94-34-52 W
Pop: 822 (1990); 789 (1980)   **Pop Density:** 27.3
Land: 30.1 sq. mi.; **Water:** 8.6 sq. mi.

Sobieski
City
ZIP: 56345   **Lat:** 45-55-27 N   **Long:** 94-28-55 W
Pop: 199 (1990); 219 (1980)   **Pop Density:** 47.4
Land: 4.2 sq. mi.; **Water:** 0.0 sq. mi.   **Elev:** 1133 ft.

Swan River
Township
Lat: 45-53-13 N   **Long:** 94-26-27 W
Pop: 759 (1990); 856 (1980)   **Pop Density:** 20.6
Land: 36.9 sq. mi.; **Water:** 0.9 sq. mi.

Swanville
City
ZIP: 56382   **Lat:** 45-54-58 N   **Long:** 94-38-22 W
Pop: 324 (1990); 295 (1980)   **Pop Density:** 648.0
Land: 0.5 sq. mi.; **Water:** 0.0 sq. mi.   **Elev:** 1183 ft.
City and township not coextensive.

*Swanville
Township
ZIP: 56382   **Lat:** 45-53-42 N   **Long:** 94-34-33 W
Pop: 504 (1990); 566 (1980)   **Pop Density:** 14.2
Land: 35.4 sq. mi.; **Water:** 1.8 sq. mi.

Two Rivers
Township
ZIP: 56314   **Lat:** 45-48-07 N   **Long:** 94-23-22 W
Pop: 576 (1990); 600 (1980)   **Pop Density:** 21.3
Land: 27.1 sq. mi.; **Water:** 0.5 sq. mi.

Upsala
City
ZIP: 56384   **Lat:** 45-48-29 N   **Long:** 94-34-08 W
Pop: 371 (1990); 400 (1980)   **Pop Density:** 115.9
Land: 3.2 sq. mi.; **Water:** 0.0 sq. mi.
Name origin: For the famous university town in Sweden.

Mower County
County Seat: Austin (ZIP: 55912)

Pop: 37,385 (1990); 40,390 (1980)   **Pop Density:** 52.5
Land: 711.5 sq. mi.; **Water:** 0.2 sq. mi.   **Area Code:** 507
On the southeastern border of MN, south of Rochester; established Feb 20, 1855 (prior to statehood) from Fillmore County.
Name origin: For John Mower (1815–79), MN territorial and state legislator (1854–55; 1874–75).

Adams
City
ZIP: 55909   **Lat:** 43-33-53 N   **Long:** 92-43-06 W
Pop: 756 (1990); 797 (1980)   **Pop Density:** 756.0
Land: 1.0 sq. mi.; **Water:** 0.0 sq. mi.
City and township not coextensive
Name origin: For John Adams (1735–1826), second U.S. president.

*Adams
Township
ZIP: 55909   **Lat:** 43-32-01 N   **Long:** 92-45-06 W
Pop: 458 (1990); 514 (1980)   **Pop Density:** 13.1
Land: 34.9 sq. mi.; **Water:** 0.0 sq. mi.

Austin
City
ZIP: 55912   **Lat:** 43-40-17 N   **Long:** 92-58-14 W
Pop: 21,907 (1990); 23,020 (1980)   **Pop Density:** 2258.5
Land: 9.7 sq. mi.; **Water:** 0.1 sq. mi.
In southern MN, 34 mi. southwest of Rochester. Founded late 1850s. City and township not coextensive.
Name origin: For the first settler, Austin Nichols.

*Austin
Township
ZIP: 55912   **Lat:** 43-37-55 N   **Long:** 92-59-06 W
Pop: 1,779 (1990); 2,386 (1980)   **Pop Density:** 59.5
Land: 29.9 sq. mi.; **Water:** 0.0 sq. mi.

Bennington
Township
ZIP: 55936   **Lat:** 43-37-33 N   **Long:** 92-30-34 W
Pop: 182 (1990); 209 (1980)   **Pop Density:** 5.0
Land: 36.1 sq. mi.; **Water:** 0.0 sq. mi.

Brownsdale
City
ZIP: 55918   **Lat:** 43-44-25 N   **Long:** 92-52-02 W
Pop: 695 (1990); 691 (1980)   **Pop Density:** 1390.0
Land: 0.5 sq. mi.; **Water:** 0.0 sq. mi.
Founded 1850s; incorporated 1876.
Name origin: For the Brown brothers, founders.

Clayton
Township
Lat: 43-37-57 N   **Long:** 92-38-10 W
Pop: 192 (1990); 191 (1980)   **Pop Density:** 5.3
Land: 36.2 sq. mi.; **Water:** 0.0 sq. mi.

Dexter
City
ZIP: 55926   **Lat:** 43-43-05 N   **Long:** 92-42-08 W
Pop: 303 (1990); 279 (1980)   **Pop Density:** 216.4
Land: 1.4 sq. mi.; **Water:** 0.0 sq. mi.
City and township not coextensive.
Name origin: For first settler, Dexter Parrity, who came to the area in 1857.

*Dexter
Township
ZIP: 55926   **Lat:** 43-43-16 N   **Long:** 92-45-33 W
Pop: 285 (1990); 337 (1980)   **Pop Density:** 8.2
Land: 34.7 sq. mi.; **Water:** 0.0 sq. mi.

Elkton
City
ZIP: 55933   **Lat:** 43-39-35 N   **Long:** 92-42-31 W
Pop: 142 (1990); 139 (1980)   **Pop Density:** 109.2
Land: 1.3 sq. mi.; **Water:** 0.0 sq. mi.
Founded 1887.
Name origin: Named by officials of the Chicago Great Western Railway.

Frankford
Township
ZIP: 55936 **Lat:** 43-42-49 N **Long:** 92-30-05 W
Pop: 348 (1990); 359 (1980) **Pop Density:** 11.6
Land: 30.1 sq. mi.; **Water:** 0.0 sq. mi.

Grand Meadow
City
ZIP: 55936 **Lat:** 43-42-18 N **Long:** 92-34-18 W
Pop: 967 (1990); 965 (1980) **Pop Density:** 1934.0
Land: 0.5 sq. mi.; **Water:** 0.0 sq. mi. **Elev:** 1341 ft.
Name origin: For its location on an extensive prairie.

*Grand Meadow
Township
ZIP: 55936 **Lat:** 43-42-45 N **Long:** 92-38-01 W
Pop: 338 (1990); 364 (1980) **Pop Density:** 9.5
Land: 35.7 sq. mi.; **Water:** 0.0 sq. mi.

Lansing
Township
ZIP: 55950 **Lat:** 43-43-30 N **Long:** 92-59-14 W
Pop: 1,270 (1990); 1,558 (1980) **Pop Density:** 39.0
Land: 32.6 sq. mi.; **Water:** 0.1 sq. mi.

Le Roy
City
ZIP: 55951 **Lat:** 43-30-48 N **Long:** 92-30-28 W
Pop: 904 (1990); 930 (1980) **Pop Density:** 1506.7
Land: 0.6 sq. mi.; **Water:** 0.0 sq. mi.
City and township not coextensive.
Name origin: Named by railroad officers for the township.

*Le Roy
Township
ZIP: 55951 **Lat:** 43-32-44 N **Long:** 92-30-49 W
Pop: 392 (1990); 422 (1980) **Pop Density:** 11.1
Land: 35.4 sq. mi.; **Water:** 0.0 sq. mi.

Lodi
Township
Lat: 43-32-56 N **Long:** 92-38-19 W
Pop: 267 (1990); 309 (1980) **Pop Density:** 7.5
Land: 35.6 sq. mi.; **Water:** 0.0 sq. mi.

Lyle
City
ZIP: 55953 **Lat:** 43-30-19 N **Long:** 92-56-31 W
Pop: 504 (1990); 576 (1980) **Pop Density:** 630.0
Land: 0.8 sq. mi.; **Water:** 0.0 sq. mi.
City and township not coextensive.
Name origin: For Judge Robert Lyle, who lived in the area in the 1850s and 1860s.

*Lyle
Township
ZIP: 55953 **Lat:** 43-32-49 N **Long:** 92-59-21 W
Pop: 419 (1990); 500 (1980) **Pop Density:** 11.8
Land: 35.5 sq. mi.; **Water:** 0.0 sq. mi.

Mapleview
City
Lat: 43-41-20 N **Long:** 92-58-29 W
Pop: 206 (1990); 253 (1980) **Pop Density:** 1030.0
Land: 0.2 sq. mi.; **Water:** 0.0 sq. mi.

Marshall
Township
ZIP: 55953 **Lat:** 43-37-57 N **Long:** 92-45-22 W
Pop: 387 (1990); 411 (1980) **Pop Density:** 11.2
Land: 34.6 sq. mi.; **Water:** 0.0 sq. mi.

Nevada
Township
ZIP: 55953 **Lat:** 43-32-23 N **Long:** 92-52-26 W
Pop: 391 (1990); 467 (1980) **Pop Density:** 10.7
Land: 36.7 sq. mi.; **Water:** 0.0 sq. mi.

Pleasant Valley
Township
Lat: 43-47-36 N **Long:** 92-37-35 W
Pop: 292 (1990); 328 (1980) **Pop Density:** 9.7
Land: 30.1 sq. mi.; **Water:** 0.0 sq. mi.

Racine
City
ZIP: 55967 **Lat:** 43-46-35 N **Long:** 92-28-55 W
Pop: 288 (1990); 285 (1980) **Pop Density:** 720.0
Land: 0.4 sq. mi.; **Water:** 0.0 sq. mi.
City and township not coextensive.

*Racine
Township
ZIP: 55967 **Lat:** 43-47-29 N **Long:** 92-30-48 W
Pop: 527 (1990); 483 (1980) **Pop Density:** 14.7
Land: 35.9 sq. mi.; **Water:** 0.0 sq. mi.

Red Rock
Township
ZIP: 55918 **Lat:** 43-43-06 N **Long:** 92-52-12 W
Pop: 754 (1990); 872 (1980) **Pop Density:** 21.3
Land: 35.4 sq. mi.; **Water:** 0.0 sq. mi.

Rose Creek
City
ZIP: 55970 **Lat:** 43-36-16 N **Long:** 92-49-46 W
Pop: 363 (1990); 371 (1980) **Pop Density:** 907.5
Land: 0.4 sq. mi.; **Water:** 0.0 sq. mi.
Name origin: For nearby Rose Creek, which is a tributary of the Cedar River.

Sargeant
City
ZIP: 55973 **Lat:** 43-48-20 N **Long:** 92-48-03 W
Pop: 78 (1990); 95 (1980) **Pop Density:** 97.5
Land: 0.8 sq. mi.; **Water:** 0.0 sq. mi.
City and township not coextensive.

*Sargeant
Township
ZIP: 55973 **Lat:** 43-48-09 N **Long:** 92-44-37 W
Pop: 271 (1990); 338 (1980) **Pop Density:** 7.7
Land: 35.4 sq. mi.; **Water:** 0.0 sq. mi.

Taopi
City
ZIP: 55977 **Lat:** 43-33-30 N **Long:** 92-38-25 W
Pop: 83 (1990); 96 (1980) **Pop Density:** 207.5
Land: 0.4 sq. mi.; **Water:** 0.0 sq. mi.

Udolpho
Township
Lat: 43-48-16 N **Long:** 92-59-14 W
Pop: 487 (1990); 535 (1980) **Pop Density:** 13.5
Land: 36.0 sq. mi.; **Water:** 0.0 sq. mi.

Waltham
City
ZIP: 55982 **Lat:** 43-49-14 N **Long:** 92-52-30 W
Pop: 170 (1990); 176 (1980) **Pop Density:** 340.0
Land: 0.5 sq. mi.; **Water:** 0.0 sq. mi.
Founded 1885. City and township not coextensive.
Name origin: For Waltham, MA.

*Waltham
Township
ZIP: 55982 **Lat:** 43-48-03 N **Long:** 92-52-02 W
Pop: 391 (1990); 477 (1980) **Pop Density:** 10.9
Land: 35.9 sq. mi.; **Water:** 0.0 sq. mi.

Windom
Township
Lat: 43-37-54 N **Long:** 92-52-09 W
Pop: 589 (1990); 657 (1980) **Pop Density:** 16.3
Land: 36.1 sq. mi.; **Water:** 0.0 sq. mi.

Murray County
County Seat: Slayton (ZIP: 56172)

Pop: 9,660 (1990); 11,507 (1980) **Pop Density:** 13.7
Land: 704.5 sq. mi.; **Water:** 15.1 sq. mi. **Area Code:** 507
In southwestern MN, southwest of Mankato; established May 23, 1857 from Lyon County.
Name origin: For William Pitt Murray (1825–1910), MN legislator and St. Paul city attorney (1876–89).

Avoca — City
ZIP: 56114 **Lat:** 43-56-58 N **Long:** 95-38-43 W
Pop: 150 (1990); 201 (1980) **Pop Density:** 136.4
Land: 1.1 sq. mi.; **Water:** 0.2 sq. mi.
Name origin: For a river in Ireland made famous by poet Thomas Moore (1779–1852).

Belfast — Township
Lat: 43-53-55 N **Long:** 95-30-45 W
Pop: 214 (1990); 295 (1980) **Pop Density:** 6.0
Land: 35.9 sq. mi.; **Water:** 0.1 sq. mi.

Bondin — Township
Lat: 43-53-21 N **Long:** 95-39-05 W
Pop: 366 (1990); 404 (1980) **Pop Density:** 10.4
Land: 35.1 sq. mi.; **Water:** 0.2 sq. mi.

Cameron — Township
Lat: 44-04-03 N **Long:** 96-00-16 W
Pop: 194 (1990); 240 (1980) **Pop Density:** 5.4
Land: 35.9 sq. mi.; **Water:** 0.2 sq. mi.

Chanarambie — Township
Lat: 43-58-41 N **Long:** 95-59-38 W
Pop: 238 (1990); 311 (1980) **Pop Density:** 6.7
Land: 35.5 sq. mi.; **Water:** 0.0 sq. mi.

Chandler — City
ZIP: 56122 **Lat:** 43-55-45 N **Long:** 95-56-56 W
Pop: 316 (1990); 344 (1980) **Pop Density:** 395.0
Land: 0.8 sq. mi.; **Water:** 0.0 sq. mi. **Elev:** 1651 ft.
Name origin: For John A. Chandler, who worked for the Chicago, Milwaukee, & St. Paul Railway in the area for over forty years.

Currie — City
ZIP: 56123 **Lat:** 44-04-15 N **Long:** 95-39-59 W
Pop: 303 (1990); 359 (1980) **Pop Density:** 505.0
Land: 0.6 sq. mi.; **Water:** 0.0 sq. mi.
Founded 1872.
Name origin: For the Currie family, who founded the city and engaged in flour milling and merchandising.

Des Moines River — Township
Lat: 43-58-38 N **Long:** 95-31-10 W
Pop: 213 (1990); 293 (1980) **Pop Density:** 6.0
Land: 35.6 sq. mi.; **Water:** 0.4 sq. mi.

Dovray — City
ZIP: 56125 **Lat:** 44-03-17 N **Long:** 95-32-45 W
Pop: 60 (1990); 87 (1980) **Pop Density:** 200.0
Land: 0.3 sq. mi.; **Water:** 0.0 sq. mi.
Founded 1879. City and township not coextensive.
Name origin: Named for a Norwegian village.

*Dovray — Township
Lat: 44-03-56 N **Long:** 95-31-18 W
Pop: 217 (1990); 276 (1980) **Pop Density:** 6.1
Land: 35.3 sq. mi.; **Water:** 0.4 sq. mi.

Ellsborough — Township
Lat: 44-08-46 N **Long:** 96-00-08 W
Pop: 189 (1990); 274 (1980) **Pop Density:** 5.4
Land: 35.1 sq. mi.; **Water:** 0.7 sq. mi.

Fenton — Township
Lat: 43-53-32 N **Long:** 95-52-58 W
Pop: 241 (1990); 295 (1980) **Pop Density:** 6.7
Land: 35.8 sq. mi.; **Water:** 0.1 sq. mi.

Fulda — City
ZIP: 56131 **Lat:** 43-52-11 N **Long:** 95-36-08 W
Pop: 1,212 (1990); 1,308 (1980) **Pop Density:** 1346.7
Land: 0.9 sq. mi.; **Water:** 0.1 sq. mi. **Elev:** 1532 ft.

Hadley — City
ZIP: 56133 **Lat:** 43-59-50 N **Long:** 95-51-29 W
Pop: 94 (1990); 137 (1980) **Pop Density:** 313.3
Land: 0.3 sq. mi.; **Water:** 0.1 sq. mi.
Name origin: For an old English name found in several New England states.

Holly — Township
Lat: 44-09-16 N **Long:** 95-31-41 W
Pop: 186 (1990); 248 (1980) **Pop Density:** 5.2
Land: 35.8 sq. mi.; **Water:** 0.0 sq. mi.

Iona — City
ZIP: 56141 **Lat:** 43-54-53 N **Long:** 95-47-06 W
Pop: 158 (1990); 248 (1980) **Pop Density:** 197.5
Land: 0.8 sq. mi.; **Water:** 0.0 sq. mi.
Founded 1880. City and township not coextensive.
Name origin: For a small island off the west coast of Scotland, known for its ancient abbey.

*Iona — Township
ZIP: 56141 **Lat:** 43-53-33 N **Long:** 95-45-56 W
Pop: 276 (1990); 294 (1980) **Pop Density:** 8.0
Land: 34.4 sq. mi.; **Water:** 0.9 sq. mi.

Lake Sarah — Township
Lat: 44-09-18 N **Long:** 95-46-05 W
Pop: 289 (1990); 305 (1980) **Pop Density:** 8.8
Land: 32.9 sq. mi.; **Water:** 3.4 sq. mi.

Lake Wilson — City
ZIP: 56151 **Lat:** 43-59-41 N **Long:** 95-57-10 W
Pop: 319 (1990); 380 (1980) **Pop Density:** 797.5
Land: 0.4 sq. mi.; **Water:** 0.1 sq. mi.
Name origin: For the nearby lake, which was named by and for prominent landowner Jonathan Wilson.

Leeds Township
Lat: 43-58-27 N Long: 95-53-36 W
Pop: 239 (1990); 285 (1980) Pop Density: 6.8
Land: 35.4 sq. mi.; Water: 0.3 sq. mi.

Lime Lake Township
Lat: 43-59-08 N Long: 95-39-09 W
Pop: 209 (1990); 281 (1980) Pop Density: 6.1
Land: 34.5 sq. mi.; Water: 0.4 sq. mi.

Lowville Township
Lat: 44-04-13 N Long: 95-52-42 W
Pop: 212 (1990); 282 (1980) Pop Density: 5.9
Land: 35.8 sq. mi.; Water: 0.1 sq. mi.

Mason Township
Lat: 44-04-15 N Long: 95-45-36 W
Pop: 297 (1990); 344 (1980) Pop Density: 8.6
Land: 34.7 sq. mi.; Water: 1.3 sq. mi.

Moulton Township
Lat: 43-53-06 N Long: 96-00-49 W
Pop: 261 (1990); 312 (1980) Pop Density: 7.4
Land: 35.2 sq. mi.; Water: 0.0 sq. mi.

Murray Township
Lat: 44-03-59 N Long: 95-38-02 W
Pop: 221 (1990); 295 (1980) Pop Density: 6.4
Land: 34.6 sq. mi.; Water: 0.9 sq. mi.

Shetek Township
Lat: 44-09-09 N Long: 95-38-15 W
Pop: 259 (1990); 300 (1980) Pop Density: 8.3
Land: 31.1 sq. mi.; Water: 4.4 sq. mi.

Skandia Township
Lat: 44-08-44 N Long: 95-52-23 W
Pop: 192 (1990); 244 (1980) Pop Density: 5.5
Land: 35.2 sq. mi.; Water: 0.6 sq. mi.

Slayton City
ZIP: 56172 Lat: 43-59-25 N Long: 95-45-17 W
Pop: 2,147 (1990); 2,420 (1980) Pop Density: 1262.9
Land: 1.7 sq. mi.; Water: 0.0 sq. mi. Elev: 1608 ft.
City and township not coextensive.
Name origin: For Charles Slayton, founder and original landowner.

*Slayton Township
ZIP: 56172 Lat: 43-58-42 N Long: 95-45-46 W
Pop: 388 (1990); 445 (1980) Pop Density: 11.4
Land: 34.1 sq. mi.; Water: 0.3 sq. mi.

Nicollet County
County Seat: St. Peter (ZIP: 56082)

Pop: 28,076 (1990); 26,929 (1980) Pop Density: 62.1
Land: 452.3 sq. mi.; Water: 14.7 sq. mi. Area Code: 507
In south-central MN, northwest of Mankato; established Mar 5, 1853 (prior to statehood) from unorganized lands.
Name origin: For Joseph Nicolas Nicollet (1786–1843), French explorer who mapped areas of MN, ND, and SD; author of *Map of the Hydrographical Basin of the Upper Mississippi River*.

Belgrade Township
Lat: 44-13-31 N Long: 94-04-00 W
Pop: 1,456 (1990); 1,118 (1980) Pop Density: 40.6
Land: 35.9 sq. mi.; Water: 0.2 sq. mi.

Bernadotte Township
Lat: 44-24-26 N Long: 94-18-16 W
Pop: 334 (1990); 433 (1980) Pop Density: 9.3
Land: 35.9 sq. mi.; Water: 0.0 sq. mi.

Brighton Township
Lat: 44-20-14 N Long: 94-18-02 W
Pop: 183 (1990); 197 (1980) Pop Density: 10.2
Land: 18.0 sq. mi.; Water: 1.1 sq. mi.

Courtland City
ZIP: 56021 Lat: 44-15-59 N Long: 94-20-38 W
Pop: 412 (1990); 399 (1980) Pop Density: 216.8
Land: 1.9 sq. mi.; Water: 0.0 sq. mi.
Founded 1858. City and township not coextensive.
Name origin: For Cortland County, NY.

*Courtland Township
ZIP: 56021 Lat: 44-17-37 N Long: 94-20-08 W
Pop: 710 (1990); 751 (1980) Pop Density: 18.4
Land: 38.6 sq. mi.; Water: 4.2 sq. mi.

Granby Township
Lat: 44-19-24 N Long: 94-10-54 W
Pop: 296 (1990); 306 (1980) Pop Density: 10.7
Land: 27.6 sq. mi.; Water: 6.4 sq. mi.

Lafayette City
ZIP: 56054 Lat: 44-26-53 N Long: 94-23-35 W
Pop: 462 (1990); 507 (1980) Pop Density: 385.0
Land: 1.2 sq. mi.; Water: 0.0 sq. mi. Elev: 1014 ft.
Founded 1858. City and township not coextensive.
Name origin: For Revolutionary War hero, Marquis de Lafayette (1757–1834), who fought with the Americans during the Revolutionary War.

*Lafayette Township
ZIP: 56054 Lat: 44-24-05 N Long: 94-26-01 W
Pop: 747 (1990); 895 (1980) Pop Density: 14.8
Land: 50.4 sq. mi.; Water: 0.1 sq. mi.

Lake Prairie Township
Lat: 44-24-53 N Long: 94-02-20 W
Pop: 691 (1990); 717 (1980) Pop Density: 12.6
Land: 54.8 sq. mi.; Water: 0.5 sq. mi.

### Mankato	City
ZIP: 56001	**Lat:** 44-11-38 N **Long:** 94-00-51 W
Pop: 9 (1990); 9 (1980)	**Pop Density:** 30.0
Land: 0.3 sq. mi.; **Water:** 0.0 sq. mi.

In southern MN on the Minnesota River, 65 mi. southwest of Minneapolis. Part of the town is also in Blue Earth County.
Name origin: For the Sioux name for the Blue Earth River.

### New Sweden	Township
Lat: 44-24-48 N **Long:** 94-11-22 W
Pop: 356 (1990); 402 (1980)	**Pop Density:** 9.9
Land: 35.8 sq. mi.; **Water:** 0.2 sq. mi.

### Nicollet	City
ZIP: 56074	**Lat:** 44-16-32 N **Long:** 94-11-17 W
Pop: 795 (1990); 709 (1980)	**Pop Density:** 993.8
Land: 0.8 sq. mi.; **Water:** 0.0 sq. mi.

City and township not coextensive.
Name origin: For explorer Joseph Nicolas Nicollet (1786–1843), French explorer who mapped the area in the 1830s; author of *Map of the Hydrographical Basin of the Upper Mississippi River*.

### *Nicollet	Township
ZIP: 56074	**Lat:** 44-14-16 N **Long:** 94-11-17 W
Pop: 563 (1990); 604 (1980)	**Pop Density:** 17.0
Land: 33.2 sq. mi.; **Water:** 0.3 sq. mi.

### North Mankato	City
ZIP: 56003	**Lat:** 44-10-34 N **Long:** 94-01-51 W
Pop: 10,164 (1990); 9,145 (1980)	**Pop Density:** 2606.2
Land: 3.9 sq. mi.; **Water:** 0.1 sq. mi.

In southern MN, across the Minnesota River from Mankato. Part of the town is also in Blue Earth County.
Name origin: For its location.

### Oshawa	Township
Lat: 44-17-41 N **Long:** 94-03-57 W
Pop: 471 (1990); 528 (1980)	**Pop Density:** 16.0
Land: 29.5 sq. mi.; **Water:** 0.3 sq. mi.

### Ridgely	Township
Lat: 44-25-59 N **Long:** 94-41-21 W
Pop: 139 (1990); 174 (1980)	**Pop Density:** 7.4
Land: 18.7 sq. mi.; **Water:** 0.1 sq. mi.

### St. Peter	City
ZIP: 56082	**Lat:** 44-19-44 N **Long:** 93-57-49 W
Pop: 9,421 (1990); 9,056 (1980)	**Pop Density:** 1884.2
Land: 5.0 sq. mi.; **Water:** 0.1 sq. mi.

Name origin: For the St. Pierre or St. Peter River, as the Minnesota River was called by early explorers and fur traders.

### Traverse	Township
Lat: 44-21-25 N **Long:** 94-02-21 W
Pop: 338 (1990); 380 (1980)	**Pop Density:** 14.6
Land: 23.2 sq. mi.; **Water:** 0.6 sq. mi.

### West Newton	Township
Lat: 44-25-21 N **Long:** 94-33-18 W
Pop: 529 (1990); 599 (1980)	**Pop Density:** 14.0
Land: 37.7 sq. mi.; **Water:** 0.6 sq. mi.

Nobles County
County Seat: Worthington (ZIP: 56187)

Pop: 20,098 (1990); 21,840 (1980)	**Pop Density:** 28.1
Land: 715.5 sq. mi.; **Water:** 6.9 sq. mi.	**Area Code:** 507

On the southwestern border of MN, southwest of Mankato; established May 23, 1857 (prior to statehood) from Jackson County.
Name origin: For William H. Nobles (1816–76), MN Territory legislator (1854; 1856); discovered Nobles Pass through the Rocky Mountains.

### Adrian	City
ZIP: 56110	**Lat:** 43-38-04 N **Long:** 95-55-56 W
Pop: 1,141 (1990); 1,336 (1980)	**Pop Density:** 1141.0
Land: 1.0 sq. mi.; **Water:** 0.0 sq. mi.	**Elev:** 1541 ft.

Name origin: For the mother of prominent railroad director, Adrian Iselin.

### Bigelow	City
ZIP: 56117	**Lat:** 43-30-19 N **Long:** 95-41-20 W
Pop: 232 (1990); 249 (1980)	**Pop Density:** 580.0
Land: 0.4 sq. mi.; **Water:** 0.0 sq. mi.

City and township not coextensive.
Name origin: For prominent lumber and insurance businessman, Charles Bigelow.

### *Bigelow	Township
ZIP: 56117	**Lat:** 43-32-28 N **Long:** 95-37-25 W
Pop: 401 (1990); 434 (1980)	**Pop Density:** 11.6
Land: 34.5 sq. mi.; **Water:** 1.8 sq. mi.

### Bloom	Township
Lat: 43-47-51 N **Long:** 95-44-33 W
Pop: 242 (1990); 298 (1980)	**Pop Density:** 6.8
Land: 35.8 sq. mi.; **Water:** 0.1 sq. mi.

### Brewster	City
ZIP: 56119	**Lat:** 43-41-46 N **Long:** 95-27-53 W
Pop: 532 (1990); 559 (1980)	**Pop Density:** 443.3
Land: 1.2 sq. mi.; **Water:** 0.0 sq. mi.

Name origin: For Brewster, MA, former home of early settlers.

Dewald Township
Lat: 43-37-43 N Long: 95-45-21 W
Pop: 345 (1990); 366 (1980) Pop Density: 9.6
Land: 36.0 sq. mi.; Water: 0.0 sq. mi.

Dundee City
ZIP: 56126 Lat: 43-50-39 N Long: 95-27-57 W
Pop: 107 (1990); 129 (1980) Pop Density: 356.7
Land: 0.3 sq. mi.; Water: 0.0 sq. mi.

Elk Township
Lat: 43-42-38 N Long: 95-38-03 W
Pop: 308 (1990); 335 (1980) Pop Density: 8.5
Land: 36.1 sq. mi.; Water: 0.0 sq. mi.

Ellsworth City
ZIP: 56129 Lat: 43-31-16 N Long: 96-01-06 W
Pop: 580 (1990); 629 (1980) Pop Density: 966.7
Land: 0.6 sq. mi.; Water: 0.0 sq. mi.
Founded 1885.
Name origin: For early pioneer Eugene Ellsworth.

Graham Lakes Township
Lat: 43-48-07 N Long: 95-30-52 W
Pop: 262 (1990); 298 (1980) Pop Density: 7.9
Land: 33.0 sq. mi.; Water: 1.8 sq. mi.

Grand Prairie Township
Lat: 43-32-31 N Long: 95-59-16 W
Pop: 272 (1990); 300 (1980) Pop Density: 7.7
Land: 35.4 sq. mi.; Water: 0.0 sq. mi.

Hersey Township
Lat: 43-42-50 N Long: 95-31-22 W
Pop: 268 (1990); 281 (1980) Pop Density: 7.6
Land: 35.1 sq. mi.; Water: 0.0 sq. mi.

Indian Lake Township
Lat: 43-32-28 N Long: 95-31-14 W
Pop: 283 (1990); 314 (1980) Pop Density: 8.4
Land: 33.6 sq. mi.; Water: 1.3 sq. mi.

Kinbrae City
ZIP: 56126 Lat: 43-49-34 N Long: 95-28-48 W
Pop: 18 (1990); 40 (1980) Pop Density: 20.0
Land: 0.9 sq. mi.; Water: 0.1 sq. mi. Elev: 1464 ft.
Founded 1879.
Name origin: A Scottish name given by officers of the Dundee Land Company.

Larkin Township
Lat: 43-42-51 N Long: 95-52-14 W
Pop: 245 (1990); 312 (1980) Pop Density: 6.8
Land: 35.8 sq. mi.; Water: 0.0 sq. mi.

Leota Township
Lat: 43-48-34 N Long: 95-59-30 W
Pop: 504 (1990); 589 (1980) Pop Density: 13.9
Land: 36.2 sq. mi.; Water: 0.0 sq. mi.

Lismore City
ZIP: 56155 Lat: 43-44-57 N Long: 95-56-53 W
Pop: 248 (1990); 276 (1980) Pop Density: 826.7
Land: 0.3 sq. mi.; Water: 0.0 sq. mi.
City and township not coextensive.
Name origin: For a baronial village in Ireland.

*Lismore Township
ZIP: 56155 Lat: 43-43-01 N Long: 95-59-21 W
Pop: 246 (1990); 301 (1980) Pop Density: 6.9
Land: 35.8 sq. mi.; Water: 0.0 sq. mi.

Little Rock Township
Lat: 43-32-44 N Long: 95-51-49 W
Pop: 261 (1990); 342 (1980) Pop Density: 7.3
Land: 36.0 sq. mi.; Water: 0.0 sq. mi.

Lorain Township
Lat: 43-38-14 N Long: 95-30-53 W
Pop: 333 (1990); 392 (1980) Pop Density: 9.6
Land: 34.8 sq. mi.; Water: 0.3 sq. mi.

Olney Township
Lat: 43-37-54 N Long: 95-52-15 W
Pop: 205 (1990); 304 (1980) Pop Density: 5.8
Land: 35.4 sq. mi.; Water: 0.0 sq. mi.

Ransom Township
Lat: 43-32-31 N Long: 95-44-40 W
Pop: 332 (1990); 384 (1980) Pop Density: 9.1
Land: 36.4 sq. mi.; Water: 0.0 sq. mi.

Round Lake City
ZIP: 56167 Lat: 43-32-19 N Long: 95-28-09 W
Pop: 463 (1990); 480 (1980) Pop Density: 463.0
Land: 1.0 sq. mi.; Water: 0.0 sq. mi.
Name origin: For the nearby lake.

Rushmore City
ZIP: 56168 Lat: 43-37-12 N Long: 95-47-55 W
Pop: 381 (1990); 387 (1980) Pop Density: 1270.0
Land: 0.3 sq. mi.; Water: 0.0 sq. mi.
Name origin: For pioneer merchant S. M. Rushmore.

Seward Township
Lat: 43-47-57 N Long: 95-37-52 W
Pop: 275 (1990); 331 (1980) Pop Density: 7.7
Land: 35.6 sq. mi.; Water: 0.1 sq. mi.

Summit Lake Township
Lat: 43-43-09 N Long: 95-44-38 W
Pop: 400 (1990); 473 (1980) Pop Density: 11.1
Land: 36.1 sq. mi.; Water: 0.0 sq. mi.

Westside Township
Lat: 43-37-42 N Long: 95-59-29 W
Pop: 292 (1990); 306 (1980) Pop Density: 8.2
Land: 35.4 sq. mi.; Water: 0.0 sq. mi.

Wilmont City
ZIP: 56185 Lat: 43-45-50 N Long: 95-49-41 W
Pop: 351 (1990); 380 (1980) Pop Density: 319.1
Land: 1.1 sq. mi.; Water: 0.0 sq. mi.
Name origin: For Wilmont Township.

*Wilmont Township
ZIP: 56185 Lat: 43-48-26 N Long: 95-51-44 W
Pop: 263 (1990); 339 (1980) Pop Density: 7.4
Land: 35.6 sq. mi.; Water: 0.0 sq. mi.

Worthington City
ZIP: 56187 Lat: 43-37-37 N Long: 95-35-54 W
Pop: 9,977 (1990); 10,243 (1980) Pop Density: 1425.3
Land: 7.0 sq. mi.; Water: 1.4 sq. mi.
Founded 1872.
Name origin: For the prominent Worthington family of OH.

*Worthington Township
ZIP: 56187 Lat: 43-38-03 N Long: 95-38-36 W
Pop: 331 (1990); 433 (1980) Pop Density: 11.5
Land: 28.8 sq. mi.; Water: 0.0 sq. mi.

Norman County
County Seat: Ada (ZIP: 56510)

Pop: 7,975 (1990); 9,379 (1980)
Land: 876.3 sq. mi.; **Water:** 0.6 sq. mi.
Pop Density: 9.1
Area Code: 218

On the northwestern border of MN, north of Fargo, ND; established Feb 17, 1881 from Polk County.

Name origin: For the many Norwegians, known locally as Normans (Norsemen), living in the area and serving in the state legislature when the county was formed.

Ada
City
ZIP: 56510 **Lat:** 47-17-58 N **Long:** 96-30-50 W
Pop: 1,708 (1990); 1,971 (1980) **Pop Density:** 1423.3
Land: 1.2 sq. mi.; **Water:** 0.0 sq. mi. **Elev:** 907 ft.
Name origin: For the daughter of railroad superintendent William H. Fisher.

Anthony
Township
Lat: 47-22-05 N **Long:** 96-38-01 W
Pop: 113 (1990); 148 (1980) **Pop Density:** 3.1
Land: 36.0 sq. mi.; **Water:** 0.0 sq. mi.

Bear Park
Township
Lat: 47-27-19 N **Long:** 96-07-57 W
Pop: 223 (1990); 312 (1980) **Pop Density:** 6.2
Land: 36.2 sq. mi.; **Water:** 0.1 sq. mi.

Borup
City
ZIP: 56519 **Lat:** 47-10-50 N **Long:** 96-30-21 W
Pop: 119 (1990); 160 (1980) **Pop Density:** 595.0
Land: 0.2 sq. mi.; **Water:** 0.0 sq. mi. **Elev:** 912 ft.

Flom
Township
Lat: 47-11-55 N **Long:** 96-08-04 W
Pop: 250 (1990); 286 (1980) **Pop Density:** 6.9
Land: 36.0 sq. mi.; **Water:** 0.1 sq. mi.

Fossum
Township
ZIP: 56584 **Lat:** 47-16-49 N **Long:** 96-08-16 W
Pop: 195 (1990); 216 (1980) **Pop Density:** 5.4
Land: 36.0 sq. mi.; **Water:** 0.0 sq. mi.

Gary
City
ZIP: 56545 **Lat:** 47-22-22 N **Long:** 96-15-54 W
Pop: 200 (1990); 241 (1980) **Pop Density:** 666.7
Land: 0.3 sq. mi.; **Water:** 0.0 sq. mi.

Good Hope
Township
Lat: 47-26-54 N **Long:** 96-38-40 W
Pop: 72 (1990); 95 (1980) **Pop Density:** 2.0
Land: 36.1 sq. mi.; **Water:** 0.0 sq. mi.

Green Meadow
Township
Lat: 47-21-32 N **Long:** 96-23-35 W
Pop: 148 (1990); 159 (1980) **Pop Density:** 4.0
Land: 36.6 sq. mi.; **Water:** 0.0 sq. mi.

Halstad
City
ZIP: 56548 **Lat:** 47-21-04 N **Long:** 96-49-26 W
Pop: 611 (1990); 690 (1980) **Pop Density:** 2036.7
Land: 0.3 sq. mi.; **Water:** 0.0 sq. mi. **Elev:** 872 ft.
City and township not coextensive.
Name origin: For early pioneer farmer, Ole Halstad, who emigrated from Norway.

*Halstad
Township
ZIP: 56548 **Lat:** 47-22-18 N **Long:** 96-46-56 W
Pop: 174 (1990); 217 (1980) **Pop Density:** 4.6
Land: 37.9 sq. mi.; **Water:** 0.0 sq. mi.

Hegne
Township
Lat: 47-16-45 N **Long:** 96-37-18 W
Pop: 71 (1990); 101 (1980) **Pop Density:** 2.0
Land: 35.6 sq. mi.; **Water:** 0.0 sq. mi.

Hendrum
City
ZIP: 56550 **Lat:** 47-15-49 N **Long:** 96-48-36 W
Pop: 309 (1990); 336 (1980) **Pop Density:** 1545.0
Land: 0.2 sq. mi.; **Water:** 0.0 sq. mi.
City and township not coextensive.
Name origin: Named by Norwegian emigrant farmers for a district in Norway.

*Hendrum
Township
ZIP: 56550 **Lat:** 47-17-17 N **Long:** 96-45-41 W
Pop: 158 (1990); 162 (1980) **Pop Density:** 3.8
Land: 42.0 sq. mi.; **Water:** 0.1 sq. mi.

Home Lake
Township
Lat: 47-11-42 N **Long:** 96-15-29 W
Pop: 192 (1990); 234 (1980) **Pop Density:** 5.3
Land: 35.9 sq. mi.; **Water:** 0.2 sq. mi.

Lake Ida
Township
Lat: 47-17-07 N **Long:** 96-22-56 W
Pop: 176 (1990); 209 (1980) **Pop Density:** 5.4
Land: 32.3 sq. mi.; **Water:** 0.0 sq. mi.

Lee
Township
Lat: 47-12-02 N **Long:** 96-45-20 W
Pop: 171 (1990); 203 (1980) **Pop Density:** 4.3
Land: 39.7 sq. mi.; **Water:** 0.0 sq. mi.

Lockhart
Township
Lat: 47-27-46 N **Long:** 96-31-33 W
Pop: 83 (1990); 115 (1980) **Pop Density:** 2.3
Land: 36.3 sq. mi.; **Water:** 0.0 sq. mi.

Mary
Township
Lat: 47-11-40 N **Long:** 96-37-44 W
Pop: 134 (1990); 148 (1980) **Pop Density:** 3.8
Land: 35.4 sq. mi.; **Water:** 0.0 sq. mi.

McDonaldsville
Township
Lat: 47-17-13 N **Long:** 96-29-50 W
Pop: 260 (1990); 255 (1980) **Pop Density:** 7.4
Land: 35.0 sq. mi.; **Water:** 0.0 sq. mi.

Perley
City
ZIP: 56574 **Lat:** 47-10-35 N **Long:** 96-48-01 W
Pop: 132 (1990); 134 (1980) **Pop Density:** 660.0
Land: 0.2 sq. mi.; **Water:** 0.0 sq. mi.
Name origin: For MN lawyer and state representative George Perley.

Pleasant View
Township
Lat: 47-21-53 N **Long:** 96-31-28 W
Pop: 136 (1990); 180 (1980) **Pop Density:** 3.8
Land: 36.2 sq. mi.; **Water:** 0.0 sq. mi.

Rockwell Township
Lat: 47-11-28 N Long: 96-23-46 W
Pop: 105 (1990); 124 (1980)   **Pop Density:** 3.3
Land: 32.3 sq. mi.; **Water:** 0.0 sq. mi.

Shelly City
ZIP: 56581   Lat: 47-27-27 N Long: 96-49-12 W
Pop: 225 (1990); 276 (1980)   **Pop Density:** 750.0
Land: 0.3 sq. mi.; **Water:** 0.0 sq. mi.
City and township not coextensive.

*****Shelly** Township
ZIP: 56581   Lat: 47-27-27 N Long: 96-47-13 W
Pop: 148 (1990); 210 (1980)   **Pop Density:** 3.5
Land: 42.1 sq. mi.; **Water:** 0.0 sq. mi.

Spring Creek Township
Lat: 47-27-48 N Long: 96-23-12 W
Pop: 94 (1990); 126 (1980)   **Pop Density:** 2.6
Land: 36.0 sq. mi.; **Water:** 0.1 sq. mi.

Strand Township
Lat: 47-22-35 N Long: 96-15-13 W
Pop: 148 (1990); 212 (1980)   **Pop Density:** 4.1
Land: 36.0 sq. mi.; **Water:** 0.0 sq. mi.

Sundal Township
Lat: 47-26-57 N Long: 96-15-54 W
Pop: 184 (1990); 231 (1980)   **Pop Density:** 5.2
Land: 35.7 sq. mi.; **Water:** 0.0 sq. mi.

Twin Valley City
ZIP: 56584   Lat: 47-15-27 N Long: 96-15-30 W
Pop: 821 (1990); 907 (1980)   **Pop Density:** 912.2
Land: 0.9 sq. mi.; **Water:** 0.0 sq. mi.
Name origin: For the town's location between the Wild Rice River and a tributary creek.

Waukon Township
Lat: 47-22-10 N Long: 96-08-06 W
Pop: 170 (1990); 231 (1980)   **Pop Density:** 4.7
Land: 36.2 sq. mi.; **Water:** 0.0 sq. mi.

Wild Rice Township
Lat: 47-16-35 N Long: 96-15-21 W
Pop: 369 (1990); 376 (1980)   **Pop Density:** 10.5
Land: 35.3 sq. mi.; **Water:** 0.0 sq. mi.

Winchester Township
Lat: 47-11-53 N Long: 96-30-13 W
Pop: 76 (1990); 114 (1980)   **Pop Density:** 2.1
Land: 35.9 sq. mi.; **Water:** 0.0 sq. mi.

Olmsted County
County Seat: Rochester (ZIP: 55902)

Pop: 106,470 (1990); 92,006 (1980)   **Pop Density:** 163.0
Land: 653.0 sq. mi.; **Water:** 1.5 sq. mi.   **Area Code:** 507
In southeastern MN, southeast of Mankato; established Feb 20, 1855 (prior to statehood) from unorganized lands.
Name origin: For David Olmsted (1822–61), president of the first MN territorial legislature (1849–50) and first mayor of St. Paul. Some claim S. Baldwin Olmstead (1810–78), a member of the territorial council (1854–55) when the county was formed.

Byron City
ZIP: 55920   Lat: 44-02-00 N Long: 92-38-45 W
Pop: 2,441 (1990); 1,715 (1980)   **Pop Density:** 1877.7
Land: 1.3 sq. mi.; **Water:** 0.0 sq. mi.   **Elev:** 1262 ft.
Incorporated 1873.
Name origin: For Port Byron, NY, former hometown of a prominent businessman.

Cascade Township
Lat: 44-04-51 N Long: 92-30-48 W
Pop: 3,128 (1990); 2,384 (1980)   **Pop Density:** 146.9
Land: 21.3 sq. mi.; **Water:** 0.1 sq. mi.

Chatfield City
ZIP: 55923   Lat: 43-51-07 N Long: 92-11-16 W
Pop: 977 (1990); 895 (1980)   **Pop Density:** 1395.7
Land: 0.7 sq. mi.; **Water:** 0.0 sq. mi.
Part of the town is also in Fillmore County.
Name origin: Named 1858 for Judge Andrew Chatfield, who presided over the first court held in the county.

Dover City
ZIP: 55929   Lat: 43-58-11 N Long: 92-08-01 W
Pop: 416 (1990); 312 (1980)   **Pop Density:** 378.2
Land: 1.1 sq. mi.; **Water:** 0.0 sq. mi.
City and township not coextensive.
Name origin: Named by early settlers for their former home, Dover, NH.

*****Dover** Township
ZIP: 55929   Lat: 43-58-39 N Long: 92-08-11 W
Pop: 464 (1990); 491 (1980)   **Pop Density:** 13.4
Land: 34.6 sq. mi.; **Water:** 0.0 sq. mi.

Elmira Township
Lat: 43-53-05 N Long: 92-08-17 W
Pop: 346 (1990); 408 (1980)   **Pop Density:** 9.9
Land: 35.1 sq. mi.; **Water:** 0.0 sq. mi.

Eyota City
ZIP: 55934   Lat: 43-59-15 N Long: 92-13-41 W
Pop: 1,448 (1990); 1,244 (1980)   **Pop Density:** 1206.7
Land: 1.2 sq. mi.; **Water:** 0.0 sq. mi.   **Elev:** 1241 ft.
City and township not coextensive.
Name origin: From Dakota or Sioux Indian 'superior' or 'best.' Originally called Springfield.

MINNESOTA, Olmsted County

*Eyota
Township
ZIP: 55934   Lat: 43-58-31 N   Long: 92-15-53 W
Pop: 527 (1990); 523 (1980)   Pop Density: 15.3
Land: 34.5 sq. mi.; Water: 0.0 sq. mi.

Farmington
Township
Lat: 44-09-04 N   Long: 92-22-10 W
Pop: 571 (1990); 626 (1980)   Pop Density: 15.9
Land: 35.8 sq. mi.; Water: 0.0 sq. mi.

Haverhill
Township
Lat: 44-03-51 N   Long: 92-22-04 W
Pop: 1,467 (1990); 1,295 (1980)   Pop Density: 42.3
Land: 34.7 sq. mi.; Water: 0.0 sq. mi.

High Forest
Township
ZIP: 55976   Lat: 43-53-16 N   Long: 92-31-04 W
Pop: 964 (1990); 1,545 (1980)   Pop Density: 22.0
Land: 43.9 sq. mi.; Water: 0.1 sq. mi.

Kalmar
Township
Lat: 44-03-41 N   Long: 92-37-23 W
Pop: 1,271 (1990); 1,209 (1980)   Pop Density: 37.1
Land: 34.3 sq. mi.; Water: 0.0 sq. mi.

Marion
Township
Lat: 43-58-12 N   Long: 92-22-45 W
Pop: 5,960 (1990); 5,299 (1980)   Pop Density: 172.8
Land: 34.5 sq. mi.; Water: 0.0 sq. mi.

New Haven
Township
Lat: 44-09-30 N   Long: 92-37-03 W
Pop: 1,201 (1990); 1,131 (1980)   Pop Density: 33.5
Land: 35.9 sq. mi.; Water: 0.0 sq. mi.

Orion
Township
Lat: 43-53-33 N   Long: 92-16-08 W
Pop: 616 (1990); 602 (1980)   Pop Density: 17.3
Land: 35.7 sq. mi.; Water: 0.0 sq. mi.

Oronoco
City
ZIP: 55960   Lat: 44-09-48 N   Long: 92-32-27 W
Pop: 727 (1990); 574 (1980)   Pop Density: 403.9
Land: 1.8 sq. mi.; Water: 0.3 sq. mi.

Settled 1850s. City and township not coextensive.
Name origin: Named by Dr. Hector Galloway for the Orinoco River in South America, with a spelling variation. An allusion to the water power of the Middle Branch of the Zumbro River, which flows through the town.

*Oronoco
Township
ZIP: 55960   Lat: 44-08-54 N   Long: 92-29-45 W
Pop: 2,026 (1990); 1,696 (1980)   Pop Density: 62.1
Land: 32.6 sq. mi.; Water: 0.8 sq. mi.

Pine Island
City
ZIP: 55963   Lat: 44-11-43 N   Long: 92-38-44 W
Pop: 0 (1990); 9 (1980)
Land: 0.001 sq. mi.; Water: 0.0 sq. mi.

Settled 1854. Part of the town is also in Goodhue County.
Name origin: From an Indian term referring to a secure winter camp ground sheltered by the island's pines.

Pleasant Grove
Township
ZIP: 55976   Lat: 43-53-09 N   Long: 92-22-51 W
Pop: 741 (1990); 776 (1980)   Pop Density: 20.8
Land: 35.7 sq. mi.; Water: 0.0 sq. mi.

Quincy
Township
Lat: 44-03-51 N   Long: 92-08-46 W
Pop: 385 (1990); 435 (1980)   Pop Density: 10.8
Land: 35.7 sq. mi.; Water: 0.0 sq. mi.

Rochester
City
ZIP: 55901   Lat: 44-00-49 N   Long: 92-28-32 W
Pop: 70,745 (1990); 57,906 (1980)   Pop Density: 2398.1
Land: 29.5 sq. mi.; Water: 0.1 sq. mi.

In southeastern MN, 70 mi. southeast of St. Paul. Incorporated 1858.
Name origin: For Rochester, NY.

*Rochester
Township
Lat: 43-58-27 N   Long: 92-30-06 W
Pop: 3,226 (1990); 4,582 (1980)   Pop Density: 133.9
Land: 24.1 sq. mi.; Water: 0.0 sq. mi.

Rock Dell
Township
Lat: 43-53-56 N   Long: 92-36-29 W
Pop: 643 (1990); 706 (1980)   Pop Density: 17.9
Land: 36.0 sq. mi.; Water: 0.0 sq. mi.

Salem
Township
Lat: 43-58-39 N   Long: 92-36-45 W
Pop: 1,056 (1990); 1,133 (1980)   Pop Density: 29.6
Land: 35.7 sq. mi.; Water: 0.0 sq. mi.

Stewartville
City
ZIP: 55976   Lat: 43-51-26 N   Long: 92-29-13 W
Pop: 4,520 (1990); 3,925 (1980)   Pop Density: 2658.8
Land: 1.7 sq. mi.; Water: 0.0 sq. mi.   Elev: 1240 ft.

Name origin: For Charles Stewart, who built a mill here in 1858.

Viola
Township
Lat: 44-03-47 N   Long: 92-15-57 W
Pop: 604 (1990); 574 (1980)   Pop Density: 16.9
Land: 35.8 sq. mi.; Water: 0.0 sq. mi.

American Places Dictionary   MINNESOTA, Otter Tail County

> ### Otter Tail County
> **County Seat: Fergus Falls (ZIP: 56537)**
>
> **Pop:** 50,714 (1990); 51,937 (1980) **Pop Density:** 25.6
> **Land:** 1979.8 sq. mi.; **Water:** 245.2 sq. mi. **Area Code:** 218
> In west-central MN, southeast of Fargo, ND; established Mar 18, 1858 from Pembina and Cass counties.
> **Name origin:** For Otter Tail lake and river. The lake was named by the Ojibway *nigigwanowe*, 'otter tail,' referring to the shape of the lake.

Aastad Township
Lat: 46-09-03 N Long: 96-04-56 W
Pop: 236 (1990); 263 (1980) **Pop Density:** 6.8
Land: 34.5 sq. mi.; **Water:** 0.9 sq. mi.

Amor Township
ZIP: 56515 Lat: 46-24-28 N Long: 95-42-48 W
Pop: 422 (1990); 510 (1980) **Pop Density:** 18.2
Land: 23.2 sq. mi.; **Water:** 12.0 sq. mi.

Aurdal Township
Lat: 46-19-32 N Long: 95-58-40 W
Pop: 1,310 (1990); 1,268 (1980) **Pop Density:** 40.4
Land: 32.4 sq. mi.; **Water:** 3.1 sq. mi.

Battle Lake City
ZIP: 56515 Lat: 46-17-19 N Long: 95-42-54 W
Pop: 698 (1990); 708 (1980) **Pop Density:** 698.0
Land: 1.0 sq. mi.; **Water:** 0.0 sq. mi. **Elev:** 1372 ft.
Name origin: For its location at the western end of West Battle Lake, itself named for a battle about 1795 between the Ojibway and Sioux.

Blowers Township
Lat: 46-35-24 N Long: 95-12-57 W
Pop: 325 (1990); 401 (1980) **Pop Density:** 9.1
Land: 35.7 sq. mi.; **Water:** 0.0 sq. mi.

Bluffton City
ZIP: 56518 Lat: 46-28-09 N Long: 95-14-00 W
Pop: 187 (1990); 206 (1980) **Pop Density:** 66.8
Land: 2.8 sq. mi.; **Water:** 0.0 sq. mi.

***Bluffton** Township
ZIP: 56518 Lat: 46-30-11 N Long: 95-13-21 W
Pop: 436 (1990); 553 (1980) **Pop Density:** 13.2
Land: 33.0 sq. mi.; **Water:** 0.0 sq. mi.

Buse Township
Lat: 46-14-30 N Long: 96-04-37 W
Pop: 602 (1990); 608 (1980) **Pop Density:** 21.1
Land: 28.5 sq. mi.; **Water:** 2.4 sq. mi.

Butler Township
ZIP: 56567 Lat: 46-40-23 N Long: 95-21-05 W
Pop: 281 (1990); 286 (1980) **Pop Density:** 8.0
Land: 35.1 sq. mi.; **Water:** 0.8 sq. mi.

Candor Township
Lat: 46-40-08 N Long: 95-51-37 W
Pop: 424 (1990); 375 (1980) **Pop Density:** 13.9
Land: 30.6 sq. mi.; **Water:** 3.9 sq. mi.

Carlisle Township
Lat: 46-19-33 N Long: 96-12-25 W
Pop: 242 (1990); 208 (1980) **Pop Density:** 6.9
Land: 35.3 sq. mi.; **Water:** 0.8 sq. mi.

Clitherall City
ZIP: 56524 Lat: 46-16-27 N Long: 95-37-46 W
Pop: 109 (1990); 121 (1980) **Pop Density:** 545.0
Land: 0.2 sq. mi.; **Water:** 0.0 sq. mi. **Elev:** 1348 ft.
Name origin: For Maj. George Clitherall, who ran the U.S. Land Office in Otter Tail City in the late 1850s.

***Clitherall** Township
ZIP: 56524 Lat: 46-14-43 N Long: 95-42-38 W
Pop: 437 (1990); 488 (1980) **Pop Density:** 14.9
Land: 29.4 sq. mi.; **Water:** 6.3 sq. mi.

Compton Township
Lat: 46-24-35 N Long: 95-12-52 W
Pop: 758 (1990); 776 (1980) **Pop Density:** 21.2
Land: 35.7 sq. mi.; **Water:** 0.0 sq. mi.

Corliss Township
Lat: 46-39-47 N Long: 95-28-35 W
Pop: 415 (1990); 414 (1980) **Pop Density:** 11.9
Land: 35.0 sq. mi.; **Water:** 1.8 sq. mi.

Dalton City
ZIP: 56324 Lat: 46-10-24 N Long: 95-54-58 W
Pop: 234 (1990); 248 (1980) **Pop Density:** 1170.0
Land: 0.2 sq. mi.; **Water:** 0.0 sq. mi.
Founded 1880s.
Name origin: For Ole C. Dahl, who was the original landowner.

Dane Prairie Township
Lat: 46-13-58 N Long: 95-57-08 W
Pop: 872 (1990); 768 (1980) **Pop Density:** 27.9
Land: 31.2 sq. mi.; **Water:** 4.5 sq. mi.

Dead Lake Township
Lat: 46-29-56 N Long: 95-43-08 W
Pop: 338 (1990); 398 (1980) **Pop Density:** 13.7
Land: 24.7 sq. mi.; **Water:** 10.4 sq. mi.

Deer Creek City
ZIP: 56527 Lat: 46-23-28 N Long: 95-19-19 W
Pop: 303 (1990); 392 (1980) **Pop Density:** 75.8
Land: 4.0 sq. mi.; **Water:** 0.0 sq. mi. **Elev:** 1393 ft.
City and township not coexistent.
Name origin: For Deer Creek, which flows through the town.

***Deer Creek** Township
ZIP: 56527 Lat: 46-25-08 N Long: 95-20-33 W
Pop: 348 (1990); 372 (1980) **Pop Density:** 10.8
Land: 32.3 sq. mi.; **Water:** 0.2 sq. mi.

Dent   City
ZIP: 56528   **Lat:** 46-33-07 N **Long:** 95-43-01 W
Pop: 177 (1990); 167 (1980)   **Pop Density:** 590.0
Land: 0.3 sq. mi.; **Water:** 0.0 sq. mi.
Founded 1904.
Name origin: For a local railroad official.

Dora   Township
                   Lat: 46-35-11 N **Long:** 95-50-40 W
Pop: 494 (1990); 525 (1980)   **Pop Density:** 17.1
Land: 28.9 sq. mi.; **Water:** 6.9 sq. mi.

Dunn   Township
                   Lat: 46-40-21 N **Long:** 95-59-25 W
Pop: 602 (1990); 594 (1980)   **Pop Density:** 23.0
Land: 26.2 sq. mi.; **Water:** 10.4 sq. mi.

Eagle Lake   Township
ZIP: 56324   **Lat:** 46-08-35 N **Long:** 95-42-25 W
Pop: 326 (1990); 361 (1980)   **Pop Density:** 10.2
Land: 31.9 sq. mi.; **Water:** 4.2 sq. mi.

Eastern   Township
ZIP: 56361   **Lat:** 46-08-49 N **Long:** 95-12-13 W
Pop: 262 (1990); 341 (1980)   **Pop Density:** 7.4
Land: 35.3 sq. mi.; **Water:** 1.2 sq. mi.

Edna   Township
                   Lat: 46-35-11 N **Long:** 95-43-21 W
Pop: 725 (1990); 624 (1980)   **Pop Density:** 27.7
Land: 26.2 sq. mi.; **Water:** 8.5 sq. mi.

Effington   Township
ZIP: 56361   **Lat:** 46-09-26 N **Long:** 95-27-50 W
Pop: 304 (1990); 330 (1980)   **Pop Density:** 9.2
Land: 33.0 sq. mi.; **Water:** 2.0 sq. mi.

Elizabeth   City
ZIP: 56533   **Lat:** 46-22-45 N **Long:** 96-07-49 W
Pop: 152 (1990); 195 (1980)   **Pop Density:** 380.0
Land: 0.4 sq. mi.; **Water:** 0.0 sq. mi.
Founded 1870. City and township not coextensive.
Name origin: For the wife of merchant Rudolph Niggler.

*Elizabeth   Township
                   Lat: 46-24-51 N **Long:** 96-05-08 W
Pop: 590 (1990); 581 (1980)   **Pop Density:** 18.6
Land: 31.8 sq. mi.; **Water:** 3.8 sq. mi.

Elmo   Township
                   Lat: 46-14-00 N **Long:** 95-20-29 W
Pop: 330 (1990); 394 (1980)   **Pop Density:** 9.1
Land: 36.3 sq. mi.; **Water:** 0.5 sq. mi.

Erhard   City
ZIP: 56534   **Lat:** 46-29-02 N **Long:** 96-05-49 W
Pop: 181 (1990); 194 (1980)   **Pop Density:** 362.0
Land: 0.5 sq. mi.; **Water:** 0.0 sq. mi.
Name origin: For Alexander Erhard whose house served as the site of the town's organizational meeting and first election.

Erhards Grove   Township
                   Lat: 46-29-56 N **Long:** 96-05-28 W
Pop: 406 (1990); 406 (1980)   **Pop Density:** 12.2
Land: 33.3 sq. mi.; **Water:** 1.7 sq. mi.

Everts   Township
                   Lat: 46-19-46 N **Long:** 95-42-27 W
Pop: 586 (1990); 539 (1980)   **Pop Density:** 25.2
Land: 23.3 sq. mi.; **Water:** 11.3 sq. mi.

Fergus Falls   City
ZIP: 56537   **Lat:** 46-16-55 N **Long:** 96-04-03 W
Pop: 12,362 (1990); 12,519 (1980)   **Pop Density:** 1274.4
Land: 9.7 sq. mi.; **Water:** 0.9 sq. mi.
In west-central MN, 50 mi. southeast of Fargo, ND.
Name origin: For James Fergus, who organized and financed the original settlement of the town, which is located on the falls of the Red River.

*Fergus Falls   Township
                   Lat: 46-19-59 N **Long:** 96-06-07 W
Pop: 1,205 (1990); 1,161 (1980)   **Pop Density:** 40.6
Land: 29.7 sq. mi.; **Water:** 0.8 sq. mi.

Folden   Township
                   Lat: 46-14-14 N **Long:** 95-28-22 W
Pop: 258 (1990); 321 (1980)   **Pop Density:** 7.5
Land: 34.5 sq. mi.; **Water:** 1.1 sq. mi.

Friberg   Township
                   Lat: 46-24-41 N **Long:** 95-58-11 W
Pop: 650 (1990); 667 (1980)   **Pop Density:** 19.9
Land: 32.7 sq. mi.; **Water:** 3.0 sq. mi.

Girard   Township
                   Lat: 46-19-29 N **Long:** 95-34-56 W
Pop: 555 (1990); 563 (1980)   **Pop Density:** 21.6
Land: 25.7 sq. mi.; **Water:** 10.0 sq. mi.

Gorman   Township
                   Lat: 46-40-47 N **Long:** 95-35-43 W
Pop: 389 (1990); 445 (1980)   **Pop Density:** 12.0
Land: 32.5 sq. mi.; **Water:** 3.2 sq. mi.

Henning   City
ZIP: 56551   **Lat:** 46-19-20 N **Long:** 95-26-34 W
Pop: 738 (1990); 832 (1980)   **Pop Density:** 263.6
Land: 2.8 sq. mi.; **Water:** 0.0 sq. mi.
Founded 1878. City and township not coextensive.
Name origin: Named in 1884 for John O. Henning, the town druggist.

*Henning   Township
ZIP: 56551   **Lat:** 46-19-33 N **Long:** 95-28-05 W
Pop: 376 (1990); 394 (1980)   **Pop Density:** 11.4
Land: 32.9 sq. mi.; **Water:** 0.3 sq. mi.

Hobart   Township
                   Lat: 46-40-25 N **Long:** 95-43-25 W
Pop: 627 (1990); 625 (1980)   **Pop Density:** 21.8
Land: 28.8 sq. mi.; **Water:** 7.2 sq. mi.

Homestead   Township
                   Lat: 46-35-36 N **Long:** 95-20-53 W
Pop: 338 (1990); 374 (1980)   **Pop Density:** 9.3
Land: 36.4 sq. mi.; **Water:** 0.2 sq. mi.

Inman   Township
                   Lat: 46-19-07 N **Long:** 95-21-09 W
Pop: 278 (1990); 370 (1980)   **Pop Density:** 7.6
Land: 36.6 sq. mi.; **Water:** 0.0 sq. mi.

Leaf Lake   Township
                   Lat: 46-24-44 N **Long:** 95-28-12 W
Pop: 404 (1990); 481 (1980)   **Pop Density:** 12.3
Land: 32.8 sq. mi.; **Water:** 2.8 sq. mi.

Leaf Mountain   Township
ZIP: 56361   **Lat:** 46-09-30 N **Long:** 95-35-18 W
Pop: 301 (1990); 354 (1980)   **Pop Density:** 9.4
Land: 31.9 sq. mi.; **Water:** 4.1 sq. mi.

Lida Township
Lat: 46-34-42 N Long: 95-57-58 W
Pop: 529 (1990); 526 (1980) Pop Density: 25.7
Land: 20.6 sq. mi.; Water: 15.0 sq. mi.

Maine Township
ZIP: 56586 Lat: 46-25-09 N Long: 95-50-24 W
Pop: 572 (1990); 601 (1980) Pop Density: 19.0
Land: 30.1 sq. mi.; Water: 5.8 sq. mi.

Maplewood Township
Lat: 46-30-06 N Long: 95-57-50 W
Pop: 259 (1990); 294 (1980) Pop Density: 8.1
Land: 32.0 sq. mi.; Water: 3.6 sq. mi.

Newton Township
Lat: 46-29-50 N Long: 95-21-09 W
Pop: 738 (1990); 831 (1980) Pop Density: 21.0
Land: 35.1 sq. mi.; Water: 0.3 sq. mi.

New York Mills City
ZIP: 56567 Lat: 46-31-10 N Long: 95-22-27 W
Pop: 940 (1990); 972 (1980) Pop Density: 854.5
Land: 1.1 sq. mi.; Water: 0.0 sq. mi.

Nidaros Township
Lat: 46-14-04 N Long: 95-34-38 W
Pop: 270 (1990); 253 (1980) Pop Density: 8.7
Land: 30.9 sq. mi.; Water: 3.6 sq. mi.

Norwegian Grove Township
Lat: 46-35-23 N Long: 96-13-11 W
Pop: 339 (1990); 388 (1980) Pop Density: 10.1
Land: 33.6 sq. mi.; Water: 2.1 sq. mi.

Oak Valley Township
Lat: 46-19-21 N Long: 95-12-46 W
Pop: 378 (1990); 444 (1980) Pop Density: 10.6
Land: 35.7 sq. mi.; Water: 0.0 sq. mi.

Orwell Township
Lat: 46-13-54 N Long: 96-11-38 W
Pop: 164 (1990); 208 (1980) Pop Density: 4.8
Land: 33.9 sq. mi.; Water: 1.5 sq. mi.

Oscar Township
Lat: 46-24-34 N Long: 96-13-29 W
Pop: 213 (1990); 266 (1980) Pop Density: 6.2
Land: 34.6 sq. mi.; Water: 1.4 sq. mi.

Ottertail City
ZIP: 56571 Lat: 46-25-42 N Long: 95-33-31 W
Pop: 313 (1990); 239 (1980) Pop Density: 71.1
Land: 4.4 sq. mi.; Water: 0.8 sq. mi.
City and township not coextensive.
Name origin: For Ottertail Lake, which had a long narrow sand bar in it resembling an otter's tail.

Otter Tail Township
Lat: 46-24-36 N Long: 95-35-35 W
Pop: 363 (1990); 291 (1980) Pop Density: 22.1
Land: 16.4 sq. mi.; Water: 14.1 sq. mi.

Otto Township
Lat: 46-29-31 N Long: 95-27-36 W
Pop: 456 (1990); 503 (1980) Pop Density: 14.6
Land: 31.3 sq. mi.; Water: 4.4 sq. mi.

Paddock Township
Lat: 46-39-50 N Long: 95-13-03 W
Pop: 368 (1990); 402 (1980) Pop Density: 10.3
Land: 35.7 sq. mi.; Water: 0.1 sq. mi.

Parkers Prairie City
ZIP: 56361 Lat: 46-09-13 N Long: 95-19-45 W
Pop: 956 (1990); 917 (1980) Pop Density: 869.1
Land: 1.1 sq. mi.; Water: 0.0 sq. mi. Elev: 1464 ft.
City and township not coextensive.

***Parkers Prairie** Township
ZIP: 56361 Lat: 46-08-48 N Long: 95-19-54 W
Pop: 273 (1990); 364 (1980) Pop Density: 8.3
Land: 32.7 sq. mi.; Water: 2.4 sq. mi.

Pelican Township
Lat: 46-35-27 N Long: 96-06-02 W
Pop: 685 (1990); 593 (1980) Pop Density: 21.8
Land: 31.4 sq. mi.; Water: 2.0 sq. mi.

Pelican Rapids City
ZIP: 56572 Lat: 46-34-14 N Long: 96-05-08 W
Pop: 1,886 (1990); 1,867 (1980) Pop Density: 754.4
Land: 2.5 sq. mi.; Water: 0.0 sq. mi.
Incorporated 1882.
Name origin: For the rapids in the adjacent Pelican River.

Perham City
ZIP: 56573 Lat: 46-35-58 N Long: 95-34-24 W
Pop: 2,075 (1990); 2,086 (1980) Pop Density: 943.2
Land: 2.2 sq. mi.; Water: 0.0 sq. mi.
City and township not coextensive.
Name origin: For Josiah Perham.

***Perham** Township
ZIP: 56573 Lat: 46-34-48 N Long: 95-35-52 W
Pop: 774 (1990); 656 (1980) Pop Density: 24.3
Land: 31.9 sq. mi.; Water: 1.8 sq. mi.

Pine Lake Township
Lat: 46-35-18 N Long: 95-28-16 W
Pop: 513 (1990); 385 (1980) Pop Density: 17.6
Land: 29.2 sq. mi.; Water: 6.6 sq. mi.

Richville City
ZIP: 56576 Lat: 46-30-23 N Long: 95-37-33 W
Pop: 121 (1990); 132 (1980) Pop Density: 121.0
Land: 1.0 sq. mi.; Water: 0.0 sq. mi.

Rothsay City
ZIP: 56579 Lat: 46-28-28 N Long: 96-16-40 W
Pop: 190 (1990); 198 (1980) Pop Density: 1900.0
Land: 0.1 sq. mi.; Water: 0.0 sq. mi. Elev: 1209 ft.
Part of the town is also in Wilkin County.
Name origin: For seaport 30 mi. west of Glasgow, Scotland.

Rush Lake Township
Lat: 46-30-05 N Long: 95-35-33 W
Pop: 777 (1990); 638 (1980) Pop Density: 29.0
Land: 26.8 sq. mi.; Water: 7.9 sq. mi.

St. Olaf Township
Lat: 46-09-14 N Long: 95-49-11 W
Pop: 361 (1990); 345 (1980) Pop Density: 11.2
Land: 32.3 sq. mi.; Water: 3.8 sq. mi.

Scambler Township
Lat: 46-40-46 N Long: 96-06-45 W
Pop: 440 (1990); 433 (1980) Pop Density: 13.7
Land: 32.1 sq. mi.; Water: 4.2 sq. mi.

Star Lake Township
Lat: 46-30-21 N Long: 95-50-28 W
Pop: 330 (1990); 373 (1980) Pop Density: 13.2
Land: 25.0 sq. mi.; Water: 10.7 sq. mi.

Sverdrup
Township
Lat: 46-19-34 N Long: 95-50-23 W
Pop: 624 (1990); 614 (1980) **Pop Density:** 22.0
Land: 28.4 sq. mi.; **Water:** 7.2 sq. mi.

Tordenskjold
Township
Lat: 46-14-15 N Long: 95-50-08 W
Pop: 452 (1990); 477 (1980) **Pop Density:** 14.8
Land: 30.5 sq. mi.; **Water:** 5.6 sq. mi.

Trondhjem
Township
Lat: 46-30-21 N Long: 96-12-38 W
Pop: 168 (1990); 216 (1980) **Pop Density:** 4.8
Land: 35.0 sq. mi.; **Water:** 0.8 sq. mi.

Tumuli
Township
ZIP: 56324 Lat: 46-08-48 N Long: 95-57-29 W
Pop: 384 (1990); 387 (1980) **Pop Density:** 13.5
Land: 28.4 sq. mi.; **Water:** 7.1 sq. mi.

Underwood
City
ZIP: 56586 Lat: 46-17-06 N Long: 95-52-12 W
Pop: 284 (1990); 332 (1980) **Pop Density:** 710.0
Land: 0.4 sq. mi.; **Water:** 0.0 sq. mi.
Name origin: For newspaperman and state representative Adoniram Underwood.

Urbank
City
ZIP: 56361 Lat: 46-07-32 N Long: 95-30-38 W
Pop: 73 (1990); 95 (1980) **Pop Density:** 104.3
Land: 0.7 sq. mi.; **Water:** 0.0 sq. mi. **Elev:** 1477 ft.

Vergas
City
ZIP: 56587 Lat: 46-39-19 N Long: 95-48-13 W
Pop: 287 (1990); 287 (1980) **Pop Density:** 191.3
Land: 1.5 sq. mi.; **Water:** 0.0 sq. mi.

Vining
City
ZIP: 56588 Lat: 46-15-47 N Long: 95-32-01 W
Pop: 84 (1990); 87 (1980) **Pop Density:** 64.6
Land: 1.3 sq. mi.; **Water:** 0.0 sq. mi. **Elev:** 1387 ft.
Name origin: Named by officials of the Northern Pacific Railway for a town in IA.

Wadena
City
ZIP: 56482 Lat: 46-25-55 N Long: 95-09-36 W
Pop: 22 (1990); 4,699 (1980) **Pop Density:** 440.0
Land: 0.05 sq. mi.; **Water:** 0.0 sq. mi.
Part of the town is also in Wadena County.
Name origin: From the Ojibway Indian term meaning 'little round hill.'

Western
Township
Lat: 46-08-59 N Long: 96-12-10 W
Pop: 150 (1990); 194 (1980) **Pop Density:** 4.3
Land: 34.5 sq. mi.; **Water:** 1.2 sq. mi.

Woodside
Township
ZIP: 56361 Lat: 46-13-50 N Long: 95-12-11 W
Pop: 310 (1990); 323 (1980) **Pop Density:** 8.6
Land: 36.2 sq. mi.; **Water:** 0.0 sq. mi.

Pennington County
County Seat: Thief River Falls (ZIP: 56701)

Pop: 13,306 (1990); 15,258 (1980) **Pop Density:** 21.6
Land: 616.6 sq. mi.; **Water:** 1.8 sq. mi. **Area Code:** 218
In northwestern MN, east of Grand Forks, ND; established Nov 23, 1910 from Red Lake County.
Name origin: For Edmund Pennington (1848–1926), president of the St. Paul and Sault Ste. Marie Railroad.

Black River
Township
Lat: 48-00-19 N Long: 96-17-28 W
Pop: 89 (1990); 137 (1980) **Pop Density:** 3.7
Land: 24.0 sq. mi.; **Water:** 0.0 sq. mi.

Bray
Township
Lat: 48-04-28 N Long: 96-26-09 W
Pop: 80 (1990); 95 (1980) **Pop Density:** 2.2
Land: 35.9 sq. mi.; **Water:** 0.2 sq. mi.

Clover Leaf
Township
Lat: 48-08-43 N Long: 95-55-03 W
Pop: 70 (1990); 124 (1980) **Pop Density:** 2.6
Land: 26.9 sq. mi.; **Water:** 0.0 sq. mi.

Deer Park
Township
Lat: 47-59-11 N Long: 95-45-50 W
Pop: 147 (1990); 162 (1980) **Pop Density:** 6.4
Land: 23.0 sq. mi.; **Water:** 0.0 sq. mi.

Goodridge
City
ZIP: 56725 Lat: 48-08-40 N Long: 95-48-14 W
Pop: 115 (1990); 191 (1980) **Pop Density:** 575.0
Land: 0.2 sq. mi.; **Water:** 0.0 sq. mi. **Elev:** 1170 ft.
City and township not coextensive.

*Goodridge
Township
ZIP: 56725 Lat: 48-08-27 N Long: 95-47-53 W
Pop: 63 (1990); 74 (1980) **Pop Density:** 2.4
Land: 26.8 sq. mi.; **Water:** 0.0 sq. mi.

Hickory
Township
Lat: 47-58-41 N Long: 95-39-27 W
Pop: 105 (1990); 130 (1980) **Pop Density:** 3.0
Land: 35.1 sq. mi.; **Water:** 0.0 sq. mi.

Highlanding
Township
Lat: 48-03-23 N Long: 95-47-12 W
Pop: 188 (1990); 228 (1980) **Pop Density:** 5.2
Land: 36.1 sq. mi.; **Water:** 0.0 sq. mi.

Kratka
Township
Lat: 48-03-34 N Long: 95-55-33 W
Pop: 131 (1990); 158 (1980) **Pop Density:** 3.6
Land: 36.1 sq. mi.; **Water:** 0.0 sq. mi.

Mayfield
Township
Lat: 48-00-03 N Long: 95-53-32 W
Pop: 87 (1990); 96 (1980) **Pop Density:** 3.8
Land: 22.8 sq. mi.; **Water:** 0.0 sq. mi.

Norden — Township
Lat: 48-08-07 N Long: 96-18-06 W
Pop: 362 (1990); 388 (1980) Pop Density: 13.1
Land: 27.6 sq. mi.; Water: 0.0 sq. mi.

North — Township
Lat: 48-08-35 N Long: 96-10-25 W
Pop: 669 (1990); 700 (1980) Pop Density: 29.1
Land: 23.0 sq. mi.; Water: 0.4 sq. mi.

Numedal — Township
Lat: 48-08-36 N Long: 96-25-27 W
Pop: 119 (1990); 129 (1980) Pop Density: 4.3
Land: 27.8 sq. mi.; Water: 0.0 sq. mi.

Polk Centre — Township
Lat: 47-59-30 N Long: 96-25-03 W
Pop: 61 (1990); 87 (1980) Pop Density: 2.5
Land: 24.1 sq. mi.; Water: 0.0 sq. mi.

Reiner — Township
Lat: 48-08-11 N Long: 95-39-29 W
Pop: 110 (1990); 134 (1980) Pop Density: 4.1
Land: 27.0 sq. mi.; Water: 0.0 sq. mi.

River Falls — Township
Lat: 47-59-24 N Long: 96-08-52 W
Pop: 225 (1990); 222 (1980) Pop Density: 9.9
Land: 22.7 sq. mi.; Water: 0.0 sq. mi.

Rocksbury — Township
Lat: 48-03-57 N Long: 96-10-40 W
Pop: 1,128 (1990); 1,286 (1980) Pop Density: 32.7
Land: 34.5 sq. mi.; Water: 0.5 sq. mi.

St. Hilaire — City
Lat: 48-00-47 N Long: 96-12-49 W
Pop: 298 (1990); 388 (1980) Pop Density: 372.5
Land: 0.8 sq. mi.; Water: 0.1 sq. mi. Elev: 1089 ft.

Sanders — Township
Lat: 48-03-46 N Long: 96-18-27 W
Pop: 300 (1990); 356 (1980) Pop Density: 8.3
Land: 36.2 sq. mi.; Water: 0.0 sq. mi.

Silverton — Township
Lat: 48-08-05 N Long: 96-02-43 W
Pop: 196 (1990); 209 (1980) Pop Density: 7.4
Land: 26.6 sq. mi.; Water: 0.0 sq. mi.

Smiley — Township
Lat: 48-03-46 N Long: 96-02-43 W
Pop: 451 (1990); 539 (1980) Pop Density: 12.5
Land: 36.0 sq. mi.; Water: 0.2 sq. mi.

Star — Township
Lat: 48-03-51 N Long: 95-40-04 W
Pop: 185 (1990); 193 (1980) Pop Density: 5.1
Land: 36.3 sq. mi.; Water: 0.0 sq. mi.

Thief River Falls — City
ZIP: 56701 Lat: 48-06-48 N Long: 96-10-31 W
Pop: 8,010 (1990); 9,105 (1980) Pop Density: 1780.0
Land: 4.5 sq. mi.; Water: 0.2 sq. mi. Elev: 1133 ft.
Name origin: For the nearby falls in the Thief River.

Wyandotte — Township
Lat: 47-59-07 N Long: 96-02-15 W
Pop: 117 (1990); 127 (1980) Pop Density: 5.2
Land: 22.6 sq. mi.; Water: 0.0 sq. mi.

Pine County
County Seat: Pine City (ZIP: 55063)

Pop: 21,264 (1990); 19,871 (1980) Pop Density: 15.1
Land: 1411.2 sq. mi.; Water: 23.5 sq. mi. Area Code: 612
On the central eastern border of MN, northeast of St. Paul; established Mar 1, 1856 (prior to statehood) from unorganized lands; annexed Buchanan County in 1861.
Name origin: For the extensive forests of red (Norway) and white pine, and possibly for the Pine lakes and river in the county.

Arlone — Township
Lat: 46-01-31 N Long: 92-45-01 W
Pop: 284 (1990); 281 (1980) Pop Density: 7.8
Land: 36.6 sq. mi.; Water: 0.1 sq. mi.

Arna — Township
Lat: 46-06-29 N Long: 92-21-33 W
Pop: 85 (1990); 86 (1980) Pop Density: 2.3
Land: 37.6 sq. mi.; Water: 0.2 sq. mi.

Askov — City
ZIP: 55704 Lat: 46-11-19 N Long: 92-46-53 W
Pop: 343 (1990); 350 (1980) Pop Density: 263.8
Land: 1.3 sq. mi.; Water: 0.0 sq. mi.

Barry — Township
ZIP: 55037 Lat: 46-01-47 N Long: 92-51-59 W
Pop: 527 (1990); 436 (1980) Pop Density: 14.5
Land: 36.4 sq. mi.; Water: 0.3 sq. mi.

Birch Creek — Township
Lat: 46-23-09 N Long: 92-59-28 W
Pop: 230 (1990); 283 (1980) Pop Density: 6.6
Land: 35.1 sq. mi.; Water: 0.0 sq. mi.

Bremen — Township
ZIP: 55735 Lat: 46-17-52 N Long: 92-59-13 W
Pop: 147 (1990); 169 (1980) Pop Density: 4.1
Land: 36.0 sq. mi.; Water: 0.2 sq. mi.

Brook Park — City
ZIP: 55007 Lat: 45-56-56 N Long: 93-04-23 W
Pop: 125 (1990); 93 (1980) Pop Density: 125.0
Land: 1.0 sq. mi.; Water: 0.0 sq. mi.
City and township not coextensive.

*Brook Park — Township
ZIP: 55007 Lat: 45-56-44 N Long: 93-05-09 W
Pop: 373 (1990); 362 (1980) Pop Density: 12.4
Land: 30.1 sq. mi.; Water: 0.0 sq. mi.

MINNESOTA, Pine County

Bruno
City
ZIP: 55712 Lat: 46-16-49 N Long: 92-40-03 W
Pop: 89 (1990); 130 (1980) Pop Density: 89.0
Land: 1.0 sq. mi.; Water: 0.0 sq. mi. Elev: 1151 ft.
City and township not coextensive.

*Bruno
Township
ZIP: 55712 Lat: 46-16-54 N Long: 92-36-51 W
Pop: 138 (1990); 134 (1980) Pop Density: 4.0
Land: 34.9 sq. mi.; Water: 0.0 sq. mi.

Chengwatana
Township
ZIP: 55063 Lat: 45-51-55 N Long: 92-49-36 W
Pop: 597 (1990); 557 (1980) Pop Density: 13.1
Land: 45.7 sq. mi.; Water: 1.5 sq. mi.

Clover
Township
Lat: 46-01-45 N Long: 92-36-36 W
Pop: 163 (1990); 151 (1980) Pop Density: 4.5
Land: 35.9 sq. mi.; Water: 0.2 sq. mi.

Crosby
Township
ZIP: 55037 Lat: 45-56-45 N Long: 92-40-26 W
Pop: 71 (1990); 86 (1980) Pop Density: 1.6
Land: 43.5 sq. mi.; Water: 0.8 sq. mi.

Danforth
Township
ZIP: 55072 Lat: 46-06-32 N Long: 92-36-14 W
Pop: 65 (1990); 67 (1980) Pop Density: 1.8
Land: 36.3 sq. mi.; Water: 0.0 sq. mi.

Dell Grove
Township
ZIP: 55072 Lat: 46-06-49 N Long: 92-58-18 W
Pop: 600 (1990); 550 (1980) Pop Density: 14.5
Land: 41.3 sq. mi.; Water: 1.1 sq. mi.

Denham
City
ZIP: 55728 Lat: 46-21-44 N Long: 92-56-37 W
Pop: 36 (1990); 48 (1980) Pop Density: 27.7
Land: 1.3 sq. mi.; Water: 0.0 sq. mi. Elev: 1203 ft.
Name origin: For an early pioneer family.

Finlayson
City
ZIP: 55735 Lat: 46-12-17 N Long: 92-55-39 W
Pop: 242 (1990); 202 (1980) Pop Density: 86.4
Land: 2.8 sq. mi.; Water: 0.2 sq. mi.
Name origin: For sawmill owner David Finlayson.

*Finlayson
Township
ZIP: 55735 Lat: 46-12-16 N Long: 92-52-17 W
Pop: 401 (1990); 441 (1980) Pop Density: 11.9
Land: 33.7 sq. mi.; Water: 0.3 sq. mi.

Fleming
Township
Lat: 46-10-37 N Long: 92-36-54 W
Pop: 91 (1990); 66 (1980) Pop Density: 2.5
Land: 36.1 sq. mi.; Water: 0.0 sq. mi.

Henriette
City
ZIP: 55036 Lat: 45-52-16 N Long: 93-07-12 W
Pop: 78 (1990); 61 (1980) Pop Density: 260.0
Land: 0.3 sq. mi.; Water: 0.0 sq. mi. Elev: 996 ft.

Hinckley
City
ZIP: 55037 Lat: 46-00-52 N Long: 92-56-18 W
Pop: 946 (1990); 963 (1980) Pop Density: 556.5
Land: 1.7 sq. mi.; Water: 0.0 sq. mi. Elev: 1031 ft.
Name origin: For Isaac Hinckley, president of the Philadelphia & Baltimore Railway Company.

*Hinckley
Township
ZIP: 55037 Lat: 46-01-23 N Long: 92-59-12 W
Pop: 683 (1990); 628 (1980) Pop Density: 19.1
Land: 35.8 sq. mi.; Water: 0.0 sq. mi.

Kerrick
City
ZIP: 55756 Lat: 46-20-22 N Long: 92-35-08 W
Pop: 56 (1990); 79 (1980) Pop Density: 56.0
Land: 1.0 sq. mi.; Water: 0.0 sq. mi.
Name origin: For Cassius Kerrick, who worked for the Great Northern Railway Company.

*Kerrick
Township
ZIP: 55756 Lat: 46-22-34 N Long: 92-36-24 W
Pop: 290 (1990); 270 (1980) Pop Density: 8.6
Land: 33.9 sq. mi.; Water: 0.9 sq. mi.

Kettle River
Township
Lat: 46-17-14 N Long: 92-52-06 W
Pop: 367 (1990); 569 (1980) Pop Density: 12.2
Land: 30.2 sq. mi.; Water: 0.8 sq. mi.

Mission Creek
Township
Lat: 45-56-38 N Long: 92-57-32 W
Pop: 500 (1990); 411 (1980) Pop Density: 15.8
Land: 31.7 sq. mi.; Water: 0.1 sq. mi.

Munch
Township
Lat: 45-56-48 N Long: 92-48-46 W
Pop: 161 (1990); 155 (1980) Pop Density: 4.5
Land: 35.5 sq. mi.; Water: 0.6 sq. mi.

New Dosey
Township
Lat: 46-15-12 N Long: 92-23-00 W
Pop: 53 (1990); 88 (1980) Pop Density: 0.5
Land: 112.8 sq. mi.; Water: 0.1 sq. mi.

Nickerson
Township
Lat: 46-21-36 N Long: 92-26-07 W
Pop: 141 (1990); 121 (1980) Pop Density: 1.9
Land: 73.9 sq. mi.; Water: 0.6 sq. mi.

Norman
Township
ZIP: 55795 Lat: 46-18-26 N Long: 92-44-35 W
Pop: 165 (1990); 197 (1980) Pop Density: 4.6
Land: 35.7 sq. mi.; Water: 0.2 sq. mi.

Ogema
Township
Lat: 46-02-25 N Long: 92-27-28 W
Pop: 264 (1990); 157 (1980) Pop Density: 5.6
Land: 46.8 sq. mi.; Water: 1.2 sq. mi.

Park
Township
ZIP: 55756 Lat: 46-18-34 N Long: 92-28-25 W
Pop: 32 (1990); 60 (1980) Pop Density: 0.9
Land: 36.6 sq. mi.; Water: 0.1 sq. mi.

Partridge
Township
ZIP: 55704 Lat: 46-12-21 N Long: 92-44-20 W
Pop: 485 (1990); 503 (1980) Pop Density: 13.9
Land: 34.9 sq. mi.; Water: 0.0 sq. mi.

Pine City
City
ZIP: 55063 Lat: 45-49-51 N Long: 92-58-11 W
Pop: 2,613 (1990); 2,489 (1980) Pop Density: 1005.0
Land: 2.6 sq. mi.; Water: 0.4 sq. mi. Elev: 950 ft.
Name origin: For the extensive stands of white and red pine originally in the district.

American Places Dictionary — MINNESOTA, Pipestone County

*Pine City — Township
ZIP: 55063 Lat: 45-48-41 N Long: 92-53-18 W
Pop: 950 (1990); 876 (1980) Pop Density: 26.6
Land: 35.7 sq. mi.; Water: 0.9 sq. mi.

Pine Lake — Township
ZIP: 55735 Lat: 46-12-09 N Long: 92-59-34 W
Pop: 469 (1990); 440 (1980) Pop Density: 14.2
Land: 33.1 sq. mi.; Water: 2.0 sq. mi.

Pokegama — Township
Lat: 45-51-59 N Long: 93-02-28 W
Pop: 1,847 (1990); 1,611 (1980) Pop Density: 35.6
Land: 51.9 sq. mi.; Water: 3.4 sq. mi.

Rock Creek — City
ZIP: 55067 Lat: 45-45-33 N Long: 92-54-27 W
Pop: 1,040 (1990); 890 (1980) Pop Density: 24.2
Land: 43.0 sq. mi.; Water: 0.3 sq. mi. Elev: 938 ft.
Name origin: For a creek that flows into the St. Croix River.

Royalton — Township
Lat: 45-46-31 N Long: 93-04-24 W
Pop: 773 (1990); 688 (1980) Pop Density: 22.5
Land: 34.3 sq. mi.; Water: 0.4 sq. mi.

Rutledge — City
ZIP: 55778 Lat: 46-15-36 N Long: 92-52-09 W
Pop: 152 (1990); 185 (1980) Pop Density: 50.7
Land: 3.0 sq. mi.; Water: 0.1 sq. mi. Elev: 1032 ft.

Sandstone — City
ZIP: 55072 Lat: 46-07-30 N Long: 92-51-52 W
Pop: 2,057 (1990); 1,594 (1980) Pop Density: 478.4
Land: 4.3 sq. mi.; Water: 0.1 sq. mi.
City and township not coextensive.
Name origin: For the extensive sandstone quarries in the nearby bluffs on the Kettle River.

*Sandstone — Township
ZIP: 55072 Lat: 46-06-55 N Long: 92-47-13 W
Pop: 582 (1990); 580 (1980) Pop Density: 9.4
Land: 61.7 sq. mi.; Water: 0.2 sq. mi.

Sturgeon Lake — City
ZIP: 55783 Lat: 46-22-59 N Long: 92-49-37 W
Pop: 230 (1990); 222 (1980) Pop Density: 74.2
Land: 3.1 sq. mi.; Water: 0.0 sq. mi. Elev: 1074 ft.
City and township not coextensive.
Name origin: For the adjacent lake.

*Sturgeon Lake — Township
ZIP: 55783 Lat: 46-22-03 N Long: 92-51-37 W
Pop: 415 (1990); 607 (1980) Pop Density: 12.8
Land: 32.5 sq. mi.; Water: 0.1 sq. mi.

Willow River — City
ZIP: 55795 Lat: 46-19-11 N Long: 92-50-12 W
Pop: 284 (1990); 303 (1980) Pop Density: 177.5
Land: 1.6 sq. mi.; Water: 0.2 sq. mi. Elev: 1038 ft.
Name origin: For the river, which traverses the town and is named for the many willows along its banks.

Wilma — Township
Lat: 46-06-48 N Long: 92-28-46 W
Pop: 52 (1990); 124 (1980) Pop Density: 1.4
Land: 36.3 sq. mi.; Water: 0.4 sq. mi.

Windemere — Township
ZIP: 55783 Lat: 46-22-33 N Long: 92-44-24 W
Pop: 972 (1990); 915 (1980) Pop Density: 31.9
Land: 30.5 sq. mi.; Water: 5.2 sq. mi.

Pipestone County
County Seat: Pipestone (ZIP: 56164)

Pop: 10,491 (1990); 11,690 (1980) Pop Density: 22.5
Land: 465.9 sq. mi.; Water: 0.3 sq. mi. Area Code: 507
On the southwestern border of MN; established mistakenly as Rock County May 23, 1857 (prior to statehood) from Murray County; name changed Feb 20, 1862.
Name origin: For the red stone (catlinite) quarried by Indians to make pipe bowls.

Aetna — Township
Lat: 44-09-16 N Long: 96-07-05 W
Pop: 220 (1990); 295 (1980) Pop Density: 6.3
Land: 35.2 sq. mi.; Water: 0.0 sq. mi.

Altona — Township
Lat: 44-09-06 N Long: 96-23-05 W
Pop: 210 (1990); 237 (1980) Pop Density: 4.9
Land: 43.1 sq. mi.; Water: 0.0 sq. mi.

Burke — Township
Lat: 43-58-19 N Long: 96-07-03 W
Pop: 292 (1990); 329 (1980) Pop Density: 8.4
Land: 34.6 sq. mi.; Water: 0.0 sq. mi.

Eden — Township
Lat: 43-53-47 N Long: 96-22-45 W
Pop: 279 (1990); 361 (1980) Pop Density: 6.5
Land: 42.9 sq. mi.; Water: 0.1 sq. mi.

Edgerton — City
ZIP: 56128 Lat: 43-52-27 N Long: 96-07-50 W
Pop: 1,106 (1990); 1,123 (1980) Pop Density: 1005.5
Land: 1.1 sq. mi.; Water: 0.0 sq. mi. Elev: 1573 ft.
Name origin: For Gen. Alonzo Edgerton, who was a state senator and later a U.S. Senator in the 1880s.

Elmer — Township
Lat: 43-53-30 N Long: 96-14-28 W
Pop: 297 (1990); 344 (1980) Pop Density: 8.4
Land: 35.2 sq. mi.; Water: 0.0 sq. mi.

Fountain Prairie — Township
Lat: 44-09-09 N Long: 96-14-20 W
Pop: 200 (1990); 275 (1980) Pop Density: 5.4
Land: 37.2 sq. mi.; Water: 0.0 sq. mi.

MINNESOTA, Pipestone County

Grange
Township
Lat: 44-03-33 N Long: 96-15-16 W
Pop: 259 (1990); 309 (1980) **Pop Density:** 7.2
Land: 36.1 sq. mi.; **Water:** 0.0 sq. mi.

Gray
Township
Lat: 43-59-09 N Long: 96-14-52 W
Pop: 258 (1990); 300 (1980) **Pop Density:** 7.7
Land: 33.7 sq. mi.; **Water:** 0.0 sq. mi.

Hatfield
City
ZIP: 56135 Lat: 43-57-05 N Long: 96-11-20 W
Pop: 66 (1990); 87 (1980) **Pop Density:** 23.6
Land: 2.8 sq. mi.; **Water:** 0.0 sq. mi.
Name origin: Named by early settlers for Hatfield, MA.

Holland
City
ZIP: 56139 Lat: 44-05-27 N Long: 96-11-30 W
Pop: 216 (1990); 234 (1980) **Pop Density:** 240.0
Land: 0.9 sq. mi.; **Water:** 0.0 sq. mi.

Ihlen
City
ZIP: 56140 Lat: 43-54-36 N Long: 96-22-18 W
Pop: 101 (1990); 129 (1980) **Pop Density:** 252.5
Land: 0.4 sq. mi.; **Water:** 0.0 sq. mi.
Name origin: For Casper Ihlen, original landowner.

Jasper
City
ZIP: 56144 Lat: 43-51-09 N Long: 96-23-52 W
Pop: 524 (1990); 659 (1980) **Pop Density:** 1048.0
Land: 0.5 sq. mi.; **Water:** 0.0 sq. mi.
Incorporated 1889. Part of the town is also in Rock County.
Name origin: For the deposits of red quartzite, or jasper, found nearby.

Osborne
Township
Lat: 43-53-38 N Long: 96-07-41 W
Pop: 394 (1990); 454 (1980) **Pop Density:** 11.3
Land: 35.0 sq. mi.; **Water:** 0.0 sq. mi.

Pipestone
City
ZIP: 56164 Lat: 44-00-00 N Long: 96-18-50 W
Pop: 4,554 (1990); 4,887 (1980) **Pop Density:** 990.0
Land: 4.6 sq. mi.; **Water:** 0.0 sq. mi. **Elev:** 1738 ft.
Name origin: For the red stone (catlinite) quarried by Indians to make pipe bowls.

Rock
Township
Lat: 44-03-58 N Long: 96-07-25 W
Pop: 207 (1990); 261 (1980) **Pop Density:** 5.8
Land: 35.8 sq. mi.; **Water:** 0.1 sq. mi.

Ruthton
City
ZIP: 56170 Lat: 44-10-40 N Long: 96-06-14 W
Pop: 328 (1990); 328 (1980) **Pop Density:** 468.6
Land: 0.7 sq. mi.; **Water:** 0.0 sq. mi.

Sweet
Township
Lat: 43-58-42 N Long: 96-23-04 W
Pop: 376 (1990); 420 (1980) **Pop Density:** 9.3
Land: 40.5 sq. mi.; **Water:** 0.0 sq. mi.

Trosky
City
ZIP: 56177 Lat: 43-53-18 N Long: 96-15-20 W
Pop: 120 (1990); 113 (1980) **Pop Density:** 70.6
Land: 1.7 sq. mi.; **Water:** 0.0 sq. mi.

Troy
Township
Lat: 44-04-03 N Long: 96-22-54 W
Pop: 325 (1990); 365 (1980) **Pop Density:** 7.5
Land: 43.6 sq. mi.; **Water:** 0.0 sq. mi.

Woodstock
City
ZIP: 56186 Lat: 44-00-37 N Long: 96-05-47 W
Pop: 159 (1990); 180 (1980) **Pop Density:** 265.0
Land: 0.6 sq. mi.; **Water:** 0.0 sq. mi.
Name origin: For Woodstock, IL, and Woodstock, VT.

Polk County
County Seat: Crookston (**ZIP:** 56716)

Pop: 32,498 (1990); 34,844 (1980) **Pop Density:** 16.5
Land: 1970.5 sq. mi.; **Water:** 27.4 sq. mi. **Area Code:** 218
In northwestern MN, east of Grand Forks, ND; established Jul 20, 1858 from Indian lands.
Name origin: For James Knox Polk (1795–1849), eleventh U.S. president.

Andover
Township
Lat: 47-43-00 N Long: 96-40-20 W
Pop: 159 (1990); 176 (1980) **Pop Density:** 4.5
Land: 35.7 sq. mi.; **Water:** 0.0 sq. mi.

Angus
Township
Lat: 48-04-06 N Long: 96-41-42 W
Pop: 136 (1990); 141 (1980) **Pop Density:** 3.8
Land: 36.0 sq. mi.; **Water:** 0.0 sq. mi.

Badger
Township
Lat: 47-42-33 N Long: 96-02-27 W
Pop: 150 (1990); 173 (1980) **Pop Density:** 4.2
Land: 35.7 sq. mi.; **Water:** 0.5 sq. mi.

Belgium
Township
Lat: 47-59-05 N Long: 96-33-16 W
Pop: 106 (1990); 130 (1980) **Pop Density:** 2.9
Land: 36.4 sq. mi.; **Water:** 0.0 sq. mi.

Beltrami
City
ZIP: 56517 Lat: 47-32-35 N Long: 96-31-40 W
Pop: 137 (1990); 134 (1980) **Pop Density:** 68.5
Land: 2.0 sq. mi.; **Water:** 0.0 sq. mi. **Elev:** 903 ft.
Name origin: For Italian exile Giacomo Beltrami, who explored the area in 1823.

Brandsvold
Township
Lat: 47-37-23 N Long: 95-44-32 W
Pop: 261 (1990); 295 (1980) **Pop Density:** 7.5
Land: 34.9 sq. mi.; **Water:** 0.9 sq. mi.

Brandt Township
Lat: 48-03-53 N Long: 96-33-54 W
Pop: 65 (1990); 96 (1980) Pop Density: 1.8
Land: 36.0 sq. mi.; Water: 0.0 sq. mi.

Brislet Township
Lat: 48-08-40 N Long: 96-41-04 W
Pop: 76 (1990); 84 (1980) Pop Density: 2.8
Land: 27.0 sq. mi.; Water: 0.0 sq. mi.

Bygland Township
Lat: 47-48-33 N Long: 96-55-12 W
Pop: 300 (1990); 317 (1980) Pop Density: 10.5
Land: 28.5 sq. mi.; Water: 0.0 sq. mi.

Chester Township
ZIP: 56684 Lat: 47-48-51 N Long: 95-46-16 W
Pop: 78 (1990); 91 (1980) Pop Density: 2.2
Land: 35.9 sq. mi.; Water: 0.0 sq. mi.

Climax City
ZIP: 56523 Lat: 47-36-24 N Long: 96-48-44 W
Pop: 264 (1990); 273 (1980) Pop Density: 220.0
Land: 1.2 sq. mi.; Water: 0.0 sq. mi.
Name origin: From an advertisement for Climax tobacco.

Columbia Township
Lat: 47-32-46 N Long: 95-37-16 W
Pop: 402 (1990); 448 (1980) Pop Density: 11.7
Land: 34.5 sq. mi.; Water: 1.3 sq. mi.

Crookston City
ZIP: 56716 Lat: 47-46-27 N Long: 96-36-20 W
Pop: 8,119 (1990); 8,628 (1980) Pop Density: 1727.4
Land: 4.7 sq. mi.; Water: 0.0 sq. mi.
Name origin: For Col. William Crooks, who was the chief engineer of the first railroad through the area.

***Crookston** Township
ZIP: 56716 Lat: 47-48-26 N Long: 96-31-27 W
Pop: 484 (1990); 532 (1980) Pop Density: 12.9
Land: 37.6 sq. mi.; Water: 0.0 sq. mi.

East Grand Forks City
ZIP: 56721 Lat: 47-55-48 N Long: 97-00-57 W
Pop: 8,658 (1990); 8,537 (1980) Pop Density: 1967.7
Land: 4.4 sq. mi.; Water: 0.0 sq. mi.
Name origin: For its location on the east side of the Red River across from Grand Forks, ND.

Eden Township
ZIP: 56646 Lat: 47-42-59 N Long: 95-38-28 W
Pop: 204 (1990); 222 (1980) Pop Density: 5.8
Land: 35.1 sq. mi.; Water: 1.1 sq. mi.

Erskine City
ZIP: 56535 Lat: 47-39-48 N Long: 96-00-49 W
Pop: 422 (1990); 585 (1980) Pop Density: 602.9
Land: 0.7 sq. mi.; Water: 0.3 sq. mi.
Name origin: For prominent local banker John Quincy Erskine.

Esther Township
Lat: 48-04-17 N Long: 97-03-05 W
Pop: 209 (1990); 201 (1980) Pop Density: 10.9
Land: 19.1 sq. mi.; Water: 0.2 sq. mi.

Euclid Township
ZIP: 56712 Lat: 47-58-27 N Long: 96-40-22 W
Pop: 184 (1990); 256 (1980) Pop Density: 5.2
Land: 35.6 sq. mi.; Water: 0.0 sq. mi.

Fairfax Township
Lat: 47-42-48 N Long: 96-33-05 W
Pop: 221 (1990); 231 (1980) Pop Density: 6.1
Land: 36.0 sq. mi.; Water: 0.0 sq. mi.

Fanny Township
Lat: 47-53-25 N Long: 96-39-55 W
Pop: 126 (1990); 119 (1980) Pop Density: 3.5
Land: 35.7 sq. mi.; Water: 0.0 sq. mi.

Farley Township
Lat: 48-08-39 N Long: 96-49-49 W
Pop: 58 (1990); 87 (1980) Pop Density: 2.1
Land: 27.1 sq. mi.; Water: 0.0 sq. mi.

Fertile City
ZIP: 56540 Lat: 47-31-55 N Long: 96-17-28 W
Pop: 853 (1990); 869 (1980) Pop Density: 448.9
Land: 1.9 sq. mi.; Water: 0.0 sq. mi.
Name origin: For Fertile, IA, the former home of early settlers.

Fisher City
ZIP: 56723 Lat: 47-47-57 N Long: 96-47-58 W
Pop: 413 (1990); 453 (1980) Pop Density: 1032.5
Land: 0.4 sq. mi.; Water: 0.0 sq. mi.
Originally a steamboat port and later a railway terminal. City and township not coextensive.
Name origin: For St. Paul & Duluth Railroad president William H. Fisher.

***Fisher** Township
ZIP: 56723 Lat: 47-48-22 N Long: 96-48-14 W
Pop: 164 (1990); 155 (1980) Pop Density: 4.6
Land: 35.6 sq. mi.; Water: 0.0 sq. mi.

Fosston City
ZIP: 56542 Lat: 47-34-51 N Long: 95-44-51 W
Pop: 1,529 (1990); 1,599 (1980) Pop Density: 1390.0
Land: 1.1 sq. mi.; Water: 0.0 sq. mi. Elev: 1298 ft.
Name origin: For pioneer merchant Louis Foss.

Garden Township
Lat: 47-32-33 N Long: 96-08-09 W
Pop: 261 (1990); 296 (1980) Pop Density: 7.7
Land: 33.8 sq. mi.; Water: 1.8 sq. mi.

Garfield Township
Lat: 47-32-17 N Long: 96-15-35 W
Pop: 412 (1990); 510 (1980) Pop Density: 12.4
Land: 33.1 sq. mi.; Water: 0.8 sq. mi.

Gentilly Township
Lat: 47-48-31 N Long: 96-24-20 W
Pop: 344 (1990); 441 (1980) Pop Density: 10.8
Land: 32.0 sq. mi.; Water: 0.0 sq. mi.

Godfrey Township
Lat: 47-38-05 N Long: 96-15-47 W
Pop: 315 (1990); 297 (1980) Pop Density: 9.1
Land: 34.5 sq. mi.; Water: 1.5 sq. mi.

Grand Forks Township
Lat: 47-59-07 N Long: 97-01-51 W
Pop: 222 (1990); 275 (1980) Pop Density: 15.6
Land: 14.2 sq. mi.; Water: 0.1 sq. mi.

Grove Park Township
Lat: 47-42-26 N Long: 96-10-10 W
Pop: 269 (1990); 279 (1980) Pop Density: 8.0
Land: 33.5 sq. mi.; Water: 0.7 sq. mi.

MINNESOTA, Polk County

Gully
City
ZIP: 56646   **Lat:** 47-46-08 N   **Long:** 95-37-24 W
Pop: 128 (1990); 116 (1980)   **Pop Density:** 64.0
Land: 2.0 sq. mi.; **Water:** 0.0 sq. mi.
Cith and township not coextensive.
Name origin: For a glacier-created gully near the town.

*Gully
Township
ZIP: 56646   **Lat:** 47-48-43 N   **Long:** 95-38-41 W
Pop: 114 (1990); 128 (1980)   **Pop Density:** 3.5
Land: 32.8 sq. mi.; **Water:** 0.0 sq. mi.

Hammond
Township
                          Lat: 47-37-46 N   **Long:** 96-38-16 W
Pop: 64 (1990); 80 (1980)   **Pop Density:** 1.8
Land: 36.3 sq. mi.; **Water:** 0.0 sq. mi.

Helgeland
Township
                          Lat: 48-08-42 N   **Long:** 96-33-17 W
Pop: 59 (1990); 94 (1980)   **Pop Density:** 2.2
Land: 27.1 sq. mi.; **Water:** 0.0 sq. mi.

Higdem
Township
                          Lat: 48-08-39 N   **Long:** 97-04-26 W
Pop: 105 (1990); 125 (1980)   **Pop Density:** 4.5
Land: 23.2 sq. mi.; **Water:** 0.2 sq. mi.

Hill River
Township
                          Lat: 47-42-41 N   **Long:** 95-46-32 W
Pop: 208 (1990); 252 (1980)   **Pop Density:** 6.0
Land: 34.9 sq. mi.; **Water:** 1.3 sq. mi.

Hubbard
Township
                          Lat: 47-32-59 N   **Long:** 96-46-57 W
Pop: 113 (1990); 134 (1980)   **Pop Density:** 2.7
Land: 41.3 sq. mi.; **Water:** 0.0 sq. mi.

Huntsville
Township
                          Lat: 47-53-22 N   **Long:** 96-55-55 W
Pop: 515 (1990); 535 (1980)   **Pop Density:** 14.5
Land: 35.6 sq. mi.; **Water:** 0.2 sq. mi.

Johnson
Township
ZIP: 56684   **Lat:** 47-52-53 N   **Long:** 95-38-45 W
Pop: 65 (1990); 104 (1980)   **Pop Density:** 1.8
Land: 35.7 sq. mi.; **Water:** 0.0 sq. mi.

Kertsonville
Township
                          Lat: 47-43-07 N   **Long:** 96-25-23 W
Pop: 149 (1990); 163 (1980)   **Pop Density:** 4.1
Land: 36.5 sq. mi.; **Water:** 0.0 sq. mi.

Keystone
Township
                          Lat: 47-58-41 N   **Long:** 96-47-39 W
Pop: 109 (1990); 114 (1980)   **Pop Density:** 3.1
Land: 35.6 sq. mi.; **Water:** 0.0 sq. mi.

King
Township
                          Lat: 47-37-49 N   **Long:** 95-52-25 W
Pop: 198 (1990); 219 (1980)   **Pop Density:** 5.7
Land: 34.9 sq. mi.; **Water:** 0.3 sq. mi.

Knute
Township
                          Lat: 47-37-19 N   **Long:** 96-00-18 W
Pop: 421 (1990); 431 (1980)   **Pop Density:** 13.4
Land: 31.5 sq. mi.; **Water:** 3.3 sq. mi.

Lengby
City
ZIP: 56651   **Lat:** 47-30-53 N   **Long:** 95-38-00 W
Pop: 112 (1990); 123 (1980)   **Pop Density:** 560.0
Land: 0.2 sq. mi.; **Water:** 0.1 sq. mi.

Lessor
Township
                          Lat: 47-42-43 N   **Long:** 95-54-02 W
Pop: 225 (1990); 209 (1980)   **Pop Density:** 6.3
Land: 35.6 sq. mi.; **Water:** 0.8 sq. mi.

Liberty
Township
                          Lat: 47-32-43 N   **Long:** 96-22-56 W
Pop: 141 (1990); 156 (1980)   **Pop Density:** 3.9
Land: 36.1 sq. mi.; **Water:** 0.0 sq. mi.

Lowell
Township
                          Lat: 47-48-14 N   **Long:** 96-41-10 W
Pop: 204 (1990); 187 (1980)   **Pop Density:** 5.9
Land: 34.6 sq. mi.; **Water:** 0.0 sq. mi.

McIntosh
City
ZIP: 56556   **Lat:** 47-38-14 N   **Long:** 95-53-06 W
Pop: 665 (1990); 681 (1980)   **Pop Density:** 665.0
Land: 1.0 sq. mi.; **Water:** 0.0 sq. mi.   **Elev:** 1223 ft.
Name origin: For a hotel proprietor who was part Scottish and part Ojibway and owned the land on which the town was founded.

Mentor
City
ZIP: 56736   **Lat:** 47-41-47 N   **Long:** 96-08-40 W
Pop: 94 (1990); 219 (1980)   **Pop Density:** 49.5
Land: 1.9 sq. mi.; **Water:** 0.0 sq. mi.
Name origin: For Menton, OH.

Nesbit
Township
                          Lat: 47-53-27 N   **Long:** 96-47-38 W
Pop: 121 (1990); 153 (1980)   **Pop Density:** 3.4
Land: 36.0 sq. mi.; **Water:** 0.0 sq. mi.

Nielsville
City
ZIP: 56568   **Lat:** 47-31-43 N   **Long:** 96-48-58 W
Pop: 100 (1990); 145 (1980)   **Pop Density:** 333.3
Land: 0.3 sq. mi.; **Water:** 0.0 sq. mi.

Northland
Township
                          Lat: 48-04-18 N   **Long:** 96-56-36 W
Pop: 196 (1990); 226 (1980)   **Pop Density:** 5.4
Land: 36.2 sq. mi.; **Water:** 0.0 sq. mi.

Onstad
Township
                          Lat: 47-37-46 N   **Long:** 96-23-18 W
Pop: 111 (1990); 126 (1980)   **Pop Density:** 3.1
Land: 35.6 sq. mi.; **Water:** 0.1 sq. mi.

Parnell
Township
                          Lat: 47-54-00 N   **Long:** 96-32-43 W
Pop: 64 (1990); 96 (1980)   **Pop Density:** 1.8
Land: 36.3 sq. mi.; **Water:** 0.0 sq. mi.

Queen
Township
                          Lat: 47-37-37 N   **Long:** 95-36-55 W
Pop: 197 (1990); 265 (1980)   **Pop Density:** 6.0
Land: 32.7 sq. mi.; **Water:** 3.9 sq. mi.

Reis
Township
                          Lat: 47-32-41 N   **Long:** 96-30-40 W
Pop: 79 (1990); 115 (1980)   **Pop Density:** 2.3
Land: 34.0 sq. mi.; **Water:** 0.0 sq. mi.

Rhinehart
Township
                          Lat: 47-53-03 N   **Long:** 97-00-59 W
Pop: 132 (1990); 98 (1980)   **Pop Density:** 45.5
Land: 2.9 sq. mi.; **Water:** 0.0 sq. mi.

Roome — Township
Lat: 47-43-00 N Long: 96-48-09 W
Pop: 191 (1990); 215 (1980) Pop Density: 5.3
Land: 36.1 sq. mi.; Water: 0.0 sq. mi.

Rosebud — Township
Lat: 47-32-39 N Long: 95-44-34 W
Pop: 331 (1990); 386 (1980) Pop Density: 10.0
Land: 33.1 sq. mi.; Water: 2.1 sq. mi.

Russia — Township
Lat: 47-37-19 N Long: 96-30-50 W
Pop: 49 (1990); 71 (1980) Pop Density: 1.4
Land: 36.1 sq. mi.; Water: 0.0 sq. mi.

Sandsville — Township
Lat: 48-08-38 N Long: 96-57-18 W
Pop: 69 (1990); 71 (1980) Pop Density: 2.6
Land: 27.0 sq. mi.; Water: 0.0 sq. mi.

Scandia — Township
Lat: 47-32-33 N Long: 96-38-35 W
Pop: 86 (1990); 106 (1980) Pop Density: 2.4
Land: 36.1 sq. mi.; Water: 0.0 sq. mi.

Sletten — Township
Lat: 47-32-29 N Long: 95-52-43 W
Pop: 151 (1990); 195 (1980) Pop Density: 4.2
Land: 36.0 sq. mi.; Water: 0.1 sq. mi.

Sullivan — Township
Lat: 47-58-15 N Long: 96-55-22 W
Pop: 168 (1990); 218 (1980) Pop Density: 4.7
Land: 35.7 sq. mi.; Water: 0.1 sq. mi.

Tabor — Township
ZIP: 56712 Lat: 48-03-26 N Long: 96-50-06 W
Pop: 163 (1990); 187 (1980) Pop Density: 4.5
Land: 36.2 sq. mi.; Water: 0.0 sq. mi.

Tilden — Township
Lat: 47-42-33 N Long: 96-17-16 W
Pop: 28 (1990); 55 (1980) Pop Density: 0.8
Land: 35.8 sq. mi.; Water: 0.1 sq. mi.

Trail — City
ZIP: 56684 Lat: 47-47-01 N Long: 95-41-56 W
Pop: 67 (1990); 97 (1980) Pop Density: 67.0
Land: 1.0 sq. mi.; Water: 0.0 sq. mi.

Tynsid — Township
Lat: 47-43-28 N Long: 96-53-59 W
Pop: 71 (1990); 87 (1980) Pop Density: 5.0
Land: 14.3 sq. mi.; Water: 0.0 sq. mi.

Vineland — Township
Lat: 47-38-12 N Long: 96-47-34 W
Pop: 141 (1990); 156 (1980) Pop Density: 3.1
Land: 45.8 sq. mi.; Water: 0.0 sq. mi.

Winger — City
ZIP: 56592 Lat: 47-32-13 N Long: 95-59-06 W
Pop: 167 (1990); 200 (1980) Pop Density: 556.7
Land: 0.3 sq. mi.; Water: 0.0 sq. mi.
City and township not coextensive.
Name origin: Named by Norwegian farmers for an area in central Norway.

*Winger — Township
ZIP: 56592 Lat: 47-32-27 N Long: 96-00-12 W
Pop: 239 (1990); 264 (1980) Pop Density: 6.8
Land: 35.1 sq. mi.; Water: 0.5 sq. mi.

Woodside — Township
Lat: 47-37-29 N Long: 96-07-59 W
Pop: 287 (1990); 312 (1980) Pop Density: 9.3
Land: 30.9 sq. mi.; Water: 5.0 sq. mi.

Pope County
County Seat: Glenwood (ZIP: 56334)

Pop: 10,745 (1990); 11,657 (1980) Pop Density: 16.0
Land: 670.2 sq. mi.; Water: 47.1 sq. mi. Area Code: 612
In west-central MN, west of St. Cloud; established Feb 20, 1862 from Pierce County, which was abolished the same year.
Name origin: For explorer Gen. John Pope (1822–92), career army officer in the Mexican-American War and the Civil War.

Bangor — Township
ZIP: 56380 Lat: 45-32-31 N Long: 95-10-57 W
Pop: 232 (1990); 234 (1980) Pop Density: 6.6
Land: 35.0 sq. mi.; Water: 0.1 sq. mi.

Barsness — Township
ZIP: 56381 Lat: 45-32-18 N Long: 95-26-51 W
Pop: 160 (1990); 187 (1980) Pop Density: 4.8
Land: 33.1 sq. mi.; Water: 2.2 sq. mi.

Ben Wade — Township
ZIP: 56349 Lat: 45-43-02 N Long: 95-34-41 W
Pop: 285 (1990); 306 (1980) Pop Density: 8.4
Land: 34.0 sq. mi.; Water: 1.4 sq. mi.

Blue Mounds — Township
ZIP: 56381 Lat: 45-32-32 N Long: 95-33-40 W
Pop: 221 (1990); 284 (1980) Pop Density: 6.3
Land: 34.9 sq. mi.; Water: 1.1 sq. mi.

Brooten — City
ZIP: 56316 Lat: 45-30-34 N Long: 95-07-57 W
Pop: 0 (1990); 647 (1980)
Land: 0.01 sq. mi.; Water: 0.0 sq. mi.
Founded 1886. Part of the town is also in Stearns County.
Name origin: For one of its early Scandinavian settlers.

Chippewa Falls — Township
Lat: 45-32-22 N Long: 95-18-56 W
Pop: 295 (1990); 341 (1980) Pop Density: 8.6
Land: 34.2 sq. mi.; Water: 1.1 sq. mi.

MINNESOTA, Pope County

Cyrus — City
ZIP: 56323   Lat: 45-36-54 N   Long: 95-44-13 W
Pop: 328 (1990); 334 (1980)   Pop Density: 1093.3
Land: 0.3 sq. mi.; Water: 0.0 sq. mi.   Elev: 1138 ft.

Farwell — City
ZIP: 56327   Lat: 45-45-06 N   Long: 95-37-05 W
Pop: 74 (1990); 77 (1980)   Pop Density: 246.7
Land: 0.3 sq. mi.; Water: 0.0 sq. mi.
Founded 1887.
Name origin: Euphonious in origin.

Gilchrist — Township
ZIP: 56380   Lat: 45-27-21 N   Long: 95-19-04 W
Pop: 202 (1990); 218 (1980)   Pop Density: 6.3
Land: 32.1 sq. mi.; Water: 3.5 sq. mi.

Glenwood — City
ZIP: 56334   Lat: 45-39-11 N   Long: 95-22-58 W
Pop: 2,573 (1990); 2,523 (1980)   Pop Density: 756.8
Land: 3.4 sq. mi.; Water: 0.0 sq. mi.
Name origin: For the great valley along the south side of Lake Minnewaska.

*Glenwood — Township
ZIP: 56334   Lat: 45-37-00 N   Long: 95-19-57 W
Pop: 847 (1990); 827 (1980)   Pop Density: 20.1
Land: 42.2 sq. mi.; Water: 1.5 sq. mi.

Grove Lake — Township
ZIP: 56334   Lat: 45-37-28 N   Long: 95-12-03 W
Pop: 247 (1990); 314 (1980)   Pop Density: 7.7
Land: 32.0 sq. mi.; Water: 1.7 sq. mi.

Hoff — Township
ZIP: 56323   Lat: 45-27-23 N   Long: 95-40-43 W
Pop: 212 (1990); 241 (1980)   Pop Density: 5.9
Land: 36.0 sq. mi.; Water: 0.0 sq. mi.

Lake Johanna — Township
ZIP: 56380   Lat: 45-27-20 N   Long: 95-11-38 W
Pop: 176 (1990); 189 (1980)   Pop Density: 5.3
Land: 33.2 sq. mi.; Water: 2.7 sq. mi.

Langhei — Township
ZIP: 56334   Lat: 45-27-30 N   Long: 95-34-08 W
Pop: 196 (1990); 270 (1980)   Pop Density: 5.6
Land: 35.3 sq. mi.; Water: 0.6 sq. mi.

Leven — Township
ZIP: 56385   Lat: 45-43-25 N   Long: 95-19-09 W
Pop: 505 (1990); 488 (1980)   Pop Density: 15.4
Land: 32.7 sq. mi.; Water: 2.7 sq. mi.

Long Beach — City
ZIP: 56334   Lat: 45-38-53 N   Long: 95-25-47 W
Pop: 204 (1990); 263 (1980)   Pop Density: 170.0
Land: 1.2 sq. mi.; Water: 0.1 sq. mi.

Lowry — City
ZIP: 56349   Lat: 45-42-19 N   Long: 95-31-01 W
Pop: 233 (1990); 283 (1980)   Pop Density: 582.5
Land: 0.4 sq. mi.; Water: 0.0 sq. mi.
Name origin: For Thomas Lowry, a prominent Minneapolis civil leader in the late 1800s.

Minnewaska — Township
Lat: 45-37-56 N   Long: 95-27-40 W
Pop: 394 (1990); 490 (1980)   Pop Density: 29.8
Land: 13.2 sq. mi.; Water: 12.6 sq. mi.

New Prairie — Township
ZIP: 56323   Lat: 45-37-37 N   Long: 95-41-33 W
Pop: 221 (1990); 263 (1980)   Pop Density: 6.3
Land: 35.2 sq. mi.; Water: 0.7 sq. mi.

Nora — Township
ZIP: 56349   Lat: 45-42-59 N   Long: 95-41-47 W
Pop: 231 (1990); 306 (1980)   Pop Density: 6.8
Land: 33.8 sq. mi.; Water: 2.4 sq. mi.

Reno — Township
ZIP: 56334   Lat: 45-42-31 N   Long: 95-26-17 W
Pop: 322 (1990); 364 (1980)   Pop Density: 10.8
Land: 29.8 sq. mi.; Water: 6.1 sq. mi.

Rolling Forks — Township
ZIP: 56334   Lat: 45-27-30 N   Long: 95-26-42 W
Pop: 179 (1990); 207 (1980)   Pop Density: 5.2
Land: 34.6 sq. mi.; Water: 1.2 sq. mi.

Sedan — City
ZIP: 56380   Lat: 45-34-37 N   Long: 95-14-43 W
Pop: 63 (1990); 62 (1980)   Pop Density: 126.0
Land: 0.5 sq. mi.; Water: 0.0 sq. mi.

Starbuck — City
ZIP: 56381   Lat: 45-36-43 N   Long: 95-31-58 W
Pop: 1,143 (1990); 1,224 (1980)   Pop Density: 714.4
Land: 1.6 sq. mi.; Water: 0.0 sq. mi.   Elev: 1162 ft.
Founded 1882.
Name origin: Named by Northern Pacific Railroad officials for a company employee.

Villard — City
ZIP: 56385   Lat: 45-42-48 N   Long: 95-16-10 W
Pop: 247 (1990); 275 (1980)   Pop Density: 308.8
Land: 0.8 sq. mi.; Water: 0.0 sq. mi.
Name origin: For Henry Villard, president of the Northern Pacific Railway Company.

Walden — Township
ZIP: 56323   Lat: 45-32-46 N   Long: 95-41-09 W
Pop: 227 (1990); 261 (1980)   Pop Density: 6.9
Land: 32.9 sq. mi.; Water: 2.8 sq. mi.

Westport — City
ZIP: 56385   Lat: 45-42-52 N   Long: 95-10-02 W
Pop: 47 (1990); 50 (1980)   Pop Density: 156.7
Land: 0.3 sq. mi.; Water: 0.0 sq. mi.
Founded 1882. City and township not coextensive.
Name origin: For a common eastern town name.

*Westport — Township
ZIP: 56385   Lat: 45-43-04 N   Long: 95-12-12 W
Pop: 277 (1990); 300 (1980)   Pop Density: 8.0
Land: 34.6 sq. mi.; Water: 0.9 sq. mi.

White Bear Lake — Township
Lat: 45-37-52 N   Long: 95-34-13 W
Pop: 404 (1990); 476 (1980)   Pop Density: 12.4
Land: 32.7 sq. mi.; Water: 1.9 sq. mi.

Ramsey County
County Seat: St. Paul (ZIP: 55102)

Pop: 485,765 (1990); 459,784 (1980) **Pop Density:** 3117.5
Land: 155.8 sq. mi.; **Water:** 14.3 sq. mi. **Area Code:** 612
In east-central MN, west of Minneapolis; original county; established Oct 27, 1849 (prior to statehood).
Name origin: For Alexander Ramsey (1815–1903), PA legislator, first MN territorial governor (1849–53), state governor (1860–63), U.S. senator (1863–75), and U.S. secretary of war (1879–81).

Arden Hills — City
ZIP: 55112 **Lat:** 45-04-17 N **Long:** 93-09-55 W
Pop: 9,199 (1990); 8,012 (1980) **Pop Density:** 1033.6
Land: 8.9 sq. mi.; **Water:** 0.7 sq. mi.
Name origin: For the Ardennes forest of northern France, with spelling altered to reflect pronunciation.

Blaine — City
ZIP: 55433 **Lat:** 45-07-15 N **Long:** 93-11-41 W
Pop: 0 (1990)
Land: 0.2 sq. mi.; **Water:** 0.0 sq. mi.
Part of the town is also in Anoka County.

Falcon Heights — City
ZIP: 55113 **Lat:** 44-59-16 N **Long:** 93-10-45 W
Pop: 5,380 (1990); 5,291 (1980) **Pop Density:** 2445.5
Land: 2.2 sq. mi.; **Water:** 0.0 sq. mi.

Gem Lake — City
ZIP: 55110 **Lat:** 45-03-30 N **Long:** 93-02-29 W
Pop: 439 (1990); 394 (1980) **Pop Density:** 399.1
Land: 1.1 sq. mi.; **Water:** 0.0 sq. mi. **Elev:** 954 ft.

Lauderdale — City
ZIP: 55113 **Lat:** 44-59-39 N **Long:** 93-12-10 W
Pop: 2,700 (1990); 1,985 (1980) **Pop Density:** 6750.0
Land: 0.4 sq. mi.; **Water:** 0.0 sq. mi.

Little Canada — City
ZIP: 55110 **Lat:** 45-01-25 N **Long:** 93-05-01 W
Pop: 8,971 (1990); 7,102 (1980) **Pop Density:** 2242.8
Land: 4.0 sq. mi.; **Water:** 0.5 sq. mi.
Name origin: For the country.

Maplewood — City
ZIP: 55109 **Lat:** 44-59-34 N **Long:** 93-01-25 W
Pop: 30,954 (1990); 26,990 (1980) **Pop Density:** 1789.2
Land: 17.3 sq. mi.; **Water:** 0.7 sq. mi.
In eastern MN, north of St. Paul.

Mounds View — City
ZIP: 55432 **Lat:** 45-06-21 N **Long:** 93-12-22 W
Pop: 12,541 (1990); 12,593 (1980) **Pop Density:** 3058.8
Land: 4.1 sq. mi.; **Water:** 0.0 sq. mi.
In eastern MN, north of Minneapolis.
Name origin: For a small group of glacier-deposit hills extending through the town to a height of 200 ft. above the countryside.

New Brighton — City
ZIP: 55112 **Lat:** 45-03-55 N **Long:** 93-12-15 W
Pop: 22,207 (1990); 23,269 (1980) **Pop Density:** 3364.7
Land: 6.6 sq. mi.; **Water:** 0.5 sq. mi.
In southeast-central MN, north of Minneapolis.
Name origin: For Brighton, MA, which, like New Brighton, was a meat-packing center.

North Oaks — City
Lat: 45-06-24 N **Long:** 93-05-13 W
Pop: 3,386 (1990); 2,846 (1980) **Pop Density:** 463.8
Land: 7.3 sq. mi.; **Water:** 1.3 sq. mi.
Name origin: Named euphoniously by its founders.

North St. Paul — City
ZIP: 55109 **Lat:** 45-00-50 N **Long:** 92-59-53 W
Pop: 12,376 (1990); 11,921 (1980) **Pop Density:** 4267.6
Land: 2.9 sq. mi.; **Water:** 0.1 sq. mi.

Roseville — City
ZIP: 55113 **Lat:** 45-00-54 N **Long:** 93-09-09 W
Pop: 33,485 (1990); 35,820 (1980) **Pop Density:** 2536.7
Land: 13.2 sq. mi.; **Water:** 0.6 sq. mi. **Elev:** 950 ft.
In eastern MN, north of St. Paul.
Name origin: For early pioneer Isaac Rose, who settled here in 1843.

St. Anthony — City
Lat: 45-02-27 N **Long:** 93-13-03 W
Pop: 2,449 (1990); 2,362 (1980) **Pop Density:** 4081.7
Land: 0.6 sq. mi.; **Water:** 0.1 sq. mi. **Elev:** 920 ft.
Part of the town is also in Hennepin County.
Name origin: For an early church.

St. Paul — City
ZIP: 55101 **Lat:** 44-56-51 N **Long:** 93-06-13 W
Pop: 272,235 (1990); 270,230 (1980) **Pop Density:** 5156.0
Land: 52.8 sq. mi.; **Water:** 3.4 sq. mi.
In eastern MN on the Mississippi River, 10 mi. east of Minneapolis. State capital. Distribution and transportation center for the Midwestern farm region.
Name origin: Named at the suggestion of Father Lucian Galtier for a small chapel dedicated to Saint Paul the Apostle (?–67). Settlement first called Pig's Eye, nickname of Pierre Parrant, a French-Canadian trader who founded the first settlement.

Shoreview — City
ZIP: 55112 **Lat:** 45-05-02 N **Long:** 93-08-09 W
Pop: 24,587 (1990); 17,300 (1980) **Pop Density:** 2195.3
Land: 11.2 sq. mi.; **Water:** 1.5 sq. mi. **Elev:** 950 ft.
Name origin: For its view of the Mississippi River.

Spring Lake Park — City
Lat: 45-06-49 N **Long:** 93-13-33 W
Pop: 103 (1990); 109 (1980) **Pop Density:** 1030.0
Land: 0.1 sq. mi.; **Water:** 0.0 sq. mi.
Part of the town is also in Anoka County.

MINNESOTA, Ramsey County

Vadnais Heights — City
ZIP: 55110 Lat: 45-03-23 N Long: 93-04-22 W
Pop: 11,041 (1990); 5,111 (1980) Pop Density: 1512.5
Land: 7.3 sq. mi.; Water: 1.0 sq. mi.
Name origin: For early pioneer settler John Vadnais.

White Bear — Township
Lat: 45-06-08 N Long: 93-01-37 W
Pop: 9,424 (1990); 5,921 (1980) Pop Density: 1256.5
Land: 7.5 sq. mi.; Water: 1.6 sq. mi.

White Bear Lake — City
ZIP: 55110 Lat: 45-04-03 N Long: 93-00-45 W
Pop: 24,288 (1990); 22,528 (1980) Pop Density: 2998.5
Land: 8.1 sq. mi.; Water: 2.2 sq. mi. Elev: 950 ft.
Part of the town is also in Washington County.
Name origin: For the nearby lake, which was sacred to the Sioux.

Red Lake County
County Seat: Red Lake Falls (ZIP: 56750)

Pop: 4,525 (1990); 5,471 (1980) Pop Density: 10.5
Land: 432.4 sq. mi.; Water: 0.1 sq. mi. Area Code: 218

In northwestern MN, southeast of Grand Forks, ND; established Dec 24, 1896 from Polk County.

Name origin: For the Red Lake River, which flows through it; from a translation of the Ojibway word meaning 'red,' referring to the color of the lake when the setting sun is reflected in it.

Brooks — City
ZIP: 56715 Lat: 47-49-01 N Long: 96-00-04 W
Pop: 158 (1990); 173 (1980) Pop Density: 131.7
Land: 1.2 sq. mi.; Water: 0.0 sq. mi.
Name origin: For an early settler.

Browns Creek — Township
Lat: 47-56-52 N Long: 96-17-11 W
Pop: 65 (1990); 75 (1980) Pop Density: 5.4
Land: 12.1 sq. mi.; Water: 0.0 sq. mi.

Emardville — Township
Lat: 47-54-05 N Long: 96-01-54 W
Pop: 238 (1990); 292 (1980) Pop Density: 5.2
Land: 45.6 sq. mi.; Water: 0.0 sq. mi.

Equality — Township
Lat: 47-54-49 N Long: 95-45-48 W
Pop: 123 (1990); 206 (1980) Pop Density: 2.6
Land: 47.7 sq. mi.; Water: 0.0 sq. mi.

Garnes — Township
Lat: 47-54-49 N Long: 95-54-45 W
Pop: 209 (1990); 246 (1980) Pop Density: 4.3
Land: 48.3 sq. mi.; Water: 0.0 sq. mi.

Gervais — Township
Lat: 47-52-59 N Long: 96-09-53 W
Pop: 274 (1990); 302 (1980) Pop Density: 7.7
Land: 35.6 sq. mi.; Water: 0.0 sq. mi.

Lake Pleasant — Township
Lat: 47-48-15 N Long: 96-17-08 W
Pop: 130 (1990); 147 (1980) Pop Density: 3.6
Land: 35.9 sq. mi.; Water: 0.0 sq. mi.

Lambert — Township
Lat: 47-48-09 N Long: 95-54-18 W
Pop: 187 (1990); 226 (1980) Pop Density: 5.3
Land: 35.6 sq. mi.; Water: 0.0 sq. mi.

Louisville — Township
Lat: 47-53-27 N Long: 96-25-09 W
Pop: 217 (1990); 241 (1980) Pop Density: 6.0
Land: 36.1 sq. mi.; Water: 0.0 sq. mi.

Oklee — City
ZIP: 56742 Lat: 47-50-19 N Long: 95-51-00 W
Pop: 441 (1990); 536 (1980) Pop Density: 630.0
Land: 0.7 sq. mi.; Water: 0.0 sq. mi.
Name origin: For early Scandinavian settler Ole K. Lee.

Plummer — City
ZIP: 56748 Lat: 47-54-56 N Long: 96-02-22 W
Pop: 277 (1990); 353 (1980) Pop Density: 98.9
Land: 2.8 sq. mi.; Water: 0.0 sq. mi.

Poplar River — Township
Lat: 47-48-17 N Long: 96-01-30 W
Pop: 192 (1990); 206 (1980) Pop Density: 5.5
Land: 34.9 sq. mi.; Water: 0.0 sq. mi.

Red Lake Falls — City
ZIP: 56750 Lat: 47-53-06 N Long: 96-16-26 W
Pop: 1,481 (1990); 1,732 (1980) Pop Density: 705.2
Land: 2.1 sq. mi.; Water: 0.0 sq. mi. Elev: 1037 ft.
City and township not coextensive.
Name origin: For the falls on the Red Lake River at the site of the town.

*Red Lake Falls — Township
ZIP: 56750 Lat: 47-53-23 N Long: 96-17-25 W
Pop: 235 (1990); 318 (1980) Pop Density: 6.9
Land: 34.0 sq. mi.; Water: 0.0 sq. mi.

River — Township
Lat: 47-56-41 N Long: 96-09-43 W
Pop: 71 (1990); 87 (1980) Pop Density: 6.0
Land: 11.8 sq. mi.; Water: 0.0 sq. mi.

Terrebonne — Township
Lat: 47-48-02 N Long: 96-09-34 W
Pop: 161 (1990); 236 (1980) Pop Density: 4.5
Land: 36.0 sq. mi.; Water: 0.0 sq. mi.

Wylie — Township
Lat: 47-56-38 N Long: 96-25-35 W
Pop: 66 (1990); 95 (1980) Pop Density: 5.5
Land: 12.1 sq. mi.; Water: 0.0 sq. mi.

> # Redwood County
> ### County Seat: Redwood Falls (ZIP: 56283)
>
> **Pop:** 17,254 (1990); 19,341 (1980) **Pop Density:** 19.6
> **Land:** 879.9 sq. mi.; **Water:** 1.4 sq. mi. **Area Code:** 507
> In southwestern MN, northwest of Mankato; established Feb 6, 1862 from Brown County.
>
> **Name origin:** For the Redwood River, which flows through it; from a Dakota phrase *chan sha ayapi* 'wood-red-on the river,' which may refer to the red bark taken from a shrub, which the Indians dried and mixed with smoking tobacco; the red cedar trees lining the banks; or spots of red paint found on trees, marking an ancient trail for a war party.

Belview   City
ZIP: 56214 **Lat:** 44-36-21 N **Long:** 95-19-43 W
Pop: 383 (1990); 438 (1980) **Pop Density:** 425.6
Land: 0.9 sq. mi.; **Water:** 0.0 sq. mi.
Name origin: From French term meaning 'beautiful view,' with spelling altered to reflect pronunciation.

Brookville   Township
Lat: 44-19-42 N **Long:** 94-55-37 W
Pop: 283 (1990); 358 (1980) **Pop Density:** 7.9
Land: 35.8 sq. mi.; **Water:** 0.0 sq. mi.

Charlestown   Township
Lat: 44-14-23 N **Long:** 95-09-57 W
Pop: 281 (1990); 350 (1980) **Pop Density:** 8.3
Land: 33.8 sq. mi.; **Water:** 0.0 sq. mi.

Clements   City
ZIP: 56224 **Lat:** 44-22-47 N **Long:** 95-03-17 W
Pop: 191 (1990); 227 (1980) **Pop Density:** 477.5
Land: 0.4 sq. mi.; **Water:** 0.0 sq. mi.
Founded 1982.
Name origin: For early settler and farmer Peter O. Clements.

Delhi   City
Lat: 44-35-53 N **Long:** 95-12-46 W
Pop: 69 (1990); 96 (1980) **Pop Density:** 86.3
Land: 0.8 sq. mi.; **Water:** 0.0 sq. mi.
City and township not coextensive.
Name origin: Named by Alfred Cook, a local flour miller, for his former home of Delhi, OH.

*Delhi   Township
Lat: 44-35-19 N **Long:** 95-11-08 W
Pop: 315 (1990); 377 (1980) **Pop Density:** 9.5
Land: 33.1 sq. mi.; **Water:** 0.1 sq. mi.

Gales   Township
Lat: 44-19-54 N **Long:** 95-31-38 W
Pop: 162 (1990); 226 (1980) **Pop Density:** 4.5
Land: 36.1 sq. mi.; **Water:** 0.1 sq. mi.

Granite Rock   Township
Lat: 44-24-47 N **Long:** 95-24-16 W
Pop: 252 (1990); 330 (1980) **Pop Density:** 6.9
Land: 36.3 sq. mi.; **Water:** 0.0 sq. mi.

Honner   Township
Lat: 44-33-13 N **Long:** 95-04-00 W
Pop: 145 (1990); 133 (1980) **Pop Density:** 19.9
Land: 7.3 sq. mi.; **Water:** 0.1 sq. mi.

Johnsonville   Township
Lat: 44-19-53 N **Long:** 95-24-24 W
Pop: 181 (1990); 241 (1980) **Pop Density:** 5.0
Land: 36.5 sq. mi.; **Water:** 0.0 sq. mi.

Kintire   Township
Lat: 44-34-57 N **Long:** 95-17-52 W
Pop: 241 (1990); 258 (1980) **Pop Density:** 6.8
Land: 35.3 sq. mi.; **Water:** 0.0 sq. mi.

Lamberton   City
ZIP: 56152 **Lat:** 44-13-47 N **Long:** 95-15-50 W
Pop: 972 (1990); 1,032 (1980) **Pop Density:** 1944.0
Land: 0.5 sq. mi.; **Water:** 0.0 sq. mi. **Elev:** 1151 ft.
City and township not coextensive.
Name origin: For Henry W. Lamberton, who was a prominent civic leader.

*Lamberton   Township
ZIP: 56152 **Lat:** 44-14-08 N **Long:** 95-17-05 W
Pop: 255 (1990); 329 (1980) **Pop Density:** 7.2
Land: 35.5 sq. mi.; **Water:** 0.0 sq. mi.

Lucan   City
ZIP: 56255 **Lat:** 44-24-33 N **Long:** 95-24-45 W
Pop: 235 (1990); 262 (1980) **Pop Density:** 587.5
Land: 0.4 sq. mi.; **Water:** 0.0 sq. mi.
Name origin: Named by Irish settlers for a village near Dublin, Ireland.

Milroy   City
ZIP: 56263 **Lat:** 44-25-02 N **Long:** 95-33-14 W
Pop: 297 (1990); 242 (1980) **Pop Density:** 990.0
Land: 0.3 sq. mi.; **Water:** 0.0 sq. mi.

Morgan   City
ZIP: 56266 **Lat:** 44-24-56 N **Long:** 94-55-28 W
Pop: 965 (1990); 975 (1980) **Pop Density:** 1608.3
Land: 0.6 sq. mi.; **Water:** 0.0 sq. mi.
City and township not coextensive.
Name origin: For soldier, explorer, and ethnographer Lewis Henry Morgan (1818–81), who passed through the area in the early 1860s.

*Morgan   Township
ZIP: 56266 **Lat:** 44-24-46 N **Long:** 94-54-56 W
Pop: 339 (1990); 417 (1980) **Pop Density:** 9.5
Land: 35.5 sq. mi.; **Water:** 0.0 sq. mi.

New Avon   Township
Lat: 44-24-19 N **Long:** 95-10-17 W
Pop: 263 (1990); 328 (1980) **Pop Density:** 7.3
Land: 36.0 sq. mi.; **Water:** 0.0 sq. mi.

North Hero
Township
Lat: 44-14-49 N **Long:** 95-25-14 W
Pop: 222 (1990); 247 (1980) **Pop Density:** 6.4
Land: 34.9 sq. mi.; **Water:** 0.0 sq. mi.

North Redwood
City
Lat: 44-33-48 N **Long:** 95-05-36 W
Pop: 203 (1990); 206 (1980) **Pop Density:** 203.0
Land: 1.0 sq. mi.; **Water:** 0.0 sq. mi. **Elev:** 847 ft.

Paxton
Township
Lat: 44-29-48 N **Long:** 95-02-43 W
Pop: 527 (1990); 449 (1980) **Pop Density:** 15.2
Land: 34.6 sq. mi.; **Water:** 0.0 sq. mi.

Redwood Falls
City
ZIP: 56283 **Lat:** 44-32-29 N **Long:** 95-06-49 W
Pop: 4,859 (1990); 5,210 (1980) **Pop Density:** 1675.5
Land: 2.9 sq. mi.; **Water:** 0.1 sq. mi. **Elev:** 1044 ft.
Name origin: For the nearby falls of the Redwood River.

*Redwood Falls
Township
ZIP: 56283 **Lat:** 44-30-12 N **Long:** 95-09-30 W
Pop: 277 (1990); 333 (1980) **Pop Density:** 8.1
Land: 34.2 sq. mi.; **Water:** 0.1 sq. mi.

Revere
City
ZIP: 56166 **Lat:** 44-13-08 N **Long:** 95-21-48 W
Pop: 117 (1990); 158 (1980) **Pop Density:** 146.3
Land: 0.8 sq. mi.; **Water:** 0.0 sq. mi.

Sanborn
City
ZIP: 56083 **Lat:** 44-12-36 N **Long:** 95-07-44 W
Pop: 459 (1990); 518 (1980) **Pop Density:** 218.6
Land: 2.1 sq. mi.; **Water:** 0.0 sq. mi.
Name origin: For Sherburn Sanborn, an official of the Chicago & Northwestern Railway Company.

Seaforth
City
Lat: 44-28-36 N **Long:** 95-19-45 W
Pop: 87 (1990); 90 (1980) **Pop Density:** 87.0
Land: 1.0 sq. mi.; **Water:** 0.0 sq. mi.

Sheridan
Township
Lat: 44-29-54 N **Long:** 95-17-44 W
Pop: 240 (1990); 305 (1980) **Pop Density:** 7.1
Land: 34.0 sq. mi.; **Water:** 0.0 sq. mi.

Sherman
Township
Lat: 44-29-38 N **Long:** 94-56-10 W
Pop: 261 (1990); 260 (1980) **Pop Density:** 9.5
Land: 27.5 sq. mi.; **Water:** 0.0 sq. mi.

Springdale
Township
Lat: 44-14-22 N **Long:** 95-32-08 W
Pop: 243 (1990); 310 (1980) **Pop Density:** 6.8
Land: 35.8 sq. mi.; **Water:** 0.1 sq. mi.

Sundown
Township
Lat: 44-19-39 N **Long:** 95-03-24 W
Pop: 292 (1990); 347 (1980) **Pop Density:** 8.1
Land: 35.9 sq. mi.; **Water:** 0.0 sq. mi.

Swedes Forest
Township
Lat: 44-39-04 N **Long:** 95-18-19 W
Pop: 126 (1990); 143 (1980) **Pop Density:** 6.5
Land: 19.4 sq. mi.; **Water:** 0.1 sq. mi.

Three Lakes
Township
Lat: 44-25-13 N **Long:** 95-02-32 W
Pop: 207 (1990); 299 (1980) **Pop Density:** 5.8
Land: 35.4 sq. mi.; **Water:** 0.0 sq. mi.

Underwood
Township
Lat: 44-29-45 N **Long:** 95-32-14 W
Pop: 226 (1990); 237 (1980) **Pop Density:** 6.5
Land: 35.0 sq. mi.; **Water:** 0.0 sq. mi.

Vail
Township
Lat: 44-24-40 N **Long:** 95-17-59 W
Pop: 307 (1990); 353 (1980) **Pop Density:** 8.8
Land: 35.0 sq. mi.; **Water:** 0.2 sq. mi.

Vesta
City
ZIP: 56292 **Lat:** 44-30-23 N **Long:** 95-24-49 W
Pop: 302 (1990); 360 (1980) **Pop Density:** 755.0
Land: 0.4 sq. mi.; **Water:** 0.0 sq. mi.
Settled 1868. City and township not coextensive.
Name origin: For the ancient Roman goddess of the hearth.

*Vesta
Township
ZIP: 56292 **Lat:** 44-30-03 N **Long:** 95-24-41 W
Pop: 223 (1990); 272 (1980) **Pop Density:** 6.4
Land: 34.8 sq. mi.; **Water:** 0.1 sq. mi.

Wabasso
City
ZIP: 56293 **Lat:** 44-24-09 N **Long:** 95-15-18 W
Pop: 684 (1990); 745 (1980) **Pop Density:** 855.0
Land: 0.8 sq. mi.; **Water:** 0.0 sq. mi.
Founded 1899.
Name origin: From Longfellow's "Song of Hiawatha," an Ojibway term meaning 'rabbit.'

Walnut Grove
City
ZIP: 56180 **Lat:** 44-13-32 N **Long:** 95-28-06 W
Pop: 625 (1990); 753 (1980) **Pop Density:** 625.0
Land: 1.0 sq. mi.; **Water:** 0.0 sq. mi. **Elev:** 1212 ft.
Name origin: For a grove of black walnut trees a mile west of the village.

Wanda
City
ZIP: 56294 **Lat:** 44-18-57 N **Long:** 95-12-43 W
Pop: 103 (1990); 118 (1980) **Pop Density:** 343.3
Land: 0.3 sq. mi.; **Water:** 0.0 sq. mi.
Name origin: From an Ojibway Indian term meaning 'forgetfulness.'

Waterbury
Township
Lat: 44-19-38 N **Long:** 95-17-22 W
Pop: 296 (1990); 363 (1980) **Pop Density:** 8.2
Land: 36.2 sq. mi.; **Water:** 0.1 sq. mi.

Westline
Township
Lat: 44-24-42 N **Long:** 95-31-42 W
Pop: 241 (1990); 288 (1980) **Pop Density:** 6.7
Land: 35.8 sq. mi.; **Water:** 0.2 sq. mi.

Willow Lake
Township
Lat: 44-19-39 N **Long:** 95-09-45 W
Pop: 298 (1990); 358 (1980) **Pop Density:** 8.3
Land: 36.0 sq. mi.; **Water:** 0.1 sq. mi.

Renville County
County Seat: Olivia (ZIP: 56277)

Pop: 17,673 (1990); 20,401 (1980) **Pop Density:** 18.0
Land: 983.0 sq. mi.; **Water:** 4.3 sq. mi. **Area Code:** 612
In south-central MN, southwest of Minneapolis; established Feb 20, 1855 (prior to statehood) from unorganized lands.
Name origin: For Joseph Renville (1779?–1846), captain in the British Army during the War of 1812, fur trader, and assistant to missionaries to the Sioux.

Bandon   Township
Lat: 44-34-59 N   **Long:** 94-48-36 W
Pop: 209 (1990); 295 (1980)   **Pop Density:** 5.7
Land: 36.6 sq. mi.; **Water:** 0.0 sq. mi.

Beaver Falls   Township
Lat: 44-35-32 N   **Long:** 95-03-01 W
Pop: 252 (1990); 357 (1980)   **Pop Density:** 9.3
Land: 27.1 sq. mi.; **Water:** 0.1 sq. mi.

Birch Cooley   Township
Lat: 44-34-47 N   **Long:** 94-55-11 W
Pop: 309 (1990); 338 (1980)   **Pop Density:** 7.4
Land: 41.5 sq. mi.; **Water:** 0.0 sq. mi.

Bird Island   City
ZIP: 55310   **Lat:** 44-45-53 N   **Long:** 94-53-38 W
Pop: 1,326 (1990); 1,372 (1980)   **Pop Density:** 884.0
Land: 1.5 sq. mi.; **Water:** 0.0 sq. mi.
City and township not coextensive.
Name origin: For a nearby marshy island that sheltered a large wild bird population in pioneer days.

*Bird Island   Township
ZIP: 55310   **Lat:** 44-45-49 N   **Long:** 94-56-45 W
Pop: 255 (1990); 345 (1980)   **Pop Density:** 7.7
Land: 33.0 sq. mi.; **Water:** 0.0 sq. mi.

Boon Lake   Township
Lat: 44-50-30 N   **Long:** 94-33-42 W
Pop: 373 (1990); 452 (1980)   **Pop Density:** 10.0
Land: 37.3 sq. mi.; **Water:** 1.9 sq. mi.

Brookfield   Township
Lat: 44-50-26 N   **Long:** 94-41-58 W
Pop: 221 (1990); 315 (1980)   **Pop Density:** 6.1
Land: 36.2 sq. mi.; **Water:** 0.0 sq. mi.

Buffalo Lake   City
ZIP: 55314   **Lat:** 44-44-12 N   **Long:** 94-37-03 W
Pop: 734 (1990); 782 (1980)   **Pop Density:** 1223.3
Land: 0.6 sq. mi.; **Water:** 0.0 sq. mi.   **Elev:** 1074 ft.
Name origin: For nearby Buffalo Lake.

Cairo   Township
Lat: 44-30-16 N   **Long:** 94-40-32 W
Pop: 297 (1990); 372 (1980)   **Pop Density:** 8.7
Land: 34.0 sq. mi.; **Water:** 0.2 sq. mi.

Camp   Township
Lat: 44-30-08 N   **Long:** 94-47-42 W
Pop: 219 (1990); 305 (1980)   **Pop Density:** 7.7
Land: 28.5 sq. mi.; **Water:** 0.0 sq. mi.

Crooks   Township
Lat: 44-50-41 N   **Long:** 95-10-37 W
Pop: 204 (1990); 311 (1980)   **Pop Density:** 5.7
Land: 36.1 sq. mi.; **Water:** 0.0 sq. mi.

Danube   City
ZIP: 56230   **Lat:** 44-47-28 N   **Long:** 95-06-09 W
Pop: 562 (1990); 590 (1980)   **Pop Density:** 1124.0
Land: 0.5 sq. mi.; **Water:** 0.0 sq. mi.
Name origin: For the Danube River in Europe.

Emmet   Township
Lat: 44-46-02 N   **Long:** 95-10-32 W
Pop: 275 (1990); 323 (1980)   **Pop Density:** 8.0
Land: 34.5 sq. mi.; **Water:** 0.0 sq. mi.

Ericson   Township
Lat: 44-50-47 N   **Long:** 95-18-03 W
Pop: 289 (1990); 349 (1980)   **Pop Density:** 8.0
Land: 36.3 sq. mi.; **Water:** 0.0 sq. mi.

Fairfax   City
ZIP: 55332   **Lat:** 44-31-41 N   **Long:** 94-43-22 W
Pop: 1,276 (1990); 1,405 (1980)   **Pop Density:** 981.5
Land: 1.3 sq. mi.; **Water:** 0.0 sq. mi.
Name origin: Named by the president of the Minneapolis & St. Louis Railway for his native county in VA.

Flora   Township
Lat: 44-39-53 N   **Long:** 95-10-00 W
Pop: 233 (1990); 307 (1980)   **Pop Density:** 6.2
Land: 37.8 sq. mi.; **Water:** 0.1 sq. mi.

Franklin   City
ZIP: 55333   **Lat:** 44-31-51 N   **Long:** 94-53-10 W
Pop: 441 (1990); 512 (1980)   **Pop Density:** 400.9
Land: 1.1 sq. mi.; **Water:** 0.0 sq. mi.
Name origin: For Benjamin Franklin (1706–90), American statesman, diplomat, and patriot.

Hawk Creek   Township
Lat: 44-46-10 N   **Long:** 95-24-42 W
Pop: 228 (1990); 253 (1980)   **Pop Density:** 7.5
Land: 30.5 sq. mi.; **Water:** 0.1 sq. mi.

Hector   City
ZIP: 55342   **Lat:** 44-44-29 N   **Long:** 94-42-45 W
Pop: 1,145 (1990); 1,252 (1980)   **Pop Density:** 763.3
Land: 1.5 sq. mi.; **Water:** 0.0 sq. mi.   **Elev:** 1078 ft.
City and township not coextensive.
Name origin: For Hector, NY.

*Hector   Township
ZIP: 55342   **Lat:** 44-45-37 N   **Long:** 94-41-45 W
Pop: 288 (1990); 355 (1980)   **Pop Density:** 8.3
Land: 34.7 sq. mi.; **Water:** 0.0 sq. mi.

Henryville   Township
Lat: 44-40-19 N   **Long:** 95-03-22 W
Pop: 248 (1990); 353 (1980)   **Pop Density:** 6.8
Land: 36.3 sq. mi.; **Water:** 0.0 sq. mi.

Kingman
Township
Lat: 44-50-24 N **Long:** 94-56-08 W
Pop: 267 (1990); 354 (1980) **Pop Density:** 7.3
Land: 36.4 sq. mi.; **Water:** 0.0 sq. mi.

Martinsburg
Township
Lat: 44-40-26 N **Long:** 94-41-28 W
Pop: 242 (1990); 275 (1980) **Pop Density:** 6.6
Land: 36.5 sq. mi.; **Water:** 0.0 sq. mi.

Melville
Township
Lat: 44-45-36 N **Long:** 94-49-04 W
Pop: 239 (1990); 344 (1980) **Pop Density:** 6.6
Land: 36.3 sq. mi.; **Water:** 0.0 sq. mi.

Morton
City
ZIP: 56270 **Lat:** 44-33-10 N **Long:** 94-59-05 W
Pop: 448 (1990); 549 (1980) **Pop Density:** 373.3
Land: 1.2 sq. mi.; **Water:** 0.0 sq. mi.
Founded 1880s.
Name origin: Named by officers of the Minneapolis & St. Louis Railway.

Norfolk
Township
Lat: 44-39-57 N **Long:** 94-55-30 W
Pop: 248 (1990); 268 (1980) **Pop Density:** 6.9
Land: 35.7 sq. mi.; **Water:** 0.0 sq. mi.

Olivia
City
ZIP: 56277 **Lat:** 44-46-32 N **Long:** 94-59-49 W
Pop: 2,623 (1990); 2,802 (1980) **Pop Density:** 1140.4
Land: 2.3 sq. mi.; **Water:** 0.0 sq. mi.
Name origin: For the first railroad agent, a woman named Olive.

Osceola
Township
Lat: 44-50-56 N **Long:** 94-48-43 W
Pop: 230 (1990); 265 (1980) **Pop Density:** 6.3
Land: 36.3 sq. mi.; **Water:** 0.0 sq. mi.

Palmyra
Township
Lat: 44-40-28 N **Long:** 94-48-50 W
Pop: 278 (1990); 340 (1980) **Pop Density:** 7.7
Land: 36.3 sq. mi.; **Water:** 0.0 sq. mi.

Preston Lake
Township
Lat: 44-45-57 N **Long:** 94-34-08 W
Pop: 324 (1990); 365 (1980) **Pop Density:** 8.7
Land: 37.4 sq. mi.; **Water:** 1.5 sq. mi.

Renville
City
ZIP: 56284 **Lat:** 44-47-39 N **Long:** 95-12-39 W
Pop: 1,315 (1990); 1,493 (1980) **Pop Density:** 939.3
Land: 1.4 sq. mi.; **Water:** 0.0 sq. mi. **Elev:** 1069 ft.
Name origin: For Joseph Renville (1779?–1846), captain in the British Army during the War of 1812, fur trader, and assistant to missionaries to the Sioux.

Sacred Heart
City
ZIP: 56285 **Lat:** 44-46-59 N **Long:** 95-21-01 W
Pop: 603 (1990); 666 (1980) **Pop Density:** 603.0
Land: 1.0 sq. mi.; **Water:** 0.0 sq. mi.
City and township not coextensive.
Name origin: For an early trapper who wore a bearskin hat, sacred to the Sioux, and so he became known as 'sacred hat,' which eventually became 'sacred heart.'

*Sacred Heart
Township
ZIP: 56285 **Lat:** 44-44-26 N **Long:** 95-17-27 W
Pop: 321 (1990); 336 (1980) **Pop Density:** 6.2
Land: 51.7 sq. mi.; **Water:** 0.0 sq. mi.

Troy
Township
Lat: 44-45-07 N **Long:** 95-03-57 W
Pop: 320 (1990); 373 (1980) **Pop Density:** 9.2
Land: 34.8 sq. mi.; **Water:** 0.0 sq. mi.

Wang
Township
Lat: 44-50-33 N **Long:** 95-25-42 W
Pop: 284 (1990); 312 (1980) **Pop Density:** 7.8
Land: 36.2 sq. mi.; **Water:** 0.0 sq. mi.

Wellington
Township
Lat: 44-35-34 N **Long:** 94-41-51 W
Pop: 250 (1990); 383 (1980) **Pop Density:** 6.9
Land: 36.1 sq. mi.; **Water:** 0.2 sq. mi.

Winfield
Township
Lat: 44-51-01 N **Long:** 95-03-24 W
Pop: 297 (1990); 333 (1980) **Pop Density:** 8.1
Land: 36.5 sq. mi.; **Water:** 0.1 sq. mi.

Rice County
County Seat: Faribault (ZIP: 55021)

Pop: 49,183 (1990); 46,087 (1980) **Pop Density:** 98.8
Land: 497.6 sq. mi.; **Water:** 18.6 sq. mi. **Area Code:** 507
In south-central MN, south of Minneapolis; established Mar 5, 1853 (prior to statehood) from Nobles County.
Name origin: For Henry Mower Rice (1817–94), MN territorial delegate to Congress (1853–57) and one of its first two U.S. senators (1858–63).

Bridgewater
Township
ZIP: 55019 **Lat:** 44-24-54 N **Long:** 93-13-19 W
Pop: 1,612 (1990); 1,691 (1980) **Pop Density:** 44.2
Land: 36.5 sq. mi.; **Water:** 0.1 sq. mi.

Cannon City
Township
ZIP: 55021 **Lat:** 44-20-00 N **Long:** 93-12-44 W
Pop: 1,109 (1990); 1,099 (1980) **Pop Density:** 36.0
Land: 30.8 sq. mi.; **Water:** 0.2 sq. mi.

Dennison City
Lat: 44-24-29 N Long: 93-02-24 W
Pop: 0 (1990)
Land: 0.005 sq. mi.; **Water:** 0.0 sq. mi.
Founded 1856. Part of the town is also in Goodhue County.
Name origin: For Morris Dennison, who owned the land upon which the city was founded.

Dundas City
ZIP: 55019 Lat: 44-25-46 N Long: 93-12-17 W
Pop: 473 (1990); 422 (1980) **Pop Density:** 315.3
Land: 1.5 sq. mi.; **Water:** 0.0 sq. mi. **Elev:** 958 ft.

Erin Township
Lat: 44-24-31 N Long: 93-27-56 W
Pop: 685 (1990); 793 (1980) **Pop Density:** 19.7
Land: 34.8 sq. mi.; **Water:** 1.4 sq. mi.

Faribault City
ZIP: 55021 Lat: 44-17-50 N Long: 93-16-29 W
Pop: 17,085 (1990); 16,241 (1980) **Pop Density:** 1472.8
Land: 11.6 sq. mi.; **Water:** 0.2 sq. mi.
In southern MN, 47 mi. south of Minneapolis.
Name origin: For early settler and merchant Alexander Faribault, who arrived in the area in 1826.

Forest Township
Lat: 44-24-53 N Long: 93-20-22 W
Pop: 872 (1990); 854 (1980) **Pop Density:** 26.7
Land: 32.7 sq. mi.; **Water:** 3.0 sq. mi.

Lonsdale City
ZIP: 55046 Lat: 44-28-39 N Long: 93-25-39 W
Pop: 1,252 (1990); 1,160 (1980) **Pop Density:** 1138.2
Land: 1.1 sq. mi.; **Water:** 0.0 sq. mi.
Name origin: Named by settlers for Lonsdale, RI.

Morristown City
ZIP: 55052 Lat: 44-13-28 N Long: 93-26-41 W
Pop: 784 (1990); 639 (1980) **Pop Density:** 871.1
Land: 0.9 sq. mi.; **Water:** 0.0 sq. mi.
Settled 1850s. City and township not coextensive.
Name origin: For minister Jonathon Morris, who died here in 1856.

*Morristown Township
ZIP: 55052 Lat: 44-14-32 N Long: 93-27-30 W
Pop: 641 (1990); 693 (1980) **Pop Density:** 19.1
Land: 33.5 sq. mi.; **Water:** 1.6 sq. mi.

Nerstrand City
ZIP: 55053 Lat: 44-20-26 N Long: 93-03-44 W
Pop: 210 (1990); 255 (1980) **Pop Density:** 150.0
Land: 1.4 sq. mi.; **Water:** 0.0 sq. mi.

Northfield City
ZIP: 55057 Lat: 44-27-15 N Long: 93-09-55 W
Pop: 14,514 (1990); 12,549 (1980) **Pop Density:** 2460.0
Land: 5.9 sq. mi.; **Water:** 0.0 sq. mi.
In southern MN, south of Minneapolis. Part of the town is also in Dakota County.
Name origin: For founder John North, who later became a U.S. judge in CA.

*Northfield Township
ZIP: 55057 Lat: 44-24-54 N Long: 93-05-23 W
Pop: 781 (1990); 757 (1980) **Pop Density:** 19.8
Land: 39.4 sq. mi.; **Water:** 0.0 sq. mi.

Richland Township
ZIP: 55021 Lat: 44-14-11 N Long: 93-06-11 W
Pop: 461 (1990); 496 (1980) **Pop Density:** 12.8
Land: 36.1 sq. mi.; **Water:** 0.0 sq. mi.

Shieldsville Township
ZIP: 55021 Lat: 44-19-48 N Long: 93-27-17 W
Pop: 969 (1990); 850 (1980) **Pop Density:** 29.8
Land: 32.5 sq. mi.; **Water:** 4.1 sq. mi.

Walcott Township
ZIP: 55021 Lat: 44-14-16 N Long: 93-12-48 W
Pop: 1,584 (1990); 1,553 (1980) **Pop Density:** 46.5
Land: 34.1 sq. mi.; **Water:** 0.0 sq. mi.

Warsaw Township
ZIP: 55087 Lat: 44-14-19 N Long: 93-20-44 W
Pop: 1,284 (1990); 1,323 (1980) **Pop Density:** 39.5
Land: 32.5 sq. mi.; **Water:** 2.6 sq. mi.

Webster Township
ZIP: 55088 Lat: 44-29-56 N Long: 93-20-28 W
Pop: 1,452 (1990); 1,397 (1980) **Pop Density:** 41.4
Land: 35.1 sq. mi.; **Water:** 0.6 sq. mi.

Wells Township
ZIP: 55021 Lat: 44-19-40 N Long: 93-20-40 W
Pop: 1,677 (1990); 1,563 (1980) **Pop Density:** 59.0
Land: 28.4 sq. mi.; **Water:** 4.0 sq. mi.

Wheatland Township
Lat: 44-29-47 N Long: 93-27-59 W
Pop: 1,276 (1990); 1,230 (1980) **Pop Density:** 37.5
Land: 34.0 sq. mi.; **Water:** 0.9 sq. mi.

Wheeling Township
ZIP: 55053 Lat: 44-19-32 N Long: 93-06-12 W
Pop: 462 (1990); 522 (1980) **Pop Density:** 13.4
Land: 34.6 sq. mi.; **Water:** 0.0 sq. mi.

Rock County
County Seat: Luverne (ZIP: 56156)

Pop: 9,806 (1990); 10,703 (1980) **Pop Density:** 20.3
Land: 482.6 sq. mi.; **Water:** 0.2 sq. mi. **Area Code:** 507

In the southwestern corner of MN; established mistakenly as Pipestone County May 23, 1857 (prior to statehood) from Nobles County; name changed Feb 20, 1862.

Name origin: For the Rock River, which runs through the county; named for the outcrop of quartzite about 3 sq. mi. in area and rising 175 ft. above this prairie region; now called "the Mound."

Battle Plain
Township
Lat: 43-48-10 N **Long:** 96-06-35 W
Pop: 229 (1990); 329 (1980) **Pop Density:** 6.3
Land: 36.3 sq. mi.; **Water:** 0.0 sq. mi.

Beaver Creek
City
ZIP: 56116 **Lat:** 43-36-45 N **Long:** 96-21-42 W
Pop: 249 (1990); 260 (1980) **Pop Density:** 498.0
Land: 0.5 sq. mi.; **Water:** 0.0 sq. mi.
Founded 1872. City and township not coextensive.
Name origin: For the excellent fur trapping of that day.

*Beaver Creek
Township
ZIP: 56116 **Lat:** 43-37-46 N **Long:** 96-22-06 W
Pop: 445 (1990); 481 (1980) **Pop Density:** 9.2
Land: 48.2 sq. mi.; **Water:** 0.0 sq. mi.

Clinton
Township
Lat: 43-32-35 N **Long:** 96-13-45 W
Pop: 350 (1990); 399 (1980) **Pop Density:** 9.8
Land: 35.6 sq. mi.; **Water:** 0.0 sq. mi.

Denver
Township
Lat: 43-48-44 N **Long:** 96-14-31 W
Pop: 227 (1990); 287 (1980) **Pop Density:** 6.6
Land: 34.2 sq. mi.; **Water:** 0.0 sq. mi.

Hardwick
City
ZIP: 56134 **Lat:** 43-46-30 N **Long:** 96-11-48 W
Pop: 234 (1990); 279 (1980) **Pop Density:** 137.6
Land: 1.7 sq. mi.; **Water:** 0.0 sq. mi. **Elev:** 607 ft.
Name origin: For J. L. Hardwick, one-time master builder of the Burlington Railway Company.

Hills
City
ZIP: 56138 **Lat:** 43-31-35 N **Long:** 96-21-38 W
Pop: 607 (1990); 598 (1980) **Pop Density:** 1214.0
Land: 0.5 sq. mi.; **Water:** 0.0 sq. mi.
Name origin: For railway president Frederick Hills.

Jasper
City
ZIP: 56144 **Lat:** 43-50-47 N **Long:** 96-24-08 W
Pop: 75 (1990); 72 (1980) **Pop Density:** 150.0
Land: 0.5 sq. mi.; **Water:** 0.0 sq. mi.
Incorporated 1889. Part of the town is also in Pipestone County.
Name origin: For the deposits of red quartzite, or jasper, found nearby.

Kanaranzi
Township
Lat: 43-32-33 N **Long:** 96-06-37 W
Pop: 320 (1990); 336 (1980) **Pop Density:** 8.9
Land: 36.0 sq. mi.; **Water:** 0.0 sq. mi.

Kenneth
City
ZIP: 56147 **Lat:** 43-45-11 N **Long:** 96-04-18 W
Pop: 81 (1990); 95 (1980) **Pop Density:** 73.6
Land: 1.1 sq. mi.; **Water:** 0.0 sq. mi.
Founded 1900.
Name origin: For the son of a nearby farmer.

Luverne
City
ZIP: 56156 **Lat:** 43-39-17 N **Long:** 96-12-35 W
Pop: 4,382 (1990); 4,568 (1980) **Pop Density:** 1825.8
Land: 2.4 sq. mi.; **Water:** 0.0 sq. mi.
City and township not coextensive.
Name origin: For an early pioneer settler.

*Luverne
Township
ZIP: 56156 **Lat:** 43-37-52 N **Long:** 96-14-14 W
Pop: 477 (1990); 581 (1980) **Pop Density:** 14.2
Land: 33.6 sq. mi.; **Water:** 0.1 sq. mi.

Magnolia
City
ZIP: 56158 **Lat:** 43-38-41 N **Long:** 96-04-28 W
Pop: 155 (1990); 234 (1980) **Pop Density:** 155.0
Land: 1.0 sq. mi.; **Water:** 0.0 sq. mi.
Founded 1872. City and township not coextensive.
Name origin: For Magnolia, WI, former home of an early settler.

*Magnolia
Township
ZIP: 56158 **Lat:** 43-37-33 N **Long:** 96-06-38 W
Pop: 303 (1990); 270 (1980) **Pop Density:** 8.6
Land: 35.1 sq. mi.; **Water:** 0.0 sq. mi.

Martin
Township
Lat: 43-32-36 N **Long:** 96-22-20 W
Pop: 465 (1990); 504 (1980) **Pop Density:** 9.7
Land: 48.0 sq. mi.; **Water:** 0.0 sq. mi.

Mound
Township
Lat: 43-42-54 N **Long:** 96-14-25 W
Pop: 274 (1990); 347 (1980) **Pop Density:** 7.7
Land: 35.7 sq. mi.; **Water:** 0.1 sq. mi.

Rose Dell
Township
Lat: 43-48-22 N **Long:** 96-22-20 W
Pop: 241 (1990); 314 (1980) **Pop Density:** 5.0
Land: 48.1 sq. mi.; **Water:** 0.0 sq. mi.

Springwater
Township
Lat: 43-42-39 N **Long:** 96-22-37 W
Pop: 303 (1990); 352 (1980) **Pop Density:** 6.2
Land: 48.7 sq. mi.; **Water:** 0.0 sq. mi.

Steen
City
ZIP: 56173 **Lat:** 43-30-47 N **Long:** 96-15-43 W
Pop: 176 (1990); 153 (1980) **Pop Density:** 440.0
Land: 0.4 sq. mi.; **Water:** 0.0 sq. mi.

American Places Dictionary   MINNESOTA, Roseau County

Vienna   Township
Lat: 43-42-44 N   **Long:** 96-07-19 W
Pop: 213 (1990); 244 (1980)   **Pop Density:** 6.1
Land: 35.0 sq. mi.; **Water:** 0.0 sq. mi.

Roseau County
County Seat: Roseau (ZIP: 56751)

Pop: 15,026 (1990); 12,574 (1980)   **Pop Density:** 9.0
Land: 1662.7 sq. mi.; **Water:** 15.8 sq. mi.   **Area Code:** 218
On the northern border of MN, northeast of Grand Forks, ND; established Dec 31, 1894 from Kittson County.

Name origin: For Roseau lake and river, both in the northern part of the county; from French 'reed,' from a translation of an Ojibway word that refers to the coarse grass (Phragmites communis) growing along the banks.

Badger   City
ZIP: 56714   **Lat:** 48-46-33 N   **Long:** 96-01-14 W
Pop: 381 (1990); 320 (1980)   **Pop Density:** 293.1
Land: 1.3 sq. mi.; **Water:** 0.0 sq. mi.   **Elev:** 1082 ft.
Name origin: For nearby Badger Creek.

Barnett   Township
Lat: 48-40-49 N   **Long:** 96-04-14 W
Pop: 165 (1990); 202 (1980)   **Pop Density:** 4.5
Land: 37.0 sq. mi.; **Water:** 0.0 sq. mi.

Barto   Township
Lat: 48-45-57 N   **Long:** 96-12-20 W
Pop: 128 (1990); 164 (1980)   **Pop Density:** 3.5
Land: 36.9 sq. mi.; **Water:** 0.0 sq. mi.

Beaver   Township
Lat: 48-40-15 N   **Long:** 95-31-28 W
Pop: 91 (1990); 103 (1980)   **Pop Density:** 2.6
Land: 35.4 sq. mi.; **Water:** 0.2 sq. mi.

Cedarbend   Township
Lat: 48-50-31 N   **Long:** 95-24-24 W
Pop: 251 (1990); 134 (1980)   **Pop Density:** 7.0
Land: 36.0 sq. mi.; **Water:** 0.0 sq. mi.

Deer   Township
Lat: 48-35-08 N   **Long:** 96-11-32 W
Pop: 129 (1990); 153 (1980)   **Pop Density:** 3.6
Land: 36.1 sq. mi.; **Water:** 0.0 sq. mi.

Dewey   Township
Lat: 48-40-20 N   **Long:** 96-19-59 W
Pop: 130 (1990); 144 (1980)   **Pop Density:** 3.7
Land: 34.8 sq. mi.; **Water:** 0.0 sq. mi.

Dieter   Township
Lat: 48-56-32 N   **Long:** 95-56-32 W
Pop: 177 (1990); 216 (1980)   **Pop Density:** 4.0
Land: 44.4 sq. mi.; **Water:** 0.0 sq. mi.

Enstrom   Township
Lat: 48-50-06 N   **Long:** 95-32-54 W
Pop: 478 (1990); 263 (1980)   **Pop Density:** 13.3
Land: 36.0 sq. mi.; **Water:** 0.0 sq. mi.

Falun   Township
Lat: 48-45-24 N   **Long:** 95-32-15 W
Pop: 257 (1990); 250 (1980)   **Pop Density:** 7.2
Land: 35.6 sq. mi.; **Water:** 0.0 sq. mi.

Golden Valley   Township
Lat: 48-35-33 N   **Long:** 95-39-26 W
Pop: 200 (1990); 184 (1980)   **Pop Density:** 5.5
Land: 36.2 sq. mi.; **Water:** 0.0 sq. mi.

Greenbush   City
ZIP: 56726   **Lat:** 48-41-53 N   **Long:** 96-11-02 W
Pop: 800 (1990); 817 (1980)   **Pop Density:** 800.0
Land: 1.0 sq. mi.; **Water:** 0.0 sq. mi.
Name origin: For evergreen spruce trees visible from an early pioneer wagon road.

Grimstad   Township
Lat: 48-39-48 N   **Long:** 95-47-20 W
Pop: 169 (1990); 211 (1980)   **Pop Density:** 4.6
Land: 37.1 sq. mi.; **Water:** 0.0 sq. mi.

Hereim   Township
Lat: 48-40-50 N   **Long:** 96-11-41 W
Pop: 222 (1990); 257 (1980)   **Pop Density:** 6.6
Land: 33.6 sq. mi.; **Water:** 0.0 sq. mi.

Huss   Township
Lat: 48-35-09 N   **Long:** 96-03-22 W
Pop: 125 (1990); 165 (1980)   **Pop Density:** 3.4
Land: 36.4 sq. mi.; **Water:** 0.0 sq. mi.

Jadis   Township
Lat: 48-52-10 N   **Long:** 95-48-22 W
Pop: 545 (1990); 544 (1980)   **Pop Density:** 10.8
Land: 50.3 sq. mi.; **Water:** 0.0 sq. mi.

Lake   Township
Lat: 48-57-05 N   **Long:** 95-23-47 W
Pop: 1,836 (1990); 738 (1980)   **Pop Density:** 31.3
Land: 58.7 sq. mi.; **Water:** 0.4 sq. mi.

Laona   Township
Lat: 48-51-01 N   **Long:** 95-09-01 W
Pop: 527 (1990); 286 (1980)   **Pop Density:** 13.8
Land: 38.1 sq. mi.; **Water:** 0.0 sq. mi.

Lind   Township
Lat: 48-35-00 N   **Long:** 96-19-10 W
Pop: 63 (1990); 92 (1980)   **Pop Density:** 1.7
Land: 36.1 sq. mi.; **Water:** 0.0 sq. mi.

Malung   Township
Lat: 48-45-52 N   **Long:** 95-40-08 W
Pop: 390 (1990); 349 (1980)   **Pop Density:** 10.9
Land: 35.8 sq. mi.; **Water:** 0.0 sq. mi.

Mickinock
Township
Lat: 48-40-30 N Long: 95-39-57 W
Pop: 262 (1990); 301 (1980) **Pop Density:** 6.9
Land: 37.7 sq. mi.; **Water:** 0.0 sq. mi.

Moose
Township
Lat: 48-50-45 N Long: 96-05-04 W
Pop: 122 (1990); 150 (1980) **Pop Density:** 3.4
Land: 36.4 sq. mi.; **Water:** 0.0 sq. mi.

Moranville
Township
Lat: 48-50-35 N Long: 95-17-08 W
Pop: 789 (1990); 402 (1980) **Pop Density:** 22.2
Land: 35.5 sq. mi.; **Water:** 0.0 sq. mi.

Nereson
Township
Lat: 48-40-46 N Long: 95-55-08 W
Pop: 105 (1990); 115 (1980) **Pop Density:** 2.9
Land: 36.3 sq. mi.; **Water:** 0.0 sq. mi.

North Roseau
Pop. Place
Lat: 48-57-58 N Long: 95-40-48 W
Pop: 149 (1990); 159 (1980) **Pop Density:** 1.2
Land: 119.8 sq. mi.; **Water:** 0.0 sq. mi.

Northwest Roseau
Pop. Place
Lat: 48-55-15 N Long: 96-16-19 W
Pop: 19 (1990); 18 (1980) **Pop Density:** 0.2
Land: 114.6 sq. mi.; **Water:** 11.5 sq. mi.

Palmville
Township
Lat: 48-34-40 N Long: 95-47-49 W
Pop: 53 (1990); 58 (1980) **Pop Density:** 1.5
Land: 35.8 sq. mi.; **Water:** 0.0 sq. mi.

Pohlitz
Township
Lat: 48-56-48 N Long: 96-03-43 W
Pop: 42 (1990); 52 (1980) **Pop Density:** 1.0
Land: 42.4 sq. mi.; **Water:** 2.8 sq. mi.

Polonia
Township
Lat: 48-45-13 N Long: 96-19-40 W
Pop: 56 (1990); 71 (1980) **Pop Density:** 1.5
Land: 36.7 sq. mi.; **Water:** 0.0 sq. mi.

Poplar Grove
Township
Lat: 48-35-16 N Long: 95-55-40 W
Pop: 103 (1990); 127 (1980) **Pop Density:** 2.9
Land: 36.0 sq. mi.; **Water:** 0.0 sq. mi.

Reine
Township
Lat: 48-34-58 N Long: 95-33-26 W
Pop: 92 (1990); 89 (1980) **Pop Density:** 2.5
Land: 36.1 sq. mi.; **Water:** 0.1 sq. mi.

Roosevelt
City
ZIP: 56673 Lat: 48-48-24 N Long: 95-06-01 W
Pop: 170 (1990); 118 (1980) **Pop Density:** 170.0
Land: 1.0 sq. mi.; **Water:** 0.0 sq. mi. **Elev:** 1163 ft.
Part of the town is also in Lake of the Woods County.
Name origin: For Theodore Roosevelt (1858–1919), twenty-sixth U.S. president.

Roseau
City
ZIP: 56751 Lat: 48-50-44 N Long: 95-45-42 W
Pop: 2,396 (1990); 2,272 (1980) **Pop Density:** 1597.3
Land: 1.5 sq. mi.; **Water:** 0.0 sq. mi. **Elev:** 1048 ft.
Name origin: For the Roseau River.

Ross
Township
Lat: 48-51-18 N Long: 95-56-31 W
Pop: 342 (1990); 320 (1980) **Pop Density:** 9.6
Land: 35.8 sq. mi.; **Water:** 0.0 sq. mi.

Skagen
Township
Lat: 48-46-04 N Long: 96-04-44 W
Pop: 220 (1990); 212 (1980) **Pop Density:** 6.3
Land: 35.1 sq. mi.; **Water:** 0.0 sq. mi.

Soler
Township
Lat: 48-51-22 N Long: 96-11-43 W
Pop: 100 (1990); 110 (1980) **Pop Density:** 2.7
Land: 36.4 sq. mi.; **Water:** 0.0 sq. mi.

Southeast Roseau
Pop. Place
Lat: 48-43-01 N Long: 95-19-23 W
Pop: 207 (1990); 208 (1980) **Pop Density:** 1.2
Land: 178.8 sq. mi.; **Water:** 0.4 sq. mi.

Spruce
Township
Lat: 48-50-54 N Long: 95-40-48 W
Pop: 573 (1990); 537 (1980) **Pop Density:** 16.1
Land: 35.7 sq. mi.; **Water:** 0.1 sq. mi.

Stafford
Township
Lat: 48-45-43 N Long: 95-48-41 W
Pop: 219 (1990); 193 (1980) **Pop Density:** 6.1
Land: 36.1 sq. mi.; **Water:** 0.0 sq. mi.

Stokes
Township
Lat: 48-45-39 N Long: 95-56-33 W
Pop: 224 (1990); 207 (1980) **Pop Density:** 6.2
Land: 36.0 sq. mi.; **Water:** 0.0 sq. mi.

Strathcona
City
ZIP: 56759 Lat: 48-33-08 N Long: 96-10-04 W
Pop: 40 (1990); 47 (1980) **Pop Density:** 80.0
Land: 0.5 sq. mi.; **Water:** 0.0 sq. mi. **Elev:** 1124 ft.

Warroad
City
ZIP: 56763 Lat: 48-54-30 N Long: 95-19-14 W
Pop: 1,679 (1990); 1,216 (1980) **Pop Density:** 1049.4
Land: 1.6 sq. mi.; **Water:** 0.1 sq. mi. **Elev:** 1070 ft.
Name origin: For the nearby Warroad River.

> ## St. Louis County
> **County Seat: Duluth (ZIP: 55802)**
>
> **Pop:** 198,213 (1990); 222,229 (1980) **Pop Density:** 31.8
> **Land:** 6225.7 sq. mi.; **Water:** 634.9 sq. mi. **Area Code:** 218
>
> On the northeastern border of MN, bordered on the southeast by Lake Superior; established Mar 3, 1855 (prior to statehood) from Lake County (then called Doty County).
>
> **Name origin:** For the St. Louis River, which flows through the county; itself named for Louis IX of France (1215–70), who participated in the Sixth Crusade (1248–54) and was canonized in 1297.

Alango Township
ZIP: 55703   Lat: 47-45-52 N **Long:** 92-46-00 W
Pop: 300 (1990); 318 (1980)   **Pop Density:** 8.3
Land: 36.1 sq. mi.; **Water:** 0.0 sq. mi.

Alborn Township
ZIP: 55702   Lat: 46-59-31 N **Long:** 92-36-50 W
Pop: 323 (1990); 314 (1980)   **Pop Density:** 9.4
Land: 34.5 sq. mi.; **Water:** 0.7 sq. mi.

Alden Township
   Lat: 47-03-10 N **Long:** 91-52-03 W
Pop: 147 (1990); 161 (1980)   **Pop Density:** 4.1
Land: 35.7 sq. mi.; **Water:** 0.1 sq. mi.

Angora Township
ZIP: 55703   Lat: 47-45-34 N **Long:** 92-37-47 W
Pop: 291 (1990); 291 (1980)   **Pop Density:** 8.0
Land: 36.3 sq. mi.; **Water:** 0.1 sq. mi.

Arnold CDP
   Lat: 46-52-30 N **Long:** 92-06-28 W
Pop: 2,891 (1990)   **Pop Density:** 249.2
Land: 11.6 sq. mi.; **Water:** 0.1 sq. mi.

Arrowhead Township
ZIP: 55711   Lat: 46-51-39 N **Long:** 92-44-30 W
Pop: 151 (1990); 151 (1980)   **Pop Density:** 2.1
Land: 70.8 sq. mi.; **Water:** 0.8 sq. mi.

Ault Township
ZIP: 55602   Lat: 47-13-56 N **Long:** 91-56-03 W
Pop: 65 (1990); 119 (1980)   **Pop Density:** 0.9
Land: 70.1 sq. mi.; **Water:** 1.7 sq. mi.

Aurora City
ZIP: 55705   Lat: 47-31-55 N **Long:** 92-14-24 W
Pop: 1,965 (1990); 2,670 (1980)   **Pop Density:** 517.1
Land: 3.8 sq. mi.; **Water:** 0.1 sq. mi.   **Elev:** 1480 ft.
Name origin: From Latin 'dawn' or for the ancient Roman goddess of the dawn.

Babbitt City
ZIP: 55706   Lat: 47-38-42 N **Long:** 91-56-24 W
Pop: 1,562 (1990); 2,435 (1980)   **Pop Density:** 14.8
Land: 105.7 sq. mi.; **Water:** 1.1 sq. mi.
Name origin: For an early settler.

Balkan Township
ZIP: 55719   Lat: 47-33-44 N **Long:** 92-51-25 W
Pop: 841 (1990); 934 (1980)   **Pop Density:** 13.1
Land: 64.2 sq. mi.; **Water:** 1.1 sq. mi.

Bassett Township
ZIP: 55602   Lat: 47-29-35 N **Long:** 91-53-37 W
Pop: 37 (1990); 40 (1980)   **Pop Density:** 0.2
Land: 174.5 sq. mi.; **Water:** 7.6 sq. mi.

Beatty Township
   Lat: 47-58-15 N **Long:** 92-37-18 W
Pop: 360 (1990); 350 (1980)   **Pop Density:** 5.5
Land: 65.2 sq. mi.; **Water:** 14.7 sq. mi.

Birch Lake Pop. Place
   Lat: 47-45-55 N **Long:** 91-59-12 W
Pop: 452 (1990); 699 (1980)   **Pop Density:** 5.0
Land: 90.9 sq. mi.; **Water:** 14.9 sq. mi.

Biwabik City
ZIP: 55708   Lat: 47-32-03 N **Long:** 92-20-59 W
Pop: 1,097 (1990); 1,428 (1980)   **Pop Density:** 228.5
Land: 4.8 sq. mi.; **Water:** 0.3 sq. mi.   **Elev:** 1448 ft.
City and township not coextensive.
Name origin: From the Ojibway Indian term meaning 'iron.'

*Biwabik Township
   Lat: 47-29-33 N **Long:** 92-22-30 W
Pop: 839 (1990); 1,034 (1980)   **Pop Density:** 30.1
Land: 27.9 sq. mi.; **Water:** 2.6 sq. mi.

Breitung Township
ZIP: 55790   Lat: 47-51-00 N **Long:** 92-10-34 W
Pop: 755 (1990); 933 (1980)   **Pop Density:** 15.4
Land: 49.1 sq. mi.; **Water:** 20.6 sq. mi.

Brevator Township
ZIP: 55779   Lat: 46-48-57 N **Long:** 92-29-32 W
Pop: 1,093 (1990); 1,023 (1980)   **Pop Density:** 31.6
Land: 34.6 sq. mi.; **Water:** 1.1 sq. mi.

Brookston City
ZIP: 55711   Lat: 46-51-57 N **Long:** 92-36-11 W
Pop: 107 (1990); 124 (1980)   **Pop Density:** 178.3
Land: 0.6 sq. mi.; **Water:** 0.0 sq. mi.   **Elev:** 1228 ft.

Buhl City
ZIP: 55713   Lat: 47-29-54 N **Long:** 92-46-00 W
Pop: 915 (1990); 1,284 (1980)   **Pop Density:** 295.2
Land: 3.1 sq. mi.; **Water:** 0.2 sq. mi.   **Elev:** 1533 ft.
Name origin: For Frank Buhl, president of the Sharon Iron Ore Company.

Canosia Township
   Lat: 46-53-37 N **Long:** 92-14-55 W
Pop: 1,743 (1990); 1,562 (1980)   **Pop Density:** 57.9
Land: 30.1 sq. mi.; **Water:** 5.6 sq. mi.

Cedar Valley Township
ZIP: 55736   Lat: 47-06-52 N **Long:** 93-00-09 W
Pop: 210 (1990); 219 (1980)   **Pop Density:** 3.1
Land: 68.5 sq. mi.; **Water:** 0.9 sq. mi.

Cherry
Township
Lat: 47-24-53 N **Long:** 92-44-40 W
Pop: 929 (1990); 1,018 (1980) **Pop Density:** 28.2
Land: 32.9 sq. mi.; **Water:** 0.6 sq. mi.

Chisholm
City
ZIP: 55719 **Lat:** 47-29-15 N **Long:** 92-52-44 W
Pop: 5,290 (1990); 5,930 (1980) **Pop Density:** 1202.3
Land: 4.4 sq. mi.; **Water:** 0.3 sq. mi. **Elev:** 1578 ft.
Name origin: For Archibald Chisholm, one of the chief explorers of the Mesabi iron ore range.

Clinton
Township
Lat: 47-24-57 N **Long:** 92-37-32 W
Pop: 1,077 (1990); 1,434 (1980) **Pop Density:** 32.3
Land: 33.3 sq. mi.; **Water:** 0.7 sq. mi.

Colvin
Township
ZIP: 55763 **Lat:** 47-19-29 N **Long:** 92-14-21 W
Pop: 392 (1990); 447 (1980) **Pop Density:** 11.7
Land: 33.6 sq. mi.; **Water:** 2.3 sq. mi.

Cook
City
Lat: 47-51-11 N **Long:** 92-41-16 W
Pop: 680 (1990); 800 (1980) **Pop Density:** 850.0
Land: 0.8 sq. mi.; **Water:** 0.0 sq. mi. **Elev:** 1306 ft.
Founded 1903.
Name origin: For Wirth Cook, a lumber businessman from Duluth who was instrumental in its founding.

Cotton
Township
Lat: 47-09-44 N **Long:** 92-25-43 W
Pop: 429 (1990); 396 (1980) **Pop Density:** 6.2
Land: 69.4 sq. mi.; **Water:** 2.7 sq. mi.

Culver
Township
ZIP: 55727 **Lat:** 46-53-26 N **Long:** 92-37-07 W
Pop: 278 (1990); 332 (1980) **Pop Density:** 8.0
Land: 34.6 sq. mi.; **Water:** 0.5 sq. mi.

Duluth
City
ZIP: 55806 **Lat:** 46-46-51 N **Long:** 92-07-04 W
Pop: 85,493 (1990); 92,811 (1980) **Pop Density:** 1264.7
Land: 67.6 sq. mi.; **Water:** 19.4 sq. mi.
On the central-eastern border of MN at the west end of Lake Superior. Incorporated as a town May 19, 1857; as a city March 5, 1870. Industrial city: steel, ironworks, blast furnaces, meat packing; busiest freshwater port in North America; principal exports iron ore and grain; coal is major import.
Name origin: For Daniel Greysolon Du Luth (Du Lhut, Du Lhud, Du Lud; 1649–1710), trader and explorer.

*Duluth
Township
Lat: 46-57-23 N **Long:** 91-51-23 W
Pop: 1,561 (1990); 1,604 (1980) **Pop Density:** 33.6
Land: 46.5 sq. mi.; **Water:** 5.4 sq. mi.

Ellsburg
Township
Lat: 47-14-45 N **Long:** 92-25-33 W
Pop: 121 (1990); 139 (1980) **Pop Density:** 1.7
Land: 69.6 sq. mi.; **Water:** 2.4 sq. mi.

Elmer
Township
Lat: 47-04-34 N **Long:** 92-50-35 W
Pop: 180 (1990); 215 (1980) **Pop Density:** 4.4
Land: 40.6 sq. mi.; **Water:** 0.1 sq. mi.

Ely
City
ZIP: 55731 **Lat:** 47-54-20 N **Long:** 91-51-02 W
Pop: 3,968 (1990); 4,820 (1980) **Pop Density:** 1469.6
Land: 2.7 sq. mi.; **Water:** 0.0 sq. mi.
Name origin: For financier Arthur Ely, who helped open up the Vermillion Range.

Embarrass
Township
ZIP: 55732 **Lat:** 47-40-36 N **Long:** 92-14-56 W
Pop: 826 (1990); 1,154 (1980) **Pop Density:** 25.3
Land: 32.7 sq. mi.; **Water:** 0.1 sq. mi.
Name origin: For the Embarrass River on which it is located; from French 'snags, obstacles [to navigation].'

Eveleth
City
ZIP: 55734 **Lat:** 47-27-49 N **Long:** 92-32-34 W
Pop: 4,064 (1990); 5,042 (1980) **Pop Density:** 645.1
Land: 6.3 sq. mi.; **Water:** 0.2 sq. mi.
Name origin: For a woodsman named Eveleth, who scouted the area for lumber interests in the 1890s.

Fairbanks
Township
ZIP: 55602 **Lat:** 47-19-15 N **Long:** 91-55-09 W
Pop: 74 (1990); 75 (1980) **Pop Density:** 1.1
Land: 70.0 sq. mi.; **Water:** 2.0 sq. mi.

Fayal
Township
ZIP: 55734 **Lat:** 47-24-42 N **Long:** 92-29-37 W
Pop: 2,001 (1990); 2,175 (1980) **Pop Density:** 63.7
Land: 31.4 sq. mi.; **Water:** 3.0 sq. mi.

Field
Township
Lat: 47-52-39 N **Long:** 92-45-38 W
Pop: 425 (1990); 430 (1980) **Pop Density:** 7.8
Land: 54.2 sq. mi.; **Water:** 0.0 sq. mi.

Fine Lakes
Township
ZIP: 55711 **Lat:** 46-48-19 N **Long:** 92-51-18 W
Pop: 150 (1990); 166 (1980) **Pop Density:** 4.4
Land: 34.1 sq. mi.; **Water:** 1.8 sq. mi.

Floodwood
City
ZIP: 55736 **Lat:** 46-55-36 N **Long:** 92-54-55 W
Pop: 574 (1990); 648 (1980) **Pop Density:** 1435.0
Land: 0.4 sq. mi.; **Water:** 0.0 sq. mi. **Elev:** 1253 ft.
City and township not coextensive.
Name origin: For its location at the mouth of the Floodwood River, which was formerly blocked by large rafts of driftwood.

*Floodwood
Township
ZIP: 55736 **Lat:** 46-54-04 N **Long:** 92-52-30 W
Pop: 345 (1990); 431 (1980) **Pop Density:** 9.9
Land: 34.9 sq. mi.; **Water:** 0.6 sq. mi.

Franklin
City
ZIP: 55792 **Lat:** 47-31-25 N **Long:** 92-31-11 W
Pop: 22 (1990); 27 (1980) **Pop Density:** 11.0
Land: 2.0 sq. mi.; **Water:** 0.1 sq. mi.
Name origin: For Benjamin Franklin (1706–90), American statesman, diplomat, and patriot.

Fredenberg
Township
Lat: 46-58-50 N **Long:** 92-14-26 W
Pop: 745 (1990); 628 (1980) **Pop Density:** 29.3
Land: 25.4 sq. mi.; **Water:** 10.4 sq. mi. **Elev:** 1393 ft.

French
Township
Lat: 47-40-22 N **Long:** 92-59-26 W
Pop: 454 (1990); 439 (1980) **Pop Density:** 13.7
Land: 33.2 sq. mi.; **Water:** 4.1 sq. mi.

Gheen
Pop. Place
Lat: 47-58-18 N **Long:** 92-45-58 W
Pop: 32 (1990); 92 (1980) **Pop Density:** 1.8
Land: 17.7 sq. mi.; **Water:** 0.3 sq. mi.

Gilbert
City
ZIP: 55741 **Lat:** 47-29-30 N **Long:** 92-27-37 W
Pop: 1,934 (1990); 2,721 (1980) **Pop Density:** 163.9
Land: 11.8 sq. mi.; **Water:** 0.8 sq. mi.
Founded 1908.
Name origin: For E. A. Gilbert, well-known Duluth businessman.

Gnesen
Township
Lat: 47-01-49 N **Long:** 92-06-38 W
Pop: 1,089 (1990); 975 (1980) **Pop Density:** 17.7
Land: 61.5 sq. mi.; **Water:** 10.1 sq. mi.

Grand Lake
Township
ZIP: 55779 **Lat:** 46-55-25 N **Long:** 92-22-06 W
Pop: 2,355 (1990); 2,166 (1980) **Pop Density:** 35.7
Land: 65.9 sq. mi.; **Water:** 5.5 sq. mi.

Great Scott
Township
Lat: 47-33-12 N **Long:** 92-44-35 W
Pop: 618 (1990); 883 (1980) **Pop Density:** 9.8
Land: 63.2 sq. mi.; **Water:** 1.4 sq. mi.

Greenwood
Township
Lat: 47-52-47 N **Long:** 92-22-35 W
Pop: 515 (1990); 565 (1980) **Pop Density:** 11.1
Land: 46.2 sq. mi.; **Water:** 27.3 sq. mi.

Halden
Township
ZIP: 55736 **Lat:** 46-54-22 N **Long:** 92-59-26 W
Pop: 139 (1990); 151 (1980) **Pop Density:** 3.9
Land: 35.8 sq. mi.; **Water:** 0.0 sq. mi.

Hay Lake
Pop. Place
Lat: 47-35-22 N **Long:** 92-22-22 W
Pop: 121 (1990); 115 (1980) **Pop Density:** 3.3
Land: 36.2 sq. mi.; **Water:** 0.2 sq. mi.

Heikkila Lake
Pop. Place
Lat: 47-21-27 N **Long:** 92-24-42 W
Pop: 1,339 (1990); 1,616 (1980) **Pop Density:** 13.1
Land: 102.4 sq. mi.; **Water:** 5.0 sq. mi.

Hermantown
City
ZIP: 55811 **Lat:** 46-48-22 N **Long:** 92-14-37 W
Pop: 6,761 (1990); 6,759 (1980) **Pop Density:** 197.1
Land: 34.3 sq. mi.; **Water:** 0.0 sq. mi. **Elev:** 1365 ft.

Hibbing
City
ZIP: 55746 **Lat:** 47-23-59 N **Long:** 92-56-53 W
Pop: 18,046 (1990); 21,193 (1980) **Pop Density:** 99.3
Land: 181.7 sq. mi.; **Water:** 4.8 sq. mi. **Elev:** 1489 ft.
In northeastern MN, 58 mi. northwest of Duluth in the Mesabi Range.
Name origin: For German immigrant, Frank Hibbing, who was a large investor in the Mesabi Iron Mines.

Hoyt Lakes
City
ZIP: 55750 **Lat:** 47-33-33 N **Long:** 92-07-10 W
Pop: 2,348 (1990); 3,186 (1980) **Pop Density:** 41.9
Land: 56.0 sq. mi.; **Water:** 2.0 sq. mi. **Elev:** 1469 ft.
Name origin: For businessman Elton Hoyt II.

Industrial
Township
ZIP: 55779 **Lat:** 46-53-39 N **Long:** 92-29-15 W
Pop: 632 (1990); 617 (1980) **Pop Density:** 17.8
Land: 35.6 sq. mi.; **Water:** 0.4 sq. mi.

Iron Junction
City
Lat: 47-24-59 N **Long:** 92-36-23 W
Pop: 133 (1990); 134 (1980) **Pop Density:** 166.3
Land: 0.8 sq. mi.; **Water:** 0.0 sq. mi.
Name origin: For a railway junction for the shipment of iron ore from the Mesabi Range.

Janette Lake
Pop. Place
Lat: 47-14-18 N **Long:** 93-01-05 W
Pop: 232 (1990); 288 (1980) **Pop Density:** 6.7
Land: 34.7 sq. mi.; **Water:** 1.5 sq. mi.

Kelsey
Township
ZIP: 55755 **Lat:** 47-09-14 N **Long:** 92-37-07 W
Pop: 175 (1990); 228 (1980) **Pop Density:** 5.0
Land: 35.3 sq. mi.; **Water:** 0.4 sq. mi.

Kinney
City
ZIP: 55758 **Lat:** 47-31-20 N **Long:** 92-43-30 W
Pop: 257 (1990); 447 (1980) **Pop Density:** 45.9
Land: 5.6 sq. mi.; **Water:** 0.3 sq. mi.
Name origin: For O. D. Kinney, who discovered the iron deposits of Virginia, MN.

Kugler
Township
ZIP: 55790 **Lat:** 47-45-40 N **Long:** 92-13-37 W
Pop: 180 (1990); 230 (1980) **Pop Density:** 5.1
Land: 35.5 sq. mi.; **Water:** 0.3 sq. mi.

Lake Vermilion
Pop. Place
Lat: 47-52-49 N **Long:** 92-30-05 W
Pop: 170 (1990); 175 (1980) **Pop Density:** 1.4
Land: 124.4 sq. mi.; **Water:** 14.1 sq. mi.

Lakewood
Township
Lat: 46-54-41 N **Long:** 91-59-06 W
Pop: 1,799 (1990); 1,680 (1980) **Pop Density:** 64.0
Land: 28.1 sq. mi.; **Water:** 0.0 sq. mi.

Lavell
Township
Lat: 47-15-33 N **Long:** 92-47-03 W
Pop: 381 (1990); 481 (1980) **Pop Density:** 3.5
Land: 107.8 sq. mi.; **Water:** 0.5 sq. mi.

Leiding
Township
Lat: 48-04-00 N **Long:** 92-50-30 W
Pop: 409 (1990); 386 (1980) **Pop Density:** 3.3
Land: 122.5 sq. mi.; **Water:** 18.5 sq. mi.

Leonidas
City
ZIP: 55734 **Lat:** 47-28-02 N **Long:** 92-34-04 W
Pop: 70 (1990); 95 (1980) **Pop Density:** 53.8
Land: 1.3 sq. mi.; **Water:** 0.1 sq. mi.

Linden Grove
Township
Lat: 47-51-17 N **Long:** 92-53-03 W
Pop: 153 (1990); 160 (1980) **Pop Density:** 4.3
Land: 35.4 sq. mi.; **Water:** 0.0 sq. mi.

McCormack Lake
Pop. Place
Lat: 47-35-02 N **Long:** 93-00-08 W
Pop: 183 (1990); 178 (1980) **Pop Density:** 5.2
Land: 35.3 sq. mi.; **Water:** 1.7 sq. mi.

MINNESOTA, St. Louis County

McDavitt Township
ZIP: 55751   Lat: 47-16-36 N   Long: 92-37-27 W
Pop: 507 (1990); 557 (1980)   Pop Density: 7.1
Land: 71.2 sq. mi.; Water: 1.2 sq. mi.

McKinley City
ZIP: 55761   Lat: 47-30-52 N   Long: 92-24-26 W
Pop: 116 (1990); 230 (1980)   Pop Density: 145.0
Land: 0.8 sq. mi.; Water: 0.0 sq. mi.   Elev: 1438 ft.
Name origin: For the McKinley brothers, who owned the local iron mine.

Meadowlands City
ZIP: 55765   Lat: 47-04-22 N   Long: 92-43-53 W
Pop: 92 (1990); 135 (1980)   Pop Density: 230.0
Land: 0.4 sq. mi.; Water: 0.0 sq. mi.
City and township not coextensive.

***Meadowlands** Township
Lat: 47-04-09 N   Long: 92-44-02 W
Pop: 256 (1990); 331 (1980)   Pop Density: 9.8
Land: 26.2 sq. mi.; Water: 0.5 sq. mi.

Midway Township
ZIP: 55792   Lat: 46-43-01 N   Long: 92-16-09 W
Pop: 1,500 (1990); 1,656 (1980)   Pop Density: 83.3
Land: 18.0 sq. mi.; Water: 0.0 sq. mi.

Morcom Township
Lat: 47-46-41 N   Long: 93-01-24 W
Pop: 123 (1990); 141 (1980)   Pop Density: 3.4
Land: 35.9 sq. mi.; Water: 0.0 sq. mi.

Morse Township
ZIP: 55731   Lat: 47-53-36 N   Long: 91-55-35 W
Pop: 1,093 (1990); 1,123 (1980)   Pop Density: 9.5
Land: 115.6 sq. mi.; Water: 22.5 sq. mi.

Mountain Iron City
ZIP: 55768   Lat: 47-31-35 N   Long: 92-37-36 W
Pop: 3,362 (1990); 4,134 (1980)   Pop Density: 68.1
Land: 49.4 sq. mi.; Water: 2.9 sq. mi.   Elev: 1474 ft.
Name origin: For the first iron ore mine to ship iron from the Mesabi range in 1892.

Ness Township
Lat: 46-59-44 N   Long: 92-45-10 W
Pop: 76 (1990); 96 (1980)   Pop Density: 2.2
Land: 34.9 sq. mi.; Water: 0.3 sq. mi.

Nett Lake Pop. Place
Lat: 48-04-40 N   Long: 93-03-48 W
Pop: 289 (1990); 339 (1980)   Pop Density: 9.1
Land: 31.6 sq. mi.; Water: 3.9 sq. mi.

New Independence Township
Lat: 46-58-17 N   Long: 92-30-20 W
Pop: 278 (1990); 254 (1980)   Pop Density: 8.0
Land: 34.8 sq. mi.; Water: 0.9 sq. mi.

Normanna Township
Lat: 46-58-42 N   Long: 91-59-27 W
Pop: 462 (1990); 507 (1980)   Pop Density: 12.7
Land: 36.5 sq. mi.; Water: 0.0 sq. mi.

Northeast St. Louis Pop. Place
Lat: 48-05-03 N   Long: 92-08-12 W
Pop: 144 (1990); 162 (1980)   Pop Density: 0.2
Land: 649.2 sq. mi.; Water: 99.5 sq. mi.

Northland Township
Lat: 47-04-52 N   Long: 92-29-12 W
Pop: 129 (1990); 142 (1980)   Pop Density: 3.7
Land: 34.7 sq. mi.; Water: 0.7 sq. mi.

North Star Township
Lat: 47-04-19 N   Long: 91-58-49 W
Pop: 113 (1990)   Pop Density: 3.4
Land: 33.3 sq. mi.; Water: 2.3 sq. mi.

Northwest St. Louis Pop. Place
Lat: 48-17-56 N   Long: 92-50-18 W
Pop: 465 (1990); 571 (1980)   Pop Density: 0.7
Land: 663.4 sq. mi.; Water: 135.3 sq. mi.

Orr City
ZIP: 55771   Lat: 48-03-50 N   Long: 92-49-13 W
Pop: 265 (1990); 294 (1980)   Pop Density: 203.8
Land: 1.3 sq. mi.; Water: 0.0 sq. mi.   Elev: 1304 ft.
Name origin: For postmaster and general store owner William Orr.

Owens Township
Lat: 47-50-41 N   Long: 92-38-11 W
Pop: 322 (1990); 318 (1980)   Pop Density: 10.9
Land: 29.5 sq. mi.; Water: 0.0 sq. mi.

Payne Township
Lat: 47-04-08 N   Long: 92-36-52 W
Pop: 36 (1990); 55 (1980)   Pop Density: 1.1
Land: 33.7 sq. mi.; Water: 0.1 sq. mi.

Pequaywan Township
Lat: 47-09-14 N   Long: 91-50-20 W
Pop: 83 (1990); 69 (1980)   Pop Density: 2.4
Land: 33.9 sq. mi.; Water: 2.2 sq. mi.

Pike Township
ZIP: 55732   Lat: 47-40-35 N   Long: 92-21-55 W
Pop: 528 (1990); 600 (1980)   Pop Density: 15.7
Land: 33.6 sq. mi.; Water: 0.0 sq. mi.

Portage Township
Lat: 48-09-13 N   Long: 92-35-49 W
Pop: 170 (1990); 262 (1980)   Pop Density: 1.2
Land: 137.3 sq. mi.; Water: 5.8 sq. mi.

Potshot Lake Pop. Place
Lat: 46-58-37 N   Long: 92-59-43 W
Pop: 77 (1990); 81 (1980)   Pop Density: 2.2
Land: 35.5 sq. mi.; Water: 0.0 sq. mi.

Prairie Lake Township
ZIP: 55736   Lat: 46-47-58 N   Long: 93-00-44 W
Pop: 55 (1990); 77 (1980)   Pop Density: 1.6
Land: 35.4 sq. mi.; Water: 0.3 sq. mi.

Proctor City
ZIP: 55810   Lat: 46-44-35 N   Long: 92-13-38 W
Pop: 2,974 (1990); 3,180 (1980)   Pop Density: 991.3
Land: 3.0 sq. mi.; Water: 0.0 sq. mi.   Elev: 1248 ft.
Name origin: For James Proctor Knott, a U.S. congressman from KY who made a humorous speech to Congress in 1871 ridiculing Duluth, which helped the city by its advertisement.

Rice Lake Township
Lat: 46-53-46 N   Long: 92-06-52 W
Pop: 3,883 (1990); 3,861 (1980)   Pop Density: 119.8
Land: 32.4 sq. mi.; Water: 1.1 sq. mi.

Sand Lake — Pop. Place
Lat: 47-40-18 N Long: 92-43-39 W
Pop: 1,192 (1990); 1,401 (1980)   **Pop Density:** 10.5
Land: 113.2 sq. mi.; **Water:** 3.5 sq. mi.

Sandy — Township
ZIP: 55710   Lat: 47-40-20 N Long: 92-29-51 W
Pop: 425 (1990); 535 (1980)   **Pop Density:** 14.1
Land: 30.2 sq. mi.; **Water:** 3.3 sq. mi.

Solway — Township
Lat: 46-48-27 N Long: 92-22-07 W
Pop: 1,772 (1990); 1,663 (1980)   **Pop Density:** 49.9
Land: 35.5 sq. mi.; **Water:** 0.2 sq. mi.

Stoney Brook — Township
ZIP: 55711   Lat: 46-47-43 N Long: 92-36-48 W
Pop: 223 (1990); 238 (1980)   **Pop Density:** 6.4
Land: 35.0 sq. mi.; **Water:** 0.9 sq. mi.

Sturgeon — Township
ZIP: 55703   Lat: 47-45-51 N Long: 92-53-22 W
Pop: 205 (1990); 200 (1980)   **Pop Density:** 5.6
Land: 36.9 sq. mi.; **Water:** 0.0 sq. mi.

Toivola — Township
Lat: 47-09-12 N Long: 92-48-16 W
Pop: 246 (1990); 347 (1980)   **Pop Density:** 3.4
Land: 71.7 sq. mi.; **Water:** 0.3 sq. mi.

Tower — City
ZIP: 55790   Lat: 47-48-36 N Long: 92-17-25 W
Pop: 502 (1990); 640 (1980)   **Pop Density:** 295.3
Land: 1.7 sq. mi.; **Water:** 0.4 sq. mi.
Name origin: For Charlemagne Tower of Philadelphia, a prominent businessman in the development of MN's iron industry.

Van Buren — Township
ZIP: 55736   Lat: 46-58-23 N Long: 92-50-49 W
Pop: 178 (1990); 189 (1980)   **Pop Density:** 5.0
Land: 35.3 sq. mi.; **Water:** 0.3 sq. mi.

Vermilion Lake — Township
Lat: 47-44-50 N Long: 92-22-51 W
Pop: 328 (1990); 379 (1980)   **Pop Density:** 9.2
Land: 35.8 sq. mi.; **Water:** 0.8 sq. mi.

Virginia — City
ZIP: 55792   Lat: 47-30-56 N Long: 92-30-25 W
Pop: 9,410 (1990); 11,056 (1980)   **Pop Density:** 560.1
Land: 16.8 sq. mi.; **Water:** 0.3 sq. mi.   **Elev:** 1437 ft.
Name origin: Named by an early lumberman for the state.

Waasa — Township
ZIP: 55732   Lat: 47-40-06 N Long: 92-07-22 W
Pop: 317 (1990); 428 (1980)   **Pop Density:** 9.0
Land: 35.1 sq. mi.; **Water:** 0.2 sq. mi.

White — Township
ZIP: 55705   Lat: 47-30-08 N Long: 92-14-16 W
Pop: 3,668 (1990); 4,916 (1980)   **Pop Density:** 36.0
Land: 102.0 sq. mi.; **Water:** 3.9 sq. mi.

Whiteface Reservoir — Pop. Place
Lat: 47-11-52 N Long: 92-11-32 W
Pop: 235 (1990); 170 (1980)   **Pop Density:** 0.7
Land: 322.3 sq. mi.; **Water:** 13.9 sq. mi.

Willow Valley — Township
ZIP: 55740   Lat: 47-56-16 N Long: 92-52-57 W
Pop: 118 (1990); 133 (1980)   **Pop Density:** 3.4
Land: 34.9 sq. mi.; **Water:** 0.0 sq. mi.

Winton — City
ZIP: 55796   Lat: 47-55-44 N Long: 91-48-04 W
Pop: 169 (1990); 276 (1980)   **Pop Density:** 1690.0
Land: 0.1 sq. mi.; **Water:** 0.0 sq. mi.
Name origin: For early lumberman William Winton.

Wuori — Township
Lat: 47-35-05 N Long: 92-29-33 W
Pop: 647 (1990); 750 (1980)   **Pop Density:** 18.6
Land: 34.8 sq. mi.; **Water:** 0.1 sq. mi.

Scott County
County Seat: Shakopee (ZIP: 55379)

Pop: 57,846 (1990); 43,784 (1980)   **Pop Density:** 162.1
Land: 356.8 sq. mi.; **Water:** 11.8 sq. mi.   **Area Code:** 612

In south-central MN, south of Minneapolis; established Mar 5, 1853 (prior to statehood) from Dakota County.

Name origin: For Gen. Winfield Scott (1786–1866), officer in the War of 1812 and the Mexican-American War; general in chief of the U.S. Army (1841–61) and commander of the Union armies at the beginning of the Civil War.

Belle Plaine — City
ZIP: 56011   Lat: 44-37-24 N Long: 93-45-51 W
Pop: 3,149 (1990); 2,754 (1980)   **Pop Density:** 768.0
Land: 4.1 sq. mi.; **Water:** 0.2 sq. mi.
City and township not coextensive.
Name origin: Named by its first settlers; French 'beautiful plain.'

*Belle Plaine — Township
ZIP: 56011   Lat: 44-34-46 N Long: 93-42-34 W
Pop: 691 (1990); 765 (1980)   **Pop Density:** 17.6
Land: 39.2 sq. mi.; **Water:** 0.0 sq. mi.

Blakeley — Township
Lat: 44-34-46 N Long: 93-50-15 W
Pop: 456 (1990); 515 (1980)   **Pop Density:** 17.0
Land: 26.9 sq. mi.; **Water:** 0.7 sq. mi.

Cedar Lake — Township
Lat: 44-35-24 N Long: 93-27-28 W
Pop: 1,688 (1990); 1,507 (1980)   **Pop Density:** 48.0
Land: 35.2 sq. mi.; **Water:** 1.1 sq. mi.

Credit River
Township
Lat: 44-40-14 N **Long:** 93-21-08 W
Pop: 2,854 (1990); 2,360 (1980) **Pop Density:** 122.0
Land: 23.4 sq. mi.; **Water:** 0.4 sq. mi.

Elko
City
ZIP: 55020 **Lat:** 44-33-55 N **Long:** 93-19-28 W
Pop: 223 (1990); 274 (1980) **Pop Density:** 159.3
Land: 1.4 sq. mi.; **Water:** 0.0 sq. mi.
Name origin: Believed to be named by early pioneers for a former home.

Helena
Township
Lat: 44-35-07 N **Long:** 93-34-55 W
Pop: 1,107 (1990); 1,215 (1980) **Pop Density:** 32.8
Land: 33.7 sq. mi.; **Water:** 1.2 sq. mi.

Jackson
Township
Lat: 44-46-15 N **Long:** 93-33-03 W
Pop: 1,359 (1990); 1,483 (1980) **Pop Density:** 181.2
Land: 7.5 sq. mi.; **Water:** 0.2 sq. mi.

Jordan
City
ZIP: 55352 **Lat:** 44-40-06 N **Long:** 93-37-56 W
Pop: 2,909 (1990); 2,663 (1980) **Pop Density:** 1322.3
Land: 2.2 sq. mi.; **Water:** 0.0 sq. mi.
Founded 1872.
Name origin: For the biblical Jordan River.

Louisville
Township
Lat: 44-44-43 N **Long:** 93-34-28 W
Pop: 910 (1990); 813 (1980) **Pop Density:** 65.5
Land: 13.9 sq. mi.; **Water:** 0.7 sq. mi.

New Market
City
ZIP: 55054 **Lat:** 44-34-19 N **Long:** 93-20-58 W
Pop: 227 (1990); 286 (1980) **Pop Density:** 454.0
Land: 0.5 sq. mi.; **Water:** 0.0 sq. mi.
City and township not coextensive.

*New Market
Township
ZIP: 55054 **Lat:** 44-34-55 N **Long:** 93-20-53 W
Pop: 2,008 (1990); 1,636 (1980) **Pop Density:** 59.2
Land: 33.9 sq. mi.; **Water:** 0.1 sq. mi.

New Prague
City
ZIP: 56071 **Lat:** 44-32-58 N **Long:** 93-34-18 W
Pop: 2,356 (1990); 1,898 (1980) **Pop Density:** 1682.9
Land: 1.4 sq. mi.; **Water:** 0.0 sq. mi.
Settled 1850s. Part of the town is also in Le Sueur County.
Name origin: For the ancient European city of Prague.

Prior Lake
City
ZIP: 55372 **Lat:** 44-43-42 N **Long:** 93-26-02 W
Pop: 11,482 (1990); 7,284 (1980) **Pop Density:** 876.5
Land: 13.1 sq. mi.; **Water:** 2.4 sq. mi.
Name origin: For Charles Prior, who was superintendent (1871–86) of the MN section of the Chicago, Milwaukee, & St. Paul Railway.

St. Lawrence
Township
Lat: 44-40-04 N **Long:** 93-40-43 W
Pop: 418 (1990); 350 (1980) **Pop Density:** 28.4
Land: 14.7 sq. mi.; **Water:** 0.5 sq. mi.

Sand Creek
Township
Lat: 44-40-41 N **Long:** 93-35-14 W
Pop: 1,511 (1990); 1,516 (1980) **Pop Density:** 46.3
Land: 32.6 sq. mi.; **Water:** 0.5 sq. mi.

Savage
City
ZIP: 55378 **Lat:** 44-45-19 N **Long:** 93-21-26 W
Pop: 9,906 (1990); 3,954 (1980) **Pop Density:** 623.0
Land: 15.9 sq. mi.; **Water:** 0.6 sq. mi.
Name origin: For horsebreeder Marion W. Savage. Previously called Hamilton.

Shakopee
City
ZIP: 55379 **Lat:** 44-46-14 N **Long:** 93-28-32 W
Pop: 11,739 (1990); 9,941 (1980) **Pop Density:** 444.7
Land: 26.4 sq. mi.; **Water:** 1.5 sq. mi.
In southeastern MN on the Minnesota River, 18 mi. southwest of Minneapolis.
Name origin: For the Sioux Indian chief who lived near the townsite.

Spring Lake
Township
Lat: 44-40-07 N **Long:** 93-27-45 W
Pop: 2,853 (1990); 2,570 (1980) **Pop Density:** 92.3
Land: 30.9 sq. mi.; **Water:** 1.8 sq. mi.

Sherburne County
County Seat: Elk River (ZIP: 55330)

Pop: 41,945 (1990); 29,908 (1980) **Pop Density:** 96.1
Land: 436.6 sq. mi.; **Water:** 14.4 sq. mi. **Area Code:** 612
In east-central MN, southeast of St. Cloud; established Feb 25, 1856 (prior to statehood) from Anoka County.
Name origin: For Moses Sherburne (1808–68), associate justice of the MN Territory supreme court (1853–57) and active in the formation of the state.

Baldwin
Township
Lat: 45-31-01 N **Long:** 93-34-06 W
Pop: 2,909 (1990); 2,412 (1980) **Pop Density:** 84.8
Land: 34.3 sq. mi.; **Water:** 1.2 sq. mi.

Becker
City
ZIP: 55308 **Lat:** 45-22-16 N **Long:** 93-52-24 W
Pop: 902 (1990); 601 (1980) **Pop Density:** 103.7
Land: 8.7 sq. mi.; **Water:** 0.5 sq. mi.
City and township not coextensive.
Name origin: For attorney and mayor of St. Paul, George Becker (1829–1904).

American Places Dictionary   MINNESOTA, Sibley County

*Becker   Township
ZIP: 55308   **Lat:** 45-25-08 N   **Long:** 93-50-40 W
Pop: 2,336 (1990); 1,341 (1980)   **Pop Density:** 42.1
Land: 55.5 sq. mi.; **Water:** 0.3 sq. mi.

Big Lake   City
ZIP: 55309   **Lat:** 45-20-11 N   **Long:** 93-44-47 W
Pop: 3,113 (1990); 2,210 (1980)   **Pop Density:** 1482.4
Land: 2.1 sq. mi.; **Water:** 0.7 sq. mi.   **Elev:** 942 ft.
City and township not coextensive.
Name origin: For the adjacent lake.

*Big Lake   Township
ZIP: 55309   **Lat:** 45-20-37 N   **Long:** 93-42-45 W
Pop: 4,452 (1990); 2,679 (1980)   **Pop Density:** 101.2
Land: 44.0 sq. mi.; **Water:** 1.3 sq. mi.

Blue Hill   Township
Lat: 45-31-02 N   **Long:** 93-41-27 W
Pop: 763 (1990); 678 (1980)   **Pop Density:** 21.4
Land: 35.7 sq. mi.; **Water:** 0.7 sq. mi.

Clear Lake   City
ZIP: 55319   **Lat:** 45-26-45 N   **Long:** 93-59-52 W
Pop: 315 (1990); 266 (1980)   **Pop Density:** 393.8
Land: 0.8 sq. mi.; **Water:** 0.0 sq. mi.
City and township not coextensive.

*Clear Lake   Township
ZIP: 55319   **Lat:** 45-26-03 N   **Long:** 93-59-06 W
Pop: 1,225 (1990); 1,048 (1980)   **Pop Density:** 36.4
Land: 33.7 sq. mi.; **Water:** 3.4 sq. mi.

Elk River   City
ZIP: 55330   **Lat:** 45-19-57 N   **Long:** 93-33-56 W
Pop: 11,143 (1990); 6,785 (1980)   **Pop Density:** 261.0
Land: 42.7 sq. mi.; **Water:** 1.2 sq. mi.   **Elev:** 900 ft.
Name origin: For the river, which traverses the county and which was named by early settlers for the large elk herds in the vicinity.

Haven   Township
Lat: 45-30-29 N   **Long:** 94-04-08 W
Pop: 1,921 (1990); 1,603 (1980)   **Pop Density:** 53.4
Land: 36.0 sq. mi.; **Water:** 0.8 sq. mi.

Livonia   Township
Lat: 45-25-25 N   **Long:** 93-34-22 W
Pop: 2,288 (1990); 1,655 (1980)   **Pop Density:** 70.4
Land: 32.5 sq. mi.; **Water:** 0.9 sq. mi.

Orrock   Township
Lat: 45-25-59 N   **Long:** 93-41-34 W
Pop: 1,474 (1990); 1,140 (1980)   **Pop Density:** 42.2
Land: 34.9 sq. mi.; **Water:** 1.4 sq. mi.

Palmer   Township
Lat: 45-31-16 N   **Long:** 93-56-55 W
Pop: 1,717 (1990); 1,362 (1980)   **Pop Density:** 49.2
Land: 34.9 sq. mi.; **Water:** 1.6 sq. mi.

Princeton   City
ZIP: 55371   **Lat:** 45-33-24 N   **Long:** 93-35-52 W
Pop: 2 (1990); 2 (1980)   **Pop Density:** 4.0
Land: 0.5 sq. mi.; **Water:** 0.0 sq. mi.   **Elev:** 983 ft.
Part of the town is also in Mille Lacs County.
Name origin: For John Prince, who helped lay out the town in 1855.

St. Cloud   City
ZIP: 56301   **Lat:** 45-32-44 N   **Long:** 94-07-55 W
Pop: 5,246 (1990); 4,421 (1980)   **Pop Density:** 2498.1
Land: 2.1 sq. mi.; **Water:** 0.1 sq. mi.
In central MN on the Mississippi River, 58 mi. northwest of Minneapolis. Part of the town is also in Stearnes and Benton counties.
Name origin: Named by town founder John Wilson for Napoleon I's (1769–1821) palace of St. Cloud outside Paris.

Santiago   Township
Lat: 45-31-42 N   **Long:** 93-48-41 W
Pop: 789 (1990); 631 (1980)   **Pop Density:** 21.9
Land: 36.1 sq. mi.; **Water:** 0.2 sq. mi.

Zimmerman   City
ZIP: 55398   **Lat:** 45-26-38 N   **Long:** 93-35-32 W
Pop: 1,350 (1990); 1,074 (1980)   **Pop Density:** 642.9
Land: 2.1 sq. mi.; **Water:** 0.1 sq. mi.

Sibley County
County Seat: Gaylord (ZIP: 55334)

Pop: 14,366 (1990); 15,448 (1980)   **Pop Density:** 24.4
Land: 588.6 sq. mi.; **Water:** 11.7 sq. mi.   **Area Code:** 612
In south-central MN, southwest of Minneapolis; established Mar 5, 1853 (prior to statehood) from unorganized lands.
Name origin: For Henry Hastings Sibley (1811–91), delegate to the U.S. Congress from WI Territory (1848–49) and from MN Territory (1849–53), and first governor of MN (1858–60).

Alfsborg   Township
Lat: 44-30-10 N   **Long:** 94-18-04 W
Pop: 379 (1990); 469 (1980)   **Pop Density:** 10.8
Land: 35.2 sq. mi.; **Water:** 0.1 sq. mi.

Arlington   City
ZIP: 55307   **Lat:** 44-36-25 N   **Long:** 94-04-40 W
Pop: 1,886 (1990); 1,779 (1980)   **Pop Density:** 2095.6
Land: 0.9 sq. mi.; **Water:** 0.0 sq. mi.
City and township not coextensive.
Name origin: For the Arlington estate in Washington D.C.

MINNESOTA, Sibley County

*Arlington — Township
ZIP: 55307 Lat: 44-35-14 N Long: 94-04-15 W
Pop: 599 (1990); 677 (1980) Pop Density: 17.0
Land: 35.2 sq. mi.; Water: 0.0 sq. mi.

Bismarck — Township
Lat: 44-35-24 N Long: 94-26-33 W
Pop: 310 (1990); 348 (1980) Pop Density: 8.6
Land: 36.0 sq. mi.; Water: 0.1 sq. mi.

Cornish — Township
Lat: 44-29-44 N Long: 94-26-00 W
Pop: 330 (1990); 383 (1980) Pop Density: 9.3
Land: 35.4 sq. mi.; Water: 0.1 sq. mi.

Dryden — Township
Lat: 44-34-53 N Long: 94-11-46 W
Pop: 442 (1990); 543 (1980) Pop Density: 13.2
Land: 33.4 sq. mi.; Water: 1.7 sq. mi.

Faxon — Township
Lat: 44-38-47 N Long: 93-50-20 W
Pop: 398 (1990); 389 (1980) Pop Density: 19.0
Land: 20.9 sq. mi.; Water: 0.5 sq. mi.

Gaylord — City
ZIP: 55334 Lat: 44-33-16 N Long: 94-13-05 W
Pop: 1,935 (1990); 1,933 (1980) Pop Density: 1759.1
Land: 1.1 sq. mi.; Water: 0.0 sq. mi.

Gibbon — City
ZIP: 55335 Lat: 44-32-06 N Long: 94-31-22 W
Pop: 712 (1990); 787 (1980) Pop Density: 791.1
Land: 0.9 sq. mi.; Water: 0.0 sq. mi.

Name origin: For Gengam John Gibbon, who was stationed in MN in the 1800s.

Grafton — Township
Lat: 44-40-04 N Long: 94-34-07 W
Pop: 292 (1990); 332 (1980) Pop Density: 7.5
Land: 39.0 sq. mi.; Water: 0.2 sq. mi.

Green Isle — City
ZIP: 55338 Lat: 44-40-41 N Long: 94-00-22 W
Pop: 239 (1990); 357 (1980) Pop Density: 1195.0
Land: 0.2 sq. mi.; Water: 0.0 sq. mi. Elev: 1000 ft.

Name origin: Named by Irish immigrant, Christopher Dolan, as an allusion to Ireland.

*Green Isle — Township
ZIP: 55338 Lat: 44-40-54 N Long: 94-04-27 W
Pop: 627 (1990); 633 (1980) Pop Density: 17.7
Land: 35.5 sq. mi.; Water: 0.8 sq. mi.

Henderson — City
ZIP: 56044 Lat: 44-31-48 N Long: 93-54-28 W
Pop: 746 (1990); 739 (1980) Pop Density: 828.9
Land: 0.9 sq. mi.; Water: 0.0 sq. mi.
City and township not coextensive.

Name origin: For Andrew Henderson, grandfather of early settler and newspaperman Joseph Brown.

*Henderson — Township
ZIP: 56044 Lat: 44-29-30 N Long: 93-57-46 W
Pop: 567 (1990); 632 (1980) Pop Density: 18.5
Land: 30.6 sq. mi.; Water: 0.3 sq. mi.

Jessenland — Township
Lat: 44-35-04 N Long: 93-56-40 W
Pop: 472 (1990); 490 (1980) Pop Density: 14.2
Land: 33.2 sq. mi.; Water: 1.2 sq. mi.

Kelso — Township
Lat: 44-30-05 N Long: 94-04-37 W
Pop: 365 (1990); 428 (1980) Pop Density: 10.3
Land: 35.6 sq. mi.; Water: 0.0 sq. mi.

Moltke — Township
Lat: 44-35-01 N Long: 94-33-45 W
Pop: 353 (1990); 415 (1980) Pop Density: 9.1
Land: 39.0 sq. mi.; Water: 0.0 sq. mi.

New Auburn — City
ZIP: 55366 Lat: 44-40-22 N Long: 94-13-44 W
Pop: 363 (1990); 331 (1980) Pop Density: 726.0
Land: 0.5 sq. mi.; Water: 0.0 sq. mi. Elev: 1002 ft.
City and township not coextensive.

Name origin: Named in the late 1850s by settlers from Auburn, NY.

*New Auburn — Township
Lat: 44-40-33 N Long: 94-11-15 W
Pop: 421 (1990); 500 (1980) Pop Density: 13.2
Land: 32.0 sq. mi.; Water: 3.8 sq. mi.

Severance — Township
Lat: 44-29-45 N Long: 94-33-59 W
Pop: 361 (1990); 440 (1980) Pop Density: 9.9
Land: 36.5 sq. mi.; Water: 1.6 sq. mi.

Sibley — Township
Lat: 44-29-52 N Long: 94-11-25 W
Pop: 357 (1990); 420 (1980) Pop Density: 10.0
Land: 35.6 sq. mi.; Water: 0.0 sq. mi.

Transit — Township
Lat: 44-35-14 N Long: 94-18-48 W
Pop: 332 (1990); 417 (1980) Pop Density: 9.4
Land: 35.2 sq. mi.; Water: 0.4 sq. mi.

Washington Lake — Township
Lat: 44-40-28 N Long: 93-56-33 W
Pop: 601 (1990); 630 (1980) Pop Density: 17.3
Land: 34.8 sq. mi.; Water: 1.1 sq. mi.

Winthrop — City
ZIP: 55396 Lat: 44-32-37 N Long: 94-21-52 W
Pop: 1,279 (1990); 1,376 (1980) Pop Density: 1598.8
Land: 0.8 sq. mi.; Water: 0.0 sq. mi. Elev: 1018 ft.
Incorporated 1891.

Name origin: Named by officers of the Minneapolis & St. Louis Railway.

Stearns County
County Seat: St. Cloud (ZIP: 56302)

Pop: 118,791 (1990); 108,161 (1980)
Land: 1344.6 sq. mi.; **Water:** 45.4 sq. mi.
Pop Density: 88.3
Area Code: 612

In central MN, northwest of Minneapolis; established Feb 20, 1855 (prior to statehood) from unorganized lands.

Name origin: For Charles Thomas Stearns (1807–98), territorial legislator (1854–55). In the original bill, the county was to be named for Isaac Ingalls Stevens (1818–62), first territorial governor of WA and surveyor for the Northern Pacific Railway, but apparently a clerical error was made and allowed to stand.

Albany — City
ZIP: 56307 **Lat:** 45-37-51 N **Long:** 94-34-07 W
Pop: 1,548 (1990); 1,569 (1980) **Pop Density:** 1290.0
Land: 1.2 sq. mi.; **Water:** 0.1 sq. mi.
Settled 1863. City and township not coextensive.
Name origin: For Albany, NY.

*Albany — Township
ZIP: 56307 **Lat:** 45-37-38 N **Long:** 94-34-41 W
Pop: 918 (1990); 922 (1980) **Pop Density:** 24.5
Land: 37.4 sq. mi.; **Water:** 0.2 sq. mi.

Ashley — Township
Lat: 45-43-14 N **Long:** 95-04-38 W
Pop: 273 (1990); 362 (1980) **Pop Density:** 6.5
Land: 41.9 sq. mi.; **Water:** 0.1 sq. mi.

Avon — City
ZIP: 56310 **Lat:** 45-36-31 N **Long:** 94-27-05 W
Pop: 970 (1990); 804 (1980) **Pop Density:** 1077.8
Land: 0.9 sq. mi.; **Water:** 0.0 sq. mi. **Elev:** 1129 ft.
Name origin: For the Avon River in England.

*Avon — Township
ZIP: 56310 **Lat:** 45-37-43 N **Long:** 94-26-53 W
Pop: 3,385 (1990); 1,737 (1980) **Pop Density:** 104.5
Land: 32.4 sq. mi.; **Water:** 2.6 sq. mi.

Belgrade — City
ZIP: 56312 **Lat:** 45-26-59 N **Long:** 94-59-56 W
Pop: 700 (1990); 805 (1980) **Pop Density:** 583.3
Land: 1.2 sq. mi.; **Water:** 0.0 sq. mi. **Elev:** 1266 ft.
Name origin: For the city in Serbia.

Brockway — Township
Lat: 45-43-05 N **Long:** 94-18-34 W
Pop: 2,261 (1990); 1,915 (1980) **Pop Density:** 47.1
Land: 48.0 sq. mi.; **Water:** 0.7 sq. mi.

Brooten — City
ZIP: 56316 **Lat:** 45-30-01 N **Long:** 95-07-08 W
Pop: 589 (1990); 647 (1980) **Pop Density:** 490.8
Land: 1.2 sq. mi.; **Water:** 0.0 sq. mi.
Founded 1886. Part of the town is also in Pope County.
Name origin: For one of its early Scandinavian settlers.

Cold Spring — City
ZIP: 56320 **Lat:** 45-27-26 N **Long:** 94-25-53 W
Pop: 2,459 (1990); 2,294 (1980) **Pop Density:** 1639.3
Land: 1.5 sq. mi.; **Water:** 0.0 sq. mi. **Elev:** 1091 ft.
Name origin: For its natural mineral springs.

Collegeville — Township
Lat: 45-32-36 N **Long:** 94-26-25 W
Pop: 1,624 (1990); 3,075 (1980) **Pop Density:** 51.4
Land: 31.6 sq. mi.; **Water:** 3.5 sq. mi.

Crow Lake — Township
ZIP: 56316 **Lat:** 45-27-19 N **Long:** 95-03-31 W
Pop: 390 (1990); 444 (1980) **Pop Density:** 11.5
Land: 33.9 sq. mi.; **Water:** 1.4 sq. mi.

Crow River — Township
ZIP: 56312 **Lat:** 45-27-47 N **Long:** 94-56-47 W
Pop: 387 (1990); 417 (1980) **Pop Density:** 11.3
Land: 34.3 sq. mi.; **Water:** 0.0 sq. mi.

Eden Lake — Township
Lat: 45-22-16 N **Long:** 94-34-18 W
Pop: 1,230 (1990); 1,227 (1980) **Pop Density:** 36.4
Land: 33.8 sq. mi.; **Water:** 4.7 sq. mi.

Eden Valley — City
ZIP: 55329 **Lat:** 45-19-50 N **Long:** 94-32-37 W
Pop: 315 (1990); 291 (1980) **Pop Density:** 525.0
Land: 0.6 sq. mi.; **Water:** 0.0 sq. mi.
Part of the town is also in Meeker County.
Name origin: Named euphoniously by St. Paul, Minneapolis, & Sault Ste. Marie Railway officers.

Elrosa — City
ZIP: 56325 **Lat:** 45-33-44 N **Long:** 94-56-51 W
Pop: 205 (1990); 214 (1980) **Pop Density:** 2050.0
Land: 0.1 sq. mi.; **Water:** 0.0 sq. mi.
Founded by officials of the Soo Railway.

Fair Haven — Township
Lat: 45-21-23 N **Long:** 94-11-37 W
Pop: 1,129 (1990); 1,102 (1980) **Pop Density:** 33.2
Land: 34.0 sq. mi.; **Water:** 1.8 sq. mi.

Farming — Township
ZIP: 56368 **Lat:** 45-32-33 N **Long:** 94-34-20 W
Pop: 777 (1990); 826 (1980) **Pop Density:** 20.7
Land: 37.5 sq. mi.; **Water:** 1.4 sq. mi.

Freeport — City
ZIP: 56331 **Lat:** 45-39-46 N **Long:** 94-41-13 W
Pop: 556 (1990); 563 (1980) **Pop Density:** 617.8
Land: 0.9 sq. mi.; **Water:** 0.0 sq. mi.
Name origin: For Freeport, IL, the former home of early settlers.

Getty — Township
Lat: 45-38-30 N **Long:** 94-57-28 W
Pop: 420 (1990); 463 (1980) **Pop Density:** 11.7
Land: 36.0 sq. mi.; **Water:** 0.1 sq. mi.

MINNESOTA, Stearns County

Greenwald
City
ZIP: 56335   **Lat:** 45-36-07 N   **Long:** 94-51-32 W
Pop: 209 (1990); 259 (1980)   **Pop Density:** 261.3
Land: 0.8 sq. mi.; **Water:** 0.0 sq. mi.   **Elev:** 1263 ft.
Name origin: From German 'green forest.'

Grove
Township
Lat: 45-37-45 N   **Long:** 94-49-47 W
Pop: 629 (1990); 693 (1980)   **Pop Density:** 18.8
Land: 33.4 sq. mi.; **Water:** 0.5 sq. mi.

Holding
Township
ZIP: 56340   **Lat:** 45-43-49 N   **Long:** 94-26-55 W
Pop: 1,160 (1990); 1,133 (1980)   **Pop Density:** 28.1
Land: 41.3 sq. mi.; **Water:** 0.7 sq. mi.

Holdingford
City
ZIP: 56340   **Lat:** 45-43-51 N   **Long:** 94-28-16 W
Pop: 561 (1990); 635 (1980)   **Pop Density:** 1402.5
Land: 0.4 sq. mi.; **Water:** 0.0 sq. mi.
Name origin: Named by pioneer Randolph Holding for the fording point of the south stream of Two River.

Kimball Prairie
City
ZIP: 55353   **Lat:** 45-18-47 N   **Long:** 94-18-02 W
Pop: 690 (1990); 651 (1980)   **Pop Density:** 492.9
Land: 1.4 sq. mi.; **Water:** 0.0 sq. mi.
Name origin: For early settler Frye Kimball.

Krain
Township
ZIP: 56307   **Lat:** 45-43-15 N   **Long:** 94-34-38 W
Pop: 889 (1990); 945 (1980)   **Pop Density:** 20.5
Land: 43.4 sq. mi.; **Water:** 0.7 sq. mi.

Lake George
Township
Lat: 45-32-37 N   **Long:** 94-56-51 W
Pop: 388 (1990); 479 (1980)   **Pop Density:** 11.2
Land: 34.6 sq. mi.; **Water:** 0.7 sq. mi.

Lake Henry
City
ZIP: 56362   **Lat:** 45-27-28 N   **Long:** 94-47-49 W
Pop: 90 (1990); 90 (1980)   **Pop Density:** 900.0
Land: 0.1 sq. mi.; **Water:** 0.0 sq. mi.
City and township not coextensive.

*Lake Henry
Township
ZIP: 56362   **Lat:** 45-27-28 N   **Long:** 94-49-30 W
Pop: 349 (1990); 453 (1980)   **Pop Density:** 9.8
Land: 35.5 sq. mi.; **Water:** 0.1 sq. mi.

Le Sauk
Township
ZIP: 56377   **Lat:** 45-37-26 N   **Long:** 94-13-28 W
Pop: 2,173 (1990); 2,009 (1980)   **Pop Density:** 128.6
Land: 16.9 sq. mi.; **Water:** 0.4 sq. mi.

Luxemburg
Township
Lat: 45-22-13 N   **Long:** 94-26-41 W
Pop: 788 (1990); 912 (1980)   **Pop Density:** 22.2
Land: 35.5 sq. mi.; **Water:** 0.3 sq. mi.

Lynden
Township
Lat: 45-23-50 N   **Long:** 94-06-12 W
Pop: 1,616 (1990); 1,389 (1980)   **Pop Density:** 67.3
Land: 24.0 sq. mi.; **Water:** 1.6 sq. mi.

Maine Prairie
Township
Lat: 45-21-19 N   **Long:** 94-18-21 W
Pop: 1,536 (1990); 1,518 (1980)   **Pop Density:** 27.3
Land: 56.3 sq. mi.; **Water:** 3.0 sq. mi.

Meire Grove
City
ZIP: 56352   **Lat:** 45-37-37 N   **Long:** 94-52-08 W
Pop: 124 (1990); 174 (1980)   **Pop Density:** 248.0
Land: 0.5 sq. mi.; **Water:** 0.0 sq. mi.

Melrose
City
ZIP: 56352   **Lat:** 45-40-31 N   **Long:** 94-48-43 W
Pop: 2,561 (1990); 2,409 (1980)   **Pop Density:** 948.5
Land: 2.7 sq. mi.; **Water:** 0.1 sq. mi.   **Elev:** 1213 ft.
Boundaries in other townships.
Name origin: For pioneer Warren Adley's daughters: Melissa and Rose.

*Melrose
Township
ZIP: 56352   **Lat:** 45-43-50 N   **Long:** 94-49-53 W
Pop: 767 (1990); 902 (1980)   **Pop Density:** 19.3
Land: 39.7 sq. mi.; **Water:** 0.7 sq. mi.

Millwood
Township
Lat: 45-43-15 N   **Long:** 94-42-39 W
Pop: 884 (1990); 909 (1980)   **Pop Density:** 22.7
Land: 39.0 sq. mi.; **Water:** 2.5 sq. mi.

Munson
Township
ZIP: 56368   **Lat:** 45-26-54 N   **Long:** 94-34-13 W
Pop: 1,114 (1990); 1,189 (1980)   **Pop Density:** 31.8
Land: 35.0 sq. mi.; **Water:** 3.0 sq. mi.

New Munich
City
ZIP: 56356   **Lat:** 45-37-50 N   **Long:** 94-45-10 W
Pop: 314 (1990); 302 (1980)   **Pop Density:** 523.3
Land: 0.6 sq. mi.; **Water:** 0.0 sq. mi.

North Fork
Township
ZIP: 56316   **Lat:** 45-32-33 N   **Long:** 95-03-53 W
Pop: 289 (1990); 304 (1980)   **Pop Density:** 8.3
Land: 34.8 sq. mi.; **Water:** 0.0 sq. mi.

Oak
Township
Lat: 45-37-33 N   **Long:** 94-42-16 W
Pop: 629 (1990); 622 (1980)   **Pop Density:** 18.8
Land: 33.5 sq. mi.; **Water:** 1.1 sq. mi.

Paynesville
City
ZIP: 56362   **Lat:** 45-22-42 N   **Long:** 94-43-11 W
Pop: 2,275 (1990); 2,140 (1980)   **Pop Density:** 1625.0
Land: 1.4 sq. mi.; **Water:** 0.0 sq. mi.
City and township not coextensive.
Name origin: For settler Edwin Paynes, who arrived in the area in 1857.

*Paynesville
Township
ZIP: 56362   **Lat:** 45-22-21 N   **Long:** 94-41-56 W
Pop: 1,307 (1990); 1,167 (1980)   **Pop Density:** 43.6
Land: 30.0 sq. mi.; **Water:** 4.5 sq. mi.

Pleasant Lake
City
ZIP: 56301   **Lat:** 45-29-56 N   **Long:** 94-17-05 W
Pop: 79 (1990); 120 (1980)   **Pop Density:** 790.0
Land: 0.1 sq. mi.; **Water:** 0.0 sq. mi.

Raymond
Township
Lat: 45-37-48 N   **Long:** 95-04-17 W
Pop: 239 (1990); 308 (1980)   **Pop Density:** 6.6
Land: 36.0 sq. mi.; **Water:** 0.2 sq. mi.

Richmond
City
ZIP: 56368   **Lat:** 45-27-09 N   **Long:** 94-31-03 W
Pop: 965 (1990); 867 (1980)   **Pop Density:** 2412.5
Land: 0.4 sq. mi.; **Water:** 0.0 sq. mi.   **Elev:** 1119 ft.

MINNESOTA, Stearns County

Rockville — City
ZIP: 56369 Lat: 45-28-20 N Long: 94-20-22 W
Pop: 579 (1990); 597 (1980) Pop Density: 965.0
Land: 0.6 sq. mi.; Water: 0.0 sq. mi. Elev: 1084 ft.
City and township not coextensive.

*Rockville — Township
Lat: 45-27-08 N Long: 94-19-28 W
Pop: 1,390 (1990); 1,255 (1980) Pop Density: 41.9
Land: 33.2 sq. mi.; Water: 1.9 sq. mi.

Roscoe — City
ZIP: 56371 Lat: 45-25-56 N Long: 94-38-06 W
Pop: 141 (1990); 154 (1980) Pop Density: 235.0
Land: 0.6 sq. mi.; Water: 0.0 sq. mi.

St. Anthony — City
Lat: 45-41-21 N Long: 94-36-32 W
Pop: 81 (1990); 78 (1980) Pop Density: 162.0
Land: 0.5 sq. mi.; Water: 0.0 sq. mi.

St. Augusta — Township
Lat: 45-26-58 N Long: 94-11-37 W
Pop: 2,657 (1990); 2,169 (1980) Pop Density: 70.3
Land: 37.8 sq. mi.; Water: 0.3 sq. mi.

St. Cloud — City
ZIP: 56301 Lat: 45-33-14 N Long: 94-11-04 W
Pop: 37,616 (1990); 33,500 (1980) Pop Density: 3548.7
Land: 10.6 sq. mi.; Water: 0.3 sq. mi.
In central MN on the Mississippi River, 58 mi. northwest of Minneapolis. Part of the town is also in Sherburne and Benton counties.
Name origin: Named by town founder John Wilson for Napoleon I's (1769–1821) palace of St. Cloud outside Paris.

*St. Cloud — Township
Lat: 45-31-49 N Long: 94-12-43 W
Pop: 7,549 (1990); 5,282 (1980) Pop Density: 401.5
Land: 18.8 sq. mi.; Water: 0.3 sq. mi.

St. Joseph — City
Lat: 45-33-59 N Long: 94-19-01 W
Pop: 3,294 (1990); 2,994 (1980) Pop Density: 3660.0
Land: 0.9 sq. mi.; Water: 0.0 sq. mi.
City and township not coextensive.
Name origin: For its first church.

*St. Joseph — Township
Lat: 45-33-07 N Long: 94-19-27 W
Pop: 2,567 (1990); 2,916 (1980) Pop Density: 75.1
Land: 34.2 sq. mi.; Water: 0.5 sq. mi.

St. Martin — City
Lat: 45-30-14 N Long: 94-39-45 W
Pop: 274 (1990); 220 (1980) Pop Density: 304.4
Land: 0.9 sq. mi.; Water: 0.0 sq. mi.

*St. Martin — Township
Lat: 45-32-37 N Long: 94-41-53 W
Pop: 525 (1990); 584 (1980) Pop Density: 15.2
Land: 34.5 sq. mi.; Water: 0.1 sq. mi.

St. Rosa — City
Lat: 45-43-52 N Long: 94-42-54 W
Pop: 75 (1990); 77 (1980) Pop Density: 187.5
Land: 0.4 sq. mi.; Water: 0.0 sq. mi.

St. Stephen — City
Lat: 45-42-07 N Long: 94-16-35 W
Pop: 607 (1990); 453 (1980) Pop Density: 173.4
Land: 3.5 sq. mi.; Water: 0.0 sq. mi.

St. Wendel — Township
Lat: 45-37-24 N Long: 94-19-51 W
Pop: 1,995 (1990); 1,773 (1980) Pop Density: 55.7
Land: 35.8 sq. mi.; Water: 0.3 sq. mi.

Sartell — City
ZIP: 56377 Lat: 45-37-12 N Long: 94-12-39 W
Pop: 3,549 (1990); 2,200 (1980) Pop Density: 1690.0
Land: 2.1 sq. mi.; Water: 0.1 sq. mi.
Part of the town is also in Benton County.
Name origin: For Joseph Sartell, who settled here in 1854 and established a sawmill.

Sauk Centre — City
ZIP: 56378 Lat: 45-44-15 N Long: 94-57-26 W
Pop: 3,581 (1990); 3,709 (1980) Pop Density: 1278.9
Land: 2.8 sq. mi.; Water: 0.3 sq. mi. Elev: 1246 ft.
City and township not coextensive.
Name origin: For its position on the Sauk River.

*Sauk Centre — Township
Lat: 45-43-17 N Long: 94-57-16 W
Pop: 1,111 (1990); 1,106 (1980) Pop Density: 29.9
Land: 37.1 sq. mi.; Water: 1.8 sq. mi.

Spring Hill — City
ZIP: 56352 Lat: 45-31-24 N Long: 94-50-03 W
Pop: 77 (1990); 94 (1980) Pop Density: 110.0
Land: 0.7 sq. mi.; Water: 0.0 sq. mi.
City and township not coextensive.

*Spring Hill — Township
ZIP: 56352 Lat: 45-32-40 N Long: 94-49-19 W
Pop: 438 (1990); 499 (1980) Pop Density: 12.6
Land: 34.9 sq. mi.; Water: 0.0 sq. mi.

Waite Park — City
ZIP: 56387 Lat: 45-33-09 N Long: 94-13-24 W
Pop: 5,020 (1990); 3,496 (1980) Pop Density: 2642.1
Land: 1.9 sq. mi.; Water: 0.0 sq. mi.
Name origin: For Henry C. Waite, businessman and state representative.

Wakefield — Township
ZIP: 56320 Lat: 45-27-19 N Long: 94-26-50 W
Pop: 2,461 (1990); 2,230 (1980) Pop Density: 77.9
Land: 31.6 sq. mi.; Water: 2.4 sq. mi.

Zion — Township
Lat: 45-27-07 N Long: 94-42-24 W
Pop: 443 (1990); 519 (1980) Pop Density: 12.5
Land: 35.5 sq. mi.; Water: 0.0 sq. mi.

Steele County
County Seat: Owatonna (ZIP: 55060)

Pop: 30,729 (1990); 30,328 (1980)
Land: 429.6 sq. mi.; **Water:** 2.6 sq. mi.
Pop Density: 71.5
Area Code: 507

In southeastern MN, west of Rochester; established Feb 20, 1855 (prior to statehood) from unorganized territory.

Name origin: For Franklin Steele (1813–80), prominent civic leader and member of the first board of regents of the University of Minnesota.

Aurora Township
ZIP: 55917 **Lat:** 43-58-58 N **Long:** 93-06-11 W
Pop: 690 (1990); 739 (1980) **Pop Density:** 19.2
Land: 36.0 sq. mi.; **Water:** 0.0 sq. mi.

Berlin Township
Lat: 43-53-38 N **Long:** 93-20-48 W
Pop: 502 (1990); 570 (1980) **Pop Density:** 14.3
Land: 35.2 sq. mi.; **Water:** 0.3 sq. mi.

Blooming Prairie City
ZIP: 55917 **Lat:** 43-52-06 N **Long:** 93-03-16 W
Pop: 2,043 (1990); 1,969 (1980) **Pop Density:** 1571.5
Land: 1.3 sq. mi.; **Water:** 0.0 sq. mi.

Settled 1856. City and township not coextensive. Part of the town is also in Dodge County.

Name origin: For the abundant spring prairie flowers.

*Blooming Prairie Township
ZIP: 55917 **Lat:** 43-53-35 N **Long:** 93-06-33 W
Pop: 567 (1990); 541 (1980) **Pop Density:** 16.5
Land: 34.4 sq. mi.; **Water:** 0.5 sq. mi.

Clinton Falls Township
Lat: 44-08-00 N **Long:** 93-13-16 W
Pop: 518 (1990); 486 (1980) **Pop Density:** 29.1
Land: 17.8 sq. mi.; **Water:** 0.1 sq. mi.

Deerfield Township
ZIP: 55049 **Lat:** 44-08-51 N **Long:** 93-20-41 W
Pop: 560 (1990); 600 (1980) **Pop Density:** 15.7
Land: 35.6 sq. mi.; **Water:** 0.3 sq. mi.

Ellendale City
ZIP: 56026 **Lat:** 43-52-24 N **Long:** 93-18-04 W
Pop: 549 (1990); 555 (1980) **Pop Density:** 784.3
Land: 0.7 sq. mi.; **Water:** 0.0 sq. mi.

Name origin: For Mrs. C.J. Ives nee Ellen Dale, the wife of the president of the Chicago, Rock Island, & Pacific Railway.

Havana Township
ZIP: 55060 **Lat:** 44-04-01 N **Long:** 93-06-16 W
Pop: 651 (1990); 677 (1980) **Pop Density:** 18.6
Land: 35.0 sq. mi.; **Water:** 1.0 sq. mi.

Lemond Township
Lat: 43-58-37 N **Long:** 93-20-33 W
Pop: 520 (1990); 551 (1980) **Pop Density:** 14.4
Land: 36.0 sq. mi.; **Water:** 0.0 sq. mi.

Medford City
ZIP: 55049 **Lat:** 44-10-18 N **Long:** 93-14-40 W
Pop: 733 (1990); 775 (1980) **Pop Density:** 1466.0
Land: 0.5 sq. mi.; **Water:** 0.0 sq. mi.

City and township not coextensive.

Name origin: For the ship *Medford*, upon which the son of town organizer William Collins had been born.

*Medford Township
ZIP: 55049 **Lat:** 44-10-30 N **Long:** 93-13-29 W
Pop: 572 (1990); 515 (1980) **Pop Density:** 33.1
Land: 17.3 sq. mi.; **Water:** 0.1 sq. mi.

Meriden Township
Lat: 44-04-04 N **Long:** 93-20-30 W
Pop: 693 (1990); 719 (1980) **Pop Density:** 19.2
Land: 36.1 sq. mi.; **Water:** 0.1 sq. mi.

Merton Township
Lat: 44-08-54 N **Long:** 93-05-57 W
Pop: 395 (1990); 427 (1980) **Pop Density:** 11.0
Land: 35.8 sq. mi.; **Water:** 0.1 sq. mi.

Owatonna City
ZIP: 55060 **Lat:** 44-05-06 N **Long:** 93-13-27 W
Pop: 19,386 (1990); 18,632 (1980) **Pop Density:** 2019.4
Land: 9.6 sq. mi.; **Water:** 0.1 sq. mi.

In southern MN, west of Rochester. City and township not coextensive.

Name origin: For the Sioux Indian name for the Straight River.

*Owatonna Township
ZIP: 55060 **Lat:** 44-03-36 N **Long:** 93-13-34 W
Pop: 991 (1990); 1,087 (1980) **Pop Density:** 37.5
Land: 26.4 sq. mi.; **Water:** 0.0 sq. mi.

Somerset Township
Lat: 43-58-22 N **Long:** 93-13-51 W
Pop: 853 (1990); 905 (1980) **Pop Density:** 23.8
Land: 35.9 sq. mi.; **Water:** 0.0 sq. mi.

Summit Township
ZIP: 55917 **Lat:** 43-53-34 N **Long:** 93-13-33 W
Pop: 506 (1990); 580 (1980) **Pop Density:** 14.1
Land: 36.0 sq. mi.; **Water:** 0.0 sq. mi.

Stevens County
County Seat: Morris (ZIP: 56267)

Pop: 10,634 (1990); 11,322 (1980)   **Pop Density:** 18.9
Land: 562.1 sq. mi.; **Water:** 13.2 sq. mi.   **Area Code:** 612
In west-central MN, west of St. Cloud; established Feb 20, 1862 from Pierce County, which was abolished the same year.
Name origin: For Gen. Isaac Ingalls Stevens (1818–62), an officer in the Mexican-American War and the Civil War, first governor of WA Territory (1853–57) and surveyor for the Northern Pacific Railway.

Alberta   City
ZIP: 56207   **Lat:** 45-34-29 N **Long:** 96-03-01 W
Pop: 136 (1990); 145 (1980)   **Pop Density:** 453.3
Land: 0.3 sq. mi.; **Water:** 0.0 sq. mi.
Name origin: For Alberta Lindsey, wife of a local farmer.

Baker   Township
Lat: 45-32-46 N **Long:** 96-10-34 W
Pop: 156 (1990); 231 (1980)   **Pop Density:** 4.4
Land: 35.4 sq. mi.; **Water:** 0.2 sq. mi.

Chokio   City
ZIP: 56221   **Lat:** 45-34-25 N **Long:** 96-10-26 W
Pop: 521 (1990); 559 (1980)   **Pop Density:** 1042.0
Land: 0.5 sq. mi.; **Water:** 0.0 sq. mi.
Name origin: From a Sioux Indian term meaning 'middle.'

Darnen   Township
Lat: 45-32-17 N **Long:** 95-56-34 W
Pop: 311 (1990); 389 (1980)   **Pop Density:** 9.5
Land: 32.9 sq. mi.; **Water:** 0.3 sq. mi.

Donnelly   City
ZIP: 56235   **Lat:** 45-41-23 N **Long:** 96-00-50 W
Pop: 221 (1990); 317 (1980)   **Pop Density:** 78.9
Land: 2.8 sq. mi.; **Water:** 0.3 sq. mi.   **Elev:** 1133 ft.
City and township not coextensive.
Name origin: For politician and author Ignatius Donnelly (1831–1901), who owned a farm near the town.

*Donnelly   Township
ZIP: 56235   **Lat:** 45-42-55 N **Long:** 96-04-09 W
Pop: 179 (1990); 195 (1980)   **Pop Density:** 5.4
Land: 33.3 sq. mi.; **Water:** 0.7 sq. mi.

Eldorado   Township
Lat: 45-42-32 N **Long:** 96-10-54 W
Pop: 126 (1990); 162 (1980)   **Pop Density:** 3.5
Land: 35.9 sq. mi.; **Water:** 0.3 sq. mi.

Everglade   Township
Lat: 45-37-45 N **Long:** 96-11-35 W
Pop: 121 (1990); 160 (1980)   **Pop Density:** 3.4
Land: 36.0 sq. mi.; **Water:** 0.1 sq. mi.

Framnas   Township
Lat: 45-37-42 N **Long:** 95-48-47 W
Pop: 333 (1990); 397 (1980)   **Pop Density:** 10.0
Land: 33.4 sq. mi.; **Water:** 2.7 sq. mi.

Hancock   City
ZIP: 56244   **Lat:** 45-29-53 N **Long:** 95-47-37 W
Pop: 723 (1990); 877 (1980)   **Pop Density:** 657.3
Land: 1.1 sq. mi.; **Water:** 0.0 sq. mi.   **Elev:** 1151 ft.
Name origin: For early missionary, teacher, and local historian Joseph Hancock.

Hodges   Township
Lat: 45-32-14 N **Long:** 95-47-54 W
Pop: 261 (1990); 291 (1980)   **Pop Density:** 7.7
Land: 34.1 sq. mi.; **Water:** 1.3 sq. mi.

Horton   Township
Lat: 45-27-31 N **Long:** 95-55-49 W
Pop: 229 (1990); 267 (1980)   **Pop Density:** 6.4
Land: 35.8 sq. mi.; **Water:** 0.1 sq. mi.

Moore   Township
Lat: 45-27-24 N **Long:** 95-48-10 W
Pop: 271 (1990); 269 (1980)   **Pop Density:** 7.7
Land: 35.3 sq. mi.; **Water:** 0.0 sq. mi.

Morris   City
ZIP: 56267   **Lat:** 45-35-09 N **Long:** 95-54-19 W
Pop: 5,613 (1990); 5,367 (1980)   **Pop Density:** 1369.0
Land: 4.1 sq. mi.; **Water:** 0.3 sq. mi.   **Elev:** 1133 ft.
Founded early 1870s.
Name origin: For railroad engineer Charles Morris.

*Morris   Township
ZIP: 56267   **Lat:** 45-37-19 N **Long:** 95-56-49 W
Pop: 466 (1990); 501 (1980)   **Pop Density:** 14.0
Land: 33.4 sq. mi.; **Water:** 0.6 sq. mi.

Pepperton   Township
Lat: 45-37-45 N **Long:** 96-03-59 W
Pop: 156 (1990); 214 (1980)   **Pop Density:** 4.4
Land: 35.7 sq. mi.; **Water:** 0.5 sq. mi.

Rendsville   Township
Lat: 45-43-07 N **Long:** 95-55-55 W
Pop: 199 (1990); 250 (1980)   **Pop Density:** 5.8
Land: 34.4 sq. mi.; **Water:** 0.6 sq. mi.

Scott   Township
Lat: 45-32-36 N **Long:** 96-03-21 W
Pop: 160 (1990); 201 (1980)   **Pop Density:** 4.8
Land: 33.1 sq. mi.; **Water:** 2.2 sq. mi.

Stevens   Township
Lat: 45-27-21 N **Long:** 96-10-41 W
Pop: 108 (1990); 147 (1980)   **Pop Density:** 3.0
Land: 35.8 sq. mi.; **Water:** 0.2 sq. mi.

Swan Lake   Township
Lat: 45-43-09 N **Long:** 95-49-17 W
Pop: 228 (1990); 253 (1980)   **Pop Density:** 6.8
Land: 33.4 sq. mi.; **Water:** 2.6 sq. mi.

Synnes   Township
Lat: 45-27-34 N **Long:** 96-03-32 W
Pop: 116 (1990); 130 (1980)   **Pop Density:** 3.3
Land: 35.5 sq. mi.; **Water:** 0.3 sq. mi.

Swift County
County Seat: Benson (ZIP: 56215)

Pop: 10,724 (1990); 12,920 (1980)   **Pop Density:** 14.4
Land: 743.6 sq. mi.; **Water:** 8.8 sq. mi.   **Area Code:** 612
In west-central MN, southwest of St. Cloud; established Feb 18, 1870 from Chippewa County.

Name origin: For Henry Adoniram Swift (1823–69), MN legislator and governor (1863–64).

Appleton — City
ZIP: 56208   **Lat:** 45-12-05 N   **Long:** 96-01-22 W
Pop: 1,552 (1990); 1,842 (1980)   **Pop Density:** 912.9
Land: 1.7 sq. mi.; **Water:** 0.1 sq. mi.
City and township not coextensive.
Name origin: For Appleton, WI. Originally called Phelps.

*Appleton — Township
ZIP: 56208   **Lat:** 45-11-53 N   **Long:** 96-02-08 W
Pop: 233 (1990); 298 (1980)   **Pop Density:** 7.5
Land: 31.1 sq. mi.; **Water:** 1.1 sq. mi.

Benson — City
ZIP: 56215   **Lat:** 45-19-01 N   **Long:** 95-36-25 W
Pop: 3,235 (1990); 3,656 (1980)   **Pop Density:** 1294.0
Land: 2.5 sq. mi.; **Water:** 0.0 sq. mi.
Name origin: For Ben Benson, who settled in the area in 1869 and began a mercantile business.

*Benson — Township
ZIP: 56215   **Lat:** 45-22-29 N   **Long:** 95-33-53 W
Pop: 334 (1990); 362 (1980)   **Pop Density:** 9.7
Land: 34.3 sq. mi.; **Water:** 1.7 sq. mi.

Camp Lake — Township
Lat: 45-21-56 N   **Long:** 95-26-11 W
Pop: 254 (1990); 326 (1980)   **Pop Density:** 7.2
Land: 35.4 sq. mi.; **Water:** 0.4 sq. mi.

Cashel — Township
Lat: 45-11-38 N   **Long:** 95-33-30 W
Pop: 161 (1990); 239 (1980)   **Pop Density:** 4.5
Land: 35.9 sq. mi.; **Water:** 0.0 sq. mi.

Clontarf — City
ZIP: 56226   **Lat:** 45-22-34 N   **Long:** 95-40-37 W
Pop: 172 (1990); 196 (1980)   **Pop Density:** 81.9
Land: 2.1 sq. mi.; **Water:** 0.0 sq. mi.   **Elev:** 1050 ft
Settled 1877. City and township not coextensive.
Name origin: Named by Irish settlers for a suburb of Dublin.

*Clontarf — Township
ZIP: 56226   **Lat:** 45-21-59 N   **Long:** 95-41-08 W
Pop: 107 (1990); 144 (1980)   **Pop Density:** 3.2
Land: 33.8 sq. mi.; **Water:** 0.1 sq. mi.

Danvers — City
ZIP: 56231   **Lat:** 45-16-57 N   **Long:** 95-45-09 W
Pop: 98 (1990); 152 (1980)   **Pop Density:** 196.0
Land: 0.5 sq. mi.; **Water:** 0.0 sq. mi.   **Elev:** 1027 ft
Name origin: For Danvers, MA, the former home of early settlers.

De Graff — City
ZIP: 56233   **Lat:** 45-15-33 N   **Long:** 95-28-08 W
Pop: 149 (1990); 179 (1980)   **Pop Density:** 186.3
Land: 0.8 sq. mi.; **Water:** 0.0 sq. mi.
Name origin: For Andrew De Graff, who built the Great Northern Railroad line in this area in the post-Civil War era.

Dublin — Township
Lat: 45-11-27 N   **Long:** 95-26-25 W
Pop: 166 (1990); 230 (1980)   **Pop Density:** 4.8
Land: 34.9 sq. mi.; **Water:** 0.0 sq. mi.

Edison — Township
Lat: 45-11-48 N   **Long:** 95-55-05 W
Pop: 168 (1990); 225 (1980)   **Pop Density:** 4.7
Land: 35.7 sq. mi.; **Water:** 0.1 sq. mi.

Fairfield — Township
Lat: 45-22-07 N   **Long:** 95-55-46 W
Pop: 185 (1990); 232 (1980)   **Pop Density:** 5.2
Land: 35.9 sq. mi.; **Water:** 0.1 sq. mi.

Hayes — Township
Lat: 45-16-22 N   **Long:** 95-18-53 W
Pop: 234 (1990); 290 (1980)   **Pop Density:** 6.7
Land: 34.9 sq. mi.; **Water:** 1.0 sq. mi.

Hegbert — Township
Lat: 45-21-47 N   **Long:** 96-03-19 W
Pop: 160 (1990); 189 (1980)   **Pop Density:** 4.8
Land: 33.3 sq. mi.; **Water:** 2.3 sq. mi.

Holloway — City
ZIP: 56249   **Lat:** 45-14-51 N   **Long:** 95-54-37 W
Pop: 123 (1990); 142 (1980)   **Pop Density:** 87.9
Land: 1.4 sq. mi.; **Water:** 0.0 sq. mi.

Kerkhoven — City
ZIP: 56252   **Lat:** 45-11-34 N   **Long:** 95-19-11 W
Pop: 732 (1990); 761 (1980)   **Pop Density:** 1045.7
Land: 0.7 sq. mi.; **Water:** 0.0 sq. mi.   **Elev:** 1109 ft

*Kerkhoven — Township
ZIP: 56252   **Lat:** 45-22-11 N   **Long:** 95-18-43 W
Pop: 289 (1990); 341 (1980)   **Pop Density:** 8.1
Land: 35.5 sq. mi.; **Water:** 0.5 sq. mi.

Kildare — Township
Lat: 45-16-40 N   **Long:** 95-26-21 W
Pop: 187 (1990); 230 (1980)   **Pop Density:** 5.4
Land: 34.8 sq. mi.; **Water:** 0.4 sq. mi.

Marysland — Township
Lat: 45-16-31 N   **Long:** 95-49-09 W
Pop: 124 (1990); 219 (1980)   **Pop Density:** 3.5
Land: 35.5 sq. mi.; **Water:** 0.0 sq. mi.

Moyer — Township
Lat: 45-17-24 N Long: 95-56-33 W
Pop: 160 (1990); 200 (1980)   Pop Density: 4.6
Land: 34.8 sq. mi.; Water: 0.0 sq. mi.

Murdock — City
ZIP: 56271   Lat: 45-13-25 N Long: 95-23-38 W
Pop: 282 (1990); 343 (1980)   Pop Density: 470.0
Land: 0.6 sq. mi.; Water: 0.0 sq. mi.   Elev: 1090 ft.

Pillsbury — Township
Lat: 45-11-38 N Long: 95-18-34 W
Pop: 301 (1990); 336 (1980)   Pop Density: 8.6
Land: 34.8 sq. mi.; Water: 0.0 sq. mi.

Shible — Township
Lat: 45-17-05 N Long: 96-03-11 W
Pop: 159 (1990); 216 (1980)   Pop Density: 4.6
Land: 34.9 sq. mi.; Water: 1.0 sq. mi.

Six Mile Grove — Township
Lat: 45-17-11 N Long: 95-40-54 W
Pop: 180 (1990); 252 (1980)   Pop Density: 5.0
Land: 35.9 sq. mi.; Water: 0.0 sq. mi.

Swenoda — Township
Lat: 45-11-30 N Long: 95-40-17 W
Pop: 175 (1990); 231 (1980)   Pop Density: 4.9
Land: 35.8 sq. mi.; Water: 0.0 sq. mi.

Tara — Township
Lat: 45-22-15 N Long: 95-48-25 W
Pop: 143 (1990); 181 (1980)   Pop Density: 4.0
Land: 35.8 sq. mi.; Water: 0.0 sq. mi.

Torning — Township
Lat: 45-16-27 N Long: 95-33-06 W
Pop: 479 (1990); 634 (1980)   Pop Density: 14.1
Land: 34.0 sq. mi.; Water: 0.0 sq. mi.

West Bank — Township
Lat: 45-11-51 N Long: 95-48-02 W
Pop: 182 (1990); 274 (1980)   Pop Density: 5.0
Land: 36.2 sq. mi.; Water: 0.0 sq. mi.

Todd County
County Seat: Long Prairie (ZIP: 56347)

Pop: 23,363 (1990); 24,991 (1980)   Pop Density: 24.8
Land: 942.1 sq. mi.; Water: 37.3 sq. mi.   Area Code: 612

In central MN, northwest of St. Cloud; established Feb 20, 1855 (prior to statehood) from Stearns County.

Name origin: For John Blair Smith Todd (1814–72), army officer in the Seminole Wars, the Mexican-American War, and the Civil War; delegate to Congress for Dakota (1861–65), and Dakota Territory lawyer and legislator.

Bartlett — Township
ZIP: 56453   Lat: 46-19-40 N Long: 94-58-07 W
Pop: 404 (1990); 469 (1980)   Pop Density: 11.3
Land: 35.9 sq. mi.; Water: 0.0 sq. mi.

Bertha — City
ZIP: 56437   Lat: 46-15-57 N Long: 95-03-47 W
Pop: 507 (1990); 510 (1980)   Pop Density: 507.0
Land: 1.0 sq. mi.; Water: 0.0 sq. mi.
Incorporated 1897. City and township not coextensive.
Name origin: For Mrs. Bertha Riston, the first woman settler.

*Bertha — Township
ZIP: 56437   Lat: 46-14-14 N Long: 95-05-02 W
Pop: 403 (1990); 490 (1980)   Pop Density: 11.4
Land: 35.5 sq. mi.; Water: 0.0 sq. mi.

Birchdale — Township
ZIP: 56336   Lat: 45-48-52 N Long: 94-50-16 W
Pop: 727 (1990); 722 (1980)   Pop Density: 22.1
Land: 32.9 sq. mi.; Water: 3.1 sq. mi.

Browerville — City
ZIP: 56438   Lat: 46-05-08 N Long: 94-52-05 W
Pop: 782 (1990); 693 (1980)   Pop Density: 1303.3
Land: 0.6 sq. mi.; Water: 0.0 sq. mi.   Elev: 1283 ft.
Name origin: For early pioneer Abraham Brower.

Bruce — Township
Lat: 45-58-16 N Long: 94-42-26 W
Pop: 602 (1990); 482 (1980)   Pop Density: 17.1
Land: 35.2 sq. mi.; Water: 0.8 sq. mi.

Burleene — Township
Lat: 46-03-57 N Long: 95-05-00 W
Pop: 370 (1990); 436 (1980)   Pop Density: 10.3
Land: 35.8 sq. mi.; Water: 0.0 sq. mi.

Burnhamville — Township
ZIP: 56318   Lat: 45-53-49 N Long: 94-42-21 W
Pop: 682 (1990); 671 (1980)   Pop Density: 21.6
Land: 31.6 sq. mi.; Water: 3.4 sq. mi.

Burtrum — City
ZIP: 56318   Lat: 45-51-57 N Long: 94-41-13 W
Pop: 172 (1990); 177 (1980)   Pop Density: 286.7
Land: 0.6 sq. mi.; Water: 0.0 sq. mi.   Elev: 1285 ft.

Clarissa — City
ZIP: 56440   Lat: 46-07-45 N Long: 94-56-57 W
Pop: 637 (1990); 663 (1980)   Pop Density: 637.0
Land: 1.0 sq. mi.; Water: 0.0 sq. mi.
Name origin: For the wife of Lewis Bishoffsheim, who settled in the area in 1877.

MINNESOTA, Todd County

Eagle Bend
City
ZIP: 56446 Lat: 46-09-54 N Long: 95-02-02 W
Pop: 524 (1990); 593 (1980) Pop Density: 403.1
Land: 1.3 sq. mi.; Water: 0.0 sq. mi. Elev: 1369 ft.
Name origin: For its location at a bend in Eagle Creek.

Eagle Valley
Township
ZIP: 56440 Lat: 46-08-51 N Long: 94-57-47 W
Pop: 585 (1990); 714 (1980) Pop Density: 16.7
Land: 35.1 sq. mi.; Water: 0.0 sq. mi.

Fawn Lake
Township
Lat: 46-14-11 N Long: 94-42-38 W
Pop: 426 (1990); 358 (1980) Pop Density: 12.5
Land: 34.0 sq. mi.; Water: 1.7 sq. mi.

Germania
Township
ZIP: 56446 Lat: 46-14-16 N Long: 94-57-36 W
Pop: 455 (1990); 508 (1980) Pop Density: 12.5
Land: 36.4 sq. mi.; Water: 0.0 sq. mi.

Gordon
Township
Lat: 45-53-16 N Long: 95-04-37 W
Pop: 583 (1990); 635 (1980) Pop Density: 20.8
Land: 28.0 sq. mi.; Water: 7.1 sq. mi.

Grey Eagle
City
ZIP: 56336 Lat: 45-49-30 N Long: 94-44-55 W
Pop: 353 (1990); 338 (1980) Pop Density: 882.5
Land: 0.4 sq. mi.; Water: 0.0 sq. mi. Elev: 1222 ft.
City and township not coextensive.
Name origin: For a gray eagle shot in the area in 1868.

*Grey Eagle
Township
ZIP: 56336 Lat: 45-48-28 N Long: 94-42-20 W
Pop: 501 (1990); 571 (1980) Pop Density: 20.0
Land: 25.1 sq. mi.; Water: 4.2 sq. mi.

Hartford
Township
ZIP: 56438 Lat: 46-03-48 N Long: 94-50-28 W
Pop: 620 (1990); 669 (1980) Pop Density: 17.7
Land: 35.1 sq. mi.; Water: 0.3 sq. mi.

Hewitt
City
ZIP: 56453 Lat: 46-19-22 N Long: 95-05-16 W
Pop: 269 (1990); 299 (1980) Pop Density: 134.5
Land: 2.0 sq. mi.; Water: 0.0 sq. mi.
Name origin: For nearby farmer Henry Hewitt.

Iona
Township
Lat: 46-03-48 N Long: 94-57-21 W
Pop: 422 (1990); 525 (1980) Pop Density: 11.7
Land: 36.0 sq. mi.; Water: 0.2 sq. mi.

Kandota
Township
Lat: 45-48-51 N Long: 94-58-08 W
Pop: 607 (1990); 535 (1980) Pop Density: 27.8
Land: 21.8 sq. mi.; Water: 2.4 sq. mi.

Leslie
Township
Lat: 45-58-42 N Long: 95-05-20 W
Pop: 530 (1990); 619 (1980) Pop Density: 15.4
Land: 34.5 sq. mi.; Water: 1.7 sq. mi.

Little Elk
Township
Lat: 46-03-48 N Long: 94-42-48 W
Pop: 309 (1990); 357 (1980) Pop Density: 8.9
Land: 34.7 sq. mi.; Water: 1.2 sq. mi.

Little Sauk
Township
Lat: 45-53-04 N Long: 94-57-25 W
Pop: 639 (1990); 642 (1980) Pop Density: 18.7
Land: 34.2 sq. mi.; Water: 1.6 sq. mi.

Long Prairie
City
ZIP: 56347 Lat: 45-58-46 N Long: 94-51-46 W
Pop: 2,786 (1990); 2,859 (1980) Pop Density: 1266.4
Land: 2.2 sq. mi.; Water: 0.1 sq. mi.
City and township not coextensive.
Name origin: For the Long Prairie River that flows through the county.

*Long Prairie
Township
Lat: 45-58-36 N Long: 94-49-59 W
Pop: 820 (1990); 938 (1980) Pop Density: 24.6
Land: 33.3 sq. mi.; Water: 0.4 sq. mi.

Moran
Township
ZIP: 56479 Lat: 46-14-18 N Long: 94-50-16 W
Pop: 532 (1990); 570 (1980) Pop Density: 14.9
Land: 35.6 sq. mi.; Water: 0.5 sq. mi.

Osakis
City
ZIP: 56360 Lat: 45-51-50 N Long: 95-08-07 W
Pop: 58 (1990); 88 (1980) Pop Density: 193.3
Land: 0.3 sq. mi.; Water: 0.1 sq. mi.
Part of the town is also in Douglas County.
Name origin: For the lake, itself named for the Sauk Indians, who once lived in the area.

Reynolds
Township
Lat: 45-58-30 N Long: 94-57-41 W
Pop: 660 (1990); 662 (1980) Pop Density: 18.5
Land: 35.6 sq. mi.; Water: 0.4 sq. mi.

Round Prairie
Township
Lat: 45-53-15 N Long: 94-50-09 W
Pop: 579 (1990); 658 (1980) Pop Density: 16.5
Land: 35.1 sq. mi.; Water: 1.0 sq. mi.

Staples
City
ZIP: 56479 Lat: 46-21-29 N Long: 94-48-04 W
Pop: 2,357 (1990); 2,623 (1980) Pop Density: 1240.5
Land: 1.9 sq. mi.; Water: 0.0 sq. mi.
Part of the town is also in Wadena County.
Name origin: For an early lumberman named Staples, who established a mill in the town.

*Staples
Township
ZIP: 56479 Lat: 46-19-57 N Long: 94-50-47 W
Pop: 842 (1990); 1,011 (1980) Pop Density: 25.6
Land: 32.9 sq. mi.; Water: 1.2 sq. mi.

Stowe Prairie
Township
ZIP: 56453 Lat: 46-19-08 N Long: 95-05-53 W
Pop: 540 (1990); 595 (1980) Pop Density: 15.9
Land: 33.9 sq. mi.; Water: 0.1 sq. mi.

Turtle Creek
Township
ZIP: 56438 Lat: 46-09-28 N Long: 94-43-14 W
Pop: 248 (1990); 371 (1980) Pop Density: 7.6
Land: 32.7 sq. mi.; Water: 3.0 sq. mi.

Villard
Township
Lat: 46-19-09 N Long: 94-43-29 W
Pop: 547 (1990); 466 (1980) Pop Density: 18.2
Land: 30.1 sq. mi.; Water: 1.6 sq. mi.

Ward Township
ZIP: 56438 **Lat:** 46-08-57 N **Long:** 94-49-50 W
Pop: 468 (1990); 515 (1980) **Pop Density:** 13.0
Land: 35.9 sq. mi.; **Water:** 0.4 sq. mi.

West Union City
Lat: 45-48-05 N **Long:** 95-04-59 W
Pop: 54 (1990); 74 (1980) **Pop Density:** 180.0
Land: 0.3 sq. mi.; **Water:** 0.0 sq. mi.
Founded 1867. City and township not coextensive.
Name origin: For the American union.

*West Union Township
Lat: 45-48-43 N **Long:** 95-04-36 W
Pop: 335 (1990); 380 (1980) **Pop Density:** 11.6
Land: 28.8 sq. mi.; **Water:** 0.8 sq. mi.

Wykeham Township
ZIP: 56446 **Lat:** 46-08-33 N **Long:** 95-05-00 W
Pop: 428 (1990); 505 (1980) **Pop Density:** 12.3
Land: 34.8 sq. mi.; **Water:** 0.2 sq. mi.

Traverse County
County Seat: Wheaton (ZIP: 56296)

Pop: 4,463 (1990); 5,542 (1980) **Pop Density:** 7.8
Land: 574.1 sq. mi.; **Water:** 11.9 sq. mi. **Area Code:** 612
On the central western border of MN, south of Fargo, ND; established Feb 20, 1862 from Wilkin County (then called Toombs County).
Name origin: For Lake Traverse on the southwestern border of the county; from the French *lac travers,* a translation of the Siouan name *Mdehdakinyan* 'lake lying crosswise' [to Big Stone and Lac Qui Parle lakes].

Arthur Township
Lat: 45-37-55 N **Long:** 96-41-49 W
Pop: 114 (1990); 151 (1980) **Pop Density:** 3.2
Land: 36.1 sq. mi.; **Water:** 0.3 sq. mi.

Browns Valley City
ZIP: 56219 **Lat:** 45-35-41 N **Long:** 96-49-58 W
Pop: 804 (1990); 887 (1980) **Pop Density:** 1005.0
Land: 0.8 sq. mi.; **Water:** 0.0 sq. mi.
Founded 1866.
Name origin: For founder Joseph Brown.

Clifton Township
Lat: 45-48-10 N **Long:** 96-19-35 W
Pop: 92 (1990); 133 (1980) **Pop Density:** 2.4
Land: 38.3 sq. mi.; **Water:** 0.0 sq. mi.

Croke Township
Lat: 45-43-22 N **Long:** 96-27-28 W
Pop: 121 (1990); 156 (1980) **Pop Density:** 3.4
Land: 35.9 sq. mi.; **Water:** 0.0 sq. mi.

Dollymount Township
Lat: 45-42-57 N **Long:** 96-19-34 W
Pop: 106 (1990); 131 (1980) **Pop Density:** 2.8
Land: 38.4 sq. mi.; **Water:** 0.0 sq. mi.

Dumont City
ZIP: 56236 **Lat:** 45-43-00 N **Long:** 96-25-18 W
Pop: 126 (1990); 173 (1980) **Pop Density:** 315.0
Land: 0.4 sq. mi.; **Water:** 0.0 sq. mi.

Folsom Township
Lat: 45-37-20 N **Long:** 96-47-31 W
Pop: 149 (1990); 162 (1980) **Pop Density:** 7.5
Land: 19.9 sq. mi.; **Water:** 1.8 sq. mi.

Lake Valley Township
Lat: 45-47-40 N **Long:** 96-30-02 W
Pop: 281 (1990); 332 (1980) **Pop Density:** 4.8
Land: 58.8 sq. mi.; **Water:** 3.1 sq. mi.

Leonardsville Township
Lat: 45-37-46 N **Long:** 96-19-21 W
Pop: 156 (1990); 179 (1980) **Pop Density:** 4.1
Land: 38.5 sq. mi.; **Water:** 0.0 sq. mi.

Monson Township
Lat: 45-52-59 N **Long:** 96-28-46 W
Pop: 198 (1990); 224 (1980) **Pop Density:** 3.7
Land: 54.2 sq. mi.; **Water:** 0.0 sq. mi.

Parnell Township
Lat: 45-37-44 N **Long:** 96-33-44 W
Pop: 78 (1990); 140 (1980) **Pop Density:** 2.1
Land: 36.4 sq. mi.; **Water:** 0.0 sq. mi.

Redpath Township
Lat: 45-53-24 N **Long:** 96-18-56 W
Pop: 64 (1990); 116 (1980) **Pop Density:** 1.6
Land: 39.0 sq. mi.; **Water:** 0.0 sq. mi.

Tara Township
Lat: 45-37-33 N **Long:** 96-26-42 W
Pop: 140 (1990); 183 (1980) **Pop Density:** 3.9
Land: 36.2 sq. mi.; **Water:** 0.2 sq. mi.

Taylor Township
Lat: 45-59-08 N **Long:** 96-28-57 W
Pop: 123 (1990); 188 (1980) **Pop Density:** 2.4
Land: 52.0 sq. mi.; **Water:** 0.0 sq. mi.

Tintah City
ZIP: 56583 **Lat:** 46-00-39 N **Long:** 96-19-12 W
Pop: 74 (1990); 119 (1980) **Pop Density:** 92.5
Land: 0.8 sq. mi.; **Water:** 0.0 sq. mi.
City and township not coextensive.

*Tintah Township
ZIP: 56583 **Lat:** 45-58-42 N **Long:** 96-20-19 W
Pop: 73 (1990); 78 (1980) **Pop Density:** 2.1
Land: 34.9 sq. mi.; **Water:** 0.0 sq. mi.

Walls
Township
Lat: 45-43-00 N **Long:** 96-34-47 W
Pop: 88 (1990); 136 (1980) **Pop Density:** 2.4
Land: 36.1 sq. mi.; **Water:** 0.2 sq. mi.

Wheaton
City
ZIP: 56296 **Lat:** 45-48-20 N **Long:** 96-29-50 W
Pop: 1,615 (1990); 1,969 (1980) **Pop Density:** 897.2
Land: 1.8 sq. mi.; **Water:** 0.0 sq. mi. **Elev:** 1019 ft.
Name origin: For early surveyor Daniel T. Wheaton.

Windsor
Township
Lat: 45-41-55 N **Long:** 96-41-27 W
Pop: 61 (1990); 85 (1980) **Pop Density:** 3.9
Land: 15.7 sq. mi.; **Water:** 6.1 sq. mi.

Wabasha County
County Seat: Wabasha (ZIP: 55981)

Pop: 19,744 (1990); 19,335 (1980) **Pop Density:** 37.6
Land: 525.0 sq. mi.; **Water:** 24.8 sq. mi. **Area Code:** 612
On the southeastern border of MN, north of Rochester; original county; established Oct 27, 1849 (prior to statehood); originally spelled Wabashaw.
Name origin: The name of hereditary Sioux chiefs. The name of the chiefs has been transliterated as *Wapashaw* and is said to mean 'red leaf,' 'red hat,' or 'red battle-standard.' The origin of the latter is probably a decoration or red uniform given by the British to one of the chiefs.

Bellechester
City
ZIP: 55027 **Lat:** 44-22-02 N **Long:** 92-30-30 W
Pop: 0 (1990); 63 (1980)
Land: 0.1 sq. mi.; **Water:** 0.0 sq. mi.
Part of the town is also in Goodhue County.

Chester
Township
Lat: 44-19-05 N **Long:** 92-29-53 W
Pop: 491 (1990); 515 (1980) **Pop Density:** 13.9
Land: 35.4 sq. mi.; **Water:** 0.0 sq. mi.

Elgin
City
ZIP: 55932 **Lat:** 44-07-51 N **Long:** 92-15-14 W
Pop: 733 (1990); 667 (1980) **Pop Density:** 1832.5
Land: 0.4 sq. mi.; **Water:** 0.0 sq. mi.
Settled 1855. City and township not coextensive.
Name origin: For the town and county in Scotland.

*Elgin
Township
ZIP: 55932 **Lat:** 44-09-29 N **Long:** 92-16-10 W
Pop: 761 (1990); 751 (1980) **Pop Density:** 21.6
Land: 35.2 sq. mi.; **Water:** 0.0 sq. mi.

Gillford
Township
Lat: 44-19-43 N **Long:** 92-22-12 W
Pop: 534 (1990); 536 (1980) **Pop Density:** 15.1
Land: 35.4 sq. mi.; **Water:** 0.0 sq. mi.

Glasgow
Township
Lat: 44-20-07 N **Long:** 92-07-26 W
Pop: 332 (1990); 277 (1980) **Pop Density:** 9.4
Land: 35.2 sq. mi.; **Water:** 0.4 sq. mi.

Greenfield
Township
Lat: 44-18-59 N **Long:** 91-59-51 W
Pop: 1,078 (1990); 943 (1980) **Pop Density:** 32.7
Land: 33.0 sq. mi.; **Water:** 4.9 sq. mi.

Hammond
City
ZIP: 55938 **Lat:** 44-13-18 N **Long:** 92-22-25 W
Pop: 205 (1990); 178 (1980) **Pop Density:** 2050.0
Land: 0.1 sq. mi.; **Water:** 0.0 sq. mi.
Name origin: For pioneer farmer, Joseph Hammond, who owned the land on which the village was founded.

Highland
Township
Lat: 44-14-24 N **Long:** 92-07-23 W
Pop: 421 (1990); 447 (1980) **Pop Density:** 11.8
Land: 35.8 sq. mi.; **Water:** 0.0 sq. mi.

Hyde Park
Township
Lat: 44-15-57 N **Long:** 92-21-37 W
Pop: 266 (1990); 274 (1980) **Pop Density:** 16.7
Land: 15.9 sq. mi.; **Water:** 0.2 sq. mi.

Kellogg
City
ZIP: 55945 **Lat:** 44-18-25 N **Long:** 91-59-55 W
Pop: 423 (1990); 440 (1980) **Pop Density:** 1410.0
Land: 0.3 sq. mi.; **Water:** 0.0 sq. mi.
Name origin: Named by railroad officials for a company vendor.

Lake
Township
Lat: 44-24-30 N **Long:** 92-15-05 W
Pop: 401 (1990); 417 (1980) **Pop Density:** 16.0
Land: 25.1 sq. mi.; **Water:** 4.8 sq. mi.

Lake City
City
ZIP: 55041 **Lat:** 44-26-25 N **Long:** 92-16-29 W
Pop: 3,889 (1990); 4,035 (1980) **Pop Density:** 1143.8
Land: 3.4 sq. mi.; **Water:** 0.0 sq. mi. **Elev:** 701 ft.
Part of the town is also in Goodhue County.
Name origin: For its location next to Lake Popin.

Mazeppa — City
ZIP: 55956   **Lat:** 44-16-24 N   **Long:** 92-32-26 W
Pop: 722 (1990); 680 (1980)   **Pop Density:** 722.0
Land: 1.0 sq. mi.; **Water:** 0.0 sq. mi.   **Elev:** 931 ft.
City and township not coextensive.
Name origin: For Cossack chief Ivan Mazeppa, commemorated in a poem by Byron.

*Mazeppa — Township
ZIP: 55956   **Lat:** 44-13-49 N   **Long:** 92-29-56 W
Pop: 619 (1990); 492 (1980)   **Pop Density:** 28.4
Land: 21.8 sq. mi.; **Water:** 0.5 sq. mi.

Millville — City
ZIP: 55957   **Lat:** 44-14-42 N   **Long:** 92-17-46 W
Pop: 163 (1990); 186 (1980)   **Pop Density:** 1630.0
Land: 0.1 sq. mi.; **Water:** 0.0 sq. mi.

Minneiska — City
Lat: 44-11-57 N   **Long:** 91-52-39 W
Pop: 66 (1990); 67 (1980)   **Pop Density:** 220.0
Land: 0.3 sq. mi.; **Water:** 0.4 sq. mi.
Part of the town is also in Winona County.

*Minneiska — Township
Lat: 44-14-02 N   **Long:** 91-55-42 W
Pop: 190 (1990); 143 (1980)   **Pop Density:** 17.8
Land: 10.7 sq. mi.; **Water:** 7.2 sq. mi.

Mount Pleasant — Township
Lat: 44-24-44 N   **Long:** 92-22-52 W
Pop: 418 (1990); 451 (1980)   **Pop Density:** 11.6
Land: 36.0 sq. mi.; **Water:** 0.0 sq. mi.

Oakwood — Township
Lat: 44-13-27 N   **Long:** 92-15-15 W
Pop: 429 (1990); 437 (1980)   **Pop Density:** 12.1
Land: 35.5 sq. mi.; **Water:** 0.2 sq. mi.

Pepin — Township
Lat: 44-23-35 N   **Long:** 92-08-49 W
Pop: 369 (1990); 386 (1980)   **Pop Density:** 21.1
Land: 17.5 sq. mi.; **Water:** 4.0 sq. mi.

Plainview — City
ZIP: 55964   **Lat:** 44-09-55 N   **Long:** 92-10-08 W
Pop: 2,768 (1990); 2,416 (1980)   **Pop Density:** 1384.0
Land: 2.0 sq. mi.; **Water:** 0.0 sq. mi.   **Elev:** 1155 ft.
City and township not coextensive.
Name origin: For the plain view available of the surrounding countryside.

*Plainview — Township
ZIP: 55964   **Lat:** 44-09-05 N   **Long:** 92-08-26 W
Pop: 535 (1990); 616 (1980)   **Pop Density:** 15.9
Land: 33.6 sq. mi.; **Water:** 0.0 sq. mi.

Wabasha — City
ZIP: 55981   **Lat:** 44-22-17 N   **Long:** 92-02-42 W
Pop: 2,384 (1990); 2,372 (1980)   **Pop Density:** 290.7
Land: 8.2 sq. mi.; **Water:** 1.1 sq. mi.
Name origin: For the hereditary name of Sioux chiefs. The name of the chiefs has been transliterated as *Wapashaw* and is said to mean 'red leaf,' 'red hat,' or 'red battle-standard.' The origin of the latter is probably a decoration or red uniform given by the British to one of the chiefs.

Watopa — Township
Lat: 44-14-42 N   **Long:** 92-00-45 W
Pop: 256 (1990); 277 (1980)   **Pop Density:** 7.2
Land: 35.4 sq. mi.; **Water:** 0.2 sq. mi.

West Albany — Township
Lat: 44-19-40 N   **Long:** 92-14-27 W
Pop: 395 (1990); 462 (1980)   **Pop Density:** 11.1
Land: 35.6 sq. mi.; **Water:** 0.2 sq. mi.

Zumbro — Township
Lat: 44-13-10 N   **Long:** 92-24-43 W
Pop: 659 (1990); 599 (1980)   **Pop Density:** 20.8
Land: 31.7 sq. mi.; **Water:** 0.6 sq. mi.

Zumbro Falls — City
ZIP: 55938   **Lat:** 44-17-12 N   **Long:** 92-25-34 W
Pop: 237 (1990); 208 (1980)   **Pop Density:** 474.0
Land: 0.5 sq. mi.; **Water:** 0.0 sq. mi.
Name origin: For the adjacent falls on the Zumbro River.

Wadena County
County Seat: Wadena (ZIP: 56482)

Pop: 13,154 (1990); 14,192 (1980)   **Pop Density:** 24.6
Land: 535.5 sq. mi.; **Water:** 7.6 sq. mi.   **Area Code:** 218
In central MN, northwest of St. Cloud; established Jun 11, 1858 from Cass and Todd counties.
Name origin: For the Wadena trading post on the trail from Crow Wing to Otter Tail City; from an archaic Ojibway word meaning 'a little round hill'; possibly a reference to the Crow Wing bluffs, but also a common Ojibway personal name.

Aldrich — City
ZIP: 56434   **Lat:** 46-22-29 N   **Long:** 94-56-21 W
Pop: 70 (1990); 88 (1980)   **Pop Density:** 140.0
Land: 0.5 sq. mi.; **Water:** 0.0 sq. mi.
City and township not coextensive.

*Aldrich — Township
ZIP: 56434   **Lat:** 46-24-26 N   **Long:** 94-58-02 W
Pop: 475 (1990); 559 (1980)   **Pop Density:** 13.8
Land: 34.5 sq. mi.; **Water:** 0.0 sq. mi.

Blueberry — Township
ZIP: 56464   **Lat:** 46-45-45 N   **Long:** 95-05-53 W
Pop: 526 (1990); 567 (1980)   **Pop Density:** 17.5
Land: 30.1 sq. mi.; **Water:** 1.8 sq. mi.

Bullard — Township
Lat: 46-29-53 N   **Long:** 94-49-35 W
Pop: 156 (1990); 163 (1980)   **Pop Density:** 5.1
Land: 30.3 sq. mi.; **Water:** 0.7 sq. mi.

MINNESOTA, Wadena County

Huntersville
Township
ZIP: 56464 Lat: 46-45-07 N Long: 94-50-53 W
Pop: 105 (1990); 89 (1980) Pop Density: 3.0
Land: 34.8 sq. mi.; Water: 1.0 sq. mi.

Leaf River
Township
ZIP: 56482 Lat: 46-30-07 N Long: 95-05-49 W
Pop: 575 (1990); 663 (1980) Pop Density: 16.1
Land: 35.7 sq. mi.; Water: 0.0 sq. mi.

Lyons
Township
Lat: 46-35-29 N Long: 94-50-25 W
Pop: 162 (1990); 185 (1980) Pop Density: 4.6
Land: 34.9 sq. mi.; Water: 0.7 sq. mi.

Meadow
Township
Lat: 46-40-33 N Long: 94-57-53 W
Pop: 215 (1990); 270 (1980) Pop Density: 5.9
Land: 36.3 sq. mi.; Water: 0.2 sq. mi.

Menahga
City
ZIP: 56464 Lat: 46-44-55 N Long: 95-06-07 W
Pop: 1,076 (1990); 980 (1980) Pop Density: 290.8
Land: 3.7 sq. mi.; Water: 0.2 sq. mi.

Name origin: From an Ojibway Indian word meaning 'blueberry.'

Nimrod
City
ZIP: 56478 Lat: 46-38-16 N Long: 94-52-51 W
Pop: 65 (1990); 69 (1980) Pop Density: 72.2
Land: 0.9 sq. mi.; Water: 0.1 sq. mi.

North Germany
Township
Lat: 46-34-38 N Long: 94-57-30 W
Pop: 322 (1990); 374 (1980) Pop Density: 9.0
Land: 35.8 sq. mi.; Water: 0.0 sq. mi.

Orton
Township
Lat: 46-40-24 N Long: 94-50-52 W
Pop: 217 (1990); 234 (1980) Pop Density: 6.3
Land: 34.4 sq. mi.; Water: 0.4 sq. mi.

Red Eye
Township
Lat: 46-40-24 N Long: 95-06-12 W
Pop: 378 (1990); 406 (1980) Pop Density: 10.8
Land: 35.1 sq. mi.; Water: 0.1 sq. mi.

Rockwood
Township
Lat: 46-35-10 N Long: 95-05-16 W
Pop: 375 (1990); 491 (1980) Pop Density: 10.8
Land: 34.6 sq. mi.; Water: 0.0 sq. mi.

Sebeka
City
ZIP: 56477 Lat: 46-37-44 N Long: 95-05-17 W
Pop: 662 (1990); 774 (1980) Pop Density: 264.8
Land: 2.5 sq. mi.; Water: 0.0 sq. mi. Elev: 1385 ft.

Name origin: Named by Great Northern Railway engineer Col. William Crooks, from the Ojibway Indian term meaning 'the village beside the river.'

Shell River
Township
ZIP: 56464 Lat: 46-46-07 N Long: 94-58-30 W
Pop: 233 (1990); 220 (1980) Pop Density: 6.7
Land: 34.8 sq. mi.; Water: 1.3 sq. mi.

Staples
City
ZIP: 56479 Lat: 46-22-47 N Long: 94-48-20 W
Pop: 397 (1990); 264 (1980) Pop Density: 305.4
Land: 1.3 sq. mi.; Water: 0.0 sq. mi.

Part of the town is also in Todd County.

Name origin: For an early lumberman named Staples, who established a mill in the town.

Thomastown
Township
ZIP: 56481 Lat: 46-24-58 N Long: 94-50-08 W
Pop: 887 (1990); 987 (1980) Pop Density: 21.0
Land: 42.2 sq. mi.; Water: 1.0 sq. mi.

Verndale
City
ZIP: 56481 Lat: 46-23-50 N Long: 95-00-41 W
Pop: 560 (1990); 504 (1980) Pop Density: 622.2
Land: 0.9 sq. mi.; Water: 0.0 sq. mi. Elev: 1349 ft.

Name origin: Named by Lucas Smith, who built the first house in the area, for his granddaughter Verne.

Wadena
City
ZIP: 56482 Lat: 46-26-23 N Long: 95-08-05 W
Pop: 4,109 (1990); 4,699 (1980) Pop Density: 933.9
Land: 4.4 sq. mi.; Water: 0.0 sq. mi.

Part of the town is also in Otter Tail County.

Name origin: From the Ojibway Indian term meaning 'little round hill.'

*Wadena
Township
ZIP: 56482 Lat: 46-24-18 N Long: 95-05-34 W
Pop: 1,134 (1990); 1,094 (1980) Pop Density: 35.8
Land: 31.7 sq. mi.; Water: 0.0 sq. mi.

Wing River
Township
ZIP: 56481 Lat: 46-30-12 N Long: 94-58-42 W
Pop: 455 (1990); 512 (1980) Pop Density: 12.6
Land: 36.0 sq. mi.; Water: 0.0 sq. mi.

Waseca County
County Seat: Waseca (ZIP: 56093)

Pop: 18,079 (1990); 18,448 (1980)   **Pop Density:** 42.7
Land: 423.3 sq. mi.; **Water:** 9.6 sq. mi.   **Area Code:** 507

In south-central MN, southeast of Mankato; established Feb 27, 1857 (prior to statehood) from Steele County.
Name origin: From Dakota 'rich,' referring either to provisions or the fertile soil.

Alton — Township
Lat: 44-04-21 N   Long: 93-43-17 W
Pop: 449 (1990); 480 (1980)   **Pop Density:** 12.9
Land: 34.9 sq. mi.; **Water:** 1.4 sq. mi.

Blooming Grove — Township
Lat: 44-08-57 N   Long: 93-27-59 W
Pop: 579 (1990); 564 (1980)   **Pop Density:** 16.3
Land: 35.6 sq. mi.; **Water:** 0.4 sq. mi.

Byron — Township
Lat: 43-53-21 N   Long: 93-35-49 W
Pop: 259 (1990); 330 (1980)   **Pop Density:** 7.2
Land: 36.0 sq. mi.; **Water:** 0.2 sq. mi.

Elysian — City
ZIP: 56028   Lat: 44-11-44 N   Long: 93-40-37 W
Pop: 2 (1990); 4 (1980)   **Pop Density:** 1000.0
Land: 0.002 sq. mi.; **Water:** 0.0 sq. mi.
Settled 1858. Part of the town is also in Le Sueur County.
Name origin: For the ancient Greek heaven, the Elysian Fields.

Freedom — Township
Lat: 43-58-51 N   Long: 93-42-25 W
Pop: 413 (1990); 522 (1980)   **Pop Density:** 11.5
Land: 35.9 sq. mi.; **Water:** 0.2 sq. mi.

Iosco — Township
Lat: 44-09-13 N   Long: 93-35-06 W
Pop: 537 (1990); 520 (1980)   **Pop Density:** 15.3
Land: 35.0 sq. mi.; **Water:** 0.7 sq. mi.

Janesville — City
ZIP: 56048   Lat: 44-06-59 N   Long: 93-42-28 W
Pop: 1,969 (1990); 1,897 (1980)   **Pop Density:** 1969.0
Land: 1.0 sq. mi.; **Water:** 0.0 sq. mi.   **Elev:** 1069 ft.
Founded 1856.
Name origin: For popular local settler, Mrs. Jane Sprague.

*Janesville — Township
ZIP: 56048   Lat: 44-08-54 N   Long: 93-41-55 W
Pop: 576 (1990); 629 (1980)   **Pop Density:** 18.5
Land: 31.2 sq. mi.; **Water:** 3.8 sq. mi.

New Richland — City
ZIP: 56072   Lat: 43-53-36 N   Long: 93-29-34 W
Pop: 1,237 (1990); 1,263 (1980)   **Pop Density:** 2061.7
Land: 0.6 sq. mi.; **Water:** 0.0 sq. mi.   **Elev:** 1184 ft.
City and township not coextensive.
Name origin: Named by settlers from WI for Richland County, WI.

*New Richland — Township
ZIP: 56072   Lat: 43-53-43 N   Long: 93-28-17 W
Pop: 468 (1990); 546 (1980)   **Pop Density:** 13.2
Land: 35.4 sq. mi.; **Water:** 0.2 sq. mi.

Otisco — Township
Lat: 43-58-49 N   Long: 93-27-40 W
Pop: 623 (1990); 672 (1980)   **Pop Density:** 17.3
Land: 36.0 sq. mi.; **Water:** 0.0 sq. mi.

St. Mary — Township
Lat: 44-04-22 N   Long: 93-34-57 W
Pop: 482 (1990); 540 (1980)   **Pop Density:** 13.4
Land: 35.9 sq. mi.; **Water:** 0.0 sq. mi.

Vivian — Township
Lat: 43-53-03 N   Long: 93-42-45 W
Pop: 306 (1990); 389 (1980)   **Pop Density:** 8.5
Land: 35.9 sq. mi.; **Water:** 0.0 sq. mi.

Waldorf — City
ZIP: 56091   Lat: 43-55-57 N   Long: 93-41-48 W
Pop: 243 (1990); 249 (1980)   **Pop Density:** 607.5
Land: 0.4 sq. mi.; **Water:** 0.0 sq. mi.
Name origin: For Waldorf, MD.

Waseca — City
ZIP: 56093   Lat: 44-04-52 N   Long: 93-30-06 W
Pop: 8,385 (1990); 8,219 (1980)   **Pop Density:** 2540.9
Land: 3.3 sq. mi.; **Water:** 1.1 sq. mi.   **Elev:** 1151 ft.
Name origin: From the Dakota term meaning 'rich' or 'fertile,' referring either to provisions or the fertile soil.

Wilton — Township
Lat: 43-58-54 N   Long: 93-35-09 W
Pop: 393 (1990); 448 (1980)   **Pop Density:** 11.0
Land: 35.7 sq. mi.; **Water:** 0.4 sq. mi.

Woodville — Township
Lat: 44-03-31 N   Long: 93-27-37 W
Pop: 1,158 (1990); 1,176 (1980)   **Pop Density:** 37.8
Land: 30.6 sq. mi.; **Water:** 1.1 sq. mi.

Washington County
County Seat: Stillwater (ZIP: 55082)

Pop: 145,896 (1990); 113,571 (1980)　　**Pop Density:** 372.4
Land: 391.7 sq. mi.; **Water:** 31.5 sq. mi.　　**Area Code:** 612
On the central eastern border of MN, east of St. Paul; original county; established Oct 27, 1849 (prior to statehood).
Name origin: For George Washington (1732–99), American patriot and first U.S. president.

Afton　　City
ZIP: 55001　　Lat: 44-54-11 N　Long: 92-49-07 W
Pop: 2,645 (1990); 2,550 (1980)　　Pop Density: 105.0
Land: 25.2 sq. mi.; Water: 1.2 sq. mi.
Organized 1855.
Name origin: For Scottish poet Robert Burn's (1759–96) poem "Afton Water."

Bayport　　City
ZIP: 55003　　Lat: 45-01-04 N　Long: 92-46-48 W
Pop: 3,200 (1990); 2,932 (1980)　　Pop Density: 2133.3
Land: 1.5 sq. mi.; Water: 0.0 sq. mi.

Baytown　　Township
ZIP: 55003　　Lat: 45-01-07 N　Long: 92-49-01 W
Pop: 939 (1990); 851 (1980)　　Pop Density: 97.8
Land: 9.6 sq. mi.; Water: 1.4 sq. mi.

Birchwood Village　　City
　　Lat: 45-03-35 N　Long: 92-58-39 W
Pop: 1,042 (1990); 1,059 (1980)　　Pop Density: 2605.0
Land: 0.4 sq. mi.; Water: 0.0 sq. mi.

Cottage Grove　　City
ZIP: 55016　　Lat: 44-49-02 N　Long: 92-55-37 W
Pop: 22,935 (1990); 18,994 (1980)　　Pop Density: 674.6
Land: 34.0 sq. mi.; Water: 3.9 sq. mi.
In eastern MN, 11 mi. southeast of St. Paul. Settled 1840s.
Name origin: For the intermingled farms and groves of trees.

Dellwood　　City
　　Lat: 45-06-07 N　Long: 92-57-59 W
Pop: 887 (1990); 751 (1980)　　Pop Density: 341.2
Land: 2.6 sq. mi.; Water: 0.1 sq. mi.
Founded 1882.
Name origin: Named euphoniously.

Denmark　　Township
　　Lat: 44-48-16 N　Long: 92-49-24 W
Pop: 1,172 (1990); 1,140 (1980)　　Pop Density: 41.0
Land: 28.6 sq. mi.; Water: 1.8 sq. mi.

Forest Lake　　City
ZIP: 55025　　Lat: 45-16-32 N　Long: 92-59-08 W
Pop: 5,833 (1990); 4,596 (1980)　　Pop Density: 2083.2
Land: 2.8 sq. mi.; Water: 0.0 sq. mi.　　Elev: 909 ft.
City and township not coextensive.
Name origin: For location on the west end of a lake with great timber growth along its shores.

*Forest Lake　　Township
ZIP: 55025　　Lat: 45-15-08 N　Long: 92-57-20 W
Pop: 6,690 (1990); 5,331 (1980)　　Pop Density: 236.4
Land: 28.3 sq. mi.; Water: 4.4 sq. mi.

Grant　　Township
　　Lat: 45-05-05 N　Long: 92-54-53 W
Pop: 3,778 (1990); 3,083 (1980)　　Pop Density: 146.4
Land: 25.8 sq. mi.; Water: 1.3 sq. mi.

Grey Cloud Island　　Township
ZIP: 55071　　Lat: 44-47-56 N　Long: 93-00-24 W
Pop: 414 (1990); 351 (1980)　　Pop Density: 133.5
Land: 3.1 sq. mi.; Water: 0.7 sq. mi.

Hastings　　City
ZIP: 55033　　Lat: 44-45-11 N　Long: 92-51-14 W
Pop: 5 (1990); 16 (1980)　　Pop Density: 16.7
Land: 0.3 sq. mi.; Water: 0.1 sq. mi.　　Elev: 730 ft.
In southeastern MN on the Mississippi River, 20 mi. southeast of St. Paul. Part of the town is also in Dakota County.
Name origin: For pioneer and first Governor of MN Henry Hastings Sibley (1811–91), who defended the state during the 1862 Sioux uprising.

Hugo　　City
ZIP: 55038　　Lat: 45-09-32 N　Long: 92-57-46 W
Pop: 4,417 (1990); 3,771 (1980)　　Pop Density: 129.9
Land: 34.0 sq. mi.; Water: 2.0 sq. mi.　　Elev: 935 ft.
Name origin: For English engineer Trevanion Hugo, who settled in MN and later became mayor of Duluth.

Lake Elmo　　City
ZIP: 55042　　Lat: 44-59-43 N　Long: 92-54-27 W
Pop: 5,903 (1990); 5,296 (1980)　　Pop Density: 250.1
Land: 23.6 sq. mi.; Water: 1.6 sq. mi.
Name origin: For a popular novel of the same name. Originally called Bass Lake.

Lakeland　　City
ZIP: 55043　　Lat: 44-57-01 N　Long: 92-46-14 W
Pop: 2,000 (1990); 1,812 (1980)　　Pop Density: 952.4
Land: 2.1 sq. mi.; Water: 0.8 sq. mi.
Name origin: For its location on Lake St. Croix.

Lakeland Shores　　City
ZIP: 55043　　Lat: 44-56-57 N　Long: 92-45-47 W
Pop: 291 (1990); 171 (1980)　　Pop Density: 970.0
Land: 0.3 sq. mi.; Water: 0.4 sq. mi.

Lake St. Croix Beach　　City
　　Lat: 44-55-27 N　Long: 92-45-55 W
Pop: 1,078 (1990); 1,176 (1980)　　Pop Density: 1796.7
Land: 0.6 sq. mi.; Water: 0.4 sq. mi.

Landfall　　City
　　Lat: 44-57-00 N　Long: 92-58-38 W
Pop: 685 (1990); 679 (1980)　　Pop Density: 6850.0
Land: 0.1 sq. mi.; Water: 0.0 sq. mi.

Mahtomedi
City
ZIP: 55115 **Lat:** 45-03-21 N **Long:** 92-57-38 W
Pop: 5,569 (1990); 3,851 (1980) **Pop Density:** 1546.9
Land: 3.6 sq. mi.; **Water:** 1.4 sq. mi.

Marine on St. Croix
City
Lat: 45-11-52 N **Long:** 92-46-23 W
Pop: 602 (1990); 543 (1980) **Pop Density:** 154.4
Land: 3.9 sq. mi.; **Water:** 0.2 sq. mi.

May
Township
ZIP: 55047 **Lat:** 45-09-53 N **Long:** 92-49-52 W
Pop: 2,535 (1990); 2,076 (1980) **Pop Density:** 71.8
Land: 35.3 sq. mi.; **Water:** 2.3 sq. mi.

Newport
City
ZIP: 55055 **Lat:** 44-52-28 N **Long:** 92-59-54 W
Pop: 3,720 (1990); 3,323 (1980) **Pop Density:** 1005.4
Land: 3.7 sq. mi.; **Water:** 0.2 sq. mi. **Elev:** 743 ft.
Name origin: Named by early settler Mrs. James Hugunin, who named the town for Newport, RI.

New Scandia
Township
ZIP: 55047 **Lat:** 45-15-07 N **Long:** 92-49-37 W
Pop: 3,197 (1990); 2,858 (1980) **Pop Density:** 88.8
Land: 36.0 sq. mi.; **Water:** 3.8 sq. mi.

Oakdale
City
ZIP: 55128 **Lat:** 44-59-19 N **Long:** 92-57-58 W
Pop: 18,374 (1990); 12,123 (1980) **Pop Density:** 1856.0
Land: 9.9 sq. mi.; **Water:** 0.2 sq. mi. **Elev:** 1074 ft.
Name origin: For the abundant white and burr oak trees.

Oak Park Heights
City
Lat: 45-01-50 N **Long:** 92-48-19 W
Pop: 3,486 (1990); 2,591 (1980) **Pop Density:** 1515.7
Land: 2.3 sq. mi.; **Water:** 0.0 sq. mi.
Name origin: For its descriptive connotations.

Pine Springs
City
Lat: 45-02-11 N **Long:** 92-57-07 W
Pop: 436 (1990); 267 (1980) **Pop Density:** 545.0
Land: 0.8 sq. mi.; **Water:** 0.1 sq. mi.

St. Marys Point
City
Lat: 44-54-48 N **Long:** 92-46-08 W
Pop: 339 (1990); 348 (1980) **Pop Density:** 847.5
Land: 0.4 sq. mi.; **Water:** 0.0 sq. mi.

St. Paul Park
City
Lat: 44-50-22 N **Long:** 92-59-41 W
Pop: 4,965 (1990); 4,864 (1980) **Pop Density:** 2068.8
Land: 2.4 sq. mi.; **Water:** 0.1 sq. mi.

Stillwater
City
ZIP: 55082 **Lat:** 45-03-23 N **Long:** 92-49-19 W
Pop: 13,882 (1990); 12,290 (1980) **Pop Density:** 2570.7
Land: 5.4 sq. mi.; **Water:** 0.7 sq. mi.
In eastern MN on the St. Croix River, 15 mi. northeast of St. Paul. City and township not coextensive.
Name origin: For the calm lake nearby and for Stillwater, ME.

*Stillwater
Township
Lat: 45-05-30 N **Long:** 92-49-02 W
Pop: 2,066 (1990); 1,599 (1980) **Pop Density:** 117.4
Land: 17.6 sq. mi.; **Water:** 1.1 sq. mi.

West Lakeland
Township
Lat: 44-58-04 N **Long:** 92-49-35 W
Pop: 1,736 (1990); 1,318 (1980) **Pop Density:** 140.0
Land: 12.4 sq. mi.; **Water:** 0.3 sq. mi.

White Bear Lake
City
ZIP: 55110 **Lat:** 45-03-16 N **Long:** 92-58-56 W
Pop: 416 (1990); 10 (1980) **Pop Density:** 4160.0
Land: 0.1 sq. mi.; **Water:** 0.0 sq. mi. **Elev:** 950 ft.
Part of the town is also in Ramsey County.
Name origin: For the nearby lake, which was sacred to the Sioux.

Willernie
City
ZIP: 55090 **Lat:** 45-03-14 N **Long:** 92-57-22 W
Pop: 584 (1990); 654 (1980) **Pop Density:** 5840.0
Land: 0.1 sq. mi.; **Water:** 0.0 sq. mi.

Woodbury
City
ZIP: 55125 **Lat:** 44-54-19 N **Long:** 92-55-15 W
Pop: 20,075 (1990); 10,297 (1980) **Pop Density:** 573.6
Land: 35.0 sq. mi.; **Water:** 0.6 sq. mi. **Elev:** 1065 ft.
Name origin: For Levi Woodbury (1789–1851), U.S. senator, Supreme Court associate justice, and governor of NH.

Watonwan County
County Seat: St. James (ZIP: 56081)

Pop: 11,682 (1990); 12,361 (1980) **Pop Density:** 26.9
Land: 434.5 sq. mi.; **Water:** 5.4 sq. mi. **Area Code:** 507
In south-central MN, southwest of Mankato; established Feb 25, 1860 from Brown County.
Name origin: For the Watonwan River, whose head streams flow through the county; probably from a Dakota word meaning 'where fish bait can be found' or 'where fish abound.'

Adrian
Township
Lat: 44-04-19 N **Long:** 94-47-20 W
Pop: 203 (1990); 279 (1980) **Pop Density:** 5.9
Land: 34.7 sq. mi.; **Water:** 0.9 sq. mi.

Antrim
Township
Lat: 43-53-34 N **Long:** 94-25-51 W
Pop: 324 (1990); 383 (1980) **Pop Density:** 9.1
Land: 35.6 sq. mi.; **Water:** 0.1 sq. mi.

MINNESOTA, Watonwan County

Butterfield — City
ZIP: 56120   Lat: 43-57-29 N   Long: 94-47-34 W
Pop: 509 (1990); 634 (1980)   Pop Density: 1272.5
Land: 0.4 sq. mi.; Water: 0.0 sq. mi.
City and township not coextensive.
Name origin: For its first settler, William Butterfield.

*Butterfield — Township
ZIP: 56120   Lat: 43-58-31 N   Long: 94-47-54 W
Pop: 385 (1990); 361 (1980)   Pop Density: 10.9
Land: 35.4 sq. mi.; Water: 0.2 sq. mi.

Darfur — City
Lat: 44-03-12 N   Long: 94-50-14 W
Pop: 128 (1990); 139 (1980)   Pop Density: 320.0
Land: 0.4 sq. mi.; Water: 0.0 sq. mi.   Elev: 1148 ft.
Incorporated c. 1900.
Name origin: For an area in the Sudan.

Fieldon — Township
Lat: 43-58-41 N   Long: 94-25-39 W
Pop: 271 (1990); 305 (1980)   Pop Density: 7.6
Land: 35.7 sq. mi.; Water: 0.2 sq. mi.

La Salle — City
ZIP: 56056   Lat: 44-04-19 N   Long: 94-34-11 W
Pop: 98 (1990); 115 (1980)   Pop Density: 980.0
Land: 0.1 sq. mi.; Water: 0.0 sq. mi.
Founded 1899.
Name origin: For the French explorer, Robert de La Salle (1643–87).

Lewisville — City
ZIP: 56060   Lat: 43-55-26 N   Long: 94-26-06 W
Pop: 255 (1990); 273 (1980)   Pop Density: 850.0
Land: 0.3 sq. mi.; Water: 0.0 sq. mi.
Name origin: For an early pioneer family.

Long Lake — Township
Lat: 43-53-37 N   Long: 94-40-52 W
Pop: 413 (1990); 424 (1980)   Pop Density: 12.0
Land: 34.4 sq. mi.; Water: 1.3 sq. mi.

Madelia — City
ZIP: 56062   Lat: 44-02-57 N   Long: 94-25-01 W
Pop: 2,237 (1990); 2,130 (1980)   Pop Density: 1864.2
Land: 1.2 sq. mi.; Water: 0.0 sq. mi.   Elev: 1029 ft.
Founded 1857. City and township not coextensive.
Name origin: An elision of *Madeline*, the daughter of an original landowner.

*Madelia — Township
ZIP: 56062   Lat: 44-04-01 N   Long: 94-26-03 W
Pop: 368 (1990); 408 (1980)   Pop Density: 11.1
Land: 33.3 sq. mi.; Water: 1.2 sq. mi.

Nelson — Township
Lat: 44-03-53 N   Long: 94-40-55 W
Pop: 318 (1990); 381 (1980)   Pop Density: 8.9
Land: 35.7 sq. mi.; Water: 0.0 sq. mi.

Odin — City
ZIP: 56160   Lat: 43-52-03 N   Long: 94-44-30 W
Pop: 102 (1990); 134 (1980)   Pop Density: 255.0
Land: 0.4 sq. mi.; Water: 0.0 sq. mi.
Settled 1860s.
Name origin: For the chief god in Norse mythology.

*Odin — Township
ZIP: 56160   Lat: 43-53-39 N   Long: 94-48-06 W
Pop: 241 (1990); 276 (1980)   Pop Density: 7.0
Land: 34.6 sq. mi.; Water: 0.9 sq. mi.

Ormsby — City
ZIP: 56162   Lat: 43-51-03 N   Long: 94-41-54 W
Pop: 107 (1990); 116 (1980)   Pop Density: 356.7
Land: 0.3 sq. mi.; Water: 0.0 sq. mi.
Founded 1800s. Part of the town is also in Martin County.
Name origin: For Colonel Ormsby of IA.

Riverdale — Township
Lat: 44-03-48 N   Long: 94-33-24 W
Pop: 380 (1990); 433 (1980)   Pop Density: 9.8
Land: 38.9 sq. mi.; Water: 0.0 sq. mi.

Rosendale — Township
Lat: 43-58-16 N   Long: 94-33-50 W
Pop: 343 (1990); 479 (1980)   Pop Density: 9.0
Land: 38.3 sq. mi.; Water: 0.2 sq. mi.

St. James — City
ZIP: 56081   Lat: 43-59-05 N   Long: 94-37-31 W
Pop: 4,364 (1990); 4,346 (1980)   Pop Density: 2182.0
Land: 2.0 sq. mi.; Water: 0.0 sq. mi.
Name origin: Named by the president and director of the St. Paul & Sioux City Railway.

*St. James — Township
Lat: 43-58-23 N   Long: 94-40-26 W
Pop: 320 (1990); 355 (1980)   Pop Density: 9.5
Land: 33.8 sq. mi.; Water: 0.4 sq. mi.

South Branch — Township
Lat: 43-53-42 N   Long: 94-33-32 W
Pop: 316 (1990); 390 (1980)   Pop Density: 8.1
Land: 39.1 sq. mi.; Water: 0.0 sq. mi.

Wilkin County
County Seat: Breckenridge (ZIP: 56520)

Pop: 7,516 (1990); 8,454 (1980)   **Pop Density:** 10.0
Land: 751.5 sq. mi.; **Water:** 0.2 sq. mi.   **Area Code:** 218

On the central western border of MN, south of Fargo, ND; established Mar 8, 1858 from Cass County; name changed from Toombs County to Andy Johnson County in 1863 and from Andy Johnson County to present name Mar 6, 1868.

Name origin: For Col. Alexander Wilkin (1820–64), an officer in the Union army killed at the Battle of Tupelo. Originally for Robert Toombs (1810–85), U.S. senator from GA (1853–61), who became the Confederate secretary of state and thus angered the local residents. Changed to honor the seventeenth U.S. president, Andrew Johnson (1808–75), but his subsequent political stands also angered them.

Akron — Township
Lat: 46-24-32 N   **Long:** 96-20-35 W
Pop: 171 (1990); 162 (1980)   **Pop Density:** 4.8
Land: 35.5 sq. mi.; **Water:** 0.0 sq. mi.

Andrea — Township
Lat: 46-19-34 N   **Long:** 96-20-33 W
Pop: 79 (1990); 91 (1980)   **Pop Density:** 2.2
Land: 35.4 sq. mi.; **Water:** 0.0 sq. mi.

Atherton — Township
Lat: 46-35-33 N   **Long:** 96-27-45 W
Pop: 170 (1990); 211 (1980)   **Pop Density:** 4.7
Land: 36.1 sq. mi.; **Water:** 0.0 sq. mi.

Bradford — Township
Lat: 46-09-25 N   **Long:** 96-19-37 W
Pop: 112 (1990); 170 (1980)   **Pop Density:** 3.2
Land: 35.5 sq. mi.; **Water:** 0.0 sq. mi.

Brandrup — Township
Lat: 46-09-07 N   **Long:** 96-28-55 W
Pop: 188 (1990); 214 (1980)   **Pop Density:** 3.5
Land: 54.2 sq. mi.; **Water:** 0.0 sq. mi.

Breckenridge — City
ZIP: 56520   **Lat:** 46-15-55 N   **Long:** 96-35-07 W
Pop: 3,708 (1990); 3,909 (1980)   **Pop Density:** 1612.2
Land: 2.3 sq. mi.; **Water:** 0.0 sq. mi.
Founded 1858. City and township not coextensive.
Name origin: For John C. Breckenridge (1821–75), U.S. vice president and general in the Confederate Army.

*Breckenridge — Township
ZIP: 56520   **Lat:** 46-14-23 N   **Long:** 96-33-05 W
Pop: 216 (1990); 264 (1980)   **Pop Density:** 10.3
Land: 21.0 sq. mi.; **Water:** 0.1 sq. mi.

Campbell — City
ZIP: 56522   **Lat:** 46-05-52 N   **Long:** 96-24-19 W
Pop: 233 (1990); 286 (1980)   **Pop Density:** 1165.0
Land: 0.2 sq. mi.; **Water:** 0.0 sq. mi.
City and township not coextensive.
Name origin: Named by the Great Northern Railway Company, possibly for one of their officers.

*Campbell — Township
ZIP: 56522   **Lat:** 46-03-29 N   **Long:** 96-28-59 W
Pop: 103 (1990); 130 (1980)   **Pop Density:** 2.1
Land: 50.1 sq. mi.; **Water:** 0.0 sq. mi.

Champion — Township
Lat: 46-04-19 N   **Long:** 96-19-45 W
Pop: 90 (1990); 115 (1980)   **Pop Density:** 2.8
Land: 32.1 sq. mi.; **Water:** 0.0 sq. mi.

Connelly — Township
Lat: 46-19-59 N   **Long:** 96-34-51 W
Pop: 141 (1990); 155 (1980)   **Pop Density:** 5.7
Land: 24.6 sq. mi.; **Water:** 0.0 sq. mi.

Deerhorn — Township
Lat: 46-35-40 N   **Long:** 96-34-57 W
Pop: 108 (1990); 160 (1980)   **Pop Density:** 3.0
Land: 36.0 sq. mi.; **Water:** 0.0 sq. mi.

Doran — City
Lat: 46-11-06 N   **Long:** 96-29-08 W
Pop: 78 (1990); 77 (1980)   **Pop Density:** 390.0
Land: 0.2 sq. mi.; **Water:** 0.0 sq. mi.
Name origin: For Michael Doran, a prominent local farmer and businessman.

Foxhome — City
ZIP: 56543   **Lat:** 46-16-36 N   **Long:** 96-18-36 W
Pop: 160 (1990); 161 (1980)   **Pop Density:** 400.0
Land: 0.4 sq. mi.; **Water:** 0.0 sq. mi.   **Elev:** 1029 ft.
City and township not coextensive.
Name origin: For real estate developer Robert A. Fox, who owned the land upon which the town was founded

*Foxhome — Township
ZIP: 56543   **Lat:** 46-14-02 N   **Long:** 96-19-39 W
Pop: 149 (1990); 175 (1980)   **Pop Density:** 4.3
Land: 35.0 sq. mi.; **Water:** 0.0 sq. mi.

Kent — City
ZIP: 56553   **Lat:** 46-26-22 N   **Long:** 96-40-51 W
Pop: 131 (1990); 121 (1980)   **Pop Density:** 436.7
Land: 0.3 sq. mi.; **Water:** 0.0 sq. mi.
Name origin: Named by Great Northern Railway officers for the county in England.

Manston — Township
Lat: 46-29-59 N   **Long:** 96-28-05 W
Pop: 80 (1990); 123 (1980)   **Pop Density:** 2.2
Land: 36.1 sq. mi.; **Water:** 0.0 sq. mi.

McCauleyville — Township
Lat: 46-25-51 N   **Long:** 96-40-49 W
Pop: 37 (1990); 85 (1980)   **Pop Density:** 3.7
Land: 9.9 sq. mi.; **Water:** 0.0 sq. mi.

MINNESOTA, Wilkin County

Meadows
Township
Lat: 46-24-29 N **Long:** 96-27-58 W
Pop: 74 (1990); 72 (1980) **Pop Density:** 2.0
Land: 36.2 sq. mi.; **Water:** 0.0 sq. mi.

Mitchell
Township
Lat: 46-30-27 N **Long:** 96-35-51 W
Pop: 93 (1990); 128 (1980) **Pop Density:** 2.6
Land: 36.4 sq. mi.; **Water:** 0.0 sq. mi.

Nashua
City
ZIP: 56565 **Lat:** 46-02-09 N **Long:** 96-18-16 W
Pop: 63 (1990); 89 (1980) **Pop Density:** 18.0
Land: 3.5 sq. mi.; **Water:** 0.0 sq. mi.

Nilsen
Township
Lat: 46-19-33 N **Long:** 96-27-56 W
Pop: 83 (1990); 105 (1980) **Pop Density:** 2.3
Land: 36.2 sq. mi.; **Water:** 0.0 sq. mi.

Nordick
Township
Lat: 46-24-30 N **Long:** 96-36-08 W
Pop: 120 (1990); 152 (1980) **Pop Density:** 3.3
Land: 36.2 sq. mi.; **Water:** 0.0 sq. mi.

Prairie View
Township
Lat: 46-35-13 N **Long:** 96-20-28 W
Pop: 211 (1990); 249 (1980) **Pop Density:** 6.0
Land: 35.1 sq. mi.; **Water:** 0.0 sq. mi.

Roberts
Township
Lat: 46-30-25 N **Long:** 96-41-14 W
Pop: 104 (1990); 133 (1980) **Pop Density:** 4.7
Land: 22.3 sq. mi.; **Water:** 0.0 sq. mi.

Rothsay
City
ZIP: 56579 **Lat:** 46-28-29 N **Long:** 96-17-12 W
Pop: 253 (1990); 278 (1980) **Pop Density:** 126.5
Land: 2.0 sq. mi.; **Water:** 0.0 sq. mi. **Elev:** 1209 ft.
Part of the town is also in Otter Tail County.
Name origin: For seaport 30 mi. west of Glasgow, Scotland.

Sunnyside
Township
Lat: 46-14-13 N **Long:** 96-26-48 W
Pop: 184 (1990); 185 (1980) **Pop Density:** 5.2
Land: 35.6 sq. mi.; **Water:** 0.0 sq. mi.

Tanberg
Township
Lat: 46-30-12 N **Long:** 96-21-46 W
Pop: 94 (1990); 109 (1980) **Pop Density:** 2.8
Land: 33.3 sq. mi.; **Water:** 0.0 sq. mi.

Tenney
City
Lat: 46-02-39 N **Long:** 96-27-14 W
Pop: 4 (1990); 19 (1980) **Pop Density:** 200.0
Land: 0.02 sq. mi.; **Water:** 0.0 sq. mi.

Wolverton
City
ZIP: 56594 **Lat:** 46-33-52 N **Long:** 96-44-07 W
Pop: 158 (1990); 177 (1980) **Pop Density:** 790.0
Land: 0.2 sq. mi.; **Water:** 0.0 sq. mi.
City and township not coextensive.
Name origin: For physician W. D. Wolverton, the township's original landowner.

*Wolverton
Township
ZIP: 56594 **Lat:** 46-35-23 N **Long:** 96-42-14 W
Pop: 121 (1990); 149 (1980) **Pop Density:** 4.1
Land: 29.8 sq. mi.; **Water:** 0.0 sq. mi.

Winona County
County Seat: Winona (ZIP: 55987)

Pop: 47,828 (1990); 46,256 (1980) **Pop Density:** 76.4
Land: 626.3 sq. mi.; **Water:** 15.3 sq. mi. **Area Code:** 507
On the southeastern border of MN, east of Rochester; established Feb 23, 1854 (prior to statehood) from unorganized lands.
Name origin: For the town that became the county seat, which was named for a Dakota Indian woman active in the removal of the Winnebagos from IA to MN. Name was also popularized by H. L. Gordon's poem, "Winona" (1881).

Altura
City
ZIP: 55910 **Lat:** 44-04-11 N **Long:** 91-56-20 W
Pop: 349 (1990); 354 (1980) **Pop Density:** 116.3
Land: 3.0 sq. mi.; **Water:** 0.0 sq. mi.
Name origin: For Altura, Valencia, Spain.

Dakota
City
ZIP: 55925 **Lat:** 43-54-42 N **Long:** 91-21-30 W
Pop: 360 (1990); 350 (1980) **Pop Density:** 514.3
Land: 0.7 sq. mi.; **Water:** 0.3 sq. mi. **Elev:** 691 ft.
Name origin: From the Sioux Indian term meaning 'alliance' or 'confederation.'

Dresbach
Township
Lat: 43-52-55 N **Long:** 91-20-17 W
Pop: 307 (1990); 354 (1980) **Pop Density:** 37.9
Land: 8.1 sq. mi.; **Water:** 1.3 sq. mi.

Elba
City
ZIP: 55910 **Lat:** 44-05-13 N **Long:** 92-01-02 W
Pop: 220 (1990); 198 (1980) **Pop Density:** 110.0
Land: 2.0 sq. mi.; **Water:** 0.0 sq. mi.
City and township not coextensive.

*Elba
Township
ZIP: 55910 **Lat:** 44-04-16 N **Long:** 92-01-15 W
Pop: 260 (1990); 309 (1980) **Pop Density:** 7.8
Land: 33.4 sq. mi.; **Water:** 0.0 sq. mi.

Fremont
Township
ZIP: 55979 **Lat:** 43-52-49 N **Long:** 91-54-27 W
Pop: 389 (1990); 375 (1980) **Pop Density:** 10.8
Land: 35.9 sq. mi.; **Water:** 0.0 sq. mi.

Goodview
City
ZIP: 55987 **Lat:** 44-04-02 N **Long:** 91-42-38 W
Pop: 2,878 (1990); 2,567 (1980) **Pop Density:** 1798.8
Land: 1.6 sq. mi.; **Water:** 0.2 sq. mi.

MINNESOTA, Winona County

Hart   Township
Lat: 43-53-25 N   **Long:** 91-47-18 W
Pop: 424 (1990); 397 (1980)   **Pop Density:** 11.9
Land: 35.6 sq. mi.; **Water:** 0.0 sq. mi.

Hillsdale   Township
Lat: 44-02-34 N   **Long:** 91-47-35 W
Pop: 1,026 (1990); 704 (1980)   **Pop Density:** 63.7
Land: 16.1 sq. mi.; **Water:** 0.0 sq. mi.

Homer   Township
Lat: 43-57-45 N   **Long:** 91-33-04 W
Pop: 1,258 (1990); 1,314 (1980)   **Pop Density:** 35.4
Land: 35.5 sq. mi.; **Water:** 1.0 sq. mi.

Lewiston   City
ZIP: 55952   **Lat:** 43-59-05 N   **Long:** 91-52-04 W
Pop: 1,298 (1990); 1,226 (1980)   **Pop Density:** 1180.0
Land: 1.1 sq. mi.; **Water:** 0.0 sq. mi.
Name origin: For early settler S. J. Lewis.

Minneiska   City
ZIP: 55910   **Lat:** 44-11-25 N   **Long:** 91-51-57 W
Pop: 61 (1990); 65 (1980)   **Pop Density:** 305.0
Land: 0.2 sq. mi.; **Water:** 0.1 sq. mi.
Part of the town is also in Wabasha County.

Minnesota City   City
ZIP: 55959   **Lat:** 44-05-31 N   **Long:** 91-45-00 W
Pop: 258 (1990); 265 (1980)   **Pop Density:** 860.0
Land: 0.3 sq. mi.; **Water:** 0.0 sq. mi.
Name origin: From the Sioux Indian term meaning 'clouded water,' referring to the river at flood stage when it becomes turbid and clouded with sediment.

Mount Vernon   Township
Lat: 44-09-26 N   **Long:** 91-53-54 W
Pop: 340 (1990); 340 (1980)   **Pop Density:** 9.7
Land: 35.1 sq. mi.; **Water:** 0.2 sq. mi.

New Hartford   Township
ZIP: 55925   **Lat:** 43-53-27 N   **Long:** 91-25-48 W
Pop: 804 (1990); 738 (1980)   **Pop Density:** 22.9
Land: 35.1 sq. mi.; **Water:** 0.1 sq. mi.

Norton   Township
ZIP: 55910   **Lat:** 44-03-51 N   **Long:** 91-53-44 W
Pop: 556 (1990); 584 (1980)   **Pop Density:** 17.1
Land: 32.6 sq. mi.; **Water:** 0.0 sq. mi.

Pleasant Hill   Township
Lat: 43-53-24 N   **Long:** 91-32-36 W
Pop: 562 (1990); 616 (1980)   **Pop Density:** 15.7
Land: 35.7 sq. mi.; **Water:** 0.0 sq. mi.

Richmond   Township
Lat: 43-57-32 N   **Long:** 91-25-44 W
Pop: 731 (1990); 665 (1980)   **Pop Density:** 45.1
Land: 16.2 sq. mi.; **Water:** 2.4 sq. mi.

Rollingstone   City
ZIP: 55969   **Lat:** 44-05-59 N   **Long:** 91-49-08 W
Pop: 697 (1990); 528 (1980)   **Pop Density:** 1394.0
Land: 0.5 sq. mi.; **Water:** 0.0 sq. mi.   **Elev:** 759 ft.
City and township not coextensive.
Name origin: For its river, from a Dakota Indian term meaning 'the stream where the stone rolls.'

*Rollingstone   Township
ZIP: 55969   **Lat:** 44-05-54 N   **Long:** 91-47-06 W
Pop: 1,217 (1990); 1,403 (1980)   **Pop Density:** 40.2
Land: 30.3 sq. mi.; **Water:** 4.1 sq. mi.

St. Charles   City
Lat: 43-58-10 N   **Long:** 92-03-50 W
Pop: 2,642 (1990); 2,184 (1980)   **Pop Density:** 943.6
Land: 2.8 sq. mi.; **Water:** 0.0 sq. mi.   **Elev:** 1142 ft.
Founded 1870. City and township not coextensive.
Name origin: For St. Charles Borromeo (1538–84) of Italy.

*St. Charles   Township
Lat: 43-59-07 N   **Long:** 92-01-10 W
Pop: 520 (1990); 517 (1980)   **Pop Density:** 15.9
Land: 32.8 sq. mi.; **Water:** 0.0 sq. mi.

Saratoga   Township
ZIP: 55972   **Lat:** 43-53-31 N   **Long:** 92-01-17 W
Pop: 536 (1990); 530 (1980)   **Pop Density:** 15.0
Land: 35.7 sq. mi.; **Water:** 0.0 sq. mi.

Stockton   City
ZIP: 55988   **Lat:** 44-01-40 N   **Long:** 91-46-20 W
Pop: 529 (1990); 517 (1980)   **Pop Density:** 330.6
Land: 1.6 sq. mi.; **Water:** 0.0 sq. mi.

Utica   City
ZIP: 55979   **Lat:** 43-58-35 N   **Long:** 91-57-02 W
Pop: 220 (1990); 249 (1980)   **Pop Density:** 244.4
Land: 0.9 sq. mi.; **Water:** 0.0 sq. mi.
City and township not coextensive.
Name origin: For Utica, NY.

*Utica   Township
ZIP: 55979   **Lat:** 43-58-50 N   **Long:** 91-53-35 W
Pop: 651 (1990); 686 (1980)   **Pop Density:** 19.2
Land: 33.9 sq. mi.; **Water:** 0.0 sq. mi.

Warren   Township
Lat: 43-58-12 N   **Long:** 91-46-38 W
Pop: 639 (1990); 623 (1980)   **Pop Density:** 18.0
Land: 35.5 sq. mi.; **Water:** 0.0 sq. mi.

Whitewater   Township
Lat: 44-09-05 N   **Long:** 92-01-13 W
Pop: 229 (1990); 222 (1980)   **Pop Density:** 6.5
Land: 35.2 sq. mi.; **Water:** 0.1 sq. mi.

Wilson   Township
Lat: 43-58-43 N   **Long:** 91-39-26 W
Pop: 1,141 (1990); 1,141 (1980)   **Pop Density:** 32.6
Land: 35.0 sq. mi.; **Water:** 0.0 sq. mi.

Winona   City
ZIP: 55987   **Lat:** 44-02-51 N   **Long:** 91-39-25 W
Pop: 25,399 (1990); 25,075 (1980)   **Pop Density:** 2134.4
Land: 11.9 sq. mi.; **Water:** 2.1 sq. mi.
In southeastern MN on Mississippi River, 40 mi. east of Rochester.
Name origin: For a prominent Dakota Indian woman active in the removal of the Winnebagos from IA to MN. Name was also popularized by H. L. Gordon's poem, "Winona" (1881).

*Winona   Township
Lat: 44-03-22 N   **Long:** 91-41-48 W
Pop: 986 (1990); 815 (1980)   **Pop Density:** 151.7
Land: 6.5 sq. mi.; **Water:** 3.3 sq. mi.

Wiscoy
Township
Lat: 43-53-26 N **Long:** 91-39-59 W
Pop: 341 (1990); 345 (1980) **Pop Density:** 9.6
Land: 35.7 sq. mi.; **Water:** 0.0 sq. mi.

Wright County
County Seat: Buffalo (ZIP: 55313)

Pop: 68,710 (1990); 58,681 (1980) **Pop Density:** 104.0
Land: 660.8 sq. mi.; **Water:** 53.6 sq. mi. **Area Code:** 612
In east-central MN, northwest of Minneapolis; established Feb 20, 1855 (prior to statehood).
Name origin: For Silas Wright (1795–1847), NY governor (1845–47) and friend of a member of the county organization committee; his name was chosen "as a compromise after a somewhat animated discussion."

Albertville
City
ZIP: 55301 **Lat:** 45-14-21 N **Long:** 93-39-36 W
Pop: 1,251 (1990); 564 (1980) **Pop Density:** 403.5
Land: 3.1 sq. mi.; **Water:** 0.2 sq. mi.
Name origin: Named by the Great Northern Railway for one of its employees.

Albion
Township
Lat: 45-12-15 N **Long:** 94-04-06 W
Pop: 1,121 (1990); 1,127 (1980) **Pop Density:** 34.5
Land: 32.5 sq. mi.; **Water:** 3.0 sq. mi.

Annandale
City
ZIP: 55302 **Lat:** 45-15-43 N **Long:** 94-07-08 W
Pop: 2,054 (1990); 1,568 (1980) **Pop Density:** 1081.1
Land: 1.9 sq. mi.; **Water:** 0.0 sq. mi.
Name origin: For the Scottish seaport of Annan.

Buffalo
City
ZIP: 55313 **Lat:** 45-10-37 N **Long:** 93-52-06 W
Pop: 6,856 (1990); 4,560 (1980) **Pop Density:** 1714.0
Land: 4.0 sq. mi.; **Water:** 1.3 sq. mi. **Elev:** 967 ft.
City and township not coextensive.
Name origin: For Buffalo Lake, which was named by Indian traders for the many buffalo fish there.

*Buffalo
Township
ZIP: 55313 **Lat:** 45-11-53 N **Long:** 93-49-25 W
Pop: 2,086 (1990); 1,870 (1980) **Pop Density:** 75.0
Land: 27.8 sq. mi.; **Water:** 3.5 sq. mi.

Chatham
Township
Lat: 45-10-09 N **Long:** 93-56-47 W
Pop: 858 (1990); 1,268 (1980) **Pop Density:** 56.4
Land: 15.2 sq. mi.; **Water:** 2.3 sq. mi.

Clearwater
City
ZIP: 55320 **Lat:** 45-24-36 N **Long:** 94-02-33 W
Pop: 597 (1990); 379 (1980) **Pop Density:** 542.7
Land: 1.1 sq. mi.; **Water:** 0.1 sq. mi.
Name origin: For its location on the Clearwater River, which flows into the Mississippi River; the latter forms the eastern border of the county.

*Clearwater
Township
ZIP: 55320 **Lat:** 45-21-56 N **Long:** 94-02-41 W
Pop: 1,156 (1990); 1,153 (1980) **Pop Density:** 51.6
Land: 22.4 sq. mi.; **Water:** 1.4 sq. mi.

Cokato
City
ZIP: 55321 **Lat:** 45-04-36 N **Long:** 94-11-21 W
Pop: 2,180 (1990); 2,056 (1980) **Pop Density:** 1816.7
Land: 1.2 sq. mi.; **Water:** 0.0 sq. mi. **Elev:** 1052 ft.
Settled 1856. City and township not coextensive.
Name origin: From the Sioux Indian term meaning 'at the middle.'

*Cokato
Township
ZIP: 55321 **Lat:** 45-06-55 N **Long:** 94-11-25 W
Pop: 1,100 (1990); 947 (1980) **Pop Density:** 33.2
Land: 33.1 sq. mi.; **Water:** 1.4 sq. mi.

Corinna
Township
Lat: 45-17-14 N **Long:** 94-04-17 W
Pop: 2,053 (1990); 1,831 (1980) **Pop Density:** 81.5
Land: 25.2 sq. mi.; **Water:** 8.5 sq. mi.

Dayton
City
Lat: 45-14-26 N **Long:** 93-31-03 W
Pop: 51 (1990); 70 (1980) **Pop Density:** 1275.0
Land: 0.04 sq. mi.; **Water:** 0.0 sq. mi.
Part of the town is also in Hennepin County.
Name origin: Named in the 1850s for Lyman Dayton, railroad president and local real estate investor.

Delano
City
ZIP: 55328 **Lat:** 45-02-28 N **Long:** 93-47-07 W
Pop: 2,709 (1990); 2,480 (1980) **Pop Density:** 1425.8
Land: 1.9 sq. mi.; **Water:** 0.0 sq. mi. **Elev:** 944 ft.
Name origin: For Francis R. Delano, who served as superintendent of the St. Paul & Pacific Railroad and as a state representative in the 1860s and the 1870s.

Frankfort
Township
Lat: 45-11-56 N **Long:** 93-41-23 W
Pop: 2,935 (1990); 2,170 (1980) **Pop Density:** 91.7
Land: 32.0 sq. mi.; **Water:** 3.8 sq. mi.

Franklin
Township
Lat: 45-01-27 N **Long:** 93-49-48 W
Pop: 2,742 (1990); 2,712 (1980) **Pop Density:** 63.0
Land: 43.5 sq. mi.; **Water:** 1.1 sq. mi.

French Lake
Township
Lat: 45-11-47 N **Long:** 94-11-34 W
Pop: 945 (1990); 936 (1980) **Pop Density:** 28.2
Land: 33.5 sq. mi.; **Water:** 2.0 sq. mi.

Hanover — City
ZIP: 55341 **Lat:** 45-09-59 N **Long:** 93-39-59 W
Pop: 518 (1990); 399 (1980) **Pop Density:** 185.0
Land: 2.8 sq. mi.; **Water:** 0.2 sq. mi.
Part of the town is also in Hennepin County.
Name origin: Named by German immigrants, the Vellbrecht brothers, for their birthplace in Germany.

Howard Lake — City
ZIP: 55349 **Lat:** 45-03-34 N **Long:** 94-03-56 W
Pop: 1,343 (1990); 1,240 (1980) **Pop Density:** 1492.2
Land: 0.9 sq. mi.; **Water:** 0.3 sq. mi. **Elev:** 1018 ft.
Name origin: For Howard Lake, which was named by early surveyors for English humanitarian, John Howard (1726–90).

Maple Lake — City
ZIP: 55358 **Lat:** 45-13-52 N **Long:** 94-00-10 W
Pop: 1,394 (1990); 1,132 (1980) **Pop Density:** 733.7
Land: 1.9 sq. mi.; **Water:** 0.0 sq. mi.
Name origin: For nearby Maple Lake and the abundant woodlands of sugar maples in the area.

*Maple Lake — Township
ZIP: 55358 **Lat:** 45-14-05 N **Long:** 93-57-06 W
Pop: 1,829 (1990); 1,718 (1980) **Pop Density:** 57.5
Land: 31.8 sq. mi.; **Water:** 2.9 sq. mi.

Marysville — Township
Lat: 45-06-30 N **Long:** 93-57-15 W
Pop: 1,839 (1990); 1,944 (1980) **Pop Density:** 56.4
Land: 32.6 sq. mi.; **Water:** 1.3 sq. mi.

Middleville — Township
Lat: 45-06-17 N **Long:** 94-04-52 W
Pop: 1,017 (1990); 1,093 (1980) **Pop Density:** 29.9
Land: 34.0 sq. mi.; **Water:** 1.9 sq. mi.

Monticello — City
ZIP: 55362 **Lat:** 45-18-17 N **Long:** 93-48-07 W
Pop: 4,941 (1990); 2,830 (1980) **Pop Density:** 882.3
Land: 5.6 sq. mi.; **Water:** 0.0 sq. mi.
Settled 1850s. City and township not coextensive.
Name origin: From Italian 'little hill,' for a hill two miles from the town.

*Monticello — Township
Lat: 45-16-55 N **Long:** 93-48-41 W
Pop: 3,981 (1990); 3,588 (1980) **Pop Density:** 97.8
Land: 40.7 sq. mi.; **Water:** 3.3 sq. mi.

Montrose — City
ZIP: 55363 **Lat:** 45-04-02 N **Long:** 93-54-44 W
Pop: 1,008 (1990); 762 (1980) **Pop Density:** 1680.0
Land: 0.6 sq. mi.; **Water:** 0.0 sq. mi.

Otsego — Township
Lat: 45-15-47 N **Long:** 93-37-32 W
Pop: 5,219 (1990); 4,769 (1980) **Pop Density:** 180.0
Land: 29.0 sq. mi.; **Water:** 1.0 sq. mi. **Elev:** 889 ft.

Rockford — City
ZIP: 55373 **Lat:** 45-05-22 N **Long:** 93-44-20 W
Pop: 2,225 (1990); 2,028 (1980) **Pop Density:** 2225.0
Land: 1.0 sq. mi.; **Water:** 0.0 sq. mi. **Elev:** 916 ft.
Founded 1855. Part of the town is also in Hennepin County.
Name origin: For a rocky ford of the Crow River where a sawmill was built.

*Rockford — Township
ZIP: 55373 **Lat:** 45-07-11 N **Long:** 93-48-13 W
Pop: 3,380 (1990); 3,151 (1980) **Pop Density:** 95.2
Land: 35.5 sq. mi.; **Water:** 2.2 sq. mi.

St. Michael — City
Lat: 45-12-39 N **Long:** 93-39-49 W
Pop: 2,506 (1990); 1,519 (1980) **Pop Density:** 1139.1
Land: 2.2 sq. mi.; **Water:** 0.0 sq. mi.
Name origin: For the church built in 1856.

Silver Creek — Township
Lat: 45-19-45 N **Long:** 93-56-48 W
Pop: 1,835 (1990); 1,778 (1980) **Pop Density:** 51.0
Land: 36.0 sq. mi.; **Water:** 3.2 sq. mi.

South Haven — City
ZIP: 55382 **Lat:** 45-17-29 N **Long:** 94-12-57 W
Pop: 193 (1990); 205 (1980) **Pop Density:** 321.7
Land: 0.6 sq. mi.; **Water:** 0.0 sq. mi.
Name origin: For its location between Southside and Fair Haven townships.

Southside — Township
Lat: 45-16-32 N **Long:** 94-11-49 W
Pop: 1,241 (1990); 1,475 (1980) **Pop Density:** 50.0
Land: 24.8 sq. mi.; **Water:** 4.1 sq. mi.

Stockholm — Township
Lat: 45-01-14 N **Long:** 94-11-43 W
Pop: 773 (1990); 779 (1980) **Pop Density:** 22.4
Land: 34.5 sq. mi.; **Water:** 1.1 sq. mi.

Victor — Township
Lat: 45-01-11 N **Long:** 94-03-51 W
Pop: 1,083 (1990); 1,012 (1980) **Pop Density:** 33.3
Land: 32.5 sq. mi.; **Water:** 2.0 sq. mi.

Waverly — City
ZIP: 55390 **Lat:** 45-04-08 N **Long:** 93-58-08 W
Pop: 600 (1990); 470 (1980) **Pop Density:** 857.1
Land: 0.7 sq. mi.; **Water:** 0.7 sq. mi. **Elev:** 998 ft.
Settled 1869.
Name origin: Named by early pioneers for their former home in Waverly, NY.

Woodland — Township
Lat: 45-01-21 N **Long:** 93-57-00 W
Pop: 1,091 (1990); 1,098 (1980) **Pop Density:** 31.5
Land: 34.6 sq. mi.; **Water:** 0.8 sq. mi.

Yellow Medicine County
County Seat: Granite Falls (ZIP: 56241)

Pop: 11,684 (1990); 13,653 (1980)
Land: 758.0 sq. mi.; **Water:** 5.4 sq. mi.
Pop Density: 15.4
Area Code: 612

On the southwestern border of MN; established Mar 6, 1871 from Redwood County.

Name origin: For the Yellow Medicine River, which flows through it; from a translation of the Siouan name for moonseed, *Menispermum canadense*, a medicinal plant that grows abundantly in the area.

Burton — Township
Lat: 44-40-34 N **Long:** 96-02-23 W
Pop: 206 (1990); 290 (1980) **Pop Density:** 5.8
Land: 35.7 sq. mi.; **Water:** 0.2 sq. mi.

Canby — City
ZIP: 56220 **Lat:** 44-42-52 N **Long:** 96-16-08 W
Pop: 1,826 (1990); 2,143 (1980) **Pop Density:** 869.5
Land: 2.1 sq. mi.; **Water:** 0.0 sq. mi.
Name origin: For Gen. Edward Canby (1817–73), who served in the Civil War, the Seminole War, and the Mexican War.

Clarkfield — City
ZIP: 56223 **Lat:** 44-47-28 N **Long:** 95-48-26 W
Pop: 924 (1990); 1,171 (1980) **Pop Density:** 840.0
Land: 1.1 sq. mi.; **Water:** 0.0 sq. mi.
Founded 1884.
Name origin: For a local railroad official.

Echo — City
ZIP: 56237 **Lat:** 44-37-21 N **Long:** 95-24-40 W
Pop: 304 (1990); 334 (1980) **Pop Density:** 304.0
Land: 1.0 sq. mi.; **Water:** 0.0 sq. mi.
Founded 1874. City and township not coextensive.
Name origin: For the fact that no other town had this name.

*Echo — Township
ZIP: 56237 **Lat:** 44-35-27 N **Long:** 95-24-50 W
Pop: 216 (1990); 295 (1980) **Pop Density:** 6.2
Land: 34.9 sq. mi.; **Water:** 0.6 sq. mi.

Florida — Township
Lat: 44-45-39 N **Long:** 96-24-09 W
Pop: 177 (1990); 211 (1980) **Pop Density:** 5.3
Land: 33.4 sq. mi.; **Water:** 0.0 sq. mi.

Fortier — Township
Lat: 44-40-27 N **Long:** 96-24-00 W
Pop: 117 (1990); 178 (1980) **Pop Density:** 3.5
Land: 33.4 sq. mi.; **Water:** 0.1 sq. mi.

Friendship — Township
Lat: 44-45-38 N **Long:** 95-46-58 W
Pop: 233 (1990); 251 (1980) **Pop Density:** 6.6
Land: 35.1 sq. mi.; **Water:** 0.1 sq. mi.

Granite Falls — City
ZIP: 56241 **Lat:** 44-48-38 N **Long:** 95-33-01 W
Pop: 2,346 (1990); 2,666 (1980) **Pop Density:** 1380.0
Land: 1.7 sq. mi.; **Water:** 0.2 sq. mi. **Elev:** 920 ft.
Part of the town is also in Chippewa County.
Name origin: For the falls over large granite outcrops in the Minnesota River.

Hammer — Township
Lat: 44-45-33 N **Long:** 96-17-10 W
Pop: 374 (1990); 362 (1980) **Pop Density:** 10.4
Land: 35.8 sq. mi.; **Water:** 0.0 sq. mi.

Hanley Falls — City
ZIP: 56245 **Lat:** 44-41-30 N **Long:** 95-37-08 W
Pop: 246 (1990); 265 (1980) **Pop Density:** 820.0
Land: 0.3 sq. mi.; **Water:** 0.0 sq. mi. **Elev:** 1046 ft.
Name origin: For an officer of the Minneapolis & St. Louis Railroad Company, which reached the town in 1884.

Hazel Run — City
ZIP: 56247 **Lat:** 44-44-59 N **Long:** 95-42-58 W
Pop: 81 (1990); 93 (1980) **Pop Density:** 101.3
Land: 0.8 sq. mi.; **Water:** 0.0 sq. mi. **Elev:** 1062 ft.
City and township not coextensive.

*Hazel Run — Township
ZIP: 56247 **Lat:** 44-45-22 N **Long:** 95-39-18 W
Pop: 206 (1990); 239 (1980) **Pop Density:** 5.8
Land: 35.6 sq. mi.; **Water:** 0.0 sq. mi.

Lisbon — Township
Lat: 44-51-02 N **Long:** 95-46-56 W
Pop: 233 (1990); 270 (1980) **Pop Density:** 6.5
Land: 35.7 sq. mi.; **Water:** 0.0 sq. mi.

Minnesota Falls — Township
Lat: 44-45-42 N **Long:** 95-33-06 W
Pop: 358 (1990); 412 (1980) **Pop Density:** 11.5
Land: 31.1 sq. mi.; **Water:** 0.3 sq. mi.

Norman — Township
Lat: 44-40-33 N **Long:** 96-16-45 W
Pop: 300 (1990); 348 (1980) **Pop Density:** 8.6
Land: 34.9 sq. mi.; **Water:** 0.0 sq. mi.

Normania — Township
Lat: 44-40-29 N **Long:** 95-47-31 W
Pop: 190 (1990); 228 (1980) **Pop Density:** 5.4
Land: 35.5 sq. mi.; **Water:** 0.8 sq. mi.

Omro — Township
Lat: 44-45-13 N **Long:** 96-02-23 W
Pop: 166 (1990); 244 (1980) **Pop Density:** 4.6
Land: 36.0 sq. mi.; **Water:** 0.3 sq. mi.

Oshkosh — Township
Lat: 44-45-32 N **Long:** 96-09-52 W
Pop: 249 (1990); 286 (1980) **Pop Density:** 6.9
Land: 36.3 sq. mi.; **Water:** 0.0 sq. mi.

Porter — City
ZIP: 56280 **Lat:** 44-38-26 N **Long:** 96-10-10 W
Pop: 210 (1990); 211 (1980) **Pop Density:** 95.5
Land: 2.2 sq. mi.; **Water:** 0.0 sq. mi.

Posen
Township
Lat: 44-34-48 N **Long:** 95-32-51 W
Pop: 269 (1990); 295 (1980) **Pop Density:** 7.7
Land: 35.1 sq. mi.; **Water:** 1.0 sq. mi.

St. Leo
City
Lat: 44-42-58 N **Long:** 96-03-16 W
Pop: 111 (1990); 147 (1980) **Pop Density:** 370.0
Land: 0.3 sq. mi.; **Water:** 0.0 sq. mi. **Elev:** 1119 ft.

Sandnes
Township
Lat: 44-40-33 N **Long:** 95-40-18 W
Pop: 216 (1990); 244 (1980) **Pop Density:** 6.0
Land: 36.1 sq. mi.; **Water:** 0.0 sq. mi.

Sioux Agency
Township
Lat: 44-40-47 N **Long:** 95-25-54 W
Pop: 277 (1990); 351 (1980) **Pop Density:** 6.7
Land: 41.5 sq. mi.; **Water:** 0.6 sq. mi.

Stony Run
Township
Lat: 44-51-00 N **Long:** 95-39-30 W
Pop: 562 (1990); 615 (1980) **Pop Density:** 13.7
Land: 40.9 sq. mi.; **Water:** 0.4 sq. mi.

Swede Prairie
Township
Lat: 44-40-30 N **Long:** 95-54-24 W
Pop: 193 (1990); 243 (1980) **Pop Density:** 5.3
Land: 36.3 sq. mi.; **Water:** 0.0 sq. mi.

Tyro
Township
Lat: 44-45-36 N **Long:** 95-55-12 W
Pop: 226 (1990); 292 (1980) **Pop Density:** 6.2
Land: 36.3 sq. mi.; **Water:** 0.0 sq. mi.

Wergeland
Township
Lat: 44-40-54 N **Long:** 96-08-38 W
Pop: 215 (1990); 235 (1980) **Pop Density:** 6.3
Land: 33.9 sq. mi.; **Water:** 0.0 sq. mi.

Wood Lake
City
ZIP: 56297 **Lat:** 44-39-02 N **Long:** 95-32-05 W
Pop: 406 (1990); 420 (1980) **Pop Density:** 406.0
Land: 1.0 sq. mi.; **Water:** 0.0 sq. mi.
City and township not coextensive.
Name origin: For the nearby lake that is fringed with timber.

*Wood Lake
Township
ZIP: 56297 **Lat:** 44-40-22 N **Long:** 95-32-33 W
Pop: 247 (1990); 314 (1980) **Pop Density:** 7.2
Land: 34.1 sq. mi.; **Water:** 0.9 sq. mi.

Index to Places and Counties in Minnesota

Aastad (Otter Tail) Township............*565*
Acoma (McLeod) Township...............*550*
Acton (Meeker) Township..................*551*
Ada (Norman) City............................*562*
Adams (Mower) City..........................*556*
Adams (Mower) Township.................*556*
Adrian (Nobles) City..........................*560*
Adrian (Watonwan) Township *609*
Aetna (Pipestone) Township..............*571*
Afton (Washington) City *608*
Agassiz (Lac qui Parle) Township.....*539*
Agder (Marshall) Township...............*546*
Agram (Morrison) Township.............*554*
Aitkin (Aitkin) City...........................*483*
Aitkin (Aitkin) Township *483*
Aitkin County....................................*483*
Akeley (Hubbard) City *527*
Akeley (Hubbard) Township *527*
Akron (Big Stone) Township *491*
Akron (Wilkin) Township...................*611*
Alango (St. Louis) Township.............*587*
Alaska (Beltrami) Township..............*488*
Alba (Jackson) Township...................*532*
Albany (Stearns) City *595*
Albany (Stearns) Township................*595*
Alberta (Benton) Township *490*
Alberta (Stevens) City........................*599*
Albert Lea (Freeborn) City.................*519*
Albert Lea (Freeborn) Township........*519*
Albertville (Wright) City *614*
Albin (Brown) Township *494*
Albion (Wright) Township..................*614*
Alborn (St. Louis) Township..............*587*
Alden (Freeborn) City........................*519*
Alden (Freeborn) Township *519*
Alden (St. Louis) Township................*587*
Aldrich (Wadena) City.......................*605*
Aldrich (Wadena) Township...............*605*
Alexandria (Douglas) City.................*514*
Alexandria (Douglas) Township........*514*
Alfsborg (Sibley) Township................*593*
Alliance (Clay) Township *504*
Alma (Marshall) Township.................*546*
Almond (Big Stone) Township *491*
Alpha (Jackson) City *532*
Alta Vista (Lincoln) Township..........*543*
Alton (Waseca) Township...................*607*
Altona (Pipestone) Township.............*571*
Altura (Winona) City.........................*612*
Alvarado (Marshall) City...................*546*
Alvwood (Itasca) Township................*530*
Amador (Chisago) Township..............*503*
Amboy (Blue Earth) City...................*493*
Amboy (Cottonwood) Township........*508*
Amherst (Fillmore) Township *517*
Amiret (Lyon) Township *544*
Amo (Cottonwood) Township *508*
Amor (Otter Tail) Township...............*565*
Andover (Anoka) City *485*
Andover (Polk) Township *572*
Andrea (Wilkin) Township.................*611*
Angora (St. Louis) Township.............*587*
Angus (Polk) Township *572*
Ann (Cottonwood) Township *508*
Annandale (Wright) City...................*614*
Ann Lake (Kanabec) Township.........*534*
Anoka (Anoka) City...........................*485*
Anoka County....................................*485*
Ansel (Cass) Township *499*
Anthony (Norman) Township............*562*

Antrim (Watonwan) Township..........*609*
Appleton (Swift) City *600*
Appleton (Swift) Township...............*600*
Apple Valley (Dakota) City *511*
Arago (Hubbard) Township...............*527*
Arbo (Itasca) Township *530*
Arco (Lincoln) City............................*543*
Arctander (Kandiyohi) Township *535*
Arden Hills (Ramsey) City...............*577*
Ardenhurst (Itasca) Township *530*
Arena (Lac qui Parle) Township.......*539*
Arendahl (Fillmore) Township..........*517*
Argyle (Marshall) City *546*
Arlington (Sibley) City *593*
Arlington (Sibley) Township..............*594*
Arlone (Pine) Township.....................*569*
Arna (Pine) Township........................*569*
Arnold (St. Louis) CDP.....................*587*
Arrowhead (St. Louis) Township *587*
Arthur (Kanabec) Township..............*534*
Arthur (Traverse) Township *603*
Artichoke (Big Stone) Township *491*
Arveson (Kittson) Township *536*
Ashby (Grant) City............................*522*
Ash Lake (Lincoln) Township *543*
Ashland (Dodge) Township...............*513*
Ashley (Stearns) Township................*595*
Askov (Pine) City...............................*569*
Athens (Isanti) Township *529*
Atherton (Wilkin) Township *611*
Atkinson (Carlton) Township............*496*
Atlanta (Becker) Township................*486*
Atwater (Kandiyohi) City..................*535*
Audubon (Becker) City......................*486*
Audubon (Becker) Township.............*486*
Augsburg (Marshall) Township *546*
Augusta (Lac qui Parle) Township....*539*
Ault (St. Louis) Township *587*
Aurdal (Otter Tail) Township............*565*
Aurora (St. Louis) City......................*587*
Aurora (Steele) Township *598*
Austin (Mower) City..........................*556*
Austin (Mower) Township.................*556*
Automba (Carlton) Township............*496*
Avoca (Murray) City..........................*558*
Avon (Stearns) City *595*
Avon (Stearns) Township...................*595*
Babbitt (St. Louis) City *587*
Backus (Cass) City.............................*499*
Badger (Polk) Township *572*
Badger (Roseau) City.........................*585*
Badoura (Hubbard) Township...........*527*
Bagley (Clearwater) City...................*506*
Baker (Stevens) Township *599*
Balaton (Lyon) City...........................*544*
Baldwin (Sherburne) Township........*592*
Balkan (St. Louis) Township.............*587*
Ball Bluff (Aitkin) Township.............*483*
Balsam (Aitkin) Township.................*483*
Balsam (Itasca) Township.................*530*
Bancroft (Freeborn) Township *519*
Bandon (Renville) Township.............*581*
Bangor (Pope) Township....................*575*
Barber (Faribault) Township.............*515*
Barclay (Cass) Township *499*
Barnesville (Clay) City *504*
Barnesville (Clay) Township..............*504*
Barnett (Roseau) Township *585*
Barnum (Carlton) City *496*
Barnum (Carlton) Township *496*

Barrett (Grant) City............................*522*
Barry (Big Stone) City *492*
Barry (Pine) Township.......................*569*
Barsness (Pope) Township.................*575*
Bartlett (Todd) Township *601*
Barto (Roseau) Township *585*
Bashaw (Brown) Township................*494*
Bass Brook (Itasca) Township...........*530*
Bassett (St. Louis) Township............*587*
Bath (Freeborn) Township.................*519*
Battle (Beltrami) Township *488*
Battle Lake (Otter Tail) City *565*
Battle Plain (Rock) Township *584*
Baudette (Lake of the Woods) City...*541*
Baxter (Crow Wing) City...................*509*
Baxter (Lac qui Parle) Township *539*
Bay Lake (Crow Wing) Township.....*509*
Bayport (Washington) City................*608*
Baytown (Washington) Township......*608*
Bear Creek (Clearwater) Township ...*506*
Beardsley (Big Stone) City *492*
Bear Park (Norman) Township *562*
Bearville (Itasca) Township...............*530*
Beatty (St. Louis) Township *587*
Beauford (Blue Earth) Township.......*493*
Beaulieu (Mahnomen) Township *545*
Beaver (Aitkin) Township *483*
Beaver (Fillmore) Township..............*517*
Beaver (Roseau) Township *585*
Beaver Bay (Lake) City *540*
Beaver Bay (Lake) Township *540*
Beaver Creek (Rock) City *584*
Beaver Creek (Rock) Township.........*584*
Beaver Falls (Renville) Township *581*
Becker (Cass) Township.....................*499*
Becker (Sherburne) City....................*592*
Becker (Sherburne) Township *593*
Becker County....................................*486*
Bejou (Mahnomen) City....................*545*
Bejou (Mahnomen) Township...........*545*
Belfast (Murray) Township *558*
Belgium (Polk) Township *572*
Belgrade (Nicollet) Township...........*559*
Belgrade (Stearns) City.....................*595*
Bellechester (Goodhue) City *520*
Bellechester (Wabasha) City.............*604*
Belle Creek (Goodhue) Township *520*
Belle Plaine (Scott) City *591*
Belle Plaine (Scott) Township *591*
Belle Prairie (Morrison) Township ...*554*
Belle River (Douglas) Township *514*
Bellevue (Morrison) Township *554*
Bellingham (Lac qui Parle) City *539*
Belmont (Jackson) Township *532*
Beltrami (Polk) City *572*
Beltrami County.................................*488*
Belvidere (Goodhue) Township.........*520*
Belview (Redwood) City....................*579*
Bemidji (Beltrami) City.....................*488*
Bemidji (Beltrami) Township............*488*
Bena (Cass) City................................*499*
Bennington (Mower) Township.........*556*
Benson (Swift) City...........................*600*
Benson (Swift) Township...................*600*
Benton (Carver) Township *497*
Benton County....................................*490*
Benville (Beltrami) Township............*488*
Ben Wade (Pope) Township *575*
Bergen (McLeod) Township..............*550*
Berlin (Steele) Township....................*598*

Bernadotte (Nicollet) Township 559
Bertha (Todd) City.............................601
Bertha (Todd) Township.....................601
Beseman (Carlton) Township 496
Bethel (Anoka) City............................485
Beulah (Cass) Township 499
Big Bend (Chippewa) Township.........502
Bigelow (Nobles) City........................560
Bigelow (Nobles) Township................560
Big Falls (Koochiching) City 538
Bigfork (Itasca) City...........................530
Bigfork (Itasca) Township...................530
Big Lake (Sherburne) City..................593
Big Lake (Sherburne) Township..........593
Big Stone (Big Stone) Township.........492
Big Stone County 491
Big Woods (Marshall) Township 546
Bingham Lake (Cottonwood) City 508
Birch (Beltrami) Township 488
Birch Cooley (Renville) Township 581
Birch Creek (Pine) Township 569
Birchdale (Todd) Township 601
Birch Lake (Cass) Township 499
Birch Lake (St. Louis) Pop. Place......587
Birchwood Village (Washington)
  City..608
Bird Island (Renville) City.................581
Bird Island (Renville) Township........581
Biscay (McLeod) City........................550
Bismarck (Sibley) Township 594
Biwabik (St. Louis) City 587
Biwabik (St. Louis) Township 587
Blackberry (Itasca) Township 530
Blackduck (Beltrami) City 488
Black Hammer (Houston) Township..526
Blackhoof (Carlton) Township 496
Black River (Pennington) Township..568
Blaine (Anoka) City............................485
Blaine (Ramsey) City..........................577
Blakeley (Scott) Township 591
Blind Lake (Cass) Township...............499
Blomkest (Kandiyohi) City 535
Bloom (Nobles) Township 560
Bloomer (Marshall) Township............546
Bloomfield (Fillmore) Township 517
Blooming Grove (Waseca) Township 607
Blooming Prairie (Dodge) City 513
Blooming Prairie (Steele) City 598
Blooming Prairie (Steele) Township .598
Bloomington (Hennepin) City............523
Blowers (Otter Tail) Township............565
Blueberry (Wadena) Township 605
Blue Earth (Faribault) City................515
Blue Earth City (Faribault)
  Township..515
Blue Earth County 493
Blue Hill (Sherburne) Township 593
Blue Mounds (Pope) Township..........575
Bluffton (Otter Tail) City 565
Bluffton (Otter Tail) Township 565
Bock (Mille Lacs) City.......................553
Bogus Brook (Mille Lacs) Township.553
Bondin (Murray) Township................558
Boon Lake (Renville) Township.........581
Borgholm (Mille Lacs) Township 553
Borup (Norman) City.........................562
Bovey (Itasca) City.............................530
Bowlus (Morrison) City......................554
Bowstring (Itasca) Township 530
Bowstring Lake (Itasca) Pop. Place...530
Boxville (Marshall) Township............546
Boyd (Lac qui Parle) City..................539
Boy Lake (Cass) Township.................499
Boy River (Cass) City.........................499
Boy River (Cass) Township................499

Bradbury (Mille Lacs) Township........553
Bradford (Isanti) Township 529
Bradford (Wilkin) Township 611
Braham (Isanti) City...........................529
Braham (Kanabec) City......................534
Brainerd (Crow Wing) City................509
Branch (Chisago) City 503
Brandon (Douglas) City.....................514
Brandon (Douglas) Township............514
Brandrup (Wilkin) Township 611
Brandsvold (Polk) Township..............572
Brandt (Polk) Township......................573
Bray (Pennington) Township..............568
Breckenridge (Wilkin) City................611
Breckenridge (Wilkin) Township........611
Breezy Point (Crow Wing) City 509
Breitung (St. Louis) Township...........587
Bremen (Pine) Township 569
Brevator (St. Louis) Township 587
Brewster (Nobles) City 560
Bricelyn (Faribault) City....................515
Bridgewater (Rice) Township 582
Brighton (Nicollet) Township............559
Brislet (Polk) Township......................573
Bristol (Fillmore) Township 517
Brockway (Stearns) Township 595
Brookfield (Renville) Township 581
Brook Lake (Beltrami) Pop. Place 488
Brooklyn Center (Hennepin) City.....523
Brooklyn Park (Hennepin) City........523
Brook Park (Pine) City......................569
Brook Park (Pine) Township..............569
Brooks (Red Lake) City.....................578
Brookston (St. Louis) City.................587
Brookville (Redwood) Township 579
Brooten (Pope) City...........................575
Brooten (Stearns) City.......................595
Browerville (Todd) City.....................601
Brown County.................................494
Browns Creek (Red Lake) Township 578
Brownsdale (Mower) City..................556
Browns Valley (Big Stone) Township 492
Browns Valley (Traverse) City...........603
Brownsville (Houston) City...............526
Brownsville (Houston) Township.......526
Brownton (McLeod) City 550
Bruce (Todd) Township 601
Bruno (Pine) City 570
Bruno (Pine) Township 570
Brunswick (Kanabec) Township........534
Brush Creek (Faribault) Township 515
Buckman (Morrison) City 554
Buckman (Morrison) Township.........554
Buffalo (Wright) City.........................614
Buffalo (Wright) Township.................614
Buffalo Lake (Renville) City.............581
Buh (Morrison) Township 554
Buhl (St. Louis) City..........................587
Bullard (Wadena) Township 605
Bull Moose (Cass) Township.............499
Bungo (Cass) Township 499
Burbank (Kandiyohi) Township.........535
Burke (Pipestone) Township 571
Burleene (Todd) Township 601
Burlington (Becker) Township...........486
Burnhamville (Todd) Township 601
Burns (Anoka) Township....................485
Burnstown (Brown) Township...........494
Burnsville (Dakota) City 511
Burton (Yellow Medicine) Township 616
Burtrum (Todd) City 601
Buse (Otter Tail) Township 565
Butler (Otter Tail) Township 565
Butterfield (Watonwan) City 610
Butterfield (Watonwan) Township 610

Butternut Valley (Blue Earth)
  Township..493
Buzzle (Beltrami) Township 488
Bygland (Polk) Township 573
Byron (Cass) Township......................499
Byron (Olmsted) City 563
Byron (Waseca) Township 607
Cairo (Renville) Township 581
Caledonia (Houston) City..................526
Caledonia (Houston) Township..........526
Callaway (Becker) City......................486
Callaway (Becker) Township 486
Calumet (Itasca) City.........................530
Cambria (Blue Earth) Township 493
Cambridge (Isanti) City.....................529
Cambridge (Isanti) Township.............529
Camden (Carver) Township...............497
Cameron (Murray) Township.............558
Camp (Renville) Township.................581
Campbell (Wilkin) City......................611
Campbell (Wilkin) Township.............611
Camp Lake (Swift) Township............600
Camp Release (Lac qui Parle)
  Township..539
Canby (Yellow Medicine) City..........616
Candor (Otter Tail) Township............565
Canisteo (Dodge) Township...............513
Cannon (Kittson) Township 536
Cannon City (Rice) Township............582
Cannon Falls (Goodhue) City 520
Cannon Falls (Goodhue) Township ..521
Canosia (St. Louis) Township............587
Canton (Fillmore) City 517
Canton (Fillmore) Township 517
Caribou (Kittson) Township 536
Carimona (Fillmore) Township 517
Carlisle (Otter Tail) Township...........565
Carlos (Douglas) City 514
Carlos (Douglas) Township 514
Carlston (Freeborn) Township...........519
Carlton (Carlton) City 496
Carlton County................................496
Carpenter (Itasca) Township 530
Carrolton (Fillmore) Township 517
Carson (Cottonwood) Township 508
Carsonville (Becker) Township..........486
Carver (Carver) City..........................497
Carver County 497
Cascade (Olmsted) Township............563
Cashel (Swift) Township....................600
Cass County 499
Cass Lake (Cass) City........................499
Castle Rock (Dakota) Township 511
Cedar (Marshall) Township 546
Cedar (Martin) Township..................549
Cedarbend (Roseau) Township 585
Cedar Lake (Scott) Township............591
Cedar Mills (Meeker) City 551
Cedar Mills (Meeker) Township........551
Cedar Valley (St. Louis) Township ...587
Center (Crow Wing) Township..........509
Center City (Chisago) City................503
Center Creek (Martin) Township......549
Centerville (Anoka) City 485
Ceresco (Blue Earth) Township.........493
Cerro Gordo (Lac qui Parle)
  Township..539
Ceylon (Martin) City..........................549
Champion (Wilkin) Township............611
Champlin (Hennepin) City................523
Chanarambie (Murray) Township.....558
Chandler (Murray) City.....................558
Chanhassen (Carver) City 497
Chanhassen (Hennepin) City 523
Charlestown (Redwood) Township ...579

MINNESOTA

Chaska (Carver) City ... 497
Chaska (Carver) Township ... 498
Chatfield (Fillmore) City ... 517
Chatfield (Fillmore) Township ... 517
Chatfield (Olmsted) City ... 563
Chatham (Wright) Township ... 614
Chengwatana (Pine) Township ... 570
Cherry (St. Louis) Township ... 588
Cherry Grove (Goodhue) Township ... 521
Chester (Polk) Township ... 573
Chester (Wabasha) Township ... 604
Chickamaw Beach (Cass) City ... 499
Chief (Mahnomen) Township ... 545
Chippewa County ... 502
Chippewa Falls (Pope) Township ... 575
Chisago City (Chisago) City ... 503
Chisago County ... 503
Chisago Lake (Chisago) Township ... 503
Chisholm (St. Louis) City ... 588
Chokio (Stevens) City ... 599
Christiania (Jackson) Township ... 532
Circle Pines (Anoka) City ... 485
Clara City (Chippewa) City ... 502
Claremont (Dodge) City ... 513
Claremont (Dodge) Township ... 513
Clarissa (Todd) City ... 601
Clark (Aitkin) Township ... 483
Clark (Faribault) Township ... 515
Clarkfield (Yellow Medicine) City ... 616
Clarks Grove (Freeborn) City ... 519
Clay (Hubbard) Township ... 527
Clay County ... 504
Clayton (Mower) Township ... 556
Clearbrook (Clearwater) City ... 506
Clear Creek (Carlton) Pop. Place ... 496
Clear Lake (Sherburne) City ... 593
Clear Lake (Sherburne) Township ... 593
Clearwater (Wright) City ... 614
Clearwater (Wright) Township ... 614
Clearwater County ... 506
Clements (Redwood) City ... 579
Cleveland (Le Sueur) City ... 541
Cleveland (Le Sueur) Township ... 541
Clifton (Lyon) Township ... 544
Clifton (Traverse) Township ... 603
Climax (Polk) City ... 573
Clinton (Big Stone) City ... 492
Clinton (Rock) Township ... 584
Clinton (St. Louis) Township ... 588
Clinton Falls (Steele) Township ... 598
Clitherall (Otter Tail) City ... 565
Clitherall (Otter Tail) Township ... 565
Clontarf (Swift) City ... 600
Clontarf (Swift) Township ... 600
Cloquet (Carlton) City ... 496
Clover (Clearwater) Township ... 506
Clover (Hubbard) Township ... 527
Clover (Mahnomen) Township ... 545
Clover (Pine) Township ... 570
Clover Leaf (Pennington) Township ... 568
Clow (Kittson) Township ... 536
Coates (Dakota) City ... 511
Cobden (Brown) City ... 494
Cokato (Wright) City ... 614
Cokato (Wright) Township ... 614
Cold Spring (Stearns) City ... 595
Coleraine (Itasca) City ... 530
Colfax (Kandiyohi) Township ... 535
Collegeville (Stearns) Township ... 595
Collins (McLeod) Township ... 550
Collinwood (Meeker) Township ... 551
Cologne (Carver) City ... 498
Columbia (Polk) Township ... 573
Columbia Heights (Anoka) City ... 485
Columbus (Anoka) Township ... 485

Colvin (St. Louis) Township ... 588
Comfort (Kanabec) Township ... 534
Comfrey (Brown) City ... 495
Comfrey (Cottonwood) City ... 508
Como (Marshall) Township ... 547
Compton (Otter Tail) Township ... 565
Comstock (Clay) City ... 504
Comstock (Marshall) Township ... 547
Concord (Dodge) Township ... 513
Conger (Freeborn) City ... 519
Connelly (Wilkin) Township ... 611
Cook (St. Louis) City ... 588
Cook County ... 507
Coon Creek (Lyon) Township ... 544
Coon Rapids (Anoka) City ... 485
Copley (Clearwater) Township ... 506
Corcoran (Hennepin) City ... 523
Cordova (Le Sueur) Township ... 541
Corinna (Wright) Township ... 614
Corliss (Otter Tail) Township ... 565
Cormant (Beltrami) Township ... 488
Cormorant (Becker) Township ... 486
Cornish (Aitkin) Township ... 483
Cornish (Sibley) Township ... 594
Correll (Big Stone) City ... 492
Cosmos (Meeker) City ... 551
Cosmos (Meeker) Township ... 552
Cottage Grove (Washington) City ... 608
Cotton (St. Louis) Township ... 588
Cottonwood (Brown) Township ... 495
Cottonwood (Lyon) City ... 544
Cottonwood County ... 508
Courtland (Nicollet) City ... 559
Courtland (Nicollet) Township ... 559
Crate (Chippewa) Township ... 502
Credit River (Scott) Township ... 592
Croke (Traverse) Township ... 603
Cromwell (Carlton) City ... 496
Cromwell (Clay) Township ... 504
Crooked Creek (Houston) Township ... 526
Crooked Lake (Cass) Township ... 499
Crooks (Renville) Township ... 581
Crookston (Polk) City ... 573
Crookston (Polk) Township ... 573
Crosby (Crow Wing) City ... 509
Crosby (Pine) Township ... 570
Crosslake (Crow Wing) City ... 509
Crow Lake (Stearns) Township ... 595
Crow River (Stearns) Township ... 595
Crow Wing (Crow Wing) Township ... 509
Crow Wing County ... 509
Crow Wing Lake (Hubbard) Township ... 527
Crystal (Hennepin) City ... 523
Crystal Bay (Lake) Township ... 540
Cuba (Becker) Township ... 486
Culdrum (Morrison) Township ... 554
Culver (St. Louis) Township ... 588
Currie (Murray) City ... 558
Cushing (Morrison) Township ... 554
Custer (Lyon) Township ... 544
Cuyuna (Crow Wing) City ... 509
Cyrus (Pope) City ... 576
Daggett Brook (Crow Wing) Township ... 509
Dahlgren (Carver) Township ... 498
Dailey (Mille Lacs) Township ... 553
Dakota (Winona) City ... 612
Dakota County ... 511
Dalbo (Isanti) Township ... 529
Dale (Cottonwood) Township ... 508
Dalton (Otter Tail) City ... 565
Dane Prairie (Otter Tail) Township ... 565
Danforth (Pine) Township ... 570
Danielson (Meeker) Township ... 552

Danube (Renville) City ... 581
Danvers (Swift) City ... 600
Danville (Blue Earth) Township ... 493
Darfur (Watonwan) City ... 610
Darling (Morrison) Township ... 554
Darnen (Stevens) Township ... 599
Darwin (Meeker) City ... 552
Darwin (Meeker) Township ... 552
Dassel (Meeker) City ... 552
Dassel (Meeker) Township ... 552
Davidson (Aitkin) Pop. Place ... 483
Davis (Kittson) Township ... 537
Dawson (Lac qui Parle) City ... 539
Dayton (Hennepin) City ... 523
Dayton (Wright) City ... 614
Dead Lake (Otter Tail) Township ... 565
Dean Lake (Crow Wing) Township ... 509
Decoria (Blue Earth) Township ... 493
Deephaven (Hennepin) City ... 524
Deer (Roseau) Township ... 585
Deer Creek (Otter Tail) City ... 565
Deer Creek (Otter Tail) Township ... 565
Deerfield (Cass) Township ... 499
Deerfield (Steele) Township ... 598
Deerhorn (Wilkin) Township ... 611
Deer Lake (Itasca) Pop. Place ... 530
Deer Park (Pennington) Township ... 568
Deer River (Itasca) City ... 530
Deer River (Itasca) Township ... 530
Deerwood (Crow Wing) City ... 509
Deerwood (Crow Wing) Township ... 509
Deerwood (Kittson) Township ... 537
De Graff (Swift) City ... 600
Delafield (Jackson) Township ... 532
Delano (Wright) City ... 614
Delavan (Faribault) City ... 515
Delavan (Faribault) Township ... 515
Delaware (Grant) Township ... 522
Delhi (Redwood) City ... 579
Delhi (Redwood) Township ... 579
Dell Grove (Pine) Township ... 570
Dellwood (Washington) City ... 608
Delton (Cottonwood) Township ... 508
Denham (Pine) City ... 570
Denmark (Washington) Township ... 608
Dennison (Goodhue) City ... 521
Dennison (Rice) City ... 583
Dent (Otter Tail) City ... 566
Denver (Rock) Township ... 584
Derrynane (Le Sueur) Township ... 542
Des Moines (Jackson) Township ... 533
Des Moines River (Murray) Township ... 558
Detroit (Becker) Township ... 486
Detroit Lakes (Becker) City ... 486
Dewald (Nobles) Township ... 561
Dewey (Roseau) Township ... 585
Dexter (Mower) City ... 556
Dexter (Mower) Township ... 556
Diamond Lake (Lincoln) Township ... 543
Dieter (Roseau) Township ... 585
Dilworth (Clay) City ... 504
Dodge Center (Dodge) City ... 513
Dodge County ... 513
Dollymount (Traverse) Township ... 603
Donaldson (Kittson) City ... 537
Donnelly (Marshall) Township ... 547
Donnelly (Stevens) City ... 599
Donnelly (Stevens) Township ... 599
Dora (Otter Tail) Township ... 566
Doran (Wilkin) City ... 611
Douglas (Dakota) Township ... 511
Douglas County ... 514
Dover (Olmsted) City ... 563
Dover (Olmsted) Township ... 563

Dovray (Murray) City 558	Elko (Scott) City 592	Farden (Hubbard) Township 527
Dovray (Murray) Township.............558	Elk River (Sherburne) City 593	Faribault (Rice) City......................583
Dovre (Kandiyohi) Township..........535	Elkton (Clay) Township..................504	**Faribault County** 515
Drammen (Lincoln) Township.........543	Elkton (Mower) City......................556	Farley (Polk) Township 573
Dresbach (Winona) Township.........612	Ellendale (Steele) City 598	Farming (Stearns) Township............595
Dryden (Sibley) Township..............594	Ellington (Dodge) Township...........513	Farmington (Dakota) City...............511
Dublin (Swift) Township 600	Ellsborough (Murray) Township 558	Farmington (Olmsted) Township 564
Dudley (Clearwater) Township........506	Ellsburg (St. Louis) Township 588	Farm Island (Aitkin) Township........483
Duluth (St. Louis) City..................588	Ellsworth (Meeker) Township 552	Farwell (Pope) City.......................576
Duluth (St. Louis) Township...........588	Ellsworth (Nobles) City 561	Fawn Lake (Todd) Township...........602
Dumont (Traverse) City 603	Elm Creek (Martin) Township 549	Faxon (Sibley) Township................594
Dunbar (Faribault) Township..........515	Elmdale (Morrison) City 554	Fayal (St. Louis) Township.............588
Dundas (Rice) City.......................583	Elmdale (Morrison) Township 554	Featherstone (Goodhue) Township ...521
Dundee (Nobles) City...................561	Elmer (Pipestone) Township 571	Federal Dam (Cass) City 500
Dunn (Otter Tail) Township............566	Elmer (St. Louis) Township............588	Feeley (Itasca) Township 530
Dunnell (Martin) City 549	Elmira (Olmsted) Township 563	Felton (Clay) City 504
Durand (Beltrami) Township 488	Elmo (Otter Tail) Township 566	Felton (Clay) Township 504
Eagan (Dakota) City 511	Elmore (Faribault) City 516	Fenton (Murray) Township.............558
Eagle (Carlton) Township..............496	Elmore (Faribault) Township 516	Fergus Falls (Otter Tail) City..........566
Eagle Bend (Todd) City.................602	Elmwood (Clay) Township 504	Fergus Falls (Otter Tail) Township...566
Eagle Lake (Blue Earth) City..........493	Elrosa (Stearns) City.....................595	Fern (Hubbard) Township 527
Eagle Lake (Otter Tail) Township 566	Ely (St. Louis) City 588	Fertile (Polk) City.........................573
Eagle Point (Marshall) Township.....547	Elysian (Le Sueur) City 542	Field (St. Louis) Township 588
Eagle Valley (Todd) Township.........602	Elysian (Le Sueur) Township 542	Fieldon (Watonwan) Township 610
Eagle View (Becker) Township........486	Elysian (Waseca) City 607	Fifty Lakes (Crow Wing) City..........510
East Bethel (Anoka) City...............485	Emardville (Red Lake) Township 578	Fillmore (Fillmore) Township 517
East Cass (Cass) Pop. Place 499	Embarrass (St. Louis) Township 588	**Fillmore County** 517
East Chain (Martin) Township........549	Emerald (Faribault) Township 516	Fine Lakes (St. Louis) Township 588
East Cook (Cook) Pop. Place 507	Emily (Crow Wing) City.................509	Finlayson (Pine) City.....................570
Eastern (Otter Tail) Township.........566	Emmet (Renville) Township 581	Finlayson (Pine) Township..............570
East Grand Forks (Polk) City..........573	Emmons (Freeborn) City................519	Fisher (Polk) City 573
East Gull Lake (Cass) City 499	Empire (Dakota) Township 511	Fisher (Polk) Township 573
East Kittson (Kittson) Pop. Place.....537	Enstrom (Roseau) Township 585	Fish Lake (Chisago) Township.........503
East Koochiching (Koochiching) Pop. Place..538	Enterprise (Jackson) Township 533	Fleming (Aitkin) Township 483
East Lake Lillian (Kandiyohi) Township.....................................535	Equality (Red Lake) Township........578	Fleming (Pine) Township 570
	Erdahl (Grant) Township 522	Flensburg (Morrison) City..............554
Easton (Faribault) City 516	Erhard (Otter Tail) City..................566	Flom (Norman) Township 562
East Park (Marshall) Township........547	Erhards Grove (Otter Tail) Township.................................... 566	Floodwood (St. Louis) City.............588
East Side (Mille Lacs) Township......553		Floodwood (St. Louis) Township 588
East Valley (Marshall) Township......547	Ericson (Renville) Township 581	Flora (Renville) Township..............581
Echo (Yellow Medicine) City 616	Erie (Becker) Township 487	Florence (Goodhue) Township 521
Echo (Yellow Medicine) Township ...616	Erin (Rice) Township.....................583	Florence (Lyon) City......................544
Eckles (Beltrami) Township............488	Erskine (Polk) City 573	Florida (Yellow Medicine) Township616
Eckvoll (Marshall) Township...........547	Espelie (Marshall) Township 547	Flowing (Clay) Township................505
Eddy (Clearwater) Township..........506	Esther (Polk) Township 573	Foldahl (Marshall) Township 547
Eden (Brown) Township 495	Euclid (Polk) Township 573	Folden (Otter Tail) Township..........566
Eden (Pipestone) Township 571	Eureka (Dakota) Township.............511	Foley (Benton) City 490
Eden (Polk) Township 573	Evan (Brown) City........................495	Folsom (Traverse) Township 603
Eden Lake (Stearns) Township........595	Evansville (Douglas) City...............514	Forada (Douglas) City 514
Eden Prairie (Hennepin) City 524	Evansville (Douglas) Township 514	Ford (Kanabec) Township 534
Eden Valley (Meeker) City 552	Eveleth (St. Louis) City..................588	Forest (Becker) Township 487
Eden Valley (Stearns) City 595	Everglade (Stevens) Township........599	Forest (Rice) Township..................583
Edgerton (Pipestone) City 571	Evergreen (Becker) Township.........487	Forest City (Meeker) Township........552
Edina (Hennepin) City 524	Everts (Otter Tail) Township 566	Forest Lake (Washington) City.........608
Edison (Swift) Township 600	Ewington (Jackson) Township 533	Forest Lake (Washington) Township.608
Edna (Otter Tail) Township 566	Excel (Marshall) Township 547	Foreston (Mille Lacs) City..............553
Edwards (Kandiyohi) Township 535	Excelsior (Hennepin) City 524	Forest Prairie (Meeker) Township.....552
Effie (Itasca) City.........................530	Eyota (Olmsted) City 563	Forestville (Fillmore) Township 517
Effie (Itasca) Pop. Place.................530	Eyota (Olmsted) Township 564	Fork (Marshall) Township 547
Effington (Otter Tail) Township........566	Fahlun (Kandiyohi) Township 535	Fortier (Yellow Medicine) Township 616
Eglon (Clay) Township 504	Fairbanks (St. Louis) Township 588	Fort Ripley (Crow Wing) City 510
Eidsvold (Lyon) Township 544	Fairfax (Polk) Township 573	Fort Ripley (Crow Wing) Township..510
Eitzen (Houston) City....................526	Fairfax (Renville) City 581	Fort Snelling (Hennepin) Pop. Place 524
Elba (Winona) City.......................612	Fairfield (Crow Wing) Township 510	Fosston (Polk) City 573
Elba (Winona) Township................612	Fairfield (Swift) Township 600	Fossum (Norman) Township 562
Elbow Lake (Grant) City 522	Fair Haven (Stearns) Township 595	Foster (Big Stone) Township 492
Elbow Lake (Grant) Township..........522	Fairmont (Martin) City 549	Foster (Faribault) Township 516
Eldorado (Stevens) Township.........599	Fairmont (Martin) Township 549	Fountain (Fillmore) City 517
Elgin (Wabasha) City 604	Fairview (Cass) Township..............499	Fountain (Fillmore) Township 517
Elgin (Wabasha) Township 604	Fairview (Lyon) Township 544	Fountain Prairie (Pipestone) Township.....................................571
Elizabeth (Otter Tail) City 566	Falcon Heights (Ramsey) City.........577	
Elizabeth (Otter Tail) Township.......566	Falk (Clearwater) Township............506	Foxhome (Wilkin) City...................611
Elk (Nobles) Township 561	Fall Lake (Lake) Township 540	Foxhome (Wilkin) Township............611
Elk Lake (Grant) Township.............522	Falun (Roseau) Township 585	Fox Lake (Martin) Township 549
	Fanny (Polk) Township..................573	Framnas (Stevens) Township 599

MINNESOTA

Franconia (Chisago) Township..........*503*
Frankford (Mower) Township............*557*
Frankfort (Wright) Township............*614*
Franklin (Renville) City.....................*581*
Franklin (St. Louis) City....................*588*
Franklin (Wright) Township..............*614*
Fraser (Martin) Township..................*549*
Frazee (Becker) City..........................*487*
Fredenberg (St. Louis) Township.......*588*
Freeborn (Freeborn) City...................*519*
Freeborn (Freeborn) Township..........*519*
Freeborn County................................*519*
Freedom (Waseca) Township.............*607*
Freeland (Lac qui Parle) Township...*539*
Freeman (Freeborn) Township..........*519*
Freeport (Stearns) City......................*595*
Fremont (Winona) Township.............*612*
French (St. Louis) Township..............*588*
French Lake (Wright) Township........*614*
Friberg (Otter Tail) Township...........*566*
Fridley (Anoka) City..........................*485*
Friendship (Yellow Medicine) Township................................. *616*
Frohn (Beltrami) Township................*488*
Frost (Faribault) City........................*516*
Fulda (Murray) City...........................*558*
Funkley (Beltrami) City.....................*488*
Gail Lake (Crow Wing) Township....*510*
Galena (Martin) Township.................*549*
Gales (Redwood) Township................*579*
Garden (Polk) Township.....................*573*
Garden City (Blue Earth) Township.*493*
Garfield (Douglas) City......................*514*
Garfield (Lac qui Parle) Township ...*539*
Garfield (Polk) Township....................*573*
Garnes (Red Lake) Township.............*578*
Garrison (Crow Wing) City................*510*
Garrison (Crow Wing) Township.......*510*
Garvin (Lyon) City..............................*544*
Gary (Norman) City............................*562*
Gaylord (Sibley) City..........................*594*
Gem Lake (Ramsey) City....................*577*
Geneva (Freeborn) City......................*519*
Geneva (Freeborn) Township..............*519*
Gennessee (Kandiyohi) Township.....*535*
Genola (Morrison) City......................*554*
Gentilly (Polk) Township *573*
Georgetown (Clay) City......................*505*
Georgetown (Clay) Township..............*505*
Germania (Todd) Township................*602*
Germantown (Cottonwood) Township................................. *508*
Gervais (Red Lake) Township............*578*
Getty (Stearns) Township...................*595*
Gheen (St. Louis) Pop. Place..............*589*
Ghent (Lyon) City...............................*544*
Gibbon (Sibley) City...........................*594*
Gilbert (St. Louis) City.......................*589*
Gilchrist (Pope) Township..................*576*
Gillford (Wabasha) Township.............*604*
Gilman (Benton) City..........................*490*
Gilmanton (Benton) Township............*491*
Girard (Otter Tail) Township..............*566*
Glasgow (Wabasha) Township............*604*
Glen (Aitkin) Township......................*483*
Glencoe (McLeod) City.......................*550*
Glencoe (McLeod) Township..............*550*
Glendorado (Benton) Township..........*491*
Glenville (Freeborn) City....................*519*
Glenwood (Pope) City.........................*576*
Glenwood (Pope) Township................*576*
Glyndon (Clay) City............................*505*
Glyndon (Clay) Township....................*505*
Gnesen (St. Louis) Township..............*589*
Godfrey (Polk) Township....................*573*

Golden Valley (Hennepin) City..........*524*
Golden Valley (Roseau) Township....*585*
Gonvick (Clearwater) City.................*506*
Good Hope (Itasca) Township...........*531*
Good Hope (Norman) Township.......*562*
Goodhue (Goodhue) City....................*521*
Goodhue (Goodhue) Township...........*521*
Goodhue County.................................*520*
Goodland (Itasca) Township..............*531*
Goodridge (Pennington) City.............*568*
Goodridge (Pennington) Township...*568*
Good Thunder (Blue Earth) City......*493*
Goodview (Winona) City....................*612*
Goose Prairie (Clay) Township..........*505*
Gordon (Todd) Township....................*602*
Gorman (Otter Tail) Township..........*566*
Gorton (Grant) Township...................*522*
Gould (Cass) Township.......................*500*
Grace (Chippewa) Township..............*502*
Graceville (Big Stone) City................*492*
Graceville (Big Stone) Township.......*492*
Grafton (Sibley) Township.................*594*
Graham (Benton) Township................*491*
Graham Lakes (Nobles) Township....*561*
Granada (Martin) City.......................*549*
Granby (Nicollet) Township...............*559*
Grand Forks (Polk) Township............*573*
Grand Lake (St. Louis) Township......*589*
Grand Marais (Cook) City.................*507*
Grand Meadow (Mower) City............*557*
Grand Meadow (Mower) Township..*557*
Grand Plain (Marshall) Township....*547*
Grand Portage (Cook) Pop. Place.....*507*
Grand Prairie (Nobles) Township.....*561*
Grand Rapids (Itasca) City................*531*
Grand Rapids (Itasca) Township.......*531*
Grandview (Lyon) Township..............*544*
Grange (Pipestone) Township............*572*
Granite (Morrison) Township............*555*
Granite Falls (Chippewa) City...........*502*
Granite Falls (Chippewa) Township.*502*
Granite Falls (Yellow Medicine) City... *616*
Granite Ledge (Benton) Township....*491*
Granite Rock (Redwood) Township.*579*
Grant (Washington) Township..........*608*
Grant County.......................................*522*
Grant Valley (Beltrami) Township....*488*
Granville (Kittson) Township............*537*
Grass Lake (Kanabec) Township......*534*
Grasston (Kanabec) City....................*534*
Grattan (Itasca) Township.................*531*
Gray (Pipestone) Township................*572*
Great Bend (Cottonwood) Township*508*
Great Scott (St. Louis) Township......*589*
Greenbush (Mille Lacs) Township....*553*
Greenbush (Roseau) City....................*585*
Greenfield (Hennepin) City.................*524*
Greenfield (Wabasha) Township........*604*
Green Isle (Sibley) City......................*594*
Green Isle (Sibley) Township.............*594*
Green Lake (Kandiyohi) Township..*535*
Greenleaf (Meeker) Township............*552*
Green Meadow (Norman) Township.*562*
Green Prairie (Morrison) Township.*555*
Greenvale (Dakota) Township...........*511*
Green Valley (Becker) Township.......*487*
Greenwald (Stearns) City...................*596*
Greenway (Itasca) Township..............*531*
Greenwood (Clearwater) Township..*506*
Greenwood (Hennepin) City...............*524*
Greenwood (St. Louis) Township......*589*
Gregory (Mahnomen) Township........*545*
Grey Cloud Island (Washington) Township................................. *608*

American Places Dictionary

Grey Eagle (Todd) City......................*602*
Grey Eagle (Todd) Township.............*602*
Grimstad (Roseau) Township............*585*
Grove (Stearns) Township..................*596*
Grove City (Meeker) City...................*552*
Grove Lake (Pope) Township.............*576*
Grove Park (Polk) Township..............*573*
Grygla (Marshall) City.......................*547*
Gully (Polk) City................................*574*
Gully (Polk) Township.......................*574*
Guthrie (Hubbard) Township............*527*
Hackensack (Cass) City......................*500*
Hadley (Murray) City.........................*558*
Hagali (Beltrami) Township...............*489*
Hagen (Clay) Township.....................*505*
Halden (St. Louis) Township.............*589*
Hale (McLeod) Township..................*550*
Hallock (Kittson) City........................*537*
Hallock (Kittson) Township...............*537*
Halma (Kittson) City..........................*537*
Halstad (Norman) City.......................*562*
Halstad (Norman) Township..............*562*
Hamburg (Carver) City......................*498*
Hamden (Becker) Township...............*487*
Ham Lake (Anoka) City.....................*485*
Hamlin (Lac qui Parle) Township.....*539*
Hammer (Yellow Medicine) Township................................. *616*
Hammond (Polk) Township................*574*
Hammond (Wabasha) City.................*604*
Hampden (Kittson) Township............*537*
Hampton (Dakota) City......................*511*
Hampton (Dakota) Township.............*511*
Hamre (Beltrami) Township...............*489*
Hancock (Carver) Township...............*498*
Hancock (Stevens) Township.............*599*
Hangaard (Clearwater) Township.....*506*
Hanley Falls (Yellow Medicine) City *616*
Hanover (Hennepin) City...................*524*
Hanover (Wright) City.......................*615*
Hanska (Brown) City..........................*495*
Hansonville (Lincoln) Township........*543*
Hantho (Lac qui Parle) Township.....*539*
Harding (Morrison) City....................*555*
Hardwick (Rock) City.........................*584*
Harmony (Fillmore) City....................*517*
Harmony (Fillmore) Township...........*517*
Harris (Chisago) City..........................*503*
Harris (Itasca) Township....................*531*
Harrison (Kandiyohi) Township........*535*
Hart (Winona) Township....................*613*
Hartford (Todd) Township.................*602*
Hart Lake (Hubbard) Township........*527*
Hartland (Freeborn) City...................*519*
Hartland (Freeborn) Township..........*519*
Harvey (Meeker) Township................*552*
Hassan (Hennepin) Township............*524*
Hassan Valley (McLeod) Township..*550*
Hastings (Dakota) City.......................*512*
Hastings (Washington) City...............*608*
Hatfield (Pipestone) City....................*572*
Haugen (Aitkin) Township.................*483*
Havana (Steele) Township..................*598*
Havelock (Chippewa) Township........*502*
Haven (Sherburne) Township.............*593*
Haverhill (Olmsted) Township...........*564*
Hawk Creek (Renville) Township.....*581*
Hawley (Clay) City..............................*505*
Hawley (Clay) Township....................*505*
Hay Brook (Kanabec) Township.......*534*
Hay Creek (Goodhue) Township.......*521*
Hayes (Swift) Township......................*600*
Hayfield (Dodge) City.........................*513*
Hayfield (Dodge) Township................*513*
Hay Lake (St. Louis) Pop. Place........*589*

Hayland (Mille Lacs) Township 553	Holloway (Swift) City 600	**Jackson County** 532
Hayward (Freeborn) City 520	Holly (Murray) Township 558	Jadis (Roseau) Township 585
Hayward (Freeborn) Township 520	Hollywood (Carver) Township 498	Jamestown (Blue Earth) Township ...493
Hazel Run (Yellow Medicine) City ...616	Holmes City (Douglas) Township 514	Janesville (Waseca) City 607
Hazel Run (Yellow Medicine) Township 616	Holmesville (Becker) Township........487	Janesville (Waseca) Township 607
Hazelton (Aitkin) Township 483	Holst (Clearwater) Township.............506	Janette Lake (St. Louis) Pop. Place ..589
Hazelton (Kittson) Township 537	Holt (Fillmore) Township..................517	Jasper (Pipestone) City......................572
Hector (Renville) City 581	Holt (Marshall) City 547	Jasper (Rock) City 584
Hector (Renville) Township 581	Holt (Marshall) Township 547	Jay (Martin) Township 549
Hegbert (Swift) Township..................600	Holy Cross (Clay) Township 505	Jeffers (Cottonwood) City 508
Hegne (Norman) Township 562	Holyoke (Carlton) Township 496	Jefferson (Houston) Township 526
Heidelberg (Le Sueur) City 542	Home (Brown) Township 495	Jenkins (Crow Wing) City 510
Heier (Mahnomen) Township 545	Home Brook (Cass) Township 500	Jenkins (Crow Wing) Township 510
Height of Land (Becker) Township....487	Home Lake (Norman) Township 562	Jessenland (Sibley) Township 594
Heikkila Lake (St. Louis) Pop. Place 589	Homer (Winona) Township................613	Jevne (Aitkin) Township 483
Helen (McLeod) Township................550	Homestead (Otter Tail) Township.....566	Jewett (Aitkin) Pop. Place 483
Helena (Scott) Township 592	Honner (Redwood) Township 579	Jo Daviess (Faribault) Township........516
Helga (Hubbard) Township 527	Hope (Lincoln) Township 543	Johnson (Big Stone) City...................492
Helgeland (Polk) Township 574	Hopkins (Hennepin) City 524	Johnson (Polk) Township 574
Henderson (Sibley) City 594	Hornet (Beltrami) Township 489	Johnsonville (Redwood) Township ...579
Henderson (Sibley) Township 594	Horton (Stevens) Township 599	Jones (Beltrami) Township 489
Hendricks (Lincoln) City 543	Houston (Houston) City 526	Jordan (Fillmore) Township 517
Hendricks (Lincoln) Township 543	Houston (Houston) Township 526	Jordan (Scott) City 592
Hendrickson (Hubbard) Township.....527	**Houston County** 526	Judson (Blue Earth) Township 493
Hendrum (Norman) City 562	Howard Lake (Wright) City 615	Jupiter (Kittson) Township 537
Hendrum (Norman) Township..........562	Hoyt Lakes (St. Louis) City 589	Kalevala (Carlton) Township 496
Hennepin County 523	Hubbard (Hubbard) Township 528	Kalmar (Olmsted) Township 564
Henning (Otter Tail) City 566	Hubbard (Polk) Township 574	Kanabec (Kanabec) Township 534
Henning (Otter Tail) Township 566	**Hubbard County** 527	**Kanabec County** 534
Henrietta (Hubbard) Township..........528	Hudson (Douglas) Township 514	Kanaranzi (Rock) Township...............584
Henriette (Pine) City 570	Hugo (Washington) City....................608	Kandiyohi (Kandiyohi) City 535
Henryville (Renville) Township 581	Humboldt (Clay) Township 505	Kandiyohi (Kandiyohi) Township.....535
Hereim (Roseau) Township 585	Humboldt (Kittson) City 537	**Kandiyohi County** 535
Herman (Grant) City 522	Hunter (Jackson) Township 533	Kandota (Todd) Township 602
Hermantown (St. Louis) City 589	Huntersville (Wadena) Township......606	Karlstad (Kittson) City 537
Heron Lake (Jackson) City................533	Huntly (Marshall) Township 547	Kasota (Le Sueur) City 542
Heron Lake (Jackson) Township 533	Huntsville (Polk) Township 574	Kasota (Le Sueur) Township 542
Hersey (Nobles) Township 561	Huss (Roseau) Township 585	Kasson (Dodge) City 513
Hewitt (Todd) City 602	Hutchinson (McLeod) City 551	Kathio (Mille Lacs) Township...........553
Hibbing (St. Louis) City 589	Hutchinson (McLeod) Township......551	Keene (Clay) Township 505
Hickory (Pennington) Township 568	Hyde Park (Wabasha) Township 604	Keewatin (Itasca) City 531
Higdem (Polk) Township...................574	Ida (Douglas) Township 514	Kego (Cass) Township 500
High Forest (Olmsted) Township 564	Ideal (Crow Wing) Township 510	Kelliher (Beltrami) City 489
Highland (Wabasha) Township 604	Idun (Aitkin) Township.....................483	Kelliher (Beltrami) Township 489
Highland Grove (Clay) Township 505	Ihlen (Pipestone) City 572	Kellogg (Wabasha) City 604
Highlanding (Pennington) Township 568	Independence (Hennepin) City 524	Kelsey (St. Louis) Township 589
Highwater (Cottonwood) Township ..508	Indian Lake (Nobles) Township........561	Kelso (Sibley) Township 594
Hill (Kittson) Township 537	Industrial (St. Louis) Township 589	Kennedy (Kittson) City 537
Hill City (Aitkin) City 483	Inguadona (Cass) Township 500	Kenneth (Rock) City 584
Hill Lake (Aitkin) Township 483	Inman (Otter Tail) Township 566	Kensington (Douglas) City 514
Hillman (Kanabec) Township 534	International Falls (Koochiching) City...... 538	Kent (Wilkin) City.............................611
Hillman (Morrison) City 555	Inver Grove Heights (Dakota) City ..512	Kenyon (Goodhue) City.....................521
Hillman (Morrison) Township 555	Iona (Murray) City 558	Kenyon (Goodhue) Township 521
Hill River (Polk) Township 574	Iona (Murray) Township 558	Kerkhoven (Swift) City 600
Hills (Rock) City 584	Iona (Todd) Township 602	Kerkhoven (Swift) Township 600
Hillsdale (Winona) Township 613	Iosco (Waseca) Township 607	Kerrick (Pine) City 570
Hilltop (Anoka) City 485	Irondale (Crow Wing) Township.......510	Kerrick (Pine) Township 570
Hinckley (Pine) City 570	Iron Junction (St. Louis) City 589	Kertsonville (Polk) Township............574
Hinckley (Pine) Township 570	Iron Range (Itasca) Township 531	Kettle River (Carlton) City 496
Hines (Beltrami) Township 489	Ironton (Crow Wing) City.................510	Kettle River (Pine) Township 570
Hiram (Cass) Township 500	Irving (Kandiyohi) Township 535	Keystone (Polk) Township 574
Hitterdal (Clay) City 505	Isanti (Isanti) City 529	Kiester (Faribault) City 516
Hobart (Otter Tail) Township 566	Isanti (Isanti) Township 529	Kiester (Faribault) Township 516
Hodges (Stevens) Township 599	**Isanti County**...................................529	Kildare (Swift) Township 600
Hoff (Pope) Township 576	Island Lake (Lyon) Township 544	Kilkenny (Le Sueur) City 542
Hoffman (Grant) City 522	Island Lake (Mahnomen) Township .545	Kilkenny (Le Sueur) Township 542
Hokah (Houston) City 526	Island View (Koochiching) City........538	Kimball (Jackson) Township 533
Hokah (Houston) Township 526	Isle (Mille Lacs) City 553	Kimball Prairie (Stearns) City 596
Holden (Goodhue) Township 521	Isle Harbor (Mille Lacs) Township ...553	Kimberly (Aitkin) Township 483
Holding (Stearns) Township 596	Itasca (Clearwater) Township 506	Kinbrae (Nobles) City 561
Holdingford (Stearns) City 596	**Itasca County**..................................530	King (Polk) Township........................574
Holland (Kandiyohi) Township.........535	Ivanhoe (Lincoln) City 543	Kinghurst (Itasca) Township 531
Holland (Pipestone) City 572	Jackson (Jackson) City......................533	Kingman (Renville) Township 582
Hollandale (Freeborn) City 520	Jackson (Scott) Township 592	Kingston (Meeker) City 552
		Kingston (Meeker) Township 552

MINNESOTA

Kinney (St. Louis) City 589
Kintire (Redwood) Township............579
Kittson County 536
Knife Lake (Kanabec) Township.......534
Knute (Polk) Township 574
Koochiching County 538
Kragero (Chippewa) Township..........502
Kragnes (Clay) Township 505
Krain (Stearns) Township..................596
Kratka (Pennington) Township 568
Kroschel (Kanabec) Township 534
Kugler (St. Louis) Township 589
Kurtz (Clay) Township 505
Lac qui Parle (Lac qui Parle)
  Township 539
Lac qui Parle County 539
La Crescent (Houston) City 526
La Crescent (Houston) Township......526
La Crosse (Jackson) Township 533
Lafayette (Nicollet) City....................559
Lafayette (Nicollet) Township...........559
La Garde (Mahnomen) Township.....545
La Grand (Douglas) Township 514
Lake (Roseau) Township 585
Lake (Wabasha) Township.................604
Lake Alice (Hubbard) Township.......528
Lake Andrew (Kandiyohi) Township 535
Lake Belt (Martin) Township 549
Lake Benton (Lincoln) City 543
Lake Benton (Lincoln) Township......543
Lake Bronson (Kittson) City 537
Lake City (Goodhue) City 521
Lake City (Wabasha) City 604
Lake County 540
Lake Crystal (Blue Earth) City..........493
Lake Edwards (Crow Wing)
  Township 510
Lake Elizabeth (Kandiyohi)
  Township 535
Lake Elmo (Washington) City 608
Lake Emma (Hubbard) Township.....528
Lake Eunice (Becker) Township........487
Lakefield (Jackson) City 533
Lake Fremont (Martin) Township 549
Lake George (Hubbard) Township....528
Lake George (Stearns) Township 596
Lake Grove (Mahnomen) Township.546
Lake Hanska (Brown) Township.......495
Lake Hattie (Hubbard) Township.....528
Lake Henry (Stearns) City.................596
Lake Henry (Stearns) Township........596
Lake Ida (Norman) Township...........562
Lake Jessie (Itasca) Township 531
Lake Johanna (Pope) Township........576
Lakeland (Washington) City.............608
Lakeland Shores (Washington) City..608
Lake Lillian (Kandiyohi) City...........535
Lake Lillian (Kandiyohi) Township..535
Lake Marshall (Lyon) Township 544
Lake Mary (Douglas) Township 514
Lake No. 1 (Lake) Pop. Place 540
Lake No. 2 (Lake) Pop. Place 540
Lake of the Woods County............541
Lake Park (Becker) City 487
Lake Park (Becker) Township 487
Lake Pleasant (Red Lake) Township 578
Lakeport (Hubbard) Township.........528
Lake Prairie (Nicollet) Township......559
Lake Sarah (Murray) Township........558
Lake Shore (Cass) City 500
Lake Shore (Lac qui Parle)
  Township 539
Lakeside (Aitkin) Township 483
Lakeside (Cottonwood) Township....508
Lake Stay (Lincoln) Township 543

Lake St. Croix Beach (Washington)
  City.. 608
Laketown (Carver) Township............498
Lake Valley (Traverse) Township......603
Lake Vermilion (St. Louis) Pop.
  Place 589
Lake View (Becker) Township...........487
Lakeview (Carlton) Township 496
Lakeville (Dakota) City 512
Lake Wilson (Murray) City 558
Lakewood (St. Louis) Township........589
Lakin (Morrison) Township 555
Lambert (Red Lake) Township 578
Lamberton (Redwood) City 579
Lamberton (Redwood) Township.....579
Lammers (Beltrami) Township.........489
Lancaster (Kittson) City 537
Land (Grant) Township 522
Landfall (Washington) City 608
Lanesboro (Fillmore) City 517
Lanesburgh (Le Sueur) Township 542
Langhei (Pope) Township 576
Langola (Benton) Township 491
Langor (Beltrami) Township 489
Lansing (Mower) Township 557
Laona (Roseau) Township 585
Laporte (Hubbard) City.....................528
La Prairie (Clearwater) Township.....506
La Prairie (Itasca) City.......................531
Larkin (Nobles) Township 561
La Salle (Watonwan) City..................610
Lastrup (Morrison) City 555
Lauderdale (Ramsey) City..................577
Lavell (St. Louis) Township 589
Lawrence (Grant) Township..............522
Lawrence (Itasca) Township 531
Leaf Lake (Otter Tail) Township.......566
Leaf Mountain (Otter Tail)
  Township 566
Leaf River (Wadena) Township 606
Leaf Valley (Douglas) Township 514
Leavenworth (Brown) Township......495
Le Center (Le Sueur) City 542
Lee (Aitkin) Township.......................483
Lee (Beltrami) Township 489
Lee (Norman) Township....................562
Leech Lake (Cass) Township.............500
Leeds (Murray) Township 559
Leenthrop (Chippewa) Township......502
Leiding (St. Louis) Township 589
Leigh (Morrison) Township..............555
Lemond (Steele) Township 598
Lengby (Polk) City.............................574
Lent (Chisago) Township...................503
Leon (Clearwater) Township.............506
Leon (Goodhue) Township................521
Leonard (Clearwater) City.................507
Leonardsville (Traverse) Township...603
Leonidas (St. Louis) City 589
Leota (Nobles) Township 561
Le Ray (Blue Earth) Township..........493
Le Roy (Mower) City 557
Le Roy (Mower) Township................557
Le Sauk (Stearns) Township...............596
Leslie (Todd) Township 602
Lessor (Polk) Township......................574
Lester Prairie (McLeod) City 551
Le Sueur (Le Sueur) City 542
Le Sueur County 541
Leven (Pope) Township......................576
Lewis (Mille Lacs) Township 553
Lewiston (Winona) City....................613
Lewisville (Watonwan) City 610
Lexington (Anoka) City.....................485
Lexington (Le Sueur) Township 542

Libby (Aitkin) Township 483
Liberty (Beltrami) Township............489
Liberty (Itasca) Township 531
Liberty (Polk) Township 574
Lida (Otter Tail) Township 567
Lien (Grant) Township......................522
Lilydale (Dakota) City.......................512
Lima (Cass) Township 500
Lime (Blue Earth) Township............493
Lime Lake (Murray) Township........559
Limestone (Lincoln) Township.........543
Lincoln (Blue Earth) Township........493
Lincoln (Marshall) Township 547
Lincoln County..............................543
Lind (Roseau) Township 585
Linden (Brown) Township...............495
Linden Grove (St. Louis) Township .589
Lindstrom (Chisago) City.................503
Lino Lakes (Anoka) City 486
Linsell (Marshall) Township............547
Linwood (Anoka) Township.............486
Lisbon (Yellow Medicine) Township 616
Lismore (Nobles) City 561
Lismore (Nobles) Township.............561
Litchfield (Meeker) City 552
Litchfield (Meeker) Township 552
Little Canada (Ramsey) City............577
Little Elk (Todd) Township 602
Little Falls (Morrison) City 555
Little Falls (Morrison) Township 555
Littlefork (Koochiching) City...........538
Little Pine (Crow Wing) Township...510
Little Rock (Beltrami) CDP 489
Little Rock (Nobles) Township 561
Little Sand Lake (Itasca) Pop. Place.531
Little Sauk (Todd) Township............602
Livonia (Sherburne) Township.........593
Lockhart (Norman) Township.........562
Lodi (Mower) Township....................557
Logan (Aitkin) Township..................484
Logan (Grant) Township...................522
London (Freeborn) Township 520
Lone Pine (Itasca) Township.............531
Lone Tree (Chippewa) Township......502
Long Beach (Pope) City 576
Long Lake (Crow Wing) Township...510
Long Lake (Hennepin) City 524
Long Lake (Watonwan) Township 610
Long Prairie (Todd) City...................602
Long Prairie (Todd) Township..........602
Longville (Cass) City 500
Lonsdale (Rice) City..........................583
Loon Lake (Cass) Township..............500
Lorain (Nobles) Township 561
Loretto (Hennepin) City....................524
Louisburg (Lac qui Parle) City 539
Louisville (Red Lake) Township.......578
Louisville (Scott) Township 592
Louriston (Chippewa) Township......502
Lowell (Polk) Township.....................574
Lower Red Lake (Beltrami) Pop.
  Place 489
Lowry (Pope) City 576
Lowville (Murray) Township............559
Lucan (Redwood) City 579
Lucas (Lyon) Township 544
Lund (Douglas) Township................514
Lura (Faribault) Township 516
Lutsen (Cook) Township 507
Luverne (Rock) City..........................584
Luverne (Rock) Township 584
Luxemburg (Stearns) Township.......596
Lyle (Mower) City..............................557
Lyle (Mower) Township....................557
Lynd (Lyon) City 544

ynd (Lyon) Township...544	Mary (Norman) Township...562	Miltona (Douglas) Township...515
ynden (Stearns) Township...596	Marysland (Swift) Township...600	Minden (Benton) Township...491
ynn (McLeod) Township...551	Marysville (Wright) Township...615	Minerva (Clearwater) Township...507
yon County...544	Mason (Murray) Township...559	Minneapolis (Hennepin) City...524
yons (Lyon) Township...544	Max (Itasca) Township...531	Minneiska (Wabasha) City...605
yons (Wadena) Township...606	Maxwell (Lac qui Parle) Township...540	Minneiska (Wabasha) Township...605
yra (Blue Earth) Township...493	May (Cass) Township...500	Minneiska (Winona) City...613
label (Fillmore) City...517	May (Washington) Township...609	Minneola (Goodhue) Township...521
lacsville (Grant) Township...522	Mayer (Carver) City...498	Minneota (Jackson) Township...533
lacville (Aitkin) Township...484	Mayfield (Pennington) Township...568	Minneota (Lyon) City...544
ladelia (Watonwan) City...610	Mayhew Lake (Benton) Township...491	Minnesota City (Winona) City...613
ladelia (Watonwan) Township...610	Maynard (Chippewa) City...502	Minnesota Falls (Yellow Medicine) Township...616
ladison (Lac qui Parle) City...540	Mayville (Houston) Township...526	Minnesota Lake (Faribault) City...516
ladison (Lac qui Parle) Township...540	Maywood (Benton) Township...491	Minnesota Lake (Faribault) Township...516
ladison Lake (Blue Earth) City...493	Mazeppa (Wabasha) City...605	Minnetonka (Hennepin) City...525
lagnolia (Rock) City...584	Mazeppa (Wabasha) Township...605	Minnetonka Beach (Hennepin) City...525
lagnolia (Rock) Township...584	McCauleyville (Wilkin) Township...611	Minnetrista (Hennepin) City...525
lahnomen (Mahnomen) City...546	McCormack Lake (St. Louis) Pop. Place...589	Minnewaska (Pope) Township...576
lahnomen County...545	McCrea (Marshall) Township...547	Minnie (Beltrami) Township...489
lahtomedi (Washington) City...609	McDavitt (St. Louis) Township...590	Mission (Crow Wing) Township...510
lahtowa (Carlton) Township...496	McDonaldsville (Norman) Township...562	Mission Creek (Pine) Township...570
laine (Otter Tail) Township...567	McGrath (Aitkin) City...484	Mitchell (Wilkin) Township...612
laine Prairie (Stearns) Township...596	McGregor (Aitkin) City...484	Mizpah (Koochiching) City...538
lalmo (Aitkin) Township...484	McGregor (Aitkin) Township...484	Moe (Douglas) Township...515
lalta (Big Stone) Township...492	McIntosh (Polk) City...574	Moland (Clay) Township...505
lalung (Roseau) Township...585	McKinley (Cass) Township...500	Moltke (Sibley) Township...594
lamre (Kandiyohi) Township...535	McKinley (Kittson) Township...537	Money Creek (Houston) Township...526
lanannah (Meeker) Township...552	McKinley (St. Louis) City...590	Monroe (Lyon) Township...544
lanchester (Freeborn) City...520	McLeod County...550	Monson (Traverse) Township...603
lanchester (Freeborn) Township...520	McPherson (Blue Earth) Township...494	Montevideo (Chippewa) City...502
landt (Chippewa) Township...502	Meadow (Wadena) Township...606	Montgomery (Le Sueur) City...542
lanfred (Lac qui Parle) Township...540	Meadow Brook (Cass) Township...500	Montgomery (Le Sueur) Township...542
lanhattan Beach (Crow Wing) City...510	Meadowlands (St. Louis) City...590	Monticello (Wright) City...615
lankato (Blue Earth) City...493	Meadowlands (St. Louis) Township...590	Monticello (Wright) Township...615
lankato (Blue Earth) Township...493	Meadows (Wilkin) Township...612	Montrose (Wright) City...615
lankato (Nicollet) City...560	Medford (Steele) City...598	Moonshine (Big Stone) Township...492
lansfield (Freeborn) Township...520	Medford (Steele) Township...598	Moore (Stevens) Township...599
lanston (Wilkin) Township...611	Medicine Lake (Hennepin) City...524	Moorhead (Clay) City...505
lantorville (Dodge) City...513	Medina (Hennepin) City...524	Moorhead (Clay) Township...505
lantorville (Dodge) Township...513	Medo (Blue Earth) Township...494	Moose (Roseau) Township...586
lantrap (Hubbard) Township...528	Meeker County...551	Moose Creek (Clearwater) Township...507
lanyaska (Martin) Township...549	Mehurin (Lac qui Parle) Township...540	Moose Lake (Beltrami) Township...489
laple (Cass) Township...500	Meire Grove (Stearns) City...596	Moose Lake (Carlton) City...496
laple Grove (Becker) Township...487	Melrose (Stearns) City...596	Moose Lake (Carlton) Township...496
laple Grove (Crow Wing) Township...510	Melrose (Stearns) Township...596	Moose Lake (Cass) Township...500
laple Grove (Hennepin) City...524	Melville (Renville) Township...582	Moose Park (Itasca) Township...531
laple Lake (Wright) City...615	Menahga (Wadena) City...606	Moose River (Marshall) Township...547
laple Lake (Wright) Township...615	Mendota (Dakota) City...512	Mora (Kanabec) City...534
laple Plain (Hennepin) City...524	Mendota Heights (Dakota) City...512	Moran (Todd) Township...602
laple Ridge (Beltrami) Township...489	Mentor (Polk) City...574	Moranville (Roseau) Township...586
laple Ridge (Isanti) Township...529	Meriden (Steele) Township...598	Morcom (St. Louis) Township...590
lapleton (Blue Earth) City...494	Merton (Steele) Township...598	Morgan (Redwood) City...579
lapleton (Blue Earth) Township...494	Mickinock (Roseau) Township...586	Morgan (Redwood) Township...579
lapleview (Mower) City...557	Middle River (Marshall) City...547	Morken (Clay) Township...505
laplewood (Otter Tail) Township...567	Middle River (Marshall) Township...547	Morrill (Morrison) Township...555
laplewood (Ramsey) City...577	Middletown (Jackson) Township...533	Morris (Stevens) City...599
larble (Itasca) City...531	Middleville (Wright) Township...615	Morris (Stevens) Township...599
larble (Lincoln) Township...543	Midway (Cottonwood) Township...508	Morrison (Aitkin) Township...484
larcell (Itasca) Township...531	Midway (St. Louis) Township...590	Morrison County...554
larietta (Lac qui Parle) City...540	Miesville (Dakota) City...512	Morristown (Rice) City...583
larine on St. Croix (Washington) City...609	Milaca (Mille Lacs) City...553	Morristown (Rice) Township...583
larion (Olmsted) Township...564	Milaca (Mille Lacs) Township...553	Morse (Itasca) Township...531
larshall (Lyon) City...544	Milan (Chippewa) City...502	Morse (St. Louis) Township...590
larshall (Mower) Township...557	Milford (Brown) Township...495	Morton (Renville) City...582
Marshall County...546	Mille Lacs County...553	Moscow (Freeborn) Township...520
larshan (Dakota) Township...512	Millerville (Douglas) City...514	Motley (Cass) City...500
larsh Creek (Mahnomen) Township...546	Millerville (Douglas) Township...514	Motley (Morrison) City...555
larshfield (Lincoln) Township...543	Millville (Wabasha) City...605	Motley (Morrison) Township...555
larsh Grove (Marshall) Township...547	Millward (Aitkin) Township...484	Moulton (Murray) Township...559
lartin (Rock) Township...584	Millwood (Stearns) Township...596	Mound (Hennepin) City...525
Martin County...549	Milo (Mille Lacs) Township...553	Mound (Rock) Township...584
lartinsburg (Renville) Township...582	Milroy (Redwood) City...579	Mound Prairie (Houston) Township...527
	Milton (Dodge) Township...513	Mounds View (Ramsey) City...577
	Miltona (Douglas) City...515	

MINNESOTA

Mountain Iron (St. Louis) City..........590
Mountain Lake (Cottonwood) City...508
Mountain Lake (Cottonwood) Township..............508
Mount Morris (Morrison) Township 555
Mount Pleasant (Wabasha) Township..............605
Mount Vernon (Winona) Township..613
Mower County..............556
Moyer (Swift) Township..............601
Moylan (Marshall) Township..............547
Mudgett (Mille Lacs) Township..............553
Mud Lake (Marshall) Pop. Place..............547
Mulligan (Brown) Township..............495
Munch (Pine) Township..............570
Munson (Stearns) Township..............596
Murdock (Swift) City..............601
Murray (Murray) Township..............559
Murray County..............558
Myrtle (Freeborn) City..............520
Nashua (Wilkin) City..............612
Nashville (Martin) Township..............549
Nashwauk (Itasca) City..............531
Nashwauk (Itasca) Township..............531
Nassau (Lac qui Parle) City..............540
Naytahwaush (Mahnomen) CDP..............546
Nebish (Beltrami) Township..............489
Nelson (Douglas) City..............515
Nelson (Watonwan) Township..............610
Nelson Park (Marshall) Township..............547
Nereson (Roseau) Township..............586
Nerstrand (Rice) City..............583
Nesbit (Polk) Township..............574
Ness (St. Louis) Township..............590
Nessel (Chisago) Township..............503
Nett Lake (Koochiching) Pop. Place.538
Nett Lake (St. Louis) Pop. Place..............590
Nevada (Mower) Township..............557
Nevis (Hubbard) City..............528
Nevis (Hubbard) Township..............528
New Auburn (Sibley) City..............594
New Auburn (Sibley) Township..............594
New Avon (Redwood) Township..............579
New Brighton (Ramsey) City..............577
Newburg (Fillmore) Township..............518
New Dosey (Pine) Township..............570
Newfolden (Marshall) City..............547
New Folden (Marshall) Township..............547
New Germany (Carver) City..............498
New Hartford (Winona) Township..613
New Haven (Olmsted) Township..............564
New Hope (Hennepin) City..............525
New Independence (St. Louis) Township..............590
New London (Kandiyohi) City..............536
New London (Kandiyohi) Township 536
New Maine (Marshall) Township..............548
New Market (Scott) City..............592
New Market (Scott) Township..............592
New Munich (Stearns) City..............596
Newport (Washington) City..............609
New Prague (Le Sueur) City..............542
New Prague (Scott) City..............592
New Prairie (Pope) Township..............576
New Richland (Waseca) City..............607
New Richland (Waseca) Township..............607
Newry (Freeborn) Township..............520
New Scandia (Washington) Township..............609
New Solum (Marshall) Township..............548
New Sweden (Nicollet) Township..............560
Newton (Otter Tail) Township..............567
New Trier (Dakota) City..............512
New Ulm (Brown) City..............495
New York Mills (Otter Tail) City..............567

Nickerson (Pine) Township..............570
Nicollet (Nicollet) City..............560
Nicollet (Nicollet) Township..............560
Nicollet County..............559
Nidaros (Otter Tail) Township..............567
Nielsville (Polk) City..............574
Nilsen (Wilkin) Township..............612
Nimrod (Wadena) City..............606
Nininger (Dakota) Township..............512
Nisswa (Crow Wing) City..............510
Nobles County..............560
Nokay Lake (Crow Wing) Township 510
Nora (Clearwater) Township..............507
Nora (Pope) Township..............576
Norcross (Grant) City..............523
Norden (Pennington) Township..............569
Nordick (Wilkin) Township..............612
Nordland (Aitkin) Township..............484
Nordland (Lyon) Township..............545
Nore (Itasca) Township..............531
Norfolk (Renville) Township..............582
Norman (Pine) Township..............570
Norman (Yellow Medicine) Township..............616
Norman County..............562
Normania (Yellow Medicine) Township..............616
Normanna (St. Louis) Township..............590
North (Pennington) Township..............569
North Beltrami (Beltrami) Pop. Place..............489
North Branch (Chisago) City..............503
North Branch (Isanti) Township..............529
North Carlton (Carlton) Pop. Place..496
North Cass (Cass) Pop. Place..............500
North Central Cass (Cass) Pop. Place..............500
North Clearwater (Clearwater) Pop. Place..............507
Northeast Aitkin (Aitkin) Pop. Place 484
Northeast Itasca (Itasca) Pop. Place.531
Northeast St. Louis (St. Louis) Pop. Place..............590
Northern (Beltrami) Township..............489
Northfield (Dakota) City..............512
Northfield (Rice) City..............583
Northfield (Rice) Township..............583
North Fork (Stearns) Township..............596
North Germany (Wadena) Township 606
North Hero (Redwood) Township..............580
Northland (Polk) Township..............574
Northland (St. Louis) Township..............590
North Mankato (Blue Earth) City..............494
North Mankato (Nicollet) City..............560
North Oaks (Ramsey) City..............577
Northome (Koochiching) City..............538
Northome (Koochiching) Pop. Place 538
North Ottawa (Grant) Township..............523
North Red River (Kittson) Township..............537
North Redwood (Redwood) City..............580
Northrop (Martin) City..............549
North Roseau (Roseau) Pop. Place...586
North Star (Brown) Township..............495
North Star (St. Louis) Township..............590
North St. Paul (Ramsey) City..............577
Northwest Aitkin (Aitkin) Pop. Place..............484
Northwest Koochiching (Koochiching) Pop. Place..............539
Northwest Roseau (Roseau) Pop. Place..............586
Northwest St. Louis (St. Louis) Pop. Place..............590
Norton (Winona) Township..............613

Norway (Fillmore) Township..............518
Norway (Kittson) Township..............537
Norway Lake (Kandiyohi) Township 536
Norwegian Grove (Otter Tail) Township..............567
Norwood (Carver) City..............498
Numedal (Pennington) Township..............569
Nunda (Freeborn) Township..............520
Oak (Stearns) Township..............596
Oakdale (Washington) City..............609
Oak Grove (Anoka) Township..............486
Oakland (Freeborn) Township..............520
Oakland (Mahnomen) Township..............546
Oak Lawn (Crow Wing) Township..510
Oak Park (Marshall) Township..............548
Oak Park Heights (Washington) City 609
Oakport (Clay) Township..............505
Oak Valley (Otter Tail) Township..............567
Oakwood (Wabasha) Township..............605
O'Brien (Beltrami) Township..............489
Odessa (Big Stone) City..............492
Odessa (Big Stone) Township..............492
Odin (Watonwan) City..............610
Odin (Watonwan) Township..............610
Ogema (Becker) City..............487
Ogema (Pine) Township..............570
Ogilvie (Kanabec) City..............534
Okabena (Jackson) City..............533
Oklee (Red Lake) City..............578
Olivia (Renville) City..............582
Olmsted County..............563
Olney (Nobles) Township..............561
Omro (Yellow Medicine) Township..616
Onamia (Mille Lacs) City..............553
Onamia (Mille Lacs) Township..............553
Onstad (Polk) Township..............574
Orange (Douglas) Township..............515
Orion (Olmsted) Township..............564
Ormsby (Martin) City..............549
Ormsby (Watonwan) City..............610
Orono (Hennepin) City..............525
Oronoco (Olmsted) City..............564
Oronoco (Olmsted) Township..............564
Orr (St. Louis) City..............590
Orrock (Sherburne) Township..............593
Orton (Wadena) Township..............606
Ortonville (Big Stone) City..............492
Ortonville (Big Stone) Township..............492
Ortonville (Lac qui Parle) City..............540
Orwell (Otter Tail) Township..............567
Osage (Becker) Township..............487
Osakis (Douglas) City..............515
Osakis (Douglas) Township..............515
Osakis (Todd) City..............602
Osborne (Pipestone) Township..............572
Oscar (Otter Tail) Township..............567
Osceola (Renville) Township..............582
Oshawa (Nicollet) Township..............560
Oshkosh (Yellow Medicine) Township..............616
Oslo (Marshall) City..............548
Osseo (Hennepin) City..............525
Ostrander (Fillmore) City..............518
Oteneagen (Itasca) Township..............531
Otisco (Waseca) Township..............607
Otrey (Big Stone) Township..............492
Otsego (Wright) Township..............615
Ottawa (Le Sueur) Township..............542
Ottertail (Otter Tail) City..............567
Otter Tail (Otter Tail) Township..............567
Otter Tail County..............565
Otter Tail Peninsula (Cass) Township..............500
Otto (Otter Tail) Township..............567
Owatonna (Steele) City..............598

Owatonna (Steele) Township.............598
Owens (St. Louis) Township 590
Oxford (Isanti) Township 529
Paddock (Otter Tail) Township..........567
Page (Mille Lacs) Township 553
Palisade (Aitkin) City........................484
Palmer (Sherburne) Township 593
Palmville (Roseau) Township 586
Palmyra (Renville) Township.............582
Park (Pine) Township 570
Parke (Clay) Township 505
Parker (Marshall) Township 548
Parker (Morrison) Township 555
Parkers Prairie (Otter Tail) City 567
Parkers Prairie (Otter Tail)
 Township..567
Park Rapids (Hubbard) City 528
Parnell (Polk) Township 574
Parnell (Traverse) Township 603
Partridge (Pine) Township.................570
Paxton (Redwood) Township 580
Payne (St. Louis) Township 590
Paynesville (Stearns) City 596
Paynesville (Stearns) Township 596
Peace (Kanabec) Township 534
Pease (Mille Lacs) City......................553
Pelan (Kittson) Township..................537
Pelican (Crow Wing) Township 510
Pelican (Otter Tail) Township 567
Pelican Lake (Grant) Township 523
Pelican Rapids (Otter Tail) City 567
Pemberton (Blue Earth) City 494
Pembina (Mahnomen) Township......546
Penn (McLeod) Township 551
Pennington County.............................568
Pennock (Kandiyohi) City.................536
Pepin (Wabasha) Township 605
Pepperton (Stevens) Township 599
Pequaywan (St. Louis) Township......590
Pequot Lakes (Crow Wing) City 510
Perch Lake (Carlton) Township 497
Percy (Kittson) Township..................537
Perham (Otter Tail) City 567
Perham (Otter Tail) Township 567
Perley (Norman) City 562
Perry (Lac qui Parle) Township 540
Perry Lake (Crow Wing) Township ..510
Petersburg (Jackson) Township 533
Peterson (Fillmore) City....................518
Pickerel Lake (Freeborn) Township ..520
Pierz (Morrison) City........................555
Pierz (Morrison) Township................555
Pike (St. Louis) Township 590
Pike Bay (Cass) Township.................500
Pike Creek (Morrison) Township......555
Pillager (Cass) City...........................500
Pillsbury (Swift) Township 601
Pilot Grove (Faribault) Township......516
Pilot Mound (Fillmore) Township 518
Pine City (Pine) City........................570
Pine City (Pine) Township 571
Pine County......................................569
Pine Island (Goodhue) City 521
Pine Island (Goodhue) Township 521
Pine Island (Olmsted) City................564
Pine Lake (Cass) Township 500
Pine Lake (Clearwater) Township 507
Pine Lake (Otter Tail) Township 567
Pine Lake (Pine) Township 571
Pine Point (Becker) Township 487
Pine River (Cass) City.......................500
Pine River (Cass) Township 500
Pine Springs (Washington) City 609
Pipestone (Pipestone) City.................572
Pipestone County..............................571

Plainview (Wabasha) City 605
Plainview (Wabasha) Township 605
Plato (McLeod) City.........................551
Platte (Morrison) Township 555
Platte Lake (Crow Wing) Township..510
Pleasant Grove (Olmsted) Township 564
Pleasant Hill (Winona) Township 613
Pleasant Lake (Stearns) City 596
Pleasant Mound (Blue Earth)
 Township.. 494
Pleasant Prairie (Martin) Township..549
Pleasant Valley (Mower) Township...557
Pleasant View (Norman) Township ..562
Pliny (Aitkin) Township 484
Plummer (Red Lake) City.................578
Plymouth (Hennepin) City 525
Pohlitz (Roseau) Township 586
Pokegama (Pine) Township 571
Polk Centre (Pennington) Township.569
Polk County......................................572
Polonia (Roseau) Township 586
Pomme de Terre (Grant) Township..523
Pomroy (Itasca) Township 531
Pomroy (Kanabec) Township 534
Ponemah (Beltrami) CDP 489
Ponto Lake (Cass) Township.............500
Pope County.....................................575
Poplar (Cass) Township 501
Poplar Grove (Roseau) Township 586
Poplar River (Red Lake) Township ..578
Popple (Clearwater) Township 507
Popple Grove (Mahnomen)
 Township.. 546
Poppleton (Kittson) Township 537
Portage (St. Louis) Township 590
Porter (Yellow Medicine) City 616
Port Hope (Beltrami) Township........489
Posen (Yellow Medicine) Township..617
Potshot Lake (St. Louis) Pop. Place .590
Powers (Cass) Township....................501
Prairie Lake (St. Louis) Township 590
Prairie View (Wilkin) Township 612
Prairieville (Brown) Township..........495
Preble (Fillmore) Township...............518
Prescott (Faribault) Township 516
Preston (Fillmore) City......................518
Preston (Fillmore) Township 518
Preston Lake (Renville) Township 582
Princeton (Mille Lacs) City...............554
Princeton (Mille Lacs) Township 554
Princeton (Sherburne) City 593
Prinsburg (Kandiyohi) City...............536
Prior (Big Stone) Township 492
Prior Lake (Scott) City 592
Proctor (St. Louis) City.....................590
Providence (Lac qui Parle)
 Township.. 540
Pulaski (Morrison) Township............555
Quamba (Kanabec) City....................534
Queen (Polk) Township 574
Quincy (Olmsted) Township 564
Quiring (Beltrami) Township 489
Rabbit Lake (Crow Wing) Township 510
Racine (Mower) City 557
Racine (Mower) Township 557
Rail Prairie (Morrison) Township.....555
Rainy Lake (Koochiching) Pop.
 Place... 539
Ramsey (Anoka) City 486
Ramsey County................................577
Randall (Morrison) City....................555
Randolph (Dakota) City....................512
Randolph (Dakota) Township 512
Ranier (Koochiching) City 539
Ransom (Nobles) Township 561

Rapidan (Blue Earth) Township........494
Ravenna (Dakota) Township.............512
Raymond (Kandiyohi) City...............536
Raymond (Stearns) Township 596
Redby (Beltrami) CDP 489
Red Eye (Wadena) Township 606
Red Lake (Beltrami) CDP.................489
Red Lake County.............................578
Red Lake Falls (Red Lake) City........578
Red Lake Falls (Red Lake)
 Township..578
Redpath (Traverse) Township 603
Red Rock (Mower) Township 557
Red Wing (Goodhue) City 521
Redwood County.............................579
Redwood Falls (Redwood) City 580
Redwood Falls (Redwood)
 Township..580
Regal (Kandiyohi) City......................536
Reine (Roseau) Township 586
Reiner (Pennington) Township 569
Reis (Polk) Township 574
Remer (Cass) City..............................501
Remer (Cass) Township.....................501
Rendsville (Stevens) Township 599
Reno (Pope) Township 576
Renville (Renville) City.....................582
Renville County...............................581
Revere (Redwood) City 580
Reynolds (Todd) Township 602
Rheiderland (Chippewa) Township..502
Rhinehart (Polk) Township 574
Rice (Benton) City............................491
Rice (Clearwater) Township 507
Rice County......................................582
Rice Lake (St. Louis) Township 590
Riceland (Freeborn) Township..........520
Rice River (Aitkin) Township 484
Riceville (Becker) Township 487
Richardson (Morrison) Township 555
Richardville (Kittson) Township........537
Richfield (Hennepin) City.................525
Richland (Rice) Township 583
Richmond (Stearns) City...................596
Richmond (Winona) Township.........613
Rich Valley (McLeod) Township......551
Richville (Otter Tail) City 567
Richwood (Becker) Township 487
Ridgely (Nicollet) Township 560
Ripley (Dodge) Township 513
Ripley (Morrison) Township 555
River (Red Lake) Township 578
Riverdale (Watonwan) Township......610
River Falls (Pennington) Township ..569
Riverside (Lac qui Parle) Township .540
Riverton (Clay) Township 505
Riverton (Crow Wing) City...............510
Robbinsdale (Hennepin) City............525
Roberts (Wilkin) Township 612
Rochester (Olmsted) City..................564
Rochester (Olmsted) Township.........564
Rock (Pipestone) Township 572
Rock County.....................................584
Rock Creek (Pine) City 571
Rock Dell (Olmsted) Township.........564
Rockford (Hennepin) City.................525
Rockford (Wright) City 615
Rockford (Wright) Township 615
Rock Lake (Lyon) Township 545
Rocksbury (Pennington) Township...569
Rockville (Stearns) City.....................597
Rockville (Stearns) Township............597
Rockwell (Norman) Township 563
Rockwood (Hubbard) Township.......528
Rockwood (Wadena) Township.........606

MINNESOTA

Rogers (Cass) Township 501
Rogers (Hennepin) City 525
Rolling Forks (Pope) Township 576
Rolling Green (Martin) Township 549
Rollingstone (Winona) City 613
Rollingstone (Winona) Township 613
Rollis (Marshall) Township 548
Rome (Faribault) Township 516
Ronneby (Benton) City 491
Roome (Polk) Township 575
Roosevelt (Beltrami) Township 489
Roosevelt (Crow Wing) Township 511
Roosevelt (Lake of the Woods) City .541
Roosevelt (Roseau) City 586
Roscoe (Goodhue) Township 521
Roscoe (Stearns) City 597
Roseau (Roseau) City 586
Roseau County 585
Rosebud (Polk) Township 575
Rose Creek (Mower) City 557
Rosedale (Mahnomen) Township 546
Rose Dell (Rock) Township 584
Rose Hill (Cottonwood) Township 508
Roseland (Kandiyohi) Township 536
Rosemount (Dakota) City 512
Rosendale (Watonwan) Township 610
Roseville (Grant) Township 523
Roseville (Kandiyohi) Township 536
Roseville (Ramsey) City 577
Rosewood (Chippewa) Township 502
Rosing (Morrison) Township 555
Ross (Roseau) Township 586
Ross Lake (Crow Wing) Township ...511
Rost (Jackson) Township 533
Rothsay (Otter Tail) City 567
Rothsay (Wilkin) City 612
Round Grove (McLeod) Township 551
Round Lake (Becker) Township 487
Round Lake (Jackson) Township 533
Round Lake (Nobles) City 561
Round Prairie (Todd) Township 602
Royal (Lincoln) Township 543
Royalton (Morrison) City 555
Royalton (Pine) Township 571
Runeberg (Becker) Township 487
Rush City (Chisago) City 503
Rushford (Fillmore) City 518
Rushford Village (Fillmore) City 518
Rush Lake (Otter Tail) Township 567
Rushmore (Nobles) City 561
Rushseba (Chisago) Township 503
Russell (Lyon) City 545
Russia (Polk) Township 575
Ruthton (Pipestone) City 572
Rutland (Martin) Township 550
Rutledge (Pine) City 571
Sabin (Clay) City 505
Sacred Heart (Renville) City 582
Sacred Heart (Renville) Township 582
Sago (Itasca) Township 532
St. Anthony (Hennepin) City 525
St. Anthony (Ramsey) City 577
St. Anthony (Stearns) City 597
St. Augusta (Stearns) Township 597
St. Bonifacius (Hennepin) City 525
St. Charles (Winona) City 613
St. Charles (Winona) Township 613
St. Clair (Blue Earth) City 494
St. Cloud (Benton) City 491
St. Cloud (Sherburne) City 593
St. Cloud (Stearns) City 597
St. Cloud (Stearns) Township 597
St. Francis (Anoka) City 486
St. George (Benton) Township 491
St. Hilaire (Pennington) City 569

St. James (Watonwan) City 610
St. James (Watonwan) Township 610
St. Johns (Kandiyohi) Township 536
St. Joseph (Kittson) Township 537
St. Joseph (Stearns) City 597
St. Joseph (Stearns) Township 597
St. Lawrence (Scott) Township 592
St. Leo (Yellow Medicine) City 617
St. Louis County 587
St. Louis Park (Hennepin) City 525
St. Martin (Stearns) City 597
St. Martin (Stearns) Township 597
St. Mary (Waseca) Township 607
St. Marys Point (Washington) City ...609
St. Mathias (Crow Wing) Township ..511
St. Michael (Wright) City 615
St. Olaf (Otter Tail) Township 567
St. Paul (Ramsey) City 577
St. Paul Park (Washington) City 609
St. Peter (Nicollet) City 560
St. Rosa (Stearns) City 597
St. Stephen (Stearns) City 597
St. Vincent (Kittson) City 538
St. Vincent (Kittson) Township 538
St. Wendel (Stearns) Township 597
Salem (Cass) Township 501
Salem (Olmsted) Township 564
Salo (Aitkin) Township 484
Sanborn (Redwood) City 580
Sand Creek (Scott) Township 592
Sanders (Pennington) Township 569
Sand Lake (Itasca) Township 532
Sand Lake (St. Louis) Pop. Place 591
Sandnes (Yellow Medicine)
  Township 617
Sandstone (Pine) City 571
Sandstone (Pine) Township 571
Sandsville (Polk) Township 575
Sandy (St. Louis) Township 591
Sanford (Grant) Township 523
San Francisco (Carver) Township 498
Santiago (Sherburne) Township 593
Saratoga (Winona) Township 613
Sargeant (Mower) City 557
Sargeant (Mower) Township 557
Sartell (Benton) City 491
Sartell (Stearns) City 597
Sauk Centre (Stearns) City 597
Sauk Centre (Stearns) Township 597
Sauk Rapids (Benton) City 491
Sauk Rapids (Benton) Township 491
Savage (Scott) City 592
Savannah (Becker) Township 487
Scambler (Otter Tail) Township 567
Scandia (Polk) Township 575
Scandia Valley (Morrison) Township 556
Scanlon (Carlton) City 497
Schoolcraft (Hubbard) Township 528
Schroeder (Cook) Township 507
Sciota (Dakota) Township 512
Scott (Stevens) Township 599
Scott County 591
Seaforth (Redwood) City 580
Seavey (Aitkin) Township 484
Sebeka (Wadena) City 606
Sedan (Pope) City 576
Seely (Faribault) Township 516
Selma (Cottonwood) Township 508
Severance (Sibley) Township 594
Seward (Nobles) Township 561
Shafer (Chisago) City 504
Shafer (Chisago) Township 504
Shakopee (Scott) City 592
Shamrock (Aitkin) Township 484
Shaokatan (Lincoln) Township 543

Sharon (Le Sueur) Township 542
Shelburne (Lyon) Township 545
Shelby (Blue Earth) Township 494
Sheldon (Houston) Township 527
Shell Lake (Becker) Township 487
Shell River (Wadena) Township 606
Shell Rock (Freeborn) Township 520
Shelly (Norman) City 563
Shelly (Norman) Township 563
Sherburn (Martin) City 550
Sherburne County 592
Sheridan (Redwood) Township 580
Sherman (Redwood) Township 580
Shetek (Murray) Township 559
Shevlin (Clearwater) City 507
Shevlin (Clearwater) Township 507
Shible (Swift) Township 601
Shieldsville (Rice) Township 583
Shingobee (Cass) Township 501
Shooks (Beltrami) Township 489
Shoreview (Ramsey) City 577
Shorewood (Hennepin) City 525
Shotley (Beltrami) Township 489
Shotley Brook (Beltrami) Pop. Place 490
Sibley (Crow Wing) Township 511
Sibley (Sibley) Township 594
Sibley County 593
Sigel (Brown) Township 495
Silver (Carlton) Township 497
Silver Bay (Lake) City 541
Silver Brook (Carlton) Township 497
Silver Creek (Lake) Township 541
Silver Creek (Wright) Township 615
Silver Lake (Martin) Township 550
Silver Lake (McLeod) City 551
Silver Leaf (Becker) Township 487
Silverton (Pennington) Township 569
Sinclair (Clearwater) Township 507
Sinnott (Marshall) Township 548
Sioux Agency (Yellow Medicine)
  Township 617
Sioux Valley (Jackson) Township 533
Six Mile Grove (Swift) Township 601
Skagen (Roseau) Township 586
Skandia (Murray) Township 559
Skane (Kittson) Township 538
Skelton (Carlton) Township 497
Skree (Clay) Township 505
Skyline (Blue Earth) City 494
Slater (Cass) Township 501
Slayton (Murray) City 559
Slayton (Murray) Township 559
Sleepy Eye (Brown) City 495
Sletten (Polk) Township 575
Smiley (Pennington) Township 569
Smoky Hollow (Cass) Township 501
Sobieski (Morrison) City 556
Sodus (Lyon) Township 545
Solem (Douglas) Township 515
Soler (Roseau) Township 586
Solway (Beltrami) City 490
Solway (St. Louis) Township 591
Somerset (Steele) Township 598
South Bend (Blue Earth) Township ..494
South Branch (Watonwan)
  Township 610
Southbrook (Cottonwood) Township 508
South Clearwater (Clearwater) Pop.
  Place 507
Southeast Aitkin (Aitkin) Pop. Place 484
Southeast Mahnomen (Mahnomen)
  Pop. Place 546
Southeast Roseau (Roseau) Pop.
  Place 586
South Fork (Kanabec) Township 534

South Harbor (Mille Lacs) Township 554
South Haven (Wright) City 615
South Koochiching (Koochiching) Pop. Place 539
South Red River (Kittson) Township 538
Southside (Wright) Township 615
South St. Paul (Dakota) City 512
Spalding (Aitkin) Township 484
Spang (Itasca) Township 532
Sparta (Chippewa) Township 502
Spencer (Aitkin) Township 484
Spencer Brook (Isanti) Township 529
Spicer (Kandiyohi) City 536
Splithand (Itasca) Township 532
Split Rock (Carlton) Township 497
Spring Brook (Kittson) Township 538
Spring Creek (Becker) Township 487
Spring Creek (Norman) Township 563
Springdale (Redwood) Township 580
Springfield (Brown) City 495
Springfield (Cottonwood) Township 508
Spring Grove (Houston) City 527
Spring Grove (Houston) Township 527
Spring Hill (Stearns) City 597
Spring Hill (Stearns) Township 597
Spring Lake (Scott) Township 592
Spring Lake Park (Anoka) City 486
Spring Lake Park (Ramsey) City 577
Spring Park (Hennepin) City 525
Spring Prairie (Clay) Township 506
Springvale (Isanti) Township 529
Spring Valley (Fillmore) City 518
Spring Valley (Fillmore) Township 518
Springwater (Rock) Township 584
Spruce (Roseau) Township 586
Spruce Grove (Becker) Township 487
Spruce Grove (Beltrami) Township 490
Spruce Hill (Douglas) Township 515
Spruce Valley (Marshall) Township 548
Squaw Lake (Itasca) City 532
Stacy (Chisago) City 504
Stafford (Roseau) Township 586
Stanchfield (Isanti) Township 529
Stanford (Isanti) Township 529
Stanley (Lyon) Township 545
Stanton (Goodhue) Township 521
Staples (Todd) City 602
Staples (Todd) Township 602
Staples (Wadena) City 606
Star (Pennington) Township 569
Starbuck (Pope) City 576
Stark (Brown) Township 495
Star Lake (Otter Tail) Township 567
Stately (Brown) Township 495
Steamboat River (Hubbard) Township 528
Stearns County 595
Steele County 598
Steen (Rock) City 584
Steenerson (Beltrami) Township 490
Stephen (Marshall) City 548
Sterling (Blue Earth) Township 494
Stevens (Stevens) Township 599
Stevens County 599
Stewart (McLeod) City 551
Stewartville (Olmsted) City 564
Stillwater (Washington) City 609
Stillwater (Washington) Township 609
Stockholm (Wright) Township 615
Stockton (Winona) City 613
Stokes (Itasca) Township 532
Stokes (Roseau) Township 586
Stoneham (Chippewa) Township 502

Stoney Brook (St. Louis) Township 591
Stony Brook (Grant) Township 523
Stony River (Lake) Township 541
Stony Run (Yellow Medicine) Township 617
Storden (Cottonwood) City 508
Storden (Cottonwood) Township 509
Stowe Prairie (Todd) Township 602
Straight River (Hubbard) Township 528
Strand (Norman) Township 563
Strandquist (Marshall) City 548
Strathcona (Roseau) City 586
Sturgeon (St. Louis) Township 591
Sturgeon Lake (Pine) City 571
Sturgeon Lake (Pine) Township 571
Sugar Bush (Becker) Township 487
Sugar Bush (Beltrami) Township 490
Sullivan (Polk) Township 575
Summit (Beltrami) Township 490
Summit (Steele) Township 598
Summit Lake (Nobles) Township 561
Sumner (Fillmore) Township 518
Sumter (McLeod) Township 551
Sunburg (Kandiyohi) City 536
Sundal (Norman) Township 563
Sundown (Redwood) Township 580
Sunfish Lake (Dakota) City 512
Sunnyside (Wilkin) Township 612
Sunrise (Chisago) Township 504
Svea (Kittson) Township 538
Sverdrup (Otter Tail) Township 568
Swan Lake (Stevens) Township 599
Swan River (Morrison) Township 556
Swanville (Morrison) City 556
Swanville (Morrison) Township 556
Swede Grove (Meeker) Township 552
Swede Prairie (Yellow Medicine) Township 617
Swedes Forest (Redwood) Township 580
Sweet (Pipestone) Township 572
Swenoda (Swift) Township 601
Swift County 600
Sylvan (Cass) Township 501
Synnes (Stevens) Township 599
Tabor (Polk) Township 575
Taconite (Itasca) City 532
Tamarac (Marshall) Township 548
Tamarack (Aitkin) City 484
Tanberg (Wilkin) Township 612
Tansem (Clay) Township 506
Taopi (Mower) City 557
Tara (Swift) Township 601
Tara (Traverse) Township 603
Taunton (Lyon) City 545
Taylor (Beltrami) Township 490
Taylor (Traverse) Township 603
Taylors Falls (Chisago) City 504
Tegner (Kittson) Township 538
Teien (Kittson) Township 538
Tenhassen (Martin) Township 550
Ten Lake (Beltrami) Township 490
Ten Mile Lake (Lac qui Parle) Township 540
Tenney (Wilkin) City 612
Tenstrike (Beltrami) City 490
Terrebonne (Red Lake) Township 578
Thief Lake (Marshall) Township 548
Thief River Falls (Pennington) City 569
Third River (Itasca) Township 532
Thomastown (Wadena) Township 606
Thompson (Kittson) Township 538
Thomson (Carlton) City 497
Thomson (Carlton) Township 497
Thorpe (Hubbard) Township 528
Three Lakes (Redwood) Township 580

Thunder Lake (Cass) Township 501
Tilden (Polk) Township 575
Timothy (Crow Wing) Township 511
Tintah (Traverse) City 603
Tintah (Traverse) Township 603
Toad Lake (Becker) Township 487
Todd (Hubbard) Township 528
Todd County 601
Tofte (Cook) Township 507
Toivola (St. Louis) Township 591
Tonka Bay (Hennepin) City 525
Toqua (Big Stone) Township 492
Tordenskjold (Otter Tail) Township 568
Torning (Swift) Township 601
Torrey (Cass) Township 501
Tower (St. Louis) City 591
Tracy (Lyon) City 545
Trail (Polk) City 575
Transit (Sibley) Township 594
Traverse (Nicollet) Township 560
Traverse County 603
Trelipe (Cass) Township 501
Trimont (Martin) City 550
Trommald (Crow Wing) City 511
Trondhjem (Otter Tail) Township 568
Trosky (Pipestone) City 572
Trout Lake (Itasca) Township 532
Troy (Pipestone) Township 572
Troy (Renville) Township 582
Truman (Martin) City 550
Tumuli (Otter Tail) Township 568
Tunsberg (Chippewa) Township 502
Turner (Aitkin) Township 484
Turtle Creek (Todd) Township 602
Turtle Lake (Beltrami) Township 490
Turtle Lake (Cass) Township 501
Turtle River (Beltrami) City 490
Turtle River (Beltrami) Township 490
Twin Lakes (Carlton) Township 497
Twin Lakes (Freeborn) City 520
Twin Lakes (Mahnomen) Township 546
Twin Valley (Norman) City 563
Two Harbors (Lake) City 541
Two Inlets (Becker) Township 488
Two Rivers (Morrison) Township 556
Tyler (Lincoln) City 543
Tynsid (Polk) Township 575
Tyro (Yellow Medicine) Township 617
Tyrone (Le Sueur) Township 542
Udolpho (Mower) Township 557
Ulen (Clay) City 506
Ulen (Clay) Township 506
Underwood (Otter Tail) City 568
Underwood (Redwood) Township 580
Union (Houston) Township 527
Union Grove (Meeker) Township 552
Upper Red Lake (Beltrami) Pop. Place 490
Upsala (Morrison) City 556
Urbank (Otter Tail) City 568
Urness (Douglas) Township 515
Utica (Winona) City 613
Utica (Winona) Township 613
Vadnais Heights (Ramsey) City 578
Vail (Redwood) Township 580
Vallers (Lyon) Township 545
Valley (Marshall) Township 548
Van Buren (St. Louis) Township 591
Vasa (Goodhue) Township 521
Vega (Marshall) Township 548
Veldt (Marshall) Township 548
Verdi (Lincoln) Township 543
Verdon (Aitkin) Township 484
Vergas (Otter Tail) City 568

MINNESOTA

Vermilion Lake (St. Louis) Township 591
Vermillion (Dakota) City 512
Vermillion (Dakota) Township 512
Verndale (Wadena) City 606
Vernon (Dodge) Township 513
Vernon Center (Blue Earth) City 494
Vernon Center (Blue Earth) Township 494
Verona (Faribault) Township 516
Vesta (Redwood) City 580
Vesta (Redwood) Township 580
Victor (Wright) Township 615
Victoria (Carver) City 498
Viding (Clay) Township 506
Vienna (Rock) Township 585
Viking (Marshall) City 548
Viking (Marshall) Township 548
Villard (Pope) City 576
Villard (Todd) Township 602
Vineland (Mille Lacs) CDP 554
Vineland (Polk) Township 575
Vining (Otter Tail) City 568
Viola (Olmsted) Township 564
Virginia (St. Louis) City 591
Vivian (Waseca) Township 607
Waasa (St. Louis) Township 591
Wabana (Itasca) Township 532
Wabasha (Wabasha) City 605
Wabasha County 604
Wabasso (Redwood) City 580
Wabedo (Cass) Township 501
Waconia (Carver) City 498
Waconia (Carver) Township 498
Wacouta (Goodhue) Township 521
Wadena (Otter Tail) City 568
Wadena (Wadena) City 606
Wadena (Wadena) Township 606
Wadena County 605
Wagner (Aitkin) Township 484
Wahkon (Mille Lacs) City 554
Wahnena (Cass) Township 501
Waite Park (Stearns) City 597
Wakefield (Stearns) Township 597
Walcott (Rice) Township 583
Walden (Cass) Township 501
Walden (Pope) Township 576
Waldorf (Waseca) City 607
Walker (Cass) City 501
Walls (Traverse) Township 604
Walnut Grove (Redwood) City 580
Walnut Lake (Faribault) Township ... 516
Walter (Lac qui Parle) Township 540
Walters (Faribault) City 516
Waltham (Mower) City 557
Waltham (Mower) Township 557
Walworth (Becker) Township 488
Wanamingo (Goodhue) City 521
Wanamingo (Goodhue) Township 521
Wanda (Redwood) City 580
Wang (Renville) Township 582
Wanger (Marshall) Township 548
Warba (Itasca) City 532
Ward (Todd) Township 603
Warren (Marshall) City 548
Warren (Winona) Township 613
Warrenton (Marshall) Township 548
Warroad (Roseau) City 586
Warsaw (Goodhue) Township 522
Warsaw (Rice) Township 583
Waseca (Waseca) City 607
Waseca County 607
Washington (Le Sueur) Township ... 542
Washington County 608
Washington Lake (Sibley) Township .594

Wasioja (Dodge) Township 513
Waskish (Beltrami) Township 490
Watab (Benton) Township 491
Waterbury (Redwood) Township ... 580
Waterford (Dakota) Township 512
Watertown (Carver) City 498
Watertown (Carver) Township 498
Waterville (Le Sueur) City 542
Waterville (Le Sueur) Township 542
Watkins (Meeker) City 552
Watonwan County 609
Watopa (Wabasha) Township 605
Watson (Chippewa) City 503
Waubun (Mahnomen) City 546
Waukenabo (Aitkin) Township 484
Waukon (Norman) Township 563
Waverly (Martin) Township 550
Waverly (Wright) City 615
Wawina (Itasca) Township 532
Wayzata (Hennepin) City 525
Wealthwood (Aitkin) Township 484
Webster (Rice) Township 583
Weimer (Jackson) Township 533
Welch (Goodhue) Township 522
Welcome (Martin) City 550
Wellington (Renville) Township 582
Wells (Faribault) City 516
Wells (Rice) Township 583
Wendell (Grant) City 523
Wergeland (Yellow Medicine) Township 617
West Albany (Wabasha) Township ... 605
West Bank (Swift) Township 601
Westbrook (Cottonwood) City 509
Westbrook (Cottonwood) Township .. 509
West Concord (Dodge) City 513
West Cook (Cook) Pop. Place 507
West Crow Wing (Crow Wing) Pop. Place 511
Westerheim (Lyon) Township 545
Western (Otter Tail) Township 568
Westfield (Dodge) Township 513
Westford (Martin) Township 550
West Heron Lake (Jackson) Township 533
West Lakeland (Washington) Township 609
Westline (Redwood) Township 580
West Newton (Nicollet) Township ... 560
Westport (Pope) City 576
Westport (Pope) Township 576
Westside (Nobles) Township 561
West St. Paul (Dakota) City 512
West Union (Todd) City 603
West Union (Todd) Township 603
West Valley (Marshall) Township .. 548
Whalan (Fillmore) City 518
Wheatland (Rice) Township 583
Wheaton (Traverse) City 604
Wheeling (Rice) Township 583
White (St. Louis) Township 591
White Bear (Ramsey) Township 578
White Bear Lake (Pope) Township ... 576
White Bear Lake (Ramsey) City 578
White Bear Lake (Washington) City .609
Whited (Kanabec) Township 534
White Earth (Becker) Township 488
Whiteface Reservoir (St. Louis) Pop. Place 591
Whitefield (Kandiyohi) Township ... 536
Whiteford (Marshall) Township 548
White Oak (Hubbard) Township ... 528
White Pine (Aitkin) Township 484
Whitewater (Winona) Township ... 613
Wilder (Jackson) City 533

American Places Dictionary

Wild Rice (Norman) Township 563
Wildwood (Itasca) Township 532
Wilkin County 611
Wilkinson (Cass) Township 501
Willernie (Washington) City 609
Williams (Aitkin) Township 484
Williams (Lake of the Woods) City .. 541
Willmar (Kandiyohi) City 536
Willmar (Kandiyohi) Township 536
Willow Lake (Redwood) Township .. 580
Willow River (Pine) City 571
Willow Valley (St. Louis) Township .591
Wilma (Pine) Township 571
Wilmington (Houston) Township ... 527
Wilmont (Nobles) City 561
Wilmont (Nobles) Township 561
Wilson (Cass) Township 501
Wilson (Winona) Township 613
Wilton (Beltrami) City 490
Wilton (Waseca) Township 607
Winchester (Norman) Township ... 563
Windemere (Pine) Township 571
Windom (Cottonwood) City 509
Windom (Mower) Township 557
Windsor (Traverse) Township 604
Winfield (Renville) Township 582
Winger (Polk) City 575
Winger (Polk) Township 575
Wing River (Wadena) Township ... 606
Winnebago (Faribault) City 516
Winnebago (Houston) Township ... 527
Winnebago City (Faribault) Township 516
Winona (Winona) City 613
Winona (Winona) Township 613
Winona County 612
Winsor (Clearwater) Township 507
Winsted (McLeod) City 551
Winsted (McLeod) Township 551
Winthrop (Sibley) City 594
Winton (St. Louis) City 591
Wirt (Itasca) Township 532
Wisconsin (Jackson) Township 533
Wiscoy (Winona) Township 614
Wolf Lake (Becker) City 488
Wolf Lake (Becker) Township 488
Wolford (Crow Wing) Township ... 511
Wolverton (Wilkin) City 612
Wolverton (Wilkin) Township 612
Woodbury (Washington) City 609
Wood Lake (Yellow Medicine) City ..617
Wood Lake (Yellow Medicine) Township 617
Woodland (Hennepin) City 526
Woodland (Wright) Township 615
Woodrow (Beltrami) Township 490
Woodrow (Cass) Township 501
Woods (Chippewa) Township 503
Woodside (Otter Tail) Township ... 568
Woodside (Polk) Township 575
Woodstock (Pipestone) City 572
Woodville (Waseca) Township 607
Workman (Aitkin) Township 485
Worthington (Nobles) City 561
Worthington (Nobles) Township ... 561
Wrenshall (Carlton) City 497
Wrenshall (Carlton) Township 497
Wright (Carlton) City 497
Wright (Marshall) Township 548
Wright County 614
Wuori (St. Louis) Township 591
Wyandotte (Pennington) Township ..569
Wyanett (Isanti) Township 529
Wykeham (Todd) Township 603
Wykoff (Fillmore) City 518

Wylie (Red Lake) Township..............578
Wyoming (Chisago) City....................504
Wyoming (Chisago) Township..........504
Yellow Bank (Lac qui Parle) Township..540
Yellow Medicine County....................*616*

York (Fillmore) Township..................*518*
Young America (Carver) City..........*498*
Young America (Carver) Township...*498*
Yucatan (Houston) Township..........*527*
Zemple (Itasca) City..........................*532*
Zimmerman (Sherburne) City..........*593*

Zion (Stearns) Township....................*597*
Zumbro (Wabasha) Township..........*605*
Zumbro Falls (Wabasha) City..........*605*
Zumbrota (Goodhue) City.................*522*
Zumbrota (Goodhue) Township........*522*

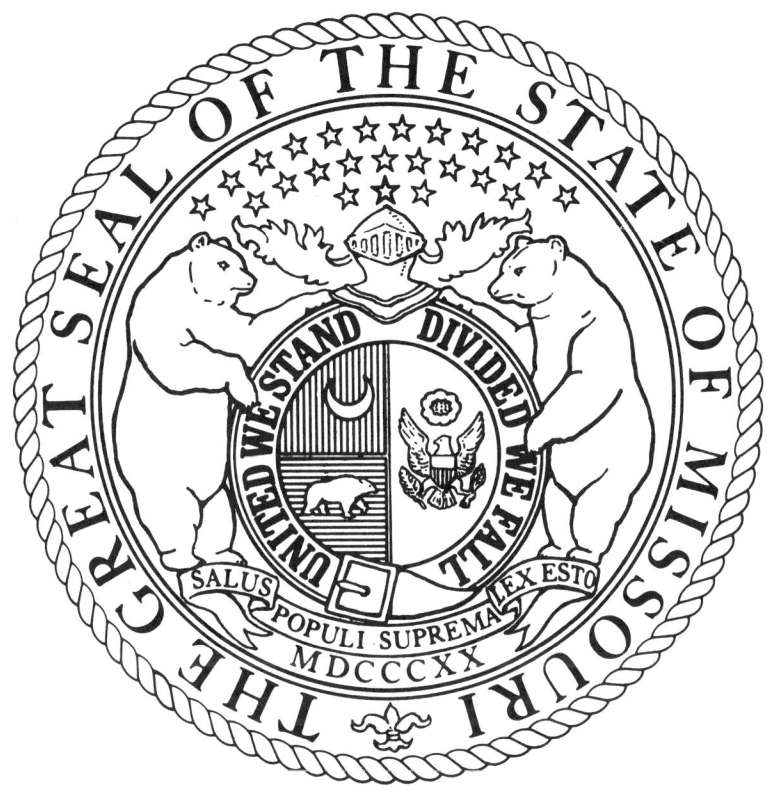

Missouri

MISSOURI

Missouri

Population: 5,117,073 (1990); 4,916,686 (1980)
Population rank (1990): 15
Percent population change (1980-1990): 4.1
Population projection: 5,369,000 (1995); 5,495,000 (2000)

Area: total 69,709 sq. mi.; 68,898 sq. mi. land, 811 sq. mi. water
Area rank: 21
Highest elevation: 1,772 ft., Taum Sauk Mountain (Iron County)
Lowest point: 230 ft. along the St. Francis River near Cardwell (Dunklin County)

State capital: Jefferson City (Cole County)
Largest city: Kansas City (435,146)
Second largest city: St. Louis (396,685)
Largest county: St. Louis (993,529)

Total housing units: 2,199,129
No. of occupied housing units: 1,961,206
Vacant housing units (%): 10.8
Distribution of population by race and Hispanic origin (%):
　White: 87.7
　Black: 10.7
　Hispanic (any race): 1.2
　Native American: 0.4
　Asian/Pacific: 0.8
　Other: 0.4

Admission date: August 10, 1821 (24th state).

Location: In the central United States, bordering Arkansas, Oklahoma, Kansas, Nebraska, Iowa, Illinois, Kentucky, and Tennessee.

Name Origin: For the Missouri River, which forms part of its western border and crosses it in an easterly direction. The name is either that of an Indian tribe that lived near the mouth of the river, or possibly a word meaning 'owners of big canoes.' As recorded in a French text in 1673, the Indian name for the river was *Pekitanoul* or *Pokitanou* 'muddy water'; its nickname is "Big Muddy."

State bird: bluebird *(Sialia sialis)*
State flower: hawthorn blossom
State fossil: crinoid
State insect: honeybee
State mineral: galena
State musical instrument: fiddle
State rock: mozarkite (chert or flint rock)
State song: "Missouri Waltz"
State tree: flowering dogwood *(Cornus florida)*

State tree nut: Eastern black walnut *(Juglans nigra)*

State motto: *Salus populi suprema lex esto* (Latin 'The welfare of the people shall be the supreme law')
State nicknames: Show Me State; Mother of the West

Area codes: 314 (St. Louis and east), 417 (Springfield and southwest), 816 (Kansas City and northwest)
Time zone: Central
Abbreviations: MO (postal); Mo. (traditional)
Part of (region): Midwest

Local Government

Counties

Missouri has 114 counties, governed by county commissioners.

Municipalities

There are 942 municipalities, most of which have a mayor-council form of government, and 325 townships in Missouri. Further local administration is provided by 557 school districts and 1,195 special districts. St. Louis is an independent city and is not part of any county.

Settlement History and Early Development

The area of present-day Missouri has been inhabited for about 4,000 years. The first Europeans, who arrived in the late seventeenth century, found Sauk, Fox, Iliniwek (Illinois), Osage, Missouri, Iowa, and Kansas Indians, most of whom had been pushed across the Mississippi River by rival eastern tribes and early European settlers.

Probably the first white men to explore the region were the French Jesuit missionary Fr. Jacques Marquette and a fur trader, Louis Jolliet, who in 1673 marked the spot where the Missouri River joins the Mississippi. In 1682 Robert Cavelier, Sieur de La Salle, claimed all the lands drained by the Mississippi for France, and named it Louisiana for King Louis XIV. They were followed by other missionaries, trappers, and lead and salt miners. About 1700 French missionaries founded the first white settlement near the present site of St. Louis, but it was abandoned three years later because of the unhealthy nearby swamps. Settlers from present-day Illinois established the first permanent white settlement in Missouri at Ste. Genevieve. In 1764, Pierre Laclède Liguest and René August Chouteau founded St. Louis.

Territorial Days and Statehood

At the end of the French and Indian Wars in 1763, France ceded all of its territory west of the Mississippi River to Spain. Spain encouraged new settlers by granting free land, relaxing restrictions against Protestants, and al-

MISSOURI

lowing slaveholders from the South to settle. One of the most notable newcomers was Daniel Boone, to whom Spain granted about 850 acres in St. Charles County in 1799 and, a year later, appointed a judge.

Spain fortified St. Louis and a few other outposts during the American Revolution and beat back a British-Indian attack on St. Louis in 1780, but otherwise the region was hardly affected by the war.

In 1800 Napoleon forced Spain to return Louisiana to France, and in 1803 the land that is now Missouri became part of the United States under the terms of the Louisiana Purchase. After Lewis and Clark's expedition in 1804-06 explored the Missouri River, St. Louis became "the gateway to the west" and was the point of departure for exploratory missions by Zebulon Pike (1805 and 1806), the Astorians (around 1811), and Stephen Long (1819). In 1812 the U.S. Congress organized the Missouri Territory, which then also included present-day Arkansas (organized separately in 1819). Farming and mining became well established.

During this period of settlement, however, the Indians became increasingly angered at the loss of their hunting grounds. When war broke out between Britain and the U.S. in 1812, the British armed the Indians and encouraged them to attack the pioneers. The raids continued even after the end of the war, and did not end until 1815. By 1836 few Indians remained, most tribes having signed treaties with the U.S. government to surrender their lands in Missouri and move into present-day Oklahoma.

Missouri petitioned for statehood in 1818, but because it expected to enter as a slave state, which would have upset the even balance in the U.S. Congress between slave and free states, permission was withheld. Three years later, Maine (a free state) and Missouri were admitted under the Missouri Compromise, which allowed slavery in the new state but banned it in the rest of the Louisiana Territory north of Missouri's southern border.

The Civil War

While black slaves comprised only five percent of Missouri's population (the lowest of any slave state except Delaware), there was nevertheless strong proslavery sentiment in the state. Those living on the western border frequently crossed into neighboring Kansas in the mid-1850s to help elect a proslavery government in that territory. Some were also active in the guerrilla warfare between proslavery and Free Stater forces, which gave the territory the nickname of "bleeding Kansas." Kansas became a free state in 1861 but the fighting continued into the Civil War.

In 1857 the U.S. Supreme Court ruled that Dred Scott, a Missouri slave temporarily brought to Minnesota, was merely property, did not have citizenship rights, and could not be freed. The decision exacerbated the slavery issue, voided the Missouri Compromise, and helped precipitate the Civil War.

Missouri remained with the Union during the war, but when it began, Gov. Claiborne Fox Jackson called out the state militia "to repel the invasion" of federal forces; he was deposed on July 30, 1861. Some 110,000 men from Missouri served with the Union and 40,000 with the Confederacy.

More battles were fought on Missouri soil than in any other states except Virginia and Tennessee. But even more destructive was the general lawlessness prevalent throughout the state. Quantrill's Raiders, Cole Younger's guerrillas, and Unionist freebooters murdered, burned, and looted without hindrance. This continued for almost twenty years after the war, when the lawlessness, typified by such outlaws as Jesse and Frank James, earned Missouri the epithet "Robber State."

At a constitutional convention in January 1865, Missouri became the first slave state to free all blacks.

Business and Industry

Fur trading, cotton, cattle, minerals (especially lead and zinc), and commerce (which grew sharply with the outfitting of wagon trains for the Santa Fe and Oregon trails) were all important to the economic development of the state. After the war, railroads replaced steamboat traffic, and the market economy shifted from St. Louis to Kansas City.

The Louisiana Purchase Exposition held in St. Louis in 1904 attracted almost 20 million visitors. In the first decade of the twentieth century Missouri passed progressive laws that regulated working conditions, child labor, and public utilities. During World War I Missouri's agriculture, mining, and manufacturing industries all provided material for the armed forces. Missouri's economy suffered during the Great Depression of the 1930s but rebounded during World War II, when Missouri developed new industries to meet military demands. Missouri's Harry S. Truman became president in 1945 when President Franklin D. Roosevelt died.

Since World War II Missouri's economy has become more diversified, with electronics, uranium-processing, and aerospace industries all being located in the state. Missouri faced serious problems in the 1970s and 1980s, including the middle-class flight from the cities to the suburbs, pollutants threatening the water supplies, and a drop in farming prices. However, the aerospace and tourism industries continue to be strong. Branson, Missouri has recently developed as a major center for musical concert theaters.

State Boundaries

Missouri was admitted to the Union with the northern, eastern, and southern boundaries as they are at present. The western boundary was along the meridian that now constitutes its western line below the Missouri River. In 1836 the Platte Country was purchased from the Indians, extending the northern part of Missouri's western border to the Missouri River, as at present.

Missouri Counties

Adair	Clay	Jackson	Morgan	Ste. Genevieve
Andrew	Clinton	Jasper	New Madrid	St. Francois
Atchison	Cole	Jefferson	Newton	St. Louis
Audrain	Cooper	Johnson	Nodaway	St. Louis Independent City
Barry	Crawford	Knox	Oregon	
Barton	Dade	Laclede	Osage	Saline
Bates	Dallas	Lafayette	Ozark	Schuyler
Benton	Daviess	Lawrence	Pemiscot	Scotland
Bollinger	DeKalb	Lewis	Perry	Scott
Boone	Dent	Lincoln	Pettis	Shannon
Buchanan	Douglas	Linn	Phelps	Shelby
Butler	Dunklin	Livingston	Pike	Stoddard
Caldwell	Franklin	Macon	Platte	Stone
Callaway	Gasconade	Madison	Polk	Sullivan
Camden	Gentry	Maries	Pulaski	Taney
Cape Girardeau	Greene	Marion	Putnam	Texas
Carroll	Grundy	McDonald	Ralls	Vernon
Carter	Harrison	Mercer	Randolph	Warren
Cass	Henry	Miller	Ray	Washington
Cedar	Hickory	Mississippi	Reynolds	Wayne
Chariton	Holt	Moniteau	Ripley	Webster
Christian	Howard	Monroe	St. Charles	Worth
Clark	Howell	Montgomery	St. Clair	Wright
	Iron			

Multi-County Places

The following Missouri places are in more than one county. Given here is the total population for each multi-county place, and the names of the counties it is in.

Argyle, pop. 178; Osage (171), Maries (7)
Belle, pop. 1,218; Maries (1,069), Osage (149)
Blackburn, pop. 308; Saline (286), Lafayette (22)
Bland, pop. 651; Gasconade (651), Osage (0)
Browning, pop. 331; Linn (255), Sullivan (76)
Bunker, pop. 390; Reynolds (231), Dent (159)
Cameron, pop. 4,831; Clinton (3,791), DeKalb (1,040)
Cape Girardeau, pop. 34,438; Cape Girardeau (34,438), Scott (0)
Centralia, pop. 3,414; Boone (3,414), Audrain (0)
Dearborn, pop. 480; Platte (480), Buchanan (0)
Drexel, pop. 936; Cass (835), Bates (101)
Emma, pop. 194; Saline (108), Lafayette (86)
Excelsior Estates, pop. 274; Ray (271), Clay (3)
Excelsior Springs, pop. 10,354; Clay (10,178), Ray (176)
Foristell, pop. 144; St. Charles (130), Warren (14)
Gilman City, pop. 393; Harrison (393), Daviess (0)
Glasgow, pop. 1,295; Howard (1,248), Chariton (47)
Gower, pop. 1,249; Clinton (1,230), Buchanan (19)
Greentop, pop. 425; Schuyler (343), Adair (82)
Hannibal, pop. 18,004; Marion (17,735), Ralls (269)
Holt, pop. 311; Clay (248), Clinton (63)
Independence, pop. 112,301; Jackson (112,301), Clay (0)
Ionia, pop. 126; Benton (126), Pettis (0)

MISSOURI

Jefferson City, pop. 35,481; Cole (35,175), Callaway (306)
Joplin, pop. 40,961; Jasper (37,032), Newton (3,929)
Kansas City, pop. 435,146; Jackson (341,179), Clay (69,316), Platte (24,609), Cass (42)
Lake Ozark, pop. 681; Miller (613), Camden (68)
Lawson, pop. 1,876; Ray (1,781), Clay (95)
Lee's Summit, pop. 46,418; Jackson (45,985), Cass (433)
Marceline, pop. 2,645; Linn (2,638), Chariton (7)
Monett, pop. 6,529; Barry (4,476), Lawrence (2,053)
Monroe City, pop. 2,701; Monroe (2,276), Marion (420), Ralls (5)
Mountain Grove, pop. 4,182; Wright (4,175), Texas (7)
Oak Grove, pop. 4,565; Jackson (4,561), Lafayette (4)
Osage Beach, pop. 2,599; Camden (2,511), Miller (88)
Osborn, pop. 400; DeKalb (355), Clinton (45)
Pacific, pop. 4,350; Franklin (4,332), St. Louis (18)
Portageville, pop. 3,401; New Madrid (3,401), Pemiscot (0)
Richland, pop. 2,029; Pulaski (1,879), Camden (95), Laclede (55)
Rogersville, pop. 995; Webster (974), Greene (21)
Scott City, pop. 4,292; Scott (4,292), Cape Girardeau (0)
Sikeston, pop. 17,641; Scott (16,909), New Madrid (732)
Springfield, pop. 140,494; Greene (140,494), Christian (0)
Stoutland, pop. 207; Camden (164), Laclede (43)
Sugar Creek, pop. 3,982; Jackson (3,982), Clay (0)
Sullivan, pop. 5,661; Franklin (4,545), Crawford (1,116)
Summersville, pop. 571; Texas (459), Shannon (112)
Sunrise Beach, pop. 181; Camden (112), Morgan (69)
Vandalia, pop. 2,683; Audrain (2,683), Ralls (0)
Windsor, pop. 3,044; Henry (2,948), Pettis (96)

Adair County
County Seat: Kirksville (ZIP: 63501)

Pop: 24,577 (1990); 24,870 (1980) **Pop Density:** 43.3
Land: 567.7 sq. mi.; **Water:** 1.6 sq. mi. **Area Code:** 816
In north-central MO; organized Jan 29, 1841 from Macon County.
Name origin: For John Adair (1757–1840), governor of KY (1820–24).

Benton
Township
Lat: 40-11-33 N Long: 92-35-29 W
Pop: 19,325 (1990); 19,204 (1980) Pop Density: 244.3
Land: 79.1 sq. mi.; Water: 1.1 sq. mi.

Brashear
City
ZIP: 63533 Lat: 40-08-52 N Long: 92-22-42 W
Pop: 318 (1990); 332 (1980) Pop Density: 795.0
Land: 0.4 sq. mi.; Water: 0.0 sq. mi.
Incorporated 1956.

Clay
Township
Lat: 40-17-02 N Long: 92-26-25 W
Pop: 576 (1990); 657 (1980) Pop Density: 7.2
Land: 79.6 sq. mi.; Water: 0.0 sq. mi.

Gibbs
Town
ZIP: 63540 Lat: 40-05-52 N Long: 92-24-58 W
Pop: 89 (1990); 107 (1980) Pop Density: 445.0
Land: 0.2 sq. mi.; Water: 0.0 sq. mi.
Incorporated 1887.

Greentop
Village
ZIP: 63546 Lat: 40-20-32 N Long: 92-33-54 W
Pop: 82 (1990); 115 (1980) Pop Density: 820.0
Land: 0.1 sq. mi.; Water: 0.0 sq. mi. Elev: 993 ft.
Incorporated 1870. Part of the town is also in Schuyler County.

Kirksville
City
ZIP: 63501 Lat: 40-11-42 N Long: 92-34-42 W
Pop: 17,152 (1990); 17,167 (1980) Pop Density: 1750.2
Land: 9.8 sq. mi.; Water: 0.0 sq. mi.
In central-northern MO, about 30 mi. south of the IA border. Founded 1841; county seat. Incorporated 1857.
Name origin: For Mr. and Mrs. Jesse Kirk, who gave the commissioners a turkey dinner on condition that the town be named for them.

Liberty
Township
Lat: 40-09-51 N Long: 92-46-29 W
Pop: 332 (1990); 399 (1980) Pop Density: 6.3
Land: 52.9 sq. mi.; Water: 0.0 sq. mi.

Millard
Village
Lat: 40-06-25 N Long: 92-32-43 W
Pop: 71 (1990); 92 (1980) Pop Density: 710.0
Land: 0.1 sq. mi.; Water: 0.0 sq. mi.
Incorporated 1976.

Morrow
Township
Lat: 40-15-53 N Long: 92-47-42 W
Pop: 353 (1990); 393 (1980) Pop Density: 6.6
Land: 53.4 sq. mi.; Water: 0.0 sq. mi.

Nineveh
Township
Lat: 40-16-26 N Long: 92-41-09 W
Pop: 1,288 (1990); 1,381 (1980) Pop Density: 23.7
Land: 54.3 sq. mi.; Water: 0.1 sq. mi.

Novinger
City
ZIP: 63559 Lat: 40-14-02 N Long: 92-42-21 W
Pop: 542 (1990); 626 (1980) Pop Density: 677.5
Land: 0.8 sq. mi.; Water: 0.0 sq. mi.
Laid out 1879. Incorporated 1879.
Name origin: For John C. Novinger, who laid out the town on his land.

Pettis
Township
Lat: 40-05-11 N Long: 92-36-25 W
Pop: 624 (1990); 666 (1980) Pop Density: 11.1
Land: 56.2 sq. mi.; Water: 0.2 sq. mi.

Polk
Township
Lat: 40-18-36 N Long: 92-34-15 W
Pop: 519 (1990); 519 (1980) Pop Density: 17.4
Land: 29.9 sq. mi.; Water: 0.0 sq. mi.

Salt River
Township
Lat: 40-09-42 N Long: 92-26-00 W
Pop: 984 (1990); 970 (1980) Pop Density: 17.5
Land: 56.2 sq. mi.; Water: 0.0 sq. mi.

Walnut
Township
Lat: 40-05-17 N Long: 92-46-22 W
Pop: 187 (1990); 218 (1980) Pop Density: 3.6
Land: 52.1 sq. mi.; Water: 0.0 sq. mi.

Wilson
Township
Lat: 40-04-49 N Long: 92-26-01 W
Pop: 389 (1990); 463 (1980) Pop Density: 7.2
Land: 54.1 sq. mi.; Water: 0.1 sq. mi.

MISSOURI, Andrew County

> ## Andrew County
> **County Seat: Savannah (ZIP: 64485)**
>
> **Pop:** 14,632 (1990); 13,980 (1980)   **Pop Density:** 33.6
> **Land:** 435.2 sq. mi.; **Water:** 1.3 sq. mi.   **Area Code:** 816
> On northwestern border of MO, north of St. Joseph; organized Jan 29, 1841 from Platte Purchase.
> **Name origin:** For either Andrew Jackson, seventh U.S. president, or Andrew Jackson Davis, a distinguished lawyer from St. Louis.

Amazonia   Town
ZIP: 64421   **Lat:** 39-53-18 N   **Long:** 94-53-30 W
Pop: 257 (1990); 314 (1980)   **Pop Density:** 642.5
Land: 0.4 sq. mi.; **Water:** 0.0 sq. mi.
Incorporated 1879.

Benton   Township
Lat: 40-03-37 N   **Long:** 94-49-42 W
Pop: 1,007 (1990); 1,103 (1980)   **Pop Density:** 20.2
Land: 49.8 sq. mi.; **Water:** 0.1 sq. mi.

Bolckow   Town
ZIP: 64427   **Lat:** 40-06-56 N   **Long:** 94-49-13 W
Pop: 253 (1990); 245 (1980)   **Pop Density:** 843.3
Land: 0.3 sq. mi.; **Water:** 0.0 sq. mi.
Platted by John Anderson and Benjamin A. Conrad. Incorporated 1982.
Name origin: Named in 1868 for a famous employee of the railroads.

Clay   Township
Lat: 40-05-17 N   **Long:** 94-57-52 W
Pop: 272 (1990); 340 (1980)   **Pop Density:** 6.0
Land: 45.3 sq. mi.; **Water:** 0.1 sq. mi.

Cosby   Town
ZIP: 64436   **Lat:** 39-51-48 N   **Long:** 94-40-46 W
Pop: 121 (1990); 148 (1980)   **Pop Density:** 1210.0
Land: 0.1 sq. mi.; **Water:** 0.0 sq. mi.
Incorporated 1905.

Country Club   Village
Lat: 39-49-39 N   **Long:** 94-49-36 W
Pop: 1,755 (1990); 1,234 (1980)   **Pop Density:** 1462.5
Land: 1.2 sq. mi.; **Water:** 0.0 sq. mi.
Incorporated 1954.

Empire   Township
Lat: 40-00-04 N   **Long:** 94-40-35 W
Pop: 345 (1990); 351 (1980)   **Pop Density:** 8.1
Land: 42.7 sq. mi.; **Water:** 0.0 sq. mi.

Fillmore   City
ZIP: 64449   **Lat:** 40-01-31 N   **Long:** 94-58-22 W
Pop: 256 (1990); 265 (1980)   **Pop Density:** 2560.0
Land: 0.1 sq. mi.; **Water:** 0.0 sq. mi.
Incorporated 1873.

Jackson   Township
Lat: 40-00-38 N   **Long:** 94-56-27 W
Pop: 549 (1990); 651 (1980)   **Pop Density:** 15.8
Land: 34.8 sq. mi.; **Water:** 0.0 sq. mi.

Jefferson   Township
Lat: 39-51-49 N   **Long:** 94-49-02 W
Pop: 3,859 (1990); 3,053 (1980)   **Pop Density:** 118.0
Land: 32.7 sq. mi.; **Water:** 0.1 sq. mi.

Lincoln   Township
Lat: 39-54-47 N   **Long:** 94-55-11 W
Pop: 864 (1990); 916 (1980)   **Pop Density:** 19.8
Land: 43.7 sq. mi.; **Water:** 0.7 sq. mi.

Monroe   Township
Lat: 39-51-02 N   **Long:** 94-41-18 W
Pop: 727 (1990); 702 (1980)   **Pop Density:** 21.4
Land: 33.9 sq. mi.; **Water:** 0.2 sq. mi.

Nodaway   Township
ZIP: 64421   **Lat:** 39-57-46 N   **Long:** 94-49-18 W
Pop: 5,446 (1990); 5,077 (1980)   **Pop Density:** 138.9
Land: 39.2 sq. mi.; **Water:** 0.1 sq. mi.

Platte   Township
Lat: 40-05-20 N   **Long:** 94-42-00 W
Pop: 496 (1990); 578 (1980)   **Pop Density:** 8.7
Land: 57.0 sq. mi.; **Water:** 0.1 sq. mi.

Rea   Town
ZIP: 64480   **Lat:** 40-03-39 N   **Long:** 94-45-50 W
Pop: 62 (1990); 78 (1980)   **Pop Density:** 620.0
Land: 0.1 sq. mi.; **Water:** 0.0 sq. mi.   **Elev:** 1059 ft.
Incorporated 1913.
Name origin: For Judge Joseph Rea.

Rochester   Township
Lat: 39-55-23 N   **Long:** 94-42-00 W
Pop: 1,067 (1990); 1,209 (1980)   **Pop Density:** 19.1
Land: 56.0 sq. mi.; **Water:** 0.0 sq. mi.

Rosendale   City
ZIP: 64483   **Lat:** 40-02-33 N   **Long:** 94-49-29 W
Pop: 186 (1990); 223 (1980)   **Pop Density:** 620.0
Land: 0.3 sq. mi.; **Water:** 0.0 sq. mi.
Incorporated 1963.

Savannah   City
ZIP: 64485   **Lat:** 39-56-19 N   **Long:** 94-49-40 W
Pop: 4,352 (1990); 4,184 (1980)   **Pop Density:** 1450.7
Land: 3.0 sq. mi.; **Water:** 0.0 sq. mi.   **Elev:** 1115 ft.
Platted 1841. Incorporated 1853.
Name origin: For Savannah, GA.

Atchison County
County Seat: Rock Port (ZIP: 64482)

Pop: 7,457 (1990); 8,605 (1980)   **Pop Density:** 13.7
Land: 544.7 sq. mi.; **Water:** 2.6 sq. mi.   **Area Code:** 816
At the northwestern tip of MO, northwest of St. Joseph; established Feb 3, 1843 from Holt County.
Name origin: For David Rice Atchison (1807–86), MO statesman and U.S. senator (1843–55).

Benton
Township
Lat: 40-19-24 N   **Long:** 95-34-41 W
Pop: 50 (1990); 61 (1980)   **Pop Density:** 2.6
Land: 19.6 sq. mi.; **Water:** 0.5 sq. mi.

Buchanan
Township
Lat: 40-33-17 N   **Long:** 95-39-22 W
Pop: 140 (1990); 182 (1980)   **Pop Density:** 3.4
Land: 41.1 sq. mi.; **Water:** 0.9 sq. mi.

Clark
Township
Lat: 40-19-18 N   **Long:** 95-26-16 W
Pop: 1,103 (1990); 1,283 (1980)   **Pop Density:** 14.8
Land: 74.7 sq. mi.; **Water:** 0.3 sq. mi.

Clay
Township
Lat: 40-24-04 N   **Long:** 95-31-00 W
Pop: 2,033 (1990); 2,293 (1980)   **Pop Density:** 48.3
Land: 42.1 sq. mi.; **Water:** 0.0 sq. mi.

Colfax
Township
Lat: 40-26-26 N   **Long:** 95-14-23 W
Pop: 108 (1990); 155 (1980)   **Pop Density:** 2.6
Land: 42.1 sq. mi.; **Water:** 0.0 sq. mi.

Dale
Township
Lat: 40-19-51 N   **Long:** 95-15-50 W
Pop: 310 (1990); 360 (1980)   **Pop Density:** 3.8
Land: 81.6 sq. mi.; **Water:** 0.0 sq. mi.

Fairfax
City
ZIP: 64446   **Lat:** 40-20-22 N   **Long:** 95-23-30 W
Pop: 699 (1990); 835 (1980)   **Pop Density:** 1398.0
Land: 0.5 sq. mi.; **Water:** 0.0 sq. mi.
Laid out 1881 by Charles E. Perkins. Incorporated 1881.

Lincoln
Township
Lat: 40-31-59 N   **Long:** 95-19-08 W
Pop: 572 (1990); 711 (1980)   **Pop Density:** 6.9
Land: 82.6 sq. mi.; **Water:** 0.0 sq. mi.

Nishnabotna
Township
Lat: 40-28-49 N   **Long:** 95-38-12 W
Pop: 215 (1990); 290 (1980)   **Pop Density:** 8.1
Land: 26.4 sq. mi.; **Water:** 0.4 sq. mi.

Phelps City
Town
Lat: 40-24-09 N   **Long:** 95-35-53 W
Pop: 32 (1990); 39 (1980)   **Pop Density:** 320.0
Land: 0.1 sq. mi.; **Water:** 0.0 sq. mi.   **Elev:** 887 ft.
Incorporated 1874.

Polk
Township
Lat: 40-30-47 N   **Long:** 95-30-24 W
Pop: 355 (1990); 442 (1980)   **Pop Density:** 5.7
Land: 62.1 sq. mi.; **Water:** 0.0 sq. mi.

Rock Port
City
ZIP: 64482   **Lat:** 40-24-40 N   **Long:** 95-30-58 W
Pop: 1,438 (1990); 1,511 (1980)   **Pop Density:** 1597.8
Land: 0.9 sq. mi.; **Water:** 0.0 sq. mi.
Incorporated 1851.

Tarkio
City
ZIP: 64491   **Lat:** 40-26-35 N   **Long:** 95-23-01 W
Pop: 2,243 (1990); 2,375 (1980)   **Pop Density:** 1602.1
Land: 1.4 sq. mi.; **Water:** 0.0 sq. mi.
Laid out August 1880 by Charles E. Perkins. Incorporated 1880.
Name origin: Probably from an Indian language; meaning unknown.

*Tarkio
Township
ZIP: 64491   **Lat:** 40-26-15 N   **Long:** 95-23-11 W
Pop: 2,445 (1990); 2,665 (1980)   **Pop Density:** 50.8
Land: 48.1 sq. mi.; **Water:** 0.0 sq. mi.

Templeton
Township
Lat: 40-23-56 N   **Long:** 95-36-17 W
Pop: 126 (1990); 163 (1980)   **Pop Density:** 5.2
Land: 24.3 sq. mi.; **Water:** 0.4 sq. mi.

Watson
Village
ZIP: 64496   **Lat:** 40-28-48 N   **Long:** 95-37-23 W
Pop: 137 (1990); 171 (1980)   **Pop Density:** 1370.0
Land: 0.1 sq. mi.; **Water:** 0.0 sq. mi.   **Elev:** 894 ft.
Incorporated 1894.

Westboro
Village
ZIP: 64498   **Lat:** 40-32-08 N   **Long:** 95-19-18 W
Pop: 182 (1990); 188 (1980)   **Pop Density:** 910.0
Land: 0.2 sq. mi.; **Water:** 0.0 sq. mi.
Laid out 1881 by Charles E. Perkins. Incorporated 1882.

MISSOURI, Audrain County

Audrain County
County Seat: Mexico (ZIP: 65265)

Pop: 23,599 (1990); 26,458 (1980)
Land: 693.4 sq. mi.; **Water:** 3.5 sq. mi.
Pop Density: 34.0
Area Code: 314

In east-central MO, northeast of Columbia; established Jan 12, 1831 from Pike, Callaway, and Ralls counties.
Name origin: For James H. Audrain (1782–1831), MO legislator.

Benton City
Town
ZIP: 65232 **Lat:** 39-08-05 N **Long:** 91-45-51 W
Pop: 139 (1990); 155 (1980) **Pop Density:** 1390.0
Land: 0.1 sq. mi.; **Water:** 0.0 sq. mi. **Elev:** 822 ft.
Incorporated 1889.

Centralia
City
ZIP: 65240 **Lat:** 39-13-04 N **Long:** 92-06-16 W
Pop: 0 (1990); 3,537 (1980)
Land: 0.01 sq. mi.; **Water:** 0.01 sq. mi. **Elev:** 891 ft.
Incorporated 1867. Part of the town is also in Boone County.

Cuivre
Township
Lat: 39-14-05 N **Long:** 91-30-46 W
Pop: 3,987 (1990); 4,864 (1980) **Pop Density:** 35.6
Land: 112.0 sq. mi.; **Water:** 0.5 sq. mi.

Farber
City
ZIP: 63345 **Lat:** 39-16-26 N **Long:** 91-34-35 W
Pop: 418 (1990); 503 (1980) **Pop Density:** 1393.3
Land: 0.3 sq. mi.; **Water:** 0.0 sq. mi. **Elev:** 767 ft.
Laid out 1872 by Thomas W. Carter. Incorporated 1955.
Name origin: For Silas W. Farber, an early settler.

Laddonia
City
ZIP: 63352 **Lat:** 39-14-29 N **Long:** 91-38-34 W
Pop: 581 (1990); 726 (1980) **Pop Density:** 1162.0
Land: 0.5 sq. mi.; **Water:** 0.0 sq. mi.
Incorporated 1871.

Linn
Township
Lat: 39-11-36 N **Long:** 91-41-06 W
Pop: 646 (1990); 773 (1980) **Pop Density:** 8.6
Land: 75.5 sq. mi.; **Water:** 0.3 sq. mi.

Loutre
Township
Lat: 39-06-32 N **Long:** 91-42-55 W
Pop: 887 (1990); 991 (1980) **Pop Density:** 15.8
Land: 56.0 sq. mi.; **Water:** 0.2 sq. mi.

Martinsburg
Town
ZIP: 65264 **Lat:** 39-06-04 N **Long:** 91-38-49 W
Pop: 337 (1990); 309 (1980) **Pop Density:** 1123.3
Land: 0.3 sq. mi.; **Water:** 0.0 sq. mi. **Elev:** 807 ft.
Founded 1857. Incorporated 1857.
Name origin: For founder William R. Martin.

Mexico
City
ZIP: 65265 **Lat:** 39-09-59 N **Long:** 91-52-14 W
Pop: 11,290 (1990); 12,276 (1980) **Pop Density:** 1140.4
Land: 9.9 sq. mi.; **Water:** 0.3 sq. mi. **Elev:** 802 ft.
In northeast-central MO, 30 mi. east-northeast of Columbia. Incorporated 1857.
Name origin: For the country.

Prairie
Township
Lat: 39-17-30 N **Long:** 91-45-11 W
Pop: 1,025 (1990); 1,269 (1980) **Pop Density:** 13.0
Land: 78.8 sq. mi.; **Water:** 0.2 sq. mi.

Rush Hill
Town
ZIP: 65280 **Lat:** 39-12-35 N **Long:** 91-43-30 W
Pop: 121 (1990); 140 (1980) **Pop Density:** 605.0
Land: 0.2 sq. mi.; **Water:** 0.0 sq. mi.
Incorporated 1881.
Name origin: Named for original owners, Reusch and Hill, with a spelling variation.

Saling
Township
Lat: 39-18-03 N **Long:** 92-12-36 W
Pop: 1,039 (1990); 1,048 (1980) **Pop Density:** 13.3
Land: 78.2 sq. mi.; **Water:** 0.2 sq. mi.

Salt River
Township
Lat: 39-11-42 N **Long:** 91-54-54 W
Pop: 10,413 (1990); 10,842 (1980) **Pop Density:** 93.2
Land: 111.7 sq. mi.; **Water:** 0.4 sq. mi.

South Fork
Township
Lat: 39-09-28 N **Long:** 91-50-07 W
Pop: 4,372 (1990); 5,219 (1980) **Pop Density:** 96.5
Land: 45.3 sq. mi.; **Water:** 0.7 sq. mi.

Vandalia
City
ZIP: 63382 **Lat:** 39-18-30 N **Long:** 91-29-23 W
Pop: 2,683 (1990); 3,170 (1980) **Pop Density:** 1578.2
Land: 1.7 sq. mi.; **Water:** 0.0 sq. mi.
Incorporated 1874. Part of the town is also in Ralls County.
Name origin: For Vandalia, IL.

Vandiver
Village
Lat: 39-09-40 N **Long:** 91-50-55 W
Pop: 75 (1990); 88 (1980) **Pop Density:** 250.0
Land: 0.3 sq. mi.; **Water:** 0.0 sq. mi.
Incorporated 1956.

Wilson
Township
Lat: 39-12-03 N **Long:** 92-02-17 W
Pop: 1,230 (1990); 1,452 (1980) **Pop Density:** 9.1
Land: 135.9 sq. mi.; **Water:** 1.0 sq. mi.

Barry County
County Seat: Cassville (ZIP: 65625)

Pop: 27,547 (1990); 24,408 (1980) **Pop Density:** 35.4
Land: 779.1 sq. mi.; **Water:** 11.8 sq. mi. **Area Code:** 417
On the southwestern border of MO, southwest of Springfield; organized Jan 5, 1835 from Greene County.
Name origin: For William Taylor Barry (1784–1835), KY legislator, U.S. senator (1814–16), and U.S. Postmaster General (1829–35).

Ash
Township
Lat: 36-33-31 N Long: 94-02-19 W
Pop: 668 (1990); 594 (1980) Pop Density: 16.2
Land: 41.3 sq. mi.; Water: 0.0 sq. mi.

Butterfield
Village
ZIP: 65623 Lat: 36-44-51 N Long: 93-54-15 W
Pop: 248 (1990); 234 (1980) Pop Density: 620.0
Land: 0.4 sq. mi.; Water: 0.0 sq. mi.
Incorporated 1966.

*Butterfield
Township
Lat: 36-44-48 N Long: 93-55-18 W
Pop: 684 (1990); 594 (1980) Pop Density: 47.2
Land: 14.5 sq. mi.; Water: 0.0 sq. mi.

Capps Creek
Township
Lat: 36-52-42 N Long: 94-01-03 W
Pop: 477 (1990); 390 (1980) Pop Density: 16.3
Land: 29.2 sq. mi.; Water: 0.0 sq. mi.

Cassville
City
ZIP: 65625 Lat: 36-40-43 N Long: 93-52-03 W
Pop: 2,371 (1990); 2,091 (1980) Pop Density: 911.9
Land: 2.6 sq. mi.; Water: 0.0 sq. mi. Elev: 1324 ft.
Incorporated 1846.
Name origin: For Lewis Cass (1782–1866), OH legislator, governor of MI Territory (1813–31), U.S. secretary of state (1831–36), and U.S. secretary of state (1857–60).

Chain-O-Lakes
Village
Lat: 36-31-59 N Long: 93-43-29 W
Pop: 111 (1990); 76 (1980) Pop Density: 1110.0
Land: 0.1 sq. mi.; Water: 0.0 sq. mi.

Corsicana
Township
Lat: 36-47-20 N Long: 93-59-05 W
Pop: 277 (1990); 307 (1980) Pop Density: 16.2
Land: 17.1 sq. mi.; Water: 0.0 sq. mi.

Crane Creek
Township
Lat: 36-52-15 N Long: 93-39-00 W
Pop: 723 (1990); 646 (1980) Pop Density: 25.6
Land: 28.2 sq. mi.; Water: 0.0 sq. mi.

Emerald Beach
Village
Lat: 36-34-26 N Long: 93-40-14 W
Pop: 172 (1990) Pop Density: 245.7
Land: 0.7 sq. mi.; Water: 0.0 sq. mi.
Incorporated 1981.

Exeter
City
ZIP: 65647 Lat: 36-40-14 N Long: 93-56-22 W
Pop: 597 (1990); 588 (1980) Pop Density: 746.3
Land: 0.8 sq. mi.; Water: 0.0 sq. mi. Elev: 1559 ft.
Laid out September 1880 for George A. Purdy. Incorporated 1881.
Name origin: For Exeter, England.

*Exeter
Township
ZIP: 65647 Lat: 36-40-16 N Long: 93-56-09 W
Pop: 1,301 (1990); 1,197 (1980) Pop Density: 55.6
Land: 23.4 sq. mi.; Water: 0.0 sq. mi.

Flat Creek
Township
Lat: 36-40-13 N Long: 93-50-55 W
Pop: 4,643 (1990); 4,091 (1980) Pop Density: 87.1
Land: 53.3 sq. mi.; Water: 0.0 sq. mi.

Jenkins
Township
Lat: 36-46-46 N Long: 93-41-42 W
Pop: 382 (1990); 344 (1980) Pop Density: 13.5
Land: 28.3 sq. mi.; Water: 0.0 sq. mi.

Kings Prairie
Township
Lat: 36-52-39 N Long: 93-51-43 W
Pop: 760 (1990); 670 (1980) Pop Density: 26.5
Land: 28.7 sq. mi.; Water: 0.0 sq. mi.

Liberty
Township
Lat: 36-41-24 N Long: 94-01-04 W
Pop: 963 (1990); 872 (1980) Pop Density: 21.3
Land: 45.2 sq. mi.; Water: 0.0 sq. mi.

McDonald
Township
Lat: 36-46-52 N Long: 93-49-32 W
Pop: 734 (1990); 625 (1980) Pop Density: 19.3
Land: 38.0 sq. mi.; Water: 0.0 sq. mi.

McDowell
Township
Lat: 36-49-16 N Long: 93-47-12 W
Pop: 241 (1990); 278 (1980) Pop Density: 10.1
Land: 23.9 sq. mi.; Water: 0.0 sq. mi.

Mineral
Township
Lat: 36-41-01 N Long: 93-44-18 W
Pop: 773 (1990); 741 (1980) Pop Density: 12.8
Land: 60.6 sq. mi.; Water: 0.0 sq. mi.

Monett
City
ZIP: 65708 Lat: 36-55-00 N Long: 93-55-28 W
Pop: 4,476 (1990); 4,367 (1980) Pop Density: 1209.7
Land: 3.7 sq. mi.; Water: 0.0 sq. mi. Elev: 1317 ft.
In southwestern MO, 35 mi. southeast of Joplin. Incorporated 1888. Part of the town is also in Lawrence County.
Name origin: Named in 1887 for the general passenger agent of the New York Central Railroad.

*Monett
Township
ZIP: 65708 Lat: 36-54-03 N Long: 93-55-55 W
Pop: 5,064 (1990); 5,010 (1980) Pop Density: 312.6
Land: 16.2 sq. mi.; Water: 0.0 sq. mi.

Mountain
Township
Lat: 36-45-35 N Long: 93-36-34 W
Pop: 199 (1990); 183 (1980) Pop Density: 5.7
Land: 34.9 sq. mi.; Water: 0.0 sq. mi.

MISSOURI, Barry County

Ozark
Township
Lat: 36-52-30 N **Long:** 93-42-41 W
Pop: 686 (1990); 504 (1980) **Pop Density:** 26.1
Land: 26.3 sq. mi.; **Water:** 0.0 sq. mi.

Pioneer
Township
Lat: 36-50-12 N **Long:** 94-02-28 W
Pop: 202 (1990); 184 (1980) **Pop Density:** 22.2
Land: 9.1 sq. mi.; **Water:** 0.0 sq. mi.

Pleasant Ridge
Township
Lat: 36-53-41 N **Long:** 93-47-41 W
Pop: 311 (1990); 344 (1980) **Pop Density:** 16.1
Land: 19.3 sq. mi.; **Water:** 0.0 sq. mi.

Purdy
City
ZIP: 65734 **Lat:** 36-49-06 N **Long:** 93-55-14 W
Pop: 977 (1990); 928 (1980) **Pop Density:** 1395.7
Land: 0.7 sq. mi.; **Water:** 0.0 sq. mi.
Founded 1880. Incorporated 1904.
Name origin: For George A. Purdy, an enterprising citizen.

*Purdy
Township
ZIP: 65734 **Lat:** 36-49-15 N **Long:** 93-55-40 W
Pop: 1,693 (1990); 1,590 (1980) **Pop Density:** 71.7
Land: 23.6 sq. mi.; **Water:** 0.0 sq. mi.

Roaring River
Township
Lat: 36-33-33 N **Long:** 93-45-20 W
Pop: 1,062 (1990); 809 (1980) **Pop Density:** 15.5
Land: 68.7 sq. mi.; **Water:** 3.4 sq. mi.

Seligman
City
ZIP: 65745 **Lat:** 36-31-21 N **Long:** 93-56-16 W
Pop: 593 (1990); 508 (1980) **Pop Density:** 539.1
Land: 1.1 sq. mi.; **Water:** 0.0 sq. mi. **Elev** 1540 ft.
Founded 1880. Incorporated 1952.
Name origin: For either a railroad official or for Mrs. Seligman, a banker's wife who made a generous gift for the building of a church.

Shell Knob
Township
ZIP: 65747 **Lat:** 36-38-23 N **Long:** 93-37-42 W
Pop: 821 (1990); 604 (1980) **Pop Density:** 22.2
Land: 36.9 sq. mi.; **Water:** 2.1 sq. mi.

Sugar Creek
Township
Lat: 36-32-36 N **Long:** 93-54-16 W
Pop: 1,332 (1990); 1,044 (1980) **Pop Density:** 33.3
Land: 40.0 sq. mi.; **Water:** 0.0 sq. mi.

Washburn
City
ZIP: 65772 **Lat:** 36-35-22 N **Long:** 93-57-58 W
Pop: 362 (1990); 289 (1980) **Pop Density:** 452.5
Land: 0.8 sq. mi.; **Water:** 0.0 sq. mi.
Settled 1840. Incorporated 1962.
Name origin: For Samuel Washburn, a pioneer who settled Washburn's prairie in 1828.

*Washburn
Township
ZIP: 65772 **Lat:** 36-35-51 N **Long:** 93-56-30 W
Pop: 918 (1990); 840 (1980) **Pop Density:** 32.1
Land: 28.6 sq. mi.; **Water:** 0.0 sq. mi.

Wheaton
City
ZIP: 64874 **Lat:** 36-45-40 N **Long:** 94-03-22 W
Pop: 637 (1990); 548 (1980) **Pop Density:** 1274.0
Land: 0.5 sq. mi.; **Water:** 0.0 sq. mi.
Incorporated 1935.

*Wheaton
Township
Lat: 36-46-36 N **Long:** 94-01-54 W
Pop: 970 (1990); 911 (1980) **Pop Density:** 66.4
Land: 14.6 sq. mi.; **Water:** 0.0 sq. mi.

White River
Township
Lat: 36-32-37 N **Long:** 93-37-37 W
Pop: 1,663 (1990); 1,036 (1980) **Pop Density:** 56.8
Land: 29.3 sq. mi.; **Water:** 6.3 sq. mi.

Barton County
County Seat: Lamar (ZIP: 64759)

Pop: 11,312 (1990); 11,292 (1980) **Pop Density:** 19.0
Land: 594.3 sq. mi.; **Water:** 2.4 sq. mi. **Area Code:** 417
On the southwestern border of MO, north of Joplin; organized Dec 12, 1855 from Jasper County.
Name origin: For David Barton (1788–1837), MO jurist, legislator, and U.S. senator (1821–31).

Barton City
Township
Lat: 37-36-02 N **Long:** 94-26-30 W
Pop: 253 (1990); 246 (1980) **Pop Density:** 6.9
Land: 36.5 sq. mi.; **Water:** 0.0 sq. mi.

Burgess
Town
Lat: 37-33-22 N **Long:** 94-36-53 W
Pop: 97 (1990); 98 (1980) **Pop Density:** 970.0
Land: 0.1 sq. mi.; **Water:** 0.0 sq. mi.
Incorporated 1893.

Central
Township
Lat: 37-31-05 N **Long:** 94-24-55 W
Pop: 509 (1990); 545 (1980) **Pop Density:** 9.4
Land: 54.3 sq. mi.; **Water:** 0.1 sq. mi.

City
Township
Lat: 37-29-37 N **Long:** 94-16-23 W
Pop: 4,168 (1990); 4,053 (1980) **Pop Density:** 1225.9
Land: 3.4 sq. mi.; **Water:** 0.3 sq. mi.

Doylesport
Township
Lat: 37-35-35 N **Long:** 94-13-04 W
Pop: 270 (1990); 260 (1980) **Pop Density:** 7.5
Land: 35.9 sq. mi.; **Water:** 0.3 sq. mi.

Golden City
City
Lat: 37-23-36 N **Long:** 94-05-35 W
Pop: 794 (1990); 900 (1980) **Pop Density:** 794.0
Land: 1.0 sq. mi.; **Water:** 0.0 sq. mi.
Laid out 1867; platted 1870 by F. C. Brock. Incorporated 1882. Not coextensive with the town of the same name.
Name origin: For some gold that was found here.

*Golden City
Township
Lat: 37-24-31 N **Long:** 94-07-34 W
Pop: 1,127 (1990); 1,252 (1980) **Pop Density:** 27.8
Land: 40.5 sq. mi.; **Water:** 0.0 sq. mi.

Lamar
City
ZIP: 64759 **Lat:** 37-29-37 N **Long:** 94-16-23 W
Pop: 4,168 (1990); 4,053 (1980) **Pop Density:** 1225.9
Land: 3.4 sq. mi.; **Water:** 0.3 sq. mi.
In southwestern MO, 30 mi. north-northeast of Joplin. Founded 1856. Incorporated 1867.
Name origin: For Mirabeau B. Lamar, president of the Republic of Texas (1838–41).

*Lamar
Township
Lat: 37-30-25 N **Long:** 94-15-18 W
Pop: 1,185 (1990); 1,053 (1980) **Pop Density:** 18.3
Land: 64.9 sq. mi.; **Water:** 0.3 sq. mi.

Lamar Heights
Village
Lat: 37-29-36 N **Long:** 94-17-52 W
Pop: 176 (1990); 171 (1980) **Pop Density:** 220.0
Land: 0.8 sq. mi.; **Water:** 0.0 sq. mi. **Elev:** 971 ft.
Incorporated 1951.

Leroy
Township
Lat: 37-36-59 N **Long:** 94-33-12 W
Pop: 226 (1990); 250 (1980) **Pop Density:** 5.6
Land: 40.1 sq. mi.; **Water:** 0.3 sq. mi.

Liberal
City
ZIP: 64762 **Lat:** 37-33-31 N **Long:** 94-30-57 W
Pop: 684 (1990); 701 (1980) **Pop Density:** 855.0
Land: 0.8 sq. mi.; **Water:** 0.0 sq. mi. **Elev:** 894 ft.
Founded 1880 and platted by G. H. Walser (1834–1910), a disciple of lawyer and lecturer on agnosticism Robert G. Ingersoll (1833–99). Incorporated 1884.

Milford
Village
ZIP: 64766 **Lat:** 37-35-10 N **Long:** 94-09-22 W
Pop: 22 (1990); 67 (1980) **Elev:** 924 ft.
Land: 0.0 sq. mi.; **Water:** 0.0 sq. mi.
Incorporated 1964. Not coextensive with the town of the same name.

*Milford
Township
Lat: 37-35-43 N **Long:** 94-07-34 W
Pop: 254 (1990); 292 (1980) **Pop Density:** 8.5
Land: 30.0 sq. mi.; **Water:** 0.0 sq. mi.

Mindenmines
City
ZIP: 64769 **Lat:** 37-28-23 N **Long:** 94-35-22 W
Pop: 346 (1990); 318 (1980) **Pop Density:** 91.1
Land: 3.8 sq. mi.; **Water:** 0.0 sq. mi. **Elev:** 968 ft.
Platted April 19, 1883, by R. J. Tucker. Incorporated 1903.

Nashville
Township
Lat: 37-25-00 N **Long:** 94-26-42 W
Pop: 346 (1990); 405 (1980) **Pop Density:** 7.1
Land: 48.5 sq. mi.; **Water:** 0.1 sq. mi.

Newport
Township
Lat: 37-30-10 N **Long:** 94-07-24 W
Pop: 286 (1990); 247 (1980) **Pop Density:** 9.4
Land: 30.5 sq. mi.; **Water:** 0.0 sq. mi.

Northfork
Township
Lat: 37-24-25 N **Long:** 94-20-42 W
Pop: 266 (1990); 256 (1980) **Pop Density:** 8.1
Land: 32.9 sq. mi.; **Water:** 0.1 sq. mi.

Ozark
Township
Lat: 37-31-41 N **Long:** 94-33-42 W
Pop: 969 (1990); 975 (1980) **Pop Density:** 25.2
Land: 38.4 sq. mi.; **Water:** 0.2 sq. mi.

Richland
Township
Lat: 37-23-56 N **Long:** 94-14-16 W
Pop: 571 (1990); 556 (1980) **Pop Density:** 11.3
Land: 50.6 sq. mi.; **Water:** 0.2 sq. mi.

South West
Township
Lat: 37-25-07 N **Long:** 94-33-46 W
Pop: 544 (1990); 538 (1980) **Pop Density:** 10.5
Land: 51.8 sq. mi.; **Water:** 0.3 sq. mi.

Union
Township
Lat: 37-35-48 N **Long:** 94-20-01 W
Pop: 338 (1990); 364 (1980) **Pop Density:** 9.4
Land: 36.1 sq. mi.; **Water:** 0.1 sq. mi.

MISSOURI, Bates County   *American Places Dictionary*

> ## Bates County
> **County Seat: Butler (ZIP: 64730)**
>
> **Pop:** 15,025 (1990); 15,873 (1980)   **Pop Density:** 17.7
> **Land:** 848.5 sq. mi.; **Water:** 2.9 sq. mi.   **Area Code:** 816
> On the central western border of MO, south of Kansas City; organized Jan 29, 1841 from Cooper County.
> **Name origin:** For Frederick Bates (1777–1825), secretary of LA Territory (1806), governor of MO Territory (1809–10), and state governor (1824–25).

Adrian — City
ZIP: 64720   **Lat:** 38-23-52 N **Long:** 94-21-03 W
Pop: 1,582 (1990); 1,484 (1980)   **Pop Density:** 1582.0
Land: 1.0 sq. mi.; **Water:** 0.0 sq. mi.   **Elev:** 871 ft.
Incorporated 1880.
Name origin: Possibly for one of the four sons of the influential Mr. Talmage, who was a General Passenger Agent for the Missouri Pacific Railroad, or for Roman Emperor Hadrian.

Amoret — City
ZIP: 64722   **Lat:** 38-15-20 N **Long:** 94-35-13 W
Pop: 212 (1990); 238 (1980)   **Pop Density:** 1060.0
Land: 0.2 sq. mi.; **Water:** 0.0 sq. mi.   **Elev:** 852 ft.
Incorporated 1891.

Amsterdam — City
ZIP: 64723   **Lat:** 38-20-57 N **Long:** 94-35-19 W
Pop: 237 (1990); 231 (1980)   **Pop Density:** 395.0
Land: 0.6 sq. mi.; **Water:** 0.0 sq. mi.
Incorporated 1971.
Name origin: Named in 1891 for Amsterdam, Holland, former home of its earliest settlers.

Butler — City
ZIP: 64730   **Lat:** 38-15-33 N **Long:** 94-20-21 W
Pop: 4,099 (1990); 4,107 (1980)   **Pop Density:** 1107.8
Land: 3.7 sq. mi.; **Water:** 0.0 sq. mi.
In western MO, southeast of Kansas City. Platted 1854. Incorporated 1873.
Name origin: For Mexican War officer William O. Butler.

Charlotte — Township
Lat: 38-16-08 N **Long:** 94-27-34 W
Pop: 277 (1990); 299 (1980)   **Pop Density:** 7.7
Land: 35.9 sq. mi.; **Water:** 0.1 sq. mi.

Deepwater — Township
Lat: 38-15-49 N **Long:** 94-07-36 W
Pop: 249 (1990); 294 (1980)   **Pop Density:** 6.9
Land: 35.9 sq. mi.; **Water:** 0.0 sq. mi.

Deer Creek — Township
Lat: 38-26-03 N **Long:** 94-20-25 W
Pop: 1,828 (1990); 1,741 (1980)   **Pop Density:** 57.7
Land: 31.7 sq. mi.; **Water:** 0.0 sq. mi.

Drexel — City
ZIP: 64742   **Lat:** 38-28-33 N **Long:** 94-36-22 W
Pop: 101 (1990); 127 (1980)   **Pop Density:** 505.0
Land: 0.2 sq. mi.; **Water:** 0.0 sq. mi.   **Elev:** 992 ft.
Incorporated 1914. Part of the town is also in Cass County.
Name origin: For the owner of a local store.

East Boone — Township
Lat: 38-26-03 N **Long:** 94-27-14 W
Pop: 426 (1990); 407 (1980)   **Pop Density:** 13.4
Land: 31.8 sq. mi.; **Water:** 0.0 sq. mi.

Elkhart — Township
Lat: 38-21-01 N **Long:** 94-27-12 W
Pop: 296 (1990); 334 (1980)   **Pop Density:** 8.3
Land: 35.5 sq. mi.; **Water:** 0.1 sq. mi.

Foster — Town
ZIP: 64745   **Lat:** 38-10-00 N **Long:** 94-30-28 W
Pop: 161 (1990); 175 (1980)   **Pop Density:** 322.0
Land: 0.5 sq. mi.; **Water:** 0.0 sq. mi.
Incorporated 1885.

Grand River — Township
Lat: 38-26-04 N **Long:** 94-14-07 W
Pop: 173 (1990); 238 (1980)   **Pop Density:** 6.9
Land: 25.1 sq. mi.; **Water:** 0.0 sq. mi.

Homer — Township
Lat: 38-15-49 N **Long:** 94-33-58 W
Pop: 409 (1990); 487 (1980)   **Pop Density:** 11.9
Land: 34.4 sq. mi.; **Water:** 0.3 sq. mi.

Howard — Township
Lat: 38-04-47 N **Long:** 94-31-32 W
Pop: 479 (1990); 535 (1980)   **Pop Density:** 13.0
Land: 36.9 sq. mi.; **Water:** 0.3 sq. mi.

Hudson — Township
Lat: 38-09-52 N **Long:** 94-06-15 W
Pop: 237 (1990); 268 (1980)   **Pop Density:** 5.2
Land: 45.9 sq. mi.; **Water:** 0.1 sq. mi.

Hume — Town
ZIP: 64752   **Lat:** 38-05-22 N **Long:** 94-34-53 W
Pop: 287 (1990); 315 (1980)   **Pop Density:** 410.0
Land: 0.7 sq. mi.; **Water:** 0.0 sq. mi.   **Elev:** 894 ft.
Incorporated 1881.

Lone Oak — Township
Lat: 38-10-22 N **Long:** 94-19-00 W
Pop: 265 (1990); 279 (1980)   **Pop Density:** 7.4
Land: 35.9 sq. mi.; **Water:** 0.0 sq. mi.

Merwin — Town
Lat: 38-24-15 N **Long:** 94-35-23 W
Pop: 75 (1990); 85 (1980)   **Pop Density:** 750.0
Land: 0.1 sq. mi.; **Water:** 0.0 sq. mi.   **Elev:** 883 ft.
Incorporated 1894.

Mingo — Township
Lat: 38-25-26 N **Long:** 94-07-44 W
Pop: 189 (1990); 177 (1980)   **Pop Density:** 7.3
Land: 25.8 sq. mi.; **Water:** 0.0 sq. mi.

Mound — Township
Lat: 38-21-01 N **Long:** 94-20-44 W
Pop: 645 (1990); 638 (1980)   **Pop Density:** 17.9
Land: 36.1 sq. mi.; **Water:** 0.1 sq. mi.

MISSOURI, Benton County

Mount Pleasant — Township
Lat: 38-15-51 N Long: 94-20-58 W
Pop: 4,848 (1990); 4,863 (1980) **Pop Density:** 135.4
Land: 35.8 sq. mi.; **Water:** 0.2 sq. mi.

New Home — Township
Lat: 38-09-48 N Long: 94-26-04 W
Pop: 198 (1990); 224 (1980) **Pop Density:** 4.4
Land: 44.5 sq. mi.; **Water:** 0.1 sq. mi. **Elev:** 795 ft.

Osage — Township
Lat: 38-05-33 N Long: 94-21-35 W
Pop: 1,630 (1990); 1,851 (1980) **Pop Density:** 36.5
Land: 44.7 sq. mi.; **Water:** 0.1 sq. mi.

Passaic — Town
ZIP: 64777 Lat: 38-19-17 N Long: 94-20-52 W
Pop: 40 (1990); 53 (1980) **Pop Density:** 400.0
Land: 0.1 sq. mi.; **Water:** 0.0 sq. mi. **Elev:** 865 ft.
Incorporated 1965.
Name origin: For Passaic, NJ.

Pleasant Gap — Township
Lat: 38-09-51 N Long: 94-13-16 W
Pop: 282 (1990); 315 (1980) **Pop Density:** 6.2
Land: 45.6 sq. mi.; **Water:** 0.0 sq. mi.

Prairie — Township
Lat: 38-04-18 N Long: 94-13-25 W
Pop: 154 (1990); 181 (1980) **Pop Density:** 5.9
Land: 25.9 sq. mi.; **Water:** 0.3 sq. mi.

Rich Hill — City
Lat: 38-05-44 N Long: 94-21-46 W
Pop: 1,317 (1990); 1,471 (1980) **Pop Density:** 940.7
Land: 1.4 sq. mi.; **Water:** 0.0 sq. mi. **Elev:** 801 ft.
Incorporated 1880.
Name origin: Named by the first postmaster, E. W. Ratekin, for the town's location on a hill underlaid with coal.

Rockville — City
ZIP: 64780 Lat: 38-04-13 N Long: 94-04-48 W
Pop: 193 (1990); 281 (1980) **Pop Density:** 643.3
Land: 0.3 sq. mi.; **Water:** 0.0 sq. mi. **Elev:** 784 ft.
Laid out 1868 by William L. Hardesty. Incorporated 1870. Not coextensive with the town of the same name.
Name origin: For the excellent white sandstone quarries in the area.

*Rockville — Township
ZIP: 64780 Lat: 38-04-22 N Long: 94-06-17 W
Pop: 302 (1990); 384 (1980) **Pop Density:** 12.2
Land: 24.7 sq. mi.; **Water:** 0.5 sq. mi.

Shawnee — Township
Lat: 38-20-52 N Long: 94-14-15 W
Pop: 254 (1990); 277 (1980) **Pop Density:** 7.1
Land: 35.8 sq. mi.; **Water:** 0.1 sq. mi.

Spruce — Township
Lat: 38-20-41 N Long: 94-07-36 W
Pop: 258 (1990); 325 (1980) **Pop Density:** 7.1
Land: 36.1 sq. mi.; **Water:** 0.0 sq. mi.

Summit — Township
Lat: 38-15-35 N Long: 94-14-52 W
Pop: 278 (1990); 278 (1980) **Pop Density:** 7.8
Land: 35.8 sq. mi.; **Water:** 0.1 sq. mi.

Walnut — Township
Lat: 38-09-59 N Long: 94-33-09 W
Pop: 464 (1990); 469 (1980) **Pop Density:** 10.2
Land: 45.7 sq. mi.; **Water:** 0.2 sq. mi.

West Boone — Township
Lat: 38-25-35 N Long: 94-33-47 W
Pop: 407 (1990); 472 (1980) **Pop Density:** 13.5
Land: 30.1 sq. mi.; **Water:** 0.2 sq. mi.

West Point — Township
Lat: 38-21-28 N Long: 94-33-28 W
Pop: 477 (1990); 537 (1980) **Pop Density:** 14.5
Land: 32.9 sq. mi.; **Water:** 0.1 sq. mi.

Benton County
County Seat: Warsaw (ZIP: 65355)

Pop: 13,859 (1990); 12,183 (1980) **Pop Density:** 19.6
Land: 705.6 sq. mi.; **Water:** 47.0 sq. mi. **Area Code:** 816
In west-central MO, southwest of Jefferson City; organized Jan 3, 1835 from Cooper County.
Name origin: For Thomas Hart Benton (1782–1858), U.S. journalist and statesman; nicknamed "Old Bullion" for championing the use of gold and silver currency rather than paper money.

Alexander — Township
Lat: 38-08-14 N Long: 93-25-35 W
Pop: 360 (1990); 274 (1980) **Pop Density:** 6.1
Land: 59.2 sq. mi.; **Water:** 12.0 sq. mi.

Cole — Township
Lat: 38-18-18 N Long: 93-10-22 W
Pop: 1,510 (1990); 1,178 (1980) **Pop Density:** 17.5
Land: 86.2 sq. mi.; **Water:** 4.0 sq. mi.

Cole Camp — City
ZIP: 65325 Lat: 38-27-34 N Long: 93-12-19 W
Pop: 1,054 (1990); 1,022 (1980) **Pop Density:** 1054.0
Land: 1.0 sq. mi.; **Water:** 0.0 sq. mi. **Elev:** 1018 ft.
Incorporated 1897.

Fristoe — Township
Lat: 38-09-32 N Long: 93-17-59 W
Pop: 1,883 (1990); 1,601 (1980) **Pop Density:** 23.3
Land: 80.7 sq. mi.; **Water:** 2.0 sq. mi.

Ionia
Town
ZIP: 65335 **Lat:** 38-30-10 N **Long:** 93-19-22 W
Pop: 126 (1990); 131 (1980) **Pop Density:** 1260.0
Land: 0.1 sq. mi.; **Water:** 0.0 sq. mi.

Laid out 1866 by Henry Pollard. Incorporated 1904. Part of the town is also in Pettis County.
Name origin: For the ancient Greek region.

Lincoln
City
ZIP: 65338 **Lat:** 38-23-38 N **Long:** 93-19-50 W
Pop: 874 (1990); 819 (1980) **Pop Density:** 971.1
Land: 0.9 sq. mi.; **Water:** 0.0 sq. mi.

Incorporated 1869.
Name origin: For Abraham Lincoln (1809–65), sixteenth U.S. president.

Lindsey
Township
Lat: 38-19-30 N **Long:** 93-23-44 W
Pop: 2,990 (1990); 2,482 (1980) **Pop Density:** 44.4
Land: 67.3 sq. mi.; **Water:** 8.2 sq. mi.

Tom
Township
Lat: 38-14-50 N **Long:** 93-27-06 W
Pop: 1,375 (1990); 894 (1980) **Pop Density:** 38.2
Land: 36.0 sq. mi.; **Water:** 17.6 sq. mi.

Union
Township
Lat: 38-09-43 N **Long:** 93-09-35 W
Pop: 1,082 (1990); 1,051 (1980) **Pop Density:** 8.9
Land: 121.5 sq. mi.; **Water:** 2.9 sq. mi.

Warsaw
City
ZIP: 65355 **Lat:** 38-14-34 N **Long:** 93-22-16 W
Pop: 1,696 (1990); 1,494 (1980) **Pop Density:** 942.2
Land: 1.8 sq. mi.; **Water:** 0.2 sq. mi. **Elev:** 709 ft.

Incorporated 1837.

White
Township
Lat: 38-26-25 N **Long:** 93-23-59 W
Pop: 1,975 (1990); 2,034 (1980) **Pop Density:** 17.2
Land: 114.8 sq. mi.; **Water:** 0.1 sq. mi.

Williams
Township
Lat: 38-26-52 N **Long:** 93-10-46 W
Pop: 2,684 (1990); 2,669 (1980) **Pop Density:** 19.2
Land: 139.9 sq. mi.; **Water:** 0.2 sq. mi.

Bollinger County
County Seat: Marble Hill (ZIP: 63764)

Pop: 10,619 (1990); 10,301 (1980) **Pop Density:** 17.1
Land: 620.8 sq. mi.; **Water:** 0.5 sq. mi. **Area Code:** 314

In southeastern MO, west of Cape Girardeau; organized Mar 1, 1851 from Cape Girardeau, Madison, Stoddard, and Wayne counties.
Name origin: For Col. George Frederick Bollinger (1770–1842), who led German settlers into MO in 1800.

Crooked Creek
Township
Lat: 37-25-03 N **Long:** 90-04-41 W
Pop: 1,042 (1990); 903 (1980) **Pop Density:** 12.3
Land: 84.7 sq. mi.; **Water:** 0.1 sq. mi.

Fillmore
Township
Lat: 37-15-01 N **Long:** 90-09-11 W
Pop: 444 (1990); 362 (1980) **Pop Density:** 7.3
Land: 60.7 sq. mi.; **Water:** 0.1 sq. mi.

Glenallen
Town
ZIP: 63751 **Lat:** 37-19-00 N **Long:** 90-01-41 W
Pop: 96 (1990); 125 (1980) **Pop Density:** 960.0
Land: 0.1 sq. mi.; **Water:** 0.0 sq. mi.

Incorporated 1906.

Liberty
Township
Lat: 37-11-14 N **Long:** 89-58-21 W
Pop: 1,068 (1990); 1,066 (1980) **Pop Density:** 11.7
Land: 91.4 sq. mi.; **Water:** 0.1 sq. mi.

Lorance
Township
Lat: 37-18-23 N **Long:** 89-58-41 W
Pop: 3,915 (1990); 3,798 (1980) **Pop Density:** 37.7
Land: 103.9 sq. mi.; **Water:** 0.1 sq. mi.

Marble Hill
City
ZIP: 63764 **Lat:** 37-18-08 N **Long:** 89-58-49 W
Pop: 1,447 (1990); 601 (1980) **Pop Density:** 964.7
Land: 1.5 sq. mi.; **Water:** 0.0 sq. mi.

Incorporated 1947.

Scopus
Township
Lat: 37-25-59 N **Long:** 89-55-48 W
Pop: 1,111 (1990); 952 (1980) **Pop Density:** 17.8
Land: 62.5 sq. mi.; **Water:** 0.0 sq. mi.

Sedgewickville
Village
ZIP: 63781 **Lat:** 37-30-54 N **Long:** 89-54-21 W
Pop: 138 (1990); 115 (1980) **Pop Density:** 276.0
Land: 0.5 sq. mi.; **Water:** 0.0 sq. mi. **Elev:** 642 ft.

Incorporated 1899.

Union
Township
Lat: 37-32-48 N **Long:** 90-04-05 W
Pop: 918 (1990); 911 (1980) **Pop Density:** 16.1
Land: 57.0 sq. mi.; **Water:** 0.0 sq. mi.

Wayne
Township
Lat: 37-07-06 N **Long:** 90-05-13 W
Pop: 1,349 (1990); 1,574 (1980) **Pop Density:** 12.4
Land: 108.8 sq. mi.; **Water:** 0.1 sq. mi.

MISSOURI, Boone County

Whitewater — Township
Lat: 37-32-43 N Long: 89-55-33 W
Pop: 772 (1990); 735 (1980) Pop Density: 14.9
Land: 51.8 sq. mi.; Water: 0.0 sq. mi.

Zalma — Village
ZIP: 63733 Lat: 37-08-36 N Long: 90-04-49 W
Pop: 83 (1990); 121 (1980) Pop Density: 830.0
Land: 0.1 sq. mi.; Water: 0.0 sq. mi.
Incorporated 1910.
Name origin: For Zalma Block, a friend of railroad builder, Louis Houck.

Boone County
County Seat: Columbia (ZIP: 65201)

Pop: 112,379 (1990); 100,376 (1980) Pop Density: 164.0
Land: 685.4 sq. mi.; Water: 5.8 sq. mi. Area Code: 314
In central MO, north of Jefferson City; organized Nov 16, 1820 (prior to statehood) from Howard County.
Name origin: For Daniel Boone (1734?–1820), U.S. frontiersman and KY pioneer.

Ashland — City
ZIP: 65010 Lat: 38-46-25 N Long: 92-15-24 W
Pop: 1,252 (1990); 1,021 (1980) Pop Density: 1565.0
Land: 0.8 sq. mi.; Water: 0.0 sq. mi.
Incorporated 1877.
Name origin: For the KY home of U.S. legislator Henry Clay (1777–1852).

Bourbon — Township
Lat: 39-12-15 N Long: 92-19-46 W
Pop: 2,140 (1990); 2,031 (1980) Pop Density: 26.3
Land: 81.3 sq. mi.; Water: 0.3 sq. mi.

Cedar — Township
Lat: 38-47-34 N Long: 92-17-48 W
Pop: 9,233 (1990); 7,797 (1980) Pop Density: 48.0
Land: 192.5 sq. mi.; Water: 3.4 sq. mi.

Centralia — City
ZIP: 65240 Lat: 39-12-41 N Long: 92-07-53 W
Pop: 3,414 (1990); 3,537 (1980) Pop Density: 1422.5
Land: 2.4 sq. mi.; Water: 0.0 sq. mi. Elev: 891 ft.
Incorporated 1867. Part of the town is also in Audrain County.

***Centralia** — Township
ZIP: 65240 Lat: 39-11-54 N Long: 92-09-16 W
Pop: 4,143 (1990); 4,238 (1980) Pop Density: 135.8
Land: 30.5 sq. mi.; Water: 0.1 sq. mi.

Columbia — City
ZIP: 65201 Lat: 38-57-14 N Long: 92-19-36 W
Pop: 69,101 (1990); 62,061 (1980) Pop Density: 1559.8
Land: 44.3 sq. mi.; Water: 0.2 sq. mi. Elev: 758 ft.
In central MO, 25 mi. north of Jefferson City. Incorporated 1821.
Name origin: Named in 1819 for Columbia, KY.

***Columbia** — Township
Lat: 38-57-00 N Long: 92-14-11 W
Pop: 38,240 (1990); 35,754 (1980) Pop Density: 476.8
Land: 80.2 sq. mi.; Water: 0.3 sq. mi.

Hallsville — City
ZIP: 65255 Lat: 39-06-56 N Long: 92-13-10 W
Pop: 917 (1990); 850 (1980) Pop Density: 1834.0
Land: 0.5 sq. mi.; Water: 0.0 sq. mi.
Incorporated 1853.

Harrisburg — Town
ZIP: 65256 Lat: 39-08-31 N Long: 92-27-34 W
Pop: 169 (1990); 283 (1980) Pop Density: 241.4
Land: 0.7 sq. mi.; Water: 0.0 sq. mi. Elev: 841 ft.
Incorporated 1890.

Hartsburg — Town
ZIP: 65039 Lat: 38-41-42 N Long: 92-18-35 W
Pop: 131 (1990); 118 (1980) Pop Density: 1310.0
Land: 0.1 sq. mi.; Water: 0.0 sq. mi. Elev: 564 ft.
Incorporated 1902.

Missouri — Township
Lat: 38-58-17 N Long: 92-25-35 W
Pop: 49,428 (1990); 41,834 (1980) Pop Density: 458.9
Land: 107.7 sq. mi.; Water: 0.9 sq. mi.

Perche — Township
Lat: 39-05-15 N Long: 92-25-13 W
Pop: 3,475 (1990); 3,199 (1980) Pop Density: 41.8
Land: 83.1 sq. mi.; Water: 0.2 sq. mi.

Rocheport — City
ZIP: 65279 Lat: 38-58-46 N Long: 92-33-47 W
Pop: 255 (1990); 272 (1980) Pop Density: 850.0
Land: 0.3 sq. mi.; Water: 0.0 sq. mi. Elev: 597 ft.
Incorporated 1835.

Rocky Fork — Township
Lat: 39-05-18 N Long: 92-13-26 W
Pop: 5,720 (1990); 5,523 (1980) Pop Density: 52.0
Land: 110.1 sq. mi.; Water: 0.5 sq. mi.

Sturgeon — City
ZIP: 65284 Lat: 39-14-01 N Long: 92-16-52 W
Pop: 838 (1990); 901 (1980) Pop Density: 1396.7
Land: 0.6 sq. mi.; Water: 0.0 sq. mi. Elev: 851 ft.
Laid out 1856 by the Sturgeon Town Co. Incorporated 1856.
Name origin: For Isaac H. Sturgeon, a superintendent of the North Missouri Railroad.

Buchanan County
County Seat: St. Joseph (ZIP: 64501)

Pop: 83,083 (1990); 87,888 (1980)
Land: 409.8 sq. mi.; **Water:** 4.8 sq. mi.
Pop Density: 202.8
Area Code: 816

On the northwestern border of MO, northwest of Kansas City; organized Dec 31, 1838 from Platte Purchase.

Name origin: For James Buchanan (1791–1868), fifteenth U.S. president.

Agency — Town
ZIP: 64401 Lat: 39-39-20 N Long: 94-44-54 W
Pop: 642 (1990); 419 (1980) Pop Density: 256.8
Land: 2.5 sq. mi.; Water: 0.0 sq. mi.
Incorporated 1903.

Name origin: Originally known as Agency Ford because the agency of the Sac and Fox Indians was located at this point, where the road from Clay County to the Blacksnake Hills crossed the ford.

*Agency — Township
ZIP: 64401 Lat: 39-40-09 N Long: 94-44-35 W
Pop: 1,177 (1990); 912 (1980) Pop Density: 73.6
Land: 16.0 sq. mi.; Water: 0.2 sq. mi.

Bloomington — Township
Lat: 39-34-15 N Long: 94-56-12 W
Pop: 584 (1990); 639 (1980) Pop Density: 16.5
Land: 35.4 sq. mi.; Water: 0.0 sq. mi.

Center — Township
Lat: 39-40-05 N Long: 94-49-20 W
Pop: 2,859 (1990); 2,756 (1980) Pop Density: 78.8
Land: 36.3 sq. mi.; Water: 0.0 sq. mi.

Crawford — Township
Lat: 39-34-14 N Long: 94-49-14 W
Pop: 954 (1990); 1,068 (1980) Pop Density: 27.0
Land: 35.3 sq. mi.; Water: 0.0 sq. mi.

Dearborn — City
Lat: 39-31-54 N Long: 94-45-51 W
Pop: 0 (1990); 547 (1980)
Land: 0.02 sq. mi.; Water: 0.0 sq. mi.
Incorporated 1882. Part of the town is also in Platte County.

Name origin: For Gen. Henry Dearborn (1751–1829), secretary of war under Thomas Jefferson (1743–1826).

De Kalb — Town
ZIP: 64440 Lat: 39-35-13 N Long: 94-55-25 W
Pop: 222 (1990); 245 (1980) Pop Density: 740.0
Land: 0.3 sq. mi.; Water: 0.0 sq. mi.
Founded 1839 by James G. Finch. Incorporated 1850.

Name origin: Named in 1851 for Baron Johann De Kalb (1721–80) of Bavaria, who fought with the Americans during the American Revolution. Previously called Bloomington.

Easton — City
ZIP: 64443 Lat: 39-43-17 N Long: 94-38-22 W
Pop: 232 (1990); 313 (1980) Pop Density: 386.7
Land: 0.6 sq. mi.; Water: 0.0 sq. mi.
Incorporated 1963.

Gower — City
Lat: 39-36-44 N Long: 94-36-10 W
Pop: 19 (1990); 87 (1980) Pop Density: 190.0
Land: 0.1 sq. mi.; Water: 0.0 sq. mi. Elev: 941 ft.
Incorporated 1946. Part of the town is also in Clinton County.

Name origin: Named in 1870 for A. G. Gower, Division Superintendent of the railroad.

Jackson — Township
Lat: 39-34-21 N Long: 94-43-53 W
Pop: 420 (1990); 464 (1980) Pop Density: 19.2
Land: 21.9 sq. mi.; Water: 0.1 sq. mi.

Lake — Township
Lat: 39-38-46 N Long: 95-01-15 W
Pop: 42 (1990); 53 (1980) Pop Density: 4.4
Land: 9.5 sq. mi.; Water: 0.4 sq. mi.

Lewis and Clark Village — Town
Lat: 39-32-23 N Long: 95-03-02 W
Pop: 142 (1990); 131 (1980) Pop Density: 236.7
Land: 0.6 sq. mi.; Water: 0.1 sq. mi.
Incorporated 1971.

Marion — Township
Lat: 39-45-42 N Long: 94-40-02 W
Pop: 1,189 (1990); 1,217 (1980) Pop Density: 24.7
Land: 48.2 sq. mi.; Water: 0.1 sq. mi.

Platte — Township
Lat: 39-34-41 N Long: 94-39-20 W
Pop: 391 (1990); 543 (1980) Pop Density: 12.7
Land: 30.8 sq. mi.; Water: 0.0 sq. mi.

Rush — Township
Lat: 39-34-04 N Long: 95-02-28 W
Pop: 1,068 (1990); 966 (1980) Pop Density: 40.5
Land: 26.4 sq. mi.; Water: 1.3 sq. mi.

Rushville — Town
ZIP: 64484 Lat: 39-35-14 N Long: 95-01-23 W
Pop: 306 (1990); 271 (1980) Pop Density: 1530.0
Land: 0.2 sq. mi.; Water: 0.0 sq. mi.
Incorporated 1847.

St. Joseph — City
ZIP: 64501 Lat: 39-45-33 N Long: 94-49-16 W
Pop: 71,852 (1990); 76,691 (1980) Pop Density: 1655.6
Land: 43.4 sq. mi.; Water: 0.7 sq. mi.
In northwest MO on the Missouri River, 45 mi. north-northwest of Kansas City. Settled 1826; laid out 1843; chartered as city 1851. Incorporated 1846.

Name origin: For Joseph, husband of the Virgin Mary.

Tremont — Township
Lat: 39-39-10 N Long: 94-39-21 W
Pop: 596 (1990); 571 (1980) Pop Density: 16.3
Land: 36.5 sq. mi.; Water: 0.1 sq. mi.

Washington Township
Lat: 39-45-29 N Long: 94-49-07 W
Pop: 73,152 (1990); 77,984 (1980)   Pop Density: 913.3
Land: 80.1 sq. mi.; Water: 2.1 sq. mi.

Wayne Township
Lat: 39-39-35 N Long: 94-56-15 W
Pop: 651 (1990); 715 (1980)   Pop Density: 19.5
Land: 33.3 sq. mi.; Water: 0.7 sq. mi.

Butler County
County Seat: Poplar Bluff (ZIP: 63901)

Pop: 38,765 (1990); 37,693 (1980)   Pop Density: 55.6
Land: 697.6 sq. mi.; Water: 1.4 sq. mi.   Area Code: 314

On the southeastern border of MO, southwest of Cape Girardeau; organized Feb 27, 1849 from Wayne County.

Name origin: For Maj. William Orlando Butler (1791–1880), officer in the War of 1812 and Mexican-American War; U.S. representative from KY (1839–43).

Ash Hill Township
Lat: 36-40-59 N Long: 90-14-45 W
Pop: 3,680 (1990); 4,199 (1980)   Pop Density: 28.1
Land: 130.9 sq. mi.; Water: 0.3 sq. mi.

Beaver Dam Township
Lat: 36-42-09 N Long: 90-31-58 W
Pop: 3,297 (1990); 2,971 (1980)   Pop Density: 43.4
Land: 75.9 sq. mi.; Water: 0.1 sq. mi.

Black River Township
Lat: 36-53-08 N Long: 90-26-37 W
Pop: 1,110 (1990); 846 (1980)   Pop Density: 21.6
Land: 51.3 sq. mi.; Water: 0.1 sq. mi.

Cane Creek Township
Lat: 36-53-31 N Long: 90-35-34 W
Pop: 378 (1990); 353 (1980)   Pop Density: 8.8
Land: 42.9 sq. mi.; Water: 0.0 sq. mi.

Coon Island Township
Lat: 36-32-34 N Long: 90-24-20 W
Pop: 221 (1990); 348 (1980)   Pop Density: 5.8
Land: 38.2 sq. mi.; Water: 0.0 sq. mi.

Epps Township
Lat: 36-48-24 N Long: 90-33-42 W
Pop: 1,944 (1990); 1,167 (1980)   Pop Density: 36.1
Land: 53.8 sq. mi.; Water: 0.1 sq. mi.

Fisk Town
ZIP: 63940   Lat: 36-46-55 N Long: 90-12-26 W
Pop: 422 (1990); 450 (1980)   Pop Density: 1406.7
Land: 0.3 sq. mi.; Water: 0.0 sq. mi.
Incorporated 1954.

Gillis Bluff Township
Lat: 36-32-31 N Long: 90-16-47 W
Pop: 712 (1990); 826 (1980)   Pop Density: 13.0
Land: 54.6 sq. mi.; Water: 0.1 sq. mi.

Neely Township
Lat: 36-33-51 N Long: 90-31-08 W
Pop: 1,212 (1990); 1,498 (1980)   Pop Density: 20.2
Land: 59.9 sq. mi.; Water: 0.0 sq. mi.

Neelyville City
ZIP: 63954   Lat: 36-33-33 N Long: 90-30-39 W
Pop: 381 (1990); 474 (1980)   Pop Density: 317.5
Land: 1.2 sq. mi.; Water: 0.0 sq. mi.
Incorporated 1883.
Name origin: For the Neely family.

Poplar Bluff City
ZIP: 63901   Lat: 36-45-50 N Long: 90-24-25 W
Pop: 16,996 (1990); 17,139 (1980)   Pop Density: 1634.2
Land: 10.4 sq. mi.; Water: 0.0 sq. mi.

In southeast MO, 65 mi. west-southwest of Cape Girardeau. Founded 1849. Incorporated 1870.

Name origin: For the trees and for its location on a bluff overlooking the Black River.

*Poplar Bluff Township
ZIP: 63901   Lat: 36-43-33 N Long: 90-23-45 W
Pop: 24,836 (1990); 24,243 (1980)   Pop Density: 179.1
Land: 138.7 sq. mi.; Water: 0.2 sq. mi.

Qulin Town
ZIP: 63961   Lat: 36-35-52 N Long: 90-14-56 W
Pop: 384 (1990); 545 (1980)   Pop Density: 960.0
Land: 0.4 sq. mi.; Water: 0.0 sq. mi.
Incorporated 1964.

St. Francois Township
Lat: 36-51-16 N Long: 90-17-10 W
Pop: 1,375 (1990); 1,242 (1980)   Pop Density: 26.7
Land: 51.5 sq. mi.; Water: 0.5 sq. mi.

Caldwell County
County Seat: Kingston (ZIP: 64650)

Pop: 8,380 (1990); 8,660 (1980)　　　　**Pop Density:** 19.5
Land: 429.4 sq. mi.; **Water:** 0.4 sq. mi.　　　　**Area Code:** 816
In northwestern MO, east of St. Joseph; organized Dec 29, 1836 from Ray County.
Name origin: For Matthew Caldwell, an officer of the KY Volunteers in the War of 1812, or for Gen. John Caldwell (?–1804), KY Indian fighter and legislator.

Braymer　　City
ZIP: 64624　　**Lat:** 39-35-24 N　**Long:** 93-47-44 W
Pop: 886 (1990); 986 (1980)　　**Pop Density:** 1476.7
Land: 0.6 sq. mi.; **Water:** 0.0 sq. mi.
Founded 1887. Incorporated 1888.
Name origin: For banker Judge Daniel Braymer.

Breckenridge　　City
ZIP: 64625　　**Lat:** 39-45-41 N　**Long:** 93-48-17 W
Pop: 418 (1990); 523 (1980)　　**Pop Density:** 696.7
Land: 0.6 sq. mi.; **Water:** 0.0 sq. mi.　　**Elev:** 927 ft.
Platted 1858. Incorporated 1865. Not coextensive with the town of the same name.
Name origin: For John C. Breckenridge (1821–75), Kentuckian, vice president under James Buchanan (1857–61), and candidate for U.S. president against Abraham Lincoln (1809–65).

*Breckenridge　　Township
ZIP: 64625　　**Lat:** 39-43-58 N　**Long:** 93-48-48 W
Pop: 608 (1990); 723 (1980)　　**Pop Density:** 17.2
Land: 35.4 sq. mi.; **Water:** 0.0 sq. mi.

Cowgill　　City
ZIP: 64637　　**Lat:** 39-33-38 N　**Long:** 93-55-32 W
Pop: 257 (1990); 267 (1980)　　**Pop Density:** 1285.0
Land: 0.2 sq. mi.; **Water:** 0.0 sq. mi.
Established 1887. Incorporated 1890.
Name origin: For prominent citizen Judge James Cowgill.

Davis　　Township
Lat: 39-34-02 N　**Long:** 93-48-48 W
Pop: 1,277 (1990); 1,377 (1980)　　**Pop Density:** 36.0
Land: 35.5 sq. mi.; **Water:** 0.0 sq. mi.

Fairview　　Township
Lat: 39-39-01 N　**Long:** 93-48-47 W
Pop: 185 (1990); 208 (1980)　　**Pop Density:** 5.2
Land: 35.9 sq. mi.; **Water:** 0.0 sq. mi.

Gomer　　Township
Lat: 39-44-21 N　**Long:** 93-55-25 W
Pop: 274 (1990); 333 (1980)　　**Pop Density:** 7.6
Land: 36.2 sq. mi.; **Water:** 0.1 sq. mi.

Grant　　Township
Lat: 39-34-19 N　**Long:** 94-01-47 W
Pop: 1,048 (1990); 1,019 (1980)　　**Pop Density:** 29.0
Land: 36.2 sq. mi.; **Water:** 0.0 sq. mi.

Hamilton　　City
ZIP: 64644　　**Lat:** 39-44-35 N　**Long:** 94-00-07 W
Pop: 1,737 (1990); 1,582 (1980)　　**Pop Density:** 1240.7
Land: 1.4 sq. mi.; **Water:** 0.0 sq. mi.　　**Elev:** 994 ft.
Incorporated 1855. Not coextensive with the town of the same name.
Name origin: Named by Albert G. Davis partly for Alexander Hamilton, first U.S. Secretary of the Treasury, and partly for lawyer and soldier Joseph Hamilton, who was killed during the War of 1812.

*Hamilton　　Township
ZIP: 64644　　**Lat:** 39-44-29 N　**Long:** 94-02-16 W
Pop: 2,191 (1990); 2,107 (1980)　　**Pop Density:** 63.0
Land: 34.8 sq. mi.; **Water:** 0.1 sq. mi.

Kidder　　City
ZIP: 64649　　**Lat:** 39-46-54 N　**Long:** 94-06-08 W
Pop: 241 (1990); 265 (1980)　　**Pop Density:** 602.5
Land: 0.4 sq. mi.; **Water:** 0.0 sq. mi.　　**Elev:** 1009 ft.
Incorporated 1976. Not coextensive with the town of the same name.

*Kidder　　Township
ZIP: 64649　　**Lat:** 39-44-11 N　**Long:** 94-08-58 W
Pop: 708 (1990); 745 (1980)　　**Pop Density:** 19.6
Land: 36.1 sq. mi.; **Water:** 0.0 sq. mi.

Kingston　　City
ZIP: 64650　　**Lat:** 39-38-32 N　**Long:** 94-02-17 W
Pop: 279 (1990); 280 (1980)　　**Pop Density:** 558.0
Land: 0.5 sq. mi.; **Water:** 0.0 sq. mi.
Incorporated 1843. Not coextensive with the town of the same name.
Name origin: For Judge Austin A. King, governor of MO (1848–52).

*Kingston　　Township
ZIP: 64650　　**Lat:** 39-39-12 N　**Long:** 94-02-35 W
Pop: 539 (1990); 546 (1980)　　**Pop Density:** 15.3
Land: 35.2 sq. mi.; **Water:** 0.0 sq. mi.

Lincoln　　Township
Lat: 39-33-57 N　**Long:** 93-55-39 W
Pop: 532 (1990); 513 (1980)　　**Pop Density:** 14.5
Land: 36.6 sq. mi.; **Water:** 0.0 sq. mi.

Mirabile　　Township
ZIP: 64671　　**Lat:** 39-39-16 N　**Long:** 94-08-24 W
Pop: 329 (1990); 386 (1980)　　**Pop Density:** 9.2
Land: 35.8 sq. mi.; **Water:** 0.1 sq. mi.

New York　　Township
Lat: 39-39-22 N　**Long:** 93-55-15 W
Pop: 241 (1990); 303 (1980)　　**Pop Density:** 6.7
Land: 36.1 sq. mi.; **Water:** 0.0 sq. mi.

Polo　　City
ZIP: 64671　　**Lat:** 39-33-07 N　**Long:** 94-02-24 W
Pop: 539 (1990); 583 (1980)　　**Pop Density:** 898.3
Land: 0.6 sq. mi.; **Water:** 0.0 sq. mi.
Settled 1867 by Isaac Webb and Groge Wilkinson. Incorporated 1866.
Name origin: For Polo, IL.

Rockford   Township
Lat: 39-34-57 N   **Long:** 94-09-13 W
Pop: 448 (1990); 400 (1980)   **Pop Density:** 12.5
Land: 35.7 sq. mi.; **Water:** 0.0 sq. mi.

Callaway County
County Seat: Fulton (ZIP: 65251)

Pop: 32,809 (1990); 32,252 (1980)   **Pop Density:** 39.1
Land: 839.1 sq. mi.; **Water:** 8.2 sq. mi.   **Area Code:** 314

In east-central MO, east of Columbia; organized Nov 25, 1820 (prior to statehood) from Howard, Boone, and Montgomery counties.

Name origin: For Capt. James Callaway (1783–1815), grandson of Daniel Boone, killed in a battle with Indians.

Auxvasse   City
ZIP: 65231   **Lat:** 39-01-02 N   **Long:** 91-53-40 W
Pop: 821 (1990); 858 (1980)   **Pop Density:** 1172.9
Land: 0.7 sq. mi.; **Water:** 0.0 sq. mi.   **Elev:** 870 ft.
Incorporated 1873.
Name origin: For the creek, itself named from French *aux vases* meaning 'at the swamp.'

***Auxvasse**   Township
ZIP: 65231   **Lat:** 38-45-34 N   **Long:** 91-44-48 W
Pop: 863 (1990); 941 (1980)   **Pop Density:** 9.7
Land: 89.2 sq. mi.; **Water:** 1.7 sq. mi.

Bourbon   Township
Lat: 38-54-41 N   **Long:** 92-05-27 W
Pop: 1,420 (1990); 1,119 (1980)   **Pop Density:** 32.0
Land: 44.4 sq. mi.; **Water:** 0.5 sq. mi.

Caldwell   Township
Lat: 38-43-32 N   **Long:** 91-59-54 W
Pop: 339 (1990); 339 (1980)   **Pop Density:** 14.5
Land: 23.3 sq. mi.; **Water:** 0.0 sq. mi.

Calwood   Township
Lat: 38-53-46 N   **Long:** 91-49-51 W
Pop: 794 (1990); 747 (1980)   **Pop Density:** 18.9
Land: 41.9 sq. mi.; **Water:** 0.2 sq. mi.

Cedar   Township
Lat: 38-42-27 N   **Long:** 92-06-58 W
Pop: 1,875 (1990); 1,571 (1980)   **Pop Density:** 39.8
Land: 47.1 sq. mi.; **Water:** 0.2 sq. mi.

Cleveland   Township
Lat: 38-59-55 N   **Long:** 92-06-37 W
Pop: 497 (1990); 499 (1980)   **Pop Density:** 20.4
Land: 24.4 sq. mi.; **Water:** 0.1 sq. mi.

Cote Sans Dessein   Township
Lat: 38-37-32 N   **Long:** 91-59-02 W
Pop: 904 (1990); 565 (1980)   **Pop Density:** 19.1
Land: 47.3 sq. mi.; **Water:** 1.5 sq. mi.

East Fulton   Township
Lat: 38-50-35 N   **Long:** 91-53-28 W
Pop: 5,954 (1990); 6,109 (1980)   **Pop Density:** 135.6
Land: 43.9 sq. mi.; **Water:** 0.1 sq. mi.

Fulton   City
ZIP: 65251   **Lat:** 38-51-11 N   **Long:** 91-56-55 W
Pop: 10,033 (1990); 11,046 (1980)   **Pop Density:** 946.5
Land: 10.6 sq. mi.; **Water:** 0.0 sq. mi.   **Elev:** 770 ft.
In central MO, 25 mi. north-northeast of Jefferson City. County seat since June 1825. Incorporated 1859.
Name origin: For American scientist, artist, and marine engineer Robert Fulton (1765–1815). Previously called Volney for Count Constantin Volney (1757–1820), French scholar and politician.

Guthrie   Township
Lat: 38-45-39 N   **Long:** 92-06-32 W
Pop: 438 (1990); 367 (1980)   **Pop Density:** 22.3
Land: 19.6 sq. mi.; **Water:** 0.0 sq. mi.

Holts Summit   City
ZIP: 65043   **Lat:** 38-38-40 N   **Long:** 92-06-57 W
Pop: 2,292 (1990); 2,540 (1980)   **Pop Density:** 694.5
Land: 3.3 sq. mi.; **Water:** 0.0 sq. mi.
Incorporated 1973.

Jackson   Township
Lat: 39-00-50 N   **Long:** 91-50-03 W
Pop: 1,637 (1990); 1,757 (1980)   **Pop Density:** 24.6
Land: 66.6 sq. mi.; **Water:** 0.3 sq. mi.

Jefferson City   City
ZIP: 65101   **Lat:** 38-35-29 N   **Long:** 92-09-34 W
Pop: 306 (1990); 25 (1980)   **Pop Density:** 87.4
Land: 3.5 sq. mi.; **Water:** 0.4 sq. mi.   **Elev:** 702 ft.
In central MO, south of Columbia. State capital since 1821; incorporated as town 1825; as city 1829. Part of the town is also in Cole County.
Name origin: For Thomas Jefferson (1743–1826), third U.S. president.

Kingdom City   Village
ZIP: 65262   **Lat:** 38-56-46 N   **Long:** 91-56-14 W
Pop: 112 (1990); 146 (1980)   **Pop Density:** 86.2
Land: 1.3 sq. mi.; **Water:** 0.0 sq. mi.   **Elev:** 862 ft.
Incorporated 1967.

Lake Mykee Town   Village
Lat: 38-40-35 N   **Long:** 92-06-02 W
Pop: 257 (1990); 188 (1980)   **Pop Density:** 1285.0
Land: 0.2 sq. mi.; **Water:** 0.1 sq. mi.
Incorporated 1978.

MISSOURI, Callaway County

Liberty
Township
Lat: 39-01-39 N **Long:** 92-01-07 W
Pop: 582 (1990); 550 (1980) **Pop Density:** 15.1
Land: 38.5 sq. mi.; **Water:** 0.1 sq. mi.

McCredie
Township
Lat: 38-57-01 N **Long:** 91-57-19 W
Pop: 550 (1990); 588 (1980) **Pop Density:** 14.1
Land: 39.1 sq. mi.; **Water:** 0.2 sq. mi.

Mokane
Town
ZIP: 65059 **Lat:** 38-40-27 N **Long:** 91-52-21 W
Pop: 186 (1990); 293 (1980) **Pop Density:** 620.0
Land: 0.3 sq. mi.; **Water:** 0.0 sq. mi. **Elev:** 534 ft.
Incorporated 1893.
Name origin: For the Missouri, Kansas and Topeka Railroad in 1849.

New Bloomfield
City
ZIP: 65063 **Lat:** 38-43-09 N **Long:** 92-05-22 W
Pop: 480 (1990); 519 (1980) **Pop Density:** 960.0
Land: 0.5 sq. mi.; **Water:** 0.0 sq. mi. **Elev:** 841 ft.
Incorporated 1959.

Nine Mile Prairie
Township
Lat: 38-53-48 N **Long:** 91-42-42 W
Pop: 634 (1990); 620 (1980) **Pop Density:** 8.7
Land: 73.0 sq. mi.; **Water:** 0.5 sq. mi.

Round Prairie
Township
Lat: 38-49-22 N **Long:** 92-04-49 W
Pop: 561 (1990); 500 (1980) **Pop Density:** 16.3
Land: 34.4 sq. mi.; **Water:** 0.1 sq. mi.

St. Aubert
Township
Lat: 38-44-31 N **Long:** 91-54-22 W
Pop: 1,491 (1990); 1,434 (1980) **Pop Density:** 26.3
Land: 56.6 sq. mi.; **Water:** 0.7 sq. mi.

Shamrock
Township
Lat: 39-00-15 N **Long:** 91-41-36 W
Pop: 332 (1990); 336 (1980) **Pop Density:** 7.7
Land: 42.9 sq. mi.; **Water:** 0.1 sq. mi.

Summit
Township
Lat: 38-37-20 N **Long:** 92-07-42 W
Pop: 6,231 (1990); 6,037 (1980) **Pop Density:** 106.1
Land: 58.7 sq. mi.; **Water:** 1.6 sq. mi.

West Fulton
Township
Lat: 38-50-42 N **Long:** 91-59-22 W
Pop: 7,707 (1990); 8,173 (1980) **Pop Density:** 159.6
Land: 48.3 sq. mi.; **Water:** 0.2 sq. mi.

Camden County
County Seat: Camdenton (ZIP: 65020)

Pop: 27,495 (1990); 20,017 (1980) **Pop Density:** 42.0
Land: 655.2 sq. mi.; **Water:** 53.7 sq. mi. **Area Code:** 314

In central MO, southwest of Jefferson City; organized Jan 29, 1841 as Kinderhook County from Pulaski, Morgan, and Benton counties; name changed Feb 23, 1843.
Name origin: For Charles Pratt (1714–94), 1st Earl of Camden, English statesman who supported the American colonies before the Revolutionary War.

Adair
Township
Lat: 38-08-18 N **Long:** 92-58-13 W
Pop: 2,059 (1990); 1,676 (1980) **Pop Density:** 20.9
Land: 98.4 sq. mi.; **Water:** 8.5 sq. mi.

Auglaize
Township
Lat: 37-54-04 N **Long:** 92-31-26 W
Pop: 2,022 (1990); 1,907 (1980) **Pop Density:** 16.5
Land: 122.6 sq. mi.; **Water:** 0.1 sq. mi.

Camdenton
City
ZIP: 65020 **Lat:** 38-00-31 N **Long:** 92-44-46 W
Pop: 2,561 (1990); 2,303 (1980) **Pop Density:** 731.7
Land: 3.5 sq. mi.; **Water:** 0.0 sq. mi. **Elev:** 1043 ft.
Incorporated 1931.
Name origin: Named in 1930 for Charles Pratt (1714–94), 1st Earl of Camden, English statesman who supported the American colonies before the Revolutionary War.

Climax Springs
Village
ZIP: 65324 **Lat:** 38-06-05 N **Long:** 93-03-05 W
Pop: 91 (1990); 87 (1980) **Pop Density:** 303.3
Land: 0.3 sq. mi.; **Water:** 0.0 sq. mi. **Elev:** 966 ft.
Incorporated 1882.

Jackson
Township
Lat: 38-01-27 N **Long:** 92-32-25 W
Pop: 536 (1990); 422 (1980) **Pop Density:** 9.7
Land: 55.5 sq. mi.; **Water:** 1.3 sq. mi.

Jasper
Township
Lat: 38-09-25 N **Long:** 92-47-20 W
Pop: 3,635 (1990); 2,425 (1980) **Pop Density:** 90.0
Land: 40.4 sq. mi.; **Water:** 14.2 sq. mi.

Kiheka
Township
Lat: 38-01-46 N **Long:** 92-41-01 W
Pop: 3,090 (1990) **Pop Density:** 74.3
Land: 41.6 sq. mi.; **Water:** 0.5 sq. mi.

Lake Ozark
City
Lat: 38-11-45 N **Long:** 92-38-39 W
Pop: 68 (1990); 98 (1980) **Pop Density:** 170.0
Land: 0.4 sq. mi.; **Water:** 0.0 sq. mi. **Elev:** 703 ft.
Incorporated 1989. Part of the town is also in Miller County.

Linn Creek
Town
ZIP: 65052 **Lat:** 38-02-38 N **Long:** 92-42-06 W
Pop: 232 (1990); 242 (1980) **Pop Density:** 210.9
Land: 1.1 sq. mi.; **Water:** 0.0 sq. mi.
Incorporated 1932.

American Places Dictionary   MISSOURI, Cape Girardeau County

Macks Creek   City
ZIP: 65786   Lat: 37-57-57 N   Long: 92-58-19 W
Pop: 272 (1990); 171 (1980)   Pop Density: 302.2
Land: 0.9 sq. mi.; Water: 0.0 sq. mi.   Elev: 875 ft.
Incorporated 1906.

Niangua   Township
Lat: 38-01-18 N   Long: 92-48-34 W
Pop: 2,922 (1990)   Pop Density: 168.9
Land: 17.3 sq. mi.; Water: 3.4 sq. mi.

Osceola   Township
Lat: 38-04-53 N   Long: 92-47-37 W
Pop: 2,411 (1990)   Pop Density: 93.8
Land: 25.7 sq. mi.; Water: 6.4 sq. mi.

Osage   Township
Lat: 38-06-07 N   Long: 92-42-07 W
Pop: 3,204 (1990); 10,642 (1980)   Pop Density: 156.3
Land: 20.5 sq. mi.; Water: 6.0 sq. mi.

Osage Beach   City
ZIP: 65065   Lat: 38-07-58 N   Long: 92-39-12 W
Pop: 2,511 (1990); 1,924 (1980)   Pop Density: 302.5
Land: 8.3 sq. mi.; Water: 0.9 sq. mi.   Elev: 895 ft.
Incorporated 1959. Part of the town is also in Miller County.

Pawhuska   Township
Lat: 38-11-10 N   Long: 92-39-36 W
Pop: 3,801 (1990)   Pop Density: 195.9
Land: 19.4 sq. mi.; Water: 10.7 sq. mi.

Richland   City
Lat: 37-51-43 N   Long: 92-24-38 W
Pop: 95 (1990); 97 (1980)   Pop Density: 475.0
Land: 0.2 sq. mi.; Water: 0.0 sq. mi.
Incorporated 1884. Part of the town is also in Pulaski and Laclede counties.

Russell   Township
Lat: 37-59-07 N   Long: 92-56-58 W
Pop: 2,035 (1990); 1,730 (1980)   Pop Density: 14.4
Land: 141.2 sq. mi.; Water: 1.6 sq. mi.

Stoutland   Village
ZIP: 65567   Lat: 37-48-54 N   Long: 92-30-55 W
Pop: 164 (1990); 240 (1980)   Pop Density: 546.7
Land: 0.3 sq. mi.; Water: 0.0 sq. mi.   Elev: 1171 ft.
Incorporated 1910. Part of the town is also in Laclede County.

Sunrise Beach   Village
ZIP: 65079   Lat: 38-10-32 N   Long: 92-46-42 W
Pop: 112 (1990); 100 (1980)   Pop Density: 124.4
Land: 0.9 sq. mi.; Water: 0.0 sq. mi.
Incorporated 1954. Part of the town is also in Morgan County.

Village of Four Seasons   Town
Lat: 38-11-53 N   Long: 92-42-55 W
Pop: 805 (1990)   Pop Density: 178.9
Land: 4.5 sq. mi.; Water: 0.1 sq. mi.

Warren   Township
Lat: 37-56-14 N   Long: 92-44-39 W
Pop: 1,780 (1990); 1,215 (1980)   Pop Density: 24.6
Land: 72.4 sq. mi.; Water: 1.1 sq. mi.

Cape Girardeau County
County Seat: Jackson (ZIP: 63755)

Pop: 61,633 (1990); 58,837 (1980)   Pop Density: 106.5
Land: 578.7 sq. mi.; Water: 7.7 sq. mi.   Area Code: 314
On the southeastern border of MO; original county; organized Oct 1, 1812 (prior to statehood).
Name origin: For Jean Girardot, a French naval officer stationed at Kaskaskia, IL (1704–20), later a trading-post operator. No explanation for the spelling variance.

Allenville   Village
Lat: 37-13-17 N   Long: 89-45-17 W
Pop: 69 (1990)   Pop Density: 345.0
Land: 0.2 sq. mi.; Water: 0.0 sq. mi.

Apple Creek   Township
ZIP: 63769   Lat: 37-32-31 N   Long: 89-45-47 W
Pop: 1,617 (1990); 1,586 (1980)   Pop Density: 19.4
Land: 83.3 sq. mi.; Water: 0.0 sq. mi.

Byrd   Township
Lat: 37-23-46 N   Long: 89-41-29 W
Pop: 12,184 (1990); 10,635 (1980)   Pop Density: 194.6
Land: 62.6 sq. mi.; Water: 0.0 sq. mi.

Cape Girardeau   City
ZIP: 63701   Lat: 37-18-46 N   Long: 89-32-57 W
Pop: 34,438 (1990); 34,361 (1980)   Pop Density: 1565.4
Land: 22.0 sq. mi.; Water: 0.0 sq. mi.
In southeastern MO on the Mississippi River, 30 mi. northwest of its confluence with the Ohio River. Incorporated 1808. Part of the town is also in Scott County.
Name origin: Named in 1812 for Jean Girardot, a French naval officer and trading-post operator.

*Cape Girardeau   Township
ZIP: 63701   Lat: 37-17-33 N   Long: 89-34-43 W
Pop: 37,092 (1990); 36,866 (1980)   Pop Density: 552.8
Land: 67.1 sq. mi.; Water: 3.4 sq. mi.

Delta   City
ZIP: 63744   Lat: 37-11-53 N   Long: 89-44-13 W
Pop: 450 (1990); 524 (1980)   Pop Density: 1500.0
Land: 0.3 sq. mi.; Water: 0.0 sq. mi.
Incorporated 1958.

MISSOURI, Cape Girardeau County

Gordonville
Town
ZIP: 63752 **Lat:** 37-18-37 N **Long:** 89-40-22 W
Pop: 345 (1990); 267 (1980) **Pop Density:** 431.3
Land: 0.8 sq. mi.; **Water:** 0.0 sq. mi.
Incorporated 1894.

Hubble
Township
Lat: 37-16-44 N **Long:** 89-43-38 W
Pop: 1,522 (1990); 1,420 (1980) **Pop Density:** 26.9
Land: 56.6 sq. mi.; **Water:** 0.1 sq. mi.

Jackson
City
ZIP: 63755 **Lat:** 37-22-49 N **Long:** 89-39-16 W
Pop: 9,256 (1990); 7,827 (1980) **Pop Density:** 1115.2
Land: 8.3 sq. mi.; **Water:** 0.0 sq. mi. **Elev:** 497 ft.
In southeastern MO, 10 mi. northwest of Cape Girardeau. Incorporated 1814.
Name origin: For Gen. Andrew Jackson (1767–1845), seventh U.S. president.

Kinder
Township
Lat: 37-21-21 N **Long:** 89-49-20 W
Pop: 819 (1990); 651 (1980) **Pop Density:** 25.5
Land: 32.1 sq. mi.; **Water:** 0.0 sq. mi.

Liberty
Township
Lat: 37-15-38 N **Long:** 89-49-50 W
Pop: 356 (1990); 325 (1980) **Pop Density:** 14.1
Land: 25.3 sq. mi.; **Water:** 0.2 sq. mi.

Oak Ridge
Town
ZIP: 63769 **Lat:** 37-29-59 N **Long:** 89-43-46 W
Pop: 202 (1990); 252 (1980) **Pop Density:** 505.0
Land: 0.4 sq. mi.; **Water:** 0.0 sq. mi.
Incorporated 1869.

Old Appleton
Town
ZIP: 63770 **Lat:** 37-35-35 N **Long:** 89-42-33 W
Pop: 82 (1990); 80 (1980) **Pop Density:** 820.0
Land: 0.1 sq. mi.; **Water:** 0.0 sq. mi.
Incorporated 1902.

Pocahontas
Town
ZIP: 63779 **Lat:** 37-30-03 N **Long:** 89-38-23 W
Pop: 90 (1990); 130 (1980) **Pop Density:** 900.0
Land: 0.1 sq. mi.; **Water:** 0.0 sq. mi.
Incorporated 1858.
Name origin: For the famous daughter (c. 1595–1617) of Indian chief Powhatan, who later prevented the execution of Capt. John Smith (c. 1580–1631).

Randol
Township
Lat: 37-23-34 N **Long:** 89-31-04 W
Pop: 3,080 (1990); 2,534 (1980) **Pop Density:** 47.2
Land: 65.3 sq. mi.; **Water:** 1.6 sq. mi.

Scott City
City
Lat: 37-14-29 N **Long:** 89-33-19 W
Pop: 0 (1990); 3,262 (1980)
Land: 0.1 sq. mi.; **Water:** 0.0 sq. mi.
Incorporated 1980. Part of the town is also in Scott County.

Shawnee
Township
Lat: 37-30-44 N **Long:** 89-34-34 W
Pop: 2,485 (1990); 2,200 (1980) **Pop Density:** 27.5
Land: 90.4 sq. mi.; **Water:** 2.0 sq. mi.

Welch
Township
Lat: 37-10-38 N **Long:** 89-46-31 W
Pop: 1,418 (1990); 1,471 (1980) **Pop Density:** 23.9
Land: 59.4 sq. mi.; **Water:** 0.1 sq. mi.

Whitewater
Town
ZIP: 63785 **Lat:** 37-14-11 N **Long:** 89-47-51 W
Pop: 103 (1990); 161 (1980) **Pop Density:** 515.0
Land: 0.2 sq. mi.; **Water:** 0.0 sq. mi. **Elev:** 370 ft.
Incorporated 1908.

*Whitewater
Township
ZIP: 63785 **Lat:** 37-26-29 N **Long:** 89-48-40 W
Pop: 1,060 (1990); 1,149 (1980) **Pop Density:** 29.0
Land: 36.5 sq. mi.; **Water:** 0.0 sq. mi.

Carroll County
County Seat: Carrollton (ZIP: 64633)

Pop: 10,748 (1990); 12,131 (1980) **Pop Density:** 15.5
Land: 694.6 sq. mi.; **Water:** 7.8 sq. mi. **Area Code:** 816
In north-central MO, northeast of Kansas City; organized Jan 2, 1833 from Ray County.
Name origin: For Charles Carroll (1737–1832), a signer of the Declaration of Independence, U.S. senator from MD (1789–92), and founder of the Baltimore and Ohio Railroad.

Bogard
City
ZIP: 64622 **Lat:** 39-27-28 N **Long:** 93-31-26 W
Pop: 228 (1990); 285 (1980) **Pop Density:** 456.0
Land: 0.5 sq. mi.; **Water:** 0.0 sq. mi.
Incorporated 1961.

Bosworth
City
ZIP: 64623 **Lat:** 39-28-11 N **Long:** 93-20-08 W
Pop: 334 (1990); 394 (1980) **Pop Density:** 556.7
Land: 0.6 sq. mi.; **Water:** 0.0 sq. mi.
Incorporated 1895.

Carrollton
City
ZIP: 64633 **Lat:** 39-21-47 N **Long:** 93-29-46 W
Pop: 4,406 (1990); 4,700 (1980) **Pop Density:** 1101.5
Land: 4.0 sq. mi.; **Water:** 0.0 sq. mi. **Elev:** 754 ft.
In northwest-central MO, northeast of Kansas City. Platted March 31, 1834; county seat. Incorporated 1833.
Name origin: For Charles Carroll (1737–1832) of Carrollton, a signer of the Declaration of Independence, U.S. senator from MD (1789–92), and founder of the Baltimore and Ohio Railroad.

MISSOURI, Carroll County

*Carrollton — Township
ZIP: 64633   Lat: 39-23-54 N   Long: 93-28-40 W
Pop: 4,520 (1990); 4,592 (1980)   Pop Density: 127.3
Land: 35.5 sq. mi.; Water: 0.1 sq. mi.

Cherry Valley — Township
Lat: 39-14-16 N   Long: 93-42-21 W
Pop: 65 (1990); 84 (1980)   Pop Density: 3.7
Land: 17.7 sq. mi.; Water: 0.8 sq. mi.

Combs — Township
Lat: 39-23-59 N   Long: 93-21-59 W
Pop: 254 (1990); 304 (1980)   Pop Density: 7.2
Land: 35.3 sq. mi.; Water: 0.0 sq. mi.

De Witt — City
ZIP: 64639   Lat: 39-23-05 N   Long: 93-13-12 W
Pop: 125 (1990); 132 (1980)   Pop Density: 625.0
Land: 0.2 sq. mi.; Water: 0.0 sq. mi.
Incorporated 1910. Not coextensive with the town of the same name.

*De Witt — Township
ZIP: 64639   Lat: 39-24-06 N   Long: 93-13-39 W
Pop: 309 (1990); 341 (1980)   Pop Density: 7.0
Land: 44.4 sq. mi.; Water: 1.7 sq. mi.

Egypt — Township
Lat: 39-18-12 N   Long: 93-42-05 W
Pop: 1,072 (1990); 1,224 (1980)   Pop Density: 29.3
Land: 36.6 sq. mi.; Water: 0.0 sq. mi.

Eugene — Township
Lat: 39-18-13 N   Long: 93-20-52 W
Pop: 283 (1990); 313 (1980)   Pop Density: 5.6
Land: 50.1 sq. mi.; Water: 2.1 sq. mi.

Fairfield — Township
Lat: 39-28-41 N   Long: 93-42-12 W
Pop: 192 (1990); 224 (1980)   Pop Density: 5.2
Land: 36.7 sq. mi.; Water: 0.0 sq. mi.

Hale — City
Lat: 39-36-18 N   Long: 93-20-35 W
Pop: 480 (1990); 529 (1980)   Pop Density: 960.0
Land: 0.5 sq. mi.; Water: 0.0 sq. mi.
Founded 1833. Incorporated 1884.
Name origin: For John P. Hale of Carrollton.

Hill — Township
Lat: 39-34-32 N   Long: 93-35-03 W
Pop: 204 (1990); 280 (1980)   Pop Density: 5.7
Land: 35.8 sq. mi.; Water: 0.0 sq. mi.

Hurricane — Township
Lat: 39-34-31 N   Long: 93-20-54 W
Pop: 771 (1990); 793 (1980)   Pop Density: 16.2
Land: 47.7 sq. mi.; Water: 0.4 sq. mi.

Leslie — Township
Lat: 39-28-50 N   Long: 93-34-59 W
Pop: 159 (1990); 212 (1980)   Pop Density: 4.4
Land: 36.1 sq. mi.; Water: 0.1 sq. mi.

Moss Creek — Township
Lat: 39-18-35 N   Long: 93-35-33 W
Pop: 131 (1990); 207 (1980)   Pop Density: 3.6
Land: 36.5 sq. mi.; Water: 0.0 sq. mi.

Norborne — City
Lat: 39-18-08 N   Long: 93-40-32 W
Pop: 856 (1990); 931 (1980)   Pop Density: 1426.7
Land: 0.6 sq. mi.; Water: 0.0 sq. mi.
Founded 1868. Incorporated 1874.
Name origin: For Norborne B. Coats, promoter of the town.

Prairie — Township
Lat: 39-23-53 N   Long: 93-41-59 W
Pop: 185 (1990); 237 (1980)   Pop Density: 5.1
Land: 36.4 sq. mi.; Water: 0.1 sq. mi.

Ridge — Township
Lat: 39-28-59 N   Long: 93-21-22 W
Pop: 496 (1990); 602 (1980)   Pop Density: 14.0
Land: 35.4 sq. mi.; Water: 0.1 sq. mi.

Rockford — Township
Lat: 39-28-33 N   Long: 93-16-43 W
Pop: 87 (1990); 119 (1980)   Pop Density: 5.7
Land: 15.2 sq. mi.; Water: 0.5 sq. mi.

Stokes Mound — Township
Lat: 39-34-15 N   Long: 93-28-43 W
Pop: 399 (1990); 458 (1980)   Pop Density: 11.3
Land: 35.2 sq. mi.; Water: 0.0 sq. mi.

Sugartree — Township
Lat: 39-14-24 N   Long: 93-33-31 W
Pop: 40 (1990); 52 (1980)   Pop Density: 2.0
Land: 20.5 sq. mi.; Water: 1.1 sq. mi.

Tina — Town
ZIP: 64682   Lat: 39-32-13 N   Long: 93-26-28 W
Pop: 199 (1990); 202 (1980)   Pop Density: 663.3
Land: 0.3 sq. mi.; Water: 0.0 sq. mi.
Incorporated 1882.
Name origin: For the daughter of railroadman, E.M. Gilchrist.

Trotter — Township
Lat: 39-23-55 N   Long: 93-35-18 W
Pop: 268 (1990); 283 (1980)   Pop Density: 7.4
Land: 36.2 sq. mi.; Water: 0.0 sq. mi.

Van Horn — Township
Lat: 39-28-57 N   Long: 93-28-37 W
Pop: 468 (1990); 617 (1980)   Pop Density: 13.1
Land: 35.6 sq. mi.; Water: 0.0 sq. mi.

Wakenda — Town
ZIP: 64687   Lat: 39-18-55 N   Long: 93-22-40 W
Pop: 89 (1990); 98 (1980)   Pop Density: 890.0
Land: 0.1 sq. mi.; Water: 0.0 sq. mi.
Incorporated 1869.

*Wakenda — Township
Lat: 39-19-00 N   Long: 93-28-11 W
Pop: 636 (1990); 868 (1980)   Pop Density: 20.1
Land: 31.7 sq. mi.; Water: 0.8 sq. mi.

Washington — Township
Lat: 39-34-04 N   Long: 93-42-03 W
Pop: 209 (1990); 257 (1980)   Pop Density: 5.8
Land: 36.0 sq. mi.; Water: 0.0 sq. mi.

Carter County
County Seat: Van Buren (ZIP: 63965)

Pop: 5,515 (1990); 5,428 (1980) **Pop Density:** 10.9
Land: 507.6 sq. mi.; **Water:** 1.4 sq. mi. **Area Code:** 314
In southeastern MO, southwest of Cape Girardeau; organized Mar 10, 1859 from Ripley, Reynolds, Shannon, and Oregon counties.
Name origin: For Zimri A. Carter, a settler from SC in 1812.

Carter   Township
Lat: 37-00-08 N **Long:** 91-01-29 W
Pop: 2,098 (1990); 2,048 (1980) **Pop Density:** 19.6
Land: 106.8 sq. mi.; **Water:** 0.4 sq. mi.

Ellsinore   Town
ZIP: 63937 **Lat:** 36-56-01 N **Long:** 90-44-45 W
Pop: 405 (1990); 362 (1980) **Pop Density:** 1012.5
Land: 0.4 sq. mi.; **Water:** 0.0 sq. mi. **Elev:** 711 ft.
Incorporated 1954.

Grandin   City
ZIP: 63943 **Lat:** 36-49-47 N **Long:** 90-49-18 W
Pop: 233 (1990); 265 (1980) **Pop Density:** 582.5
Land: 0.4 sq. mi.; **Water:** 0.0 sq. mi. **Elev:** 585 ft.
Incorporated 1963.

Jackson   Township
Lat: 36-59-20 N **Long:** 90-47-58 W
Pop: 575 (1990); 588 (1980) **Pop Density:** 7.9
Land: 73.2 sq. mi.; **Water:** 0.1 sq. mi.

Johnson   Township
Lat: 36-52-24 N **Long:** 90-46-52 W
Pop: 2,201 (1990); 2,097 (1980) **Pop Density:** 19.6
Land: 112.3 sq. mi.; **Water:** 0.2 sq. mi.

Kelly   Township
Lat: 36-53-15 N **Long:** 91-01-58 W
Pop: 216 (1990); 311 (1980) **Pop Density:** 1.7
Land: 130.2 sq. mi.; **Water:** 0.7 sq. mi.

Pike   Township
Lat: 36-59-19 N **Long:** 91-09-21 W
Pop: 425 (1990); 384 (1980) **Pop Density:** 5.0
Land: 85.0 sq. mi.; **Water:** 0.0 sq. mi.

Van Buren   Town
ZIP: 63965 **Lat:** 37-00-26 N **Long:** 91-00-43 W
Pop: 893 (1990); 850 (1980) **Pop Density:** 446.5
Land: 2.0 sq. mi.; **Water:** 0.0 sq. mi. **Elev:** 475 ft.
Incorporated 1927.
Name origin: For Martin Van Buren (1782–1862), eighth U.S. president.

Cass County
County Seat: Harrisonville (ZIP: 64701)

Pop: 63,808 (1990); 51,029 (1980) **Pop Density:** 91.3
Land: 699.1 sq. mi.; **Water:** 3.6 sq. mi. **Area Code:** 816
On the central western border of MO, south of Kansas City; organized as Van Buren County Mar 3, 1835 from Jackson County; name changed in 1849.
Name origin: For Gen. Lewis Cass (1782–1866), OH legislator, governor of MI Territory (1813–31), U.S. secretary of war (1831–36), and U.S. secretary of state (1857–60).

Archie   City
ZIP: 64725 **Lat:** 38-28-58 N **Long:** 94-20-56 W
Pop: 799 (1990); 753 (1980) **Pop Density:** 799.0
Land: 1.0 sq. mi.; **Water:** 0.0 sq. mi. **Elev:** 832 ft.
Incorporated 1962.
Name origin: For one of the four sons of Mr. Talmage, who was a General Passenger Agent for the Missouri Pacific Railroad.

Austin   Township
Lat: 38-30-46 N **Long:** 94-19-29 W
Pop: 1,531 (1990); 1,450 (1980) **Pop Density:** 30.0
Land: 51.1 sq. mi.; **Water:** 0.1 sq. mi.

Baldwin Park   Village
Lat: 38-47-43 N **Long:** 94-14-43 W
Pop: 85 (1990); 126 (1980) **Pop Density:** 850.0
Land: 0.1 sq. mi.; **Water:** 0.0 sq. mi.
Incorporated 1971.

Belton   City
ZIP: 64012 **Lat:** 38-49-10 N **Long:** 94-31-52 W
Pop: 18,150 (1990); 12,708 (1980) **Pop Density:** 1500.0
Land: 12.1 sq. mi.; **Water:** 0.1 sq. mi. **Elev:** 1102 ft.
In western MO, 10 mi. south of Kansas City. Platted 1871. Incorporated 1873.
Name origin: For Marcus Lindsey Belt (?–1921) a friend of the founder.

MISSOURI, Cass County

Big Creek
Township
Lat: 38-47-43 N Long: 94-20-23 W
Pop: 2,246 (1990); 1,698 (1980) Pop Density: 64.4
Land: 34.9 sq. mi.; Water: 1.5 sq. mi.

Camp Branch
Township
Lat: 38-38-05 N Long: 94-14-11 W
Pop: 2,002 (1990); 1,735 (1980) Pop Density: 37.8
Land: 52.9 sq. mi.; Water: 0.4 sq. mi.

Cleveland
Town
ZIP: 64734 Lat: 38-40-40 N Long: 94-35-49 W
Pop: 506 (1990); 485 (1980) Pop Density: 337.3
Land: 1.5 sq. mi.; Water: 0.0 sq. mi.
Incorporated 1910.
Name origin: Named in 1900 for Grover Cleveland (1837–1908), twenty-fourth U.S. president.

Coldwater
Township
Lat: 38-30-53 N Long: 94-33-36 W
Pop: 1,181 (1990); 1,068 (1980) Pop Density: 35.1
Land: 33.6 sq. mi.; Water: 0.1 sq. mi.

Creighton
City
ZIP: 64739 Lat: 38-29-47 N Long: 94-04-18 W
Pop: 289 (1990); 301 (1980) Pop Density: 963.3
Land: 0.3 sq. mi.; Water: 0.0 sq. mi.
Incorporated 1885.
Name origin: Named in 1855 for an early settler, John Creighton.

Dayton
Township
Lat: 38-30-21 N Long: 94-11-58 W
Pop: 599 (1990); 648 (1980) Pop Density: 16.5
Land: 36.4 sq. mi.; Water: 0.0 sq. mi.

Dolan
Township
Lat: 38-37-00 N Long: 94-29-39 W
Pop: 1,509 (1990); 1,376 (1980) Pop Density: 42.0
Land: 35.9 sq. mi.; Water: 0.2 sq. mi.

Drexel
City
Lat: 38-29-07 N Long: 94-36-24 W
Pop: 835 (1990); 781 (1980) Pop Density: 1391.7
Land: 0.6 sq. mi.; Water: 0.0 sq. mi. Elev: 992 ft.
Incorporated 1914. Part of the town is also in Bates County.
Name origin: For the owner of a local store.

East Lynne
Town
ZIP: 64743 Lat: 38-40-05 N Long: 94-13-45 W
Pop: 289 (1990); 286 (1980) Pop Density: 963.3
Land: 0.3 sq. mi.; Water: 0.0 sq. mi.
Incorporated 1871.

Everett
Township
Lat: 38-31-18 N Long: 94-27-29 W
Pop: 381 (1990); 395 (1980) Pop Density: 10.6
Land: 36.1 sq. mi.; Water: 0.1 sq. mi.

Freeman
City
ZIP: 64746 Lat: 38-37-07 N Long: 94-30-20 W
Pop: 480 (1990); 485 (1980) Pop Density: 960.0
Land: 0.5 sq. mi.; Water: 0.0 sq. mi. Elev: 349 ft.
Incorporated 1967.

Garden City
City
ZIP: 64747 Lat: 38-33-38 N Long: 94-11-18 W
Pop: 1,225 (1990); 1,021 (1980) Pop Density: 1020.8
Land: 1.2 sq. mi.; Water: 0.0 sq. mi. Elev: 916 ft.
Incorporated 1898.

Grand River
Township
Lat: 38-36-38 N Long: 94-21-51 W
Pop: 9,196 (1990); 7,932 (1980) Pop Density: 143.5
Land: 64.1 sq. mi.; Water: 0.1 sq. mi.

Gunn City
Village
ZIP: 64760 Lat: 38-39-58 N Long: 94-09-49 W
Pop: 65 (1990); 58 (1980) Pop Density: 650.0
Land: 0.1 sq. mi.; Water: 0.0 sq. mi.
Incorporated 1880.

Harrisonville
City
ZIP: 64701 Lat: 38-39-19 N Long: 94-20-57 W
Pop: 7,683 (1990); 6,372 (1980) Pop Density: 1146.7
Land: 6.7 sq. mi.; Water: 0.1 sq. mi. Elev: 904 ft.
In western MO, 30 mi. south of Kansas City. Incorporated 1857.

Index
Township
Lat: 38-37-20 N Long: 94-09-48 W
Pop: 1,238 (1990); 1,264 (1980) Pop Density: 33.6
Land: 36.9 sq. mi.; Water: 0.2 sq. mi.

Kansas City
City
Lat: 38-50-05 N Long: 94-33-29 W
Pop: 42 (1990); 448,028 (1980) Pop Density: 42.0
Land: 1.0 sq. mi.; Water: 0.0 sq. mi.
In western MO at the confluence of the Missouri and Kansas (or Kaw) rivers; on the western bank is Kansas City, KS. Established 1821; founded 1833; laid out 1838; developed 1836. Called *The Heart of America* for its location. Largest winter-wheat market; one of the largest livestock exchanges in U.S.; wheat flour production second only to Buffalo. Manufacturing (printing and publishing, food processing, automobile assembly) and industrial (chemicals, electric equipment, farm machinery) city. Site of University of Missouri. Incorporated 1850. Part of the town is also in Clay, Jackson, and Platte counties.
Name origin: Named in 1889 from the old Siouan language Kansa 'people of the south wind.' Previously called City of Kansas (1853).

Lake Annette
Village
Lat: 38-39-19 N Long: 94-30-28 W
Pop: 157 (1990) Pop Density: 785.0
Land: 0.2 sq. mi.; Water: 0.1 sq. mi.

Lake Winnebago
City
Lat: 38-49-17 N Long: 94-21-25 W
Pop: 748 (1990); 681 (1980) Pop Density: 415.6
Land: 1.8 sq. mi.; Water: 0.4 sq. mi.
Incorporated 1964.

Lee's Summit
City
Lat: 38-49-59 N Long: 94-23-28 W
Pop: 433 (1990); 50 (1980) Pop Density: 541.3
Land: 0.8 sq. mi.; Water: 0.3 sq. mi.
In western MO, 20 mi. southeast of Kansas City. Incorporated 1868. Part of the town is also in Jackson County.

Mount Pleasant
Township
Lat: 38-48-17 N Long: 94-33-19 W
Pop: 16,674 (1990); 12,771 (1980) Pop Density: 537.9
Land: 31.0 sq. mi.; Water: 0.1 sq. mi.

MISSOURI, Cass County

Peculiar
City
ZIP: 64078 **Lat:** 38-43-23 N **Long:** 94-27-28 W
Pop: 1,777 (1990); 1,571 (1980) **Pop Density:** 1269.3
Land: 1.4 sq. mi.; **Water:** 0.0 sq. mi. **Elev:** 1004 ft.
In western MO, southwest of Independence. Incorporated 1953.
Name origin: According to one story, George Moore, Carry Nation's (1846–1911) father, took Mrs. Jane Hawkins and her group of spiritualists to look at a farm as a possible home. As they came over a hilltop and saw the valley below, Mrs. Hawkins exclaimed: "That's peculiar! It is the very place I saw in a vision in Connecticut." Another story concerns the postmaster, E.T. Thompson, who sent word to the P.O. Dept. that any name would do so long as it was different or 'peculiar.'

*Peculiar
Township
ZIP: 64078 **Lat:** 38-41-55 N **Long:** 94-21-16 W
Pop: 2,031 (1990); 1,680 (1980) **Pop Density:** 56.4
Land: 36.0 sq. mi.; **Water:** 0.1 sq. mi.

Pleasant Hill
City
ZIP: 64080 **Lat:** 38-47-47 N **Long:** 94-15-56 W
Pop: 3,827 (1990); 3,301 (1980) **Pop Density:** 933.4
Land: 4.1 sq. mi.; **Water:** 0.0 sq. mi. **Elev:** 909 ft.
Incorporated 1859.
Name origin: For its descriptive connotations.

*Pleasant Hill
Township
ZIP: 64080 **Lat:** 38-46-20 N **Long:** 94-15-38 W
Pop: 4,598 (1990); 4,022 (1980) **Pop Density:** 166.6
Land: 27.6 sq. mi.; **Water:** 0.1 sq. mi.

Polk
Township
Lat: 38-45-40 N **Long:** 94-10-39 W
Pop: 1,459 (1990); 1,378 (1980) **Pop Density:** 26.4
Land: 55.3 sq. mi.; **Water:** 0.0 sq. mi.

Raymore
City
ZIP: 64083 **Lat:** 38-48-40 N **Long:** 94-27-26 W
Pop: 5,592 (1990); 3,154 (1980) **Pop Density:** 408.2
Land: 13.7 sq. mi.; **Water:** 0.1 sq. mi. **Elev:** 1104 ft.
Incorporated 1879.
Name origin: For two St. Louis railroad men, the Messrs. Ray and Moore.

*Raymore
Township
ZIP: 64083 **Lat:** 38-47-54 N **Long:** 94-27-23 W
Pop: 11,646 (1990); 7,332 (1980) **Pop Density:** 322.6
Land: 36.1 sq. mi.; **Water:** 0.2 sq. mi.

Sherman
Township
Lat: 38-30-26 N **Long:** 94-06-20 W
Pop: 711 (1990); 701 (1980) **Pop Density:** 18.8
Land: 37.9 sq. mi.; **Water:** 0.1 sq. mi.

Strasburg
Town
ZIP: 64090 **Lat:** 38-45-33 N **Long:** 94-09-52 W
Pop: 124 (1990); 170 (1980) **Pop Density:** 620.0
Land: 0.2 sq. mi.; **Water:** 0.0 sq. mi.
Incorporated 1966.

Union
Township
Lat: 38-42-43 N **Long:** 94-34-00 W
Pop: 1,788 (1990); 1,506 (1980) **Pop Density:** 59.4
Land: 30.1 sq. mi.; **Water:** 0.1 sq. mi.

West Dolan
Township
Lat: 38-37-17 N **Long:** 94-34-41 W
Pop: 798 (1990); 703 (1980) **Pop Density:** 29.0
Land: 27.5 sq. mi.; **Water:** 0.1 sq. mi.

West Line
Village
Lat: 38-37-57 N **Long:** 94-35-06 W
Pop: 98 (1990); 109 (1980) **Pop Density:** 980.0
Land: 0.1 sq. mi.; **Water:** 0.0 sq. mi.
Incorporated 1975.

West Peculiar
Township
Lat: 38-42-32 N **Long:** 94-27-44 W
Pop: 4,220 (1990); 3,370 (1980) **Pop Density:** 117.5
Land: 35.9 sq. mi.; **Water:** 0.1 sq. mi.

Cedar County
County Seat: Stockton (ZIP: 65785)

Pop: 12,093 (1990); 11,894 (1980) **Pop Density:** 25.4
Land: 476.0 sq. mi.; **Water:** 22.6 sq. mi. **Area Code:** 417
In southwestern MO, northwest of Springfield; organized Feb 14, 1845 from Dade and St. Clair counties.
Name origin: For the many cedar trees found by early settlers.

Benton
Township
Lat: 37-40-17 N **Long:** 94-00-24 W
Pop: 933 (1990); 934 (1980) **Pop Density:** 11.1
Land: 84.3 sq. mi.; **Water:** 0.0 sq. mi.

Box
Township
Lat: 37-49-12 N **Long:** 93-59-32 W
Pop: 5,903 (1990); 5,923 (1980) **Pop Density:** 71.6
Land: 82.5 sq. mi.; **Water:** 0.1 sq. mi.

Cedar
Township
Lat: 37-50-28 N **Long:** 93-52-04 W
Pop: 510 (1990); 487 (1980) **Pop Density:** 12.5
Land: 40.8 sq. mi.; **Water:** 0.1 sq. mi.

El Dorado Springs
City
ZIP: 64744 **Lat:** 37-52-10 N **Long:** 94-01-10 W
Pop: 3,830 (1990); 3,868 (1980) **Pop Density:** 1235.5
Land: 3.1 sq. mi.; **Water:** 0.0 sq. mi.
In western MO northwest of Springfield. Incorporated 1881.

Jefferson — Township
Lat: 37-42-55 N Long: 93-40-52 W
Pop: 569 (1990); 565 (1980) Pop Density: 11.4
Land: 50.1 sq. mi.; Water: 0.4 sq. mi.

Jerico Springs — Village
ZIP: 64756 Lat: 37-37-07 N Long: 94-00-37 W
Pop: 247 (1990); 208 (1980) Pop Density: 352.9
Land: 0.7 sq. mi.; Water: 0.0 sq. mi.
Incorporated 1881.

Linn — Township
Lat: 37-39-42 N Long: 93-51-37 W
Pop: 2,883 (1990); 2,679 (1980) Pop Density: 26.1
Land: 110.5 sq. mi.; Water: 7.7 sq. mi.

Madison — Township
Lat: 37-38-01 N Long: 93-41-37 W
Pop: 622 (1990); 572 (1980) Pop Density: 13.6
Land: 45.6 sq. mi.; Water: 14.1 sq. mi.

Stockton — City
ZIP: 65785 Lat: 37-41-48 N Long: 93-47-44 W
Pop: 1,579 (1990); 1,432 (1980) Pop Density: 789.5
Land: 2.0 sq. mi.; Water: 0.0 sq. mi. Elev: 965 ft.
Incorporated 1850.
Name origin: For Commodore Robert Field Stockton (1795–1866), a naval officer and U.S. senator (1851–53) who served in the War of 1812 and claimed California (1847) for the U.S.

Umber View Heights — Village
Lat: 37-37-27 N Long: 93-48-13 W
Pop: 34 (1990); 41 (1980) Pop Density: 340.0
Land: 0.1 sq. mi.; Water: 0.0 sq. mi.
Incorporated 1975.

Washington — Township
Lat: 37-47-44 N Long: 93-45-54 W
Pop: 673 (1990); 734 (1980) Pop Density: 10.8
Land: 62.1 sq. mi.; Water: 0.1 sq. mi.

Chariton County
County Seat: Keytesville (ZIP: 65216)

Pop: 9,202 (1990); 10,489 (1980) Pop Density: 12.2
Land: 755.9 sq. mi.; Water: 12.4 sq. mi. Area Code: 816

In north-central MO, northwest of Columbia; organized Nov 16, 1820 (prior to statehood) from Howard County.
Name origin: For a French fur trader, probably Jean Chariton, who was also called Joseph or John Chorette. During the 1700s he established a trading post on the north bank of the Missouri River in what is now IA.

Bee Branch — Township
Lat: 39-39-29 N Long: 92-46-39 W
Pop: 416 (1990); 449 (1980) Pop Density: 7.7
Land: 54.2 sq. mi.; Water: 0.2 sq. mi.

Bowling Green — Township
Lat: 39-22-41 N Long: 92-59-40 W
Pop: 210 (1990); 272 (1980) Pop Density: 5.3
Land: 39.4 sq. mi.; Water: 1.7 sq. mi.

Brunswick — City
ZIP: 65236 Lat: 39-25-26 N Long: 93-07-33 W
Pop: 1,074 (1990); 1,272 (1980) Pop Density: 895.0
Land: 1.2 sq. mi.; Water: 0.1 sq. mi.
In north-central MO on the Missouri River. Laid out 1836. Incorporated 1836. Not coextensive with the town of the same name.
Name origin: For Brunswick Terrace, the former English home of the Rev. James Keyte.

***Brunswick** — Township
ZIP: 65236 Lat: 39-27-06 N Long: 93-05-20 W
Pop: 1,610 (1990); 1,929 (1980) Pop Density: 23.0
Land: 70.1 sq. mi.; Water: 1.3 sq. mi.

Chariton — Township
Lat: 39-17-41 N Long: 92-52-40 W
Pop: 416 (1990); 451 (1980) Pop Density: 7.7
Land: 54.1 sq. mi.; Water: 1.8 sq. mi.

Clark — Township
Lat: 39-39-25 N Long: 92-54-53 W
Pop: 375 (1990); 412 (1980) Pop Density: 10.4
Land: 36.2 sq. mi.; Water: 0.0 sq. mi.

Cockrell — Township
Lat: 39-34-24 N Long: 92-48-26 W
Pop: 188 (1990); 238 (1980) Pop Density: 5.4
Land: 34.8 sq. mi.; Water: 0.2 sq. mi.

Cunningham — Township
Lat: 39-38-43 N Long: 93-12-19 W
Pop: 307 (1990); 389 (1980) Pop Density: 5.3
Land: 58.1 sq. mi.; Water: 3.9 sq. mi.

Dalton — Town
ZIP: 65246 Lat: 39-23-53 N Long: 92-59-31 W
Pop: 38 (1990); 76 (1980) Pop Density: 190.0
Land: 0.2 sq. mi.; Water: 0.0 sq. mi. Elev: 725 ft.
Incorporated 1872.

Glasgow — City
ZIP: 65254 Lat: 39-14-07 N Long: 92-50-45 W
Pop: 47 (1990); 52 (1980) Pop Density: 470.0
Land: 0.1 sq. mi.; Water: 0.0 sq. mi. Elev: 650 ft.
Laid out in 1836 after three earlier attempts to establish a river port in the vicinity had failed. Incorporated 1936. Part of the town is also in Howard County.
Name origin: For James Glasgow, a St. Louis merchant.

Keytesville — City
ZIP: 65261 Lat: 39-25-57 N Long: 92-56-12 W
Pop: 564 (1990); 689 (1980) Pop Density: 805.7
Land: 0.7 sq. mi.; Water: 0.0 sq. mi. Elev: 709 ft.
Platted in 1830 by the Rev. James Keyte. County seat. Incorporated 1868. Not coextensive with the town of the same name.

MISSOURI, Chariton County

*Keytesville
ZIP: 65261   **Lat:** 39-27-01 N   **Long:** 92-55-59 W   Township
Pop: 985 (1990); 1,233 (1980)   **Pop Density:** 13.2
Land: 74.6 sq. mi.; **Water:** 0.1 sq. mi.

Marceline
ZIP: 64658   **Lat:** 39-42-00 N   **Long:** 92-56-53 W   City
Pop: 7 (1990); 2,938 (1980)   **Pop Density:** 70.0
Land: 0.1 sq. mi.; **Water:** 0.0 sq. mi.

Founded 1887. Incorporated 1888. Part of the town is also in Linn County.

Name origin: For the wife of a railroad official.

Mendon
ZIP: 64660   **Lat:** 39-35-27 N   **Long:** 93-08-00 W   Town
Pop: 207 (1990); 252 (1980)   **Pop Density:** 1035.0
Land: 0.2 sq. mi.; **Water:** 0.0 sq. mi.

Founded 1871. Incorporated 1890. Not coextensive with the town of the same name.

*Mendon
ZIP: 64660   **Lat:** 39-34-11 N   **Long:** 93-08-36 W   Township
Pop: 351 (1990); 469 (1980)   **Pop Density:** 9.9
Land: 35.5 sq. mi.; **Water:** 1.6 sq. mi.

Musselfork
Lat: 39-33-52 N   **Long:** 92-55-22 W   Township
Pop: 369 (1990); 353 (1980)   **Pop Density:** 9.9
Land: 37.2 sq. mi.; **Water:** 0.4 sq. mi.

Rothville
ZIP: 64676   **Lat:** 39-39-16 N   **Long:** 93-03-39 W   Village
Pop: 100 (1990); 118 (1980)   **Pop Density:** 333.3
Land: 0.3 sq. mi.; **Water:** 0.0 sq. mi.

Incorporated 1907.

Salisbury
ZIP: 65281   **Lat:** 39-25-24 N   **Long:** 92-48-08 W   City
Pop: 1,881 (1990); 1,975 (1980)   **Pop Density:** 1446.9
Land: 1.3 sq. mi.; **Water:** 0.0 sq. mi.

Incorporated 1882. Not coextensive with the town of the same name.

Name origin: For Judge Lucien Salsbury, a founder.

*Salisbury
ZIP: 65281   **Lat:** 39-25-02 N   **Long:** 92-47-01 W   Township
Pop: 2,896 (1990); 2,978 (1980)   **Pop Density:** 31.0
Land: 93.3 sq. mi.; **Water:** 0.1 sq. mi.

Salt Creek
Lat: 39-34-04 N   **Long:** 93-01-47 W   Township
Pop: 217 (1990); 244 (1980)   **Pop Density:** 5.8
Land: 37.3 sq. mi.; **Water:** 0.0 sq. mi.

Sumner
ZIP: 64681   **Lat:** 39-39-20 N   **Long:** 93-14-35 W   Town
Pop: 140 (1990); 182 (1980)   **Pop Density:** 466.7
Land: 0.3 sq. mi.; **Water:** 0.0 sq. mi.   **Elev:** 682 ft.

Incorporated 1882.

Triplett
ZIP: 65286   **Lat:** 39-29-51 N   **Long:** 93-11-36 W   City
Pop: 58 (1990); 137 (1980)   **Pop Density:** 290.0
Land: 0.2 sq. mi.; **Water:** 0.0 sq. mi.

Incorporated 1881. Not coextensive with the town of the same name.

*Triplett
ZIP: 65286   **Lat:** 39-30-24 N   **Long:** 93-12-56 W   Township
Pop: 192 (1990); 314 (1980)   **Pop Density:** 4.3
Land: 45.1 sq. mi.; **Water:** 0.8 sq. mi.

Wayland
Lat: 39-31-34 N   **Long:** 92-44-47 W   Township
Pop: 230 (1990); 255 (1980)   **Pop Density:** 6.2
Land: 37.1 sq. mi.; **Water:** 0.1 sq. mi.

Yellow Creek
Lat: 39-39-29 N   **Long:** 93-02-57 W   Township
Pop: 440 (1990); 461 (1980)   **Pop Density:** 9.0
Land: 49.1 sq. mi.; **Water:** 0.0 sq. mi.

Christian County
County Seat: Ozark (ZIP: 65721)

Pop: 32,644 (1990); 22,402 (1980)   **Pop Density:** 58.0
Land: 563.2 sq. mi.; **Water:** 0.9 sq. mi.   **Area Code:** 417

In southwestern MO, south of Springfield; organized Mar 8, 1859 from Taney, Greene, and Webster counties.

Name origin: For Col. William Christian (1743–86), army officer, Indian fighter, and legislator; brother-in-law of Revolutionary leader Patrick Henry (1736–99).

Billings
ZIP: 65610   **Lat:** 37-03-48 N   **Long:** 93-33-20 W   City
Pop: 989 (1990); 911 (1980)   **Pop Density:** 1236.3
Land: 0.8 sq. mi.; **Water:** 0.0 sq. mi.

Founded 1872. Incorporated 1871.

Name origin: For a Mr. Billings, who paid $1000 to local churches for the honor.

Bruner
ZIP: 65620   **Lat:** 37-00-48 N   **Long:** 92-57-17 W   Township
Pop: 603 (1990); 519 (1980)   **Pop Density:** 19.4
Land: 31.1 sq. mi.; **Water:** 0.0 sq. mi.

Cassidy
Lat: 37-03-35 N   **Long:** 93-14-32 W   Township
Pop: 2,069 (1990)   **Pop Density:** 181.5
Land: 11.4 sq. mi.; **Water:** 0.0 sq. mi.

MISSOURI, Christian County

Chadwick — Township
ZIP: 65629 Lat: 36-55-02 N Long: 93-01-56 W
Pop: 326 (1990); 437 (1980) Pop Density: 16.4
Land: 19.9 sq. mi.; Water: 0.0 sq. mi.

Clever — City
ZIP: 65631 Lat: 37-01-47 N Long: 93-28-16 W
Pop: 580 (1990); 551 (1980) Pop Density: 966.7
Land: 0.6 sq. mi.; Water: 0.0 sq. mi. Elev: 1398 ft.
Incorporated 1909.

East Benton — Township
Lat: 37-03-56 N Long: 92-56-58 W
Pop: 305 (1990); 292 (1980) Pop Density: 19.8
Land: 15.4 sq. mi.; Water: 0.0 sq. mi.

East Finley — Township
Lat: 36-58-35 N Long: 93-12-28 W
Pop: 3,389 (1990) Pop Density: 313.8
Land: 10.8 sq. mi.; Water: 0.0 sq. mi.

East Polk — Township
Lat: 37-02-32 N Long: 93-31-46 W
Pop: 1,531 (1990) Pop Density: 58.4
Land: 26.2 sq. mi.; Water: 0.0 sq. mi.

Fremont Hills — City
Lat: 37-03-56 N Long: 93-15-09 W
Pop: 201 (1990) Pop Density: 402.0
Land: 0.5 sq. mi.; Water: 0.0 sq. mi.

Garden Grove — Township
Lat: 37-01-08 N Long: 93-17-14 W
Pop: 765 (1990) Pop Density: 170.0
Land: 4.5 sq. mi.; Water: 0.0 sq. mi.

Garrison — Township
ZIP: 65657 Lat: 36-51-31 N Long: 93-00-47 W
Pop: 267 (1990); 152 (1980) Pop Density: 7.7
Land: 34.9 sq. mi.; Water: 0.0 sq. mi.

Lead Hill — Township
Lat: 36-56-38 N Long: 92-56-38 W
Pop: 134 (1990); 158 (1980) Pop Density: 6.6
Land: 20.2 sq. mi.; Water: 0.0 sq. mi.

Lincoln — Township
Lat: 37-02-14 N Long: 93-26-11 W
Pop: 1,728 (1990); 1,499 (1980) Pop Density: 40.9
Land: 42.3 sq. mi.; Water: 0.2 sq. mi.

Linden — Township
Lat: 37-04-03 N Long: 93-07-12 W
Pop: 1,067 (1990); 657 (1980) Pop Density: 48.3
Land: 22.1 sq. mi.; Water: 0.1 sq. mi.

McCracken — Township
Lat: 36-59-39 N Long: 93-09-15 W
Pop: 1,076 (1990); 575 (1980) Pop Density: 55.5
Land: 19.4 sq. mi.; Water: 0.1 sq. mi.

Nixa — City
ZIP: 65714 Lat: 37-02-49 N Long: 93-17-52 W
Pop: 4,707 (1990); 2,662 (1980) Pop Density: 1569.0
Land: 3.0 sq. mi.; Water: 0.0 sq. mi.
Incorporated 1946.

North Galloway — Township
Lat: 36-56-23 N Long: 93-16-25 W
Pop: 2,219 (1990); 1,307 (1980) Pop Density: 60.5
Land: 36.7 sq. mi.; Water: 0.0 sq. mi.

North Linn — Township
Lat: 36-54-19 N Long: 93-09-36 W
Pop: 470 (1990); 301 (1980) Pop Density: 16.5
Land: 28.4 sq. mi.; Water: 0.0 sq. mi.

North View — Township
Lat: 37-03-54 N Long: 93-17-01 W
Pop: 2,755 (1990) Pop Density: 459.2
Land: 6.0 sq. mi.; Water: 0.0 sq. mi.

Oldfield — Township
ZIP: 65720 Lat: 36-57-42 N Long: 93-01-12 W
Pop: 409 (1990); 316 (1980) Pop Density: 27.4
Land: 14.9 sq. mi.; Water: 0.0 sq. mi.

Ozark — City
ZIP: 65721 Lat: 37-01-10 N Long: 93-12-28 W
Pop: 4,243 (1990); 2,980 (1980) Pop Density: 1285.8
Land: 3.3 sq. mi.; Water: 0.0 sq. mi. Elev: 1178 ft.
Incorporated 1888.

Riverside — Township
Lat: 37-03-41 N Long: 93-12-07 W
Pop: 1,325 (1990) Pop Density: 125.0
Land: 10.6 sq. mi.; Water: 0.1 sq. mi.

Rosedale — Township
Lat: 37-00-41 N Long: 93-19-38 W
Pop: 2,102 (1990) Pop Density: 127.4
Land: 16.5 sq. mi.; Water: 0.1 sq. mi.

Seneca — Township
Lat: 36-52-25 N Long: 92-55-45 W
Pop: 95 (1990); 106 (1980) Pop Density: 5.2
Land: 18.2 sq. mi.; Water: 0.0 sq. mi.

South Galloway — Township
Lat: 36-51-28 N Long: 93-15-39 W
Pop: 968 (1990); 767 (1980) Pop Density: 20.4
Land: 47.5 sq. mi.; Water: 0.0 sq. mi.

South Linn — Township
Lat: 36-51-30 N Long: 93-07-08 W
Pop: 188 (1990); 192 (1980) Pop Density: 5.4
Land: 34.5 sq. mi.; Water: 0.0 sq. mi.

Sparta — City
ZIP: 65753 Lat: 37-00-06 N Long: 93-04-59 W
Pop: 751 (1990); 743 (1980) Pop Density: 1072.9
Land: 0.7 sq. mi.; Water: 0.0 sq. mi. Elev: 1407 ft.
Incorporated 1885.

*Sparta — Township
ZIP: 65753 Lat: 36-59-26 N Long: 93-04-59 W
Pop: 1,411 (1990); 1,213 (1980) Pop Density: 57.4
Land: 24.6 sq. mi.; Water: 0.0 sq. mi.

Springfield — City
Lat: 37-05-21 N Long: 93-16-19 W
Pop: 0 (1990); 133,116 (1980)
Land: 0.03 sq. mi.; Water: 0.0 sq. mi.

In southwestern MO, 145 mi. south-southeast of Kansas City. Settled 1829. Part of the town is also in Greene County. Commercial center for farming, lumbering, and mining areas; agriculture (fruit orchards, dairy processing, poultry); commercial (flour mills, meat-packing, electronics equipment, machine shops). Incorporated 1838.

Name origin: For either the former home of one of the early settlers, or named by John Polk Campbell, who staked an early claim here, and chose the name because there was a field on a hill with a spring under it.

MISSOURI, Christian County

Union Chapel
Township
Lat: 37-04-28 N Long: 93-20-54 W
Pop: 4,094 (1990) Pop Density: 206.8
Land: 19.8 sq. mi.; Water: 0.2 sq. mi.

West Benton
Township
Lat: 37-03-45 N Long: 93-02-05 W
Pop: 281 (1990); 222 (1980) Pop Density: 19.1
Land: 14.7 sq. mi.; Water: 0.0 sq. mi.

West Finley
Township
Lat: 36-59-38 N Long: 93-14-36 W
Pop: 2,190 (1990) Pop Density: 172.4
Land: 12.7 sq. mi.; Water: 0.1 sq. mi.

West Polk
Township
Lat: 37-03-07 N Long: 93-34-52 W
Pop: 877 (1990) Pop Density: 44.5
Land: 19.7 sq. mi.; Water: 0.0 sq. mi.

Clark County
County Seat: Kahoka (ZIP: 63445)

Pop: 7,547 (1990); 8,493 (1980) **Pop Density:** 14.9
Land: 507.3 sq. mi.; **Water:** 4.6 sq. mi. **Area Code:** 816
On the northeastern tip of MO; organized Dec 16, 1836 from Lewis County.
Name origin: For William Clark (1770–1838), explorer and co-leader of the Lewis and Clark Expedition (1803–06).

Alexandria
City
ZIP: 63430 Lat: 40-21-35 N Long: 91-27-33 W
Pop: 341 (1990); 417 (1980) Pop Density: 852.5
Land: 0.4 sq. mi.; Water: 0.0 sq. mi.
Incorporated 1947.
Name origin: For Alexandria, Egypt.

Clay
Township
Lat: 40-19-12 N Long: 91-33-02 W
Pop: 367 (1990); 402 (1980) Pop Density: 6.8
Land: 53.8 sq. mi.; Water: 0.2 sq. mi.

Des Moines
Township
Lat: 40-25-16 N Long: 91-34-01 W
Pop: 842 (1990); 953 (1980) Pop Density: 29.8
Land: 28.3 sq. mi.; Water: 0.8 sq. mi.

Folker
Township
Lat: 40-32-22 N Long: 91-53-40 W
Pop: 266 (1990); 302 (1980) Pop Density: 5.0
Land: 53.6 sq. mi.; Water: 0.1 sq. mi.

Grant
Township
Lat: 40-34-44 N Long: 91-45-59 W
Pop: 167 (1990); 192 (1980) Pop Density: 6.8
Land: 24.4 sq. mi.; Water: 0.3 sq. mi.

Jackson
Township
Lat: 40-19-02 N Long: 91-40-00 W
Pop: 455 (1990); 571 (1980) Pop Density: 8.5
Land: 53.7 sq. mi.; Water: 0.1 sq. mi.

Jefferson
Township
Lat: 40-30-47 N Long: 91-46-37 W
Pop: 200 (1990); 220 (1980) Pop Density: 5.5
Land: 36.4 sq. mi.; Water: 0.0 sq. mi.

Kahoka
City
ZIP: 63445 Lat: 40-25-25 N Long: 91-43-06 W
Pop: 2,195 (1990); 2,101 (1980) Pop Density: 1463.3
Land: 1.5 sq. mi.; Water: 0.0 sq. mi. Elev: 703 ft.
Platted 1856. Incorporated 1885.
Name origin: A variant form of *Cahokia*, the name of an Indian tribe; meaning of the name is unknown.

Lincoln
Township
Lat: 40-25-52 N Long: 91-46-15 W
Pop: 2,703 (1990); 2,977 (1980) Pop Density: 64.1
Land: 42.2 sq. mi.; Water: 0.1 sq. mi.

Luray
Town
ZIP: 63453 Lat: 40-27-09 N Long: 91-53-03 W
Pop: 70 (1990); 175 (1980) Pop Density: 350.0
Land: 0.2 sq. mi.; Water: 0.0 sq. mi.

Madison
Township
Lat: 40-25-23 N Long: 91-38-58 W
Pop: 552 (1990); 524 (1980) Pop Density: 18.2
Land: 30.4 sq. mi.; Water: 0.1 sq. mi.

Revere
Town
ZIP: 63465 Lat: 40-29-39 N Long: 91-40-33 W
Pop: 133 (1990); 191 (1980) Pop Density: 665.0
Land: 0.2 sq. mi.; Water: 0.0 sq. mi. Elev: 680 ft.
Incorporated 1887.

Sweet Home
Township
Lat: 40-30-35 N Long: 91-40-07 W
Pop: 411 (1990); 463 (1980) Pop Density: 13.3
Land: 30.9 sq. mi.; Water: 0.4 sq. mi.

Union
Township
Lat: 40-19-28 N Long: 91-46-48 W
Pop: 300 (1990); 328 (1980) Pop Density: 5.5
Land: 54.7 sq. mi.; Water: 0.0 sq. mi.

Vernon
Township
Lat: 40-20-47 N Long: 91-28-12 W
Pop: 385 (1990); 469 (1980) Pop Density: 38.9
Land: 9.9 sq. mi.; Water: 2.3 sq. mi.

Washington
Township
Lat: 40-19-05 N Long: 91-53-34 W
Pop: 256 (1990); 293 (1980) Pop Density: 4.8
Land: 53.5 sq. mi.; Water: 0.1 sq. mi.

Wayland
City
ZIP: 63472 Lat: 40-23-42 N Long: 91-34-54 W
Pop: 391 (1990); 498 (1980) Pop Density: 1303.3
Land: 0.3 sq. mi.; Water: 0.0 sq. mi. Elev: 535 ft.
Founded 1880. Incorporated 1962.
Name origin: For pioneer Jerre Wayland.

Wyaconda — City
ZIP: 63474   Lat: 40-23-34 N   Long: 91-55-34 W
Pop: 347 (1990); 359 (1980)   Pop Density: 578.3
Land: 0.6 sq. mi.; Water: 0.0 sq. mi.   Elev: 756 ft.
Founded 1888. Incorporated 1892.
Name origin: From the Siouan Indian term meaning 'sacred being' or 'spirit.'

*Wyaconda — Township
ZIP: 63474   Lat: 40-25-42 N   Long: 91-53-32 W
Pop: 643 (1990); 799 (1980)   Pop Density: 18.1
Land: 35.5 sq. mi.; Water: 0.0 sq. mi.

Clay County
County Seat: Liberty (ZIP: 64068)

Pop: 153,411 (1990); 136,488 (1980)   Pop Density: 387.0
Land: 396.5 sq. mi.; Water: 12.7 sq. mi.   Area Code: 816
In west-central MO, north of Kansas City; organized Jun 2, 1822 from Ray County.
Name origin: For Henry Clay (1777–1852), U.S. senator from KY, known as the "Great Pacificator" for his advocacy of compromise to avert national crises.

Avondale — City
Lat: 39-09-12 N   Long: 94-32-41 W
Pop: 550 (1990); 612 (1980)   Pop Density: 5500.0
Land: 0.1 sq. mi.; Water: 0.0 sq. mi.
Incorporated 1913.

Birmingham — Village
Lat: 39-09-59 N   Long: 94-27-01 W
Pop: 222 (1990); 240 (1980)   Pop Density: 370.0
Land: 0.6 sq. mi.; Water: 0.0 sq. mi.
Incorporated 1888.

Chouteau — Township
Lat: 39-12-49 N   Long: 94-30-09 W
Pop: 34,755 (1990); 29,923 (1980)   Pop Density: 681.5
Land: 51.0 sq. mi.; Water: 1.4 sq. mi.

Claycomo — Village
Lat: 39-11-58 N   Long: 94-28-36 W
Pop: 1,668 (1990); 1,671 (1980)   Pop Density: 667.2
Land: 2.5 sq. mi.; Water: 0.0 sq. mi.
Incorporated 1946.

Excelsior Estates — Village
Lat: 39-23-28 N   Long: 94-12-46 W
Pop: 3 (1990)   Pop Density: 100.0
Land: 0.03 sq. mi.; Water: 0.0 sq. mi.
Part of the town is also in Ray County.

Excelsior Springs — City
ZIP: 64024   Lat: 39-20-20 N   Long: 94-14-22 W
Pop: 10,178 (1990); 10,268 (1980)   Pop Density: 1183.5
Land: 8.6 sq. mi.; Water: 0.0 sq. mi.
In northwestern MO, a northeastern suburb of Kansas City. Incorporated 1881. Part of the town is also in Ray County.

Fishing River — Township
Lat: 39-16-39 N   Long: 94-17-44 W
Pop: 10,538 (1990); 10,987 (1980)   Pop Density: 151.0
Land: 69.8 sq. mi.; Water: 1.7 sq. mi.

Gallatin — Township
Lat: 39-10-54 N   Long: 94-34-05 W
Pop: 64,251 (1990); 61,511 (1980)   Pop Density: 2185.4
Land: 29.4 sq. mi.; Water: 1.0 sq. mi.

Gladstone — City
ZIP: 64118   Lat: 39-12-46 N   Long: 94-33-32 W
Pop: 26,243 (1990); 24,990 (1980)   Pop Density: 3280.4
Land: 8.0 sq. mi.; Water: 0.0 sq. mi.
In northwestern MO, north of Kansas City. Incorporated 1952.
Name origin: For William Ewart Gladstone (1809–98), prime minister of England, who supported the American colonies.

Glenaire — Village
Lat: 39-13-12 N   Long: 94-26-59 W
Pop: 597 (1990); 541 (1980)   Pop Density: 1990.0
Land: 0.3 sq. mi.; Water: 0.0 sq. mi.
Incorporated 1950.

Holt — City
ZIP: 64048   Lat: 39-27-10 N   Long: 94-20-39 W
Pop: 248 (1990); 276 (1980)   Pop Density: 1240.0
Land: 0.2 sq. mi.; Water: 0.0 sq. mi.
Incorporated 1878. Part of the town is also in Clinton County.
Name origin: For either Dr. David Rice Holt, a member of the State Legislature, or early settler Jerre A. Holt.

Independence — City
Lat: 39-07-29 N   Long: 94-27-39 W
Pop: 0 (1990); 111,797 (1980)
Land: 0.2 sq. mi.; Water: 0.1 sq. mi.
In northwestern MO, 10 mi. east of Kansas City. Incorporated 1849. Part of the town is also in Jackson County.
Name origin: Locally believed to be in recognition of Andrew Jackson's (1767–1845) independent character. Another plausible story is that those in Jackson County noted that their rival county, Clay, had a county seat named Liberty. There can be no liberty without independence; thus the reasoning and the name.

Kansas City — City
ZIP: 64108   Lat: 39-13-48 N   Long: 94-31-30 W
Pop: 69,316 (1990); 60,574 (1980)   Pop Density: 782.3
Land: 88.6 sq. mi.; Water: 2.1 sq. mi.
In western MO at the confluence of the Missouri and Kansas (or Kaw) rivers; on the western bank is Kansas City, KS. Established 1821; founded 1833; laid out 1838; developed 1836. Called *The Heart of America* for its location. Largest winter-wheat market; one of the largest livestock exchanges

MISSOURI, Clay County

in U.S.; wheat flour production second only to Buffalo. Manufacturing (printing and publishing, food processing, automobile assembly) and industrial (chemicals, electric equipment, farm machinery) city. Site of University of Missouri. Incorporated 1850. Part of the town is also in Cass, Jackson, and Platte counties.

Name origin: Named in 1889 from the old Siouan language Kansa 'people of the south wind.' Previously called City of Kansas (1853).

Kearney — City
ZIP: 64060　　Lat: 39-21-51 N　Long: 94-21-41 W
Pop: 1,790 (1990); 1,433 (1980)　Pop Density: 426.2
Land: 4.2 sq. mi.; Water: 0.0 sq. mi.　Elev: 849 ft.
Founded 1867. Incorporated 1883.

*Kearney — Township
ZIP: 64060　　Lat: 39-23-32 N　Long: 94-23-19 W
Pop: 5,951 (1990); 4,680 (1980)　Pop Density: 92.8
Land: 64.1 sq. mi.; Water: 0.5 sq. mi.

Lawson — City
ZIP: 64062　　Lat: 39-26-10 N　Long: 94-13-02 W
Pop: 95 (1990); 72 (1980)　Pop Density: 86.4
Land: 1.1 sq. mi.; Water: 0.1 sq. mi.
Founded June 1870 by the St. Joseph Land Company. Incorporated 1871. Part of the town is also in Ray County.

Name origin: For L. M. Lawson of Donnell, Lawson & Company, a NY banking house that helped finance the venture.

Liberty — City
ZIP: 64068　　Lat: 39-14-31 N　Long: 94-25-08 W
Pop: 20,459 (1990); 16,251 (1980)　Pop Density: 760.6
Land: 26.9 sq. mi.; Water: 0.1 sq. mi.
In northwestern MO, 15 mi. north-northeast of Kansas City. Incorporated 1822.

*Liberty — Township
ZIP: 64068　　Lat: 39-15-38 N　Long: 94-25-55 W
Pop: 26,606 (1990); 20,895 (1980)　Pop Density: 369.5
Land: 72.0 sq. mi.; Water: 0.4 sq. mi.

Missouri City — City
ZIP: 64072　　Lat: 39-14-17 N　Long: 94-18-03 W
Pop: 348 (1990); 343 (1980)　Pop Density: 348.0
Land: 1.0 sq. mi.; Water: 0.1 sq. mi.
Incorporated 1859.

Mosby — City
Lat: 39-19-10 N　Long: 94-18-02 W
Pop: 194 (1990); 284 (1980)　Pop Density: 129.3
Land: 1.5 sq. mi.; Water: 0.0 sq. mi.
Incorporated 1914.

Name origin: For the Mosby family.

North Kansas City — City
ZIP: 64116　　Lat: 39-08-20 N　Long: 94-33-50 W
Pop: 4,130 (1990); 4,507 (1980)　Pop Density: 938.6
Land: 4.4 sq. mi.; Water: 0.3 sq. mi.
Incorporated 1912.

Oaks — Village
Lat: 39-11-49 N　Long: 94-34-18 W
Pop: 130 (1990); 126 (1980)　Pop Density: 1300.0
Land: 0.1 sq. mi.; Water: 0.0 sq. mi.
Incorporated 1952.

Oakview — Village
Lat: 39-12-28 N　Long: 94-34-14 W
Pop: 351 (1990); 497 (1980)　Pop Density: 1755.0
Land: 0.2 sq. mi.; Water: 0.0 sq. mi.
Incorporated 1949.

Oakwood — Village
Lat: 39-12-01 N　Long: 94-34-19 W
Pop: 212 (1990); 227 (1980)　Pop Density: 1060.0
Land: 0.2 sq. mi.; Water: 0.0 sq. mi.
Incorporated 1952.

Oakwood Park — Village
Lat: 39-12-20 N　Long: 94-34-22 W
Pop: 213 (1990); 231 (1980)　Pop Density: 2130.0
Land: 0.1 sq. mi.; Water: 0.0 sq. mi.
Incorporated 1949.

Platte — Township
Lat: 39-22-34 N　Long: 94-32-23 W
Pop: 7,196 (1990); 4,972 (1980)　Pop Density: 106.3
Land: 67.7 sq. mi.; Water: 7.4 sq. mi.

Pleasant Valley — City
Lat: 39-13-06 N　Long: 94-28-52 W
Pop: 2,731 (1990); 1,545 (1980)　Pop Density: 2100.8
Land: 1.3 sq. mi.; Water: 0.0 sq. mi.
Incorporated 1955.

Prathersville — Village
Lat: 39-18-50 N　Long: 94-16-34 W
Pop: 130 (1990); 141 (1980)　Pop Density: 56.5
Land: 2.3 sq. mi.; Water: 0.0 sq. mi.
Incorporated 1957.

Randolph — Village
Lat: 39-09-22 N　Long: 94-29-26 W
Pop: 60 (1990); 91 (1980)　Pop Density: 200.0
Land: 0.3 sq. mi.; Water: 0.0 sq. mi.

Smithville — City
ZIP: 64089　　Lat: 39-22-53 N　Long: 94-34-26 W
Pop: 2,525 (1990); 1,873 (1980)　Pop Density: 336.7
Land: 7.5 sq. mi.; Water: 0.0 sq. mi.
Incorporated 1867.

Name origin: For pioneer Humphrey Smith, who settled here in 1822.

Sugar Creek — City
ZIP: 64054　　Lat: 39-07-36 N　Long: 94-27-06 W
Pop: 0 (1990); 4,305 (1980)
Land: 0.04 sq. mi.; Water: 0.1 sq. mi.
In northwestern MO, 10 mi. east of Kansas City. Incorporated 1920. Part of the town is also in Jackson County.

Name origin: For the sugar maple trees found in the area.

Washington — Township
Lat: 39-24-10 N　Long: 94-16-07 W
Pop: 4,114 (1990); 3,520 (1980)　Pop Density: 96.8
Land: 42.5 sq. mi.; Water: 0.3 sq. mi.

Clinton County
County Seat: Plattsburg (ZIP: 64477)

Pop: 16,595 (1990); 15,916 (1980)   **Pop Density:** 39.6
Land: 418.8 sq. mi.; **Water:** 4.7 sq. mi.   **Area Code:** 816
In west-central MO, north of Kansas City; organized Jan 2, 1833 from Clay and Ray counties.
Name origin: For DeWitt Clinton (1769–1828), governor of NY (1817–21; 1825–28) and supporter of the Erie Canal.

Atchison
Township
Lat: 39-35-22 N **Long:** 94-32-29 W
Pop: 1,724 (1990); 1,659 (1980)   **Pop Density:** 39.8
Land: 43.3 sq. mi.; **Water:** 0.0 sq. mi.

Cameron
City
ZIP: 64429   **Lat:** 39-44-11 N **Long:** 94-14-21 W
Pop: 3,791 (1990); 3,829 (1980)   **Pop Density:** 1648.3
Land: 2.3 sq. mi.; **Water:** 0.0 sq. mi.   **Elev:** 1036 ft.
In northwestern MO, 45 mi. north-northeast of Kansas City. Platted 1855. Incorporated 1867. Part of the town is also in DeKalb County.
Name origin: For Col. Elisha Cameron of Clay County, father-in-law of Samuel McCorkle, one of the town's founders.

Clinton
Township
Lat: 39-29-24 N **Long:** 94-24-44 W
Pop: 545 (1990); 430 (1980)   **Pop Density:** 17.8
Land: 30.7 sq. mi.; **Water:** 0.0 sq. mi.

Concord
Township
Lat: 39-35-37 N **Long:** 94-25-32 W
Pop: 2,843 (1990); 2,712 (1980)   **Pop Density:** 49.9
Land: 57.0 sq. mi.; **Water:** 0.2 sq. mi.

Gower
City
ZIP: 64454   **Lat:** 39-36-44 N **Long:** 94-35-33 W
Pop: 1,230 (1990); 1,189 (1980)   **Pop Density:** 1366.7
Land: 0.9 sq. mi.; **Water:** 0.0 sq. mi.   **Elev:** 941 ft.
Incorporated 1946. Part of the town is also in Buchanan County.
Name origin: Named in 1870 for A. G. Gower, division superintendent of the railroad.

Hardin
Township
Lat: 39-30-04 N **Long:** 94-32-27 W
Pop: 944 (1990); 796 (1980)   **Pop Density:** 26.8
Land: 35.2 sq. mi.; **Water:** 4.0 sq. mi.

Holt
City
ZIP: 64048   **Lat:** 39-27-24 N **Long:** 94-20-29 W
Pop: 63 (1990)   **Pop Density:** 2100.0
Land: 0.03 sq. mi.; **Water:** 0.0 sq. mi.
Incorporated 1878. Part of the town is also in Clay County.
Name origin: For either Dr. David Rice Holt, a member of the State Legislature, or early settler Jerre A. Holt.

Jackson
Township
Lat: 39-29-13 N **Long:** 94-16-43 W
Pop: 2,144 (1990); 1,826 (1980)   **Pop Density:** 54.0
Land: 39.7 sq. mi.; **Water:** 0.2 sq. mi.

Lafayette
Township
Lat: 39-42-00 N **Long:** 94-32-09 W
Pop: 698 (1990); 690 (1980)   **Pop Density:** 14.1
Land: 49.6 sq. mi.; **Water:** 0.0 sq. mi.

Lathrop
City
ZIP: 64465   **Lat:** 39-32-56 N **Long:** 94-19-46 W
Pop: 1,794 (1990); 1,732 (1980)   **Pop Density:** 1495.0
Land: 1.2 sq. mi.; **Water:** 0.0 sq. mi.
Founded 1857 by J. S. Harris, land commissioner of the Hannibal and St. Joseph Railroad. Incorporated 1881. Part of the town is also in Johnson County.
Name origin: For the township (see below).

*Lathrop
Township
ZIP: 64465   **Lat:** 39-34-43 N **Long:** 94-17-14 W
Pop: 2,636 (1990); 2,625 (1980)   **Pop Density:** 41.3
Land: 63.8 sq. mi.; **Water:** 0.1 sq. mi.

Osborn
City
ZIP: 64474   **Lat:** 39-44-42 N **Long:** 94-21-33 W
Pop: 45 (1990); 58 (1980)   **Pop Density:** 450.0
Land: 0.1 sq. mi.; **Water:** 0.0 sq. mi.   **Elev:** 1035 ft.
Founded by the Hannibal and St. Joseph Railroad. Incorporated 1887. Part of the town is also in DeKalb County.
Name origin: For Col. William Osborn of Waterville, NY.

Platte
Township
Lat: 39-42-15 N **Long:** 94-24-14 W
Pop: 398 (1990); 427 (1980)   **Pop Density:** 8.0
Land: 50.0 sq. mi.; **Water:** 0.0 sq. mi.

Plattsburg
City
ZIP: 64477   **Lat:** 39-33-54 N **Long:** 94-27-44 W
Pop: 2,248 (1990); 2,095 (1980)   **Pop Density:** 661.2
Land: 3.4 sq. mi.; **Water:** 0.0 sq. mi.   **Elev:** 953 ft.
Incorporated 1861.

Shoal
Township
Lat: 39-41-17 N **Long:** 94-16-13 W
Pop: 4,663 (1990); 4,751 (1980)   **Pop Density:** 94.2
Land: 49.5 sq. mi.; **Water:** 0.1 sq. mi.

Trimble
Town
ZIP: 64492   **Lat:** 39-28-28 N **Long:** 94-33-39 W
Pop: 405 (1990); 262 (1980)   **Pop Density:** 810.0
Land: 0.5 sq. mi.; **Water:** 0.0 sq. mi.   **Elev:** 931 ft.
Incorporated 1898.

Turney
Town
ZIP: 64493   **Lat:** 39-38-12 N **Long:** 94-19-14 W
Pop: 155 (1990); 379 (1980)   **Pop Density:** 310.0
Land: 0.5 sq. mi.; **Water:** 0.0 sq. mi.
Incorporated 1879.

Cole County
County Seat: Jefferson City (ZIP: 65101)

Pop: 63,579 (1990); 56,663 (1980)   **Pop Density:** 162.4
Land: 391.6 sq. mi.; **Water:** 7.6 sq. mi.   **Area Code:** 314

In central MO, south of Columbia; organized Nov 16, 1820 (prior to statehood) from Cooper County,

Name origin: For Capt. Stephen Cole (?–1822), an Indian fighter.

Centertown
Town
ZIP: 65023   **Lat:** 38-37-08 N   **Long:** 92-24-33 W
Pop: 356 (1990); 304 (1980)   **Pop Density:** 395.6
Land: 0.9 sq. mi.; **Water:** 0.0 sq. mi.   **Elev:** 848 ft.
Incorporated 1901.

Clark
Township
Lat: 38-25-05 N   **Long:** 92-19-46 W
Pop: 3,329 (1990); 2,935 (1980)   **Pop Density:** 38.0
Land: 87.6 sq. mi.; **Water:** 0.5 sq. mi.

Eugene
Town
ZIP: 65032   **Lat:** 38-21-13 N   **Long:** 92-24-12 W
Pop: 141 (1990); 220 (1980)   **Pop Density:** 705.0
Land: 0.2 sq. mi.; **Water:** 0.0 sq. mi.
Incorporated 1904.

Jefferson
Township
Lat: 38-34-12 N   **Long:** 92-13-43 W
Pop: 48,050 (1990); 43,271 (1980)   **Pop Density:** 629.8
Land: 76.3 sq. mi.; **Water:** 2.2 sq. mi.

Jefferson City
City
ZIP: 65101   **Lat:** 38-34-10 N   **Long:** 92-11-48 W
Pop: 35,175 (1990); 33,594 (1980)   **Pop Density:** 1522.7
Land: 23.1 sq. mi.; **Water:** 0.6 sq. mi.   **Elev:** 702 ft.
In central MO, south of Columbia. State capital since 1821; incorporated as town 1825; as city 1829. Part of the town is also in Callaway County.
Name origin: For Thomas Jefferson (1743–1826), third U.S. president.

Liberty
Township
Lat: 38-30-22 N   **Long:** 92-04-37 W
Pop: 4,157 (1990); 3,210 (1980)   **Pop Density:** 108.8
Land: 38.2 sq. mi.; **Water:** 2.1 sq. mi.

Lohman
Town
ZIP: 65053   **Lat:** 38-32-32 N   **Long:** 92-21-48 W
Pop: 154 (1990); 168 (1980)   **Pop Density:** 385.0
Land: 0.4 sq. mi.; **Water:** 0.0 sq. mi.   **Elev:** 649 ft.
Incorporated 1910.

Marion
Township
Lat: 38-37-56 N   **Long:** 92-22-11 W
Pop: 2,932 (1990); 2,851 (1980)   **Pop Density:** 49.2
Land: 59.6 sq. mi.; **Water:** 1.1 sq. mi.

Moreau
Township
Lat: 38-30-29 N   **Long:** 92-24-23 W
Pop: 2,523 (1990); 2,032 (1980)   **Pop Density:** 38.9
Land: 64.8 sq. mi.; **Water:** 0.0 sq. mi.

Osage
Township
Lat: 38-26-18 N   **Long:** 92-11-29 W
Pop: 2,588 (1990); 2,364 (1980)   **Pop Density:** 39.8
Land: 65.1 sq. mi.; **Water:** 1.6 sq. mi.

Russellville
City
ZIP: 65074   **Lat:** 38-30-45 N   **Long:** 92-26-16 W
Pop: 869 (1990); 667 (1980)   **Pop Density:** 1086.3
Land: 0.8 sq. mi.; **Water:** 0.0 sq. mi.   **Elev:** 888 ft.
Incorporated 1895.

St. Martins
City
Lat: 38-35-44 N   **Long:** 92-20-00 W
Pop: 717 (1990); 739 (1980)   **Pop Density:** 448.1
Land: 1.6 sq. mi.; **Water:** 0.0 sq. mi.
Incorporated 1972.

St. Thomas
Town
Lat: 38-22-07 N   **Long:** 92-12-56 W
Pop: 263 (1990); 337 (1980)   **Pop Density:** 239.1
Land: 1.1 sq. mi.; **Water:** 0.0 sq. mi.
Incorporated 1962.

Taos
City
Lat: 38-29-52 N   **Long:** 92-04-50 W
Pop: 802 (1990); 759 (1980)   **Pop Density:** 348.7
Land: 2.3 sq. mi.; **Water:** 0.1 sq. mi.   **Elev:** 728 ft.
Incorporated 1972.

Wardsville
Town
Lat: 38-29-16 N   **Long:** 92-10-24 W
Pop: 513 (1990); 535 (1980)   **Pop Density:** 223.0
Land: 2.3 sq. mi.; **Water:** 0.0 sq. mi.   **Elev:** 803 ft.
Incorporated 1965.

Cooper County
County Seat: Boonville (ZIP: 65233)

Pop: 14,835 (1990); 14,643 (1980) **Pop Density:** 26.3
Land: 565.1 sq. mi.; **Water:** 5.2 sq. mi. **Area Code:** 816
In central MO, west of Columbia; organized Dec 17, 1818 (prior to statehood) from Howard County.
Name origin: For Sarshel Cooper (?–1814), an early settler.

Blackwater — City
ZIP: 65322 **Lat:** 38-58-45 N **Long:** 92-59-26 W
Pop: 221 (1990); 290 (1980) **Pop Density:** 736.7
Land: 0.3 sq. mi.; **Water:** 0.0 sq. mi. **Elev:** 610 ft.
Incorporated 1888.

*Blackwater — Township
ZIP: 65322 **Lat:** 38-56-30 N **Long:** 93-00-06 W
Pop: 430 (1990); 533 (1980) **Pop Density:** 17.3
Land: 24.9 sq. mi.; **Water:** 0.4 sq. mi.

Boonville — City
ZIP: 65233 **Lat:** 38-57-51 N **Long:** 92-44-52 W
Pop: 7,095 (1990); 6,959 (1980) **Pop Density:** 1244.7
Land: 5.7 sq. mi.; **Water:** 0.4 sq. mi. **Elev:** 660 ft.
In central MO, 25 mi. west of Columbia. Incorporated 1839.
Name origin: For Booneville, KY.

*Boonville — Township
ZIP: 65233 **Lat:** 38-56-52 N **Long:** 92-45-11 W
Pop: 8,393 (1990); 7,849 (1980) **Pop Density:** 162.0
Land: 51.8 sq. mi.; **Water:** 1.7 sq. mi.

Bunceton — City
ZIP: 65237 **Lat:** 38-47-22 N **Long:** 92-47-54 W
Pop: 341 (1990); 419 (1980) **Pop Density:** 378.9
Land: 0.9 sq. mi.; **Water:** 0.0 sq. mi.
Incorporated 1886.

Clark Fork — Township
Lat: 38-51-06 N **Long:** 92-41-42 W
Pop: 556 (1990); 524 (1980) **Pop Density:** 10.6
Land: 52.6 sq. mi.; **Water:** 0.0 sq. mi.

Clear Creek — Township
Lat: 38-50-53 N **Long:** 92-59-07 W
Pop: 434 (1990); 440 (1980) **Pop Density:** 8.6
Land: 50.3 sq. mi.; **Water:** 0.1 sq. mi.

Kelly — Township
Lat: 38-44-36 N **Long:** 92-48-13 W
Pop: 686 (1990); 771 (1980) **Pop Density:** 10.3
Land: 66.6 sq. mi.; **Water:** 0.1 sq. mi.

Lamine — Township
Lat: 38-59-11 N **Long:** 92-55-55 W
Pop: 283 (1990); 322 (1980) **Pop Density:** 7.2
Land: 39.5 sq. mi.; **Water:** 1.4 sq. mi.

Lebanon — Township
Lat: 38-44-17 N **Long:** 92-56-08 W
Pop: 301 (1990); 364 (1980) **Pop Density:** 7.1
Land: 42.3 sq. mi.; **Water:** 0.0 sq. mi.

North Moniteau — Township
Lat: 38-45-16 N **Long:** 92-39-10 W
Pop: 154 (1990); 159 (1980) **Pop Density:** 5.7
Land: 26.8 sq. mi.; **Water:** 0.0 sq. mi.

Otterville — City
ZIP: 65348 **Lat:** 38-42-08 N **Long:** 93-00-10 W
Pop: 507 (1990); 472 (1980) **Pop Density:** 1267.5
Land: 0.4 sq. mi.; **Water:** 0.0 sq. mi. **Elev:** 722 ft.
Incorporated 1857.

*Otterville — Township
ZIP: 65348 **Lat:** 38-44-31 N **Long:** 93-00-56 W
Pop: 853 (1990); 811 (1980) **Pop Density:** 31.4
Land: 27.2 sq. mi.; **Water:** 0.0 sq. mi.

Palestine — Township
Lat: 38-50-30 N **Long:** 92-50-17 W
Pop: 375 (1990); 398 (1980) **Pop Density:** 8.4
Land: 44.9 sq. mi.; **Water:** 0.1 sq. mi.

Pilot Grove — City
ZIP: 65276 **Lat:** 38-52-25 N **Long:** 92-54-43 W
Pop: 714 (1990); 745 (1980) **Pop Density:** 1785.0
Land: 0.4 sq. mi.; **Water:** 0.0 sq. mi.
Incorporated 1880.

*Pilot Grove — Township
ZIP: 65276 **Lat:** 38-53-12 N **Long:** 92-54-01 W
Pop: 1,065 (1990); 1,158 (1980) **Pop Density:** 29.7
Land: 35.9 sq. mi.; **Water:** 0.2 sq. mi.

Prairie Home — City
ZIP: 65068 **Lat:** 38-48-53 N **Long:** 92-35-22 W
Pop: 215 (1990); 279 (1980) **Pop Density:** 537.5
Land: 0.4 sq. mi.; **Water:** 0.0 sq. mi.
Incorporated 1956.

*Prairie Home — Township
ZIP: 65068 **Lat:** 38-49-33 N **Long:** 92-35-50 W
Pop: 533 (1990); 553 (1980) **Pop Density:** 16.2
Land: 33.0 sq. mi.; **Water:** 0.0 sq. mi.

Saline — Township
Lat: 38-55-07 N **Long:** 92-35-08 W
Pop: 570 (1990); 545 (1980) **Pop Density:** 12.2
Land: 46.7 sq. mi.; **Water:** 1.2 sq. mi.

South Moniteau — Township
Lat: 38-42-27 N **Long:** 92-39-38 W
Pop: 202 (1990); 216 (1980) **Pop Density:** 9.0
Land: 22.4 sq. mi.; **Water:** 0.0 sq. mi.

Wooldridge — Town
ZIP: 65287 **Lat:** 38-54-23 N **Long:** 92-31-18 W
Pop: 54 (1990); 79 (1980) **Pop Density:** 540.0
Land: 0.1 sq. mi.; **Water:** 0.0 sq. mi.
Incorporated 1902.

Crawford County
County Seat: Steelville (ZIP: 65565)

Pop: 19,173 (1990); 18,300 (1980) **Pop Density:** 25.8
Land: 742.6 sq. mi.; **Water:** 1.3 sq. mi. **Area Code:** 314

In east-central MO, southwest of St. Louis; organized Jan 23, 1829 from Gasconade County.

Name origin: For William Harris Crawford (1772–1834), U.S. senator from GA (1807–13), U.S. Secretary of War (1815–16), and U.S. Secretary of Treasury (1816–25).

Benton
Township
Lat: 38-04-37 N **Long:** 91-22-25 W
Pop: 4,783 (1990); 4,617 (1980) **Pop Density:** 97.6
Land: 49.0 sq. mi.; **Water:** 0.2 sq. mi.

Boone
Township
Lat: 38-09-46 N **Long:** 91-12-10 W
Pop: 4,530 (1990); 4,315 (1980) **Pop Density:** 67.3
Land: 67.3 sq. mi.; **Water:** 0.1 sq. mi.

Bourbon
City
ZIP: 65441 **Lat:** 38-09-05 N **Long:** 91-14-50 W
Pop: 1,188 (1990); 1,259 (1980) **Pop Density:** 1080.0
Land: 1.1 sq. mi.; **Water:** 0.0 sq. mi. **Elev:** 932 ft.
Incorporated 1907.

Name origin: Named in 1825 for either Bourbon, KY, or for an old local post office, which had been named Bourbon for the corn whiskey.

Courtois
Township
Lat: 37-55-59 N **Long:** 91-12-21 W
Pop: 1,177 (1990); 1,139 (1980) **Pop Density:** 11.5
Land: 102.0 sq. mi.; **Water:** 0.1 sq. mi.

Cuba
City
ZIP: 65453 **Lat:** 38-03-46 N **Long:** 91-23-59 W
Pop: 2,537 (1990); 2,120 (1980) **Pop Density:** 1153.2
Land: 2.2 sq. mi.; **Water:** 0.0 sq. mi. **Elev:** 1015 ft.
Incorporated 1857.

Name origin: Named by two former gold miners from CA, who wished to perpetuate the memory of a holiday they had spent in Cuba.

Knobview
Township
Lat: 38-03-34 N **Long:** 91-29-14 W
Pop: 1,241 (1990); 986 (1980) **Pop Density:** 25.5
Land: 48.6 sq. mi.; **Water:** 0.4 sq. mi.

Leasburg
Village
ZIP: 65535 **Lat:** 38-05-39 N **Long:** 91-17-42 W
Pop: 289 (1990); 304 (1980) **Pop Density:** 722.5
Land: 0.4 sq. mi.; **Water:** 0.0 sq. mi.
Incorporated 1919.

Liberty
Township
Lat: 38-03-45 N **Long:** 91-11-42 W
Pop: 1,061 (1990); 1,040 (1980) **Pop Density:** 11.8
Land: 89.9 sq. mi.; **Water:** 0.1 sq. mi.

Meramec
Township
Lat: 37-57-41 N **Long:** 91-23-30 W
Pop: 3,146 (1990); 2,855 (1980) **Pop Density:** 38.6
Land: 81.5 sq. mi.; **Water:** 0.0 sq. mi.

Oak Hill
Township
Lat: 38-10-17 N **Long:** 91-24-38 W
Pop: 1,281 (1990); 1,260 (1980) **Pop Density:** 19.8
Land: 64.8 sq. mi.; **Water:** 0.2 sq. mi.

Osage
Township
Lat: 37-47-29 N **Long:** 91-12-10 W
Pop: 1,147 (1990); 1,286 (1980) **Pop Density:** 8.8
Land: 130.5 sq. mi.; **Water:** 0.1 sq. mi.

St. Cloud
Village
Lat: 38-10-21 N **Long:** 91-12-45 W
Pop: 59 (1990); 40 (1980) **Pop Density:** 53.6
Land: 1.1 sq. mi.; **Water:** 0.0 sq. mi.
Incorporated 1963.

Steelville
City
ZIP: 65565 **Lat:** 37-58-09 N **Long:** 91-21-19 W
Pop: 1,465 (1990); 1,470 (1980) **Pop Density:** 665.9
Land: 2.2 sq. mi.; **Water:** 0.0 sq. mi. **Elev:** 750 ft.
Incorporated 1850.

Name origin: For James Steel, a landowner.

Sullivan
City
ZIP: 63080 **Lat:** 38-11-52 N **Long:** 91-10-02 W
Pop: 1,116 (1990); 1,025 (1980) **Pop Density:** 465.0
Land: 2.4 sq. mi.; **Water:** 0.0 sq. mi. **Elev:** 987 ft.
Established 1856. Incorporated 1883. Part of the town is also in Franklin County.

Name origin: Named in 1860 for Stephen Sullivan, who had donated the right of way through the village. Previously called Mt. Helicon.

Union
Township
Lat: 37-51-22 N **Long:** 91-24-48 W
Pop: 807 (1990); 802 (1980) **Pop Density:** 7.4
Land: 109.0 sq. mi.; **Water:** 0.1 sq. mi.

Dade County
County Seat: Greenfield (ZIP: 65661)

Pop: 7,449 (1990); 7,383 (1980)
Land: 490.4 sq. mi.; **Water:** 16.0 sq. mi.
Pop Density: 15.2
Area Code: 417

In southwestern MO, northwest of Springfield; organized Jan 29, 1841 from Polk and Barry counties.
Name origin: For Francis Langhorne Dade (1793–1835), officer killed in the Seminole War (1835–42).

Arcola — Village
ZIP: 65603 **Lat:** 37-32-59 N **Long:** 93-52-32 W
Pop: 72 (1990); 136 (1980) **Pop Density:** 240.0
Land: 0.3 sq. mi.; **Water:** 0.0 sq. mi.
Incorporated 1967.

Cedar — Township
Lat: 37-31-47 N **Long:** 94-01-52 W
Pop: 346 (1990); 364 (1980) **Pop Density:** 7.2
Land: 48.2 sq. mi.; **Water:** 0.1 sq. mi.

Center — Township
Lat: 37-25-34 N **Long:** 93-50-36 W
Pop: 2,041 (1990); 2,040 (1980) **Pop Density:** 47.5
Land: 43.0 sq. mi.; **Water:** 0.4 sq. mi.

Dadeville — Village
ZIP: 65635 **Lat:** 37-28-47 N **Long:** 93-40-29 W
Pop: 220 (1990); 216 (1980) **Pop Density:** 220.0
Land: 1.0 sq. mi.; **Water:** 0.0 sq. mi.
Incorporated 1895.
Name origin: For Francis Langhorne Dade (1793–1835), officer killed in the Seminole War (1835–42).

Ernest — Township
Lat: 37-29-00 N **Long:** 93-56-31 W
Pop: 113 (1990); 118 (1980) **Pop Density:** 4.5
Land: 25.1 sq. mi.; **Water:** 0.0 sq. mi.

Everton — City
ZIP: 65646 **Lat:** 37-20-36 N **Long:** 93-42-08 W
Pop: 325 (1990); 317 (1980) **Pop Density:** 1083.3
Land: 0.3 sq. mi.; **Water:** 0.0 sq. mi. **Elev:** 1038 ft.
Incorporated 1892.

Grant — Township
Lat: 37-20-00 N **Long:** 94-01-09 W
Pop: 247 (1990); 339 (1980) **Pop Density:** 6.4
Land: 38.3 sq. mi.; **Water:** 0.1 sq. mi.

Greenfield — City
ZIP: 65661 **Lat:** 37-24-58 N **Long:** 93-50-33 W
Pop: 1,416 (1990); 1,394 (1980) **Pop Density:** 1287.3
Land: 1.1 sq. mi.; **Water:** 0.0 sq. mi. **Elev:** 1087 ft.
Incorporated 1870.

Lockwood — City
ZIP: 65682 **Lat:** 37-23-13 N **Long:** 93-57-31 W
Pop: 1,041 (1990); 971 (1980) **Pop Density:** 1156.7
Land: 0.9 sq. mi.; **Water:** 0.0 sq. mi.
Incorporated 1883. Not coextensive with the town of the same name.

*Lockwood — Township
ZIP: 65682 **Lat:** 37-23-31 N **Long:** 93-56-56 W
Pop: 1,344 (1990); 1,273 (1980) **Pop Density:** 42.9
Land: 31.3 sq. mi.; **Water:** 0.1 sq. mi.

Marion — Township
Lat: 37-24-47 N **Long:** 94-02-02 W
Pop: 210 (1990); 201 (1980) **Pop Density:** 7.0
Land: 30.1 sq. mi.; **Water:** 0.1 sq. mi.

North — Township
Lat: 37-32-24 N **Long:** 93-53-39 W
Pop: 301 (1990); 293 (1980) **Pop Density:** 9.2
Land: 32.8 sq. mi.; **Water:** 0.5 sq. mi.

North Morgan — Township
Lat: 37-32-34 N **Long:** 93-40-19 W
Pop: 172 (1990); 153 (1980) **Pop Density:** 8.3
Land: 20.7 sq. mi.; **Water:** 3.6 sq. mi.

Pilgrim — Township
Lat: 37-21-51 N **Long:** 93-45-49 W
Pop: 128 (1990); 156 (1980) **Pop Density:** 11.5
Land: 11.1 sq. mi.; **Water:** 0.0 sq. mi.

Polk — Township
Lat: 37-24-52 N **Long:** 93-41-30 W
Pop: 489 (1990); 410 (1980) **Pop Density:** 10.8
Land: 45.4 sq. mi.; **Water:** 1.2 sq. mi.

Rock Prairie — Township
Lat: 37-19-38 N **Long:** 93-40-50 W
Pop: 816 (1990); 812 (1980) **Pop Density:** 22.4
Land: 36.5 sq. mi.; **Water:** 0.0 sq. mi.

Sac — Township
Lat: 37-31-25 N **Long:** 93-47-06 W
Pop: 278 (1990); 201 (1980) **Pop Density:** 7.3
Land: 37.9 sq. mi.; **Water:** 9.8 sq. mi.

Smith — Township
Lat: 37-19-25 N **Long:** 93-54-05 W
Pop: 192 (1990); 199 (1980) **Pop Density:** 7.6
Land: 25.4 sq. mi.; **Water:** 0.0 sq. mi.

South — Township
Lat: 37-18-26 N **Long:** 93-47-23 W
Pop: 157 (1990); 194 (1980) **Pop Density:** 6.7
Land: 23.6 sq. mi.; **Water:** 0.0 sq. mi.

South Greenfield — Village
ZIP: 65752 **Lat:** 37-22-33 N **Long:** 93-50-32 W
Pop: 112 (1990); 110 (1980) **Pop Density:** 560.0
Land: 0.2 sq. mi.; **Water:** 0.0 sq. mi. **Elev:** 943 ft.
Incorporated 1882.

South Morgan — Township
Lat: 37-29-10 N **Long:** 93-40-31 W
Pop: 367 (1990); 369 (1980) **Pop Density:** 15.3
Land: 24.0 sq. mi.; **Water:** 0.0 sq. mi.

MISSOURI, Dade County

Washington
Township
Lat: 37-22-11 N Long: 93-50-49 W
Pop: 248 (1990); 261 (1980)   **Pop Density:** 14.4
Land: 17.2 sq. mi.; **Water:** 0.0 sq. mi.

Dallas County
County Seat: Buffalo (ZIP: 65622)

Pop: 12,646 (1990); 12,096 (1980)   **Pop Density:** 23.3
Land: 541.6 sq. mi.; **Water:** 1.3 sq. mi.   **Area Code:** 417

In south-central MO, northeast of Springfield; organized as Niangua County Jan 29, 1841 from Polk County; name changed Dec 16, 1844.

Name origin: For George Mifflin Dallas (1792–1864), U.S. senator from PA (1831–33), U.S. vice president (1845–49), and U.S. Minister to Russia (1837–39) and Great Britain (1856–61).

Buffalo
City
ZIP: 65622   Lat: 37-38-39 N Long: 93-05-39 W
Pop: 2,414 (1990); 2,217 (1980)   **Pop Density:** 1420.0
Land: 1.7 sq. mi.; **Water:** 0.0 sq. mi.   **Elev:** 1200 ft.
Incorporated 1896.
Name origin: For the large herds of buffalo that once lived in the territory.

Grant
Township
Lat: 37-46-41 N Long: 93-05-54 W
Pop: 986 (1990); 1,088 (1980)   **Pop Density:** 18.0
Land: 54.8 sq. mi.; **Water:** 0.1 sq. mi.

Jackson
Township
Lat: 37-31-37 N Long: 93-05-37 W
Pop: 1,454 (1990); 1,373 (1980)   **Pop Density:** 26.8
Land: 54.2 sq. mi.; **Water:** 0.0 sq. mi.

Jasper
Township
Lat: 37-43-03 N Long: 92-55-58 W
Pop: 769 (1990); 863 (1980)   **Pop Density:** 11.7
Land: 65.8 sq. mi.; **Water:** 0.6 sq. mi.

Lincoln
Township
Lat: 37-51-42 N Long: 93-07-57 W
Pop: 755 (1990); 779 (1980)   **Pop Density:** 20.8
Land: 36.3 sq. mi.; **Water:** 0.0 sq. mi.

Louisburg
Village
ZIP: 65685   Lat: 37-45-17 N Long: 93-08-24 W
Pop: 115 (1990); 140 (1980)   **Pop Density:** 230.0
Land: 0.5 sq. mi.; **Water:** 0.0 sq. mi.
Incorporated 1962.

Miller
Township
Lat: 37-49-44 N Long: 92-55-04 W
Pop: 428 (1990); 393 (1980)   **Pop Density:** 6.9
Land: 62.4 sq. mi.; **Water:** 0.6 sq. mi.

North Benton
Township
Lat: 37-40-54 N Long: 93-05-38 W
Pop: 3,544 (1990); 3,223 (1980)   **Pop Density:** 63.6
Land: 55.7 sq. mi.; **Water:** 0.0 sq. mi.

Sheridan
Township
Lat: 37-27-14 N Long: 93-08-07 W
Pop: 917 (1990); 805 (1980)   **Pop Density:** 30.5
Land: 30.1 sq. mi.; **Water:** 0.0 sq. mi.

Sherman
Township
Lat: 37-50-55 N Long: 93-01-41 W
Pop: 399 (1990); 376 (1980)   **Pop Density:** 11.0
Land: 36.3 sq. mi.; **Water:** 0.0 sq. mi.

South Benton
Township
Lat: 37-36-06 N Long: 93-05-50 W
Pop: 1,805 (1990); 1,634 (1980)   **Pop Density:** 47.0
Land: 38.4 sq. mi.; **Water:** 0.0 sq. mi.

Urbana
City
ZIP: 65767   Lat: 37-50-38 N Long: 93-09-58 W
Pop: 350 (1990); 329 (1980)   **Pop Density:** 318.2
Land: 1.1 sq. mi.; **Water:** 0.0 sq. mi.
Incorporated 1960.
Name origin: For Urbana, IL.

Washington
Township
Lat: 37-31-16 N Long: 92-55-25 W
Pop: 638 (1990); 648 (1980)   **Pop Density:** 11.8
Land: 54.0 sq. mi.; **Water:** 0.0 sq. mi.

Wilson
Township
Lat: 37-36-50 N Long: 92-56-02 W
Pop: 951 (1990); 914 (1980)   **Pop Density:** 17.7
Land: 53.6 sq. mi.; **Water:** 0.0 sq. mi.

> ### Daviess County
> **County Seat: Gallatin (ZIP: 64640)**
>
> **Pop:** 7,865 (1990); 8,905 (1980) **Pop Density:** 13.9
> **Land:** 567.0 sq. mi.; **Water:** 2.1 sq. mi. **Area Code:** 816
> In north-central MO, northeast of St. Joseph; organized Dec 29, 1836 from Ray County.
> **Name origin:** For Col. Joseph Hamilton Daviess (1774–1811), VA soldier and jurist who unsuccessfully attempted to indict Aaron Burr for treason (1806). According to Jacob Piatt Dunn, "The Colonel's name was Daveiss and he always wrote it that way"; however, the name is sometimes spelled 'Daviess' in biographical entries and in places named for him.

Altamont
Town
ZIP: 64620 **Lat:** 39-53-19 N **Long:** 94-05-12 W
Pop: 188 (1990); 192 (1980) **Pop Density:** 626.7
Land: 0.3 sq. mi.; **Water:** 0.0 sq. mi. **Elev:** 1004 ft.
Incorporated 1896.

Benton
Township
Lat: 40-04-59 N **Long:** 94-09-07 W
Pop: 635 (1990); 761 (1980) **Pop Density:** 15.1
Land: 42.1 sq. mi.; **Water:** 0.1 sq. mi.

Coffey
Town
ZIP: 64636 **Lat:** 40-06-18 N **Long:** 94-00-22 W
Pop: 131 (1990); 165 (1980) **Pop Density:** 655.0
Land: 0.2 sq. mi.; **Water:** 0.0 sq. mi. **Elev:** 290 ft.
Incorporated 1965.

Colfax
Township
Lat: 39-49-53 N **Long:** 94-08-57 W
Pop: 567 (1990); 614 (1980) **Pop Density:** 15.8
Land: 35.9 sq. mi.; **Water:** 0.0 sq. mi.

Gallatin
City
ZIP: 64640 **Lat:** 39-54-37 N **Long:** 93-57-49 W
Pop: 1,864 (1990); 2,063 (1980) **Pop Density:** 716.9
Land: 2.6 sq. mi.; **Water:** 0.0 sq. mi. **Elev:** 931 ft.
In northwestern MO on the south bank of the Grand River, northeast of Kansas City. Platted 1837. Incorporated 1856.
Name origin: For Albert Gallatin (1761–1849), U.S. secretary of the treasury (1801–14).

Gilman City
City
ZIP: 64642 **Lat:** 40-07-57 N **Long:** 93-52-39 W
Pop: 0 (1990); 2 (1980)
Land: 0.01 sq. mi.; **Water:** 0.0 sq. mi. **Elev:** 979 ft.
Incorporated 1898. Part of the town is also in Harrison County.

Grand River
Township
Lat: 40-00-31 N **Long:** 93-57-47 W
Pop: 401 (1990); 500 (1980) **Pop Density:** 7.6
Land: 52.9 sq. mi.; **Water:** 0.1 sq. mi.

Harrison
Township
Lat: 39-49-02 N **Long:** 93-49-44 W
Pop: 92 (1990); 103 (1980) **Pop Density:** 4.2
Land: 21.7 sq. mi.; **Water:** 0.0 sq. mi.

Jackson
Township
Lat: 39-54-13 N **Long:** 93-48-20 W
Pop: 576 (1990); 728 (1980) **Pop Density:** 11.8
Land: 48.8 sq. mi.; **Water:** 0.3 sq. mi.

Jameson
Town
ZIP: 64647 **Lat:** 40-00-19 N **Long:** 93-59-15 W
Pop: 149 (1990); 172 (1980) **Pop Density:** 745.0
Land: 0.2 sq. mi.; **Water:** 0.0 sq. mi. **Elev:** 797 ft.
Incorporated 1876.

Jamesport
City
ZIP: 64648 **Lat:** 39-58-28 N **Long:** 93-48-07 W
Pop: 570 (1990); 651 (1980) **Pop Density:** 950.0
Land: 0.6 sq. mi.; **Water:** 0.0 sq. mi. **Elev:** 990 ft.
Incorporated 1872. Not coextensive with the town of the same name.

*Jamesport
Township
ZIP: 64648 **Lat:** 40-00-07 N **Long:** 93-48-51 W
Pop: 1,049 (1990); 1,183 (1980) **Pop Density:** 30.5
Land: 34.4 sq. mi.; **Water:** 0.1 sq. mi.

Jefferson
Township
Lat: 39-54-46 N **Long:** 94-08-52 W
Pop: 331 (1990); 378 (1980) **Pop Density:** 9.2
Land: 35.9 sq. mi.; **Water:** 0.0 sq. mi.

Liberty
Township
Lat: 39-55-23 N **Long:** 94-02-01 W
Pop: 811 (1990); 706 (1980) **Pop Density:** 24.5
Land: 33.1 sq. mi.; **Water:** 0.9 sq. mi.

Lincoln
Township
Lat: 40-05-17 N **Long:** 93-48-57 W
Pop: 139 (1990); 192 (1980) **Pop Density:** 3.9
Land: 36.0 sq. mi.; **Water:** 0.0 sq. mi.

Lock Springs
Town
ZIP: 64654 **Lat:** 39-50-56 N **Long:** 93-46-33 W
Pop: 57 (1990); 85 (1980) **Pop Density:** 570.0
Land: 0.1 sq. mi.; **Water:** 0.0 sq. mi. **Elev:** 717 ft.
Incorporated 1872.

Marion
Township
Lat: 39-59-35 N **Long:** 94-06-43 W
Pop: 220 (1990); 249 (1980) **Pop Density:** 4.8
Land: 46.3 sq. mi.; **Water:** 0.1 sq. mi.

Monroe
Township
Lat: 39-49-18 N **Long:** 93-55-30 W
Pop: 127 (1990); 210 (1980) **Pop Density:** 3.5
Land: 36.5 sq. mi.; **Water:** 0.0 sq. mi.

Pattonsburg
City
ZIP: 64670 **Lat:** 40-02-52 N **Long:** 94-08-15 W
Pop: 414 (1990); 502 (1980) **Pop Density:** 591.4
Land: 0.7 sq. mi.; **Water:** 0.0 sq. mi. **Elev:** 776 ft.
Incorporated 1904.

MISSOURI, Daviess County

Salem
Township
Lat: 40-05-36 N **Long:** 94-02-22 W
Pop: 359 (1990); 396 (1980) **Pop Density:** 9.9
Land: 36.4 sq. mi.; **Water:** 0.0 sq. mi.

Sheridan
Township
Lat: 39-50-00 N **Long:** 94-02-00 W
Pop: 276 (1990); 316 (1980) **Pop Density:** 8.0
Land: 34.4 sq. mi.; **Water:** 0.0 sq. mi.

Union
Township
Lat: 39-54-51 N **Long:** 93-55-49 W
Pop: 2,156 (1990); 2,378 (1980) **Pop Density:** 59.1
Land: 36.5 sq. mi.; **Water:** 0.4 sq. mi.

Washington
Township
Lat: 40-05-39 N **Long:** 93-56-06 W
Pop: 126 (1990); 191 (1980) **Pop Density:** 3.5
Land: 36.0 sq. mi.; **Water:** 0.0 sq. mi.

Winston
Town
ZIP: 64689 **Lat:** 39-52-11 N **Long:** 94-08-29 W
Pop: 251 (1990); 246 (1980) **Pop Density:** 836.7
Land: 0.3 sq. mi.; **Water:** 0.0 sq. mi.
Incorporated 1878.

DeKalb County
County Seat: Maysville (ZIP: 64469)

Pop: 9,967 (1990); 8,222 (1980) **Pop Density:** 23.5
Land: 424.2 sq. mi.; **Water:** 1.6 sq. mi. **Area Code:** 816
In northwestern MO, east of St. Joseph; organized Feb 25, 1845 from Clinton County.
Name origin: For Johann, Baron de Kalb (1721–1780), German-born French soldier who fought with the Americans during the Revolutionary War.

Adams
Township
Lat: 39-53-14 N **Long:** 94-15-23 W
Pop: 540 (1990); 564 (1980) **Pop Density:** 12.8
Land: 42.3 sq. mi.; **Water:** 0.0 sq. mi.

Amity
Town
ZIP: 64422 **Lat:** 39-52-06 N **Long:** 94-26-04 W
Pop: 99 (1990); 74 (1980) **Pop Density:** 495.0
Land: 0.2 sq. mi.; **Water:** 0.0 sq. mi.
Incorporated 1907.

Camden
Township
Lat: 39-53-18 N **Long:** 94-23-01 W
Pop: 1,586 (1990); 1,700 (1980) **Pop Density:** 31.7
Land: 50.0 sq. mi.; **Water:** 0.2 sq. mi.

Cameron
City
Lat: 39-45-03 N **Long:** 94-13-54 W
Pop: 1,040 (1990); 690 (1980) **Pop Density:** 611.8
Land: 1.7 sq. mi.; **Water:** 0.0 sq. mi.
In northwestern MO, 45 mi. north-northeast of Kansas City. Platted 1855. Incorporated 1867. Part of the town is also in Clinton County.
Name origin: For Col. Elisha Cameron of Clay County, father-in-law of Samuel McCorkle, one of the town's founders.

Clarksdale
City
ZIP: 64430 **Lat:** 39-48-48 N **Long:** 94-33-00 W
Pop: 287 (1990); 278 (1980) **Pop Density:** 956.7
Land: 0.3 sq. mi.; **Water:** 0.0 sq. mi.
Incorporated 1962.

Colfax
Township
Lat: 39-47-33 N **Long:** 94-23-00 W
Pop: 671 (1990); 660 (1980) **Pop Density:** 15.9
Land: 42.2 sq. mi.; **Water:** 0.5 sq. mi.

Dallas
Township
Lat: 39-58-47 N **Long:** 94-15-18 W
Pop: 223 (1990); 256 (1980) **Pop Density:** 5.3
Land: 42.3 sq. mi.; **Water:** 0.0 sq. mi.

Grand River
Township
Lat: 39-47-05 N **Long:** 94-15-57 W
Pop: 3,587 (1990); 1,384 (1980) **Pop Density:** 99.9
Land: 35.9 sq. mi.; **Water:** 0.2 sq. mi.

Grant
Township
Lat: 39-59-04 N **Long:** 94-23-11 W
Pop: 302 (1990); 335 (1980) **Pop Density:** 6.0
Land: 50.1 sq. mi.; **Water:** 0.4 sq. mi.

Maysville
City
ZIP: 64469 **Lat:** 39-53-13 N **Long:** 94-21-40 W
Pop: 1,176 (1990); 1,187 (1980) **Pop Density:** 980.0
Land: 1.2 sq. mi.; **Water:** 0.0 sq. mi. **Elev:** 974 ft.
Established 1845 as county seat; located and surveyed by G. W. McPherson. Incorporated 1907.

Osborn
City
ZIP: 64474 **Lat:** 39-45-00 N **Long:** 94-21-20 W
Pop: 355 (1990); 323 (1980) **Pop Density:** 710.0
Land: 0.5 sq. mi.; **Water:** 0.0 sq. mi. **Elev:** 1035 ft.
Founded by the Hannibal and St. Joseph Railroad. Incorporated 1887. Part of the town is also in Clinton County.
Name origin: For Col. William Osborn of Waterville, NY.

Polk
Township
Lat: 39-59-17 N **Long:** 94-31-08 W
Pop: 793 (1990); 805 (1980) **Pop Density:** 13.9
Land: 56.9 sq. mi.; **Water:** 0.0 sq. mi.

Sherman
Township
Lat: 39-53-09 N **Long:** 94-31-09 W
Pop: 484 (1990); 582 (1980) **Pop Density:** 8.6
Land: 56.3 sq. mi.; **Water:** 0.0 sq. mi.

Stewartsville — City
ZIP: 64490 **Lat:** 39-45-15 N **Long:** 94-29-55 W
Pop: 732 (1990); 832 (1980) **Pop Density:** 732.0
Land: 1.0 sq. mi.; **Water:** 0.0 sq. mi.
Laid out 1854. Incorporated 1869.
Name origin: For Robert M. Stewart, governor of MO in 1857.

Union Star — Town
ZIP: 64494 **Lat:** 39-58-45 N **Long:** 94-35-52 W
Pop: 432 (1990); 423 (1980) **Pop Density:** 1440.0
Land: 0.3 sq. mi.; **Water:** 0.0 sq. mi.
Incorporated 1935.

Washington — Township
Lat: 39-47-02 N **Long:** 94-31-28 W
Pop: 1,781 (1990); 1,936 (1980) **Pop Density:** 36.9
Land: 48.3 sq. mi.; **Water:** 0.1 sq. mi.

Weatherby — Town
ZIP: 64497 **Lat:** 39-54-33 N **Long:** 94-14-28 W
Pop: 91 (1990); 121 (1980) **Pop Density:** 910.0
Land: 0.1 sq. mi.; **Water:** 0.0 sq. mi. **Elev:** 885 ft.
Incorporated 1887.

Dent County
County Seat: Salem (ZIP: 65560)

Pop: 13,702 (1990); 14,517 (1980) **Pop Density:** 18.2
Land: 753.6 sq. mi.; **Water:** 1.0 sq. mi. **Area Code:** 314
In south-central MO, northwest of Cape Girardeau; organized Feb 10, 1851 from Shannon and Crawford counties.
Name origin: For Lewis Dent (1808–80), landowner and MO legislator.

Bunker — City
ZIP: 63629 **Lat:** 37-27-46 N **Long:** 91-12-50 W
Pop: 159 (1990); 268 (1980) **Pop Density:** 397.5
Land: 0.4 sq. mi.; **Water:** 0.0 sq. mi.
Incorporated 1907. Part of the town is also in Reynolds County.

Current — Township
Lat: 37-28-13 N **Long:** 91-40-43 W
Pop: 408 (1990); 434 (1980) **Pop Density:** 7.5
Land: 54.5 sq. mi.; **Water:** 0.0 sq. mi.

Franklin — Township
Lat: 37-32-41 N **Long:** 91-31-21 W
Pop: 839 (1990); 933 (1980) **Pop Density:** 14.0
Land: 60.0 sq. mi.; **Water:** 0.0 sq. mi.

Gladden — Township
ZIP: 65560 **Lat:** 37-27-39 N **Long:** 91-30-46 W
Pop: 374 (1990); 390 (1980) **Pop Density:** 6.8
Land: 54.6 sq. mi.; **Water:** 0.0 sq. mi.

Linn — Township
Lat: 37-33-20 N **Long:** 91-21-47 W
Pop: 137 (1990); 152 (1980) **Pop Density:** 3.7
Land: 37.5 sq. mi.; **Water:** 0.0 sq. mi.

Meramec — Township
Lat: 37-38-54 N **Long:** 91-21-37 W
Pop: 223 (1990); 228 (1980) **Pop Density:** 4.8
Land: 46.4 sq. mi.; **Water:** 0.1 sq. mi.

Norman — Township
Lat: 37-45-04 N **Long:** 91-35-27 W
Pop: 632 (1990); 707 (1980) **Pop Density:** 17.4
Land: 36.3 sq. mi.; **Water:** 0.1 sq. mi.

Osage — Township
Lat: 37-39-04 N **Long:** 91-14-30 W
Pop: 457 (1990); 504 (1980) **Pop Density:** 7.1
Land: 64.2 sq. mi.; **Water:** 0.1 sq. mi.

Salem — City
ZIP: 65560 **Lat:** 37-38-23 N **Long:** 91-31-59 W
Pop: 4,486 (1990); 4,454 (1980) **Pop Density:** 1602.1
Land: 2.8 sq. mi.; **Water:** 0.0 sq. mi. **Elev:** 1182 ft.
In southeast-central MO, southeast of Jefferson City. Incorporated 1881.

Short Bend — Township
Lat: 37-44-21 N **Long:** 91-25-04 W
Pop: 429 (1990); 465 (1980) **Pop Density:** 6.0
Land: 72.1 sq. mi.; **Water:** 0.3 sq. mi.

Sinking — Township
Lat: 37-27-26 N **Long:** 91-18-28 W
Pop: 315 (1990); 436 (1980) **Pop Density:** 4.4
Land: 71.4 sq. mi.; **Water:** 0.0 sq. mi.

Spring Creek — Township
Lat: 37-38-54 N **Long:** 91-32-01 W
Pop: 7,998 (1990); 8,333 (1980) **Pop Density:** 90.7
Land: 88.2 sq. mi.; **Water:** 0.2 sq. mi.

Texas — Township
Lat: 37-34-07 N **Long:** 91-40-36 W
Pop: 663 (1990); 702 (1980) **Pop Density:** 12.4
Land: 53.6 sq. mi.; **Water:** 0.0 sq. mi.

Watkins — Township
Lat: 37-42-00 N **Long:** 91-43-13 W
Pop: 1,227 (1990); 1,233 (1980) **Pop Density:** 10.7
Land: 114.7 sq. mi.; **Water:** 0.1 sq. mi.

MISSOURI, Douglas County — *American Places Dictionary*

Douglas County
County Seat: Ava (ZIP: 65608)

Pop: 11,876 (1990); 11,594 (1980) **Pop Density:** 14.6
Land: 814.6 sq. mi.; **Water:** 0.1 sq. mi. **Area Code:** 417
In south-central MO, southeast of Springfield; organized Oct 29, 1857 from Ozark County.
Name origin: For Stephen Arnold Douglas (1813–61), U.S. orator and statesman.

Ava City
ZIP: 65608 **Lat:** 36-57-11 N **Long:** 92-39-54 W
Pop: 2,938 (1990); 2,761 (1980) **Pop Density:** 1013.1
Land: 2.9 sq. mi.; **Water:** 0.0 sq. mi. **Elev:** 1283 ft.
Incorporated 1909.

Benton Township
Lat: 36-55-54 N **Long:** 92-40-43 W
Pop: 4,094 (1990); 3,837 (1980) **Pop Density:** 112.8
Land: 36.3 sq. mi.; **Water:** 0.0 sq. mi.

Boone Township
Lat: 36-55-42 N **Long:** 92-35-04 W
Pop: 542 (1990); 534 (1980) **Pop Density:** 14.9
Land: 36.4 sq. mi.; **Water:** 0.0 sq. mi.

Brown Township
Lat: 36-50-25 N **Long:** 92-28-04 W
Pop: 236 (1990); 194 (1980) **Pop Density:** 6.6
Land: 35.8 sq. mi.; **Water:** 0.0 sq. mi.

Brush Creek Township
Lat: 36-50-53 N **Long:** 92-15-31 W
Pop: 314 (1990); 315 (1980) **Pop Density:** 8.6
Land: 36.6 sq. mi.; **Water:** 0.0 sq. mi.

Bryan Township
Lat: 36-55-30 N **Long:** 92-15-23 W
Pop: 277 (1990); 320 (1980) **Pop Density:** 7.6
Land: 36.3 sq. mi.; **Water:** 0.0 sq. mi.

Buchanan Township
Lat: 36-52-31 N **Long:** 92-52-45 W
Pop: 220 (1990); 247 (1980) **Pop Density:** 8.1
Land: 27.1 sq. mi.; **Water:** 0.0 sq. mi.

Campbell Township
Lat: 36-51-11 N **Long:** 92-48-17 W
Pop: 377 (1990); 326 (1980) **Pop Density:** 10.4
Land: 36.1 sq. mi.; **Water:** 0.0 sq. mi.

Cass Township
Lat: 37-01-08 N **Long:** 92-21-49 W
Pop: 258 (1990); 285 (1980) **Pop Density:** 7.1
Land: 36.4 sq. mi.; **Water:** 0.0 sq. mi.

Champion Township
Lat: 36-55-49 N **Long:** 92-21-30 W
Pop: 229 (1990); 209 (1980) **Pop Density:** 6.3
Land: 36.5 sq. mi.; **Water:** 0.0 sq. mi.

Clay Township
Lat: 37-01-11 N **Long:** 92-28-00 W
Pop: 223 (1990); 196 (1980) **Pop Density:** 6.2
Land: 35.9 sq. mi.; **Water:** 0.0 sq. mi.

Clinton Township
Lat: 37-00-50 N **Long:** 92-08-28 W
Pop: 221 (1990); 247 (1980) **Pop Density:** 6.1
Land: 36.0 sq. mi.; **Water:** 0.0 sq. mi.

Findley Township
Lat: 37-01-15 N **Long:** 92-41-16 W
Pop: 588 (1990); 527 (1980) **Pop Density:** 16.4
Land: 35.8 sq. mi.; **Water:** 0.0 sq. mi.

Jackson Township
Lat: 36-50-24 N **Long:** 92-22-21 W
Pop: 248 (1990); 302 (1980) **Pop Density:** 6.8
Land: 36.5 sq. mi.; **Water:** 0.0 sq. mi.

Lincoln Township
Lat: 37-01-14 N **Long:** 92-47-14 W
Pop: 351 (1990); 433 (1980) **Pop Density:** 9.7
Land: 36.2 sq. mi.; **Water:** 0.0 sq. mi.

McKinley Township
Lat: 36-55-53 N **Long:** 92-08-59 W
Pop: 182 (1990); 179 (1980) **Pop Density:** 5.1
Land: 36.0 sq. mi.; **Water:** 0.0 sq. mi.

McMurtrey Township
Lat: 36-56-12 N **Long:** 92-28-28 W
Pop: 326 (1990); 315 (1980) **Pop Density:** 9.1
Land: 35.9 sq. mi.; **Water:** 0.0 sq. mi.

Miller Township
Lat: 37-01-17 N **Long:** 92-34-35 W
Pop: 537 (1990); 545 (1980) **Pop Density:** 14.8
Land: 36.4 sq. mi.; **Water:** 0.0 sq. mi.

Richland Township
Lat: 36-49-56 N **Long:** 92-08-54 W
Pop: 289 (1990); 216 (1980) **Pop Density:** 8.0
Land: 36.3 sq. mi.; **Water:** 0.0 sq. mi.

Spencer Township
Lat: 36-59-30 N **Long:** 92-52-49 W
Pop: 262 (1990); 263 (1980) **Pop Density:** 9.7
Land: 27.0 sq. mi.; **Water:** 0.0 sq. mi.

Spring Creek Township
Lat: 36-50-54 N **Long:** 92-41-42 W
Pop: 624 (1990); 567 (1980) **Pop Density:** 17.2
Land: 36.3 sq. mi.; **Water:** 0.0 sq. mi.

Walls Township
Lat: 36-50-51 N **Long:** 92-35-16 W
Pop: 536 (1990); 523 (1980) **Pop Density:** 14.8
Land: 36.3 sq. mi.; **Water:** 0.0 sq. mi.

Washington Township
Lat: 36-56-12 N **Long:** 92-47-18 W
Pop: 574 (1990); 655 (1980) **Pop Density:** 15.9
Land: 36.2 sq. mi.; **Water:** 0.0 sq. mi.

Wood Township
Lat: 37-01-13 N **Long:** 92-14-56 W
Pop: 368 (1990); 359 (1980) **Pop Density:** 10.1
Land: 36.3 sq. mi.; **Water:** 0.0 sq. mi.

Dunklin County
County Seat: Kennett (ZIP: 63857)

Pop: 33,112 (1990); 36,324 (1980)   **Pop Density:** 60.7
Land: 545.6 sq. mi.; **Water:** 1.5 sq. mi.   **Area Code:** 314

On the southern border of MO, southwest of Cape Girardeau; organized Feb 14, 1845 from Stoddard County.

Name origin: For Daniel Dunklin (1790–1844), governor of MO (1833–36) and surveyor-general of MO, IL, and AR.

Arbyrd   City
ZIP: 63821   **Lat:** 36-03-09 N   **Long:** 90-14-23 W
Pop: 597 (1990); 704 (1980)   **Pop Density:** 597.0
Land: 1.0 sq. mi.; **Water:** 0.0 sq. mi.
Incorporated 1919.
Name origin: Named in 1915 by and for landowner A. R. Byrd.

Buffalo   Township
Lat: 36-02-53 N   **Long:** 90-17-42 W
Pop: 1,552 (1990); 1,766 (1980)   **Pop Density:** 37.9
Land: 40.9 sq. mi.; **Water:** 0.0 sq. mi.

Campbell   City
ZIP: 63933   **Lat:** 36-29-31 N   **Long:** 90-04-27 W
Pop: 2,165 (1990); 2,134 (1980)   **Pop Density:** 1665.4
Land: 1.3 sq. mi.; **Water:** 0.0 sq. mi.
Incorporated 1892.
Name origin: Named in 1886 for Judge Alexander Campbell.

Cardwell   City
ZIP: 63829   **Lat:** 36-02-50 N   **Long:** 90-17-28 W
Pop: 792 (1990); 831 (1980)   **Pop Density:** 1320.0
Land: 0.6 sq. mi.; **Water:** 0.0 sq. mi.
Incorporated 1904.

Clarkton   City
ZIP: 63837   **Lat:** 36-27-08 N   **Long:** 89-57-54 W
Pop: 1,113 (1990); 1,228 (1980)   **Pop Density:** 1236.7
Land: 0.9 sq. mi.; **Water:** 0.0 sq. mi.
Platted 1860. Incorporated 1926.
Name origin: For Henry E. Clark, one of the contractors of the old Weaverville-Clarkton plank road, sometimes called the Devil's Washboard. Previously called Bach.

Clay   Township
Lat: 36-04-16 N   **Long:** 90-04-09 W
Pop: 1,685 (1990); 2,047 (1980)   **Pop Density:** 14.3
Land: 117.9 sq. mi.; **Water:** 0.3 sq. mi.

Cotton Hill   Township
Lat: 36-33-43 N   **Long:** 89-59-43 W
Pop: 6,735 (1990); 7,808 (1980)   **Pop Density:** 189.2
Land: 35.6 sq. mi.; **Water:** 0.0 sq. mi.

Freeborn   Township
ZIP: 63837   **Lat:** 36-26-38 N   **Long:** 89-59-13 W
Pop: 1,672 (1990); 1,865 (1980)   **Pop Density:** 57.9
Land: 28.9 sq. mi.; **Water:** 0.0 sq. mi.

Holcomb   City
ZIP: 63852   **Lat:** 36-24-00 N   **Long:** 90-01-22 W
Pop: 531 (1990); 632 (1980)   **Pop Density:** 885.0
Land: 0.6 sq. mi.; **Water:** 0.0 sq. mi.
Incorporated 1891. Not coextensive with the town of the same name.

*Holcomb   Township
ZIP: 63852   **Lat:** 36-23-43 N   **Long:** 90-03-15 W
Pop: 1,103 (1990); 1,454 (1980)   **Pop Density:** 27.5
Land: 40.1 sq. mi.; **Water:** 0.0 sq. mi.

Hornersville   City
ZIP: 63855   **Lat:** 36-02-24 N   **Long:** 90-06-53 W
Pop: 629 (1990); 704 (1980)   **Pop Density:** 786.3
Land: 0.8 sq. mi.; **Water:** 0.0 sq. mi.
Incorporated 1845.

Independence   Township
Lat: 36-14-11 N   **Long:** 90-02-16 W
Pop: 12,882 (1990); 13,284 (1980)   **Pop Density:** 116.1
Land: 111.0 sq. mi.; **Water:** 0.3 sq. mi.

Kennett   City
ZIP: 63857   **Lat:** 36-14-23 N   **Long:** 90-02-55 W
Pop: 10,941 (1990); 10,145 (1980)   **Pop Density:** 1736.7
Land: 6.3 sq. mi.; **Water:** 0.0 sq. mi.
In southeastern MO near the St. Francis River, the AR border. Incorporated 1873.
Name origin: For Dr. Luther M. Kennett, mayor of St. Louis (1849–52). Previously called Chilletecaux and Butler.

Malden   City
ZIP: 63863   **Lat:** 36-35-05 N   **Long:** 89-58-32 W
Pop: 5,123 (1990); 6,096 (1980)   **Pop Density:** 839.8
Land: 6.1 sq. mi.; **Water:** 0.0 sq. mi.
In southeastern MO, 30 mi. east-southeast of Poplar Bluff. Incorporated 1878.
Name origin: For Malden, MA.

Salem   Township
Lat: 36-06-40 N   **Long:** 90-11-34 W
Pop: 3,125 (1990); 3,590 (1980)   **Pop Density:** 46.3
Land: 67.5 sq. mi.; **Water:** 0.2 sq. mi.

Senath   City
ZIP: 63876   **Lat:** 36-08-00 N   **Long:** 90-09-39 W
Pop: 1,622 (1990); 1,728 (1980)   **Pop Density:** 853.7
Land: 1.9 sq. mi.; **Water:** 0.0 sq. mi.
Established 1882 by first postmaster, A. W. Douglass. Incorporated 1882.
Name origin: For the wife of A. W. Douglass.

Union   Township
Lat: 36-32-25 N   **Long:** 90-06-43 W
Pop: 4,358 (1990); 4,510 (1980)   **Pop Density:** 42.0
Land: 103.7 sq. mi.; **Water:** 0.7 sq. mi.

Franklin County
County Seat: Union (ZIP: 63084)

Pop: 80,603 (1990); 71,233 (1980)   **Pop Density:** 87.4
Land: 922.1 sq. mi.; **Water:** 7.6 sq. mi.   **Area Code:** 314

In central-eastern MO, west of St. Louis; organized Dec 11, 1818 (prior to statehood) from Saint Louis County.

Name origin: For Benjamin Franklin (1706–90), U.S. patriot, diplomat, and statesman.

Berger — City
ZIP: 63014   **Lat:** 38-40-26 N   **Long:** 91-20-06 W
Pop: 247 (1990); 214 (1980)   **Pop Density:** 1235.0
Land: 0.2 sq. mi.; **Water:** 0.0 sq. mi.   **Elev:** 512 ft.
Incorporated 1928.

Boeuf — Township
Lat: 38-36-20 N   **Long:** 91-16-30 W
Pop: 1,980 (1990); 1,883 (1980)   **Pop Density:** 23.5
Land: 84.2 sq. mi.; **Water:** 1.9 sq. mi.

Boles — Township
Lat: 38-30-49 N   **Long:** 90-48-54 W
Pop: 14,215 (1990); 12,913 (1980)   **Pop Density:** 157.1
Land: 90.5 sq. mi.; **Water:** 1.8 sq. mi.

Boone — Township
Lat: 38-18-41 N   **Long:** 91-16-58 W
Pop: 4,616 (1990); 4,156 (1980)   **Pop Density:** 34.4
Land: 134.1 sq. mi.; **Water:** 0.3 sq. mi.

Calvey — Township
Lat: 38-23-07 N   **Long:** 90-47-54 W
Pop: 4,588 (1990); 3,856 (1980)   **Pop Density:** 81.6
Land: 56.2 sq. mi.; **Water:** 0.6 sq. mi.

Central — Township
Lat: 38-21-12 N   **Long:** 90-59-00 W
Pop: 11,755 (1990); 9,956 (1980)   **Pop Density:** 115.2
Land: 102.0 sq. mi.; **Water:** 0.2 sq. mi.

Gerald — City
ZIP: 63037   **Lat:** 38-23-57 N   **Long:** 91-19-52 W
Pop: 888 (1990); 921 (1980)   **Pop Density:** 634.3
Land: 1.4 sq. mi.; **Water:** 0.0 sq. mi.   **Elev:** 895 ft.
Incorporated 1907.

Gray Summit — CDP
ZIP: 63039   **Lat:** 38-29-41 N   **Long:** 90-48-54 W
Pop: 2,505 (1990)   **Pop Density:** 321.2
Land: 7.8 sq. mi.; **Water:** 0.0 sq. mi.

Leslie — Village
ZIP: 63056   **Lat:** 38-25-03 N   **Long:** 91-13-52 W
Pop: 134 (1990); 108 (1980)   **Pop Density:** 1340.0
Land: 0.1 sq. mi.; **Water:** 0.0 sq. mi.
Incorporated 1912.

Lyon — Township
ZIP: 63068   **Lat:** 38-29-40 N   **Long:** 91-15-04 W
Pop: 3,423 (1990); 3,175 (1980)   **Pop Density:** 27.9
Land: 122.5 sq. mi.; **Water:** 0.2 sq. mi.

Meramec — Township
Lat: 38-16-08 N   **Long:** 91-06-23 W
Pop: 7,335 (1990); 6,949 (1980)   **Pop Density:** 77.4
Land: 94.8 sq. mi.; **Water:** 0.0 sq. mi.

New Haven — City
ZIP: 63068   **Lat:** 38-36-26 N   **Long:** 91-13-05 W
Pop: 1,757 (1990); 1,581 (1980)   **Pop Density:** 627.5
Land: 2.8 sq. mi.; **Water:** 0.2 sq. mi.
Incorporated 1858.
Name origin: Named in 1858 for New Haven, CT.

*New Haven — Township
ZIP: 63068   **Lat:** 38-36-43 N   **Long:** 91-13-09 W
Pop: 1,751 (1990); 1,581 (1980)   **Pop Density:** 625.4
Land: 2.8 sq. mi.; **Water:** 0.4 sq. mi.

Oak Grove — City
Lat: 38-13-36 N   **Long:** 91-09-04 W
Pop: 402 (1990); 386 (1980)   **Pop Density:** 804.0
Land: 0.5 sq. mi.; **Water:** 0.0 sq. mi.
Incorporated 1953.

Pacific — City
ZIP: 63069   **Lat:** 38-28-41 N   **Long:** 90-45-10 W
Pop: 4,332 (1990); 4,398 (1980)   **Pop Density:** 1353.8
Land: 3.2 sq. mi.; **Water:** 0.0 sq. mi.   **Elev:** 466 ft.
In eastern MO, 35 mi. west of St. Louis. Incorporated 1859. Part of the town is also in St. Louis County.

Parkway — Village
Lat: 38-20-18 N   **Long:** 90-58-25 W
Pop: 277 (1990); 254 (1980)   **Pop Density:** 923.3
Land: 0.3 sq. mi.; **Water:** 0.0 sq. mi.   **Elev:** 748 ft.
Incorporated 1943.

Prairie — Township
Lat: 38-16-20 N   **Long:** 90-51-29 W
Pop: 3,172 (1990); 2,794 (1980)   **Pop Density:** 37.0
Land: 85.8 sq. mi.; **Water:** 0.2 sq. mi.

St. Clair — City
Lat: 38-21-03 N   **Long:** 90-58-51 W
Pop: 3,917 (1990); 3,485 (1980)   **Pop Density:** 1398.9
Land: 2.8 sq. mi.; **Water:** 0.0 sq. mi.   **Elev:** 769 ft.
In eastern MO, 50 mi. southwest of St. Louis. Incorporated 1882.
Name origin: For Gen. Arthur St. Clair (1736–1818), first governor of the Northwest Territory (1787–1802).

St. Johns — Township
Lat: 38-32-12 N   **Long:** 91-02-31 W
Pop: 5,108 (1990); 3,919 (1980)   **Pop Density:** 94.9
Land: 53.8 sq. mi.; **Water:** 1.4 sq. mi.

Sullivan — City
ZIP: 63080   **Lat:** 38-13-01 N   **Long:** 91-09-48 W
Pop: 4,545 (1990); 4,436 (1980)   **Pop Density:** 909.0
Land: 5.0 sq. mi.; **Water:** 0.0 sq. mi.   **Elev:** 987 ft.
Established 1856. Incorporated 1883. Part of the town is also in Crawford County.
Name origin: Named in 1860 for Stephen Sullivan, who had

donated the right of way through the village. Previously called Mt. Helicon.

Union
City
ZIP: 63084 Lat: 38-26-53 N Long: 91-00-45 W
Pop: 5,909 (1990); 5,506 (1980) Pop Density: 1515.1
Land: 3.9 sq. mi.; Water: 0.0 sq. mi. Elev: 545 ft.

In eastern MO, 50 mi. west-southwest of St. Louis. Incorporated 1848.

Name origin: Named by the Missourians for the high ideals they had and for which they were fond of naming places.

*Union
Township
ZIP: 63084 Lat: 38-26-20 N Long: 91-03-58 W
Pop: 12,331 (1990); 10,800 (1980) Pop Density: 136.7
Land: 90.2 sq. mi.; Water: 0.1 sq. mi.

Villa Ridge
CDP
ZIP: 63089 Lat: 38-28-16 N Long: 90-53-00 W
Pop: 1,865 (1990) Pop Density: 380.6
Land: 4.9 sq. mi.; Water: 0.1 sq. mi.

Washington
City
ZIP: 63090 Lat: 38-33-11 N Long: 91-00-45 W
Pop: 10,704 (1990); 9,251 (1980) Pop Density: 1574.1
Land: 6.8 sq. mi.; Water: 0.5 sq. mi.

In eastern MO on the Missouri River, 50 mi. east of St. Louis. Incorporated 1839.

Name origin: For George Washington (1732–99), American patriot and first U.S. president.

*Washington
Township
ZIP: 63090 Lat: 38-33-10 N Long: 91-00-33 W
Pop: 10,329 (1990); 9,251 (1980) Pop Density: 1986.3
Land: 5.2 sq. mi.; Water: 0.5 sq. mi.

Gasconade County
County Seat: Hermann (ZIP: 65041)

Pop: 14,006 (1990); 13,181 (1980) Pop Density: 27.0
Land: 519.5 sq. mi.; Water: 5.0 sq. mi. Area Code: 314

In east-central MO, west of St. Louis; organized Nov 25, 1820 (prior to statehood) from Franklin County.

Name origin: For the Gasconade River, which runs through it. It is believed that French residents of St. Louis gave this name to the river and general area for the bragging of the inhabitants when they went to St. Louis; an allusion to the residents of the French province of Gascony, supposed to be boastful.

Bland
City
ZIP: 65014 Lat: 38-18-02 N Long: 91-37-57 W
Pop: 651 (1990); 662 (1980) Pop Density: 1085.0
Land: 0.6 sq. mi.; Water: 0.0 sq. mi. Elev: 1023 ft.

Incorporated 1902. Part of the town is also in Osage County.

Name origin: For U.S. Congressman Richard P. Bland (1835–99).

Boeuf
Township
Lat: 38-30-40 N Long: 91-25-49 W
Pop: 899 (1990); 851 (1980) Pop Density: 12.4
Land: 72.6 sq. mi.; Water: 0.1 sq. mi.

Boulware
Township
Lat: 38-30-33 N Long: 91-33-50 W
Pop: 528 (1990); 545 (1980) Pop Density: 7.8
Land: 67.4 sq. mi.; Water: 0.5 sq. mi.

Bourbois
Township
Lat: 38-11-59 N Long: 91-35-15 W
Pop: 361 (1990); 398 (1980) Pop Density: 9.7
Land: 37.1 sq. mi.; Water: 0.0 sq. mi.

Brush Creek
Township
Lat: 38-15-01 N Long: 91-26-48 W
Pop: 678 (1990); 596 (1980) Pop Density: 12.7
Land: 53.4 sq. mi.; Water: 0.1 sq. mi.

Canaan
Township
Lat: 38-22-07 N Long: 91-26-19 W
Pop: 4,821 (1990); 4,396 (1980) Pop Density: 63.2
Land: 76.3 sq. mi.; Water: 0.3 sq. mi.

Clay
Township
Lat: 38-17-46 N Long: 91-34-49 W
Pop: 1,512 (1990); 1,407 (1980) Pop Density: 30.7
Land: 49.3 sq. mi.; Water: 0.1 sq. mi.

Gasconade
City
ZIP: 65036 Lat: 38-40-09 N Long: 91-33-37 W
Pop: 253 (1990); 250 (1980) Pop Density: 1265.0
Land: 0.2 sq. mi.; Water: 0.0 sq. mi. Elev: 527 ft.

Incorporated 1958.

Hermann
City
ZIP: 65041 Lat: 38-41-56 N Long: 91-26-06 W
Pop: 2,754 (1990); 2,695 (1980) Pop Density: 1311.4
Land: 2.1 sq. mi.; Water: 0.2 sq. mi. Elev: 519 ft.

Founded by the German Settlement Association of Philadelphia in 1837. Incorporated 1845.

Name origin: For Hermann, Germany.

Morrison
City
ZIP: 65036 Lat: 38-40-14 N Long: 91-37-58 W
Pop: 160 (1990); 169 (1980) Pop Density: 320.0
Land: 0.5 sq. mi.; Water: 0.0 sq. mi.

Incorporated 1899.

Owensville
City
ZIP: 65066 Lat: 38-20-51 N Long: 91-29-51 W
Pop: 2,325 (1990); 2,241 (1980) Pop Density: 1453.1
Land: 1.6 sq. mi.; Water: 0.0 sq. mi. Elev: 935 ft.

Incorporated 1900.

Name origin: For a storekeeper named Owen.

MISSOURI, Gasconade County

Richland
Township
Lat: 38-36-50 N Long: 91-35-40 W
Pop: 855 (1990); 882 (1980)   Pop Density: 17.3
Land: 49.5 sq. mi.; Water: 2.4 sq. mi.

Roark
Township
Lat: 38-39-00 N Long: 91-26-43 W
Pop: 3,868 (1990); 3,757 (1980)   Pop Density: 53.9
Land: 71.7 sq. mi.; Water: 1.3 sq. mi.

Rosebud
City
ZIP: 63091   Lat: 38-23-11 N Long: 91-24-10 W
Pop: 380 (1990); 326 (1980)   Pop Density: 1266.7
Land: 0.3 sq. mi.; Water: 0.0 sq. mi.   Elev: 883 ft.
Incorporated 1911.

Third Creek
Township
Lat: 38-23-51 N Long: 91-34-41 W
Pop: 484 (1990); 349 (1980)   Pop Density: 11.5
Land: 42.1 sq. mi.; Water: 0.2 sq. mi.

Gentry County
County Seat: Albany (ZIP: 64402)

Pop: 6,848 (1990); 7,887 (1980)   Pop Density: 13.9
Land: 491.6 sq. mi.; Water: 0.3 sq. mi.   Area Code: 816

In northwestern MO, northeast of St. Joseph; established Feb 12, 1841 from Clinton County.

Name origin: For Richard Gentry (1788-1837), officer in the Black Hawk War who died fighting the Seminoles in Florida.

Albany
City
ZIP: 64402   Lat: 40-14-53 N Long: 94-20-01 W
Pop: 1,958 (1990); 2,152 (1980)   Pop Density: 783.2
Land: 2.5 sq. mi.; Water: 0.0 sq. mi.   Elev: 915 ft.
Incorporated 1845.

Name origin: Previously called Ashton. Named in 1857 by an act of the legislature for Albany, NY.

Athens
Township
Lat: 40-14-27 N Long: 94-17-48 W
Pop: 2,387 (1990); 2,649 (1980)   Pop Density: 31.4
Land: 76.0 sq. mi.; Water: 0.1 sq. mi.

Bogle
Township
Lat: 40-21-03 N Long: 94-24-31 W
Pop: 256 (1990); 303 (1980)   Pop Density: 5.8
Land: 44.3 sq. mi.; Water: 0.0 sq. mi.

Cooper
Township
Lat: 40-12-40 N Long: 94-29-52 W
Pop: 1,869 (1990); 2,167 (1980)   Pop Density: 26.9
Land: 69.4 sq. mi.; Water: 0.0 sq. mi.

Darlington
Town
ZIP: 64438   Lat: 40-11-55 N Long: 94-24-00 W
Pop: 76 (1990); 131 (1980)   Pop Density: 190.0
Land: 0.4 sq. mi.; Water: 0.0 sq. mi.   Elev: 836 ft.
Incorporated 1892.

Ford City
Town
Lat: 40-06-44 N Long: 94-27-53 W
Pop: 29 (1990); 30 (1980)   Pop Density: 145.0
Land: 0.2 sq. mi.; Water: 0.0 sq. mi.   Elev: 1043 ft.

Gentry
Village
ZIP: 64453   Lat: 40-19-59 N Long: 94-25-24 W
Pop: 95 (1990); 126 (1980)   Pop Density: 475.0
Land: 0.2 sq. mi.; Water: 0.0 sq. mi.   Elev: 888 ft.
Incorporated 1902.

Name origin: For Richard Gentry (1788–1837), officer in the Black Hawk war who died fighting the Seminoles in Florida.

Howard
Township
Lat: 40-20-27 N Long: 94-17-01 W
Pop: 98 (1990); 164 (1980)   Pop Density: 2.5
Land: 39.9 sq. mi.; Water: 0.0 sq. mi.

Huggins
Township
Lat: 40-16-16 N Long: 94-25-54 W
Pop: 115 (1990); 170 (1980)   Pop Density: 3.8
Land: 30.1 sq. mi.; Water: 0.0 sq. mi.

Jackson
Township
Lat: 40-06-03 N Long: 94-31-41 W
Pop: 1,382 (1990); 1,544 (1980)   Pop Density: 18.1
Land: 76.2 sq. mi.; Water: 0.2 sq. mi.

King City
City
ZIP: 64463   Lat: 40-03-02 N Long: 94-31-28 W
Pop: 986 (1990); 1,063 (1980)   Pop Density: 704.3
Land: 1.4 sq. mi.; Water: 0.0 sq. mi.
Incorporated 1881.

McFall
City
Lat: 40-06-42 N Long: 94-13-21 W
Pop: 142 (1990); 139 (1980)   Pop Density: 473.3
Land: 0.3 sq. mi.; Water: 0.0 sq. mi.
Incorporated 1852.

Miller
Township
Lat: 40-05-19 N Long: 94-19-19 W
Pop: 547 (1990); 613 (1980)   Pop Density: 5.1
Land: 106.5 sq. mi.; Water: 0.0 sq. mi.

Stanberry
City
ZIP: 64489   Lat: 40-13-00 N Long: 94-32-16 W
Pop: 1,310 (1990); 1,387 (1980)   Pop Density: 1091.7
Land: 1.2 sq. mi.; Water: 0.0 sq. mi.   Elev: 886 ft.
Incorporated 1879.

Name origin: For John J. Stanberry, original owner of the townsite.

Wilson
Township
Lat: 40-19-41 N Long: 94-32-19 W
Pop: 194 (1990); 277 (1980)   Pop Density: 4.0
Land: 49.1 sq. mi.; Water: 0.0 sq. mi.

> ## Greene County
> **County Seat: Springfield (ZIP: 65802)**
>
> **Pop:** 207,949 (1990); 185,302 (1980)   **Pop Density:** 308.1
> **Land:** 675.0 sq. mi.; **Water:** 2.8 sq. mi.   **Area Code:** 417
> In south-central MO, northeast of Joplin; organized Jan 2, 1833 from Wayne and Crawford counties.
> **Name origin:** For Gen. Nathanael Greene (1742–1786), hero of the Revolutionary War, quartermaster general (1778–80), and commander of the Army of the South.

Ash Grove — City
ZIP: 65604   **Lat:** 37-19-02 N   **Long:** 93-34-49 W
Pop: 1,128 (1990); 1,157 (1980)   **Pop Density:** 1128.0
Land: 1.0 sq. mi.; **Water:** 0.0 sq. mi.   **Elev:** 1042 ft.
Incorporated 1871.
Name origin: Named in 1853 for its descriptive connotations.

Battlefield — Town
ZIP: 65619   **Lat:** 37-07-05 N   **Long:** 93-22-04 W
Pop: 1,526 (1990); 1,227 (1980)   **Pop Density:** 1090.0
Land: 1.4 sq. mi.; **Water:** 0.0 sq. mi.
Incorporated 1971.

Boone No. 1 — Township
Lat: 37-20-32 N   **Long:** 93-33-39 W
Pop: 1,063 (1990); 1,002 (1980)   **Pop Density:** 56.2
Land: 18.9 sq. mi.; **Water:** 0.0 sq. mi.

Boone No. 2 — Township
Lat: 37-17-17 N   **Long:** 93-34-49 W
Pop: 846 (1990); 799 (1980)   **Pop Density:** 42.1
Land: 20.1 sq. mi.; **Water:** 0.0 sq. mi.

Brookline — Village
Lat: 37-10-15 N   **Long:** 93-24-36 W
Pop: 283 (1990); 211 (1980)   **Pop Density:** 67.4
Land: 4.2 sq. mi.; **Water:** 0.0 sq. mi.   **Elev:** 1286 ft.
Incorporated 1968.

*Brookline — Township
Lat: 37-08-57 N   **Long:** 93-25-06 W
Pop: 1,623 (1990); 1,250 (1980)   **Pop Density:** 74.8
Land: 21.7 sq. mi.; **Water:** 0.0 sq. mi.

Campbell No. 1 — Township
Lat: 37-11-43 N   **Long:** 93-11-34 W
Pop: 2,569 (1990); 1,861 (1980)   **Pop Density:** 383.4
Land: 6.7 sq. mi.; **Water:** 0.0 sq. mi.

Campbell No. 2 — Township
Lat: 37-09-43 N   **Long:** 93-21-43 W
Pop: 5,261 (1990); 1,880 (1980)   **Pop Density:** 536.8
Land: 9.8 sq. mi.; **Water:** 0.0 sq. mi.

Cass — Township
Lat: 37-22-29 N   **Long:** 93-27-14 W
Pop: 975 (1990); 851 (1980)   **Pop Density:** 31.2
Land: 31.3 sq. mi.; **Water:** 0.0 sq. mi.

Center No. 1 — Township
Lat: 37-14-23 N   **Long:** 93-25-24 W
Pop: 1,856 (1990); 1,885 (1980)   **Pop Density:** 120.5
Land: 15.4 sq. mi.; **Water:** 0.0 sq. mi.

Center No. 2 — Township
Lat: 37-13-05 N   **Long:** 93-34-30 W
Pop: 230 (1990); 434 (1980)   **Pop Density:** 20.7
Land: 11.1 sq. mi.; **Water:** 0.0 sq. mi.

Center No. 3 — Township
Lat: 37-14-49 N   **Long:** 93-30-12 W
Pop: 1,281 (1990); 1,247 (1980)   **Pop Density:** 43.4
Land: 29.5 sq. mi.; **Water:** 0.0 sq. mi.

Clay — Township
Lat: 37-07-17 N   **Long:** 93-13-06 W
Pop: 6,799 (1990); 4,437 (1980)   **Pop Density:** 291.8
Land: 23.3 sq. mi.; **Water:** 0.2 sq. mi.

East Republic — Township
Lat: 37-08-31 N   **Long:** 93-27-40 W
Pop: 5,093 (1990); 3,257 (1980)   **Pop Density:** 382.9
Land: 13.3 sq. mi.; **Water:** 0.0 sq. mi.

Fair Grove — City
ZIP: 65648   **Lat:** 37-22-57 N   **Long:** 93-09-04 W
Pop: 919 (1990); 863 (1980)   **Pop Density:** 306.3
Land: 3.0 sq. mi.; **Water:** 0.0 sq. mi.
Incorporated 1965.

Franklin No. 1 — Township
Lat: 37-22-07 N   **Long:** 93-12-40 W
Pop: 1,241 (1990); 996 (1980)   **Pop Density:** 58.3
Land: 21.3 sq. mi.; **Water:** 0.5 sq. mi.

Franklin No. 2 — Township
Lat: 37-18-51 N   **Long:** 93-15-15 W
Pop: 2,449 (1990); 2,378 (1980)   **Pop Density:** 88.7
Land: 27.6 sq. mi.; **Water:** 0.8 sq. mi.

Jackson No. 1 — Township
Lat: 37-22-09 N   **Long:** 93-08-16 W
Pop: 2,079 (1990); 1,939 (1980)   **Pop Density:** 60.1
Land: 34.6 sq. mi.; **Water:** 0.1 sq. mi.

Jackson No. 2 — Township
Lat: 37-17-03 N   **Long:** 93-07-12 W
Pop: 2,819 (1990); 2,672 (1980)   **Pop Density:** 71.2
Land: 39.6 sq. mi.; **Water:** 0.1 sq. mi.

Murray — Township
Lat: 37-18-04 N   **Long:** 93-27-12 W
Pop: 3,198 (1990); 2,756 (1980)   **Pop Density:** 114.6
Land: 27.9 sq. mi.; **Water:** 0.0 sq. mi.

North Campbell No. 1 — Township
Lat: 37-14-59 N   **Long:** 93-12-36 W
Pop: 2,941 (1990); 2,101 (1980)   **Pop Density:** 201.4
Land: 14.6 sq. mi.; **Water:** 0.0 sq. mi.

MISSOURI, Greene County

North Campbell No. 2 Township
Lat: 37-15-01 N Long: 93-21-36 W
Pop: 1,557 (1990); 1,193 (1980) **Pop Density:** 115.3
Land: 13.5 sq. mi.; **Water:** 0.0 sq. mi.

North Campbell No. 3 Township
Lat: 37-16-04 N Long: 93-18-40 W
Pop: 1,035 (1990); 812 (1980) **Pop Density:** 646.9
Land: 1.6 sq. mi.; **Water:** 0.0 sq. mi.

Pond Creek Township
Lat: 37-08-55 N Long: 93-33-51 W
Pop: 1,073 (1990); 713 (1980) **Pop Density:** 30.5
Land: 35.2 sq. mi.; **Water:** 0.0 sq. mi.

Republic City
ZIP: 65738 Lat: 37-07-02 N Long: 93-28-30 W
Pop: 6,292 (1990); 4,485 (1980) **Pop Density:** 1498.1
Land: 4.2 sq. mi.; **Water:** 0.0 sq. mi.
Incorporated 1891.

Robberson No. 1 Township
Lat: 37-23-42 N Long: 93-19-42 W
Pop: 1,598 (1990); 1,545 (1980) **Pop Density:** 43.2
Land: 37.0 sq. mi.; **Water:** 0.0 sq. mi.

Robberson No. 2 Township
Lat: 37-19-41 N Long: 93-20-50 W
Pop: 2,215 (1990); 1,900 (1980) **Pop Density:** 67.5
Land: 32.8 sq. mi.; **Water:** 0.3 sq. mi.

Rogersville Town
ZIP: 65742 Lat: 37-06-58 N Long: 93-03-54 W
Pop: 21 (1990); 35 (1980) **Pop Density:** 210.0
Land: 0.1 sq. mi.; **Water:** 0.0 sq. mi.
Incorporated 1947. Part of the town is also in Webster County.
Name origin: For Dr. Rogers, a pioneer.

Springfield City
ZIP: 65801 Lat: 37-11-46 N Long: 93-17-09 W
Pop: 140,494 (1990); 133,116 (1980) **Pop Density:** 2069.1
Land: 67.9 sq. mi.; **Water:** 0.6 sq. mi.
In southwestern MO, 145 mi. south-southeast of Kansas City. Settled 1829. Part of the town is also in Christian County. Commercial center for farming, lumbering, and mining areas; agriculture (fruit orchards, dairy processing, poultry); commercial (flour mills, meat-packing, electronics equipment, machine shops). Incorporated 1838.
Name origin: For either the former home of one of the early settlers, or named by John Polk Campbell, who staked an early claim here, and chose the name because there was a field on a hill with a spring under it.

Strafford City
ZIP: 65757 Lat: 37-16-11 N Long: 93-07-03 W
Pop: 1,166 (1990); 1,121 (1980) **Pop Density:** 613.7
Land: 1.9 sq. mi.; **Water:** 0.0 sq. mi. **Elev:** 1482 ft.
Incorporated 1964.

Taylor Township
Lat: 37-12-07 N Long: 93-07-10 W
Pop: 1,960 (1990); 1,799 (1980) **Pop Density:** 66.2
Land: 29.6 sq. mi.; **Water:** 0.1 sq. mi.

Walnut Grove City
ZIP: 65770 Lat: 37-24-42 N Long: 93-32-53 W
Pop: 549 (1990); 504 (1980) **Pop Density:** 1098.0
Land: 0.5 sq. mi.; **Water:** 0.0 sq. mi.
Incorporated 1934.
Name origin: For the many walnut trees found in the area.

*Walnut Grove Township
ZIP: 65770 Lat: 37-23-39 N Long: 93-33-55 W
Pop: 1,237 (1990); 1,187 (1980) **Pop Density:** 41.4
Land: 29.9 sq. mi.; **Water:** 0.0 sq. mi.

Washington Township
Lat: 37-07-21 N Long: 93-07-16 W
Pop: 2,113 (1990); 1,854 (1980) **Pop Density:** 70.4
Land: 30.0 sq. mi.; **Water:** 0.0 sq. mi.

West Republic Township
Lat: 37-09-09 N Long: 93-29-42 W
Pop: 2,414 (1990); 2,113 (1980) **Pop Density:** 164.2
Land: 14.7 sq. mi.; **Water:** 0.0 sq. mi.

Willard City
ZIP: 65781 Lat: 37-17-36 N Long: 93-24-39 W
Pop: 2,177 (1990); 1,799 (1980) **Pop Density:** 463.2
Land: 4.7 sq. mi.; **Water:** 0.0 sq. mi.
Incorporated 1949.

Wilson Township
Lat: 37-06-59 N Long: 93-20-16 W
Pop: 9,930 (1990); 7,284 (1980) **Pop Density:** 613.0
Land: 16.2 sq. mi.; **Water:** 0.1 sq. mi.

Grundy County
County Seat: Trenton (ZIP: 64683)

Pop: 10,536 (1990); 11,959 (1980) **Pop Density:** 24.2
Land: 435.9 sq. mi.; **Water:** 2.2 sq. mi. **Area Code:** 816
In north-central MO, northeast of St. Joseph; organized Jan 29, 1841 from Livingston and Ray counties.
Name origin: For Felix Grundy (1777–1840), chief justice of KY supreme court, U.S. senator from TN (1829–38; 1839–40), and U.S. Attorney General (1838–39).

Brimson — Village
Lat: 40-08-39 N Long: 93-44-15 W
Pop: 72 (1990); 104 (1980) **Pop Density:** 720.0
Land: 0.1 sq. mi.; **Water:** 0.0 sq. mi. **Elev:** 776 ft.
Incorporated 1906.

Franklin — Township
Lat: 40-14-19 N Long: 93-34-45 W
Pop: 497 (1990); 566 (1980) **Pop Density:** 15.3
Land: 32.5 sq. mi.; **Water:** 0.0 sq. mi.

Galt — City
ZIP: 64641 Lat: 40-07-37 N Long: 93-23-15 W
Pop: 296 (1990); 323 (1980) **Pop Density:** 986.7
Land: 0.3 sq. mi.; **Water:** 0.0 sq. mi.
Incorporated 1894.

Harrison — Township
Lat: 40-10-00 N Long: 93-40-25 W
Pop: 123 (1990); 189 (1980) **Pop Density:** 5.7
Land: 21.6 sq. mi.; **Water:** 0.4 sq. mi.

Jackson — Township
Lat: 39-59-22 N Long: 93-33-44 W
Pop: 143 (1990); 190 (1980) **Pop Density:** 4.8
Land: 29.6 sq. mi.; **Water:** 0.3 sq. mi.

Jefferson — Township
Lat: 39-59-46 N Long: 93-41-17 W
Pop: 410 (1990); 419 (1980) **Pop Density:** 11.3
Land: 36.3 sq. mi.; **Water:** 0.0 sq. mi.

Laredo — City
ZIP: 64652 Lat: 40-01-34 N Long: 93-26-50 W
Pop: 205 (1990); 340 (1980) **Pop Density:** 683.3
Land: 0.3 sq. mi.; **Water:** 0.0 sq. mi. **Elev:** 808 ft.
Incorporated 1890.

Liberty — Township
Lat: 40-09-28 N Long: 93-25-57 W
Pop: 506 (1990); 561 (1980) **Pop Density:** 14.4
Land: 35.2 sq. mi.; **Water:** 0.0 sq. mi.

Lincoln — Township
Lat: 40-09-44 N Long: 93-34-28 W
Pop: 398 (1990); 549 (1980) **Pop Density:** 8.2
Land: 48.4 sq. mi.; **Water:** 0.0 sq. mi.

Madison — Township
Lat: 40-04-26 N Long: 93-41-59 W
Pop: 561 (1990); 633 (1980) **Pop Density:** 16.1
Land: 34.8 sq. mi.; **Water:** 0.2 sq. mi.

Marion — Township
Lat: 40-04-34 N Long: 93-26-06 W
Pop: 281 (1990); 355 (1980) **Pop Density:** 6.6
Land: 42.4 sq. mi.; **Water:** 0.0 sq. mi.

Myers — Township
Lat: 40-13-44 N Long: 93-26-01 W
Pop: 162 (1990); 202 (1980) **Pop Density:** 4.6
Land: 35.2 sq. mi.; **Water:** 0.0 sq. mi.

Spickard — City
Lat: 40-14-33 N Long: 93-35-31 W
Pop: 326 (1990); 389 (1980) **Pop Density:** 407.5
Land: 0.8 sq. mi.; **Water:** 0.0 sq. mi. **Elev:** 260 ft.
Incorporated 1871.
Name origin: For pioneer W.W. Spickard.

Taylor — Township
Lat: 40-09-40 N Long: 93-44-24 W
Pop: 147 (1990); 223 (1980) **Pop Density:** 8.4
Land: 17.5 sq. mi.; **Water:** 0.2 sq. mi.

Tindall — Town
Lat: 40-09-37 N Long: 93-36-33 W
Pop: 46 (1990); 104 (1980) **Pop Density:** 460.0
Land: 0.1 sq. mi.; **Water:** 0.0 sq. mi. **Elev:** 787 ft.
Incorporated 1920.

Trenton — City
ZIP: 64683 Lat: 40-04-52 N Long: 93-36-16 W
Pop: 6,129 (1990); 6,811 (1980) **Pop Density:** 1075.3
Land: 5.7 sq. mi.; **Water:** 0.3 sq. mi. **Elev:** 841 ft.
In northern MO, 20 mi. north of Chillicothe. Incorporated 1857. Not coextensive with the town of the same name.
Name origin: For Trenton, NJ.

*Trenton — Township
ZIP: 64683 Lat: 40-04-38 N Long: 93-34-35 W
Pop: 6,749 (1990); 7,317 (1980) **Pop Density:** 141.8
Land: 47.6 sq. mi.; **Water:** 0.8 sq. mi.

Washington — Township
Lat: 40-14-08 N Long: 93-42-20 W
Pop: 74 (1990); 145 (1980) **Pop Density:** 3.5
Land: 20.9 sq. mi.; **Water:** 0.1 sq. mi.

Wilson — Township
Lat: 40-00-10 N Long: 93-26-03 W
Pop: 485 (1990); 610 (1980) **Pop Density:** 14.3
Land: 34.0 sq. mi.; **Water:** 0.0 sq. mi.

MISSOURI, Harrison County

Harrison County
County Seat: Bethany (ZIP: 64424)

Pop: 8,469 (1990); 9,890 (1980)
Land: 725.2 sq. mi.; **Water:** 1.3 sq. mi.
Pop Density: 11.7
Area Code: 816

On the central northern border of MO, northeast of St. Joseph; organized Feb 14, 1845 from Daviess and Ray counties.

Name origin: For Albert Galliton Harrison (1800–39), U.S. representative from MO (1835–39).

Adams
Township
Lat: 40-10-12 N **Long:** 93-55-31 W
Pop: 187 (1990); 224 (1980) **Pop Density:** 6.3
Land: 29.7 sq. mi.; **Water:** 0.0 sq. mi.

Bethany
City
ZIP: 64424 **Lat:** 40-16-03 N **Long:** 94-01-41 W
Pop: 3,005 (1990); 3,095 (1980) **Pop Density:** 683.0
Land: 4.4 sq. mi.; **Water:** 0.0 sq. mi. **Elev:** 904 ft.
In northern MO, 45 mi. northeast of Kansas City. Incorporated 1857. Not coextensive with the town of the same name.

*Bethany
Township
ZIP: 64424 **Lat:** 40-15-04 N **Long:** 94-02-54 W
Pop: 3,295 (1990); 3,535 (1980) **Pop Density:** 91.3
Land: 36.1 sq. mi.; **Water:** 0.1 sq. mi.

Blythedale
Village
ZIP: 64426 **Lat:** 40-28-30 N **Long:** 93-55-37 W
Pop: 130 (1990); 219 (1980) **Pop Density:** 433.3
Land: 0.3 sq. mi.; **Water:** 0.0 sq. mi. **Elev:** 1087 ft.
Incorporated 1891.

Butler
Township
Lat: 40-10-11 N **Long:** 94-09-52 W
Pop: 125 (1990); 184 (1980) **Pop Density:** 4.1
Land: 30.2 sq. mi.; **Water:** 0.0 sq. mi.

Cainsville
City
ZIP: 64632 **Lat:** 40-26-24 N **Long:** 93-46-28 W
Pop: 387 (1990); 496 (1980) **Pop Density:** 276.4
Land: 1.4 sq. mi.; **Water:** 0.0 sq. mi.
Founded 1837 by James Nash. Incorporated 1875.

Clay
Township
Lat: 40-31-41 N **Long:** 93-49-34 W
Pop: 103 (1990); 160 (1980) **Pop Density:** 2.4
Land: 43.6 sq. mi.; **Water:** 0.0 sq. mi.

Colfax
Township
Lat: 40-30-57 N **Long:** 93-56-48 W
Pop: 482 (1990); 540 (1980) **Pop Density:** 11.2
Land: 42.9 sq. mi.; **Water:** 0.1 sq. mi.

Cypress
Township
Lat: 40-10-25 N **Long:** 94-03-17 W
Pop: 122 (1990); 155 (1980) **Pop Density:** 4.0
Land: 30.2 sq. mi.; **Water:** 0.0 sq. mi.

Dallas
Township
Lat: 40-20-21 N **Long:** 94-09-30 W
Pop: 173 (1990); 221 (1980) **Pop Density:** 4.8
Land: 36.2 sq. mi.; **Water:** 0.0 sq. mi.

Eagleville
Town
ZIP: 64442 **Lat:** 40-28-07 N **Long:** 93-59-17 W
Pop: 275 (1990); 364 (1980) **Pop Density:** 343.8
Land: 0.8 sq. mi.; **Water:** 0.0 sq. mi. **Elev:** 1097 ft.
Incorporated 1877.

Fox Creek
Township
Lat: 40-15-14 N **Long:** 93-49-31 W
Pop: 98 (1990); 158 (1980) **Pop Density:** 2.7
Land: 36.6 sq. mi.; **Water:** 0.1 sq. mi.

Gilman City
City
Lat: 40-08-17 N **Long:** 93-52-20 W
Pop: 393 (1990); 412 (1980) **Pop Density:** 982.5
Land: 0.4 sq. mi.; **Water:** 0.0 sq. mi. **Elev:** 979 ft.
Incorporated 1898. Part of the town is also in Daviess County.

Grant
Township
Lat: 40-20-05 N **Long:** 93-55-48 W
Pop: 455 (1990); 557 (1980) **Pop Density:** 13.2
Land: 34.4 sq. mi.; **Water:** 0.0 sq. mi.

Hamilton
Township
Lat: 40-31-38 N **Long:** 94-03-26 W
Pop: 124 (1990); 149 (1980) **Pop Density:** 2.9
Land: 42.6 sq. mi.; **Water:** 0.0 sq. mi.

Jefferson
Township
Lat: 40-20-38 N **Long:** 94-02-14 W
Pop: 181 (1990); 235 (1980) **Pop Density:** 5.0
Land: 36.0 sq. mi.; **Water:** 0.1 sq. mi.

Lincoln
Township
Lat: 40-31-38 N **Long:** 94-10-16 W
Pop: 141 (1990); 169 (1980) **Pop Density:** 3.3
Land: 42.2 sq. mi.; **Water:** 0.0 sq. mi.

Madison
Township
Lat: 40-25-31 N **Long:** 93-49-13 W
Pop: 589 (1990); 727 (1980) **Pop Density:** 15.3
Land: 38.5 sq. mi.; **Water:** 0.2 sq. mi.

Marion
Township
Lat: 40-25-27 N **Long:** 93-56-13 W
Pop: 418 (1990); 517 (1980) **Pop Density:** 11.9
Land: 35.0 sq. mi.; **Water:** 0.2 sq. mi.

Mount Moriah
Town
ZIP: 64665 **Lat:** 40-19-45 N **Long:** 93-47-50 W
Pop: 104 (1990); 162 (1980) **Pop Density:** 104.0
Land: 1.0 sq. mi.; **Water:** 0.0 sq. mi.
Incorporated 1897.

New Hampton City
ZIP: 64471 Lat: 40-15-54 N Long: 94-11-44 W
Pop: 320 (1990); 358 (1980) Pop Density: 457.1
Land: 0.7 sq. mi.; Water: 0.0 sq. mi. Elev: 958 ft.
Incorporated 1886.

Ridgeway City
ZIP: 64481 Lat: 40-22-40 N Long: 93-56-15 W
Pop: 379 (1990); 516 (1980) Pop Density: 315.8
Land: 1.2 sq. mi.; Water: 0.0 sq. mi. Elev: 1057 ft.
Incorporated 1884.

Sherman Township
Lat: 40-15-05 N Long: 93-55-46 W
Pop: 181 (1990); 211 (1980) Pop Density: 5.2
Land: 35.1 sq. mi.; Water: 0.0 sq. mi.

Sugar Creek Township
Lat: 40-09-52 N Long: 93-48-41 W
Pop: 533 (1990); 621 (1980) Pop Density: 17.5
Land: 30.4 sq. mi.; Water: 0.0 sq. mi.

Trail Creek Township
Lat: 40-20-29 N Long: 93-48-54 W
Pop: 247 (1990); 328 (1980) Pop Density: 6.8
Land: 36.5 sq. mi.; Water: 0.3 sq. mi.

Union Township
Lat: 40-26-05 N Long: 94-02-41 W
Pop: 376 (1990); 451 (1980) Pop Density: 10.2
Land: 36.9 sq. mi.; Water: 0.0 sq. mi.

Washington Township
Lat: 40-25-15 N Long: 94-09-20 W
Pop: 98 (1990); 173 (1980) Pop Density: 2.7
Land: 36.1 sq. mi.; Water: 0.0 sq. mi.

White Oak Township
Lat: 40-15-16 N Long: 94-09-06 W
Pop: 541 (1990); 575 (1980) Pop Density: 15.0
Land: 36.1 sq. mi.; Water: 0.0 sq. mi.

Henry County
County Seat: Clinton (ZIP: 64735)

Pop: 20,044 (1990); 19,672 (1980) Pop Density: 28.5
Land: 702.5 sq. mi.; Water: 30.1 sq. mi. Area Code: 816
In west-central MO, southeast of Kansas City; organized as Rives County Dec 13, 1834 from Lafayette County; name changed Feb 15, 1841.
Name origin: For Patrick Henry (1736–99), patriot, governor of VA (1776–79; 1784–86), and statesman, famous for proclaiming "Give me liberty or give me death."

Bear Creek Township
Lat: 38-14-47 N Long: 93-53-55 W
Pop: 206 (1990); 243 (1980) Pop Density: 5.7
Land: 35.9 sq. mi.; Water: 0.2 sq. mi.

Bethlehem Township
Lat: 38-19-24 N Long: 93-40-39 W
Pop: 538 (1990); 477 (1980) Pop Density: 12.5
Land: 43.2 sq. mi.; Water: 3.5 sq. mi.

Big Creek Township
Lat: 38-30-48 N Long: 93-53-55 W
Pop: 259 (1990); 267 (1980) Pop Density: 6.2
Land: 41.5 sq. mi.; Water: 0.5 sq. mi.

Blairstown City
ZIP: 64726 Lat: 38-33-26 N Long: 93-57-26 W
Pop: 185 (1990); 144 (1980) Pop Density: 925.0
Land: 0.2 sq. mi.; Water: 0.0 sq. mi. Elev: 760 ft.
Incorporated 1959.

Bogard Township
Lat: 38-31-13 N Long: 94-00-52 W
Pop: 544 (1990); 502 (1980) Pop Density: 12.9
Land: 42.1 sq. mi.; Water: 0.0 sq. mi.

Brownington Town
Lat: 38-14-44 N Long: 93-43-20 W
Pop: 84 (1990); 112 (1980) Pop Density: 420.0
Land: 0.2 sq. mi.; Water: 0.0 sq. mi. Elev: 721 ft.
Incorporated 1870.

Calhoun City
ZIP: 65323 Lat: 38-28-04 N Long: 93-37-28 W
Pop: 450 (1990); 427 (1980) Pop Density: 450.0
Land: 1.0 sq. mi.; Water: 0.0 sq. mi.
Incorporated 1870.

Clinton City
ZIP: 64735 Lat: 38-22-16 N Long: 93-46-05 W
Pop: 8,703 (1990); 8,366 (1980) Pop Density: 1000.3
Land: 8.7 sq. mi.; Water: 0.1 sq. mi. Elev: 803 ft.
In western MO, southeast of Kansas City. Incorporated 1836.
Name origin: Named in 1833 for NY Gov. DeWitt Clinton, supporter of the Erie Canal.

***Clinton** Township
ZIP: 64735 Lat: 38-19-56 N Long: 93-47-13 W
Pop: 8,089 (1990); 8,001 (1980) Pop Density: 231.1
Land: 35.0 sq. mi.; Water: 6.7 sq. mi.

Davis Township
Lat: 38-20-21 N Long: 93-54-03 W
Pop: 208 (1990); 258 (1980) Pop Density: 6.2
Land: 33.7 sq. mi.; Water: 2.1 sq. mi.

Deepwater City
ZIP: 64740 Lat: 38-15-33 N Long: 93-46-25 W
Pop: 441 (1990); 475 (1980) Pop Density: 490.0
Land: 0.9 sq. mi.; Water: 0.0 sq. mi.
Incorporated 1865.

MISSOURI, Henry County

*Deepwater — Township
ZIP: 64740 Lat: 38-15-23 N Long: 94-01-04 W
Pop: 643 (1990); 752 (1980) Pop Density: 17.9
Land: 35.9 sq. mi.; Water: 0.3 sq. mi.

Deer Creek — Township
Lat: 38-25-36 N Long: 93-40-56 W
Pop: 275 (1990); 327 (1980) Pop Density: 8.3
Land: 33.2 sq. mi.; Water: 0.1 sq. mi.

Fairview — Township
Lat: 38-15-11 N Long: 93-47-43 W
Pop: 750 (1990); 728 (1980) Pop Density: 23.7
Land: 31.7 sq. mi.; Water: 1.3 sq. mi.

Fields Creek — Township
Lat: 38-25-18 N Long: 93-47-22 W
Pop: 1,306 (1990); 1,033 (1980) Pop Density: 41.1
Land: 31.8 sq. mi.; Water: 0.2 sq. mi.

Hartwell — Village
ZIP: 64788 Lat: 38-26-05 N Long: 93-56-02 W
Pop: 14 (1990); 13 (1980) Pop Density: 28.0
Land: 0.5 sq. mi.; Water: 0.0 sq. mi.

Honey Creek — Township
Lat: 38-25-55 N Long: 93-54-05 W
Pop: 221 (1990); 228 (1980) Pop Density: 7.2
Land: 30.7 sq. mi.; Water: 1.3 sq. mi.

La Due — Village
Lat: 38-18-45 N Long: 93-52-39 W
Pop: 20 (1990) Pop Density: 200.0
Land: 0.1 sq. mi.; Water: 0.0 sq. mi.

Leesville — Township
Lat: 38-19-02 N Long: 93-33-57 W
Pop: 768 (1990); 663 (1980) Pop Density: 18.3
Land: 42.0 sq. mi.; Water: 4.6 sq. mi.

Montrose — City
ZIP: 64770 Lat: 38-15-33 N Long: 93-58-55 W
Pop: 440 (1990); 498 (1980) Pop Density: 733.3
Land: 0.6 sq. mi.; Water: 0.0 sq. mi. Elev: 836 ft.
Incorporated 1871.

Osage — Township
Lat: 38-13-54 N Long: 93-37-32 W
Pop: 483 (1990); 397 (1980) Pop Density: 12.1
Land: 39.8 sq. mi.; Water: 7.1 sq. mi.

Shawnee — Township
Lat: 38-31-03 N Long: 93-47-36 W
Pop: 384 (1990); 383 (1980) Pop Density: 9.2
Land: 41.9 sq. mi.; Water: 0.1 sq. mi.

Springfield — Township
Lat: 38-25-03 N Long: 93-34-16 W
Pop: 259 (1990); 247 (1980) Pop Density: 7.8
Land: 33.0 sq. mi.; Water: 0.2 sq. mi.

Tebo — Township
Lat: 38-31-06 N Long: 93-40-26 W
Pop: 795 (1990); 768 (1980) Pop Density: 16.4
Land: 48.4 sq. mi.; Water: 0.8 sq. mi.

Tightwad — Village
Lat: 38-18-40 N Long: 93-32-29 W
Pop: 50 (1990) Pop Density: 50.0
Land: 1.0 sq. mi.; Water: 0.0 sq. mi.

Urich — City
ZIP: 64788 Lat: 38-27-35 N Long: 93-59-56 W
Pop: 498 (1990); 509 (1980) Pop Density: 1245.0
Land: 0.4 sq. mi.; Water: 0.0 sq. mi.
Founded 1871. Incorporated 1885.
Name origin: For the French Gen. Uhrich, who defended Strasburg against the Prussians; with a spelling variation.

Walker — Township
Lat: 38-20-33 N Long: 94-00-57 W
Pop: 226 (1990); 252 (1980) Pop Density: 6.4
Land: 35.5 sq. mi.; Water: 0.7 sq. mi.

White Oak — Township
Lat: 38-25-48 N Long: 94-00-31 W
Pop: 728 (1990); 785 (1980) Pop Density: 22.5
Land: 32.3 sq. mi.; Water: 0.2 sq. mi.

Windsor — City
ZIP: 65360 Lat: 38-31-56 N Long: 93-31-29 W
Pop: 2,948 (1990); 2,940 (1980) Pop Density: 1474.0
Land: 2.0 sq. mi.; Water: 0.0 sq. mi.
Founded 1855. Incorporated 1855. Part of the town is also in Pettis County.
Name origin: Named Dec 9, 1859, for Windsor Castle in England. Previously called Belmont.

*Windsor — Township
ZIP: 65360 Lat: 38-30-45 N Long: 93-33-35 W
Pop: 3,362 (1990); 3,361 (1980) Pop Density: 96.6
Land: 34.8 sq. mi.; Water: 0.2 sq. mi.

Hickory County
County Seat: Hermitage (ZIP: 65668)

Pop: 7,335 (1990); 6,367 (1980)
Land: 398.7 sq. mi.; **Water:** 13.1 sq. mi.
Pop Density: 18.4
Area Code: 417

In west-central MO, north of Springfield; organized Feb 14, 1845 from Benton and Polk counties.
Name origin: For "Old Hickory," the nickname of Andrew Jackson (1767–1845), seventh U.S. president.

Center — Township
Lat: 37-56-12 N **Long:** 93-18-56 W
Pop: 1,595 (1990); 1,154 (1980) **Pop Density:** 41.0
Land: 38.9 sq. mi.; **Water:** 2.6 sq. mi.

Cross Timbers — City
ZIP: 65634 **Lat:** 38-01-27 N **Long:** 93-13-43 W
Pop: 168 (1990); 217 (1980) **Pop Density:** 336.0
Land: 0.5 sq. mi.; **Water:** 0.0 sq. mi.
Incorporated 1948.

*Cross Timbers — Township
ZIP: 65634 **Lat:** 38-01-26 N **Long:** 93-15-33 W
Pop: 405 (1990); 471 (1980) **Pop Density:** 8.6
Land: 47.3 sq. mi.; **Water:** 0.4 sq. mi.

Green — Township
Lat: 37-50-44 N **Long:** 93-16-13 W
Pop: 1,590 (1990); 1,223 (1980) **Pop Density:** 33.0
Land: 48.2 sq. mi.; **Water:** 7.3 sq. mi.

Hermitage — City
ZIP: 65668 **Lat:** 37-56-41 N **Long:** 93-19-23 W
Pop: 512 (1990); 384 (1980) **Pop Density:** 365.7
Land: 1.4 sq. mi.; **Water:** 0.0 sq. mi. **Elev:** 822 ft.
Incorporated 1958.

Jordan — Township
Lat: 38-01-29 N **Long:** 93-07-03 W
Pop: 207 (1990); 190 (1980) **Pop Density:** 7.0
Land: 29.7 sq. mi.; **Water:** 0.1 sq. mi.

Montgomery — Township
Lat: 38-00-46 N **Long:** 93-28-43 W
Pop: 240 (1990); 244 (1980) **Pop Density:** 5.8
Land: 41.4 sq. mi.; **Water:** 0.0 sq. mi.

Preston — Town
ZIP: 65732 **Lat:** 37-56-24 N **Long:** 93-12-48 W
Pop: 136 (1990); 149 (1980) **Pop Density:** 680.0
Land: 0.2 sq. mi.; **Water:** 0.0 sq. mi. **Elev:** 1046 ft.
Incorporated 1947.

Stark — Township
Lat: 37-56-28 N **Long:** 93-09-39 W
Pop: 753 (1990); 701 (1980) **Pop Density:** 12.6
Land: 59.8 sq. mi.; **Water:** 0.1 sq. mi.

Tyler — Township
Lat: 37-51-36 N **Long:** 93-25-54 W
Pop: 928 (1990); 675 (1980) **Pop Density:** 22.0
Land: 42.1 sq. mi.; **Water:** 2.0 sq. mi.

Weaubleau — City
ZIP: 65774 **Lat:** 37-53-29 N **Long:** 93-32-26 W
Pop: 436 (1990); 464 (1980) **Pop Density:** 545.0
Land: 0.8 sq. mi.; **Water:** 0.0 sq. mi.
Incorporated 1914.

*Weaubleau — Township
ZIP: 65774 **Lat:** 37-51-58 N **Long:** 93-30-57 W
Pop: 814 (1990); 921 (1980) **Pop Density:** 21.4
Land: 38.0 sq. mi.; **Water:** 0.2 sq. mi.

Wheatland — City
ZIP: 65779 **Lat:** 37-56-36 N **Long:** 93-24-14 W
Pop: 363 (1990); 364 (1980) **Pop Density:** 907.5
Land: 0.4 sq. mi.; **Water:** 0.0 sq. mi.
Founded 1869. Incorporated 1964.
Name origin: For its descriptive connotations.

*Wheatland — Township
ZIP: 65779 **Lat:** 37-59-16 N **Long:** 93-23-23 W
Pop: 803 (1990); 788 (1980) **Pop Density:** 15.1
Land: 53.1 sq. mi.; **Water:** 0.5 sq. mi.

Holt County
County Seat: Oregon (ZIP: 64473)

Pop: 6,034 (1990); 6,882 (1980)   **Pop Density:** 13.1
Land: 461.9 sq. mi.; **Water:** 7.2 sq. mi.   **Area Code:** 816
On northwestern border of MO, northwest of St. Joseph; organized as Nodaway County Jan 29, 1841 from Platte Purchase; name changed Feb 15, 1841.
Name origin: For David Rice Holt (1803–40), MO legislator.

Benton
Township
Lat: 40-07-20 N   **Long:** 95-13-45 W
Pop: 1,655 (1990); 1,902 (1980)   **Pop Density:** 33.2
Land: 49.9 sq. mi.; **Water:** 0.4 sq. mi.

Bigelow
Village
ZIP: 64425   **Lat:** 40-06-33 N   **Long:** 95-17-18 W
Pop: 32 (1990); 67 (1980)   **Pop Density:** 320.0
Land: 0.1 sq. mi.; **Water:** 0.0 sq. mi.   **Elev:** 858 ft.
Incorporated 1868.

*Bigelow
Township
ZIP: 64425   **Lat:** 40-06-19 N   **Long:** 95-19-01 W
Pop: 271 (1990); 321 (1980)   **Pop Density:** 9.4
Land: 28.7 sq. mi.; **Water:** 1.0 sq. mi.

Big Lake
Village
Lat: 40-04-26 N   **Long:** 95-21-05 W
Pop: 170 (1990)   **Pop Density:** 100.0
Land: 1.7 sq. mi.; **Water:** 1.0 sq. mi.
Incorporated 1983.

Clay
Township
Lat: 40-11-58 N   **Long:** 95-06-45 W
Pop: 582 (1990); 728 (1980)   **Pop Density:** 12.5
Land: 46.4 sq. mi.; **Water:** 0.1 sq. mi.

Corning
Town
ZIP: 64435   **Lat:** 40-14-55 N   **Long:** 95-27-17 W
Pop: 88 (1990); 126 (1980)   **Pop Density:** 880.0
Land: 0.1 sq. mi.; **Water:** 0.0 sq. mi.
Incorporated 1910.

Craig
City
ZIP: 64437   **Lat:** 40-11-32 N   **Long:** 95-22-24 W
Pop: 346 (1990); 379 (1980)   **Pop Density:** 1153.3
Land: 0.3 sq. mi.; **Water:** 0.0 sq. mi.   **Elev:** 868 ft.
Established 1868. Incorporated 1879.
Name origin: For Gen. James Craig, a member of Congress.

Forbes
Township
Lat: 39-54-17 N   **Long:** 95-04-05 W
Pop: 224 (1990); 222 (1980)   **Pop Density:** 5.1
Land: 43.9 sq. mi.; **Water:** 0.8 sq. mi.

Forest
Township
Lat: 39-59-06 N   **Long:** 95-13-18 W
Pop: 450 (1990); 499 (1980)   **Pop Density:** 12.8
Land: 35.2 sq. mi.; **Water:** 0.9 sq. mi.

Forest City
City
ZIP: 64451   **Lat:** 39-58-57 N   **Long:** 95-11-16 W
Pop: 380 (1990); 387 (1980)   **Pop Density:** 380.0
Land: 1.0 sq. mi.; **Water:** 0.0 sq. mi.   **Elev:** 856 ft.
Incorporated 1857.

Fortescue
Town
ZIP: 64452   **Lat:** 40-03-07 N   **Long:** 95-19-02 W
Pop: 46 (1990); 51 (1980)   **Pop Density:** 460.0
Land: 0.1 sq. mi.; **Water:** 0.0 sq. mi.   **Elev:** 860 ft.
Incorporated 1892.

Hickory
Township
Lat: 40-05-33 N   **Long:** 95-06-05 W
Pop: 272 (1990); 362 (1980)   **Pop Density:** 7.0
Land: 38.9 sq. mi.; **Water:** 0.1 sq. mi.

Lewis
Township
Lat: 39-58-42 N   **Long:** 95-08-38 W
Pop: 1,202 (1990); 1,234 (1980)   **Pop Density:** 34.3
Land: 35.0 sq. mi.; **Water:** 0.2 sq. mi.

Liberty
Township
Lat: 40-13-08 N   **Long:** 95-14-20 W
Pop: 239 (1990); 311 (1980)   **Pop Density:** 4.9
Land: 48.3 sq. mi.; **Water:** 0.0 sq. mi.

Lincoln
Township
Lat: 40-13-49 N   **Long:** 95-26-25 W
Pop: 178 (1990); 213 (1980)   **Pop Density:** 7.4
Land: 23.9 sq. mi.; **Water:** 0.6 sq. mi.

Maitland
City
ZIP: 64466   **Lat:** 40-12-11 N   **Long:** 95-04-43 W
Pop: 338 (1990); 415 (1980)   **Pop Density:** 1126.7
Land: 0.3 sq. mi.; **Water:** 0.0 sq. mi.
Incorporated 1880.

Minton
Township
Lat: 40-02-47 N   **Long:** 95-19-18 W
Pop: 206 (1990); 201 (1980)   **Pop Density:** 6.3
Land: 32.9 sq. mi.; **Water:** 2.5 sq. mi.

Mound City
City
ZIP: 64470   **Lat:** 40-08-09 N   **Long:** 95-14-03 W
Pop: 1,273 (1990); 1,447 (1980)   **Pop Density:** 979.2
Land: 1.3 sq. mi.; **Water:** 0.0 sq. mi.
Incorporated 1857.
Name origin: For a low mound or hill upon which a portion of the town is built.

Nodaway
Township
Lat: 40-00-23 N   **Long:** 95-03-32 W
Pop: 175 (1990); 210 (1980)   **Pop Density:** 6.5
Land: 26.9 sq. mi.; **Water:** 0.0 sq. mi.

Oregon
City
ZIP: 64473   **Lat:** 39-59-04 N   **Long:** 95-08-37 W
Pop: 935 (1990); 901 (1980)   **Pop Density:** 850.0
Land: 1.1 sq. mi.; **Water:** 0.0 sq. mi.   **Elev:** 1094 ft.
Laid out June 1841. Incorporated 1841.
Name origin: For Oregon Territory, which was then attracting the first of a long procession of immigrants.

Union
Township
Lat: 40-11-10 N **Long:** 95-22-28 W
Pop: 580 (1990); 679 (1980) **Pop Density:** 11.2
Land: 51.9 sq. mi.; **Water:** 0.6 sq. mi.

Howard County
County Seat: Fayette (ZIP: 65248)

Pop: 9,631 (1990); 10,008 (1980) **Pop Density:** 20.7
Land: 465.8 sq. mi.; **Water:** 4.8 sq. mi. **Area Code:** 816
In north-central MO, northwest of Columbia; organized Jan 13, 1816 (prior to statehood) from St. Louis and St. Charles counties.
Name origin: For Gen. Benjamin Howard (1760–1814), KY legislator and U.S. representative (1807–10), governor of LA Territory (1810–12), and commander of the Eighth Military Department, territory west of the Mississippi River.

Armstrong
City
ZIP: 65230 **Lat:** 39-16-09 N **Long:** 92-42-18 W
Pop: 310 (1990); 360 (1980) **Pop Density:** 387.5
Land: 0.8 sq. mi.; **Water:** 0.0 sq. mi. **Elev:** 830 ft.
Incorporated 1953.

Bonne Femme
Township
Lat: 39-12-49 N **Long:** 92-31-12 W
Pop: 353 (1990); 366 (1980) **Pop Density:** 7.4
Land: 47.6 sq. mi.; **Water:** 0.1 sq. mi.

Boons Lick
Township
Lat: 39-04-15 N **Long:** 92-52-05 W
Pop: 440 (1990); 437 (1980) **Pop Density:** 8.3
Land: 52.7 sq. mi.; **Water:** 1.1 sq. mi.

Burton
Township
Lat: 39-14-55 N **Long:** 92-37-00 W
Pop: 162 (1990); 131 (1980) **Pop Density:** 5.3
Land: 30.3 sq. mi.; **Water:** 0.0 sq. mi.

Chariton
Township
Lat: 39-12-35 N **Long:** 92-48-44 W
Pop: 1,761 (1990); 1,879 (1980) **Pop Density:** 27.0
Land: 65.2 sq. mi.; **Water:** 0.9 sq. mi.

Fayette
City
ZIP: 65248 **Lat:** 39-08-51 N **Long:** 92-41-08 W
Pop: 2,888 (1990); 2,983 (1980) **Pop Density:** 1255.7
Land: 2.3 sq. mi.; **Water:** 0.0 sq. mi. **Elev:** 700 ft.
In north-central MO, 25 mi. northwest of Columbia. Incorporated 1823.
Name origin: For the Marquis de Lafayette (1757–1834) of France, who fought with the Americans during the American Revolution.

Franklin
City
ZIP: 65250 **Lat:** 39-00-40 N **Long:** 92-45-16 W
Pop: 181 (1990); 196 (1980) **Pop Density:** 905.0
Land: 0.2 sq. mi.; **Water:** 0.0 sq. mi.
Incorporated 1894.

*Franklin
Township
ZIP: 65250 **Lat:** 39-01-35 N **Long:** 92-45-08 W
Pop: 1,835 (1990); 1,986 (1980) **Pop Density:** 28.1
Land: 65.2 sq. mi.; **Water:** 1.3 sq. mi.

Glasgow
City
ZIP: 65254 **Lat:** 39-13-37 N **Long:** 92-50-16 W
Pop: 1,248 (1990); 1,284 (1980) **Pop Density:** 1040.0
Land: 1.2 sq. mi.; **Water:** 0.1 sq. mi. **Elev:** 650 ft.
Laid out in 1836 after three earlier attempts to establish a river port in the vicinity had failed. Incorporated 1936. Part of the town is also in Chariton County.
Name origin: For James Glasgow, a St. Louis merchant.

Moniteau
Township
Lat: 39-04-17 N **Long:** 92-34-49 W
Pop: 644 (1990); 578 (1980) **Pop Density:** 8.1
Land: 79.6 sq. mi.; **Water:** 0.7 sq. mi.

New Franklin
City
ZIP: 65274 **Lat:** 39-01-07 N **Long:** 92-44-26 W
Pop: 1,107 (1990); 1,228 (1980) **Pop Density:** 851.5
Land: 1.3 sq. mi.; **Water:** 0.0 sq. mi.
Incorporated 1835.

Prairie
Township
Lat: 39-15-49 N **Long:** 92-42-32 W
Pop: 773 (1990); 845 (1980) **Pop Density:** 15.2
Land: 51.0 sq. mi.; **Water:** 0.0 sq. mi.

Richmond
Township
Lat: 39-08-28 N **Long:** 92-40-54 W
Pop: 3,663 (1990); 3,786 (1980) **Pop Density:** 49.4
Land: 74.2 sq. mi.; **Water:** 0.6 sq. mi.

Howell County
County Seat: West Plains (ZIP: 65775)

Pop: 31,447 (1990); 28,807 (1980)   **Pop Density:** 33.9
Land: 927.8 sq. mi.; **Water:** 0.6 sq. mi.   **Area Code:** 417
On the central southern border of MO; organized Mar 2, 1857 from Oregon County.
Name origin: For Thomas Jefferson Howell, MO legislator; or for James Howell, a prominent citizen; or for Josiah Howell.

Benton   Township
Lat: 36-34-22 N   **Long:** 92-02-07 W
Pop: 1,739 (1990); 1,587 (1980)   **Pop Density:** 17.7
Land: 98.3 sq. mi.; **Water:** 0.0 sq. mi.

Brandsville   City
ZIP: 65688   **Lat:** 36-39-01 N   **Long:** 91-41-48 W
Pop: 167 (1990); 133 (1980)   **Pop Density:** 334.0
Land: 0.5 sq. mi.; **Water:** 0.0 sq. mi.   **Elev:** 949 ft.
Incorporated 1917.

Chapel   Township
Lat: 36-55-29 N   **Long:** 91-42-37 W
Pop: 518 (1990); 511 (1980)   **Pop Density:** 13.6
Land: 38.0 sq. mi.; **Water:** 0.0 sq. mi.

Dry Creek   Township
Lat: 36-50-27 N   **Long:** 91-55-10 W
Pop: 1,309 (1990); 1,312 (1980)   **Pop Density:** 25.4
Land: 51.5 sq. mi.; **Water:** 0.0 sq. mi.

Goldsberry   Township
Lat: 37-00-06 N   **Long:** 91-43-15 W
Pop: 3,324 (1990); 2,858 (1980)   **Pop Density:** 73.2
Land: 45.4 sq. mi.; **Water:** 0.0 sq. mi.

Howell   Township
Lat: 36-42-22 N   **Long:** 91-49-06 W
Pop: 15,125 (1990); 13,417 (1980)   **Pop Density:** 81.5
Land: 185.5 sq. mi.; **Water:** 0.2 sq. mi.

Hutton Valley   Township
Lat: 36-57-01 N   **Long:** 91-50-55 W
Pop: 822 (1990); 833 (1980)   **Pop Density:** 14.9
Land: 55.0 sq. mi.; **Water:** 0.0 sq. mi.

Mountain View   City
ZIP: 65548   **Lat:** 36-59-41 N   **Long:** 91-41-55 W
Pop: 2,036 (1990); 1,664 (1980)   **Pop Density:** 702.1
Land: 2.9 sq. mi.; **Water:** 0.0 sq. mi.   **Elev:** 1144 ft.
Incorporated 1917.

Myatt   Township
Lat: 36-33-28 N   **Long:** 91-45-04 W
Pop: 529 (1990); 473 (1980)   **Pop Density:** 8.3
Land: 63.7 sq. mi.; **Water:** 0.1 sq. mi.

Siloam Springs   Township
Lat: 36-49-27 N   **Long:** 92-02-30 W
Pop: 498 (1990); 466 (1980)   **Pop Density:** 9.4
Land: 52.9 sq. mi.; **Water:** 0.0 sq. mi.

Sisson   Township
Lat: 36-50-19 N   **Long:** 91-45-50 W
Pop: 1,074 (1990); 1,148 (1980)   **Pop Density:** 14.2
Land: 75.6 sq. mi.; **Water:** 0.0 sq. mi.

South Fork   Township
Lat: 36-33-42 N   **Long:** 91-53-22 W
Pop: 729 (1990); 695 (1980)   **Pop Density:** 10.9
Land: 66.7 sq. mi.; **Water:** 0.1 sq. mi.

Spring Creek   Township
Lat: 36-42-48 N   **Long:** 92-02-27 W
Pop: 1,387 (1990); 1,276 (1980)   **Pop Density:** 20.2
Land: 68.6 sq. mi.; **Water:** 0.0 sq. mi.

West Plains   City
ZIP: 65775   **Lat:** 36-44-28 N   **Long:** 91-51-46 W
Pop: 8,913 (1990); 7,741 (1980)   **Pop Density:** 1048.6
Land: 8.5 sq. mi.; **Water:** 0.0 sq. mi.   **Elev:** 991 ft.
In southern MO, 90 mi. east-southeast of Springfield. Incorporated 1883.
Name origin: For its level site.

Willow Springs   City
ZIP: 65793   **Lat:** 36-59-39 N   **Long:** 91-58-11 W
Pop: 2,038 (1990); 2,215 (1980)   **Pop Density:** 1019.0
Land: 2.0 sq. mi.; **Water:** 0.0 sq. mi.   **Elev:** 1257 ft.
Incorporated 1888.
Name origin: For the many willow trees found in the area.

*Willow Springs   Township
ZIP: 65793   **Lat:** 36-58-54 N   **Long:** 91-58-57 W
Pop: 4,393 (1990); 4,231 (1980)   **Pop Density:** 34.7
Land: 126.6 sq. mi.; **Water:** 0.2 sq. mi.

Iron County
County Seat: Ironton (ZIP: 63650)

Pop: 10,726 (1990); 11,084 (1980)   **Pop Density:** 19.5
Land: 551.4 sq. mi.; **Water:** 0.7 sq. mi.   **Area Code:** 314
In southeastern MO, northwest of Cape Girardeau; organized Feb 17, 1857 from Madison, St. Francois, Wayne, Washington, and Reynolds counties.
Name origin: For the rich iron deposits.

Annapolis — City
ZIP: 63620   **Lat:** 37-21-35 N   **Long:** 90-41-53 W
Pop: 363 (1990); 370 (1980)   **Pop Density:** 1210.0
Land: 0.3 sq. mi.; **Water:** 0.0 sq. mi.
Incorporated 1955.
Name origin: Named in 1876 for Annapolis, MD.

Arcadia — City
ZIP: 63621   **Lat:** 37-35-07 N   **Long:** 90-37-42 W
Pop: 609 (1990); 683 (1980)   **Pop Density:** 761.3
Land: 0.8 sq. mi.; **Water:** 0.0 sq. mi.
Incorporated 1923.
Name origin: For the region in ancient Greece.

*Arcadia — Township
ZIP: 63621   **Lat:** 37-34-25 N   **Long:** 90-39-37 W
Pop: 5,603 (1990); 5,517 (1980)   **Pop Density:** 49.5
Land: 113.2 sq. mi.; **Water:** 0.3 sq. mi.

Dent — Township
Lat: 37-40-18 N   **Long:** 91-04-45 W
Pop: 1,317 (1990); 1,621 (1980)   **Pop Density:** 14.2
Land: 92.6 sq. mi.; **Water:** 0.0 sq. mi.

Des Arc — Village
ZIP: 63636   **Lat:** 37-17-03 N   **Long:** 90-38-05 W
Pop: 173 (1990); 237 (1980)   **Pop Density:** 865.0
Land: 0.2 sq. mi.; **Water:** 0.0 sq. mi.
Incorporated 1901.
Name origin: For a big bend in the railroad near town. From French 'of the bend.'

Iron — Township
Lat: 37-41-37 N   **Long:** 90-43-49 W
Pop: 1,223 (1990); 1,273 (1980)   **Pop Density:** 20.4
Land: 60.0 sq. mi.; **Water:** 0.2 sq. mi.

Ironton — City
ZIP: 63650   **Lat:** 37-35-48 N   **Long:** 90-38-08 W
Pop: 1,539 (1990); 1,743 (1980)   **Pop Density:** 1099.3
Land: 1.4 sq. mi.; **Water:** 0.0 sq. mi.
Incorporated 1859.
Name origin: For the large iron ore deposits found here.

Kaolin — Township
Lat: 37-40-07 N   **Long:** 90-53-39 W
Pop: 508 (1990); 496 (1980)   **Pop Density:** 5.5
Land: 91.7 sq. mi.; **Water:** 0.0 sq. mi.

Liberty — Township
Lat: 37-27-32 N   **Long:** 90-39-46 W
Pop: 445 (1990); 466 (1980)   **Pop Density:** 5.0
Land: 88.2 sq. mi.; **Water:** 0.2 sq. mi.

Pilot Knob — City
ZIP: 63663   **Lat:** 37-37-24 N   **Long:** 90-38-36 W
Pop: 783 (1990); 722 (1980)   **Pop Density:** 978.8
Land: 0.8 sq. mi.; **Water:** 0.0 sq. mi.
Incorporated 1946.

Union — Township
Lat: 37-20-06 N   **Long:** 90-39-34 W
Pop: 1,630 (1990); 1,711 (1980)   **Pop Density:** 15.4
Land: 105.8 sq. mi.; **Water:** 0.0 sq. mi.

Viburnum — Town
ZIP: 65566   **Lat:** 37-42-56 N   **Long:** 91-07-44 W
Pop: 743 (1990); 836 (1980)   **Pop Density:** 437.1
Land: 1.7 sq. mi.; **Water:** 0.0 sq. mi.
Incorporated 1959.

Jackson County
County Seat: Kansas City (ZIP: 64106)

Pop: 633,232 (1990); 629,266 (1980)   **Pop Density:** 1047.0
Land: 604.8 sq. mi.; **Water:** 11.3 sq. mi.   **Area Code:** 816
On central western border of MO; organized Dec 15, 1826 from Lafayette County.
Name origin: For Andrew Jackson (1767–1845), seventh U.S. president.

Blue — Township
Lat: 39-06-41 N   **Long:** 94-23-53 W
Pop: 164,071 (1990); 165,441 (1980)   **Pop Density:** 1482.1
Land: 110.7 sq. mi.; **Water:** 2.6 sq. mi.

Blue Springs — City
ZIP: 64015   **Lat:** 39-01-19 N   **Long:** 94-16-25 W
Pop: 40,153 (1990); 25,936 (1980)   **Pop Density:** 2494.0
Land: 16.1 sq. mi.; **Water:** 0.0 sq. mi.
In western MO, 10 mi. southeast of Independence. Incorporated 1904.
Name origin: For a spring falling from the hillside into a tributary of the Little Blue River.

MISSOURI, Jackson County

Brooking
Township
Lat: 38-59-31 N **Long:** 94-28-11 W
Pop: 78,461 (1990); 87,265 (1980) **Pop Density:** 1683.7
Land: 46.6 sq. mi.; **Water:** 0.2 sq. mi.

Buckner
City
ZIP: 64016 **Lat:** 39-08-05 N **Long:** 94-11-52 W
Pop: 2,873 (1990); 2,848 (1980) **Pop Density:** 2611.8
Land: 1.1 sq. mi.; **Water:** 0.0 sq. mi.

Began in 1875 as a station on the Missouri Pacific railroad. Incorporated 1930.

Name origin: For Mr. Buckner, who lived on a hill nearby.

Fort Osage
Township
Lat: 39-08-18 N **Long:** 94-12-52 W
Pop: 5,985 (1990); 5,628 (1980) **Pop Density:** 86.1
Land: 69.5 sq. mi.; **Water:** 1.0 sq. mi.

Grain Valley
City
ZIP: 64029 **Lat:** 39-00-25 N **Long:** 94-12-24 W
Pop: 1,898 (1990); 1,327 (1980) **Pop Density:** 612.3
Land: 3.1 sq. mi.; **Water:** 0.0 sq. mi.

Surveyed in 1878 for Joseph Peters. Incorporated 1945.

Name origin: For the grain production in the area.

Grandview
City
ZIP: 64030 **Lat:** 38-52-52 N **Long:** 94-31-20 W
Pop: 24,967 (1990); 24,561 (1980) **Pop Density:** 1698.4
Land: 14.7 sq. mi.; **Water:** 0.1 sq. mi.

In western MO, 5 mi. south of Kansas City. Incorporated 1929.

Greenwood
City
ZIP: 64034 **Lat:** 38-51-04 N **Long:** 94-20-31 W
Pop: 1,505 (1990); 1,315 (1980) **Pop Density:** 376.3
Land: 4.0 sq. mi.; **Water:** 0.0 sq. mi. **Elev:** 953 ft.

Incorporated 1963.

Independence
City
ZIP: 64050 **Lat:** 39-05-28 N **Long:** 94-21-02 W
Pop: 112,301 (1990); 111,797 (1980) **Pop Density:** 1441.6
Land: 77.9 sq. mi.; **Water:** 0.0 sq. mi.

In northwestern MO, 10 mi. east of Kansas City. Incorporated 1849. Part of the town is also in Clay County.

Name origin: Locally believed to be in recognition of Andrew Jackson's (1767–1845) independent character. Another plausible story is that those in Jackson County noted that their rival county, Clay, had a county seat named Liberty. There can be no liberty without independence; thus the reasoning and the name.

Kansas City
City
ZIP: 64108 **Lat:** 38-59-39 N **Long:** 94-31-18 W
Pop: 341,179 (1990); 371,860 (1980) **Pop Density:** 2205.4
Land: 154.7 sq. mi.; **Water:** 2.4 sq. mi.

In western MO at the confluence of the Missouri and Kansas (or Kaw) rivers; on the western bank is Kansas City, KS. Established 1821; founded 1833; laid out 1838; developed 1836. Called *The Heart of America* for its location. Largest winter-wheat market; one of the largest livestock exchanges in U.S.; wheat flour production second only to Buffalo. Manufacturing (printing and publishing, food processing, automobile assembly) and industrial (chemicals, electric equipment, farm machinery) city. Site of University of Missouri. Incorporated 1850. Jackson is the county in which Kansas City has its greatest population. Part of the city is also in Cass, Clay, and Platte counties.

Name origin: Named in 1889 from the old Siouan language Kansa 'people of the south wind.' Previously called City of Kansas (1853).

Kaw
Township
Lat: 38-59-52 N **Long:** 94-34-20 W
Pop: 199,499 (1990); 220,142 (1980) **Pop Density:** 3518.5
Land: 56.7 sq. mi.; **Water:** 0.5 sq. mi.

Lake Lotawana
City
ZIP: 64063 **Lat:** 38-55-46 N **Long:** 94-15-28 W
Pop: 2,141 (1990); 1,875 (1980) **Pop Density:** 1427.3
Land: 1.5 sq. mi.; **Water:** 0.8 sq. mi.

Incorporated 1958.

Lake Tapawingo
City
Lat: 39-01-05 N **Long:** 94-18-37 W
Pop: 761 (1990); 925 (1980) **Pop Density:** 2536.7
Land: 0.3 sq. mi.; **Water:** 0.1 sq. mi.

Incorporated 1963.

Lee's Summit
City
ZIP: 64063 **Lat:** 38-55-11 N **Long:** 94-23-14 W
Pop: 45,985 (1990); 28,691 (1980) **Pop Density:** 788.8
Land: 58.3 sq. mi.; **Water:** 1.9 sq. mi.

In western MO, 20 mi. southeast of Kansas City. Incorporated 1868. Part of the town is also in Cass County.

Levasy
City
Lat: 39-07-59 N **Long:** 94-07-56 W
Pop: 279 (1990); 235 (1980) **Pop Density:** 38.8
Land: 7.2 sq. mi.; **Water:** 0.1 sq. mi.

Incorporated 1901.

Lone Jack
Village
ZIP: 64070 **Lat:** 38-52-13 N **Long:** 94-09-59 W
Pop: 392 (1990); 420 (1980) **Pop Density:** 126.5
Land: 3.1 sq. mi.; **Water:** 0.0 sq. mi.

Founded 1841. Incorporated 1965.

Name origin: For a single blackjack (oak) tree *Quercus marilandica* near a spring that served as a prairie landmark.

Oak Grove
City
ZIP: 64075 **Lat:** 39-00-10 N **Long:** 94-07-41 W
Pop: 4,561 (1990); 4,067 (1980) **Pop Density:** 1303.1
Land: 3.5 sq. mi.; **Water:** 0.0 sq. mi.

Incorporated 1881. Part of the town is also in Lafayette County.

Prairie
Township
Lat: 38-54-53 N **Long:** 94-21-12 W
Pop: 50,137 (1990); 31,712 (1980) **Pop Density:** 511.6
Land: 98.0 sq. mi.; **Water:** 3.2 sq. mi.

Raytown
City
ZIP: 64133 **Lat:** 38-59-41 N **Long:** 94-27-54 W
Pop: 30,601 (1990); 31,831 (1980) **Pop Density:** 3091.0
Land: 9.9 sq. mi.; **Water:** 0.0 sq. mi.

In western MO, a southeastern suburb of Kansas City. Incorporated 1951.

Name origin: Possibly for John Ray, a legislator. Once a postal station and assembly place for wagon trains on the Santa Fe Trail and in 1840 a crossroads trading village.

Sibley
Village
ZIP: 64088 **Lat:** 39-10-45 N **Long:** 94-11-48 W
Pop: 367 (1990); 382 (1980) **Pop Density:** 524.3
Land: 0.7 sq. mi.; **Water:** 0.0 sq. mi.
Incorporated 1957.
Name origin: For Gen. George C. Sibley, early factor of Fort Osage and a surveyor of the Santa Fe Trail.

Sni-A-Bar
Township
Lat: 39-02-09 N **Long:** 94-12-49 W
Pop: 53,714 (1990); 38,534 (1980) **Pop Density:** 522.5
Land: 102.8 sq. mi.; **Water:** 1.7 sq. mi.

Sugar Creek
City
ZIP: 64054 **Lat:** 39-08-17 N **Long:** 94-24-40 W
Pop: 3,982 (1990); 4,305 (1980) **Pop Density:** 497.8
Land: 8.0 sq. mi.; **Water:** 0.2 sq. mi.
In northwestern MO, 10 mi. east of Kansas City. Incorporated 1920. Part of the town is also in Clay County.
Name origin: For the sugar maple trees found in the area.

Unity Village
Town
Lat: 38-57-01 N **Long:** 94-24-05 W
Pop: 138 (1990); 202 (1980) **Pop Density:** 72.6
Land: 1.9 sq. mi.; **Water:** 0.1 sq. mi.
Incorporated 1953.

Van Buren
Township
Lat: 38-53-46 N **Long:** 94-11-22 W
Pop: 6,012 (1990); 4,953 (1980) **Pop Density:** 84.9
Land: 70.8 sq. mi.; **Water:** 0.9 sq. mi.

Washington
Township
Lat: 38-54-30 N **Long:** 94-30-36 W
Pop: 75,353 (1990); 75,591 (1980) **Pop Density:** 1513.1
Land: 49.8 sq. mi.; **Water:** 1.4 sq. mi.

Jasper County
County Seat: Carthage (ZIP: 64836)

Pop: 90,465 (1990); 86,958 (1980) **Pop Density:** 141.4
Land: 639.8 sq. mi.; **Water:** 1.6 sq. mi. **Area Code:** 417
On the southwestern border of MO, west of Springfield; organized Jan 29, 1841 from Barry County.
Name origin: For Sgt. William Jasper (1750–79), Revolutionary War soldier from SC.

Airport Drive
Village
Lat: 37-08-20 N **Long:** 94-30-56 W
Pop: 818 (1990); 502 (1980) **Pop Density:** 355.7
Land: 2.3 sq. mi.; **Water:** 0.0 sq. mi. **Elev:** 964 ft.
Incorporated 1947.

Alba
City
ZIP: 64830 **Lat:** 37-14-13 N **Long:** 94-25-01 W
Pop: 465 (1990); 474 (1980) **Pop Density:** 1550.0
Land: 0.3 sq. mi.; **Water:** 0.0 sq. mi. **Elev:** 989 ft.
Founded 1882. Incorporated 1902.
Name origin: For its first postmaster.

Asbury
City
ZIP: 64832 **Lat:** 37-16-25 N **Long:** 94-36-10 W
Pop: 220 (1990); 210 (1980) **Pop Density:** 733.3
Land: 0.3 sq. mi.; **Water:** 0.0 sq. mi.
Incorporated 1920.

Avilla
Town
ZIP: 64833 **Lat:** 37-11-39 N **Long:** 94-07-48 W
Pop: 99 (1990); 151 (1980) **Pop Density:** 495.0
Land: 0.2 sq. mi.; **Water:** 0.0 sq. mi.
Incorporated 1874.

Brooklyn Heights
Village
ZIP: 64836 **Lat:** 37-10-13 N **Long:** 94-23-10 W
Pop: 116 (1990); 126 (1980) **Pop Density:** 1160.0
Land: 0.1 sq. mi.; **Water:** 0.0 sq. mi.
Incorporated 1967.

Carl Junction
City
ZIP: 64834 **Lat:** 37-09-49 N **Long:** 94-32-44 W
Pop: 4,123 (1990); 3,937 (1980) **Pop Density:** 916.2
Land: 4.5 sq. mi.; **Water:** 0.1 sq. mi.
Incorporated 1884.

Carterville
City
ZIP: 64835 **Lat:** 37-09-03 N **Long:** 94-26-18 W
Pop: 2,013 (1990); 1,973 (1980) **Pop Density:** 649.4
Land: 3.1 sq. mi.; **Water:** 0.0 sq. mi.
Incorporated 1877.

Carthage
City
ZIP: 64836 **Lat:** 37-10-03 N **Long:** 94-18-48 W
Pop: 10,747 (1990); 11,104 (1980) **Pop Density:** 1733.4
Land: 6.2 sq. mi.; **Water:** 0.0 sq. mi. **Elev:** 1002 ft.
In southwestern MO, 15 mi. northeast of Joplin. County seat; platted 1842. Incorporated 1868.
Name origin: For the ancient commercial center of North Africa.

Carytown
City
ZIP: 64836 **Lat:** 37-14-56 N **Long:** 94-20-03 W
Pop: 149 (1990); 150 (1980) **Pop Density:** 16.2
Land: 9.2 sq. mi.; **Water:** 0.0 sq. mi.
Incorporated 1971.

Duenweg
City
ZIP: 64841 **Lat:** 37-04-44 N **Long:** 94-24-37 W
Pop: 940 (1990); 703 (1980) **Pop Density:** 2350.0
Land: 0.4 sq. mi.; **Water:** 0.0 sq. mi. **Elev:** 1074 ft.
Incorporated 1959.

MISSOURI, Jasper County

Duquesne — Village
Lat: 37-04-16 N Long: 94-27-31 W
Pop: 1,229 (1990); 1,252 (1980) Pop Density: 877.9
Land: 1.4 sq. mi.; Water: 0.0 sq. mi. Elev: 1072 ft.
Incorporated 1959.

Duval — Township
Lat: 37-18-01 N Long: 94-27-04 W
Pop: 653 (1990); 599 (1980) Pop Density: 15.7
Land: 41.5 sq. mi.; Water: 0.2 sq. mi.

Fidelity — Town
ZIP: 64836 Lat: 37-04-55 N Long: 94-18-34 W
Pop: 235 (1990); 274 (1980) Pop Density: 235.0
Land: 1.0 sq. mi.; Water: 0.0 sq. mi. Elev: 1121 ft.
Incorporated 1966.

Galena — Township
Lat: 37-06-02 N Long: 94-34-00 W
Pop: 22,074 (1990); 21,819 (1980) Pop Density: 533.2
Land: 41.4 sq. mi.; Water: 0.0 sq. mi.

Iron Gates — Village
Lat: 37-03-48 N Long: 94-33-25 W
Pop: 309 (1990); 314 (1980) Pop Density: 1030.0
Land: 0.3 sq. mi.; Water: 0.0 sq. mi.
Incorporated 1956.

Jackson — Township
Lat: 37-06-13 N Long: 94-20-04 W
Pop: 3,464 (1990); 3,184 (1980) Pop Density: 81.7
Land: 42.4 sq. mi.; Water: 0.0 sq. mi.

Jasper — City
ZIP: 64755 Lat: 37-20-04 N Long: 94-18-09 W
Pop: 994 (1990); 1,012 (1980) Pop Density: 994.0
Land: 1.0 sq. mi.; Water: 0.0 sq. mi. Elev: 946 ft.
Incorporated 1881.

*Jasper — Township
ZIP: 64755 Lat: 37-18-42 N Long: 94-33-53 W
Pop: 603 (1990); 589 (1980) Pop Density: 13.8
Land: 43.7 sq. mi.; Water: 0.6 sq. mi.

Joplin — City
ZIP: 64801 Lat: 37-05-33 N Long: 94-30-09 W
Pop: 37,032 (1990); 36,695 (1980) Pop Density: 1569.2
Land: 23.6 sq. mi.; Water: 0.0 sq. mi.
In southwestern MO, 70 mi. west of Springfield. Founded 1839; chartered 1874. Incorporated 1954. Part of the town is also in Newton County.
Name origin: For Methodist minister Harris G. Joplin.

*Joplin — Township
Lat: 37-06-27 N Long: 94-27-22 W
Pop: 34,574 (1990); 32,912 (1980) Pop Density: 825.2
Land: 41.9 sq. mi.; Water: 0.0 sq. mi.

La Russell — City
ZIP: 64848 Lat: 37-08-26 N Long: 94-03-39 W
Pop: 114 (1990); 126 (1980) Pop Density: 380.0
Land: 0.3 sq. mi.; Water: 0.0 sq. mi.
Incorporated 1903.

Lincoln — Township
Lat: 37-17-29 N Long: 94-07-25 W
Pop: 274 (1990); 286 (1980) Pop Density: 7.1
Land: 38.7 sq. mi.; Water: 0.0 sq. mi.

Madison — Township
Lat: 37-12-31 N Long: 94-13-59 W
Pop: 1,858 (1990); 1,630 (1980) Pop Density: 40.5
Land: 45.9 sq. mi.; Water: 0.1 sq. mi.

Marion — Township
Lat: 37-12-26 N Long: 94-21-01 W
Pop: 12,617 (1990); 12,302 (1980) Pop Density: 298.3
Land: 42.3 sq. mi.; Water: 0.1 sq. mi.

McDonald — Township
Lat: 37-12-21 N Long: 94-07-04 W
Pop: 678 (1990); 734 (1980) Pop Density: 15.0
Land: 45.3 sq. mi.; Water: 0.1 sq. mi.

Mineral — Township
Lat: 37-12-23 N Long: 94-27-33 W
Pop: 3,618 (1990); 3,244 (1980) Pop Density: 87.0
Land: 41.6 sq. mi.; Water: 0.0 sq. mi.

Neck City — City
Lat: 37-15-22 N Long: 94-26-36 W
Pop: 132 (1990); 151 (1980) Pop Density: 1320.0
Land: 0.1 sq. mi.; Water: 0.0 sq. mi. Elev: 934 ft.
Incorporated 1899.

Oakland Park — Village
Lat: 37-06-36 N Long: 94-28-21 W
Pop: 89 (1990); 143 (1980) Pop Density: 296.7
Land: 0.3 sq. mi.; Water: 0.0 sq. mi.
Incorporated 1958.

Oronogo — City
ZIP: 64855 Lat: 37-11-16 N Long: 94-28-09 W
Pop: 595 (1990); 525 (1980) Pop Density: 371.9
Land: 1.6 sq. mi.; Water: 0.0 sq. mi.
Incorporated 1906.

Preston — Township
Lat: 37-18-24 N Long: 94-20-57 W
Pop: 1,424 (1990); 1,418 (1980) Pop Density: 34.6
Land: 41.2 sq. mi.; Water: 0.1 sq. mi.

Purcell — City
ZIP: 64857 Lat: 37-14-35 N Long: 94-26-19 W
Pop: 359 (1990); 322 (1980) Pop Density: 897.5
Land: 0.4 sq. mi.; Water: 0.0 sq. mi.
Incorporated 1904.

Reeds — Town
ZIP: 64859 Lat: 37-06-59 N Long: 94-10-02 W
Pop: 88 (1990); 105 (1980) Pop Density: 440.0
Land: 0.2 sq. mi.; Water: 0.0 sq. mi.
Incorporated 1872.

Sarcoxie — City
ZIP: 64862 Lat: 37-04-00 N Long: 94-07-20 W
Pop: 1,330 (1990); 1,381 (1980) Pop Density: 1330.0
Land: 1.0 sq. mi.; Water: 0.0 sq. mi.
Founded 1834. Incorporated 1869.
Name origin: Named in 1839 by the Hon. James S. Rains for an old Shawnee chief who lived near a spring in the present town limits. The name means 'Rising Sun.' Previously called Centerville for its location on Center Creek.

*Sarcoxie — Township
ZIP: 64862 Lat: 37-06-17 N Long: 94-07-15 W
Pop: 2,506 (1990); 2,509 (1980) Pop Density: 55.0
Land: 45.6 sq. mi.; Water: 0.1 sq. mi.

Sheridan — Township
Lat: 37-18-06 N Long: 94-14-21 W
Pop: 387 (1990); 408 (1980) Pop Density: 9.6
Land: 40.3 sq. mi.; Water: 0.0 sq. mi.

Twin Groves — Township
Lat: 37-12-30 N Long: 94-33-47 W
Pop: 4,158 (1990); 3,844 (1980) Pop Density: 99.0
Land: 42.0 sq. mi.; Water: 0.3 sq. mi.

Union — Township
Lat: 37-06-26 N Long: 94-13-58 W
Pop: 1,577 (1990); 1,480 (1980) Pop Density: 34.4
Land: 45.9 sq. mi.; Water: 0.0 sq. mi.

Waco — Town
ZIP: 64869 Lat: 37-14-46 N Long: 94-35-59 W
Pop: 86 (1990); 129 (1980) Pop Density: 286.7
Land: 0.3 sq. mi.; Water: 0.0 sq. mi.
Incorporated 1919.
Name origin: For Waco, TX.

Webb City — City
ZIP: 64870 Lat: 37-08-28 N Long: 94-28-16 W
Pop: 7,449 (1990); 7,309 (1980) Pop Density: 1128.6
Land: 6.6 sq. mi.; Water: 0.0 sq. mi.
Incorporated 1890.
Name origin: For John C. Webb, whose land made up part of the town.

Jefferson County
County Seat: Hillsboro (ZIP: 63050)

Pop: 171,380 (1990); 146,183 (1980) Pop Density: 260.9
Land: 656.8 sq. mi.; Water: 7.3 sq. mi. Area Code: 314

On the central eastern border of MO, south of St. Louis; organized Dec 8, 1818 (prior to statehood) from Ste. Genevieve and St. Louis counties.

Name origin: For Thomas Jefferson (1743–1826), U.S. patriot and statesman; third U.S. president.

Arnold — City
ZIP: 63010 Lat: 38-25-42 N Long: 90-22-09 W
Pop: 18,828 (1990); 19,141 (1980) Pop Density: 1681.1
Land: 11.2 sq. mi.; Water: 0.3 sq. mi.
Incorporated 1972.
Name origin: Named in 1915 for early landowner J. L. Arnold.

Barnhart — CDP
ZIP: 63012 Lat: 38-20-03 N Long: 90-24-14 W
Pop: 4,911 (1990) Pop Density: 962.9
Land: 5.1 sq. mi.; Water: 0.1 sq. mi.

Big River — Township
Lat: 38-14-17 N Long: 90-42-05 W
Pop: 5,195 (1990); 4,439 (1980) Pop Density: 54.8
Land: 94.8 sq. mi.; Water: 0.2 sq. mi.

Byrnes Mill — City
Lat: 38-26-21 N Long: 90-34-25 W
Pop: 1,578 (1990) Pop Density: 322.0
Land: 4.9 sq. mi.; Water: 0.1 sq. mi. Elev: 458 ft.
Incorporated 1986.

Cedar Hill — CDP
ZIP: 63016 Lat: 38-21-22 N Long: 90-38-29 W
Pop: 1,966 (1990); 1,512 (1980) Pop Density: 854.8
Land: 2.3 sq. mi.; Water: 0.0 sq. mi.

Cedar Hill Lakes — Village
Lat: 38-19-49 N Long: 90-39-26 W
Pop: 227 (1990); 200 (1980) Pop Density: 1135.0
Land: 0.2 sq. mi.; Water: 0.0 sq. mi.
Incorporated 1973.

Central — Township
Lat: 38-14-31 N Long: 90-34-08 W
Pop: 10,314 (1990); 8,868 (1980) Pop Density: 140.5
Land: 73.4 sq. mi.; Water: 0.6 sq. mi.

Crystal City — City
ZIP: 63019 Lat: 38-13-33 N Long: 90-22-58 W
Pop: 4,088 (1990); 3,618 (1980) Pop Density: 1572.3
Land: 2.6 sq. mi.; Water: 0.0 sq. mi. Elev: 432 ft.
In eastern MO, 30 mi. south of St. Louis. Incorporated 1911.

De Soto — City
ZIP: 63020 Lat: 38-08-20 N Long: 90-33-37 W
Pop: 5,993 (1990); 5,993 (1980) Pop Density: 1816.1
Land: 3.3 sq. mi.; Water: 0.0 sq. mi. Elev: 503 ft.
In eastern MO, 40 mi. south-southwest of St. Louis. Incorporated 1869.
Name origin: Named in 1857 for Spanish explorer Hernando de Soto (c. 1500–42), who discovered the Mississippi River in 1540.

Festus — City
ZIP: 63028 Lat: 38-13-22 N Long: 90-24-19 W
Pop: 8,105 (1990); 7,574 (1980) Pop Density: 2315.7
Land: 3.5 sq. mi.; Water: 0.0 sq. mi.
In eastern MO, 30 mi. south of St. Louis. Platted 1878. Incorporated 1887.
Name origin: For the village fathers who opened a Bible at random, and the first passage a finger came to rest on was "then Agrippa said unto Festus, I would also hear the man myself." Previously called Tanglefoot for the gait of homeward-bound roisterers or for the town's principal product, which caused it.

Herculaneum — City
ZIP: 63048 Lat: 38-15-33 N Long: 90-23-15 W
Pop: 2,263 (1990); 2,293 (1980) Pop Density: 707.2
Land: 3.2 sq. mi.; Water: 0.0 sq. mi. Elev: 422 ft.
Incorporated 1972.

High Ridge — Township
ZIP: 63049 Lat: 38-25-59 N Long: 90-33-44 W
Pop: 15,741 (1990) Pop Density: 432.4
Land: 36.4 sq. mi.; Water: 0.3 sq. mi.

MISSOURI, Jefferson County

Hillsboro
City
ZIP: 63050 **Lat:** 38-13-56 N **Long:** 90-34-00 W
Pop: 1,625 (1990); 1,508 (1980) **Pop Density:** 812.5
Land: 2.0 sq. mi.; **Water:** 0.0 sq. mi. **Elev:** 802 ft.
County seat 1839. Incorporated 1839.
Name origin: Previously called Monticello for the hill just to the south.

Horine
CDP
ZIP: 63070 **Lat:** 38-15-57 N **Long:** 90-25-48 W
Pop: 1,043 (1990) **Pop Density:** 1158.9
Land: 0.9 sq. mi.; **Water:** 0.0 sq. mi.

Imperial
CDP
Lat: 38-22-03 N **Long:** 90-22-19 W
Pop: 4,156 (1990) **Pop Density:** 769.6
Land: 5.4 sq. mi.; **Water:** 0.7 sq. mi.

*Imperial
Township
Lat: 38-21-53 N **Long:** 90-26-54 W
Pop: 14,856 (1990) **Pop Density:** 349.6
Land: 42.5 sq. mi.; **Water:** 0.2 sq. mi.

Joachim
Township
Lat: 38-15-40 N **Long:** 90-27-04 W
Pop: 13,116 (1990); 25,617 (1980) **Pop Density:** 216.4
Land: 60.6 sq. mi.; **Water:** 0.9 sq. mi.

Kimmswick
City
ZIP: 63053 **Lat:** 38-22-00 N **Long:** 90-21-54 W
Pop: 135 (1990); 207 (1980) **Pop Density:** 1350.0
Land: 0.1 sq. mi.; **Water:** 0.0 sq. mi. **Elev:** 411 ft.
Founded October 1859. Incorporated 1879.
Name origin: For founder Theodoro Kimm.

Meramec
Township
Lat: 38-23-38 N **Long:** 90-38-30 W
Pop: 14,816 (1990); 25,396 (1980) **Pop Density:** 154.3
Land: 96.0 sq. mi.; **Water:** 1.1 sq. mi.

Murphy
CDP
ZIP: 63049 **Lat:** 38-29-34 N **Long:** 90-29-11 W
Pop: 9,342 (1990); 8,121 (1980) **Pop Density:** 2335.5
Land: 4.0 sq. mi.; **Water:** 0.0 sq. mi.

Olympian Village
City
ZIP: 63020 **Lat:** 38-08-04 N **Long:** 90-27-26 W
Pop: 752 (1990); 774 (1980) **Pop Density:** 1253.3
Land: 0.6 sq. mi.; **Water:** 0.0 sq. mi. **Elev:** 600 ft.
Incorporated 1969.

Parkdale
Town
Lat: 38-28-44 N **Long:** 90-31-35 W
Pop: 212 (1990); 270 (1980) **Pop Density:** 2120.0
Land: 0.1 sq. mi.; **Water:** 0.0 sq. mi. **Elev:** 750 ft.
Incorporated 1957.

Pevely
City
ZIP: 63070 **Lat:** 38-17-20 N **Long:** 90-23-52 W
Pop: 2,831 (1990); 2,732 (1980) **Pop Density:** 1490.0
Land: 1.9 sq. mi.; **Water:** 0.0 sq. mi. **Elev:** 440 ft.
Incorporated 1953.

Plattin
Township
ZIP: 63028 **Lat:** 38-07-22 N **Long:** 90-23-26 W
Pop: 8,654 (1990); 6,046 (1980) **Pop Density:** 85.3
Land: 101.5 sq. mi.; **Water:** 1.6 sq. mi.

River View
Township
Lat: 38-13-18 N **Long:** 90-23-48 W
Pop: 13,568 (1990) **Pop Density:** 1169.7
Land: 11.6 sq. mi.; **Water:** 0.4 sq. mi.

Rock
Township
Lat: 38-27-42 N **Long:** 90-28-24 W
Pop: 25,362 (1990); 63,052 (1980) **Pop Density:** 1010.4
Land: 25.1 sq. mi.; **Water:** 0.3 sq. mi.

Scotsdale
Town
Lat: 38-23-45 N **Long:** 90-35-22 W
Pop: 193 (1990); 183 (1980) **Pop Density:** 482.5
Land: 0.4 sq. mi.; **Water:** 0.0 sq. mi.
Not coextensive with the town of the same name.

Valle
Township
Lat: 38-05-26 N **Long:** 90-34-12 W
Pop: 13,333 (1990); 12,765 (1980) **Pop Density:** 152.4
Land: 87.5 sq. mi.; **Water:** 0.6 sq. mi.

Windsor
Township
Lat: 38-24-19 N **Long:** 90-23-57 W
Pop: 17,597 (1990) **Pop Density:** 1099.8
Land: 16.0 sq. mi.; **Water:** 0.8 sq. mi.

Johnson County
County Seat: Warrensburg (ZIP: 64093)

Pop: 42,514 (1990); 39,059 (1980) **Pop Density:** 51.2
Land: 830.6 sq. mi.; **Water:** 2.5 sq. mi. **Area Code:** 816
In west-central MO, southeast of Kansas City; organized Dec 13, 1834 from Lafayette County.
Name origin: For Col. Richard Mentor Johnson (1781–1850), officer in the War of 1812, U.S. senator from KY (1819–29), and U.S. vice president under Van Buren (1837–41).

Centerview
Town
ZIP: 64019 **Lat:** 38-44-44 N **Long:** 93-50-44 W
Pop: 214 (1990); 223 (1980) **Pop Density:** 2140.0
Land: 0.1 sq. mi.; **Water:** 0.0 sq. mi.
Incorporated 1914.

*Centerview
Township
ZIP: 64019 **Lat:** 38-45-01 N **Long:** 93-51-27 W
Pop: 1,203 (1990); 1,134 (1980) **Pop Density:** 19.2
Land: 62.5 sq. mi.; **Water:** 0.1 sq. mi.

Chilhowee — Town
ZIP: 64733 Lat: 38-35-20 N Long: 93-51-22 W
Pop: 335 (1990); 349 (1980) Pop Density: 837.5
Land: 0.4 sq. mi.; Water: 0.0 sq. mi. Elev: 885 ft.
Incorporated 1907.

*Chilhowee — Township
ZIP: 64733 Lat: 38-36-51 N Long: 93-52-28 W
Pop: 927 (1990); 1,048 (1980) Pop Density: 13.1
Land: 71.0 sq. mi.; Water: 0.1 sq. mi.

Columbus — Township
Lat: 38-51-33 N Long: 93-53-42 W
Pop: 711 (1990); 707 (1980) Pop Density: 17.0
Land: 41.9 sq. mi.; Water: 0.1 sq. mi.

Grover — Township
Lat: 38-52-40 N Long: 93-33-08 W
Pop: 377 (1990); 489 (1980) Pop Density: 7.7
Land: 48.7 sq. mi.; Water: 0.1 sq. mi.

Hazel Hill — Township
Lat: 38-52-30 N Long: 93-46-49 W
Pop: 1,217 (1990); 975 (1980) Pop Density: 25.4
Land: 47.9 sq. mi.; Water: 0.1 sq. mi.

Holden — City
ZIP: 64040 Lat: 38-42-48 N Long: 93-59-20 W
Pop: 2,389 (1990); 2,195 (1980) Pop Density: 995.4
Land: 2.4 sq. mi.; Water: 0.0 sq. mi.
Incorporated 1861.
Name origin: For Maj. N. B. Holden, member of the state legislature.

Jackson — Township
Lat: 38-51-07 N Long: 94-01-38 W
Pop: 2,282 (1990); 1,848 (1980) Pop Density: 29.9
Land: 76.2 sq. mi.; Water: 0.3 sq. mi.

Jefferson — Township
Lat: 38-36-57 N Long: 93-34-15 W
Pop: 453 (1990); 458 (1980) Pop Density: 7.6
Land: 59.7 sq. mi.; Water: 0.2 sq. mi.

Kingsville — City
ZIP: 64061 Lat: 38-44-34 N Long: 94-04-07 W
Pop: 279 (1990); 365 (1980) Pop Density: 930.0
Land: 0.3 sq. mi.; Water: 0.0 sq. mi. Elev: 914 ft.
Incorporated 1885.

*Kingsville — Township
ZIP: 64061 Lat: 38-44-38 N Long: 94-04-28 W
Pop: 1,165 (1990); 1,119 (1980) Pop Density: 28.6
Land: 40.8 sq. mi.; Water: 0.7 sq. mi.

Knob Noster — City
ZIP: 65305 Lat: 38-46-04 N Long: 93-33-57 W
Pop: 2,261 (1990); 2,040 (1980) Pop Density: 1413.1
Land: 1.6 sq. mi.; Water: 0.0 sq. mi. Elev: 793 ft.
Founded 1856. Incorporated 1890.
Name origin: A pseudo-Latin term for 'Our Knobs,' two prominent mounds or knobs on the prairie nearby.

La Tour — Town
Lat: 38-38-02 N Long: 94-06-08 W
Pop: 87 (1990); 84 (1980) Pop Density: 870.0
Land: 0.1 sq. mi.; Water: 0.0 sq. mi. Elev: 781 ft.
Incorporated 1912.

Leeton — City
ZIP: 64761 Lat: 38-35-01 N Long: 93-41-42 W
Pop: 632 (1990); 604 (1980) Pop Density: 1264.0
Land: 0.5 sq. mi.; Water: 0.0 sq. mi. Elev: 955 ft.
Incorporated 1946.

Madison — Township
Lat: 38-43-40 N Long: 93-58-20 W
Pop: 3,088 (1990); 2,825 (1980) Pop Density: 71.0
Land: 43.5 sq. mi.; Water: 0.2 sq. mi.

Montserrat — Township
Lat: 38-45-15 N Long: 93-37-51 W
Pop: 1,071 (1990); 917 (1980) Pop Density: 26.3
Land: 40.8 sq. mi.; Water: 0.1 sq. mi.

Post Oak — Township
Lat: 38-37-22 N Long: 93-42-24 W
Pop: 1,723 (1990); 1,491 (1980) Pop Density: 24.6
Land: 70.0 sq. mi.; Water: 0.1 sq. mi.

Rose Hill — Township
Lat: 38-37-38 N Long: 94-01-56 W
Pop: 745 (1990); 798 (1980) Pop Density: 10.3
Land: 72.1 sq. mi.; Water: 0.1 sq. mi.

Simpson — Township
Lat: 38-52-33 N Long: 93-40-13 W
Pop: 489 (1990); 472 (1980) Pop Density: 10.8
Land: 45.1 sq. mi.; Water: 0.0 sq. mi.

Warrensburg — City
ZIP: 64093 Lat: 38-45-35 N Long: 93-43-43 W
Pop: 15,244 (1990); 13,807 (1980) Pop Density: 1836.6
Land: 8.3 sq. mi.; Water: 0.1 sq. mi.
In western MO, southeast of Kansas City. Incorporated 1865.
Name origin: For early settler and founder Martin Warren.

*Warrensburg — Township
ZIP: 64093 Lat: 38-45-11 N Long: 93-44-05 W
Pop: 18,839 (1990); 16,880 (1980) Pop Density: 289.4
Land: 65.1 sq. mi.; Water: 0.2 sq. mi.

Washington — Township
Lat: 38-44-54 N Long: 93-32-57 W
Pop: 8,224 (1990); 7,898 (1980) Pop Density: 181.1
Land: 45.4 sq. mi.; Water: 0.1 sq. mi.

Whiteman Air Force Base — Military Facility
Lat: 38-43-57 N Long: 93-33-16 W
Pop: 4,174 (1990) Pop Density: 818.4
Land: 5.1 sq. mi.; Water: 0.0 sq. mi.

Knox County
County Seat: Edina (ZIP: 63537)

Pop: 4,482 (1990); 5,508 (1980)   **Pop Density:** 8.9
Land: 505.7 sq. mi.; **Water:** 1.1 sq. mi.   **Area Code:** 816
In northeastern MO, north of Columbia; organized Feb 14, 1845 from Scotland County.
Name origin: For Gen. Henry Knox (1750–1806), Revolutionary War officer and first U.S. Secretary of War (1785–95).

Baring — City
ZIP: 63531   **Lat:** 40-14-40 N **Long:** 92-12-20 W
Pop: 182 (1990); 206 (1980)   **Pop Density:** 1820.0
Land: 0.1 sq. mi.; **Water:** 0.0 sq. mi.
Incorporated 1959.
Name origin: Named in 1889 for the Baring brothers of England, who made a large loan to establish this town.

Bee Ridge — Township
Lat: 40-04-44 N **Long:** 92-07-23 W
Pop: 134 (1990); 154 (1980)   **Pop Density:** 3.7
Land: 36.5 sq. mi.; **Water:** 0.0 sq. mi.

Benton — Township
Lat: 40-15-33 N **Long:** 92-07-00 W
Pop: 192 (1990); 239 (1980)   **Pop Density:** 5.3
Land: 36.4 sq. mi.; **Water:** 0.1 sq. mi.

Bourbon — Township
Lat: 39-59-22 N **Long:** 92-07-21 W
Pop: 149 (1990); 198 (1980)   **Pop Density:** 4.2
Land: 35.6 sq. mi.; **Water:** 0.1 sq. mi.

Center — Township
Lat: 40-10-04 N **Long:** 92-10-23 W
Pop: 1,283 (1990); 1,520 (1980)   **Pop Density:** 986.9
Land: 1.3 sq. mi.; **Water:** 0.0 sq. mi.

Colony — Township
Lat: 40-15-17 N **Long:** 92-00-40 W
Pop: 175 (1990); 282 (1980)   **Pop Density:** 4.9
Land: 35.6 sq. mi.; **Water:** 0.1 sq. mi.

Edina — City
ZIP: 63537   **Lat:** 40-10-04 N **Long:** 92-10-23 W
Pop: 1,283 (1990); 1,520 (1980)   **Pop Density:** 986.9
Land: 1.3 sq. mi.; **Water:** 0.0 sq. mi.   **Elev:** 816 ft.
County seat 1845. Incorporated 1879.
Name origin: Named in 1839 for the town of Edina, Scotland.

Fabius — Township
Lat: 39-59-12 N **Long:** 92-00-18 W
Pop: 195 (1990); 265 (1980)   **Pop Density:** 5.6
Land: 34.7 sq. mi.; **Water:** 0.2 sq. mi.

Greensburg — Township
Lat: 40-15-19 N **Long:** 92-15-33 W
Pop: 440 (1990); 544 (1980)   **Pop Density:** 8.2
Land: 53.9 sq. mi.; **Water:** 0.2 sq. mi.

Hurdland — City
ZIP: 63547   **Lat:** 40-09-02 N **Long:** 92-18-08 W
Pop: 212 (1990); 227 (1980)   **Pop Density:** 1060.0
Land: 0.2 sq. mi.; **Water:** 0.0 sq. mi.   **Elev:** 889 ft.
Incorporated 1965.

Jeddo — Township
Lat: 40-04-19 N **Long:** 92-00-05 W
Pop: 102 (1990); 111 (1980)   **Pop Density:** 3.0
Land: 34.5 sq. mi.; **Water:** 0.0 sq. mi.

Knox City — City
ZIP: 63446   **Lat:** 40-08-37 N **Long:** 92-00-36 W
Pop: 262 (1990); 281 (1980)   **Pop Density:** 1310.0
Land: 0.2 sq. mi.; **Water:** 0.0 sq. mi.
Incorporated 1859.

Liberty — Township
Lat: 40-10-31 N **Long:** 92-07-01 W
Pop: 317 (1990); 337 (1980)   **Pop Density:** 8.2
Land: 38.8 sq. mi.; **Water:** 0.0 sq. mi.

Lyon — Township
Lat: 40-10-12 N **Long:** 92-15-46 W
Pop: 508 (1990); 633 (1980)   **Pop Density:** 9.0
Land: 56.3 sq. mi.; **Water:** 0.2 sq. mi.

Myrtle — Township
Lat: 40-10-16 N **Long:** 91-59-56 W
Pop: 445 (1990); 490 (1980)   **Pop Density:** 12.3
Land: 36.1 sq. mi.; **Water:** 0.0 sq. mi.

Newark — Town
ZIP: 63458   **Lat:** 39-59-39 N **Long:** 91-58-23 W
Pop: 82 (1990); 105 (1980)   **Pop Density:** 273.3
Land: 0.3 sq. mi.; **Water:** 0.0 sq. mi.
Incorporated 1872.
Name origin: Named in 1837 for Newark, NJ.

Novelty — Town
ZIP: 63460   **Lat:** 40-00-45 N **Long:** 92-12-26 W
Pop: 143 (1990); 187 (1980)   **Pop Density:** 476.7
Land: 0.3 sq. mi.; **Water:** 0.0 sq. mi.
Incorporated 1896.

Salt River — Township
Lat: 39-59-54 N **Long:** 92-15-17 W
Pop: 322 (1990); 460 (1980)   **Pop Density:** 6.3
Land: 51.5 sq. mi.; **Water:** 0.0 sq. mi.

Shelton — Township
Lat: 40-04-44 N **Long:** 92-15-40 W
Pop: 220 (1990); 275 (1980)   **Pop Density:** 4.0
Land: 54.4 sq. mi.; **Water:** 0.1 sq. mi.

> ## Laclede County
> **County Seat: Lebanon (ZIP: 65536)**
>
> **Pop:** 27,158 (1990); 24,323 (1980)   **Pop Density:** 35.5
> **Land:** 765.9 sq. mi.; **Water:** 2.1 sq. mi.   **Area Code:** 417
>
> In south-central MO, northeast of Springfield; organized Feb 24, 1849 from Pulaski, Wright, and Camden counties.
>
> **Name origin:** For Pierre Laclède Liguest (1724–78), French fur trader who established the site of St. Louis (Dec 1763).

Auglaize   Township
Lat: 37-48-18 N **Long:** 92-37-34 W
Pop: 1,483 (1990); 1,324 (1980)   **Pop Density:** 24.8
Land: 59.9 sq. mi.; **Water:** 0.0 sq. mi.

Conway   City
ZIP: 65632   **Lat:** 37-30-02 N **Long:** 92-49-27 W
Pop: 629 (1990); 601 (1980)   **Pop Density:** 786.3
Land: 0.8 sq. mi.; **Water:** 0.0 sq. mi.
Incorporated 1914.

Eldridge   Township
ZIP: 65463   **Lat:** 37-51-10 N **Long:** 92-45-53 W
Pop: 636 (1990); 468 (1980)   **Pop Density:** 11.5
Land: 55.3 sq. mi.; **Water:** 0.1 sq. mi.

Franklin   Township
Lat: 37-32-49 N **Long:** 92-29-28 W
Pop: 692 (1990); 691 (1980)   **Pop Density:** 9.7
Land: 71.3 sq. mi.; **Water:** 0.2 sq. mi.

Gasconade   Township
Lat: 37-34-41 N **Long:** 92-20-08 W
Pop: 847 (1990); 853 (1980)   **Pop Density:** 6.7
Land: 127.1 sq. mi.; **Water:** 0.6 sq. mi.

Hooker   Township
Lat: 37-45-50 N **Long:** 92-46-42 W
Pop: 1,071 (1990); 701 (1980)   **Pop Density:** 19.5
Land: 55.0 sq. mi.; **Water:** 0.2 sq. mi.

Lebanon   City
ZIP: 65536   **Lat:** 37-40-13 N **Long:** 92-39-39 W
Pop: 9,983 (1990); 9,507 (1980)   **Pop Density:** 818.3
Land: 12.2 sq. mi.; **Water:** 0.0 sq. mi.
In south-central MO, 25 mi. south of the east end of the Lake of the Ozarks. Incorporated 1877.
Name origin: For Lebanon, TN.

*Lebanon   Township
ZIP: 65536   **Lat:** 37-40-32 N **Long:** 92-39-11 W
Pop: 14,852 (1990); 13,676 (1980)   **Pop Density:** 180.9
Land: 82.1 sq. mi.; **Water:** 0.1 sq. mi.

Mayfield   Township
Lat: 37-48-46 N **Long:** 92-27-33 W
Pop: 415 (1990); 331 (1980)   **Pop Density:** 20.9
Land: 19.9 sq. mi.; **Water:** 0.1 sq. mi.

Osage   Township
Lat: 37-39-42 N **Long:** 92-29-39 W
Pop: 1,284 (1990); 1,167 (1980)   **Pop Density:** 19.0
Land: 67.5 sq. mi.; **Water:** 0.2 sq. mi.

Phillipsburg   Town
ZIP: 65722   **Lat:** 37-33-13 N **Long:** 92-47-06 W
Pop: 170 (1990); 134 (1980)   **Pop Density:** 340.0
Land: 0.5 sq. mi.; **Water:** 0.0 sq. mi.
Incorporated 1912.

*Phillipsburg   Township
ZIP: 65722   **Lat:** 37-34-22 N **Long:** 92-46-22 W
Pop: 1,106 (1990); 863 (1980)   **Pop Density:** 24.4
Land: 45.4 sq. mi.; **Water:** 0.0 sq. mi.

Richland   City
ZIP: 65556   **Lat:** 37-51-28 N **Long:** 92-24-44 W
Pop: 55 (1990); 22 (1980)   **Pop Density:** 550.0
Land: 0.1 sq. mi.; **Water:** 0.0 sq. mi.
Incorporated 1884. Part of the town is also in Camden and Pulaski counties.

Smith   Township
Lat: 37-45-11 N **Long:** 92-29-23 W
Pop: 602 (1990); 674 (1980)   **Pop Density:** 14.7
Land: 40.9 sq. mi.; **Water:** 0.5 sq. mi.

Spring Hollow   Township
Lat: 37-39-56 N **Long:** 92-47-39 W
Pop: 1,332 (1990); 955 (1980)   **Pop Density:** 31.8
Land: 41.9 sq. mi.; **Water:** 0.0 sq. mi.

Stoutland   Village
ZIP: 65567   **Lat:** 37-48-36 N **Long:** 92-30-45 W
Pop: 43 (1990); 46 (1980)   **Pop Density:** 143.3
Land: 0.3 sq. mi.; **Water:** 0.0 sq. mi.   **Elev:** 1171 ft.
Incorporated 1910. Part of the town is also in Camden County.

Twin Bridges   Town
Lat: 37-33-07 N **Long:** 92-35-49 W
Pop: 44 (1990)   **Pop Density:** 5.2
Land: 8.5 sq. mi.; **Water:** 0.1 sq. mi.

Union   Township
Lat: 37-30-25 N **Long:** 92-46-52 W
Pop: 1,143 (1990); 1,098 (1980)   **Pop Density:** 41.7
Land: 27.4 sq. mi.; **Water:** 0.0 sq. mi.

Washington   Township
Lat: 37-32-51 N **Long:** 92-37-39 W
Pop: 1,695 (1990); 1,522 (1980)   **Pop Density:** 23.5
Land: 72.1 sq. mi.; **Water:** 0.1 sq. mi.

Lafayette County
County Seat: Lexington (ZIP: 64067)

Pop: 31,107 (1990); 29,931 (1980) **Pop Density:** 49.4
Land: 629.4 sq. mi.; **Water:** 9.5 sq. mi. **Area Code:** 816
In west-central MO, east of Kansas City; organized as Lillard County Nov 16, 1820 (prior to statehood) from Cooper County; name changed Feb 16, 1825.
Name origin: For Marquis de Lafayette (1757–1834), French statesman and soldier who fought with the Americans during the Revolutionary War.

Alma — City
ZIP: 64001 **Lat:** 39-05-44 N **Long:** 93-32-52 W
Pop: 446 (1990); 445 (1980) **Pop Density:** 1486.7
Land: 0.3 sq. mi.; **Water:** 0.0 sq. mi.
Incorporated 1878.
Name origin: Named in 1879 for the daughter of founder John M. Woodson.

Aullville — Village
Lat: 39-01-05 N **Long:** 93-40-38 W
Pop: 72 (1990); 92 (1980) **Pop Density:** 240.0
Land: 0.3 sq. mi.; **Water:** 0.0 sq. mi.

Bates City — Village
ZIP: 64011 **Lat:** 39-00-22 N **Long:** 94-04-12 W
Pop: 197 (1990); 199 (1980) **Pop Density:** 656.7
Land: 0.3 sq. mi.; **Water:** 0.0 sq. mi. **Elev:** 880 ft.
Incorporated 1905.

Blackburn — City
ZIP: 65321 **Lat:** 39-06-16 N **Long:** 93-29-24 W
Pop: 22 (1990); 6 (1980) **Pop Density:** 220.0
Land: 0.1 sq. mi.; **Water:** 0.0 sq. mi. **Elev:** 805 ft.
Incorporated 1909. Part of the town is also in Saline County.

Clay — Township
Lat: 39-04-50 N **Long:** 94-01-02 W
Pop: 4,598 (1990); 4,036 (1980) **Pop Density:** 47.9
Land: 95.9 sq. mi.; **Water:** 1.9 sq. mi.

Concordia — City
ZIP: 64020 **Lat:** 38-59-15 N **Long:** 93-34-06 W
Pop: 2,160 (1990); 2,129 (1980) **Pop Density:** 1350.0
Land: 1.6 sq. mi.; **Water:** 0.0 sq. mi. **Elev:** 787 ft.
Incorporated 1877.

Corder — City
ZIP: 64021 **Lat:** 39-05-58 N **Long:** 93-38-18 W
Pop: 485 (1990); 483 (1980) **Pop Density:** 1212.5
Land: 0.4 sq. mi.; **Water:** 0.0 sq. mi.
Incorporated 1881.

Davis — Township
Lat: 39-02-39 N **Long:** 93-38-45 W
Pop: 4,662 (1990); 4,519 (1980) **Pop Density:** 64.2
Land: 72.6 sq. mi.; **Water:** 0.6 sq. mi.

Dover — Town
ZIP: 64022 **Lat:** 39-11-40 N **Long:** 93-41-22 W
Pop: 115 (1990); 126 (1980) **Pop Density:** 575.0
Land: 0.2 sq. mi.; **Water:** 0.0 sq. mi. **Elev:** 817 ft.
Incorporated 1900.

*Dover — Township
ZIP: 64022 **Lat:** 39-09-13 N **Long:** 93-39-58 W
Pop: 2,447 (1990); 2,523 (1980) **Pop Density:** 29.9
Land: 81.8 sq. mi.; **Water:** 1.7 sq. mi.

Emma — City
ZIP: 65327 **Lat:** 38-58-35 N **Long:** 93-29-43 W
Pop: 86 (1990); 109 (1980) **Pop Density:** 286.
Land: 0.3 sq. mi.; **Water:** 0.0 sq. mi. **Elev:** 759 ft
Incorporated 1958. Part of the town is also in Saline County
Name origin: Named in 1895 for the daughter of a Lutheran minister at Concordia.

Freedom — Township
Lat: 38-58-19 N **Long:** 93-37-16 W
Pop: 3,289 (1990); 3,255 (1980) **Pop Density:** 41.
Land: 80.0 sq. mi.; **Water:** 0.6 sq. mi.

Higginsville — City
ZIP: 64037 **Lat:** 39-03-53 N **Long:** 93-43-35 W
Pop: 4,693 (1990); 4,595 (1980) **Pop Density:** 1303.
Land: 3.6 sq. mi.; **Water:** 0.0 sq. mi. **Elev:** 836 ft
In western MO, east of Kansas City. Incorporated 1886.

Lexington — City
ZIP: 64067 **Lat:** 39-10-55 N **Long:** 93-52-29 W
Pop: 4,860 (1990); 5,063 (1980) **Pop Density:** 1429.4
Land: 3.4 sq. mi.; **Water:** 0.2 sq. mi. **Elev:** 849 ft
In western MO, 35 mi. east of Independence. Incorporated 1845.
Name origin: For Lexington, KY, former home of many of its settlers.

*Lexington — Township
ZIP: 64067 **Lat:** 39-08-44 N **Long:** 93-50-30 W
Pop: 6,294 (1990); 6,601 (1980) **Pop Density:** 78.9
Land: 79.8 sq. mi.; **Water:** 2.4 sq. mi.

Mayview — City
ZIP: 64071 **Lat:** 39-03-09 N **Long:** 93-50-01 W
Pop: 279 (1990); 291 (1980) **Pop Density:** 1395.0
Land: 0.2 sq. mi.; **Water:** 0.0 sq. mi.
Incorporated 1957.

Middleton — Township
Lat: 39-09-28 N **Long:** 93-32-38 W
Pop: 1,754 (1990); 1,841 (1980) **Pop Density:** 27.1
Land: 64.7 sq. mi.; **Water:** 1.1 sq. mi.

Napoleon — City
ZIP: 64074 **Lat:** 39-07-56 N **Long:** 94-05-18 W
Pop: 233 (1990); 271 (1980) **Pop Density:** 137.1
Land: 1.7 sq. mi.; **Water:** 0.0 sq. mi. **Elev:** 768 ft.
Incorporated 1888.

Oak Grove — City
ZIP: 64075 **Lat:** 38-59-52 N **Long:** 94-06-15 W
Pop: 4 (1990) **Pop Density:** 13.3
Land: 0.3 sq. mi.; **Water:** 0.0 sq. mi.
Incorporated 1881. Part of the town is also in Jackson County.

American Places Dictionary   MISSOURI, Lawrence County

Odessa — City
ZIP: 64076   **Lat:** 38-59-49 N **Long:** 93-57-17 W
Pop: 3,695 (1990); 3,088 (1980)   **Pop Density:** 1606.5
Land: 2.3 sq. mi.; **Water:** 0.0 sq. mi.

In western MO, 30 mi. east of Independence. Incorporated 1880.

Sni-A-Bar — Township
Lat: 38-57-14 N **Long:** 94-01-59 W
Pop: 5,708 (1990); 4,802 (1980)   **Pop Density:** 105.5
Land: 54.1 sq. mi.; **Water:** 0.3 sq. mi.

Washington — Township
Lat: 39-00-11 N **Long:** 93-51-45 W
Pop: 2,355 (1990); 2,354 (1980)   **Pop Density:** 23.5
Land: 100.4 sq. mi.; **Water:** 0.8 sq. mi.

Waverly — Town
ZIP: 64096   **Lat:** 39-12-23 N **Long:** 93-31-11 W
Pop: 837 (1990); 941 (1980)   **Pop Density:** 837.0
Land: 1.0 sq. mi.; **Water:** 0.1 sq. mi.

Incorporated 1882.

Name origin: For the novel by Sir Walter Scott (1771–1832), published in 1814.

Wellington — City
ZIP: 64097   **Lat:** 39-08-10 N **Long:** 93-59-15 W
Pop: 779 (1990); 780 (1980)   **Pop Density:** 708.2
Land: 1.1 sq. mi.; **Water:** 0.0 sq. mi.

Platted 1837. Incorporated 1891.

Lawrence County
County Seat: Mount Vernon (ZIP: 65712)

Pop: 30,236 (1990); 28,973 (1980)   **Pop Density:** 49.3
Land: 613.1 sq. mi.; **Water:** 0.3 sq. mi.   **Area Code:** 417

In southwestern MO, west of Springfield; organized Feb 14, 1845 from Dade and Barry counties.

Name origin: For Capt. James Lawrence (1781–1813), U.S. naval officer in the war with Barbary pirates near Tripoli and commander of the U.S.S. *Chesapeake* in the War of 1812, who said, "Don't give up the ship!"

Aurora — City
ZIP: 65605   **Lat:** 36-58-11 N **Long:** 93-43-13 W
Pop: 6,459 (1990); 6,437 (1980)   **Pop Density:** 1242.1
Land: 5.2 sq. mi.; **Water:** 0.0 sq. mi.   **Elev:** 1368 ft.

In southwestern MO, 30 mi. southwest of Springfield. Incorporated 1886.

Name origin: For the ancient Roman goddess of the morning.

*Aurora — Township
ZIP: 65605   **Lat:** 36-59-29 N **Long:** 93-43-18 W
Pop: 7,994 (1990); 7,631 (1980)   **Pop Density:** 207.6
Land: 38.5 sq. mi.; **Water:** 0.0 sq. mi.

Buck Prairie — Township
Lat: 36-59-47 N **Long:** 93-38-42 W
Pop: 3,186 (1990); 3,147 (1980)   **Pop Density:** 79.7
Land: 40.0 sq. mi.; **Water:** 0.0 sq. mi.

Freistatt — Town
ZIP: 65654   **Lat:** 37-01-16 N **Long:** 93-53-46 W
Pop: 166 (1990); 139 (1980)   **Pop Density:** 830.0
Land: 0.2 sq. mi.; **Water:** 0.0 sq. mi.

Incorporated 1916.

*Freistatt — Township
Lat: 37-00-50 N **Long:** 93-53-18 W
Pop: 515 (1990); 458 (1980)   **Pop Density:** 24.5
Land: 21.0 sq. mi.; **Water:** 0.0 sq. mi.

Green — Township
Lat: 37-14-18 N **Long:** 93-54-20 W
Pop: 426 (1990); 416 (1980)   **Pop Density:** 10.1
Land: 42.1 sq. mi.; **Water:** 0.0 sq. mi.

Halltown — Town
ZIP: 65664   **Lat:** 37-11-39 N **Long:** 93-37-43 W
Pop: 161 (1990); 149 (1980)   **Pop Density:** 805.0
Land: 0.2 sq. mi.; **Water:** 0.0 sq. mi.

Incorporated 1972.

Hoberg — Village
ZIP: 65712   **Lat:** 37-04-06 N **Long:** 93-50-57 W
Pop: 62 (1990); 77 (1980)   **Pop Density:** 620.0
Land: 0.1 sq. mi.; **Water:** 0.0 sq. mi.

Incorporated 1927.

*Hoberg — Township
ZIP: 65712   **Lat:** 37-03-44 N **Long:** 93-51-33 W
Pop: 375 (1990); 418 (1980)   **Pop Density:** 17.0
Land: 22.1 sq. mi.; **Water:** 0.0 sq. mi.

Lincoln — Township
Lat: 37-14-02 N **Long:** 93-48-04 W
Pop: 1,560 (1990); 1,598 (1980)   **Pop Density:** 34.1
Land: 45.7 sq. mi.; **Water:** 0.0 sq. mi.

Marionville — City
ZIP: 65705   **Lat:** 37-00-01 N **Long:** 93-38-12 W
Pop: 1,920 (1990); 1,920 (1980)   **Pop Density:** 1476.9
Land: 1.3 sq. mi.; **Water:** 0.0 sq. mi.   **Elev:** 1359 ft.

Incorporated 1885.

Miller — City
ZIP: 65707   **Lat:** 37-12-55 N **Long:** 93-50-25 W
Pop: 753 (1990); 795 (1980)   **Pop Density:** 941.3
Land: 0.8 sq. mi.; **Water:** 0.0 sq. mi.

Incorporated 1915.

MISSOURI, Lawrence County

Monett
City
ZIP: 65708 **Lat:** 36-56-05 N **Long:** 93-55-22 W
Pop: 2,053 (1990); 1,781 (1980) **Pop Density:** 1710.8
Land: 1.2 sq. mi.; **Water:** 0.0 sq. mi. **Elev:** 1317 ft.

In southwestern MO, 35 mi. southeast of Joplin. Incorporated 1888. Part of the town is also in Barry County.
Name origin: Named in 1887 for the general passenger agent of the New York Central Railroad.

Mount Pleasant
Township
Lat: 37-01-54 N **Long:** 93-59-47 W
Pop: 749 (1990); 716 (1980) **Pop Density:** 17.8
Land: 42.0 sq. mi.; **Water:** 0.0 sq. mi.

Mount Vernon
City
ZIP: 65712 **Lat:** 37-06-05 N **Long:** 93-49-04 W
Pop: 3,726 (1990); 3,341 (1980) **Pop Density:** 1284.8
Land: 2.9 sq. mi.; **Water:** 0.0 sq. mi.

In southwestern MO, 30 mi. west-southwest of Springfield. Incorporated 1848.
Name origin: Named in 1845 for the VA home of George Washington (1732–99), first president of the U.S.

*Mount Vernon
Township
ZIP: 65712 **Lat:** 37-06-50 N **Long:** 93-48-11 W
Pop: 5,570 (1990); 5,058 (1980) **Pop Density:** 67.4
Land: 82.7 sq. mi.; **Water:** 0.0 sq. mi.

Ozark
Township
Lat: 37-13-41 N **Long:** 93-40-22 W
Pop: 1,306 (1990); 1,196 (1980) **Pop Density:** 21.8
Land: 59.8 sq. mi.; **Water:** 0.0 sq. mi.

Pierce
Township
Lat: 36-57-33 N **Long:** 93-58-17 W
Pop: 5,042 (1990); 4,741 (1980) **Pop Density:** 126.1
Land: 40.0 sq. mi.; **Water:** 0.0 sq. mi.

Pierce City
City
ZIP: 65723 **Lat:** 36-56-48 N **Long:** 94-00-07 W
Pop: 1,382 (1990); 1,391 (1980) **Pop Density:** 1151.7
Land: 1.2 sq. mi.; **Water:** 0.0 sq. mi. **Elev:** 1199 ft.

Founded 1870. Incorporated 1870.
Name origin: For Andrew Pierce of Boston, president of the St. Louis and San Francisco Railroad.

Red Oak
Township
Lat: 37-13-56 N **Long:** 94-00-04 W
Pop: 338 (1990); 385 (1980) **Pop Density:** 8.2
Land: 41.4 sq. mi.; **Water:** 0.2 sq. mi.

Spring River
Township
Lat: 36-58-18 N **Long:** 93-48-55 W
Pop: 1,469 (1990); 1,491 (1980) **Pop Density:** 36.5
Land: 40.2 sq. mi.; **Water:** 0.0 sq. mi.

Stotts City
City
ZIP: 65756 **Lat:** 37-06-06 N **Long:** 93-56-51 W
Pop: 235 (1990); 232 (1980) **Pop Density:** 470.0
Land: 0.5 sq. mi.; **Water:** 0.0 sq. mi.

Incorporated 1895.

Turnback
Township
Lat: 37-06-57 N **Long:** 93-39-35 W
Pop: 881 (1990); 922 (1980) **Pop Density:** 21.1
Land: 41.7 sq. mi.; **Water:** 0.0 sq. mi.

Verona
Town
ZIP: 65769 **Lat:** 36-57-46 N **Long:** 93-47-38 W
Pop: 546 (1990); 592 (1980) **Pop Density:** 606.7
Land: 0.9 sq. mi.; **Water:** 0.0 sq. mi.

Incorporated 1868.
Name origin: For Verona, Italy.

Vineyard
Township
ZIP: 65756 **Lat:** 37-07-37 N **Long:** 93-59-16 W
Pop: 825 (1990); 796 (1980) **Pop Density:** 14.8
Land: 55.8 sq. mi.; **Water:** 0.0 sq. mi.

Lewis County
County Seat: Monticello (ZIP: 63457)

Pop: 10,233 (1990); 10,901 (1980) **Pop Density:** 20.3
Land: 505.1 sq. mi.; **Water:** 5.8 sq. mi. **Area Code:** 314

On the northeastern border of MO, northeast of Columbia; organized Jan 2, 1833 from Marion County.
Name origin: For Meriwether Lewis (1774–1809), co-leader of the Lewis and Clark Expedition (1804–06).

Canton
City
ZIP: 63435 **Lat:** 40-07-46 N **Long:** 91-31-25 W
Pop: 2,623 (1990); 2,435 (1980) **Pop Density:** 1380.5
Land: 1.9 sq. mi.; **Water:** 0.3 sq. mi.

Established 1830. Incorporated 1967.
Name origin: For Canton, OH.

*Canton
Township
ZIP: 63435 **Lat:** 40-10-39 N **Long:** 91-33-30 W
Pop: 3,484 (1990); 3,141 (1980) **Pop Density:** 63.0
Land: 55.3 sq. mi.; **Water:** 1.9 sq. mi.

Dickerson
Township
Lat: 40-06-24 N **Long:** 91-42-18 W
Pop: 515 (1990); 646 (1980) **Pop Density:** 8.1
Land: 63.6 sq. mi.; **Water:** 0.1 sq. mi.

Ewing
City
ZIP: 63440 **Lat:** 40-00-30 N **Long:** 91-42-51 W
Pop: 463 (1990); 400 (1980) **Pop Density:** 771.7
Land: 0.6 sq. mi.; **Water:** 0.0 sq. mi.

Incorporated 1970.

Highland
Township
Lat: 40-00-06 N **Long:** 91-42-16 W
Pop: 1,411 (1990); 1,631 (1980) **Pop Density:** 22.3
Land: 63.3 sq. mi.; **Water:** 0.1 sq. mi.

La Belle — City
ZIP: 63447 Lat: 40-06-59 N Long: 91-54-49 W
Pop: 655 (1990); 845 (1980) Pop Density: 1091.7
Land: 0.6 sq. mi.; Water: 0.0 sq. mi.
Laid out November 1871. Incorporated 1892.
Name origin: From French 'the beautiful,' probably suggested by the town's location.

*La Belle — Township
ZIP: 63447 Lat: 40-06-03 N Long: 91-52-06 W
Pop: 1,717 (1990); 1,945 (1980) Pop Density: 28.0
Land: 61.3 sq. mi.; Water: 0.2 sq. mi.

La Grange — City
ZIP: 63448 Lat: 40-02-52 N Long: 91-30-01 W
Pop: 1,102 (1990); 1,217 (1980) Pop Density: 787.1
Land: 1.4 sq. mi.; Water: 0.3 sq. mi.
Incorporated 1853.

Lewistown — Town
ZIP: 63452 Lat: 40-05-02 N Long: 91-48-45 W
Pop: 453 (1990); 502 (1980) Pop Density: 1510.0
Land: 0.3 sq. mi.; Water: 0.0 sq. mi. Elev: 725 ft.
Surveyed July 1, 1871, by Charles Peter. Incorporated 1924.
Name origin: For Lewis County.

Lyon — Township
Lat: 40-12-03 N Long: 91-41-55 W
Pop: 338 (1990); 377 (1980) Pop Density: 5.3
Land: 63.6 sq. mi.; Water: 0.2 sq. mi.

Monticello — Town
ZIP: 63457 Lat: 40-07-08 N Long: 91-42-45 W
Pop: 106 (1990); 134 (1980) Pop Density: 530.0
Land: 0.2 sq. mi.; Water: 0.0 sq. mi.
County seat since Sep 1833. Incorporated 1833.
Name origin: For third U.S. president Thomas Jefferson's (1743–1826) home in VA.

Reddish — Township
Lat: 40-12-38 N Long: 91-52-23 W
Pop: 343 (1990); 452 (1980) Pop Density: 5.5
Land: 62.9 sq. mi.; Water: 0.4 sq. mi.

Salem — Township
Lat: 40-00-02 N Long: 91-52-04 W
Pop: 310 (1990); 392 (1980) Pop Density: 5.1
Land: 61.3 sq. mi.; Water: 0.0 sq. mi.

Union — Township
Lat: 40-00-57 N Long: 91-32-37 W
Pop: 2,115 (1990); 2,317 (1980) Pop Density: 28.7
Land: 73.8 sq. mi.; Water: 2.9 sq. mi.

Lincoln County
County Seat: Troy (ZIP: 63379)

Pop: 28,892 (1990); 22,193 (1980) Pop Density: 45.8
Land: 630.5 sq. mi.; Water: 9.9 sq. mi. Area Code: 314
On the central eastern border of MO, north of St. Louis; organized Dec 14, 1818 (prior to statehood) from St. Charles County.
Name origin: For Gen. Benjamin Lincoln (1733–1810), Revolutionary War officer, U.S. Secretary of War (1781–83), and Lt. Gov. of MA (1788).

Bedford — Township
Lat: 39-00-01 N Long: 91-00-33 W
Pop: 5,851 (1990); 4,194 (1980) Pop Density: 138.6
Land: 42.2 sq. mi.; Water: 0.0 sq. mi.

Burr Oak — Township
Lat: 39-04-04 N Long: 90-46-03 W
Pop: 2,518 (1990); 1,724 (1980) Pop Density: 48.3
Land: 52.1 sq. mi.; Water: 4.1 sq. mi.

Cave — Town
Lat: 39-01-25 N Long: 91-02-42 W
Pop: 10 (1990) Pop Density: 10.0
Land: 1.0 sq. mi.; Water: 0.0 sq. mi.

Clark — Township
Lat: 38-54-34 N Long: 90-58-27 W
Pop: 3,538 (1990); 2,126 (1980) Pop Density: 53.3
Land: 66.4 sq. mi.; Water: 0.1 sq. mi.

Elsberry — City
ZIP: 63343 Lat: 39-10-12 N Long: 90-47-23 W
Pop: 1,898 (1990); 1,272 (1980) Pop Density: 1581.7
Land: 1.2 sq. mi.; Water: 0.0 sq. mi.
Incorporated 1883.
Name origin: Named in 1879 for Robert T. Elsberry, one of the early homesteaders.

Foley — City
ZIP: 63347 Lat: 39-02-44 N Long: 90-44-28 W
Pop: 209 (1990); 216 (1980) Pop Density: 2090.0
Land: 0.1 sq. mi.; Water: 0.0 sq. mi.
Incorporated 1900.

Hawk Point — City
ZIP: 63349 Lat: 38-58-16 N Long: 91-08-01 W
Pop: 472 (1990); 386 (1980) Pop Density: 2360.0
Land: 0.2 sq. mi.; Water: 0.0 sq. mi.
Incorporated 1908.

*Hawk Point — Township
ZIP: 63349 Lat: 38-58-42 N Long: 91-07-29 W
Pop: 1,550 (1990); 1,305 (1980) Pop Density: 30.5
Land: 50.8 sq. mi.; Water: 0.0 sq. mi.

Hurricane — Township
Lat: 39-09-36 N Long: 90-49-43 W
Pop: 3,739 (1990); 3,255 (1980) Pop Density: 37.2
Land: 100.6 sq. mi.; Water: 3.9 sq. mi.

Millwood — Township
ZIP: 63377 Lat: 39-05-38 N Long: 91-05-52 W
Pop: 665 (1990); 595 (1980) Pop Density: 16.1
Land: 41.2 sq. mi.; Water: 0.0 sq. mi.

MISSOURI, Lincoln County

Monroe
Township
Lat: 38-58-06 N **Long:** 90-48-02 W
Pop: 6,382 (1990); 5,254 (1980) **Pop Density:** 74.9
Land: 85.2 sq. mi.; **Water:** 1.5 sq. mi.

Moscow Mills
City
ZIP: 63362 **Lat:** 38-56-45 N **Long:** 90-55-09 W
Pop: 924 (1990); 484 (1980) **Pop Density:** 1540.0
Land: 0.6 sq. mi.; **Water:** 0.0 sq. mi.
Incorporated 1821.

Nineveh
Township
Lat: 39-05-16 N **Long:** 91-12-43 W
Pop: 351 (1990); 415 (1980) **Pop Density:** 9.5
Land: 37.0 sq. mi.; **Water:** 0.0 sq. mi.

Old Monroe
City
ZIP: 63369 **Lat:** 38-55-52 N **Long:** 90-44-49 W
Pop: 242 (1990); 272 (1980) **Pop Density:** 2420.0
Land: 0.1 sq. mi.; **Water:** 0.0 sq. mi.
Incorporated 1960.

Prairie
Township
Lat: 39-00-55 N **Long:** 91-13-24 W
Pop: 266 (1990); 248 (1980) **Pop Density:** 15.6
Land: 17.1 sq. mi.; **Water:** 0.0 sq. mi.

Silex
Village
ZIP: 63377 **Lat:** 39-07-34 N **Long:** 91-03-26 W
Pop: 197 (1990); 287 (1980) **Pop Density:** 985.0
Land: 0.2 sq. mi.; **Water:** 0.0 sq. mi. **Elev:** 508 ft.
Incorporated 1886.

Snow Hill
Township
Lat: 39-03-01 N **Long:** 90-53-53 W
Pop: 1,851 (1990); 1,247 (1980) **Pop Density:** 51.3
Land: 36.1 sq. mi.; **Water:** 0.2 sq. mi.

Troy
City
ZIP: 63379 **Lat:** 38-58-36 N **Long:** 90-58-31 W
Pop: 3,811 (1990); 2,624 (1980) **Pop Density:** 1190.9
Land: 3.2 sq. mi.; **Water:** 0.0 sq. mi.
Platted in 1819. Incorporated 1881.
Name origin: Named by Joshua N. Robbins for Troy, NY.

Truxton
Village
ZIP: 63381 **Lat:** 39-00-07 N **Long:** 91-14-26 W
Pop: 90 (1990) **Pop Density:** 450.0
Land: 0.2 sq. mi.; **Water:** 0.0 sq. mi.

Union
Township
Lat: 39-08-45 N **Long:** 91-00-25 W
Pop: 1,865 (1990); 1,532 (1980) **Pop Density:** 29.4
Land: 63.5 sq. mi.; **Water:** 0.1 sq. mi.

Waverly
Township
Lat: 39-10-40 N **Long:** 91-07-25 W
Pop: 316 (1990); 298 (1980) **Pop Density:** 8.2
Land: 38.5 sq. mi.; **Water:** 0.0 sq. mi.

Whiteside
Village
ZIP: 63387 **Lat:** 39-11-00 N **Long:** 91-00-59 W
Pop: 79 (1990); 97 (1980) **Pop Density:** 790.0
Land: 0.1 sq. mi.; **Water:** 0.0 sq. mi.
Incorporated 1907.

Winfield
City
ZIP: 63389 **Lat:** 38-59-43 N **Long:** 90-44-23 W
Pop: 672 (1990); 592 (1980) **Pop Density:** 1680.0
Land: 0.4 sq. mi.; **Water:** 0.0 sq. mi. **Elev:** 446 ft.
Incorporated 1882.

Linn County
County Seat: Linneus (ZIP: 64653)

Pop: 13,885 (1990); 15,495 (1980) **Pop Density:** 22.4
Land: 620.4 sq. mi.; **Water:** 1.1 sq. mi. **Area Code:** 816
In north-central MO, east of St. Joseph; organized Jan 6, 1837 from Chariton County.
Name origin: For Lewis Fields Linn (1795–1843), U.S. senator from MO (1833–43).

Baker
Township
Lat: 39-55-05 N **Long:** 92-55-23 W
Pop: 252 (1990); 311 (1980) **Pop Density:** 5.3
Land: 47.2 sq. mi.; **Water:** 0.0 sq. mi.

Benton
Township
Lat: 39-59-36 N **Long:** 93-10-23 W
Pop: 650 (1990); 719 (1980) **Pop Density:** 20.6
Land: 31.6 sq. mi.; **Water:** 0.0 sq. mi.

Brookfield
City
ZIP: 64628 **Lat:** 39-47-08 N **Long:** 93-04-34 W
Pop: 4,888 (1990); 5,555 (1980) **Pop Density:** 1163.8
Land: 4.2 sq. mi.; **Water:** 0.0 sq. mi. **Elev:** 767 ft.
In northern MO, 25 mi. east of Chillicothe. Incorporated 1865. Not coextensive with the town of the same name.

*Brookfield
Township
ZIP: 64628 **Lat:** 39-46-21 N **Long:** 93-04-22 W
Pop: 5,494 (1990); 6,136 (1980) **Pop Density:** 122.6
Land: 44.8 sq. mi.; **Water:** 0.2 sq. mi.

Browning
City
ZIP: 64630 **Lat:** 40-02-02 N **Long:** 93-09-36 W
Pop: 255 (1990); 281 (1980) **Pop Density:** 637.5
Land: 0.4 sq. mi.; **Water:** 0.0 sq. mi.
Founded 1872. Incorporated 1878. Part of the town is also in Sullivan County.
Name origin: For Mrs. Browning, the wife of an official of the C, B & Q Railroad. Previously called Linnivan, since it was located near the Linn and Sullivan County lines.

MISSOURI, Livingston County

Bucklin — City
ZIP: 64631 Lat: 39-46-56 N Long: 92-53-21 W
Pop: 616 (1990); 713 (1980) Pop Density: 560.0
Land: 1.1 sq. mi.; Water: 0.0 sq. mi. Elev: 910 ft.
Founded 1854. Incorporated 1866. Not coextensive with the town of the same name.
Name origin: For Maj. James H. Bucklin, chief engineer of the J. & St. J. Railway Company.

*Bucklin — Township
ZIP: 64631 Lat: 39-48-39 N Long: 92-54-18 W
Pop: 899 (1990); 1,029 (1980) Pop Density: 20.2
Land: 44.5 sq. mi.; Water: 0.0 sq. mi.

Clay — Township
Lat: 39-52-26 N Long: 93-17-42 W
Pop: 245 (1990); 292 (1980) Pop Density: 4.9
Land: 50.3 sq. mi.; Water: 0.0 sq. mi.

Enterprise — Township
Lat: 40-00-09 N Long: 93-03-51 W
Pop: 108 (1990); 144 (1980) Pop Density: 4.3
Land: 25.2 sq. mi.; Water: 0.0 sq. mi.

Grantsville — Township
Lat: 39-55-32 N Long: 93-03-44 W
Pop: 202 (1990); 267 (1980) Pop Density: 4.4
Land: 45.9 sq. mi.; Water: 0.0 sq. mi.

Jackson — Township
Lat: 39-59-02 N Long: 93-17-11 W
Pop: 222 (1990); 266 (1980) Pop Density: 3.9
Land: 56.3 sq. mi.; Water: 0.0 sq. mi.

Jefferson — Township
Lat: 39-46-12 N Long: 93-10-42 W
Pop: 793 (1990); 825 (1980) Pop Density: 14.2
Land: 56.0 sq. mi.; Water: 0.1 sq. mi.

Laclede — City
ZIP: 64651 Lat: 39-47-17 N Long: 93-10-10 W
Pop: 410 (1990); 445 (1980) Pop Density: 341.7
Land: 1.2 sq. mi.; Water: 0.0 sq. mi.
Incorporated 1866.

Linneus — City
ZIP: 64653 Lat: 39-52-36 N Long: 93-11-14 W
Pop: 364 (1990); 421 (1980) Pop Density: 330.9
Land: 1.1 sq. mi.; Water: 0.0 sq. mi. Elev: 837 ft.
Incorporated 1859.

Locust Creek — Township
Lat: 39-53-12 N Long: 93-09-12 W
Pop: 642 (1990); 762 (1980) Pop Density: 12.9
Land: 49.8 sq. mi.; Water: 0.0 sq. mi.

Marceline — City
ZIP: 64658 Lat: 39-43-01 N Long: 92-56-50 W
Pop: 2,638 (1990); 2,938 (1980) Pop Density: 824.4
Land: 3.2 sq. mi.; Water: 0.0 sq. mi.
Founded 1887. Incorporated 1888. Part of the town is also in Chariton County.
Name origin: For the wife of a railroad official.

*Marceline — Township
ZIP: 64658 Lat: 39-43-34 N Long: 92-56-40 W
Pop: 3,113 (1990); 3,368 (1980) Pop Density: 102.7
Land: 30.3 sq. mi.; Water: 0.2 sq. mi.

Meadville — City
ZIP: 64659 Lat: 39-47-15 N Long: 93-18-09 W
Pop: 360 (1990); 416 (1980) Pop Density: 900.0
Land: 0.4 sq. mi.; Water: 0.0 sq. mi. Elev: 756 ft.
Incorporated 1859.

North Salem — Township
Lat: 40-00-02 N Long: 92-56-12 W
Pop: 142 (1990); 194 (1980) Pop Density: 3.2
Land: 44.4 sq. mi.; Water: 0.0 sq. mi.

Parson Creek — Township
Lat: 39-46-13 N Long: 93-17-44 W
Pop: 774 (1990); 797 (1980) Pop Density: 13.7
Land: 56.7 sq. mi.; Water: 0.5 sq. mi.

Purdin — City
ZIP: 64674 Lat: 39-57-00 N Long: 93-10-01 W
Pop: 217 (1990); 243 (1980) Pop Density: 723.3
Land: 0.3 sq. mi.; Water: 0.0 sq. mi.
Incorporated 1969.
Name origin: For Allen W. Purdin, owner of the land on which the town was laid out.

Yellow Creek — Township
Lat: 39-48-52 N Long: 92-59-28 W
Pop: 349 (1990); 385 (1980) Pop Density: 9.4
Land: 37.2 sq. mi.; Water: 0.1 sq. mi.

Livingston County
County Seat: Chillicothe (ZIP: 64601)

Pop: 14,592 (1990); 15,739 (1980) Pop Density: 27.3
Land: 534.6 sq. mi.; Water: 3.9 sq. mi. Area Code: 816
In north-central MO, east of St. Joseph; organized Jan 6, 1837 from Carroll County.
Name origin: For Edward Livingston (1764–1836), NY legislator, LA legislator and U.S. senator (1829–31), and U.S. Secretary of State (1831–33).

Blue Mound — Township
Lat: 39-40-07 N Long: 93-35-28 W
Pop: 468 (1990); 544 (1980) Pop Density: 11.1
Land: 42.3 sq. mi.; Water: 0.2 sq. mi.

Chillicothe — City
ZIP: 64601 Lat: 39-47-29 N Long: 93-33-14 W
Pop: 8,804 (1990); 9,089 (1980) Pop Density: 2201.0
Land: 4.0 sq. mi.; Water: 0.0 sq. mi. Elev: 798 ft.
In northern MO, 75 mi. northeast of Kansas City. County

MISSOURI, Livingston County

seat; platted 1837. Incorporated 1855. Not coextensive with the town of the same name.
Name origin: For Chillicothe, OH; from the Shawnee Indian term meaning 'village.'

*Chillicothe — Township
Lat: 39-46-57 N **Long:** 93-31-39 W
Pop: 9,833 (1990); 10,081 (1980) **Pop Density:** 180.1
Land: 54.6 sq. mi.; **Water:** 0.8 sq. mi.

Chula — City
ZIP: 64635 **Lat:** 39-55-17 N **Long:** 93-28-34 W
Pop: 183 (1990); 244 (1980) **Pop Density:** 915.0
Land: 0.2 sq. mi.; **Water:** 0.0 sq. mi.
Incorporated 1885.

Cream Ridge — Township
Lat: 39-55-32 N **Long:** 93-31-31 W
Pop: 551 (1990); 638 (1980) **Pop Density:** 12.1
Land: 45.7 sq. mi.; **Water:** 0.2 sq. mi.

Fairview — Township
Lat: 39-40-19 N **Long:** 93-29-16 W
Pop: 388 (1990); 473 (1980) **Pop Density:** 8.4
Land: 46.2 sq. mi.; **Water:** 0.6 sq. mi.

Grand River — Township
Lat: 39-39-54 N **Long:** 93-21-26 W
Pop: 250 (1990); 306 (1980) **Pop Density:** 4.7
Land: 53.3 sq. mi.; **Water:** 0.9 sq. mi.

Green — Township
Lat: 39-43-24 N **Long:** 93-37-11 W
Pop: 361 (1990); 418 (1980) **Pop Density:** 16.9
Land: 21.3 sq. mi.; **Water:** 0.2 sq. mi.

Jackson — Township
Lat: 39-53-32 N **Long:** 93-40-18 W
Pop: 424 (1990); 431 (1980) **Pop Density:** 6.1
Land: 69.9 sq. mi.; **Water:** 0.6 sq. mi.

Ludlow — Town
ZIP: 64656 **Lat:** 39-39-12 N **Long:** 93-42-11 W
Pop: 147 (1990); 178 (1980) **Pop Density:** 1470.0
Land: 0.1 sq. mi.; **Water:** 0.0 sq. mi.
Incorporated 1922.

Medicine — Township
Lat: 39-55-16 N **Long:** 93-24-10 W
Pop: 134 (1990); 176 (1980) **Pop Density:** 4.5
Land: 29.9 sq. mi.; **Water:** 0.0 sq. mi.

Monroe — Township
Lat: 39-39-19 N **Long:** 93-42-16 W
Pop: 355 (1990); 438 (1980) **Pop Density:** 10.2
Land: 34.9 sq. mi.; **Water:** 0.0 sq. mi.

Mooresville — Village
ZIP: 64664 **Lat:** 39-44-46 N **Long:** 93-43-12 W
Pop: 100 (1990); 129 (1980) **Pop Density:** 500.0
Land: 0.2 sq. mi.; **Water:** 0.0 sq. mi. **Elev:** 920 ft.
Incorporated 1874. Not coextensive with the town of the same name.

*Mooresville — Township
ZIP: 64664 **Lat:** 39-44-31 N **Long:** 93-42-58 W
Pop: 320 (1990); 386 (1980) **Pop Density:** 11.5
Land: 27.9 sq. mi.; **Water:** 0.1 sq. mi.

Rich Hill — Township
Lat: 39-50-18 N **Long:** 93-29-03 W
Pop: 808 (1990); 996 (1980) **Pop Density:** 22.0
Land: 36.8 sq. mi.; **Water:** 0.1 sq. mi.

Sampsel — Township
Lat: 39-49-34 N **Long:** 93-41-32 W
Pop: 219 (1990); 283 (1980) **Pop Density:** 5.6
Land: 38.8 sq. mi.; **Water:** 0.2 sq. mi.

Utica — Village
ZIP: 64686 **Lat:** 39-44-44 N **Long:** 93-37-45 W
Pop: 299 (1990) **Pop Density:** 332.2
Land: 0.9 sq. mi.; **Water:** 0.0 sq. mi.
Incorporated 1885.

Wheeling — City
Lat: 39-47-11 N **Long:** 93-23-11 W
Pop: 284 (1990); 379 (1980) **Pop Density:** 946.7
Land: 0.3 sq. mi.; **Water:** 0.0 sq. mi. **Elev:** 749 ft.
Incorporated 1964. Not coextensive with the town of the same name.

*Wheeling — Township
Lat: 39-48-34 N **Long:** 93-23-34 W
Pop: 481 (1990); 569 (1980) **Pop Density:** 14.6
Land: 33.0 sq. mi.; **Water:** 0.0 sq. mi.

> **Macon County**
> **County Seat: Macon (ZIP: 63552)**
>
> **Pop:** 15,345 (1990); 16,313 (1980)   **Pop Density:** 19.1
> **Land:** 803.8 sq. mi.; **Water:** 8.8 sq. mi.   **Area Code:** 816
> In north-central MO, northwest of Columbia; organized Jan 6, 1837 from Randolph and Chariton counties.
> **Name origin:** For Nathaniel Macon (1757–1837), Revolutionary War soldier, NC legislator, U.S. representative (1791–1815), U.S. senator (1815–28), and president of the NC constitutional convention (1835).

Atlanta City
ZIP: 63530   **Lat:** 39-53-52 N **Long:** 92-28-47 W
Pop: 411 (1990); 441 (1980)   **Pop Density:** 1370.0
Land: 0.3 sq. mi.; **Water:** 0.0 sq. mi.
Incorporated 1858.

Bevier City
ZIP: 63532   **Lat:** 39-44-56 N **Long:** 92-33-49 W
Pop: 643 (1990); 733 (1980)   **Pop Density:** 714.4
Land: 0.9 sq. mi.; **Water:** 0.0 sq. mi.   **Elev:** 791 ft.
Incorporated 1881.
Name origin: For Confederate leader Col. Robert Bevier of KY.

*Bevier Township
ZIP: 63532   **Lat:** 39-44-25 N **Long:** 92-33-58 W
Pop: 1,130 (1990); 1,274 (1980)   **Pop Density:** 38.4
Land: 29.4 sq. mi.; **Water:** 0.4 sq. mi.

Callao City
ZIP: 63534   **Lat:** 39-45-43 N **Long:** 92-37-23 W
Pop: 332 (1990); 326 (1980)   **Pop Density:** 664.0
Land: 0.5 sq. mi.; **Water:** 0.0 sq. mi.   **Elev:** 819 ft.
Incorporated 1889.

*Callao Township
ZIP: 63534   **Lat:** 39-44-25 N **Long:** 92-39-38 W
Pop: 553 (1990); 567 (1980)   **Pop Density:** 18.6
Land: 29.8 sq. mi.; **Water:** 0.2 sq. mi.

Chariton Township
Lat: 39-39-27 N **Long:** 92-34-14 W
Pop: 332 (1990); 349 (1980)   **Pop Density:** 11.4
Land: 29.1 sq. mi.; **Water:** 0.8 sq. mi.

Drake Township
Lat: 40-00-20 N **Long:** 92-47-29 W
Pop: 55 (1990); 79 (1980)   **Pop Density:** 1.8
Land: 31.3 sq. mi.; **Water:** 0.0 sq. mi.

Eagle Township
Lat: 39-49-22 N **Long:** 92-27-50 W
Pop: 376 (1990); 390 (1980)   **Pop Density:** 10.8
Land: 34.8 sq. mi.; **Water:** 1.2 sq. mi.

Easley Township
Lat: 39-59-59 N **Long:** 92-40-32 W
Pop: 218 (1990); 286 (1980)   **Pop Density:** 6.9
Land: 31.7 sq. mi.; **Water:** 0.1 sq. mi.

Elmer City
ZIP: 63538   **Lat:** 39-57-27 N **Long:** 92-38-59 W
Pop: 91 (1990); 180 (1980)   **Pop Density:** 455.0
Land: 0.2 sq. mi.; **Water:** 0.0 sq. mi.
Incorporated 1960.

Ethel Town
ZIP: 63539   **Lat:** 39-53-36 N **Long:** 92-44-25 W
Pop: 71 (1990); 145 (1980)   **Pop Density:** 355.0
Land: 0.2 sq. mi.; **Water:** 0.0 sq. mi.   **Elev:** 850 ft.
Incorporated 1896.

Hudson Township
Lat: 39-44-16 N **Long:** 92-27-52 W
Pop: 6,846 (1990); 6,752 (1980)   **Pop Density:** 199.0
Land: 34.4 sq. mi.; **Water:** 1.4 sq. mi.

Independence Township
Lat: 39-55-05 N **Long:** 92-33-57 W
Pop: 165 (1990); 202 (1980)   **Pop Density:** 4.6
Land: 36.0 sq. mi.; **Water:** 0.0 sq. mi.

Jackson Township
Lat: 39-54-39 N **Long:** 92-20-49 W
Pop: 107 (1990); 154 (1980)   **Pop Density:** 3.0
Land: 36.2 sq. mi.; **Water:** 0.0 sq. mi.

Johnston Township
Lat: 39-59-32 N **Long:** 92-21-47 W
Pop: 52 (1990); 79 (1980)   **Pop Density:** 3.0
Land: 17.1 sq. mi.; **Water:** 0.0 sq. mi.

La Plata City
ZIP: 63549   **Lat:** 40-01-30 N **Long:** 92-29-27 W
Pop: 1,401 (1990); 1,423 (1980)   **Pop Density:** 1167.5
Land: 1.2 sq. mi.; **Water:** 0.0 sq. mi.   **Elev:** 941 ft.
Laid out 1855. Incorporated 1881.
Name origin: From Spanish 'the silver,' for silver deposits found here.

*La Plata Township
ZIP: 63549   **Lat:** 39-59-27 N **Long:** 92-27-15 W
Pop: 1,673 (1990); 1,833 (1980)   **Pop Density:** 50.1
Land: 33.4 sq. mi.; **Water:** 0.1 sq. mi.

Liberty Township
Lat: 39-49-32 N **Long:** 92-34-22 W
Pop: 174 (1990); 219 (1980)   **Pop Density:** 5.1
Land: 34.4 sq. mi.; **Water:** 1.5 sq. mi.

Lingo Township
Lat: 39-44-20 N **Long:** 92-46-26 W
Pop: 583 (1990); 649 (1980)   **Pop Density:** 12.0
Land: 48.4 sq. mi.; **Water:** 0.0 sq. mi.

Lyda Township
Lat: 39-54-22 N **Long:** 92-27-14 W
Pop: 625 (1990); 694 (1980)   **Pop Density:** 17.5
Land: 35.7 sq. mi.; **Water:** 0.1 sq. mi.

Macon
City
ZIP: 63552   Lat: 39-44-19 N   Long: 92-28-13 W
Pop: 5,571 (1990); 5,680 (1980)   Pop Density: 1114.2
Land: 5.0 sq. mi.; Water: 0.0 sq. mi.
Incorporated 1859.
Name origin: For Nathaniel Macon (1757–1837), Revolutionary War soldier, NC legislator, U.S. representative (1791–1815), U.S. senator (1815–28), and president of the NC constitutional convention (1835).

Middle Fork
Township
Lat: 39-38-57 N   Long: 92-20-40 W
Pop: 220 (1990); 227 (1980)   Pop Density: 6.2
Land: 35.7 sq. mi.; Water: 0.0 sq. mi.

Morrow
Township
Lat: 39-39-43 N   Long: 92-39-24 W
Pop: 164 (1990); 196 (1980)   Pop Density: 7.5
Land: 21.8 sq. mi.; Water: 2.2 sq. mi.

Narrows
Township
Lat: 39-39-10 N   Long: 92-28-18 W
Pop: 332 (1990); 363 (1980)   Pop Density: 9.3
Land: 35.8 sq. mi.; Water: 0.0 sq. mi.

New Cambria
Town
ZIP: 63558   Lat: 39-46-30 N   Long: 92-45-04 W
Pop: 223 (1990); 246 (1980)   Pop Density: 446.0
Land: 0.5 sq. mi.; Water: 0.0 sq. mi.   Elev: 855 ft.
Incorporated 1960.

Richland
Township
Lat: 39-59-59 N   Long: 92-34-16 W
Pop: 292 (1990); 247 (1980)   Pop Density: 8.8
Land: 33.0 sq. mi.; Water: 0.0 sq. mi.

Round Grove
Township
Lat: 39-44-15 N   Long: 92-21-16 W
Pop: 309 (1990); 371 (1980)   Pop Density: 8.6
Land: 35.8 sq. mi.; Water: 0.0 sq. mi.

Russell
Township
Lat: 39-49-34 N   Long: 92-47-47 W
Pop: 173 (1990); 222 (1980)   Pop Density: 4.7
Land: 36.5 sq. mi.; Water: 0.0 sq. mi.

South Gifford
Village
Lat: 40-01-33 N   Long: 92-40-56 W
Pop: 64 (1990); 98 (1980)   Pop Density: 320.0
Land: 0.2 sq. mi.; Water: 0.0 sq. mi.
Incorporated 1905.

Ten Mile
Township
Lat: 39-49-23 N   Long: 92-20-58 W
Pop: 352 (1990); 356 (1980)   Pop Density: 9.9
Land: 35.7 sq. mi.; Water: 0.0 sq. mi.

Valley
Township
Lat: 39-49-13 N   Long: 92-41-21 W
Pop: 162 (1990); 193 (1980)   Pop Density: 4.5
Land: 36.1 sq. mi.; Water: 0.3 sq. mi.

Walnut Creek
Township
Lat: 39-54-57 N   Long: 92-40-52 W
Pop: 257 (1990); 351 (1980)   Pop Density: 7.2
Land: 35.7 sq. mi.; Water: 0.4 sq. mi.

White
Township
Lat: 39-55-40 N   Long: 92-47-55 W
Pop: 195 (1990); 260 (1980)   Pop Density: 5.4
Land: 36.1 sq. mi.; Water: 0.0 sq. mi.

Madison County
County Seat: Fredericktown (ZIP: 63645)

Pop: 11,127 (1990); 10,725 (1980)   Pop Density: 22.4
Land: 496.8 sq. mi.; Water: 0.9 sq. mi.   Area Code: 314
In southeastern MO, northwest of Cape Girardeau; organized Dec 14, 1818 (prior to statehood) from Ste. Genevieve and Cape Girardeau counties.
Name origin: For James Madison (1751–1836), fourth U.S. president.

Big Creek
Township
ZIP: 63655   Lat: 37-20-08 N   Long: 90-15-10 W
Pop: 209 (1990); 204 (1980)   Pop Density: 5.2
Land: 40.3 sq. mi.; Water: 0.0 sq. mi.

Castor
Township
Lat: 37-32-40 N   Long: 90-11-19 W
Pop: 742 (1990); 686 (1980)   Pop Density: 13.7
Land: 54.3 sq. mi.; Water: 0.0 sq. mi.

Central
Township
Lat: 37-26-10 N   Long: 90-22-22 W
Pop: 508 (1990); 485 (1980)   Pop Density: 9.4
Land: 54.0 sq. mi.; Water: 0.0 sq. mi.

Cobalt City
Village
ZIP: 63645   Lat: 37-32-41 N   Long: 90-17-12 W
Pop: 254 (1990); 272 (1980)   Pop Density: 2540.0
Land: 0.1 sq. mi.; Water: 0.0 sq. mi.
Incorporated 1952.

Fredericktown
City
ZIP: 63645   Lat: 37-33-52 N   Long: 90-17-47 W
Pop: 3,950 (1990); 4,036 (1980)   Pop Density: 1161.8
Land: 3.4 sq. mi.; Water: 0.1 sq. mi.   Elev: 743 ft.
In southeastern MO, 45 mi. west-northwest of Cape Girardeau. Incorporated 1818.

Junction City
Village
ZIP: 63645   Lat: 37-34-26 N   Long: 90-17-38 W
Pop: 326 (1990); 238 (1980)   Pop Density: 815.0
Land: 0.4 sq. mi.; Water: 0.0 sq. mi.
Incorporated 1951.

Liberty
Township
Lat: 37-25-48 N   Long: 90-30-01 W
Pop: 281 (1990); 368 (1980)   Pop Density: 4.3
Land: 64.8 sq. mi.; Water: 0.0 sq. mi.

Marquand City
ZIP: 63655 Lat: 37-25-43 N Long: 90-10-01 W
Pop: 278 (1990); 397 (1980) Pop Density: 1390.0
Land: 0.2 sq. mi.; Water: 0.0 sq. mi. Elev: 571 ft.
Incorporated 1967.
Name origin: For W. G. Marquand, who donated to the local church.

*Marquand Township
ZIP: 63655 Lat: 37-25-42 N Long: 90-13-11 W
Pop: 745 (1990); 924 (1980) Pop Density: 12.6
Land: 59.2 sq. mi.; Water: 0.0 sq. mi.

Mine La Motte Township
Lat: 37-37-04 N Long: 90-17-22 W
Pop: 620 (1990); 408 (1980) Pop Density: 29.1
Land: 21.3 sq. mi.; Water: 0.4 sq. mi.

Polk Township
Lat: 37-35-37 N Long: 90-27-05 W
Pop: 809 (1990); 741 (1980) Pop Density: 10.3
Land: 78.6 sq. mi.; Water: 0.1 sq. mi.

St. Francois Township
Lat: 37-30-31 N Long: 90-24-21 W
Pop: 249 (1990); 331 (1980) Pop Density: 11.0
Land: 22.7 sq. mi.; Water: 0.0 sq. mi.

St. Michael Township
Lat: 37-32-43 N Long: 90-17-37 W
Pop: 6,698 (1990); 6,272 (1980) Pop Density: 125.4
Land: 53.4 sq. mi.; Water: 0.2 sq. mi.

Twelvemile Township
Lat: 37-21-33 N Long: 90-24-12 W
Pop: 266 (1990); 306 (1980) Pop Density: 5.5
Land: 48.1 sq. mi.; Water: 0.0 sq. mi.

Maries County
County Seat: Vienna (ZIP: 65582)

Pop: 7,976 (1990); 7,551 (1980) Pop Density: 15.1
Land: 527.8 sq. mi.; Water: 2.2 sq. mi. Area Code: 314
In east-central MO, southwest of St. Louis; established Mar 2, 1855 from Osage and Pulaski counties.
Name origin: For the Maries River, which runs through it; a corruption of French *marais* 'swamp.'

Argyle Town
Lat: 38-17-16 N Long: 92-01-26 W
Pop: 7 (1990); 10 (1980) Pop Density: 233.3
Land: 0.03 sq. mi.; Water: 0.0 sq. mi.
Incorporated 1908. Part of the town is also in Osage County.
Name origin: Named by early settlers for their homeland in Scotland.

Belle City
ZIP: 65013 Lat: 38-16-59 N Long: 91-43-26 W
Pop: 1,069 (1990); 1,099 (1980) Pop Density: 1069.0
Land: 1.0 sq. mi.; Water: 0.0 sq. mi. Elev: 1039 ft.
Incorporated 1901. Part of the town is also in Osage County.

Boone Township
Lat: 38-13-42 N Long: 92-06-59 W
Pop: 672 (1990); 700 (1980) Pop Density: 8.3
Land: 81.4 sq. mi.; Water: 0.0 sq. mi.

Dry Creek Township
Lat: 38-04-10 N Long: 91-59-00 W
Pop: 539 (1990); 428 (1980) Pop Density: 9.8
Land: 55.2 sq. mi.; Water: 0.4 sq. mi.

Jackson Township
Lat: 38-12-05 N Long: 91-56-31 W
Pop: 2,009 (1990); 1,897 (1980) Pop Density: 16.0
Land: 125.5 sq. mi.; Water: 1.2 sq. mi.

Jefferson Township
Lat: 38-12-58 N Long: 91-44-19 W
Pop: 2,399 (1990); 2,310 (1980) Pop Density: 25.7
Land: 93.3 sq. mi.; Water: 0.3 sq. mi.

Johnson Township
Lat: 38-06-20 N Long: 91-43-10 W
Pop: 1,128 (1990); 1,047 (1980) Pop Density: 17.2
Land: 65.5 sq. mi.; Water: 0.0 sq. mi.

Miller Township
Lat: 38-05-36 N Long: 92-07-26 W
Pop: 946 (1990); 867 (1980) Pop Density: 13.1
Land: 72.0 sq. mi.; Water: 0.1 sq. mi.

Spring Creek Township
Lat: 38-06-02 N Long: 91-50-17 W
Pop: 283 (1990); 302 (1980) Pop Density: 8.1
Land: 34.9 sq. mi.; Water: 0.2 sq. mi.

Vienna City
ZIP: 65582 Lat: 38-11-15 N Long: 91-56-52 W
Pop: 611 (1990); 514 (1980) Pop Density: 763.8
Land: 0.8 sq. mi.; Water: 0.0 sq. mi. Elev: 873 ft.
County seat 1855. Incorporated 1953.
Name origin: For Vienna, Austria.

Marion County
County Seat: Palmyra (ZIP: 63461)

Pop: 27,682 (1990); 28,638 (1980)   **Pop Density:** 63.2
Land: 438.1 sq. mi.; **Water:** 6.0 sq. mi.   **Area Code:** 314

On the northeastern border of MO, north of St. Louis; established Dec 14, 1822 from Ralls County.

Name origin: For Gen. Francis Marion (c. 1732–95), SC soldier and legislator, known as "The Swamp Fox" for his tactics in the Carolina swamps during the Revolutionary War.

Fabius — Township
Lat: 39-53-07 N   Long: 91-32-27 W
Pop: 1,207 (1990); 1,279 (1980)   **Pop Density:** 15.0
Land: 80.5 sq. mi.; **Water:** 2.2 sq. mi.

Hannibal — City
ZIP: 63401   Lat: 39-42-34 N   Long: 91-22-49 W
Pop: 17,735 (1990); 18,639 (1980)   **Pop Density:** 1689.0
Land: 10.5 sq. mi.; **Water:** 0.5 sq. mi.   **Elev:** 491 ft.

In northeastern MO on the Mississippi River. Incorporated 1845. Part of the town is also in Ralls County.

Name origin: Named in 1819 for the Carthaginian general (247–183 B.C.), who invaded Roman territory by crossing the Alps.

Liberty — Township
Lat: 39-47-37 N   Long: 91-29-27 W
Pop: 4,096 (1990); 4,099 (1980)   **Pop Density:** 78.6
Land: 52.1 sq. mi.; **Water:** 2.0 sq. mi.

Mason — Township
Lat: 39-43-21 N   Long: 91-22-59 W
Pop: 18,385 (1990); 19,074 (1980)   **Pop Density:** 1004.6
Land: 18.3 sq. mi.; **Water:** 1.7 sq. mi.

Miller — Township
Lat: 39-43-27 N   Long: 91-27-52 W
Pop: 967 (1990); 877 (1980)   **Pop Density:** 32.1
Land: 30.1 sq. mi.; **Water:** 0.0 sq. mi.

Monroe City — City
Lat: 39-39-39 N   Long: 91-43-56 W
Pop: 420 (1990); 370 (1980)   **Pop Density:** 466.7
Land: 0.9 sq. mi.; **Water:** 0.0 sq. mi.   **Elev:** 749 ft.

Incorporated 1857. Part of the town is also in Monroe and Ralls counties.

Name origin: For James Monroe (1758–1831), fifth U.S. president.

Palmyra — City
ZIP: 63461   Lat: 39-47-47 N   Long: 91-31-28 W
Pop: 3,371 (1990); 3,469 (1980)   **Pop Density:** 1532.3
Land: 2.2 sq. mi.; **Water:** 0.0 sq. mi.   **Elev:** 641 ft.

In northeast MO, 10 mi. northwest of Hannibal. Platted 1819. Incorporated 1855.

Name origin: For the Syrian city built by King Solomon, probably because it, too, was founded in the wilderness.

Round Grove — Township
Lat: 39-54-28 N   Long: 91-42-27 W
Pop: 780 (1990); 833 (1980)   **Pop Density:** 13.2
Land: 59.2 sq. mi.; **Water:** 0.0 sq. mi.

South River — Township
Lat: 39-43-14 N   Long: 91-33-48 W
Pop: 254 (1990); 350 (1980)   **Pop Density:** 9.3
Land: 27.2 sq. mi.; **Water:** 0.0 sq. mi.

Union — Township
Lat: 39-50-20 N   Long: 91-44-06 W
Pop: 675 (1990); 748 (1980)   **Pop Density:** 11.2
Land: 60.1 sq. mi.; **Water:** 0.0 sq. mi.

Warren — Township
Lat: 39-43-54 N   Long: 91-45-05 W
Pop: 1,318 (1990); 1,378 (1980)   **Pop Density:** 11.9
Land: 110.6 sq. mi.; **Water:** 0.0 sq. mi.

McDonald County
County Seat: Pineville (ZIP: 64856)

Pop: 16,938 (1990); 14,917 (1980)　　**Pop Density:** 31.4
Land: 539.5 sq. mi.; **Water:** 0.2 sq. mi.　　**Area Code:** 417
In southwestern corner of MO, south of Joplin; organized Mar 3, 1849 from Newton County.
Name origin: For Sgt. Alexander McDonald, a soldier in the American Revolution.

Anderson　　City
ZIP: 64831　　**Lat:** 36-39-17 N **Long:** 94-26-54 W
Pop: 1,432 (1990); 1,237 (1980)　　**Pop Density:** 753.7
Land: 1.9 sq. mi.; **Water:** 0.0 sq. mi.　　**Elev:** 890 ft.
Incorporated 1909.

Anderson East　　Township
　　Lat: 36-39-06 N **Long:** 94-25-24 W
Pop: 1,390 (1990); 1,241 (1980)　　**Pop Density:** 93.3
Land: 14.9 sq. mi.; **Water:** 0.0 sq. mi.

Anderson West　　Township
　　Lat: 36-39-58 N **Long:** 94-27-53 W
Pop: 1,451 (1990); 1,387 (1980)　　**Pop Density:** 72.9
Land: 19.9 sq. mi.; **Water:** 0.0 sq. mi.

Buffalo Hart　　Township
　　Lat: 36-44-26 N **Long:** 94-35-22 W
Pop: 311 (1990); 319 (1980)　　**Pop Density:** 24.5
Land: 12.7 sq. mi.; **Water:** 0.0 sq. mi.

Buffalo May　　Township
　　Lat: 36-44-05 N **Long:** 94-30-38 W
Pop: 445 (1990); 404 (1980)　　**Pop Density:** 17.8
Land: 25.0 sq. mi.; **Water:** 0.0 sq. mi.

Center　　Township
　　Lat: 36-37-00 N **Long:** 94-09-38 W
Pop: 575 (1990); 431 (1980)　　**Pop Density:** 11.3
Land: 50.8 sq. mi.; **Water:** 0.0 sq. mi.

Elk Horn　　Township
　　Lat: 36-41-32 N **Long:** 94-14-17 W
Pop: 870 (1990); 863 (1980)　　**Pop Density:** 15.2
Land: 57.4 sq. mi.; **Water:** 0.0 sq. mi.

Elk River East　　Township
　　Lat: 36-31-58 N **Long:** 94-27-54 W
Pop: 1,122 (1990); 1,132 (1980)　　**Pop Density:** 114.5
Land: 9.8 sq. mi.; **Water:** 0.0 sq. mi.

Elk River West　　Township
　　Lat: 36-32-32 N **Long:** 94-30-21 W
Pop: 1,117 (1990); 978 (1980)　　**Pop Density:** 41.5
Land: 26.9 sq. mi.; **Water:** 0.1 sq. mi.

Erie Goodman　　Township
　　Lat: 36-43-45 N **Long:** 94-23-43 W
Pop: 1,748 (1990); 1,617 (1980)　　**Pop Density:** 98.2
Land: 17.8 sq. mi.; **Water:** 0.0 sq. mi.

Erie McNatt　　Township
　　Lat: 36-42-34 N **Long:** 94-20-05 W
Pop: 277 (1990); 296 (1980)　　**Pop Density:** 10.7
Land: 25.8 sq. mi.; **Water:** 0.0 sq. mi.

Goodman　　Town
ZIP: 64843　　**Lat:** 36-44-16 N **Long:** 94-24-33 W
Pop: 1,094 (1990); 1,030 (1980)　　**Pop Density:** 911.7
Land: 1.2 sq. mi.; **Water:** 0.0 sq. mi.　　**Elev:** 1254 ft.
Incorporated 1856.

Lanagan　　Town
ZIP: 64847　　**Lat:** 36-36-24 N **Long:** 94-27-02 W
Pop: 501 (1990); 440 (1980)　　**Pop Density:** 501.0
Land: 1.0 sq. mi.; **Water:** 0.0 sq. mi.
Incorporated 1963.

McMillen Coy　　Township
　　Lat: 36-38-57 N **Long:** 94-31-56 W
Pop: 880 (1990); 724 (1980)　　**Pop Density:** 27.8
Land: 31.7 sq. mi.; **Water:** 0.0 sq. mi.

McMillen Tiff　　Township
　　Lat: 36-39-44 N **Long:** 94-35-27 W
Pop: 364 (1990); 335 (1980)　　**Pop Density:** 20.6
Land: 17.7 sq. mi.; **Water:** 0.0 sq. mi.

Mountain　　Township
　　Lat: 36-32-23 N **Long:** 94-08-05 W
Pop: 693 (1990); 630 (1980)　　**Pop Density:** 20.3
Land: 34.2 sq. mi.; **Water:** 0.0 sq. mi.

Noel　　City
ZIP: 64854　　**Lat:** 36-32-42 N **Long:** 94-29-13 W
Pop: 1,169 (1990); 1,161 (1980)　　**Pop Density:** 584.5
Land: 2.0 sq. mi.; **Water:** 0.1 sq. mi.
Incorporated 1946.
Name origin: For C.W. and W.J. Noel, livestock raisers and sawmill owners.

Pineville　　Town
ZIP: 64856　　**Lat:** 36-35-35 N **Long:** 94-23-01 W
Pop: 580 (1990); 504 (1980)　　**Pop Density:** 966.7
Land: 0.6 sq. mi.; **Water:** 0.0 sq. mi.　　**Elev:** 899 ft.
Incorporated 1919.
Name origin: For nearby pine forests.

Pineville Lanagan　　Township
　　Lat: 36-35-58 N **Long:** 94-27-28 W
Pop: 755 (1990); 584 (1980)　　**Pop Density:** 85.8
Land: 8.8 sq. mi.; **Water:** 0.0 sq. mi.

Pineville North　　Township
　　Lat: 36-37-20 N **Long:** 94-21-13 W
Pop: 1,304 (1990); 1,055 (1980)　　**Pop Density:** 49.2
Land: 26.5 sq. mi.; **Water:** 0.0 sq. mi.

Pineville South　　Township
　　Lat: 36-33-16 N **Long:** 94-21-57 W
Pop: 766 (1990); 542 (1980)　　**Pop Density:** 16.2
Land: 47.3 sq. mi.; **Water:** 0.0 sq. mi.

MISSOURI, McDonald County

Prairie
Township
Lat: 36-33-30 N Long: 94-34-58 W
Pop: 1,201 (1990); 1,103 (1980) **Pop Density:** 41.6
Land: 28.9 sq. mi.; **Water:** 0.0 sq. mi.

Richwood
Township
Lat: 36-41-45 N Long: 94-06-54 W
Pop: 543 (1990); 609 (1980) **Pop Density:** 14.2
Land: 38.2 sq. mi.; **Water:** 0.0 sq. mi.

South West City
City
ZIP: 64863 Lat: 36-31-25 N Long: 94-36-31 W
Pop: 600 (1990); 516 (1980) **Pop Density:** 428.6
Land: 1.4 sq. mi.; **Water:** 0.0 sq. mi. **Elev:** 949 ft.
Founded 1870. Incorporated 1870.
Name origin: For the location of the town in the southwest corner of the county and state.

White Rock
Township
Lat: 36-32-37 N Long: 94-16-35 W
Pop: 1,126 (1990); 667 (1980) **Pop Density:** 25.0
Land: 45.1 sq. mi.; **Water:** 0.0 sq. mi.

Mercer County
County Seat: Princeton (ZIP: 64673)

Pop: 3,723 (1990); 4,685 (1980) **Pop Density:** 8.2
Land: 454.5 sq. mi.; **Water:** 0.8 sq. mi. **Area Code:** 816

On the central northern border of MO, northeast of St. Joseph; organized Feb 14, 1845 from Grundy and Livingston counties.

Name origin: For Lt. Col. John Francis Mercer (1759–1821), officer in the Revolutionary War, MD legislator, and governor of MD (1801–13); or possibly for Gen. Hugh Mercer (1721–77), Revolutionary War officer and physician.

Harrison
Township
Lat: 40-25-26 N Long: 93-42-42 W
Pop: 216 (1990); 299 (1980) **Pop Density:** 5.0
Land: 43.6 sq. mi.; **Water:** 0.4 sq. mi.

Lindley
Township
Lat: 40-31-38 N Long: 93-41-49 W
Pop: 213 (1990); 299 (1980) **Pop Density:** 3.7
Land: 58.0 sq. mi.; **Water:** 0.0 sq. mi.

Madison
Township
Lat: 40-18-41 N Long: 93-41-41 W
Pop: 179 (1990); 226 (1980) **Pop Density:** 4.3
Land: 41.4 sq. mi.; **Water:** 0.0 sq. mi.

Marion
Township
Lat: 40-31-20 N Long: 93-32-57 W
Pop: 828 (1990); 1,002 (1980) **Pop Density:** 16.0
Land: 51.8 sq. mi.; **Water:** 0.2 sq. mi.

Medicine
Township
Lat: 40-19-12 N Long: 93-25-47 W
Pop: 156 (1990); 248 (1980) **Pop Density:** 3.2
Land: 49.3 sq. mi.; **Water:** 0.0 sq. mi.

Mercer
Town
ZIP: 64661 Lat: 40-30-39 N Long: 93-31-45 W
Pop: 297 (1990); 442 (1980) **Pop Density:** 742.5
Land: 0.4 sq. mi.; **Water:** 0.0 sq. mi. **Elev:** 1074 ft.
Incorporated 1886.

Morgan
Township
Lat: 40-25-27 N Long: 93-35-32 W
Pop: 1,446 (1990); 1,697 (1980) **Pop Density:** 28.1
Land: 51.4 sq. mi.; **Water:** 0.1 sq. mi.

Princeton
City
ZIP: 64673 Lat: 40-23-49 N Long: 93-35-17 W
Pop: 1,021 (1990); 1,264 (1980) **Pop Density:** 638.1
Land: 1.6 sq. mi.; **Water:** 0.0 sq. mi. **Elev:** 932 ft.
Platted 1846; incorporated 1853; county seat.
Name origin: For the Battle of Princeton, which took place January 3, 1777.

Ravanna
Township
Lat: 40-25-29 N Long: 93-26-48 W
Pop: 254 (1990); 293 (1980) **Pop Density:** 4.4
Land: 57.5 sq. mi.; **Water:** 0.0 sq. mi.

Somerset
Township
Lat: 40-31-44 N Long: 93-25-44 W
Pop: 147 (1990); 205 (1980) **Pop Density:** 3.3
Land: 44.7 sq. mi.; **Water:** 0.0 sq. mi.

South Lineville
Town
Lat: 40-34-40 N Long: 93-31-25 W
Pop: 40 (1990); 55 (1980) **Pop Density:** 400.0
Land: 0.1 sq. mi.; **Water:** 0.0 sq. mi.
Incorporated 1905.

Washington
Township
Lat: 40-18-49 N Long: 93-34-30 W
Pop: 284 (1990); 416 (1980) **Pop Density:** 5.0
Land: 56.8 sq. mi.; **Water:** 0.0 sq. mi.

> ## Miller County
> **County Seat: Tuscumbia (ZIP: 65082)**
>
> **Pop:** 20,700 (1990); 18,539 (1980) **Pop Density:** 34.9
> **Land:** 592.3 sq. mi.; **Water:** 7.7 sq. mi. **Area Code:** 314
> In central MO, south of Jefferson City; organized Feb 6, 1837 from Cole and Pulaski counties.
> **Name origin:** For Col. John Miller (1781–1846), officer in the War of 1812, governor of MO (1825–32), and U.S. representative (1837–43).

Bagnell   Town
Lat: 38-13-43 N Long: 92-36-18 W
Pop: 89 (1990); 71 (1980) **Pop Density:** 178.0
Land: 0.5 sq. mi.; **Water:** 0.1 sq. mi. **Elev:** 586 ft.
Founded 1882; incorporated 1874.
Name origin: For railroad contractor William Bagnell.

Brumley   Town
ZIP: 65017 Lat: 38-05-14 N Long: 92-29-10 W
Pop: 81 (1990); 109 (1980) **Pop Density:** 162.0
Land: 0.5 sq. mi.; **Water:** 0.0 sq. mi. **Elev:** 751 ft.
Founded 1869. Incorporated 1926.
Name origin: For early settler John Brumley.

Eldon   City
ZIP: 65026 Lat: 38-21-03 N Long: 92-34-35 W
Pop: 4,419 (1990); 4,342 (1980) **Pop Density:** 1425.5
Land: 3.1 sq. mi.; **Water:** 0.0 sq. mi. **Elev:** 933 ft.
In central MO, 25 mi. southwest of Jefferson City. Incorporated 1904.
Name origin: Named in 1881 for a railroad official.

Equality   Township
Lat: 38-14-20 N Long: 92-28-51 W
Pop: 1,183 (1990); 1,275 (1980) **Pop Density:** 18.3
Land: 64.8 sq. mi.; **Water:** 1.0 sq. mi.

Franklin   Township
Lat: 38-17-35 N Long: 92-37-19 W
Pop: 1,982 (1990); 2,879 (1980) **Pop Density:** 41.1
Land: 48.2 sq. mi.; **Water:** 0.3 sq. mi.

Glaze   Township
Lat: 38-07-59 N Long: 92-31-34 W
Pop: 5,065 (1990); 2,556 (1980) **Pop Density:** 41.3
Land: 122.5 sq. mi.; **Water:** 4.5 sq. mi.

Iberia   City
ZIP: 65486 Lat: 38-05-19 N Long: 92-17-40 W
Pop: 650 (1990); 852 (1980) **Pop Density:** 812.5
Land: 0.8 sq. mi.; **Water:** 0.0 sq. mi. **Elev:** 932 ft.
Incorporated 1953.
Name origin: For Iberia, LA.

Jim Henry   Township
Lat: 38-17-58 N Long: 92-17-58 W
Pop: 1,187 (1990); 1,243 (1980) **Pop Density:** 18.8
Land: 63.3 sq. mi.; **Water:** 1.2 sq. mi.

Lakeland   Town
Lat: 38-13-10 N Long: 92-37-51 W
Pop: 351 (1990); 197 (1980) **Pop Density:** 140.4
Land: 2.5 sq. mi.; **Water:** 0.2 sq. mi. **Elev:** 853 ft.
Incorporated 1964.

Lake Ozark   City
Lat: 38-11-34 N Long: 92-37-18 W
Pop: 613 (1990); 436 (1980) **Pop Density:** 197.7
Land: 3.1 sq. mi.; **Water:** 0.5 sq. mi. **Elev:** 703 ft.
Incorporated 1989. Part of the town is also in Camden County.

Lakeside   City
Lat: 38-12-14 N Long: 92-37-21 W
Pop: 38 (1990); 115 (1980) **Pop Density:** 126.7
Land: 0.3 sq. mi.; **Water:** 0.3 sq. mi. **Elev:** 836 ft.
Incorporated 1981.

Lakeview   Village
Lat: 38-12-49 N Long: 92-37-37 W
Pop: 110 (1990); 119 (1980) **Pop Density:** 1100.0
Land: 0.1 sq. mi.; **Water:** 0.0 sq. mi. **Elev:** 804 ft.

Olean   Town
ZIP: 65064 Lat: 38-24-37 N Long: 92-31-48 W
Pop: 106 (1990); 128 (1980) **Pop Density:** 530.0
Land: 0.2 sq. mi.; **Water:** 0.0 sq. mi. **Elev:** 769 ft.
Incorporated 1891.

Osage   Township
Lat: 38-12-44 N Long: 92-18-17 W
Pop: 911 (1990); 770 (1980) **Pop Density:** 11.9
Land: 76.3 sq. mi.; **Water:** 0.4 sq. mi.

Osage Beach   City
ZIP: 65065 Lat: 38-09-32 N Long: 92-35-56 W
Pop: 88 (1990); 68 (1980) **Pop Density:** 293.3
Land: 0.3 sq. mi.; **Water:** 0.0 sq. mi. **Elev:** 895 ft.
Incorporated 1959. Part of the town is also in Camden County.

Richwoods   Township
Lat: 38-05-26 N Long: 92-17-33 W
Pop: 2,793 (1990); 2,876 (1980) **Pop Density:** 23.4
Land: 119.4 sq. mi.; **Water:** 0.0 sq. mi.

St. Elizabeth   Town
Lat: 38-15-22 N Long: 92-15-57 W
Pop: 257 (1990); 312 (1980) **Pop Density:** 285.6
Land: 0.9 sq. mi.; **Water:** 0.0 sq. mi. **Elev:** 812 ft.
Incorporated 1948.

Saline   Township
Lat: 38-22-02 N Long: 92-30-40 W
Pop: 7,579 (1990); 6,940 (1980) **Pop Density:** 77.5
Land: 97.8 sq. mi.; **Water:** 0.1 sq. mi.

Tuscumbia
Town
ZIP: 65082 **Lat:** 38-14-07 N **Long:** 92-27-34 W
Pop: 148 (1990); 241 (1980) **Pop Density:** 370.0
Land: 0.4 sq. mi.; **Water:** 0.0 sq. mi. **Elev:** 742 ft.
In central MO, located in the Osage River Valley. Incorporated 1857.

Name origin: For Tuscumbia, AL.

Mississippi County
County Seat: Charleston (ZIP: 63834)

Pop: 14,442 (1990); 15,726 (1980) **Pop Density:** 35.0
Land: 413.2 sq. mi.; **Water:** 15.8 sq. mi. **Area Code:** 314
On the southeastern border of MO, south of Cape Girardeau; established Feb 14, 1845 from Scott County.

Name origin: For its location on the Mississippi River.

Anniston
Town
ZIP: 63820 **Lat:** 36-49-28 N **Long:** 89-19-34 W
Pop: 288 (1990); 320 (1980) **Pop Density:** 720.0
Land: 0.4 sq. mi.; **Water:** 0.0 sq. mi.
Incorporated 1913.

Name origin: Named in 1895 for Anniston, AL.

Bertrand
City
ZIP: 63823 **Lat:** 36-54-32 N **Long:** 89-26-58 W
Pop: 692 (1990); 688 (1980) **Pop Density:** 988.6
Land: 0.7 sq. mi.; **Water:** 0.0 sq. mi.
Incorporated 1962.

Charleston
City
ZIP: 63834 **Lat:** 36-55-08 N **Long:** 89-20-16 W
Pop: 5,085 (1990); 5,230 (1980) **Pop Density:** 1452.9
Land: 3.5 sq. mi.; **Water:** 0.0 sq. mi.
In southeastern MO, 30 mi. south-southeast of Cape Girardeau. Incorporated 1872.

Name origin: Named in 1837 for Charleston, SC.

East Prairie
City
ZIP: 63845 **Lat:** 36-46-44 N **Long:** 89-23-02 W
Pop: 3,416 (1990); 3,713 (1980) **Pop Density:** 2627.7
Land: 1.3 sq. mi.; **Water:** 0.0 sq. mi. **Elev:** 307 ft.
In southeastern MO, 40 mi. south of Cape Girardeau. Incorporated 1883.

James Bayou
Township
Lat: 36-38-35 N **Long:** 89-16-18 W
Pop: 158 (1990); 282 (1980) **Pop Density:** 3.2
Land: 50.1 sq. mi.; **Water:** 5.1 sq. mi.

Long Prairie
Township
Lat: 36-52-49 N **Long:** 89-27-36 W
Pop: 1,248 (1990); 1,300 (1980) **Pop Density:** 33.7
Land: 37.0 sq. mi.; **Water:** 0.0 sq. mi.

Mississippi
Township
Lat: 36-49-22 N **Long:** 89-12-25 W
Pop: 91 (1990); 164 (1980) **Pop Density:** 1.8
Land: 50.9 sq. mi.; **Water:** 2.0 sq. mi.

Ohio
Township
Lat: 36-55-52 N **Long:** 89-11-12 W
Pop: 895 (1990); 1,127 (1980) **Pop Density:** 16.2
Land: 55.4 sq. mi.; **Water:** 4.3 sq. mi.

St. James
Township
Lat: 36-47-20 N **Long:** 89-22-27 W
Pop: 5,830 (1990); 6,139 (1980) **Pop Density:** 96.8
Land: 60.2 sq. mi.; **Water:** 0.1 sq. mi.

Tywappity
Township
Lat: 36-56-06 N **Long:** 89-19-12 W
Pop: 5,967 (1990); 6,291 (1980) **Pop Density:** 58.3
Land: 102.4 sq. mi.; **Water:** 3.7 sq. mi.

Wilson City
Town
Lat: 36-55-22 N **Long:** 89-13-22 W
Pop: 210 (1990); 309 (1980) **Pop Density:** 2100.0
Land: 0.1 sq. mi.; **Water:** 0.0 sq. mi.
Incorporated 1954.

Wolf Island
Township
Lat: 36-43-10 N **Long:** 89-15-20 W
Pop: 253 (1990); 423 (1980) **Pop Density:** 4.4
Land: 57.2 sq. mi.; **Water:** 0.5 sq. mi.

Wyatt
City
ZIP: 63882 **Lat:** 36-54-43 N **Long:** 89-13-24 W
Pop: 376 (1990); 441 (1980) **Pop Density:** 1253.3
Land: 0.3 sq. mi.; **Water:** 0.0 sq. mi.
Incorporated 1954.

Moniteau County
County Seat: California (ZIP: 65018)

Pop: 12,298 (1990); 12,068 (1980)   **Pop Density:** 29.5
Land: 416.5 sq. mi.; **Water:** 2.3 sq. mi.   **Area Code:** 314
In central MO, west of Jefferson City; organized Feb 14, 1845 from Cole and Morgan counties, annexed small part of Morgan County in 1881.
Name origin: A French transliteration of an Algonquian word meaning 'God spirit' or 'great spirit.'

Burris Fork — Township
Lat: 38-30-09 N   Long: 92-31-02 W
Pop: 533 (1990); 506 (1980)   **Pop Density:** 14.3
Land: 37.4 sq. mi.; **Water:** 0.0 sq. mi.

California — City
ZIP: 65018   Lat: 38-37-53 N   Long: 92-34-00 W
Pop: 3,465 (1990); 3,381 (1980)   **Pop Density:** 1386.0
Land: 2.5 sq. mi.; **Water:** 0.0 sq. mi.   **Elev:** 874 ft.
In central MO, 20 mi. west of Jefferson City. Incorporated 1857.
Name origin: Named in 1856 by prospectors returning from the California gold rush.

Clarksburg — City
ZIP: 65025   Lat: 38-39-40 N   Long: 92-39-58 W
Pop: 358 (1990); 352 (1980)   **Pop Density:** 596.7
Land: 0.6 sq. mi.; **Water:** 0.0 sq. mi.   **Elev:** 897 ft.
Incorporated 1882.
Name origin: For pioneer and first postmaster Hiram Clark.

Harrison — Township
Lat: 38-28-46 N   Long: 92-36-27 W
Pop: 509 (1990); 572 (1980)   **Pop Density:** 12.4
Land: 40.9 sq. mi.; **Water:** 0.1 sq. mi.

Jamestown — Town
ZIP: 65046   Lat: 38-45-56 N   Long: 92-28-39 W
Pop: 298 (1990); 317 (1980)   **Pop Density:** 298.0
Land: 1.0 sq. mi.; **Water:** 0.0 sq. mi.
Incorporated 1873.

Linn — Township
Lat: 38-47-23 N   Long: 92-29-11 W
Pop: 1,018 (1990); 1,045 (1980)   **Pop Density:** 11.7
Land: 87.2 sq. mi.; **Water:** 1.9 sq. mi.

Lupus — Town
Lat: 38-50-44 N   Long: 92-27-15 W
Pop: 39 (1990); 50 (1980)   **Pop Density:** 195.0
Land: 0.2 sq. mi.; **Water:** 0.0 sq. mi.   **Elev:** 574 ft.
Incorporated 1901.
Name origin: From Latin 'wolf.' Previously called Wolf's Point.

Moreau — Township
Lat: 38-37-51 N   Long: 92-40-50 W
Pop: 784 (1990); 798 (1980)   **Pop Density:** 19.4
Land: 40.4 sq. mi.; **Water:** 0.0 sq. mi.

Pilot Grove — Township
Lat: 38-32-46 N   Long: 92-39-38 W
Pop: 937 (1990); 848 (1980)   **Pop Density:** 17.9
Land: 52.3 sq. mi.; **Water:** 0.0 sq. mi.

Tipton — City
ZIP: 65081   Lat: 38-39-11 N   Long: 92-46-48 W
Pop: 2,026 (1990); 2,155 (1980)   **Pop Density:** 1066.3
Land: 1.9 sq. mi.; **Water:** 0.0 sq. mi.   **Elev:** 926 ft.
Incorporated 1899.
Name origin: For Tipton Sealey, who donated land for the townsite.

Walker — Township
Lat: 38-38-58 N   Long: 92-31-07 W
Pop: 5,691 (1990); 5,322 (1980)   **Pop Density:** 53.1
Land: 107.2 sq. mi.; **Water:** 0.3 sq. mi.

Willow Fork — Township
Lat: 38-37-35 N   Long: 92-47-07 W
Pop: 2,826 (1990); 2,977 (1980)   **Pop Density:** 55.2
Land: 51.2 sq. mi.; **Water:** 0.1 sq. mi.

Monroe County
County Seat: Paris (ZIP: 65275)

Pop: 9,104 (1990); 9,716 (1980)   **Pop Density:** 14.1
Land: 646.0 sq. mi.; **Water:** 24.2 sq. mi.   **Area Code:** 816
In northeastern MO, northeast of Columbia; organized Jan 6, 1831 from Ralls County.
Name origin: For James Monroe (1758–1831), fifth U.S. president.

Clay — Township
Lat: 39-35-30 N   Long: 92-05-23 W
Pop: 293 (1990); 367 (1980)   **Pop Density:** 5.5
Land: 53.7 sq. mi.; **Water:** 0.1 sq. mi.

Florida — Village
Lat: 39-29-35 N   Long: 91-47-24 W
Pop: 2 (1990)   **Pop Density:** 20.0
Land: 0.1 sq. mi.; **Water:** 0.0 sq. mi.

MISSOURI, Monroe County

Holliday
Village
ZIP: 65258 Lat: 39-29-36 N Long: 92-07-54 W
Pop: 139 (1990); 168 (1980) Pop Density: 463.3
Land: 0.3 sq. mi.; Water: 0.0 sq. mi. Elev: 788 ft.
Incorporated 1890.

Indian Creek
Township
Lat: 39-35-03 N Long: 91-48-26 W
Pop: 190 (1990); 193 (1980) Pop Density: 10.2
Land: 18.6 sq. mi.; Water: 0.0 sq. mi.

Jackson
Township
Lat: 39-27-03 N Long: 92-00-53 W
Pop: 2,630 (1990); 2,913 (1980) Pop Density: 17.6
Land: 149.1 sq. mi.; Water: 1.5 sq. mi.

Jefferson
Township
Lat: 39-29-10 N Long: 91-48-41 W
Pop: 327 (1990); 372 (1980) Pop Density: 4.9
Land: 67.2 sq. mi.; Water: 19.9 sq. mi.

Madison
City
ZIP: 65263 Lat: 39-28-23 N Long: 92-12-42 W
Pop: 518 (1990); 656 (1980) Pop Density: 1295.0
Land: 0.4 sq. mi.; Water: 0.0 sq. mi. Elev: 796 ft.
Incorporated 1894.

Marion
Township
Lat: 39-29-26 N Long: 92-12-49 W
Pop: 1,264 (1990); 1,460 (1980) Pop Density: 18.7
Land: 67.5 sq. mi.; Water: 0.0 sq. mi.

Monroe
Township
Lat: 39-36-21 N Long: 91-45-46 W
Pop: 2,590 (1990); 2,462 (1980) Pop Density: 67.4
Land: 38.4 sq. mi.; Water: 1.1 sq. mi.

Monroe City
City
ZIP: 63456 Lat: 39-39-05 N Long: 91-44-07 W
Pop: 2,276 (1990); 2,187 (1980) Pop Density: 1138.0
Land: 2.0 sq. mi.; Water: 0.0 sq. mi. Elev: 749 ft.
Incorporated 1857. Part of the town is also in Marion and Ralls counties.
Name origin: For James Monroe (1758–1831), fifth U.S. president.

Paris
City
ZIP: 65275 Lat: 39-28-37 N Long: 92-00-14 W
Pop: 1,486 (1990); 1,598 (1980) Pop Density: 1143.1
Land: 1.3 sq. mi.; Water: 0.0 sq. mi. Elev: 696 ft.
Incorporated 1842.
Name origin: For Paris, France.

South Fork
Township
Lat: 39-23-02 N Long: 91-50-16 W
Pop: 497 (1990); 577 (1980) Pop Density: 6.5
Land: 76.2 sq. mi.; Water: 0.7 sq. mi.

Stoutsville
Village
ZIP: 65283 Lat: 39-33-06 N Long: 91-51-10 W
Pop: 26 (1990); 34 (1980) Pop Density: 32.5
Land: 0.8 sq. mi.; Water: 0.0 sq. mi. Elev: 613 ft.
Incorporated 1871.

Union
Township
Lat: 39-23-17 N Long: 92-12-38 W
Pop: 732 (1990); 685 (1980) Pop Density: 10.6
Land: 68.8 sq. mi.; Water: 0.1 sq. mi.

Washington
Township
Lat: 39-36-55 N Long: 91-56-29 W
Pop: 291 (1990); 327 (1980) Pop Density: 4.9
Land: 59.7 sq. mi.; Water: 0.8 sq. mi.

Woodlawn
Township
Lat: 39-35-08 N Long: 92-12-29 W
Pop: 290 (1990); 360 (1980) Pop Density: 6.2
Land: 46.9 sq. mi.; Water: 0.0 sq. mi.

Montgomery County
County Seat: Montgomery City (ZIP: 63361)

Pop: 11,355 (1990); 11,537 (1980) Pop Density: 21.1
Land: 538.7 sq. mi.; Water: 3.3 sq. mi. Area Code: 314
In east-central MO, northwest of St. Louis; organized Dec 14, 1818 (prior to statehood) from St. Charles County.
Name origin: For Gen. Richard Montgomery (1736–75), American Revolutionary War officer who captured Montreal, Canada.

Bear Creek
Township
Lat: 38-56-04 N Long: 91-20-17 W
Pop: 2,358 (1990); 2,409 (1980) Pop Density: 22.7
Land: 103.9 sq. mi.; Water: 0.6 sq. mi.

Bellflower
City
ZIP: 63333 Lat: 39-00-13 N Long: 91-21-09 W
Pop: 413 (1990); 403 (1980) Pop Density: 826.0
Land: 0.5 sq. mi.; Water: 0.0 sq. mi.
Incorporated 1963.

Danville
Township
ZIP: 63361 Lat: 38-53-33 N Long: 91-31-32 W
Pop: 1,745 (1990); 1,653 (1980) Pop Density: 16.6
Land: 105.4 sq. mi.; Water: 0.3 sq. mi.

High Hill
City
ZIP: 63350 Lat: 38-52-31 N Long: 91-22-32 W
Pop: 204 (1990); 254 (1980) Pop Density: 510.0
Land: 0.4 sq. mi.; Water: 0.0 sq. mi. Elev: 894 ft.
Incorporated 1947.

Jonesburg
City
ZIP: 63351 **Lat:** 38-51-12 N **Long:** 91-18-23 W
Pop: 630 (1990); 614 (1980) **Pop Density:** 700.0
Land: 0.9 sq. mi.; **Water:** 0.0 sq. mi. **Elev:** 897 ft.
Incorporated 1897.

Loutre
Township
Lat: 38-45-53 N **Long:** 91-31-30 W
Pop: 1,340 (1990); 1,406 (1980) **Pop Density:** 12.2
Land: 109.8 sq. mi.; **Water:** 1.9 sq. mi.

McKittrick
Town
Lat: 38-44-06 N **Long:** 91-26-33 W
Pop: 66 (1990); 87 (1980) **Pop Density:** 330.0
Land: 0.2 sq. mi.; **Water:** 0.0 sq. mi. **Elev:** 550 ft.
Incorporated 1909.

Middletown
Town
ZIP: 63359 **Lat:** 39-07-42 N **Long:** 91-24-52 W
Pop: 217 (1990); 268 (1980) **Pop Density:** 723.3
Land: 0.3 sq. mi.; **Water:** 0.0 sq. mi. **Elev:** 713 ft.
Incorporated 1864.

Montgomery
Township
ZIP: 63361 **Lat:** 39-00-05 N **Long:** 91-30-51 W
Pop: 3,160 (1990); 2,965 (1980) **Pop Density:** 39.4
Land: 80.3 sq. mi.; **Water:** 0.1 sq. mi.

Montgomery City
City
ZIP: 63361 **Lat:** 38-58-32 N **Long:** 91-30-18 W
Pop: 2,281 (1990); 2,101 (1980) **Pop Density:** 1036.8
Land: 2.2 sq. mi.; **Water:** 0.0 sq. mi. **Elev:** 816 ft.
Incorporated 1857.

New Florence
City
ZIP: 63363 **Lat:** 38-54-29 N **Long:** 91-26-59 W
Pop: 801 (1990); 731 (1980) **Pop Density:** 534.0
Land: 1.5 sq. mi.; **Water:** 0.0 sq. mi.
Founded 1857. Incorporated 1869.
Name origin: Named by Judge Lewis for his only daughter, Florence.

Prairie
Township
Lat: 39-05-45 N **Long:** 91-22-02 W
Pop: 853 (1990); 974 (1980) **Pop Density:** 11.2
Land: 76.2 sq. mi.; **Water:** 0.1 sq. mi.

Rhineland
Town
ZIP: 65069 **Lat:** 38-43-06 N **Long:** 91-31-02 W
Pop: 157 (1990); 172 (1980) **Pop Density:** 785.0
Land: 0.2 sq. mi.; **Water:** 0.0 sq. mi. **Elev:** 517 ft.
Founded 1853 by Germans. Incorporated 1896.
Name origin: For the Rhine River.

Upper Loutre
Township
Lat: 39-04-52 N **Long:** 91-33-43 W
Pop: 1,899 (1990); 2,130 (1980) **Pop Density:** 30.0
Land: 63.2 sq. mi.; **Water:** 0.3 sq. mi.

Wellsville
City
ZIP: 63384 **Lat:** 39-04-25 N **Long:** 91-34-04 W
Pop: 1,430 (1990); 1,546 (1980) **Pop Density:** 1021.4
Land: 1.4 sq. mi.; **Water:** 0.0 sq. mi.
Founded 1856. Incorporated 1890.
Name origin: For founder Judge Wells.

Morgan County
County Seat: Versailles (ZIP: 65084)

Pop: 15,574 (1990); 13,807 (1980) **Pop Density:** 26.1
Land: 597.5 sq. mi.; **Water:** 16.5 sq. mi. **Area Code:** 314
In central MO, west of Jefferson City; organized Jan 5, 1833 from Cooper County.
Name origin: For Gen. Daniel Morgan (1736–1802), an officer in the Revolutionary War and U.S. representative from VA (1797–99).

Barnett
City
ZIP: 65011 **Lat:** 38-22-37 N **Long:** 92-40-26 W
Pop: 215 (1990); 203 (1980) **Pop Density:** 716.7
Land: 0.3 sq. mi.; **Water:** 0.0 sq. mi. **Elev:** 970 ft.
Incorporated 1904.

Buffalo
Township
Lat: 38-16-58 N **Long:** 92-57-27 W
Pop: 1,246 (1990); 851 (1980) **Pop Density:** 11.5
Land: 108.1 sq. mi.; **Water:** 5.4 sq. mi.

Gravois Mills
Village
ZIP: 65037 **Lat:** 38-18-34 N **Long:** 92-49-28 W
Pop: 101 (1990); 101 (1980) **Pop Density:** 336.7
Land: 0.3 sq. mi.; **Water:** 0.1 sq. mi.

Haw Creek
Township
Lat: 38-26-22 N **Long:** 92-57-28 W
Pop: 3,228 (1990); 3,216 (1980) **Pop Density:** 23.2
Land: 139.4 sq. mi.; **Water:** 0.4 sq. mi.

Laurie
Village
ZIP: 65038 **Lat:** 38-12-13 N **Long:** 92-49-44 W
Pop: 507 (1990); 154 (1980) **Pop Density:** 107.9
Land: 4.7 sq. mi.; **Water:** 0.0 sq. mi. **Elev:** 965 ft.
Incorporated 1966.

Mill Creek
Township
Lat: 38-35-49 N **Long:** 92-52-42 W
Pop: 904 (1990); 902 (1980) **Pop Density:** 14.0
Land: 64.4 sq. mi.; **Water:** 0.0 sq. mi.

Moreau
Township
Lat: 38-25-36 N **Long:** 92-45-07 W
Pop: 4,785 (1990); 4,519 (1980) **Pop Density:** 37.5
Land: 127.5 sq. mi.; **Water:** 0.1 sq. mi.

Osage
Township
Lat: 38-16-21 N **Long:** 92-46-53 W
Pop: 4,564 (1990); 3,392 (1980) **Pop Density:** 56.9
Land: 80.2 sq. mi.; **Water:** 10.4 sq. mi.

Richland
Township
Lat: 38-36-31 N **Long:** 92-59-48 W
Pop: 847 (1990); 927 (1980) **Pop Density:** 10.9
Land: 78.0 sq. mi.; **Water:** 0.0 sq. mi.

Stover
City
ZIP: 65078 **Lat:** 38-26-31 N **Long:** 92-59-23 W
Pop: 964 (1990); 1,041 (1980) **Pop Density:** 1071.1
Land: 0.9 sq. mi.; **Water:** 0.0 sq. mi. **Elev:** 1052 ft.
Incorporated 1903.
Name origin: For Col. John Stover, U.S. congressman.

Sunrise Beach
Village
ZIP: 65079 **Lat:** 38-11-29 N **Long:** 92-46-13 W
Pop: 69 (1990); 48 (1980) **Pop Density:** 230.0
Land: 0.3 sq. mi.; **Water:** 0.0 sq. mi.
Incorporated 1954. Part of the town is also in Camden County.

Syracuse
City
ZIP: 65354 **Lat:** 38-40-09 N **Long:** 92-52-32 W
Pop: 185 (1990); 222 (1980) **Pop Density:** 462.5
Land: 0.4 sq. mi.; **Water:** 0.0 sq. mi.
Incorporated 1894.

Versailles
City
ZIP: 65084 **Lat:** 38-25-59 N **Long:** 92-50-45 W
Pop: 2,365 (1990); 2,406 (1980) **Pop Density:** 1028.3
Land: 2.3 sq. mi.; **Water:** 0.0 sq. mi. **Elev:** 1036 ft.
Founded 1834. Incorporated 1878.
Name origin: For Versailles, France.

New Madrid County
County Seat: New Madrid (ZIP: 63869)

Pop: 20,928 (1990); 22,945 (1980) **Pop Density:** 30.9
Land: 678.1 sq. mi.; **Water:** 20.0 sq. mi. **Area Code:** 314

On the southeastern border of MO, south of Cape Girardeau; original county; organized Oct 1, 1812 (prior to statehood).

Name origin: For the city, named for the capital of Spain. Originally called *Nuevo Madrid* by Col. George Morgan who founded the city in 1788.

Anderson
Township
Lat: 36-26-47 N **Long:** 89-54-23 W
Pop: 1,599 (1990); 1,862 (1980) **Pop Density:** 29.0
Land: 55.2 sq. mi.; **Water:** 0.0 sq. mi.

Big Prairie
Township
Lat: 36-46-57 N **Long:** 89-33-27 W
Pop: 2,626 (1990); 2,340 (1980) **Pop Density:** 25.8
Land: 101.9 sq. mi.; **Water:** 0.0 sq. mi.

Canalou
City
ZIP: 63828 **Lat:** 36-45-15 N **Long:** 89-41-14 W
Pop: 319 (1990); 369 (1980) **Pop Density:** 1063.3
Land: 0.3 sq. mi.; **Water:** 0.0 sq. mi. **Elev:** 289 ft.
Incorporated 1909.

Catron
Town
ZIP: 63833 **Lat:** 36-36-44 N **Long:** 89-42-22 W
Pop: 81 (1990); 180 (1980) **Pop Density:** 202.5
Land: 0.4 sq. mi.; **Water:** 0.0 sq. mi.
Incorporated 1924.

Como
Township
Lat: 36-34-22 N **Long:** 89-49-49 W
Pop: 2,308 (1990); 3,036 (1980) **Pop Density:** 20.1
Land: 114.8 sq. mi.; **Water:** 0.2 sq. mi.

Gideon
City
ZIP: 63848 **Lat:** 36-27-02 N **Long:** 89-54-38 W
Pop: 1,104 (1990); 1,240 (1980) **Pop Density:** 613.3
Land: 1.8 sq. mi.; **Water:** 0.0 sq. mi. **Elev:** 269 ft.
Incorporated 1909.
Name origin: For merchant Frank Gideon.

Hough
Township
Lat: 36-43-02 N **Long:** 89-27-01 W
Pop: 49 (1990); 54 (1980) **Pop Density:** 2.7
Land: 18.4 sq. mi.; **Water:** 0.0 sq. mi.

Howardville
City
ZIP: 63869 **Lat:** 36-34-06 N **Long:** 89-35-50 W
Pop: 440 (1990); 536 (1980) **Pop Density:** 2200.0
Land: 0.2 sq. mi.; **Water:** 0.0 sq. mi.
Incorporated 1966.

La Font
Township
Lat: 36-30-21 N **Long:** 89-38-45 W
Pop: 1,160 (1990); 1,493 (1980) **Pop Density:** 21.6
Land: 53.6 sq. mi.; **Water:** 1.3 sq. mi.

Le Sieur
Township
Lat: 36-25-30 N **Long:** 89-34-36 W
Pop: 623 (1990); 752 (1980) **Pop Density:** 14.2
Land: 43.8 sq. mi.; **Water:** 7.0 sq. mi.

Lewis
Township
Lat: 36-35-43 N **Long:** 89-38-34 W
Pop: 2,258 (1990); 2,664 (1980) **Pop Density:** 73.6
Land: 30.7 sq. mi.; **Water:** 0.0 sq. mi.

Lilbourn
City
ZIP: 63862 **Lat:** 36-35-26 N **Long:** 89-36-49 W
Pop: 1,378 (1990); 1,463 (1980) **Pop Density:** 1531.1
Land: 0.9 sq. mi.; **Water:** 0.0 sq. mi.
Incorporated 1904.

Marston
City
ZIP: 63866 **Lat:** 36-31-03 N **Long:** 89-36-31 W
Pop: 691 (1990); 742 (1980) **Pop Density:** 863.8
Land: 0.8 sq. mi.; **Water:** 0.0 sq. mi.
Incorporated 1898.

American Places Dictionary
MISSOURI, Newton County

Matthews — City
ZIP: 63867   Lat: 36-45-33 N   Long: 89-35-01 W
Pop: 614 (1990); 547 (1980)   Pop Density: 614.0
Land: 1.0 sq. mi.; Water: 0.0 sq. mi.   Elev: 310 ft.
Incorporated 1906.

Morehouse — City
ZIP: 63868   Lat: 36-50-45 N   Long: 89-41-27 W
Pop: 1,068 (1990); 1,220 (1980)   Pop Density: 1335.0
Land: 0.8 sq. mi.; Water: 0.0 sq. mi.   Elev: 302 ft.
Incorporated 1908.

New Madrid — City
ZIP: 63869   Lat: 36-35-21 N   Long: 89-32-55 W
Pop: 3,350 (1990); 3,204 (1980)   Pop Density: 744.4
Land: 4.5 sq. mi.; Water: 0.0 sq. mi.   Elev: 305 ft.
Incorporated 1879.

*New Madrid — Township
ZIP: 63869   Lat: 36-38-31 N   Long: 89-33-22 W
Pop: 4,212 (1990); 4,131 (1980)   Pop Density: 39.0
Land: 108.0 sq. mi.; Water: 1.8 sq. mi.

North Lilbourn — Village
ZIP: 63862   Lat: 36-36-06 N   Long: 89-37-18 W
Pop: 157 (1990); 237 (1980)   Pop Density: 785.0
Land: 0.2 sq. mi.; Water: 0.0 sq. mi.
Incorporated 1954.

Parma — City
ZIP: 63870   Lat: 36-36-39 N   Long: 89-49-05 W
Pop: 995 (1990); 1,081 (1980)   Pop Density: 1658.3
Land: 0.6 sq. mi.; Water: 0.0 sq. mi.   Elev: 281 ft.
Incorporated 1903.
Name origin: For Parma, Italy.

Portage — Township
Lat: 36-27-00 N   Long: 89-46-28 W
Pop: 4,160 (1990); 4,173 (1980)   Pop Density: 66.9
Land: 62.2 sq. mi.; Water: 0.1 sq. mi.

Portageville — City
ZIP: 63873   Lat: 36-25-48 N   Long: 89-41-55 W
Pop: 3,401 (1990); 3,470 (1980)   Pop Density: 2000.6
Land: 1.7 sq. mi.; Water: 0.0 sq. mi.   Elev: 281 ft.
In southeastern MO, 19 mi. north of Caruthersville. Incorporated 1900. Part of the town is also in Pemiscot County.

Risco — City
ZIP: 63874   Lat: 36-33-05 N   Long: 89-49-07 W
Pop: 434 (1990); 446 (1980)   Pop Density: 868.0
Land: 0.5 sq. mi.; Water: 0.0 sq. mi.
Incorporated 1924.

St. John — Township
Lat: 36-35-27 N   Long: 89-25-15 W
Pop: 77 (1990); 97 (1980)   Pop Density: 1.4
Land: 54.9 sq. mi.; Water: 9.5 sq. mi.

Sikeston — City
ZIP: 63801   Lat: 36-52-07 N   Long: 89-34-09 W
Pop: 732 (1990); 668 (1980)   Pop Density: 209.1
Land: 3.5 sq. mi.; Water: 0.0 sq. mi.
In southeastern MO, 30 mi. south of Cape Girardeau. Incorporated 1874. Part of the town is also in Scott County.
Name origin: For John Sikes, who laid out the town.

Tallapoosa — City
Lat: 36-30-26 N   Long: 89-49-07 W
Pop: 174 (1990); 197 (1980)   Pop Density: 435.0
Land: 0.4 sq. mi.; Water: 0.0 sq. mi.
Incorporated 1926.

West — Township
Lat: 36-47-15 N   Long: 89-40-31 W
Pop: 1,856 (1990); 2,343 (1980)   Pop Density: 53.8
Land: 34.5 sq. mi.; Water: 0.1 sq. mi.

Newton County
County Seat: Neosho (ZIP: 64850)

Pop: 44,445 (1990); 40,555 (1980)   Pop Density: 70.9
Land: 626.5 sq. mi.; Water: 0.2 sq. mi.   Area Code: 417
On the southwestern border of MO, south of Joplin; organized Dec 30, 1838 from Barry County.
Name origin: For Sgt. John Newton (1752–80), soldier under Gen. Francis Marion in the Revolutionary War, who saved several colonial patriots from execution by surprising and capturing the British soldiers guarding them.

Benton — Township
Lat: 36-47-48 N   Long: 94-15-39 W
Pop: 426 (1990); 420 (1980)   Pop Density: 13.1
Land: 32.5 sq. mi.; Water: 0.0 sq. mi.

Berwick — Township
Lat: 36-54-04 N   Long: 94-06-36 W
Pop: 272 (1990); 238 (1980)   Pop Density: 14.2
Land: 19.2 sq. mi.; Water: 0.0 sq. mi.

Buffalo — Township
Lat: 36-47-59 N   Long: 94-31-49 W
Pop: 1,555 (1990); 1,575 (1980)   Pop Density: 32.1
Land: 48.5 sq. mi.; Water: 0.0 sq. mi.

Cliff Village — Village
Lat: 37-01-31 N   Long: 94-31-00 W
Pop: 19 (1990); 24 (1980)   Pop Density: 475.0
Land: 0.04 sq. mi.; Water: 0.0 sq. mi.
Incorporated 1959.

Dayton — Township
Lat: 36-52-29 N   Long: 94-30-40 W
Pop: 1,161 (1990); 1,089 (1980)   Pop Density: 48.8
Land: 23.8 sq. mi.; Water: 0.0 sq. mi.

MISSOURI, Newton County

Dennis Acres — Village
Lat: 37-02-44 N Long: 94-30-14 W
Pop: 157 (1990); 56 (1980) **Pop Density:** 3140.0
Land: 0.05 sq. mi.; **Water:** 0.0 sq. mi. **Elev:** 1060 ft.
Incorporated 1956.

Diamond — Town
ZIP: 64840 Lat: 36-59-43 N Long: 94-18-54 W
Pop: 775 (1990); 766 (1980) **Pop Density:** 1291.7
Land: 0.6 sq. mi.; **Water:** 0.0 sq. mi. **Elev:** 1180 ft.
Incorporated 1950.
Name origin: Original name, Adam-Ondi-Ahman, was coined by Mormon founder Joseph Smith (1805–44), but the Mormon settlement shortened it to Di-amon, Diamong or Diamond.

Fairview — Town
ZIP: 64842 Lat: 36-49-00 N Long: 94-05-05 W
Pop: 298 (1990); 282 (1980) **Pop Density:** 745.0
Land: 0.4 sq. mi.; **Water:** 0.0 sq. mi.
Incorporated 1907.

Five Mile — Township
Lat: 36-57-42 N Long: 94-33-16 W
Pop: 2,801 (1990); 2,013 (1980) **Pop Density:** 74.1
Land: 37.8 sq. mi.; **Water:** 0.0 sq. mi.

Franklin — Township
Lat: 36-47-42 N Long: 94-08-18 W
Pop: 1,426 (1990); 1,405 (1980) **Pop Density:** 25.4
Land: 56.2 sq. mi.; **Water:** 0.0 sq. mi.

Granby — City
ZIP: 64844 Lat: 36-55-01 N Long: 94-15-36 W
Pop: 1,945 (1990); 1,908 (1980) **Pop Density:** 442.0
Land: 4.4 sq. mi.; **Water:** 0.0 sq. mi.
Incorporated 1875.
Name origin: For Granby, MA.

*Granby — Township
ZIP: 64844 Lat: 36-53-58 N Long: 94-15-46 W
Pop: 3,571 (1990); 3,367 (1980) **Pop Density:** 66.0
Land: 54.1 sq. mi.; **Water:** 0.0 sq. mi.

Joplin — City
ZIP: 64801 Lat: 37-02-31 N Long: 94-30-11 W
Pop: 3,929 (1990); 2,431 (1980) **Pop Density:** 644.1
Land: 6.1 sq. mi.; **Water:** 0.1 sq. mi.
In southwestern MO, 70 mi. west of Springfield. Founded 1839; chartered 1874. Incorporated 1954. Part of the town is also in Jasper County.
Name origin: For Methodist minister Harris G. Joplin.

Leawood — Village
Lat: 37-02-00 N Long: 94-29-25 W
Pop: 736 (1990); 509 (1980) **Pop Density:** 490.7
Land: 1.5 sq. mi.; **Water:** 0.0 sq. mi.
Incorporated 1956.

Marion — Township
Lat: 37-00-34 N Long: 94-18-51 W
Pop: 2,736 (1990); 2,579 (1980) **Pop Density:** 37.5
Land: 73.0 sq. mi.; **Water:** 0.0 sq. mi.

Neosho — City
ZIP: 64850 Lat: 36-50-40 N Long: 94-22-30 W
Pop: 9,254 (1990); 9,493 (1980) **Pop Density:** 701.1
Land: 13.2 sq. mi.; **Water:** 0.0 sq. mi.
In southwestern MO, 15 mi. south-southeast of Joplin. Incorporated 1878.
Name origin: The Osage term meaning 'clear water,' a reference to the large spring near the center of the town.

*Neosho — Township
ZIP: 64850 Lat: 36-54-23 N Long: 94-23-58 W
Pop: 14,351 (1990); 13,780 (1980) **Pop Density:** 169.2
Land: 84.8 sq. mi.; **Water:** 0.0 sq. mi.

Newtonia — Town
ZIP: 64853 Lat: 36-52-46 N Long: 94-11-02 W
Pop: 204 (1990); 224 (1980) **Pop Density:** 510.0
Land: 0.4 sq. mi.; **Water:** 0.0 sq. mi. **Elev:** 1203 ft.
Incorporated 1968.

*Newtonia — Township
Lat: 36-51-55 N Long: 94-10-25 W
Pop: 695 (1990); 749 (1980) **Pop Density:** 27.3
Land: 25.5 sq. mi.; **Water:** 0.0 sq. mi.

Redings Mill — Village
Lat: 37-01-10 N Long: 94-30-59 W
Pop: 204 (1990); 222 (1980) **Pop Density:** 1020.0
Land: 0.2 sq. mi.; **Water:** 0.0 sq. mi.
Incorporated 1955.

Ritchey — Town
ZIP: 64844 Lat: 36-56-37 N Long: 94-11-08 W
Pop: 62 (1990); 126 (1980) **Pop Density:** 620.0
Land: 0.1 sq. mi.; **Water:** 0.0 sq. mi. **Elev:** 1086 ft.
Incorporated 1871.

Saginaw — Village
ZIP: 64864 Lat: 37-01-35 N Long: 94-28-10 W
Pop: 384 (1990); 293 (1980) **Pop Density:** 480.0
Land: 0.8 sq. mi.; **Water:** 0.0 sq. mi.
Incorporated 1957.
Name origin: For Saginaw, MI.

Seneca — City
ZIP: 64865 Lat: 36-50-16 N Long: 94-36-30 W
Pop: 1,885 (1990); 1,853 (1980) **Pop Density:** 1108.8
Land: 1.7 sq. mi.; **Water:** 0.0 sq. mi. **Elev:** 853 ft.
Incorporated 1868.
Name origin: For an Indian tribe that was moved to Indian Territory a few miles west of the town.

*Seneca — Township
ZIP: 64865 Lat: 36-52-23 N Long: 94-35-23 W
Pop: 2,703 (1990); 2,469 (1980) **Pop Density:** 103.2
Land: 26.2 sq. mi.; **Water:** 0.0 sq. mi.

Shoal Creek — Township
Lat: 37-01-16 N Long: 94-30-49 W
Pop: 10,025 (1990); 8,341 (1980) **Pop Density:** 218.9
Land: 45.8 sq. mi.; **Water:** 0.1 sq. mi.

Shoal Creek Drive — Village
Lat: 37-02-15 N Long: 94-31-23 W
Pop: 296 (1990); 374 (1980) **Pop Density:** 592.0
Land: 0.5 sq. mi.; **Water:** 0.0 sq. mi.
Incorporated 1956.

Shoal Creek Estates Town
Lat: 37-01-07 N **Long:** 94-29-38 W
Pop: 21 (1990); 89 (1980) **Pop Density:** 210.0
Land: 0.1 sq. mi.; **Water:** 0.0 sq. mi.
Incorporated 1976.

Silver Creek Village
Lat: 37-02-19 N **Long:** 94-28-18 W
Pop: 513 (1990); 519 (1980) **Pop Density:** 641.3
Land: 0.8 sq. mi.; **Water:** 0.0 sq. mi.
Incorporated 1960.

Stark City Town
ZIP: 64866 **Lat:** 36-51-36 N **Long:** 94-11-19 W
Pop: 127 (1990); 132 (1980) **Pop Density:** 1270.0
Land: 0.1 sq. mi.; **Water:** 0.0 sq. mi.
Incorporated 1910.

Stella Town
ZIP: 64867 **Lat:** 36-45-44 N **Long:** 94-11-25 W
Pop: 132 (1990); 230 (1980) **Pop Density:** 660.0
Land: 0.2 sq. mi.; **Water:** 0.0 sq. mi.
Incorporated 1953.

Van Buren Township
Lat: 36-59-08 N **Long:** 94-08-34 W
Pop: 1,211 (1990); 1,287 (1980) **Pop Density:** 18.0
Land: 67.1 sq. mi.; **Water:** 0.0 sq. mi.

Wentworth Village
ZIP: 64873 **Lat:** 36-59-35 N **Long:** 94-04-29 W
Pop: 138 (1990); 138 (1980) **Pop Density:** 690.0
Land: 0.2 sq. mi.; **Water:** 0.0 sq. mi.
Incorporated 1895.

West Benton Township
Lat: 36-48-10 N **Long:** 94-22-48 W
Pop: 1,512 (1990); 1,243 (1980) **Pop Density:** 47.4
Land: 31.9 sq. mi.; **Water:** 0.0 sq. mi.

Nodaway County
County Seat: Maryville (ZIP: 64468)

Pop: 21,709 (1990); 21,996 (1980) **Pop Density:** 24.8
Land: 876.7 sq. mi.; **Water:** 1.1 sq. mi. **Area Code:** 816
On the northwestern border of MO, north of St. Joseph; established Jan 29, 1841 from Andrew County.
Name origin: A Potawatomi Indian word whose meaning is unclear, possibly 'placid.'

Arkoe Town
Lat: 40-15-31 N **Long:** 94-49-46 W
Pop: 64 (1990); 63 (1980) **Pop Density:** 640.0
Land: 0.1 sq. mi.; **Water:** 0.0 sq. mi.
Incorporated 1906.

Atchison Township
Lat: 40-31-39 N **Long:** 94-58-34 W
Pop: 524 (1990); 672 (1980) **Pop Density:** 9.5
Land: 55.4 sq. mi.; **Water:** 0.1 sq. mi.

Barnard City
ZIP: 64423 **Lat:** 40-10-32 N **Long:** 94-49-21 W
Pop: 234 (1990); 234 (1980) **Pop Density:** 1170.0
Land: 0.2 sq. mi.; **Water:** 0.0 sq. mi.
Incorporated 1881.

Burlington Junction City
ZIP: 64428 **Lat:** 40-26-50 N **Long:** 95-04-02 W
Pop: 634 (1990); 657 (1980) **Pop Density:** 576.4
Land: 1.1 sq. mi.; **Water:** 0.0 sq. mi. **Elev:** 944 ft.
Incorporated 1879.

Clearmont City
ZIP: 64431 **Lat:** 40-30-26 N **Long:** 95-01-58 W
Pop: 175 (1990); 261 (1980) **Pop Density:** 875.0
Land: 0.2 sq. mi.; **Water:** 0.0 sq. mi.
Incorporated 1964.

Clyde Village
ZIP: 64432 **Lat:** 40-15-58 N **Long:** 94-40-12 W
Pop: 71 (1990); 61 (1980) **Pop Density:** 355.0
Land: 0.2 sq. mi.; **Water:** 0.0 sq. mi. **Elev:** 986 ft.
Incorporated 1879.

Conception Junction Town
ZIP: 64434 **Lat:** 40-16-05 N **Long:** 94-41-26 W
Pop: 236 (1990); 252 (1980) **Pop Density:** 786.7
Land: 0.3 sq. mi.; **Water:** 0.0 sq. mi. **Elev:** 1001 ft.
Incorporated 1915.

Elmo City
ZIP: 64445 **Lat:** 40-31-07 N **Long:** 95-07-01 W
Pop: 179 (1990); 215 (1980) **Pop Density:** 895.0
Land: 0.2 sq. mi.; **Water:** 0.0 sq. mi.
Incorporated 1879.

Graham Town
ZIP: 64455 **Lat:** 40-12-05 N **Long:** 95-02-23 W
Pop: 204 (1990); 253 (1980) **Pop Density:** 680.0
Land: 0.3 sq. mi.; **Water:** 0.0 sq. mi.
Incorporated 1929.

Grant Township
Lat: 40-11-32 N **Long:** 94-47-25 W
Pop: 561 (1990); 675 (1980) **Pop Density:** 12.0
Land: 46.6 sq. mi.; **Water:** 0.0 sq. mi.

Green Township
Lat: 40-21-52 N **Long:** 95-04-40 W
Pop: 302 (1990); 375 (1980) **Pop Density:** 4.5
Land: 67.1 sq. mi.; **Water:** 0.2 sq. mi.

Guilford Town
ZIP: 64457 **Lat:** 40-10-08 N **Long:** 94-44-09 W
Pop: 93 (1990); 87 (1980) **Pop Density:** 930.0
Land: 0.1 sq. mi.; **Water:** 0.0 sq. mi.
Incorporated 1899.

MISSOURI, Nodaway County

Hopkins — City
ZIP: 64461 **Lat:** 40-33-04 N **Long:** 94-48-58 W
Pop: 575 (1990); 634 (1980) **Pop Density:** 821.4
Land: 0.7 sq. mi.; **Water:** 0.0 sq. mi. **Elev:** 1046 ft.
Founded 1871. Incorporated 1872. Not coextensive with the town of the same name.
Name origin: For railroad agent A.L. Hopkins.

*Hopkins — Township
ZIP: 64461 **Lat:** 40-32-39 N **Long:** 94-49-23 W
Pop: 869 (1990); 956 (1980) **Pop Density:** 22.5
Land: 38.7 sq. mi.; **Water:** 0.1 sq. mi.

Hughes — Township
Lat: 40-11-45 N **Long:** 95-00-04 W
Pop: 543 (1990); 666 (1980) **Pop Density:** 8.5
Land: 64.2 sq. mi.; **Water:** 0.1 sq. mi.

Independence — Township
Lat: 40-29-50 N **Long:** 94-40-44 W
Pop: 456 (1990); 616 (1980) **Pop Density:** 7.5
Land: 61.1 sq. mi.; **Water:** 0.0 sq. mi.

Jackson — Township
Lat: 40-21-35 N **Long:** 94-40-41 W
Pop: 977 (1990); 985 (1980) **Pop Density:** 13.1
Land: 74.8 sq. mi.; **Water:** 0.0 sq. mi.

Jefferson — Township
Lat: 40-15-35 N **Long:** 94-40-38 W
Pop: 836 (1990); 945 (1980) **Pop Density:** 18.9
Land: 44.3 sq. mi.; **Water:** 0.0 sq. mi.

Lincoln — Township
Lat: 40-30-46 N **Long:** 95-07-31 W
Pop: 481 (1990); 563 (1980) **Pop Density:** 7.3
Land: 65.9 sq. mi.; **Water:** 0.1 sq. mi.

Maryville — City
ZIP: 64468 **Lat:** 40-20-36 N **Long:** 94-52-15 W
Pop: 10,663 (1990); 9,558 (1980) **Pop Density:** 2423.4
Land: 4.4 sq. mi.; **Water:** 0.1 sq. mi. **Elev:** 1136 ft.
In northwestern MO, 40 mi. north of St. Joseph. County seat since September 1845. Incorporated 1854.
Name origin: For Mrs. Mary Graham, the first white woman to live within the town limits.

Monroe — Township
Lat: 40-17-22 N **Long:** 95-04-28 W
Pop: 638 (1990); 738 (1980) **Pop Density:** 14.4
Land: 44.2 sq. mi.; **Water:** 0.1 sq. mi.

Nodaway — Township
Lat: 40-26-30 N **Long:** 95-00-53 W
Pop: 922 (1990); 998 (1980) **Pop Density:** 19.8
Land: 46.6 sq. mi.; **Water:** 0.1 sq. mi.

Parnell — City
ZIP: 64475 **Lat:** 40-26-24 N **Long:** 94-37-18 W
Pop: 157 (1990); 223 (1980) **Pop Density:** 785.0
Land: 0.2 sq. mi.; **Water:** 0.0 sq. mi.
Incorporated 1988.

Pickering — Town
ZIP: 64476 **Lat:** 40-27-01 N **Long:** 94-50-30 W
Pop: 171 (1990); 215 (1980) **Pop Density:** 855.0
Land: 0.2 sq. mi.; **Water:** 0.0 sq. mi. **Elev:** 1022 ft.
Incorporated 1879.
Name origin: For railroad official Pickering Clark.

Polk — Township
Lat: 40-21-03 N **Long:** 94-51-53 W
Pop: 13,175 (1990); 12,237 (1980) **Pop Density:** 109.5
Land: 120.3 sq. mi.; **Water:** 0.3 sq. mi.
In northwestern MO.

Quitman — Town
ZIP: 64478 **Lat:** 40-22-23 N **Long:** 95-04-35 W
Pop: 47 (1990); 66 (1980) **Pop Density:** 470.0
Land: 0.1 sq. mi.; **Water:** 0.0 sq. mi. **Elev:** 913 ft.
Incorporated 1875.

Ravenwood — Town
ZIP: 64479 **Lat:** 40-21-09 N **Long:** 94-40-16 W
Pop: 409 (1990); 436 (1980) **Pop Density:** 1363.3
Land: 0.3 sq. mi.; **Water:** 0.0 sq. mi.
Incorporated 1898.

Skidmore — City
ZIP: 64487 **Lat:** 40-17-14 N **Long:** 95-04-43 W
Pop: 404 (1990); 437 (1980) **Pop Density:** 1346.7
Land: 0.3 sq. mi.; **Water:** 0.0 sq. mi. **Elev:** 925 ft.
Incorporated 1933.

Union — Township
Lat: 40-27-56 N **Long:** 94-50-08 W
Pop: 525 (1990); 588 (1980) **Pop Density:** 11.1
Land: 47.2 sq. mi.; **Water:** 0.1 sq. mi.

Washington — Township
Lat: 40-10-37 N **Long:** 94-40-45 W
Pop: 388 (1990); 405 (1980) **Pop Density:** 8.2
Land: 47.3 sq. mi.; **Water:** 0.0 sq. mi.

White Cloud — Township
Lat: 40-12-14 N **Long:** 94-52-38 W
Pop: 512 (1990); 577 (1980) **Pop Density:** 9.7
Land: 53.0 sq. mi.; **Water:** 0.0 sq. mi.

Oregon County
County Seat: Alton (ZIP: 65606)

Pop: 9,470 (1990); 10,238 (1980)
Land: 791.5 sq. mi.; **Water:** 0.2 sq. mi.
Pop Density: 12.0
Area Code: 417

On the central southern border of MO, southwest of Cape Girardeau; organized Feb 14, 1845 from Ripley County.

Name origin: For OR Territory, named during the dispute with Great Britain over its possession.

Alton
City
ZIP: 65606   **Lat:** 36-41-37 N   **Long:** 91-23-56 W
Pop: 692 (1990); 721 (1980)   **Pop Density:** 865.0
Land: 0.8 sq. mi.; **Water:** 0.0 sq. mi.   **Elev:** 779 ft.
Incorporated 1929.

Big Apple
Township
Lat: 36-36-53 N   **Long:** 91-36-56 W
Pop: 727 (1990); 689 (1980)   **Pop Density:** 13.3
Land: 54.6 sq. mi.; **Water:** 0.0 sq. mi.

Billmore
Township
Lat: 36-34-00 N   **Long:** 91-12-56 W
Pop: 109 (1990); 105 (1980)   **Pop Density:** 8.7
Land: 12.5 sq. mi.; **Water:** 0.0 sq. mi.

Black Pond
Township
Lat: 36-51-46 N   **Long:** 91-33-16 W
Pop: 169 (1990); 215 (1980)   **Pop Density:** 3.9
Land: 43.5 sq. mi.; **Water:** 0.0 sq. mi.

Cedar Bluff
Township
Lat: 36-33-08 N   **Long:** 91-09-14 W
Pop: 84 (1990); 140 (1980)   **Pop Density:** 3.3
Land: 25.1 sq. mi.; **Water:** 0.0 sq. mi.

Couch
Township
ZIP: 65690   **Lat:** 36-36-08 N   **Long:** 91-22-47 W
Pop: 398 (1990); 466 (1980)   **Pop Density:** 8.7
Land: 45.7 sq. mi.; **Water:** 0.0 sq. mi.

Falling Spring
Township
Lat: 36-50-01 N   **Long:** 91-16-54 W
Pop: 59 (1990); 56 (1980)   **Pop Density:** 1.5
Land: 40.1 sq. mi.; **Water:** 0.0 sq. mi.

Goebel
Township
Lat: 36-43-23 N   **Long:** 91-16-21 W
Pop: 210 (1990); 251 (1980)   **Pop Density:** 6.6
Land: 31.7 sq. mi.; **Water:** 0.0 sq. mi.

Highland
Township
Lat: 36-42-50 N   **Long:** 91-35-45 W
Pop: 370 (1990); 374 (1980)   **Pop Density:** 7.0
Land: 52.9 sq. mi.; **Water:** 0.0 sq. mi.

Jeff
Township
Lat: 36-31-37 N   **Long:** 91-22-59 W
Pop: 288 (1990); 284 (1980)   **Pop Density:** 10.2
Land: 28.1 sq. mi.; **Water:** 0.0 sq. mi.

Jobe
Township
Lat: 36-35-07 N   **Long:** 91-15-24 W
Pop: 116 (1990); 155 (1980)   **Pop Density:** 5.6
Land: 20.9 sq. mi.; **Water:** 0.0 sq. mi.

Johnson
Township
Lat: 36-39-31 N   **Long:** 91-14-35 W
Pop: 241 (1990); 259 (1980)   **Pop Density:** 7.9
Land: 30.5 sq. mi.; **Water:** 0.0 sq. mi.

King
Township
Lat: 36-46-37 N   **Long:** 91-10-38 W
Pop: 91 (1990); 117 (1980)   **Pop Density:** 2.0
Land: 45.9 sq. mi.; **Water:** 0.0 sq. mi.

Koshkonong
Town
ZIP: 65692   **Lat:** 36-35-39 N   **Long:** 91-38-43 W
Pop: 198 (1990); 245 (1980)   **Pop Density:** 990.0
Land: 0.2 sq. mi.; **Water:** 0.0 sq. mi.   **Elev:** 970 ft.
Incorporated 1899.

Moore
Township
Lat: 36-49-11 N   **Long:** 91-29-37 W
Pop: 387 (1990); 404 (1980)   **Pop Density:** 3.6
Land: 108.3 sq. mi.; **Water:** 0.0 sq. mi.

Myrtle
Township
ZIP: 65778   **Lat:** 36-31-17 N   **Long:** 91-15-01 W
Pop: 404 (1990); 549 (1980)   **Pop Density:** 15.6
Land: 25.9 sq. mi.; **Water:** 0.0 sq. mi.

Ozark
Township
Lat: 36-40-36 N   **Long:** 91-09-16 W
Pop: 91 (1990); 84 (1980)   **Pop Density:** 2.8
Land: 33.0 sq. mi.; **Water:** 0.0 sq. mi.

Piney
Township
Lat: 36-41-16 N   **Long:** 91-24-23 W
Pop: 1,977 (1990); 1,976 (1980)   **Pop Density:** 25.2
Land: 78.3 sq. mi.; **Water:** 0.0 sq. mi.

Thayer
City
ZIP: 65791   **Lat:** 36-31-28 N   **Long:** 91-32-28 W
Pop: 1,996 (1990); 2,211 (1980)   **Pop Density:** 950.5
Land: 2.1 sq. mi.; **Water:** 0.0 sq. mi.   **Elev:** 532 ft.
Incorporated 1890.
Name origin: For stockholder Nathaniel Thayer of Boston.

*Thayer
Township
ZIP: 65791   **Lat:** 36-33-30 N   **Long:** 91-31-56 W
Pop: 3,473 (1990); 3,776 (1980)   **Pop Density:** 41.5
Land: 83.6 sq. mi.; **Water:** 0.0 sq. mi.

Woodside
Township
Lat: 36-46-10 N   **Long:** 91-22-58 W
Pop: 276 (1990); 338 (1980)   **Pop Density:** 8.9
Land: 31.0 sq. mi.; **Water:** 0.0 sq. mi.

MISSOURI, Osage County

Osage County
County Seat: Linn (ZIP: 65051)

Pop: 12,018 (1990); 12,014 (1980)
Land: 606.1 sq. mi.; **Water:** 7.3 sq. mi.
Pop Density: 19.8
Area Code: 314

In east-central MO, west of St. Louis; organized Jan 29, 1841 from Gasconade County.

Name origin: For the Osage Indians, a tribe of Siouan linguistic stock. Name is a corruption of their name in their language, *Wazhazhe*, meaning unknown.

Argyle
Town
ZIP: 65001 **Lat:** 38-17-43 N **Long:** 92-01-31 W
Pop: 171 (1990); 206 (1980) **Pop Density:** 427.5
Land: 0.4 sq. mi.; **Water:** 0.0 sq. mi. **Elev:** 719 ft.
Incorporated 1908. Part of the town is also in Maries County.
Name origin: Named by early settlers for their homeland in Scotland.

Belle
City
ZIP: 65013 **Lat:** 38-17-33 N **Long:** 91-42-53 W
Pop: 149 (1990); 134 (1980) **Pop Density:** 745.0
Land: 0.2 sq. mi.; **Water:** 0.0 sq. mi. **Elev:** 1039 ft.
Incorporated 1901. Part of the town is also in Maries County.

Benton
Township
Lat: 38-37-18 N **Long:** 91-44-41 W
Pop: 1,197 (1990); 1,412 (1980) **Pop Density:** 11.1
Land: 107.4 sq. mi.; **Water:** 1.7 sq. mi.

Bland
City
ZIP: 65014 **Lat:** 38-18-05 N **Long:** 91-38-43 W
Pop: 0 (1990)
Land: 0.02 sq. mi.; **Water:** 0.0 sq. mi. **Elev:** 1023 ft.
Incorporated 1902. Part of the town is also in Gasconade County.
Name origin: For U.S. Congressman Richard P. Bland (1835–99).

Chamois
City
ZIP: 65024 **Lat:** 38-40-37 N **Long:** 91-46-12 W
Pop: 449 (1990); 546 (1980) **Pop Density:** 1122.5
Land: 0.4 sq. mi.; **Water:** 0.0 sq. mi. **Elev:** 530 ft.
Incorporated 1868.

Crawford
Township
Lat: 38-29-12 N **Long:** 91-45-41 W
Pop: 3,452 (1990); 3,359 (1980) **Pop Density:** 28.8
Land: 119.9 sq. mi.; **Water:** 0.8 sq. mi.

Freeburg
Village
ZIP: 65035 **Lat:** 38-18-55 N **Long:** 91-55-20 W
Pop: 446 (1990); 554 (1980) **Pop Density:** 557.5
Land: 0.8 sq. mi.; **Water:** 0.0 sq. mi. **Elev:** 899 ft.
Incorporated 1909.

Jackson
Township
Lat: 38-22-05 N **Long:** 92-05-50 W
Pop: 1,235 (1990); 1,374 (1980) **Pop Density:** 13.5
Land: 91.6 sq. mi.; **Water:** 1.4 sq. mi.

Jefferson
Township
Lat: 38-21-10 N **Long:** 91-43-47 W
Pop: 1,034 (1990); 1,032 (1980) **Pop Density:** 11.6
Land: 89.2 sq. mi.; **Water:** 0.6 sq. mi.

Linn
City
ZIP: 65051 **Lat:** 38-28-50 N **Long:** 91-50-39 W
Pop: 1,148 (1990); 1,211 (1980) **Pop Density:** 1435.0
Land: 0.8 sq. mi.; **Water:** 0.0 sq. mi.
Incorporated 1911.
Name origin: For U. S. Senator Lewis F. Linn.

*Linn
Township
ZIP: 65051 **Lat:** 38-32-59 N **Long:** 91-56-06 W
Pop: 2,122 (1990); 1,903 (1980) **Pop Density:** 28.4
Land: 74.8 sq. mi.; **Water:** 2.4 sq. mi.

Meta
City
ZIP: 65058 **Lat:** 38-18-44 N **Long:** 92-09-59 W
Pop: 249 (1990); 336 (1980) **Pop Density:** 830.0
Land: 0.3 sq. mi.; **Water:** 0.0 sq. mi. **Elev:** 610 ft.
Incorporated 1959.

Washington
Township
Lat: 38-22-49 N **Long:** 91-55-36 W
Pop: 2,978 (1990); 2,934 (1980) **Pop Density:** 24.2
Land: 123.2 sq. mi.; **Water:** 0.3 sq. mi.

Westphalia
City
ZIP: 65085 **Lat:** 38-26-28 N **Long:** 92-00-01 W
Pop: 287 (1990); 285 (1980) **Pop Density:** 717.5
Land: 0.4 sq. mi.; **Water:** 0.0 sq. mi. **Elev:** 622 ft.
Incorporated 1905.
Name origin: For Westphalia, Germany.

> ## Ozark County
> **County Seat: Gainesville (ZIP: 65655)**
>
> **Pop:** 8,598 (1990); 7,961 (1980) **Pop Density:** 11.5
> **Land:** 746.8 sq. mi.; **Water:** 8.3 sq. mi. **Area Code:** 417
> On the central southern border of MO, southeast of Springfield; organized Jan 29, 1841 from Taney County.
> **Name origin:** For the Ozark Mountains, whose name derives from the anglicized phonetic spelling of French *aux arcs* or *aux Arks* 'in the country of the Arkansas Indians.'

Bakersfield — Village
ZIP: 65609 **Lat:** 36-31-26 N **Long:** 92-08-39 W
Pop: 292 (1990); 241 (1980) **Pop Density:** 208.6
Land: 1.4 sq. mi.; **Water:** 0.0 sq. mi. **Elev:** 718 ft.
Incorporated 1967.

Barren Fork — Township
Lat: 36-44-46 N **Long:** 92-29-29 W
Pop: 455 (1990); 427 (1980) **Pop Density:** 9.0
Land: 50.3 sq. mi.; **Water:** 0.0 sq. mi.

Bayou — Township
Lat: 36-34-27 N **Long:** 92-11-16 W
Pop: 1,455 (1990); 1,197 (1980) **Pop Density:** 17.7
Land: 82.3 sq. mi.; **Water:** 0.6 sq. mi.

Big Creek — Township
Lat: 36-33-26 N **Long:** 92-42-26 W
Pop: 855 (1990); 766 (1980) **Pop Density:** 15.0
Land: 57.0 sq. mi.; **Water:** 1.5 sq. mi.

Bridges — Township
Lat: 36-35-54 N **Long:** 92-26-53 W
Pop: 1,918 (1990); 1,922 (1980) **Pop Density:** 19.5
Land: 98.5 sq. mi.; **Water:** 0.0 sq. mi.

Dawt — Township
Lat: 36-35-29 N **Long:** 92-17-04 W
Pop: 263 (1990); 237 (1980) **Pop Density:** 14.4
Land: 18.3 sq. mi.; **Water:** 0.0 sq. mi.

Gainesville — City
ZIP: 65655 **Lat:** 36-36-20 N **Long:** 92-25-25 W
Pop: 659 (1990); 707 (1980) **Pop Density:** 263.6
Land: 2.5 sq. mi.; **Water:** 0.0 sq. mi. **Elev:** 759 ft.
Incorporated 1896.

Jackson — Township
Lat: 36-45-18 N **Long:** 92-23-00 W
Pop: 198 (1990); 197 (1980) **Pop Density:** 4.7
Land: 41.7 sq. mi.; **Water:** 0.0 sq. mi.

Jasper — Township
Lat: 36-34-55 N **Long:** 92-36-13 W
Pop: 571 (1990); 422 (1980) **Pop Density:** 17.9
Land: 31.9 sq. mi.; **Water:** 2.9 sq. mi.

Lick Creek — Township
Lat: 36-32-17 N **Long:** 92-20-18 W
Pop: 386 (1990); 413 (1980) **Pop Density:** 9.9
Land: 39.0 sq. mi.; **Water:** 0.5 sq. mi.

Longrun — Township
ZIP: 65761 **Lat:** 36-39-25 N **Long:** 92-43-31 W
Pop: 99 (1990); 91 (1980) **Pop Density:** 5.0
Land: 19.7 sq. mi.; **Water:** 0.0 sq. mi.

Noble — Township
ZIP: 65715 **Lat:** 36-45-30 N **Long:** 92-35-21 W
Pop: 318 (1990); 346 (1980) **Pop Density:** 11.1
Land: 28.7 sq. mi.; **Water:** 0.0 sq. mi.

Nottinghill — Township
Lat: 36-40-10 N **Long:** 92-34-41 W
Pop: 142 (1990); 155 (1980) **Pop Density:** 3.7
Land: 38.9 sq. mi.; **Water:** 0.0 sq. mi.

Pine Creek — Township
Lat: 36-41-13 N **Long:** 92-20-43 W
Pop: 371 (1990); 288 (1980) **Pop Density:** 7.9
Land: 46.9 sq. mi.; **Water:** 0.0 sq. mi.

Pontiac — Township
ZIP: 65729 **Lat:** 36-30-52 N **Long:** 92-33-27 W
Pop: 243 (1990); 185 (1980) **Pop Density:** 13.2
Land: 18.4 sq. mi.; **Water:** 2.7 sq. mi.

Richland — Township
Lat: 36-43-54 N **Long:** 92-14-43 W
Pop: 763 (1990); 742 (1980) **Pop Density:** 10.7
Land: 71.6 sq. mi.; **Water:** 0.0 sq. mi.

Spring Creek — Township
Lat: 36-43-04 N **Long:** 92-09-21 W
Pop: 86 (1990); 89 (1980) **Pop Density:** 2.8
Land: 31.1 sq. mi.; **Water:** 0.0 sq. mi.

Sundown — Village
Lat: 36-33-55 N **Long:** 92-38-14 W
Pop: 35 (1990); 39 (1980) **Pop Density:** 35.0
Land: 1.0 sq. mi.; **Water:** 0.0 sq. mi.
Incorporated 1976.

Theodosia — Village
ZIP: 65761 **Lat:** 36-34-47 N **Long:** 92-39-54 W
Pop: 235 (1990); 204 (1980) **Pop Density:** 180.8
Land: 1.3 sq. mi.; **Water:** 0.2 sq. mi.
Incorporated 1963.

Thornfield — Township
ZIP: 65762 **Lat:** 36-43-19 N **Long:** 92-41-40 W
Pop: 475 (1990); 484 (1980) **Pop Density:** 6.5
Land: 72.8 sq. mi.; **Water:** 0.0 sq. mi.

Pemiscot County
County Seat: Caruthersville (ZIP: 63830)

Pop: 21,921 (1990); 24,987 (1980)
Land: 493.1 sq. mi.; **Water:** 19.3 sq. mi.
Pop Density: 44.5
Area Code: 314

On southeastern tip of MO, south of Cape Girardeau; organized Feb 19, 1851 from New Madrid County.

Name origin: From an Indian name of uncertain origin and meaning: 'at the long place,' 'running beside,' and 'liquid mud' have been suggested.

Braggadocio — Township
Lat: 36-11-25 N Long: 89-53-02 W
Pop: 980 (1990); 1,243 (1980) Pop Density: 19.1
Land: 51.4 sq. mi.; Water: 0.0 sq. mi.

Bragg City — Town
ZIP: 63827 Lat: 36-16-06 N Long: 89-54-41 W
Pop: 117 (1990); 200 (1980) Pop Density: 585.0
Land: 0.2 sq. mi.; Water: 0.0 sq. mi.
Incorporated 1970.

Butler — Township
Lat: 36-22-07 N Long: 89-37-35 W
Pop: 248 (1990); 400 (1980) Pop Density: 9.0
Land: 27.7 sq. mi.; Water: 2.9 sq. mi.

Caruthersville — City
ZIP: 63830 Lat: 36-10-44 N Long: 89-39-54 W
Pop: 7,389 (1990); 7,958 (1980) Pop Density: 1508.0
Land: 4.9 sq. mi.; Water: 0.0 sq. mi. Elev: 282 ft.
Incorporated 1874.

Concord — Township
Lat: 36-16-58 N Long: 89-39-53 W
Pop: 401 (1990); 357 (1980) Pop Density: 7.4
Land: 54.4 sq. mi.; Water: 6.3 sq. mi.

Cooter — Town
ZIP: 63839 Lat: 36-02-49 N Long: 89-48-34 W
Pop: 451 (1990); 479 (1980) Pop Density: 1503.3
Land: 0.3 sq. mi.; Water: 0.0 sq. mi.
Incorporated 1964.

Name origin: Named in 1854 for the Coutre family, one of whom was a merchant in New Madrid in 1795; with a spelling variation.

*Cooter — Township
Lat: 36-03-01 N Long: 89-48-41 W
Pop: 3,353 (1990); 3,519 (1980) Pop Density: 108.2
Land: 31.0 sq. mi.; Water: 0.0 sq. mi.

Godair — Township
Lat: 36-22-17 N Long: 89-42-53 W
Pop: 369 (1990); 500 (1980) Pop Density: 13.2
Land: 27.9 sq. mi.; Water: 0.0 sq. mi.

Hayti — City
ZIP: 63851 Lat: 36-13-56 N Long: 89-44-54 W
Pop: 3,280 (1990); 3,964 (1980) Pop Density: 1490.9
Land: 2.2 sq. mi.; Water: 0.0 sq. mi. Elev: 273 ft.
In southeastern MO near the TN border. Incorporated 1896.

Name origin: A variant spelling for Haiti, the island country in the West Indies.

*Hayti — Township
ZIP: 63851 Lat: 36-13-28 N Long: 89-45-17 W
Pop: 4,672 (1990); 5,319 (1980) Pop Density: 198.8
Land: 23.5 sq. mi.; Water: 0.2 sq. mi.

Hayti Heights — City
Lat: 36-13-56 N Long: 89-46-06 W
Pop: 893 (1990); 1,023 (1980) Pop Density: 893.0
Land: 1.0 sq. mi.; Water: 0.0 sq. mi.
Incorporated 1972.

Hayward — Town
Lat: 36-23-46 N Long: 89-39-57 W
Pop: 103 (1990); 123 (1980) Pop Density: 515.0
Land: 0.2 sq. mi.; Water: 0.0 sq. mi.

Holland — Town
ZIP: 63853 Lat: 36-03-26 N Long: 89-52-13 W
Pop: 237 (1990); 295 (1980) Pop Density: 1185.0
Land: 0.2 sq. mi.; Water: 0.0 sq. mi.
Incorporated 1903.

*Holland — Township
Lat: 36-02-06 N Long: 89-54-00 W
Pop: 613 (1990); 727 (1980) Pop Density: 23.4
Land: 26.2 sq. mi.; Water: 0.0 sq. mi.

Homestown — City
Lat: 36-19-54 N Long: 89-49-28 W
Pop: 230 (1990); 306 (1980) Pop Density: 2300.0
Land: 0.1 sq. mi.; Water: 0.0 sq. mi.
Incorporated 1954.

Little Prairie — Township
Lat: 36-09-28 N Long: 89-42-14 W
Pop: 8,376 (1990); 9,204 (1980) Pop Density: 131.3
Land: 63.8 sq. mi.; Water: 4.8 sq. mi.

Little River — Township
Lat: 36-21-14 N Long: 89-51-34 W
Pop: 1,095 (1990); 1,303 (1980) Pop Density: 21.1
Land: 51.8 sq. mi.; Water: 0.0 sq. mi.

North Wardell — Village
Lat: 36-21-27 N Long: 89-48-55 W
Pop: 135 (1990); 184 (1980) Pop Density: 1350.0
Land: 0.1 sq. mi.; Water: 0.0 sq. mi.
Incorporated 1946.

Pascola — Town
ZIP: 63871 Lat: 36-15-57 N Long: 89-49-35 W
Pop: 120 (1990); 211 (1980) Pop Density: 600.0
Land: 0.2 sq. mi.; Water: 0.0 sq. mi. Elev: 268 ft.
Incorporated 1800.

*Pascola — Township
Lat: 36-16-41 N Long: 89-52-39 W
Pop: 711 (1990); 991 (1980) Pop Density: 12.4
Land: 57.3 sq. mi.; Water: 0.0 sq. mi.

Pemiscot — Township
Lat: 36-04-07 N Long: 89-43-48 W
Pop: 459 (1990); 571 (1980) **Pop Density:** 12.6
Land: 36.5 sq. mi.; **Water:** 4.9 sq. mi.

Portageville — City
ZIP: 63873 Lat: 36-25-04 N Long: 89-42-30 W
Pop: 0 (1990) **Elev:** 281 ft.
Land: 0.2 sq. mi.; **Water:** 0.0 sq. mi.
In southeastern MO, 19 mi. north of Caruthersville. Incorporated 1900. Part of the town is also in New Madrid County.

Steele — City
ZIP: 63877 Lat: 36-05-05 N Long: 89-50-48 W
Pop: 2,395 (1990); 2,419 (1980) **Pop Density:** 1330.6
Land: 1.8 sq. mi.; **Water:** 0.0 sq. mi.
Incorporated 1901.
Name origin: For merchant L. L. Steele.

Virginia — Township
Lat: 36-06-02 N Long: 89-53-52 W
Pop: 644 (1990); 853 (1980) **Pop Density:** 15.5
Land: 41.6 sq. mi.; **Water:** 0.1 sq. mi.

Wardell — Town
ZIP: 63879 Lat: 36-21-02 N Long: 89-49-00 W
Pop: 325 (1990); 299 (1980) **Pop Density:** 1625.0
Land: 0.2 sq. mi.; **Water:** 0.0 sq. mi.
Incorporated 1912.

Perry County
County Seat: Perryville (ZIP: 63775)

Pop: 16,648 (1990); 16,784 (1980) **Pop Density:** 35.1
Land: 474.7 sq. mi.; **Water:** 9.6 sq. mi. **Area Code:** 314

On the southeastern border of MO, north of Cape Girardeau; organized Nov 16, 1820 (prior to statehood) from Ste. Genevieve County.

Name origin: For Oliver Hazard Perry (1785–1819), U.S. naval officer who won the Battle of Lake Erie during the War of 1812, famous for the message, "We have met the enemy and they are ours."

Altenburg — City
ZIP: 63732 Lat: 37-37-52 N Long: 89-34-53 W
Pop: 307 (1990); 280 (1980) **Pop Density:** 341.1
Land: 0.9 sq. mi.; **Water:** 0.0 sq. mi.
Incorporated 1870.
Name origin: Named by settlers in 1839 for the capital of the Duchy of Saxe-Altenburg, Germany.

Bois Brule — Township
Lat: 37-49-00 N Long: 89-47-19 W
Pop: 612 (1990); 696 (1980) **Pop Density:** 10.1
Land: 60.5 sq. mi.; **Water:** 2.8 sq. mi.

Brazeau — Township
Lat: 37-38-34 N Long: 89-34-14 W
Pop: 1,129 (1990); 1,173 (1980) **Pop Density:** 17.7
Land: 63.8 sq. mi.; **Water:** 4.3 sq. mi.

Central — Township
Lat: 37-43-54 N Long: 89-51-44 W
Pop: 9,318 (1990); 9,582 (1980) **Pop Density:** 169.1
Land: 55.1 sq. mi.; **Water:** 0.2 sq. mi.

Cinque Hommes — Township
Lat: 37-38-18 N Long: 89-51-46 W
Pop: 1,137 (1990); 1,178 (1980) **Pop Density:** 20.5
Land: 55.5 sq. mi.; **Water:** 0.0 sq. mi.

Frohna — City
ZIP: 63748 Lat: 37-38-11 N Long: 89-37-13 W
Pop: 162 (1990); 265 (1980) **Pop Density:** 270.0
Land: 0.6 sq. mi.; **Water:** 0.0 sq. mi.
Incorporated 1946.

Lithium — Village
Lat: 37-49-55 N Long: 89-53-01 W
Pop: 75 (1990); 81 (1980) **Pop Density:** 750.0
Land: 0.1 sq. mi.; **Water:** 0.0 sq. mi.
Founded 1882.
Name origin: For the metal found here.

Longtown — Town
Lat: 37-40-11 N Long: 89-46-24 W
Pop: 107 (1990); 121 (1980) **Pop Density:** 1070.0
Land: 0.1 sq. mi.; **Water:** 0.0 sq. mi.
Incorporated 1871.

Perryville — City
ZIP: 63775 Lat: 37-43-33 N Long: 89-52-19 W
Pop: 6,933 (1990); 7,343 (1980) **Pop Density:** 1019.6
Land: 6.8 sq. mi.; **Water:** 0.0 sq. mi.
In southeastern MO, 35 mi. north-northwest of Cape Girardeau. Incorporated 1831.
Name origin: For Oliver Hazard Perry (1785–1819), U.S. naval officer who won the Battle of Lake Erie during the War of 1812, famous for the message, "We have met the enemy and they are ours."

St. Marys — Township
Lat: 37-39-48 N Long: 90-01-40 W
Pop: 1,326 (1990); 1,017 (1980) **Pop Density:** 13.0
Land: 101.8 sq. mi.; **Water:** 0.7 sq. mi.

Salem — Township
Lat: 37-43-09 N Long: 89-42-23 W
Pop: 694 (1990); 789 (1980) **Pop Density:** 14.8
Land: 47.0 sq. mi.; **Water:** 1.5 sq. mi.

MISSOURI, Perry County

Saline
Township
Lat: 37-48-53 N **Long:** 89-56-15 W
Pop: 1,383 (1990); 1,305 (1980) **Pop Density:** 30.5
Land: 45.3 sq. mi.; **Water:** 0.0 sq. mi.

Union
Township
Lat: 37-38-33 N **Long:** 89-42-50 W
Pop: 1,049 (1990); 1,044 (1980) **Pop Density:** 23.0
Land: 45.6 sq. mi.; **Water:** 0.0 sq. mi.

Pettis County
County Seat: Sedalia (ZIP: 65301)

Pop: 35,437 (1990); 36,378 (1980) **Pop Density:** 51.7
Land: 685.0 sq. mi.; **Water:** 1.4 sq. mi. **Area Code:** 816

In west-central MO, southwest of Columbia; organized Jan 26, 1833 from Saline and Cooper counties.

Name origin: For Spencer Darwin Pettis (1802–31), U.S. representative from MO (1829–31) killed in a duel with Maj. Thomas Biddle.

Blackwater
Township
Lat: 38-52-32 N **Long:** 93-26-31 W
Pop: 353 (1990); 432 (1980) **Pop Density:** 6.5
Land: 54.5 sq. mi.; **Water:** 0.0 sq. mi.

Bowling Green
Township
Lat: 38-45-16 N **Long:** 93-06-17 W
Pop: 805 (1990); 745 (1980) **Pop Density:** 21.6
Land: 37.2 sq. mi.; **Water:** 0.0 sq. mi.

Cedar
Township
Lat: 38-45-43 N **Long:** 93-13-27 W
Pop: 707 (1990); 614 (1980) **Pop Density:** 23.7
Land: 29.8 sq. mi.; **Water:** 0.0 sq. mi.

Dresden
Township
Lat: 38-45-32 N **Long:** 93-20-02 W
Pop: 610 (1990); 631 (1980) **Pop Density:** 16.8
Land: 36.3 sq. mi.; **Water:** 0.0 sq. mi.

Elk Fork
Township
Lat: 38-40-42 N **Long:** 93-27-04 W
Pop: 332 (1990); 383 (1980) **Pop Density:** 9.2
Land: 36.0 sq. mi.; **Water:** 0.0 sq. mi.

Flat Creek
Township
Lat: 38-35-21 N **Long:** 93-13-30 W
Pop: 1,418 (1990); 1,291 (1980) **Pop Density:** 27.8
Land: 51.0 sq. mi.; **Water:** 0.3 sq. mi.

Green Ridge
Town
ZIP: 65332 **Lat:** 38-37-12 N **Long:** 93-24-35 W
Pop: 452 (1990); 488 (1980) **Pop Density:** 1130.0
Land: 0.4 sq. mi.; **Water:** 0.0 sq. mi.
Incorporated 1903.

*Green Ridge
Township
ZIP: 65332 **Lat:** 38-34-12 N **Long:** 93-27-03 W
Pop: 957 (1990); 1,104 (1980) **Pop Density:** 18.8
Land: 50.9 sq. mi.; **Water:** 0.0 sq. mi.

Heaths Creek
Township
Lat: 38-52-05 N **Long:** 93-07-01 W
Pop: 461 (1990); 482 (1980) **Pop Density:** 8.3
Land: 55.7 sq. mi.; **Water:** 0.0 sq. mi.

Houstonia
City
ZIP: 65333 **Lat:** 38-53-57 N **Long:** 93-21-35 W
Pop: 283 (1990); 327 (1980) **Pop Density:** 1415.0
Land: 0.2 sq. mi.; **Water:** 0.0 sq. mi.
Incorporated 1879.

*Houstonia
Township
ZIP: 65333 **Lat:** 38-53-45 N **Long:** 93-20-38 W
Pop: 534 (1990); 552 (1980) **Pop Density:** 17.6
Land: 30.3 sq. mi.; **Water:** 0.1 sq. mi.

Hughesville
Village
ZIP: 65334 **Lat:** 38-50-16 N **Long:** 93-17-45 W
Pop: 174 (1990); 152 (1980) **Pop Density:** 1740.0
Land: 0.1 sq. mi.; **Water:** 0.0 sq. mi. **Elev:** 808 ft.
Incorporated 1905.

*Hughesville
Township
ZIP: 65334 **Lat:** 38-50-24 N **Long:** 93-17-36 W
Pop: 502 (1990); 446 (1980) **Pop Density:** 12.6
Land: 39.7 sq. mi.; **Water:** 0.0 sq. mi.

Ionia
Town
ZIP: 65335 **Lat:** 38-30-27 N **Long:** 93-19-21 W
Pop: 0 (1990)
Land: 0.006 sq. mi.; **Water:** 0.0 sq. mi.
Laid out 1866 by Henry Pollard. Incorporated 1904. Part of the town is also in Benton County.
Name origin: For the ancient Greek region.

Lake Creek
Township
Lat: 38-34-38 N **Long:** 93-06-54 W
Pop: 408 (1990); 394 (1980) **Pop Density:** 10.9
Land: 37.5 sq. mi.; **Water:** 0.0 sq. mi.

La Monte
City
ZIP: 65337 **Lat:** 38-46-16 N **Long:** 93-25-21 W
Pop: 995 (1990); 1,054 (1980) **Pop Density:** 995.0
Land: 1.0 sq. mi.; **Water:** 0.0 sq. mi.
Incorporated 1880.

*La Monte
Township
ZIP: 65337 **Lat:** 38-45-47 N **Long:** 93-26-33 W
Pop: 1,384 (1990); 1,474 (1980) **Pop Density:** 38.0
Land: 36.4 sq. mi.; **Water:** 0.1 sq. mi.

Longwood
Township
Lat: 38-52-38 N **Long:** 93-12-43 W
Pop: 414 (1990); 364 (1980) **Pop Density:** 10.8
Land: 38.5 sq. mi.; **Water:** 0.0 sq. mi.

Prairie
Township
Lat: 38-40-21 N **Long:** 93-20-31 W
Pop: 1,143 (1990); 936 (1980) **Pop Density:** 31.7
Land: 36.1 sq. mi.; **Water:** 0.1 sq. mi.

Sedalia City
ZIP: 65301   **Lat:** 38-42-10 N   **Long:** 93-13-59 W
Pop: 19,800 (1990); 20,927 (1980)   **Pop Density:** 1767.9
Land: 11.2 sq. mi.; **Water:** 0.0 sq. mi.   **Elev:** 919 ft.

In west-central MO, 60 mi. west of Jefferson City. Founded 1860; platted by pioneer George Smith. Incorporated 1864.

Name origin: Named October 16, 1860, by Gen. George R. Smith, for his daughter, Sarah Elvira, nicknamed *Sed*. Originally called Sedville.

Sedalia Township
ZIP: 65301   **Lat:** 38-41-31 N   **Long:** 93-13-47 W
Pop: 22,297 (1990); 23,183 (1980)   **Pop Density:** 779.6
Land: 28.6 sq. mi.; **Water:** 0.1 sq. mi.

Smithton City
ZIP: 65350   **Lat:** 38-40-53 N   **Long:** 93-05-32 W
Pop: 532 (1990); 559 (1980)   **Pop Density:** 1773.3
Land: 0.3 sq. mi.; **Water:** 0.0 sq. mi.   **Elev:** 888 ft.

Incorporated 1955.

*Smithton Township
ZIP: 65350   **Lat:** 38-40-03 N   **Long:** 93-06-55 W
Pop: 2,474 (1990); 2,710 (1980)   **Pop Density:** 67.4
Land: 36.7 sq. mi.; **Water:** 0.1 sq. mi.

Washington Township
   Lat: 38-34-16 N   **Long:** 93-20-39 W
Pop: 638 (1990); 637 (1980)   **Pop Density:** 12.8
Land: 50.0 sq. mi.; **Water:** 0.2 sq. mi.

Windsor City
ZIP: 65360   **Lat:** 38-32-06 N   **Long:** 93-30-34 W
Pop: 96 (1990); 118 (1980)   **Pop Density:** 320.0
Land: 0.3 sq. mi.; **Water:** 0.0 sq. mi.

Founded 1855. Incorporated 1855. Part of the town is also in Henry County.

Name origin: Named Dec 9, 1859, for Windsor Castle in England. Previously called Belmont.

Phelps County
County Seat: Rolla (ZIP: 65401)

Pop: 35,248 (1990); 33,633 (1980)   **Pop Density:** 52.4
Land: 672.9 sq. mi.; **Water:** 1.4 sq. mi.   **Area Code:** 314

In south-central MO, southwest of St. Louis; organized Nov 13, 1857 from Crawford County.

Name origin: For John Smith Phelps (1814–86), MO legislator, U.S. representative (1845–63), and governor (1876–80).

Arlington Township
   Lat: 37-56-01 N   **Long:** 91-56-53 W
Pop: 2,385 (1990); 2,424 (1980)   **Pop Density:** 39.0
Land: 61.2 sq. mi.; **Water:** 0.5 sq. mi.

Cold Spring Township
   Lat: 37-50-00 N   **Long:** 91-44-17 W
Pop: 1,787 (1990); 1,676 (1980)   **Pop Density:** 24.3
Land: 73.4 sq. mi.; **Water:** 0.0 sq. mi.

Dawson Township
   Lat: 38-05-47 N   **Long:** 91-34-47 W
Pop: 518 (1990); 490 (1980)   **Pop Density:** 12.6
Land: 41.1 sq. mi.; **Water:** 0.0 sq. mi.

Dillon Township
ZIP: 65401   **Lat:** 37-57-46 N   **Long:** 91-41-40 W
Pop: 6,453 (1990); 5,423 (1980)   **Pop Density:** 85.9
Land: 75.1 sq. mi.; **Water:** 0.2 sq. mi.

Doolittle City
ZIP: 65401   **Lat:** 37-56-29 N   **Long:** 91-53-16 W
Pop: 599 (1990); 701 (1980)   **Pop Density:** 239.6
Land: 2.5 sq. mi.; **Water:** 0.0 sq. mi.   **Elev:** 1008 ft.

Incorporated 1941.

Edgar Springs City
ZIP: 65462   **Lat:** 37-42-06 N   **Long:** 91-51-56 W
Pop: 215 (1990); 271 (1980)   **Pop Density:** 430.0
Land: 0.5 sq. mi.; **Water:** 0.0 sq. mi.

Incorporated 1974.

Liberty Township
   Lat: 37-50-22 N   **Long:** 91-56-21 W
Pop: 293 (1990); 314 (1980)   **Pop Density:** 5.5
Land: 53.5 sq. mi.; **Water:** 0.0 sq. mi.

Meramec Township
   Lat: 37-52-44 N   **Long:** 91-34-44 W
Pop: 671 (1990); 581 (1980)   **Pop Density:** 9.5
Land: 70.4 sq. mi.; **Water:** 0.0 sq. mi.

Miller Township
   Lat: 38-00-22 N   **Long:** 91-51-07 W
Pop: 2,428 (1990); 2,085 (1980)   **Pop Density:** 36.0
Land: 67.5 sq. mi.; **Water:** 0.3 sq. mi.

Newburg City
ZIP: 65550   **Lat:** 37-55-00 N   **Long:** 91-54-04 W
Pop: 589 (1990); 743 (1980)   **Pop Density:** 981.7
Land: 0.6 sq. mi.; **Water:** 0.0 sq. mi.   **Elev:** 711 ft.

Incorporated 1888.

Rolla City
ZIP: 65401   **Lat:** 37-56-55 N   **Long:** 91-45-56 W
Pop: 14,090 (1990); 13,303 (1980)   **Pop Density:** 1761.3
Land: 8.0 sq. mi.; **Water:** 0.0 sq. mi.   **Elev:** 1119 ft.

In south-central MO, southeast of Jefferson City. Organized 1855. Incorporated 1861.

Name origin: Origin debatable: possibly a phonetic spelling of Raleigh, NC, former home of many of the settlers; or from Irish dramatist Richard B. Sheridan's (1751–1816) popular translation of August von Kotzebue's (1761–1819) play *Pizarro*, subtitled "The Death of Rolla" (1799).

MISSOURI, Phelps County

*Rolla
ZIP: 65401   Lat: 37-55-28 N   Long: 91-48-19 W   Township
Pop: 14,625 (1990); 14,698 (1980)   Pop Density: 404.0
Land: 36.2 sq. mi.; Water: 0.2 sq. mi.

St. James
Lat: 38-00-03 N   Long: 91-36-50 W   City
Pop: 3,256 (1990); 3,328 (1980)   Pop Density: 1252.3
Land: 2.6 sq. mi.; Water: 0.0 sq. mi.   Elev: 1088 ft.

In south-central MO, southeast of Jefferson City. Incorporated 1892.

Name origin: For St. James the Apostle, but indirectly for founder Thomas James.

*St. James
Lat: 38-00-38 N   Long: 91-34-46   Township
Pop: 4,416 (1990); 4,263 (1980)   Pop Density: 126
Land: 34.8 sq. mi.; Water: 0.1 sq. mi.

Spring Creek
Lat: 37-41-50 N   Long: 91-55-28   Township
Pop: 1,672 (1990); 1,679 (1980)   Pop Density: 10
Land: 159.6 sq. mi.; Water: 0.0 sq. mi.

Pike County
County Seat: Bowling Green (ZIP: 63334)

Pop: 15,969 (1990); 17,568 (1980)   Pop Density: 23.7
Land: 672.9 sq. mi.; Water: 11.9 sq. mi.   Area Code: 314

On the central eastern border of MO, north of St. Louis; organized Dec 14, 1818 (prior to statehood) from St. Charles County.

Name origin: For Zebulon Montgomery Pike (1779–1813), U.S. army officer and discoverer of Pikes Peak, CO.

Annada
ZIP: 63330   Lat: 39-15-43 N   Long: 90-49-42 W   Town
Pop: 70 (1990); 70 (1980)   Pop Density: 700.0
Land: 0.1 sq. mi.; Water: 0.0 sq. mi.   Elev: 449 ft.
Incorporated 1912.

Ashburn
ZIP: 63433   Lat: 39-32-46 N   Long: 91-10-15 W   Town
Pop: 51 (1990); 89 (1980)   Pop Density: 510.0
Land: 0.1 sq. mi.; Water: 0.0 sq. mi.

Ashley
Lat: 39-15-15 N   Long: 91-13-01 W   Township
Pop: 567 (1990); 725 (1980)   Pop Density: 16.2
Land: 35.0 sq. mi.; Water: 0.0 sq. mi.

Bowling Green
ZIP: 63334   Lat: 39-20-20 N   Long: 91-11-44 W   City
Pop: 2,976 (1990); 3,022 (1980)   Pop Density: 1566.3
Land: 1.9 sq. mi.; Water: 0.0 sq. mi.   Elev: 899 ft.
Platted 1826. Incorporated 1823.

Name origin: For the former KY home of many of the town's early residents.

Buffalo
Lat: 39-24-46 N   Long: 91-05-46 W   Township
Pop: 5,676 (1990); 6,018 (1980)   Pop Density: 59.3
Land: 95.7 sq. mi.; Water: 2.5 sq. mi.

Calumet
Lat: 39-18-25 N   Long: 90-52-50 W   Township
Pop: 1,418 (1990); 1,657 (1980)   Pop Density: 13.2
Land: 107.8 sq. mi.; Water: 5.0 sq. mi.

Clarksville
ZIP: 63336   Lat: 39-22-18 N   Long: 90-54-20 W   City
Pop: 480 (1990); 585 (1980)   Pop Density: 960.0
Land: 0.5 sq. mi.; Water: 0.4 sq. mi.
Incorporated 1887.

Cuivre
Lat: 39-20-01 N   Long: 91-11-23 W   Township
Pop: 4,694 (1990); 4,856 (1980)   Pop Density: 45.
Land: 103.1 sq. mi.; Water: 0.1 sq. mi.

Curryville
ZIP: 63339   Lat: 39-20-45 N   Long: 91-20-33 W   City
Pop: 261 (1990); 323 (1980)   Pop Density: 1305.0
Land: 0.2 sq. mi.; Water: 0.0 sq. mi.   Elev: 816 ft
Incorporated 1874.

Name origin: For Perry A. Curry, who laid out the town in 1867.

Eolia
ZIP: 63344   Lat: 39-14-23 N   Long: 91-00-40 W   Village
Pop: 389 (1990); 401 (1980)   Pop Density: 324.2
Land: 1.2 sq. mi.; Water: 0.0 sq. mi.   Elev: 833 ft.
Incorporated 1964.

Frankford
ZIP: 63441   Lat: 39-29-35 N   Long: 91-19-14 W   City
Pop: 396 (1990); 443 (1980)   Pop Density: 792.0
Land: 0.5 sq. mi.; Water: 0.0 sq. mi.   Elev: 600 ft.
Incorporated 1889.

Hartford
ZIP: 63364   Lat: 39-10-53 N   Long: 91-18-12 W   Township
Pop: 489 (1990); 558 (1980)   Pop Density: 6.7
Land: 72.7 sq. mi.; Water: 0.1 sq. mi.

Indian
Lat: 39-16-44 N   Long: 91-21-30 W   Township
Pop: 619 (1990); 808 (1980)   Pop Density: 13.9
Land: 44.6 sq. mi.; Water: 0.1 sq. mi.

Louisiana
City
ZIP: 63353 **Lat:** 39-26-36 N **Long:** 91-03-33 W
Pop: 3,967 (1990); 4,261 (1980) **Pop Density:** 1525.8
Land: 2.6 sq. mi.; **Water:** 0.3 sq. mi. **Elev:** 1477 ft.
In eastern MO, northwest of St. Louis. Laid out 1818 by Samuel K. Caldwell and Joel Shaw. Incorporated 1849.
Name origin: For the state.

Paynesville
Town
ZIP: 63371 **Lat:** 39-15-43 N **Long:** 90-53-58 W
Pop: 54 (1990); 85 (1980) **Pop Density:** 180.0
Land: 0.3 sq. mi.; **Water:** 0.0 sq. mi.
Incorporated 1966.

Peno
Township
Lat: 39-29-40 N **Long:** 91-16-41 W
Pop: 836 (1990); 1,067 (1980) **Pop Density:** 13.1
Land: 63.8 sq. mi.; **Water:** 0.3 sq. mi.

Prairieville
Township
ZIP: 63344 **Lat:** 39-15-24 N **Long:** 91-00-28 W
Pop: 688 (1990); 721 (1980) **Pop Density:** 18.4
Land: 37.3 sq. mi.; **Water:** 0.1 sq. mi.

Salt River
Township
Lat: 39-32-32 N **Long:** 91-10-03 W
Pop: 163 (1990); 212 (1980) **Pop Density:** 5.5
Land: 29.7 sq. mi.; **Water:** 3.6 sq. mi.

Spencer
Township
Lat: 39-23-31 N **Long:** 91-22-13 W
Pop: 819 (1990); 946 (1980) **Pop Density:** 9.8
Land: 83.2 sq. mi.; **Water:** 0.2 sq. mi.

Tarrants
Village
ZIP: 63334 **Lat:** 39-21-29 N **Long:** 91-11-00 W
Pop: 43 (1990); 50 (1980) **Pop Density:** 1075.0
Land: 0.04 sq. mi.; **Water:** 0.0 sq. mi.
Incorporated 1964.

Platte County
County Seat: Platte City (ZIP: 64079)

Pop: 57,867 (1990); 46,341 (1980) **Pop Density:** 137.7
Land: 420.4 sq. mi.; **Water:** 6.9 sq. mi. **Area Code:** 816
On the northwestern border of MO, northwest of Kansas City; organized Dec 31, 1838 from Platte Purchase.
Name origin: For the Platte River, which runs through it; French 'flat' or 'still.'

Camden Point
City
ZIP: 64018 **Lat:** 39-27-09 N **Long:** 94-44-49 W
Pop: 373 (1990); 263 (1980) **Pop Density:** 746.0
Land: 0.5 sq. mi.; **Water:** 0.0 sq. mi.
Incorporated 1962.

Carroll
Township
Lat: 39-20-18 N **Long:** 94-42-46 W
Pop: 7,144 (1990); 5,649 (1980) **Pop Density:** 98.1
Land: 72.8 sq. mi.; **Water:** 0.4 sq. mi.

Dearborn
City
ZIP: 64439 **Lat:** 39-31-29 N **Long:** 94-46-22 W
Pop: 480 (1990); 547 (1980) **Pop Density:** 800.0
Land: 0.6 sq. mi.; **Water:** 0.0 sq. mi.
Incorporated 1882. Part of the town is also in Buchanan County.
Name origin: For Gen. Henry Dearborn (1751–1829), secretary of war under Thomas Jefferson (1743–1826).

Edgerton
City
ZIP: 64444 **Lat:** 39-30-18 N **Long:** 94-37-50 W
Pop: 565 (1990); 584 (1980) **Pop Density:** 1412.5
Land: 0.4 sq. mi.; **Water:** 0.0 sq. mi.
Incorporated 1883.

Fair
Township
Lat: 39-23-48 N **Long:** 94-47-46 W
Pop: 760 (1990); 725 (1980) **Pop Density:** 22.8
Land: 33.3 sq. mi.; **Water:** 0.3 sq. mi.

Farley
Village
ZIP: 64028 **Lat:** 39-16-56 N **Long:** 94-49-42 W
Pop: 217 (1990); 184 (1980) **Pop Density:** 434.0
Land: 0.5 sq. mi.; **Water:** 0.0 sq. mi.
Incorporated 1850.

Ferrelview
Village
Lat: 39-18-49 N **Long:** 94-39-55 W
Pop: 338 (1990); 447 (1980) **Pop Density:** 3380.0
Land: 0.1 sq. mi.; **Water:** 0.0 sq. mi.
Incorporated 1948.

Fox
Township
Lat: 39-12-51 N **Long:** 94-39-07 W
Pop: 9,553 (1990); 7,226 (1980) **Pop Density:** 1736.9
Land: 5.5 sq. mi.; **Water:** 0.0 sq. mi.

Green
Township
Lat: 39-29-31 N **Long:** 94-45-08 W
Pop: 1,937 (1990); 1,739 (1980) **Pop Density:** 33.0
Land: 58.7 sq. mi.; **Water:** 0.0 sq. mi.

Houston Lake
City
Lat: 39-11-30 N **Long:** 94-37-24 W
Pop: 303 (1990); 280 (1980) **Pop Density:** 3030.0
Land: 0.1 sq. mi.; **Water:** 0.0 sq. mi.
Incorporated 1960.

Iatan
Village
Lat: 39-28-30 N **Long:** 94-58-53 W
Pop: 47 (1990); 64 (1980) **Pop Density:** 1175.0
Land: 0.04 sq. mi.; **Water:** 0.0 sq. mi.
Incorporated 1974.

MISSOURI, Platte County

Kansas City *City*
ZIP: 64108   **Lat:** 39-16-50 N   **Long:** 94-40-15 W
Pop: 24,609 (1990); 15,594 (1980)   **Pop Density:** 365.7
Land: 67.3 sq. mi.; **Water:** 0.1 sq. mi.

In western MO at the confluence of the Missouri and Kansas (or Kaw) rivers; on the western bank is Kansas City, KS. Established 1821; founded 1833; laid out 1838; developed 1836. Called *The Heart of America* for its location. Largest winter-wheat market; one of the largest livestock exchanges in U.S.; wheat flour production second only to Buffalo. Manufacturing (printing and publishing, food processing, automobile assembly) and industrial (chemicals, electric equipment, farm machinery) city. Site of University of Missouri. Incorporated 1850. Part of the town is also in Cass, Clay, and Jackson counties.

Name origin: Named in 1889 from the old Siouan language Kansa 'people of the south wind.' Previously called City of Kansas (1853).

Kickapoo *Township*
Lat: 39-14-58 N   **Long:** 94-44-58 W
Pop: 4,514 (1990); 4,053 (1980)   **Pop Density:** 293.1
Land: 15.4 sq. mi.; **Water:** 0.0 sq. mi.

Lake Waukomis *City*
Lat: 39-13-49 N   **Long:** 94-38-11 W
Pop: 1,027 (1990); 1,050 (1980)   **Pop Density:** 3423.3
Land: 0.3 sq. mi.; **Water:** 0.2 sq. mi.
Incorporated 1956.

Lee *Township*
Lat: 39-19-04 N   **Long:** 94-51-15 W
Pop: 563 (1990); 587 (1980)   **Pop Density:** 22.3
Land: 25.2 sq. mi.; **Water:** 1.4 sq. mi.

Marshall *Township*
Lat: 39-29-39 N   **Long:** 94-57-09 W
Pop: 1,046 (1990); 1,082 (1980)   **Pop Density:** 17.2
Land: 60.9 sq. mi.; **Water:** 1.5 sq. mi.

May *Township*
Lat: 39-16-40 N   **Long:** 94-38-30 W
Pop: 11,221 (1990); 5,819 (1980)   **Pop Density:** 354.0
Land: 31.7 sq. mi.; **Water:** 0.2 sq. mi.

Northmoor *City*
Lat: 39-11-03 N   **Long:** 94-36-23 W
Pop: 441 (1990); 506 (1980)   **Pop Density:** 2205.0
Land: 0.2 sq. mi.; **Water:** 0.0 sq. mi.
Incorporated 1954.

Parkville *City*
ZIP: 64152   **Lat:** 39-11-42 N   **Long:** 94-40-26 W
Pop: 2,402 (1990); 2,091 (1980)   **Pop Density:** 667.2
Land: 3.6 sq. mi.; **Water:** 0.5 sq. mi.
Incorporated 1858.

Pawnee *Township*
Lat: 39-12-42 N   **Long:** 94-37-14 W
Pop: 5,679 (1990); 4,503 (1980)   **Pop Density:** 1320.7
Land: 4.3 sq. mi.; **Water:** 0.0 sq. mi.

Pettis *Township*
Lat: 39-10-25 N   **Long:** 94-37-49 W
Pop: 4,728 (1990); 5,318 (1980)   **Pop Density:** 716.4
Land: 6.6 sq. mi.; **Water:** 0.3 sq. mi.

Platte City *City*
ZIP: 64079   **Lat:** 39-21-41 N   **Long:** 94-46-39 W
Pop: 2,947 (1990); 2,114 (1980)   **Pop Density:** 1403.3
Land: 2.1 sq. mi.; **Water:** 0.0 sq. mi.
Incorporated 1882.

Platte Woods *City*
Lat: 39-13-45 N   **Long:** 94-39-07 W
Pop: 427 (1990); 467 (1980)   **Pop Density:** 1067.5
Land: 0.4 sq. mi.; **Water:** 0.0 sq. mi.
Incorporated 1946.

Preston *Township*
Lat: 39-27-07 N   **Long:** 94-38-22 W
Pop: 1,427 (1990); 1,427 (1980)   **Pop Density:** 37.3
Land: 38.3 sq. mi.; **Water:** 0.0 sq. mi.

Ridgely *Town*
Lat: 39-27-07 N   **Long:** 94-38-22 W
Pop: 57 (1990); 78 (1980)   **Pop Density:** 51.8
Land: 1.1 sq. mi.; **Water:** 0.0 sq. mi.   **Elev:** 955 ft.
Incorporated 1852.

Riverside *City*
ZIP: 64150   **Lat:** 39-10-02 N   **Long:** 94-38-01 W
Pop: 3,010 (1990); 3,206 (1980)   **Pop Density:** 567.9
Land: 5.3 sq. mi.; **Water:** 0.3 sq. mi.
Incorporated 1951.

Sioux *Township*
Lat: 39-12-05 N   **Long:** 94-42-08 W
Pop: 6,617 (1990); 5,688 (1980)   **Pop Density:** 735.2
Land: 9.0 sq. mi.; **Water:** 0.5 sq. mi.

Tracy *City*
ZIP: 64079   **Lat:** 39-22-42 N   **Long:** 94-47-34 W
Pop: 287 (1990); 310 (1980)   **Pop Density:** 1435.0
Land: 0.2 sq. mi.; **Water:** 0.0 sq. mi.
Founded 1872. Incorporated 1883.

Name origin: For J. W. Tracey, a Rock Island Railroad superintendent.

Waldron *Township*
Lat: 39-13-30 N   **Long:** 94-46-39 W
Pop: 484 (1990); 437 (1980)   **Pop Density:** 22.1
Land: 21.9 sq. mi.; **Water:** 1.2 sq. mi.

Weatherby Lake *City*
ZIP: 64152   **Lat:** 39-14-18 N   **Long:** 94-41-51 W
Pop: 1,613 (1990); 1,446 (1980)   **Pop Density:** 1613.0
Land: 1.0 sq. mi.; **Water:** 0.3 sq. mi.
Incorporated 1961.

Weston *City*
ZIP: 64098   **Lat:** 39-24-52 N   **Long:** 94-53-47 W
Pop: 1,528 (1990); 1,440 (1980)   **Pop Density:** 955.0
Land: 1.6 sq. mi.; **Water:** 0.0 sq. mi.

In northwestern MO, half-hidden in a pinched little valley between Missouri River bluffs northwest of Kansas City. Incorporated 1842.

*Weston *Township*
ZIP: 64098   **Lat:** 39-25-32 N   **Long:** 94-53-25 W
Pop: 2,194 (1990); 2,088 (1980)   **Pop Density:** 59.5
Land: 36.9 sq. mi.; **Water:** 0.8 sq. mi.

Polk County
County Seat: Bolivar (ZIP: 65613)

Pop: 21,826 (1990); 18,822 (1980) **Pop Density:** 34.3
Land: 637.2 sq. mi.; **Water:** 5.3 sq. mi. **Area Code:** 417
In south-central MO, north of Springfield; organized Jan 5, 1835 from Greene and Laclede counties.
Name origin: For James Knox Polk (1795–1849), eleventh U.S. president.

Aldrich — Village
ZIP: 65601 **Lat:** 37-32-56 N **Long:** 93-33-08 W
Pop: 76 (1990); 53 (1980) **Pop Density:** 380.0
Land: 0.2 sq. mi.; **Water:** 0.0 sq. mi.
Incorporated 1889.

Bolivar — City
ZIP: 65613 **Lat:** 37-36-34 N **Long:** 93-24-51 W
Pop: 6,845 (1990); 5,919 (1980) **Pop Density:** 1521.1
Land: 4.5 sq. mi.; **Water:** 0.0 sq. mi. **Elev:** 1056 ft.
Incorporated 1835.
Name origin: Named in 1840 for Bolivar, TN.

Campbell — Township
Lat: 37-42-11 N **Long:** 93-33-41 W
Pop: 369 (1990); 323 (1980) **Pop Density:** 15.7
Land: 23.5 sq. mi.; **Water:** 0.0 sq. mi.

Cliquot — Township
ZIP: 65640 **Lat:** 37-41-57 N **Long:** 93-28-37 W
Pop: 386 (1990); 304 (1980) **Pop Density:** 16.7
Land: 23.1 sq. mi.; **Water:** 0.0 sq. mi.

East Looney — Township
Lat: 37-28-39 N **Long:** 93-21-55 W
Pop: 920 (1990); 786 (1980) **Pop Density:** 28.8
Land: 32.0 sq. mi.; **Water:** 0.0 sq. mi.

East Madison — Township
Lat: 37-37-40 N **Long:** 93-32-28 W
Pop: 474 (1990); 418 (1980) **Pop Density:** 20.0
Land: 23.7 sq. mi.; **Water:** 0.0 sq. mi.

Fair Play — City
ZIP: 65649 **Lat:** 37-38-01 N **Long:** 93-34-31 W
Pop: 442 (1990); 384 (1980) **Pop Density:** 1473.3
Land: 0.3 sq. mi.; **Water:** 0.0 sq. mi. **Elev:** 994 ft.
Incorporated 1898.

Flemington — Village
ZIP: 65650 **Lat:** 37-48-13 N **Long:** 93-29-59 W
Pop: 141 (1990); 140 (1980) **Pop Density:** 470.0
Land: 0.3 sq. mi.; **Water:** 0.0 sq. mi.
Incorporated 1945.

*Flemington — Township
ZIP: 65650 **Lat:** 37-46-19 N **Long:** 93-29-50 W
Pop: 242 (1990); 243 (1980) **Pop Density:** 16.2
Land: 14.9 sq. mi.; **Water:** 0.0 sq. mi.

Halfway — Village
Lat: 37-36-57 N **Long:** 93-14-08 W
Pop: 171 (1990); 157 (1980) **Pop Density:** 81.4
Land: 2.1 sq. mi.; **Water:** 0.0 sq. mi.
Incorporated 1967.

Humansville — City
ZIP: 65674 **Lat:** 37-47-44 N **Long:** 93-34-33 W
Pop: 1,084 (1990); 907 (1980) **Pop Density:** 903.3
Land: 1.2 sq. mi.; **Water:** 0.0 sq. mi.
Incorporated 1872.

Jackson — Township
Lat: 37-28-11 N **Long:** 93-32-59 W
Pop: 763 (1990); 661 (1980) **Pop Density:** 16.6
Land: 46.1 sq. mi.; **Water:** 0.0 sq. mi.

Jefferson — Township
Lat: 37-46-12 N **Long:** 93-25-43 W
Pop: 400 (1990); 310 (1980) **Pop Density:** 13.8
Land: 28.9 sq. mi.; **Water:** 1.0 sq. mi.

Johnson — Township
Lat: 37-46-55 N **Long:** 93-34-42 W
Pop: 1,541 (1990); 1,383 (1980) **Pop Density:** 50.0
Land: 30.8 sq. mi.; **Water:** 0.1 sq. mi.

McKinley — Township
Lat: 37-44-37 N **Long:** 93-19-53 W
Pop: 485 (1990); 455 (1980) **Pop Density:** 12.8
Land: 38.0 sq. mi.; **Water:** 0.7 sq. mi.

Mooney — Township
Lat: 37-28-36 N **Long:** 93-14-55 W
Pop: 2,079 (1990); 1,861 (1980) **Pop Density:** 32.5
Land: 63.9 sq. mi.; **Water:** 0.0 sq. mi.

Morrisville — Town
ZIP: 65710 **Lat:** 37-28-50 N **Long:** 93-25-42 W
Pop: 293 (1990); 331 (1980) **Pop Density:** 976.7
Land: 0.3 sq. mi.; **Water:** 0.0 sq. mi.
Founded 1870. Incorporated 1908.
Name origin: For founder Morris Mitchell.

North Benton — Township
Lat: 37-38-58 N **Long:** 93-15-21 W
Pop: 427 (1990); 440 (1980) **Pop Density:** 13.8
Land: 30.9 sq. mi.; **Water:** 0.0 sq. mi.

Northeast Marion — Township
Lat: 37-40-04 N **Long:** 93-22-50 W
Pop: 2,692 (1990); 2,265 (1980) **Pop Density:** 62.9
Land: 42.8 sq. mi.; **Water:** 0.0 sq. mi.

North Green — Township
Lat: 37-46-07 N **Long:** 93-13-45 W
Pop: 240 (1990); 236 (1980) **Pop Density:** 11.1
Land: 21.7 sq. mi.; **Water:** 0.0 sq. mi.

Northwest Marion — Township
Lat: 37-38-12 N **Long:** 93-27-54 W
Pop: 1,875 (1990); 1,773 (1980) **Pop Density:** 117.9
Land: 15.9 sq. mi.; **Water:** 0.0 sq. mi.

MISSOURI, Polk County

Pleasant Hope
City
ZIP: 65725 Lat: 37-27-42 N Long: 93-16-24 W
Pop: 360 (1990); 354 (1980) Pop Density: 450.0
Land: 0.8 sq. mi.; Water: 0.0 sq. mi.
Incorporated 1946.

South Benton
Township
Lat: 37-33-58 N Long: 93-14-59 W
Pop: 843 (1990); 754 (1980) Pop Density: 18.7
Land: 45.0 sq. mi.; Water: 0.0 sq. mi.

Southeast Marion
Township
Lat: 37-34-34 N Long: 93-21-47 W
Pop: 2,737 (1990); 3,024 (1980) Pop Density: 138.9
Land: 19.7 sq. mi.; Water: 0.0 sq. mi.

South Green
Township
Lat: 37-42-15 N Long: 93-14-19 W
Pop: 379 (1990); 318 (1980) Pop Density: 13.6
Land: 27.8 sq. mi.; Water: 0.0 sq. mi.

Southwest Marion
Township
Lat: 37-34-57 N Long: 93-26-22 W
Pop: 2,972 (1990); 1,551 (1980) Pop Density: 113.9
Land: 26.1 sq. mi.; Water: 0.0 sq. mi.

Union
Township
Lat: 37-32-47 N Long: 93-33-47 W
Pop: 405 (1990); 321 (1980) Pop Density: 14.9
Land: 27.1 sq. mi.; Water: 3.2 sq. mi.

West Looney
Township
Lat: 37-28-01 N Long: 93-25-45 W
Pop: 689 (1990); 538 (1980) Pop Density: 30.6
Land: 22.5 sq. mi.; Water: 0.0 sq. mi.

West Madison
Township
Lat: 37-37-48 N Long: 93-35-51 W
Pop: 513 (1990); 463 (1980) Pop Density: 41.7
Land: 12.3 sq. mi.; Water: 0.0 sq. mi.

Wishart
Township
Lat: 37-31-19 N Long: 93-27-44 W
Pop: 395 (1990); 395 (1980) Pop Density: 19.2
Land: 20.6 sq. mi.; Water: 0.0 sq. mi.

Pulaski County
County Seat: Waynesville (ZIP: 65583)

Pop: 41,307 (1990); 42,011 (1980) Pop Density: 75.5
Land: 547.0 sq. mi.; Water: 4.4 sq. mi. Area Code: 314
In south-central MO, northeast of Springfield; organized Jan 19, 1833 from Crawford County.

Name origin: For Count Casimir Pulaski (1747–79), Polish soldier who fought for America during the Revolutionary War.

Crocker
City
ZIP: 65452 Lat: 37-56-56 N Long: 92-16-02 W
Pop: 1,077 (1990); 979 (1980) Pop Density: 979.1
Land: 1.1 sq. mi.; Water: 0.0 sq. mi. Elev: 1124 ft.
Incorporated 1911.

Cullen
Township
Lat: 37-48-37 N Long: 92-09-08 W
Pop: 27,761 (1990); 31,050 (1980) Pop Density: 195.8
Land: 141.8 sq. mi.; Water: 1.6 sq. mi.

Dixon
City
ZIP: 65459 Lat: 37-59-42 N Long: 92-05-44 W
Pop: 1,585 (1990); 1,402 (1980) Pop Density: 1585.0
Land: 1.0 sq. mi.; Water: 0.0 sq. mi. Elev: 1167 ft.
Incorporated 1869.

Fort Leonard Wood
Military Facility
ZIP: 65473 Lat: 37-42-18 N Long: 92-09-28 W
Pop: 15,863 (1990); 21,181 (1980) Pop Density: 163.2
Land: 97.2 sq. mi.; Water: 0.4 sq. mi.

Liberty
Township
Lat: 37-49-07 N Long: 92-21-10 W
Pop: 4,413 (1990); 4,132 (1980) Pop Density: 42.2
Land: 104.6 sq. mi.; Water: 1.1 sq. mi.

Piney
Township
Lat: 37-40-30 N Long: 92-05-59 W
Pop: 1,660 (1990); 352 (1980) Pop Density: 25.7
Land: 64.5 sq. mi.; Water: 0.5 sq. mi.

Richland
City
ZIP: 65556 Lat: 37-51-41 N Long: 92-23-50 W
Pop: 1,879 (1990); 1,803 (1980) Pop Density: 939.5
Land: 2.0 sq. mi.; Water: 0.0 sq. mi.
Incorporated 1884. Part of the town is also in Camden and Laclede counties.

Roubidoux
Township
Lat: 37-40-42 N Long: 92-13-30 W
Pop: 188 (1990); 132 (1980) Pop Density: 3.0
Land: 62.9 sq. mi.; Water: 0.2 sq. mi.

St. Robert
City
Lat: 37-49-16 N Long: 92-09-20 W
Pop: 1,730 (1990); 1,735 (1980) Pop Density: 480.6
Land: 3.6 sq. mi.; Water: 0.0 sq. mi.
Incorporated 1951.

Tavern
Township
Lat: 37-57-22 N Long: 92-17-27 W
Pop: 2,954 (1990); 2,619 (1980) Pop Density: 33.9
Land: 87.1 sq. mi.; Water: 0.2 sq. mi.

Union
Township
Lat: 37-57-04 N Long: 92-06-42 W
Pop: 4,331 (1990); 3,726 (1980) Pop Density: 50.2
Land: 86.2 sq. mi.; Water: 0.7 sq. mi.

Waynesville — City
ZIP: 65583 **Lat:** 37-49-39 N **Long:** 92-13-00 W
Pop: 3,207 (1990); 2,879 (1980) **Pop Density:** 654.5
Land: 4.9 sq. mi.; **Water:** 0.0 sq. mi.

Platted 1839. Incorporated 1931.
Name origin: For General "Mad Anthony" Wayne (1745–1796), noted for his exploits during the American Revolution.

Putnam County
County Seat: Unionville (ZIP: 63565)

Pop: 5,079 (1990); 6,092 (1980) **Pop Density:** 9.8
Land: 518.0 sq. mi.; **Water:** 1.7 sq. mi. **Area Code:** 816

On the central northern border of MO; established Feb 22, 1843 from Adair, Sullivan, and Linn counties, annexed Dodge County in 1853.
Name origin: For Gen. Israel Putnam (1718–90), Revolutionary War officer and American commander at the Battle of Bunker Hill.

Elm — Township
Lat: 40-24-33 N **Long:** 92-46-12 W
Pop: 605 (1990); 762 (1980) **Pop Density:** 7.7
Land: 78.2 sq. mi.; **Water:** 0.0 sq. mi.

Grant — Township
Lat: 40-31-29 N **Long:** 92-43-03 W
Pop: 309 (1990); 332 (1980) **Pop Density:** 13.4
Land: 23.1 sq. mi.; **Water:** 0.0 sq. mi.

Jackson — Township
Lat: 40-26-05 N **Long:** 93-08-36 W
Pop: 176 (1990); 208 (1980) **Pop Density:** 4.3
Land: 40.8 sq. mi.; **Water:** 0.0 sq. mi.

Liberty — Township
Lat: 40-32-00 N **Long:** 92-48-45 W
Pop: 239 (1990); 344 (1980) **Pop Density:** 5.0
Land: 48.0 sq. mi.; **Water:** 0.0 sq. mi.

Lincoln — Township
Lat: 40-31-32 N **Long:** 92-55-04 W
Pop: 250 (1990); 322 (1980) **Pop Density:** 5.2
Land: 48.0 sq. mi.; **Water:** 0.0 sq. mi.

Livonia — Village
ZIP: 63551 **Lat:** 40-29-29 N **Long:** 92-41-58 W
Pop: 126 (1990); 162 (1980) **Pop Density:** 420.0
Land: 0.3 sq. mi.; **Water:** 0.0 sq. mi.
Incorporated 1911.

Lucerne — Village
ZIP: 64655 **Lat:** 40-27-49 N **Long:** 93-17-29 W
Pop: 51 (1990); 130 (1980) **Pop Density:** 255.0
Land: 0.2 sq. mi.; **Water:** 0.0 sq. mi.
Incorporated 1905.

Medicine — Township
Lat: 40-25-41 N **Long:** 93-16-44 W
Pop: 209 (1990); 328 (1980) **Pop Density:** 3.8
Land: 54.5 sq. mi.; **Water:** 0.0 sq. mi.

Powersville — Village
ZIP: 64672 **Lat:** 40-32-59 N **Long:** 93-18-02 W
Pop: 38 (1990); 116 (1980) **Pop Density:** 63.3
Land: 0.6 sq. mi.; **Water:** 0.0 sq. mi.
Incorporated 1911.

Richland — Township
Lat: 40-25-14 N **Long:** 92-54-19 W
Pop: 249 (1990); 263 (1980) **Pop Density:** 7.0
Land: 35.8 sq. mi.; **Water:** 0.0 sq. mi.

Sherman — Township
Lat: 40-32-12 N **Long:** 93-09-00 W
Pop: 99 (1990); 131 (1980) **Pop Density:** 2.5
Land: 40.1 sq. mi.; **Water:** 0.0 sq. mi.

Union — Township
Lat: 40-31-55 N **Long:** 93-01-36 W
Pop: 2,053 (1990); 2,266 (1980) **Pop Density:** 45.3
Land: 45.3 sq. mi.; **Water:** 1.7 sq. mi.

Unionville — City
ZIP: 63565 **Lat:** 40-28-32 N **Long:** 93-00-13 W
Pop: 1,989 (1990); 2,178 (1980) **Pop Density:** 994.5
Land: 2.0 sq. mi.; **Water:** 0.0 sq. mi. **Elev:** 1067 ft.
Incorporated 1857.

Wilson — Township
Lat: 40-25-42 N **Long:** 93-01-44 W
Pop: 606 (1990); 753 (1980) **Pop Density:** 16.7
Land: 36.3 sq. mi.; **Water:** 0.0 sq. mi.

Worthington — Village
ZIP: 63567 **Lat:** 40-24-28 N **Long:** 92-41-19 W
Pop: 86 (1990); 105 (1980) **Pop Density:** 860.0
Land: 0.1 sq. mi.; **Water:** 0.0 sq. mi.

York — Township
Lat: 40-31-28 N **Long:** 93-17-36 W
Pop: 284 (1990); 383 (1980) **Pop Density:** 4.2
Land: 67.9 sq. mi.; **Water:** 0.0 sq. mi.

MISSOURI, Ralls County

Ralls County
County Seat: New London (ZIP: 63459)

Pop: 8,476 (1990); 8,984 (1980)
Land: 471.0 sq. mi.; **Water:** 12.8 sq. mi.
Pop Density: 18.0
Area Code: 314

On northeastern border of MO; northeast of Columbia; organized Nov 16, 1820 (prior to statehood) from Pike County.

Name origin: For Daniel Ralls (1785–1820), a MO legislator who died the year the county was formed.

Center — City
ZIP: 63436 **Lat:** 39-30-35 N **Long:** 91-31-42 W
Pop: 552 (1990); 669 (1980) **Pop Density:** 1380.0
Land: 0.4 sq. mi.; **Water:** 0.0 sq. mi. **Elev:** 719 ft.
Incorporated 1882.

*Center — Township
ZIP: 63436 **Lat:** 39-30-52 N **Long:** 91-33-35 W
Pop: 971 (1990); 1,037 (1980) **Pop Density:** 20.1
Land: 48.4 sq. mi.; **Water:** 0.4 sq. mi.

Clay — Township
Lat: 39-38-57 N **Long:** 91-27-56 W
Pop: 1,873 (1990); 1,799 (1980) **Pop Density:** 34.5
Land: 54.3 sq. mi.; **Water:** 0.5 sq. mi.

Hannibal — City
ZIP: 63401 **Lat:** 39-40-51 N **Long:** 91-24-15 W
Pop: 269 (1990); 172 (1980) **Pop Density:** 336.3
Land: 0.8 sq. mi.; **Water:** 0.0 sq. mi. **Elev:** 491 ft.
In northeastern MO on the Mississippi River. Incorporated 1845. Part of the town is also in Marion County.

Name origin: Named in 1819 for the Carthaginian general (247–183 B.C.), who invaded Roman territory by crossing the Alps.

Jasper — Township
Lat: 39-24-08 N **Long:** 91-31-39 W
Pop: 592 (1990); 767 (1980) **Pop Density:** 5.7
Land: 103.2 sq. mi.; **Water:** 0.1 sq. mi.

Monroe City — City
Lat: 39-39-12 N **Long:** 91-42-38 W
Pop: 5 (1990) **Pop Density:** 16.7
Land: 0.3 sq. mi.; **Water:** 0.0 sq. mi. **Elev:** 749 ft.
Incorporated 1857. Part of the town is also in Marion and Monroe counties.

Name origin: For James Monroe (1758–1831), fifth U.S. president.

New London — City
ZIP: 63459 **Lat:** 39-35-03 N **Long:** 91-23-55 W
Pop: 988 (1990); 1,161 (1980) **Pop Density:** 1411.4
Land: 0.7 sq. mi.; **Water:** 0.0 sq. mi.
Incorporated 1870.

Name origin: Named in 1819 for London, England.

Perry — City
ZIP: 63462 **Lat:** 39-25-47 N **Long:** 91-40-04 W
Pop: 711 (1990); 836 (1980) **Pop Density:** 646.4
Land: 1.1 sq. mi.; **Water:** 0.0 sq. mi. **Elev:** 683 ft.
Incorporated 1891.

Saline — Township
Lat: 39-36-53 N **Long:** 91-38-25 W
Pop: 517 (1990); 488 (1980) **Pop Density:** 6.8
Land: 76.4 sq. mi.; **Water:** 4.4 sq. mi.

Salt River — Township
Lat: 39-25-27 N **Long:** 91-40-03 W
Pop: 1,213 (1990); 1,323 (1980) **Pop Density:** 18.7
Land: 65.0 sq. mi.; **Water:** 4.3 sq. mi.

Saverton — Township
ZIP: 63467 **Lat:** 39-37-00 N **Long:** 91-17-49 W
Pop: 1,654 (1990); 1,645 (1980) **Pop Density:** 30.7
Land: 53.9 sq. mi.; **Water:** 2.6 sq. mi.

Spencer — Township
Lat: 39-33-10 N **Long:** 91-24-54 W
Pop: 1,656 (1990); 1,925 (1980) **Pop Density:** 23.7
Land: 69.8 sq. mi.; **Water:** 0.6 sq. mi.

The Landing — Village
Lat: 39-33-33 N **Long:** 91-39-32 W
Pop: 8 (1990) **Pop Density:** 40.0
Land: 0.2 sq. mi.; **Water:** 0.0 sq. mi.

Vandalia — City
Lat: 39-19-15 N **Long:** 91-29-01 W
Pop: 0 (1990)
Land: 0.03 sq. mi.; **Water:** 0.0 sq. mi.
Incorporated 1874. Part of the town is also in Audrain County.

Name origin: For Vandalia, IL.

Randolph County
County Seat: Huntsville (ZIP: 65259)

Pop: 24,370 (1990); 25,460 (1980) **Pop Density:** 50.5
Land: 482.4 sq. mi.; **Water:** 5.3 sq. mi. **Area Code:** 816
In north-central MO, north of Columbia; organized Jan 22, 1829 from Chariton and Ralls counties.
Name origin: For John Randolph (1773–1833), VA statesman and U.S. Minister to Russia (1830).

Cairo — Village
ZIP: 65239 **Lat:** 39-30-43 N **Long:** 92-26-26 W
Pop: 282 (1990); 315 (1980) **Pop Density:** 1410.0
Land: 0.2 sq. mi.; **Water:** 0.0 sq. mi. **Elev:** 864 ft.
Incorporated 1886.

*Cairo — Township
ZIP: 65239 **Lat:** 39-31-01 N **Long:** 92-26-30 W
Pop: 1,089 (1990); 959 (1980) **Pop Density:** 25.7
Land: 42.4 sq. mi.; **Water:** 0.7 sq. mi.

Chariton — Township
Lat: 39-33-14 N **Long:** 92-36-44 W
Pop: 286 (1990); 378 (1980) **Pop Density:** 4.8
Land: 59.4 sq. mi.; **Water:** 3.7 sq. mi.

Clark — City
ZIP: 65243 **Lat:** 39-16-50 N **Long:** 92-20-30 W
Pop: 257 (1990); 304 (1980) **Pop Density:** 1285.0
Land: 0.2 sq. mi.; **Water:** 0.0 sq. mi. **Elev:** 867 ft.
Incorporated 1928.

Clifton — Township
Lat: 39-27-38 N **Long:** 92-39-36 W
Pop: 236 (1990); 344 (1980) **Pop Density:** 8.6
Land: 27.4 sq. mi.; **Water:** 0.0 sq. mi.

Clifton Hill — City
ZIP: 65244 **Lat:** 39-26-21 N **Long:** 92-40-01 W
Pop: 108 (1990); 152 (1980) **Pop Density:** 1080.0
Land: 0.1 sq. mi.; **Water:** 0.0 sq. mi. **Elev:** 722 ft.
Incorporated 1876.

Higbee — City
ZIP: 65257 **Lat:** 39-18-23 N **Long:** 92-30-43 W
Pop: 639 (1990); 817 (1980) **Pop Density:** 1597.5
Land: 0.4 sq. mi.; **Water:** 0.0 sq. mi.
Incorporated 1891.

Huntsville — City
ZIP: 65259 **Lat:** 39-26-14 N **Long:** 92-32-37 W
Pop: 1,567 (1990); 1,657 (1980) **Pop Density:** 681.3
Land: 2.3 sq. mi.; **Water:** 0.0 sq. mi. **Elev:** 800 ft.
Platted 1831. Incorporated 1905.
Name origin: For Daniel Hunt, one of the first settlers in the vicinity and one of the donors of the town site.

Jackson — Township
Lat: 39-34-55 N **Long:** 92-28-10 W
Pop: 306 (1990); 348 (1980) **Pop Density:** 13.1
Land: 23.4 sq. mi.; **Water:** 0.2 sq. mi.

Jacksonville — Village
ZIP: 65260 **Lat:** 39-35-14 N **Long:** 92-28-22 W
Pop: 115 (1990); 130 (1980) **Pop Density:** 1150.0
Land: 0.1 sq. mi.; **Water:** 0.0 sq. mi. **Elev:** 867 ft.
Established as a railroad stop 1858. Incorporated 1865.
Name origin: For Hancock Jackson, pre-Civil War governor of MO and Randolph County resident.

Moberly — City
ZIP: 65270 **Lat:** 39-25-11 N **Long:** 92-26-10 W
Pop: 12,839 (1990); 13,418 (1980) **Pop Density:** 1271.2
Land: 10.1 sq. mi.; **Water:** 0.0 sq. mi.
In north-central MO, 35 mi. north of Columbia. Incorporated 1868.
Name origin: For Col. William E. Moberly, president of the railway which is now part of the Wabash Railroad.

Moniteau — Township
Lat: 39-18-44 N **Long:** 92-31-02 W
Pop: 962 (1990); 1,144 (1980) **Pop Density:** 32.7
Land: 29.4 sq. mi.; **Water:** 0.1 sq. mi.

North Sugar Creek — Township
Lat: 39-26-49 N **Long:** 92-27-20 W
Pop: 6,947 (1990); 6,754 (1980) **Pop Density:** 482.4
Land: 14.4 sq. mi.; **Water:** 0.1 sq. mi.

Prairie — Township
Lat: 39-19-16 N **Long:** 92-23-28 W
Pop: 3,468 (1990); 3,144 (1980) **Pop Density:** 38.7
Land: 89.5 sq. mi.; **Water:** 0.1 sq. mi.

Renick — Village
ZIP: 65278 **Lat:** 39-20-31 N **Long:** 92-24-38 W
Pop: 195 (1990); 195 (1980) **Pop Density:** 975.0
Land: 0.2 sq. mi.; **Water:** 0.0 sq. mi. **Elev:** 874 ft.
Incorporated 1886.

Salt River — Township
Lat: 39-33-48 N **Long:** 92-20-50 W
Pop: 221 (1990); 267 (1980) **Pop Density:** 6.9
Land: 31.8 sq. mi.; **Water:** 0.0 sq. mi.

Salt Springs — Township
Lat: 39-26-14 N **Long:** 92-33-14 W
Pop: 2,639 (1990); 2,803 (1980) **Pop Density:** 41.0
Land: 64.4 sq. mi.; **Water:** 0.2 sq. mi.

Silver Creek — Township
Lat: 39-20-49 N **Long:** 92-38-12 W
Pop: 279 (1990); 322 (1980) **Pop Density:** 5.9
Land: 47.4 sq. mi.; **Water:** 0.1 sq. mi.

South Sugar Creek — Township
Lat: 39-24-03 N **Long:** 92-24-10 W
Pop: 7,135 (1990); 8,222 (1980) **Pop Density:** 320.0
Land: 22.3 sq. mi.; **Water:** 0.1 sq. mi.

MISSOURI, Randolph County

Union
Township
Lat: 39-28-04 N **Long:** 92-21-50 W
Pop: 802 (1990); 775 (1980) **Pop Density:** 26.2
Land: 30.6 sq. mi.; **Water:** 0.0 sq. mi.

Ray County
County Seat: Richmond (ZIP: 64085)

Pop: 21,971 (1990); 21,378 (1980) **Pop Density:** 38.6
Land: 569.5 sq. mi.; **Water:** 4.1 sq. mi. **Area Code:** 816

In west-central MO, northeast of Kansas City; organized Nov 16, 1820 (prior to statehood) from Howard County.

Name origin: For John Ray, a MO legislator when the county was named.

Camden
City
ZIP: 64017 **Lat:** 39-12-00 N **Long:** 94-01-07 W
Pop: 238 (1990); 219 (1980) **Pop Density:** 297.5
Land: 0.8 sq. mi.; **Water:** 0.0 sq. mi. **Elev:** 713 ft.
Laid out by Edward M. and Elizabeth R. Samuel and Amos and Judith C. Rees. Incorporated 1836.
Name origin: Named in 1845 for the Earl of Camden, a leader of the Whig Party in England.

*Camden
Township
ZIP: 64017 **Lat:** 39-11-37 N **Long:** 94-01-25 W
Pop: 618 (1990); 685 (1980) **Pop Density:** 16.5
Land: 37.5 sq. mi.; **Water:** 1.6 sq. mi.

Crooked River
Township
Lat: 39-16-53 N **Long:** 93-49-58 W
Pop: 1,092 (1990); 1,273 (1980) **Pop Density:** 14.7
Land: 74.5 sq. mi.; **Water:** 0.9 sq. mi.

Crystal Lakes
Village
Lat: 39-21-29 N **Long:** 94-11-23 W
Pop: 255 (1990) **Pop Density:** 255.0
Land: 1.0 sq. mi.; **Water:** 0.2 sq. mi.

Elmira
Village
Lat: 39-30-30 N **Long:** 94-09-10 W
Pop: 70 (1990); 109 (1980) **Pop Density:** 350.0
Land: 0.2 sq. mi.; **Water:** 0.0 sq. mi.
Incorporated 1921.

Excelsior Estates
Village
Lat: 39-23-24 N **Long:** 94-12-27 W
Pop: 271 (1990) **Pop Density:** 1355.0
Land: 0.2 sq. mi.; **Water:** 0.0 sq. mi.
Part of the town is also in Clay County.

Excelsior Springs
City
Lat: 39-20-14 N **Long:** 94-12-17 W
Pop: 176 (1990); 156 (1980) **Pop Density:** 160.0
Land: 1.1 sq. mi.; **Water:** 0.0 sq. mi.
In northwestern MO, a northeastern suburb of Kansas City. Incorporated 1881. Part of the town is also in Clay County.

Fishing River
Township
Lat: 39-19-45 N **Long:** 94-09-12 W
Pop: 4,872 (1990); 4,386 (1980) **Pop Density:** 89.4
Land: 54.5 sq. mi.; **Water:** 0.3 sq. mi.

Fleming
City
Lat: 39-11-34 N **Long:** 94-03-04 W
Pop: 130 (1990); 144 (1980) **Pop Density:** 260.0
Land: 0.5 sq. mi.; **Water:** 0.0 sq. mi.
Incorporated 1964.

Grape Grove
Township
Lat: 39-26-42 N **Long:** 93-51-00 W
Pop: 927 (1990); 991 (1980) **Pop Density:** 8.0
Land: 116.0 sq. mi.; **Water:** 0.1 sq. mi.

Hardin
City
ZIP: 64035 **Lat:** 39-16-03 N **Long:** 93-49-49 W
Pop: 598 (1990); 688 (1980) **Pop Density:** 996.7
Land: 0.6 sq. mi.; **Water:** 0.0 sq. mi.
Incorporated 1888.
Name origin: For Charles H. Hardin, who later became governor of MO.

Henrietta
City
ZIP: 64036 **Lat:** 39-14-14 N **Long:** 93-56-16 W
Pop: 412 (1990); 424 (1980) **Pop Density:** 686.7
Land: 0.6 sq. mi.; **Water:** 0.0 sq. mi. **Elev:** 702 ft.
Incorporated 1868.

Homestead
Village
Lat: 39-21-34 N **Long:** 94-12-06 W
Pop: 177 (1990); 138 (1980) **Pop Density:** 885.0
Land: 0.2 sq. mi.; **Water:** 0.0 sq. mi.

Knoxville
Township
Lat: 39-27-17 N **Long:** 94-00-54 W
Pop: 571 (1990); 698 (1980) **Pop Density:** 8.9
Land: 63.9 sq. mi.; **Water:** 0.0 sq. mi.

Lawson
City
ZIP: 64062 **Lat:** 39-26-16 N **Long:** 94-12-12 W
Pop: 1,781 (1990); 1,671 (1980) **Pop Density:** 2226.3
Land: 0.8 sq. mi.; **Water:** 0.0 sq. mi.
Founded June 1870 by the St. Joseph Land Company. Incorporated 1871. Part of the town is also in Clay County.
Name origin: For L. M. Lawson of Donnell, Lawson & Company, a NY banking house that helped finance the venture.

Orrick
City
ZIP: 64077 **Lat:** 39-12-48 N **Long:** 94-07-30 W
Pop: 935 (1990); 922 (1980) **Pop Density:** 667.9
Land: 1.4 sq. mi.; **Water:** 0.0 sq. mi.
Laid out by the North Missouri Railroad Company March 1869. Incorporated 1873.
Name origin: For W. W. Orrick, who worked for the railroad.

*Orrick Township
ZIP: 64077   Lat: 39-13-06 N   Long: 94-08-05 W
Pop: 1,425 (1990); 1,421 (1980)   Pop Density: 33.5
Land: 42.6 sq. mi.; Water: 0.6 sq. mi.

Polk Township
Lat: 39-27-23 N   Long: 94-08-38 W
Pop: 3,792 (1990); 3,363 (1980)   Pop Density: 60.8
Land: 62.4 sq. mi.; Water: 0.1 sq. mi.

Rayville Town
ZIP: 64084   Lat: 39-20-52 N   Long: 94-03-48 W
Pop: 170 (1990); 197 (1980)   Pop Density: 850.0
Land: 0.2 sq. mi.; Water: 0.0 sq. mi.
Founded 1871. Incorporated 1903.
Name origin: For the county. Previously called Hallard or Haller Station.

Richmond City
ZIP: 64085   Lat: 39-16-43 N   Long: 93-58-24 W
Pop: 5,738 (1990); 5,499 (1980)   Pop Density: 1024.6
Land: 5.6 sq. mi.; Water: 0.0 sq. mi.   Elev: 826 ft.
In northwest MO, 40 mi. east-northeast of Kansas City. Founded 1733 by Col. William Byrd. Incorporated 1835.
Name origin: For the city of Richmond, VA.

*Richmond Township
ZIP: 64085   Lat: 39-18-24 N   Long: 93-59-41 W
Pop: 8,674 (1990); 8,561 (1980)   Pop Density: 73.5
Land: 118.0 sq. mi.; Water: 0.5 sq. mi.

Woods Heights City
Lat: 39-20-24 N   Long: 94-09-44 W
Pop: 708 (1990); 747 (1980)   Pop Density: 307.8
Land: 2.3 sq. mi.; Water: 0.0 sq. mi.
Incorporated 1959.

Reynolds County
County Seat: Centerville (ZIP: 63633)

Pop: 6,661 (1990); 7,230 (1980)   Pop Density: 8.2
Land: 811.3 sq. mi.; Water: 3.2 sq. mi.   Area Code: 314
In southeastern MO, west of Cape Girardeau; organized Feb 25, 1845 from Shannon County.
Name origin: For Thomas Reynolds (1796–1844), IL legislator, MO legislator, and governor (1840–44).

Black River Township
Lat: 37-32-02 N   Long: 90-58-56 W
Pop: 648 (1990); 728 (1980)   Pop Density: 7.3
Land: 89.0 sq. mi.; Water: 0.0 sq. mi.

Bunker City
ZIP: 63629   Lat: 37-27-09 N   Long: 91-12-33 W
Pop: 231 (1990); 405 (1980)   Pop Density: 770.0
Land: 0.3 sq. mi.; Water: 0.0 sq. mi.
Incorporated 1907. Part of the town is also in Dent County.

Carroll Township
Lat: 37-29-00 N   Long: 91-06-39 W
Pop: 1,366 (1990); 1,738 (1980)   Pop Density: 7.4
Land: 183.6 sq. mi.; Water: 0.1 sq. mi.

Centerville City
ZIP: 63633   Lat: 37-26-10 N   Long: 90-57-37 W
Pop: 89 (1990); 241 (1980)   Pop Density: 296.7
Land: 0.3 sq. mi.; Water: 0.0 sq. mi.   Elev: 742 ft.
Selected as county seat by Ayers Hudspeth, John Miller, and Moses Carty. Incorporated 1976.
Name origin: Named in 1847 for its central location in the county.

Ellington City
ZIP: 63638   Lat: 37-14-07 N   Long: 90-58-19 W
Pop: 994 (1990); 1,215 (1980)   Pop Density: 764.6
Land: 1.3 sq. mi.; Water: 0.0 sq. mi.
Incorporated 1911.

Jackson Township
Lat: 37-19-53 N   Long: 91-07-02 W
Pop: 448 (1990); 415 (1980)   Pop Density: 5.8
Land: 77.8 sq. mi.; Water: 0.0 sq. mi.

Lesterville Township
ZIP: 63654   Lat: 37-28-37 N   Long: 90-50-02 W
Pop: 733 (1990); 795 (1980)   Pop Density: 6.6
Land: 110.3 sq. mi.; Water: 0.6 sq. mi.

Logan Township
Lat: 37-14-10 N   Long: 90-57-53 W
Pop: 2,731 (1990); 2,898 (1980)   Pop Density: 12.9
Land: 211.1 sq. mi.; Water: 0.0 sq. mi.

Webb Township
Lat: 37-11-37 N   Long: 90-49-32 W
Pop: 735 (1990); 656 (1980)   Pop Density: 5.3
Land: 139.5 sq. mi.; Water: 2.5 sq. mi.

MISSOURI, Ripley County — *American Places Dictionary*

Ripley County
County Seat: Doniphan (ZIP: 63935)

Pop: 12,303 (1990); 12,458 (1980)
Land: 629.5 sq. mi.; **Water:** 2.2 sq. mi.
Pop Density: 19.5
Area Code: 314

On the southeastern border of MO, southwest of Cape Girardeau; organized Jan 5, 1833 from Wayne County.

Name origin: For Gen. Eleazar Wheelock Ripley (1782–1839), officer in the War of 1812, MA legislator, and U.S. representative from LA (1835–39).

Current River — Township
ZIP: 63935
Lat: 36-31-36 N Long: 90-50-00 W
Pop: 156 (1990); 119 (1980) Pop Density: 13.3
Land: 11.7 sq. mi.; Water: 0.2 sq. mi.

Doniphan — City
ZIP: 63935
Lat: 36-37-22 N Long: 90-49-19 W
Pop: 1,713 (1990); 1,921 (1980) Pop Density: 1317.7
Land: 1.3 sq. mi.; Water: 0.0 sq. mi.
Settled 1847. Incorporated 1891.
Name origin: For Mexican War hero Col. Alexander Doniphan.

*Doniphan — Township
ZIP: 63935
Lat: 36-37-56 N Long: 90-47-37 W
Pop: 4,874 (1990); 4,918 (1980) Pop Density: 74.3
Land: 65.6 sq. mi.; Water: 0.5 sq. mi.

Flatwoods — Township
Lat: 36-39-45 N Long: 90-42-02 W
Pop: 469 (1990); 388 (1980) Pop Density: 37.2
Land: 12.6 sq. mi.; Water: 0.0 sq. mi.

Gatewood — Township
ZIP: 63942
Lat: 36-33-11 N Long: 91-04-29 W
Pop: 342 (1990); 346 (1980) Pop Density: 6.4
Land: 53.6 sq. mi.; Water: 0.0 sq. mi.

Harris — Township
Lat: 36-31-58 N Long: 90-45-35 W
Pop: 663 (1990); 540 (1980) Pop Density: 21.3
Land: 31.1 sq. mi.; Water: 0.1 sq. mi.

Johnson — Township
ZIP: 63935
Lat: 36-43-49 N Long: 90-41-52 W
Pop: 376 (1990); 315 (1980) Pop Density: 6.2
Land: 61.0 sq. mi.; Water: 0.0 sq. mi.

Jordan — Township
Lat: 36-45-01 N Long: 90-50-14 W
Pop: 827 (1990); 809 (1980) Pop Density: 10.6
Land: 77.9 sq. mi.; Water: 0.3 sq. mi.

Kelley — Township
Lat: 36-44-37 N Long: 90-57-37 W
Pop: 57 (1990); 65 (1980) Pop Density: 1.4
Land: 39.9 sq. mi.; Water: 0.3 sq. mi.

Naylor — City
ZIP: 63953
Lat: 36-34-26 N Long: 90-36-19 W
Pop: 642 (1990); 602 (1980) Pop Density: 1284.0
Land: 0.5 sq. mi.; Water: 0.0 sq. mi. Elev: 304 ft.
Incorporated 1909.

Pine — Township
ZIP: 63935
Lat: 36-44-01 N Long: 91-04-34 W
Pop: 216 (1990); 379 (1980) Pop Density: 3.2
Land: 68.5 sq. mi.; Water: 0.0 sq. mi.

Poynor — Township
Lat: 36-31-47 N Long: 90-54-13 W
Pop: 258 (1990); 326 (1980) Pop Density: 12.5
Land: 20.6 sq. mi.; Water: 0.0 sq. mi.

Shirley — Township
Lat: 36-38-20 N Long: 90-57-40 W
Pop: 617 (1990); 626 (1980) Pop Density: 9.5
Land: 65.0 sq. mi.; Water: 0.3 sq. mi.

Thomas — Township
Lat: 36-32-42 N Long: 90-37-37 W
Pop: 1,003 (1990); 1,043 (1980) Pop Density: 26.6
Land: 37.7 sq. mi.; Water: 0.1 sq. mi.

Union — Township
Lat: 36-32-52 N Long: 90-57-27 W
Pop: 375 (1990); 387 (1980) Pop Density: 11.2
Land: 33.4 sq. mi.; Water: 0.0 sq. mi.

Varner — Township
Lat: 36-35-04 N Long: 90-40-56 W
Pop: 596 (1990); 700 (1980) Pop Density: 24.8
Land: 24.0 sq. mi.; Water: 0.0 sq. mi.

Washington — Township
Lat: 36-38-50 N Long: 90-37-36 W
Pop: 829 (1990); 728 (1980) Pop Density: 45.3
Land: 18.3 sq. mi.; Water: 0.0 sq. mi.

West Doniphan — Township
Lat: 36-35-49 N Long: 90-52-29 W
Pop: 645 (1990); 769 (1980) Pop Density: 75.0
Land: 8.6 sq. mi.; Water: 0.2 sq. mi.

St. Charles County
County Seat: St. Charles (ZIP: 63301)

Pop: 212,907 (1990); 144,107 (1980)
Land: 561.4 sq. mi.; **Water:** 32.1 sq. mi.
Pop Density: 379.2
Area Code: 314

On central eastern border of MO, north of St. Louis; original county; organized Oct 1, 1812 (prior to statehood).

Name origin: For St. Carlo Borromeo (1538–84), archbishop of Milan and founder of the religious order of the Oblates of St. Ambrose.

Augusta — City
ZIP: 63332 Lat: 38-34-22 N Long: 90-52-58 W
Pop: 263 (1990); 308 (1980) Pop Density: 876.7
Land: 0.3 sq. mi.; Water: 0.0 sq. mi.
Incorporated 1855.

Blanchette — Township
Lat: 38-48-40 N Long: 90-29-53 W
Pop: 11,368 (1990) Pop Density: 3072.4
Land: 3.7 sq. mi.; Water: 0.0 sq. mi.

Boone — Township
Lat: 38-40-09 N Long: 90-49-43 W
Pop: 14,752 (1990); 7,164 (1980) Pop Density: 78.3
Land: 188.3 sq. mi.; Water: 6.8 sq. mi.

Cottleville — Town
ZIP: 63338 Lat: 38-45-14 N Long: 90-39-13 W
Pop: 2,936 (1990); 184 (1980) Pop Density: 1223.3
Land: 2.4 sq. mi.; Water: 0.0 sq. mi.
Established 1839. Incorporated 1853.
Name origin: For Capt. Lorenzo Cottle, who served in the Black Hawk and Florida Wars.

*Cottleville — Township
Lat: 38-45-43 N Long: 90-40-10 W
Pop: 25,290 (1990) Pop Density: 1109.2
Land: 22.8 sq. mi.; Water: 0.0 sq. mi.

Dardenne — Township
Lat: 38-45-55 N Long: 90-45-55 W
Pop: 18,198 (1990); 14,971 (1980) Pop Density: 610.7
Land: 29.8 sq. mi.; Water: 0.9 sq. mi.

Dardenne Prairie — Town
Lat: 38-45-15 N Long: 90-43-55 W
Pop: 1,769 (1990) Pop Density: 453.6
Land: 3.9 sq. mi.; Water: 0.0 sq. mi.

Flint Hill — Village
Lat: 38-51-17 N Long: 90-51-19 W
Pop: 229 (1990); 219 (1980) Pop Density: 190.8
Land: 1.2 sq. mi.; Water: 0.0 sq. mi. Elev: 516 ft.
Incorporated 1976.

Foristell — City
ZIP: 63348 Lat: 38-48-49 N Long: 90-57-15 W
Pop: 130 (1990); 119 (1980) Pop Density: 144.4
Land: 0.9 sq. mi.; Water: 0.0 sq. mi. Elev: 707 ft.
Incorporated 1980. Part of the town is also in Warren County.

Friedens — Township
Lat: 38-45-57 N Long: 90-31-28 W
Pop: 17,131 (1990); 13,725 (1980) Pop Density: 2635.5
Land: 6.5 sq. mi.; Water: 0.3 sq. mi.

Frontier — Township
Lat: 38-47-12 N Long: 90-29-06 W
Pop: 10,693 (1990) Pop Density: 3449.4
Land: 3.1 sq. mi.; Water: 0.5 sq. mi.

Harvester — Township
Lat: 38-43-24 N Long: 90-33-30 W
Pop: 16,991 (1990) Pop Density: 1258.6
Land: 13.5 sq. mi.; Water: 1.0 sq. mi.

Josephville — Village
ZIP: 63385 Lat: 38-49-51 N Long: 90-47-34 W
Pop: 445 (1990); 58 (1980) Pop Density: 317.9
Land: 1.4 sq. mi.; Water: 0.0 sq. mi.

Lake St. Louis — City
ZIP: 63367 Lat: 38-47-20 N Long: 90-46-57 W
Pop: 7,400 (1990); 3,843 (1980) Pop Density: 1451.0
Land: 5.1 sq. mi.; Water: 0.8 sq. mi.

Lindenwood — Township
Lat: 38-47-52 N Long: 90-30-48 W
Pop: 9,062 (1990) Pop Density: 4119.1
Land: 2.2 sq. mi.; Water: 0.0 sq. mi.

New Melle — Village
ZIP: 63365 Lat: 38-42-36 N Long: 90-52-48 W
Pop: 486 (1990); 168 (1980) Pop Density: 1620.0
Land: 0.3 sq. mi.; Water: 0.0 sq. mi. Elev: 789 ft.
Incorporated 1979.

O'Fallon — City
ZIP: 63366 Lat: 38-47-03 N Long: 90-42-28 W
Pop: 18,698 (1990); 8,677 (1980) Pop Density: 1176.0
Land: 15.9 sq. mi.; Water: 0.0 sq. mi. Elev: 543 ft.
In eastern MO, 30 mi. northwest of St. Louis. Founded 1857. Incorporated 1912.
Name origin: For Col. John O'Fallon, St. Louis capitalist and director of the Old North Missouri Railway.

*O'Fallon — Township
Lat: 38-50-59 N Long: 90-44-11 W
Pop: 11,918 (1990); 10,271 (1980) Pop Density: 377.2
Land: 31.6 sq. mi.; Water: 0.0 sq. mi.

Portage Des Sioux — City
ZIP: 63373 Lat: 38-55-33 N Long: 90-20-31 W
Pop: 503 (1990); 488 (1980) Pop Density: 1257.5
Land: 0.4 sq. mi.; Water: 0.0 sq. mi.
Incorporated 1834.
Name origin: For the portage of canoes across the peninsula here between the Mississippi and Missouri rivers.

Rivers — Township
Lat: 38-52-43 N Long: 90-26-59 W
Pop: 7,298 (1990) Pop Density: 44.2
Land: 165.3 sq. mi.; Water: 22.5 sq. mi.

St. Charles — City
ZIP: 63301 Lat: 38-47-25 N Long: 90-30-59 W
Pop: 54,555 (1990); 37,379 (1980) Pop Density: 3286.4
Land: 16.6 sq. mi.; Water: 0.5 sq. mi. Elev: 536 ft.

In eastern MO on the Missouri River, 20 mi. northwest of St. Louis. First capital of state 1821–26; incorporated as city 1849.

Name origin:

Name origin: For St. Carlo Borromeo (1538–84), archbishop of Milan and founder of the religious order of the Oblates of St. Ambrose; it was the purpose of the vicar of Pontoise to establish a seminary here where Indians could be educated.

St. Paul — Village
Lat: 38-50-59 N Long: 90-44-11 W
Pop: 1,192 (1990); 607 (1980) Pop Density: 229.2
Land: 5.2 sq. mi.; Water: 0.0 sq. mi.

Incorporated 1976.

St. Peters — City
ZIP: 63376 Lat: 38-46-42 N Long: 90-36-19 W
Pop: 45,779 (1990); 15,700 (1980) Pop Density: 2897.4
Land: 15.8 sq. mi.; Water: 0.0 sq. mi.

Established 1820; platted 1868. Incorporated 1910.

Name origin: For a Jesuit mission established here.

*St. Peters — Township
Lat: 38-47-04 N Long: 90-36-53 W
Pop: 24,217 (1990); 24,130 (1980) Pop Density: 3104.7
Land: 7.8 sq. mi.; Water: 0.0 sq. mi.

Spencer Creek — Township
Lat: 38-46-11 N Long: 90-34-37 W
Pop: 24,515 (1990) Pop Density: 2918.5
Land: 8.4 sq. mi.; Water: 0.0 sq. mi.

Weldon Spring — Town
ZIP: 63303 Lat: 38-42-59 N Long: 90-38-56 W
Pop: 1,470 (1990) Pop Density: 245.0
Land: 6.0 sq. mi.; Water: 0.0 sq. mi.

Incorporated 1984. Not coextensive with the town of the same name.

Weldon Spring Heights — Town
Lat: 38-42-14 N Long: 90-41-04 W
Pop: 82 (1990); 144 (1980) Pop Density: 820.0
Land: 0.1 sq. mi.; Water: 0.0 sq. mi.

Incorporated 1951.

Name origin: For settlers Joseph and John Weldon.

Wentzville — City
ZIP: 63385 Lat: 38-48-48 N Long: 90-51-34 W
Pop: 5,088 (1990); 3,193 (1980) Pop Density: 524.5
Land: 9.7 sq. mi.; Water: 0.0 sq. mi. Elev: 603 ft.

Founded 1855. Incorporated 1872.

Name origin: For the chief of the St. Louis, Kansas City & Northern Railway.

*Wentzville — Township
Lat: 38-50-07 N Long: 90-51-58 W
Pop: 9,878 (1990); 7,163 (1980) Pop Density: 133.1
Land: 74.2 sq. mi.; Water: 0.1 sq. mi.

Zumbehl — Township
Lat: 38-47-52 N Long: 90-32-29 W
Pop: 11,596 (1990) Pop Density: 2696.7
Land: 4.3 sq. mi.; Water: 0.0 sq. mi.

St. Clair County
County Seat: Osceola (ZIP: 64776)

Pop: 8,457 (1990); 8,622 (1980) Pop Density: 12.5
Land: 676.7 sq. mi.; Water: 25.2 sq. mi. Area Code: 417

In west-central MO, northwest of Springfield; organized Jan 29, 1841 from Rives County.

Name origin: For Gen. Arthur St. Clair (1736?–1818), an officer in the French and Indian War and the Revolutionary War, president of the Continental Congress (1787), and governor of the Northwest Territory (1788–1802).

Appleton — Township
Lat: 38-09-10 N Long: 93-59-17 W
Pop: 1,584 (1990); 1,593 (1980) Pop Density: 34.8
Land: 45.5 sq. mi.; Water: 0.2 sq. mi.

Appleton City — City
ZIP: 64724 Lat: 38-11-23 N Long: 94-01-49 W
Pop: 1,280 (1990); 1,257 (1980) Pop Density: 1163.6
Land: 1.1 sq. mi.; Water: 0.0 sq. mi. Elev: 836 ft.

Incorporated 1870.

Name origin: For the publishing house of D. Appleton, through William H. Appleton of NY, who made a large donation for a public library.

Butler — Township
Lat: 38-08-45 N Long: 93-41-33 W
Pop: 1,345 (1990); 1,213 (1980) Pop Density: 23.6
Land: 57.1 sq. mi.; Water: 3.0 sq. mi.

Center — Township
Lat: 38-03-08 N Long: 93-48-00 W
Pop: 203 (1990); 335 (1980) Pop Density: 8.8
Land: 23.0 sq. mi.; Water: 1.3 sq. mi.

Chalk Level — Township
Lat: 38-09-30 N Long: 93-47-42 W
Pop: 150 (1990); 278 (1980) Pop Density: 4.9
Land: 30.6 sq. mi.; Water: 0.1 sq. mi.

Collins — Village
ZIP: 64738 Lat: 37-53-24 N Long: 93-37-14 W
Pop: 144 (1990); 145 (1980) Pop Density: 720.0
Land: 0.2 sq. mi.; Water: 0.0 sq. mi. Elev: 851 ft.

Incorporated 1885.

*Collins
Township
ZIP: 64738　**Lat:** 37-52-19 N　**Long:** 93-37-46 W
Pop: 604 (1990); 557 (1980)　**Pop Density:** 15.4
Land: 39.3 sq. mi.; **Water:** 0.0 sq. mi.

Dallas
Township
Lat: 37-57-07 N　**Long:** 93-34-06 W
Pop: 326 (1990); 330 (1980)　**Pop Density:** 8.9
Land: 36.8 sq. mi.; **Water:** 0.0 sq. mi.

Doyal
Township
Lat: 37-57-33 N　**Long:** 93-41-03 W
Pop: 496 (1990); 547 (1980)　**Pop Density:** 12.1
Land: 41.1 sq. mi.; **Water:** 0.9 sq. mi.

Gerster
Town
Lat: 37-57-14 N　**Long:** 93-34-35 W
Pop: 40 (1990); 45 (1980)　**Pop Density:** 400.0
Land: 0.1 sq. mi.; **Water:** 0.0 sq. mi.
Incorporated 1986.

Jackson
Township
Lat: 38-08-47 N　**Long:** 93-34-07 W
Pop: 260 (1990); 184 (1980)　**Pop Density:** 6.1
Land: 42.6 sq. mi.; **Water:** 8.5 sq. mi.

Lowry City
City
ZIP: 64763　**Lat:** 38-08-27 N　**Long:** 93-43-36 W
Pop: 723 (1990); 676 (1980)　**Pop Density:** 657.3
Land: 1.1 sq. mi.; **Water:** 0.0 sq. mi.　**Elev:** 885 ft.
Incorporated 1898.

Monegaw
Township
Lat: 38-09-27 N　**Long:** 93-53-23 W
Pop: 285 (1990); 315 (1980)　**Pop Density:** 6.3
Land: 45.6 sq. mi.; **Water:** 0.0 sq. mi.

Osage
Township
Lat: 38-03-00 N　**Long:** 93-53-30 W
Pop: 204 (1990); 154 (1980)　**Pop Density:** 5.4
Land: 37.5 sq. mi.; **Water:** 1.0 sq. mi.

Osceola
City
ZIP: 64776　**Lat:** 38-02-47 N　**Long:** 93-41-52 W
Pop: 755 (1990); 841 (1980)　**Pop Density:** 838.9
Land: 0.9 sq. mi.; **Water:** 0.0 sq. mi.　**Elev:** 763 ft.
Incorporated 1841.
Name origin: For Osceola (c. 1804–38), the Seminole Indian chief who was captured in 1837 when he attended a conference after the two-year Second Seminole War with the U.S.

*Osceola
Township
Lat: 38-02-58 N　**Long:** 93-41-18 W
Pop: 1,429 (1990); 1,438 (1980)　**Pop Density:** 34.6
Land: 41.3 sq. mi.; **Water:** 5.3 sq. mi.

Polk
Township
Lat: 38-02-54 N　**Long:** 93-33-35 W
Pop: 179 (1990); 157 (1980)　**Pop Density:** 5.0
Land: 35.7 sq. mi.; **Water:** 1.0 sq. mi.

Roscoe
Village
ZIP: 64781　**Lat:** 37-58-36 N　**Long:** 93-48-44 W
Pop: 100 (1990); 91 (1980)　**Pop Density:** 71.4
Land: 1.4 sq. mi.; **Water:** 0.2 sq. mi.　**Elev:** 763 ft.
Incorporated 1869.

*Roscoe
Township
Lat: 37-57-12 N　**Long:** 93-49-10 W
Pop: 503 (1990); 551 (1980)　**Pop Density:** 8.0
Land: 63.0 sq. mi.; **Water:** 2.6 sq. mi.

Speedwell
Township
Lat: 37-57-13 N　**Long:** 93-58-42 W
Pop: 437 (1990); 473 (1980)　**Pop Density:** 6.6
Land: 66.6 sq. mi.; **Water:** 0.8 sq. mi.

Taber
Township
Lat: 38-02-50 N　**Long:** 93-59-25 W
Pop: 212 (1990); 240 (1980)　**Pop Density:** 5.5
Land: 38.6 sq. mi.; **Water:** 0.3 sq. mi.

Vista
Village
ZIP: 64789　**Lat:** 37-59-19 N　**Long:** 93-39-49 W
Pop: 50 (1990); 73 (1980)　**Pop Density:** 500.0
Land: 0.1 sq. mi.; **Water:** 0.0 sq. mi.
Incorporated 1952.

Washington
Township
Lat: 37-51-58 N　**Long:** 93-44-36 W
Pop: 240 (1990); 257 (1980)　**Pop Density:** 7.4
Land: 32.4 sq. mi.; **Water:** 0.1 sq. mi.

Ste. Genevieve County
County Seat: Ste. Genevieve (ZIP: 63670)

Pop: 16,037 (1990); 15,180 (1980)　**Pop Density:** 31.9
Land: 502.4 sq. mi.; **Water:** 6.5 sq. mi.　**Area Code:** 314
On southeastern border of MO, south of St. Louis; original county; organized Oct 1, 1812 (prior to statehood).
Name origin: For the city, the oldest white settlement in MO; itself named for Ste. Genevieve (c. 422–c. 500), French nun and patron saint of Paris.

Beauvais
Township
Lat: 37-49-42 N　**Long:** 90-04-03 W
Pop: 1,772 (1990); 1,801 (1980)　**Pop Density:** 21.8
Land: 81.1 sq. mi.; **Water:** 0.3 sq. mi.

Bloomsdale
City
ZIP: 63627　**Lat:** 38-00-41 N　**Long:** 90-13-09 W
Pop: 353 (1990); 397 (1980)　**Pop Density:** 353.0
Land: 1.0 sq. mi.; **Water:** 0.0 sq. mi.　**Elev:** 506 ft.
Incorporated 1962.

MISSOURI, Ste. Genevieve County

Jackson
Township
Lat: 38-01-58 N Long: 90-16-20 W
Pop: 2,629 (1990); 2,355 (1980) **Pop Density:** 27.0
Land: 97.4 sq. mi.; **Water:** 2.7 sq. mi.

Rocky Ridge
Village
ZIP: 63670 Lat: 37-56-00 N Long: 90-14-33 W
Pop: 362 (1990) **Pop Density:** 116.8
Land: 3.1 sq. mi.; **Water:** 0.4 sq. mi.

St. Mary
City
Lat: 37-52-33 N Long: 89-56-55 W
Pop: 461 (1990); 565 (1980) **Pop Density:** 1152.5
Land: 0.4 sq. mi.; **Water:** 0.0 sq. mi.
Incorporated 1892.

Ste. Genevieve
City
Lat: 37-58-29 N Long: 90-02-58 W
Pop: 4,411 (1990); 4,481 (1980) **Pop Density:** 2005.0
Land: 2.2 sq. mi.; **Water:** 0.0 sq. mi. **Elev:** 401 ft.

*Ste. Genevieve
Township
Lat: 37-56-53 N Long: 90-07-02 W
Pop: 8,707 (1990); 8,602 (1980) **Pop Density:** 70.0
Land: 124.3 sq. mi.; **Water:** 2.7 sq. mi.

Saline
Township
Lat: 37-45-50 N Long: 90-12-18 W
Pop: 887 (1990); 813 (1980) **Pop Density:** 8.2
Land: 107.8 sq. mi.; **Water:** 0.4 sq. mi.

Union
Township
Lat: 37-52-57 N Long: 90-19-47 W
Pop: 2,042 (1990); 1,609 (1980) **Pop Density:** 22.2
Land: 91.9 sq. mi.; **Water:** 0.6 sq. mi.

St. Francois County
County Seat: Farmington (ZIP: 63640)

Pop: 48,904 (1990); 42,600 (1980) **Pop Density:** 108.8
Land: 449.5 sq. mi.; **Water:** 2.9 sq. mi. **Area Code:** 314

In southeastern MO, south of St. Louis; established Dec 19, 1821 from Ste. Genevieve, Jefferson, and Washington counties.

Name origin: For the St. Francois Mountains, part of which are in the county; French for St. Francis.

Big River
Township
Lat: 38-00-07 N Long: 90-33-51 W
Pop: 1,435 (1990); 986 (1980) **Pop Density:** 44.3
Land: 32.4 sq. mi.; **Water:** 0.2 sq. mi.

Bismarck
City
ZIP: 63624 Lat: 37-46-02 N Long: 90-37-21 W
Pop: 1,579 (1990); 1,625 (1980) **Pop Density:** 1579.0
Land: 1.0 sq. mi.; **Water:** 0.0 sq. mi.
Incorporated 1877.

Name origin: Named by German-Americans for the city in Germany.

Bonne Terre
City
ZIP: 63628 Lat: 37-55-21 N Long: 90-32-59 W
Pop: 3,871 (1990); 3,797 (1980) **Pop Density:** 1488.8
Land: 2.6 sq. mi.; **Water:** 0.1 sq. mi.

In eastern MO, 50 mi. south-southwest of St. Louis. Incorporated 1917.

Name origin: From French meaning 'good earth.'

Desloge
City
ZIP: 63601 Lat: 37-52-25 N Long: 90-31-14 W
Pop: 4,150 (1990); 3,481 (1980) **Pop Density:** 1886.4
Land: 2.2 sq. mi.; **Water:** 0.0 sq. mi.
Incorporated 1941.

Name origin: For the president of a mining company, Firmin Desloge.

Elvins
City
ZIP: 63601 Lat: 37-50-07 N Long: 90-32-05 W
Pop: 1,391 (1990); 1,548 (1980) **Pop Density:** 2318.3
Land: 0.6 sq. mi.; **Water:** 0.0 sq. mi. **Elev:** 765 ft.
Incorporated 1902.

Name origin: For Politte Elvins, a member of Congress.

Esther
City
ZIP: 63601 Lat: 37-51-07 N Long: 90-29-40 W
Pop: 1,071 (1990); 1,038 (1980) **Pop Density:** 2677.5
Land: 0.4 sq. mi.; **Water:** 0.0 sq. mi.
Incorporated 1952.

Name origin: Named in 1901 for the daughter of businessman Harry Cantwell.

Farmington
City
ZIP: 63640 Lat: 37-46-48 N Long: 90-25-33 W
Pop: 11,598 (1990); 8,270 (1980) **Pop Density:** 1812.2
Land: 6.4 sq. mi.; **Water:** 0.0 sq. mi. **Elev:** 918 ft.

In eastern MO, 60 mi. south of St. Louis. Incorporated 1879.

Flat River
City
ZIP: 63601 Lat: 37-51-12 N Long: 90-30-59 W
Pop: 4,823 (1990); 4,443 (1980) **Pop Density:** 1378.0
Land: 3.5 sq. mi.; **Water:** 0.0 sq. mi.

In eastern MO, 55 mi. south-southwest of St. Louis. Incorporated 1934.

Iron
Township
Lat: 37-42-39 N Long: 90-35-50 W
Pop: 2,921 (1990); 2,880 (1980) **Pop Density:** 60.6
Land: 48.2 sq. mi.; **Water:** 0.7 sq. mi.

Iron Mountain Lake   City
ZIP: 63624   **Lat:** 37-41-06 N **Long:** 90-36-52 W
Pop: 632 (1990)   **Pop Density:** 316.0
Land: 2.0 sq. mi.; **Water:** 0.1 sq. mi.

Leadington   City
ZIP: 63601   **Lat:** 37-50-03 N **Long:** 90-28-53 W
Pop: 201 (1990); 238 (1980)   **Pop Density:** 287.1
Land: 0.7 sq. mi.; **Water:** 0.0 sq. mi.
Incorporated 1958.

Leadwood   City
ZIP: 63653   **Lat:** 37-51-44 N **Long:** 90-35-21 W
Pop: 1,247 (1990); 1,371 (1980)   **Pop Density:** 1039.2
Land: 1.2 sq. mi.; **Water:** 0.0 sq. mi.
Incorporated 1964.

Liberty   Township
Lat: 37-41-19 N **Long:** 90-17-34 W
Pop: 1,482 (1990); 1,425 (1980)   **Pop Density:** 17.7
Land: 83.9 sq. mi.; **Water:** 0.4 sq. mi.

Marion   Township
Lat: 37-58-50 N **Long:** 90-25-28 W
Pop: 1,495 (1990); 1,115 (1980)   **Pop Density:** 27.1
Land: 55.1 sq. mi.; **Water:** 0.5 sq. mi.

Pendleton   Township
Lat: 37-41-46 N **Long:** 90-29-13 W
Pop: 2,338 (1990); 2,112 (1980)   **Pop Density:** 37.3
Land: 62.7 sq. mi.; **Water:** 0.1 sq. mi.

Perry   Township
Lat: 37-54-52 N **Long:** 90-32-47 W
Pop: 7,610 (1990); 6,908 (1980)   **Pop Density:** 127.0
Land: 59.9 sq. mi.; **Water:** 0.7 sq. mi.

Randolph   Township
Lat: 37-49-45 N **Long:** 90-34-36 W
Pop: 8,841 (1990); 7,615 (1980)   **Pop Density:** 203.2
Land: 43.5 sq. mi.; **Water:** 0.1 sq. mi.

Rivermines   Village
ZIP: 63601   **Lat:** 37-50-38 N **Long:** 90-31-47 W
Pop: 459 (1990); 414 (1980)   **Pop Density:** 655.7
Land: 0.7 sq. mi.; **Water:** 0.0 sq. mi.
Incorporated 1911.

St. Francois   Township
Lat: 37-47-52 N **Long:** 90-26-35 W
Pop: 22,782 (1990); 19,559 (1980)   **Pop Density:** 357.1
Land: 63.8 sq. mi.; **Water:** 0.2 sq. mi.

St. Louis (Independent City)
County Seat: St. Louis (Independent City) (ZIP: 63166)

Lat: 38-38-09 N **Long:** 90-14-39 W
Pop: 396,685 (1990); 452,801 (1980)   **Pop Density:** 6408.5
Land: 61.9 sq. mi.; **Water:** 4.2 sq. mi.

On the central-eastern border of MO on the Mississippi River, 11 mi. below its confluence with the Missouri River. In 1763 site was selected by Pierre Laclède Liguest (1724?–78), partner in Maxent, Laclede and Company; settled 1764; chartered as city 1822. Busiest inland port on the Mississippi River; in early 1800s known as the "Gateway to the West." Manufacturing city (transportation equipment, automobile production); home of Anheuser-Busch, largest beer-producer in U.S.

Name origin: For Louis IX (1214–70), crusader king of France, canonized in 1297.

St. Louis County
County Seat: Clayton (ZIP: 63105)

Pop: 993,529 (1990); 974,180 (1980)   **Pop Density:** 1956.7
Land: 507.8 sq. mi.; **Water:** 15.9 sq. mi.   **Area Code:** 314

On the central-eastern border of MO on the Mississippi River, 11 mi. below its confluence with the Missouri River. Organized 1812; original county.

Name origin: For Louis IX (1214–70), crusader king of France, canonized in 1297.

Affton   CDP
ZIP: 63123   **Lat:** 38-32-58 N **Long:** 90-19-44 W
Pop: 21,106 (1990); 10,897 (1980)   **Pop Density:** 4307.3
Land: 4.9 sq. mi.; **Water:** 0.0 sq. mi.

Airport   Township
Lat: 38-44-10 N **Long:** 90-21-24 W
Pop: 33,279 (1990); 42,212 (1980)   **Pop Density:** 2919.2
Land: 11.4 sq. mi.; **Water:** 0.0 sq. mi.

Ballwin   City
ZIP: 63011   **Lat:** 38-35-38 N **Long:** 90-33-08 W
Pop: 21,816 (1990); 12,656 (1980)   **Pop Density:** 3462.9
Land: 6.3 sq. mi.; **Water:** 0.0 sq. mi.   **Elev:** 659 ft.
In eastern MO, a southwestern suburb of St. Louis. Incorporated 1950.

Name origin: For John Ball, who settled the area in 1804 and owned the land on which the town was laid out.

Bella Villa — City
ZIP: 63125 **Lat:** 38-32-36 N **Long:** 90-17-10 W
Pop: 708 (1990); 758 (1980) **Pop Density:** 7080.0
Land: 0.1 sq. mi.; **Water:** 0.0 sq. mi.
Incorporated 1947.

Bellefontaine Neighbors — City
ZIP: 63137 **Lat:** 38-45-07 N **Long:** 90-13-36 W
Pop: 10,922 (1990); 12,082 (1980) **Pop Density:** 2482.3
Land: 4.4 sq. mi.; **Water:** 0.0 sq. mi.
In eastern MO, a northern suburb of St. Louis. Incorporated 1950.
Name origin: From French meaning 'beautiful spring' or 'fountain.'

Bellerive — Village
ZIP: 63121 **Lat:** 38-42-46 N **Long:** 90-18-35 W
Pop: 238 (1990); 255 (1980) **Pop Density:** 595.0
Land: 0.4 sq. mi.; **Water:** 0.0 sq. mi.
Incorporated 1934.

Bel-Nor — Village
Lat: 38-42-11 N **Long:** 90-18-58 W
Pop: 2,935 (1990); 2,047 (1980) **Pop Density:** 4192.9
Land: 0.7 sq. mi.; **Water:** 0.0 sq. mi.
Incorporated 1937.

Bel-Ridge — Village
Lat: 38-42-50 N **Long:** 90-19-40 W
Pop: 3,199 (1990); 3,682 (1980) **Pop Density:** 3998.8
Land: 0.8 sq. mi.; **Water:** 0.0 sq. mi.
Incorporated 1947.

Berkeley — City
ZIP: 63134 **Lat:** 38-44-35 N **Long:** 90-20-08 W
Pop: 12,450 (1990); 15,922 (1980) **Pop Density:** 2540.8
Land: 4.9 sq. mi.; **Water:** 0.0 sq. mi.
In eastern MO, a northwestern suburb of St. Louis. Incorporated 1937.
Name origin: For the person who planned the subdivision.

Beverly Hills — City
ZIP: 63121 **Lat:** 38-41-51 N **Long:** 90-17-25 W
Pop: 660 (1990); 712 (1980) **Pop Density:** 6600.0
Land: 0.1 sq. mi.; **Water:** 0.0 sq. mi.
Incorporated 1933.

Black Jack — City
ZIP: 63031 **Lat:** 38-47-53 N **Long:** 90-15-48 W
Pop: 6,128 (1990); 5,293 (1980) **Pop Density:** 2269.6
Land: 2.7 sq. mi.; **Water:** 0.0 sq. mi. **Elev:** 596 ft.
Incorporated 1970.

Bonhomme — Township
Lat: 38-32-56 N **Long:** 90-25-39 W
Pop: 37,896 (1990); 36,578 (1980) **Pop Density:** 1592.3
Land: 23.8 sq. mi.; **Water:** 0.5 sq. mi.

Breckenridge Hills — Village
ZIP: 63114 **Lat:** 38-42-55 N **Long:** 90-22-02 W
Pop: 5,404 (1990); 5,666 (1980) **Pop Density:** 6755.0
Land: 0.8 sq. mi.; **Water:** 0.0 sq. mi.
Incorporated 1950.

Brentwood — City
ZIP: 63144 **Lat:** 38-37-08 N **Long:** 90-20-54 W
Pop: 8,150 (1990); 8,209 (1980) **Pop Density:** 4289.5
Land: 1.9 sq. mi.; **Water:** 0.0 sq. mi. **Elev:** 493 ft.
In eastern MO, 10 mi. west of St. Louis. Incorporated 1919.
Name origin: For Mr. Brent, who laid out the town.

Bridgeton — City
ZIP: 63044 **Lat:** 38-45-58 N **Long:** 90-25-35 W
Pop: 17,779 (1990); 18,445 (1980) **Pop Density:** 1226.1
Land: 14.5 sq. mi.; **Water:** 0.6 sq. mi.
In eastern MO on the Coldwater River, a northwestern suburb of St. Louis. Incorporated 1794.
Name origin: Previously called Marais des Liards and Bridgetown.

Calverton Park — Village
Lat: 38-45-59 N **Long:** 90-18-31 W
Pop: 1,404 (1990); 1,717 (1980) **Pop Density:** 3510.0
Land: 0.4 sq. mi.; **Water:** 0.0 sq. mi.
Incorporated 1940.

Castle Point — CDP
Lat: 38-45-28 N **Long:** 90-14-53 W
Pop: 4,975 (1990) **Pop Density:** 7107.1
Land: 0.7 sq. mi.; **Water:** 0.0 sq. mi.

Champ — Village
Lat: 38-44-37 N **Long:** 90-26-57 W
Pop: 11 (1990); 28 (1980) **Pop Density:** 18.3
Land: 0.6 sq. mi.; **Water:** 0.0 sq. mi. **Elev:** 607 ft.
Incorporated 1959.

Charlack — City
ZIP: 63114 **Lat:** 38-42-12 N **Long:** 90-20-33 W
Pop: 1,388 (1990); 1,537 (1980) **Pop Density:** 4626.7
Land: 0.3 sq. mi.; **Water:** 0.0 sq. mi.
Incorporated 1974.

Chesterfield — City
ZIP: 63017 **Lat:** 38-39-15 N **Long:** 90-34-52 W
Pop: 37,991 (1990) **Pop Density:** 1266.4
Land: 30.0 sq. mi.; **Water:** 1.2 sq. mi.

Clarkson Valley — City
ZIP: 63017 **Lat:** 38-37-30 N **Long:** 90-35-38 W
Pop: 2,508 (1990); 1,435 (1980) **Pop Density:** 928.9
Land: 2.7 sq. mi.; **Water:** 0.1 sq. mi.
Incorporated 1950.

Clayton — City
ZIP: 63105 **Lat:** 38-38-39 N **Long:** 90-19-42 W
Pop: 13,874 (1990); 14,306 (1980) **Pop Density:** 5549.6
Land: 2.5 sq. mi.; **Water:** 0.0 sq. mi.
In eastern MO, 10 mi. west of St. Louis. Incorporated 1913.
Name origin: Named in 1877 for landowner Ralph Clayton, who donated one hundred acres of his farm to the new county.

*Clayton — Township
Lat: 38-37-50 N **Long:** 90-24-03 W
Pop: 34,887 (1990); 35,650 (1980) **Pop Density:** 1744.3
Land: 20.0 sq. mi.; **Water:** 0.0 sq. mi.

Concord — CDP
ZIP: 63128 **Lat:** 38-30-51 N **Long:** 90-21-12 W
Pop: 19,859 (1990); 20,896 (1980) **Pop Density:** 2878.1
Land: 6.9 sq. mi.; **Water:** 0.0 sq. mi.

MISSOURI, St. Louis County

*Concord Township
Lat: 38-30-28 N Long: 90-21-57 W
Pop: 58,311 (1990); 59,424 (1980) **Pop Density:** 2662.6
Land: 21.9 sq. mi.; **Water:** 0.2 sq. mi.

Cool Valley City
Lat: 38-43-29 N Long: 90-18-17 W
Pop: 1,407 (1990); 2,084 (1980) **Pop Density:** 2814.0
Land: 0.5 sq. mi.; **Water:** 0.0 sq. mi.
Incorporated 1951.

Country Club Hills City
ZIP: 63136 Lat: 38-43-14 N Long: 90-16-29 W
Pop: 1,316 (1990); 1,315 (1980) **Pop Density:** 6580.0
Land: 0.2 sq. mi.; **Water:** 0.0 sq. mi.
Incorporated 1943.

Country Life Acres Village
ZIP: 63131 Lat: 38-37-29 N Long: 90-27-21 W
Pop: 101 (1990); 77 (1980) **Pop Density:** 1010.0
Land: 0.1 sq. mi.; **Water:** 0.0 sq. mi.
Incorporated 1945.

Crestwood City
ZIP: 63126 Lat: 38-33-20 N Long: 90-22-53 W
Pop: 11,234 (1990); 12,815 (1980) **Pop Density:** 3510.6
Land: 3.2 sq. mi.; **Water:** 0.0 sq. mi. **Elev:** 621 ft.
Incorporated 1949.
Name origin: Descriptive and promotional.

Creve Coeur City
ZIP: 63141 Lat: 38-39-37 N Long: 90-26-07 W
Pop: 12,304 (1990); 11,743 (1980) **Pop Density:** 1618.9
Land: 7.6 sq. mi.; **Water:** 0.0 sq. mi. **Elev:** 644 ft.
In eastern MO, a western suburb of St. Louis. Incorporated 1949.
Name origin: For Creve Coeur, IL.

*Creve Coeur Township
Lat: 38-40-26 N Long: 90-23-29 W
Pop: 55,422 (1990); 56,778 (1980) **Pop Density:** 3358.9
Land: 16.5 sq. mi.; **Water:** 0.0 sq. mi.

Crystal Lake Park City
ZIP: 63131 Lat: 38-37-13 N Long: 90-25-51 W
Pop: 506 (1990); 496 (1980) **Pop Density:** 5060.0
Land: 0.1 sq. mi.; **Water:** 0.0 sq. mi.
Incorporated 1939.

Dellwood City
ZIP: 63136 Lat: 38-45-18 N Long: 90-16-39 W
Pop: 5,245 (1990); 6,200 (1980) **Pop Density:** 5245.0
Land: 1.0 sq. mi.; **Water:** 0.0 sq. mi. **Elev:** 537 ft.
Incorporated 1951.

Des Peres City
ZIP: 63131 Lat: 38-35-45 N Long: 90-26-49 W
Pop: 8,395 (1990); 7,953 (1980) **Pop Density:** 1998.8
Land: 4.2 sq. mi.; **Water:** 0.0 sq. mi.
In eastern MO, 10 mi. west of St. Louis. Incorporated 1934.

Edmundson Village
ZIP: 63134 Lat: 38-44-03 N Long: 90-21-57 W
Pop: 1,111 (1990); 1,374 (1980) **Pop Density:** 3703.3
Incorporated 1948.

Ellisville City
ZIP: 63011 Lat: 38-35-20 N Long: 90-35-09 W
Pop: 7,545 (1990); 6,233 (1980) **Pop Density:** 1840.2
Land: 4.1 sq. mi.; **Water:** 0.0 sq. mi.
In eastern MO, a western suburb of St. Louis. Settled c. 1836 by Capt. Harvey Ferris, who came from KY. Incorporated 1932.
Name origin: For Vespuccio Ellis, U.S. Consul to Venezuela.

Eureka City
ZIP: 63025 Lat: 38-30-10 N Long: 90-38-33 W
Pop: 4,683 (1990); 3,862 (1980) **Pop Density:** 503.5
Land: 9.3 sq. mi.; **Water:** 0.1 sq. mi.
Incorporated 1954.
Name origin: From Greek 'I have found it!' Named by the surveying engineer of the Missouri Pacific Railroad who found that a route through this valley would eliminate many cuts and grades.

Fenton City
ZIP: 63026 Lat: 38-32-09 N Long: 90-27-04 W
Pop: 3,346 (1990); 2,417 (1980) **Pop Density:** 669.2
Land: 5.0 sq. mi.; **Water:** 0.1 sq. mi.
Incorporated 1874.

Ferguson City
ZIP: 63135 Lat: 38-44-55 N Long: 90-17-44 W
Pop: 22,286 (1990); 24,549 (1980) **Pop Density:** 3594.5
Land: 6.2 sq. mi.; **Water:** 0.0 sq. mi.
In eastern MO, a northwestern suburb of St. Louis. Incorporated 1894.
Name origin: Named in 1876 for one of the early settlers, William B. Ferguson.

*Ferguson Township
Lat: 38-44-47 N Long: 90-17-20 W
Pop: 43,991 (1990); 48,187 (1980) **Pop Density:** 3963.2
Land: 11.1 sq. mi.; **Water:** 0.0 sq. mi.

Flordell Hills City
ZIP: 63136 Lat: 38-43-03 N Long: 90-15-54 W
Pop: 950 (1990); 919 (1980) **Pop Density:** 9500.0
Land: 0.1 sq. mi.; **Water:** 0.0 sq. mi. **Elev:** 493 ft.
Incorporated 1945.

Florissant City
ZIP: 63033 Lat: 38-47-50 N Long: 90-19-27 W
Pop: 51,206 (1990); 55,721 (1980) **Pop Density:** 5020.2
Land: 10.2 sq. mi.; **Water:** 0.0 sq. mi.
In eastern MO, northwest of St. Louis. Incorporated 1786.
Name origin: From French 'prosperous.' Previously called St. Ferdinand by Spanish authorities and known as St. Ferdinand de Florissant.

*Florissant Township
Lat: 38-47-22 N Long: 90-18-32 W
Pop: 33,816 (1990); 37,028 (1980) **Pop Density:** 4508.8
Land: 7.5 sq. mi.; **Water:** 0.0 sq. mi.

Frontenac City
ZIP: 63131 Lat: 38-37-50 N Long: 90-24-57 W
Pop: 3,374 (1990); 3,654 (1980) **Pop Density:** 1163.4
Land: 2.9 sq. mi.; **Water:** 0.0 sq. mi.
In eastern MO, 10 mi. west of St. Louis. Incorporated 1947.

Glasgow Village CDP
ZIP: 63137 Lat: 38-45-29 N Long: 90-11-48 W
Pop: 5,199 (1990) **Pop Density:** 5776.7
Land: 0.9 sq. mi.; **Water:** 0.0 sq. mi.

MISSOURI, St. Louis County

Glendale City
ZIP: 63122 **Lat:** 38-35-34 N **Long:** 90-22-52 W
Pop: 5,945 (1990); 6,035 (1980) **Pop Density:** 4573.1
Land: 1.3 sq. mi.; **Water:** 0.0 sq. mi. **Elev:** 585 ft.
In eastern MO, 10 mi. southwest of St. Louis. Incorporated 1912.

Glen Echo Park Village
Lat: 38-42-03 N **Long:** 90-17-43 W
Pop: 304 (1990); 249 (1980) **Pop Density:** 3040.0
Land: 0.1 sq. mi.; **Water:** 0.0 sq. mi.
Incorporated 1937.

Grantwood Village Town
Lat: 38-33-01 N **Long:** 90-21-15 W
Pop: 904 (1990); 1,002 (1980) **Pop Density:** 1130.0
Land: 0.8 sq. mi.; **Water:** 0.0 sq. mi. **Elev:** 605 ft.
Incorporated 1937.

Gravois Township
ZIP: 63116 **Lat:** 38-33-48 N **Long:** 90-21-15 W
Pop: 49,605 (1990); 51,883 (1980) **Pop Density:** 3647.4
Land: 13.6 sq. mi.; **Water:** 0.0 sq. mi.

Greendale City
ZIP: 63133 **Lat:** 38-41-29 N **Long:** 90-18-44 W
Pop: 426 (1990); 853 (1980) **Pop Density:** 2130.0
Land: 0.2 sq. mi.; **Water:** 0.0 sq. mi.
Incorporated 1950.

Hadley Township
Lat: 38-38-09 N **Long:** 90-19-04 W
Pop: 38,769 (1990); 41,320 (1980) **Pop Density:** 6923.0
Land: 5.6 sq. mi.; **Water:** 0.0 sq. mi.

Hanley Hills Village
ZIP: 63133 **Lat:** 38-41-05 N **Long:** 90-19-27 W
Pop: 2,325 (1990); 2,439 (1980) **Pop Density:** 5812.5
Land: 0.4 sq. mi.; **Water:** 0.0 sq. mi.
Incorporated 1948.

Hazelwood City
ZIP: 63042 **Lat:** 38-46-39 N **Long:** 90-21-34 W
Pop: 15,324 (1990); 13,098 (1980) **Pop Density:** 3127.3
Land: 4.9 sq. mi.; **Water:** 0.0 sq. mi.
In eastern MO, northwest of St. Louis. Incorporated 1949.
Name origin: For its descriptive connotations.

Hillsdale Village
Lat: 38-41-06 N **Long:** 90-17-18 W
Pop: 1,948 (1990); 2,247 (1980) **Pop Density:** 6493.3
Land: 0.3 sq. mi.; **Water:** 0.0 sq. mi.
Incorporated 1947.

Huntleigh City
ZIP: 63131 **Lat:** 38-36-48 N **Long:** 90-24-27 W
Pop: 392 (1990); 428 (1980) **Pop Density:** 392.0
Land: 1.0 sq. mi.; **Water:** 0.0 sq. mi.
Incorporated 1929.

Jefferson Township
Lat: 38-36-36 N **Long:** 90-21-25 W
Pop: 33,937 (1990); 34,175 (1980) **Pop Density:** 3360.1
Land: 10.1 sq. mi.; **Water:** 0.0 sq. mi.

Jennings City
ZIP: 63136 **Lat:** 38-43-24 N **Long:** 90-15-52 W
Pop: 15,905 (1990); 16,934 (1980) **Pop Density:** 4298.6
Land: 3.7 sq. mi.; **Water:** 0.0 sq. mi.
In eastern MO, 5 mi. north of St. Louis. Incorporated 1946.
Name origin: For landowner and prominent citizen James Jennings (?–1855).

Kinloch City
ZIP: 63140 **Lat:** 38-44-17 N **Long:** 90-19-31 W
Pop: 2,702 (1990); 4,455 (1980) **Pop Density:** 3860.0
Land: 0.7 sq. mi.; **Water:** 0.0 sq. mi.
Incorporated 1948.

Kirkwood City
ZIP: 63122 **Lat:** 38-34-49 N **Long:** 90-25-12 W
Pop: 27,291 (1990); 27,739 (1980) **Pop Density:** 3032.3
Land: 9.0 sq. mi.; **Water:** 0.0 sq. mi.
In eastern MO, 15 mi. west of St. Louis. Incorporated 1865. Incorporated 1865.
Name origin: For James P. Kirkwood, chief engineer of the railroad.

Ladue City
ZIP: 63124 **Lat:** 38-38-12 N **Long:** 90-22-53 W
Pop: 8,847 (1990); 9,369 (1980) **Pop Density:** 1028.7
Land: 8.6 sq. mi.; **Water:** 0.0 sq. mi.
In eastern MO, 40 mi. west of St. Louis. Incorporated 1936.

Lakeshire City
Lat: 38-32-28 N **Long:** 90-20-13 W
Pop: 1,467 (1990); 1,593 (1980) **Pop Density:** 7335.0
Land: 0.2 sq. mi.; **Water:** 0.0 sq. mi.
Incorporated 1951.

Lemay CDP
ZIP: 63125 **Lat:** 38-31-54 N **Long:** 90-17-02 W
Pop: 18,005 (1990); 1,198 (1980) **Pop Density:** 4391.5
Land: 4.1 sq. mi.; **Water:** 0.2 sq. mi.

*Lemay Township
Lat: 38-28-23 N **Long:** 90-18-48 W
Pop: 79,806 (1990); 72,216 (1980) **Pop Density:** 2557.9
Land: 31.2 sq. mi.; **Water:** 3.0 sq. mi.

Lewis and Clark Township
Lat: 38-49-03 N **Long:** 90-21-29 W
Pop: 46,935 (1990); 44,472 (1980) **Pop Density:** 3352.5
Land: 14.0 sq. mi.; **Water:** 1.6 sq. mi.

Mac Kenzie Village
Lat: 38-34-49 N **Long:** 90-18-59 W
Pop: 148 (1990); 186 (1980) **Pop Density:** 4933.3
Land: 0.03 sq. mi.; **Water:** 0.0 sq. mi.
Incorporated 1946.

Manchester City
ZIP: 63011 **Lat:** 38-35-33 N **Long:** 90-30-53 W
Pop: 6,542 (1990); 6,351 (1980) **Pop Density:** 2973.6
Land: 2.2 sq. mi.; **Water:** 0.0 sq. mi.
In eastern MO, 15 mi. west of St. Louis. Incorporated 1960.
Name origin: Probably for old Mr. Manchester, who lived in the vicinity as early as 1795.

Maplewood City
ZIP: 63143 **Lat:** 38-36-43 N **Long:** 90-19-27 W
Pop: 9,962 (1990); 10,960 (1980) **Pop Density:** 6641.3
Land: 1.5 sq. mi.; **Water:** 0.0 sq. mi.
In eastern MO, 5 mi. west of St. Louis. Incorporated 1908.

Marlborough
Village
Lat: 38-34-04 N **Long:** 90-20-20 W
Pop: 1,949 (1990); 2,012 (1980) **Pop Density:** 9745.0
Land: 0.2 sq. mi.; **Water:** 0.0 sq. mi.
Incorporated 1938.

Maryland Heights
City
ZIP: 63043 **Lat:** 38-43-20 N **Long:** 90-28-38 W
Pop: 25,407 (1990); 839 (1980) **Pop Density:** 1209.9
Land: 21.0 sq. mi.; **Water:** 2.2 sq. mi.
Incorporated 1985.

Mehlville
CDP
ZIP: 63129 **Lat:** 38-30-04 N **Long:** 90-18-56 W
Pop: 27,557 (1990) **Pop Density:** 3723.9
Land: 7.4 sq. mi.; **Water:** 0.2 sq. mi.

Meramec
Township
Lat: 38-34-31 N **Long:** 90-38-59 W
Pop: 36,441 (1990); 20,667 (1980) **Pop Density:** 321.1
Land: 113.5 sq. mi.; **Water:** 1.9 sq. mi.

Midland
Township
Lat: 38-42-13 N **Long:** 90-21-59 W
Pop: 39,601 (1990); 42,632 (1980) **Pop Density:** 4400.1
Land: 9.0 sq. mi.; **Water:** 0.0 sq. mi.

Missouri River
Township
Lat: 38-40-14 N **Long:** 90-30-21 W
Pop: 81,448 (1990); 72,463 (1980) **Pop Density:** 1810.0
Land: 45.0 sq. mi.; **Water:** 1.9 sq. mi.

Moline Acres
City
ZIP: 63136 **Lat:** 38-44-42 N **Long:** 90-14-32 W
Pop: 2,710 (1990); 2,774 (1980) **Pop Density:** 4516.7
Land: 0.6 sq. mi.; **Water:** 0.0 sq. mi.
Incorporated 1949.

Normandy
City
ZIP: 63121 **Lat:** 38-42-27 N **Long:** 90-18-01 W
Pop: 4,480 (1990); 5,174 (1980) **Pop Density:** 2488.9
Land: 1.8 sq. mi.; **Water:** 0.0 sq. mi.
In eastern MO, 5 mi. northwest of St. Louis. Incorporated 1977.
Name origin: For Normandy, France.

*Normandy
Township
ZIP: 63121 **Lat:** 38-41-34 N **Long:** 90-18-21 W
Pop: 42,917 (1990); 48,347 (1980) **Pop Density:** 4379.3
Land: 9.8 sq. mi.; **Water:** 0.0 sq. mi.

Northwest
Township
Lat: 38-45-56 N **Long:** 90-25-36 W
Pop: 45,389 (1990); 47,066 (1980) **Pop Density:** 1247.0
Land: 36.4 sq. mi.; **Water:** 1.8 sq. mi.

Northwoods
City
ZIP: 63121 **Lat:** 38-42-11 N **Long:** 90-16-56 W
Pop: 5,106 (1990); 5,831 (1980) **Pop Density:** 7294.3
Land: 0.7 sq. mi.; **Water:** 0.0 sq. mi.
Incorporated 1950.

Norwood Court
Town
Lat: 38-42-56 N **Long:** 90-17-25 W
Pop: 888 (1990); 881 (1980) **Pop Density:** 8880.0
Land: 0.1 sq. mi.; **Water:** 0.0 sq. mi. **Elev:** 622 ft.
Incorporated 1949.

Oakland
City
ZIP: 63122 **Lat:** 38-34-32 N **Long:** 90-23-03 W
Pop: 1,593 (1990); 1,728 (1980) **Pop Density:** 2655.0
Land: 0.6 sq. mi.; **Water:** 0.0 sq. mi. **Elev:** 616 ft.
Incorporated 1946.

Oakville
CDP
Lat: 38-26-38 N **Long:** 90-19-00 W
Pop: 31,750 (1990) **Pop Density:** 1972.0
Land: 16.1 sq. mi.; **Water:** 2.0 sq. mi.

Olivette
City
ZIP: 63132 **Lat:** 38-40-20 N **Long:** 90-22-38 W
Pop: 7,573 (1990); 7,952 (1980) **Pop Density:** 2704.6
Land: 2.8 sq. mi.; **Water:** 0.0 sq. mi. **Elev:** 660 ft.
Incorporated 1950.

Overland
City
ZIP: 63114 **Lat:** 38-41-45 N **Long:** 90-22-05 W
Pop: 17,987 (1990); 19,620 (1980) **Pop Density:** 4088.0
Land: 4.4 sq. mi.; **Water:** 0.0 sq. mi. **Elev:** 641 ft.
In eastern MO, 10 mi. west-northwest of St. Louis. Incorporated 1939.

Pacific
City
ZIP: 63069 **Lat:** 38-28-53 N **Long:** 90-43-55 W
Pop: 18 (1990); 12 (1980) **Pop Density:** 90.0
Land: 0.2 sq. mi.; **Water:** 0.0 sq. mi. **Elev:** 466 ft.
In eastern MO, 35 mi. west of St. Louis. Incorporated 1859. Part of the town is also in Franklin County.

Pagedale
City
ZIP: 63133 **Lat:** 38-40-51 N **Long:** 90-18-30 W
Pop: 3,771 (1990); 4,590 (1980) **Pop Density:** 3142.5
Land: 1.2 sq. mi.; **Water:** 0.0 sq. mi.
Incorporated 1950.

Pasadena Hills
Village
ZIP: 63121 **Lat:** 38-42-30 N **Long:** 90-17-28 W
Pop: 1,165 (1990); 1,221 (1980) **Pop Density:** 5825.0
Land: 0.2 sq. mi.; **Water:** 0.0 sq. mi.
Incorporated 1982.

Pasadena Park
Village
ZIP: 63121 **Lat:** 38-42-36 N **Long:** 90-17-48 W
Pop: 532 (1990); 531 (1980) **Pop Density:** 5320.0
Land: 0.1 sq. mi.; **Water:** 0.0 sq. mi.
Incorporated 1935.

Peerless Park
Village
Lat: 38-32-32 N **Long:** 90-30-03 W
Pop: 33 (1990); 79 (1980) **Pop Density:** 36.7
Land: 0.9 sq. mi.; **Water:** 0.0 sq. mi.
Incorporated 1935.

Pine Lawn
City
ZIP: 63120 **Lat:** 38-41-42 N **Long:** 90-16-31 W
Pop: 5,092 (1990); 6,570 (1980) **Pop Density:** 8486.7
Land: 0.6 sq. mi.; **Water:** 0.0 sq. mi.
Incorporated 1947.
Name origin: For its descriptive connotations.

Queeny
Township
Lat: 38-33-42 N **Long:** 90-30-53 W
Pop: 92,030 (1990); 76,822 (1980) **Pop Density:** 1811.6
Land: 50.8 sq. mi.; **Water:** 0.5 sq. mi.

Richmond Heights
City
ZIP: 63117   **Lat:** 38-37-48 N **Long:** 90-19-54 W
Pop: 10,448 (1990); 11,516 (1980)   **Pop Density:** 4542.6
Land: 2.3 sq. mi.; **Water:** 0.0 sq. mi.   **Elev:** 469 ft.
In eastern MO, 5 mi. west of St. Louis. Incorporated 1913.
Name origin: For its descriptive connotations.

Riverview
Village
ZIP: 63137   **Lat:** 38-44-37 N **Long:** 90-12-42 W
Pop: 3,242 (1990); 3,367 (1980)   **Pop Density:** 4052.5
Land: 0.8 sq. mi.; **Water:** 0.0 sq. mi.
Incorporated 1950.

Rock Hill
City
ZIP: 63124   **Lat:** 38-36-32 N **Long:** 90-22-00 W
Pop: 5,217 (1990); 5,702 (1980)   **Pop Density:** 4742.7
Land: 1.1 sq. mi.; **Water:** 0.0 sq. mi.
In eastern MO, 10 mi. west of St. Louis. Incorporated 1929.

St. Ann
City
ZIP: 63073   **Lat:** 38-43-33 N **Long:** 90-23-16 W
Pop: 14,489 (1990); 15,523 (1980)   **Pop Density:** 4673.9
Land: 3.1 sq. mi.; **Water:** 0.0 sq. mi.
In eastern MO, a northwestern suburb of St. Louis. Incorporated 1948.
Name origin: For St. Anne, mother of the Virgin Mary.

St. Ferdinand
Township
     Lat: 38-44-36 N **Long:** 90-14-06 W
Pop: 48,125 (1990); 51,428 (1980)   **Pop Density:** 4184.8
Land: 11.5 sq. mi.; **Water:** 0.0 sq. mi.

St. George
City
     Lat: 38-32-16 N **Long:** 90-18-47 W
Pop: 1,270 (1990); 1,545 (1980)   **Pop Density:** 6350.0
Land: 0.2 sq. mi.; **Water:** 0.0 sq. mi.
Incorporated 1948.

St. John
City
ZIP: 63114   **Lat:** 38-42-52 N **Long:** 90-20-45 W
Pop: 7,466 (1990); 7,854 (1980)   **Pop Density:** 5332.9
Land: 1.4 sq. mi.; **Water:** 0.0 sq. mi.
Incorporated 1945.
Name origin: For old Fort San Juan del Misuri built by the Spaniards.

Sappington
CDP
ZIP: 63126   **Lat:** 38-31-11 N **Long:** 90-23-08 W
Pop: 10,917 (1990); 666 (1980)   **Pop Density:** 2021.7
Land: 5.4 sq. mi.; **Water:** 0.1 sq. mi.

Shrewsbury
City
ZIP: 63119   **Lat:** 38-35-13 N **Long:** 90-19-40 W
Pop: 6,416 (1990); 5,077 (1980)   **Pop Density:** 4582.9
Land: 1.4 sq. mi.; **Water:** 0.0 sq. mi.
Incorporated 1915.

Spanish Lake
CDP
ZIP: 63138   **Lat:** 38-47-12 N **Long:** 90-12-27 W
Pop: 20,322 (1990); 20,632 (1980)   **Pop Density:** 2746.2
Land: 7.4 sq. mi.; **Water:** 0.2 sq. mi.

*Spanish Lake
Township
     Lat: 38-49-00 N **Long:** 90-14-25 W
Pop: 60,924 (1990); 54,832 (1980)   **Pop Density:** 1356.9
Land: 44.9 sq. mi.; **Water:** 4.4 sq. mi.

Sunset Hills
City
     Lat: 38-32-14 N **Long:** 90-24-58 W
Pop: 4,915 (1990); 4,363 (1980)   **Pop Density:** 792.7
Land: 6.2 sq. mi.; **Water:** 0.0 sq. mi.
Incorporated 1957.

Sycamore Hills
Village
     Lat: 38-42-03 N **Long:** 90-20-55 W
Pop: 667 (1990); 741 (1980)   **Pop Density:** 6670.0
Land: 0.1 sq. mi.; **Water:** 0.0 sq. mi.   **Elev:** 655 ft.
Incorporated 1941.

Town and Country
City
ZIP: 63131   **Lat:** 38-37-29 N **Long:** 90-28-34 W
Pop: 9,519 (1990); 3,187 (1980)   **Pop Density:** 1002.0
Land: 9.5 sq. mi.; **Water:** 0.0 sq. mi.
Incorporated 1950.

Twin Oaks
Village
ZIP: 63088   **Lat:** 38-33-59 N **Long:** 90-30-01 W
Pop: 506 (1990); 426 (1980)   **Pop Density:** 1686.7
Land: 0.3 sq. mi.; **Water:** 0.0 sq. mi.
Incorporated 1938.

University City
City
ZIP: 63130   **Lat:** 38-39-58 N **Long:** 90-19-51 W
Pop: 40,087 (1990); 42,690 (1980)   **Pop Density:** 6794.4
Land: 5.9 sq. mi.; **Water:** 0.0 sq. mi.   **Elev:** 550 ft.
In eastern MO, 9 mi. west-northwest of St. Louis. Incorporated 1906.

Uplands Park
Village
     Lat: 38-41-33 N **Long:** 90-16-56 W
Pop: 499 (1990); 576 (1980)   **Pop Density:** 4990.0
Land: 0.1 sq. mi.; **Water:** 0.0 sq. mi.
Incorporated 1941.

Valley Park
City
ZIP: 63088   **Lat:** 38-33-16 N **Long:** 90-28-56 W
Pop: 4,165 (1990); 3,232 (1980)   **Pop Density:** 1666.0
Land: 2.5 sq. mi.; **Water:** 0.1 sq. mi.   **Elev:** 421 ft.
In eastern MO, 15 mi. west of St. Louis. Incorporated 1917.
Name origin: For its descriptive connotations.

Velda Village
City
     Lat: 38-41-38 N **Long:** 90-17-38 W
Pop: 1,597 (1990); 1,979 (1980)   **Pop Density:** 7985.0
Land: 0.2 sq. mi.; **Water:** 0.0 sq. mi.

Velda Village Hills
Village
ZIP: 63121   **Lat:** 38-41-32 N **Long:** 90-17-12 W
Pop: 1,315 (1990); 1,432 (1980)   **Pop Density:** 13150.0
Land: 0.1 sq. mi.; **Water:** 0.0 sq. mi.
Incorporated 1945.

Vinita Park
City
ZIP: 63114   **Lat:** 38-41-24 N **Long:** 90-20-22 W
Pop: 2,001 (1990); 2,283 (1980)   **Pop Density:** 2858.6
Land: 0.7 sq. mi.; **Water:** 0.0 sq. mi.
Incorporated 1949.

Vinita Terrace
Village
     Lat: 38-41-05 N **Long:** 90-19-46 W
Pop: 338 (1990); 349 (1980)   **Pop Density:** 3380.0
Land: 0.1 sq. mi.; **Water:** 0.0 sq. mi.
Incorporated 1940.

Warson Woods — City
ZIP: 63122　Lat: 38-36-24 N　Long: 90-23-29 W
Pop: 2,049 (1990); 2,127 (1980)　Pop Density: 3415.0
Land: 0.6 sq. mi.; Water: 0.0 sq. mi.
Incorporated 1936.

Webster Groves — City
ZIP: 63119　Lat: 38-35-08 N　Long: 90-21-16 W
Pop: 22,987 (1990); 23,097 (1980)　Pop Density: 3896.1
Land: 5.9 sq. mi.; Water: 0.0 sq. mi.
In eastern MO, 10 mi. west of St. Louis. Incorporated 1896.
Name origin: For Daniel Webster (1782–1852) of Marshfield, MA, famous U.S. statesman.

Wellston — City
Lat: 38-40-29 N　Long: 90-17-36 W
Pop: 3,612 (1990); 4,495 (1980)　Pop Density: 4013.3
Land: 0.9 sq. mi.; Water: 0.0 sq. mi.
Incorporated 1949.
Name origin: For Erastus Wells, who developed the streetcar system of St. Louis.

Westwood — Village
ZIP: 63131　Lat: 38-38-48 N　Long: 90-26-03 W
Pop: 309 (1990); 335 (1980)　Pop Density: 515.0
Land: 0.6 sq. mi.; Water: 0.0 sq. mi.
Incorporated 1952.

Wilbur Park — Village
Lat: 38-33-09 N　Long: 90-18-26 W
Pop: 522 (1990); 564 (1980)　Pop Density: 5220.0
Land: 0.1 sq. mi.; Water: 0.0 sq. mi.
Incorporated 1941.

Winchester — City
ZIP: 63011　Lat: 38-35-23 N　Long: 90-31-32 W
Pop: 1,678 (1990); 2,077 (1980)　Pop Density: 8390.0
Land: 0.2 sq. mi.; Water: 0.0 sq. mi.
Incorporated 1935.

Woodson Terrace — City
ZIP: 63134　Lat: 38-43-42 N　Long: 90-21-36 W
Pop: 4,362 (1990); 4,788 (1980)　Pop Density: 5452.5
Land: 0.8 sq. mi.; Water: 0.0 sq. mi.
Incorporated 1954.

Saline County
County Seat: Marshall (ZIP: 65340)

Pop: 23,523 (1990); 24,913 (1980)　Pop Density: 31.1
Land: 755.6 sq. mi.; Water: 9.0 sq. mi.　Area Code: 816
In central MO, east of Kansas City; organized Nov 25, 1820 (prior to statehood) from Cooper County.
Name origin: French 'salt spring' or 'lick.'

Arrow Rock — Town
ZIP: 65320　Lat: 39-04-11 N　Long: 92-56-52 W
Pop: 70 (1990); 82 (1980)　Pop Density: 700.0
Land: 0.1 sq. mi.; Water: 0.0 sq. mi.
Incorporated 1829.

*Arrow Rock — Township
ZIP: 65320　Lat: 39-04-27 N　Long: 93-01-05 W
Pop: 736 (1990); 878 (1980)　Pop Density: 12.5
Land: 58.7 sq. mi.; Water: 0.7 sq. mi.

Blackburn — City
ZIP: 65321　Lat: 39-06-14 N　Long: 93-29-04 W
Pop: 286 (1990); 308 (1980)　Pop Density: 953.3
Land: 0.3 sq. mi.; Water: 0.0 sq. mi.　Elev: 805 ft.
Incorporated 1909. Part of the town is also in Lafayette County.

Blackwater — Township
Lat: 38-57-46 N　Long: 93-08-37 W
Pop: 345 (1990); 346 (1980)　Pop Density: 7.6
Land: 45.1 sq. mi.; Water: 0.1 sq. mi.

Cambridge — Township
Lat: 39-15-30 N　Long: 93-00-59 W
Pop: 2,890 (1990); 3,221 (1980)　Pop Density: 35.7
Land: 80.9 sq. mi.; Water: 2.4 sq. mi.

Clay — Township
Lat: 39-09-42 N　Long: 93-00-02 W
Pop: 458 (1990); 485 (1980)　Pop Density: 7.2
Land: 63.4 sq. mi.; Water: 1.1 sq. mi.

Elmwood — Township
Lat: 39-04-59 N　Long: 93-23-51 W
Pop: 777 (1990); 998 (1980)　Pop Density: 11.1
Land: 69.9 sq. mi.; Water: 0.2 sq. mi.

Emma — City
Lat: 38-58-21 N　Long: 93-29-38 W
Pop: 108 (1990); 158 (1980)　Pop Density: 540.0
Land: 0.2 sq. mi.; Water: 0.0 sq. mi.　Elev: 759 ft.
Incorporated 1958. Part of the town is also in Lafayette County.
Name origin: Named in 1895 for the daughter of a Lutheran minister at Concordia.

Gilliam — Town
ZIP: 65330　Lat: 39-13-57 N　Long: 93-00-13 W
Pop: 212 (1990); 227 (1980)　Pop Density: 1060.0
Land: 0.2 sq. mi.; Water: 0.0 sq. mi.
Incorporated 1899.

Grand Pass — Town
ZIP: 65339　Lat: 39-12-18 N　Long: 93-26-35 W
Pop: 53 (1990); 71 (1980)　Pop Density: 530.0
Land: 0.1 sq. mi.; Water: 0.0 sq. mi.　Elev: 666 ft.
Incorporated 1889.

*Grand Pass — Township
Lat: 39-12-57 N　Long: 93-22-54 W
Pop: 622 (1990); 743 (1980)　Pop Density: 7.5
Land: 83.1 sq. mi.; Water: 1.9 sq. mi.

MISSOURI, Saline County

Liberty
Township
Lat: 38-59-39 N **Long:** 93-17-22 W
Pop: 479 (1990); 572 (1980) **Pop Density:** 8.7
Land: 55.0 sq. mi.; **Water:** 0.0 sq. mi.

Malta Bend
Town
ZIP: 65339 **Lat:** 39-11-39 N **Long:** 93-21-50 W
Pop: 289 (1990); 292 (1980) **Pop Density:** 963.3
Land: 0.3 sq. mi.; **Water:** 0.0 sq. mi. **Elev:** 684 ft.
Incorporated 1956.

Marshall
City
ZIP: 65340 **Lat:** 39-06-53 N **Long:** 93-12-07 W
Pop: 12,711 (1990); 12,781 (1980) **Pop Density:** 1324.1
Land: 9.6 sq. mi.; **Water:** 0.1 sq. mi.
In west-central MO, east of Kansas City. Settled 1839. Incorporated 1839.
Name origin: For John Marshall (1755–1835), Chief Justice of the U. S. Supreme Court. Originally known as Elk's Hill.

*Marshall
Township
ZIP: 65340 **Lat:** 39-07-20 N **Long:** 93-11-59 W
Pop: 14,135 (1990); 14,232 (1980) **Pop Density:** 129.9
Land: 108.8 sq. mi.; **Water:** 0.3 sq. mi.

Miami
City
ZIP: 65344 **Lat:** 39-19-18 N **Long:** 93-13-31 W
Pop: 142 (1990); 177 (1980) **Pop Density:** 236.7
Land: 0.6 sq. mi.; **Water:** 0.1 sq. mi.
In west-central MO, northeast of Kansas City. Established before 1810 by a group of Miami Indians. Incorporated 1860.
Name origin: For the Miami tribe of Algonquin Indians formerly living in WI and IL. Origin of name is uncertain: probably from Ojibway *oumaumeg* 'people of the peninsula,' or from Delaware *we-mi-a-mik* 'all friends'; or possibly, Ottawa 'mother.'

*Miami
Township
ZIP: 65344 **Lat:** 39-16-44 N **Long:** 93-11-19 W
Pop: 569 (1990); 778 (1980) **Pop Density:** 5.2
Land: 109.5 sq. mi.; **Water:** 1.9 sq. mi.

Mount Leonard
Town
Lat: 39-07-29 N **Long:** 93-23-40 W
Pop: 96 (1990); 131 (1980) **Pop Density:** 960.0
Land: 0.1 sq. mi.; **Water:** 0.0 sq. mi.
Incorporated 1881.

Nelson
City
ZIP: 65347 **Lat:** 38-59-36 N **Long:** 93-01-49 W
Pop: 181 (1990); 248 (1980) **Pop Density:** 603.3
Land: 0.3 sq. mi.; **Water:** 0.0 sq. mi.
Incorporated 1892.

Salt Fork
Township
Lat: 39-00-54 N **Long:** 93-08-01 W
Pop: 289 (1990); 313 (1980) **Pop Density:** 9.0
Land: 32.1 sq. mi.; **Water:** 0.1 sq. mi.

Salt Pond
Township
Lat: 38-59-25 N **Long:** 93-25-34 W
Pop: 2,223 (1990); 2,347 (1980) **Pop Density:** 45.4
Land: 49.0 sq. mi.; **Water:** 0.4 sq. mi.

Slater
City
ZIP: 65349 **Lat:** 39-13-21 N **Long:** 93-03-52 W
Pop: 2,186 (1990); 2,492 (1980) **Pop Density:** 1561.4
Land: 1.4 sq. mi.; **Water:** 0.0 sq. mi. **Elev:** 853 ft.
Founded 1880. Incorporated 1878.
Name origin: For Col. John F. Slater of Chicago, a director of the C & A Railroad.

Sweet Springs
City
ZIP: 65351 **Lat:** 38-57-51 N **Long:** 93-24-59 W
Pop: 1,595 (1990); 1,694 (1980) **Pop Density:** 996.9
Land: 1.6 sq. mi.; **Water:** 0.0 sq. mi. **Elev:** 683 ft.
Incorporated 1887.

Schuyler County
County Seat: Lancaster (ZIP: 63548)

Pop: 4,236 (1990); 4,979 (1980) **Pop Density:** 13.8
Land: 307.9 sq. mi.; **Water:** 0.3 sq. mi. **Area Code:** 816
On the northeastern border of MO; organized Feb 14, 1845 from Adair County.
Name origin: For Gen. Philip John Schuyler (1733–1804), an officer in the Revolutionary War, member of the Continental Congress (1775–77; 1778–81), and U.S. senator from NY (1789–91; 1797–98).

Chariton
Township
Lat: 40-33-59 N **Long:** 92-38-11 W
Pop: 148 (1990); 174 (1980) **Pop Density:** 5.6
Land: 26.5 sq. mi.; **Water:** 0.0 sq. mi.

Downing
City
ZIP: 63536 **Lat:** 40-29-11 N **Long:** 92-22-06 W
Pop: 359 (1990); 462 (1980) **Pop Density:** 398.9
Land: 0.9 sq. mi.; **Water:** 0.0 sq. mi. **Elev:** 873 ft.
Incorporated 1896.
Name origin: Founded by and named for Henry Downing.

Fabius
Township
Lat: 40-31-58 N **Long:** 92-24-40 W
Pop: 684 (1990); 833 (1980) **Pop Density:** 13.0
Land: 52.8 sq. mi.; **Water:** 0.1 sq. mi.

Glenwood
Village
ZIP: 63541 **Lat:** 40-31-24 N **Long:** 92-34-34 W
Pop: 195 (1990); 218 (1980) **Pop Density:** 278.6
Land: 0.7 sq. mi.; **Water:** 0.0 sq. mi.
Incorporated 1869.

*Glenwood
Township
ZIP: 63541   **Lat:** 40-30-27 N   **Long:** 92-37-17 W
Pop: 333 (1990); 385 (1980)   **Pop Density:** 10.7
Land: 31.0 sq. mi.; **Water:** 0.0 sq. mi.

Greentop
Village
Lat: 40-21-07 N   **Long:** 92-33-57 W
Pop: 343 (1990); 423 (1980)   **Pop Density:** 428.8
Land: 0.8 sq. mi.; **Water:** 0.0 sq. mi.   **Elev:** 993 ft.
Incorporated 1870. Part of the town is also in Adair County.

Independence
Township
Lat: 40-25-04 N   **Long:** 92-24-47 W
Pop: 263 (1990); 335 (1980)   **Pop Density:** 4.7
Land: 56.2 sq. mi.; **Water:** 0.0 sq. mi.

Lancaster
City
ZIP: 63548   **Lat:** 40-31-21 N   **Long:** 92-31-49 W
Pop: 785 (1990); 855 (1980)   **Pop Density:** 523.3
Land: 1.5 sq. mi.; **Water:** 0.0 sq. mi.
County seat 1845. Incorporated 1857.

Liberty
Township
Lat: 40-31-49 N   **Long:** 92-31-03 W
Pop: 1,066 (1990); 1,241 (1980)   **Pop Density:** 29.2
Land: 36.5 sq. mi.; **Water:** 0.1 sq. mi.

Prairie
Township
Lat: 40-26-12 N   **Long:** 92-34-58 W
Pop: 1,186 (1990); 1,359 (1980)   **Pop Density:** 16.8
Land: 70.4 sq. mi.; **Water:** 0.0 sq. mi.

Queen City
City
ZIP: 63561   **Lat:** 40-24-49 N   **Long:** 92-33-59 W
Pop: 704 (1990); 783 (1980)   **Pop Density:** 704.0
Land: 1.0 sq. mi.; **Water:** 0.0 sq. mi.   **Elev:** 1003 ft.
Founded 1867. Incorporated 1883.
Name origin: Named by founder Dr. George W. Wilson, with the hope that it would be queen of the prairies.

Salt River
Township
Lat: 40-22-07 N   **Long:** 92-34-17 W
Pop: 556 (1990); 652 (1980)   **Pop Density:** 16.2
Land: 34.4 sq. mi.; **Water:** 0.1 sq. mi.

Scotland County
County Seat: Memphis (ZIP: 63555)

Pop: 4,822 (1990); 5,415 (1980)   **Pop Density:** 11.0
Land: 438.5 sq. mi.; **Water:** 0.8 sq. mi.   **Area Code:** 816
On the northeastern border of MO; organized Jan 29, 1841 from Clark, Lewis, and Shelby counties.
Name origin: For the country, the former home of early settlers.

Arbela
Town
ZIP: 63432   **Lat:** 40-27-46 N   **Long:** 92-00-57 W
Pop: 40 (1990); 67 (1980)   **Pop Density:** 400.0
Land: 0.1 sq. mi.; **Water:** 0.0 sq. mi.
Incorporated 1877.

Granger
Town
ZIP: 63442   **Lat:** 40-28-03 N   **Long:** 91-58-23 W
Pop: 63 (1990); 91 (1980)   **Pop Density:** 315.0
Land: 0.2 sq. mi.; **Water:** 0.0 sq. mi.   **Elev:** 760 ft.
Incorporated 1912.

Harrison
Township
Lat: 40-21-04 N   **Long:** 91-59-43 W
Pop: 428 (1990); 507 (1980)   **Pop Density:** 10.3
Land: 41.7 sq. mi.; **Water:** 0.0 sq. mi.

Jefferson
Township
Lat: 40-27-00 N   **Long:** 92-09-51 W
Pop: 2,672 (1990); 2,716 (1980)   **Pop Density:** 34.5
Land: 77.5 sq. mi.; **Water:** 0.5 sq. mi.

Johnson
Township
Lat: 40-33-09 N   **Long:** 91-59-39 W
Pop: 187 (1990); 224 (1980)   **Pop Density:** 4.7
Land: 40.0 sq. mi.; **Water:** 0.0 sq. mi.

Memphis
City
ZIP: 63555   **Lat:** 40-27-39 N   **Long:** 92-10-11 W
Pop: 2,094 (1990); 2,105 (1980)   **Pop Density:** 1308.8
Land: 1.6 sq. mi.; **Water:** 0.0 sq. mi.   **Elev:** 801 ft.
Settled 1838; built on land donated by Samuel Cecil for the county seat. Incorporated 1853.

Miller
Township
Lat: 40-32-40 N   **Long:** 92-18-20 W
Pop: 134 (1990); 165 (1980)   **Pop Density:** 3.8
Land: 35.7 sq. mi.; **Water:** 0.0 sq. mi.

Mount Pleasant
Township
Lat: 40-21-02 N   **Long:** 92-18-02 W
Pop: 133 (1990); 201 (1980)   **Pop Density:** 4.0
Land: 33.3 sq. mi.; **Water:** 0.0 sq. mi.

Rutledge
Town
ZIP: 63563   **Lat:** 40-18-46 N   **Long:** 92-05-14 W
Pop: 74 (1990); 128 (1980)   **Pop Density:** 740.0
Land: 0.1 sq. mi.; **Water:** 0.0 sq. mi.
Incorporated 1888.

Sand Hill
Township
Lat: 40-20-42 N   **Long:** 92-07-03 W
Pop: 284 (1990); 326 (1980)   **Pop Density:** 9.4
Land: 30.2 sq. mi.; **Water:** 0.0 sq. mi.

South Gorin
Town
Lat: 40-21-36 N   **Long:** 92-01-26 W
Pop: 130 (1990); 212 (1980)   **Pop Density:** 650.0
Land: 0.2 sq. mi.; **Water:** 0.0 sq. mi.

Thomson
Township
Lat: 40-27-21 N   **Long:** 92-00-14 W
Pop: 377 (1990); 485 (1980)   **Pop Density:** 8.7
Land: 43.3 sq. mi.; **Water:** 0.1 sq. mi.

Tobin
Township
Lat: 40-20-47 N   **Long:** 92-12-08 W
Pop: 115 (1990); 153 (1980)   **Pop Density:** 4.1
Land: 28.1 sq. mi.; **Water:** 0.0 sq. mi.

MISSOURI, Scotland County

Union Township
Lat: 40-33-05 N Long: 92-09-08 W
Pop: 356 (1990); 432 (1980) **Pop Density:** 4.8
Land: 73.5 sq. mi.; **Water:** 0.1 sq. mi.

Vest Township
Lat: 40-27-38 N Long: 92-18-17 W
Pop: 136 (1990); 206 (1980) **Pop Density:** 3.9
Land: 35.3 sq. mi.; **Water:** 0.0 sq. mi.

Scott County
County Seat: Benton (ZIP: 63736)

Pop: 39,376 (1990); 39,647 (1980) **Pop Density:** 93.5
Land: 421.0 sq. mi.; **Water:** 5.0 sq. mi. **Area Code:** 314

On the southeastern border of MO, south of Cape Girardeau; established Dec 28, 1821 from New Madrid County.

Name origin: For John Scott (1785–1861), lawyer and U.S. representative from MO (1821–27).

Benton City
ZIP: 63736 Lat: 37-05-52 N Long: 89-33-43 W
Pop: 575 (1990); 674 (1980) **Pop Density:** 1437.5
Land: 0.4 sq. mi.; **Water:** 0.0 sq. mi. **Elev:** 440 ft.
Incorporated 1953.
Name origin: For U.S. senator, Thomas Hart Benton (1782–1858).

Blodgett Town
ZIP: 63824 Lat: 37-00-15 N Long: 89-31-34 W
Pop: 202 (1990); 255 (1980) **Pop Density:** 2020.0
Land: 0.1 sq. mi.; **Water:** 0.0 sq. mi. **Elev:** 325 ft.
Incorporated 1900.

Chaffee City
ZIP: 63740 Lat: 37-10-49 N Long: 89-39-40 W
Pop: 3,059 (1990); 3,241 (1980) **Pop Density:** 1699.4
Land: 1.8 sq. mi.; **Water:** 0.0 sq. mi.
In southeastern MO, 10 mi. southwest of Cape Girardeau. Incorporated 1907.
Name origin: For Gen. Adna Romanza Chaffee (1842–1914), officer in the Spanish-American War.

Commerce Town
ZIP: 63742 Lat: 37-09-29 N Long: 89-26-47 W
Pop: 173 (1990); 199 (1980) **Pop Density:** 576.7
Land: 0.3 sq. mi.; **Water:** 0.0 sq. mi.
Incorporated 1834.

*Commerce Township
Lat: 37-07-29 N Long: 89-27-20 W
Pop: 735 (1990); 666 (1980) **Pop Density:** 17.1
Land: 43.0 sq. mi.; **Water:** 2.1 sq. mi.

Diehlstadt Town
Lat: 36-57-33 N Long: 89-25-56 W
Pop: 145 (1990); 170 (1980) **Pop Density:** 1450.0
Land: 0.1 sq. mi.; **Water:** 0.0 sq. mi.
Incorporated 1901.

Hay-Wood City Village
Lat: 37-00-42 N Long: 89-36-00 W
Pop: 263 (1990); 425 (1980) **Pop Density:** 657.5
Land: 0.4 sq. mi.; **Water:** 0.0 sq. mi.
Incorporated 1949.

Kelso Town
ZIP: 63758 Lat: 37-11-24 N Long: 89-33-01 W
Pop: 526 (1990); 455 (1980) **Pop Density:** 2630.0
Land: 0.2 sq. mi.; **Water:** 0.0 sq. mi.
Incorporated 1905.

*Kelso Township
Lat: 37-11-58 N Long: 89-34-24 W
Pop: 9,730 (1990); 9,910 (1980) **Pop Density:** 172.2
Land: 56.5 sq. mi.; **Water:** 1.4 sq. mi.

Lambert Village
ZIP: 63736 Lat: 37-05-37 N Long: 89-33-20 W
Pop: 36 (1990); 34 (1980) **Pop Density:** 360.0
Land: 0.1 sq. mi.; **Water:** 0.0 sq. mi.

Miner City
Lat: 36-53-37 N Long: 89-32-04 W
Pop: 1,218 (1990); 1,182 (1980) **Pop Density:** 320.5
Land: 3.8 sq. mi.; **Water:** 0.0 sq. mi.
Incorporated 1951.

Moreland Township
Lat: 37-05-49 N Long: 89-33-24 W
Pop: 2,511 (1990); 2,417 (1980) **Pop Density:** 41.8
Land: 60.1 sq. mi.; **Water:** 0.1 sq. mi.

Morley Town
ZIP: 63767 Lat: 37-02-35 N Long: 89-36-45 W
Pop: 683 (1990); 745 (1980) **Pop Density:** 975.7
Land: 0.7 sq. mi.; **Water:** 0.0 sq. mi.
Incorporated 1868.

*Morley Township
Lat: 37-01-15 N Long: 89-39-22 W
Pop: 1,657 (1990); 2,120 (1980) **Pop Density:** 41.8
Land: 39.6 sq. mi.; **Water:** 0.0 sq. mi.

Oran City
ZIP: 63771 Lat: 37-05-06 N Long: 89-39-10 W
Pop: 1,164 (1990); 1,266 (1980) **Pop Density:** 1058.2
Land: 1.1 sq. mi.; **Water:** 0.0 sq. mi. **Elev:** 347 ft.
Founded 1869. Incorporated 1869.
Name origin: Named by a retired sea captain who once visited the Algerian city.

Richland Township
Lat: 36-55-08 N Long: 89-37-04 W
Pop: 20,783 (1990); 20,313 (1980) **Pop Density:** 283.1
Land: 73.4 sq. mi.; **Water:** 0.2 sq. mi.

Sandywoods
Township
Lat: 36-59-00 N Long: 89-30-53 W
Pop: 1,423 (1990); 1,371 (1980)   **Pop Density:** 26.0
Land: 54.7 sq. mi.; **Water:** 0.1 sq. mi.

Scott City
City
ZIP: 63780   Lat: 37-13-21 N Long: 89-31-55 W
Pop: 4,292 (1990); 3,262 (1980)   **Pop Density:** 1046.8
Land: 4.1 sq. mi.; **Water:** 0.0 sq. mi.

Incorporated 1980. Part of the town is also in Cape Girardeau County.

Sikeston
City
ZIP: 63801   Lat: 36-53-07 N Long: 89-35-05 W
Pop: 16,909 (1990); 16,763 (1980)   **Pop Density:** 1537.2
Land: 11.0 sq. mi.; **Water:** 0.2 sq. mi.

In southeastern MO, 30 mi. south of Cape Girardeau. Incorporated 1874. Part of the town is also in New Madrid County.
Name origin: For John Sikes, who laid out the town.

Sylvania
Township
Lat: 37-05-38 N Long: 89-42-06 W
Pop: 2,131 (1990); 2,406 (1980)   **Pop Density:** 38.8
Land: 54.9 sq. mi.; **Water:** 0.0 sq. mi.

Tywappity
Township
Lat: 37-00-31 N Long: 89-24-36 W
Pop: 406 (1990); 444 (1980)   **Pop Density:** 10.4
Land: 38.9 sq. mi.; **Water:** 1.2 sq. mi.

Vanduser
Village
ZIP: 63784   Lat: 36-59-28 N Long: 89-41-11 W
Pop: 187 (1990); 320 (1980)   **Pop Density:** 1870.0
Land: 0.1 sq. mi.; **Water:** 0.0 sq. mi.   **Elev:** 313 ft.

Incorporated 1903.

Shannon County
County Seat: Eminence (ZIP: 65466)

Pop: 7,613 (1990); 7,885 (1980)   **Pop Density:** 7.6
Land: 1003.9 sq. mi.; **Water:** 0.2 sq. mi.   **Area Code:** 314

In south-central MO, east of Springfield; organized Jan 29, 1841 from Ripley County.

Name origin: For George F. "Peg-leg" Shannon (1785–1836), a member of the Lewis and Clark expedition.

Bartlett
Township
Lat: 36-58-01 N Long: 91-25-19 W
Pop: 401 (1990); 388 (1980)   **Pop Density:** 8.9
Land: 45.3 sq. mi.; **Water:** 0.0 sq. mi.

Birch Tree
City
ZIP: 65438   Lat: 36-59-29 N Long: 91-29-32 W
Pop: 599 (1990); 622 (1980)   **Pop Density:** 855.7
Land: 0.7 sq. mi.; **Water:** 0.0 sq. mi.   **Elev:** 991 ft.

Incorporated 1908.
Name origin: For a large birch that stood on the bank of a creek near the site of an early post office.

*Birch Tree
Township
ZIP: 65438   Lat: 36-58-52 N Long: 91-29-48 W
Pop: 1,217 (1990); 1,216 (1980)   **Pop Density:** 24.8
Land: 49.1 sq. mi.; **Water:** 0.0 sq. mi.

Bowlan
Township
Lat: 37-09-32 N Long: 91-07-02 W
Pop: 61 (1990); 75 (1980)   **Pop Density:** 0.9
Land: 66.6 sq. mi.; **Water:** 0.0 sq. mi.

Buckeye
Township
Lat: 37-06-50 N Long: 91-13-27 W
Pop: 209 (1990); 169 (1980)   **Pop Density:** 3.8
Land: 54.4 sq. mi.; **Water:** 0.0 sq. mi.

Delaware
Township
Lat: 37-04-51 N Long: 91-26-02 W
Pop: 103 (1990); 103 (1980)   **Pop Density:** 2.4
Land: 42.3 sq. mi.; **Water:** 0.0 sq. mi.

Eminence
City
ZIP: 65466   Lat: 37-08-46 N Long: 91-21-30 W
Pop: 582 (1990); 614 (1980)   **Pop Density:** 582.0
Land: 1.0 sq. mi.; **Water:** 0.0 sq. mi.   **Elev:** 677 ft.

Incorporated 1946.

*Eminence
Township
ZIP: 65466   Lat: 37-10-56 N Long: 91-23-24 W
Pop: 1,614 (1990); 1,649 (1980)   **Pop Density:** 11.5
Land: 140.9 sq. mi.; **Water:** 0.0 sq. mi.

Jackson
Township
Lat: 37-22-15 N Long: 91-33-30 W
Pop: 155 (1990); 137 (1980)   **Pop Density:** 2.2
Land: 70.3 sq. mi.; **Water:** 0.0 sq. mi.

Montier
Township
Lat: 37-00-16 N Long: 91-35-53 W
Pop: 573 (1990); 661 (1980)   **Pop Density:** 16.6
Land: 34.5 sq. mi.; **Water:** 0.0 sq. mi.

Moore
Township
Lat: 37-17-54 N Long: 91-13-56 W
Pop: 151 (1990); 173 (1980)   **Pop Density:** 1.3
Land: 117.1 sq. mi.; **Water:** 0.0 sq. mi.

Newton
Township
Lat: 37-21-01 N Long: 91-24-31 W
Pop: 189 (1990); 220 (1980)   **Pop Density:** 2.0
Land: 93.7 sq. mi.; **Water:** 0.0 sq. mi.

Spring Creek
Township
Lat: 36-55-54 N Long: 91-34-56 W
Pop: 309 (1990); 338 (1980)   **Pop Density:** 7.2
Land: 43.1 sq. mi.; **Water:** 0.0 sq. mi.

MISSOURI, Shannon County   *American Places Dictionary*

Spring Valley
Township
Lat: 37-10-45 N **Long:** 91-34-21 W
Pop: 836 (1990); 921 (1980)   **Pop Density:** 5.9
Land: 141.4 sq. mi.; **Water:** 0.0 sq. mi.

Summersville
City
ZIP: 65571   **Lat:** 37-10-40 N **Long:** 91-39-02 W
Pop: 112 (1990); 98 (1980)   **Pop Density:** 373.3
Land: 0.3 sq. mi.; **Water:** 0.0 sq. mi.
Incorporated 1924. Part of the town is also in Texas County.

Winona
City
ZIP: 65588   **Lat:** 37-00-22 N **Long:** 91-19-55 W
Pop: 1,081 (1990); 1,050 (1980)   **Pop Density:** 400.4
Land: 2.7 sq. mi.; **Water:** 0.0 sq. mi.
Incorporated 1888.
Name origin: For the Winnebago Indian woman active in removing the tribe from IA.

*Winona
Township
ZIP: 65588   **Lat:** 36-58-32 N **Long:** 91-17-52 W
Pop: 1,795 (1990); 1,835 (1980)   **Pop Density:** 17.0
Land: 105.3 sq. mi.; **Water:** 0.0 sq. mi.

Shelby County
County Seat: Shelbyville (ZIP: 63469)

Pop: 6,942 (1990); 7,826 (1980)   **Pop Density:** 13.9
Land: 500.9 sq. mi.; **Water:** 1.5 sq. mi.   **Area Code:** 314
In northeastern MO, northeast of Columbia; organized Jan 2, 1835 from Marion County.
Name origin: For Gen. Isaac Shelby (1750–1826), officer in the Revolutionary War, NC legislator, and governor of KY (1792–96; 1812–16).

Bethel
Town
ZIP: 63434   **Lat:** 39-52-41 N **Long:** 92-01-21 W
Pop: 117 (1990); 132 (1980)   **Pop Density:** 1170.0
Land: 0.1 sq. mi.; **Water:** 0.0 sq. mi.
Incorporated 1883.

*Bethel
Township
ZIP: 63434   **Lat:** 39-54-23 N **Long:** 92-01-46 W
Pop: 377 (1990); 465 (1980)   **Pop Density:** 7.0
Land: 53.8 sq. mi.; **Water:** 0.1 sq. mi.

Black Creek
Township
Lat: 39-49-02 N **Long:** 92-04-00 W
Pop: 929 (1990); 1,114 (1980)   **Pop Density:** 12.9
Land: 71.9 sq. mi.; **Water:** 0.1 sq. mi.

Clarence
City
ZIP: 63437   **Lat:** 39-44-34 N **Long:** 92-15-36 W
Pop: 1,026 (1990); 1,147 (1980)   **Pop Density:** 855.0
Land: 1.2 sq. mi.; **Water:** 0.0 sq. mi.
Platted 1857 by John Duff. Incorporated 1866.
Name origin: For one of the children of railroad contractor John Duff.

Clay
Township
Lat: 39-48-09 N **Long:** 92-14-20 W
Pop: 1,291 (1990); 1,433 (1980)   **Pop Density:** 24.5
Land: 52.7 sq. mi.; **Water:** 0.6 sq. mi.

Hunnewell
City
ZIP: 63443   **Lat:** 39-40-05 N **Long:** 91-51-31 W
Pop: 219 (1990); 235 (1980)   **Pop Density:** 365.0
Land: 0.6 sq. mi.; **Water:** 0.0 sq. mi.
Incorporated 1915.

Jackson
Township
Lat: 39-43-35 N **Long:** 91-55-03 W
Pop: 578 (1990); 677 (1980)   **Pop Density:** 10.0
Land: 57.9 sq. mi.; **Water:** 0.4 sq. mi.

Jefferson
Township
Lat: 39-40-13 N **Long:** 92-14-18 W
Pop: 309 (1990); 393 (1980)   **Pop Density:** 5.7
Land: 54.1 sq. mi.; **Water:** 0.0 sq. mi.

Lentner
Township
ZIP: 63450   **Lat:** 39-43-06 N **Long:** 92-08-47 W
Pop: 198 (1990); 244 (1980)   **Pop Density:** 6.3
Land: 31.6 sq. mi.; **Water:** 0.0 sq. mi.

Leonard
Town
ZIP: 63451   **Lat:** 39-53-42 N **Long:** 92-10-50 W
Pop: 90 (1990); 109 (1980)   **Pop Density:** 300.0
Land: 0.3 sq. mi.; **Water:** 0.0 sq. mi.

North River
Township
Lat: 39-48-07 N **Long:** 91-52-06 W
Pop: 132 (1990); 179 (1980)   **Pop Density:** 7.9
Land: 16.8 sq. mi.; **Water:** 0.0 sq. mi.

Salt River
Township
Lat: 39-42-56 N **Long:** 92-02-18 W
Pop: 2,619 (1990); 2,714 (1980)   **Pop Density:** 45.4
Land: 57.7 sq. mi.; **Water:** 0.1 sq. mi.

Shelbina
City
ZIP: 63468   **Lat:** 39-41-32 N **Long:** 92-02-22 W
Pop: 2,172 (1990); 2,169 (1980)   **Pop Density:** 987.3
Land: 2.2 sq. mi.; **Water:** 0.0 sq. mi.   **Elev:** 779 ft.
Incorporated 1867.
Name origin: For Gen. Isaac Shelby (1750–1826), officer in the Revolutionary War, NC legislator, and governor of KY (1792–96; 1812–16).

Shelbyville
City
ZIP: 63469   **Lat:** 39-48-25 N **Long:** 92-02-23 W
Pop: 582 (1990); 645 (1980)   **Pop Density:** 727.5
Land: 0.8 sq. mi.; **Water:** 0.0 sq. mi.   **Elev:** 768 ft.
Incorporated 1867.

Taylor
Township
Lat: 39-54-54 N **Long:** 92-12-19 W
Pop: 312 (1990); 390 (1980) **Pop Density:** 5.9
Land: 53.2 sq. mi.; **Water:** 0.1 sq. mi.

Tiger Fork
Township
Lat: 39-53-17 N **Long:** 91-54-04 W
Pop: 197 (1990); 217 (1980) **Pop Density:** 3.9
Land: 51.1 sq. mi.; **Water:** 0.0 sq. mi.

Stoddard County
County Seat: Bloomfield (ZIP: 63825)

Pop: 28,895 (1990); 29,009 (1980) **Pop Density:** 34.9
Land: 827.2 sq. mi.; **Water:** 1.8 sq. mi. **Area Code:** 314

In southeastern MO, southwest of Cape Girardeau; organized Jun 21, 1835 from Cape Girardeau County.

Name origin: For Capt. Amos Stoddard (1762–1813), an officer in the Revolutionary War and acting governor of LA Territory (1804–05).

Advance
City
ZIP: 63730 **Lat:** 37-06-12 N **Long:** 89-54-52 W
Pop: 1,139 (1990); 1,054 (1980) **Pop Density:** 1423.8
Land: 0.8 sq. mi.; **Water:** 0.0 sq. mi. **Elev:** 361 ft.
Founded 1810; incorporated 1883.
Name origin: For an ideal, from which many MO place names are derived.

Baker
Village
Lat: 36-46-24 N **Long:** 89-45-41 W
Pop: 8 (1990); 31 (1980) **Pop Density:** 40.0
Land: 0.2 sq. mi.; **Water:** 0.0 sq. mi. **Elev:** 292 ft.

Bell City
City
ZIP: 63735 **Lat:** 37-01-25 N **Long:** 89-49-09 W
Pop: 469 (1990); 539 (1980) **Pop Density:** 781.7
Land: 0.6 sq. mi.; **Water:** 0.0 sq. mi. **Elev:** 326 ft.
Incorporated 1922.

Bernie
City
ZIP: 63822 **Lat:** 36-40-19 N **Long:** 89-58-13 W
Pop: 1,847 (1990); 1,975 (1980) **Pop Density:** 1539.2
Land: 1.2 sq. mi.; **Water:** 0.0 sq. mi.
Incorporated 1898.

Bloomfield
City
ZIP: 63825 **Lat:** 36-53-19 N **Long:** 89-55-53 W
Pop: 1,800 (1990); 1,795 (1980) **Pop Density:** 1285.7
Land: 1.4 sq. mi.; **Water:** 0.0 sq. mi. **Elev:** 497 ft.
Incorporated 1835.
Name origin: Named in 1835 for its descriptive connotations.

Castor
Township
Lat: 36-53-08 N **Long:** 89-56-28 W
Pop: 4,390 (1990); 4,647 (1980) **Pop Density:** 40.5
Land: 108.5 sq. mi.; **Water:** 0.4 sq. mi.

Dexter
City
ZIP: 63841 **Lat:** 36-47-25 N **Long:** 89-57-37 W
Pop: 7,559 (1990); 7,043 (1980) **Pop Density:** 1453.7
Land: 5.2 sq. mi.; **Water:** 0.1 sq. mi.
In southeastern MO, southwest of Cape Girardeau. Incorporated 1873.
Name origin: Named in 1873 for a race horse.

Duck Creek
Township
Lat: 36-53-14 N **Long:** 90-09-09 W
Pop: 3,274 (1990); 3,221 (1980) **Pop Density:** 23.5
Land: 139.2 sq. mi.; **Water:** 0.1 sq. mi.

Dudley
City
ZIP: 63936 **Lat:** 36-47-20 N **Long:** 90-05-29 W
Pop: 271 (1990); 287 (1980) **Pop Density:** 677.5
Land: 0.4 sq. mi.; **Water:** 0.0 sq. mi. **Elev:** 343 ft.
Incorporated 1915.

Elk
Township
Lat: 36-41-49 N **Long:** 89-48-19 W
Pop: 575 (1990); 764 (1980) **Pop Density:** 5.3
Land: 108.8 sq. mi.; **Water:** 0.1 sq. mi.

Essex
City
ZIP: 63846 **Lat:** 36-48-43 N **Long:** 89-51-44 W
Pop: 531 (1990); 545 (1980) **Pop Density:** 1770.0
Land: 0.3 sq. mi.; **Water:** 0.0 sq. mi. **Elev:** 300 ft.
Incorporated 1876.

Liberty
Township
Lat: 36-43-02 N **Long:** 90-01-22 W
Pop: 14,435 (1990); 13,583 (1980) **Pop Density:** 96.2
Land: 150.0 sq. mi.; **Water:** 0.5 sq. mi.
In southeastern MO.

New Lisbon
Township
Lat: 36-58-43 N **Long:** 90-02-14 W
Pop: 809 (1990); 905 (1980) **Pop Density:** 12.0
Land: 67.6 sq. mi.; **Water:** 0.3 sq. mi.

Penermon
Village
Lat: 36-47-36 N **Long:** 89-49-46 W
Pop: 94 (1990); 136 (1980) **Pop Density:** 470.0
Land: 0.2 sq. mi.; **Water:** 0.0 sq. mi.
Incorporated 1968.

Pike
Township
Lat: 37-01-55 N **Long:** 89-50-46 W
Pop: 3,615 (1990); 3,869 (1980) **Pop Density:** 25.3
Land: 142.7 sq. mi.; **Water:** 0.5 sq. mi.

Puxico
City
ZIP: 63960 **Lat:** 36-57-02 N **Long:** 90-09-32 W
Pop: 819 (1990); 833 (1980) **Pop Density:** 1638.0
Land: 0.5 sq. mi.; **Water:** 0.0 sq. mi. **Elev:** 370 ft.
Incorporated 1884.
Name origin: For a well-known Indian chief.

Richland
Township
Lat: 36-50-00 N **Long:** 89-47-11 W
Pop: 1,797 (1990); 2,020 (1980) **Pop Density:** 16.3
Land: 110.3 sq. mi.; **Water:** 0.0 sq. mi.

MISSOURI, Stone County

Stone County
County Seat: Galena (ZIP: 65656)

Pop: 19,078 (1990); 15,587 (1980)
Land: 463.3 sq. mi.; **Water:** 47.7 sq. mi.
Pop Density: 41.2
Area Code: 417

On the southwestern border of MO, south of Springfield; organized Feb 10, 1851 from Taney County.

Name origin: For either William Stone, a prominent judge, or John W. Stone, an early settler.

Alpine — Township
Lat: 36-37-21 N **Long:** 93-32-42 W
Pop: 440 (1990); 443 (1980) **Pop Density:** 26.7
Land: 16.5 sq. mi.; **Water:** 8.0 sq. mi.

Blue Eye — Town
ZIP: 65611 **Lat:** 36-29-59 N **Long:** 93-23-47 W
Pop: 112 (1990); 94 (1980) **Pop Density:** 224.0
Land: 0.5 sq. mi.; **Water:** 0.0 sq. mi. **Elev:** 1290 ft.
Incorporated 1946.

Cass — Township
Lat: 36-57-36 N **Long:** 93-22-57 W
Pop: 445 (1990); 352 (1980) **Pop Density:** 21.4
Land: 20.8 sq. mi.; **Water:** 0.0 sq. mi.

Crane — City
ZIP: 65633 **Lat:** 36-54-11 N **Long:** 93-34-16 W
Pop: 1,218 (1990); 1,185 (1980) **Pop Density:** 1107.3
Land: 1.1 sq. mi.; **Water:** 0.0 sq. mi. **Elev:** 1122 ft.
Incorporated 1906.

Flat Creek A — Township
Lat: 36-43-29 N **Long:** 93-31-20 W
Pop: 954 (1990); 704 (1980) **Pop Density:** 26.6
Land: 35.8 sq. mi.; **Water:** 3.5 sq. mi.

Flat Creek B — Township
Lat: 36-40-58 N **Long:** 93-30-21 W
Pop: 389 (1990); 369 (1980) **Pop Density:** 49.2
Land: 7.9 sq. mi.; **Water:** 3.1 sq. mi.

Galena — City
ZIP: 65656 **Lat:** 36-48-16 N **Long:** 93-28-12 W
Pop: 401 (1990); 423 (1980) **Pop Density:** 572.9
Land: 0.7 sq. mi.; **Water:** 0.0 sq. mi. **Elev:** 985 ft.
Incorporated 1903.
Name origin: Named in 1853 for the large amounts of the lead sulfide mined here.

Grant — Township
Lat: 36-57-25 N **Long:** 93-34-00 W
Pop: 445 (1990); 502 (1980) **Pop Density:** 17.8
Land: 25.0 sq. mi.; **Water:** 0.0 sq. mi.

Hurley — City
ZIP: 65675 **Lat:** 36-55-51 N **Long:** 93-29-47 W
Pop: 87 (1990); 125 (1980) **Pop Density:** 435.0
Land: 0.2 sq. mi.; **Water:** 0.0 sq. mi. **Elev:** 1080 ft.
Incorporated 1955.

*Hurley — Township
Lat: 36-55-04 N **Long:** 93-28-06 W
Pop: 766 (1990); 689 (1980) **Pop Density:** 23.3
Land: 32.9 sq. mi.; **Water:** 0.0 sq. mi.

Indian Point — Village
Lat: 36-38-26 N **Long:** 93-20-48 W
Pop: 435 (1990) **Pop Density:** 155.4
Land: 2.8 sq. mi.; **Water:** 1.1 sq. mi.

Kimberling City — City
ZIP: 65686 **Lat:** 36-38-30 N **Long:** 93-25-26 W
Pop: 1,590 (1990); 1,285 (1980) **Pop Density:** 512.9
Land: 3.1 sq. mi.; **Water:** 0.5 sq. mi. **Elev:** 1050 ft.
Incorporated 1973.

Lakeview — City
ZIP: 65737 **Lat:** 36-41-51 N **Long:** 93-21-58 W
Pop: 37 (1990); 58 (1980) **Pop Density:** 123.3
Land: 0.3 sq. mi.; **Water:** 0.0 sq. mi. **Elev:** 1362 ft.
Incorporated 1988.

Lincoln — Township
Lat: 36-50-52 N **Long:** 93-32-17 W
Pop: 668 (1990); 742 (1980) **Pop Density:** 23.2
Land: 28.8 sq. mi.; **Water:** 0.0 sq. mi.

McKinley — Township
Lat: 36-50-34 N **Long:** 93-23-14 W
Pop: 294 (1990); 278 (1980) **Pop Density:** 25.3
Land: 11.6 sq. mi.; **Water:** 0.0 sq. mi.

Pierce — Township
Lat: 36-53-17 N **Long:** 93-33-31 W
Pop: 1,726 (1990); 1,460 (1980) **Pop Density:** 98.6
Land: 17.5 sq. mi.; **Water:** 0.0 sq. mi.

Pine A — Township
Lat: 36-32-29 N **Long:** 93-22-39 W
Pop: 1,294 (1990); 1,055 (1980) **Pop Density:** 35.0
Land: 37.0 sq. mi.; **Water:** 7.4 sq. mi.

Pine B — Township
Lat: 36-34-52 N **Long:** 93-27-00 W
Pop: 1,219 (1990); 1,077 (1980) **Pop Density:** 69.7
Land: 17.5 sq. mi.; **Water:** 6.7 sq. mi.

Ponce de Leon — Township
ZIP: 65728 **Lat:** 36-53-43 N **Long:** 93-22-27 W
Pop: 435 (1990); 355 (1980) **Pop Density:** 19.8
Land: 22.0 sq. mi.; **Water:** 0.0 sq. mi.

Reeds Spring — City
ZIP: 65737 **Lat:** 36-45-00 N **Long:** 93-22-51 W
Pop: 411 (1990); 461 (1980) **Pop Density:** 822.0
Land: 0.5 sq. mi.; **Water:** 0.0 sq. mi. **Elev:** 1199 ft.
Incorporated 1947.

Ruth A — Township
Lat: 36-44-31 N **Long:** 93-22-37 W
Pop: 2,300 (1990); 1,672 (1980) **Pop Density:** 39.6
Land: 58.1 sq. mi.; **Water:** 1.2 sq. mi.

Ruth B — Township
Lat: 36-38-30 N Long: 93-25-26 W
Pop: 1,590 (1990); 2,190 (1980) Pop Density: 512.9
Land: 3.1 sq. mi.; Water: 0.5 sq. mi.

Ruth B Rural — Township
Lat: 36-38-12 N Long: 93-26-42 W
Pop: 1,618 (1990) Pop Density: 161.8
Land: 10.0 sq. mi.; Water: 4.2 sq. mi.

Ruth C — Township
Lat: 36-38-28 N Long: 93-22-22 W
Pop: 1,372 (1990); 1,578 (1980) Pop Density: 60.7
Land: 22.6 sq. mi.; Water: 5.8 sq. mi.

Ruth C Rural — Township
Lat: 36-38-42 N Long: 93-19-56 W
Pop: 754 (1990) Pop Density: 100.5
Land: 7.5 sq. mi.; Water: 2.3 sq. mi.

Union — Township
Lat: 36-58-20 N Long: 93-28-41 W
Pop: 302 (1990); 312 (1980) Pop Density: 21.3
Land: 14.2 sq. mi.; Water: 0.0 sq. mi.

Washington — Township
Lat: 36-48-11 N Long: 93-28-29 W
Pop: 1,345 (1990); 1,254 (1980) Pop Density: 30.8
Land: 43.6 sq. mi.; Water: 0.8 sq. mi.

Williams — Township
Lat: 36-32-30 N Long: 93-31-31 W
Pop: 722 (1990); 555 (1980) Pop Density: 23.4
Land: 30.9 sq. mi.; Water: 4.2 sq. mi.

Sullivan County
County Seat: Milan (ZIP: 63556)

Pop: 6,326 (1990); 7,434 (1980) Pop Density: 9.7
Land: 651.0 sq. mi.; Water: 0.5 sq. mi. Area Code: 816

In north-central MO; organized Feb 14, 1845 from Linn County.

Name origin: For either James Sullivan, a prominent local resident, or for Sullivan County, TN, which was named for Gen. John Sullivan (1740–95), Revolutionary War officer, member of the Continental Congress, chief executive and governor (1786–87, 1789) of NH.

Bowman — Township
Lat: 40-10-04 N Long: 93-16-37 W
Pop: 382 (1990); 516 (1980) Pop Density: 7.1
Land: 54.1 sq. mi.; Water: 0.0 sq. mi.

Browning — City
ZIP: 64630 Lat: 40-02-12 N Long: 93-09-39 W
Pop: 76 (1990); 87 (1980) Pop Density: 380.0
Land: 0.2 sq. mi.; Water: 0.0 sq. mi.
Founded 1872. Incorporated 1878. Part of the town is also in Linn County.
Name origin: For Mrs. Browning, the wife of an official of the C, B & Q Railroad. Previously called Linnivan, since it was located near the Linn and Sullivan County lines.

Buchanan — Township
Lat: 40-20-24 N Long: 92-56-32 W
Pop: 171 (1990); 237 (1980) Pop Density: 3.2
Land: 54.2 sq. mi.; Water: 0.0 sq. mi.

Clay — Township
Lat: 40-20-16 N Long: 93-16-28 W
Pop: 440 (1990); 524 (1980) Pop Density: 8.1
Land: 54.5 sq. mi.; Water: 0.0 sq. mi.

Duncan — Township
Lat: 40-05-19 N Long: 93-11-22 W
Pop: 368 (1990); 500 (1980) Pop Density: 7.3
Land: 50.4 sq. mi.; Water: 0.0 sq. mi.

Greencastle — City
Lat: 40-15-41 N Long: 92-52-42 W
Pop: 254 (1990); 285 (1980) Pop Density: 508.0
Land: 0.5 sq. mi.; Water: 0.0 sq. mi.

Green City — City
ZIP: 63545 Lat: 40-15-56 N Long: 92-57-25 W
Pop: 671 (1990); 719 (1980) Pop Density: 479.3
Land: 1.4 sq. mi.; Water: 0.0 sq. mi. Elev: 1059 ft.
Incorporated 1880.

Harris — Town
ZIP: 64645 Lat: 40-18-23 N Long: 93-21-00 W
Pop: 102 (1990); 116 (1980) Pop Density: 510.0
Land: 0.2 sq. mi.; Water: 0.0 sq. mi.
Incorporated 1887.

Humphreys — Town
ZIP: 64646 Lat: 40-07-30 N Long: 93-19-06 W
Pop: 98 (1990); 133 (1980) Pop Density: 490.0
Land: 0.2 sq. mi.; Water: 0.0 sq. mi. Elev: 928 ft.
Incorporated 1881.

Jackson — Township
Lat: 40-19-09 N Long: 93-06-40 W
Pop: 529 (1990); 637 (1980) Pop Density: 6.5
Land: 80.9 sq. mi.; Water: 0.1 sq. mi.

Liberty — Township
Lat: 40-15-10 N Long: 93-16-54 W
Pop: 181 (1990); 229 (1980) Pop Density: 3.3
Land: 54.5 sq. mi.; Water: 0.0 sq. mi.

Milan — City
ZIP: 63556 Lat: 40-12-11 N Long: 93-07-26 W
Pop: 1,767 (1990); 1,947 (1980) Pop Density: 981.7
Land: 1.8 sq. mi.; Water: 0.0 sq. mi. Elev: 969 ft.
Surveyed 1845 by Wilson Baldridge as the county seat. Incorporated 1877.

Morris
Township
Lat: 40-04-49 N **Long:** 92-55-42 W
Pop: 193 (1990); 255 (1980) **Pop Density:** 4.0
Land: 48.1 sq. mi.; **Water:** 0.0 sq. mi.

Newtown
Town
ZIP: 64667 **Lat:** 40-22-35 N **Long:** 93-19-58 W
Pop: 115 (1990); 170 (1980) **Pop Density:** 383.3
Land: 0.3 sq. mi.; **Water:** 0.0 sq. mi.
Incorporated 1961.

Osgood
Town
Lat: 40-11-53 N **Long:** 93-21-02 W
Pop: 53 (1990); 93 (1980) **Pop Density:** 265.0
Land: 0.2 sq. mi.; **Water:** 0.0 sq. mi.
Incorporated 1909.

Penn
Township
Lat: 40-15-28 N **Long:** 92-56-50 W
Pop: 1,186 (1990); 1,328 (1980) **Pop Density:** 21.9
Land: 54.1 sq. mi.; **Water:** 0.1 sq. mi.

Pleasant Hill
Township
Lat: 40-05-45 N **Long:** 93-03-54 W
Pop: 163 (1990); 231 (1980) **Pop Density:** 3.4
Land: 48.5 sq. mi.; **Water:** 0.0 sq. mi.

Polk
Township
Lat: 40-12-05 N **Long:** 93-06-45 W
Pop: 2,400 (1990); 2,589 (1980) **Pop Density:** 37.9
Land: 63.3 sq. mi.; **Water:** 0.2 sq. mi.

Pollock
Village
ZIP: 63560 **Lat:** 40-21-32 N **Long:** 93-05-02 W
Pop: 66 (1990); 102 (1980) **Pop Density:** 660.0
Land: 0.1 sq. mi.; **Water:** 0.0 sq. mi.

Taylor
Township
Lat: 40-04-30 N **Long:** 93-18-55 W
Pop: 146 (1990); 153 (1980) **Pop Density:** 4.0
Land: 36.2 sq. mi.; **Water:** 0.0 sq. mi.

Union
Township
Lat: 40-09-47 N **Long:** 92-56-16 W
Pop: 167 (1990); 235 (1980) **Pop Density:** 3.2
Land: 52.2 sq. mi.; **Water:** 0.0 sq. mi.

Taney County
County Seat: Forsyth (ZIP: 65653)

Pop: 25,561 (1990); 20,467 (1980) **Pop Density:** 40.4
Land: 632.4 sq. mi.; **Water:** 19.1 sq. mi. **Area Code:** 417
On southwestern border of MO, south of Springfield; organized Jan 6, 1837 from Greene County.
Name origin: For Roger Brooke Taney (1777–1864), Chief Justice of the U.S. Supreme Court (1836–64), who wrote the decision in the Dred Scott Case.

Beaver
Township
Lat: 36-42-31 N **Long:** 92-52-25 W
Pop: 758 (1990); 803 (1980) **Pop Density:** 4.8
Land: 159.3 sq. mi.; **Water:** 0.0 sq. mi.

Big Creek
Township
Lat: 36-33-12 N **Long:** 92-50-48 W
Pop: 375 (1990); 382 (1980) **Pop Density:** 5.2
Land: 72.6 sq. mi.; **Water:** 1.5 sq. mi.

Branson
City
ZIP: 65616 **Lat:** 36-38-44 N **Long:** 93-14-42 W
Pop: 3,706 (1990); 2,550 (1980) **Pop Density:** 650.2
Land: 5.7 sq. mi.; **Water:** 0.0 sq. mi. **Elev:** 722 ft.
Incorporated 1912.
Name origin: Named in 1881 for the first postmaster, R. S. Branson.

*Branson
Township
ZIP: 65616 **Lat:** 36-41-16 N **Long:** 93-15-39 W
Pop: 7,658 (1990); 5,926 (1980) **Pop Density:** 137.7
Land: 55.6 sq. mi.; **Water:** 0.9 sq. mi.

Cedar Creek
Township
Lat: 36-34-00 N **Long:** 92-59-49 W
Pop: 407 (1990); 377 (1980) **Pop Density:** 7.3
Land: 55.9 sq. mi.; **Water:** 4.5 sq. mi.

Forsyth
City
ZIP: 65653 **Lat:** 36-41-14 N **Long:** 93-06-29 W
Pop: 1,175 (1990); 1,010 (1980) **Pop Density:** 691.2
Land: 1.7 sq. mi.; **Water:** 0.0 sq. mi. **Elev:** 947 ft.
Incorporated 1928.

Hollister
City
ZIP: 65672 **Lat:** 36-37-08 N **Long:** 93-13-13 W
Pop: 2,628 (1990); 1,439 (1980) **Pop Density:** 821.3
Land: 3.2 sq. mi.; **Water:** 0.1 sq. mi. **Elev:** 733 ft.
Incorporated 1910.

Jasper
Township
Lat: 36-46-24 N **Long:** 93-12-43 W
Pop: 2,076 (1990); 1,833 (1980) **Pop Density:** 42.6
Land: 48.7 sq. mi.; **Water:** 0.2 sq. mi.

Merriam Woods
Village
Lat: 36-43-00 N **Long:** 93-10-14 W
Pop: 601 (1990) **Pop Density:** 429.3
Land: 1.4 sq. mi.; **Water:** 0.0 sq. mi.

Oliver
Township
Lat: 36-33-49 N **Long:** 93-14-04 W
Pop: 6,324 (1990); 6,131 (1980) **Pop Density:** 89.8
Land: 70.4 sq. mi.; **Water:** 5.3 sq. mi.

Rockaway Beach — Town
ZIP: 65740 Lat: 36-42-06 N Long: 93-09-32 W
Pop: 275 (1990); 292 (1980) Pop Density: 550.0
Land: 0.5 sq. mi.; Water: 0.1 sq. mi.
Incorporated 1955.

Scott — Township
Lat: 36-35-22 N Long: 93-07-33 W
Pop: 1,794 (1990); 123 (1980) Pop Density: 30.6
Land: 58.7 sq. mi.; Water: 3.4 sq. mi.

Swan — Township
ZIP: 65759 Lat: 36-43-17 N Long: 93-03-33 W
Pop: 6,169 (1990); 4,892 (1980) Pop Density: 55.4
Land: 111.3 sq. mi.; Water: 3.4 sq. mi.

Table Rock — Village
Lat: 36-36-15 N Long: 93-18-01 W
Pop: 100 (1990); 58 (1980) Pop Density: 500.0
Land: 0.2 sq. mi.; Water: 0.0 sq. mi. Elev: 900 ft.
Incorporated 1968.

Taneyville — Village
ZIP: 65759 Lat: 36-44-14 N Long: 93-02-05 W
Pop: 279 (1990); 300 (1980) Pop Density: 697.5
Land: 0.4 sq. mi.; Water: 0.0 sq. mi. Elev: 1075 ft.
Incorporated 1900.
Name origin: For the county.

Texas County
County Seat: Houston (ZIP: 65483)

Pop: 21,476 (1990); 21,070 (1980) Pop Density: 18.2
Land: 1178.6 sq. mi.; Water: 0.7 sq. mi. Area Code: 417
In south-central MO, east of Springfield; organized as Ashley County Feb 17, 1843 from Shannon and Wright counties; name changed Feb 14, 1845.
Name origin: Probably in honor of the admission of the state of TX.

Boone — Township
Lat: 37-33-01 N Long: 92-00-33 W
Pop: 223 (1990); 235 (1980) Pop Density: 4.5
Land: 49.1 sq. mi.; Water: 0.4 sq. mi.

Burdine — Township
Lat: 37-07-16 N Long: 92-05-24 W
Pop: 3,123 (1990); 3,126 (1980) Pop Density: 58.3
Land: 53.6 sq. mi.; Water: 0.0 sq. mi.

Cabool — City
ZIP: 65689 Lat: 37-07-36 N Long: 92-06-14 W
Pop: 2,006 (1990); 2,090 (1980) Pop Density: 542.2
Land: 3.7 sq. mi.; Water: 0.0 sq. mi. Elev: 1253 ft.
Incorporated 1884.

Carroll — Township
Lat: 37-11-56 N Long: 91-42-27 W
Pop: 950 (1990); 959 (1980) Pop Density: 20.5
Land: 46.3 sq. mi.; Water: 0.0 sq. mi.

Cass — Township
ZIP: 65464 Lat: 37-12-41 N Long: 91-58-14 W
Pop: 1,149 (1990); 1,152 (1980) Pop Density: 12.8
Land: 89.5 sq. mi.; Water: 0.0 sq. mi.

Clinton — Township
Lat: 37-08-25 N Long: 92-11-30 W
Pop: 1,264 (1990); 1,165 (1980) Pop Density: 19.3
Land: 65.5 sq. mi.; Water: 0.1 sq. mi.

Current — Township
Lat: 37-17-38 N Long: 91-42-21 W
Pop: 306 (1990); 353 (1980) Pop Density: 8.7
Land: 35.1 sq. mi.; Water: 0.0 sq. mi.

Date — Township
Lat: 37-05-17 N Long: 91-42-27 W
Pop: 498 (1990); 507 (1980) Pop Density: 13.8
Land: 36.2 sq. mi.; Water: 0.0 sq. mi.

Houston — City
ZIP: 65483 Lat: 37-19-21 N Long: 91-57-34 W
Pop: 2,118 (1990); 2,157 (1980) Pop Density: 641.8
Land: 3.3 sq. mi.; Water: 0.0 sq. mi.
Established 1845; county seat. Incorporated 1872.
Name origin: For Gen. Samuel Houston (1793–1863), first president of the Republic of Texas (1836–38; 1841–44) and governor of Texas (1859–61).

Jackson — Township
Lat: 37-22-12 N Long: 91-45-53 W
Pop: 1,145 (1990); 1,153 (1980) Pop Density: 11.8
Land: 96.8 sq. mi.; Water: 0.0 sq. mi.

Licking — City
ZIP: 65542 Lat: 37-29-46 N Long: 91-51-38 W
Pop: 1,328 (1990); 1,272 (1980) Pop Density: 885.3
Land: 1.5 sq. mi.; Water: 0.0 sq. mi. Elev: 1259 ft.
Surveyed 1878. Incorporated 1935.
Name origin: For a salt lick frequented by buffalo.

Lynch — Township
Lat: 37-26-50 N Long: 91-59-28 W
Pop: 1,078 (1990); 1,067 (1980) Pop Density: 10.9
Land: 99.0 sq. mi.; Water: 0.1 sq. mi.

Morris — Township
Lat: 37-16-11 N Long: 92-10-18 W
Pop: 752 (1990); 731 (1980) Pop Density: 9.0
Land: 83.3 sq. mi.; Water: 0.0 sq. mi.

Mountain Grove — City
Lat: 37-08-28 N Long: 92-14-53 W
Pop: 7 (1990); 3,974 (1980) Pop Density: 350.0
Land: 0.02 sq. mi.; Water: 0.0 sq. mi.
In southern MO, east of Springfield. Incorporated 1886. Part of the town is also in Wright County.
Name origin: For its descriptive connotations.

Ozark
Township
Lat: 37-13-02 N **Long:** 91-49-22 W
Pop: 476 (1990); 497 (1980) **Pop Density:** 8.1
Land: 58.7 sq. mi.; **Water:** 0.0 sq. mi.

Pierce
Township
Lat: 37-05-30 N **Long:** 91-50-23 W
Pop: 480 (1990); 534 (1980) **Pop Density:** 8.8
Land: 54.4 sq. mi.; **Water:** 0.1 sq. mi.

Piney
Township
Lat: 37-19-19 N **Long:** 91-58-22 W
Pop: 4,427 (1990); 4,449 (1980) **Pop Density:** 42.4
Land: 104.3 sq. mi.; **Water:** 0.0 sq. mi.

Raymondville
Town
ZIP: 65555 **Lat:** 37-20-23 N **Long:** 91-50-08 W
Pop: 425 (1990); 388 (1980) **Pop Density:** 146.6
Land: 2.9 sq. mi.; **Water:** 0.0 sq. mi.
Incorporated 1942.

Roubidoux
Township
Lat: 37-32-21 N **Long:** 92-09-58 W
Pop: 1,321 (1990); 1,068 (1980) **Pop Density:** 16.1
Land: 82.0 sq. mi.; **Water:** 0.0 sq. mi.

Sargent
Township
Lat: 37-06-17 N **Long:** 91-58-42 W
Pop: 275 (1990); 275 (1980) **Pop Density:** 7.7
Land: 35.5 sq. mi.; **Water:** 0.0 sq. mi.

Sherrill
Township
Lat: 37-31-09 N **Long:** 91-50-26 W
Pop: 3,388 (1990); 3,161 (1980) **Pop Density:** 31.7
Land: 106.8 sq. mi.; **Water:** 0.0 sq. mi.

Summersville
City
ZIP: 65571 **Lat:** 37-10-41 N **Long:** 91-39-37 W
Pop: 459 (1990); 453 (1980) **Pop Density:** 573.8
Land: 0.8 sq. mi.; **Water:** 0.0 sq. mi.
Incorporated 1924. Part of the town is also in Shannon County.

Upton
Township
Lat: 37-24-19 N **Long:** 92-10-01 W
Pop: 621 (1990); 638 (1980) **Pop Density:** 7.5
Land: 82.5 sq. mi.; **Water:** 0.0 sq. mi.

Vernon County
County Seat: Nevada (ZIP: 64772)

Pop: 19,041 (1990); 19,806 (1980) **Pop Density:** 22.8
Land: 834.0 sq. mi.; **Water:** 3.1 sq. mi. **Area Code:** 417
On central western border of MO, north of Joplin; organized Feb 17, 1851 from Bates County.

Name origin: For Col. Miles Vernon (1786–1866), veteran of the Battle of New Orleans and MO legislator.

Bacon
Township
Lat: 37-59-08 N **Long:** 94-07-05 W
Pop: 701 (1990); 818 (1980) **Pop Density:** 14.9
Land: 47.2 sq. mi.; **Water:** 1.0 sq. mi.

Badger
Township
Lat: 37-48-41 N **Long:** 94-14-43 W
Pop: 389 (1990); 370 (1980) **Pop Density:** 10.7
Land: 36.2 sq. mi.; **Water:** 0.1 sq. mi.

Blue Mound
Township
Lat: 37-59-28 N **Long:** 94-13-22 W
Pop: 297 (1990); 290 (1980) **Pop Density:** 6.4
Land: 46.2 sq. mi.; **Water:** 0.2 sq. mi.

Bronaugh
Town
ZIP: 64728 **Lat:** 37-41-40 N **Long:** 94-28-04 W
Pop: 211 (1990); 209 (1980) **Pop Density:** 703.3
Land: 0.3 sq. mi.; **Water:** 0.0 sq. mi.
Incorporated 1887.
Name origin: Named in 1886 for landowner W. C. Bronaugh.

Center
Township
Lat: 37-48-26 N **Long:** 94-20-43 W
Pop: 9,159 (1990); 9,227 (1980) **Pop Density:** 253.0
Land: 36.2 sq. mi.; **Water:** 0.1 sq. mi.

Clear Creek
Township
Lat: 37-53-08 N **Long:** 94-07-36 W
Pop: 563 (1990); 560 (1980) **Pop Density:** 15.5
Land: 36.3 sq. mi.; **Water:** 0.1 sq. mi.

Coal
Township
Lat: 37-48-54 N **Long:** 94-33-32 W
Pop: 285 (1990); 283 (1980) **Pop Density:** 8.4
Land: 34.1 sq. mi.; **Water:** 0.1 sq. mi.

Deerfield
Village
ZIP: 64741 **Lat:** 37-50-20 N **Long:** 94-30-23 W
Pop: 85 (1990); 95 (1980) **Pop Density:** 850.0
Land: 0.1 sq. mi.; **Water:** 0.0 sq. mi. **Elev:** 785 ft.
Incorporated 1963. Not coextensive with the town of the same name.

*Deerfield
Township
ZIP: 64741 **Lat:** 37-48-36 N **Long:** 94-26-52 W
Pop: 683 (1990); 629 (1980) **Pop Density:** 19.1
Land: 35.7 sq. mi.; **Water:** 0.0 sq. mi.

Dover
Township
Lat: 37-41-36 N **Long:** 94-13-02 W
Pop: 360 (1990); 398 (1980) **Pop Density:** 7.6
Land: 47.6 sq. mi.; **Water:** 0.0 sq. mi.

Drywood
Township
Lat: 37-42-44 N **Long:** 94-20-00 W
Pop: 1,127 (1990); 1,108 (1980) **Pop Density:** 23.8
Land: 47.3 sq. mi.; **Water:** 0.0 sq. mi.

Harrison
Township
Lat: 37-42-52 N **Long:** 94-33-09 W
Pop: 216 (1990); 268 (1980) **Pop Density:** 3.9
Land: 56.0 sq. mi.; **Water:** 0.1 sq. mi.

MISSOURI, Vernon County

Harwood
Town
ZIP: 64750   **Lat:** 37-57-24 N   **Long:** 94-09-13 W
Pop: 89 (1990); 104 (1980)   **Pop Density:** 890.0
Land: 0.1 sq. mi.; **Water:** 0.0 sq. mi.   **Elev:** 840 ft.
Incorporated 1822.

Henry
Township
Lat: 38-00-00 N   **Long:** 94-33-24 W
Pop: 249 (1990); 257 (1980)   **Pop Density:** 5.1
Land: 48.9 sq. mi.; **Water:** 0.1 sq. mi.

Lake
Township
Lat: 37-53-21 N   **Long:** 94-26-37 W
Pop: 144 (1990); 189 (1980)   **Pop Density:** 4.0
Land: 35.7 sq. mi.; **Water:** 0.2 sq. mi.

Metz
Town
ZIP: 64765   **Lat:** 37-59-46 N   **Long:** 94-26-31 W
Pop: 91 (1990); 136 (1980)   **Pop Density:** 910.0
Land: 0.1 sq. mi.; **Water:** 0.0 sq. mi.
Incorporated 1907. Not coextensive with the town of the same name.

*Metz
Township
Lat: 37-59-52 N   **Long:** 94-26-44 W
Pop: 289 (1990); 346 (1980)   **Pop Density:** 6.0
Land: 48.0 sq. mi.; **Water:** 0.1 sq. mi.

Milo
Town
ZIP: 64767   **Lat:** 37-45-18 N   **Long:** 94-18-18 W
Pop: 76 (1990); 78 (1980)   **Pop Density:** 760.0
Land: 0.1 sq. mi.; **Water:** 0.0 sq. mi.   **Elev:** 878 ft.
Incorporated 1884.

Montevallo
Township
Lat: 37-41-41 N   **Long:** 94-06-59 W
Pop: 233 (1990); 304 (1980)   **Pop Density:** 5.9
Land: 39.4 sq. mi.; **Water:** 0.1 sq. mi.

Moundville
Town
ZIP: 64771   **Lat:** 37-45-57 N   **Long:** 94-27-04 W
Pop: 140 (1990); 149 (1980)   **Pop Density:** 700.0
Land: 0.2 sq. mi.; **Water:** 0.0 sq. mi.
Incorporated 1860. Not coextensive with the town of the same name.

*Moundville
Township
ZIP: 64771   **Lat:** 37-42-36 N   **Long:** 94-26-39 W
Pop: 753 (1990); 739 (1980)   **Pop Density:** 15.6
Land: 48.4 sq. mi.; **Water:** 0.2 sq. mi.

Nevada
City
ZIP: 64772   **Lat:** 37-50-28 N   **Long:** 94-21-10 W
Pop: 8,597 (1990); 9,044 (1980)   **Pop Density:** 1409.3
Land: 6.1 sq. mi.; **Water:** 0.0 sq. mi.   **Elev:** 880 ft.
In western MO, 55 mi. north of Joplin. Incorporated 1880.

Osage
Township
Lat: 37-59-36 N   **Long:** 94-20-39 W
Pop: 262 (1990); 328 (1980)   **Pop Density:** 5.6
Land: 47.1 sq. mi.; **Water:** 0.4 sq. mi.

Richards
Town
ZIP: 64778   **Lat:** 37-54-35 N   **Long:** 94-33-25 W
Pop: 106 (1990); 117 (1980)   **Pop Density:** 353.3
Land: 0.3 sq. mi.; **Water:** 0.0 sq. mi.
Incorporated 1894.

Richland
Township
Lat: 37-54-06 N   **Long:** 94-33-36 W
Pop: 207 (1990); 262 (1980)   **Pop Density:** 5.9
Land: 35.3 sq. mi.; **Water:** 0.1 sq. mi.

Schell City
City
ZIP: 64783   **Lat:** 38-01-08 N   **Long:** 94-06-59 W
Pop: 292 (1990); 327 (1980)   **Pop Density:** 486.7
Land: 0.6 sq. mi.; **Water:** 0.0 sq. mi.   **Elev:** 747 ft.
Incorporated 1879.

Sheldon
City
ZIP: 64784   **Lat:** 37-39-30 N   **Long:** 94-17-44 W
Pop: 464 (1990); 491 (1980)   **Pop Density:** 928.0
Land: 0.5 sq. mi.; **Water:** 0.0 sq. mi.   **Elev:** 915 ft.
Incorporated 1881.

Stotesbury
Town
Lat: 37-58-27 N   **Long:** 94-33-53 W
Pop: 42 (1990); 48 (1980)   **Pop Density:** 420.0
Land: 0.1 sq. mi.; **Water:** 0.0 sq. mi.
Incorporated 1895.

Virgil
Township
Lat: 37-48-14 N   **Long:** 94-07-52 W
Pop: 354 (1990); 381 (1980)   **Pop Density:** 9.8
Land: 36.3 sq. mi.; **Water:** 0.0 sq. mi.

Walker
Town
ZIP: 64790   **Lat:** 37-53-58 N   **Long:** 94-13-49 W
Pop: 283 (1990); 325 (1980)   **Pop Density:** 943.3
Land: 0.3 sq. mi.; **Water:** 0.0 sq. mi.   **Elev:** 852 ft.
Platted 1870. Incorporated 1870. Not coextensive with the town of the same name.
Name origin: For early resident Hiram F. Walker.

*Walker
Township
ZIP: 64790   **Lat:** 37-53-43 N   **Long:** 94-13-58 W
Pop: 544 (1990); 600 (1980)   **Pop Density:** 15.0
Land: 36.2 sq. mi.; **Water:** 0.1 sq. mi.

Washington
Township
Lat: 37-53-19 N   **Long:** 94-20-19 W
Pop: 2,226 (1990); 2,449 (1980)   **Pop Density:** 62.0
Land: 35.9 sq. mi.; **Water:** 0.1 sq. mi.

Warren County
County Seat: Warrenton (ZIP: 63383)

Pop: 19,534 (1990); 14,900 (1980)   **Pop Density:** 45.2
Land: 431.7 sq. mi.; **Water:** 6.1 sq. mi.   **Area Code:** 314

In east-central MO, west of St. Louis; organized Jan 5, 1833 from Montgomery County.

Name origin: For Gen. Joseph Warren (1741–75), Revolutionary War patriot and member of the Committee of Safety who dispatched Paul Revere (1735–1818) on his famous ride (1775).

Bridgeport — Township
Lat: 38-45-49 N Long: 91-21-31 W
Pop: 510 (1990); 446 (1980)   **Pop Density:** 8.6
Land: 59.0 sq. mi.; **Water:** 1.0 sq. mi.

Camp Branch — Township
ZIP: 63383   Lat: 38-55-11 N Long: 91-11-50 W
Pop: 870 (1990); 618 (1980)   **Pop Density:** 17.2
Land: 50.5 sq. mi.; **Water:** 0.1 sq. mi.

Charrette — Township
Lat: 38-39-38 N Long: 91-05-10 W
Pop: 3,974 (1990); 3,157 (1980)   **Pop Density:** 36.2
Land: 109.7 sq. mi.; **Water:** 2.5 sq. mi.

Foristell — City
Lat: 38-49-15 N Long: 90-58-50 W
Pop: 14 (1990)   **Pop Density:** 10.0
Land: 1.4 sq. mi.; **Water:** 0.1 sq. mi.
Incorporated 1980. Part of the town is also in St. Charles County.

Hickory Grove — Township
Lat: 38-47-19 N Long: 91-01-08 W
Pop: 4,872 (1990); 3,511 (1980)   **Pop Density:** 65.5
Land: 74.4 sq. mi.; **Water:** 0.9 sq. mi.

Marthasville — City
ZIP: 63357   Lat: 38-37-42 N Long: 91-03-11 W
Pop: 674 (1990); 543 (1980)   **Pop Density:** 1123.3
Land: 0.6 sq. mi.; **Water:** 0.0 sq. mi.   **Elev:** 496 ft.
Incorporated 1920.

North Elkhorn — Township
Lat: 38-49-57 N Long: 91-11-35 W
Pop: 4,730 (1990); 3,630 (1980)   **Pop Density:** 82.5
Land: 57.3 sq. mi.; **Water:** 0.3 sq. mi.

Pinckney — Township
Lat: 38-43-08 N Long: 91-13-25 W
Pop: 672 (1990); 537 (1980)   **Pop Density:** 12.4
Land: 54.1 sq. mi.; **Water:** 1.1 sq. mi.

South Elkhorn — Township
Lat: 38-47-06 N Long: 91-08-05 W
Pop: 3,906 (1990); 3,001 (1980)   **Pop Density:** 146.3
Land: 26.7 sq. mi.; **Water:** 0.2 sq. mi.

Truesdale — City
ZIP: 63383   Lat: 38-48-39 N Long: 91-07-30 W
Pop: 285 (1990); 297 (1980)   **Pop Density:** 316.7
Land: 0.9 sq. mi.; **Water:** 0.0 sq. mi.
Incorporated 1927.

Warrenton — City
ZIP: 63383   Lat: 38-49-16 N Long: 91-08-24 W
Pop: 3,564 (1990); 3,219 (1980)   **Pop Density:** 698.8
Land: 5.1 sq. mi.; **Water:** 0.0 sq. mi.   **Elev:** 828 ft.
Incorporated 1864.

Wright City — City
ZIP: 63390   Lat: 38-49-39 N Long: 91-01-27 W
Pop: 1,250 (1990); 1,179 (1980)   **Pop Density:** 568.2
Land: 2.2 sq. mi.; **Water:** 0.0 sq. mi.   **Elev:** 727 ft.
Founded 1857. Incorporated 1869.
Name origin: For early settler H.C. Wright.

> ## Washington County
> **County Seat:** Potosi (ZIP: 63664)
>
> **Pop:** 20,380 (1990); 17,983 (1980) **Pop Density:** 26.8
> **Land:** 759.8 sq. mi.; **Water:** 2.7 sq. mi. **Area Code:** 314
>
> In east-central MO, southwest of St. Louis; organized Aug 21, 1813 (prior to statehood) from Ste. Genevieve County.
>
> **Name origin:** For George Washington (1732–99), American patriot and first U.S. president.

Belgrade
Township
ZIP: 63622 **Lat:** 37-48-07 N **Long:** 90-51-59 W
Pop: 1,000 (1990); 969 (1980) **Pop Density:** 13.3
Land: 75.0 sq. mi.; **Water:** 0.1 sq. mi.

Belleview
Township
Lat: 37-46-10 N **Long:** 90-43-56 W
Pop: 808 (1990); 802 (1980) **Pop Density:** 27.4
Land: 29.5 sq. mi.; **Water:** 0.1 sq. mi.

Breton
Township
Lat: 37-55-24 N **Long:** 90-45-22 W
Pop: 8,782 (1990); 7,527 (1980) **Pop Density:** 111.7
Land: 78.6 sq. mi.; **Water:** 0.7 sq. mi.

Caledonia
Village
ZIP: 63631 **Lat:** 37-45-48 N **Long:** 90-46-15 W
Pop: 142 (1990); 162 (1980) **Pop Density:** 1420.0
Land: 0.1 sq. mi.; **Water:** 0.0 sq. mi.
Incorporated 1874.
Name origin: For Caledonia, Scotland.

Concord
Township
Lat: 37-49-35 N **Long:** 90-42-44 W
Pop: 2,123 (1990); 2,011 (1980) **Pop Density:** 41.5
Land: 51.1 sq. mi.; **Water:** 0.0 sq. mi.

Harmony
Township
Lat: 37-48-28 N **Long:** 91-00-29 W
Pop: 389 (1990); 347 (1980) **Pop Density:** 4.9
Land: 80.2 sq. mi.; **Water:** 0.4 sq. mi.

Irondale
City
ZIP: 63648 **Lat:** 37-50-03 N **Long:** 90-40-15 W
Pop: 474 (1990); 349 (1980) **Pop Density:** 948.0
Land: 0.5 sq. mi.; **Water:** 0.0 sq. mi.
Incorporated 1910.

Johnson
Township
Lat: 38-05-02 N **Long:** 91-01-21 W
Pop: 699 (1990); 496 (1980) **Pop Density:** 5.4
Land: 130.2 sq. mi.; **Water:** 0.2 sq. mi.

Kingston
Township
Lat: 38-05-14 N **Long:** 90-43-45 W
Pop: 889 (1990); 619 (1980) **Pop Density:** 22.8
Land: 39.0 sq. mi.; **Water:** 0.1 sq. mi.

Liberty
Township
Lat: 38-00-37 N **Long:** 90-52-27 W
Pop: 971 (1990); 848 (1980) **Pop Density:** 15.2
Land: 63.7 sq. mi.; **Water:** 0.2 sq. mi.

Mineral Point
Town
ZIP: 63660 **Lat:** 37-56-42 N **Long:** 90-43-27 W
Pop: 384 (1990); 358 (1980) **Pop Density:** 1280.0
Land: 0.3 sq. mi.; **Water:** 0.0 sq. mi.
Incorporated 1904.

Potosi
City
ZIP: 63664 **Lat:** 37-56-09 N **Long:** 90-46-55 W
Pop: 2,683 (1990); 2,528 (1980) **Pop Density:** 1676.9
Land: 1.6 sq. mi.; **Water:** 0.0 sq. mi.
In eastern MO, 60 mi. southwest of St. Louis. Incorporated 1826.
Name origin: For Potosi, Bolivia, a silver-mining center.

Richwoods
Township
ZIP: 63071 **Lat:** 38-08-28 N **Long:** 90-50-40 W
Pop: 1,079 (1990); 1,020 (1980) **Pop Density:** 12.2
Land: 88.7 sq. mi.; **Water:** 0.3 sq. mi.

Union
Township
Lat: 38-00-35 N **Long:** 90-42-38 W
Pop: 2,801 (1990); 2,451 (1980) **Pop Density:** 59.5
Land: 47.1 sq. mi.; **Water:** 0.3 sq. mi.

Walton
Township
Lat: 37-55-22 N **Long:** 90-58-40 W
Pop: 839 (1990); 893 (1980) **Pop Density:** 10.9
Land: 76.7 sq. mi.; **Water:** 0.3 sq. mi.

MISSOURI, Wayne County

Wayne County
County Seat: Greenville (ZIP: 63944)

Pop: 11,543 (1990); 11,277 (1980)
Land: 761.1 sq. mi.; **Water:** 13.1 sq. mi.
Pop Density: 15.2
Area Code: 314

In southeastern MO, southwest of Cape Girardeau; organized Dec 11, 1818 (prior to statehood) from Cape Girardeau and Lawrence counties.

Name origin: For Gen. Anthony Wayne (1745–96), PA soldier and statesman, nicknamed "Mad Anthony" for his daring during the Revolutionary War.

Benton
Township
Lat: 37-10-36 N **Long:** 90-41-30 W
Pop: 3,631 (1990); 3,528 (1980) **Pop Density:** 57.5
Land: 63.2 sq. mi.; **Water:** 0.3 sq. mi.

Black River
Township
Lat: 36-58-02 N **Long:** 90-25-04 W
Pop: 486 (1990); 378 (1980) **Pop Density:** 8.6
Land: 56.4 sq. mi.; **Water:** 3.7 sq. mi.

Cedar Creek
Township
Lat: 37-16-53 N **Long:** 90-23-48 W
Pop: 406 (1990); 473 (1980) **Pop Density:** 5.4
Land: 74.9 sq. mi.; **Water:** 0.3 sq. mi.

Cowan
Township
Lat: 37-12-06 N **Long:** 90-17-42 W
Pop: 538 (1990); 498 (1980) **Pop Density:** 5.7
Land: 94.2 sq. mi.; **Water:** 0.2 sq. mi.

Greenville
City
ZIP: 63944 **Lat:** 37-07-36 N **Long:** 90-26-45 W
Pop: 437 (1990); 393 (1980) **Pop Density:** 624.3
Land: 0.7 sq. mi.; **Water:** 0.0 sq. mi. **Elev:** 406 ft.
Incorporated 1819.

Jefferson
Township
Lat: 37-01-50 N **Long:** 90-11-20 W
Pop: 308 (1990); 341 (1980) **Pop Density:** 8.1
Land: 37.8 sq. mi.; **Water:** 0.0 sq. mi.

Logan
Township
Lat: 37-12-26 N **Long:** 90-34-34 W
Pop: 1,318 (1990); 1,289 (1980) **Pop Density:** 16.5
Land: 79.7 sq. mi.; **Water:** 0.6 sq. mi.

Lost Creek
Township
Lat: 37-01-52 N **Long:** 90-17-53 W
Pop: 1,395 (1990); 1,037 (1980) **Pop Density:** 16.2
Land: 86.2 sq. mi.; **Water:** 5.4 sq. mi.

Mill Spring
Village
ZIP: 63952 **Lat:** 37-03-52 N **Long:** 90-40-53 W
Pop: 252 (1990); 257 (1980) **Pop Density:** 1260.0
Land: 0.2 sq. mi.; **Water:** 0.0 sq. mi.
Established November 1871. Incorporated 1957.
Name origin: For the large spring that powered the local mill.

*Mill Spring
Township
ZIP: 63952 **Lat:** 37-03-06 N **Long:** 90-39-57 W
Pop: 820 (1990); 867 (1980) **Pop Density:** 9.6
Land: 85.6 sq. mi.; **Water:** 0.4 sq. mi.

Piedmont
City
ZIP: 63957 **Lat:** 37-08-52 N **Long:** 90-41-54 W
Pop: 2,166 (1990); 2,359 (1980) **Pop Density:** 1140.0
Land: 1.9 sq. mi.; **Water:** 0.0 sq. mi. **Elev:** 502 ft.
Laid out by the railroad. Incorporated 1855.
Name origin: From French 'foot of the mountain.'

St. Francois
Township
Lat: 37-06-51 N **Long:** 90-27-03 W
Pop: 1,769 (1990); 1,971 (1980) **Pop Density:** 14.8
Land: 119.3 sq. mi.; **Water:** 2.1 sq. mi.

Williams
Township
Lat: 36-58-38 N **Long:** 90-35-10 W
Pop: 872 (1990); 895 (1980) **Pop Density:** 13.6
Land: 63.9 sq. mi.; **Water:** 0.1 sq. mi.

Williamsville
City
ZIP: 63967 **Lat:** 36-58-24 N **Long:** 90-32-52 W
Pop: 391 (1990); 418 (1980) **Pop Density:** 1303.3
Land: 0.3 sq. mi.; **Water:** 0.0 sq. mi. **Elev:** 392 ft.
Founded 1822. Incorporated 1887.
Name origin: For founder Asa E. Williams.

Webster County
County Seat: Marshfield (ZIP: 65706)

Pop: 23,753 (1990); 20,414 (1980)
Land: 593.4 sq. mi.; **Water:** 0.3 sq. mi.
Pop Density: 40.0
Area Code: 417
In south-central MO, east of Springfield; organized Mar 3, 1855 from Greene County.
Name origin: For Daniel Webster (1782–1852), U.S. statesman and orator from MA.

Diggins — Village
ZIP: 65636 **Lat:** 37-10-26 N **Long:** 92-51-08 W
Pop: 258 (1990); 245 (1980) **Pop Density:** 368.6
Land: 0.7 sq. mi.; **Water:** 0.0 sq. mi. **Elev:** 1651 ft.
Incorporated 1929.

East Benton — Township
Lat: 37-07-29 N **Long:** 92-54-38 W
Pop: 2,080 (1990); 1,581 (1980) **Pop Density:** 51.7
Land: 40.2 sq. mi.; **Water:** 0.0 sq. mi.

East Dallas — Township
Lat: 37-13-13 N **Long:** 92-53-40 W
Pop: 1,292 (1990); 1,038 (1980) **Pop Density:** 31.7
Land: 40.8 sq. mi.; **Water:** 0.0 sq. mi.

Finley — Township
Lat: 37-06-21 N **Long:** 92-46-03 W
Pop: 2,500 (1990); 2,373 (1980) **Pop Density:** 45.9
Land: 54.5 sq. mi.; **Water:** 0.0 sq. mi.

Fordland — City
ZIP: 65652 **Lat:** 37-09-24 N **Long:** 92-56-33 W
Pop: 523 (1990); 569 (1980) **Pop Density:** 581.1
Land: 0.9 sq. mi.; **Water:** 0.0 sq. mi. **Elev:** 1608 ft.
Founded 1881. Incorporated 1953.
Name origin: For J. S. Ford of the Kansas City, Ft. Scott Railroad.

Grant — Township
Lat: 37-19-55 N **Long:** 93-01-04 W
Pop: 1,741 (1990); 1,448 (1980) **Pop Density:** 36.0
Land: 48.4 sq. mi.; **Water:** 0.1 sq. mi.

Hazelwood — Township
Lat: 37-12-03 N **Long:** 92-45-51 W
Pop: 1,336 (1990); 1,104 (1980) **Pop Density:** 24.5
Land: 54.5 sq. mi.; **Water:** 0.0 sq. mi.

High Prairie — Township
Lat: 37-18-00 N **Long:** 92-45-07 W
Pop: 788 (1990); 694 (1980) **Pop Density:** 15.8
Land: 50.0 sq. mi.; **Water:** 0.0 sq. mi.

Jackson — Township
Lat: 37-26-02 N **Long:** 93-01-03 W
Pop: 1,136 (1990); 1,077 (1980) **Pop Density:** 27.0
Land: 42.1 sq. mi.; **Water:** 0.0 sq. mi.

Marshfield — City
ZIP: 65706 **Lat:** 37-20-21 N **Long:** 92-54-37 W
Pop: 4,374 (1990); 3,871 (1980) **Pop Density:** 994.1
Land: 4.4 sq. mi.; **Water:** 0.0 sq. mi. **Elev:** 1494 ft.
In southern MO, 25 mi. east-northeast of Springfield. Incorporated 1856.
Name origin: For the MA home of Daniel Webster.

Niangua — City
ZIP: 65713 **Lat:** 37-23-15 N **Long:** 92-49-47 W
Pop: 459 (1990); 376 (1980) **Pop Density:** 1147.5
Land: 0.4 sq. mi.; **Water:** 0.0 sq. mi. **Elev:** 1435 ft.
Incorporated 1964.
Name origin: For the nearby Niangua River.

*Niangua — Township
ZIP: 65713 **Lat:** 37-23-03 N **Long:** 92-47-47 W
Pop: 1,065 (1990); 972 (1980) **Pop Density:** 33.8
Land: 31.5 sq. mi.; **Water:** 0.0 sq. mi.

Ozark — Township
Lat: 37-19-32 N **Long:** 92-53-19 W
Pop: 7,414 (1990); 6,457 (1980) **Pop Density:** 100.5
Land: 73.8 sq. mi.; **Water:** 0.1 sq. mi.

Rogersville — Town
ZIP: 65742 **Lat:** 37-06-55 N **Long:** 93-03-25 W
Pop: 974 (1990); 706 (1980) **Pop Density:** 1623.3
Land: 0.6 sq. mi.; **Water:** 0.0 sq. mi.
Incorporated 1947. Part of the town is also in Greene County.
Name origin: For Dr. Rogers, a pioneer.

Seymour — City
ZIP: 65746 **Lat:** 37-08-54 N **Long:** 92-46-01 W
Pop: 1,636 (1990); 1,535 (1980) **Pop Density:** 681.7
Land: 2.4 sq. mi.; **Water:** 0.0 sq. mi. **Elev:** 1653 ft.
Incorporated 1895.

Union — Township
Lat: 37-26-11 N **Long:** 92-44-48 W
Pop: 669 (1990); 656 (1980) **Pop Density:** 14.6
Land: 45.7 sq. mi.; **Water:** 0.0 sq. mi.

Washington — Township
Lat: 37-26-47 N **Long:** 92-54-10 W
Pop: 869 (1990); 793 (1980) **Pop Density:** 21.6
Land: 40.2 sq. mi.; **Water:** 0.0 sq. mi.

West Benton — Township
Lat: 37-07-23 N **Long:** 93-00-55 W
Pop: 2,010 (1990); 1,506 (1980) **Pop Density:** 71.3
Land: 28.2 sq. mi.; **Water:** 0.0 sq. mi.

West Dallas — Township
Lat: 37-12-42 N **Long:** 93-00-33 W
Pop: 853 (1990); 715 (1980) **Pop Density:** 19.7
Land: 43.4 sq. mi.; **Water:** 0.0 sq. mi.

Worth County
County Seat: Grant City (ZIP: 64456)

Pop: 2,440 (1990); 3,008 (1980)
Land: 266.5 sq. mi.; **Water:** 0.2 sq. mi.
Pop Density: 9.2
Area Code: 816

On the northwestern border of MO, northeast of St. Joseph; organized Feb 8, 1861 from Gentry County.

Name origin: For Gen. William Jenkins Worth (1794–1849), officer in the War of 1812, Seminole War, and the Mexican-American War; cited by Congress for bravery.

Allen — Township
Lat: 40-25-48 N **Long:** 94-17-06 W
Pop: 181 (1990); 268 (1980) **Pop Density:** 3.9
Land: 46.8 sq. mi.; **Water:** 0.0 sq. mi.

Allendale — Town
ZIP: 64420 **Lat:** 40-29-10 N **Long:** 94-17-19 W
Pop: 58 (1990); 95 (1980) **Pop Density:** 96.7
Land: 0.6 sq. mi.; **Water:** 0.0 sq. mi.
Incorporated 1928.

Denver — Village
ZIP: 64441 **Lat:** 40-23-56 N **Long:** 94-19-25 W
Pop: 53 (1990); 74 (1980) **Pop Density:** 132.5
Land: 0.4 sq. mi.; **Water:** 0.0 sq. mi. **Elev:** 898 ft.
Incorporated 1945.

Fletchall — Township
Lat: 40-31-11 N **Long:** 94-23-57 W
Pop: 1,218 (1990); 1,309 (1980) **Pop Density:** 29.1
Land: 41.8 sq. mi.; **Water:** 0.0 sq. mi.

Grant City — City
ZIP: 64456 **Lat:** 40-29-09 N **Long:** 94-24-49 W
Pop: 998 (1990); 1,068 (1980) **Pop Density:** 767.7
Land: 1.3 sq. mi.; **Water:** 0.0 sq. mi. **Elev:** 1136 ft.
Incorporated 1863.

Name origin: Named in 1863 for Ulysses S. Grant (1822–85), commander in chief of Union forces during the Civil War, and eighteenth U.S. president.

Greene — Township
Lat: 40-25-44 N **Long:** 94-32-37 W
Pop: 144 (1990); 175 (1980) **Pop Density:** 3.6
Land: 39.9 sq. mi.; **Water:** 0.0 sq. mi.

Middlefork — Township
Lat: 40-25-36 N **Long:** 94-25-40 W
Pop: 229 (1990); 353 (1980) **Pop Density:** 6.6
Land: 34.5 sq. mi.; **Water:** 0.0 sq. mi.

Sheridan — Town
ZIP: 64486 **Lat:** 40-31-02 N **Long:** 94-36-52 W
Pop: 174 (1990); 220 (1980) **Pop Density:** 870.0
Land: 0.2 sq. mi.; **Water:** 0.0 sq. mi.
Incorporated 1899.

Smith — Township
Lat: 40-31-19 N **Long:** 94-17-36 W
Pop: 183 (1990); 296 (1980) **Pop Density:** 4.4
Land: 41.9 sq. mi.; **Water:** 0.1 sq. mi.

Union — Township
Lat: 40-30-46 N **Long:** 94-32-42 W
Pop: 485 (1990); 607 (1980) **Pop Density:** 7.9
Land: 61.6 sq. mi.; **Water:** 0.1 sq. mi.

Worth — Town
ZIP: 64499 **Lat:** 40-24-19 N **Long:** 94-26-48 W
Pop: 103 (1990); 137 (1980) **Pop Density:** 515.0
Land: 0.2 sq. mi.; **Water:** 0.0 sq. mi. **Elev:** 923 ft.
Incorporated 1911.

Wright County
County Seat: Hartville (ZIP: 65667)

Pop: 16,758 (1990); 16,188 (1980)
Land: 682.3 sq. mi.; **Water:** 0.9 sq. mi.
Pop Density: 24.6
Area Code: 417

In south-central MO, east of Springfield; organized Jan 29, 1841 from Pulaski County.

Name origin: For Silas Wright (1795–1847), NY governor (1844–46), U.S. representative, and senator (1833–45).

Boone — Township
Lat: 37-18-30 N **Long:** 92-36-35 W
Pop: 893 (1990); 886 (1980) **Pop Density:** 16.4
Land: 54.6 sq. mi.; **Water:** 0.0 sq. mi.

Brush Creek — Township
Lat: 37-18-18 N **Long:** 92-28-41 W
Pop: 510 (1990); 440 (1980) **Pop Density:** 14.1
Land: 36.2 sq. mi.; **Water:** 0.0 sq. mi.

Clark — Township
Lat: 37-06-20 N **Long:** 92-27-59 W
Pop: 1,061 (1990); 1,024 (1980) **Pop Density:** 29.4
Land: 36.1 sq. mi.; **Water:** 0.0 sq. mi.

Elk Creek — Township
Lat: 37-24-30 N **Long:** 92-28-09 W
Pop: 382 (1990); 448 (1980) **Pop Density:** 7.1
Land: 53.6 sq. mi.; **Water:** 0.1 sq. mi.

Gasconade
Township
Lat: 37-12-34 N **Long:** 92-35-48 W
Pop: 1,051 (1990); 1,042 (1980) **Pop Density:** 15.5
Land: 67.6 sq. mi.; **Water:** 0.0 sq. mi.

Hart
Township
Lat: 37-12-02 N **Long:** 92-28-01 W
Pop: 1,068 (1990); 1,107 (1980) **Pop Density:** 24.0
Land: 44.5 sq. mi.; **Water:** 0.0 sq. mi.

Hartville
City
ZIP: 65667 **Lat:** 37-15-00 N **Long:** 92-30-42 W
Pop: 495 (1990); 576 (1980) **Pop Density:** 825.0
Land: 0.6 sq. mi.; **Water:** 0.0 sq. mi.
Incorporated 1905.
Name origin: For early settler Isaac Hart.

Mansfield
City
ZIP: 65704 **Lat:** 37-06-35 N **Long:** 92-34-51 W
Pop: 1,429 (1990); 1,423 (1980) **Pop Density:** 840.6
Land: 1.7 sq. mi.; **Water:** 0.0 sq. mi. **Elev:** 1488 ft.
Incorporated 1900.

Montgomery
Township
Lat: 37-24-16 N **Long:** 92-20-06 W
Pop: 533 (1990); 603 (1980) **Pop Density:** 6.7
Land: 79.7 sq. mi.; **Water:** 0.5 sq. mi.

Mountain Grove
City
ZIP: 65711 **Lat:** 37-07-55 N **Long:** 92-15-53 W
Pop: 4,175 (1990); 3,974 (1980) **Pop Density:** 1265.2
Land: 3.3 sq. mi.; **Water:** 0.1 sq. mi.
In southern MO, east of Springfield. Incorporated 1886. Not coextensive with the town of the same name. Part of the town is also in Texas County.
Name origin: For its descriptive connotations.

*Mountain Grove
Township
ZIP: 65711 **Lat:** 37-06-19 N **Long:** 92-19-39 W
Pop: 5,698 (1990); 5,343 (1980) **Pop Density:** 105.3
Land: 54.1 sq. mi.; **Water:** 0.1 sq. mi.

Norwood
City
ZIP: 65717 **Lat:** 37-06-24 N **Long:** 92-25-00 W
Pop: 449 (1990); 391 (1980) **Pop Density:** 408.2
Land: 1.1 sq. mi.; **Water:** 0.0 sq. mi. **Elev:** 1496 ft.
Incorporated 1882.

Pleasant Valley
Township
Lat: 37-06-30 N **Long:** 92-36-07 W
Pop: 2,702 (1990); 2,530 (1980) **Pop Density:** 49.7
Land: 54.4 sq. mi.; **Water:** 0.1 sq. mi.

Union
Township
Lat: 37-24-56 N **Long:** 92-36-37 W
Pop: 1,045 (1990); 970 (1980) **Pop Density:** 12.8
Land: 81.4 sq. mi.; **Water:** 0.0 sq. mi.

Van Buren
Township
Lat: 37-18-04 N **Long:** 92-19-57 W
Pop: 550 (1990); 515 (1980) **Pop Density:** 10.1
Land: 54.5 sq. mi.; **Water:** 0.1 sq. mi.

Wood
Township
Lat: 37-12-07 N **Long:** 92-19-43 W
Pop: 1,265 (1990); 1,280 (1980) **Pop Density:** 19.3
Land: 65.6 sq. mi.; **Water:** 0.0 sq. mi.

MISSOURI

Index to Places and Counties in Missouri

Adair (Camden) Township 654
Adair County 639
Adams (DeKalb) Township 674
Adams (Harrison) Township 684
Adrian (Bates) City 646
Advance (Stoddard) City 757
Affton (St. Louis) CDP 745
Agency (Buchanan) Town 650
Agency (Buchanan) Township 650
Airport (St. Louis) Township 745
Airport Drive (Jasper) Village 693
Alba (Jasper) City 693
Albany (Gentry) City 680
Aldrich (Polk) Village 733
Alexander (Benton) Township 647
Alexandria (Clark) City 664
Allen (Worth) Township 768
Allendale (Worth) Town 768
Allenville (Cape Girardeau) Village .. 655
Alma (Lafayette) City 700
Alpine (Stone) Township 758
Altamont (Daviess) Town 673
Altenburg (Perry) City 727
Alton (Oregon) City 723
Amazonia (Andrew) Town 640
Amity (DeKalb) Town 674
Amoret (Bates) City 646
Amsterdam (Bates) City 646
Anderson (McDonald) City 711
Anderson (New Madrid) Township .. 718
Anderson East (McDonald)
  Township 711
Anderson West (McDonald)
  Township 711
Andrew County 640
Annada (Pike) Town 730
Annapolis (Iron) City 691
Anniston (Mississippi) Town 714
Apple Creek (Cape Girardeau)
  Township 655
Appleton (St. Clair) Township 742
Appleton City (St. Clair) City 742
Arbela (Scotland) Town 753
Arbyrd (Dunklin) City 677
Arcadia (Iron) City 691
Arcadia (Iron) Township 691
Archie (Cass) City 658
Arcola (Dade) Village 671
Argyle (Maries) Town 709
Argyle (Osage) Town 724
Arkoe (Nodaway) Town 721
Arlington (Phelps) Township 729
Armstrong (Howard) City 689
Arnold (Jefferson) City 695
Arrow Rock (Saline) Town 751
Arrow Rock (Saline) Township 751
Asbury (Jasper) City 693
Ash (Barry) Township 643
Ashburn (Pike) Town 730
Ash Grove (Greene) City 681
Ash Hill (Butler) Township 651
Ashland (Boone) City 649
Ashley (Pike) Township 730
Atchison (Clinton) Township 667
Atchison (Nodaway) Township 721
Atchison County 641
Athens (Gentry) Township 680
Atlanta (Macon) City 707
Audrain County 642
Auglaize (Camden) Township 654

Auglaize (Laclede) Township 699
Augusta (St. Charles) City 741
Aullville (Lafayette) Village 700
Aurora (Lawrence) City 701
Aurora (Lawrence) Township 701
Austin (Cass) Township 658
Auxvasse (Callaway) City 653
Auxvasse (Callaway) Township 653
Ava (Douglas) City 676
Avilla (Jasper) Town 693
Avondale (Clay) City 665
Bacon (Vernon) Township 762
Badger (Vernon) Township 762
Bagnell (Miller) Town 713
Baker (Linn) Township 704
Baker (Stoddard) Village 757
Bakersfield (Ozark) Village 725
Baldwin Park (Cass) Village 658
Ballwin (St. Louis) City 745
Baring (Knox) City 698
Barnard (Nodaway) City 721
Barnett (Morgan) City 717
Barnhart (Jefferson) CDP 695
Barren Fork (Ozark) Township 725
Barry County 643
Bartlett (Shannon) Township 755
Barton City (Barton) Township 644
Barton County 644
Bates City (Lafayette) Village 700
Bates County 646
Battlefield (Greene) Town 681
Bayou (Ozark) Township 725
Bear Creek (Henry) Township 685
Bear Creek (Montgomery) Township 716
Beauvais (Ste. Genevieve) Township 743
Beaver (Taney) Township 760
Beaver Dam (Butler) Township 651
Bedford (Lincoln) Township 703
Bee Branch (Chariton) Township ... 661
Bee Ridge (Knox) Township 698
Belgrade (Washington) Township ... 765
Bella Villa (St. Louis) City 746
Bell City (Stoddard) City 757
Belle (Maries) City 709
Belle (Osage) City 724
Bellefontaine Neighbors (St. Louis)
  City 746
Bellerive (St. Louis) Village 746
Belleview (Washington) Township .. 765
Bellflower (Montgomery) City 716
Bel-Nor (St. Louis) Village 746
Bel-Ridge (St. Louis) Village 746
Belton (Cass) City 658
Benton (Adair) Township 639
Benton (Andrew) Township 640
Benton (Atchison) Township 641
Benton (Cedar) Township 660
Benton (Crawford) Township 670
Benton (Daviess) Township 673
Benton (Douglas) Township 676
Benton (Holt) Township 688
Benton (Howell) Township 690
Benton (Knox) Township 698
Benton (Linn) Township 704
Benton (Newton) Township 719
Benton (Osage) Township 724
Benton (Scott) City 754
Benton (Wayne) Township 766
Benton City (Audrain) Town 642
Benton County 647

Berger (Franklin) City 678
Berkeley (St. Louis) City 746
Bernie (Stoddard) City 757
Bertrand (Mississippi) City 714
Berwick (Newton) Township 719
Bethany (Harrison) City 684
Bethany (Harrison) Township 684
Bethel (Shelby) Town 756
Bethel (Shelby) Township 756
Bethlehem (Henry) Township 685
Beverly Hills (St. Louis) City 746
Bevier (Macon) City 707
Bevier (Macon) Township 707
Big Apple (Oregon) Township 723
Big Creek (Cass) Township 659
Big Creek (Henry) Township 685
Big Creek (Madison) Township 708
Big Creek (Ozark) Township 725
Big Creek (Taney) Township 760
Bigelow (Holt) Township 688
Bigelow (Holt) Village 688
Big Lake (Holt) Village 688
Big Prairie (New Madrid) Township 718
Big River (Jefferson) Township 695
Big River (St. Francois) Township .. 744
Billings (Christian) City 662
Billmore (Oregon) Township 723
Birch Tree (Shannon) City 755
Birch Tree (Shannon) Township 755
Birmingham (Clay) Village 665
Bismarck (St. Francois) City 744
Blackburn (Lafayette) City 700
Blackburn (Saline) City 751
Black Creek (Shelby) Township 756
Black Jack (St. Louis) City 746
Black Pond (Oregon) Township 723
Black River (Butler) Township 651
Black River (Reynolds) Township .. 739
Black River (Wayne) Township 766
Blackwater (Cooper) City 669
Blackwater (Cooper) Township 669
Blackwater (Pettis) Township 728
Blackwater (Saline) Township 751
Blairstown (Henry) City 685
Blanchette (St. Charles) Township .. 741
Bland (Gasconade) City 679
Bland (Osage) City 724
Blodgett (Scott) Town 754
Bloomfield (Stoddard) City 757
Bloomington (Buchanan) Township .. 650
Bloomsdale (Ste. Genevieve) City .. 743
Blue (Jackson) Township 691
Blue Eye (Stone) Town 758
Blue Mound (Livingston) Township 705
Blue Mound (Vernon) Township ... 762
Blue Springs (Jackson) City 691
Blythedale (Harrison) Village 684
Boeuf (Franklin) Township 678
Boeuf (Gasconade) Township 679
Bogard (Carroll) City 656
Bogard (Henry) Township 685
Bogle (Gentry) Township 680
Bois Brule (Perry) Township 727
Bolckow (Andrew) Town 640
Boles (Franklin) Township 678
Bolivar (Polk) City 733
Bollinger County 648
Bonhomme (St. Louis) Township .. 746
Bonne Femme (Howard) Township .. 689
Bonne Terre (St. Francois) City 744

770

Boone (Crawford) Township 670	Buffalo (Newton) Township 719	Carterville (Jasper) City 693
Boone (Douglas) Township 676	Buffalo (Pike) Township 730	Carthage (Jasper) City 693
Boone (Franklin) Township................678	Buffalo Hart (McDonald) Township.711	Caruthersville (Pemiscot) City 726
Boone (Maries) Township 709	Buffalo May (McDonald) Township.711	Carytown (Jasper) City......................693
Boone (St. Charles) Township 741	Bunceton (Cooper) City.....................669	Cass (Douglas) Township 676
Boone (Texas) Township 761	Bunker (Dent) City 675	Cass (Greene) Township....................681
Boone (Wright) Township 768	Bunker (Reynolds) City 739	Cass (Stone) Township 758
Boone County 649	Burdine (Texas) Township.................761	Cass (Texas) Township 761
Boone No. 1 (Greene) Township 681	Burgess (Barton) Town 644	**Cass County** 658
Boone No. 2 (Greene) Township 681	Burlington Junction (Nodaway) City 721	Cassidy (Christian) Township 662
Boons Lick (Howard) Township 689	Burris Fork (Moniteau) Township 715	Cassville (Barry) City 643
Boonville (Cooper) City 669	Burr Oak (Lincoln) Township 703	Castle Point (St. Louis) CDP 746
Boonville (Cooper) Township............669	Burton (Howard) Township 689	Castor (Madison) Township 708
Bosworth (Carroll) City 656	Butler (Bates) City 646	Castor (Stoddard) Township 757
Boulware (Gasconade) Township......679	Butler (Harrison) Township 684	Catron (New Madrid) Town..............718
Bourbois (Gasconade) Township.......679	Butler (Pemiscot) Township 726	Cave (Lincoln) Town 703
Bourbon (Boone) Township 649	Butler (St. Clair) Township 742	Cedar (Boone) Township...................649
Bourbon (Callaway) Township 653	**Butler County** 651	Cedar (Callaway) Township 653
Bourbon (Crawford) City 670	Butterfield (Barry) Township 643	Cedar (Cedar) Township 660
Bourbon (Knox) Township................698	Butterfield (Barry) Village 643	Cedar (Dade) Township 671
Bowlan (Shannon) Township.............755	Byrd (Cape Girardeau) Township......655	Cedar (Pettis) Township 728
Bowling Green (Chariton) Township 661	Byrnes Mill (Jefferson) City..............695	Cedar Bluff (Oregon) Township 723
Bowling Green (Pettis) Township 728	Cabool (Texas) City 761	**Cedar County** 660
Bowling Green (Pike) City 730	Cainsville (Harrison) City 684	Cedar Creek (Taney) Township.........760
Bowman (Sullivan) Township 759	Cairo (Randolph) Township...............737	Cedar Creek (Wayne) Township........766
Box (Cedar) Township.......................660	Cairo (Randolph) Village 737	Cedar Hill (Jefferson) CDP 695
Braggadocio (Pemiscot) Township 726	Caldwell (Callaway) Township 653	Cedar Hill Lakes (Jefferson) Village .695
Bragg City (Pemiscot) Town 726	**Caldwell County** 652	Center (Buchanan) Township............650
Brandsville (Howell) City..................690	Caledonia (Washington) Village........765	Center (Dade) Township 671
Branson (Taney) City 760	Calhoun (Henry) City........................685	Center (Hickory) Township 687
Branson (Taney) Township................760	California (Moniteau) City................715	Center (Knox) Township 698
Brashear (Adair) City 639	Callao (Macon) City 707	Center (McDonald) Township............711
Braymer (Caldwell) City 652	Callao (Macon) Township 707	Center (Ralls) City 736
Brazeau (Perry) Township 727	**Callaway County** 653	Center (Ralls) Township 736
Breckenridge (Caldwell) City............652	Calumet (Pike) Township...................730	Center (St. Clair) Township 742
Breckenridge (Caldwell) Township....652	Calverton Park (St. Louis) Village 746	Center (Vernon) Township 762
Breckenridge Hills (St. Louis) Village 746	Calvey (Franklin) Township 678	Center No. 1 (Greene) Township......681
Brentwood (St. Louis) City 746	Calwood (Callaway) Township..........653	Center No. 2 (Greene) Township......681
Breton (Washington) Township..........765	Cambridge (Saline) Township 751	Center No. 3 (Greene) Township......681
Bridgeport (Warren) Township..........764	Camden (DeKalb) Township..............674	Centertown (Cole) Town 668
Bridges (Ozark) Township 725	Camden (Ray) City 738	Centerview (Johnson) Town 696
Bridgeton (St. Louis) City 746	Camden (Ray) Township 738	Centerview (Johnson) Township 696
Brimson (Grundy) Village 683	**Camden County** 654	Centerville (Reynolds) City 739
Bronaugh (Vernon) Town 762	Camden Point (Platte) City................731	Central (Barton) Township................644
Brookfield (Linn) City 704	Camdenton (Camden) City 654	Central (Franklin) Township 678
Brookfield (Linn) Township 704	Cameron (Clinton) City......................667	Central (Jefferson) Township 695
Brooking (Jackson) Township 692	Cameron (DeKalb) City 674	Central (Madison) Township..............708
Brookline (Greene) Township 681	Campbell (Douglas) Township 676	Central (Perry) Township 727
Brookline (Greene) Village 681	Campbell (Dunklin) City 677	Centralia (Audrain) City 642
Brooklyn Heights (Jasper) Village.....693	Campbell (Polk) Township 733	Centralia (Boone) City.......................649
Brown (Douglas) Township 676	Campbell No. 1 (Greene) Township .681	Centralia (Boone) Township..............649
Browning (Linn) City 704	Campbell No. 2 (Greene) Township .681	Chadwick (Christian) Township........663
Browning (Sullivan) City...................759	Camp Branch (Cass) Township..........659	Chaffee (Scott) City 754
Brownington (Henry) Town 685	Camp Branch (Warren) Township 764	Chain-O-Lakes (Barry) Village 643
Brumley (Miller) Town 713	Canaan (Gasconade) Township..........679	Chalk Level (St. Clair) Township......742
Bruner (Christian) Township.............662	Canalou (New Madrid) City 718	Chamois (Osage) City........................724
Brunswick (Chariton) City 661	Cane Creek (Butler) Township 651	Champ (St. Louis) Village 746
Brunswick (Chariton) Township 661	Canton (Lewis) City 702	Champion (Douglas) Township..........676
Brush Creek (Douglas) Township......676	Canton (Lewis) Township..................702	Chapel (Howell) Township................690
Brush Creek (Gasconade) Township.679	Cape Girardeau (Cape Girardeau) City........................... 655	Chariton (Chariton) Township 661
Brush Creek (Wright) Township 768	Cape Girardeau (Cape Girardeau) Township......................... 655	Chariton (Howard) Township 689
Bryan (Douglas) Township 676	**Cape Girardeau County**................655	Chariton (Macon) Township 707
Buchanan (Atchison) Township 641	Capps Creek (Barry) Township 643	Chariton (Randolph) Township 737
Buchanan (Douglas) Township..........676	Cardwell (Dunklin) City....................677	Chariton (Schuyler) Township...........752
Buchanan (Sullivan) Township 759	Carl Junction (Jasper) City 693	**Chariton County** 661
Buchanan County 650	Carroll (Platte) Township 731	Charlack (St. Louis) City...................746
Buckeye (Shannon) Township 755	Carroll (Reynolds) Township 739	Charleston (Mississippi) City 714
Bucklin (Linn) City............................705	Carroll (Texas) Township 761	Charlotte (Bates) Township 646
Bucklin (Linn) Township...................705	**Carroll County** 656	Charrette (Warren) Township............764
Buckner (Jackson) City......................692	Carrollton (Carroll) City 656	Cherry Valley (Carroll) Township 657
Buck Prairie (Lawrence) Township...701	Carrollton (Carroll) Township 657	Chesterfield (St. Louis) City..............746
Buffalo (Dallas) City..........................672	Carter (Carter) Township 658	Chilhowee (Johnson) Town 697
Buffalo (Dunklin) Township..............677	**Carter County** 658	Chilhowee (Johnson) Township.........697
Buffalo (Morgan) Township 717		Chillicothe (Livingston) City.............705
		Chillicothe (Livingston) Township....706

MISSOURI

Chouteau (Clay) Township................665
Christian County................662
Chula (Livingston) City................706
Cinque Hommes (Perry) Township..727
City (Barton) Township................644
Clarence (Shelby) City................756
Clark (Atchison) Township................641
Clark (Chariton) Township................661
Clark (Cole) Township................668
Clark (Lincoln) Township................703
Clark (Randolph) City................737
Clark (Wright) Township................768
Clark County................664
Clark Fork (Cooper) Township................669
Clarksburg (Moniteau) City................715
Clarksdale (DeKalb) City................674
Clarkson Valley (St. Louis) City................746
Clarksville (Pike) City................730
Clarkton (Dunklin) City................677
Clay (Adair) Township................639
Clay (Andrew) Township................640
Clay (Atchison) Township................641
Clay (Clark) Township................664
Clay (Douglas) Township................676
Clay (Dunklin) Township................677
Clay (Gasconade) Township................679
Clay (Greene) Township................681
Clay (Harrison) Township................684
Clay (Holt) Township................688
Clay (Lafayette) Township................700
Clay (Linn) Township................705
Clay (Monroe) Township................715
Clay (Ralls) Township................736
Clay (Saline) Township................751
Clay (Shelby) Township................756
Clay (Sullivan) Township................759
Claycomo (Clay) Village................665
Clay County................665
Clayton (St. Louis) City................746
Clayton (St. Louis) Township................746
Clear Creek (Cooper) Township................669
Clear Creek (Vernon) Township................762
Clearmont (Nodaway) City................721
Cleveland (Callaway) Township................653
Cleveland (Cass) Town................659
Clever (Christian) City................663
Cliff Village (Newton) Village................719
Clifton (Randolph) Township................737
Clifton Hill (Randolph) City................737
Climax Springs (Camden) Village................654
Clinton (Clinton) Township................667
Clinton (Douglas) Township................676
Clinton (Henry) City................685
Clinton (Henry) Township................685
Clinton (Texas) Township................761
Clinton County................667
Cliquot (Polk) Township................733
Clyde (Nodaway) Village................721
Coal (Vernon) Township................762
Cobalt City (Madison) Village................708
Cockrell (Chariton) Township................661
Coffey (Daviess) Town................673
Cold Spring (Phelps) Township................729
Coldwater (Cass) Township................659
Cole (Benton) Township................647
Cole Camp (Benton) City................647
Cole County................668
Colfax (Atchison) Township................641
Colfax (Daviess) Township................673
Colfax (DeKalb) Township................674
Colfax (Harrison) Township................684
Collins (St. Clair) Township................743
Collins (St. Clair) Village................742
Colony (Knox) Township................698
Columbia (Boone) City................649

Columbia (Boone) Township................649
Columbus (Johnson) Township................697
Combs (Carroll) Township................657
Commerce (Scott) Town................754
Commerce (Scott) Township................754
Como (New Madrid) Township................718
Conception Junction (Nodaway) Town................721
Concord (Clinton) Township................667
Concord (Pemiscot) Township................726
Concord (St. Louis) CDP................746
Concord (St. Louis) Township................747
Concord (Washington) Township................765
Concordia (Lafayette) City................700
Conway (Laclede) City................699
Cool Valley (St. Louis) City................747
Coon Island (Butler) Township................651
Cooper (Gentry) Township................680
Cooper County................669
Cooter (Pemiscot) Town................726
Cooter (Pemiscot) Township................726
Corder (Lafayette) City................700
Corning (Holt) Town................688
Corsicana (Barry) Township................643
Cosby (Andrew) Town................640
Cote Sans Dessein (Callaway) Township................653
Cottleville (St. Charles) Town................741
Cottleville (St. Charles) Township................741
Cotton Hill (Dunklin) Township................677
Couch (Oregon) Township................723
Country Club (Andrew) Village................640
Country Club Hills (St. Louis) City..747
Country Life Acres (St. Louis) Village................747
Courtois (Crawford) Township................670
Cowan (Wayne) Township................766
Cowgill (Caldwell) City................652
Craig (Holt) City................688
Crane (Stone) City................758
Crane Creek (Barry) Township................643
Crawford (Buchanan) Township................650
Crawford (Osage) Township................724
Crawford County................670
Cream Ridge (Livingston) Township 706
Creighton (Cass) City................659
Crestwood (St. Louis) City................747
Creve Coeur (St. Louis) City................747
Creve Coeur (St. Louis) Township................747
Crocker (Pulaski) City................734
Crooked Creek (Bollinger) Township648
Crooked River (Ray) Township................738
Cross Timbers (Hickory) City................687
Cross Timbers (Hickory) Township................687
Crystal City (Jefferson) City................695
Crystal Lake Park (St. Louis) City....747
Crystal Lakes (Ray) Village................738
Cuba (Crawford) City................670
Cuivre (Audrain) Township................642
Cuivre (Pike) Township................730
Cullen (Pulaski) Township................734
Cunningham (Chariton) Township..661
Current (Dent) Township................675
Current (Texas) Township................761
Current River (Ripley) Township................740
Curryville (Pike) City................730
Cypress (Harrison) Township................684
Dade County................671
Dadeville (Dade) Village................671
Dale (Atchison) Township................641
Dallas (DeKalb) Township................674
Dallas (Harrison) Township................684
Dallas (St. Clair) Township................743
Dallas County................672
Dalton (Chariton) Town................661

Danville (Montgomery) Township....716
Dardenne (St. Charles) Township.....741
Dardenne Prairie (St. Charles) Town741
Darlington (Gentry) Town................680
Date (Texas) Township................761
Daviess County................673
Davis (Caldwell) Township................652
Davis (Henry) Township................685
Davis (Lafayette) Township................700
Dawson (Phelps) Township................729
Dawt (Ozark) Township................725
Dayton (Cass) Township................659
Dayton (Newton) Township................719
Dearborn (Buchanan) Township................650
Dearborn (Platte) City................731
Deepwater (Bates) Township................646
Deepwater (Henry) City................685
Deepwater (Henry) Township................686
Deer Creek (Bates) Township................646
Deer Creek (Henry) Township................686
Deerfield (Vernon) Township................762
Deerfield (Vernon) Village................762
De Kalb (Buchanan) Town................650
DeKalb County................674
Delaware (Shannon) Township................755
Dellwood (St. Louis) City................747
Delta (Cape Girardeau) City................655
Dennis Acres (Newton) Village................720
Dent (Iron) Township................691
Dent County................675
Denver (Worth) Village................768
Des Arc (Iron) Village................691
Desloge (St. Francois) City................744
Des Moines (Clark) Township................664
De Soto (Jefferson) City................695
Des Peres (St. Louis) City................747
De Witt (Carroll) City................657
De Witt (Carroll) Township................657
Dexter (Stoddard) City................757
Diamond (Newton) Town................720
Dickerson (Lewis) Township................702
Diehlstadt (Scott) Town................754
Diggins (Webster) Village................767
Dillon (Phelps) Township................729
Dixon (Pulaski) City................734
Dolan (Cass) Township................659
Doniphan (Ripley) City................740
Doniphan (Ripley) Township................740
Doolittle (Phelps) City................729
Douglas County................676
Dover (Lafayette) Town................700
Dover (Lafayette) Township................700
Dover (Vernon) Township................762
Downing (Schuyler) City................752
Doyal (St. Clair) Township................743
Doylesport (Barton) Township................644
Drake (Macon) Township................707
Dresden (Pettis) Township................728
Drexel (Bates) City................646
Drexel (Cass) City................659
Dry Creek (Howell) Township................690
Dry Creek (Maries) Township................709
Drywood (Vernon) Township................762
Duck Creek (Stoddard) Township.....757
Dudley (Stoddard) City................757
Duenweg (Jasper) City................693
Duncan (Sullivan) Township................759
Dunklin County................677
Duquesne (Jasper) Village................694
Duval (Jasper) Township................694
Eagle (Macon) Township................707
Eagleville (Harrison) Town................684
Easley (Macon) Township................707
East Benton (Christian) Township....663
East Benton (Webster) Township......767

East Boone (Bates) Township............646	Fairview (Caldwell) Township............652	Friedens (St. Charles) Township........741
East Dallas (Webster) Township........767	Fairview (Henry) Township...............686	Fristoe (Benton) Township................647
East Finley (Christian) Township.....663	Fairview (Livingston) Township........706	Frohna (Perry) City............................727
East Fulton (Callaway) Township.....653	Fairview (Newton) Town...................720	Frontenac (St. Louis) City.................747
East Looney (Polk) Township............733	Falling Spring (Oregon) Township....723	Frontier (St. Charles) Township.......741
East Lynne (Cass) Town.....................659	Farber (Audrain) City........................642	Fulton (Callaway) City......................653
East Madison (Polk) Township.........733	Farley (Platte) Village.......................731	Gainesville (Ozark) City....................725
Easton (Buchanan) City....................650	Farmington (St. Francois) City.........744	Galena (Jasper) Township.................694
East Polk (Christian) Township........663	Fayette (Howard) City.......................689	Galena (Stone) City..........................758
East Prairie (Mississippi) City..........714	Fenton (St. Louis) City......................747	Gallatin (Clay) Township..................665
East Republic (Greene) Township....681	Ferguson (St. Louis) City..................747	Gallatin (Daviess) City......................673
Edgar Springs (Phelps) City..............729	Ferguson (St. Louis) Township.........747	Galt (Grundy) City............................683
Edgerton (Platte) City.......................731	Ferrelview (Platte) Village................731	Garden City (Cass) City....................659
Edina (Knox) City.............................698	Festus (Jefferson) City......................695	Garden Grove (Christian) Township 663
Edmundson (St. Louis) Village.........747	Fidelity (Jasper) Town......................694	Garrison (Christian) Township.........663
Egypt (Carroll) Township.................657	Fields Creek (Henry) Township........686	Gasconade (Gasconade) City............679
Eldon (Miller) City............................713	Fillmore (Andrew) City.....................640	Gasconade (Laclede) Township........699
El Dorado Springs (Cedar) City........660	Fillmore (Bollinger) Township..........648	Gasconade (Wright) Township.........769
Eldridge (Laclede) Township............699	Findley (Douglas) Township.............676	**Gasconade County**............................679
Elk (Stoddard) Township..................757	Finley (Webster) Township...............767	Gatewood (Ripley) Township............740
Elk Creek (Wright) Township...........768	Fishing River (Clay) Township.........665	Gentry (Gentry) Village....................680
Elk Fork (Pettis) Township................728	Fishing River (Ray) Township..........738	**Gentry County**..................................680
Elkhart (Bates) Township.................646	Fisk (Butler) Town............................651	Gerald (Franklin) City.......................678
Elk Horn (McDonald) Township......711	Five Mile (Newton) Township..........720	Gerster (St. Clair) Town....................743
Elk River East (McDonald)	Flat Creek (Barry) Township............643	Gibbs (Adair) Town..........................639
Township....................................711	Flat Creek (Pettis) Township............728	Gideon (New Madrid) City...............718
Elk River West (McDonald)	Flat Creek A (Stone) Township........758	Gilliam (Saline) Town.......................751
Township....................................711	Flat Creek B (Stone) Township........758	Gillis Bluff (Butler) Township...........651
Ellington (Reynolds) City..................739	Flat River (St. Francois) City...........744	Gilman City (Daviess) City...............673
Ellisville (St. Louis) City...................747	Flatwoods (Ripley) Township...........740	Gilman City (Harrison) City.............684
Ellsinore (Carter) Town....................658	Fleming (Ray) City...........................738	Gladden (Dent) Township................675
Elm (Putnam) Township..................735	Flemington (Polk) Township............733	Gladstone (Clay) City.......................665
Elmer (Macon) City..........................707	Flemington (Polk) Village.................733	Glasgow (Chariton) City...................661
Elmira (Ray) Village.........................738	Fletchall (Worth) Township..............768	Glasgow (Howard) City....................689
Elmo (Nodaway) City.......................721	Flint Hill (St. Charles) Village..........741	Glasgow Village (St. Louis) CDP......747
Elmwood (Saline) Township.............751	Flordell Hills (St. Louis) City............747	Glaze (Miller) Township...................713
Elsberry (Lincoln) City.....................703	Florida (Monroe) Village...................715	Glenaire (Clay) Village.....................665
Elvins (St. Francois) City..................744	Florissant (St. Louis) City.................747	Glenallen (Bollinger) Town...............648
Emerald Beach (Barry) Village.........643	Florissant (St. Louis) Township........747	Glendale (St. Louis) City...................748
Eminence (Shannon) City.................755	Foley (Lincoln) City..........................703	Glen Echo Park (St. Louis) Village...748
Eminence (Shannon) Township........755	Folker (Clark) Township...................664	Glenwood (Schuyler) Township........753
Emma (Lafayette) City.....................700	Forbes (Holt) Township....................688	Glenwood (Schuyler) Village............752
Emma (Saline) City..........................751	Ford City (Gentry) Town..................680	Godair (Pemiscot) Township............726
Empire (Andrew) Township..............640	Fordland (Webster) City...................767	Goebel (Oregon) Township..............723
Enterprise (Linn) Township..............705	Forest (Holt) Township.....................688	Golden City (Barton) City................645
Eolia (Pike) Village...........................730	Forest City (Holt) City......................688	Golden City (Barton) Township.......645
Epps (Butler) Township....................651	Foristell (St. Charles) City................741	Goldsberry (Howell) Township.........690
Equality (Miller) Township...............713	Foristell (Warren) City......................764	Gomer (Caldwell) Township.............652
Erie Goodman (McDonald)	Forsyth (Taney) City.........................760	Goodman (McDonald) Town...........711
Township....................................711	Fortescue (Holt) Town......................688	Gordonville (Cape Girardeau) Town 656
Erie McNatt (McDonald) Township.711	Fort Leonard Wood (Pulaski) Military	Gower (Buchanan) City....................650
Ernest (Dade) Township...................671	Facility......................................734	Gower (Clinton) City........................667
Essex (Stoddard) City.......................757	Fort Osage (Jackson) Township........692	Graham (Nodaway) Town................721
Esther (St. Francois) City.................744	Foster (Bates) Town..........................646	Grain Valley (Jackson) City..............692
Ethel (Macon) Town.........................707	Fox (Platte) Township......................731	Granby (Newton) City......................720
Eugene (Carroll) Township...............657	Fox Creek (Harrison) Township.......684	Granby (Newton) Township.............720
Eugene (Cole) Town..........................668	Frankford (Pike) City.......................730	Grandin (Carter) City.......................658
Eureka (St. Louis) City.....................747	Franklin (Dent) Township................675	Grand Pass (Saline) Town.................751
Everett (Cass) Township...................659	Franklin (Grundy) Township............683	Grand Pass (Saline) Township..........751
Everton (Dade) City..........................671	Franklin (Howard) City....................689	Grand River (Bates) Township.........646
Ewing (Lewis) City............................702	Franklin (Howard) Township...........689	Grand River (Cass) Township..........659
Excelsior Estates (Clay) Village........665	Franklin (Laclede) Township............699	Grand River (Daviess) Township.....673
Excelsior Estates (Ray) Village.........738	Franklin (Miller) Township..............713	Grand River (DeKalb) Township.....674
Excelsior Springs (Clay) City............665	Franklin (Newton) Township...........720	Grand River (Livingston) Township.706
Excelsior Springs (Ray) City.............738	**Franklin County**................................678	Grandview (Jackson) City................692
Exeter (Barry) City...........................643	Franklin No. 1 (Greene) Township...681	Granger (Scotland) Town.................753
Exeter (Barry) Township..................643	Franklin No. 2 (Greene) Township...681	Grant (Caldwell) Township..............652
Fabius (Knox) Township..................698	Fredericktown (Madison) City..........708	Grant (Clark) Township...................664
Fabius (Marion) Township...............710	Freeborn (Dunklin) Township..........677	Grant (Dade) Township....................671
Fabius (Schuyler) Township.............752	Freeburg (Osage) Village..................724	Grant (Dallas) Township..................672
Fair (Platte) Township......................731	Freedom (Lafayette) Township.........700	Grant (DeKalb) Township................674
Fairfax (Atchison) City.....................641	Freeman (Cass) City.........................659	Grant (Harrison) Township..............684
Fairfield (Carroll) Township.............657	Freistatt (Lawrence) Town................701	Grant (Nodaway) Township.............721
Fair Grove (Greene) City..................681	Freistatt (Lawrence) Township.........701	Grant (Putnam) Township................735
Fair Play (Polk) City.........................733	Fremont Hills (Christian) City..........663	Grant (Stone) Township...................758

MISSOURI

Grant (Webster) Township 767
Grant City (Worth) City 768
Grantsville (Linn) Township 705
Grantwood Village (St. Louis) Town 748
Grape Grove (Ray) Township 738
Gravois (St. Louis) Township 748
Gravois Mills (Morgan) Village 717
Gray Summit (Franklin) CDP 678
Green (Hickory) Township 687
Green (Lawrence) Township 701
Green (Livingston) Township 706
Green (Nodaway) Township 721
Green (Platte) Township 731
Greencastle (Sullivan) City 759
Green City (Sullivan) City 759
Greendale (St. Louis) City 748
Greene (Worth) Township 768
Greene County 681
Greenfield (Dade) City 671
Green Ridge (Pettis) Town 728
Green Ridge (Pettis) Township 728
Greensburg (Knox) Township 698
Greentop (Adair) Village 639
Greentop (Schuyler) Village 753
Greenville (Wayne) City 766
Greenwood (Jackson) City 692
Grover (Johnson) Township 697
Grundy County 683
Guilford (Nodaway) Town 721
Gunn City (Cass) Village 659
Guthrie (Callaway) Township 653
Hadley (St. Louis) Township 748
Hale (Carroll) City 657
Halfway (Polk) Village 733
Hallsville (Boone) City 649
Halltown (Lawrence) Town 701
Hamilton (Caldwell) City 652
Hamilton (Caldwell) Township 652
Hamilton (Harrison) Township 684
Hanley Hills (St. Louis) Village 748
Hannibal (Marion) City 710
Hannibal (Ralls) City 736
Hardin (Clinton) Township 667
Hardin (Ray) City 738
Harmony (Washington) Township 765
Harris (Ripley) Township 740
Harris (Sullivan) Town 759
Harrisburg (Boone) Town 649
Harrison (Daviess) Township 673
Harrison (Grundy) Township 683
Harrison (Mercer) Township 712
Harrison (Moniteau) Township 715
Harrison (Scotland) Township 753
Harrison (Vernon) Township 762
Harrison County 684
Harrisonville (Cass) City 659
Hart (Wright) Township 769
Hartford (Pike) Township 730
Hartsburg (Boone) Town 649
Hartville (Wright) City 769
Hartwell (Henry) Village 686
Harvester (St. Charles) Township 741
Harwood (Vernon) Town 763
Haw Creek (Morgan) Township 717
Hawk Point (Lincoln) City 703
Hawk Point (Lincoln) Township 703
Hayti (Pemiscot) City 726
Hayti (Pemiscot) Township 726
Hayti Heights (Pemiscot) City 726
Hayward (Pemiscot) Town 726
Hay-Wood City (Scott) Village 754
Hazel Hill (Johnson) Township 697
Hazelwood (St. Louis) City 748
Hazelwood (Webster) Township 767
Heaths Creek (Pettis) Township 728

Henrietta (Ray) City 738
Henry (Vernon) Township 763
Henry County 685
Herculaneum (Jefferson) City 695
Hermann (Gasconade) City 679
Hermitage (Hickory) City 687
Hickory (Holt) Township 688
Hickory County 687
Hickory Grove (Warren) Township .. 764
Higbee (Randolph) City 737
Higginsville (Lafayette) City 700
High Hill (Montgomery) City 716
Highland (Lewis) Township 702
Highland (Oregon) Township 723
High Prairie (Webster) Township 767
High Ridge (Jefferson) Township 695
Hill (Carroll) Township 657
Hillsboro (Jefferson) City 696
Hillsdale (St. Louis) Village 748
Hoberg (Lawrence) Township 701
Hoberg (Lawrence) Village 701
Holcomb (Dunklin) City 677
Holcomb (Dunklin) Township 677
Holden (Johnson) City 697
Holland (Pemiscot) Town 726
Holland (Pemiscot) Township 726
Holliday (Monroe) Village 716
Hollister (Taney) City 760
Holt (Clay) City 665
Holt (Clinton) City 667
Holt County 688
Holts Summit (Callaway) City 653
Homer (Bates) Township 646
Homestead (Ray) Village 738
Homestown (Pemiscot) City 726
Honey Creek (Henry) Township 686
Hooker (Laclede) Township 699
Hopkins (Nodaway) City 722
Hopkins (Nodaway) Township 722
Horine (Jefferson) CDP 696
Hornersville (Dunklin) City 677
Hough (New Madrid) Township 718
Houston (Texas) City 761
Houstonia (Pettis) City 728
Houstonia (Pettis) Township 728
Houston Lake (Platte) City 731
Howard (Bates) Township 646
Howard (Gentry) Township 680
Howard County 689
Howardville (New Madrid) City 718
Howell (Howell) Township 690
Howell County 690
Hubble (Cape Girardeau) Township . 656
Hudson (Bates) Township 646
Hudson (Macon) Township 707
Huggins (Gentry) Township 680
Hughes (Nodaway) Township 722
Hughesville (Pettis) Township 728
Hughesville (Pettis) Village 728
Humansville (Polk) City 733
Hume (Bates) Town 646
Humphreys (Sullivan) Town 759
Hunnewell (Shelby) City 756
Huntleigh (St. Louis) City 748
Huntsville (Randolph) City 737
Hurdland (Knox) City 698
Hurley (Stone) City 758
Hurley (Stone) Township 758
Hurricane (Carroll) Township 657
Hurricane (Lincoln) Township 703
Hutton Valley (Howell) Township 690
Iatan (Platte) Village 731
Iberia (Miller) City 713
Imperial (Jefferson) CDP 696
Imperial (Jefferson) Township 696

American Places Dictionary

Independence (Clay) City 665
Independence (Dunklin) Township ... 677
Independence (Jackson) City 692
Independence (Macon) Township 707
Independence (Nodaway) Township . 722
Independence (Schuyler) Township .. 753
Index (Cass) Township 659
Indian (Pike) Township 730
Indian Creek (Monroe) Township 716
Indian Point (Stone) Village 758
Ionia (Benton) Town 648
Ionia (Pettis) Town 728
Iron (Iron) Township 691
Iron (St. Francois) Township 744
Iron County 691
Irondale (Washington) City 765
Iron Gates (Jasper) Village 694
Iron Mountain Lake (St. Francois)
  City 745
Ironton (Iron) City 691
Jackson (Andrew) Township 640
Jackson (Buchanan) Township 650
Jackson (Callaway) Township 653
Jackson (Camden) Township 654
Jackson (Cape Girardeau) City 656
Jackson (Carter) Township 658
Jackson (Clark) Township 664
Jackson (Clinton) Township 667
Jackson (Dallas) Township 672
Jackson (Daviess) Township 673
Jackson (Douglas) Township 676
Jackson (Gentry) Township 680
Jackson (Grundy) Township 683
Jackson (Jasper) Township 694
Jackson (Johnson) Township 697
Jackson (Linn) Township 705
Jackson (Livingston) Township 706
Jackson (Macon) Township 707
Jackson (Maries) Township 709
Jackson (Monroe) Township 716
Jackson (Nodaway) Township 722
Jackson (Osage) Township 724
Jackson (Ozark) Township 725
Jackson (Polk) Township 733
Jackson (Putnam) Township 735
Jackson (Randolph) Township 737
Jackson (Reynolds) Township 739
Jackson (Shannon) Township 755
Jackson (Shelby) Township 756
Jackson (St. Clair) Township 743
Jackson (Ste. Genevieve) Township .. 744
Jackson (Sullivan) Township 759
Jackson (Texas) Township 761
Jackson (Webster) Township 767
Jackson County 691
Jackson No. 1 (Greene) Township 681
Jackson No. 2 (Greene) Township 681
Jacksonville (Randolph) Village 737
James Bayou (Mississippi)
  Township 714
Jameson (Daviess) Town 673
Jamesport (Daviess) City 673
Jamesport (Daviess) Township 673
Jamestown (Moniteau) Town 715
Jasper (Camden) Township 654
Jasper (Dallas) Township 672
Jasper (Jasper) City 694
Jasper (Jasper) Township 694
Jasper (Ozark) Township 725
Jasper (Ralls) Township 736
Jasper (Taney) Township 760
Jasper County 693
Jeddo (Knox) Township 698
Jeff (Oregon) Township 723
Jefferson (Andrew) Township 640

Jefferson (Cedar) Township............661	Kingsville (Johnson) Township.........697	Lentner (Shelby) Township...............756
Jefferson (Clark) Township..............664	Kinloch (St. Louis) City....................748	Leonard (Shelby) Town.....................756
Jefferson (Cole) Township................668	Kirksville (Adair) City......................639	Leroy (Barton) Township..................645
Jefferson (Daviess) Township...........673	Kirkwood (St. Louis) City.................748	Le Sieur (New Madrid) Township....718
Jefferson (Grundy) Township...........683	Knob Noster (Johnson) City.............697	Leslie (Carroll) Township.................657
Jefferson (Harrison) Township.........684	Knobview (Crawford) Township.......670	Leslie (Franklin) Village...................678
Jefferson (Johnson) Township..........697	Knox City (Knox) City......................698	Lesterville (Reynolds) Township.......739
Jefferson (Linn) Township................705	**Knox County**..................................698	Levasy (Jackson) City.......................692
Jefferson (Maries) Township............709	Knoxville (Ray) Township................738	Lewis (Holt) Township......................688
Jefferson (Monroe) Township..........716	Koshkonong (Oregon) Town............723	Lewis (New Madrid) Township........718
Jefferson (Nodaway) Township........722	La Belle (Lewis) City.......................703	Lewis and Clark (St. Louis)
Jefferson (Osage) Township.............724	La Belle (Lewis) Township...............703	Township..748
Jefferson (Polk) Township................733	Laclede (Linn) City...........................705	Lewis and Clark Village (Buchanan)
Jefferson (Scotland) Township.........753	**Laclede County**.............................699	Town...650
Jefferson (Shelby) Township............756	Laddonia (Audrain) City...................642	**Lewis County**................................702
Jefferson (St. Louis) Township.........748	La Due (Henry) Village....................686	Lewistown (Lewis) Town..................703
Jefferson (Wayne) Township............766	Ladue (St. Louis) City.......................748	Lexington (Lafayette) City...............700
Jefferson City (Callaway) City..........653	Lafayette (Clinton) Township...........667	Lexington (Lafayette) Township........700
Jefferson City (Cole) City.................668	**Lafayette County**..........................700	Liberal (Barton) City........................645
Jefferson County...........................695	La Font (New Madrid) Township.....718	Liberty (Adair) Township.................639
Jenkins (Barry) Township.................643	La Grange (Lewis) City....................703	Liberty (Barry) Township.................643
Jennings (St. Louis) City...................748	Lake (Buchanan) Township..............650	Liberty (Bollinger) Township............648
Jerico Springs (Cedar) Village..........661	Lake (Vernon) Township..................763	Liberty (Callaway) Township............654
Jim Henry (Miller) Township...........713	Lake Annette (Cass) Village.............659	Liberty (Cape Girardeau) Township.656
Joachim (Jefferson) Township..........696	Lake Creek (Pettis) Township..........728	Liberty (Clay) City............................666
Jobe (Oregon) Township..................723	Lakeland (Miller) Town....................713	Liberty (Clay) Township...................666
Johnson (Carter) Township..............658	Lake Lotawana (Jackson) City..........692	Liberty (Cole) Township...................668
Johnson (Maries) Township.............709	Lake Mykee Town (Callaway)	Liberty (Crawford) Township...........670
Johnson (Oregon) Township............723	Village..653	Liberty (Daviess) Township..............673
Johnson (Polk) Township.................733	Lake Ozark (Camden) City...............654	Liberty (Grundy) Township..............683
Johnson (Ripley) Township..............740	Lake Ozark (Miller) City...................713	Liberty (Holt) Township...................688
Johnson (Scotland) Township...........753	Lakeshire (St. Louis) City.................748	Liberty (Iron) Township...................691
Johnson (Washington) Township.....765	Lakeside (Miller) City.......................713	Liberty (Knox) Township.................698
Johnson County............................696	Lake St. Louis (St. Charles) City......741	Liberty (Macon) Township...............707
Johnston (Macon) Township............707	Lake Tapawingo (Jackson) City........692	Liberty (Madison) Township............708
Jonesburg (Montgomery) City.........717	Lakeview (Miller) Village.................713	Liberty (Marion) Township..............710
Joplin (Jasper) City...........................694	Lakeview (Stone) City......................758	Liberty (Phelps) Township...............729
Joplin (Jasper) Township..................694	Lake Waukomis (Platte) City...........732	Liberty (Pulaski) Township..............734
Joplin (Newton) City........................720	Lake Winnebago (Cass) City............659	Liberty (Putnam) Township.............735
Jordan (Hickory) Township.............687	Lamar (Barton) City.........................645	Liberty (Saline) Township................752
Jordan (Ripley) Township................740	Lamar (Barton) Township................645	Liberty (Schuyler) Township............753
Josephville (St. Charles) Village........741	Lamar Heights (Barton) Village........645	Liberty (St. Francois) Township.......745
Junction City (Madison) Village.......708	Lambert (Scott) Village....................754	Liberty (Stoddard) Township...........757
Kahoka (Clark) City.........................664	Lamine (Cooper) Township..............669	Liberty (Sullivan) Township.............759
Kansas City (Cass) City....................659	La Monte (Pettis) City......................728	Liberty (Washington) Township.......765
Kansas City (Clay) City....................665	La Monte (Pettis) Township.............728	Lick Creek (Ozark) Township..........725
Kansas City (Jackson) City...............692	Lanagan (McDonald) Town..............711	Licking (Texas) City.........................761
Kansas City (Platte) City..................732	Lancaster (Schuyler) City..................753	Lilbourn (New Madrid) City............718
Kaolin (Iron) Township....................691	The Landing (Ralls) Village..............736	Lincoln (Andrew) Township............640
Kaw (Jackson) Township..................692	La Plata (Macon) City......................707	Lincoln (Atchison) Township..........641
Kearney (Clay) City..........................666	La Plata (Macon) Township.............707	Lincoln (Benton) City......................648
Kearney (Clay) Township.................666	Laredo (Grundy) City.......................683	Lincoln (Caldwell) Township...........652
Kelley (Ripley) Township.................740	La Russell (Jasper) City....................694	Lincoln (Christian) Township..........663
Kelly (Carter) Township...................658	Lathrop (Clinton) City.....................667	Lincoln (Clark) Township................664
Kelly (Cooper) Township.................669	Lathrop (Clinton) Township............667	Lincoln (Dallas) Township...............672
Kelso (Scott) Town..........................754	La Tour (Johnson) Town..................697	Lincoln (Daviess) Township.............673
Kelso (Scott) Township...................754	Laurie (Morgan) Village...................717	Lincoln (Douglas) Township............676
Kennett (Dunklin) City....................677	**Lawrence County**.........................701	Lincoln (Grundy) Township............683
Keytesville (Chariton) City...............661	Lawson (Clay) City...........................666	Lincoln (Harrison) Township..........684
Keytesville (Chariton) Township......662	Lawson (Ray) City............................738	Lincoln (Holt) Township..................688
Kickapoo (Platte) Township.............732	Lead Hill (Christian) Township........663	Lincoln (Jasper) Township...............694
Kidder (Caldwell) City.....................652	Leadington (St. Francois) City.........745	Lincoln (Lawrence) Township..........701
Kidder (Caldwell) Township............652	Leadwood (St. Francois) City...........745	Lincoln (Nodaway) Township..........722
Kiheka (Camden) Township............654	Leasburg (Crawford) Village.............670	Lincoln (Putnam) Township............735
Kimberling City (Stone) City...........758	Leawood (Newton) Village...............720	Lincoln (Stone) Township................758
Kimmswick (Jefferson) City.............696	Lebanon (Cooper) Township............669	**Lincoln County**.............................703
Kinder (Cape Girardeau) Township.656	Lebanon (Laclede) City....................699	Linden (Christian) Township...........663
King (Oregon) Township.................723	Lebanon (Laclede) Township...........699	Lindenwood (St. Charles) Township.741
King City (Gentry) City...................680	Lee (Platte) Township......................732	Lindley (Mercer) Township..............712
Kingdom City (Callaway) Village.....653	Lee's Summit (Cass) City..................659	Lindsey (Benton) Township.............648
Kings Prairie (Barry) Township........643	Lee's Summit (Jackson) City............692	Lingo (Macon) Township.................707
Kingston (Caldwell) City..................652	Leesville (Henry) Township.............686	Linn (Audrain) Township.................642
Kingston (Caldwell) Township.........652	Leeton (Johnson) City.......................697	Linn (Cedar) Township....................661
Kingston (Washington) Township....765	Lemay (St. Louis) CDP.....................748	Linn (Dent) Township......................675
Kingsville (Johnson) City..................697	Lemay (St. Louis) Township............748	Linn (Moniteau) Township...............715

MISSOURI

Linn (Osage) City 724
Linn (Osage) Township 724
Linn County 704
Linn Creek (Camden) Town 654
Linneus (Linn) City 705
Lithium (Perry) Village 727
Little Prairie (Pemiscot) Township ... 726
Little River (Pemiscot) Township 726
Livingston County 705
Livonia (Putnam) Village 735
Lock Springs (Daviess) Town 673
Lockwood (Dade) City 671
Lockwood (Dade) Township 671
Locust Creek (Linn) Township 705
Logan (Reynolds) Township 739
Logan (Wayne) Township 766
Lohman (Cole) Town 668
Lone Jack (Jackson) Village 692
Lone Oak (Bates) Township 646
Long Prairie (Mississippi) Township 714
Longrun (Ozark) Township 725
Longtown (Perry) Town 727
Longwood (Pettis) Township 728
Lorance (Bollinger) Township 648
Lost Creek (Wayne) Township 766
Louisburg (Dallas) Village 672
Louisiana (Pike) City 731
Loutre (Audrain) Township 642
Loutre (Montgomery) Township 717
Lowry City (St. Clair) City 743
Lucerne (Putnam) Village 735
Ludlow (Livingston) Town 706
Lupus (Moniteau) Town 715
Luray (Clark) Town 664
Lyda (Macon) Township 707
Lynch (Texas) Township 761
Lyon (Franklin) Township 678
Lyon (Knox) Township 698
Lyon (Lewis) Township 703
Mac Kenzie (St. Louis) Village 748
Macks Creek (Camden) City 655
Macon (Macon) City 708
Macon County 707
Madison (Cedar) Township 661
Madison (Clark) Township 664
Madison (Grundy) Township 683
Madison (Harrison) Township 684
Madison (Jasper) Township 694
Madison (Johnson) Township 697
Madison (Mercer) Township 712
Madison (Monroe) City 716
Madison County 708
Maitland (Holt) City 688
Malden (Dunklin) City 677
Malta Bend (Saline) Town 752
Manchester (St. Louis) City 748
Mansfield (Wright) City 769
Maplewood (St. Louis) City 748
Marble Hill (Bollinger) City 648
Marceline (Chariton) City 662
Marceline (Linn) City 705
Marceline (Linn) Township 705
Maries County 709
Marion (Buchanan) Township 650
Marion (Cole) Township 668
Marion (Dade) Township 671
Marion (Daviess) Township 673
Marion (Grundy) Township 683
Marion (Harrison) Township 684
Marion (Jasper) Township 694
Marion (Mercer) Township 712
Marion (Monroe) Township 716
Marion (Newton) Township 720
Marion (St. Francois) Township 745
Marion County 710

Marionville (Lawrence) City 701
Marlborough (St. Louis) Village 749
Marquand (Madison) City 709
Marquand (Madison) Township 709
Marshall (Platte) Township 732
Marshall (Saline) City 752
Marshall (Saline) Township 752
Marshfield (Webster) City 767
Marston (New Madrid) City 718
Marthasville (Warren) City 764
Martinsburg (Audrain) Town 642
Maryland Heights (St. Louis) City 749
Maryville (Nodaway) City 722
Mason (Marion) Township 710
Matthews (New Madrid) City 719
May (Platte) Township 732
Mayfield (Laclede) Township 699
Maysville (DeKalb) City 674
Mayview (Lafayette) City 700
McCracken (Christian) Township 663
McCredie (Callaway) Township 654
McDonald (Barry) Township 643
McDonald (Jasper) Township 694
McDonald County 711
McDowell (Barry) Township 643
McFall (Gentry) City 680
McKinley (Douglas) Township 676
McKinley (Polk) Township 733
McKinley (Stone) Township 758
McKittrick (Montgomery) Town 717
McMillen Coy (McDonald) Township 711
McMillen Tiff (McDonald) Township 711
McMurtrey (Douglas) Township 676
Meadville (Linn) City 705
Medicine (Livingston) Township 706
Medicine (Mercer) Township 712
Medicine (Putnam) Township 735
Mehlville (St. Louis) CDP 749
Memphis (Scotland) City 753
Mendon (Chariton) City 662
Mendon (Chariton) Township 662
Meramec (Crawford) Township 670
Meramec (Dent) Township 675
Meramec (Franklin) Township 678
Meramec (Jefferson) Township 696
Meramec (Phelps) Township 729
Meramec (St. Louis) Township 749
Mercer (Mercer) Town 712
Mercer County 712
Merriam Woods (Taney) Village 760
Merwin (Bates) Town 646
Meta (Osage) City 724
Metz (Vernon) Town 763
Metz (Vernon) Township 763
Mexico (Audrain) City 642
Miami (Saline) City 752
Miami (Saline) Township 752
Middle Fork (Macon) Township 708
Middlefork (Worth) Township 768
Middleton (Lafayette) Township 700
Middletown (Montgomery) Town 717
Midland (St. Louis) Township 749
Milan (Sullivan) City 759
Milford (Barton) Township 645
Milford (Barton) Village 645
Millard (Adair) Village 639
Mill Creek (Morgan) Township 717
Miller (Dallas) Township 672
Miller (Douglas) Township 676
Miller (Gentry) Township 680
Miller (Lawrence) City 701
Miller (Maries) Township 709
Miller (Marion) Township 710

Miller (Phelps) Township 729
Miller (Scotland) Township 753
Miller County 713
Mill Spring (Wayne) Township 766
Mill Spring (Wayne) Village 766
Millwood (Lincoln) Township 703
Milo (Vernon) Town 763
Mindenmines (Barton) City 645
Mine La Motte (Madison) Township 709
Miner (Scott) City 754
Mineral (Barry) Township 643
Mineral (Jasper) Township 694
Mineral Point (Washington) Town 765
Mingo (Bates) Township 646
Minton (Holt) Township 688
Mirabile (Caldwell) Township 652
Mississippi (Mississippi) Township .. 714
Mississippi County 714
Missouri (Boone) Township 649
Missouri City (Clay) City 666
Missouri River (St. Louis) Township 749
Moberly (Randolph) City 737
Mokane (Callaway) City 654
Moline Acres (St. Louis) City 749
Monegaw (St. Clair) Township 743
Monett (Barry) City 643
Monett (Barry) Township 643
Monett (Lawrence) City 702
Moniteau (Howard) Township 689
Moniteau (Randolph) Township 737
Moniteau County 715
Monroe (Andrew) Township 640
Monroe (Daviess) Township 673
Monroe (Lincoln) Township 704
Monroe (Livingston) Township 706
Monroe (Monroe) Township 716
Monroe (Nodaway) Township 722
Monroe City (Marion) City 710
Monroe City (Monroe) City 716
Monroe City (Ralls) City 736
Monroe County 715
Montevallo (Vernon) Township 763
Montgomery (Hickory) Township 687
Montgomery (Montgomery) Township 717
Montgomery (Wright) Township 769
Montgomery City (Montgomery) City 717
Montgomery County 716
Monticello (Lewis) Town 703
Montier (Shannon) Township 755
Montrose (Henry) City 686
Montserrat (Johnson) Township 697
Mooney (Polk) Township 733
Moore (Oregon) Township 723
Moore (Shannon) Township 755
Mooresville (Livingston) Township .. 706
Mooresville (Livingston) Village 706
Moreau (Cole) Township 668
Moreau (Moniteau) Township 715
Moreau (Morgan) Township 717
Morehouse (New Madrid) City 719
Moreland (Scott) Township 754
Morgan (Mercer) Township 712
Morgan County 717
Morley (Scott) Town 754
Morley (Scott) Township 754
Morris (Sullivan) Township 760
Morris (Texas) Township 761
Morrison (Gasconade) City 679
Morrisville (Polk) Town 733
Morrow (Adair) Township 639
Morrow (Macon) Township 708
Mosby (Clay) City 666
Moscow Mills (Lincoln) City 704

Moss Creek (Carroll) Township 657	Nodaway (Holt) Township 688	Osage (Camden) Township................655
Mound (Bates) Township 646	Nodaway (Nodaway) Township 722	Osage (Cole) Township 668
Mound City (Holt) City 688	**Nodaway County** 721	Osage (Crawford) Township 670
Moundville (Vernon) Town 763	Nocl (McDonald) City 711	Osage (Dent) Township 675
Moundville (Vernon) Township 763	Norborne (Carroll) City 657	Osage (Henry) Township 686
Mountain (Barry) Township...............643	Norman (Dent) Township 675	Osage (Laclede) Township 699
Mountain (McDonald) Township 711	Normandy (St. Louis) City 749	Osage (Miller) Township 713
Mountain Grove (Texas) City 761	Normandy (St. Louis) Township........749	Osage (Morgan) Township 717
Mountain Grove (Wright) City 769	North (Dade) Township 671	Osage (St. Clair) Township 743
Mountain Grove (Wright) Township 769	North Benton (Dallas) Township 672	Osage (Vernon) Township 763
Mountain View (Howell) City 690	North Benton (Polk) Township...........733	Osage Beach (Camden) City 655
Mount Leonard (Saline) Town 752	North Campbell No. 1 (Greene)	Osage Beach (Miller) City 713
Mount Moriah (Harrison) Town 684	Township............................ 681	**Osage County** 724
Mount Pleasant (Bates) Township 647	North Campbell No. 2 (Greene)	Osborn (Clinton) City.........................667
Mount Pleasant (Cass) Township.....659	Township.............................682	Osborn (DeKalb) City 674
Mount Pleasant (Lawrence)	North Campbell No. 3 (Greene)	Osceola (Camden) Township 655
Township... 702	Township.............................682	Osceola (St. Clair) City 743
Mount Pleasant (Scotland)	Northeast Marion (Polk) Township ..733	Osceola (St. Clair) Township 743
Township.. 753	North Elkhorn (Warren) Township ...764	Osgood (Sullivan) Town 760
Mount Vernon (Lawrence) City 702	Northfork (Barton) Township 645	Otterville (Cooper) City 669
Mount Vernon (Lawrence)	North Galloway (Christian)	Otterville (Cooper) Township............669
Township.. 702	Township.. 663	Overland (St. Louis) City...................749
Murphy (Jefferson) CDP.....................696	North Green (Polk) Township 733	Owensville (Gasconade) City 679
Murray (Greene) Township................681	North Kansas City (Clay) City...........666	Ozark (Barry) Township 644
Musselfork (Chariton) Township 662	North Lilbourn (New Madrid)	Ozark (Barton) Township 645
Myatt (Howell) Township..................690	Village 719	Ozark (Christian) City........................663
Myers (Grundy) Township.................683	North Linn (Christian) Township 663	Ozark (Lawrence) Township..............702
Myrtle (Knox) Township 698	North Moniteau (Cooper) Township 669	Ozark (Oregon) Township 723
Myrtle (Oregon) Township 723	Northmoor (Platte) City.....................732	Ozark (Texas) Township 762
Napoleon (Lafayette) City..................700	North Morgan (Dade) Township........671	Ozark (Webster) Township 767
Narrows (Macon) Township...............708	North River (Shelby) Township 756	**Ozark County** 725
Nashville (Barton) Township.............645	North Salem (Linn) Township 705	Pacific (Franklin) City........................678
Naylor (Ripley) City...........................740	North Sugar Creek (Randolph)	Pacific (St. Louis) City 749
Neck City (Jasper) City 694	Township.. 737	Pagedale (St. Louis) City 749
Neely (Butler) Township....................651	North View (Christian) Township.....663	Palestine (Cooper) Township 669
Neelyville (Butler) City 651	North Wardell (Pemiscot) Village 726	Palmyra (Marion) City.......................710
Nelson (Saline) City............................752	Northwest (St. Louis) Township 749	Paris (Monroe) City............................716
Neosho (Newton) City 720	Northwest Marion (Polk) Township .733	Parkdale (Jefferson) Town 696
Neosho (Newton) Township 720	Northwoods (St. Louis) City 749	Parkville (Platte) City.........................732
Nevada (Vernon) City 763	Norwood (Wright) City 769	Parkway (Franklin) Village.................678
Newark (Knox) Town 698	Norwood Court (St. Louis) Town 749	Parma (New Madrid) City 719
New Bloomfield (Callaway) City 654	Nottinghill (Ozark) Township 725	Parnell (Nodaway) City 722
Newburg (Phelps) City 729	Novelty (Knox) Town 698	Parson Creek (Linn) Township 705
New Cambria (Macon) Town............708	Novinger (Adair) City 639	Pasadena Hills (St. Louis) Village 749
New Florence (Montgomery) City 717	Oak Grove (Franklin) City.................678	Pasadena Park (St. Louis) Village......749
New Franklin (Howard) City 689	Oak Grove (Jackson) City..................692	Pascola (Pemiscot) Town 726
New Hampton (Harrison) City 685	Oak Grove (Lafayette) City................700	Pascola (Pemiscot) Township 726
New Haven (Franklin) City................678	Oak Hill (Crawford) Township 670	Passaic (Bates) Town 647
New Haven (Franklin) Township.......678	Oakland (St. Louis) City 749	Pattonsburg (Daviess) City.................673
New Home (Bates) Township............647	Oakland Park (Jasper) Village 694	Pawhuska (Camden) Township..........655
New Lisbon (Stoddard) Township 757	Oak Ridge (Cape Girardeau) Town ..656	Pawnee (Platte) Township 732
New London (Ralls) City 736	Oaks (Clay) Village 666	Paynesville (Pike) Town 731
New Madrid (New Madrid) City 719	Oakview (Clay) Village......................666	Peculiar (Cass) City............................660
New Madrid (New Madrid)	Oakville (St. Louis) CDP 749	Peculiar (Cass) Township...................660
Township... 719	Oakwood (Clay) Village.....................666	Peerless Park (St. Louis) Village 749
New Madrid County.........................718	Oakwood Park (Clay) Village............666	Pemiscot (Pemiscot) Township 727
New Melle (St. Charles) Village 741	Odessa (Lafayette) City......................701	**Pemiscot County**..............................726
Newport (Barton) Township...............645	O'Fallon (St. Charles) City 741	Pendleton (St. Francois) Township ...745
Newton (Shannon) Township.............755	O'Fallon (St. Charles) Township.......741	Penermon (Stoddard) Village 757
Newton County................................719	Ohio (Mississippi) Township.............714	Penn (Sullivan) Township 760
Newtonia (Newton) Town 720	Old Appleton (Cape Girardeau)	Peno (Pike) Township........................731
Newtonia (Newton) Township 720	Town.. 656	Perche (Boone) Township..................649
Newtown (Sullivan) Town 760	Oldfield (Christian) Township...........663	Perry (Ralls) City................................736
New York (Caldwell) Township.........652	Old Monroe (Lincoln) City 704	Perry (St. Francois) Township...........745
Niangua (Camden) Township............655	Olean (Miller) Town 713	**Perry County** 727
Niangua (Webster) City......................767	Oliver (Taney) Township 760	Perryville (Perry) City........................727
Niangua (Webster) Township 767	Olivette (St. Louis) City 749	Pettis (Adair) Township.....................639
Nine Mile Prairie (Callaway)	Olympian Village (Jefferson) City....696	Pettis (Platte) Township.....................732
Township.. 654	Oran (Scott) City 754	**Pettis County** 728
Nineveh (Adair) Township.................639	**Oregon County** 723	Pevely (Jefferson) City 696
Nineveh (Lincoln) Township..............704	Oronogo (Jasper) City 694	Phelps City (Atchison) Town 641
Nishnabotna (Atchison) Township.....641	Orrick (Ray) City................................738	**Phelps County** 729
Nixa (Christian) City..........................663	Orrick (Ray) Township 739	Phillipsburg (Laclede) Town..............699
Noble (Ozark) Township 725	Osage (Bates) Township 647	Phillipsburg (Laclede) Township.......699
Nodaway (Andrew) Township............640		Pickering (Nodaway) Town 722

MISSOURI

Piedmont (Wayne) City 766
Pierce (Lawrence) Township 702
Pierce (Stone) Township 758
Pierce (Texas) Township 762
Pierce City (Lawrence) City 702
Pike (Carter) Township 658
Pike (Stoddard) Township 757
Pike County 730
Pilgrim (Dade) Township 671
Pilot Grove (Cooper) City 669
Pilot Grove (Cooper) Township 669
Pilot Grove (Moniteau) Township 715
Pilot Knob (Iron) City 691
Pinckney (Warren) Township 764
Pine (Ripley) Township 740
Pine A (Stone) Township 758
Pine B (Stone) Township 758
Pine Creek (Ozark) Township 725
Pine Lawn (St. Louis) City 749
Pineville (McDonald) Town 711
Pineville Lanagan (McDonald)
    Township 711
Pineville North (McDonald)
    Township 711
Pineville South (McDonald)
    Township 711
Piney (Oregon) Township 723
Piney (Pulaski) Township 734
Piney (Texas) Township 762
Pioneer (Barry) Township 644
Platte (Andrew) Township 640
Platte (Buchanan) Township 650
Platte (Clay) Township 666
Platte (Clinton) Township 667
Platte City (Platte) City 732
Platte County 731
Platte Woods (Platte) City 732
Plattin (Jefferson) Township 696
Plattsburg (Clinton) City 667
Pleasant Gap (Bates) Township 647
Pleasant Hill (Cass) City 660
Pleasant Hill (Cass) Township 660
Pleasant Hill (Sullivan) Township 760
Pleasant Hope (Polk) City 734
Pleasant Ridge (Barry) Township 644
Pleasant Valley (Clay) City 666
Pleasant Valley (Wright) Township 769
Pocahontas (Cape Girardeau) Town 656
Polk (Adair) Township 639
Polk (Atchison) Township 641
Polk (Cass) Township 660
Polk (Dade) Township 671
Polk (DeKalb) Township 674
Polk (Madison) Township 709
Polk (Nodaway) Township 722
Polk (Ray) Township 739
Polk (St. Clair) Township 743
Polk (Sullivan) Township 760
Polk County 733
Pollock (Sullivan) Village 760
Polo (Caldwell) City 652
Ponce de Leon (Stone) Township 758
Pond Creek (Greene) Township 682
Pontiac (Ozark) Township 725
Poplar Bluff (Butler) City 651
Poplar Bluff (Butler) Township 651
Portage (New Madrid) Township 719
Portage Des Sioux (St. Charles) City ... 741
Portageville (New Madrid) City 719
Portageville (Pemiscot) City 727
Post Oak (Johnson) Township 697
Potosi (Washington) City 765
Powersville (Putnam) Village 735
Poynor (Ripley) Township 740
Prairie (Audrain) Township 642

Prairie (Bates) Township 647
Prairie (Carroll) Township 657
Prairie (Franklin) Township 678
Prairie (Howard) Township 689
Prairie (Jackson) Township 692
Prairie (Lincoln) Township 704
Prairie (McDonald) Township 712
Prairie (Montgomery) Township 717
Prairie (Pettis) Township 728
Prairie (Randolph) Township 737
Prairie (Schuyler) Township 753
Prairie Home (Cooper) City 669
Prairie Home (Cooper) Township 669
Prairieville (Pike) Township 731
Prathersville (Clay) Village 666
Preston (Hickory) Town 687
Preston (Jasper) Township 694
Preston (Platte) Township 732
Princeton (Mercer) City 712
Pulaski County 734
Purcell (Jasper) City 694
Purdin (Linn) City 705
Purdy (Barry) City 644
Purdy (Barry) Township 644
Putnam County 735
Puxico (Stoddard) City 757
Queen City (Schuyler) City 753
Queeny (St. Louis) Township 749
Quitman (Nodaway) Town 722
Qulin (Butler) Town 651
Ralls County 736
Randol (Cape Girardeau) Township 656
Randolph (Clay) Village 666
Randolph (St. Francois) Township 745
Randolph County 737
Ravanna (Mercer) Township 712
Ravenwood (Nodaway) Town 722
Ray County 738
Raymondville (Texas) Town 762
Raymore (Cass) City 660
Raymore (Cass) Township 660
Raytown (Jackson) City 692
Rayville (Ray) Town 739
Rea (Andrew) Town 640
Reddish (Lewis) Township 703
Redings Mill (Newton) Village 720
Red Oak (Lawrence) Township 702
Reeds (Jasper) Town 694
Reeds Spring (Stone) City 758
Renick (Randolph) Village 737
Republic (Greene) City 682
Revere (Clark) Town 664
Reynolds County 739
Rhineland (Montgomery) Town 717
Richards (Vernon) Town 763
Rich Hill (Bates) City 647
Rich Hill (Livingston) Township 706
Richland (Barton) Township 645
Richland (Camden) City 655
Richland (Douglas) Township 676
Richland (Gasconade) Township 680
Richland (Laclede) City 699
Richland (Macon) Township 708
Richland (Morgan) Township 718
Richland (Ozark) Township 725
Richland (Pulaski) City 734
Richland (Putnam) Township 735
Richland (Scott) Township 754
Richland (Stoddard) Township 757
Richland (Vernon) Township 763
Richmond (Howard) Township 689
Richmond (Ray) City 739
Richmond (Ray) Township 739
Richmond Heights (St. Louis) City 750
Richwood (McDonald) Township 712

American Places Dictionary

Richwoods (Miller) Township 713
Richwoods (Washington) Township 765
Ridge (Carroll) Township 657
Ridgely (Platte) Town 732
Ridgeway (Harrison) City 685
Ripley County 740
Risco (New Madrid) City 719
Ritchey (Newton) Town 720
Rivermines (St. Francois) Village 745
Rivers (St. Charles) Township 741
Riverside (Christian) Township 663
Riverside (Platte) City 732
River View (Jefferson) Township 696
Riverview (St. Louis) Village 750
Roaring River (Barry) Township 644
Roark (Gasconade) Township 680
Robberson No. 1 (Greene)
    Township 682
Robberson No. 2 (Greene)
    Township 682
Rocheport (Boone) City 649
Rochester (Andrew) Township 640
Rock (Jefferson) Township 696
Rockaway Beach (Taney) Town 761
Rockford (Caldwell) Township 653
Rockford (Carroll) Township 657
Rock Hill (St. Louis) City 750
Rock Port (Atchison) City 641
Rock Prairie (Dade) Township 671
Rockville (Bates) City 647
Rockville (Bates) Township 647
Rocky Fork (Boone) Township 649
Rocky Ridge (Ste. Genevieve)
    Village 744
Rogersville (Greene) Town 682
Rogersville (Webster) Town 767
Rolla (Phelps) City 729
Rolla (Phelps) Township 730
Roscoe (St. Clair) Township 743
Roscoe (St. Clair) Village 743
Rosebud (Gasconade) City 680
Rosedale (Christian) Township 663
Rose Hill (Johnson) Township 697
Rosendale (Andrew) City 640
Rothville (Chariton) Village 662
Roubidoux (Pulaski) Township 734
Roubidoux (Texas) Township 762
Round Grove (Macon) Township 708
Round Grove (Marion) Township 710
Round Prairie (Callaway) Township 654
Rush (Buchanan) Township 650
Rush Hill (Audrain) Town 642
Rushville (Buchanan) Town 650
Russell (Camden) Township 655
Russell (Macon) Township 708
Russellville (Cole) City 668
Ruth A (Stone) Township 758
Ruth B (Stone) Township 759
Ruth B Rural (Stone) Township 759
Ruth C (Stone) Township 759
Ruth C Rural (Stone) Township 759
Rutledge (Scotland) Town 753
Sac (Dade) Township 671
Saginaw (Newton) Village 720
St. Ann (St. Louis) City 750
St. Aubert (Callaway) Township 654
St. Charles (St. Charles) City 742
St. Charles County 741
St. Clair (Franklin) City 678
St. Clair County 742
St. Cloud (Crawford) Village 670
Ste. Genevieve (Ste. Genevieve)
    City 744
Ste. Genevieve (Ste. Genevieve)
    Township 744

MISSOURI

Ste. Genevieve County 743
St. Elizabeth (Miller) Town 713
St. Ferdinand (St. Louis) Township .. 750
St. Francois (Butler) Township 651
St. Francois (Madison) Township 709
St. Francois (St. Francois) Township 745
St. Francois (Wayne) Township 766
St. Francois County 744
St. George (St. Louis) City 750
St. James (Mississippi) Township 714
St. James (Phelps) City 730
St. James (Phelps) Township 730
St. John (New Madrid) Township 719
St. John (St. Louis) City 750
St. Johns (Franklin) Township 678
St. Joseph (Buchanan) City 650
St. Louis County 745
St. Louis (Independent City) 745
St. Martins (Cole) City 668
St. Mary (Ste. Genevieve) City 744
St. Marys (Perry) Township 727
St. Michael (Madison) Township 709
St. Paul (St. Charles) Village 742
St. Peters (St. Charles) City 742
St. Peters (St. Charles) Township 742
St. Robert (Pulaski) City 734
St. Thomas (Cole) Town 668
Salem (Daviess) Township 674
Salem (Dent) City 675
Salem (Dunklin) Township 677
Salem (Lewis) Township 703
Salem (Perry) Township 727
Saline (Cooper) Township 669
Saline (Miller) Township 713
Saline (Perry) Township 728
Saline (Ralls) Township 736
Saline (Ste. Genevieve) Township 744
Saline County 751
Saling (Audrain) Township 642
Salisbury (Chariton) City 662
Salisbury (Chariton) Township 662
Salt Creek (Chariton) Township 662
Salt Fork (Saline) Township 752
Salt Pond (Saline) Township 752
Salt River (Adair) Township 639
Salt River (Audrain) Township 642
Salt River (Knox) Township 698
Salt River (Pike) Township 731
Salt River (Ralls) Township 736
Salt River (Randolph) Township 737
Salt River (Schuyler) Township 753
Salt River (Shelby) Township 756
Salt Springs (Randolph) Township 737
Sampsel (Livingston) Township 706
Sand Hill (Scotland) Township 753
Sandywoods (Scott) Township 755
Sappington (St. Louis) CDP 750
Sarcoxie (Jasper) City 694
Sarcoxie (Jasper) Township 694
Sargent (Texas) Township 762
Savannah (Andrew) City 640
Saverton (Ralls) Township 736
Schell City (Vernon) City 763
Schuyler County 752
Scopus (Bollinger) Township 648
Scotland County 753
Scotsdale (Jefferson) Town 696
Scott (Taney) Township 761
Scott City (Cape Girardeau) City 656
Scott City (Scott) City 755
Scott County 754
Sedalia (Pettis) City 729
Sedalia (Pettis) Township 729
Sedgewickville (Bollinger) Village 648
Seligman (Barry) City 644

Senath (Dunklin) City 677
Seneca (Christian) Township 663
Seneca (Newton) City 720
Seneca (Newton) Township 720
Seymour (Webster) City 767
Shamrock (Callaway) Township 654
Shannon County 755
Shawnee (Bates) Township 647
Shawnee (Cape Girardeau) Township 656
Shawnee (Henry) Township 686
Shelbina (Shelby) City 756
Shelby County 756
Shelbyville (Shelby) City 756
Sheldon (Vernon) City 763
Shell Knob (Barry) Township 644
Shelton (Knox) Township 698
Sheridan (Dallas) Township 672
Sheridan (Daviess) Township 674
Sheridan (Jasper) Township 695
Sheridan (Worth) Town 768
Sherman (Cass) Township 660
Sherman (Dallas) Township 672
Sherman (DeKalb) Township 674
Sherman (Harrison) Township 685
Sherman (Putnam) Township 735
Sherrill (Texas) Township 762
Shirley (Ripley) Township 740
Shoal (Clinton) Township 667
Shoal Creek (Newton) Township 720
Shoal Creek Drive (Newton) Village 720
Shoal Creek Estates (Newton) Town. 721
Short Bend (Dent) Township 675
Shrewsbury (St. Louis) City 750
Sibley (Jackson) Village 693
Sikeston (New Madrid) City 719
Sikeston (Scott) City 755
Silex (Lincoln) Village 704
Siloam Springs (Howell) Township 690
Silver Creek (Newton) Village 721
Silver Creek (Randolph) Township 737
Simpson (Johnson) Township 697
Sinking (Dent) Township 675
Sioux (Platte) Township 732
Sisson (Howell) Township 690
Skidmore (Nodaway) City 722
Slater (Saline) City 752
Smith (Dade) Township 671
Smith (Laclede) Township 699
Smith (Worth) Township 768
Smithton (Pettis) City 729
Smithton (Pettis) Township 729
Smithville (Clay) City 666
Sni-A-Bar (Jackson) Township 693
Sni-A-Bar (Lafayette) Township 701
Snow Hill (Lincoln) Township 704
Somerset (Mercer) Township 712
South (Dade) Township 671
South Benton (Dallas) Township 672
South Benton (Polk) Township 734
Southeast Marion (Polk) Township 734
South Elkhorn (Warren) Township 764
South Fork (Audrain) Township 642
South Fork (Howell) Township 690
South Fork (Monroe) Township 716
South Galloway (Christian) Township 663
South Gifford (Macon) Village 708
South Gorin (Scotland) Town 753
South Green (Polk) Township 734
South Greenfield (Dade) Village 671
South Lineville (Mercer) Town 712
South Linn (Christian) Township 663
South Moniteau (Cooper) Township. 669
South Morgan (Dade) Township 671

South River (Marion) Township 710
South Sugar Creek (Randolph) Township 737
South West (Barton) Township 645
South West City (McDonald) City 712
Southwest Marion (Polk) Township .. 734
Spanish Lake (St. Louis) CDP 750
Spanish Lake (St. Louis) Township .. 750
Sparta (Christian) City 663
Sparta (Christian) Township 663
Speedwell (St. Clair) Township 743
Spencer (Douglas) Township 676
Spencer (Pike) Township 731
Spencer (Ralls) Township 736
Spencer Creek (St. Charles) Township 742
Spickard (Grundy) City 683
Spring Creek (Dent) Township 675
Spring Creek (Douglas) Township 676
Spring Creek (Howell) Township 690
Spring Creek (Maries) Township 709
Spring Creek (Ozark) Township 725
Spring Creek (Phelps) Township 730
Spring Creek (Shannon) Township 755
Springfield (Christian) City 663
Springfield (Greene) City 682
Springfield (Henry) Township 686
Spring Hollow (Laclede) Township 699
Spring River (Lawrence) Township 702
Spring Valley (Shannon) Township 756
Spruce (Bates) Township 647
Stanberry (Gentry) City 680
Stark (Hickory) Township 687
Stark City (Newton) Town 721
Steele (Pemiscot) City 727
Steelville (Crawford) City 670
Stella (Newton) Town 721
Stewartsville (DeKalb) City 675
Stockton (Cedar) City 661
Stoddard County 757
Stokes Mound (Carroll) Township 657
Stone County 758
Stotesbury (Vernon) Town 763
Stotts City (Lawrence) City 702
Stoutland (Camden) Village 655
Stoutland (Laclede) Village 699
Stoutsville (Monroe) Village 716
Stover (Morgan) City 718
Strafford (Greene) City 682
Strasburg (Cass) Town 660
Sturgeon (Boone) City 649
Sugar Creek (Barry) Township 644
Sugar Creek (Clay) City 666
Sugar Creek (Harrison) Township 685
Sugar Creek (Jackson) City 693
Sugartree (Carroll) Township 657
Sullivan (Crawford) City 670
Sullivan (Franklin) City 678
Sullivan County 759
Summersville (Shannon) City 756
Summersville (Texas) City 762
Summit (Bates) Township 647
Summit (Callaway) Township 654
Sumner (Chariton) Town 662
Sundown (Ozark) Village 725
Sunrise Beach (Camden) Village 655
Sunrise Beach (Morgan) Village 718
Sunset Hills (St. Louis) City 750
Swan (Taney) Township 761
Sweet Home (Clark) Township 664
Sweet Springs (Saline) City 752
Sycamore Hills (St. Louis) Village 750
Sylvania (Scott) Township 755
Syracuse (Morgan) City 718
Taber (St. Clair) Township 743

MISSOURI

American Places Dictionary

Table Rock (Taney) Village *761*
Tallapoosa (New Madrid) City *719*
Taney County *760*
Taneyville (Taney) Village *761*
Taos (Cole) City *668*
Tarkio (Atchison) City *641*
Tarkio (Atchison) Township *641*
Tarrants (Pike) Village *731*
Tavern (Pulaski) Township *734*
Taylor (Greene) Township *682*
Taylor (Grundy) Township *683*
Taylor (Shelby) Township *757*
Taylor (Sullivan) Township *760*
Tebo (Henry) Township *686*
Templeton (Atchison) Township *641*
Ten Mile (Macon) Township *708*
Texas (Dent) Township *675*
Texas County *761*
Thayer (Oregon) City *723*
Thayer (Oregon) Township *723*
Theodosia (Ozark) Village *725*
Third Creek (Gasconade) Township .. *680*
Thomas (Ripley) Township *740*
Thomson (Scotland) Township *753*
Thornfield (Ozark) Township *725*
Tiger Fork (Shelby) Township *757*
Tightwad (Henry) Village *686*
Tina (Carroll) Town *657*
Tindall (Grundy) Town *683*
Tipton (Moniteau) City *715*
Tobin (Scotland) Township *753*
Tom (Benton) Township *648*
Town and Country (St. Louis) City .. *750*
Tracy (Platte) City *732*
Trail Creek (Harrison) Township *685*
Tremont (Buchanan) Township *650*
Trenton (Grundy) City *683*
Trenton (Grundy) Township *683*
Trimble (Clinton) Town *667*
Triplett (Chariton) City *662*
Triplett (Chariton) Township *662*
Trotter (Carroll) Township *657*
Troy (Lincoln) City *704*
Truesdale (Warren) City *764*
Truxton (Lincoln) Village *704*
Turnback (Lawrence) Township *702*
Turney (Clinton) Town *667*
Tuscumbia (Miller) Town *714*
Twelvemile (Madison) Township *709*
Twin Bridges (Laclede) Town *699*
Twin Groves (Jasper) Township *695*
Twin Oaks (St. Louis) Village *750*
Tyler (Hickory) Township *687*
Tywappity (Mississippi) Township *714*
Tywappity (Scott) Township *755*
Umber View Heights (Cedar) Village *661*
Union (Barton) Township *645*
Union (Benton) Township *648*
Union (Bollinger) Township *648*
Union (Cass) Township *660*
Union (Clark) Township *664*
Union (Crawford) Township *670*
Union (Daviess) Township *674*
Union (Dunklin) Township *677*
Union (Franklin) City *679*
Union (Franklin) Township *679*
Union (Harrison) Township *685*
Union (Holt) Township *689*
Union (Iron) Township *691*
Union (Jasper) Township *695*
Union (Laclede) Township *699*
Union (Lewis) Township *703*
Union (Lincoln) Township *704*
Union (Marion) Township *710*

Union (Monroe) Township *716*
Union (Nodaway) Township *722*
Union (Perry) Township *728*
Union (Polk) Township *734*
Union (Pulaski) Township *734*
Union (Putnam) Township *735*
Union (Randolph) Township *738*
Union (Ripley) Township *740*
Union (Scotland) Township *754*
Union (Ste. Genevieve) Township *744*
Union (Stone) Township *759*
Union (Sullivan) Township *760*
Union (Washington) Township *765*
Union (Webster) Township *767*
Union (Worth) Township *768*
Union (Wright) Township *769*
Union Chapel (Christian) Township .*664*
Union Star (DeKalb) Town *675*
Unionville (Putnam) City *735*
Unity Village (Jackson) Town *693*
University City (St. Louis) City *750*
Uplands Park (St. Louis) Village *750*
Upper Loutre (Montgomery) Township *717*
Upton (Texas) Township *762*
Urbana (Dallas) City *672*
Urich (Henry) City *686*
Utica (Livingston) Village *706*
Valle (Jefferson) Township *696*
Valley (Macon) Township *708*
Valley Park (St. Louis) City *750*
Van Buren (Carter) Town *658*
Van Buren (Jackson) Township *693*
Van Buren (Newton) Township *721*
Van Buren (Wright) Township *769*
Vandalia (Audrain) City *642*
Vandalia (Ralls) City *736*
Vandiver (Audrain) Village *642*
Vanduser (Scott) Village *755*
Van Horn (Carroll) Township *657*
Varner (Ripley) Township *740*
Velda Village (St. Louis) City *750*
Velda Village Hills (St. Louis) Village *750*
Vernon (Clark) Township *664*
Vernon County *762*
Verona (Lawrence) Town *702*
Versailles (Morgan) City *718*
Vest (Scotland) Township *754*
Viburnum (Iron) Town *691*
Vienna (Maries) City *709*
Village of Four Seasons (Camden) Town *655*
Villa Ridge (Franklin) CDP *679*
Vineyard (Lawrence) Township *702*
Vinita Park (St. Louis) City *750*
Vinita Terrace (St. Louis) Village *750*
Virgil (Vernon) Township *763*
Virginia (Pemiscot) Township *727*
Vista (St. Clair) Village *743*
Waco (Jasper) Town *695*
Wakenda (Carroll) Town *657*
Wakenda (Carroll) Township *657*
Waldron (Platte) Township *732*
Walker (Henry) Township *686*
Walker (Moniteau) Township *715*
Walker (Vernon) Town *763*
Walker (Vernon) Township *763*
Walls (Douglas) Township *676*
Walnut (Adair) Township *639*
Walnut (Bates) Township *647*
Walnut Creek (Macon) Township *708*
Walnut Grove (Greene) City *682*
Walnut Grove (Greene) Township ... *682*
Walton (Washington) Township *765*

Wardell (Pemiscot) Town *727*
Wardsville (Cole) Town *668*
Warren (Camden) Township *655*
Warren (Marion) Township *710*
Warren County *764*
Warrensburg (Johnson) City *697*
Warrensburg (Johnson) Township *697*
Warrenton (Warren) City *764*
Warsaw (Benton) City *648*
Warson Woods (St. Louis) City *751*
Washburn (Barry) City *644*
Washburn (Barry) Township *644*
Washington (Buchanan) Township ... *651*
Washington (Carroll) Township *657*
Washington (Cedar) Township *661*
Washington (Clark) Township *664*
Washington (Clay) Township *666*
Washington (Dade) Township *672*
Washington (Dallas) Township *672*
Washington (Daviess) Township *674*
Washington (DeKalb) Township *675*
Washington (Douglas) Township *676*
Washington (Franklin) City *679*
Washington (Franklin) Township *679*
Washington (Greene) Township *682*
Washington (Grundy) Township *683*
Washington (Harrison) Township *685*
Washington (Jackson) Township *693*
Washington (Johnson) Township *697*
Washington (Laclede) Township *699*
Washington (Lafayette) Township *701*
Washington (Mercer) Township *712*
Washington (Monroe) Township *716*
Washington (Nodaway) Township *722*
Washington (Osage) Township *724*
Washington (Pettis) Township *729*
Washington (Ripley) Township *740*
Washington (St. Clair) Township *743*
Washington (Stone) Township *759*
Washington (Vernon) Township *763*
Washington (Webster) Township *767*
Washington County *765*
Watkins (Dent) Township *675*
Watson (Atchison) Village *641*
Waverly (Lafayette) Town *701*
Waverly (Lincoln) Township *704*
Wayland (Chariton) Township *662*
Wayland (Clark) City *664*
Wayne (Bollinger) Township *648*
Wayne (Buchanan) Township *651*
Wayne County *766*
Waynesville (Pulaski) City *735*
Weatherby (DeKalb) Town *675*
Weatherby Lake (Platte) City *732*
Weaubleau (Hickory) City *687*
Weaubleau (Hickory) Township *687*
Webb (Reynolds) Township *739*
Webb City (Jasper) City *695*
Webster County *767*
Webster Groves (St. Louis) City *751*
Welch (Cape Girardeau) Township ... *656*
Weldon Spring (St. Charles) Town ... *742*
Weldon Spring Heights (St. Charles) Town *742*
Wellington (Lafayette) City *701*
Wellston (St. Louis) City *751*
Wellsville (Montgomery) City *717*
Wentworth (Newton) Village *721*
Wentzville (St. Charles) City *742*
Wentzville (St. Charles) Township *742*
West (New Madrid) Township *719*
West Benton (Christian) Township ... *664*
West Benton (Newton) Township *721*
West Benton (Webster) Township *767*
West Boone (Bates) Township *647*

American Places Dictionary   MISSOURI

Westboro (Atchison) Village............*641*	White Oak (Harrison) Township........*685*	Windsor (Jefferson) Township *696*
West Dallas (Webster) Township.......*767*	White Oak (Henry) Township...........*686*	Windsor (Pettis) City........................*729*
West Dolan (Cass) Township *660*	White River (Barry) Township..........*644*	Winfield (Lincoln) City *704*
West Doniphan (Ripley) Township...*740*	White Rock (McDonald) Township..*712*	Winona (Shannon) City....................*756*
West Finley (Christian) Township.....*664*	Whiteside (Lincoln) Village...............*704*	Winona (Shannon) Township...........*756*
West Fulton (Callaway) Township *654*	Whitewater (Bollinger) Township *649*	Winston (Daviess) Town *674*
West Line (Cass) Village....................*660*	Whitewater (Cape Girardeau) Town.*656*	Wishart (Polk) Township...................*734*
West Looney (Polk) Township *734*	Whitewater (Cape Girardeau)	Wolf Island (Mississippi) Township..*714*
West Madison (Polk) Township *734*	Township.. *656*	Wood (Douglas) Township *676*
Weston (Platte) City *732*	Wilbur Park (St. Louis) Village..........*751*	Wood (Wright) Township..................*769*
Weston (Platte) Township..................*732*	Willard (Greene) City........................*682*	Woodlawn (Monroe) Township.........*716*
West Peculiar (Cass) Township *660*	Williams (Benton) Township.............*648*	Woods Heights (Ray) City.................*739*
Westphalia (Osage) City *724*	Williams (Stone) Township *759*	Woodside (Oregon) Township *723*
West Plains (Howell) City *690*	Williams (Wayne) Township *766*	Woodson Terrace (St. Louis) City.....*751*
West Point (Bates) Township *647*	Williamsville (Wayne) City *766*	Wooldridge (Cooper) Town *669*
West Polk (Christian) Township *664*	Willow Fork (Moniteau) Township...*715*	Worth (Worth) Town *768*
West Republic (Greene) Township....*682*	Willow Springs (Howell) City *690*	**Worth County**....................................*768*
Westwood (St. Louis) Village *751*	Willow Springs (Howell) Township...*690*	Worthington (Putnam) Village *735*
Wheatland (Hickory) City.................*687*	Wilson (Adair) Township *639*	Wright City (Warren) City *764*
Wheatland (Hickory) Township *687*	Wilson (Audrain) Township *642*	**Wright County**...................................*768*
Wheaton (Barry) City *644*	Wilson (Dallas) Township *672*	Wyaconda (Clark) City......................*665*
Wheaton (Barry) Township *644*	Wilson (Gentry) Township *680*	Wyaconda (Clark) Township............*665*
Wheeling (Livingston) City *706*	Wilson (Greene) Township................*682*	Wyatt (Mississippi) City....................*714*
Wheeling (Livingston) Township *706*	Wilson (Grundy) Township...............*683*	Yellow Creek (Chariton) Township...*662*
White (Benton) Township *648*	Wilson (Putnam) Township...............*735*	Yellow Creek (Linn) Township..........*705*
White (Macon) Township..................*708*	Wilson City (Mississippi) Town........*714*	York (Putnam) Township *735*
White Cloud (Nodaway) Township...*722*	Winchester (St. Louis) City...............*751*	Zalma (Bollinger) Village *649*
Whiteman Air Force Base (Johnson)	Windsor (Henry) City........................*686*	Zumbehl (St. Charles) Township.......*742*
Military Facility............................. *697*	Windsor (Henry) Township...............*686*	

Ohio

OHIO

Ohio

Population: 10,847,115 (1990); 10,797,630 (1980)
Population rank (1990): 7
Percent population change (1980-1990): 0.5
Population projection: 11,027,000 (1995); 11,096,000 (2000)

Area: total 44,828 sq. mi.; 40,953 sq. mi. land, 3,875 sq. mi. water
Area rank: 34
Highest elevation: 1,550 ft., Campbell Hill (Logan County)
Lowest point: 433 ft. along the Ohio River (Hamilton County)

State capital: Columbus (Franklin County)
Largest city: Columbus (632,910)
Second largest city: Cleveland (505,616)
Largest county: Cuyahoga (1,412,140)

Total housing units: 4,371,945
No. of occupied housing units: 4,087,546
Vacant housing units (%): 6.5
Distribution of population by race and Hispanic origin (%):
  White: 87.8
  Black: 10.6
  Hispanic (any race): 1.3
  Native American: 0.2
  Asian/Pacific: 0.8
  Other: 0.5

Admission date: March 1, 1803 (17th state).

Location: In the east-central United States, bordering West Virginia, Kentucky, Indiana, Michigan, Lake Erie, and Pennsylvania.

Name Origin: For the Ohio River, which forms the southern boundary of the state and also marked the southern boundary of the Northwest Territory, from which Ohio was the first portion to achieve statehood. The name is either from Iroquoian *oheo* 'beautiful' or *ohion-hiio* 'beautiful river'; or possibly Wyandot *ohezuh* 'great; fair to look upon.'

State animal: white-tailed deer *(Odocoileus virginianus)*
State beverage: tomato juice
State bird: cardinal *(Cardinalis cardinalis)*
State flower: scarlet carnation *(Dianthus caryophyllus)*
State fossil: trilobite
State gemstone: Ohio flint
State insect: ladybird beetle (ladybug; *Hippodamia convergens*)
State song: "Beautiful Ohio"
State rock song: "Hang on Sloopy"

State tree: buckeye *(Aesculus glabra)*

State motto: With God All Things Are Possible
State nicknames: Buckeye State; Mother of Presidents; Gateway State

Area codes: 216 (Cleveland and northeast), 419 (Toledo and northwest), 513 (Cincinnati and southwest), 614 (Columbus and southeast)
Time zone: Eastern
Abbreviations: OH (postal); O. (traditional)
Part of (region): Great Lakes, Midwest

Local Government

Counties

Ohio has 88 counties. Each of them except for Summit County is governed by an elected board of commissioners. Summit County has elected to have home rule.

Municipalities

Ohio has 941 incorporated cities and villages, and 1,317 townships. When the population of a village reaches 5,000 it automatically becomes a city and must, by law, establish executive and legislative bodies.

Settlement History and Early Development

Ohio has been inhabited for about 11,000 years; first by the prehistoric ancestors of the Mound Builders, who left many burial mounds and forts in the Ohio area. The Adena and Hopewell Indians lived in Ohio from about 600 B.C. to about A.D. 500. When the first Europeans arrived in the region, they found Wyandot (Huron), Delaware, Ohio, Miami, and Shawnee Indians.

Robert Cavelier, Sieur de La Salle, was the first European to reach the area of present-day Ohio. Historians believe he discovered the Ohio River about 1670, but his first well-documented exploration was in 1679 when he sailed along the south shore of Lake Erie. He was followed in the early 1700s by French and British traders. Both countries claimed the area. The British claimed all territory inland from their Atlantic colonies, and the French claimed the entire Northwest based on La Salle's exploration. This dispute led to the French and Indian Wars (1754-1763), which the French lost, ceding to Britain most of the territory east of the Mississippi River.

The American Revolution

A Moravian mission settlement, established in 1772 by David Zeisberger near present-day New Philadelphia, was forced to close down in 1776 by fighting during the war. In 1780 George Rogers Clark and his band of Virginia frontiersmen, called "Big Knives," seized British posts and trading stations, and in the Battle of Piqua, near present-day Springfield, defeated Shawnee Indian allies of the British, thus helping secure the region for the U.S.

The Northwest Territory

All the newly acquired land between the Alleghenies and the Mississippi River became the Northwest Territory in 1787. The U.S. Congress enacted the Land Ordinance of 1785, which created a survey system of rectangular sections and townships to aid the development of the territory northwest of the Ohio River. In 1787 the Northwest Ordinance was enacted, providing a system of government under which new territories could become states on an equal basis with the original colonies.

Ohio's first permanent white settlement, Marietta, was established April 7, 1788, by an organization of Revolutionary War veterans who had been given land warrants in payment for their military service. Later that year a party from Lexington, Kentucky, founded Losantiville, now Cincinnati. Other settlers arrived and new towns were established, leading to conflict with the Indians, who wanted to protect their land. In 1794 General "Mad Anthony" Wayne defeated the Indians in the Battle of Fallen Timbers near present-day Toledo. The following year, in the Treaty of Greenville, the Indians ceded the southern half of what is now Ohio to the U.S. In 1800 Connecticut ceded to the U.S. a strip of land along Lake Erie, called the Western Reserve, which was added to the Northwest Territory.

Statehood and the War of 1812

The cessation of Indian raids, the fertile soil, mild climate, and abundant water all brought thousands of settlers from the East. By 1802 Ohio had enough population to seek statehood, and by November of that year had framed a constitution. On March 1, 1803, Ohio became the seventeenth state and the first to be carved out of the Northwest Territory. Trading thrived when the Louisiana Purchase in 1803 gave settlers access, via the Ohio River, to the Mississippi River and the port of New Orleans.

In 1811 Tecumseh, a powerful Shawnee chief, led tribal resistance (supported by the British) against white advances into the territory beyond Ohio's western border. General William Henry Harrison led Ohio militia regiments and repulsed an Indian invasion near Toledo in the Battle of Tippecanoe, November 7, 1811. During the War of 1812, Commodore Oliver Hazard Perry won a decisive victory over a British fleet on Lake Erie, which secured U.S. control of the lake and thus secured Great Lakes commerce.

At the end of the war in 1815, "Ohio fever" spread through New England. Thousands of settlers came from the East, and thousands of immigrants arrived from England, Ireland, and Germany. By 1850 Ohio was the third most populous state in the Union, and Cincinnati the sixth most populous city.

Ohio needed transportation routes to the East to ship its surplus production. The Ohio canal system, completed in 1841, linked the Ohio River and Lake Erie and provided a route to the Atlantic via the Erie Canal. It served as a busy trade route for more than 25 years, and the Great Lakes served as a waterway to the West, giving Ohio one of its nicknames, "The Gateway State." By 1860 railroads crisscrossed the state.

The Civil War

Northern Ohio was populated mainly by New Englanders who were anti-slavery. Southern Ohio, however, had close ties with Kentucky and Virginia and was opposed to President Lincoln's policies. Nevertheless, Ohio provided more than its quota and sent 320,000 men to the Union armies. The state was involved directly in the war only for two weeks in 1863 when Confederate General John Hunt Morgan brought Civil War fighting to its northernmost point, leading his Kentucky force on an ineffectual raid through the southern counties.

Generals Ulysses S. Grant, William Tecumseh Sherman, and Philip H. Sheridan were all Ohio men, as were Lincoln's Secretary of the Treasury, Salmon P. Chase, and his Secretary of War, Edwin M. Stanton.

Business and Industry

Until the Civil War, Ohio had been primarily an agricultural state, producing wheat, corn, pork, beef, salt, wool, and leather. The demands of the war, though, spurred the development of industry, and Ohio became a top manufacturing state. Shipping of coal, iron ore, and other bulk goods on Lake Erie increased. In 1870 Benjamin F. Goodrich began manufacturing rubber products in Akron. Later, Charles F. Kettering of Dayton developed a self-starter for automobiles, and the aluminum-refining process was discovered by Charles M. Hall of Oberlin. Cleveland became an important rail terminus and manufacturing center, producing iron, steel, heavy equipment, and automobile parts. Cleveland also became the headquarters of John D. Rockefeller's Standard Oil.

Seven U.S. presidents were born in Ohio, more than any other state except Virginia: Ulysses S. Grant, Rutherford B. Hayes, James A. Garfield, Benjamin Harrison, William McKinley, William Howard Taft, and Warren G. Harding. William Henry Harrison, born in Virginia, was living in Ohio when he became U.S. president. Ohio claims the nickname "Mother of Presidents," as does Virginia.

Twentieth Century

Ohio suffered a devastating flood in the spring of 1913, a disaster that led to the state's passage of the Conservancy Act, the first legislation in the United States to provide for flood-control districts based on entire river systems. Many dams and reservoirs were built. The state supplied many war materials during World War I and continued its industrial development in the decade following the war. Cities such as Dayton, Cleveland, Toledo, and Cincinnati grew rapidly while much of the state's farming areas declined in importance. The cities suffered greatly during the depression of the 1930s, but the state rebounded during World War II, when it supplied aircraft, ships, weapons, steel, tires, and other materials to the armed services. In the decades following World War II, Ohio's industrial growth continued, spurred by the construction of atomic energy installations, a space propulsion research center, aluminum plants, and chemical factories. Ohio was also able to export its products internationally after the opening of the St. Lawrence Seaway in 1959 allowed ocean-going vessels access to Ohio's ports on Lake Erie.

In recent decades, Ohio has faced such problems as a lack of funding for education, decreasing energy resources, pollution of Lake Erie and the state's rivers, and foreign competition for many of Ohio's industries. Recovery from the recession of the 1980s has seen the growth of the state capital, Columbus, into an industrial and technology center; the revitalization of Cleveland; and the continued thriving of Cincinnati.

State Boundaries

Ohio's present boundaries were fixed in 1802, with the exception of the northern boundary west of Lake Erie, which was established in 1836 as it now stands.

Ohio Counties

Adams	Darke	Hocking	Miami	Sandusky
Allen	Defiance	Holmes	Monroe	Scioto
Ashland	Delaware	Huron	Montgomery	Seneca
Ashtabula	Erie	Jackson	Morgan	Shelby
Athens	Fairfield	Jefferson	Morrow	Stark
Auglaize	Fayette	Knox	Muskingum	Summit
Belmont	Franklin	Lake	Noble	Trumbull
Brown	Fulton	Lawrence	Ottawa	Tuscarawas
Butler	Gallia	Licking	Paulding	Union
Carroll	Geauga	Logan	Perry	Van Wert
Champaign	Greene	Lorain	Pickaway	Vinton
Clark	Guernsey	Lucas	Pike	Warren
Clermont	Hamilton	Madison	Portage	Washington
Clinton	Hancock	Mahoning	Preble	Wayne
Columbiana	Hardin	Marion	Putnam	Williams
Coshocton	Harrison	Medina	Richland	Wood
Crawford	Henry	Meigs	Ross	Wyandot
Cuyahoga	Highland	Mercer		

Multi-County Places

The following Ohio places are in more than one county. Given here is the total population for each multi-county place, and the names of the counties it is in.

Adena, pop. 842; Jefferson (692), Harrison (150)
Alliance, pop. 23,376; Stark (23,304), Mahoning (72)
Baltic, pop. 659; Tuscarawas (561), Holmes (98), Coshocton (0)
Bellevue, pop. 8,146; Sandusky (4,236), Huron (3,910)
Blanchester, pop. 4,206; Clinton (4,206), Warren (0)
Bluffton, pop. 3,367; Allen (3,206), Hancock (161)
Bradford, pop. 2,005; Miami (1,111), Darke (894)
Burkettsville, pop. 268; Mercer (181), Darke (87)
Canal Winchester, pop. 2,617; Franklin (2,617), Fairfield (0)
Carlisle, pop. 4,872; Warren (4,610), Montgomery (262)
Clifton, pop. 165; Greene (113), Clark (52)
College Corner, pop. 379; Preble (274), Butler (105)
Columbiana, pop. 4,961; Columbiana (4,948), Mahoning (13)
Columbus, pop. 632,910; Franklin (632,270), Fairfield (640)
Crestline, pop. 4,934; Crawford (4,925), Richland (9)
Delphos, pop. 7,093; Allen (3,901), Van Wert (3,192)
Dublin, pop. 16,366; Franklin (12,551), Delaware (3,811), Union (4)
Fairfield, pop. 39,729; Butler (39,729), Hamilton (0)
Fairview, pop. 79; Guernsey (79), Belmont (0)

Fostoria, pop. 14,983; Seneca (10,848), Hancock (3,091), Wood (1,044)
Gratiot, pop. 195; Licking (111), Muskingum (84)
Green Springs, pop. 1,446; Seneca (731), Sandusky (715)
Harrisburg, pop. 340; Franklin (340), Pickaway (0)
Huber Heights, pop. 38,696; Montgomery (38,686), Miami (10)
Hunting Valley, pop. 799; Cuyahoga (648), Geauga (151)
Kettering, pop. 60,569; Montgomery (60,569), Greene (0)
Loudonville, pop. 2,915; Ashland (2,844), Holmes (71)
Loveland, pop. 9,990; Hamilton (8,263), Clermont (1,695), Warren (32)
Loveland Park, pop. 1,357; Warren (1,130), Hamilton (227)
Magnolia, pop. 937; Stark (591), Carroll (346)
Middletown, pop. 46,022; Butler (45,991), Warren (31)
Milan, pop. 1,464; Erie (1,056), Huron (408)
Milford, pop. 5,660; Clermont (5,655), Hamilton (5)
Mineral Ridge, pop. 3,928; Trumbull (2,862), Mahoning (1,066)
Minerva, pop. 4,318; Stark (2,226), Carroll (2,086), Columbiana (6)
Mogadore, pop. 4,008; Summit (2,967), Portage (1,041)
Monroe, pop. 4,490; Butler (4,438), Warren (52)
New Holland, pop. 841; Pickaway (739), Fayette (102)
Norton, pop. 11,477; Summit (11,475), Wayne (2)
Pickerington, pop. 5,668; Fairfield (5,645), Franklin (23)
Plain City, pop. 2,278; Madison (1,302), Union (976)
Plymouth, pop. 1,942; Richland (1,013), Huron (929)
Reynoldsburg, pop. 25,748; Franklin (24,483), Licking (1,265), Fairfield (0)
Ridgeway, pop. 378; Hardin (250), Logan (128)
Rittman, pop. 6,147; Wayne (6,037), Medina (110)
Roseville, pop. 1,847; Perry (982), Muskingum (865)
Salineville, pop. 1,474; Columbiana (1,474), Jefferson (0)
Scott, pop. 339; Van Wert (201), Paulding (138)
Sharonville, pop. 13,153; Hamilton (11,312), Butler (1,841)
Springboro, pop. 6,590; Warren (6,590), Montgomery (0)
Swanton, pop. 3,557; Fulton (3,378), Lucas (179)
Utica, pop. 1,997; Licking (1,980), Knox (17)
Vermilion, pop. 11,127; Lorain (5,644), Erie (5,483)
Verona, pop. 472; Preble (387), Montgomery (85)
Washingtonville, pop. 894; Columbiana (482), Mahoning (412)
Westerville, pop. 30,269; Franklin (29,092), Delaware (1,177)
Wilson, pop. 136; Monroe (109), Belmont (27)
Wright-Patterson AFB, pop. 8,579; Montgomery (4,947), Greene (3,632)
Yorkville, pop. 1,246; Jefferson (758), Belmont (488)
Youngstown, pop. 95,732; Mahoning (95,706), Trumbull (26)

Adams County
County Seat: West Union (ZIP: 45693)

Pop: 25,371 (1990); 24,328 (1980)   **Pop Density:** 43.4
Land: 584.0 sq. mi.; **Water:** 1.9 sq. mi.   **Area Code:** 513
On the south-central border of OH; original county; organized Jul 10, 1797 (prior to statehood).
Name origin: For John Adams (1735–1826), second U.S. president.

Bratton   Township
Lat: 39-00-13 N   Long: 83-26-36 W
Pop: 862 (1990); 699 (1980)   **Pop Density:** 26.8
Land: 32.2 sq. mi.; **Water:** 0.0 sq. mi.

Brush Creek   Township
Lat: 38-47-37 N   Long: 83-23-38 W
Pop: 1,195 (1990); 1,278 (1980)   **Pop Density:** 28.8
Land: 41.5 sq. mi.; **Water:** 0.0 sq. mi.

Cherry Fork   Village
ZIP: 45618   Lat: 38-53-18 N   Long: 83-36-48 W
Pop: 178 (1990); 210 (1980)   **Pop Density:** 1780.0
Land: 0.1 sq. mi.; **Water:** 0.0 sq. mi.

Franklin   Township
Lat: 38-58-58 N   Long: 83-20-02 W
Pop: 1,098 (1990); 1,002 (1980)   **Pop Density:** 20.3
Land: 54.2 sq. mi.; **Water:** 0.0 sq. mi.

Green   Township
ZIP: 45684   Lat: 38-40-57 N   Long: 83-20-50 W
Pop: 704 (1990); 795 (1980)   **Pop Density:** 12.8
Land: 55.1 sq. mi.; **Water:** 0.5 sq. mi.

Jefferson   Township
ZIP: 45684   Lat: 38-46-54 N   Long: 83-18-42 W
Pop: 1,022 (1990); 981 (1980)   **Pop Density:** 23.7
Land: 43.1 sq. mi.; **Water:** 0.0 sq. mi.

Liberty   Township
ZIP: 45693   Lat: 38-48-19 N   Long: 83-37-53 W
Pop: 1,400 (1990); 1,247 (1980)   **Pop Density:** 32.4
Land: 43.2 sq. mi.; **Water:** 0.0 sq. mi.

Manchester   Village
ZIP: 45144   Lat: 38-41-29 N   Long: 83-36-18 W
Pop: 2,223 (1990); 2,313 (1980)   **Pop Density:** 2470.0
Land: 0.9 sq. mi.; **Water:** 0.0 sq. mi.
Not coextensive with the town of the same name.
Name origin: For Manchester, England.

*Manchester   Township
ZIP: 45144   Lat: 38-41-45 N   Long: 83-35-54 W
Pop: 2,393 (1990); 2,319 (1980)   **Pop Density:** 1087.7
Land: 2.2 sq. mi.; **Water:** 0.0 sq. mi.

Meigs   Township
Lat: 38-54-39 N   Long: 83-23-19 W
Pop: 3,701 (1990); 3,473 (1980)   **Pop Density:** 58.9
Land: 62.8 sq. mi.; **Water:** 0.3 sq. mi.

Monroe   Township
Lat: 38-43-03 N   Long: 83-30-57 W
Pop: 657 (1990); 796 (1980)   **Pop Density:** 24.0
Land: 27.4 sq. mi.; **Water:** 0.8 sq. mi.

Oliver   Township
Lat: 38-53-04 N   Long: 83-30-30 W
Pop: 865 (1990); 715 (1980)   **Pop Density:** 29.8
Land: 29.0 sq. mi.; **Water:** 0.0 sq. mi.

Peebles   Village
ZIP: 45660   Lat: 38-56-49 N   Long: 83-24-29 W
Pop: 1,782 (1990); 1,790 (1980)   **Pop Density:** 1620.0
Land: 1.1 sq. mi.; **Water:** 0.0 sq. mi.   **Elev:** 829 ft.
In southern OH, 30 mi. northwest of Portsmouth.

Rome   Village
ZIP: 45684   Lat: 38-39-53 N   Long: 83-22-44 W
Pop: 99 (1990); 135 (1980)   **Pop Density:** 330.0
Land: 0.3 sq. mi.; **Water:** 0.0 sq. mi.

Scott   Township
Lat: 38-58-44 N   Long: 83-32-47 W
Pop: 1,920 (1990); 1,929 (1980)   **Pop Density:** 51.3
Land: 37.4 sq. mi.; **Water:** 0.0 sq. mi.

Seaman   Village
ZIP: 45679   Lat: 38-56-19 N   Long: 83-34-23 W
Pop: 1,013 (1990); 1,039 (1980)   **Pop Density:** 1688.3
Land: 0.6 sq. mi.; **Water:** 0.0 sq. mi.

Sprigg   Township
Lat: 38-42-25 N   Long: 83-38-47 W
Pop: 1,499 (1990); 1,659 (1980)   **Pop Density:** 34.1
Land: 44.0 sq. mi.; **Water:** 0.1 sq. mi.

Tiffin   Township
ZIP: 45693   Lat: 38-48-18 N   Long: 83-29-40 W
Pop: 5,144 (1990); 4,549 (1980)   **Pop Density:** 100.7
Land: 51.1 sq. mi.; **Water:** 0.1 sq. mi.

Wayne   Township
Lat: 38-53-16 N   Long: 83-36-45 W
Pop: 1,147 (1990); 1,110 (1980)   **Pop Density:** 41.0
Land: 28.0 sq. mi.; **Water:** 0.0 sq. mi.

West Union   Village
ZIP: 45693   Lat: 38-47-35 N   Long: 83-32-37 W
Pop: 3,096 (1990); 2,791 (1980)   **Pop Density:** 1407.3
Land: 2.2 sq. mi.; **Water:** 0.0 sq. mi.   **Elev:** 967 ft.
In southern OH, 55 mi. southeast of Cincinnati and 10 mi. north of the KY border.

Winchester   Village
ZIP: 45697   Lat: 38-56-33 N   Long: 83-39-12 W
Pop: 978 (1990); 1,080 (1980)   **Pop Density:** 376.2
Land: 2.6 sq. mi.; **Water:** 0.0 sq. mi.
In southern OH, 45 mi. east of Cincinnati. Not coextensive with the town of the same name.

*Winchester   Township
ZIP: 45697   Lat: 38-57-55 N   Long: 83-38-28 W
Pop: 1,764 (1990); 1,776 (1980)   **Pop Density:** 53.9
Land: 32.7 sq. mi.; **Water:** 0.0 sq. mi.

Allen County
County Seat: Lima (ZIP: 45801)

Pop: 109,755 (1990); 112,241 (1980) **Pop Density:** 271.4
Land: 404.5 sq. mi.; **Water:** 2.5 sq. mi. **Area Code:** 419
In west-central OH, north of Dayton; organized Feb 12, 1820 from Mercer County.
Name origin: For Ethan Allen (1738–89), leader of the Green Mountain Boys of VT in the Revolutionary War.

Amanda
Township
Lat: 40-44-10 N **Long:** 84-16-19 W
Pop: 1,773 (1990); 1,769 (1980) **Pop Density:** 52.9
Land: 33.5 sq. mi.; **Water:** 0.9 sq. mi.

American
Township
ZIP: 45807 **Lat:** 40-46-09 N **Long:** 84-10-32 W
Pop: 12,407 (1990); 12,825 (1980) **Pop Density:** 506.4
Land: 24.5 sq. mi.; **Water:** 0.0 sq. mi.
In northwestern OH, northwest of Lima.

Auglaize
Township
Lat: 40-40-53 N **Long:** 83-56-24 W
Pop: 2,778 (1990); 2,548 (1980) **Pop Density:** 77.0
Land: 36.1 sq. mi.; **Water:** 0.0 sq. mi.

Bath
Township
ZIP: 45801 **Lat:** 40-46-57 N **Long:** 84-02-35 W
Pop: 10,105 (1990); 9,997 (1980) **Pop Density:** 326.0
Land: 31.0 sq. mi.; **Water:** 1.1 sq. mi.
In northwestern OH, north of Lima.

Beaverdam
Village
Lat: 40-49-58 N **Long:** 83-58-34 W
Pop: 467 (1990); 492 (1980) **Pop Density:** 934.0
Land: 0.5 sq. mi.; **Water:** 0.0 sq. mi. **Elev:** 860 ft.

Bluffton
Village
ZIP: 45817 **Lat:** 40-53-31 N **Long:** 83-53-33 W
Pop: 3,206 (1990); 3,237 (1980) **Pop Density:** 1603.0
Land: 2.0 sq. mi.; **Water:** 0.0 sq. mi. **Elev:** 824 ft.
In northwestern OH, 14 mi. northeast of Lima. Founded 1833. Part of the town is also in Hancock County.
Name origin: For a Mennonite community in IN.

Cairo
Village
ZIP: 45820 **Lat:** 40-49-52 N **Long:** 84-05-04 W
Pop: 473 (1990); 596 (1980) **Pop Density:** 2365.0
Land: 0.2 sq. mi.; **Water:** 0.0 sq. mi. **Elev:** 815 ft.

Delphos
City
ZIP: 45833 **Lat:** 40-50-39 N **Long:** 84-20-01 W
Pop: 3,901 (1990); 3,984 (1980) **Pop Density:** 3546.4
Land: 1.1 sq. mi.; **Water:** 0.0 sq. mi. **Elev:** 780 ft.
In northwestern OH, 10 mi. northwest of Lima. Part of the town is also in Van Wert County.

Elida
Village
ZIP: 45807 **Lat:** 40-47-09 N **Long:** 84-11-59 W
Pop: 1,486 (1990); 1,349 (1980) **Pop Density:** 1857.5
Land: 0.8 sq. mi.; **Water:** 0.0 sq. mi.
In western OH, 7 mi. northwest of Lima.

Fort Shawnee
Village
Lat: 40-40-52 N **Long:** 84-07-53 W
Pop: 4,128 (1990); 4,541 (1980) **Pop Density:** 573.3
Land: 7.2 sq. mi.; **Water:** 0.0 sq. mi. **Elev:** 866 ft.
In northwestern OH, near Shawnee State Forest, the largest forested area in OH.

Harrod
Village
ZIP: 45850 **Lat:** 40-42-30 N **Long:** 83-55-13 W
Pop: 537 (1990); 506 (1980) **Pop Density:** 2685.0
Land: 0.2 sq. mi.; **Water:** 0.0 sq. mi. **Elev:** 991 ft.

Jackson
Township
Lat: 40-46-39 N **Long:** 83 56 00 W
Pop: 2,737 (1990); 2,702 (1980) **Pop Density:** 76.5
Land: 35.8 sq. mi.; **Water:** 0.2 sq. mi.

Lafayette
Village
Lat: 40-45-30 N **Long:** 83-56-58 W
Pop: 449 (1990); 488 (1980) **Pop Density:** 2245.0
Land: 0.2 sq. mi.; **Water:** 0.0 sq. mi. **Elev:** 927 ft.

Lima
City
ZIP: 45802 **Lat:** 40-44-35 N **Long:** 84-06-41 W
Pop: 45,549 (1990); 47,827 (1980) **Pop Density:** 3586.5
Land: 12.7 sq. mi.; **Water:** 0.1 sq. mi.
In northwest OH, north of Dayton. Founded 1831; incorporated 1841.
Name origin: For Lima, Peru.

Marion
Township
ZIP: 45833 **Lat:** 40-48-42 N **Long:** 84-17-32 W
Pop: 6,676 (1990); 6,718 (1980) **Pop Density:** 156.7
Land: 42.6 sq. mi.; **Water:** 0.0 sq. mi.

Monroe
Township
Lat: 40-51-42 N **Long:** 84-03-02 W
Pop: 2,095 (1990); 2,217 (1980) **Pop Density:** 57.9
Land: 36.2 sq. mi.; **Water:** 0.0 sq. mi.

Perry
Township
Lat: 40-40-41 N **Long:** 84-03-17 W
Pop: 3,577 (1990); 3,586 (1980) **Pop Density:** 106.8
Land: 33.5 sq. mi.; **Water:** 0.0 sq. mi.

Richland
Township
ZIP: 45817 **Lat:** 40-52-08 N **Long:** 83-56-12 W
Pop: 5,494 (1990); 5,357 (1980) **Pop Density:** 131.1
Land: 41.9 sq. mi.; **Water:** 0.1 sq. mi.

Shawnee
Township
ZIP: 45805 **Lat:** 40-41-35 N **Long:** 84-10-00 W
Pop: 12,133 (1990); 12,344 (1980) **Pop Density:** 414.1
Land: 29.3 sq. mi.; **Water:** 0.0 sq. mi.
In west-central OH, 4 mi. south of Lima.
Name origin: For the Indian tribe.

Spencer — Township
Lat: 40-43-56 N Long: 84-21-35 W
Pop: 3,120 (1990); 3,109 (1980)   Pop Density: 133.9
Land: 23.3 sq. mi.; Water: 0.0 sq. mi.

Spencerville — Village
ZIP: 45887   Lat: 40-42-28 N Long: 84-21-11 W
Pop: 2,288 (1990); 2,184 (1980)   Pop Density: 2542.2
Land: 0.9 sq. mi.; Water: 0.0 sq. mi.   Elev: 833 ft.

Sugar Creek — Township
Lat: 40-50-09 N Long: 84-09-40 W
Pop: 1,311 (1990); 1,242 (1980)   Pop Density: 54.4
Land: 24.1 sq. mi.; Water: 0.1 sq. mi.

Ashland County
County Seat: Ashland (ZIP: 44805)

Pop: 47,507 (1990); 46,178 (1980)   Pop Density: 111.9
Land: 424.4 sq. mi.; Water: 2.5 sq. mi.   Area Code: 419

In north-central OH, southwest of Akron; organized Feb 24, 1846 from the counties of Huron (Ruggles twp), Lorain (Sullivan and Troy twps), Richland (Vermillion, Montgomery, Orange, Green, Hanover, and parts of Monroe, Mifflin, and Clear Fork twps), and Wayne (Jackson, Perry, Mohican, and Lake twps).

Name origin: Named in 1822 for the home of Henry Clay (1777–1852) at Lexington, KY.

Ashland — City
ZIP: 44805   Lat: 40-52-01 N Long: 82-19-03 W
Pop: 20,079 (1990); 20,326 (1980)   Pop Density: 2113.6
Land: 9.5 sq. mi.; Water: 0.0 sq. mi.
In north-central OH, northeast of Mansfield.
Name origin: Named in 1822 for Henry Clay's (1777–1852) estate at Lexington, KY.

Bailey Lakes — Village
ZIP: 44805   Lat: 40-56-50 N Long: 82-21-19 W
Pop: 367 (1990); 397 (1980)   Pop Density: 917.5
Land: 0.4 sq. mi.; Water: 0.1 sq. mi.

Clear Creek — Township
Lat: 40-56-27 N Long: 82-22-40 W
Pop: 1,798 (1990); 1,702 (1980)   Pop Density: 71.1
Land: 25.3 sq. mi.; Water: 0.1 sq. mi.

Green — Township
Lat: 40-40-46 N Long: 82-17-10 W
Pop: 3,965 (1990); 3,867 (1980)   Pop Density: 106.3
Land: 37.3 sq. mi.; Water: 0.3 sq. mi.

Hanover — Township
Lat: 40-35-59 N Long: 82-17-05 W
Pop: 2,377 (1990); 2,383 (1980)   Pop Density: 73.4
Land: 32.4 sq. mi.; Water: 0.2 sq. mi.

Hayesville — Village
ZIP: 44838   Lat: 40-46-29 N Long: 82-15-38 W
Pop: 457 (1990); 518 (1980)   Pop Density: 652.9
Land: 0.7 sq. mi.; Water: 0.0 sq. mi.   Elev: 1244 ft.
Laid out 1830.
Name origin: For tavern owner Linus Hayes, who, with the Rev. John Cox, laid it out.

Jackson — Township
Lat: 40-56-45 N Long: 82-10-25 W
Pop: 2,439 (1990); 1,841 (1980)   Pop Density: 77.7
Land: 31.4 sq. mi.; Water: 0.3 sq. mi.

Jeromesville — Village
ZIP: 44840   Lat: 40-48-13 N Long: 82-11-46 W
Pop: 582 (1990); 582 (1980)   Pop Density: 1455.0
Land: 0.4 sq. mi.; Water: 0.0 sq. mi.   Elev: 1012 ft.

Lake — Township
Lat: 40-41-47 N Long: 82-10-29 W
Pop: 543 (1990); 529 (1980)   Pop Density: 27.1
Land: 20.0 sq. mi.; Water: 0.1 sq. mi.

Loudonville — Village
ZIP: 44842   Lat: 40-38-01 N Long: 82-14-07 W
Pop: 2,844 (1990); 2,878 (1980)   Pop Density: 1422.0
Land: 2.0 sq. mi.; Water: 0.0 sq. mi.   Elev: 974 ft.
Laid out 1814. Part of the town is also in Holmes County.
Name origin: For James Loudon Priest who, with Stephen Butler, laid it out.

Mifflin — Village
ZIP: 44805   Lat: 40-46-27 N Long: 82-21-51 W
Pop: 162 (1990); 203 (1980)   Pop Density: 540.0
Land: 0.3 sq. mi.; Water: 0.0 sq. mi.
Not coextensive with the town of the same name.

*Mifflin — Township
ZIP: 44805   Lat: 40-46-24 N Long: 82-21-42 W
Pop: 1,016 (1990); 1,060 (1980)   Pop Density: 81.9
Land: 12.4 sq. mi.; Water: 1.2 sq. mi.

Milton — Township
Lat: 40-51-40 N Long: 82-22-33 W
Pop: 2,059 (1990); 2,044 (1980)   Pop Density: 88.8
Land: 23.2 sq. mi.; Water: 0.0 sq. mi.

Mohican — Township
Lat: 40-46-32 N Long: 82-10-12 W
Pop: 1,786 (1990); 1,650 (1980)   Pop Density: 59.3
Land: 30.1 sq. mi.; Water: 0.0 sq. mi.

Montgomery — Township
Lat: 40-51-22 N Long: 82-16-16 W
Pop: 2,231 (1990); 2,236 (1980)   Pop Density: 77.2
Land: 28.9 sq. mi.; Water: 0.1 sq. mi.

OHIO, Ashland County

Orange
Township
Lat: 40-56-51 N Long: 82-16-53 W
Pop: 2,113 (1990); 1,968 (1980) **Pop Density:** 55.5
Land: 38.1 sq. mi.; **Water:** 0.1 sq. mi.

Perry
Township
Lat: 40-51-29 N Long: 82-10-18 W
Pop: 1,791 (1990); 1,594 (1980) **Pop Density:** 58.9
Land: 30.4 sq. mi.; **Water:** 0.0 sq. mi.

Perrysville
Village
ZIP: 44864 Lat: 40-39-24 N Long: 82-18-44 W
Pop: 691 (1990); 836 (1980) **Pop Density:** 2303.3
Land: 0.3 sq. mi.; **Water:** 0.0 sq. mi.

Polk
Village
ZIP: 44866 Lat: 40-56-42 N Long: 82-12-51 W
Pop: 355 (1990); 351 (1980) **Pop Density:** 355.0
Land: 1.0 sq. mi.; **Water:** 0.0 sq. mi.

Ruggles
Township
Lat: 41-01-30 N Long: 82-22-56 W
Pop: 678 (1990); 696 (1980) **Pop Density:** 26.2
Land: 25.9 sq. mi.; **Water:** 0.1 sq. mi.

Savannah
Village
ZIP: 44874 Lat: 40-58-02 N Long: 82-21-51 W
Pop: 363 (1990); 351 (1980) **Pop Density:** 907.5
Land: 0.4 sq. mi.; **Water:** 0.0 sq. mi. **Elev:** 1101 ft.

Sullivan
Township
ZIP: 44880 Lat: 41-01-41 N Long: 82-13-18 W
Pop: 1,491 (1990); 1,311 (1980) **Pop Density:** 58.5
Land: 25.5 sq. mi.; **Water:** 0.0 sq. mi.

Troy
Township
Lat: 41-01-46 N Long: 82-18-12 W
Pop: 887 (1990); 853 (1980) **Pop Density:** 52.8
Land: 16.8 sq. mi.; **Water:** 0.0 sq. mi.

Vermillion
Township
Lat: 40-46-23 N Long: 82-16-56 W
Pop: 2,254 (1990); 2,118 (1980) **Pop Density:** 60.6
Land: 37.2 sq. mi.; **Water:** 0.0 sq. mi.

Ashtabula County
County Seat: Jefferson (ZIP: 44047)

Pop: 99,821 (1990); 104,215 (1980) **Pop Density:** 142.1
Land: 702.7 sq. mi.; **Water:** 666.1 sq. mi. **Area Code:** 216

In the northeastern corner of OH, bordered on north by Lake Erie; organized Jun 7, 1807 from Trumbull county.

Name origin: For the Ashtabula River, which runs through the northeastern part of the county; from an Algonquian name thought to mean 'fish river' or 'there are always enough moving,' possibly referring to the fish.

Andover
Village
ZIP: 44003 Lat: 41-36-26 N Long: 80-34-10 W
Pop: 1,216 (1990); 1,205 (1980) **Pop Density:** 868.6
Land: 1.4 sq. mi.; **Water:** 0.0 sq. mi.

Not coextensive with the town of the same name.

Name origin: For Andover, ME.

*Andover
Township
ZIP: 44003 Lat: 41-36-27 N Long: 80-34-11 W
Pop: 2,481 (1990); 2,424 (1980) **Pop Density:** 111.8
Land: 22.2 sq. mi.; **Water:** 4.1 sq. mi.

Ashtabula
City
ZIP: 44004 Lat: 41-52-46 N Long: 80-47-53 W
Pop: 21,633 (1990); 23,449 (1980) **Pop Density:** 2846.4
Land: 7.6 sq. mi.; **Water:** 0.2 sq. mi.

In northeastern OH on Lake Erie, 50 mi. northeast of Cleveland. Settled 1803; incorporated 1831; chartered as a city 1812. Not coextensive with the town of the same name.

Name origin: From an Algonquian name thought to mean 'fish river' or 'there are always enough moving,' possibly referring to the fish.

*Ashtabula
Township
ZIP: 44004 Lat: 41-52-54 N Long: 80-46-00 W
Pop: 23,989 (1990); 26,247 (1980) **Pop Density:** 1193.5
Land: 20.1 sq. mi.; **Water:** 0.2 sq. mi.

Austinburg
Township
ZIP: 44010 Lat: 41-45-04 N Long: 80-51-32 W
Pop: 1,902 (1990); 1,869 (1980) **Pop Density:** 76.7
Land: 24.8 sq. mi.; **Water:** 0.2 sq. mi.

Cherry Valley
Township
ZIP: 44003 Lat: 41-36-26 N Long: 80-40-07 W
Pop: 738 (1990); 765 (1980) **Pop Density:** 30.6
Land: 24.1 sq. mi.; **Water:** 0.1 sq. mi.

Colebrook
Township
Lat: 41-32-09 N Long: 80-45-44 W
Pop: 747 (1990); 731 (1980) **Pop Density:** 30.5
Land: 24.5 sq. mi.; **Water:** 0.1 sq. mi.

Conneaut
City
ZIP: 44030 Lat: 41-55-34 N Long: 80-34-12 W
Pop: 13,241 (1990); 13,835 (1980) **Pop Density:** 501.6
Land: 26.4 sq. mi.; **Water:** 0.1 sq. mi. **Elev:** 662 ft.

In northeastern OH on Lake Erie. Ore and coal port.

Name origin: For the nearby creek; derivation of the name is in dispute.

Dorset
Township
ZIP: 44032 Lat: 41-40-40 N Long: 80-40-08 W
Pop: 850 (1990); 952 (1980) **Pop Density:** 36.8
Land: 23.1 sq. mi.; **Water:** 0.0 sq. mi.

Edgewood CDP
ZIP: 44004 **Lat:** 41-52-43 N **Long:** 80-44-26 W
Pop: 5,189 (1990); 3,099 (1980) **Pop Density:** 774.5
Land: 6.7 sq. mi.; **Water:** 0.0 sq. mi.

Geneva City
ZIP: 44041 **Lat:** 41-47-59 N **Long:** 80-56-54 W
Pop: 6,597 (1990); 6,655 (1980) **Pop Density:** 1884.9
Land: 3.5 sq. mi.; **Water:** 0.0 sq. mi. **Elev:** 673 ft.

In northeastern OH, 10 mi. southwest of Astabula. Not coextensive with the town of the same name.
Name origin: For Geneva, Switzerland.

*Geneva Township
ZIP: 44041 **Lat:** 41-49-13 N **Long:** 80-56-53 W
Pop: 11,912 (1990); 12,017 (1980) **Pop Density:** 458.2
Land: 26.0 sq. mi.; **Water:** 0.0 sq. mi.

Geneva-on-the-Lake Village
Lat: 41-51-23 N **Long:** 80-56-45 W
Pop: 1,626 (1990); 1,634 (1980) **Pop Density:** 813.0
Land: 2.0 sq. mi.; **Water:** 0.0 sq. mi. **Elev:** 605 ft.

In northeastern OH on Lake Erie, north of Geneva.

Harpersfield Township
ZIP: 44041 **Lat:** 41-44-57 N **Long:** 80-57-22 W
Pop: 2,496 (1990); 2,331 (1980) **Pop Density:** 94.2
Land: 26.5 sq. mi.; **Water:** 0.1 sq. mi.

Hartsgrove Township
ZIP: 44085 **Lat:** 41-36-20 N **Long:** 80-57-12 W
Pop: 1,157 (1990); 1,214 (1980) **Pop Density:** 46.7
Land: 24.8 sq. mi.; **Water:** 0.0 sq. mi.

Jefferson Village
ZIP: 44047 **Lat:** 41-44-19 N **Long:** 80-46-07 W
Pop: 3,331 (1990); 2,952 (1980) **Pop Density:** 1448.3
Land: 2.3 sq. mi.; **Water:** 0.0 sq. mi. **Elev:** 967 ft.

In the northeastern corner of OH, 10 mi. south of Ashtabula. Not coextensive with the town of the same name.
Name origin: For Thomas Jefferson (1743–1826), third U.S. president.

*Jefferson Township
ZIP: 44047 **Lat:** 41-44-59 N **Long:** 80-46-00 W
Pop: 5,355 (1990); 4,987 (1980) **Pop Density:** 208.4
Land: 25.7 sq. mi.; **Water:** 0.1 sq. mi.

Kingsville Township
ZIP: 44048 **Lat:** 41-53-15 N **Long:** 80-39-55 W
Pop: 2,007 (1990); 2,162 (1980) **Pop Density:** 155.6
Land: 12.9 sq. mi.; **Water:** 0.1 sq. mi.

Lenox Township
ZIP: 44047 **Lat:** 41-40-45 N **Long:** 80-45-51 W
Pop: 1,266 (1990); 1,291 (1980) **Pop Density:** 52.1
Land: 24.3 sq. mi.; **Water:** 0.1 sq. mi.

Monroe Township
Lat: 41-50-33 N **Long:** 80-34-36 W
Pop: 1,883 (1990); 2,079 (1980) **Pop Density:** 48.8
Land: 38.6 sq. mi.; **Water:** 0.0 sq. mi.

Morgan Township
Lat: 41-40-40 N **Long:** 80-51-13 W
Pop: 1,593 (1990); 1,359 (1980) **Pop Density:** 66.7
Land: 23.9 sq. mi.; **Water:** 0.3 sq. mi.

New Lyme Township
ZIP: 44047 **Lat:** 41-36-32 N **Long:** 80-45-22 W
Pop: 1,015 (1990); 1,058 (1980) **Pop Density:** 40.9
Land: 24.8 sq. mi.; **Water:** 0.0 sq. mi.

North Kingsville Village
Lat: 41-55-01 N **Long:** 80-40-12 W
Pop: 2,672 (1990); 2,939 (1980) **Pop Density:** 300.2
Land: 8.9 sq. mi.; **Water:** 0.0 sq. mi. **Elev:** 715 ft.

In northeastern OH, just south of Lake Erie.

Orwell Village
ZIP: 44076 **Lat:** 41-32-09 N **Long:** 80-51-30 W
Pop: 1,258 (1990); 1,067 (1980) **Pop Density:** 1143.6
Land: 1.1 sq. mi.; **Water:** 0.0 sq. mi. **Elev:** 902 ft.

Not coextensive with the town of the same name.

*Orwell Township
ZIP: 44076 **Lat:** 41-32-09 N **Long:** 80-51-30 W
Pop: 2,421 (1990); 2,220 (1980) **Pop Density:** 101.7
Land: 23.8 sq. mi.; **Water:** 0.0 sq. mi.

Pierpont Township
ZIP: 44082 **Lat:** 41-45-11 N **Long:** 80-34-17 W
Pop: 1,042 (1990); 1,074 (1980) **Pop Density:** 37.1
Land: 28.1 sq. mi.; **Water:** 0.0 sq. mi.

Plymouth Township
ZIP: 44004 **Lat:** 41-49-31 N **Long:** 80-45-26 W
Pop: 2,020 (1990); 2,029 (1980) **Pop Density:** 90.6
Land: 22.3 sq. mi.; **Water:** 0.1 sq. mi.

Richmond Township
Lat: 41-40-51 N **Long:** 80-34-18 W
Pop: 850 (1990); 887 (1980) **Pop Density:** 33.7
Land: 25.2 sq. mi.; **Water:** 0.3 sq. mi.

Roaming Shores Village
ZIP: 44084 **Lat:** 41-38-12 N **Long:** 80-49-42 W
Pop: 775 (1990); 581 (1980) **Pop Density:** 369.0
Land: 2.1 sq. mi.; **Water:** 0.7 sq. mi.

Rock Creek Village
ZIP: 44084 **Lat:** 41-39-38 N **Long:** 80-51-13 W
Pop: 553 (1990); 652 (1980) **Pop Density:** 614.4
Land: 0.9 sq. mi.; **Water:** 0.0 sq. mi.

Rome Township
ZIP: 44085 **Lat:** 41-36-21 N **Long:** 80-51-30 W
Pop: 1,256 (1990); 863 (1980) **Pop Density:** 53.4
Land: 23.5 sq. mi.; **Water:** 0.6 sq. mi.

Saybrook Township
ZIP: 44004 **Lat:** 41-50-11 N **Long:** 80-51-17 W
Pop: 10,164 (1990); 11,279 (1980) **Pop Density:** 319.6
Land: 31.8 sq. mi.; **Water:** 0.0 sq. mi.

In northeastern OH, 4 mi. south of Ashtabula.

Sheffield Township
Lat: 41-49-26 N **Long:** 80-39-59 W
Pop: 1,362 (1990); 1,513 (1980) **Pop Density:** 58.7
Land: 23.2 sq. mi.; **Water:** 0.0 sq. mi.

Trumbull Township
ZIP: 44041 **Lat:** 41-40-29 N **Long:** 80-57-09 W
Pop: 1,286 (1990); 1,330 (1980) **Pop Density:** 51.0
Land: 25.2 sq. mi.; **Water:** 0.0 sq. mi.

Wayne Township
ZIP: 44093 **Lat:** 41-32-09 N **Long:** 80-39-53 W
Pop: 610 (1990); 652 (1980) **Pop Density:** 25.4
Land: 24.0 sq. mi.; **Water:** 0.1 sq. mi.

OHIO, Ashtabula County

Williamsfield
Township
ZIP: 44093 Lat: 41-32-10 N Long: 80-34-20 W
Pop: 1,319 (1990); 1,224 (1980) Pop Density: 53.2
Land: 24.8 sq. mi.; Water: 0.7 sq. mi.

Windsor
Township
ZIP: 44099 Lat: 41-31-52 N Long: 80-57-12 W
Pop: 1,481 (1990); 1,485 (1980) Pop Density: 59.5
Land: 24.9 sq. mi.; Water: 0.0 sq. mi.

Athens County
County Seat: Athens (ZIP: 45701)

Pop: 59,549 (1990); 56,399 (1980) Pop Density: 117.5
Land: 506.8 sq. mi.; Water: 1.8 sq. mi. Area Code: 614
In southeastern OH, southeast of Columbus; organized Mar 1, 1805 from Washington County.
Name origin: For Athens, Greece.

Albany
Village
ZIP: 45710 Lat: 39-13-25 N Long: 82-11-55 W
Pop: 795 (1990); 905 (1980) Pop Density: 662.5
Land: 1.2 sq. mi.; Water: 0.0 sq. mi. Elev: 755 ft.

Alexander
Township
ZIP: 45701 Lat: 39-14-23 N Long: 82-07-56 W
Pop: 2,366 (1990); 2,096 (1980) Pop Density: 63.3
Land: 37.4 sq. mi.; Water: 0.1 sq. mi.

Ames
Township
Lat: 39-25-08 N Long: 82-00-22 W
Pop: 1,128 (1990); 1,014 (1980) Pop Density: 29.8
Land: 37.9 sq. mi.; Water: 0.0 sq. mi.

Amesville
Village
Lat: 39-24-05 N Long: 81-57-18 W
Pop: 250 (1990); 247 (1980) Pop Density: 1250.0
Land: 0.2 sq. mi.; Water: 0.0 sq. mi.

Athens
City
ZIP: 45701 Lat: 39-19-27 N Long: 82-05-45 W
Pop: 21,265 (1990); 19,743 (1980) Pop Density: 3127.2
Land: 6.8 sq. mi.; Water: 0.0 sq. mi. Elev: 723 ft.
In southeastern OH, west of Parkersburg, WV. County seat (1805). Settled 1797. Site of Ohio University. Not coextensive with the town of the same name.
Name origin: For Athens, Greece.

*Athens
Township
ZIP: 45701 Lat: 39-19-50 N Long: 82-07-25 W
Pop: 27,428 (1990); 25,706 (1980) Pop Density: 739.3
Land: 37.1 sq. mi.; Water: 0.0 sq. mi.

Bern
Township
Lat: 39-24-25 N Long: 81-54-27 W
Pop: 543 (1990); 538 (1980) Pop Density: 17.3
Land: 31.3 sq. mi.; Water: 0.0 sq. mi.

Buchtel
Village
ZIP: 45716 Lat: 39-27-45 N Long: 82-10-56 W
Pop: 640 (1990); 585 (1980) Pop Density: 1600.0
Land: 0.4 sq. mi.; Water: 0.0 sq. mi.

Canaan
Township
Lat: 39-19-52 N Long: 82-00-27 W
Pop: 1,568 (1990); 1,430 (1980) Pop Density: 40.8
Land: 38.4 sq. mi.; Water: 0.3 sq. mi.

Carthage
Township
ZIP: 45735 Lat: 39-13-46 N Long: 81-53-33 W
Pop: 1,360 (1990); 1,090 (1980) Pop Density: 35.1
Land: 38.8 sq. mi.; Water: 0.0 sq. mi.

Chauncey
Village
ZIP: 45719 Lat: 39-23-58 N Long: 82-07-40 W
Pop: 980 (1990); 1,050 (1980) Pop Density: 1633.3
Land: 0.6 sq. mi.; Water: 0.0 sq. mi. Elev: 659 ft.

Coolville
Village
ZIP: 45723 Lat: 39-13-13 N Long: 81-47-53 W
Pop: 663 (1990); 649 (1980) Pop Density: 828.8
Land: 0.8 sq. mi.; Water: 0.0 sq. mi.

Dover
Township
ZIP: 45761 Lat: 39-25-08 N Long: 82-06-54 W
Pop: 3,595 (1990); 3,429 (1980) Pop Density: 98.8
Land: 36.4 sq. mi.; Water: 0.0 sq. mi.

Glouster
Village
ZIP: 45732 Lat: 39-30-10 N Long: 82-05-05 W
Pop: 2,001 (1990); 2,211 (1980) Pop Density: 1539.2
Land: 1.3 sq. mi.; Water: 0.0 sq. mi.

Jacksonville
Village
ZIP: 45740 Lat: 39-28-32 N Long: 82-04-48 W
Pop: 544 (1990); 651 (1980) Pop Density: 1813.3
Land: 0.3 sq. mi.; Water: 0.0 sq. mi.
In southeast-central OH in central Wayne National Forest, 15 mi. north of Athens.
Name origin: For Gen. Andrew Jackson (1767–1845), hero of the War of 1812 and seventh U.S. president.

Lee
Township
Lat: 39-15-07 N Long: 82-13-55 W
Pop: 2,233 (1990); 2,066 (1980) Pop Density: 89.0
Land: 25.1 sq. mi.; Water: 0.3 sq. mi.

Lodi
Township
Lat: 39-13-52 N Long: 82-01-07 W
Pop: 1,238 (1990); 1,112 (1980) Pop Density: 31.6
Land: 39.2 sq. mi.; Water: 0.0 sq. mi.

Nelsonville
City
ZIP: 45764 Lat: 39-27-31 N Long: 82-13-33 W
Pop: 4,563 (1990); 4,567 (1980) Pop Density: 1140.8
Land: 4.0 sq. mi.; Water: 0.0 sq. mi. Elev: 680 ft.
Name origin: Named in 1824 for Daniel Nelson, its most enterprising citizen. Originally called Englishtown.

Rome
Township
Lat: 39-18-36 N Long: 81-53-34 W
Pop: 1,429 (1990); 1,452 (1980) Pop Density: 38.7
Land: 36.9 sq. mi.; Water: 0.1 sq. mi.

American Places Dictionary   OHIO, Auglaize County

The Plains   CDP
ZIP: 45780   **Lat:** 39-21-56 N   **Long:** 82-08-02 W
Pop: 2,644 (1990); 1,671 (1980)   **Pop Density:** 1101.7
Land: 2.4 sq. mi.; **Water:** 0.0 sq. mi.

Trimble   Village
ZIP: 45782   **Lat:** 39-29-11 N   **Long:** 82-04-47 W
Pop: 441 (1990); 579 (1980)   **Pop Density:** 630.0
Land: 0.7 sq. mi.; **Water:** 0.0 sq. mi.
Not coextensive with the town of the same name.

*Trimble   Township
Lat: 39-30-26 N   **Long:** 82-06-39 W
Pop: 4,716 (1990); 5,063 (1980)   **Pop Density:** 126.8
Land: 37.2 sq. mi.; **Water:** 0.3 sq. mi.

Troy   Township
Lat: 39-13-28 N   **Long:** 81-47-11 W
Pop: 2,588 (1990); 2,340 (1980)   **Pop Density:** 71.3
Land: 36.3 sq. mi.; **Water:** 0.5 sq. mi.

Waterloo   Township
Lat: 39-20-15 N   **Long:** 82-14-14 W
Pop: 2,321 (1990); 1,934 (1980)   **Pop Density:** 61.4
Land: 37.8 sq. mi.; **Water:** 0.1 sq. mi.

York   Township
ZIP: 45764   **Lat:** 39-25-34 N   **Long:** 82-13-49 W
Pop: 7,036 (1990); 7,129 (1980)   **Pop Density:** 189.1
Land: 37.2 sq. mi.; **Water:** 0.0 sq. mi.

Auglaize County
County Seat: Wapakoneta (ZIP: 45895)

Pop: 44,585 (1990); 42,554 (1980)   **Pop Density:** 111.1
Land: 401.3 sq. mi.; **Water:** 0.5 sq. mi.   **Area Code:** 419
In west-central OH, south of Lima; organized Feb 14, 1848 from Allen and Mercer counties.
Name origin: For the Auglaize River, which traverses it; from French 'at the stream' or 'at the lick,' with possible reference to a salt lick; or from an Indian word meaning 'fallen timbers.'

Buckland   Village
ZIP: 45819   **Lat:** 40-37-27 N   **Long:** 84-15-38 W
Pop: 239 (1990); 271 (1980)   **Pop Density:** 1195.0
Land: 0.2 sq. mi.; **Water:** 0.0 sq. mi.

Clay   Township
Lat: 40-31-08 N   **Long:** 84-02-50 W
Pop: 923 (1990); 832 (1980)   **Pop Density:** 30.5
Land: 30.3 sq. mi.; **Water:** 0.0 sq. mi.

Cridersville   Village
ZIP: 45806   **Lat:** 40-39-09 N   **Long:** 84-08-45 W
Pop: 1,885 (1990); 1,843 (1980)   **Pop Density:** 2094.4
Land: 0.9 sq. mi.; **Water:** 0.0 sq. mi.   **Elev:** 890 ft.
In west-central OH, 10 mi. south of Lima.

Duchouquet   Township
ZIP: 45895   **Lat:** 40-36-52 N   **Long:** 84-09-56 W
Pop: 14,196 (1990); 13,371 (1980)   **Pop Density:** 336.4
Land: 42.2 sq. mi.; **Water:** 0.1 sq. mi.
In northwest-central OH, 8 mi. south of Lima.

German   Township
Lat: 40-26-24 N   **Long:** 84-23-38 W
Pop: 3,400 (1990); 3,171 (1980)   **Pop Density:** 183.8
Land: 18.5 sq. mi.; **Water:** 0.0 sq. mi.

Goshen   Township
Lat: 40-33-31 N   **Long:** 83-56-27 W
Pop: 487 (1990); 517 (1980)   **Pop Density:** 27.2
Land: 17.9 sq. mi.; **Water:** 0.0 sq. mi.

Jackson   Township
Lat: 40-23-52 N   **Long:** 84-24-06 W
Pop: 3,415 (1990); 3,298 (1980)   **Pop Density:** 167.4
Land: 20.4 sq. mi.; **Water:** 0.0 sq. mi.

Logan   Township
Lat: 40-38-57 N   **Long:** 84-16-53 W
Pop: 1,028 (1990); 1,051 (1980)   **Pop Density:** 36.8
Land: 27.9 sq. mi.; **Water:** 0.0 sq. mi.

Minster   Village
ZIP: 45865   **Lat:** 40-23-39 N   **Long:** 84-22-46 W
Pop: 2,650 (1990); 2,557 (1980)   **Pop Density:** 1656.3
Land: 1.6 sq. mi.; **Water:** 0.0 sq. mi.   **Elev:** 967 ft.
In western OH, southwest of Lima.

Moulton   Township
Lat: 40-35-06 N   **Long:** 84-17-03 W
Pop: 1,618 (1990); 1,365 (1980)   **Pop Density:** 58.0
Land: 27.9 sq. mi.; **Water:** 0.0 sq. mi.

New Bremen   Village
ZIP: 45869   **Lat:** 40-26-14 N   **Long:** 84-22-50 W
Pop: 2,558 (1990); 2,393 (1980)   **Pop Density:** 2131.7
Land: 1.2 sq. mi.; **Water:** 0.0 sq. mi.   **Elev:** 941 ft.
Name origin: For Bremen, Germany.

New Knoxville   Village
ZIP: 45871   **Lat:** 40-29-39 N   **Long:** 84-19-06 W
Pop: 838 (1990); 760 (1980)   **Pop Density:** 1197.1
Land: 0.7 sq. mi.; **Water:** 0.0 sq. mi.   **Elev:** 903 ft.

Noble   Township
Lat: 40-35-16 N   **Long:** 84-23-54 W
Pop: 1,070 (1990); 1,081 (1980)   **Pop Density:** 35.1
Land: 30.5 sq. mi.; **Water:** 0.1 sq. mi.

Pusheta   Township
Lat: 40-31-14 N   **Long:** 84-09-48 W
Pop: 1,175 (1990); 1,108 (1980)   **Pop Density:** 38.9
Land: 30.2 sq. mi.; **Water:** 0.1 sq. mi.

OHIO, Auglaize County

St. Marys — City
ZIP: 45885   Lat: 40-32-38 N   Long: 84-23-27 W
Pop: 8,441 (1990); 8,414 (1980)   Pop Density: 2557.9
Land: 3.3 sq. mi.; Water: 0.0 sq. mi.   Elev: 871 ft.
In western OH, 80 mi. northwest of Columbus. Not coextensive with the town of the same name.
Name origin: For an early church.

*St. Marys — Township
ZIP: 45885   Lat: 40-30-31 N   Long: 84-23-25 W
Pop: 11,562 (1990); 11,214 (1980)   Pop Density: 313.3
Land: 36.9 sq. mi.; Water: 0.1 sq. mi.   Elev: 871 ft.

Salem — Township
Lat: 40-39-06 N   Long: 84-24-05 W
Pop: 516 (1990); 515 (1980)   Pop Density: 20.8
Land: 24.8 sq. mi.; Water: 0.0 sq. mi.

Union — Township
Lat: 40-35-58 N   Long: 84-02-48 W
Pop: 1,695 (1990); 1,667 (1980)   Pop Density: 47.2
Land: 35.9 sq. mi.; Water: 0.0 sq. mi.

Uniopolis — Village
ZIP: 45888   Lat: 40-36-06 N   Long: 84-05-11 W
Pop: 261 (1990); 259 (1980)   Pop Density: 2610.0
Land: 0.1 sq. mi.; Water: 0.0 sq. mi.   Elev: 935 ft.

Wapakoneta — City
ZIP: 45895   Lat: 40-34-12 N   Long: 84-11-32 W
Pop: 9,214 (1990); 8,402 (1980)   Pop Density: 2094.1
Land: 4.4 sq. mi.; Water: 0.1 sq. mi.   Elev: 901 ft.
Name origin: According to local history, from a combination of the names of Indian chief Wapaugh and his wife, Konetta. Originally called Wapaghkonetta.

Washington — Township
Lat: 40-31-11 N   Long: 84-16-47 W
Pop: 1,852 (1990); 1,706 (1980)   Pop Density: 59.7
Land: 31.0 sq. mi.; Water: 0.0 sq. mi.

Wayne — Township
Lat: 40-36-28 N   Long: 83-56-31 W
Pop: 1,648 (1990); 1,658 (1980)   Pop Density: 61.3
Land: 26.9 sq. mi.; Water: 0.0 sq. mi.

Waynesfield — Village
ZIP: 45896   Lat: 40-36-06 N   Long: 83-58-25 W
Pop: 831 (1990); 826 (1980)   Pop Density: 1187.1
Land: 0.7 sq. mi.; Water: 0.0 sq. mi.   Elev: 1054 ft.

Belmont County
County Seat: Saint Clairsville (ZIP: 43950)

Pop: 71,074 (1990); 82,569 (1980)   Pop Density: 132.3
Land: 537.3 sq. mi.; Water: 4.1 sq. mi.   Area Code: 614
On the central eastern border of OH, west of Wheeling, WV; organized Sep 7, 1801 (prior to statehood) from Jefferson County.
Name origin: French 'beautiful mountain.'

Barnesville — Village
ZIP: 43713   Lat: 39-59-20 N   Long: 81-10-24 W
Pop: 4,326 (1990); 4,633 (1980)   Pop Density: 2276.8
Land: 1.9 sq. mi.; Water: 0.0 sq. mi.
In southeastern OH in a hilly region, 40 mi. southwest of Steubenville. Founded 1808.
Name origin: For its founder, James Barnes.

Bellaire — City
ZIP: 43906   Lat: 40-01-00 N   Long: 80-44-47 W
Pop: 6,028 (1990); 8,241 (1980)   Pop Density: 3172.6
Land: 1.9 sq. mi.; Water: 0.0 sq. mi.   Elev: 653 ft.
In eastern OH on the Ohio River, 35 mi. south of Steubenville.

Belmont — Village
ZIP: 43718   Lat: 40-01-40 N   Long: 81-02-28 W
Pop: 471 (1990); 714 (1980)   Pop Density: 1570.0
Land: 0.3 sq. mi.; Water: 0.0 sq. mi.

Bethesda — Village
ZIP: 43719   Lat: 40-00-58 N   Long: 81-04-22 W
Pop: 1,161 (1990); 1,429 (1980)   Pop Density: 1935.0
Land: 0.6 sq. mi.; Water: 0.0 sq. mi.

Bridgeport — Village
ZIP: 43912   Lat: 40-03-59 N   Long: 80-44-48 W
Pop: 2,318 (1990); 2,642 (1980)   Pop Density: 1655.7
Land: 1.4 sq. mi.; Water: 0.0 sq. mi.
In eastern OH on the Ohio River, across from Wheeling, WV.

Brookside — Village
ZIP: 43912   Lat: 40-04-16 N   Long: 80-45-42 W
Pop: 703 (1990); 887 (1980)   Pop Density: 3515.0
Land: 0.2 sq. mi.; Water: 0.0 sq. mi.

Colerain — Township
Lat: 40-07-12 N   Long: 80-50-12 W
Pop: 4,602 (1990); 5,316 (1980)   Pop Density: 182.6
Land: 25.2 sq. mi.; Water: 0.0 sq. mi.

Fairview — Village
ZIP: 43736   Lat: 40-03-21 N   Long: 81-13-47 W
Pop: 79 (1990); 4 (1980)   Pop Density: 2633.3
Land: 0.03 sq. mi.; Water: 0.0 sq. mi.   Elev: 1238 ft.
Part of the town is also in Guernsey County.

Flushing — Village
ZIP: 43977   Lat: 40-08-54 N   Long: 81-03-55 W
Pop: 1,042 (1990); 1,266 (1980)   Pop Density: 1736.7
Land: 0.6 sq. mi.; Water: 0.0 sq. mi.   Elev: 1132 ft.
In eastern OH, 40 mi. southwest of Steubenville. Not coextensive with the town of the same name.
Name origin: For the city in Holland.

OHIO, Belmont County

***Flushing** — Township
ZIP: 43977 Lat: 40-09-16 N Long: 81-07-41 W
Pop: 2,081 (1990); 2,394 (1980) Pop Density: 72.3
Land: 28.8 sq. mi.; Water: 2.2 sq. mi.

Goshen — Township
Lat: 39-59-19 N Long: 81-04-00 W
Pop: 2,972 (1990); 3,412 (1980) Pop Density: 81.6
Land: 36.4 sq. mi.; Water: 0.1 sq. mi.

Holloway — Village
ZIP: 43985 Lat: 40-09-37 N Long: 81-07-35 W
Pop: 354 (1990); 459 (1980) Pop Density: 321.8
Land: 1.1 sq. mi.; Water: 0.0 sq. mi.
In eastern OH, 40 mi. southwest of Steubenville. Platted 1883 by Isaac Holloway.
Name origin: Named in 1827 for the Holloway family from VA.

Kirkwood — Township
Lat: 40-04-54 N Long: 81-10-20 W
Pop: 334 (1990); 360 (1980) Pop Density: 9.3
Land: 36.0 sq. mi.; Water: 0.7 sq. mi.

Martins Ferry — City
ZIP: 43935 Lat: 40-06-04 N Long: 80-43-25 W
Pop: 7,990 (1990); 9,331 (1980) Pop Density: 3804.8
Land: 2.1 sq. mi.; Water: 0.0 sq. mi.
On the central eastern border of OH, along the Ohio River, north of Wheeling, WV.
Name origin: Named in 1835 for Ebenezer Martin, who laid out the town. Previously called Jefferson and Martinsville.

Mead — Township
ZIP: 43947 Lat: 39-56-59 N Long: 80-49-57 W
Pop: 6,166 (1990); 7,038 (1980) Pop Density: 193.3
Land: 31.9 sq. mi.; Water: 0.0 sq. mi.

Morristown — Village
ZIP: 43759 Lat: 40-03-46 N Long: 81-04-17 W
Pop: 296 (1990); 463 (1980) Pop Density: 592.0
Land: 0.5 sq. mi.; Water: 0.0 sq. mi.

Neffs — CDP
Lat: 40-01-44 N Long: 80-48-55 W
Pop: 1,213 (1990); 1,106 (1980) Pop Density: 303.3
Land: 4.0 sq. mi.; Water: 0.0 sq. mi.

Pease — Township
ZIP: 43935 Lat: 40-06-23 N Long: 80-45-17 W
Pop: 16,368 (1990); 19,471 (1980) Pop Density: 572.3
Land: 28.6 sq. mi.; Water: 0.0 sq. mi.
In east-central OH, 4 mi. north of Wheeling.

Powhatan Point — Village
ZIP: 43942 Lat: 39-51-40 N Long: 80-48-33 W
Pop: 1,807 (1990); 2,181 (1980) Pop Density: 1129.4
Land: 1.6 sq. mi.; Water: 0.2 sq. mi.

Pultney — Township
ZIP: 43906 Lat: 40-01-00 N Long: 80-47-00 W
Pop: 11,107 (1990); 13,675 (1980) Pop Density: 425.6
Land: 26.1 sq. mi.; Water: 0.0 sq. mi.
In southeastern OH, 5 mi. southwest of Wheeling, WV.

Richland — Township
ZIP: 43950 Lat: 40-03-27 N Long: 80-54-28 W
Pop: 11,318 (1990); 12,614 (1980) Pop Density: 192.8
Land: 58.7 sq. mi.; Water: 0.1 sq. mi.
In southeastern OH, 8 mi. west of Wheeling, WV.

St. Clairsville — City
ZIP: 43950 Lat: 40-04-41 N Long: 80-53-56 W
Pop: 5,162 (1990); 5,452 (1980) Pop Density: 2581.0
Land: 2.0 sq. mi.; Water: 0.0 sq. mi. Elev: 1284 ft.
Name origin: For Arthur St. Clair (1736–1818), first governor of the Northwest Territory.

Shadyside — Village
ZIP: 43947 Lat: 39-58-16 N Long: 80-45-03 W
Pop: 3,934 (1990); 4,315 (1980) Pop Density: 3934.0
Land: 1.0 sq. mi.; Water: 0.0 sq. mi.

Smith — Township
Lat: 39-59-12 N Long: 80-56-59 W
Pop: 1,624 (1990); 1,883 (1980) Pop Density: 44.7
Land: 36.3 sq. mi.; Water: 0.0 sq. mi.

Somerset — Township
Lat: 39-54-44 N Long: 81-11-07 W
Pop: 1,029 (1990); 1,062 (1980) Pop Density: 29.7
Land: 34.6 sq. mi.; Water: 0.2 sq. mi.

Union — Township
Lat: 40-04-56 N Long: 81-03-44 W
Pop: 2,029 (1990); 2,263 (1980) Pop Density: 57.6
Land: 35.2 sq. mi.; Water: 0.3 sq. mi.

Warren — Township
ZIP: 43713 Lat: 39-59-42 N Long: 81-10-32 W
Pop: 5,887 (1990); 6,427 (1980) Pop Density: 167.7
Land: 35.1 sq. mi.; Water: 0.1 sq. mi.

Washington — Township
Lat: 39-54-09 N Long: 80-57-12 W
Pop: 602 (1990); 741 (1980) Pop Density: 16.8
Land: 35.8 sq. mi.; Water: 0.0 sq. mi.

Wayne — Township
Lat: 39-54-15 N Long: 81-04-18 W
Pop: 579 (1990); 677 (1980) Pop Density: 16.3
Land: 35.5 sq. mi.; Water: 0.1 sq. mi.

Wheeling — Township
Lat: 40-08-42 N Long: 80-57-20 W
Pop: 1,578 (1990); 1,823 (1980) Pop Density: 57.4
Land: 27.5 sq. mi.; Water: 0.0 sq. mi.

Wilson — Village
ZIP: 43716 Lat: 39-51-50 N Long: 81-04-13 W
Pop: 27 (1990); 20 (1980) Pop Density: 270.0
Land: 0.1 sq. mi.; Water: 0.1 sq. mi. Elev: 1247 ft.
Part of the town is also in Monroe County.

York — Township
Lat: 39-53-11 N Long: 80-51-19 W
Pop: 2,798 (1990); 3,413 (1980) Pop Density: 108.9
Land: 25.7 sq. mi.; Water: 0.3 sq. mi.

Yorkville — Village
Lat: 40-09-00 N Long: 80-42-32 W
Pop: 488 (1990); 492 (1980) Pop Density: 1220.0
Land: 0.4 sq. mi.; Water: 0.0 sq. mi.
Part of the town is also in Jefferson County.
Name origin: For York, PA, former home of early settlers.

OHIO, Brown County

Brown County
County Seat: Georgetown (ZIP: 45121)

Pop: 34,966 (1990); 31,920 (1980)   **Pop Density:** 71.1
Land: 491.8 sq. mi.; **Water:** 3.5 sq. mi.   **Area Code:** 513
On the southwestern border of OH, east of Cincinnati; organized Mar 1, 1818 from Adams and Clermont counties.
Name origin: For Gen. Jacob Jennings Brown (1775–1828), an officer in the War of 1812 and commander of the U.S. Army (1821–28).

Aberdeen — Village
ZIP: 45101   **Lat:** 38-40-00 N   **Long:** 83-46-11 W
Pop: 1,329 (1990); 1,566 (1980)   **Pop Density:** 1329.0
Land: 1.0 sq. mi.; **Water:** 0.2 sq. mi.
Name origin: For Aberdeen, Scotland.

Byrd — Township
Lat: 38-49-12 N   **Long:** 83-43-31 W
Pop: 697 (1990); 653 (1980)   **Pop Density:** 27.4
Land: 25.4 sq. mi.; **Water:** 0.0 sq. mi.

Clark — Township
Lat: 38-55-39 N   **Long:** 83-59-33 W
Pop: 2,831 (1990); 2,858 (1980)   **Pop Density:** 94.1
Land: 30.1 sq. mi.; **Water:** 0.0 sq. mi.

Eagle — Township
Lat: 38-59-24 N   **Long:** 83-43-38 W
Pop: 1,080 (1990); 941 (1980)   **Pop Density:** 42.4
Land: 25.5 sq. mi.; **Water:** 0.0 sq. mi.

Fayetteville — Village
ZIP: 45118   **Lat:** 39-11-10 N   **Long:** 83-55-55 W
Pop: 393 (1990); 478 (1980)   **Pop Density:** 982.5
Land: 0.4 sq. mi.; **Water:** 0.0 sq. mi.   **Elev:** 944 ft.

Franklin — Township
Lat: 38-55-07 N   **Long:** 83-49-40 W
Pop: 1,061 (1990); 925 (1980)   **Pop Density:** 39.4
Land: 26.9 sq. mi.; **Water:** 0.4 sq. mi.

Georgetown — Village
ZIP: 45121   **Lat:** 38-52-00 N   **Long:** 83-54-09 W
Pop: 3,627 (1990); 3,467 (1980)   **Pop Density:** 1295.4
Land: 2.8 sq. mi.; **Water:** 0.0 sq. mi.   **Elev:** 930 ft.
In southwestern OH near the Ohio River. Surveyed 1819.
Name origin: For Georgetown, KY.

Green — Township
Lat: 39-04-17 N   **Long:** 83-54-14 W
Pop: 2,860 (1990); 2,415 (1980)   **Pop Density:** 110.9
Land: 25.8 sq. mi.; **Water:** 0.0 sq. mi.

Hamersville — Village
ZIP: 45130   **Lat:** 38-55-05 N   **Long:** 83-59-05 W
Pop: 586 (1990); 688 (1980)   **Pop Density:** 1465.0
Land: 0.4 sq. mi.; **Water:** 0.0 sq. mi.   **Elev:** 968 ft.

Higginsport — Village
ZIP: 45131   **Lat:** 38-47-26 N   **Long:** 83-58-06 W
Pop: 298 (1990); 343 (1980)   **Pop Density:** 1490.0
Land: 0.2 sq. mi.; **Water:** 0.0 sq. mi.
Name origin: For Robert Higgins, who settled here in 1894. Also known as Ginsport.

Huntington — Township
Lat: 38-42-36 N   **Long:** 83-44-13 W
Pop: 2,704 (1990); 2,534 (1980)   **Pop Density:** 80.5
Land: 33.6 sq. mi.; **Water:** 0.6 sq. mi.

Jackson — Township
Lat: 38-54-42 N   **Long:** 83-43-57 W
Pop: 806 (1990); 747 (1980)   **Pop Density:** 28.9
Land: 27.9 sq. mi.; **Water:** 0.2 sq. mi.

Jefferson — Township
Lat: 38-50-59 N   **Long:** 83-47-26 W
Pop: 1,168 (1990); 1,092 (1980)   **Pop Density:** 49.9
Land: 23.4 sq. mi.; **Water:** 0.0 sq. mi.

Lewis — Township
Lat: 38-50-34 N   **Long:** 83-59-47 W
Pop: 1,676 (1990); 1,498 (1980)   **Pop Density:** 39.3
Land: 42.7 sq. mi.; **Water:** 0.6 sq. mi.

Mount Orab — Village
ZIP: 45154   **Lat:** 39-01-45 N   **Long:** 83-55-25 W
Pop: 1,929 (1990); 1,573 (1980)   **Pop Density:** 1015.3
Land: 1.9 sq. mi.; **Water:** 0.0 sq. mi.   **Elev:** 922 ft.
In southwestern OH, southeast of Cincinnati.

Perry — Township
ZIP: 45118   **Lat:** 39-11-20 N   **Long:** 83-56-00 W
Pop: 3,805 (1990); 3,288 (1980)   **Pop Density:** 64.6
Land: 58.9 sq. mi.; **Water:** 0.3 sq. mi.

Pike — Township
Lat: 39-00-40 N   **Long:** 83-57-03 W
Pop: 2,901 (1990); 2,447 (1980)   **Pop Density:** 117.9
Land: 24.6 sq. mi.; **Water:** 0.3 sq. mi.

Pleasant — Township
Lat: 38-50-24 N   **Long:** 83-54-04 W
Pop: 4,819 (1990); 4,552 (1980)   **Pop Density:** 133.9
Land: 36.0 sq. mi.; **Water:** 0.4 sq. mi.

Ripley — Village
ZIP: 45167   **Lat:** 38-44-22 N   **Long:** 83-50-24 W
Pop: 1,816 (1990); 2,174 (1980)   **Pop Density:** 1650.9
Land: 1.1 sq. mi.; **Water:** 0.1 sq. mi.
Name origin: For Gen. Eleazer Wheelock Ripley, officer in the War of 1812.

Russellville — Village
ZIP: 45168   **Lat:** 38-52-02 N   **Long:** 83-47-15 W
Pop: 459 (1990); 445 (1980)   **Pop Density:** 573.8
Land: 0.8 sq. mi.; **Water:** 0.0 sq. mi.   **Elev:** 975 ft.

St. Martin — Village
Lat: 39-12-52 N   **Long:** 83-53-16 W
Pop: 141 (1990); 126 (1980)   **Pop Density:** 117.5
Land: 1.2 sq. mi.; **Water:** 0.0 sq. mi.   **Elev:** 979 ft.

OHIO, Butler County

Sardinia
Village
ZIP: 45171 **Lat:** 39-00-24 N **Long:** 83-48-25 W
Pop: 792 (1990); 826 (1980) **Pop Density:** 2640.0
Land: 0.3 sq. mi.; **Water:** 0.0 sq. mi. **Elev:** 962 ft.

Scott
Township
Lat: 38-57-03 N **Long:** 83-54-35 W
Pop: 1,001 (1990); 963 (1980) **Pop Density:** 47.4
Land: 21.1 sq. mi.; **Water:** 0.0 sq. mi.

Sterling
Township
Lat: 39-05-13 N **Long:** 83-58-21 W
Pop: 2,377 (1990); 1,532 (1980) **Pop Density:** 81.7
Land: 29.1 sq. mi.; **Water:** 0.0 sq. mi.

Union
Township
Lat: 38-46-00 N **Long:** 83-49-38 W
Pop: 3,068 (1990); 3,503 (1980) **Pop Density:** 80.7
Land: 38.0 sq. mi.; **Water:** 0.7 sq. mi.

Washington
Township
Lat: 38-59-26 N **Long:** 83-49-10 W
Pop: 2,112 (1990); 1,972 (1980) **Pop Density:** 93.0
Land: 22.7 sq. mi.; **Water:** 0.0 sq. mi.

Butler County
County Seat: Hamilton (ZIP: 45011)

Pop: 291,479 (1990); 258,787 (1980) **Pop Density:** 623.7
Land: 467.3 sq. mi.; **Water:** 2.9 sq. mi. **Area Code:** 513

On the southwestern border of OH, north of Cincinnati; organized May 1, 1803 from Hamilton County.

Name origin: For Maj. Gen. Richard Butler (1743–91), an officer in the Revolutionary War, PA legislator, and Indian commissioner.

Beckett Ridge
CDP
Lat: 39-20-49 N **Long:** 84-26-07 W
Pop: 4,505 (1990) **Pop Density:** 919.4
Land: 4.9 sq. mi.; **Water:** 0.0 sq. mi.

College Corner
Village
ZIP: 45003 **Lat:** 39-33-55 N **Long:** 84-48-45 W
Pop: 105 (1990); 116 (1980) **Pop Density:** 2100.0
Land: 0.05 sq. mi.; **Water:** 0.0 sq. mi.

Part of the town is also in Preble County.

Fairfield
City
ZIP: 45014 **Lat:** 39-19-51 N **Long:** 84-32-34 W
Pop: 39,729 (1990); 30,777 (1980) **Pop Density:** 1910.0
Land: 20.8 sq. mi.; **Water:** 0.1 sq. mi.

In southwestern OH, 20 mi. north of Cincinnati. Not coextensive with the town of the same name. Part of the town is also in Hamilton County.

Name origin: For its descriptive connotations.

*Fairfield
Township
ZIP: 45014 **Lat:** 39-21-18 N **Long:** 84-31-41 W
Pop: 49,373 (1990); 38,707 (1980) **Pop Density:** 1371.5
Land: 36.0 sq. mi.; **Water:** 0.3 sq. mi.

Hamilton
City
ZIP: 45011 **Lat:** 39-23-26 N **Long:** 84-33-50 W
Pop: 61,368 (1990); 63,189 (1980) **Pop Density:** 3068.4
Land: 20.0 sq. mi.; **Water:** 0.5 sq. mi.

In southwestern OH on the Great Miami River, 20 mi. north of Cincinnati. Settled 1803; incorporated 1810.

Name origin: For Alexander Hamilton (1757–1804), first U.S. secretary of the treasury.

Hanover
Township
ZIP: 45013 **Lat:** 39-26-14 N **Long:** 84-39-26 W
Pop: 7,653 (1990); 7,290 (1980) **Pop Density:** 231.9
Land: 33.0 sq. mi.; **Water:** 0.1 sq. mi.

Jacksonburg
Village
ZIP: 45067 **Lat:** 39-32-16 N **Long:** 84-30-13 W
Pop: 50 (1990); 58 (1980) **Pop Density:** 2500.0
Land: 0.02 sq. mi.; **Water:** 0.0 sq. mi.

Lemon
Township
ZIP: 45050 **Lat:** 39-27-07 N **Long:** 84-23-27 W
Pop: 12,172 (1990); 12,782 (1980) **Pop Density:** 728.9
Land: 16.7 sq. mi.; **Water:** 0.4 sq. mi.

In southwestern OH, 8 mi. northwest of Hamilton.

Liberty
Township
ZIP: 45011 **Lat:** 39-23-59 N **Long:** 84-24-38 W
Pop: 9,249 (1990); 6,508 (1980) **Pop Density:** 317.8
Land: 29.1 sq. mi.; **Water:** 0.0 sq. mi.

Madison
Township
ZIP: 45042 **Lat:** 39-32-20 N **Long:** 84-25-29 W
Pop: 8,547 (1990); 8,596 (1980) **Pop Density:** 231.0
Land: 37.0 sq. mi.; **Water:** 0.5 sq. mi.

Middletown
City
ZIP: 45042 **Lat:** 39-30-20 N **Long:** 84-22-24 W
Pop: 45,991 (1990); 43,719 (1980) **Pop Density:** 2276.8
Land: 20.2 sq. mi.; **Water:** 0.1 sq. mi.

In southwestern OH on the Miami River, 35 mi. north of Cincinnati. Founded 1802; incorporated as city 1883. Part of the town is also in Warren County.

Name origin: For its location between Dayton and Cincinnati.

Milford
Township
Lat: 39-31-37 N **Long:** 84-38-48 W
Pop: 2,651 (1990); 2,550 (1980) **Pop Density:** 71.8
Land: 36.9 sq. mi.; **Water:** 0.1 sq. mi.

Millville
Village
ZIP: 45013 **Lat:** 39-23-30 N **Long:** 84-39-12 W
Pop: 755 (1990); 809 (1980) **Pop Density:** 1510.0
Land: 0.5 sq. mi.; **Water:** 0.0 sq. mi.

OHIO, Butler County

Monroe — Village
ZIP: 45050 Lat: 39-26-38 N Long: 84-21-36 W
Pop: 4,438 (1990); 4,188 (1980) Pop Density: 672.4
Land: 6.6 sq. mi.; Water: 0.0 sq. mi. Elev: 823 ft.
In southwestern OH, 30 mi. north of Cincinnati. Part of the town is also in Warren County.
Name origin: For James Monroe (1758–1831), fifth U.S. president.

Morgan — Township
Lat: 39-20-43 N Long: 84-45-46 W
Pop: 4,972 (1990); 4,076 (1980) Pop Density: 134.7
Land: 36.9 sq. mi.; Water: 0.0 sq. mi.

New Miami — Village
ZIP: 45011 Lat: 39-25-53 N Long: 84-32-27 W
Pop: 2,555 (1990); 2,980 (1980) Pop Density: 2838.9
Land: 0.9 sq. mi.; Water: 0.0 sq. mi.
Name origin: For the local Miami Indians.

Oxford — City
ZIP: 45056 Lat: 39-30-20 N Long: 84-44-50 W
Pop: 18,937 (1990); 17,655 (1980) Pop Density: 4303.9
Land: 4.4 sq. mi.; Water: 0.0 sq. mi. Elev: 972 ft.
In southwest OH, 25 mi. southwest of Dayton. Site of Miami Univ.
Name origin: For Oxford, England.

*Oxford — Township
ZIP: 45056 Lat: 39-31-18 N Long: 84-45-33 W
Pop: 23,092 (1990); 21,714 (1980) Pop Density: 625.8
Land: 36.9 sq. mi.; Water: 0.3 sq. mi.

Reily — Township
ZIP: 45056 Lat: 39-25-59 N Long: 84-45-32 W
Pop: 2,521 (1990); 2,177 (1980) Pop Density: 69.3
Land: 36.4 sq. mi.; Water: 0.0 sq. mi.

Ross — Township
ZIP: 45061 Lat: 39-20-59 N Long: 84-38-50 W
Pop: 6,383 (1990); 5,626 (1980) Pop Density: 207.9
Land: 30.7 sq. mi.; Water: 0.2 sq. mi.

St. Clair — Township
ZIP: 45011 Lat: 39-26-57 N Long: 84-32-00 W
Pop: 7,718 (1990); 8,223 (1980) Pop Density: 357.3
Land: 21.6 sq. mi.; Water: 0.3 sq. mi.

Seven Mile — Village
ZIP: 45062 Lat: 39-28-45 N Long: 84-33-08 W
Pop: 804 (1990); 841 (1980) Pop Density: 2010.0
Land: 0.4 sq. mi.; Water: 0.0 sq. mi. Elev: 655 ft

Sharonville — City
Lat: 39-17-46 N Long: 84-21-58 W
Pop: 1,841 (1990); 10,108 (1980) Pop Density: 3068.3
Land: 0.6 sq. mi.; Water: 0.0 sq. mi.
In southwestern OH, 15 mi. northeast of Cincinnati. Part of the town is also in Hamilton County.
Name origin: For Sharon, PA.

Somerville — Village
ZIP: 45064 Lat: 39-33-48 N Long: 84-38-18 W
Pop: 279 (1990); 357 (1980) Pop Density: 930.0
Land: 0.3 sq. mi.; Water: 0.0 sq. mi.

South Middletown — CDP
Lat: 39-28-52 N Long: 84-24-02 W
Pop: 3,491 (1990) Pop Density: 3491.0
Land: 1.0 sq. mi.; Water: 0.0 sq. mi.

Trenton — City
ZIP: 45067 Lat: 39-28-37 N Long: 84-27-44 W
Pop: 6,189 (1990); 6,401 (1980) Pop Density: 1875.5
Land: 3.3 sq. mi.; Water: 0.0 sq. mi. Elev: 653 ft.
In southwestern OH, 35 mi. north of Cincinnati.
Name origin: For Trenton, NJ.

Union — Township
ZIP: 45069 Lat: 39-20-01 N Long: 84-24-50 W
Pop: 39,703 (1990); 23,553 (1980) Pop Density: 1105.9
Land: 35.9 sq. mi.; Water: 0.0 sq. mi.
In southwestern OH, 6 mi. southeast of Hamilton.

Wayne — Township
Lat: 39-31-29 N Long: 84-31-33 W
Pop: 3,897 (1990); 3,676 (1980) Pop Density: 106.2
Land: 36.7 sq. mi.; Water: 0.0 sq. mi.

Carroll County
County Seat: Carrollton (ZIP: 44615)

Pop: 26,521 (1990); 25,598 (1980) Pop Density: 67.2
Land: 394.7 sq. mi.; Water: 4.3 sq. mi. Area Code: 216
In east-central OH, southeast of Canton; organized Jan 1, 1833 from Columbiana, Stark, Harrison, and Jefferson counties.
Name origin: For Charles Carroll (1737–1832), a signer of the Declaration of Independence, U.S. senator from MD (1789–92), and founder of the Baltimore and Ohio Railroad.

Augusta — Township
Lat: 40-41-26 N Long: 81-02-33 W
Pop: 1,369 (1990); 1,394 (1980) Pop Density: 49.2
Land: 27.8 sq. mi.; Water: 0.0 sq. mi.

Brown — Township
ZIP: 44644 Lat: 40-41-20 N Long: 81-09-49 W
Pop: 7,958 (1990); 7,568 (1980) Pop Density: 189.0
Land: 42.1 sq. mi.; Water: 0.8 sq. mi.

Carrollton
Village
ZIP: 44615   **Lat:** 40-34-47 N **Long:** 81-05-28 W
Pop: 3,042 (1990); 3,065 (1980)   **Pop Density:** 1601.1
Land: 1.9 sq. mi.; **Water:** 0.0 sq. mi.   **Elev:** 1130 ft.
In eastern OH, 20 mi. southeast of Canton.
Name origin: For Charles Carroll (1737–1832), signer of the Declaration of Independence, U.S. senator from MD (1789–92), and founder of the Baltimore and Ohio Railroad.

Center
Township
Lat: 40-34-42 N **Long:** 81-04-37 W
Pop: 4,434 (1990); 4,526 (1980)   **Pop Density:** 299.6
Land: 14.8 sq. mi.; **Water:** 0.0 sq. mi.

Dellroy
Village
ZIP: 44620   **Lat:** 40-33-20 N **Long:** 81-11-57 W
Pop: 314 (1990); 368 (1980)   **Pop Density:** 1570.0
Land: 0.2 sq. mi.; **Water:** 0.0 sq. mi.

East
Township
Lat: 40-41-03 N **Long:** 80-57-13 W
Pop: 734 (1990); 742 (1980)   **Pop Density:** 31.8
Land: 23.1 sq. mi.; **Water:** 0.0 sq. mi.

Fox
Township
Lat: 40-36-04 N **Long:** 80-55-38 W
Pop: 1,033 (1990); 994 (1980)   **Pop Density:** 28.6
Land: 36.1 sq. mi.; **Water:** 0.0 sq. mi.

Harrison
Township
Lat: 40-36-17 N **Long:** 81-09-27 W
Pop: 2,127 (1990); 1,807 (1980)   **Pop Density:** 68.0
Land: 31.3 sq. mi.; **Water:** 0.1 sq. mi.

Lee
Township
Lat: 40-31-53 N **Long:** 80-59-13 W
Pop: 1,046 (1990); 1,000 (1980)   **Pop Density:** 33.0
Land: 31.7 sq. mi.; **Water:** 0.0 sq. mi.

Leesville
Village
ZIP: 44639   **Lat:** 40-27-03 N **Long:** 81-12-34 W
Pop: 156 (1990); 233 (1980)   **Pop Density:** 520.0
Land: 0.3 sq. mi.; **Water:** 0.0 sq. mi.   **Elev:** 985 ft.

Loudon
Township
Lat: 40-27-49 N **Long:** 80-59-25 W
Pop: 933 (1990); 976 (1980)   **Pop Density:** 36.9
Land: 25.3 sq. mi.; **Water:** 0.0 sq. mi.

Magnolia
Village
ZIP: 44643   **Lat:** 40-38-52 N **Long:** 81-17-39 W
Pop: 346 (1990); 309 (1980)   **Pop Density:** 1730.0
Land: 0.2 sq. mi.; **Water:** 0.0 sq. mi.
In northeastern OH along Sandy Creek, 15 mi. south of Canton. Founded 1834. Part of the town is also in Stark County.
Name origin: Named by founder and mill owner Richard Elson, for the flower.

Malvern
Village
ZIP: 44644   **Lat:** 40-41-20 N **Long:** 81-10-54 W
Pop: 1,112 (1990); 1,032 (1980)   **Pop Density:** 1853.3
Land: 0.6 sq. mi.; **Water:** 0.0 sq. mi.   **Elev:** 997 ft.
In eastern OH on Sandy Creek, 16 mi. southeast of Canton.
Name origin: Named by landowners Joseph Tidbald and Lewis Vail for Malvern, PA.

Minerva
Village
ZIP: 44657   **Lat:** 40-43-18 N **Long:** 81-06-37 W
Pop: 2,086 (1990); 2,145 (1980)   **Pop Density:** 2086.0
Land: 1.0 sq. mi.; **Water:** 0.0 sq. mi.
Part of the town is also in Columbiana and Stark counties.
Name origin: For the niece of founder John Whitacre.

Monroe
Township
Lat: 40-31-44 N **Long:** 81-12-29 W
Pop: 1,755 (1990); 1,633 (1980)   **Pop Density:** 70.2
Land: 25.0 sq. mi.; **Water:** 2.0 sq. mi.

Orange
Township
Lat: 40-27-55 N **Long:** 81-13-03 W
Pop: 1,123 (1990); 1,171 (1980)   **Pop Density:** 43.7
Land: 25.7 sq. mi.; **Water:** 1.1 sq. mi.

Perry
Township
Lat: 40-27-50 N **Long:** 81-05-49 W
Pop: 912 (1990); 896 (1980)   **Pop Density:** 32.8
Land: 27.8 sq. mi.; **Water:** 0.2 sq. mi.

Rose
Township
Lat: 40-36-32 N **Long:** 81-15-35 W
Pop: 1,384 (1990); 1,289 (1980)   **Pop Density:** 39.0
Land: 35.5 sq. mi.; **Water:** 0.0 sq. mi.

Sherrodsville
Village
ZIP: 44675   **Lat:** 40-29-40 N **Long:** 81-14-40 W
Pop: 284 (1990); 396 (1980)   **Pop Density:** 946.7
Land: 0.3 sq. mi.; **Water:** 0.0 sq. mi.

Union
Township
Lat: 40-31-37 N **Long:** 81-06-02 W
Pop: 900 (1990); 830 (1980)   **Pop Density:** 40.0
Land: 22.5 sq. mi.; **Water:** 0.1 sq. mi.

Washington
Township
Lat: 40-36-42 N **Long:** 81-01-32 W
Pop: 813 (1990); 772 (1980)   **Pop Density:** 31.3
Land: 26.0 sq. mi.; **Water:** 0.0 sq. mi.

Champaign County
County Seat: Urbana (ZIP: 43078)

Pop: 36,019 (1990); 33,649 (1980)
Land: 428.6 sq. mi.; **Water:** 1.1 sq. mi.
Pop Density: 84.0
Area Code: 513

In west-central OH, west of Columbus; organized Mar 1, 1805 from Greene and Franklin counties.

Name origin: Variation of French *campagne* 'field' or 'plain,' referring to the flatness of the country.

Adams
Township
Lat: 40-13-56 N **Long:** 83-57-48 W
Pop: 1,114 (1990); 1,146 (1980) **Pop Density:** 35.8
Land: 31.1 sq. mi.; **Water:** 0.0 sq. mi.

Christiansburg
Village
Lat: 40-03-24 N **Long:** 84-01-30 W
Pop: 599 (1990); 593 (1980) **Pop Density:** 2995.0
Land: 0.2 sq. mi.; **Water:** 0.0 sq. mi. **Elev:** 1116 ft.

Concord
Township
Lat: 40-10-12 N **Long:** 83-51-02 W
Pop: 1,122 (1990); 1,042 (1980) **Pop Density:** 37.4
Land: 30.0 sq. mi.; **Water:** 0.1 sq. mi.

Goshen
Township
ZIP: 43044 **Lat:** 40-04-16 N **Long:** 83-33-15 W
Pop: 3,172 (1990); 3,255 (1980) **Pop Density:** 84.6
Land: 37.5 sq. mi.; **Water:** 0.0 sq. mi.

Harrison
Township
Lat: 40-13-56 N **Long:** 83-50-50 W
Pop: 713 (1990); 596 (1980) **Pop Density:** 29.2
Land: 24.4 sq. mi.; **Water:** 0.1 sq. mi.

Jackson
Township
Lat: 40-04-35 N **Long:** 83-58-42 W
Pop: 2,244 (1990); 2,148 (1980) **Pop Density:** 60.0
Land: 37.4 sq. mi.; **Water:** 0.0 sq. mi.

Johnson
Township
Lat: 40-09-38 N **Long:** 83-58-09 W
Pop: 3,171 (1990); 2,950 (1980) **Pop Density:** 105.3
Land: 30.1 sq. mi.; **Water:** 0.6 sq. mi.

Mad River
Township
Lat: 40-04-28 N **Long:** 83-51-38 W
Pop: 2,353 (1990); 2,203 (1980) **Pop Density:** 55.1
Land: 42.7 sq. mi.; **Water:** 0.1 sq. mi.

Mechanicsburg
Village
ZIP: 43044 **Lat:** 40-04-27 N **Long:** 83-33-28 W
Pop: 1,803 (1990); 1,792 (1980) **Pop Density:** 1803.0
Land: 1.0 sq. mi.; **Water:** 0.0 sq. mi.

In western OH, 30 mi. west of Columbus.

Mutual
Village
ZIP: 43044 **Lat:** 40-04-44 N **Long:** 83-38-14 W
Pop: 126 (1990); 159 (1980) **Pop Density:** 1260.0
Land: 0.1 sq. mi.; **Water:** 0.0 sq. mi.

North Lewisburg
Village
ZIP: 43060 **Lat:** 40-13-25 N **Long:** 83-33-28 W
Pop: 1,160 (1990); 1,072 (1980) **Pop Density:** 2320.0
Land: 0.5 sq. mi.; **Water:** 0.0 sq. mi. **Elev:** 1087 ft.

Rush
Township
Lat: 40-10-29 N **Long:** 83-32-46 W
Pop: 2,248 (1990); 2,055 (1980) **Pop Density:** 70.9
Land: 31.7 sq. mi.; **Water:** 0.0 sq. mi.

St. Paris
Village
Lat: 40-07-40 N **Long:** 83-57-28 W
Pop: 1,842 (1990); 1,742 (1980) **Pop Density:** 2631.4
Land: 0.7 sq. mi.; **Water:** 0.0 sq. mi.

Salem
Township
Lat: 40-11-01 N **Long:** 83-43-37 W
Pop: 2,045 (1990); 1,970 (1980) **Pop Density:** 40.7
Land: 50.3 sq. mi.; **Water:** 0.0 sq. mi.

Union
Township
Lat: 40-04-39 N **Long:** 83-38-24 W
Pop: 1,651 (1990); 1,529 (1980) **Pop Density:** 44.0
Land: 37.5 sq. mi.; **Water:** 0.0 sq. mi.

Urbana
City
ZIP: 43078 **Lat:** 40-06-31 N **Long:** 83-45-06 W
Pop: 11,353 (1990); 10,762 (1980) **Pop Density:** 1831.1
Land: 6.2 sq. mi.; **Water:** 0.0 sq. mi.

In west-central OH, 12 mi. north of Springfield.

Name origin: From Latin *urbanus* 'citified.' The addition of *a* is a common practice in the United States to designate a place.

*Urbana
Township
ZIP: 43078 **Lat:** 40-04-06 N **Long:** 83-44-49 W
Pop: 14,770 (1990); 13,541 (1980) **Pop Density:** 340.3
Land: 43.4 sq. mi.; **Water:** 0.2 sq. mi.

In west-central OH, 14 mi. north of Springfield.

Wayne
Township
Lat: 40-10-53 N **Long:** 83-37-29 W
Pop: 1,416 (1990); 1,214 (1980) **Pop Density:** 43.7
Land: 32.4 sq. mi.; **Water:** 0.0 sq. mi.

Woodstock
Village
ZIP: 43084 **Lat:** 40-10-24 N **Long:** 83-31-40 W
Pop: 296 (1990); 292 (1980) **Pop Density:** 986.7
Land: 0.3 sq. mi.; **Water:** 0.0 sq. mi. **Elev:** 1042 ft.

Clark County
County Seat: Springfield (ZIP: 45502)

Pop: 147,548 (1990); 150,236 (1980)   **Pop Density:** 368.8
Land: 400.0 sq. mi.; **Water:** 3.8 sq. mi.   **Area Code:** 513
In west-central OH, west of Columbus; organized Mar 1, 1817 from Champaign, Madison, and Greene counties.
Name origin: For Gen. George Rogers Clark (1752–1818), officer in the Revolutionary War and frontiersman in the Northwest Territory.

Bethel — Township
ZIP: 45344   **Lat:** 39-54-43 N **Long:** 83-59-08 W
Pop: 19,580 (1990); 20,128 (1980)   **Pop Density:** 519.4
Land: 37.7 sq. mi.; **Water:** 0.3 sq. mi.
In west-central OH, west of Springfield.

Catawba — Village
ZIP: 43010   **Lat:** 39-59-59 N **Long:** 83-37-20 W
Pop: 268 (1990); 317 (1980)   **Pop Density:** 893.3
Land: 0.3 sq. mi.; **Water:** 0.0 sq. mi.

Clifton — Village
Lat: 39-47-55 N **Long:** 83-49-32 W
Pop: 52 (1990); 45 (1980)   **Pop Density:** 520.0
Land: 0.1 sq. mi.; **Water:** 0.0 sq. mi.
In southwest-central OH on the Little Miami River. Part of the town is also in Greene County.
Name origin: For the cliffs that surround the river.

Crystal Lakes — CDP
Lat: 39-53-05 N **Long:** 84-01-31 W
Pop: 1,613 (1990); 1,463 (1980)   **Pop Density:** 3226.0
Land: 0.5 sq. mi.; **Water:** 0.0 sq. mi.

Donnelsville — Village
ZIP: 45319   **Lat:** 39-55-05 N **Long:** 83-56-47 W
Pop: 276 (1990); 219 (1980)   **Pop Density:** 1380.0
Land: 0.2 sq. mi.; **Water:** 0.0 sq. mi.

Enon — Village
ZIP: 45323   **Lat:** 39-51-55 N **Long:** 83-56-07 W
Pop: 2,605 (1990); 2,597 (1980)   **Pop Density:** 2003.8
Land: 1.3 sq. mi.; **Water:** 0.0 sq. mi.
In western OH, 10 mi. southwest of Springfield.

German — Township
ZIP: 45504   **Lat:** 39-59-06 N **Long:** 83-52-29 W
Pop: 7,467 (1990); 7,397 (1980)   **Pop Density:** 222.2
Land: 33.6 sq. mi.; **Water:** 0.1 sq. mi.

Green — Township
Lat: 39-50-06 N **Long:** 83-47-05 W
Pop: 2,861 (1990); 2,907 (1980)   **Pop Density:** 79.7
Land: 35.9 sq. mi.; **Water:** 0.0 sq. mi.

Green Meadows — CDP
Lat: 39-52-07 N **Long:** 83-56-39 W
Pop: 2,526 (1990); 2,689 (1980)   **Pop Density:** 4210.0
Land: 0.6 sq. mi.; **Water:** 0.0 sq. mi.

Harmony — Township
Lat: 39-53-58 N **Long:** 83-37-40 W
Pop: 3,395 (1990); 3,253 (1980)   **Pop Density:** 66.2
Land: 51.3 sq. mi.; **Water:** 0.0 sq. mi.

Holiday Valley — CDP
Lat: 39-50-51 N **Long:** 83-57-59 W
Pop: 1,243 (1990)   **Pop Density:** 591.9
Land: 2.1 sq. mi.; **Water:** 0.0 sq. mi.

Lawrenceville — Village
Lat: 39-59-06 N **Long:** 83-52-29 W
Pop: 304 (1990); 307 (1980)   **Pop Density:** 3040.0
Land: 0.1 sq. mi.; **Water:** 0.0 sq. mi.

Madison — Township
Lat: 39-49-05 N **Long:** 83-38-50 W
Pop: 2,482 (1990); 2,649 (1980)   **Pop Density:** 60.1
Land: 41.3 sq. mi.; **Water:** 0.0 sq. mi.

Mad River — Township
ZIP: 45324   **Lat:** 39-51-48 N **Long:** 83-55-24 W
Pop: 11,819 (1990); 11,623 (1980)   **Pop Density:** 346.6
Land: 34.1 sq. mi.; **Water:** 0.2 sq. mi.
In west-central OH, 5 mi. southwest of Springfield.

Moorefield — Township
ZIP: 45502   **Lat:** 39-59-05 N **Long:** 83-44-38 W
Pop: 9,621 (1990); 9,823 (1980)   **Pop Density:** 299.7
Land: 32.1 sq. mi.; **Water:** 2.8 sq. mi.

New Carlisle — City
ZIP: 45344   **Lat:** 39-56-36 N **Long:** 84-01-41 W
Pop: 6,049 (1990); 6,498 (1980)   **Pop Density:** 3360.6
Land: 1.8 sq. mi.; **Water:** 0.0 sq. mi.   **Elev:** 906 ft.
In west-central OH, 12 mi. west of Springfield.
Name origin: For Carlisle, NJ.

North Hampton — Village
ZIP: 45349   **Lat:** 39-59-25 N **Long:** 83-56-30 W
Pop: 417 (1990); 421 (1980)   **Pop Density:** 1390.0
Land: 0.3 sq. mi.; **Water:** 0.0 sq. mi.   **Elev:** 1083 ft.

Northridge — CDP
ZIP: 45502   **Lat:** 39-59-49 N **Long:** 83-46-32 W
Pop: 5,939 (1990); 5,559 (1980)   **Pop Density:** 1915.8
Land: 3.1 sq. mi.; **Water:** 0.0 sq. mi.

Park Layne — CDP
Lat: 39-53-11 N **Long:** 84-02-22 W
Pop: 4,795 (1990); 5,372 (1980)   **Pop Density:** 3196.7
Land: 1.5 sq. mi.; **Water:** 0.0 sq. mi.

Pike — Township
Lat: 39-59-25 N **Long:** 83-59-12 W
Pop: 3,784 (1990); 3,469 (1980)   **Pop Density:** 102.3
Land: 37.0 sq. mi.; **Water:** 0.0 sq. mi.

Pleasant — Township
Lat: 39-59-07 N **Long:** 83-36-04 W
Pop: 2,700 (1990); 2,760 (1980)   **Pop Density:** 63.2
Land: 42.7 sq. mi.; **Water:** 0.2 sq. mi.

OHIO, Clark County   *American Places Dictionary*

South Charleston — Village
ZIP: 45368 Lat: 39-49-28 N Long: 83-38-40 W
Pop: 1,626 (1990); 1,682 (1980) Pop Density: 1250.8
Land: 1.3 sq. mi.; Water: 0.0 sq. mi. Elev: 1124 ft.

South Vienna — Village
ZIP: 45369 Lat: 39-55-43 N Long: 83-36-42 W
Pop: 550 (1990); 464 (1980) Pop Density: 1375.0
Land: 0.4 sq. mi.; Water: 0.0 sq. mi.

Springfield — City
ZIP: 45501 Lat: 39-55-36 N Long: 83-47-47 W
Pop: 70,487 (1990); 72,563 (1980) Pop Density: 3614.7
Land: 19.5 sq. mi.; Water: 0.0 sq. mi.

In west-central OH, 24 mi. northeast of Dayton. Incorporated as a town 1801; as a city 1850.

Name origin: For the spring water flowing down the hills that border the valley of Buck Creek.

*Springfield — Township
ZIP: 45505 Lat: 39-54-09 N Long: 83-47-20 W
Pop: 13,352 (1990); 13,664 (1980) Pop Density: 382.6
Land: 34.9 sq. mi.; Water: 0.1 sq. mi.

Tremont City — Village
ZIP: 45372 Lat: 40-00-52 N Long: 83-50-09 W
Pop: 493 (1990); 374 (1980) Pop Density: 1643.3
Land: 0.3 sq. mi.; Water: 0.0 sq. mi.

Clermont County
County Seat: Batavia (ZIP: 45103)

Pop: 150,187 (1990); 128,483 (1980) Pop Density: 332.2
Land: 452.1 sq. mi.; Water: 5.7 sq. mi. Area Code: 513

On the southwestern border of OH, east of Cincinnati; original county; organized Dec 6, 1800 (prior to statehood).

Name origin: For the province in France, former home of some early settlers; French 'clear mountain.'

Amelia — Village
ZIP: 45102 Lat: 39-01-32 N Long: 84-13-00 W
Pop: 1,837 (1990); 1,108 (1980) Pop Density: 2624.3
Land: 0.7 sq. mi.; Water: 0.0 sq. mi.

In southwestern OH, 21 mi. southeast of Cincinnati.

Batavia — Village
ZIP: 45103 Lat: 39-04-42 N Long: 84-10-52 W
Pop: 1,700 (1990); 1,896 (1980) Pop Density: 1133.3
Land: 1.5 sq. mi.; Water: 0.0 sq. mi. Elev: 594 ft.

In southwestern OH on the east fork of the Miami River, 20 mi. east of Cincinnati. Not coextensive with the town of the same name.

*Batavia — Township
ZIP: 45103 Lat: 39-03-42 N Long: 84-10-09 W
Pop: 13,673 (1990); 10,523 (1980) Pop Density: 344.4
Land: 39.7 sq. mi.; Water: 1.6 sq. mi.

Bethel — Village
ZIP: 45106 Lat: 38-57-44 N Long: 84-05-04 W
Pop: 2,407 (1990); 2,231 (1980) Pop Density: 2188.2
Land: 1.1 sq. mi.; Water: 0.0 sq. mi. Elev: 892 ft.

In southwestern OH, 30 mi. southeast of Cincinnati.

Name origin: For the biblical name.

Chilo — Village
ZIP: 45112 Lat: 38-47-37 N Long: 84-08-17 W
Pop: 130 (1990); 173 (1980) Pop Density: 650.0
Land: 0.2 sq. mi.; Water: 0.0 sq. mi.

Day Heights — CDP
Lat: 39-10-26 N Long: 84-13-34 W
Pop: 2,812 (1990) Pop Density: 2343.3
Land: 1.2 sq. mi.; Water: 0.0 sq. mi.

Felicity — Village
ZIP: 45120 Lat: 38-50-23 N Long: 84-05-52 W
Pop: 856 (1990); 929 (1980) Pop Density: 4280.0
Land: 0.2 sq. mi.; Water: 0.0 sq. mi.

Franklin — Township
Lat: 38-50-03 N Long: 84-05-41 W
Pop: 3,803 (1990); 3,191 (1980) Pop Density: 96.8
Land: 39.3 sq. mi.; Water: 0.7 sq. mi.

Goshen — Township
ZIP: 45122 Lat: 39-13-52 N Long: 84-09-32 W
Pop: 12,697 (1990); 12,442 (1980) Pop Density: 368.0
Land: 34.5 sq. mi.; Water: 0.0 sq. mi.

In southwestern OH, 21 mi. northeast of Cincinnati.

Jackson — Township
Lat: 39-07-44 N Long: 84-03-12 W
Pop: 2,461 (1990); 2,221 (1980) Pop Density: 80.4
Land: 30.6 sq. mi.; Water: 0.2 sq. mi.

Loveland — City
ZIP: 45140 Lat: 39-15-45 N Long: 84-15-02 W
Pop: 1,695 (1990); 1,643 (1980) Pop Density: 1695.0
Land: 1.0 sq. mi.; Water: 0.0 sq. mi. Elev: 890 ft.

In southwestern OH on the Little Miami River, 16 mi. northeast of Cincinnati. Part of the town is also in Hamilton and Warren counties.

Name origin: For Col. James Loveland, first storeowner.

Miami — Township
ZIP: 45147 Lat: 39-11-53 N Long: 84-14-45 W
Pop: 28,199 (1990); 28,587 (1980) Pop Density: 849.4
Land: 33.2 sq. mi.; Water: 0.3 sq. mi.

In southwest OH, 15 mi. east-northeast of Cincinnati.

OHIO, Clermont County

Milford — Village
ZIP: 45150 Lat: 39-10-15 N Long: 84-16-53 W
Pop: 5,655 (1990); 5,205 (1980) Pop Density: 1615.7
Land: 3.5 sq. mi.; Water: 0.0 sq. mi.

In southwestern OH, 12 mi. northeast of Cincinnati. Part of the town is also in Hamilton County.

Monroe — Township
ZIP: 45148 Lat: 38-56-42 N Long: 84-12-11 W
Pop: 7,762 (1990); 6,133 (1980) Pop Density: 245.6
Land: 31.6 sq. mi.; Water: 0.1 sq. mi.

Moscow — Village
ZIP: 45153 Lat: 38-51-37 N Long: 84-13-42 W
Pop: 279 (1990); 324 (1980) Pop Density: 697.5
Land: 0.4 sq. mi.; Water: 0.0 sq. mi.

Mount Carmel — CDP
Lat: 39-05-47 N Long: 84-17-54 W
Pop: 4,462 (1990) Pop Density: 2624.7
Land: 1.7 sq. mi.; Water: 0.0 sq. mi.

Mount Repose — CDP
Lat: 39-11-07 N Long: 84-13-28 W
Pop: 3,093 (1990) Pop Density: 2062.0
Land: 1.5 sq. mi.; Water: 0.0 sq. mi.

Mulberry — CDP
Lat: 39-11-50 N Long: 84-14-56 W
Pop: 2,856 (1990) Pop Density: 1904.0
Land: 1.5 sq. mi.; Water: 0.0 sq. mi.

Neville — Village
ZIP: 45156 Lat: 38-48-47 N Long: 84-12-38 W
Pop: 226 (1990); 142 (1980) Pop Density: 565.0
Land: 0.4 sq. mi.; Water: 0.0 sq. mi.

New Richmond — Village
ZIP: 45157 Lat: 38-57-44 N Long: 84-16-47 W
Pop: 2,408 (1990); 2,769 (1980) Pop Density: 708.2
Land: 3.4 sq. mi.; Water: 0.1 sq. mi.

Newtonsville — Village
ZIP: 45158 Lat: 39-10-58 N Long: 84-05-14 W
Pop: 427 (1990); 434 (1980) Pop Density: 2135.0
Land: 0.2 sq. mi.; Water: 0.0 sq. mi.

Ohio — Township
ZIP: 45157 Lat: 38-57-53 N Long: 84-15-00 W
Pop: 5,310 (1990); 5,222 (1980) Pop Density: 390.4
Land: 13.6 sq. mi.; Water: 0.1 sq. mi.

Owensville — Village
ZIP: 45160 Lat: 39-07-25 N Long: 84-08-07 W
Pop: 1,019 (1990); 858 (1980) Pop Density: 2547.5
Land: 0.4 sq. mi.; Water: 0.0 sq. mi. Elev: 862 ft.

Pierce — Township
ZIP: 45245 Lat: 39-01-22 N Long: 84-15-53 W
Pop: 9,589 (1990); 7,262 (1980) Pop Density: 422.4
Land: 22.7 sq. mi.; Water: 0.1 sq. mi.

Stonelick — Township
ZIP: 45103 Lat: 39-08-44 N Long: 84-08-48 W
Pop: 5,597 (1990); 5,133 (1980) Pop Density: 188.5
Land: 29.7 sq. mi.; Water: 0.1 sq. mi.

Summerside — CDP
Lat: 39-07-22 N Long: 84-17-11 W
Pop: 4,573 (1990) Pop Density: 1988.3
Land: 2.3 sq. mi.; Water: 0.0 sq. mi.

Tate — Township
ZIP: 45106 Lat: 38-57-07 N Long: 84-05-20 W
Pop: 8,399 (1990); 7,946 (1980) Pop Density: 181.4
Land: 46.3 sq. mi.; Water: 0.6 sq. mi.

Union — Township
ZIP: 45245 Lat: 39-06-02 N Long: 84-16-04 W
Pop: 33,368 (1990); 28,225 (1980) Pop Density: 1150.6
Land: 29.0 sq. mi.; Water: 0.1 sq. mi.

In southwestern OH, 13 mi. east of Cincinnati.

Washington — Township
Lat: 38-51-42 N Long: 84-10-34 W
Pop: 2,441 (1990); 2,066 (1980) Pop Density: 68.0
Land: 35.9 sq. mi.; Water: 0.4 sq. mi.

Wayne — Township
Lat: 39-12-24 N Long: 84-03-21 W
Pop: 4,749 (1990); 3,352 (1980) Pop Density: 150.3
Land: 31.6 sq. mi.; Water: 0.2 sq. mi.

Williamsburg — Village
ZIP: 45176 Lat: 39-03-11 N Long: 84-03-02 W
Pop: 2,322 (1990); 1,952 (1980) Pop Density: 1451.3
Land: 1.6 sq. mi.; Water: 0.0 sq. mi.

In southwestern OH on the east fork of the Miami River, 25 mi. east of Cincinnati. Not coextensive with the town of the same name.

Name origin: For Williamsburg, VA.

*Williamsburg — Township
ZIP: 45176 Lat: 39-02-09 N Long: 84-03-48 W
Pop: 4,789 (1990); 4,537 (1980) Pop Density: 160.2
Land: 29.9 sq. mi.; Water: 1.0 sq. mi.

Withamsville — CDP
Lat: 39-03-30 N Long: 84-16-11 W
Pop: 2,834 (1990) Pop Density: 1574.4
Land: 1.8 sq. mi.; Water: 0.0 sq. mi.

Clinton County
County Seat: Wilmington (ZIP: 45177)

Pop: 35,415 (1990); 34,603 (1980) **Pop Density:** 86.2
Land: 410.9 sq. mi.; **Water:** 1.4 sq. mi. **Area Code:** 513

In southwestern OH, northeast of Cincinnati; organized Mar 1, 1810 from Highland County.

Name origin: For George Clinton (1739–1812), first governor of NY and vice president of the U.S. (1805–12).

Adams Township
Lat: 39-26-19 N Long: 83-55-49 W
Pop: 1,592 (1990); 1,371 (1980) **Pop Density:** 73.4
Land: 21.7 sq. mi.; **Water:** 0.0 sq. mi.

Blanchester Village
ZIP: 45107 Lat: 39-17-22 N Long: 83-58-46 W
Pop: 4,206 (1990); 3,202 (1980) **Pop Density:** 1450.3
Land: 2.9 sq. mi.; **Water:** 0.1 sq. mi. **Elev:** 971 ft.

In southwestern OH, 30 mi. northeast of Cincinnati. Settled 1832. Part of the town is also in Warren County.

Chester Township
Lat: 39-31-05 N Long: 83-56-22 W
Pop: 1,200 (1990); 1,080 (1980) **Pop Density:** 37.7
Land: 31.8 sq. mi.; **Water:** 0.1 sq. mi.

Clark Township
Lat: 39-17-36 N Long: 83-48-05 W
Pop: 1,581 (1990); 1,672 (1980) **Pop Density:** 43.1
Land: 36.7 sq. mi.; **Water:** 0.0 sq. mi.

Clarksville Village
ZIP: 45113 Lat: 39-24-08 N Long: 83-58-58 W
Pop: 485 (1990); 525 (1980) **Pop Density:** 970.0
Land: 0.5 sq. mi.; **Water:** 0.0 sq. mi.

Green Township
Lat: 39-22-16 N Long: 83-42-08 W
Pop: 2,007 (1990); 2,093 (1980) **Pop Density:** 47.6
Land: 42.2 sq. mi.; **Water:** 0.0 sq. mi.

Jefferson Township
Lat: 39-16-53 N Long: 83-53-10 W
Pop: 1,312 (1990); 1,326 (1980) **Pop Density:** 56.6
Land: 23.2 sq. mi.; **Water:** 0.0 sq. mi.

Liberty Township
Lat: 39-32-31 N Long: 83-48-58 W
Pop: 840 (1990); 953 (1980) **Pop Density:** 33.9
Land: 24.8 sq. mi.; **Water:** 0.0 sq. mi.

Marion Township
ZIP: 45107 Lat: 39-17-57 N Long: 83-57-49 W
Pop: 5,184 (1990); 5,311 (1980) **Pop Density:** 204.1
Land: 25.4 sq. mi.; **Water:** 0.1 sq. mi.

Martinsville Village
ZIP: 45146 Lat: 39-19-22 N Long: 83-48-39 W
Pop: 476 (1990); 539 (1980) **Pop Density:** 1190.0
Land: 0.4 sq. mi.; **Water:** 0.0 sq. mi. **Elev:** 1087 ft.

Midland Village
ZIP: 45148 Lat: 39-18-21 N Long: 83-54-37 W
Pop: 319 (1990); 365 (1980) **Pop Density:** 1063.3
Land: 0.3 sq. mi.; **Water:** 0.0 sq. mi. **Elev:** 994 ft.

New Vienna Village
ZIP: 45159 Lat: 39-19-28 N Long: 83-41-32 W
Pop: 932 (1990); 1,133 (1980) **Pop Density:** 1331.4
Land: 0.7 sq. mi.; **Water:** 0.0 sq. mi.

In southwest-central OH, east of Hamilton.

Name origin: For Vienna, Austria.

Port William Village
ZIP: 45164 Lat: 39-33-06 N Long: 83-47-08 W
Pop: 242 (1990); 300 (1980) **Pop Density:** 2420.0
Land: 0.1 sq. mi.; **Water:** 0.0 sq. mi. **Elev:** 1028 ft.

Richland Township
Lat: 39-29-10 N Long: 83-38-47 W
Pop: 3,626 (1990); 3,735 (1980) **Pop Density:** 107.3
Land: 33.8 sq. mi.; **Water:** 0.0 sq. mi.

Sabina Village
ZIP: 45169 Lat: 39-29-24 N Long: 83-38-01 W
Pop: 2,662 (1990); 2,799 (1980) **Pop Density:** 2047.7
Land: 1.3 sq. mi.; **Water:** 0.0 sq. mi. **Elev:** 1045 ft.

In southwestern OH, southeast of Dayton.

Union Township
ZIP: 45177 Lat: 39-27-21 N Long: 83-49-02 W
Pop: 13,379 (1990); 12,702 (1980) **Pop Density:** 221.5
Land: 60.4 sq. mi.; **Water:** 0.1 sq. mi.

In southwestern OH, 37 mi. east of Hamilton.

Vernon Township
Lat: 39-22-51 N Long: 83-56-46 W
Pop: 2,015 (1990); 1,845 (1980) **Pop Density:** 74.1
Land: 27.2 sq. mi.; **Water:** 0.9 sq. mi.

Washington Township
Lat: 39-21-36 N Long: 83-50-30 W
Pop: 1,475 (1990); 1,296 (1980) **Pop Density:** 53.8
Land: 27.4 sq. mi.; **Water:** 0.2 sq. mi.

Wayne Township
Lat: 39-25-00 N Long: 83-38-02 W
Pop: 681 (1990); 708 (1980) **Pop Density:** 21.6
Land: 31.6 sq. mi.; **Water:** 0.0 sq. mi.

Wilmington City
ZIP: 45177 Lat: 39-26-37 N Long: 83-49-51 W
Pop: 11,199 (1990); 10,431 (1980) **Pop Density:** 2239.8
Land: 5.0 sq. mi.; **Water:** 0.0 sq. mi.

In southwestern OH, 30 mi. southeast of Dayton. Founded 1810.

Name origin: For either Wilmington, NC, or for Spencer Compton (c. 1673–1743), the Earl of Wilmington.

Wilson Township
Lat: 39-31-51 N Long: 83-41-34 W
Pop: 523 (1990); 511 (1980) **Pop Density:** 21.3
Land: 24.6 sq. mi.; **Water:** 0.1 sq. mi.

Columbiana County
County Seat: Lisbon (ZIP: 44432)

Pop: 108,276 (1990); 113,572 (1980)   **Pop Density:** 203.3
Land: 532.5 sq. mi.; **Water:** 2.7 sq. mi.   **Area Code:** 216

On the northeastern border of OH, east of Canton; organized May 1, 1803 from Jefferson and Washington counties.

Name origin: A variation of Columbus or Columbia, for Christopher Columbus (1451–1506). The ending '-iana' may be the feminine form, which was considered appropriate for place names, or it may refer to an unidentified person named Anne or Anna.

Butler   Township
Lat: 40-51-07 N   Long: 80-55-16 W
Pop: 3,265 (1990); 3,228 (1980)   Pop Density: 98.9
Land: 33.0 sq. mi.; Water: 0.1 sq. mi.

Calcutta   CDP
Lat: 40-40-33 N   Long: 80-34-42 W
Pop: 1,212 (1990); 1,121 (1980)   Pop Density: 932.3
Land: 1.3 sq. mi.; Water: 0.0 sq. mi.

Center   Township
ZIP: 44432   Lat: 40-46-11 N   Long: 80-48-19 W
Pop: 6,235 (1990); 6,549 (1980)   Pop Density: 176.6
Land: 35.3 sq. mi.; Water: 0.2 sq. mi.

Columbiana   Village
ZIP: 44408   Lat: 40-53-05 N   Long: 80-41-20 W
Pop: 4,948 (1990); 4,986 (1980)   Pop Density: 1499.4
Land: 3.3 sq. mi.; Water: 0.0 sq. mi.   Elev: 1118 ft.
Part of the town is also in Mahoning County.

East Liverpool   City
ZIP: 43920   Lat: 40-37-58 N   Long: 80-34-10 W
Pop: 13,654 (1990); 16,687 (1980)   Pop Density: 3103.2
Land: 4.4 sq. mi.; Water: 0.2 sq. mi.   Elev: 689 ft.
In eastern OH on the Ohio River, north of Steubenville. Settled 1798; incorporated 1834.
Name origin: For Liverpool, England, former home of early settlers. Previously named Liverpool.

East Palestine   City
ZIP: 44413   Lat: 40-50-14 N   Long: 80-32-41 W
Pop: 5,168 (1990); 5,306 (1980)   Pop Density: 1845.7
Land: 2.8 sq. mi.; Water: 0.0 sq. mi.
In eastern OH, 20 mi. south of Youngstown. Established 1828 by Thomas McCalla and William Grate.

Elkrun   Township
Lat: 40-46-07 N   Long: 80-41-23 W
Pop: 2,186 (1990); 2,288 (1980)   Pop Density: 61.1
Land: 35.8 sq. mi.; Water: 0.0 sq. mi.

Fairfield   Township
ZIP: 44408   Lat: 40-51-24 N   Long: 80-41-18 W
Pop: 8,981 (1990); 8,996 (1980)   Pop Density: 250.2
Land: 35.9 sq. mi.; Water: 0.1 sq. mi.

Franklin   Township
Lat: 40-41-03 N   Long: 80-52-58 W
Pop: 777 (1990); 831 (1980)   Pop Density: 33.8
Land: 23.0 sq. mi.; Water: 0.0 sq. mi.

Glenmoor   CDP
Lat: 40-39-54 N   Long: 80-36-47 W
Pop: 2,307 (1990); 2,588 (1980)   Pop Density: 823.9
Land: 2.8 sq. mi.; Water: 0.0 sq. mi.

Hanover   Township
Lat: 40-45-59 N   Long: 80-55-15 W
Pop: 3,467 (1990); 3,288 (1980)   Pop Density: 96.8
Land: 35.8 sq. mi.; Water: 0.5 sq. mi.

Hanoverton   Village
ZIP: 44423   Lat: 40-45-18 N   Long: 80-56-08 W
Pop: 434 (1990); 490 (1980)   Pop Density: 620.0
Land: 0.7 sq. mi.; Water: 0.0 sq. mi.   Elev: 1137 ft.

Knox   Township
Lat: 40-51-35 N   Long: 81-01-50 W
Pop: 4,449 (1990); 4,486 (1980)   Pop Density: 124.6
Land: 35.7 sq. mi.; Water: 0.2 sq. mi.

La Croft   CDP
Lat: 40-38-49 N   Long: 80-36-04 W
Pop: 1,427 (1990); 1,508 (1980)   Pop Density: 1297.3
Land: 1.1 sq. mi.; Water: 0.0 sq. mi.

Leetonia   Village
ZIP: 44431   Lat: 40-52-42 N   Long: 80-45-39 W
Pop: 2,070 (1990); 2,121 (1980)   Pop Density: 985.7
Land: 2.1 sq. mi.; Water: 0.0 sq. mi.   Elev: 1021 ft.

Lisbon   Village
ZIP: 44432   Lat: 40-46-33 N   Long: 80-46-09 W
Pop: 3,037 (1990); 3,159 (1980)   Pop Density: 2760.9
Land: 1.1 sq. mi.; Water: 0.0 sq. mi.   Elev: 968 ft.
In eastern OH, southeast of Canton. Founded 1802.
Name origin: For Lisbon, Portugal.

Liverpool   Township
Lat: 40-38-30 N   Long: 80-35-14 W
Pop: 4,746 (1990); 4,921 (1980)   Pop Density: 624.5
Land: 7.6 sq. mi.; Water: 0.1 sq. mi.

Madison   Township
Lat: 40-40-56 N   Long: 80-41-59 W
Pop: 3,385 (1990); 3,387 (1980)   Pop Density: 95.1
Land: 35.6 sq. mi.; Water: 0.1 sq. mi.

Middleton   Township
ZIP: 44408   Lat: 40-45-52 N   Long: 80-34-25 W
Pop: 3,422 (1990); 3,426 (1980)   Pop Density: 97.2
Land: 35.2 sq. mi.; Water: 0.2 sq. mi.

Minerva   Village
ZIP: 44657   Lat: 40-44-41 N   Long: 81-05-04 W
Pop: 6 (1990); 7 (1980)   Pop Density: 60.0
Land: 0.1 sq. mi.; Water: 0.0 sq. mi.
Part of the town is also in Carroll and Stark counties.
Name origin: For the niece of founder John Whitacre.

OHIO, Columbiana County

New Waterford
Village
ZIP: 44445 **Lat:** 40-50-54 N **Long:** 80-37-13 W
Pop: 1,278 (1990); 1,314 (1980) **Pop Density:** 1420.0
Land: 0.9 sq. mi.; **Water:** 0.0 sq. mi. **Elev:** 1053 ft.

Perry
Township
ZIP: 44460 **Lat:** 40-54-01 N **Long:** 80-51-30 W
Pop: 17,215 (1990); 17,886 (1980) **Pop Density:** 1089.6
Land: 15.8 sq. mi.; **Water:** 0.0 sq. mi.
In northeastern OH, 27 mi. east-northeast of Canton.

Rogers
Village
ZIP: 44455 **Lat:** 40-47-24 N **Long:** 80-37-37 W
Pop: 247 (1990); 298 (1980) **Pop Density:** 1235.0
Land: 0.2 sq. mi.; **Water:** 0.0 sq. mi. **Elev:** 1023 ft.

St. Clair
Township
ZIP: 43920 **Lat:** 40-41-37 N **Long:** 80-34-28 W
Pop: 7,705 (1990); 8,080 (1980) **Pop Density:** 261.2
Land: 29.5 sq. mi.; **Water:** 0.1 sq. mi.

Salem
City
ZIP: 44460 **Lat:** 40-54-09 N **Long:** 80-51-13 W
Pop: 12,233 (1990); 12,869 (1980) **Pop Density:** 2659.3
Land: 4.6 sq. mi.; **Water:** 0.0 sq. mi. **Elev:** 1226 ft.
In eastern OH, 20 mi. southwest of Youngstown. Founded 1801.
Name origin: For Salem, MA.

*Salem
Township
ZIP: 44460 **Lat:** 40-51-07 N **Long:** 80-47-43 W
Pop: 5,523 (1990); 5,365 (1980) **Pop Density:** 177.0
Land: 31.2 sq. mi.; **Water:** 0.1 sq. mi.

Salineville
Village
ZIP: 43945 **Lat:** 40-37-15 N **Long:** 80-49-58 W
Pop: 1,474 (1990); 1,629 (1980) **Pop Density:** 670.0
Land: 2.2 sq. mi.; **Water:** 0.0 sq. mi. **Elev:** 1084 ft.
In eastern OH, northwest of Steubenville. Part of the town is also in Jefferson County.
Name origin: For the area's salt springs.

Summitville
Village
ZIP: 43962 **Lat:** 40-40-37 N **Long:** 80-53-09 W
Pop: 125 (1990); 146 (1980) **Pop Density:** 138.9
Land: 0.9 sq. mi.; **Water:** 0.0 sq. mi.

Unity
Township
ZIP: 44413 **Lat:** 40-51-42 N **Long:** 80-34-05 W
Pop: 10,129 (1990); 10,220 (1980) **Pop Density:** 286.9
Land: 35.3 sq. mi.; **Water:** 0.2 sq. mi.
In northeastern OH, 15 mi. southeast of Youngstown.

Washington
Township
Lat: 40-37-18 N **Long:** 80-47-51 W
Pop: 2,464 (1990); 2,618 (1980) **Pop Density:** 112.0
Land: 22.0 sq. mi.; **Water:** 0.3 sq. mi.

Washingtonville
Village
ZIP: 44490 **Lat:** 40-53-54 N **Long:** 80-45-52 W
Pop: 482 (1990); 532 (1980) **Pop Density:** 1205.0
Land: 0.4 sq. mi.; **Water:** 0.0 sq. mi. **Elev:** 1069 ft.
Part of the town is also in Mahoning County.

Wayne
Township
Lat: 40-41-20 N **Long:** 80-47-59 W
Pop: 771 (1990); 741 (1980) **Pop Density:** 30.8
Land: 25.0 sq. mi.; **Water:** 0.0 sq. mi.

Wellsville
City
ZIP: 43968 **Lat:** 40-36-09 N **Long:** 80-39-22 W
Pop: 4,532 (1990); 5,095 (1980) **Pop Density:** 2665.9
Land: 1.7 sq. mi.; **Water:** 0.1 sq. mi.

West
Township
Lat: 40-46-17 N **Long:** 81-02-01 W
Pop: 3,162 (1990); 3,022 (1980) **Pop Density:** 90.6
Land: 34.9 sq. mi.; **Water:** 0.2 sq. mi.

Yellow Creek
Township
Lat: 40-36-55 N **Long:** 80-41-51 W
Pop: 2,208 (1990); 2,458 (1980) **Pop Density:** 111.5
Land: 19.8 sq. mi.; **Water:** 0.1 sq. mi.

Coshocton County
County Seat: Coshocton (ZIP: 43812)

Pop: 35,427 (1990); 36,024 (1980) **Pop Density:** 62.8
Land: 564.1 sq. mi.; **Water:** 3.5 sq. mi. **Area Code:** 614
In central OH, southwest of Canton; organized Jan 31, 1810 from Muskingum County.

Name origin: From Delaware Indian *goschachgunk*, thought to mean 'union of waters,' referring to the confluence of the Tuscarawas and Muskingum rivers; 'crossing' or 'ford,' or 'black bear town.'

Adams
Township
Lat: 40-20-16 N **Long:** 81-39-54 W
Pop: 595 (1990); 580 (1980) **Pop Density:** 23.2
Land: 25.7 sq. mi.; **Water:** 0.0 sq. mi.

Baltic
Village
ZIP: 43804 **Lat:** 40-26-34 N **Long:** 81-42-35 W
Pop: 0 (1990); 563 (1980)
Land: 0.004 sq. mi.; **Water:** 0.0 sq. mi. **Elev:** 1041 ft.
Part of the town is also in Holmes and Tuscarawas counties.

Bedford
Township
Lat: 40-15-36 N **Long:** 82-02-07 W
Pop: 499 (1990); 405 (1980) **Pop Density:** 18.7
Land: 26.7 sq. mi.; **Water:** 0.0 sq. mi.

Bethlehem
Township
Lat: 40-20-16 N **Long:** 81-56-57 W
Pop: 1,163 (1990); 1,094 (1980) **Pop Density:** 46.3
Land: 25.1 sq. mi.; **Water:** 0.3 sq. mi.

Clark
Township
ZIP: 43812 **Lat:** 40-24-47 N **Long:** 81-56-39 W
Pop: 578 (1990); 526 (1980) **Pop Density:** 22.8
Land: 25.4 sq. mi.; **Water:** 0.0 sq. mi.

Conesville
Village
ZIP: 43811 **Lat:** 40-11-05 N **Long:** 81-53-32 W
Pop: 420 (1990); 451 (1980) **Pop Density:** 2100.0
Land: 0.2 sq. mi.; **Water:** 0.0 sq. mi.

Coshocton
City
ZIP: 43812 **Lat:** 40-15-49 N **Long:** 81-50-58 W
Pop: 12,193 (1990); 13,405 (1980) **Pop Density:** 1625.7
Land: 7.5 sq. mi.; **Water:** 0.1 sq. mi.
In southeast-central OH, northeast of Zanesville.
Name origin: From Delaware Indian *goschachgunk*, thought to mean 'union of waters,' referring to the confluence of the Tuscarawas and Muskingum rivers; 'crossing' or 'ford,' or 'black bear town.'

Crawford
Township
Lat: 40-24-42 N **Long:** 81-45-03 W
Pop: 1,221 (1990); 1,020 (1980) **Pop Density:** 48.1
Land: 25.4 sq. mi.; **Water:** 0.0 sq. mi.

Franklin
Township
Lat: 40-11-33 N **Long:** 81-51-42 W
Pop: 1,376 (1990); 1,338 (1980) **Pop Density:** 56.4
Land: 24.4 sq. mi.; **Water:** 0.7 sq. mi.

Jackson
Township
Lat: 40-15-54 N **Long:** 81-56-16 W
Pop: 1,947 (1990); 1,947 (1980) **Pop Density:** 61.6
Land: 31.6 sq. mi.; **Water:** 0.2 sq. mi.

Jefferson
Township
Lat: 40-20-25 N **Long:** 82-02-23 W
Pop: 1,383 (1990); 1,421 (1980) **Pop Density:** 52.4
Land: 26.4 sq. mi.; **Water:** 0.0 sq. mi.

Keene
Township
Lat: 40-20-13 N **Long:** 81-50-47 W
Pop: 1,583 (1990); 1,523 (1980) **Pop Density:** 66.2
Land: 23.9 sq. mi.; **Water:** 0.1 sq. mi.

Lafayette
Township
Lat: 40-15-43 N **Long:** 81-45-55 W
Pop: 4,140 (1990); 4,275 (1980) **Pop Density:** 167.6
Land: 24.7 sq. mi.; **Water:** 0.4 sq. mi.

Linton
Township
Lat: 40-11-39 N **Long:** 81-44-07 W
Pop: 611 (1990); 716 (1980) **Pop Density:** 16.9
Land: 36.1 sq. mi.; **Water:** 0.4 sq. mi.

Mill Creek
Township
Lat: 40-25-00 N **Long:** 81-51-00 W
Pop: 540 (1990); 529 (1980) **Pop Density:** 22.8
Land: 23.7 sq. mi.; **Water:** 0.0 sq. mi.

Monroe
Township
Lat: 40-25-36 N **Long:** 82-02-11 W
Pop: 399 (1990); 381 (1980) **Pop Density:** 15.2
Land: 26.2 sq. mi.; **Water:** 0.0 sq. mi.

Nellie
Village
ZIP: 43844 **Lat:** 40-20-17 N **Long:** 82-04-06 W
Pop: 130 (1990); 150 (1980) **Pop Density:** 185.7
Land: 0.7 sq. mi.; **Water:** 0.0 sq. mi. **Elev:** 817 ft.

Newcastle
Township
ZIP: 43843 **Lat:** 40-20-08 N **Long:** 82-08-45 W
Pop: 387 (1990); 358 (1980) **Pop Density:** 15.0
Land: 25.8 sq. mi.; **Water:** 0.0 sq. mi.

Oxford
Township
ZIP: 43845 **Lat:** 40-15-51 N **Long:** 81-40-13 W
Pop: 1,512 (1990); 1,521 (1980) **Pop Density:** 59.8
Land: 25.3 sq. mi.; **Water:** 0.5 sq. mi.

Perry
Township
ZIP: 43843 **Lat:** 40-16-38 N **Long:** 82-08-55 W
Pop: 408 (1990); 343 (1980) **Pop Density:** 15.9
Land: 25.7 sq. mi.; **Water:** 0.0 sq. mi.

Pike
Township
Lat: 40-12-00 N **Long:** 82-08-17 W
Pop: 411 (1990); 415 (1980) **Pop Density:** 16.7
Land: 24.6 sq. mi.; **Water:** 0.0 sq. mi.

Plainfield
Village
ZIP: 43836 **Lat:** 40-12-22 N **Long:** 81-43-08 W
Pop: 178 (1990); 221 (1980) **Pop Density:** 445.0
Land: 0.4 sq. mi.; **Water:** 0.0 sq. mi.

Tiverton
Township
Lat: 40-25-24 N **Long:** 82-08-14 W
Pop: 291 (1990); 322 (1980) **Pop Density:** 11.1
Land: 26.2 sq. mi.; **Water:** 0.0 sq. mi.

Tuscarawas
Township
Lat: 40-16-44 N **Long:** 81-50-37 W
Pop: 2,151 (1990); 2,010 (1980) **Pop Density:** 231.3
Land: 9.3 sq. mi.; **Water:** 0.4 sq. mi.

Virginia
Township
Lat: 40-11-49 N **Long:** 81-57-15 W
Pop: 525 (1990); 516 (1980) **Pop Density:** 21.2
Land: 24.8 sq. mi.; **Water:** 0.2 sq. mi.

Warsaw
Village
ZIP: 43844 **Lat:** 40-20-07 N **Long:** 82-00-05 W
Pop: 699 (1990); 765 (1980) **Pop Density:** 1747.5
Land: 0.4 sq. mi.; **Water:** 0.0 sq. mi.

Washington
Township
Lat: 40-12-02 N **Long:** 82-02-39 W
Pop: 533 (1990); 452 (1980) **Pop Density:** 22.1
Land: 24.1 sq. mi.; **Water:** 0.0 sq. mi.

West Lafayette
Village
ZIP: 43845 **Lat:** 40-16-25 N **Long:** 81-45-03 W
Pop: 2,129 (1990); 2,225 (1980) **Pop Density:** 3548.3
Land: 0.6 sq. mi.; **Water:** 0.0 sq. mi. **Elev:** 807 ft.

White Eyes
Township
Lat: 40-19-49 N **Long:** 81-45-44 W
Pop: 981 (1990); 927 (1980) **Pop Density:** 38.3
Land: 25.6 sq. mi.; **Water:** 0.0 sq. mi.

Crawford County
County Seat: Bucyrus (ZIP: 44820)

Pop: 47,870 (1990); 50,075 (1980)   **Pop Density:** 119.0
Land: 402.3 sq. mi.; **Water:** 0.5 sq. mi.   **Area Code:** 419

In north-central OH, north of Columbus; organized Apr 1, 1820 from Old Indian Territory.

Name origin: For Col. William Crawford (1732–82), VA officer in the Revolutionary War, Indian fighter, and surveyor.

Auburn — Township
Lat: 40-57-13 N Long: 82-45-27 W
Pop: 840 (1990); 989 (1980)   **Pop Density:** 34.0
Land: 24.7 sq. mi.; **Water:** 0.1 sq. mi.

Bucyrus — City
ZIP: 44820   Lat: 40-48-10 N Long: 82-58-24 W
Pop: 13,496 (1990); 13,433 (1980)   **Pop Density:** 2212.5
Land: 6.1 sq. mi.; **Water:** 0.0 sq. mi.

In north-central OH on the Sandusky River, 20 mi. northeast of Marion. County seat since 1830. Settled 1818. Industrial city (farm equipment, construction machinery). Not coextensive with the town of the same name.

Name origin: Named by James Kilbourne, its founder, either for Busiris, the ancient Egyptian city, with a spelling variation; or for Cyrus, king of Persia (c. 558–c. 529 B.C.), and prefixed with *bu* for the 'beautiful' countryside.

*Bucyrus — Township
ZIP: 44820   Lat: 40-46-18 N Long: 83-01-19 W
Pop: 1,105 (1990); 12,274 (1980)   **Pop Density:** 34.9
Land: 31.7 sq. mi.; **Water:** 0.0 sq. mi.

Chatfield — Village
ZIP: 44825   Lat: 40-57-09 N Long: 82-56-29 W
Pop: 206 (1990); 228 (1980)   **Pop Density:** 686.7
Land: 0.3 sq. mi.; **Water:** 0.0 sq. mi.

Not coextensive with the town of the same name.

*Chatfield — Township
Lat: 40-57-09 N Long: 82-55-41 W
Pop: 796 (1990); 880 (1980)   **Pop Density:** 26.6
Land: 29.9 sq. mi.; **Water:** 0.0 sq. mi.

Cranberry — Township
Lat: 40-57-10 N Long: 82-50-21 W
Pop: 1,714 (1990); 1,943 (1980)   **Pop Density:** 60.8
Land: 28.2 sq. mi.; **Water:** 0.0 sq. mi.

Crestline — City
ZIP: 44827   Lat: 40-47-08 N Long: 82-44-19 W
Pop: 4,925 (1990); 5,392 (1980)   **Pop Density:** 2141.3
Land: 2.3 sq. mi.; **Water:** 0.0 sq. mi.

In north-central OH, 10 mi. west of Mansfield. Part of the town is also in Richland County.

Name origin: For its location on the watershed.

Dallas — Township
Lat: 40-43-11 N Long: 83-03-03 W
Pop: 456 (1990); 482 (1980)   **Pop Density:** 20.6
Land: 22.1 sq. mi.; **Water:** 0.0 sq. mi.

Galion — City
ZIP: 44833   Lat: 40-43-54 N Long: 82-47-25 W
Pop: 11,859 (1990); 12,391 (1980)   **Pop Density:** 2420.2
Land: 4.9 sq. mi.; **Water:** 0.0 sq. mi.   **Elev:** 1166 ft.

In north-central OH, 15 mi. west of Mansfield. Settled 1831 by Michael and Jacob Ruhl, German Lutherans from PA.

Name origin: Given this name by the Post Office for reasons unknown.

Holmes — Township
Lat: 40-52-04 N Long: 83-00-37 W
Pop: 1,397 (1990); 2,551 (1980)   **Pop Density:** 39.0
Land: 35.8 sq. mi.; **Water:** 0.0 sq. mi.

Jackson — Township
ZIP: 44827   Lat: 40-47-32 N Long: 82-44-38 W
Pop: 5,392 (1990); 5,800 (1980)   **Pop Density:** 523.5
Land: 10.3 sq. mi.; **Water:** 0.0 sq. mi.

Jefferson — Township
Lat: 40-47-06 N Long: 82-48-45 W
Pop: 1,662 (1990); 1,731 (1980)   **Pop Density:** 86.6
Land: 19.2 sq. mi.; **Water:** 0.1 sq. mi.

Liberty — Township
Lat: 40-52-12 N Long: 82-54-41 W
Pop: 1,470 (1990); 1,489 (1980)   **Pop Density:** 44.8
Land: 32.8 sq. mi.; **Water:** 0.1 sq. mi.

Lykens — Township
Lat: 40-57-23 N Long: 83-01-27 W
Pop: 637 (1990); 694 (1980)   **Pop Density:** 21.1
Land: 30.2 sq. mi.; **Water:** 0.0 sq. mi.

New Washington — Village
ZIP: 44854   Lat: 40-57-41 N Long: 82-51-15 W
Pop: 1,057 (1990); 1,213 (1980)   **Pop Density:** 813.1
Land: 1.3 sq. mi.; **Water:** 0.0 sq. mi.

In north-central OH, 20 mi. northwest of Mansfield.

Name origin: For George Washington (1732–99), patriot and first U.S. president.

North Robinson — Village
Lat: 40-47-31 N Long: 82-51-22 W
Pop: 216 (1990); 302 (1980)   **Pop Density:** 2160.0
Land: 0.1 sq. mi.; **Water:** 0.0 sq. mi.

Polk — Township
Lat: 40-44-48 N Long: 82-47-36 W
Pop: 2,321 (1990); 2,770 (1980)   **Pop Density:** 146.9
Land: 15.8 sq. mi.; **Water:** 0.0 sq. mi.

Sandusky — Township
Lat: 40-51-33 N Long: 82-49-56 W
Pop: 473 (1990); 497 (1980)   **Pop Density:** 26.4
Land: 17.9 sq. mi.; **Water:** 0.0 sq. mi.

Texas — Township
Lat: 40-57-26 N **Long:** 83-05-33 W
Pop: 420 (1990); 458 (1980) **Pop Density:** 35.0
Land: 12.0 sq. mi.; **Water:** 0.0 sq. mi.

Tiro — Village
ZIP: 44887 **Lat:** 40-54-21 N **Long:** 82-46-05 W
Pop: 246 (1990); 279 (1980) **Pop Density:** 615.0
Land: 0.4 sq. mi.; **Water:** 0.0 sq. mi.

Tod — Township
Lat: 40-50-29 N **Long:** 83-05-37 W
Pop: 746 (1990); 755 (1980) **Pop Density:** 41.0
Land: 18.2 sq. mi.; **Water:** 0.0 sq. mi.

Vernon — Township
Lat: 40-51-25 N **Long:** 82-45-47 W
Pop: 768 (1990); 804 (1980) **Pop Density:** 35.7
Land: 21.5 sq. mi.; **Water:** 0.0 sq. mi.

Whetstone — Township
Lat: 40-45-13 N **Long:** 82-54-12 W
Pop: 2,318 (1990); 3,567 (1980) **Pop Density:** 56.7
Land: 40.9 sq. mi.; **Water:** 0.1 sq. mi.

Cuyahoga County
County Seat: Cleveland (ZIP: 44113)

Pop: 1,412,140 (1990); 1,498,400 (1980) **Pop Density:** 3081.4
Land: 458.3 sq. mi.; **Water:** 787.3 sq. mi. **Area Code:** 216

On the northeastern border of OH, bordered on north by Lake Erie; organized Jun 7, 1808 from Geauga County.

Name origin: For the Cuyahoga River, which runs through it; from an Indian word, exact origin uncertain. Possibly from *Cayahaga* 'crooked,' or *Cuyahoganuk* 'lake river,' or the Iroquoian word for 'river.'

Bay Village — City
ZIP: 44140 **Lat:** 41-29-23 N **Long:** 81-55-45 W
Pop: 17,000 (1990); 17,846 (1980) **Pop Density:** 3695.7
Land: 4.6 sq. mi.; **Water:** 2.5 sq. mi.

In northeastern OH overlooking Lake Erie, a suburb of Cleveland.

Beachwood — City
ZIP: 44122 **Lat:** 41-28-43 N **Long:** 81-30-08 W
Pop: 10,677 (1990); 9,983 (1980) **Pop Density:** 2321.1
Land: 4.6 sq. mi.; **Water:** 0.0 sq. mi.

In northeastern OH on Lake Erie, a suburb of Cleveland.

Bedford — City
ZIP: 44146 **Lat:** 41-23-28 N **Long:** 81-32-14 W
Pop: 14,822 (1990); 15,056 (1980) **Pop Density:** 2796.6
Land: 5.3 sq. mi.; **Water:** 0.0 sq. mi.

In northeastern OH, a residential suburb 10 mi. southeast of Cleveland. Site of a temporary settlement by Moravian missionaries in 1786.
Name origin: For Bedford, CT.

Bedford Heights — City
ZIP: 44146 **Lat:** 41-24-18 N **Long:** 81-30-22 W
Pop: 12,131 (1990); 13,214 (1980) **Pop Density:** 2695.8
Land: 4.5 sq. mi.; **Water:** 0.0 sq. mi.

In northeastern OH, 11 mi. southeast of Cleveland.
Name origin: For Bedford, Bedfordshire, England.

Bentleyville — Village
ZIP: 44022 **Lat:** 41-24-48 N **Long:** 81-24-47 W
Pop: 674 (1990); 381 (1980) **Pop Density:** 259.2
Land: 2.6 sq. mi.; **Water:** 0.0 sq. mi. **Elev:** 938 ft.

Berea — City
ZIP: 44017 **Lat:** 41-22-11 N **Long:** 81-51-45 W
Pop: 19,051 (1990); 19,567 (1980) **Pop Density:** 3463.8
Land: 5.5 sq. mi.; **Water:** 0.1 sq. mi.

In northern OH, 10 mi. southeast of Cleveland. Industrial city (greenhouse horticulture and research).
Name origin: For the biblical city in ancient Syria; name chosen by a committee (including two clergymen) instructed to select a biblical name for a new post office.

Bratenahl — Village
ZIP: 44108 **Lat:** 41-33-27 N **Long:** 81-35-49 W
Pop: 1,356 (1990); 1,485 (1980) **Pop Density:** 1356.0
Land: 1.0 sq. mi.; **Water:** 0.6 sq. mi.

In northeastern OH on Lake Erie.

Brecksville — City
ZIP: 44141 **Lat:** 41-18-27 N **Long:** 81-37-06 W
Pop: 11,818 (1990); 10,132 (1980) **Pop Density:** 603.0
Land: 19.6 sq. mi.; **Water:** 0.0 sq. mi.

In northern OH, 12 mi. south of Cleveland. Settled c. 1811.
Name origin: For early landowners John and Robert Breck.

Broadview Heights — City
ZIP: 44141 **Lat:** 41-19-09 N **Long:** 81-40-47 W
Pop: 12,219 (1990); 10,920 (1980) **Pop Density:** 932.7
Land: 13.1 sq. mi.; **Water:** 0.0 sq. mi.

In northeastern OH, a southern suburb of Cleveland.

Brooklyn — City
ZIP: 44144 **Lat:** 41-26-04 N **Long:** 81-44-58 W
Pop: 11,706 (1990); 12,342 (1980) **Pop Density:** 2722.3
Land: 4.3 sq. mi.; **Water:** 0.0 sq. mi. **Elev:** 765 ft.

In northeastern OH, a southern suburb of Cleveland.
Name origin: Named for reasons of euphony, not for Brooklyn, NY.

OHIO, Cuyahoga County

Brooklyn Heights Village
ZIP: 44131 Lat: 41-24-56 N Long: 81-39-55 W
Pop: 1,450 (1990); 1,653 (1980) Pop Density: 805.6
Land: 1.8 sq. mi.; Water: 0.0 sq. mi.

Brook Park City
ZIP: 44142 Lat: 41-24-00 N Long: 81-49-36 W
Pop: 22,865 (1990); 26,195 (1980) Pop Density: 2931.4
Land: 7.8 sq. mi.; Water: 0.0 sq. mi.

In northeastern OH near a branch of the Rocky River. A southwestern suburb of Cleveland.

Name origin: Descriptive and promotional.

Chagrin Falls City
ZIP: 44022 Lat: 41-25-52 N Long: 81-23-22 W
Pop: 4,146 (1990); 4,335 (1980) Pop Density: 1974.3
Land: 2.1 sq. mi.; Water: 0.0 sq. mi.

In northeastern OH in a wide loop of the Chagrin River. An eastern suburb of Cleveland.

Name origin: Named by Moses Cleaveland (1754–1806) and his party of surveyors for the river, itself possibly named from an Indian term meaning 'clear water.'

*Chagrin Falls Township
  Lat: 41-26-01 N Long: 81-23-26 W
Pop: 4,348 (1990); 4,471 (1980) Pop Density: 1672.3
Land: 2.6 sq. mi.; Water: 0.0 sq. mi.

Cleveland City
ZIP: 44101 Lat: 41-28-46 N Long: 81-40-42 W
Pop: 505,616 (1990); 573,822 (1980) Pop Density: 6566.4
Land: 77.0 sq. mi.; Water: 5.1 sq. mi.

In northern OH at the mouth of the Cuyahoga River on Lake Erie. State's largest city. Incorporated as a village 1814, as a city 1836. International port via the St. Lawrence Seaway; commercial and industrial city (iron, steel, chemicals, oil refining). Site of Case Western Reserve Univ.

Name origin: For Gen. Moses Cleaveland (1754–1806), who platted the town site in 1796 for the Connecticut Land Company. The spelling was altered soon after by map makers, was gradually adopted by others, and by the time of incorporation in 1814 so appeared in the Law.

Cleveland Heights City
ZIP: 44118 Lat: 41-30-34 N Long: 81-33-48 W
Pop: 54,052 (1990); 56,438 (1980) Pop Density: 6673.1
Land: 8.1 sq. mi.; Water: 0.0 sq. mi.

In northeastern OH on an Appalachian plateau above Lake Erie, 10 mi. east of Cleveland.

Cuyahoga Heights Village
ZIP: 44125 Lat: 41-26-10 N Long: 81-39-11 W
Pop: 682 (1990); 739 (1980) Pop Density: 213.1
Land: 3.2 sq. mi.; Water: 0.0 sq. mi. Elev: 4718 ft.

East Cleveland City
ZIP: 44112 Lat: 41-31-52 N Long: 81-34-48 W
Pop: 33,096 (1990); 36,957 (1980) Pop Density: 10676.1
Land: 3.1 sq. mi.; Water: 0.0 sq. mi.

In northeastern OH, 4 mi. northeast of Cleveland.

Euclid City
ZIP: 44117 Lat: 41-35-32 N Long: 81-31-09 W
Pop: 54,875 (1990); 59,999 (1980) Pop Density: 5128.5
Land: 10.7 sq. mi.; Water: 0.9 sq. mi. Elev: 618 ft.

In northern OH on Lake Erie, a suburb of Cleveland. Settled 1798.

Name origin: Named for the Greek mathematician (fl. c. 300 B.C.) by surveyors in the party of Moses Cleaveland (1754–1806).

Fairview Park City
ZIP: 44126 Lat: 41-26-26 N Long: 81-51-14 W
Pop: 18,028 (1990); 19,311 (1980) Pop Density: 3835.7
Land: 4.7 sq. mi.; Water: 0.0 sq. mi.

In northeastern OH, 10 mi. southwest of Cleveland city center.

Garfield Heights City
ZIP: 44125 Lat: 41-25-10 N Long: 81-36-14 W
Pop: 31,739 (1990); 34,938 (1980) Pop Density: 4408.2
Land: 7.2 sq. mi.; Water: 0.1 sq. mi.

In northeastern OH on the Cuyahoga River-Ohio Canal, a southern suburb of Cleveland.

Gates Mills Village
ZIP: 44040 Lat: 41-31-57 N Long: 81-24-38 W
Pop: 2,508 (1990); 2,236 (1980) Pop Density: 275.6
Land: 9.1 sq. mi.; Water: 0.0 sq. mi.

In northeastern OH, east of Cleveland.

Name origin: For Halsey Gates, who settled here in 1812.

Glenwillow Village
  Lat: 41-21-38 N Long: 81-28-20 W
Pop: 455 (1990); 492 (1980) Pop Density: 156.9
Land: 2.9 sq. mi.; Water: 0.0 sq. mi.

Highland Heights City
ZIP: 44124 Lat: 41-32-56 N Long: 81-28-17 W
Pop: 6,249 (1990); 5,739 (1980) Pop Density: 1225.3
Land: 5.1 sq. mi.; Water: 0.0 sq. mi. Elev: 934 ft.

Hunting Valley Village
ZIP: 44022 Lat: 41-28-36 N Long: 81-25-11 W
Pop: 648 (1990); 633 (1980) Pop Density: 92.6
Land: 7.0 sq. mi.; Water: 0.0 sq. mi. Elev: 772 ft.

Part of the town is also in Geauga County.

Independence City
ZIP: 44131 Lat: 41-22-49 N Long: 81-38-29 W
Pop: 6,500 (1990); 6,607 (1980) Pop Density: 677.1
Land: 9.6 sq. mi.; Water: 0.0 sq. mi. Elev: 728 ft.

Lakewood City
ZIP: 44107 Lat: 41-29-01 N Long: 81-48-05 W
Pop: 59,718 (1990); 61,963 (1980) Pop Density: 10857.8
Land: 5.5 sq. mi.; Water: 1.1 sq. mi.

In northeastern OH on Lake Erie. A residential suburb of Cleveland.

Name origin: For its setting along the wooded shore of Lake Erie. Originally known as East Rockport.

Linndale Village
  Lat: 41-26-42 N Long: 81-45-59 W
Pop: 159 (1990); 129 (1980) Pop Density: 1590.0
Land: 0.1 sq. mi.; Water: 0.0 sq. mi.

Lyndhurst City
ZIP: 44124 Lat: 41-30-55 N Long: 81-29-33 W
Pop: 15,982 (1990); 18,092 (1980) Pop Density: 3632.3
Land: 4.4 sq. mi.; Water: 0.0 sq. mi.

In northeastern OH, 10 mi. east of downtown Cleveland.

Maple Heights City
ZIP: 44137 **Lat:** 41-24-31 N **Long:** 81-33-46 W
Pop: 27,089 (1990); 29,735 (1980) **Pop Density:** 5209.4
Land: 5.2 sq. mi.; **Water:** 0.0 sq. mi.

In northeastern OH, 8 mi. southeast of Cleveland.

Name origin: For the trees that line many of the streets.

Mayfield Village
Lat: 41-33-12 N **Long:** 81-26-07 W
Pop: 3,462 (1990); 3,577 (1980) **Pop Density:** 887.7
Land: 3.9 sq. mi.; **Water:** 0.0 sq. mi. **Elev:** 927 ft.

In northeastern OH, 15 mi. east of Cleveland.

Mayfield Heights City
ZIP: 44124 **Lat:** 41-31-02 N **Long:** 81-27-14 W
Pop: 19,847 (1990); 21,550 (1980) **Pop Density:** 4725.5
Land: 4.2 sq. mi.; **Water:** 0.0 sq. mi.

In northeastern OH, south of the village of Mayfield, and 15 mi. east of Cleveland.

Name origin: Possibly for Mayfield, Derby, England, but the pleasant associations of the month of May may have had some influence.

Middleburg Heights City
ZIP: 44130 **Lat:** 41-22-03 N **Long:** 81-48-53 W
Pop: 14,702 (1990); 16,218 (1980) **Pop Density:** 1815.1
Land: 8.1 sq. mi.; **Water:** 0.0 sq. mi.

In northwestern OH, 15 mi. southwest of Cleveland, a suburban-residential area.

Moreland Hills Village
ZIP: 44022 **Lat:** 41-26-40 N **Long:** 81-25-51 W
Pop: 3,354 (1990); 3,083 (1980) **Pop Density:** 465.8
Land: 7.2 sq. mi.; **Water:** 0.0 sq. mi. **Elev:** 1037 ft.

Newburgh Heights Village
Lat: 41-27-09 N **Long:** 81-39-44 W
Pop: 2,310 (1990); 2,678 (1980) **Pop Density:** 3850.0
Land: 0.6 sq. mi.; **Water:** 0.0 sq. mi.

In northeast OH, just south of downtown Cleveland.

North Olmsted City
ZIP: 44070 **Lat:** 41-24-52 N **Long:** 81-55-13 W
Pop: 34,204 (1990); 36,486 (1980) **Pop Density:** 2974.3
Land: 11.5 sq. mi.; **Water:** 0.0 sq. mi.

In northeastern OH just south of the Lake Erie shoreline, 15 mi. west of Cleveland.

North Randall Village
ZIP: 44128 **Lat:** 41-25-52 N **Long:** 81-31-50 W
Pop: 977 (1990); 1,054 (1980) **Pop Density:** 1221.3
Land: 0.8 sq. mi.; **Water:** 0.0 sq. mi.

North Royalton City
ZIP: 44133 **Lat:** 41-18-44 N **Long:** 81-44-42 W
Pop: 23,197 (1990); 17,671 (1980) **Pop Density:** 1089.1
Land: 21.3 sq. mi.; **Water:** 0.0 sq. mi. **Elev:** 1197 ft.

In northeastern OH, 20 mi. south of Cleveland in a residential area.

Oakwood Village
Lat: 41-22-01 N **Long:** 81-30-14 W
Pop: 3,392 (1990); 3,786 (1980) **Pop Density:** 969.1
Land: 3.5 sq. mi.; **Water:** 0.0 sq. mi. **Elev:** 64 ft.

In northeastern OH, 15 mi. southeast of Cleveland.

Olmsted Township
ZIP: 44138 **Lat:** 41-22-46 N **Long:** 81-55-59 W
Pop: 8,380 (1990); 6,976 (1980) **Pop Density:** 829.7
Land: 10.1 sq. mi.; **Water:** 0.0 sq. mi.

Olmsted Falls City
ZIP: 44138 **Lat:** 41-22-03 N **Long:** 81-54-17 W
Pop: 6,741 (1990); 5,868 (1980) **Pop Density:** 1644.1
Land: 4.1 sq. mi.; **Water:** 0.0 sq. mi. **Elev:** 774 ft.

In northeastern OH along Rocky Creek, 15 mi. southwest of Cleveland.

Orange Village
ZIP: 44022 **Lat:** 41-26-18 N **Long:** 81-28-19 W
Pop: 2,810 (1990); 2,376 (1980) **Pop Density:** 780.6
Land: 3.6 sq. mi.; **Water:** 0.0 sq. mi. **Elev:** 1158 ft.

Parma City
ZIP: 44129 **Lat:** 41-23-00 N **Long:** 81-43-45 W
Pop: 87,876 (1990); 92,548 (1980) **Pop Density:** 4393.8
Land: 20.0 sq. mi.; **Water:** 0.0 sq. mi.

In northern OH, 10 mi. south of Cleveland. Incorporated as a city 1932.

Name origin: For Parma, Italy.

Parma Heights City
ZIP: 44130 **Lat:** 41-23-09 N **Long:** 81-45-48 W
Pop: 21,448 (1990); 23,112 (1980) **Pop Density:** 5106.7
Land: 4.2 sq. mi.; **Water:** 0.0 sq. mi.

In northeastern OH, 7 mi. southwest of Cleveland.

Pepper Pike City
ZIP: 44124 **Lat:** 41-28-46 N **Long:** 81-27-36 W
Pop: 6,185 (1990); 6,177 (1980) **Pop Density:** 871.1
Land: 7.1 sq. mi.; **Water:** 0.0 sq. mi. **Elev:** 1050 ft.

In northern OH, 10 mi. east of Cleveland.

Richmond Heights City
ZIP: 44143 **Lat:** 41-33-29 N **Long:** 81-30-13 W
Pop: 9,611 (1990); 10,095 (1980) **Pop Density:** 2184.3
Land: 4.4 sq. mi.; **Water:** 0.0 sq. mi.

In northeastern OH just south of Lake Erie, 15 mi. northeast of Cleveland.

Riveredge Township
Lat: 41-25-14 N **Long:** 81-51-04 W
Pop: 0 (1990); 477 (1980)
Land: 0.1 sq. mi.; **Water:** 0.0 sq. mi.

Rocky River City
ZIP: 44116 **Lat:** 41-28-22 N **Long:** 81-51-15 W
Pop: 20,410 (1990); 21,084 (1980) **Pop Density:** 4252.1
Land: 4.8 sq. mi.; **Water:** 0.9 sq. mi.

In northeastern OH at the mouth of the Rocky River on Lake Erie, 10 mi. west of Cleveland city center.

Seven Hills City
ZIP: 44131 **Lat:** 41-22-46 N **Long:** 81-40-30 W
Pop: 12,339 (1990); 13,650 (1980) **Pop Density:** 2467.8
Land: 5.0 sq. mi.; **Water:** 0.0 sq. mi.

In northeastern OH, 7 mi. south of Cleveland.

Name origin: For the Seven Hills of Rome.

Shaker Heights City
ZIP: 44120 **Lat:** 41-28-32 N **Long:** 81-32-52 W
Pop: 30,831 (1990); 32,487 (1980) **Pop Density:** 4893.8
Land: 6.3 sq. mi.; **Water:** 0.0 sq. mi.

In northeastern OH, 8 mi. east of Cleveland.

Name origin: For a former religious colony of Shakers.

OHIO, Cuyahoga County

Solon
City
ZIP: 44139 **Lat:** 41-23-10 N **Long:** 81-26-27 W
Pop: 18,548 (1990); 14,341 (1980) **Pop Density:** 909.2
Land: 20.4 sq. mi.; **Water:** 0.0 sq. mi. **Elev:** 1036 ft.
In northern OH, 12 mi. southeast of Cleveland.
Name origin: For one of the early settlers, Solon Bull (c. 1800-50).

South Euclid
City
ZIP: 44121 **Lat:** 41-31-27 N **Long:** 81-31-30 W
Pop: 23,866 (1990); 25,713 (1980) **Pop Density:** 5077.9
Land: 4.7 sq. mi.; **Water:** 0.0 sq. mi.
In northern OH, 9 mi. east of Cleveland.

Strongsville
City
ZIP: 44136 **Lat:** 41-18-45 N **Long:** 81-49-55 W
Pop: 35,308 (1990); 28,577 (1980) **Pop Density:** 1435.3
Land: 24.6 sq. mi.; **Water:** 0.0 sq. mi. **Elev:** 932 ft.
In northern OH, 13 mi. southwest of Cleveland.
Name origin: For MA statesman Caleb Strong (1745-1819).

University Heights
City
ZIP: 44118 **Lat:** 41-29-40 N **Long:** 81-32-07 W
Pop: 14,790 (1990); 15,401 (1980) **Pop Density:** 8216.7
Land: 1.8 sq. mi.; **Water:** 0.0 sq. mi.
In northeastern OH, 10 mi. west of Cleveland.
Name origin: Originally known as Idlewood.

Valley View
Village
ZIP: 44131 **Lat:** 41-23-10 N **Long:** 81-36-24 W
Pop: 2,137 (1990); 1,576 (1980) **Pop Density:** 381.6
Land: 5.6 sq. mi.; **Water:** 0.0 sq. mi.

Walton Hills
Village
ZIP: 44146 **Lat:** 41-21-51 N **Long:** 81-33-16 W
Pop: 2,371 (1990); 2,199 (1980) **Pop Density:** 343.6
Land: 6.9 sq. mi.; **Water:** 0.0 sq. mi. **Elev:** 989 ft.

Warrensville
Township
Lat: 41-26-58 N **Long:** 81-30-39 W
Pop: 1,934 (1990); 1,640 (1980) **Pop Density:** 644.7
Land: 3.0 sq. mi.; **Water:** 0.0 sq. mi.

Warrensville Heights
City
ZIP: 44122 **Lat:** 41-26-18 N **Long:** 81-31-24 W
Pop: 15,745 (1990); 16,565 (1980) **Pop Density:** 3936.3
Land: 4.0 sq. mi.; **Water:** 0.0 sq. mi. **Elev:** 1039 ft.
In northwestern OH, 11 mi. southeast of Cleveland.
Name origin: For the David Warren family. Originally known as Warrensville.

Westlake
City
ZIP: 44145 **Lat:** 41-27-15 N **Long:** 81-55-43 W
Pop: 27,018 (1990); 19,483 (1980) **Pop Density:** 1699.2
Land: 15.9 sq. mi.; **Water:** 0.0 sq. mi.
In northern OH, 11 mi. west of Cleveland.
Name origin: Probably for its location near Lake Erie and west of Cleveland.

Woodmere
Village
ZIP: 44122 **Lat:** 41-27-33 N **Long:** 81-28-45 W
Pop: 834 (1990); 877 (1980) **Pop Density:** 2780.0
Land: 0.3 sq. mi.; **Water:** 0.0 sq. mi. **Elev:** 171 ft.

Darke County
County Seat: Greenville (ZIP: 45331)

Pop: 53,619 (1990); 55,096 (1980) **Pop Density:** 89.4
Land: 599.9 sq. mi.; **Water:** 0.5 sq. mi. **Area Code:** 513

On the central western border of OH, northwest of Dayton; organized Jan 3, 1809 from Miami County.

Name origin: For Gen. William Darke (1736-1801), an officer in the French and Indian War and the Revolutionary War.

Adams
Township
Lat: 40-07-46 N **Long:** 84-29-17 W
Pop: 3,477 (1990); 3,563 (1980) **Pop Density:** 92.7
Land: 37.5 sq. mi.; **Water:** 0.1 sq. mi.

Allen
Township
Lat: 40-18-08 N **Long:** 84-39-59 W
Pop: 1,276 (1990); 1,441 (1980) **Pop Density:** 44.2
Land: 28.9 sq. mi.; **Water:** 0.1 sq. mi.

Ansonia
Village
ZIP: 45303 **Lat:** 40-12-52 N **Long:** 84-38-07 W
Pop: 1,279 (1990); 1,267 (1980) **Pop Density:** 1827.1
Land: 0.7 sq. mi.; **Water:** 0.0 sq. mi. **Elev:** 1009 ft.

Arcanum
Village
ZIP: 45304 **Lat:** 39-59-29 N **Long:** 84-33-13 W
Pop: 1,953 (1990); 2,002 (1980) **Pop Density:** 1953.0
Land: 1.0 sq. mi.; **Water:** 0.0 sq. mi.
In western OH along Twin Creek, northwest of Dayton.

Bradford
Village
ZIP: 45308 **Lat:** 40-07-53 N **Long:** 84-26-03 W
Pop: 894 (1990); 994 (1980) **Pop Density:** 2980.0
Land: 0.3 sq. mi.; **Water:** 0.0 sq. mi. **Elev:** 989 ft.
In west-central OH, northwest of Dayton. Part of the town is also in Miami County.

Brown
Township
Lat: 40-13-06 N **Long:** 84-39-47 W
Pop: 2,211 (1990); 2,199 (1980) **Pop Density:** 74.4
Land: 29.7 sq. mi.; **Water:** 0.0 sq. mi.

Burkettsville
Village
Lat: 40-21-04 N **Long:** 84-38-37 W
Pop: 87 (1990); 97 (1980) **Pop Density:** 870.0
Land: 0.1 sq. mi.; **Water:** 0.0 sq. mi.
Part of the town is also in Mercer County.

Butler
Township
Lat: 39-57-41 N **Long:** 84-39-02 W
Pop: 1,729 (1990); 1,842 (1980) **Pop Density:** 50.0
Land: 34.6 sq. mi.; **Water:** 0.0 sq. mi.

OHIO, Darke County

Castine
Village
ZIP: 45304 Lat: 39-55-50 N Long: 84-37-28 W
Pop: 163 (1990); 147 (1980) Pop Density: 1630.0
Land: 0.1 sq. mi.; Water: 0.0 sq. mi.

Franklin
Township
Lat: 40-03-07 N Long: 84-28-16 W
Pop: 1,267 (1990); 1,341 (1980) Pop Density: 50.1
Land: 25.3 sq. mi.; Water: 0.0 sq. mi.

Gettysburg
Village
ZIP: 45328 Lat: 40-06-56 N Long: 84-29-45 W
Pop: 539 (1990); 545 (1980) Pop Density: 1347.5
Land: 0.4 sq. mi.; Water: 0.0 sq. mi.
Name origin: For Gettysburg, PA.

Gordon
Village
ZIP: 45304 Lat: 39-55-47 N Long: 84-30-30 W
Pop: 206 (1990); 230 (1980) Pop Density: 1030.0
Land: 0.2 sq. mi.; Water: 0.0 sq. mi.
In western OH near the IN border, northwest of Dayton.

Greenville
City
ZIP: 45331 Lat: 40-06-10 N Long: 84-37-29 W
Pop: 12,863 (1990); 12,999 (1980) Pop Density: 2625.1
Land: 4.9 sq. mi.; Water: 0.0 sq. mi.
In western OH, 30 mi. northwest of Dayton. County seat since 1809. Site of a fort built in 1793 by Gen. Anthony Wayne (1745–96), which two years later became the scene of the Greenville Treaty which led to the opening of the Northwest Territory to European settlement. Once the home of Tecumseh (1768–1813), Shawnee chief. Not coextensive with the town of the same name.
Name origin: For Gen. Nathanael Greene (1742–86).

*Greenville
Township
ZIP: 45331 Lat: 40-07-01 N Long: 84-38-23 W
Pop: 17,302 (1990); 17,470 (1980) Pop Density: 300.4
Land: 57.6 sq. mi.; Water: 0.0 sq. mi.

Harrison
Township
Lat: 39-57-36 N Long: 84-45-28 W
Pop: 2,315 (1990); 2,402 (1980) Pop Density: 67.9
Land: 34.1 sq. mi.; Water: 0.0 sq. mi.

Hollansburg
Village
ZIP: 45332 Lat: 39-59-54 N Long: 84-47-34 W
Pop: 300 (1990); 339 (1980) Pop Density: 3000.0
Land: 0.1 sq. mi.; Water: 0.0 sq. mi.

Ithaca
Village
ZIP: 45304 Lat: 39-56-17 N Long: 84-33-12 W
Pop: 119 (1990); 130 (1980) Pop Density: 3966.7
Land: 0.03 sq. mi.; Water: 0.0 sq. mi.
In western OH, 15 mi. south of Greenville.

Jackson
Township
Lat: 40-12-55 N Long: 84-45-39 W
Pop: 3,356 (1990); 3,569 (1980) Pop Density: 107.9
Land: 31.1 sq. mi.; Water: 0.0 sq. mi.

Liberty
Township
Lat: 40-03-19 N Long: 84-45-26 W
Pop: 1,141 (1990); 1,218 (1980) Pop Density: 34.4
Land: 33.2 sq. mi.; Water: 0.0 sq. mi.

Mississinawa
Township
Lat: 40-18-45 N Long: 84-45-07 W
Pop: 795 (1990); 855 (1980) Pop Density: 27.0
Land: 29.4 sq. mi.; Water: 0.0 sq. mi.

Monroe
Township
Lat: 39-57-44 N Long: 84-27-53 W
Pop: 1,731 (1990); 1,824 (1980) Pop Density: 67.4
Land: 25.7 sq. mi.; Water: 0.0 sq. mi.

Neave
Township
Lat: 40-01-35 N Long: 84-39-21 W
Pop: 2,442 (1990); 2,288 (1980) Pop Density: 106.2
Land: 23.0 sq. mi.; Water: 0.1 sq. mi.

New Madison
Village
ZIP: 45346 Lat: 39-58-06 N Long: 84-42-29 W
Pop: 928 (1990); 1,008 (1980) Pop Density: 2320.0
Land: 0.4 sq. mi.; Water: 0.0 sq. mi.
In western OH, 11 mi. south of Greenville.

New Weston
Village
ZIP: 45348 Lat: 40-20-13 N Long: 84-38-38 W
Pop: 148 (1990); 184 (1980) Pop Density: 493.3
Land: 0.3 sq. mi.; Water: 0.0 sq. mi.

North Star
Village
ZIP: 45350 Lat: 40-19-26 N Long: 84-34-04 W
Pop: 246 (1990); 254 (1980) Pop Density: 492.0
Land: 0.5 sq. mi.; Water: 0.0 sq. mi.
Elev: 1006 ft.

Osgood
Village
ZIP: 45351 Lat: 40-20-24 N Long: 84-29-39 W
Pop: 255 (1990); 306 (1980) Pop Density: 850.0
Land: 0.3 sq. mi.; Water: 0.0 sq. mi.
Elev: 961 ft.

Palestine
Village
ZIP: 45352 Lat: 40-03-00 N Long: 84-44-40 W
Pop: 197 (1990); 213 (1980) Pop Density: 1970.0
Land: 0.1 sq. mi.; Water: 0.0 sq. mi.

Patterson
Township
Lat: 40-19-03 N Long: 84-28-42 W
Pop: 1,394 (1990); 1,434 (1980) Pop Density: 51.6
Land: 27.0 sq. mi.; Water: 0.0 sq. mi.

Pitsburg
Village
ZIP: 45358 Lat: 39-59-12 N Long: 84-29-15 W
Pop: 425 (1990); 460 (1980) Pop Density: 2125.0
Land: 0.2 sq. mi.; Water: 0.0 sq. mi.

Richland
Township
Lat: 40-11-40 N Long: 84-34-04 W
Pop: 906 (1990); 924 (1980) Pop Density: 42.7
Land: 21.2 sq. mi.; Water: 0.0 sq. mi.

Rossburg
Village
ZIP: 45348 Lat: 40-16-47 N Long: 84-38-17 W
Pop: 250 (1990); 260 (1980) Pop Density: 2500.0
Land: 0.1 sq. mi.; Water: 0.0 sq. mi.
Elev: 1036 ft.

Twin
Township
Lat: 39-57-48 N Long: 84-32-36 W
Pop: 3,899 (1990); 4,063 (1980) Pop Density: 134.0
Land: 29.1 sq. mi.; Water: 0.0 sq. mi.

Union City
Village
ZIP: 45390 Lat: 40-11-53 N Long: 84-47-41 W
Pop: 1,984 (1990); 1,985 (1980) Pop Density: 2204.4
Land: 0.9 sq. mi.; Water: 0.0 sq. mi.
Elev: 1114 ft.

Van Buren
Township
Lat: 40-02-29 N Long: 84-33-10 W
Pop: 1,652 (1990); 1,741 (1980) Pop Density: 65.0
Land: 25.4 sq. mi.; Water: 0.0 sq. mi.

OHIO, Darke County

Versailles
Village
ZIP: 45380 **Lat:** 40-13-22 N **Long:** 84-29-02 W
Pop: 2,351 (1990); 2,384 (1980) **Pop Density:** 1679.3
Land: 1.4 sq. mi.; **Water:** 0.0 sq. mi. **Elev:** 978 ft.
In western OH, 40 mi. northwest of Dayton.
Name origin: For Versailles, France.

Wabash
Township
Lat: 40-19-26 N **Long:** 84-34-04 W
Pop: 931 (1990); 958 (1980) **Pop Density:** 42.5
Land: 21.9 sq. mi.; **Water:** 0.0 sq. mi.

Washington
Township
Lat: 40-07-43 N **Long:** 84-45-33 W
Pop: 1,311 (1990); 1,390 (1980) **Pop Density:** 41.4
Land: 31.7 sq. mi.; **Water:** 0.0 sq. mi.

Wayne
Township
Lat: 40-13-25 N **Long:** 84-28-58 W
Pop: 3,927 (1990); 4,005 (1980) **Pop Density:** 122.7
Land: 32.0 sq. mi.; **Water:** 0.0 sq. mi.

Wayne Lakes
Village
ZIP: 45331 **Lat:** 40-01-16 N **Long:** 84-39-44 W
Pop: 671 (1990) **Pop Density:** 1118.3
Land: 0.6 sq. mi.; **Water:** 0.1 sq. mi.

York
Township
Lat: 40-15-24 N **Long:** 84-34-29 W
Pop: 557 (1990); 569 (1980) **Pop Density:** 25.7
Land: 21.7 sq. mi.; **Water:** 0.0 sq. mi.

Yorkshire
Village
ZIP: 45388 **Lat:** 40-19-31 N **Long:** 84-29-45 W
Pop: 126 (1990); 146 (1980) **Pop Density:** 420.0
Land: 0.3 sq. mi.; **Water:** 0.0 sq. mi. **Elev:** 988 ft.

Defiance County
County Seat: Defiance (ZIP: 43512)

Pop: 39,350 (1990); 39,987 (1980) **Pop Density:** 95.7
Land: 411.2 sq. mi.; **Water:** 3.0 sq. mi. **Area Code:** 419
On the northwestern border of OH; organized Apr 7, 1845 from Williams, Henry, and Paulding counties.
Name origin: For Fort Defiance, built here 1794 by Gen. "Mad Anthony" Wayne (1745–96), and which he described as being so strong that he "defied hell and all her emissaries..." to take it.

Adams
Township
Lat: 41-22-49 N **Long:** 84-17-10 W
Pop: 980 (1990); 1,038 (1980) **Pop Density:** 27.5
Land: 35.6 sq. mi.; **Water:** 0.0 sq. mi.

Defiance
City
ZIP: 43512 **Lat:** 41-16-52 N **Long:** 84-21-42 W
Pop: 16,768 (1990); 16,810 (1980) **Pop Density:** 1927.4
Land: 8.7 sq. mi.; **Water:** 0.5 sq. mi.
In northwestern OH at the junction of the Auglaize and Maumee rivers, 40 mi. northwest of Lima. Incorporated as a village 1836, as a city 1881. Not coextensive with the town of the same name.
Name origin: For Fort Defiance, built here 1794 by Gen. "Mad Anthony" Wayne (1745–96), and which he described as being so strong that he "defied hell and all her emissaries..." to take it.

*Defiance
Township
ZIP: 43512 **Lat:** 41-14-42 N **Long:** 84-23-54 W
Pop: 13,743 (1990); 13,613 (1980) **Pop Density:** 462.7
Land: 29.7 sq. mi.; **Water:** 1.2 sq. mi.

Delaware
Township
Lat: 41-17-41 N **Long:** 84-31-10 W
Pop: 2,025 (1990); 2,100 (1980) **Pop Density:** 57.2
Land: 35.4 sq. mi.; **Water:** 0.6 sq. mi.

Farmer
Township
Lat: 41-23-25 N **Long:** 84-38-09 W
Pop: 808 (1990); 832 (1980) **Pop Density:** 22.1
Land: 36.5 sq. mi.; **Water:** 0.0 sq. mi.

Hicksville
Village
ZIP: 43526 **Lat:** 41-17-40 N **Long:** 84-45-59 W
Pop: 3,664 (1990); 3,929 (1980) **Pop Density:** 1465.6
Land: 2.5 sq. mi.; **Water:** 0.0 sq. mi. **Elev:** 766 ft.
In northwestern OH just west of the IN border, 20 mi. west of Defiance. Laid out 1836. Not coextensive with the town of the same name.
Name origin: For Henry W. Wicks who, with the American Land Company from NY, laid it out.

*Hicksville
Township
ZIP: 43526 **Lat:** 41-17-42 N **Long:** 84-44-52 W
Pop: 4,923 (1990); 5,286 (1980) **Pop Density:** 138.3
Land: 35.6 sq. mi.; **Water:** 0.0 sq. mi.

Highland
Township
Lat: 41-12-39 N **Long:** 84-17-24 W
Pop: 2,612 (1990); 2,642 (1980) **Pop Density:** 72.6
Land: 36.0 sq. mi.; **Water:** 0.0 sq. mi.

Mark
Township
Lat: 41-17-40 N **Long:** 84-38-01 W
Pop: 963 (1990); 1,019 (1980) **Pop Density:** 26.2
Land: 36.7 sq. mi.; **Water:** 0.0 sq. mi.

Milford
Township
Lat: 41-22-33 N **Long:** 84-45-11 W
Pop: 947 (1990); 898 (1980) **Pop Density:** 26.8
Land: 35.4 sq. mi.; **Water:** 0.1 sq. mi.

Ney Village
ZIP: 43549 Lat: 41-22-50 N Long: 84-31-15 W
Pop: 331 (1990); 379 (1980) Pop Density: 827.5
Land: 0.4 sq. mi.; Water: 0.0 sq. mi. Elev: 714 ft.

Noble Township
ZIP: 43512 Lat: 41-18-44 N Long: 84-24-07 W
Pop: 6,249 (1990); 6,340 (1980) Pop Density: 267.1
Land: 23.4 sq. mi.; Water: 0.2 sq. mi.

Richland Township
Lat: 41-17-38 N Long: 84-17-06 W
Pop: 2,791 (1990); 2,946 (1980) Pop Density: 80.0
Land: 34.9 sq. mi.; Water: 0.8 sq. mi.

Sherwood Village
ZIP: 43556 Lat: 41-17-24 N Long: 84-33-10 W
Pop: 828 (1990); 915 (1980) Pop Density: 591.4
Land: 1.4 sq. mi.; Water: 0.0 sq. mi. Elev: 709 ft.

Tiffin Township
Lat: 41-23-01 N Long: 84-23-54 W
Pop: 1,772 (1990); 1,691 (1980) Pop Density: 48.8
Land: 36.3 sq. mi.; Water: 0.1 sq. mi.

Washington Township
Lat: 41-23-01 N Long: 84-30-57 W
Pop: 1,537 (1990); 1,582 (1980) Pop Density: 43.1
Land: 35.7 sq. mi.; Water: 0.0 sq. mi.

Delaware County
County Seat: Delaware (ZIP: 43015)

Pop: 66,929 (1990); 53,840 (1980) Pop Density: 151.2
Land: 442.5 sq. mi.; Water: 13.5 sq. mi. Area Code: 614
In central OH, north of Columbus; organized Apr 1, 1808 from Franklin County.
Name origin: For the Delaware Indians (also called Leni-Lenape), named for the Delaware Bay.

Ashley Village
ZIP: 43003 Lat: 40-24-32 N Long: 82-57-16 W
Pop: 1,059 (1990); 1,057 (1980) Pop Density: 2118.0
Land: 0.5 sq. mi.; Water: 0.0 sq. mi. Elev: 989 ft.
In central OH on the eastern shore of the Delaware Reservoir, 40 mi. north of Columbus.

Berkshire Township
ZIP: 43074 Lat: 40-14-38 N Long: 82-54-08 W
Pop: 2,074 (1990); 1,630 (1980) Pop Density: 92.2
Land: 22.5 sq. mi.; Water: 0.3 sq. mi.

Berlin Township
Lat: 40-14-44 N Long: 82-59-03 W
Pop: 1,978 (1990); 1,625 (1980) Pop Density: 87.9
Land: 22.5 sq. mi.; Water: 3.6 sq. mi.

Brown Township
Lat: 40-19-02 N Long: 82-58-45 W
Pop: 1,164 (1990); 1,007 (1980) Pop Density: 46.4
Land: 25.1 sq. mi.; Water: 0.7 sq. mi.

Concord Township
ZIP: 43015 Lat: 40-12-23 N Long: 83-08-39 W
Pop: 7,597 (1990); 3,791 (1980) Pop Density: 323.3
Land: 23.5 sq. mi.; Water: 1.2 sq. mi.

Delaware City
ZIP: 43015 Lat: 40-17-55 N Long: 83-04-52 W
Pop: 20,030 (1990); 18,780 (1980) Pop Density: 1926.0
Land: 10.4 sq. mi.; Water: 0.1 sq. mi.
In central OH, 21 mi. north of Columbus. Founded 1808. Birthplace of Pres. Rutherford B. Hayes (1822-93). Not coextensive with the town of the same name.
Name origin: For the Delaware Indians (also called Leni-Lenape), who had a village here.

Delaware Township
ZIP: 43015 Lat: 40-17-29 N Long: 83-04-39 W
Pop: 21,028 (1990); 20,127 (1980) Pop Density: 841.1
Land: 25.0 sq. mi.; Water: 0.2 sq. mi.

Dublin Village
ZIP: 43017 Lat: 40-08-54 N Long: 83-08-41 W
Pop: 3,811 (1990); 595 (1980) Pop Density: 2117.2
Land: 1.8 sq. mi.; Water: 0.0 sq. mi.
In central OH on the west bank of the Scioto River. Part of the town is also in Franklin and Union counties.
Name origin: For Dublin, Ireland.

Galena Village
ZIP: 43021 Lat: 40-13-13 N Long: 82-52-55 W
Pop: 361 (1990); 358 (1980) Pop Density: 601.7
Land: 0.6 sq. mi.; Water: 0.0 sq. mi.
In central OH on the Hoover Reservoir, north of Columbus.

Genoa Township
Lat: 40-10-48 N Long: 82-54-03 W
Pop: 4,053 (1990); 4,065 (1980) Pop Density: 215.6
Land: 18.8 sq. mi.; Water: 3.3 sq. mi.

Harlem Township
Lat: 40-09-59 N Long: 82-48-34 W
Pop: 3,391 (1990); 2,981 (1980) Pop Density: 129.4
Land: 26.2 sq. mi.; Water: 0.0 sq. mi.

Kingston Township
Lat: 40-19-05 N Long: 82-53-43 W
Pop: 1,136 (1990); 959 (1980) Pop Density: 48.1
Land: 23.6 sq. mi.; Water: 0.0 sq. mi.

Liberty Township
ZIP: 43065 Lat: 40-11-14 N Long: 83-05-02 W
Pop: 5,944 (1990); 3,325 (1980) Pop Density: 180.7
Land: 32.9 sq. mi.; Water: 0.4 sq. mi.

Marlboro Township
Lat: 40-24-44 N Long: 83-04-15 W
Pop: 213 (1990); 227 (1980) Pop Density: 18.7
Land: 11.4 sq. mi.; Water: 0.6 sq. mi.

Orange Township
Lat: 40-09-57 N Long: 83-00-00 W
Pop: 3,789 (1990); 1,941 (1980) Pop Density: 152.8
Land: 24.8 sq. mi.; Water: 1.6 sq. mi.

OHIO, Delaware County

Ostrander — Village
ZIP: 43061 Lat: 40-15-54 N Long: 83-12-43 W
Pop: 431 (1990); 397 (1980) Pop Density: 1436.7
Land: 0.3 sq. mi.; Water: 0.0 sq. mi. Elev: 937 ft.

Oxford — Township
Lat: 40-23-14 N Long: 82-58-31 W
Pop: 901 (1990); 723 (1980) Pop Density: 46.2
Land: 19.5 sq. mi.; Water: 0.0 sq. mi.

Porter — Township
ZIP: 43074 Lat: 40-18-37 N Long: 82-48-13 W
Pop: 1,345 (1990); 1,160 (1980) Pop Density: 52.1
Land: 25.8 sq. mi.; Water: 0.0 sq. mi.

Powell — Village
ZIP: 43065 Lat: 40-09-37 N Long: 83-03-56 W
Pop: 2,154 (1990); 387 (1980) Pop Density: 1133.7
Land: 1.9 sq. mi.; Water: 0.0 sq. mi. Elev: 922 ft.
In central OH, 15 mi. north of downtown Columbus.

Radnor — Township
ZIP: 43066 Lat: 40-23-01 N Long: 83-09-03 W
Pop: 1,156 (1990); 1,123 (1980) Pop Density: 36.9
Land: 31.3 sq. mi.; Water: 0.1 sq. mi.

Scioto — Township
Lat: 40-17-07 N Long: 83-12-15 W
Pop: 2,129 (1990); 1,832 (1980) Pop Density: 61.4
Land: 34.7 sq. mi.; Water: 0.4 sq. mi.

Shawnee Hills — Village
ZIP: 43065 Lat: 40-09-33 N Long: 83-08-07 W
Pop: 423 (1990); 430 (1980) Pop Density: 1057.5
Land: 0.4 sq. mi.; Water: 0.0 sq. mi.

Sunbury — Village
ZIP: 43074 Lat: 40-14-42 N Long: 82-51-53 W
Pop: 2,046 (1990); 2,101 (1980) Pop Density: 1203.5
Land: 1.7 sq. mi.; Water: 0.0 sq. mi.
In central OH, north of Columbus.

Thompson — Township
Lat: 40-23-52 N Long: 83-12-35 W
Pop: 582 (1990); 566 (1980) Pop Density: 29.0
Land: 20.1 sq. mi.; Water: 0.0 sq. mi.

Trenton — Township
Lat: 40-14-09 N Long: 82-48-09 W
Pop: 1,906 (1990); 1,722 (1980) Pop Density: 71.7
Land: 26.6 sq. mi.; Water: 0.0 sq. mi.

Troy — Township
Lat: 40-21-46 N Long: 83-04-40 W
Pop: 2,261 (1990); 1,878 (1980) Pop Density: 95.4
Land: 23.7 sq. mi.; Water: 1.1 sq. mi.

Westerville — City
ZIP: 43081 Lat: 40-08-18 N Long: 82-54-29 W
Pop: 1,177 (1990); 387 (1980) Pop Density: 511.7
Land: 2.3 sq. mi.; Water: 0.0 sq. mi.
In central OH, 11 mi. north of Columbus. Part of the town is also in Franklin County.
Name origin: For prominent farmers in the area, the Westervelt family.

Erie County
County Seat: Sandusky (ZIP: 44870)

Pop: 76,779 (1990); 79,655 (1980) Pop Density: 301.7
Land: 254.5 sq. mi.; Water: 371.3 sq. mi. Area Code: 419
On the north-central coast of OH, bordered on north by Lake Erie; organized Mar 15, 1838 from Huron and Sandusky counties.
Name origin: For Lake Erie.

Bay View — Village
ZIP: 44870 Lat: 41-28-07 N Long: 82-49-25 W
Pop: 739 (1990); 804 (1980) Pop Density: 2463.3
Land: 0.3 sq. mi.; Water: 0.0 sq. mi.

Berlin — Township
Lat: 41-19-43 N Long: 82-29-44 W
Pop: 3,319 (1990); 3,481 (1980) Pop Density: 108.5
Land: 30.6 sq. mi.; Water: 1.0 sq. mi.

Berlin Heights — Village
ZIP: 44814 Lat: 41-19-15 N Long: 82-29-33 W
Pop: 691 (1990); 756 (1980) Pop Density: 431.9
Land: 1.6 sq. mi.; Water: 0.0 sq. mi. Elev: 777 ft.

Castalia — Village
ZIP: 44824 Lat: 41-24-04 N Long: 82-48-33 W
Pop: 915 (1990); 973 (1980) Pop Density: 915.0
Land: 1.0 sq. mi.; Water: 0.0 sq. mi.

Fairview Lanes — CDP
Lat: 41-25-37 N Long: 82-39-24 W
Pop: 1,120 (1990); 1,244 (1980) Pop Density: 2800.0
Land: 0.4 sq. mi.; Water: 0.0 sq. mi.

Florence — Township
Lat: 41-19-22 N Long: 82-23-18 W
Pop: 2,101 (1990); 2,119 (1980) Pop Density: 81.1
Land: 25.9 sq. mi.; Water: 0.1 sq. mi.

Groton — Township
Lat: 41-19-35 N Long: 82-47-44 W
Pop: 1,245 (1990); 1,235 (1980) Pop Density: 48.1
Land: 25.9 sq. mi.; Water: 0.1 sq. mi.

Huron — City
ZIP: 44839 Lat: 41-23-47 N Long: 82-33-43 W
Pop: 7,030 (1990); 7,123 (1980) Pop Density: 1434.7
Land: 4.9 sq. mi.; Water: 2.8 sq. mi.
In northern OH at the mouth of the Huron River, 10 mi.

American Places Dictionary   OHIO, Fairfield County

southeast of Sandusky. Not coextensive with the town of the same name.
Name origin: For the Indian tribe.

*Huron — Township
ZIP: 44839   **Lat:** 41-23-20 N **Long:** 82-35-25 W
Pop: 9,297 (1990); 9,279 (1980)   **Pop Density:** 392.3
Land: 23.7 sq. mi.; **Water:** 4.1 sq. mi.

Kelleys Island — Village
ZIP: **Lat:** 41-36-09 N **Long:** 82-42-21 W
Pop: 172 (1990); 121 (1980)   **Pop Density:** 37.4
Land: 4.6 sq. mi.; **Water:** 0.1 sq. mi.   **Elev:** 598 ft.

Margaretta — Township
ZIP: 44824   **Lat:** 41-25-35 N **Long:** 82-49-43 W
Pop: 6,255 (1990); 6,536 (1980)   **Pop Density:** 184.0
Land: 34.0 sq. mi.; **Water:** 16.2 sq. mi.

Milan — Village
ZIP: 44846   **Lat:** 41-17-34 N **Long:** 82-36-21 W
Pop: 1,056 (1990); 1,181 (1980)   **Pop Density:** 1508.6
Land: 0.7 sq. mi.; **Water:** 0.0 sq. mi.

Part of the town is also in Huron County.
Name origin: For Milan, Italy.

*Milan — Township
ZIP: 44846   **Lat:** 41-19-16 N **Long:** 82-35-40 W
Pop: 3,149 (1990); 3,310 (1980)   **Pop Density:** 121.6
Land: 25.9 sq. mi.; **Water:** 0.0 sq. mi.

Oxford — Township
   Lat: 41-19-16 N **Long:** 82-41-45 W
Pop: 1,150 (1990); 1,198 (1980)   **Pop Density:** 44.2
Land: 26.0 sq. mi.; **Water:** 0.1 sq. mi.

Perkins — Township
ZIP: 44870   **Lat:** 41-23-55 N **Long:** 82-41-42 W
Pop: 10,793 (1990); 10,989 (1980)   **Pop Density:** 416.7
Land: 25.9 sq. mi.; **Water:** 0.1 sq. mi.

In north-central OH, 3 mi. south of Sandusky.

Sandusky — City
ZIP: 44870   **Lat:** 41-27-21 N **Long:** 82-42-51 W
Pop: 29,764 (1990); 31,360 (1980)   **Pop Density:** 2976.4
Land: 10.0 sq. mi.; **Water:** 11.9 sq. mi.

In northern OH on Lake Erie, 48 mi. west of Cleveland. Platted 1818; incorporated 1824.
Name origin: From the Wyandot Indian term probably meaning 'cold water' or 'pure water.'

Sandusky South — CDP
ZIP: 44870   **Lat:** 41-24-57 N **Long:** 82-41-13 W
Pop: 6,336 (1990); 6,548 (1980)   **Pop Density:** 1545.4
Land: 4.1 sq. mi.; **Water:** 0.0 sq. mi.

Vermilion — City
ZIP: 44089   **Lat:** 41-24-57 N **Long:** 82-21-40 W
Pop: 5,483 (1990); 5,634 (1980)   **Pop Density:** 2741.5
Land: 2.0 sq. mi.; **Water:** 0.0 sq. mi.

In northern OH on Lake Erie and the Vermilion River, just east of Sandusky. Settled 1808. Part of the town is also in Lorain County.
Name origin: For the river.

*Vermilion — Township
ZIP: 44089   **Lat:** 41-23-22 N **Long:** 82-24-06 W
Pop: 9,534 (1990); 10,027 (1980)   **Pop Density:** 433.4
Land: 22.0 sq. mi.; **Water:** 2.3 sq. mi.

In north-central OH, 35 mi. west of Cleveland.

Fairfield County
County Seat: Lancaster (ZIP: 43130)

Pop: 103,461 (1990); 93,678 (1980)   **Pop Density:** 204.6
Land: 505.7 sq. mi.; **Water:** 2.8 sq. mi.   **Area Code:** 614

In central OH, southeast of Columbus; organized Dec 9, 1800 (prior to statehood) from Franklin County.
Name origin: Descriptive name for the rich farmland in the area.

Amanda — Village
ZIP: 43102   **Lat:** 39-39-01 N **Long:** 82-44-35 W
Pop: 729 (1990); 720 (1980)   **Pop Density:** 3645.0
Land: 0.2 sq. mi.; **Water:** 0.0 sq. mi.

In central OH, 30 mi. southeast of Columbus.
Name origin: Named by surveyor William Hamilton.

*Amanda — Township
ZIP: 43102   **Lat:** 39-41-28 N **Long:** 82-46-17 W
Pop: 2,262 (1990); 2,331 (1980)   **Pop Density:** 61.3
Land: 36.9 sq. mi.; **Water:** 0.0 sq. mi.

Baltimore — Village
ZIP: 43105   **Lat:** 39-50-46 N **Long:** 82-36-27 W
Pop: 2,971 (1990); 2,689 (1980)   **Pop Density:** 1747.6
Land: 1.7 sq. mi.; **Water:** 0.0 sq. mi.

In south-central OH, 30 mi. southeast of Columbus.

Berne — Township
ZIP: 43155   **Lat:** 39-39-46 N **Long:** 82-32-40 W
Pop: 4,690 (1990); 4,588 (1980)   **Pop Density:** 105.6
Land: 44.4 sq. mi.; **Water:** 0.1 sq. mi.

Bloom — Township
ZIP: 43136   **Lat:** 39-47-05 N **Long:** 82-45-58 W
Pop: 5,788 (1990); 5,657 (1980)   **Pop Density:** 155.6
Land: 37.2 sq. mi.; **Water:** 0.0 sq. mi.

Bremen — Village
ZIP: 43107   **Lat:** 39-42-21 N **Long:** 82-25-52 W
Pop: 1,386 (1990); 1,432 (1980)   **Pop Density:** 1980.0
Land: 0.7 sq. mi.; **Water:** 0.0 sq. mi.

In central OH, 10 mi. east of Lancaster.
Name origin: For the city in Germany.

Carroll — Village
ZIP: 43112   **Lat:** 39-47-59 N **Long:** 82-42-12 W
Pop: 558 (1990); 641 (1980)   **Pop Density:** 2790.0
Land: 0.2 sq. mi.; **Water:** 0.0 sq. mi.

OHIO, Fairfield County

Clear Creek
Township
Lat: 39-36-24 N Long: 82-47-12 W
Pop: 3,040 (1990); 2,609 (1980) Pop Density: 84.0
Land: 36.2 sq. mi.; Water: 0.0 sq. mi.

Columbus
City
ZIP: 43201-99 Lat: 39-55-19 N Long: 82-48-00 W
Pop: 640 (1990); 45 (1980) Pop Density: 376.5
Land: 1.7 sq. mi.; Water: 0.0 sq. mi.

In central OH on the Scioto River, 98 mi. northeast of Cincinnati. State capital. County seat since 1824. Incorporated as a city 1834. Diverse manufacturing city (airplanes and automobile parts); computer services; site of Battelle Memorial Institute, largest independent research laboratories in the world; site of Ohio State Univ. Part of the town is also in Franklin County.

Name origin: Named in 1816 by Joseph Foos, a senator from Franklin County, for Christopher Columbus (1451–1506). Name is part Latinized, part anglicized form of Cristoforo Colombo.

Fairfield Beach
CDP
Lat: 39-55-04 N Long: 82-28-52 W
Pop: 1,084 (1990) Pop Density: 1806.7
Land: 0.6 sq. mi.; Water: 0.3 sq. mi.

Greenfield
Township
Lat: 39-46-17 N Long: 82-39-11 W
Pop: 4,581 (1990); 4,322 (1980) Pop Density: 139.7
Land: 32.8 sq. mi.; Water: 0.1 sq. mi.

Hocking
Township
Lat: 39-40-49 N Long: 82-40-03 W
Pop: 4,331 (1990); 2,864 (1980) Pop Density: 128.5
Land: 33.7 sq. mi.; Water: 0.0 sq. mi.

Lancaster
City
ZIP: 43130 Lat: 39-43-20 N Long: 82-35-57 W
Pop: 34,507 (1990); 34,953 (1980) Pop Density: 2197.9
Land: 15.7 sq. mi.; Water: 0.0 sq. mi.

In south-central OH, southeast of Columbus. Founded 1800; incorporated 1831.

Name origin: For Lancaster, PA. Previously called New Lancaster.

Liberty
Township
ZIP: 43105 Lat: 39-52-25 N Long: 82-38-10 W
Pop: 6,758 (1990); 6,221 (1980) Pop Density: 134.1
Land: 50.4 sq. mi.; Water: 0.0 sq. mi.

Lithopolis
Village
ZIP: 43136 Lat: 39-48-17 N Long: 82-48-40 W
Pop: 563 (1990); 652 (1980) Pop Density: 1407.5
Land: 0.4 sq. mi.; Water: 0.0 sq. mi.

Madison
Township
Lat: 39-36-04 N Long: 82-40-08 W
Pop: 1,218 (1990); 1,147 (1980) Pop Density: 41.3
Land: 29.5 sq. mi.; Water: 0.0 sq. mi.

Millersport
Village
ZIP: 43046 Lat: 39-53-46 N Long: 82-32-31 W
Pop: 1,010 (1990); 844 (1980) Pop Density: 1122.2
Land: 0.9 sq. mi.; Water: 0.0 sq. mi. Elev: 904 ft.

Pickerington
Village
ZIP: 43147 Lat: 39-53-25 N Long: 82-46-06 W
Pop: 5,645 (1990); 3,886 (1980) Pop Density: 956.8
Land: 5.9 sq. mi.; Water: 0.0 sq. mi. Elev: 842 ft.

In central OH, 10 mi. northwest of Lancaster. Part of the town is also in Franklin County.

Name origin: For Abraham Pickerington, who bought land here 1811.

Pleasant
Township
ZIP: 43130 Lat: 39-46-05 N Long: 82-32-09 W
Pop: 5,623 (1990); 5,551 (1980) Pop Density: 159.7
Land: 35.2 sq. mi.; Water: 0.1 sq. mi.

Pleasantville
Village
ZIP: 43148 Lat: 39-48-32 N Long: 82-31-21 W
Pop: 926 (1990); 780 (1980) Pop Density: 3086.7
Land: 0.3 sq. mi.; Water: 0.0 sq. mi. Elev: 912 ft.

Reynoldsburg
City
ZIP: 43068 Lat: 39-56-19 N Long: 82-47-44 W
Pop: 0 (1990); 20,661 (1980)
Land: 0.8 sq. mi.; Water: 0.0 sq. mi.

In central OH, 10 mi. east of Columbus. Founded by John French in 1831. Part of the town is also in Franklin and Licking counties.

Name origin: For John C. Reynolds. Previously called French Town.

Richland
Township
Lat: 39-47-21 N Long: 82-26-09 W
Pop: 1,840 (1990); 1,616 (1980) Pop Density: 73.0
Land: 25.2 sq. mi.; Water: 0.0 sq. mi.

Rush Creek
Township
Lat: 39-42-04 N Long: 82-25-44 W
Pop: 3,388 (1990); 3,300 (1980) Pop Density: 90.3
Land: 37.5 sq. mi.; Water: 0.0 sq. mi.

Rushville
Village
ZIP: 43150 Lat: 39-45-45 N Long: 82-25-52 W
Pop: 229 (1990); 299 (1980) Pop Density: 1145.0
Land: 0.2 sq. mi.; Water: 0.0 sq. mi.

Stoutsville
Village
ZIP: 43154 Lat: 39-36-23 N Long: 82-49-28 W
Pop: 518 (1990); 537 (1980) Pop Density: 398.5
Land: 1.3 sq. mi.; Water: 0.0 sq. mi.

Sugar Grove
Village
ZIP: 43155 Lat: 39-37-36 N Long: 82-32-49 W
Pop: 465 (1990); 407 (1980) Pop Density: 2325.0
Land: 0.2 sq. mi.; Water: 0.0 sq. mi.

Thurston
Village
ZIP: 43157 Lat: 39-50-28 N Long: 82-32-41 W
Pop: 539 (1990); 527 (1980) Pop Density: 2695.0
Land: 0.2 sq. mi.; Water: 0.0 sq. mi. Elev: 881 ft.

Violet
Township
ZIP: 43147 Lat: 39-52-48 N Long: 82-45-12 W
Pop: 19,253 (1990); 12,613 (1980) Pop Density: 445.7
Land: 43.2 sq. mi.; Water: 0.1 sq. mi.

In central OH, 15 mi. southeast of Columbus.

Walnut
Township
ZIP: 43046 Lat: 39-51-56 N Long: 82-31-37 W
Pop: 6,182 (1990); 5,906 (1980) Pop Density: 129.1
Land: 47.9 sq. mi.; Water: 2.4 sq. mi.

West Rushville — Village
ZIP: 43163 Lat: 39-45-45 N Long: 82-26-54 W
Pop: 134 (1990); 159 (1980) Pop Density: 1340.0
Land: 0.1 sq. mi.; Water: 0.0 sq. mi.

Fayette County
County Seat: Washington Court House (ZIP: 43160)

Pop: 27,466 (1990); 27,467 (1980) Pop Density: 67.5
Land: 406.6 sq. mi.; Water: 0.5 sq. mi. Area Code: 614
In central OH, east of Dayton; organized Mar 1, 1810 from Ross and Highland counties.
Name origin: For the Marquis de Lafayette (1757–1834), French statesman and soldier who fought with the Americans during the Revolutionary War.

Bloomingburg — Village
ZIP: 43106 Lat: 39-36-28 N Long: 83-23-43 W
Pop: 769 (1990); 869 (1980) Pop Density: 1098.6
Land: 0.7 sq. mi.; Water: 0.0 sq. mi. Elev: 998 ft.

Concord — Township
ZIP: 43160 Lat: 39-28-34 N Long: 83-32-20 W
Pop: 1,015 (1990); 1,078 (1980) Pop Density: 35.4
Land: 28.7 sq. mi.; Water: 0.0 sq. mi.

Green — Township
Lat: 39-24-01 N Long: 83-30-59 W
Pop: 451 (1990); 469 (1980) Pop Density: 20.4
Land: 22.1 sq. mi.; Water: 0.0 sq. mi.

Jasper — Township
Lat: 39-33-40 N Long: 83-35-19 W
Pop: 839 (1990); 897 (1980) Pop Density: 20.5
Land: 41.0 sq. mi.; Water: 0.1 sq. mi.

Jefferson — Township
ZIP: 43128 Lat: 39-39-06 N Long: 83-34-20 W
Pop: 2,814 (1990); 2,712 (1980) Pop Density: 46.1
Land: 61.0 sq. mi.; Water: 0.1 sq. mi.

Jeffersonville — Village
ZIP: 43128 Lat: 39-39-07 N Long: 83-33-24 W
Pop: 1,281 (1990); 1,252 (1980) Pop Density: 854.0
Land: 1.5 sq. mi.; Water: 0.0 sq. mi. Elev: 1049 ft.
In southwest-central OH, near Paint Creek.
Name origin: For Thomas Jefferson (1743–1826), third U.S. president.

Madison — Township
ZIP: 43160 Lat: 39-39-48 N Long: 83-19-24 W
Pop: 1,022 (1990); 1,071 (1980) Pop Density: 28.9
Land: 35.4 sq. mi.; Water: 0.2 sq. mi.

Marion — Township
Lat: 39-34-48 N Long: 83-18-48 W
Pop: 713 (1990); 749 (1980) Pop Density: 20.8
Land: 34.2 sq. mi.; Water: 0.0 sq. mi.

Milledgeville — Village
ZIP: 43142 Lat: 39-35-36 N Long: 83-35-16 W
Pop: 120 (1990); 162 (1980) Pop Density: 1200.0
Land: 0.1 sq. mi.; Water: 0.0 sq. mi.

New Holland — Village
ZIP: 43145 Lat: 39-33-27 N Long: 83-16-09 W
Pop: 102 (1990); 116 (1980) Pop Density: 255.0
Land: 0.4 sq. mi.; Water: 0.0 sq. mi. Elev: 851 ft.
Part of the town is also in Pickaway County.

Octa — Village
ZIP: 43160 Lat: 39-36-54 N Long: 83-36-30 W
Pop: 78 (1990); 74 (1980) Pop Density: 260.0
Land: 0.3 sq. mi.; Water: 0.0 sq. mi.

Paint — Township
Lat: 39-39-31 N Long: 83-27-20 W
Pop: 1,711 (1990); 1,845 (1980) Pop Density: 33.1
Land: 51.7 sq. mi.; Water: 0.0 sq. mi.

Perry — Township
Lat: 39-24-58 N Long: 83-26-35 W
Pop: 896 (1990); 904 (1980) Pop Density: 31.2
Land: 28.7 sq. mi.; Water: 0.0 sq. mi.

Union — Township
ZIP: 43160 Lat: 39-32-49 N Long: 83-26-21 W
Pop: 3,718 (1990); 3,691 (1980) Pop Density: 71.0
Land: 52.4 sq. mi.; Water: 0.1 sq. mi.

Washington Court House — City
ZIP: 43160 Lat: 39-32-15 N Long: 83-25-52 W
Pop: 12,983 (1990); 12,682 (1980) Pop Density: 2496.7
Land: 5.2 sq. mi.; Water: 0.1 sq. mi.
In southwestern OH, 26 mi. northwest of Chillicothe.
Name origin: For George Washington (1732–99), patriot and first U.S. president.

Wayne — Township
Lat: 39-28-20 N Long: 83-21-00 W
Pop: 1,304 (1990); 1,369 (1980) Pop Density: 28.3
Land: 46.1 sq. mi.; Water: 0.0 sq. mi.

Franklin County
County Seat: Columbus (ZIP: 43215)

Pop: 961,437 (1990); 869,126 (1980)   **Pop Density:** 1780.5
Land: 540.0 sq. mi.; **Water:** 3.4 sq. mi.   **Area Code:** 614
In central OH; organized Apr 30, 1803 from Ross County.
Name origin: For Benjamin Franklin (1706–90), author, inventor, founder of the Philadelphia Library, scientist, and statesman.

Bexley   City
ZIP: 43209   Lat: 39-57-52 N   Long: 82-56-04 W
Pop: 13,088 (1990); 13,405 (1980)   Pop Density: 5235.2
Land: 2.5 sq. mi.; Water: 0.0 sq. mi.
In central OH, east of Columbus.
Name origin: For Bexley, England.

Blacklick Estates   CDP
ZIP: 43227   Lat: 39-54-17 N   Long: 82-51-52 W
Pop: 10,080 (1990); 9,761 (1980)   Pop Density: 4200.0
Land: 2.4 sq. mi.; Water: 0.0 sq. mi.

Blendon   Township
ZIP: 43081   Lat: 40-05-27 N   Long: 82-53-44 W
Pop: 11,194 (1990); 11,124 (1980)   Pop Density: 1576.6
Land: 7.1 sq. mi.; Water: 0.7 sq. mi.
In central OH, northeast of Columbus.

Brice   Village
ZIP: 43109   Lat: 39-54-59 N   Long: 82-49-55 W
Pop: 109 (1990); 93 (1980)   Pop Density: 1090.0
Land: 0.1 sq. mi.; Water: 0.0 sq. mi.

Brown   Township
Lat: 40-00-10 N   Long: 83-13-40 W
Pop: 1,825 (1990); 1,538 (1980)   Pop Density: 84.1
Land: 21.7 sq. mi.; Water: 0.0 sq. mi.

Canal Winchester   Village
ZIP: 43110   Lat: 39-50-48 N   Long: 82-49-16 W
Pop: 2,617 (1990); 2,712 (1980)   Pop Density: 484.6
Land: 5.4 sq. mi.; Water: 0.0 sq. mi.
Part of the town is also in Fairfield County.

Clinton   Township
Lat: 40-02-02 N   Long: 82-58-15 W
Pop: 4,579 (1990); 5,300 (1980)   Pop Density: 3052.7
Land: 1.5 sq. mi.; Water: 0.0 sq. mi.

Columbus   City
ZIP: 43216   Lat: 39-59-20 N   Long: 82-59-14 W
Pop: 632,270 (1990); 564,976 (1980)   Pop Density: 3340.0
Land: 189.3 sq. mi.; Water: 2.1 sq. mi.
In central OH on the Scioto River, 98 mi. northeast of Cincinnati. State capital. County seat since 1824. Incorporated as a city 1834. Diverse manufacturing city (airplanes and automobile parts); computer services; site of Battelle Memorial Institute, largest independent research laboratories in the world; site of Ohio State Univ. Part of the town is also in Fairfield County.
Name origin: Named in 1816 by Joseph Foos, a senator from Franklin County, for Christopher Columbus (1451–1506). Name is part Latinized, part anglicized form of Cristoforo Colombo.

Dublin   Village
ZIP: 43016   Lat: 40-06-49 N   Long: 83-07-57 W
Pop: 12,551 (1990); 3,260 (1980)   Pop Density: 799.4
Land: 15.7 sq. mi.; Water: 0.0 sq. mi.
In central OH on the west bank of the Scioto River. Part of the town is also in Delaware and Union counties.
Name origin: For Dublin, Ireland.

Franklin   Township
ZIP: 43204   Lat: 39-55-55 N   Long: 83-03-50 W
Pop: 14,757 (1990); 14,395 (1980)   Pop Density: 1676.9
Land: 8.8 sq. mi.; Water: 0.0 sq. mi.
In central OH, 4 mi. west of Columbus.

Gahanna   City
ZIP: 43230   Lat: 40-01-30 N   Long: 82-52-30 W
Pop: 27,791 (1990); 18,001 (1980)   Pop Density: 2105.4
Land: 13.2 sq. mi.; Water: 0.0 sq. mi.
In south-central OH, 8 mi. northeast of Columbus.
Name origin: From Algonquian Indian term *hanna* probably meaning 'stream.'

Grandview Heights   City
ZIP: 43212   Lat: 39-58-46 N   Long: 83-02-23 W
Pop: 7,010 (1990); 7,420 (1980)   Pop Density: 5392.3
Land: 1.3 sq. mi.; Water: 0.0 sq. mi.
In central OH on the Olentangy River, just west of downtown Columbus.

Grove City   City
ZIP: 43123   Lat: 39-52-23 N   Long: 83-04-28 W
Pop: 19,661 (1990); 16,816 (1980)   Pop Density: 1946.6
Land: 10.1 sq. mi.; Water: 0.0 sq. mi.
In central OH, just south of Columbus.
Name origin: Named by William F. Bruck for its descriptive connotations.

Groveport   Village
ZIP: 43125   Lat: 39-51-41 N   Long: 82-53-50 W
Pop: 2,948 (1990); 3,286 (1980)   Pop Density: 427.2
Land: 6.9 sq. mi.; Water: 0.0 sq. mi.   Elev: 745 ft.
In central OH between the Hocking River and Big Walnut Creek, 9 mi. southeast of Columbus.
Name origin: Originally called Wert's Grove for Jacob Wert and the walnut groves here. In 1846 present name coined from a combination of Wert's *Grove* and Rareys*port*, for John Rareys, who in 1844 had started a settlement nearby.

Hamilton   Township
ZIP: 43137   Lat: 39-50-19 N   Long: 82-57-47 W
Pop: 9,746 (1990); 10,161 (1980)   Pop Density: 487.3
Land: 20.0 sq. mi.; Water: 0.3 sq. mi.
In central OH, 9 mi. south of Columbus.

OHIO, Franklin County

Harrisburg — Village
ZIP: 43126 Lat: 39-48-39 N Long: 83-10-17 W
Pop: 340 (1990); 356 (1980) Pop Density: 3400.0
Land: 0.1 sq. mi.; Water: 0.0 sq. mi.
Part of the town is also in Pickaway County.

Hilliard — City
ZIP: 43026 Lat: 40-02-16 N Long: 83-08-33 W
Pop: 11,796 (1990); 8,131 (1980) Pop Density: 1371.6
Land: 8.6 sq. mi.; Water: 0.0 sq. mi.
In south-central OH, west of Columbus. Laid out 1853.
Name origin: For John Hilliard, who laid it out.

Huber Ridge — CDP
ZIP: 43081 Lat: 40-05-24 N Long: 82-55-06 W
Pop: 5,255 (1990); 5,835 (1980) Pop Density: 4379.2
Land: 1.2 sq. mi.; Water: 0.0 sq. mi.

Jackson — Township
ZIP: 43123 Lat: 39-51-18 N Long: 83-04-07 W
Pop: 25,265 (1990); 23,024 (1980) Pop Density: 684.7
Land: 36.9 sq. mi.; Water: 0.0 sq. mi.
In central OH, 9 mi. south of Columbus.

Jefferson — Township
Lat: 40-00-59 N Long: 82-48-15 W
Pop: 3,983 (1990); 4,061 (1980) Pop Density: 220.1
Land: 18.1 sq. mi.; Water: 0.0 sq. mi.

Lake Darby — CDP
Lat: 39-57-26 N Long: 83-13-44 W
Pop: 2,798 (1990); 2,304 (1980) Pop Density: 822.9
Land: 3.4 sq. mi.; Water: 0.0 sq. mi.

Lincoln Village — CDP
ZIP: 43228 Lat: 39-57-16 N Long: 83-07-51 W
Pop: 9,958 (1990); 10,548 (1980) Pop Density: 5241.1
Land: 1.9 sq. mi.; Water: 0.0 sq. mi.

Lockbourne — Village
ZIP: 43137 Lat: 39-48-32 N Long: 82-58-13 W
Pop: 173 (1990); 373 (1980) Pop Density: 1730.0
Land: 0.1 sq. mi.; Water: 0.0 sq. mi.

Madison — Township
ZIP: 43125 Lat: 39-50-53 N Long: 82-52-09 W
Pop: 18,749 (1990); 20,274 (1980) Pop Density: 415.7
Land: 45.1 sq. mi.; Water: 0.0 sq. mi.
In central OH, 9 mi. southeast of Columbus.

Marble Cliff — Village
ZIP: 43212 Lat: 39-59-06 N Long: 83-03-37 W
Pop: 633 (1990); 630 (1980) Pop Density: 2110.0
Land: 0.3 sq. mi.; Water: 0.0 sq. mi.

Mifflin — Township
ZIP: 43230 Lat: 40-01-19 N Long: 82-52-45 W
Pop: 28,449 (1990); 22,832 (1980) Pop Density: 1962.0
Land: 14.5 sq. mi.; Water: 0.0 sq. mi.
In central OH, 5 mi. northeast of Columbus.

Minerva Park — Village
ZIP: 43229 Lat: 40-04-39 N Long: 82-56-36 W
Pop: 1,463 (1990); 1,618 (1980) Pop Density: 2926.0
Land: 0.5 sq. mi.; Water: 0.0 sq. mi.

New Albany — Village
ZIP: 43054 Lat: 40-04-46 N Long: 82-48-31 W
Pop: 1,621 (1990); 409 (1980) Pop Density: 279.5
Land: 5.8 sq. mi.; Water: 0.0 sq. mi.
In central OH, 13 mi. northeast of Columbus.
Name origin: For Albany, NY.

New Rome — Village
ZIP: 43228 Lat: 39-57-05 N Long: 83-08-28 W
Pop: 111 (1990); 63 (1980) Pop Density: 3700.0
Land: 0.03 sq. mi.; Water: 0.0 sq. mi.

Norwich — Township
ZIP: 43026 Lat: 40-01-59 N Long: 83-08-52 W
Pop: 15,960 (1990); 13,258 (1980) Pop Density: 1071.1
Land: 14.9 sq. mi.; Water: 0.0 sq. mi.
In central OH, 5 mi. northwest of Columbus.

Obetz — Village
ZIP: 43207 Lat: 39-52-36 N Long: 82-56-26 W
Pop: 3,167 (1990); 3,095 (1980) Pop Density: 1131.1
Land: 2.8 sq. mi.; Water: 0.0 sq. mi.

Perry — Township
ZIP: 43017 Lat: 40-06-33 N Long: 83-05-07 W
Pop: 5,933 (1990); 6,402 (1980) Pop Density: 847.6
Land: 7.0 sq. mi.; Water: 0.0 sq. mi.
In central OH, 9 mi. northwest of Columbus.

Pickerington — Village
Lat: 39-54-13 N Long: 82-47-59 W
Pop: 23 (1990); 31 (1980) Pop Density: 76.7
Land: 0.3 sq. mi.; Water: 0.0 sq. mi. Elev: 842 ft.
In central OH, 10 mi. northwest of Lancaster. Part of the town is also in Fairfield County.
Name origin: For Abraham Pickerington, who bought land here 1811.

Plain — Township
Lat: 40-05-48 N Long: 82-48-33 W
Pop: 4,366 (1990); 4,572 (1980) Pop Density: 189.0
Land: 23.1 sq. mi.; Water: 0.0 sq. mi.

Pleasant — Township
ZIP: 43123 Lat: 39-51-34 N Long: 83-11-08 W
Pop: 6,678 (1990); 6,068 (1980) Pop Density: 153.9
Land: 43.4 sq. mi.; Water: 0.2 sq. mi.

Prairie — Township
ZIP: 43119 Lat: 39-56-18 N Long: 83-11-09 W
Pop: 16,945 (1990); 16,340 (1980) Pop Density: 770.2
Land: 22.0 sq. mi.; Water: 0.0 sq. mi.
In central OH, 8 mi. west of Columbus.

Reynoldsburg — City
ZIP: 43068 Lat: 39-57-22 N Long: 82-48-22 W
Pop: 24,483 (1990); 19,668 (1980) Pop Density: 3654.2
Land: 6.7 sq. mi.; Water: 0.0 sq. mi.
In central OH, 10 mi. east of Columbus. Founded by John French in 1831. Part of the town is also in Fairfield and Licking counties.
Name origin: For John C. Reynolds. Previously called French Town.

Riverlea — Village
ZIP: 43085 Lat: 40-04-49 N Long: 83-01-32 W
Pop: 503 (1990); 528 (1980) Pop Density: 2515.0
Land: 0.2 sq. mi.; Water: 0.0 sq. mi.

Sharon
Township
ZIP: 43085 **Lat:** 40-06-04 N **Long:** 83-00-45 W
Pop: 17,493 (1990); 18,129 (1980) **Pop Density:** 1841.4
Land: 9.5 sq. mi.; **Water:** 0.0 sq. mi.

In central OH, 9 mi. north of Columbus.

Truro
Township
ZIP: 43068 **Lat:** 39-57-21 N **Long:** 82-48-34 W
Pop: 26,265 (1990); 21,551 (1980) **Pop Density:** 3455.9
Land: 7.6 sq. mi.; **Water:** 0.0 sq. mi.

In central OH, 7 mi. east of Columbus.

Upper Arlington
City
ZIP: 43221 **Lat:** 40-01-35 N **Long:** 83-04-13 W
Pop: 34,128 (1990); 35,648 (1980) **Pop Density:** 3555.0
Land: 9.6 sq. mi.; **Water:** 0.0 sq. mi.

In central OH, northwest of Columbus.

Name origin: For a development organization, the Upper Arlington Company.

Urbancrest
Village
ZIP: 43123 **Lat:** 39-53-57 N **Long:** 83-05-20 W
Pop: 862 (1990); 880 (1980) **Pop Density:** 2155.0
Land: 0.4 sq. mi.; **Water:** 0.0 sq. mi.

Valleyview
Village
ZIP: 43204 **Lat:** 39-57-53 N **Long:** 83-04-22 W
Pop: 604 (1990); 730 (1980) **Pop Density:** 3020.0
Land: 0.2 sq. mi.; **Water:** 0.0 sq. mi.

Washington
Township
ZIP: 43017 **Lat:** 40-05-40 N **Long:** 83-09-25 W
Pop: 13,090 (1990); 4,322 (1980) **Pop Density:** 579.2
Land: 22.6 sq. mi.; **Water:** 0.0 sq. mi.

In central OH, 4 mi. southwest of Columbus.

Westerville
City
ZIP: 43081 **Lat:** 40-06-59 N **Long:** 82-55-08 W
Pop: 29,092 (1990); 23,027 (1980) **Pop Density:** 3547.8
Land: 8.2 sq. mi.; **Water:** 0.0 sq. mi.

In central OH, 11 mi. north of Columbus. Part of the town is also in Delaware County.

Name origin: For prominent farmers in the area, the Westervelt family.

Whitehall
City
ZIP: 43213 **Lat:** 39-58-06 N **Long:** 82-53-01 W
Pop: 20,572 (1990); 21,299 (1980) **Pop Density:** 4033.7
Land: 5.1 sq. mi.; **Water:** 0.0 sq. mi.

In central OH on Big Walnut Creek, 6 mi. east of Columbus.

Name origin: For the site of the main government offices in London, England.

Worthington
City
ZIP: 43085 **Lat:** 40-05-51 N **Long:** 83-01-15 W
Pop: 14,869 (1990); 15,016 (1980) **Pop Density:** 2655.2
Land: 5.6 sq. mi.; **Water:** 0.0 sq. mi.

In central OH, 10 mi. north of Columbus.

Name origin: Named in 1803 for the Worthington family, who were active in OH government.

Fulton County
County Seat: Wauseon (ZIP: 43567)

Pop: 38,498 (1990); 37,751 (1980) **Pop Density:** 94.6
Land: 406.8 sq. mi.; **Water:** 0.5 sq. mi. **Area Code:** 419

On the northwestern border of OH, west of Toledo; organized Apr 1, 1850 from Lucas, Henry, and Williams counties.

Name origin: For Robert Fulton (1765–1815), builder of the *Clermont*, the first commercially successful steamboat.

Amboy
Township
Lat: 41-41-29 N **Long:** 83-56-36 W
Pop: 1,531 (1990); 1,596 (1980) **Pop Density:** 58.9
Land: 26.0 sq. mi.; **Water:** 0.0 sq. mi.

Archbold
Village
ZIP: 43502 **Lat:** 41-30-55 N **Long:** 84-18-15 W
Pop: 3,440 (1990); 3,318 (1980) **Pop Density:** 1228.6
Land: 2.8 sq. mi.; **Water:** 0.1 sq. mi. **Elev:** 734 ft.

Chesterfield
Township
Lat: 41-40-45 N **Long:** 84-09-48 W
Pop: 1,055 (1990); 1,044 (1980) **Pop Density:** 36.1
Land: 29.2 sq. mi.; **Water:** 0.0 sq. mi.

Clinton
Township
ZIP: 43567 **Lat:** 41-32-20 N **Long:** 84-10-25 W
Pop: 8,327 (1990); 8,122 (1980) **Pop Density:** 200.7
Land: 41.5 sq. mi.; **Water:** 0.1 sq. mi.

Delta
Village
ZIP: 43515 **Lat:** 41-34-26 N **Long:** 84-00-09 W
Pop: 2,849 (1990); 2,831 (1980) **Pop Density:** 1295.0
Land: 2.2 sq. mi.; **Water:** 0.0 sq. mi.

In northwestern OH, 25 mi. west of Toledo.

Dover
Township
Lat: 41-36-34 N **Long:** 84-09-48 W
Pop: 1,111 (1990); 1,125 (1980) **Pop Density:** 51.7
Land: 21.5 sq. mi.; **Water:** 0.0 sq. mi.

Fayette
Village
ZIP: 43521 **Lat:** 41-40-21 N **Long:** 84-19-44 W
Pop: 1,248 (1990); 1,222 (1980) **Pop Density:** 1386.7
Land: 0.9 sq. mi.; **Water:** 0.0 sq. mi.

Franklin
Township
Lat: 41-36-44 N **Long:** 84-18-17 W
Pop: 740 (1990); 737 (1980) **Pop Density:** 25.8
Land: 28.7 sq. mi.; **Water:** 0.1 sq. mi.

Fulton
Township
Lat: 41-37-18 N **Long:** 83-56-15 W
Pop: 3,193 (1990); 3,226 (1980) **Pop Density:** 111.3
Land: 28.7 sq. mi.; **Water:** 0.0 sq. mi.

German
Township
ZIP: 43502 **Lat:** 41-32-30 N **Long:** 84-18-10 W
Pop: 5,477 (1990); 5,432 (1980) **Pop Density:** 108.0
Land: 50.7 sq. mi.; **Water:** 0.1 sq. mi.

Gorham
Township
Lat: 41-40-21 N **Long:** 84-18-36 W
Pop: 2,248 (1990); 2,304 (1980) **Pop Density:** 51.8
Land: 43.4 sq. mi.; **Water:** 0.1 sq. mi.

Lyons
Village
ZIP: 43533 **Lat:** 41-41-58 N **Long:** 84-04-22 W
Pop: 579 (1990); 596 (1980) **Pop Density:** 827.1
Land: 0.7 sq. mi.; **Water:** 0.0 sq. mi. **Elev:** 771 ft.
In northwestern OH, just south of the MI border, 50 mi. west of Toledo.

Metamora
Village
ZIP: 43540 **Lat:** 41-42-39 N **Long:** 83-54-28 W
Pop: 543 (1990); 556 (1980) **Pop Density:** 1810.0
Land: 0.3 sq. mi.; **Water:** 0.0 sq. mi.

Pike
Township
Lat: 41-37-22 N **Long:** 84-03-36 W
Pop: 1,542 (1990); 1,436 (1980) **Pop Density:** 54.9
Land: 28.1 sq. mi.; **Water:** 0.1 sq. mi.

Royalton
Township
Lat: 41-41-07 N **Long:** 84-03-31 W
Pop: 1,395 (1990); 1,441 (1980) **Pop Density:** 56.5
Land: 24.7 sq. mi.; **Water:** 0.0 sq. mi.

Swan Creek
Township
ZIP: 43558 **Lat:** 41-32-21 N **Long:** 83-56-06 W
Pop: 7,699 (1990); 7,307 (1980) **Pop Density:** 182.4
Land: 42.2 sq. mi.; **Water:** 0.0 sq. mi.

Swanton
Village
ZIP: 43558 **Lat:** 41-34-59 N **Long:** 83-53-34 W
Pop: 3,378 (1990); 3,424 (1980) **Pop Density:** 1777.9
Land: 1.9 sq. mi.; **Water:** 0.0 sq. mi.
Part of the town is also in Lucas County.

Wauseon
Village
ZIP: 43567 **Lat:** 41-33-12 N **Long:** 84-08-30 W
Pop: 6,322 (1990); 6,173 (1980) **Pop Density:** 1404.9
Land: 4.5 sq. mi.; **Water:** 0.0 sq. mi. **Elev:** 757 ft.
In northwestern OH, west of Toledo.

York
Township
Lat: 41-32-12 N **Long:** 84-03-41 W
Pop: 4,180 (1990); 3,981 (1980) **Pop Density:** 99.3
Land: 42.1 sq. mi.; **Water:** 0.0 sq. mi.

Gallia County
County Seat: Gallipolis (ZIP: 45631)

Pop: 30,954 (1990); 30,098 (1980) **Pop Density:** 66.0
Land: 468.8 sq. mi.; **Water:** 2.4 sq. mi. **Area Code:** 614
On the southeastern border of OH; organized in Apr 30, 1803 from Washington County.
Name origin: For Gaul, the Latin name for France, chosen by French colonists.

Addison
Township
ZIP: 45631 **Lat:** 38-53-36 N **Long:** 82-10-14 W
Pop: 2,422 (1990); 2,495 (1980) **Pop Density:** 88.7
Land: 27.3 sq. mi.; **Water:** 0.2 sq. mi.

Centerville
Village
ZIP: 45685 **Lat:** 38-53-54 N **Long:** 82-26-42 W
Pop: 128 (1990); 148 (1980) **Pop Density:** 1280.0
Land: 0.1 sq. mi.; **Water:** 0.0 sq. mi.

Cheshire
Village
ZIP: 45620 **Lat:** 38-56-38 N **Long:** 82-06-44 W
Pop: 250 (1990); 297 (1980) **Pop Density:** 1250.0
Land: 0.2 sq. mi.; **Water:** 0.0 sq. mi. **Elev:** 573 ft.
Not coextensive with the town of the same name.

*Cheshire
Township
ZIP: 45620 **Lat:** 38-58-13 N **Long:** 82-09-18 W
Pop: 1,245 (1990); 1,232 (1980) **Pop Density:** 41.0
Land: 30.4 sq. mi.; **Water:** 0.4 sq. mi.

Clay
Township
ZIP: 45631 **Lat:** 38-42-53 N **Long:** 82-13-29 W
Pop: 1,912 (1990); 1,593 (1980) **Pop Density:** 86.5
Land: 22.1 sq. mi.; **Water:** 0.5 sq. mi.

Crown City
Village
ZIP: 45623 **Lat:** 38-35-17 N **Long:** 82-17-22 W
Pop: 445 (1990); 513 (1980) **Pop Density:** 404.5
Land: 1.1 sq. mi.; **Water:** 0.0 sq. mi.

Gallipolis
City
ZIP: 45631 **Lat:** 38-49-11 N **Long:** 82-11-29 W
Pop: 4,831 (1990); 5,576 (1980) **Pop Density:** 1420.9
Land: 3.4 sq. mi.; **Water:** 0.1 sq. mi. **Elev:** 576 ft.
In southern OH on the Ohio River near the WV border, northeast of Ironton. Established 1790. Not coextensive with the town of the same name.

*Gallipolis
Township
ZIP: 45631 **Lat:** 38-49-20 N **Long:** 82-11-53 W
Pop: 6,500 (1990); 7,228 (1980) **Pop Density:** 643.6
Land: 10.1 sq. mi.; **Water:** 0.3 sq. mi.

Green
Township
ZIP: 45658 **Lat:** 38-48-17 N **Long:** 82-17-28 W
Pop: 5,189 (1990); 4,907 (1980) **Pop Density:** 135.8
Land: 38.2 sq. mi.; **Water:** 0.0 sq. mi.

Greenfield
Township
ZIP: 45658 Lat: 38-48-30 N Long: 82-31-26 W
Pop: 437 (1990); 399 (1980) Pop Density: 13.1
Land: 33.3 sq. mi.; Water: 0.0 sq. mi.

Guyan
Township
ZIP: 45623 Lat: 38-37-42 N Long: 82-18-45 W
Pop: 1,181 (1990); 1,346 (1980) Pop Density: 37.4
Land: 31.6 sq. mi.; Water: 0.0 sq. mi.

Harrison
Township
Lat: 38-42-29 N Long: 82-17-56 W
Pop: 970 (1990); 780 (1980) Pop Density: 31.0
Land: 31.3 sq. mi.; Water: 0.0 sq. mi.

Huntington
Township
Lat: 38-59-39 N Long: 82-23-06 W
Pop: 1,445 (1990); 1,520 (1980) Pop Density: 39.2
Land: 36.9 sq. mi.; Water: 0.0 sq. mi.

Morgan
Township
Lat: 38-58-37 N Long: 82-16-20 W
Pop: 1,332 (1990); 1,115 (1980) Pop Density: 43.0
Land: 31.0 sq. mi.; Water: 0.0 sq. mi.

Ohio
Township
Lat: 38-37-44 N Long: 82-13-12 W
Pop: 1,006 (1990); 1,002 (1980) Pop Density: 43.2
Land: 23.3 sq. mi.; Water: 0.3 sq. mi.

Perry
Township
ZIP: 45658 Lat: 38-48-53 N Long: 82-24-04 W
Pop: 1,029 (1990); 946 (1980) Pop Density: 26.9
Land: 38.3 sq. mi.; Water: 0.0 sq. mi.

Raccoon
Township
Lat: 38-53-48 N Long: 82-23-46 W
Pop: 2,247 (1990); 1,884 (1980) Pop Density: 60.2
Land: 37.3 sq. mi.; Water: 0.4 sq. mi.

Rio Grande
Village
ZIP: 45674 Lat: 38-52-53 N Long: 82-22-43 W
Pop: 995 (1990); 864 (1980) Pop Density: 1105.6
Land: 0.9 sq. mi.; Water: 0.0 sq. mi.

Springfield
Township
Lat: 38-53-39 N Long: 82-16-34 W
Pop: 3,204 (1990); 2,792 (1980) Pop Density: 87.1
Land: 36.8 sq. mi.; Water: 0.1 sq. mi.

Vinton
Village
ZIP: 45686 Lat: 38-58-38 N Long: 82-20-25 W
Pop: 293 (1990); 375 (1980) Pop Density: 266.4
Land: 1.1 sq. mi.; Water: 0.0 sq. mi.

Walnut
Township
ZIP: 45658 Lat: 38-43-09 N Long: 82-24-45 W
Pop: 835 (1990); 859 (1980) Pop Density: 20.4
Land: 41.0 sq. mi.; Water: 0.0 sq. mi.

Geauga County
County Seat: Chardon (ZIP: 44024)

Pop: 81,129 (1990); 74,474 (1980) Pop Density: 200.7
Land: 404.1 sq. mi.; Water: 4.6 sq. mi. Area Code: 216

In northeastern OH, east of Cleveland; organized Mar 1, 1806 from Trumbull County.

Name origin: Meaning of name is unclear: possibly from Iroquoian *sheauga* 'raccoon,' or for an Indian chief.

Aquilla
Village
Lat: 41-32-45 N Long: 81-10-16 W
Pop: 360 (1990); 355 (1980) Pop Density: 3600.0
Land: 0.1 sq. mi.; Water: 0.0 sq. mi.

Auburn
Township
Lat: 41-22-47 N Long: 81-14-44 W
Pop: 3,298 (1990); 2,351 (1980) Pop Density: 118.2
Land: 27.9 sq. mi.; Water: 2.1 sq. mi.

Bainbridge
CDP
Lat: 41-23-36 N Long: 81-20-13 W
Pop: 3,602 (1990) Pop Density: 1059.4
Land: 3.4 sq. mi.; Water: 0.1 sq. mi.

*Bainbridge
Township
ZIP: 44022 Lat: 41-23-12 N Long: 81-20-46 W
Pop: 9,694 (1990); 8,207 (1980) Pop Density: 377.2
Land: 25.7 sq. mi.; Water: 0.2 sq. mi.

Burton
Village
ZIP: 44021 Lat: 41-28-13 N Long: 81-08-47 W
Pop: 1,349 (1990); 1,401 (1980) Pop Density: 1226.4
Land: 1.1 sq. mi.; Water: 0.0 sq. mi.

In northeastern OH near the Cuyahoga River. Not coextensive with the town of the same name.
Name origin: For the son of founder Titus Street.

*Burton
Township
ZIP: 44021 Lat: 41-27-48 N Long: 81-08-38 W
Pop: 4,187 (1990); 4,180 (1980) Pop Density: 172.3
Land: 24.3 sq. mi.; Water: 0.1 sq. mi.

Chardon
Village
ZIP: 44024 Lat: 41-34-44 N Long: 81-12-30 W
Pop: 4,446 (1990); 4,434 (1980) Pop Density: 966.5
Land: 4.6 sq. mi.; Water: 0.0 sq. mi.

In northeastern OH, 25 mi. northeast of Cleveland.
Name origin: For Peter Chardon Brooks, first owner of the site.

*Chardon
Township
ZIP: 44024 Lat: 41-37-08 N Long: 81-15-03 W
Pop: 4,037 (1990); 7,907 (1980) Pop Density: 176.3
Land: 22.9 sq. mi.; Water: 0.0 sq. mi.

Chester
Township
ZIP: 44026 Lat: 41-31-52 N Long: 81-20-37 W
Pop: 11,049 (1990); 11,212 (1980) Pop Density: 470.2
Land: 23.5 sq. mi.; Water: 0.0 sq. mi.

In northeastern OH, 18 mi. northeast of Cleveland.

American Places Dictionary   OHIO, Greene County

Chesterland   CDP
ZIP: 44026   **Lat:** 41-31-27 N   **Long:** 81-20-34 W
Pop: 2,078 (1990); 2,301 (1980)   **Pop Density:** 742.1
Land: 2.8 sq. mi.; **Water:** 0.0 sq. mi.

Claridon   Township
Lat: 41-32-07 N   **Long:** 81-09-08 W
Pop: 3,016 (1990); 2,812 (1980)   **Pop Density:** 132.9
Land: 22.7 sq. mi.; **Water:** 0.1 sq. mi.

Hambden   Township
Lat: 41-36-22 N   **Long:** 81-09-17 W
Pop: 3,311 (1990); 2,934 (1980)   **Pop Density:** 147.2
Land: 22.5 sq. mi.; **Water:** 0.0 sq. mi.

Hunting Valley   Village
ZIP: 44022   **Lat:** 41-28-50 N   **Long:** 81-23-12 W
Pop: 151 (1990); 153 (1980)   **Pop Density:** 151.0
Land: 1.0 sq. mi.; **Water:** 0.0 sq. mi.   **Elev:** 772 ft.
Part of the town is also in Cuyahoga County.

Huntsburg   Township
ZIP: 44046   **Lat:** 41-32-03 N   **Long:** 81-03-08 W
Pop: 2,642 (1990); 2,201 (1980)   **Pop Density:** 112.9
Land: 23.4 sq. mi.; **Water:** 0.5 sq. mi.

Middlefield   Village
ZIP: 44062   **Lat:** 41-27-32 N   **Long:** 81 04-30 W
Pop: 1,898 (1990); 1,997 (1980)   **Pop Density:** 825.2
Land: 2.3 sq. mi.; **Water:** 0.0 sq. mi.   **Elev:** 1126 ft.
Not coextensive with the town of the same name.
Name origin: For its location between Warren and Painesville.

*Middlefield   Township
ZIP: 44062   **Lat:** 41-27-31 N   **Long:** 81-03-25 W
Pop: 6,009 (1990); 5,569 (1980)   **Pop Density:** 227.6
Land: 26.4 sq. mi.; **Water:** 0.0 sq. mi.

Montville   Township
ZIP: 44064   **Lat:** 41-36-09 N   **Long:** 81-03-16 W
Pop: 1,682 (1990); 1,722 (1980)   **Pop Density:** 68.9
Land: 24.4 sq. mi.; **Water:** 0.1 sq. mi.

Munson   Township
ZIP: 44024   **Lat:** 41-32-06 N   **Long:** 81-14-23 W
Pop: 5,775 (1990); 5,286 (1980)   **Pop Density:** 225.6
Land: 25.6 sq. mi.; **Water:** 0.3 sq. mi.

Newbury   Township
ZIP: 44065   **Lat:** 41-28-11 N   **Long:** 81-14-45 W
Pop: 5,611 (1990); 5,337 (1980)   **Pop Density:** 199.0
Land: 28.2 sq. mi.; **Water:** 0.4 sq. mi.

Parkman   Township
Lat: 41-23-18 N   **Long:** 81-03-28 W
Pop: 3,083 (1990); 2,638 (1980)   **Pop Density:** 113.3
Land: 27.2 sq. mi.; **Water:** 0.0 sq. mi.

Russell   Township
ZIP: 44072   **Lat:** 41-28-03 N   **Long:** 81-20-38 W
Pop: 5,765 (1990); 8,300 (1980)   **Pop Density:** 285.4
Land: 20.2 sq. mi.; **Water:** 0.1 sq. mi.

South Russell   Village
Lat: 41-26-04 N   **Long:** 81-19-58 W
Pop: 3,402 (1990); 2,784 (1980)   **Pop Density:** 872.3
Land: 3.9 sq. mi.; **Water:** 0.0 sq. mi.

Thompson   Township
ZIP: 44086   **Lat:** 41-40-27 N   **Long:** 81-03-27 W
Pop: 2,219 (1990); 2,083 (1980)   **Pop Density:** 86.3
Land: 25.7 sq. mi.; **Water:** 0.0 sq. mi.

Troy   Township
ZIP: 44021   **Lat:** 41-23-00 N   **Long:** 81-09-03 W
Pop: 1,903 (1990); 1,735 (1980)   **Pop Density:** 75.2
Land: 25.3 sq. mi.; **Water:** 0.4 sq. mi.

Greene County
County Seat: Xenia (ZIP: 45385)

Pop: 136,731 (1990); 129,769 (1980)   **Pop Density:** 329.5
Land: 414.9 sq. mi.; **Water:** 1.3 sq. mi.   **Area Code:** 513
In west-central OH, east of Dayton; organized May 1, 1803 from Hamilton and Ross counties.
Name origin: For Gen. Nathanael Greene (1742–86), hero of the Revolutionary War, quartermaster general (1778–80), and commander of the Army of the South (1780).

Bath   Township
ZIP: 45324   **Lat:** 39-48-39 N   **Long:** 84-01-06 W
Pop: 38,277 (1990); 36,865 (1980)   **Pop Density:** 1020.7
Land: 37.5 sq. mi.; **Water:** 0.4 sq. mi.
In northwestern OH, 11 mi. northeast of Dayton.

Beavercreek   City
ZIP: 45434   **Lat:** 39-43-45 N   **Long:** 84-03-44 W
Pop: 33,626 (1990); 31,589 (1980)   **Pop Density:** 1308.4
Land: 25.7 sq. mi.; **Water:** 0.0 sq. mi.   **Elev:** 850 ft.
In west-central OH, 8 mi. southeast of Dayton.

*Beavercreek   Township
ZIP: 45401   **Lat:** 39-43-37 N   **Long:** 84-02-01 W
Pop: 35,536 (1990); 33,364 (1980)   **Pop Density:** 722.3
Land: 49.2 sq. mi.; **Water:** 0.2 sq. mi.

Bellbrook   City
ZIP: 45305   **Lat:** 39-38-23 N   **Long:** 84-05-08 W
Pop: 6,511 (1990); 5,174 (1980)   **Pop Density:** 2100.3
Land: 3.1 sq. mi.; **Water:** 0.0 sq. mi.   **Elev:** 796 ft.
In southwestern OH, 14 mi. southeast of Dayton.
Name origin: Named in 1816 for Stephen Bell.

Bowersville   Village
ZIP: 45307   **Lat:** 39-34-48 N   **Long:** 83-43-25 W
Pop: 225 (1990); 329 (1980)   **Pop Density:** 2250.0
Land: 0.1 sq. mi.; **Water:** 0.0 sq. mi.

Caesars Creek   Township
Lat: 39-35-54 N   **Long:** 83-51-35 W
Pop: 1,170 (1990); 1,181 (1980)   **Pop Density:** 42.4
Land: 27.6 sq. mi.; **Water:** 0.0 sq. mi.

OHIO, Greene County

Cedarville
Village
ZIP: 45314 Lat: 39-44-41 N Long: 83-48-37 W
Pop: 3,210 (1990); 2,799 (1980) Pop Density: 3210.0
Land: 1.0 sq. mi.; Water: 0.0 sq. mi. Elev: 1055 ft.

In southwest-central OH, south of Springfield. Not coextensive with the town of the same name.

Name origin: For its descriptive connotations. Formerly called Milford.

*Cedarville
Township
ZIP: 45314 Lat: 39-44-40 N Long: 83-47-49 W
Pop: 4,297 (1990); 3,711 (1980) Pop Density: 109.9
Land: 39.1 sq. mi.; Water: 0.0 sq. mi.

Clifton
Village
Lat: 39-47-42 N Long: 83-49-32 W
Pop: 113 (1990); 137 (1980) Pop Density: 1130.0
Land: 0.1 sq. mi.; Water: 0.0 sq. mi.

In southwest-central OH on the Little Miami River. Part of the town is also in Clark County.

Name origin: For the cliffs that surround the river.

Fairborn
City
ZIP: 45324 Lat: 39-48-16 N Long: 84-01-02 W
Pop: 31,300 (1990); 29,702 (1980) Pop Density: 2794.6
Land: 11.2 sq. mi.; Water: 0.0 sq. mi.

In southwestern OH, 10 mi. northeast of Dayton.

Name origin: Named Jan 1, 1950, at the merger of the twin towns of *Fair*field and O*sborn*.

Jamestown
Village
ZIP: 45335 Lat: 39-39-31 N Long: 83-44-23 W
Pop: 1,794 (1990); 1,702 (1980) Pop Density: 1993.3
Land: 0.9 sq. mi.; Water: 0.0 sq. mi.

Name origin: For Jamestown, VA.

Jefferson
Township
Lat: 39-35-11 N Long: 83-43-56 W
Pop: 997 (1990); 1,016 (1980) Pop Density: 34.6
Land: 28.8 sq. mi.; Water: 0.0 sq. mi.

Kettering
City
Lat: 39-40-05 N Long: 84-06-27 W
Pop: 0 (1990); 61,186 (1980)
Land: 0.003 sq. mi.; Water: 0.0 sq. mi.

In southwestern OH, on the southern outskirts of Dayton. Part of the town is also in Montgomery County.

Name origin: For engineer Charles F. Kettering (1876–1958), who developed the automobile self-starting ignition system.

Miami
Township
ZIP: 45387 Lat: 39-47-57 N Long: 83-52-29 W
Pop: 5,162 (1990); 5,208 (1980) Pop Density: 187.0
Land: 27.6 sq. mi.; Water: 0.1 sq. mi.

New Jasper
Township
Lat: 39-39-29 N Long: 83-49-27 W
Pop: 2,393 (1990); 2,281 (1980) Pop Density: 112.3
Land: 21.3 sq. mi.; Water: 0.1 sq. mi.

Ross
Township
Lat: 39-43-14 N Long: 83-41-34 W
Pop: 705 (1990); 684 (1980) Pop Density: 19.4
Land: 36.3 sq. mi.; Water: 0.0 sq. mi.

Shawnee Hills
CDP
Lat: 39-39-08 N Long: 83-46-57 W
Pop: 2,199 (1990); 1,355 (1980) Pop Density: 814.4
Land: 2.7 sq. mi.; Water: 0.2 sq. mi.

Silver Creek
Township
Lat: 39-38-58 N Long: 83-43-23 W
Pop: 3,373 (1990); 3,326 (1980) Pop Density: 127.8
Land: 26.4 sq. mi.; Water: 0.1 sq. mi.

Spring Valley
Village
ZIP: 45370 Lat: 39-36-36 N Long: 84-00-21 W
Pop: 507 (1990); 541 (1980) Pop Density: 1690.0
Land: 0.3 sq. mi.; Water: 0.0 sq. mi.

*Spring Valley
Township
ZIP: 45370 Lat: 39-36-51 N Long: 83-59-04 W
Pop: 2,613 (1990); 2,492 (1980) Pop Density: 74.4
Land: 35.1 sq. mi.; Water: 0.1 sq. mi.

Sugar Creek
Township
Lat: 39-37-50 N Long: 84-04-00 W
Pop: 3,400 (1990); 7,670 (1980) Pop Density: 127.3
Land: 26.7 sq. mi.; Water: 0.0 sq. mi.

Wilberforce
CDP
Lat: 39-42-59 N Long: 83-53-00 W
Pop: 2,639 (1990); 2,512 (1980) Pop Density: 851.3
Land: 3.1 sq. mi.; Water: 0.1 sq. mi.

Wright-Patterson Air Force Base
Military Facility
Lat: 39-48-29 N Long: 84-03-37 W
Pop: 3,632 (1990) Pop Density: 366.9
Land: 9.9 sq. mi.; Water: 0.1 sq. mi.

Part of the facility is also in Montgomery County.

Xenia
City
ZIP: 45385 Lat: 39-41-06 N Long: 83-56-26 W
Pop: 24,664 (1990); 24,653 (1980) Pop Density: 2740.4
Land: 9.0 sq. mi.; Water: 0.0 sq. mi.

In southwestern OH, 15 mi. southeast of Dayton and 3 mi. east of the Little Miami River.

Name origin: From Greek 'hospitality.'

*Xenia
Township
ZIP: 45385 Lat: 39-42-06 N Long: 83-54-49 W
Pop: 7,633 (1990); 7,318 (1980) Pop Density: 161.4
Land: 47.3 sq. mi.; Water: 0.3 sq. mi.

Yellow Springs
Village
ZIP: 45387 Lat: 39-47-58 N Long: 83-53-40 W
Pop: 3,973 (1990); 4,077 (1980) Pop Density: 2207.2
Land: 1.8 sq. mi.; Water: 0.0 sq. mi.

In southwestern OH, 9 mi. south of Springfield. Founded 1804.

Name origin: From the yellow discharges of the neighboring iron springs whose health-giving waters attracted visitors for several decades.

Guernsey County
County Seat: Cambridge (ZIP: 43725)

Pop: 39,024 (1990); 42,024 (1980) **Pop Density:** 74.8
Land: 522.0 sq. mi.; **Water:** 6.3 sq. mi. **Area Code:** 614
In east-central OH, south of Canton; organized Mar 1, 1810 from Belmont County.
Name origin: For the British island in the English Channel.

Adams
Township
ZIP: 43725 Lat: 40-02-22 N Long: 81-40-34 W
Pop: 1,877 (1990); 1,759 (1980) Pop Density: 74.5
Land: 25.2 sq. mi.; Water: 0.0 sq. mi.

Byesville
Village
ZIP: 43723 Lat: 39-58-04 N Long: 81-32-33 W
Pop: 2,435 (1990); 2,572 (1980) Pop Density: 3043.8
Land: 0.8 sq. mi.; Water: 0.0 sq. mi.
Name origin: For Jonathan Bye, who built the first flour mill in the vicinity early in the 19th century.

Cambridge
City
ZIP: 43725 Lat: 40-01-30 N Long: 81-35-12 W
Pop: 11,748 (1990); 13,573 (1980) Pop Density: 2259.2
Land: 5.2 sq. mi.; Water: 0.0 sq. mi. Elev: 805 ft.
In eastern OH, 20 mi. northeast of Zanesville. Laid out 1806 by Jacob Gomer and Zacheus Beatty. Industrial city (coal, pottery clay, oil). Not coextensive with the town of the same name.
Name origin: Named by Gomber and Beatty for either Cambridge, MD, former home of many early settlers, or for Cambridge, MA.

*Cambridge
Township
ZIP: 43725 Lat: 40-02-23 N Long: 81-34-56 W
Pop: 16,126 (1990); 18,359 (1980) Pop Density: 463.4
Land: 34.8 sq. mi.; Water: 0.1 sq. mi.

Center
Township
ZIP: 43725 Lat: 40-01-49 N Long: 81-29-44 W
Pop: 1,597 (1990); 1,564 (1980) Pop Density: 66.3
Land: 24.1 sq. mi.; Water: 0.2 sq. mi.

Cumberland
Village
ZIP: 43732 Lat: 39-51-08 N Long: 81-39-31 W
Pop: 318 (1990); 461 (1980) Pop Density: 636.0
Land: 0.5 sq. mi.; Water: 0.0 sq. mi. Elev: 857 ft.

Fairview
Village
ZIP: 43772 Lat: 40-03-26 N Long: 81-14-14 W
Pop: 79 (1990); 121 (1980) Pop Density: 197.5
Land: 0.4 sq. mi.; Water: 0.0 sq. mi.
Part of the town is also in Belmont County.

Jackson
Township
ZIP: 43723 Lat: 39-57-45 N Long: 81-33-46 W
Pop: 5,298 (1990); 5,584 (1980) Pop Density: 218.9
Land: 24.2 sq. mi.; Water: 0.1 sq. mi.

Jefferson
Township
Lat: 40-06-25 N Long: 81-29-12 W
Pop: 72 (1990); 51 (1980) Pop Density: 3.2
Land: 22.4 sq. mi.; Water: 3.1 sq. mi.

Kimbolton
Village
ZIP: 43749 Lat: 40-09-14 N Long: 81-34-27 W
Pop: 134 (1990); 255 (1980) Pop Density: 670.0
Land: 0.2 sq. mi.; Water: 0.0 sq. mi.

Knox
Township
ZIP: 43725 Lat: 40-06-27 N Long: 81-40-15 W
Pop: 504 (1990); 486 (1980) Pop Density: 20.2
Land: 25.0 sq. mi.; Water: 0.0 sq. mi.

Liberty
Township
ZIP: 43725 Lat: 40-07-16 N Long: 81-34-40 W
Pop: 1,012 (1990); 1,142 (1980) Pop Density: 42.2
Land: 24.0 sq. mi., Water: 1.3 sq. mi.

Londonderry
Township
Lat: 40-07-57 N Long: 81-17-08 W
Pop: 653 (1990); 689 (1980) Pop Density: 17.9
Land: 36.4 sq. mi.; Water: 0.0 sq. mi.

Lore City
Village
ZIP: 43755 Lat: 39-59-02 N Long: 81-27-34 W
Pop: 384 (1990); 443 (1980) Pop Density: 1280.0
Land: 0.3 sq. mi.; Water: 0.0 sq. mi.

Madison
Township
ZIP: 43773 Lat: 40-06-23 N Long: 81-23-30 W
Pop: 703 (1990); 661 (1980) Pop Density: 28.2
Land: 24.9 sq. mi.; Water: 0.0 sq. mi.

Millwood
Township
ZIP: 43773 Lat: 39-58-50 N Long: 81-18-05 W
Pop: 1,069 (1990); 1,336 (1980) Pop Density: 39.3
Land: 27.2 sq. mi.; Water: 0.0 sq. mi.

Monroe
Township
ZIP: 43749 Lat: 40-10-44 N Long: 81-28-58 W
Pop: 614 (1990); 590 (1980) Pop Density: 24.6
Land: 25.0 sq. mi.; Water: 0.1 sq. mi.

Old Washington
Village
Lat: 40-02-14 N Long: 81-26-39 W
Pop: 281 (1990); 279 (1980) Pop Density: 401.4
Land: 0.7 sq. mi.; Water: 0.0 sq. mi. Elev: 1008 ft.

Oxford
Township
ZIP: 43773 Lat: 40-02-50 N Long: 81-16-34 W
Pop: 512 (1990); 632 (1980) Pop Density: 17.0
Land: 30.1 sq. mi.; Water: 0.0 sq. mi.

Pleasant City
Village
ZIP: 43772 Lat: 39-54-12 N Long: 81-32-40 W
Pop: 419 (1990); 481 (1980) Pop Density: 2095.0
Land: 0.2 sq. mi.; Water: 0.0 sq. mi.

Quaker City
Village
ZIP: 43736 Lat: 39-58-08 N Long: 81-17-47 W
Pop: 560 (1990); 698 (1980) Pop Density: 1120.0
Land: 0.5 sq. mi.; Water: 0.0 sq. mi.
In eastern OH, 16 mi. east of Cambridge.

Richland
Township
ZIP: 43780 Lat: 39-57-05 N Long: 81-26-29 W
Pop: 1,525 (1990); 1,511 (1980) Pop Density: 54.5
Land: 28.0 sq. mi.; Water: 1.1 sq. mi.

OHIO, Guernsey County

Salesville — Village
ZIP: 43778　　Lat: 39-58-24 N　Long: 81-20-13 W
Pop: 84 (1990); 139 (1980)　　Pop Density: 840.0
Land: 0.1 sq. mi.; Water: 0.0 sq. mi.

Senecaville — Village
ZIP: 43780　　Lat: 39-56-04 N　Long: 81-27-35 W
Pop: 434 (1990); 458 (1980)　　Pop Density: 868.0
Land: 0.5 sq. mi.; Water: 0.0 sq. mi.

Spencer — Township
Lat: 39-53-03 N　Long: 81-38-40 W
Pop: 929 (1990); 1,014 (1980)　　Pop Density: 31.5
Land: 29.5 sq. mi.; Water: 0.1 sq. mi.

Valley — Township
ZIP: 43772　　Lat: 39-54-41 N　Long: 81-33-31 W
Pop: 2,354 (1990); 2,567 (1980)　　Pop Density: 104.2
Land: 22.6 sq. mi.; Water: 0.0 sq. mi.

Washington — Township
ZIP: 43749　　Lat: 40-10-37 N　Long: 81-23-16 W
Pop: 441 (1990); 491 (1980)　　Pop Density: 17.9
Land: 24.6 sq. mi.; Water: 0.0 sq. mi.

Westland — Township
ZIP: 43725　　Lat: 39-58-01 N　Long: 81-40-19 W
Pop: 1,750 (1990); 1,624 (1980)　　Pop Density: 69.2
Land: 25.3 sq. mi.; Water: 0.1 sq. mi.

Wheeling — Township
Lat: 40-11-33 N　Long: 81-36-18 W
Pop: 592 (1990); 611 (1980)　　Pop Density: 18.3
Land: 32.3 sq. mi.; Water: 0.0 sq. mi.

Wills — Township
Lat: 40-01-18 N　Long: 81-23-59 W
Pop: 1,396 (1990); 1,353 (1980)　　Pop Density: 38.4
Land: 36.4 sq. mi.; Water: 0.0 sq. mi.

Hamilton County
County Seat: Cincinnati (ZIP: 45202)

Pop: 866,228 (1990); 873,203 (1980)　　Pop Density: 2126.3
Land: 407.4 sq. mi.; Water: 5.4 sq. mi.　　Area Code: 513

In the southwest corner of OH; original county; organized Jan 2, 1790 (prior to statehood).

Name origin: For Alexander Hamilton (1757–1804), first U.S. secretary of the treasury (1789–95).

Addyston — Village
ZIP: 45001　　Lat: 39-08-17 N　Long: 84-42-38 W
Pop: 1,198 (1990); 1,195 (1980)　　Pop Density: 1331.1
Land: 0.9 sq. mi.; Water: 0.0 sq. mi.　　Elev: 492 ft.

Settled as early as 1789; became a town 1871 when Matthew Addy of Cincinnati established a large pipe foundry here.
Name origin: For founder Matthew Addy.

Amberley — Village
Lat: 39-12-08 N　Long: 84-25-59 W
Pop: 3,108 (1990); 3,442 (1980)　　Pop Density: 888.0
Land: 3.5 sq. mi.; Water: 0.0 sq. mi.　　Elev: 803 ft.

In southwestern OH, 10 mi. northeast of Cincinnati.
Name origin: For Amberley, England.

Anderson — Township
ZIP: 45230　　Lat: 39-05-15 N　Long: 84-21-13 W
Pop: 39,939 (1990); 34,510 (1980)　　Pop Density: 1300.9
Land: 30.7 sq. mi.; Water: 0.5 sq. mi.

In southwestern OH, 10 mi. east of Cincinnati.

Arlington Heights — Village
ZIP: 45215　　Lat: 39-12-54 N　Long: 84-27-20 W
Pop: 1,084 (1990); 1,082 (1980)　　Pop Density: 3613.3
Land: 0.3 sq. mi.; Water: 0.0 sq. mi.

Blue Ash — City
ZIP: 45242　　Lat: 39-14-48 N　Long: 84-22-50 W
Pop: 11,860 (1990); 9,510 (1980)　　Pop Density: 1540.3
Land: 7.7 sq. mi.; Water: 0.0 sq. mi.

In southwestern OH, a residential suburb northeast of Cincinnati.
Name origin: For a species of ash tree (Fraxinus quadrangulata).

Bridgetown North — CDP
ZIP: 45211　　Lat: 39-09-29 N　Long: 84-38-08 W
Pop: 11,748 (1990); 11,460 (1980)　　Pop Density: 3455.3
Land: 3.4 sq. mi.; Water: 0.0 sq. mi.

Cherry Grove — CDP
Lat: 39-04-46 N　Long: 84-19-22 W
Pop: 4,972 (1990)　　Pop Density: 4520.0
Land: 1.1 sq. mi.; Water: 0.0 sq. mi.

Cheviot — City
ZIP: 45211　　Lat: 39-09-27 N　Long: 84-36-49 W
Pop: 9,616 (1990); 9,888 (1980)　　Pop Density: 8013.3
Land: 1.2 sq. mi.; Water: 0.0 sq. mi.

In southwestern OH, 10 mi. northwest of Cincinnati.

Cincinnati — City
ZIP: 45202　　Lat: 39-08-23 N　Long: 84-30-21 W
Pop: 364,040 (1990); 385,409 (1980)　　Pop Density: 4715.5
Land: 77.2 sq. mi.; Water: 1.6 sq. mi.　　Elev: 683 ft.

In the southwest corner of OH on the Ohio River. Incorporated as a town 1802, as a city 1819. Nicknamed "Queen City" and "Queen of the West." Commercial and manufacturing city; railroad center; distribution port (brewing, meatpacking). Birthplace of Pres. William H. Taft (1857–1930).

Name origin: Named in 1709 by Gen. Arthur St. Clair (1736–1818), governor of the Northwest Territory, for the Society of Cincinnati, an association of Revolutionary War veterans, which was named for Cincinnatus (fl. 5th century B.C.), farmer-soldier of the Roman Empire.

Cleves — Village
ZIP: 45002   Lat: 39-09-44 N   Long: 84-44-57 W
Pop: 2,208 (1990); 2,094 (1980)   Pop Density: 1698.5
Land: 1.3 sq. mi.; Water: 0.0 sq. mi.   Elev: 496 ft.
Name origin: For early proprietor John Cleves Symmes.

Colerain — Township
ZIP: 45251   Lat: 39-15-21 N   Long: 84-37-36 W
Pop: 56,781 (1990); 56,536 (1980)   Pop Density: 1323.6
Land: 42.9 sq. mi.; Water: 0.3 sq. mi.

In southwestern OH, 11 mi. northwest of Cincinnati.

Columbia — Township
ZIP: 45243   Lat: 39-09-19 N   Long: 84-22-33 W
Pop: 6,298 (1990); 6,428 (1980)   Pop Density: 1908.5
Land: 3.3 sq. mi.; Water: 0.2 sq. mi.

Covedale — CDP
ZIP: 45238   Lat: 39-07-25 N   Long: 84-38-26 W
Pop: 6,669 (1990), 5,830 (1980)   Pop Density: 2381.8
Land: 2.8 sq. mi.; Water: 0.0 sq. mi.

Crosby — Township
ZIP: 45030   Lat: 39-16-27 N   Long: 84-42-50 W
Pop: 2,665 (1990); 2,470 (1980)   Pop Density: 133.3
Land: 20.0 sq. mi.; Water: 0.2 sq. mi.

Deer Park — City
ZIP: 45236   Lat: 39-12-12 N   Long: 84-23-49 W
Pop: 6,181 (1990); 6,745 (1980)   Pop Density: 6867.8
Land: 0.9 sq. mi.; Water: 0.0 sq. mi.

In the southwestern corner of OH, 10 mi. northeast of Cincinnati.

Delhi — Township
ZIP: 45238   Lat: 39-06-06 N   Long: 84-37-53 W
Pop: 30,250 (1990); 29,099 (1980)   Pop Density: 3025.0
Land: 10.0 sq. mi.; Water: 0.0 sq. mi.

In southwestern OH, 2 mi. north of Cincinnati.

Dent — CDP
ZIP: 45211   Lat: 39-11-37 N   Long: 84-39-39 W
Pop: 6,416 (1990)   Pop Density: 1087.5
Land: 5.9 sq. mi.; Water: 0.0 sq. mi.

Dillonvale — CDP
Lat: 39-13-04 N   Long: 84-24-07 W
Pop: 4,209 (1990)   Pop Density: 4676.7
Land: 0.9 sq. mi.; Water: 0.0 sq. mi.

Dry Run — CDP
Lat: 39-06-15 N   Long: 84-19-50 W
Pop: 5,389 (1990)   Pop Density: 1122.7
Land: 4.8 sq. mi.; Water: 0.0 sq. mi.

Elmwood Place — Village
ZIP: 45216   Lat: 39-11-05 N   Long: 84-29-18 W
Pop: 2,937 (1990); 2,840 (1980)   Pop Density: 9790.0
Land: 0.3 sq. mi.; Water: 0.0 sq. mi.

In southwestern OH on Mill Creek, just north of downtown Cincinnati.

Evendale — Village
Lat: 39-15-13 N   Long: 84-25-32 W
Pop: 3,175 (1990); 1,954 (1980)   Pop Density: 661.5
Land: 4.8 sq. mi.; Water: 0.0 sq. mi.   Elev: 584 ft.

Fairfax — Village
ZIP: 45227   Lat: 39-08-33 N   Long: 84-23-46 W
Pop: 2,029 (1990); 2,222 (1980)   Pop Density: 2536.3
Land: 0.8 sq. mi.; Water: 0.0 sq. mi.

In southwestern OH, north of Cincinnati.

Fairfield — City
Lat: 39-18-06 N   Long: 84-31-23 W
Pop: 0 (1990)
Land: 0.01 sq. mi.; Water: 0.0 sq. mi.

In southwestern OH, 20 mi. north of Cincinnati. Part of the town is also in Butler County.
Name origin: For its descriptive connotations.

Finneytown — CDP
ZIP: 45224   Lat: 39-13-00 N   Long: 84-30-51 W
Pop: 13,096 (1990)   Pop Density: 3274.0
Land: 4.0 sq. mi.; Water: 0.0 sq. mi.

Forest Park — City
ZIP: 45240   Lat: 39-17-13 N   Long: 84-31-36 W
Pop: 18,609 (1990); 18,566 (1980)   Pop Density: 2953.8
Land: 6.3 sq. mi.; Water: 0.0 sq. mi.   Elev: 836 ft.

In southwestern OH, 20 mi. north of downtown Cincinnati.

Forestville — CDP
ZIP: 45230   Lat: 39-04-12 N   Long: 84-20-19 W
Pop: 9,185 (1990)   Pop Density: 2482.4
Land: 3.7 sq. mi.; Water: 0.0 sq. mi.

Fruit Hill — CDP
Lat: 39-04-04 N   Long: 84-21-58 W
Pop: 4,101 (1990)   Pop Density: 3154.6
Land: 1.3 sq. mi.; Water: 0.0 sq. mi.

Glendale — Village
ZIP: 45246   Lat: 39-16-14 N   Long: 84-27-30 W
Pop: 2,445 (1990); 2,368 (1980)   Pop Density: 1438.2
Land: 1.7 sq. mi.; Water: 0.0 sq. mi.   Elev: 630 ft.

In southwestern OH, 15 mi. north of Cincinnati.

Golf Manor — City
ZIP: 45237   Lat: 39-11-13 N   Long: 84-26-47 W
Pop: 4,154 (1990); 4,317 (1980)   Pop Density: 6923.3
Land: 0.6 sq. mi.; Water: 0.0 sq. mi.

In southwestern OH, just north of downtown Cincinnati.
Name origin: For its descriptive connotations.

Grandview — CDP
Lat: 39-11-39 N   Long: 84-43-27 W
Pop: 1,301 (1990)   Pop Density: 295.7
Land: 4.4 sq. mi.; Water: 0.3 sq. mi.

Green — Township
Lat: 39-10-07 N   Long: 84-38-18 W
Pop: 52,687 (1990); 50,764 (1980)   Pop Density: 1835.8
Land: 28.7 sq. mi.; Water: 0.0 sq. mi.

In southwestern OH, 7 mi. northwest of Cincinnati.

Greenhills — City
ZIP: 45218   Lat: 39-15-53 N   Long: 84-31-03 W
Pop: 4,393 (1990); 4,927 (1980)   Pop Density: 3660.8
Land: 1.2 sq. mi.; Water: 0.0 sq. mi.

In southwestern OH, a northern suburb of Cincinnati. Developed in 1937 by the Federal Works Project Administration as a model community.

OHIO, Hamilton County

Groesbeck
CDP
ZIP: 45239 Lat: 39-13-43 N Long: 84-35-39 W
Pop: 6,684 (1990); 9,594 (1980) Pop Density: 2304.8
Land: 2.9 sq. mi.; Water: 0.0 sq. mi.

Harrison
Village
ZIP: 45030 Lat: 39-14-59 N Long: 84-47-34 W
Pop: 7,518 (1990); 5,855 (1980) Pop Density: 2148.0
Land: 3.5 sq. mi.; Water: 0.0 sq. mi. Elev: 528 ft.
Not coextensive with the town of the same name.
Name origin: For William Henry Harrison (1773–1841), ninth U.S. president.

*Harrison
Township
ZIP: 45030 Lat: 39-15-44 N Long: 84-47-23 W
Pop: 12,145 (1990); 9,310 (1980) Pop Density: 686.2
Land: 17.7 sq. mi.; Water: 0.2 sq. mi.

Kenwood
CDP
ZIP: 45236 Lat: 39-12-20 N Long: 84-22-26 W
Pop: 7,469 (1990); 9,928 (1980) Pop Density: 3112.1
Land: 2.4 sq. mi.; Water: 0.0 sq. mi.

Lincoln Heights
City
ZIP: 45215 Lat: 39-14-38 N Long: 84-27-29 W
Pop: 4,805 (1990); 5,259 (1980) Pop Density: 6864.3
Land: 0.7 sq. mi.; Water: 0.0 sq. mi.
In southwestern OH, north of Cincinnati in the hills encircling the city.

Lockland
City
ZIP: 45215 Lat: 39-13-39 N Long: 84-27-26 W
Pop: 4,357 (1990); 4,292 (1980) Pop Density: 3630.8
Land: 1.2 sq. mi.; Water: 0.0 sq. mi.
In southwestern OH on Mill Creek, just north of Cincinnati.

Loveland
City
ZIP: 45111 Lat: 39-16-00 N Long: 84-17-08 W
Pop: 8,263 (1990); 7,385 (1980) Pop Density: 2849.3
Land: 2.9 sq. mi.; Water: 0.0 sq. mi. Elev: 890 ft.
In southwestern OH on the Little Miami River, 16 mi. northeast of Cincinnati. Part of the town is also in Clermont and Warren counties.
Name origin: For Col. James Loveland, first storeowner.

Loveland Park
CDP
Lat: 39-16-45 N Long: 84-16-02 W
Pop: 227 (1990); 215 (1980) Pop Density: 756.7
Land: 0.3 sq. mi.; Water: 0.0 sq. mi.
Part of the town is also in Warren County.

Mack North
CDP
Lat: 39-10-00 N Long: 84-40-23 W
Pop: 2,816 (1990) Pop Density: 908.4
Land: 3.1 sq. mi.; Water: 0.0 sq. mi.

Mack South
CDP
Lat: 39-08-31 N Long: 84-40-23 W
Pop: 5,767 (1990) Pop Density: 1558.6
Land: 3.7 sq. mi.; Water: 0.0 sq. mi.

Madeira
City
ZIP: 45243 Lat: 39-11-03 N Long: 84-22-29 W
Pop: 9,141 (1990); 9,341 (1980) Pop Density: 2688.5
Land: 3.4 sq. mi.; Water: 0.0 sq. mi. Elev: 772 ft.
In southwestern OH, 15 mi. northeast of Cincinnati.

Mariemont
Village
ZIP: 45227 Lat: 39-08-31 N Long: 84-22-44 W
Pop: 3,118 (1990); 3,295 (1980) Pop Density: 3464.4
Land: 0.9 sq. mi.; Water: 0.0 sq. mi.
In southwestern OH overlooking the Little Miami River. Laid out 1922.
Name origin: For Marie Emery of Cincinnati, on whose land it was laid out.

Miami
Township
ZIP: 45002 Lat: 39-09-32 N Long: 84-44-24 W
Pop: 11,552 (1990); 9,941 (1980) Pop Density: 508.9
Land: 22.7 sq. mi.; Water: 1.1 sq. mi.
In southwest OH, 10 mi. northwest of Cincinnati.

Milford
Village
ZIP: 45150 Lat: 39-10-18 N Long: 84-17-57 W
Pop: 5 (1990); 27 (1980) Pop Density: 50.0
Land: 0.1 sq. mi.; Water: 0.0 sq. mi.
In southwestern OH, 12 mi. northeast of Cincinnati. Part of the town is also in Clermont County.

Monfort Heights East
CDP
Lat: 39-10-55 N Long: 84-35-02 W
Pop: 3,661 (1990) Pop Density: 1926.8
Land: 1.9 sq. mi.; Water: 0.0 sq. mi.

Monfort Heights South
CDP
Lat: 39-10-23 N Long: 84-36-22 W
Pop: 4,587 (1990) Pop Density: 1310.6
Land: 3.5 sq. mi.; Water: 0.0 sq. mi.

Montgomery
City
ZIP: 45242 Lat: 39-14-50 N Long: 84-20-51 W
Pop: 9,753 (1990); 10,084 (1980) Pop Density: 1950.6
Land: 5.0 sq. mi.; Water: 0.0 sq. mi.
In southwestern OH, 15 mi. northeast of Cincinnati in a residential area.
Name origin: For Revolutionary War general, Richard Montgomery (1738–75).

Mount Healthy
City
ZIP: 45231 Lat: 39-13-57 N Long: 84-32-49 W
Pop: 7,580 (1990); 7,562 (1980) Pop Density: 5414.3
Land: 1.4 sq. mi.; Water: 0.0 sq. mi. Elev: 855 ft.
In southwestern OH, 14 mi. north of Cincinnati.
Name origin: Descriptive and promotional.

Mount Healthy Heights
CDP
Lat: 39-16-12 N Long: 84-34-05 W
Pop: 3,863 (1990) Pop Density: 4828.8
Land: 0.8 sq. mi.; Water: 0.0 sq. mi.

Newtown
Village
Lat: 39-07-20 N Long: 84-21-01 W
Pop: 1,589 (1990); 1,817 (1980) Pop Density: 690.9
Land: 2.3 sq. mi.; Water: 0.0 sq. mi.
In southwestern OH, just east of Cincinnati.
Name origin: For its descriptive connotations.

North Bend
Village
ZIP: 45052 Lat: 39-08-54 N Long: 84-44-29 W
Pop: 541 (1990); 546 (1980) Pop Density: 491.8
Land: 1.1 sq. mi.; Water: 0.1 sq. mi.
In southwestern OH on a bend in the Ohio River, 10 mi. west of Cincinnati.
Name origin: For the river's northernmost bend.

OHIO, Hamilton County

Northbrook — CDP
ZIP: 45231 Lat: 39-14-50 N Long: 84-34-44 W
Pop: 11,471 (1990); 8,357 (1980) Pop Density: 6037.4
Land: 1.9 sq. mi.; Water: 0.0 sq. mi.

North College Hill — City
ZIP: 45239 Lat: 39-13-01 N Long: 84-33-05 W
Pop: 11,002 (1990); 11,114 (1980) Pop Density: 6112.2
Land: 1.8 sq. mi.; Water: 0.0 sq. mi.
In southwestern OH, 10 mi. north of Cincinnati.
Name origin: Promotionally named.

Northgate — CDP
Lat: 39-15-09 N Long: 84-35-32 W
Pop: 7,864 (1990) Pop Density: 3145.6
Land: 2.5 sq. mi.; Water: 0.0 sq. mi.

Norwood — City
ZIP: 45212 Lat: 39-09-34 N Long: 84-27-13 W
Pop: 23,674 (1990); 26,342 (1980) Pop Density: 7636.8
Land: 3.1 sq. mi.; Water: 0.0 sq. mi.
In southwestern OH surrounded by the city of Cincinnati.

Pleasant Run — CDP
Lat: 39-17-27 N Long: 84-34-20 W
Pop: 4,964 (1990) Pop Density: 2363.8
Land: 2.1 sq. mi.; Water: 0.0 sq. mi.

Pleasant Run Farm — CDP
Lat: 39-18-10 N Long: 84-32-52 W
Pop: 4,545 (1990) Pop Density: 4131.8
Land: 1.1 sq. mi.; Water: 0.0 sq. mi.

Reading — City
ZIP: 45215 Lat: 39-13-27 N Long: 84-25-53 W
Pop: 12,038 (1990); 12,843 (1980) Pop Density: 4151.0
Land: 2.9 sq. mi.; Water: 0.0 sq. mi.
In southwestern OH, 10 mi. northeast of Cincinnati in a residential area.
Name origin: For Reading, Berkshire, England.

St. Bernard — City
ZIP: 45217 Lat: 39-10-15 N Long: 84-29-43 W
Pop: 5,344 (1990); 5,396 (1980) Pop Density: 3562.7
Land: 1.5 sq. mi.; Water: 0.0 sq. mi.

Sharonville — City
ZIP: 45241 Lat: 39-16-44 N Long: 84-24-36 W
Pop: 11,312 (1990); 10,108 (1980) Pop Density: 1229.6
Land: 9.2 sq. mi.; Water: 0.1 sq. mi. Elev: 589 ft.
In southwestern OH, 15 mi. northeast of Cincinnati. Part of the town is also in Butler County.
Name origin: For Sharon, PA.

Sherwood — CDP
Lat: 39-05-05 N Long: 84-21-38 W
Pop: 3,709 (1990) Pop Density: 3371.8
Land: 1.1 sq. mi.; Water: 0.0 sq. mi.

Silverton — City
ZIP: 45236 Lat: 39-11-21 N Long: 84-24-04 W
Pop: 5,859 (1990); 6,172 (1980) Pop Density: 5326.4
Land: 1.1 sq. mi.; Water: 0.0 sq. mi.

Springdale — City
ZIP: 45246 Lat: 39-17-29 N Long: 84-28-31 W
Pop: 10,621 (1990); 10,111 (1980) Pop Density: 2167.6
Land: 4.9 sq. mi.; Water: 0.0 sq. mi.
In southwestern OH, 13 mi. north of Cincinnati.
Name origin: For a spring or springs in the area.

Springfield — Township
ZIP: 45239 Lat: 39-14-45 N Long: 84-31-29 W
Pop: 38,509 (1990); 42,133 (1980) Pop Density: 2319.8
Land: 16.6 sq. mi.; Water: 0.3 sq. mi.
In southwestern OH, 10 mi. north of Cincinnati.

Sycamore — Township
ZIP: 45242 Lat: 39-13-30 N Long: 84-22-00 W
Pop: 20,074 (1990); 29,137 (1980) Pop Density: 2996.1
Land: 6.7 sq. mi.; Water: 0.0 sq. mi.
In southwestern OH, 11 mi. northeast of Cincinnati.

Symmes — Township
ZIP: 45242 Lat: 39-15-35 N Long: 84-18-11 W
Pop: 11,769 (1990); 7,566 (1980) Pop Density: 1293.3
Land: 9.1 sq. mi.; Water: 0.2 sq. mi.

Terrace Park — Village
ZIP: 45174 Lat: 39-09-28 N Long: 84-18-43 W
Pop: 2,133 (1990); 2,044 (1980) Pop Density: 1777.5
Land: 1.2 sq. mi.; Water: 0.1 sq. mi.

The Village of Indian Hill — City
ZIP: 45243 Lat: 39-11-22 N Long: 84-20-05 W
Pop: 5,383 (1990); 5,521 (1980) Pop Density: 291.0
Land: 18.5 sq. mi.; Water: 0.1 sq. mi.

Turpin Hills — CDP
Lat: 39-06-25 N Long: 84-22-23 W
Pop: 4,927 (1990) Pop Density: 1642.3
Land: 3.0 sq. mi.; Water: 0.0 sq. mi.

White Oak — CDP
ZIP: 45239 Lat: 39-13-12 N Long: 84-36-19 W
Pop: 12,430 (1990); 9,563 (1980) Pop Density: 3031.7
Land: 4.1 sq. mi.; Water: 0.0 sq. mi.

White Oak East — CDP
Lat: 39-12-07 N Long: 84-35-24 W
Pop: 3,544 (1990) Pop Density: 4430.0
Land: 0.8 sq. mi.; Water: 0.0 sq. mi.

White Oak West — CDP
Lat: 39-11-57 N Long: 84-36-51 W
Pop: 2,879 (1990) Pop Density: 2214.6
Land: 1.3 sq. mi.; Water: 0.0 sq. mi.

Whitewater — Township
ZIP: 45002 Lat: 39-11-49 N Long: 84-45-50 W
Pop: 5,178 (1990); 4,662 (1980) Pop Density: 202.3
Land: 25.6 sq. mi.; Water: 0.7 sq. mi.

Woodlawn — Village
ZIP: 45215 Lat: 39-15-24 N Long: 84-28-03 W
Pop: 2,674 (1990); 2,715 (1980) Pop Density: 1028.5
Land: 2.6 sq. mi.; Water: 0.0 sq. mi. Elev: 586 ft.

Wyoming — City
ZIP: 45215 Lat: 39-13-46 N Long: 84-28-53 W
Pop: 8,128 (1990); 8,282 (1980) Pop Density: 2902.9
Land: 2.8 sq. mi.; Water: 0.0 sq. mi.
In southwestern OH, 10 mi. north of Cincinnati.
Name origin: For Wyoming County, PA.

Hancock County
County Seat: Findlay (ZIP: 45840)

Pop: 65,536 (1990); 64,581 (1980) **Pop Density:** 123.3
Land: 531.4 sq. mi.; **Water:** 2.2 sq. mi. **Area Code:** 419
In north-central OH, south of Toledo; organized Apr 1, 1820 from Indian lands.
Name origin: For John Hancock (1737–93), noted signer of the Declaration of Independence, governor of MA (1780–85; 1787–93), and statesman.

Allen
Township
Lat: 41-07-31 N **Long:** 83-38-53 W
Pop: 1,980 (1990); 1,884 (1980) **Pop Density:** 82.8
Land: 23.9 sq. mi.; **Water:** 0.1 sq. mi.

Amanda
Township
Lat: 40-56-58 N **Long:** 83-30-50 W
Pop: 992 (1990); 1,041 (1980) **Pop Density:** 35.8
Land: 27.7 sq. mi.; **Water:** 0.0 sq. mi.

Arcadia
Village
ZIP: 44804 **Lat:** 41-06-40 N **Long:** 83-30-40 W
Pop: 546 (1990); 580 (1980) **Pop Density:** 1820.0
Land: 0.3 sq. mi.; **Water:** 0.0 sq. mi. **Elev:** 808 ft.

Arlington
Village
ZIP: 45814 **Lat:** 40-53-33 N **Long:** 83-39-13 W
Pop: 1,267 (1990); 1,187 (1980) **Pop Density:** 1583.8
Land: 0.8 sq. mi.; **Water:** 0.0 sq. mi. **Elev:** 869 ft.
Name origin: For the city in VA.

Benton Ridge
Village
ZIP: 45816 **Lat:** 41-00-17 N **Long:** 83-47-31 W
Pop: 351 (1990); 343 (1980) **Pop Density:** 702.0
Land: 0.5 sq. mi.; **Water:** 0.0 sq. mi. **Elev:** 778 ft.

Biglick
Township
Lat: 41-02-07 N **Long:** 83-28-47 W
Pop: 933 (1990); 1,019 (1980) **Pop Density:** 25.9
Land: 36.0 sq. mi.; **Water:** 0.0 sq. mi.

Blanchard
Township
Lat: 41-01-47 N **Long:** 83-49-14 W
Pop: 1,100 (1990); 1,068 (1980) **Pop Density:** 30.4
Land: 36.2 sq. mi.; **Water:** 0.0 sq. mi.

Bluffton
Village
ZIP: 45817 **Lat:** 40-53-24 N **Long:** 83-52-30 W
Pop: 161 (1990); 73 (1980) **Pop Density:** 161.0
Land: 1.0 sq. mi.; **Water:** 0.0 sq. mi. **Elev:** 824 ft.
In northwestern OH, 14 mi. northeast of Lima. Founded 1833. Part of the town is also in Allen County.
Name origin: For a Mennonite community in IN.

Cass
Township
Lat: 41-07-33 N **Long:** 83-34-39 W
Pop: 1,023 (1990); 922 (1980) **Pop Density:** 42.6
Land: 24.0 sq. mi.; **Water:** 0.0 sq. mi.

Delaware
Township
Lat: 40-51-27 N **Long:** 83-33-49 W
Pop: 1,196 (1990); 1,233 (1980) **Pop Density:** 38.3
Land: 31.2 sq. mi.; **Water:** 0.0 sq. mi.

Eagle
Township
Lat: 40-57-00 N **Long:** 83-42-25 W
Pop: 1,106 (1990); 1,077 (1980) **Pop Density:** 30.9
Land: 35.8 sq. mi.; **Water:** 0.0 sq. mi.

Findlay
City
ZIP: 45840 **Lat:** 41-02-34 N **Long:** 83-38-31 W
Pop: 35,703 (1990); 35,594 (1980) **Pop Density:** 2625.2
Land: 13.6 sq. mi.; **Water:** 0.1 sq. mi. **Elev:** 780 ft.
In northwestern OH, 41 mi. south of Toledo.
Name origin: For Fort Findlay, one of the outposts built here under the direction of Gen. William Hull (1753–1825) during his march to Detroit in the War of 1812.

Fostoria
City
ZIP: 44830 **Lat:** 41-09-12 N **Long:** 83-25-50 W
Pop: 3,091 (1990); 3,412 (1980) **Pop Density:** 1931.9
Land: 1.6 sq. mi.; **Water:** 0.2 sq. mi. **Elev:** 780 ft.
In northern OH, 14 mi. northeast of Findlay. Part of the town is also in Seneca and Wood counties.
Name origin: For local developer, businessman, and banker, C. W. Foster.

Jackson
Township
Lat: 40-57-00 N **Long:** 83-36-07 W
Pop: 971 (1990); 953 (1980) **Pop Density:** 32.8
Land: 29.6 sq. mi.; **Water:** 0.1 sq. mi.

Jenera
Village
ZIP: 45841 **Lat:** 40-53-59 N **Long:** 83-43-38 W
Pop: 285 (1990); 302 (1980) **Pop Density:** 712.5
Land: 0.4 sq. mi.; **Water:** 0.0 sq. mi. **Elev:** 859 ft.

Liberty
Township
Lat: 41-02-30 N **Long:** 83-42-54 W
Pop: 4,871 (1990); 3,940 (1980) **Pop Density:** 158.7
Land: 30.7 sq. mi.; **Water:** 0.1 sq. mi.

Madison
Township
Lat: 40-51-28 N **Long:** 83-38-57 W
Pop: 2,028 (1990); 1,872 (1980) **Pop Density:** 85.6
Land: 23.7 sq. mi.; **Water:** 0.0 sq. mi.

Marion
Township
Lat: 41-02-00 N **Long:** 83-35-09 W
Pop: 2,204 (1990); 2,088 (1980) **Pop Density:** 82.2
Land: 26.8 sq. mi.; **Water:** 1.3 sq. mi.

McComb
Village
ZIP: 45858 **Lat:** 41-06-23 N **Long:** 83-47-22 W
Pop: 1,544 (1990); 1,608 (1980) **Pop Density:** 1715.6
Land: 0.9 sq. mi.; **Water:** 0.0 sq. mi. **Elev:** 778 ft.
In northwestern OH, southwest of Toledo.

Mount Blanchard
Village
ZIP: 45867 **Lat:** 40-53-54 N **Long:** 83-33-26 W
Pop: 491 (1990); 492 (1980) **Pop Density:** 982.0
Land: 0.5 sq. mi.; **Water:** 0.0 sq. mi. **Elev:** 835 ft.

Mount Cory
Village
ZIP: 45868 **Lat:** 40-56-05 N **Long:** 83-49-27 W
Pop: 245 (1990); 276 (1980) **Pop Density:** 612.5
Land: 0.4 sq. mi.; **Water:** 0.0 sq. mi. **Elev:** 820 ft.

Orange
Township
Lat: 40-51-50 N **Long:** 83-49-14 W
Pop: 1,191 (1990); 1,108 (1980) **Pop Density:** 32.8
Land: 36.3 sq. mi.; **Water:** 0.0 sq. mi.

Pleasant
Township
Lat: 41-07-25 N **Long:** 83-49-32 W
Pop: 2,298 (1990); 2,419 (1980) **Pop Density:** 63.0
Land: 36.5 sq. mi.; **Water:** 0.0 sq. mi.

Portage
Township
Lat: 41-07-16 N **Long:** 83-44-01 W
Pop: 555 (1990); 557 (1980) **Pop Density:** 23.1
Land: 24.0 sq. mi.; **Water:** 0.0 sq. mi.

Rawson
Village
ZIP: 45841 **Lat:** 40-57-24 N **Long:** 83-47-08 W
Pop: 482 (1990); 477 (1980) **Pop Density:** 1205.0
Land: 0.4 sq. mi.; **Water:** 0.0 sq. mi. **Elev:** 817 ft.

Union
Township
Lat: 40-57-02 N **Long:** 83-49-21 W
Pop: 1,800 (1990); 1,808 (1980) **Pop Density:** 50.6
Land: 35.6 sq. mi.; **Water:** 0.0 sq. mi.

Van Buren
Village
ZIP: 45889 **Lat:** 41-08-20 N **Long:** 83-38-57 W
Pop: 337 (1990); 342 (1980) **Pop Density:** 1685.0
Land: 0.2 sq. mi.; **Water:** 0.0 sq. mi.
Not coextensive with the town of the same name.

*Van Buren
Township
ZIP: 45889 **Lat:** 40-51-49 N **Long:** 83-43-32 W
Pop: 910 (1990); 902 (1980) **Pop Density:** 37.3
Land: 24.4 sq. mi.; **Water:** 0.0 sq. mi.

Vanlue
Village
ZIP: 45890 **Lat:** 40-58-35 N **Long:** 83-28-54 W
Pop: 373 (1990); 390 (1980) **Pop Density:** 1243.3
Land: 0.3 sq. mi.; **Water:** 0.0 sq. mi.

Washington
Township
Lat: 41-07-15 N **Long:** 83-29-00 W
Pop: 4,675 (1990); 5,096 (1980) **Pop Density:** 132.1
Land: 35.4 sq. mi.; **Water:** 0.4 sq. mi.

Hardin County
County Seat: Kenton (**ZIP:** 43326)

Pop: 31,111 (1990); 32,719 (1980) **Pop Density:** 66.2
Land: 470.3 sq. mi.; **Water:** 0.2 sq. mi. **Area Code:** 419
In west-central OH, northwest of Columbus; organized Apr 1, 1820 from Indian lands.
Name origin: For Gen. John Hardin (1753–92), Revolutionary War officer and Indian fighter with George Rogers Clark (1752–1818) in the trans-Ohio campaigns; killed while on a peace mission to the Miami Indians.

Ada
Village
ZIP: 45810 **Lat:** 40-46-07 N **Long:** 83-49-25 W
Pop: 5,413 (1990); 5,669 (1980) **Pop Density:** 3383.1
Land: 1.6 sq. mi.; **Water:** 0.0 sq. mi.
In northwestern OH, 6 mi. east of Lima. Established 1853.
Name origin: Originally called Johnstown.

Alger
Village
ZIP: 45812 **Lat:** 40-42-34 N **Long:** 83-50-40 W
Pop: 864 (1990); 992 (1980) **Pop Density:** 2880.0
Land: 0.3 sq. mi.; **Water:** 0.0 sq. mi. **Elev:** 978 ft.

Blanchard
Township
Lat: 40-46-42 N **Long:** 83-36-41 W
Pop: 1,522 (1990); 1,614 (1980) **Pop Density:** 63.4
Land: 24.0 sq. mi.; **Water:** 0.1 sq. mi.

Buck
Township
ZIP: 43326 **Lat:** 40-36-35 N **Long:** 83-36-25 W
Pop: 2,776 (1990); 2,907 (1980) **Pop Density:** 90.7
Land: 30.6 sq. mi.; **Water:** 0.1 sq. mi.

Cessna
Township
ZIP: 43326 **Lat:** 40-41-48 N **Long:** 83-42-06 W
Pop: 430 (1990); 546 (1980) **Pop Density:** 18.9
Land: 22.8 sq. mi.; **Water:** 0.0 sq. mi.

Dudley
Township
ZIP: 43326 **Lat:** 40-35-50 N **Long:** 83-28-59 W
Pop: 1,092 (1990); 1,199 (1980) **Pop Density:** 29.2
Land: 37.4 sq. mi.; **Water:** 0.0 sq. mi.

Dunkirk
Village
ZIP: 45836 **Lat:** 40-47-15 N **Long:** 83-38-33 W
Pop: 869 (1990); 954 (1980) **Pop Density:** 1448.3
Land: 0.6 sq. mi.; **Water:** 0.1 sq. mi. **Elev:** 951 ft.

Forest
Village
ZIP: 45843 **Lat:** 40-48-11 N **Long:** 83-30-42 W
Pop: 1,594 (1990); 1,633 (1980) **Pop Density:** 1328.3
Land: 1.2 sq. mi.; **Water:** 0.0 sq. mi.

Goshen
Township
ZIP: 43326 **Lat:** 40-40-45 N **Long:** 83-29-12 W
Pop: 560 (1990); 649 (1980) **Pop Density:** 19.7
Land: 28.4 sq. mi.; **Water:** 0.0 sq. mi.

Hale
Township
Lat: 40-32-00 N **Long:** 83-30-44 W
Pop: 1,371 (1990); 1,434 (1980) **Pop Density:** 37.6
Land: 36.5 sq. mi.; **Water:** 0.0 sq. mi.

Jackson
Township
Lat: 40-46-07 N **Long:** 83-31-59 W
Pop: 2,210 (1990); 2,328 (1980) **Pop Density:** 87.4
Land: 25.3 sq. mi.; **Water:** 0.0 sq. mi.

Kenton
City
ZIP: 43326 **Lat:** 40-38-40 N **Long:** 83-36-37 W
Pop: 8,356 (1990); 8,605 (1980) **Pop Density:** 2695.5
Land: 3.1 sq. mi.; **Water:** 0.1 sq. mi. **Elev:** 991 ft.

OHIO, Hardin County

Liberty Township
ZIP: 45810 Lat: 40-46-32 N Long: 83-49-25 W
Pop: 6,788 (1990); 7,046 (1980) Pop Density: 189.6
Land: 35.8 sq. mi.; Water: 0.0 sq. mi.

Lynn Township
ZIP: 43326 Lat: 40-37-59 N Long: 83-41-57 W
Pop: 629 (1990); 645 (1980) Pop Density: 25.1
Land: 25.1 sq. mi.; Water: 0.0 sq. mi.

Marion Township
Lat: 40-41-21 N Long: 83-49-24 W
Pop: 2,357 (1990); 2,583 (1980) Pop Density: 71.0
Land: 33.2 sq. mi.; Water: 0.0 sq. mi.

McDonald Township
ZIP: 43326 Lat: 40-35-27 N Long: 83-46-41 W
Pop: 921 (1990); 958 (1980) Pop Density: 21.5
Land: 42.9 sq. mi.; Water: 0.0 sq. mi.

McGuffey Village
ZIP: 45859 Lat: 40-41-35 N Long: 83-47-09 W
Pop: 550 (1990); 646 (1980) Pop Density: 1375.0
Land: 0.4 sq. mi.; Water: 0.0 sq. mi. Elev: 973 ft.

Mount Victory Village
ZIP: 43340 Lat: 40-32-02 N Long: 83-31-12 W
Pop: 551 (1990); 667 (1980) Pop Density: 688.8
Land: 0.8 sq. mi.; Water: 0.0 sq. mi. Elev: 1033 ft.

Patterson Village
ZIP: 45843 Lat: 40-46-54 N Long: 83-31-33 W
Pop: 145 (1990); 153 (1980) Pop Density: 1450.0
Land: 0.1 sq. mi.; Water: 0.0 sq. mi.

Pleasant Township
ZIP: 43326 Lat: 40-41-13 N Long: 83-35-22 W
Pop: 8,469 (1990); 8,648 (1980) Pop Density: 218.8
Land: 38.7 sq. mi.; Water: 0.0 sq. mi.

Ridgeway Village
ZIP: 43345 Lat: 40-30-54 N Long: 83-34-06 W
Pop: 250 (1990); 284 (1980) Pop Density: 833.3
Land: 0.3 sq. mi.; Water: 0.0 sq. mi. Elev: 1053 ft.
Part of the town is also in Logan County.

Roundhead Township
Lat: 40-35-31 N Long: 83-51-08 W
Pop: 721 (1990); 708 (1980) Pop Density: 27.8
Land: 25.9 sq. mi.; Water: 0.0 sq. mi.

Taylor Creek Township
Lat: 40-33-00 N Long: 83-40-24 W
Pop: 460 (1990); 559 (1980) Pop Density: 16.5
Land: 27.8 sq. mi.; Water: 0.0 sq. mi.

Washington Township
Lat: 40-46-44 N Long: 83-42-34 W
Pop: 805 (1990); 895 (1980) Pop Density: 22.4
Land: 35.9 sq. mi.; Water: 0.0 sq. mi.

Harrison County
County Seat: Cadiz (ZIP: 43907)

Pop: 16,085 (1990); 18,152 (1980) Pop Density: 39.9
Land: 403.6 sq. mi.; Water: 7.2 sq. mi. Area Code: 614
In east-central OH, southeast of Canton; organized Feb 1, 1813 from Jefferson and Tuscarawas counties.
Name origin: For William Henry Harrison (1773–1841), ninth U.S. president.

Adena Village
Lat: 40-12-48 N Long: 80-53-06 W
Pop: 150 (1990); 153 (1980) Pop Density: 1500.0
Land: 0.1 sq. mi.; Water: 0.0 sq. mi. Elev: 884 ft.
Part of the town is also in Jefferson County.

Archer Township
Lat: 40-19-29 N Long: 81-01-03 W
Pop: 299 (1990); 337 (1980) Pop Density: 11.9
Land: 25.1 sq. mi.; Water: 0.0 sq. mi.

Athens Township
Lat: 40-11-27 N Long: 81-02-12 W
Pop: 534 (1990); 605 (1980) Pop Density: 21.1
Land: 25.3 sq. mi.; Water: 0.2 sq. mi.

Bowerston Village
ZIP: 44695 Lat: 40-25-36 N Long: 81-11-15 W
Pop: 343 (1990); 487 (1980) Pop Density: 686.0
Land: 0.5 sq. mi.; Water: 0.0 sq. mi.

Cadiz Village
ZIP: 43907 Lat: 40-16-00 N Long: 80-59-32 W
Pop: 3,439 (1990); 4,058 (1980) Pop Density: 477.6
Land: 7.2 sq. mi.; Water: 0.1 sq. mi. Elev: 1280 ft.
In eastern OH, 20 mi. southwest of Steubenville. Not coextensive with the town of the same name.
Name origin: For Cadiz, Spain.

***Cadiz** Township
ZIP: 43907 Lat: 40-15-51 N Long: 81-02-28 W
Pop: 3,907 (1990); 4,643 (1980) Pop Density: 113.6
Land: 34.4 sq. mi.; Water: 0.5 sq. mi.

Deersville Village
ZIP: 44693 Lat: 40-18-29 N Long: 81-11-15 W
Pop: 86 (1990); 109 (1980) Pop Density: 286.7
Land: 0.3 sq. mi.; Water: 0.0 sq. mi. Elev: 1254 ft.

Franklin Township
ZIP: 44699 Lat: 40-20-26 N Long: 81-14-02 W
Pop: 609 (1990); 628 (1980) Pop Density: 29.7
Land: 20.5 sq. mi.; Water: 2.0 sq. mi.

Freeport Village
ZIP: 43973 **Lat:** 40-12-38 N **Long:** 81-16-05 W
Pop: 475 (1990); 525 (1980) **Pop Density:** 791.7
Land: 0.6 sq. mi.; **Water:** 0.0 sq. mi.
Not coextensive with the town of the same name.

*Freeport Township
ZIP: 43973 **Lat:** 40-11-51 N **Long:** 81-16-46 W
Pop: 914 (1990); 961 (1980) **Pop Density:** 37.9
Land: 24.1 sq. mi.; **Water:** 0.0 sq. mi.

German Township
Lat: 40 23-29 N **Long:** 80-54-49 W
Pop: 695 (1990); 872 (1980) **Pop Density:** 27.6
Land: 25.2 sq. mi.; **Water:** 0.0 sq. mi.

Green Township
Lat: 40-18-10 N **Long:** 80-55-21 W
Pop: 1,723 (1990); 2,062 (1980) **Pop Density:** 48.4
Land: 35.6 sq. mi.; **Water:** 0.0 sq. mi.

Harrisville Village
ZIP: 43974 **Lat:** 40-10-54 N **Long:** 80-53-13 W
Pop: 308 (1990); 324 (1980) **Pop Density:** 1540.0
Land: 0.2 sq. mi.; **Water:** 0.0 sq. mi.

Hopedale Village
ZIP: 43976 **Lat:** 40-19-23 N **Long:** 80-53-56 W
Pop: 685 (1990); 857 (1980) **Pop Density:** 1712.5
Land: 0.4 sq. mi.; **Water:** 0.0 sq. mi.

Jewett Village
ZIP: 43986 **Lat:** 40-22-05 N **Long:** 81-00-09 W
Pop: 778 (1990); 972 (1980) **Pop Density:** 1556.0
Land: 0.5 sq. mi.; **Water:** 0.0 sq. mi.
In eastern OH, 25 mi. west of Steubenville. Coal-mining area.

Monroe Township
ZIP: 44695 **Lat:** 40-24-03 N **Long:** 81-13-20 W
Pop: 1,171 (1990); 1,145 (1980) **Pop Density:** 44.5
Land: 26.3 sq. mi.; **Water:** 0.0 sq. mi.

Moorefield Township
Lat: 40-11-53 N **Long:** 81-09-22 W
Pop: 441 (1990); 563 (1980) **Pop Density:** 16.4
Land: 26.9 sq. mi.; **Water:** 0.6 sq. mi.

New Athens Village
ZIP: 43981 **Lat:** 40-11-03 N **Long:** 80-59-43 W
Pop: 370 (1990); 440 (1980) **Pop Density:** 1233.3
Land: 0.3 sq. mi.; **Water:** 0.0 sq. mi.

North Township
Lat: 40-23-50 N **Long:** 81-06-10 W
Pop: 1,822 (1990); 1,979 (1980) **Pop Density:** 78.5
Land: 23.2 sq. mi.; **Water:** 0.0 sq. mi.

Nottingham Township
ZIP: 43907 **Lat:** 40-16-02 N **Long:** 81-10-03 W
Pop: 248 (1990); 351 (1980) **Pop Density:** 8.8
Land: 28.1 sq. mi.; **Water:** 1.3 sq. mi.

Rumley Township
ZIP: 43986 **Lat:** 40-23-25 N **Long:** 81-00-53 W
Pop: 1,530 (1990); 1,693 (1980) **Pop Density:** 65.7
Land: 23.3 sq. mi.; **Water:** 0.0 sq. mi.

Scio Village
ZIP: 43988 **Lat:** 40-23-55 N **Long:** 81-05-15 W
Pop: 856 (1990); 1,003 (1980) **Pop Density:** 1426.7
Land: 0.6 sq. mi.; **Water:** 0.0 sq. mi.

Short Creek Township
Lat: 40-12-14 N **Long:** 80-55-36 W
Pop: 1,157 (1990); 1,337 (1980) **Pop Density:** 37.9
Land: 30.5 sq. mi.; **Water:** 0.1 sq. mi.

Stock Township
Lat: 40-20-01 N **Long:** 81-07-35 W
Pop: 409 (1990); 441 (1980) **Pop Density:** 16.6
Land: 24.6 sq. mi.; **Water:** 1.2 sq. mi.

Washington Township
ZIP: 44699 **Lat:** 40-15-59 N **Long:** 81-16-37 W
Pop: 626 (1990); 535 (1980) **Pop Density:** 20.7
Land: 30.3 sq. mi.; **Water:** 1.3 sq. mi.

Henry County
County Seat: Napoleon (ZIP: 43545)

Pop: 29,108 (1990); 28,383 (1980) **Pop Density:** 69.9
Land: 416.5 sq. mi.; **Water:** 3.5 sq. mi. **Area Code:** 419
In northwestern OH, southwest of Toledo; organized Feb 12, 1820 from Wood County.
Name origin: For Patrick Henry (1736-99), patriot, governor of VA (1776-79; 1784-86), and statesman, famous for proclaiming, "Give me liberty or give me death."

Bartlow Township
Lat: 41-12-41 N **Long:** 83-56-22 W
Pop: 2,554 (1990); 2,628 (1980) **Pop Density:** 70.4
Land: 36.3 sq. mi.; **Water:** 0.0 sq. mi.

Damascus Township
Lat: 41-22-41 N **Long:** 83-56-22 W
Pop: 1,876 (1990); 1,627 (1980) **Pop Density:** 62.1
Land: 30.2 sq. mi.; **Water:** 0.6 sq. mi.

Deshler Village
ZIP: 43516 **Lat:** 41-12-28 N **Long:** 83-54-20 W
Pop: 1,876 (1990); 1,870 (1980) **Pop Density:** 852.7
Land: 2.2 sq. mi.; **Water:** 0.0 sq. mi. **Elev:** 715 ft.

Flatrock Township
Lat: 41-17-50 N **Long:** 84-10-20 W
Pop: 1,370 (1990); 1,369 (1980) **Pop Density:** 39.1
Land: 35.0 sq. mi.; **Water:** 0.5 sq. mi.

OHIO, Henry County

Florida — Village
ZIP: 43545 Lat: 41-19-22 N Long: 84-12-02 W
Pop: 304 (1990); 294 (1980) Pop Density: 1520.0
Land: 0.2 sq. mi.; Water: 0.0 sq. mi.

Freedom — Township
Lat: 41-27-31 N Long: 84-10-09 W
Pop: 853 (1990); 784 (1980) Pop Density: 36.1
Land: 23.6 sq. mi.; Water: 0.0 sq. mi.

Hamler — Village
ZIP: 43524 Lat: 41-13-48 N Long: 84-01-59 W
Pop: 623 (1990); 625 (1980) Pop Density: 1038.3
Land: 0.6 sq. mi.; Water: 0.0 sq. mi. Elev: 714 ft.
In northwestern OH, 20 mi. east of Defiance.

Harrison — Township
Lat: 41-22-17 N Long: 84-03-10 W
Pop: 1,253 (1990); 1,298 (1980) Pop Density: 46.4
Land: 27.0 sq. mi.; Water: 0.5 sq. mi.

Holgate — Village
ZIP: 43527 Lat: 41-14-55 N Long: 84-07-42 W
Pop: 1,290 (1990); 1,315 (1980) Pop Density: 1290.0
Land: 1.0 sq. mi.; Water: 0.0 sq. mi. Elev: 714 ft.
In northwestern OH, southwest of Toledo.

Liberty — Township
Lat: 41-26-37 N Long: 84-03-19 W
Pop: 2,434 (1990); 2,304 (1980) Pop Density: 75.8
Land: 32.1 sq. mi.; Water: 0.6 sq. mi.

Liberty Center — Village
ZIP: 43532 Lat: 41-26-36 N Long: 84-00-29 W
Pop: 1,084 (1990); 1,111 (1980) Pop Density: 1084.0
Land: 1.0 sq. mi.; Water: 0.0 sq. mi.

Malinta — Village
ZIP: 43535 Lat: 41-19-10 N Long: 84-02-13 W
Pop: 294 (1990); 327 (1980) Pop Density: 367.5
Land: 0.8 sq. mi.; Water: 0.0 sq. mi. Elev: 686 ft.

Marion — Township
Lat: 41-12-40 N Long: 84-03-23 W
Pop: 1,439 (1990); 1,443 (1980) Pop Density: 39.6
Land: 36.3 sq. mi.; Water: 0.0 sq. mi.

McClure — Village
ZIP: 43534 Lat: 41-22-13 N Long: 83-56-31 W
Pop: 781 (1990); 694 (1980) Pop Density: 1562.0
Land: 0.5 sq. mi.; Water: 0.0 sq. mi.

Monroe — Township
Lat: 41-17-59 N Long: 84-03-24 W
Pop: 1,221 (1990); 1,310 (1980) Pop Density: 33.4
Land: 36.6 sq. mi.; Water: 0.0 sq. mi.

Napoleon — City
ZIP: 43545 Lat: 41-23-41 N Long: 84-07-35 W
Pop: 8,884 (1990); 8,614 (1980) Pop Density: 1850.8
Land: 4.8 sq. mi.; Water: 0.3 sq. mi. Elev: 677 ft.
Not coextensive with the town of the same name.
Name origin: For Napoleon Bonaparte (1769–1821), emperor of France.

***Napoleon** — Township
ZIP: 43545 Lat: 41-23-07 N Long: 84-10-18 W
Pop: 10,033 (1990); 9,656 (1980) Pop Density: 289.1
Land: 34.7 sq. mi.; Water: 0.4 sq. mi.

New Bavaria — Village
ZIP: 43548 Lat: 41-12-12 N Long: 84-10-01 W
Pop: 92 (1990); 135 (1980) Pop Density: 920.0
Land: 0.1 sq. mi.; Water: 0.0 sq. mi. Elev: 732 ft.

Pleasant — Township
Lat: 41-12-48 N Long: 84-10-06 W
Pop: 2,399 (1990); 2,457 (1980) Pop Density: 66.6
Land: 36.0 sq. mi.; Water: 0.0 sq. mi.

Richfield — Township
Lat: 41-18-19 N Long: 83-56-28 W
Pop: 724 (1990); 665 (1980) Pop Density: 19.8
Land: 36.5 sq. mi.; Water: 0.0 sq. mi.

Ridgeville — Township
Lat: 41-27-27 N Long: 84-17-12 W
Pop: 1,129 (1990); 1,054 (1980) Pop Density: 47.8
Land: 23.6 sq. mi.; Water: 0.0 sq. mi.

Washington — Township
Lat: 41-27-10 N Long: 83-56-28 W
Pop: 1,823 (1990); 1,788 (1980) Pop Density: 63.3
Land: 28.8 sq. mi.; Water: 0.7 sq. mi.

Highland County
County Seat: Hillsboro (ZIP: 45133)

Pop: 35,728 (1990); 33,477 (1980) Pop Density: 64.6
Land: 553.3 sq. mi.; Water: 4.6 sq. mi. Area Code: 513
In southwest OH; organized May 1, 1805 from Ross, Adams, and Clermont counties.
Name origin: For the terrain.

Brush Creek — Township
Lat: 39-06-20 N Long: 83-25-30 W
Pop: 1,103 (1990); 1,033 (1980) Pop Density: 25.5
Land: 43.3 sq. mi.; Water: 0.0 sq. mi.

Clay — Township
Lat: 39-04-29 N Long: 83-49-52 W
Pop: 1,219 (1990); 1,200 (1980) Pop Density: 43.4
Land: 28.1 sq. mi.; Water: 0.0 sq. mi.

Concord — Township
Lat: 39-03-16 N Long: 83-38-52 W
Pop: 995 (1990); 852 (1980) Pop Density: 29.5
Land: 33.7 sq. mi.; Water: 0.0 sq. mi.

Dodson — Township
Lat: 39-12-46 N Long: 83-48-27 W
Pop: 2,304 (1990); 2,305 (1980) Pop Density: 87.6
Land: 26.3 sq. mi.; Water: 0.0 sq. mi.

Fairfield
Township
Lat: 39-20-19 N **Long:** 83-33-10 W
Pop: 2,616 (1990); 2,473 (1980) **Pop Density:** 65.9
Land: 39.7 sq. mi.; **Water:** 0.0 sq. mi.

Greenfield
City
ZIP: 45123 **Lat:** 39-21-15 N **Long:** 83-23-20 W
Pop: 5,172 (1990); 5,150 (1980) **Pop Density:** 2722.1
Land: 1.9 sq. mi.; **Water:** 0.0 sq. mi.
In southern OH on Paint Creek, 20 mi. west of Chillicothe.
Name origin: For its descriptive connotations.

Hamer
Township
Lat: 39-09-21 N **Long:** 83-44-46 W
Pop: 802 (1990); 732 (1980) **Pop Density:** 35.5
Land: 22.6 sq. mi.; **Water:** 0.1 sq. mi.

Highland
Village
ZIP: 45132 **Lat:** 39-20-36 N **Long:** 83-35-58 W
Pop: 275 (1990); 284 (1980) **Pop Density:** 1375.0
Land: 0.2 sq. mi.; **Water:** 0.0 sq. mi.

Hillsboro
City
ZIP: 45133 **Lat:** 39-12-33 N **Long:** 83-36-45 W
Pop: 6,235 (1990); 6,356 (1980) **Pop Density:** 1558.8
Land: 4.0 sq. mi.; **Water:** 0.0 sq. mi. **Elev:** 1132 ft.

Jackson
Township
Lat: 39-03-45 N **Long:** 83-31-54 W
Pop: 743 (1990); 639 (1980) **Pop Density:** 28.8
Land: 25.8 sq. mi.; **Water:** 0.0 sq. mi.

Leesburg
Village
ZIP: 45135 **Lat:** 39-20-44 N **Long:** 83-33-16 W
Pop: 1,063 (1990); 1,019 (1980) **Pop Density:** 1518.6
Land: 0.7 sq. mi.; **Water:** 0.0 sq. mi.
In southwest-central OH, northeast of Cincinnati.

Liberty
Township
ZIP: 45133 **Lat:** 39-12-32 N **Long:** 83-35-29 W
Pop: 9,184 (1990); 8,806 (1980) **Pop Density:** 156.2
Land: 58.8 sq. mi.; **Water:** 0.5 sq. mi.

Lynchburg
Village
ZIP: 45142 **Lat:** 39-14-39 N **Long:** 83-47-19 W
Pop: 1,212 (1990); 1,205 (1980) **Pop Density:** 2424.0
Land: 0.5 sq. mi.; **Water:** 0.0 sq. mi. **Elev:** 1009 ft.
In southern OH, 15 mi. northwest of Hillsboro.
Name origin: Named by early settlers for Lynchburg, VA, their former home.

Madison
Township
ZIP: 45123 **Lat:** 39-20-22 N **Long:** 83-25-42 W
Pop: 6,987 (1990); 6,982 (1980) **Pop Density:** 203.1
Land: 34.4 sq. mi.; **Water:** 0.4 sq. mi.

Marshall
Township
ZIP: 45133 **Lat:** 39-08-31 N **Long:** 83-29-23 W
Pop: 830 (1990); 773 (1980) **Pop Density:** 37.9
Land: 21.9 sq. mi.; **Water:** 0.7 sq. mi.

Mowrystown
Village
ZIP: 45155 **Lat:** 39-02-19 N **Long:** 83-45-09 W
Pop: 460 (1990); 475 (1980) **Pop Density:** 920.0
Land: 0.5 sq. mi.; **Water:** 0.0 sq. mi. **Elev:** 997 ft.

New Market
Township
ZIP: 45133 **Lat:** 39-09-23 N **Long:** 83-40-17 W
Pop: 1,480 (1990); 1,182 (1980) **Pop Density:** 55.4
Land: 26.7 sq. mi.; **Water:** 0.0 sq. mi.

Paint
Township
Lat: 39-13-28 N **Long:** 83-26-33 W
Pop: 2,908 (1990); 2,362 (1980) **Pop Density:** 52.1
Land: 55.8 sq. mi.; **Water:** 2.8 sq. mi.

Penn
Township
Lat: 39-17-17 N **Long:** 83-35-49 W
Pop: 882 (1990); 890 (1980) **Pop Density:** 27.5
Land: 32.1 sq. mi.; **Water:** 0.0 sq. mi.

Salem
Township
Lat: 39-08-32 N **Long:** 83-49-31 W
Pop: 587 (1990); 561 (1980) **Pop Density:** 29.9
Land: 19.6 sq. mi.; **Water:** 0.0 sq. mi.

Sinking Spring
Village
ZIP: 45172 **Lat:** 39-04-30 N **Long:** 83-23-13 W
Pop: 189 (1990); 239 (1980) **Pop Density:** 378.0
Land: 0.5 sq. mi.; **Water:** 0.0 sq. mi.

Union
Township
Lat: 39-15-22 N **Long:** 83-42-56 W
Pop: 1,037 (1990); 827 (1980) **Pop Density:** 34.8
Land: 29.8 sq. mi.; **Water:** 0.0 sq. mi.

Washington
Township
Lat: 39-07-31 N **Long:** 83-34-13 W
Pop: 694 (1990); 646 (1980) **Pop Density:** 28.4
Land: 24.4 sq. mi.; **Water:** 0.0 sq. mi.

White Oak
Township
Lat: 39-03-54 N **Long:** 83-44-57 W
Pop: 1,357 (1990); 1,214 (1980) **Pop Density:** 44.8
Land: 30.3 sq. mi.; **Water:** 0.0 sq. mi.

OHIO, Hocking County

Hocking County
County Seat: Logan (ZIP: 43138)

Pop: 25,533 (1990); 24,304 (1980)
Land: 422.8 sq. mi.; **Water:** 0.8 sq. mi.
Pop Density: 60.4
Area Code: 614

In central OH, southeast of Columbus; organized Jan 3, 1818 from Athens and Ross counties.

Name origin: For the Hocking River, which runs through it; from anglicized Algonquian word whose meaning is uncertain, perhaps referring to cleared fields.

Benton
Township
Lat: 39-24-31 N **Long:** 82-34-39 W
Pop: 763 (1990); 724 (1980) **Pop Density:** 20.2
Land: 37.8 sq. mi.; **Water:** 0.0 sq. mi.

Falls
Township
ZIP: 43138 **Lat:** 39-32-21 N **Long:** 82-24-56 W
Pop: 10,878 (1990); 10,984 (1980) **Pop Density:** 219.3
Land: 49.6 sq. mi.; **Water:** 0.5 sq. mi.
In south-central OH, 15 mi. south of Lancaster.

Good Hope
Township
ZIP: 43149 **Lat:** 39-34-53 N **Long:** 82-33-18 W
Pop: 1,247 (1990); 1,337 (1980) **Pop Density:** 47.4
Land: 26.3 sq. mi.; **Water:** 0.0 sq. mi.

Green
Township
Lat: 39-31-29 N **Long:** 82-20-20 W
Pop: 2,217 (1990); 2,077 (1980) **Pop Density:** 59.9
Land: 37.0 sq. mi.; **Water:** 0.1 sq. mi.

Laurel
Township
ZIP: 43149 **Lat:** 39-29-58 N **Long:** 82-33-53 W
Pop: 968 (1990); 931 (1980) **Pop Density:** 25.2
Land: 38.4 sq. mi.; **Water:** 0.0 sq. mi.

Laurelville
Village
Lat: 39-28-17 N **Long:** 82-44-14 W
Pop: 605 (1990); 591 (1980) **Pop Density:** 3025.0
Land: 0.2 sq. mi.; **Water:** 0.0 sq. mi. **Elev:** 741 ft.

Logan
City
ZIP: 43138 **Lat:** 39-32-12 N **Long:** 82-24-06 W
Pop: 6,725 (1990); 6,557 (1980) **Pop Density:** 2319.0
Land: 2.9 sq. mi.; **Water:** 0.0 sq. mi. **Elev:** 741 ft.
Name origin: For Logan, a Mingo chief.

Marion
Township
ZIP: 43138 **Lat:** 39-36-52 N **Long:** 82-26-31 W
Pop: 1,950 (1990); 1,643 (1980) **Pop Density:** 52.6
Land: 37.1 sq. mi.; **Water:** 0.2 sq. mi.

Murray City
Village
ZIP: 43144 **Lat:** 39-30-38 N **Long:** 82-10-01 W
Pop: 499 (1990); 579 (1980) **Pop Density:** 1663.3
Land: 0.3 sq. mi.; **Water:** 0.0 sq. mi. **Elev:** 712 ft.

Perry
Township
Lat: 39-30-55 N **Long:** 82-40-44 W
Pop: 2,225 (1990); 1,978 (1980) **Pop Density:** 52.9
Land: 42.1 sq. mi.; **Water:** 0.0 sq. mi.

Salt Creek
Township
Lat: 39-25-00 N **Long:** 82-41-04 W
Pop: 1,172 (1990); 961 (1980) **Pop Density:** 27.8
Land: 42.1 sq. mi.; **Water:** 0.0 sq. mi.

Starr
Township
Lat: 39-26-08 N **Long:** 82-20-38 W
Pop: 1,278 (1990); 1,244 (1980) **Pop Density:** 34.5
Land: 37.0 sq. mi.; **Water:** 0.0 sq. mi.

Ward
Township
Lat: 39-31-04 N **Long:** 82-13-17 W
Pop: 1,857 (1990); 1,706 (1980) **Pop Density:** 49.0
Land: 37.9 sq. mi.; **Water:** 0.0 sq. mi.

Washington
Township
ZIP: 43138 **Lat:** 39-26-24 N **Long:** 82-27-00 W
Pop: 978 (1990); 719 (1980) **Pop Density:** 26.2
Land: 37.3 sq. mi.; **Water:** 0.0 sq. mi.

Holmes County
County Seat: Millersburg (ZIP: 44654)

Pop: 32,849 (1990); 29,416 (1980)
Land: 423.0 sq. mi.; **Water:** 1.0 sq. mi.
Pop Density: 77.7
Area Code: 216

In central OH, southwest of Canton; organized Jan 20, 1824 from Coshocton County.

Name origin: For Maj. Andrew Hunter Holmes (?–1814), officer in the War of 1812.

Baltic
Village
ZIP: 43804 **Lat:** 40-26-48 N **Long:** 81-42-02 W
Pop: 98 (1990); 40 (1980) **Pop Density:** 980.0
Land: 0.1 sq. mi.; **Water:** 0.0 sq. mi. **Elev:** 1041 ft.
Part of the town is also in Coshocton and Tuscarawas counties.

Berlin
Township
Lat: 40-33-25 N **Long:** 81-48-46 W
Pop: 3,457 (1990); 2,996 (1980) **Pop Density:** 132.5
Land: 26.1 sq. mi.; **Water:** 0.0 sq. mi.

Clark
Township
Lat: 40-28-58 N **Long:** 81-44-13 W
Pop: 2,940 (1990); 2,763 (1980) **Pop Density:** 85.2
Land: 34.5 sq. mi.; **Water:** 0.0 sq. mi.

Glenmont
Village
ZIP: 44628 **Lat:** 40-31-01 N **Long:** 82-05-33 W
Pop: 233 (1990); 270 (1980) **Pop Density:** 776.7
Land: 0.3 sq. mi.; **Water:** 0.0 sq. mi. **Elev:** 881 ft.
In northeast-central OH, southwest of Canton.

Hardy
Township
ZIP: 44654 **Lat:** 40-33-33 N **Long:** 81-55-15 W
Pop: 5,261 (1990); 5,266 (1980) **Pop Density:** 160.4
Land: 32.8 sq. mi.; **Water:** 0.0 sq. mi.

Holmesville
Village
ZIP: 44633 **Lat:** 40-37-42 N **Long:** 81-55-24 W
Pop: 419 (1990); 436 (1980) **Pop Density:** 2095.0
Land: 0.2 sq. mi.; **Water:** 0.0 sq. mi. **Elev:** 880 ft.

Killbuck
Village
ZIP: 44637 **Lat:** 40-29-49 N **Long:** 81-59-01 W
Pop: 809 (1990); 937 (1980) **Pop Density:** 2696.7
Land: 0.3 sq. mi.; **Water:** 0.0 sq. mi.
Settled 1811. Not coextensive with the town of the same name.
Name origin: For Killbuck, an Indian who figured in the region's history.

*Killbuck
Township
ZIP: 44637 **Lat:** 40-29-12 N **Long:** 81-59-02 W
Pop: 1,829 (1990); 1,941 (1980) **Pop Density:** 60.6
Land: 30.2 sq. mi.; **Water:** 0.0 sq. mi.

Knox
Township
ZIP: 44638 **Lat:** 40-34-12 N **Long:** 82-08-28 W
Pop: 977 (1990); 708 (1980) **Pop Density:** 35.0
Land: 27.9 sq. mi.; **Water:** 0.0 sq. mi.

Loudonville
Village
ZIP: 44842 **Lat:** 40-38-05 N **Long:** 82-12-56 W
Pop: 71 (1990); 67 (1980) **Pop Density:** 236.7
Land: 0.3 sq. mi.; **Water:** 0.0 sq. mi. **Elev:** 974 ft.
Laid out 1814. Part of the town is also in Ashland County.
Name origin: For James Loudon Priest who, with Stephen Butler, laid it out.

Mechanic
Township
Lat: 40-28-53 N **Long:** 81-52-07 W
Pop: 2,052 (1990); 1,640 (1980) **Pop Density:** 60.7
Land: 33.8 sq. mi.; **Water:** 0.2 sq. mi.

Millersburg
Village
ZIP: 44654 **Lat:** 40-33-12 N **Long:** 81-54-56 W
Pop: 3,051 (1990); 3,247 (1980) **Pop Density:** 1906.9
Land: 1.6 sq. mi.; **Water:** 0.0 sq. mi. **Elev:** 906 ft.
Name origin: For Charles Miller, who with Adam Johnson, settled here in 1824.

Monroe
Township
Lat: 40-33-17 N **Long:** 82-01-37 W
Pop: 1,062 (1990); 811 (1980) **Pop Density:** 44.1
Land: 24.1 sq. mi.; **Water:** 0.0 sq. mi.

Nashville
Village
ZIP: 44661 **Lat:** 40-35-45 N **Long:** 82-06-47 W
Pop: 181 (1990); 211 (1980) **Pop Density:** 1810.0
Land: 0.1 sq. mi.; **Water:** 0.0 sq. mi. **Elev:** 1220 ft.

Paint
Township
Lat: 40-37-41 N **Long:** 81-42-55 W
Pop: 2,825 (1990); 2,325 (1980) **Pop Density:** 97.4
Land: 29.0 sq. mi.; **Water:** 0.0 sq. mi.

Prairie
Township
Lat: 40-37-50 N **Long:** 81-56-08 W
Pop: 2,265 (1990); 2,000 (1980) **Pop Density:** 73.8
Land: 30.7 sq. mi.; **Water:** 0.0 sq. mi.

Richland
Township
ZIP: 44628 **Lat:** 40-29-48 N **Long:** 82-07-02 W
Pop: 892 (1990); 936 (1980) **Pop Density:** 23.9
Land: 37.3 sq. mi.; **Water:** 0.0 sq. mi.

Ripley
Township
Lat: 40-37-33 N **Long:** 82-02-56 W
Pop: 1,730 (1990); 1,564 (1980) **Pop Density:** 58.8
Land: 29.4 sq. mi.; **Water:** 0.1 sq. mi.

Salt Creek
Township
Lat: 40-37-43 N **Long:** 81-49-21 W
Pop: 3,061 (1990); 2,577 (1980) **Pop Density:** 102.4
Land: 29.9 sq. mi.; **Water:** 0.0 sq. mi.

Walnut Creek
Township
Lat: 40-32-59 N **Long:** 81-42-30 W
Pop: 3,044 (1990); 2,629 (1980) **Pop Density:** 111.1
Land: 27.4 sq. mi.; **Water:** 0.5 sq. mi.

Washington
Township
ZIP: 44638 **Lat:** 40-37-49 N **Long:** 82-09-25 W
Pop: 1,454 (1990); 1,260 (1980) **Pop Density:** 48.8
Land: 29.8 sq. mi.; **Water:** 0.2 sq. mi.

OHIO, Huron County   *American Places Dictionary*

Huron County
County Seat: Norwalk (ZIP: 44857)

Pop: 56,240 (1990); 54,608 (1980)   **Pop Density:** 114.1
Land: 493.1 sq. mi.; **Water:** 1.8 sq. mi.   **Area Code:** 419
In north-central OH, west of Akron; organized Feb 7, 1809 from Indian lands.

Name origin: For the Huron Indians, a tribe of Iroquoian linguistic stock, later known as the Wyandot. Name from a French word for 'rough,' with a derogatory suffix, *-on*, probably indicating that they were formidable opponents.

Bellevue   City
ZIP: 44811   Lat: 41-16-29 N Long: 82-49-50 W
Pop: 3,910 (1990); 3,950 (1980)   Pop Density: 2300.0
Land: 1.7 sq. mi.; Water: 0.0 sq. mi.

In northern OH, 15 mi. southwest of Sandusky. Settled 1815. Part of the town is also in Sandusky County.

Name origin: Named in 1839 by James Bell, who was then building the Mad River & Lake Erie Railroad from Sandusky.

Bronson   Township
ZIP: 44857   Lat: 41-10-38 N Long: 82-35-07 W
Pop: 1,683 (1990); 1,591 (1980)   Pop Density: 64.2
Land: 26.2 sq. mi.; Water: 0.0 sq. mi.

Clarksfield   Township
ZIP: 44889   Lat: 41-10-03 N Long: 82-23-09 W
Pop: 1,302 (1990); 1,289 (1980)   Pop Density: 48.0
Land: 27.1 sq. mi.; Water: 0.0 sq. mi.

Fairfield   Township
                    Lat: 41-05-56 N Long: 82-35-14 W
Pop: 1,229 (1990); 1,198 (1980)   Pop Density: 47.3
Land: 26.0 sq. mi.; Water: 0.0 sq. mi.

Fitchville   Township
ZIP: 44851   Lat: 41-05-56 N Long: 82-29-18 W
Pop: 889 (1990); 938 (1980)   Pop Density: 34.3
Land: 25.9 sq. mi.; Water: 0.0 sq. mi.

Greenfield   Township
                    Lat: 41-06-21 N Long: 82-41-13 W
Pop: 1,422 (1990); 1,144 (1980)   Pop Density: 56.2
Land: 25.3 sq. mi.; Water: 0.3 sq. mi.

Greenwich   Village
ZIP: 44837   Lat: 41-01-52 N Long: 82-31-04 W
Pop: 1,442 (1990); 1,458 (1980)   Pop Density: 1030.0
Land: 1.4 sq. mi.; Water: 0.0 sq. mi.

Not coextensive with the town of the same name.

Name origin: For Greenwich, CT.

*Greenwich   Township
ZIP: 44837   Lat: 41-01-44 N Long: 82-29-07 W
Pop: 785 (1990); 2,185 (1980)   Pop Density: 31.4
Land: 25.0 sq. mi.; Water: 0.0 sq. mi.

Hartland   Township
ZIP: 44857   Lat: 41-10-18 N Long: 82-29-05 W
Pop: 934 (1990); 899 (1980)   Pop Density: 36.5
Land: 25.6 sq. mi.; Water: 0.0 sq. mi.

Lyme   Township
                    Lat: 41-15-11 N Long: 82-47-20 W
Pop: 908 (1990); 954 (1980)   Pop Density: 37.4
Land: 24.3 sq. mi.; Water: 0.1 sq. mi.

Milan   Village
ZIP: 44846   Lat: 41-16-59 N Long: 82-35-40 W
Pop: 408 (1990); 388 (1980)   Pop Density: 816.0
Land: 0.5 sq. mi.; Water: 0.0 sq. mi.

Part of the town is also in Erie County.

Name origin: For Milan, Italy.

Monroeville   Village
ZIP: 44847   Lat: 41-14-38 N Long: 82-42-04 W
Pop: 1,381 (1990); 1,329 (1980)   Pop Density: 986.4
Land: 1.4 sq. mi.; Water: 0.0 sq. mi.   Elev: 723 ft.

New Haven   Township
                    Lat: 41-01-57 N Long: 82-40-50 W
Pop: 3,049 (1990); 3,043 (1980)   Pop Density: 130.9
Land: 23.3 sq. mi.; Water: 0.3 sq. mi.

New London   Village
ZIP: 44851   Lat: 41-04-45 N Long: 82-24-22 W
Pop: 2,642 (1990); 2,449 (1980)   Pop Density: 1258.1
Land: 2.1 sq. mi.; Water: 0.4 sq. mi.   Elev: 980 ft.

In north-central OH near the Vermillion River, 45 mi. southwest of Cleveland. Not coextensive with the town of the same name.

Name origin: For New London, CT.

*New London   Township
ZIP: 44851   Lat: 41-05-54 N Long: 82-23-26 W
Pop: 3,417 (1990); 3,159 (1980)   Pop Density: 131.9
Land: 25.9 sq. mi.; Water: 0.4 sq. mi.

North Fairfield   Village
ZIP: 44855   Lat: 41-06-17 N Long: 82-36-46 W
Pop: 504 (1990); 525 (1980)   Pop Density: 1008.0
Land: 0.5 sq. mi.; Water: 0.0 sq. mi.   Elev: 932 ft.

Norwalk   City
ZIP: 44857   Lat: 41-14-31 N Long: 82-36-37 W
Pop: 14,731 (1990); 14,358 (1980)   Pop Density: 1841.4
Land: 8.0 sq. mi.; Water: 0.2 sq. mi.   Elev: 731 ft.

In north-central OH, southwest of Cleveland. Founded 1816.

Name origin: For Norwalk, CT, because many of its settlers left there to settle here on their "Firelands" grants, having been burned out of their New England homes by the British.

*Norwalk   Township
ZIP: 44857   Lat: 41-15-05 N Long: 82-35-05 W
Pop: 3,276 (1990); 3,106 (1980)   Pop Density: 176.1
Land: 18.6 sq. mi.; Water: 0.0 sq. mi.

Norwich   Township
                    Lat: 41-06-30 N Long: 82-47-09 W
Pop: 958 (1990); 892 (1980)   Pop Density: 36.8
Land: 26.0 sq. mi.; Water: 0.0 sq. mi.

Peru Township
Lat: 41-10-44 N Long: 82-41-29 W
Pop: 928 (1990); 1,033 (1980)   **Pop Density:** 36.1
Land: 25.7 sq. mi.; **Water:** 0.0 sq. mi.

Plymouth Village
Lat: 40-59-56 N Long: 82-40-04 W
Pop: 929 (1990); 969 (1980)   **Pop Density:** 929.0
Land: 1.0 sq. mi.; **Water:** 0.0 sq. mi.   **Elev:** 1029 ft.
In north-central OH on the west branch of the Huron River. Part of the town is also in Richland County.
Name origin: For Plymouth, MA.

Richmond Township
ZIP: 44890   Lat: 41-01-58 N Long: 82-46-44 W
Pop: 1,169 (1990); 1,221 (1980)   **Pop Density:** 45.5
Land: 25.7 sq. mi.; **Water:** 0.1 sq. mi.

Ridgefield Township
ZIP: 44847   Lat: 41-15-01 N Long: 82-41-21 W
Pop: 2,512 (1990); 2,466 (1980)   **Pop Density:** 98.1
Land: 25.6 sq. mi.; **Water:** 0.0 sq. mi.

Ripley Township
Lat: 41-01-35 N Long: 82-34-19 W
Pop: 867 (1990); 924 (1980)   **Pop Density:** 33.9
Land: 25.6 sq. mi.; **Water:** 0.0 sq. mi.

Sherman Township
Lat: 41-10-42 N Long: 82-47-10 W
Pop: 530 (1990); 521 (1980)   **Pop Density:** 20.5
Land: 25.9 sq. mi.; **Water:** 0.1 sq. mi.

Townsend Township
Lat: 41-14-40 N Long: 82-29-24 W
Pop: 1,571 (1990); 1,571 (1980)   **Pop Density:** 61.1
Land: 25.7 sq. mi.; **Water:** 0.0 sq. mi.

Wakeman Village
ZIP: 44889   Lat: 41-15-21 N Long: 82-24-14 W
Pop: 948 (1990); 906 (1980)   **Pop Density:** 1185.0
Land: 0.8 sq. mi.; **Water:** 0.0 sq. mi.   **Elev:** 856 ft.
Not coextensive with the town of the same name.

*Wakeman Township
ZIP: 44889   Lat: 41-14-59 N Long: 82-23-19 W
Pop: 2,518 (1990); 2,446 (1980)   **Pop Density:** 98.4
Land: 25.6 sq. mi.; **Water:** 0.1 sq. mi.

Willard City
ZIP: 44890   Lat: 41-03-02 N Long: 82-43-21 W
Pop: 6,210 (1990); 5,720 (1980)   **Pop Density:** 1940.6
Land: 3.2 sq. mi.; **Water:** 0.0 sq. mi.   **Elev:** 955 ft.
In north-central OH, 20 mi. north of Mansfield.

Jackson County
County Seat: Jackson (ZIP: 45640)

Pop: 30,230 (1990); 30,592 (1980)   **Pop Density:** 71.9
Land: 420.3 sq. mi.; **Water:** 1.2 sq. mi.   **Area Code:** 614
In south-central OH; organized Mar 1, 1816 from Pike County.
Name origin: For Andrew Jackson (1767–1845), seventh U.S. president.

Bloomfield Township
Lat: 38-59-32 N Long: 82-30-07 W
Pop: 817 (1990); 705 (1980)   **Pop Density:** 21.1
Land: 38.7 sq. mi.; **Water:** 0.0 sq. mi.

Coal Township
Lat: 39-06-29 N Long: 82-36-40 W
Pop: 1,825 (1990); 2,118 (1980)   **Pop Density:** 94.1
Land: 19.4 sq. mi.; **Water:** 0.0 sq. mi.

Coalton Village
ZIP: 45621   Lat: 39-06-44 N Long: 82-36-40 W
Pop: 553 (1990); 639 (1980)   **Pop Density:** 921.7
Land: 0.6 sq. mi.; **Water:** 0.0 sq. mi.

Franklin Township
Lat: 38-58-39 N Long: 82-36-42 W
Pop: 1,420 (1990); 1,384 (1980)   **Pop Density:** 38.1
Land: 37.3 sq. mi.; **Water:** 0.0 sq. mi.

Hamilton Township
ZIP: 45656   Lat: 38-54-07 N Long: 82-43-14 W
Pop: 453 (1990); 426 (1980)   **Pop Density:** 17.8
Land: 25.5 sq. mi.; **Water:** 0.0 sq. mi.

Jackson City
ZIP: 45640   Lat: 39-02-44 N Long: 82-37-45 W
Pop: 6,144 (1990); 6,675 (1980)   **Pop Density:** 1307.2
Land: 4.7 sq. mi.; **Water:** 0.0 sq. mi.   **Elev:** 680 ft.
In southern OH, northeast of Portsmouth. Platted 1817.
Name origin: For Gen. Andrew Jackson (1767–1845), seventh U.S. president.

*Jackson Township
ZIP: 45640   Lat: 39-09-55 N Long: 82-43-06 W
Pop: 1,113 (1990); 1,147 (1980)   **Pop Density:** 28.7
Land: 38.8 sq. mi.; **Water:** 0.0 sq. mi.

Jefferson Township
ZIP: 45656   Lat: 38-53-29 N Long: 82-37-51 W
Pop: 3,132 (1990); 3,475 (1980)   **Pop Density:** 85.6
Land: 36.6 sq. mi.; **Water:** 0.3 sq. mi.

Liberty Township
Lat: 39-04-20 N Long: 82-43-54 W
Pop: 1,431 (1990); 1,250 (1980)   **Pop Density:** 33.4
Land: 42.9 sq. mi.; **Water:** 0.4 sq. mi.

Lick Township
ZIP: 45640   Lat: 39-03-12 N Long: 82-36-30 W
Pop: 8,564 (1990); 9,054 (1980)   **Pop Density:** 343.9
Land: 24.9 sq. mi.; **Water:** 0.0 sq. mi.

Madison
Township
ZIP: 45656 **Lat:** 38-54-14 N **Long:** 82-30-23 W
Pop: 2,179 (1990); 2,139 (1980) **Pop Density:** 48.1
Land: 45.3 sq. mi.; **Water:** 0.1 sq. mi.

Milton
Township
Lat: 39-05-09 N **Long:** 82-28-36 W
Pop: 1,090 (1990); 985 (1980) **Pop Density:** 27.7
Land: 39.4 sq. mi.; **Water:** 0.1 sq. mi.

Oak Hill
Village
ZIP: 45656 **Lat:** 38-53-45 N **Long:** 82-34-09 W
Pop: 1,831 (1990); 1,713 (1980) **Pop Density:** 1664.5
Land: 1.1 sq. mi.; **Water:** 0.0 sq. mi.

In southern OH on Jackson Lake, northeast of Portsmouth.

Scioto
Township
Lat: 38-59-11 N **Long:** 82-44-06 W
Pop: 1,432 (1990); 1,280 (1980) **Pop Density:** 33.9
Land: 42.3 sq. mi.; **Water:** 0.1 sq. mi.

Washington
Township
ZIP: 45656 **Lat:** 39-09-37 N **Long:** 82-35-31 W
Pop: 725 (1990); 613 (1980) **Pop Density:** 32.4
Land: 22.4 sq. mi.; **Water:** 0.0 sq. mi.

Wellston
City
ZIP: 45692 **Lat:** 39-07-01 N **Long:** 82-32-18 W
Pop: 6,049 (1990); 6,016 (1980) **Pop Density:** 876.7
Land: 6.9 sq. mi.; **Water:** 0.1 sq. mi.

Jefferson County
County Seat: Steubenville (ZIP: 43952)

Pop: 80,298 (1990); 91,564 (1980) **Pop Density:** 196.0
Land: 409.6 sq. mi.; **Water:** 1.3 sq. mi. **Area Code:** 614

On east-central border of OH, southeast of Canton; original county; organized Jul 27, 1797 (prior to statehood).

Name origin: For Thomas Jefferson (1743–1826), U.S. patriot and statesman; third U.S. president.

Adena
Village
ZIP: 43901 **Lat:** 40-13-02 N **Long:** 80-52-23 W
Pop: 692 (1990); 909 (1980) **Pop Density:** 1730.0
Land: 0.4 sq. mi.; **Water:** 0.0 sq. mi. **Elev:** 884 ft.

Part of the town is also in Harrison County.

Amsterdam
Village
ZIP: 43903 **Lat:** 40-28-16 N **Long:** 80-55-16 W
Pop: 669 (1990); 783 (1980) **Pop Density:** 2230.0
Land: 0.3 sq. mi.; **Water:** 0.0 sq. mi.

In eastern OH, 21 mi. northwest of Steubenville.
Name origin: For the Dutch city.

Bergholz
Village
ZIP: 43908 **Lat:** 40-31-15 N **Long:** 80-53-05 W
Pop: 713 (1990); 914 (1980) **Pop Density:** 1188.3
Land: 0.6 sq. mi.; **Water:** 0.0 sq. mi.

Bloomingdale
Village
ZIP: 43910 **Lat:** 40-20-30 N **Long:** 80-49-02 W
Pop: 227 (1990); 254 (1980) **Pop Density:** 2270.0
Land: 0.1 sq. mi.; **Water:** 0.0 sq. mi. **Elev:** 1277 ft.

Brentwood
CDP
Lat: 40-21-10 N **Long:** 80-43-50 W
Pop: 3,568 (1990); 3,636 (1980) **Pop Density:** 849.5
Land: 4.2 sq. mi.; **Water:** 0.0 sq. mi.

Brilliant
Village
ZIP: 43913 **Lat:** 40-16-06 N **Long:** 80-37-29 W
Pop: 1,672 (1990); 1,751 (1980) **Pop Density:** 1857.8
Land: 0.9 sq. mi.; **Water:** 0.0 sq. mi.

In eastern OH on the Ohio River, 7 mi. south of Steubenville.

Brush Creek
Township
Lat: 40-33-50 N **Long:** 80-48-15 W
Pop: 461 (1990); 470 (1980) **Pop Density:** 19.5
Land: 23.7 sq. mi.; **Water:** 0.0 sq. mi.

Cross Creek
Township
ZIP: 43952 **Lat:** 40-20-04 N **Long:** 80-42-05 W
Pop: 9,305 (1990); 10,372 (1980) **Pop Density:** 283.7
Land: 32.8 sq. mi.; **Water:** 0.0 sq. mi.

Dillonvale
Village
ZIP: 43917 **Lat:** 40-11-54 N **Long:** 80-46-31 W
Pop: 857 (1990); 912 (1980) **Pop Density:** 2142.5
Land: 0.4 sq. mi.; **Water:** 0.0 sq. mi.

Empire
Village
Lat: 40-30-39 N **Long:** 80-37-30 W
Pop: 364 (1990); 484 (1980) **Pop Density:** 1213.3
Land: 0.3 sq. mi.; **Water:** 0.0 sq. mi. **Elev:** 682 ft.

Irondale
Village
ZIP: 43932 **Lat:** 40-34-21 N **Long:** 80-43-33 W
Pop: 382 (1990); 535 (1980) **Pop Density:** 272.9
Land: 1.4 sq. mi.; **Water:** 0.0 sq. mi. **Elev:** 718 ft.

Island Creek
Township
ZIP: 43964 **Lat:** 40-25-59 N **Long:** 80-40-44 W
Pop: 11,649 (1990); 12,954 (1980) **Pop Density:** 270.3
Land: 43.1 sq. mi.; **Water:** 0.0 sq. mi.

Knox
Township
ZIP: 43964 **Lat:** 40-29-41 N **Long:** 80-40-31 W
Pop: 5,506 (1990); 5,912 (1980) **Pop Density:** 187.3
Land: 29.4 sq. mi.; **Water:** 0.3 sq. mi.

Mingo Junction
City
ZIP: 43938 **Lat:** 40-19-14 N **Long:** 80-36-48 W
Pop: 4,297 (1990); 4,834 (1980) **Pop Density:** 1953.2
Land: 2.2 sq. mi.; **Water:** 0.0 sq. mi. **Elev:** 675 ft.

In eastern OH on the Ohio River, south of Steubenville.

Mount Pleasant
Village
ZIP: 43939 **Lat:** 40-10-33 N **Long:** 80-47-59 W
Pop: 498 (1990); 616 (1980) **Pop Density:** 1660.0
Land: 0.3 sq. mi.; **Water:** 0.0 sq. mi.

Not coextensive with the town of the same name.

OHIO, Jefferson County

***Mount Pleasant** — Township
Lat: 40-10-31 N Long: 80-49-37 W
Pop: 2,695 (1990); 3,153 (1980) Pop Density: 141.1
Land: 19.1 sq. mi.; Water: 0.0 sq. mi.

New Alexandria — Village
ZIP: 43938 Lat: 40-17-28 N Long: 80-40-31 W
Pop: 257 (1990); 410 (1980) Pop Density: 642.5
Land: 0.4 sq. mi.; Water: 0.0 sq. mi. Elev: 1250 ft.

Rayland — Village
ZIP: 43943 Lat: 40-11-00 N Long: 80-41-29 W
Pop: 490 (1990); 566 (1980) Pop Density: 980.0
Land: 0.5 sq. mi.; Water: 0.0 sq. mi.

Richmond — Village
ZIP: 43944 Lat: 40-25-58 N Long: 80-46-19 W
Pop: 446 (1990); 624 (1980) Pop Density: 892.0
Land: 0.5 sq. mi.; Water: 0.0 sq. mi.

Ross — Township
Lat: 40-29-59 N Long: 80-48-32 W
Pop: 595 (1990); 601 (1980) Pop Density: 19.3
Land: 30.9 sq. mi.; Water: 0.0 sq. mi.

Salem — Township
Lat: 40-25-42 N Long: 80-48-10 W
Pop: 3,739 (1990); 3,569 (1980) Pop Density: 102.4
Land: 36.5 sq. mi.; Water: 0.1 sq. mi.

Saline — Township
Lat: 40-33-03 N Long: 80-41-45 W
Pop: 1,467 (1990); 1,823 (1980) Pop Density: 69.5
Land: 21.1 sq. mi.; Water: 0.4 sq. mi.

Salineville — Village
ZIP: 43945 Lat: 40-35-52 N Long: 80-49-14 W
Pop: 0 (1990)
Land: 0.01 sq. mi.; Water: 0.0 sq. mi. Elev: 1084 ft.
In eastern OH, northwest of Steubenville. Part of the town is also in Columbiana County.
Name origin: For the area's salt springs.

Smithfield — Village
ZIP: 43948 Lat: 40-16-21 N Long: 80-46-36 W
Pop: 722 (1990); 1,308 (1980) Pop Density: 802.2
Land: 0.9 sq. mi.; Water: 0.0 sq. mi.

***Smithfield** — Township
Lat: 40-14-44 N Long: 80-49-08 W
Pop: 3,810 (1990); 4,802 (1980) Pop Density: 101.6
Land: 37.5 sq. mi.; Water: 0.2 sq. mi.

Springfield — Township
Lat: 40-29-17 N Long: 80-53-51 W
Pop: 2,644 (1990); 3,042 (1980) Pop Density: 86.1
Land: 30.7 sq. mi.; Water: 0.0 sq. mi.

Steubenville — City
ZIP: 43952 Lat: 40-22-01 N Long: 80-38-47 W
Pop: 22,125 (1990); 26,400 (1980) Pop Density: 2731.5
Land: 8.1 sq. mi.; Water: 0.0 sq. mi.
In eastern OH on the Ohio River, 48 mi. south of Youngstown. Settled 1797; incorporated 1805.
Name origin: For Fort Steuben, which was named after Baron von Steuben (1730–94), a Prussian drill master who trained and fought with the soldiers in the American Revolution.

***Steubenville** — Township
ZIP: 43952 Lat: 40-19-20 N Long: 80-37-19 W
Pop: 5,513 (1990); 6,247 (1980) Pop Density: 697.8
Land: 7.9 sq. mi.; Water: 0.0 sq. mi.

Stratton — Village
ZIP: 43961 Lat: 40-31-29 N Long: 80-37-49 W
Pop: 278 (1990); 356 (1980) Pop Density: 556.0
Land: 0.5 sq. mi.; Water: 0.0 sq. mi. Elev: 676 ft.

Tiltonsville — Village
ZIP: 43963 Lat: 40-10-21 N Long: 80-41-51 W
Pop: 1,517 (1990); 1,750 (1980) Pop Density: 2528.3
Land: 0.6 sq. mi.; Water: 0.0 sq. mi.
In eastern OH on the Ohio River, 20 mi. south of Steubenville. Platted 1806.
Name origin: For John Tilton, who platted it.

Toronto — City
ZIP: 43964 Lat: 40-27-32 N Long: 80-36-22 W
Pop: 6,127 (1990); 6,934 (1980) Pop Density: 3224.7
Land: 1.9 sq. mi.; Water: 0.0 sq. mi.
Name origin: For Toronto, Ontario, Canada.

Warren — Township
Lat: 40-11-30 N Long: 80-43-04 W
Pop: 4,964 (1990); 5,709 (1980) Pop Density: 214.0
Land: 23.2 sq. mi.; Water: 0.0 sq. mi.

Wayne — Township
Lat: 40-20-16 N Long: 80-48-53 W
Pop: 2,576 (1990); 2,839 (1980) Pop Density: 66.7
Land: 38.6 sq. mi.; Water: 0.2 sq. mi.

Wells — Township
Lat: 40-15-28 N Long: 80-41-28 W
Pop: 3,249 (1990); 3,671 (1980) Pop Density: 119.9
Land: 27.1 sq. mi.; Water: 0.0 sq. mi.

Wintersville — Village
ZIP: 43952 Lat: 40-22-44 N Long: 80-42-23 W
Pop: 4,102 (1990); 4,724 (1980) Pop Density: 1640.8
Land: 2.5 sq. mi.; Water: 0.0 sq. mi. Elev: 262 ft.

Yorkville — Village
ZIP: 43971 Lat: 40-09-45 N Long: 80-42-19 W
Pop: 758 (1990); 955 (1980) Pop Density: 3790.0
Land: 0.2 sq. mi.; Water: 0.0 sq. mi.
Part of the town is also in Belmont County.
Name origin: For York, PA, former home of early settlers.

OHIO, Knox County   *American Places Dictionary*

Knox County
County Seat: Mount Vernon (ZIP: 43050)

Pop: 47,473 (1990); 46,304 (1980)   **Pop Density:** 90.1
Land: 527.2 sq. mi.; **Water:** 2.4 sq. mi.   **Area Code:** 614

In central OH, northeast of Columbus; organized Mar 1, 1808 from Fairfield County.

Name origin: For Gen. Henry Knox (1750–1806), Revolutionary War officer and first U.S. secretary of war (1785–95).

Berlin   Township
Lat: 40-31-05 N **Long:** 82-29-52 W
Pop: 1,388 (1990); 1,452 (1980)   **Pop Density:** 75.4
Land: 18.4 sq. mi.; **Water:** 0.8 sq. mi.

Brown   Township
Lat: 40-30-23 N **Long:** 82-19-05 W
Pop: 1,019 (1990); 1,000 (1980)   **Pop Density:** 34.0
Land: 30.0 sq. mi.; **Water:** 0.0 sq. mi.

Butler   Township
Lat: 40-20-52 N **Long:** 82-13-54 W
Pop: 504 (1990); 449 (1980)   **Pop Density:** 20.7
Land: 24.4 sq. mi.; **Water:** 0.0 sq. mi.

Centerburg   Village
ZIP: 43011   **Lat:** 40-18-13 N **Long:** 82-41-47 W
Pop: 1,323 (1990); 1,275 (1980)   **Pop Density:** 2205.0
Land: 0.6 sq. mi.; **Water:** 0.0 sq. mi.

Clay   Township
Lat: 40-16-23 N **Long:** 82-19-41 W
Pop: 1,084 (1990); 1,040 (1980)   **Pop Density:** 43.0
Land: 25.2 sq. mi.; **Water:** 0.0 sq. mi.

Clinton   Township
Lat: 40-22-16 N **Long:** 82-30-43 W
Pop: 3,502 (1990); 3,600 (1980)   **Pop Density:** 212.2
Land: 16.5 sq. mi.; **Water:** 0.1 sq. mi.

College   Township
Lat: 40-22-17 N **Long:** 82-23-42 W
Pop: 2,421 (1990); 2,363 (1980)   **Pop Density:** 378.3
Land: 6.4 sq. mi.; **Water:** 0.0 sq. mi.

Danville   Village
ZIP: 43014   **Lat:** 40-26-52 N **Long:** 82-15-36 W
Pop: 1,001 (1990); 1,127 (1980)   **Pop Density:** 2002.0
Land: 0.5 sq. mi.; **Water:** 0.0 sq. mi.   **Elev:** 966 ft.

Fredericktown   Village
ZIP: 43019   **Lat:** 40-28-43 N **Long:** 82-32-43 W
Pop: 2,443 (1990); 2,299 (1980)   **Pop Density:** 1879.2
Land: 1.3 sq. mi.; **Water:** 0.0 sq. mi.   **Elev:** 1130 ft.

Gambier   Village
ZIP: 43022   **Lat:** 40-22-34 N **Long:** 82-23-41 W
Pop: 2,073 (1990); 2,056 (1980)   **Pop Density:** 2303.3
Land: 0.9 sq. mi.; **Water:** 0.0 sq. mi.

In north-central OH on the Walhonding River, 5 mi. east of Mount Vernon.
Name origin: For English admiral Lord James Gambier (1756–1833).

Gann   Village
ZIP: 43006   **Lat:** 40-28-08 N **Long:** 82-11-25 W
Pop: 179 (1990); 173 (1980)   **Pop Density:** 895.0
Land: 0.2 sq. mi.; **Water:** 0.0 sq. mi.

Harrison   Township
Lat: 40-21-21 N **Long:** 82-19-40 W
Pop: 586 (1990); 559 (1980)   **Pop Density:** 24.3
Land: 24.1 sq. mi.; **Water:** 0.0 sq. mi.

Hilliar   Township
Lat: 40-18-31 N **Long:** 82-41-54 W
Pop: 2,645 (1990); 2,337 (1980)   **Pop Density:** 101.7
Land: 26.0 sq. mi.; **Water:** 0.0 sq. mi.

Howard   Township
ZIP: 43028   **Lat:** 40-25-23 N **Long:** 82-19-07 W
Pop: 2,149 (1990); 1,557 (1980)   **Pop Density:** 95.1
Land: 22.6 sq. mi.; **Water:** 0.8 sq. mi.

Jackson   Township
Lat: 40-16-44 N **Long:** 82-13-59 W
Pop: 680 (1990); 674 (1980)   **Pop Density:** 28.8
Land: 23.6 sq. mi.; **Water:** 0.0 sq. mi.

Jefferson   Township
Lat: 40-31-07 N **Long:** 82-13-37 W
Pop: 524 (1990); 558 (1980)   **Pop Density:** 16.0
Land: 32.8 sq. mi.; **Water:** 0.0 sq. mi.

Liberty   Township
Lat: 40-22-49 N **Long:** 82-35-33 W
Pop: 1,213 (1990); 1,277 (1980)   **Pop Density:** 47.0
Land: 25.8 sq. mi.; **Water:** 0.0 sq. mi.

Martinsburg   Village
ZIP: 43037   **Lat:** 40-16-09 N **Long:** 82-21-17 W
Pop: 213 (1990); 240 (1980)   **Pop Density:** 1065.0
Land: 0.2 sq. mi.; **Water:** 0.0 sq. mi.   **Elev:** 1167 ft.

Middlebury   Township
Lat: 40-30-54 N **Long:** 82-35-25 W
Pop: 849 (1990); 950 (1980)   **Pop Density:** 41.4
Land: 20.5 sq. mi.; **Water:** 0.4 sq. mi.

Milford   Township
Lat: 40-18-34 N **Long:** 82-36-06 W
Pop: 1,175 (1990); 1,075 (1980)   **Pop Density:** 45.7
Land: 25.7 sq. mi.; **Water:** 0.0 sq. mi.

Miller   Township
Lat: 40-18-23 N **Long:** 82-30-23 W
Pop: 717 (1990); 722 (1980)   **Pop Density:** 34.6
Land: 20.7 sq. mi.; **Water:** 0.0 sq. mi.

Monroe   Township
Lat: 40-25-38 N **Long:** 82-24-56 W
Pop: 2,062 (1990); 2,172 (1980)   **Pop Density:** 82.8
Land: 24.9 sq. mi.; **Water:** 0.0 sq. mi.

Morgan   Township
Lat: 40-16-51 N **Long:** 82-25-17 W
Pop: 624 (1990); 636 (1980)   **Pop Density:** 24.0
Land: 26.0 sq. mi.; **Water:** 0.0 sq. mi.

Morris
Township
Lat: 40-26-39 N **Long:** 82-30-01 W
Pop: 1,801 (1990); 1,896 (1980) **Pop Density:** 85.4
Land: 21.1 sq. mi.; **Water:** 0.0 sq. mi.

Mount Vernon
City
ZIP: 43050 **Lat:** 40-23-25 N **Long:** 82-28-30 W
Pop: 14,550 (1990); 14,323 (1980) **Pop Density:** 2385.2
Land: 6.1 sq. mi.; **Water:** 0.0 sq. mi.

In central OH on the Kokosing River, 35 northeast of Columbus.

Name origin: For George Washington's (1732–99) estate in VA.

Pike
Township
Lat: 40-30-38 N **Long:** 82-24-40 W
Pop: 1,065 (1990); 1,057 (1980) **Pop Density:** 35.0
Land: 30.4 sq. mi.; **Water:** 0.0 sq. mi.

Pleasant
Township
Lat: 40-20-26 N **Long:** 82-25-48 W
Pop: 1,454 (1990); 1,321 (1980) **Pop Density:** 76.5
Land: 19.0 sq. mi.; **Water:** 0.0 sq. mi.

Union
Township
Lat: 40-25-28 N **Long:** 82-13-52 W
Pop: 2,150 (1990); 2,124 (1980) **Pop Density:** 71.2
Land: 30.2 sq. mi.; **Water:** 0.0 sq. mi.

Utica
Village
ZIP: 43080 **Lat:** 40-14-44 N **Long:** 82-26-19 W
Pop: 17 (1990); 17 (1980) **Pop Density:** 340.0
Land: 0.05 sq. mi.; **Water:** 0.0 sq. mi. **Elev:** 967 ft.

In central OH on the Licking River, northeast of Columbus. Part of the town is also in Licking County.

Name origin: For Utica, NY. Previously named Wilmington in 1815.

Wayne
Township
Lat: 40-27-01 N **Long:** 82-35-10 W
Pop: 868 (1990); 863 (1980) **Pop Density:** 34.4
Land: 25.2 sq. mi.; **Water:** 0.0 sq. mi.

Lake County
County Seat: Painesville (ZIP: 44077)

Pop: 215,499 (1990); 212,801 (1980) **Pop Density:** 944.2
Land: 228.2 sq. mi.; **Water:** 750.8 sq. mi. **Area Code:** 216

On the northeastern border of OH, bounded on the north by Lake Erie; organized Mar 6, 1840 from Geauga and Cuyahoga counties.

Name origin: For its location on Lake Erie.

Concord
Township
ZIP: 44077 **Lat:** 41-39-55 N **Long:** 81-13-57 W
Pop: 12,432 (1990); 10,335 (1980) **Pop Density:** 538.2
Land: 23.1 sq. mi.; **Water:** 0.1 sq. mi.

In northeastern OH, 28 mi. northwest of Cleveland.

Eastlake
City
ZIP: 44095 **Lat:** 41-39-34 N **Long:** 81-25-49 W
Pop: 21,161 (1990); 22,104 (1980) **Pop Density:** 3306.4
Land: 6.4 sq. mi.; **Water:** 0.1 sq. mi.

In northeastern OH on Lake Erie, 20 mi. northeast of Cleveland.

Fairport Harbor
Village
Lat: 41-44-51 N **Long:** 81-16-23 W
Pop: 2,978 (1990); 3,357 (1980) **Pop Density:** 2978.0
Land: 1.0 sq. mi.; **Water:** 0.1 sq. mi.

Grand River
Village
Lat: 41-44-32 N **Long:** 81-17-09 W
Pop: 297 (1990); 412 (1980) **Pop Density:** 594.0
Land: 0.5 sq. mi.; **Water:** 0.1 sq. mi.

In northeastern OH, 2 mi. south of Lake Erie and just west of the mouth of the Grand River.

Kirtland
City
ZIP: 44094 **Lat:** 41-35-54 N **Long:** 81-20-16 W
Pop: 5,881 (1990); 5,969 (1980) **Pop Density:** 354.3
Land: 16.6 sq. mi.; **Water:** 0.1 sq. mi.

In northeastern OH, on the brow of a hill overlooking the Chagrin River; a northeastern suburb of Cleveland.

Name origin: For Turhand Kirtland, resident general agent of the Connecticut Land Company.

Kirtland Hills
Village
ZIP: 44060 **Lat:** 41-38-32 N **Long:** 81-19-04 W
Pop: 628 (1990); 506 (1980) **Pop Density:** 112.1
Land: 5.6 sq. mi.; **Water:** 0.1 sq. mi.

Lakeline
Village
Lat: 41-39-30 N **Long:** 81-27-14 W
Pop: 210 (1990); 258 (1980) **Pop Density:** 2100.0
Land: 0.1 sq. mi.; **Water:** 0.0 sq. mi. **Elev:** 617 ft.

Leroy
Township
ZIP: 44077 **Lat:** 41-42-05 N **Long:** 81-08-30 W
Pop: 2,581 (1990); 2,505 (1980) **Pop Density:** 101.2
Land: 25.5 sq. mi.; **Water:** 0.2 sq. mi.

Madison
Village
ZIP: 44057 **Lat:** 41-46-18 N **Long:** 81-03-11 W
Pop: 2,477 (1990); 2,291 (1980) **Pop Density:** 563.0
Land: 4.4 sq. mi.; **Water:** 0.0 sq. mi. **Elev:** 744 ft.

In northeastern OH, 15 mi. southwest of Ashtabula. Not coextensive with the town of the same name.

Name origin: For James Madison (1751–1836), fourth U.S. president.

OHIO, Lake County *American Places Dictionary*

*Madison Township
ZIP: 44057   **Lat:** 42-03-47 N   **Long:** 81-03-30 W
Pop: 17,954 (1990); 17,669 (1980)   **Pop Density:** 410.8
Land: 43.7 sq. mi.; **Water:** 140.7 sq. mi.

Mentor City
ZIP: 44060   **Lat:** 41-41-29 N   **Long:** 81-20-04 W
Pop: 47,358 (1990); 42,065 (1980)   **Pop Density:** 1767.1
Land: 26.8 sq. mi.; **Water:** 1.3 sq. mi.

In northeastern OH, just south of Lake Erie.

Name origin: Possibly for early settler, Hiram Mentor, or for the mythological Greek teacher from the *Odyssey*.

Mentor-on-the-Lake City
ZIP: 44060   **Lat:** 41-42-49 N   **Long:** 81-21-53 W
Pop: 8,271 (1990); 7,919 (1980)   **Pop Density:** 5169.4
Land: 1.6 sq. mi.; **Water:** 0.0 sq. mi.

In northeastern OH on the Lake Erie shoreline.

North Madison CDP
ZIP: 44057   **Lat:** 41-49-47 N   **Long:** 81-03-17 W
Pop: 8,699 (1990); 8,741 (1980)   **Pop Density:** 2174.8
Land: 4.0 sq. mi.; **Water:** 0.0 sq. mi.

North Perry Village
ZIP: 44081   **Lat:** 41-48-24 N   **Long:** 81-07-31 W
Pop: 824 (1990); 897 (1980)   **Pop Density:** 216.8
Land: 3.8 sq. mi.; **Water:** 0.0 sq. mi.   **Elev:** 680 ft.

Painesville City
ZIP: 44077   **Lat:** 41-43-37 N   **Long:** 81-14-53 W
Pop: 15,699 (1990); 16,391 (1980)   **Pop Density:** 3019.0
Land: 5.2 sq. mi.; **Water:** 0.7 sq. mi.   **Elev:** 677 ft.

In northeastern OH, 30 mi. northeast of Cleveland.

Name origin: For Revolutionary War officer, Gen. Edward Paine, who arrived here in the early 1800s.

*Painesville Township
ZIP: 44077   **Lat:** 42-03-00 N   **Long:** 81-14-27 W
Pop: 16,493 (1990); 16,117 (1980)   **Pop Density:** 921.4
Land: 17.9 sq. mi.; **Water:** 160.7 sq. mi.

In northeastern OH, 28 mi. northeast of Cleveland.

Perry Village
ZIP: 44081   **Lat:** 41-46-02 N   **Long:** 81-08-34 W
Pop: 1,012 (1990); 961 (1980)   **Pop Density:** 506.0
Land: 2.0 sq. mi.; **Water:** 0.0 sq. mi.   **Elev:** 706 ft.

*Perry Township
ZIP: 44081   **Lat:** 42-03-22 N   **Long:** 81-08-55 W
Pop: 6,780 (1990); 6,984 (1980)   **Pop Density:** 289.7
Land: 23.4 sq. mi.; **Water:** 128.3 sq. mi.

Timberlake Village
         Lat: 41-39-52 N   **Long:** 81-26-34 W
Pop: 833 (1990); 885 (1980)   **Pop Density:** 4165.0
Land: 0.2 sq. mi.; **Water:** 0.0 sq. mi.

Waite Hill Village
ZIP: 44094   **Lat:** 41-36-35 N   **Long:** 81-23-16 W
Pop: 454 (1990); 529 (1980)   **Pop Density:** 108.1
Land: 4.2 sq. mi.; **Water:** 0.1 sq. mi.

Wickliffe City
ZIP: 44092   **Lat:** 41-36-29 N   **Long:** 81-28-03 W
Pop: 14,558 (1990); 16,790 (1980)   **Pop Density:** 3097.4
Land: 4.7 sq. mi.; **Water:** 0.0 sq. mi.

In northeastern OH on Lake Erie, 14 mi. northeast of Cleveland.

Name origin: For a prominent KY family, most notably Charles A. Wickliffe.

Willoughby City
ZIP: 44094   **Lat:** 41-38-46 N   **Long:** 81-24-33 W
Pop: 20,510 (1990); 19,329 (1980)   **Pop Density:** 2010.8
Land: 10.2 sq. mi.; **Water:** 0.1 sq. mi.   **Elev:** 665 ft.

In northeastern OH, 20 mi. northeast of Cleveland.

Name origin: For an instructor at the Willoughby Medical College. Originally called Chagrin.

Willoughby Hills City
ZIP: 44092   **Lat:** 41-35-05 N   **Long:** 81-26-06 W
Pop: 8,427 (1990); 8,612 (1980)   **Pop Density:** 780.3
Land: 10.8 sq. mi.; **Water:** 0.1 sq. mi.

Willowick City
ZIP: 44092   **Lat:** 41-38-06 N   **Long:** 81-28-06 W
Pop: 15,269 (1990); 17,834 (1980)   **Pop Density:** 6107.6
Land: 2.5 sq. mi.; **Water:** 0.0 sq. mi.

In northeastern OH on Lake Erie, a suburb 10 mi. northeast of Cleveland.

Name origin: Named in 1951 by combining two personal names, Willoughby and Wickliffe.

Lawrence County
County Seat: Ironton (ZIP: 45638)

Pop: 61,834 (1990); 63,849 (1980)   **Pop Density:** 135.8
Land: 455.4 sq. mi.; **Water:** 1.9 sq. mi.   **Area Code:** 614
On the southeastern border of OH; organized Dec 21, 1815 from Gallia County.

Name origin: For Capt. James Lawrence (1781-1813), U.S. naval officer in the war with Barbary pirates near Tripoli and commander of the U.S.S. *Chesapeake* in the War of 1812, who said, "Don't give up the ship!"

Aid Township
         Lat: 38-37-52 N   **Long:** 82-32-02 W
Pop: 811 (1990); 861 (1980)   **Pop Density:** 19.8
Land: 40.9 sq. mi.; **Water:** 0.0 sq. mi.

Athalia Village
ZIP: 45669   **Lat:** 38-30-43 N   **Long:** 82-18-27 W
Pop: 346 (1990); 367 (1980)   **Pop Density:** 494.3
Land: 0.7 sq. mi.; **Water:** 0.0 sq. mi.

Burlington CDP
ZIP: 45680 **Lat:** 38-24-33 N **Long:** 82-31-44 W
Pop: 3,003 (1990) **Pop Density:** 2145.0
Land: 1.4 sq. mi.; **Water:** 0.0 sq. mi.

Chesapeake Village
ZIP: 45619 **Lat:** 38-25-49 N **Long:** 82-27-01 W
Pop: 1,073 (1990); 1,370 (1980) **Pop Density:** 1788.3
Land: 0.6 sq. mi.; **Water:** 0.0 sq. mi.

In southern OH on the Ohio River across from Huntington, WV.

Name origin: For Chesapeake Bay.

Coal Grove Village
ZIP: 45638 **Lat:** 38-29-52 N **Long:** 82-38-33 W
Pop: 2,251 (1990); 2,602 (1980) **Pop Density:** 1125.5
Land: 2.0 sq. mi.; **Water:** 0.2 sq. mi.

Decatur Township
Lat: 38-42-49 N **Long:** 82-38-14 W
Pop: 870 (1990); 895 (1980) **Pop Density:** 26.0
Land: 33.4 sq. mi.; **Water:** 0.1 sq. mi.

Elizabeth Township
Lat: 38-37-53 N **Long:** 82-40-34 W
Pop: 2,515 (1990); 2,315 (1980) **Pop Density:** 48.3
Land: 52.1 sq. mi.; **Water:** 0.3 sq. mi.

Fayette Township
ZIP: 45680 **Lat:** 38-27-28 N **Long:** 82-31-38 W
Pop: 9,181 (1990); 8,826 (1980) **Pop Density:** 332.6
Land: 27.6 sq. mi.; **Water:** 0.0 sq. mi.

Hamilton Township
Lat: 38-34-15 N **Long:** 82-44-44 W
Pop: 1,899 (1990); 2,089 (1980) **Pop Density:** 169.6
Land: 11.2 sq. mi.; **Water:** 0.4 sq. mi.

Hanging Rock Village
ZIP: 45638 **Lat:** 38-33-32 N **Long:** 82-43-34 W
Pop: 306 (1990); 353 (1980) **Pop Density:** 510.0
Land: 0.6 sq. mi.; **Water:** 0.1 sq. mi.

In southern OH on the Ohio River southeast of Portsmouth. Founded 1820.

Name origin: For the cornicelike jut at the top of a 400-ft-high sandstone cliff.

Ironton City
ZIP: 45638 **Lat:** 38-31-56 N **Long:** 82-40-42 W
Pop: 12,751 (1990); 14,290 (1980) **Pop Density:** 3110.0
Land: 4.1 sq. mi.; **Water:** 0.3 sq. mi.

In southern OH on the Ohio River. Founded 1848.

Name origin: For iron ore discovered here in 1826.

Lawrence Township
Lat: 38-33-25 N **Long:** 82-32-15 W
Pop: 2,484 (1990); 2,275 (1980) **Pop Density:** 74.4
Land: 33.4 sq. mi.; **Water:** 0.0 sq. mi.

Mason Township
Lat: 38-37-57 N **Long:** 82-24-46 W
Pop: 1,036 (1990); 1,064 (1980) **Pop Density:** 26.2
Land: 39.6 sq. mi.; **Water:** 0.0 sq. mi.

Perry Township
ZIP: 45638 **Lat:** 38-29-22 N **Long:** 82-35-19 W
Pop: 6,584 (1990); 6,298 (1980) **Pop Density:** 257.2
Land: 25.6 sq. mi.; **Water:** 0.0 sq. mi.

Proctorville Village
ZIP: 45669 **Lat:** 38-26-15 N **Long:** 82-22-51 W
Pop: 765 (1990); 975 (1980) **Pop Density:** 3825.0
Land: 0.2 sq. mi.; **Water:** 0.0 sq. mi.

Rome Township
ZIP: 45669 **Lat:** 38-30-58 N **Long:** 82-20-31 W
Pop: 7,579 (1990); 7,496 (1980) **Pop Density:** 224.9
Land: 33.7 sq. mi.; **Water:** 0.3 sq. mi.

South Point Village
ZIP: 45680 **Lat:** 38-25-09 N **Long:** 82-34-27 W
Pop: 3,823 (1990); 3,918 (1980) **Pop Density:** 1592.9
Land: 2.4 sq. mi.; **Water:** 0.0 sq. mi.

Symmes Township
Lat: 38-44-00 N **Long:** 82-32-04 W
Pop: 412 (1990); 488 (1980) **Pop Density:** 10.9
Land: 37.7 sq. mi.; **Water:** 0.0 sq. mi.

Union Township
ZIP: 45619 **Lat:** 38-28-06 N **Long:** 82-26-00 W
Pop: 9,139 (1990); 9,695 (1980) **Pop Density:** 282.9
Land: 32.3 sq. mi.; **Water:** 0.3 sq. mi.

Upper Township
ZIP: 45645 **Lat:** 38-32-55 N **Long:** 82-39-00 W
Pop: 17,136 (1990); 19,089 (1980) **Pop Density:** 699.4
Land: 24.5 sq. mi.; **Water:** 0.4 sq. mi.

In south-central OH, 16 mi. northwest of Huntington, WV.

Washington Township
Lat: 38-47-53 N **Long:** 82-36-59 W
Pop: 302 (1990); 414 (1980) **Pop Density:** 12.5
Land: 24.2 sq. mi.; **Water:** 0.0 sq. mi.

Windsor Township
Lat: 38-33-03 N **Long:** 82-25-20 W
Pop: 1,886 (1990); 2,044 (1980) **Pop Density:** 48.2
Land: 39.1 sq. mi.; **Water:** 0.0 sq. mi.

OHIO, Licking County

Licking County
County Seat: Newark (ZIP: 43055)

Pop: 128,300 (1990); 120,981 (1980)   **Pop Density:** 186.9
Land: 686.5 sq. mi.; **Water:** 1.9 sq. mi.   **Area Code:** 614
In central OH, east of Columbus; organized Mar 1, 1808 from Fairfield County.
Name origin: For the salt licks in the area.

Alexandria
Village
ZIP: 43001   **Lat:** 40-05-23 N **Long:** 82-36-47 W
Pop: 468 (1990); 489 (1980)   **Pop Density:** 2340.0
Land: 0.2 sq. mi.; **Water:** 0.0 sq. mi.

Beechwood Trails
CDP
Lat: 40-01-25 N **Long:** 82-39-03 W
Pop: 1,875 (1990)   **Pop Density:** 436.0
Land: 4.3 sq. mi.; **Water:** 0.0 sq. mi.

Bennington
Township
Lat: 40-14-18 N **Long:** 82-36-13 W
Pop: 971 (1990); 837 (1980)   **Pop Density:** 35.8
Land: 27.1 sq. mi.; **Water:** 0.0 sq. mi.

Bowling Green
Township
Lat: 39-56-05 N **Long:** 82-18-39 W
Pop: 1,292 (1990); 1,052 (1980)   **Pop Density:** 60.7
Land: 21.3 sq. mi.; **Water:** 0.0 sq. mi.

Buckeye Lake
Village
ZIP: 43008   **Lat:** 39-56-13 N **Long:** 82-28-45 W
Pop: 2,986 (1990); 2,521 (1980)   **Pop Density:** 1658.9
Land: 1.8 sq. mi.; **Water:** 0.0 sq. mi.

Burlington
Township
Lat: 40-13-26 N **Long:** 82-30-54 W
Pop: 966 (1990); 904 (1980)   **Pop Density:** 37.7
Land: 25.6 sq. mi.; **Water:** 0.0 sq. mi.

Eden
Township
ZIP: 43071   **Lat:** 40-12-18 N **Long:** 82-19-36 W
Pop: 1,135 (1990); 971 (1980)   **Pop Density:** 53.0
Land: 21.4 sq. mi.; **Water:** 0.0 sq. mi.

Etna
Township
ZIP: 43018   **Lat:** 39-57-13 N **Long:** 82-41-34 W
Pop: 6,439 (1990); 6,107 (1980)   **Pop Density:** 275.2
Land: 23.4 sq. mi.; **Water:** 0.0 sq. mi.

Fallsbury
Township
Lat: 40-12-12 N **Long:** 82-14-21 W
Pop: 739 (1990); 653 (1980)   **Pop Density:** 29.8
Land: 24.8 sq. mi.; **Water:** 0.0 sq. mi.

Franklin
Township
Lat: 39-59-46 N **Long:** 82-19-52 W
Pop: 1,349 (1990); 1,306 (1980)   **Pop Density:** 54.4
Land: 24.8 sq. mi.; **Water:** 0.0 sq. mi.

Granville
Village
ZIP: 43023   **Lat:** 40-04-15 N **Long:** 82-30-05 W
Pop: 4,353 (1990); 3,851 (1980)   **Pop Density:** 1061.7
Land: 4.1 sq. mi.; **Water:** 0.0 sq. mi.

In central OH, east of Columbus. Not coextensive with the town of the same name.
Name origin: For Granville, MA.

*Granville
Township
ZIP: 43023   **Lat:** 40-04-37 N **Long:** 82-31-18 W
Pop: 7,819 (1990); 7,515 (1980)   **Pop Density:** 293.9
Land: 26.6 sq. mi.; **Water:** 0.1 sq. mi.

Granville South
CDP
Lat: 40-03-10 N **Long:** 82-32-24 W
Pop: 1,124 (1990)   **Pop Density:** 184.3
Land: 6.1 sq. mi.; **Water:** 0.0 sq. mi.

Gratiot
Village
ZIP: 43740   **Lat:** 39-57-08 N **Long:** 82-12-57 W
Pop: 111 (1990); 101 (1980)   **Pop Density:** 1110.0
Land: 0.1 sq. mi.; **Water:** 0.0 sq. mi.   **Elev:** 988 ft.

In southeast-central OH, 10 mi. west of Zanesville. Part of the town is also in Muskingum County.
Name origin: For Gen. Charles Gratiot, a chief army engineer for the National Road between Columbus and Zanesville.

Hanover
Village
ZIP: 43055   **Lat:** 40-04-45 N **Long:** 82-16-13 W
Pop: 803 (1990); 926 (1980)   **Pop Density:** 1147.1
Land: 0.7 sq. mi.; **Water:** 0.0 sq. mi.

Not coextensive with the town of the same name.

*Hanover
Township
Lat: 40-03-46 N **Long:** 82-14-07 W
Pop: 2,551 (1990); 2,501 (1980)   **Pop Density:** 102.0
Land: 25.0 sq. mi.; **Water:** 0.0 sq. mi.

Harbor Hills
CDP
ZIP: 43025   **Lat:** 39-56-12 N **Long:** 82-26-06 W
Pop: 1,372 (1990)   **Pop Density:** 508.1
Land: 2.7 sq. mi.; **Water:** 0.7 sq. mi.

Harrison
Township
ZIP: 43033   **Lat:** 39-59-49 N **Long:** 82-37-04 W
Pop: 5,041 (1990); 4,278 (1980)   **Pop Density:** 175.6
Land: 28.7 sq. mi.; **Water:** 0.0 sq. mi.

Hartford
Village
Lat: 40-14-21 N **Long:** 82-41-15 W
Pop: 418 (1990); 444 (1980)   **Pop Density:** 836.0
Land: 0.5 sq. mi.; **Water:** 0.0 sq. mi.

In east-central OH, northeast of Columbus. Land deeded in 1798 to Ephriam Root and Urial Holmes.
Name origin: For Hartford, CT.

*Hartford
Township
Lat: 40-14-09 N **Long:** 82-42-00 W
Pop: 1,197 (1990); 1,080 (1980)   **Pop Density:** 42.6
Land: 28.1 sq. mi.; **Water:** 0.0 sq. mi.

Heath
City
ZIP: 43056   **Lat:** 40-01-36 N **Long:** 82-26-14 W
Pop: 7,231 (1990); 6,969 (1980)   **Pop Density:** 812.5
Land: 8.9 sq. mi.; **Water:** 0.0 sq. mi.

In south-central OH, just west of Newark.

OHIO, Licking County

Hebron
Village
ZIP: 43025 **Lat:** 39-57-45 N **Long:** 82-29-29 W
Pop: 2,076 (1990); 2,035 (1980) **Pop Density:** 943.6
Land: 2.2 sq. mi.; **Water:** 0.0 sq. mi. **Elev:** 889 ft.

In south-central OH on a branch of the Licking River, 9 mi. southwest of Newark.
Name origin: For the biblical city in Palestine.

Hopewell
Township
Lat: 39-59-04 N **Long:** 82-14-35 W
Pop: 1,089 (1990); 961 (1980) **Pop Density:** 42.9
Land: 25.4 sq. mi.; **Water:** 0.0 sq. mi.

Jersey
Township
ZIP: 43062 **Lat:** 40-04-50 N **Long:** 82-42-24 W
Pop: 2,432 (1990); 2,196 (1980) **Pop Density:** 90.7
Land: 26.8 sq. mi.; **Water:** 0.0 sq. mi.

Johnstown
Village
ZIP: 43031 **Lat:** 40-09-04 N **Long:** 82-41-15 W
Pop: 3,237 (1990); 3,158 (1980) **Pop Density:** 1798.3
Land: 1.8 sq. mi.; **Water:** 0.0 sq. mi.

In north-central OH, 20 mi. northeast of Columbus.
Name origin: For Capt. James Johnston, an early landowner.

Kirkersville
Village
ZIP: 43033 **Lat:** 39-57-00 N **Long:** 82-35-52 W
Pop: 563 (1990); 626 (1980) **Pop Density:** 296.3
Land: 1.9 sq. mi.; **Water:** 0.0 sq. mi.

In central OH along a branch of the Licking River, 22 mi. east of Columbus.

Liberty
Township
Lat: 40-09-25 N **Long:** 82-36-37 W
Pop: 1,470 (1990); 1,300 (1980) **Pop Density:** 56.1
Land: 26.2 sq. mi.; **Water:** 0.1 sq. mi.

Licking
Township
Lat: 39-58-37 N **Long:** 82-25-05 W
Pop: 3,945 (1990); 4,128 (1980) **Pop Density:** 149.4
Land: 26.4 sq. mi.; **Water:** 0.7 sq. mi.

Lima
Township
Lat: 40-00-43 N **Long:** 82-43-20 W
Pop: 4,408 (1990); 4,343 (1980) **Pop Density:** 170.2
Land: 25.9 sq. mi.; **Water:** 0.0 sq. mi.

Madison
Township
Lat: 40-03-56 N **Long:** 82-19-56 W
Pop: 2,716 (1990); 2,758 (1980) **Pop Density:** 120.7
Land: 22.5 sq. mi.; **Water:** 0.0 sq. mi.

Mary Ann
Township
Lat: 40-08-05 N **Long:** 82-19-52 W
Pop: 1,927 (1990); 1,747 (1980) **Pop Density:** 83.1
Land: 23.2 sq. mi.; **Water:** 0.0 sq. mi.

McKean
Township
Lat: 40-08-58 N **Long:** 82-31-11 W
Pop: 1,357 (1990); 1,197 (1980) **Pop Density:** 52.8
Land: 25.7 sq. mi.; **Water:** 0.0 sq. mi.

Monroe
Township
ZIP: 43031 **Lat:** 40-09-48 N **Long:** 82-42-52 W
Pop: 5,151 (1990); 5,057 (1980) **Pop Density:** 187.3
Land: 27.5 sq. mi.; **Water:** 0.0 sq. mi.

Newark
City
ZIP: 43055 **Lat:** 40-04-03 N **Long:** 82-25-24 W
Pop: 44,389 (1990); 41,200 (1980) **Pop Density:** 2466.1
Land: 18.0 sq. mi.; **Water:** 0.2 sq. mi. **Elev:** 829 ft.

In central OH, 35 mi. east of Columbus. Founded 1802 by Gen. William Schenck.
Name origin: For Newark, NJ.

*Newark
Township
Lat: 40-05-26 N **Long:** 82-25-52 W
Pop: 2,496 (1990); 3,179 (1980) **Pop Density:** 328.4
Land: 7.6 sq. mi.; **Water:** 0.0 sq. mi.

Newton
Township
Lat: 40-08-31 N **Long:** 82-25-23 W
Pop: 3,092 (1990); 3,309 (1980) **Pop Density:** 126.2
Land: 24.5 sq. mi.; **Water:** 0.0 sq. mi.

Pataskala
Village
ZIP: 43062 **Lat:** 40-00-02 N **Long:** 82-40-24 W
Pop: 3,046 (1990); 2,284 (1980) **Pop Density:** 1384.5
Land: 2.2 sq. mi.; **Water:** 0.0 sq. mi.

In central OH, 20 mi. east of Columbus.
Name origin: From an Indian term meaning 'salt lick.'

Perry
Township
Lat: 40-07-47 N **Long:** 82-14-15 W
Pop: 1,202 (1990); 1,128 (1980) **Pop Density:** 48.1
Land: 25.0 sq. mi.; **Water:** 0.0 sq. mi.

Reynoldsburg
City
ZIP: 43068 **Lat:** 39-57-52 N **Long:** 82-46-32 W
Pop: 1,265 (1990); 993 (1980) **Pop Density:** 665.8
Land: 1.9 sq. mi.; **Water:** 0.0 sq. mi.

In central OH, 10 mi. east of Columbus. Founded by John French in 1831. Part of the town is also in Franklin and Fairfield counties.
Name origin: For John C. Reynolds. Previously called French Town.

St. Albans
Township
Lat: 40-04-51 N **Long:** 82-36-53 W
Pop: 2,136 (1990); 1,946 (1980) **Pop Density:** 80.0
Land: 26.7 sq. mi.; **Water:** 0.0 sq. mi.

St. Louisville
Village
Lat: 40-10-17 N **Long:** 82-25-08 W
Pop: 372 (1990); 375 (1980) **Pop Density:** 1860.0
Land: 0.2 sq. mi.; **Water:** 0.0 sq. mi. **Elev:** 905 ft.

Summit Station
CDP
Lat: 40-00-17 N **Long:** 82-45-02 W
Pop: 1,380 (1990) **Pop Density:** 345.0
Land: 4.0 sq. mi.; **Water:** 0.0 sq. mi.

Union
Township
ZIP: 43025 **Lat:** 39-58-50 N **Long:** 82-31-19 W
Pop: 7,730 (1990); 7,054 (1980) **Pop Density:** 178.5
Land: 43.3 sq. mi.; **Water:** 0.5 sq. mi.

Utica
Village
ZIP: 43080 **Lat:** 40-14-00 N **Long:** 82-26-36 W
Pop: 1,980 (1990); 2,221 (1980) **Pop Density:** 1414.3
Land: 1.4 sq. mi.; **Water:** 0.0 sq. mi. **Elev:** 967 ft.

In central OH on the Licking River, northeast of Columbus. Part of the town is also in Knox County.
Name origin: For Utica, NY. Previously named Wilmington in 1815.

OHIO, Licking County

Washington
Township
Lat: 40-12-44 N **Long:** 82-24-52 W
Pop: 2,984 (1990); 3,021 (1980) **Pop Density:** 125.9
Land: 23.7 sq. mi.; **Water:** 0.0 sq. mi.

Logan County
County Seat: Bellefontaine (ZIP: 43311)

Pop: 42,310 (1990); 39,155 (1980) **Pop Density:** 92.3
Land: 458.5 sq. mi.; **Water:** 8.3 sq. mi. **Area Code:** 513

In west-central OH, northwest of Columbus; organized Mar 1, 1817 from Champaign County.

Name origin: For Gen. Benjamin Logan (c. 1743–1802), VA patriot and soldier active in the West during the Revolutionary War.

Belle Center
Village
ZIP: 43310 **Lat:** 40-30-32 N **Long:** 83-44-41 W
Pop: 796 (1990); 930 (1980) **Pop Density:** 1137.1
Land: 0.7 sq. mi.; **Water:** 0.0 sq. mi. **Elev:** 1045 ft.

Bellefontaine
City
ZIP: 43311 **Lat:** 40-21-35 N **Long:** 83-45-25 W
Pop: 12,142 (1990); 11,888 (1980) **Pop Density:** 1990.5
Land: 6.1 sq. mi.; **Water:** 0.0 sq. mi. **Elev:** 1251 ft.

In western OH, 30 mi. north of Springfield. Settled 1806. Agricultural region.

Name origin: From French 'beautiful spring,' so named for its natural springs.

Bloomfield
Township
Lat: 40-24-30 N **Long:** 83-58-00 W
Pop: 395 (1990); 403 (1980) **Pop Density:** 17.2
Land: 22.9 sq. mi.; **Water:** 0.0 sq. mi.

Bokes Creek
Township
ZIP: 43358 **Lat:** 40-27-17 N **Long:** 83-33-57 W
Pop: 1,417 (1990); 1,354 (1980) **Pop Density:** 42.0
Land: 33.7 sq. mi.; **Water:** 0.0 sq. mi.

De Graff
Village
ZIP: 43318 **Lat:** 40-18-36 N **Long:** 83-54-52 W
Pop: 1,331 (1990); 1,358 (1980) **Pop Density:** 1478.9
Land: 0.9 sq. mi.; **Water:** 0.0 sq. mi. **Elev:** 1007 ft.

In west-central OH, north of Springfield.

Harrison
Township
ZIP: 43311 **Lat:** 40-22-09 N **Long:** 83-49-06 W
Pop: 2,077 (1990); 1,706 (1980) **Pop Density:** 80.8
Land: 25.7 sq. mi.; **Water:** 0.1 sq. mi.

Huntsville
Village
ZIP: 43324 **Lat:** 40-26-32 N **Long:** 83-48-13 W
Pop: 343 (1990); 489 (1980) **Pop Density:** 1143.3
Land: 0.3 sq. mi.; **Water:** 0.0 sq. mi. **Elev:** 1069 ft.

Jefferson
Township
ZIP: 43311 **Lat:** 40-21-42 N **Long:** 83-40-50 W
Pop: 2,104 (1990); 1,807 (1980) **Pop Density:** 56.3
Land: 37.4 sq. mi.; **Water:** 0.1 sq. mi.

Lake
Township
ZIP: 43311 **Lat:** 40-22-26 N **Long:** 83-45-05 W
Pop: 12,227 (1990); 12,134 (1980) **Pop Density:** 1018.9
Land: 12.0 sq. mi.; **Water:** 0.0 sq. mi.

In west-central OH, 30 mi. north of Springfield.

Lakeview
Village
ZIP: 43331 **Lat:** 40-29-16 N **Long:** 83-55-32 W
Pop: 1,056 (1990); 1,089 (1980) **Pop Density:** 1760.0
Land: 0.6 sq. mi.; **Water:** 0.0 sq. mi.

In western OH on Indian Lake, 15 mi. northwest of Bellefontaine.

Name origin: For its lakeside location.

Liberty
Township
Lat: 40-17-08 N **Long:** 83-45-57 W
Pop: 2,999 (1990); 2,858 (1980) **Pop Density:** 197.3
Land: 15.2 sq. mi.; **Water:** 0.0 sq. mi.

McArthur
Township
Lat: 40-26-23 N **Long:** 83-47-48 W
Pop: 1,746 (1990); 1,693 (1980) **Pop Density:** 62.8
Land: 27.8 sq. mi.; **Water:** 0.1 sq. mi.

Miami
Township
Lat: 40-17-35 N **Long:** 83-56-28 W
Pop: 2,352 (1990); 2,251 (1980) **Pop Density:** 102.3
Land: 23.0 sq. mi.; **Water:** 0.0 sq. mi.

Monroe
Township
Lat: 40-16-21 N **Long:** 83-41-18 W
Pop: 1,274 (1990); 925 (1980) **Pop Density:** 40.8
Land: 31.2 sq. mi.; **Water:** 0.0 sq. mi.

Perry
Township
Lat: 40-21-18 N **Long:** 83-35-04 W
Pop: 905 (1990); 872 (1980) **Pop Density:** 33.8
Land: 26.8 sq. mi.; **Water:** 0.0 sq. mi.

Pleasant
Township
Lat: 40-20-20 N **Long:** 83-56-22 W
Pop: 889 (1990); 887 (1980) **Pop Density:** 36.7
Land: 24.2 sq. mi.; **Water:** 0.0 sq. mi.

Quincy
Village
ZIP: 43343 **Lat:** 40-17-45 N **Long:** 83-58-10 W
Pop: 697 (1990); 633 (1980) **Pop Density:** 633.6
Land: 1.1 sq. mi.; **Water:** 0.0 sq. mi. **Elev:** 1055 ft.

Richland
Township
ZIP: 43310 **Lat:** 40-29-53 N **Long:** 83-47-56 W
Pop: 2,132 (1990); 2,015 (1980) **Pop Density:** 73.3
Land: 29.1 sq. mi.; **Water:** 0.8 sq. mi.

Ridgeway — Village
ZIP: 43345　**Lat:** 40-30-36 N　**Long:** 83-34-16 W
Pop: 128 (1990); 104 (1980)　**Pop Density:** 426.7
Land: 0.3 sq. mi.; **Water:** 0.0 sq. mi.　**Elev:** 1053 ft.
Part of the town is also in Hardin County.

Rushcreek — Township
ZIP: 43347　**Lat:** 40-27-35 N　**Long:** 83-39-57 W
Pop: 1,944 (1990); 2,075 (1980)　**Pop Density:** 39.5
Land: 49.2 sq. mi.; **Water:** 0.1 sq. mi.

Rushsylvania — Village
ZIP: 43347　**Lat:** 40-27-40 N　**Long:** 83-40-15 W
Pop: 573 (1990); 610 (1980)　**Pop Density:** 716.3
Land: 0.8 sq. mi.; **Water:** 0.0 sq. mi.　**Elev:** 1238 ft.

Russells Point — Village
ZIP: 43348　**Lat:** 40-28-04 N　**Long:** 83-53-35 W
Pop: 1,504 (1990); 1,156 (1980)　**Pop Density:** 1671.1
Land: 0.9 sq. mi.; **Water:** 0.1 sq. mi.
In western OH on south Indian Lake, southeast of Lima.

Stokes — Township
Lat: 40-29-38 N　**Long:** 83-56-08 W
Pop: 4,991 (1990); 4,157 (1980)　**Pop Density:** 153.6
Land: 32.5 sq. mi.; **Water:** 5.6 sq. mi.

Union — Township
ZIP: 43311　**Lat:** 40-18-19 N　**Long:** 83-50-05 W
Pop: 668 (1990); 674 (1980)　**Pop Density:** 29.0
Land: 23.0 sq. mi.; **Water:** 0.1 sq. mi.

Valley Hi — Village
Lat: 40-18-58 N　**Long:** 83-40-22 W
Pop: 217 (1990); 60 (1980)　**Pop Density:** 310.0
Land: 0.7 sq. mi.; **Water:** 0.0 sq. mi.

Washington — Township
Lat: 40-25-06 N　**Long:** 83-53-24 W
Pop: 3,486 (1990); 2,776 (1980)　**Pop Density:** 152.9
Land: 22.8 sq. mi.; **Water:** 1.4 sq. mi.

West Liberty — Village
ZIP: 43357　**Lat:** 40-15-13 N　**Long:** 83-45-28 W
Pop: 1,613 (1990); 1,653 (1980)　**Pop Density:** 1613.0
Land: 1.0 sq. mi.; **Water:** 0.0 sq. mi.　**Elev:** 1111 ft.

West Mansfield — Village
ZIP: 43358　**Lat:** 40-23-58 N　**Long:** 83-32-42 W
Pop: 830 (1990); 716 (1980)　**Pop Density:** 1037.5
Land: 0.8 sq. mi.; **Water:** 0.0 sq. mi.

Zane — Township
Lat: 40-16-05 N　**Long:** 83-35-20 W
Pop: 704 (1990); 568 (1980)　**Pop Density:** 32.0
Land: 22.0 sq. mi.; **Water:** 0.0 sq. mi.

Zanesfield — Village
ZIP: 43360　**Lat:** 40-20-17 N　**Long:** 83-40-41 W
Pop: 183 (1990); 269 (1980)　**Pop Density:** 1830.0
Land: 0.1 sq. mi.; **Water:** 0.0 sq. mi.

Lorain County
County Seat: Elyria (ZIP: 44035)

Pop: 271,126 (1990); 274,909 (1980)　**Pop Density:** 550.4
Land: 492.6 sq. mi.; **Water:** 430.5 sq. mi.　**Area Code:** 216
On the northern coast of OH, bordered on the north by Lake Erie; organized Dec 26, 1822 from Huron, Cuyahoga, and Medina counties.
Name origin: For the province of Lorraine, France, former home of early settlers.

Amherst — City
ZIP: 44001　**Lat:** 41-24-00 N　**Long:** 82-13-50 W
Pop: 10,332 (1990); 10,638 (1980)　**Pop Density:** 1476.0
Land: 7.0 sq. mi.; **Water:** 0.0 sq. mi.
In northern OH, 25 mi. southwest of Cleveland. Noted for its sandstone quarries.
Name origin: For Amherst, NJ.

*Amherst — Township
ZIP: 44001　**Lat:** 41-22-44 N　**Long:** 82-12-27 W
Pop: 7,060 (1990); 7,016 (1980)　**Pop Density:** 455.5
Land: 15.5 sq. mi.; **Water:** 0.1 sq. mi.

Avon — City
ZIP: 44011　**Lat:** 41-27-04 N　**Long:** 82-01-24 W
Pop: 7,337 (1990); 7,241 (1980)　**Pop Density:** 351.1
Land: 20.9 sq. mi.; **Water:** 0.0 sq. mi.　**Elev:** 670 ft.
In northern OH, south of Lake Erie.
Name origin: For the English river.

Avon Lake — City
ZIP: 44012　**Lat:** 41-29-37 N　**Long:** 82-00-57 W
Pop: 15,066 (1990); 13,222 (1980)　**Pop Density:** 1357.3
Land: 11.1 sq. mi.; **Water:** 0.0 sq. mi.
In northeastern OH, 19 mi. west of Cleveland.

Brighton — Township
Lat: 41-10-06 N　**Long:** 82-18-12 W
Pop: 812 (1990); 728 (1980)　**Pop Density:** 50.1
Land: 16.2 sq. mi.; **Water:** 0.0 sq. mi.

Brownhelm — Township
ZIP: 44001　**Lat:** 41-23-36 N　**Long:** 82-18-50 W
Pop: 7,060 (1990); 6,705 (1980)　**Pop Density:** 353.0
Land: 20.0 sq. mi.; **Water:** 0.1 sq. mi.

Camden — Township
Lat: 41-14-27 N　**Long:** 82-18-46 W
Pop: 1,522 (1990); 1,522 (1980)　**Pop Density:** 76.1
Land: 20.0 sq. mi.; **Water:** 0.1 sq. mi.　**Elev:** 872 ft.

Carlisle — Township
ZIP: 44035　**Lat:** 41-18-55 N　**Long:** 82-07-14 W
Pop: 7,554 (1990); 7,689 (1980)　**Pop Density:** 307.1
Land: 24.6 sq. mi.; **Water:** 0.2 sq. mi.

Columbia — Township
ZIP: 44028　**Lat:** 41-18-33 N　**Long:** 81-55-32 W
Pop: 6,594 (1990); 6,494 (1980)　**Pop Density:** 260.6
Land: 25.3 sq. mi.; **Water:** 0.3 sq. mi.

Eaton
Township
ZIP: 44035 **Lat:** 41-18-43 N **Long:** 82-01-29 W
Pop: 8,821 (1990); 7,803 (1980) **Pop Density:** 326.7
Land: 27.0 sq. mi.; **Water:** 0.0 sq. mi.

Eaton Estates
CDP
Lat: 41-18-19 N **Long:** 82-00-34 W
Pop: 1,586 (1990); 1,806 (1980) **Pop Density:** 1762.2
Land: 0.9 sq. mi.; **Water:** 0.0 sq. mi.

Elyria
City
ZIP: 44035 **Lat:** 41-22-47 N **Long:** 82-06-20 W
Pop: 56,746 (1990); 57,538 (1980) **Pop Density:** 2925.1
Land: 19.4 sq. mi.; **Water:** 0.0 sq. mi. **Elev:** 733 ft.

In northern OH on the Black River, 22 mi. southwest of Cleveland. Settled 1817.
Name origin: Named by first settler, Herman Ely, a New Englander who acquired 12,500 acres around the falls of the river and combined *Ely* with *ria* for his wife, Maria.

*Elyria
Township
Lat: 41-23-52 N **Long:** 82-08-51 W
Pop: 3,699 (1990); 4,576 (1980) **Pop Density:** 616.5
Land: 6.0 sq. mi.; **Water:** 0.0 sq. mi.

Grafton
Village
ZIP: 44044 **Lat:** 41-16-49 N **Long:** 82-01-59 W
Pop: 3,344 (1990); 2,231 (1980) **Pop Density:** 777.7
Land: 4.3 sq. mi.; **Water:** 0.0 sq. mi.

In northern OH on the Black River, a southwestern suburb of Cleveland. Not coextensive with the town of the same name.

*Grafton
Township
ZIP: 44044 **Lat:** 41-14-16 N **Long:** 82-01-15 W
Pop: 3,052 (1990); 3,021 (1980) **Pop Density:** 115.6
Land: 26.4 sq. mi.; **Water:** 0.0 sq. mi.

Henrietta
Township
ZIP: 44001 **Lat:** 41-19-43 N **Long:** 82-18-31 W
Pop: 1,795 (1990); 1,864 (1980) **Pop Density:** 84.3
Land: 21.3 sq. mi.; **Water:** 0.0 sq. mi.

Huntington
Township
Lat: 41-06-15 N **Long:** 82-13-15 W
Pop: 1,172 (1990); 1,057 (1980) **Pop Density:** 45.1
Land: 26.0 sq. mi.; **Water:** 0.3 sq. mi.

Kipton
Village
ZIP: 44049 **Lat:** 41-16-01 N **Long:** 82-18-17 W
Pop: 283 (1990); 352 (1980) **Pop Density:** 566.0
Land: 0.5 sq. mi.; **Water:** 0.0 sq. mi. **Elev:** 857 ft.

Lagrange
Village
ZIP: 44050 **Lat:** 41-14-19 N **Long:** 82-07-13 W
Pop: 1,199 (1990); 1,258 (1980) **Pop Density:** 856.4
Land: 1.4 sq. mi.; **Water:** 0.0 sq. mi. **Elev:** 825 ft.

In northern OH near the Black River, 10 mi. south of Elyria. Not coextensive with the town of the same name.

*Lagrange
Township
ZIP: 44050 **Lat:** 41-14-12 N **Long:** 82-07-14 W
Pop: 4,644 (1990); 4,477 (1980) **Pop Density:** 180.7
Land: 25.7 sq. mi.; **Water:** 0.2 sq. mi.

Lorain
City
ZIP: 44052 **Lat:** 41-26-29 N **Long:** 82-11-00 W
Pop: 71,245 (1990); 75,416 (1980) **Pop Density:** 2956.2
Land: 24.1 sq. mi.; **Water:** 0.2 sq. mi.

In northern OH where the Black River flows into Lake Erie, 25 mi. west of Cleveland. Settled 1807; incorporated 1874.
Name origin: Named by Judge Herman Ely for the French region of Lorraine, with a spelling variation. Previously called the Black River Settlement and Charleston.

North Ridgeville
City
ZIP: 44039 **Lat:** 41-23-16 N **Long:** 82-00-54 W
Pop: 21,564 (1990); 21,522 (1980) **Pop Density:** 921.5
Land: 23.4 sq. mi.; **Water:** 0.1 sq. mi.

In northern OH, a northern residential suburb of Elyria.

Oberlin
City
ZIP: 44074 **Lat:** 41-17-25 N **Long:** 82-13-00 W
Pop: 8,191 (1990); 8,660 (1980) **Pop Density:** 2155.5
Land: 3.8 sq. mi.; **Water:** 0.0 sq. mi.

In northern OH, 20 mi. southwest of Cleveland. Antebellum center of antislavery. Site of Oberlin College (1832), one of the first U.S. colleges to admit blacks.
Name origin: For Rev. Johann Friedrich Oberlin (1740–1826), pastor in Alsace-Lorraine for thirty years; his church was an asylum for refugees of the French Revolution.

Penfield
Township
Lat: 41-09-58 N **Long:** 82-07-04 W
Pop: 1,312 (1990); 1,253 (1980) **Pop Density:** 59.6
Land: 22.0 sq. mi.; **Water:** 0.1 sq. mi.

Pittsfield
Township
Lat: 41-14-14 N **Long:** 82-13-11 W
Pop: 1,546 (1990); 1,436 (1980) **Pop Density:** 57.7
Land: 26.8 sq. mi.; **Water:** 0.0 sq. mi.

Rochester
Village
ZIP: 44090 **Lat:** 41-07-29 N **Long:** 82-18-22 W
Pop: 206 (1990); 207 (1980) **Pop Density:** 187.3
Land: 1.1 sq. mi.; **Water:** 0.0 sq. mi.

Not coextensive with the town of the same name.

*Rochester
Township
ZIP: 44090 **Lat:** 41-06-16 N **Long:** 82-18-23 W
Pop: 627 (1990); 627 (1980) **Pop Density:** 35.6
Land: 17.6 sq. mi.; **Water:** 0.0 sq. mi.

Russia
Township
ZIP: 44074 **Lat:** 41-18-19 N **Long:** 82-13-07 W
Pop: 10,661 (1990); 11,116 (1980) **Pop Density:** 382.1
Land: 27.9 sq. mi.; **Water:** 0.1 sq. mi.

In northeastern OH, 25 mi. southwest of Cleveland.

Sheffield
Village
ZIP: 44054 **Lat:** 41-27-24 N **Long:** 82-05-40 W
Pop: 1,943 (1990); 1,886 (1980) **Pop Density:** 179.9
Land: 10.8 sq. mi.; **Water:** 0.0 sq. mi. **Elev:** 673 ft.

*Sheffield
Township
Lat: 41-25-15 N **Long:** 82-08-24 W
Pop: 3,751 (1990); 4,170 (1980) **Pop Density:** 1562.9
Land: 2.4 sq. mi.; **Water:** 0.0 sq. mi.

Sheffield Lake
City
ZIP: 44054 **Lat:** 41-29-19 N **Long:** 82-05-52 W
Pop: 9,825 (1990); 10,484 (1980) **Pop Density:** 3930.0
Land: 2.5 sq. mi.; **Water:** 0.0 sq. mi.

In northern OH on Lake Erie, 19 mi. west of Cleveland.
Name origin: For Sheffield, Yorkshire, England.

South Amherst
Village
ZIP: 44001 **Lat:** 41-21-14 N **Long:** 82-14-17 W
Pop: 1,765 (1990); 1,848 (1980) **Pop Density:** 735.4
Land: 2.4 sq. mi.; **Water:** 0.0 sq. mi. **Elev:** 803 ft.

Vermilion City
ZIP: 44089 Lat: 41-24-11 N Long: 82-18-43 W
Pop: 5,644 (1990); 5,378 (1980) Pop Density: 648.7
Land: 8.7 sq. mi.; Water: 0.0 sq. mi.
In northern OH on Lake Erie and the Vermilion River, just east of Sandusky. Settled 1808. Part of the town is also in Erie County.
Name origin: For the river.

Wellington Village
ZIP: 44090 Lat: 41-09-52 N Long: 82-13-24 W
Pop: 4,140 (1990); 4,146 (1980) Pop Density: 1478.6
Land: 2.8 sq. mi.; Water: 0.0 sq. mi. Elev: 854 ft.
Not coextensive with the town of the same name.

*Wellington Township
ZIP: 44090 Lat: 41-10-02 N Long: 82-13-13 W
Pop: 5,386 (1990); 5,408 (1980) Pop Density: 239.4
Land: 22.5 sq. mi.; Water: 0.1 sq. mi.

Lucas County
County Seat: Toledo (ZIP: 43604)

Pop: 462,361 (1990); 471,741 (1980) Pop Density: 1358.3
Land: 340.4 sq. mi.; Water: 220.2 sq. mi. Area Code: 419

On the northwest coast of OH, bordered on the north by Lake Erie; organized Jun 20, 1835 from Wood County.
Name origin: For Col. Robert Lucas (1781–1853), governor of OH (1832–36) and first territorial governor of IA (1838–41).

Berkey Village
ZIP: 43504 Lat: 41-42-51 N Long: 83-50-00 W
Pop: 264 (1990); 306 (1980) Pop Density: 62.9
Land: 4.2 sq. mi.; Water: 0.0 sq. mi.

Harbor View Village
ZIP: 43434 Lat: 41-41-33 N Long: 83-26-40 W
Pop: 122 (1990); 164 (1980) Pop Density: 4066.7
Land: 0.03 sq. mi.; Water: 0.0 sq. mi.

Harding Township
Lat: 41-37-23 N Long: 83-50-46 W
Pop: 593 (1990); 631 (1980) Pop Density: 63.1
Land: 9.4 sq. mi.; Water: 0.0 sq. mi.

Holland Village
ZIP: 43528 Lat: 41-37-13 N Long: 83-42-34 W
Pop: 1,210 (1990); 1,048 (1980) Pop Density: 1728.6
Land: 0.7 sq. mi.; Water: 0.0 sq. mi.

Jerusalem Township
Lat: 41-42-44 N Long: 83-15-08 W
Pop: 3,253 (1990); 3,327 (1980) Pop Density: 106.7
Land: 30.5 sq. mi.; Water: 200.2 sq. mi.

Maumee City
ZIP: 43537 Lat: 41-34-27 N Long: 83-39-12 W
Pop: 15,561 (1990); 15,747 (1980) Pop Density: 1852.5
Land: 8.4 sq. mi.; Water: 0.6 sq. mi.
In northwestern OH on the Maumee River, 10 mi. southwest of Toledo. Early trading post and fort (1680), later the British Ft. Miami (1764). Settled 1817.
Name origin: From the Ojibway Indian term, *omaumeeg*, meaning 'people who live on the peninsula'; it is a variation of *Miami*.

Monclova Township
ZIP: 43542 Lat: 41-33-28 N Long: 83-44-50 W
Pop: 4,547 (1990); 4,285 (1980) Pop Density: 193.5
Land: 23.5 sq. mi.; Water: 0.1 sq. mi.

Oregon City
ZIP: 43616 Lat: 41-40-01 N Long: 83-25-09 W
Pop: 18,334 (1990); 18,675 (1980) Pop Density: 627.9
Land: 29.2 sq. mi.; Water: 8.7 sq. mi.
In northwest OH just south of Maumee Bay, 10 mi. east of Toledo.
Name origin: For the state.

Ottawa Hills Village
Lat: 41-40-03 N Long: 83-38-42 W
Pop: 4,543 (1990); 4,065 (1980) Pop Density: 2391.1
Land: 1.9 sq. mi.; Water: 0.0 sq. mi.

Providence Township
Lat: 41-27-50 N Long: 83-50-39 W
Pop: 3,016 (1990); 2,702 (1980) Pop Density: 115.6
Land: 26.1 sq. mi.; Water: 0.4 sq. mi. Elev: 663 ft.

Richfield Township
Lat: 41-41-33 N Long: 83-49-46 W
Pop: 1,442 (1990); 1,401 (1980) Pop Density: 63.8
Land: 22.6 sq. mi.; Water: 0.0 sq. mi.

Spencer Township
Lat: 41-38-24 N Long: 83-48-39 W
Pop: 1,665 (1990); 1,744 (1980) Pop Density: 137.6
Land: 12.1 sq. mi.; Water: 0.0 sq. mi.

Springfield Township
ZIP: 43528 Lat: 41-37-01 N Long: 83-43-43 W
Pop: 20,045 (1990); 16,091 (1980) Pop Density: 932.3
Land: 21.5 sq. mi.; Water: 0.0 sq. mi.
In northwestern OH, 9 mi. southwest of Toledo.

Swanton Village
Lat: 41-34-43 N Long: 83-52-51 W
Pop: 179 (1990) Pop Density: 1790.0
Land: 0.1 sq. mi.; Water: 0.0 sq. mi.
Part of the town is also in Fulton County.

*Swanton Township
Lat: 41-33-29 N Long: 83-50-50 W
Pop: 3,508 (1990); 3,379 (1980) Pop Density: 158.7
Land: 22.1 sq. mi.; Water: 0.1 sq. mi.

OHIO, Lucas County

Sylvania — City
ZIP: 43560 Lat: 41-42-52 N Long: 83-42-21 W
Pop: 17,301 (1990); 15,527 (1980) Pop Density: 2982.9
Land: 5.8 sq. mi.; Water: 0.0 sq. mi.

In western OH, 11 mi. northwest of Toledo, just south of the MI state line. Not coextensive with the town of the same name.
Name origin: Poetic name, from Latin *silva* or *sylva* meaning 'woods' or 'grove.'

*Sylvania — Township
ZIP: 43560 Lat: 41-41-33 N Long: 83-43-03 W
Pop: 39,983 (1990); 33,061 (1980) Pop Density: 1402.9
Land: 28.5 sq. mi.; Water: 0.1 sq. mi.

Toledo — City
ZIP: 43601 Lat: 41-39-50 N Long: 83-34-53 W
Pop: 332,943 (1990); 354,635 (1980) Pop Density: 4130.8
Land: 80.6 sq. mi.; Water: 3.5 sq. mi.

In northwestern OH on both banks of the Maumee River, near Lake Erie. Formed by the union of two villages 1833; incorporated 1837. Major Great Lakes port, major shipper of coal; diverse manufacturing city: transportation equipment, glass products, and nonelectrical machinery; trading center for agricultural region. Headquarters for Champion Spark Plug Co.
Name origin: For Toledo, Spain. Originally known as Port Lawrence.

Washington — Township
Lat: 41-42-56 N Long: 83-26-16 W
Pop: 3,803 (1990); 4,000 (1980) Pop Density: 4225.6
Land: 0.9 sq. mi.; Water: 5.7 sq. mi.

Waterville — Village
ZIP: 43566 Lat: 41-29-52 N Long: 83-43-59 W
Pop: 4,517 (1990); 3,884 (1980) Pop Density: 1290.6
Land: 3.5 sq. mi.; Water: 0.1 sq. mi.

In northwestern OH. Platted 1818 by John Pray. Not coextensive with the town of the same name.

*Waterville — Township
ZIP: 43566 Lat: 41-30-21 N Long: 83-46-29 W
Pop: 9,003 (1990); 7,834 (1980) Pop Density: 388.1
Land: 23.2 sq. mi.; Water: 0.8 sq. mi.

Whitehouse — Village
ZIP: 43571 Lat: 41-31-07 N Long: 83-48-09 W
Pop: 2,528 (1990); 2,137 (1980) Pop Density: 766.1
Land: 3.3 sq. mi.; Water: 0.0 sq. mi.

In northwestern OH, 20 mi. southwest of Toledo.

Madison County
County Seat: London (ZIP: 43140)

Pop: 37,068 (1990); 33,004 (1980) Pop Density: 79.7
Land: 465.2 sq. mi.; Water: 0.7 sq. mi. Area Code: 614

In west-central OH, west of Columbus; organized Mar 1, 1810 from Fayette County.
Name origin: For James Madison (1751–1836), fourth U.S. president.

Canaan — Township
ZIP: 43064 Lat: 40-02-43 N Long: 83-18-05 W
Pop: 2,309 (1990); 2,210 (1980) Pop Density: 66.0
Land: 35.0 sq. mi.; Water: 0.0 sq. mi.

Chocktou Lake — CDP
Lat: 39-57-36 N Long: 83-29-06 W
Pop: 1,234 (1990) Pop Density: 1542.5
Land: 0.8 sq. mi.; Water: 0.4 sq. mi.

Darby — Township
ZIP: 43064 Lat: 40-05-26 N Long: 83-18-09 W
Pop: 2,225 (1990); 2,015 (1980) Pop Density: 104.5
Land: 21.3 sq. mi.; Water: 0.0 sq. mi.

Deer Creek — Township
ZIP: 43140 Lat: 39-56-19 N Long: 83-24-22 W
Pop: 1,038 (1990); 1,020 (1980) Pop Density: 31.4
Land: 33.1 sq. mi.; Water: 0.0 sq. mi.

Fairfield — Township
Lat: 39-50-44 N Long: 83-17-23 W
Pop: 1,331 (1990); 1,293 (1980) Pop Density: 42.1
Land: 31.6 sq. mi.; Water: 0.0 sq. mi.

Jefferson — Village
ZIP: 43162 Lat: 39-56-28 N Long: 83-17-39 W
Pop: 4,505 (1990); 4,448 (1980) Pop Density: 1802.0
Land: 2.5 sq. mi.; Water: 0.0 sq. mi.

*Jefferson — Township
ZIP: 43162 Lat: 39-57-09 N Long: 83-17-59 W
Pop: 6,987 (1990); 7,055 (1980) Pop Density: 165.6
Land: 42.2 sq. mi.; Water: 0.0 sq. mi.

London — City
ZIP: 43140 Lat: 39-53-21 N Long: 83-26-27 W
Pop: 7,807 (1990); 6,958 (1980) Pop Density: 1561.4
Land: 5.0 sq. mi.; Water: 0.0 sq. mi. Elev: 1054 ft.

In southwest-central OH, southwest of Columbus.
Name origin: For London, England.

Midway — Village
Lat: 39-43-57 N Long: 83-28-34 W
Pop: 289 (1990); 339 (1980) Pop Density: 963.3
Land: 0.3 sq. mi.; Water: 0.0 sq. mi. Elev: 1070 ft.

Monroe — Township
ZIP: 43140 Lat: 40-01-36 N Long: 83-24-11 W
Pop: 1,467 (1990); 1,066 (1980) Pop Density: 64.3
Land: 22.8 sq. mi.; Water: 0.0 sq. mi.

Mount Sterling — Village
ZIP: 43143 Lat: 39-43-10 N Long: 83-16-05 W
Pop: 1,647 (1990); 1,623 (1980) Pop Density: 1647.0
Land: 1.0 sq. mi.; Water: 0.0 sq. mi. Elev: 906 ft.

In southwest-central OH on Deer Creek, 23 mi. southwest of Columbus.

Oak Run
Township
ZIP: 43143   **Lat:** 39-49-18 N   **Long:** 83-22-20 W
Pop: 415 (1990); 363 (1980)   **Pop Density:** 14.8
Land: 28.0 sq. mi.; **Water:** 0.0 sq. mi.

Paint
Township
ZIP: 43140   **Lat:** 39-49-07 N   **Long:** 83-30-45 W
Pop: 595 (1990); 607 (1980)   **Pop Density:** 16.2
Land: 36.7 sq. mi.; **Water:** 0.0 sq. mi.

Pike
Township
Lat: 40-04-46 N   **Long:** 83-26-36 W
Pop: 506 (1990); 438 (1980)   **Pop Density:** 19.5
Land: 26.0 sq. mi.; **Water:** 0.0 sq. mi.

Plain City
Village
ZIP: 43064   **Lat:** 40-06-15 N   **Long:** 83-16-15 W
Pop: 1,302 (1990); 1,222 (1980)   **Pop Density:** 1860.0
Land: 0.7 sq. mi.; **Water:** 0.0 sq. mi.   **Elev:** 934 ft.
Laid out 1818 by Issac Bigelow. Part of the town is also in Union County.
Name origin: Named in 1851 for its location on Big Darby Plain.

Pleasant
Township
ZIP: 43143   **Lat:** 39-44-28 N   **Long:** 83-17-24 W
Pop: 2,812 (1990); 2,768 (1980)   **Pop Density:** 89.8
Land: 31.3 sq. mi.; **Water:** 0.0 sq. mi.

Range
Township
ZIP: 43143   **Lat:** 39-45-02 N   **Long:** 83-25-26 W
Pop: 1,082 (1990); 1,085 (1980)   **Pop Density:** 22.4
Land: 48.2 sq. mi.; **Water:** 0.0 sq. mi.

Somerford
Township
Lat: 39-58-42 N   **Long:** 83-29-30 W
Pop: 2,544 (1990); 2,172 (1980)   **Pop Density:** 86.5
Land: 29.4 sq. mi.; **Water:** 0.4 sq. mi.

South Solon
Village
ZIP: 43153   **Lat:** 39-44-13 N   **Long:** 83-36-48 W
Pop: 379 (1990); 416 (1980)   **Pop Density:** 1895.0
Land: 0.2 sq. mi.; **Water:** 0.0 sq. mi.

Stokes
Township
Lat: 39-44-44 N   **Long:** 83-34-16 W
Pop: 747 (1990); 787 (1980)   **Pop Density:** 21.5
Land: 34.8 sq. mi.; **Water:** 0.0 sq. mi.

Union
Township
ZIP: 43140   **Lat:** 39-52-27 N   **Long:** 83-27-36 W
Pop: 5,203 (1990); 3,167 (1980)   **Pop Density:** 130.4
Land: 39.9 sq. mi.; **Water:** 0.2 sq. mi.

Mahoning County
County Seat: Youngstown (ZIP: 44503)

Pop: 264,806 (1990); 289,487 (1980)   **Pop Density:** 637.7
Land: 415.3 sq. mi.; **Water:** 8.1 sq. mi.   **Area Code:** 216
On the northeastern border of OH, northeast of Canton; organized Feb 16, 1846 from Columbiana and Trumbull counties.
Name origin: From Delaware Indian *mahanoi* or *m'hoani* 'salt lick'; also spelled *Mahanoy*.

Alliance
City
ZIP: 44601   **Lat:** 40-54-48 N   **Long:** 81-05-07 W
Pop: 72 (1990); 24,315 (1980)   **Pop Density:** 720.0
Land: 0.1 sq. mi.; **Water:** 0.0 sq. mi.   **Elev:** 1174 ft.
In northeast-central OH on the Mahoning River, 14 mi. northeast of Canton. Settled 1805 by Quakers; united with nearby Greedom, Williamsport, and Mount Union in 1854; incorporated as a city 1889. Part of the town is also in Stark County.
Name origin: Named by railroad official Gen. Robinson either for its having been a grouping of small villages or for the junction here of two railroads.

Austintown
CDP
ZIP: 44512   **Lat:** 41-05-29 N   **Long:** 80-44-17 W
Pop: 32,371 (1990); 33,636 (1980)   **Pop Density:** 2766.8
Land: 11.7 sq. mi.; **Water:** 0.0 sq. mi.

*Austintown
Township
ZIP: 44515   **Lat:** 41-06-02 N   **Long:** 80-45-43 W
Pop: 36,740 (1990); 37,664 (1980)   **Pop Density:** 1481.5
Land: 24.8 sq. mi.; **Water:** 1.5 sq. mi.
In northeastern OH, northwest of Youngstown.

Beaver
Township
ZIP: 44408   **Lat:** 40-56-42 N   **Long:** 80-41-08 W
Pop: 5,433 (1990); 5,401 (1980)   **Pop Density:** 154.3
Land: 35.2 sq. mi.; **Water:** 0.8 sq. mi.

Beloit
Village
ZIP: 44609   **Lat:** 40-55-13 N   **Long:** 81-00-01 W
Pop: 1,037 (1990); 1,093 (1980)   **Pop Density:** 1296.3
Land: 0.8 sq. mi.; **Water:** 0.0 sq. mi.   **Elev:** 1132 ft.
In eastern OH, 30 mi. southwest of Youngstown.

Berlin
Township
ZIP: 44401   **Lat:** 41-01-51 N   **Long:** 80-57-02 W
Pop: 2,070 (1990); 2,047 (1980)   **Pop Density:** 85.9
Land: 24.1 sq. mi.; **Water:** 1.0 sq. mi.

Boardman
Township
ZIP: 44512   **Lat:** 41-01-17 N   **Long:** 80-39-54 W
Pop: 41,796 (1990); 41,758 (1980)   **Pop Density:** 1763.5
Land: 23.7 sq. mi.; **Water:** 0.1 sq. mi.
In northeastern OH, 6 mi. south of Youngstown.
Name origin: For Frederick Boardman, its original proprietor.

OHIO, Mahoning County

Campbell
City
ZIP: 44405 Lat: 41-04-38 N Long: 80-35-26 W
Pop: 10,038 (1990); 11,619 (1980) Pop Density: 2713.0
Land: 3.7 sq. mi.; Water: 0.0 sq. mi.

In northeastern OH on the Mahoning River, 5 mi. southeast of Youngstown. A residential and industrial (iron-steel) suburb.
Name origin: For James A. Campbell, former president of Youngstown Sheet and Tube Company, now Youngstown Steel Company. Previously named East Youngstown.

Canfield
City
ZIP: 44406 Lat: 41-01-46 N Long: 80-46-02 W
Pop: 5,409 (1990); 5,535 (1980) Pop Density: 1229.3
Land: 4.4 sq. mi.; Water: 0.0 sq. mi. Elev: 1161 ft.

In northeastern OH, 10 mi. southwest of Youngstown. Not coextensive with the town of the same name.
Name origin: For early landowner Johnathan Canfield.

*Canfield
Township
ZIP: 44406 Lat: 41-01-33 N Long: 80-45-38 W
Pop: 10,831 (1990); 10,350 (1980) Pop Density: 415.0
Land: 26.1 sq. mi.; Water: 0.0 sq. mi.

Coitsville
Township
ZIP: 44436 Lat: 41-06-05 N Long: 80-32-26 W
Pop: 1,841 (1990); 2,105 (1980) Pop Density: 142.7
Land: 12.9 sq. mi.; Water: 0.0 sq. mi.

Columbiana
Village
ZIP: 44408 Lat: 40-54-27 N Long: 80-41-27 W
Pop: 13 (1990); 1 (1980) Pop Density: 65.0
Land: 0.2 sq. mi.; Water: 0.0 sq. mi. Elev: 1118 ft.

Part of the town is also in Columbiana County.

Craig Beach
Village
ZIP: 44429 Lat: 41-07-06 N Long: 80-58-56 W
Pop: 1,402 (1990); 1,657 (1980) Pop Density: 1557.8
Land: 0.9 sq. mi.; Water: 0.8 sq. mi.

In northeastern OH on a widened area of the Mahoning River, west of Youngstown.

Ellsworth
Township
Lat: 41-01-14 N Long: 80-50-57 W
Pop: 2,103 (1990); 2,310 (1980) Pop Density: 82.8
Land: 25.4 sq. mi.; Water: 0.0 sq. mi.

Goshen
Township
Lat: 40-56-58 N Long: 80-55-14 W
Pop: 3,314 (1990); 3,481 (1980) Pop Density: 100.4
Land: 33.0 sq. mi.; Water: 0.0 sq. mi.

Green
Township
Lat: 40-57-02 N Long: 80-47-50 W
Pop: 3,321 (1990); 3,329 (1980) Pop Density: 106.1
Land: 31.3 sq. mi.; Water: 0.0 sq. mi.

In northeast OH, 23 mi. east of Canton.

Jackson
Township
ZIP: 44451 Lat: 41-06-14 N Long: 80-51-28 W
Pop: 2,164 (1990); 2,141 (1980) Pop Density: 90.2
Land: 24.0 sq. mi.; Water: 0.3 sq. mi.

Lowellville
Village
ZIP: 44436 Lat: 41-02-24 N Long: 80-32-53 W
Pop: 1,349 (1990); 1,558 (1980) Pop Density: 963.6
Land: 1.4 sq. mi.; Water: 0.0 sq. mi.

In northeastern OH, 5 mi. southeast of Youngstown.

Maple Ridge
CDP
Lat: 40-54-58 N Long: 81-02-59 W
Pop: 1,018 (1990) Pop Density: 509.0
Land: 2.0 sq. mi.; Water: 0.0 sq. mi.

Milton
Township
Lat: 41-06-05 N Long: 80-57-07 W
Pop: 4,068 (1990); 4,444 (1980) Pop Density: 184.1
Land: 22.1 sq. mi.; Water: 2.7 sq. mi.

Mineral Ridge
CDP
Lat: 41-07-42 N Long: 80-45-58 W
Pop: 1,066 (1990) Pop Density: 761.4
Land: 1.4 sq. mi.; Water: 0.0 sq. mi.

Part of the town is also in Trumbull County.

New Middletown
Village
ZIP: 44442 Lat: 40-57-49 N Long: 80-33-35 W
Pop: 1,912 (1990); 2,195 (1980) Pop Density: 2124.4
Land: 0.9 sq. mi.; Water: 0.0 sq. mi.

In northeastern OH, 12 mi. southeast of Youngstown.

Poland
Village
ZIP: 44514 Lat: 41-01-26 N Long: 80-36-50 W
Pop: 2,992 (1990); 3,084 (1980) Pop Density: 2493.3
Land: 1.2 sq. mi.; Water: 0.0 sq. mi.

Not coextensive with the town of the same name.

*Poland
Township
ZIP: 44514 Lat: 41-01-07 N Long: 80-33-30 W
Pop: 13,993 (1990); 15,198 (1980) Pop Density: 663.2
Land: 21.1 sq. mi.; Water: 0.1 sq. mi.

Sebring
City
ZIP: 44672 Lat: 40-55-24 N Long: 81-01-20 W
Pop: 4,848 (1990); 5,078 (1980) Pop Density: 2424.0
Land: 2.0 sq. mi.; Water: 0.0 sq. mi.

Smith
Township
Lat: 40-56-57 N Long: 81-01-25 W
Pop: 4,892 (1990); 5,321 (1980) Pop Density: 153.4
Land: 31.9 sq. mi.; Water: 0.2 sq. mi.

Springfield
Township
ZIP: 44442 Lat: 40-56-46 N Long: 80-34-28 W
Pop: 6,031 (1990); 5,920 (1980) Pop Density: 177.4
Land: 34.0 sq. mi.; Water: 0.8 sq. mi.

Struthers
City
ZIP: 44471 Lat: 41-03-04 N Long: 80-35-35 W
Pop: 12,284 (1990); 13,624 (1980) Pop Density: 3320.0
Land: 3.7 sq. mi.; Water: 0.0 sq. mi.

In northeastern OH on the Mahoning River, 4 mi. southeast of Youngstown.

Washingtonville
Village
ZIP: 44490 Lat: 40-54-03 N Long: 80-46-23 W
Pop: 412 (1990); 333 (1980) Pop Density: 2060.0
Land: 0.2 sq. mi.; Water: 0.0 sq. mi. Elev: 1069 ft.

Part of the town is also in Columbiana County.

Youngstown
City
ZIP: 44501 Lat: 41-05-56 N Long: 80-38-47 W
Pop: 95,706 (1990); 115,502 (1980) Pop Density: 2848.4
Land: 33.6 sq. mi.; Water: 0.4 sq. mi. Elev: 861 ft.

In northeastern OH on the Mahoning River, 45 mi. east of Akron. Platted 1802; incorporated 1859. Industrial city;

prior to late 1970s, a leading steel-producer. Part of the town is also in Trumbull County.
Name origin: For pioneer John Young of Whitestown, NY, who arrived with settlers in 1797.

Marion County
County Seat: Marion (ZIP: 43302)

Pop: 64,274 (1990); 67,974 (1980) **Pop Density:** 159.1
Land: 403.9 sq. mi.; **Water:** 0.3 sq. mi. **Area Code:** 614
In central OH, north of Columbus; organized Apr 1, 1820 from Crawford County.
Name origin: For Gen. Francis Marion (c. 1732–95), SC soldier and legislator, known as "The Swamp Fox" for his tactics in the Carolina swamps during the Revolutionary War.

Big Island Township
Lat: 40-36-08 N Long: 83-14-46 W
Pop: 1,271 (1990); 1,317 (1980) **Pop Density:** 36.0
Land: 35.3 sq. mi.; **Water:** 0.0 sq. mi.

Bowling Green Township
ZIP: 43332 Lat: 40-32-28 N Long: 83-21-52 W
Pop: 699 (1990); 576 (1980) **Pop Density:** 25.3
Land: 27.6 sq. mi.; **Water:** 0.0 sq. mi.

Caledonia Village
ZIP: 43314 Lat: 40-38-09 N Long: 82-58-09 W
Pop: 644 (1990); 759 (1980) **Pop Density:** 3220.0
Land: 0.2 sq. mi.; **Water:** 0.0 sq. mi. **Elev:** 998 ft.

Claridon Township
ZIP: 43314 Lat: 40-36-12 N Long: 83-01-08 W
Pop: 2,498 (1990); 2,660 (1980) **Pop Density:** 67.9
Land: 36.8 sq. mi.; **Water:** 0.0 sq. mi.

Grand Township
Lat: 40-40-05 N Long: 83-22-18 W
Pop: 340 (1990); 370 (1980) **Pop Density:** 18.7
Land: 18.2 sq. mi.; **Water:** 0.0 sq. mi.

Grand Prairie Township
Lat: 40-40-07 N Long: 83-07-54 W
Pop: 1,697 (1990); 1,828 (1980) **Pop Density:** 69.8
Land: 24.3 sq. mi.; **Water:** 0.0 sq. mi.

Green Camp Village
ZIP: 43322 Lat: 40-31-58 N Long: 83-12-28 W
Pop: 393 (1990); 475 (1980) **Pop Density:** 1310.0
Land: 0.3 sq. mi.; **Water:** 0.0 sq. mi.
In central OH at the confluence of the Scioto and Little Scioto rivers. Not coextensive with the town of the same name.

*Green Camp Township
Lat: 40-31-41 N Long: 83-15-01 W
Pop: 1,188 (1990); 1,162 (1980) **Pop Density:** 48.7
Land: 24.4 sq. mi.; **Water:** 0.0 sq. mi.

La Rue Village
ZIP: 43332 Lat: 40-34-40 N Long: 83-22-56 W
Pop: 802 (1990); 861 (1980) **Pop Density:** 1604.0
Land: 0.5 sq. mi.; **Water:** 0.0 sq. mi. **Elev:** 926 ft.
In central OH on the Scioto River, 13 mi. west of Marion.
Name origin: For landowner William LaRue.

Marion City
ZIP: 43302 Lat: 40-35-05 N Long: 83-07-40 W
Pop: 34,075 (1990); 37,040 (1980) **Pop Density:** 4259.4
Land: 8.0 sq. mi.; **Water:** 0.0 sq. mi. **Elev:** 956 ft.
In central OH, 45 mi. north of Columbus. Settled 1821; incorporated as a village 1830, as a city 1890. Not coextensive with the town of the same name.
Name origin: For Revolutionary War hero and legislator from SC, Gen. Francis Marion (c. 1732–95) nicknamed "The Swamp Fox" for his exploits in the Carolina swamps during the American Revolution.

*Marion Township
ZIP: 43302 Lat: 40-36-02 N Long: 83-07-49 W
Pop: 43,564 (1990); 46,388 (1980) **Pop Density:** 1187.0
Land: 36.7 sq. mi.; **Water:** 0.1 sq. mi.

Montgomery Township
ZIP: 43332 Lat: 40-36-24 N Long: 83-21-35 W
Pop: 2,316 (1990); 2,466 (1980) **Pop Density:** 81.5
Land: 28.4 sq. mi.; **Water:** 0.0 sq. mi.

Morral Village
ZIP: 43337 Lat: 40-41-23 N Long: 83-12-47 W
Pop: 373 (1990); 454 (1980) **Pop Density:** 138.1
Land: 2.7 sq. mi.; **Water:** 0.0 sq. mi. **Elev:** 912 ft.

New Bloomington Village
ZIP: 43341 Lat: 40-35-07 N Long: 83-18-55 W
Pop: 282 (1990); 303 (1980) **Pop Density:** 1410.0
Land: 0.2 sq. mi.; **Water:** 0.0 sq. mi. **Elev:** 945 ft.

Pleasant Township
Lat: 40-31-35 N Long: 83-08-05 W
Pop: 4,107 (1990); 4,425 (1980) **Pop Density:** 145.1
Land: 28.3 sq. mi.; **Water:** 0.0 sq. mi.

Prospect Village
ZIP: 43342 Lat: 40-27-08 N Long: 83-11-08 W
Pop: 1,148 (1990); 1,159 (1980) **Pop Density:** 1913.3
Land: 0.6 sq. mi.; **Water:** 0.0 sq. mi.
In central OH along the Scioto River, 12 mi. south of Marion. Not coextensive with the town of the same name.

*Prospect Township
ZIP: 43342 Lat: 40-27-47 N Long: 83-11-06 W
Pop: 2,050 (1990); 1,978 (1980) **Pop Density:** 84.7
Land: 24.2 sq. mi.; **Water:** 0.1 sq. mi.

OHIO, Marion County

Richland — Township
Lat: 40-31-15 N Long: 83-01-03 W
Pop: 1,531 (1990); 1,644 (1980) Pop Density: 49.9
Land: 30.7 sq. mi.; Water: 0.0 sq. mi.

Salt Rock — Township
Lat: 40-39-57 N Long: 83-14-57 W
Pop: 706 (1990); 768 (1980) Pop Density: 28.8
Land: 24.5 sq. mi.; Water: 0.0 sq. mi.

Scott — Township
Lat: 40-40-43 N Long: 83-01-24 W
Pop: 498 (1990); 518 (1980) Pop Density: 20.3
Land: 24.5 sq. mi.; Water: 0.0 sq. mi.

Tully — Township
Lat: 40-40-32 N Long: 82-54-40 W
Pop: 744 (1990); 809 (1980) Pop Density: 35.4
Land: 21.0 sq. mi.; Water: 0.0 sq. mi.

Waldo — Village
ZIP: 43356 Lat: 40-27-41 N Long: 83-05-08 W
Pop: 340 (1990); 347 (1980) Pop Density: 485.7
Land: 0.7 sq. mi.; Water: 0.0 sq. mi.
Not coextensive with the town of the same name.

*Waldo — Township
ZIP: 43356 Lat: 40-27-41 N Long: 83-04-20 W
Pop: 1,065 (1990); 1,065 (1980) Pop Density: 56.3
Land: 18.9 sq. mi.; Water: 0.0 sq. mi.

Medina County
County Seat: Medina (ZIP: 44256)

Pop: 122,354 (1990); 113,150 (1980) Pop Density: 290.2
Land: 421.6 sq. mi.; Water: 1.6 sq. mi. Area Code: 216
In north-central OH, northwest of Akron; organized Feb 18, 1812 from Portage County.

Name origin: Named for the city in Saudi Arabia to which Muhammad (c. 570–632), founder of Islam, fled from Mecca in 622.

Briarwood Beach — Village
ZIP: 44215 Lat: 41-04-29 N Long: 81-54-17 W
Pop: 682 (1990); 628 (1980) Pop Density: 3410.0
Land: 0.2 sq. mi.; Water: 0.0 sq. mi.

Brunswick — City
ZIP: 44212 Lat: 41-14-44 N Long: 81-49-16 W
Pop: 28,230 (1990); 28,104 (1980) Pop Density: 2454.8
Land: 11.5 sq. mi.; Water: 0.0 sq. mi.
In northern OH, 25 mi. southwest of Cleveland.

Brunswick Hills — Township
Lat: 41-13-41 N Long: 81-51-01 W
Pop: 4,328 (1990); 3,324 (1980) Pop Density: 320.6
Land: 13.5 sq. mi.; Water: 0.0 sq. mi.

Chatham — Township
ZIP: 44275 Lat: 41-05-53 N Long: 82-01-30 W
Pop: 1,799 (1990); 1,825 (1980) Pop Density: 68.1
Land: 26.4 sq. mi.; Water: 0.0 sq. mi.

Chippewa-on-the-Lake — Village
Lat: 41-04-12 N Long: 81-54-13 W
Pop: 271 (1990); 245 (1980) Pop Density: 2710.0
Land: 0.1 sq. mi.; Water: 0.0 sq. mi.

Gloria Glens Park — Village
Lat: 41-03-29 N Long: 81-54-03 W
Pop: 446 (1990); 435 (1980) Pop Density: 4460.0
Land: 0.1 sq. mi.; Water: 0.0 sq. mi.

Granger — Township
Lat: 41-10-03 N Long: 81-44-06 W
Pop: 2,932 (1990); 2,660 (1980) Pop Density: 125.8
Land: 23.3 sq. mi.; Water: 0.1 sq. mi.

Guilford — Township
ZIP: 44273 Lat: 41-01-42 N Long: 81-50-27 W
Pop: 4,773 (1990); 4,230 (1980) Pop Density: 190.2
Land: 25.1 sq. mi.; Water: 0.0 sq. mi.

Harrisville — Township
Lat: 41-01-32 N Long: 82-01-30 W
Pop: 4,776 (1990); 4,563 (1980) Pop Density: 182.3
Land: 26.2 sq. mi.; Water: 0.0 sq. mi.

Hinckley — Township
ZIP: 44233 Lat: 41-14-31 N Long: 81-44-08 W
Pop: 5,845 (1990); 5,174 (1980) Pop Density: 218.9
Land: 26.7 sq. mi.; Water: 0.1 sq. mi.

Homer — Township
ZIP: 44235 Lat: 41-01-45 N Long: 82-07-38 W
Pop: 1,196 (1990); 1,077 (1980) Pop Density: 49.0
Land: 24.4 sq. mi.; Water: 0.0 sq. mi.

Lafayette — Township
Lat: 41-06-16 N Long: 81-55-37 W
Pop: 4,804 (1990); 4,614 (1980) Pop Density: 204.4
Land: 23.5 sq. mi.; Water: 0.5 sq. mi.

Litchfield — Township
ZIP: 44253 Lat: 41-10-06 N Long: 82-01-28 W
Pop: 2,506 (1990); 2,329 (1980) Pop Density: 111.9
Land: 22.4 sq. mi.; Water: 0.0 sq. mi.

Liverpool — Township
ZIP: 44280 Lat: 41-14-15 N Long: 81-55-44 W
Pop: 3,713 (1990); 3,664 (1980) Pop Density: 143.4
Land: 25.9 sq. mi.; Water: 0.0 sq. mi.

Lodi — Village
ZIP: 44254 Lat: 41-02-01 N Long: 82-00-47 W
Pop: 3,042 (1990); 2,942 (1980) Pop Density: 1382.7
Land: 2.2 sq. mi.; Water: 0.0 sq. mi. Elev: 924 ft.
Name origin: For the Bridge of Lodi, Italy, site of Napoleon Bonaparte's (1769–1821) defeat of the Austrians in 1796.

American Places Dictionary   OHIO, Meigs County

Medina   City
ZIP: 44256   **Lat:** 41-08-10 N **Long:** 81-52-02 W
Pop: 19,231 (1990); 15,268 (1980)   **Pop Density:** 1885.4
Land: 10.2 sq. mi.; **Water:** 0.2 sq. mi.   **Elev:** 1092 ft.
In northern OH, 20 mi. northwest of Akron.
Name origin: Named in 1825 for the city in Saudi Arabia to which Muhammad (c. 570–632), the founder of Islam, made his famous flight from Mecca in 622.

*Medina   Township
Lat: 41-10-40 N **Long:** 81-49-20 W
Pop: 4,864 (1990); 3,561 (1980)   **Pop Density:** 270.2
Land: 18.0 sq. mi.; **Water:** 0.1 sq. mi.

Montville   Township
Lat: 41-05-31 N **Long:** 81-49-37 W
Pop: 3,371 (1990); 2,999 (1980)   **Pop Density:** 157.5
Land: 21.4 sq. mi.; **Water:** 0.1 sq. mi.

Rittman   City
ZIP: 44270   **Lat:** 40-59-33 N **Long:** 81-47-27 W
Pop: 110 (1990); 65 (1980)   **Pop Density:** 220.0
Land: 0.5 sq. mi.; **Water:** 0.0 sq. mi.   **Elev:** 979 ft.
In northeast-central OH, 16 mi. southwest of Akron. Part of the town is also in Wayne County.
Name origin: For Frederick B. Rittman, treasurer of the Atlanta & Great Western Railroad.

Seville   Village
ZIP: 44273   **Lat:** 41-01-20 N **Long:** 81-52-03 W
Pop: 1,810 (1990); 1,568 (1980)   **Pop Density:** 905.0
Land: 2.0 sq. mi.; **Water:** 0.0 sq. mi.

Sharon   Township
Lat: 41-05-56 N **Long:** 81-44-08 W
Pop: 3,234 (1990); 3,398 (1980)   **Pop Density:** 123.9
Land: 26.1 sq. mi.; **Water:** 0.0 sq. mi.

Spencer   Village
ZIP: 44275   **Lat:** 41-05-51 N **Long:** 82-07-21 W
Pop: 726 (1990); 764 (1980)   **Pop Density:** 726.0
Land: 1.0 sq. mi.; **Water:** 0.0 sq. mi.

*Spencer   Township
ZIP: 44275   **Lat:** 41-06-01 N **Long:** 82-07-22 W
Pop: 1,786 (1990); 1,859 (1980)   **Pop Density:** 71.2
Land: 25.1 sq. mi.; **Water:** 0.1 sq. mi.

Wadsworth   City
ZIP: 44281   **Lat:** 41-01-25 N **Long:** 81-43-54 W
Pop: 15,718 (1990); 15,166 (1980)   **Pop Density:** 1871.2
Land: 8.4 sq. mi.; **Water:** 0.0 sq. mi.
In northeast-central OH, 35 mi. south of Cleveland. Settled 1814. Not coextensive with the town of the same name.
Name origin: For Wadsworth Township (see below), itself named for Gen. Elijah Wadsworth, the largest landowner in the Western Reserve.

*Wadsworth   Township
ZIP: 44281   **Lat:** 41-01-32 N **Long:** 81-44-16 W
Pop: 19,093 (1990); 18,729 (1980)   **Pop Density:** 734.3
Land: 26.0 sq. mi.; **Water:** 0.0 sq. mi.

Westfield   Township
Lat: 41-01-28 N **Long:** 81-55-37 W
Pop: 3,394 (1990); 3,242 (1980)   **Pop Density:** 133.6
Land: 25.4 sq. mi.; **Water:** 0.1 sq. mi.

Westfield Center   Village
Lat: 41-01-35 N **Long:** 81-56-00 W
Pop: 784 (1990); 791 (1980)   **Pop Density:** 603.1
Land: 1.3 sq. mi.; **Water:** 0.0 sq. mi.

York   Township
Lat: 41-10-10 N **Long:** 81-55-59 W
Pop: 2,479 (1990); 2,530 (1980)   **Pop Density:** 120.3
Land: 20.6 sq. mi.; **Water:** 0.1 sq. mi.

Meigs County
County Seat: Pomeroy (ZIP: 45769)

Pop: 22,987 (1990); 23,641 (1980)   **Pop Density:** 53.5
Land: 429.5 sq. mi.; **Water:** 3.0 sq. mi.   **Area Code:** 614
On the southeastern border of OH; organized Jan 21, 1819 from Gallia and Athens counties.
Name origin: For Return Jonathan Meigs (1764–1824), OH governor (1810–14) and U.S. Postmaster General (1814–23).

Bedford   Township
Lat: 39-08-43 N **Long:** 82-01-21 W
Pop: 1,097 (1990); 1,004 (1980)   **Pop Density:** 27.9
Land: 39.3 sq. mi.; **Water:** 0.0 sq. mi.

Chester   Township
Lat: 39-04-52 N **Long:** 81-55-21 W
Pop: 2,131 (1990); 2,090 (1980)   **Pop Density:** 46.8
Land: 45.5 sq. mi.; **Water:** 0.0 sq. mi.

Columbia   Township
Lat: 39-09-27 N **Long:** 82-15-00 W
Pop: 801 (1990); 753 (1980)   **Pop Density:** 21.3
Land: 37.6 sq. mi.; **Water:** 0.0 sq. mi.

Lebanon   Township
ZIP: 45770   **Lat:** 38-59-47 N **Long:** 81-48-51 W
Pop: 905 (1990); 830 (1980)   **Pop Density:** 25.3
Land: 35.8 sq. mi.; **Water:** 0.7 sq. mi.

Letart   Township
ZIP: 45771   **Lat:** 38-55-12 N **Long:** 81-52-50 W
Pop: 689 (1990); 800 (1980)   **Pop Density:** 41.5
Land: 16.6 sq. mi.; **Water:** 0.9 sq. mi.

Middleport   Village
ZIP: 45760   **Lat:** 38-59-59 N **Long:** 82-03-24 W
Pop: 2,725 (1990); 2,971 (1980)   **Pop Density:** 2477.3
Land: 1.1 sq. mi.; **Water:** 0.0 sq. mi.
In southeastern OH, 40 mi. southwest of Marietta.

Olive
Township
ZIP: 45743 Lat: 39-07-55 N Long: 81-48-24 W
Pop: 1,727 (1990); 1,661 (1980) Pop Density: 44.4
Land: 38.9 sq. mi.; Water: 0.7 sq. mi.

Orange
Township
Lat: 39-09-00 N Long: 81-54-12 W
Pop: 970 (1990); 898 (1980) Pop Density: 37.6
Land: 25.8 sq. mi.; Water: 0.0 sq. mi.

Pomeroy
Village
ZIP: 45769 Lat: 39-01-39 N Long: 82-01-59 W
Pop: 2,259 (1990); 2,728 (1980) Pop Density: 705.9
Land: 3.2 sq. mi.; Water: 0.0 sq. mi.

In southeastern OH, 40 mi. southeast of Marietta.
Name origin: For Samuel Pomeroy, a Boston merchant who purchased 262 acres of land here 1804.

Racine
Village
ZIP: 45771 Lat: 38-58-05 N Long: 81-54-45 W
Pop: 729 (1990); 908 (1980) Pop Density: 1822.5
Land: 0.4 sq. mi.; Water: 0.0 sq. mi. Elev: 601 ft.

In southeast OH on the Ohio River, southwest of Parkersburg, WV.

Rutland
Village
ZIP: 45775 Lat: 39-02-31 N Long: 82-07-44 W
Pop: 469 (1990); 635 (1980) Pop Density: 586.3
Land: 0.8 sq. mi.; Water: 0.0 sq. mi.

Not coextensive with the town of the same name.

*Rutland
Township
ZIP: 45775 Lat: 39-03-08 N Long: 82-08-42 W
Pop: 2,243 (1990); 2,434 (1980) Pop Density: 51.0
Land: 44.0 sq. mi.; Water: 0.0 sq. mi.

Salem
Township
Lat: 39-03-42 N Long: 82-15-31 W
Pop: 1,018 (1990); 1,003 (1980) Pop Density: 23.4
Land: 43.5 sq. mi.; Water: 0.0 sq. mi.

Salisbury
Township
ZIP: 45769 Lat: 39-02-47 N Long: 82-02-56 W
Pop: 7,227 (1990); 8,037 (1980) Pop Density: 212.6
Land: 34.0 sq. mi.; Water: 0.2 sq. mi.

Scipio
Township
Lat: 39-08-49 N Long: 82-08-17 W
Pop: 1,094 (1990); 1,026 (1980) Pop Density: 29.2
Land: 37.5 sq. mi.; Water: 0.0 sq. mi.

Sutton
Township
Lat: 38-59-58 N Long: 81-54-53 W
Pop: 3,085 (1990); 3,105 (1980) Pop Density: 99.2
Land: 31.1 sq. mi.; Water: 0.4 sq. mi.

Syracuse
Village
ZIP: 45779 Lat: 38-59-58 N Long: 81-58-22 W
Pop: 827 (1990); 946 (1980) Pop Density: 1033.8
Land: 0.8 sq. mi.; Water: 0.0 sq. mi.

Name origin: For Syracuse, NY.

Mercer County
County Seat: Celina (ZIP: 45822)

Pop: 39,443 (1990); 38,334 (1980) Pop Density: 85.1
Land: 463.3 sq. mi.; Water: 10.0 sq. mi. Area Code: 419

On the central-western border of OH, southwest of Lima; organized Feb 12, 1820 from Darke County.

Name origin: For Gen. Hugh Mercer (1721–77), Revolutionary War officer and physician.

Black Creek
Township
Lat: 40-41-06 N Long: 84-44-35 W
Pop: 619 (1990); 647 (1980) Pop Density: 17.3
Land: 35.8 sq. mi.; Water: 0.0 sq. mi.

Burkettsville
Village
Lat: 40-21-14 N Long: 84-38-33 W
Pop: 181 (1990); 198 (1980) Pop Density: 1810.0
Land: 0.1 sq. mi.; Water: 0.0 sq. mi.

Part of the town is also in Darke County.

Butler
Township
ZIP: 45828 Lat: 40-28-57 N Long: 84-37-53 W
Pop: 6,181 (1990); 6,049 (1980) Pop Density: 186.7
Land: 33.1 sq. mi.; Water: 0.1 sq. mi.

Celina
City
ZIP: 45822 Lat: 40-33-12 N Long: 84-34-12 W
Pop: 9,650 (1990); 9,137 (1980) Pop Density: 2680.6
Land: 3.6 sq. mi.; Water: 0.0 sq. mi.

In western OH on the western end of Lake St. Marys, southwest of Lima. Settled 1834.
Name origin: For Salina, NY, with a spelling variation.

Center
Township
Lat: 40-36-25 N Long: 84-30-38 W
Pop: 937 (1990); 917 (1980) Pop Density: 30.7
Land: 30.5 sq. mi.; Water: 0.0 sq. mi.

Chickasaw
Village
ZIP: 45826 Lat: 40-26-10 N Long: 84-29-38 W
Pop: 378 (1990); 381 (1980) Pop Density: 1890.0
Land: 0.2 sq. mi.; Water: 0.0 sq. mi. Elev: 946 ft.

Coldwater
Village
ZIP: 45828 Lat: 40-28-57 N Long: 84-37-53 W
Pop: 4,335 (1990); 4,220 (1980) Pop Density: 2709.4
Land: 1.6 sq. mi.; Water: 0.0 sq. mi. Elev: 912 ft.

Dublin
Township
Lat: 40-41-10 N Long: 84-37-41 W
Pop: 2,244 (1990); 2,235 (1980) Pop Density: 60.0
Land: 37.4 sq. mi.; Water: 0.0 sq. mi.

Fort Recovery — Village
ZIP: 45846   Lat: 40-24-39 N   Long: 84-46-30 W
Pop: 1,313 (1990); 1,370 (1980)   Pop Density: 1458.9
Land: 0.9 sq. mi.; Water: 0.0 sq. mi.   Elev: 948 ft.
In western OH, 40 mi. southwest of Lima.
Name origin: For the site of Gen. Arthur St. Clair's (1736–1818) defeat in 1791, and of Gen. Anthony Wayne's (1745–96) recovery of the area in 1793, after the erection of a fort here.

Franklin — Township
Lat: 40-29-01 N   Long: 84-31-05 W
Pop: 2,126 (1990); 1,790 (1980)   Pop Density: 84.7
Land: 25.1 sq. mi.; Water: 2.3 sq. mi.

Gibson — Township
Lat: 40-22-48 N   Long: 84-45-02 W
Pop: 1,855 (1990); 1,872 (1980)   Pop Density: 82.1
Land: 22.6 sq. mi.; Water: 0.0 sq. mi.

Granville — Township
Lat: 40-23-38 N   Long: 84-37-46 W
Pop: 3,615 (1990); 3,591 (1980)   Pop Density: 92.2
Land: 39.2 sq. mi.; Water: 0.0 sq. mi.

Hopewell — Township
Lat: 40-36-11 N   Long: 84-38-16 W
Pop: 968 (1990); 977 (1980)   Pop Density: 30.9
Land: 31.3 sq. mi.; Water: 0.0 sq. mi.

Jefferson — Township
ZIP: 45822   Lat: 40-32-36 N   Long: 84-34-05 W
Pop: 12,983 (1990); 12,151 (1980)   Pop Density: 384.1
Land: 33.8 sq. mi.; Water: 7.6 sq. mi.
In west-central OH, 30 mi. southwest of Lima.

Liberty — Township
Lat: 40-35-46 N   Long: 84-44-47 W
Pop: 964 (1990); 1,014 (1980)   Pop Density: 26.9
Land: 35.9 sq. mi.; Water: 0.0 sq. mi.

Marion — Township
Lat: 40-24-01 N   Long: 84-31-02 W
Pop: 2,784 (1990); 2,753 (1980)   Pop Density: 67.1
Land: 41.5 sq. mi.; Water: 0.0 sq. mi.

Mendon — Village
ZIP: 45862   Lat: 40-40-16 N   Long: 84-31-04 W
Pop: 717 (1990); 749 (1980)   Pop Density: 1792.5
Land: 0.4 sq. mi.; Water: 0.0 sq. mi.
In western OH, just south of the Saint Marys River, southwest of Lima.

Montezuma — Village
ZIP: 45866   Lat: 40-29-21 N   Long: 84-32-56 W
Pop: 199 (1990); 200 (1980)   Pop Density: 1990.0
Land: 0.1 sq. mi.; Water: 0.0 sq. mi.   Elev: 884 ft.

Recovery — Township
Lat: 40-26-22 N   Long: 84-44-28 W
Pop: 1,381 (1990); 1,447 (1980)   Pop Density: 56.6
Land: 24.4 sq. mi.; Water: 0.0 sq. mi.

Rockford — Village
ZIP: 45882   Lat: 40-41-31 N   Long: 84-38-55 W
Pop: 1,119 (1990); 1,245 (1980)   Pop Density: 1865.0
Land: 0.6 sq. mi.; Water: 0.0 sq. mi.   Elev: 813 ft.

St. Henry — Village
Lat: 40-25-15 N   Long: 84-38-01 W
Pop: 1,907 (1990); 1,596 (1980)   Pop Density: 1466.9
Land: 1.3 sq. mi.; Water: 0.0 sq. mi.   Elev: 967 ft.

Union — Township
Lat: 40-41-07 N   Long: 84-30-47 W
Pop: 1,527 (1990); 1,626 (1980)   Pop Density: 42.0
Land: 36.4 sq. mi.; Water: 0.0 sq. mi.

Washington — Township
Lat: 40-30-30 N   Long: 84-44-48 W
Pop: 1,259 (1990); 1,265 (1980)   Pop Density: 34.7
Land: 36.3 sq. mi.; Water: 0.0 sq. mi.

Miami County
County Seat: Troy (ZIP: 45373)

Pop: 93,182 (1990); 90,381 (1980)   Pop Density: 228.9
Land: 407.0 sq. mi.; Water: 2.2 sq. mi.   Area Code: 513
In west-central OH, north of Dayton; organized Mar 1, 1807 from Montgomery County.
Name origin: For the Miami Indians, an Algonquin Indian tribe. Origin of the name uncertain, probably from Ojibway *oumaumeg* 'people of the peninsula,' or from Delaware *we-mi-a-mik* 'all friends.'

Bethel — Township
Lat: 39-55-47 N   Long: 84-05-38 W
Pop: 4,812 (1990); 4,709 (1980)   Pop Density: 137.9
Land: 34.9 sq. mi.; Water: 0.1 sq. mi.

Bradford — Village
ZIP: 45308   Lat: 40-07-51 N   Long: 84-25-34 W
Pop: 1,111 (1990); 1,172 (1980)   Pop Density: 2222.0
Land: 0.5 sq. mi.; Water: 0.0 sq. mi.   Elev: 989 ft.
In west-central OH, northwest of Dayton. Part of the town is also in Darke County.

Brown — Township
Lat: 40-09-00 N   Long: 84-04-27 W
Pop: 1,594 (1990); 1,515 (1980)   Pop Density: 52.8
Land: 30.2 sq. mi.; Water: 0.0 sq. mi.

Casstown — Village
ZIP: 45312   Lat: 40-03-09 N   Long: 84-07-43 W
Pop: 246 (1990); 331 (1980)   Pop Density: 2460.0
Land: 0.1 sq. mi.; Water: 0.0 sq. mi.   Elev: 937 ft.

OHIO, Miami County

Concord
Township
ZIP: 45373 Lat: 40-02-40 N Long: 84-14-26 W
Pop: 24,392 (1990); 23,392 (1980) Pop Density: 681.3
Land: 35.8 sq. mi.; Water: 0.1 sq. mi.

In southwest-central OH, 20 mi. north of Dayton.

Covington
Village
ZIP: 45318 Lat: 40-07-08 N Long: 84-21-03 W
Pop: 2,603 (1990); 2,610 (1980) Pop Density: 2603.0
Land: 1.0 sq. mi.; Water: 0.0 sq. mi. Elev: 930 ft.

In southwestern OH on Stillwater Creek, northwest of Dayton.

Elizabeth
Township
Lat: 40-00-02 N Long: 84-05-47 W
Pop: 1,620 (1990); 1,661 (1980) Pop Density: 54.2
Land: 29.9 sq. mi.; Water: 0.0 sq. mi.

Fletcher
Village
ZIP: 45326 Lat: 40-08-39 N Long: 84-06-42 W
Pop: 545 (1990); 498 (1980) Pop Density: 1816.7
Land: 0.3 sq. mi.; Water: 0.0 sq. mi.

Huber Heights
City
Lat: 39-53-18 N Long: 84-08-54 W
Pop: 10 (1990); 35,480 (1980) Pop Density: 50.0
Land: 0.2 sq. mi.; Water: 0.0 sq. mi.

In southwestern OH, 7 mi. northeast of Dayton. Part of the town is also in Montgomery County.

Laura
Village
ZIP: 45337 Lat: 39-59-36 N Long: 84-24-32 W
Pop: 483 (1990); 501 (1980) Pop Density: 2415.0
Land: 0.2 sq. mi.; Water: 0.0 sq. mi.

Lostcreek
Township
Lat: 40-04-44 N Long: 84-05-08 W
Pop: 1,534 (1990); 1,523 (1980) Pop Density: 51.1
Land: 30.0 sq. mi.; Water: 0.0 sq. mi.

Ludlow Falls
Village
ZIP: 45339 Lat: 39-59-54 N Long: 84-20-20 W
Pop: 300 (1990); 248 (1980) Pop Density: 1500.0
Land: 0.2 sq. mi.; Water: 0.0 sq. mi.

Monroe
Township
ZIP: 45371 Lat: 39-57-21 N Long: 84-12-56 W
Pop: 12,690 (1990); 11,469 (1980) Pop Density: 414.7
Land: 30.6 sq. mi.; Water: 0.2 sq. mi.

In west-central OH, 12 mi. north of Dayton.

Newberry
Township
ZIP: 45318 Lat: 40-08-39 N Long: 84-22-30 W
Pop: 6,460 (1990); 6,517 (1980) Pop Density: 152.4
Land: 42.4 sq. mi.; Water: 0.4 sq. mi.

Newton
Township
Lat: 40-03-17 N Long: 84-21-43 W
Pop: 3,221 (1990); 3,116 (1980) Pop Density: 77.2
Land: 41.7 sq. mi.; Water: 0.3 sq. mi.

Piqua
City
ZIP: 45356 Lat: 40-08-47 N Long: 84-15-03 W
Pop: 20,612 (1990); 20,480 (1980) Pop Density: 2785.4
Land: 7.4 sq. mi.; Water: 0.2 sq. mi. Elev: 869 ft.

In western OH on the Great Miami River, 25 mi. north of Dayton. Settled 1797.

Name origin: From the French translation of the name of a tribe of Shawnee Indians who established themselves in this region after 1763. Name is thought to mean 'a man risen out of the ashes.'

Pleasant Hill
Village
ZIP: 45359 Lat: 40-03-04 N Long: 84-20-41 W
Pop: 1,066 (1990); 1,051 (1980) Pop Density: 2132.0
Land: 0.5 sq. mi.; Water: 0.0 sq. mi.

Potsdam
Village
ZIP: 45361 Lat: 39-57-55 N Long: 84-24-43 W
Pop: 250 (1990); 289 (1980) Pop Density: 500.0
Land: 0.5 sq. mi.; Water: 0.0 sq. mi.

Springcreek
Township
Lat: 40-09-21 N Long: 84-10-58 W
Pop: 1,883 (1990); 1,864 (1980) Pop Density: 75.0
Land: 25.1 sq. mi.; Water: 0.1 sq. mi.

Staunton
Township
Lat: 40-03-42 N Long: 84-11-00 W
Pop: 2,040 (1990); 2,054 (1980) Pop Density: 77.3
Land: 26.4 sq. mi.; Water: 0.3 sq. mi.

Tipp City
City
ZIP: 45371 Lat: 39-57-49 N Long: 84-11-01 W
Pop: 6,027 (1990); 5,595 (1980) Pop Density: 1230.0
Land: 4.9 sq. mi.; Water: 0.0 sq. mi.

In west-central OH along the Miami River, a northern suburb of Dayton.

Troy
City
ZIP: 45373 Lat: 40-02-39 N Long: 84-13-09 W
Pop: 19,478 (1990); 19,086 (1980) Pop Density: 2264.9
Land: 8.6 sq. mi.; Water: 0.1 sq. mi.

In west-central OH, 20 mi. north of Dayton.

Name origin: For Troy, NY.

Union
Township
ZIP: 45383 Lat: 39-57-55 N Long: 84-20-43 W
Pop: 10,331 (1990); 10,222 (1980) Pop Density: 213.0
Land: 48.5 sq. mi.; Water: 0.3 sq. mi.

In southwestern OH, 14 mi. northwest of Dayton.

Washington
Township
ZIP: 45356 Lat: 40-08-53 N Long: 84-16-24 W
Pop: 22,595 (1990); 22,339 (1980) Pop Density: 719.6
Land: 31.4 sq. mi.; Water: 0.4 sq. mi.

In west-central OH, 28 mi. northwest of Springfield.

West Milton
Village
ZIP: 45383 Lat: 39-57-10 N Long: 84-19-30 W
Pop: 4,348 (1990); 4,119 (1980) Pop Density: 2557.6
Land: 1.7 sq. mi.; Water: 0.0 sq. mi.

Monroe County
County Seat: Woodsfield (ZIP: 43793)

Pop: 15,497 (1990); 17,382 (1980)
Land: 455.6 sq. mi.; **Water:** 1.9 sq. mi.
Pop Density: 34.0
Area Code: 614

On the central-eastern border of OH; organized Jan 29, 1813 from Belmont, Washington, and Guernsey counties.

Name origin: For James Monroe (1758–1831), fifth U.S. president.

Adams
Township
Lat: 39-46-30 N Long: 80-59-42 W
Pop: 595 (1990); 699 (1980) **Pop Density:** 26.4
Land: 22.5 sq. mi.; **Water:** 0.0 sq. mi.

Antioch
Village
Lat: 39-39-41 N Long: 81-04-03 W
Pop: 68 (1990); 113 (1980) **Pop Density:** 680.0
Land: 0.1 sq. mi.; **Water:** 0.0 sq. mi.
Name origin: For the biblical city in Syria.

Beallsville
Village
ZIP: 43716 Lat: 39-50-53 N Long: 81-02-07 W
Pop: 464 (1990); 601 (1980) **Pop Density:** 1160.0
Land: 0.4 sq. mi.; **Water:** 0.0 sq. mi. **Elev:** 1263 ft.

Benton
Township
Lat: 39-36-25 N Long: 81-05-08 W
Pop: 409 (1990); 466 (1980) **Pop Density:** 18.1
Land: 22.6 sq. mi.; **Water:** 0.0 sq. mi.

Bethel
Township
Lat: 39-37-44 N Long: 81-14-41 W
Pop: 433 (1990); 421 (1980) **Pop Density:** 18.4
Land: 23.5 sq. mi.; **Water:** 0.0 sq. mi.

Center
Township
ZIP: 43793 Lat: 39-45-25 N Long: 81-06-18 W
Pop: 3,955 (1990); 4,304 (1980) **Pop Density:** 95.5
Land: 41.4 sq. mi.; **Water:** 0.0 sq. mi.

Clarington
Village
ZIP: 43915 Lat: 39-46-36 N Long: 80-51-54 W
Pop: 406 (1990); 558 (1980) **Pop Density:** 369.1
Land: 1.1 sq. mi.; **Water:** 0.1 sq. mi.

Franklin
Township
Lat: 39-43-54 N Long: 81-16-28 W
Pop: 436 (1990); 429 (1980) **Pop Density:** 17.4
Land: 25.0 sq. mi.; **Water:** 0.0 sq. mi.

Graysville
Village
ZIP: 45734 Lat: 39-39-39 N Long: 81-10-15 W
Pop: 89 (1990); 112 (1980) **Pop Density:** 89.0
Land: 1.0 sq. mi.; **Water:** 0.0 sq. mi.
In southeastern OH in Wayne National Forest.

Green
Township
ZIP: 43793 Lat: 39-41-43 N Long: 81-00-35 W
Pop: 442 (1990); 400 (1980) **Pop Density:** 16.0
Land: 27.7 sq. mi.; **Water:** 0.0 sq. mi.

Jackson
Township
Lat: 39-36-34 N Long: 81-00-02 W
Pop: 388 (1990); 448 (1980) **Pop Density:** 19.5
Land: 19.9 sq. mi.; **Water:** 0.3 sq. mi.

Jerusalem
Village
ZIP: 43747 Lat: 39-51-07 N Long: 81-05-43 W
Pop: 144 (1990); 237 (1980) **Pop Density:** 480.0
Land: 0.3 sq. mi.; **Water:** 0.0 sq. mi.
Name origin: For the biblical city.

Lee
Township
Lat: 39-38-32 N Long: 80-56-03 W
Pop: 1,237 (1990); 1,311 (1980) **Pop Density:** 71.1
Land: 17.4 sq. mi.; **Water:** 0.2 sq. mi.

Lewisville
Village
ZIP: 43754 Lat: 39-45-57 N Long: 81-13-07 W
Pop: 261 (1990); 285 (1980) **Pop Density:** 652.5
Land: 0.4 sq. mi.; **Water:** 0.0 sq. mi. **Elev:** 1187 ft.

Malaga
Township
Lat: 39-50-01 N Long: 81-09-53 W
Pop: 978 (1990); 1,113 (1980) **Pop Density:** 33.4
Land: 29.3 sq. mi.; **Water:** 0.1 sq. mi.

Miltonsburg
Village
ZIP: 43793 Lat: 39-49-54 N Long: 81-09-51 W
Pop: 56 (1990); 109 (1980) **Pop Density:** 560.0
Land: 0.1 sq. mi.; **Water:** 0.0 sq. mi.

Ohio
Township
Lat: 39-40-53 N Long: 80-54-33 W
Pop: 1,134 (1990); 1,318 (1980) **Pop Density:** 49.1
Land: 23.1 sq. mi.; **Water:** 0.3 sq. mi.

Perry
Township
ZIP: 43793 Lat: 39-39-40 N Long: 81-04-10 W
Pop: 496 (1990); 600 (1980) **Pop Density:** 20.3
Land: 24.4 sq. mi.; **Water:** 0.0 sq. mi.

Salem
Township
Lat: 39-45-24 N Long: 80-53-37 W
Pop: 996 (1990); 1,162 (1980) **Pop Density:** 38.8
Land: 25.7 sq. mi.; **Water:** 0.7 sq. mi.

Seneca
Township
Lat: 39-49-47 N Long: 81-16-42 W
Pop: 386 (1990); 485 (1980) **Pop Density:** 17.2
Land: 22.5 sq. mi.; **Water:** 0.0 sq. mi.

Stafford
Village
ZIP: 43786 Lat: 39-42-47 N Long: 81-16-39 W
Pop: 89 (1990); 98 (1980) **Pop Density:** 296.7
Land: 0.3 sq. mi.; **Water:** 0.0 sq. mi.

Summit
Township
Lat: 39-47-04 N Long: 81-13-01 W
Pop: 728 (1990); 767 (1980) **Pop Density:** 33.4
Land: 21.8 sq. mi.; **Water:** 0.0 sq. mi.

Sunsbury
Township
Lat: 39-50-13 N Long: 81-01-56 W
Pop: 1,486 (1990); 1,804 (1980) **Pop Density:** 52.3
Land: 28.4 sq. mi.; **Water:** 0.0 sq. mi.

OHIO, Monroe County

Switzerland
Township
Lat: 39-49-34 N **Long:** 80-54-12 W
Pop: 501 (1990); 575 (1980) **Pop Density:** 18.4
Land: 27.2 sq. mi.; **Water:** 0.1 sq. mi.

Washington
Township
ZIP: 43716 **Lat:** 39-38-17 N **Long:** 81-10-25 W
Pop: 518 (1990); 604 (1980) **Pop Density:** 16.8
Land: 30.9 sq. mi.; **Water:** 0.0 sq. mi.

Wayne
Township
Lat: 39-43-09 N **Long:** 81-10-57 W
Pop: 379 (1990); 476 (1980) **Pop Density:** 16.9
Land: 22.4 sq. mi.; **Water:** 0.0 sq. mi.

Wilson
Village
ZIP: 43716 **Lat:** 39-51-19 N **Long:** 81-04-04 W
Pop: 109 (1990); 116 (1980) **Pop Density:** 363.3
Land: 0.3 sq. mi.; **Water:** 0.0 sq. mi. **Elev:** 1247 ft.
Part of the town is also in Belmont County.

Woodsfield
Village
ZIP: 43793 **Lat:** 39-45-46 N **Long:** 81-07-00 W
Pop: 2,832 (1990); 3,145 (1980) **Pop Density:** 1416.0
Land: 2.0 sq. mi.; **Water:** 0.0 sq. mi. **Elev:** 1213 ft.
In southeastern OH, 30 mi. northeast of Marietta. Founded 1815.
Name origin: For its founder, Archibald Woods.

Montgomery County
County Seat: Dayton (ZIP: 45422)

Pop: 573,809 (1990); 571,697 (1980) **Pop Density:** 1242.8
Land: 461.7 sq. mi.; **Water:** 2.7 sq. mi. **Area Code:** 513
In west-central OH, north of Cincinnati; organized Mar 24, 1803 from Hamilton and Ross counties.
Name origin: For Gen. Richard Montgomery (1736–75), American Revolutionary War officer who captured Montreal, Canada.

Brookville
Village
ZIP: 45309 **Lat:** 39-50-08 N **Long:** 84-24-54 W
Pop: 4,621 (1990); 4,322 (1980) **Pop Density:** 2100.5
Land: 2.2 sq. mi.; **Water:** 0.0 sq. mi. **Elev:** 1033 ft.
In western OH, 20 mi. northwest of Dayton.

Butler
Township
ZIP: 45337 **Lat:** 39-53-12 N **Long:** 84-14-42 W
Pop: 8,634 (1990); 9,365 (1980) **Pop Density:** 417.1
Land: 20.7 sq. mi.; **Water:** 0.3 sq. mi.

Carlisle
Village
ZIP: 45005 **Lat:** 39-35-22 N **Long:** 84-19-03 W
Pop: 262 (1990); 308 (1980) **Pop Density:** 1310.0
Land: 0.2 sq. mi.; **Water:** 0.0 sq. mi.
In southwestern OH between the Twin and Miami rivers, 15 mi. southwest of Dayton. Part of the town is also in Warren County.

Centerville
City
ZIP: 45459 **Lat:** 39-38-27 N **Long:** 84-08-24 W
Pop: 21,082 (1990); 18,886 (1980) **Pop Density:** 2368.8
Land: 8.9 sq. mi.; **Water:** 0.0 sq. mi. **Elev:** 1020 ft.
In southwest OH, 10 mi. south of Dayton.
Name origin: For its geographical position between Springfield and Hamilton.

Clay
Township
ZIP: 45354 **Lat:** 39-51-59 N **Long:** 84-25-34 W
Pop: 8,310 (1990); 7,959 (1980) **Pop Density:** 219.8
Land: 37.8 sq. mi.; **Water:** 0.0 sq. mi.

Clayton
Village
ZIP: 45315 **Lat:** 39-51-38 N **Long:** 84-21-18 W
Pop: 713 (1990); 752 (1980) **Pop Density:** 594.2
Land: 1.2 sq. mi.; **Water:** 0.0 sq. mi.

Dayton
City
ZIP: 45401 **Lat:** 39-46-44 N **Long:** 84-11-50 W
Pop: 182,044 (1990); 193,536 (1980) **Pop Density:** 3309.9
Land: 55.0 sq. mi.; **Water:** 0.9 sq. mi.
Part of the town is also in Greene County.

Drexel
CDP
ZIP: 45427 **Lat:** 39-44-38 N **Long:** 84-17-30 W
Pop: 5,143 (1990) **Pop Density:** 1254.4
Land: 4.1 sq. mi.; **Water:** 0.0 sq. mi.

Englewood
City
ZIP: 45315 **Lat:** 39-51-38 N **Long:** 84-18-24 W
Pop: 11,432 (1990); 11,329 (1980) **Pop Density:** 2198.5
Land: 5.2 sq. mi.; **Water:** 0.0 sq. mi. **Elev:** 920 ft.
In southwestern OH, 10 mi. northwest of Dayton.
Name origin: Possibly named by an early settler for a place mentioned in a novel he was reading at the time, or for an Engle family prominent in the community.

Farmersville
Village
ZIP: 45325 **Lat:** 39-40-43 N **Long:** 84-25-37 W
Pop: 932 (1990); 950 (1980) **Pop Density:** 1331.4
Land: 0.7 sq. mi.; **Water:** 0.0 sq. mi. **Elev:** 882 ft.

Fort McKinley
CDP
ZIP: 45426 **Lat:** 39-48-21 N **Long:** 84-15-23 W
Pop: 9,740 (1990); 4,604 (1980) **Pop Density:** 3358.6
Land: 2.9 sq. mi.; **Water:** 0.0 sq. mi.

German
Township
ZIP: 45327 **Lat:** 39-37-44 N **Long:** 84-24-09 W
Pop: 7,712 (1990); 7,910 (1980) **Pop Density:** 202.9
Land: 38.0 sq. mi.; **Water:** 0.0 sq. mi.

Germantown — Village
ZIP: 45325 **Lat:** 39-38-05 N **Long:** 84-21-44 W
Pop: 4,916 (1990); 5,015 (1980) **Pop Density:** 1365.6
Land: 3.6 sq. mi.; **Water:** 0.0 sq. mi.
In southwest-central OH, 15 mi. southwest of Dayton.
Name origin: Named by early German settlers for Germantown, PA.

Harrison — Township
ZIP: 45415 **Lat:** 39-48-46 N **Long:** 84-13-00 W
Pop: 26,026 (1990); 26,986 (1980) **Pop Density:** 2891.8
Land: 9.0 sq. mi.; **Water:** 0.1 sq. mi.
In southwest OH, 3 mi. north of Dayton.

Huber Heights — City
ZIP: 45424 **Lat:** 39-51-21 N **Long:** 84-06-44 W
Pop: 38,686 (1990); 35,480 (1980) **Pop Density:** 1878.0
Land: 20.6 sq. mi.; **Water:** 0.1 sq. mi.
In southwestern OH, 7 mi. northeast of Dayton. Part of the town is also in Miami County.

Jackson — Township
ZIP: 45325 **Lat:** 39-42-12 N **Long:** 84-25-49 W
Pop: 6,390 (1990); 6,517 (1980) **Pop Density:** 174.1
Land: 36.7 sq. mi.; **Water:** 0.2 sq. mi.

Jefferson — Township
ZIP: 45345 **Lat:** 39-42-27 N **Long:** 84-19-25 W
Pop: 8,652 (1990); 9,379 (1980) **Pop Density:** 311.2
Land: 27.8 sq. mi.; **Water:** 0.0 sq. mi.

Kettering — City
ZIP: 45429 **Lat:** 39-41-45 N **Long:** 84-09-00 W
Pop: 60,569 (1990); 61,186 (1980) **Pop Density:** 3239.0
Land: 18.7 sq. mi.; **Water:** 0.0 sq. mi.
In southwestern OH, on the southern outskirts of Dayton. Part of the town is also in Greene County.
Name origin: For engineer Charles F. Kettering (1876–1958), who developed the automobile self-starting ignition system.

Madison — Township
ZIP: 45426 **Lat:** 39-47-30 N **Long:** 84-18-51 W
Pop: 29,421 (1990); 30,586 (1980) **Pop Density:** 952.1
Land: 30.9 sq. mi.; **Water:** 0.0 sq. mi.
In west-central OH, 6 mi. northwest of Dayton.

Mad River — Township
ZIP: 45424 **Lat:** 39-46-53 N **Long:** 84-07-15 W
Pop: 30,195 (1990); 32,711 (1980) **Pop Density:** 3081.1
Land: 9.8 sq. mi.; **Water:** 0.0 sq. mi.
In west-central OH, 4 mi. northeast of Dayton.

Miami — Township
ZIP: 45342 **Lat:** 39-37-48 N **Long:** 84-15-54 W
Pop: 40,700 (1990); 33,688 (1980) **Pop Density:** 1190.1
Land: 34.2 sq. mi.; **Water:** 0.4 sq. mi.
In southwestern OH, 9 mi. south of Dayton.

Miamisburg — City
ZIP: 45343 **Lat:** 39-38-07 N **Long:** 84-16-28 W
Pop: 17,834 (1990); 15,304 (1980) **Pop Density:** 1877.3
Land: 9.5 sq. mi.; **Water:** 0.2 sq. mi.
In southwestern OH on the Great Miami River, south of Dayton.

Moraine — City
ZIP: 45439 **Lat:** 39-42-14 N **Long:** 84-13-42 W
Pop: 5,989 (1990); 5,325 (1980) **Pop Density:** 868.0
Land: 6.9 sq. mi.; **Water:** 0.3 sq. mi.
In southwestern OH, 5 mi. south of Dayton.
Name origin: For its prominent moraine (glacial deposit).

New Lebanon — Village
ZIP: 45345 **Lat:** 39-44-42 N **Long:** 84-24-01 W
Pop: 4,323 (1990); 4,501 (1980) **Pop Density:** 2401.7
Land: 1.8 sq. mi.; **Water:** 0.0 sq. mi.
In southwestern OH, 10 mi. west of Dayton.
Name origin: For the biblical mountain noted for its cedar trees.

Northridge — CDP
ZIP: 45414 **Lat:** 39-48-37 N **Long:** 84-11-30 W
Pop: 9,448 (1990); 9,720 (1980) **Pop Density:** 4107.8
Land: 2.3 sq. mi.; **Water:** 0.0 sq. mi.

Northview — CDP
ZIP: 45322 **Lat:** 39-50-35 N **Long:** 84-16-46 W
Pop: 10,337 (1990); 9,973 (1980) **Pop Density:** 2793.8
Land: 3.7 sq. mi.; **Water:** 0.1 sq. mi.

Oakwood — City
ZIP: 45419 **Lat:** 39-43-11 N **Long:** 84-10-24 W
Pop: 8,957 (1990); 9,372 (1980) **Pop Density:** 4071.4
Land: 2.2 sq. mi.; **Water:** 0.0 sq. mi.
In southwest-central OH, a suburb of Dayton.

Overlook-Page Manor — CDP
ZIP: 45431 **Lat:** 39-45-14 N **Long:** 84-06-55 W
Pop: 13,242 (1990); 14,825 (1980) **Pop Density:** 4566.2
Land: 2.9 sq. mi.; **Water:** 0.0 sq. mi.

Perry — Township
ZIP: 45309 **Lat:** 39-47-27 N **Long:** 84-25-09 W
Pop: 6,172 (1990); 6,441 (1980) **Pop Density:** 168.2
Land: 36.7 sq. mi.; **Water:** 0.0 sq. mi.

Phillipsburg — Village
ZIP: 45354 **Lat:** 39-54-15 N **Long:** 84-24-02 W
Pop: 644 (1990); 705 (1980) **Pop Density:** 2146.7
Land: 0.3 sq. mi.; **Water:** 0.0 sq. mi.

Randolph — Township
ZIP: 45322 **Lat:** 39-52-17 N **Long:** 84-19-27 W
Pop: 30,458 (1990); 29,196 (1980) **Pop Density:** 1072.5
Land: 28.4 sq. mi.; **Water:** 0.2 sq. mi.
In southwestern OH, 12 mi. northwest of Dayton.

Riverside — Village
Lat: 39-46-50 N **Long:** 84-07-26 W
Pop: 1,471 (1990); 1,475 (1980) **Pop Density:** 3677.5
Land: 0.4 sq. mi.; **Water:** 0.0 sq. mi.

Shiloh — CDP
ZIP: 45415 **Lat:** 39-48-48 N **Long:** 84-13-54 W
Pop: 11,607 (1990); 11,735 (1980) **Pop Density:** 2976.2
Land: 3.9 sq. mi., **Water:** 0.1 sq. mi.

Springboro — City
Lat: 39-35-12 N **Long:** 84-13-01 W
Pop: 0 (1990); 4,962 (1980)
Land: 0.2 sq. mi.; **Water:** 0.0 sq. mi.
Part of the town is also in Warren County.

OHIO, Montgomery County *American Places Dictionary*

Trotwood
City
ZIP: 45426 Lat: 39-48-10 N Long: 84-18-16 W
Pop: 8,816 (1990); 7,802 (1980) Pop Density: 1469.3
Land: 6.0 sq. mi.; Water: 0.0 sq. mi.

Union
Village
ZIP: 45322 Lat: 39-54-09 N Long: 84-18-35 W
Pop: 5,501 (1990); 5,219 (1980) Pop Density: 2292.1
Land: 2.4 sq. mi.; Water: 0.0 sq. mi.

Vandalia
City
ZIP: 45377 Lat: 39-52-41 N Long: 84-11-38 W
Pop: 13,882 (1990); 13,161 (1980) Pop Density: 1273.6
Land: 10.9 sq. mi.; Water: 0.0 sq. mi.
In southwestern OH, 7 mi. north of Dayton. Settled 1838.
Name origin: For Vandalia, IL.

Verona
Village
ZIP: 45378 Lat: 39-54-06 N Long: 84-28-58 W
Pop: 85 (1990); 90 (1980) Pop Density: 850.0
Land: 0.1 sq. mi.; Water: 0.0 sq. mi.
Part of the town is also in Preble County.

Washington
Township
ZIP: 45459 Lat: 39-37-34 N Long: 84-09-33 W
Pop: 46,609 (1990); 39,751 (1980) Pop Density: 1493
Land: 31.2 sq. mi.; Water: 0.0 sq. mi.
In southwestern OH, 12 mi. south of Dayton.

West Carrollton City
City
ZIP: 45449 Lat: 39-40-10 N Long: 84-15-09 W
Pop: 14,403 (1990); 13,148 (1980) Pop Density: 2286.
Land: 6.3 sq. mi.; Water: 0.2 sq. mi.
In southwestern OH on the Miami River, 7 mi. south of Dayton.

Woodbourne-Hyde Park
CD
ZIP: 45429 Lat: 39-39-38 N Long: 84-10-25 W
Pop: 7,837 (1990); 8,826 (1980) Pop Density: 1703.
Land: 4.6 sq. mi.; Water: 0.0 sq. mi.

Wright-Patterson Air Force Base
Military Facility
Lat: 39-46-28 N Long: 84-06-37 W
Pop: 4,947 (1990) Pop Density: 2603.
Land: 1.9 sq. mi.; Water: 0.0 sq. mi.
Part of the facility is also in Greene County.

Morgan County
County Seat: McConnelsville (ZIP: 43756)

Pop: 14,194 (1990); 14,241 (1980) Pop Density: 34.0
Land: 417.7 sq. mi.; Water: 4.2 sq. mi. Area Code: 614
In east-central OH, southeast of Columbus; organized Dec 29, 1817 from Washington County.
Name origin: For Gen. Daniel Morgan (1736–1802), an officer in the Revolutionary War and U.S. representative from VA (1797–99).

Bloom
Township
Lat: 39-44-12 N Long: 81-52-09 W
Pop: 1,003 (1990); 1,026 (1980) Pop Density: 40.0
Land: 25.1 sq. mi.; Water: 0.5 sq. mi.

Bristol
Township
Lat: 39-42-50 N Long: 81-45-15 W
Pop: 173 (1990); 216 (1980) Pop Density: 4.6
Land: 37.7 sq. mi.; Water: 0.9 sq. mi.

Center
Township
Lat: 39-37-48 N Long: 81-38-49 W
Pop: 593 (1990); 615 (1980) Pop Density: 18.4
Land: 32.2 sq. mi.; Water: 0.1 sq. mi.

Chesterhill
Village
ZIP: 43728 Lat: 39-29-23 N Long: 81-51-57 W
Pop: 309 (1990); 395 (1980) Pop Density: 618.0
Land: 0.5 sq. mi.; Water: 0.0 sq. mi.

Deerfield
Township
ZIP: 43758 Lat: 39-40-50 N Long: 81-58-18 W
Pop: 683 (1990); 549 (1980) Pop Density: 20.7
Land: 33.0 sq. mi.; Water: 0.0 sq. mi.

Homer
Township
Lat: 39-29-59 N Long: 82-00-10 W
Pop: 763 (1990); 683 (1980) Pop Density: 20.2
Land: 37.7 sq. mi.; Water: 0.6 sq. mi.

Malta
Village
ZIP: 43758 Lat: 39-39-01 N Long: 81-51-52 W
Pop: 802 (1990); 956 (1980) Pop Density: 2673.
Land: 0.3 sq. mi.; Water: 0.0 sq. mi. Elev: 671 ft
In southeastern OH across the Muskingum River from McConnelsville. Not coextensive with the town of the same name.
Name origin: For the Mediterranean island.

*Malta
Township
ZIP: 43758 Lat: 39-38-28 N Long: 81-53-42 W
Pop: 1,992 (1990); 2,065 (1980) Pop Density: 76.9
Land: 25.9 sq. mi.; Water: 0.3 sq. mi.

Manchester
Township
Lat: 39-42-17 N Long: 81-40-37 W
Pop: 149 (1990); 134 (1980) Pop Density: 8.1
Land: 18.3 sq. mi.; Water: 0.3 sq. mi.

Marion
Township
Lat: 39-30-02 N Long: 81-53-07 W
Pop: 1,215 (1990); 1,290 (1980) Pop Density: 32.2
Land: 37.7 sq. mi.; Water: 0.0 sq. mi.

McConnelsville
Village
ZIP: 43756 Lat: 39-39-14 N Long: 81-50-39 W
Pop: 1,804 (1990); 2,018 (1980) Pop Density: 1202.7
Land: 1.5 sq. mi.; Water: 0.1 sq. mi.

Meigsville — Township
Lat: 39-38-12 N Long: 81-45-24 W
Pop: 774 (1990); 761 (1980) Pop Density: 24.7
Land: 31.3 sq. mi.; Water: 0.1 sq. mi.

Morgan — Township
Lat: 39-39-31 N Long: 81-50-42 W
Pop: 2,646 (1990); 2,621 (1980) Pop Density: 218.7
Land: 12.1 sq. mi.; Water: 0.3 sq. mi.

Penn — Township
Lat: 39-34-21 N Long: 81-52-16 W
Pop: 784 (1990); 720 (1980) Pop Density: 34.2
Land: 22.9 sq. mi.; Water: 0.0 sq. mi.

Stockport — Village
ZIP: 43770 Lat: 39-32-57 N Long: 81-47-41 W
Pop: 462 (1990); 558 (1980) Pop Density: 1540.0
Land: 0.3 sq. mi.; Water: 0.0 sq. mi.

Union — Township
Lat: 39-35-25 N Long: 81-58-32 W
Pop: 531 (1990); 596 (1980) Pop Density: 14.5
Land: 36.5 sq. mi.; Water: 0.2 sq. mi.

Windsor — Township
ZIP: 43787 Lat: 39-32-18 N Long: 81-45-43 W
Pop: 1,939 (1990); 1,997 (1980) Pop Density: 45.4
Land: 42.7 sq. mi.; Water: 1.0 sq. mi.

York — Township
Lat: 39-44-52 N Long: 82-00-06 W
Pop: 949 (1990); 968 (1980) Pop Density: 38.7
Land: 24.5 sq. mi.; Water: 0.0 sq. mi.

Morrow County
County Seat: Mount Gilead (ZIP: 43338)

Pop: 27,749 (1990); 26,480 (1980) Pop Density: 68.4
Land: 405.5 sq. mi.; Water: 1.8 sq. mi. Area Code: 419

In central OH, north of Columbus; organized Mar 1, 1848 from Knox, Marion, Delaware, and Richland counties.

Name origin: For Jeremiah Morrow (1771–1852), OH legislator, U.S. senator (1813–19), and governor (1822–36).

Bennington — Township
Lat: 40-23-02 N Long: 82-47-40 W
Pop: 2,377 (1990); 2,223 (1980) Pop Density: 94.3
Land: 25.2 sq. mi.; Water: 0.0 sq. mi.

Canaan — Township
Lat: 40-36-31 N Long: 82-54-33 W
Pop: 844 (1990); 872 (1980) Pop Density: 30.7
Land: 27.5 sq. mi.; Water: 0.0 sq. mi.

Cardington — Village
ZIP: 43315 Lat: 40-29-56 N Long: 82-53-37 W
Pop: 1,770 (1990); 1,665 (1980) Pop Density: 1264.3
Land: 1.4 sq. mi.; Water: 0.0 sq. mi. Elev: 1014 ft.
In north-central OH, 14 mi. southeast of Marion. Not coextensive with the town of the same name.

***Cardington** — Township
ZIP: 43315 Lat: 40-31-01 N Long: 82-54-38 W
Pop: 2,651 (1990); 2,574 (1980) Pop Density: 111.4
Land: 23.8 sq. mi.; Water: 0.0 sq. mi.

Chester — Township
Lat: 40-27-29 N Long: 82-41-16 W
Pop: 1,613 (1990); 1,283 (1980) Pop Density: 61.1
Land: 26.4 sq. mi.; Water: 0.1 sq. mi.

Chesterville — Village
ZIP: 43317 Lat: 40-28-48 N Long: 82-40-58 W
Pop: 286 (1990); 242 (1980) Pop Density: 2860.0
Land: 0.1 sq. mi.; Water: 0.0 sq. mi. Elev: 1142 ft.

Congress — Township
Lat: 40-36-08 N Long: 82-44-26 W
Pop: 1,442 (1990); 1,200 (1980) Pop Density: 46.1
Land: 31.3 sq. mi.; Water: 0.3 sq. mi.

Edison — Village
ZIP: 43320 Lat: 40-33-28 N Long: 82-51-48 W
Pop: 488 (1990); 504 (1980) Pop Density: 1626.7
Land: 0.3 sq. mi.; Water: 0.0 sq. mi. Elev: 1062 ft.

Franklin — Township
Lat: 40-31-39 N Long: 82-42-23 W
Pop: 972 (1990); 918 (1980) Pop Density: 35.5
Land: 27.4 sq. mi.; Water: 0.1 sq. mi.

Fulton — Village
ZIP: 43321 Lat: 40-27-44 N Long: 82-49-42 W
Pop: 325 (1990); 378 (1980) Pop Density: 1625.0
Land: 0.2 sq. mi.; Water: 0.0 sq. mi. Elev: 1057 ft.

Gilead — Township
ZIP: 43338 Lat: 40-33-14 N Long: 82-49-41 W
Pop: 5,512 (1990); 5,571 (1980) Pop Density: 161.2
Land: 34.2 sq. mi.; Water: 0.1 sq. mi.

Harmony — Township
Lat: 40-28-05 N Long: 82-46-17 W
Pop: 1,594 (1990); 1,338 (1980) Pop Density: 66.4
Land: 24.0 sq. mi.; Water: 0.0 sq. mi.

Lincoln — Township
ZIP: 43321 Lat: 40-27-48 N Long: 82-51-47 W
Pop: 1,682 (1990); 1,546 (1980) Pop Density: 72.5
Land: 23.2 sq. mi.; Water: 0.0 sq. mi.

Marengo — Village
ZIP: 43334 Lat: 40-24-04 N Long: 82-48-36 W
Pop: 393 (1990); 329 (1980) Pop Density: 1965.0
Land: 0.2 sq. mi.; Water: 0.0 sq. mi. Elev: 1119 ft.

OHIO, Morrow County

Mount Gilead — Village
ZIP: 43338   **Lat:** 40-33-03 N   **Long:** 82-50-09 W
Pop: 2,846 (1990); 2,911 (1980)   **Pop Density:** 1497.9
Land: 1.9 sq. mi.; **Water:** 0.0 sq. mi.
Name origin: For Mt. Gilead, VA.

North Bloomfield — Township
Lat: 40-40-34 N   **Long:** 82-44-50 W
Pop: 1,808 (1990); 1,861 (1980)   **Pop Density:** 60.9
Land: 29.7 sq. mi.; **Water:** 0.0 sq. mi.

Perry — Township
Lat: 40-35-51 N   **Long:** 82-39-21 W
Pop: 1,646 (1990); 1,614 (1980)   **Pop Density:** 78.8
Land: 20.9 sq. mi.; **Water:** 0.0 sq. mi.

Peru — Township
ZIP: 43334   **Lat:** 40-23-23 N   **Long:** 82-53-07 W
Pop: 955 (1990); 921 (1980)   **Pop Density:** 40.8
Land: 23.4 sq. mi.; **Water:** 0.0 sq. mi.

South Bloomfield — Township
Lat: 40-22-48 N   **Long:** 82-41-26 W
Pop: 1,340 (1990); 1,314 (1980)   **Pop Density:** 51.7
Land: 25.9 sq. mi.; **Water:** 0.0 sq. mi.

Sparta — Village
ZIP: 43350   **Lat:** 40-23-40 N   **Long:** 82-41-58 W
Pop: 201 (1990); 219 (1980)   **Pop Density:** 2010.0
Land: 0.1 sq. mi.; **Water:** 0.0 sq. mi.

Troy — Township
Lat: 40-40-38 N   **Long:** 82-39-17 W
Pop: 1,096 (1990); 1,012 (1980)   **Pop Density:** 76.6
Land: 14.3 sq. mi.; **Water:** 0.4 sq. mi.

Washington — Township
Lat: 40-39-25 N   **Long:** 82-49-50 W
Pop: 1,159 (1990); 1,140 (1980)   **Pop Density:** 52.2
Land: 22.2 sq. mi.; **Water:** 0.1 sq. mi.

Westfield — Township
Lat: 40-27-05 N   **Long:** 82-58-32 W
Pop: 1,058 (1990); 1,093 (1980)   **Pop Density:** 40.7
Land: 26.0 sq. mi.; **Water:** 0.7 sq. mi.

Muskingum County
County Seat: Zanesville (ZIP: 43702)

Pop: 82,068 (1990); 83,340 (1980)   **Pop Density:** 123.5
Land: 664.6 sq. mi.; **Water:** 8.0 sq. mi.   **Area Code:** 614

In central OH, east of Columbus; organized Mar 1, 1804 from Washington and Fairfield counties.

Name origin: For the Muskingum River, which flows through it; from Algonquian but the meaning is uncertain, possibly 'by the river.'

Adams — Township
ZIP: 43821   **Lat:** 40-07-33 N   **Long:** 81-52-08 W
Pop: 397 (1990); 426 (1980)   **Pop Density:** 15.8
Land: 25.1 sq. mi.; **Water:** 0.3 sq. mi.

Adamsville — Village
ZIP: 43802   **Lat:** 40-04-07 N   **Long:** 81-52-59 W
Pop: 151 (1990); 229 (1980)   **Pop Density:** 1510.0
Land: 0.1 sq. mi.; **Water:** 0.0 sq. mi.

Blue Rock — Township
ZIP: 43720   **Lat:** 39-48-14 N   **Long:** 81-51-13 W
Pop: 519 (1990); 550 (1980)   **Pop Density:** 19.2
Land: 27.0 sq. mi.; **Water:** 0.3 sq. mi.

Brush Creek — Township
Lat: 39-49-16 N   **Long:** 81-58-40 W
Pop: 1,215 (1990); 1,256 (1980)   **Pop Density:** 40.1
Land: 30.3 sq. mi.; **Water:** 0.1 sq. mi.

Cass — Township
ZIP: 43821   **Lat:** 40-07-57 N   **Long:** 82-01-36 W
Pop: 1,197 (1990); 1,097 (1980)   **Pop Density:** 42.4
Land: 28.2 sq. mi.; **Water:** 0.4 sq. mi.

Clay — Township
Lat: 39-47-36 N   **Long:** 82-02-43 W
Pop: 1,126 (1990); 1,143 (1980)   **Pop Density:** 119.8
Land: 9.4 sq. mi.; **Water:** 0.0 sq. mi.

Dresden — Village
ZIP: 43821   **Lat:** 40-07-18 N   **Long:** 82-00-40 W
Pop: 1,581 (1990); 1,646 (1980)   **Pop Density:** 1437.3
Land: 1.1 sq. mi.; **Water:** 0.0 sq. mi.

Falls — Township
ZIP: 43701   **Lat:** 39-59-16 N   **Long:** 82-03-16 W
Pop: 8,524 (1990); 8,733 (1980)   **Pop Density:** 331.7
Land: 25.7 sq. mi.; **Water:** 1.3 sq. mi.

Frazeysburg — Village
ZIP: 43822   **Lat:** 40-06-58 N   **Long:** 82-07-07 W
Pop: 1,165 (1990); 1,025 (1980)   **Pop Density:** 1456.3
Land: 0.8 sq. mi.; **Water:** 0.0 sq. mi.
In southeast-central OH, 15 mi. north of Zanesville.
Name origin: For Samuel Frazey, who purchased the town site of Knoxville in 1828 and gave it the present name.

Fultonham — Village
Lat: 39-51-21 N   **Long:** 82-08-34 W
Pop: 178 (1990); 281 (1980)   **Pop Density:** 890.0
Land: 0.2 sq. mi.; **Water:** 0.0 sq. mi.

OHIO, Muskingum County

Gratiot — Village
ZIP: 43740   Lat: 39-57-01 N   Long: 82-13-05 W
Pop: 84 (1990); 126 (1980)   Pop Density: 2100.0
Land: 0.04 sq. mi.; Water: 0.0 sq. mi.   Elev: 988 ft.
In southeast-central OH, 10 mi. west of Zanesville. Part of the town is also in Licking County.
Name origin: For Gen. Charles Gratiot, a chief army engineer for the National Road between Columbus and Zanesville.

Harrison — Township
ZIP: 43771   Lat: 39-48-29 N   Long: 81-55-15 W
Pop: 1,508 (1990); 1,418 (1980)   Pop Density: 91.4
Land: 16.5 sq. mi.; Water: 0.4 sq. mi.

Highland — Township
Lat: 40-02-17 N   Long: 81-45-59 W
Pop: 820 (1990); 761 (1980)   Pop Density: 32.5
Land: 25.2 sq. mi.; Water: 0.0 sq. mi.

Hopewell — Township
ZIP: 43746   Lat: 39-57-36 N   Long: 82-09-40 W
Pop: 2,648 (1990); 2,371 (1980)   Pop Density: 69.1
Land: 38.3 sq. mi.; Water: 0.5 sq. mi.

Jackson — Township
Lat: 40-07-42 N   Long: 82-08-21 W
Pop: 2,076 (1990); 1,912 (1980)   Pop Density: 85.1
Land: 24.4 sq. mi.; Water: 0.0 sq. mi.

Jefferson — Township
ZIP: 43821   Lat: 40-06-49 N   Long: 82-00-43 W
Pop: 1,879 (1990); 1,917 (1980)   Pop Density: 894.8
Land: 2.1 sq. mi.; Water: 0.1 sq. mi.

Licking — Township
ZIP: 43830   Lat: 40-03-18 N   Long: 82-08-43 W
Pop: 1,878 (1990); 1,661 (1980)   Pop Density: 74.8
Land: 25.1 sq. mi.; Water: 0.7 sq. mi.

Madison — Township
ZIP: 43821   Lat: 40-05-45 N   Long: 81-57-10 W
Pop: 388 (1990); 378 (1980)   Pop Density: 13.8
Land: 28.1 sq. mi.; Water: 0.6 sq. mi.

Meigs — Township
Lat: 39-47-40 N   Long: 81-45-02 W
Pop: 165 (1990); 208 (1980)   Pop Density: 4.5
Land: 36.8 sq. mi.; Water: 0.6 sq. mi.

Monroe — Township
Lat: 40-07-06 N   Long: 81-45-53 W
Pop: 371 (1990); 378 (1980)   Pop Density: 15.0
Land: 24.7 sq. mi.; Water: 0.2 sq. mi.

Muskingum — Township
Lat: 40-03-24 N   Long: 82-02-18 W
Pop: 3,343 (1990); 2,712 (1980)   Pop Density: 110.3
Land: 30.3 sq. mi.; Water: 0.4 sq. mi.

New Concord — Village
ZIP: 43762   Lat: 39-59-50 N   Long: 81-44-08 W
Pop: 2,086 (1990); 1,860 (1980)   Pop Density: 2317.8
Land: 0.9 sq. mi.; Water: 0.0 sq. mi.
In southeast-central OH, 8 mi. west of Cambridge.
Name origin: For Concord, MA.

Newton — Township
ZIP: 43735   Lat: 39-51-38 N   Long: 82-05-08 W
Pop: 5,205 (1990); 5,230 (1980)   Pop Density: 112.4
Land: 46.3 sq. mi.; Water: 0.4 sq. mi.

North Zanesville — CDP
Lat: 39-58-55 N   Long: 82-00-00 W
Pop: 2,121 (1990); 2,166 (1980)   Pop Density: 1325.6
Land: 1.6 sq. mi.; Water: 0.0 sq. mi.

Norwich — Village
ZIP: 43767   Lat: 39-59-04 N   Long: 81-47-33 W
Pop: 133 (1990); 170 (1980)   Pop Density: 1330.0
Land: 0.1 sq. mi.; Water: 0.0 sq. mi.

Perry — Township
Lat: 39-58-25 N   Long: 81-52-03 W
Pop: 2,086 (1990); 1,959 (1980)   Pop Density: 81.5
Land: 25.6 sq. mi.; Water: 0.0 sq. mi.

Philo — Village
ZIP: 43771   Lat: 39-51-40 N   Long: 81-54-33 W
Pop: 810 (1990); 799 (1980)   Pop Density: 2025.0
Land: 0.4 sq. mi.; Water: 0.0 sq. mi.

Pleasant Grove — CDP
Lat: 39-56-58 N   Long: 81-57-34 W
Pop: 2,001 (1990)   Pop Density: 625.3
Land: 3.2 sq. mi.; Water: 0.0 sq. mi.

Rich Hill — Township
Lat: 39-53-06 N   Long: 81-44-32 W
Pop: 409 (1990); 381 (1980)   Pop Density: 11.3
Land: 36.3 sq. mi.; Water: 0.5 sq. mi.

Roseville — Village
ZIP: 43777   Lat: 39-48-24 N   Long: 82-04-15 W
Pop: 865 (1990); 896 (1980)   Pop Density: 2883.3
Land: 0.3 sq. mi.; Water: 0.0 sq. mi.   Elev: 737 ft.
Part of the town is also in Perry County.

Salem — Township
Lat: 40-02-53 N   Long: 81-51-34 W
Pop: 878 (1990); 936 (1980)   Pop Density: 34.8
Land: 25.2 sq. mi.; Water: 0.0 sq. mi.

Salt Creek — Township
Lat: 39-53-27 N   Long: 81-51-11 W
Pop: 965 (1990); 966 (1980)   Pop Density: 34.6
Land: 27.9 sq. mi.; Water: 0.0 sq. mi.

South Zanesville — Village
ZIP: 43701   Lat: 39-54-12 N   Long: 82-01-10 W
Pop: 1,969 (1990); 1,739 (1980)   Pop Density: 2812.9
Land: 0.7 sq. mi.; Water: 0.0 sq. mi.

Springfield — Township
ZIP: 43701   Lat: 39-55-22 N   Long: 82-04-05 W
Pop: 5,290 (1990); 5,607 (1980)   Pop Density: 284.4
Land: 18.6 sq. mi.; Water: 0.1 sq. mi.

Union — Township
Lat: 39-58-15 N   Long: 81-46-52 W
Pop: 3,687 (1990); 3,821 (1980)   Pop Density: 145.2
Land: 25.4 sq. mi.; Water: 0.0 sq. mi.

Washington — Township
Lat: 39-59-39 N   Long: 81-56-54 W
Pop: 4,202 (1990); 4,409 (1980)   Pop Density: 153.9
Land: 27.3 sq. mi.; Water: 0.4 sq. mi.

Wayne — Township
Lat: 39-54-04 N   Long: 81-56-31 W
Pop: 4,514 (1990); 4,455 (1980)   Pop Density: 185.8
Land: 24.3 sq. mi.; Water: 0.3 sq. mi.

Zanesville
City
ZIP: 43701 **Lat:** 39-57-08 N **Long:** 82-00-43 W
Pop: 26,778 (1990); 28,655 (1980) **Pop Density:** 2574.8
Land: 10.4 sq. mi.; **Water:** 0.3 sq. mi.

In southeast-central OH on the Muskingum River, 50 mi. east of Columbus.

Name origin: For Ebenezer Zane, who founded a settlement here he named Westbourne. It came to be known as Zane's Town, and the post office was established as Zanesville in 1800.

Noble County
County Seat: Caldwell (ZIP: 43724)

Pop: 11,336 (1990); 11,310 (1980) **Pop Density:** 28.4
Land: 399.0 sq. mi.; **Water:** 5.6 sq. mi. **Area Code:** 614

In east-central OH, south of Canton; organized Apr 1, 1851 from Monroe, Morgan, Guernsey, and Washington counties.

Name origin: For James and Warren P. Noble, early settlers.

Batesville
Village
Lat: 39-54-51 N **Long:** 81-16-52 W
Pop: 95 (1990); 129 (1980) **Pop Density:** 475.0
Land: 0.2 sq. mi.; **Water:** 0.0 sq. mi.

Beaver
Township
Lat: 39-54-37 N **Long:** 81-17-05 W
Pop: 572 (1990); 679 (1980) **Pop Density:** 19.5
Land: 29.3 sq. mi.; **Water:** 0.1 sq. mi.

Belle Valley
Village
ZIP: 43717 **Lat:** 39-47-19 N **Long:** 81-33-18 W
Pop: 267 (1990); 329 (1980) **Pop Density:** 890.0
Land: 0.3 sq. mi.; **Water:** 0.0 sq. mi.

Brookfield
Township
Lat: 39-47-35 N **Long:** 81-38-37 W
Pop: 119 (1990); 144 (1980) **Pop Density:** 4.0
Land: 29.8 sq. mi.; **Water:** 0.7 sq. mi.

Buffalo
Township
Lat: 39-52-05 N **Long:** 81-31-19 W
Pop: 645 (1990); 572 (1980) **Pop Density:** 26.3
Land: 24.5 sq. mi.; **Water:** 0.0 sq. mi.

Caldwell
Village
ZIP: 43724 **Lat:** 39-44-44 N **Long:** 81-30-47 W
Pop: 1,786 (1990); 1,935 (1980) **Pop Density:** 1984.4
Land: 0.9 sq. mi.; **Water:** 0.0 sq. mi. **Elev:** 744 ft.

In southeastern OH, southeast of Zanesville. Founded 1857. Rich coal-mining region.

Name origin: For the owners of the land on which the town was laid out.

Center
Township
Lat: 39-47-45 N **Long:** 81-27-20 W
Pop: 993 (1990); 935 (1980) **Pop Density:** 35.1
Land: 28.3 sq. mi.; **Water:** 0.0 sq. mi.

Dexter City
Village
ZIP: 45727 **Lat:** 39-39-33 N **Long:** 81-28-29 W
Pop: 161 (1990); 173 (1980) **Pop Density:** 805.0
Land: 0.2 sq. mi.; **Water:** 0.0 sq. mi.

Elk
Township
Lat: 39-38-36 N **Long:** 81-18-58 W
Pop: 378 (1990); 359 (1980) **Pop Density:** 13.0
Land: 29.1 sq. mi.; **Water:** 0.0 sq. mi.

Enoch
Township
Lat: 39-42-16 N **Long:** 81-26-01 W
Pop: 406 (1990); 419 (1980) **Pop Density:** 15.4
Land: 26.4 sq. mi.; **Water:** 0.0 sq. mi.

Jackson
Township
ZIP: 45727 **Lat:** 39-37-29 N **Long:** 81-32-16 W
Pop: 478 (1990); 536 (1980) **Pop Density:** 14.8
Land: 32.4 sq. mi.; **Water:** 0.0 sq. mi.

Jefferson
Township
Lat: 39-38-23 N **Long:** 81-23-32 W
Pop: 297 (1990); 297 (1980) **Pop Density:** 12.5
Land: 23.7 sq. mi.; **Water:** 0.0 sq. mi.

Marion
Township
Lat: 39-48-38 N **Long:** 81-21-21 W
Pop: 729 (1990); 678 (1980) **Pop Density:** 30.0
Land: 24.3 sq. mi.; **Water:** 0.0 sq. mi.

Noble
Township
Lat: 39-47-38 N **Long:** 81-33-16 W
Pop: 1,981 (1990); 1,903 (1980) **Pop Density:** 66.3
Land: 29.9 sq. mi.; **Water:** 0.5 sq. mi.

Olive
Township
Lat: 39-42-12 N **Long:** 81-30-41 W
Pop: 3,333 (1990); 3,383 (1980) **Pop Density:** 120.3
Land: 27.7 sq. mi.; **Water:** 0.0 sq. mi.

Sarahsville
Village
ZIP: 43779 **Lat:** 39-48-27 N **Long:** 81-28-10 W
Pop: 162 (1990); 226 (1980) **Pop Density:** 810.0
Land: 0.2 sq. mi.; **Water:** 0.0 sq. mi.

Seneca
Township
Lat: 39-51-58 N **Long:** 81-24-18 W
Pop: 357 (1990); 368 (1980) **Pop Density:** 15.1
Land: 23.7 sq. mi.; **Water:** 0.8 sq. mi.

Sharon
Township
ZIP: 43724 **Lat:** 39-42-07 N **Long:** 81-35-30 W
Pop: 338 (1990); 325 (1980) **Pop Density:** 12.4
Land: 27.3 sq. mi.; **Water:** 0.0 sq. mi.

Stock
Township
Lat: 39-44-03 N **Long:** 81-21-35 W
Pop: 354 (1990); 344 (1980) **Pop Density:** 14.4
Land: 24.6 sq. mi.; **Water:** 0.0 sq. mi.

Summerfield — Village
ZIP: 43788 Lat: 39-47-51 N Long: 81-20-09 W
Pop: 295 (1990); 299 (1980) Pop Density: 737.5
Land: 0.4 sq. mi.; Water: 0.0 sq. mi.

Wayne — Township
Lat: 39-54-47 N Long: 81-22-36 W
Pop: 356 (1990); 368 (1980) Pop Density: 19.9
Land: 17.9 sq. mi.; Water: 3.5 sq. mi.

Ottawa County
County Seat: Port Clinton (ZIP: 43452)

Pop: 40,029 (1990); 40,076 (1980) Pop Density: 156.9
Land: 255.1 sq. mi.; Water: 365.3 sq. mi. Area Code: 419
On the northern coast of Ohio, bordered on the north by Lake Erie; organized Mar 6, 1840 from Erie, Sandusky, and Lucas counties.
Name origin: For the Ottawa Indians, a tribe of Algonquian linguistic stock. Tribal name is derived from *adawe* 'to trade,' for their ability as intertribal traders and barterers.

Allen — Township
Lat: 41-35-17 N Long: 83-21-27 W
Pop: 3,177 (1990); 3,322 (1980) Pop Density: 125.6
Land: 25.3 sq. mi.; Water: 0.0 sq. mi.

Bay — Township
Lat: 41-29-02 N Long: 83-00-57 W
Pop: 1,276 (1990); 1,815 (1980) Pop Density: 78.8
Land: 16.2 sq. mi.; Water: 5.7 sq. mi.

Benton — Township
Lat: 41-34-06 N Long: 83-14-24 W
Pop: 2,471 (1990); 2,446 (1980) Pop Density: 55.9
Land: 44.2 sq. mi.; Water: 0.2 sq. mi.

Carroll — Township
Lat: 41-34-44 N Long: 83-07-34 W
Pop: 1,735 (1990); 1,706 (1980) Pop Density: 51.3
Land: 33.8 sq. mi.; Water: 2.5 sq. mi.

Catawba Island — Township
ZIP: 43452 Lat: 41-34-18 N Long: 82-50-29 W
Pop: 3,148 (1990); 3,402 (1980) Pop Density: 552.3
Land: 5.7 sq. mi.; Water: 12.4 sq. mi.

Clay — Township
ZIP: 43430 Lat: 41-31-37 N Long: 83-21-18 W
Pop: 5,267 (1990); 5,359 (1980) Pop Density: 202.6
Land: 26.0 sq. mi.; Water: 0.0 sq. mi.

Clay Center — Village
ZIP: 43408 Lat: 41-34-07 N Long: 83-21-39 W
Pop: 289 (1990); 327 (1980) Pop Density: 361.3
Land: 0.8 sq. mi.; Water: 0.0 sq. mi.

Danbury — Township
Lat: 41-31-31 N Long: 82-45-17 W
Pop: 4,410 (1990); 4,414 (1980) Pop Density: 242.3
Land: 18.2 sq. mi.; Water: 38.2 sq. mi.

Elmore — Village
ZIP: 43416 Lat: 41-28-22 N Long: 83-17-30 W
Pop: 1,334 (1990); 1,271 (1980) Pop Density: 2223.3
Land: 0.6 sq. mi.; Water: 0.0 sq. mi.
In northern OH on the Portage River.

Erie — Township
Lat: 41-31-50 N Long: 83-01-35 W
Pop: 1,454 (1990); 1,518 (1980) Pop Density: 118.2
Land: 12.3 sq. mi.; Water: 1.4 sq. mi.

Genoa — Village
ZIP: 43430 Lat: 41-31-06 N Long: 83-21-39 W
Pop: 2,262 (1990); 2,213 (1980) Pop Density: 2262.0
Land: 1.0 sq. mi.; Water: 0.0 sq. mi.
In northern OH, 15 mi. south of Lake Erie and 20 mi. southeast of Toledo.

Harris — Township
Lat: 41-28-56 N Long: 83-15-07 W
Pop: 2,765 (1990); 2,688 (1980) Pop Density: 98.0
Land: 28.2 sq. mi.; Water: 0.2 sq. mi.

Marblehead — Village
ZIP: 43440 Lat: 41-31-54 N Long: 82-43-17 W
Pop: 745 (1990); 679 (1980) Pop Density: 392.1
Land: 1.9 sq. mi.; Water: 0.9 sq. mi.

Oak Harbor — Village
ZIP: 43449 Lat: 41-30-41 N Long: 83-08-47 W
Pop: 2,637 (1990); 2,678 (1980) Pop Density: 2028.5
Land: 1.3 sq. mi.; Water: 0.1 sq. mi. Elev: 585 ft.
In northern OH on the Portage River, southeast of Toledo.
Name origin: For the many oaks once in the area and for the harbor of Sandusky Bay.

Portage — Township
Lat: 41-29-26 N Long: 82-53-53 W
Pop: 1,600 (1990); 7,916 (1980) Pop Density: 177.8
Land: 9.0 sq. mi.; Water: 12.6 sq. mi.

Port Clinton — City
ZIP: 43452 Lat: 41-30-34 N Long: 82-56-18 W
Pop: 7,106 (1990); 7,223 (1980) Pop Density: 3383.8
Land: 2.1 sq. mi.; Water: 0.2 sq. mi.
In northern OH, 30 mi. southeast of Toledo.
Name origin: For DeWitt Clinton (1769–1828), NY governor (1817–23, 1825–28) and supporter of the Erie Canal.

Put-in-Bay — Village
Lat: 41-39-11 N Long: 82-48-54 W
Pop: 141 (1990); 146 (1980) Pop Density: 352.5
Land: 0.4 sq. mi.; Water: 0.2 sq. mi.
Not coextensive with the town of the same name.

*Put-in-Bay — Township
Lat: 41-40-30 N Long: 82-48-52 W
Pop: 556 (1990); 556 (1980) Pop Density: 111.2
Land: 5.0 sq. mi.; Water: 0.3 sq. mi.

OHIO, Ottawa County

Rocky Ridge   Village
ZIP: 43458   **Lat:** 41-31-49 N   **Long:** 83-12-48 W
Pop: 425 (1990); 457 (1980)   **Pop Density:** 425.0
Land: 1.0 sq. mi.; **Water:** 0.0 sq. mi.   **Elev:** 608 ft.

Salem   Township
ZIP: 43449   **Lat:** 41-29-39 N   **Long:** 83-07-37 W
Pop: 5,064 (1990); 4,934 (1980)   **Pop Density:** 174.0
Land: 29.1 sq. mi.; **Water:** 1.2 sq. mi.

Paulding County
County Seat: Paulding (ZIP: 45879)

Pop: 20,488 (1990); 21,302 (1980)   **Pop Density:** 49.2
Land: 416.3 sq. mi.; **Water:** 2.6 sq. mi.   **Area Code:** 419
On the northwest coast of OH; organized Feb 12, 1820 from Indian lands.
Name origin: For John Paulding (1758–1818) of Peekskill, NY, one of the captors (1780) of British spy John André (1750–80) during the Revolutionary War.

Antwerp   Village
ZIP: 45813   **Lat:** 41-10-50 N   **Long:** 84-44-20 W
Pop: 1,677 (1990); 1,765 (1980)   **Pop Density:** 1524.5
Land: 1.1 sq. mi.; **Water:** 0.0 sq. mi.   **Elev:** 732 ft.
Name origin: Named by Dutch and German settlers, probably for the Belgian city.

Auglaize   Township
Lat: 41-11-06 N   **Long:** 84-24-32 W
Pop: 1,521 (1990); 1,427 (1980)   **Pop Density:** 70.7
Land: 21.5 sq. mi.; **Water:** 0.7 sq. mi.

Benton   Township
Lat: 41-02-25 N   **Long:** 84-44-45 W
Pop: 1,054 (1990); 1,168 (1980)   **Pop Density:** 28.9
Land: 36.5 sq. mi.; **Water:** 0.0 sq. mi.

Blue Creek   Township
Lat: 41-01-56 N   **Long:** 84-37-29 W
Pop: 828 (1990); 829 (1980)   **Pop Density:** 22.9
Land: 36.2 sq. mi.; **Water:** 0.0 sq. mi.

Broughton   Village
Lat: 41-05-16 N   **Long:** 84-32-09 W
Pop: 151 (1990); 171 (1980)   **Pop Density:** 755.0
Land: 0.2 sq. mi.; **Water:** 0.0 sq. mi.   **Elev:** 726 ft.

Brown   Township
Lat: 41-07-10 N   **Long:** 84-23-28 W
Pop: 2,408 (1990); 2,594 (1980)   **Pop Density:** 64.7
Land: 37.2 sq. mi.; **Water:** 0.5 sq. mi.

Carryall   Township
Lat: 41-12-38 N   **Long:** 84-44-18 W
Pop: 3,039 (1990); 3,016 (1980)   **Pop Density:** 85.4
Land: 35.6 sq. mi.; **Water:** 0.6 sq. mi.

Cecil   Village
ZIP: 45821   **Lat:** 41-13-08 N   **Long:** 84-36-05 W
Pop: 249 (1990); 267 (1980)   **Pop Density:** 166.0
Land: 1.5 sq. mi.; **Water:** 0.0 sq. mi.   **Elev:** 725 ft.

Crane   Township
Lat: 41-12-31 N   **Long:** 84-37-59 W
Pop: 1,527 (1990); 1,613 (1980)   **Pop Density:** 42.4
Land: 36.0 sq. mi.; **Water:** 0.5 sq. mi.

Emerald   Township
Lat: 41-12-44 N   **Long:** 84-31-30 W
Pop: 766 (1990); 852 (1980)   **Pop Density:** 23.4
Land: 32.7 sq. mi.; **Water:** 0.0 sq. mi.

Grover Hill   Village
ZIP: 45849   **Lat:** 41-01-07 N   **Long:** 84-28-37 W
Pop: 518 (1990); 486 (1980)   **Pop Density:** 1726.7
Land: 0.3 sq. mi.; **Water:** 0.0 sq. mi.
In northwest OH, 20 mi. southwest of Defiance.

Harrison   Township
Lat: 41-07-42 N   **Long:** 84-45-04 W
Pop: 1,712 (1990); 1,720 (1980)   **Pop Density:** 47.3
Land: 36.2 sq. mi.; **Water:** 0.0 sq. mi.

Haviland   Village
ZIP: 45851   **Lat:** 41-01-06 N   **Long:** 84-34-52 W
Pop: 210 (1990); 219 (1980)   **Pop Density:** 700.0
Land: 0.3 sq. mi.; **Water:** 0.0 sq. mi.   **Elev:** 736 ft.

Jackson   Township
Lat: 41-06-56 N   **Long:** 84-30-37 W
Pop: 1,821 (1990); 1,952 (1980)   **Pop Density:** 49.5
Land: 36.8 sq. mi.; **Water:** 0.1 sq. mi.

Latty   Village
ZIP: 45855   **Lat:** 41-05-17 N   **Long:** 84-35-00 W
Pop: 205 (1990); 261 (1980)   **Pop Density:** 683.3
Land: 0.3 sq. mi.; **Water:** 0.0 sq. mi.   **Elev:** 730 ft.

***Latty**   Township
Lat: 41-01-58 N   **Long:** 84-30-36 W
Pop: 1,113 (1990); 1,101 (1980)   **Pop Density:** 30.6
Land: 36.4 sq. mi.; **Water:** 0.0 sq. mi.

Melrose   Village
ZIP: 45861   **Lat:** 41-05-22 N   **Long:** 84-25-10 W
Pop: 307 (1990); 315 (1980)   **Pop Density:** 341.1
Land: 0.9 sq. mi.; **Water:** 0.0 sq. mi.

Oakwood   Village
ZIP: 45873   **Lat:** 41-05-33 N   **Long:** 84-22-34 W
Pop: 709 (1990); 886 (1980)   **Pop Density:** 1181.7
Land: 0.6 sq. mi.; **Water:** 0.0 sq. mi.   **Elev:** 1079 ft.

Paulding   Village
ZIP: 45879   **Lat:** 41-08-12 N   **Long:** 84-34-57 W
Pop: 2,605 (1990); 2,754 (1980)   **Pop Density:** 2003.8
Land: 1.3 sq. mi.; **Water:** 0.1 sq. mi.   **Elev:** 723 ft.
In northwestern OH, 40 mi. northwest of Lima. Not coextensive with the town of the same name.
Name origin: For John Paulding (1758–1818) of Peekskill, NY, one of the captors (1780) of British spy John André (1750–80), during the Revolutionary War.

Paulding Township
ZIP: 45879 Lat: 41-07-13 N Long: 84-38-02 W
Pop: 3,978 (1990); 4,288 (1980) Pop Density: 110.2
Land: 36.1 sq. mi.; Water: 0.1 sq. mi.

Payne Village
ZIP: 45880 Lat: 41-04-45 N Long: 84-43-38 W
Pop: 1,244 (1990); 1,399 (1980) Pop Density: 2488.0
Land: 0.5 sq. mi.; Water: 0.0 sq. mi. Elev: 753 ft.
In northwestern OH, 35 mi. east of Fort Wayne, IN.

Scott Village
ZIP: 45886 Lat: 40-59-36 N Long: 84-35-10 W
Pop: 138 (1990); 135 (1980) Pop Density: 460.0
Land: 0.3 sq. mi.; Water: 0.0 sq. mi. Elev: 742 ft.
Part of the town is also in Van Wert County.

Washington Township
Lat: 41-01-59 N Long: 84-23-54 W
Pop: 721 (1990); 742 (1980) Pop Density: 20.6
Land: 35.0 sq. mi.; Water: 0.1 sq. mi.

Perry County
County Seat: New Lexington (ZIP: 43764)

Pop: 31,557 (1990); 31,032 (1980) Pop Density: 77.0
Land: 410.0 sq. mi.; Water: 2.6 sq. mi. Area Code: 614

In central OH, southeast of Columbus; organized Mar 1, 1818 from Washington, Fairfield, and Muskingum counties.

Name origin: For Oliver Hazard Perry (1785–1819), U.S. naval officer during the War of 1812, famous for the message, "We have met the enemy and they are ours."

Bearfield Township
Lat: 39-41-32 N Long: 82-04-43 W
Pop: 1,267 (1990); 1,261 (1980) Pop Density: 46.2
Land: 27.4 sq. mi.; Water: 0.2 sq. mi.

Clayton Township
ZIP: 43764 Lat: 39-47-00 N Long: 82-11-39 W
Pop: 1,121 (1990); 1,038 (1980) Pop Density: 35.8
Land: 31.3 sq. mi.; Water: 0.3 sq. mi.

Coal Township
ZIP: 43766 Lat: 39-34-36 N Long: 82-12-55 W
Pop: 1,156 (1990); 1,257 (1980) Pop Density: 82.6
Land: 14.0 sq. mi.; Water: 0.0 sq. mi.

Corning Village
ZIP: 43730 Lat: 39-36-08 N Long: 82-05-19 W
Pop: 703 (1990); 789 (1980) Pop Density: 1757.5
Land: 0.4 sq. mi.; Water: 0.0 sq. mi. Elev: 732 ft.
In southeast-central OH in Wayne National Forest.

Crooksville Village
ZIP: 43731 Lat: 39-46-05 N Long: 82-05-41 W
Pop: 2,601 (1990); 2,766 (1980) Pop Density: 1734.0
Land: 1.5 sq. mi.; Water: 0.0 sq. mi.
In southeast-central OH, 10 mi. south of Zanesville.

Glenford Village
ZIP: 43739 Lat: 39-53-10 N Long: 82-19-11 W
Pop: 208 (1990); 173 (1980) Pop Density: 2080.0
Land: 0.1 sq. mi.; Water: 0.0 sq. mi. Elev: 844 ft.

Harrison Township
ZIP: 43731 Lat: 39-46-20 N Long: 82-06-47 W
Pop: 5,235 (1990); 5,364 (1980) Pop Density: 225.6
Land: 23.2 sq. mi.; Water: 0.1 sq. mi.

Hemlock Village
Lat: 39-35-20 N Long: 82-09-19 W
Pop: 203 (1990); 197 (1980) Pop Density: 507.5
Land: 0.4 sq. mi.; Water: 0.0 sq. mi. Elev: 765 ft.

Hopewell Township
Lat: 39-52-31 N Long: 82-17-48 W
Pop: 1,724 (1990); 1,512 (1980) Pop Density: 45.7
Land: 37.7 sq. mi.; Water: 0.0 sq. mi.

Jackson Township
ZIP: 43748 Lat: 39-42-10 N Long: 82-18-34 W
Pop: 2,266 (1990); 2,040 (1980) Pop Density: 59.8
Land: 37.9 sq. mi.; Water: 0.0 sq. mi.

Junction City Village
ZIP: 43748 Lat: 39-43-17 N Long: 82-18-00 W
Pop: 770 (1990); 754 (1980) Pop Density: 1283.3
Land: 0.6 sq. mi.; Water: 0.0 sq. mi.
In southeast-central OH, 18 mi. east of Lancaster.
Name origin: For its location at a railroad junction.

Madison Township
ZIP: 43760 Lat: 39-52-03 N Long: 82-11-57 W
Pop: 908 (1990); 774 (1980) Pop Density: 39.0
Land: 23.3 sq. mi.; Water: 0.0 sq. mi.

Monday Creek Township
Lat: 39-37-25 N Long: 82-19-21 W
Pop: 501 (1990); 567 (1980) Pop Density: 19.8
Land: 25.3 sq. mi.; Water: 0.0 sq. mi.

Monroe Township
Lat: 39-35-45 N Long: 82-05-23 W
Pop: 1,514 (1990); 1,628 (1980) Pop Density: 45.2
Land: 33.5 sq. mi.; Water: 0.1 sq. mi.

New Lexington Village
ZIP: 43764 Lat: 39-42-47 N Long: 82-12-29 W
Pop: 5,117 (1990); 5,179 (1980) Pop Density: 3010.0
Land: 1.7 sq. mi.; Water: 0.0 sq. mi. Elev: 958 ft.
In southeast-central OH, 19 mi. southwest of Zanesville.
Name origin: For Lexington, MA.

New Straitsville Village
ZIP: 43766 Lat: 39-34-40 N Long: 82-14-09 W
Pop: 865 (1990); 937 (1980) Pop Density: 665.4
Land: 1.3 sq. mi.; Water: 0.0 sq. mi. Elev: 862 ft.

Pike Township
ZIP: 43764 Lat: 39-41-30 N Long: 82-12-07 W
Pop: 6,821 (1990); 6,697 (1980) Pop Density: 213.2
Land: 32.0 sq. mi.; Water: 0.6 sq. mi.

OHIO, Perry County

Pleasant
Township
ZIP: 43731   **Lat:** 39-39-22 N   **Long:** 82-07-28 W
Pop: 782 (1990); 817 (1980)   **Pop Density:** 49.5
Land: 15.8 sq. mi.; **Water:** 0.4 sq. mi.

Reading
Township
ZIP: 43783   **Lat:** 39-47-06 N   **Long:** 82-19-08 W
Pop: 3,546 (1990); 3,484 (1980)   **Pop Density:** 70.1
Land: 50.6 sq. mi.; **Water:** 0.1 sq. mi.

Rendville
Village
ZIP: 43730   **Lat:** 39-37-09 N   **Long:** 82-05-24 W
Pop: 32 (1990); 68 (1980)   **Pop Density:** 106.7
Land: 0.3 sq. mi.; **Water:** 0.0 sq. mi.

Roseville
Village
ZIP: 43777   **Lat:** 39-48-27 N   **Long:** 82-04-31 W
Pop: 982 (1990); 1,019 (1980)   **Pop Density:** 3273.3
Land: 0.3 sq. mi.; **Water:** 0.0 sq. mi.   **Elev:** 737 ft.
Part of the town is also in Muskingum County.

Salt Lick
Township
Lat: 39-36-59 N   **Long:** 82-12-13 W
Pop: 1,262 (1990); 1,444 (1980)   **Pop Density:** 61.0
Land: 20.7 sq. mi.; **Water:** 0.0 sq. mi.

Shawnee
Village
ZIP: 43782   **Lat:** 39-36-37 N   **Long:** 82-12-26 W
Pop: 742 (1990); 924 (1980)   **Pop Density:** 371.0
Land: 2.0 sq. mi.; **Water:** 0.0 sq. mi.

Somerset
Village
ZIP: 43783   **Lat:** 39-48-20 N   **Long:** 82-18-00 W
Pop: 1,390 (1990); 1,432 (1980)   **Pop Density:** 1263.6
Land: 1.1 sq. mi.; **Water:** 0.0 sq. mi.   **Elev:** 1065 ft

Thorn
Township
Lat: 39-52-54 N   **Long:** 82-24-24 W
Pop: 3,454 (1990); 3,149 (1980)   **Pop Density:** 92.6
Land: 37.3 sq. mi.; **Water:** 0.7 sq. mi.

Thornville
Village
ZIP: 43076   **Lat:** 39-53-45 N   **Long:** 82-25-09 W
Pop: 758 (1990); 838 (1980)   **Pop Density:** 2526.7
Land: 0.3 sq. mi.; **Water:** 0.0 sq. mi.

Pickaway County
County Seat: Circleville (ZIP: 43113)

Pop: 48,255 (1990); 43,662 (1980)   **Pop Density:** 96.1
Land: 502.2 sq. mi.; **Water:** 4.7 sq. mi.   **Area Code:** 614

In central OH, south of Columbus; organized Jan 12, 1810 from Ross, Fairfield, and Franklin counties.

Name origin: A folk etymological form of *Piqua*, believed to be the name of the Shawnee subtribe to which Tecumseh (1768–1813) belonged. Name is thought to mean 'ashes,' referring to the myth that the first man of their tribe rose out of ashes.

Ashville
Village
ZIP: 43103   **Lat:** 39-43-03 N   **Long:** 82-57-18 W
Pop: 2,254 (1990); 2,046 (1980)   **Pop Density:** 2504.4
Land: 0.9 sq. mi.; **Water:** 0.0 sq. mi.   **Elev:** 709 ft.
In south-central OH, 30 mi. south of Columbus.

Circleville
City
ZIP: 43113   **Lat:** 39-36-06 N   **Long:** 82-56-20 W
Pop: 11,666 (1990); 11,700 (1980)   **Pop Density:** 2845.4
Land: 4.1 sq. mi.; **Water:** 0.0 sq. mi.   **Elev:** 702 ft.
In south-central OH on the Scioto River, 25 mi. south of Columbus. Settled 1806; incorporated as a village 1814, as a city 1853.
Name origin: For the ancient circular Mound Builders' earthworks at the site. The mounds contain prehistoric bones and artifacts.

*Circleville
Township
ZIP: 43113   **Lat:** 39-36-42 N   **Long:** 82-56-32 W
Pop: 15,154 (1990); 15,039 (1980)   **Pop Density:** 977.7
Land: 15.5 sq. mi.; **Water:** 0.3 sq. mi.

Commercial Point
Village
ZIP: 43116   **Lat:** 39-46-09 N   **Long:** 83-03-28 W
Pop: 405 (1990); 316 (1980)   **Pop Density:** 1012.5
Land: 0.4 sq. mi.; **Water:** 0.0 sq. mi.

Darby
Township
Lat: 39-45-47 N   **Long:** 83-12-03 W
Pop: 3,484 (1990); 3,268 (1980)   **Pop Density:** 101.6
Land: 34.3 sq. mi.; **Water:** 0.1 sq. mi.

Darbyville
Village
ZIP: 43146   **Lat:** 39-41-44 N   **Long:** 83-06-51 W
Pop: 272 (1990); 282 (1980)   **Pop Density:** 544.0
Land: 0.5 sq. mi.; **Water:** 0.0 sq. mi.

Deer Creek
Township
Lat: 39-33-17 N   **Long:** 83-07-00 W
Pop: 1,431 (1990); 1,438 (1980)   **Pop Density:** 39.4
Land: 36.3 sq. mi.; **Water:** 0.0 sq. mi.

Harrisburg
Village
ZIP: 43126   **Lat:** 39-48-31 N   **Long:** 83-10-15 W
Pop: 0 (1990); 7 (1980)
Land: 0.006 sq. mi.; **Water:** 0.0 sq. mi.
Part of the town is also in Franklin County.

Harrison
Township
ZIP: 43103   **Lat:** 39-44-48 N   **Long:** 82-58-32 W
Pop: 5,292 (1990); 5,001 (1980)   **Pop Density:** 191.0
Land: 27.7 sq. mi.; **Water:** 0.4 sq. mi.

Jackson
Township
ZIP: 43113   **Lat:** 39-38-22 N   **Long:** 83-01-56 W
Pop: 911 (1990); 839 (1980)   **Pop Density:** 21.4
Land: 42.5 sq. mi.; **Water:** 0.2 sq. mi.

Logan Elm Village
CDP
ZIP: 43113 **Lat:** 39-34-18 N **Long:** 82-56-50 W
Pop: 1,287 (1990) **Pop Density:** 2574.0
Land: 0.5 sq. mi.; **Water:** 0.0 sq. mi.

Madison
Township
Lat: 39-45-53 N **Long:** 82-52-31 W
Pop: 1,586 (1990); 1,485 (1980) **Pop Density:** 61.0
Land: 26.0 sq. mi.; **Water:** 0.1 sq. mi.

Monroe
Township
Lat: 39-39-31 N **Long:** 83-11-13 W
Pop: 1,124 (1990); 1,128 (1980) **Pop Density:** 27.8
Land: 40.4 sq. mi.; **Water:** 1.2 sq. mi.

Muhlenberg
Township
Lat: 39-41-52 N **Long:** 83-07-01 W
Pop: 664 (1990); 734 (1980) **Pop Density:** 29.5
Land: 22.5 sq. mi.; **Water:** 0.2 sq. mi.

New Holland
Village
ZIP: 43145 **Lat:** 39-33-05 N **Long:** 83-15-18 W
Pop: 739 (1990); 667 (1980) **Pop Density:** 568.5
Land: 1.3 sq. mi.; **Water:** 0.0 sq. mi. **Elev:** 851 ft.
Part of the town is also in Fayette County.

Orient
Village
ZIP: 43146 **Lat:** 39-48-20 N **Long:** 83-09-05 W
Pop: 273 (1990); 283 (1980) **Pop Density:** 2730.0
Land: 0.1 sq. mi.; **Water:** 0.0 sq. mi. **Elev:** 841 ft.

Perry
Township
ZIP: 43145 **Lat:** 39-33-44 N **Long:** 83-12-49 W
Pop: 1,326 (1990); 1,427 (1980) **Pop Density:** 36.0
Land: 36.8 sq. mi.; **Water:** 1.0 sq. mi.

Pickaway
Township
ZIP: 43113 **Lat:** 39-31-32 N **Long:** 82-55-13 W
Pop: 1,642 (1990); 1,608 (1980) **Pop Density:** 33.7
Land: 48.7 sq. mi.; **Water:** 0.3 sq. mi.

Salt Creek
Township
Lat: 39-30-47 N **Long:** 82-47-36 W
Pop: 2,069 (1990); 1,936 (1980) **Pop Density:** 57.6
Land: 35.9 sq. mi.; **Water:** 0.0 sq. mi.

Scioto
Township
ZIP: 43103 **Lat:** 39-46-08 N **Long:** 83-04-17 W
Pop: 8,231 (1990); 4,458 (1980) **Pop Density:** 184.1
Land: 44.7 sq. mi.; **Water:** 0.3 sq. mi.

South Bloomfield
Village
ZIP: 43103 **Lat:** 39-42-57 N **Long:** 82-59-24 W
Pop: 900 (1990); 934 (1980) **Pop Density:** 1125.0
Land: 0.8 sq. mi.; **Water:** 0.0 sq. mi.

Tarlton
Village
Lat: 39-33-15 N **Long:** 82-46-38 W
Pop: 315 (1990); 394 (1980) **Pop Density:** 787.5
Land: 0.4 sq. mi.; **Water:** 0.0 sq. mi. **Elev:** 892 ft.

Walnut
Township
Lat: 39-41-26 N **Long:** 82-53-56 W
Pop: 2,179 (1990); 2,104 (1980) **Pop Density:** 55.4
Land: 39.3 sq. mi.; **Water:** 0.1 sq. mi.

Washington
Township
ZIP: 43113 **Lat:** 39-36-20 N **Long:** 82-52-27 W
Pop: 2,662 (1990); 2,666 (1980) **Pop Density:** 106.9
Land: 24.9 sq. mi.; **Water:** 0.3 sq. mi.

Wayne
Township
ZIP: 43113 **Lat:** 39-34-17 N **Long:** 83-01-22 W
Pop: 500 (1990); 531 (1980) **Pop Density:** 18.6
Land: 26.9 sq. mi.; **Water:** 0.2 sq. mi.

Williamsport
Village
ZIP: 43164 **Lat:** 39-35-00 N **Long:** 83-07-00 W
Pop: 851 (1990); 792 (1980) **Pop Density:** 654.6
Land: 1.3 sq. mi.; **Water:** 0.0 sq. mi. **Elev:** 771 ft.

Pike County
County Seat: Waverly City (ZIP: 45690)

Pop: 24,249 (1990); 22,802 (1980) **Pop Density:** 54.9
Land: 441.5 sq. mi.; **Water:** 2.5 sq. mi. **Area Code:** 614
In south-central OH, south of Columbus; organized Jan 4, 1815 from Ross, Highland, and Scioto counties.
Name origin: For Gen. Zebulon Montgomery Pike (1779–1813), U.S. army officer and discoverer of Pikes Peak, CO.

Beaver
Village
ZIP: 45613 **Lat:** 39-01-56 N **Long:** 82-49-30 W
Pop: 336 (1990); 330 (1980) **Pop Density:** 840.0
Land: 0.4 sq. mi.; **Water:** 0.0 sq. mi.
Not coextensive with the town of the same name.

*Beaver
Township
ZIP: 45613 **Lat:** 39-03-12 N **Long:** 82-51-38 W
Pop: 1,335 (1990); 1,115 (1980) **Pop Density:** 56.1
Land: 23.8 sq. mi.; **Water:** 0.0 sq. mi.

Benton
Township
Lat: 39-07-46 N **Long:** 83-11-56 W
Pop: 1,312 (1990); 1,147 (1980) **Pop Density:** 34.0
Land: 38.6 sq. mi.; **Water:** 0.0 sq. mi.

Camp Creek
Township
Lat: 38-58-47 N **Long:** 83-07-59 W
Pop: 724 (1990); 706 (1980) **Pop Density:** 26.5
Land: 27.3 sq. mi.; **Water:** 0.1 sq. mi.

Jackson
Township
Lat: 39-07-56 N **Long:** 82-52-07 W
Pop: 1,298 (1990); 1,174 (1980) **Pop Density:** 25.2
Land: 51.5 sq. mi.; **Water:** 0.6 sq. mi.

Marion
Township
Lat: 38-59-33 N **Long:** 82-50-15 W
Pop: 1,024 (1990); 1,163 (1980) **Pop Density:** 45.3
Land: 22.6 sq. mi.; **Water:** 0.0 sq. mi.

Mifflin
Township
ZIP: 45646 Lat: 39-05-16 N Long: 83-17-34 W
Pop: 1,146 (1990); 1,051 (1980) Pop Density: 24.9
Land: 46.1 sq. mi.; Water: 0.1 sq. mi.

Newton
Township
Lat: 39-02-33 N Long: 83-05-27 W
Pop: 1,587 (1990); 1,476 (1980) Pop Density: 51.9
Land: 30.6 sq. mi.; Water: 0.2 sq. mi.

Pebble
Township
Lat: 39-08-03 N Long: 83-05-55 W
Pop: 1,625 (1990); 1,342 (1980) Pop Density: 44.0
Land: 36.9 sq. mi.; Water: 0.0 sq. mi.

Pee Pee
Township
ZIP: 45690 Lat: 39-07-39 N Long: 83-00-24 W
Pop: 7,481 (1990); 6,986 (1980) Pop Density: 236.0
Land: 31.7 sq. mi.; Water: 0.7 sq. mi.

Perry
Township
Lat: 39-09-39 N Long: 83-19-26 W
Pop: 690 (1990); 785 (1980) Pop Density: 30.0
Land: 23.0 sq. mi.; Water: 0.0 sq. mi.

Piketon
Village
ZIP: 45661 Lat: 39-04-05 N Long: 82-59-59 W
Pop: 1,717 (1990); 1,726 (1980) Pop Density: 817.6
Land: 2.1 sq. mi.; Water: 0.1 sq. mi. Elev: 578 ft.
In southern OH, 10 mi. south of Waverley.
Name origin: For Gen. Zebulon Montgomery Pike (1779–1813), U.S. army officer and discoverer of Pikes Peak, CO.

Scioto
Township
Lat: 38-59-40 N Long: 82-59-55 W
Pop: 1,170 (1990); 1,049 (1980) Pop Density: 47.6
Land: 24.6 sq. mi.; Water: 0.4 sq. mi.

Seal
Township
Lat: 39-03-57 N Long: 82-58-34 W
Pop: 2,619 (1990); 2,754 (1980) Pop Density: 91.9
Land: 28.5 sq. mi.; Water: 0.4 sq. mi.

Sunfish
Township
Lat: 39-02-16 N Long: 83-12-26 W
Pop: 1,091 (1990); 1,031 (1980) Pop Density: 33.4
Land: 32.7 sq. mi.; Water: 0.0 sq. mi.

Union
Township
Lat: 39-00-07 N Long: 82-55-08 W
Pop: 1,147 (1990); 1,023 (1980) Pop Density: 48.6
Land: 23.6 sq. mi.; Water: 0.0 sq. mi.

Waverly City
City
ZIP: 45690 Lat: 39-07-31 N Long: 82-58-56 W
Pop: 4,477 (1990); 4,603 (1980) Pop Density: 1119.3
Land: 4.0 sq. mi.; Water: 0.0 sq. mi.
In southern OH, 15 mi. south of Chillicothe. Founded 1829.
Name origin: For Sir Walter Scott's (1771–1832) novel *Waverly* (1814).

Portage County
County Seat: Ravenna (ZIP: 44266)

Pop: 142,585 (1990); 135,856 (1980) Pop Density: 289.6
Land: 492.4 sq. mi.; Water: 14.7 sq. mi. Area Code: 216

In northeastern OH, east of Akron; organized Jun 7, 1807 from Trumbull and Jackson counties.

Name origin: For the portage of canoes or other craft between the Cuyahoga and Mahoning rivers.

Atwater
Township
ZIP: 44201 Lat: 41-01-28 N Long: 81-09-05 W
Pop: 2,663 (1990); 2,691 (1980) Pop Density: 102.8
Land: 25.9 sq. mi.; Water: 0.1 sq. mi.

Aurora
City
ZIP: 44202 Lat: 41-18-43 N Long: 81-20-40 W
Pop: 9,192 (1990); 8,177 (1980) Pop Density: 394.5
Land: 23.3 sq. mi.; Water: 0.9 sq. mi. Elev: 1130 ft.
In northeastern OH, 21 mi. southeast of Cleveland.
Name origin: For the ancient Roman goddess of the dawn.

Brady Lake
Village
Lat: 41-09-45 N Long: 81-18-50 W
Pop: 490 (1990); 470 (1980) Pop Density: 1633.3
Land: 0.3 sq. mi.; Water: 0.1 sq. mi.

Brimfield
Township
ZIP: 44240 Lat: 41-06-01 N Long: 81-20-45 W
Pop: 8,389 (1990); 7,868 (1980) Pop Density: 377.9
Land: 22.2 sq. mi.; Water: 0.8 sq. mi.

Charlestown
Township
ZIP: 44266 Lat: 41-09-48 N Long: 81-08-52 W
Pop: 1,903 (1990); 1,693 (1980) Pop Density: 93.7
Land: 20.3 sq. mi.; Water: 2.8 sq. mi.

Deerfield
Township
ZIP: 44411 Lat: 41-01-28 N Long: 81-03-01 W
Pop: 2,764 (1990); 2,710 (1980) Pop Density: 121.8
Land: 22.7 sq. mi.; Water: 3.7 sq. mi.

Edinburg
Township
ZIP: 44272 Lat: 41-05-57 N Long: 81-08-49 W
Pop: 1,978 (1990); 1,943 (1980) Pop Density: 81.7
Land: 24.2 sq. mi.; Water: 0.3 sq. mi.

Franklin
Township
ZIP: 44240 Lat: 41-10-12 N Long: 81-20-58 W
Pop: 34,968 (1990); 31,206 (1980) Pop Density: 1714.1
Land: 20.4 sq. mi.; Water: 1.6 sq. mi.
In northeastern OH, 10 mi. northeast of Akron.

Freedom Township
ZIP: 44288 Lat: 41-14-09 N Long: 81-08-49 W
Pop: 2,530 (1990); 2,398 (1980) Pop Density: 105.4
Land: 24.0 sq. mi.; Water: 0.0 sq. mi.

Garrettsville Village
ZIP: 44231 Lat: 41-17-02 N Long: 81-05-43 W
Pop: 2,014 (1990); 1,769 (1980) Pop Density: 875.7
Land: 2.3 sq. mi.; Water: 0.0 sq. mi.
In northeastern OH, northwest of Youngstown.
Name origin: For Col. John Garrett, its first settler.

Hiram Village
ZIP: 44234 Lat: 41-18-36 N Long: 81-08-40 W
Pop: 1,330 (1990); 1,360 (1980) Pop Density: 1477.8
Land: 0.9 sq. mi.; Water: 0.0 sq. mi.
Not coextensive with the town of the same name.

Hiram Township
ZIP: 44234 Lat: 41-18-41 N Long: 81-08-46 W
Pop: 3,218 (1990); 3,041 (1980) Pop Density: 133.5
Land: 24.1 sq. mi.; Water: 0.0 sq. mi.

Kent City
ZIP: 44240 Lat: 41-08-49 N Long: 81-21-44 W
Pop: 28,835 (1990); 26,164 (1980) Pop Density: 3314.4
Land: 8.7 sq. mi.; Water: 0.0 sq. mi. Elev: 1097 ft.
In northeast-central OH on the Cuyahoga River, 10 mi. east of Akron. Kent State Univ. established here 1910.
Name origin: For railway investor Marvin Kent.

Mantua Village
ZIP: 44255 Lat: 41-16-53 N Long: 81-13-21 W
Pop: 1,178 (1990); 1,041 (1980) Pop Density: 841.4
Land: 1.4 sq. mi.; Water: 0.0 sq. mi.
In northeastern OH on the Cuyahoga River, 30 mi. southeast of Cleveland. Not coextensive with the town of the same name.
Name origin: Named by John Leavitt for Mantua, Italy.

Mantua Township
ZIP: 44255 Lat: 41-18-24 N Long: 81-15-17 W
Pop: 5,596 (1990); 5,418 (1980) Pop Density: 201.3
Land: 27.8 sq. mi.; Water: 0.1 sq. mi.

Mogadore Village
ZIP: 44260 Lat: 41-03-01 N Long: 81-23-23 W
Pop: 1,041 (1990); 1,129 (1980) Pop Density: 2082.0
Land: 0.5 sq. mi.; Water: 0.0 sq. mi.
Part of the town is also in Summit County.
Name origin: For Mogador, Morocco, with an added *e*.

Nelson Township
ZIP: 44231 Lat: 41-18-35 N Long: 81-03-00 W
Pop: 2,778 (1990); 2,424 (1980) Pop Density: 112.0
Land: 24.8 sq. mi.; Water: 0.0 sq. mi.

Palmyra Township
ZIP: 44412 Lat: 41-06-19 N Long: 81-03-09 W
Pop: 2,531 (1990); 2,436 (1980) Pop Density: 97.7
Land: 25.9 sq. mi.; Water: 0.0 sq. mi.

Paris Township
ZIP: 44266 Lat: 41-09-57 N Long: 81-02-16 W
Pop: 1,785 (1990); 1,629 (1980) Pop Density: 78.6
Land: 22.7 sq. mi.; Water: 1.2 sq. mi.

Randolph Township
  Lat: 41-01-30 N Long: 81-15-12 W
Pop: 4,970 (1990); 5,093 (1980) Pop Density: 170.8
Land: 29.1 sq. mi.; Water: 0.1 sq. mi.

Ravenna City
ZIP: 44266 Lat: 41-09-35 N Long: 81-14-33 W
Pop: 12,069 (1990); 11,987 (1980) Pop Density: 2514.4
Land: 4.8 sq. mi.; Water: 0.0 sq. mi. Elev: 1128 ft.
In northeastern OH, 14 mi. northeast of Akron. Settled 1799. Not coextensive with the town of the same name.
Name origin: For the Italian city.

*Ravenna Township
ZIP: 44266 Lat: 41-10-06 N Long: 81-14-43 W
Pop: 21,030 (1990); 21,182 (1980) Pop Density: 818.3
Land: 25.7 sq. mi.; Water: 0.2 sq. mi.

Rootstown Township
ZIP: 44272 Lat: 41-06-01 N Long: 81-14-54 W
Pop: 6,612 (1990); 6,585 (1980) Pop Density: 249.5
Land: 26.5 sq. mi.; Water: 0.7 sq. mi.

Shalersville Township
ZIP: 44255 Lat: 41-14-31 N Long: 81-15-03 W
Pop: 5,270 (1990); 5,268 (1980) Pop Density: 191.6
Land: 27.5 sq. mi.; Water: 0.1 sq. mi.

Streetsboro City
ZIP: 44241 Lat: 41-14-19 N Long: 81-20-44 W
Pop: 9,932 (1990); 9,055 (1980) Pop Density: 413.8
Land: 24.0 sq. mi.; Water: 0.4 sq. mi. Elev: 1137 ft.

Suffield Township
ZIP: 44260 Lat: 41-01-39 N Long: 81-21-01 W
Pop: 6,312 (1990); 6,211 (1980) Pop Density: 275.6
Land: 22.9 sq. mi.; Water: 1.8 sq. mi.

Sugar Bush Knolls Village
  Lat: 41-12-17 N Long: 81-20-48 W
Pop: 211 (1990); 201 (1980) Pop Density: 1055.0
Land: 0.2 sq. mi.; Water: 0.0 sq. mi.

Windham Village
ZIP: 44288 Lat: 41-14-10 N Long: 81-02-10 W
Pop: 2,943 (1990); 3,721 (1980) Pop Density: 1401.4
Land: 2.1 sq. mi.; Water: 0.0 sq. mi.

*Windham Township
ZIP: 44288 Lat: 41-14-03 N Long: 81-02-50 W
Pop: 4,898 (1990); 5,729 (1980) Pop Density: 195.1
Land: 25.1 sq. mi.; Water: 0.0 sq. mi.

OHIO, Preble County

Preble County
County Seat: Eaton (ZIP: 45320)

Pop: 40,113 (1990); 38,223 (1980)   **Pop Density:** 94.4
Land: 424.8 sq. mi.; **Water:** 1.5 sq. mi.   **Area Code:** 513
On the southwestern border of OH, west of Dayton; organized Mar 1, 1808 from Montgomery and Butler counties.
Name origin: For Capt. Edward Preble (1761–1807), commander of the *U.S.S. Constitution*, which bombarded Tripoli in 1804 during the war against the Barbary pirates.

Camden — Village
ZIP: 45311   **Lat:** 39-38-13 N **Long:** 84-38-47 W
Pop: 2,210 (1990); 1,971 (1980)   **Pop Density:** 1841.7
Land: 1.2 sq. mi.; **Water:** 0.0 sq. mi.
In southwestern OH on Seven Mile Creek, southwest of Dayton.
Name origin: For Camden, NJ.

College Corner — Village
Lat: 39-34-08 N **Long:** 84-48-45 W
Pop: 274 (1990); 248 (1980)   **Pop Density:** 2740.0
Land: 0.1 sq. mi.; **Water:** 0.0 sq. mi.
Part of the town is also in Butler County.

Dixon — Township
Lat: 39-41-57 N **Long:** 84-45-42 W
Pop: 604 (1990); 657 (1980)   **Pop Density:** 16.9
Land: 35.7 sq. mi.; **Water:** 0.0 sq. mi.

Eaton — City
ZIP: 45320   **Lat:** 39-44-54 N **Long:** 84-38-01 W
Pop: 7,396 (1990); 6,839 (1980)   **Pop Density:** 1450.2
Land: 5.1 sq. mi.; **Water:** 0.0 sq. mi.   **Elev:** 1046 ft.
In southwestern OH, 20 mi. west of Dayton. Founded 1806.
Name origin: For Gen. William Eaton (1764–1811), U.S. army officer in the Tripolitan War of 1805.

Eldorado — Village
ZIP: 45321   **Lat:** 39-54-13 N **Long:** 84-40-32 W
Pop: 549 (1990); 509 (1980)   **Pop Density:** 2745.0
Land: 0.2 sq. mi.; **Water:** 0.0 sq. mi.

Gasper — Township
Lat: 39-40-51 N **Long:** 84-38-44 W
Pop: 1,638 (1990); 1,114 (1980)   **Pop Density:** 73.8
Land: 22.2 sq. mi.; **Water:** 0.5 sq. mi.

Gratis — Village
ZIP: 45330   **Lat:** 39-38-54 N **Long:** 84-31-43 W
Pop: 998 (1990); 809 (1980)   **Pop Density:** 1108.9
Land: 0.9 sq. mi.; **Water:** 0.0 sq. mi.   **Elev:** 876 ft.
Not coextensive with the town of the same name.

*Gratis — Township
Lat: 39-36-59 N **Long:** 84-32-31 W
Pop: 4,474 (1990); 4,140 (1980)   **Pop Density:** 121.6
Land: 36.8 sq. mi.; **Water:** 0.0 sq. mi.

Harrison — Township
Lat: 39-52-51 N **Long:** 84-31-57 W
Pop: 4,365 (1990); 4,297 (1980)   **Pop Density:** 121.6
Land: 35.9 sq. mi.; **Water:** 0.0 sq. mi.

Israel — Township
Lat: 39-36-28 N **Long:** 84-45-20 W
Pop: 1,397 (1990); 1,404 (1980)   **Pop Density:** 39.1
Land: 35.7 sq. mi.; **Water:** 0.8 sq. mi.

Jackson — Township
Lat: 39-47-15 N **Long:** 84-45-34 W
Pop: 1,222 (1990); 1,314 (1980)   **Pop Density:** 35.5
Land: 34.4 sq. mi.; **Water:** 0.0 sq. mi.

Jefferson — Township
Lat: 39-52-13 N **Long:** 84-45-55 W
Pop: 3,783 (1990); 3,831 (1980)   **Pop Density:** 107.2
Land: 35.3 sq. mi.; **Water:** 0.1 sq. mi.

Lanier — Township
Lat: 39-41-48 N **Long:** 84-32-59 W
Pop: 3,734 (1990); 3,621 (1980)   **Pop Density:** 102.6
Land: 36.4 sq. mi.; **Water:** 0.0 sq. mi.

Lewisburg — Village
ZIP: 45338   **Lat:** 39-50-56 N **Long:** 84-32-26 W
Pop: 1,584 (1990); 1,450 (1980)   **Pop Density:** 2640.0
Land: 0.6 sq. mi.; **Water:** 0.0 sq. mi.
In southwestern OH, 22 mi. northwest of Dayton.

Monroe — Township
Lat: 39-52-18 N **Long:** 84-39-06 W
Pop: 2,474 (1990); 2,496 (1980)   **Pop Density:** 70.3
Land: 35.2 sq. mi.; **Water:** 0.0 sq. mi.

New Paris — Village
ZIP: 45347   **Lat:** 39-51-25 N **Long:** 84-47-36 W
Pop: 1,801 (1990); 1,709 (1980)   **Pop Density:** 2572.9
Land: 0.7 sq. mi.; **Water:** 0.0 sq. mi.

Somers — Township
Lat: 39-36-59 N **Long:** 84-38-59 W
Pop: 4,226 (1990); 3,824 (1980)   **Pop Density:** 115.8
Land: 36.5 sq. mi.; **Water:** 0.0 sq. mi.

Twin — Township
Lat: 39-47-01 N **Long:** 84-32-12 W
Pop: 2,826 (1990); 2,745 (1980)   **Pop Density:** 80.7
Land: 35.0 sq. mi.; **Water:** 0.0 sq. mi.

Verona — Village
ZIP: 45378   **Lat:** 39-54-13 N **Long:** 84-29-21 W
Pop: 387 (1990); 481 (1980)   **Pop Density:** 3870.0
Land: 0.1 sq. mi.; **Water:** 0.0 sq. mi.
Part of the town is also in Montgomery County.

Washington — Township
Lat: 39-45-56 N **Long:** 84-39-06 W
Pop: 1,974 (1990); 1,941 (1980)   **Pop Density:** 48.6
Land: 40.6 sq. mi.; **Water:** 0.0 sq. mi.

West Alexandria — Village
ZIP: 45381   **Lat:** 39-44-34 N **Long:** 84-32-00 W
Pop: 1,460 (1990); 1,313 (1980)   **Pop Density:** 2085.7
Land: 0.7 sq. mi.; **Water:** 0.0 sq. mi.   **Elev:** 900 ft.

West Elkton — Village
ZIP: 45070   **Lat:** 39-35-19 N   **Long:** 84-33-15 W
Pop: 208 (1990); 277 (1980)   **Pop Density:** 2080.0
Land: 0.1 sq. mi.; **Water:** 0.0 sq. mi.

West Manchester — Village
ZIP: 45382   **Lat:** 39-54-08 N   **Long:** 84-37-34 W
Pop: 464 (1990); 448 (1980)   **Pop Density:** 2320.0
Land: 0.2 sq. mi.; **Water:** 0.0 sq. mi.   **Elev:** 1093 ft.

Putnam County
County Seat: Ottawa (ZIP: 45875)

Pop: 33,819 (1990); 32,991 (1980)   **Pop Density:** 69.9
Land: 483.9 sq. mi.; **Water:** 0.4 sq. mi.   **Area Code:** 419
In northwestern OH, north of Lima; organized Apr 1, 1820 from Indian Territory.
Name origin: For Gen. Israel Putnam, (1718–90), Revolutionary War officer and and American commander at the Battle of Bunker Hill.

Belmore — Village
ZIP: 45815   **Lat:** 41-09-15 N   **Long:** 83-56-28 W
Pop: 161 (1990); 205 (1980)   **Pop Density:** 402.5
Land: 0.4 sq. mi.; **Water:** 0.0 sq. mi.   **Elev:** 736 ft.
In northwestern OH, north of Lima.

Blanchard — Township
Lat: 41-02-04 N   **Long:** 83-56-02 W
Pop: 1,344 (1990); 1,272 (1980)   **Pop Density:** 37.1
Land: 36.2 sq. mi.; **Water:** 0.0 sq. mi.

Cloverdale — Village
ZIP: 45827   **Lat:** 41-01-10 N   **Long:** 84-18-15 W
Pop: 270 (1990); 304 (1980)   **Pop Density:** 450.0
Land: 0.6 sq. mi.; **Water:** 0.0 sq. mi.

Columbus Grove — Village
ZIP: 45830   **Lat:** 40-55-09 N   **Long:** 84-03-29 W
Pop: 2,231 (1990); 2,313 (1980)   **Pop Density:** 2478.9
Land: 0.9 sq. mi.; **Water:** 0.0 sq. mi.   **Elev:** 773 ft.

Continental — Village
ZIP: 45831   **Lat:** 41-05-55 N   **Long:** 84-16-00 W
Pop: 1,214 (1990); 1,179 (1980)   **Pop Density:** 2023.3
Land: 0.6 sq. mi.; **Water:** 0.0 sq. mi.   **Elev:** 723 ft.

Dupont — Village
ZIP: 45837   **Lat:** 41-03-17 N   **Long:** 84-18-07 W
Pop: 279 (1990); 308 (1980)   **Pop Density:** 310.0
Land: 0.9 sq. mi.; **Water:** 0.0 sq. mi.

Fort Jennings — Village
ZIP: 45844   **Lat:** 40-54-22 N   **Long:** 84-17-57 W
Pop: 436 (1990); 538 (1980)   **Pop Density:** 872.0
Land: 0.5 sq. mi.; **Water:** 0.0 sq. mi.

Gilboa — Village
Lat: 41-01-08 N   **Long:** 83-55-16 W
Pop: 208 (1990); 220 (1980)   **Pop Density:** 2080.0
Land: 0.1 sq. mi.; **Water:** 0.0 sq. mi.

Glandorf — Village
ZIP: 45848   **Lat:** 41-01-49 N   **Long:** 84-04-45 W
Pop: 829 (1990); 746 (1980)   **Pop Density:** 552.7
Land: 1.5 sq. mi.; **Water:** 0.0 sq. mi.
In northwest-central OH on the Ottawa River, north of Lima.
Name origin: Named by early German settlers for Glandorf, Germany.

Greensburg — Township
Lat: 41-02-55 N   **Long:** 84-10-16 W
Pop: 1,244 (1990); 1,116 (1980)   **Pop Density:** 41.2
Land: 30.2 sq. mi.; **Water:** 0.0 sq. mi.

Jackson — Township
Lat: 40-58-07 N   **Long:** 84-16-13 W
Pop: 974 (1990); 914 (1980)   **Pop Density:** 37.8
Land: 25.8 sq. mi.; **Water:** 0.0 sq. mi.

Jennings — Township
Lat: 40-53-24 N   **Long:** 84-16-52 W
Pop: 1,806 (1990); 1,761 (1980)   **Pop Density:** 63.8
Land: 28.3 sq. mi.; **Water:** 0.0 sq. mi.

Kalida — Village
ZIP: 45853   **Lat:** 40-59-09 N   **Long:** 84-11-43 W
Pop: 947 (1990); 1,019 (1980)   **Pop Density:** 1183.8
Land: 0.8 sq. mi.; **Water:** 0.0 sq. mi.   **Elev:** 727 ft.
In northwestern OH along the Ottawa River, 20 mi. north of Lima.
Name origin: From the Greek term meaning 'beautiful.'

Leipsic — Village
ZIP: 45856   **Lat:** 41-05-57 N   **Long:** 83-59-04 W
Pop: 2,203 (1990); 2,171 (1980)   **Pop Density:** 2447.8
Land: 0.9 sq. mi.; **Water:** 0.0 sq. mi.   **Elev:** 766 ft.
In northwestern OH, 30 mi. north of Lima.
Name origin: Named by its settlers for Leipsic, Germany, their former home.

Liberty — Township
Lat: 41-07-34 N   **Long:** 84-03-13 W
Pop: 1,497 (1990); 1,556 (1980)   **Pop Density:** 41.1
Land: 36.4 sq. mi.; **Water:** 0.0 sq. mi.

Miller City — Village
Lat: 41-06-06 N   **Long:** 84-07-55 W
Pop: 173 (1990); 168 (1980)   **Pop Density:** 1730.0
Land: 0.1 sq. mi.; **Water:** 0.0 sq. mi.   **Elev:** 732 ft.

Monroe — Township
Lat: 41-07-27 N   **Long:** 84-16-53 W
Pop: 2,254 (1990); 2,189 (1980)   **Pop Density:** 62.8
Land: 35.9 sq. mi.; **Water:** 0.0 sq. mi.

Monterey — Township
Lat: 40-56-50 N   **Long:** 84-21-36 W
Pop: 1,972 (1990); 1,893 (1980)   **Pop Density:** 80.2
Land: 24.6 sq. mi.; **Water:** 0.0 sq. mi.

OHIO, Putnam County

Ottawa — Village
ZIP: 45875   Lat: 41-01-15 N   Long: 84-02-28 W
Pop: 3,999 (1990); 3,874 (1980)   Pop Density: 1428.2
Land: 2.8 sq. mi.; Water: 0.0 sq. mi.

In northwestern OH, 20 mi. north of Lima. Established 1822, shortly after the last of the Ottawa Indians had been removed to their western reservation. Not coextensive with the town of the same name.
Name origin: For the Indian tribe.

*Ottawa — Township
ZIP: 45875   Lat: 41-02-11 N   Long: 84-03-04 W
Pop: 7,589 (1990); 7,223 (1980)   Pop Density: 209.6
Land: 36.2 sq. mi.; Water: 0.1 sq. mi.

Ottoville — Village
ZIP: 45876   Lat: 40-55-53 N   Long: 84-20-19 W
Pop: 842 (1990); 833 (1980)   Pop Density: 2105.0
Land: 0.4 sq. mi.; Water: 0.0 sq. mi.   Elev: 743 ft.

Palmer — Township
Lat: 41-07-06 N   Long: 84-10-11 W
Pop: 1,264 (1990); 1,266 (1980)   Pop Density: 34.8
Land: 36.3 sq. mi.; Water: 0.0 sq. mi.

Pandora — Village
ZIP: 45877   Lat: 40-56-51 N   Long: 83-57-40 W
Pop: 1,009 (1990); 977 (1980)   Pop Density: 1681.7
Land: 0.6 sq. mi.; Water: 0.0 sq. mi.   Elev: 773 ft.

In northwestern OH, 18 mi. northeast of Lima.
Name origin: For the mythological Greek character.

Perry — Township
Lat: 41-02-34 N   Long: 84-16-38 W
Pop: 1,225 (1990); 1,216 (1980)   Pop Density: 40.8
Land: 30.0 sq. mi.; Water: 0.2 sq. mi.

Pleasant — Township
Lat: 40-57-02 N   Long: 84-03-14 W
Pop: 3,856 (1990); 3,873 (1980)   Pop Density: 105.6
Land: 36.5 sq. mi.; Water: 0.0 sq. mi.

Riley — Township
Lat: 40-57-25 N   Long: 83-56-17 W
Pop: 2,026 (1990); 1,975 (1980)   Pop Density: 67.1
Land: 30.2 sq. mi.; Water: 0.0 sq. mi.

Sugar Creek — Township
Lat: 40-53-39 N   Long: 84-10-06 W
Pop: 1,131 (1990); 1,126 (1980)   Pop Density: 37.1
Land: 30.5 sq. mi.; Water: 0.0 sq. mi.

Union — Township
Lat: 40-58-03 N   Long: 84-09-51 W
Pop: 2,477 (1990); 2,368 (1980)   Pop Density: 81.5
Land: 30.4 sq. mi.; Water: 0.0 sq. mi.

Van Buren — Township
Lat: 41-07-29 N   Long: 83-56-33 W
Pop: 3,160 (1990); 3,243 (1980)   Pop Density: 87.3
Land: 36.2 sq. mi.; Water: 0.0 sq. mi.

West Leipsic — Village
ZIP: 45856   Lat: 41-06-19 N   Long: 84-00-06 W
Pop: 244 (1990); 298 (1980)   Pop Density: 1220.0
Land: 0.2 sq. mi.; Water: 0.0 sq. mi.

Richland County
County Seat: Mansfield (ZIP: 44902)

Pop: 126,137 (1990); 131,205 (1980)   Pop Density: 253.8
Land: 497.0 sq. mi.; Water: 3.3 sq. mi.   Area Code: 419

In north-central OH, west of Canton; organized Mar 1, 1808 from Knox County.
Name origin: For the fertile soil in the area.

Bellville — Village
ZIP: 44813   Lat: 40-37-14 N   Long: 82-30-39 W
Pop: 1,568 (1990); 1,714 (1980)   Pop Density: 1206.2
Land: 1.3 sq. mi.; Water: 0.0 sq. mi.

Blooming Grove — Township
Lat: 40-56-58 N   Long: 82-31-48 W
Pop: 1,061 (1990); 1,092 (1980)   Pop Density: 41.8
Land: 25.4 sq. mi.; Water: 0.0 sq. mi.

Butler — Village
ZIP: 44822   Lat: 40-35-11 N   Long: 82-25-12 W
Pop: 968 (1990); 991 (1980)   Pop Density: 880.0
Land: 1.1 sq. mi.; Water: 0.0 sq. mi.   Elev: 1073 ft.

*Butler — Township
ZIP: 44822   Lat: 40-57-01 N   Long: 82-27-06 W
Pop: 1,122 (1990); 899 (1980)   Pop Density: 44.0
Land: 25.5 sq. mi.; Water: 0.0 sq. mi.

Cass — Township
Lat: 40-57-08 N   Long: 82-36-23 W
Pop: 1,626 (1990); 1,746 (1980)   Pop Density: 63.0
Land: 25.8 sq. mi.; Water: 0.0 sq. mi.

Crestline — City
ZIP: 44827   Lat: 40-47-12 N   Long: 82-43-20 W
Pop: 9 (1990); 14 (1980)   Pop Density: 225.0
Land: 0.04 sq. mi.; Water: 0.0 sq. mi.

In north-central OH, 10 mi. west of Mansfield. Part of the town is also in Crawford County.
Name origin: For its location on the watershed.

Franklin — Township
Lat: 40-51-37 N   Long: 82-32-21 W
Pop: 1,713 (1990); 1,689 (1980)   Pop Density: 78.2
Land: 21.9 sq. mi.; Water: 0.0 sq. mi.

Jackson — Township
ZIP: 44875   Lat: 40-51-18 N   Long: 82-36-12 W
Pop: 3,602 (1990); 3,660 (1980)   Pop Density: 147.6
Land: 24.4 sq. mi.; Water: 0.0 sq. mi.

Jefferson — Township
Lat: 40-35-44 N   Long: 82-30-31 W
Pop: 4,258 (1990); 4,002 (1980)   Pop Density: 116.7
Land: 36.5 sq. mi.; Water: 0.0 sq. mi.

Lexington
Village
ZIP: 44904 **Lat:** 40-40-41 N **Long:** 82-35-12 W
Pop: 4,124 (1990); 3,823 (1980) **Pop Density:** 1527.4
Land: 2.7 sq. mi.; **Water:** 0.0 sq. mi.

In north-central OH, 10 mi. southwest of Mansfield. Laid out 1812.
Name origin: For Lexington, MA.

Lucas
Village
ZIP: 44843 **Lat:** 40-42-10 N **Long:** 82-25-16 W
Pop: 730 (1990); 753 (1980) **Pop Density:** 1460.0
Land: 0.5 sq. mi.; **Water:** 0.0 sq. mi. **Elev:** 1105 ft.

Madison
Township
ZIP: 44903 **Lat:** 40-46-44 N **Long:** 82-29-44 W
Pop: 13,286 (1990); 14,624 (1980) **Pop Density:** 790.8
Land: 16.8 sq. mi.; **Water:** 0.0 sq. mi.

In north-central OH, just south of Mansfield.

Mansfield
City
ZIP: 44901 **Lat:** 40-45-46 N **Long:** 82-31-36 W
Pop: 50,627 (1990); 53,927 (1980) **Pop Density:** 1814.6
Land: 27.9 sq. mi.; **Water:** 0.0 sq. mi.

In north-central OH, 55 mi. southwest of Akron.
Name origin: Named in 1808 for Jared Mansfield, U.S. Surveyor General, who directed the platting of the town.

Mifflin
Township
ZIP: 44843 **Lat:** 40-46-14 N **Long:** 82-25-15 W
Pop: 6,859 (1990); 6,698 (1980) **Pop Density:** 310.4
Land: 22.1 sq. mi.; **Water:** 1.0 sq. mi.

Monroe
Township
Lat: 40-40-43 N **Long:** 82-23-41 W
Pop: 2,646 (1990); 2,654 (1980) **Pop Density:** 72.7
Land: 36.4 sq. mi.; **Water:** 0.7 sq. mi.

Ontario
Village
ZIP: 44862 **Lat:** 40-45-57 N **Long:** 82-36-27 W
Pop: 4,026 (1990); 4,123 (1980) **Pop Density:** 398.6
Land: 10.1 sq. mi.; **Water:** 0.0 sq. mi.

In north-central OH, just west of Mansfield.
Name origin: For Ontario, Canada.

Perry
Township
Lat: 40-35-40 N **Long:** 82-35-53 W
Pop: 1,272 (1990); 1,204 (1980) **Pop Density:** 71.1
Land: 17.9 sq. mi.; **Water:** 0.0 sq. mi.

Plymouth
Village
ZIP: 44865 **Lat:** 40-59-27 N **Long:** 82-40-07 W
Pop: 1,013 (1990); 970 (1980) **Pop Density:** 1125.6
Land: 0.9 sq. mi.; **Water:** 0.0 sq. mi. **Elev:** 1029 ft.

In north-central OH on the west branch of the Huron River. Part of the town is also in Huron County.
Name origin: For Plymouth, MA.

*Plymouth
Township
ZIP: 44865 **Lat:** 40-56-45 N **Long:** 82-41-08 W
Pop: 2,233 (1990); 2,277 (1980) **Pop Density:** 86.6
Land: 25.8 sq. mi.; **Water:** 0.1 sq. mi.

Sandusky
Township
Lat: 40-45-34 N **Long:** 82-42-36 W
Pop: 940 (1990); 1,118 (1980) **Pop Density:** 65.7
Land: 14.3 sq. mi.; **Water:** 0.0 sq. mi.

Sharon
Township
ZIP: 44875 **Lat:** 40-51-06 N **Long:** 82-40-54 W
Pop: 9,812 (1990); 9,967 (1980) **Pop Density:** 407.1
Land: 24.1 sq. mi.; **Water:** 0.1 sq. mi.

In north-central OH, 10 mi. northwest of Mansfield.

Shelby
City
ZIP: 44875 **Lat:** 40-52-55 N **Long:** 82-39-41 W
Pop: 9,564 (1990); 9,703 (1980) **Pop Density:** 2034.9
Land: 4.7 sq. mi.; **Water:** 0.1 sq. mi. **Elev:** 1102 ft.

In north-central OH, 19 mi. northwest of Mansfield.
Name origin: For Isaac Shelby (1750–1826), hero of the American Revolution and the War of 1812.

Shiloh
Village
ZIP: 44878 **Lat:** 40-58-07 N **Long:** 82-36-07 W
Pop: 778 (1990); 857 (1980) **Pop Density:** 972.5
Land: 0.8 sq. mi.; **Water:** 0.0 sq. mi.

Springfield
Township
ZIP: 44906 **Lat:** 40-46-02 N **Long:** 82-38-01 W
Pop: 8,460 (1990); 8,596 (1980) **Pop Density:** 231.1
Land: 36.6 sq. mi.; **Water:** 0.0 sq. mi.

Troy
Township
ZIP: 44904 **Lat:** 40-40-59 N **Long:** 82-36-17 W
Pop: 6,179 (1990); 5,880 (1980) **Pop Density:** 277.1
Land: 22.3 sq. mi.; **Water:** 1.2 sq. mi.

Washington
Township
ZIP: 44906 **Lat:** 40-40-43 N **Long:** 82-30-12 W
Pop: 6,474 (1990); 7,150 (1980) **Pop Density:** 198.6
Land: 32.6 sq. mi.; **Water:** 0.0 sq. mi.

Weller
Township
Lat: 40-51-43 N **Long:** 82-27-02 W
Pop: 1,462 (1990); 1,466 (1980) **Pop Density:** 59.4
Land: 24.6 sq. mi.; **Water:** 0.0 sq. mi.

Worthington
Township
Lat: 40-36-11 N **Long:** 82-23-50 W
Pop: 2,505 (1990); 2,556 (1980) **Pop Density:** 69.8
Land: 35.9 sq. mi.; **Water:** 0.2 sq. mi.

Ross County
County Seat: Chillicothe (ZIP: 45601)

Pop: 69,330 (1990); 65,004 (1980) **Pop Density:** 100.7
Land: 688.5 sq. mi.; **Water:** 4.5 sq. mi. **Area Code:** 614
In south-central OH, south of Columbus; original county; organized Aug 20, 1798 (prior to statehood).
Name origin: For James Ross (1762–1847), U.S. senator from PA (1794–1803).

Adelphi Village
ZIP: 43101 **Lat:** 39-27-52 N **Long:** 82-44-46 W
Pop: 398 (1990); 472 (1980) **Pop Density:** 1326.7
Land: 0.3 sq. mi.; **Water:** 0.0 sq. mi. **Elev:** 838 ft.

Bainbridge Village
ZIP: 45612 **Lat:** 39-13-35 N **Long:** 83-16-10 W
Pop: 968 (1990); 1,042 (1980) **Pop Density:** 1936.0
Land: 0.5 sq. mi.; **Water:** 0.0 sq. mi.
Name origin: For William Bainbridge (1774–1833), War of 1812 naval hero.

Buckskin Township
Lat: 39-21-13 N **Long:** 83-18-15 W
Pop: 1,416 (1990); 1,340 (1980) **Pop Density:** 28.2
Land: 50.3 sq. mi.; **Water:** 0.0 sq. mi.

Chillicothe City
ZIP: 45601 **Lat:** 39-20-08 N **Long:** 82-59-17 W
Pop: 21,923 (1990); 23,420 (1980) **Pop Density:** 2775.1
Land: 7.9 sq. mi.; **Water:** 0.2 sq. mi.
In southern OH on the Scioto River, 44 mi. south of Columbus. The state's first capital (1803–16). Settled and laid out 1796. An industrial (shoes, paper and aluminum products), agricultural, and coal-mining region.
Name origin: Possibly from Shawnee 'village.'

Clarksburg Village
ZIP: 43115 **Lat:** 39-30-22 N **Long:** 83-09-16 W
Pop: 523 (1990); 483 (1980) **Pop Density:** 2615.0
Land: 0.2 sq. mi.; **Water:** 0.0 sq. mi. **Elev:** 772 ft.

Colerain Township
Lat: 39-25-30 N **Long:** 82-48-01 W
Pop: 1,609 (1990); 1,485 (1980) **Pop Density:** 45.6
Land: 35.3 sq. mi.; **Water:** 0.0 sq. mi.

Concord Township
Lat: 39-25-01 N **Long:** 83-12-49 W
Pop: 3,599 (1990); 3,234 (1980) **Pop Density:** 47.5
Land: 75.7 sq. mi.; **Water:** 0.0 sq. mi.

Deerfield Township
Lat: 39-29-24 N **Long:** 83-09-44 W
Pop: 1,077 (1990); 1,095 (1980) **Pop Density:** 35.0
Land: 30.8 sq. mi.; **Water:** 0.0 sq. mi.

Frankfort Village
ZIP: 45628 **Lat:** 39-24-28 N **Long:** 83-10-58 W
Pop: 1,065 (1990); 1,008 (1980) **Pop Density:** 2130.0
Land: 0.5 sq. mi.; **Water:** 0.0 sq. mi.

Franklin Township
Lat: 39-12-33 N **Long:** 82-55-32 W
Pop: 1,655 (1990); 1,588 (1980) **Pop Density:** 45.3
Land: 36.5 sq. mi.; **Water:** 0.4 sq. mi.

Green Township
Lat: 39-25-57 N **Long:** 82-55-26 W
Pop: 3,696 (1990); 3,380 (1980) **Pop Density:** 85.8
Land: 43.1 sq. mi.; **Water:** 0.4 sq. mi.

Harrison Township
Lat: 39-20-26 N **Long:** 82-48-24 W
Pop: 1,084 (1990); 1,007 (1980) **Pop Density:** 29.9
Land: 36.2 sq. mi.; **Water:** 0.0 sq. mi.

Huntington Township
ZIP: 45601 **Lat:** 39-14-27 N **Long:** 83-03-31 W
Pop: 5,102 (1990); 4,726 (1980) **Pop Density:** 85.7
Land: 59.5 sq. mi.; **Water:** 0.1 sq. mi.

Jefferson Township
Lat: 39-12-33 N **Long:** 82-48-37 W
Pop: 1,026 (1990); 1,048 (1980) **Pop Density:** 41.9
Land: 24.5 sq. mi.; **Water:** 0.3 sq. mi.

Kingston Village
ZIP: 45644 **Lat:** 39-28-19 N **Long:** 82-54-42 W
Pop: 1,153 (1990); 1,208 (1980) **Pop Density:** 2882.5
Land: 0.4 sq. mi.; **Water:** 0.0 sq. mi. **Elev:** 797 ft.
In south-central OH, 11 mi. northeast of Chillicothe.

Liberty Township
Lat: 39-15-55 N **Long:** 82-50-25 W
Pop: 2,126 (1990); 1,939 (1980) **Pop Density:** 61.8
Land: 34.4 sq. mi.; **Water:** 0.2 sq. mi.

North Folk Village CDP
Lat: 39-20-10 N **Long:** 83-01-39 W
Pop: 1,247 (1990) **Pop Density:** 2494.0
Land: 0.5 sq. mi.; **Water:** 0.0 sq. mi.

Paint Township
ZIP: 45612 **Lat:** 39-16-41 N **Long:** 83-18-54 W
Pop: 1,125 (1990); 988 (1980) **Pop Density:** 31.7
Land: 35.5 sq. mi.; **Water:** 0.6 sq. mi.

Paxton Township
ZIP: 45612 **Lat:** 39-13-33 N **Long:** 83-15-41 W
Pop: 1,962 (1990); 1,876 (1980) **Pop Density:** 61.9
Land: 31.7 sq. mi.; **Water:** 0.1 sq. mi.

Scioto Township
ZIP: 45601 **Lat:** 39-18-50 N **Long:** 82-59-43 W
Pop: 30,654 (1990); 31,469 (1980) **Pop Density:** 806.7
Land: 38.0 sq. mi.; **Water:** 1.4 sq. mi.
In southern OH, 47 mi. south of Columbus.

South Salem Village
ZIP: 45681 **Lat:** 39-20-10 N **Long:** 83-18-26 W
Pop: 227 (1990); 252 (1980) **Pop Density:** 1135.0
Land: 0.2 sq. mi.; **Water:** 0.0 sq. mi.

Springfield
Township
Lat: 39-21-12 N **Long:** 82-55-07 W
Pop: 2,284 (1990); 1,805 (1980) **Pop Density:** 75.1
Land: 30.4 sq. mi.; **Water:** 0.4 sq. mi.

Twin
Township
Lat: 39-16-54 N **Long:** 83-09-24 W
Pop: 2,755 (1990); 2,616 (1980) **Pop Density:** 45.8
Land: 60.2 sq. mi.; **Water:** 0.1 sq. mi.

Union
Township
ZIP: 45628 **Lat:** 39-25-43 N **Long:** 83-03-30 W
Pop: 8,160 (1990); 5,408 (1980) **Pop Density:** 122.9
Land: 66.4 sq. mi.; **Water:** 0.5 sq. mi.

Sandusky County
County Seat: Fremont (ZIP: 43420)

Pop: 61,963 (1990); 63,267 (1980) **Pop Density:** 151.4
Land: 409.2 sq. mi.; **Water:** 8.6 sq. mi. **Area Code:** 419

In north-central OH, southeast of Toledo; organized Feb 12, 1820 from Huron County.

Name origin: For the Sandusky River, which flows through it. From a Wyandot word, now lost, which seems to have meant 'cold water' or 'pure water.'

Ballville
Township
ZIP: 43420 **Lat:** 41-17-51 N **Long:** 83-07-55 W
Pop: 6,049 (1990); 6,182 (1980) **Pop Density:** 177.9
Land: 34.0 sq. mi.; **Water:** 0.4 sq. mi.

Bellevue
City
ZIP: 44811 **Lat:** 41-16-27 N **Long:** 82-51-07 W
Pop: 4,236 (1990); 4,237 (1980) **Pop Density:** 2353.3
Land: 1.8 sq. mi.; **Water:** 0.0 sq. mi.

In northern OH, 15 mi. southwest of Sandusky. Settled 1815. Part of the town is also in Huron County.

Name origin: Named in 1839 by James Bell, who was then building the Mad River & Lake Erie Railroad from Sandusky.

Burgoon
Village
ZIP: 43407 **Lat:** 41-16-02 N **Long:** 83-15-02 W
Pop: 224 (1990); 244 (1980) **Pop Density:** 2240.0
Land: 0.1 sq. mi.; **Water:** 0.0 sq. mi.

Clyde
City
ZIP: 43410 **Lat:** 41-18-18 N **Long:** 82-58-39 W
Pop: 5,776 (1990); 5,489 (1980) **Pop Density:** 1698.8
Land: 3.4 sq. mi.; **Water:** 0.1 sq. mi.

Fremont
City
ZIP: 43420 **Lat:** 41-21-01 N **Long:** 83-06-46 W
Pop: 17,648 (1990); 17,834 (1980) **Pop Density:** 2846.5
Land: 6.2 sq. mi.; **Water:** 0.2 sq. mi. **Elev:** 636 ft.

In northern OH on the Sandusky River, 45 mi. west of Cleveland.

Name origin: For explorer and army officer John C. Frémont (1813–90).

Gibsonburg
Village
ZIP: 43431 **Lat:** 41-23-11 N **Long:** 83-19-22 W
Pop: 2,579 (1990); 2,479 (1980) **Pop Density:** 1228.1
Land: 2.1 sq. mi.; **Water:** 0.0 sq. mi.

In northern OH, 24 mi. southeast of Toledo.

Green Creek
Township
ZIP: 43410 **Lat:** 41-18-15 N **Long:** 83-00-50 W
Pop: 9,792 (1990); 9,681 (1980) **Pop Density:** 279.0
Land: 35.1 sq. mi.; **Water:** 0.1 sq. mi.

Green Springs
Village
Lat: 41-15-35 N **Long:** 83-03-04 W
Pop: 715 (1990); 627 (1980) **Pop Density:** 1191.7
Land: 0.6 sq. mi.; **Water:** 0.0 sq. mi.

In northern OH, southeast of Toledo. Part of the town is also in Seneca County.

Helena
Village
ZIP: 43435 **Lat:** 41-20-23 N **Long:** 83-17-30 W
Pop: 267 (1990); 307 (1980) **Pop Density:** 890.0
Land: 0.3 sq. mi.; **Water:** 0.0 sq. mi.

Jackson
Township
Lat: 41-18-05 N **Long:** 83-14-50 W
Pop: 1,614 (1990); 1,757 (1980) **Pop Density:** 44.8
Land: 36.0 sq. mi.; **Water:** 0.0 sq. mi.

Lindsey
Village
ZIP: 43442 **Lat:** 41-25-14 N **Long:** 83-13-14 W
Pop: 529 (1990); 571 (1980) **Pop Density:** 352.7
Land: 1.5 sq. mi.; **Water:** 0.0 sq. mi.

In northern OH, 10 mi. west of Sandusky Bay and 30 mi. southeast of Toledo.

Madison
Township
Lat: 41-22-26 N **Long:** 83-21-22 W
Pop: 3,687 (1990); 3,662 (1980) **Pop Density:** 135.6
Land: 27.2 sq. mi.; **Water:** 0.1 sq. mi.

Rice
Township
Lat: 41-26-14 N **Long:** 83-06-49 W
Pop: 1,467 (1990); 1,505 (1980) **Pop Density:** 67.9
Land: 21.6 sq. mi.; **Water:** 1.6 sq. mi.

Riley
Township
Lat: 41-23-39 N **Long:** 83-00-37 W
Pop: 1,449 (1990); 1,633 (1980) **Pop Density:** 37.5
Land: 38.6 sq. mi.; **Water:** 4.2 sq. mi.

Sandusky
Township
Lat: 41-22-55 N **Long:** 83-07-56 W
Pop: 4,441 (1990); 4,773 (1980) **Pop Density:** 187.4
Land: 23.7 sq. mi.; **Water:** 0.5 sq. mi.

Scott
Township
Lat: 41-17-40 N Long: 83-22-08 W
Pop: 1,540 (1990); 1,539 (1980) **Pop Density:** 42.3
Land: 36.4 sq. mi.; **Water:** 0.0 sq. mi.

Stony Prairie
CDP
Lat: 41-21-04 N Long: 83-09-18 W
Pop: 1,536 (1990); 1,767 (1980) **Pop Density:** 667.8
Land: 2.3 sq. mi.; **Water:** 0.0 sq. mi.

Townsend
Township
Lat: 41-23-18 N Long: 82-53-45 W
Pop: 1,528 (1990); 1,700 (1980) **Pop Density:** 47.0
Land: 32.5 sq. mi.; **Water:** 1.3 sq. mi.

Washington
Township
Lat: 41-24-00 N Long: 83-14-29 W
Pop: 2,308 (1990); 2,571 (1980) **Pop Density:** 47.5
Land: 48.6 sq. mi.; **Water:** 0.1 sq. mi.

Woodville
Village
ZIP: 43469 Lat: 41-27-04 N Long: 83-21-46 W
Pop: 1,953 (1990); 2,050 (1980) **Pop Density:** 1627.5
Land: 1.2 sq. mi.; **Water:** 0.0 sq. mi.

In northern OH, 25 mi. southeast of Toledo. Laid out 1838. Not coextensive with the town of the same name.
Name origin: For Amos Wood, who laid it out.

*Woodville
Township
ZIP: 43469 Lat: 41-26-56 N Long: 83-21-50 W
Pop: 3,088 (1990); 3,234 (1980) **Pop Density:** 93.3
Land: 33.1 sq. mi.; **Water:** 0.1 sq. mi.

York
Township
Lat: 41-17-33 N Long: 82-53-44 W
Pop: 2,401 (1990); 2,332 (1980) **Pop Density:** 70.8
Land: 33.9 sq. mi.; **Water:** 0.0 sq. mi.

Scioto County
County Seat: Portsmouth (ZIP: 45662)

Pop: 80,327 (1990); 84,545 (1980) **Pop Density:** 131.2
Land: 612.3 sq. mi.; **Water:** 3.8 sq. mi. **Area Code:** 614

On the southern border of OH; organized May 1, 1803 from Indian Territory.
Name origin: For the Scioto River, which flows through it; from an Iroquoian word of uncertain meaning, said by some scholars to be Wyandot 'deer.'

Bloom
Township
Lat: 38-48-22 N Long: 82-43-29 W
Pop: 3,216 (1990); 3,263 (1980) **Pop Density:** 66.0
Land: 48.7 sq. mi.; **Water:** 0.0 sq. mi.

Brush Creek
Township
ZIP: 45657 Lat: 38-50-47 N Long: 83-12-35 W
Pop: 1,123 (1990); 1,102 (1980) **Pop Density:** 22.1
Land: 50.9 sq. mi.; **Water:** 0.0 sq. mi.

Clay
Township
Lat: 38-47-58 N Long: 82-58-06 W
Pop: 4,000 (1990); 4,047 (1980) **Pop Density:** 185.2
Land: 21.6 sq. mi.; **Water:** 0.5 sq. mi.

Franklin Furnace
CDP
ZIP: 45629 Lat: 38-36-28 N Long: 82-50-47 W
Pop: 1,212 (1990); 1,093 (1980) **Pop Density:** 505.0
Land: 2.4 sq. mi.; **Water:** 0.4 sq. mi.

Green
Township
Lat: 38-38-33 N Long: 82-48-17 W
Pop: 3,758 (1990); 3,880 (1980) **Pop Density:** 96.9
Land: 38.8 sq. mi.; **Water:** 0.5 sq. mi.

Harrison
Township
Lat: 38-48-36 N Long: 82-51-42 W
Pop: 4,316 (1990); 4,288 (1980) **Pop Density:** 112.4
Land: 38.4 sq. mi.; **Water:** 0.0 sq. mi.

Jefferson
Township
Lat: 38-53-16 N Long: 82-56-08 W
Pop: 2,536 (1990); 2,500 (1980) **Pop Density:** 103.1
Land: 24.6 sq. mi.; **Water:** 0.0 sq. mi.

Lucasville
CDP
Lat: 38-52-44 N Long: 82-59-42 W
Pop: 1,575 (1990); 3,349 (1980) **Pop Density:** 630.0
Land: 2.5 sq. mi.; **Water:** 0.0 sq. mi.

Madison
Township
Lat: 38-54-19 N Long: 82-50-24 W
Pop: 3,351 (1990); 3,325 (1980) **Pop Density:** 64.8
Land: 51.7 sq. mi.; **Water:** 0.0 sq. mi.

Morgan
Township
Lat: 38-55-25 N Long: 83-04-57 W
Pop: 2,030 (1990); 1,952 (1980) **Pop Density:** 67.9
Land: 29.9 sq. mi.; **Water:** 0.3 sq. mi.

New Boston
Village
ZIP: 45662 Lat: 38-45-07 N Long: 82-56-05 W
Pop: 2,717 (1990); 3,188 (1980) **Pop Density:** 2470.0
Land: 1.1 sq. mi.; **Water:** 0.1 sq. mi.

In southern OH on the Ohio River, 5 mi. east of Portsmouth.
Name origin: For Boston, MA.

Nile
Township
Lat: 38-41-23 N Long: 83-10-36 W
Pop: 2,302 (1990); 2,568 (1980) **Pop Density:** 26.8
Land: 85.9 sq. mi.; **Water:** 0.7 sq. mi.

Otway
Village
ZIP: 45657 Lat: 38-51-54 N Long: 83-11-17 W
Pop: 105 (1990); 161 (1980) **Pop Density:** 525.0
Land: 0.2 sq. mi.; **Water:** 0.0 sq. mi.

Porter
Township
ZIP: 45694 Lat: 38-44-00 N Long: 82-50-27 W
Pop: 9,687 (1990); 9,529 (1980) **Pop Density:** 486.8
Land: 19.9 sq. mi.; **Water:** 0.2 sq. mi.

Portsmouth — City
ZIP: 45662 **Lat:** 38-45-18 N **Long:** 82-57-02 W
Pop: 22,676 (1990); 25,943 (1980) **Pop Density:** 2099.6
Land: 10.8 sq. mi.; **Water:** 0.3 sq. mi.
In southern OH on the Scioto River, where it joins the Ohio River. Founded 1803.
Name origin: For Portsmouth, Hampshire, England.

Rarden — Village
ZIP: 45671 **Lat:** 38-55-21 N **Long:** 83-14-34 W
Pop: 184 (1990); 199 (1980) **Pop Density:** 920.0
Land: 0.2 sq. mi.; **Water:** 0.0 sq. mi.
Not coextensive with the town of the same name.

*Rarden — Township
ZIP: 45671 **Lat:** 38-56-32 N **Long:** 83-14-07 W
Pop: 948 (1990); 853 (1980) **Pop Density:** 29.8
Land: 31.8 sq. mi.; **Water:** 0.0 sq. mi.

Rosemount — CDP
Lat: 38-47-16 N **Long:** 82-58-18 W
Pop: 1,926 (1990); 1,747 (1980) **Pop Density:** 469.8
Land: 4.1 sq. mi.; **Water:** 0.0 sq. mi.

Rush — Township
Lat: 38-50-17 N **Long:** 83-02-44 W
Pop: 2,887 (1990); 3,048 (1980) **Pop Density:** 122.9
Land: 23.5 sq. mi.; **Water:** 0.3 sq. mi.

Sciotodale — CDP
Lat: 38-45-19 N **Long:** 82-51-39 W
Pop: 1,128 (1990); 1,191 (1980) **Pop Density:** 564.0
Land: 2.0 sq. mi.; **Water:** 0.0 sq. mi.

South Webster — Village
ZIP: 45682 **Lat:** 38-48-56 N **Long:** 82-43-40 W
Pop: 806 (1990); 886 (1980) **Pop Density:** 620.0
Land: 1.3 sq. mi.; **Water:** 0.0 sq. mi. **Elev:** 702 ft.

Union — Township
Lat: 38-49-09 N **Long:** 83-07-49 W
Pop: 1,960 (1990); 1,978 (1980) **Pop Density:** 39.4
Land: 49.8 sq. mi.; **Water:** 0.0 sq. mi.

Valley — Township
Lat: 38-54-15 N **Long:** 83-00-01 W
Pop: 4,785 (1990); 4,387 (1980) **Pop Density:** 193.7
Land: 24.7 sq. mi.; **Water:** 0.5 sq. mi.

Vernon — Township
Lat: 38-43-21 N **Long:** 82-44-59 W
Pop: 1,864 (1990); 1,800 (1980) **Pop Density:** 52.8
Land: 35.3 sq. mi.; **Water:** 0.0 sq. mi.

Washington — Township
ZIP: 45663 **Lat:** 38-44-43 N **Long:** 83-02-56 W
Pop: 6,171 (1990); 6,894 (1980) **Pop Density:** 247.8
Land: 24.9 sq. mi.; **Water:** 0.5 sq. mi.

West Portsmouth — CDP
Lat: 38-45-46 N **Long:** 83-02-17 W
Pop: 3,551 (1990); 4,095 (1980) **Pop Density:** 755.5
Land: 4.7 sq. mi.; **Water:** 0.0 sq. mi.

Wheelersburg — CDP
ZIP: 45694 **Lat:** 38-44-02 N **Long:** 82-50-43 W
Pop: 5,113 (1990); 4,796 (1980) **Pop Density:** 1247.1
Land: 4.1 sq. mi.; **Water:** 0.1 sq. mi.

Seneca County
County Seat: Tiffin (ZIP: **44883**)

Pop: 59,733 (1990); 61,901 (1980) **Pop Density:** 108.5
Land: 550.6 sq. mi.; **Water:** 1.8 sq. mi. **Area Code:** 419
In north-central OH, southeast of Toledo; organized Feb 12, 1820 from Sandusky County.
Name origin: For the Seneca Indians, one of the Five Nations of the Iroquois; name probably means 'stony area.'

Adams — Township
Lat: 41-12-24 N **Long:** 83-01-05 W
Pop: 1,285 (1990); 1,338 (1980) **Pop Density:** 35.7
Land: 36.0 sq. mi.; **Water:** 0.2 sq. mi.

Attica — Village
ZIP: 44807 **Lat:** 41-03-54 N **Long:** 82-53-10 W
Pop: 944 (1990); 865 (1980) **Pop Density:** 1888.0
Land: 0.5 sq. mi.; **Water:** 0.0 sq. mi.
In northern OH, south of Sandusky on a branch of the Sandusky River.
Name origin: For Attica, NY.

Bettsville — Village
ZIP: 44815 **Lat:** 41-14-38 N **Long:** 83-14-00 W
Pop: 752 (1990); 752 (1980) **Pop Density:** 1504.0
Land: 0.5 sq. mi.; **Water:** 0.0 sq. mi. **Elev:** 707 ft.

Big Spring — Township
Lat: 41-01-56 N **Long:** 83-21-28 W
Pop: 1,746 (1990); 1,873 (1980) **Pop Density:** 48.0
Land: 36.4 sq. mi.; **Water:** 0.0 sq. mi.

Bloom — Township
Lat: 41-02-18 N **Long:** 83-00-40 W
Pop: 1,799 (1990); 1,881 (1980) **Pop Density:** 49.4
Land: 36.4 sq. mi.; **Water:** 0.1 sq. mi.

Bloomville — Village
ZIP: 44818 **Lat:** 41-03-03 N **Long:** 83-00-47 W
Pop: 949 (1990); 1,019 (1980) **Pop Density:** 1581.7
Land: 0.6 sq. mi.; **Water:** 0.0 sq. mi.

Clinton — Township
Lat: 41-07-36 N **Long:** 83-07-31 W
Pop: 4,055 (1990); 4,028 (1980) **Pop Density:** 130.0
Land: 31.2 sq. mi.; **Water:** 0.1 sq. mi.

Eden — Township
Lat: 41-02-10 N **Long:** 83-08-05 W
Pop: 1,996 (1990); 2,045 (1980) **Pop Density:** 55.0
Land: 36.3 sq. mi.; **Water:** 0.1 sq. mi.

OHIO, Seneca County   *American Places Dictionary*

Fostoria
City
ZIP: 44830　　　**Lat:** 41-09-35 N　**Long:** 83-24-23 W
Pop: 10,848 (1990); 11,260 (1980)　**Pop Density:** 2213.9
Land: 4.9 sq. mi.; **Water:** 0.0 sq. mi.　**Elev:** 780 ft.
In northern OH, 14 mi. northeast of Findlay. Part of the town is also in Hancock and Wood counties.
Name origin: For local developer, businessman, and banker, C. W. Foster.

Green Springs
Village
ZIP: 44836　　　**Lat:** 41-15-09 N　**Long:** 83-03-12 W
Pop: 731 (1990); 941 (1980)　**Pop Density:** 1462.0
Land: 0.5 sq. mi.; **Water:** 0.0 sq. mi.
In northern OH, southeast of Toledo. Part of the town is also in Sandusky County.

Hopewell
Township
Lat: 41-07-24 N　**Long:** 83-14-47 W
Pop: 2,976 (1990); 3,035 (1980)　**Pop Density:** 86.3
Land: 34.5 sq. mi.; **Water:** 0.1 sq. mi.

Jackson
Township
Lat: 41-12-51 N　**Long:** 83-21-53 W
Pop: 1,747 (1990); 1,808 (1980)　**Pop Density:** 50.1
Land: 34.9 sq. mi.; **Water:** 0.0 sq. mi.

Liberty
Township
Lat: 41-12-37 N　**Long:** 83-14-43 W
Pop: 2,358 (1990); 2,350 (1980)　**Pop Density:** 64.8
Land: 36.4 sq. mi.; **Water:** 0.0 sq. mi.

Loudon
Township
Lat: 41-07-11 N　**Long:** 83-21-48 W
Pop: 2,475 (1990); 2,507 (1980)　**Pop Density:** 73.7
Land: 33.6 sq. mi.; **Water:** 0.0 sq. mi.

New Riegel
Village
ZIP: 44853　　　**Lat:** 41-03-05 N　**Long:** 83-19-08 W
Pop: 298 (1990); 329 (1980)　**Pop Density:** 1490.0
Land: 0.2 sq. mi.; **Water:** 0.0 sq. mi.　**Elev:** 824 ft.

Pleasant
Township
Lat: 41-12-44 N　**Long:** 83-08-09 W
Pop: 1,594 (1990); 1,711 (1980)　**Pop Density:** 44.8
Land: 35.6 sq. mi.; **Water:** 0.5 sq. mi.

Reed
Township
ZIP: 44807　　　**Lat:** 41-07-54 N　**Long:** 82-53-24 W
Pop: 966 (1990); 955 (1980)　**Pop Density:** 25
Land: 38.5 sq. mi.; **Water:** 0.0 sq. mi.

Republic
Village
ZIP: 44867　　　**Lat:** 41-07-29 N　**Long:** 83-00-57 W
Pop: 611 (1990); 656 (1980)　**Pop Density:** 611.
Land: 1.0 sq. mi.; **Water:** 0.0 sq. mi.　**Elev:** 884 f

Scipio
Township
Lat: 41-07-29 N　**Long:** 83-00-57 W
Pop: 1,735 (1990); 1,718 (1980)　**Pop Density:** 47.
Land: 36.9 sq. mi.; **Water:** 0.0 sq. mi.

Seneca
Township
Lat: 41-02-31 N　**Long:** 83-14-48 W
Pop: 1,515 (1990); 1,500 (1980)　**Pop Density:** 42.
Land: 35.6 sq. mi.; **Water:** 0.5 sq. mi.

Thompson
Township
Lat: 41-12-16 N　**Long:** 82-53-59 W
Pop: 1,477 (1990); 1,533 (1980)　**Pop Density:** 39.
Land: 37.3 sq. mi.; **Water:** 0.0 sq. mi.

Tiffin
City
ZIP: 44883　　　**Lat:** 41-07-00 N　**Long:** 83-10-39 W
Pop: 18,604 (1990); 19,549 (1980)　**Pop Density:** 3049.
Land: 6.1 sq. mi.; **Water:** 0.1 sq. mi.
In northern OH on the Sandusky River, southeast of Toledo. Settled 1817.
Name origin: For first governor of OH, Edward Tiffin (1766-1829).

Venice
Township
Lat: 41-02-18 N　**Long:** 82-53-36 W
Pop: 1,826 (1990); 1,869 (1980)　**Pop Density:** 46.
Land: 39.6 sq. mi.; **Water:** 0.0 sq. mi.

Shelby County
County Seat: Sidney (ZIP: 45365)

Pop: 44,915 (1990); 43,089 (1980)　　**Pop Density:** 109.7
Land: 409.3 sq. mi.; **Water:** 1.8 sq. mi.　　**Area Code:** 513
In west-central OH, north of Dayton; organized Jan 7, 1819 from Miami County.
Name origin: For Gen. Isaac Shelby (1750–1826), officer in the Revolutionary War, NC legislator, and governor of KY (1792–96; 1812–16).

Anna
Village
ZIP: 45302　　　**Lat:** 40-23-44 N　**Long:** 84-10-22 W
Pop: 1,164 (1990); 1,038 (1980)　**Pop Density:** 1662.9
Land: 0.7 sq. mi.; **Water:** 0.0 sq. mi.

Botkins
Village
ZIP: 45306　　　**Lat:** 40-28-02 N　**Long:** 84-10-57 W
Pop: 1,340 (1990); 1,372 (1980)　**Pop Density:** 2680.0
Land: 0.5 sq. mi.; **Water:** 0.0 sq. mi.　**Elev:** 1011 ft.

Clinton
Township
ZIP: 45365　　　**Lat:** 40-17-12 N　**Long:** 84-10-14 W
Pop: 19,755 (1990); 18,919 (1980)　**Pop Density:** 1182.9
Land: 16.7 sq. mi.; **Water:** 0.1 sq. mi.
In west-central OH, 28 mi. south of Lima.

Cynthian
Township
Lat: 40-17-57 N　**Long:** 84-21-13 W
Pop: 1,762 (1990); 1,808 (1980)　**Pop Density:** 56.3
Land: 31.3 sq. mi.; **Water:** 0.1 sq. mi.

Dinsmore — Township
Lat: 40-26-18 N Long: 84-10-06 W
Pop: 3,313 (1990); 3,179 (1980) Pop Density: 91.3
Land: 36.3 sq. mi.; Water: 0.0 sq. mi.

Fort Loramie — Village
ZIP: 45845 Lat: 40-20-46 N Long: 84-22-13 W
Pop: 1,042 (1990); 977 (1980) Pop Density: 2084.0
Land: 0.5 sq. mi.; Water: 0.0 sq. mi. Elev: 953 ft.

Franklin — Township
Lat: 40-21-37 N Long: 84-10-06 W
Pop: 2,375 (1990); 2,142 (1980) Pop Density: 95.8
Land: 24.8 sq. mi.; Water: 0.0 sq. mi.

Green — Township
Lat: 40-13-12 N Long: 84-03-52 W
Pop: 973 (1990); 975 (1980) Pop Density: 38.6
Land: 25.2 sq. mi.; Water: 0.0 sq. mi.

Jackson — Township
Lat: 40-25-55 N Long: 84-03-05 W
Pop: 2,393 (1990); 2,225 (1980) Pop Density: 64.0
Land: 37.4 sq. mi.; Water: 0.0 sq. mi.

Jackson Center — Village
ZIP: 45334 Lat: 40-26-20 N Long: 84-02-22 W
Pop: 1,398 (1990); 1,310 (1980) Pop Density: 1270.9
Land: 1.1 sq. mi.; Water: 0.0 sq. mi.

Kettlersville — Village
ZIP: 45336 Lat: 40-26-19 N Long: 84-15-39 W
Pop: 194 (1990); 199 (1980) Pop Density: 194.0
Land: 1.0 sq. mi.; Water: 0.0 sq. mi. Elev: 980 ft.

Lockington — Village
Lat: 40-12-27 N Long: 84-14-07 W
Pop: 214 (1990); 203 (1980) Pop Density: 2140.0
Land: 0.1 sq. mi.; Water: 0.0 sq. mi.

Loramie — Township
Lat: 40-14-23 N Long: 84-22-05 W
Pop: 2,190 (1990); 2,169 (1980) Pop Density: 61.7
Land: 35.5 sq. mi.; Water: 0.0 sq. mi.

McLean — Township
Lat: 40-21-46 N Long: 84-21-21 W
Pop: 2,692 (1990); 2,653 (1980) Pop Density: 83.3
Land: 32.3 sq. mi.; Water: 1.2 sq. mi.

Orange — Township
Lat: 40-13-14 N Long: 84-08-51 W
Pop: 1,183 (1990); 1,167 (1980) Pop Density: 52.1
Land: 22.7 sq. mi.; Water: 0.1 sq. mi.

Perry — Township
Lat: 40-17-49 N Long: 84-04-14 W
Pop: 1,227 (1990); 1,293 (1980) Pop Density: 43.7
Land: 28.1 sq. mi.; Water: 0.0 sq. mi.

Port Jefferson — Village
ZIP: 45360 Lat: 40-19-47 N Long: 84-05-31 W
Pop: 381 (1990); 482 (1980) Pop Density: 1905.0
Land: 0.2 sq. mi.; Water: 0.0 sq. mi. Elev: 974 ft.

Russia — Village
ZIP: 45363 Lat: 40-13-56 N Long: 84-24-39 W
Pop: 442 (1990); 438 (1980) Pop Density: 1105.0
Land: 0.4 sq. mi.; Water: 0.0 sq. mi.

Salem — Township
Lat: 40-20-45 N Long: 84-04-16 W
Pop: 2,080 (1990); 1,888 (1980) Pop Density: 77.9
Land: 26.7 sq. mi.; Water: 0.0 sq. mi.

Sidney — City
ZIP: 45365 Lat: 40-17-19 N Long: 84-09-47 W
Pop: 18,710 (1990); 17,657 (1980) Pop Density: 2175.6
Land: 8.6 sq. mi.; Water: 0.0 sq. mi.

In western OH, 28 mi. northwest of Springfield.

Name origin: For English poet, politician and soldier Sir Philip Sidney (1554–86), "the great light of chivalry," brought to mind by someone because of the beauty of the site. Also possibly influenced by the middle name of Charles Sidney Starrett, who donated the land for the townsite.

Turtle Creek — Township
Lat: 40-19-46 N Long: 84-14-57 W
Pop: 1,301 (1990); 1,319 (1980) Pop Density: 42.9
Land: 30.3 sq. mi.; Water: 0.0 sq. mi.

Van Buren — Township
Lat: 40-26-11 N Long: 84-16-18 W
Pop: 1,816 (1990); 1,709 (1980) Pop Density: 49.1
Land: 37.0 sq. mi.; Water: 0.1 sq. mi.

Washington — Township
Lat: 40-14-08 N Long: 84-15-14 W
Pop: 1,855 (1990); 1,643 (1980) Pop Density: 74.2
Land: 25.0 sq. mi.; Water: 0.1 sq. mi.

Stark County
County Seat: Canton (ZIP: 44702)

Pop: 367,585 (1990); 378,823 (1980) Pop Density: 638.0
Land: 576.2 sq. mi.; Water: 4.8 sq. mi. Area Code: 216

In northeastern OH, south of Akron; organized Feb 13, 1808 from Indian Territory.

Name origin: For Gen. John Stark (1728–1822), officer in the French and Indian war and the Revolutionary War.

Alliance — City
ZIP: 44601 Lat: 40-54-39 N Long: 81-07-01 W
Pop: 23,304 (1990); 24,315 (1980) Pop Density: 2842.0
Land: 8.2 sq. mi.; Water: 0.0 sq. mi. Elev: 1174 ft.

In northeast-central OH on the Mahoning River, 14 mi. northeast of Canton. Settled 1805 by Quakers; united with nearby Greedom, Williamsport, and Mount Union in 1854; incorporated as a city 1889. Part of the town is also in Mahoning County.

Name origin: Named by railroad official Gen. Robinson either for its having been a grouping of small villages or for the junction here of two railroads.

Beach City — Village
ZIP: 44608   **Lat:** 40-39-09 N   **Long:** 81-34-48 W
Pop: 1,051 (1990); 1,083 (1980)   **Pop Density:** 2102.0
Land: 0.5 sq. mi.; **Water:** 0.0 sq. mi.   **Elev:** 970 ft.

Bethlehem — Township
ZIP: 44662   **Lat:** 40-41-29 N   **Long:** 81-29-43 W
Pop: 5,803 (1990); 5,892 (1980)   **Pop Density:** 174.3
Land: 33.3 sq. mi.; **Water:** 0.1 sq. mi.

Brewster — Village
ZIP: 44613   **Lat:** 40-42-45 N   **Long:** 81-36-02 W
Pop: 2,307 (1990); 2,321 (1980)   **Pop Density:** 1153.5
Land: 2.0 sq. mi.; **Water:** 0.0 sq. mi.

In northeastern OH along Sugar Creek, 18 mi. southwest of Canton.

Canal Fulton — Village
ZIP: 44614   **Lat:** 40-53-24 N   **Long:** 81-35-04 W
Pop: 4,157 (1990); 3,481 (1980)   **Pop Density:** 1807.4
Land: 2.3 sq. mi.; **Water:** 0.0 sq. mi.

Name origin: For Robert Fulton (1765–1815), inventor of the *Clermont*, the first commercially successful steamboat. Formerly called Milan.

Canton — City
ZIP: 44711   **Lat:** 40-48-43 N   **Long:** 81-22-23 W
Pop: 84,161 (1990); 93,077 (1980)   **Pop Density:** 4166.4
Land: 20.2 sq. mi.; **Water:** 0.0 sq. mi.

In northeastern OH, 20 mi. southeast of Akron. Incorporated as a village 1822, as a city 1854. Industrial city (steel, office equipment). Home of William McKinley (1843–1901), twenty-fifth president of the U.S., buried here in National McKinley Memorial.

Name origin: Named by Bezaleel Wells for his friend Capt. John O'Donnell's Baltimore estate, which was named for Canton, China.

*Canton — Township
ZIP: 44701   **Lat:** 40-45-43 N   **Long:** 81-21-54 W
Pop: 14,050 (1990); 15,193 (1980)   **Pop Density:** 553.1
Land: 25.4 sq. mi.; **Water:** 0.1 sq. mi.

East Canton — Village
ZIP: 44730   **Lat:** 40-47-20 N   **Long:** 81-17-00 W
Pop: 1,742 (1990); 1,721 (1980)   **Pop Density:** 1340.0
Land: 1.3 sq. mi.; **Water:** 0.0 sq. mi.   **Elev:** 1146 ft.

In northeastern OH, 5 mi. east of Canton.

Name origin: Named in 1918 for its location. Formerly called Osnaburg.

East Sparta — Village
ZIP: 44626   **Lat:** 40-40-11 N   **Long:** 81-21-13 W
Pop: 771 (1990); 868 (1980)   **Pop Density:** 1285.0
Land: 0.6 sq. mi.; **Water:** 0.0 sq. mi.

Greentown — CDP
Lat: 40-55-39 N   **Long:** 81-24-06 W
Pop: 1,856 (1990)   **Pop Density:** 687.4
Land: 2.7 sq. mi.; **Water:** 0.0 sq. mi.

Hartville — Village
ZIP: 44632   **Lat:** 40-57-39 N   **Long:** 81-20-02 W
Pop: 2,031 (1990); 1,772 (1980)   **Pop Density:** 1269.4
Land: 1.6 sq. mi.; **Water:** 0.0 sq. mi.

Hills and Dales — Village
ZIP: 44708   **Lat:** 40-49-41 N   **Long:** 81-26-41 W
Pop: 297 (1990); 281 (1980)   **Pop Density:** 990.0
Land: 0.3 sq. mi.; **Water:** 0.0 sq. mi.

Jackson — Township
ZIP: 44646   **Lat:** 40-51-45 N   **Long:** 81-28-52 W
Pop: 32,071 (1990); 29,001 (1980)   **Pop Density:** 876.3
Land: 36.6 sq. mi.; **Water:** 0.6 sq. mi.

In northeastern OH, just outside Massillon.

Lake — Township
ZIP: 44720   **Lat:** 40-56-46 N   **Long:** 81-21-39 W
Pop: 22,343 (1990); 20,559 (1980)   **Pop Density:** 642.0
Land: 34.8 sq. mi.; **Water:** 0.4 sq. mi.

In northeastern OH, 9 mi. north of Canton.

Lawrence — Township
ZIP: 44614   **Lat:** 40-51-50 N   **Long:** 81-35-32 W
Pop: 12,047 (1990); 11,380 (1980)   **Pop Density:** 348.2
Land: 34.6 sq. mi.; **Water:** 0.3 sq. mi.

In northeastern OH, 11 mi. northwest of Canton.

Lexington — Township
ZIP: 44601   **Lat:** 40-57-11 N   **Long:** 81-08-23 W
Pop: 5,291 (1990); 6,351 (1980)   **Pop Density:** 229.0
Land: 23.1 sq. mi.; **Water:** 1.7 sq. mi.

Limaville — Village
ZIP: 44640   **Lat:** 40-59-02 N   **Long:** 81-08-53 W
Pop: 152 (1990); 164 (1980)   **Pop Density:** 506.7
Land: 0.3 sq. mi.; **Water:** 0.0 sq. mi.

Louisville — City
ZIP: 44641   **Lat:** 40-50-14 N   **Long:** 81-15-39 W
Pop: 8,087 (1990); 7,996 (1980)   **Pop Density:** 1797.1
Land: 4.5 sq. mi.; **Water:** 0.0 sq. mi.

In north-central OH, 5 mi. northeast of Canton.

Name origin: Named Lewisville by landowner Henry Loutzenheiser for his son, Lewis. Spelling was changed because another OH town had a prior claim.

Magnolia — Village
ZIP: 44643   **Lat:** 40-39-11 N   **Long:** 81-17-24 W
Pop: 591 (1990); 677 (1980)   **Pop Density:** 985.0
Land: 0.6 sq. mi.; **Water:** 0.0 sq. mi.

In northeastern OH along Sandy Creek, 15 mi. south of Canton. Founded 1834. Part of the town is also in Carroll County.

Name origin: Named by founder and mill owner Richard Elson, for the flower.

Marlboro — Township
Lat: 40-56-44 N   **Long:** 81-14-30 W
Pop: 3,687 (1990); 3,748 (1980)   **Pop Density:** 103.0
Land: 35.8 sq. mi.; **Water:** 0.6 sq. mi.

Massillon — City
ZIP: 44646   **Lat:** 40-47-11 N   **Long:** 81-31-12 W
Pop: 31,007 (1990); 30,557 (1980)   **Pop Density:** 2349.0
Land: 13.2 sq. mi.; **Water:** 0.1 sq. mi.   **Elev:** 951 ft.

In northeast-central OH, 10 mi. west of Canton. Founded 1826; incorporated 1853.

Name origin: For the French divine, Jean Batiste Massillon (1663–1742), whose works were favorites of the wife of the town founder.

Meyers Lake — Village
Lat: 40-48-49 N   **Long:** 81-25-05 W
Pop: 493 (1990); 222 (1980)   **Pop Density:** 2465.0
Land: 0.2 sq. mi.; **Water:** 0.2 sq. mi.

Minerva — Village
ZIP: 44657   Lat: 40-44-07 N   Long: 81-05-46 W
Pop: 2,226 (1990); 2,397 (1980)   Pop Density: 2023.6
Land: 1.1 sq. mi.; Water: 0.0 sq. mi.
Part of the town is also in Carroll and Columbiana counties.
Name origin: For the niece of founder John Whitacre.

Navarre — Village
ZIP: 44662   Lat: 40-43-21 N   Long: 81-31-21 W
Pop: 1,635 (1990); 1,343 (1980)   Pop Density: 3270.0
Land: 0.5 sq. mi.; Water: 0.0 sq. mi.
Name origin: Named by the French-speaking wife of James Duncan, for Henry IV (1553–1610), king of Navarre and France. Previously named Bethelehem.

Nimishillen — Township
ZIP: 44641   Lat: 40-51-26 N   Long: 81-14-49 W
Pop: 9,492 (1990); 10,436 (1980)   Pop Density: 293.9
Land: 32.3 sq. mi.; Water: 0.1 sq. mi.
In northeastern OH, 5 mi. northeast of Canton.

North Canton — City
ZIP: 44720   Lat: 40-52-23 N   Long: 81-23-54 W
Pop: 14,748 (1990); 14,228 (1980)   Pop Density: 2681.5
Land: 5.5 sq. mi.; Water: 0.0 sq. mi.   Elev: 1160 ft.
In northeast-central OH, just north of Canton. Site of Walsh College (1960).

Osnaburg — Township
ZIP: 44730   Lat: 40-45-58 N   Long: 81-15-01 W
Pop: 5,781 (1990); 5,867 (1980)   Pop Density: 155.8
Land: 37.1 sq. mi.; Water: 0.0 sq. mi.

Paris — Township
ZIP: 44669   Lat: 40-46-20 N   Long: 81-08-25 W
Pop: 5,907 (1990); 6,374 (1980)   Pop Density: 175.3
Land: 33.7 sq. mi.; Water: 0.1 sq. mi.

Perry — Township
ZIP: 44708   Lat: 40-46-21 N   Long: 81-28-37 W
Pop: 30,307 (1990); 32,675 (1980)   Pop Density: 1148.0
Land: 26.4 sq. mi.; Water: 0.3 sq. mi.
In northeastern OH, 9 mi. west-southwest of Canton.

Perry Heights — CDP
ZIP: 44646   Lat: 40-47-48 N   Long: 81-28-08 W
Pop: 9,055 (1990); 9,206 (1980)   Pop Density: 3233.9
Land: 2.8 sq. mi.; Water: 0.0 sq. mi.

Pike — Township
Lat: 40-40-59 N   Long: 81-22-25 W
Pop: 3,931 (1990); 4,179 (1980)   Pop Density: 123.6
Land: 31.8 sq. mi.; Water: 0.1 sq. mi.

Plain — Township
ZIP: 44708   Lat: 40-52-08 N   Long: 81-21-46 W
Pop: 49,181 (1990); 48,318 (1980)   Pop Density: 1731.7
Land: 28.4 sq. mi.; Water: 0.2 sq. mi.
In northeastern OH, 5 mi. north of Canton.

Sandy — Township
Lat: 40-41-17 N   Long: 81-16-29 W
Pop: 3,630 (1990); 3,724 (1980)   Pop Density: 176.2
Land: 20.6 sq. mi.; Water: 0.0 sq. mi.

Sugar Creek — Township
ZIP: 44662   Lat: 40-41-22 N   Long: 81-36-09 W
Pop: 6,489 (1990); 6,636 (1980)   Pop Density: 191.4
Land: 33.9 sq. mi.; Water: 0.1 sq. mi.

Tuscarawas — Township
ZIP: 44646   Lat: 40-46-51 N   Long: 81-35-37 W
Pop: 6,251 (1990); 7,369 (1980)   Pop Density: 199.1
Land: 31.4 sq. mi.; Water: 0.0 sq. mi.

Uniontown — CDP
ZIP: 44685   Lat: 40-58-24 N   Long: 81-24-12 W
Pop: 3,074 (1990)   Pop Density: 1229.6
Land: 2.5 sq. mi.; Water: 0.0 sq. mi.

Washington — Township
Lat: 40-51-13 N   Long: 81-08-28 W
Pop: 4,765 (1990); 5,176 (1980)   Pop Density: 153.7
Land: 31.0 sq. mi.; Water: 0.0 sq. mi.

Waynesburg — Village
ZIP: 44688   Lat: 40-40-05 N   Long: 81-15-33 W
Pop: 1,068 (1990); 1,160 (1980)   Pop Density: 2136.0
Land: 0.5 sq. mi.; Water: 0.0 sq. mi.

Wilmot — Village
ZIP: 44689   Lat: 40-39-21 N   Long: 81-38-06 W
Pop: 261 (1990); 329 (1980)   Pop Density: 1305.0
Land: 0.2 sq. mi.; Water: 0.0 sq. mi.   Elev: 1093 ft.

Summit County
County Seat: Akron (ZIP: 44308)

Pop: 514,990 (1990); 524,472 (1980)   Pop Density: 1247.5
Land: 412.8 sq. mi.; Water: 7.3 sq. mi.   Area Code: 216
In northeastern OH, south of Cleveland; organized Mar 3, 1840 from Portage, Medina, and Stark counties.
Name origin: From the Greek 'summit,' because the highest point on the Ohio Canal is at the county seat, Akron.

Akron — City
ZIP: 44309   Lat: 41-04-49 N   Long: 81-31-17 W
Pop: 223,019 (1990); 237,177 (1980)   Pop Density: 3585.5
Land: 62.2 sq. mi.; Water: 0.4 sq. mi.
In northeastern OH on the Little Cuyahoga River, 35 mi. southeast of Cleveland. County seat (1842). Settled 1825; incorporated as a village 1836; granted charter as a city 1865. Old Indian portage trail between the Cuyahoga and Tuscarawas rivers. Diverse rubber industries (first rubber factory founded by B. F. Goodrich in 1869). Main office of

Goodyear Tire & Rubber Co. here. Site of Univ. of Akron (1913).

Name origin: From Greek 'summit,' for the name of its county.

Barberton
City
ZIP: 44203   **Lat:** 41-00-43 N **Long:** 81-36-20 W
Pop: 27,623 (1990); 29,751 (1980)   **Pop Density:** 3634.6
Land: 7.6 sq. mi.; **Water:** 0.2 sq. mi.   **Elev:** 969 ft.

In northeastern OH, 7 mi. southwest of Akron. Laid out 1891 by Ohio Columbus Barber, president of the Diamond Match Company. Industrial city (tires, chemicals).

Name origin: For Ohio Columbus Barber.

Bath
Township
ZIP: 44210   **Lat:** 41-10-18 N **Long:** 81-38-18 W
Pop: 9,015 (1990); 8,476 (1980)   **Pop Density:** 398.9
Land: 22.6 sq. mi.; **Water:** 0.2 sq. mi.

Boston
Township
ZIP: 44264   **Lat:** 41-14-03 N **Long:** 81-33-04 W
Pop: 1,879 (1990); 2,064 (1980)   **Pop Density:** 95.9
Land: 19.6 sq. mi.; **Water:** 0.1 sq. mi.

Boston Heights
Village
Lat: 41-15-20 N **Long:** 81-30-16 W
Pop: 733 (1990); 781 (1980)   **Pop Density:** 107.8
Land: 6.8 sq. mi.; **Water:** 0.0 sq. mi.   **Elev:** 1064 ft.

Clinton
Village
ZIP: 44216   **Lat:** 40-55-44 N **Long:** 81-37-52 W
Pop: 1,175 (1990); 1,277 (1980)   **Pop Density:** 326.4
Land: 3.6 sq. mi.; **Water:** 0.1 sq. mi.

In northeast-central OH, just southwest of Akron.

Name origin: For NY Gov. DeWitt Clinton (1769–1828), supporter of the Erie Canal.

Copley
Township
ZIP: 44321   **Lat:** 41-05-35 N **Long:** 81-38-37 W
Pop: 11,130 (1990); 15,910 (1980)   **Pop Density:** 545.6
Land: 20.4 sq. mi.; **Water:** 0.3 sq. mi.

In northeastern OH, 5 mi. east of Akron.

Coventry
Township
ZIP: 44319   **Lat:** 41-00-19 N **Long:** 81-32-18 W
Pop: 11,295 (1990); 11,951 (1980)   **Pop Density:** 1298.3
Land: 8.7 sq. mi.; **Water:** 1.0 sq. mi.

In northeastern OH, 5 mi. south of Akron.

Cuyahoga Falls
City
ZIP: 44222   **Lat:** 41-10-08 N **Long:** 81-31-21 W
Pop: 48,950 (1990); 43,890 (1980)   **Pop Density:** 1919.6
Land: 25.5 sq. mi.; **Water:** 0.1 sq. mi.

In northeastern OH on the Cuyahoga River, 5 mi. north of Akron.

Name origin: For its location along a falls of the river.

Fairlawn
City
ZIP: 44313   **Lat:** 41-07-29 N **Long:** 81-37-16 W
Pop: 5,779 (1990); 6,100 (1980)   **Pop Density:** 1376.0
Land: 4.2 sq. mi.; **Water:** 0.0 sq. mi.   **Elev:** 1005 ft.

Name origin: In northeast-central OH, a residential area on the Cuyahoga River, just north of Akron.

Franklin
Township
ZIP: 44216   **Lat:** 40-57-15 N **Long:** 81-35-05 W
Pop: 14,910 (1990); 16,142 (1980)   **Pop Density:** 573.5
Land: 26.0 sq. mi.; **Water:** 1.6 sq. mi.

In northeastern OH, 12 mi. south of Akron.

Green
Village
Lat: 40-56-51 N **Long:** 81-29-11 W
Pop: 3,553 (1990)   **Pop Density:** 1184.3
Land: 3.0 sq. mi.; **Water:** 0.0 sq. mi.

*Green
Township
ZIP: 44720   **Lat:** 40-56-50 N **Long:** 81-28-32 W
Pop: 19,179 (1990); 17,625 (1980)   **Pop Density:** 599.3
Land: 32.0 sq. mi.; **Water:** 1.5 sq. mi.   **Elev:** 1150 ft.

In northeast OH, 12 mi. northwest of Canton.

Greensburg
CDP
Lat: 40-56-10 N **Long:** 81-26-11 W
Pop: 3,306 (1990)   **Pop Density:** 359.3
Land: 9.2 sq. mi.; **Water:** 0.0 sq. mi.

Hudson
Village
ZIP: 44236   **Lat:** 41-14-40 N **Long:** 81-27-04 W
Pop: 5,159 (1990); 4,615 (1980)   **Pop Density:** 1289.8
Land: 4.0 sq. mi.; **Water:** 0.1 sq. mi.

In northeastern OH, 10 mi. northeast of Akron. Settled 1799 by a group from CT. Not coextensive with the town of the same name.

Name origin: For David Hudson, an original settler.

*Hudson
Township
ZIP: 44236   **Lat:** 41-14-23 N **Long:** 81-26-27 W
Pop: 17,128 (1990); 12,645 (1980)   **Pop Density:** 669.1
Land: 25.6 sq. mi.; **Water:** 0.3 sq. mi.

Lakemore
Village
ZIP: 44250   **Lat:** 41-01-16 N **Long:** 81-25-39 W
Pop: 2,684 (1990); 2,744 (1980)   **Pop Density:** 1789.3
Land: 1.5 sq. mi.; **Water:** 0.2 sq. mi.

In northeastern OH at the northern tip of Springfield Lake, just southeast of Akron.

Macedonia
City
ZIP: 44056   **Lat:** 41-18-39 N **Long:** 81-29-50 W
Pop: 7,509 (1990); 6,571 (1980)   **Pop Density:** 782.2
Land: 9.6 sq. mi.; **Water:** 0.0 sq. mi.   **Elev:** 989 ft.

In northeastern OH, midway between Cleveland and Akron.

Name origin: For the ancient European kingdom.

Mogadore
Village
ZIP: 44260   **Lat:** 41-03-15 N **Long:** 81-24-04 W
Pop: 2,967 (1990); 3,061 (1980)   **Pop Density:** 1854.4
Land: 1.6 sq. mi.; **Water:** 0.0 sq. mi.

Part of the town is also in Portage County.

Name origin: For Mogador, Morocco, with an added *e*.

Montrose-Ghent
CDP
Lat: 41-09-26 N **Long:** 81-38-32 W
Pop: 4,906 (1990)   **Pop Density:** 511.0
Land: 9.6 sq. mi.; **Water:** 0.1 sq. mi.

Munroe Falls
Village
ZIP: 44262   **Lat:** 41-08-22 N **Long:** 81-26-10 W
Pop: 5,359 (1990); 4,731 (1980)   **Pop Density:** 1984.8
Land: 2.7 sq. mi.; **Water:** 0.1 sq. mi.

In northeastern OH, northeast of Akron.

Name origin: For founder Edmund Munroe and for the falls on the Cuyahoga River.

American Places Dictionary   OHIO, Trumbull County

Northfield   Village
ZIP: 44056   **Lat:** 41-20-37 N **Long:** 81-31-47 W
Pop: 3,624 (1990); 3,913 (1980)   **Pop Density:** 3294.5
Land: 1.1 sq. mi.; **Water:** 0.0 sq. mi.
In northeastern OH, 20 mi. south of Cleveland.
Name origin: Named by its settlers for Northfield, MA, their former home.

Northfield Center   Township
ZIP: 44067   **Lat:** 41-17-38 N **Long:** 81-31-21 W
Pop: 3,982 (1990); 4,294 (1980)   **Pop Density:** 737.4
Land: 5.4 sq. mi.; **Water:** 0.0 sq. mi.

Norton   City
ZIP: 44203   **Lat:** 41-01-43 N **Long:** 81-38-44 W
Pop: 11,475 (1990); 12,242 (1980)   **Pop Density:** 573.8
Land: 20.0 sq. mi.; **Water:** 0.2 sq. mi.   **Elev:** 1050 ft.
In northeast-central OH, a residential suburb just south of Akron. Part of the town is also in Wayne County.

Peninsula   Village
ZIP: 44264   **Lat:** 41-14-12 N **Long:** 81-33-10 W
Pop: 562 (1990); 604 (1980)   **Pop Density:** 119.6
Land: 4.7 sq. mi.; **Water:** 0.0 sq. mi.

Pigeon Creek   CDP
Lat: 41-06-39 N **Long:** 81-40-23 W
Pop: 1,008 (1990)   **Pop Density:** 1120.0
Land: 0.9 sq. mi.; **Water:** 0.0 sq. mi.

Portage Lakes   CDP
ZIP: 44319   **Lat:** 40-59-13 N **Long:** 81-32-11 W
Pop: 13,373 (1990); 7,312 (1980)   **Pop Density:** 1592.0
Land: 8.4 sq. mi.; **Water:** 1.8 sq. mi.

Reminderville   Village
Lat: 41-19-38 N **Long:** 81-23-50 W
Pop: 2,163 (1990); 1,960 (1980)   **Pop Density:** 1081.5
Land: 2.0 sq. mi.; **Water:** 0.0 sq. mi.

Richfield   Village
ZIP: 44286   **Lat:** 41-13-53 N **Long:** 81-38-14 W
Pop: 3,117 (1990); 3,437 (1980)   **Pop Density:** 394.6
Land: 7.9 sq. mi.; **Water:** 0.0 sq. mi.
Not coextensive with the town of the same name.

*Richfield   Township
ZIP: 44286   **Lat:** 41-14-38 N **Long:** 81-38-00 W
Pop: 5,010 (1990); 4,941 (1980)   **Pop Density:** 196.5
Land: 25.5 sq. mi.; **Water:** 0.0 sq. mi.

Sagamore Hills   Township
ZIP: 44067   **Lat:** 41-19-00 N **Long:** 81-33-33 W
Pop: 6,503 (1990); 7,189 (1980)   **Pop Density:** 575.5
Land: 11.3 sq. mi.; **Water:** 0.0 sq. mi.

Silver Lake   Village
Lat: 41-09-23 N **Long:** 81-27-34 W
Pop: 3,052 (1990); 2,915 (1980)   **Pop Density:** 2180.0
Land: 1.4 sq. mi.; **Water:** 0.2 sq. mi.

Springfield   Township
ZIP: 44312   **Lat:** 41-00-52 N **Long:** 81-26-36 W
Pop: 14,773 (1990); 16,125 (1980)   **Pop Density:** 998.2
Land: 14.8 sq. mi.; **Water:** 0.3 sq. mi.
In northeastern OH, 5 mi. southeast of Akron.

Stow   City
ZIP: 44224   **Lat:** 41-10-35 N **Long:** 81-26-11 W
Pop: 27,702 (1990); 25,303 (1980)   **Pop Density:** 1620.0
Land: 17.1 sq. mi.; **Water:** 0.2 sq. mi.   **Elev:** 1091 ft.
In northeastern OH, 6 mi. northeast of Akron.
Name origin: For landowner Joshua Stow.

Tallmadge   City
ZIP: 44278   **Lat:** 41-06-12 N **Long:** 81-25-23 W
Pop: 14,870 (1990); 15,269 (1980)   **Pop Density:** 1101.5
Land: 13.5 sq. mi.; **Water:** 0.0 sq. mi.   **Elev:** 1114 ft.
In northeast-central OH, just east of Akron.
Name origin: For founder, Col. Benjamin Tallmadge.

Twinsburg   City
ZIP: 44087   **Lat:** 41-19-27 N **Long:** 81-27-10 W
Pop: 9,606 (1990); 7,632 (1980)   **Pop Density:** 787.4
Land: 12.2 sq. mi.; **Water:** 0.0 sq. mi.   **Elev:** 1004 ft.
Name origin: For the Wilcox twins, Moses and Aaron, who donated the 6-acre village square.

*Twinsburg   Township
ZIP: 44087   **Lat:** 41-17-44 N **Long:** 81-25-29 W
Pop: 1,896 (1990); 1,257 (1980)   **Pop Density:** 225.7
Land: 8.4 sq. mi.; **Water:** 0.1 sq. mi.

Trumbull County
County Seat: Warren (ZIP: 44481)

Pop: 227,813 (1990); 241,863 (1980)   **Pop Density:** 369.9
Land: 615.8 sq. mi.; **Water:** 18.2 sq. mi.   **Area Code:** 216
On the northeastern border of OH; organized Jul 10, 1800 from Jefferson County (prior to statehood).
Name origin: For Jonathan Trumbull (1740–1809), aide-de-camp to Gen. George Washington (1780–83), governor of CT (1798–1809), and son of the colonial governor of the same name.

Bazetta   Township
ZIP: 44410   **Lat:** 41-18-26 N **Long:** 80-46-04 W
Pop: 5,414 (1990); 10,107 (1980)   **Pop Density:** 257.8
Land: 21.0 sq. mi.; **Water:** 3.5 sq. mi.

Bloomfield   Township
ZIP: 44450   **Lat:** 41-28-13 N **Long:** 80-51-28 W
Pop: 1,117 (1990); 1,078 (1980)   **Pop Density:** 44.0
Land: 25.4 sq. mi.; **Water:** 0.0 sq. mi.

Bolindale
CDP
Lat: 41-12-26 N Long: 80-46-39 W
Pop: 2,827 (1990) **Pop Density:** 2827.0
Land: 1.0 sq. mi.; **Water:** 0.0 sq. mi.

Braceville
Township
ZIP: 44444 Lat: 41-14-09 N Long: 80-57-20 W
Pop: 2,972 (1990); 3,132 (1980) **Pop Density:** 127.0
Land: 23.4 sq. mi.; **Water:** 0.2 sq. mi.

Bristol
Township
ZIP: 44402 Lat: 41-22-58 N Long: 80-51-44 W
Pop: 3,026 (1990); 3,151 (1980) **Pop Density:** 116.4
Land: 26.0 sq. mi.; **Water:** 0.0 sq. mi.

Brookfield
Township
ZIP: 44403 Lat: 41-14-01 N Long: 80-34-08 W
Pop: 10,562 (1990); 10,935 (1980) **Pop Density:** 429.3
Land: 24.6 sq. mi.; **Water:** 0.1 sq. mi.

In northeastern OH, northeast of Youngstown.

Champion
Township
ZIP: 44481 Lat: 41-18-39 N Long: 80-51-22 W
Pop: 9,189 (1990); 9,504 (1980) **Pop Density:** 356.2
Land: 25.8 sq. mi.; **Water:** 0.0 sq. mi.

Champion Heights
CDP
Lat: 41-17-17 N Long: 80-50-55 W
Pop: 4,665 (1990) **Pop Density:** 1372.1
Land: 3.4 sq. mi.; **Water:** 0.0 sq. mi.

Churchill
CDP
Lat: 41-10-24 N Long: 80-40-02 W
Pop: 2,691 (1990) **Pop Density:** 1076.4
Land: 2.5 sq. mi.; **Water:** 0.0 sq. mi.

Cortland
Village
ZIP: 44410 Lat: 41-19-53 N Long: 80-43-24 W
Pop: 5,666 (1990); 5,011 (1980) **Pop Density:** 1573.9
Land: 3.6 sq. mi.; **Water:** 0.0 sq. mi.

In northeastern OH, north of Youngstown.

Name origin: Named by the Company Railroad, which came through in the 1800s. Originally known as Baconsburgh, for Enos Bacon, who owned a store here in 1829.

Farmington
Township
ZIP: 44491 Lat: 41-23-20 N Long: 80-57-03 W
Pop: 1,897 (1990); 1,747 (1980) **Pop Density:** 70.3
Land: 27.0 sq. mi.; **Water:** 0.0 sq. mi.

Fowler
Township
ZIP: 44418 Lat: 41-17-58 N Long: 80-40-25 W
Pop: 2,868 (1990); 3,066 (1980) **Pop Density:** 110.3
Land: 26.0 sq. mi.; **Water:** 0.0 sq. mi.

Girard
City
ZIP: 44420 Lat: 41-09-16 N Long: 80-41-51 W
Pop: 11,304 (1990); 12,517 (1980) **Pop Density:** 2355.0
Land: 4.8 sq. mi.; **Water:** 0.0 sq. mi.

In northeastern OH, 6 mi. northwest of Youngstown.

Name origin: For Stephen Girard (1750–1831), philanthropist and founder of Girard College in Philadelphia, PA.

Greene
Township
ZIP: 44450 Lat: 41-27-46 N Long: 80-45-39 W
Pop: 940 (1990); 903 (1980) **Pop Density:** 39.0
Land: 24.1 sq. mi.; **Water:** 2.4 sq. mi. **Elev:** 929 ft.

Gustavus
Township
ZIP: 44417 Lat: 41-28-10 N Long: 80-40-27 W
Pop: 1,031 (1990); 1,108 (1980) **Pop Density:** 41.2
Land: 25.0 sq. mi.; **Water:** 0.0 sq. mi.

Hartford
Township
Lat: 41-18-42 N Long: 80-34-15 W
Pop: 2,157 (1990); 2,236 (1980) **Pop Density:** 81.4
Land: 26.5 sq. mi.; **Water:** 0.1 sq. mi.

Howland
Township
ZIP: 44484 Lat: 41-14-05 N Long: 80-45-14 W
Pop: 20,096 (1990); 20,586 (1980) **Pop Density:** 1135.4
Land: 17.7 sq. mi.; **Water:** 0.0 sq. mi.

In northeastern OH, just east of Warren.

Hubbard
City
ZIP: 44425 Lat: 41-09-35 N Long: 80-34-10 W
Pop: 8,248 (1990); 9,245 (1980) **Pop Density:** 2660.6
Land: 3.1 sq. mi.; **Water:** 0.0 sq. mi.

In northeastern OH just west of the PA border, 10 mi. north of Youngstown. Not coextensive with the town of the same name.

Name origin: For Nehemiah Hubbard, who purchased the surrounding township in 1801.

*Hubbard
Township
ZIP: 44425 Lat: 41-10-04 N Long: 80-34-05 W
Pop: 14,863 (1990); 16,520 (1980) **Pop Density:** 606.7
Land: 24.5 sq. mi.; **Water:** 0.1 sq. mi.

Johnston
Township
ZIP: 44410 Lat: 41-23-21 N Long: 80-39-51 W
Pop: 1,931 (1990); 2,012 (1980) **Pop Density:** 78.2
Land: 24.7 sq. mi.; **Water:** 0.0 sq. mi.

Kinsman
Township
ZIP: 44428 Lat: 41-27-47 N Long: 80-34-15 W
Pop: 2,099 (1990); 2,120 (1980) **Pop Density:** 79.2
Land: 26.5 sq. mi.; **Water:** 0.4 sq. mi.

Liberty
Township
ZIP: 44420 Lat: 41-10-04 N Long: 80-39-36 W
Pop: 24,453 (1990); 26,827 (1980) **Pop Density:** 1072.5
Land: 22.8 sq. mi.; **Water:** 0.4 sq. mi.

In northeastern OH, 4 mi. north of Youngstown.

Lordstown
Village
ZIP: 44481 Lat: 41-09-55 N Long: 80-51-15 W
Pop: 3,404 (1990); 3,280 (1980) **Pop Density:** 147.4
Land: 23.1 sq. mi.; **Water:** 0.0 sq. mi. **Elev:** 957 ft.

McDonald
Village
ZIP: 44437 Lat: 41-09-51 N Long: 80-43-25 W
Pop: 3,526 (1990); 3,744 (1980) **Pop Density:** 2074.1
Land: 1.7 sq. mi.; **Water:** 0.0 sq. mi.

In northeastern OH, just south of Niles and Warren.

Mecca
Township
ZIP: 44410 Lat: 41-23-40 N Long: 80-46-09 W
Pop: 2,602 (1990); 2,695 (1980) **Pop Density:** 128.2
Land: 20.3 sq. mi.; **Water:** 6.5 sq. mi.

Mesopotamia
Township
Lat: 41-27-43 N Long: 80-57-12 W
Pop: 2,533 (1990); 1,966 (1980) **Pop Density:** 94.2
Land: 26.9 sq. mi.; **Water:** 0.0 sq. mi.

OHIO, Trumbull County

Mineral Ridge — CDP
ZIP: 44440 Lat: 41-08-41 N Long: 80-45-55 W
Pop: 2,862 (1990) Pop Density: 1506.3
Land: 1.9 sq. mi.; Water: 0.0 sq. mi.
Part of the town is also in Mahoning County.

Newton — Township
ZIP: 44444 Lat: 41-10-08 N Long: 80-57-10 W
Pop: 9,541 (1990); 9,797 (1980) Pop Density: 413.0
Land: 23.1 sq. mi.; Water: 0.2 sq. mi.

Newton Falls — City
ZIP: 44444 Lat: 41-11-20 N Long: 80-58-11 W
Pop: 4,866 (1990); 4,960 (1980) Pop Density: 2115.7
Land: 2.3 sq. mi.; Water: 0.1 sq. mi. Elev: 924 ft.
In northeastern OH on the Mahoning River, 10 mi. west of Warren.

Niles — City
ZIP: 44446 Lat: 41-11-16 N Long: 80-45-11 W
Pop: 21,128 (1990); 23,088 (1980) Pop Density: 2485.6
Land: 8.5 sq. mi.; Water: 0.0 sq. mi.
In northeast-central OH, just south of Warren.
Name origin: For Baltimore newspaper editor Niles Hezeklah (1777–1830), publisher and author of several books on American government.

Orangeville — Village
ZIP: 44453 Lat: 41-20-35 N Long: 80-31-45 W
Pop: 253 (1990); 223 (1980) Pop Density: 316.3
Land: 0.8 sq. mi.; Water: 0.3 sq. mi.

South Canal — CDP
Lat: 41-10-38 N Long: 80-59-12 W
Pop: 1,319 (1990) Pop Density: 824.4
Land: 1.6 sq. mi.; Water: 0.0 sq. mi.

Southington — Township
ZIP: 44470 Lat: 41-18-22 N Long: 80-56-49 W
Pop: 3,610 (1990); 3,723 (1980) Pop Density: 139.4
Land: 25.9 sq. mi.; Water: 0.0 sq. mi.

Turnpike Interchange — CDP
Lat: 41-12-58 N Long: 80-56-03 W
Pop: 1,188 (1990) Pop Density: 172.2
Land: 6.9 sq. mi.; Water: 0.1 sq. mi.

Vernon — Township
ZIP: 44428 Lat: 41-23-13 N Long: 80-34-07 W
Pop: 1,690 (1990); 1,635 (1980) Pop Density: 71.6
Land: 23.6 sq. mi.; Water: 2.7 sq. mi.

Vienna — Township
ZIP: 44473 Lat: 41-14-06 N Long: 80-39-53 W
Pop: 4,180 (1990); 4,344 (1980) Pop Density: 178.6
Land: 23.4 sq. mi.; Water: 0.1 sq. mi.

Warren — City
ZIP: 44481 Lat: 41-14-16 N Long: 80-49-00 W
Pop: 50,793 (1990); 56,629 (1980) Pop Density: 3174.6
Land: 16.0 sq. mi.; Water: 0.0 sq. mi. Elev: 893 ft.
In northeastern OH, 15 mi. northwest of Youngstown. Incorporated as a city 1869.
Name origin: Named in 1798 for county surveyor, Moses Warren.

*Warren — Township
ZIP: 44430 Lat: 41-14-16 N Long: 80-52-00 W
Pop: 6,867 (1990); 7,940 (1980) Pop Density: 470.3
Land: 14.6 sq. mi.; Water: 0.1 sq. mi.

Weathersfield — Township
ZIP: 44420 Lat: 41-10-07 N Long: 80-45-49 W
Pop: 28,507 (1990); 34,590 (1980) Pop Density: 1295.8
Land: 22.0 sq. mi.; Water: 1.3 sq. mi.

West Farmington — Village
ZIP: 44491 Lat: 41-23-27 N Long: 80-58-24 W
Pop: 542 (1990); 563 (1980) Pop Density: 602.2
Land: 0.9 sq. mi.; Water: 0.0 sq. mi.

West Hill — CDP
Lat: 41-13-51 N Long: 80-31-38 W
Pop: 2,954 (1990) Pop Density: 1846.3
Land: 1.6 sq. mi.; Water: 0.0 sq. mi.

Yankee Lake — Village
ZIP: 44403 Lat: 41-16-17 N Long: 80-34-14 W
Pop: 88 (1990); 99 (1980) Pop Density: 176.0
Land: 0.5 sq. mi.; Water: 0.0 sq. mi.

Youngstown — City
ZIP: 44501 Lat: 41-08-05 N Long: 80-39-13 W
Pop: 26 (1990); 9 (1980) Pop Density: 478660.0
Land: 0.2 sq. mi.; Water: 0.0 sq. mi. Elev: 861 ft.
In northeastern OH on the Mahoning River, 45 mi. east of Akron. Platted 1802; incorporated 1859. Industrial city; prior to late 1970s, a leading steel-producer. Part of the town is also in Mahoning County.
Name origin: For pioneer John Young of Whitestown, NY, who arrived with settlers in 1797.

Tuscarawas County
County Seat: New Philadelphia (ZIP: 44663)

Pop: 84,090 (1990); 84,614 (1980)   **Pop Density:** 148.1
Land: 567.6 sq. mi.; **Water:** 3.9 sq. mi.   **Area Code:** 216

In east-central OH, south of Canton; organized Mar 15, 1808 from Jefferson County.

Name origin: For the Tuscarawas River, which flows through it; from an Indian word thought to mean 'open mouth.'

Auburn — Township
ZIP: 44681   Lat: 40-27-40 N   Long: 81-37-15 W
Pop: 820 (1990); 788 (1980)   Pop Density: 36.4
Land: 22.5 sq. mi.; Water: 0.0 sq. mi.

Baltic — Village
ZIP: 43804   Lat: 40-26-24 N   Long: 81-42-05 W
Pop: 561 (1990); 523 (1980)   Pop Density: 1402.5
Land: 0.4 sq. mi.; Water: 0.0 sq. mi.   Elev: 1041 ft.

Part of the town is also in Holmes and Coshocton counties.

Barnhill — Village
Lat: 40-26-53 N   Long: 81-22-03 W
Pop: 313 (1990); 327 (1980)   Pop Density: 782.5
Land: 0.4 sq. mi.; Water: 0.0 sq. mi.

Bolivar — Village
ZIP: 44612   Lat: 40-38-59 N   Long: 81-27-17 W
Pop: 914 (1990); 989 (1980)   Pop Density: 1828.0
Land: 0.5 sq. mi.; Water: 0.0 sq. mi.

Name origin: For Simon Bolívar (1783–1830), the great South American liberator.

Bucks — Township
ZIP: 43804   Lat: 40-24-21 N   Long: 81-40-19 W
Pop: 1,298 (1990); 1,139 (1980)   Pop Density: 57.4
Land: 22.6 sq. mi.; Water: 0.0 sq. mi.

Clay — Township
Lat: 40-20-37 N   Long: 81-27-34 W
Pop: 1,929 (1990); 2,016 (1980)   Pop Density: 79.7
Land: 24.2 sq. mi.; Water: 0.5 sq. mi.

Dennison — Village
ZIP: 44621   Lat: 40-23-49 N   Long: 81-19-40 W
Pop: 3,282 (1990); 3,398 (1980)   Pop Density: 2344.3
Land: 1.4 sq. mi.; Water: 0.0 sq. mi.   Elev: 862 ft.

In eastern OH, 30 mi. south of Canton.

Name origin: For William Dennison, a Civil War governor of OH.

Dover — City
ZIP: 44622   Lat: 40-31-47 N   Long: 81-28-47 W
Pop: 11,329 (1990); 11,782 (1980)   Pop Density: 2360.2
Land: 4.8 sq. mi.; Water: 0.1 sq. mi.   Elev: 898 ft.

In eastern OH, south of Canton.

Name origin: For Dover, England.

*Dover — Township
ZIP: 44622   Lat: 40-31-49 N   Long: 81-29-56 W
Pop: 4,506 (1990); 4,055 (1980)   Pop Density: 121.8
Land: 37.0 sq. mi.; Water: 0.3 sq. mi.

Fairfield — Township
Lat: 40-32-37 N   Long: 81-22-42 W
Pop: 1,238 (1990); 1,269 (1980)   Pop Density: 56.0
Land: 22.1 sq. mi.; Water: 0.1 sq. mi.

Franklin — Township
ZIP: 44680   Lat: 40-35-56 N   Long: 81-32-39 W
Pop: 3,532 (1990); 3,558 (1980)   Pop Density: 153.6
Land: 23.0 sq. mi.; Water: 0.3 sq. mi.

Gnadenhutten — Village
ZIP: 44629   Lat: 40-21-33 N   Long: 81-25-52 W
Pop: 1,226 (1990); 1,320 (1980)   Pop Density: 1362.2
Land: 0.9 sq. mi.; Water: 0.0 sq. mi.

In east-central OH on the Tuscarawas River, south of Canton. Founded 1772.

Name origin: Named by a group of Christian Indians led by Joshua, a Mohican elder, from German for 'tents of grace,' which they had learned from Moravian missionaries.

Goshen — Township
ZIP: 44663   Lat: 40-28-05 N   Long: 81-24-01 W
Pop: 5,718 (1990); 4,551 (1980)   Pop Density: 205.7
Land: 27.8 sq. mi.; Water: 0.4 sq. mi.

Jefferson — Township
ZIP: 43840   Lat: 40-23-48 N   Long: 81-33-42 W
Pop: 868 (1990); 753 (1980)   Pop Density: 38.9
Land: 22.3 sq. mi.; Water: 0.0 sq. mi.

Lawrence — Township
Lat: 40-37-05 N   Long: 81-27-40 W
Pop: 4,296 (1990); 4,148 (1980)   Pop Density: 162.1
Land: 26.5 sq. mi.; Water: 0.1 sq. mi.

Midvale — Village
ZIP: 44653   Lat: 40-26-13 N   Long: 81-22-19 W
Pop: 575 (1990); 654 (1980)   Pop Density: 958.3
Land: 0.6 sq. mi.; Water: 0.0 sq. mi.

Mill — Township
ZIP: 44683   Lat: 40-22-55 N   Long: 81-19-52 W
Pop: 10,315 (1990); 11,158 (1980)   Pop Density: 404.5
Land: 25.5 sq. mi.; Water: 0.1 sq. mi.

In northwestern OH, 27 mi. south of Canton.

Mineral City — Village
ZIP: 44656   Lat: 40-36-08 N   Long: 81-21-41 W
Pop: 725 (1990); 884 (1980)   Pop Density: 906.3
Land: 0.8 sq. mi.; Water: 0.0 sq. mi.

Newcomerstown — Village
ZIP: 43832   Lat: 40-16-28 N   Long: 81-35-55 W
Pop: 4,012 (1990); 3,986 (1980)   Pop Density: 1744.3
Land: 2.3 sq. mi.; Water: 0.1 sq. mi.   Elev: 806 ft.

In eastern OH, 28 mi. northeast of Zanesville.

Name origin: For Chief Eagle Feather's second wife, who was called "the newcomer" by his first wife and who fled after circumstantial evidence pointed to her guilt in his murder.

OHIO, Tuscarawas County

New Philadelphia — City
ZIP: 44663 Lat: 40-29-11 N Long: 81-26-28 W
Pop: 15,698 (1990); 16,883 (1980) Pop Density: 2308.5
Land: 6.8 sq. mi.; Water: 0.1 sq. mi.
In eastern OH, 18 mi. south of Canton. Founded 1804 by John Kinisely.

Oxford — Township
ZIP: 43832 Lat: 40-15-42 N Long: 81-34-46 W
Pop: 5,149 (1990); 5,153 (1980) Pop Density: 209.3
Land: 24.6 sq. mi.; Water: 0.3 sq. mi.

Parral — Village
ZIP: 44622 Lat: 40-33-40 N Long: 81-29-42 W
Pop: 255 (1990); 259 (1980) Pop Density: 1275.0
Land: 0.2 sq. mi.; Water: 0.0 sq. mi.

Perry — Township
Lat: 40-15-39 N Long: 81-23-12 W
Pop: 382 (1990); 362 (1980) Pop Density: 14.9
Land: 25.7 sq. mi.; Water: 0.0 sq. mi.

Port Washington — Village
ZIP: 43837 Lat: 40-19-36 N Long: 81-31-10 W
Pop: 513 (1990); 622 (1980) Pop Density: 1026.0
Land: 0.5 sq. mi.; Water: 0.0 sq. mi.

Roswell — Village
Lat: 40-28-31 N Long: 81-20-47 W
Pop: 257 (1990); 264 (1980) Pop Density: 856.7
Land: 0.3 sq. mi.; Water: 0.0 sq. mi.

Rush — Township
ZIP: 44683 Lat: 40-19-03 N Long: 81-21-57 W
Pop: 855 (1990); 830 (1980) Pop Density: 28.8
Land: 29.7 sq. mi.; Water: 0.0 sq. mi.

Salem — Township
ZIP: 43832 Lat: 40-19-44 N Long: 81-33-09 W
Pop: 1,510 (1990); 1,629 (1980) Pop Density: 44.7
Land: 33.8 sq. mi.; Water: 0.3 sq. mi.

Sandy — Township
Lat: 40-36-53 N Long: 81-21-39 W
Pop: 3,162 (1990); 3,131 (1980) Pop Density: 130.7
Land: 24.2 sq. mi.; Water: 0.0 sq. mi.

Stone Creek — Village
ZIP: 43840 Lat: 40-23-55 N Long: 81-33-31 W
Pop: 181 (1990); 150 (1980) Pop Density: 452.5
Land: 0.4 sq. mi.; Water: 0.0 sq. mi.

Strasburg — Village
ZIP: 44680 Lat: 40-36-08 N Long: 81-31-45 W
Pop: 1,995 (1990); 2,091 (1980) Pop Density: 1813.6
Land: 1.1 sq. mi.; Water: 0.0 sq. mi.

Sugarcreek — Village
ZIP: 44681 Lat: 40-30-23 N Long: 81-38-30 W
Pop: 2,062 (1990); 1,966 (1980) Pop Density: 1085.3
Land: 1.9 sq. mi.; Water: 0.0 sq. mi.
In eastern OH along a branch of Sugar Creek, southwest of Canton.
Name origin: Named in 1818 for its township (see below).

Sugar Creek — Township
Lat: 40-31-06 N Long: 81-37-15 W
Pop: 3,666 (1990); 3,375 (1980) Pop Density: 156.7
Land: 23.4 sq. mi.; Water: 0.0 sq. mi.

Tuscarawas — Village
ZIP: 44682 Lat: 40-23-50 N Long: 81-24-15 W
Pop: 826 (1990); 917 (1980) Pop Density: 2065.0
Land: 0.4 sq. mi.; Water: 0.0 sq. mi.
In east-central OH, south of Canton.
Name origin: For the river, which traverses the county; from an Indian word thought to mean 'open mouth.'

Uhrichsville — City
ZIP: 44683 Lat: 40-24-00 N Long: 81-21-03 W
Pop: 5,604 (1990); 6,130 (1980) Pop Density: 2001.4
Land: 2.8 sq. mi.; Water: 0.0 sq. mi.
Settled 1804.
Name origin: For its first settler, Michael Uhrich of PA.

Union — Township
Lat: 40-26-32 N Long: 81-18-13 W
Pop: 1,207 (1990); 1,275 (1980) Pop Density: 54.4
Land: 22.2 sq. mi.; Water: 0.0 sq. mi.

Warren — Township
Lat: 40-31-11 N Long: 81-18-19 W
Pop: 1,034 (1990); 980 (1980) Pop Density: 47.4
Land: 21.8 sq. mi.; Water: 0.7 sq. mi.

Warwick — Township
Lat: 40-24-09 N Long: 81-25-11 W
Pop: 2,532 (1990); 2,714 (1980) Pop Density: 118.3
Land: 21.4 sq. mi.; Water: 0.4 sq. mi.

Washington — Township
ZIP: 43832 Lat: 40-15-21 N Long: 81-28-36 W
Pop: 612 (1990); 670 (1980) Pop Density: 23.8
Land: 25.7 sq. mi.; Water: 0.0 sq. mi.

Wayne — Township
ZIP: 44624 Lat: 40-35-37 N Long: 81-37-02 W
Pop: 1,255 (1990); 1,223 (1980) Pop Density: 47.2
Land: 26.6 sq. mi.; Water: 0.1 sq. mi.

York — Township
Lat: 40-26-46 N Long: 81-30-37 W
Pop: 1,179 (1990); 1,172 (1980) Pop Density: 50.0
Land: 23.6 sq. mi.; Water: 0.0 sq. mi.

Zoar — Village
ZIP: 44697 Lat: 40-36-50 N Long: 81-25-27 W
Pop: 177 (1990); 264 (1980) Pop Density: 354.0
Land: 0.5 sq. mi.; Water: 0.1 sq. mi.
In east-central OH along the Tuscarawas River, 15 mi. south of Canton.
Name origin: For the biblical city to which Lot fled from Sodom.

OHIO, Union County

Union County
County Seat: Marysville (ZIP: 43040)

Pop: 31,969 (1990); 29,536 (1980) **Pop Density:** 73.2
Land: 436.7 sq. mi.; **Water:** 0.3 sq. mi. **Area Code:** 513
In central OH, northwest of Columbus; organized Apr 1, 1820 from Franklin, Madison, and Logan counties.
Name origin: For the union of parts of four counties.

Allen
Township
Lat: 40-14-58 N Long: 83-29-24 W
Pop: 901 (1990); 1,133 (1980) **Pop Density:** 29.9
Land: 30.1 sq. mi.; **Water:** 0.0 sq. mi.

Claibourne
Township
ZIP: 43344 Lat: 40-25-15 N Long: 83-18-33 W
Pop: 3,299 (1990); 3,321 (1980) **Pop Density:** 95.1
Land: 34.7 sq. mi.; **Water:** 0.0 sq. mi.

Darby
Township
Lat: 40-09-27 N Long: 83-20-22 W
Pop: 1,530 (1990); 1,569 (1980) **Pop Density:** 48.6
Land: 31.5 sq. mi.; **Water:** 0.0 sq. mi.

Dover
Township
Lat: 40-15-41 N Long: 83-17-03 W
Pop: 2,067 (1990); 1,499 (1980) **Pop Density:** 90.3
Land: 22.9 sq. mi.; **Water:** 0.0 sq. mi.

Dublin
City
ZIP: 43017 Lat: 40-06-32 N Long: 83-10-46 W
Pop: 4 (1990) **Pop Density:** 81830.0
Land: 0.2 sq. mi.; **Water:** 0.0 sq. mi.
In central OH on the west bank of the Scioto River. Part of the town is also in Delaware and Franklin counties.
Name origin: For Dublin, Ireland.

Jackson
Township
Lat: 40-28-43 N Long: 83-19-21 W
Pop: 757 (1990); 690 (1980) **Pop Density:** 27.0
Land: 28.0 sq. mi.; **Water:** 0.0 sq. mi.

Jerome
Township
Lat: 40-09-06 N Long: 83-13-36 W
Pop: 3,499 (1990); 3,290 (1980) **Pop Density:** 96.4
Land: 36.3 sq. mi.; **Water:** 0.0 sq. mi.

Leesburg
Township
Lat: 40-20-28 N Long: 83-18-14 W
Pop: 1,373 (1990); 1,285 (1980) **Pop Density:** 44.9
Land: 30.6 sq. mi.; **Water:** 0.0 sq. mi.

Liberty
Township
Lat: 40-20-01 N Long: 83-28-51 W
Pop: 1,221 (1990); 1,136 (1980) **Pop Density:** 33.3
Land: 36.7 sq. mi.; **Water:** 0.0 sq. mi.

Magnetic Springs
Village
Lat: 40-21-13 N Long: 83-15-46 W
Pop: 373 (1990); 314 (1980) **Pop Density:** 1865.0
Land: 0.2 sq. mi.; **Water:** 0.0 sq. mi. **Elev:** 944 ft.

Marysville
City
ZIP: 43040 Lat: 40-14-15 N Long: 83-22-28 W
Pop: 9,656 (1990); 7,414 (1980) **Pop Density:** 1636.6
Land: 5.9 sq. mi.; **Water:** 0.0 sq. mi. **Elev:** 991 ft.
Settled 1816 by Jonathan Summers. Platted 1820 by Samuel Culbertson.
Name origin: Named by Culbertson for his daughter Mary.

Milford Center
Village
ZIP: 43045 Lat: 40-10-44 N Long: 83-26-13 W
Pop: 651 (1990); 764 (1980) **Pop Density:** 1627.5
Land: 0.4 sq. mi.; **Water:** 0.0 sq. mi.

Millcreek
Township
Lat: 40-12-11 N Long: 83-13-59 W
Pop: 815 (1990); 834 (1980) **Pop Density:** 37.9
Land: 21.5 sq. mi.; **Water:** 0.0 sq. mi.

Paris
Township
ZIP: 43040 Lat: 40-14-45 N Long: 83-22-24 W
Pop: 12,024 (1990); 10,542 (1980) **Pop Density:** 331.2
Land: 36.3 sq. mi.; **Water:** 0.1 sq. mi.
In west-central OH, 28 mi. northwest of Columbus.

Plain City
Village
ZIP: 43064 Lat: 40-06-39 N Long: 83-16-26 W
Pop: 976 (1990); 880 (1980) **Pop Density:** 3253.3
Land: 0.3 sq. mi.; **Water:** 0.0 sq. mi. **Elev:** 934 ft.
Laid out 1818 by Issac Bigelow. Part of the town is also in Madison County.
Name origin: Named in 1851 for its location on Big Darby Plain.

Richwood
Village
ZIP: 43344 Lat: 40-25-37 N Long: 83-17-46 W
Pop: 2,186 (1990); 2,181 (1980) **Pop Density:** 1987.3
Land: 1.1 sq. mi.; **Water:** 0.0 sq. mi.
In west-central OH, 15 mi. south of Marion.

Taylor
Township
Lat: 40-20-25 N Long: 83-23-14 W
Pop: 1,266 (1990); 1,076 (1980) **Pop Density:** 47.4
Land: 26.7 sq. mi.; **Water:** 0.0 sq. mi.

Union
Township
Lat: 40-09-13 N Long: 83-27-11 W
Pop: 1,658 (1990); 1,681 (1980) **Pop Density:** 46.1
Land: 36.0 sq. mi.; **Water:** 0.1 sq. mi.

Unionville Center
Village
Lat: 40-08-10 N Long: 83-20-29 W
Pop: 238 (1990); 272 (1980) **Pop Density:** 1190.0
Land: 0.2 sq. mi.; **Water:** 0.0 sq. mi.

Washington
Township
Lat: 40-28-29 N Long: 83-27-10 W
Pop: 634 (1990); 582 (1980) **Pop Density:** 22.8
Land: 27.8 sq. mi.; **Water:** 0.0 sq. mi.

York   Township
Lat: 40-24-34 N **Long:** 83-27-00 W
Pop: 925 (1990); 898 (1980) **Pop Density:** 24.7
Land: 37.5 sq. mi.; **Water:** 0.0 sq. mi.

Van Wert County
County Seat: Van Wert (ZIP: 45891)

Pop: 30,464 (1990); 30,458 (1980) **Pop Density:** 74.3
Land: 410.1 sq. mi.; **Water:** 0.4 sq. mi. **Area Code:** 419
On the western border of OH, west of Lima; organized Apr 1, 1820 from Indian Territory.
Name origin: For Isaac Van Wert (?–1828), a captor of John André (1750–80), a British spy, during the Revolutionary War.

Convoy   Village
ZIP: 45832 **Lat:** 40-55-01 N **Long:** 84-42-22 W
Pop: 1,200 (1990); 1,140 (1980) **Pop Density:** 2400.0
Land: 0.5 sq. mi.; **Water:** 0.0 sq. mi. **Elev:** 787 ft.

Delphos   City
ZIP: 45833 **Lat:** 40-50-39 N **Long:** 84-20-44 W
Pop: 3,192 (1990); 3,330 (1980) **Pop Density:** 3546.7
Land: 0.9 sq. mi.; **Water:** 0.0 sq. mi. **Elev:** 780 ft.
In northwestern OH, 10 mi. northwest of Lima. Part of the town is also in Allen County.

Elgin   Village
ZIP: 45838 **Lat:** 40-44-29 N **Long:** 84-28-33 W
Pop: 71 (1990); 96 (1980) **Pop Density:** 355.0
Land: 0.2 sq. mi.; **Water:** 0.0 sq. mi. **Elev:** 819 ft.

Harrison   Township
Lat: 40-51-09 N **Long:** 84-44-57 W
Pop: 1,019 (1990); 992 (1980) **Pop Density:** 28.3
Land: 36.0 sq. mi.; **Water:** 0.0 sq. mi.

Hoaglin   Township
Lat: 40-56-20 N **Long:** 84-31-26 W
Pop: 624 (1990); 598 (1980) **Pop Density:** 19.4
Land: 32.2 sq. mi.; **Water:** 0.0 sq. mi.

Jackson   Township
Lat: 40-56-58 N **Long:** 84-25-56 W
Pop: 505 (1990); 518 (1980) **Pop Density:** 22.6
Land: 22.3 sq. mi.; **Water:** 0.0 sq. mi.

Jennings   Township
Lat: 40-45-00 N **Long:** 84-25-53 W
Pop: 739 (1990); 749 (1980) **Pop Density:** 26.3
Land: 28.1 sq. mi.; **Water:** 0.0 sq. mi.

Liberty   Township
Lat: 40-46-20 N **Long:** 84-37-58 W
Pop: 2,051 (1990); 1,789 (1980) **Pop Density:** 55.3
Land: 37.1 sq. mi.; **Water:** 0.0 sq. mi.

Middle Point   Village
ZIP: 45863 **Lat:** 40-51-21 N **Long:** 84-26-48 W
Pop: 639 (1990); 709 (1980) **Pop Density:** 1278.0
Land: 0.5 sq. mi.; **Water:** 0.0 sq. mi. **Elev:** 779 ft.
In northwestern OH on the Auglaize River, northwest of Lima.
Name origin: For its location at the midpoint of a large bend in the river.

Ohio City   Village
ZIP: 45874 **Lat:** 40-46-12 N **Long:** 84-36-57 W
Pop: 899 (1990); 881 (1980) **Pop Density:** 1798.0
Land: 0.5 sq. mi.; **Water:** 0.0 sq. mi. **Elev:** 822 ft.

Pleasant   Township
ZIP: 45891 **Lat:** 40-51-37 N **Long:** 84-37-37 W
Pop: 11,237 (1990); 12,985 (1980) **Pop Density:** 307.0
Land: 36.6 sq. mi.; **Water:** 0.2 sq. mi.
In northwestern OH, 25 mi. west-northwest of Lima.

Ridge   Township
Lat: 40-51-26 N **Long:** 84-30-34 W
Pop: 2,964 (1990); 1,369 (1980) **Pop Density:** 81.7
Land: 36.3 sq. mi.; **Water:** 0.1 sq. mi.

Scott   Village
ZIP: 45886 **Lat:** 40-59-13 N **Long:** 84-34-58 W
Pop: 201 (1990); 205 (1980) **Pop Density:** 402.0
Land: 0.5 sq. mi.; **Water:** 0.0 sq. mi. **Elev:** 742 ft.
Part of the town is also in Paulding County.

Tully   Township
Lat: 40-56-51 N **Long:** 84-44-31 W
Pop: 2,134 (1990); 2,093 (1980) **Pop Density:** 59.0
Land: 36.2 sq. mi.; **Water:** 0.0 sq. mi.

Union   Township
Lat: 40-56-42 N **Long:** 84-37-26 W
Pop: 1,032 (1990); 976 (1980) **Pop Density:** 28.3
Land: 36.5 sq. mi.; **Water:** 0.0 sq. mi.

Van Wert   City
ZIP: 45891 **Lat:** 40-51-52 N **Long:** 84-34-54 W
Pop: 10,891 (1990); 11,035 (1980) **Pop Density:** 2178.2
Land: 5.0 sq. mi.; **Water:** 0.2 sq. mi. **Elev:** 788 ft.
In northwestern OH, 70 mi. southwest of Toledo. Settled 1835.
Name origin: For Issac Van Wert (?–1828), one of the captors of John André (1750–80), British spy, during the Revolutionary War.

Venedocia   Village
ZIP: 45894 **Lat:** 40-47-07 N **Long:** 84-27-19 W
Pop: 158 (1990); 161 (1980) **Pop Density:** 1580.0
Land: 0.1 sq. mi.; **Water:** 0.0 sq. mi.

Washington   Township
ZIP: 45833 **Lat:** 40-51-23 N **Long:** 84-24-06 W
Pop: 5,392 (1990); 5,671 (1980) **Pop Density:** 146.9
Land: 36.7 sq. mi.; **Water:** 0.0 sq. mi.

Willshire
Village
ZIP: 45898 Lat: 40-44-47 N Long: 84-47-31 W
Pop: 541 (1990); 564 (1980) Pop Density: 1352.5
Land: 0.4 sq. mi.; Water: 0.0 sq. mi. Elev: 798 ft.
Not coextensive with the town of the same name.

*Willshire
Township
ZIP: 45898 Lat: 40-46-26 N Long: 84-44-43 W
Pop: 1,807 (1990); 1,874 (1980) Pop Density: 50.6
Land: 35.7 sq. mi.; Water: 0.0 sq. mi.

Wren
Village
ZIP: 45899 Lat: 40-48-00 N Long: 84-46-26 W
Pop: 190 (1990); 282 (1980) Pop Density: 633.3
Land: 0.3 sq. mi.; Water: 0.0 sq. mi. Elev: 813 ft.

York
Township
Lat: 40-46-18 N Long: 84-30-54 W
Pop: 960 (1990); 844 (1980) Pop Density: 26.3
Land: 36.5 sq. mi.; Water: 0.0 sq. mi.

Vinton County
County Seat: McArthur (ZIP: 45651)

Pop: 11,098 (1990); 11,584 (1980) Pop Density: 26.8
Land: 414.1 sq. mi.; Water: 0.9 sq. mi. Area Code: 614
In south-central OH; organized Mar 23, 1850 from Gallia, Athens, Ross, Hocking, Meigs, and Jackson counties.
Name origin: For Samuel Finley Vinton (1792–1862), U.S. representative from OH (1823–37; 1843–51).

Brown
Township
ZIP: 45654 Lat: 39-20-25 N Long: 82-21-24 W
Pop: 248 (1990); 263 (1980) Pop Density: 6.7
Land: 36.8 sq. mi.; Water: 0.2 sq. mi.

Clinton
Township
Lat: 39-10-26 N Long: 82-28-31 W
Pop: 1,761 (1990); 1,977 (1980) Pop Density: 56.8
Land: 31.0 sq. mi.; Water: 0.6 sq. mi.

Eagle
Township
Lat: 39-19-17 N Long: 82-41-56 W
Pop: 521 (1990); 430 (1980) Pop Density: 15.9
Land: 32.7 sq. mi.; Water: 0.0 sq. mi.

Elk
Township
Lat: 39-15-28 N Long: 82-28-06 W
Pop: 2,684 (1990); 2,839 (1980) Pop Density: 70.6
Land: 38.0 sq. mi.; Water: 0.0 sq. mi.

Hamden
Village
ZIP: 45634 Lat: 39-09-36 N Long: 82-31-31 W
Pop: 877 (1990); 1,010 (1980) Pop Density: 1461.7
Land: 0.6 sq. mi.; Water: 0.0 sq. mi.

Harrison
Township
Lat: 39-15-00 N Long: 82-41-57 W
Pop: 938 (1990); 984 (1980) Pop Density: 27.5
Land: 34.1 sq. mi.; Water: 0.0 sq. mi.

Jackson
Township
Lat: 39-19-22 N Long: 82-35-00 W
Pop: 541 (1990); 567 (1980) Pop Density: 14.4
Land: 37.5 sq. mi.; Water: 0.0 sq. mi.

Knox
Township
Lat: 39-15-12 N Long: 82-18-19 W
Pop: 443 (1990); 508 (1980) Pop Density: 17.6
Land: 25.1 sq. mi.; Water: 0.0 sq. mi.

Madison
Township
Lat: 39-15-19 N Long: 82-22-43 W
Pop: 612 (1990); 691 (1980) Pop Density: 25.0
Land: 24.5 sq. mi.; Water: 0.0 sq. mi.

McArthur
Village
ZIP: 45651 Lat: 39-14-49 N Long: 82-28-42 W
Pop: 1,541 (1990); 1,912 (1980) Pop Density: 1185.4
Land: 1.3 sq. mi.; Water: 0.0 sq. mi. Elev: 767 ft.
Name origin: For Gen. Duncan McArthur, officer in the War of 1812 and OH governor. Originally called McArthurstown.

Richland
Township
Lat: 39-14-22 N Long: 82-35-45 W
Pop: 1,241 (1990); 1,272 (1980) Pop Density: 28.7
Land: 43.2 sq. mi.; Water: 0.0 sq. mi.

Swan
Township
Lat: 39-20-32 N Long: 82-27-58 W
Pop: 696 (1990); 699 (1980) Pop Density: 18.5
Land: 37.6 sq. mi.; Water: 0.0 sq. mi.

Vinton
Township
Lat: 39-09-36 N Long: 82-22-27 W
Pop: 512 (1990); 516 (1980) Pop Density: 13.9
Land: 36.9 sq. mi.; Water: 0.0 sq. mi.

Wilkesville
Village
ZIP: 45695 Lat: 39-04-35 N Long: 82-19-35 W
Pop: 151 (1990); 189 (1980) Pop Density: 503.3
Land: 0.3 sq. mi.; Water: 0.0 sq. mi.
Not coextensive with the town of the same name.

*Wilkesville
Township
Lat: 39-04-31 N Long: 82-22-49 W
Pop: 901 (1990); 838 (1980) Pop Density: 24.6
Land: 36.7 sq. mi.; Water: 0.0 sq. mi.

Zaleski
Village
ZIP: 45698 Lat: 39-16-50 N Long: 82-23-46 W
Pop: 294 (1990); 347 (1980) Pop Density: 588.0
Land: 0.5 sq. mi.; Water: 0.0 sq. mi. Elev: 713 ft.

OHIO, Warren County

> ## Warren County
> **County Seat: Lebanon (ZIP: 45036)**
>
> **Pop:** 113,909 (1990); 99,276 (1980) **Pop Density:** 284.9
> **Land:** 399.9 sq. mi.; **Water:** 7.3 sq. mi. **Area Code:** 513
>
> In southwestern OH, northeast of Cincinnati; organized Mar 24, 1803 from Hamilton County.
>
> **Name origin:** For Gen. Joseph Warren (1741–75), Revolutionary War patriot and member of the Committee of Safety, who dispatched Paul Revere (1735–1818) on his famous ride.

Blanchester   Village
ZIP: 45107   **Lat:** 39-17-26 N **Long:** 84-00-14 W
Pop: 4,206 (1990)   **Pop Density:** 42,060.0
Land: 0.01 sq. mi.; **Water:** 0.0 sq. mi.   **Elev:** 971 ft.
In southwestern OH, 30 mi. northeast of Cincinnati. Settled 1832. Part of the town is also in Clinton County.

Butlerville   Village
ZIP: 45162   **Lat:** 39-18-07 N **Long:** 84-05-20 W
Pop: 188 (1990); 223 (1980)   **Pop Density:** 1880.0
Land: 0.1 sq. mi.; **Water:** 0.0 sq. mi.   **Elev:** 856 ft.

Carlisle   Village
ZIP: 45005   **Lat:** 39-34-42 N **Long:** 84-19-32 W
Pop: 4,610 (1990); 3,968 (1980)   **Pop Density:** 1844.0
Land: 2.5 sq. mi.; **Water:** 0.0 sq. mi.
In southwestern OH between the Twin and Miami rivers, 15 mi. southwest of Dayton. Part of the town is also in Montgomery County.

Clear Creek   Township
ZIP: 45066   **Lat:** 39-32-07 N **Long:** 84-11-48 W
Pop: 13,347 (1990); 10,566 (1980)   **Pop Density:** 294.6
Land: 45.3 sq. mi.; **Water:** 0.0 sq. mi.
In west-central OH, 14 mi. south of Dayton.

Corwin   Village
ZIP: 45068   **Lat:** 39-31-30 N **Long:** 84-04-23 W
Pop: 225 (1990); 276 (1980)   **Pop Density:** 1125.0
Land: 0.2 sq. mi.; **Water:** 0.0 sq. mi.   **Elev:** 732 ft.

Deerfield   Township
ZIP: 45040   **Lat:** 39-20-27 N **Long:** 84-18-28 W
Pop: 26,359 (1990); 16,697 (1980)   **Pop Density:** 801.2
Land: 32.9 sq. mi.; **Water:** 0.2 sq. mi.
In southwestern OH, 18 mi. northeast of Cincinnati.

Five Points   CDP
    Lat: 39-33-41 N **Long:** 84-11-49 W
Pop: 1,554 (1990)   **Pop Density:** 535.9
Land: 2.9 sq. mi.; **Water:** 0.0 sq. mi.

Franklin   City
ZIP: 45005   **Lat:** 39-33-14 N **Long:** 84-18-04 W
Pop: 11,026 (1990); 10,711 (1980)   **Pop Density:** 1361.2
Land: 8.1 sq. mi.; **Water:** 0.2 sq. mi.
In southwestern OH on the Miami River, 13 mi. south of Dayton. Not coextensive with the town of the same name.

*Franklin   Township
ZIP: 45005   **Lat:** 39-32-30 N **Long:** 84-18-16 W
Pop: 27,476 (1990); 28,159 (1980)   **Pop Density:** 825.1
Land: 33.3 sq. mi.; **Water:** 0.5 sq. mi.

Hamilton   Township
ZIP: 45039   **Lat:** 39-19-11 N **Long:** 84-12-15 W
Pop: 5,900 (1990); 5,819 (1980)   **Pop Density:** 166.7
Land: 35.4 sq. mi.; **Water:** 0.3 sq. mi.

Harlan   Township
    Lat: 39-18-19 N **Long:** 84-03-37 W
Pop: 3,268 (1990); 3,262 (1980)   **Pop Density:** 72.3
Land: 45.2 sq. mi.; **Water:** 0.0 sq. mi.

Harveysburg   Village
ZIP: 45032   **Lat:** 39-30-01 N **Long:** 84-00-08 W
Pop: 437 (1990); 425 (1980)   **Pop Density:** 728.3
Land: 0.6 sq. mi.; **Water:** 0.0 sq. mi.
In southwestern OH along Caesar's Creek, 29 mi. southeast of Dayton. Platted 1815.
Name origin: For George Harvey.

Landen   CDP
ZIP: 45040   **Lat:** 39-18-28 N **Long:** 84-16-46 W
Pop: 9,263 (1990); 2,870 (1980)   **Pop Density:** 1929.8
Land: 4.8 sq. mi.; **Water:** 0.1 sq. mi.

Lebanon   City
ZIP: 45036   **Lat:** 39-25-35 N **Long:** 84-12-45 W
Pop: 10,453 (1990); 9,636 (1980)   **Pop Density:** 1124.0
Land: 9.3 sq. mi.; **Water:** 0.0 sq. mi.   **Elev:** 769 ft.
In southwestern OH, 20 mi. east of Hamilton.
Name origin: For the biblical mountain famous for its cedar trees.

Loveland   City
    Lat: 39-16-21 N **Long:** 84-15-12 W
Pop: 32 (1990); 78 (1980)   **Pop Density:** 320.0
Land: 0.1 sq. mi.; **Water:** 0.0 sq. mi.   **Elev:** 890 ft.
In southwestern OH on the Little Miami River, 16 mi. northeast of Cincinnati. Part of the town is also in Clermont and Hamilton counties.
Name origin: For Col. James Loveland, first storeowner.

Loveland Park   CDP
    Lat: 39-18-13 N **Long:** 84-15-45 W
Pop: 1,130 (1990); 1,438 (1980)   **Pop Density:** 1027.3
Land: 1.1 sq. mi.; **Water:** 0.0 sq. mi.
Part of the town is also in Hamilton County.

Maineville   Village
ZIP: 45039   **Lat:** 39-18-56 N **Long:** 84-13-23 W
Pop: 359 (1990); 307 (1980)   **Pop Density:** 1795.0
Land: 0.2 sq. mi.; **Water:** 0.0 sq. mi.   **Elev:** 805 ft.

OHIO, Warren County

Mason
City
ZIP: 45040   **Lat:** 39-21-36 N   **Long:** 84-18-25 W
Pop: 11,452 (1990); 8,692 (1980)   **Pop Density:** 938.7
Land: 12.2 sq. mi.; **Water:** 0.0 sq. mi.

In southwestern OH in a hilly residential area, 20 mi. east of Cincinnati.

Massie
Township
Lat: 39-29-20 N   **Long:** 84-01-04 W
Pop: 885 (1990); 802 (1980)   **Pop Density:** 51.8
Land: 17.1 sq. mi.; **Water:** 4.1 sq. mi.

Middletown
City
ZIP: 45042   **Lat:** 39-30-55 N   **Long:** 84-20-02 W
Pop: 31 (1990); 43,719 (1980)   **Pop Density:** 1033.3
Land: 0.03 sq. mi.; **Water:** 0.0 sq. mi.

In southwestern OH on the Miami River, 35 mi. north of Cincinnati. Founded 1802; incorporated as city 1883. Part of the town is also in Butler County.
Name origin: For its location between Dayton and Cincinnati.

Monroe
Village
ZIP: 45050   **Lat:** 39-27-09 N   **Long:** 84-19-58 W
Pop: 52 (1990); 68 (1980)   **Pop Density:** 19.3
Land: 2.7 sq. mi.; **Water:** 0.0 sq. mi.   **Elev:** 823 ft.

In southwestern OH, 30 mi. north of Cincinnati. Part of the town is also in Butler County.
Name origin: For James Monroe (1758–1831), fifth U.S. president.

Morrow
Village
ZIP: 45152   **Lat:** 39-20-56 N   **Long:** 84-07-35 W
Pop: 1,206 (1990); 1,254 (1980)   **Pop Density:** 709.4
Land: 1.7 sq. mi.; **Water:** 0.0 sq. mi.

Settled 1844.
Name origin: For Jeremiah Morrow, OH governor (1822–26).

Pleasant Plain
Village
ZIP: 45162   **Lat:** 39-16-47 N   **Long:** 84-06-33 W
Pop: 138 (1990); 210 (1980)   **Pop Density:** 1380.0
Land: 0.1 sq. mi.; **Water:** 0.0 sq. mi.   **Elev:** 886 ft.

Salem
Township
Lat: 39-21-18 N   **Long:** 84-07-10 W
Pop: 4,038 (1990); 3,812 (1980)   **Pop Density:** 185.2
Land: 21.8 sq. mi.; **Water:** 0.1 sq. mi.

South Lebanon
Village
ZIP: 45065   **Lat:** 39-22-16 N   **Long:** 84-12-40 W
Pop: 2,696 (1990); 2,700 (1980)   **Pop Density:** 3370.0
Land: 0.8 sq. mi.; **Water:** 0.0 sq. mi.

Springboro
City
ZIP: 45066   **Lat:** 39-33-48 N   **Long:** 84-14-15 W
Pop: 6,590 (1990); 4,962 (1980)   **Pop Density:** 1013.8
Land: 6.5 sq. mi.; **Water:** 0.0 sq. mi.

Part of the town is also in Montgomery County.

Turtle Creek
Township
ZIP: 45036   **Lat:** 39-26-21 N   **Long:** 84-13-43 W
Pop: 10,391 (1990); 8,444 (1980)   **Pop Density:** 164.4
Land: 63.2 sq. mi.; **Water:** 0.3 sq. mi.

Union
Township
Lat: 39-23-01 N   **Long:** 84-13-14 W
Pop: 4,631 (1990); 4,899 (1980)   **Pop Density:** 270.8
Land: 17.1 sq. mi.; **Water:** 0.1 sq. mi.

Washington
Township
Lat: 39-25-10 N   **Long:** 84-03-08 W
Pop: 1,354 (1990); 1,258 (1980)   **Pop Density:** 39.5
Land: 34.3 sq. mi.; **Water:** 0.1 sq. mi.

Wayne
Township
ZIP: 45068   **Lat:** 39-31-49 N   **Long:** 84-04-24 W
Pop: 5,744 (1990); 5,844 (1980)   **Pop Density:** 128.2
Land: 44.8 sq. mi.; **Water:** 1.5 sq. mi.

Waynesville
Village
ZIP: 45068   **Lat:** 39-32-02 N   **Long:** 84-05-11 W
Pop: 1,949 (1990); 1,796 (1980)   **Pop Density:** 1771.8
Land: 1.1 sq. mi.; **Water:** 0.0 sq. mi.   **Elev:** 754 ft.

Washington County
County Seat: Marietta (ZIP: 45750)

Pop: 62,254 (1990); 64,266 (1980)   **Pop Density:** 98.0
Land: 635.2 sq. mi.; **Water:** 4.9 sq. mi.   **Area Code:** 614

On the southeastern border of OH; original county; organized Jul 27, 1788 (prior to statehood).
Name origin: For George Washington (1732–99), American patriot and first U.S. president.

Adams
Township
Lat: 39-32-42 N   **Long:** 81-31-18 W
Pop: 1,741 (1990); 1,921 (1980)   **Pop Density:** 55.8
Land: 31.2 sq. mi.; **Water:** 0.5 sq. mi.

Aurelius
Township
Lat: 39-36-24 N   **Long:** 81-26-40 W
Pop: 445 (1990); 538 (1980)   **Pop Density:** 31.6
Land: 14.1 sq. mi.; **Water:** 0.0 sq. mi.

Barlow
Township
Lat: 39-23-52 N   **Long:** 81-38-33 W
Pop: 1,982 (1990); 1,981 (1980)   **Pop Density:** 61.9
Land: 32.0 sq. mi.; **Water:** 0.0 sq. mi.

Belpre
City
ZIP: 45714   **Lat:** 39-16-41 N   **Long:** 81-35-19 W
Pop: 6,796 (1990); 7,193 (1980)   **Pop Density:** 2517.0
Land: 2.7 sq. mi.; **Water:** 0.0 sq. mi.

Name origin: From French 'beautiful prairie.'

OHIO, Washington County

*Belpre — Township
ZIP: 45714 Lat: 39-17-00 N Long: 81-39-48 W
Pop: 4,208 (1990); 4,343 (1980) Pop Density: 171.8
Land: 24.5 sq. mi.; Water: 0.5 sq. mi.

Beverly — Village
ZIP: 45715 Lat: 39-32-58 N Long: 81-38-10 W
Pop: 1,444 (1990); 1,471 (1980) Pop Density: 2062.9
Land: 0.7 sq. mi.; Water: 0.1 sq. mi.
Settled 1789.

Decatur — Township
Lat: 39-18-46 N Long: 81-46-49 W
Pop: 1,114 (1990); 983 (1980) Pop Density: 31.7
Land: 35.1 sq. mi.; Water: 0.0 sq. mi.

Devola — CDP
ZIP: 45750 Lat: 39-28-23 N Long: 81-28-10 W
Pop: 2,736 (1990); 2,708 (1980) Pop Density: 536.5
Land: 5.1 sq. mi.; Water: 0.2 sq. mi.

Dunham — Township
Lat: 39-19-52 N Long: 81-38-25 W
Pop: 2,224 (1990); 2,042 (1980) Pop Density: 95.0
Land: 23.4 sq. mi.; Water: 0.3 sq. mi.

Fairfield — Township
ZIP: 45724 Lat: 39-22-13 N Long: 81-44-14 W
Pop: 874 (1990); 778 (1980) Pop Density: 35.5
Land: 24.6 sq. mi.; Water: 0.0 sq. mi.

Fearing — Township
Lat: 39-28-52 N Long: 81-24-07 W
Pop: 825 (1990); 917 (1980) Pop Density: 34.8
Land: 23.7 sq. mi.; Water: 0.2 sq. mi.

Grandview — Township
ZIP: 45767 Lat: 39-31-44 N Long: 81-06-42 W
Pop: 1,965 (1990); 2,119 (1980) Pop Density: 55.8
Land: 35.2 sq. mi.; Water: 0.3 sq. mi.

Independence — Township
Lat: 39-28-45 N Long: 81-12-28 W
Pop: 358 (1990); 462 (1980) Pop Density: 12.6
Land: 28.5 sq. mi.; Water: 0.0 sq. mi.

Lawrence — Township
Lat: 39-28-09 N Long: 81-18-13 W
Pop: 885 (1990); 879 (1980) Pop Density: 25.1
Land: 35.2 sq. mi.; Water: 0.0 sq. mi.

Liberty — Township
ZIP: 45745 Lat: 39-33-21 N Long: 81-18-34 W
Pop: 575 (1990); 540 (1980) Pop Density: 19.5
Land: 29.5 sq. mi.; Water: 0.0 sq. mi.

Lowell — Village
ZIP: 45744 Lat: 39-31-44 N Long: 81-30-27 W
Pop: 617 (1990); 729 (1980) Pop Density: 2056.7
Land: 0.3 sq. mi.; Water: 0.0 sq. mi.

Lower Salem — Village
ZIP: 45745 Lat: 39-33-48 N Long: 81-23-40 W
Pop: 103 (1990); 110 (1980) Pop Density: 1030.0
Land: 0.1 sq. mi.; Water: 0.0 sq. mi. Elev: 653 ft.

Ludlow — Township
Lat: 39-32-40 N Long: 81-11-48 W
Pop: 350 (1990); 419 (1980) Pop Density: 15.6
Land: 22.5 sq. mi.; Water: 0.0 sq. mi.

Macksburg — Village
ZIP: 45746 Lat: 39-37-52 N Long: 81-27-24 W
Pop: 218 (1990); 295 (1980) Pop Density: 1090.0
Land: 0.2 sq. mi.; Water: 0.0 sq. mi.

Marietta — City
ZIP: 45750 Lat: 39-25-16 N Long: 81-26-48 W
Pop: 15,026 (1990); 16,467 (1980) Pop Density: 1951.4
Land: 7.7 sq. mi.; Water: 0.3 sq. mi. Elev: 616 ft.
In southeast OH where the Ohio and Muskingum rivers merge, 45 mi. southeast of Zanesville.
Name origin: Named by Gen. Rufus Putnam (1738–1824) and a group of officers for Queen Marie-Antoinette (1755–93) of France for her assistance in the Revolutionary War.

*Marietta — Township
ZIP: 45750 Lat: 39-23-29 N Long: 81-23-17 W
Pop: 4,453 (1990); 4,333 (1980) Pop Density: 291.0
Land: 15.3 sq. mi.; Water: 0.4 sq. mi.

Matamoras — Village
Lat: 39-31-07 N Long: 81-04-13 W
Pop: 1,002 (1990); 1,172 (1980) Pop Density: 2505.0
Land: 0.4 sq. mi.; Water: 0.0 sq. mi.

Muskingum — Township
Lat: 39-29-06 N Long: 81-28-38 W
Pop: 4,764 (1990); 4,625 (1980) Pop Density: 222.6
Land: 21.4 sq. mi.; Water: 0.8 sq. mi.

Newport — Township
ZIP: 45768 Lat: 39-23-50 N Long: 81-17-19 W
Pop: 2,077 (1990); 2,185 (1980) Pop Density: 58.3
Land: 35.6 sq. mi.; Water: 0.1 sq. mi.

Palmer — Township
Lat: 39-27-19 N Long: 81-43-25 W
Pop: 597 (1990); 547 (1980) Pop Density: 26.7
Land: 22.4 sq. mi.; Water: 0.0 sq. mi.

Salem — Township
ZIP: 45745 Lat: 39-33-13 N Long: 81-24-31 W
Pop: 1,124 (1990); 1,085 (1980) Pop Density: 40.3
Land: 27.9 sq. mi.; Water: 0.0 sq. mi.

Warren — Township
Lat: 39-24-04 N Long: 81-32-15 W
Pop: 3,872 (1990); 3,635 (1980) Pop Density: 103.0
Land: 37.6 sq. mi.; Water: 0.4 sq. mi.

Waterford — Township
ZIP: 45786 Lat: 39-33-00 N Long: 81-38-53 W
Pop: 3,701 (1990); 3,930 (1980) Pop Density: 98.4
Land: 37.6 sq. mi.; Water: 1.2 sq. mi.

Watertown — Township
Lat: 39-29-18 N Long: 81-36-37 W
Pop: 1,498 (1990); 1,467 (1980) Pop Density: 41.0
Land: 36.5 sq. mi.; Water: 0.0 sq. mi.

Wesley — Township
Lat: 39-25-33 N Long: 81-48-36 W
Pop: 800 (1990); 877 (1980) Pop Density: 25.6
Land: 31.2 sq. mi.; Water: 0.0 sq. mi.

OHIO, Wayne County *American Places Dictionary*

Wayne County
County Seat: Wooster (ZIP: 44691)

Pop: 101,461 (1990); 97,408 (1980) **Pop Density:** 182.7
Land: 555.4 sq. mi.; **Water:** 0.9 sq. mi. **Area Code:** 216

In north-central OH, west of Canton; original county; organized Aug 15, 1796 (prior to statehood).

Name origin: For Gen. Anthony Wayne (1745–96), PA soldier and statesman, nicknamed "Mad Anthony" for his daring during the Revolutionary War.

Apple Creek — Village
ZIP: 44606 **Lat:** 40-44-53 N **Long:** 81-50-00 W
Pop: 860 (1990); 741 (1980) **Pop Density:** 1433.3
Land: 0.6 sq. mi.; **Water:** 0.0 sq. mi.

In northeastern OH, southeast of Canton.
Name origin: For the creek.

Baughman — Township
Lat: 40-51-46 N **Long:** 81-42-31 W
Pop: 4,408 (1990); 4,539 (1980) **Pop Density:** 121.8
Land: 36.2 sq. mi.; **Water:** 0.1 sq. mi.

Burbank — Village
ZIP: 44214 **Lat:** 40-59-15 N **Long:** 81-59-40 W
Pop: 289 (1990); 365 (1980) **Pop Density:** 963.3
Land: 0.3 sq. mi.; **Water:** 0.0 sq. mi.

Canaan — Township
ZIP: 44217 **Lat:** 40-56-46 N **Long:** 81-56-13 W
Pop: 3,996 (1990); 4,092 (1980) **Pop Density:** 108.0
Land: 37.0 sq. mi.; **Water:** 0.0 sq. mi.

Chester — Township
Lat: 40-51-17 N **Long:** 82-03-31 W
Pop: 2,581 (1990); 2,680 (1980) **Pop Density:** 61.9
Land: 41.7 sq. mi.; **Water:** 0.0 sq. mi.

Chippewa — Township
ZIP: 44230 **Lat:** 40-56-40 N **Long:** 81-42-13 W
Pop: 9,329 (1990); 9,250 (1980) **Pop Density:** 259.9
Land: 35.9 sq. mi.; **Water:** 0.2 sq. mi.

Clinton — Township
ZIP: 44676 **Lat:** 40-42-01 N **Long:** 82-03-18 W
Pop: 3,028 (1990); 2,913 (1980) **Pop Density:** 109.3
Land: 27.7 sq. mi.; **Water:** 0.1 sq. mi.

Congress — Village
ZIP: 44287 **Lat:** 40-55-34 N **Long:** 82-03-19 W
Pop: 162 (1990); 178 (1980) **Pop Density:** 810.0
Land: 0.2 sq. mi.; **Water:** 0.0 sq. mi.

Not coextensive with the town of the same name.

*Congress — Township
ZIP: 44287 **Lat:** 40-56-36 N **Long:** 82-03-45 W
Pop: 4,159 (1990); 3,724 (1980) **Pop Density:** 95.8
Land: 43.4 sq. mi.; **Water:** 0.0 sq. mi.

Creston — Village
ZIP: 44217 **Lat:** 40-58-45 N **Long:** 81-54-01 W
Pop: 1,848 (1990); 1,828 (1980) **Pop Density:** 1026.7
Land: 1.8 sq. mi.; **Water:** 0.0 sq. mi. **Elev:** 985 ft.

Dalton — Village
ZIP: 44618 **Lat:** 40-47-57 N **Long:** 81-41-49 W
Pop: 1,377 (1990); 1,357 (1980) **Pop Density:** 1377.0
Land: 1.0 sq. mi.; **Water:** 0.0 sq. mi.

In northeast-central OH, 7 mi. west of Massillon.

Doylestown — Village
ZIP: 44230 **Lat:** 40-58-13 N **Long:** 81-41-48 W
Pop: 2,668 (1990); 2,493 (1980) **Pop Density:** 1667.5
Land: 1.6 sq. mi.; **Water:** 0.0 sq. mi.

East Union — Township
ZIP: 44606 **Lat:** 40-46-17 N **Long:** 81-49-28 W
Pop: 5,833 (1990); 5,887 (1980) **Pop Density:** 163.8
Land: 35.6 sq. mi.; **Water:** 0.0 sq. mi.

Franklin — Township
Lat: 40-42-57 N **Long:** 81-55-40 W
Pop: 2,747 (1990); 2,815 (1980) **Pop Density:** 75.7
Land: 36.3 sq. mi.; **Water:** 0.1 sq. mi.

Fredericksburg — Village
ZIP: 44627 **Lat:** 40-40-38 N **Long:** 81-52-11 W
Pop: 502 (1990); 511 (1980) **Pop Density:** 1673.3
Land: 0.3 sq. mi.; **Water:** 0.0 sq. mi. **Elev:** 972 ft.

Green — Township
ZIP: 44667 **Lat:** 40-51-23 N **Long:** 81-49-05 W
Pop: 11,356 (1990); 10,980 (1980) **Pop Density:** 315.4
Land: 36.0 sq. mi.; **Water:** 0.0 sq. mi.

Marshallville — Village
ZIP: 44645 **Lat:** 40-54-01 N **Long:** 81-43-59 W
Pop: 758 (1990); 788 (1980) **Pop Density:** 1516.0
Land: 0.5 sq. mi.; **Water:** 0.0 sq. mi.

In northeastern OH, 25 mi. southwest of Akron.

Milton — Township
ZIP: 44270 **Lat:** 40-56-35 N **Long:** 81-49-22 W
Pop: 9,023 (1990); 8,872 (1980) **Pop Density:** 251.3
Land: 35.9 sq. mi.; **Water:** 0.2 sq. mi.

Mount Eaton — Village
ZIP: 44659 **Lat:** 40-41-41 N **Long:** 81-42-10 W
Pop: 236 (1990); 289 (1980) **Pop Density:** 2360.0
Land: 0.1 sq. mi.; **Water:** 0.0 sq. mi.

Norton — City
Lat: 40-59-16 N **Long:** 81-38-55 W
Pop: 2 (1990) **Pop Density:** 222.2
Land: 0.009 sq. mi.; **Water:** 0.0 sq. mi.

In northeast-central OH, a residential suburb just south of Akron. Part of the town is also in Summit County.

Orrville — City
ZIP: 44667 **Lat:** 40-50-48 N **Long:** 81-46-16 W
Pop: 7,712 (1990); 7,511 (1980) **Pop Density:** 1836.2
Land: 4.2 sq. mi.; **Water:** 0.0 sq. mi. **Elev:** 1064 ft.

In northeastern OH, 44 mi. south of Cleveland.

Paint — Township
Lat: 40-41-45 N **Long:** 81-42-20 W
Pop: 2,506 (1990); 2,107 (1980) **Pop Density:** 102.7
Land: 24.4 sq. mi.; **Water:** 0.0 sq. mi.

Plain
Township
Lat: 40-46-06 N **Long:** 82-03-45 W
Pop: 2,499 (1990); 2,336 (1980) **Pop Density:** 59.9
Land: 41.7 sq. mi.; **Water:** 0.0 sq. mi.

Rittman
City
ZIP: 44270 **Lat:** 40-58-10 N **Long:** 81-46-58 W
Pop: 6,037 (1990); 5,998 (1980) **Pop Density:** 1183.7
Land: 5.1 sq. mi.; **Water:** 0.2 sq. mi. **Elev:** 979 ft.

In northeast-central OH, 16 mi. southwest of Akron. Part of the town is also in Medina County.
Name origin: For Frederick B. Rittman, treasurer of the Atlanta & Great Western Railroad.

Salt Creek
Township
Lat: 40-41-50 N **Long:** 81-49-21 W
Pop: 3,137 (1990); 2,709 (1980) **Pop Density:** 131.8
Land: 23.8 sq. mi.; **Water:** 0.0 sq. mi.

Shreve
Village
ZIP: 44676 **Lat:** 40-40-55 N **Long:** 82-01-20 W
Pop: 1,584 (1990); 1,608 (1980) **Pop Density:** 1980.0
Land: 0.8 sq. mi.; **Water:** 0.0 sq. mi. **Elev:** 914 ft.

Smithville
Village
ZIP: 44677 **Lat:** 40-51-46 N **Long:** 81-51-35 W
Pop: 1,354 (1990); 1,467 (1980) **Pop Density:** 1128.3
Land: 1.2 sq. mi.; **Water:** 0.0 sq. mi.

Sugar Creek
Township
ZIP: 44618 **Lat:** 40-46-28 N **Long:** 81-42-30 W
Pop: 5,790 (1990); 5,576 (1980) **Pop Density:** 155.2
Land: 37.3 sq. mi.; **Water:** 0.0 sq. mi.

Wayne
Township
Lat: 40-51-41 N **Long:** 81-56-03 W
Pop: 3,958 (1990); 5,538 (1980) **Pop Density:** 134.2
Land: 29.5 sq. mi.; **Water:** 0.0 sq. mi.

West Salem
Village
ZIP: 44287 **Lat:** 40-58-10 N **Long:** 82-06-28 W
Pop: 1,534 (1990); 1,357 (1980) **Pop Density:** 1534.0
Land: 1.0 sq. mi.; **Water:** 0.0 sq. mi. **Elev:** 1120 ft.

Laid out 1834 by the Rickel brothers.

Wooster
City
ZIP: 44691 **Lat:** 40-49-06 N **Long:** 81-55-58 W
Pop: 22,191 (1990); 19,289 (1980) **Pop Density:** 1880.6
Land: 11.8 sq. mi.; **Water:** 0.0 sq. mi.

In northeast-central OH, 25 mi. west of Canton. Settled 1807.
Name origin: For Revolutionary War general, David Wooster (1711–77).

*Wooster
Township
ZIP: 44691 **Lat:** 40-46-22 N **Long:** 81-57-03 W
Pop: 4,918 (1990); 4,101 (1980) **Pop Density:** 234.2
Land: 21.0 sq. mi.; **Water:** 0.1 sq. mi.

Williams County
County Seat: Bryan (ZIP: 43506)

Pop: 36,956 (1990); 36,369 (1980) **Pop Density:** 87.6
Land: 421.8 sq. mi.; **Water:** 1.3 sq. mi. **Area Code:** 419

In the northwestern corner of OH; organized Feb 12, 1820 from Henry County.
Name origin: For David Williams, a captor of British spy John André (1750–80), in the Revolutionary War.

Alvordton
Village
ZIP: 43501 **Lat:** 41-39-55 N **Long:** 84-26-03 W
Pop: 298 (1990); 362 (1980) **Pop Density:** 993.3
Land: 0.3 sq. mi.; **Water:** 0.0 sq. mi. **Elev:** 847 ft.

Blakeslee
Village
Lat: 41-31-25 N **Long:** 84-43-51 W
Pop: 128 (1990); 136 (1980) **Pop Density:** 1280.0
Land: 0.1 sq. mi.; **Water:** 0.0 sq. mi.

Brady
Township
Lat: 41-33-54 N **Long:** 84-24-58 W
Pop: 2,582 (1990); 2,528 (1980) **Pop Density:** 90.3
Land: 28.6 sq. mi.; **Water:** 0.0 sq. mi.

Bridgewater
Township
Lat: 41-39-32 N **Long:** 84-37-55 W
Pop: 1,103 (1990); 1,106 (1980) **Pop Density:** 32.9
Land: 33.5 sq. mi.; **Water:** 0.4 sq. mi.

Bryan
City
ZIP: 43506 **Lat:** 41-28-12 N **Long:** 84-32-52 W
Pop: 8,348 (1990); 7,879 (1980) **Pop Density:** 2087.0
Land: 4.0 sq. mi.; **Water:** 0.0 sq. mi.

In northwestern OH, 50 mi. west of Toledo.
Name origin: For the Hon. John A. Bryan, who held state offices and helped develop this area.

Center
Township
Lat: 41-28-15 N **Long:** 84-37-58 W
Pop: 3,055 (1990); 3,046 (1980) **Pop Density:** 84.2
Land: 36.3 sq. mi.; **Water:** 0.0 sq. mi.

Edgerton
Village
ZIP: 43517 **Lat:** 41-26-48 N **Long:** 84-44-59 W
Pop: 1,896 (1990); 1,813 (1980) **Pop Density:** 1354.3
Land: 1.4 sq. mi.; **Water:** 0.0 sq. mi.

In northwestern OH, 40 mi. northeast of Fort Wayne, IN.
Name origin: For land developer Alfred P. Edgerton.

Edon
Village
ZIP: 43518 **Lat:** 41-33-23 N **Long:** 84-46-05 W
Pop: 880 (1990); 947 (1980) **Pop Density:** 1100.0
Land: 0.8 sq. mi.; **Water:** 0.0 sq. mi.

Florence
Township
Lat: 41-34-20 N **Long:** 84-45-12 W
Pop: 1,956 (1990); 2,133 (1980) **Pop Density:** 45.5
Land: 43.0 sq. mi.; **Water:** 0.0 sq. mi.

Jefferson
Township
Lat: 41-34-08 N **Long:** 84-30-59 W
Pop: 1,795 (1990); 1,857 (1980) **Pop Density:** 42.1
Land: 42.6 sq. mi.; **Water:** 0.1 sq. mi.

OHIO, Williams County

Madison
Township
Lat: 41-39-29 N Long: 84-31-28 W
Pop: 2,350 (1990); 2,207 (1980)   Pop Density: 77.8
Land: 30.2 sq. mi.; Water: 0.1 sq. mi.

Mill Creek
Township
Lat: 41-39-36 N Long: 84-26-19 W
Pop: 954 (1990); 1,015 (1980)   Pop Density: 39.4
Land: 24.2 sq. mi.; Water: 0.0 sq. mi.

Montpelier
Village
ZIP: 43543   Lat: 41-34-53 N Long: 84-36-01 W
Pop: 4,299 (1990); 4,431 (1980)   Pop Density: 1592.2
Land: 2.7 sq. mi.; Water: 0.0 sq. mi.   Elev: 850 ft.
In northwestern OH on the St. Joseph River, 50 mi. west of Toledo.
Name origin: For Montpelier, France.

Northwest
Township
Lat: 41-39-27 N Long: 84-44-43 W
Pop: 1,198 (1990); 1,055 (1980)   Pop Density: 36.7
Land: 32.6 sq. mi.; Water: 0.3 sq. mi.

Pioneer
Village
ZIP: 43554   Lat: 41-40-40 N Long: 84-33-07 W
Pop: 1,287 (1990); 1,133 (1980)   Pop Density: 858.0
Land: 1.5 sq. mi.; Water: 0.1 sq. mi.   Elev: 874 ft.
In the northwestern corner of OH, just south of the MI border.

Pulaski
Township
Lat: 41-27-55 N Long: 84-31-00 W
Pop: 2,647 (1990); 2,539 (1980)   Pop Density: 83.0
Land: 31.9 sq. mi.; Water: 0.0 sq. mi.

St. Joseph
Township
Lat: 41-28-23 N Long: 84-44-38 W
Pop: 2,790 (1990); 2,756 (1980)   Pop Density: 79.5
Land: 35.1 sq. mi.; Water: 0.1 sq. mi.

Springfield
Township
Lat: 41-28-26 N Long: 84-24-24 W
Pop: 2,607 (1990); 2,517 (1980)   Pop Density: 71.8
Land: 36.3 sq. mi.; Water: 0.0 sq. mi.

Stryker
Village
ZIP: 43557   Lat: 41-30-11 N Long: 84-25-03 W
Pop: 1,468 (1990); 1,423 (1980)   Pop Density: 1835.0
Land: 0.8 sq. mi.; Water: 0.0 sq. mi.   Elev: 719 ft.
In northwestern OH on Tiffin Creek.
Name origin: For an early settler.

Superior
Township
ZIP: 43543   Lat: 41-34-07 N Long: 84-38-03 W
Pop: 5,571 (1990); 5,731 (1980)   Pop Density: 127.8
Land: 43.6 sq. mi.; Water: 0.2 sq. mi.

West Unity
Village
ZIP: 43570   Lat: 41-35-09 N Long: 84-26-03 W
Pop: 1,677 (1990); 1,639 (1980)   Pop Density: 1677.0
Land: 1.0 sq. mi.; Water: 0.0 sq. mi.   Elev: 788 ft.

Wood County
County Seat: Bowling Green (ZIP: 43402)

Pop: 113,269 (1990); 107,372 (1980)   Pop Density: 183.5
Land: 617.4 sq. mi.; Water: 3.2 sq. mi.   Area Code: 419
In west-central OH, south of Toledo; organized Feb 12, 1820 from Indian lands.
Name origin: For Capt. Eleazer Derby Wood (1783–1814), an officer in the War of 1812 and builder of Fort Meigs.

Bairdstown
Village
ZIP: 45872   Lat: 41-10-15 N Long: 83-36-25 W
Pop: 130 (1990); 151 (1980)   Pop Density: 433.3
Land: 0.3 sq. mi.; Water: 0.0 sq. mi.

Bloom
Township
Lat: 41-12-34 N Long: 83-35-27 W
Pop: 2,402 (1990); 2,665 (1980)   Pop Density: 67.5
Land: 35.6 sq. mi.; Water: 0.0 sq. mi.

Bloomdale
Village
ZIP: 44817   Lat: 41-10-15 N Long: 83-33-12 W
Pop: 632 (1990); 744 (1980)   Pop Density: 902.9
Land: 0.7 sq. mi.; Water: 0.0 sq. mi.

Bowling Green
City
ZIP: 43402   Lat: 41-22-35 N Long: 83-38-58 W
Pop: 28,176 (1990); 25,728 (1980)   Pop Density: 3566.6
Land: 7.9 sq. mi.; Water: 0.0 sq. mi.
In northwest-central OH, 20 mi. southwest of Toledo. Laid out 1835. Industrial city (meatpacking; oil wells). Site of Bowling Green State Univ. (1910).
Name origin: Named by Joseph Gordon for Bowling Green, KY, his former home.

Bradner
Village
ZIP: 43406   Lat: 41-19-25 N Long: 83-26-11 W
Pop: 1,093 (1990); 1,175 (1980)   Pop Density: 1821.7
Land: 0.6 sq. mi.; Water: 0.0 sq. mi.

Center
Township
Lat: 41-23-05 N Long: 83-36-01 W
Pop: 1,158 (1990); 1,334 (1980)   Pop Density: 42.7
Land: 27.1 sq. mi.; Water: 0.1 sq. mi.

Custar
Village
ZIP: 43511   Lat: 41-17-03 N Long: 83-50-36 W
Pop: 209 (1990); 254 (1980)   Pop Density: 696.7
Land: 0.3 sq. mi.; Water: 0.0 sq. mi.
In northwestern OH, 17 mi. southwest of Bowling Green.

Cygnet
Village
ZIP: 43413   Lat: 41-14-24 N Long: 83-38-37 W
Pop: 560 (1990); 646 (1980)   Pop Density: 1866.7
Land: 0.3 sq. mi.; Water: 0.0 sq. mi.
In central OH, 10 mi. south of Bowling Green.

Fostoria — City
ZIP: 44830 **Lat:** 41-10-18 N **Long:** 83-25-31 W
Pop: 1,044 (1990); 1,071 (1980) **Pop Density:** 1740.0
Land: 0.6 sq. mi.; **Water:** 0.0 sq. mi. **Elev:** 780 ft.
In northern OH, 14 mi. northeast of Findlay. Part of the town is also in Hancock and Seneca counties.
Name origin: For local developer, businessman, and banker, C. W. Foster.

Freedom — Township
Lat: 41-22-51 N **Long:** 83-28-03 W
Pop: 2,520 (1990); 2,536 (1980) **Pop Density:** 83.2
Land: 30.3 sq. mi.; **Water:** 0.0 sq. mi.

Grand Rapids — Village
ZIP: 43522 **Lat:** 41-24-37 N **Long:** 83-51-56 W
Pop: 955 (1990); 962 (1980) **Pop Density:** 2387.5
Land: 0.4 sq. mi.; **Water:** 0.1 sq. mi. **Elev:** 654 ft.
In northwestern OH on the Maumee River, 7 mi. west of Bowling Green. Not coextensive with the town of the same name.

*Grand Rapids — Township
ZIP: 43522 **Lat:** 41-23-50 N **Long:** 83-50-39 W
Pop: 1,539 (1990); 1,510 (1980) **Pop Density:** 114.0
Land: 13.5 sq. mi.; **Water:** 0.4 sq. mi.

Haskins — Village
ZIP: 43525 **Lat:** 41-27-49 N **Long:** 83-42-14 W
Pop: 549 (1990); 568 (1980) **Pop Density:** 366.0
Land: 1.5 sq. mi.; **Water:** 0.0 sq. mi.

Henry — Township
Lat: 41-13-04 N **Long:** 83-42-34 W
Pop: 3,820 (1990); 3,835 (1980) **Pop Density:** 106.1
Land: 36.0 sq. mi.; **Water:** 0.1 sq. mi.

Hoytville — Village
ZIP: 43529 **Lat:** 41-11-25 N **Long:** 83-47-01 W
Pop: 301 (1990); 315 (1980) **Pop Density:** 376.3
Land: 0.8 sq. mi.; **Water:** 0.0 sq. mi. **Elev:** 714 ft.

Jackson — Township
Lat: 41-12-41 N **Long:** 83-49-23 W
Pop: 765 (1990); 812 (1980) **Pop Density:** 21.0
Land: 36.5 sq. mi.; **Water:** 0.0 sq. mi.

Jerry City — Village
ZIP: 43437 **Lat:** 41-15-11 N **Long:** 83-36-09 W
Pop: 517 (1990); 512 (1980) **Pop Density:** 517.0
Land: 1.0 sq. mi.; **Water:** 0.0 sq. mi.

Lake — Township
ZIP: 43447 **Lat:** 41-33-32 N **Long:** 83-28-11 W
Pop: 10,449 (1990); 10,899 (1980) **Pop Density:** 301.1
Land: 34.7 sq. mi.; **Water:** 0.1 sq. mi.

Liberty — Township
Lat: 41-18-06 N **Long:** 83-42-38 W
Pop: 1,875 (1990); 1,947 (1980) **Pop Density:** 51.0
Land: 36.8 sq. mi.; **Water:** 0.0 sq. mi.

Luckey — Village
ZIP: 43443 **Lat:** 41-27-08 N **Long:** 83-29-01 W
Pop: 848 (1990); 895 (1980) **Pop Density:** 1211.4
Land: 0.7 sq. mi.; **Water:** 0.0 sq. mi.

Middleton — Township
Lat: 41-27-58 N **Long:** 83-40-04 W
Pop: 2,460 (1990); 2,448 (1980) **Pop Density:** 75.0
Land: 32.8 sq. mi.; **Water:** 0.3 sq. mi.

Millbury — Village
ZIP: 43447 **Lat:** 41-33-50 N **Long:** 83-25-32 W
Pop: 1,081 (1990); 955 (1980) **Pop Density:** 1081.0
Land: 1.0 sq. mi.; **Water:** 0.0 sq. mi.

Milton — Township
Lat: 41-17-49 N **Long:** 83-49-29 W
Pop: 1,297 (1990); 1,234 (1980) **Pop Density:** 35.4
Land: 36.6 sq. mi.; **Water:** 0.0 sq. mi.

Milton Center — Village
Lat: 41-18-05 N **Long:** 83-49-46 W
Pop: 200 (1990); 181 (1980) **Pop Density:** 500.0
Land: 0.4 sq. mi.; **Water:** 0.0 sq. mi.

Montgomery — Township
Lat: 41-17-55 N **Long:** 83-28-37 W
Pop: 4,450 (1990); 4,637 (1980) **Pop Density:** 122.3
Land: 36.4 sq. mi.; **Water:** 0.0 sq. mi.

North Baltimore — Village
ZIP: 45872 **Lat:** 41-10-49 N **Long:** 83-40-32 W
Pop: 3,139 (1990); 3,127 (1980) **Pop Density:** 1846.5
Land: 1.7 sq. mi.; **Water:** 0.0 sq. mi.
In northwestern OH, 20 mi. south of Bowling Green.

Northwood — Village
ZIP: 43619 **Lat:** 41-36-37 N **Long:** 83-28-49 W
Pop: 5,506 (1990); 5,495 (1980) **Pop Density:** 679.8
Land: 8.1 sq. mi.; **Water:** 0.0 sq. mi.
In northwestern OH across the Maumee River from Toledo.

Pemberville — Village
ZIP: 43450 **Lat:** 41-24-35 N **Long:** 83-27-28 W
Pop: 1,279 (1990); 1,321 (1980) **Pop Density:** 1279.0
Land: 1.0 sq. mi.; **Water:** 0.0 sq. mi.

Perry — Township
Lat: 41-12-08 N **Long:** 83-28-49 W
Pop: 1,822 (1990); 1,862 (1980) **Pop Density:** 51.6
Land: 35.3 sq. mi.; **Water:** 0.0 sq. mi.

Perrysburg — City
ZIP: 43551 **Lat:** 41-33-10 N **Long:** 83-37-25 W
Pop: 12,551 (1990); 10,215 (1980) **Pop Density:** 2670.4
Land: 4.7 sq. mi.; **Water:** 0.2 sq. mi. **Elev:** 632 ft.
In northwestern OH, overlooking the Maumee River and the city of Maumee, 9 mi. southwest of Toledo.
Name origin: For Oliver Hazard Perry (1785–1819), naval officer and hero of the War of 1812, famous for his message, "We have met the enemy and they are ours."

*Perrysburg — Township
ZIP: 43551 **Lat:** 41-31-31 N **Long:** 83-35-48 W
Pop: 13,176 (1990); 10,651 (1980) **Pop Density:** 292.8
Land: 45.0 sq. mi.; **Water:** 0.8 sq. mi.

Plain — Township
Lat: 41-22-51 N **Long:** 83-42-31 W
Pop: 2,021 (1990); 2,460 (1980) **Pop Density:** 75.4
Land: 26.8 sq. mi.; **Water:** 0.0 sq. mi.

Portage — Village
ZIP: 43451 **Lat:** 41-19-25 N **Long:** 83-38-52 W
Pop: 469 (1990); 479 (1980) **Pop Density:** 312.7
Land: 1.5 sq. mi.; **Water:** 0.0 sq. mi.
Not coextensive with the town of the same name.

OHIO, Wood County

*Portage
Township
ZIP: 43451 Lat: 41-17-48 N Long: 83-35-35 W
Pop: 1,547 (1990); 1,690 (1980) Pop Density: 42.4
Land: 36.5 sq. mi.; Water: 0.1 sq. mi.

Risingsun
Village
ZIP: 43457 Lat: 41-16-07 N Long: 83-25-35 W
Pop: 659 (1990); 698 (1980) Pop Density: 1098.3
Land: 0.6 sq. mi.; Water: 0.0 sq. mi.

Rossford
City
ZIP: 43460 Lat: 41-36-13 N Long: 83-33-43 W
Pop: 5,861 (1990); 5,978 (1980) Pop Density: 2254.2
Land: 2.6 sq. mi.; Water: 0.3 sq. mi.

Tontogany
Village
ZIP: 43565 Lat: 41-25-12 N Long: 83-44-24 W
Pop: 364 (1990); 367 (1980) Pop Density: 1820.0
Land: 0.2 sq. mi.; Water: 0.0 sq. mi.

Troy
Township
Lat: 41-28-37 N Long: 83-27-41 W
Pop: 3,848 (1990); 3,558 (1980) Pop Density: 129.6
Land: 29.7 sq. mi.; Water: 0.1 sq. mi.

Walbridge
Village
ZIP: 43465 Lat: 41-35-08 N Long: 83-29-21 W
Pop: 2,736 (1990); 2,900 (1980) Pop Density: 1954.3
Land: 1.4 sq. mi.; Water: 0.0 sq. mi. Elev: 617 ft.

Washington
Township
Lat: 41-25-22 N Long: 83-45-35 W
Pop: 1,559 (1990); 1,500 (1980) Pop Density: 74.6
Land: 20.9 sq. mi.; Water: 0.6 sq. mi.

Wayne
Village
ZIP: 43466 Lat: 41-18-04 N Long: 83-28-20 W
Pop: 803 (1990); 894 (1980) Pop Density: 2676.7
Land: 0.3 sq. mi.; Water: 0.0 sq. mi.

Webster
Township
Lat: 41-25-40 N Long: 83-32-24 W
Pop: 1,111 (1990); 1,082 (1980) Pop Density: 38.6
Land: 28.8 sq. mi.; Water: 0.0 sq. mi.

West Millgrove
Village
ZIP: 43467 Lat: 41-14-37 N Long: 83-29-31 W
Pop: 171 (1990); 205 (1980) Pop Density: 570.0
Land: 0.3 sq. mi.; Water: 0.0 sq. mi.

Weston
Village
ZIP: 43569 Lat: 41-20-44 N Long: 83-47-40 W
Pop: 1,716 (1990); 1,708 (1980) Pop Density: 1560.0
Land: 1.1 sq. mi.; Water: 0.0 sq. mi.

In northwestern OH, 8 mi. west of Bowling Green. Not coextensive with the town of the same name.

*Weston
Township
ZIP: 43569 Lat: 41-21-43 N Long: 83-48-43 W
Pop: 2,312 (1990); 2,225 (1980) Pop Density: 160.6
Land: 14.4 sq. mi.; Water: 0.0 sq. mi.

Wyandot County
County Seat: Upper Sandusky (ZIP: 43351)

Pop: 22,254 (1990); 22,651 (1980) Pop Density: 54.9
Land: 405.6 sq. mi.; Water: 2.0 sq. mi. Area Code: 419

In west-central OH; organized Feb 3, 1845 from Marion, Crawford, Hardin, and Hancock counties.

Name origin: For the Wyandot Indians, a tribe of Iroquoian linguistic stock. Name is thought to mean 'islanders' or 'those who live on a peninsula,' from their original home on islands in the St. Lawrence River and on a peninsula. Also spelled **Wyandotte**.

Antrim
Township
ZIP: 43323 Lat: 40-45-49 N Long: 83-08-53 W
Pop: 1,322 (1990); 1,414 (1980) Pop Density: 40.9
Land: 32.3 sq. mi.; Water: 0.0 sq. mi.

Carey
Village
ZIP: 43316 Lat: 40-57-05 N Long: 83-22-54 W
Pop: 3,684 (1990); 3,674 (1980) Pop Density: 2167.1
Land: 1.7 sq. mi.; Water: 0.0 sq. mi.

In northwest-central OH, northwest of Marion.
Name origin: For Judge John Carey, president of the Indiana, Bloomington and Western Railroad.

Crane
Township
ZIP: 43351 Lat: 40-50-57 N Long: 83-15-28 W
Pop: 6,935 (1990); 7,064 (1980) Pop Density: 176.0
Land: 39.4 sq. mi.; Water: 0.2 sq. mi.

Crawford
Township
ZIP: 43316 Lat: 40-56-57 N Long: 83-21-42 W
Pop: 4,949 (1990); 5,021 (1980) Pop Density: 137.1
Land: 36.1 sq. mi.; Water: 0.0 sq. mi.

Eden
Township
ZIP: 44849 Lat: 40-51-39 N Long: 83-09-21 W
Pop: 979 (1990); 1,082 (1980) Pop Density: 32.3
Land: 30.3 sq. mi.; Water: 0.0 sq. mi.

Harpster
Village
ZIP: 43323 Lat: 40-44-18 N Long: 83-15-02 W
Pop: 233 (1990); 239 (1980) Pop Density: 122.6
Land: 1.9 sq. mi.; Water: 0.0 sq. mi.

Jackson
Township
Lat: 40-46-08 N Long: 83-27-28 W
Pop: 586 (1990); 545 (1980) Pop Density: 21.6
Land: 27.1 sq. mi.; Water: 0.0 sq. mi.

Kirby Village
ZIP: 43330 Lat: 40-48-48 N Long: 83-25-07 W
Pop: 155 (1990); 158 (1980) Pop Density: 1550.0
Land: 0.1 sq. mi.; Water: 0.0 sq. mi.

Marseilles Village
ZIP: 43351 Lat: 40-42-04 N Long: 83-23-33 W
Pop: 130 (1990); 164 (1980) Pop Density: 1300.0
Land: 0.1 sq. mi.; Water: 0.0 sq. mi.
Not coextensive with the town of the same name.

*Marseilles Township
ZIP: 43351 Lat: 40-42-30 N Long: 83-22-48 W
Pop: 520 (1990); 487 (1980) Pop Density: 22.0
Land: 23.6 sq. mi.; Water: 0.5 sq. mi.

Mifflin Township
Lat: 40-46-30 N Long: 83-21-46 W
Pop: 833 (1990); 816 (1980) Pop Density: 22.8
Land: 36.5 sq. mi.; Water: 0.0 sq. mi.

Nevada Village
ZIP: 44849 Lat: 40-49-06 N Long: 83-07-52 W
Pop: 849 (1990); 945 (1980) Pop Density: 849.0
Land: 1.0 sq. mi.; Water: 0.0 sq. mi.
In northwest-central OH, 10 mi. west of Bucyrus.
Name origin: Named in 1852 for the Nevada Territory.

Pitt Township
ZIP: 43323 Lat: 40-44-52 N Long: 83-14-56 W
Pop: 1,009 (1990); 945 (1980) Pop Density: 26.3
Land: 38.4 sq. mi.; Water: 1.2 sq. mi.

Richland Township
Lat: 40-51-39 N Long: 83-27-59 W
Pop: 934 (1990); 893 (1980) Pop Density: 30.7
Land: 30.4 sq. mi.; Water: 0.0 sq. mi.

Ridge Township
ZIP: 43316 Lat: 40-56-28 N Long: 83-26-48 W
Pop: 537 (1990); 492 (1980) Pop Density: 36.3
Land: 14.8 sq. mi.; Water: 0.0 sq. mi.

Salem Township
Lat: 40-51-25 N Long: 83-21-51 W
Pop: 963 (1990); 984 (1980) Pop Density: 26.5
Land: 36.4 sq. mi.; Water: 0.0 sq. mi.

Sycamore Village
ZIP: 44882 Lat: 40-57-03 N Long: 83-10-15 W
Pop: 919 (1990); 1,059 (1980) Pop Density: 1531.7
Land: 0.6 sq. mi.; Water: 0.0 sq. mi.
In northwest-central OH, north of Marion. Not coextensive with the town of the same name.
Name origin: For the creek that runs through it.

*Sycamore Township
ZIP: 44882 Lat: 40-57-03 N Long: 83-08-57 W
Pop: 1,560 (1990); 1,722 (1980) Pop Density: 64.5
Land: 24.2 sq. mi.; Water: 0.0 sq. mi.

Tymochtee Township
Lat: 40-56-50 N Long: 83-15-02 W
Pop: 1,127 (1990); 1,186 (1980) Pop Density: 31.1
Land: 36.2 sq. mi.; Water: 0.0 sq. mi.

Upper Sandusky City
ZIP: 43351 Lat: 40-49-51 N Long: 83-16-50 W
Pop: 5,906 (1990); 5,967 (1980) Pop Density: 1845.6
Land: 3.2 sq. mi.; Water: 0.0 sq. mi. Elev: 861 ft.

Wharton Village
ZIP: 43359 Lat: 40-51-43 N Long: 83-27-53 W
Pop: 378 (1990); 432 (1980) Pop Density: 290.8
Land: 1.3 sq. mi.; Water: 0.0 sq. mi.

OHIO — *American Places Dictionary*

Index to Places and Counties in Ohio

Aberdeen (Brown) Village 798
Ada (Hardin) Village 835
Adams (Champaign) Township 802
Adams (Clinton) Township 806
Adams (Coshocton) Township 808
Adams (Darke) Township 814
Adams (Defiance) Township 816
Adams (Guernsey) Township 829
Adams (Monroe) Township 865
Adams (Muskingum) Township 870
Adams (Seneca) Township 887
Adams (Washington) Township 902
Adams County 789
Adamsville (Muskingum) Village 870
Addison (Gallia) Township 825
Addyston (Hamilton) Village 830
Adelphi (Ross) Village 884
Adena (Harrison) Village 836
Adena (Jefferson) Village 844
Aid (Lawrence) Township 848
Akron (Summit) City 891
Albany (Athens) Village 794
Alexander (Athens) Township 794
Alexandria (Licking) Village 850
Alger (Hardin) Village 835
Allen (Darke) Township 814
Allen (Hancock) Township 834
Allen (Ottawa) Township 873
Allen (Union) Township 898
Allen County 790
Alliance (Mahoning) City 857
Alliance (Stark) City 889
Alvordton (Williams) Village 905
Amanda (Allen) Township 790
Amanda (Fairfield) Township 819
Amanda (Fairfield) Village 819
Amanda (Hancock) Township 834
Amberley (Hamilton) Village 830
Amboy (Fulton) Township 824
Amelia (Clermont) Village 804
American (Allen) Township 790
Ames (Athens) Township 794
Amesville (Athens) Village 794
Amherst (Lorain) City 853
Amherst (Lorain) Township 853
Amsterdam (Jefferson) Village 844
Anderson (Hamilton) Township 830
Andover (Ashtabula) Township 792
Andover (Ashtabula) Village 792
Anna (Shelby) Village 888
Ansonia (Darke) Village 814
Antioch (Monroe) Village 865
Antrim (Wyandot) Township 908
Antwerp (Paulding) Village 874
Apple Creek (Wayne) Village 904
Aquilla (Geauga) Village 826
Arcadia (Hancock) Village 834
Arcanum (Darke) Village 814
Archbold (Fulton) Village 824
Archer (Harrison) Township 836
Arlington (Hancock) Village 834
Arlington Heights (Hamilton)
  Village 830
Ashland (Ashland) City 791
Ashland County 791
Ashley (Delaware) Village 817
Ashtabula (Ashtabula) City 792
Ashtabula (Ashtabula) Township 792
Ashtabula County 792
Ashville (Pickaway) Village 876

Athalia (Lawrence) Village 848
Athens (Athens) City 794
Athens (Athens) Township 794
Athens (Harrison) Township 836
Athens County 794
Attica (Seneca) Village 887
Atwater (Portage) Township 878
Auburn (Crawford) Township 810
Auburn (Geauga) Township 826
Auburn (Tuscarawas) Township 896
Auglaize (Allen) Township 790
Auglaize (Paulding) Township 874
Auglaize County 795
Augusta (Carroll) Township 800
Aurelius (Washington) Township 902
Aurora (Portage) City 878
Austinburg (Ashtabula) Township ... 792
Austintown (Mahoning) CDP 857
Austintown (Mahoning) Township ... 857
Avon (Lorain) City 853
Avon Lake (Lorain) City 853
Bailey Lakes (Ashland) Village 791
Bainbridge (Geauga) CDP 826
Bainbridge (Geauga) Township 826
Bainbridge (Ross) Village 884
Bairdstown (Wood) Village 906
Ballville (Sandusky) Township 885
Baltic (Coshocton) Village 808
Baltic (Holmes) Village 840
Baltic (Tuscarawas) Village 896
Baltimore (Fairfield) Village 819
Barberton (Summit) City 892
Barlow (Washington) Township 902
Barnesville (Belmont) Village 796
Barnhill (Tuscarawas) Village 896
Bartlow (Henry) Township 837
Batavia (Clermont) Township 804
Batavia (Clermont) Village 804
Batesville (Noble) Village 872
Bath (Allen) Township 790
Bath (Greene) Township 827
Bath (Summit) Township 892
Baughman (Wayne) Township 904
Bay (Ottawa) Township 873
Bay View (Erie) Village 818
Bay Village (Cuyahoga) City 811
Bazetta (Trumbull) Township 893
Beach City (Stark) Village 890
Beachwood (Cuyahoga) City 811
Beallsville (Monroe) Village 865
Bearfield (Perry) Township 875
Beaver (Mahoning) Township 857
Beaver (Noble) Township 872
Beaver (Pike) Township 877
Beaver (Pike) Village 877
Beavercreek (Greene) City 827
Beavercreek (Greene) Township 827
Beaverdam (Allen) Village 790
Beckett Ridge (Butler) CDP 799
Bedford (Coshocton) Township 808
Bedford (Cuyahoga) City 811
Bedford (Meigs) Township 861
Bedford Heights (Cuyahoga) City 811
Beechwood Trails (Licking) CDP 850
Bellaire (Belmont) City 796
Bellbrook (Greene) Village 827
Belle Center (Logan) Village 852
Bellefontaine (Logan) City 852
Belle Valley (Noble) Village 872
Bellevue (Huron) City 842

Bellevue (Sandusky) City 885
Bellville (Richland) Village 882
Belmont (Belmont) Village 796
Belmont County 796
Belmore (Putnam) Village 881
Beloit (Mahoning) Village 857
Belpre (Washington) City 902
Belpre (Washington) Township 903
Bennington (Licking) Township 850
Bennington (Morrow) Township 869
Bentleyville (Cuyahoga) Village 811
Benton (Hocking) Township 840
Benton (Monroe) Township 865
Benton (Ottawa) Township 873
Benton (Paulding) Township 874
Benton (Pike) Township 877
Benton Ridge (Hancock) Village 834
Berea (Cuyahoga) City 811
Bergholz (Jefferson) Village 844
Berkey (Lucas) Village 855
Berkshire (Delaware) Township 817
Berlin (Delaware) Township 817
Berlin (Erie) Township 818
Berlin (Holmes) Township 840
Berlin (Knox) Township 846
Berlin (Mahoning) Township 857
Berlin Heights (Erie) Village 818
Bern (Athens) Township 794
Berne (Fairfield) Township 819
Bethel (Clark) Township 803
Bethel (Clermont) Village 804
Bethel (Miami) Township 863
Bethel (Monroe) Township 865
Bethesda (Belmont) Village 796
Bethlehem (Coshocton) Township ... 808
Bethlehem (Stark) Township 890
Bettsville (Seneca) Village 887
Beverly (Washington) Village 903
Bexley (Franklin) City 822
Big Island (Marion) Township 859
Biglick (Hancock) Township 834
Big Spring (Seneca) Township 887
Black Creek (Mercer) Township 862
Blacklick Estates (Franklin) CDP 822
Blakeslee (Williams) Village 905
Blanchard (Hancock) Township 834
Blanchard (Hardin) Township 835
Blanchard (Putnam) Township 881
Blanchester (Clinton) Village 806
Blanchester (Warren) Village 901
Blendon (Franklin) Township 822
Bloom (Fairfield) Township 819
Bloom (Morgan) Township 868
Bloom (Scioto) Township 886
Bloom (Seneca) Township 887
Bloom (Wood) Township 906
Bloomdale (Wood) Village 906
Bloomfield (Jackson) Township 843
Bloomfield (Logan) Township 852
Bloomfield (Trumbull) Township ... 893
Bloomingburg (Fayette) Village 821
Bloomingdale (Jefferson) Village 844
Blooming Grove (Richland)
  Township 882
Bloomville (Seneca) Village 887
Blue Ash (Hamilton) City 830
Blue Creek (Paulding) Township 874
Blue Rock (Muskingum) Township .. 870
Bluffton (Allen) Village 790
Bluffton (Hancock) Village 834

910

OHIO

oardman (Mahoning) Township 857
okes Creek (Logan) Township.........852
olindale (Trumbull) CDP 894
olivar (Tuscarawas) Village 896
oston (Summit) Township................892
oston Heights (Summit) Village......892
otkins (Shelby) Village 888
owerston (Harrison) Village 836
owersville (Greene) Village............827
owling Green (Licking) Township ..850
owling Green (Marion) Township ..859
owling Green (Wood) City..............906
raceville (Trumbull) Township........894
radford (Darke) Village...................814
radford (Miami) Village...................863
radner (Wood) Village.....................906
rady (Williams) Township................905
rady Lake (Portage) Village............878
ratenahl (Cuyahoga) Village............811
ratton (Adams) Township 789
recksville (Cuyahoga) City.............811
remen (Fairfield) Village 819
rentwood (Jefferson) CDP 844
rewster (Stark) Village....................890
riarwood Beach (Medina) Village ...860
rice (Franklin) Village 822
ridgeport (Belmont) Village 796
ridgetown North (Hamilton) CDP .830
ridgewater (Williams) Township.....905
righton (Lorain) Township 853
rilliant (Jefferson) Village................844
rimfield (Portage) Township...........878
ristol (Morgan) Township................868
ristol (Trumbull) Township..............894
roadview Heights (Cuyahoga) City.811
ronson (Huron) Township................842
rookfield (Noble) Township 872
rookfield (Trumbull) Township........894
rooklyn (Cuyahoga) City 811
rooklyn Heights (Cuyahoga)
   Village 812
rook Park (Cuyahoga) City 812
rookside (Belmont) Village 796
rookville (Montgomery) Village......866
roughton (Paulding) Village............874
rown (Carroll) Township.................800
rown (Darke) Township 814
rown (Delaware) Township 817
rown (Franklin) Township 822
rown (Knox) Township....................846
rown (Miami) Township..................863
rown (Paulding) Township..............874
rown (Vinton) Township..................900
Brown County.................................798
rownhelm (Lorain) Township 853
runswick (Medina) City..................860
runswick Hills (Medina) Township 860
rush Creek (Adams) Township 789
rush Creek (Highland) Township....838
rush Creek (Jefferson) Township 844
Brush Creek (Muskingum)
   Township..................................870
rush Creek (Scioto) Township.........886
ryan (Williams) City........................905
uchtel (Athens) Village....................794
uck (Hardin) Township....................835
uckeye Lake (Licking) Village.........850
uckland (Auglaize) Village...............795
ucks (Tuscarawas) Township...........896
uckskin (Ross) Township 884
ucyrus (Crawford) City....................810
ucyrus (Crawford) Township 810
uffalo (Noble) Township 872
urbank (Wayne) Village....................904
urgoon (Sandusky) Village 885

Burkettsville (Darke) Village............814
Burkettsville (Mercer) Village..........862
Burlington (Lawrence) CDP.............849
Burlington (Licking) Township 850
Burton (Geauga) Township 826
Burton (Geauga) Village...................826
Butler (Columbiana) Township 807
Butler (Darke) Township 814
Butler (Knox) Township....................846
Butler (Mercer) Township 862
Butler (Montgomery) Township........866
Butler (Richland) Township 882
Butler (Richland) Village..................882
Butler County.................................799
Butlerville (Warren) Village..............901
Byesville (Guernsey) Village............829
Byrd (Brown) Township....................798
Cadiz (Harrison) Township 836
Cadiz (Harrison) Village...................836
Caesars Creek (Greene) Township....827
Cairo (Allen) Village.........................790
Calcutta (Columbiana) CDP.............807
Caldwell (Noble) Village..................872
Caledonia (Marion) Village 859
Cambridge (Guernsey) City..............829
Cambridge (Guernsey) Township.....829
Camden (Lorain) Township 853
Camden (Preble) Village...................880
Campbell (Mahoning) City...............858
Camp Creek (Pike) Township...........877
Canaan (Athens) Township 794
Canaan (Madison) Township 856
Canaan (Morrow) Township 869
Canaan (Wayne) Township...............904
Canal Fulton (Stark) Village.............890
Canal Winchester (Franklin) Village.822
Canfield (Mahoning) City.................858
Canfield (Mahoning) Township.........858
Canton (Stark) City 890
Canton (Stark) Township 890
Cardington (Morrow) Township 869
Cardington (Morrow) Village 869
Carey (Wyandot) Village..................908
Carlisle (Lorain) Township...............853
Carlisle (Montgomery) Village 866
Carlisle (Warren) Village 901
Carroll (Fairfield) Village 819
Carroll (Ottawa) Township 873
Carroll County................................800
Carrollton (Carroll) Village...............801
Carryall (Paulding) Township...........874
Carthage (Athens) Township 794
Cass (Hancock) Township 834
Cass (Muskingum) Township 870
Cass (Richland) Township................882
Casstown (Miami) Village................863
Castalia (Erie) Village......................818
Castine (Darke) Village 815
Catawba (Clark) Village 803
Catawba Island (Ottawa) Township ..873
Cecil (Paulding) Village...................874
Cedarville (Greene) Township..........828
Cedarville (Greene) Village..............828
Celina (Mercer) City.........................862
Center (Carroll) Township................801
Center (Columbiana) Township 807
Center (Guernsey) Township............829
Center (Mercer) Township 862
Center (Monroe) Township...............865
Center (Morgan) Township...............868
Center (Noble) Township..................872
Center (Williams) Township 905
Center (Wood) Township..................906
Centerburg (Knox) Village................846
Centerville (Gallia) Village...............825

Centerville (Montgomery) City.........866
Cessna (Hardin) Township................835
Chagrin Falls (Cuyahoga) City 812
Chagrin Falls (Cuyahoga) Township .812
Champaign County........................802
Champion (Trumbull) Township.......894
Champion Heights (Trumbull) CDP.894
Chardon (Geauga) Township............826
Chardon (Geauga) Village.................826
Charlestown (Portage) Township 878
Chatfield (Crawford) Township 810
Chatfield (Crawford) Village.............810
Chatham (Medina) Township 860
Chauncey (Athens) Village 794
Cherry Fork (Adams) Village 789
Cherry Grove (Hamilton) CDP 830
Cherry Valley (Ashtabula) Township 792
Chesapeake (Lawrence) Village........849
Cheshire (Gallia) Township...............825
Cheshire (Gallia) Village...................825
Chester (Clinton) Township..............806
Chester (Geauga) Township 826
Chester (Meigs) Township 861
Chester (Morrow) Township 869
Chester (Wayne) Township...............904
Chesterfield (Fulton) Township.........824
Chesterhill (Morgan) Village 868
Chesterland (Geauga) CDP 827
Chesterville (Morrow) Village 869
Cheviot (Hamilton) City 830
Chickasaw (Mercer) Village.............862
Chillicothe (Ross) City 884
Chilo (Clermont) Village 804
Chippewa (Wayne) Township...........904
Chippewa-on-the-Lake (Medina)
   Village 860
Chocktou Lake (Madison) CDP........856
Christiansburg (Champaign) Village.802
Churchill (Trumbull) CDP 894
Cincinnati (Hamilton) City 830
Circleville (Pickaway) City...............876
Circleville (Pickaway) Township 876
Claibourne (Union) Township..........898
Claridon (Geauga) Township 827
Claridon (Marion) Township............859
Clarington (Monroe) Village 865
Clark (Brown) Township 798
Clark (Clinton) Township.................806
Clark (Coshocton) Township 809
Clark (Holmes) Township.................841
Clark County..................................803
Clarksburg (Ross) Village 884
Clarksfield (Huron) Township..........842
Clarksville (Clinton) Village.............806
Clay (Auglaize) Township.................795
Clay (Gallia) Township.....................825
Clay (Highland) Township................838
Clay (Knox) Township......................846
Clay (Montgomery) Township..........866
Clay (Muskingum) Township 870
Clay (Ottawa) Township...................873
Clay (Scioto) Township 886
Clay (Tuscarawas) Township............896
Clay Center (Ottawa) Village............873
Clayton (Montgomery) Village.........866
Clayton (Perry) Township 875
Clear Creek (Ashland) Township 791
Clear Creek (Fairfield) Township......820
Clear Creek (Warren) Township........901
Clermont County...........................804
Cleveland (Cuyahoga) City...............812
Cleveland Heights (Cuyahoga) City ..812
Cleves (Hamilton) Village 831
Clifton (Clark) Village 803
Clifton (Greene) Village 828

911

Clinton (Franklin) Township............822
Clinton (Fulton) Township...............824
Clinton (Knox) Township...................846
Clinton (Seneca) Township................887
Clinton (Shelby) Township..................888
Clinton (Summit) Village 892
Clinton (Vinton) Township 900
Clinton (Wayne) Township....................904
Clinton County..806
Cloverdale (Putnam) Village 881
Clyde (Sandusky) City........................885
Coal (Jackson) Township...................843
Coal (Perry) Township........................875
Coal Grove (Lawrence) Village..........849
Coalton (Jackson) Village....................843
Coitsville (Mahoning) Township.......858
Coldwater (Mercer) Village 862
Colebrook (Ashtabula) Township......792
Colerain (Belmont) Township............796
Colerain (Hamilton) Township..........831
Colerain (Ross) Township....................884
College (Knox) Township...................846
College Corner (Butler) Village.........799
College Corner (Preble) Village..........880
Columbia (Hamilton) Township........831
Columbia (Lorain) Township..............853
Columbia (Meigs) Township..............861
Columbiana (Columbiana) Village....807
Columbiana (Mahoning) Village........858
Columbiana County.................................807
Columbus (Fairfield) City 820
Columbus (Franklin) City 822
Columbus Grove (Putnam) Village....881
Commercial Point (Pickaway)
   Village 876
Concord (Champaign) Township 802
Concord (Delaware) Township..........817
Concord (Fayette) Township 821
Concord (Highland) Township..........838
Concord (Lake) Township 847
Concord (Miami) Township...............864
Concord (Ross) Township....................884
Conesville (Coshocton) Village.........809
Congress (Morrow) Township 869
Congress (Wayne) Township 904
Congress (Wayne) Village 904
Conneaut (Ashtabula) City..................792
Continental (Putnam) Village 881
Convoy (Van Wert) Village 899
Coolville (Athens) Village..................794
Copley (Summit) Township................892
Corning (Perry) Village......................875
Cortland (Trumbull) Village..............894
Corwin (Warren) Village....................901
Coshocton (Coshocton) City..............809
Coshocton County 808
Covedale (Hamilton) CDP..................831
Coventry (Summit) Township...........892
Covington (Miami) Village................864
Craig Beach (Mahoning) Village 858
Cranberry (Crawford) Township........810
Crane (Paulding) Township.................874
Crane (Wyandot) Township................908
Crawford (Coshocton) Township 809
Crawford (Wyandot) Township..........908
Crawford County 810
Crestline (Crawford) City 810
Crestline (Richland) City...................882
Creston (Wayne) Village.....................904
Cridersville (Auglaize) Village...........795
Crooksville (Perry) Village..................875
Crosby (Hamilton) Township............831
Cross Creek (Jefferson) Township.....844
Crown City (Gallia) Village...............825
Crystal Lakes (Clark) CDP.................803

Cumberland (Guernsey) Village........829
Custar (Wood) Village 906
Cuyahoga County 811
Cuyahoga Falls (Summit) City 892
Cuyahoga Heights (Cuyahoga)
   Village 812
Cygnet (Wood) Village......................906
Cynthian (Shelby) Township.............888
Dallas (Crawford) Township 810
Dalton (Wayne) Village.....................904
Damascus (Henry) Township 837
Danbury (Ottawa) Township.............873
Danville (Knox) Village.....................846
Darby (Madison) Township 856
Darby (Pickaway) Township 876
Darby (Union) Township 898
Darbyville (Pickaway) Village...........876
Darke County...814
Day Heights (Clermont) CDP............804
Dayton (Montgomery) City................866
Decatur (Lawrence) Township 849
Decatur (Washington) Township.......903
Deer Creek (Madison) Township 856
Deer Creek (Pickaway) Township......876
Deerfield (Morgan) Township............868
Deerfield (Portage) Township.............878
Deerfield (Ross) Township..................884
Deerfield (Warren) Township..............901
Deer Park (Hamilton) City.................831
Deersville (Harrison) Village..............836
Defiance (Defiance) City....................816
Defiance (Defiance) Township..........816
Defiance County..816
De Graff (Logan) Village....................852
Delaware (Defiance) Township..........816
Delaware (Delaware) City...................817
Delaware (Delaware) Township.........817
Delaware (Hancock) Township..........834
Delaware County 817
Delhi (Hamilton) Township 831
Dellroy (Carroll) Village.....................801
Delphos (Allen) City..........................790
Delphos (Van Wert) City 899
Delta (Fulton) Village.........................824
Dennison (Tuscarawas) Village 896
Dent (Hamilton) CDP.........................831
Deshler (Henry) Village.....................837
Devola (Washington) CDP................903
Dexter City (Noble) Village 872
Dillonvale (Hamilton) CDP...............831
Dillonvale (Jefferson) Village............844
Dinsmore (Shelby) Township............889
Dixon (Preble) Township 880
Dodson (Highland) Township...........838
Donnelsville (Clark) Village..............803
Dorset (Ashtabula) Township............792
Dover (Athens) Township 794
Dover (Fulton) Township...................824
Dover (Tuscarawas) City 896
Dover (Tuscarawas) Township..........896
Dover (Union) Township 898
Doylestown (Wayne) Village 904
Dresden (Muskingum) Village..........870
Drexel (Montgomery) CDP...............866
Dry Run (Hamilton) CDP 831
Dublin (Delaware) Village.................817
Dublin (Franklin) Village 822
Dublin (Mercer) Township 862
Dublin (Union) City...........................898
Duchouquet (Auglaize) Township.....795
Dudley (Hardin) Township................835
Dunham (Washington) Township 903
Dunkirk (Hardin) Village...................835
Dupont (Putnam) Village 881
Eagle (Brown) Township....................798

Eagle (Hancock) Township................834
Eagle (Vinton) Township...................900
East (Carroll) Township.......................801
East Canton (Stark) Village................890
East Cleveland (Cuyahoga) City 812
Eastlake (Lake) City 847
East Liverpool (Columbiana) City....807
East Palestine (Columbiana) City.....807
East Sparta (Stark) Village.................890
East Union (Wayne) Township 904
Eaton (Lorain) Township 854
Eaton (Preble) City.............................880
Eaton Estates (Lorain) CDP...............854
Eden (Licking) Township 850
Eden (Seneca) Township....................887
Eden (Wyandot) Township................908
Edgerton (Williams) Village..............905
Edgewood (Ashtabula) CDP..............793
Edinburg (Portage) Township............878
Edison (Morrow) Village 869
Edon (Williams) Village....................905
Eldorado (Preble) Village 880
Elgin (Van Wert) Village....................899
Elida (Allen) Village 790
Elizabeth (Lawrence) Township 849
Elizabeth (Miami) Township.............864
Elk (Noble) Township........................872
Elk (Vinton) Township......................900
Elkrun (Columbiana) Township........807
Ellsworth (Mahoning) Township......858
Elmore (Ottawa) Village....................873
Elmwood Place (Hamilton) Village...831
Elyria (Lorain) City 854
Elyria (Lorain) Township 854
Emerald (Paulding) Township...........874
Empire (Jefferson) Village 844
Englewood (Montgomery) City 866
Enoch (Noble) Township...................872
Enon (Clark) Village..........................803
Erie (Ottawa) Township.....................873
Erie County..818
Etna (Licking) Township 850
Euclid (Cuyahoga) City 812
Evendale (Hamilton) Village.............831
Fairborn (Greene) City.......................828
Fairfax (Hamilton) Village 831
Fairfield (Butler) City 799
Fairfield (Butler) Township 799
Fairfield (Columbiana) Township 807
Fairfield (Hamilton) City 831
Fairfield (Highland) Township 839
Fairfield (Huron) Township 842
Fairfield (Madison) Township...........856
Fairfield (Tuscarawas) Township.......896
Fairfield (Washington) Township 903
Fairfield Beach (Fairfield) CDP 820
Fairfield County..819
Fairlawn (Summit) City.....................892
Fairport Harbor (Lake) Village 847
Fairview (Belmont) Village...............796
Fairview (Guernsey) Village 829
Fairview Lanes (Erie) CDP................818
Fairview Park (Cuyahoga) City.........812
Falls (Hocking) Township.................840
Falls (Muskingum) Township............870
Fallsbury (Licking) Township...........850
Farmer (Defiance) Township.............816
Farmersville (Montgomery) Village ..866
Farmington (Trumbull) Township.....894
Fayette (Fulton) Village.....................824
Fayette (Lawrence) Township............849
Fayette County..821
Fayetteville (Brown) Village 798
Fearing (Washington) Township........903
Felicity (Clermont) Village................804

OHIO

Findlay (Hancock) City 834
Finneytown (Hamilton) CDP 831
Fitchville (Huron) Township 842
Five Points (Warren) CDP 901
Flatrock (Henry) Township 837
Fletcher (Miami) Village 864
Florence (Erie) Township 818
Florence (Williams) Township 905
Florida (Henry) Village 838
Flushing (Belmont) Township 797
Flushing (Belmont) Village 796
Forest (Hardin) Village 835
Forest Park (Hamilton) City 831
Forestville (Hamilton) CDP 831
Fort Jennings (Putnam) Village 881
Fort Loramie (Shelby) Village 889
Fort McKinley (Montgomery) CDP .. 866
Fort Recovery (Mercer) Village 863
Fort Shawnee (Allen) Village 790
Fostoria (Hancock) City 834
Fostoria (Seneca) City 888
Fostoria (Wood) City 907
Fowler (Trumbull) Township 894
Fox (Carroll) Township 801
Frankfort (Ross) Village 884
Franklin (Adams) Township 789
Franklin (Brown) Township 798
Franklin (Clermont) Township 804
Franklin (Columbiana) Township 807
Franklin (Coshocton) Township 809
Franklin (Darke) Township 815
Franklin (Franklin) Township 822
Franklin (Fulton) Township 824
Franklin (Harrison) Township 836
Franklin (Jackson) Township 843
Franklin (Licking) Township 850
Franklin (Mercer) Township 863
Franklin (Monroe) Township 865
Franklin (Morrow) Township 869
Franklin (Portage) Township 878
Franklin (Richland) Township 882
Franklin (Ross) Township 884
Franklin (Shelby) Township 889
Franklin (Summit) Township 892
Franklin (Tuscarawas) Township 896
Franklin (Warren) City 901
Franklin (Warren) Township 901
Franklin (Wayne) Township 904
Franklin County 822
Franklin Furnace (Scioto) CDP 886
Frazeysburg (Muskingum) Village 870
Fredericksburg (Wayne) Village 904
Fredericktown (Knox) Village 846
Freedom (Henry) Township 838
Freedom (Portage) Township 879
Freedom (Wood) Township 907
Freeport (Harrison) Township 837
Freeport (Harrison) Village 837
Fremont (Sandusky) City 885
Fruit Hill (Hamilton) CDP 831
Fulton (Fulton) Township 825
Fulton (Morrow) Village 869
Fulton County 824
Fultonham (Muskingum) Village 870
Gahanna (Franklin) City 822
Galena (Delaware) Village 817
Galion (Crawford) City 810
Gallia County 825
Gallipolis (Gallia) City 825
Gallipolis (Gallia) Township 825
Gambier (Knox) Village 846
Gann (Knox) Village 846
Garfield Heights (Cuyahoga) City 812
Garrettsville (Portage) Village 879
Gasper (Preble) Township 880

Gates Mills (Cuyahoga) Village 812
Geauga County 826
Geneva (Ashtabula) City 793
Geneva (Ashtabula) Township 793
Geneva-on-the-Lake (Ashtabula)
  Village 793
Genoa (Delaware) Township 817
Genoa (Ottawa) Village 873
Georgetown (Brown) Village 798
German (Auglaize) Township 795
German (Clark) Township 803
German (Fulton) Township 825
German (Harrison) Township 837
German (Montgomery) Township 866
Germantown (Montgomery) Village . 867
Gettysburg (Darke) Village 815
Gibson (Mercer) Township 863
Gibsonburg (Sandusky) Village 885
Gilboa (Putnam) Village 881
Gilead (Morrow) Township 869
Girard (Trumbull) City 894
Glandorf (Putnam) Village 881
Glendale (Hamilton) Village 831
Glenford (Perry) Village 875
Glenmont (Holmes) Village 841
Glenmoor (Columbiana) CDP 807
Glenwillow (Cuyahoga) Village 812
Gloria Glens Park (Medina) Village .. 860
Glouster (Athens) Village 794
Gnadenhutten (Tuscarawas) Village .. 896
Golf Manor (Hamilton) City 831
Good Hope (Hocking) Township 840
Gordon (Darke) Village 815
Gorham (Fulton) Township 825
Goshen (Auglaize) Township 795
Goshen (Belmont) Township 797
Goshen (Champaign) Township 802
Goshen (Clermont) Township 804
Goshen (Hardin) Township 835
Goshen (Mahoning) Township 858
Goshen (Tuscarawas) Township 896
Grafton (Lorain) Township 854
Grafton (Lorain) Village 854
Grand (Marion) Township 859
Grand Prairie (Marion) Township 859
Grand Rapids (Wood) Township 907
Grand Rapids (Wood) Village 907
Grand River (Lake) Village 847
Grandview (Hamilton) CDP 831
Grandview (Washington) Township .. 903
Grandview Heights (Franklin) City .. 822
Granger (Medina) Township 860
Granville (Licking) Township 850
Granville (Licking) Village 850
Granville (Mercer) Township 863
Granville South (Licking) CDP 850
Gratiot (Licking) Village 850
Gratiot (Muskingum) Village 871
Gratis (Preble) Township 880
Gratis (Preble) Village 880
Graysville (Monroe) Village 865
Green (Adams) Township 789
Green (Ashland) Township 791
Green (Brown) Township 798
Green (Clark) Township 803
Green (Clinton) Township 806
Green (Fayette) Township 821
Green (Gallia) Township 825
Green (Hamilton) Township 831
Green (Harrison) Township 837
Green (Hocking) Township 840
Green (Mahoning) Township 858
Green (Monroe) Township 865
Green (Ross) Township 884
Green (Scioto) Township 886

Green (Shelby) Township 889
Green (Summit) Township 892
Green (Summit) Village 892
Green (Wayne) Township 904
Green Camp (Marion) Township 859
Green Camp (Marion) Village 859
Green Creek (Sandusky) Township ... 885
Greene (Trumbull) Township 894
Greene County 827
Greenfield (Fairfield) Township 820
Greenfield (Gallia) Township 826
Greenfield (Highland) City 839
Greenfield (Huron) Township 842
Greenhills (Hamilton) City 831
Green Meadows (Clark) CDP 803
Greensburg (Putnam) Township 881
Greensburg (Summit) CDP 892
Green Springs (Sandusky) Village 885
Green Springs (Seneca) Village 888
Greentown (Stark) CDP 890
Greenville (Darke) City 815
Greenville (Darke) Township 815
Greenwich (Huron) Township 842
Greenwich (Huron) Village 842
Groesbeck (Hamilton) CDP 832
Groton (Erie) Township 818
Grove City (Franklin) City 822
Groveport (Franklin) Village 822
Grover Hill (Paulding) Village 874
Guernsey County 829
Guilford (Medina) Township 860
Gustavus (Trumbull) Township 894
Guyan (Gallia) Township 826
Hale (Hardin) Township 835
Hambden (Geauga) Township 827
Hamden (Vinton) Village 900
Hamer (Highland) Township 839
Hamersville (Brown) Village 798
Hamilton (Butler) City 799
Hamilton (Franklin) Township 822
Hamilton (Jackson) Township 843
Hamilton (Lawrence) Township 849
Hamilton (Warren) Township 901
Hamilton County 830
Hamler (Henry) Village 838
Hancock County 834
Hanging Rock (Lawrence) Village ... 849
Hanover (Ashland) Township 791
Hanover (Butler) Township 799
Hanover (Columbiana) Township 807
Hanover (Licking) Township 850
Hanover (Licking) Village 850
Hanoverton (Columbiana) Village 807
Harbor Hills (Licking) CDP 850
Harbor View (Lucas) Village 855
Hardin County 835
Harding (Lucas) Township 855
Hardy (Holmes) Township 841
Harlan (Warren) Township 901
Harlem (Delaware) Township 817
Harmony (Clark) Township 803
Harmony (Morrow) Township 869
Harpersfield (Ashtabula) Township .. 793
Harpster (Wyandot) Village 908
Harris (Ottawa) Township 873
Harrisburg (Franklin) Village 823
Harrisburg (Pickaway) Village 876
Harrison (Carroll) Township 801
Harrison (Champaign) Township 802
Harrison (Darke) Township 815
Harrison (Gallia) Township 826
Harrison (Hamilton) Township 832
Harrison (Hamilton) Village 832
Harrison (Henry) Township 838
Harrison (Knox) Township 846

OHIO

American Places Dictionary

Harrison (Licking) Township *850*
Harrison (Logan) Township *852*
Harrison (Montgomery) Township...*867*
Harrison (Muskingum) Township.....*871*
Harrison (Paulding) Township *874*
Harrison (Perry) Township................*875*
Harrison (Pickaway) Township *876*
Harrison (Preble) Township *880*
Harrison (Ross) Township *884*
Harrison (Scioto) Township *886*
Harrison (Van Wert) Township.........*899*
Harrison (Vinton) Township *900*
Harrison County.................................*836*
Harrisville (Harrison) Village.............*837*
Harrisville (Medina) Township *860*
Harrod (Allen) Village *790*
Hartford (Licking) Township *850*
Hartford (Licking) Village..................*850*
Hartford (Trumbull) Township *894*
Hartland (Huron) Township................*842*
Hartsgrove (Ashtabula) Township.....*793*
Hartville (Stark) Village *890*
Harveysburg (Warren) Village *901*
Haskins (Wood) Village *907*
Haviland (Paulding) Village *874*
Hayesville (Ashland) Village *791*
Heath (Licking) City..........................*850*
Hebron (Licking) Village....................*851*
Helena (Sandusky) Village..................*885*
Hemlock (Perry) Village *875*
Henrietta (Lorain) Township...............*854*
Henry (Wood) Township *907*
Henry County.....................................*837*
Hicksville (Defiance) Township *816*
Hicksville (Defiance) Village.............*816*
Higginsport (Brown) Village...............*798*
Highland (Defiance) Township *816*
Highland (Highland) Village *839*
Highland (Muskingum) Township.....*871*
Highland County................................*838*
Highland Heights (Cuyahoga) City ...*812*
Hilliar (Knox) Township *846*
Hilliard (Franklin) City......................*823*
Hills and Dales (Stark) Village...........*890*
Hillsboro (Highland) City...................*839*
Hinckley (Medina) Township *860*
Hiram (Portage) Township *879*
Hiram (Portage) Village *879*
Hoaglin (Van Wert) Township...........*899*
Hocking (Fairfield) Township *820*
Hocking County.................................*840*
Holgate (Henry) Village......................*838*
Holiday Valley (Clark) CDP..............*803*
Holland (Lucas) Village......................*855*
Hollansburg (Darke) Village...............*815*
Holloway (Belmont) Village...............*797*
Holmes (Crawford) Township............*810*
Holmes County..................................*840*
Holmesville (Holmes) Village............*841*
Homer (Medina) Township *860*
Homer (Morgan) Township *868*
Hopedale (Harrison) Village...............*837*
Hopewell (Licking) Township *851*
Hopewell (Mercer) Township *863*
Hopewell (Muskingum) Township....*871*
Hopewell (Perry) Township *875*
Hopewell (Seneca) Township *888*
Howard (Knox) Township *846*
Howland (Trumbull) Township *894*
Hoytville (Wood) Village *907*
Hubbard (Trumbull) City *894*
Hubbard (Trumbull) Township *894*
Huber Heights (Miami) City..............*864*
Huber Heights (Montgomery) City...*867*
Huber Ridge (Franklin) CDP..............*823*

Hudson (Summit) Township *892*
Hudson (Summit) Village...................*892*
Huntington (Brown) Township *798*
Huntington (Gallia) Township *826*
Huntington (Lorain) Township *854*
Huntington (Ross) Township *884*
Hunting Valley (Cuyahoga) Village...*812*
Hunting Valley (Geauga) Village.......*827*
Huntsburg (Geauga) Township...........*827*
Huntsville (Logan) Village..................*852*
Huron (Erie) City *818*
Huron (Erie) Township.......................*819*
Huron County....................................*842*
Independence (Cuyahoga) City *812*
Independence (Washington)
    Township.......................................*903*
Irondale (Jefferson) Village *844*
Ironton (Lawrence) City *849*
Island Creek (Jefferson) Township....*844*
Israel (Preble) Township *880*
Ithaca (Darke) Village *815*
Jackson (Allen) Township *790*
Jackson (Ashland) Township *791*
Jackson (Auglaize) Township *795*
Jackson (Brown) Township *798*
Jackson (Champaign) Township.........*802*
Jackson (Clermont) Township............*804*
Jackson (Coshocton) Township *809*
Jackson (Crawford) Township............*810*
Jackson (Darke) Township *815*
Jackson (Franklin) Township *823*
Jackson (Guernsey) Township............*829*
Jackson (Hancock) Township.............*834*
Jackson (Hardin) Township................*835*
Jackson (Highland) Township *839*
Jackson (Jackson) City *843*
Jackson (Jackson) Township *843*
Jackson (Knox) Township *846*
Jackson (Mahoning) Township...........*858*
Jackson (Monroe) Township *865*
Jackson (Montgomery) Township.....*867*
Jackson (Muskingum) Township.......*871*
Jackson (Noble) Township *872*
Jackson (Paulding) Township.............*874*
Jackson (Perry) Township *875*
Jackson (Pickaway) Township *876*
Jackson (Pike) Township *877*
Jackson (Preble) Township *880*
Jackson (Putnam) Township *881*
Jackson (Richland) Township *882*
Jackson (Sandusky) Township............*885*
Jackson (Seneca) Township *888*
Jackson (Shelby) Township.................*889*
Jackson (Stark) Township...................*890*
Jackson (Union) Township *898*
Jackson (Van Wert) Township............*899*
Jackson (Vinton) Township *900*
Jackson (Wood) Township *907*
Jackson (Wyandot) Township *908*
Jacksonburg (Butler) Village...............*799*
Jackson Center (Shelby) Village.........*889*
Jackson County.................................*843*
Jacksonville (Athens) Village.............*794*
Jamestown (Greene) Village...............*828*
Jasper (Fayette) Township *821*
Jefferson (Adams) Township *789*
Jefferson (Ashtabula) Township *793*
Jefferson (Ashtabula) Village.............*793*
Jefferson (Brown) Township *798*
Jefferson (Clinton) Township.............*806*
Jefferson (Coshocton) Township *809*
Jefferson (Crawford) Township..........*810*
Jefferson (Fayette) Township *821*
Jefferson (Franklin) Township *823*
Jefferson (Greene) Township..............*828*

Jefferson (Guernsey) Township.........*829*
Jefferson (Jackson) Township *843*
Jefferson (Knox) Township *846*
Jefferson (Logan) Township *852*
Jefferson (Madison) Township...........*856*
Jefferson (Madison) Village...............*856*
Jefferson (Mercer) Township..............*863*
Jefferson (Montgomery) Township ...*867*
Jefferson (Muskingum) Township.....*871*
Jefferson (Noble) Township *872*
Jefferson (Preble) Township *880*
Jefferson (Richland) Township..........*882*
Jefferson (Ross) Township *884*
Jefferson (Scioto) Township *886*
Jefferson (Tuscarawas) Township......*896*
Jefferson (Williams) Township..........*905*
Jefferson County...............................*844*
Jeffersonville (Fayette) Village *821*
Jenera (Hancock) Village....................*834*
Jennings (Putnam) Township *881*
Jennings (Van Wert) Township..........*899*
Jerome (Union) Township *898*
Jeromesville (Ashland) Village *791*
Jerry City (Wood) Village...................*907*
Jersey (Licking) Township *851*
Jerusalem (Lucas) Township *855*
Jerusalem (Monroe) Village *865*
Jewett (Harrison) Village....................*837*
Johnson (Champaign) Township........*802*
Johnston (Trumbull) Township *894*
Johnstown (Licking) Village...............*851*
Junction City (Perry) Village *875*
Kalida (Putnam) Village.....................*881*
Keene (Coshocton) Township *809*
Kelleys Island (Erie) Village..............*819*
Kent (Portage) City.............................*879*
Kenton (Hardin) City..........................*835*
Kenwood (Hamilton) CDP *832*
Kettering (Greene) City......................*828*
Kettering (Montgomery) City............*867*
Kettlersville (Shelby) Village.............*889*
Killbuck (Holmes) Township.............*841*
Killbuck (Holmes) Village..................*841*
Kimbolton (Guernsey) Village *829*
Kingston (Delaware) Township..........*817*
Kingston (Ross) Village *884*
Kingsville (Ashtabula) Township *793*
Kinsman (Trumbull) Township *894*
Kipton (Lorain) Village *854*
Kirby (Wyandot) Village *909*
Kirkersville (Licking) Village *851*
Kirkwood (Belmont) Township..........*797*
Kirtland (Lake) City............................*847*
Kirtland Hills (Lake) Village *847*
Knox (Columbiana) Township *807*
Knox (Guernsey) Township................*829*
Knox (Holmes) Township *841*
Knox (Jefferson) Township *844*
Knox (Vinton) Township....................*900*
Knox County.....................................*846*
La Croft (Columbiana) CDP..............*807*
Lafayette (Allen) Village *790*
Lafayette (Coshocton) Township *809*
Lafayette (Medina) Township *860*
Lagrange (Lorain) Township *854*
Lagrange (Lorain) Village...................*854*
Lake (Ashland) Township *791*
Lake (Logan) Township *852*
Lake (Stark) Township........................*890*
Lake (Wood) Township.......................*907*
Lake County......................................*847*
Lake Darby (Franklin) CDP *823*
Lakeline (Lake) Village......................*847*
Lakemore (Summit) Village...............*892*
Lakeview (Logan) Village..................*852*

Lakewood (Cuyahoga) City 812	Litchfield (Medina) Township 860	Mad River (Clark) Township 803
Lancaster (Fairfield) City 820	Lithopolis (Fairfield) Village 820	Mad River (Montgomery) Township 867
Landen (Warren) CDP 901	Liverpool (Columbiana) Township ... 807	Magnetic Springs (Union) Village 898
Lanier (Preble) Township 880	Liverpool (Medina) Township 860	Magnolia (Carroll) Village 801
La Rue (Marion) Village 859	Lockbourne (Franklin) Village 823	Magnolia (Stark) Village 890
Latty (Paulding) Township 874	Lockington (Shelby) Village 889	**Mahoning County** 857
Latty (Paulding) Village 874	Lockland (Hamilton) City 832	Maineville (Warren) Village 901
Laura (Miami) Village 864	Lodi (Athens) Township 794	Malaga (Monroe) Township 865
Laurel (Hocking) Township 840	Lodi (Medina) Village 860	Malinta (Henry) Village 838
Laurelville (Hocking) Village 840	Logan (Auglaize) Township 795	Malta (Morgan) Township 868
Lawrence (Lawrence) Township 849	Logan (Hocking) City 840	Malta (Morgan) Village 868
Lawrence (Stark) Township 890	**Logan County** 852	Malvern (Carroll) Village 801
Lawrence (Tuscarawas) Township 896	Logan Elm Village (Pickaway) CDP .877	Manchester (Adams) Township 789
Lawrence (Washington) Township .. 903	London (Madison) City 856	Manchester (Adams) Village 789
Lawrence County 848	Londonderry (Guernsey) Township .. 829	Manchester (Morgan) Township 868
Lawrenceville (Clark) Village 803	Lorain (Lorain) City 854	Mansfield (Richland) City 883
Lebanon (Meigs) Township 861	**Lorain County** 853	Mantua (Portage) Township 879
Lebanon (Warren) City 901	Loramie (Shelby) Township 889	Mantua (Portage) Village 879
Lee (Athens) Township 794	Lordstown (Trumbull) Village 894	Maple Heights (Cuyahoga) City 813
Lee (Carroll) Township 801	Lore City (Guernsey) Village 829	Maple Ridge (Mahoning) CDP 858
Lee (Monroe) Township 865	Lostcreek (Miami) Township 864	Marble Cliff (Franklin) Village 823
Leesburg (Highland) Village 839	Loudon (Carroll) Township 801	Marblehead (Ottawa) Village 873
Leesburg (Union) Township 898	Loudon (Seneca) Township 888	Marengo (Morrow) Village 869
Leesville (Carroll) Village 801	Loudonville (Ashland) Village 791	Margaretta (Erie) Township 819
Leetonia (Columbiana) Village 807	Loudonville (Holmes) Village 841	Mariemont (Hamilton) Village 832
Leipsic (Putnam) Village 881	Louisville (Stark) City 890	Marietta (Washington) City 903
Lemon (Butler) Township 799	Loveland (Clermont) City 804	Marietta (Washington) Township 903
Lenox (Ashtabula) Township 793	Loveland (Hamilton) City 832	Marion (Allen) Township 790
Leroy (Lake) Township 847	Loveland (Warren) City 901	Marion (Clinton) Township 806
Letart (Meigs) Township 861	Loveland Park (Hamilton) CDP 832	Marion (Fayette) Township 821
Lewis (Brown) Township 798	Loveland Park (Warren) CDP 901	Marion (Hancock) Township 834
Lewisburg (Preble) Village 880	Lowell (Washington) Village 903	Marion (Hardin) Township 836
Lewisville (Monroe) Village 865	Lowellville (Mahoning) Village 858	Marion (Henry) Township 838
Lexington (Richland) Village 883	Lower Salem (Washington) Village ... 903	Marion (Hocking) Township 840
Lexington (Stark) Township 890	Lucas (Richland) Village 883	Marion (Marion) City 859
Liberty (Adams) Township 789	**Lucas County** 855	Marion (Marion) Township 859
Liberty (Butler) Township 799	Lucasville (Scioto) CDP 886	Marion (Mercer) Township 863
Liberty (Clinton) Township 806	Luckey (Wood) Village 907	Marion (Morgan) Township 868
Liberty (Crawford) Township 810	Ludlow (Washington) Township 903	Marion (Noble) Township 872
Liberty (Darke) Township 815	Ludlow Falls (Miami) Village 864	Marion (Pike) Township 877
Liberty (Delaware) Township 817	Lykens (Crawford) Township 810	**Marion County** 859
Liberty (Fairfield) Township 820	Lyme (Huron) Township 842	Mark (Defiance) Township 816
Liberty (Guernsey) Township 829	Lynchburg (Highland) Village 839	Marlboro (Delaware) Township 817
Liberty (Hancock) Township 834	Lyndhurst (Cuyahoga) City 812	Marlboro (Stark) Township 890
Liberty (Hardin) Township 836	Lynn (Hardin) Township 836	Marseilles (Wyandot) Township 909
Liberty (Henry) Township 838	Lyons (Fulton) Village 825	Marseilles (Wyandot) Village 909
Liberty (Highland) Township 839	Macedonia (Summit) City 892	Marshall (Highland) Township 839
Liberty (Jackson) Township 843	Mack North (Hamilton) CDP 832	Marshallville (Wayne) Village 904
Liberty (Knox) Township 846	Macksburg (Washington) Village 903	Martinsburg (Knox) Village 846
Liberty (Licking) Township 851	Mack South (Hamilton) CDP 832	Martins Ferry (Belmont) City 797
Liberty (Logan) Township 852	Madeira (Hamilton) City 832	Martinsville (Clinton) Village 806
Liberty (Mercer) Township 863	Madison (Butler) Township 799	Mary Ann (Licking) Township 851
Liberty (Putnam) Township 881	Madison (Clark) Township 803	Marysville (Union) City 898
Liberty (Ross) Township 884	Madison (Columbiana) Township 807	Mason (Lawrence) Township 849
Liberty (Seneca) Township 888	Madison (Fairfield) Township 820	Mason (Warren) City 902
Liberty (Trumbull) Township 894	Madison (Fayette) Township 821	Massie (Warren) Township 902
Liberty (Union) Township 898	Madison (Franklin) Township 823	Massillon (Stark) City 890
Liberty (Van Wert) Township 899	Madison (Guernsey) Township 829	Matamoras (Washington) Village 903
Liberty (Washington) Township 903	Madison (Hancock) Township 834	Maumee (Lucas) City 855
Liberty (Wood) Township 907	Madison (Highland) Township 839	Mayfield (Cuyahoga) Village 813
Liberty Center (Henry) Village 838	Madison (Jackson) Township 844	Mayfield Heights (Cuyahoga) City 813
Lick (Jackson) Township 843	Madison (Lake) Township 848	McArthur (Logan) Township 852
Licking (Licking) Township 851	Madison (Lake) Village 847	McArthur (Vinton) Village 900
Licking (Muskingum) Township 871	Madison (Licking) Township 851	McClure (Henry) Village 838
Licking County 850	Madison (Montgomery) Township ... 867	McComb (Hancock) Village 834
Lima (Allen) City 790	Madison (Muskingum) Township 871	McConnelsville (Morgan) Village 868
Lima (Licking) Township 851	Madison (Perry) Township 875	McDonald (Hardin) Township 836
Limaville (Stark) Village 890	Madison (Pickaway) Township 877	McDonald (Trumbull) Village 894
Lincoln (Morrow) Township 869	Madison (Richland) Township 883	McGuffey (Hardin) Village 836
Lincoln Heights (Hamilton) City 832	Madison (Sandusky) Township 885	McKean (Licking) Township 851
Lincoln Village (Franklin) CDP 823	Madison (Scioto) Township 886	McLean (Shelby) Township 889
Lindsey (Sandusky) Village 885	Madison (Vinton) Township 900	Mead (Belmont) Township 797
Linndale (Cuyahoga) Village 812	Madison (Williams) Township 906	Mecca (Trumbull) Township 894
Linton (Coshocton) Township 809	**Madison County** 856	Mechanic (Holmes) Township 841
Lisbon (Columbiana) Village 807	Mad River (Champaign) Township .. 802	Mechanicsburg (Champaign) Village 802

OHIO

Medina (Medina) City...... 861
Medina (Medina) Township...... 861
Medina County...... 860
Meigs (Adams) Township...... 789
Meigs (Muskingum) Township...... 871
Meigs County...... 861
Meigsville (Morgan) Township...... 869
Melrose (Paulding) Village...... 874
Mendon (Mercer) Village...... 863
Mentor (Lake) City...... 848
Mentor-on-the-Lake (Lake) City...... 848
Mercer County...... 862
Mesopotamia (Trumbull) Township...... 894
Metamora (Fulton) Village...... 825
Meyers Lake (Stark) Village...... 890
Miami (Clermont) Township...... 804
Miami (Greene) Township...... 828
Miami (Hamilton) Township...... 832
Miami (Logan) Township...... 852
Miami (Montgomery) Township...... 867
Miami County...... 863
Miamisburg (Montgomery) City...... 867
Middleburg Heights (Cuyahoga) City...... 813
Middlebury (Knox) Township...... 846
Middlefield (Geauga) Township...... 827
Middlefield (Geauga) Village...... 827
Middle Point (Van Wert) Village...... 899
Middleport (Meigs) Village...... 861
Middleton (Columbiana) Township...... 807
Middleton (Wood) Township...... 907
Middletown (Butler) City...... 799
Middletown (Warren) City...... 902
Midland (Clinton) Village...... 806
Midvale (Tuscarawas) Village...... 896
Midway (Madison) Village...... 856
Mifflin (Ashland) Township...... 791
Mifflin (Ashland) Village...... 791
Mifflin (Franklin) Township...... 823
Mifflin (Pike) Township...... 878
Mifflin (Richland) Township...... 883
Mifflin (Wyandot) Township...... 909
Milan (Erie) Township...... 819
Milan (Erie) Village...... 819
Milan (Huron) Village...... 842
Milford (Butler) Township...... 799
Milford (Clermont) Village...... 805
Milford (Defiance) Township...... 816
Milford (Hamilton) Village...... 832
Milford (Knox) Township...... 846
Milford Center (Union) Village...... 898
Mill (Tuscarawas) Township...... 896
Millbury (Wood) Village...... 907
Mill Creek (Coshocton) Township...... 809
Millcreek (Union) Township...... 898
Mill Creek (Williams) Township...... 906
Milledgeville (Fayette) Village...... 821
Miller (Knox) Township...... 846
Miller City (Putnam) Village...... 881
Millersburg (Holmes) Village...... 841
Millersport (Fairfield) Village...... 820
Millville (Butler) Village...... 799
Millwood (Guernsey) Township...... 829
Milton (Ashland) Township...... 791
Milton (Jackson) Township...... 844
Milton (Mahoning) Township...... 858
Milton (Wayne) Township...... 904
Milton (Wood) Township...... 907
Milton Center (Wood) Village...... 907
Miltonsburg (Monroe) Village...... 865
Mineral City (Tuscarawas) Village...... 896
Mineral Ridge (Mahoning) CDP...... 858
Mineral Ridge (Trumbull) CDP...... 895
Minerva (Carroll) Village...... 801
Minerva (Columbiana) Village...... 807

Minerva (Stark) Village...... 891
Minerva Park (Franklin) Village...... 823
Mingo Junction (Jefferson) City...... 844
Minster (Auglaize) Village...... 795
Mississinawa (Darke) Township...... 815
Mogadore (Portage) Village...... 879
Mogadore (Summit) Village...... 892
Mohican (Ashland) Township...... 791
Monclova (Lucas) Township...... 855
Monday Creek (Perry) Township...... 875
Monfort Heights East (Hamilton) CDP...... 832
Monfort Heights South (Hamilton) CDP...... 832
Monroe (Adams) Township...... 789
Monroe (Allen) Township...... 790
Monroe (Ashtabula) Township...... 793
Monroe (Butler) Village...... 800
Monroe (Carroll) Township...... 801
Monroe (Clermont) Township...... 805
Monroe (Coshocton) Township...... 809
Monroe (Darke) Township...... 815
Monroe (Guernsey) Township...... 829
Monroe (Harrison) Township...... 837
Monroe (Henry) Township...... 838
Monroe (Holmes) Township...... 841
Monroe (Knox) Township...... 846
Monroe (Licking) Township...... 851
Monroe (Logan) Township...... 852
Monroe (Madison) Township...... 856
Monroe (Miami) Township...... 864
Monroe (Muskingum) Township...... 871
Monroe (Perry) Township...... 875
Monroe (Pickaway) Township...... 877
Monroe (Preble) Township...... 880
Monroe (Putnam) Township...... 881
Monroe (Richland) Township...... 883
Monroe (Warren) Village...... 902
Monroe County...... 865
Monroeville (Huron) Village...... 842
Monterey (Putnam) Township...... 881
Montezuma (Mercer) Village...... 863
Montgomery (Ashland) Township...... 791
Montgomery (Hamilton) City...... 832
Montgomery (Marion) Township...... 859
Montgomery (Wood) Township...... 907
Montgomery County...... 866
Montpelier (Williams) Village...... 906
Montrose-Ghent (Summit) CDP...... 892
Montville (Geauga) Township...... 827
Montville (Medina) Township...... 861
Moorefield (Clark) Township...... 803
Moorefield (Harrison) Township...... 837
Moraine (Montgomery) City...... 867
Moreland Hills (Cuyahoga) Village...... 813
Morgan (Ashtabula) Township...... 793
Morgan (Butler) Township...... 800
Morgan (Gallia) Township...... 826
Morgan (Knox) Township...... 846
Morgan (Morgan) Township...... 869
Morgan (Scioto) Township...... 886
Morgan County...... 868
Morral (Marion) Village...... 859
Morris (Knox) Township...... 847
Morristown (Belmont) Village...... 797
Morrow (Warren) Village...... 902
Morrow County...... 869
Moscow (Clermont) Village...... 805
Moulton (Auglaize) Township...... 795
Mount Blanchard (Hancock) Village...... 834
Mount Carmel (Clermont) CDP...... 805
Mount Cory (Hancock) Village...... 834
Mount Eaton (Wayne) Village...... 904
Mount Gilead (Morrow) Village...... 870
Mount Healthy (Hamilton) City...... 832

Mount Healthy Heights (Hamilton) CDP...... 832
Mount Orab (Brown) Village...... 798
Mount Pleasant (Jefferson) Township...... 845
Mount Pleasant (Jefferson) Village...... 844
Mount Repose (Clermont) CDP...... 805
Mount Sterling (Madison) Village...... 856
Mount Vernon (Knox) City...... 847
Mount Victory (Hardin) Village...... 836
Mowrystown (Highland) Village...... 839
Muhlenberg (Pickaway) Township...... 877
Mulberry (Clermont) CDP...... 805
Munroe Falls (Summit) Village...... 892
Munson (Geauga) Township...... 827
Murray City (Hocking) Village...... 840
Muskingum (Muskingum) Township...... 871
Muskingum (Washington) Township...... 903
Muskingum County...... 870
Mutual (Champaign) Village...... 802
Napoleon (Henry) City...... 838
Napoleon (Henry) Township...... 838
Nashville (Holmes) Village...... 841
Navarre (Stark) Village...... 891
Neave (Darke) Township...... 815
Neffs (Belmont) CDP...... 797
Nellie (Coshocton) Village...... 809
Nelson (Portage) Township...... 879
Nelsonville (Athens) City...... 794
Nevada (Wyandot) Village...... 909
Neville (Clermont) Village...... 805
New Albany (Franklin) Village...... 823
New Alexandria (Jefferson) Village...... 845
Newark (Licking) City...... 851
Newark (Licking) Township...... 851
New Athens (Harrison) Village...... 837
New Bavaria (Henry) Village...... 838
Newberry (Miami) Township...... 864
New Bloomington (Marion) Village...... 859
New Boston (Scioto) Village...... 886
New Bremen (Auglaize) Village...... 795
Newburgh Heights (Cuyahoga) Village...... 813
Newbury (Geauga) Township...... 827
New Carlisle (Clark) City...... 803
Newcastle (Coshocton) Township...... 809
Newcomerstown (Tuscarawas) Village...... 896
New Concord (Muskingum) Village...... 871
New Haven (Huron) Township...... 842
New Holland (Fayette) Village...... 821
New Holland (Pickaway) Village...... 877
New Jasper (Greene) Township...... 828
New Knoxville (Auglaize) Village...... 795
New Lebanon (Montgomery) Village...... 867
New Lexington (Perry) Village...... 875
New London (Huron) Township...... 842
New London (Huron) Village...... 842
New Lyme (Ashtabula) Township...... 793
New Madison (Darke) Village...... 815
New Market (Highland) Township...... 839
New Miami (Butler) Village...... 800
New Middletown (Mahoning) Village...... 858
New Paris (Preble) Village...... 880
New Philadelphia (Tuscarawas) City...... 897
Newport (Washington) Township...... 903
New Richmond (Clermont) Village...... 805
New Riegel (Seneca) Village...... 888
New Rome (Franklin) Village...... 823
New Straitsville (Perry) Village...... 875
Newton (Licking) Township...... 851
Newton (Miami) Township...... 864
Newton (Muskingum) Township...... 871
Newton (Pike) Township...... 878

Newton (Trumbull) Township 895
Newton Falls (Trumbull) City 895
Newtonsville (Clermont) Village 805
Newtown (Hamilton) Village 832
New Vienna (Clinton) Village 806
New Washington (Crawford) Village 810
New Waterford (Columbiana)
  Village 808
New Weston (Darke) Village 815
Ney (Defiance) Village 817
Nile (Scioto) Township 886
Niles (Trumbull) City 895
Nimishillen (Stark) Township 891
Noble (Auglaize) Township 795
Noble (Defiance) Township 817
Noble (Noble) Township 872
Noble County 872
North (Harrison) Township 837
North Baltimore (Wood) Village 907
North Bend (Hamilton) Village 832
North Bloomfield (Morrow)
  Township 870
Northbrook (Hamilton) CDP 833
North Canton (Stark) City 891
North College Hill (Hamilton) City .. 833
North Fairfield (Huron) Village 842
Northfield (Summit) Village 893
Northfield Center (Summit)
  Township 893
North Fork Village (Ross) CDP 884
Northgate (Hamilton) CDP 833
North Hampton (Clark) Village 803
North Kingsville (Ashtabula) Village 793
North Lewisburg (Champaign)
  Village 802
North Madison (Lake) CDP 848
North Olmsted (Cuyahoga) City 813
North Perry (Lake) Village 848
North Randall (Cuyahoga) Village 813
Northridge (Clark) CDP 803
Northridge (Montgomery) CDP 867
North Ridgeville (Lorain) City 854
North Robinson (Crawford) Village . 810
North Royalton (Cuyahoga) City 813
North Star (Darke) Village 815
Northview (Montgomery) CDP 867
Northwest (Williams) Township 906
Northwood (Wood) Village 907
North Zanesville (Muskingum) CDP 871
Norton (Summit) City 893
Norton (Wayne) City 904
Norwalk (Huron) City 842
Norwalk (Huron) Township 842
Norwich (Franklin) Township 823
Norwich (Huron) Township 842
Norwich (Muskingum) Village 871
Norwood (Hamilton) City 833
Nottingham (Harrison) Township 837
Oak Harbor (Ottawa) Village 873
Oak Hill (Jackson) Village 844
Oak Run (Madison) Township 857
Oakwood (Cuyahoga) Village 813
Oakwood (Montgomery) City 867
Oakwood (Paulding) Village 874
Oberlin (Lorain) City 854
Obetz (Franklin) Village 823
Octa (Fayette) Village 821
Ohio (Clermont) Township 805
Ohio (Gallia) Township 826
Ohio (Monroe) Township 865
Ohio City (Van Wert) Village 899
Old Washington (Guernsey) Village . 829
Olive (Meigs) Township 862
Olive (Noble) Township 872
Oliver (Adams) Township 789

Olmsted (Cuyahoga) Township 813
Olmsted Falls (Cuyahoga) City 813
Ontario (Richland) Village 883
Orange (Ashland) Township 792
Orange (Carroll) Township 801
Orange (Cuyahoga) Village 813
Orange (Delaware) Township 817
Orange (Hancock) Township 835
Orange (Meigs) Township 862
Orange (Shelby) Township 889
Orangeville (Trumbull) Village 895
Oregon (Lucas) City 855
Orient (Pickaway) Village 877
Orrville (Wayne) City 904
Orwell (Ashtabula) Township 793
Orwell (Ashtabula) Village 793
Osgood (Darke) Village 815
Osnaburg (Stark) Township 891
Ostrander (Delaware) Village 818
Ottawa (Putnam) Township 882
Ottawa (Putnam) Village 882
Ottawa County 873
Ottawa Hills (Lucas) Village 855
Ottoville (Putnam) Village 882
Otway (Scioto) Village 886
Overlook-Page Manor (Montgomery)
  CDP 867
Owensville (Clermont) Village 805
Oxford (Butler) City 800
Oxford (Butler) Township 800
Oxford (Coshocton) Township 809
Oxford (Delaware) Township 818
Oxford (Erie) Township 819
Oxford (Guernsey) Township 829
Oxford (Tuscarawas) Township 897
Painesville (Lake) City 848
Painesville (Lake) Township 848
Paint (Fayette) Township 821
Paint (Highland) Township 839
Paint (Holmes) Township 841
Paint (Madison) Township 857
Paint (Ross) Township 884
Paint (Wayne) Township 904
Palestine (Darke) Village 815
Palmer (Putnam) Township 882
Palmer (Washington) Township 903
Palmyra (Portage) Township 879
Pandora (Putnam) Village 882
Paris (Portage) Township 879
Paris (Stark) Township 891
Paris (Union) Township 898
Park Layne (Clark) CDP 803
Parkman (Geauga) Township 827
Parma (Cuyahoga) City 813
Parma Heights (Cuyahoga) City 813
Parral (Tuscarawas) Village 897
Pataskala (Licking) Village 851
Patterson (Darke) Township 815
Patterson (Hardin) Village 836
Paulding (Paulding) Township 875
Paulding (Paulding) Village 874
Paulding County 874
Paxton (Ross) Township 884
Payne (Paulding) Village 875
Pease (Belmont) Township 797
Pebble (Pike) Township 878
Peebles (Adams) Village 789
Pee Pee (Pike) Township 878
Pemberville (Wood) Village 907
Penfield (Lorain) Township 854
Peninsula (Summit) Village 893
Penn (Highland) Township 839
Penn (Morgan) Township 869
Pepper Pike (Cuyahoga) City 813
Perkins (Erie) Township 819

Perry (Allen) Township 790
Perry (Ashland) Township 792
Perry (Brown) Township 798
Perry (Carroll) Township 801
Perry (Columbiana) Township 808
Perry (Coshocton) Township 809
Perry (Fayette) Township 821
Perry (Franklin) Township 823
Perry (Gallia) Township 826
Perry (Hocking) Township 840
Perry (Lake) Township 848
Perry (Lake) Village 848
Perry (Lawrence) Township 849
Perry (Licking) Township 851
Perry (Logan) Township 852
Perry (Monroe) Township 865
Perry (Montgomery) Township 867
Perry (Morrow) Township 870
Perry (Muskingum) Township 871
Perry (Pickaway) Township 877
Perry (Pike) Township 878
Perry (Putnam) Township 882
Perry (Richland) Township 883
Perry (Shelby) Township 889
Perry (Stark) Township 891
Perry (Tuscarawas) Township 897
Perry (Wood) Township 907
Perry County 875
Perry Heights (Stark) CDP 891
Perrysburg (Wood) City 907
Perrysburg (Wood) Township 907
Perrysville (Ashland) Village 792
Peru (Huron) Township 843
Peru (Morrow) Township 870
Phillipsburg (Montgomery) Village .. 867
Philo (Muskingum) Village 871
Pickaway (Pickaway) Township 877
Pickaway County 876
Pickerington (Fairfield) Village 820
Pickerington (Franklin) Village 823
Pierce (Clermont) Township 805
Pierpont (Ashtabula) Township 793
Pigeon Creek (Summit) CDP 893
Pike (Brown) Township 798
Pike (Clark) Township 803
Pike (Coshocton) Township 809
Pike (Fulton) Township 825
Pike (Knox) Township 847
Pike (Madison) Township 857
Pike (Perry) Township 875
Pike (Stark) Township 891
Pike County 877
Piketon (Pike) Village 878
Pioneer (Williams) Village 906
Piqua (Miami) City 864
Pitsburg (Darke) Village 815
Pitt (Wyandot) Township 909
Pittsfield (Lorain) Township 854
Plain (Franklin) Township 823
Plain (Stark) Township 891
Plain (Wayne) Township 905
Plain (Wood) Township 907
Plain City (Madison) Village 857
Plain City (Union) Village 898
Plainfield (Coshocton) Village 809
The Plains (Athens) CDP 795
Pleasant (Brown) Township 798
Pleasant (Clark) Township 803
Pleasant (Fairfield) Township 820
Pleasant (Franklin) Township 823
Pleasant (Hancock) Township 835
Pleasant (Hardin) Township 836
Pleasant (Henry) Township 838
Pleasant (Knox) Township 847
Pleasant (Logan) Township 852

Pleasant (Madison) Township *857*
Pleasant (Marion) Township *859*
Pleasant (Perry) Township *876*
Pleasant (Putnam) Township *882*
Pleasant (Seneca) Township *888*
Pleasant (Van Wert) Township *899*
Pleasant City (Guernsey) Village *829*
Pleasant Grove (Muskingum) CDP .. *871*
Pleasant Hill (Miami) Village *864*
Pleasant Plain (Warren) Village *902*
Pleasant Run (Hamilton) CDP *833*
Pleasant Run Farm (Hamilton) CDP *833*
Pleasantville (Fairfield) Village *820*
Plymouth (Ashtabula) Township *793*
Plymouth (Huron) Village *843*
Plymouth (Richland) Township *883*
Plymouth (Richland) Village *883*
Poland (Mahoning) Township *858*
Poland (Mahoning) Village *858*
Polk (Ashland) Village *792*
Polk (Crawford) Township *810*
Pomeroy (Meigs) Village *862*
Portage (Hancock) Township *835*
Portage (Ottawa) Township *873*
Portage (Wood) Township *908*
Portage (Wood) Village *907*
Portage County *878*
Portage Lakes (Summit) CDP *893*
Port Clinton (Ottawa) City *873*
Porter (Delaware) Township *818*
Porter (Scioto) Township *886*
Port Jefferson (Shelby) Village *889*
Portsmouth (Scioto) City *887*
Port Washington (Tuscarawas) Village *897*
Port William (Clinton) Village *806*
Potsdam (Miami) Village *864*
Powell (Delaware) Village *818*
Powhatan Point (Belmont) Village ... *797*
Prairie (Franklin) Township *823*
Prairie (Holmes) Township *841*
Preble County *880*
Proctorville (Lawrence) Village *849*
Prospect (Marion) Township *859*
Prospect (Marion) Village *859*
Providence (Lucas) Township *855*
Pulaski (Williams) Township *906*
Pultney (Belmont) Township *797*
Pusheta (Auglaize) Township *795*
Put-in-Bay (Ottawa) Township *873*
Put-in-Bay (Ottawa) Village *873*
Putnam County *881*
Quaker City (Guernsey) Village *829*
Quincy (Logan) Village *852*
Raccoon (Gallia) Township *826*
Racine (Meigs) Village *862*
Radnor (Delaware) Township *818*
Randolph (Montgomery) Township .. *867*
Randolph (Portage) Township *879*
Range (Madison) Township *857*
Rarden (Scioto) Township *887*
Rarden (Scioto) Village *887*
Ravenna (Portage) City *879*
Ravenna (Portage) Township *879*
Rawson (Hancock) Village *835*
Rayland (Jefferson) Village *845*
Reading (Hamilton) City *833*
Reading (Perry) Township *876*
Recovery (Mercer) Township *863*
Reed (Seneca) Township *888*
Reily (Butler) Township *800*
Reminderville (Summit) Village *893*
Rendville (Perry) Village *876*
Republic (Seneca) Village *888*

Reynoldsburg (Fairfield) City *820*
Reynoldsburg (Franklin) City *823*
Reynoldsburg (Licking) City *851*
Rice (Sandusky) Township *885*
Richfield (Henry) Township *838*
Richfield (Lucas) Township *855*
Richfield (Summit) Township *893*
Richfield (Summit) Village *893*
Rich Hill (Muskingum) Township ... *871*
Richland (Allen) Township *790*
Richland (Belmont) Township *797*
Richland (Clinton) Township *806*
Richland (Darke) Township *815*
Richland (Defiance) Township *817*
Richland (Fairfield) Township *820*
Richland (Guernsey) Township *829*
Richland (Holmes) Township *841*
Richland (Logan) Township *852*
Richland (Marion) Township *860*
Richland (Vinton) Township *900*
Richland (Wyandot) Township *909*
Richland County *882*
Richmond (Ashtabula) Township *793*
Richmond (Huron) Township *843*
Richmond (Jefferson) Village *845*
Richmond Heights (Cuyahoga) City *813*
Richwood (Union) Village *898*
Ridge (Van Wert) Township *899*
Ridge (Wyandot) Township *909*
Ridgefield (Huron) Township *843*
Ridgeville (Henry) Township *838*
Ridgeway (Hardin) Village *836*
Ridgeway (Logan) Village *853*
Riley (Putnam) Township *882*
Riley (Sandusky) Township *885*
Rio Grande (Gallia) Village *826*
Ripley (Brown) Village *798*
Ripley (Holmes) Township *841*
Ripley (Huron) Township *843*
Risingsun (Wood) Village *908*
Rittman (Medina) City *861*
Rittman (Wayne) City *905*
Riveredge (Cuyahoga) Township *813*
Riverlea (Franklin) Village *823*
Riverside (Montgomery) Village *867*
Roaming Shores (Ashtabula) Village *793*
Rochester (Lorain) Township *854*
Rochester (Lorain) Village *854*
Rock Creek (Ashtabula) Village *793*
Rockford (Mercer) Village *863*
Rocky Ridge (Ottawa) Village *874*
Rocky River (Cuyahoga) City *813*
Rogers (Columbiana) Village *808*
Rome (Adams) Village *789*
Rome (Ashtabula) Township *793*
Rome (Athens) Township *794*
Rome (Lawrence) Township *849*
Rootstown (Portage) Township *879*
Rose (Carroll) Township *801*
Rosemount (Scioto) CDP *887*
Roseville (Muskingum) Village *871*
Roseville (Perry) Village *876*
Ross (Butler) Township *800*
Ross (Greene) Township *828*
Ross (Jefferson) Township *845*
Rossburg (Darke) Village *815*
Ross County *884*
Rossford (Wood) City *908*
Roswell (Tuscarawas) Village *897*
Roundhead (Hardin) Township *836*
Royalton (Fulton) Township *825*
Ruggles (Ashland) Township *792*
Rumley (Harrison) Township *837*
Rush (Champaign) Township *802*
Rush (Scioto) Township *887*

Rush (Tuscarawas) Township *897*
Rush Creek (Fairfield) Township *820*
Rushcreek (Logan) Township *853*
Rushsylvania (Logan) Village *853*
Rushville (Fairfield) Village *820*
Russell (Geauga) Township *827*
Russells Point (Logan) Village *853*
Russellville (Brown) Village *798*
Russia (Lorain) Township *854*
Russia (Shelby) Village *889*
Rutland (Meigs) Township *862*
Rutland (Meigs) Village *862*
Sabina (Clinton) Village *806*
Sagamore Hills (Summit) Township *893*
St. Albans (Licking) Township *851*
St. Bernard (Hamilton) City *833*
St. Clair (Butler) Township *800*
St. Clair (Columbiana) Township *808*
St. Clairsville (Belmont) City *797*
St. Henry (Mercer) Village *863*
St. Joseph (Williams) Township *906*
St. Louisville (Licking) Village *851*
St. Martin (Brown) Village *798*
St. Marys (Auglaize) City *796*
St. Marys (Auglaize) Township *796*
St. Paris (Champaign) Village *802*
Salem (Auglaize) Township *796*
Salem (Champaign) Township *802*
Salem (Columbiana) City *808*
Salem (Columbiana) Township *808*
Salem (Highland) Township *839*
Salem (Jefferson) Township *845*
Salem (Meigs) Township *862*
Salem (Monroe) Township *865*
Salem (Muskingum) Township *871*
Salem (Ottawa) Township *874*
Salem (Shelby) Township *889*
Salem (Tuscarawas) Township *897*
Salem (Warren) Township *902*
Salem (Washington) Township *903*
Salem (Wyandot) Township *909*
Salesville (Guernsey) Village *830*
Saline (Jefferson) Township *845*
Salineville (Columbiana) Village *808*
Salineville (Jefferson) Village *845*
Salisbury (Meigs) Township *862*
Salt Creek (Hocking) Township *840*
Salt Creek (Holmes) Township *841*
Salt Creek (Muskingum) Township .. *871*
Salt Creek (Pickaway) Township *877*
Salt Creek (Wayne) Township *905*
Salt Lick (Perry) Township *876*
Salt Rock (Marion) Township *860*
Sandusky (Crawford) Township *810*
Sandusky (Erie) City *819*
Sandusky (Richland) Township *883*
Sandusky (Sandusky) Township *885*
Sandusky County *885*
Sandusky South (Erie) CDP *819*
Sandy (Stark) Township *891*
Sandy (Tuscarawas) Township *897*
Sarahsville (Noble) Village *872*
Sardinia (Brown) Village *799*
Savannah (Ashland) Village *792*
Saybrook (Ashtabula) Township *793*
Scio (Harrison) Village *837*
Scioto (Delaware) Township *818*
Scioto (Jackson) Township *844*
Scioto (Pickaway) Township *877*
Scioto (Pike) Township *878*
Scioto (Ross) Township *884*
Scioto County *886*
Sciotodale (Scioto) CDP *887*
Scipio (Meigs) Township *862*
Scipio (Seneca) Township *888*

Scott (Adams) Township 789	South Vienna (Clark) Village 804	Swan (Vinton) Township...................900
Scott (Brown) Township 799	South Webster (Scioto) Village..........887	Swan Creek (Fulton) Township..........825
Scott (Marion) Township 860	South Zanesville (Muskingum)	Swanton (Fulton) Village....................825
Scott (Paulding) Village 875	Village 871	Swanton (Lucas) Township 855
Scott (Sandusky) Township 886	Sparta (Morrow) Village 870	Swanton (Lucas) Village 855
Scott (Van Wert) Village 899	Spencer (Allen) Township..................791	Switzerland (Monroe) Township 866
Seal (Pike) Township 878	Spencer (Guernsey) Township...........830	Sycamore (Hamilton) Township........833
Seaman (Adams) Village 789	Spencer (Lucas) Township 855	Sycamore (Wyandot) Township 909
Sebring (Mahoning) City 858	Spencer (Medina) Township 861	Sycamore (Wyandot) Village.............909
Seneca (Monroe) Township 865	Spencer (Medina) Village 861	Sylvania (Lucas) City........................856
Seneca (Noble) Township 872	Spencerville (Allen) Village 791	Sylvania (Lucas) Township...............856
Seneca (Seneca) Township 888	Sprigg (Adams) Township 789	Symmes (Hamilton) Township..........833
Seneca County................................887	Springboro (Montgomery) City.........867	Symmes (Lawrence) Township..........849
Senecaville (Guernsey) Village 830	Springboro (Warren) City..................902	Syracuse (Meigs) Village...................862
Seven Hills (Cuyahoga) City 813	Springcreek (Miami) Township.........864	Tallmadge (Summit) City 893
Seven Mile (Butler) Village 800	Springdale (Hamilton) City 833	Tarlton (Pickaway) Village 877
Seville (Medina) Village 861	Springfield (Clark) City 804	Tate (Clermont) Township 805
Shadyside (Belmont) Village 797	Springfield (Clark) Township 804	Taylor (Union) Township...................898
Shaker Heights (Cuyahoga) City 813	Springfield (Gallia) Township 826	Taylor Creek (Hardin) Township.......836
Shalersville (Portage) Township 879	Springfield (Hamilton) Township......833	Terrace Park (Hamilton) Village 833
Sharon (Franklin) Township 824	Springfield (Jefferson) Township.......845	Texas (Crawford) Township 811
Sharon (Medina) Township................861	Springfield (Lucas) Township 855	Thompson (Delaware) Township.......818
Sharon (Noble) Township 872	Springfield (Mahoning) Township.....858	Thompson (Geauga) Township..........827
Sharon (Richland) Township 883	Springfield (Muskingum) Township..871	Thompson (Seneca) Township 888
Sharonville (Butler) City 800	Springfield (Richland) Township 883	Thorn (Perry) Township 876
Sharonville (Hamilton) City...............833	Springfield (Ross) Township 885	Thornville (Perry) Village..................876
Shawnee (Allen) Township 790	Springfield (Summit) Township 893	Thurston (Fairfield) Village...............820
Shawnee (Perry) Village.....................876	Springfield (Williams) Township.......906	Tiffin (Adams) Township 789
Shawnee Hills (Delaware) Village 818	Spring Valley (Greene) Township 828	Tiffin (Defiance) Township................817
Shawnee Hills (Greene) CDP.............828	Spring Valley (Greene) Village 828	Tiffin (Seneca) City 888
Sheffield (Ashtabula) Township 793	Stafford (Monroe) Village 865	Tiltonsville (Jefferson) Village 845
Sheffield (Lorain) Township 854	**Stark County**..................................889	Timberlake (Lake) Village 848
Sheffield (Lorain) Village 854	Starr (Hocking) Township 840	Tipp City (Miami) City......................864
Sheffield Lake (Lorain) City 854	Staunton (Miami) Township 864	Tiro (Crawford) Village......................811
Shelby (Richland) City 883	Sterling (Brown) Township 799	Tiverton (Coshocton) Township 809
Shelby County................................888	Steubenville (Jefferson) City 845	Tod (Crawford) Township 811
Sherman (Huron) Township 843	Steubenville (Jefferson) Township.....845	Toledo (Lucas) City...........................856
Sherrodsville (Carroll) Village 801	Stock (Harrison) Township 837	Tontogany (Wood) Village.................908
Sherwood (Defiance) Village 817	Stock (Noble) Township 872	Toronto (Jefferson) City 845
Sherwood (Hamilton) CDP 833	Stockport (Morgan) Village 869	Townsend (Huron) Township............843
Shiloh (Montgomery) CDP 867	Stokes (Logan) Township 853	Townsend (Sandusky) Township.......886
Shiloh (Richland) Village...................883	Stokes (Madison) Township 857	Tremont City (Clark) Village.............804
Short Creek (Harrison) Township......837	Stone Creek (Tuscarawas) Village 897	Trenton (Butler) City.........................800
Shreve (Wayne) Village 905	Stonelick (Clermont) Township.........805	Trenton (Delaware) Township...........818
Sidney (Shelby) City 889	Stony Prairie (Sandusky) CDP 886	Trimble (Athens) Township...............795
Silver Creek (Greene) Township 828	Stoutsville (Fairfield) Village.............820	Trimble (Athens) Village 795
Silver Lake (Summit) Village 893	Stow (Summit) City 893	Trotwood (Montgomery) City 868
Silverton (Hamilton) City 833	Strasburg (Tuscarawas) Village.........897	Troy (Ashland) Township..................792
Sinking Spring (Highland) Village 839	Stratton (Jefferson) Village................845	Troy (Athens) Township....................795
Smith (Belmont) Township 797	Streetsboro (Portage) City 879	Troy (Delaware) Township................818
Smith (Mahoning) Township..............858	Strongsville (Cuyahoga) City.............814	Troy (Geauga) Township 827
Smithfield (Jefferson) Township 845	Struthers (Mahoning) City.................858	Troy (Miami) City 864
Smithfield (Jefferson) Village.............845	Stryker (Williams) Village 906	Troy (Morrow) Township...................870
Smithville (Wayne) Village 905	Suffield (Portage) Township 879	Troy (Richland) Township.................883
Solon (Cuyahoga) City.......................814	Sugar Bush Knolls (Portage) Village .879	Troy (Wood) Township......................908
Somerford (Madison) Township.........857	Sugar Creek (Allen) Township...........791	Trumbull (Ashtabula) Township 793
Somers (Preble) Township 880	Sugar Creek (Greene) Township........828	**Trumbull County** 893
Somerset (Belmont) Township 797	Sugar Creek (Putnam) Township.......882	Truro (Franklin) Township................824
Somerset (Perry) Village....................876	Sugar Creek (Stark) Township...........891	Tully (Marion) Township...................860
Somerville (Butler) Village 800	Sugar Creek (Tuscarawas) Township.897	Tully (Van Wert) Township 899
South Amherst (Lorain) Village.........854	Sugarcreek (Tuscarawas) Village 897	Turnpike Interchange (Trumbull)
South Bloomfield (Morrow)	Sugar Creek (Wayne) Township 905	CDP 895
Township..870	Sugar Grove (Fairfield) Village 820	Turpin Hills (Hamilton) CDP 833
South Bloomfield (Pickaway)	Sullivan (Ashland) Township 792	Turtle Creek (Shelby) Township........889
Village 877	Summerfield (Noble) Village..............873	Turtle Creek (Warren) Township.......902
South Canal (Trumbull) CDP 895	Summerside (Clermont) CDP 805	Tuscarawas (Coshocton) Township ...809
South Charleston (Clark) Village 804	Summit (Monroe) Township..............865	Tuscarawas (Stark) Township............891
South Euclid (Cuyahoga) City...........814	**Summit County**..............................891	Tuscarawas (Tuscarawas) Village......897
Southington (Trumbull) Township....895	Summit Station (Licking) CDP..........851	**Tuscarawas County**........................896
South Lebanon (Warren) Village........902	Summitville (Columbiana) Village.....808	Twin (Darke) Township 815
South Middletown (Butler) CDP........800	Sunbury (Delaware) Village...............818	Twin (Preble) Township.....................880
South Point (Lawrence) Village..........849	Sunfish (Pike) Township 878	Twin (Ross) Township 885
South Russell (Geauga) Village 827	Sunsbury (Monroe) Township 865	Twinsburg (Summit) City 893
South Salem (Ross) Village 884	Superior (Williams) Township...........906	Twinsburg (Summit) Township 893
South Solon (Madison) Village 857	Sutton (Meigs) Township...................862	Tymochtee (Wyandot) Township......909

OHIO

Column 1	Column 2	Column 3
Uhrichsville (Tuscarawas) City 897	Vinton (Gallia) Village 826	Washington (Warren) Township........902
Union (Auglaize) Township................796	Vinton (Vinton) Township 900	Washington (Wood) Township 908
Union (Belmont) Township................797	**Vinton County**..................................900	**Washington County**..............................902
Union (Brown) Township..................799	Violet (Fairfield) Township 820	Washington Court House (Fayette) City... 821
Union (Butler) Township 800	Virginia (Coshocton) Township 809	Washingtonville (Columbiana) Village 808
Union (Carroll) Township..................801	Wabash (Darke) Township 816	Washingtonville (Mahoning) Village .858
Union (Champaign) Township..........802	Wadsworth (Medina) City 861	Waterford (Washington) Township ...903
Union (Clermont) Township 805	Wadsworth (Medina) Township 861	Waterloo (Athens) Township.............795
Union (Clinton) Township 806	Waite Hill (Lake) Village...................848	Watertown (Washington) Township ..903
Union (Fayette) Township.................821	Wakeman (Huron) Township 843	Waterville (Lucas) Township............856
Union (Hancock) Township 835	Wakeman (Huron) Village.................843	Waterville (Lucas) Village................856
Union (Highland) Township 839	Walbridge (Wood) Village.................908	Wauseon (Fulton) Village 825
Union (Knox) Township....................847	Waldo (Marion) Township 860	Waverly City (Pike) City 878
Union (Lawrence) Township.............849	Waldo (Marion) Village 860	Wayne (Adams) Township................789
Union (Licking) Township 851	Walnut (Fairfield) Township 820	Wayne (Ashtabula) Township............793
Union (Logan) Township 853	Walnut (Gallia) Township 826	Wayne (Auglaize) Township.............796
Union (Madison) Township...............857	Walnut (Pickaway) Township............877	Wayne (Belmont) Township 797
Union (Mercer) Township.................863	Walnut Creek (Holmes) Township....841	Wayne (Butler) Township 800
Union (Miami) Township..................864	Walton Hills (Cuyahoga) Village.......814	Wayne (Champaign) Township 802
Union (Montgomery) Village 868	Wapakoneta (Auglaize) City..............796	Wayne (Clermont) Township 805
Union (Morgan) Township................869	Ward (Hocking) Township 840	Wayne (Clinton) Township 806
Union (Muskingum) Township.........871	Warren (Belmont) Township 797	Wayne (Columbiana) Township........808
Union (Pike) Township 878	Warren (Jefferson) Township 845	Wayne (Darke) Township 816
Union (Putnam) Township.................882	Warren (Trumbull) City.....................895	Wayne (Fayette) Township 821
Union (Ross) Township.....................885	Warren (Trumbull) Township............895	Wayne (Jefferson) Township 845
Union (Scioto) Township 887	Warren (Tuscarawas) Township 897	Wayne (Knox) Township 847
Union (Tuscarawas) Township..........897	Warren (Washington) Township........903	Wayne (Monroe) Township...............866
Union (Union) Township...................898	**Warren County**..................................901	Wayne (Muskingum) Township........871
Union (Van Wert) Township.............899	Warrensville (Cuyahoga) Township...814	Wayne (Noble) Township 873
Union (Warren) Township.................902	Warrensville Heights (Cuyahoga) City... 814	Wayne (Pickaway) Township............877
Union City (Darke) Village 815	Warsaw (Coshocton) Village..............809	Wayne (Tuscarawas) Township 897
Union County..................................898	Warwick (Tuscarawas) Township 897	Wayne (Warren) Township 902
Uniontown (Stark) CDP.....................891	Washington (Auglaize) Township......796	Wayne (Wayne) Township 905
Unionville Center (Union) Village....898	Washington (Belmont) Township......797	Wayne (Wood) Village 908
Uniopolis (Auglaize) Village.............796	Washington (Brown) Township.........799	**Wayne County**..................................904
Unity (Columbiana) Township..........808	Washington (Carroll) Township 801	Wayne Lakes (Darke) Village 816
University Heights (Cuyahoga) City.814	Washington (Clermont) Township 805	Waynesburg (Stark) Village 891
Upper (Lawrence) Township 849	Washington (Clinton) Township........806	Waynesfield (Auglaize) Village 796
Upper Arlington (Franklin) City.......824	Washington (Columbiana) Township 808	Waynesville (Warren) Village 902
Upper Sandusky (Wyandot) City......909	Washington (Coshocton) Township...809	Weathersfield (Trumbull) Township..895
Urbana (Champaign) City..................802	Washington (Darke) Township..........816	Webster (Wood) Township 908
Urbana (Champaign) Township.........802	Washington (Defiance) Township 817	Weller (Richland) Township.............883
Urbancrest (Franklin) Village............824	Washington (Franklin) Township......824	Wellington (Lorain) Township..........855
Utica (Knox) Village.........................847	Washington (Guernsey) Township 830	Wellington (Lorain) Village 855
Utica (Licking) Village 851	Washington (Hancock) Township......835	Wells (Jefferson) Township...............845
Valley (Guernsey) Township..............830	Washington (Hardin) Township 836	Wellston (Jackson) City 844
Valley (Scioto) Township 887	Washington (Harrison) Township 837	Wellsville (Columbiana) City 808
Valley Hi (Logan) Village 853	Washington (Henry) Township 838	Wesley (Washington) Township.......903
Valley View (Cuyahoga) Village 814	Washington (Highland) Township.....839	West (Columbiana) Township 808
Valleyview (Franklin) Village............824	Washington (Hocking) Township......840	West Alexandria (Preble) Village 880
Van Buren (Darke) Township 815	Washington (Holmes) Township 841	West Carrollton City (Montgomery) City... 868
Van Buren (Hancock) Township 835	Washington (Jackson) Township.......844	West Elkton (Preble) Village 881
Van Buren (Hancock) Village............835	Washington (Lawrence) Township 849	Westerville (Delaware) City..............818
Van Buren (Putnam) Township..........882	Washington (Licking) Township.......852	Westerville (Franklin) City...............824
Van Buren (Shelby) Township...........889	Washington (Logan) Township 853	West Farmington (Trumbull) Village 895
Vandalia (Montgomery) City............868	Washington (Lucas) Township 856	Westfield (Medina) Township 861
Vanlue (Hancock) Village 835	Washington (Mercer) Township........863	Westfield (Morrow) Township..........870
Van Wert (Van Wert) City 899	Washington (Miami) Township.........864	Westfield Center (Medina) Village....861
Van Wert County..............................899	Washington (Monroe) Township.......866	West Hill (Trumbull) CDP 895
Venedocia (Van Wert) Village 899	Washington (Montgomery) Township... 868	West Lafayette (Coshocton) Village..809
Venice (Seneca) Township 888	Washington (Morrow) Township.......870	Westlake (Cuyahoga) City.................814
Vermilion (Erie) City.........................819	Washington (Muskingum) Township 871	Westland (Guernsey) Township.........830
Vermilion (Erie) Township 819	Washington (Paulding) Township 875	West Leipsic (Putnam) Village 882
Vermilion (Lorain) City.....................855	Washington (Pickaway) Township 877	West Liberty (Logan) Village............853
Vermillion (Ashland) Township 792	Washington (Preble) Township..........880	West Manchester (Preble) Village 881
Vernon (Clinton) Township...............806	Washington (Richland) Township.....883	West Mansfield (Logan) Village........853
Vernon (Crawford) Township............811	Washington (Sandusky) Township 886	West Millgrove (Wood) Village 908
Vernon (Scioto) Township 887	Washington (Scioto) Township 887	West Milton (Miami) Village............864
Vernon (Trumbull) Township............895	Washington (Shelby) Township.........889	Weston (Wood) Township 908
Verona (Montgomery) Village...........868	Washington (Stark) Township 891	Weston (Wood) Village 908
Verona (Preble) Village.....................880	Washington (Tuscarawas) Township .897	West Portsmouth (Scioto) CDP 887
Versailles (Darke) Village 816	Washington (Union) Township.........898	West Rushville (Fairfield) Village 821
Vienna (Trumbull) Township............895	Washington (Van Wert) Township 899	
The Village of Indian Hill (Hamilton) City... 833		

West Salem (Wayne) Village..............905
West Union (Adams) Village.............789
West Unity (Williams) Village...........906
Wharton (Wyandot) Village..............909
Wheelersburg (Scioto) CDP..............887
Wheeling (Belmont) Township..........797
Wheeling (Guernsey) Township........830
Whetstone (Crawford) Township......811
White Eyes (Coshocton) Township...809
Whitehall (Franklin) City....................824
Whitehouse (Lucas) Village...............856
White Oak (Hamilton) CDP..............833
White Oak (Highland) Township......839
White Oak East (Hamilton) CDP.....833
White Oak West (Hamilton) CDP....833
Whitewater (Hamilton) Township.....833
Wickliffe (Lake) City.........................848
Wilberforce (Greene) CDP................828
Wilkesville (Vinton) Township..........900
Wilkesville (Vinton) Village...............900
Willard (Huron) City..........................843
Williamsburg (Clermont) Township..805
Williamsburg (Clermont) Village......805
Williams County...............................905
Williamsfield (Ashtabula) Township.794
Williamsport (Pickaway) Village.......877
Willoughby (Lake) City.....................848
Willoughby Hills (Lake) City............848
Willowick (Lake) City........................848
Wills (Guernsey) Township...............830
Willshire (Van Wert) Township.........900

Willshire (Van Wert) Village.............900
Wilmington (Clinton) City................806
Wilmot (Stark) Village.......................891
Wilson (Belmont) Village..................797
Wilson (Clinton) Township...............806
Wilson (Monroe) Village...................866
Winchester (Adams) Township.........789
Winchester (Adams) Village..............789
Windham (Portage) Township..........879
Windham (Portage) Village...............879
Windsor (Ashtabula) Township.........794
Windsor (Lawrence) Township.........849
Windsor (Morgan) Township............869
Wintersville (Jefferson) Village.........845
Withamsville (Clermont) CDP..........805
Woodbourne-Hyde Park (Montgomery) CDP..............868
Wood County......................................906
Woodlawn (Hamilton) Village...........833
Woodmere (Cuyahoga) Village.........814
Woodsfield (Monroe) Village............866
Woodstock (Champaign) Village......802
Woodville (Sandusky) Township......886
Woodville (Sandusky) Village..........886
Wooster (Wayne) City.......................905
Wooster (Wayne) Township...............905
Worthington (Franklin) City.............824
Worthington (Richland) Township...883
Wren (Van Wert) Village...................900
Wright-Patterson Air Force Base (Greene) Military Facility..............828

Wright-Patterson Air Force Base (Montgomery) Military Facility...............868
Wyandot County...................................908
Wyoming (Hamilton) City................833
Xenia (Greene) City...........................828
Xenia (Greene) Township..................828
Yankee Lake (Trumbull) Village.......895
Yellow Creek (Columbiana) Township..................................808
Yellow Springs (Greene) Village........828
York (Athens) Township....................795
York (Belmont) Township.................797
York (Darke) Township.....................816
York (Fulton) Township....................825
York (Medina) Township...................861
York (Morgan) Township..................869
York (Sandusky) Township................886
York (Tuscarawas) Township.............897
York (Union) Township.....................899
York (Van Wert) Township................900
Yorkshire (Darke) Village..................816
Yorkville (Belmont) Village...............797
Yorkville (Jefferson) Village..............845
Youngstown (Mahoning) City...........858
Youngstown (Trumbull) City.............895
Zaleski (Vinton) Village....................900
Zane (Logan) Township....................853
Zanesfield (Logan) Village.................853
Zanesville (Muskingum) City............872
Zoar (Tuscarawas) Village.................897

WISCONSIN

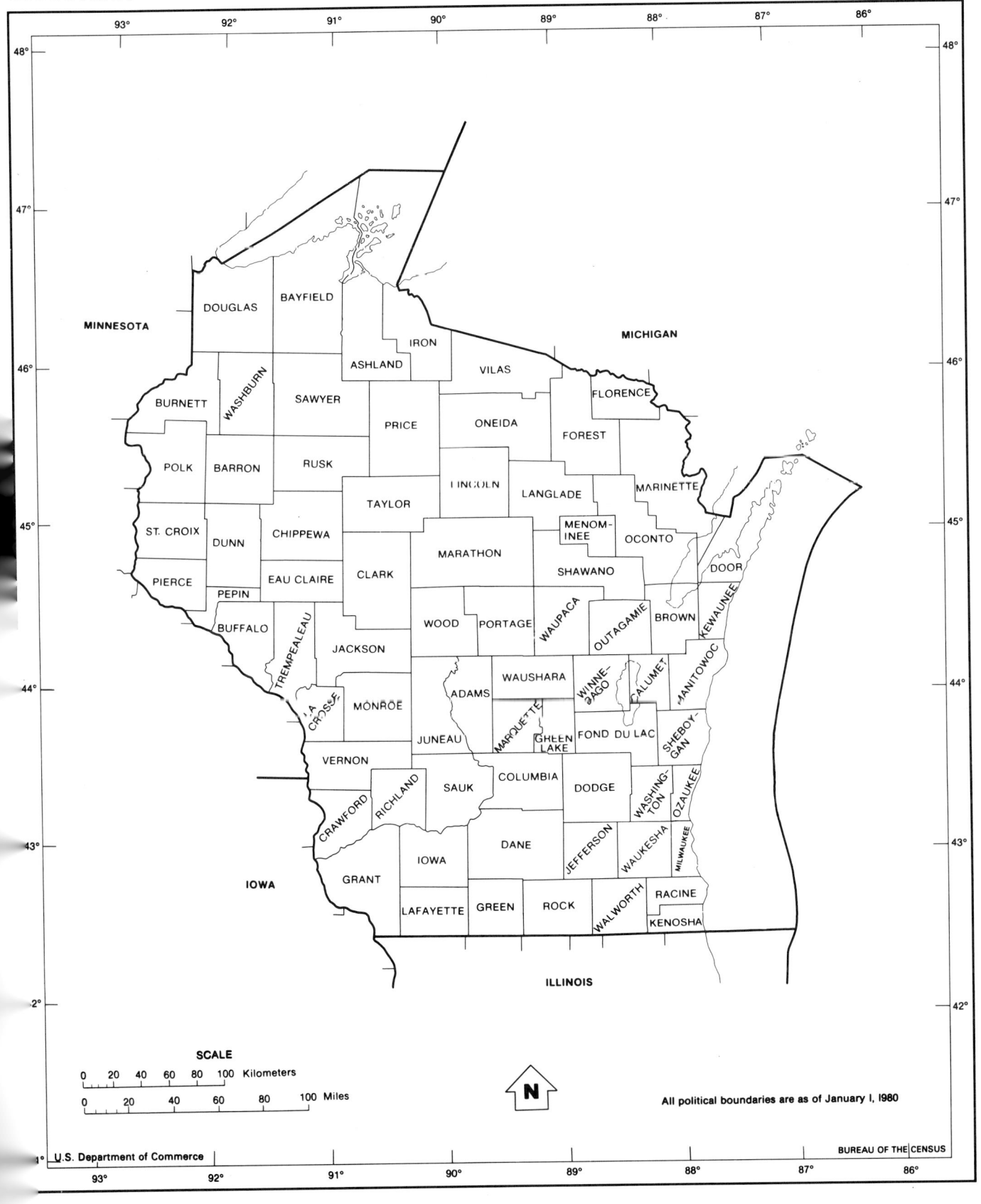

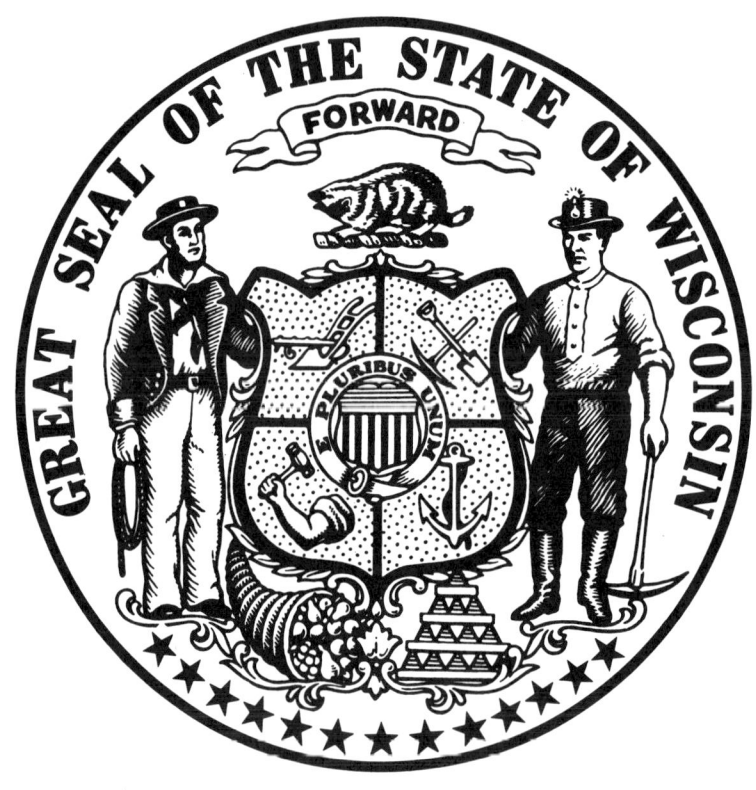

Wisconsin

Wisconsin

Population: 4,891,769 (1990); 4,705,767 (1980)
Population rank (1990): 16
Percent population change (1980-1990): 4.0
Population projection: 4,954,000 (1995); 4,993,000 (2000)

Area: total 65,503 sq. mi.; 54,314 sq. mi. land, 11,190 sq. mi. water
Area rank: 23
Highest elevation: 1,952 ft., Timms Hill (Price County)
Lowest point: 581 ft. along shore of Lake Michigan

State capital: Madison (Dane County)
Largest city: Milwaukee (628,088)
Second largest city: Madison (191,262)
Largest county: Milwaukee (959,275)

Total housing units: 2,055,774
No. of occupied housing units: 1,822,118
Vacant housing units (%): 11.4
Distribution of population by race and Hispanic origin (%):
  White: 92.2
  Black: 5.0
  Hispanic (any race): 1.9
  Native American: 0.8
  Asian/Pacific: 1.1
  Other: 0.9

Admission date: May 29, 1848 (30th state).

Location: In the north-central United States, bordering Illinois, Iowa, Minnesota, Lake Superior, Michigan (Upper Peninsula), and Lake Michigan.

Name Origin: For the Wisconsin River, which flows through the central part of the state, itself named probably from Ojibwa *Wees-kon-san* 'the gathering of the waters.'

State animal: badger *(Taxidea taxus)* ; **wildlife animal—** white-tailed deer *(Odocoileus virginianus)* ; **domestic—** dairy cow *(Bos taurus)*
State beverage: milk
State bird: robin *(Turdus migratorius)*
State dog: American water spaniel
State fish: muskellunge (muskie; *Esox masquinongy)*
State flower: wood violet *(Viola papilionacea)*
State fossil: trilobite
State grain: corn *(Zea mays)*
State insect: honeybee *(Apis mellifera)*
State mineral: galena
State rock: red granite
State soil: Antigo silt loam

State song: "On, Wisconsin!"
State symbol of peace: mourning dove *(Zenaidura macroura)*
State tree: sugar maple *(Acer saccharum)*

State motto: Forward
State nicknames: Badger State; America's Dairyland

Area codes: 414 (Milwaukee and east), 608 (Madison and southwest), 715 (Eau Claire and northern half)
Time zone: Central
Abbreviations: WI (postal); Wis. (traditional)
Part of (region): Great Lakes, Midwest

Local Government

Counties

Wisconsin has 72 counties, each governed by a board of elected supervisors.

Municipalities

Wisconsin has 188 incorporated cities, 397 incorporated villages, and 1,269 towns. Towns are civil subdivisions of counties, equivalent to townships in other states.

Settlement History and Early Development

Wisconsin is believed to have been inhabited for about 10,000 years. Some of the earliest inhabitants were ancestors of the Menominee and later the Winnebago Indians. The first Europeans to arrive found Ojibwa, Sauk, Fox, Potawatomi, Chippewa, Kickapoo, and Dakota Indians. These tribes all hunted, fished, and farmed, but with the arrival of the Europeans, they became dependent on the fur trade.

Jean Nicolet, a French explorer in the service of Samuel de Champlain, was the first white man known to have reached the region. He landed on the shores of Green Bay in 1634. About twenty-five years later, Médard Chouart des Groseilliers and Pierre Esprit Radisson, fur traders, explored northern Wisconsin. In 1673 the French Jesuit missionary Fr. Jacques Marquette and the explorer Louis Jolliet crossed Wisconsin on their way to the Mississippi. They were followed by other Jesuits who established missions, and by French fur traders who set up trading posts.

Rival British claims to the area resulted in the French and Indian Wars. Following the British victory in 1763 France ceded Canada and almost all its possessions east of the Mississippi River. The British ruled the area as part of Quebec Province from 1774 to 1783. At the end of the Revolutionary War, England relinquished all of its land east of the Mississippi and south of the Great Lakes, and the territory that is now Wisconsin became part of the United States.

Territorial Days and Statehood

Wisconsin became part of the Northwest Territory, established in 1787. It was subsequently included in the Indiana Territory, the Territory of Illinois, and then the Michigan Territory.

In the early 1820s the population boomed with the arrival of white settlers attracted by the rich deposits of lead ore. Some of the miners lived in shelters burrowed out of the hillside, and in time became known as *badgers* (for the burrowing mammal that is native to the area), the present nickname for all Wisconsinites.

The Black Hawk Indians led the resistance against further white incursion, but they were defeated in 1832 at the battle of Bad Axe, which ended the Black Hawk War.

In 1836 the Wisconsin Territory was formed and included Iowa and Minnesota, plus a portion of the Dakotas, but in 1838 those areas became part of the newly organized Iowa Territory. In the 1830s there was another land boom and migrating Yankees from New England and Southerners helped the economy expand. By 1846 the voters endorsed statehood, and in 1848 Wisconsin became the thirtieth state of the Union, with its boundaries set as they are at present.

The Civil War

Wisconsinites were for the most part abolitionist, and opposed the Kansas-Nebraska Act in Congress in 1854. The act allowed these two new territories to decide for themselves if they wished to permit slavery; Wisconsin did not believe slavery should be allowed in new territories. A protest meeting against the bill in Ripon in February 1854, ultimately led to the establishment of the Republican Party.

While Wisconsin sent 96,000 men to the Union armies, and the Iron Brigade, one of the Union's outstanding fighting groups, consisted largely of Wisconsin regiments, no battles were fought on any of the state's land.

Business and Industry

The newly formed Republican Party helped the railroads and the lumber industry to get financial backing, and they both grew in importance after the Civil War. During the late nineteenth century Wisconsin prospered in general, with dairying, food processing, and lumbering as the major industries, while Milwaukee grew into an important industrial center. Wisconsin suffered its worst natural disaster in 1871, when the Peshtigo forest fire destroyed the town of Peshtigo and killed about 1,200 people, devastating much of six counties.

At the turn of the century Robert M. La Follette, Sr. ("Fighting Bob"), became Wisconsin's governor and led a Progressive Party fight to rid the state of political bosses and pass legislation furthering social, political, and economic reforms. Wisconsin became a leader in progressivism, fostering the "Wisconsin Idea," in which the University of Wisconsin lent its brainpower and facilities to the formulation of social and political reforms. Wisconsin passed a Workman's Compensation Act as well as laws providing for industrial safety codes, a state income tax, and state forest and water conservation. During the Great Depression of the 1930s, Philip F. La Follette, the son of Robert, was elected governor three times and urged legislation, including the first state unemployment compensation act, to alleviate the problems of the Depression.

The state's economy improved during World War II, and after the war the state began to move from an agricultural to an industrial economy. Robert M. La Follette, Jr., lost his U.S. Senate seat (after 21 years) to Joseph R. McCarthy, who became infamous in the early 1950s for his allegations of widespread Communist activity in the U.S. government.

In recent decades Wisconsin has seen some decline in the market for its dairy products, which nevertheless remain the state's most important agricultural resource. Many smaller farms have been consolidated into larger agribusinesses. Wisconsin manufacturing industries include engines and turbines, farm machinery, construction equipment, food products, and paper products.

State Boundaries

Wisconsin's present borders were set at the time of statehood.

Wisconsin Counties

Adams	Douglas	Kewaunee	Outagamie	Shawano
Ashland	Dunn	La Crosse	Ozaukee	Sheboygan
Barron	Eau Claire	Lafayette	Pepin	Taylor
Bayfield	Florence	Langlade	Pierce	Trempealeau
Brown	Fond du Lac	Lincoln	Polk	Vernon
Buffalo	Forest	Manitowoc	Portage	Vilas
Burnett	Grant	Marathon	Price	Walworth
Calumet	Green	Marinette	Racine	Washburn
Chippewa	Green Lake	Marquette	Richland	Washington
Clark	Iowa	Menominee	Rock	Waukesha
Columbia	Iron	Milwaukee	Rusk	Waupaca
Crawford	Jackson	Monroe	St. Croix	Waushara
Dane	Jefferson	Oconto	Sauk	Winnebago
Dodge	Juneau	Oneida	Sawyer	Wood
Door	Kenosha			

Multi-County Places

The following Wisconsin places are in more than one county. Given here is the total population for each multi-county place, and the names of the counties it is in.

Abbotsford, pop. 1,916; Clark (1,409), Marathon (507)
Appleton, pop. 65,695; Outagamie (56,177), Calumet (9,075), Winnebago (443)
Bayside, pop. 4,789; Milwaukee (4,681), Ozaukee (108)
Belleville, pop. 1,456; Dane (1,349), Green (107)
Berlin, pop. 5,371; Green Lake (5,304), Waushara (67)
Birnamwood, pop. 693; Shawano (687), Marathon (6)
Blanchardville, pop. 802; Lafayette (635), Iowa (167)
Brooklyn, pop. 789; Dane (406), Green (383)
Burlington, pop. 8,855; Racine (8,851), Walworth (4)
Cambridge, pop. 963; Dane (883), Jefferson (80)
Cazenovia, pop. 288; Richland (288), Sauk (0)
Colby, pop. 1,532; Clark (1,116), Marathon (416)
Columbus, pop. 4,093; Columbia (4,083), Dodge (10)
Cuba City, pop. 2,024; Grant (1,863), Lafayette (161)
De Soto, pop. 326; Vernon (253), Crawford (73)
Eau Claire, pop. 56,856; Eau Claire (55,180), Chippewa (1,676)
Genoa City, pop. 1,277; Walworth (1,277), Kenosha (0)
Hartford, pop. 8,188; Washington (8,179), Dodge (9)
Hazel Green, pop. 1,171; Grant (1,171), Lafayette (0)
Kewaskum, pop. 2,515; Washington (2,514), Fond du Lac (1)
Kiel, pop. 2,910; Manitowoc (2,534), Calumet (376)
Lake Wisconsin, pop. 2,268; Columbia (2,178), Sauk (90)
Livingston, pop. 576; Grant (566), Iowa (10)
Marshfield, pop. 19,291; Wood (18,859), Marathon (432)
Menasha, pop. 14,711; Winnebago (14,638), Calumet (73)
Milladore, pop. 314; Wood (314), Portage (0)
Milwaukee, pop. 628,088; Milwaukee (628,088), Washington (0), Waukesha (0)
Montfort, pop. 676; Grant (580), Iowa (96)
Muscoda, pop. 1,287; Grant (1,283), Iowa (4)
New Auburn, pop. 485; Chippewa (459), Barron (26)
Newburg, pop. 875; Washington (853), Ozaukee (22)
New London, pop. 6,658; Waupaca (5,321), Outagamie (1,337)

Powers Lake, pop. 1,044; Kenosha (752), Walworth (292)
Randolph, pop. 1,729; Dodge (1,227), Columbia (502)
River Falls, pop. 10,610; Pierce (8,841), St. Croix (1,769)
Spring Valley, pop. 1,051; Pierce (1,051), St. Croix (0)
Turtle Lake, pop. 817; Barron (811), Polk (6)
Unity, pop. 452; Marathon (256), Clark (196)
Viola, pop. 644; Richland (437), Vernon (207)
Watertown, pop. 19,142; Jefferson (12,388), Dodge (6,754)
Waupun, pop. 8,207; Dodge (5,490), Fond du Lac (2,717)
Whitewater, pop. 12,636; Walworth (10,170), Jefferson (2,466)
Wisconsin Dells, pop. 2,393; Columbia (2,261), Sauk (132), Adams (0)

Adams County
County Seat: Friendship (ZIP: 53934)

Pop: 15,682 (1990); 13,457 (1980) **Pop Density:** 24.2
Land: 647.8 sq. mi.; **Water:** 40.8 sq. mi. **Area Code:** 608
In south-central WI, west of Oshkosh; organized Mar 11, 1848 (prior to statehood) from Portage County.
Name origin: For John Adams (1735–1826), second U.S. president.

Adams — City
ZIP: 53910 **Lat:** 43-57-19 N **Long:** 89-49-00 W
Pop: 1,715 (1990); 1,744 (1980) **Pop Density:** 591.4
Land: 2.9 sq. mi.; **Water:** 0.0 sq. mi. **Elev:** 960 ft.
Incorporated 1926.
Name origin: For John Quincy Adams (1767–1848), sixth U.S. president. Previously called South Friendship.

*Adams — Town
ZIP: 53910 **Lat:** 43-56-18 N **Long:** 89-48-27 W
Pop: 1,170 (1990); 961 (1980) **Pop Density:** 23.1
Land: 50.6 sq. mi.; **Water:** 0.1 sq. mi.

Big Flats — Town
ZIP: 54613 **Lat:** 44-06-22 N **Long:** 89-47-56 W
Pop: 731 (1990); 694 (1980) **Pop Density:** 15.2
Land: 48.1 sq. mi.; **Water:** 0.0 sq. mi.

Colburn — Town
Lat: 44-06-44 N **Long:** 89-39-22 W
Pop: 154 (1990); 177 (1980) **Pop Density:** 4.3
Land: 35.9 sq. mi.; **Water:** 0.0 sq. mi.

Dell Prairie — Town
Lat: 43-41-22 N **Long:** 89-44-53 W
Pop: 1,063 (1990); 856 (1980) **Pop Density:** 31.8
Land: 33.4 sq. mi.; **Water:** 1.2 sq. mi.

Easton — Town
Lat: 43-51-25 N **Long:** 89-46-56 W
Pop: 824 (1990); 858 (1980) **Pop Density:** 22.8
Land: 36.1 sq. mi.; **Water:** 0.0 sq. mi.

Friendship — Village
ZIP: 53934 **Lat:** 43-58-18 N **Long:** 89-49-11 W
Pop: 728 (1990); 744 (1980) **Pop Density:** 808.9
Land: 0.9 sq. mi.; **Water:** 0.0 sq. mi.
Incorporated 1907.
Name origin: Named by settlers for their hometown of Friendship, NY.

Jackson — Town
Lat: 43-45-55 N **Long:** 89-39-29 W
Pop: 641 (1990); 640 (1980) **Pop Density:** 18.4
Land: 34.8 sq. mi.; **Water:** 1.0 sq. mi.

Leola — Town
Lat: 44-11-58 N **Long:** 89-39-23 W
Pop: 217 (1990); 237 (1980) **Pop Density:** 5.8
Land: 37.2 sq. mi.; **Water:** 0.0 sq. mi.

Lincoln — Town
Lat: 43-56-28 N **Long:** 89-39-31 W
Pop: 318 (1990); 289 (1980) **Pop Density:** 8.8
Land: 36.2 sq. mi.; **Water:** 0.0 sq. mi.

Monroe — Town
Lat: 44-06-15 N **Long:** 89-56-58 W
Pop: 305 (1990); 288 (1980) **Pop Density:** 13.9
Land: 21.9 sq. mi.; **Water:** 16.6 sq. mi.

New Chester — Town
Lat: 43-51-33 N **Long:** 89-39-05 W
Pop: 1,675 (1990); 1,088 (1980) **Pop Density:** 53.7
Land: 31.2 sq. mi.; **Water:** 0.2 sq. mi.

New Haven — Town
Lat: 43-40-43 N **Long:** 89-38-57 W
Pop: 511 (1990); 522 (1980) **Pop Density:** 17.4
Land: 29.3 sq. mi.; **Water:** 1.1 sq. mi.

Preston — Town
Lat: 44-01-20 N **Long:** 89-46-30 W
Pop: 1,057 (1990); 967 (1980) **Pop Density:** 29.9
Land: 35.4 sq. mi.; **Water:** 0.5 sq. mi.

Quincy — Town
Lat: 43-53-34 N **Long:** 89-54-44 W
Pop: 927 (1990); 639 (1980) **Pop Density:** 28.3
Land: 32.8 sq. mi.; **Water:** 6.8 sq. mi.

Richfield — Town
Lat: 44-01-45 N **Long:** 89-39-36 W
Pop: 159 (1990); 183 (1980) **Pop Density:** 4.5
Land: 35.5 sq. mi.; **Water:** 0.0 sq. mi.

Rome — Town
Lat: 44-12-09 N **Long:** 89-49-06 W
Pop: 1,674 (1990); 1,110 (1980) **Pop Density:** 30.8
Land: 54.3 sq. mi.; **Water:** 8.1 sq. mi.

Springville — Town
Lat: 43-46-40 N **Long:** 89-47-14 W
Pop: 785 (1990); 584 (1980) **Pop Density:** 17.9
Land: 43.9 sq. mi.; **Water:** 0.7 sq. mi.

Strongs Prairie — Town
Lat: 44-01-20 N **Long:** 89-55-41 W
Pop: 1,028 (1990); 876 (1980) **Pop Density:** 21.7
Land: 47.4 sq. mi.; **Water:** 4.5 sq. mi.

Wisconsin Dells — City
Lat: 43-38-30 N **Long:** 89-46-40 W
Pop: 0 (1990); 2,521 (1980)
Land: 0.004 sq. mi.; **Water:** 0.0 sq. mi.
Incorporated 1925. Part of the town is also in Columbia and Sauk counties.
Name origin: Named in 1931 for its descriptive connotations. Previously called Kilbourn, for Byron Kilbourne.

Ashland County
County Seat: Ashland (ZIP: 54806)

Pop: 16,307 (1990); 16,783 (1980)   **Pop Density:** 15.6
Land: 1043.9 sq. mi.; **Water:** 1250.2 sq. mi.   **Area Code:** 715

On central northern border of WI, bordered on north by Lake Superior; organized Mar 27, 1860 from unorganized territory.

Name origin: For the abundant ash trees, probably *Fraxinus americana*, or for the KY home of Henry Clay (1777–1852), U.S. senator known as the "Great Pacificator" for his advocacy of compromise to avert national crises.

Agenda   Town
Lat: 46-03-45 N   Long: 90-22-17 W
Pop: 591 (1990); 623 (1980)   **Pop Density:** 6.7
Land: 88.7 sq. mi.; **Water:** 0.9 sq. mi.

Ashland   City
ZIP: 54806   Lat: 46-34-48 N   Long: 90-52-26 W
Pop: 8,695 (1990); 9,115 (1980)   **Pop Density:** 658.7
Land: 13.2 sq. mi.; **Water:** 0.3 sq. mi.   **Elev:** 671 ft.
Incorporated 1887.

Name origin: Named in 1885 for U.S. Sen. Henry Clay's (1777–1852) home in KY. Previously called Zham-a-wa-mik, an Ojibway Indian term meaning 'the long stretched beaver,' and Whittlesey for the first postmaster, Adolph Whittlesey.

*Ashland   Town
ZIP: 54806   Lat: 46-22-58 N   Long: 90-44-01 W
Pop: 567 (1990); 596 (1980)   **Pop Density:** 13.8
Land: 41.2 sq. mi.; **Water:** 0.1 sq. mi.

Butternut   Village
ZIP: 54514   Lat: 46-00-49 N   Long: 90-29-51 W
Pop: 416 (1990); 438 (1980)   **Pop Density:** 260.0
Land: 1.6 sq. mi.; **Water:** 0.0 sq. mi.   **Elev:** 1503 ft.
Incorporated 1903.

Name origin: For a grove of huge butternut trees that grew here.

Chippewa   Town
Lat: 46-01-39 N   Long: 90-42-02 W
Pop: 405 (1990); 402 (1980)   **Pop Density:** 3.3
Land: 124.4 sq. mi.; **Water:** 1.1 sq. mi.

Gingles   Town
Lat: 46-32-39 N   Long: 90-50-02 W
Pop: 492 (1990); 545 (1980)   **Pop Density:** 12.6
Land: 39.2 sq. mi.; **Water:** 0.0 sq. mi.

Gordon   Town
Lat: 46-12-23 N   Long: 90-44-43 W
Pop: 301 (1990); 333 (1980)   **Pop Density:** 2.9
Land: 104.4 sq. mi.; **Water:** 2.6 sq. mi.

Jacobs   Town
Lat: 46-10-24 N   Long: 90-30-24 W
Pop: 885 (1990); 907 (1980)   **Pop Density:** 17.3
Land: 51.1 sq. mi.; **Water:** 0.3 sq. mi.

La Pointe   Town
Lat: 46-55-09 N   Long: 90-38-23 W
Pop: 147 (1990); 156 (1980)   **Pop Density:** 1.9
Land: 77.6 sq. mi.; **Water:** 0.4 sq. mi.

Marengo   Town
ZIP: 54855   Lat: 46-19-47 N   Long: 90-51-08 W
Pop: 284 (1990); 276 (1980)   **Pop Density:** 4.0
Land: 71.3 sq. mi.; **Water:** 1.0 sq. mi.

Mellen   City
ZIP: 54546   Lat: 46-19-23 N   Long: 90-39-39 W
Pop: 935 (1990); 1,046 (1980)   **Pop Density:** 492.1
Land: 1.9 sq. mi.; **Water:** 0.0 sq. mi.
Incorporated 1907.

Name origin: For railroad official, Charles Sanger Mellen. Previously called Iron City.

Morse   Town
ZIP: 54546   Lat: 46-18-41 N   Long: 90-39-28 W
Pop: 481 (1990); 469 (1980)   **Pop Density:** 4.7
Land: 102.8 sq. mi.; **Water:** 1.6 sq. mi.

Odanah   CDP
Lat: 46-36-16 N   Long: 90-41-00 W
Pop: 190 (1990)   **Pop Density:** 126.7
Land: 1.5 sq. mi.; **Water:** 0.0 sq. mi.

Peeksville   Town
Lat: 46-06-29 N   Long: 90-30-06 W
Pop: 167 (1990); 184 (1980)   **Pop Density:** 4.5
Land: 36.8 sq. mi.; **Water:** 0.1 sq. mi.

Sanborn   Town
Lat: 46-32-28 N   Long: 90-40-17 W
Pop: 998 (1990); 834 (1980)   **Pop Density:** 6.4
Land: 156.4 sq. mi.; **Water:** 4.3 sq. mi.

Shanagolden   Town
Lat: 46-06-52 N   Long: 90-46-30 W
Pop: 172 (1990); 174 (1980)   **Pop Density:** 1.9
Land: 89.3 sq. mi.; **Water:** 0.6 sq. mi.

White River   Town
Lat: 46-26-26 N   Long: 90-50-53 W
Pop: 771 (1990); 685 (1980)   **Pop Density:** 17.5
Land: 44.0 sq. mi.; **Water:** 0.1 sq. mi.

> ## Barron County
> **County Seat: Barron (ZIP: 54812)**
>
> **Pop:** 40,750 (1990); 38,730 (1980)　　**Pop Density:** 47.2
> **Land:** 862.9 sq. mi.; **Water:** 27.2 sq. mi.　　**Area Code:** 715
> In west-central WI, east of St. Paul, MN; organized as Dallas County Mar 19, 1859; name changed Mar 4, 1869.
> **Name origin:** For Henry D. Barron, state senator and judge of the WI circuit court. Originally for George Dallas (1792–1864), U.S. vice president (1845–49).

Almena — Village
ZIP: 54805　　Lat: 45-24-52 N　Long: 92-02-11 W
Pop: 625 (1990); 526 (1980)　　Pop Density: 625.0
Land: 1.0 sq. mi.; Water: 0.0 sq. mi.　　Elev: 1187 ft.
Incorporated 1945.
Name origin: Named in 1887 for storekeepers, Albert and Wilhelmena Koehler. Originally known as Lightning City or Lightning Creek.

*Almena — Town
ZIP: 54805　　Lat: 45-25-27 N　Long: 92-05-30 W
Pop: 773 (1990); 776 (1980)　　Pop Density: 25.2
Land: 30.7 sq. mi.; Water: 1.9 sq. mi.

Arland — Town
ZIP: 54004　　Lat: 45-20-15 N　Long: 91-58-15 W
Pop: 609 (1990); 692 (1980)　　Pop Density: 17.3
Land: 35.3 sq. mi.; Water: 0.0 sq. mi.

Barron — City
ZIP: 54812　　Lat: 45-24-02 N　Long: 91-50-47 W
Pop: 2,986 (1990); 2,595 (1980)　　Pop Density: 1148.5
Land: 2.6 sq. mi.; Water: 0.1 sq. mi.　　Elev: 1115 ft.
Incorporated 1887.
Name origin: For Henry D. Barron, a judge and state senator. Originally known as Quaderer's Camp for John Quaderer, foreman of the lumber camp here.

*Barron — Town
ZIP: 54812　　Lat: 45-25-05 N　Long: 91-51-10 W
Pop: 1,015 (1990); 977 (1980)　　Pop Density: 30.7
Land: 33.1 sq. mi.; Water: 0.1 sq. mi.

Bear Lake — Town
Lat: 45-35-38 N　Long: 91-50-18 W
Pop: 530 (1990); 521 (1980)　　Pop Density: 16.1
Land: 32.9 sq. mi.; Water: 2.3 sq. mi.

Cameron — Village
ZIP: 54822　　Lat: 45-24-12 N　Long: 91-44-36 W
Pop: 1,273 (1990); 1,115 (1980)　　Pop Density: 530.4
Land: 2.4 sq. mi.; Water: 0.1 sq. mi.　　Elev: 1097 ft.
Settled 1879. Incorporated 1894.
Name origin: For WI state Senator Cameron of La Crosse.

Cedar Lake — Town
Lat: 45-35-33 N　Long: 91-36-06 W
Pop: 741 (1990); 617 (1980)　　Pop Density: 23.7
Land: 31.3 sq. mi.; Water: 4.1 sq. mi.

Chetek — City
ZIP: 54728　　Lat: 45-18-57 N　Long: 91-39-11 W
Pop: 1,953 (1990); 1,931 (1980)　　Pop Density: 813.7
Land: 2.4 sq. mi.; Water: 0.7 sq. mi.
Incorporated 1891.
Name origin: Probably for an Ojibway Indian chief, the name probably meaning 'pelican.'

*Chetek — Town
ZIP: 54728　　Lat: 45-20-16 N　Long: 91-35-49 W
Pop: 1,446 (1990); 1,210 (1980)　　Pop Density: 47.6
Land: 30.4 sq. mi.; Water: 3.1 sq. mi.

Clinton — Town
Lat: 45-25-38 N　Long: 91-57-59 W
Pop: 849 (1990); 851 (1980)　　Pop Density: 24.2
Land: 35.1 sq. mi.; Water: 0.3 sq. mi.

Crystal Lake — Town
Lat: 45-30-28 N　Long: 92-05-53 W
Pop: 700 (1990); 756 (1980)　　Pop Density: 20.8
Land: 33.6 sq. mi.; Water: 1.8 sq. mi.

Cumberland — City
ZIP: 54829　　Lat: 45-32-09 N　Long: 92-01-23 W
Pop: 2,163 (1990); 1,983 (1980)　　Pop Density: 865.2
Land: 2.5 sq. mi.; Water: 0.6 sq. mi.　　Elev: 1251 ft.
Incorporated 1885.
Name origin: Named in 1879 by John A. Humbird for his hometown of Cumberland, MD. Originally called Lakeland.

*Cumberland — Town
ZIP: 54829　　Lat: 45-30-30 N　Long: 91-58-00 W
Pop: 884 (1990); 909 (1980)　　Pop Density: 27.5
Land: 32.1 sq. mi.; Water: 0.9 sq. mi.

Dallas — Village
ZIP: 54733　　Lat: 45-15-29 N　Long: 91-48-52 W
Pop: 452 (1990); 477 (1980)　　Pop Density: 301.3
Land: 1.5 sq. mi.; Water: 0.0 sq. mi.　　Elev: 1054 ft.
Incorporated 1903.
Name origin: For George Dallas (1792–1864), U.S. vice president (1845–49).

*Dallas — Town
ZIP: 54733　　Lat: 45-15-06 N　Long: 91-51-17 W
Pop: 548 (1990); 567 (1980)　　Pop Density: 16.2
Land: 33.9 sq. mi.; Water: 0.0 sq. mi.

Dovre — Town
Lat: 45-15-05 N　Long: 91-36-03 W
Pop: 561 (1990); 526 (1980)　　Pop Density: 16.0
Land: 35.1 sq. mi.; Water: 0.1 sq. mi.

Doyle — Town
Lat: 45-30-52 N　Long: 91-36-38 W
Pop: 460 (1990); 455 (1980)　　Pop Density: 12.9
Land: 35.6 sq. mi.; Water: 0.0 sq. mi.

Haugen — Village
ZIP: 54841　　Lat: 45-36-27 N　Long: 91-46-42 W
Pop: 305 (1990); 251 (1980)　　Pop Density: 610.0
Land: 0.5 sq. mi.; Water: 0.0 sq. mi.　　Elev: 1229 ft.
Incorporated 1918.

Lakeland
Town
Lat: 45-35-54 N Long: 91-58-14 W
Pop: 789 (1990); 672 (1980) **Pop Density:** 23.9
Land: 33.0 sq. mi.; **Water:** 2.3 sq. mi.

Maple Grove
Town
Lat: 45-20-12 N Long: 91-51-03 W
Pop: 926 (1990); 948 (1980) **Pop Density:** 26.1
Land: 35.5 sq. mi.; **Water:** 0.0 sq. mi.

Maple Plain
Town
Lat: 45-35-27 N Long: 92-05-52 W
Pop: 610 (1990); 577 (1980) **Pop Density:** 18.3
Land: 33.3 sq. mi.; **Water:** 2.7 sq. mi.

New Auburn
Village
ZIP: 54757 Lat: 45-12-30 N Long: 91-32-59 W
Pop: 26 (1990); 14 (1980) **Pop Density:** 130.0
Land: 0.2 sq. mi.; **Water:** 0.0 sq. mi.
Incorporated 1902. Part of the town is also in Chippewa County.
Name origin: Previously called Cartwright's Mills and Cartwright.

Prairie Farm
Village
ZIP: 54762 Lat: 45-14-15 N Long: 91-58-50 W
Pop: 494 (1990); 387 (1980) **Pop Density:** 494.0
Land: 1.0 sq. mi.; **Water:** 0.0 sq. mi.
Incorporated 1901.
Name origin: For farms established here on the prairie by the Knapp Stout Lumber Company.

*Prairie Farm
Town
ZIP: 54762 Lat: 45-15-07 N Long: 91-58-38 W
Pop: 567 (1990); 634 (1980) **Pop Density:** 16.5
Land: 34.4 sq. mi.; **Water:** 0.0 sq. mi.

Prairie Lake
Town
Lat: 45-20-00 N Long: 91-44-08 W
Pop: 1,129 (1990); 1,076 (1980) **Pop Density:** 34.1
Land: 33.1 sq. mi.; **Water:** 1.8 sq. mi.

Rice Lake
City
ZIP: 54868 Lat: 45-29-48 N Long: 91-44-21 W
Pop: 7,998 (1990); 7,691 (1980) **Pop Density:** 1230.5
Land: 6.5 sq. mi.; **Water:** 1.0 sq. mi.
Incorporated 1887.
Name origin: For a swamp where Indians gathered wild rice that was turned into a lake around 1868 when the Knapp Stout Lumber Company built a dam here.

*Rice Lake
Town
ZIP: 54868 Lat: 45-30-42 N Long: 91-43-07 W
Pop: 2,473 (1990); 2,372 (1980) **Pop Density:** 91.6
Land: 27.0 sq. mi.; **Water:** 1.2 sq. mi.

Sioux Creek
Town
Lat: 45-15-00 N Long: 91-43-22 W
Pop: 635 (1990); 643 (1980) **Pop Density:** 18.2
Land: 34.9 sq. mi.; **Water:** 0.3 sq. mi.

Stanfold
Town
Lat: 45-30-33 N Long: 91-50-51 W
Pop: 644 (1990); 721 (1980) **Pop Density:** 17.9
Land: 35.9 sq. mi.; **Water:** 0.0 sq. mi.

Stanley
Town
Lat: 45-25-48 N Long: 91-43-28 W
Pop: 2,087 (1990); 1,813 (1980) **Pop Density:** 64.0
Land: 32.6 sq. mi.; **Water:** 0.6 sq. mi.

Sumner
Town
Lat: 45-25-19 N Long: 91-35-59 W
Pop: 550 (1990); 556 (1980) **Pop Density:** 15.4
Land: 35.7 sq. mi.; **Water:** 0.0 sq. mi. **Elev:** 1089 ft.

Turtle Lake
Village
ZIP: 54004 Lat: 45-23-36 N Long: 92-08-28 W
Pop: 811 (1990); 762 (1980) **Pop Density:** 368.6
Land: 2.2 sq. mi.; **Water:** 0.1 sq. mi. **Elev:** 1264 ft.
Incorporated 1898. Part of the town is also in Polk County.
Name origin: For the nearby lake that was named for turtle's eggs found on its shore. Originally called Skowhagen for Skowhagen, ME, the former home of settler Joel Richardson.

*Turtle Lake
Town
ZIP: 54004 Lat: 45-20-38 N Long: 92-05-58 W
Pop: 621 (1990); 587 (1980) **Pop Density:** 17.6
Land: 35.2 sq. mi.; **Water:** 0.4 sq. mi.

Vance Creek
Town
Lat: 45-14-44 N Long: 92-05-15 W
Pop: 611 (1990); 650 (1980) **Pop Density:** 17.2
Land: 35.5 sq. mi.; **Water:** 0.0 sq. mi.

Bayfield County
County Seat: Washburn (ZIP: 54891)

Pop: 14,008 (1990); 13,822 (1980) **Pop Density:** 9.5
Land: 1476.4 sq. mi.; **Water:** 565.3 sq. mi. **Area Code:** 715

On northwestern border of WI, east of Duluth, MN; organized as LaPointe County Feb 19, 1845 (prior to statehood) from Ashland County; name changed Apr 12, 1866.

Name origin: For Henry W. Bayfield, an admiral in the British navy.

Barksdale
Town
Lat: 46-37-09 N Long: 91-04-15 W
Pop: 756 (1990); 762 (1980) **Pop Density:** 13.6
Land: 55.5 sq. mi.; **Water:** 11.1 sq. mi.

Barnes
Town
Lat: 46-18-20 N Long: 91-29-16 W
Pop: 473 (1990); 493 (1980) **Pop Density:** 4.0
Land: 117.5 sq. mi.; **Water:** 6.7 sq. mi.

Bayfield — City
ZIP: 54814 Lat: 46-48-41 N Long: 90-49-17 W
Pop: 686 (1990); 778 (1980) Pop Density: 980.0
Land: 0.7 sq. mi.; Water: 0.0 sq. mi.
Established 1665. Incorporated 1913.
Name origin: For Adm. Henry W. Bayfield of the Royal Navy. Originally a Jesuit mission called La Pointe du Saint Esprit, and then La Pointe.

*Bayfield — Town
ZIP: 54814 Lat: 46-53-26 N Long: 90-57-10 W
Pop: 603 (1990); 607 (1980) Pop Density: 6.8
Land: 89.3 sq. mi.; Water: 44.9 sq. mi.

Bayview — Town
Lat: 46-45-01 N Long: 90-55-19 W
Pop: 402 (1990); 343 (1980) Pop Density: 9.7
Land: 41.5 sq. mi.; Water: 14.6 sq. mi.

Bell — Town
Lat: 46-47-28 N Long: 91-06-36 W
Pop: 237 (1990); 247 (1980) Pop Density: 4.0
Land: 59.6 sq. mi.; Water: 0.8 sq. mi.

Cable — Village
ZIP: 54821 Lat: 46-12-08 N Long: 91-17-53 W
Pop: 817 (1990); 604 (1980) Pop Density: 11.8
Land: 69.2 sq. mi.; Water: 2.2 sq. mi.
Name origin: For the first engineer to pull a train into this stop, which, in 1878, was the end of the line.

Clover — Town
Lat: 46-45-58 N Long: 91-14-13 W
Pop: 213 (1990); 254 (1980) Pop Density: 3.6
Land: 59.6 sq. mi.; Water: 0.3 sq. mi.

Delta — Town
Lat: 46-27-13 N Long: 91-17-51 W
Pop: 215 (1990); 205 (1980) Pop Density: 3.1
Land: 69.6 sq. mi.; Water: 2.7 sq. mi.

Drummond — Town
ZIP: 54832 Lat: 46-19-34 N Long: 91-17-46 W
Pop: 417 (1990); 442 (1980) Pop Density: 3.0
Land: 137.2 sq. mi.; Water: 6.0 sq. mi.

Eileen — Town
Lat: 46-32-24 N Long: 90-59-33 W
Pop: 665 (1990); 664 (1980) Pop Density: 18.9
Land: 35.2 sq. mi.; Water: 0.1 sq. mi.

Grand View — Town
ZIP: 54839 Lat: 46-18-35 N Long: 91-04-34 W
Pop: 419 (1990); 440 (1980) Pop Density: 4.0
Land: 104.3 sq. mi.; Water: 2.8 sq. mi.

Hughes — Town
Lat: 46-31-29 N Long: 91-29-31 W
Pop: 334 (1990); 290 (1980) Pop Density: 6.4
Land: 52.0 sq. mi.; Water: 1.5 sq. mi.

Iron River — Town
ZIP: 54847 Lat: 46-32-55 N Long: 91-21-53 W
Pop: 901 (1990); 991 (1980) Pop Density: 28.7
Land: 31.4 sq. mi.; Water: 3.4 sq. mi.

Kelly — Town
Lat: 46-27-08 N Long: 90-59-11 W
Pop: 383 (1990); 354 (1980) Pop Density: 10.4
Land: 36.7 sq. mi.; Water: 0.0 sq. mi.

Keystone — Town
Lat: 46-31-50 N Long: 91-11-03 W
Pop: 320 (1990); 344 (1980) Pop Density: 8.9
Land: 35.8 sq. mi.; Water: 0.3 sq. mi.

Lincoln — Town
Lat: 46-21-57 N Long: 90-58-00 W
Pop: 294 (1990); 280 (1980) Pop Density: 8.3
Land: 35.5 sq. mi.; Water: 0.4 sq. mi.

Mason — Village
ZIP: 54856 Lat: 46-26-07 N Long: 91-03-44 W
Pop: 102 (1990); 102 (1980) Pop Density: 204.0
Land: 0.5 sq. mi.; Water: 0.0 sq. mi.
Incorporated 1925.

*Mason — Town
ZIP: 54856 Lat: 46-27-55 N Long: 91-06-42 W
Pop: 296 (1990); 304 (1980) Pop Density: 8.2
Land: 35.9 sq. mi.; Water: 0.0 sq. mi.

Namakagon — Town
Lat: 46-12-07 N Long: 91-02-57 W
Pop: 276 (1990); 286 (1980) Pop Density: 4.2
Land: 65.0 sq. mi.; Water: 7.2 sq. mi.

Orienta — Town
Lat: 46-42-36 N Long: 91-26-32 W
Pop: 114 (1990); 109 (1980) Pop Density: 2.1
Land: 54.1 sq. mi.; Water: 0.2 sq. mi.

Oulu — Town
Lat: 46-37-44 N Long: 91-28-57 W
Pop: 513 (1990); 547 (1980) Pop Density: 14.5
Land: 35.5 sq. mi.; Water: 0.0 sq. mi.

Pilsen — Town
Lat: 46-33-53 N Long: 91-10-35 W
Pop: 203 (1990); 222 (1980) Pop Density: 5.9
Land: 34.6 sq. mi.; Water: 0.2 sq. mi.

Port Wing — Town
ZIP: 54865 Lat: 46-44-56 N Long: 91-20-06 W
Pop: 434 (1990); 525 (1980) Pop Density: 9.3
Land: 46.6 sq. mi.; Water: 0.1 sq. mi.

Russell — Town
Lat: 46-56-42 N Long: 90-50-23 W
Pop: 978 (1990); 791 (1980) Pop Density: 19.6
Land: 49.8 sq. mi.; Water: 50.3 sq. mi.

Tripp — Town
Lat: 46-37-41 N Long: 91-21-27 W
Pop: 182 (1990); 145 (1980) Pop Density: 5.2
Land: 34.7 sq. mi.; Water: 0.2 sq. mi.

Washburn — City
ZIP: 54891 Lat: 46-40-25 N Long: 90-53-36 W
Pop: 2,285 (1990); 2,080 (1980) Pop Density: 585.9
Land: 3.9 sq. mi.; Water: 2.2 sq. mi.
Incorporated 1904.

*Washburn — Town
ZIP: 54891 Lat: 46-39-49 N Long: 91-05-24 W
Pop: 490 (1990); 386 (1980) Pop Density: 5.8
Land: 85.0 sq. mi.; Water: 0.2 sq. mi.

WISCONSIN, Brown County

Brown County
County Seat: Green Bay (ZIP: 54305)

Pop: 194,594 (1990); 175,280 (1980)   **Pop Density:** 368.1
Land: 528.7 sq. mi.; **Water:** 86.8 sq. mi.   **Area Code:** 414

In central-eastern WI, at southern end of Green Bay; organized Oct 26, 1818 (prior to statehood) from a territorial county; annexed part of Shawano and Oconto counties in 1919.

Name origin: For Gen. Jacob Jennings Brown (1775–1828), an officer in the War of 1812 and commander of the U.S. Army (1821–28).

Allouez — Village
ZIP: 54301   **Lat:** 44-28-20 N   **Long:** 88-01-33 W
Pop: 14,431 (1990); 14,882 (1980)   **Pop Density:** 3137.2
Land: 4.6 sq. mi.; **Water:** 0.5 sq. mi.

Ashwaubenon — Village
ZIP: 54304   **Lat:** 44-29-08 N   **Long:** 88-05-00 W
Pop: 16,376 (1990); 14,486 (1980)   **Pop Density:** 1574.6
Land: 10.4 sq. mi.; **Water:** 0.4 sq. mi.   **Elev:** 590 ft.
Incorporated 1977.

Name origin: For the great Menominee Chief, Ashwaubamic, who left this land to his descendants, the Franks and La Rose families.

Bellevue — Town
ZIP: 54311   **Lat:** 44-27-34 N   **Long:** 87-57-21 W
Pop: 7,541 (1990); 4,101 (1980)   **Pop Density:** 531.1
Land: 14.2 sq. mi.; **Water:** 0.1 sq. mi.

Denmark — Village
ZIP: 54208   **Lat:** 44-20-53 N   **Long:** 87-49-46 W
Pop: 1,612 (1990); 1,475 (1980)   **Pop Density:** 1074.7
Land: 1.5 sq. mi.; **Water:** 0.0 sq. mi.
Incorporated 1915.

Name origin: Settled and named by immigrants from Denmark.

De Pere — City
ZIP: 54115   **Lat:** 44-26-18 N   **Long:** 88-04-18 W
Pop: 16,569 (1990); 14,892 (1980)   **Pop Density:** 1996.3
Land: 8.3 sq. mi.; **Water:** 0.7 sq. mi.
In eastern WI on the Fox River, 5 mi. south of Green Bay. Incorporated 1883.

Name origin: Named by Fr. Claude Allouez as *Rapides des Peres* 'Rapids of the Fathers,' for its location on the Fox river.

*De Pere — Town
ZIP: 54115   **Lat:** 44-25-34 N   **Long:** 87-58-17 W
Pop: 1,558 (1990); 1,535 (1980)   **Pop Density:** 87.5
Land: 17.8 sq. mi.; **Water:** 0.1 sq. mi.

Eaton — Town
Lat: 44-26-42 N   **Long:** 87-49-32 W
Pop: 1,128 (1990); 1,106 (1980)   **Pop Density:** 46.6
Land: 24.2 sq. mi.; **Water:** 0.1 sq. mi.

Glenmore — Town
Lat: 44-22-21 N   **Long:** 87-56-52 W
Pop: 1,057 (1990); 1,046 (1980)   **Pop Density:** 32.3
Land: 32.7 sq. mi.; **Water:** 0.0 sq. mi.   **Elev:** 924 ft.

Green Bay — City
ZIP: 54303   **Lat:** 44-31-17 N   **Long:** 87-59-23 W
Pop: 96,466 (1990); 87,899 (1980)   **Pop Density:** 2202.4
Land: 43.8 sq. mi.; **Water:** 10.5 sq. mi.   **Elev:** 594 ft.
In eastern WI on the south end of Green Bay, an arm of Lake Michigan, at the mouth of the Fox River. Incorporated 1854.

Name origin: For Green Bay; from French *La Baie Verte*.

*Green Bay — Town
Lat: 44-35-59 N   **Long:** 87-47-49 W
Pop: 1,292 (1990); 1,106 (1980)   **Pop Density:** 58.5
Land: 22.1 sq. mi.; **Water:** 8.5 sq. mi.

Hobart — Town
Lat: 44-29-37 N   **Long:** 88-09-35 W
Pop: 4,284 (1990); 3,765 (1980)   **Pop Density:** 128.6
Land: 33.3 sq. mi.; **Water:** 0.1 sq. mi.

Holland — Town
Lat: 44-16-23 N   **Long:** 88-05-57 W
Pop: 1,237 (1990); 1,268 (1980)   **Pop Density:** 34.4
Land: 36.0 sq. mi.; **Water:** 0.0 sq. mi.

Howard — Village
ZIP: 54303   **Lat:** 44-34-24 N   **Long:** 88-04-36 W
Pop: 9,874 (1990); 8,240 (1980)   **Pop Density:** 548.6
Land: 18.0 sq. mi.; **Water:** 5.0 sq. mi.
Incorporated 1959.

Name origin: For Brig. Gen. Benjamin Howard, who fought in the War of 1812.

Humboldt — Town
Lat: 44-30-07 N   **Long:** 87-49-24 W
Pop: 1,334 (1990); 1,281 (1980)   **Pop Density:** 55.6
Land: 24.0 sq. mi.; **Water:** 0.0 sq. mi.

Lawrence — Town
Lat: 44-24-23 N   **Long:** 88-08-31 W
Pop: 1,363 (1990); 1,431 (1980)   **Pop Density:** 70.6
Land: 19.3 sq. mi.; **Water:** 0.6 sq. mi.

Morrison — Town
Lat: 44-17-04 N   **Long:** 87-56-55 W
Pop: 1,493 (1990); 1,565 (1980)   **Pop Density:** 42.5
Land: 35.1 sq. mi.; **Water:** 1.4 sq. mi.

New Denmark — Town
Lat: 44-22-12 N   **Long:** 87-49-44 W
Pop: 1,370 (1990); 1,420 (1980)   **Pop Density:** 39.5
Land: 34.7 sq. mi.; **Water:** 0.1 sq. mi.

Pittsfield — Town
Lat: 44-37-51 N   **Long:** 88-11-05 W
Pop: 2,165 (1990); 2,219 (1980)   **Pop Density:** 66.6
Land: 32.5 sq. mi.; **Water:** 0.0 sq. mi.

WISCONSIN, Buffalo County

Pulaski — Village
ZIP: 54162 Lat: 44-40-09 N Long: 88-14-12 W
Pop: 2,200 (1990); 1,875 (1980) Pop Density: 1222.2
Land: 1.8 sq. mi.; Water: 0.0 sq. mi.
Incorporated 1910.
Name origin: For Polish Count Casimir Pulaski (1747–79), who fought with the Americans during the Revolutionary War.

Rockland — Town
Lat: 44-22-55 N Long: 88-03-19 W
Pop: 974 (1990); 882 (1980) Pop Density: 43.7
Land: 22.3 sq. mi.; Water: 0.6 sq. mi.

Scott — Town
Lat: 44-36-30 N Long: 87-51-52 W
Pop: 2,044 (1990); 1,929 (1980) Pop Density: 103.8
Land: 19.7 sq. mi.; Water: 34.6 sq. mi.

Suamico — Town
ZIP: 54173 Lat: 44-37-59 N Long: 88-01-54 W
Pop: 5,214 (1990); 4,003 (1980) Pop Density: 144.0
Land: 36.2 sq. mi.; Water: 23.1 sq. mi.

Wrightstown — Village
ZIP: 54180 Lat: 44-19-29 N Long: 88-10-27 W
Pop: 1,262 (1990); 1,169 (1980) Pop Density: 631.0
Land: 2.0 sq. mi.; Water: 0.2 sq. mi.
Incorporated 1901.
Name origin: For Hoel S. Wright, who settled here around 1833. Previously called Wright's Ferry.

*Wrightstown — Town
ZIP: 54180 Lat: 44-19-33 N Long: 88-05-31 W
Pop: 1,750 (1990); 1,705 (1980) Pop Density: 51.5
Land: 34.0 sq. mi.; Water: 0.2 sq. mi.

Buffalo County
County Seat: Alma (ZIP: 54610)

Pop: 13,584 (1990); 14,309 (1980) Pop Density: 19.8
Land: 684.5 sq. mi.; Water: 25.1 sq. mi. Area Code: 608
On central western border of WI, southeast of St. Paul, MN; organized Jul 6, 1853.
Name origin: For the herds of buffalo that once roamed here.

Alma — City
ZIP: 54610 Lat: 44-19-51 N Long: 91-55-19 W
Pop: 790 (1990); 848 (1980) Pop Density: 136.2
Land: 5.8 sq. mi.; Water: 1.9 sq. mi. Elev: 687 ft.
Incorporated 1885.
Name origin: Named by W.H. Gates for the Alma River in Russia.

*Alma — Town
ZIP: 54610 Lat: 44-22-38 N Long: 91-50-15 W
Pop: 479 (1990); 397 (1980) Pop Density: 11.2
Land: 42.8 sq. mi.; Water: 0.1 sq. mi.

Belvidere — Town
Lat: 44-15-27 N Long: 91-50-46 W
Pop: 505 (1990); 425 (1980) Pop Density: 15.3
Land: 33.0 sq. mi.; Water: 1.4 sq. mi.

Buffalo — City
Lat: 44-13-24 N Long: 91-52-09 W
Pop: 915 (1990); 894 (1980) Pop Density: 457.5
Land: 2.0 sq. mi.; Water: 3.9 sq. mi.
Incorporated 1859.
Name origin: For the buffalo that once roamed here.

*Buffalo — Town
Lat: 44-05-22 N Long: 91-36-23 W
Pop: 686 (1990); 821 (1980) Pop Density: 22.9
Land: 29.9 sq. mi.; Water: 4.3 sq. mi.

Canton — Town
Lat: 44-33-16 N Long: 91-49-17 W
Pop: 309 (1990); 359 (1980) Pop Density: 8.6
Land: 35.8 sq. mi.; Water: 0.0 sq. mi.

Cochrane — Village
ZIP: 54622 Lat: 44-13-43 N Long: 91-50-11 W
Pop: 475 (1990); 512 (1980) Pop Density: 678.6
Land: 0.7 sq. mi.; Water: 0.0 sq. mi.
Incorporated 1910.
Name origin: For an officer of the railroad.

Cross — Town
Lat: 44-10-04 N Long: 91-38-27 W
Pop: 307 (1990); 393 (1980) Pop Density: 8.1
Land: 37.7 sq. mi.; Water: 0.0 sq. mi.

Dover — Town
Lat: 44-27-49 N Long: 91-35-28 W
Pop: 451 (1990); 455 (1980) Pop Density: 12.5
Land: 36.2 sq. mi.; Water: 0.0 sq. mi.

Fountain City — City
ZIP: 54629 Lat: 44-07-11 N Long: 91-41-51 W
Pop: 938 (1990); 963 (1980) Pop Density: 208.4
Land: 4.5 sq. mi.; Water: 1.1 sq. mi. Elev: 663 ft.
Incorporated 1889.
Name origin: Named in 1855 for the many springs along the bluffs near here. Previously called Wha-ma-dee by the Sioux and Holmes' Landing for pioneer Thomas A. Holmes.

Gilmanton — Town
Lat: 44-28-06 N Long: 91-42-26 W
Pop: 469 (1990); 498 (1980) Pop Density: 12.9
Land: 36.3 sq. mi.; Water: 0.0 sq. mi.

Glencoe — Town
Lat: 44-16-30 N Long: 91-35-41 W
Pop: 502 (1990); 558 (1980) Pop Density: 11.2
Land: 44.7 sq. mi.; Water: 0.0 sq. mi.

WISCONSIN, Buffalo County

Lincoln
Town
Lat: 44-20-37 N **Long:** 91-44-44 W
Pop: 250 (1990); 272 (1980) **Pop Density:** 6.7
Land: 37.2 sq. mi.; **Water:** 0.0 sq. mi.

Maxville
Town
Lat: 44-33-48 N **Long:** 91-58-09 W
Pop: 370 (1990); 403 (1980) **Pop Density:** 8.8
Land: 42.0 sq. mi.; **Water:** 0.7 sq. mi.

Milton
Town
Lat: 44-10-26 N **Long:** 91-45-39 W
Pop: 450 (1990); 416 (1980) **Pop Density:** 18.0
Land: 25.0 sq. mi.; **Water:** 4.5 sq. mi.

Modena
Town
Lat: 44-28-08 N **Long:** 91-49-59 W
Pop: 360 (1990); 436 (1980) **Pop Density:** 10.0
Land: 36.1 sq. mi.; **Water:** 0.0 sq. mi.

Mondovi
City
ZIP: 54755 **Lat:** 44-34-08 N **Long:** 91-40-10 W
Pop: 2,491 (1990); 2,545 (1980) **Pop Density:** 778.4
Land: 3.2 sq. mi.; **Water:** 0.0 sq. mi.
Incorporated 1889.
Name origin: For Mondavi, Italy, where Napoleon (1769–1821) won a victory against the Sardinians. Previously called Pan Cake Valley and Farringtons, for first settler Harvey Farrington.

*Mondovi
Town
Lat: 44-32-58 N **Long:** 91-42-49 W
Pop: 545 (1990); 511 (1980) **Pop Density:** 16.7
Land: 32.7 sq. mi.; **Water:** 0.0 sq. mi.

Montana
Town
Lat: 44-23-17 N **Long:** 91-36-36 W
Pop: 316 (1990); 337 (1980) **Pop Density:** 6.7
Land: 47.2 sq. mi.; **Water:** 0.0 sq. mi.

Naples
Town
Lat: 44-33-16 N **Long:** 91-35-12 W
Pop: 496 (1990); 580 (1980) **Pop Density:** 13.9
Land: 35.8 sq. mi.; **Water:** 0.0 sq. mi.

Nelson
Village
ZIP: 54756 **Lat:** 44-25-24 N **Long:** 92-00-17 W
Pop: 388 (1990); 389 (1980) **Pop Density:** 258.7
Land: 1.5 sq. mi.; **Water:** 0.0 sq. mi.
Incorporated 1978.
Name origin: For settler James Nelson. Previously called Nelson's Landing and eventually shortened to Nelson.

*Nelson
Town
ZIP: 54756 **Lat:** 44-26-20 N **Long:** 91-58-21 W
Pop: 571 (1990); 703 (1980) **Pop Density:** 8.1
Land: 70.7 sq. mi.; **Water:** 6.9 sq. mi.

Waumandee
Town
Lat: 44-15-57 N **Long:** 91-42-13 W
Pop: 521 (1990); 594 (1980) **Pop Density:** 11.9
Land: 43.8 sq. mi.; **Water:** 0.0 sq. mi.

Burnett County
County Seat: Siren (ZIP: 54872)

Pop: 13,084 (1990); 12,340 (1980) **Pop Density:** 15.9
Land: 821.5 sq. mi.; **Water:** 58.9 sq. mi. **Area Code:** 715
On northwestern border of WI; organized Mar 31, 1856 from Polk County.
Name origin: For Thomas P. Burnett (?–1846), lawyer and WI territorial legislator.

Anderson
Town
Lat: 45-41-59 N **Long:** 92-46-11 W
Pop: 324 (1990); 265 (1980) **Pop Density:** 5.2
Land: 62.8 sq. mi.; **Water:** 1.2 sq. mi.

Blaine
Town
Lat: 46-06-51 N **Long:** 92-10-36 W
Pop: 172 (1990); 151 (1980) **Pop Density:** 2.5
Land: 68.8 sq. mi.; **Water:** 1.4 sq. mi.

Daniels
Town
Lat: 45-46-18 N **Long:** 92-27-57 W
Pop: 602 (1990); 607 (1980) **Pop Density:** 17.9
Land: 33.7 sq. mi.; **Water:** 2.1 sq. mi.

Dewey
Town
Lat: 45-46-31 N **Long:** 92-04-59 W
Pop: 482 (1990); 520 (1980) **Pop Density:** 13.3
Land: 36.3 sq. mi.; **Water:** 0.6 sq. mi.

Grantsburg
Village
ZIP: 54840 **Lat:** 45-46-50 N **Long:** 92-41-04 W
Pop: 1,144 (1990); 1,153 (1980) **Pop Density:** 394.5
Land: 2.9 sq. mi.; **Water:** 0.0 sq. mi.
Incorporated 1887.
Name origin: For Ulysses S. Grant (1822–85), eighteenth U.S. president.

*Grantsburg
Town
ZIP: 54840 **Lat:** 45-45-57 N **Long:** 92-43-14 W
Pop: 860 (1990); 677 (1980) **Pop Density:** 24.1
Land: 35.7 sq. mi.; **Water:** 0.7 sq. mi.

Jackson
Town
Lat: 45-56-32 N **Long:** 92-13-09 W
Pop: 457 (1990); 331 (1980) **Pop Density:** 15.7
Land: 29.1 sq. mi.; **Water:** 5.8 sq. mi.

La Follette
Town
Lat: 45-46-22 N **Long:** 92-13-03 W
Pop: 416 (1990); 388 (1980) **Pop Density:** 11.2
Land: 37.0 sq. mi.; **Water:** 2.0 sq. mi.

Lincoln
Town
Lat: 45-51-21 N **Long:** 92-28-10 W
Pop: 228 (1990); 215 (1980) **Pop Density:** 6.6
Land: 34.8 sq. mi.; **Water:** 0.4 sq. mi.

Meenon
Town
Lat: 45-51-17 N **Long:** 92-20-15 W
Pop: 956 (1990); 838 (1980) **Pop Density:** 29.9
Land: 32.0 sq. mi.; **Water:** 1.4 sq. mi.

Oakland
Town
Lat: 45-56-34 N **Long:** 92-20-39 W
Pop: 480 (1990); 486 (1980) **Pop Density:** 18.5
Land: 26.0 sq. mi.; **Water:** 6.9 sq. mi.

Roosevelt
Town
Lat: 45-41-04 N **Long:** 92-05-41 W
Pop: 175 (1990); 178 (1980) **Pop Density:** 5.0
Land: 35.1 sq. mi.; **Water:** 0.2 sq. mi.

Rusk
Town
Lat: 45-51-50 N **Long:** 92-05-10 W
Pop: 396 (1990); 349 (1980) **Pop Density:** 12.1
Land: 32.6 sq. mi.; **Water:** 2.1 sq. mi.

Sand Lake
Town
Lat: 45-51-40 N **Long:** 92-12-32 W
Pop: 439 (1990); 422 (1980) **Pop Density:** 13.4
Land: 32.8 sq. mi.; **Water:** 3.4 sq. mi.

Scott
Town
Lat: 45-56-39 N **Long:** 92-05-18 W
Pop: 419 (1990); 409 (1980) **Pop Density:** 15.1
Land: 27.7 sq. mi.; **Water:** 6.5 sq. mi.

Siren
Village
ZIP: 54872 **Lat:** 45-47-01 N **Long:** 92-22-47 W
Pop: 863 (1990); 896 (1980) **Pop Density:** 863.0
Land: 1.0 sq. mi.; **Water:** 0.0 sq. mi. **Elev** 996 ft.
Incorporated 1948.
Name origin: From Swedish *syren* 'lilacs,' so named by postmaster Charles F. Segerstrom, because his house was surrounded by the flowers; with a spelling variation.

*Siren
Town
ZIP: 54872 **Lat:** 45-46-09 N **Long:** 92-20-31 W
Pop: 910 (1990); 887 (1980) **Pop Density:** 28.9
Land: 31.5 sq. mi.; **Water:** 4.6 sq. mi.

Swiss
Town
Lat: 46-01-24 N **Long:** 92-17-21 W
Pop: 645 (1990); 587 (1980) **Pop Density:** 11.2
Land: 57.4 sq. mi.; **Water:** 3.3 sq. mi.

Trade Lake
Town
Lat: 45-41-08 N **Long:** 92-35-27 W
Pop: 831 (1990); 824 (1980) **Pop Density:** 25.6
Land: 32.5 sq. mi.; **Water:** 3.0 sq. mi.

Union
Town
Lat: 45-56-31 N **Long:** 92-28-38 W
Pop: 221 (1990); 199 (1980) **Pop Density:** 6.4
Land: 34.5 sq. mi.; **Water:** 3.4 sq. mi.

Webb Lake
Town
Lat: 46-01-58 N **Long:** 92-06-47 W
Pop: 200 (1990); 256 (1980) **Pop Density:** 6.3
Land: 32.0 sq. mi.; **Water:** 4.2 sq. mi.

Webster
Village
ZIP: 54893 **Lat:** 45-52-42 N **Long:** 92-21-43 W
Pop: 623 (1990); 610 (1980) **Pop Density:** 366.5
Land: 1.7 sq. mi.; **Water:** 0.0 sq. mi.
Incorporated 1916.
Name origin: For Noah Webster (1758–1843), the famous lexicographer. Previously called Clam River.

West Marshland
Town
Lat: 45-51-55 N **Long:** 92-37-21 W
Pop: 293 (1990); 209 (1980) **Pop Density:** 4.2
Land: 69.3 sq. mi.; **Water:** 4.1 sq. mi.

Wood River
Town
Lat: 45-46-19 N **Long:** 92-35-15 W
Pop: 948 (1990); 883 (1980) **Pop Density:** 27.8
Land: 34.1 sq. mi.; **Water:** 1.6 sq. mi.

Calumet County
County Seat: Chilton (ZIP: 53014)

Pop: 34,291 (1990); 30,867 (1980) **Pop Density:** 107.2
Land: 319.9 sq. mi.; **Water:** 77.2 sq. mi. **Area Code:** 414
In east-central WI, east of Lake Winnebago; organized Dec 7, 1836 (prior to statehood) from a territorial county.
Name origin: French *chalumet* 'tube' or 'little reed'; extended to the Indians' 'peace pipe.'

Appleton
City
ZIP: 54911 **Lat:** 44-14-12 N **Long:** 88-23-10 W
Pop: 9,075 (1990); 5,484 (1980) **Pop Density:** 4125.0
Land: 2.2 sq. mi.; **Water:** 0.0 sq. mi.
In eastern WI on the Fox River, 17 mi. north of Oshkosh. Incorporated 1857. Part of the town is also in Outagamie and Winnebago counties.
Name origin: For Samuel Appleton, one of the founders of Lawrence University.

Brillion
City
ZIP: 54110 **Lat:** 44-10-36 N **Long:** 88-04-09 W
Pop: 2,840 (1990); 2,907 (1980) **Pop Density:** 1234.8
Land: 2.3 sq. mi.; **Water:** 0.0 sq. mi.
Incorporated 1944.
Name origin: Originally called Brandon but renamed in 1854 because there was already another Brandon in the state.

*Brillion
Town
ZIP: 54110 **Lat:** 44-11-48 N **Long:** 88-06-29 W
Pop: 1,300 (1990); 1,191 (1980) **Pop Density:** 38.7
Land: 33.6 sq. mi.; **Water:** 0.0 sq. mi.

Brothertown
Town
Lat: 43-57-46 N **Long:** 88-16-34 W
Pop: 1,409 (1990); 1,494 (1980) **Pop Density:** 38.3
Land: 36.8 sq. mi.; **Water:** 17.7 sq. mi.

Charlestown
Town
Lat: 44-01-03 N **Long:** 88-06-26 W
Pop: 875 (1990); 1,090 (1980) **Pop Density:** 27.3
Land: 32.1 sq. mi.; **Water:** 0.0 sq. mi.

Chilton
City
ZIP: 53014 **Lat:** 44-01-46 N **Long:** 88-09-52 W
Pop: 3,240 (1990); 2,965 (1980) **Pop Density:** 900.0
Land: 3.6 sq. mi.; **Water:** 0.0 sq. mi. **Elev:** 902 ft.
Incorporated 1877.

Name origin: For John Marygold's home, Chillington, in England, altered in spelling during the recording. Originally known as Chillington.

*Chilton
Town
ZIP: 53014 **Lat:** 44-03-56 N **Long:** 88-11-36 W
Pop: 998 (1990); 1,120 (1980) **Pop Density:** 30.7
Land: 32.5 sq. mi.; **Water:** 0.0 sq. mi.

Harrison
Town
Lat: 44-11-30 N **Long:** 88-19-06 W
Pop: 3,195 (1990); 3,541 (1980) **Pop Density:** 89.7
Land: 35.6 sq. mi.; **Water:** 25.9 sq. mi.

Hilbert
Village
ZIP: 54129 **Lat:** 44-08-24 N **Long:** 88-09-32 W
Pop: 1,211 (1990); 1,176 (1980) **Pop Density:** 1211.0
Land: 1.0 sq. mi.; **Water:** 0.0 sq. mi. **Elev:** 839 ft.
Incorporated 1898.

Name origin: Previously called Hilbert Junction.

Kiel
City
ZIP: 53042 **Lat:** 43-54-53 N **Long:** 88-02-39 W
Pop: 376 (1990); 429 (1980) **Pop Density:** 1253.3
Land: 0.3 sq. mi.; **Water:** 0.0 sq. mi. **Elev:** 933 ft.
Incorporated 1920. Part of the town is also in Manitowoc County.

Name origin: For Col. Belitz's home in Kiel, Germany. Previously called Abel, for first settler D. Abel, and Schleswig.

Menasha
City
ZIP: 54952 **Lat:** 44-13-19 N **Long:** 88-24-00 W
Pop: 73 (1990); 14,728 (1980) **Pop Density:** 243.3
Land: 0.3 sq. mi.; **Water:** 0.0 sq. mi.

In eastern WI on Lake Winnebago and Fox River, 5 mi. south of Appleton. Incorporated 1874. Part of the town is also in Winnebago County.

Name origin: From the Menominee Indian term possibly meaning 'thorn' or 'island.'

New Holstein
City
ZIP: 53061 **Lat:** 43-56-57 N **Long:** 88-05-41 W
Pop: 3,342 (1990); 3,412 (1980) **Pop Density:** 1591.4
Land: 2.1 sq. mi.; **Water:** 0.0 sq. mi. **Elev:** 935 ft.
Incorporated 1926.

Name origin: For the former home of settler Ferdinand Ostenfeld in Schleswig-Holstein, Germany.

*New Holstein
Town
ZIP: 53061 **Lat:** 43-56-05 N **Long:** 88-06-10 W
Pop: 1,406 (1990); 1,527 (1980) **Pop Density:** 43.7
Land: 32.2 sq. mi.; **Water:** 0.1 sq. mi.

Potter
Village
ZIP: 54160 **Lat:** 44-07-10 N **Long:** 88-05-51 W
Pop: 252 (1990) **Pop Density:** 504.0
Land: 0.5 sq. mi.; **Water:** 0.0 sq. mi.
Incorporated 1980.

Rantoul
Town
Lat: 44-06-37 N **Long:** 88-05-59 W
Pop: 895 (1990); 1,184 (1980) **Pop Density:** 27.6
Land: 32.4 sq. mi.; **Water:** 0.1 sq. mi.

Sherwood
Village
ZIP: 54169 **Lat:** 44-10-24 N **Long:** 88-16-30 W
Pop: 837 (1990); 372 (1980) **Pop Density:** 348.8
Land: 2.4 sq. mi.; **Water:** 0.0 sq. mi.
Incorporated 1968.

Name origin: Established 1858. For a Civil War veteran named Sherwood. Formerly called Lima and Nicolai's Corners for settler Steven Nicolai.

Stockbridge
Village
ZIP: 53088 **Lat:** 44-04-26 N **Long:** 88-18-57 W
Pop: 579 (1990); 567 (1980) **Pop Density:** 180.9
Land: 3.2 sq. mi.; **Water:** 0.0 sq. mi.
Incorporated 1908.

Name origin: For the Stockbridge Indians, who migrated from the east coast to this area around 1830.

*Stockbridge
Town
Lat: 44-03-29 N **Long:** 88-19-07 W
Pop: 1,317 (1990); 1,248 (1980) **Pop Density:** 39.0
Land: 33.8 sq. mi.; **Water:** 33.3 sq. mi.

Woodville
Town
Lat: 44-10-46 N **Long:** 88-12-21 W
Pop: 1,071 (1990); 1,160 (1980) **Pop Density:** 32.5
Land: 33.0 sq. mi.; **Water:** 0.0 sq. mi.

Chippewa County
County Seat: Chippewa Falls (ZIP: 54729)

Pop: 52,360 (1990); 52,127 (1980) **Pop Density:** 51.8
Land: 1010.5 sq. mi.; **Water:** 30.9 sq. mi. **Area Code:** 715

In west-central WI, east of St. Paul, MN; organized Feb 3, 1845 (prior to statehood) from Crawford County. (A former county of the same name existed at the time of the 1830 census, covering much of what is now Douglas, Bayfield, Ashland, Iron, and Vilas counties).

Name origin: For the Chippewa River, which flows through it and near whose headwaters lived the Chippewa (properly Ojibway) Indians. Name means 'puckered', and refers to the seam in their moccasins.

Anson Town
Lat: 45-01-13 N Long: 91-16-10 W
Pop: 1,634 (1990); 1,590 (1980) **Pop Density:** 43.7
Land: 37.4 sq. mi.; **Water:** 2.1 sq. mi.

Arthur Town
Lat: 45-04-18 N Long: 91-09-17 W
Pop: 756 (1990); 856 (1980) **Pop Density:** 17.6
Land: 42.9 sq. mi.; **Water:** 0.2 sq. mi.

Auburn Town
Lat: 45-09-34 N Long: 91-36-19 W
Pop: 474 (1990); 456 (1980) **Pop Density:** 13.3
Land: 35.7 sq. mi.; **Water:** 0.0 sq. mi.

Birch Creek Town
Lat: 45-14-18 N Long: 91-13-16 W
Pop: 500 (1990); 540 (1980) **Pop Density:** 11.2
Land: 44.6 sq. mi.; **Water:** 2.1 sq. mi.

Bloomer City
ZIP: 54724 Lat: 45-06-08 N Long: 91-29-26 W
Pop: 3,085 (1990); 3,342 (1980) **Pop Density:** 1285.4
Land: 2.4 sq. mi.; **Water:** 0.1 sq. mi. **Elev:** 1011 ft.
Incorporated 1920.

Name origin: For an IL merchant, Mr. Bloomer, who came to build a sawmill on the Chippewa River and scouted for hay from the nearby prairie. Originally known as Bloomer Prairie.

*Bloomer Town
ZIP: 54724 Lat: 45-10-01 N Long: 91-27-26 W
Pop: 880 (1990); 930 (1980) **Pop Density:** 18.7
Land: 47.1 sq. mi.; **Water:** 0.7 sq. mi.

Boyd Village
ZIP: 54726 Lat: 44-57-12 N Long: 91-02-24 W
Pop: 683 (1990); 660 (1980) **Pop Density:** 379.4
Land: 1.8 sq. mi.; **Water:** 0.0 sq. mi. **Elev:** 1105 ft.
Incorporated 1891.

Name origin: For Mr. Boyd, who surveyed for the railroad around 1893.

Cadott Village
ZIP: 54727 Lat: 44-57-04 N Long: 91-09-04 W
Pop: 1,328 (1990); 1,247 (1980) **Pop Density:** 457.9
Land: 2.9 sq. mi.; **Water:** 0.0 sq. mi. **Elev:** 979 ft.
Incorporated 1895.

Name origin: For Jean Baptiste Cadotte, who ran a trading post near here. Originally known as Cadotte Falls.

Chippewa Falls City
ZIP: 54729 Lat: 44-55-57 N Long: 91-23-28 W
Pop: 12,727 (1990); 12,270 (1980) **Pop Density:** 1298.7
Land: 9.8 sq. mi.; **Water:** 0.6 sq. mi.

In western WI on the Chippewa River, 10 mi. northeast of Eau Claire. Incorporated 1869.

Name origin: For its location at the falls on the river.

Cleveland Town
Lat: 45-09-29 N Long: 91-16-44 W
Pop: 758 (1990); 732 (1980) **Pop Density:** 14.0
Land: 54.1 sq. mi.; **Water:** 2.2 sq. mi.

Colburn Town
Lat: 45-05-29 N Long: 91-00-24 W
Pop: 731 (1990); 760 (1980) **Pop Density:** 11.2
Land: 65.0 sq. mi.; **Water:** 1.3 sq. mi.

Cooks Valley Town
Lat: 45-04-38 N Long: 91-34-58 W
Pop: 594 (1990); 603 (1980) **Pop Density:** 17.3
Land: 34.3 sq. mi.; **Water:** 0.0 sq. mi.

Cornell City
ZIP: 54732 Lat: 45-09-44 N Long: 91-09-08 W
Pop: 1,541 (1990); 1,583 (1980) **Pop Density:** 428.1
Land: 3.6 sq. mi.; **Water:** 0.5 sq. mi.
Incorporated 1956.

Name origin: For Ezra Cornell (1807–74), president of Cornell University, which had large land holdings in WI. Previously called Brunet's Falls for Jean Brunet, who ran a trading post here.

Delmar Town
Lat: 44-58-50 N Long: 91-00-52 W
Pop: 994 (1990); 1,062 (1980) **Pop Density:** 22.9
Land: 43.5 sq. mi.; **Water:** 0.0 sq. mi.

Eagle Point Town
Lat: 45-02-32 N Long: 91-20-15 W
Pop: 2,542 (1990); 2,750 (1980) **Pop Density:** 40.9
Land: 62.1 sq. mi.; **Water:** 5.1 sq. mi.

Eau Claire City
ZIP: 54701 Lat: 44-52-00 N Long: 91-28-18 W
Pop: 1,676 (1990); 1,657 (1980) **Pop Density:** 465.6
Land: 3.6 sq. mi.; **Water:** 0.1 sq. mi.

In western WI on the Chippewa River. Platted 1855. Incorporated 1872. Part of the town is also in Eau Claire County.

Name origin: Named in 1855 for the nearby Eau Claire River; from French 'clear water.'

Edson
Town
ZIP: 54726   Lat: 44-53-45 N   Long: 91-01-19 W
Pop: 913 (1990); 1,061 (1980)   Pop Density: 16.9
Land: 54.0 sq. mi.; Water: 0.0 sq. mi.

Estella
Town
Lat: 45-09-21 N   Long: 91-07-06 W
Pop: 449 (1990); 483 (1980)   Pop Density: 14.1
Land: 31.8 sq. mi.; Water: 0.5 sq. mi.

Goet
Town
Lat: 44-59-18 N   Long: 91-09-05 W
Pop: 640 (1990); 607 (1980)   Pop Density: 21.4
Land: 29.9 sq. mi.; Water: 0.0 sq. mi.

Hallie
Town
Lat: 44-52-57 N   Long: 91-23-52 W
Pop: 4,531 (1990); 4,275 (1980)   Pop Density: 208.8
Land: 21.7 sq. mi.; Water: 0.5 sq. mi.

Howard
Town
Lat: 44-59-03 N   Long: 91-35-16 W
Pop: 625 (1990); 660 (1980)   Pop Density: 17.5
Land: 35.8 sq. mi.; Water: 0.0 sq. mi.

Lafayette
Town
Lat: 44-54-22 N   Long: 91-16-54 W
Pop: 4,448 (1990); 4,181 (1980)   Pop Density: 128.2
Land: 34.7 sq. mi.; Water: 4.5 sq. mi.

Lake Holcombe
Town
ZIP: 54745   Lat: 45-14-52 N   Long: 91-06-06 W
Pop: 920 (1990); 791 (1980)   Pop Density: 34.2
Land: 26.9 sq. mi.; Water: 3.7 sq. mi.

Lake Wissota
CDP
Lat: 44-55-12 N   Long: 91-18-09 W
Pop: 2,175 (1990); 1,788 (1980)   Pop Density: 572.4
Land: 3.8 sq. mi.; Water: 0.6 sq. mi.

New Auburn
Village
ZIP: 54757   Lat: 45-11-53 N   Long: 91-33-54 W
Pop: 459 (1990); 452 (1980)   Pop Density: 143.4
Land: 3.2 sq. mi.; Water: 0.0 sq. mi.
Incorporated 1902. Part of the town is also in Barron County.
Name origin: Previously called Cartwright's Mills and Cartwright.

Ruby
Town
Lat: 45-14-17 N   Long: 90-59-02 W
Pop: 464 (1990); 514 (1980)   Pop Density: 8.7
Land: 53.5 sq. mi.; Water: 0.1 sq. mi.

Sampson
Town
Lat: 45-14-51 N   Long: 91-25-18 W
Pop: 817 (1990); 805 (1980)   Pop Density: 13.1
Land: 62.5 sq. mi.; Water: 5.7 sq. mi.

Sigel
Town
Lat: 44-54-09 N   Long: 91-10-20 W
Pop: 736 (1990); 782 (1980)   Pop Density: 20.3
Land: 36.2 sq. mi.; Water: 0.1 sq. mi.

Stanley
City
ZIP: 54768   Lat: 44-57-45 N   Long: 90-56-33 W
Pop: 2,011 (1990); 2,095 (1980)   Pop Density: 670.3
Land: 3.0 sq. mi.; Water: 0.1 sq. mi.
Platted 1881; incorporated 1898.
Name origin: For L.C. Stanley of the Northwest Lumber Company.

Tilden
Town
Lat: 44-59-41 N   Long: 91-28-06 W
Pop: 1,079 (1990); 1,088 (1980)   Pop Density: 30.0
Land: 36.0 sq. mi.; Water: 0.1 sq. mi.

Wheaton
Town
Lat: 44-54-11 N   Long: 91-33-32 W
Pop: 2,279 (1990); 2,328 (1980)   Pop Density: 41.5
Land: 54.9 sq. mi.; Water: 0.4 sq. mi.

Woodmohr
Town
Lat: 45-04-40 N   Long: 91-27-50 W
Pop: 1,086 (1990); 967 (1980)   Pop Density: 30.6
Land: 35.5 sq. mi.; Water: 0.1 sq. mi.

Clark County
County Seat: Neillsville (ZIP: 54456)

Pop: 31,647 (1990); 32,910 (1980)   Pop Density: 26.0
Land: 1215.7 sq. mi.; Water: 3.4 sq. mi.   Area Code: 715
In west-central WI; organized 1853 from Marathon County.
Name origin: For Gen. George Rogers Clark (1752–1818), officer in the Revolutionary War and frontiersman in the Northwest Territory.

Abbotsford
City
ZIP: 54405   Lat: 44-56-56 N   Long: 90-19-38 W
Pop: 1,409 (1990); 1,401 (1980)   Pop Density: 1280.9
Land: 1.1 sq. mi.; Water: 0.0 sq. mi.
Incorporated 1965. Part of the town is also in Marathon County.
Name origin: For Edwin H. Abbot, an official of the Wisconsin Central Railway.

Beaver
Town
Lat: 44-48-36 N   Long: 90-30-00 W
Pop: 703 (1990); 777 (1980)   Pop Density: 19.5
Land: 36.1 sq. mi.; Water: 0.0 sq. mi.

Butler
Town
Lat: 44-48-52 N   Long: 90-51-33 W
Pop: 91 (1990); 81 (1980)   Pop Density: 2.5
Land: 36.0 sq. mi.; Water: 0.0 sq. mi.

WISCONSIN, Clark County

Colby
City
ZIP: 54421　　Lat: 44-54-41 N　Long: 90-19-16 W
Pop: 1,116 (1990); 1,151 (1980)　Pop Density: 1395.0
Land: 0.8 sq. mi.; Water: 0.0 sq. mi.　Elev: 1350 ft.
Incorporated 1891. Part of the town is also in Marathon County.
Name origin: For Charles L. Colby, president of the Wisconsin Central Railroad.

*Colby
Town
ZIP: 54421　　Lat: 44-53-41 N　Long: 90-22-51 W
Pop: 846 (1990); 800 (1980)　Pop Density: 25.0
Land: 33.8 sq. mi.; Water: 0.0 sq. mi.

Curtiss
Village
ZIP: 54422　　Lat: 44-57-13 N　Long: 90-26-06 W
Pop: 173 (1990); 127 (1980)　Pop Density: 247.1
Land: 0.7 sq. mi.; Water: 0.0 sq. mi.
Incorporated 1917.
Name origin: Named in 1882 for Charles Curtiss, civil engineer for the railroad. Previously called Quar.

Dewhurst
Town
Lat: 44-27-44 N　Long: 90-44-08 W
Pop: 197 (1990); 132 (1980)　Pop Density: 3.6
Land: 35.4 sq. mi.; Water: 0.7 sq. mi.

Dorchester
Village
ZIP: 54425　　Lat: 45-00-08 N　Long: 90-20-00 W
Pop: 697 (1990); 613 (1980)　Pop Density: 580.8
Land: 1.2 sq. mi.; Water: 0.0 sq. mi.
Incorporated 1901.

Eaton
Town
ZIP: 54437　　Lat: 44-43-19 N　Long: 90-37-21 W
Pop: 640 (1990); 663 (1980)　Pop Density: 18.8
Land: 34.0 sq. mi.; Water: 0.1 sq. mi.

Foster
Town
Lat: 44-40-06 N　Long: 90-51-51 W
Pop: 85 (1990); 111 (1980)　Pop Density: 1.2
Land: 71.3 sq. mi.; Water: 0.2 sq. mi.

Fremont
Town
Lat: 44-38-30 N　Long: 90-22-54 W
Pop: 963 (1990); 982 (1980)　Pop Density: 27.4
Land: 35.2 sq. mi.; Water: 0.0 sq. mi.

Grant
Town
ZIP: 54436　　Lat: 44-32-35 N　Long: 90-30-18 W
Pop: 890 (1990); 882 (1980)　Pop Density: 24.9
Land: 35.8 sq. mi.; Water: 0.0 sq. mi.

Granton
Village
ZIP: 54436　　Lat: 44-35-18 N　Long: 90-27-43 W
Pop: 379 (1990); 399 (1980)　Pop Density: 758.0
Land: 0.5 sq. mi.; Water: 0.0 sq. mi.
Incorporated 1916.
Name origin: For Grant township, which was named for Ulysses S. Grant (1822–85), eighteenth U.S. president.

Green Grove
Town
ZIP: 54460　　Lat: 44-53-54 N　Long: 90-29-49 W
Pop: 628 (1990); 678 (1980)　Pop Density: 17.2
Land: 36.5 sq. mi.; Water: 0.0 sq. mi.

Greenwood
City
ZIP: 54437　　Lat: 44-45-55 N　Long: 90-35-55 W
Pop: 969 (1990); 1,124 (1980)　Pop Density: 372.7
Land: 2.6 sq. mi.; Water: 0.0 sq. mi.　Elev: 1168 ft.
Incorporated 1891.
Name origin: For the numerous pine and hardwood trees in the area.

Hendren
Town
ZIP: 54493　　Lat: 44-43-40 N　Long: 90-44-22 W
Pop: 542 (1990); 570 (1980)　Pop Density: 15.1
Land: 35.8 sq. mi.; Water: 0.0 sq. mi.

Hewett
Town
Lat: 44-33-05 N　Long: 90-44-10 W
Pop: 314 (1990); 301 (1980)　Pop Density: 8.8
Land: 35.8 sq. mi.; Water: 0.0 sq. mi.

Hixon
Town
Lat: 44-59-25 N　Long: 90-37-05 W
Pop: 673 (1990); 810 (1980)　Pop Density: 20.1
Land: 33.5 sq. mi.; Water: 0.4 sq. mi.

Hoard
Town
ZIP: 54422　　Lat: 44-59-25 N　Long: 90-29-15 W
Pop: 805 (1990); 881 (1980)　Pop Density: 22.8
Land: 35.3 sq. mi.; Water: 0.0 sq. mi.

Levis
Town
Lat: 44-27-51 N　Long: 90-37-29 W
Pop: 492 (1990); 433 (1980)　Pop Density: 13.7
Land: 35.9 sq. mi.; Water: 0.3 sq. mi.

Longwood
Town
ZIP: 54498　　Lat: 44-54-16 N　Long: 90-36-29 W
Pop: 661 (1990); 673 (1980)　Pop Density: 18.4
Land: 35.9 sq. mi.; Water: 0.0 sq. mi.

Loyal
City
ZIP: 54446　　Lat: 44-44-10 N　Long: 90-29-47 W
Pop: 1,244 (1990); 1,252 (1980)　Pop Density: 956.9
Land: 1.3 sq. mi.; Water: 0.0 sq. mi.
Incorporated 1948.
Name origin: For the townsmen who fought in the Civil War, every eligible one of which, it is claimed, enlisted.

*Loyal
Town
ZIP: 54446　　Lat: 44-43-22 N　Long: 90-30-22 W
Pop: 718 (1990); 882 (1980)　Pop Density: 20.6
Land: 34.8 sq. mi.; Water: 0.0 sq. mi.

Lynn
Town
ZIP: 54436　　Lat: 44-33-19 N　Long: 90-21-50 W
Pop: 703 (1990); 587 (1980)　Pop Density: 19.8
Land: 35.5 sq. mi.; Water: 0.1 sq. mi.

Mayville
Town
Lat: 44-59-21 N　Long: 90-22-24 W
Pop: 932 (1990); 962 (1980)　Pop Density: 28.7
Land: 32.5 sq. mi.; Water: 0.1 sq. mi.

Mead
Town
Lat: 44-49-17 N　Long: 90-44-13 W
Pop: 249 (1990); 303 (1980)　Pop Density: 7.1
Land: 35.1 sq. mi.; Water: 0.5 sq. mi.

Mentor
Town
Lat: 44-33-18 N　Long: 90-52-00 W
Pop: 521 (1990); 596 (1980)　Pop Density: 14.6
Land: 35.7 sq. mi.; Water: 0.1 sq. mi.

Neillsville   City
ZIP: 54456   Lat: 44-33-37 N   Long: 90-35-27 W
Pop: 2,680 (1990); 2,780 (1980)   Pop Density: 992.6
Land: 2.7 sq. mi.; Water: 0.0 sq. mi.
Incorporated 1882.
Name origin: For James O'Neill, who ran a sawmill here. Originally known as O'Neill's Mills.

Owen   City
ZIP: 54460   Lat: 44-56-57 N   Long: 90-34-04 W
Pop: 895 (1990); 998 (1980)   Pop Density: 526.5
Land: 1.7 sq. mi.; Water: 0.0 sq. mi.   Elev: 1245 ft.
Incorporated 1925.

Pine Valley   Town
Lat: 44-33-20 N   Long: 90-37-06 W
Pop: 1,032 (1990); 1,137 (1980)   Pop Density: 30.9
Land: 33.4 sq. mi.; Water: 0.2 sq. mi.

Reseburg   Town
Lat: 44-53-51 N   Long: 90-44-27 W
Pop: 687 (1990); 761 (1980)   Pop Density: 19.1
Land: 35.9 sq. mi.; Water: 0.0 sq. mi.

Seif   Town
Lat: 44-37-58 N   Long: 90-43-46 W
Pop: 211 (1990); 254 (1980)   Pop Density: 5.9
Land: 36.0 sq. mi.; Water: 0.0 sq. mi.

Sherman   Town
Lat: 44-43-46 N   Long: 90-22-49 W
Pop: 736 (1990); 766 (1980)   Pop Density: 21.0
Land: 35.0 sq. mi.; Water: 0.0 sq. mi.

Sherwood   Town
Lat: 44-27-43 N   Long: 90-22-14 W
Pop: 195 (1990); 173 (1980)   Pop Density: 5.5
Land: 35.7 sq. mi.; Water: 0.2 sq. mi.

Thorp   City
ZIP: 54771   Lat: 44-57-35 N   Long: 90-48-03 W
Pop: 1,657 (1990); 1,635 (1980)   Pop Density: 1506.4
Land: 1.1 sq. mi.; Water: 0.0 sq. mi.
Incorporated 1948.

*Thorp   Town
ZIP: 54771   Lat: 44-59-04 N   Long: 90-51-27 W
Pop: 710 (1990); 743 (1980)   Pop Density: 20.1
Land: 35.4 sq. mi.; Water: 0.0 sq. mi.

Unity   Town
Lat: 44-48-50 N   Long: 90-22-31 W
Pop: 735 (1990); 815 (1980)   Pop Density: 21.1
Land: 34.8 sq. mi.; Water: 0.0 sq. mi.

*Unity   Village
Lat: 44-51-07 N   Long: 90-19-01 W
Pop: 196 (1990); 166 (1980)   Pop Density: 490.0
Land: 0.4 sq. mi.; Water: 0.0 sq. mi.
Incorporated 1903. Part of the town is also in Marathon County.
Name origin: Named by Mrs. Edmund Creed for the fact that the community was very united.

Warner   Town
Lat: 44-48-38 N   Long: 90-36-57 W
Pop: 599 (1990); 668 (1980)   Pop Density: 17.2
Land: 34.9 sq. mi.; Water: 0.1 sq. mi.

Washburn   Town
Lat: 44-27-35 N   Long: 90-29-34 W
Pop: 310 (1990); 276 (1980)   Pop Density: 8.5
Land: 36.3 sq. mi.; Water: 0.1 sq. mi.

Weston   Town
Lat: 44-38-19 N   Long: 90-36-46 W
Pop: 662 (1990); 646 (1980)   Pop Density: 18.3
Land: 36.1 sq. mi.; Water: 0.1 sq. mi.

Withee   Village
ZIP: 54498   Lat: 44-57-10 N   Long: 90-35-49 W
Pop: 503 (1990); 509 (1980)   Pop Density: 838.3
Land: 0.6 sq. mi.; Water: 0.0 sq. mi.   Elev: 1272 ft.
Incorporated 1901.
Name origin: For Niran H. Withee, a school teacher who was influential in village affairs.

*Withee   Town
ZIP: 54498   Lat: 44-59-26 N   Long: 90-43-51 W
Pop: 767 (1990); 859 (1980)   Pop Density: 21.8
Land: 35.2 sq. mi.; Water: 0.0 sq. mi.

Worden   Town
Lat: 44-53-53 N   Long: 90-51-18 W
Pop: 575 (1990); 650 (1980)   Pop Density: 15.9
Land: 36.1 sq. mi.; Water: 0.0 sq. mi.

York   Town
ZIP: 54436   Lat: 44-38-37 N   Long: 90-30-06 W
Pop: 857 (1990); 903 (1980)   Pop Density: 23.7
Land: 36.1 sq. mi.; Water: 0.0 sq. mi.

Columbia County
County Seat: Portage (ZIP: 53901)

Pop: 45,088 (1990); 43,222 (1980)
Land: 773.9 sq. mi.; **Water:** 21.9 sq. mi.
Pop Density: 58.3
Area Code: 608

In south-central WI, northwest of Milwaukee; organized Feb 3, 1846 (prior to statehood) from Portage, Brown, and Crawford counties.

Name origin: Feminine form of Columbus, a poetic and honorific reference to Christopher Columbus (1451–1506) and America.

Arlington — Village
ZIP: 53911 **Lat:** 43-20-18 N **Long:** 89-22-35 W
Pop: 440 (1990); 440 (1980) **Pop Density:** 1466.7
Land: 0.3 sq. mi.; **Water:** 0.0 sq. mi. **Elev:** 1052 ft.
Settled c. 1838. Incorporated 1945.

*Arlington — Town
ZIP: 53911 **Lat:** 43-20-07 N **Long:** 89-24-47 W
Pop: 748 (1990); 752 (1980) **Pop Density:** 21.0
Land: 35.6 sq. mi.; **Water:** 0.0 sq. mi.

Caledonia — Town
Lat: 43-28-39 N **Long:** 89-31-49 W
Pop: 1,031 (1990); 923 (1980) **Pop Density:** 17.3
Land: 59.5 sq. mi.; **Water:** 4.1 sq. mi.

Cambria — Village
ZIP: 53923 **Lat:** 43-32-27 N **Long:** 89-06-49 W
Pop: 768 (1990); 680 (1980) **Pop Density:** 960.0
Land: 0.8 sq. mi.; **Water:** 0.0 sq. mi. **Elev:** 868 ft.
Incorporated 1866.

Name origin: Named c. 1851 by Welsh settlers for the old Roman name for Wales. Originally known as Langdon's Saw Mill, Florence, and Bellville.

Columbus — City
ZIP: 53925 **Lat:** 43-20-09 N **Long:** 89-01-47 W
Pop: 4,083 (1990); 4,049 (1980) **Pop Density:** 1103.5
Land: 3.7 sq. mi.; **Water:** 0.0 sq. mi. **Elev:** 871 ft.
Incorporated 1874. Part of the town is also in Dodge County.

Name origin: Named by Maj. Dickason, one of the first white men in the area, probably for Christopher Columbus (1451–1506).

*Columbus — Town
ZIP: 53925 **Lat:** 43-19-32 N **Long:** 89-04-44 W
Pop: 838 (1990); 704 (1980) **Pop Density:** 26.0
Land: 32.2 sq. mi.; **Water:** 0.0 sq. mi.

Courtland — Town
Lat: 43-29-51 N **Long:** 89-03-31 W
Pop: 528 (1990); 601 (1980) **Pop Density:** 15.0
Land: 35.3 sq. mi.; **Water:** 0.1 sq. mi.

Dekorra — Town
Lat: 43-25-04 N **Long:** 89-26-42 W
Pop: 1,829 (1990); 1,914 (1980) **Pop Density:** 44.4
Land: 41.2 sq. mi.; **Water:** 3.8 sq. mi.

Doylestown — Village
ZIP: 53928 **Lat:** 43-25-39 N **Long:** 89-08-46 W
Pop: 316 (1990); 294 (1980) **Pop Density:** 81.0
Land: 3.9 sq. mi.; **Water:** 0.1 sq. mi.
Platted 1865. Incorporated 1907.

Name origin: For Lemuel H. Doyle, who bought land here. Previously called Ostego by settlers from Ostego, NY.

Fall River — Village
ZIP: 53932 **Lat:** 43-23-06 N **Long:** 89-02-51 W
Pop: 842 (1990); 850 (1980) **Pop Density:** 647.7
Land: 1.3 sq. mi.; **Water:** 0.0 sq. mi. **Elev:** 858 ft.
Incorporated 1903.

Name origin: Named by settler Alfred Brayton for the hometown of his father's family in Fall River, MA.

Fort Winnebago — Town
Lat: 43-36-39 N **Long:** 89-25-00 W
Pop: 825 (1990); 860 (1980) **Pop Density:** 24.6
Land: 33.5 sq. mi.; **Water:** 0.5 sq. mi.

Fountain Prairie — Town
Lat: 43-24-56 N **Long:** 89-03-31 W
Pop: 743 (1990); 771 (1980) **Pop Density:** 21.3
Land: 34.9 sq. mi.; **Water:** 0.3 sq. mi.

Friesland — Village
ZIP: 53935 **Lat:** 43-35-20 N **Long:** 89-04-03 W
Pop: 271 (1990); 267 (1980) **Pop Density:** 271.0
Land: 1.0 sq. mi.; **Water:** 0.0 sq. mi.
Incorporated 1946.

Name origin: Previously called Randolph Center, because it was at the center of Randolph township. Renamed by Dutch settlers for the province of Friesland in Holland.

Hampden — Town
Lat: 43-19-13 N **Long:** 89-11-12 W
Pop: 566 (1990); 650 (1980) **Pop Density:** 15.9
Land: 35.7 sq. mi.; **Water:** 0.0 sq. mi.

Lake Wisconsin — CDP
Lat: 43-22-24 N **Long:** 89-34-31 W
Pop: 2,178 (1990) **Pop Density:** 177.1
Land: 12.3 sq. mi.; **Water:** 8.7 sq. mi.
Part of the town is also in Sauk County.

Leeds — Town
Lat: 43-19-16 N **Long:** 89-17-42 W
Pop: 809 (1990); 845 (1980) **Pop Density:** 22.8
Land: 35.5 sq. mi.; **Water:** 0.3 sq. mi.

Lewiston — Town
Lat: 43-35-54 N **Long:** 89-33-55 W
Pop: 1,123 (1990); 1,122 (1980) **Pop Density:** 20.8
Land: 54.0 sq. mi.; **Water:** 1.0 sq. mi.

Lodi — City
ZIP: 53555 **Lat:** 43-18-59 N **Long:** 89-31-55 W
Pop: 2,093 (1990); 1,959 (1980) **Pop Density:** 1744.2
Land: 1.2 sq. mi.; **Water:** 0.0 sq. mi. **Elev:** 833 ft.
Incorporated 1941.

Name origin: Possibly for Lodi, Italy, or Lodi, NY.

WISCONSIN, Columbia County

*Lodi
Town
ZIP: 53555 Lat: 43-20-18 N Long: 89-32-11 W
Pop: 1,913 (1990); 1,855 (1980) Pop Density: 70.1
Land: 27.3 sq. mi.; Water: 1.8 sq. mi.

Lowville
Town
Lat: 43-24-21 N Long: 89-18-26 W
Pop: 938 (1990); 976 (1980) Pop Density: 27.3
Land: 34.4 sq. mi.; Water: 1.5 sq. mi. Elev: 967 ft.

Marcellon
Town
Lat: 43-35-57 N Long: 89-18-37 W
Pop: 880 (1990); 809 (1980) Pop Density: 24.8
Land: 35.5 sq. mi.; Water: 0.3 sq. mi.

Newport
Town
Lat: 43-36-27 N Long: 89-42-32 W
Pop: 536 (1990); 657 (1980) Pop Density: 24.9
Land: 21.5 sq. mi.; Water: 0.6 sq. mi.

Otsego
Town
Lat: 43-24-16 N Long: 89-11-15 W
Pop: 647 (1990); 767 (1980) Pop Density: 21.2
Land: 30.5 sq. mi.; Water: 0.5 sq. mi.

Pacific
Town
Lat: 43-30-42 N Long: 89-24-12 W
Pop: 1,944 (1990); 1,215 (1980) Pop Density: 95.8
Land: 20.3 sq. mi.; Water: 1.3 sq. mi.

Pardeeville
Village
ZIP: 53954 Lat: 43-32-02 N Long: 89-18-01 W
Pop: 1,630 (1990); 1,594 (1980) Pop Density: 815.0
Land: 2.0 sq. mi.; Water: 0.3 sq. mi. Elev: 815 ft.
Incorporated 1894.
Name origin: For Milwaukee merchant John S. Pardee, who was the U.S. consul to San Juan del Sur, Nicaragua.

Portage
City
ZIP: 53901 Lat: 43-32-52 N Long: 89-27-57 W
Pop: 8,640 (1990); 7,896 (1980) Pop Density: 1053.7
Land: 8.2 sq. mi.; Water: 0.7 sq. mi.
Incorporated 1854.
Name origin: Named by the French for its importance as a portage from the Fox to the Wisconsin rivers.

Poynette
Village
ZIP: 53955 Lat: 43-23-27 N Long: 89-24-29 W
Pop: 1,662 (1990); 1,447 (1980) Pop Density: 692.5
Land: 2.4 sq. mi.; Water: 0.0 sq. mi. Elev: 847 ft.
Incorporated 1892.
Name origin: From a post office corruption of Pauquette, for Pierre Pauquette, an Indian interpreter and trader.

Randolph
Village
ZIP: 53956 Lat: 43-32-25 N Long: 89-00-34 W
Pop: 502 (1990); 485 (1980) Pop Density: 2510.0
Land: 0.2 sq. mi.; Water: 0.0 sq. mi. Elev: 964 ft.
Incorporated 1870. Part of the town is also in Dodge County.
Name origin: For Randolph, VT. Previously called LeRoy; Conversville for settler Jon Converse; and Westford.

*Randolph
Town
ZIP: 53956 Lat: 43-34-48 N Long: 89-03-41 W
Pop: 676 (1990); 700 (1980) Pop Density: 19.2
Land: 35.3 sq. mi.; Water: 0.0 sq. mi.

Rio
Village
ZIP: 53960 Lat: 43-27-00 N Long: 89-14-15 W
Pop: 768 (1990); 785 (1980) Pop Density: 698.2
Land: 1.1 sq. mi.; Water: 0.0 sq. mi. Elev: 974 ft.
Incorporated 1887.

Scott
Town
Lat: 43-36-23 N Long: 89-11-21 W
Pop: 639 (1990); 602 (1980) Pop Density: 17.8
Land: 35.8 sq. mi.; Water: 0.0 sq. mi.

Springvale
Town
Lat: 43-30-09 N Long: 89-11-22 W
Pop: 466 (1990); 521 (1980) Pop Density: 11.4
Land: 41.0 sq. mi.; Water: 0.0 sq. mi.

West Point
Town
Lat: 43-19-33 N Long: 89-38-43 W
Pop: 1,285 (1990); 1,122 (1980) Pop Density: 44.5
Land: 28.9 sq. mi.; Water: 3.6 sq. mi.

Wisconsin Dells
City
ZIP: 53965 Lat: 43-37-30 N Long: 89-45-54 W
Pop: 2,261 (1990); 2,337 (1980) Pop Density: 1076.7
Land: 2.1 sq. mi.; Water: 0.1 sq. mi. Elev: 912 ft.
Incorporated 1925. Part of the town is also in Sauk and Adams counties.
Name origin: Named in 1931 for its descriptive connotations. Previously called Kilbourn, for Byron Kilbourne.

Wyocena
Village
ZIP: 53969 Lat: 43-29-35 N Long: 89-18-36 W
Pop: 620 (1990); 548 (1980) Pop Density: 442.9
Land: 1.4 sq. mi.; Water: 0.1 sq. mi. Elev: 826 ft.
Incorporated 1909.
Name origin: From a Potawatomi Indian term probably meaning 'somebody else,' the name was said to have belonged to an Indian girl in a dream Maj. Dickason, an early settler, had.

*Wyocena
Town
Lat: 43-29-58 N Long: 89-17-40 W
Pop: 1,228 (1990); 1,225 (1980) Pop Density: 33.8
Land: 36.3 sq. mi.; Water: 0.8 sq. mi.

Crawford County
County Seat: Prairie du Chien (ZIP: 53821)

Pop: 15,940 (1990); 16,556 (1980)   **Pop Density:** 27.8
Land: 572.8 sq. mi.; **Water:** 26.5 sq. mi.   **Area Code:** 608

On southwestern border of WI; organized Oct 26, 1818 (prior to statehood) from a territorial county.

Name origin: For Fort Crawford, or possibly for William Harris Crawford (1772–1834), U.S. senator from GA (1807-13), U.S. secretary of war (1815–16), and U.S. secretary of the treasury (1816–25).

Bell Center   Village
ZIP: 54631   **Lat:** 43-17-31 N   **Long:** 90-49-31 W
Pop: 127 (1990); 124 (1980)   **Pop Density:** 23.1
Land: 5.5 sq. mi.; **Water:** 0.0 sq. mi.
Incorporated 1901.
Name origin: For resident Daniel Bell and for its central location in the township.

Bridgeport   Town
Lat: 43-01-06 N   **Long:** 91-04-54 W
Pop: 753 (1990); 708 (1980)   **Pop Density:** 36.0
Land: 20.9 sq. mi.; **Water:** 3.0 sq. mi.

Clayton   Town
Lat: 43-21-27 N   **Long:** 90-44-48 W
Pop: 794 (1990); 927 (1980)   **Pop Density:** 11.5
Land: 69.2 sq. mi.; **Water:** 0.0 sq. mi.
Part of the town is also in Vernon County.

De Soto   Village
Lat: 43-25-09 N   **Long:** 91-11-40 W
Pop: 73 (1990); 66 (1980)   **Pop Density:** 243.3
Land: 0.3 sq. mi.; **Water:** 0.0 sq. mi.
Incorporated 1886. Part of the town is also in Vernon County.
Name origin: For Hernando de Soto (c. 1500–42), the Spanish explorer who discovered the Mississippi River. Originally known as Winneshiek's Landing for a Winnebago Indian chief.

Eastman   Village
ZIP: 54626   **Lat:** 43-09-44 N   **Long:** 91-01-13 W
Pop: 369 (1990); 371 (1980)   **Pop Density:** 102.5
Land: 3.6 sq. mi.; **Water:** 0.0 sq. mi.   **Elev:** 1224 ft.
Incorporated 1909.
Name origin: For the surname of several residents. Previously called Batavia.

*Eastman   Town
ZIP: 54626   **Lat:** 43-09-10 N   **Long:** 91-00-32 W
Pop: 745 (1990); 840 (1980)   **Pop Density:** 10.4
Land: 71.5 sq. mi.; **Water:** 1.1 sq. mi.

Ferryville   Village
ZIP: 54628   **Lat:** 43-20-35 N   **Long:** 91-05-00 W
Pop: 154 (1990); 227 (1980)   **Pop Density:** 61.6
Land: 2.5 sq. mi.; **Water:** 0.0 sq. mi.   **Elev:** 634 ft.
Incorporated 1912.
Name origin: For the ferry service begun here where settlers often crossed the Mississippi River. Previously called Big Landing or Landing.

Freeman   Town
Lat: 43-22-30 N   **Long:** 91-04-58 W
Pop: 692 (1990); 796 (1980)   **Pop Density:** 10.1
Land: 68.2 sq. mi.; **Water:** 9.5 sq. mi.

Gays Mills   Village
ZIP: 54631   **Lat:** 43-19-12 N   **Long:** 90-51-01 W
Pop: 578 (1990); 627 (1980)   **Pop Density:** 125.7
Land: 4.6 sq. mi.; **Water:** 0.0 sq. mi.
Incorporated 1900.
Name origin: For James Gay, a settler from VA who built a sawmill here around 1848.

Haney   Town
Lat: 43-14-29 N   **Long:** 90-51-09 W
Pop: 384 (1990); 404 (1980)   **Pop Density:** 11.7
Land: 32.7 sq. mi.; **Water:** 0.0 sq. mi.

Lynxville   Village
ZIP: 54640   **Lat:** 43-14-52 N   **Long:** 91-02-52 W
Pop: 153 (1990); 174 (1980)   **Pop Density:** 109.3
Land: 1.4 sq. mi.; **Water:** 0.0 sq. mi.   **Elev:** 638 ft.
Incorporated 1899.
Name origin: For the steamboat, *Lynx*, on which surveyors arrived to lay out the village.

Marietta   Town
Lat: 43-09-23 N   **Long:** 90-47-02 W
Pop: 532 (1990); 568 (1980)   **Pop Density:** 11.3
Land: 47.0 sq. mi.; **Water:** 1.0 sq. mi.

Mount Sterling   Village
ZIP: 54645   **Lat:** 43-18-51 N   **Long:** 90-55-50 W
Pop: 217 (1990); 223 (1980)   **Pop Density:** 155.0
Land: 1.4 sq. mi.; **Water:** 0.0 sq. mi.
Incorporated 1936.
Name origin: For settler William Sterling, and for the high hill north of the village.

Prairie du Chien   City
ZIP: 53821   **Lat:** 43-02-35 N   **Long:** 91-08-23 W
Pop: 5,659 (1990); 5,859 (1980)   **Pop Density:** 1286.1
Land: 4.4 sq. mi.; **Water:** 0.7 sq. mi.   **Elev:** 632 ft.
Incorporated 1872.
Name origin: From French 'dog's prairie' for Fox Indian chief, Dog.

*Prairie du Chien   Town
ZIP: 53821   **Lat:** 43-04-21 N   **Long:** 91-06-27 W
Pop: 927 (1990); 694 (1980)   **Pop Density:** 27.1
Land: 34.2 sq. mi.; **Water:** 2.8 sq. mi.

Scott   Town
Lat: 43-15-03 N   **Long:** 90-43-39 W
Pop: 453 (1990); 472 (1980)   **Pop Density:** 12.7
Land: 35.7 sq. mi.; **Water:** 0.0 sq. mi.

Seneca
Town
Lat: 43-15-51 N **Long:** 90-59-39 W
Pop: 873 (1990); 832 (1980) **Pop Density:** 14.9
Land: 58.6 sq. mi.; **Water:** 6.9 sq. mi.

Soldiers Grove
Village
ZIP: 54655 **Lat:** 43-23-32 N **Long:** 90-46-24 W
Pop: 564 (1990); 622 (1980) **Pop Density:** 156.7
Land: 3.6 sq. mi.; **Water:** 0.0 sq. mi.
Incorporated 1888.

Name origin: Originally known as Pine Grove, the name was changed because there was already another Pine Grove in the state.

Steuben
Village
ZIP: 54657 **Lat:** 43-10-52 N **Long:** 90-51-26 W
Pop: 161 (1990); 175 (1980) **Pop Density:** 26.0
Land: 6.2 sq. mi.; **Water:** 0.0 sq. mi. **Elev:** 675 ft.
Incorporated 1900.

Name origin: For Prussian Baron Friedrich von Steuben (1730–94), who trained and fought with the Americans during the Revolutionary War. Previously called Farris' Landing.

Utica
Town
Lat: 43-22-04 N **Long:** 90-54-13 W
Pop: 738 (1990); 822 (1980) **Pop Density:** 13.6
Land: 54.2 sq. mi.; **Water:** 0.0 sq. mi.

Wauzeka
Village
ZIP: 53826 **Lat:** 43-05-03 N **Long:** 90-53-43 W
Pop: 595 (1990); 580 (1980) **Pop Density:** 124.0
Land: 4.8 sq. mi.; **Water:** 0.0 sq. mi. **Elev:** 657 ft.
Incorporated 1890.

Name origin: Probably for Wauzega, an Indian who lived in the area. The name may mean either 'white pine' or 'wrinkled.'

*Wauzeka
Town
ZIP: 53826 **Lat:** 43-04-58 N **Long:** 90-55-51 W
Pop: 399 (1990); 445 (1980) **Pop Density:** 9.4
Land: 42.4 sq. mi.; **Water:** 1.4 sq. mi.

Dane County
County Seat: Madison (ZIP: 53709)

Pop: 367,085 (1990); 323,545 (1980) **Pop Density:** 305.4
Land: 1202.2 sq. mi.; **Water:** 36.3 sq. mi. **Area Code:** 608

In south-central WI, west of Milwaukee; organized Dec 7, 1836 (prior to statehood) from Iowa County.

Name origin: For Nathan Dane (1725–1835), U.S. representative from MA (1782–85) who proposed the Ordinance of 1787 establishing the Northwest Territory.

Albion
Town
Lat: 42-53-30 N **Long:** 89-04-44 W
Pop: 1,964 (1990); 1,918 (1980) **Pop Density:** 55.2
Land: 35.6 sq. mi.; **Water:** 0.6 sq. mi.

Belleville
Village
ZIP: 53508 **Lat:** 42-51-42 N **Long:** 89-32-11 W
Pop: 1,349 (1990); 1,203 (1980) **Pop Density:** 1498.9
Land: 0.9 sq. mi.; **Water:** 0.2 sq. mi. **Elev:** 870 ft.
Founded c. 1845. Incorporated 1892. Part of the town is also in Green County.

Name origin: For founder John Frederick's former home of Belleville, Canada.

Berry
Town
Lat: 43-09-53 N **Long:** 89-39-46 W
Pop: 1,248 (1990); 1,116 (1980) **Pop Density:** 34.8
Land: 35.9 sq. mi.; **Water:** 0.1 sq. mi.

Black Earth
Village
ZIP: 53515 **Lat:** 43-08-11 N **Long:** 89-44-45 W
Pop: 1,248 (1990); 1,145 (1980) **Pop Density:** 2080.0
Land: 0.6 sq. mi.; **Water:** 0.0 sq. mi. **Elev:** 818 ft.
Incorporated 1901.

Name origin: Named in 1851 for the creek that runs through the town. Previously called Berry and Ray.

*Black Earth
Town
ZIP: 53515 **Lat:** 43-07-45 N **Long:** 89-46-43 W
Pop: 365 (1990); 406 (1980) **Pop Density:** 21.1
Land: 17.3 sq. mi.; **Water:** 0.0 sq. mi.

Blooming Grove
Town
Lat: 43-03-05 N **Long:** 89-16-42 W
Pop: 2,079 (1990); 1,965 (1980) **Pop Density:** 203.8
Land: 10.2 sq. mi.; **Water:** 1.3 sq. mi.

Blue Mounds
Village
ZIP: 53517 **Lat:** 43-01-14 N **Long:** 89-49-34 W
Pop: 446 (1990); 387 (1980) **Pop Density:** 557.5
Land: 0.8 sq. mi.; **Water:** 0.0 sq. mi. **Elev:** 1261 ft.
Incorporated 1912.

Name origin: Named by French missionaries for the bluish color of the earth, caused by the presence of copper, and for three mounds here.

*Blue Mounds
Town
ZIP: 53517 **Lat:** 42-59-07 N **Long:** 89-46-35 W
Pop: 667 (1990); 637 (1980) **Pop Density:** 20.1
Land: 33.2 sq. mi.; **Water:** 0.0 sq. mi.

Bristol
Town
Lat: 43-14-45 N **Long:** 89-10-43 W
Pop: 1,850 (1990); 1,723 (1980) **Pop Density:** 52.9
Land: 35.0 sq. mi.; **Water:** 0.0 sq. mi.

Brooklyn
Village
ZIP: 53521 **Lat:** 42-51-13 N **Long:** 89-21-59 W
Pop: 406 (1990); 250 (1980) **Pop Density:** 812.0
Land: 0.5 sq. mi.; **Water:** 0.0 sq. mi.
Incorporated 1905. Part of the town is also in Green County.

Name origin: Named by engineer John E. Glunt, for the city of Brooklyn, NY.

Burke
Town
Lat: 43-09-40 N **Long:** 89-17-55 W
Pop: 3,004 (1990); 2,967 (1980) **Pop Density:** 123.1
Land: 24.4 sq. mi.; **Water:** 0.0 sq. mi.

Cambridge
Village
ZIP: 53523 **Lat:** 43-00-16 N **Long:** 89-01-07 W
Pop: 883 (1990); 785 (1980) **Pop Density:** 1766.0
Land: 0.5 sq. mi.; **Water:** 0.0 sq. mi.

Incorporated 1891. Part of the town is also in Jefferson County.

Name origin: Named in 1847 by landowner Alvin B. Carpenter for Cambridge, NY, the hometown of his sweetheart.

Christiana
Town
Lat: 42-58-51 N **Long:** 89-04-03 W
Pop: 1,182 (1990); 1,209 (1980) **Pop Density:** 33.3
Land: 35.5 sq. mi.; **Water:** 0.1 sq. mi.

Cottage Grove
Village
ZIP: 53527 **Lat:** 43-05-06 N **Long:** 89-12-08 W
Pop: 1,131 (1990); 888 (1980) **Pop Density:** 1256.7
Land: 0.9 sq. mi.; **Water:** 0.0 sq. mi. **Elev:** 888 ft.

Incorporated 1924.

Name origin: For a grove of burr oaks that surrounded the house of settler William C. Wells.

*Cottage Grove
Town
ZIP: 53527 **Lat:** 43-03-54 N **Long:** 89-11-20 W
Pop: 3,525 (1990); 2,952 (1980) **Pop Density:** 101.9
Land: 34.6 sq. mi.; **Water:** 0.0 sq. mi.

Cross Plains
Village
ZIP: 53528 **Lat:** 43-06-50 N **Long:** 89-38-46 W
Pop: 2,098 (1990); 2,156 (1980) **Pop Density:** 2098.0
Land: 1.0 sq. mi.; **Water:** 0.0 sq. mi. **Elev:** 859 ft.

Incorporated 1920.

Name origin: Named in 1838 by Postmaster Derry Haney for his hometown in TN.

*Cross Plains
Town
ZIP: 53528 **Lat:** 43-04-57 N **Long:** 89-39-56 W
Pop: 1,320 (1990); 1,003 (1980) **Pop Density:** 37.2
Land: 35.5 sq. mi.; **Water:** 0.0 sq. mi.

Dane
Village
ZIP: 53529 **Lat:** 43-15-01 N **Long:** 89-30-01 W
Pop: 621 (1990); 518 (1980) **Pop Density:** 621.0
Land: 1.0 sq. mi.; **Water:** 0.0 sq. mi.

Incorporated 1899.

Name origin: For the county.

*Dane
Town
ZIP: 53529 **Lat:** 43-15-16 N **Long:** 89-33-00 W
Pop: 921 (1990); 945 (1980) **Pop Density:** 26.2
Land: 35.2 sq. mi.; **Water:** 0.0 sq. mi.

Deerfield
Village
ZIP: 53531 **Lat:** 43-03-05 N **Long:** 89-04-27 W
Pop: 1,617 (1990); 1,466 (1980) **Pop Density:** 1470.0
Land: 1.1 sq. mi.; **Water:** 0.0 sq. mi.

Incorporated 1891.

Name origin: For the many deer that lived in the area.

*Deerfield
Town
ZIP: 53531 **Lat:** 43-04-00 N **Long:** 89-04-26 W
Pop: 1,181 (1990); 1,111 (1980) **Pop Density:** 34.4
Land: 34.3 sq. mi.; **Water:** 0.2 sq. mi.

De Forest
Village
ZIP: 53532 **Lat:** 43-14-44 N **Long:** 89-20-44 W
Pop: 4,882 (1990); 3,367 (1980) **Pop Density:** 2034.2
Land: 2.4 sq. mi.; **Water:** 0.0 sq. mi. **Elev:** 949 ft.

Incorporated 1903.

Name origin: For Isaac DeForest, who purchased land here in 1854.

Dunkirk
Town
Lat: 42-52-53 N **Long:** 89-11-23 W
Pop: 2,121 (1990); 2,098 (1980) **Pop Density:** 64.9
Land: 32.7 sq. mi.; **Water:** 0.4 sq. mi. **Elev:** 843 ft.

Dunn
Town
ZIP: 53558 **Lat:** 42-58-19 N **Long:** 89-18-17 W
Pop: 5,274 (1990); 4,966 (1980) **Pop Density:** 183.8
Land: 28.7 sq. mi.; **Water:** 5.8 sq. mi.

Fitchburg
City
ZIP: 53713 **Lat:** 42-59-09 N **Long:** 89-25-30 W
Pop: 15,648 (1990); 11,965 (1980) **Pop Density:** 448.4
Land: 34.9 sq. mi.; **Water:** 0.0 sq. mi.

Incorporated 1983.

Madison
City
ZIP: 53714 **Lat:** 43-04-47 N **Long:** 89-23-15 W
Pop: 191,262 (1990); 170,616 (1980) **Pop Density:** 3309.0
Land: 57.8 sq. mi.; **Water:** 16.0 sq. mi. **Elev:** 863 ft.

In southern WI on the isthmus between Lake Monona and Lake Mendota. State capital, second largest city. Winnebago Indians had a village here called *Dejop* 'four lakes.' Farming and cattle raising area; food processing industry; site of Univ. of Wisconsin. Incorporated 1856.

Name origin: For James Madison (1751–1836), fourth U.S. president.

*Madison
Town
ZIP: 53701 **Lat:** 43-02-38 N **Long:** 89-24-34 W
Pop: 6,442 (1990); 6,162 (1980) **Pop Density:** 1952.1
Land: 3.3 sq. mi.; **Water:** 0.5 sq. mi.

Maple Bluff
Village
ZIP: 53704 **Lat:** 43-06-35 N **Long:** 89-22-09 W
Pop: 1,352 (1990); 1,351 (1980) **Pop Density:** 1931.4
Land: 0.7 sq. mi.; **Water:** 0.0 sq. mi.

Incorporated 1930.

Name origin: For the maple trees growing on a bluff near the lake. Previously called Lakewood Bluff.

Marshall
Village
ZIP: 53559 **Lat:** 43-10-21 N **Long:** 89-03-50 W
Pop: 2,329 (1990); 2,363 (1980) **Pop Density:** 1552.7
Land: 1.5 sq. mi.; **Water:** 0.1 sq. mi.

Incorporated 1905.

Name origin: For property buyers, Porter and Marshall. Previously called Bird's Ruins, after the settlement started by A. A. Bird and Zenas Bird burned in a prairie fire; Hanchettville, for postmaster Hanchett; and Howard City, for a contractor.

Mazomanie
Village
ZIP: 53560 **Lat:** 43-10-27 N **Long:** 89-47-41 W
Pop: 1,377 (1990); 1,248 (1980) **Pop Density:** 1377.0
Land: 1.0 sq. mi.; **Water:** 0.0 sq. mi.

Incorporated 1885.

Name origin: From one of several Indian terms: *May-Zhee-Mau-nee* meaning 'Walking Mat,' a Winnebago chief; *mo-zo-*

mee-nan meaning 'mooseberries'; or *mo-so-min-um* meaning 'moon berries.'

⋏Mazomanie — Town
ZIP: 53560 **Lat:** 43-12-10 N **Long:** 89-46-23 W
Pop: 982 (1990); 1,007 (1980) **Pop Density:** 32.2
Land: 30.5 sq. mi.; **Water:** 0.8 sq. mi.

McFarland — Village
ZIP: 53558 **Lat:** 43-01-07 N **Long:** 89-17-37 W
Pop: 5,232 (1990); 3,783 (1980) **Pop Density:** 1687.7
Land: 3.1 sq. mi.; **Water:** 0.0 sq. mi.
Incorporated 1920.
Name origin: For William H. McFarland, who bought land here and laid out the village. Previously called MacFarland.

Medina — Town
Lat: 43-08-33 N **Long:** 89-03-59 W
Pop: 1,124 (1990); 1,019 (1980) **Pop Density:** 33.4
Land: 33.7 sq. mi.; **Water:** 0.3 sq. mi.

Middleton — City
ZIP: 53562 **Lat:** 43-06-10 N **Long:** 89-30-22 W
Pop: 13,289 (1990); 11,851 (1980) **Pop Density:** 2076.4
Land: 6.4 sq. mi.; **Water:** 0.0 sq. mi.
Incorporated 1963.
Name origin: For the town of Middleton, VT.

*Middleton — Town
Lat: 43-04-42 N **Long:** 89-33-22 W
Pop: 3,628 (1990); 2,595 (1980) **Pop Density:** 161.2
Land: 22.5 sq. mi.; **Water:** 0.0 sq. mi.

Monona — City
ZIP: 53716 **Lat:** 43-03-15 N **Long:** 89-19-59 W
Pop: 8,637 (1990); 8,809 (1980) **Pop Density:** 2617.3
Land: 3.3 sq. mi.; **Water:** 0.1 sq. mi.
Incorporated 1969.
Name origin: From an Indian term whose meaning is in dispute: possibly 'beautiful'; an Indian divinity; or a legendary maiden, who leaped into the Mississippi River when she believed her lover had been killed.

Montrose — Town
Lat: 42-54-06 N **Long:** 89-32-48 W
Pop: 1,032 (1990) **Pop Density:** 30.0
Land: 34.4 sq. mi.; **Water:** 0.2 sq. mi.

Mount Horeb — Village
ZIP: 53572 **Lat:** 43-00-32 N **Long:** 89-44-01 W
Pop: 4,182 (1990); 3,251 (1980) **Pop Density:** 1900.9
Land: 2.2 sq. mi.; **Water:** 0.0 sq. mi.
Incorporated 1899.
Name origin: Named for the biblical site by Mr. Wright, a Methodist minister who was also the town's first postmaster.

Oregon — Village
ZIP: 53575 **Lat:** 42-55-34 N **Long:** 89-22-55 W
Pop: 4,519 (1990); 3,876 (1980) **Pop Density:** 1673.7
Land: 2.7 sq. mi.; **Water:** 0.0 sq. mi. **Elev:** 949 ft.
Incorporated 1883.
Name origin: Named in 1847 for the state. Previously called Rome Corners.

*Oregon — Town
ZIP: 53575 **Lat:** 42-54-01 N **Long:** 89-25-44 W
Pop: 2,428 (1990); 1,798 (1980) **Pop Density:** 74.7
Land: 32.5 sq. mi.; **Water:** 0.1 sq. mi.

Perry — Town
Lat: 42-53-53 N **Long:** 89-46-39 W
Pop: 646 (1990); 632 (1980) **Pop Density:** 17.9
Land: 36.1 sq. mi.; **Water:** 0.0 sq. mi.

Pleasant Springs — Town
Lat: 42-58-18 N **Long:** 89-11-24 W
Pop: 2,660 (1990); 2,529 (1980) **Pop Density:** 79.4
Land: 33.5 sq. mi.; **Water:** 2.2 sq. mi.

Primrose — Town
Lat: 42-54-27 N **Long:** 89-40-03 W
Pop: 595 (1990); 654 (1980) **Pop Density:** 16.6
Land: 35.8 sq. mi.; **Water:** 0.0 sq. mi. **Elev:** 1002 ft.

Rockdale — Village
Lat: 42-58-20 N **Long:** 89-01-57 W
Pop: 235 (1990); 200 (1980) **Pop Density:** 1175.0
Land: 0.2 sq. mi.; **Water:** 0.0 sq. mi.
Incorporated 1914.
Name origin: For its location in a valley between two rock ridges. Previously called Clinton.

Roxbury — Town
Lat: 43-14-47 N **Long:** 89-39-28 W
Pop: 1,536 (1990); 1,491 (1980) **Pop Density:** 44.4
Land: 34.6 sq. mi.; **Water:** 1.3 sq. mi.

Rutland — Town
Lat: 42-53-41 N **Long:** 89-18-38 W
Pop: 1,584 (1990); 1,393 (1980) **Pop Density:** 44.9
Land: 35.3 sq. mi.; **Water:** 0.1 sq. mi.

Shorewood Hills — Village
ZIP: 53705 **Lat:** 43-04-39 N **Long:** 89-26-47 W
Pop: 1,680 (1990); 1,837 (1980) **Pop Density:** 2100.0
Land: 0.8 sq. mi.; **Water:** 0.0 sq. mi.
Incorporated 1927.
Name origin: For its wooded location near hills on the shore of Lake Mendota.

Springdale — Town
Lat: 42-59-51 N **Long:** 89-39-51 W
Pop: 1,258 (1990); 1,279 (1980) **Pop Density:** 35.1
Land: 35.8 sq. mi.; **Water:** 0.0 sq. mi.

Springfield — Town
Lat: 43-09-43 N **Long:** 89-32-41 W
Pop: 2,650 (1990); 2,379 (1980) **Pop Density:** 73.2
Land: 36.2 sq. mi.; **Water:** 0.2 sq. mi.

Stoughton — City
ZIP: 53589 **Lat:** 42-55-15 N **Long:** 89-13-21 W
Pop: 8,786 (1990); 7,589 (1980) **Pop Density:** 2928.7
Land: 3.0 sq. mi.; **Water:** 0.1 sq. mi.
Incorporated 1882.
Name origin: For Luke Stoughton, who bought the land in 1847 and platted the village.

Sun Prairie — City
ZIP: 53590 **Lat:** 43-11-01 N **Long:** 89-13-56 W
Pop: 15,333 (1990); 12,931 (1980) **Pop Density:** 2190.4
Land: 7.0 sq. mi.; **Water:** 0.0 sq. mi. **Elev:** 951 ft.
In southern WI, 11 mi. northeast of Madison. Incorporated 1958.
Name origin: For a group of workmen traveling out of Milwaukee in 1837 and breaking the wilderness, this was the first time they saw sun on their ten-day trip.

American Places Dictionary WISCONSIN, Dodge County

***Sun Prairie** Town
Lat: 43-09-22 N Long: 89-10-38 W
Pop: 1,839 (1990); 1,990 (1980) **Pop Density:** 58.2
Land: 31.6 sq. mi.; **Water:** 0.0 sq. mi.

Vermont Town
Lat: 43-04-19 N Long: 89-47-08 W
Pop: 678 (1990); 634 (1980) **Pop Density:** 18.9
Land: 35.8 sq. mi.; **Water:** 0.0 sq. mi.

Verona City
ZIP: 53593 Lat: 42-59-19 N Long: 89-32-07 W
Pop: 5,374 (1990); 3,336 (1980) **Pop Density:** 2687.0
Land: 2.0 sq. mi., **Water:** 0.0 sq. mi.
Incorporated 1977.
Name origin: Named by settlers for Verona, NY. Originally known as The Corners, because two main roads crossed here, and then Verona Corners.

***Verona** Town
Lat: 42-59-16 N Long: 89-32-49 W
Pop: 2,137 (1990); 2,259 (1980) **Pop Density:** 66.0
Land: 32.4 sq. mi.; **Water:** 0.0 sq. mi.

Vienna Town
Lat: 43-14-40 N Long: 89-25-43 W
Pop: 1,351 (1990); 1,365 (1980) **Pop Density:** 37.6
Land: 35.9 sq. mi.; **Water:** 0.0 sq. mi.

Waunakee Village
ZIP: 53597 Lat: 43-11-11 N Long: 89-27-07 W
Pop: 5,897 (1990); 3,866 (1980) **Pop Density:** 2268.1
Land: 2.6 sq. mi.; **Water:** 0.0 sq. mi. **Elev:** 925 ft.
Incorporated 1893.
Name origin: For either a friendly Indian who camped near here, or from an Indian term of disputed meaning: possibly 'you win,' 'sharp-shooter,' 'he lies,' or 'he lives in peace.'

Westport Town
Lat: 43-09-33 N Long: 89-25-32 W
Pop: 2,732 (1990); 2,748 (1980) **Pop Density:** 105.1
Land: 26.0 sq. mi.; **Water:** 5.0 sq. mi.

Windsor Town
ZIP: 53598 Lat: 43-13-45 N Long: 89-18-04 W
Pop: 4,620 (1990); 3,812 (1980) **Pop Density:** 140.4
Land: 32.9 sq. mi.; **Water:** 0.1 sq. mi.

York Town
Lat: 43-14-22 N Long: 89-04-00 W
Pop: 649 (1990); 714 (1980) **Pop Density:** 18.1
Land: 35.9 sq. mi.; **Water:** 0.0 sq. mi.

Dodge County
County Seat: Juneau (ZIP: 53039)

Pop: 76,559 (1990); 75,064 (1980) **Pop Density:** 86.8
Land: 882.4 sq. mi.; **Water:** 24.7 sq. mi. **Area Code:** 414
In southeastern WI, west of Milwaukee; organized Dec 7, 1836 (prior to statehood) from territorial county.
Name origin: For Gen. Henry Dodge (1782–1867), an officer in the War of 1812 and Black Hawk War, first governor of WI Territory (1836–41; 1845–48), and U.S. senator from WI (1848–57).

Ashippun Town
Lat: 43-14-25 N Long: 88-28-26 W
Pop: 1,783 (1990); 1,929 (1980) **Pop Density:** 50.1
Land: 35.6 sq. mi.; **Water:** 0.1 sq. mi.

Beaver Dam City
ZIP: 53916 Lat: 43-27-50 N Long: 88-50-13 W
Pop: 14,196 (1990); 14,149 (1980) **Pop Density:** 2957.5
Land: 4.8 sq. mi.; **Water:** 1.3 sq. mi. **Elev:** 879 ft.
In southeast-central WI, 29 mi. southwest of Fond du Lac. Incorporated 1856.
Name origin: Named by James P. Brower for the many beaver that built dams in nearby streams.

***Beaver Dam** Town
ZIP: 53916 Lat: 43-26-33 N Long: 88-48-56 W
Pop: 3,097 (1990); 3,030 (1980) **Pop Density:** 89.3
Land: 34.7 sq. mi.; **Water:** 2.8 sq. mi.

Brownsville Village
ZIP: 53006 Lat: 43-36-56 N Long: 88-29-28 W
Pop: 415 (1990); 433 (1980) **Pop Density:** 2075.0
Land: 0.2 sq. mi.; **Water:** 0.0 sq. mi.
Incorporated 1952.
Name origin: For Alfred D. Brown, an English immigrant who settled here about 1850.

Burnett Town
ZIP: 53922 Lat: 43-30-13 N Long: 88-42-12 W
Pop: 915 (1990); 917 (1980) **Pop Density:** 25.3
Land: 36.2 sq. mi.; **Water:** 0.3 sq. mi.

Calamus Town
Lat: 43-24-28 N Long: 88-57-12 W
Pop: 1,009 (1990); 1,077 (1980) **Pop Density:** 28.0
Land: 36.1 sq. mi.; **Water:** 0.5 sq. mi.

Chester Town
Lat: 43-35-31 N Long: 88-42-18 W
Pop: 1,393 (1990); 981 (1980) **Pop Density:** 41.5
Land: 33.6 sq. mi.; **Water:** 1.2 sq. mi.

WISCONSIN, Dodge County

Clyman
Village
ZIP: 53016   Lat: 43-18-43 N   **Long:** 88-43-09 W
Pop: 370 (1990); 317 (1980)   **Pop Density:** 1850.0
Land: 0.2 sq. mi.; **Water:** 0.0 sq. mi.
Incorporated 1924.
Name origin: For frontiersman Col. Clyman.

*Clyman
Town
Lat: 43-19-48 N   **Long:** 88-42-56 W
Pop: 742 (1990); 815 (1980)   **Pop Density:** 21.0
Land: 35.4 sq. mi.; **Water:** 0.0 sq. mi.

Columbus
City
ZIP: 53925   Lat: 43-19-49 N   **Long:** 89-00-29 W
Pop: 10 (1990)   **Pop Density:** 200.0
Land: 0.05 sq. mi.; **Water:** 0.0 sq. mi.   **Elev:** 871 ft.
Incorporated 1874. Part of the town is also in Columbia County.
Name origin: Named by Maj. Dickason, one of the first white men in the area, probably for Christopher Columbus (1451–1506).

Elba
Town
Lat: 43-19-40 N   **Long:** 88-57-02 W
Pop: 964 (1990); 1,028 (1980)   **Pop Density:** 27.2
Land: 35.4 sq. mi.; **Water:** 0.0 sq. mi.

Emmet
Town
Lat: 43-14-23 N   **Long:** 88-42-40 W
Pop: 1,014 (1990); 1,089 (1980)   **Pop Density:** 31.6
Land: 32.1 sq. mi.; **Water:** 0.0 sq. mi.

Fox Lake
City
ZIP: 53933   Lat: 43-33-48 N   **Long:** 88-54-45 W
Pop: 1,269 (1990); 1,373 (1980)   **Pop Density:** 906.4
Land: 1.4 sq. mi.; **Water:** 0.1 sq. mi.   **Elev:** 920 ft.
Incorporated 1938.
Name origin: Translation of the Indian term *Hos-a-rac-a-tah* probably meaning 'fox.'

*Fox Lake
Town
ZIP: 53933   Lat: 43-35-04 N   **Long:** 88-56-31 W
Pop: 1,938 (1990); 1,674 (1980)   **Pop Density:** 60.0
Land: 32.3 sq. mi.; **Water:** 6.0 sq. mi.

Hartford
City
Lat: 43-19-59 N   **Long:** 88-25-25 W
Pop: 9 (1990); 7,159 (1980)   **Pop Density:** 18.0
Land: 0.5 sq. mi.; **Water:** 0.0 sq. mi.
Incorporated 1883. Part of the town is also in Washington County.
Name origin: Possibly for the ford at heart-shaped Pike Lake nearby or for Hartford, CT. Previously called Wright after a Mr. Wright.

Herman
Town
Lat: 43-24-47 N   **Long:** 88-27-27 W
Pop: 1,127 (1990); 1,131 (1980)   **Pop Density:** 31.0
Land: 36.4 sq. mi.; **Water:** 0.0 sq. mi.

Horicon
City
ZIP: 53032   Lat: 43-26-41 N   **Long:** 88-38-13 W
Pop: 3,873 (1990); 3,584 (1980)   **Pop Density:** 1173.6
Land: 3.3 sq. mi.; **Water:** 0.0 sq. mi.   **Elev:** 884 ft.
Incorporated 1897.
Name origin: For the settlers' home at Lake Horicon (now Lake George), NY; name means 'clear water.' Previously called *Maunk-shak-kah,* or 'White Breast,' Elk Village, Indian Ford, and Hubbard's Ford.

Hubbard
Town
Lat: 43-24-20 N   **Long:** 88-35-07 W
Pop: 1,390 (1990); 1,508 (1980)   **Pop Density:** 43.7
Land: 31.8 sq. mi.; **Water:** 1.6 sq. mi.

Hustisford
Village
ZIP: 53034   Lat: 43-20-43 N   **Long:** 88-36-13 W
Pop: 979 (1990); 874 (1980)   **Pop Density:** 1398.6
Land: 0.7 sq. mi.; **Water:** 0.1 sq. mi.
Incorporated 1870.
Name origin: For John Hustis, the first settler and because the Indians had used a fording place here. Previously called Rock River Rapids for the half mile of rapids here.

*Hustisford
Town
Lat: 43-19-47 N   **Long:** 88-35-51 W
Pop: 1,209 (1990); 1,262 (1980)   **Pop Density:** 35.7
Land: 33.9 sq. mi.; **Water:** 1.3 sq. mi.

Iron Ridge
Village
ZIP: 53035   Lat: 43-23-51 N   **Long:** 88-31-55 W
Pop: 887 (1990); 766 (1980)   **Pop Density:** 1267.1
Land: 0.7 sq. mi.; **Water:** 0.0 sq. mi.
Incorporated 1913.
Name origin: For iron ore mines in the vicinity.

Juneau
City
ZIP: 53039   Lat: 43-24-22 N   **Long:** 88-42-11 W
Pop: 2,157 (1990); 2,045 (1980)   **Pop Density:** 1540.7
Land: 1.4 sq. mi.; **Water:** 0.0 sq. mi.
Incorporated 1887.
Name origin: For Solomon Juneau (1793–1856), founder of Milwaukee. Previously called Victory and Dodge Center.

Kekoskee
Village
Lat: 43-31-39 N   **Long:** 88-33-42 W
Pop: 188 (1990); 224 (1980)   **Pop Density:** 940.0
Land: 0.2 sq. mi.; **Water:** 0.0 sq. mi.   **Elev:** 909 ft.
Incorporated 1958.
Name origin: From a Winnebago Indian term probably meaning 'friendly village.'

Lebanon
Town
Lat: 43-14-27 N   **Long:** 88-35-35 W
Pop: 1,630 (1990); 1,518 (1980)   **Pop Density:** 45.5
Land: 35.8 sq. mi.; **Water:** 0.2 sq. mi.

Leroy
Town
Lat: 43-35-32 N   **Long:** 88-35-34 W
Pop: 1,025 (1990); 1,110 (1980)   **Pop Density:** 28.0
Land: 36.6 sq. mi.; **Water:** 0.8 sq. mi.

Lomira
Village
ZIP: 53048   Lat: 43-35-19 N   **Long:** 88-26-40 W
Pop: 1,542 (1990); 1,446 (1980)   **Pop Density:** 1101.4
Land: 1.4 sq. mi.; **Water:** 0.0 sq. mi.   **Elev:** 1039 ft.
Incorporated 1899.
Name origin: Named in 1849 for either Lomira Schoonover or the loamy soil here. Previously called Springfield.

*Lomira
Town
ZIP: 53048   Lat: 43-35-40 N   **Long:** 88-27-55 W
Pop: 1,280 (1990); 1,391 (1980)   **Pop Density:** 36.5
Land: 35.1 sq. mi.; **Water:** 0.0 sq. mi.

Lowell — Village
ZIP: 53557   **Lat:** 43-20-16 N   **Long:** 88-49-15 W
Pop: 300 (1990); 326 (1980)   **Pop Density:** 300.0
Land: 1.0 sq. mi.; **Water:** 0.0 sq. mi.
Established 1830s. Incorporated 1894.
Name origin: For Lowell, MA, the hometown of mill owner Clark Lawton. Previously called Town Ten.

*Lowell — Town
ZIP: 53557   **Lat:** 43-19-46 N   **Long:** 88-50-19 W
Pop: 1,146 (1990); 1,205 (1980)   **Pop Density:** 22.3
Land: 51.5 sq. mi.; **Water:** 0.4 sq. mi.

Mayville — City
ZIP: 53050   **Lat:** 43-29-53 N   **Long:** 88-32-46 W
Pop: 4,374 (1990); 4,333 (1980)   **Pop Density:** 1562.1
Land: 2.8 sq. mi.; **Water:** 0.0 sq. mi.
Incorporated 1885.
Name origin: For Eli P. May, who established a trading post here in 1845.

Neosho — Village
ZIP: 53059   **Lat:** 43-18-35 N   **Long:** 88-31-04 W
Pop: 658 (1990); 575 (1980)   **Pop Density:** 1096.7
Land: 0.6 sq. mi.; **Water:** 0.0 sq. mi.   **Elev:** 883 ft.
Incorporated 1902.
Name origin: From an Indian term probably meaning 'point of land projecting into a lake.' Previously called Cotton's Mill.

Oak Grove — Town
Lat: 43-25-37 N   **Long:** 88-41-59 W
Pop: 1,200 (1990); 1,333 (1980)   **Pop Density:** 34.9
Land: 34.4 sq. mi.; **Water:** 0.1 sq. mi.

Portland — Town
Lat: 43-14-22 N   **Long:** 88-57-09 W
Pop: 994 (1990); 976 (1980)   **Pop Density:** 28.2
Land: 35.3 sq. mi.; **Water:** 0.4 sq. mi.

Randolph — Village
ZIP: 53956   **Lat:** 43-32-15 N   **Long:** 88-59-59 W
Pop: 1,227 (1990); 1,206 (1980)   **Pop Density:** 1752.9
Land: 0.7 sq. mi.; **Water:** 0.0 sq. mi.   **Elev:** 964 ft.
Incorporated 1870. Part of the town is also in Columbia County.
Name origin: For Randolph, VT. Previously called LeRoy; Conversville for settler Jon Converse; and Westford.

Reeseville — Village
ZIP: 53579   **Lat:** 43-18-21 N   **Long:** 88-50-42 W
Pop: 673 (1990); 649 (1980)   **Pop Density:** 1121.7
Land: 0.6 sq. mi.; **Water:** 0.0 sq. mi.   **Elev:** 856 ft.
Incorporated 1899.
Name origin: For Samuel Reese, the father of Adam Reese, who platted and surveyed the village.

Rubicon — Town
ZIP: 53078   **Lat:** 43-19-58 N   **Long:** 88-28-25 W
Pop: 1,709 (1990); 1,759 (1980)   **Pop Density:** 49.5
Land: 34.5 sq. mi.; **Water:** 0.4 sq. mi.

Shields — Town
Lat: 43-14-02 N   **Long:** 88-49-01 W
Pop: 500 (1990); 584 (1980)   **Pop Density:** 18.9
Land: 26.5 sq. mi.; **Water:** 0.4 sq. mi.

Theresa — Village
ZIP: 53091   **Lat:** 43-31-04 N   **Long:** 88-27-09 W
Pop: 771 (1990); 766 (1980)   **Pop Density:** 1285.0
Land: 0.6 sq. mi.; **Water:** 0.0 sq. mi.
Incorporated 1898.
Name origin: For the mother of founder of Milwaukee Solomon Juneau (1793–1856).

*Theresa — Town
ZIP: 53091   **Lat:** 43-29-56 N   **Long:** 88-27-53 W
Pop: 1,083 (1990); 1,152 (1980)   **Pop Density:** 30.7
Land: 35.3 sq. mi.; **Water:** 0.5 sq. mi.

Trenton — Town
Lat: 43-34-02 N   **Long:** 88-49-51 W
Pop: 1,299 (1990); 1,319 (1980)   **Pop Density:** 24.1
Land: 53.9 sq. mi.; **Water:** 0.5 sq. mi.

Watertown — City
ZIP: 53094   **Lat:** 43-12-26 N   **Long:** 88-43-31 W
Pop: 6,754 (1990); 5,911 (1980)   **Pop Density:** 1929.7
Land: 3.5 sq. mi.; **Water:** 0.2 sq. mi.   **Elev:** 823 ft.
In southeastern WI, 32 mi. east of Madison. Incorporated 1853. Part of the town is also in Jefferson County.
Name origin: For Watertown, NY. Previously called Johnson's Rapids.

Waupun — City
ZIP: 53963   **Lat:** 43-37-31 N   **Long:** 88-44-03 W
Pop: 5,490 (1990); 5,439 (1980)   **Pop Density:** 3050.0
Land: 1.8 sq. mi.; **Water:** 0.0 sq. mi.   **Elev:** 904 ft.
Incorporated 1878. Part of the town is also in Fond du Lac County.
Name origin: From the Indian term *Waubun* probably meaning 'dawn' or 'early light of day.' Originally known as Madrid, for Madrid, VT.

Westford — Town
Lat: 43-29-17 N   **Long:** 88-56-24 W
Pop: 1,248 (1990); 1,203 (1980)   **Pop Density:** 41.2
Land: 30.3 sq. mi.; **Water:** 4.6 sq. mi.

Williamstown — Town
Lat: 43-30-06 N   **Long:** 88-35-08 W
Pop: 722 (1990); 657 (1980)   **Pop Density:** 21.7
Land: 33.2 sq. mi.; **Water:** 0.7 sq. mi.

Door County
County Seat: Sturgeon Bay (ZIP: 54235)

Pop: 25,690 (1990); 25,029 (1980) **Pop Density:** 53.2
Land: 482.7 sq. mi.; **Water:** 1887.2 sq. mi. **Area Code:** 414

On the peninsula in northeast WI, bordered on west by Green Bay and on east by Lake Michigan; organized Feb 11, 1851 from Brown County.

Name origin: Origin uncertain. A legendary incident involving Indians is said to be the reason the strait between Washington Island and the peninsula is named in French *La Porte des Morts*, 'Door of the Dead.' Or possibly "the door" refers to the entrance to Green Bay. The county later took the name from the strait.

Baileys Harbor Town
ZIP: 54202 **Lat:** 45-03-48 N **Long:** 87-05-41 W
Pop: 780 (1990); 799 (1980) **Pop Density:** 26.4
Land: 29.5 sq. mi.; **Water:** 39.2 sq. mi.

Brussels Town
ZIP: 54204 **Lat:** 44-42-30 N **Long:** 87-34-50 W
Pop: 1,042 (1990); 1,097 (1980) **Pop Density:** 28.9
Land: 36.1 sq. mi.; **Water:** 0.0 sq. mi.

Claybanks Town
Lat: 44-45-27 N **Long:** 87-19-30 W
Pop: 379 (1990); 409 (1980) **Pop Density:** 25.4
Land: 14.9 sq. mi.; **Water:** 32.2 sq. mi.

Egg Harbor Village
ZIP: 54209 **Lat:** 45-02-44 N **Long:** 87-17-28 W
Pop: 183 (1990); 238 (1980) **Pop Density:** 101.7
Land: 1.8 sq. mi.; **Water:** 0.0 sq. mi.
Incorporated 1964.

Name origin: Possibly for a nest of duck's eggs discovered at the harbor here.

*Egg Harbor Town
ZIP: 54209 **Lat:** 44-59-38 N **Long:** 87-21-14 W
Pop: 1,019 (1990); 825 (1980) **Pop Density:** 27.8
Land: 36.7 sq. mi.; **Water:** 66.4 sq. mi.

Ephraim Village
ZIP: 54211 **Lat:** 45-09-27 N **Long:** 87-09-58 W
Pop: 261 (1990); 319 (1980) **Pop Density:** 66.9
Land: 3.9 sq. mi.; **Water:** 0.0 sq. mi.
Settled 1853. Incorporated 1919.

Name origin: For the biblical name meaning 'doubly fruitful.'

Forestville Village
ZIP: 54213 **Lat:** 44-41-27 N **Long:** 87-28-42 W
Pop: 470 (1990); 455 (1980) **Pop Density:** 940.0
Land: 0.5 sq. mi.; **Water:** 0.0 sq. mi. **Elev:** 633 ft.
Incorporated 1960.

*Forestville Town
ZIP: 54213 **Lat:** 44-42-55 N **Long:** 87-28-08 W
Pop: 999 (1990); 1,035 (1980) **Pop Density:** 28.2
Land: 35.4 sq. mi.; **Water:** 0.1 sq. mi.

Gardner Town
Lat: 44-50-50 N **Long:** 87-35-13 W
Pop: 1,025 (1990); 1,084 (1980) **Pop Density:** 29.9
Land: 34.3 sq. mi.; **Water:** 79.2 sq. mi.

Gibraltar Town
Lat: 45-09-32 N **Long:** 87-15-55 W
Pop: 939 (1990); 742 (1980) **Pop Density:** 27.7
Land: 33.9 sq. mi.; **Water:** 117.6 sq. mi.

Jacksonport Town
ZIP: 54235 **Lat:** 44-59-06 N **Long:** 87-10-39 W
Pop: 689 (1990); 707 (1980) **Pop Density:** 23.8
Land: 29.0 sq. mi.; **Water:** 29.3 sq. mi.

Liberty Grove Town
Lat: 45-15-44 N **Long:** 87-03-33 W
Pop: 1,506 (1990); 1,313 (1980) **Pop Density:** 28.1
Land: 53.6 sq. mi.; **Water:** 136.9 sq. mi.

Nasewaupee Town
Lat: 44-50-59 N **Long:** 87-27-50 W
Pop: 1,798 (1990); 1,899 (1980) **Pop Density:** 41.7
Land: 43.1 sq. mi.; **Water:** 28.1 sq. mi.

Sevastopol Town
ZIP: 54235 **Lat:** 44-53-22 N **Long:** 87-15-55 W
Pop: 2,552 (1990); 2,520 (1980) **Pop Density:** 49.2
Land: 51.9 sq. mi.; **Water:** 38.2 sq. mi.

Sister Bay Village
ZIP: 54234 **Lat:** 45-11-12 N **Long:** 87-07-38 W
Pop: 675 (1990); 564 (1980) **Pop Density:** 259.6
Land: 2.6 sq. mi.; **Water:** 0.5 sq. mi. **Elev:** 587 ft.
Incorporated 1912.

Name origin: For two "sister islands" in the bay. Originally known as Pebble Beach for the round pebbles found here.

Sturgeon Bay City
ZIP: 54235 **Lat:** 44-49-17 N **Long:** 87-22-05 W
Pop: 9,176 (1990); 8,847 (1980) **Pop Density:** 955.8
Land: 9.6 sq. mi.; **Water:** 1.7 sq. mi. **Elev:** 588 ft.
In northeastern WI, on the peninsula bound on the north by Green Bay and on the south by Lake Michigan. Incorporated 1883.

Name origin: Named in 1860 for the abundant sturgeon in the bay off of Green Bay. Previously called Graham and Ottumba.

*Sturgeon Bay Town
ZIP: 54235 **Lat:** 44-48-33 N **Long:** 87-17-25 W
Pop: 853 (1990); 863 (1980) **Pop Density:** 44.0
Land: 19.4 sq. mi.; **Water:** 15.9 sq. mi.

Union Town
Lat: 44-43-33 N **Long:** 87-42-00 W
Pop: 721 (1990); 755 (1980) **Pop Density:** 34.0
Land: 21.2 sq. mi.; **Water:** 14.7 sq. mi.

Washington Town
Lat: 45-23-08 N **Long:** 86-55-33 W
Pop: 623 (1990); 558 (1980) **Pop Density:** 24.4
Land: 25.5 sq. mi.; **Water:** 99.0 sq. mi.

Douglas County
County Seat: Superior (ZIP: 54880)

Pop: 41,758 (1990); 44,421 (1980) **Pop Density:** 31.9
Land: 1309.3 sq. mi.; **Water:** 170.8 sq. mi. **Area Code:** 715
On northwestern border of WI, at southwestern end of Lake Superior; organized Feb 9, 1854 from unorganized territory.
Name origin: For Stephen Arnold Douglas (1813–61), U.S. orator and statesman.

Amnicon Town
Lat: 46-35-21 N **Long:** 91-51-12 W
Pop: 929 (1990); 916 (1980) **Pop Density:** 23.8
Land: 39.1 sq. mi.; **Water:** 0.0 sq. mi.

Bennett Town
Lat: 46-26-27 N **Long:** 91-49-27 W
Pop: 525 (1990); 501 (1980) **Pop Density:** 11.1
Land: 47.5 sq. mi.; **Water:** 0.8 sq. mi.

Brule Town
ZIP: 54820 **Lat:** 46-35-25 N **Long:** 91-36-18 W
Pop: 527 (1990); 544 (1980) **Pop Density:** 9.5
Land: 55.7 sq. mi.; **Water:** 0.2 sq. mi.

Cloverland Town
Lat: 46-41-58 N **Long:** 91-37-43 W
Pop: 246 (1990); 263 (1980) **Pop Density:** 5.3
Land: 46.2 sq. mi.; **Water:** 0.0 sq. mi.

Dairyland Town
Lat: 46-14-52 N **Long:** 92-10-03 W
Pop: 222 (1990); 258 (1980) **Pop Density:** 1.6
Land: 140.2 sq. mi.; **Water:** 0.6 sq. mi.

Gordon Town
ZIP: 54838 **Lat:** 46-17-42 N **Long:** 91-49-36 W
Pop: 553 (1990); 627 (1980) **Pop Density:** 3.6
Land: 151.8 sq. mi.; **Water:** 5.6 sq. mi.

Hawthorne Town
Lat: 46-30-44 N **Long:** 91-50-04 W
Pop: 1,049 (1990); 902 (1980) **Pop Density:** 23.0
Land: 45.6 sq. mi.; **Water:** 0.5 sq. mi.

Highland Town
Lat: 46-25-16 N **Long:** 91-37-45 W
Pop: 207 (1990); 190 (1980) **Pop Density:** 2.7
Land: 76.5 sq. mi.; **Water:** 1.6 sq. mi.

Lake Nebagamon Village
ZIP: 54849 **Lat:** 46-30-28 N **Long:** 91-41-40 W
Pop: 900 (1990); 780 (1980) **Pop Density:** 70.9
Land: 12.7 sq. mi.; **Water:** 1.7 sq. mi.
Incorporated 1907.
Name origin: From the Chippewa term *nee-bay-go-mow-win* probably meaning 'place to still hunt deer by water.'

Lakeside Town
Lat: 46-39-37 N **Long:** 91-49-17 W
Pop: 569 (1990); 572 (1980) **Pop Density:** 14.3
Land: 39.9 sq. mi.; **Water:** 0.0 sq. mi.

Maple Town
ZIP: 54854 **Lat:** 46-36-17 N **Long:** 91-41-49 W
Pop: 667 (1990); 685 (1980) **Pop Density:** 20.8
Land: 32.1 sq. mi.; **Water:** 0.0 sq. mi.

Oakland Town
Lat: 46-29-39 N **Long:** 91-59-23 W
Pop: 993 (1990); 938 (1980) **Pop Density:** 15.5
Land: 63.9 sq. mi.; **Water:** 1.1 sq. mi.

Oliver Village
Lat: 46-38-59 N **Long:** 92-11-23 W
Pop: 265 (1990); 253 (1980) **Pop Density:** 132.5
Land: 2.0 sq. mi.; **Water:** 0.0 sq. mi. **Elev:** 649 ft.
Platted 1911. Incorporated 1917.
Name origin: For Henry W. Oliver. Previously called Freedom.

Parkland Town
Lat: 46-37-11 N **Long:** 91-59-14 W
Pop: 1,326 (1990); 1,496 (1980) **Pop Density:** 37.4
Land: 35.5 sq. mi.; **Water:** 0.0 sq. mi. **Elev:** 693 ft.

Poplar Village
ZIP: 54864 **Lat:** 46-34-54 N **Long:** 91-47-16 W
Pop: 516 (1990); 569 (1980) **Pop Density:** 43.4
Land: 11.9 sq. mi.; **Water:** 0.0 sq. mi.
Incorporated 1917.
Name origin: For the poplar trees that grew up quickly here after the land had been logged. Originally part of the town of Brule.

Solon Springs Village
ZIP: 54873 **Lat:** 46-20-58 N **Long:** 91-49-11 W
Pop: 575 (1990); 590 (1980) **Pop Density:** 359.4
Land: 1.6 sq. mi.; **Water:** 0.7 sq. mi.
Established 1888. Incorporated 1920.
Name origin: For Tom Solon, a settler who bottled water from a spring on his land. Originally known as White Birch.

*Solon Springs Town
ZIP: 54873 **Lat:** 46-21-54 N **Long:** 91-49-07 W
Pop: 619 (1990); 553 (1980) **Pop Density:** 7.5
Land: 83.0 sq. mi.; **Water:** 1.5 sq. mi.

Summit Town
Lat: 46-25-39 N **Long:** 92-10-33 W
Pop: 1,009 (1990); 1,057 (1980) **Pop Density:** 6.9
Land: 146.6 sq. mi.; **Water:** 1.0 sq. mi.

Superior City
ZIP: 54880 **Lat:** 46-41-48 N **Long:** 92-03-34 W
Pop: 27,134 (1990); 29,571 (1980) **Pop Density:** 735.3
Land: 36.9 sq. mi.; **Water:** 18.5 sq. mi. **Elev:** 642 ft.
In northwestern WI at the extreme west end of Lake Superior opposite Duluth, MN. Incorporated 1949.
Name origin: For Lake Superior. Previously called Grand Lac, by the explorer Samuel de Champlain (c. 1567–1635) and Lac Superieur de Tracy, by Father Marquette (1637–75).

WISCONSIN, Douglas County

*Superior — Village
ZIP: 54880 Lat: 46-39-13 N Long: 92-06-19 W
Pop: 481 (1990); 580 (1980) Pop Density: 400.8
Land: 1.2 sq. mi.; Water: 0.0 sq. mi.

*Superior — Town
ZIP: 54880 Lat: 46-34-59 N Long: 92-09-52 W
Pop: 1,911 (1990); 2,065 (1980) Pop Density: 18.0
Land: 106.2 sq. mi.; Water: 1.6 sq. mi.

Wascott — Town
Lat: 46-12-07 N Long: 91-47-54 W
Pop: 535 (1990); 511 (1980) Pop Density: 4.0
Land: 133.0 sq. mi.; Water: 8.1 sq. mi.

Dunn County
County Seat: Menomonie (ZIP: 54751)

Pop: 35,909 (1990); 34,314 (1980) Pop Density: 42.1
Land: 852.1 sq. mi.; Water: 11.9 sq. mi. Area Code: 715

In west-central WI, east of St. Paul, MN; organized Feb 3, 1854 from Chippewa County.

Name origin: For Charles Dunn, a legislator and first chief justice of WI Territory.

Boyceville — Village
ZIP: 54725 Lat: 45-02-33 N Long: 92-02-23 W
Pop: 913 (1990); 862 (1980) Pop Density: 228.3
Land: 4.0 sq. mi.; Water: 0.0 sq. mi. Elev: 948 ft.
Incorporated 1922.
Name origin: For the Boyce family that owned a mill here.

Colfax — Village
ZIP: 54730 Lat: 44-59-48 N Long: 91-43-33 W
Pop: 1,110 (1990); 1,149 (1980) Pop Density: 792.9
Land: 1.4 sq. mi.; Water: 0.0 sq. mi.
Incorporated 1904.
Name origin: Named c. 1868 for Sen. Schuyler Colfax (1823–85). Previously called Begga Town for the "rutabeggas" raised here.

*Colfax — Town
ZIP: 54730 Lat: 44-59-11 N Long: 91-42-26 W
Pop: 691 (1990); 660 (1980) Pop Density: 20.2
Land: 34.2 sq. mi.; Water: 0.3 sq. mi.

Downing — Village
ZIP: 54734 Lat: 45-02-54 N Long: 92-07-26 W
Pop: 250 (1990); 242 (1980) Pop Density: 83.3
Land: 3.0 sq. mi.; Water: 0.0 sq. mi. Elev: 983 ft.
Incorporated 1909.
Name origin: For settler James Downing.

Dunn — Town
Lat: 44-45-22 N Long: 91-54-47 W
Pop: 1,315 (1990); 1,294 (1980) Pop Density: 23.6
Land: 55.7 sq. mi.; Water: 1.4 sq. mi.

Eau Galle — Town
ZIP: 54737 Lat: 44-43-28 N Long: 92-03-12 W
Pop: 854 (1990); 944 (1980) Pop Density: 18.0
Land: 47.4 sq. mi.; Water: 0.6 sq. mi.

Elk Mound — Village
ZIP: 54739 Lat: 44-52-30 N Long: 91-41-15 W
Pop: 765 (1990); 737 (1980) Pop Density: 332.6
Land: 2.3 sq. mi.; Water: 0.0 sq. mi.
Incorporated 1909.
Name origin: For a 1,220-foot bluff here, from which elk were sometimes seen.

*Elk Mound — Town
ZIP: 54739 Lat: 44-54-10 N Long: 91-42-28 W
Pop: 749 (1990); 668 (1980) Pop Density: 22.2
Land: 33.7 sq. mi.; Water: 0.0 sq. mi.

Grant — Town
Lat: 45-04-48 N Long: 91-42-41 W
Pop: 412 (1990); 443 (1980) Pop Density: 11.2
Land: 36.9 sq. mi.; Water: 0.5 sq. mi.

Hay River — Town
Lat: 45-04-19 N Long: 91-57-00 W
Pop: 510 (1990); 433 (1980) Pop Density: 14.1
Land: 36.1 sq. mi.; Water: 0.0 sq. mi.

Knapp — Village
ZIP: 54749 Lat: 44-57-14 N Long: 92-04-37 W
Pop: 419 (1990); 419 (1980) Pop Density: 261.9
Land: 1.6 sq. mi.; Water: 0.0 sq. mi.
Incorporated 1905.
Name origin: For John H. Knapp, who with William Wilson, started the Knapp Stout and Company lumbering firm. Originally known as Knapp Station.

Lucas — Town
Lat: 44-54-07 N Long: 92-04-13 W
Pop: 644 (1990); 699 (1980) Pop Density: 18.0
Land: 35.7 sq. mi.; Water: 0.0 sq. mi.

Menomonie — City
ZIP: 54751 Lat: 44-53-16 N Long: 91-54-50 W
Pop: 13,547 (1990); 12,769 (1980) Pop Density: 1198.8
Land: 11.3 sq. mi.; Water: 1.7 sq. mi. Elev: 877 ft.
In western WI, 21 mi. west of Eau Claire. Incorporated 1882.
Name origin: A variant spelling of the Indian tribal name *Menomonee*.

*Menomonie — Town
ZIP: 54751 Lat: 44-52-53 N Long: 91-57-35 W
Pop: 2,732 (1990); 2,453 (1980) Pop Density: 65.2
Land: 41.9 sq. mi.; Water: 0.2 sq. mi.

New Haven — Town
Lat: 45-09-58 N Long: 92-05-44 W
Pop: 658 (1990); 707 (1980) Pop Density: 18.1
Land: 36.4 sq. mi.; Water: 0.0 sq. mi.

Otter Creek — Town
Lat: 45-04-28 N Long: 91-50-03 W
Pop: 339 (1990); 337 (1980)   Pop Density: 9.2
Land: 36.9 sq. mi.; Water: 0.0 sq. mi.

Peru — Town
Lat: 44-42-47 N Long: 91-48-54 W
Pop: 203 (1990); 194 (1980)   Pop Density: 10.9
Land: 18.7 sq. mi.; Water: 0.9 sq. mi.

Red Cedar — Town
Lat: 44-53-10 N Long: 91-50-03 W
Pop: 1,417 (1990); 1,278 (1980)   Pop Density: 34.3
Land: 41.3 sq. mi.; Water: 0.9 sq. mi.

Ridgeland — Village
ZIP: 54763   Lat: 45-12-07 N Long: 91-53-50 W
Pop: 246 (1990); 300 (1980)   Pop Density: 615.0
Land: 0.4 sq. mi.; Water: 0.0 sq. mi.
Incorporated 1921.
Name origin: For the ridges on either side of town.

Rock Creek — Town
Lat: 44-43-05 N Long: 91-42-59 W
Pop: 696 (1990); 668 (1980)   Pop Density: 22.6
Land: 30.8 sq. mi.; Water: 0.8 sq. mi.

Sand Creek — Town
Lat: 45-09-56 N Long: 91-43-17 W
Pop: 568 (1990); 575 (1980)   Pop Density: 15.9
Land: 35.8 sq. mi.; Water: 0.4 sq. mi.

Sheridan — Town
Lat: 45-09-43 N Long: 91-58-22 W
Pop: 468 (1990); 476 (1980)   Pop Density: 13.0
Land: 36.1 sq. mi.; Water: 0.0 sq. mi.

Sherman — Town
Lat: 44-59-30 N Long: 91-57-30 W
Pop: 725 (1990); 666 (1980)   Pop Density: 20.5
Land: 35.3 sq. mi.; Water: 0.1 sq. mi.

Spring Brook — Town
Lat: 44-48-25 N Long: 91-44-29 W
Pop: 1,293 (1990); 1,293 (1980)   Pop Density: 21.3
Land: 60.8 sq. mi.; Water: 1.4 sq. mi.

Stanton — Town
Lat: 44-59-23 N Long: 92-04-51 W
Pop: 637 (1990); 553 (1980)   Pop Density: 18.8
Land: 33.9 sq. mi.; Water: 0.0 sq. mi.

Tainter — Town
Lat: 44-58-53 N Long: 91-50-03 W
Pop: 1,756 (1990); 1,507 (1980)   Pop Density: 53.2
Land: 33.0 sq. mi.; Water: 2.7 sq. mi.

Tainter Lake — CDP
Lat: 44-59-21 N Long: 91-50-51 W
Pop: 1,716 (1990)   Pop Density: 92.3
Land: 18.6 sq. mi.; Water: 2.8 sq. mi.

Tiffany — Town
Lat: 45-04-55 N Long: 92-04-29 W
Pop: 594 (1990); 639 (1980)   Pop Density: 19.9
Land: 29.8 sq. mi.; Water: 0.0 sq. mi.

Weston — Town
Lat: 44-48-51 N Long: 92-04-04 W
Pop: 560 (1990); 654 (1980)   Pop Density: 13.5
Land: 41.5 sq. mi.; Water: 0.0 sq. mi.

Wheeler — Village
ZIP: 54772   Lat: 45-02-37 N Long: 91-54-19 W
Pop: 348 (1990); 231 (1980)   Pop Density: 435.0
Land: 0.8 sq. mi.; Water: 0.0 sq. mi.   Elev: 938 ft.
Incorporated 1922.
Name origin: For first postmaster, H. D. Wheeler. Previously called Lochiel and Welton, for homesteader Maria L. Welton.

Wilson — Town
Lat: 45-09-54 N Long: 91-50-37 W
Pop: 490 (1990); 464 (1980)   Pop Density: 13.8
Land: 35.5 sq. mi.; Water: 0.0 sq. mi.

Eau Claire County
County Seat: Eau Claire (ZIP: 54703)

Pop: 85,183 (1990); 78,805 (1980)   Pop Density: 133.6
Land: 637.7 sq. mi.; Water: 7.6 sq. mi.   Area Code: 715
In west-central WI, east of St. Paul, MN; organized Oct 6, 1856 from Clark County.
Name origin: For Eau Claire River, which runs through it; French transliteration of an Indian word meaning 'clear water.'

Altoona — City
ZIP: 54720   Lat: 44-48-18 N Long: 91-26-31 W
Pop: 5,889 (1990); 4,393 (1980)   Pop Density: 1436.3
Land: 4.1 sq. mi.; Water: 0.2 sq. mi.
Platted 1881. Incorporated 1887.
Name origin: For Mr. Beal's hometown of Altoona, PA. Originally known as East Eau Claire.

Augusta — City
ZIP: 54722   Lat: 44-40-43 N Long: 91-07-16 W
Pop: 1,510 (1990); 1,560 (1980)   Pop Density: 794.7
Land: 1.9 sq. mi.; Water: 0.0 sq. mi.
Incorporated 1885.
Name origin: For either Augusta, ME, Charles Buckman's hometown, or for Augusta Rickard, who was voted the prettiest girl in town. Originally known as Ridge Creek.

Bridge Creek — Town
Lat: 44-41-11 N Long: 91-03-59 W
Pop: 1,440 (1990); 1,206 (1980)   Pop Density: 14.0
Land: 102.5 sq. mi.; Water: 1.8 sq. mi.

Brunswick — Town
Lat: 44-43-55 N Long: 91-35-14 W
Pop: 1,506 (1990); 1,411 (1980)   Pop Density: 41.3
Land: 36.5 sq. mi.; Water: 0.8 sq. mi.

WISCONSIN, Eau Claire County

Clear Creek   Town
Lat: 44-37-55 N Long: 91-20-30 W
Pop: 692 (1990); 798 (1980)   **Pop Density:** 19.3
Land: 35.9 sq. mi.; **Water:** 0.0 sq. mi.

Drammen   Town
Lat: 44-38-07 N Long: 91-35-36 W
Pop: 767 (1990); 725 (1980)   **Pop Density:** 21.4
Land: 35.9 sq. mi.; **Water:** 0.0 sq. mi.

Eau Claire   City
ZIP: 54703   Lat: 44-48-51 N Long: 91-29-46 W
Pop: 55,180 (1990); 49,852 (1980)   **Pop Density:** 2289.6
Land: 24.1 sq. mi.; **Water:** 2.0 sq. mi.

In western WI on the Chippewa River. Platted 1855. Incorporated 1872. Part of the town is also in Chippewa County.
Name origin: Named in 1855 for the nearby Eau Claire River; from French 'clear water.'

Fairchild   Village
ZIP: 54741   Lat: 44-36-19 N Long: 90-57-23 W
Pop: 504 (1990); 577 (1980)   **Pop Density:** 336.0
Land: 1.5 sq. mi.; **Water:** 0.0 sq. mi.   **Elev:** 1080 ft.

Incorporated 1880.
Name origin: For Lucius Fairchild, governor of WI (1866–72).

*Fairchild   Town
ZIP: 54741   Lat: 44-38-14 N Long: 90-59-02 W
Pop: 312 (1990); 278 (1980)   **Pop Density:** 9.0
Land: 34.5 sq. mi.; **Water:** 0.0 sq. mi.

Fall Creek   Village
ZIP: 54742   Lat: 44-45-43 N Long: 91-16-26 W
Pop: 1,034 (1990); 1,148 (1980)   **Pop Density:** 689.3
Land: 1.5 sq. mi.; **Water:** 0.0 sq. mi.

Incorporated 1906.
Name origin: For the creek that runs by the village. Previously called Cousins, for Henry Cousins.

Lincoln   Town
Lat: 44-44-32 N Long: 91-14-40 W
Pop: 1,002 (1990); 1,012 (1980)   **Pop Density:** 17.2
Land: 58.3 sq. mi.; **Water:** 0.5 sq. mi.

Ludington   Town
Lat: 44-48-31 N Long: 91-09-37 W
Pop: 906 (1990); 969 (1980)   **Pop Density:** 19.8
Land: 45.8 sq. mi.; **Water:** 0.2 sq. mi.

Otter Creek   Town
Lat: 44-38-07 N Long: 91-13-06 W
Pop: 459 (1990); 497 (1980)   **Pop Density:** 12.9
Land: 35.6 sq. mi.; **Water:** 0.0 sq. mi.

Pleasant Valley   Town
Lat: 44-39-40 N Long: 91-27-42 W
Pop: 2,076 (1990); 1,908 (1980)   **Pop Density:** 38.3
Land: 54.2 sq. mi.; **Water:** 0.0 sq. mi.

Seymour   Town
Lat: 44-50-08 N Long: 91-20-12 W
Pop: 2,757 (1990); 2,824 (1980)   **Pop Density:** 88.1
Land: 31.3 sq. mi.; **Water:** 1.1 sq. mi.

Union   Town
Lat: 44-49-18 N Long: 91-35-58 W
Pop: 2,446 (1990); 2,689 (1980)   **Pop Density:** 83.5
Land: 29.3 sq. mi.; **Water:** 0.5 sq. mi.

Washington   Town
ZIP: 54742   Lat: 44-45-13 N Long: 91-24-24 W
Pop: 6,226 (1990); 6,489 (1980)   **Pop Density:** 109.2
Land: 57.0 sq. mi.; **Water:** 0.5 sq. mi.

Wilson   Town
Lat: 44-48-37 N Long: 91-00-42 W
Pop: 477 (1990); 469 (1980)   **Pop Density:** 10.0
Land: 47.7 sq. mi.; **Water:** 0.0 sq. mi.

Florence County
County Seat: Florence (ZIP: 54121)

Pop: 4,590 (1990); 4,172 (1980)   **Pop Density:** 9.4
Land: 488.1 sq. mi.; **Water:** 9.4 sq. mi.   **Area Code:** 715

On northeastern border of WI; organized Mar 18, 1882 from Marinette and Oconto counties.

Name origin: For Florence Terry Hulst, wife of an early developer and mine owner, Dr. N. P. Hulst.

Aurora   Town
Lat: 45-46-10 N Long: 88-08-23 W
Pop: 1,036 (1990); 1,050 (1980)   **Pop Density:** 27.3
Land: 38.0 sq. mi.; **Water:** 0.4 sq. mi.

Commonwealth   Town
Lat: 45-51-16 N Long: 88-14-19 W
Pop: 407 (1990); 369 (1980)   **Pop Density:** 9.6
Land: 42.3 sq. mi.; **Water:** 0.6 sq. mi.

Fence   Town
ZIP: 54120   Lat: 45-45-44 N Long: 88-31-44 W
Pop: 222 (1990); 192 (1980)   **Pop Density:** 2.5
Land: 89.5 sq. mi.; **Water:** 0.6 sq. mi.

Fern   Town
Lat: 45-50-29 N Long: 88-21-50 W
Pop: 112 (1990); 111 (1980)   **Pop Density:** 3.3
Land: 34.0 sq. mi.; **Water:** 1.2 sq. mi.

Florence   Town
ZIP: 54121   Lat: 45-54-56 N Long: 88-23-23 W
Pop: 2,097 (1990); 1,809 (1980)   **Pop Density:** 13.6
Land: 153.7 sq. mi.; **Water:** 4.0 sq. mi.

Homestead   Town
Lat: 45-45-56 N Long: 88-15-56 W
Pop: 337 (1990); 272 (1980)   **Pop Density:** 6.3
Land: 53.9 sq. mi.; **Water:** 0.5 sq. mi.   **Elev:** 1225 ft.

Long Lake Town
ZIP: 54542 Lat: 45-51-14 N Long: 88-37-21 W
Pop: 205 (1990); 199 (1980) **Pop Density:** 6.0
Land: 34.0 sq. mi.; **Water:** 1.9 sq. mi.

Tipler Town
Lat: 45-57-08 N Long: 88-36-09 W
Pop: 174 (1990); 170 (1980) **Pop Density:** 4.1
Land: 42.8 sq. mi.; **Water:** 0.3 sq. mi.

Fond du Lac County
County Seat: Fond du Lac (ZIP: 54935)

Pop: 90,083 (1990); 88,964 (1980) **Pop Density:** 124.6
Land: 723.0 sq. mi.; **Water:** 42.9 sq. mi. **Area Code:** 414

In east-central WI; organized Dec 7, 1836 (prior to statehood) from a territorial county.

Name origin: For its location at the southern end of Lake Winnebago; French 'end of the lake,' transliterated from *Wanikamiu*, name of an Indian village, with the similar meaning 'farthest point of the lake.'

Alto Town
Lat: 43-40-26 N Long: 88-49-10 W
Pop: 1,145 (1990); 1,176 (1980) **Pop Density:** 31.5
Land: 36.3 sq. mi.; **Water:** 0.0 sq. mi.

Ashford Town
Lat: 43-35-26 N Long: 88-20-26 W
Pop: 1,598 (1990); 1,506 (1980) **Pop Density:** 44.6
Land: 35.8 sq. mi.; **Water:** 0.1 sq. mi.

Auburn Town
Lat: 43-34-47 N Long: 88-13-18 W
Pop: 1,790 (1990); 1,803 (1980) **Pop Density:** 50.7
Land: 35.3 sq. mi.; **Water:** 0.6 sq. mi.

Brandon Village
ZIP: 53919 Lat: 43-44-14 N Long: 88-47-01 W
Pop: 872 (1990); 862 (1980) **Pop Density:** 1453.3
Land: 0.6 sq. mi.; **Water:** 0.0 sq. mi. **Elev:** 999 ft.
Incorporated 1881.
Name origin: Previously called Bungtown. Named by settler William Locklin for Brandon, VT.

Byron Town
Lat: 43-40-05 N Long: 88-28-01 W
Pop: 1,634 (1990); 1,681 (1980) **Pop Density:** 45.0
Land: 36.3 sq. mi.; **Water:** 0.0 sq. mi.

Calumet Town
Lat: 43-54-58 N Long: 88-17-10 W
Pop: 1,444 (1990); 1,609 (1980) **Pop Density:** 47.8
Land: 30.2 sq. mi.; **Water:** 13.9 sq. mi.

Campbellsport Village
ZIP: 53010 Lat: 43-35-57 N Long: 88-16-52 W
Pop: 1,732 (1990); 1,740 (1980) **Pop Density:** 1924.4
Land: 0.9 sq. mi.; **Water:** 0.0 sq. mi.
Incorporated 1902.
Name origin: For landowner Stuart Campbell. Previously called Crouchville and New Cassel, after Hesse-Cassel, Germany.

Eden Village
ZIP: 53019 Lat: 43-41-32 N Long: 88-21-46 W
Pop: 610 (1990); 534 (1980) **Pop Density:** 2033.3
Land: 0.3 sq. mi.; **Water:** 0.0 sq. mi.
Incorporated 1912.
Name origin: For either the Garden of Eden in the Bible, or for early settler John Eden.

*Eden Town
ZIP: 53019 Lat: 43-40-37 N Long: 88-20-42 W
Pop: 1,037 (1990); 1,130 (1980) **Pop Density:** 28.6
Land: 36.2 sq. mi.; **Water:** 0.0 sq. mi.

Eldorado Town
ZIP: 54932 Lat: 43-51-08 N Long: 88-34-57 W
Pop: 1,409 (1990); 1,502 (1980) **Pop Density:** 39.4
Land: 35.8 sq. mi.; **Water:** 0.5 sq. mi.

Empire Town
Lat: 43-45-14 N Long: 88-20-40 W
Pop: 2,485 (1990); 2,359 (1980) **Pop Density:** 82.6
Land: 30.1 sq. mi.; **Water:** 0.1 sq. mi.

Fairwater Village
Lat: 43-44-27 N Long: 88-52-07 W
Pop: 302 (1990); 310 (1980) **Pop Density:** 431.4
Land: 0.7 sq. mi.; **Water:** 0.0 sq. mi.
Incorporated 1921.
Name origin: For its favorable location on the Grand River.

Fond du Lac City
ZIP: 54935 Lat: 43-46-23 N Long: 88-26-43 W
Pop: 37,757 (1990); 35,863 (1980) **Pop Density:** 2949.8
Land: 12.8 sq. mi.; **Water:** 0.9 sq. mi. **Elev:** 760 ft.
In east-central WI, at the southern end of Lake Winnebago. Incorporated 1852.
Name origin: French 'end of the lake,' translated from Indian *Wanikamiu*, name of an Indian village with the similar meaning of 'farthest end of the lake.'

*Fond du Lac Town
Lat: 43-45-23 N Long: 88-28-07 W
Pop: 2,308 (1990); 3,001 (1980) **Pop Density:** 104.9
Land: 22.0 sq. mi.; **Water:** 1.1 sq. mi.

Forest Town
Lat: 43-46-07 N Long: 88-13-33 W
Pop: 1,094 (1990); 1,098 (1980) **Pop Density:** 31.1
Land: 35.2 sq. mi.; **Water:** 0.9 sq. mi.

Friendship Town
Lat: 43-51-11 N Long: 88-27-44 W
Pop: 2,220 (1990); 2,321 (1980) **Pop Density:** 128.3
Land: 17.3 sq. mi.; **Water:** 17.9 sq. mi.

WISCONSIN, Fond du Lac County

Kewaskum
Village
ZIP: 53040 **Lat:** 43-32-42 N **Long:** 88-16-04 W
Pop: 1 (1990); 13 (1980) **Pop Density:** 10.0
Land: 0.1 sq. mi.; **Water:** 0.0 sq. mi.

Incorporated 1895. Part of the town is also in Washington County.

Name origin: From a Potawatomi chief's name that may mean either 'a man able to turn fate whichever way he wants' or 'his tracks are toward home.'

Lamartine
Town
Lat: 43-45-34 N **Long:** 88-34-53 W
Pop: 1,607 (1990); 1,749 (1980) **Pop Density:** 44.0
Land: 36.5 sq. mi.; **Water:** 0.1 sq. mi.

Marshfield
Town
Lat: 43-51-21 N **Long:** 88-13-20 W
Pop: 1,130 (1990); 1,214 (1980) **Pop Density:** 33.0
Land: 34.2 sq. mi.; **Water:** 0.2 sq. mi.

Metomen
Town
Lat: 43-46-08 N **Long:** 88-50-04 W
Pop: 685 (1990); 792 (1980) **Pop Density:** 19.7
Land: 34.8 sq. mi.; **Water:** 0.0 sq. mi.

Mount Calvary
Village
ZIP: 53057 **Lat:** 43-49-35 N **Long:** 88-14-48 W
Pop: 558 (1990); 585 (1980) **Pop Density:** 558.0
Land: 1.0 sq. mi.; **Water:** 0.0 sq. mi.

Incorporated 1962.

Name origin: Named in 1853 by Bishop Henni for its location at the foot of a hill on which a cross had been erected. Previously called St. Nicholas Congregation.

North Fond du Lac
Village
Lat: 43-48-32 N **Long:** 88-28-59 W
Pop: 4,292 (1990); 3,844 (1980) **Pop Density:** 2524.7
Land: 1.7 sq. mi.; **Water:** 0.0 sq. mi.

Incorporated 1903.

Oakfield
Village
ZIP: 53065 **Lat:** 43-41-04 N **Long:** 88-32-48 W
Pop: 1,003 (1990); 990 (1980) **Pop Density:** 1114.4
Land: 0.9 sq. mi.; **Water:** 0.0 sq. mi. **Elev:** 894 ft.

Incorporated 1903.

Name origin: For its descriptive connotations. Previously called Avoca and Lime, for the limestone quarries.

*Oakfield
Town
ZIP: 53065 **Lat:** 43-40-39 N **Long:** 88-34-56 W
Pop: 822 (1990); 833 (1980) **Pop Density:** 23.0
Land: 35.8 sq. mi.; **Water:** 0.1 sq. mi.

Osceola
Town
Lat: 43-39-46 N **Long:** 88-13-25 W
Pop: 1,588 (1990); 1,569 (1980) **Pop Density:** 45.2
Land: 35.1 sq. mi.; **Water:** 1.2 sq. mi.

Ripon
City
ZIP: 54971 **Lat:** 43-50-44 N **Long:** 88-50-29 W
Pop: 7,241 (1990); 7,111 (1980) **Pop Density:** 1766.1
Land: 4.1 sq. mi.; **Water:** 0.0 sq. mi. **Elev:** 943 ft.

Incorporated 1858.

*Ripon
Town
ZIP: 54971 **Lat:** 43-51-33 N **Long:** 88-49-26 W
Pop: 1,419 (1990); 1,411 (1980) **Pop Density:** 44.3
Land: 32.0 sq. mi.; **Water:** 0.1 sq. mi.

Rosendale
Village
ZIP: 54974 **Lat:** 43-48-29 N **Long:** 88-40-32 W
Pop: 777 (1990); 725 (1980) **Pop Density:** 777.0
Land: 1.0 sq. mi.; **Water:** 0.0 sq. mi.

Incorporated 1915.

Name origin: For its descriptive connotations.

*Rosendale
Town
ZIP: 54974 **Lat:** 43-50-37 N **Long:** 88-42-02 W
Pop: 770 (1990); 763 (1980) **Pop Density:** 21.6
Land: 35.7 sq. mi.; **Water:** 0.0 sq. mi.

St. Cloud
Village
Lat: 43-49-21 N **Long:** 88-10-02 W
Pop: 494 (1990); 560 (1980) **Pop Density:** 548.9
Land: 0.9 sq. mi.; **Water:** 0.0 sq. mi. **Elev:** 930 ft.

Incorporated 1909.

Name origin: For St. Cloud, France.

Springvale
Town
Lat: 43-45-49 N **Long:** 88-42-18 W
Pop: 750 (1990); 808 (1980) **Pop Density:** 20.8
Land: 36.0 sq. mi.; **Water:** 0.0 sq. mi.

Taycheedah
Town
Lat: 43-50-04 N **Long:** 88-20-33 W
Pop: 3,383 (1990); 3,227 (1980) **Pop Density:** 109.5
Land: 30.9 sq. mi.; **Water:** 5.2 sq. mi.

Waupun
City
ZIP: 53963 **Lat:** 43-38-12 N **Long:** 88-44-09 W
Pop: 2,717 (1990); 2,693 (1980) **Pop Density:** 2090.0
Land: 1.3 sq. mi.; **Water:** 0.0 sq. mi. **Elev:** 904 ft.

Incorporated 1878. Part of the town is also in Dodge County.

Name origin: From the Indian term *Waubun* probably meaning 'dawn' or 'early light of day.' Originally known as Madrid, for Madrid, VT.

*Waupun
Town
ZIP: 53963 **Lat:** 43-40-50 N **Long:** 88-42-27 W
Pop: 1,409 (1990); 1,492 (1980) **Pop Density:** 40.1
Land: 35.1 sq. mi.; **Water:** 0.0 sq. mi.

Forest County
County Seat: Crandon (ZIP: 54520)

Pop: 8,776 (1990); 9,044 (1980)
Land: 1014.1 sq. mi.; **Water:** 32.3 sq. mi.
Pop Density: 8.7
Area Code: 715

On northeastern border of WI; organized Apr 11, 1885 from Langlade and Oconto counties.

Name origin: Descriptively named for the forests in the area.

Alvin — Town
Lat: 45-57-53 N **Long:** 88-49-19 W
Pop: 145 (1990); 195 (1980) **Pop Density:** 1.3
Land: 115.0 sq. mi.; **Water:** 1.0 sq. mi.

Argonne — Town
ZIP: 54511 **Lat:** 45-46-52 N **Long:** 88-51-32 W
Pop: 497 (1990); 469 (1980) **Pop Density:** 4.6
Land: 108.2 sq. mi.; **Water:** 0.1 sq. mi.

Armstrong Creek — Town
ZIP: 54103 **Lat:** 45-40-05 N **Long:** 88-29-49 W
Pop: 460 (1990); 501 (1980) **Pop Density:** 9.6
Land: 48.0 sq. mi.; **Water:** 0.7 sq. mi.

Blackwell — Town
ZIP: 54541 **Lat:** 45-33-00 N **Long:** 88-31-33 W
Pop: 384 (1990); 384 (1980) **Pop Density:** 5.8
Land: 66.0 sq. mi.; **Water:** 0.4 sq. mi.

Caswell — Town
Lat: 45-40-39 N **Long:** 88-39-57 W
Pop: 94 (1990); 85 (1980) **Pop Density:** 2.0
Land: 47.7 sq. mi.; **Water:** 0.2 sq. mi.

Crandon — City
ZIP: 54520 **Lat:** 45-34-11 N **Long:** 88-53-50 W
Pop: 1,958 (1990); 1,969 (1980) **Pop Density:** 376.5
Land: 5.2 sq. mi.; **Water:** 1.0 sq. mi.
Incorporated 1898.
Name origin: Originally known as Ayr, for Ayr, Scotland. Renamed in 1885 for Maj. Frank P. Crandon of the Chicago and North Western Railway.

*Crandon — Town
ZIP: 54520 **Lat:** 45-36-17 N **Long:** 88-59-12 W
Pop: 529 (1990); 569 (1980) **Pop Density:** 15.7
Land: 33.8 sq. mi.; **Water:** 2.0 sq. mi.

Freedom — Town
ZIP: 54566 **Lat:** 45-25-33 N **Long:** 88-45-04 W
Pop: 296 (1990); 307 (1980) **Pop Density:** 8.7
Land: 34.1 sq. mi.; **Water:** 2.0 sq. mi.

Hiles — Town
ZIP: 54511 **Lat:** 45-48-13 N **Long:** 88-58-50 W
Pop: 312 (1990); 327 (1980) **Pop Density:** 2.4
Land: 131.5 sq. mi.; **Water:** 9.5 sq. mi.

Laona — Town
ZIP: 54541 **Lat:** 45-33-53 N **Long:** 88-41-51 W
Pop: 1,387 (1990); 1,474 (1980) **Pop Density:** 13.4
Land: 103.4 sq. mi.; **Water:** 4.1 sq. mi.

Lincoln — Town
Lat: 45-32-43 N **Long:** 88-51-13 W
Pop: 630 (1990); 577 (1980) **Pop Density:** 10.8
Land: 58.1 sq. mi.; **Water:** 4.8 sq. mi.

Nashville — Town
ZIP: 54520 **Lat:** 45-28-00 N **Long:** 88-55-32 W
Pop: 871 (1990); 703 (1980) **Pop Density:** 13.0
Land: 67.2 sq. mi.; **Water:** 5.2 sq. mi. **Elev:** 1700 ft.

Popple River — Town
Lat: 45-49-53 N **Long:** 88-43-27 W
Pop: 12 (1990); 59 (1980) **Pop Density:** 0.0
Land: 50.1 sq. mi.; **Water:** 0.4 sq. mi.

Ross — Town
Lat: 45-44-27 N **Long:** 88-43-52 W
Pop: 159 (1990); 203 (1980) **Pop Density:** 4.1
Land: 38.5 sq. mi.; **Water:** 0.1 sq. mi.

Wabeno — Town
ZIP: 54566 **Lat:** 45-25-58 N **Long:** 88-33-10 W
Pop: 1,012 (1990); 1,222 (1980) **Pop Density:** 9.4
Land: 107.3 sq. mi.; **Water:** 0.9 sq. mi.

WISCONSIN, Grant County — *American Places Dictionary*

Grant County
County Seat: Lancaster (ZIP: 53813)

Pop: 49,264 (1990); 51,736 (1980)
Land: 1147.9 sq. mi.; **Water:** 35.5 sq. mi.
Pop Density: 42.9
Area Code: 608

On southwestern border of WI; organized Dec 8, 1836 (prior to statehood) from Iowa County.

Name origin: For the Grant River, which runs through it; itself named for a trapper and Indian trader who lived on the banks.

Bagley — Village
ZIP: 53801 **Lat:** 42-54-12 N **Long:** 91-05-53 W
Pop: 306 (1990); 317 (1980) **Pop Density:** 510.0
Land: 0.6 sq. mi.; **Water:** 0.0 sq. mi.

Platted c. 1884. Incorporated 1919.

Name origin: For Mary Bagley, who owned the land on which the village was built.

Beetown — Town
Lat: 42-48-43 N **Long:** 90-51-38 W
Pop: 782 (1990); 933 (1980) **Pop Density:** 16.2
Land: 48.4 sq. mi.; **Water:** 0.0 sq. mi.

Bloomington — Village
ZIP: 53804 **Lat:** 42-53-31 N **Long:** 90-55-38 W
Pop: 776 (1990); 743 (1980) **Pop Density:** 596.9
Land: 1.3 sq. mi.; **Water:** 0.0 sq. mi.

Incorporated 1880.

Name origin: For a surge in agriculture triggered when a local blacksmith patented a new device for sowing oats. Previously called Taft, for a local mill owner, and then Blooming.

*Bloomington — Town
ZIP: 53804 **Lat:** 42-52-34 N **Long:** 91-00-18 W
Pop: 364 (1990); 567 (1980) **Pop Density:** 10.0
Land: 36.4 sq. mi.; **Water:** 3.6 sq. mi.

Blue River — Village
ZIP: 53518 **Lat:** 43-11-10 N **Long:** 90-34-20 W
Pop: 438 (1990); 412 (1980) **Pop Density:** 625.7
Land: 0.7 sq. mi.; **Water:** 0.0 sq. mi. **Elev:** 676 ft.

Incorporated 1916.

Name origin: For the river, named because it ran through a nearby farm belonging to Mr. Blue. Previously called Minnehaha.

Boscobel — City
ZIP: 53805 **Lat:** 43-08-22 N **Long:** 90-42-16 W
Pop: 2,706 (1990); 2,662 (1980) **Pop Density:** 1503.3
Land: 1.8 sq. mi.; **Water:** 0.0 sq. mi.

Incorporated 1873.

Name origin: For either the Boscobel Wood in England, or from Spanish *bosque bello* 'beautiful woods.'

*Boscobel — Town
ZIP: 53805 **Lat:** 43-08-20 N **Long:** 90-41-42 W
Pop: 426 (1990); 494 (1980) **Pop Density:** 54.6
Land: 7.8 sq. mi.; **Water:** 0.4 sq. mi.

Cassville — Village
ZIP: 53806 **Lat:** 42-42-56 N **Long:** 90-59-25 W
Pop: 1,144 (1990); 1,270 (1980) **Pop Density:** 1040.0
Land: 1.1 sq. mi.; **Water:** 0.0 sq. mi. **Elev:** 621 ft.

Founded 1827. Incorporated 1882.

Name origin: For Lewis Cass (1782-1866), governor of the MI Territory, which at that time encompassed WI.

*Cassville — Town
ZIP: 53806 **Lat:** 42-44-02 N **Long:** 90-57-52 W
Pop: 554 (1990); 633 (1980) **Pop Density:** 16.5
Land: 33.5 sq. mi.; **Water:** 2.9 sq. mi.

Castle Rock — Town
Lat: 43-04-44 N **Long:** 90-29-09 W
Pop: 311 (1990); 339 (1980) **Pop Density:** 8.7
Land: 35.8 sq. mi.; **Water:** 0.0 sq. mi.

Clifton — Town
Lat: 42-53-57 N **Long:** 90-29-18 W
Pop: 306 (1990); 404 (1980) **Pop Density:** 8.6
Land: 35.7 sq. mi.; **Water:** 0.0 sq. mi.

Cuba City — City
ZIP: 53807 **Lat:** 42-36-11 N **Long:** 90-25-57 W
Pop: 1,863 (1990); 1,928 (1980) **Pop Density:** 1863.0
Land: 1.0 sq. mi.; **Water:** 0.0 sq. mi. **Elev:** 1012 ft.

Incorporated 1925. Part of the town is also in Lafayette County.

Name origin: A substitution for Yuba, because there was another Yuba in the state. Previously called Western, Yuba, and Cuba.

Dickeyville — Village
ZIP: 53808 **Lat:** 42-37-32 N **Long:** 90-35-31 W
Pop: 862 (1990); 1,156 (1980) **Pop Density:** 957.8
Land: 0.9 sq. mi.; **Water:** 0.0 sq. mi. **Elev:** 957 ft.

Settled c. 1849. Incorporated 1947.

Name origin: For early resident, Mr. Dickey.

Ellenboro — Town
Lat: 42-48-30 N **Long:** 90-35-57 W
Pop: 521 (1990); 544 (1980) **Pop Density:** 14.4
Land: 36.2 sq. mi.; **Water:** 0.0 sq. mi.

Fennimore — City
ZIP: 53809 **Lat:** 42-58-50 N **Long:** 90-39-02 W
Pop: 2,378 (1990); 2,212 (1980) **Pop Density:** 1585.3
Land: 1.5 sq. mi.; **Water:** 0.0 sq. mi.

Incorporated 1919.

Name origin: For John Fennimore, who farmed in the area, and disappeared during the Black Hawk War. Previously called Fennimore Center.

WISCONSIN, Grant County

*Fennimore — Town
ZIP: 53809   Lat: 42-59-07 N   Long: 90-36-21 W
Pop: 556 (1990); 726 (1980)   Pop Density: 16.0
Land: 34.8 sq. mi.; Water: 0.0 sq. mi.

Glen Haven — Town
ZIP: 53810   Lat: 42-48-40 N   Long: 91-00-30 W
Pop: 548 (1990); 596 (1980)   Pop Density: 16.0
Land: 34.3 sq. mi.; Water: 1.1 sq. mi.

Harrison — Town
Lat: 42-43-33 N   Long: 90-36-18 W
Pop: 544 (1990); 600 (1980)   Pop Density: 15.1
Land: 36.1 sq. mi.; Water: 0.0 sq. mi.

Hazel Green — Village
ZIP: 53811   Lat: 42-32-04 N   Long: 90-26-10 W
Pop: 1,171 (1990); 1,270 (1980)   Pop Density: 1064.5
Land: 1.1 sq. mi.; Water: 0.0 sq. mi.
Incorporated 1867. Part of the town is also in Lafayette County.
Name origin: For either Capt. Charles McCoy's hometown of Hazel Green, KY, or for the hazel bushes in the area. Previously called Hardy's Scrape and Hard Scrabble.

*Hazel Green — Town
ZIP: 53811   Lat: 42-32-55 N   Long: 90-29-18 W
Pop: 1,108 (1990); 1,228 (1980)   Pop Density: 31.4
Land: 35.3 sq. mi.; Water: 0.0 sq. mi.

Hickory Grove — Town
Lat: 43-04-26 N   Long: 90-36-31 W
Pop: 409 (1990); 423 (1980)   Pop Density: 11.2
Land: 36.4 sq. mi.; Water: 0.0 sq. mi.   Elev: 1106 ft.

Jamestown — Town
Lat: 42-33-21 N   Long: 90-35-26 W
Pop: 2,175 (1990); 2,369 (1980)   Pop Density: 72.3
Land: 30.1 sq. mi.; Water: 2.6 sq. mi.   Elev: 923 ft.

Lancaster — City
ZIP: 53813   Lat: 42-50-54 N   Long: 90-42-28 W
Pop: 4,192 (1990); 4,076 (1980)   Pop Density: 1552.6
Land: 2.7 sq. mi.; Water: 0.0 sq. mi.
Platted 1837. Incorporated 1878.
Name origin: For Lancaster, PA, the hometown of one of the settlers.

Liberty — Town
Lat: 42-53-33 N   Long: 90-36-32 W
Pop: 569 (1990); 609 (1980)   Pop Density: 15.6
Land: 36.5 sq. mi.; Water: 0.0 sq. mi.

Lima — Town
Lat: 42-48-59 N   Long: 90-29-18 W
Pop: 691 (1990); 750 (1980)   Pop Density: 18.9
Land: 36.5 sq. mi.; Water: 0.0 sq. mi.

Little Grant — Town
Lat: 42-54-00 N   Long: 90-50-24 W
Pop: 375 (1990); 347 (1980)   Pop Density: 10.4
Land: 36.0 sq. mi.; Water: 0.0 sq. mi.

Livingston — Village
ZIP: 53554   Lat: 42-54-02 N   Long: 90-26-09 W
Pop: 566 (1990); 626 (1980)   Pop Density: 707.5
Land: 0.8 sq. mi.; Water: 0.0 sq. mi.   Elev: 1164 ft.
Incorporated 1914. Part of the town is also in Iowa County.
Name origin: For Hugh Livingston, who donated his farmland to the railroad. Previously called Dublin by Irish settlers.

Marion — Town
Lat: 43-04-31 N   Long: 90-43-25 W
Pop: 484 (1990); 463 (1980)   Pop Density: 13.6
Land: 35.5 sq. mi.; Water: 0.3 sq. mi.

Millville — Town
Lat: 43-01-22 N   Long: 90-57-26 W
Pop: 169 (1990); 152 (1980)   Pop Density: 8.0
Land: 21.0 sq. mi.; Water: 0.8 sq. mi.

Montfort — Village
ZIP: 53569   Lat: 42-58-11 N   Long: 90-26-02 W
Pop: 580 (1990); 516 (1980)   Pop Density: 1160.0
Land: 0.5 sq. mi.; Water: 0.0 sq. mi.
Incorporated 1893. Part of the town is also in Iowa County.
Name origin: For a small fort that miners built here to protect themselves during the Black Hawk War. Previously called Wingville and Podunk.

Mount Hope — Village
ZIP: 53816   Lat: 42-58-10 N   Long: 90-51-30 W
Pop: 173 (1990); 197 (1980)   Pop Density: 576.7
Land: 0.3 sq. mi.; Water: 0.0 sq. mi.
Incorporated 1919.
Name origin: For its location on a hill and the community's hope at the time of attracting an institution of higher learning.

*Mount Hope — Town
ZIP: 53816   Lat: 42-58-51 N   Long: 90-50-03 W
Pop: 240 (1990); 343 (1980)   Pop Density: 8.0
Land: 29.9 sq. mi.; Water: 0.0 sq. mi.

Mount Ida — Town
Lat: 42-59-10 N   Long: 90-43-29 W
Pop: 510 (1990); 544 (1980)   Pop Density: 14.0
Land: 36.3 sq. mi.; Water: 0.0 sq. mi.

Muscoda — Village
ZIP: 53573   Lat: 43-11-18 N   Long: 90-26-26 W
Pop: 1,283 (1990); 1,331 (1980)   Pop Density: 1425.6
Land: 0.9 sq. mi.; Water: 0.0 sq. mi.
Incorporated 1894. Part of the town is also in Iowa County.
Name origin: From *mash-ko-deng*, an Indian word for 'meadow' or 'prairie.' Previously called English Prairie or English Meadow because an English trader and his son were murdered here.

*Muscoda — Town
ZIP: 53573   Lat: 43-09-30 N   Long: 90-29-29 W
Pop: 566 (1990); 566 (1980)   Pop Density: 16.9
Land: 33.5 sq. mi.; Water: 1.1 sq. mi.

North Lancaster — Town
Lat: 42-53-48 N   Long: 90-43-32 W
Pop: 548 (1990); 506 (1980)   Pop Density: 15.2
Land: 36.0 sq. mi.; Water: 0.0 sq. mi.

Paris — Town
Lat: 42-38-06 N   Long: 90-35-48 W
Pop: 749 (1990); 842 (1980)   Pop Density: 21.3
Land: 35.1 sq. mi.; Water: 0.4 sq. mi.

Patch Grove — Village
ZIP: 53817   Lat: 42-56-21 N   Long: 90-58-21 W
Pop: 202 (1990); 259 (1980)   Pop Density: 505.0
Land: 0.4 sq. mi.; Water: 0.0 sq. mi.
Incorporated 1921.
Name origin: For Henry Patch, who built a cabin near a grove

of trees and often accommodated travelers. Originally known as Finntown, for settler Enos Finn.

### *Patch Grove	Town
Lat: 42-56-52 N   **Long:** 90-57-45 W
Pop: 378 (1990); 421 (1980)   **Pop Density:** 11.5
Land: 32.9 sq. mi.; **Water:** 0.0 sq. mi.

### Platteville	City
ZIP: 53818   **Lat:** 42-44-06 N   **Long:** 90-28-36 W
Pop: 9,708 (1990); 9,580 (1980)   **Pop Density:** 2427.0
Land: 4.0 sq. mi.; **Water:** 0.0 sq. mi.   **Elev:** 994 ft.
Incorporated 1876.
Name origin: For the Platte River, which flows through the southeastern part of the county. Previously called Platte River Diggings and Lebanon.

### *Platteville	Town
ZIP: 53818   **Lat:** 42-43-29 N   **Long:** 90-29-06 W
Pop: 1,415 (1990); 1,309 (1980)   **Pop Density:** 43.8
Land: 32.3 sq. mi.; **Water:** 0.0 sq. mi.

### Potosi	Village
ZIP: 53820   **Lat:** 42-41-21 N   **Long:** 90-42-39 W
Pop: 654 (1990); 736 (1980)   **Pop Density:** 467.1
Land: 1.4 sq. mi.; **Water:** 0.0 sq. mi.
Incorporated 1887.
Name origin: Possibly for the famous Potosi Mine in South America. Previously called Snake Hollow.

### *Potosi	Town
ZIP: 53820   **Lat:** 42-41-49 N   **Long:** 90-43-15 W
Pop: 963 (1990); 1,104 (1980)   **Pop Density:** 20.6
Land: 46.7 sq. mi.; **Water:** 11.2 sq. mi.

### Smelser	Town
Lat: 42-38-20 N   **Long:** 90-29-31 W
Pop: 763 (1990); 970 (1980)   **Pop Density:** 21.7
Land: 35.1 sq. mi.; **Water:** 0.0 sq. mi.

### South Lancaster	Town
Lat: 42-48-41 N   **Long:** 90-43-37 W
Pop: 905 (1990); 1,032 (1980)   **Pop Density:** 26.5
Land: 34.1 sq. mi.; **Water:** 0.0 sq. mi.

### Tennyson	Village
Lat: 42-41-22 N   **Long:** 90-41-11 W
Pop: 378 (1990); 476 (1980)   **Pop Density:** 945.0
Land: 0.4 sq. mi.; **Water:** 0.0 sq. mi.
Incorporated 1940.
Name origin: Previously called Dutch Hollow by settlers from Holland.

### Waterloo	Town
Lat: 42-43-29 N   **Long:** 90-50-29 W
Pop: 588 (1990); 615 (1980)   **Pop Density:** 15.4
Land: 38.2 sq. mi.; **Water:** 6.4 sq. mi.

### Watterstown	Town
Lat: 43-09-42 N   **Long:** 90-35-57 W
Pop: 361 (1990); 348 (1980)   **Pop Density:** 13.0
Land: 27.8 sq. mi.; **Water:** 1.0 sq. mi.

### Wingville	Town
Lat: 42-59-29 N   **Long:** 90-29-29 W
Pop: 340 (1990); 417 (1980)   **Pop Density:** 9.6
Land: 35.5 sq. mi.; **Water:** 0.0 sq. mi.

### Woodman	Village
ZIP: 53827   **Lat:** 43-05-26 N   **Long:** 90-47-52 W
Pop: 120 (1990); 116 (1980)   **Pop Density:** 600.0
Land: 0.2 sq. mi.; **Water:** 0.0 sq. mi.
Incorporated 1917.
Name origin: For Cyrus Woodman, who laid out the village in 1864.

### *Woodman	Town
ZIP: 53827   **Lat:** 43-03-13 N   **Long:** 90-50-22 W
Pop: 182 (1990); 216 (1980)   **Pop Density:** 6.8
Land: 26.7 sq. mi.; **Water:** 0.8 sq. mi.

### Wyalusing	Town
Lat: 42-57-10 N   **Long:** 91-05-23 W
Pop: 364 (1990); 443 (1980)   **Pop Density:** 9.1
Land: 39.9 sq. mi.; **Water:** 2.7 sq. mi.

Green County
County Seat: Monroe (ZIP: 53566)

Pop: 30,339 (1990); 30,012 (1980)   **Pop Density:** 51.9
Land: 584.0 sq. mi.; **Water:** 0.6 sq. mi.   **Area Code:** 608
On central southern border of WI, south of Madison; organized Dec 8, 1836 (prior to statehood) from Iowa County.
Name origin: For Gen. Nathanael Greene (1742–86), Revolutionary War officer and quartermaster general (1778–80). The missing *e* not explained.

### Adams	Town
Lat: 42-43-48 N   **Long:** 89-46-50 W
Pop: 452 (1990); 484 (1980)   **Pop Density:** 12.5
Land: 36.2 sq. mi.; **Water:** 0.0 sq. mi.

### Albany	Village
ZIP: 53502   **Lat:** 42-42-25 N   **Long:** 89-26-12 W
Pop: 1,140 (1990); 1,051 (1980)   **Pop Density:** 876.9
Land: 1.3 sq. mi.; **Water:** 0.0 sq. mi.
Incorporated 1883.
Name origin: For Albany, NY, so named by settlers for their former hometown.

WISCONSIN, Green County

***Albany** — Town
ZIP: 53502 Lat: 42-43-25 N Long: 89-25-41 W
Pop: 598 (1990); 657 (1980) Pop Density: 17.5
Land: 34.2 sq. mi.; Water: 0.2 sq. mi.
Part of the town is also in Dane County.

Belleville — Village
ZIP: 53508 Lat: 42-51-22 N Long: 89-31-55 W
Pop: 107 (1990); 99 (1980) Pop Density: 1070.0
Land: 0.1 sq. mi.; Water: 0.0 sq. mi. Elev: 870 ft.
Founded c. 1845. Incorporated 1892. Part of the town is also in Dane County.
Name origin: For founder John Frederick's former home of Belleville, Canada.

Brodhead — City
ZIP: 53520 Lat: 42-37-00 N Long: 89-22-34 W
Pop: 3,165 (1990); 3,153 (1980) Pop Density: 1978.1
Land: 1.6 sq. mi.; Water: 0.0 sq. mi. Elev: 798 ft.
Incorporated 1891.
Name origin: For Edward H. Broadhead of the Chicago, Milwaukee and St. Paul Railway, with a spelling variation.

Brooklyn — Village
ZIP: 53521 Lat: 42-50-59 N Long: 89-22-33 W
Pop: 383 (1990); 377 (1980) Pop Density: 638.3
Land: 0.6 sq. mi.; Water: 0.0 sq. mi.
Incorporated 1905. Part of the town is also in Dane County.
Name origin: Named by engineer John E. Glunt, for the city of Brooklyn, NY.

***Brooklyn** — Town
ZIP: 53521 Lat: 42-49-27 N Long: 89-25-27 W
Pop: 764 (1990); 760 (1980) Pop Density: 21.5
Land: 35.5 sq. mi.; Water: 0.0 sq. mi.

Browntown — Village
ZIP: 53522 Lat: 42-34-40 N Long: 89-47-28 W
Pop: 256 (1990); 284 (1980) Pop Density: 256.0
Land: 1.0 sq. mi.; Water: 0.0 sq. mi.
Incorporated 1890.
Name origin: For William G. Brown, who helped build the mill here. Originally known as Irion, Wood's Mill, and Brown.

Cadi — Town
Lat: 42-32-51 N Long: 89-46-39 W
Pop: 913 (1990); 891 (1980) Pop Density: 25.0
Land: 36.5 sq. mi.; Water: 0.1 sq. mi.

Clarno — Town
Lat: 42-32-46 N Long: 89-39-18 W
Pop: 1,011 (1990); 1,069 (1980) Pop Density: 27.6
Land: 36.6 sq. mi.; Water: 0.0 sq. mi.

Decatur — Town
Lat: 42-38-36 N Long: 89-25-40 W
Pop: 1,076 (1990); 1,035 (1980) Pop Density: 31.5
Land: 34.2 sq. mi.; Water: 0.2 sq. mi.

Exeter — Town
Lat: 42-48-36 N Long: 89-32-53 W
Pop: 756 (1990); 709 (1980) Pop Density: 21.5
Land: 35.1 sq. mi.; Water: 0.0 sq. mi.

Jefferson — Town
Lat: 42-33-14 N Long: 89-32-30 W
Pop: 1,130 (1990); 1,204 (1980) Pop Density: 29.1
Land: 38.8 sq. mi.; Water: 0.0 sq. mi.

Jordan — Town
Lat: 42-38-26 N Long: 89-46-53 W
Pop: 545 (1990); 585 (1980) Pop Density: 15.1
Land: 36.0 sq. mi.; Water: 0.0 sq. mi.

Monroe — City
ZIP: 53566 Lat: 42-35-59 N Long: 89-38-37 W
Pop: 10,241 (1990); 10,027 (1980) Pop Density: 2560.3
Land: 4.0 sq. mi.; Water: 0.0 sq. mi. Elev: 1099 ft.
In southern WI, 30 mi. west of Beloit. Incorporated 1882.
Name origin: For James Monroe (1758–1831), fifth U.S. president.

***Monroe** — Town
ZIP: 53566 Lat: 42-38-34 N Long: 89-39-43 W
Pop: 1,066 (1990); 1,054 (1980) Pop Density: 32.0
Land: 33.3 sq. mi.; Water: 0.0 sq. mi.

Monticello — Village
ZIP: 53570 Lat: 42-44-44 N Long: 89-35-22 W
Pop: 1,140 (1990); 1,021 (1980) Pop Density: 1036.4
Land: 1.1 sq. mi.; Water: 0.0 sq. mi. Elev: 84 ft.
Incorporated 1891.
Name origin: For the mounds or bluffs along the Long Hollow valley. From a term meaning 'little mountain.'

Mount Pleasant — Town
Lat: 42-43-23 N Long: 89-32-21 W
Pop: 539 (1990); 567 (1980) Pop Density: 15.7
Land: 34.3 sq. mi.; Water: 0.0 sq. mi.

New Glarus — Village
ZIP: 53574 Lat: 42-48-47 N Long: 89-38-04 W
Pop: 1,899 (1990); 1,763 (1980) Pop Density: 1356.4
Land: 1.4 sq. mi.; Water: 0.0 sq. mi.
Incorporated 1901.
Name origin: Named by Swiss settlers for Canton Glarus, from which Swiss authorities decided to send families to the U.S. to escape the famine and unemployment in their homeland.

***New Glarus** — Town
ZIP: 53574 Lat: 42-48-29 N Long: 89-39-38 W
Pop: 571 (1990); 510 (1980) Pop Density: 16.5
Land: 34.7 sq. mi.; Water: 0.0 sq. mi.

Spring Grove — Town
Lat: 42-32-53 N Long: 89-25-40 W
Pop: 745 (1990); 819 (1980) Pop Density: 18.7
Land: 39.8 sq. mi.; Water: 0.0 sq. mi.

Sylvester — Town
Lat: 42-38-16 N Long: 89-32-34 W
Pop: 746 (1990); 786 (1980) Pop Density: 20.8
Land: 35.9 sq. mi.; Water: 0.0 sq. mi.

Washington — Town
Lat: 42-43-43 N Long: 89-39-14 W
Pop: 587 (1990); 555 (1980) Pop Density: 16.4
Land: 35.8 sq. mi.; Water: 0.0 sq. mi.

York — Town
Lat: 42-48-42 N Long: 89-46-36 W
Pop: 509 (1990); 552 (1980) Pop Density: 14.1
Land: 36.0 sq. mi.; Water: 0.0 sq. mi.

Green Lake County
County Seat: Green Lake (ZIP: 54941)

Pop: 18,651 (1990); 18,370 (1980)   **Pop Density:** 52.6
Land: 354.3 sq. mi.; **Water:** 26.2 sq. mi.   **Area Code:** 414

In east-central WI, west of Lake Winnebago; organized Mar 5, 1858 from Marquette District.

Name origin: For the large lake in the middle of the county, named for the color of the water.

Berlin — City
ZIP: 54923   Lat: 43-58-04 N   Long: 88-57-04 W
Pop: 5,304 (1990); 5,387 (1980)   Pop Density: 1020.0
Land: 5.2 sq. mi.; Water: 0.3 sq. mi.   Elev: 764 ft.
Incorporated 1857. Part of the town is also in Waushara County.
Name origin: Named in 1851 for Berlin, Germany. Previously called Strong's Landing, and then Strongville.

*Berlin — Town
ZIP: 54923   Lat: 43-56-10 N   Long: 88-56-11 W
Pop: 996 (1990); 1,065 (1980)   Pop Density: 33.5
Land: 29.7 sq. mi.; Water: 0.3 sq. mi.

Brooklyn — Town
Lat: 43-50-38 N   Long: 88-58-02 W
Pop: 1,798 (1990); 1,431 (1980)   Pop Density: 50.6
Land: 35.5 sq. mi.; Water: 11.8 sq. mi.

Green Lake — City
ZIP: 54941   Lat: 43-50-33 N   Long: 88-57-20 W
Pop: 1,064 (1990); 1,208 (1980)   Pop Density: 818.5
Land: 1.3 sq. mi.; Water: 0.2 sq. mi.   Elev: 828 ft.
Incorporated 1962.
Name origin: For the lake with green water at the center of the county. Previously called Dartford, for a Mr. Dart, who built a dam and a ford across the Puckyan River, the lake's outlet.

*Green Lake — Town
ZIP: 54941   Lat: 43-44-56 N   Long: 88-58-51 W
Pop: 1,335 (1990); 1,307 (1980)   Pop Density: 28.2
Land: 47.3 sq. mi.; Water: 1.3 sq. mi.

Kingston — Village
ZIP: 53939   Lat: 43-41-36 N   Long: 89-07-52 W
Pop: 346 (1990); 328 (1980)   Pop Density: 247.1
Land: 1.4 sq. mi.; Water: 0.2 sq. mi.
Incorporated 1923.
Name origin: For Kingston, Canada, the hometown of the wife of J. E. Millard, who owned a grist mill here.

*Kingston — Town
Lat: 43-40-51 N   Long: 89-11-12 W
Pop: 776 (1990); 708 (1980)   Pop Density: 26.9
Land: 28.8 sq. mi.; Water: 0.6 sq. mi.

Mackford — Town
Lat: 43-40-11 N   Long: 88-56-44 W
Pop: 616 (1990); 622 (1980)   Pop Density: 18.3
Land: 33.6 sq. mi.; Water: 0.7 sq. mi.

Manchester — Town
Lat: 43-40-29 N   Long: 89-04-03 W
Pop: 774 (1990); 812 (1980)   Pop Density: 22.2
Land: 34.9 sq. mi.; Water: 0.5 sq. mi.

Markesan — City
ZIP: 53946   Lat: 43-42-33 N   Long: 88-59-22 W
Pop: 1,496 (1990); 1,446 (1980)   Pop Density: 650.4
Land: 2.3 sq. mi.; Water: 0.0 sq. mi.   Elev: 847 ft.
Incorporated 1959.
Name origin: For the Marquesas Islands. Originally known as Granville.

Marquette — Village
ZIP: 53947   Lat: 43-44-31 N   Long: 89-08-19 W
Pop: 182 (1990); 204 (1980)   Pop Density: 227.5
Land: 0.8 sq. mi.; Water: 0.0 sq. mi.
Incorporated 1958.
Name origin: For Father Jacques Marquette (1637–75), a French missionary who explored this area around 1673.

*Marquette — Town
Lat: 43-44-16 N   Long: 89-08-46 W
Pop: 400 (1990); 393 (1980)   Pop Density: 13.2
Land: 30.4 sq. mi.; Water: 9.9 sq. mi.

Princeton — City
ZIP: 54968   Lat: 43-51-08 N   Long: 89-07-46 W
Pop: 1,458 (1990); 1,479 (1980)   Pop Density: 911.3
Land: 1.6 sq. mi.; Water: 0.0 sq. mi.
Incorporated 1920.
Name origin: Named by settler Royal C. Treat when he and his brother obtained title to 132 acres and laid out the town; no reason known for the name. Previously called Treat's Landing.

*Princeton — Town
ZIP: 54968   Lat: 43-49-49 N   Long: 89-07-43 W
Pop: 1,363 (1990); 1,287 (1980)   Pop Density: 38.6
Land: 35.3 sq. mi.; Water: 0.3 sq. mi.

St. Marie — Town
Lat: 43-53-05 N   Long: 89-05-08 W
Pop: 348 (1990); 310 (1980)   Pop Density: 10.4
Land: 33.5 sq. mi.; Water: 0.0 sq. mi.

Seneca — Town
Lat: 43-56-48 N   Long: 89-05-21 W
Pop: 395 (1990); 383 (1980)   Pop Density: 12.1
Land: 32.7 sq. mi.; Water: 0.1 sq. mi.

Iowa County
County Seat: Dodgeville (ZIP: 53533)

Pop: 20,150 (1990); 19,802 (1980) **Pop Density:** 26.4
Land: 762.7 sq. mi.; **Water:** 5.4 sq. mi. **Area Code:** 608

In southwestern WI, west of Madison; organized Oct 9, 1829 (prior to statehood) from a territorial county.

Name origin: For either the Iowa River, or the Iowa Indians. Name is a French version of the Dakota name for the tribe, variously *Ayuhwa, Ouaouia, Aiouez,* and *Ioways* 'the sleepy ones.'

Arena — Village
ZIP: 53503 Lat: 43-09-47 N Long: 89-54-47 W
Pop: 525 (1990); 451 (1980) Pop Density: 656.3
Land: 0.8 sq. mi.; Water: 0.0 sq. mi. Elev: 735 ft.
Incorporated 1923.

*Arena — Town
ZIP: 53503 Lat: 43-07-38 N Long: 89-55-57 W
Pop: 1,301 (1990); 1,292 (1980) Pop Density: 16.6
Land: 78.3 sq. mi.; Water: 1.5 sq. mi.

Avoca — Village
ZIP: 53506 Lat: 43-11-17 N Long: 90-19-30 W
Pop: 474 (1990); 505 (1980) Pop Density: 206.1
Land: 2.3 sq. mi.; Water: 0.1 sq. mi. Elev: 698 ft.
Incorporated 1870.
Name origin: For the valley of Avoca in Thomas Moore's (1779–1852) poem, or named in 1857 by an Irishman who was homesick for the vale of Avoca in Ireland.

Barneveld — Village
ZIP: 53507 Lat: 43-00-52 N Long: 89-53-45 W
Pop: 660 (1990); 579 (1980) Pop Density: 507.7
Land: 1.3 sq. mi.; Water: 0.0 sq. mi.
Incorporated 1906.
Name origin: Named by a native of Holland for Dutch leader, Jonna (Johan van Olden) Barneveld (1547–1619).

Blanchardville — Village
ZIP: 53516 Lat: 42-48-56 N Long: 89-51-36 W
Pop: 167 (1990); 139 (1980) Pop Density: 1670.0
Land: 0.1 sq. mi.; Water: 0.0 sq. mi. Elev: 833 ft.
Incorporated 1890. Part of the town is also in Lafayette County.
Name origin: For Alvin Blanchard, who bought a mill here in 1855. Previously called Zarahamia by local members of the Latter Day Saints.

Brigham — Town
Lat: 42-59-41 N Long: 89-53-45 W
Pop: 692 (1990); 821 (1980) Pop Density: 10.8
Land: 64.1 sq. mi.; Water: 0.0 sq. mi.

Clyde — Town
Lat: 43-07-53 N Long: 90-13-12 W
Pop: 391 (1990); 381 (1980) Pop Density: 11.5
Land: 34.1 sq. mi.; Water: 0.5 sq. mi.

Cobb — Village
ZIP: 53526 Lat: 42-57-54 N Long: 90-19-45 W
Pop: 440 (1990); 409 (1980) Pop Density: 488.9
Land: 0.9 sq. mi.; Water: 0.0 sq. mi. Elev: 1165 ft.
Incorporated 1902.
Name origin: For Capt. Amasa Cobb, a congressman who was influential in establishing the post office and railroad. Previously called Cross Plains for the road that crossed the prairie here.

Dodgeville — City
ZIP: 53533 Lat: 42-57-49 N Long: 90-07-48 W
Pop: 3,882 (1990); 3,458 (1980) Pop Density: 1176.4
Land: 3.3 sq. mi.; Water: 0.0 sq. mi. Elev: 1222 ft.
Incorporated 1889.
Name origin: For settler Henry Dodge (1782–1867), who in 1836 became the first governor of the WI Territory. Previously called Minersville.

*Dodgeville — Town
ZIP: 53533 Lat: 43-00-41 N Long: 90-07-23 W
Pop: 1,172 (1990); 1,234 (1980) Pop Density: 13.0
Land: 90.1 sq. mi.; Water: 0.4 sq. mi.

Eden — Town
Lat: 42-58-27 N Long: 90-20-57 W
Pop: 381 (1990); 419 (1980) Pop Density: 10.8
Land: 35.2 sq. mi.; Water: 0.1 sq. mi.

Highland — Village
ZIP: 53543 Lat: 43-02-46 N Long: 90-22-44 W
Pop: 799 (1990); 860 (1980) Pop Density: 726.4
Land: 1.1 sq. mi.; Water: 0.0 sq. mi.
Incorporated 1873.
Name origin: Named in 1846. Previously called Franklin.

*Highland — Town
ZIP: 53543 Lat: 43-03-58 N Long: 90-20-38 W
Pop: 756 (1990); 844 (1980) Pop Density: 11.7
Land: 64.7 sq. mi.; Water: 0.2 sq. mi.

Hollandale — Village
ZIP: 53544 Lat: 42-52-34 N Long: 89-55-59 W
Pop: 256 (1990); 271 (1980) Pop Density: 365.7
Land: 0.7 sq. mi.; Water: 0.0 sq. mi. Elev: 862 ft.
Incorporated 1910.
Name origin: For Bjorn Holland, who ran a small supply store for railroad construction crews. Previously called Bennville.

Linden — Village
ZIP: 53553 Lat: 42-55-09 N Long: 90-16-26 W
Pop: 429 (1990); 395 (1980) Pop Density: 536.3
Land: 0.8 sq. mi.; Water: 0.0 sq. mi. Elev: 1101 ft.
Incorporated 1900.
Name origin: Named in 1855 for a big linden tree that grew outside the general store. Previously called Peddler's Creek, after a nearby stream.

*Linden — Town
ZIP: 53553 Lat: 42-55-02 N Long: 90-15-36 W
Pop: 773 (1990); 828 (1980) Pop Density: 12.7
Land: 60.7 sq. mi.; Water: 0.0 sq. mi.

WISCONSIN, Iowa County

Livingston
Village
ZIP: 53554   **Lat:** 42-53-59 N   **Long:** 90-25-31 W
Pop: 10 (1990); 16 (1980)   **Pop Density:** 50.0
Land: 0.2 sq. mi.; **Water:** 0.0 sq. mi.   **Elev:** 1164 ft.
Incorporated 1914. Part of the town is also in Grant County.
Name origin: For Hugh Livingston, who donated his farmland to the railroad. Previously called Dublin by Irish settlers.

Mifflin
Town
Lat: 42-52-46 N   **Long:** 90-21-52 W
Pop: 564 (1990); 591 (1980)   **Pop Density:** 11.1
Land: 50.7 sq. mi.; **Water:** 0.0 sq. mi.

Mineral Point
City
ZIP: 53565   **Lat:** 42-51-42 N   **Long:** 90-10-59 W
Pop: 2,428 (1990); 2,259 (1980)   **Pop Density:** 837.2
Land: 2.9 sq. mi.; **Water:** 0.0 sq. mi.   **Elev:** 1135 ft.
Incorporated 1857.
Name origin: For the lead and zinc found at a high rocky point between two streams.

*Mineral Point
Town
ZIP: 53565   **Lat:** 42-52-01 N   **Long:** 90-09-07 W
Pop: 851 (1990); 792 (1980)   **Pop Density:** 14.4
Land: 59.1 sq. mi.; **Water:** 0.1 sq. mi.

Montfort
Village
ZIP: 53569   **Lat:** 42-58-10 N   **Long:** 90-25-35 W
Pop: 96 (1990); 100 (1980)   **Pop Density:** 4800.0
Land: 0.02 sq. mi.; **Water:** 0.0 sq. mi.
Incorporated 1893. Part of the town is also in Grant County.
Name origin: For a small fort that miners built here to protect themselves during the Black Hawk War. Previously called Wingville and Podunk.

Moscow
Town
Lat: 42-52-05 N   **Long:** 89-54-08 W
Pop: 528 (1990); 568 (1980)   **Pop Density:** 12.8
Land: 41.4 sq. mi.; **Water:** 0.0 sq. mi.

Muscoda
Village
ZIP: 53573   **Lat:** 43-10-47 N   **Long:** 90-25-08 W
Pop: 4 (1990)   **Pop Density:** 10.0
Land: 0.4 sq. mi.; **Water:** 0.0 sq. mi.
Incorporated 1894. Part of the town is also in Grant County.
Name origin: From *mash-ko-deng*, an Indian word for 'meadow' or 'prairie.' Previously called English Prairie or English Meadow because an English trader and his son were murdered here.

Pulaski
Town
Lat: 43-09-33 N   **Long:** 90-21-00 W
Pop: 392 (1990); 462 (1980)   **Pop Density:** 9.1
Land: 43.3 sq. mi.; **Water:** 1.3 sq. mi.

Rewey
Village
ZIP: 53580   **Lat:** 42-50-30 N   **Long:** 90-23-46 W
Pop: 220 (1990); 233 (1980)   **Pop Density:** 440.0
Land: 0.5 sq. mi.; **Water:** 0.0 sq. mi.   **Elev:** 1140 ft.
Platted 1880. Incorporated 1902.
Name origin: For J. W. Rewey.

Ridgeway
Village
ZIP: 53582   **Lat:** 42-59-56 N   **Long:** 89-59-31 W
Pop: 577 (1990); 503 (1980)   **Pop Density:** 443.8
Land: 1.3 sq. mi.; **Water:** 0.0 sq. mi.
Incorporated 1902.

*Ridgeway
Town
ZIP: 53582   **Lat:** 42-59-26 N   **Long:** 89-59-29 W
Pop: 557 (1990); 564 (1980)   **Pop Density:** 13.0
Land: 42.7 sq. mi.; **Water:** 0.0 sq. mi.

Waldwick
Town
Lat: 42-51-26 N   **Long:** 90-01-20 W
Pop: 487 (1990); 503 (1980)   **Pop Density:** 11.6
Land: 41.9 sq. mi.; **Water:** 0.0 sq. mi.

Wyoming
Town
Lat: 43-07-18 N   **Long:** 90-06-32 W
Pop: 338 (1990); 325 (1980)   **Pop Density:** 8.5
Land: 39.8 sq. mi.; **Water:** 1.1 sq. mi.

Iron County
County Seat: Hurley (ZIP: 54534)

Pop: 6,153 (1990); 6,730 (1980)   **Pop Density:** 8.1
Land: 757.3 sq. mi.; **Water:** 162.0 sq. mi.   **Area Code:** 715
On central northern border of WI; organized Mar 1, 1893 from Ashland and Oneida counties.
Name origin: For the huge deposits of iron ore found in the Mesabi Range.

Anderson
Town
Lat: 46-20-37 N   **Long:** 90-27-55 W
Pop: 69 (1990); 91 (1980)   **Pop Density:** 0.8
Land: 83.2 sq. mi.; **Water:** 0.4 sq. mi.

Carey
Town
Lat: 46-18-56 N   **Long:** 90-13-49 W
Pop: 175 (1990); 179 (1980)   **Pop Density:** 4.2
Land: 41.6 sq. mi.; **Water:** 1.5 sq. mi.

Gurney
Town
Lat: 46-28-41 N   **Long:** 90-30-22 W
Pop: 143 (1990); 153 (1980)   **Pop Density:** 3.9
Land: 37.1 sq. mi.; **Water:** 0.0 sq. mi.

Hurley
City
ZIP: 54534   **Lat:** 46-26-39 N   **Long:** 90-11-47 W
Pop: 1,782 (1990); 2,015 (1980)   **Pop Density:** 574.8
Land: 3.1 sq. mi.; **Water:** 0.2 sq. mi.
Platted 1885. Incorporated 1918.
Name origin: For Judge M. A. Hurley, a lawyer and iron ore mine operator.

Kimball
Town
Lat: 46-28-28 N   **Long:** 90-16-53 W
Pop: 513 (1990); 499 (1980)   **Pop Density:** 13.8
Land: 37.1 sq. mi.; **Water:** 0.0 sq. mi.

Knight — Town
Lat: 46-15-51 N Long: 90-21-38 W
Pop: 265 (1990); 294 (1980) Pop Density: 2.8
Land: 94.1 sq. mi.; Water: 1.0 sq. mi.

Mercer — Town
ZIP: 54547 Lat: 46-09-48 N Long: 90-07-29 W
Pop: 1,325 (1990); 1,425 (1980) Pop Density: 7.9
Land: 168.1 sq. mi.; Water: 16.7 sq. mi.

Montreal — City
ZIP: 54550 Lat: 46-25-49 N Long: 90-14-19 W
Pop: 838 (1990); 887 (1980) Pop Density: 380.9
Land: 2.2 sq. mi.; Water: 0.0 sq. mi.
Incorporated 1924.

Oma — Town
Lat: 46-17-01 N Long: 90-05-17 W
Pop: 260 (1990); 298 (1980) Pop Density: 3.5
Land: 74.7 sq. mi.; Water: 3.0 sq. mi.

Pence — Town
Lat: 46-21-36 N Long: 90-16-25 W
Pop: 181 (1990); 191 (1980) Pop Density: 5.6
Land: 32.2 sq. mi.; Water: 3.9 sq. mi.

Saxon — Town
ZIP: 54559 Lat: 46-30-02 N Long: 90-25-21 W
Pop: 335 (1990); 362 (1980) Pop Density: 5.1
Land: 66.0 sq. mi.; Water: 0.1 sq. mi.

Sherman — Town
Lat: 46-02-53 N Long: 90-05-02 W
Pop: 267 (1990); 336 (1980) Pop Density: 2.3
Land: 118.0 sq. mi.; Water: 18.6 sq. mi.

Jackson County
County Seat: Black River Falls (ZIP: 54615)

Pop: 16,588 (1990); 16,831 (1980) Pop Density: 16.8
Land: 987.3 sq. mi.; Water: 12.8 sq. mi. Area Code: 715
In west-central WI, northwest of Madison; organized Feb 11, 1853 from Crawford County.
Name origin: For Andrew Jackson (1767–1845), seventh U.S. president.

Adams — Town
Lat: 44-21-11 N Long: 90-49-49 W
Pop: 1,167 (1990); 1,300 (1980) Pop Density: 32.3
Land: 36.1 sq. mi.; Water: 1.0 sq. mi.

Albion — Town
Lat: 44-16-56 N Long: 90-57-33 W
Pop: 904 (1990); 976 (1980) Pop Density: 19.8
Land: 45.6 sq. mi.; Water: 0.2 sq. mi.

Alma — Town
Lat: 44-25-49 N Long: 90-51-45 W
Pop: 831 (1990); 696 (1980) Pop Density: 14.4
Land: 57.9 sq. mi.; Water: 0.0 sq. mi.

Alma Center — Village
ZIP: 54611 Lat: 44-26-11 N Long: 90-54-46 W
Pop: 416 (1990); 454 (1980) Pop Density: 416.0
Land: 1.0 sq. mi.; Water: 0.0 sq. mi.
Incorporated 1902.

Bear Bluff — Town
Lat: 44-13-25 N Long: 90-22-59 W
Pop: 149 (1990); 133 (1980) Pop Density: 2.8
Land: 53.1 sq. mi.; Water: 3.0 sq. mi.

Black River Falls — City
ZIP: 54615 Lat: 44-17-55 N Long: 90-50-49 W
Pop: 3,490 (1990); 3,434 (1980) Pop Density: 1203.4
Land: 2.9 sq. mi.; Water: 0.1 sq. mi. Elev: 796 ft.
Incorporated 1883.

Brockway — Town
Lat: 44-17-16 N Long: 90-46-17 W
Pop: 1,222 (1990); 1,053 (1980) Pop Density: 25.6
Land: 47.8 sq. mi.; Water: 0.8 sq. mi.

City Point — Town
Lat: 44-21-27 N Long: 90-25-50 W
Pop: 193 (1990); 196 (1980) Pop Density: 2.2
Land: 89.1 sq. mi.; Water: 1.1 sq. mi.

Cleveland — Town
Lat: 44-33-12 N Long: 90-58-20 W
Pop: 452 (1990); 422 (1980) Pop Density: 12.6
Land: 35.9 sq. mi.; Water: 0.0 sq. mi.

Curran — Town
Lat: 44-22-30 N Long: 91-06-07 W
Pop: 351 (1990); 410 (1980) Pop Density: 9.7
Land: 36.2 sq. mi.; Water: 0.0 sq. mi.

Franklin — Town
Lat: 44-12-35 N Long: 91-05-05 W
Pop: 431 (1990); 417 (1980) Pop Density: 11.8
Land: 36.6 sq. mi.; Water: 0.0 sq. mi.

Garden Valley — Town
Lat: 44-28-00 N Long: 90-59-19 W
Pop: 386 (1990); 421 (1980) Pop Density: 10.7
Land: 36.2 sq. mi.; Water: 0.0 sq. mi.

Garfield — Town
Lat: 44-32-43 N Long: 91-06-17 W
Pop: 421 (1990); 423 (1980) Pop Density: 11.7
Land: 36.0 sq. mi.; Water: 0.0 sq. mi.

Hixton — Village
ZIP: 54635 Lat: 44-23-02 N Long: 91-00-39 W
Pop: 345 (1990); 364 (1980) Pop Density: 431.3
Land: 0.8 sq. mi.; Water: 0.0 sq. mi.
Platted 1860. Incorporated 1920.
Name origin: For settler, John L. Hicks. Previously called

Williamsport and Hick's Town. Originally part of the town of Alma.

*Hixton — Town
ZIP: 54635 Lat: 44-22-26 N Long: 90-58-53 W
Pop: 652 (1990); 646 (1980) Pop Density: 18.6
Land: 35.1 sq. mi.; Water: 0.0 sq. mi.

Irving — Town
Lat: 44-12-22 N Long: 90-57-59 W
Pop: 565 (1990); 618 (1980) Pop Density: 12.9
Land: 43.9 sq. mi.; Water: 0.5 sq. mi.

Knapp — Town
Lat: 44-15-21 N Long: 90-30-15 W
Pop: 257 (1990); 201 (1980) Pop Density: 3.7
Land: 69.1 sq. mi.; Water: 2.4 sq. mi.

Komensky — Town
Lat: 44-22-59 N Long: 90-39-16 W
Pop: 292 (1990); 449 (1980) Pop Density: 5.0
Land: 58.9 sq. mi.; Water: 0.5 sq. mi.

Manchester — Town
Lat: 44-12-14 N Long: 90-46-49 W
Pop: 563 (1990); 590 (1980) Pop Density: 8.8
Land: 64.3 sq. mi.; Water: 0.2 sq. mi.

Melrose — Village
ZIP: 54642 Lat: 44-07-55 N Long: 90-59-48 W
Pop: 551 (1990); 507 (1980) Pop Density: 688.8
Land: 0.8 sq. mi.; Water: 0.0 sq. mi.
Incorporated 1914.
Name origin: Named in 1860 for Melrose Abbey in Scotland. Previously called Bristol for Bristol, England.

*Melrose — Town
ZIP: 54642 Lat: 44-06-56 N Long: 91-00-33 W
Pop: 357 (1990); 338 (1980) Pop Density: 13.3
Land: 26.8 sq. mi.; Water: 0.6 sq. mi.

Merrillan — Village
ZIP: 54754 Lat: 44-27-03 N Long: 90-50-11 W
Pop: 553 (1990); 587 (1980) Pop Density: 425.4
Land: 1.3 sq. mi.; Water: 0.1 sq. mi. Elev: 937 ft.
Incorporated 1881.
Name origin: For founders Benjamin H. and Leander G. Merrill.

Millston — Town
Lat: 44-14-31 N Long: 90-37-36 W
Pop: 154 (1990); 202 (1980) Pop Density: 2.2
Land: 70.9 sq. mi.; Water: 1.5 sq. mi.

North Bend — Town
ZIP: 54642 Lat: 44-07-15 N Long: 91-06-06 W
Pop: 419 (1990); 456 (1980) Pop Density: 15.1
Land: 27.8 sq. mi.; Water: 0.5 sq. mi.

Northfield — Town
Lat: 44-28-16 N Long: 91-06-00 W
Pop: 572 (1990); 652 (1980) Pop Density: 15.9
Land: 36.0 sq. mi.; Water: 0.0 sq. mi.

Springfield — Town
Lat: 44-17-20 N Long: 91-06-29 W
Pop: 476 (1990); 475 (1980) Pop Density: 13.0
Land: 36.5 sq. mi.; Water: 0.0 sq. mi.

Taylor — Village
ZIP: 54659 Lat: 44-19-19 N Long: 91-07-16 W
Pop: 419 (1990); 411 (1980) Pop Density: 598.6
Land: 0.7 sq. mi.; Water: 0.0 sq. mi.
Settled c. 1854. Incorporated 1919.
Name origin: For a railroad official.

Jefferson County
County Seat: Jefferson (ZIP: 53549)

Pop: 67,783 (1990); 66,152 (1980) Pop Density: 121.7
Land: 557.1 sq. mi.; Water: 25.7 sq. mi. Area Code: 414

In southeastern WI, east of Milwaukee; organized Dec 7, 1836 from Dodge and Waukesha counties.

Name origin: For Thomas Jefferson (1743–1826), U.S. patriot and statesman; third U.S. president. Others claim it was named for Jefferson County, NY, former home of some prominent early settlers.

Aztalan — Town
Lat: 43-03-15 N Long: 88-50-13 W
Pop: 1,476 (1990); 1,752 (1980) Pop Density: 58.3
Land: 25.3 sq. mi.; Water: 0.6 sq. mi.

Cambridge — Village
Lat: 43-00-42 N Long: 89-00-40 W
Pop: 80 (1990); 59 (1980) Pop Density: 400.0
Land: 0.2 sq. mi.; Water: 0.0 sq. mi.
Incorporated 1891. Part of the town is also in Dane County.
Name origin: Named in 1847 by landowner Alvin B. Carpenter for Cambridge, NY, the hometown of his sweetheart.

Cold Spring — Town
Lat: 42-52-50 N Long: 88-43-03 W
Pop: 683 (1990); 684 (1980) Pop Density: 28.0
Land: 24.4 sq. mi.; Water: 0.1 sq. mi.

Concord — Town
Lat: 43-04-10 N Long: 88-35-58 W
Pop: 1,896 (1990); 1,805 (1980) Pop Density: 52.7
Land: 36.0 sq. mi.; Water: 0.6 sq. mi.

Farmington — Town
Lat: 43-03-37 N Long: 88-42-50 W
Pop: 1,404 (1990); 1,528 (1980) Pop Density: 38.4
Land: 36.6 sq. mi.; Water: 0.1 sq. mi.

Fort Atkinson — City
ZIP: 53538 Lat: 42-55-36 N Long: 88-50-29 W
Pop: 10,227 (1990); 9,785 (1980) Pop Density: 2378.4
Land: 4.3 sq. mi.; Water: 0.1 sq. mi. Elev: 790 ft.
Incorporated 1878.
Name origin: Named in 1836 by settlers for Brig. Gen. Henry Atkinson (1782–1842). Originally known as Fort Koshkonong.

Hebron — Town
Lat: 42-55-55 N Long: 88-43-07 W
Pop: 975 (1990); 1,104 (1980) Pop Density: 33.9
Land: 28.8 sq. mi.; Water: 0.1 sq. mi.

Ixonia — Town
ZIP: 53036 Lat: 43-08-52 N Long: 88-35-47 W
Pop: 2,789 (1990); 2,905 (1980) Pop Density: 77.7
Land: 35.9 sq. mi.; Water: 0.6 sq. mi.

Jefferson — City
ZIP: 53549 Lat: 43-00-23 N Long: 88-48-29 W
Pop: 6,078 (1990); 5,647 (1980) Pop Density: 1447.1
Land: 4.2 sq. mi.; Water: 0.2 sq. mi.
Incorporated 1878.
Name origin: For Thomas Jefferson (1743–1826), third U.S. president.

*Jefferson — Town
ZIP: 53549 Lat: 42-59-13 N Long: 88-47-26 W
Pop: 2,673 (1990); 2,891 (1980) Pop Density: 61.3
Land: 43.6 sq. mi.; Water: 0.5 sq. mi.

Johnson Creek — Village
ZIP: 53038 Lat: 43-04-47 N Long: 88-46-26 W
Pop: 1,259 (1990); 1,136 (1980) Pop Density: 1049.2
Land: 1.2 sq. mi.; Water: 0.0 sq. mi. Elev: 812 ft.
Incorporated 1903.
Name origin: For Timothy Johnson, who had an early land claim here. Previously called Belleville.

Koshkonong — Town
Lat: 42-53-00 N Long: 88-50-51 W
Pop: 2,984 (1990); 2,979 (1980) Pop Density: 69.2
Land: 43.1 sq. mi.; Water: 0.9 sq. mi. Elev: 820 ft.

Lake Mills — City
ZIP: 53551 Lat: 43-04-26 N Long: 88-54-28 W
Pop: 4,143 (1990); 3,670 (1980) Pop Density: 1479.6
Land: 2.8 sq. mi.; Water: 0.4 sq. mi.
Incorporated 1905.
Name origin: Named by Capt. Joseph Keyes, who owned mills here. Previously called Keyes Mills and Tyranena.

*Lake Mills — Town
ZIP: 53551 Lat: 43-03-49 N Long: 88-57-46 W
Pop: 1,584 (1990); 1,515 (1980) Pop Density: 50.9
Land: 31.1 sq. mi.; Water: 2.1 sq. mi.

Lake Ripley — CDP
Lat: 43-00-20 N Long: 88-59-09 W
Pop: 1,218 (1990) Pop Density: 641.1
Land: 1.9 sq. mi.; Water: 0.6 sq. mi.

Milford — Town
Lat: 43-08-36 N Long: 88-50-17 W
Pop: 1,007 (1990); 1,066 (1980) Pop Density: 29.7
Land: 33.9 sq. mi.; Water: 1.2 sq. mi.

Oakland — Town
Lat: 42-58-19 N Long: 88-57-30 W
Pop: 2,526 (1990); 2,240 (1980) Pop Density: 72.4
Land: 34.9 sq. mi.; Water: 1.3 sq. mi.

Palmyra — Village
ZIP: 53156 Lat: 42-52-44 N Long: 88-35-17 W
Pop: 1,539 (1990); 1,515 (1980) Pop Density: 1282.5
Land: 1.2 sq. mi.; Water: 0.0 sq. mi. Elev: 848 ft.
Incorporated 1866.
Name origin: For Palmyra, Syria, the oasis city mentioned in the Bible.

*Palmyra — Town
ZIP: 53156 Lat: 42-53-00 N Long: 88-35-56 W
Pop: 1,177 (1990); 1,069 (1980) Pop Density: 33.8
Land: 34.8 sq. mi.; Water: 0.4 sq. mi.

Sullivan — Village
ZIP: 53178 Lat: 43-00-45 N Long: 88-35-22 W
Pop: 432 (1990); 434 (1980) Pop Density: 392.7
Land: 1.1 sq. mi.; Water: 0.0 sq. mi. Elev: 860 ft.
Incorporated 1915.
Name origin: Named in 1883, possibly for John Sullivan, a transient workman. Originally known as Winfield because a field between the woods here was open to the wind.

*Sullivan — Town
ZIP: 53178 Lat: 42-58-29 N Long: 88-36-05 W
Pop: 1,929 (1990); 1,646 (1980) Pop Density: 55.6
Land: 34.7 sq. mi.; Water: 0.9 sq. mi.

Sumner — Town
Lat: 42-53-37 N Long: 88-57-45 W
Pop: 822 (1990); 973 (1980) Pop Density: 50.4
Land: 16.3 sq. mi.; Water: 15.0 sq. mi.

Waterloo — City
ZIP: 53594 Lat: 43-10-58 N Long: 88-59-23 W
Pop: 2,712 (1990); 2,393 (1980) Pop Density: 695.4
Land: 3.9 sq. mi.; Water: 0.0 sq. mi. Elev: 819 ft.
Incorporated 1962.
Name origin: Named by settler Bradford Hill for the battle of Waterloo at which Napoleon I (1769–1821) was decisively defeated. Originally known as Maunesha by the Indians.

*Waterloo — Town
ZIP: 53594 Lat: 43-08-47 N Long: 88-56-32 W
Pop: 694 (1990); 811 (1980) Pop Density: 21.5
Land: 32.3 sq. mi.; Water: 0.0 sq. mi.

Watertown — City
ZIP: 53094 Lat: 43-10-57 N Long: 88-43-28 W
Pop: 12,388 (1990); 12,202 (1980) Pop Density: 1966.3
Land: 6.3 sq. mi.; Water: 0.2 sq. mi. Elev: 823 ft.
In southeastern WI, 32 mi. east of Madison. Incorporated 1853. Part of the town is also in Dodge County.
Name origin: For Watertown, NY. Previously called Johnson's Rapids.

*Watertown — Town
ZIP: 53094 Lat: 43-08-53 N Long: 88-43-56 W
Pop: 1,840 (1990); 1,921 (1980) Pop Density: 47.1
Land: 39.1 sq. mi.; Water: 0.5 sq. mi.

WISCONSIN, Jefferson County *American Places Dictionary*

Whitewater City
ZIP: 53190 **Lat:** 42-50-44 N **Long:** 88-44-39 W
Pop: 2,466 (1990); 2,422 (1980) **Pop Density:** 2466.0
Land: 1.0 sq. mi.; **Water:** 0.0 sq. mi.

In southern WI, 18 mi. northeast of Janesville. Incorporated 1885. Part of the town is also in Walworth County.

Name origin: From the Indian term for the river, *Wau-be-gan-naw-o-cat* probably meaning 'white water.'

Juneau County
County Seat: Mauston (ZIP: 53948)

Pop: 21,650 (1990); 21,037 (1980) **Pop Density:** 28.2
Land: 767.7 sq. mi.; **Water:** 36.5 sq. mi. **Area Code:** 608

In south-central WI, northwest of Madison; organized Oct 13, 1856 from Adams County.

Name origin: For Solomon Juneau (1793–1856), early French trader, the first postmaster and first mayor of Milwaukee, called "the father of the city."

Armenia Town
Lat: 44-10-43 N **Long:** 90-00-38 W
Pop: 592 (1990); 545 (1980) **Pop Density:** 9.0
Land: 66.0 sq. mi.; **Water:** 11.7 sq. mi.

Camp Douglas Village
ZIP: 54618 **Lat:** 43-55-08 N **Long:** 90-16-08 W
Pop: 512 (1990); 589 (1980) **Pop Density:** 512.0
Land: 1.0 sq. mi.; **Water:** 0.0 sq. mi. **Elev:** 933 ft.
Incorporated 1893.

Name origin: For a railroad camp run by James Douglas that supplied cut wood for locomotives.

Clearfield Town
Lat: 43-56-42 N **Long:** 90-08-15 W
Pop: 502 (1990); 538 (1980) **Pop Density:** 14.0
Land: 35.8 sq. mi.; **Water:** 0.0 sq. mi.

Cutler Town
ZIP: 54646 **Lat:** 44-02-41 N **Long:** 90-15-12 W
Pop: 314 (1990); 369 (1980) **Pop Density:** 6.0
Land: 52.2 sq. mi.; **Water:** 1.9 sq. mi.

Elroy City
ZIP: 53929 **Lat:** 43-44-33 N **Long:** 90-16-20 W
Pop: 1,533 (1990); 1,504 (1980) **Pop Density:** 901.8
Land: 1.7 sq. mi.; **Water:** 0.0 sq. mi. **Elev:** 959 ft.
Incorporated 1885.

Name origin: From a reversal of the *Le* in LeRoy, because there was already another LeRoy in WI. Originally named by James Madison Brintnall for his hometown of LeRoy, NY.

Finley Town
Lat: 44-12-01 N **Long:** 90-08-16 W
Pop: 66 (1990); 72 (1980) **Pop Density:** 1.7
Land: 38.3 sq. mi.; **Water:** 0.3 sq. mi.

Fountain Town
Lat: 43-51-13 N **Long:** 90-15-29 W
Pop: 633 (1990); 598 (1980) **Pop Density:** 20.4
Land: 31.0 sq. mi.; **Water:** 0.0 sq. mi.

Germantown Town
Lat: 43-54-56 N **Long:** 90-01-19 W
Pop: 615 (1990); 638 (1980) **Pop Density:** 18.5
Land: 33.2 sq. mi.; **Water:** 11.8 sq. mi.

Hustler Village
ZIP: 54637 **Lat:** 43-52-45 N **Long:** 90-16-05 W
Pop: 156 (1990); 170 (1980) **Pop Density:** 312.0
Land: 0.5 sq. mi.; **Water:** 0.0 sq. mi. **Elev:** 929 ft.
Incorporated 1914.

Name origin: Probably for Hustler Street, an important road in the village.

Kildare Town
Lat: 43-43-43 N **Long:** 89-54-31 W
Pop: 491 (1990); 465 (1980) **Pop Density:** 17.7
Land: 27.8 sq. mi.; **Water:** 0.5 sq. mi.

Kingston Town
Lat: 44-10-36 N **Long:** 90-15-10 W
Pop: 57 (1990); 64 (1980) **Pop Density:** 1.0
Land: 54.6 sq. mi.; **Water:** 2.5 sq. mi.

Lemonweir Town
Lat: 43-47-04 N **Long:** 90-01-03 W
Pop: 1,707 (1990); 1,317 (1980) **Pop Density:** 39.7
Land: 43.0 sq. mi.; **Water:** 0.0 sq. mi.

Lindina Town
Lat: 43-47-03 N **Long:** 90-08-04 W
Pop: 796 (1990); 816 (1980) **Pop Density:** 23.8
Land: 33.5 sq. mi.; **Water:** 0.0 sq. mi.

Lisbon Town
Lat: 43-51-24 N **Long:** 90-07-56 W
Pop: 862 (1990); 903 (1980) **Pop Density:** 30.2
Land: 28.5 sq. mi.; **Water:** 0.0 sq. mi.

Lyndon Town
Lat: 43-40-06 N **Long:** 89-52-05 W
Pop: 790 (1990); 701 (1980) **Pop Density:** 27.9
Land: 28.3 sq. mi.; **Water:** 1.3 sq. mi.

Lyndon Station Village
ZIP: 53944 **Lat:** 43-42-36 N **Long:** 89-53-39 W
Pop: 474 (1990); 375 (1980) **Pop Density:** 237.0
Land: 2.0 sq. mi.; **Water:** 0.0 sq. mi.
Incorporated 1903.

American Places Dictionary
WISCONSIN, Kenosha County

Marion
Town
Lat: 43-49-15 N **Long:** 89-56-34 W
Pop: 351 (1990); 362 (1980) **Pop Density:** 14.9
Land: 23.5 sq. mi.; **Water:** 0.9 sq. mi.

Mauston
City
ZIP: 53948 **Lat:** 43-48-02 N **Long:** 90-04-51 W
Pop: 3,439 (1990); 3,284 (1980) **Pop Density:** 1185.9
Land: 2.9 sq. mi.; **Water:** 0.4 sq. mi. **Elev:** 883 ft.
Platted 1834. Incorporated 1883.
Name origin: For M. M. Maughes, who managed a mill here; with a spelling variation. Previously called To-ko-nee and Maugha Mills.

Necedah
Village
ZIP: 54646 **Lat:** 44-01-28 N **Long:** 90-04-18 W
Pop: 743 (1990); 773 (1980) **Pop Density:** 285.8
Land: 2.6 sq. mi.; **Water:** 0.3 sq. mi.
Incorporated 1870.
Name origin: From an Indian name thought to mean either 'let there be three of us' or 'land of the yellow waters,' referring to the Yellow River.

*Necedah
Town
ZIP: 54646 **Lat:** 44-03-45 N **Long:** 90-06-18 W
Pop: 1,601 (1990); 1,394 (1980) **Pop Density:** 20.4
Land: 78.4 sq. mi.; **Water:** 4.6 sq. mi.

New Lisbon
City
ZIP: 53950 **Lat:** 43-52-42 N **Long:** 90-09-52 W
Pop: 1,491 (1990); 1,390 (1980) **Pop Density:** 621.3
Land: 2.4 sq. mi.; **Water:** 0.2 sq. mi. **Elev:** 891 ft.
Incorporated 1889.
Name origin: Probably for Lisbon, OH. Previously called Wa-du-shudan and Mill Haven.

Orange
Town
Lat: 43-56-29 N **Long:** 90-15-01 W
Pop: 581 (1990); 607 (1980) **Pop Density:** 16.6
Land: 35.1 sq. mi.; **Water:** 0.0 sq. mi.

Plymouth
Town
Lat: 43-46-52 N **Long:** 90-14-59 W
Pop: 601 (1990); 644 (1980) **Pop Density:** 17.4
Land: 34.6 sq. mi.; **Water:** 0.0 sq. mi.

Seven Mile Creek
Town
Lat: 43-40-57 N **Long:** 90-01-01 W
Pop: 383 (1990); 362 (1980) **Pop Density:** 10.5
Land: 36.4 sq. mi.; **Water:** 0.0 sq. mi.

Summit
Town
Lat: 43-41-03 N **Long:** 90-08-11 W
Pop: 600 (1990); 721 (1980) **Pop Density:** 16.3
Land: 36.9 sq. mi.; **Water:** 0.0 sq. mi.

Union Center
Village
ZIP: 53962 **Lat:** 43-41-02 N **Long:** 90-15-47 W
Pop: 197 (1990); 216 (1980) **Pop Density:** 281.4
Land: 0.7 sq. mi.; **Water:** 0.0 sq. mi. **Elev:** 922 ft.
Incorporated 1913.

Wonewoc
Village
ZIP: 53968 **Lat:** 43-39-11 N **Long:** 90-13-26 W
Pop: 793 (1990); 842 (1980) **Pop Density:** 793.0
Land: 1.0 sq. mi.; **Water:** 0.0 sq. mi. **Elev:** 938 ft.
Incorporated 1878.
Name origin: From a Chippewa term thought to mean 'to howl,' probably referring to the wolves in the area.

*Wonewoc
Town
ZIP: 53968 **Lat:** 43-41-27 N **Long:** 90-15-18 W
Pop: 770 (1990); 778 (1980) **Pop Density:** 21.5
Land: 35.8 sq. mi.; **Water:** 0.0 sq. mi.

Kenosha County
County Seat: Kenosha (ZIP: 53140)

Pop: 128,181 (1990); 123,137 (1980) **Pop Density:** 469.8
Land: 272.8 sq. mi.; **Water:** 481.5 sq. mi. **Area Code:** 414
On southeastern border of WI; organized Jan 30, 1850 from Racine County.
Name origin: For the name of Potawatomi (Algonquian) Indian villages, meaning 'pike' or 'pickerel,' for the abundance of this fish in the local creeks.

Brighton
Town
Lat: 42-37-43 N **Long:** 88-07-29 W
Pop: 1,264 (1990); 1,180 (1980) **Pop Density:** 35.3
Land: 35.8 sq. mi.; **Water:** 0.2 sq. mi.

Bristol
Town
ZIP: 53104 **Lat:** 42-32-34 N **Long:** 88-00-57 W
Pop: 3,968 (1990); 3,599 (1980) **Pop Density:** 110.2
Land: 36.0 sq. mi.; **Water:** 0.3 sq. mi.

Camp Lake
CDP
Lat: 42-31-50 N **Long:** 88-08-45 W
Pop: 2,291 (1990); 2,060 (1980) **Pop Density:** 509.1
Land: 4.5 sq. mi.; **Water:** 0.9 sq. mi.

Genoa City
Village
Lat: 42-29-47 N **Long:** 88-18-05 W
Pop: 0 (1990); 1,202 (1980)
Land: 0.1 sq. mi.; **Water:** 0.0 sq. mi.
Incorporated 1901. Part of the town is also in Walworth County.
Name origin: For Genoa, NY.

Kenosha
City
ZIP: 53140 **Lat:** 42-35-02 N **Long:** 87-51-16 W
Pop: 80,352 (1990); 77,685 (1980) **Pop Density:** 3737.3
Land: 21.5 sq. mi.; **Water:** 3.5 sq. mi.
In southeastern WI on Lake Michigan, 10 mi. south of Racine. Incorporated 1850.
Name origin: From a Potawatomi Indian term for villages meaning 'pike' or 'pickerel' for the abundance of this fish in local creeks. Previously called Southport.

Paddock Lake
Village
Lat: 42-34-17 N **Long:** 88-06-08 W
Pop: 2,662 (1990); 2,207 (1980) **Pop Density:** 1663.8
Land: 1.6 sq. mi.; **Water:** 0.2 sq. mi.
Incorporated 1960.

Paris
Town
Lat: 42-37-01 N **Long:** 88-00-46 W
Pop: 1,482 (1990); 1,612 (1980) **Pop Density:** 40.6
Land: 36.5 sq. mi.; **Water:** 0.0 sq. mi.

Pleasant Prairie
Village
ZIP: 53158 **Lat:** 42-31-26 N **Long:** 87-52-54 W
Pop: 11,961 (1990) **Pop Density:** 370.0
Land: 32.3 sq. mi.; **Water:** 0.1 sq. mi.

*Pleasant Prairie
Town
Lat: 42-31-06 N **Long:** 87-48-09 W
Pop: 37 (1990); 12,703 (1980) **Pop Density:** 3700.0
Land: 0.01 sq. mi.; **Water:** 3.0 sq. mi.

Powers Lake
CDP
Lat: 42-32-44 N **Long:** 88-17-44 W
Pop: 752 (1990); 740 (1980) **Pop Density:** 683.6
Land: 1.1 sq. mi.; **Water:** 0.7 sq. mi.
Part of the town is also in Walworth County.

Randall
Town
Lat: 42-32-14 N **Long:** 88-14-14 W
Pop: 2,395 (1990); 2,155 (1980) **Pop Density:** 147.8
Land: 16.2 sq. mi.; **Water:** 0.7 sq. mi.

Salem
Town
ZIP: 53168 **Lat:** 42-32-22 N **Long:** 88-07-55 W
Pop: 7,146 (1990); 6,292 (1980) **Pop Density:** 238.2
Land: 30.0 sq. mi.; **Water:** 2.7 sq. mi.

Silver Lake
Village
ZIP: 53170 **Lat:** 42 33 06 N **Long:** 88-10-03 W
Pop: 1,801 (1990); 1,598 (1980) **Pop Density:** 1200.7
Land: 1.5 sq. mi.; **Water:** 0.0 sq. mi.
Incorporated 1926.

Name origin: For the silvery sheen on the water here.

Somers
Town
ZIP: 53171 **Lat:** 42-38-02 N **Long:** 87-53-32 W
Pop: 7,861 (1990); 7,724 (1980) **Pop Density:** 241.1
Land: 32.6 sq. mi.; **Water:** 0.0 sq. mi.

Twin Lakes
Village
ZIP: 53181 **Lat:** 42-31-07 N **Long:** 88-15-31 W
Pop: 3,989 (1990); 3,474 (1980) **Pop Density:** 782.2
Land: 5.1 sq. mi.; **Water:** 1.5 sq. mi.
Incorporated 1937.

Wheatland
Town
Lat: 42-34-53 N **Long:** 88-14-50 W
Pop: 3,263 (1990); 2,908 (1980) **Pop Density:** 138.3
Land: 23.6 sq. mi.; **Water:** 0.5 sq. mi.

Kewaunee County
County Seat: Kewaunee (ZIP: 54216)

Pop: 18,878 (1990); 19,539 (1980) **Pop Density:** 55.1
Land: 342.7 sq. mi.; **Water:** 742.0 sq. mi. **Area Code:** 414

On the peninsula in eastern WI, bordered on west by Green Bay and on east by Lake Michigan; organized Apr 16, 1852 from Manitowoc County.

Name origin: A Potawatomi word whose meaning is unclear: possibly 'to cross a point,' referring to the river between Green Bay and Lake Michigan or 'prairie hen' or 'wild duck.'

Ahnapee
Town
Lat: 44-38-34 N **Long:** 87-27-53 W
Pop: 941 (1990); 948 (1980) **Pop Density:** 30.4
Land: 31.0 sq. mi.; **Water:** 0.2 sq. mi.

Algoma
City
ZIP: 54201 **Lat:** 44-36-21 N **Long:** 87-26-43 W
Pop: 3,353 (1990); 3,656 (1980) **Pop Density:** 1397.1
Land: 2.4 sq. mi.; **Water:** 0.0 sq. mi. **Elev:** 600 ft.
Incorporated 1879.

Name origin: Coined by explorer and legislator Henry Rowe Schoolcraft (1793–1834) to describe the area surrounding Lake Superior. *Al* for 'Algonquin' and *goma* from Ojibway Indian 'waters,' thus "the Algonquin Sea."

Carlton
Town
Lat: 44-22-41 N **Long:** 87-35-15 W
Pop: 1,041 (1990); 1,140 (1980) **Pop Density:** 29.2
Land: 35.6 sq. mi.; **Water:** 0.0 sq. mi.

Casco
Village
ZIP: 54205 **Lat:** 44-33-13 N **Long:** 87-37-06 W
Pop: 544 (1990); 484 (1980) **Pop Density:** 1088.0
Land: 0.5 sq. mi.; **Water:** 0.0 sq. mi.
Incorporated 1920.

Name origin: Named by settler Edward Decker for his hometown of Casco, ME.

*Casco
Town
ZIP: 54205 **Lat:** 44-32-46 N **Long:** 87-34-59 W
Pop: 1,010 (1990); 1,001 (1980) **Pop Density:** 28.3
Land: 35.7 sq. mi.; **Water:** 0.0 sq. mi.

Franklin
Town
Lat: 44-22-24 N **Long:** 87-41-59 W
Pop: 990 (1990); 1,062 (1980) **Pop Density:** 27.9
Land: 35.5 sq. mi.; **Water:** 0.7 sq. mi.

American Places Dictionary   WISCONSIN, La Crosse County

Kewaunee City
ZIP: 54216　　**Lat:** 44-27-37 N　**Long:** 87-30-40 W
Pop: 2,750 (1990); 2,801 (1980)　**Pop Density:** 833.3
Land: 3.3 sq. mi.; **Water:** 0.7 sq. mi.
Incorporated 1883.
Name origin: From a Potawatomi word possibly meaning either 'prairie chicken,' 'wild duck,' or 'to cross a point.'

Lincoln Town
　　Lat: 44-37-56 N　**Long:** 87-35-00 W
Pop: 996 (1990); 967 (1980)　**Pop Density:** 27.9
Land: 35.7 sq. mi.; **Water:** 0.0 sq. mi.

Luxemburg Village
ZIP: 54217　　**Lat:** 44-32-33 N　**Long:** 87-42-18 W
Pop: 1,151 (1990); 1,040 (1980)　**Pop Density:** 719.4
Land: 1.6 sq. mi.; **Water:** 0.0 sq. mi.
Incorporated 1908.
Name origin: Named by settlers for Luxemburg, Belgium.

*Luxemburg Town
ZIP: 54217　　**Lat:** 44-32-55 N　**Long:** 87-42-27 W
Pop: 1,387 (1990); 1,468 (1980)　**Pop Density:** 40.0
Land: 34.7 sq. mi.; **Water:** 0.0 sq. mi.

Montpelier Town
　　Lat: 44-27-32 N　**Long:** 87-42-25 W
Pop: 1,369 (1990); 1,457 (1980)　**Pop Density:** 37.8
Land: 36.2 sq. mi.; **Water:** 0.0 sq. mi.

Pierce Town
　　Lat: 44-32-43 N　**Long:** 87-29-31 W
Pop: 724 (1990); 790 (1980)　**Pop Density:** 38.7
Land: 18.7 sq. mi.; **Water:** 3.2 sq. mi.

Red River Town
　　Lat: 44-37-51 N　**Long:** 87-42-20 W
Pop: 1,407 (1990); 1,431 (1980)　**Pop Density:** 40.5
Land: 34.7 sq. mi.; **Water:** 1.4 sq. mi.

West Kewaunee Town
　　Lat: 44-27-20 N　**Long:** 87-35-11 W
Pop: 1,215 (1990); 1,294 (1980)　**Pop Density:** 32.9
Land: 36.9 sq. mi.; **Water:** 0.1 sq. mi.

La Crosse County
County Seat: La Crosse (ZIP: 54601)

Pop: 97,904 (1990); 91,056 (1980)　**Pop Density:** 216.2
Land: 452.8 sq. mi.; **Water:** 27.2 sq. mi.　**Area Code:** 608
On southwestern border of WI, northwest of Madison; organized Mar 1, 1851 from unorganized territory.
Name origin: For the village of the same name, from the French name for an Indian game *baggataway*, from a resemblance they saw to their tennis game, played with a racquet that resembled a bishop's crozier or cross.

Bangor Village
ZIP: 54614　　**Lat:** 43-53-31 N　**Long:** 90-59-28 W
Pop: 1,076 (1990); 1,012 (1980)　**Pop Density:** 1076.0
Land: 1.0 sq. mi.; **Water:** 0.0 sq. mi.
Incorporated 1899.
Name origin: Named by Welsh settlers for the town of Bangor, Wales.

*Bangor Town
ZIP: 54614　　**Lat:** 43-50-57 N　**Long:** 90-58-39 W
Pop: 598 (1990); 572 (1980)　**Pop Density:** 17.0
Land: 35.1 sq. mi.; **Water:** 0.0 sq. mi.

Barre Town
　　Lat: 43-49-59 N　**Long:** 91-05-23 W
Pop: 909 (1990); 901 (1980)　**Pop Density:** 43.9
Land: 20.7 sq. mi.; **Water:** 0.0 sq. mi.

Brice Prairie CDP
　　Lat: 43-56-19 N　**Long:** 91-17-58 W
Pop: 1,031 (1990)　**Pop Density:** 343.7
Land: 3.0 sq. mi.; **Water:** 0.0 sq. mi.

Burns Town
　　Lat: 43-57-59 N　**Long:** 90-57-38 W
Pop: 977 (1990); 988 (1980)　**Pop Density:** 20.2
Land: 48.4 sq. mi.; **Water:** 0.0 sq. mi.

Campbell Town
　　Lat: 43-53-09 N　**Long:** 91-17-39 W
Pop: 4,478 (1990); 4,118 (1980)　**Pop Density:** 1119.5
Land: 4.0 sq. mi.; **Water:** 8.9 sq. mi.

Farmington Town
　　Lat: 44-01-25 N　**Long:** 91-04-53 W
Pop: 1,576 (1990); 1,603 (1980)　**Pop Density:** 20.9
Land: 75.4 sq. mi.; **Water:** 0.2 sq. mi.

French Island CDP
　　Lat: 43-51-29 N　**Long:** 91-15-37 W
Pop: 4,478 (1990); 4,118 (1980)　**Pop Density:** 2132.4
Land: 2.1 sq. mi.; **Water:** 0.6 sq. mi.

Greenfield Town
　　Lat: 43-46-43 N　**Long:** 91-04-38 W
Pop: 1,617 (1990); 1,537 (1980)　**Pop Density:** 53.7
Land: 30.1 sq. mi.; **Water:** 0.0 sq. mi.

Hamilton Town
　　Lat: 43-55-14 N　**Long:** 91-06-04 W
Pop: 1,633 (1990); 1,472 (1980)　**Pop Density:** 32.3
Land: 50.6 sq. mi.; **Water:** 1.0 sq. mi.

Holland Town
　　Lat: 44-00-22 N　**Long:** 91-17-43 W
Pop: 2,172 (1990); 1,776 (1980)　**Pop Density:** 50.4
Land: 43.1 sq. mi.; **Water:** 3.1 sq. mi.

Holmen
Village
ZIP: 54636 **Lat:** 43-57-24 N **Long:** 91-15-32 W
Pop: 3,220 (1990); 2,411 (1980) **Pop Density:** 1694.7
Land: 1.9 sq. mi.; **Water:** 0.0 sq. mi. **Elev:** 718 ft.
Incorporated 1946.
Name origin: Probably for Sen. Holmen of IN, who once surveyed this territory. Previously called Frederickstown and Cricken.

La Crosse
City
ZIP: 54601 **Lat:** 43-49-37 N **Long:** 91-14-02 W
Pop: 51,003 (1990); 48,347 (1980) **Pop Density:** 2771.9
Land: 18.4 sq. mi.; **Water:** 1.8 sq. mi. **Elev:** 669 ft.
In western WI, at the junction of the Black and Mississippi rivers. Incorporated 1856.
Name origin: For *baggataway,* a game the Indians played that reminded the French explorers of their tennis game, played with a racquet that resembled a bishop's crozier or cross.

Medary
Town
Lat: 43-51-15 N **Long:** 91-10-52 W
Pop: 1,585 (1990); 1,794 (1980) **Pop Density:** 109.3
Land: 14.5 sq. mi.; **Water:** 0.1 sq. mi.

Onalaska
City
ZIP: 54650 **Lat:** 43-53-13 N **Long:** 91-13-07 W
Pop: 11,284 (1990); 9,249 (1980) **Pop Density:** 1763.1
Land: 6.4 sq. mi.; **Water:** 0.6 sq. mi. **Elev:** 716 ft.
In western WI, 5 mi. north of La Crosse. Incorporated 1887.
Name origin: From an Aleut term *lulaq* probably meaning 'living together happily,' a name that appears in Thomas Campbell's (1777–1844) poem "Pleasure of Hope."

*Onalaska
Town
ZIP: 54650 **Lat:** 43-56-35 N **Long:** 91-14-55 W
Pop: 5,907 (1990); 5,386 (1980) **Pop Density:** 152.2
Land: 38.8 sq. mi.; **Water:** 7.9 sq. mi.

Rockland
Village
ZIP: 54653 **Lat:** 43-54-22 N **Long:** 90-55-05 W
Pop: 509 (1990); 383 (1980) **Pop Density:** 1018.0
Land: 0.5 sq. mi.; **Water:** 0.0 sq. mi. **Elev:** 752 ft.
Incorporated 1919.
Name origin: For a prominent rock ledge.

Shelby
Town
ZIP: 54601 **Lat:** 43-45-35 N **Long:** 91-10-54 W
Pop: 5,151 (1990); 5,620 (1980) **Pop Density:** 197.4
Land: 26.1 sq. mi.; **Water:** 3.6 sq. mi.

Washington
Town
Lat: 43-46-44 N **Long:** 90-58-14 W
Pop: 598 (1990); 611 (1980) **Pop Density:** 16.6
Land: 36.1 sq. mi.; **Water:** 0.0 sq. mi.

West Salem
Village
ZIP: 54669 **Lat:** 43-53-54 N **Long:** 91-04-54 W
Pop: 3,611 (1990); 3,276 (1980) **Pop Density:** 2006.1
Land: 1.8 sq. mi.; **Water:** 0.0 sq. mi. **Elev:** 742 ft.
Incorporated 1893.
Name origin: For 'peace,' the meaning of Salem, and *West* to distinguish it from Salem in Kenosha County.

Lafayette County
County Seat: Darlington (ZIP: 53530)

Pop: 16,076 (1990); 17,412 (1980) **Pop Density:** 25.4
Land: 633.6 sq. mi.; **Water:** 1.0 sq. mi. **Area Code:** 608
On southwestern border of WI, southwest of Madison; organized Jan 31, 1846 (prior to statehood) from Iowa County.
Name origin: For the Marquis de Lafayette (1757–1834), French statesman and soldier who fought with the Americans during the Revolutionary War.

Argyle
Village
ZIP: 53504 **Lat:** 42-42-02 N **Long:** 89-51-58 W
Pop: 798 (1990); 720 (1980) **Pop Density:** 1330.0
Land: 0.6 sq. mi.; **Water:** 0.0 sq. mi. **Elev:** 810 ft.
Incorporated 1903.
Name origin: Named in 1844 by Scotsman Allen Wright for County Argyll in Scotland, with spelling change.

*Argyle
Town
ZIP: 53504 **Lat:** 42-43-35 N **Long:** 89-53-56 W
Pop: 424 (1990); 498 (1980) **Pop Density:** 11.9
Land: 35.6 sq. mi.; **Water:** 0.1 sq. mi.

Belmont
Village
ZIP: 53510 **Lat:** 42-44-16 N **Long:** 90-19-57 W
Pop: 823 (1990); 826 (1980) **Pop Density:** 1371.7
Land: 0.6 sq. mi.; **Water:** 0.0 sq. mi.
Incorporated 1894.
Name origin: For its location near three mounds and from the French 'beautiful mountain.'

*Belmont
Town
ZIP: 53510 **Lat:** 42-46-07 N **Long:** 90-21-44 W
Pop: 737 (1990); 716 (1980) **Pop Density:** 17.8
Land: 41.3 sq. mi.; **Water:** 0.1 sq. mi.

Benton
Village
ZIP: 53803 **Lat:** 42-34-15 N **Long:** 90-22-55 W
Pop: 898 (1990); 983 (1980) **Pop Density:** 1496.7
Land: 0.6 sq. mi.; **Water:** 0.0 sq. mi. **Elev:** 932 ft.
Incorporated 1892.
Name origin: For Sen. Thomas Hart Benton (1782–1858) of MO. Originally known as Swindler's Ridge.

*Benton
Town
ZIP: 53803 **Lat:** 42-34-27 N **Long:** 90-23-34 W
Pop: 507 (1990); 524 (1980) **Pop Density:** 18.0
Land: 28.2 sq. mi.; **Water:** 0.0 sq. mi.

Blanchard
Town
Lat: 42-47-31 N **Long:** 89-54-03 W
Pop: 220 (1990); 209 (1980) **Pop Density:** 12.6
Land: 17.5 sq. mi.; **Water:** 0.0 sq. mi.

WISCONSIN, Lafayette County

Blanchardville — Village
ZIP: 53516 Lat: 42-48-28 N Long: 89-51-36 W
Pop: 635 (1990); 664 (1980) Pop Density: 2116.7
Land: 0.3 sq. mi.; Water: 0.0 sq. mi. Elev: 833 ft.
Incorporated 1890. Part of the town is also in Iowa County.
Name origin: For Alvin Blanchard, who bought a mill here in 1855. Previously called Zarahamia by local members of the Latter Day Saints.

Cuba City — City
ZIP: 53807 Lat: 42-36-17 N Long: 90-25-27 W
Pop: 161 (1990); 201 (1980) Pop Density: 1610.0
Land: 0.1 sq. mi.; Water: 0.0 sq. mi. Elev: 1012 ft.
Incorporated 1925. Part of this town is also in Grant County.
Name origin: A substitution for Yuba, because there was another Yuba in the state. Previously called Western, Yuba, and Cuba.

Darlington — City
ZIP: 53530 Lat: 42-40-49 N Long: 90-07-01 W
Pop: 2,235 (1990); 2,300 (1980) Pop Density: 2031.8
Land: 1.1 sq. mi.; Water: 0.0 sq. mi. Elev: 817 ft.
Purchased 1850. Incorporated 1877.
Name origin: For land agent Joshua Darling of NY.

*Darlington — Town
ZIP: 53530 Lat: 42-38-45 N Long: 90-06-46 W
Pop: 867 (1990); 842 (1980) Pop Density: 18.7
Land: 46.4 sq. mi.; Water: 0.0 sq. mi.

Elk Grove — Town
Lat: 42-40-52 N Long: 90-21-58 W
Pop: 476 (1990); 522 (1980) Pop Density: 13.1
Land: 36.3 sq. mi.; Water: 0.0 sq. mi.

Fayette — Town
Lat: 42-46-01 N Long: 90-01-20 W
Pop: 390 (1990); 447 (1980) Pop Density: 11.1
Land: 35.2 sq. mi.; Water: 0.7 sq. mi.

Gratiot — Village
ZIP: 53541 Lat: 42-34-46 N Long: 90-01-22 W
Pop: 207 (1990); 280 (1980) Pop Density: 345.0
Land: 0.6 sq. mi.; Water: 0.0 sq. mi.
Incorporated 1891.
Name origin: For Henry Gratiot, who came here in 1824. Originally known as Gratiot's Grove.

*Gratiot — Town
ZIP: 53541 Lat: 42-33-54 N Long: 90-01-41 W
Pop: 709 (1990); 706 (1980) Pop Density: 13.1
Land: 54.3 sq. mi.; Water: 0.0 sq. mi.

Hazel Green — Village
ZIP: 53811 Lat: 42-31-49 N Long: 90-25-25 W
Pop: 0 (1990); 12 (1980)
Land: 0.04 sq. mi.; Water: 0.0 sq. mi.
Incorporated 1867. Part of the town is also in Grant County.
Name origin: For either Capt. Charles McCoy's hometown of Hazel Green, KY, or for the hazel bushes in the area. Previously called Hardy's Scrape and Hard Scrabble.

Kendall — Town
Lat: 42-44-48 N Long: 90-14-30 W
Pop: 363 (1990); 432 (1980) Pop Density: 8.5
Land: 42.6 sq. mi.; Water: 0.0 sq. mi.

Lamont — Town
Lat: 42-42-06 N Long: 90-00-27 W
Pop: 254 (1990); 341 (1980) Pop Density: 12.8
Land: 19.9 sq. mi.; Water: 0.0 sq. mi.

Monticello — Town
Lat: 42-31-27 N Long: 90-08-26 W
Pop: 182 (1990); 202 (1980) Pop Density: 9.3
Land: 19.6 sq. mi.; Water: 0.0 sq. mi.

New Diggings — Town
Lat: 42-34-15 N Long: 90-20-01 W
Pop: 485 (1990); 556 (1980) Pop Density: 19.2
Land: 25.3 sq. mi.; Water: 0.0 sq. mi.

Seymour — Town
Lat: 42-39-09 N Long: 90-14-57 W
Pop: 401 (1990); 497 (1980) Pop Density: 11.1
Land: 36.1 sq. mi.; Water: 0.0 sq. mi.

Shullsburg — City
ZIP: 53586 Lat: 42-34-23 N Long: 90-13-53 W
Pop: 1,236 (1990); 1,484 (1980) Pop Density: 1123.6
Land: 1.1 sq. mi.; Water: 0.0 sq. mi. Elev: 1021 ft.
Founded c. 1827. Incorporated 1889.
Name origin: For Jesse W. Shull, who came to the area in 1818 and established a settlement called Old Shullsburg.

*Shullsburg — Town
ZIP: 53586 Lat: 42-34-49 N Long: 90-13-09 W
Pop: 363 (1990); 455 (1980) Pop Density: 10.4
Land: 35.0 sq. mi.; Water: 0.0 sq. mi.

South Wayne — Village
ZIP: 53587 Lat: 42-33-59 N Long: 89-52-49 W
Pop: 478 (1990); 495 (1980) Pop Density: 956.0
Land: 0.5 sq. mi.; Water: 0.0 sq. mi. Elev: 803 ft.
Incorporated 1911.
Name origin: For Gen. "Mad Anthony" Wayne (1745–96), of Revolutionary War fame; so named by settlers who were descendants of men who had served under him. Originally known as Lost Township.

Wayne — Town
Lat: 42-32-55 N Long: 89-54-01 W
Pop: 510 (1990); 559 (1980) Pop Density: 13.8
Land: 37.0 sq. mi.; Water: 0.0 sq. mi.

White Oak Springs — Town
Lat: 42-31-53 N Long: 90-15-37 W
Pop: 116 (1990); 165 (1980) Pop Density: 7.0
Land: 16.5 sq. mi.; Water: 0.0 sq. mi.

Willow Springs — Town
Lat: 42-45-07 N Long: 90-07-48 W
Pop: 656 (1990); 685 (1980) Pop Density: 13.6
Land: 48.3 sq. mi.; Water: 0.0 sq. mi.

Wiota — Town
Lat: 42-38-17 N Long: 89-55-28 W
Pop: 945 (1990); 1,091 (1980) Pop Density: 17.9
Land: 52.8 sq. mi.; Water: 0.0 sq. mi.

WISCONSIN, Langlade County

Langlade County
County Seat: Antigo (ZIP: 54409)

Pop: 19,505 (1990); 19,978 (1980)
Land: 872.7 sq. mi.; **Water:** 15.2 sq. mi.
Pop Density: 22.3
Area Code: 715

In northeastern WI, northeast of Wausau; organized Feb 27, 1879 as New County from Oconto County; name changed Feb 19, 1880.

Name origin: For Charles Michael de Langlade (1729–1800), an Indian leader who fought with the French against the British in the French and Indian War and with the British against the Americans during the Revolutionary War; he established the first permanent settlement at Green Bay (1764). Some claim for his father, Augustin de Langlade (1695–1771), a French settler who married an Indian woman.

Ackley — Town
Lat: 45-08-52 N Long: 89-17-18 W
Pop: 550 (1990); 639 (1980) **Pop Density:** 7.7
Land: 71.0 sq. mi.; **Water:** 0.1 sq. mi.

Ainsworth — Town
Lat: 45-22-26 N Long: 88-59-07 W
Pop: 474 (1990); 447 (1980) **Pop Density:** 6.8
Land: 69.5 sq. mi.; **Water:** 2.5 sq. mi.

Antigo — City
ZIP: 54409 Lat: 45-08-38 N Long: 89-09-18 W
Pop: 8,276 (1990); 8,653 (1980) **Pop Density:** 1451.9
Land: 5.7 sq. mi.; **Water:** 0.0 sq. mi.
Incorporated 1885.

Name origin: From a Chippewa Indian term possibly meaning 'balsam evergreen river' or 'place where evergreens can be found.'

*Antigo — Town
Lat: 45-09-36 N Long: 89-06-28 W
Pop: 1,406 (1990); 1,661 (1980) **Pop Density:** 44.9
Land: 31.3 sq. mi.; **Water:** 0.0 sq. mi.

Elcho — Town
ZIP: 54428 Lat: 45-25-19 N Long: 89-10-57 W
Pop: 1,075 (1990); 1,078 (1980) **Pop Density:** 15.1
Land: 71.4 sq. mi.; **Water:** 3.9 sq. mi.

Evergreen — Town
Lat: 45-10-07 N Long: 88-52-01 W
Pop: 483 (1990); 515 (1980) **Pop Density:** 13.5
Land: 35.8 sq. mi.; **Water:** 0.4 sq. mi.

Langlade — Town
ZIP: 54465 Lat: 45-17-28 N Long: 88-51-31 W
Pop: 415 (1990); 413 (1980) **Pop Density:** 5.8
Land: 71.5 sq. mi.; **Water:** 1.0 sq. mi.

Neva — Town
Lat: 45-14-54 N Long: 89-07-27 W
Pop: 910 (1990); 970 (1980) **Pop Density:** 24.3
Land: 37.4 sq. mi.; **Water:** 0.3 sq. mi.

Norwood — Town
Lat: 45-04-45 N Long: 89-02-28 W
Pop: 842 (1990) **Pop Density:** 23.5
Land: 35.8 sq. mi.; **Water:** 0.4 sq. mi.

Parrish — Town
Lat: 45-25-12 N Long: 89-22-09 W
Pop: 81 (1990); 87 (1980) **Pop Density:** 2.2
Land: 36.3 sq. mi.; **Water:** 0.3 sq. mi.

Peck — Town
Lat: 45-14-57 N Long: 89-14-26 W
Pop: 402 (1990); 424 (1980) **Pop Density:** 10.8
Land: 37.2 sq. mi.; **Water:** 0.1 sq. mi.

Polar — Town
ZIP: 54418 Lat: 45-09-38 N Long: 88-59-20 W
Pop: 900 (1990); 827 (1980) **Pop Density:** 25.3
Land: 35.6 sq. mi.; **Water:** 0.3 sq. mi.

Price — Town
Lat: 45-15-32 N Long: 88-59-06 W
Pop: 248 (1990); 243 (1980) **Pop Density:** 6.9
Land: 36.2 sq. mi.; **Water:** 0.2 sq. mi.

Rolling — Town
Lat: 45-04-35 N Long: 89-09-31 W
Pop: 1,316 (1990); 1,236 (1980) **Pop Density:** 36.2
Land: 36.4 sq. mi.; **Water:** 0.0 sq. mi.

Summit — Town
Lat: 45-19-53 N Long: 89-22-01 W
Pop: 190 (1990); 197 (1980) **Pop Density:** 5.2
Land: 36.4 sq. mi.; **Water:** 0.0 sq. mi.

Upham — Town
Lat: 45-20-17 N Long: 89-11-22 W
Pop: 626 (1990); 545 (1980) **Pop Density:** 8.9
Land: 70.5 sq. mi.; **Water:** 3.4 sq. mi.

Vilas — Town
Lat: 45-15-10 N Long: 89-21-37 W
Pop: 257 (1990); 264 (1980) **Pop Density:** 7.2
Land: 35.9 sq. mi.; **Water:** 0.0 sq. mi.

White Lake — Village
ZIP: 54491 Lat: 45-09-48 N Long: 88-45-59 W
Pop: 304 (1990); 309 (1980) **Pop Density:** 138.2
Land: 2.2 sq. mi.; **Water:** 0.3 sq. mi. **Elev:** 1286 ft.
Incorporated 1926.

Name origin: For the lake which, before the advent of the lumber mills, had a white sand bottom.

Wolf River — Town
Lat: 45-14-41 N Long: 88-44-04 W
Pop: 750 (1990); 604 (1980) **Pop Density:** 6.4
Land: 116.6 sq. mi.; **Water:** 2.2 sq. mi.

> ## Lincoln County
> **County Seat: Merrill (ZIP: 54452)**
>
> **Pop:** 26,993 (1990); 26,555 (1980) **Pop Density:** 30.6
> **Land:** 883.0 sq. mi.; **Water:** 23.9 sq. mi. **Area Code:** 715
>
> In northeastern WI, north of Wausau; organized Mar 4, 1874 from Marathon County.
> **Name origin:** For Abraham Lincoln (1809–65), sixteenth U.S. president.

Birch   Town
ZIP: 54442   **Lat:** 45-19-30 N   **Long:** 89-36-47 W
Pop: 675 (1990); 689 (1980)   **Pop Density:** 18.9
Land: 35.8 sq. mi.; **Water:** 0.4 sq. mi.

Bradley   Town
  Lat: 45-27-11 N   **Long:** 89-44-22 W
Pop: 2,231 (1990); 2,235 (1980)   **Pop Density:** 40.1
Land: 55.7 sq. mi.; **Water:** 7.8 sq. mi.

Corning   Town
ZIP: 54452   **Lat:** 45-14-13 N   **Long:** 89-57-57 W
Pop: 795 (1990); 807 (1980)   **Pop Density:** 5.4
Land: 146.5 sq. mi.; **Water:** 0.1 sq. mi.

Harding   Town
ZIP: 54452   **Lat:** 45-17-13 N   **Long:** 89-51-25 W
Pop: 283 (1990); 261 (1980)   **Pop Density:** 3.9
Land: 72.1 sq. mi.; **Water:** 0.7 sq. mi.

Harrison   Town
ZIP: 54435   **Lat:** 45-28-05 N   **Long:** 89-28-57 W
Pop: 660 (1990); 693 (1980)   **Pop Density:** 9.5
Land: 69.5 sq. mi.; **Water:** 2.9 sq. mi.

King   Town
  Lat: 45-30-25 N   **Long:** 89-36-53 W
Pop: 675 (1990); 597 (1980)   **Pop Density:** 19.9
Land: 33.9 sq. mi.; **Water:** 3.0 sq. mi.

Merrill   City
ZIP: 54452   **Lat:** 45-10-55 N   **Long:** 89-42-12 W
Pop: 9,860 (1990); 9,578 (1980)   **Pop Density:** 1471.6
Land: 6.7 sq. mi.; **Water:** 0.5 sq. mi.

In northern WI on Wisconsin River, 15 mi. north of Wausau. Incorporated 1883.
Name origin: Named in 1881 for S. S. Merrill, general manager of the Wisconsin Central Railroad. Originally known as Jenny Bull Falls, shortened to Jenny Falls and then Jenny, for the daughter of a Potawatomi chief.

*Merrill   Town
ZIP: 54452   **Lat:** 45-14-42 N   **Long:** 89-40-31 W
Pop: 2,716 (1990); 2,591 (1980)   **Pop Density:** 52.1
Land: 52.1 sq. mi.; **Water:** 1.3 sq. mi.

Pine River   Town
ZIP: 54452   **Lat:** 45-09-53 N   **Long:** 89-32-03 W
Pop: 1,552 (1990); 1,463 (1980)   **Pop Density:** 24.3
Land: 64.0 sq. mi.; **Water:** 0.3 sq. mi.

Rock Falls   Town
ZIP: 54442   **Lat:** 45-18-46 N   **Long:** 89-44-39 W
Pop: 463 (1990); 434 (1980)   **Pop Density:** 9.7
Land: 47.8 sq. mi.; **Water:** 1.4 sq. mi.

Russell   Town
  Lat: 45-20-38 N   **Long:** 89-29-10 W
Pop: 671 (1990); 668 (1980)   **Pop Density:** 18.5
Land: 36.2 sq. mi.; **Water:** 0.2 sq. mi.

Schley   Town
ZIP: 54452   **Lat:** 45-14-58 N   **Long:** 89-30-29 W
Pop: 838 (1990); 818 (1980)   **Pop Density:** 17.4
Land: 48.1 sq. mi.; **Water:** 0.2 sq. mi.

Scott   Town
ZIP: 54452   **Lat:** 45-09-39 N   **Long:** 89-43-36 W
Pop: 1,210 (1990); 1,149 (1980)   **Pop Density:** 39.7
Land: 30.5 sq. mi.; **Water:** 0.5 sq. mi.

Skanawan   Town
ZIP: 54442   **Lat:** 45-25-34 N   **Long:** 89-36-56 W
Pop: 312 (1990); 256 (1980)   **Pop Density:** 8.8
Land: 35.4 sq. mi.; **Water:** 0.5 sq. mi.

Somo   Town
  Lat: 45-31-38 N   **Long:** 89-58-05 W
Pop: 116 (1990); 150 (1980)   **Pop Density:** 3.2
Land: 36.2 sq. mi.; **Water:** 0.0 sq. mi.

Tomahawk   City
ZIP: 54487   **Lat:** 45-28-24 N   **Long:** 89-43-26 W
Pop: 3,328 (1990); 3,527 (1980)   **Pop Density:** 449.7
Land: 7.4 sq. mi.; **Water:** 1.4 sq. mi.

Incorporated 1891.
Name origin: For the Tomahawk River, which got its name when warring Sioux and Chippewa Indians buried a tomahawk, or Indian hatchet, here as a symbol of peace between the two tribes.

*Tomahawk   Town
  Lat: 45-26-00 N   **Long:** 89-54-29 W
Pop: 370 (1990); 383 (1980)   **Pop Density:** 5.3
Land: 70.1 sq. mi.; **Water:** 1.5 sq. mi.

Wilson   Town
  Lat: 45-30-39 N   **Long:** 89-51-16 W
Pop: 238 (1990); 256 (1980)   **Pop Density:** 6.8
Land: 35.2 sq. mi.; **Water:** 1.2 sq. mi.

Manitowoc County
County Seat: Manitowoc (ZIP: 54220)

Pop: 80,421 (1990); 82,918 (1980)
Land: 591.6 sq. mi.; **Water:** 902.3 sq. mi.
Pop Density: 135.9
Area Code: 414

On central eastern coast of WI, south of Green Bay; organized Dec 7, 1836 (prior to statehood) from a territorial county.

Name origin: From an Indian name probably meaning 'land of the spirit,' possibly with a connotation of evil.

Cato — Town
ZIP: 54206   Lat: 44-06-21 N Long: 87-51-58 W
Pop: 1,503 (1990); 1,653 (1980)   Pop Density: 42.7
Land: 35.2 sq. mi.; Water: 0.2 sq. mi.

Centerville — Town
Lat: 43-56-31 N Long: 87-45-11 W
Pop: 685 (1990); 796 (1980)   Pop Density: 28.3
Land: 24.2 sq. mi.; Water: 2.7 sq. mi.

Cleveland — Village
ZIP: 53015   Lat: 43-55-09 N Long: 87-44-52 W
Pop: 1,398 (1990); 1,270 (1980)   Pop Density: 822.4
Land: 1.7 sq. mi.; Water: 0.0 sq. mi.   Elev: 640 ft.
Founded 1850. Incorporated 1958.

Name origin: Named in 1885 for Grover Cleveland (1837–1908), twenty-second U.S. president. Originally known as Birch for the area's birch trees.

Cooperstown — Town
Lat: 44-16-48 N Long: 87-49-51 W
Pop: 1,320 (1990); 1,249 (1980)   Pop Density: 37.6
Land: 35.1 sq. mi.; Water: 0.0 sq. mi.

Eaton — Town
Lat: 44-01-56 N Long: 87-59-19 W
Pop: 761 (1990); 764 (1980)   Pop Density: 21.6
Land: 35.2 sq. mi.; Water: 0.2 sq. mi.

Francis Creek — Village
ZIP: 54214   Lat: 44-12-05 N Long: 87-43-19 W
Pop: 562 (1990); 589 (1980)   Pop Density: 624.4
Land: 0.9 sq. mi.; Water: 0.0 sq. mi.
Incorporated 1960.

Name origin: For a substitution for French Creek, because there was already a French Creek in the state. Originally so named for a French settlement at a nearby stream.

Franklin — Town
Lat: 44-11-45 N Long: 87-51-24 W
Pop: 1,325 (1990); 1,372 (1980)   Pop Density: 36.6
Land: 36.2 sq. mi.; Water: 0.0 sq. mi.

Gibson — Town
Lat: 44-17-04 N Long: 87-42-14 W
Pop: 1,445 (1990); 1,416 (1980)   Pop Density: 40.9
Land: 35.3 sq. mi.; Water: 0.1 sq. mi.

Kellnersville — Village
ZIP: 54215   Lat: 44-13-27 N Long: 87-48-11 W
Pop: 350 (1990); 369 (1980)   Pop Density: 700.0
Land: 0.5 sq. mi.; Water: 0.0 sq. mi.   Elev: 827 ft.
Incorporated 1971.

Name origin: For John (or Michele) Kellner, who built a sawmill here in 1849. Previously called Kellner's Corners.

Kiel — City
ZIP: 53042   Lat: 43-55-02 N Long: 88-01-39 W
Pop: 2,534 (1990); 2,654 (1980)   Pop Density: 1583.8
Land: 1.6 sq. mi.; Water: 0.1 sq. mi.   Elev: 933 ft.
Incorporated 1920. Part of the town is also in Calumet County.

Name origin: For Col. Belitz's home in Kiel, Germany. Previously called Abel, for first settler D. Abel, and Schleswig.

Kossuth — Town
Lat: 44-11-47 N Long: 87-43-51 W
Pop: 1,951 (1990); 2,097 (1980)   Pop Density: 50.2
Land: 38.9 sq. mi.; Water: 0.0 sq. mi.

Liberty — Town
Lat: 44-01-50 N Long: 87-51-37 W
Pop: 1,218 (1990); 1,170 (1980)   Pop Density: 34.5
Land: 35.3 sq. mi.; Water: 0.3 sq. mi.

Manitowoc — City
ZIP: 54220   Lat: 44-05-55 N Long: 87-40-38 W
Pop: 32,520 (1990); 32,547 (1980)   Pop Density: 2258.3
Land: 14.4 sq. mi.; Water: 0.3 sq. mi.   Elev: 606 ft.
In eastern WI on Lake Michigan, 25 mi. north of Sheboygan. Incorporated 1870.

Name origin: From an Indian name probably meaning 'land of the spirit,' possibly with a connotation of evil.

*Manitowoc — Town
ZIP: 54220   Lat: 44-07-03 N Long: 87-39-38 W
Pop: 937 (1990); 1,177 (1980)   Pop Density: 128.4
Land: 7.3 sq. mi.; Water: 0.0 sq. mi.

Manitowoc Rapids — Town
Lat: 44-06-35 N Long: 87-45-33 W
Pop: 2,579 (1990); 3,186 (1980)   Pop Density: 88.6
Land: 29.1 sq. mi.; Water: 0.3 sq. mi.

Maple Grove — Town
Lat: 44-11-36 N Long: 87-59-40 W
Pop: 888 (1990); 962 (1980)   Pop Density: 25.1
Land: 35.4 sq. mi.; Water: 0.0 sq. mi.

Maribel — Village
ZIP: 54227   Lat: 44-16-45 N Long: 87-48-07 W
Pop: 372 (1990); 363 (1980)   Pop Density: 310.0
Land: 1.2 sq. mi.; Water: 0.0 sq. mi.   Elev: 861 ft.
Incorporated 1963.

Meeme — Town
Lat: 43-56-03 N Long: 87-51-45 W
Pop: 1,516 (1990); 1,535 (1980)   Pop Density: 41.9
Land: 36.2 sq. mi.; Water: 0.1 sq. mi.

Mishicot   Village
ZIP: 54228   Lat: 44-13-50 N   **Long:** 87-38-36 W
Pop: 1,296 (1990); 1,503 (1980)   **Pop Density:** 518.4
Land: 2.5 sq. mi.; **Water:** 0.0 sq. mi.
Incorporated 1950.
Name origin: Probably for Chief Mishicot of the Ottawa Indians, whose name probably means 'hairy legs.'

*Mishicot   Town
ZIP: 54228   **Lat:** 44-15-44 N   **Long:** 87-37-44 W
Pop: 1,344 (1990); 1,334 (1980)   **Pop Density:** 48.5
Land: 27.7 sq. mi.; **Water:** 0.0 sq. mi.

Newton   Town
ZIP: 53063   **Lat:** 44-01-19 N   **Long:** 87-44-40 W
Pop: 2,242 (1990); 2,332 (1980)   **Pop Density:** 65.6
Land: 34.2 sq. mi.; **Water:** 1.4 sq. mi.

Reedsville   Village
ZIP: 54230   **Lat:** 44-09-12 N   **Long:** 87-57-11 W
Pop: 1,182 (1990); 1,134 (1980)   **Pop Density:** 1313.3
Land: 0.9 sq. mi.; **Water:** 0.0 sq. mi.
Incorporated 1892.
Name origin: For Judge George Reed of Manitowoc. Previously called Mud Creek.

Rockland   Town
   Lat: 44-06-54 N   **Long:** 87-59-09 W
Pop: 911 (1990); 936 (1980)   **Pop Density:** 26.4
Land: 34.5 sq. mi.; **Water:** 1.0 sq. mi.

St. Nazianz   Village
   Lat: 44-00-25 N   **Long:** 87-55-27 W
Pop: 693 (1990); 738 (1980)   **Pop Density:** 866.3
Land: 0.8 sq. mi.; **Water:** 0.0 sq. mi.
Incorporated 1956.
Name origin: Named by founding German immigrants for St. Gregory Nazianz (c. 330–c. 389).

Schleswig   Town
   Lat: 43-56-08 N   **Long:** 87-58-42 W
Pop: 1,641 (1990); 1,633 (1980)   **Pop Density:** 48.8
Land: 33.6 sq. mi.; **Water:** 0.7 sq. mi.

Two Creeks   Town
   Lat: 44-16-29 N   **Long:** 87-33-20 W
Pop: 466 (1990); 489 (1980)   **Pop Density:** 31.3
Land: 14.9 sq. mi.; **Water:** 0.0 sq. mi.

Two Rivers   City
ZIP: 54241   **Lat:** 44-09-22 N   **Long:** 87-34-52 W
Pop: 13,030 (1990); 13,354 (1980)   **Pop Density:** 2369.1
Land: 5.5 sq. mi.; **Water:** 0.4 sq. mi.
In eastern WI on Lake Michigan, 7 mi. northeast of Manitowoc. Incorporated 1878.
Name origin: For its location between the North and South Twin rivers.

*Two Rivers   Town
ZIP: 54241   **Lat:** 44-11-34 N   **Long:** 87-34-35 W
Pop: 2,147 (1990); 2,663 (1980)   **Pop Density:** 67.3
Land: 31.9 sq. mi.; **Water:** 0.1 sq. mi.

Valders   Village
ZIP: 54245   **Lat:** 44-03-57 N   **Long:** 87-53-08 W
Pop: 905 (1990); 984 (1980)   **Pop Density:** 1131.3
Land: 0.8 sq. mi.; **Water:** 0.0 sq. mi.   **Elev:** 840 ft.
Incorporated 1919.
Name origin: Named by settlers for Valders, Norway.

Whitelaw   Village
ZIP: 54247   **Lat:** 44-08-42 N   **Long:** 87-49-39 W
Pop: 700 (1990); 649 (1980)   **Pop Density:** 1166.7
Land: 0.6 sq. mi.; **Water:** 0.0 sq. mi.   **Elev:** 857 ft.
Incorporated 1958.
Name origin: For either Whitelaw Reed, a railroad official, or for a Mr. White, who established the post office here in 1892. Previously called Pine Grove Siding.

Marathon County
County Seat: Wausau (ZIP: 54401)

Pop: 115,400 (1990); 111,270 (1980)   **Pop Density:** 74.7
Land: 1545.1 sq. mi.; **Water:** 31.2 sq. mi.   **Area Code:** 715
In central WI, east of Eau Claire; organized Feb 9, 1850 from Portage County.
Name origin: For the site of the famous battle in Greece (490 B.C.).

Abbotsford   City
ZIP: 54405   **Lat:** 44-56-46 N   **Long:** 90-18-29 W
Pop: 507 (1990); 500 (1980)   **Pop Density:** 633.8
Land: 0.8 sq. mi.; **Water:** 0.0 sq. mi.
Incorporated 1965. Part of the town is also in Clark County.
Name origin: For Edwin H. Abbot, an official of the Wisconsin Central Railway.

Athens   Village
ZIP: 54411   **Lat:** 45-02-01 N   **Long:** 90-04-34 W
Pop: 951 (1990); 988 (1980)   **Pop Density:** 528.3
Land: 1.8 sq. mi.; **Water:** 0.0 sq. mi.
Incorporated 1901.
Name origin: Probably for Athens, Greece.

Bergen   Town
   Lat: 44-44-10 N   **Long:** 89-47-06 W
Pop: 499 (1990); 478 (1980)   **Pop Density:** 18.5
Land: 27.0 sq. mi.; **Water:** 7.8 sq. mi.

Berlin   Town
   Lat: 45-04-34 N   **Long:** 89-47-21 W
Pop: 849 (1990); 820 (1980)   **Pop Density:** 24.5
Land: 34.7 sq. mi.; **Water:** 0.0 sq. mi.

Bern   Town
   Lat: 45-04-36 N   **Long:** 90-08-29 W
Pop: 550 (1990); 487 (1980)   **Pop Density:** 15.9
Land: 34.5 sq. mi.; **Water:** 0.0 sq. mi.

Bevent
Town
ZIP: 54440 Lat: 44-44-00 N Long: 89-25-13 W
Pop: 978 (1990); 983 (1980) Pop Density: 23.2
Land: 42.1 sq. mi.; Water: 0.6 sq. mi.

Birnamwood
Village
Lat: 44-55-35 N Long: 89-13-34 W
Pop: 6 (1990); 688 (1980) Pop Density: 60.0
Land: 0.1 sq. mi.; Water: 0.0 sq. mi.
Incorporated 1895. Part of the town is also in Shawano County.
Name origin: Named by the son of a railroad official, who saw large piles of brush burning near the tracks here. They were described by an Indian as 'heap big burn-em-wood,' which reminded the young man of Birnamwood mentioned in Shakespeare's *Macbeth*.

Brighton
Town
Lat: 44-48-53 N Long: 90-15-28 W
Pop: 610 (1990); 600 (1980) Pop Density: 17.8
Land: 34.2 sq. mi.; Water: 0.0 sq. mi.

Brokaw
Village
ZIP: 54417 Lat: 45-01-38 N Long: 89-39-09 W
Pop: 224 (1990); 298 (1980) Pop Density: 280.0
Land: 0.8 sq. mi.; Water: 0.2 sq. mi.
Incorporated 1903.

Cassel
Town
Lat: 44-54-03 N Long: 89-54-28 W
Pop: 816 (1990); 899 (1980) Pop Density: 24.6
Land: 33.2 sq. mi.; Water: 0.0 sq. mi.

Cleveland
Town
Lat: 44-49-13 N Long: 90-01-09 W
Pop: 982 (1990); 958 (1980) Pop Density: 33.1
Land: 29.7 sq. mi.; Water: 0.9 sq. mi.

Colby
City
ZIP: 54421 Lat: 44-54-25 N Long: 90-18-47 W
Pop: 416 (1990); 345 (1980) Pop Density: 832.0
Land: 0.5 sq. mi.; Water: 0.0 sq. mi. Elev: 1350 ft.
Incorporated 1891. Part of the town is also in Clark County.
Name origin: For Charles L. Colby, president of the Wisconsin Central Railroad.

Day
Town
Lat: 44-44-00 N Long: 90-01-22 W
Pop: 1,010 (1990); 989 (1980) Pop Density: 30.0
Land: 33.7 sq. mi.; Water: 0.2 sq. mi.

Easton
Town
Lat: 44-59-08 N Long: 89-25-11 W
Pop: 1,039 (1990); 1,046 (1980) Pop Density: 24.2
Land: 43.0 sq. mi.; Water: 0.0 sq. mi.

Eau Pleine
Town
Lat: 44-48-58 N Long: 90-08-50 W
Pop: 688 (1990); 759 (1980) Pop Density: 20.7
Land: 33.2 sq. mi.; Water: 0.0 sq. mi.

Edgar
Village
ZIP: 54426 Lat: 44-55-22 N Long: 89-57-46 W
Pop: 1,318 (1990); 1,194 (1980) Pop Density: 775.3
Land: 1.7 sq. mi.; Water: 0.0 sq. mi.
Platted 1891. Incorporated 1898.
Name origin: For railroad employee William Edgar.

Elderon
Village
ZIP: 54429 Lat: 44-46-59 N Long: 89 15 01 W
Pop: 175 (1990); 191 (1980) Pop Density: 159.1
Land: 1.1 sq. mi.; Water: 0.1 sq. mi. Elev: 1199 ft.
Incorporated 1917.
Name origin: For the beauty of the elderberry bushes that blossomed here.

*Elderon
Town
Lat: 44-48-41 N Long: 89-17-08 W
Pop: 605 (1990); 628 (1980) Pop Density: 17.5
Land: 34.6 sq. mi.; Water: 0.3 sq. mi.

Emmet
Town
Lat: 44-48-47 N Long: 89-53-56 W
Pop: 732 (1990); 757 (1980) Pop Density: 18.4
Land: 39.8 sq. mi.; Water: 0.4 sq. mi.

Evergreen
CDP
Lat: 44-50-32 N Long: 89-38-14 W
Pop: 3,423 (1990); 1,842 (1980) Pop Density: 834.9
Land: 4.1 sq. mi.; Water: 0.0 sq. mi.

Fenwood
Village
Lat: 44-51-55 N Long: 90-00-49 W
Pop: 214 (1990); 165 (1980) Pop Density: 214.0
Land: 1.0 sq. mi.; Water: 0.0 sq. mi.
Incorporated 1904.
Name origin: For the marshy woodlands or fens in this area.

Frankfort
Town
Lat: 44-54-23 N Long: 90-07-43 W
Pop: 606 (1990); 743 (1980) Pop Density: 17.2
Land: 35.2 sq. mi.; Water: 0.0 sq. mi.

Franzen
Town
Lat: 44-43-35 N Long: 89-17-49 W
Pop: 532 (1990); 571 (1980) Pop Density: 14.6
Land: 36.4 sq. mi.; Water: 0.2 sq. mi.

Green Valley
Town
Lat: 44-43-40 N Long: 89-54-58 W
Pop: 396 (1990); 355 (1980) Pop Density: 13.7
Land: 28.9 sq. mi.; Water: 6.2 sq. mi.

Guenther
Town
Lat: 44-43-43 N Long: 89-32-45 W
Pop: 258 (1990); 297 (1980) Pop Density: 7.5
Land: 34.4 sq. mi.; Water: 0.0 sq. mi.

Halsey
Town
Lat: 45-04-52 N Long: 90-01-29 W
Pop: 512 (1990); 548 (1980) Pop Density: 15.5
Land: 33.1 sq. mi.; Water: 0.0 sq. mi.

Hamburg
Town
Lat: 45-04-47 N Long: 89-53-44 W
Pop: 768 (1990); 749 (1980) Pop Density: 21.7
Land: 35.4 sq. mi.; Water: 0.0 sq. mi.

Harrison
Town
Lat: 45-04-18 N Long: 89-16-42 W
Pop: 383 (1990); 354 (1980) Pop Density: 10.4
Land: 36.7 sq. mi.; Water: 0.0 sq. mi.

Hatley Village
ZIP: 54440 Lat: 44-53-13 N Long: 89-20-13 W
Pop: 295 (1990); 300 (1980) Pop Density: 327.8
Land: 0.9 sq. mi.; **Water:** 0.0 sq. mi.
Incorporated 1912.
Name origin: Named by Matthew LaBarian for his hometown of Hatley, Quebec.

Hewitt Town
Lat: 45-04-28 N Long: 89-25-02 W
Pop: 508 (1990); 496 (1980) Pop Density: 11.7
Land: 43.4 sq. mi.; **Water:** 0.0 sq. mi.

Holton Town
Lat: 44-59-04 N Long: 90-15-48 W
Pop: 971 (1990); 945 (1980) Pop Density: 28.1
Land: 34.6 sq. mi.; **Water:** 0.0 sq. mi.

Hull Town
Lat: 44-53-42 N Long: 90-14-52 W
Pop: 836 (1990); 1,402 (1980) Pop Density: 25.0
Land: 33.5 sq. mi.; **Water:** 0.1 sq. mi.

Johnson Town
Lat: 44-59-20 N Long: 90-08-17 W
Pop: 923 (1990); 933 (1980) Pop Density: 26.4
Land: 35.0 sq. mi.; **Water:** 0.0 sq. mi.

Knowlton Town
ZIP: 54455 Lat: 44-43-48 N Long: 89-39-53 W
Pop: 1,414 (1990); 1,153 (1980) Pop Density: 48.6
Land: 29.1 sq. mi.; **Water:** 5.1 sq. mi.

Kronenwetter Town
ZIP: 54455 Lat: 44-49-20 N Long: 89-35-25 W
Pop: 4,850 (1990); 5,012 (1980) Pop Density: 93.1
Land: 52.1 sq. mi.; **Water:** 0.4 sq. mi.

Maine Town
Lat: 45-03-10 N Long: 89-40-55 W
Pop: 2,206 (1990); 2,163 (1980) Pop Density: 51.5
Land: 42.8 sq. mi.; **Water:** 0.5 sq. mi.

Marathon Town
ZIP: 54448 Lat: 44-54-02 N Long: 89-47-07 W
Pop: 978 (1990); 1,114 (1980) Pop Density: 29.5
Land: 33.2 sq. mi.; **Water:** 0.0 sq. mi.

Marathon City Village
ZIP: 54448 Lat: 44-55-56 N Long: 89-50-30 W
Pop: 1,606 (1990); 1,552 (1980) Pop Density: 944.7
Land: 1.7 sq. mi.; **Water:** 0.0 sq. mi.

Marshfield City
ZIP: 54449 Lat: 44-41-30 N Long: 90-12-05 W
Pop: 432 (1990); 237 (1980) Pop Density: 308.6
Land: 1.4 sq. mi.; **Water:** 0.0 sq. mi.
Incorporated 1883. Part of the town is also in Wood County.
Name origin: For J.J. Marsh, or for his uncle, Samuel Marsh, one of the early owners of the land.

McMillan Town
Lat: 44-43-47 N Long: 90-08-32 W
Pop: 1,697 (1990); 1,433 (1980) Pop Density: 49.0
Land: 34.6 sq. mi.; **Water:** 0.2 sq. mi.

Mosinee City
ZIP: 54455 Lat: 44-47-13 N Long: 89-41-00 W
Pop: 3,820 (1990); 3,015 (1980) Pop Density: 496.1
Land: 7.7 sq. mi.; **Water:** 0.8 sq. mi. Elev: 1153 ft.
Incorporated 1931.
Name origin: For Old Chief Mosinee. Previously called Little Bull Falls, because the rapids on the river here sounded like a roaring bull.

*Mosinee Town
ZIP: 54455 Lat: 44-49-22 N Long: 89-45-46 W
Pop: 1,638 (1990); 1,464 (1980) Pop Density: 44.0
Land: 37.2 sq. mi.; **Water:** 1.3 sq. mi.

Norrie Town
Lat: 44-54-47 N Long: 89-16-57 W
Pop: 874 (1990); 808 (1980) Pop Density: 25.2
Land: 34.7 sq. mi.; **Water:** 0.6 sq. mi.

Plover Town
Lat: 44-59-23 N Long: 89-16-48 W
Pop: 568 (1990); 553 (1980) Pop Density: 15.7
Land: 36.2 sq. mi.; **Water:** 0.0 sq. mi.

Reid Town
Lat: 44-48-38 N Long: 89-25-11 W
Pop: 1,057 (1990); 957 (1980) Pop Density: 25.4
Land: 41.6 sq. mi.; **Water:** 0.6 sq. mi.

Rib Falls Town
ZIP: 54426 Lat: 44-59-36 N Long: 89-54-22 W
Pop: 860 (1990); 851 (1980) Pop Density: 24.0
Land: 35.9 sq. mi.; **Water:** 0.0 sq. mi.

Rib Mountain Town
ZIP: 54401 Lat: 44-53-47 N Long: 89-41-01 W
Pop: 5,605 (1990); 5,344 (1980) Pop Density: 227.8
Land: 24.6 sq. mi.; **Water:** 1.0 sq. mi.

Rietbrock Town
Lat: 44-59-22 N Long: 90-00-52 W
Pop: 888 (1990); 981 (1980) Pop Density: 26.1
Land: 34.0 sq. mi.; **Water:** 0.0 sq. mi.

Ringle Town
ZIP: 54471 Lat: 44-53-33 N Long: 89-25-16 W
Pop: 1,279 (1990); 1,097 (1980) Pop Density: 30.4
Land: 42.1 sq. mi.; **Water:** 0.1 sq. mi.

Rothschild Village
ZIP: 54474 Lat: 44-53-12 N Long: 89-37-15 W
Pop: 3,310 (1990); 3,338 (1980) Pop Density: 1838.9
Land: 1.8 sq. mi.; **Water:** 0.3 sq. mi.
Incorporated 1917.
Name origin: For a local man who was nicknamed Baron de Rothschild.

Schofield City
ZIP: 54476 Lat: 44-54-54 N Long: 89-36-42 W
Pop: 2,415 (1990); 2,226 (1980) Pop Density: 1341.7
Land: 1.8 sq. mi.; **Water:** 1.1 sq. mi. Elev: 1198 ft.
Incorporated 1951.
Name origin: For Dr. William Scholfield, who built a sawmill here. The *l* was later dropped from the name. Previously called Scholfield Mill.

WISCONSIN, Marathon County

Spencer
Village
ZIP: 54479 Lat: 44-45-19 N Long: 90-17-53 W
Pop: 1,757 (1990); 1,754 (1980) Pop Density: 976.1
Land: 1.8 sq. mi.; Water: 0.0 sq. mi.
Incorporated 1902.
Name origin: For Spencer, MA. Originally known as Waltham and Irene, for the wife of sawmill owner James L. Robinson.

*Spencer
Town
ZIP: 54479 Lat: 44-43-40 N Long: 90-15-22 W
Pop: 1,036 (1990); 989 (1980) Pop Density: 32.7
Land: 31.7 sq. mi.; Water: 0.2 sq. mi.

Stettin
Town
Lat: 44-58-52 N Long: 89-46-42 W
Pop: 2,191 (1990); 4,436 (1980) Pop Density: 57.7
Land: 38.0 sq. mi.; Water: 0.2 sq. mi.

Stratford
Village
ZIP: 54484 Lat: 44-48-04 N Long: 90-04-19 W
Pop: 1,515 (1990); 1,385 (1980) Pop Density: 285.8
Land: 5.3 sq. mi.; Water: 0.0 sq. mi.
Incorporated 1910.
Name origin: For Stratford, Ontario, the original home of land and mill owners, the Connors family.

Texas
Town
Lat: 45-04-21 N Long: 89-33-38 W
Pop: 1,643 (1990); 1,634 (1980) Pop Density: 36.8
Land: 44.6 sq. mi.; Water: 0.5 sq. mi.

Unity
Village
ZIP: 54488 Lat: 44-50-52 N Long: 90-18-31 W
Pop: 256 (1990); 252 (1980) Pop Density: 426.7
Land: 0.6 sq. mi.; Water: 0.0 sq. mi. Elev: 1338 ft.
Incorporated 1903. Part of the town is also in Clark County.
Name origin: Named by Mrs. Edmund Creed for the fact that the community was very united.

Wausau
City
ZIP: 54401 Lat: 44-57-42 N Long: 89-38-40 W
Pop: 37,060 (1990); 32,426 (1980) Pop Density: 2628.4
Land: 14.1 sq. mi.; Water: 1.2 sq. mi.
In central WI on the Wisconsin River, 84 mi. northwest of Green Bay. Incorporated 1872.
Name origin: From a Chippewa Indian term probably meaning 'far away.'

*Wausau
Town
Lat: 44-58-53 N Long: 89-33-18 W
Pop: 2,133 (1990); 2,215 (1980) Pop Density: 62.7
Land: 34.0 sq. mi.; Water: 0.0 sq. mi.

Weston
Town
ZIP: 54474 Lat: 44-53-47 N Long: 89-32-57 W
Pop: 11,450 (1990); 11,342 (1980) Pop Density: 318.9
Land: 35.9 sq. mi.; Water: 0.2 sq. mi.
Name origin: For Charles Weston, a sawmill owner in the early 1850s.

Wien
Town
Lat: 44-53-46 N Long: 90-01-23 W
Pop: 705 (1990); 761 (1980) Pop Density: 22.3
Land: 31.6 sq. mi.; Water: 0.0 sq. mi. Elev: 1320 ft.

Marinette County
County Seat: Marinette (ZIP: 54143)

Pop: 40,548 (1990); 39,314 (1980) Pop Density: 28.9
Land: 1402.0 sq. mi.; Water: 148.3 sq. mi. Area Code: 715
On northeastern border of WI, north of Green Bay; organized Feb 27, 1879 from Oconto County.
Name origin: For Marguerite Chevallier (1784–1865), a successful female fur trader, also known as *Marinette*, a combined form of Marie Antoinette (1755–93), then Queen of France.

Amberg
Town
ZIP: 54102 Lat: 45-29-47 N Long: 87-56-05 W
Pop: 917 (1990); 852 (1980) Pop Density: 12.8
Land: 71.8 sq. mi.; Water: 0.9 sq. mi.

Athelstane
Town
ZIP: 54104 Lat: 45-28-43 N Long: 88-09-37 W
Pop: 437 (1990); 364 (1980) Pop Density: 4.1
Land: 106.2 sq. mi.; Water: 0.8 sq. mi.

Beaver
Town
Lat: 45-09-09 N Long: 88-04-35 W
Pop: 1,041 (1990); 1,042 (1980) Pop Density: 15.2
Land: 68.6 sq. mi.; Water: 0.9 sq. mi.

Beecher
Town
ZIP: 54156 Lat: 45-33-54 N Long: 87-56-10 W
Pop: 626 (1990); 521 (1980) Pop Density: 12.9
Land: 48.5 sq. mi.; Water: 0.9 sq. mi.

Coleman
Village
ZIP: 54112 Lat: 45-04-13 N Long: 88-02-00 W
Pop: 839 (1990); 852 (1980) Pop Density: 762.7
Land: 1.1 sq. mi.; Water: 0.0 sq. mi.
Incorporated 1903.

Crivitz
Village
ZIP: 54114 Lat: 45-14-05 N Long: 88-00-24 W
Pop: 996 (1990); 1,041 (1980) Pop Density: 711.4
Land: 1.4 sq. mi.; Water: 0.0 sq. mi. Elev: 681 ft.
Incorporated 1974.

Dunbar
Town
Lat: 45-38-04 N Long: 88-08-59 W
Pop: 838 (1990); 522 (1980) Pop Density: 8.0
Land: 104.4 sq. mi.; Water: 0.8 sq. mi.

Goodman — Town
ZIP: 54125 **Lat:** 45-37-58 N **Long:** 88-20-16 W
Pop: 758 (1990); 803 (1980) **Pop Density:** 7.2
Land: 105.9 sq. mi.; **Water:** 1.7 sq. mi.

Grover — Town
Lat: 45-03-31 N **Long:** 87-51-37 W
Pop: 1,670 (1990); 1,709 (1980) **Pop Density:** 22.8
Land: 73.1 sq. mi.; **Water:** 0.2 sq. mi.

Lake — Town
Lat: 45-11-56 N **Long:** 87-53-07 W
Pop: 989 (1990); 915 (1980) **Pop Density:** 17.7
Land: 55.8 sq. mi.; **Water:** 3.8 sq. mi.

Marinette — City
ZIP: 54143 **Lat:** 45-05-18 N **Long:** 87-37-36 W
Pop: 11,843 (1990); 11,965 (1980) **Pop Density:** 1767.6
Land: 6.7 sq. mi.; **Water:** 1.2 sq. mi. **Elev:** 598 ft.
On Green Bay, 44 mi. northeast of Green Bay. Incorporated 1887.
Name origin: For the nickname—a combined form of Marie Antoinette (1755–93), Queen of France—of Marguerite Chevallier (1784–1865) who started a fur trading business on the banks of the Menominee River.

Middle Inlet — Town
Lat: 45-18-25 N **Long:** 87-56-24 W
Pop: 744 (1990); 681 (1980) **Pop Density:** 14.7
Land: 50.7 sq. mi.; **Water:** 0.8 sq. mi.

Niagara — Village
ZIP: 54151 **Lat:** 45-46-48 N **Long:** 88-00-07 W
Pop: 1,999 (1990); 2,079 (1980) **Pop Density:** 740.4
Land: 2.7 sq. mi.; **Water:** 0.3 sq. mi.
Incorporated 1914.
Name origin: Probably from the Iroquois term *oh-nia-ga* thought to mean 'bisected bottom land.'

*Niagara — Town
ZIP: 54151 **Lat:** 45-42-45 N **Long:** 87-55-50 W
Pop: 891 (1990); 717 (1980) **Pop Density:** 13.3
Land: 67.1 sq. mi.; **Water:** 1.3 sq. mi.

Pembine — Town
ZIP: 54119 **Lat:** 45-38-21 N **Long:** 87-56-06 W
Pop: 817 (1990); 773 (1980) **Pop Density:** 12.3
Land: 66.3 sq. mi.; **Water:** 1.0 sq. mi.

Peshtigo — City
ZIP: 54157 **Lat:** 45-03-19 N **Long:** 87-44-45 W
Pop: 3,154 (1990); 2,807 (1980) **Pop Density:** 1051.3
Land: 3.0 sq. mi.; **Water:** 0.2 sq. mi.
Incorporated 1903.
Name origin: From an Indian term possibly meaning either 'snapping turtle' or 'wild goose.'

*Peshtigo — Town
ZIP: 54157 **Lat:** 45-00-10 N **Long:** 87-38-49 W
Pop: 3,564 (1990); 3,566 (1980) **Pop Density:** 60.0
Land: 59.4 sq. mi.; **Water:** 121.0 sq. mi.

Porterfield — Town
ZIP: 54159 **Lat:** 45-10-30 N **Long:** 87-45-29 W
Pop: 1,805 (1990); 1,857 (1980) **Pop Density:** 34.8
Land: 51.8 sq. mi.; **Water:** 1.5 sq. mi.

Pound — Village
ZIP: 54161 **Lat:** 45-05-45 N **Long:** 88-01-58 W
Pop: 434 (1990); 407 (1980) **Pop Density:** 542.5
Land: 0.8 sq. mi.; **Water:** 0.0 sq. mi.
Incorporated 1914.
Name origin: For Thaddeus C. Pound, U.S. representative from WI. Previously called Beaver Creek.

*Pound — Town
ZIP: 54161 **Lat:** 45-03-39 N **Long:** 88-01-54 W
Pop: 1,386 (1990); 1,412 (1980) **Pop Density:** 27.7
Land: 50.0 sq. mi.; **Water:** 0.3 sq. mi.

Silver Cliff — Town
Lat: 45-26-36 N **Long:** 88-18-58 W
Pop: 259 (1990); 267 (1980) **Pop Density:** 2.4
Land: 106.4 sq. mi.; **Water:** 0.6 sq. mi.

Stephenson — Town
Lat: 45-16-48 N **Long:** 88-08-55 W
Pop: 2,288 (1990); 2,137 (1980) **Pop Density:** 13.5
Land: 169.7 sq. mi.; **Water:** 7.2 sq. mi.

Wagner — Town
Lat: 45-19-14 N **Long:** 87-44-19 W
Pop: 660 (1990); 624 (1980) **Pop Density:** 12.4
Land: 53.2 sq. mi.; **Water:** 1.4 sq. mi.

Wausaukee — Village
ZIP: 54177 **Lat:** 45-22-42 N **Long:** 87-57-17 W
Pop: 656 (1990); 648 (1980) **Pop Density:** 468.6
Land: 1.4 sq. mi.; **Water:** 0.0 sq. mi. **Elev:** 744 ft.
Incorporated 1924.
Name origin: From the Indian term meaning possibly 'river among the hills,' 'beyond the hill,' or 'far away land.' Previously called Big Wausaukee.

*Wausaukee — Town
ZIP: 54177 **Lat:** 45-23-53 N **Long:** 87-57-04 W
Pop: 937 (1990); 753 (1980) **Pop Density:** 12.4
Land: 75.7 sq. mi.; **Water:** 1.7 sq. mi.

Marquette County
County Seat: Montello (ZIP: 53949)

Pop: 12,321 (1990); 11,672 (1980) **Pop Density:** 27.0
Land: 455.5 sq. mi.; **Water:** 8.9 sq. mi. **Area Code:** 608

In south-central WI, west of Lake Winnebago; established Dec 7, 1836 (prior to statehood) from Marquette District.

Name origin: For Jacques Marquette (1637–75), French missionary known as Père Marquette; explorer with Louis Jolliet (1645–1700) of the Wisconsin and Mississippi rivers.

Buffalo — Town
Lat: 43-41-10 N Long: 89-19-44 W
Pop: 792 (1990); 745 (1980) **Pop Density:** 16.3
Land: 48.5 sq. mi.; **Water:** 0.8 sq. mi.

Crystal Lake — Town
Lat: 43-55-56 N Long: 89-18-33 W
Pop: 400 (1990); 332 (1980) **Pop Density:** 11.3
Land: 35.3 sq. mi.; **Water:** 0.6 sq. mi.

Douglas — Town
Lat: 43-41-25 N Long: 89-32-58 W
Pop: 684 (1990); 764 (1980) **Pop Density:** 23.8
Land: 28.8 sq. mi.; **Water:** 0.4 sq. mi.

Endeavor — Village
ZIP: 53930 Lat: 43-42-52 N Long: 89-28-08 W
Pop: 316 (1990); 335 (1980) **Pop Density:** 526.7
Land: 0.6 sq. mi.; **Water:** 0.1 sq. mi. **Elev:** 785 ft.
Incorporated 1946.

Name origin: For the Christian Endeavor Academy, established here in 1891, and named for the Christian Endeavor Society. Previously called Merritt's Landing.

Harris — Town
Lat: 43-51-20 N Long: 89-25-47 W
Pop: 715 (1990); 657 (1980) **Pop Density:** 23.4
Land: 30.6 sq. mi.; **Water:** 0.3 sq. mi.

Mecan — Town
Lat: 43-49-31 N Long: 89-12-34 W
Pop: 541 (1990); 599 (1980) **Pop Density:** 19.7
Land: 27.5 sq. mi.; **Water:** 0.1 sq. mi.

Montello — City
ZIP: 53949 Lat: 43-47-39 N Long: 89-20-03 W
Pop: 1,329 (1990); 1,273 (1980) **Pop Density:** 738.3
Land: 1.8 sq. mi.; **Water:** 0.2 sq. mi. **Elev:** 782 ft.
Incorporated 1938.

Name origin: From French *Mont l'eau* meaning 'hill by the water.' Previously called Serairo and Hill River.

*Montello — Town
ZIP: 53949 Lat: 43-46-33 N Long: 89-17-51 W
Pop: 940 (1990); 640 (1980) **Pop Density:** 28.8
Land: 32.6 sq. mi.; **Water:** 1.5 sq. mi.

Moundville — Town
Lat: 43-40-35 N Long: 89-27-26 W
Pop: 457 (1990); 470 (1980) **Pop Density:** 20.0
Land: 22.9 sq. mi.; **Water:** 0.3 sq. mi.

Neshkoro — Village
ZIP: 54960 Lat: 43-57-54 N Long: 89-12-49 W
Pop: 384 (1990); 386 (1980) **Pop Density:** 167.
Land: 2.3 sq. mi.; **Water:** 0.1 sq. mi. **Elev:** 800 f
Incorporated 1906.

Name origin: From a Winnebago Indian term possibly meaning either 'salt' or 'sweet water,' or, by combining Nash and Kora, for two settlers.

*Neshkoro — Town
ZIP: 54960 Lat: 43-55-51 N Long: 89-12-21 W
Pop: 489 (1990); 370 (1980) **Pop Density:** 23.
Land: 21.0 sq. mi.; **Water:** 0.4 sq. mi.

Newton — Town
Lat: 43-56-15 N Long: 89-25-52 W
Pop: 470 (1990); 460 (1980) **Pop Density:** 13.
Land: 35.5 sq. mi.; **Water:** 0.1 sq. mi.

Oxford — Village
ZIP: 53952 Lat: 43-46-48 N Long: 89-33-45 W
Pop: 499 (1990); 432 (1980) **Pop Density:** 499.
Land: 1.0 sq. mi.; **Water:** 0.0 sq. mi. **Elev:** 857 f
Incorporated 1912.

*Oxford — Town
ZIP: 53952 Lat: 43-46-33 N Long: 89-32-26 W
Pop: 637 (1990); 720 (1980) **Pop Density:** 19.
Land: 33.4 sq. mi.; **Water:** 0.2 sq. mi.

Packwaukee — Town
Lat: 43-46-01 N Long: 89-25-30 W
Pop: 1,135 (1990); 998 (1980) **Pop Density:** 29.
Land: 38.1 sq. mi.; **Water:** 2.8 sq. mi.

Shields — Town
Lat: 43-50-51 N Long: 89-18-28 W
Pop: 408 (1990); 419 (1980) **Pop Density:** 13.
Land: 31.2 sq. mi.; **Water:** 0.3 sq. mi.

Springfield — Town
Lat: 43-55-49 N Long: 89-31-56 W
Pop: 480 (1990); 501 (1980) **Pop Density:** 13.9
Land: 34.6 sq. mi.; **Water:** 0.3 sq. mi.

Westfield — Village
ZIP: 53964 Lat: 43-53-04 N Long: 89-29-38 W
Pop: 1,125 (1990); 1,033 (1980) **Pop Density:** 803.
Land: 1.4 sq. mi.; **Water:** 0.0 sq. mi. **Elev:** 865 ft
Incorporated 1902.

Name origin: Named by founder Robert Cochrane for his former home of Westfield, NY.

*Westfield — Town
ZIP: 53964 Lat: 43-51-03 N Long: 89-33-09 W
Pop: 520 (1990); 538 (1980) **Pop Density:** 18.3
Land: 28.4 sq. mi.; **Water:** 0.5 sq. mi.

> ## Menominee County
> **County Seat: Keshena (ZIP: 54135)**
>
> **Pop:** 3,890 (1990); 3,373 (1980) **Pop Density:** 10.9
> **Land:** 358.8 sq. mi.; **Water:** 7.0 sq. mi. **Area Code:** 715
>
> In east-central WI, northwest of Lake Winnebago; organized May 1, 1961 from Shawano and Oconto counties.
>
> **Name origin:** For the Menominee Indians, a tribe of Algonquian linguistic stock, who lived in the lake region where wild rice grows. The name probably means 'wild rice people.'

Keshena CDP
ZIP: 54135   **Lat:** 44-53-01 N **Long:** 88-38-10 W
Pop: 685 (1990)   **Pop Density:** 1141.7
Land: 0.6 sq. mi.; **Water:** 0.0 sq. mi.

Menominee Town
   Lat: 45-01-08 N **Long:** 88-41-59 W
Pop: 3,890 (1990); 3,373 (1980)   **Pop Density:** 10.9
Land: 358.0 sq. mi.; **Water:** 7.0 sq. mi.

Neopit CDP
ZIP: 54150   **Lat:** 44-58-52 N **Long:** 88-49-35 W
Pop: 615 (1990); 1,065 (1980)   **Pop Density:** 3075.0
Land: 0.2 sq. mi.; **Water:** 0.0 sq. mi.

> ## Milwaukee County
> **County Seat: Milwaukee (ZIP: 53233)**
>
> **Pop:** 959,275 (1990); 964,988 (1980) **Pop Density:** 3971.1
> **Land:** 241.6 sq. mi.; **Water:** 948.2 sq. mi. **Area Code:** 414
>
> On southeastern coast of WI; organized Aug 25, 1835 (prior to statehood).
>
> **Name origin:** An Algonquian word of uncertain meaning; possibly 'rich beautiful land' or 'gathering place by the river.' The area had long been a council ground for different tribes.

Bayside Village
ZIP: 53217   **Lat:** 43-10-49 N **Long:** 87-54-11 W
Pop: 4,681 (1990); 4,612 (1980)   **Pop Density:** 2035.2
Land: 2.3 sq. mi.; **Water:** 0.0 sq. mi.
Incorporated 1953. Part of the town is also in Ozaukee County.
Name origin: For its geographical location on Lake Michigan.

Brown Deer Village
ZIP: 53209   **Lat:** 43-10-29 N **Long:** 87-58-29 W
Pop: 12,236 (1990); 12,921 (1980)   **Pop Density:** 2780.9
Land: 4.4 sq. mi.; **Water:** 0.0 sq. mi.   **Elev:** 679 ft.
In southeastern WI, north of Milwaukee. Incorporated 1955.
Name origin: For brown deer common to the vicinity. Previously called White Deer after an albino deer was seen in the area.

Cudahy City
ZIP: 53110   **Lat:** 42-56-47 N **Long:** 87-51-53 W
Pop: 18,659 (1990); 19,547 (1980)   **Pop Density:** 3887.3
Land: 4.8 sq. mi.; **Water:** 0.0 sq. mi.
In southeastern WI on Lake Michigan, 7 mi. south of Milwaukee. Incorporated 1906.
Name origin: For Patrick Cudahy, who grew up in the area and, with his brother John, started the meat-packing firm of Cudahy Brothers.

Fox Point Village
ZIP: 53217   **Lat:** 43-09-30 N **Long:** 87-54-06 W
Pop: 7,238 (1990); 7,649 (1980)   **Pop Density:** 2495.9
Land: 2.9 sq. mi.; **Water:** 0.0 sq. mi.   **Elev:** 672 ft.
Incorporated 1926.
Name origin: A surveyor's name for the point of land at Doctor's Park. Previously called Dutch Settlement by Dutch immigrants.

Franklin City
ZIP: 53132   **Lat:** 42-53-10 N **Long:** 88-00-35 W
Pop: 21,855 (1990); 16,871 (1980)   **Pop Density:** 631.6
Land: 34.6 sq. mi.; **Water:** 0.1 sq. mi.
In southeastern WI, a southwest suburb of Milwaukee. Incorporated 1956.
Name origin: For Benjamin Franklin (1706–90), one of the most popular and versatile of American Revolutionary patriots.

Glendale City
ZIP: 53209   **Lat:** 43-07-48 N **Long:** 87-55-39 W
Pop: 14,088 (1990); 13,882 (1980)   **Pop Density:** 2429.0
Land: 5.8 sq. mi.; **Water:** 0.2 sq. mi.
Incorporated 1950.
Name origin: Descriptively named by townspeople. Previously called Lake; at one time part of the city of Milwaukee.

Greendale
Village
ZIP: 53129 **Lat:** 42-56-08 N **Long:** 88-00-05 W
Pop: 15,128 (1990); 16,928 (1980) **Pop Density:** 2701.4
Land: 5.6 sq. mi.; **Water:** 0.0 sq. mi.

In southeastern WI, a southwestern suburb of Milwaukee. One of the Greenbelt Towns built c. 1936 by the Resettlement Administration. Incorporated 1939.

Greenfield
City
ZIP: 53220 **Lat:** 42-57-45 N **Long:** 88-00-20 W
Pop: 33,403 (1990); 31,353 (1980) **Pop Density:** 2904.6
Land: 11.5 sq. mi.; **Water:** 0.0 sq. mi.

In western WI, southeast of Winona, MN. Incorporated 1857.

Name origin: Named by Nathan Dennison for his hometown of Greenfield, MA.

Hales Corners
Village
ZIP: 53130 **Lat:** 42-56-25 N **Long:** 88-02-57 W
Pop: 7,623 (1990); 7,110 (1980) **Pop Density:** 2382.2
Land: 3.2 sq. mi.; **Water:** 0.0 sq. mi.

Incorporated 1952.

Name origin: For William Hale, who built the first log cabin here in 1837.

Milwaukee
City
ZIP: 53201 **Lat:** 43-03-48 N **Long:** 87-57-59 W
Pop: 628,088 (1990); 636,295 (1980) **Pop Density:** 6542.6
Land: 96.0 sq. mi.; **Water:** 0.8 sq. mi. **Elev:** 634 ft.

On the southeastern coast of WI, on Lake Michigan. Platted 1835; settled 1836; incorporated 1846. Largest city in WI, a major U.S. industrial center, important Great Lakes port. Diverse manufacturing city (automobile parts, beer, electrical equipment, farm and factory machinery); insurance and banking; trade (beer, dairy products, and machinery). Milwaukee is the county in which the city of Milwaukee has its greatest population. Part of the city is also in Washington and Waukesha counties.

Name origin: From an Algonquian word of uncertain meaning; possibly 'rich beautiful land' or 'gathering place by the river.'

Oak Creek
City
ZIP: 53154 **Lat:** 42-52-56 N **Long:** 87-53-50 W
Pop: 19,513 (1990); 16,932 (1980) **Pop Density:** 682.3
Land: 28.6 sq. mi.; **Water:** 0.0 sq. mi.

In southeastern WI, southeast of Milwaukee. Incorporated 1955.

River Hills
Village
ZIP: 53217 **Lat:** 43-10-24 N **Long:** 87-56-06 W
Pop: 1,612 (1990); 1,642 (1980) **Pop Density:** 316.1
Land: 5.1 sq. mi.; **Water:** 0.2 sq. mi.

Incorporated 1930.

Name origin: For its descriptive connotations.

St. Francis
City
ZIP: 53207 **Lat:** 42-58-14 N **Long:** 87-52-18 W
Pop: 9,245 (1990); 10,095 (1980) **Pop Density:** 3698.0
Land: 2.5 sq. mi.; **Water:** 0.0 sq. mi.

Incorporated 1951.

Name origin: For St. Francis of Sales (1567–1622), French bishop and theologian. Previously called by the Indian name *No-gosh-ing* possibly meaning 'snake' or 'enemies.'

Shorewood
Village
ZIP: 53211 **Lat:** 43-05-28 N **Long:** 87-53-10 W
Pop: 14,116 (1990); 14,327 (1980) **Pop Density:** 8822.5
Land: 1.6 sq. mi.; **Water:** 0.0 sq. mi. **Elev:** 679 ft.

In southeastern WI, 4 mi. north of Milwaukee. Platted 1836; incorporated 1900.

Name origin: For its location on the shore of Lake Michigan. Previously called Mechanicsville and East Milwaukee.

South Milwaukee
City
ZIP: 53172 **Lat:** 42-54-46 N **Long:** 87-51-43 W
Pop: 20,958 (1990); 21,069 (1980) **Pop Density:** 4366.3
Land: 4.8 sq. mi.; **Water:** 0.0 sq. mi.

In southeastern WI on Lake Michigan, 9 mi. south of Milwaukee. Incorporated 1897.

Name origin: For its location.

Wauwatosa
City
ZIP: 53213 **Lat:** 43-03-43 N **Long:** 88-02-00 W
Pop: 49,366 (1990); 51,308 (1980) **Pop Density:** 3739.8
Land: 13.2 sq. mi.; **Water:** 0.0 sq. mi. **Elev:** 672 ft.

In southeastern WI, 5 mi. west of Milwaukee. Incorporated 1897.

Name origin: From Algonquian *wauwautaesie* 'firefly;' also the name of a legendary Indian chief. Originally known as Hart's Mills, for mill owner Charles Hart.

West Allis
City
ZIP: 53214 **Lat:** 43-00-26 N **Long:** 88-01-48 W
Pop: 63,221 (1990); 63,982 (1980) **Pop Density:** 5594.8
Land: 11.3 sq. mi.; **Water:** 0.0 sq. mi. **Elev:** 730 ft.

In southeastern WI, 6 mi. southwest of Milwaukee. Incorporated 1906.

Name origin: For Allis-Chalmers, a manufacturing plant established here. Parts of this city were previously called North Greenfield and Honey Creek.

West Milwaukee
Village
ZIP: 53214 **Lat:** 43-00-46 N **Long:** 87-58-12 W
Pop: 3,973 (1990); 3,535 (1980) **Pop Density:** 3611.8
Land: 1.1 sq. mi.; **Water:** 0.0 sq. mi.

Incorporated 1906.

Name origin: For its location, west of the city of Milwaukee.

Whitefish Bay
Village
ZIP: 53217 **Lat:** 43-06-45 N **Long:** 87-54-03 W
Pop: 14,272 (1990); 14,930 (1980) **Pop Density:** 6796.2
Land: 2.1 sq. mi.; **Water:** 0.0 sq. mi.

In southeastern WI on Lake Michigan, 5 mi. north of Milwaukee. Incorporated 1892.

Name origin: For the many whitefish found in the bay.

Monroe County
County Seat: Sparta (ZIP: 54656)

Pop: 36,633 (1990); 35,074 (1980) **Pop Density:** 40.7
Land: 900.9 sq. mi.; **Water:** 7.5 sq. mi. **Area Code:** 608
In southwestern WI, east of La Crosse; organized Mar 21, 1854 from unorganized territory.
Name origin: For James Monroe (1758–1831), fifth U.S. president.

Adrian — Town
Lat: 43-56-49 N Long: 90-36-43 W
Pop: 520 (1990); 403 (1980) **Pop Density:** 14.7
Land: 35.3 sq. mi.; **Water:** 0.0 sq. mi.

Angelo — Town
Lat: 43-56-47 N Long: 90-43-49 W
Pop: 1,219 (1990); 1,189 (1980) **Pop Density:** 34.7
Land: 35.1 sq. mi.; **Water:** 0.1 sq. mi.

Byron — Town
Lat: 44-01-37 N Long: 90-22-23 W
Pop: 1,250 (1990); 1,162 (1980) **Pop Density:** 35.2
Land: 35.5 sq. mi.; **Water:** 0.6 sq. mi.

Cashton — Village
ZIP: 54619 Lat: 43-44-35 N Long: 90-46-53 W
Pop: 780 (1990); 827 (1980) **Pop Density:** 1114.3
Land: 0.7 sq. mi.; **Water:** 0.0 sq. mi.
Incorporated 1901.
Name origin: Named in 1879 for Henry Harrison Cash, who built the railroad through town. Previously called Mt. Pisgah and Hazen's Corner.

Clifton — Town
Lat: 43-51-47 N Long: 90-22-25 W
Pop: 587 (1990); 610 (1980) **Pop Density:** 17.2
Land: 34.1 sq. mi.; **Water:** 0.0 sq. mi.

Glendale — Town
Lat: 43-46-19 N Long: 90-22-36 W
Pop: 564 (1990); 558 (1980) **Pop Density:** 15.8
Land: 35.6 sq. mi.; **Water:** 0.0 sq. mi.

Grant — Town
Lat: 44-06-37 N Long: 90-37-33 W
Pop: 346 (1990); 312 (1980) **Pop Density:** 9.7
Land: 35.7 sq. mi.; **Water:** 0.2 sq. mi.

Greenfield — Town
Lat: 44-01-36 N Long: 90-36-48 W
Pop: 556 (1990); 536 (1980) **Pop Density:** 15.8
Land: 35.3 sq. mi.; **Water:** 0.1 sq. mi.

Jefferson — Town
Lat: 43-46-09 N Long: 90-43-17 W
Pop: 815 (1990); 710 (1980) **Pop Density:** 23.3
Land: 35.0 sq. mi.; **Water:** 0.0 sq. mi.

Kendall — Village
ZIP: 54638 Lat: 43-47-35 N Long: 90-22-03 W
Pop: 453 (1990); 486 (1980) **Pop Density:** 647.1
Land: 0.7 sq. mi.; **Water:** 0.0 sq. mi. **Elev:** 1021 ft.
Incorporated 1894.
Name origin: For contractor L. G. Kendall, who purchased right-of-way for the railroad.

Lafayette — Town
Lat: 44-01-46 N Long: 90-43-21 W
Pop: 298 (1990); 256 (1980) **Pop Density:** 8.4
Land: 35.3 sq. mi.; **Water:** 0.0 sq. mi.

La Grange — Town
Lat: 44-01-26 N Long: 90-29-11 W
Pop: 1,507 (1990); 1,728 (1980) **Pop Density:** 49.4
Land: 30.5 sq. mi.; **Water:** 1.6 sq. mi.

Leon — Town
Lat: 43-51-34 N Long: 90-51-15 W
Pop: 746 (1990); 751 (1980) **Pop Density:** 20.8
Land: 35.8 sq. mi.; **Water:** 0.0 sq. mi.

Lincoln — Town
Lat: 44-07-05 N Long: 90-29-21 W
Pop: 765 (1990); 644 (1980) **Pop Density:** 22.4
Land: 34.1 sq. mi.; **Water:** 0.8 sq. mi.

Little Falls — Town
Lat: 44-06-12 N Long: 90-52-14 W
Pop: 1,137 (1990); 1,228 (1980) **Pop Density:** 16.6
Land: 68.5 sq. mi.; **Water:** 0.4 sq. mi.

Melvina — Village
ZIP: 54619 Lat: 43-48-15 N Long: 90-46-48 W
Pop: 115 (1990); 117 (1980) **Pop Density:** 230.0
Land: 0.5 sq. mi.; **Water:** 0.0 sq. mi.
Incorporated 1922.

New Lyme — Town
Lat: 44-06-09 N Long: 90-44-01 W
Pop: 156 (1990); 123 (1980) **Pop Density:** 4.4
Land: 35.6 sq. mi.; **Water:** 0.5 sq. mi.

Norwalk — Village
ZIP: 54648 Lat: 43-49-59 N Long: 90-37-31 W
Pop: 564 (1990); 517 (1980) **Pop Density:** 564.0
Land: 1.0 sq. mi.; **Water:** 0.0 sq. mi. **Elev:** 1030 ft.
Incorporated 1894.
Name origin: Named by early settler S. McGary for Norwalk, OH.

Oakdale — Village
Lat: 43-57-45 N Long: 90-22-42 W
Pop: 162 (1990) **Pop Density:** 202.5
Land: 0.8 sq. mi.; **Water:** 0.0 sq. mi.

*Oakdale — Town
Lat: 43-56-45 N Long: 90-22-09 W
Pop: 643 (1990); 759 (1980) **Pop Density:** 18.0
Land: 35.7 sq. mi.; **Water:** 0.1 sq. mi.
Incorporated 1988.

Portland — Town
Lat: 43-46-22 N Long: 90-51-12 W
Pop: 733 (1990); 755 (1980) **Pop Density:** 20.3
Land: 36.1 sq. mi.; **Water:** 0.0 sq. mi.

WISCONSIN, Monroe County

Ridgeville
Town
Lat: 43-51-14 N **Long:** 90-37-36 W
Pop: 497 (1990); 530 (1980) **Pop Density:** 14.5
Land: 34.2 sq. mi.; **Water:** 0.0 sq. mi.

Scott
Town
Lat: 44-07-19 N **Long:** 90-22-47 W
Pop: 120 (1990); 117 (1980) **Pop Density:** 3.5
Land: 33.9 sq. mi.; **Water:** 2.6 sq. mi.

Sheldon
Town
Lat: 43-46-00 N **Long:** 90-37-10 W
Pop: 521 (1990); 524 (1980) **Pop Density:** 14.8
Land: 35.3 sq. mi.; **Water:** 0.0 sq. mi.

Sparta
City
ZIP: 54656 **Lat:** 43-56-33 N **Long:** 90-48-35 W
Pop: 7,788 (1990); 6,934 (1980) **Pop Density:** 1589.4
Land: 4.9 sq. mi.; **Water:** 0.1 sq. mi. **Elev:** 793 ft.
Incorporated 1883.
Name origin: For the ancient city in Greece.

*Sparta
Town
ZIP: 54656 **Lat:** 43-58-13 N **Long:** 90-52-18 W
Pop: 2,385 (1990); 2,317 (1980) **Pop Density:** 48.3
Land: 49.4 sq. mi.; **Water:** 0.0 sq. mi.

Tomah
City
ZIP: 54660 **Lat:** 43-59-22 N **Long:** 90-30-11 W
Pop: 7,570 (1990); 7,204 (1980) **Pop Density:** 1182.8
Land: 6.4 sq. mi.; **Water:** 0.4 sq. mi.
Incorporated 1883.
Name origin: From the French pronunciation of *Thomas*, for Chief Thomas Carron of the Menominee Indians.

*Tomah
Town
ZIP: 54660 **Lat:** 43-56-13 N **Long:** 90-29-46 W
Pop: 1,076 (1990); 1,089 (1980) **Pop Density:** 33.8
Land: 31.8 sq. mi.; **Water:** 0.0 sq. mi.

Warrens
Village
ZIP: 54666 **Lat:** 44-07-49 N **Long:** 90-30-02 W
Pop: 343 (1990); 300 (1980) **Pop Density:** 686.0
Land: 0.5 sq. mi.; **Water:** 0.0 sq. mi.
Incorporated 1973.
Name origin: For George Warren, who started a sawmill here. Originally called Warren's Mills.

Wellington
Town
Lat: 43-45-42 N **Long:** 90-29-25 W
Pop: 566 (1990); 616 (1980) **Pop Density:** 16.0
Land: 35.4 sq. mi.; **Water:** 0.0 sq. mi.

Wells
Town
Lat: 43-51-45 N **Long:** 90-44-08 W
Pop: 442 (1990); 474 (1980) **Pop Density:** 12.4
Land: 35.7 sq. mi.; **Water:** 0.0 sq. mi.

Wilton
Village
ZIP: 54670 **Lat:** 43-48-52 N **Long:** 90-31-38 W
Pop: 478 (1990); 465 (1980) **Pop Density:** 531.1
Land: 0.9 sq. mi.; **Water:** 0.0 sq. mi. **Elev:** 995 ft.
Settled c. 1842. Incorporated 1890.

*Wilton
Town
ZIP: 54670 **Lat:** 43-50-42 N **Long:** 90-29-24 W
Pop: 777 (1990); 670 (1980) **Pop Density:** 22.3
Land: 34.9 sq. mi.; **Water:** 0.0 sq. mi.

Wyeville
Village
ZIP: 54671 **Lat:** 44-01-39 N **Long:** 90-23-08 W
Pop: 154 (1990); 163 (1980) **Pop Density:** 256.7
Land: 0.6 sq. mi.; **Water:** 0.0 sq. mi.
Incorporated 1923.

Oconto County
County Seat: Oconto (ZIP: 54153)

Pop: 30,226 (1990); 28,947 (1980) **Pop Density:** 30.3
Land: 998.1 sq. mi.; **Water:** 151.1 sq. mi. **Area Code:** 414
On northeastern coast of WI, bordered on east by Green Bay; organized Feb 6, 1851 from unorganized territory.
Name origin: For the Oconto River, which flows through it; from a Menominee word of unclear meaning, possibly 'place of the pike fish' or 'red river.'

Abrams
Town
ZIP: 54101 **Lat:** 44-47-55 N **Long:** 88-04-32 W
Pop: 1,347 (1990); 1,181 (1980) **Pop Density:** 35.9
Land: 37.5 sq. mi.; **Water:** 0.1 sq. mi.

Armstrong
Town
Lat: 45-09-25 N **Long:** 88-25-47 W
Pop: 730 (1990); 735 (1980) **Pop Density:** 10.2
Land: 71.6 sq. mi.; **Water:** 1.1 sq. mi.

Bagley
Town
Lat: 45-04-18 N **Long:** 88-17-31 W
Pop: 271 (1990); 272 (1980) **Pop Density:** 7.8
Land: 34.8 sq. mi.; **Water:** 0.9 sq. mi.

Brazeau
Town
Lat: 45-06-31 N **Long:** 88-12-38 W
Pop: 1,169 (1990); 1,039 (1980) **Pop Density:** 17.1
Land: 68.5 sq. mi.; **Water:** 3.0 sq. mi.

Breed
Town
Lat: 45-04-20 N **Long:** 88-25-28 W
Pop: 564 (1990); 563 (1980) **Pop Density:** 15.8
Land: 35.6 sq. mi.; **Water:** 0.2 sq. mi.

Chase
Town
Lat: 44-43-07 N **Long:** 88-11-39 W
Pop: 1,375 (1990); 1,256 (1980) **Pop Density:** 38.8
Land: 35.4 sq. mi.; **Water:** 0.1 sq. mi.

WISCONSIN, Oconto County

Doty — Town
Lat: 45-12-17 N Long: 88-36-53 W
Pop: 184 (1990); 154 (1980) Pop Density: 3.5
Land: 52.2 sq. mi.; Water: 2.2 sq. mi.

Gillett — City
ZIP: 54124 Lat: 44-53-23 N Long: 88-18-22 W
Pop: 1,303 (1990); 1,356 (1980) Pop Density: 1002.3
Land: 1.3 sq. mi.; Water: 0.0 sq. mi. Elev: 812 ft.
Incorporated 1944.
Name origin: For Rodney and Mary Roblee Gillett, who settled here in 1858. Previously called Gillett Center.

*Gillett — Town
Lat: 44-53-51 N Long: 88-18-30 W
Pop: 1,026 (1990); 1,059 (1980) Pop Density: 30.7
Land: 33.4 sq. mi.; Water: 0.9 sq. mi.

How — Town
Lat: 44-59-22 N Long: 88-26-13 W
Pop: 564 (1990); 592 (1980) Pop Density: 16.2
Land: 34.9 sq. mi.; Water: 0.1 sq. mi.

Lakewood — Town
ZIP: 54138 Lat: 45-20-24 N Long: 88-26-09 W
Pop: 607 (1990); 516 (1980) Pop Density: 8.6
Land: 70.8 sq. mi.; Water: 1.6 sq. mi.

Lena — Village
ZIP: 54139 Lat: 44-57-09 N Long: 88-03-00 W
Pop: 590 (1990); 585 (1980) Pop Density: 655.6
Land: 0.9 sq. mi.; Water: 0.0 sq. mi. Elev: 714 ft.
Incorporated 1921.
Name origin: For the wife of postmaster George R. Hall. Previously called Maple Valley.

*Lena — Town
ZIP: 54139 Lat: 44-58-32 N Long: 88-03-23 W
Pop: 790 (1990); 851 (1980) Pop Density: 23.7
Land: 33.4 sq. mi.; Water: 0.0 sq. mi.

Little River — Town
Lat: 44-57-52 N Long: 87-54-23 W
Pop: 1,003 (1990); 940 (1980) Pop Density: 19.5
Land: 51.5 sq. mi.; Water: 0.0 sq. mi.

Little Suamico — Town
ZIP: 54141 Lat: 44-42-39 N Long: 88-03-20 W
Pop: 2,637 (1990); 1,969 (1980) Pop Density: 70.7
Land: 37.3 sq. mi.; Water: 0.1 sq. mi.

Maple Valley — Town
Lat: 44-59-05 N Long: 88-18-55 W
Pop: 690 (1990); 715 (1980) Pop Density: 19.5
Land: 35.3 sq. mi.; Water: 0.1 sq. mi.

Morgan — Town
Lat: 44-48-33 N Long: 88-12-02 W
Pop: 815 (1990); 726 (1980) Pop Density: 22.9
Land: 35.6 sq. mi.; Water: 0.1 sq. mi.

Oconto — City
ZIP: 54153 Lat: 44-53-28 N Long: 87-52-05 W
Pop: 4,474 (1990); 4,505 (1980) Pop Density: 648.4
Land: 6.9 sq. mi.; Water: 0.5 sq. mi. Elev: 591 ft.
Incorporated 1869.
Name origin: For the river, itself named from a Menominee Indian word of unclear meaning, possibly 'red river,' or 'place of the pike fish.'

*Oconto — Town
ZIP: 54153 Lat: 44-53-15 N Long: 87-56-28 W
Pop: 999 (1990); 937 (1980) Pop Density: 27.5
Land: 36.3 sq. mi.; Water: 0.4 sq. mi.

Oconto Falls — City
ZIP: 54154 Lat: 44-52-21 N Long: 88-08-42 W
Pop: 2,584 (1990); 2,500 (1980) Pop Density: 1076.7
Land: 2.4 sq. mi.; Water: 0.2 sq. mi. Elev: 735 ft.
Incorporated 1919.
Name origin: For the falls on the Oconto River.

*Oconto Falls — Town
ZIP: 54154 Lat: 44-54-00 N Long: 88-11-31 W
Pop: 1,014 (1990); 1,033 (1980) Pop Density: 31.2
Land: 32.5 sq. mi.; Water: 0.5 sq. mi.

Pensaukee — Town
ZIP: 54153 Lat: 44-48-29 N Long: 87-58-10 W
Pop: 979 (1990); 1,000 (1980) Pop Density: 27.6
Land: 35.5 sq. mi.; Water: 0.1 sq. mi.

Riverview — Town
Lat: 45-14-23 N Long: 88-26-31 W
Pop: 483 (1990); 417 (1980) Pop Density: 6.9
Land: 69.7 sq. mi.; Water: 2.0 sq. mi.

Spruce — Town
Lat: 44-59-21 N Long: 88-11-04 W
Pop: 776 (1990); 805 (1980) Pop Density: 22.0
Land: 35.2 sq. mi.; Water: 0.5 sq. mi.

Stiles — Town
Lat: 44-53-20 N Long: 88-03-57 W
Pop: 1,243 (1990); 1,261 (1980) Pop Density: 36.1
Land: 34.4 sq. mi.; Water: 0.8 sq. mi.

Suring — Village
ZIP: 54174 Lat: 45-00-01 N Long: 88-22-13 W
Pop: 626 (1990); 581 (1980) Pop Density: 626.0
Land: 1.0 sq. mi.; Water: 0.0 sq. mi. Elev: 804 ft.
Incorporated 1914.
Name origin: For John Suring and his wife, pioneer settlers who built a sawmill here.

Townsend — Town
ZIP: 54175 Lat: 45-19-24 N Long: 88-36-42 W
Pop: 715 (1990); 735 (1980) Pop Density: 18.3
Land: 39.0 sq. mi.; Water: 3.5 sq. mi.

Underhill — Town
Lat: 44-53-47 N Long: 88-26-04 W
Pop: 668 (1990); 664 (1980) Pop Density: 19.0
Land: 35.1 sq. mi.; Water: 0.5 sq. mi.

WISCONSIN, Oneida County

Oneida County
County Seat: Rhinelander (ZIP: 54501)

Pop: 31,679 (1990); 31,216 (1980)
Land: 1124.7 sq. mi.; **Water:** 111.4 sq. mi.
Pop Density: 28.2
Area Code: 815
In north-central WI; organized Apr 11, 1885 from Lincoln County.

Name origin: For the Oneida Indians, one of the Five Nations of the Iroquois. The name is thought to mean 'stone people,' perhaps in praise of their bravery.

Cassian   Town
ZIP: 54529   **Lat:** 45-41-24 N **Long:** 89-40-58 W
Pop: 668 (1990); 585 (1980)   **Pop Density:** 10.3
Land: 65.0 sq. mi.; **Water:** 3.4 sq. mi.

Crescent   Town
ZIP: 54501   **Lat:** 45-36-01 N **Long:** 89-29-06 W
Pop: 1,790 (1990); 1,702 (1980)   **Pop Density:** 56.8
Land: 31.5 sq. mi.; **Water:** 3.3 sq. mi.

Enterprise   Town
                    Lat: 45-30-30 N **Long:** 89-19-32 W
Pop: 271 (1990); 277 (1980)   **Pop Density:** 4.8
Land: 56.7 sq. mi.; **Water:** 2.2 sq. mi.

Hazelhurst   Town
ZIP: 54531   **Lat:** 45-46-40 N **Long:** 89-43-45 W
Pop: 927 (1990); 780 (1980)   **Pop Density:** 29.5
Land: 31.4 sq. mi.; **Water:** 3.9 sq. mi.

Lake Tomahawk   Town
ZIP: 54539   **Lat:** 45-46-17 N **Long:** 89-36-29 W
Pop: 851 (1990); 738 (1980)   **Pop Density:** 24.8
Land: 34.3 sq. mi.; **Water:** 4.9 sq. mi.

Little Rice   Town
                    Lat: 45-38-20 N **Long:** 89-51-23 W
Pop: 196 (1990); 172 (1980)   **Pop Density:** 2.9
Land: 68.1 sq. mi.; **Water:** 5.6 sq. mi.

Lynne   Town
                    Lat: 45-37-58 N **Long:** 89-57-59 W
Pop: 157 (1990); 185 (1980)   **Pop Density:** 2.2
Land: 70.6 sq. mi.; **Water:** 1.5 sq. mi.

Minocqua   Town
ZIP: 54548   **Lat:** 45-49-28 N **Long:** 89-53-09 W
Pop: 3,486 (1990); 3,328 (1980)   **Pop Density:** 23.1
Land: 150.6 sq. mi.; **Water:** 17.3 sq. mi.

Monico   Town
                    Lat: 45-36-01 N **Long:** 89-08-36 W
Pop: 294 (1990); 291 (1980)   **Pop Density:** 5.4
Land: 54.1 sq. mi.; **Water:** 0.5 sq. mi.

Newbold   Town
ZIP: 54501   **Lat:** 45-46-52 N **Long:** 89-29-32 W
Pop: 2,281 (1990); 2,171 (1980)   **Pop Density:** 28.8
Land: 79.1 sq. mi.; **Water:** 13.9 sq. mi.

Nokomis   Town
                    Lat: 45-36-14 N **Long:** 89-43-54 W
Pop: 999 (1990); 883 (1980)   **Pop Density:** 29.9
Land: 33.4 sq. mi.; **Water:** 3.6 sq. mi.

Pelican   Town
ZIP: 54501   **Lat:** 45-36-05 N **Long:** 89-19-54 W
Pop: 3,202 (1990); 3,387 (1980)   **Pop Density:** 61.9
Land: 51.7 sq. mi.; **Water:** 2.7 sq. mi.

Piehl   Town
                    Lat: 45-41-04 N **Long:** 89-06-34 W
Pop: 66 (1990); 94 (1980)   **Pop Density:** 1.8
Land: 37.4 sq. mi.; **Water:** 0.6 sq. mi.

Pine Lake   Town
ZIP: 54501   **Lat:** 45-41-20 N **Long:** 89-23-50 W
Pop: 2,445 (1990); 2,656 (1980)   **Pop Density:** 60.1
Land: 40.7 sq. mi.; **Water:** 4.4 sq. mi.

Rhinelander   City
ZIP: 54501   **Lat:** 45-38-22 N **Long:** 89-24-43 W
Pop: 7,427 (1990); 7,873 (1980)   **Pop Density:** 1456.3
Land: 5.1 sq. mi.; **Water:** 0.1 sq. mi.   **Elev:** 1554 ft.
Incorporated 1894.

Name origin: For F. W. Rhineland, president of the railroad company. Previously called Pelican Rapids.

Schoepke   Town
                    Lat: 45-30-46 N **Long:** 89-08-45 W
Pop: 378 (1990); 399 (1980)   **Pop Density:** 8.2
Land: 46.1 sq. mi.; **Water:** 4.5 sq. mi.

Stella   Town
ZIP: 54501   **Lat:** 45-40-38 N **Long:** 89-14-11 W
Pop: 525 (1990); 489 (1980)   **Pop Density:** 14.9
Land: 35.3 sq. mi.; **Water:** 2.0 sq. mi.

Sugar Camp   Town
ZIP: 54501   **Lat:** 45-48-15 N **Long:** 89-20-24 W
Pop: 1,375 (1990); 1,337 (1980)   **Pop Density:** 15.5
Land: 88.8 sq. mi.; **Water:** 9.1 sq. mi.

Three Lakes   Town
ZIP: 54562   **Lat:** 45-48-04 N **Long:** 89-07-59 W
Pop: 2,004 (1990); 1,864 (1980)   **Pop Density:** 24.6
Land: 81.5 sq. mi.; **Water:** 18.4 sq. mi.

Woodboro   Town
ZIP: 54501   **Lat:** 45-35-48 N **Long:** 89-36-52 W
Pop: 703 (1990); 547 (1980)   **Pop Density:** 20.3
Land: 34.7 sq. mi.; **Water:** 2.5 sq. mi.

Woodruff   Town
ZIP: 54568   **Lat:** 45-51-24 N **Long:** 89-37-27 W
Pop: 1,634 (1990); 1,458 (1980)   **Pop Density:** 57.3
Land: 28.5 sq. mi.; **Water:** 7.0 sq. mi.

Outagamie County
County Seat: Appleton (ZIP: 54911)

Pop: 140,510 (1990); 128,730 (1980)   **Pop Density:** 219.4
Land: 640.4 sq. mi.; **Water:** 4.1 sq. mi.   **Area Code:** 414
In east-central WI, west of Green Bay; organized Feb 17, 1851 from Brown County.
Name origin: Ojibway *O-dug-am-eeg* 'dwellers on the other side,' in reference to the Fox Indians.

Appleton   City
ZIP: 54911   **Lat:** 44-16-19 N   **Long:** 88-23-50 W
Pop: 56,177 (1990); 53,424 (1980)   **Pop Density:** 3847.7
Land: 14.6 sq. mi.; **Water:** 0.5 sq. mi.
In eastern WI on the Fox River, 17 mi. north of Oshkosh. Incorporated 1857. Outagamie is the county in which the city of Appleton has its greatest population. Part of the town is also in Calumet and Winnebago counties.
Name origin: For Samuel Appleton, one of the founders of Lawrence University.

Bear Creek   Village
ZIP: 54922   **Lat:** 44-31-51 N   **Long:** 88-43-36 W
Pop: 418 (1990); 454 (1980)   **Pop Density:** 464.4
Land: 0.9 sq. mi.; **Water:** 0.0 sq. mi.   **Elev:** 817 ft.
Incorporated 1902.
Name origin: Named in 1885 for nearby Bear Creek. Previously called Welcome, for lumberman Welcome Hyde.

Black Creek   Village
ZIP: 54106   **Lat:** 44-28-28 N   **Long:** 88-27-00 W
Pop: 1,152 (1990); 1,097 (1980)   **Pop Density:** 1152.0
Land: 1.0 sq. mi.; **Water:** 0.0 sq. mi.   **Elev:** 790 ft.
Incorporated 1904.
Name origin: For a creek with dark water on the edge of town. Originally called Middleburg.

*Black Creek   Town
ZIP: 54106   **Lat:** 44-27-34 N   **Long:** 88-26-26 W
Pop: 1,169 (1990); 1,149 (1980)   **Pop Density:** 33.3
Land: 35.1 sq. mi.; **Water:** 0.0 sq. mi.

Bovina   Town
Lat: 44-27-28 N   **Long:** 88-33-03 W
Pop: 957 (1990); 822 (1980)   **Pop Density:** 28.4
Land: 33.7 sq. mi.; **Water:** 0.1 sq. mi.

Buchanan   Town
Lat: 44-15-47 N   **Long:** 88-14-54 W
Pop: 2,484 (1990); 1,742 (1980)   **Pop Density:** 135.0
Land: 18.4 sq. mi.; **Water:** 0.4 sq. mi.

Center   Town
Lat: 44-22-13 N   **Long:** 88-26-26 W
Pop: 2,716 (1990); 2,570 (1980)   **Pop Density:** 76.1
Land: 35.7 sq. mi.; **Water:** 0.0 sq. mi.

Cicero   Town
Lat: 44-32-54 N   **Long:** 88-25-59 W
Pop: 1,126 (1990); 1,062 (1980)   **Pop Density:** 31.7
Land: 35.5 sq. mi.; **Water:** 0.0 sq. mi.

Combined Locks   Village
ZIP: 54113   **Lat:** 44-16-07 N   **Long:** 88-18-39 W
Pop: 2,190 (1990); 2,573 (1980)   **Pop Density:** 1825.0
Land: 1.2 sq. mi.; **Water:** 0.2 sq. mi.
Incorporated 1920.
Name origin: For the canal locks on the Fox River.

Dale   Town
Lat: 44-16-37 N   **Long:** 88-40-45 W
Pop: 1,818 (1990); 1,620 (1980)   **Pop Density:** 59.8
Land: 30.4 sq. mi.; **Water:** 0.0 sq. mi.

Deer Creek   Town
Lat: 44-32-18 N   **Long:** 88-40-07 W
Pop: 724 (1990); 826 (1980)   **Pop Density:** 20.4
Land: 35.5 sq. mi.; **Water:** 0.0 sq. mi.

Ellington   Town
Lat: 44-22-13 N   **Long:** 88-33-30 W
Pop: 2,099 (1990); 1,865 (1980)   **Pop Density:** 60.1
Land: 34.9 sq. mi.; **Water:** 0.2 sq. mi.

Freedom   Town
Lat: 44-22-29 N   **Long:** 88-18-41 W
Pop: 4,114 (1990); 3,746 (1980)   **Pop Density:** 114.9
Land: 35.8 sq. mi.; **Water:** 0.0 sq. mi.

Grand Chute   Town
ZIP: 54911   **Lat:** 44-17-41 N   **Long:** 88-26-12 W
Pop: 14,490 (1990); 9,529 (1980)   **Pop Density:** 526.9
Land: 27.5 sq. mi.; **Water:** 0.1 sq. mi.

Greenville   Town
ZIP: 54942   **Lat:** 44-17-15 N   **Long:** 88-33-30 W
Pop: 3,806 (1990); 3,310 (1980)   **Pop Density:** 106.3
Land: 35.8 sq. mi.; **Water:** 0.0 sq. mi.

Hortonia   Town
Lat: 44-20-46 N   **Long:** 88-40-57 W
Pop: 883 (1990); 869 (1980)   **Pop Density:** 45.5
Land: 19.4 sq. mi.; **Water:** 0.2 sq. mi.

Hortonville   Village
ZIP: 54944   **Lat:** 44-20-19 N   **Long:** 88-37-58 W
Pop: 2,029 (1990); 2,016 (1980)   **Pop Density:** 780.4
Land: 2.6 sq. mi.; **Water:** 0.1 sq. mi.   **Elev:** 794 ft.
Incorporated 1894.
Name origin: For Alonzo Erastus Horton, who founded the village in 1849.

Kaukauna   City
ZIP: 54130   **Lat:** 44-16-44 N   **Long:** 88-16-06 W
Pop: 11,982 (1990); 11,310 (1980)   **Pop Density:** 2549.4
Land: 4.7 sq. mi.; **Water:** 0.4 sq. mi.
In eastern WI. Incorporated 1885.
Name origin: From the Menominee term *okakaning* or *kakaning* referring to the rapids in the Fox River.

*Kaukauna   Town
ZIP: 54130   **Lat:** 44-20-59 N   **Long:** 88-13-17 W
Pop: 939 (1990); 998 (1980)   **Pop Density:** 52.2
Land: 18.0 sq. mi.; **Water:** 0.3 sq. mi.

WISCONSIN, Outagamie County

Kimberly
Village
ZIP: 54136 **Lat:** 44-16-12 N **Long:** 88-20-26 W
Pop: 5,406 (1990); 5,881 (1980) **Pop Density:** 3180.0
Land: 1.7 sq. mi.; **Water:** 0.2 sq. mi. **Elev:** 734 ft.
Incorporated 1910.
Name origin: For Kimberly Clark, a company that built a pulp and paper mill here in 1889. Originally known as The Cedars, because the Treaty of Cedars was signed here.

Liberty
Town
Lat: 44-24-57 N **Long:** 88-39-14 W
Pop: 702 (1990); 609 (1980) **Pop Density:** 23.0
Land: 30.5 sq. mi.; **Water:** 0.1 sq. mi.

Little Chute
Village
ZIP: 54140 **Lat:** 44-17-08 N **Long:** 88-18-48 W
Pop: 9,207 (1990); 7,907 (1980) **Pop Density:** 2630.6
Land: 3.5 sq. mi.; **Water:** 0.3 sq. mi. **Elev:** 728 ft.
Incorporated 1899.
Name origin: From a translation of the French name for the falls in the Fox River *La Petite Chute* by Father Vanden Broek, who built the first church here in 1836.

Maine
Town
Lat: 44-32-44 N **Long:** 88-33-15 W
Pop: 791 (1990); 816 (1980) **Pop Density:** 21.6
Land: 36.6 sq. mi.; **Water:** 0.8 sq. mi.

Maple Creek
Town
Lat: 44-27-46 N **Long:** 88-41-46 W
Pop: 695 (1990); 652 (1980) **Pop Density:** 31.3
Land: 22.2 sq. mi.; **Water:** 0.1 sq. mi.

New London
City
ZIP: 54961 **Lat:** 44-23-31 N **Long:** 88-43-44 W
Pop: 1,337 (1990); 1,269 (1980) **Pop Density:** 703.7
Land: 1.9 sq. mi.; **Water:** 0.0 sq. mi. **Elev:** 789 ft.
Established 1852. Incorporated 1877. Part of the town is also in Waupaca County.
Name origin: For New London, CT, the birthplace of the father of Reeder Smith, one of the city developers.

Nichols
Village
ZIP: 54152 **Lat:** 44-33-55 N **Long:** 88-28-01 W
Pop: 254 (1990); 267 (1980) **Pop Density:** 282.2
Land: 0.9 sq. mi.; **Water:** 0.0 sq. mi.
Incorporated 1967.
Name origin: For Albert L. Nichols, who established the town.

Oneida
Town
ZIP: 54155 **Lat:** 44-28-20 N **Long:** 88-14-32 W
Pop: 3,858 (1990); 3,499 (1980) **Pop Density:** 63.5
Land: 60.8 sq. mi.; **Water:** 0.0 sq. mi.

Osborn
Town
Lat: 44-27-20 N **Long:** 88-20-24 W
Pop: 784 (1990); 786 (1980) **Pop Density:** 46.4
Land: 16.9 sq. mi.; **Water:** 0.0 sq. mi.

Seymour
City
ZIP: 54165 **Lat:** 44-30-52 N **Long:** 88-19-38 W
Pop: 2,782 (1990); 2,530 (1980) **Pop Density:** 1112.8
Land: 2.5 sq. mi.; **Water:** 0.0 sq. mi.
Incorporated 1879.
Name origin: For Horatio Seymour (1810–66), governor of NY.

*Seymour
Town
ZIP: 54165 **Lat:** 44-32-37 N **Long:** 88-18-48 W
Pop: 1,217 (1990); 1,189 (1980) **Pop Density:** 39.9
Land: 30.5 sq. mi.; **Water:** 0.0 sq. mi.

Shiocton
Village
ZIP: 54170 **Lat:** 44-26-42 N **Long:** 88-34-35 W
Pop: 913 (1990); 805 (1980) **Pop Density:** 570.6
Land: 1.6 sq. mi.; **Water:** 0.0 sq. mi.
Incorporated 1903.
Name origin: For Chief Shioc of the Menominees whose name meant 'by force of wind.' Previously called Jordan's Landing or Jordanville, for Dominicus Jordan.

Vandenbroek
Town
Lat: 44-18-42 N **Long:** 88-17-52 W
Pop: 1,291 (1990); 1,538 (1980) **Pop Density:** 127.8
Land: 10.1 sq. mi.; **Water:** 0.0 sq. mi.

Ozaukee County
County Seat: Port Washington (ZIP: 53074)

Pop: 72,831 (1990); 66,981 (1980) **Pop Density:** 314.0
Land: 232.0 sq. mi.; **Water:** 884.3 sq. mi. **Area Code:** 414
On southeastern coast of WI, north of Milwaukee; organized Mar 7, 1853 from Milwaukee County.
Name origin: Said to be the true name of the main Sauk Indian tribe; meaning is either 'people at the mouth of the river' (the Ojibway name for the tribe), or 'yellow earth,' from their tradition that the first Sauk male sprang from yellow earth.

Bayside
Village
ZIP: 53217 **Lat:** 43-11-34 N **Long:** 87-53-46 W
Pop: 108 (1990); 112 (1980) **Pop Density:** 1080.0
Land: 0.1 sq. mi.; **Water:** 0.0 sq. mi.
Incorporated 1953. Part of the town is also in Milwaukee County.
Name origin: For its geographical location on Lake Michigan.

Belgium
Village
ZIP: 53004 **Lat:** 43-30-02 N **Long:** 87-51-01 W
Pop: 928 (1990); 892 (1980) **Pop Density:** 928.0
Land: 1.0 sq. mi.; **Water:** 0.0 sq. mi. **Elev:** 736 ft.
Established 1864. Incorporated 1922.
Name origin: For the country, so named when the federal government confused it with the desired name of Luxembourg.

WISCONSIN, Ozaukee County

*Belgium — Town
ZIP: 53004 Lat: 43-29-38 N Long: 87-51-32 W
Pop: 1,405 (1990); 1,424 (1980) Pop Density: 38.8
Land: 36.2 sq. mi.; Water: 1.1 sq. mi.

Cedarburg — City
ZIP: 53012 Lat: 43-17-47 N Long: 87-59-17 W
Pop: 9,895 (1990); 9,005 (1980) Pop Density: 2748.6
Land: 3.6 sq. mi.; Water: 0.0 sq. mi.
Incorporated 1885.
Name origin: Possibly for the house of Dr. Fred Luening, which stood on a hill surrounded by cedars.

*Cedarburg — Town
ZIP: 53012 Lat: 43-19-28 N Long: 88-00-58 W
Pop: 5,334 (1990); 5,244 (1980) Pop Density: 205.9
Land: 25.9 sq. mi.; Water: 0.2 sq. mi.

Fredonia — Village
ZIP: 53021 Lat: 43-28-06 N Long: 87-57-06 W
Pop: 1,558 (1990); 1,437 (1980) Pop Density: 1112.9
Land: 1.4 sq. mi.; Water: 0.0 sq. mi.
Incorporated 1922.
Name origin: For the town of Fredonia, NY. Previously called Stoney Creek.

*Fredonia — Town
ZIP: 53021 Lat: 43-29-28 N Long: 87-59-07 W
Pop: 2,043 (1990); 2,144 (1980) Pop Density: 58.9
Land: 34.7 sq. mi.; Water: 0.3 sq. mi.

Grafton — Village
ZIP: 53024 Lat: 43-19-07 N Long: 87-57-16 W
Pop: 9,340 (1990); 8,381 (1980) Pop Density: 3220.7
Land: 2.9 sq. mi.; Water: 0.0 sq. mi.
Incorporated 1896.
Name origin: Possibly for Grafton Street in Dublin, Ireland, or the Grafton in NH, MA, or WV. Originally known as Hamburg and Manchester (1857–1862).

*Grafton — Town
ZIP: 53024 Lat: 43-19-31 N Long: 87-55-22 W
Pop: 3,745 (1990); 3,588 (1980) Pop Density: 180.0
Land: 20.8 sq. mi.; Water: 1.6 sq. mi.

Mequon — City
ZIP: 53092 Lat: 43-14-09 N Long: 87-59-21 W
Pop: 18,885 (1990); 16,193 (1980) Pop Density: 408.8
Land: 46.2 sq. mi.; Water: 0.6 sq. mi.
In eastern WI, south of Sheboygan. Incorporated 1957.
Name origin: For Wau-Mequon or 'White Feather,' the name of Chief Waubaka's daughter.

Newburg — Village
ZIP: 53060 Lat: 43-25-53 N Long: 88-02-03 W
Pop: 22 (1990); 95 (1980) Pop Density: 220.0
Land: 0.1 sq. mi.; Water: 0.0 sq. mi. Elev: 850 ft.
Incorporated 1973. Part of the town is also in Washington County.

Port Washington — City
ZIP: 53074 Lat: 43-23-37 N Long: 87-52-47 W
Pop: 9,338 (1990); 8,612 (1980) Pop Density: 2668.0
Land: 3.5 sq. mi.; Water: 0.0 sq. mi. Elev: 612 ft.
Incorporated 1822.
Name origin: For George Washington (1732–99), patriot and first U.S. president. *Port* was added when a pier was built and the city became a center of commerce. Previously called Green Bay and Wisconsin Bay.

*Port Washington — Town
ZIP: 53074 Lat: 43-25-07 N Long: 87-52-23 W
Pop: 1,480 (1990); 1,436 (1980) Pop Density: 77.9
Land: 19.0 sq. mi.; Water: 2.6 sq. mi.

Saukville — Village
ZIP: 53080 Lat: 43-23-01 N Long: 87-56-29 W
Pop: 3,695 (1990); 3,494 (1980) Pop Density: 1539.6
Land: 2.4 sq. mi.; Water: 0.0 sq. mi.
Incorporated 1915.
Name origin: For a Sauk Indian village once located here. The present town encompasses the early settlements of Voelker's Mills, Schmit's Mill, Mechanicsville, and St. Finbars.

*Saukville — Town
ZIP: 53080 Lat: 43-24-31 N Long: 87-59-16 W
Pop: 1,754 (1990); 1,583 (1980) Pop Density: 52.8
Land: 33.2 sq. mi.; Water: 0.7 sq. mi.

Thiensville — Village
ZIP: 53092 Lat: 43-14-12 N Long: 87-58-47 W
Pop: 3,301 (1990); 3,341 (1980) Pop Density: 3000.9
Land: 1.1 sq. mi.; Water: 0.0 sq. mi.
Incorporated 1910.
Name origin: For Joachim Heinrich Thein, a German settler who built the first mill and laid out the village. Originally known as Mequon River.

WISCONSIN, Pepin County   *American Places Dictionary*

Pepin County
County Seat: Durand (ZIP: 54736)

Pop: 7,107 (1990); 7,477 (1980) **Pop Density:** 30.6
Land: 232.3 sq. mi.; **Water:** 16.4 sq. mi. **Area Code:** 715
On central western border of WI, southeast of St. Paul, MN; organized Feb 25, 1858 from Chippewa County.

Name origin: For Pepin Lake, a widening of the Mississippi River. Named before 1700 by French explorers either for a member of the Duluth expedition, or for the French king, Pepin le Bref (715–768), the father of Charlemagne (742–814).

Albany   Town
Lat: 44-38-06 N **Long:** 91-43-09 W
Pop: 507 (1990); 586 (1980) **Pop Density:** 14.1
Land: 36.0 sq. mi.; **Water:** 0.0 sq. mi.

Durand   City
ZIP: 54736 **Lat:** 44-37-44 N **Long:** 91-57-38 W
Pop: 2,003 (1990); 2,047 (1980) **Pop Density:** 1251.9
Land: 1.6 sq. mi.; **Water:** 0.1 sq. mi. **Elev:** 721 ft.
Incorporated 1887.

Name origin: For Miles Durand Prindle, who with Charles Billings, platted the town in 1856.

*Durand   Town
ZIP: 54736 **Lat:** 44-37-59 N **Long:** 91-55-56 W
Pop: 604 (1990); 591 (1980) **Pop Density:** 32.6
Land: 18.5 sq. mi.; **Water:** 0.6 sq. mi.

Frankfort   Town
Lat: 44-33-27 N **Long:** 92-05-57 W
Pop: 322 (1990); 397 (1980) **Pop Density:** 10.7
Land: 30.1 sq. mi.; **Water:** 0.9 sq. mi.

Lima   Town
Lat: 44-38-26 N **Long:** 91-50-01 W
Pop: 649 (1990); 631 (1980) **Pop Density:** 18.1
Land: 35.9 sq. mi.; **Water:** 0.0 sq. mi.

Pepin   Village
ZIP: 54759 **Lat:** 44-26-32 N **Long:** 92-08-46 W
Pop: 873 (1990); 890 (1980) **Pop Density:** 1247.1
Land: 0.7 sq. mi.; **Water:** 0.0 sq. mi. **Elev:** 720 ft.
Incorporated 1860.

Name origin: For the lake, which was named by early French explorers either for a companion of Duluth, who came here in 1679, or for a French king, Pepin le Bref (715–768), father of Charlemagne (742–814).

*Pepin   Town
ZIP: 54759 **Lat:** 44-28-42 N **Long:** 92-08-25 W
Pop: 696 (1990); 749 (1980) **Pop Density:** 15.3
Land: 45.4 sq. mi.; **Water:** 7.1 sq. mi.

Stockholm   Village
ZIP: 54769 **Lat:** 44-29-00 N **Long:** 92-15-37 W
Pop: 89 (1990); 104 (1980) **Pop Density:** 98.9
Land: 0.9 sq. mi.; **Water:** 0.0 sq. mi. **Elev:** 690 ft.
Incorporated 1903.

Name origin: Named by Swedish settlers for the capital city of Sweden.

*Stockholm   Town
ZIP: 54769 **Lat:** 44-30-17 N **Long:** 92-15-23 W
Pop: 173 (1990); 168 (1980) **Pop Density:** 11.2
Land: 15.4 sq. mi.; **Water:** 6.4 sq. mi.

Waterville   Town
Lat: 44-38-30 N **Long:** 92-03-45 W
Pop: 875 (1990); 1,075 (1980) **Pop Density:** 24.2
Land: 36.2 sq. mi.; **Water:** 0.5 sq. mi.

Waubeek   Town
Lat: 44-39-39 N **Long:** 91-58-26 W
Pop: 316 (1990); 239 (1980) **Pop Density:** 27.5
Land: 11.5 sq. mi.; **Water:** 0.8 sq. mi.

Pierce County
County Seat: Ellsworth (ZIP: 54011)

Pop: 32,765 (1990); 31,149 (1980) **Pop Density:** 56.8
Land: 576.5 sq. mi.; **Water:** 15.1 sq. mi. **Area Code:** 715
On central western border of WI, east of St. Paul, MN; organized Mar 14, 1853 from Saint Croix County.

Name origin: For Franklin Pierce (1804–69), fourteenth U.S. president.

Bay City   Village
ZIP: 54723 **Lat:** 44-35-07 N **Long:** 92-27-09 W
Pop: 578 (1990); 543 (1980) **Pop Density:** 1156.0
Land: 0.5 sq. mi.; **Water:** 0.0 sq. mi.
Incorporated 1909.

Clifton   Town
ZIP: 54022 **Lat:** 44-48-36 N **Long:** 92-43-42 W
Pop: 1,119 (1990); 975 (1980) **Pop Density:** 32.5
Land: 34.4 sq. mi.; **Water:** 1.2 sq. mi.

WISCONSIN, Pierce County

Diamond Bluff — Town
ZIP: 54014 Lat: 44-39-15 N Long: 92-37-25 W
Pop: 492 (1990); 458 (1980) Pop Density: 29.5
Land: 16.7 sq. mi.; Water: 1.7 sq. mi.

Ellsworth — Village
ZIP: 54003 Lat: 44-44-14 N Long: 92-28-47 W
Pop: 2,706 (1990); 2,143 (1980) Pop Density: 751.7
Land: 3.6 sq. mi.; Water: 0.0 sq. mi. Elev: 1226 ft.
Incorporated 1887.
Name origin: For Col. E. E. Ellsworth. Previously called Perry.

*Ellsworth — Town
ZIP: 54003 Lat: 44-44-07 N Long: 92-25-48 W
Pop: 1,030 (1990); 1,408 (1980) Pop Density: 32.0
Land: 32.2 sq. mi.; Water: 0.0 sq. mi.

Elmwood — Village
ZIP: 54740 Lat: 44-46-48 N Long: 92-08-57 W
Pop: 775 (1990); 885 (1980) Pop Density: 516.7
Land: 1.5 sq. mi.; Water: 0.0 sq. mi.
Incorporated 1905.

El Paso — Town
ZIP: 54003 Lat: 44-43-35 N Long: 92-19-21 W
Pop: 641 (1990); 689 (1980) Pop Density: 18.3
Land: 35.1 sq. mi.; Water: 0.0 sq. mi.

Gilman — Town
Lat: 44-48-48 N Long: 92-19-28 W
Pop: 762 (1990); 914 (1980) Pop Density: 22.5
Land: 33.9 sq. mi.; Water: 0.0 sq. mi.

Hartland — Town
ZIP: 54011 Lat: 44-38-43 N Long: 92-26-28 W
Pop: 766 (1990); 821 (1980) Pop Density: 21.3
Land: 36.0 sq. mi.; Water: 0.0 sq. mi.

Isabelle — Town
Lat: 44-34-58 N Long: 92-26-20 W
Pop: 196 (1990); 190 (1980) Pop Density: 18.8
Land: 10.4 sq. mi.; Water: 5.2 sq. mi.

Maiden Rock — Village
ZIP: 54750 Lat: 44-34-04 N Long: 92-18-30 W
Pop: 146 (1990); 172 (1980) Pop Density: 132.7
Land: 1.1 sq. mi.; Water: 0.0 sq. mi. Elev: 689 ft.
Incorporated 1887.
Name origin: For a rocky bluff that towers over the river here, said to be where Dakota maiden, Winona, jumped to her death.

*Maiden Rock — Town
ZIP: 54750 Lat: 44-34-15 N Long: 92-14-36 W
Pop: 649 (1990); 641 (1980) Pop Density: 16.1
Land: 40.3 sq. mi.; Water: 3.7 sq. mi.

Martell — Town
ZIP: 54767 Lat: 44-49-19 N Long: 92-26-17 W
Pop: 866 (1990); 864 (1980) Pop Density: 24.2
Land: 35.8 sq. mi.; Water: 0.0 sq. mi.

Oak Grove — Town
ZIP: 54021 Lat: 44-44-24 N Long: 92-41-39 W
Pop: 1,120 (1990); 936 (1980) Pop Density: 28.5
Land: 39.3 sq. mi.; Water: 0.5 sq. mi.

Plum City — Village
ZIP: 54761 Lat: 44-37-58 N Long: 92-11-30 W
Pop: 534 (1990); 505 (1980) Pop Density: 534.0
Land: 1.0 sq. mi.; Water: 0.0 sq. mi.
Incorporated 1909.
Name origin: For nearby Plum Creek, which was named for the many plum trees on its banks.

Prescott — City
ZIP: 54021 Lat: 44-45-02 N Long: 92-47-24 W
Pop: 3,243 (1990); 2,654 (1980) Pop Density: 1621.5
Land: 2.0 sq. mi.; Water: 0.4 sq. mi.
Incorporated 1857.
Name origin: For Philander Prescott, an Indian interpreter. Previously called Mouth of the St. Croix, Lake Mouth, and Elizabeth, for Elizabeth Schasser.

River Falls — City
ZIP: 54022 Lat: 44-51-07 N Long: 92-37-18 W
Pop: 8,841 (1990); 7,521 (1980) Pop Density: 3157.5
Land: 2.8 sq. mi.; Water: 0.0 sq. mi.
Incorporated 1875. Part of the town is also in St. Croix County.
Name origin: For the falls in the Kinnickinic River, after it was discovered there was already a Greenwood in the state. Previously called Kinnickinnic and Greenwood.

*River Falls — Town
ZIP: 54022 Lat: 44-48-50 N Long: 92-34-29 W
Pop: 1,944 (1990); 2,168 (1980) Pop Density: 43.1
Land: 45.1 sq. mi.; Water: 0.0 sq. mi.

Rock Elm — Town
Lat: 44-43-18 N Long: 92-11-56 W
Pop: 519 (1990); 654 (1980) Pop Density: 14.5
Land: 35.8 sq. mi.; Water: 0.0 sq. mi.

Salem — Town
Lat: 44-38-33 N Long: 92-18-36 W
Pop: 514 (1990); 616 (1980) Pop Density: 14.5
Land: 35.4 sq. mi.; Water: 0.0 sq. mi. Elev: 1027 ft.

Spring Lake — Town
Lat: 44-48-57 N Long: 92-11-45 W
Pop: 565 (1990); 613 (1980) Pop Density: 18.0
Land: 31.4 sq. mi.; Water: 0.0 sq. mi.

Spring Valley — Village
ZIP: 54767 Lat: 44-50-44 N Long: 92-14-27 W
Pop: 1,051 (1990); 982 (1980) Pop Density: 350.3
Land: 3.0 sq. mi.; Water: 0.1 sq. mi.
Incorporated 1895. Part of the town is also in St. Croix County.
Name origin: Probably for two principal streams in this valley: Eagle and Berghardt springs.

Trenton — Town
ZIP: 54014 Lat: 44-38-11 N Long: 92-31-58 W
Pop: 1,583 (1990); 1,624 (1980) Pop Density: 56.3
Land: 28.1 sq. mi.; Water: 2.0 sq. mi.

Trimbelle — Town
ZIP: 54011 Lat: 44-43-54 N Long: 92-33-21 W
Pop: 1,482 (1990); 1,420 (1980) Pop Density: 40.9
Land: 36.2 sq. mi.; Water: 0.0 sq. mi.

Union — Town
Lat: 44-38-38 N Long: 92-12-18 W
Pop: 643 (1990); 753 (1980) Pop Density: 18.4
Land: 34.9 sq. mi.; Water: 0.2 sq. mi.

WISCONSIN, Polk County

Polk County
County Seat: Balsam Lake (ZIP: 54810)

Pop: 34,773 (1990); 32,351 (1980)   **Pop Density:** 37.9
Land: 917.3 sq. mi.; **Water:** 39.0 sq. mi.   **Area Code:** 715
On central western border of WI, northeast of St. Paul, MN; organized Mar 14, 1853 from Saint Croix County.
Name origin: For James Knox Polk (1795–1849), eleventh U.S. president.

Alden — Town
Lat: 45-15-00 N   Long: 92-30-08 W
Pop: 2,133 (1990); 1,862 (1980)   **Pop Density:** 38.0
Land: 56.1 sq. mi.; **Water:** 3.0 sq. mi.

Amery — City
ZIP: 54001   Lat: 45-18-16 N   Long: 92-21-47 W
Pop: 2,657 (1990); 2,404 (1980)   **Pop Density:** 885.7
Land: 3.0 sq. mi.; **Water:** 0.6 sq. mi.
Incorporated 1919.
Name origin: Named in 1887 for William Amery, an Englishman who settled in St. Croix, WI.

Apple River — Town
Lat: 45-25-55 N   Long: 92-20-44 W
Pop: 815 (1990); 819 (1980)   **Pop Density:** 24.0
Land: 34.0 sq. mi.; **Water:** 2.0 sq. mi.

Balsam Lake — Village
ZIP: 54810   Lat: 45-27-29 N   Long: 92-27-16 W
Pop: 792 (1990); 749 (1980)   **Pop Density:** 396.0
Land: 2.0 sq. mi.; **Water:** 1.2 sq. mi.   **Elev:** 1155 ft.
Incorporated 1905.
Name origin: Named by the Chippewa Indians for its natural surroundings.

*Balsam Lake — Town
ZIP: 54024   Lat: 45-25-27 N   Long: 92-28-11 W
Pop: 1,067 (1990); 960 (1980)   **Pop Density:** 35.9
Land: 29.7 sq. mi.; **Water:** 2.5 sq. mi.

Beaver — Town
Lat: 45-25-27 N   Long: 92-13-13 W
Pop: 663 (1990); 755 (1980)   **Pop Density:** 18.5
Land: 35.8 sq. mi.; **Water:** 1.6 sq. mi.

Black Brook — Town
ZIP: 54005   Lat: 45-14-56 N   Long: 92-21-07 W
Pop: 964 (1990); 949 (1980)   **Pop Density:** 28.1
Land: 34.3 sq. mi.; **Water:** 0.7 sq. mi.

Bone Lake — Town
Lat: 45-36-02 N   Long: 92-20-06 W
Pop: 503 (1990); 466 (1980)   **Pop Density:** 15.0
Land: 33.6 sq. mi.; **Water:** 1.9 sq. mi.

Centuria — Village
ZIP: 54824   Lat: 45-26-58 N   Long: 92-33-20 W
Pop: 790 (1990); 711 (1980)   **Pop Density:** 526.7
Land: 1.5 sq. mi.; **Water:** 0.0 sq. mi.
Incorporated 1904.
Name origin: For its founding date, 1900, at the turn of the century.

Clam Falls — Town
Lat: 45-41-00 N   Long: 92-20-41 W
Pop: 596 (1990); 614 (1980)   **Pop Density:** 17.2
Land: 34.7 sq. mi.; **Water:** 0.7 sq. mi.

Clayton — Village
Lat: 45-19-25 N   Long: 92-10-12 W
Pop: 450 (1990); 425 (1980)   **Pop Density:** 145.2
Land: 3.1 sq. mi.; **Water:** 0.1 sq. mi.
Incorporated 1909.
Name origin: For Clayton Rogers, who was in charge of a mill at the time of settlement.

*Clayton — Town
Lat: 45-20-28 N   Long: 92-13-54 W
Pop: 780 (1990); 789 (1980)   **Pop Density:** 23.5
Land: 33.2 sq. mi.; **Water:** 0.6 sq. mi.

Clear Lake — Village
ZIP: 54005   Lat: 45-15-00 N   Long: 92-16-07 W
Pop: 932 (1990); 899 (1980)   **Pop Density:** 358.5
Land: 2.6 sq. mi.; **Water:** 0.0 sq. mi.   **Elev:** 1201 ft.
Incorporated 1894.
Name origin: A substitution for Clark's Lake named for one of the town's oldest families, because there was already a Clark's Lake in the state.

*Clear Lake — Town
ZIP: 54005   Lat: 45-15-06 N   Long: 92-12-49 W
Pop: 744 (1990); 777 (1980)   **Pop Density:** 21.6
Land: 34.5 sq. mi.; **Water:** 0.1 sq. mi.

Dresser — Village
ZIP: 54009   Lat: 45-21-41 N   Long: 92-38-01 W
Pop: 614 (1990); 670 (1980)   **Pop Density:** 361.2
Land: 1.7 sq. mi.; **Water:** 0.0 sq. mi.
Incorporated 1919.
Name origin: For Samuel Dresser, who donated land for the railroad. Previously called Dresser Junction.

Eureka — Town
ZIP: 54024   Lat: 45-30-57 N   Long: 92-37-18 W
Pop: 1,201 (1990); 1,135 (1980)   **Pop Density:** 22.3
Land: 53.9 sq. mi.; **Water:** 0.9 sq. mi.

Farmington — Town
Lat: 45-15-37 N   Long: 92-41-04 W
Pop: 1,267 (1990); 1,195 (1980)   **Pop Density:** 28.7
Land: 44.2 sq. mi.; **Water:** 0.9 sq. mi.

Frederic — Village
ZIP: 54837   Lat: 45-39-23 N   Long: 92-27-50 W
Pop: 1,124 (1990); 1,039 (1980)   **Pop Density:** 749.3
Land: 1.5 sq. mi.; **Water:** 0.1 sq. mi.
Incorporated 1903.
Name origin: Named by landowner William J. Starr for his son.

Garfield — Town
Lat: 45-20-11 N   Long: 92-29-00 W
Pop: 1,107 (1990); 1,010 (1980)   **Pop Density:** 33.5
Land: 33.0 sq. mi.; **Water:** 2.1 sq. mi.

WISCONSIN, Polk County

Georgetown
Town
Lat: 45-30-43 N　Long: 92-20-46 W
Pop: 780 (1990); 746 (1980)　Pop Density: 25.7
Land: 30.3 sq. mi.; Water: 4.8 sq. mi.

Johnstown
Town
Lat: 45-30-19 N　Long: 92-13-00 W
Pop: 410 (1990); 401 (1980)　Pop Density: 11.5
Land: 35.8 sq. mi.; Water: 1.3 sq. mi.

Laketown
Town
ZIP: 54006　Lat: 45-36-24 N　Long: 92-35-22 W
Pop: 921 (1990); 909 (1980)　Pop Density: 26.9
Land: 34.2 sq. mi.; Water: 1.5 sq. mi.

Lincoln
Town
ZIP: 54001　Lat: 45-20-21 N　Long: 92-21-23 W
Pop: 1,835 (1990); 1,683 (1980)　Pop Density: 51.4
Land: 35.7 sq. mi.; Water: 2.7 sq. mi.

Lorain
Town
Lat: 45-41-07 N　Long: 92-13-11 W
Pop: 299 (1990); 280 (1980)　Pop Density: 8.1
Land: 36.9 sq. mi.; Water: 0.1 sq. mi.

Luck
Village
ZIP: 54853　Lat: 45-34-30 N　Long: 92-28-02 W
Pop: 1,022 (1990); 997 (1980)　Pop Density: 601.2
Land: 1.7 sq. mi.; Water: 0.6 sq. mi.
Incorporated 1905.
Name origin: Named by settlers for the "luck" said to be had if they reached here by nightfall on their way to MN for supplies.

*Luck
Town
ZIP: 54853　Lat: 45-35-51 N　Long: 92-28-28 W
Pop: 880 (1990); 863 (1980)　Pop Density: 27.2
Land: 32.3 sq. mi.; Water: 0.6 sq. mi.

McKinley
Town
Lat: 45-36-10 N　Long: 92-12-53 W
Pop: 327 (1990); 337 (1980)　Pop Density: 9.1
Land: 36.0 sq. mi.; Water: 1.1 sq. mi.

Milltown
Village
ZIP: 54858　Lat: 45-31-36 N　Long: 92-29-58 W
Pop: 786 (1990); 732 (1980)　Pop Density: 436.7
Land: 1.8 sq. mi.; Water: 0.0 sq. mi.　Elev: 1246 ft.
Incorporated 1910.
Name origin: Named in 1839 either for Milton, PA, or John Milton (1608–74), the author of *Paradise Lost*, with a spelling variation. Previously called Grainfield.

*Milltown
Town
ZIP: 54858　Lat: 45-30-23 N　Long: 92-28-10 W
Pop: 949 (1990); 943 (1980)　Pop Density: 30.4
Land: 31.2 sq. mi.; Water: 2.2 sq. mi.

Osceola
Village
ZIP: 54020　Lat: 45-19-09 N　Long: 92-41-45 W
Pop: 2,075 (1990); 1,581 (1980)　Pop Density: 715.5
Land: 2.9 sq. mi.; Water: 0.1 sq. mi.
Incorporated 1886.

*Osceola
Town
ZIP: 54020　Lat: 45-20-21 N　Long: 92-36-39 W
Pop: 1,337 (1990); 1,066 (1980)　Pop Density: 37.6
Land: 35.6 sq. mi.; Water: 1.8 sq. mi.

St. Croix Falls
City
Lat: 45-24-33 N　Long: 92-38-01 W
Pop: 1,640 (1990); 1,497 (1980)　Pop Density: 565.5
Land: 2.9 sq. mi.; Water: 0.1 sq. mi.
Incorporated 1958.
Name origin: For a waterfall here on the St. Croix River, now altered by a power company dam.

*St. Croix Falls
Town
Lat: 45-25-46 N　Long: 92-36-01 W
Pop: 1,034 (1990); 873 (1980)　Pop Density: 32.9
Land: 31.4 sq. mi.; Water: 0.9 sq. mi.

Sterling
Town
ZIP: 54006　Lat: 45-35-59 N　Long: 92-45-52 W
Pop: 591 (1990); 497 (1980)　Pop Density: 9.3
Land: 63.4 sq. mi.; Water: 1.0 sq. mi.

Turtle Lake
Village
ZIP: 54889　Lat: 45-23-23 N　Long: 92-09-31 W
Pop: 6 (1990)　Pop Density: 120.0
Land: 0.05 sq. mi.; Water: 0.0 sq. mi.　Elev: 1264 ft.
Incorporated 1898. Part of the town is also in Barron County.
Name origin: For the nearby lake that was named for turtle's eggs found on its shore. Originally called Skowhagen for Skowhagen, ME, the former home of settler Joel Richardson.

West Sweden
Town
Lat: 45-41-16 N　Long: 92-28-12 W
Pop: 682 (1990); 718 (1980)　Pop Density: 20.9
Land: 32.7 sq. mi.; Water: 1.0 sq. mi.

Portage County

County Seat: Stevens Point (ZIP: 54481)

Pop: 61,405 (1990); 57,420 (1980)
Land: 806.4 sq. mi.; **Water:** 16.5 sq. mi.
Pop Density: 76.2
Area Code: 715

In east-central WI, northwest of Lake Winnebago; organized Dec 7, 1836 (prior to statehood) from territorial county in the area now occupied by much of Columbia County, expanded northward in 1841 (into territory from Crawford County); Columbia County detached in 1846.

Name origin: For the portage of canoes or other craft between the Fox and Wisconsin rivers.

Alban — Town
ZIP: 54473 Lat: 44-38-03 N Long: 89-16-36 W
Pop: 860 (1990); 768 (1980) Pop Density: 24.2
Land: 35.5 sq. mi.; Water: 0.6 sq. mi.

Almond — Village
ZIP: 54909 Lat: 44-15-40 N Long: 89-24-31 W
Pop: 455 (1990); 477 (1980) Pop Density: 455.0
Land: 1.0 sq. mi.; Water: 0.0 sq. mi.
Founded 1849. Incorporated 1905.

Name origin: Named by settlers for their hometown of Almond, NY.

*Almond — Town
ZIP: 54909 Lat: 44-17-41 N Long: 89-25-27 W
Pop: 590 (1990); 624 (1980) Pop Density: 13.7
Land: 43.1 sq. mi.; Water: 0.1 sq. mi.

Amherst — Village
ZIP: 54406 Lat: 44-26-53 N Long: 89-17-05 W
Pop: 792 (1990); 701 (1980) Pop Density: 660.0
Land: 1.2 sq. mi.; Water: 0.0 sq. mi.
Incorporated 1899.

Name origin: Named by Judge Gilbert Park and Adam Uline for British Commander Jeffery Amherst (1717–97).

*Amherst — Town
ZIP: 54406 Lat: 44-27-41 N Long: 89-17-41 W
Pop: 1,335 (1990); 1,215 (1980) Pop Density: 35.0
Land: 38.1 sq. mi.; Water: 0.5 sq. mi.

Amherst Junction — Village
ZIP: 54407 Lat: 44-28-10 N Long: 89-19-00 W
Pop: 269 (1990); 225 (1980) Pop Density: 244.5
Land: 1.1 sq. mi.; Water: 0.0 sq. mi. Elev: 1126 ft.
Incorporated 1912.

Name origin: For its location, two miles from the village of Amherst. Previously called Groversberg, and then Junction, for the railroad crossing here.

Belmont — Town
Lat: 44-17-10 N Long: 89-17-49 W
Pop: 540 (1990); 496 (1980) Pop Density: 15.0
Land: 36.1 sq. mi.; Water: 0.2 sq. mi.

Buena Vista — Town
ZIP: 54467 Lat: 44-22-38 N Long: 89-27-24 W
Pop: 1,170 (1990); 1,023 (1980) Pop Density: 19.1
Land: 61.2 sq. mi.; Water: 0.0 sq. mi.

Carson — Town
ZIP: 54443 Lat: 44-33-40 N Long: 89-44-13 W
Pop: 1,327 (1990); 1,441 (1980) Pop Density: 24.6
Land: 53.9 sq. mi.; Water: 1.1 sq. mi.

Dewey — Town
Lat: 44-38-19 N Long: 89-34-32 W
Pop: 849 (1990); 803 (1980) Pop Density: 18.7
Land: 45.3 sq. mi.; Water: 1.7 sq. mi.

Eau Pleine — Town
ZIP: 54443 Lat: 44-37-39 N Long: 89-44-34 W
Pop: 944 (1990); 963 (1980) Pop Density: 17.0
Land: 55.5 sq. mi.; Water: 2.3 sq. mi.

Grant — Town
Lat: 44-20-18 N Long: 89-40-25 W
Pop: 1,673 (1990); 1,593 (1980) Pop Density: 23.5
Land: 71.2 sq. mi.; Water: 0.0 sq. mi.

Hull — Town
ZIP: 54481 Lat: 44-33-40 N Long: 89-33-34 W
Pop: 5,559 (1990); 5,122 (1980) Pop Density: 189.1
Land: 29.4 sq. mi.; Water: 3.6 sq. mi.

Junction City — Village
ZIP: 54443 Lat: 44-35-28 N Long: 89-45-57 W
Pop: 502 (1990); 523 (1980) Pop Density: 418.3
Land: 1.2 sq. mi.; Water: 0.0 sq. mi.
Incorporated 1911.

Name origin: For its location at the junction of the Wisconsin Valley Railroad and Wisconsin Central Railroad. City was added later.

Lanark — Town
Lat: 44-22-02 N Long: 89-17-22 W
Pop: 1,154 (1990); 1,043 (1980) Pop Density: 32.1
Land: 35.9 sq. mi.; Water: 0.2 sq. mi.

Linwood — Town
Lat: 44-29-05 N Long: 89-39-58 W
Pop: 1,035 (1990); 1,082 (1980) Pop Density: 32.4
Land: 31.9 sq. mi.; Water: 1.8 sq. mi.

Milladore — Village
ZIP: 54454 Lat: 44-36-32 N Long: 89-50-39 W
Pop: 0 (1990); 10 (1980)
Land: 0.004 sq. mi.; Water: 0.0 sq. mi.
Incorporated 1933. Part of the town is also in Wood County.

Name origin: From a word coined by the residents of Mill Creek who had to change their village's name because there was already a Mill Creek in the state.

Nelsonville — Village
ZIP: 54458 Lat: 44-29-41 N Long: 89-18-36 W
Pop: 171 (1990); 199 (1980) Pop Density: 171.0
Land: 1.0 sq. mi.; Water: 0.0 sq. mi.
Incorporated 1913.

Name origin: For Jerome Nelson, who purchased land and built a grist mill here.

New Hope
Town
Lat: 44-33-00 N **Long:** 89-16-47 W
Pop: 694 (1990); 625 (1980) **Pop Density:** 19.3
Land: 35.9 sq. mi.; **Water:** 0.5 sq. mi.

Park Ridge
Village
ZIP: 54481 **Lat:** 44-31-12 N **Long:** 89-32-46 W
Pop: 546 (1990); 643 (1980) **Pop Density:** 2730.0
Land: 0.2 sq. mi.; **Water:** 0.0 sq. mi.
Incorporated 1938.
Name origin: For its location on a ridge by the Plover River. Originally spelled Parkridge.

Pine Grove
Town
Lat: 44-17-29 N **Long:** 89-32-19 W
Pop: 949 (1990); 762 (1980) **Pop Density:** 25.1
Land: 37.8 sq. mi.; **Water:** 0.0 sq. mi.

Plover
Village
ZIP: 54467 **Lat:** 44-27-45 N **Long:** 89-32-34 W
Pop: 8,176 (1990); 5,310 (1980) **Pop Density:** 1048.2
Land: 7.8 sq. mi.; **Water:** 0.3 sq. mi. **Elev:** 1075 ft.
Incorporated 1971.
Name origin: For the Plover River. Originally called by a Chippewa term meaning 'prairie.'

*Plover
Town
ZIP: 54467 **Lat:** 44-26-00 N **Long:** 89-34-17 W
Pop: 2,223 (1990); 2,330 (1980) **Pop Density:** 50.6
Land: 43.9 sq. mi.; **Water:** 1.4 sq. mi.

Rosholt
Village
ZIP: 54473 **Lat:** 44-37-48 N **Long:** 89-18-17 W
Pop: 512 (1990); 520 (1980) **Pop Density:** 465.5
Land: 1.1 sq. mi.; **Water:** 0.0 sq. mi.
Incorporated 1907.
Name origin: For J.G. Rosholt, who platted the village.

Sharon
Town
ZIP: 54473 **Lat:** 44-37-34 N **Long:** 89-24-39 W
Pop: 1,742 (1990); 1,694 (1980) **Pop Density:** 27.1
Land: 64.3 sq. mi.; **Water:** 0.6 sq. mi.

Stevens Point
City
ZIP: 54481 **Lat:** 44-31-39 N **Long:** 89-33-37 W
Pop: 23,006 (1990); 22,970 (1980) **Pop Density:** 1716.9
Land: 13.4 sq. mi.; **Water:** 0.9 sq. mi. **Elev:** 1093 ft.
In central WI, 30 mi. south of Wausau. Incorporated 1858.
Name origin: For George Stevens, who started the settlement here. Previously called Hemlock Island and First Island.

Stockton
Town
Lat: 44-29-16 N **Long:** 89-26-12 W
Pop: 2,494 (1990); 2,208 (1980) **Pop Density:** 43.2
Land: 57.7 sq. mi.; **Water:** 0.1 sq. mi.

Whiting
Village
ZIP: 54481 **Lat:** 44-29-20 N **Long:** 89-33-42 W
Pop: 1,838 (1990); 2,050 (1980) **Pop Density:** 1021.1
Land: 1.8 sq. mi.; **Water:** 0.3 sq. mi. **Elev:** 1069 ft.
Incorporated 1947.

Price County
County Seat: Phillips (ZIP: 54555)

Pop: 15,600 (1990); 15,788 (1980) **Pop Density:** 12.5
Land: 1252.7 sq. mi.; **Water:** 25.9 sq. mi. **Area Code:** 715
In north-central WI, northwest of Wausau; organized Feb 26, 1879 from Chippewa and Lincoln counties.
Name origin: For William Thompson Price (1824–86), WI jurist, legislator, and U.S. representative (1883–86).

Catawba
Village
ZIP: 54515 **Lat:** 45-32-09 N **Long:** 90-31-58 W
Pop: 178 (1990); 205 (1980) **Pop Density:** 39.6
Land: 4.5 sq. mi.; **Water:** 0.0 sq. mi.
Incorporated 1922.
Name origin: Probably from the Choctaw Indian term *katapa* thought to mean 'divided' or 'departed.'

*Catawba
Town
ZIP: 54515 **Lat:** 45-29-16 N **Long:** 90-29-43 W
Pop: 276 (1990); 319 (1980) **Pop Density:** 5.5
Land: 50.0 sq. mi.; **Water:** 0.0 sq. mi.

Eisenstein
Town
ZIP: 54552 **Lat:** 45-56-16 N **Long:** 90-17-57 W
Pop: 679 (1990); 728 (1980) **Pop Density:** 9.1
Land: 74.9 sq. mi.; **Water:** 1.4 sq. mi.

Elk
Town
ZIP: 54555 **Lat:** 45-41-52 N **Long:** 90-32-09 W
Pop: 1,059 (1990); 996 (1980) **Pop Density:** 20.8
Land: 50.8 sq. mi.; **Water:** 2.7 sq. mi.

Emery
Town
Lat: 45-42-21 N **Long:** 90-08-23 W
Pop: 322 (1990); 308 (1980) **Pop Density:** 3.0
Land: 108.1 sq. mi.; **Water:** 0.1 sq. mi.

Fifield
Town
ZIP: 54524 **Lat:** 45-51-15 N **Long:** 90-13-35 W
Pop: 863 (1990); 805 (1980) **Pop Density:** 5.8
Land: 149.4 sq. mi.; **Water:** 7.1 sq. mi.

Flambeau
Town
ZIP: 54555 **Lat:** 45-46-32 N **Long:** 90-33-58 W
Pop: 459 (1990); 389 (1980) **Pop Density:** 4.8
Land: 95.8 sq. mi.; **Water:** 2.6 sq. mi.

Georgetown
Town
Lat: 45-36-59 N **Long:** 90-36-38 W
Pop: 195 (1990); 166 (1980) **Pop Density:** 3.6
Land: 53.6 sq. mi.; **Water:** 0.1 sq. mi.

Hackett
Town
ZIP: 54555 **Lat:** 45-35-49 N **Long:** 90-15-15 W
Pop: 214 (1990); 179 (1980) **Pop Density:** 3.1
Land: 69.5 sq. mi.; **Water:** 1.4 sq. mi.

WISCONSIN, Price County

Harmony
Town
Lat: 45-36-15 N **Long:** 90-29-49 W
Pop: 203 (1990); 268 (1980) **Pop Density:** 5.8
Land: 35.0 sq. mi.; **Water:** 0.6 sq. mi.

Hill
Town
Lat: 45-25-55 N **Long:** 90-13-34 W
Pop: 360 (1990); 349 (1980) **Pop Density:** 10.3
Land: 35.1 sq. mi.; **Water:** 0.7 sq. mi.

Kennan
Village
ZIP: 54537 **Lat:** 45-31-51 N **Long:** 90-35-09 W
Pop: 169 (1990); 194 (1980) **Pop Density:** 84.5
Land: 2.0 sq. mi.; **Water:** 0.0 sq. mi.
Incorporated 1903.
Name origin: For a railroad tax lawyer, K. K. Kennan, who built a log house station here. Previously called Ripley.

*Kennan
Town
ZIP: 54537 **Lat:** 45-27-35 N **Long:** 90-36-37 W
Pop: 330 (1990); 387 (1980) **Pop Density:** 4.7
Land: 69.9 sq. mi.; **Water:** 0.1 sq. mi.

Knox
Town
Lat: 45-32-46 N **Long:** 90-06-33 W
Pop: 420 (1990); 542 (1980) **Pop Density:** 8.7
Land: 48.1 sq. mi.; **Water:** 0.0 sq. mi.

Lake
Town
ZIP: 54552 **Lat:** 45-55-28 N **Long:** 90-33-55 W
Pop: 1,333 (1990); 1,369 (1980) **Pop Density:** 15.0
Land: 88.6 sq. mi.; **Water:** 3.6 sq. mi.

Ogema
Town
ZIP: 54459 **Lat:** 45-26-27 N **Long:** 90-23-00 W
Pop: 860 (1990); 850 (1980) **Pop Density:** 10.6
Land: 81.3 sq. mi.; **Water:** 0.1 sq. mi.

Park Falls
City
ZIP: 54552 **Lat:** 45-56-00 N **Long:** 90-26-45 W
Pop: 3,104 (1990); 3,192 (1980) **Pop Density:** 886.9
Land: 3.5 sq. mi.; **Water:** 0.3 sq. mi. **Elev:** 1490 ft.
Incorporated 1912.
Name origin: Named in 1885 for the falls on the Flambeau River and for the parklike landscape in the area. Previously called Muskallonge Falls.

Phillips
City
ZIP: 54555 **Lat:** 45-41-44 N **Long:** 90-23-51 W
Pop: 1,592 (1990); 1,522 (1980) **Pop Density:** 612.3
Land: 2.6 sq. mi.; **Water:** 0.7 sq. mi.
Platted 1876. Incorporated 1891.
Name origin: For Elijah B. Phillips, general manager of the Wisconsin Central Railroad Company.

Prentice
Village
ZIP: 54556 **Lat:** 45-32-30 N **Long:** 90-17-17 W
Pop: 571 (1990); 605 (1980) **Pop Density:** 300.5
Land: 1.9 sq. mi.; **Water:** 0.0 sq. mi.
Incorporated 1899.
Name origin: For Alexander Prentice, the town's first postmaster, or Jackson L. Prentice, an early surveyor.

*Prentice
Town
ZIP: 54556 **Lat:** 45-32-04 N **Long:** 90-15-58 W
Pop: 486 (1990); 547 (1980) **Pop Density:** 7.0
Land: 69.4 sq. mi.; **Water:** 0.2 sq. mi.

Spirit
Town
Lat: 45-25-49 N **Long:** 90-05-54 W
Pop: 345 (1990); 379 (1980) **Pop Density:** 8.4
Land: 41.1 sq. mi.; **Water:** 0.5 sq. mi.

Worcester
Town
ZIP: 54555 **Lat:** 45-44-03 N **Long:** 90-19-04 W
Pop: 1,582 (1990); 1,489 (1980) **Pop Density:** 13.5
Land: 117.4 sq. mi.; **Water:** 3.7 sq. mi.

Racine County
County Seat: Racine (ZIP: 53403)

Pop: 175,034 (1990); 173,132 (1980) **Pop Density:** 525.4
Land: 333.1 sq. mi.; **Water:** 458.8 sq. mi. **Area Code:** 414
On southeastern coast of WI, south of Milwaukee; organized Dec 7, 1836 (prior to statehood) from territorial county.
Name origin: French 'root,' referring to the county's principal town, located on the Root River, which had so many roots growing out of its banks that navigation was difficult.

Bohners Lake
CDP
Lat: 42-37-22 N **Long:** 88-16-48 W
Pop: 1,553 (1990); 1,507 (1980) **Pop Density:** 1194.6
Land: 1.3 sq. mi.; **Water:** 0.2 sq. mi.

Browns Lake
CDP
Lat: 42-41-32 N **Long:** 88-13-51 W
Pop: 1,725 (1990); 1,648 (1980) **Pop Density:** 784.1
Land: 2.2 sq. mi.; **Water:** 0.6 sq. mi.

Burlington
City
ZIP: 53105 **Lat:** 42-40-41 N **Long:** 88-16-37 W
Pop: 8,851 (1990); 8,385 (1980) **Pop Density:** 2458.6
Land: 3.6 sq. mi.; **Water:** 0.2 sq. mi.
Incorporated 1900. Part of the town is also in Walworth County.
Name origin: Named by E. D. Putnam for Burlington, VT.

*Burlington
Town
ZIP: 53105 **Lat:** 42-39-28 N **Long:** 88-15-06 W
Pop: 5,833 (1990); 5,629 (1980) **Pop Density:** 158.9
Land: 36.7 sq. mi.; **Water:** 1.4 sq. mi.

Caledonia
Town
ZIP: 53108 **Lat:** 42-48-05 N **Long:** 87-52-15 W
Pop: 20,999 (1990); 20,940 (1980) **Pop Density:** 461.5
Land: 45.5 sq. mi.; **Water:** 3.2 sq. mi.

Dover
Town
Lat: 42-42-42 N **Long:** 88-07-34 W
Pop: 3,631 (1990); 3,419 (1980) **Pop Density:** 102.6
Land: 35.4 sq. mi.; **Water:** 0.8 sq. mi.

Eagle Lake
CDP
Lat: 42-42-25 N **Long:** 88-07-41 W
Pop: 1,196 (1990) **Pop Density:** 543.6
Land: 2.2 sq. mi.; **Water:** 0.8 sq. mi.

Elmwood Park
Village
Lat: 42-41-34 N **Long:** 87-49-20 W
Pop: 534 (1990); 483 (1980) **Pop Density:** 5340.0
Land: 0.1 sq. mi.; **Water:** 0.0 sq. mi.
Incorporated 1960.

Mount Pleasant
Town
ZIP: 53401 **Lat:** 42-42-54 N **Long:** 87-53-15 W
Pop: 20,084 (1990); 19,340 (1980) **Pop Density:** 561.0
Land: 35.8 sq. mi.; **Water:** 1.6 sq. mi.

North Bay
Village
Lat: 42-45-53 N **Long:** 87-46-50 W
Pop: 246 (1990); 219 (1980) **Pop Density:** 2460.0
Land: 0.1 sq. mi.; **Water:** 0.0 sq. mi.
On the southeastern coast of WI, a southeastern suburb of Milwaukee. Platted 1926. Incorporated 1951.
Name origin: For its location on a bay in Lake Michigan.

Norway
Town
ZIP: 53182 **Lat:** 42-47-46 N **Long:** 88-07-21 W
Pop: 5,493 (1990); 4,619 (1980) **Pop Density:** 163.0
Land: 33.7 sq. mi.; **Water:** 1.9 sq. mi.

Racine
City
ZIP: 53401 **Lat:** 42-43-41 N **Long:** 87-48-25 W
Pop: 84,298 (1990); 85,725 (1980) **Pop Density:** 5473.9
Land: 15.4 sq. mi.; **Water:** 3.1 sq. mi.
On Lake Michigan, 23 mi. south of Milwaukee. Incorporated 1848.
Name origin: For the Root River. French 'root,' referring to the county's principal town, located on the Root River, which had so many roots growing out of its banks that navigation was difficult. Originally known as Belle City of the Great Lakes.

Raymond
Town
Lat: 42-48-05 N **Long:** 88-00-38 W
Pop: 3,243 (1990); 3,610 (1980) **Pop Density:** 91.1
Land: 35.6 sq. mi.; **Water:** 0.0 sq. mi.

Rochester
Village
ZIP: 53167 **Lat:** 42-44-26 N **Long:** 88-13-26 W
Pop: 978 (1990); 746 (1980) **Pop Density:** 1956.0
Land: 0.5 sq. mi.; **Water:** 0.0 sq. mi. **Elev:** 777 ft.
Incorporated 1912.
Name origin: Named by settlers for their former home of Rochester, NY.

*Rochester
Town
Lat: 42-44-27 N **Long:** 88-14-37 W
Pop: 1,844 (1990); 1,478 (1980) **Pop Density:** 107.8
Land: 17.1 sq. mi.; **Water:** 0.2 sq. mi.

Sturtevant
Village
ZIP: 53177 **Lat:** 42-42-01 N **Long:** 87-53-56 W
Pop: 3,803 (1990); 4,130 (1980) **Pop Density:** 1653.5
Land: 2.3 sq. mi.; **Water:** 0.0 sq. mi. **Elev:** 727 ft.
Incorporated 1907.
Name origin: For the B.F. Sturtevant Company. Previously called Johnson, for postmaster William M. Johnson; Western Union; and Corliss.

Union Grove
Village
ZIP: 53182 **Lat:** 42-41-03 N **Long:** 88-03-03 W
Pop: 3,669 (1990); 3,517 (1980) **Pop Density:** 3335.5
Land: 1.1 sq. mi.; **Water:** 0.0 sq. mi.
Incorporated 1893.
Name origin: For the Union School established here in 1846, and for a grove of burr oak trees nearby, so named by Gov. Henry Dodge (1782–1867).

Waterford
Village
ZIP: 53185 **Lat:** 42-45-46 N **Long:** 88-12-55 W
Pop: 2,431 (1990); 2,051 (1980) **Pop Density:** 1350.6
Land: 1.8 sq. mi.; **Water:** 0.1 sq. mi.
Incorporated 1906.
Name origin: For an old Indian ford across the Fox River at this site.

*Waterford
Town
ZIP: 53185 **Lat:** 42-47-25 N **Long:** 88-14-43 W
Pop: 4,255 (1990); 3,984 (1980) **Pop Density:** 132.1
Land: 32.2 sq. mi.; **Water:** 2.0 sq. mi.

Waterford North
CDP
Lat: 42-47-35 N **Long:** 88-13-19 W
Pop: 1,604 (1990) **Pop Density:** 297.0
Land: 5.4 sq. mi.; **Water:** 1.1 sq. mi.

Wind Lake
CDP
Lat: 42-49-20 N **Long:** 88-09-24 W
Pop: 3,748 (1990) **Pop Density:** 797.4
Land: 4.7 sq. mi.; **Water:** 1.9 sq. mi.

Wind Point
Village
Lat: 42-46-53 N **Long:** 87-46-22 W
Pop: 1,941 (1990); 1,695 (1980) **Pop Density:** 1617.5
Land: 1.2 sq. mi.; **Water:** 0.2 sq. mi.
Incorporated 1954.

Yorkville
Town
Lat: 42-42-36 N **Long:** 88-00-51 W
Pop: 2,901 (1990); 3,162 (1980) **Pop Density:** 83.1
Land: 34.9 sq. mi.; **Water:** 0.0 sq. mi.

Richland County
County Seat: Richland Center (ZIP: 53581)

Pop: 17,521 (1990); 17,476 (1980)
Land: 586.3 sq. mi.; **Water:** 3.2 sq. mi.
Pop Density: 29.9
Area Code: 608

In southwestern WI, northwest of Madison; organized Feb 18, 1842 (prior to statehood) from Crawford, Sauk, and Iowa counties.

Name origin: For the fertile soil, and possibly because an early settler came from Richland Co., IA.

Akan
Town
Lat: 43-19-53 N **Long:** 90-36-17 W
Pop: 444 (1990); 483 (1980) **Pop Density:** 12.3
Land: 36.1 sq. mi.; **Water:** 0.0 sq. mi.

Bloom
Town
Lat: 43-30-51 N **Long:** 90-29-21 W
Pop: 540 (1990); 565 (1980) **Pop Density:** 15.0
Land: 36.1 sq. mi.; **Water:** 0.0 sq. mi.

Boaz
Village
Lat: 43-19-50 N **Long:** 90-31-37 W
Pop: 131 (1990); 161 (1980) **Pop Density:** 327.5
Land: 0.4 sq. mi.; **Water:** 0.0 sq. mi. **Elev:** 740 ft.
Platted 1857. Incorporated 1939.

Name origin: For the local Boaz Sawmill, which had taken its name from the Bible.

Buena Vista
Town
Lat: 43-14-53 N **Long:** 90-15-17 W
Pop: 1,547 (1990) **Pop Density:** 37.4
Land: 41.4 sq. mi.; **Water:** 1.0 sq. mi.

Cazenovia
Village
ZIP: 53924 **Lat:** 43-31-31 N **Long:** 90-11-55 W
Pop: 288 (1990); 245 (1980) **Pop Density:** 320.0
Land: 0.9 sq. mi.; **Water:** 0.1 sq. mi. **Elev:** 951 ft.
Incorporated 1902. Part of the town is also in Sauk County.

Name origin: For Cazenovia, NY.

Dayton
Town
Lat: 43-20-19 N **Long:** 90-29-45 W
Pop: 706 (1990); 709 (1980) **Pop Density:** 20.1
Land: 35.1 sq. mi.; **Water:** 0.0 sq. mi.

Eagle
Town
Lat: 43-14-59 N **Long:** 90-29-05 W
Pop: 611 (1990); 634 (1980) **Pop Density:** 17.6
Land: 34.8 sq. mi.; **Water:** 0.9 sq. mi.

Forest
Town
Lat: 43-30-09 N **Long:** 90-36-35 W
Pop: 339 (1990); 351 (1980) **Pop Density:** 9.5
Land: 35.5 sq. mi.; **Water:** 0.0 sq. mi.

Henrietta
Town
Lat: 43-30-34 N **Long:** 90-22-33 W
Pop: 617 (1990); 606 (1980) **Pop Density:** 17.2
Land: 35.9 sq. mi.; **Water:** 0.0 sq. mi.

Ithaca
Town
Lat: 43-20-24 N **Long:** 90-15-11 W
Pop: 632 (1990); 702 (1980) **Pop Density:** 17.6
Land: 36.0 sq. mi.; **Water:** 0.0 sq. mi.

Lone Rock
Village
ZIP: 53556 **Lat:** 43-11-04 N **Long:** 90-12-06 W
Pop: 641 (1990); 577 (1980) **Pop Density:** 712.2
Land: 0.9 sq. mi.; **Water:** 0.0 sq. mi. **Elev:** 706 ft.
Laid out 1856. Incorporated 1886.

Name origin: For a large sandstone landmark that once stood near the Wisconsin River.

Marshall
Town
Lat: 43-25-11 N **Long:** 90-29-47 W
Pop: 550 (1990); 558 (1980) **Pop Density:** 15.3
Land: 36.0 sq. mi.; **Water:** 0.0 sq. mi.

Orion
Town
Lat: 43-15-24 N **Long:** 90-22-22 W
Pop: 604 (1990); 644 (1980) **Pop Density:** 16.9
Land: 35.8 sq. mi.; **Water:** 0.4 sq. mi.

Richland
Town
Lat: 43-20-03 N **Long:** 90-22-18 W
Pop: 1,423 (1990); 1,442 (1980) **Pop Density:** 43.8
Land: 32.5 sq. mi.; **Water:** 0.0 sq. mi.

Richland Center
City
ZIP: 53581 **Lat:** 43-20-16 N **Long:** 90-22-59 W
Pop: 5,018 (1990); 4,997 (1980) **Pop Density:** 1433.7
Land: 3.5 sq. mi.; **Water:** 0.1 sq. mi. **Elev:** 731 ft.
Incorporated 1887.

Name origin: For its location at the center of Richland County.

Richwood
Town
Lat: 43-14-11 N **Long:** 90-36-33 W
Pop: 662 (1990); 654 (1980) **Pop Density:** 15.9
Land: 41.7 sq. mi.; **Water:** 0.7 sq. mi.

Rockbridge
Town
Lat: 43-25-22 N **Long:** 90-22-13 W
Pop: 662 (1990); 662 (1980) **Pop Density:** 18.3
Land: 36.2 sq. mi.; **Water:** 0.0 sq. mi.

Sylvan
Town
Lat: 43-24-54 N **Long:** 90-36-48 W
Pop: 507 (1990); 487 (1980) **Pop Density:** 14.0
Land: 36.1 sq. mi.; **Water:** 0.0 sq. mi.

Viola
Village
Lat: 43-30-34 N **Long:** 90-39-59 W
Pop: 437 (1990); 473 (1980) **Pop Density:** 1092.5
Land: 0.4 sq. mi.; **Water:** 0.0 sq. mi.
Incorporated 1899. Part of the town is also in Vernon County.

Westford
Town
Lat: 43-30-14 N **Long:** 90-14-49 W
Pop: 513 (1990); 558 (1980) **Pop Density:** 14.7
Land: 34.9 sq. mi.; **Water:** 0.0 sq. mi.

Willow — Town
Lat: 43-25-42 N Long: 90-15-03 W
Pop: 572 (1990); 527 (1980)   Pop Density: 16.0
Land: 35.8 sq. mi.; Water: 0.0 sq. mi.

Yuba — Village
Lat: 43-32-10 N Long: 90-25-40 W
Pop: 77 (1990); 72 (1980)   Pop Density: 256.7
Land: 0.3 sq. mi.; Water: 0.0 sq. mi.   Elev: 1868 ft.
Laid out 1856. Incorporated 1935.
Name origin: Possibly for the gold mining area in CA.

Rock County
County Seat: Janesville (ZIP: 53545)

Pop: 139,510 (1990); 139,420 (1980)   Pop Density: 193.6
Land: 720.3 sq. mi.; Water: 5.7 sq. mi.   Area Code: 608
On central southern border of WI, southeast of Madison; organized Dec 7, 1836 (prior to statehood) from a territorial county.
Name origin: For the Rock River, which flows through it.

Avon — Town
Lat: 42-32-26 N Long: 89-18-41 W
Pop: 570 (1990); 555 (1980)   Pop Density: 15.8
Land: 36.1 sq. mi.; Water: 0.0 sq. mi.

Beloit — City
ZIP: 53511   Lat: 42-31-25 N Long: 89-01-12 W
Pop: 35,573 (1990); 35,207 (1980)   Pop Density: 2195.9
Land: 16.2 sq. mi.; Water: 0.2 sq. mi.
In southern WI on the Rock River on the IL border. Incorporated 1857.
Name origin: Named c. 1837 by settler Maj. Johnston because he liked a name similar to Detroit. Originally known as Turtle Creek and New Albany.

*Beloit — Town
ZIP: 53511   Lat: 42-32-17 N Long: 89-04-47 W
Pop: 6,778 (1990); 8,382 (1980)   Pop Density: 255.8
Land: 26.5 sq. mi.; Water: 0.7 sq. mi.

Bradford — Town
Lat: 42-37-24 N Long: 88-49-45 W
Pop: 1,030 (1990); 1,100 (1980)   Pop Density: 28.4
Land: 36.3 sq. mi.; Water: 0.0 sq. mi.

Center — Town
Lat: 42-42-54 N Long: 89-11-06 W
Pop: 861 (1990); 908 (1980)   Pop Density: 24.2
Land: 35.6 sq. mi.; Water: 0.0 sq. mi.   Elev: 974 ft.

Clinton — Village
ZIP: 53525   Lat: 42-33-23 N Long: 88-51-58 W
Pop: 1,849 (1990); 1,751 (1980)   Pop Density: 2311.3
Land: 0.8 sq. mi.; Water: 0.0 sq. mi.   Elev: 949 ft.
Incorporated 1882.
Name origin: Probably for DeWitt Clinton (1769–1828), governor of NY and supporter of the Erie Canal.

*Clinton — Town
ZIP: 53525   Lat: 42-32-14 N Long: 88-50-16 W
Pop: 899 (1990); 925 (1980)   Pop Density: 25.0
Land: 35.9 sq. mi.; Water: 0.0 sq. mi.

Edgerton — City
ZIP: 53534   Lat: 42-50-16 N Long: 89-04-21 W
Pop: 4,254 (1990); 4,335 (1980)   Pop Density: 1372.3
Land: 3.1 sq. mi.; Water: 0.0 sq. mi.
Incorporated 1883.
Name origin: For Benjamin Edgerton, chief surveyor for the railroad.

Evansville — City
ZIP: 53536   Lat: 42-46-47 N Long: 89-17-55 W
Pop: 3,174 (1990); 2,835 (1980)   Pop Density: 1670.5
Land: 1.9 sq. mi.; Water: 0.0 sq. mi.   Elev: 897 ft.
Incorporated 1896.
Name origin: For physician, Dr. Calvin (or J. M.) Evans. Previously called The Grove.

Footville — Village
ZIP: 53537   Lat: 42-40-17 N Long: 89-12-32 W
Pop: 764 (1990); 794 (1980)   Pop Density: 764.0
Land: 1.0 sq. mi.; Water: 0.0 sq. mi.
Incorporated 1918.
Name origin: For settler, Ezra A. Foot. Previously called Bachelor's Grove for Mr. Watson, a real estate agent who was unmarried.

Fulton — Town
Lat: 42-48-19 N Long: 89-04-08 W
Pop: 2,867 (1990); 2,866 (1980)   Pop Density: 89.3
Land: 32.1 sq. mi.; Water: 1.0 sq. mi.

Harmony — Town
Lat: 42-43-27 N Long: 88-56-40 W
Pop: 2,138 (1990); 2,090 (1980)   Pop Density: 81.0
Land: 26.4 sq. mi.; Water: 0.1 sq. mi.

Janesville — City
ZIP: 53545   Lat: 42-41-04 N Long: 89-00-55 W
Pop: 52,133 (1990); 51,071 (1980)   Pop Density: 2218.4
Land: 23.5 sq. mi.; Water: 0.6 sq. mi.   Elev: 858 ft.
In southern WI, 12 mi. north of Beloit. Incorporated 1853.
Name origin: Previously called by Winnebago Indians *E-nee-poro-poro* probably meaning 'round rock,' referring to the large stone outcrop in the Rock River.

*Janesville — Town
Lat: 42-43-08 N Long: 89-04-37 W
Pop: 3,198 (1990); 3,068 (1980)   Pop Density: 110.7
Land: 28.9 sq. mi.; Water: 0.5 sq. mi.

Johnstown
Town
Lat: 42-43-02 N Long: 88-50-02 W
Pop: 850 (1990); 844 (1980) **Pop Density:** 23.5
Land: 36.2 sq. mi.; **Water:** 0.0 sq. mi.

La Prairie
Town
Lat: 42-37-37 N Long: 88-56-35 W
Pop: 943 (1990); 1,099 (1980) **Pop Density:** 27.0
Land: 34.9 sq. mi.; **Water:** 0.0 sq. mi.

Lima
Town
Lat: 42-47-37 N Long: 88-50-31 W
Pop: 1,285 (1990); 1,179 (1980) **Pop Density:** 35.3
Land: 36.4 sq. mi.; **Water:** 0.0 sq. mi.

Magnolia
Town
Lat: 42-42-57 N Long: 89-18-28 W
Pop: 717 (1990); 746 (1980) **Pop Density:** 19.9
Land: 36.0 sq. mi.; **Water:** 0.0 sq. mi.

Milton
City
ZIP: 53563 Lat: 42-46-44 N Long: 88-56-57 W
Pop: 4,434 (1990); 4,092 (1980) **Pop Density:** 1642.2
Land: 2.7 sq. mi.; **Water:** 0.0 sq. mi.
Incorporated 1969.

*Milton
Town
ZIP: 53563 Lat: 42-48-34 N Long: 88-57-09 W
Pop: 2,363 (1990); 2,306 (1980) **Pop Density:** 74.1
Land: 31.9 sq. mi.; **Water:** 1.7 sq. mi.

Newark
Town
Lat: 42-32-21 N Long: 89-11-17 W
Pop: 1,514 (1990); 1,574 (1980) **Pop Density:** 41.6
Land: 36.4 sq. mi.; **Water:** 0.0 sq. mi.

Orfordville
Village
ZIP: 53576 Lat: 42-37-44 N Long: 89-15-26 W
Pop: 1,219 (1990); 1,143 (1980) **Pop Density:** 1015.8
Land: 1.2 sq. mi.; **Water:** 0.0 sq. mi.
Incorporated 1900.
Name origin: For Orford, NH. To avoid confusion with Oxford, the *ville* was added later.

Plymouth
Town
Lat: 42-37-44 N Long: 89-11-10 W
Pop: 1,189 (1990); 1,267 (1980) **Pop Density:** 33.4
Land: 35.6 sq. mi.; **Water:** 0.0 sq. mi.

Porter
Town
Lat: 42-48-03 N Long: 89-10-53 W
Pop: 953 (1990); 940 (1980) **Pop Density:** 26.4
Land: 36.1 sq. mi.; **Water:** 0.4 sq. mi.

Rock
Town
Lat: 42-37-19 N Long: 89-04-14 W
Pop: 3,172 (1990); 3,399 (1980) **Pop Density:** 105.4
Land: 30.1 sq. mi.; **Water:** 0.5 sq. mi.

Spring Valley
Town
Lat: 42-37-45 N Long: 89-18-49 W
Pop: 790 (1990); 912 (1980) **Pop Density:** 22.5
Land: 35.1 sq. mi.; **Water:** 0.0 sq. mi.

Turtle
Town
Lat: 42-32-25 N Long: 88-56-49 W
Pop: 2,456 (1990); 2,703 (1980) **Pop Density:** 83.3
Land: 29.5 sq. mi.; **Water:** 0.0 sq. mi.

Union
Town
Lat: 42-47-58 N Long: 89-18-51 W
Pop: 1,537 (1990); 1,329 (1980) **Pop Density:** 44.8
Land: 34.3 sq. mi.; **Water:** 0.1 sq. mi.

Rusk County
County Seat: Ladysmith (ZIP: 54848)

Pop: 15,079 (1990); 15,589 (1980) **Pop Density:** 16.5
Land: 913.2 sq. mi.; **Water:** 17.8 sq. mi. **Area Code:** 715

In northwestern WI, northeast of St. Paul, MN; organized May 15, 1901 as Gates County from Chippewa County; name changed Jun 19, 1905.

Name origin: For Col. Jeremiah McLain Rusk (1830–93), an officer in the Civil War, statesman, governor of WI (1882–89), and U.S. secretary of agriculture (1889–93).

Atlanta
Town
Lat: 45-30-36 N Long: 91-19-51 W
Pop: 585 (1990); 586 (1980) **Pop Density:** 11.5
Land: 50.8 sq. mi.; **Water:** 0.2 sq. mi.

Big Bend
Town
Lat: 45-20-29 N Long: 91-21-49 W
Pop: 386 (1990); 398 (1980) **Pop Density:** 11.8
Land: 32.6 sq. mi.; **Water:** 2.7 sq. mi.

Big Falls
Town
Lat: 45-34-45 N Long: 90-59-05 W
Pop: 107 (1990); 122 (1980) **Pop Density:** 3.0
Land: 35.4 sq. mi.; **Water:** 0.6 sq. mi.

Bruce
Village
ZIP: 54819 Lat: 45-27-30 N Long: 91-16-22 W
Pop: 844 (1990); 905 (1980) **Pop Density:** 367.0
Land: 2.3 sq. mi.; **Water:** 0.1 sq. mi. **Elev:** 1106 ft.
Incorporated 1901.
Name origin: For a son of the Weyerhauser lumber family.

Cedar Rapids
Town
ZIP: 54526 Lat: 45-35-38 N Long: 90-50-38 W
Pop: 30 (1990); 30 (1980) **Pop Density:** 0.9
Land: 35.2 sq. mi.; **Water:** 0.5 sq. mi.

WISCONSIN, Rusk County

Conrath — Village
ZIP: 54731 Lat: 45-23-04 N Long: 91-02-08 W
Pop: 92 (1990); 86 (1980) Pop Density: 184.0
Land: 0.5 sq. mi.; Water: 0.0 sq. mi. Elev: 1136 ft.
Incorporated 1915.
Name origin: For Frank and Charles Conrath, loggers who settled here.

Dewey — Town
Lat: 45-30-07 N Long: 90-58-37 W
Pop: 487 (1990); 399 (1980) Pop Density: 15.7
Land: 31.0 sq. mi.; Water: 3.0 sq. mi.

Flambeau — Town
Lat: 45-30-28 N Long: 91-07-01 W
Pop: 1,018 (1990); 1,086 (1980) Pop Density: 29.4
Land: 34.6 sq. mi.; Water: 0.3 sq. mi.

Glen Flora — Village
ZIP: 54526 Lat: 45-29-48 N Long: 90-53-34 W
Pop: 108 (1990); 83 (1980) Pop Density: 180.0
Land: 0.6 sq. mi.; Water: 0.0 sq. mi. Elev: 1276 ft.
Incorporated 1915.
Name origin: Named in 1887 by Mr. Miller for his two children. Previously called Miller's Spur.

Grant — Town
Lat: 45-25-38 N Long: 91-06-19 W
Pop: 847 (1990); 998 (1980) Pop Density: 25.3
Land: 33.5 sq. mi.; Water: 0.4 sq. mi.

Grow — Town
Lat: 45-25-19 N Long: 90-59-20 W
Pop: 450 (1990); 560 (1980) Pop Density: 12.7
Land: 35.4 sq. mi.; Water: 0.0 sq. mi.

Hawkins — Village
ZIP: 54530 Lat: 45-30-42 N Long: 90-42-47 W
Pop: 375 (1990); 407 (1980) Pop Density: 170.5
Land: 2.2 sq. mi.; Water: 0.0 sq. mi. Elev: 1369 ft.
Incorporated 1922.
Name origin: For Mr. Hawkins, who was either a lumberjack or a railroad official. Previously called Main Creek.

*Hawkins — Town
ZIP: 54530 Lat: 45-28-14 N Long: 90-42-49 W
Pop: 163 (1990); 184 (1980) Pop Density: 3.6
Land: 45.6 sq. mi.; Water: 0.1 sq. mi.

Hubbard — Town
Lat: 45-36-09 N Long: 91-07-56 W
Pop: 216 (1990); 185 (1980) Pop Density: 4.9
Land: 44.1 sq. mi.; Water: 0.6 sq. mi.

Ingram — Village
Lat: 45-30-19 N Long: 90-48-47 W
Pop: 91 (1990); 61 (1980) Pop Density: 91.0
Land: 1.0 sq. mi.; Water: 0.0 sq. mi.
Incorporated 1907.

Ladysmith — City
ZIP: 54848 Lat: 45-27-45 N Long: 91-05-45 W
Pop: 3,938 (1990); 3,826 (1980) Pop Density: 1064.3
Land: 3.7 sq. mi.; Water: 0.4 sq. mi. Elev: 1144 ft.
Incorporated 1905.
Name origin: Named in 1900 for Lady Smith, the wife of a factory manager, as an enticement for him to move his woodenware company to the town. Previously called Corbett, Flambeau Falls, and Warner.

Lawrence — Town
Lat: 45-26-08 N Long: 90-51-09 W
Pop: 240 (1990); 240 (1980) Pop Density: 5.0
Land: 47.7 sq. mi.; Water: 0.0 sq. mi.

Marshall — Town
Lat: 45-20-11 N Long: 90-59-04 W
Pop: 630 (1990); 697 (1980) Pop Density: 17.6
Land: 35.8 sq. mi.; Water: 0.0 sq. mi.

Murry — Town
Lat: 45-35-57 N Long: 91-18-48 W
Pop: 291 (1990); 301 (1980) Pop Density: 4.7
Land: 61.9 sq. mi.; Water: 0.3 sq. mi.

Richland — Town
Lat: 45-30-43 N Long: 90-47-53 W
Pop: 185 (1990); 217 (1980) Pop Density: 8.0
Land: 23.0 sq. mi.; Water: 0.1 sq. mi.

Rusk — Town
Lat: 45-20-18 N Long: 91-28-42 W
Pop: 443 (1990); 422 (1980) Pop Density: 13.2
Land: 33.5 sq. mi.; Water: 2.3 sq. mi.

Sheldon — Village
ZIP: 54766 Lat: 45-18-39 N Long: 90-57-26 W
Pop: 268 (1990); 292 (1980) Pop Density: 382.9
Land: 0.7 sq. mi.; Water: 0.0 sq. mi. Elev: 1129 ft.
Incorporated 1917.
Name origin: For an official of the Wisconsin Central Railroad.

South Fork — Town
ZIP: 54530 Lat: 45-35-33 N Long: 90-43-52 W
Pop: 119 (1990); 146 (1980) Pop Density: 3.4
Land: 35.4 sq. mi.; Water: 0.4 sq. mi.

Strickland — Town
Lat: 45-25-20 N Long: 91-28-57 W
Pop: 262 (1990); 281 (1980) Pop Density: 7.6
Land: 34.7 sq. mi.; Water: 0.4 sq. mi. Elev: 1275 ft.

Stubbs — Town
Lat: 45-25-07 N Long: 91-20-42 W
Pop: 573 (1990); 612 (1980) Pop Density: 16.0
Land: 35.9 sq. mi.; Water: 0.8 sq. mi.

Thornapple — Town
Lat: 45-27-30 N Long: 91-13-35 W
Pop: 757 (1990); 740 (1980) Pop Density: 14.7
Land: 51.4 sq. mi.; Water: 1.2 sq. mi.

Tony — Village
ZIP: 54563 Lat: 45-28-52 N Long: 90-59-44 W
Pop: 114 (1990); 146 (1980) Pop Density: 57.0
Land: 2.0 sq. mi.; Water: 0.0 sq. mi.
Incorporated 1911.
Name origin: For Tony Hein of the Hein Lumber Company. Previously called Deer Tail, for a nearby creek.

True — Town
Lat: 45-30-26 N Long: 90-53-14 W
Pop: 310 (1990); 332 (1980) Pop Density: 13.3
Land: 23.3 sq. mi.; Water: 0.2 sq. mi.

Washington — Town
Lat: 45-20-05 N Long: 91-14-12 W
Pop: 301 (1990); 318 (1980) Pop Density: 8.9
Land: 33.7 sq. mi.; Water: 1.9 sq. mi.

Weyerhaeuser — Village
ZIP: 54895 Lat: 45-25-25 N Long: 91-24-51 W
Pop: 283 (1990); 313 (1980) Pop Density: 314.4
Land: 0.9 sq. mi.; Water: 0.0 sq. mi.
Incorporated 1906.

Name origin: For Frederick Weyerhaeuser (1834–1914), of the Weyerhaeuser Lumber Company, which located one of its headquarters here.

Wilkinson — Town
Lat: 45-30-18 N Long: 91-28-15 W
Pop: 51 (1990); 63 (1980) Pop Density: 1.4
Land: 35.2 sq. mi.; Water: 0.3 sq. mi.

Willard — Town
Lat: 45-19-42 N Long: 91-07-06 W
Pop: 448 (1990); 481 (1980) Pop Density: 12.6
Land: 35.6 sq. mi.; Water: 0.6 sq. mi.

Wilson — Town
Lat: 45-36-17 N Long: 91-28-52 W
Pop: 67 (1990); 72 (1980) Pop Density: 2.0
Land: 34.1 sq. mi.; Water: 0.3 sq. mi.

St. Croix County
County Seat: Hudson (ZIP: 54016)

Pop: 50,251 (1990); 43,262 (1980) Pop Density: 69.6
Land: 722.0 sq. mi.; Water: 13.9 sq. mi. Area Code: 715

On central western border of WI, east of St. Paul, MN; organized Jan 9, 1840 (prior to statehood) from a territorial county.

Name origin: For the river, which flows through it; French 'holy cross,' probably for an early French explorer of that name who drowned in it.

Baldwin — Village
ZIP: 54002 Lat: 44-57-46 N Long: 92-22-15 W
Pop: 2,022 (1990); 1,620 (1980) Pop Density: 1189.4
Land: 1.7 sq. mi.; Water: 0.0 sq. mi.
Incorporated 1875.

Name origin: For early settler D. A. Baldwin or for D. H. Baldwin of the West Wisconsin Railway Company. Originally known as Clarksville.

*Baldwin — Town
ZIP: 54002 Lat: 44-59-07 N Long: 92-18-48 W
Pop: 911 (1990); 943 (1980) Pop Density: 28.4
Land: 32.1 sq. mi.; Water: 0.1 sq. mi.

Cady — Town
ZIP: 54027 Lat: 44-54-11 N Long: 92-11-25 W
Pop: 643 (1990); 724 (1980) Pop Density: 18.6
Land: 34.5 sq. mi.; Water: 0.4 sq. mi.

Cylon — Town
ZIP: 54017 Lat: 45-09-48 N Long: 92-20-27 W
Pop: 639 (1990); 717 (1980) Pop Density: 18.1
Land: 35.3 sq. mi.; Water: 0.1 sq. mi.

Deer Park — Village
ZIP: 54007 Lat: 45-11-19 N Long: 92-23-11 W
Pop: 237 (1990); 232 (1980) Pop Density: 263.3
Land: 0.9 sq. mi.; Water: 0.0 sq. mi.
Incorporated 1913.

Name origin: For a 160-acre enclosure built by Otto Neitge as a park for deer.

Eau Galle — Town
ZIP: 54028 Lat: 44-54-27 N Long: 92-18-32 W
Pop: 756 (1990); 897 (1980) Pop Density: 22.2
Land: 34.1 sq. mi.; Water: 0.2 sq. mi.

Emerald — Town
Lat: 45-04-24 N Long: 92-18-31 W
Pop: 630 (1990); 638 (1980) Pop Density: 18.1
Land: 34.8 sq. mi.; Water: 0.1 sq. mi.

Erin Prairie — Town
ZIP: 54002 Lat: 45-04-36 N Long: 92-26-17 W
Pop: 647 (1990); 661 (1980) Pop Density: 18.2
Land: 35.5 sq. mi.; Water: 0.2 sq. mi.

Forest — Town
ZIP: 54012 Lat: 45-10-22 N Long: 92-13-45 W
Pop: 614 (1990); 631 (1980) Pop Density: 16.5
Land: 37.2 sq. mi.; Water: 0.1 sq. mi.

Glenwood — Town
ZIP: 54012 Lat: 45-04-28 N Long: 92-12-09 W
Pop: 700 (1990); 715 (1980) Pop Density: 20.3
Land: 34.4 sq. mi.; Water: 0.1 sq. mi.

Glenwood City — City
ZIP: 54012 Lat: 45-03-26 N Long: 92-10-17 W
Pop: 1,026 (1990); 950 (1980) Pop Density: 427.5
Land: 2.4 sq. mi.; Water: 0.0 sq. mi.
Incorporated 1895.

Name origin: For the Glenwood Manufacturing Company, which came to the area in 1885.

Hammond — Village
ZIP: 54002 Lat: 44-58-22 N Long: 92-26-13 W
Pop: 1,097 (1990); 991 (1980) Pop Density: 914.2
Land: 1.2 sq. mi.; Water: 0.0 sq. mi.
Incorporated 1880.

Name origin: For R.B. Hammond, who built the first sawmill here.

*Hammond — Town
ZIP: 54002 Lat: 44-59-31 N Long: 92-26-13 W
Pop: 819 (1990); 822 (1980) Pop Density: 24.2
Land: 33.9 sq. mi.; Water: 0.2 sq. mi.

Hudson
City
ZIP: 54016   Lat: 44-58-01 N   **Long:** 92-44-31 W
Pop: 6,378 (1990); 5,434 (1980)   **Pop Density:** 1594.5
Land: 4.0 sq. mi.; **Water:** 0.9 sq. mi.
Incorporated 1856.
Name origin: Named by travelers for the resemblance of the St. Croix River to the Hudson River in NY. Previously called Willow River.

*Hudson
Town
ZIP: 54016   Lat: 44-59-18 N   **Long:** 92-40-45 W
Pop: 3,692 (1990); 2,012 (1980)   **Pop Density:** 138.3
Land: 26.7 sq. mi.; **Water:** 0.5 sq. mi.

Kinnickinnic
Town
Lat: 44-54-25 N   **Long:** 92-33-30 W
Pop: 1,139 (1990); 1,051 (1980)   **Pop Density:** 32.1
Land: 35.5 sq. mi.; **Water:** 0.0 sq. mi.

New Richmond
City
ZIP: 54017   Lat: 45-07-19 N   **Long:** 92-32-12 W
Pop: 5,106 (1990); 4,306 (1980)   **Pop Density:** 1547.3
Land: 3.3 sq. mi.; **Water:** 0.1 sq. mi.   **Elev:** 982 ft.
Incorporated 1885.
Name origin: For town surveyor Richmond Day. Previously called Foster's Crossing.

North Hudson
Village
ZIP: 54016   Lat: 44-59-44 N   **Long:** 92-45-32 W
Pop: 3,101 (1990); 2,218 (1980)   **Pop Density:** 2385.4
Land: 1.3 sq. mi.; **Water:** 0.8 sq. mi.
Incorporated 1912.

Pleasant Valley
Town
ZIP: 54015   Lat: 44-54-14 N   **Long:** 92-27-47 W
Pop: 384 (1990); 360 (1980)   **Pop Density:** 21.3
Land: 18.0 sq. mi.; **Water:** 0.0 sq. mi.

Richmond
Town
ZIP: 54017   Lat: 45-04-48 N   **Long:** 92-33-39 W
Pop: 1,400 (1990); 1,338 (1980)   **Pop Density:** 41.2
Land: 34.0 sq. mi.; **Water:** 0.2 sq. mi.

River Falls
City
ZIP: 54022   Lat: 44-52-05 N   **Long:** 92-37-20 W
Pop: 1,769 (1990); 1,498 (1980)   **Pop Density:** 1474.2
Land: 1.2 sq. mi.; **Water:** 0.0 sq. mi.
Incorporated 1875. Part of the town is also in Pierce County.
Name origin: For the falls in the Kinnickinic River, after it was discovered there was already a Greenwood in the state. Previously called Kinnickinnic and Greenwood.

Roberts
Village
ZIP: 54023   Lat: 44-59-06 N   **Long:** 92-33-07 W
Pop: 1,043 (1990); 833 (1980)   **Pop Density:** 2607.5
Land: 0.4 sq. mi.; **Water:** 0.0 sq. mi.
Incorporated 1945.
Name origin: For a railroad man. Originally located in Warren Township.

Rush River
Town
ZIP: 54002   Lat: 44-54-28 N   **Long:** 92-24-28 W
Pop: 419 (1990); 476 (1980)   **Pop Density:** 23.4
Land: 17.9 sq. mi.; **Water:** 0.0 sq. mi.

St. Joseph
Town
Lat: 45-02-53 N   **Long:** 92-42-03 W
Pop: 2,657 (1990); 2,180 (1980)   **Pop Density:** 82.8
Land: 32.1 sq. mi.; **Water:** 2.4 sq. mi.

Somerset
Village
ZIP: 54025   Lat: 45-07-38 N   **Long:** 92-40-33 W
Pop: 1,065 (1990); 860 (1980)   **Pop Density:** 626.5
Land: 1.7 sq. mi.; **Water:** 0.0 sq. mi.
Incorporated 1915.
Name origin: For Somerset County, England, the home of founder Gen. Samuel Harriman's father.

*Somerset
Town
Lat: 45-08-30 N   **Long:** 92-42-08 W
Pop: 1,975 (1990); 1,833 (1980)   **Pop Density:** 41.1
Land: 48.1 sq. mi.; **Water:** 2.0 sq. mi.

Springfield
Town
ZIP: 54013   Lat: 44-59-19 N   **Long:** 92-11-48 W
Pop: 772 (1990); 816 (1980)   **Pop Density:** 22.5
Land: 34.3 sq. mi.; **Water:** 0.2 sq. mi.

Spring Valley
Village
ZIP: 54767   Lat: 44-51-58 N   **Long:** 92-14-39 W
Pop: 0 (1990); 5 (1980)
Land: 0.5 sq. mi.; **Water:** 0.7 sq. mi.
Incorporated 1895. Part of the town is also in Pierce County.
Name origin: Probably for two principal streams in this valley: Eagle and Berghardt springs.

Stanton
Town
ZIP: 54017   Lat: 45-10-01 N   **Long:** 92-28-38 W
Pop: 1,042 (1990); 1,083 (1980)   **Pop Density:** 30.4
Land: 34.3 sq. mi.; **Water:** 0.9 sq. mi.

Star Prairie
Village
Lat: 45-11-53 N   **Long:** 92-31-54 W
Pop: 507 (1990); 420 (1980)   **Pop Density:** 253.5
Land: 2.0 sq. mi.; **Water:** 0.0 sq. mi.
Incorporated 1900.
Name origin: Poetically named by Maj. Edmund Otis.

*Star Prairie
Town
Lat: 45-09-44 N   **Long:** 92-35-36 W
Pop: 2,098 (1990); 1,900 (1980)   **Pop Density:** 64.8
Land: 32.4 sq. mi.; **Water:** 1.3 sq. mi.

Troy
Town
Lat: 44-55-08 N   **Long:** 92-41-51 W
Pop: 2,850 (1990); 2,326 (1980)   **Pop Density:** 73.5
Land: 38.8 sq. mi.; **Water:** 2.0 sq. mi.

Warren
Town
ZIP: 54023   Lat: 44-59-22 N   **Long:** 92-33-19 W
Pop: 1,008 (1990); 897 (1980)   **Pop Density:** 28.8
Land: 35.0 sq. mi.; **Water:** 0.5 sq. mi.

Wilson
Village
ZIP: 54027   Lat: 44-57-20 N   **Long:** 92-10-20 W
Pop: 163 (1990); 155 (1980)   **Pop Density:** 116.4
Land: 1.4 sq. mi.; **Water:** 0.0 sq. mi.
Incorporated 1911.

Woodville
Village
ZIP: 54028   Lat: 44-57-09 N   **Long:** 92-17-10 W
Pop: 942 (1990); 725 (1980)   **Pop Density:** 856.4
Land: 1.1 sq. mi.; **Water:** 0.0 sq. mi.
Incorporated 1911.
Name origin: For either an early settler, or the abundant woodlands before the logging companies came. Originally known as Kelly's Switch.

WISCONSIN, Sauk County

Sauk County
County Seat: Baraboo (ZIP: 53913)

Pop: 46,975 (1990); 43,469 (1980) **Pop Density:** 56.1
Land: 837.7 sq. mi.; **Water:** 10.8 sq. mi. **Area Code:** 608

In south-central WI, northwest of Madison; organized Jan 11, 1840 (prior to statehood) from a territorial county.

Name origin: Shortened form of Saukie, a local Indian tribe; French form is *Sac*. Meaning of the name is unclear: possibly 'something sprouting up' or 'yellow earth' from which their tradition says their first male sprang.

Baraboo City
ZIP: 53913 **Lat:** 43-28-06 N **Long:** 89-44-29 W
Pop: 9,203 (1990); 8,081 (1980) **Pop Density:** 1958.1
Land: 4.7 sq. mi.; **Water:** 0.0 sq. mi. **Elev:** 894 ft.
Incorporated 1882.

Name origin: For the Baraboo River, which traverses the county; itself named for any of three Frenchmen called Baribeau: two brothers who had a mill at the mouth of the Baraboo River, or another Baribeau who later had a trading post there.

*Baraboo Town
ZIP: 53913 **Lat:** 43-27-40 N **Long:** 89-47-23 W
Pop: 1,503 (1990); 1,545 (1980) **Pop Density:** 46.1
Land: 32.6 sq. mi.; **Water:** 0.6 sq. mi.

Bear Creek Town
Lat: 43-18-43 N **Long:** 90-08-36 W
Pop: 521 (1990); 537 (1980) **Pop Density:** 10.5
Land: 49.7 sq. mi.; **Water:** 0.0 sq. mi.

Cazenovia Village
ZIP: 53924 **Lat:** 43-31-24 N **Long:** 90-11-28 W
Pop: 0 (1990); 14 (1980)
Land: 0.004 sq. mi.; **Water:** 0.0 sq. mi. **Elev:** 951 ft.
Incorporated 1902. Part of the town is also in Richland County.

Name origin: For Cazenovia, NY.

Dellona Town
Lat: 43-36-26 N **Long:** 89-53-47 W
Pop: 768 (1990); 705 (1980) **Pop Density:** 21.9
Land: 35.1 sq. mi.; **Water:** 0.0 sq. mi.

Delton Town
Lat: 43-33-52 N **Long:** 89-47-44 W
Pop: 1,599 (1990); 1,426 (1980) **Pop Density:** 50.6
Land: 31.6 sq. mi.; **Water:** 0.6 sq. mi.

Excelsior Town
Lat: 43-30-43 N **Long:** 89-53-59 W
Pop: 1,194 (1990); 1,266 (1980) **Pop Density:** 35.2
Land: 33.9 sq. mi.; **Water:** 0.1 sq. mi.

Fairfield Town
Lat: 43-32-25 N **Long:** 89-40-22 W
Pop: 826 (1990); 819 (1980) **Pop Density:** 23.6
Land: 35.0 sq. mi.; **Water:** 0.6 sq. mi.

Franklin Town
Lat: 43-18-20 N **Long:** 90-02-19 W
Pop: 668 (1990); 747 (1980) **Pop Density:** 13.6
Land: 49.2 sq. mi.; **Water:** 0.2 sq. mi.

Freedom Town
Lat: 43-25-19 N **Long:** 89-53-39 W
Pop: 422 (1990); 405 (1980) **Pop Density:** 12.2
Land: 34.6 sq. mi.; **Water:** 0.1 sq. mi.

Greenfield Town
Lat: 43-27-59 N **Long:** 89-39-49 W
Pop: 758 (1990); 719 (1980) **Pop Density:** 25.5
Land: 29.7 sq. mi.; **Water:** 0.0 sq. mi.

Honey Creek Town
Lat: 43-19-54 N **Long:** 89-55-18 W
Pop: 725 (1990); 774 (1980) **Pop Density:** 15.3
Land: 47.5 sq. mi.; **Water:** 0.0 sq. mi.

Ironton Village
ZIP: 53941 **Lat:** 43-32-41 N **Long:** 90-08-29 W
Pop: 200 (1990); 206 (1980) **Pop Density:** 666.7
Land: 0.3 sq. mi.; **Water:** 0.0 sq. mi. **Elev:** 954 ft.
Incorporated 1914.

Name origin: Named and platted by miner Jonas Tower for the iron ore discovered nearby.

*Ironton Town
ZIP: 53941 **Lat:** 43-30-11 N **Long:** 90-08-12 W
Pop: 585 (1990); 643 (1980) **Pop Density:** 16.6
Land: 35.2 sq. mi.; **Water:** 0.0 sq. mi.

Lake Delton Village
ZIP: 53940 **Lat:** 43-35-35 N **Long:** 89-46-49 W
Pop: 1,470 (1990); 1,158 (1980) **Pop Density:** 341.9
Land: 4.3 sq. mi.; **Water:** 0.5 sq. mi. **Elev:** 894 ft.
Incorporated 1954.

Lake Wisconsin CDP
Lat: 43-23-03 N **Long:** 89-36-31 W
Pop: 90 (1990) **Pop Density:** 225.0
Land: 0.4 sq. mi.; **Water:** 0.3 sq. mi.
Part of the town is also in Columbia County.

La Valle Village
ZIP: 53941 **Lat:** 43-34-57 N **Long:** 90-07-50 W
Pop: 446 (1990); 412 (1980) **Pop Density:** 1115.0
Land: 0.4 sq. mi.; **Water:** 0.0 sq. mi. **Elev:** 896 ft.
Incorporated 1883.

Name origin: For a fur trapper who settled here.

*La Valle Town
ZIP: 53941 **Lat:** 43-35-49 N **Long:** 90-08-00 W
Pop: 1,005 (1990); 929 (1980) **Pop Density:** 29.4
Land: 34.2 sq. mi.; **Water:** 1.1 sq. mi.

Lime Ridge
Village
Lat: 43-28-05 N **Long:** 90-09-23 W
Pop: 152 (1990); 191 (1980) **Pop Density:** 152.0
Land: 1.0 sq. mi.; **Water:** 0.0 sq. mi.

Incorporated 1910.

Name origin: For the location of the town on a ridge with limestone outcroppings.

Loganville
Village
ZIP: 53943 **Lat:** 43-26-23 N **Long:** 90-02-13 W
Pop: 228 (1990); 239 (1980) **Pop Density:** 1140.0
Land: 0.2 sq. mi.; **Water:** 0.0 sq. mi.

Incorporated 1917.

Name origin: For Chauncey P. Logan, an early settler who was instrumental in starting the village.

Merrimac
Village
ZIP: 53561 **Lat:** 43-22-25 N **Long:** 89-37-31 W
Pop: 392 (1990); 365 (1980) **Pop Density:** 490.0
Land: 0.8 sq. mi.; **Water:** 0.6 sq. mi.

Incorporated 1899.

Name origin: For either the Merrimack River and county in NH, or from the Indian term meaning 'sturgeon' or 'swift water.' Previously called Matt's Ferry, for settler Chester Mattson, and Colomar.

*Merrimac
Town
ZIP: 53561 **Lat:** 43-23-25 N **Long:** 89-40-14 W
Pop: 737 (1990); 661 (1980) **Pop Density:** 30.1
Land: 24.5 sq. mi.; **Water:** 1.8 sq. mi.

North Freedom
Village
ZIP: 53951 **Lat:** 43-27-31 N **Long:** 89-51-47 W
Pop: 591 (1990); 616 (1980) **Pop Density:** 656.7
Land: 0.9 sq. mi.; **Water:** 0.0 sq. mi. **Elev:** 867 ft.

Incorporated 1893.

Plain
Village
ZIP: 53577 **Lat:** 43-16-41 N **Long:** 90-02-31 W
Pop: 691 (1990); 676 (1980) **Pop Density:** 987.1
Land: 0.7 sq. mi.; **Water:** 0.0 sq. mi.

Incorporated 1912.

Name origin: For its resemblance to Maria Von Plain in Austria. Previously called Cramers Corners for settlers John and Adam Cramer.

Prairie du Sac
Village
ZIP: 53578 **Lat:** 43-17-27 N **Long:** 89-43-42 W
Pop: 2,380 (1990); 2,145 (1980) **Pop Density:** 1830.8
Land: 1.3 sq. mi.; **Water:** 0.1 sq. mi.

Incorporated 1885.

Name origin: From French for a Sauk Indian village once located here on the prairie.

*Prairie du Sac
Town
ZIP: 53578 **Lat:** 43-16-43 N **Long:** 89-47-15 W
Pop: 1,271 (1990); 1,010 (1980) **Pop Density:** 42.8
Land: 29.7 sq. mi.; **Water:** 0.9 sq. mi.

Reedsburg
City
ZIP: 53959 **Lat:** 43-32-05 N **Long:** 89-59-56 W
Pop: 5,834 (1990); 5,038 (1980) **Pop Density:** 1576.8
Land: 3.7 sq. mi.; **Water:** 0.0 sq. mi. **Elev:** 926 ft.

Founded 1850. Incorporated 1887.

Name origin: For founder David C. Reed.

*Reedsburg
Town
ZIP: 53959 **Lat:** 43-30-22 N **Long:** 90-01-02 W
Pop: 1,367 (1990); 1,468 (1980) **Pop Density:** 42.5
Land: 32.2 sq. mi.; **Water:** 0.0 sq. mi.

Rock Springs
Village
ZIP: 53961 **Lat:** 43-28-47 N **Long:** 89-55-04 W
Pop: 432 (1990); 426 (1980) **Pop Density:** 332.3
Land: 1.3 sq. mi.; **Water:** 0.0 sq. mi.

Incorporated 1894.

Name origin: For natural springs in the rocks here. Previously called Excelsior, Ableman's Mills, and Ableman.

Sauk City
Village
ZIP: 53583 **Lat:** 43-16-19 N **Long:** 89-43-42 W
Pop: 3,019 (1990); 2,703 (1980) **Pop Density:** 2156.4
Land: 1.4 sq. mi.; **Water:** 0.1 sq. mi. **Elev:** 757 ft.

Incorporated 1854.

Name origin: Previously called Harszthy, after Count Augustine Harszthy, who platted the town in 1840. That name was too difficult to remember so it was changed to Westfield and then to its present name.

Spring Green
Village
ZIP: 53588 **Lat:** 43-10-32 N **Long:** 90-04-01 W
Pop: 1,283 (1990); 1,265 (1980) **Pop Density:** 1069.2
Land: 1.2 sq. mi.; **Water:** 0.0 sq. mi. **Elev:** 729 ft.

Incorporated 1869.

Name origin: For nearby hollows that became green earlier in spring than did the rest of the surrounding country, as suggested by Mrs. Turner Williams.

*Spring Green
Town
ZIP: 53588 **Lat:** 43-11-52 N **Long:** 90-06-11 W
Pop: 1,329 (1990); 1,139 (1980) **Pop Density:** 29.9
Land: 44.5 sq. mi.; **Water:** 1.8 sq. mi.

Sumpter
Town
Lat: 43-22-09 N **Long:** 89-46-20 W
Pop: 747 (1990); 720 (1980) **Pop Density:** 19.8
Land: 37.7 sq. mi.; **Water:** 0.1 sq. mi.

Troy
Town
Lat: 43-14-45 N **Long:** 89-55-18 W
Pop: 867 (1990); 799 (1980) **Pop Density:** 16.3
Land: 53.1 sq. mi.; **Water:** 1.2 sq. mi.

Washington
Town
Lat: 43-25-23 N **Long:** 90-07-55 W
Pop: 798 (1990); 741 (1980) **Pop Density:** 22.4
Land: 35.6 sq. mi.; **Water:** 0.0 sq. mi.

West Baraboo
Village
ZIP: 53913 **Lat:** 43-28-33 N **Long:** 89-46-04 W
Pop: 1,021 (1990); 846 (1980) **Pop Density:** 1276.3
Land: 0.8 sq. mi.; **Water:** 0.0 sq. mi. **Elev:** 886 ft.

Incorporated 1956.

Westfield
Town
Lat: 43-25-12 N **Long:** 90-00-54 W
Pop: 578 (1990); 633 (1980) **Pop Density:** 16.1
Land: 35.8 sq. mi.; **Water:** 0.0 sq. mi.

Winfield
Town
Lat: 43-35-52 N **Long:** 90-00-51 W
Pop: 649 (1990); 624 (1980) **Pop Density:** 18.3
Land: 35.4 sq. mi.; **Water:** 0.0 sq. mi.

Wisconsin Dells
City
Lat: 43-37-30 N **Long:** 89-47-32 W
Pop: 132 (1990); 184 (1980) **Pop Density:** 69.5
Land: 1.9 sq. mi.; **Water:** 0.1 sq. mi. **Elev:** 912 ft.
Incorporated 1925. Part of the town is also in Columbia and Adams counties.

Name origin: Named in 1931 for its descriptive connotations. Previously called Kilbourn, for Byron Kilbourne.

Woodland
Town
Lat: 43-35-58 N **Long:** 90-15-12 W
Pop: 584 (1990); 594 (1980) **Pop Density:** 16.2
Land: 36.1 sq. mi.; **Water:** 0.1 sq. mi.

Sawyer County
County Seat: Hayward (ZIP: 54843)

Pop: 14,181 (1990); 12,843 (1980) **Pop Density:** 11.3
Land: 1256.5 sq. mi.; **Water:** 93.9 sq. mi. **Area Code:** 715

In northwestern WI, north of Eau Claire; organized Mar 10, 1883 from Ashland and Chippewa counties.

Name origin: For Philetus Sawyer (1816–1900), U.S. representative from WI (1865–75) and U.S. senator (1881–93).

Bass Lake
Town
Lat: 45-55-57 N **Long:** 91-27-02 W
Pop: 1,717 (1990); 1,288 (1980) **Pop Density:** 37.3
Land: 46.0 sq. mi.; **Water:** 15.7 sq. mi.

Chief Lake
CDP
Lat: 45-55-35 N **Long:** 91-19-57 W
Pop: 570 (1990) **Pop Density:** 27.0
Land: 21.1 sq. mi.; **Water:** 2.5 sq. mi.

Couderay
Village
ZIP: 54828 **Lat:** 45-47-46 N **Long:** 91-17-56 W
Pop: 92 (1990); 114 (1980) **Pop Density:** 92.0
Land: 1.0 sq. mi.; **Water:** 0.0 sq. mi. **Elev:** 1265 ft.
Incorporated 1922.

Name origin: An anglicization of French *court oreilles* 'short ears,' the Europeans' name for the Ottawa Indians.

*Couderay
Town
ZIP: 54828 **Lat:** 45-48-17 N **Long:** 91-20-49 W
Pop: 386 (1990); 394 (1980) **Pop Density:** 5.8
Land: 66.5 sq. mi.; **Water:** 0.8 sq. mi.

Draper
Town
Lat: 45-55-01 N **Long:** 90-48-45 W
Pop: 208 (1990); 242 (1980) **Pop Density:** 1.5
Land: 136.1 sq. mi.; **Water:** 2.1 sq. mi.

Edgewater
Town
Lat: 45-41-49 N **Long:** 91-28-06 W
Pop: 509 (1990); 441 (1980) **Pop Density:** 10.8
Land: 47.2 sq. mi.; **Water:** 5.1 sq. mi.

Exeland
Village
ZIP: 54835 **Lat:** 45-40-04 N **Long:** 91-14-24 W
Pop: 180 (1990); 219 (1980) **Pop Density:** 180.0
Land: 1.0 sq. mi.; **Water:** 0.0 sq. mi.
Incorporated 1920.

Name origin: For the crossing or X in the tracks of the Wisconsin Central Railroad and an Arpin Lumber Company line.

Hayward
City
ZIP: 54843 **Lat:** 46-00-36 N **Long:** 91-28-49 W
Pop: 1,897 (1990); 1,698 (1980) **Pop Density:** 729.6
Land: 2.6 sq. mi.; **Water:** 0.2 sq. mi. **Elev:** 1198 ft.
Incorporated 1915.

Name origin: For sawmill owner Judson Hayward.

*Hayward
Town
ZIP: 54843 **Lat:** 45-59-52 N **Long:** 91-24-06 W
Pop: 3,017 (1990); 2,331 (1980) **Pop Density:** 52.3
Land: 57.7 sq. mi.; **Water:** 6.6 sq. mi.

Hunter
Town
Lat: 45-56-07 N **Long:** 91-10-27 W
Pop: 557 (1990); 594 (1980) **Pop Density:** 10.7
Land: 52.1 sq. mi.; **Water:** 23.9 sq. mi.

Lenroot
Town
Lat: 46-06-01 N **Long:** 91-26-05 W
Pop: 966 (1990); 926 (1980) **Pop Density:** 11.8
Land: 81.7 sq. mi.; **Water:** 6.3 sq. mi.

Little Round Lake
CDP
Lat: 45-57-53 N **Long:** 91-22-04 W
Pop: 871 (1990) **Pop Density:** 99.0
Land: 8.8 sq. mi.; **Water:** 0.2 sq. mi.

Meadowbrook
Town
Lat: 45-41-22 N **Long:** 91-06-35 W
Pop: 192 (1990); 202 (1980) **Pop Density:** 5.3
Land: 36.0 sq. mi.; **Water:** 0.3 sq. mi.

Meteor
Town
Lat: 45-41-09 N **Long:** 91-21-03 W
Pop: 111 (1990); 105 (1980) **Pop Density:** 3.2
Land: 34.4 sq. mi.; **Water:** 0.8 sq. mi.

New Post
CDP
Lat: 45-53-49 N **Long:** 91-11-31 W
Pop: 243 (1990) **Pop Density:** 12.0
Land: 20.2 sq. mi.; **Water:** 7.1 sq. mi.

Ojibwa
Town
Lat: 45-50-19 N **Long:** 91-06-50 W
Pop: 250 (1990); 264 (1980) **Pop Density:** 4.9
Land: 50.8 sq. mi.; **Water:** 0.6 sq. mi.

Radisson — Village
ZIP: 54867 Lat: 45-46-06 N Long: 91-13-07 W
Pop: 237 (1990); 280 (1980) Pop Density: 592.5
Land: 0.4 sq. mi.; Water: 0.0 sq. mi. Elev: 1245 ft.
Incorporated 1953.
Name origin: For Pierre Esprit Radisson (c. 1636–c. 1710), who explored this area c. 1659.

Radisson — Town
ZIP: 54867 Lat: 45-46-55 N Long: 91-11-53 W
Pop: 412 (1990); 394 (1980) Pop Density: 5.6
Land: 74.1 sq. mi.; Water: 1.1 sq. mi.

Reserve — CDP
Lat: 45-49-42 N Long: 91-21-36 W
Pop: 371 (1990) Pop Density: 7.0
Land: 52.9 sq. mi.; Water: 0.7 sq. mi.

Round Lake — Town
Lat: 46-01-34 N Long: 91-07-40 W
Pop: 727 (1990); 786 (1980) Pop Density: 6.7
Land: 109.3 sq. mi.; Water: 8.9 sq. mi.

Sand Lake — Town
Lat: 45-49-53 N Long: 91-28-07 W
Pop: 821 (1990); 768 (1980) Pop Density: 17.7
Land: 46.4 sq. mi.; Water: 5.2 sq. mi.

Spider Lake — Town
Lat: 46-07-13 N Long: 91-06-54 W
Pop: 362 (1990); 331 (1980) Pop Density: 3.6
Land: 99.3 sq. mi.; Water: 9.6 sq. mi.

Weirgor — Town
Lat: 45-41-29 N Long: 91-14-46 W
Pop: 356 (1990); 386 (1980) Pop Density: 10.6
Land: 33.6 sq. mi.; Water: 0.9 sq. mi.

Winter — Village
ZIP: 54862 Lat: 45-49-15 N Long: 91-00-43 W
Pop: 383 (1990); 376 (1980) Pop Density: 478.8
Land: 0.8 sq. mi.; Water: 0.0 sq. mi.
Incorporated 1973.
Name origin: For John Winter, an official of the Omaha Railroad. Originally known as LeBoef.

*Winter — Town
ZIP: 54862 Lat: 45-45-58 N Long: 90-53-05 W
Pop: 801 (1990); 704 (1980) Pop Density: 2.9
Land: 279.5 sq. mi.; Water: 5.8 sq. mi.

Shawano County
County Seat: Shawano (ZIP: 54166)

Pop: 37,157 (1990); 35,928 (1980) Pop Density: 41.6
Land: 892.6 sq. mi.; Water: 16.8 sq. mi. Area Code: 715
In east-central WI, northwest of Green Bay; organized Feb 16, 1853 from Oconto County.
Name origin: For Shawano Lake, a Menominee word probably meaning 'to the south.'

Almon — Town
Lat: 44-53-38 N Long: 89-02-07 W
Pop: 557 (1990); 632 (1980) Pop Density: 15.9
Land: 35.1 sq. mi.; Water: 0.1 sq. mi.

Angelica — Town
Lat: 44-43-09 N Long: 88-18-36 W
Pop: 1,417 (1990); 1,522 (1980) Pop Density: 38.7
Land: 36.6 sq. mi.; Water: 0.0 sq. mi.

Aniwa — Village
ZIP: 54408 Lat: 45-00-35 N Long: 89-12-29 W
Pop: 249 (1990); 273 (1980) Pop Density: 118.6
Land: 2.1 sq. mi.; Water: 0.0 sq. mi. Elev: 1414 ft.
Incorporated 1899.
Name origin: From a Chippewa Indian term for 'those,' possibly a prefix that signifies superiority.

Aniwa — Town
ZIP: 54408 Lat: 44-59-44 N Long: 89-09-58 W
Pop: 601 (1990); 612 (1980) Pop Density: 18.1
Land: 33.2 sq. mi.; Water: 0.3 sq. mi.

Bartelme — Town
Lat: 44-54-13 N Long: 88-55-34 W
Pop: 618 (1990); 583 (1980) Pop Density: 17.4
Land: 35.5 sq. mi.; Water: 0.1 sq. mi.

Belle Plaine — Town
Lat: 44-43-37 N Long: 88-40-03 W
Pop: 1,792 (1990); 1,626 (1980) Pop Density: 46.7
Land: 38.4 sq. mi.; Water: 0.8 sq. mi.

Birnamwood — Village
ZIP: 54414 Lat: 44-55-52 N Long: 89-12-30 W
Pop: 687 (1990); 688 (1980) Pop Density: 327.1
Land: 2.1 sq. mi.; Water: 0.0 sq. mi.
Incorporated 1895. Part of the town is also in Marathon County.
Name origin: Named by the son of a railroad official, who saw large piles of brush burning near the tracks here. They were described by an Indian as 'heap big burn-em-wood,' which reminded the young man of Birnamwood mentioned in Shakespeare's *Macbeth*.

*Birnamwood — Town
ZIP: 54414 Lat: 44-53-23 N Long: 89-09-27 W
Pop: 632 (1990); 570 (1980) Pop Density: 20.1
Land: 31.4 sq. mi.; Water: 0.0 sq. mi.

WISCONSIN, Shawano County

Bonduel — Village
ZIP: 54107   **Lat:** 44-44-28 N   **Long:** 88-26-54 W
Pop: 1,210 (1990); 1,160 (1980)   **Pop Density:** 711.8
Land: 1.7 sq. mi.; **Water:** 0.0 sq. mi.
Incorporated 1916
Name origin: For Father Floribrant Bonduel, a Jesuit priest who started a chapel here for the Menominee Indians.

Bowler — Village
ZIP: 54416   **Lat:** 44-51-48 N   **Long:** 88-58-55 W
Pop: 279 (1990); 339 (1980)   **Pop Density:** 279.0
Land: 1.0 sq. mi.; **Water:** 0.0 sq. mi.   **Elev:** 1080 ft.
Incorporated 1923.
Name origin: For Mr. Bowler, a lawyer for the Chicago and North Western Railway Company, who helped purchase a right-of-way for the railroad here.

Cecil — Village
ZIP: 54111   **Lat:** 44-48-44 N   **Long:** 88-26-56 W
Pop: 373 (1990); 445 (1980)   **Pop Density:** 266.4
Land: 1.4 sq. mi.; **Water:** 0.0 sq. mi.   **Elev:** 811 ft.
Incorporated 1905.
Name origin: Named in 1884 for railroad man Cecil Leavitt.

Eland — Village
ZIP: 54427   **Lat:** 44-51-57 N   **Long:** 89-12-40 W
Pop: 247 (1990); 230 (1980)   **Pop Density:** 112.3
Land: 2.2 sq. mi.; **Water:** 0.0 sq. mi.
Incorporated 1905.
Name origin: For the eland, an African variety of antelope. The herds of wild deer in the area may have suggested some similarity.

Fairbanks — Town
Lat: 44-43-56 N   **Long:** 89-02-43 W
Pop: 600 (1990); 608 (1980)   **Pop Density:** 17.0
Land: 35.2 sq. mi.; **Water:** 0.1 sq. mi.

Germania — Town
Lat: 44-43-24 N   **Long:** 89-10-01 W
Pop: 410 (1990); 392 (1980)   **Pop Density:** 11.3
Land: 36.2 sq. mi.; **Water:** 0.0 sq. mi.

Grant — Town
Lat: 44-43-15 N   **Long:** 88-55-20 W
Pop: 946 (1990); 976 (1980)   **Pop Density:** 25.6
Land: 36.9 sq. mi.; **Water:** 0.1 sq. mi.

Green Valley — Town
Lat: 44-48-33 N   **Long:** 88-18-42 W
Pop: 984 (1990); 1,054 (1980)   **Pop Density:** 27.6
Land: 35.7 sq. mi.; **Water:** 0.1 sq. mi.

Gresham — Village
ZIP: 54128   **Lat:** 44-50-54 N   **Long:** 88-47-09 W
Pop: 515 (1990); 534 (1980)   **Pop Density:** 468.2
Land: 1.1 sq. mi.; **Water:** 0.1 sq. mi.   **Elev:** 9554 ft.
Incorporated 1908.
Name origin: For Postmaster-Gen. Gresham of Pres. Chester A. Arthur's (1829–86) cabinet.

Hartland — Town
Lat: 44-43-02 N   **Long:** 88-25-38 W
Pop: 764 (1990); 872 (1980)   **Pop Density:** 21.8
Land: 35.1 sq. mi.; **Water:** 0.2 sq. mi.

Herman — Town
Lat: 44-48-32 N   **Long:** 88-47-29 W
Pop: 739 (1990); 834 (1980)   **Pop Density:** 21.0
Land: 35.2 sq. mi.; **Water:** 0.2 sq. mi.

Hutchins — Town
Lat: 44-59-25 N   **Long:** 89-02-05 W
Pop: 523 (1990); 467 (1980)   **Pop Density:** 15.6
Land: 33.6 sq. mi.; **Water:** 0.1 sq. mi.

Lessor — Town
Lat: 44-38-18 N   **Long:** 88-25-38 W
Pop: 892 (1990); 955 (1980)   **Pop Density:** 24.8
Land: 35.9 sq. mi.; **Water:** 0.2 sq. mi.

Maple Grove — Town
Lat: 44-37-45 N   **Long:** 88-18-32 W
Pop: 1,159 (1990); 1,271 (1980)   **Pop Density:** 32.7
Land: 35.4 sq. mi.; **Water:** 0.0 sq. mi.

Mattoon — Village
ZIP: 54450   **Lat:** 45-00-17 N   **Long:** 89-02-33 W
Pop: 431 (1990); 382 (1980)   **Pop Density:** 287.3
Land: 1.5 sq. mi.; **Water:** 0.0 sq. mi.
Incorporated 1901.

Morris — Town
ZIP: 54486   **Lat:** 44-48-35 N   **Long:** 89-02-10 W
Pop: 453 (1990); 447 (1980)   **Pop Density:** 12.5
Land: 36.2 sq. mi.; **Water:** 0.0 sq. mi.

Navarino — Town
Lat: 44-38-13 N   **Long:** 88-32-56 W
Pop: 439 (1990); 456 (1980)   **Pop Density:** 12.5
Land: 35.2 sq. mi.; **Water:** 0.5 sq. mi.

Pella — Town
Lat: 44-43-17 N   **Long:** 88-47-43 W
Pop: 885 (1990); 788 (1980)   **Pop Density:** 24.3
Land: 36.4 sq. mi.; **Water:** 0.3 sq. mi.

Red Springs — Town
Lat: 44-53-42 N   **Long:** 88-47-19 W
Pop: 614 (1990); 524 (1980)   **Pop Density:** 17.2
Land: 35.8 sq. mi.; **Water:** 0.7 sq. mi.

Richmond — Town
Lat: 44-48-38 N   **Long:** 88-40-49 W
Pop: 1,587 (1990); 1,543 (1980)   **Pop Density:** 47.2
Land: 33.6 sq. mi.; **Water:** 0.8 sq. mi.

Seneca — Town
Lat: 44-48-52 N   **Long:** 88-54-58 W
Pop: 538 (1990); 525 (1980)   **Pop Density:** 14.7
Land: 36.6 sq. mi.; **Water:** 0.1 sq. mi.

Shawano — City
ZIP: 54166   **Lat:** 44-46-35 N   **Long:** 88-35-19 W
Pop: 7,598 (1990); 7,013 (1980)   **Pop Density:** 1461.2
Land: 5.2 sq. mi.; **Water:** 0.1 sq. mi.   **Elev:** 821 ft.
Incorporated 1874.
Name origin: For Shawano Lake, a Menominee word probably meaning 'to the south'

Tigerton — Village
ZIP: 54486   **Lat:** 44-44-25 N   **Long:** 89-03-39 W
Pop: 815 (1990); 865 (1980)   **Pop Density:** 905.6
Land: 0.9 sq. mi.; **Water:** 0.0 sq. mi.
Incorporated 1896.

Washington
Town
Lat: 44-48-08 N **Long:** 88-26-36 W
Pop: 1,620 (1990); 1,374 (1980) **Pop Density:** 45.8
Land: 35.4 sq. mi.; **Water:** 3.6 sq. mi.

Waukechon
Town
Lat: 44-43-32 N **Long:** 88-33-04 W
Pop: 876 (1990); 874 (1980) **Pop Density:** 24.5
Land: 35.8 sq. mi.; **Water:** 0.5 sq. mi.

Wescott
Town
Lat: 44-49-06 N **Long:** 88-33-32 W
Pop: 3,085 (1990); 2,668 (1980) **Pop Density:** 134.1
Land: 23.0 sq. mi.; **Water:** 7.7 sq. mi.

Wittenberg
Village
ZIP: 54499 **Lat:** 44-49-35 N **Long:** 89-10-14 W
Pop: 1,145 (1990); 997 (1980) **Pop Density:** 817.9
Land: 1.4 sq. mi.; **Water:** 0.0 sq. mi.
Incorporated 1893.
Name origin: For a suggestion by Pastor E. J. Homme, who came here with the intention of establishing a home for orphans and the aged. Previously called Carbenaro for charcoal kilns.

*Wittenberg
Town
ZIP: 54499 **Lat:** 44-48-54 N **Long:** 89-10-20 W
Pop: 877 (1990); 829 (1980) **Pop Density:** 25.5
Land: 34.4 sq. mi.; **Water:** 0.1 sq. mi.

Sheboygan County
County Seat: Sheboygan (ZIP: 53081)

Pop: 103,877 (1990); 100,935 (1980) **Pop Density:** 202.2
Land: 513.7 sq. mi.; **Water:** 757.4 sq. mi. **Area Code:** 414

On central eastern coast of WI, southeast of Lake Winnebago; organized Dec 7, 1836 (prior to statehood) from a territorial county.

Name origin: For the Sheboygan River, from an Algonquian word whose meaning is unclear: possibly either 'reed like,' 'something that pierces,' or 'thundering under the ground.'

Adell
Village
ZIP: 53001 **Lat:** 43-37-14 N **Long:** 87-56-46 W
Pop: 510 (1990); 545 (1980) **Pop Density:** 1020.0
Land: 0.5 sq. mi.; **Water:** 0.0 sq. mi.
Incorporated 1918.
Name origin: Previously called Sherman's Station.

Cascade
Village
ZIP: 53011 **Lat:** 43-39-33 N **Long:** 88-00-30 W
Pop: 620 (1990); 615 (1980) **Pop Density:** 885.7
Land: 0.7 sq. mi.; **Water:** 0.0 sq. mi.
Located near the rapids in the north fork of the Milwaukee River. Incorporated 1914.
Name origin: For Cascade Falls in CO. Previously called Nineveh.

Cedar Grove
Village
ZIP: 53013 **Lat:** 43-34-01 N **Long:** 87-49-25 W
Pop: 1,521 (1990); 1,420 (1980) **Pop Density:** 760.5
Land: 2.0 sq. mi.; **Water:** 0.0 sq. mi. **Elev:** 711 ft.
Incorporated 1899.
Name origin: For a forty-acre tract of cedar trees at the south end of town.

Elkhart Lake
Village
ZIP: 53020 **Lat:** 43-49-58 N **Long:** 88-00-52 W
Pop: 1,019 (1990); 1,054 (1980) **Pop Density:** 926.4
Land: 1.1 sq. mi.; **Water:** 0.0 sq. mi. **Elev:** 938 ft.
Incorporated 1894.
Name origin: For its descriptive connotations. Originally known as the Rhine by German settlers.

Glenbeulah
Village
ZIP: 53023 **Lat:** 43-47-55 N **Long:** 88-02-47 W
Pop: 386 (1990); 423 (1980) **Pop Density:** 551.4
Land: 0.7 sq. mi.; **Water:** 0.0 sq. mi.
Incorporated 1913.
Name origin: Named by Edward Appleton for its location in a glen, combined with Beulah, his mother's name. Previously called Clark's Mill, for Hazel P. Clark, who owned a sawmill here.

Greenbush
Town
Lat: 43-46-39 N **Long:** 88-06-03 W
Pop: 1,943 (1990); 1,665 (1980) **Pop Density:** 41.2
Land: 47.2 sq. mi.; **Water:** 0.3 sq. mi.

Herman
Town
Lat: 43-51-11 N **Long:** 87-51-39 W
Pop: 1,820 (1990); 2,095 (1980) **Pop Density:** 53.2
Land: 34.2 sq. mi.; **Water:** 0.1 sq. mi.

Holland
Town
Lat: 43-35-22 N **Long:** 87-50-35 W
Pop: 2,567 (1990); 2,504 (1980) **Pop Density:** 61.3
Land: 41.9 sq. mi.; **Water:** 0.0 sq. mi.

Howards Grove
Village
Lat: 43-49-46 N **Long:** 87-49-33 W
Pop: 2,329 (1990); 1,838 (1980) **Pop Density:** 1109.0
Land: 2.1 sq. mi.; **Water:** 0.0 sq. mi.
Incorporated 1967.
Name origin: For H. B. Howard, who established a trading post here in 1850. Previously called Pitchville.

Kohler
Village
ZIP: 53044 **Lat:** 43-44-07 N **Long:** 87-46-44 W
Pop: 1,817 (1990); 1,651 (1980) **Pop Density:** 336.5
Land: 5.4 sq. mi.; **Water:** 0.1 sq. mi. **Elev:** 676 ft.
Incorporated 1912.
Name origin: For the Kohler Manufacturing Company,

which moved its plant here in 1912. Previously called Riverside.

Lima
Town
Lat: 43-40-30 N Long: 87-51-45 W
Pop: 2,715 (1990); 2,809 (1980)   **Pop Density:** 74.2
Land: 36.6 sq. mi.; **Water:** 0.1 sq. mi.

Lyndon
Town
Lat: 43-40-27 N Long: 87-58-48 W
Pop: 1,432 (1990); 1,342 (1980)   **Pop Density:** 41.9
Land: 34.2 sq. mi.; **Water:** 0.2 sq. mi.

Mitchell
Town
Lat: 43-40-26 N Long: 88-05-58 W
Pop: 944 (1990); 900 (1980)   **Pop Density:** 26.1
Land: 36.1 sq. mi.; **Water:** 0.0 sq. mi.

Mosel
Town
Lat: 43-50-28 N Long: 87-45-56 W
Pop: 918 (1990); 1,035 (1980)   **Pop Density:** 43.5
Land: 21.1 sq. mi.; **Water:** 0.0 sq. mi.

Oostburg
Village
ZIP: 53070   Lat: 43-37-27 N Long: 87-47-51 W
Pop: 1,931 (1990); 1,647 (1980)   **Pop Density:** 2413.8
Land: 0.8 sq. mi.; **Water:** 0.0 sq. mi.
Incorporated 1909.

Name origin: Named by Dutch settlers for Oostburg, Holland.

Plymouth
City
ZIP: 53073   Lat: 43-44-49 N Long: 87-58-19 W
Pop: 6,769 (1990); 6,027 (1980)   **Pop Density:** 1880.3
Land: 3.6 sq. mi.; **Water:** 0.1 sq. mi.
Settled 1845. Incorporated 1877.

Name origin: For Plymouth, MA, the hometown of the girlfriend of settler Thomas Davidson.

*Plymouth
Town
ZIP: 53073   Lat: 43-45-48 N Long: 87-58-52 W
Pop: 2,911 (1990); 3,068 (1980)   **Pop Density:** 91.0
Land: 32.0 sq. mi.; **Water:** 0.0 sq. mi.

Random Lake
Village
ZIP: 53075   Lat: 43-33-17 N Long: 87-57-21 W
Pop: 1,439 (1990); 1,287 (1980)   **Pop Density:** 1106.9
Land: 1.3 sq. mi.; **Water:** 0.3 sq. mi.   **Elev:** 901 ft.
Incorporated 1907.

Name origin: For nearby Random Lake. Originally known as Greenleaf, for E. D. Greenleaf, a financial agent for the railroad company.

Rhine
Town
Lat: 43-50-52 N Long: 87-58-54 W
Pop: 2,235 (1990); 1,910 (1980)   **Pop Density:** 66.1
Land: 33.8 sq. mi.; **Water:** 0.9 sq. mi.

Russell
Town
Lat: 43-51-13 N Long: 88-06-02 W
Pop: 362 (1990), 429 (1980)   **Pop Density:** 15.7
Land: 23.1 sq. mi.; **Water:** 1.0 sq. mi.

Scott
Town
Lat: 43-35-01 N Long: 88-06-14 W
Pop: 1,671 (1990); 1,625 (1980)   **Pop Density:** 46.2
Land: 36.2 sq. mi.; **Water:** 0.4 sq. mi.

Sheboygan
City
ZIP: 53081   Lat: 43-44-44 N Long: 87-43-48 W
Pop: 49,676 (1990); 48,085 (1980)   **Pop Density:** 3763.3
Land: 13.2 sq. mi.; **Water:** 0.1 sq. mi.
In eastern WI on Lake Michigan, 51 mi. north of Milwaukee. Incorporated 1853.

Name origin: For the Sheboygan River, which runs through the county; from an Algonquian Indian word of uncertain meaning, possibly either 'reed-like,' 'something that pierces,' or 'thundering under the ground.'

*Sheboygan
Town
Lat: 43-47-05 N Long: 87-45-59 W
Pop: 3,866 (1990); 3,962 (1980)   **Pop Density:** 339.1
Land: 11.4 sq. mi.; **Water:** 0.0 sq. mi.

Sheboygan Falls
City
ZIP: 53085   Lat: 43-43-47 N Long: 87-49-21 W
Pop: 5,823 (1990); 5,253 (1980)   **Pop Density:** 2007.9
Land: 2.9 sq. mi.; **Water:** 0.1 sq. mi.   **Elev:** 659 ft.
Incorporated 1913.

Name origin: For falls on the Sheboygan River. Previously called Rochester for Rochester, NY.

*Sheboygan Falls
Town
ZIP: 53085   Lat: 43-45-39 N Long: 87-51-30 W
Pop: 1,908 (1990); 2,281 (1980)   **Pop Density:** 57.5
Land: 33.2 sq. mi.; **Water:** 0.0 sq. mi.

Sherman
Town
Lat: 43-35-14 N Long: 87-58-55 W
Pop: 1,461 (1990); 1,445 (1980)   **Pop Density:** 42.6
Land: 34.3 sq. mi.; **Water:** 0.0 sq. mi.

Waldo
Village
ZIP: 53093   Lat: 43-40-32 N Long: 87-56-47 W
Pop: 442 (1990); 416 (1980)   **Pop Density:** 552.5
Land: 0.8 sq. mi.; **Water:** 0.0 sq. mi.   **Elev:** 838 ft.
Incorporated 1922.

Name origin: For O. H. Waldo, president of the Milwaukee and Northern Railroad. Previously called Lora and Lyndon Station.

Wilson
Town
Lat: 43-40-27 N Long: 87-45-28 W
Pop: 2,842 (1990); 3,604 (1980)   **Pop Density:** 122.0
Land: 23.3 sq. mi.; **Water:** 0.0 sq. mi.

Taylor County
County Seat: Medford (ZIP: 54451)

Pop: 18,901 (1990); 18,817 (1980) **Pop Density:** 19.4
Land: 975.0 sq. mi.; **Water:** 9.6 sq. mi. **Area Code:** 715
In north-central WI, northwest of Wausau; organized Mar 4, 1875 from Clark and Lincoln counties.
Name origin: For William Robert Taylor (1820–1909), governor of WI (1874–76), known as the "farmer governor."

Aurora   Town
Lat: 45-09-51 N Long: 90-51-51 W
Pop: 473 (1990); 461 (1980) Pop Density: 13.8
Land: 34.2 sq. mi.; Water: 0.0 sq. mi.

Browning   Town
Lat: 45-09-59 N Long: 90-13-56 W
Pop: 740 (1990); 702 (1980) Pop Density: 20.3
Land: 36.5 sq. mi.; Water: 0.0 sq. mi.

Chelsea   Town
ZIP: 54451 Lat: 45-14-39 N Long: 90-22-06 W
Pop: 731 (1990); 677 (1980) Pop Density: 18.1
Land: 40.4 sq. mi.; Water: 0.5 sq. mi.

Cleveland   Town
Lat: 45-14-39 N Long: 90-43-33 W
Pop: 235 (1990); 286 (1980) Pop Density: 6.9
Land: 33.9 sq. mi.; Water: 1.8 sq. mi.

Deer Creek   Town
ZIP: 54480 Lat: 45-04-54 N Long: 90-15-45 W
Pop: 738 (1990); 747 (1980) Pop Density: 21.6
Land: 34.2 sq. mi.; Water: 0.0 sq. mi.

Ford   Town
Lat: 45-09-15 N Long: 90-43-57 W
Pop: 254 (1990); 274 (1980) Pop Density: 7.7
Land: 32.8 sq. mi.; Water: 2.3 sq. mi.

Gilman   Village
ZIP: 54433 Lat: 45-10-00 N Long: 90-48-24 W
Pop: 412 (1990); 436 (1980) Pop Density: 179.1
Land: 2.3 sq. mi.; Water: 0.0 sq. mi.
Incorporated 1914.
Name origin: For Gilman Moore, whose father had an interest in the S.M. & P. Railroad.

Goodrich   Town
ZIP: 54451 Lat: 45-09-24 N Long: 90-05-43 W
Pop: 454 (1990); 408 (1980) Pop Density: 12.5
Land: 36.3 sq. mi.; Water: 0.0 sq. mi.

Greenwood   Town
Lat: 45-14-51 N Long: 90-11-09 W
Pop: 634 (1990); 705 (1980) Pop Density: 11.7
Land: 54.3 sq. mi.; Water: 0.0 sq. mi.

Grover   Town
Lat: 45-12-24 N Long: 90-37-04 W
Pop: 214 (1990); 229 (1980) Pop Density: 3.0
Land: 70.7 sq. mi.; Water: 0.7 sq. mi.

Hammel   Town
Lat: 45-09-32 N Long: 90-29-14 W
Pop: 633 (1990); 562 (1980) Pop Density: 17.8
Land: 35.5 sq. mi.; Water: 0.2 sq. mi.

Holway   Town
Lat: 45-04-50 N Long: 90-29-34 W
Pop: 779 (1990); 903 (1980) Pop Density: 21.4
Land: 36.4 sq. mi.; Water: 0.0 sq. mi.

Jump River   Town
Lat: 45-20-47 N Long: 90-44-30 W
Pop: 330 (1990); 365 (1980) Pop Density: 9.2
Land: 36.0 sq. mi.; Water: 0.0 sq. mi.

Little Black   Town
ZIP: 54451 Lat: 45-04-39 N Long: 90-22-40 W
Pop: 1,195 (1990); 1,169 (1980) Pop Density: 34.0
Land: 35.1 sq. mi.; Water: 0.0 sq. mi.

Lublin   Village
ZIP: 54447 Lat: 45-04-30 N Long: 90-43-26 W
Pop: 129 (1990); 142 (1980) Pop Density: 86.0
Land: 1.5 sq. mi.; Water: 0.0 sq. mi. Elev: 1289 ft.
Incorporated 1915.
Name origin: For Lublin, Poland, the home of land agent, Marvin Durski.

Maplehurst   Town
Lat: 45-03-37 N Long: 90-37-03 W
Pop: 300 (1990); 345 (1980) Pop Density: 8.4
Land: 35.9 sq. mi.; Water: 0.0 sq. mi.

McKinley   Town
Lat: 45-20-22 N Long: 90-51-30 W
Pop: 403 (1990); 416 (1980) Pop Density: 11.3
Land: 35.7 sq. mi.; Water: 0.1 sq. mi.

Medford   City
ZIP: 54451 Lat: 45-08-19 N Long: 90-20-52 W
Pop: 4,283 (1990); 4,035 (1980) Pop Density: 1338.4
Land: 3.2 sq. mi.; Water: 0.0 sq. mi.
Incorporated 1889.
Name origin: Possibly for Medford, MA, the hometown of a young man who passed through here in 1873.

*Medford   Town
ZIP: 54451 Lat: 45-10-14 N Long: 90-21-59 W
Pop: 1,961 (1990); 1,809 (1980) Pop Density: 51.7
Land: 37.9 sq. mi.; Water: 0.1 sq. mi.

Molitor   Town
Lat: 45-15-14 N Long: 90-28-59 W
Pop: 183 (1990); 212 (1980) Pop Density: 5.2
Land: 35.3 sq. mi.; Water: 0.7 sq. mi.

Pershing   Town
Lat: 45-15-05 N Long: 90-51-36 W
Pop: 217 (1990); 276 (1980) Pop Density: 6.1
Land: 35.7 sq. mi.; Water: 0.2 sq. mi.

WISCONSIN, Taylor County   *American Places Dictionary*

Rib Lake
Village
ZIP: 54470　　　Lat: 45-19-07 N　Long: 90-12-12 W
Pop: 887 (1990); 945 (1980)　　　Pop Density: 466.8
Land: 1.9 sq. mi.; Water: 0.5 sq. mi.
Incorporated 1902.
Name origin: For the lake here that is said to be shaped like a rib.

*Rib Lake
Town
ZIP: 54470　　　Lat: 45-19-33 N　Long: 90-08-01 W
Pop: 746 (1990); 682 (1980)　　　Pop Density: 10.1
Land: 74.0 sq. mi.; Water: 0.8 sq. mi.

Roosevelt
Town
　　　　　　　Lat: 45-05-01 N　Long: 90-44-11 W
Pop: 429 (1990); 491 (1980)　　　Pop Density: 12.5
Land: 34.4 sq. mi.; Water: 0.1 sq. mi.

Stetsonville
Village
ZIP: 54480　　　Lat: 45-04-35 N　Long: 90-18-45 W
Pop: 511 (1990); 487 (1980)　　　Pop Density: 1277.5
Land: 0.4 sq. mi.; Water: 0.0 sq. mi.
Incorporated 1949.
Name origin: For Isaiah F. Stetson, who built the first sawmill here in 1875.

Taft
Town
　　　　　　　Lat: 45-04-27 N　Long: 90-51-46 W
Pop: 367 (1990); 347 (1980)　　　Pop Density: 10.1
Land: 36.5 sq. mi.; Water: 0.1 sq. mi.

Westboro
Town
ZIP: 54490　　　Lat: 45-19-52 N　Long: 90-27-47 W
Pop: 663 (1990); 706 (1980)　　　Pop Density: 5.3
Land: 124.1 sq. mi.; Water: 1.3 sq. mi.

Trempealeau County
County Seat: Whitehall (ZIP: 54773)

Pop: 25,263 (1990); 26,158 (1980)　　　Pop Density: 34.4
Land: 734.1 sq. mi.; Water: 7.9 sq. mi.　　　Area Code: 715

On central western border of WI, southeast of St. Paul, MN; organized Jan 27, 1854 from Chippewa County.

Name origin: For the town at the foot of a high elevation surrounded by water; French transliteration *la montagne qui trempe a l'eau* of an Indian word probably meaning 'mountain drenched with water.' The Trempealeau River forms the lower western border of the county.

Albion
Town
　　　　　　　Lat: 44-32-48 N　Long: 91-27-57 W
Pop: 696 (1990); 605 (1980)　　　Pop Density: 19.7
Land: 35.3 sq. mi.; Water: 0.0 sq. mi.

Arcadia
City
ZIP: 54612　　　Lat: 44-15-08 N　Long: 91-29-36 W
Pop: 2,166 (1990); 2,109 (1980)　　　Pop Density: 1203.3
Land: 1.8 sq. mi.; Water: 0.0 sq. mi.　　　Elev: 728 ft.
Incorporated 1925.
Name origin: For the region in ancient Greece.

*Arcadia
Town
ZIP: 54612　　　Lat: 44-14-23 N　Long: 91-27-46 W
Pop: 1,710 (1990); 1,919 (1980)　　　Pop Density: 14.3
Land: 119.7 sq. mi.; Water: 0.2 sq. mi.

Blair
City
ZIP: 54616　　　Lat: 44-17-45 N　Long: 91-13-47 W
Pop: 1,126 (1990); 1,142 (1980)　　　Pop Density: 1251.1
Land: 0.9 sq. mi.; Water: 0.1 sq. mi.　　　Elev: 859 ft.
Incorporated 1949.
Name origin: Named in 1873 for John Insley Blair, a stockholder in the railroad company. Originally called Porterville for the Porter family.

Burnside
Town
　　　　　　　Lat: 44-22-53 N　Long: 91-28-44 W
Pop: 653 (1990); 639 (1980)　　　Pop Density: 18.6
Land: 35.2 sq. mi.; Water: 0.0 sq. mi.

Caledonia
Town
　　　　　　　Lat: 44-01-52 N　Long: 91-21-38 W
Pop: 555 (1990); 507 (1980)　　　Pop Density: 26.6
Land: 20.9 sq. mi.; Water: 0.4 sq. mi.

Chimney Rock
Town
　　　　　　　Lat: 44-27-57 N　Long: 91-28-41 W
Pop: 267 (1990); 390 (1980)　　　Pop Density: 7.4
Land: 36.1 sq. mi.; Water: 0.0 sq. mi.

Dodge
Town
ZIP: 54625　　　Lat: 44-07-39 N　Long: 91-30-30 W
Pop: 397 (1990); 399 (1980)　　　Pop Density: 18.6
Land: 21.4 sq. mi.; Water: 0.0 sq. mi.

Eleva
Village
ZIP: 54738　　　Lat: 44-34-35 N　Long: 91-28-13 W
Pop: 491 (1990); 593 (1980)　　　Pop Density: 982.0
Land: 0.5 sq. mi.; Water: 0.0 sq. mi.
Incorporated 1902.
Name origin: Named by R. P. Goddard for the French town of Eleva. Previously called New Chicago and Dogtown.

Ettrick
Village
ZIP: 54627　　　Lat: 44-10-11 N　Long: 91-15-58 W
Pop: 461 (1990); 462 (1980)　　　Pop Density: 658.6
Land: 0.7 sq. mi.; Water: 0.0 sq. mi.　　　Elev: 771 ft.
Incorporated 1948.
Name origin: Named by Scotsman John Chance, for the Ettrick Forest in Sir Walter Scott's (1771–1832) "Marmion."

*Ettrick
Town
ZIP: 54627　　　Lat: 44-11-38 N　Long: 91-14-52 W
Pop: 1,339 (1990); 1,420 (1980)　　　Pop Density: 17.4
Land: 77.1 sq. mi.; Water: 0.0 sq. mi.

Gale
Town
　　　　　　　Lat: 44-06-07 N　Long: 91-17-43 W
Pop: 1,563 (1990); 1,553 (1980)　　　Pop Density: 25.8
Land: 60.5 sq. mi.; Water: 0.6 sq. mi.

Galesville
City
ZIP: 54630 **Lat:** 44-05-03 N **Long:** 91-21-22 W
Pop: 1,278 (1990); 1,239 (1980) **Pop Density:** 1161.8
Land: 1.1 sq. mi.; **Water:** 0.1 sq. mi. **Elev:** 712 ft.
Incorporated 1942.
Name origin: For Judge George Gale, who purchased land here and founded Gale College.

Hale
Town
Lat: 44-27-49 N **Long:** 91-18-26 W
Pop: 971 (1990); 983 (1980) **Pop Density:** 13.9
Land: 69.7 sq. mi.; **Water:** 0.0 sq. mi.

Independence
City
ZIP: 54747 **Lat:** 44-21-43 N **Long:** 91-25-09 W
Pop: 1,041 (1990); 1,180 (1980) **Pop Density:** 1041.0
Land: 1.0 sq. mi.; **Water:** 0.0 sq. mi. **Elev:** 782 ft.
Platted 1876. Incorporated 1942.
Name origin: The town was platted the year of the centennial celebration of American independence.

Lincoln
Town
Lat: 44-22-18 N **Long:** 91-21-07 W
Pop: 894 (1990); 935 (1980) **Pop Density:** 31.5
Land: 28.4 sq. mi.; **Water:** 0.0 sq. mi.

Osseo
City
ZIP: 54758 **Lat:** 44-34-42 N **Long:** 91-13-05 W
Pop: 1,551 (1990); 1,474 (1980) **Pop Density:** 1034.0
Land: 1.5 sq. mi.; **Water:** 0.0 sq. mi. **Elev:** 959 ft.
Incorporated 1941.

Pigeon
Town
Lat: 44-23-32 N **Long:** 91-13-40 W
Pop: 845 (1990); 876 (1980) **Pop Density:** 21.9
Land: 38.6 sq. mi.; **Water:** 0.0 sq. mi.

Pigeon Falls
Village
ZIP: 54760 **Lat:** 44-25-28 N **Long:** 91-12-29 W
Pop: 289 (1990); 338 (1980) **Pop Density:** 578.0
Land: 0.5 sq. mi.; **Water:** 0.0 sq. mi. **Elev:** 882 ft.
Incorporated 1956.
Name origin: For the falls in Pigeon Creek, and for wild passenger pigeons that were once abundant.

Preston
Town
Lat: 44-18-01 N **Long:** 91-15-29 W
Pop: 963 (1990); 1,112 (1980) **Pop Density:** 16.2
Land: 59.3 sq. mi.; **Water:** 0.0 sq. mi.

Strum
Village
ZIP: 54770 **Lat:** 44-33-10 N **Long:** 91-23-10 W
Pop: 949 (1990); 944 (1980) **Pop Density:** 862.7
Land: 1.1 sq. mi.; **Water:** 0.1 sq. mi.
Incorporated 1948.
Name origin: Named in 1890 for Louis (or Peter) Strum, who was later a state senator from this district. Originally known as Tilden, for statesman Samuel J. Tilden.

Sumner
Town
Lat: 44-33-30 N **Long:** 91-13-41 W
Pop: 711 (1990); 785 (1980) **Pop Density:** 20.7
Land: 34.4 sq. mi.; **Water:** 0.0 sq. mi.

Trempealeau
Village
ZIP: 54661 **Lat:** 44-00-25 N **Long:** 91-26-09 W
Pop: 1,039 (1990); 956 (1980) **Pop Density:** 944.5
Land: 1.1 sq. mi.; **Water:** 0.1 sq. mi. **Elev:** 691 ft.
Incorporated 1867.
Name origin: From French translation, *la montagne qui trempe a l'eau*, of an Indian word probably meaning 'mountain drenched with water.' Originally known as Reed's Landing, Reed's Town, Montoville, and Mountainville.

*Trempealeau
Town
ZIP: 54661 **Lat:** 44-04-15 N **Long:** 91-27-47 W
Pop: 1,341 (1990); 1,504 (1980) **Pop Density:** 26.2
Land: 51.2 sq. mi.; **Water:** 6.2 sq. mi.

Unity
Town
Lat: 44-33-17 N **Long:** 91-20-51 W
Pop: 473 (1990); 564 (1980) **Pop Density:** 13.7
Land: 34.6 sq. mi.; **Water:** 0.0 sq. mi.

Whitehall
City
ZIP: 54773 **Lat:** 44-21-56 N **Long:** 91-18-49 W
Pop: 1,494 (1990); 1,530 (1980) **Pop Density:** 933.8
Land: 1.6 sq. mi.; **Water:** 0.0 sq. mi. **Elev:** 820 ft.
Incorporated 1941.
Name origin: For Whitehall, IL.

WISCONSIN, Vernon County

Vernon County
County Seat: Viroqua (ZIP: 54665)

Pop: 25,617 (1990); 25,642 (1980)   **Pop Density:** 32.2
Land: 795.0 sq. mi.; **Water:** 21.5 sq. mi.   **Area Code:** 608

On southwestern border of WI, southwest of Madison; organized as Bad Axe County Mar 1, 1851 from Richland and Crawford counties; name changed Mar 22, 1862.

Name origin: For either Mount Vernon, first U.S. President George Washington's (1732–99) home overlooking the Potomac River in VA, or for George Vernon Weeks, a friend of the county judge. Originally for the Bad Ax River, which traverses it.

Bergen — Town
Lat: 43-39-33 N   **Long:** 91-12-27 W
Pop: 1,223 (1990); 1,117 (1980)   **Pop Density:** 35.8
Land: 34.2 sq. mi.; **Water:** 18.6 sq. mi.

Chaseburg — Village
ZIP: 54621   **Lat:** 43-39-17 N   **Long:** 91-05-59 W
Pop: 365 (1990); 279 (1980)   **Pop Density:** 608.3
Land: 0.6 sq. mi.; **Water:** 0.0 sq. mi.   **Elev:** 728 ft.
Incorporated 1922.

Name origin: For P. E. Chase, who settled here in 1854 and started a mill.

Christiana — Town
Lat: 43-41-06 N   **Long:** 90-50-41 W
Pop: 851 (1990); 823 (1980)   **Pop Density:** 25.2
Land: 33.8 sq. mi.; **Water:** 0.1 sq. mi.

Clinton — Town
Lat: 43-41-09 N   **Long:** 90-43-45 W
Pop: 1,093 (1990); 920 (1980)   **Pop Density:** 30.4
Land: 35.9 sq. mi.; **Water:** 0.0 sq. mi.

Coon — Town
Lat: 43-40-50 N   **Long:** 90-58-17 W
Pop: 701 (1990); 757 (1980)   **Pop Density:** 20.1
Land: 34.9 sq. mi.; **Water:** 0.0 sq. mi.

Coon Valley — Village
ZIP: 54623   **Lat:** 43-42-06 N   **Long:** 91-00-36 W
Pop: 817 (1990); 758 (1980)   **Pop Density:** 817.0
Land: 1.0 sq. mi.; **Water:** 0.0 sq. mi.   **Elev:** 735 ft.
Incorporated 1907.

Name origin: For the many raccoons in the area. Originally known as Helgedalen (Helge Valley) for founder Helge Gulbrandson.

De Soto — Village
ZIP: 54624   **Lat:** 43-25-44 N   **Long:** 91-11-45 W
Pop: 253 (1990); 252 (1980)   **Pop Density:** 281.1
Land: 0.9 sq. mi.; **Water:** 0.1 sq. mi.
Incorporated 1886. Part of the town is also in Crawford County.

Name origin: For Hernando de Soto (c. 1500–42), the Spanish explorer who discovered the Mississippi River. Originally known as Winneshiek's Landing for a Winnebago Indian chief.

Forest — Town
Lat: 43-40-43 N   **Long:** 90-29-39 W
Pop: 543 (1990); 551 (1980)   **Pop Density:** 15.1
Land: 36.0 sq. mi.; **Water:** 0.0 sq. mi.

Franklin — Town
Lat: 43-28-35 N   **Long:** 90-54-24 W
Pop: 926 (1990); 1,047 (1980)   **Pop Density:** 18.0
Land: 51.5 sq. mi.; **Water:** 0.0 sq. mi.

Genoa — Village
ZIP: 54632   **Lat:** 43-34-24 N   **Long:** 91-13-32 W
Pop: 266 (1990); 283 (1980)   **Pop Density:** 886.7
Land: 0.3 sq. mi.; **Water:** 0.0 sq. mi.
Incorporated 1935.

Name origin: Named by Italian immigrants who thought the region resembled the Genoa Valley. Previously called Bad Ax, after the river.

*Genoa — Town
ZIP: 54632   **Lat:** 43-32-55 N   **Long:** 91-10-05 W
Pop: 661 (1990); 787 (1980)   **Pop Density:** 18.9
Land: 35.0 sq. mi.; **Water:** 1.3 sq. mi.

Greenwood — Town
Lat: 43-35-46 N   **Long:** 90-22-05 W
Pop: 574 (1990); 546 (1980)   **Pop Density:** 16.0
Land: 35.8 sq. mi.; **Water:** 0.0 sq. mi.

Hamburg — Town
Lat: 43-40-39 N   **Long:** 91-05-23 W
Pop: 712 (1990); 774 (1980)   **Pop Density:** 19.9
Land: 35.8 sq. mi.; **Water:** 0.0 sq. mi.

Harmony — Town
Lat: 43-35-01 N   **Long:** 91-05-21 W
Pop: 551 (1990); 636 (1980)   **Pop Density:** 12.8
Land: 42.9 sq. mi.; **Water:** 0.0 sq. mi.

Hillsboro — City
ZIP: 54634   **Lat:** 43-39-14 N   **Long:** 90-20-15 W
Pop: 1,288 (1990); 1,263 (1980)   **Pop Density:** 1073.3
Land: 1.2 sq. mi.; **Water:** 0.0 sq. mi.   **Elev:** 1001 ft.
Incorporated 1885.

Name origin: For Vilentia Hill, who laid the first claim here in 1850. Originally spelled Hillsborough.

*Hillsboro — Town
ZIP: 54634   **Lat:** 43-41-22 N   **Long:** 90-21-58 W
Pop: 642 (1990); 763 (1980)   **Pop Density:** 18.0
Land: 35.6 sq. mi.; **Water:** 0.0 sq. mi.

Jefferson — Town
Lat: 43-35-00 N   **Long:** 90-58-29 W
Pop: 915 (1990); 919 (1980)   **Pop Density:** 19.5
Land: 46.9 sq. mi.; **Water:** 0.1 sq. mi.

WISCONSIN, Vernon County

Kickapoo — Town
Lat: 43-27-42 N Long: 90-45-00 W
Pop: 472 (1990); 523 (1980) Pop Density: 12.5
Land: 37.9 sq. mi.; Water: 0.0 sq. mi.

La Farge — Village
ZIP: 54639 Lat: 43-34-39 N Long: 90-38-17 W
Pop: 766 (1990); 746 (1980) Pop Density: 766.0
Land: 1.0 sq. mi.; Water: 0.0 sq. mi.
Incorporated 1899.
Name origin: Randomly selected from a list of United States place names. Previously called Corners.

Liberty — Town
Lat: 43-31-42 N Long: 90-44-09 W
Pop: 189 (1990); 171 (1980) Pop Density: 8.2
Land: 23.1 sq. mi.; Water: 0.0 sq. mi.

Ontario — Village
ZIP: 54651 Lat: 43-43-19 N Long: 90-35-34 W
Pop: 407 (1990); 398 (1980) Pop Density: 407.0
Land: 1.0 sq. mi.; Water: 0.0 sq. mi.
Incorporated 1890.
Name origin: Named by O. H. Millard for Ontario County in NY.

Readstown — Village
ZIP: 54652 Lat: 43-26-55 N Long: 90-45-32 W
Pop: 420 (1990); 396 (1980) Pop Density: 233.3
Land: 1.8 sq. mi.; Water: 0.0 sq. mi. Elev: 760 ft.
Platted 1855. Incorporated 1898.
Name origin: For Daniel Read, who platted the village.

Stark — Town
Lat: 43-35-44 N Long: 90-36-34 W
Pop: 259 (1990); 322 (1980) Pop Density: 7.5
Land: 34.4 sq. mi.; Water: 0.0 sq. mi.

Sterling — Town
Lat: 43-28-13 N Long: 91-02-06 W
Pop: 598 (1990); 626 (1980) Pop Density: 13.1
Land: 45.5 sq. mi.; Water: 0.0 sq. mi.

Stoddard — Village
ZIP: 54658 Lat: 43-39-40 N Long: 91-13-06 W
Pop: 775 (1990); 762 (1980) Pop Density: 1291.7
Land: 0.6 sq. mi.; Water: 0.1 sq. mi. Elev: 646 ft.
Incorporated 1911.
Name origin: Named by Henry Hewitt White for Col. S. Stoddard, former mayor of La Crosse, WI.

Union — Town
Lat: 43-36-14 N Long: 90-29-05 W
Pop: 420 (1990); 405 (1980) Pop Density: 11.7
Land: 35.8 sq. mi.; Water: 0.0 sq. mi.

Viola — Village
ZIP: 54664 Lat: 43-30-24 N Long: 90-40-32 W
Pop: 207 (1990); 223 (1980) Pop Density: 345.0
Land: 0.6 sq. mi.; Water: 0.0 sq. mi.
Incorporated 1899. Part of the town is also in Richland County.

Viroqua — City
ZIP: 54665 Lat: 43-33-29 N Long: 90-53-10 W
Pop: 3,922 (1990); 3,716 (1980) Pop Density: 1265.2
Land: 3.1 sq. mi.; Water: 0.0 sq. mi.
Platted 1850. Incorporated 1885.
Name origin: Named in 1854 possibly for the name of an Indian girl. Originally called Farwell for Gov. Farwell.

*Viroqua — Town
ZIP: 54665 Lat: 43-34-58 N Long: 90-50-45 W
Pop: 1,499 (1990); 1,663 (1980) Pop Density: 30.9
Land: 48.5 sq. mi.; Water: 0.0 sq. mi.

Webster — Town
Lat: 43-35-46 N Long: 90-43-34 W
Pop: 529 (1990); 594 (1980) Pop Density: 14.9
Land: 35.4 sq. mi.; Water: 0.0 sq. mi.

Westby — City
ZIP: 54667 Lat: 43-39-10 N Long: 90-51-25 W
Pop: 1,866 (1990); 1,797 (1980) Pop Density: 811.3
Land: 2.3 sq. mi.; Water: 0.0 sq. mi. Elev: 1298 ft.
Incorporated 1920.
Name origin: For Ole T. Westby, who built a store here in 1867.

Wheatland — Town
Lat: 43-27-10 N Long: 91-09-21 W
Pop: 436 (1990); 407 (1980) Pop Density: 16.4
Land: 26.6 sq. mi.; Water: 1.1 sq. mi.

Whitestown — Town
Lat: 43-40-42 N Long: 90-36-32 W
Pop: 471 (1990); 418 (1980) Pop Density: 13.5
Land: 35.0 sq. mi.; Water: 0.0 sq. mi.

WISCONSIN, Vilas County

Vilas County
County Seat: Eagle River (ZIP: 54521)

Pop: 17,707 (1990); 16,535 (1980)   **Pop Density:** 20.3
Land: 872.8 sq. mi.; **Water:** 145.1 sq. mi.   **Area Code:** 715

On central northern border of WI; organized Apr 12, 1893 from Oneida County.
Name origin: For Col. William Freeman Vilas (1840–1908), officer in the Civil War, U.S. postmaster general (1885–88), U.S. secretary of the interior (1888–89), and U.S. senator from WI (1891–97).

Arbor Vitae   Town
Lat: 45-57-30 N   **Long:** 89-40-40 W
Pop: 2,531 (1990); 2,303 (1980)   **Pop Density:** 40.4
Land: 62.6 sq. mi.; **Water:** 8.7 sq. mi.

Boulder Junction   Town
ZIP: 54512   **Lat:** 46-05-37 N   **Long:** 89-40-48 W
Pop: 884 (1990); 934 (1980)   **Pop Density:** 10.8
Land: 81.9 sq. mi.; **Water:** 18.5 sq. mi.

Cloverland   Town
ZIP: 54521   **Lat:** 45-56-39 N   **Long:** 89-22-02 W
Pop: 768 (1990); 692 (1980)   **Pop Density:** 24.5
Land: 31.4 sq. mi.; **Water:** 3.8 sq. mi.

Conover   Town
ZIP: 54519   **Lat:** 46-03-04 N   **Long:** 89-15-52 W
Pop: 932 (1990); 826 (1980)   **Pop Density:** 11.6
Land: 80.6 sq. mi.; **Water:** 7.1 sq. mi.

Eagle River   City
ZIP: 54521   **Lat:** 45-55-28 N   **Long:** 89-15-28 W
Pop: 1,374 (1990); 1,326 (1980)   **Pop Density:** 572.5
Land: 2.4 sq. mi.; **Water:** 0.2 sq. mi.   **Elev:** 1647 ft.
Incorporated 1937.

Lac du Flambeau   Town
ZIP: 54538   **Lat:** 45-58-05 N   **Long:** 89-52-52 W
Pop: 2,433 (1990); 2,190 (1980)   **Pop Density:** 24.3
Land: 100.3 sq. mi.; **Water:** 27.4 sq. mi.

Land O'Lakes   Town
Lat: 46-09-35 N   **Long:** 89-24-10 W
Pop: 839 (1990); 803 (1980)   **Pop Density:** 10.1
Land: 83.0 sq. mi.; **Water:** 12.3 sq. mi.

Lincoln   Town
ZIP: 54521   **Lat:** 45-54-39 N   **Long:** 89-14-49 W
Pop: 2,310 (1990); 2,262 (1980)   **Pop Density:** 70.6
Land: 32.7 sq. mi.; **Water:** 4.6 sq. mi.

Manitowish Waters   Town
ZIP: 54545   **Lat:** 46-06-44 N   **Long:** 89-52-01 W
Pop: 651 (1990); 625 (1980)   **Pop Density:** 21.4
Land: 30.4 sq. mi.; **Water:** 6.1 sq. mi.

Phelps   Town
ZIP: 54554   **Lat:** 46-02-51 N   **Long:** 89-04-10 W
Pop: 1,187 (1990); 1,129 (1980)   **Pop Density:** 12.6
Land: 94.3 sq. mi.; **Water:** 14.0 sq. mi.

Plum Lake   Town
ZIP: 54560   **Lat:** 46-02-53 N   **Long:** 89-28-55 W
Pop: 465 (1990); 408 (1980)   **Pop Density:** 5.2
Land: 88.9 sq. mi.; **Water:** 11.1 sq. mi.

Presque Isle   Town
ZIP: 54557   **Lat:** 46-12-30 N   **Long:** 89-41-55 W
Pop: 471 (1990); 390 (1980)   **Pop Density:** 7.7
Land: 61.4 sq. mi.; **Water:** 13.0 sq. mi.

St. Germain   Town
Lat: 45-56-32 N   **Long:** 89-29-40 W
Pop: 1,319 (1990); 1,176 (1980)   **Pop Density:** 39.5
Land: 33.4 sq. mi.; **Water:** 6.7 sq. mi.

Washington   Town
ZIP: 54521   **Lat:** 45-56-46 N   **Long:** 89-08-12 W
Pop: 1,189 (1990); 1,100 (1980)   **Pop Density:** 28.7
Land: 41.4 sq. mi.; **Water:** 6.1 sq. mi.

Winchester   Town
Lat: 46-13-26 N   **Long:** 89-52-06 W
Pop: 354 (1990); 371 (1980)   **Pop Density:** 7.4
Land: 48.1 sq. mi.; **Water:** 5.5 sq. mi.

Walworth County
County Seat: Elkhorn (ZIP: 53121)

Pop: 75,000 (1990); 71,507 (1980)   **Pop Density:** 135.0
Land: 555.4 sq. mi.; **Water:** 21.2 sq. mi.   **Area Code:** 414
On southeastern border of WI, southwest of Milwaukee; organized Dec 7, 1836 (prior to statehood) from a territorial county.
Name origin: For Col. Reuben Hyde Walworth (1788–1867), officer in the War of 1812, jurist, and U.S. representative from NY (1821–23); unconfirmed nominee to the U.S. Supreme Court (1844).

Bloomfield Town
Lat: 42-32-19 N **Long:** 88-21-54 W
Pop: 3,723 (1990); 3,277 (1980)   **Pop Density:** 111.5
Land: 33.4 sq. mi.; **Water:** 0.8 sq. mi.

Burlington City
ZIP: 53105   **Lat:** 42-41-39 N **Long:** 88-18-44 W
Pop: 4 (1990)   **Pop Density:** 40.0
Land: 0.1 sq. mi.; **Water:** 0.0 sq. mi.
Incorporated 1900. Part of the town is also in Racine County.
Name origin: Named by E. D. Putnam for Burlington, VT.

Como CDP
Lat: 42-36-33 N **Long:** 88-29-42 W
Pop: 1,353 (1990); 1,376 (1980)   **Pop Density:** 451.0
Land: 3.0 sq. mi.; **Water:** 0.5 sq. mi.

Darien Village
ZIP: 53114   **Lat:** 42-36-03 N **Long:** 88-42-36 W
Pop: 1,158 (1990); 1,152 (1980)   **Pop Density:** 1447.5
Land: 0.8 sq. mi.; **Water:** 0.0 sq. mi.   **Elev:** 948 ft.
Incorporated 1951.
Name origin: Originally known as Bruceville, after landowner John Bruce. Renamed about 1838 by settlers for Darien, NY.

*Darien Town
ZIP: 53114   **Lat:** 42-37-10 N **Long:** 88-43-28 W
Pop: 1,490 (1990); 1,495 (1980)   **Pop Density:** 42.7
Land: 34.9 sq. mi.; **Water:** 0.0 sq. mi.

Delavan City
ZIP: 53115   **Lat:** 42-37-36 N **Long:** 88-37-57 W
Pop: 6,073 (1990); 5,684 (1980)   **Pop Density:** 1190.8
Land: 5.1 sq. mi.; **Water:** 0.4 sq. mi.   **Elev:** 940 ft.
Incorporated 1897.
Name origin: For Edward Cornelius Delavan, a prominent temperance leader from NY.

*Delavan Town
ZIP: 53115   **Lat:** 42-37-43 N **Long:** 88-35-23 W
Pop: 4,195 (1990); 4,182 (1980)   **Pop Density:** 156.5
Land: 26.8 sq. mi.; **Water:** 2.8 sq. mi.

Delavan Lake CDP
Lat: 42-36-09 N **Long:** 88-37-08 W
Pop: 2,177 (1990); 1,936 (1980)   **Pop Density:** 622.0
Land: 3.5 sq. mi.; **Water:** 2.4 sq. mi.

East Troy Village
ZIP: 53120   **Lat:** 42-47-20 N **Long:** 88-23-57 W
Pop: 2,664 (1990); 2,385 (1980)   **Pop Density:** 1024.6
Land: 2.6 sq. mi.; **Water:** 0.0 sq. mi.
Incorporated 1900.
Name origin: Named by settlers for their hometown of Troy, NY. Originally part of a larger township of Troy, it split and became East Troy.

*East Troy Town
ZIP: 53120   **Lat:** 42-48-10 N **Long:** 88-21-39 W
Pop: 3,687 (1990); 3,583 (1980)   **Pop Density:** 117.4
Land: 31.4 sq. mi.; **Water:** 1.8 sq. mi.

Elkhorn City
ZIP: 53121   **Lat:** 42-40-15 N **Long:** 88-32-24 W
Pop: 5,337 (1990); 4,605 (1980)   **Pop Density:** 1111.9
Land: 4.8 sq. mi.; **Water:** 0.1 sq. mi.   **Elev:** 1033 ft.
Incorporated 1897.
Name origin: Named in 1836 by Col. Samuel F. Phoenix, who, while traveling through here, saw the horns of an elk that someone had hung in a tree.

Fontana-on-Geneva Lake Village
Lat: 42-32-43 N **Long:** 88-33-59 W
Pop: 1,635 (1990); 1,764 (1980)   **Pop Density:** 563.8
Land: 2.9 sq. mi.; **Water:** 1.1 sq. mi.
Incorporated 1924.
Name origin: Named by pioneers from what they thought was a French term meaning 'place of many springs.'

Geneva Town
Lat: 42-37-43 N **Long:** 88-28-45 W
Pop: 3,472 (1990); 3,933 (1980)   **Pop Density:** 113.8
Land: 30.5 sq. mi.; **Water:** 1.5 sq. mi.

Genoa City Village
ZIP: 53128   **Lat:** 42-30-01 N **Long:** 88-19-34 W
Pop: 1,277 (1990); 1,202 (1980)   **Pop Density:** 912.1
Land: 1.4 sq. mi.; **Water:** 0.0 sq. mi.
Incorporated 1901. Part of the town is also in Kenosha County.
Name origin: For Genoa, NY.

Lafayette Town
Lat: 42-43-01 N **Long:** 88-29-12 W
Pop: 1,276 (1990); 1,024 (1980)   **Pop Density:** 36.8
Land: 34.7 sq. mi.; **Water:** 0.0 sq. mi.

La Grange Town
Lat: 42-48-10 N **Long:** 88-35-20 W
Pop: 1,643 (1990); 1,661 (1980)   **Pop Density:** 47.9
Land: 34.3 sq. mi.; **Water:** 1.4 sq. mi.

Lake Geneva City
ZIP: 53147   **Lat:** 42-35-19 N **Long:** 88-25-46 W
Pop: 5,979 (1990); 5,612 (1980)   **Pop Density:** 1272.1
Land: 4.7 sq. mi.; **Water:** 0.8 sq. mi.
Incorporated 1883.
Name origin: Named by settler John Brink, for the village of Geneva on Seneca Lake in NY. Previously called Muck-Suck

or Big Foot, for a Potawatomi chief, and Gros Pied by the French.

Linn
Town
Lat: 42-32-20 N Long: 88-28-53 W
Pop: 2,062 (1990); 2,064 (1980) Pop Density: 71.8
Land: 28.7 sq. mi.; Water: 5.1 sq. mi.

Lyons
Town
Lat: 42-37-38 N Long: 88-22-10 W
Pop: 2,579 (1990); 2,659 (1980) Pop Density: 74.3
Land: 34.7 sq. mi.; Water: 0.2 sq. mi.

Pell Lake
CDP
Lat: 42-32-27 N Long: 88-21-28 W
Pop: 2,018 (1990); 1,826 (1980) Pop Density: 531.1
Land: 3.8 sq. mi.; Water: 0.2 sq. mi.

Potter Lake
CDP
Lat: 42-49-17 N Long: 88-20-55 W
Pop: 1,096 (1990); 1,068 (1980) Pop Density: 782.9
Land: 1.4 sq. mi.; Water: 0.2 sq. mi.

Powers Lake
CDP
Lat: 42-32-26 N Long: 88-18-34 W
Pop: 292 (1990); 320 (1980) Pop Density: 365.0
Land: 0.8 sq. mi.; Water: 0.2 sq. mi.
Part of the town is also in Kenosha County.

Richmond
Town
Lat: 42-42-51 N Long: 88-43-45 W
Pop: 1,405 (1990); 1,649 (1980) Pop Density: 39.8
Land: 35.3 sq. mi.; Water: 0.7 sq. mi.

Sharon
Village
ZIP: 53585 Lat: 42-30-05 N Long: 88-43-48 W
Pop: 1,250 (1990); 1,280 (1980) Pop Density: 1388.9
Land: 0.9 sq. mi.; Water: 0.0 sq. mi. Elev: 1027 ft.
Incorporated 1892.

Name origin: Probably for Sharon, NY, former home of settlers.

*Sharon
Town
ZIP: 53585 Lat: 42-32-26 N Long: 88-43-03 W
Pop: 1,016 (1990); 945 (1980) Pop Density: 28.5
Land: 35.6 sq. mi.; Water: 0.0 sq. mi.

Spring Prairie
Town
Lat: 42-42-34 N Long: 88-22-14 W
Pop: 1,752 (1990); 1,777 (1980) Pop Density: 48.9
Land: 35.8 sq. mi.; Water: 0.1 sq. mi.

Sugar Creek
Town
Lat: 42-42-38 N Long: 88-35-51 W
Pop: 2,661 (1990); 2,599 (1980) Pop Density: 78.5
Land: 33.9 sq. mi.; Water: 0.8 sq. mi.

Troy
Town
Lat: 42-48-13 N Long: 88-28-44 W
Pop: 2,051 (1990); 1,794 (1980) Pop Density: 58.9
Land: 34.8 sq. mi.; Water: 0.7 sq. mi.

Walworth
Village
ZIP: 53184 Lat: 42-31-49 N Long: 88-35-50 W
Pop: 1,614 (1990); 1,607 (1980) Pop Density: 1241.5
Land: 1.3 sq. mi.; Water: 0.0 sq. mi. Elev: 998 ft.
Incorporated 1901.

Name origin: For the county, which was named for soldier and statesman Reuben Hyde Walworth (1788–1867). Previously called Douglass Corners, for settler Christopher Douglass.

*Walworth
Town
ZIP: 53184 Lat: 42-32-18 N Long: 88-36-25 W
Pop: 1,341 (1990); 1,443 (1980) Pop Density: 46.1
Land: 29.1 sq. mi.; Water: 0.6 sq. mi.

Whitewater
City
ZIP: 53190 Lat: 42-49-53 N Long: 88-44-07 W
Pop: 10,170 (1990); 9,098 (1980) Pop Density: 2676.3
Land: 3.8 sq. mi.; Water: 0.3 sq. mi.

In southern WI, 18 mi. northeast of Janesville. Incorporated 1885. Part of the town is also in Jefferson County.

Name origin: From the Indian term for the river, *Wau-be-gan-naw-o-cat* probably meaning 'white water.'

*Whitewater
Town
ZIP: 53190 Lat: 42-47-50 N Long: 88-42-19 W
Pop: 1,378 (1990); 1,270 (1980) Pop Density: 44.7
Land: 30.8 sq. mi.; Water: 1.0 sq. mi.

Williams Bay
Village
ZIP: 53191 Lat: 42-34-35 N Long: 88-32-34 W
Pop: 2,108 (1990); 1,763 (1980) Pop Density: 878.3
Land: 2.4 sq. mi.; Water: 0.8 sq. mi.
Incorporated 1919.

Name origin: For settler Israel Williams.

Washburn County
County Seat: Shell Lake (ZIP: 54871)

Pop: 13,772 (1990); 13,174 (1980)
Land: 809.7 sq. mi.; **Water:** 43.4 sq. mi.
Pop Density: 17.0
Area Code: 715
In northwestern WI; organized Mar 27, 1883 from Burnett County.
Name origin: For Cadwallader Colden Washburn (1818–82), U.S. representative (1855–61; 1867–71) and governor of WI (1872–74).

Barronett — Town
Lat: 45-40-40 N Long: 91-57-59 W
Pop: 373 (1990); 371 (1980) **Pop Density:** 11.4
Land: 32.8 sq. mi.; **Water:** 0.9 sq. mi.

Bashaw — Town
Lat: 45-46-18 N Long: 91-58-32 W
Pop: 756 (1990); 724 (1980) **Pop Density:** 22.6
Land: 33.5 sq. mi.; **Water:** 0.4 sq. mi.

Bass Lake — Town
Lat: 45-56-43 N Long: 91-36-10 W
Pop: 337 (1990); 252 (1980) **Pop Density:** 10.4
Land: 32.3 sq. mi.; **Water:** 0.8 sq. mi.

Beaver Brook — Town
Lat: 45-46-22 N Long: 91-50-29 W
Pop: 580 (1990); 603 (1980) **Pop Density:** 17.9
Land: 32.4 sq. mi.; **Water:** 0.5 sq. mi.

Birchwood — Village
ZIP: 54817 Lat: 45-39-25 N Long: 91-33-07 W
Pop: 443 (1990); 437 (1980) **Pop Density:** 402.7
Land: 1.1 sq. mi.; **Water:** 0.2 sq. mi. **Elev:** 1264 ft.
Incorporated 1921.
Name origin: Named by George M. Huss, president of the Soo Line Railroad, for the many white birch trees that grew along the lakeshore here.

*Birchwood — Town
ZIP: 54817 Lat: 45-43-57 N Long: 91-36-27 W
Pop: 329 (1990); 252 (1980) **Pop Density:** 5.2
Land: 63.8 sq. mi.; **Water:** 6.1 sq. mi.

Brooklyn — Town
Lat: 46-00-30 N Long: 91-51-10 W
Pop: 276 (1990); 273 (1980) **Pop Density:** 7.7
Land: 35.7 sq. mi.; **Water:** 0.6 sq. mi.

Casey — Town
Lat: 45-56-43 N Long: 91-58-07 W
Pop: 401 (1990); 404 (1980) **Pop Density:** 12.9
Land: 31.1 sq. mi.; **Water:** 3.0 sq. mi.

Chicog — Town
Lat: 46-01-47 N Long: 91-57-57 W
Pop: 182 (1990); 168 (1980) **Pop Density:** 4.2
Land: 43.6 sq. mi.; **Water:** 2.0 sq. mi.

Crystal — Town
Lat: 45-51-16 N Long: 91-43-04 W
Pop: 279 (1990); 276 (1980) **Pop Density:** 7.9
Land: 35.1 sq. mi.; **Water:** 0.6 sq. mi.

Evergreen — Town
Lat: 45-51-37 N Long: 91-58-34 W
Pop: 910 (1990); 798 (1980) **Pop Density:** 27.1
Land: 33.6 sq. mi.; **Water:** 1.3 sq. mi.

Frog Creek — Town
Lat: 46-07-31 N Long: 91-41-12 W
Pop: 155 (1990); 142 (1980) **Pop Density:** 2.2
Land: 71.0 sq. mi.; **Water:** 0.6 sq. mi.

Gull Lake — Town
Lat: 46-00-35 N Long: 91-43-31 W
Pop: 148 (1990); 141 (1980) **Pop Density:** 4.2
Land: 35.1 sq. mi.; **Water:** 1.2 sq. mi.

Long Lake — Town
Lat: 45-41-08 N Long: 91-43-20 W
Pop: 583 (1990); 508 (1980) **Pop Density:** 17.9
Land: 32.6 sq. mi.; **Water:** 5.1 sq. mi.

Madge — Town
Lat: 45-46-34 N Long: 91-43-58 W
Pop: 349 (1990); 317 (1980) **Pop Density:** 10.9
Land: 32.0 sq. mi.; **Water:** 2.1 sq. mi.

Minong — Village
ZIP: 54859 Lat: 46-05-54 N Long: 91-49-26 W
Pop: 521 (1990); 557 (1980) **Pop Density:** 434.2
Land: 1.2 sq. mi.; **Water:** 0.0 sq. mi. **Elev:** 1064 ft.
Incorporated 1915.
Name origin: From an Indian term meaning either 'a good high place,' 'a place where blueberries grow,' or 'a pleasant valley.'

*Minong — Town
ZIP: 54859 Lat: 46-06-58 N Long: 91-55-36 W
Pop: 730 (1990); 761 (1980) **Pop Density:** 11.3
Land: 64.5 sq. mi.; **Water:** 6.8 sq. mi.

Sarona — Town
ZIP: 54870 Lat: 45-41-20 N Long: 91-51-16 W
Pop: 391 (1990); 394 (1980) **Pop Density:** 12.3
Land: 31.9 sq. mi.; **Water:** 1.4 sq. mi.

Shell Lake — City
ZIP: 54871 Lat: 45-44-18 N Long: 91-53-56 W
Pop: 1,161 (1990); 1,135 (1980) **Pop Density:** 187.3
Land: 6.2 sq. mi.; **Water:** 4.0 sq. mi.
Incorporated 1961.
Name origin: For the nearby lake, shaped like a shell. Previously called *Mokokesese Sahkiagin* 'frog's navel,' Frog Lake, and Summit.

Spooner — City
ZIP: 54801 Lat: 45-49-28 N Long: 91-53-36 W
Pop: 2,464 (1990); 2,365 (1980) **Pop Density:** 849.7
Land: 2.9 sq. mi.; **Water:** 0.1 sq. mi. **Elev:** 1065 ft.
Incorporated 1909.
Name origin: For John C. Spooner (1843–1919), a lawyer for the Chicago, St. Paul, Minneapolis and Omaha Railroad Corporation, who later became a U.S. senator.

WISCONSIN, Washburn County

*Spooner — Town
ZIP: 54801 Lat: 45-50-48 N Long: 91-50-37 W
Pop: 644 (1990); 600 (1980) Pop Density: 33.9
Land: 19.0 sq. mi.; Water: 2.0 sq. mi.

Springbrook — Town
ZIP: 54875 Lat: 45-56-26 N Long: 91-43-25 W
Pop: 403 (1990); 441 (1980) Pop Density: 11.8
Land: 34.2 sq. mi.; Water: 0.5 sq. mi.

Stinnett — Town
Lat: 46-01-36 N Long: 91-36-40 W
Pop: 202 (1990); 179 (1980) Pop Density: 5.9
Land: 34.4 sq. mi.; Water: 1.2 sq. mi.

Stone Lake — Town
Lat: 45-51-30 N Long: 91-35-39 W
Pop: 446 (1990); 379 (1980) Pop Density: 13.2
Land: 33.7 sq. mi.; Water: 1.2 sq. mi.

Trego — Town
ZIP: 54888 Lat: 45-55-10 N Long: 91-50-59 W
Pop: 709 (1990); 697 (1980) Pop Density: 19.7
Land: 35.9 sq. mi.; Water: 0.8 sq. mi.

Washington County
County Seat: West Bend (ZIP: 53095)

Pop: 95,328 (1990); 84,848 (1980) Pop Density: 221.3
Land: 430.8 sq. mi.; Water: 5.1 sq. mi. Area Code: 414
In southeastern WI, northwest of Milwaukee; organized Dec 7, 1836 (prior to statehood) from a territorial county.
Name origin: For George Washington (1732–99), American patriot and first U.S. president.

Addison — Town
Lat: 43-24-46 N Long: 88-20-25 W
Pop: 3,051 (1990); 2,834 (1980) Pop Density: 84.3
Land: 36.2 sq. mi.; Water: 0.0 sq. mi.

Barton — Town
Lat: 43-27-15 N Long: 88-13-49 W
Pop: 2,637 (1990); 2,493 (1980) Pop Density: 131.2
Land: 20.1 sq. mi.; Water: 0.2 sq. mi.

Erin — Town
Lat: 43-14-16 N Long: 88-21-10 W
Pop: 2,817 (1990); 2,455 (1980) Pop Density: 78.5
Land: 35.9 sq. mi.; Water: 0.4 sq. mi.

Farmington — Town
Lat: 43-30-20 N Long: 88-06-20 W
Pop: 2,523 (1990); 2,386 (1980) Pop Density: 69.3
Land: 36.4 sq. mi.; Water: 0.3 sq. mi.

Germantown — Village
ZIP: 53022 Lat: 43-14-09 N Long: 88-07-13 W
Pop: 13,658 (1990); 10,729 (1980) Pop Density: 397.0
Land: 34.4 sq. mi.; Water: 0.0 sq. mi. Elev: 863 ft.
In southeastern WI, 17 mi. northwest of Milwaukee. Incorporated 1927.
Name origin: For the German settlers who made up the entire village.

*Germantown — Town
ZIP: 53022 Lat: 43-16-14 N Long: 88-09-21 W
Pop: 258 (1990); 267 (1980) Pop Density: 151.8
Land: 1.7 sq. mi.; Water: 0.0 sq. mi.

Hartford — City
ZIP: 53027 Lat: 43-19-26 N Long: 88-23-04 W
Pop: 8,179 (1990); 7,159 (1980) Pop Density: 1902.1
Land: 4.3 sq. mi.; Water: 0.1 sq. mi.
Incorporated 1883. Part of the town is also in Dodge County.
Name origin: Possibly for the ford at heart-shaped Pike Lake nearby or for Hartford, CT. Previously called Wright after a Mr. Wright.

*Hartford — Town
ZIP: 53027 Lat: 43-19-33 N Long: 88-21-17 W
Pop: 3,243 (1990); 3,269 (1980) Pop Density: 103.0
Land: 31.5 sq. mi.; Water: 0.7 sq. mi.

Jackson — Village
ZIP: 53037 Lat: 43-19-15 N Long: 88-09-49 W
Pop: 2,486 (1990); 1,817 (1980) Pop Density: 1462.4
Land: 1.7 sq. mi.; Water: 0.0 sq. mi. Elev: 896 ft.
Incorporated 1912.
Name origin: For Stonewall Jackson (1824–63), Confederate general who stood "firm as a stone wall" against the Union forces in the Civil War.

*Jackson — Town
ZIP: 53037 Lat: 43-18-57 N Long: 88-07-01 W
Pop: 3,172 (1990); 3,180 (1980) Pop Density: 91.1
Land: 34.8 sq. mi.; Water: 0.1 sq. mi.

Kewaskum — Village
ZIP: 53040 Lat: 43-31-13 N Long: 88-13-38 W
Pop: 2,514 (1990); 2,381 (1980) Pop Density: 1795.7
Land: 1.4 sq. mi.; Water: 0.0 sq. mi.
Incorporated 1895. Part of the town is also in Fond du Lac County.
Name origin: From a Potawatomi chief's name that may mean either 'a man able to turn fate whichever way he wants' or 'his tracks are toward home.'

*Kewaskum — Town
ZIP: 53040 Lat: 43-30-43 N Long: 88-13-14 W
Pop: 1,139 (1990); 1,243 (1980) Pop Density: 49.7
Land: 22.9 sq. mi.; Water: 0.0 sq. mi.

Milwaukee — City
ZIP: 53201 **Lat:** 43-11-40 N **Long:** 88-03-55 W
Pop: 0 (1990); 2 (1980)
Land: 0.03 sq. mi.; **Water:** 0.0 sq. mi. **Elev:** 634 ft.
On the southeastern coast of WI, on Lake Michigan. Platted 1835; settled 1836; incorporated 1846. Largest city in WI, a major U.S. industrial center, important Great Lakes port. Diverse manufacturing city (automobile parts, beer, electrical equipment, farm and factory machinery); insurance and banking; trade (beer, dairy products, and machinery). Part of the city is also in Milwaukee and Waukesha counties.
Name origin: From an Algonquian word of uncertain meaning; possibly 'rich beautiful land' or 'gathering place by the river.'

Newburg — Village
ZIP: 53060 **Lat:** 43-25-53 N **Long:** 88-02-51 W
Pop: 853 (1990); 688 (1980) **Pop Density:** 1218.6
Land: 0.7 sq. mi.; **Water:** 0.0 sq. mi. **Elev:** 850 ft.
Incorporated 1973. Part of the town is also in Ozaukee County.

Polk — Town
Lat: 43-19-18 N **Long:** 88-14-09 W
Pop: 3,540 (1990); 3,486 (1980) **Pop Density:** 105.4
Land: 33.6 sq. mi.; **Water:** 0.3 sq. mi.

Richfield — Town
ZIP: 53076 **Lat:** 43-14-03 N **Long:** 88-14-25 W
Pop: 8,993 (1990); 8,390 (1980) **Pop Density:** 250.5
Land: 35.9 sq. mi.; **Water:** 0.5 sq. mi.

Slinger — Village
ZIP: 53086 **Lat:** 43-19-55 N **Long:** 88-17-08 W
Pop: 2,340 (1990); 1,612 (1980) **Pop Density:** 1063.6
Land: 2.2 sq. mi.; **Water:** 0.0 sq. mi. **Elev:** 1069 ft.
Incorporated 1869.
Name origin: For B. Schleisinger Weil, who purchased land here. Previously called Schleisingerville, the name was shortened to Slinger in 1921.

Trenton — Town
Lat: 43-24-01 N **Long:** 88-05-44 W
Pop: 4,028 (1990); 3,914 (1980) **Pop Density:** 117.4
Land: 34.3 sq. mi.; **Water:** 0.1 sq. mi.

Wayne — Town
Lat: 43-30-16 N **Long:** 88-21-06 W
Pop: 1,374 (1990); 1,471 (1980) **Pop Density:** 38.4
Land: 35.8 sq. mi.; **Water:** 0.0 sq. mi.

West Bend — City
ZIP: 53095 **Lat:** 43-25-22 N **Long:** 88-11-03 W
Pop: 23,916 (1990); 21,484 (1980) **Pop Density:** 2391.6
Land: 10.0 sq. mi.; **Water:** 0.2 sq. mi. **Elev:** 893 ft.
In southeastern WI, 29 mi. northwest of Milwaukee. Incorporated 1885.
Name origin: For a bend in the Milwaukee River. The city combines the early settlements of Salisbury's Mills (later called Barton) and West Bend.

*West Bend — Town
ZIP: 53095 **Lat:** 43-23-44 N **Long:** 88-13-54 W
Pop: 4,607 (1990); 3,588 (1980) **Pop Density:** 267.8
Land: 17.2 sq. mi.; **Water:** 2.0 sq. mi.

Waukesha County
County Seat: Waukesha (**ZIP:** 53188)

Pop: 304,715 (1990), 280,203 (1980) **Pop Density:** 548.4
Land: 555.6 sq. mi.; **Water:** 24.9 sq. mi. **Area Code:** 414
In southeastern WI, west of Milwaukee; organized Jan 31, 1846 (prior to statehood) from Milwaukee County.
Name origin: For the Fox River and the Fox Indian tribe, from Potawatomi *wakusheg* 'foxes.'

Big Bend — Village
ZIP: 53103 **Lat:** 42-52-56 N **Long:** 88-12-14 W
Pop: 1,299 (1990); 1,345 (1980) **Pop Density:** 1623.8
Land: 0.8 sq. mi.; **Water:** 0.0 sq. mi.
Incorporated 1928.
Name origin: Named by the Indians for the bend in the Fox River, which flows on the west side of the village.

Brookfield — City
ZIP: 53045 **Lat:** 43-03-46 N **Long:** 88-07-11 W
Pop: 35,184 (1990); 34,035 (1980) **Pop Density:** 1312.8
Land: 26.8 sq. mi.; **Water:** 0.0 sq. mi. **Elev:** 828 ft.
In southeastern WI, a western suburb of Milwaukee. Incorporated 1954.
Name origin: For its descriptive connotations.

*Brookfield — Town
Lat: 43-03-01 N **Long:** 88-10-19 W
Pop: 4,232 (1990); 4,364 (1980) **Pop Density:** 729.7
Land: 5.8 sq. mi.; **Water:** 0.0 sq. mi.

Butler — Village
ZIP: 53007 **Lat:** 43-06-30 N **Long:** 88-04-20 W
Pop: 2,079 (1990); 2,059 (1980) **Pop Density:** 2598.8
Land: 0.8 sq. mi.; **Water:** 0.0 sq. mi.
Incorporated 1913.

Chenequa — Village
Lat: 43-07-24 N **Long:** 88-22-51 W
Pop: 601 (1990); 532 (1980) **Pop Density:** 171.7
Land: 3.5 sq. mi.; **Water:** 1.1 sq. mi.
Incorporated 1928.
Name origin: Possibly from a Potawatomi Indian term meaning 'big tree grove,' a Winnebago Indian term meaning 'village,' or a Chippewa Indian term meaning 'Indian maiden.'

WISCONSIN, Waukesha County

Delafield — City
ZIP: 53018 **Lat:** 43-04-10 N **Long:** 88-23-30 W
Pop: 5,347 (1990); 4,083 (1980) **Pop Density:** 574.9
Land: 9.3 sq. mi.; **Water:** 1.6 sq. mi.
Incorporated 1959.

Name origin: For Charles Delafield, who started a mulberry grove here in 1843. Originally known as Nehaamabin or Nemahbin by the Indians and Hayopolis by its settlers.

*Delafield — Town
ZIP: 53018 **Lat:** 43-02-52 N **Long:** 88-20-39 W
Pop: 5,735 (1990); 4,597 (1980) **Pop Density:** 294.1
Land: 19.5 sq. mi.; **Water:** 2.1 sq. mi.

Dousman — Village
ZIP: 53118 **Lat:** 43-00-53 N **Long:** 88-28-16 W
Pop: 1,277 (1990); 1,153 (1980) **Pop Density:** 1277.0
Land: 1.0 sq. mi.; **Water:** 0.0 sq. mi.
Incorporated 1917.

Name origin: For either Talbot C. or Col. John Dousman. Previously called Bull Frog Station, for the marshy land at the railroad station here.

Eagle — Village
ZIP: 53119 **Lat:** 42-52-46 N **Long:** 88-28-16 W
Pop: 1,182 (1990); 1,008 (1980) **Pop Density:** 1182.0
Land: 1.0 sq. mi.; **Water:** 0.0 sq. mi. **Elev:** 949 ft.
Incorporated 1899.

Name origin: For a bald eagle seen by prospectors on the prairie here in 1836. Previously called Eagle Prairie, Eagleville, and Eagle Center.

*Eagle — Town
ZIP: 53119 **Lat:** 42-52-55 N **Long:** 88-29-25 W
Pop: 2,028 (1990); 1,758 (1980) **Pop Density:** 58.1
Land: 34.9 sq. mi.; **Water:** 0.4 sq. mi.

Elm Grove — Village
ZIP: 53122 **Lat:** 43-02-51 N **Long:** 88-05-11 W
Pop: 6,261 (1990); 6,735 (1980) **Pop Density:** 1897.3
Land: 3.3 sq. mi.; **Water:** 0.0 sq. mi. **Elev:** 746 ft.
Incorporated 1955.

Name origin: For its descriptive connotations.

Genesee — Town
ZIP: 53149 **Lat:** 42-58-22 N **Long:** 88-21-59 W
Pop: 5,986 (1990); 5,126 (1980) **Pop Density:** 183.1
Land: 32.7 sq. mi.; **Water:** 0.1 sq. mi.

Hartland — Village
ZIP: 53029 **Lat:** 43-05-53 N **Long:** 88-20-40 W
Pop: 6,906 (1990); 5,559 (1980) **Pop Density:** 2227.7
Land: 3.1 sq. mi.; **Water:** 0.0 sq. mi.
Incorporated 1891.

Name origin: Probably for its descriptive connotations, the heartland, with a spelling variation. Previously called Warren, for settler Steve Warren; and Hersheyville and Hershey's Mills, for Mr. Christ Hershey.

Lac La Belle — Village
Lat: 43-08-43 N **Long:** 88-31-32 W
Pop: 258 (1990); 289 (1980) **Pop Density:** 516.0
Land: 0.5 sq. mi.; **Water:** 0.0 sq. mi.
Incorporated 1931.

Name origin: From French 'beautiful lake.'

Lannon — Village
ZIP: 53046 **Lat:** 43-09-04 N **Long:** 88-09-44 W
Pop: 924 (1990); 987 (1980) **Pop Density:** 385.0
Land: 2.4 sq. mi.; **Water:** 0.0 sq. mi.
Incorporated 1930.

Name origin: For Bill Lannon, who built a farm and the post office around 1840. Originally known as Lannon Springs and Stone City, for the limestone quarries here.

Lisbon — Town
ZIP: 53089 **Lat:** 43-09-04 N **Long:** 88-14-45 W
Pop: 8,277 (1990); 8,352 (1980) **Pop Density:** 258.7
Land: 32.0 sq. mi.; **Water:** 0.0 sq. mi.

Menomonee Falls — Village
ZIP: 53051 **Lat:** 43-08-49 N **Long:** 88-07-33 W
Pop: 26,840 (1990); 27,845 (1980) **Pop Density:** 806.0
Land: 33.3 sq. mi.; **Water:** 0.0 sq. mi.

In southeastern WI, northwest of Milwaukee. Incorporated 1892.

Name origin: For the Indian tribe that lived here; name may mean 'wild rice.'

Merton — Village
ZIP: 53056 **Lat:** 43-08-27 N **Long:** 88-18-48 W
Pop: 1,199 (1990); 1,045 (1980) **Pop Density:** 521.3
Land: 2.3 sq. mi.; **Water:** 0.0 sq. mi.
Incorporated 1922.

Name origin: Named in 1849 for Moreton, England, with a spelling variation. Originally called Warren, for Sylvanus Warren and his family.

*Merton — Town
ZIP: 53029 **Lat:** 43-09-24 N **Long:** 88-21-31 W
Pop: 6,430 (1990); 6,025 (1980) **Pop Density:** 243.6
Land: 26.4 sq. mi.; **Water:** 2.5 sq. mi.

Milwaukee — City
Lat: 43-07-19 N **Long:** 88-04-05 W
Pop: 0 (1990)
Land: 0.1 sq. mi.; **Water:** 0.0 sq. mi.

On the southeastern coast of WI, on Lake Michigan. Platted 1835; settled 1836; incorporated 1846. Largest city in WI, a major U.S. industrial center, important Great Lakes port. Diverse manufacturing city (automobile parts, beer, electrical equipment, farm and factory machinery); insurance and banking; trade (beer, dairy products, and machinery). Part of the city is also in Milwaukee and Washington counties.

Name origin: From an Algonquian word of uncertain meaning; possibly 'rich beautiful land' or 'gathering place by the river.'

Mukwonago — Village
ZIP: 53149 **Lat:** 42-51-58 N **Long:** 88-19-52 W
Pop: 4,457 (1990); 4,014 (1980) **Pop Density:** 1782.8
Land: 2.5 sq. mi.; **Water:** 0.1 sq. mi. **Elev:** 837 ft.
Incorporated 1905.

Name origin: From an Indian term probably meaning 'place of the bear.' Previously spelled Mequanigo.

*Mukwonago — Town
ZIP: 53149 **Lat:** 42-53-07 N **Long:** 88-22-04 W
Pop: 5,974 (1990); 4,979 (1980) **Pop Density:** 179.9
Land: 33.2 sq. mi.; **Water:** 1.1 sq. mi.

Muskego
City
ZIP: 53150 **Lat:** 42-53-27 N **Long:** 88-07-22 W
Pop: 16,813 (1990); 15,277 (1980) **Pop Density:** 538.9
Land: 31.2 sq. mi.; **Water:** 4.7 sq. mi.
Incorporated 1964.
Name origin: From the original Potawatomi settlement here, the name possibly meaning 'fishing place,' 'sunfish,' 'swamp,' or 'cranberry bog.'

Nashotah
Village
ZIP: 53058 **Lat:** 43-05-34 N **Long:** 88-24-04 W
Pop: 567 (1990); 513 (1980) **Pop Density:** 354.4
Land: 1.6 sq. mi.; **Water:** 0.0 sq. mi.
Incorporated 1957.
Name origin: For the Upper and Lower Nashotah lakes, from an Indian term meaning 'twins.'

New Berlin
City
ZIP: 53151 **Lat:** 42-58-22 N **Long:** 88-07-45 W
Pop: 33,592 (1990); 30,529 (1980) **Pop Density:** 912.8
Land: 36.8 sq. mi.; **Water:** 0.1 sq. mi.
In southeastern WI, west of Milwaukee. Incorporated 1959.
Name origin: Named in 1840 for the NY hometown of settler Sidney Evans.

North Prairie
Village
ZIP: 53153 **Lat:** 42-56-13 N **Long:** 88-23-44 W
Pop: 1,322 (1990); 938 (1980) **Pop Density:** 944.3
Land: 1.4 sq. mi.; **Water:** 0.0 sq. mi.
Settled 1836. Incorporated 1919.
Name origin: For the beautiful prairie land here. *North* was added to distinguish it from another prairie two miles to the south.

Oconomowoc
City
ZIP: 53066 **Lat:** 43-06-09 N **Long:** 88-29-48 W
Pop: 10,993 (1990); 9,909 (1980) **Pop Density:** 1895.3
Land: 5.8 sq. mi.; **Water:** 0.5 sq. mi. **Elev:** 873 ft.
In southeastern WI, 13 mi. southeast of Watertown. Incorporated 1875.
Name origin: Probably from the Indian term *Coo-no-mo-wauk,* possibly meaning 'beaver dam.' Other interpretations include 'waterfall,' 'beautiful waters,' or 'river of lakes' referring to the string of lakes joined by the Oconomowoc River.

*Oconomowoc
Town
ZIP: 53066 **Lat:** 43-09-28 N **Long:** 88-28-17 W
Pop: 7,323 (1990); 7,340 (1980) **Pop Density:** 244.1
Land: 30.0 sq. mi.; **Water:** 3.3 sq. mi.

Oconomowoc Lake
Village
Lat: 43-05-55 N **Long:** 88-27-18 W
Pop: 493 (1990); 524 (1980) **Pop Density:** 273.9
Land: 1.8 sq. mi.; **Water:** 1.3 sq. mi.
Incorporated 1959.

Okauchee Lake
CDP
Lat: 43-07-24 N **Long:** 88-26-26 W
Pop: 3,819 (1990); 3,958 (1980) **Pop Density:** 1091.1
Land: 3.5 sq. mi.; **Water:** 1.5 sq. mi.

Ottawa
Town
Lat: 42-58-36 N **Long:** 88-29-08 W
Pop: 2,988 (1990); 2,795 (1980) **Pop Density:** 85.9
Land: 34.8 sq. mi.; **Water:** 0.6 sq. mi. **Elev:** 927 ft.

Pewaukee
Village
ZIP: 53072 **Lat:** 43-05-08 N **Long:** 88-15-07 W
Pop: 4,941 (1990); 4,637 (1980) **Pop Density:** 1235.3
Land: 4.0 sq. mi.; **Water:** 0.3 sq. mi.
Incorporated 1876.
Name origin: For the lake, from the Potawatomi term *Pewaukeewinick* probably meaning 'snail lake.'

*Pewaukee
Town
ZIP: 53072 **Lat:** 43-03-53 N **Long:** 88-14-36 W
Pop: 9,621 (1990); 8,922 (1980) **Pop Density:** 407.7
Land: 23.6 sq. mi.; **Water:** 1.5 sq. mi.

Summit
Town
Lat: 43-03-04 N **Long:** 88-28-43 W
Pop: 4,003 (1990); 4,050 (1980) **Pop Density:** 152.8
Land: 26.2 sq. mi.; **Water:** 2.8 sq. mi.

Sussex
Village
ZIP: 53089 **Lat:** 43-08-09 N **Long:** 88-13-04 W
Pop: 5,039 (1990); 3,482 (1980) **Pop Density:** 1292.1
Land: 3.9 sq. mi.; **Water:** 0.0 sq. mi.
Incorporated 1924.
Name origin: For Sussex, England, the former home of the Weaver brothers, who laid out the village.

Vernon
Town
ZIP: 53103 **Lat:** 42-53-28 N **Long:** 88-14-44 W
Pop: 7,549 (1990); 6,372 (1980) **Pop Density:** 222.7
Land: 33.9 sq. mi.; **Water:** 0.5 sq. mi.

Wales
Village
ZIP: 53183 **Lat:** 43-00-17 N **Long:** 88-22-39 W
Pop: 2,471 (1990); 1,992 (1980) **Pop Density:** 1074.3
Land: 2.3 sq. mi.; **Water:** 0.0 sq. mi. **Elev:** 1002 ft.
Incorporated 1922.
Name origin: For the home country of Welsh immigrants.

Waukesha
City
ZIP: 53186 **Lat:** 43-00-44 N **Long:** 88-14-17 W
Pop: 56,958 (1990); 50,365 (1980) **Pop Density:** 3292.4
Land: 17.3 sq. mi.; **Water:** 0.0 sq. mi. **Elev:** 821 ft.
In southeastern WI, 15 mi. west of Milwaukee. Incorporated 1895.
Name origin: County seat. From Potawatomi Indian *wakusheg,* 'foxes,' for the Fox Indian tribe. Previously called Prairieville.

*Waukesha
Town
ZIP: 53186 **Lat:** 42-57-52 N **Long:** 88-14-56 W
Pop: 7,566 (1990); 6,668 (1980) **Pop Density:** 295.5
Land: 25.6 sq. mi.; **Water:** 0.1 sq. mi.

WISCONSIN, Waupaca County — *American Places Dictionary*

Waupaca County
County Seat: Waupaca (ZIP: 54981)

Pop: 46,104 (1990); 42,831 (1980) **Pop Density:** 61.4
Land: 751.1 sq. mi.; **Water:** 14.2 sq. mi. **Area Code:** 715

In east-central WI, west of Green Bay; organized Feb 17, 1851 from Winnebago and Brown counties.

Name origin: From an Indian name of various interpretations; the most probable is 'place of clear water.'

Bear Creek — Town
Lat: 44-32-47 N Long: 88-48-10 W
Pop: 787 (1990); 820 (1980) **Pop Density:** 21.4
Land: 36.7 sq. mi.; **Water:** 0.0 sq. mi.

Big Falls — Village
ZIP: 54926 Lat: 44-37-10 N Long: 89-01-00 W
Pop: 75 (1990); 107 (1980) **Pop Density:** 150.0
Land: 0.5 sq. mi.; **Water:** 0.0 sq. mi.
Founded 1862. Incorporated 1925.

Name origin: For the falls in the Little Wolf River, which runs through the village.

Caledonia — Town
Lat: 44-17-39 N Long: 88-47-22 W
Pop: 1,177 (1990); 1,040 (1980) **Pop Density:** 42.3
Land: 27.8 sq. mi.; **Water:** 0.2 sq. mi.

Chain o' Lakes-King — CDP
Lat: 44-19-50 N Long: 89-10-04 W
Pop: 1,667 (1990) **Pop Density:** 396.9
Land: 4.2 sq. mi.; **Water:** 1.3 sq. mi.

Clintonville — City
ZIP: 54929 Lat: 44-37-17 N Long: 88-45-03 W
Pop: 4,351 (1990); 4,567 (1980) **Pop Density:** 1087.8
Land: 4.0 sq. mi.; **Water:** 0.1 sq. mi. **Elev:** 825 ft.
Incorporated 1887.

Name origin: For the first permanent settlers, the Norman Clinton family. Previously called Pigeon Lake.

Dayton — Town
Lat: 44-17-27 N Long: 89-09-52 W
Pop: 1,992 (1990); 1,514 (1980) **Pop Density:** 56.6
Land: 35.2 sq. mi.; **Water:** 1.2 sq. mi.

Dupont — Town
Lat: 44-38-12 N Long: 88-55-22 W
Pop: 634 (1990); 615 (1980) **Pop Density:** 18.2
Land: 34.9 sq. mi.; **Water:** 0.3 sq. mi.

Embarrass — Village
ZIP: 54933 Lat: 44-40-14 N Long: 88-42-12 W
Pop: 461 (1990); 496 (1980) **Pop Density:** 384.2
Land: 1.2 sq. mi.; **Water:** 0.0 sq. mi.
Incorporated 1895.

Name origin: For the Embarrass River, a mistranslation of French *Rivière Embarrass,* 'obstacle river,' referring to the roots and snags that impeded the flow of logs.

Farmington — Town
Lat: 44-22-38 N Long: 89-09-53 W
Pop: 3,602 (1990); 2,959 (1980) **Pop Density:** 103.2
Land: 34.9 sq. mi.; **Water:** 1.0 sq. mi.

Fremont — Village
ZIP: 54940 Lat: 44-15-34 N Long: 88-52-14 W
Pop: 632 (1990); 510 (1980) **Pop Density:** 632.0
Land: 1.0 sq. mi.; **Water:** 0.1 sq. mi.
Incorporated 1882.

Name origin: For Col. John C. Frémont (1813–90), who explored CA and fought in the Mexican War.

*Fremont — Town
ZIP: 54940 Lat: 44-15-49 N Long: 88-53-27 W
Pop: 561 (1990); 618 (1980) **Pop Density:** 29.4
Land: 19.1 sq. mi.; **Water:** 1.0 sq. mi.

Harrison — Town
Lat: 44-38-19 N Long: 89-10-13 W
Pop: 432 (1990); 450 (1980) **Pop Density:** 11.7
Land: 36.9 sq. mi.; **Water:** 0.1 sq. mi.

Helvetia — Town
Lat: 44-32-40 N Long: 89-02-11 W
Pop: 587 (1990); 568 (1980) **Pop Density:** 16.4
Land: 35.9 sq. mi.; **Water:** 0.3 sq. mi.

Iola — Village
ZIP: 54945 Lat: 44-30-33 N Long: 89-07-34 W
Pop: 1,125 (1990); 957 (1980) **Pop Density:** 803.6
Land: 1.4 sq. mi.; **Water:** 0.2 sq. mi. **Elev:** 955 ft.
Incorporated 1892.

Name origin: For a Potawatomi Indian girl, Iola, who was said to be the daughter of Old Red Bird, brother of Chief Waupaca.

*Iola — Town
ZIP: 54945 Lat: 44-33-04 N Long: 89-10-18 W
Pop: 637 (1990); 702 (1980) **Pop Density:** 18.8
Land: 33.8 sq. mi.; **Water:** 0.8 sq. mi.

Larrabee — Town
Lat: 44-38-07 N Long: 88-48-00 W
Pop: 1,388 (1990); 1,254 (1980) **Pop Density:** 41.3
Land: 33.6 sq. mi.; **Water:** 0.2 sq. mi.

Lebanon — Town
Lat: 44-27-29 N Long: 88-47-55 W
Pop: 1,290 (1990); 1,168 (1980) **Pop Density:** 35.7
Land: 36.1 sq. mi.; **Water:** 0.0 sq. mi.

Lind — Town
Lat: 44-17-10 N Long: 89-02-36 W
Pop: 1,157 (1990); 1,038 (1980) **Pop Density:** 32.2
Land: 35.9 sq. mi.; **Water:** 0.2 sq. mi.

Little Wolf — Town
Lat: 44-27-24 N Long: 88-55-49 W
Pop: 1,326 (1990); 1,138 (1980) **Pop Density:** 39.5
Land: 33.6 sq. mi.; **Water:** 0.4 sq. mi.

Manawa — City
ZIP: 54949 Lat: 44-27-40 N Long: 88-55-13 W
Pop: 1,169 (1990); 1,205 (1980) Pop Density: 730.6
Land: 1.6 sq. mi.; Water: 0.1 sq. mi.
Incorporated 1954.
Name origin: For the hero of an Indian legend. Previously called Brickley and Elberton, for postmaster Elbert Scott.

Marion — City
ZIP: 54950 Lat: 44-40-16 N Long: 88-53-14 W
Pop: 1,242 (1990); 1,348 (1980) Pop Density: 653.7
Land: 1.9 sq. mi.; Water: 0.1 sq. mi.
Name origin: Either for Marion, OH; Gen. Francis Marion (c. 1732–95) of the Revolutionary War; or for settler Marion Ransdell. Previously called Perry's Mills for J.W. Perry, who had a sawmill here.

Matteson — Town
Lat: 44-37-55 N Long: 88-40-07 W
Pop: 889 (1990); 844 (1980) Pop Density: 24.2
Land: 36.7 sq. mi.; Water: 0.5 sq. mi.

Mukwa — Town
Lat: 44-22-23 N Long: 88-48-04 W
Pop: 2,304 (1990); 1,946 (1980) Pop Density: 73.1
Land: 31.5 sq. mi.; Water: 1.7 sq. mi.

New London — City
ZIP: 54961 Lat: 44-23-40 N Long: 88-44-49 W
Pop: 5,321 (1990); 4,941 (1980) Pop Density: 1773.7
Land: 3.0 sq. mi.; Water: 0.0 sq. mi. Elev: 789 ft.
Established 1852. Incorporated 1877. Part of the town is also in Outagamie County.
Name origin: For New London, CT, the birthplace of the father of Reeder Smith, one of the city developers.

Ogdensburg — Village
ZIP: 54962 Lat: 44-27-14 N Long: 89-01-55 W
Pop: 220 (1990); 214 (1980) Pop Density: 220.0
Land: 1.0 sq. mi.; Water: 0.1 sq. mi. Elev: 861 ft.
Founded 1848. Incorporated 1912.
Name origin: For founder Judge Ogden.

Royalton — Town
Lat: 44-22-22 N Long: 88-54-49 W
Pop: 1,458 (1990); 1,432 (1980) Pop Density: 43.1
Land: 33.8 sq. mi.; Water: 2.3 sq. mi.

St. Lawrence — Town
Lat: 44-27-26 N Long: 89-02-38 W
Pop: 697 (1990); 608 (1980) Pop Density: 20.1
Land: 34.7 sq. mi.; Water: 0.3 sq. mi.

Scandinavia — Village
ZIP: 54977 Lat: 44-27-38 N Long: 89-08-47 W
Pop: 298 (1990); 292 (1980) Pop Density: 331.1
Land: 0.9 sq. mi.; Water: 0.1 sq. mi. Elev: 931 ft.
Incorporated 1894.
Name origin: For the former home of most of the early settlers.

*Scandinavia — Town
ZIP: 54977 Lat: 44-27-23 N Long: 89-09-35 W
Pop: 890 (1990); 772 (1980) Pop Density: 26.2
Land: 34.0 sq. mi.; Water: 0.4 sq. mi.

Union — Town
Lat: 44-32-57 N Long: 88-55-20 W
Pop: 733 (1990); 784 (1980) Pop Density: 20.4
Land: 35.9 sq. mi.; Water: 0.2 sq. mi.

Waupaca — City
ZIP: 54981 Lat: 44-21-16 N Long: 89-04-31 W
Pop: 4,957 (1990); 4,472 (1980) Pop Density: 953.3
Land: 5.2 sq. mi.; Water: 0.1 sq. mi.
Incorporated 1875.
Name origin: From an Indian term of disputed meaning, the most probable being 'place of clear water.'

*Waupaca — Town
ZIP: 54981 Lat: 44-23-20 N Long: 89-01-39 W
Pop: 1,111 (1990); 1,040 (1980) Pop Density: 35.6
Land: 31.2 sq. mi.; Water: 0.1 sq. mi.

Weyauwega — City
ZIP: 54983 Lat: 44-19-21 N Long: 88-55-43 W
Pop: 1,665 (1990); 1,549 (1980) Pop Density: 1513.6
Land: 1.1 sq. mi.; Water: 0.1 sq. mi.
Incorporated 1939.
Name origin: From an Indian term probably meaning 'here we rest.'

*Weyauwega — Town
ZIP: 54983 Lat: 44-18-11 N Long: 88-55-34 W
Pop: 653 (1990); 559 (1980) Pop Density: 32.5
Land: 20.1 sq. mi.; Water: 1.9 sq. mi.

Wyoming — Town
Lat: 44-38-00 N Long: 89-02-40 W
Pop: 283 (1990); 304 (1980) Pop Density: 7.8
Land: 36.1 sq. mi.; Water: 0.1 sq. mi.

Waushara County
County Seat: Wautoma (ZIP: 54982)

Pop: 19,385 (1990); 18,526 (1980) **Pop Density:** 31.0
Land: 626.1 sq. mi.; **Water:** 11.4 sq. mi. **Area Code:** 414

In east-central WI, west of Lake Winnebago; organized Feb 15, 1851 from Marquette County.

Name origin: From an Indian word possibly meaning 'good land river' or for a Winnebago word meaning 'foxes.' Corruption of the name of a Winnebago chief, an ancient Winnebago village, and the Indian name for Fox Lake.

Aurora — Town
Lat: 44-01-14 N **Long:** 88-56-25 W
Pop: 846 (1990); 890 (1980) **Pop Density:** 24.6
Land: 34.4 sq. mi.; **Water:** 0.4 sq. mi.

Berlin — City
ZIP: 54923 **Lat:** 43-59-24 N **Long:** 88-56-20 W
Pop: 67 (1990); 91 (1980) **Pop Density:** 111.7
Land: 0.6 sq. mi.; **Water:** 0.1 sq. mi. **Elev:** 764 ft.
Incorporated 1857. Part of the town is also in Green Lake County.
Name origin: Named in 1851 for Berlin, Germany. Previously called Strong's Landing, and then Strongville.

Bloomfield — Town
Lat: 44-12-17 N **Long:** 88-56-59 W
Pop: 922 (1990); 931 (1980) **Pop Density:** 26.0
Land: 35.4 sq. mi.; **Water:** 0.5 sq. mi.

Coloma — Village
ZIP: 54930 **Lat:** 44-02-00 N **Long:** 89-31-15 W
Pop: 383 (1990); 367 (1980) **Pop Density:** 348.2
Land: 1.1 sq. mi.; **Water:** 0.0 sq. mi. **Elev:** 1044 ft.
Incorporated 1939.
Name origin: For Coloma, CA, where gold was discovered. Previously called Coloma Corners and Coloma Station.

*Coloma — Town
ZIP: 54930 **Lat:** 44-01-45 N **Long:** 89-32-41 W
Pop: 499 (1990); 437 (1980) **Pop Density:** 15.1
Land: 33.1 sq. mi.; **Water:** 0.2 sq. mi.

Dakota — Town
Lat: 44-01-06 N **Long:** 89-18-11 W
Pop: 1,092 (1990); 994 (1980) **Pop Density:** 32.6
Land: 33.5 sq. mi.; **Water:** 0.6 sq. mi.

Deerfield — Town
Lat: 44-06-30 N **Long:** 89-25-30 W
Pop: 454 (1990); 445 (1980) **Pop Density:** 13.1
Land: 34.7 sq. mi.; **Water:** 0.3 sq. mi.

Hancock — Village
ZIP: 54943 **Lat:** 44-08-04 N **Long:** 89-31-12 W
Pop: 382 (1990); 419 (1980) **Pop Density:** 347.3
Land: 1.1 sq. mi.; **Water:** 0.1 sq. mi. **Elev:** 1089 ft.
Settled 1854. Incorporated 1902.
Name origin: Reason for the present name is unknown. Previously called Sylvester after a man by that name.

*Hancock — Town
ZIP: 54943 **Lat:** 44-06-40 N **Long:** 89-32-29 W
Pop: 467 (1990); 426 (1980) **Pop Density:** 14.0
Land: 33.4 sq. mi.; **Water:** 0.3 sq. mi.

Leon — Town
Lat: 44-06-32 N **Long:** 89-04-02 W
Pop: 992 (1990); 844 (1980) **Pop Density:** 27.6
Land: 36.0 sq. mi.; **Water:** 0.3 sq. mi.

Lohrville — Village
ZIP: 54970 **Lat:** 44-02-16 N **Long:** 89-07-15 W
Pop: 368 (1990); 336 (1980) **Pop Density:** 306.7
Land: 1.2 sq. mi.; **Water:** 0.0 sq. mi. **Elev:** 802 ft.
Incorporated 1910.
Name origin: For Lohr Granite Company, a customer of the Rothman Quarry, which was located here.

Marion — Town
Lat: 44-00-56 N **Long:** 89-11-22 W
Pop: 1,478 (1990); 1,333 (1980) **Pop Density:** 44.0
Land: 33.6 sq. mi.; **Water:** 1.4 sq. mi.

Mount Morris — Town
Lat: 44-06-42 N **Long:** 89-11-14 W
Pop: 767 (1990); 685 (1980) **Pop Density:** 22.4
Land: 34.2 sq. mi.; **Water:** 1.0 sq. mi.

Oasis — Town
Lat: 44-11-47 N **Long:** 89-25-14 W
Pop: 389 (1990); 403 (1980) **Pop Density:** 11.1
Land: 35.0 sq. mi.; **Water:** 0.3 sq. mi.

Plainfield — Village
ZIP: 54966 **Lat:** 44-12-50 N **Long:** 89-29-39 W
Pop: 839 (1990); 813 (1980) **Pop Density:** 645.4
Land: 1.3 sq. mi.; **Water:** 0.0 sq. mi.
Incorporated 1882.
Name origin: For Elijah C. Waterman's former home in Plainfield, VT. Originally known as Norwich.

*Plainfield — Town
ZIP: 54966 **Lat:** 44-11-57 N **Long:** 89-32-15 W
Pop: 529 (1990); 574 (1980) **Pop Density:** 15.6
Land: 34.0 sq. mi.; **Water:** 0.0 sq. mi.

Poysippi — Town
ZIP: 54967 **Lat:** 44-06-27 N **Long:** 88-56-55 W
Pop: 929 (1990); 913 (1980) **Pop Density:** 28.8
Land: 32.3 sq. mi.; **Water:** 3.6 sq. mi.
Name origin: For the stream running through the town; an Indian name probably meaning 'pine river.'

Redgranite — Village
ZIP: 54970 **Lat:** 44-03-01 N **Long:** 89-06-09 W
Pop: 1,009 (1990); 976 (1980) **Pop Density:** 504.5
Land: 2.0 sq. mi.; **Water:** 0.0 sq. mi. **Elev:** 789 ft.
Incorporated 1904.
Name origin: For the red granite stone in the quarry around which the village is built.

Richford
Town
ZIP: 54930   **Lat:** 44-01-27 N   **Long:** 89-25-48 W
Pop: 455 (1990); 404 (1980)   **Pop Density:** 13.2
Land: 34.6 sq. mi.; **Water:** 0.2 sq. mi.

Rose
Town
Lat: 44-11-57 N   **Long:** 89-19-11 W
Pop: 486 (1990); 515 (1980)   **Pop Density:** 13.9
Land: 34.9 sq. mi.; **Water:** 0.1 sq. mi.

Saxeville
Town
Lat: 44-12-40 N   **Long:** 89-04-20 W
Pop: 846 (1990); 776 (1980)   **Pop Density:** 23.4
Land: 36.1 sq. mi.; **Water:** 0.5 sq. mi.

Springwater
Town
Lat: 44-11-57 N   **Long:** 89-10-49 W
Pop: 1,088 (1990); 924 (1980)   **Pop Density:** 32.4
Land: 33.6 sq. mi.; **Water:** 1.3 sq. mi.

Warren
Town
Lat: 44-01-40 N   **Long:** 89-04-11 W
Pop: 550 (1990); 573 (1980)   **Pop Density:** 16.8
Land: 32.7 sq. mi.; **Water:** 0.1 sq. mi.

Wautoma
City
ZIP: 54982   **Lat:** 44-04-11 N   **Long:** 89-17-33 W
Pop: 1,784 (1990); 1,629 (1980)   **Pop Density:** 938.9
Land: 1.9 sq. mi.; **Water:** 0.0 sq. mi.   **Elev:** 867 ft.
Incorporated 1902.
Name origin: From the Indian term *wau* meaning 'good,' 'life,' or 'earth,' and *tomah* probably meaning 'land of Tomah,' an Indian chief.

*Wautoma
Town
ZIP: 54982   **Lat:** 44-06-21 N   **Long:** 89-18-35 W
Pop: 1,088 (1990); 1,087 (1980)   **Pop Density:** 31.8
Land: 34.2 sq. mi.; **Water:** 0.1 sq. mi.

Wild Rose
Village
ZIP: 54984   **Lat:** 44-10-34 N   **Long:** 89-14-52 W
Pop: 676 (1990); 741 (1980)   **Pop Density:** 520.0
Land: 1.3 sq. mi.; **Water:** 0.0 sq. mi.
Incorporated 1904.
Name origin: Named by settlers from Rose, NY.

Winnebago County
County Seat: Oshkosh (ZIP: 54901)

Pop: 140,320 (1990); 131,772 (1980)   **Pop Density:** 319.9
Land: 438.6 sq. mi.; **Water:** 140.1 sq. mi.   **Area Code:** 414
In east-central WI, west of Lake Winnebago; organized Jan 6, 1840 (prior to statehood) from Brown County.
Name origin: For the Winnebago Indians, a tribe of Siouan linguistic stock; their name believed to mean 'fish eaters.'

Algoma
Town
Lat: 44-01-45 N   **Long:** 88-36-59 W
Pop: 3,442 (1990); 3,249 (1980)   **Pop Density:** 315.8
Land: 10.9 sq. mi.; **Water:** 2.6 sq. mi.

Appleton
City
ZIP: 54911   **Lat:** 44-14-25 N   **Long:** 88-24-57 W
Pop: 443 (1990); 5 (1980)   **Pop Density:** 1476.7
Land: 0.3 sq. mi.; **Water:** 0.0 sq. mi.
In eastern WI on the Fox River, 17 mi. north of Oshkosh. Incorporated 1857. Part of the town is also in Calumet and Outagamie counties.
Name origin: For Samuel Appleton, one of the founders of Lawrence University.

Black Wolf
Town
Lat: 43-56-09 N   **Long:** 88-28-42 W
Pop: 2,154 (1990); 2,318 (1980)   **Pop Density:** 137.2
Land: 15.7 sq. mi.; **Water:** 26.3 sq. mi.

Clayton
Town
Lat: 44-11-31 N   **Long:** 88-35-04 W
Pop: 2,264 (1990); 2,353 (1980)   **Pop Density:** 62.0
Land: 36.5 sq. mi.; **Water:** 0.0 sq. mi.

Menasha
City
ZIP: 54952   **Lat:** 44-12-41 N   **Long:** 88-26-18 W
Pop: 14,638 (1990); 14,728 (1980)   **Pop Density:** 3404.2
Land: 4.3 sq. mi.; **Water:** 1.4 sq. mi.
In eastern WI on Lake Winnebago and Fox River, 5 mi. south of Appleton. Incorporated 1874. Part of the town is also in Calumet County.
Name origin: From the Menominee Indian term possibly meaning 'thorn' or 'island.'

*Menasha
Town
ZIP: 54952   **Lat:** 44-13-17 N   **Long:** 88-28-22 W
Pop: 13,975 (1990); 12,307 (1980)   **Pop Density:** 1109.1
Land: 12.6 sq. mi.; **Water:** 1.6 sq. mi.

Neenah
City
ZIP: 54956   **Lat:** 44-10-10 N   **Long:** 88-28-19 W
Pop: 23,219 (1990); 22,432 (1980)   **Pop Density:** 3137.7
Land: 7.4 sq. mi.; **Water:** 0.5 sq. mi.
In eastern WI on Lake Winnebago, 7 mi. south of Appleton. Incorporated 1873.
Name origin: Previously called Winnebago Rapids. From the Winnebago Indian term probably meaning 'running water.'

*Neenah
Town
ZIP: 54956   **Lat:** 44-09-18 N   **Long:** 88-27-50 W
Pop: 2,691 (1990); 2,864 (1980)   **Pop Density:** 274.6
Land: 9.8 sq. mi.; **Water:** 8.9 sq. mi.

Nekimi
Town
Lat: 43-56-20 N   **Long:** 88-35-22 W
Pop: 1,525 (1990); 1,516 (1980)   **Pop Density:** 50.7
Land: 30.1 sq. mi.; **Water:** 0.0 sq. mi.

Nepeuskun
Town
Lat: 43-56-40 N Long: 88-49-36 W
Pop: 647 (1990); 682 (1980)   Pop Density: 20.3
Land: 31.9 sq. mi.; Water: 4.2 sq. mi.

Omro
City
ZIP: 54963   Lat: 44-02-20 N Long: 88-44-29 W
Pop: 2,836 (1990); 2,763 (1980)   Pop Density: 1418.0
Land: 2.0 sq. mi.; Water: 0.1 sq. mi.
Platted 1849. Incorporated 1944.
Name origin: For Indian trader Charles Omro. Previously called Smalley's Landing and Beckwith Town, for settler Nelson Beckwith.

*Omro
Town
ZIP: 54963   Lat: 44-01-50 N Long: 88-42-44 W
Pop: 1,616 (1990); 1,684 (1980)   Pop Density: 48.7
Land: 33.2 sq. mi.; Water: 2.5 sq. mi.

Oshkosh
City
ZIP: 54901   Lat: 44-01-03 N Long: 88-33-14 W
Pop: 55,006 (1990); 49,620 (1980)   Pop Density: 3073.0
Land: 17.9 sq. mi.; Water: 2.1 sq. mi.
In east-central WI on the western shore of Lake Winnebago. Incorporated 1853.
Name origin: For Oskosh (1759–1858), Menominee Indian chief and leader of a band by this name.

*Oshkosh
Town
Lat: 44-03-02 N Long: 88-30-26 W
Pop: 4,655 (1990); 4,420 (1980)   Pop Density: 334.9
Land: 13.9 sq. mi.; Water: 49.2 sq. mi.

Poygan
Town
Lat: 44-07-27 N Long: 88-49-20 W
Pop: 824 (1990); 898 (1980)   Pop Density: 35.4
Land: 23.3 sq. mi.; Water: 18.3 sq. mi.

Rushford
Town
Lat: 44-01-17 N Long: 88-48-59 W
Pop: 1,361 (1990); 1,420 (1980)   Pop Density: 38.8
Land: 35.1 sq. mi.; Water: 0.5 sq. mi.

Utica
Town
Lat: 43-56-18 N Long: 88-42-09 W
Pop: 1,046 (1990); 1,038 (1980)   Pop Density: 29.1
Land: 35.9 sq. mi.; Water: 0.0 sq. mi.

Vinland
Town
Lat: 44-07-35 N Long: 88-32-01 W
Pop: 1,688 (1990); 1,632 (1980)   Pop Density: 58.2
Land: 29.0 sq. mi.; Water: 7.3 sq. mi.

Winchester
Town
ZIP: 54947   Lat: 44-12-24 N Long: 88-42-41 W
Pop: 1,433 (1990); 1,261 (1980)   Pop Density: 40.0
Land: 35.8 sq. mi.; Water: 0.7 sq. mi.

Winneconne
Village
ZIP: 54986   Lat: 44-06-43 N Long: 88-42-42 W
Pop: 2,059 (1990); 1,935 (1980)   Pop Density: 1470.7
Land: 1.4 sq. mi.; Water: 0.4 sq. mi.   Elev: 753 ft.
Incorporated 1887.
Name origin: From an Indian term probaly meaning 'place of skulls,' which came from a battle here in which the Sauk and Fox Indians fought against the French and the Menominee and Chippewa Indians.

*Winneconne
Town
ZIP: 54986   Lat: 44-07-12 N Long: 88-42-23 W
Pop: 1,761 (1990); 1,595 (1980)   Pop Density: 79.7
Land: 22.1 sq. mi.; Water: 11.5 sq. mi.

Wolf River
Town
Lat: 44-12-56 N Long: 88-49-39 W
Pop: 1,037 (1990); 1,052 (1980)   Pop Density: 35.3
Land: 29.4 sq. mi.; Water: 1.1 sq. mi.

Wood County
County Seat: Wisconsin Rapids (ZIP: 54494)

Pop: 73,605 (1990); 72,799 (1980)   Pop Density: 92.8
Land: 792.9 sq. mi.; Water: 16.7 sq. mi.   Area Code: 715
In central WI, southwest of Wausau; organized Mar 29, 1856 from Portage County.
Name origin: For Joseph Wood, legislator, county judge, and mayor of Grand Rapids.

Arpin
Village
ZIP: 54410   Lat: 44-32-28 N Long: 90-01-57 W
Pop: 312 (1990); 361 (1980)   Pop Density: 390.0
Land: 0.8 sq. mi.; Water: 0.0 sq. mi.
Incorporated 1978.
Name origin: For John D. and Antoine Arpin, who settled about one mile east of the present village site.

*Arpin
Town
ZIP: 54410   Lat: 44-33-19 N Long: 90-01-22 W
Pop: 806 (1990); 764 (1980)   Pop Density: 24.4
Land: 33.0 sq. mi.; Water: 0.0 sq. mi.

Auburndale
Village
ZIP: 54412   Lat: 44-37-41 N Long: 90-00-53 W
Pop: 665 (1990); 641 (1980)   Pop Density: 316.7
Land: 2.1 sq. mi.; Water: 0.0 sq. mi.   Elev: 1220 ft.
Incorporated 1881.
Name origin: For an English name brought by settlers or possibly for the auburn-haired daughters of prominent resident W.D. Connors.

*Auburndale
Town
ZIP: 54412   Lat: 44-38-11 N Long: 90-00-54 W
Pop: 844 (1990); 942 (1980)   Pop Density: 26.1
Land: 32.3 sq. mi.; Water: 0.0 sq. mi.

WISCONSIN, Wood County

Biron
Village
ZIP: 54494   Lat: 44-25-42 N   Long: 89-45-51 W
Pop: 794 (1990); 698 (1980)   Pop Density: 189.0
Land: 4.2 sq. mi.; Water: 1.7 sq. mi.   Elev: 1026 ft.
Incorporated 1910.
Name origin: For Francis Biron, who purchased a mill here in 1848.

Cameron
Town
Lat: 44-37-10 N   Long: 90-10-20 W
Pop: 522 (1990); 590 (1980)   Pop Density: 68.7
Land: 7.6 sq. mi.; Water: 0.0 sq. mi.

Cary
Town
Lat: 44-28-09 N   Long: 90-15-18 W
Pop: 385 (1990); 382 (1980)   Pop Density: 11.0
Land: 35.0 sq. mi.; Water: 0.1 sq. mi.

Cranmoor
Town
Lat: 44-20-41 N   Long: 90-00-56 W
Pop: 185 (1990); 234 (1980)   Pop Density: 5.0
Land: 36.7 sq. mi.; Water: 5.6 sq. mi.

Dexter
Town
Lat: 44-22-39 N   Long: 90-08-14 W
Pop: 354 (1990); 429 (1980)   Pop Density: 10.4
Land: 34.2 sq. mi.; Water: 1.3 sq. mi.

Grand Rapids
Town
ZIP: 54494   Lat: 44-22-39 N   Long: 89-45-59 W
Pop: 7,071 (1990); 7,319 (1980)   Pop Density: 312.9
Land: 22.6 sq. mi.; Water: 0.2 sq. mi.

Hansen
Town
ZIP: 54489   Lat: 44-27-49 N   Long: 90-01-31 W
Pop: 698 (1990); 705 (1980)   Pop Density: 20.6
Land: 33.9 sq. mi.; Water: 0.0 sq. mi.

Hewitt
Village
ZIP: 54441   Lat: 44-38-42 N   Long: 90-06-18 W
Pop: 595 (1990); 470 (1980)   Pop Density: 743.8
Land: 0.8 sq. mi.; Water: 0.0 sq. mi.
Incorporated 1973.
Name origin: For a lumberman named Hewitt, who had a railroad sidetrack built here. Previously called Number 28, Kreuser, and Hewitt Side Track.

Hiles
Town
Lat: 44-22-52 N   Long: 90-15-09 W
Pop: 144 (1990); 194 (1980)   Pop Density: 4.1
Land: 34.8 sq. mi.; Water: 0.5 sq. mi.

Lake Wazeecha
CDP
Lat: 44-22-16 N   Long: 89-45-22 W
Pop: 2,278 (1990); 2,176 (1980)   Pop Density: 599.5
Land: 3.8 sq. mi.; Water: 0.2 sq. mi.

Lincoln
Town
Lat: 44-38-26 N   Long: 90-15-18 W
Pop: 1,429 (1990); 1,269 (1980)   Pop Density: 41.7
Land: 34.3 sq. mi.; Water: 0.0 sq. mi.

Marshfield
City
ZIP: 54449   Lat: 44-39-39 N   Long: 90-10-18 W
Pop: 18,859 (1990); 18,053 (1980)   Pop Density: 1848.9
Land: 10.2 sq. mi.; Water: 0.0 sq. mi.
Incorporated 1883. Part of the town is also in Marathon County.
Name origin: For J.J. Marsh, or for his uncle, Samuel Marsh, one of the early owners of the land.

*Marshfield
Town
Lat: 44-38-43 N   Long: 90-06-53 W
Pop: 769 (1990); 784 (1980)   Pop Density: 45.0
Land: 17.1 sq. mi.; Water: 0.0 sq. mi.

Milladore
Village
ZIP: 54454   Lat: 44-36-16 N   Long: 89-51-14 W
Pop: 314 (1990); 240 (1980)   Pop Density: 314.0
Land: 1.0 sq. mi.; Water: 0.0 sq. mi.
Incorporated 1933. Part of the town is also in Portage County.
Name origin: From a word coined by the residents of Mill Creek who had to change their village's name because there was already a Mill Creek in the state.

*Milladore
Town
ZIP: 54454   Lat: 44-38-39 N   Long: 89-53-45 W
Pop: 719 (1990); 760 (1980)   Pop Density: 21.1
Land: 34.0 sq. mi.; Water: 0.0 sq. mi.

Nekoosa
City
ZIP: 54457   Lat: 44-18-47 N   Long: 89-54-28 W
Pop: 2,557 (1990); 2,519 (1980)   Pop Density: 752.1
Land: 3.4 sq. mi.; Water: 0.0 sq. mi.
Incorporated 1926.
Name origin: Named in 1893 from an Indian term probably meaning 'running water.' Previously called Whitney's Rapids, Point Boss, Point Basse, and Boss.

Pittsville
City
ZIP: 54466   Lat: 44-26-25 N   Long: 90-07-47 W
Pop: 838 (1990); 810 (1980)   Pop Density: 419.0
Land: 2.0 sq. mi.; Water: 0.0 sq. mi.   Elev: 1032 ft.
Incorporated 1887.
Name origin: For Oliver Wright Pitts, who settled here in 1856 and built a sawmill. Previously called Pitt's Mill.

Port Edwards
Village
ZIP: 54469   Lat: 44-20-47 N   Long: 89-50-46 W
Pop: 1,848 (1990); 2,077 (1980)   Pop Density: 308.0
Land: 6.0 sq. mi.; Water: 1.3 sq. mi.   Elev: 975 ft.
Incorporated 1902.
Name origin: For John Edwards, Sr., who built a sawmill here in 1840. Previously called Frenchtown for the large French population.

*Port Edwards
Town
ZIP: 54469   Lat: 44-17-07 N   Long: 89-58-45 W
Pop: 1,351 (1990); 1,387 (1980)   Pop Density: 35.0
Land: 38.6 sq. mi.; Water: 0.6 sq. mi.

Remington
Town
Lat: 44-17-53 N   Long: 90-12-09 W
Pop: 304 (1990); 299 (1980)   Pop Density: 4.4
Land: 69.4 sq. mi.; Water: 2.2 sq. mi.

Richfield
Town
Lat: 44-33-17 N   Long: 90-09-00 W
Pop: 1,344 (1990); 1,235 (1980)   Pop Density: 38.6
Land: 34.8 sq. mi.; Water: 0.0 sq. mi.

Rock
Town
Lat: 44-33-41 N   Long: 90-15-06 W
Pop: 764 (1990); 745 (1980)   Pop Density: 22.1
Land: 34.5 sq. mi.; Water: 0.0 sq. mi.

WISCONSIN, Wood County

Rudolph
Village
ZIP: 54475 **Lat:** 44-29-50 N **Long:** 89-48-06 W
Pop: 451 (1990); 392 (1980) **Pop Density:** 451.0
Land: 1.0 sq. mi.; **Water:** 0.0 sq. mi. **Elev:** 1138 ft.
Settled c. 1840. Incorporated 1960.
Name origin: Named in 1856 for Frederick Rudolph Hecox, the first white boy born here.

*Rudolph
Town
ZIP: 54475 **Lat:** 44-28-21 N **Long:** 89-47-33 W
Pop: 1,180 (1990); 1,385 (1980) **Pop Density:** 39.6
Land: 29.8 sq. mi.; **Water:** 0.0 sq. mi.

Saratoga
Town
Lat: 44-17-33 N **Long:** 89-48-39 W
Pop: 4,775 (1990); 4,363 (1980) **Pop Density:** 96.7
Land: 49.4 sq. mi.; **Water:** 1.8 sq. mi.

Seneca
Town
Lat: 44-23-43 N **Long:** 89-56-48 W
Pop: 1,133 (1990); 1,245 (1980) **Pop Density:** 35.1
Land: 32.3 sq. mi.; **Water:** 0.2 sq. mi.

Sherry
Town
ZIP: 54454 **Lat:** 44-33-36 N **Long:** 89-53-51 W
Pop: 787 (1990); 790 (1980) **Pop Density:** 22.3
Land: 35.3 sq. mi.; **Water:** 0.1 sq. mi.

Sigel
Town
Lat: 44-28-05 N **Long:** 89-54-04 W
Pop: 1,192 (1990); 1,332 (1980) **Pop Density:** 33.
Land: 35.5 sq. mi.; **Water:** 0.0 sq. mi.

Vesper
Village
ZIP: 54489 **Lat:** 44-28-51 N **Long:** 89-58-02 W
Pop: 598 (1990); 554 (1980) **Pop Density:** 543.
Land: 1.1 sq. mi.; **Water:** 0.0 sq. mi. **Elev:** 1110 ft
Incorporated 1948.
Name origin: Named by the post office c. 1882 as a replacement for the suggested name of Hardscrabble.

Wisconsin Rapids
City
ZIP: 54494 **Lat:** 44-23-40 N **Long:** 89-49-58 W
Pop: 18,245 (1990); 17,995 (1980) **Pop Density:** 1559.
Land: 11.7 sq. mi.; **Water:** 0.9 sq. mi.
In central WI on Wisconsin River rapids, 40 mi. south of Wausau. Incorporated 1869.
Name origin: Previously called 'rabbit's place' by Indians.

Wood
Town
Lat: 44-28-19 N **Long:** 90-08-31 W
Pop: 773 (1990); 836 (1980) **Pop Density:** 23.2
Land: 33.3 sq. mi.; **Water:** 0.0 sq. mi.

Index to Places and Counties in Wisconsin

Abbotsford (Clark) City 940
Abbotsford (Marathon) City 979
Abrams (Oconto) Town 988
Ackley (Langlade) Town 976
Adams (Adams) City 929
Adams (Adams) Town 929
Adams (Green) Town 962
Adams (Jackson) Town 967
Adams County 929
Addison (Washington) Town 1024
Adell (Sheboygan) Village 1013
Adrian (Monroe) Town 987
Agenda (Ashland) Town 930
Ahnapee (Kewaunee) Town 972
Ainsworth (Langlade) Town 976
Akan (Richland) Town 1002
Alban (Portage) Town 998
Albany (Green) Town 963
Albany (Green) Village 962
Albany (Pepin) Town 994
Albion (Dane) Town 946
Albion (Jackson) Town 967
Albion (Trempealeau) Town 1016
Alden (Polk) Town 996
Algoma (Kewaunee) City 972
Algoma (Winnebago) Town 1031
Allouez (Brown) Village 934
Alma (Buffalo) City 935
Alma (Buffalo) Town 935
Alma (Jackson) Town 967
Alma Center (Jackson) Village 967
Almena (Barron) Town 931
Almena (Barron) Village 931
Almon (Shawano) Town 1011
Almond (Portage) Town 998
Almond (Portage) Village 998
Alto (Fond du Lac) Town 957
Altoona (Eau Claire) City 955
Alvin (Forest) Town 959
Amberg (Marinette) Town 982
Amery (Polk) City 996
Amherst (Portage) Town 998
Amherst (Portage) Village 998
Amherst Junction (Portage) Village .. 998
Amnicon (Douglas) Town 953
Anderson (Burnett) Town 936
Anderson (Iron) Town 966
Angelica (Shawano) Town 1011
Angelo (Monroe) Town 987
Aniwa (Shawano) Town 1011
Aniwa (Shawano) Village 1011
Anson (Chippewa) Town 939
Antigo (Langlade) City 976
Antigo (Langlade) Town 976
Apple River (Polk) Town 996
Appleton (Calumet) City 937
Appleton (Outagamie) City 991
Appleton (Winnebago) City 1031
Arbor Vitae (Vilas) Town 1020
Arcadia (Trempealeau) City 1016
Arcadia (Trempealeau) Town 1016
Arena (Iowa) Town 965
Arena (Iowa) Village 965
Argonne (Forest) Town 959
Argyle (Lafayette) Town 974
Argyle (Lafayette) Village 974
Arland (Barron) Town 931
Arlington (Columbia) Town 943
Arlington (Columbia) Village 943
Armenia (Juneau) Town 970

Armstrong (Oconto) Town 988
Armstrong Creek (Forest) Town 959
Arpin (Wood) Town 1032
Arpin (Wood) Village 1032
Arthur (Chippewa) Town 939
Ashford (Fond du Lac) Town 957
Ashippun (Dodge) Town 949
Ashland (Ashland) City 930
Ashland (Ashland) Town 930
Ashland County 930
Ashwaubenon (Brown) Village 934
Athelstane (Marinette) Town 982
Athens (Marathon) Village 979
Atlanta (Rusk) Town 1004
Auburn (Chippewa) Town 939
Auburn (Fond du Lac) Town 957
Auburndale (Wood) Town 1032
Auburndale (Wood) Village 1032
Augusta (Eau Claire) City 955
Aurora (Florence) Town 956
Aurora (Taylor) Town 1015
Aurora (Waushara) Town 1030
Avoca (Iowa) Village 965
Avon (Rock) Town 1003
Aztalan (Jefferson) Town 968
Bagley (Grant) Village 960
Bagley (Oconto) Town 988
Baileys Harbor (Door) Town 952
Baldwin (St. Croix) Town 1006
Baldwin (St. Croix) Village 1006
Balsam Lake (Polk) Town 996
Balsam Lake (Polk) Village 996
Bangor (La Crosse) Town 973
Bangor (La Crosse) Village 973
Baraboo (Sauk) City 1008
Baraboo (Sauk) Town 1008
Barksdale (Bayfield) Town 932
Barnes (Bayfield) Town 932
Barneveld (Iowa) Village 965
Barre (La Crosse) Town 973
Barron (Barron) City 931
Barron (Barron) Town 931
Barron County 931
Barronett (Washburn) Town 1023
Bartelme (Shawano) Town 1011
Barton (Washington) Town 1024
Bashaw (Washburn) Town 1023
Bass Lake (Sawyer) Town 1010
Bass Lake (Washburn) Town 1023
Bay City (Pierce) Village 994
Bayfield (Bayfield) City 933
Bayfield (Bayfield) Town 933
Bayfield County 932
Bayside (Milwaukee) Village 985
Bayside (Ozaukee) Village 992
Bayview (Bayfield) Town 933
Bear Bluff (Jackson) Town 967
Bear Creek (Outagamie) Village 991
Bear Creek (Sauk) Town 1008
Bear Creek (Waupaca) Town 1028
Bear Lake (Barron) Town 931
Beaver (Clark) Town 940
Beaver (Marinette) Town 982
Beaver (Polk) Town 996
Beaver Brook (Washburn) Town ... 1023
Beaver Dam (Dodge) City 949
Beaver Dam (Dodge) Town 949
Beecher (Marinette) Town 982
Beetown (Grant) Town 960
Belgium (Ozaukee) Town 993

Belgium (Ozaukee) Village 992
Bell (Bayfield) Town 933
Bell Center (Crawford) Village 945
Belle Plaine (Shawano) Town 1011
Belleville (Dane) Village 946
Belleville (Green) Village 963
Bellevue (Brown) Town 934
Belmont (Lafayette) Town 974
Belmont (Lafayette) Village 974
Belmont (Portage) Town 998
Beloit (Rock) City 1003
Beloit (Rock) Town 1003
Belvidere (Buffalo) Town 935
Bennett (Douglas) Town 953
Benton (Lafayette) Town 974
Benton (Lafayette) Village 974
Bergen (Marathon) Town 979
Bergen (Vernon) Town 1018
Berlin (Green Lake) City 964
Berlin (Green Lake) Town 964
Berlin (Marathon) Town 979
Berlin (Waushara) City 1030
Bern (Marathon) Town 979
Berry (Dane) Town 946
Bevent (Marathon) Town 980
Big Bend (Rusk) Town 1004
Big Bend (Waukesha) Village 1025
Big Falls (Rusk) Town 1004
Big Falls (Waupaca) Village 1028
Big Flats (Adams) Town 929
Birch (Lincoln) Town 977
Birch Creek (Chippewa) Town 939
Birchwood (Washburn) Town 1023
Birchwood (Washburn) Village 1023
Birnamwood (Marathon) Village 980
Birnamwood (Shawano) Town 1011
Birnamwood (Shawano) Village 1011
Biron (Wood) Village 1033
Black Brook (Polk) Town 996
Black Creek (Outagamie) Town 991
Black Creek (Outagamie) Village 991
Black Earth (Dane) Town 946
Black Earth (Dane) Village 946
Black River Falls (Jackson) City 967
Blackwell (Forest) Town 959
Black Wolf (Winnebago) Town 1031
Blaine (Burnett) Town 936
Blair (Trempealeau) City 1016
Blanchard (Lafayette) Town 974
Blanchardville (Iowa) Village 965
Blanchardville (Lafayette) Village ... 975
Bloom (Richland) Town 1002
Bloomer (Chippewa) City 939
Bloomer (Chippewa) Town 939
Bloomfield (Walworth) Town 1021
Bloomfield (Waushara) Town 1030
Blooming Grove (Dane) Town 946
Bloomington (Grant) Town 960
Bloomington (Grant) Village 960
Blue Mounds (Dane) Town 946
Blue Mounds (Dane) Village 946
Blue River (Grant) Village 960
Boaz (Richland) Village 1002
Bohners Lake (Racine) CDP 1000
Bonduel (Shawano) Village 1012
Bone Lake (Polk) Town 996
Boscobel (Grant) City 960
Boscobel (Grant) Town 960
Boulder Junction (Vilas) Town 1020
Bovina (Outagamie) Town 991

WISCONSIN

Bowler (Shawano) Village.............*1012*
Boyceville (Dunn) Village *954*
Boyd (Chippewa) Village................*939*
Bradford (Rock) Town....................*1003*
Bradley (Lincoln) Town..................*977*
Brandon (Fond du Lac) Village.......*957*
Brazeau (Oconto) Town..................*988*
Breed (Oconto) Town.....................*988*
Brice Prairie (La Crosse) CDP........*973*
Bridge Creek (Eau Claire) Town......*955*
Bridgeport (Crawford) Town............*945*
Brigham (Iowa) Town.....................*965*
Brighton (Kenosha) Town................*971*
Brighton (Marathon) Town...............*980*
Brillion (Calumet) City....................*937*
Brillion (Calumet) Town..................*937*
Bristol (Dane) Town *946*
Bristol (Kenosha) Town..................*971*
Brockway (Jackson) Town................*967*
Brodhead (Green) City...................*963*
Brokaw (Marathon) Village.............*980*
Brookfield (Waukesha) City *1025*
Brookfield (Waukesha) Town *1025*
Brooklyn (Dane) Village.................*946*
Brooklyn (Green) Town..................*963*
Brooklyn (Green) Village................*963*
Brooklyn (Green Lake) Town...........*964*
Brooklyn (Washburn) Town.............*1023*
Brothertown (Calumet) Town *938*
Brown County................................*934*
Brown Deer (Milwaukee) Village......*985*
Browning (Taylor) Town..................*1015*
Browns Lake (Racine) CDP *1000*
Brownsville (Dodge) Village...........*949*
Browntown (Green) Village.............*963*
Bruce (Rusk) Village......................*1004*
Brule (Douglas) Town.....................*953*
Brunswick (Eau Claire) Town *955*
Brussels (Door) Town.....................*952*
Buchanan (Outagamie) Town...........*991*
Buena Vista (Portage) Town............*998*
Buena Vista (Richland) Town *1002*
Buffalo (Buffalo) City......................*935*
Buffalo (Buffalo) Town....................*935*
Buffalo (Marquette) Town................*984*
Buffalo County..............................*935*
Burke (Dane) Town *947*
Burlington (Racine) City *1000*
Burlington (Racine) Town................*1000*
Burlington (Walworth) City.............*1021*
Burnett (Dodge) Town.....................*949*
Burnett County..............................*936*
Burns (La Crosse) Town..................*973*
Burnside (Trempealeau) Town *1016*
Butler (Clark) Town........................*940*
Butler (Waukesha) Village *1025*
Butternut (Ashland) Village.............*930*
Byron (Fond du Lac) Town..............*957*
Byron (Monroe) Town.....................*987*
Cable (Bayfield) Village..................*933*
Cadi (Green) Town.........................*963*
Cadott (Chippewa) Village...............*939*
Cady (St. Croix) Town....................*1006*
Calamus (Dodge) Town...................*949*
Caledonia (Columbia) Town *943*
Caledonia (Racine) Town................*1001*
Caledonia (Trempealeau) Town *1016*
Caledonia (Waupaca) Town.............*1028*
Calumet (Fond du Lac) Town...........*957*
Calumet County..............................*937*
Cambria (Columbia) Village *943*
Cambridge (Dane) Village................*947*
Cambridge (Jefferson) Village..........*968*
Cameron (Barron) Village................*931*
Cameron (Wood) Town *1033*

Campbell (La Crosse) Town *973*
Campbellsport (Fond du Lac)
   Village *957*
Camp Douglas (Juneau) Village........*970*
Camp Lake (Kenosha) CDP............*971*
Canton (Buffalo) Town....................*935*
Carey (Iron) Town *966*
Carlton (Kewaunee) Town................*972*
Carson (Portage) Town...................*998*
Cary (Wood) Town *1033*
Cascade (Sheboygan) Village...........*1013*
Casco (Kewaunee) Town *972*
Casco (Kewaunee) Village...............*972*
Casey (Washburn) Town..................*1023*
Cashton (Monroe) Village................*987*
Cassel (Marathon) Town..................*980*
Cassian (Oneida) Town *990*
Cassville (Grant) Town....................*960*
Cassville (Grant) Village..................*960*
Castle Rock (Grant) Town *960*
Caswell (Forest) Town *959*
Catawba (Price) Town....................*999*
Catawba (Price) Village...................*999*
Cato (Manitowoc) Town...................*978*
Cazenovia (Richland) Village..........*1002*
Cazenovia (Sauk) Village................*1008*
Cecil (Shawano) Village..................*1012*
Cedarburg (Ozaukee) City...............*993*
Cedarburg (Ozaukee) Town..............*993*
Cedar Grove (Sheboygan) Village ...*1013*
Cedar Lake (Barron) Town..............*931*
Cedar Rapids (Rusk) Town *1004*
Center (Outagamie) Town *991*
Center (Rock) Town *1003*
Centerville (Manitowoc) Town.........*978*
Centuria (Polk) Village....................*996*
Chain o' Lakes-King (Waupaca)
   CDP *1028*
Charlestown (Calumet) Town............*938*
Chase (Oconto) Town *988*
Chaseburg (Vernon) Village.............*1018*
Chelsea (Taylor) Town *1015*
Chenequa (Waukesha) Village..........*1025*
Chester (Dodge) Town....................*949*
Chetek (Barron) City *931*
Chetek (Barron) Town *931*
Chicog (Washburn) Town.................*1023*
Chief Lake (Sawyer) CDP *1010*
Chilton (Calumet) City....................*938*
Chilton (Calumet) Town..................*938*
Chimney Rock (Trempealeau)
   Town *1016*
Chippewa (Ashland) Town...............*930*
Chippewa County...........................*939*
Chippewa Falls (Chippewa) City......*939*
Christiana (Dane) Town..................*947*
Christiana (Vernon) Town *1018*
Cicero (Outagamie) Town *991*
City Point (Jackson) Town...............*967*
Clam Falls (Polk) Town...................*996*
Clark County..................................*940*
Clarno (Green) Town......................*963*
Claybanks (Door) Town...................*952*
Clayton (Crawford) Town.................*945*
Clayton (Polk) Town.......................*996*
Clayton (Polk) Village.....................*996*
Clayton (Winnebago) Town...............*1031*
Clear Creek (Eau Claire) Town *956*
Clearfield (Juneau) Town.................*970*
Clear Lake (Polk) Town *996*
Clear Lake (Polk) Village.................*996*
Cleveland (Chippewa) Town *939*
Cleveland (Jackson) Town................*967*
Cleveland (Manitowoc) Village..........*978*
Cleveland (Marathon) Town..............*980*

American Places Dictionary

Cleveland (Taylor) Town *1015*
Clifton (Grant) Town.......................*960*
Clifton (Monroe) Town....................*987*
Clifton (Pierce) Town......................*995*
Clinton (Barron) Town *931*
Clinton (Rock) Town *1003*
Clinton (Rock) Village.....................*1003*
Clinton (Vernon) Town....................*1018*
Clintonville (Waupaca) City.............*1028*
Clover (Bayfield) Town...................*933*
Cloverland (Douglas) Town..............*953*
Cloverland (Vilas) Town..................*1020*
Clyde (Iowa) Town *965*
Clyman (Dodge) Town....................*950*
Clyman (Dodge) Village..................*950*
Cobb (Iowa) Village.......................*965*
Cochrane (Buffalo) Village *935*
Colburn (Adams) Town....................*929*
Colburn (Chippewa) Town *939*
Colby (Clark) City *940*
Colby (Clark) Town *940*
Colby (Marathon) City....................*980*
Cold Spring (Jefferson) Town...........*968*
Coleman (Marinette) Village............*981*
Colfax (Dunn) Town.......................*954*
Colfax (Dunn) Village *954*
Coloma (Waushara) Town................*1030*
Coloma (Waushara) Village..............*1030*
Columbia County............................*942*
Columbus (Columbia) City...............*943*
Columbus (Columbia) Town *943*
Columbus (Dodge) City...................*950*
Combined Locks (Outagamie)
   Village *991*
Commonwealth (Florence) Town.......*956*
Como (Walworth) CDP *1021*
Concord (Jefferson) Town *968*
Conover (Vilas) Town.....................*1020*
Conrath (Rusk) Village....................*1004*
Cooks Valley (Chippewa) Town *939*
Coon (Vernon) Town *1018*
Coon Valley (Vernon) Village..........*1018*
Cooperstown (Manitowoc) Town *978*
Cornell (Chippewa) City..................*939*
Corning (Lincoln) Town *977*
Cottage Grove (Dane) Town *947*
Cottage Grove (Dane) Village...........*947*
Couderay (Sawyer) Town.................*1010*
Couderay (Sawyer) Village...............*1010*
Courtland (Columbia) Town.............*943*
Crandon (Forest) City.....................*959*
Crandon (Forest) Town *959*
Cranmoor (Wood) Town *1033*
Crawford County............................*945*
Crescent (Oneida) Town..................*990*
Crivitz (Marinette) Village *982*
Cross (Buffalo) Town......................*935*
Cross Plains (Dane) Town................*947*
Cross Plains (Dane) Village.............*947*
Crystal (Washburn) Town *1023*
Crystal Lake (Barron) Town.............*931*
Crystal Lake (Marquette) Town *984*
Cuba City (Grant) City *960*
Cuba City (Lafayette) City..............*975*
Cudahy (Milwaukee) City *985*
Cumberland (Barron) City...............*931*
Cumberland (Barron) Town..............*931*
Curran (Jackson) Town...................*967*
Curtiss (Clark) Village....................*941*
Cutler (Juneau) Town.....................*970*
Cylon (St. Croix) Town *1006*
Dairyland (Douglas) Town................*953*
Dakota (Waushara) Town.................*1030*
Dale (Outagamie) Town *991*
Dallas (Barron) Town *931*

WISCONSIN

Dallas (Barron) Village...........931	Eagle Point (Chippewa) Town...........939	Fairchild (Eau Claire) Village...........956
Dane (Dane) Town...........947	Eagle River (Vilas) City...........1020	Fairfield (Sauk) Town...........1008
Dane (Dane) Village...........947	Eastman (Crawford) Town...........945	Fairwater (Fond du Lac) Village...........957
Dane County...........946	Eastman (Crawford) Village...........945	Fall Creek (Eau Claire) Village...........956
Daniels (Burnett) Town...........936	Easton (Adams) Town...........929	Fall River (Columbia) Village...........943
Darien (Walworth) Town...........1021	Easton (Marathon) Town...........980	Farmington (Jefferson) Town...........968
Darien (Walworth) Village...........1021	East Troy (Walworth) Town...........1021	Farmington (La Crosse) Town...........973
Darlington (Lafayette) City...........975	East Troy (Walworth) Village...........1021	Farmington (Polk) Town...........996
Darlington (Lafayette) Town...........975	Eaton (Brown) Town...........934	Farmington (Washington) Town...........1024
Day (Marathon) Town...........980	Eaton (Clark) Town...........941	Farmington (Waupaca) Town...........1028
Dayton (Richland) Town...........1002	Eaton (Manitowoc) Town...........978	Fayette (Lafayette) Town...........975
Dayton (Waupaca) Town...........1028	Eau Claire (Chippewa) City...........939	Fence (Florence) Town...........956
Decatur (Green) Town...........963	Eau Claire (Eau Claire) City...........956	Fennimore (Grant) City...........960
Deer Creek (Outagamie) Town...........991	**Eau Claire County**...........955	Fennimore (Grant) Town...........961
Deer Creek (Taylor) Town...........1015	Eau Galle (Dunn) Town...........954	Fenwood (Marathon) Village...........980
Deerfield (Dane) Town...........947	Eau Galle (St. Croix) Town...........1006	Fern (Florence) Town...........956
Deerfield (Dane) Village...........947	Eau Pleine (Marathon) Town...........980	Ferryville (Crawford) Village...........945
Deerfield (Waushara) Town...........1030	Eau Pleine (Portage) Town...........998	Fifield (Price) Town...........999
Deer Park (St. Croix) Village...........1006	Eden (Fond du Lac) Town...........957	Finley (Juneau) Town...........970
De Forest (Dane) Village...........947	Eden (Fond du Lac) Village...........957	Fitchburg (Dane) City...........947
Dekorra (Columbia) Town...........943	Eden (Iowa) Town...........965	Flambeau (Price) Town...........999
Delafield (Waukesha) City...........1026	Edgar (Marathon) Village...........980	Flambeau (Rusk) Town...........1005
Delafield (Waukesha) Town...........1026	Edgerton (Rock) City...........1003	Florence (Florence) Town...........956
Delavan (Walworth) City...........1021	Edgewater (Sawyer) Town...........1010	**Florence County**...........956
Delavan (Walworth) Town...........1021	Edson (Chippewa) Town...........940	Fond du Lac (Fond du Lac) City...........957
Delavan Lake (Walworth) CDP...........1021	Egg Harbor (Door) Town...........952	Fond du Lac (Fond du Lac) Town...........957
Dellona (Sauk) Town...........1008	Egg Harbor (Door) Village...........952	**Fond du Lac County**...........957
Dell Prairie (Adams) Town...........929	Eileen (Bayfield) Town...........933	Fontana-on-Geneva Lake (Walworth) Village...........1021
Delmar (Chippewa) Town...........939	Eisenstein (Price) Town...........999	Footville (Rock) Village...........1003
Delta (Bayfield) Town...........933	Eland (Shawano) Village...........1012	Ford (Taylor) Town...........1015
Delton (Sauk) Town...........1008	Elba (Dodge) Town...........950	Forest (Fond du Lac) Town...........957
Denmark (Brown) Village...........934	Elcho (Langlade) Town...........976	Forest (Richland) Town...........1002
De Pere (Brown) City...........934	Elderon (Marathon) Town...........980	Forest (St. Croix) Town...........1006
De Pere (Brown) Town...........934	Elderon (Marathon) Village...........980	Forest (Vernon) Town...........1018
De Soto (Crawford) Village...........945	Eldorado (Fond du Lac) Town...........957	**Forest County**...........959
De Soto (Vernon) Village...........1018	Eleva (Trempealeau) Village...........1016	Forestville (Door) Town...........952
Dewey (Burnett) Town...........936	Elk (Price) Town...........999	Forestville (Door) Village...........952
Dewey (Portage) Town...........998	Elk Grove (Lafayette) Town...........975	Fort Atkinson (Jefferson) City...........969
Dewey (Rusk) Town...........1005	Elkhart Lake (Sheboygan) Village...........1013	Fort Winnebago (Columbia) Town...........943
Dewhurst (Clark) Town...........941	Elkhorn (Walworth) City...........1021	Foster (Clark) Town...........941
Dexter (Wood) Town...........1033	Elk Mound (Dunn) Town...........954	Fountain (Juneau) Town...........970
Diamond Bluff (Pierce) Town...........995	Elk Mound (Dunn) Village...........954	Fountain City (Buffalo) City...........935
Dickeyville (Grant) Village...........960	Ellenboro (Grant) Town...........960	Fountain Prairie (Columbia) Town...........943
Dodge (Trempealeau) Town...........1016	Ellington (Outagamie) Town...........991	Fox Lake (Dodge) City...........950
Dodge County...........949	Ellsworth (Pierce) Town...........995	Fox Lake (Dodge) Town...........950
Dodgeville (Iowa) City...........965	Ellsworth (Pierce) Village...........995	Fox Point (Milwaukee) Village...........985
Dodgeville (Iowa) Town...........965	Elm Grove (Waukesha) Village...........1026	Francis Creek (Manitowoc) Village...........978
Door County...........952	Elmwood (Pierce) Village...........995	Frankfort (Marathon) Town...........980
Dorchester (Clark) Village...........941	Elmwood Park (Racine) Village...........1001	Frankfort (Pepin) Town...........994
Doty (Oconto) Town...........989	El Paso (Pierce) Town...........995	Franklin (Jackson) Town...........967
Douglas (Marquette) Town...........984	Elroy (Juneau) City...........970	Franklin (Kewaunee) Town...........972
Douglas County...........953	Embarrass (Waupaca) Village...........1028	Franklin (Manitowoc) Town...........978
Dousman (Waukesha) Village...........1026	Emerald (St. Croix) Town...........1006	Franklin (Milwaukee) City...........985
Dover (Buffalo) Town...........935	Emery (Price) Town...........999	Franklin (Sauk) Town...........1008
Dover (Racine) Town...........1001	Emmet (Dodge) Town...........950	Franklin (Vernon) Town...........1018
Dovre (Barron) Town...........931	Emmet (Marathon) Town...........980	Franzen (Marathon) Town...........980
Downing (Dunn) Village...........954	Empire (Fond du Lac) Town...........957	Frederic (Polk) Village...........996
Doyle (Barron) Town...........931	Endeavor (Marquette) Village...........984	Fredonia (Ozaukee) Town...........993
Doylestown (Columbia) Village...........943	Enterprise (Oneida) Town...........990	Fredonia (Ozaukee) Village...........993
Drammen (Eau Claire) Town...........956	Ephraim (Door) Village...........952	Freedom (Forest) Town...........959
Draper (Sawyer) Town...........1010	Erin (Washington) Town...........1024	Freedom (Outagamie) Town...........991
Dresser (Polk) Village...........996	Erin Prairie (St. Croix) Town...........1006	Freedom (Sauk) Town...........1008
Drummond (Bayfield) Town...........933	Estella (Chippewa) Town...........940	Freeman (Crawford) Town...........945
Dunbar (Marinette) Town...........982	Ettrick (Trempealeau) Town...........1016	Fremont (Clark) Town...........941
Dunkirk (Dane) Town...........947	Ettrick (Trempealeau) Village...........1016	Fremont (Waupaca) Town...........1028
Dunn (Dane) Town...........947	Eureka (Polk) Town...........996	Fremont (Waupaca) Village...........1028
Dunn (Dunn) Town...........954	Evansville (Rock) City...........1003	French Island (La Crosse) CDP...........973
Dunn County...........954	Evergreen (Langlade) Town...........976	Friendship (Adams) Village...........929
Dupont (Waupaca) Town...........1028	Evergreen (Marathon) CDP...........980	Friendship (Fond du Lac) Town...........957
Durand (Pepin) City...........994	Evergreen (Washburn) Town...........1023	Friesland (Columbia) Village...........943
Durand (Pepin) Town...........994	Excelsior (Sauk) Town...........1008	Frog Creek (Washburn) Town...........1023
Eagle (Richland) Town...........1002	Exeland (Sawyer) Village...........1010	Fulton (Rock) Town...........1003
Eagle (Waukesha) Town...........1026	Exeter (Green) Town...........963	Gale (Trempealeau) Town...........1016
Eagle (Waukesha) Village...........1026	Fairbanks (Shawano) Town...........1012	Galesville (Trempealeau) City...........1017
Eagle Lake (Racine) CDP...........1001	Fairchild (Eau Claire) Town...........956	

WISCONSIN   *American Places Dictionary*

Garden Valley (Jackson) Town..........*967*	Gresham (Shawano) Village............*1012*	Hobart (Brown) Town......................*934*
Gardner (Door) Town...................*952*	Grover (Marinette) Town.................*983*	Holland (Brown) Town....................*934*
Garfield (Jackson) Town...................*967*	Grover (Taylor) Town....................*1015*	Holland (La Crosse) Town................*973*
Garfield (Polk) Town....................*996*	Grow (Rusk) Town........................*1005*	Holland (Sheboygan) Town...............*1013*
Gays Mills (Crawford) Village............*945*	Guenther (Marathon) Town................*980*	Hollandale (Iowa) Village................*965*
Genesee (Waukesha) Town................*1026*	Gull Lake (Washburn) Town..............*1023*	Holmen (La Crosse) Village...............*974*
Geneva (Walworth) Town..................*1021*	Gurney (Iron) Town........................*966*	Holton (Marathon) Town..................*981*
Genoa (Vernon) Town....................*1018*	Hackett (Price) Town......................*999*	Holway (Taylor) Town...................*1015*
Genoa (Vernon) Village..................*1018*	Hale (Trempealeau) Town................*1017*	Homestead (Florence) Town...............*956*
Genoa City (Kenosha) Village............*971*	Hales Corners (Milwaukee) Village...*986*	Honey Creek (Sauk) Town................*1008*
Genoa City (Walworth) Village.........*1021*	Hallie (Chippewa) Town...................*940*	Horicon (Dodge) City.....................*950*
Georgetown (Polk) Town..................*997*	Halsey (Marathon) Town..................*980*	Hortonia (Outagamie) Town...............*991*
Georgetown (Price) Town.................*999*	Hamburg (Marathon) Town................*980*	Hortonville (Outagamie) Village........*991*
Germania (Shawano) Town...............*1012*	Hamburg (Vernon) Town..................*1018*	How (Oconto) Town........................*989*
Germantown (Juneau) Town..............*970*	Hamilton (La Crosse) Town................*973*	Howard (Brown) Village...................*934*
Germantown (Washington) Town...*1024*	Hammel (Taylor) Town....................*1015*	Howard (Chippewa) Town..................*940*
Germantown (Washington) Village.*1024*	Hammond (St. Croix) Town.............*1006*	Howards Grove (Sheboygan)
Gibraltar (Door) Town.....................*952*	Hammond (St. Croix) Village............*1006*	Village.. *1013*
Gibson (Manitowoc) Town................*978*	Hampden (Columbia) Town................*943*	Hubbard (Dodge) Town....................*950*
Gillett (Oconto) City.......................*989*	Hancock (Waushara) Town...............*1030*	Hubbard (Rusk) Town....................*1005*
Gillett (Oconto) Town.....................*989*	Hancock (Waushara) Village...............*1030*	Hudson (St. Croix) City..................*1007*
Gilman (Pierce) Town.....................*995*	Haney (Crawford) Town..................*945*	Hudson (St. Croix) Town..................*1007*
Gilman (Taylor) Village..................*1015*	Hansen (Wood) Town.....................*1033*	Hughes (Bayfield) Town..................*933*
Gilmanton (Buffalo) Town................*935*	Harding (Lincoln) Town....................*977*	Hull (Marathon) Town....................*981*
Gingles (Ashland) Town...................*930*	Harmony (Price) Town....................*1000*	Hull (Portage) Town.......................*998*
Glenbeulah (Sheboygan) Village......*1013*	Harmony (Rock) Town...................*1003*	Humboldt (Brown) Town..................*934*
Glencoe (Buffalo) Town...................*935*	Harmony (Vernon) Town..................*1018*	Hunter (Sawyer) Town...................*1010*
Glendale (Milwaukee) City...............*985*	Harris (Marquette) Town..................*984*	Hurley (Iron) City..........................*966*
Glendale (Monroe) Town..................*987*	Harrison (Calumet) Town.................*938*	Hustisford (Dodge) Town..................*950*
Glen Flora (Rusk) Village...............*1005*	Harrison (Grant) Town....................*961*	Hustisford (Dodge) Village................*950*
Glen Haven (Grant) Town................*961*	Harrison (Lincoln) Town..................*977*	Hustler (Juneau) Village..................*970*
Glenmore (Brown) Town..................*934*	Harrison (Marathon) Town................*980*	Hutchins (Shawano) Town..............*1012*
Glenwood (St. Croix) Town..............*1006*	Harrison (Waupaca) Town...............*1028*	Independence (Trempealeau) City ..*1017*
Glenwood City (St. Croix) City.......*1006*	Hartford (Dodge) City.....................*950*	Ingram (Rusk) Village....................*1005*
Goet (Chippewa) Town...................*940*	Hartford (Washington) City..............*1024*	Iola (Waupaca) Town....................*1028*
Goodman (Marinette) Town...............*983*	Hartford (Washington) Town............*1024*	Iola (Waupaca) Village...................*1028*
Goodrich (Taylor) Town..................*1015*	Hartland (Pierce) Town....................*995*	**Iowa County**................................*965*
Gordon (Ashland) Town...................*930*	Hartland (Shawano) Town..............*1012*	**Iron County**..................................*966*
Gordon (Douglas) Town...................*953*	Hartland (Waukesha) Village...........*1026*	Iron Ridge (Dodge) Village..............*950*
Grafton (Ozaukee) Town..................*993*	Hatley (Marathon) Village................*981*	Iron River (Bayfield) Town...............*933*
Grafton (Ozaukee) Village................*993*	Haugen (Barron) Village...................*931*	Ironton (Sauk) Town....................*1008*
Grand Chute (Outagamie) Town......*991*	Hawkins (Rusk) Town...................*1005*	Ironton (Sauk) Village...................*1008*
Grand Rapids (Wood) Town............*1033*	Hawkins (Rusk) Village..................*1005*	Irving (Jackson) Town....................*968*
Grand View (Bayfield) Town............*933*	Hawthorne (Douglas) Town...............*953*	Isabelle (Pierce) Town....................*995*
Grant (Clark) Town.......................*941*	Hay River (Dunn) Town...................*954*	Ithaca (Richland) Town..................*1002*
Grant (Dunn) Town........................*954*	Hayward (Sawyer) City..................*1010*	Ixonia (Jefferson) Town..................*969*
Grant (Monroe) Town.....................*987*	Hayward (Sawyer) Town.................*1010*	Jackson (Adams) Town...................*929*
Grant (Portage) Town.....................*998*	Hazel Green (Grant) Town................*961*	Jackson (Burnett) Town...................*936*
Grant (Rusk) Town.......................*1005*	Hazel Green (Grant) Village..............*961*	Jackson (Washington) Town............*1024*
Grant (Shawano) Town..................*1012*	Hazel Green (Lafayette) Village........*975*	Jackson (Washington) Village..........*1024*
Grant County................................*960*	Hazelhurst (Oneida) Town................*990*	**Jackson County**...............................*967*
Granton (Clark) Village....................*941*	Hebron (Jefferson) Town..................*969*	Jacksonport (Door) Town.................*952*
Grantsburg (Burnett) Town..............*936*	Helvetia (Waupaca) Town...............*1028*	Jacobs (Ashland) Town...................*930*
Grantsburg (Burnett) Village.............*936*	Hendren (Clark) Town....................*941*	Jamestown (Grant) Town.................*961*
Gratiot (Lafayette) Town.................*975*	Henrietta (Richland) Town..............*1002*	Janesville (Rock) City....................*1003*
Gratiot (Lafayette) Village................*975*	Herman (Dodge) Town....................*950*	Janesville (Rock) Town..................*1003*
Green Bay (Brown) City..................*934*	Herman (Shawano) Town...............*1012*	Jefferson (Green) Town...................*963*
Green Bay (Brown) Town................*934*	Herman (Sheboygan) Town..............*1013*	Jefferson (Jefferson) City.................*969*
Greenbush (Sheboygan) Town.........*1013*	Hewett (Clark) Town....................*941*	Jefferson (Jefferson) Town...............*969*
Green County.................................*962*	Hewitt (Marathon) Town..................*981*	Jefferson (Monroe) Town.................*987*
Greendale (Milwaukee) Village.........*986*	Hewitt (Wood) Village....................*1033*	Jefferson (Vernon) Town................*1018*
Greenfield (La Crosse) Town............*973*	Hickory Grove (Grant) Town............*961*	**Jefferson County**............................*968*
Greenfield (Milwaukee) City.............*986*	Highland (Douglas) Town.................*953*	Johnson (Marathon) Town...............*981*
Greenfield (Monroe) Town...............*987*	Highland (Iowa) Town....................*965*	Johnson Creek (Jefferson) Village.....*969*
Greenfield (Sauk) Town.................*1008*	Highland (Iowa) Village..................*965*	Johnstown (Polk) Town...................*997*
Green Grove (Clark) Town...............*941*	Hilbert (Calumet) Village.................*938*	Johnstown (Rock) Town.................*1004*
Green Lake (Green Lake) City..........*964*	Hiles (Forest) Town........................*959*	Jordan (Green) Town......................*963*
Green Lake (Green Lake) Town........*964*	Hiles (Wood) Town.......................*1033*	Jump River (Taylor) Town..............*1015*
Green Lake County........................*964*	Hill (Price) Town..........................*1000*	Junction City (Portage) Village........*998*
Green Valley (Marathon) Town.........*980*	Hillsboro (Vernon) City..................*1018*	Juneau (Dodge) City......................*950*
Green Valley (Shawano) Town........*1012*	Hillsboro (Vernon) Town................*1018*	**Juneau County**..............................*970*
Greenville (Outagamie) Town..........*991*	Hixon (Clark) Town......................*941*	Kaukauna (Outagamie) City............*991*
Greenwood (Clark) City.................*941*	Hixton (Jackson) Town..................*968*	Kaukauna (Outagamie) Town..........*991*
Greenwood (Taylor) Town..............*1015*	Hixton (Jackson) Village.................*967*	Kekoskee (Dodge) Village................*950*
Greenwood (Vernon) Town.............*1018*	Hoard (Clark) Town.......................*941*	Kellnersville (Manitowoc) Village.....*978*

WISCONSIN

Kelly (Bayfield) Town 933
Kendall (Lafayette) Town 975
Kendall (Monroe) Village 987
Kennan (Price) Town 1000
Kennan (Price) Village 1000
Kenosha (Kenosha) City 971
Kenosha County 971
Keshena (Menominee) CDP 985
Kewaskum (Fond du Lac) Village 958
Kewaskum (Washington) Town 1024
Kewaskum (Washington) Village 1024
Kewaunee (Kewaunee) City 973
Kewaunee County 972
Keystone (Bayfield) Town 933
Kickapoo (Vernon) Town 1019
Kiel (Calumet) City 938
Kiel (Manitowoc) City 978
Kildare (Juneau) Town 970
Kimball (Iron) Town 966
Kimberly (Outagamie) Village 992
King (Lincoln) Town 977
Kingston (Green Lake) Town 964
Kingston (Green Lake) Village 964
Kingston (Juneau) Town 970
Kinnickinnic (St. Croix) Town 1007
Knapp (Dunn) Village 954
Knapp (Jackson) Town 968
Knight (Iron) Town 967
Knowlton (Marathon) Town 981
Knox (Price) Town 1000
Kohler (Sheboygan) Village 1013
Komensky (Jackson) Town 968
Koshkonong (Jefferson) Town 969
Kossuth (Manitowoc) Town 978
Kronenwetter (Marathon) Town 981
Lac du Flambeau (Vilas) Town 1020
Lac La Belle (Waukesha) Village 1026
La Crosse (La Crosse) City 974
La Crosse County 973
Ladysmith (Rusk) City 1005
La Farge (Vernon) Village 1019
Lafayette (Chippewa) Town 940
Lafayette (Monroe) Town 987
Lafayette (Walworth) Town 1021
Lafayette County 974
La Follette (Burnett) Town 936
La Grange (Monroe) Town 987
La Grange (Walworth) Town 1021
Lake (Marinette) Town 983
Lake (Price) Town 1000
Lake Delton (Sauk) Village 1008
Lake Geneva (Walworth) City 1021
Lake Holcombe (Chippewa) Town 940
Lakeland (Barron) Town 932
Lake Mills (Jefferson) City 969
Lake Mills (Jefferson) Town 969
Lake Nebagamon (Douglas) Village 953
Lake Ripley (Jefferson) CDP 969
Lakeside (Douglas) Town 953
Lake Tomahawk (Oneida) Town 990
Laketown (Polk) Town 997
Lake Wazeecha (Wood) CDP 1033
Lake Wisconsin (Columbia) CDP 943
Lake Wisconsin (Sauk) CDP 1008
Lake Wissota (Chippewa) CDP 940
Lakewood (Oconto) Town 989
Lamartine (Fond du Lac) Town 958
Lamont (Lafayette) Town 975
Lanark (Portage) Town 998
Lancaster (Grant) City 961
Land O'Lakes (Vilas) Town 1020
Langlade (Langlade) Town 976
Langlade County 976
Lannon (Waukesha) Village 1026
Laona (Forest) Town 959

La Pointe (Ashland) Town 930
La Prairie (Rock) Town 1004
Larrabee (Waupaca) Town 1028
La Valle (Sauk) Town 1008
La Valle (Sauk) Village 1008
Lawrence (Brown) Town 934
Lawrence (Rusk) Town 1005
Lebanon (Dodge) Town 950
Lebanon (Waupaca) Town 1028
Leeds (Columbia) Town 943
Lemonweir (Juneau) Town 970
Lena (Oconto) Town 989
Lena (Oconto) Village 989
Lenroot (Sawyer) Town 1010
Leola (Adams) Town 929
Leon (Monroe) Town 987
Leon (Waushara) Town 1030
Leroy (Dodge) Town 950
Lessor (Shawano) Town 1012
Levis (Clark) Town 941
Lewiston (Columbia) Town 943
Liberty (Grant) Town 961
Liberty (Manitowoc) Town 978
Liberty (Outagamie) Town 992
Liberty (Vernon) Town 1019
Liberty Grove (Door) Town 952
Lima (Grant) Town 961
Lima (Pepin) Town 994
Lima (Rock) Town 1004
Lima (Sheboygan) Town 1014
Lime Ridge (Sauk) Village 1009
Lincoln (Adams) Town 929
Lincoln (Bayfield) Town 933
Lincoln (Buffalo) Town 936
Lincoln (Burnett) Town 937
Lincoln (Eau Claire) Town 956
Lincoln (Forest) Town 959
Lincoln (Kewaunee) Town 973
Lincoln (Monroe) Town 987
Lincoln (Polk) Town 997
Lincoln (Trempealeau) Town 1017
Lincoln (Vilas) Town 1020
Lincoln (Wood) Town 1033
Lincoln County 977
Lind (Waupaca) Town 1028
Linden (Iowa) Town 965
Linden (Iowa) Village 965
Lindina (Juneau) Town 970
Linn (Walworth) Town 1022
Linwood (Portage) Town 998
Lisbon (Juneau) Town 970
Lisbon (Waukesha) Town 1026
Little Black (Taylor) Town 1015
Little Chute (Outagamie) Village 992
Little Falls (Monroe) Town 987
Little Grant (Grant) Town 961
Little Rice (Oneida) Town 990
Little River (Oconto) Town 989
Little Round Lake (Sawyer) CDP 1010
Little Suamico (Oconto) Town 989
Little Wolf (Waupaca) Town 1028
Livingston (Grant) Village 961
Livingston (Iowa) Village 966
Lodi (Columbia) City 943
Lodi (Columbia) Town 944
Loganville (Sauk) Village 1009
Lohrville (Waushara) Village 1030
Lomira (Dodge) Town 950
Lomira (Dodge) Village 950
Lone Rock (Richland) Village 1002
Long Lake (Florence) Town 957
Long Lake (Washburn) Town 1023
Longwood (Clark) Town 941
Lorain (Polk) Town 997
Lowell (Dodge) Town 951

Lowell (Dodge) Village 951
Lowville (Columbia) Town 944
Loyal (Clark) City 941
Loyal (Clark) Town 941
Lublin (Taylor) Village 1015
Lucas (Dunn) Town 954
Luck (Polk) Town 997
Luck (Polk) Village 997
Ludington (Eau Claire) Town 956
Luxemburg (Kewaunee) Town 973
Luxemburg (Kewaunee) Village 973
Lyndon (Juneau) Town 970
Lyndon (Sheboygan) Town 1014
Lyndon Station (Juneau) Village 970
Lynn (Clark) Town 941
Lynne (Oneida) Town 990
Lynxville (Crawford) Village 945
Lyons (Walworth) Town 1022
Mackford (Green Lake) Town 964
Madge (Washburn) Town 1023
Madison (Dane) City 947
Madison (Dane) Town 947
Magnolia (Rock) Town 1004
Maiden Rock (Pierce) Town 995
Maiden Rock (Pierce) Village 995
Maine (Marathon) Town 981
Maine (Outagamie) Town 992
Manawa (Waupaca) City 1029
Manchester (Green Lake) Town 964
Manchester (Jackson) Town 968
Manitowish Waters (Vilas) Town 1020
Manitowoc (Manitowoc) City 978
Manitowoc (Manitowoc) Town 978
Manitowoc County 978
Manitowoc Rapids (Manitowoc)
  Town 978
Maple (Douglas) Town 953
Maple Bluff (Dane) Village 947
Maple Creek (Outagamie) Town 992
Maple Grove (Barron) Town 932
Maple Grove (Manitowoc) Town 978
Maple Grove (Shawano) Town 1012
Maplehurst (Taylor) Town 1015
Maple Plain (Barron) Town 932
Maple Valley (Oconto) Town 989
Marathon (Marathon) Town 981
Marathon City (Marathon) Village 981
Marathon County 979
Marcellon (Columbia) Town 944
Marengo (Ashland) Town 930
Maribel (Manitowoc) Village 978
Marietta (Crawford) Town 945
Marinette (Marinette) City 983
Marinette County 982
Marion (Grant) Town 961
Marion (Juneau) Town 971
Marion (Waupaca) City 1029
Marion (Waushara) Town 1030
Markesan (Green Lake) City 964
Marquette (Green Lake) Town 964
Marquette (Green Lake) Village 964
Marquette County 984
Marshall (Dane) Village 947
Marshall (Richland) Town 1002
Marshall (Rusk) Town 1005
Marshfield (Fond du Lac) Town 958
Marshfield (Marathon) City 981
Marshfield (Wood) City 1033
Marshfield (Wood) Town 1033
Martell (Pierce) Town 995
Mason (Bayfield) Town 933
Mason (Bayfield) Village 933
Matteson (Waupaca) Town 1029
Mattoon (Shawano) Village 1012
Mauston (Juneau) City 971

WISCONSIN

Maxville (Buffalo) Town.....................936
Mayville (Clark) Town........................941
Mayville (Dodge) City........................951
Mazomanie (Dane) Town...................948
Mazomanie (Dane) Village..................947
McFarland (Dane) Village...................948
McKinley (Polk) Town.........................997
McKinley (Taylor) Town....................1015
McMillan (Marathon) Town................981
Mead (Clark) Town..............................941
Meadowbrook (Sawyer) Town..........1010
Mecan (Marquette) Town....................984
Medary (La Crosse) Town...................974
Medford (Taylor) City.......................1015
Medford (Taylor) Town.....................1015
Medina (Dane) Town...........................948
Meeme (Manitowoc) Town..................978
Meenon (Burnett) Town......................937
Mellen (Ashland) City.........................930
Melrose (Jackson) Town......................968
Melrose (Jackson) Village...................968
Melvina (Monroe) Village...................987
Menasha (Calumet) City.....................938
Menasha (Winnebago) City..............1031
Menasha (Winnebago) Town............1031
Menominee (Menominee) Town........985
Menominee County...........................985
Menomonee Falls (Waukesha)
 Village..1026
Menomonie (Dunn) City.....................954
Menomonie (Dunn) Town...................954
Mentor (Clark) Town..........................941
Mequon (Ozaukee) City......................993
Mercer (Iron) Town.............................967
Merrill (Lincoln) City..........................977
Merrill (Lincoln) Town........................977
Merrillan (Jackson) Village.................968
Merrimac (Sauk) Town......................1009
Merrimac (Sauk) Village...................1009
Merton (Waukesha) Town.................1026
Merton (Waukesha) Village...............1026
Meteor (Sawyer) Town......................1010
Metomen (Fond du Lac) Town...........958
Middle Inlet (Marinette) Town...........983
Middleton (Dane) City........................948
Middleton (Dane) Town......................948
Mifflin (Iowa) Town............................966
Milford (Jefferson) Town....................969
Milladore (Portage) Village................998
Milladore (Wood) Town....................1033
Milladore (Wood) Village.................1033
Millston (Jackson) Town.....................968
Milltown (Polk) Town.........................997
Milltown (Polk) Village.......................997
Millville (Grant) Town........................961
Milton (Buffalo) Town........................936
Milton (Rock) City............................1004
Milton (Rock) Town..........................1004
Milwaukee (Milwaukee) City.............986
Milwaukee (Washington) City.........1025
Milwaukee (Waukesha) City............1026
Milwaukee County............................985
Mineral Point (Iowa) City...................966
Mineral Point (Iowa) Town.................966
Minocqua (Oneida) Town...................990
Minong (Washburn) Town................1023
Minong (Washburn) Village.............1023
Mishicot (Manitowoc) Town..............979
Mishicot (Manitowoc) Village............979
Mitchell (Sheboygan) Town..............1014
Modena (Buffalo) Town......................936
Molitor (Taylor) Town......................1015
Mondovi (Buffalo) City......................936
Mondovi (Buffalo) Town....................936
Monico (Oneida) Town.......................990

Monona (Dane) City...........................948
Monroe (Adams) Town.......................929
Monroe (Green) City...........................963
Monroe (Green) Town.........................963
Monroe County..................................987
Montana (Buffalo) Town.....................936
Montello (Marquette) City..................984
Montello (Marquette) Town................984
Montfort (Grant) Village.....................961
Montfort (Iowa) Village......................966
Monticello (Green) Village..................963
Monticello (Lafayette) Town..............975
Montpelier (Kewaunee) Town............973
Montreal (Iron) City............................967
Montrose (Dane) Town.......................948
Morgan (Oconto) Town.......................989
Morris (Shawano) Town....................1012
Morrison (Brown) Town......................934
Morse (Ashland) Town........................930
Moscow (Iowa) Town.........................966
Mosel (Sheboygan) Town.................1014
Mosinee (Marathon) City....................981
Mosinee (Marathon) Town..................981
Moundville (Marquette) Town...........984
Mount Calvary (Fond du Lac)
 Village...958
Mount Hope (Grant) Town..................961
Mount Hope (Grant) Village...............961
Mount Horeb (Dane) Village..............948
Mount Ida (Grant) Town.....................961
Mount Morris (Waushara) Town.....1030
Mount Pleasant (Green) Town............963
Mount Pleasant (Racine) Town........1001
Mount Sterling (Crawford) Village....945
Mukwa (Waupaca) Town..................1029
Mukwonago (Waukesha) Town.......1026
Mukwonago (Waukesha) Village.....1026
Murry (Rusk) Town...........................1005
Muscoda (Grant) Town.......................961
Muscoda (Grant) Village.....................961
Muscoda (Iowa) Village......................966
Muskego (Waukesha) City...............1027
Namakagon (Bayfield) Town.............933
Naples (Buffalo) Town........................936
Nasewaupee (Door) Town..................952
Nashotah (Waukesha) Village..........1027
Nashville (Forest) Town......................959
Navarino (Shawano) Town...............1012
Necedah (Juneau) Town......................971
Necedah (Juneau) Village...................971
Neenah (Winnebago) City................1031
Neenah (Winnebago) Town..............1031
Neillsville (Clark) City........................942
Nekimi (Winnebago) Town..............1031
Nekoosa (Wood) City........................1033
Nelson (Buffalo) Town........................936
Nelson (Buffalo) Village......................936
Nelsonville (Portage) Village.............998
Neopit (Menominee) CDP..................985
Neosho (Dodge) Village......................951
Nepeuskun (Winnebago) Town........1032
Neshkoro (Marquette) Town..............984
Neshkoro (Marquette) Village............984
Neva (Langlade) Town........................976
Newark (Rock) Town........................1004
New Auburn (Barron) Village............932
New Auburn (Chippewa) Village......940
New Berlin (Waukesha) City...........1027
Newbold (Oneida) Town.....................990
Newburg (Ozaukee) Village................993
Newburg (Washington) Village.......1025
New Chester (Adams) Town..............929
New Denmark (Brown) Town............934
New Diggings (Lafayette) Town........975
New Glarus (Green) Town..................963

American Places Dictionary

New Glarus (Green) Village................96.
New Haven (Adams) Town................92.
New Haven (Dunn) Town...................95.
New Holstein (Calumet) City.............938
New Holstein (Calumet) Town..........93.
New Hope (Portage) Town.................99.
New Lisbon (Juneau) City..................97.
New London (Outagamie) City.........99.
New London (Waupaca) City..........102.
New Lyme (Monroe) Town.................98.
Newport (Columbia) Town.................94.
New Post (Sawyer) CDP...................101.
New Richmond (St. Croix) City......100.
Newton (Manitowoc) Town................979
Newton (Marquette) Town..................984
Niagara (Marinette) Town..................98.
Niagara (Marinette) Village................98.
Nichols (Outagamie) Village..............992
Nokomis (Oneida) Town....................990
Norrie (Marathon) Town.....................98.
North Bay (Racine) Village..............100.
North Bend (Jackson) Town...............968
Northfield (Jackson) Town.................968
North Fond du Lac (Fond du Lac)
 Village...958
North Freedom (Sauk) Village........1009
North Hudson (St. Croix) Village...1007
North Lancaster (Grant) Town..........96.
North Prairie (Waukesha) Village...102.
Norwalk (Monroe) Village.................98.
Norway (Racine) Town.....................100.
Norwood (Langlade) Town................976
Oak Creek (Milwaukee) City.............986
Oakdale (Monroe) Town.....................987
Oakdale (Monroe) Village..................987
Oakfield (Fond du Lac) Town............958
Oakfield (Fond du Lac) Village.........958
Oak Grove (Dodge) Town...................951
Oak Grove (Pierce) Town...................995
Oakland (Burnett) Town.....................937
Oakland (Douglas) Town....................953
Oakland (Jefferson) Town..................969
Oasis (Waushara) Town....................1030
Oconomowoc (Waukesha) City......1027
Oconomowoc (Waukesha) Town....1027
Oconomowoc Lake (Waukesha)
 Village..1027
Oconto (Oconto) City..........................989
Oconto (Oconto) Town........................989
Oconto County...................................988
Oconto Falls (Oconto) City.................989
Oconto Falls (Oconto) Town...............989
Odanah (Ashland) CDP.......................930
Ogdensburg (Waupaca) Village.......1029
Ogema (Price) Town.........................1000
Ojibwa (Sawyer) Town.....................1010
Okauchee Lake (Waukesha) CDP...1027
Oliver (Douglas) Village.....................953
Oma (Iron) Town.................................967
Omro (Winnebago) City...................1032
Omro (Winnebago) Town.................1032
Onalaska (La Crosse) City..................974
Onalaska (La Crosse) Town................974
Oneida (Outagamie) Town..................992
Oneida County..................................990
Ontario (Vernon) Village..................1019
Oostburg (Sheboygan) Village.........1014
Orange (Juneau) Town.......................971
Oregon (Dane) Town..........................948
Oregon (Dane) Village........................948
Orfordville (Rock) Village...............1004
Orienta (Bayfield) Town.....................933
Orion (Richland) Town.....................1002
Osborn (Outagamie) Town.................992
Osceola (Fond du Lac) Town.............958

1040

Osceola (Polk) Town..........................997
Osceola (Polk) Village........................997
Oshkosh (Winnebago) City..............1032
Oshkosh (Winnebago) Town............1032
Osseo (Trempealeau) City................1017
Otsego (Columbia) Town....................944
Ottawa (Waukesha) Town.................1027
Otter Creek (Dunn) Town....................955
Otter Creek (Eau Claire) Town............956
Oulu (Bayfield) Town...........................933
Outagamie County.............................991
Owen (Clark) City................................942
Oxford (Marquette) Town....................984
Oxford (Marquette) Village..................984
Ozaukee County................................992
Pacific (Columbia) Town.....................944
Packwaukee (Marquette) Town...........984
Paddock Lake (Kenosha) Village........972
Palmyra (Jefferson) Town...................969
Palmyra (Jefferson) Village.................969
Pardeeville (Columbia) Village............944
Paris (Grant) Town..............................961
Paris (Kenosha) Town.........................972
Park Falls (Price) City.......................1000
Parkland (Douglas) Town....................953
Park Ridge (Portage) Village..............999
Parrish (Langlade) Town.....................976
Patch Grove (Grant) Town..................962
Patch Grove (Grant) Village................961
Peck (Langlade) Town........................976
Peeksville (Ashland) Town..................930
Pelican (Oneida) Town........................990
Pella (Shawano) Town......................1012
Pell Lake (Walworth) CDP................1022
Pembine (Marinette) Town..................983
Pence (Iron) Town...............................967
Pensaukee (Oconto) Town..................989
Pepin (Pepin) Town.............................994
Pepin (Pepin) Village..........................994
Pepin County......................................994
Perry (Dane) Town..............................948
Pershing (Taylor) Town.....................1015
Peru (Dunn) Town...............................955
Peshtigo (Marinette) City....................983
Peshtigo (Marinette) Town..................983
Pewaukee (Waukesha) Town............1027
Pewaukee (Waukesha) Village.........1027
Phelps (Vilas) Town..........................1020
Phillips (Price) City...........................1000
Piehl (Oneida) Town...........................990
Pierce (Kewaunee) Town....................973
Pierce County....................................994
Pigeon (Trempealeau) Town.............1017
Pigeon Falls (Trempealeau) Village.1017
Pilsen (Bayfield) Town........................933
Pine Grove (Portage) Town.................999
Pine Lake (Oneida) Town....................990
Pine River (Lincoln) Town....................977
Pine Valley (Clark) Town.....................942
Pittsfield (Brown) Town........................934
Pittsville (Wood) City.........................1033
Plain (Sauk) Village...........................1009
Plainfield (Waushara) Town..............1030
Plainfield (Waushara) Village............1030
Platteville (Grant) City.........................962
Platteville (Grant) Town.......................962
Pleasant Prairie (Kenosha) Town.......972
Pleasant Prairie (Kenosha) Village ...972
Pleasant Springs (Dane) Town...........948
Pleasant Valley (Eau Claire) Town....956
Pleasant Valley (St. Croix) Town 1007
Plover (Marathon) Town......................981
Plover (Portage) Town........................999
Plover (Portage) Village......................999
Plum City (Pierce) Village...................995

Plum Lake (Vilas) Town....................1020
Plymouth (Juneau) Town....................971
Plymouth (Rock) Town.....................1004
Plymouth (Sheboygan) City..............1014
Plymouth (Sheboygan) Town............1014
Polar (Langlade) Town........................976
Polk (Washington) Town...................1025
Polk County......................................996
Poplar (Douglas) Village.....................953
Popple River (Forest) Town................959
Portage (Columbia) City......................944
Portage County................................998
Port Edwards (Wood) Town..............1033
Port Edwards (Wood) Village...........1033
Porter (Rock) Town...........................1004
Porterfield (Marinette) Town...............983
Portland (Dodge) Town.......................951
Portland (Monroe) Town......................987
Port Washington (Ozaukee) City........993
Port Washington (Ozaukee) Town 993
Port Wing (Bayfield) Town...................933
Potosi (Grant) Town............................962
Potosi (Grant) Village..........................962
Potter (Calumet) Village......................938
Potter Lake (Walworth) CDP............1022
Pound (Marinette) Town.....................983
Pound (Marinette) Village...................983
Powers Lake (Kenosha) CDP.............972
Powers Lake (Walworth) CDP..........1022
Poygan (Winnebago) Town..............1032
Poynette (Columbia) Village...............944
Poysippi (Waushara) Town...............1030
Prairie du Chien (Crawford) City.....945
Prairie du Chien (Crawford) Town...945
Prairie du Sac (Sauk) Town.............1009
Prairie du Sac (Sauk) Village...........1009
Prairie Farm (Barron) Town................932
Prairie Farm (Barron) Village..............932
Prairie Lake (Barron) Town.................932
Prentice (Price) Town.......................1000
Prentice (Price) Village.....................1000
Prescott (Pierce) City..........................995
Presque Isle (Vilas) Town................1020
Preston (Adams) Town.......................929
Preston (Trempealeau) Town...........1017
Price (Langlade) Town........................976
Price County......................................999
Primrose (Dane) Town........................948
Princeton (Green Lake) City...............964
Princeton (Green Lake) Town.............964
Pulaski (Brown) Village.......................935
Pulaski (Iowa) Town............................966
Quincy (Adams) Town........................929
Racine (Racine) City.........................1001
Racine County................................1000
Radisson (Sawyer) Town.................1011
Radisson (Sawyer) Village...............1011
Randall (Kenosha) Town.....................972
Randolph (Columbia) Town.................944
Randolph (Columbia) Village..............944
Randolph (Dodge) Village...................951
Random Lake (Sheboygan) Village.1014
Rantoul (Calumet) Town.....................938
Raymond (Racine) Town...................1001
Readstown (Vernon) Village.............1019
Red Cedar (Dunn) Town.....................955
Redgranite (Waushara) Village........1030
Red River (Kewaunee) Town..............973
Red Springs (Shawano) Town..........1012
Reedsburg (Sauk) City......................1009
Reedsburg (Sauk) Town...................1009
Reedsville (Manitowoc) Village..........979
Reeseville (Dodge) Village.................951
Reid (Marathon) Town.........................981
Remington (Wood) Town..................1033

Reseburg (Clark) Town.......................942
Reserve (Sawyer) CDP....................1011
Rewey (Iowa) Village..........................966
Rhine (Sheboygan) Town.................1014
Rhinelander (Oneida) City..................990
Rib Falls (Marathon) Town..................981
Rib Lake (Taylor) Town....................1016
Rib Lake (Taylor) Village..................1016
Rib Mountain (Marathon) Town..........981
Rice Lake (Barron) City......................932
Rice Lake (Barron) Town....................932
Richfield (Adams) Town......................929
Richfield (Washington) Town...........1025
Richfield (Wood) Town.....................1033
Richford (Waushara) Town...............1031
Richland (Richland) Town.................1002
Richland (Rusk) Town......................1005
Richland Center (Richland) City 1002
Richland County..............................1002
Richmond (Shawano) Town.............1012
Richmond (St. Croix) Town..............1007
Richmond (Walworth) Town.............1022
Richwood (Richland) Town...............1002
Ridgeland (Dunn) Village....................955
Ridgeville (Monroe) Town...................988
Ridgeway (Iowa) Town.......................966
Ridgeway (Iowa) Village.....................966
Rietbrock (Marathon) Town................981
Ringle (Marathon) Town.....................981
Rio (Columbia) Village........................944
Ripon (Fond du Lac) City...................958
Ripon (Fond du Lac) Town.................958
River Falls (Pierce) City......................995
River Falls (Pierce) Town...................995
River Falls (St. Croix) City...............1007
River Hills (Milwaukee) Village..........986
Riverview (Oconto) Town...................989
Roberts (St. Croix) Village...............1007
Rochester (Racine) Town.................1001
Rochester (Racine) Village...............1001
Rock (Rock) Town............................1004
Rock (Wood) Town...........................1033
Rockbridge (Richland) Town............1002
Rock County...................................1003
Rock Creek (Dunn) Town...................955
Rockdale (Dane) Village.....................948
Rock Elm (Pierce) Town.....................995
Rock Falls (Lincoln) Town..................977
Rockland (Brown) Town......................935
Rockland (La Crosse) Village............974
Rockland (Manitowoc) Town..............979
Rock Springs (Sauk) Village.............1009
Rolling (Langlade) Town.....................976
Rome (Adams) Town..........................929
Roosevelt (Burnett) Town...................937
Roosevelt (Taylor) Town..................1016
Rose (Waushara) Town....................1031
Rosendale (Fond du Lac) Town.........958
Rosendale (Fond du Lac) Village......958
Rosholt (Portage) Village....................999
Ross (Forest) Town............................959
Rothschild (Marathon) Village............981
Round Lake (Sawyer) Town.............1011
Roxbury (Dane) Town.........................948
Royalton (Waupaca) Town...............1029
Rubicon (Dodge) Town.......................951
Ruby (Chippewa) Town......................940
Rudolph (Wood) Town......................1034
Rudolph (Wood) Village....................1034
Rushford (Winnebago) Town............1032
Rush River (St. Croix) Town............1007
Rusk (Burnett) Town...........................937
Rusk (Rusk) Town............................1005
Rusk County...................................1004
Russell (Bayfield) Town......................933

Entry	Page
Russell (Lincoln) Town	977
Russell (Sheboygan) Town	1014
Rutland (Dane) Town	948
St. Cloud (Fond du Lac) Village	958
St. Croix County	1006
St. Croix Falls (Polk) City	997
St. Croix Falls (Polk) Town	997
St. Francis (Milwaukee) City	986
St. Germain (Vilas) Town	1020
St. Joseph (St. Croix) Town	1007
St. Lawrence (Waupaca) Town	1029
St. Marie (Green Lake) Town	964
St. Nazianz (Manitowoc) Village	979
Salem (Kenosha) Town	972
Salem (Pierce) Town	995
Sampson (Chippewa) Town	940
Sanborn (Ashland) Town	930
Sand Creek (Dunn) Town	955
Sand Lake (Burnett) Town	937
Sand Lake (Sawyer) Town	1011
Saratoga (Wood) Town	1034
Sarona (Washburn) Town	1023
Sauk City (Sauk) Village	1009
Sauk County	1008
Saukville (Ozaukee) Town	993
Saukville (Ozaukee) Village	993
Sawyer County	1010
Saxeville (Waushara) Town	1031
Saxon (Iron) Town	967
Scandinavia (Waupaca) Town	1029
Scandinavia (Waupaca) Village	1029
Schleswig (Manitowoc) Town	979
Schley (Lincoln) Town	977
Schoepke (Oneida) Town	990
Schofield (Marathon) City	981
Scott (Brown) Town	935
Scott (Burnett) Town	937
Scott (Columbia) Town	944
Scott (Crawford) Town	945
Scott (Lincoln) Town	977
Scott (Monroe) Town	988
Scott (Sheboygan) Town	1014
Seif (Clark) Town	942
Seneca (Crawford) Town	946
Seneca (Green Lake) Town	964
Seneca (Shawano) Town	1012
Seneca (Wood) Town	1034
Sevastopol (Door) Town	952
Seven Mile Creek (Juneau) Town	971
Seymour (Eau Claire) Town	956
Seymour (Lafayette) Town	975
Seymour (Outagamie) City	992
Seymour (Outagamie) Town	992
Shanagolden (Ashland) Town	930
Sharon (Portage) Town	999
Sharon (Walworth) Town	1022
Sharon (Walworth) Village	1022
Shawano (Shawano) City	1012
Shawano County	1011
Sheboygan (Sheboygan) City	1014
Sheboygan (Sheboygan) Town	1014
Sheboygan County	1013
Sheboygan Falls (Sheboygan) City	1014
Sheboygan Falls (Sheboygan) Town	1014
Shelby (La Crosse) Town	974
Sheldon (Monroe) Town	988
Sheldon (Rusk) Village	1005
Shell Lake (Washburn) City	1023
Sheridan (Dunn) Town	955
Sherman (Clark) Town	942
Sherman (Dunn) Town	955
Sherman (Iron) Town	967
Sherman (Sheboygan) Town	1014
Sherry (Wood) Town	1034
Sherwood (Calumet) Village	938
Sherwood (Clark) Town	942
Shields (Dodge) Town	951
Shields (Marquette) Town	984
Shiocton (Outagamie) Village	992
Shorewood (Milwaukee) Village	986
Shorewood Hills (Dane) Village	948
Shullsburg (Lafayette) City	975
Shullsburg (Lafayette) Town	975
Sigel (Chippewa) Town	940
Sigel (Wood) Town	1034
Silver Cliff (Marinette) Town	983
Silver Lake (Kenosha) Village	972
Sioux Creek (Barron) Town	932
Siren (Burnett) Town	937
Siren (Burnett) Village	937
Sister Bay (Door) Village	952
Skanawan (Lincoln) Town	977
Slinger (Washington) Village	1025
Smelser (Grant) Town	962
Soldiers Grove (Crawford) Village	946
Solon Springs (Douglas) Town	953
Solon Springs (Douglas) Village	953
Somers (Kenosha) Town	972
Somerset (St. Croix) Town	1007
Somerset (St. Croix) Village	1007
Somo (Lincoln) Town	977
South Fork (Rusk) Town	1005
South Lancaster (Grant) Town	962
South Milwaukee (Milwaukee) City	986
South Wayne (Lafayette) Village	975
Sparta (Monroe) City	988
Sparta (Monroe) Town	988
Spencer (Marathon) Town	982
Spencer (Marathon) Village	982
Spider Lake (Sawyer) Town	1011
Spirit (Price) Town	1000
Spooner (Washburn) City	1023
Spooner (Washburn) Town	1024
Spring Brook (Dunn) Town	955
Springbrook (Washburn) Town	1024
Springdale (Dane) Town	948
Springfield (Dane) Town	948
Springfield (Jackson) Town	968
Springfield (Marquette) Town	984
Springfield (St. Croix) Town	1007
Spring Green (Sauk) Town	1009
Spring Green (Sauk) Village	1009
Spring Grove (Green) Town	963
Spring Lake (Pierce) Town	995
Spring Prairie (Walworth) Town	1022
Springvale (Columbia) Town	944
Springvale (Fond du Lac) Town	958
Spring Valley (Pierce) Village	995
Spring Valley (Rock) Town	1004
Spring Valley (St. Croix) Village	1007
Springville (Adams) Town	929
Springwater (Waushara) Town	1031
Spruce (Oconto) Town	989
Stanfold (Barron) Town	932
Stanley (Barron) Town	932
Stanley (Chippewa) City	940
Stanton (Dunn) Town	955
Stanton (St. Croix) Town	1007
Stark (Vernon) Town	1019
Star Prairie (St. Croix) Town	1007
Star Prairie (St. Croix) Village	1007
Stella (Oneida) Town	990
Stephenson (Marinette) Town	983
Sterling (Polk) Town	997
Sterling (Vernon) Town	1019
Stetsonville (Taylor) Village	1016
Stettin (Marathon) Town	982
Steuben (Crawford) Village	946
Stevens Point (Portage) City	999
Stiles (Oconto) Town	989
Stinnett (Washburn) Town	1024
Stockbridge (Calumet) Town	938
Stockbridge (Calumet) Village	938
Stockholm (Pepin) Town	994
Stockholm (Pepin) Village	994
Stockton (Portage) Town	999
Stoddard (Vernon) Village	1019
Stone Lake (Washburn) Town	1024
Stoughton (Dane) City	948
Stratford (Marathon) Village	982
Strickland (Rusk) Town	1005
Strongs Prairie (Adams) Town	929
Strum (Trempealeau) Village	1017
Stubbs (Rusk) Town	1005
Sturgeon Bay (Door) City	952
Sturgeon Bay (Door) Town	952
Sturtevant (Racine) Village	1001
Suamico (Brown) Town	935
Sugar Camp (Oneida) Town	990
Sugar Creek (Walworth) Town	1022
Sullivan (Jefferson) Town	969
Sullivan (Jefferson) Village	969
Summit (Douglas) Town	953
Summit (Juneau) Town	971
Summit (Langlade) Town	976
Summit (Waukesha) Town	1027
Sumner (Barron) Town	932
Sumner (Jefferson) Town	969
Sumner (Trempealeau) Town	1017
Sumpter (Sauk) Town	1009
Sun Prairie (Dane) City	948
Sun Prairie (Dane) Town	949
Superior (Douglas) City	953
Superior (Douglas) Town	954
Superior (Douglas) Village	954
Suring (Oconto) Village	989
Sussex (Waukesha) Village	1027
Swiss (Burnett) Town	937
Sylvan (Richland) Town	1002
Sylvester (Green) Town	963
Taft (Taylor) Town	1016
Tainter (Dunn) Town	955
Tainter Lake (Dunn) CDP	955
Taycheedah (Fond du Lac) Town	958
Taylor (Jackson) Village	968
Taylor County	1015
Tennyson (Grant) Village	962
Texas (Marathon) Town	982
Theresa (Dodge) Town	951
Theresa (Dodge) Village	951
Thiensville (Ozaukee) Village	993
Thornapple (Rusk) Town	1005
Thorp (Clark) City	942
Thorp (Clark) Town	942
Three Lakes (Oneida) Town	990
Tiffany (Dunn) Town	955
Tigerton (Shawano) Village	1012
Tilden (Chippewa) Town	940
Tipler (Florence) Town	957
Tomah (Monroe) City	988
Tomah (Monroe) Town	988
Tomahawk (Lincoln) City	977
Tomahawk (Lincoln) Town	977
Tony (Rusk) Village	1005
Townsend (Oconto) Town	989
Trade Lake (Burnett) Town	937
Trego (Washburn) Town	1024
Trempealeau (Trempealeau) Town	1017
Trempealeau (Trempealeau) Village	1017
Trempealeau County	1016
Trenton (Dodge) Town	951
Trenton (Pierce) Town	995
Trenton (Washington) Town	1025
Trimbelle (Pierce) Town	995
Tripp (Bayfield) Town	933

Troy (Sauk) Town 1009
Troy (St. Croix) Town 1007
Troy (Walworth) Town 1022
True (Rusk) Town 1005
Turtle (Rock) Town 1004
Turtle Lake (Barron) Town..............932
Turtle Lake (Barron) Village 932
Turtle Lake (Polk) Village 997
Twin Lakes (Kenosha) Village..............972
Two Creeks (Manitowoc) Town 979
Two Rivers (Manitowoc) City..............979
Two Rivers (Manitowoc) Town..............979
Underhill (Oconto) Town 989
Union (Burnett) Town 937
Union (Door) Town..............953
Union (Eau Claire) Town 956
Union (Pierce) Town 995
Union (Rock) Town 1004
Union (Vernon) Town 1019
Union (Waupaca) Town..............1029
Union Center (Juneau) Village 971
Union Grove (Racine) Village 1001
Unity (Clark) Town 942
Unity (Clark) Village 942
Unity (Marathon) Village 982
Unity (Trempealeau) Town 1017
Upham (Langlade) Town..............976
Utica (Crawford) Town 946
Utica (Winnebago) Town 1032
Valders (Manitowoc) Village 979
Vance Creek (Barron) Town..............932
Vandenbroek (Outagamie) Town..............992
Vermont (Dane) Town 949
Vernon (Waukesha) Town 1027
Vernon County 1018
Verona (Dane) City..............949
Verona (Dane) Town 949
Vesper (Wood) Village 1034
Vienna (Dane) Town 949
Vilas (Langlade) Town..............976
Vilas County..............1020
Vinland (Winnebago) Town 1032
Viola (Richland) Village 1002
Viola (Vernon) Village 1019
Viroqua (Vernon) City..............1019
Viroqua (Vernon) Town..............1019
Wabeno (Forest) Town..............959
Wagner (Marinette) Town..............983
Waldo (Sheboygan) Village..............1014
Waldwick (Iowa) Town 966
Wales (Waukesha) Village..............1027
Walworth (Walworth) Town 1022
Walworth (Walworth) Village 1022
Walworth County 1021
Warner (Clark) Town 942
Warren (St. Croix) Town 1007
Warren (Waushara) Town 1031
Warrens (Monroe) Village 988
Wascott (Douglas) Town..............954
Washburn (Bayfield) City..............933
Washburn (Bayfield) Town..............933
Washburn (Clark) Town 942
Washburn County..............1023
Washington (Door) Town 952
Washington (Eau Claire) Town 956
Washington (Green) Town..............963
Washington (La Crosse) Town 974
Washington (Rusk) Town 1005
Washington (Sauk) Town 1009
Washington (Shawano) Town 1013
Washington (Vilas) Town 1020
Washington County 1024
Waterford (Racine) Town 1001
Waterford (Racine) Village..............1001

Waterford North (Racine) CDP 1001
Waterloo (Grant) Town 962
Waterloo (Jefferson) City..............969
Waterloo (Jefferson) Town..............969
Watertown (Dodge) City..............951
Watertown (Jefferson) City..............969
Watertown (Jefferson) Town..............969
Waterville (Pepin) Town..............994
Watterstown (Grant) Town..............962
Waubeek (Pepin) Town..............994
Waukechon (Shawano) Town 1013
Waukesha (Waukesha) City 1027
Waukesha (Waukesha) Town 1027
Waukesha County 1025
Waumandee (Buffalo) Town 936
Waunakee (Dane) Village 949
Waupaca (Waupaca) City 1029
Waupaca (Waupaca) Town 1029
Waupaca County 1028
Waupun (Dodge) City..............951
Waupun (Fond du Lac) City 958
Waupun (Fond du Lac) Town 958
Wausau (Marathon) City..............982
Wausau (Marathon) Town..............982
Wausaukee (Marinette) Town..............983
Wausaukee (Marinette) Village..............983
Waushara County 1030
Wautoma (Waushara) City 1031
Wautoma (Waushara) Town 1031
Wauwatosa (Milwaukee) City..............986
Wauzeka (Crawford) Town 946
Wauzeka (Crawford) Village..............946
Wayne (Lafayette) Town..............975
Wayne (Washington) Town 1025
Webb Lake (Burnett) Town..............937
Webster (Burnett) Village 937
Webster (Vernon) Town 1019
Weirgor (Sawyer) Town 1011
Wellington (Monroe) Town 988
Wells (Monroe) Town 988
Wescott (Shawano) Town 1013
West Allis (Milwaukee) City..............986
West Baraboo (Sauk) Village 1009
West Bend (Washington) City 1025
West Bend (Washington) Town 1025
Westboro (Taylor) Town 1016
Westby (Vernon) City 1019
Westfield (Marquette) Town..............984
Westfield (Marquette) Village 984
Westfield (Sauk) Town 1009
Westford (Dodge) Town 951
Westford (Richland) Town 1002
West Kewaunee (Kewaunee) Town ...973
West Marshland (Burnett) Town..............937
West Milwaukee (Milwaukee) Village 986
Weston (Clark) Town 942
Weston (Dunn) Town 955
Weston (Marathon) Town..............982
West Point (Columbia) Town..............944
Westport (Dane) Town 949
West Salem (La Crosse) Village 974
West Sweden (Polk) Town 997
Weyauwega (Waupaca) City 1029
Weyauwega (Waupaca) Town 1029
Weyerhaeuser (Rusk) Village..............1006
Wheatland (Kenosha) Town..............972
Wheatland (Vernon) Town 1019
Wheaton (Chippewa) Town..............940
Wheeler (Dunn) Village..............955
Whitefish Bay (Milwaukee) Village...986
Whitehall (Trempealeau) City 1017
White Lake (Langlade) Village..............976
Whitelaw (Manitowoc) Village..............979

White Oak Springs (Lafayette) Town 975
White River (Ashland) Town 930
Whitestown (Vernon) Town 1019
Whitewater (Jefferson) City 970
Whitewater (Walworth) City 1022
Whitewater (Walworth) Town 1022
Whiting (Portage) Village 999
Wien (Marathon) Town 982
Wild Rose (Waushara) Village 1031
Wilkinson (Rusk) Town 1006
Willard (Rusk) Town 1006
Williams Bay (Walworth) Village..............1022
Williamstown (Dodge) Town 951
Willow (Richland) Town 1003
Willow Springs (Lafayette) Town..............975
Wilson (Dunn) Town 955
Wilson (Eau Claire) Town..............956
Wilson (Lincoln) Town 977
Wilson (Rusk) Town 1006
Wilson (Sheboygan) Town 1014
Wilson (St. Croix) Village 1007
Wilton (Monroe) Town 988
Wilton (Monroe) Village 988
Winchester (Vilas) Town 1020
Winchester (Winnebago) Town 1032
Wind Lake (Racine) CDP 1001
Wind Point (Racine) Village 1001
Windsor (Dane) Town 949
Winfield (Sauk) Town 1009
Wingville (Grant) Town 962
Winnebago County 1031
Winneconne (Winnebago) Town 1032
Winneconne (Winnebago) Village 1032
Winter (Sawyer) Town 1011
Winter (Sawyer) Village..............1011
Wiota (Lafayette) Town..............975
Wisconsin Dells (Adams) City 929
Wisconsin Dells (Columbia) City 944
Wisconsin Dells (Sauk) City..............1010
Wisconsin Rapids (Wood) City..............1034
Withee (Clark) Town 942
Withee (Clark) Village 942
Wittenberg (Shawano) Town 1013
Wittenberg (Shawano) Village 1013
Wolf River (Langlade) Town 976
Wolf River (Winnebago) Town 1032
Wonewoc (Juneau) Town..............971
Wonewoc (Juneau) Village 971
Wood (Wood) Town 1034
Woodboro (Oneida) Town 990
Wood County 1032
Woodland (Sauk) Town 1010
Woodman (Grant) Town 962
Woodman (Grant) Village 962
Woodmohr (Chippewa) Town 940
Wood River (Burnett) Town 937
Woodruff (Oneida) Town 990
Woodville (Calumet) Town 938
Woodville (St. Croix) Village 1007
Worcester (Price) Town 1000
Worden (Clark) Town 942
Wrightstown (Brown) Town 935
Wrightstown (Brown) Village 935
Wyalusing (Grant) Town 962
Wyeville (Monroe) Village 988
Wyocena (Columbia) Town 944
Wyocena (Columbia) Village 944
Wyoming (Iowa) Town 966
Wyoming (Waupaca) Town..............1029
York (Clark) Town 942
York (Dane) Town 949
York (Green) Town 963
Yorkville (Racine) Town 1001
Yuba (Richland) Village 1003